Pocket
Oxford–Duden
German Dictionary

Third Edition

German ⤍ English
English ⤍ German

Edited by
the Dudenredaktion
and the German Section of
the Oxford University Press
Dictionary Department

Chief Editors
M. Clark
O. Thyen

OXFORD
UNIVERSITY PRESS

OXFORD
UNIVERSITY PRESS

Great Clarendon Street, Oxford OX2 6DP

Oxford University Press is a department of the University of Oxford.
It furthers the University's objective of excellence in research, scholarship,
and education by publishing worldwide in

Oxford New York

Auckland Cape Town Dar es Salaam Hong Kong Karachi
Kuala Lumpur Madrid Melbourne Mexico City Nairobi
New Delhi Shanghai Taipei Toronto

With offices in

Argentina Austria Brazil Chile Czech Republic France Greece
Guatemala Hungary Italy Japan Poland Portugal Singapore
South Korea Switzerland Thailand Turkey Ukraine Vietnam

Oxford is a registered trade mark of Oxford University Press
in the UK and in certain other countries

Published in the United States
by Oxford University Press Inc., New York

First edition published 1992
Revised edition published 1997
Second edition published 2000
Revised second edition published 2003
Third edition published 2006

British Library Cataloguing in Publication Data
Data available

Library of Congress Cataloging in Publication Data
Data available

Designed by Information Design Unit, Newport Pagnell
Typeset in Nimrod, Arial and Meta by Tradespools
Printed in Great Britain by Clays Ltd, Bungay, Suffolk

ISBN 0-19-861435-7
ISBN 978-0-19861435-7

3

Preface

This new edition of the *Pocket Oxford-Duden German Dictionary* has been enlarged and updated to take account of new vocabulary and recent developments in German, with the needs of both the general and school user in mind. New words and phrases reflect scientific and technological innovations as well as changes in politics, culture, and society. Reforms to the spelling of German ratified by the governments of Germany, Austria, and Switzerland in 1996 have been fully incorporated and are clearly signposted.

Combining the authority of the *Oxford-Duden German Dictionary* with the convenience of a smaller format and quick-access layout, this easy-to-use pocket dictionary is the ideal reference tool for all those requiring quick and reliable answers to their translation questions. It provides clear guidance on selecting the most appropriate translation, numerous examples to help with problems of usage and construction, and precise information on grammar, style, and pronunciation. All grammatical terms used are explained in a glossary at the back of the dictionary.

New features of the dictionary include an expanded and updated A–Z of life and culture, giving essential encyclopedic and cultural information about contemporary Germany and German-speaking countries, and a practical guide to letter-writing in German, including sample letters, e-mails, and CVs, with practical tips about key differences between German and English letter styles and layout, and a new section on text messaging.

Designed to meet the needs of a wide range of users, from the student at intermediate level and above to the enthusiastic traveller and business professional, the *Pocket Oxford-Duden German Dictionary* is an invaluable practical resource for learners of modern, idiomatic German.

Michael Clark
Oxford University Press

Editors and contributors

Oxford University Press
Michael Clark
Bernadette Mohan
Robin Sawers
Gunhild Prowe

Dudenverlag
Olaf Thyen
Werner Scholze-Stubenrecht
Magdalena Seubel

Data input
Susan Wilkin
Anne McConnell
Anna Cotgreave

**A-Z of German culture
Calendar of traditions,
festivals, and holidays**
Ella Associates
Valerie Grundy
Eva Vennebusch
Neil Morris
Roswitha Morris
Penelope Isaac

**Summary of German
Grammar**
Nicholas Rollin
Marie-Louise Wasmeier

Key to English-German Entries / Erläuterungen zum englisch-deutschen Text

Headword
Stichwort

barber /'bɑːbə(r)/ *n.* [Herren]friseur, *der;* ∼'s **shop** (Brit.) Friseursalon, *der*
barbiturate /bɑːˈbɪtjʊrət/ *n.* (Chem.) Barbiturat, *das*

bar: ∼**chart** *n.* Stabdiagramm, *das;* ∼**code** *n.* Strichcode, *der*

Compound block with a swung dash representing the first element of each compound
Kompositablock. Eine Tilde ersetzt jeweils den gemeinsamen ersten Bestandteil der Komposita

bear[2] [1] *v.t.,* **bore** /bɔː(r)/, **borne** /bɔːn/ ...
■ **bear 'out** *v.t.* (fig.) bestätigen ⟨*Bericht, Erklärung*⟩; ∼ **sb. out** jmdm. Recht geben.
■ **'bear with** *v.t.* Nachsicht haben mit

Each phrasal verb is entered on a new line immediately following the entry for the first element
Die *Phrasal Verbs* folgen, jedes auf einer neuen Zeile, direkt auf den Eintrag zu ihrem Grundverb

bemused /bɪˈmjuːzd/ *adj.* verwirrt

Pronunciation shown in IPA (see p. xiii).
Ausspracheangaben (in IPA-Lautschrift) (s. S. xiii)

'bin liner *n.* Müllbeutel, *der*

Stress mark, showing stress on the following syllable
Betonungszeichen vor der betonten Silbe

cart /kɑːt/ [1] *n.* Wagen, *der* [2] *v.t.* (coll.) schleppen

Grammatical categories and parts of speech
Grammatische Gliederungspunkte und Wortartangaben

Irregular tenses of a verb
Unregelmäßige Verbformen

choose /tʃuːz/ [1] *v.t.,* **chose** /tʃəʊz/, **chosen** /'tʃəʊzn/ (a) wählen

dub /dʌb/ *v.t.,* **-bb-** (Cinemat.) synchronisieren

Doubling of a final consonant of a verb before -ed or -ing
Verdoppelung des Endkonsonanten eines Verbs vor -ed oder -ing

Irregular comparative and superlative forms of an adjective
Unregelmäßige Steigerungsformen eines Adjektivs

good /gʊd/ [1] *adj.,* **better** /'betə(r)/, **best** /best/ (a) gut; günstig ⟨*Gelegenheit, Angebot*⟩; ...

groom /gruːm, grʊm/ [1] *n.* (a) (stable boy) Stallbursche, *der* (b) (bride∼) Bräutigam, *der*

Sense categories and sense indicators
Semantische Gliederungspunkte und Bedeutungsindikatoren

Subject labels
Bereichsangaben

HTML *abbr.* (Comp.) **hypertext markup language** HTML
immobilizer /ɪˈməʊbɪlaɪzə(r)/ *n.* (Motor Veh.) Wegfahrsperre, *die*

Key to English-German entries

• •

Style labels •————— **jam-packed** *adj.* (coll.) knallvoll (ugs.),
Stilistische proppenvoll (ugs.) (**with** von)
Kennzeichnungen

loch /lɒx, lɒk/ *n.* (Scot.) See, *der* ————• **Regional labels**
Medicare /'medɪkeə(r)/ *n.* (Amer.) Angaben zur
[*bundes*]staatliches räumlichen
Krankenversicherungssystem für Personen Zuordnung
über 65 Jahre

oppress /ə'pres/ *v.t.* unterdrücken; (fig.)
Collocators • ‹*Gefühl:*› bedrücken
—**words often used** **oppressive** /ə'presɪv/ *adj.* repressiv; (fig.)
with the headword, bedrückend ‹*Ängste, Atmosphäre*›; (hot and
shown to help select close) drückend ‹*Wetter, Klima, Tag*›
the correct transla-
tion for each context.
Kollokatoren (Wörter,
mit denen zusammen
das Stichwort häufig
vorkommt) als Hilfe
zur Auswahl der für
den jeweiligen Kontext **price** /praɪs/ *n.* (lit. or fig.) Preis, *der;* **at a**
passenden ~ **of** zum Preis von; **what is the** ~ **of this?** ————• **Examples (with a**
Übersetzung was kostet das?; **at/not at any** ~: um jeden/ **swung dash**
keinen Preis **representing the**
headword)
Beispiele (jeweils mit
einer Tilde an Stelle
des Stichworts)

An arrow directs •——— **sitcom** /'sɪtkɒm/ (coll.) ▶ SITUATION COMEDY
the user to another
headword with the
same meaning **Sunday** /'sʌndeɪ, 'sʌndɪ/ *n.* Sonntag, *der;*
Ein Pfeil verweist auf ~ **opening** die sonntägliche Öffnung;
ein bedeutungsglei- ~ **trading** sonntägliche Ladenöffnung; *see*
ches anderes *also* FRIDAY
Stichwort
————• *see also* **directs the**
user to another
headword where
additional
information can be
found
Mit *see also* wird auf
ein Stichwort
verwiesen, unter dem
noch zusätzliche
Informationen zu
finden sind

Phonetic symbols used in transcriptions of German words

Phonetic information given in the German-English section

The pronunciation of German is largely regular, and phonetic transcriptions have only been given where additional help is needed. In all other cases only the position of the stressed syllable and the length of the vowel in that syllable are shown: a long vowel is indicated by an underline, e.g. **Maß**, a short vowel by a dot placed underneath, e.g. **Masse**.

a	*hạt*	hat
aː	*Bạhn*	baːn
ɐ	*Ober*	ˈoːbɐ
ɐ̯	*Uhr*	uːɐ̯
ã	*Ensemble*	ãˈsãːbl̩
ãː	*Abonnement*	abɔnəˈmãː
ai̯	*weit*	vai̯t
au̯	*Haut*	hau̯t
b	*Bạll*	bal
ç	*ịch*	ɪç
d	*dạnn*	dan
dʒ	*Gịn*	dʒɪn
e	*egạl*	eˈgaːl
eː	*Beet*	beːt
ɛ	*mạ̈sten*	ˈmɛstn̩
ɛː	*wählen*	ˈvɛːlən
ɛ̃	*Mạnnequin*	ˈmanəkɛ̃
ɛ̃ː	*Cousin*	kuˈzɛ̃ː
ə	*Nạse*	ˈnaːzə
f	*Fạß*	fas
g	*Gạst*	gast
h	*hạt*	hat
i	*vitạl*	viˈtaːl
iː	*viel*	fiːl
i̯	*Studie*	ˈʃtuːdi̯ə
ɪ	*Bịrke*	ˈbɪrkə
j	*ja*	jaː
k	*kạlt*	kalt
l	*Lạst*	last
l̩	*Nạbel*	ˈnaːbl̩

m	*Mast*	mast	l	Glottal stop, e.g. beachten /bə|axtn̩/	
n	*Naht*	na:t			
n̩	*baden*	'ba:dn̩	:	Length sign, indicating that the preceding vowel is long, e.g. Chrom /kro:m/	
ŋ	*lang*	laŋ			
o	*Moral*	mo'ra:l			
o:	*Boot*	bo:t	~	Indicates a nasal vowel, e.g. Fond /fõ:/	
o̯	*loyal*	lo̯a'ja:l			
õ	*Fondue*	fõ'dy:	'	Stress mark, immediately preceding a stressed syllable, e.g. Ballon /ba'lɔn/	
õ:	*Fond*	fõ:			
ɔ	*Post*	pɔst			
ø	*Ökonom*	øko'no:m			
ø:	*Öl*	ø:l			
œ	*göttlich*	'gœtlɪç			
œ̃	*Parfum*	par'fœ̃:			
ɔy	*Heu*	hɔy			
p	*Pakt*	pakt			
pf	*Pfahl*	pfa:l			
r	*Rast*	rast			
s	*Hast*	hast			
ʃ	*schal*	ʃa:l			
t	*Tal*	ta:l			
ts	*Zahl*	tsa:l			
tʃ	*Matsch*	matʃ			
u	*kulant*	ku'lant			
u:	*Hut*	hu:t			
u̯	*aktuell*	ak'tu̯ɛl			
ʊ	*Pult*	pʊlt			
v	*was*	vas			
x	*Bach*	bax			
y	*Physik*	fy'zi:k			
y:	*Rübe*	'ry:bə			
y̆	*Nuance*	'ny̆ã:sə			
ʏ	*Fülle*	'fʏlə			
z	*Hase*	'ha:zə			
ʒ	*Genie*	ʒe'ni:			

Die für das Englische verwendeten Zeichen der Lautschrift

ɑ	*barb*	bɑːb	p	*pet*	pet
ãː	*séance*	ˈseɪãs	r	*rat*	ræt
æ	*fat*	fæt	s	*sip*	sɪp
æ̃	*lingerie*	ˈlæ̃ʒərɪ	ʃ	*ship*	ʃɪp
aɪ	*fine*	faɪn	t	*tip*	tɪp
aʊ	*now*	naʊ	tʃ	*chin*	tʃɪn
b	*bat*	bæt	θ	*thin*	θɪn
d	*dog*	dɒg	ð	*the*	ðə
dʒ	*jam*	dʒæm	uː	*boot*	buːt
e	*met*	met	ʊ	*book*	bʊk
eɪ	*fate*	feɪt	ʊə	*tourist*	ˈtʊərɪst
eə	*fairy*	ˈfeərɪ	ʌ	*dug*	dʌg
əʊ	*goat*	gəʊt	v	*van*	væn
ə	*ago*	əˈgəʊ	w	*win*	wɪn
ɜː	*fur*	fɜː(r)	x	*loch*	lɒx
f	*fat*	fæt	z	*zip*	zɪp
g	*good*	gʊd	ʒ	*vision*	ˈvɪʒn
h	*hat*	hæt	ː	Längezeichen, bezeichnet Länge des unmittelbar davor stehenden Vokals, z. B. boot /buːt/	
ɪ	*bit, lately*	bɪt, ˈleɪtlɪ			
ɪə	*nearly*	ˈnɪəlɪ			
iː	*meet*	miːt	ˈ	Betonung, steht unmittelbar vor einer betonten Silbe, z. B. ago /əˈgəʊ/	
j	*yet*	jet			
k	*kit*	kɪt			
l	*lot*	lɒt	(r)	Ein „r" in runden Klammern wird nur gesprochen, wenn im Textzusammenhang ein Vokal unmittelbar folgt, z. B. pare /peə(r)/; pare away /peər əˈweɪ/	
m	*mat*	mæt			
n	*not*	nɒt			
ŋ	*sing*	sɪŋ			
ɒ	*got*	gɒt			
ɔː	*paw*	pɔː			
ɔɪ	*boil*	bɔɪl			

German spellings in this dictionary

German spellings in this dictionary are in accordance with the reforms ratified by the governments of Germany, Austria, and Switzerland in July 1996 and in force since August 1998. Key points of the reforms are summarized below. In cases of doubt the editors have followed *Duden— Rechtschreibung der deutschen Sprache*, twenty-first edition, 1996.

To help the user who may not yet be familiar with the reforms, the German-English section of the dictionary gives both the new spellings and the old versions which became 'invalid' in 2005. The old spellings are marked with an asterisk and are cross-referred where necessary to the new. For example, the translations of the compound verb *wiedererkennen* will no longer be found at this headword, since under the new spelling rules the word vanishes from the language. Instead they are covered by two phrases at the entry for *wieder: jemanden/etwas wieder erkennen* (in the form *jmdn./etw. ~ erkennen*) and *er war kaum wieder zu erkennen* (in the form *er war kaum ~ zu erkennen*). Similarly, the translations of the adjective previously written *belemmert* will be found at the new entry for the headword *belämmert*.

In a number of cases, however, implementing the new spelling rules has meant that just some, but not all, uses of a word have had to be transferred from one entry to another. In these cases the headword is not marked with an asterisk, but the entry is provided with a cross-reference to where the transferred information is now to be found. So, for example, the user who consults the entry for *leid* looking for a translation of the phrase previously written *jemandem leid tun* will find a cross-reference to the entry for the noun *Leid*, since according to the new spelling rules the word is written with a capital *L* in this expression. The headword *leid* itself is not marked with an asterisk, since it continues to exist in its own right as an adjective.

The following summary lists the most important changes:

1 The ß character The ß character, which is generally replaced in Switzerland by a double s, is retained in Germany and Austria, but is only be written after a long vowel (as in Fuß, Füße) and after a diphthong (as in Strauß, Sträuße).

Fluß, Baß, keß, läßt, Nußknacker become: *Fluss, Bass, kess, lässt, Nussknacker*

2 Nominalized adjectives Nominalized adjectives is written with a capital even in set phrases.

sein Schäfchen ins trockene bringen, im trüben fischen, im allgemeinen become: *sein Schäfchen ins Trockene bringen, im Trüben fischen, im Allgemeinen*

3 Words from the same word family
In certain cases the spelling of words belonging to the same family have been made uniform.

numerieren, überschwenglich become: *nummerieren* (like Nummer), *überschwänglich* (being related to Überschwang)

4 The same consonant repeated three times
When the same consonant repeated three times occurs in compounds, all three are written even when a vowel follows.

Brennessel, Schiffahrt become: *Brennnessel, Schifffahrt* (exceptions are dennoch, Drittel, Mittag)

5 Verb, adjective and participle compounds
Verb, adjective and participle compounds are written more frequently than previously in two words.

spazierengehen, radfahren, ernstgemeint, erdölexportierend become: *spazieren gehen, Rad fahren, ernst gemeint, Erdöl exportierend*

6 Compounds containing numbers in figures
Compounds containing numbers in figures are now written with a hyphen.

24karätig, 8pfünder become: *24-karätig, 8-Pfünder*

7 The division of words containing st
st is treated like a normal combination of consonants and is no longer be indivisible.

Ha-stig, Ki-ste become: *has-tig, Kis-te*

8 The division of words containing ck
The combination ck is not be divided and goes on to the next line.

Bäk-ker, schik-ken become: *Bä-cker, schi-cken*

9 The division of foreign words
Compound foreign words which are hardly recognized as such today may be divided by syllables, without regard to their original components.

He-li-ko-pter (from the Greek helix and pteron) may also be written: *He-li-kop-ter*

10 The comma before und
Where two complete clauses are connected by *und* a comma is no longer obligatory.

Karl war in Schwierigkeiten, und niemand konnte ihm helfen. may also be written: *Karl war in Schwierigkeiten und niemand konnte ihm helfen.*

11 The comma with infinitives and participles
Even longer clauses containing an infinitive or participle do not have to be divided off with a comma.

Er begann sofort, das neue Buch zu lesen. Ungläubig den Kopf schüttelnd, verließ er das Zimmer. may also be written: *Er begann sofort das neue Buch zu lesen. Ungläubig den Kopf schüttelnd verließ er das Zimmer.*

Abkürzungen / Abbreviations

anderes, andere	a.	other, others
ähnliches, ähnliche	ä.	similar
Abkürzung	abbr.	abbreviation
Abkürzung	Abk.	abbreviation
absolut	abs.	absolute
adjektivisch	adj.	adjective, adjectival
Adjektiv	Adj.	adjective
Verwaltungssprache	Admin.	Administration, Administrative
adverbial	adv.	adverb, adverbial
Adverb	Adv.	adverb
Flugwesen	Aeronaut.	Aeronautics
Landwirtschaft	Agric.	Agriculture
Akkusativ	Akk.	accusative
Amerika	Amer.	American, America
amerikanisch	amerik.	American
Amtssprache	Amtsspr.	official language
Anatomie	Anat.	Anatomy
Anthropologie	Anthrop.	Anthropology
veraltet	arch.	archaic
Archäologie	Archaeol.	Archaeology
Architektur	Archit.	Architecture
Artikel	art.	article
Astrologie	Astrol.	Astrology
Astronomie	Astron.	Astronomy
Raumfahrt	Astronaut.	Astronautics
Altes Testament	A. T.	Old Testament
attributiv	attr., attrib.	attributive
Australien	Austral.	Australian, Australia
Bauwesen	Bauw.	Construction
Bergmannssprache	Berg-mannsspr.	Mining terminology
besonders	bes.	especially
Bezeichnung	Bez.	name
biblisch	bibl.	biblical
Biologie	Biol.	Biology
Buchführung	Bookk.	Bookkeeping
Börsenwesen	Börsenw.	Stock Market
Botanik	Bot.	Botany
Bundesrepublik Deutschland	BRD	Federal Republic of Germany
britisch, Großbritannien	Brit.	British, Britain
britisch	brit.	British
Bruchzahl	Bruchz.	fraction
Buchführung	Buchf.	Bookkeeping
Buchwesen	Buchw.	Book Trade
Chemie	Chem.	Chemistry
chemisch	chem.	chemical
Kindersprache	child lang.	child language
christlich	christl.	Christian
Kinematographie	Cinemat.	Cinematography
umgangssprachlich	coll.	colloquial
Kollektivum	collect.	collective
Kombination	comb.	combination
Handel, Handels-	Commerc.	Commerce, Commercial
elektronische Datenverarbeitung	Comp.	Computing
Komparativ, komparativ	compar.	comparative
Konditional, konditional	condit.	conditional
Konjunktion	conj.	conjunction
Dativ	Dat.	dative
Deutsche Demokratische Republik	DDR	German Democratic Republic
bestimmt	def.	definite
Deklination	Dekl.	declension
Demonstrativpronomen	Demonstra-tivpron.	demonstrative pronoun
Zahnmedizin	Dent.	Dentistry
abwertend	derog.	derogatory
das heißt	d. h.	that is [to say]
Dialekt	dial.	dialect
dichterisch	dichter.	poetic
Damenschneiderei	Dressm.	Dressmaking
Druckwesen	Druckw.	Printing
deutsch	dt.	German
Datenverarbeitung	DV	Data Processing
kirchlich	Eccl.	Ecclesiastical
Ökologie	Ecol.	Ecology
Ökonomik	Econ.	Economics
Bildungswesen	Educ.	Education
ehemals, ehemalig	ehem.	former, formerly
Eisenbahn	Eisenb.	Railways
Elektrizität	Electr.	Electricity
Elektrotechnik	Elektrot.	Electrical Engineering
elektrisch	elektr.	electrical
elliptisch	ellipt.	elliptical
emphatisch	emphat.	emphatic
besonders	esp.	especially
etwas	etw.	something
euphemistisch	euphem.	euphemistic
evangelisch	ev.	Evangelical
ausdrückend	expr.	expressing

Abkürzungen / Abbreviations

fachsprachlich	fachspr.	technical	Kindersprache	Kinderspr.	child language
familiär	fam.	familiar	Kochkunst	Kochk.	Cookery
feminin	fem.	feminine	Komparativ	Komp.	Comparative
Fernsehen	Ferns.	Television	Konjunktion	Konj.	conjunction
Fernsprechwesen	Fernspr.	Telephony	landschaftlich	landsch.	regional
figurativ	fig.	figurative	Landwirtschaft	Landw.	Agriculture
Finanzwesen	Finanzw.	Finance	Linguistik	Ling.	Linguistics
Flugwesen	Flugw.	Aeronautics	wortwörtlich	lit.	literal
Fußball	Footb.	Football	Literatur	Lit.	Literature
Forstwesen	Forstw.	Forestry	Literaturwissen-	Literaturw.	Literary Studies
Fotografie	Fot.	Photography	schaft		
Gastronomie	Gastr.	Gastronomy	Luftfahrt	Luftf.	Aeronautics
gehoben	geh.	elevated	mittelalterlich	ma.	medieval
Genitiv	Gen.	genitive	Mittelalter	MA.	Middle Ages
Geographie	Geog.	Geography	marxistisch	marx.	Marxist
Geologie	Geol.	Geology	maskulin	masc.	masculine
Geometrie	Geom.	Geometry	Mathematik	Math.	Mathematics
Handarbeit	Handarb.	Handicraft	Maschinenbau	Mech.	Mechanical
Heraldik	Her.	Heraldry		Engin.	Engineering
Hilfsverb	Hilfsv.	auxiliary verb	Medizin	Med.	Medicine
historisch	hist.	historical	Meereskunde	Meeresk.	oceanography
Geschichte,	Hist.	History, historical	Meteorologie	Met.	Meteorology
historisch			Metallurgie	Metall.	Metallurgy
Hochschulwesen	Hoch-	Higher Education	Metallbearbeitung	Metall-	Metalwork
	schulw.			bearb.	
Gartenbau	Hort.	Horticultural	Metallbearbeitung	Metalw.	Metalwork
Imperativ,	imper.	imperative	Meteorologie	Meteorol.	Meteorology
imperativisch			Militär	Mil., Milit.	Military
unpersönlich	impers.	impersonal	modifizierend	mod.	modifying
unbestimmt	indef.	indefinite	Modalverb	Modalv.	modal verb
Indefinitpronomen	Indefinit	indefinite	Kraftfahrzeug-	Motor Veh.	Motor Vehicles
	-pron.	pronoun	wesen		
Indeklinabel	Indekl.	indeclinable	Musik	Mus.	Music
Indikativ	Indik.	indicative	Mythologie	Mythol.	Mythology
Infinitiv	Inf.	infinitive	Substantiv	n.	noun
Interjektion	Interj., int.	interjection	Seemannssprache	Naut.	Nautical
interrogativ	interrog.	interrogative	negativ	neg.	negative
intransitiv	intr.	intransitive	Nominativ	Nom.	nominative
irisch, Irland	Ir.	Irish, Ireland	norddeutsch	nordd.	North German
ironisch	iron.	ironical	nordostdeutsch	nordostd.	North-East
Jägersprache	Jägerspr.	hunting language			German
jemand	jmd.	somebody	Substantive	ns.	nouns
jemandem	jmdm.	somebody		(English)	
jemanden	jmdn.	somebody	nationalsozialis-	ns.	National
jemandes	jmds.	somebody	tisch	(Deutsch)	Socialist
scherzhaft	joc.	jocular	Neues Testament	N. T.	New Testament
Journalismus	Journ.	Journalism	Kernphysik	Nucl. Phys.	Nuclear Physics
Jugendsprache	Jugend-	young people's	ohne; oben	o.	without; above
	spr.	language	Objekt	obj.	object
juristisch	jur.	legal	oder	od.	or
Kardinalzahl	Kardinalz.	cardinal number	Ordinalzahl	Ordinalz.	ordinal number
katholisch	kath.	Catholic	Ornithologie	Ornith.	Ornithology
Kaufmanns-	Kauf-	business	österreichisch	österr.	Austrian
sprache	mannsspr.	language	Papierdeutsch	Papierdt.	officialese
Kraftfahrzeug-	Kfz-W.	Motor Vehicles	Parlament	Parl.	Parliament
wesen			Partizip	Part.	participle

• •

Passiv	pass.	passive
Perfekt	Perf.	perfect
Person	Pers.	person
Philosophie	Philos.	Philosophy
Fotografie	Photog.	Photography
Phrase(n)	phr(s).	Phrase(s)
Physik	Phys.	Physics
Physiologie	Physiol.	Physiology
Plural	Pl., pl.	plural
Plusquamperfekt	Plusq.	pluperfect
dichterisch	poet.	poetical
Politik	Polit.	Politics
possessiv, Possessiv-	poss.	possessive
nachgestellt	postpos.	postpositive
Postwesen	Postw.	Post Office
zweites Partizip	p.p.	past participle
prädikativ	präd.	predicative
Präposition	Präp.	preposition
Präsens	Präs.	present
Präteritum	Prät.	preterite
prädikativ	pred.	predicative
Präfix	pref.	prefix
Präposition	prep.	preposition
Präsens	pres.	present
erstes Partizip	pres. p.	present participle
Eigenname	pr. n.	proper noun
Pronomen	Pron., pron.	pronoun
sprichwörtlich	prov.	proverbial
Psychologie	Psych.	Psychology
Präteritum	p.t.	past tense
Warenzeichen	®	Registered Trade Mark
Eisenbahn	Railw.	Railways
Raumfahrt	Raumf.	Space Travel
römisch-katho- lische Kirche	RC Ch.	Roman Catholic Church
Rechtssprache	Rechtsspr.	legal terminology
Rechtswesen	Rechtsw.	Law
reflexiv	refl.	reflexive
regelmäßig	regelm.	regular
relativ	rel.	relative
Religion	Rel.	Religion
Relativpronomen	Relativ- pron.	relative pronoun
römisch	röm.	Roman
römisch-katholisch	röm-kath.	Roman Catholic
Rundfunk	Rundf.	Radio
siehe	s.	see
Seite	S.	page
jemand	sb.	somebody
Schule	Sch.	School
scherzhaft	scherzh.	jocular
Schülersprache	Schüler- spr.	school slang
schweizerisch	schweiz.	Swiss

Wissenschaft	Sci.	Science
schottisch	Scot.	Scottish, Scotland
Schulwesen	Schulw.	School System
Seemannssprache	Seemanns- spr.	Nautical
Seewesen	Seew.	maritime affairs
Singular	Sg., sing.	singular
salopp	sl.	slang
siehe oben	s. o.	see above
Soziologie	Sociol.	Sociology
Soldatensprache	Soldaten- spr.	army slang
Soziologie	Soziol.	Sociology
spöttisch	spött.	derisive
Sprichwort	Spr.	proverb
Sprach- wissenschaft	Sprachw.	Linguistics
Börsenwesen	St. Exch.	Stock Exchange
Steuerwesen	Steuerw.	Taxation
etwas	sth.	something
Studentensprache	Studen- tenspr.	student slang
siehe unten	s. u.	see below
Subjekt	Subj.	subject
substantivisch; substantiviert	subst.	nominal; nominalized
Substantiv	Subst.	noun
süddeutsch	südd.	South German
südwestdeutsch	südwestd.	South-West German
Suffix	suf.	suffix
Superlativ	Sup., superl.	superlative
Landvermessung	Surv.	Surveying
Symbol	symb.	symbol
fachsprachlich	tech.	technical
Fernsprechwesen	Teleph.	Telephony
Fernsehen	Telev.	Television
Textilwesen	Textilw.	Textiles
Theologie	Theol.	Theology
Tiermedizin	Tiermed.	Veterinary Medicine
transitiv	tr.	transitive
Trennung	Trenn.	division
und	u.	and
und Ähnliches	u. Ä.	and similar
umgangssprachlich	ugs.	colloquial
unbestimmt	unbest.	indefinite
Universität	Univ.	University
unpersönlich	unpers.	impersonal
unregelmäßig	unr.	irregular
gewöhnlich	usu.	usually
und so weiter	usw.	et cetera
von	v.	of
Verb	V.	verb
Hilfsverb	v. aux.	auxiliary verb

veraltet; veraltend	**veralt.**	obsolete; obsolescent
Verhaltensforschung	**Verhaltensf.**	Behavioural Research
verhüllend	**verhüll.**	euphemistic
Verkehrswesen	**Verkehrsw.**	Transport
Versicherungswesen	**Versicherungsw.**	Insurance
Tiermedizin	**Vet. Med.**	Veterinary Medicine
vergleiche	**vgl.**	compare
intransitives Verb	**v. i.**	intransitive verb
Verkleinerungsform	**Vkl.**	diminutive
Völkerkunde	**Völkerk.**	Ethnology
volkstümlich	**volkst.**	popular, vernacular
reflexives Verb	**v. refl.**	reflexive verb
transitives Verb	**v. t.**	transitive verb

transitives und intransitives Verb	**v. t. & i.**	transitive and intransitive verb
vulgär	**vulg.**	vulgar
Werbesprache	**Werbespr.**	advertising jargon
westdeutsch	**westd.**	western German
Wirtschaft	**Wirtsch.**	Commerce and Industry
Wissenschaft	**Wissensch.**	Science
Warenzeichen	**Wz.**	Registered Trade Mark
Zahnmedizin	**Zahnmed.**	Dentistry
zum Beispiel	**z. B.**	for example
Zeitungswesen	**Zeitungsw.**	Newspaper Industry
Zoologie	**Zool.**	Zoology
Zusammensetzung	**Zus.**	compound
Zusammenschreibung	**Zusschr.**	writing as one word

Aa

a, A /aː/ *das;* ~, ~ **(a)** (Buchstabe) a/A; **das A und O** (fig.) the essential thing/things (*Gen.* for); **von A bis Z** (fig. ugs.) from beginning to end
(b) (Musik) [key of] A

a *Abk.* = **Ar**

à /a/ *Präp. mit Nom., Akk.* (Kaufmannsspr.) **zehn Marken à 0,56 Euro** ten stamps at 0·56 euro each

A *Abk.* = **Autobahn** ≈ M

Aal *der;* ~[e]s, ~e eel; ~ **grün** (Kochk.) green eels; stewed eels

aalen *refl. V.* (ugs.) stretch out

aal·glatt (abwertend) ⒈ *Adj.* slippery; ~ **sein** be as slippery as an eel ⒉ *adv.* smoothly

Aas *das;* ~es, ~e *od.* Äser **(a)** *Pl.* ~e carrion *no art.;* (Kadaver) [rotting] carcass **(b)** *Pl.* **Äser** (salopp abwertend) swine; (anerkennend) devil

ab ⒈ *Präp. mit Dat.* **(a)** from; **ab 1980** as from 1980; **ab Werk** (Kaufmannsspr.) ex works; **ab Frankfurt fliegen** fly from Frankfurt **(b)** ([Rang]folge) from … on[wards]; **ab 20 Euro** from 20 euros [upwards] ⒉ *Adv.* **(a)** (weg) off; away; **[an etw. (*Dat.*)] ab sein** (ugs.: sich [von etw.] gelöst haben) have come off [sth.] **(b)** (ugs.: Aufforderung) off; away; **ab nach Hause** get off home **(c)** **Gewehr ab!** (milit. Kommando) order arms! **(d)** **ab und zu** *od.* **an** now and then

ab|ändern *tr. V.* alter; amend ⟨*text*⟩

Ab·änderung *die* alteration; (eines Textes) amendment

ab|arbeiten *tr. V.* work for ⟨*meal*⟩; work off ⟨*debt, amount*⟩

Ab·art *die* variety

ab·artig *Adj.* deviant; abnormal

Ab·artigkeit *die;* ~, ~en abnormality; deviancy

Abb. *Abk.* = **Abbildung** Fig.

Ab·bau *der* **(a)** dismantling; (von Zelten, Lagern) striking **(b)** ▶ ABBAUEN C: cutback (*Gen.* in); pruning; reduction **(c)** (Bergbau) mining; (von Stein) quarrying

ab|bauen *tr. V.* **(a)** dismantle; strike ⟨*tent, camp*⟩ **(b)** (beseitigen) gradually remove; break down ⟨*prejudices, inhibitions*⟩ **(c)** (verringern) cut back ⟨*staff*⟩; prune ⟨*jobs*⟩; reduce ⟨*wages*⟩ **(d)** (Bergbau) mine; quarry ⟨*stone*⟩

ab|beißen ⒈ *unr. tr. V.* bite off ⒉ *unr. itr. V.* have a bite

ab|bekommen *unr. tr. V.* **(a)** get **(b)** **einen Schlag/ein paar Kratzer** ~: get hit/ get a few scratches; **etwas** ~ (getroffen werden) be hit; (verletzt werden) be hurt **(c)** (los-, herunterbekommen) get ⟨*paint, lid, chain*⟩ off

ab|berufen *unr. tr. V.* recall ⟨*ambassador, envoy*⟩ (aus, von from)

ab|bestellen *tr. V.* cancel

ab|bezahlen *tr. V.* pay off

ab|biegen *unr. itr. V.; mit sein* turn off; **links/rechts** ~: turn [off] left/right

Abbieger *der;* ~s, ~, **Abbiegerin** *die;* ~, ~nen (Verkehrsw.) motorist/cyclist/car *etc.* turning off

Ab·bild *das* (eines Menschen) likeness; (eines Gegenstandes) copy; (fig.) portrayal

ab|bilden *tr. V.* copy; reproduce ⟨*object, picture*⟩; depict ⟨*person, landscape*⟩; (fig.) portray

Abbildung *die* illustration

ab|binden *unr. tr. V.* **(a)** (losbinden) untie; undo **(b)** (abschnüren) put a tourniquet on ⟨*artery, arm, leg, etc.*⟩; tie ⟨*umbilical cord*⟩

ab|blasen *unr. tr. V.* (ugs.) call off

ab|blättern *itr. V.; mit sein* flake off

ab|blenden *tr., itr. V.* black out; dip (Brit.), dim (Amer.) ⟨*headlights*⟩; **bei Gegenverkehr frühzeitig** ~: dip *or* (Amer.) dim one's headlights promptly when there is oncoming traffic

ab|blitzen *itr. V.; mit sein* (ugs.) **sie ließ alle Verehrer** ~: she gave all her admirers the brush-off

ab|brausen *tr. V.* ▶ ABDUSCHEN

ab|brechen ⒈ *unr. tr. V.* **(a)** break off; break ⟨*needle, pencil*⟩ **(b)** (zerlegen) strike ⟨*tent, camp*⟩ **(c)** (abreißen) demolish, pull down ⟨*building*⟩ **(d)** (beenden) break off ⟨*negotiations, [diplomatic] relations, discussion, activity*⟩; (vorzeitig) cut short ⟨*conversation, holiday, activity*⟩ **(e)** (DV) cancel ⒉ *unr. itr. V.* **(a)** *mit sein* break [off] **(b)** (aufhören) break off

ab|bremsen ⒈ *tr. V.* **(a)** brake **(b)** retard ⟨*motion*⟩ ⒉ *itr. V.* brake

ab|brennen ⒈ *unr. itr. V.; mit sein* **(a)** be burned down; **das Haus ist abgebrannt** the house has burned down **(b)** ⟨*fuse*⟩ burn away; ⟨*candle*⟩ burn down ⒉ *unr. tr. V.* **(a)** let off ⟨*firework*⟩ **(b)** burn down ⟨*building*⟩

ạb|bringen *unr. tr. V.* jmdn. davon ~, etw. zu tun dissuade sb. from doing sth; jmdn. vom Kurs ~: make sb. change course

ạb|bröckeln *itr. V.; mit sein* (auch fig.) crumble away

Ạb·bruch *der* **(a)** (Abriss) demolition; pulling down **(b)** (Beendigung) breaking-off; (einer Schwangerschaft) termination **(c)** einer Sache (*Dat.*) [keinen] ~ tun do [no] harm to sth.

ạb|buchen *tr. V.* ⟨bank⟩ debit (von to); ⟨creditor⟩ claim by direct debit (von to); etw. ~ lassen (durch die Bank) pay sth. by standing order; (durch Gläubiger) pay sth. by direct debit

ạb|bügeln *tr. V.* (ugs.) reject, brush aside ⟨warning, question, criticism⟩; rebuff ⟨person⟩

ạb|bürsten *tr. V.* **(a)** brush off **(b)** (säubern) brush ⟨garment⟩

ạb|büßen *tr. V.* serve [out] ⟨prison sentence⟩

Abc /a(:)be(:)'tse:/ *das;* ~ (auch fig.) ABC

Abc-Schütze *der,* **Abc-Schützin** *die* child just starting school

ạb|dampfen *itr. V.; mit sein* (ugs.: abfahren) set off

ạb|danken *itr. V.* ⟨ruler⟩ abdicate; ⟨government, minister⟩ resign

Ạbdankung *die;* ~, ~en ▶ ABDANKEN: abdication; resignation

ạb|decken *tr. V.* **(a)** open up; ⟨gale⟩ take the roof/roofs off ⟨house⟩, take the tiles off ⟨roof⟩ **(b)** (herunternehmen, -reißen) take off **(c)** (abräumen) clear ⟨table⟩; clear away ⟨dishes⟩ **(d)** (schützen) cover ⟨person⟩

ạb|dichten *tr. V.* seal

ạb|drängen *tr. V.* push away

ạb|drehen ①*tr. V.* **(a)** (ausschalten) turn off; den Hahn ~ (fig.) turn off the supply **(b)** (abtrennen) twist off ②*itr. V.; meist mit sein* turn off

Ạb·druck *der; Pl.* Abdrücke mark; (Fuß~) footprint; (Wachs~) impression; (Gips~) cast

ạb|drücken ①*itr. V.* pull the trigger; shoot ②*tr. V.* (zudrücken) constrict

ạb|dunkeln *tr. V.* darken ⟨room⟩; dim ⟨light⟩

ạb|duschen *tr. V.* sich/jmdn. [warm] ~: take/give sb. a [hot] shower

ạb|düsen *itr. V.* (ugs.) zoom off

*****abend** ▶ ABEND A

Ạbend *der;* ~s, ~e evening; guten ~! good evening; am [frühen/späten] ~: [early/late] in the evening; heute/morgen/gestern ~: this/tomorrow/yesterday evening; zu ~ essen have dinner; (allgemeiner) have one's evening meal; ein bunter ~: a social [evening]

abend-, Ạbend-: ~akademie *die*

―――――――――――――――――
*****old spelling - see note on page xiv

evening school; ~anzug *der* evening suit; ~blatt *das* evening [news]paper; ~brot *das* supper; ~dämmerung *die* [evening] twilight; ~essen *das* dinner; ~füllend *Adj.* occupying a whole evening *postpos.*, *not pred.*; ein ~füllendes Programm a full evening's programme; ~gymnasium *das* night school, evening classes *pl.* (*leading to the 'Abitur'*); ~kasse *die* box office (*open on the evening of the performance*); ~kleid *das* evening dress; ~kurs[us] *der* evening class

Ạbend·land *das;* ~[e]s West

ạbendlich *Adj.* evening; ⟨quiet, coolness⟩ of the evening

Ạbend-: ~mahl *das* (Rel.) Communion; (N.T.) Last Supper; ~programm *das* evening programmes *pl.;* ~rot *das* red glow of the sunset sky

ạbends *Adv.* in the evenings; um sechs Uhr ~: at six o'clock in the evening

Ạbend-: ~schule *die* night school; ~sonne *die* evening sun; ~stern *der* evening star; ~stunde *die* evening hour; in den frühen/späten ~stunden early/late in the evening; ~vorstellung *die* evening performance; ~zeitung *die* ▶ ~BLATT

Abenteuer *das;* ~s, ~ **(a)** (auch fig.) adventure **(b)** (Unternehmen) venture **(c)** (Liebesaffäre) affair

abenteuerlich *Adj.* **(a)** (riskant) risky **(b)** (bizarr) bizarre

Abenteuer-: ~lust *die* thirst for adventure; ~roman *der* adventure novel

Abenteurer *der;* ~s, ~: adventurer

Abenteurerin *die;* ~, ~nen adventuress

aber ① *Konj.* but ② *Partikel* ~ ja/nein! why, yes/no! ~ natürlich! but of course!; du bist ~ groß! aren't you tall!

Aber·glaube[n] *der* superstition

aber·gläubisch *Adj.* superstitious

abermals *Adv.* once again; once more

Abf. *Abk.* = **Abfahrt** dep.

ạb|fahren ① *unr. itr. V.; mit sein* **(a)** (wegfahren) leave; wo fährt der Zug nach Paris ab? where does the Paris train leave from? **(b)** (hinunterfahren) drive down; (Skisport) ski down **(c)** (salopp: sich begeistern) auf jmdn./etw. [voll] ~: be mad about sb./sth. **(d)** (salopp: abgewiesen werden) jmdn. ~ lassen tell sb. where he/she can go (sl.) ② *unr. tr. V.* **(a)** (abtransportieren) take away **(b)** (abnutzen) wear out; abgefahrene Reifen worn tyres

Ạb·fahrt *die* **(a)** departure **(b)** (Skisport) descent; (Strecke) run

Ạbfahrts-: ~lauf *der* (Skisport) downhill [racing]; ~läufer *der,* ~läuferin *die*

(Skisport) downhill racer; **~rennen** *das*
(Skisport) downhill [racing]; **~zeit** *die* time
of departure; departure time

Ab·fall *der* (Küchen~ o Ä.) rubbish, (Amer.)
trash *no indef. art., no pl.;* (Fleisch~) offal *no
indef. art., no pl.;* (Industrie~) waste *no indef.
art.;* (auf der Straße) litter *no indef. art., no pl.*

Abfall: ~beseitigung *die* refuse
disposal; (industriell) waste disposal; **~eimer**
der rubbish bin; trash can (Amer.); (auf der
Straße) litter bin; trash can (Amer.)

ab|fallen *unr. itr. V.; mit sein* **(a)** fall off
(b) (abschüssig sein) 〈*land, road, etc.*〉 drop
away, slope
(c) (übrigbleiben) be left [over]; **für dich wird
[dabei] auch etwas ~**: you'll get something
out of it too
(d) von jmdm. ~: leave sb.; **vom Glauben ~**:
desert the faith

ab·fällig ① *Adj.* disparaging
② *adv.* **sich ~ über jmdn. äußern** make
disparaging remarks about sb.

Abfall-: ~produkt *das* (auch fig.) by-
product; (Sekundärstoff) secondary product;
~vermeidung *die* waste avoidance

ab|fangen *unr. tr. V.* **(a)** catch; intercept
〈*agent, message, aircraft*〉
(b) repel 〈*charge, assault*〉; ward off 〈*blow,
attack*〉

ab|färben *itr. V.* **(a)** 〈*colour, garment, etc.*〉
run
(b) auf jmdn./etw. ~ (fig.) rub off on sb./sth.

ab|fassen *tr. V.* write 〈*report, letter, etc.*〉;
draw up 〈*will*〉

ab|fegen *tr. V.* **(a)** brush off; **etw. von etw.
~**: brush sth. off sth.
(b) (säubern) **etw. ~**: brush sth. clean

ab|feiern *tr. V.* use up 〈*excess hours
worked*〉 (by taking time off)

ab|fertigen *tr. V.* dispatch 〈*mail*〉; deal
with 〈*applicant*〉; handle 〈*passengers*〉; serve
〈*customer*〉; clear 〈*ship*〉 for sailing; clear
〈*aircraft*〉 for take-off; clear 〈*lorry*〉 for
departure

ab|feuern *tr. V.* fire

ab|finden ① *unr. tr. V.* **jmdn. mit etw. ~**:
compensate sb. with sth.; **seine Gläubiger ~**:
settle with one's creditors
② *unr. refl. V.* **sich ~**: resign oneself; **sich
~ mit** come to terms with; learn to live with
〈*noise, heat*〉

Abfindung *die* **~, ~en** settlement; **eine ~
in Höhe von … zahlen** make a settlement of
…

Abfindungs-summe *die* ▶ ABFINDUNG

ab|flauen *itr. V.; mit sein* die down;
subside; 〈*interest, conversation*〉 flag;
〈*business*〉 become slack; 〈*noise*〉 abate

ab|fliegen *unr. itr. V.; mit sein* leave

ab|fließen *unr. itr. V.; mit sein* flow off

Ab·flug *der* departure

Abflug·zeit *die* departure time

Ab·fluss, *Ab·fluß *der* drain; (Rohr)
drainpipe; (für Abwasser) waste pipe

Ab·folge *die* sequence; **die ~ der
Jahreszeiten** the cycle of the seasons

ab|fotografieren *tr. V.* take pictures of

ab|fragen *tr. V.* test; **jmdm. od. jmdm. die
Vokabeln ~**: test sb. on his/her vocabulary

Abfuhr *die;* **~, ~en (a)** removal
(b) jmdm. eine ~ erteilen (fig. ugs.) rebuff sb.

ab|führen ① *tr. V.* **(a)** (nach Festnahme) take
away
(b) (zahlen) pay out
(c) (abbringen) take away
② *itr. V.* (für Stuhlgang sorgen) be a laxative

Abführ·mittel *das* laxative

ab|füllen *tr. V.* (in Flaschen) bottle; (in Dosen)
can

Ab·gabe *die* **(a)** handing in; (eines Briefes,
Pakets, Telegramms) delivery; (eines Gesuchs,
Antrags) submission
(b) (Steuer, Gebühr) tax; (auf Produkte) duty
(c) (Ausstrahlung) release; emission
(d) (Sport: Abspiel) pass

Ab·gang *der* **(a)** leaving; departure; (Abfahrt)
departure; (Theater) exit
(b) (jmd., der ausscheidet) departure; (Schule)
leaver
(c) (bes. Amtsspr.: Todesfall) death
(d) (Turnen) dismount

Ab·gas *das* exhaust

Abgas·katalysator *der* (Kfz-W.) catalytic
converter

abgearbeitet *Adj.* work-worn 〈*hands*〉

ab|geben ① *unr. tr. V.* **(a)** (aushändigen)
hand over; deliver 〈*letter, parcel, telegram*〉;
hand in, submit 〈*application*〉; hand in
〈*school work*〉; **den Mantel in der Garderobe
~**: leave one's coat in the cloakroom
(b) *auch itr.* **jmdm. [etwas] von etw. ~**: let
sb. have some of sth.
(c) (abfeuern) fire
② *unr. refl. V.* **sich mit jmdm./etw. ~**: spend
time on sb./sth.; (geringschätzig) waste one's
time on sb./sth.

ab·gebrannt *Adj.* (ugs.) broke (coll.)

abgebrüht *Adj.* (ugs.) hardened

ab·gedroschen *Adj.* (ugs.) hackneyed

ab·gegriffen *Adj.* battered

ab|gehen *unr. itr. V.; mit sein* **(a)** (sich
entfernen) leave; (Theater) exit
(b) (ausscheiden) leave
(c) (abfahren) 〈*train, ship, bus*〉 leave, depart
(d) (abgeschickt werden) 〈*message, letter*〉 be
sent [off]
(e) (abzweigen) branch off
(f) (sich lösen) come off

abgehetzt *Adj.* exhausted

ab·gelegen *Adj.* remote; (einsam) isolated;
out-of-the-way 〈*district*〉

abgemagert *Adj.* emaciated; wasted

ab·geneigt *Adj.* averse (*Dat.* to); **[nicht] ~
sein, etw. zu tun** [not] be averse to doing sth.

Abgeordnete der/die; adj. Dekl. member [of parliament]; (z.B. in Frankreich) deputy

ạb·gerissen Adj. ragged

ạb·geschieden Adj. secluded; (abgelegen) isolated

ạb·geschlagen Adj. (Sport) [well] beaten

ạb·geschlossen Adj. secluded

ạb·geschnitten Adj. isolated; **von der Außenwelt** ∼: cut off from the outside world

ạb·gesehen Adv. ∼ **von** apart from; ∼ **davon, dass …** apart from the fact that …

ạb·gespannt Adj. weary; exhausted

ạb·gestanden Adj. flat

ạb·gestorben Adj. dead ⟨branch, tree⟩; numb ⟨fingers, legs, etc.⟩

ạb·getreten Adj. worn down

ạbgewetzt Adj. well-worn; battered ⟨case etc.⟩

ạb|gewöhnen tr. V.: jmdm. etw. ∼: make sb. give up sth.; **sich** (Dat.) **etw.** ∼: give up sth.

ạb|gießen unr. tr. V. pour away ⟨liquid⟩; drain ⟨potatoes⟩

ạbgöttisch Adj. idolatrous

ạb|grenzen tr. V. (a) bound; **etw. gegen** od. **von etw.** ∼: separate sth. from sth. (b) (unterscheiden) distinguish

Ạb·grund der abyss; chasm; (Abhang) precipice

ạb|hacken tr. V. chop off; **jmdm. die Hand** usw. ∼: chop sb.'s hand etc. off

ạb|haken tr. V. tick off; check off (Amer.)

ạb|halten unr. tr. V. (a) jmdn./etw. [von jmdm./etw.] ∼: keep sb./sth. off [sb./sth.] (b) jmdn. davon ∼, etw. zu tun stop sb. doing sth. (c) (durchführen) hold ⟨elections, meeting, referendum⟩

ạb|handeln tr. V. (a) jmdm. etw. ∼: do a deal with sb. for sth. (b) (darstellen) deal with

abhạnden Adv. ∼ **kommen** get lost; go astray; **etw. kommt jmdm.** ∼: sb. loses sth.

Ạb·handlung die treatise (**über** + Akk. on)

Ạb·hang der slope; incline

ạb|hängen¹ unr. itr. V. **von jmdm./etw.** ∼: depend on sb./sth.

ạb|hängen² 1 tr. V. (a) take down (b) (abkuppeln) uncouple (c) (ugs.) shake off ⟨pursuer, competitor⟩ 2 itr. V. (den Hörer auflegen) hang up

ạbhängig Adj. dependent (**von** on); (süchtig) addicted (**von** to); **von jmdm./etw.** ∼ **sein** depend on sb./sth.

Ạbhängige der/die; adj. Dekl. (Rechtsspr.) dependant; (Untergebene) subordinate

Ạbhängigkeit die; ∼, ∼en dependence; (Sucht) addiction

Ạbhängigkeits·verhältnis das relationship of dependence (**zu** on)

ạb|härten tr. V. harden

ạb|hauen 1 unr. tr. V. (a) Prät. **haute ab** knock off (b) Prät. **hieb** (geh.) od. **haute ab** (mit Schwert, Axt usw.) chop off 2 unr. itr. V.; mit sein; Prät. **haute ab** (salopp) beat it (coll.)

ạb|heben 1 unr. tr. V. (a) lift off ⟨lid, cover, etc.⟩; [**den Hörer**] ∼: answer [the telephone] (b) (von einem Konto) withdraw ⟨money⟩ 2 unr. itr. V. ⟨balloon⟩ rise; ⟨aircraft, bird⟩ take off; ⟨rocket⟩ lift off 3 unr. refl. V. stand out (**von** against)

ạb|heften tr. V. file

ạb|hetzen refl. V. rush [around]; s. auch ABGEHETZT

Ạb·hilfe die action to improve matters; ∼ **schaffen** put things right

ạb|holen tr. V. collect; pick up ⟨parcel, book, tickets, etc.⟩; pick up ⟨person⟩

ạb|hören tr. V. (a) jmdm. od. jmdn. **Vokabeln** ∼: test sb.'s vocabulary [orally]; **das Einmaleins** ∼: ask questions on the multiplication tables (b) tap ⟨telephone conversation, telephone⟩; bug (coll.) ⟨conversation, premises⟩; jmdn. ∼: tap sb.'s telephone

ạbhör·sicher Adj. bug-proof (coll.); tap-proof ⟨telephone⟩

Ạbi das; ∼s, ∼s (Schülerspr.), **Abitur** das; ∼s, ∼e Abitur (school-leaving examination at grammar school needed for entry to higher education); ≈ A levels (Brit.)

Abiturient der; ∼en, ∼en, **Abiturientin** die; ∼, ∼nen sb. who is taking/has passed the 'Abitur'

ạb|jagen tr. V. jmdm. etw. ∼: finally get sth. away from sb.

Abk. Abk. = **Abkürzung** abbr.

ạb|kapseln tr. V. encapsulate; **sich gegen die Umwelt** ∼ (fig.) isolate oneself from one's surroundings

ạb|kaufen tr. V. jmdm. etw. ∼: buy sth. from sb.

Ạb·klatsch der (abwertend) pale imitation; poor copy

ạb|klopfen tr. V. (a) knock off (b) (säubern) knock the dirt/snow/crumbs etc. off (c) (untersuchen) tap

ạb|knallen tr. V. (salopp) shoot down; gun down

ạb|knicken 1 tr. V. snap off 2 itr. V.; mit sein snap

ạb|kochen tr. V. boil

ạb|kommen unr. itr. V.; mit sein (a) vom **Weg** ∼: lose one's way; **vom Kurs** ∼: go off course; **von der Fahrbahn** ∼: leave the road; **vom Thema** ∼: stray from the topic (b) **von einem Plan** ∼: abandon a plan

Ạb·kommen das; ∼s, ∼: agreement

ạbkömmlich Adj. free; available

---

ab|können *unr. tr. V.* (nordd.: mögen) stand; (vertragen) take

ab|kratzen ⓵ *tr. V.* (a) (mit den Fingern) scratch off; (mit einem Werkzeug) scrape off
(b) (säubern) scrape [clean]
⓶ *itr. V.; mit sein* (derb) snuff it (sl.)

ab|kriegen *tr. V.* (ugs.) ▶ ABBEKOMMEN

ab|kühlen ⓵ *tr. V.* cool down
⓶ *itr., refl. V.; itr. meist mit sein* cool down

Ab-kühlung *die* cooling

ab|kupfern *tr. V.* (ugs.) copy mechanically (**bei** from)

ab|kürzen *tr., itr. V.* (a) (räumlich) shorten; **den Weg** ∼: take a shorter route
(b) (zeitlich) cut short
(c) (kürzer schreiben) abbreviate (**mit** to)

Ab-kürzung *die* (a) (Weg) short cut
(b) (Wort) abbreviation

ab|küssen *tr. V.* cover with kisses

ab|laden *unr. tr., itr. V.* unload

Ab-lage *die* (a) storage place
(b) (Raum) storage room
(c) (Bürow.) filing

ab|lagern *tr. V.* deposit

ab|lassen ⓵ *unr. tr. V.* let out (**aus** of); let off ⟨steam⟩
⓶ *unr. itr. V.* (a) **von jmdm./etw.** ∼: leave sb./sth. alone
(b) **von etw.** ∼ (etw. aufgeben) give sth. up

Ab-lauf *der* (a) (Verlauf) course; (einer Veranstaltung) passing off
(b) (Ende) **nach** ∼ **eines Jahres** after a year; **nach** ∼ **einer Frist** at the end of a period of time

ab|laufen *unr. itr. V.; mit sein* (a) flow away; (aus einem Behälter) run out
(b) (verlaufen) pass off
(c) ⟨alarm clock⟩ run down; ⟨parking meter⟩ expire
(d) ⟨period, contract, passport⟩ expire

ab|lecken *tr. V.* (a) lick off
(b) (säubern) lick clean

ab|legen ⓵ *tr. V.* (a) lay *or* put down
(b) (Bürow.) file
(c) stop wearing ⟨clothes⟩
(d) give up ⟨habit⟩; lose ⟨shyness⟩
(e) swear ⟨oath⟩; sit ⟨examination⟩; make ⟨confession⟩
⓶ *tr., itr. V.* take off; **möchten Sie** ∼? would you like to take your coat off?
⓷ *itr. V.* [**vom Kai**] ∼: cast off

Ableger *der;* ∼**s,** ∼: layer; (Steckling) cutting

ab|lehnen *tr. V.* (a) decline; decline, turn down ⟨money, invitation, position⟩; reject ⟨suggestion, applicant⟩
(b) (missbilligen) disapprove of

Ablehnung *die;* ∼, ∼**en** (a) rejection
(b) (Missbilligung) disapproval

ab|leiten *tr. V.* (a) divert
(b) (herleiten) **etw. aus/von etw.** ∼: derive sth. from sth.

Ab-leitung *die* derivation

ab|lenken *tr. V.* (a) deflect
(b) **jmdn. von etw.** ∼: distract sb. from sth.
(c) (zerstreuen) divert; **sich** ∼: amuse oneself

Ab-lenkung *die* ▶ ABLENKEN: deflection; distraction; diversion

Ablenkungs-manöver *das* diversion[ary tactic]

ab|lesen *unr. tr. V.* (a) read ⟨speech, lecture⟩; **werden Sie frei sprechen oder** ∼? will you be talking from notes or reading your speech?
(b) read ⟨gas meter, thermometer, etc.⟩; check ⟨time, speed, temperature⟩
(c) (erkennen) see

ab|lichten *tr. V.* (a) (fotokopieren) photocopy
(b) (fotografieren) take a photograph of

Ab-lichtung *die* (a) (das Fotografieren) photographing; (das Fotokopieren) photocopying
(b) (Fotokopie) photocopy

ab|liefern *tr., itr. V.* hand in; deliver ⟨goods⟩

ab|lösen ⓵ *tr. V.* (a) etw. [**von etw.**] ∼: get sth. off [sth.]
(b) **jmdn.** ∼: relieve sb.; **sich** *od.* **einander** ∼: take turns
⓶ *refl. V.* **sich** [**von etw.**] ∼: come off [sth.]

Ab-lösung *die* (eines Postens) changing; **ich schicke Ihnen jemanden zur** ∼: I'll send someone to relieve you

ab|machen *tr. V.* (a) (ugs.) take off; take down ⟨sign, rope⟩
(b) (vereinbaren) agree

Abmachung *die;* ∼, ∼**en** agreement

ab|magern *itr. V.; mit sein* become thin; (absichtlich) slim

Abmagerungs-kur *die* reducing diet

ab|marschieren *itr. V.; mit sein* depart; (Milit.) march off

ab|melden *tr. V.* (a) **sich/jmdn.** ∼: report that one/sb. is leaving
(b) (Umzug melden) notify the authorities that one is moving from an address;
(c) **ein Auto** ∼: cancel a car's registration
(d) (DV) ▶ AUSLOGGEN

Ab-meldung *die* (a) (beim Weggehen) report that one is leaving
(b) (beim Umzug) registration of a move with the authorities at one's old address;
(c) ∼ **eines Autos** cancellation of a car's registration

Ab-messung *die* (Dimension) dimension; measurement

ab|montieren *tr. V.* take off ⟨part⟩; dismantle ⟨machine, equipment⟩

ab|mühen *refl. V.* toil; **sie mühte sich mit dem schweren Koffer ab** she struggled with the heavy suitcase

ab|murksen *tr. V.* (salopp) do in (sl.)

Abnahme *die;* ∼, ∼**n** (a) (das Entfernen) removal
(b) (Verminderung) decrease

ab|nehmen 1 *unr. tr. V.* (a) (entfernen)
take off; take down ⟨*picture, curtain, lamp*⟩
(b) jmdm. den Koffer ∼: take sb.'s suitcase;
jmdm. eine Arbeit ∼: save sb. a job
(c) jmdm. ein Versprechen/einen Eid ∼:
make sb. give a promise/swear an oath
(d) (prüfen) inspect and approve; test and
pass ⟨*vehicle*⟩
(e) jmdm. etw. ∼ (wegnehmen) take sth. off sb.
(f) (beim Telefon) answer ⟨*telephone*⟩; pick up
⟨*receiver*⟩
(g) (Handarb.) decrease
(h) das nehme ich dir/ihm *usw.* nicht ab I
won't buy that (coll.)
2 *unr. itr. V.* (a) (Gewicht verlieren) lose
weight
(b) (sich verringern) decrease; drop; ⟨*attention,
interest*⟩ flag; ⟨*brightness*⟩ diminish; wir
haben ∼den Mond there is a waning moon
(c) (beim Telefon) answer the telephone

Ab·neigung *die* dislike (gegen for)

ab|nutzen, (landsch.:) **ab|nützen** *tr., refl.*
V. wear out; abgenutzt worn

Abonnement /abɔnəˈmãː/ *das;* ∼s, ∼s
subscription (*Gen.* to)

Abonnent *der;* ∼en, ∼en, **Abonnentin**
die; ∼, ∼nen subscriber (+ *Gen.* to); (Theater,
Oper) season ticket holder

abonnieren *tr. V.* subscribe to

Ab·ordnung *die* delegation

ab|packen *tr. V.* pack; wrap ⟨*bread*⟩;
abgepacktes Obst/abgepackte
Fleischportionen packaged fruit/pieces of
meat

ab|passen *tr. V.* (a) (abwarten) wait for
(b) (aufhalten) catch

ab|pausen *tr. V.* trace

ab|pfeifen (Sport) 1 *itr. V.* blow the whistle
2 *tr. V.* [blow the whistle to] stop

Ab·pfiff *der* (Sport) final whistle; (Halbzeit∼)
half-time whistle

ab|pflücken *tr. V.* pick

ab|plagen *refl. V.* slave away

ab|prallen *itr. V.; mit sein* rebound; ⟨*bullet,
missile*⟩ ricochet

Ab·produkt *das* waste product

ab|putzen *tr. V.* (ugs.) (a) wipe off
(b) (säubern) wipe; jmdm./sich das Gesicht ∼:
clean sb.'s/one's face

ab|quälen *refl. V.* sich [mit etw.] ∼:
struggle [with sth.]

ab|rackern *refl. V.* (ugs.) flog oneself to
death (coll.)

ab|rasieren *tr. V.* shave off

ab|raten *unr. itr. V.* jmdm. von etw. ∼:
advise sb. against sth.

ab|räumen *tr. V.* (a) clear away
(b) (leer machen) clear ⟨*table*⟩

ab|rechnen 1 *itr. V.* cash up; mit jmdm.
∼ (fig.) call sb. to account

2 *tr. V.* die Kasse ∼: reckon up the till;
seine Spesen ∼: claim one's expenses

Ab·rechnung *die* (a) cashing up *no art.;*
(Aufstellung) statement
(b) (fig.: Vergeltung) reckoning

Ab·rede *die* (a) arrangement; agreement
(b) etw. in ∼ stellen deny sth.

ab|regen *refl. V.* (ugs.) calm down; reg dich
ab! cool it! (coll.); calm down!

ab|reiben *unr. tr. V.* (a) rub off
(b) (säubern) rub

Ab·reise *die* departure (nach for); bei
meiner ∼: when I left/leave

ab|reisen *itr. V.; mit sein* leave (nach for)

ab|reißen 1 *unr. tr. V.* (a) tear off; tear
down ⟨*poster, notice*⟩; pull off ⟨*button*⟩
(b) (niederreißen) demolish, pull down
⟨*building*⟩
2 *unr. itr. V.; mit sein* (a) fly off; ⟨*shoelace*⟩
break off
(b) (aufhören) come to an end; ⟨*connection,
contact*⟩ be broken off

ab|richten *tr. V.* train

Ab·riss, *Ab·riß *der* (a) ▶ ABREISSEN 1B:
demolition; pulling down
(b) (knappe Darstellung) outline

ab|rollen 1 *tr. V.* unwind
2 *itr. V.; mit sein* unwind [itself]

ab|rücken 1 *tr. V.* (wegschieben) move
away
2 *itr. V.; mit sein* move away

Ab·ruf *der:* auf ∼: on call; (DV) in
retrievable form

ab|rufen *unr. tr. V.* summon; call

ab|runden *tr. V.* (a) (auch fig.) round off
(b) round ⟨*figure*⟩ up/down (auf + Akk. to);
etw. nach oben/unten ∼: round sth. up/down

abrupt 1 *Adj.* abrupt
2 *adv.* abruptly

ab|rüsten *itr., tr. V.* disarm

Ab·rüstung *die;* ∼: disarmament

ab|rutschen *itr. V.; mit sein* (a) slip
(b) (nach unten rutschen) slide down

Abs. *Abk.* (a) = **Absender;**
(b) = **Absatz**

ABS *Abk.* = **Antiblockiersystem** ABS

Ab·sage *die* (auf eine Einladung) refusal; (auf
eine Bewerbung) rejection

ab|sagen 1 *tr. V.* cancel; withdraw
⟨*participation*⟩
2 *itr. V.* jmdm. ∼: tell sb. one cannot come

ab|sägen *tr. V.* saw off

Ab·satz *der* (a) (am Schuh) heel
(b) (Textunterbrechung) break
(c) (Textabschnitt) paragraph
(d) (Kaufmannsspr.) sales *pl.*

Absatz-: ∼**chance** *die* (Kaufmannsspr.)
sales prospect; ∼**förderung** *die*
(Kaufmannsspr.) sales promotion; ∼**markt** *der*
(Kaufmannsspr.) market; ∼**steigerung** *die*
(Kaufmannsspr.) increase in sales

absaufen ···⊱ Abschuss · · · ·

ab|saufen *unr. itr. V.; mit sein* (ugs.)
⟨*engine, car*⟩ flood

ab|saugen *tr. V.* (a) suck away
(b) (säubern) hoover (Brit.)

ab|schaben *tr. V.* (a) scrape off
(b) (säubern) scrape [clean]

ab|schaffen *tr. V.* (a) (beseitigen) abolish
⟨*capital punishment, regulation, customs
duty, institution*⟩; repeal ⟨*law*⟩; put an end to
⟨*injustice, abuse*⟩
(b) (weggeben) get rid of

Ab·schaffung *die* abolition; (von Gesetzen)
repeal; (von Unrecht, Missstand) ending

ab|schalten *tr., itr. V.* switch off; shut
down ⟨*power station*⟩

abschätzig ① *Adj.* derogatory
② *adv.* derogatorily

Ab·scheu *der;* ∼s detestation; abhorrence

abscheulich ① *Adj.* (a) disgusting
⟨*smell, taste*⟩; repulsive ⟨*sight*⟩
(b) (verwerflich) disgraceful ⟨*behaviour*⟩;
abominable ⟨*crime*⟩
② *adv.* disgracefully

ab|schicken *tr. V.* send [off]

ab|schieben *unr. tr. V.* (a) push away
(b) (abwälzen) shift ⟨*responsibility, blame*⟩
(c) (außer Landes bringen) deport

Ab·schiebung *die* (Rechtsw.) deportation

Abschiebungs·haft *die* (Rechtsw.)
detention prior to deportation

Abschied *der;* ∼[e]s, ∼e parting (von
from); farewell (von to); ∼ **nehmen** take
one's leave (von of)

Abschieds-: ∼**brief** *der* farewell letter;
∼**geschenk** *das* parting gift; ∼**gruß** *der*
goodbye; farewell

ab|schießen *unr. tr. V.* (a) shoot down
⟨*aeroplane*⟩
(b) fire ⟨*arrow*⟩; launch ⟨*spacecraft*⟩
(c) (töten) take

ab|schirmen *tr. V.* (a) (schützen) shield
(b) (fernhalten) screen off ⟨*light, radiation*⟩

ab|schlachten *tr. V.* slaughter

Ab·schlag *der* (a) (Kaufmannsspr.) discount
(b) (Teilzahlung) interim payment; (Vorschuss)
advance
(c) (Fußball) goalkeeper's kick out

ab|schlagen ① *unr. tr. V.* (a) knock off;
(mit dem Beil, Schwert usw.) chop off
(b) (ablehnen) refuse
(c) (abwehren) beat off
② *unr. itr. V.* (Fußball) kick the ball out

ab|schleifen *unr. tr. V.* (von Holz) sand off;
(von Metall, Glas usw.) grind off

Abschlepp·dienst *der* breakdown
recovery service; tow[ing] service (Amer.)

ab|schleppen tow away; take ⟨*ship*⟩ in
tow; **ein Auto zur Werkstatt** ∼: tow a car to
the garage

Abschlepp: ∼**seil** *das* tow rope; (aus
Draht) towing cable; ∼**stange** *die* tow bar;
∼**wagen** *der* breakdown vehicle; tow
truck (Amer.); (der Polizei) tow-away vehicle

ab|schließen ① *unr. tr. V.* (a) auch itr.
(zuschließen) lock ⟨*door, gate, cupboard*⟩; lock
[up] ⟨*house, flat, room, park*⟩
(b) (verschließen) seal; **etw. luftdicht** ∼: seal
sth. hermetically
(c) (begrenzen) border
(d) (zum Abschluss bringen) conclude; **sein
Studium** ∼: finish one's studies; **Bewerber
mit abgeschlossenem Universitätsstudium**
applicants with a degree
(e) (vereinbaren) strike ⟨*bargain, deal*⟩; make
⟨*purchase*⟩; enter into ⟨*agreement*⟩
② *unr. itr. V.* (aufhören, enden) end; ∼**d sagte
er ...:** in conclusion he said ...

Ab·schluss, *Ab·schluß *der* (a)
(Verschluss) seal
(b) (Beendigung) conclusion; end
(c) (eines Geschäfts, Vertrags) conclusion

Abschluss-, *Abschluß-: ∼**ball** *der*
final dance; ∼**prüfung** *die* (a) (Schulw.)
leaving *or* (Amer.) final examination;
(Hochschulw.) final examination; finals *pl.;* (b)
(Wirtsch.) audit

ab|schmecken *tr. V.* (a) (kosten) taste; try
(b) (würzen) season

ab|schmieren *tr. V.* (Technik) grease

ab|schminken *tr. V.* jmdn./sich ∼:
remove sb.'s/one's make-up

ab|schmirgeln *tr. V.* rub off with emery;
(mit Sandpapier) sand off

ab|schnallen *tr. V.* unfasten

ab|schneiden ① *unr. tr. V.* (a) (auch fig.:
isolieren) cut off; cut down ⟨*sth. hanging*⟩; **etw.
von etw.** ∼: cut sth. off sth.; **sich** (*Dat.*) **eine
Scheibe Brot** ∼: cut oneself a slice of bread
(b) (kürzer schneiden) cut
(c) jmdm. den Weg ∼: take a short cut to
get ahead of sb.
② *unr. itr. V.* **bei etw. gut/schlecht** ∼: do
well/badly in sth.

Ab·schnitt *der* (a) (Kapitel) section
(b) (Zeitspanne) phase
(c) (Teil eines Formulars) [detachable] portion

ab|schrauben *tr. V.* unscrew [and
remove]

ab|schrecken *tr. V.* (a) deter
(b) (fernhalten) scare off
(c) (Kochk.) pour cold water over

Abschreckung *die;* ∼, ∼**en** deterrence;
(Mittel zur Abschreckung) deterrent

ab|schreiben ① *unr. tr. V.* (a) copy out;
etw. bei *od.* **von jmdm.** ∼ (in der Schule) copy
sth. off sb.; (als Plagiator) plagiarize sth. from
sb.
(b) (Wirtsch.) amortize
② *unr. itr. V.* **bei** *od.* **von jmdm.** ∼ (in der
Schule) copy off sb.; (als Plagiator) copy from
sb.

Ab·schreibung *die* (Wirtsch.) amortization

Ab·schrift *die* copy

ab|schürfen *tr. V.* graze

Ab·schuss, *Ab·schuß *der* (a) (eines
Flugzeugs) shooting down ···⊱

a

(b) (von Geschossen) firing; (eines Raumschiffs) launching

abschüssig *Adj.* downward sloping ‹*land*›

ab|schütteln *tr. V.* shake off; (herunterschütteln) shake down

ab|schwächen 1 *tr. V.* **(a)** (mildern) tone down ‹*statement, criticism*›
(b) (verringern) lessen ‹*effect, impression*›; cushion ‹*blow, impact*›
2 *refl. V.* ‹*interest, demand*› wane

Abschwächung *die;* ~ **(a)** (Milderung) toning down
(b) (eines Aufpralls, Stoßes usw.) cushioning

ab|schweifen *itr. V.; mit sein* digress

Abschweifung *die;* ~, ~en digression

ab|schwören *unr. itr. V.* dem Teufel/ seinem Glauben ~: renounce the Devil/one's faith; dem Alkohol/Laster ~: forswear alcohol/vice

absehbar *Adj.* foreseeable; in ~er Zeit within the foreseeable future

ab|sehen 1 *unr. tr. V.* **(a)** (voraussehen) predict; foresee ‹*event*›
(b) es auf etw. (*Akk.*) abgesehen haben be after sth.; er hat es darauf abgesehen, uns zu ärgern he's out to annoy us; der Chef hat es auf ihn abgesehen the boss has got it in for him
2 *unr. itr. V.* **(a)** von etw. ~ (etw. nicht beachten) leave aside sth.; *s. auch* ABGESEHEN;
(b) von etw. ~ (auf etw. verzichten) refrain from sth

ab|seilen 1 *tr. V.* lower [with a rope]
2 *refl. V.* (Bergsteigen) abseil

***ab|sein** ▸ AB 2A

abseits 1 *Präp. mit Gen.* away from
2 *Adv.* **(a)** far away
(b) (Ballspiele) ~ sein *od.* stehen be offside

Abseits *das;* ~, ~: das war ein klares ~: that was clearly offside

ab|senden *unr. od. regelm. tr. V.* dispatch

Ab·sender *der,* **Ab·senderin** *die;* ~, ~nen sender; (Anschrift) sender's address

ab|setzen 1 *tr. V.* **(a)** take off ‹*hat, glasses, etc.*›
(b) (hinstellen) put down ‹*bag, suitcase*›
(c) (aussteigen lassen) jmdn. ~ (im öffentlichen Verkehr) put sb. down; let sb. out (Amer.); (im privaten Verkehr) drop sb. [off]
(d) remove ‹*chancellor, judge*› from office; depose ‹*king, emperor*›
2 *refl. V.* **(a)** (sich ablagern) be deposited
(b) (flüchten) get away

Absetzung *die;* ~, ~en ▸ ABSETZEN 1D: removal; deposition

ab|sichern 1 *tr. V.* make safe
2 *refl. V.* safeguard oneself

Ab·sicht *die* intention; etw. mit ~ tun do sth. intentionally; etw. ohne *od.* nicht mit ~ tun do sth. unintentionally

ab·sichtlich 1 *Adj.* intentional; deliberate

2 *adv.* intentionally; deliberately

ab|sinken *unr. itr. V.; mit sein* sink

absolut *Adj.* absolute

Absolutismus *der;* ~ (hist.) absolutism *no art.*

Absolvent /...'vɛnt/ *der;* ~en, ~en, **Absolventin** *die;* ~, ~nen (einer Schule) one who has taken the leaving *or* (Amer.) final examination; (einer Akademie) graduate

absolvieren *tr. V.* complete

Absolvierung *die;* ~: completion

ab·sonderlich *Adj.* strange; odd

ab|sondern 1 *tr. V.* exude; (Physiol.) secrete
2 *refl. V.* isolate oneself

absorbieren *tr. V.* absorb

ab|speisen *tr. V.* jmdn. mit etw. ~: fob sb. off with sth.

abspenstig *Adj.* jmdm. etw. ~ machen get sb. to part with sth.

ab|sperren *tr. V.* seal off; close off

Ab·spiel *das* (Ballspiele) passing

ab|spielen 1 *tr. V.* **(a)** play ‹*record, tape*›
(b) vom Blatt ~: ‹*piece of music*› play at sight
(c) (Ballspiele) pass
2 *refl. V.* take place

Ab·sprache *die* arrangement; eine ~ treffen make an arrangement

ab|sprechen *unr. tr. V.* **(a)** jmdm. etw. ~: deny that sb. has sth.
(b) (vereinbaren) arrange

ab|springen *unr. itr. V.; mit sein* jump off; (herunterspringen) jump down; vom Fahrrad ~: jump off one's bicycle

Ab·sprung *der* take-off; (das Herunterspringen) jump

ab|spülen 1 *tr. V.* **(a)** wash off
(b) (reinigen) rinse off; sich (*Dat.*) die Hände usw. ~: rinse one's hands *etc.*; das Geschirr ~ (bes. südd.) wash the dishes
2 *itr. V.* (bes. südd.) wash up

ab|stammen *itr. V.* be descended (von from)

Abstammung *die;* ~, ~en descent

Ab·stand *der* **(a)** distance; in 20 Meter ~: at a distance of 20 metres
(b) (Unterschied) gap

ab|stauben *tr., itr. V.* dust

Abstecher *der;* ~s, ~: side trip

ab|stehen *unr. itr. V.* ‹*hair*› stand up; ‹*pigtail[s]*› stick out; ~de Ohren protruding ears

Ab·steige *die;* ~, ~n (ugs. abwertend) cheap and crummy hotel (coll. derog.)

ab|steigen *unr. itr. V.; mit sein* **(a)** [vom Pferd/Fahrrad] ~: get off [one's horse/ bicycle]
(b) (abwärts gehen) go down

ab|stellen *tr. V.* **(a)** put down
(b) (unterbringen) put; (parken) park
(c) (ausschalten, abdrehen) turn off

(d) (unterbinden) put a stop to
Abstell-: ~**kammer** die, ~**raum** der lumber room
ab|stempeln tr. V. **(a)** frank ⟨letter⟩; cancel ⟨stamp⟩
(b) (fig.) label, brand (**zu, als** as)
ab|sterben unr. itr. V.; mit sein **(a)** [gradually] die
(b) (gefühllos werden) go numb
Abstieg der; ~[e]s, ~e **(a)** descent
(b) (Niedergang) decline
ab|stimmen ① itr. V. vote (**über** + Akk. on)
② tr. V. etw. mit jmdm. ~: discuss and agree on sth. with sb.
Ab·stimmung die **(a)** vote; **während der** ~: during the voting
(b) (Absprache) agreement
abstinent /apstiˈnɛnt/ Adj. teetotal; ~ **sein** be a teetotaler
Abstinenz die; ~: teetotalism
Abstinenzler der; ~s, ~,
Abstinenzlerin die; ~, ~nen teetotaller
ab|stoppen ① tr. V. halt; stop; check ⟨advance⟩
② itr. V. come to a halt; ⟨person⟩ stop
Ab·stoß der (Fußball) goal kick
ab|stoßen unr. tr. V. **(a)** push off
(b) (beschädigen) chip ⟨crockery, paintwork, plaster⟩
(c) (verkaufen) sell off
(d) (anwidern) repel; put off
abstoßend Adj. repulsive
abstrakt /apˈstrakt/ Adj. abstract
ab|streifen tr. V. pull off; strip off ⟨berries⟩; **die Asche [von der Zigarette/ Zigarre]** ~: remove the ash [from one's cigarette/cigar]
ab|streiten unr. tr. V. deny
Ab·strich der **(a)** (Med.) swab; **einen** ~ **machen** take a swab
(b) (Streichung, Kürzung) cut; ~**e machen** make cuts (**an** + Dat. in)
ab|stumpfen itr. V.; mit sein jmd. **stumpft ab** (wird unsensibel) sb.'s mind becomes deadened
Ab·sturz der fall; (eines Flugzeugs) crash
ab|stürzen itr. V.; mit sein fall; ⟨aircraft, pilot, passenger⟩ crash
Absturz·ursache die cause of the crash
ab|stützen ① refl. V. support oneself (**mit on, an** + Dat. against)
② tr. V. support
ab|suchen tr. V. search (**nach** for)
absurd Adj. absurd
absurderweise Adv. absurdly enough
Absurdität die; ~, ~en absurdity; (Ungereimtheit) inconsistency
Abszess, *Abszeß der; Abszesses, Abszesse **(a)** (Med.) abscess
(b) (Geschwür) ulcer
Abszisse die; ~, ~n (Math.) abscissa

Abt der; ~[e]s, Äbte abbot
Abt. Abk. = **Abteilung**
ab|tasten tr. V. etw. ~: feel sth. all over
ab|tauen ① itr. V.; mit sein (eis-/schneefrei werden) become clear of ice/snow; ⟨refrigerator⟩ defrost
② tr. V. melt; thaw; defrost ⟨refrigerator⟩
Abtei die; ~, ~en abbey
Abteil das; ~[e]s, ~e compartment
Ab·teilung die department
Abteilungs·leiter der,
Abteilungs·leiterin die head of department
ab|tippen tr. V. (ugs.) type out
Äbtissin die; ~, ~nen abbess
ab|tönen tr. V. tint
ab|töten tr. V. destroy ⟨parasites, germs⟩; deaden ⟨nerve, feeling⟩
ab|tragen unr. tr. V. (abnutzen) wear out; **abgetragen** well worn
abträglich Adj. (geh.) **einer Sache** (Dat.) ~ **sein** be detrimental to sth.
Ab·transport der ▶ ABTRANSPORTIEREN: taking away; removal
ab|transportieren tr. V. take away; remove ⟨dead, injured⟩
ab|treiben ① unr. tr. V. **(a)** carry away; **jmdn./ein Schiff vom Kurs** ~: drive sb./a ship off course
(b) abort ⟨foetus⟩; **ein Kind** ~ **lassen** have an abortion
② unr. itr. V.; mit sein be carried away; ⟨ship⟩ be driven off course
Abtreibung die; ~, ~en abortion
ab|trennen tr. V. detach
ab|treten ① unr. tr. V. **(a) sich** (Dat.) **die Füße/Schuhe** ~: wipe one's feet
(b) jmdm. etw. ~: let sb. have sth.
② unr. itr. V.; mit sein **(a)** (Theater) exit; (fig.) make one's exit
(b) (zurücktreten) step down; ⟨monarch⟩ abdicate
Abtreter der; ~s, ~: doormat
ab|trocknen tr. V. dry; **sich** (Dat.) **die Hände/die Tränen** ~: dry one's hands/tears
ab|tropfen itr. V.; mit sein drip off
abtrünnig Adj. (einer Partei) renegade; (einer Religion, Sekte) apostate; **der Kirche/dem Glauben** ~ **werden** desert the Church/the faith
ab|tun unr. tr. V. dismiss
ab|wägen unr. od. regelm. tr., itr. V. weigh up; **abgewogen** carefully weighted; balanced ⟨judgement⟩
ab|wählen tr. V. vote out; drop ⟨school subject⟩
ab|wandeln tr. V. adapt
ab|wandern itr. V.; mit sein migrate; (in ein anderes Land) emigrate
Abwanderung die migration; (in ein anderes Land) emigration
Ab·wandlung die adaptation

Ab·wärme die (Technik) waste heat

ab|warten ⓵ itr. V. wait; **sie warteten ab** they awaited events; **warte ab!** wait and see; (als Drohung) just you wait!
⓶ tr. V. wait for

abwärts Adv. downwards; (bergab) downhill; **den Fluss ∼:** downstream

Abwärts·trend der downward trend

Abwasch der; ∼[e]s washing-up (Brit.); washing dishes (Amer.); **den ∼ machen** do the washing-up/wash the dishes

abwaschbar Adj. washable

ab|waschen ⓵ unr. tr. V. (a) wash off (b) (reinigen) wash down; wash [up] ‹dishes›
⓶ unr. itr. V. wash up (Brit.); wash the dishes (Amer.)

Ab·wasser das; Pl. Abwässer sewage

Abwasser: ∼aufbereitung die; ∼∼: sewage treatment; **∼kanal** der sewer

ab|watschen tr. V. (ugs.) lambaste (coll.)

ab|wechseln refl., itr. V. alternate; **wir wechselten uns ab** we took turns

abwechselnd Adv. alternately

Abwechslung die; ∼, ∼en variety; (Wechsel) change; **zur ∼:** for a change

Ab·weg der: **auf ∼e kommen** od. **geraten** go astray

abwegig erroneous; false ‹suspicion›

Ab·wehr die; ∼ (a) repulsion; (von Schlägen) fending off; (Sport) clearance; clearing (Amer.)
(b) (Sport: Hintermannschaft) defence

ab|wehren tr. V. (a) repulse; fend off ‹blow›; (Sport) clear ‹ball, shot›
(b) avert ‹danger, consequences›

Abwehr: ∼kraft die power of resistance; **∼spieler** der, **∼spielerin** die (Sport) defender

ab|weichen unr. itr. V.; mit sein (a) deviate
(b) (sich unterscheiden) differ

Abweichung die; ∼, ∼en (a) deviation
(b) (Unterschied) difference

ab|weisen unr. tr. V. turn away; turn down ‹applicant, suitor›

abweisend Adj. cold ‹look, tone of voice›; **in ∼em Ton** coldly

Ab·weisung die; ▶ ABWEISEN: turning away; turning down

ab|wenden ⓵ unr. od. regelm. tr. V. (a) turn away
(b) nur regelm. (verhindern) avert
⓶ unr. od. regelm. refl. V. turn away

ab|werben unr. tr. V. lure away

ab|werfen ⓵ unr. tr. V. (a) drop; throw off ‹clothing›; jettison ‹ballast›; throw ‹rider›
(b) (ins Spielfeld werfen) throw out ‹ball›
(c) (einbringen) bring in; **Profit ∼:** make a profit
⓶ unr. itr. V. (Sport) throw the ball out

ab|werten tr., itr. V. devalue

abwertend Adj. derogatory ‹term›

Ab·wertung die devaluation

abwesend Adj. absent

Abwesenheit die; ∼: absence

ab|wickeln tr. V. (a) unwind
(b) (erledigen) deal with ‹case›; do ‹business›

Abwicklung die; ∼, ∼en ▶ ABWICKELN 1B: dealing (Gen. with); doing

ab|wiegen unr. tr. V. weigh out; weigh ‹single item›

ab|wimmeln tr. V. (ugs.) get rid of

ab|winken itr. V. uninteressiert ∼: wave it/them aside uninterestedly; **Skat dreschen bis zum Abwinken** (ugs.) play skat till you can't stand any more (coll.); **Champagner bis zum Abwinken** (ugs.) more champagne than you can drink

ab|wischen tr. V. (a) wipe away
(b) (säubern) wipe

Ab·wurf der (a) dropping; (von Ballast) jettisoning
(b) beim ∼ stolperte der Torwart the goalkeeper stumbled as he threw the ball out

ab|zahlen tr. V. pay off ‹debt, loan›

ab|zählen tr. V. count

Ab·zahlung die paying off; **etw. auf ∼ kaufen/verkaufen** buy/sell sth. on easy terms

Ab·zeichen das emblem; (Ansteckbadel, Plakette) badge

ab|zeichnen ⓵ tr. V. (a) (kopieren) copy
(b) (signieren) initial
⓶ refl. V. stand out; (fig.) begin to emerge

Abzieh·bild das transfer

ab|ziehen ⓵ unr. tr. V. (a) pull off; peel off ‹skin›; strip ‹bed›
(b) (Fot.) make a print/prints of
(c) (Milit., auch fig.) withdraw
(d) (subtrahieren) subtract; take away; (abrechnen) deduct
⓶ unr. itr. V.; mit sein (a) (sich verflüchtigen) escape
(b) (Milit.) withdraw

Ab·zug der (a) (an einer Schusswaffe) trigger
(b) (Fot.) print
(c) (Verminderung) deduction

abzüglich Präp. mit Gen. (Kaufmannsspr.) less

ab|zweigen ⓵ itr. V.; mit sein branch off
⓶ tr. V. put aside

Abzweigung die; ∼, ∼en turn-off; (Gabelung) fork

ach Interj. (a) (betroffen, mitleidig) oh [dear]
(b) (bedauernd, unwirsch) oh
(c) (klagend) ah
(d) (erstaunt) oh; ∼, **wirklich?** no, really?; ∼, **der!** oh, him!
(e) ∼ **so!** oh, I see; ∼ **was** od. **wo!** of course not

Achat der; ∼[e]s, ∼e (Min.) agate

Achse die; ∼, ∼n (a) (Rad∼) axle
(b) (Dreh∼, Math., Astron.) axis

---

*old spelling - see note on page xiv

Achsel *die;* ~, ~n (Schulter) shoulder; (~höhle) armpit

Achsel-: ~**haare** *Pl.* armpit hair *sing.;* ~**höhle** *die* armpit

acht¹ *Kardinalz.* eight; um ~ [Uhr] at eight [o'clock]; um halb ~: at half past seven; drei viertel ~, Viertel vor ~: [a] quarter to eight; es steht ~ zu ~/~ zu zwei (Sport) the score is eight all/eight to two

acht²: sie waren zu ~: there were eight of them

acht... *Ordinalz.* eighth; der ~e September the eighth of September; München, [den] 8. Mai 1984 Munich, 8 May 1984

Acht¹ *die;* ~, ~en (a) eight
(b) (Figur) figure eight
(c) (Verbiegung) buckle; mein Rad hat eine ~: my wheel is buckled

Acht² *etw.* außer ~ lassen disregard sth.; sich in ~ nehmen be careful; sich vor jmdm./etw. in ~ nehmen be wary of sb./sth.; auf jmdn./etw. ~ geben take care of sb./sth.; ~ geben be careful

Achte *der/die; adj. Dekl.* eighth

acht-, Acht-: ~**eck** *das* octagon; ~**eckig** *Adj.* octagonal; ~**einhalb** *Bruchz.* eight and a half

achtel *Bruchz.* eighth

Achtel *das* (schweiz. meist *der*); ~s, ~: eighth

Achtel·note *die* (Musik) quaver

achten ① *tr. V.* respect
② *itr. V.* auf etw. (*Akk.*) ~: pay heed to sth.

achtens *Adv.* eighthly

Achterbahn *die* roller coaster

acht·fach *Vervielfältigungsz.* eightfold; die ~fache Menge eight times the quantity; ~fach vergrößert/verkleinert magnified/reduced eight times; das Achtfache kosten cost eight times as much

*****acht|geben ▶ ACHT²

acht-: ~**hundert** *Kardinalz.* eight hundred; ~**jährig** *Adj.* (8 Jahre alt) eight-year-old *attrib.;* eight years old *pred.;* (8 Jahre dauernd) eight-year *attrib.;* ~**köpfig** *Adj.* ⟨family, committee⟩ of eight

acht·los ① *Adj.* heedless
② *adv.* heedlessly

Achtlosigkeit *die;* ~: heedlessness

acht-: ~**mal** *Adv.* eight times; ~**spurig** *Adj.* eight-lane ⟨road⟩; eight-track ⟨cassette⟩; ~**stellig** *Adj.* eight-figure *attrib.;* ~stellig sein have eight figures; ~**stimmig** ① *Adj.* eight-part *attrib.;* ② *adv.* in eight parts; ~**stöckig** *Adj.* eight-storey *attrib.;* ~**tägig** *Adj.* (8 Tage alt) eight-day-old *attrib.;* (8 Tage dauernd) eight-day[-long] *attrib.;* ~**tausend** *Kardinalz.* eight thousand; ~**teilig** *Adj.* eight-piece ⟨tea service, tool set, etc.⟩; eight-part ⟨series, serial⟩

Achtung *die;* ~ (a) respect (vor + *Dat.,* Gen.* for)

(b) ~! watch out!; ~, fertig, los! on your marks, get set, go!

acht·zehn *Kardinalz.* eighteen; **18 Uhr 33** 6.33p.m.; (auf der 24-Stunden-Uhr) 1833

achtzehn·jährig *Adj.* (18 Jahre alt) eighteen-year-old *attrib.;* eighteen years old *pred.;* (18 Jahre dauernd) eighteen-year *attrib.*

achtzig *Kardinalz.* eighty; [mit] ~ [km/h] fahren drive at *or* (coll.) do eighty [k.p.h.]; über/etwa ~ [Jahre alt] sein be over/about eighty [years old]; mit ~ [Jahren] at eighty [years of age]

achtzig·jährig *Adj.* (80 Jahre alt) eighty-year-old *attrib.;* eighty years old *pred.;* (80 Jahre dauernd) eighty-year *attrib.*

ächzen *itr. V.* groan

Acker *der;* ~s, Äcker field

Acker: ~**bau** *der* arable farming; ~**land** *das* farmland

A.D. *Abk.* = **Anno Domini** AD

ADAC *Abk.* = **Allgemeiner Deutscher Automobilclub**

Adams·apfel *der* (ugs.) Adam's apple

adäquat /atɛ'kvaːt/ *Adj.* appropriate (*Dat.* to); suitable (*Dat.* for)

addieren ① *tr. V.* add [up]
② *itr. V.* add

Addition *die;* ~, ~en addition

ade *Interj.* (veralt., landsch.) farewell (dated); bye (coll.); jmdm. ~ *od.* Ade sagen bid farewell to sb.

Adel *der;* ~s nobility; der niedere/hohe ~: the lesser nobility/the aristocracy

adelig ▶ ADLIG

Adelige ▶ ADLIGE

adeln *tr. V.* jmdn. ~: give sb. a title; (in den hohen Adel erheben) raise sb. to the peerage

Adels-: ~**geschlecht** *das* noble family; ~**stand** *der* nobility; (hoher Adel) nobility; ~**titel** *der* title of nobility

Ader *die;* ~, ~n (a) blood vessel
(b) (Anlage, Begabung) streak
(c) (Bot., Geol.) vein
(d) (Elektrot.) core

adieu /a'djøː/ *Interj.* (veralt.) adieu

Adjektiv *das;* ~s, ~e (Sprachw.) adjective

Adjutant *der;* ~en, ~en, **Adjutantin** *die;* ~, ~nen adjutant

Adler *der;* ~s, ~: eagle

adlig *Adj.* noble; ~ sein be a noble [man/woman]

Adlige *der/die; adj. Dekl.* noble [man/woman]

Admiral *der;* ~s, ~e *od.* Admiräle admiral

adoptieren *tr. V.* adopt

Adoption *die;* ~, ~en adoption

Adoptiv-: ~**eltern** *Pl.* adoptive parents; ~**kind** *das* adopted child; ~**mutter** *die;* *Pl.* ~mütter adoptive mother; ~**sohn** *der* adoptive *or* adopted son; ~**tochter** *die* adoptive *or* adopted daughter; ~**vater** *der* adoptive father

Adressat *der;* ~en, ~en, **Adressatin** *die;* ~, ~nen addressee

Adress·buch, *****Adreß·buch** *das* directory

Adresse *die;* ~, ~n address; **bei jmdm. an die falsche ~ kommen** *od.* **geraten** (fig. ugs.) come to the wrong address (fig.)

adressieren *tr. V.* address

adrett 1 *Adj.* smart
2 *adv.* smartly

Advent /at'vɛnt/ *der;* ~s (a) Advent
(b) (Adventssonntag) Sunday in Advent

Advents-: ~**kalender** *der* Advent calendar; ~**kranz** *der:* garland of evergreens with four candles for the Sundays in Advent

Adverb /at'vɛrp/ *das;* ~s, ~ien (Sprachw.) adverb

adverbial (Sprachw.) 1 *Adj.* adverbial
2 *adv.* adverbially

Advokat /atvo'ka:t/ *der;* ~en, ~en, **Advokatin** *die;* ~, ~nen (österr., schweiz., sonst veralt.) lawyer; advocate (arch.)

Aero- /aero- *od.* ɛ:ro-/: ~**gramm** *das* air[mail] letter; ~**sol** *das;* ~~s, ~~e aerosol

Affäre *die;* ~, ~n affair; **sich aus der ~ ziehen** (ugs.) get out of it

Affe *der;* ~n, ~n (a) monkey; (Menschen~) ape
(b) (salopp) (dummer Kerl) oaf; clot (Brit. coll.); (Geck) dandy

Affekt *der;* ~[e]s, ~e emotion; **im ~:** in the heat of the moment

affektiert (abwertend) 1 *Adj.* affected
2 *adv.* affectedly

Affen·theater *das* (salopp) farce

Afghane /af'ga:nə/ *der;* ~n, ~n (a) Afghan
(b) (Hund) Afghan hound

Afghanin *die;* ~, ~nen Afghan

afghanisch *Adj.* Afghan

Afghanistan /af'ga:nɪsta:n/ *(das);* ~s Afghanistan

Afrika *(das)* ~s Africa

Afrikaner *der;* ~s, ~, **Afrikanerin** *die;* ~, ~nen African

afrikanisch *Adj.* African

After *der;* ~s, ~: anus

AG *Abk.* (a) = **Aktiengesellschaft** PLC (Brit.); Ltd. (*private company*) (Brit.); Inc. (Amer.)
(b) = **Arbeitsgemeinschaft**

Agent *der;* ~en, ~en, **Agentin** *die;* ~, ~nen agent

Agentur *die;* ~, ~en agency

Agentur·bericht *der,*
Agentur·meldung *die* agency report

Aggregat *das;* ~[e]s, ~e (Technik) unit; (Elektrot.) set

Aggregat·zustand *der* (Chemie) state

Aggression *die;* ~, ~en aggression

aggressiv 1 *Adj.* aggressive
2 *adv.* aggressively

Aggressivität *die;* ~: aggressiveness

Aggressor *der;* ~s, ~en, **Aggressorin** *die;* ~, ~nen aggressor

Agitation *die;* ~: agitation

agitieren *itr. V.* agitate

Agrar·land *das* agrarian country

Ägypten *(das);* ~s Egypt

Ägypter *der;* ~s, ~, **Ägypterin** *die;* ~, ~nen Egyptian

ägyptisch *Adj.* Egyptian

ah *Interj.* (verwundert) oh; (freudig, genießerisch) ah; (verstehend) oh; ah

äh /ɛ(:)/ *Interj.* (a) (angeekelt) ugh
(b) (stotternd) er; hum

aha /a'ha(:)/ *Interj.* (verstehend) oh[, I see]; (triumphierend) aha

Ahn *der;* ~[e]s, *od.* ~en, ~en (geh.), **Ahne** *der;* ~n, ~n forebear; ancestor

ähneln *itr. V.* jmdm. ~: resemble *or* be like sb.; **jmdm. sehr/wenig ~:** strongly resemble *or* be very like sb./bear little resemblance to sb.; **einer Sache** (*Dat.*) **~:** be similar to sth.; be like sth.; **sich** (*Dat.*) **~:** resemble one another; be alike

ahnen *tr. V.* (a) (im Voraus fühlen) have a premonition of
(b) (vermuten) suspect; **das konnte ich doch nicht ~!** I had no way of knowing that

Ahnin *die;* ~, ~nen ▶ AHN

ähnlich 1 *Adj.* similar; **jmdm. ~ sein** be like sb.; **~ wie** like
2 *adv.* similarly; ‹answer, react› in a similar way
3 *Präp. mit Dat.* like

Ähnlichkeit *die;* ~, ~en similarity; **mit jmdm. ~ haben** be like sb.

Ahnung *die;* ~, ~en (a) (Vorgefühl) premonition
(b) (ugs.: Kenntnisse) knowledge; **von etw. [viel] ~ haben** know [a lot] about sth.; **keine ~!** [I've] no idea

ahnungs·los *Adj.* (nichts ahnend) unsuspecting; (naiv, unwissend) naïve

Ahnungslosigkeit *die;* ~ (Naivität, Unschuld) naïvety; innocence; (Unwissenheit) naïvety

ahoi *Interj.* (Seemannsspr.) ahoy

Ahorn /'a:hɔrn/ *der;* ~s, ~e maple

Ähre *die;* ~, ~n ear

Aids /e:ts/ *das;* ~: Aids

Aids-: ~**kranke** *der/die* person suffering from Aids; ~**test** *der* Aids test

Airbag /'ɛːɡbɛk/ *der;* ~s, ~s (Kfz.-W.) air bag

Akademie *die;* ~, ~n academy; (Bergbau, Forstw., Bauw.) school; college

Akademiker *der;* ~s, ~,
Akademikerin *die;* ~, ~nen [university/college] graduate

akademisch 1 *Adj.* academic

---

*alte Schreibung - vgl. Hinweis auf S. xiv

2 *adv.* academically

Akazie /aˈkaːtsjə/ *die;* ~, ~n acacia

akklimatisieren *refl. V.* become *or* get acclimatized

Akkord *der;* ~[e]s, ~e (a) (Musik) chord (b) (Wirtsch.) (Arbeit) piecework; (Lohn) piecework pay *no indef. art., no pl.;* (Satz) piece rate

Akkordeon *das;* ~s, ~s accordion

Akku *der;* ~s, ~s, **Akkumulator** *der;* ~s, ~en accumulator (Brit.); storage battery

akkurat 1 *Adj.* meticulous
2 *adv.* meticulously

Akkusativ *der;* ~s, ~e (Sprachw.) accusative [case]

Akkusativ-objekt *das* (Sprachw.) accusative *or* direct object

Akne *die;* ~, ~n (Med.) acne

Akribie /akriˈbiː/ *die;* ~ (geh.) meticulousness; meticulous precision

akribisch /aˈkriːbɪʃ/ 1 *Adj.* meticulous; meticulously precise
2 *adv.* meticulously; with meticulous precision

Akrobat *der;* ~en, ~en acrobat

Akrobatik *die;* ~: acrobatics *pl.*

Akrobatin *die;* ~, ~nen acrobat

akrobatisch *Adj.* acrobatic

Akt *der;* ~[e]s, ~e (a) (auch Theater, Zirkus-, Varieteeakt) act
(b) (Zeremonie) ceremony
(c) (Geschlechtsakt) sexual act
(d) (Kunst) nude

Akt-: ~**aufnahme** *die* nude photograph; ~**bild** *das* nude [picture]

Akte *die;* ~, ~n file

Akten-: ~**deckel** *der* folder; ~**koffer** *der* attaché case; ~**mappe** *die* briefcase; ~**notiz** *die* note [for the files]; ~**ordner** *der* file; ~**tasche** *die* briefcase; ~**zeichen** *das* reference

Akteur /akˈtøːɐ̯/ *der;* ~s, ~e, **Akteurin** *die;* ~, ~nen person involved

Akt-foto *das* nude photo

Aktie /ˈaktsjə/ *die;* ~, ~n (Wirtsch.) share; ~n shares (Brit.); stock (Amer.); **die** ~**n fallen/ steigen** share *or* stock prices are falling/ rising

Aktien-: ~**gesellschaft** *die* joint stock company; ~**kapital** *das* share capital; ~**mehrheit** *die* majority shareholding (*Gen.* in); ~**paket** *das* block of shares

Aktion *die;* ~, ~en (a) action *no indef. art.;* (militärisch) operation
(b) (Kampagne) campaign

Aktionär *der;* ~s, ~e, **Aktionärin** *die;* ~, ~nen shareholder

aktiv 1 *Adj.* (a) active
(b) (Milit.) serving *attrib.* (officer, soldier)
2 *adv.* actively

Aktiv *das;* ~s, ~e (Sprachw.) active

Aktive *der/die; adj. Dekl.* (Sport) participant

aktivieren *tr. V.* (a) mobilize (party members, group, class, etc.); **den Kreislauf** ~: stimulate the circulation
(b) (DV) activate

Aktivität *die;* ~, ~en activity

Akt-modell *das* nude model

aktualisieren *tr. V.* update

Aktualität *die;* ~, ~en (a) (Gegenwartsbezug) relevance [to the present]
(b) (von Nachrichten usw.) topicality

aktuell *Adj.* topical; (gegenwärtig) current; (neu) up-to-the-minute; **eine** ~**e Sendung** (Ferns., Rundf.) a [news and] current affairs programme

Akupunktur *die;* ~, ~en (Med.) acupuncture

Akustik *die;* ~ (a) (Lehre vom Schall) acoustics *sing., no art.;*
(b) (Schallverhältnisse) acoustics *pl.*

akustisch 1 *Adj.* acoustic
2 *adv.* acoustically

akut *Adj.* (auch Med.) acute; pressing, urgent (question, issue)

AKW *Abk.* = **Atomkraftwerk**

Akzent *der;* ~[e]s, ~e (a) (Sprachw.) (Betonung) stress; (Betonungszeichen) accent
(b) (Sprachmelodie, Aussprache) accent

akzeptabel 1 *Adj.* acceptable
2 *adv.* acceptably

akzeptieren *tr. V.* accept

à la /ala/ (Gastr., ugs.) à la

Alabaster *der;* ~s, ~: alabaster

à la carte /alaˈkart/ (Gastr.) à la carte

Alarm *der;* ~[e]s, ~e alarm; (Flieger~) air-raid warning; ~ **geben**/(fig. ugs.) **schlagen** raise the alarm; **blinder** ~: false alarm

alarm-, Alarm-: ~**anlage** *die* alarm system; ~**bereit** *Adj.* on alert *postpos.;* ~**bereitschaft** *die* alert

alarmieren *tr. V.* (a) alarm
(b) (zu Hilfe rufen) call [out] (doctor, police, fire brigade, etc.)

Alarm-: ~**sirene** *die* warning siren; ~**stufe** *die* alert stage

Albaner *der;* ~s, ~, **Albanerin** *die;* ~, ~nen Albanian

Albanien /alˈbaːnjən/ (*das);* ~s Albania

albanisch *Adj.* Albanian

Albatros *der;* ~, ~se (Zool.) albatross

Alben ▶ ALBUM

albern *Adj.* (a) silly; **sich** ~ **benehmen** act silly
(b) (ugs.: nebensächlich) silly; stupid

Albernheit *die;* ~, ~en silliness

Albino *der;* ~s, ~s albino

Alb-traum *der* nightmare

Album *das;* ~s, Alben album

Alge *die;* ~, ~n alga

Algebra /österr.: alˈgeːbra/ *die;* ~: algebra

Algerien /alˈgeːrjən/ (*das);* ~s Algeria

Algerier der; ~s, ~, **Algerierin** die; ~, ~nen Algerian

algerisch Adj. Algerian

alias Adv. alias

Alibi das; ~s, ~s alibi

Alkohol der; ~s, ~e alcohol

alkohol-, Alkohol-: ~**abhängig** Adj. dependent on alcohol postpos.; ~**abhängigkeit** die dependence on alcohol; alcohol dependence; ~**ein·fluss,** *~**ein·fluß** der, ~**ein·wirkung** die influence of alcohol or drink; unter ~einfluss od. ~einwirkung [stehen] [be] under the influence of alcohol or drink; ~**fahne** die smell of alcohol [on one's breath]; eine ~fahne haben smell of alcohol; ~**frei** Adj. non-alcoholic

Alkoholiker der; ~s, ~, **Alkoholikerin** die; ~, ~nen alcoholic

alkoholisch Adj. alcoholic

Alkoholismus der; ~: alcoholism no art.

alkohol-, Alkohol-: ~**konsum** der consumption of alcohol; ~**missbrauch,** *~**mißbrauch** der alcohol abuse; ~**sucht** die alcohol addiction; alcoholism; ~**süchtig** Adj. addicted to alcohol postpos.; alcoholic; ~**süchtige** der/die; adj. Dekl. alcoholic; ~**sünder** der, ~**sünderin** die (ugs.) drunk[en] driver; ~**vergiftung** die alcohol[ic] poisoning

all Indefinitpron. u. unbest. Zahlw. **1** attr. (ganz, gesamt...) all; ~es andere/Weitere/ Übrige everything else; ~es Schöne everything or all that is beautiful; ~es Gute! all the best!; wir/ihr/sie ~ all of us/you/ them; ~e Anwesenden all those present; ~e Bewohner der Stadt all the inhabitants of the town; ~e Jahre wieder every year; ~e fünf Minuten/Meter every five minutes/metres; in ~er Ruhe in peace and quiet **2** allein stehend (a) ~e all; ~e, die ...: all those who ... **(b)** ~es (auf Sachen bezogen) everything; (auf Personen bezogen) everybody; das ~es all that; trotz ~em in spite of everything; ~es in ~em all in all; vor ~em above all; das ist ~es that's all or (coll.) it; ist das ~es? is that all or (coll.) it?; ~es mal herhören! (ugs.) listen everybody!; ~es aussteigen! (ugs.) everyone out!; (vom Schaffner gesagt) all change!

All das; ~s ▶ WELTALL

alle Adj. ~ sein be all gone; ~ werden run out

alle·dem Pron. trotz ~: in spite of or despite all that

Allee die; ~, ~n avenue

allein **1** Adj. (a) (für sich) alone; on one's/its own; by oneself/itself; ganz ~: all on one's/ its own **(b)** (einsam) alone **2** adv. (ohne Hilfe) by oneself/itself; on one's/ its own; etw. ~ tun do sth. oneself; von ~ (ugs.) by oneself/itself

3 Adv. (a) (geh.: ausschließlich) alone **(b)** [schon] ~ der Gedanke, [schon] der Gedanke ~: the mere thought [of it]

alleine (ugs.) ▶ ALLEIN 1A, 2, 3B

allein-, Allein-: *~**erziehend** Adj. single (mother, father, parent); ~**erziehende** der/die; adj. Dekl. single parent; ~**gang** der (fig.) independent initiative; im ~gang off one's own bat

alleinig Adj. sole

*allein·stehend Adj. (person) living alone; (ledig) single (person)

Alleinstehende der/die; adj. Dekl. person living alone; (Ledige[r]) single person

alle·mal Adv. (ugs.) any time (coll.); was der kann, das kann ich doch ~: anything he can do, I can do too; s. auch EIN[1] 1

allen·falls Adv. (a) (höchstens) at [the] most **(b)** (bestenfalls) at best

aller-: ~**dings** Adv. (a) (einschränkend) though; es stimmt ~dings, dass ...: it's true though that ...; **(b)** (zustimmend) [yes,] certainly; das war ~dings Pech that was bad luck, to be sure; ~**erst...** Adj. (a) very first; der/die/das ~erste the very first; **(b)** (best...) very best

Allergen /alɛrˈgeːn/ das; ~s, ~e (Med.) allergen

Allergie die; ~, ~n (Med.) allergy

allergisch **1** Adj. (Med.) allergic (gegen) **2** adv. auf etw. (Akk.) ~ reagieren have an allergic reaction to sth

aller-, Aller-: ~**größt...** Adj. utmost (trouble, care, etc.); biggest (car, house, town, etc.) of all; tallest (person) of all; am ~größten sein be [the] biggest/tallest of all; ~**hand** indekl. Adj. (ugs.) (a) attr. all kinds or sorts of; **(b)** allein stehend all kinds or sorts of things; das ist ~hand (viel) that's a lot; das ist ja ~hand! that's just not on! (Brit. coll.); ~**heiligen** das; ~~s (bes. kath. Kirche) All Saints' Day; ~**herzlichst** **1** Adj. warmest (thanks, greetings, congratulations); most cordial (reception, welcome, invitation); **2** most warmly; ~**höchst...** **1** Adj. highest (building, tree, etc.) of all; **2** adv. am ~höchsten (fly, jump, etc.) the highest of all; ~**höchstens** Adv. at the very most

allerlei indekl. Adj. all kinds or sorts of; allein stehend all kinds or sorts of things

Allerlei das; ~s, ~s (Gemisch) pot-pourri; (Durcheinander) jumble

aller-: ~**letzt...** Adj. (a) very last; **(b)** (ugs. abwertend) most dreadful (coll.); das ist das Allerletzte that is the absolute limit; ~**liebst...** **1** Adj. most favourite; es wäre mir am ~liebsten od. das Allerliebste, wenn ...: I should like it best of all if ...; **2** adv. etw. am ~liebsten tun like doing sth. best of all; ~**meist...** **1** Indefinitpron. u. unbest. Zahlw. by far the most attrib.; das ~meiste/ am ~meisten most of all/by far the most; **2** Adv. am ~meisten most of all;

~**mindest...** *Adj.* slightest; least; **das** ~**mindeste** the very least; ~**nächst...** [1] *Adj.* very nearest *attrib.;* (Reihenfolge ausdrückend) very next *attrib.;* [2] *adv.* **am** ~**nächsten** nearest of all; ~**neu[e]st...** *Adj.* very latest *attrib.;* **das Allerneu[e]ste** the very latest; ~**schlimmst...** *Adj.* very worst *attrib.;* ~**schönst...** [1] *Adj.* most beautiful *attrib.;* loveliest *attrib.;* (angenehmst...) very nicest *attrib.;* [2] *adv.* **er singt am** ~**schönsten** his singing is the most beautiful of all; ~**seits** *Adv.* **guten Morgen** ~**seits!** good morning everyone

Allerwelts-: ~**gesicht** *das* nondescript face; ~**wort** *das* hackneyed word

allerwenigst... [1] *Adj.* lest ... of all; *Pl.* fewest ... of all
[2] *adv.* **am** ~**wenigsten** least of all

alle·samt *Indefinitpron. u. unbest. Zahlw.* (ugs.) all [of you/us/them]; **wir** ~: we all

Alles·kleber *der* all-purpose adhesive

all·gemein [1] *Adj.* general; universal ⟨*conscription, suffrage*⟩; **im** ~**en Interesse** in the common interest; **im Allgemein, ***~**en** in general
[2] *adv.* **(a)** generally; (ausnahmslos) universally; **es ist** ~ **bekannt, dass ...:** it is common knowledge that ...
(b) (unverbindlich) ⟨*write, talk, discuss*⟩ in general terms

Allgemein-: ~**befinden** *das* (Med.) general state of health; ~**bildung** *die* general education

Allgemeinheit *die;* ~ **(a)** generality
(b) die ~: the general public

Allgemein-: ~**medizin** *die* general medicine; ~**wohl** *das* public good

All·heilmittel *das* (auch fig.) cure-all; panacea

Alligator *der;* ~**s**, ~**en** alligator

Alliierte *der; adj. Dekl.* ally; **die** ~**n** the Allies

all-: ~**jährlich** [1] *Adj.* annual; yearly;
[2] *adv.* annually; every year; ~**mächtig** *Adj.* all-powerful

all·mählich [1] *Adj.* gradual
[2] *adv.* gradually
[3] *Adv.* **wir sollten** ~ **gehen** it's time we got going

all-, All-: ~**morgendlich** [1] *Adj.* regular morning; [2] *adv.* every morning;
~**seitig** [1] *Adj.* general; all-round, (Amer.) all-around *attrib.;* [2] *adv.* generally;
~**seits** *Adv.* on all sides; ~**tag** *der* **(a)** (Werktag) weekday; **(b)** (Einerlei) daily routine; **der graue** ~: the dull routine of everyday life; ~**täglich** *Adj.* ordinary ⟨*face, person, appearance, etc.*⟩; everyday ⟨*topic, event, sight*⟩; commonplace ⟨*remark*⟩; **ein nicht** ~**täglicher Anblick** a sight one doesn't see every day; ~**tags** *Adv.* [on] weekdays; ~**zu** *Adv.* all too; ~**zu bald/früh** all too

soon/early; ~**zu lange/oft/sehr** too long/often/much; ~**zu viel** too much; **nicht** ~**zu viele** not too many

*allzu·bald *usw.* ▶ ALLZU

Alm *die;* ~, ~**en** mountain pasture; Alpine pasture

Alm·hütte *die* Alpine hut

Almosen *das;* ~**s**, ~: alms *pl.*

Alp *die;* ~, ~**en** (bes. schweiz.) ▶ ALM

Alpaka *das;* ~**s**, ~**s** alpaca

Alpen *Pl. die* ~: the Alps

Alpen-: ~**rose** *die* rhododendron; ~**veilchen** *das* cyclamen

Alpha *das;* ~**[s]**, ~**[s]** alpha

Alphabet *das;* ~**[e]s**, ~**e** alphabet

alphabetisch [1] *Adj.* alphabetical
[2] *adv.* alphabetically

Alp·horn *das* alpenhorn

alpin *Adj.* Alpine

Alpinist *der;* ~**en**, ~**en**, **Alpinistin** *die;* ~, ~**nen** Alpinist

Alp·traum ▶ ALBTRAUM

als *Konj.* **(a)** (zeitlich) when; **damals,** ~: [in the days] when; **gerade** ~: just as
(b) (kausal) **um so mehr,** ~: all the more **since** *or* in that
(c) *Vergleichspartikel* **größer/älter/mehr/weniger** ~: bigger/older/more/less than; **anders** ~ **wir sein/leben** be different/live differently from us; **so viel/so weit** ~ **möglich** as much/as far as possible; **so bald/schnell** ~ **möglich** as soon/as quickly as possible; ~ **[wenn od. ob]** (+ *Konjunktiv II*) as if; as though; ~ **ob ich das nicht wüsste!** as if I didn't know
(d) ~ **Rentner/Arzt** as a pensioner/a doctor; **sich** ~ **wahr/Lüge erweisen** prove to be true/a lie

also [1] *Adv.* so; therefore
[2] *Partikel* **(a)** (das heißt) that is
(b) (nach Unterbrechung) well [then]
(c) (verstärkend) **na** ~! there you are[, you see]; ~ **schön** well all right then

alt, älter, ältest... *Adj.* **(a)** old; **Alt und Jung** old and young; **seine** ~**en Eltern** his aged parents; **wie** ~ **bist du?** how old are you?; **mein älterer/ältester Bruder** my elder/eldest brother
(b) (nicht mehr frisch) old; ~**es Brot** stale bread
(c) (vom letzten Jahr) old; ~**e Äpfel/Kartoffeln** last year's apples/potatoes
(d) (langjährig) long-standing ⟨*acquaintance*⟩
(e) (antik, klassisch) ancient
(f) (vertraut) old familiar ⟨*streets, sights, etc.*⟩; **ganz der/die Alte sein** be just the same

Alt¹ *der;* ~**s**, ~**e** (Musik) alto; (Frauenstimme) contralto; (im Chor) contraltos *pl.*

Alt² *das;* ~**[s]**, ~: *top fermented, dark beer*

Altar *der;* ~**[e]s**, **Altäre** altar

alt-, Alt-: ~**bau·wohnung** *die* flat (Brit.) *or* (Amer.) apartment in an old building; ~**bekannt** *Adj.* well-known; ~**bier** *das* ▶ ALT²

Alte *der/die; adj. Dekl.* **(a)** (alter Mensch) old man/woman; *Pl.* old people **(b)** (salopp) (Vater, Ehemann) old man (coll.); (Mutter, Ehefrau) old woman (coll.); (Chef) governor (coll.); (Chefin) boss (coll.); **die ~n** (Eltern) my/his *etc.* old man and old woman (coll.) **(c)** *Pl.* (Tiereltern) parents

alt·ehrwürdig *Adj.* (geh.) venerable; time-honoured ‹customs›

Alt·englisch *das* Old English

Alten-: **~pfleger** *der,* **~pflegerin** *die* geriatric nurse; **~tages·stätte** *die* old people's day centre

Alter *das;* ~s, ~: age; (hohes ~) old age; **im ~:** in one's old age; **im ~ von** at the age of

älter 1 ▶ ALT
2 *Adj.* (nicht mehr jung) elderly

altern *itr. V.; mit sein* age

alters-, Alters-: **~beschwerden** *Pl.* complaints of old age; **~genosse** *der,* **~genossin** *die* contemporary; person/child of the same age; **meine ~genossen** my contemporaries; people of my age; **~gruppe** *die* age group; **~heim** *das* old people's home; old-age home (Amer.); **~rente** *die* old-age pension; **~ruhe·geld** *das* retirement pension; **~schwach** *Adj.* old and infirm ‹person›; old and weak ‹animal›; **~schwäche** *die* (bei Menschen) [old] age and infirmity; (bei Tieren) [old] age and weakness; **~starrsinn** *der* obstinacy of old age; **~stufe** *die* age; **~unterschied** *der* age difference; **~versorgung** *die* provision for one's old age; (System) pension scheme

Altertum *das;* ~s antiquity *no art.*

Älteste *der/die; adj. Dekl.* **(a)** (Dorf-, Vereins-, Kirchenälteste usw.) elder **(b)** (Sohn, Tochter) eldest

alt-, Alt-: **~glas·behälter** *der* bottle bank; **~griechisch** *das* classical *or* ancient Greek; **~hochdeutsch** *das* Old High German; **~klug;** ~kluger, ~klugst... 1 *Adj.* precocious; 2 *adv.* precociously; **~last** *die* (Ökologie) old, improperly disposed of harmful waste; (fig.) inherited problem

ältlich *Adj.* rather elderly

alt-, Alt-: **~metall** *das* scrap metal; **~modisch** 1 *Adj.* old-fashioned; 2 *adv.* in an old-fashioned way; **~papier** *das* waste paper; **~rosa** *Adj.* old rose; **~stadt** *die* old [part of the] town; **~waren·händler** *der,* **~waren·händlerin** *die* second-hand dealer

Alu *das;* ~s (ugs.) aluminium

Alu·folie *die* aluminium foil

Aluminium *das;* ~s aluminium; aluminum (Amer.)

am *Präp. + Art.* **(a)** = **an dem;** **(b) Frankfurt am Main** Frankfurt on [the]

Main; **am Marktplatz** on the market square; **am Meer/Fluss** by the sea/on *or* by the river; **am Anfang/Ende** at the beginning/end; **am 19. November** on 19 November; **am schnellsten laufen** run [the] fastest; **am Verwelken sein** be wilting

Amalgam *das;* ~s, ~e (Chemie, auch fig.) amalgam

Amalgam·füllung *die* (Zahnmed.) amalgam filling

Amateur /amaˈtøːɐ̯/ *der;* ~s, ~e, **Amateurin** *die;* ~, ~nen amateur

Amazonas *der;* ~: Amazon

Amboss, *Amboß *der;* Ambosse, Ambosse anvil

ambulant (Med.) 1 *Adj.* outpatient *attrib.;* 2 *adv.* jmdn. ~ **behandeln** give sb. outpatient treatment

Ambulanz *die;* ~, ~en **(a)** (in Kliniken) outpatient[s'] department **(b)** (Krankenwagen) ambulance

Ameise *die;* ~, ~n ant

Ameisen-: **~bär** *der* anteater; **~haufen** *der* anthill

amen *Adv.* amen

Amen *das;* ~s, ~: Amen

Amerika (*das*); ~s America

Amerikaner *der;* ~s, ~ **(a)** American **(b)** (Gebäck) *small, flat iced cake*

Amerikanerin *die;* ~, ~nen American

amerikanisch *Adj.* American

Amino·säure *die* (Chemie) amino acid

Ammann *der;* ~[e]s, Ammänner (schweiz.) (Gemeinde-, Bezirksamman) ≈ mayor; (Landamman) cantonal president

Amme *die;* ~, ~n wet nurse

Amnestie /amnɛsˈtiː/ *die;* ~, ~n amnesty

amnestieren *tr. V.* grant an amnesty to

Amöbe *die;* ~, ~n (Biol.) amoeba

Amok *der;* ~ **laufen** run amok

Amok·läufer *der* madman

Amok·läuferin *die* madwoman

Ampel *die;* ~, ~n **(a)** traffic lights *pl.* **(b)** (für Pflanzen) hanging flowerpot

Amphibie /amˈfiːbi̯ə/ *die;* ~, ~n (Zool.) amphibian

Amphibien·fahrzeug *das* amphibious vehicle

Amphi·theater *das* amphitheatre

Ampulle *die;* ~, ~n (Med.) ampoule

Amputation *die;* ~, ~en (Med.) amputation

amputieren *tr. V.* amputate

Amsel *die;* ~, ~n blackbird

Amt *das;* ~[e]s, Ämter **(a)** (Stellung) post; position; (hohes politisches od. kirchliches ~) office; **im ~ sein** be in office **(b)** (Aufgabe) task; job **(c)** (Behörde) office **(d)** (Fernsprechvermittlung) exchange

amtieren *itr. V.* **(a)** hold office

---

*alte Schreibung - vgl. Hinweis auf S. xiv

(b) (vorübergehend) act (**als** as)
amtlich ⟨1⟩ *Adj.* official; (ugs.: sicher) definite
⟨2⟩ *adv.* officially
Amt·mann *der; Pl.* ...**männer** *od.* ...**leute**,
Amt·männin *die;* ~, ~**nen** senior civil
servant
Amts-: ~**anmaßung** *die* (Rechtsw.)
unauthorized assumption of authority;
~**arzt** *der,* ~**ärztin** *die* medical officer;
~**eid** *der* oath of office; ~**gericht** *das*
local *or* district court; ~**geschäfte** *Pl.*
official duties; ~**handlung** *die* official act
or duty; ~**leitung** *die* (Fernspr.) exchange
line
Amulett *das;* ~[e]**s,** ~**e** amulet; charm
amüsant ⟨1⟩ *Adj.* entertaining; amusing
⟨2⟩ *adv.* in an entertaining *or* amusing way
amüsieren ⟨1⟩ *refl. V.* **(a)** (sich vergnügen)
enjoy oneself; **sich mit jmdm.** ~: have fun *or*
a good time with sb.
(b) (belustigt sein) be amused; **sich über jmdn./
etw.** ~: find sb./sth. funny
⟨2⟩ *tr. V.* amuse
an ⟨1⟩ *Präp. mit Dat.* **(a)** (räumlich) at; (auf) on;
Frankfurt an der Oder Frankfurt on [the]
Oder; **Tür an Tür** next door to one another;
an ... vorbei past
(b) (zeitlich) on; **an jedem Sonntag** every
Sunday; **an Ostern** (bes. südd.) at Easter
(c) arm/reich **an Vitaminen** low/rich in
vitamins; **jmdn. an etw. erkennen** recognize
sb. by sth.; **an etw. leiden** suffer from sth.;
an einer Krankheit sterben die of a disease
(d) an [und für] sich actually
⟨2⟩ *Präp. mit Akk.* **(a)** to; (auf, gegen) on
(b) an etw./jmdn. **glauben** believe in sth./sb.;
an etw. denken think of sth.; **sich an etw.
erinnern** remember sth.
⟨3⟩ *Adv.* **(a)** (Verkehrsw.) **Köln an: 9.15** arriving
Cologne 09.15
(b) (ugs.: in Betrieb) on; **die Waschmaschine/
der Fernseher/das Licht/das Gas ist an** the
washing machine/television/light/gas is on
(c) (ugs.: ungefähr) around; about; **an [die]
2 000 Euro** around *or* about 2,000 euros
Anabolikum *das;* ~**s, Anabolika** (Med.)
anabolic steroid
analog ⟨1⟩ *Adj.* **(a)** (gleichartig) analogous; ~
[**zu**] **diesem Fall** analogous to this case
(b) (Technik, DV) analogue
⟨2⟩ *adv.* **(a)** (gleichartig) analogously
(b) (Technik, DV) ⟨display, reproduce⟩ in
analogue form
Analog-: ~**rechner** *der* (DV) analogue
computer; ~**uhr** *die* analogue clock;
(Armbanduhr) analogue watch
Analphabet *der;* ~**en,** ~**en,**
Analphabetin *die;* ~, ~**nen** illiterate
[person]; ~ **sein** be illiterate
Analyse *die;* ~, ~**n** analysis
analysieren *tr. V.* analyse
Analyst *der;* ~**en, Analystin,** *die;*
~, ~**nen** (Börsenw.) analyst
analytisch ⟨1⟩ *Adj.* analytical

⟨2⟩ *adv.* analytically
Ananas *die;* ~, ~ *od.* ~**se** pineapple
Anarchie *die;* ~, ~**n** anarchy
Anarchist *der;* ~**en,** ~**en, Anarchistin**
die; ~, ~**nen** anarchist
Anästhesie *die;* ~, ~**n** (Med.) anaesthesia
anästhesieren *tr. V.* (Med.) anaesthetize
Anästhesist *der;* ~**en,** ~**en,**
Anästhesistin *die;* ~, ~**nen** (Med.)
anaesthetist
Anatomie *die;* ~, ~**n** anatomy
anatomisch *Adj.* anatomical
an|bahnen ⟨1⟩ *tr. V.* initiate ⟨negotiations,
talks, process, etc.⟩; develop ⟨relationship,
connection⟩
⟨2⟩ *refl. V.* ⟨development⟩ be in the offing;
⟨friendship, relationship⟩ start to develop
an|bändeln *itr. V.* **mit jmdm.** ~ (ugs.) get
off with sb. (Brit. coll.); pick sb. up
An-bau *der; Pl.* ~**ten (a)** building
(b) (Gebäude) extension
(c) (das Anpflanzen) growing
an|bauen ⟨1⟩ *tr. V.* **(a)** build on
(b) (anpflanzen) grow
⟨2⟩ *itr. V.* (das Haus vergrößern) build an
extension
an-bei *Adv.* (Amtsspr.) herewith; **Rückporto**
~: return postage enclosed
an|beißen ⟨1⟩ *unr. tr. V.* bite into; take a
bite of
⟨2⟩ *unr. itr. V.* (auch fig. ugs.) bite
an|belangen *tr. V.* **was mich/dies** *usw.*
anbelangt as far as I am/this matter is *etc.*
concerned
an|beten *tr. V.* (auch fig.) worship
An-betracht *der:* **in** ~ **einer Sache** (*Gen.*)
in view of sth.
an|betreffen *unr. tr. V.* ▶ ANBELANGEN
an|betteln *tr. V.* **jmdn.** ~: beg from sb.;
jmdn. um etw. ~: beg sb. for sth.
Anbetung *die;* ~, ~**en** (auch fig.) worship
an|biedern *refl. V.* **sich [bei jmdm.]** ~:
curry favour [with sb.]
an|bieten ⟨1⟩ *unr. tr. V.* offer; **jmdm. etw.**
~: offer sb. sth.
⟨2⟩ *unr. refl. V.* **(a)** (offer one's services; **sich**
~, **etw. zu tun** offer to do sth.
(b) (fig.) ⟨possibility, solution⟩ suggest itself
An-bieter *der,* **An-bieterin** *die* (Wirtsch.)
supplier
an|binden *unr. tr. V.* tie [up] (**an** + *Dat. od.
Akk.* to); tie up, moor ⟨boat⟩ (**an** + *Dat. od.
Akk.* to); tether ⟨animal⟩ (**an** + *Dat. od. Akk.*
to)
an|blasen *unr. tr. V.* **(a)** blow at
(b) (anfachen) blow on
An-blick *der* sight
an|blicken *tr. V.* look at
an|blinzeln *tr. V.* **(a)** blink at
(b) (zuzwinkern) wink at
an|brechen ⟨1⟩ *unr. tr. V.* **(a)** crack
(b) (öffnen) open ···>

(c) (zu verbrauchen beginnen) break into ⟨supplies, reserves⟩
[2] *unr. itr. V.; mit sein* (geh.: beginnen) ⟨dawn, day⟩ break; ⟨age, epoch⟩ dawn

an|brennen [1] *unr. tr. V.* (anzünden) light
[2] *unr. itr. V.; mit sein* burn

an|bringen *unr. tr. V.* **(a)** (befestigen) put up ⟨sign, aerial, curtain, plaque⟩ (**an** + *Dat.* on)
(b) (äußern) make ⟨request, complaint, comment⟩
(c) (zeigen) demonstrate ⟨knowledge, experience⟩
(d) (ugs.: herbeibringen) bring

An·bruch *der* (geh.: Beginn) dawn[ing]; **der ~ des Tages** daybreak

an|brüllen *tr. V.* (ugs.) bellow at

Andacht *die;* ~, ~**en (a)** (Sammlung) rapt attention; (im Gebet) silent worship *or* prayer
(b) (Gottesdienst) prayers *pl.*

andächtig [1] *Adj.* rapt; (ins Gebet versunken) devout
[2] *adv.* with rapt attention; (ins Gebet versunken) devoutly

an|dauern *itr. V.* ⟨negotiations⟩ continue, go on; ⟨weather, rain⟩ last

andauernd [1] *Adj.* continual; constant
[2] *adv.* continually; constantly

Anden *Pl. die* ~: the Andes

An·denken *das;* ~**s,** ~ **(a)** memory; **zum ~ an jmdn./etw.** to remind you/us *etc.* of sb./sth.
(b) (Erinnerungsstück) memento; (Reise~) souvenir

ander... *Indefinitpron.* [1] *attr.* **(a)** other; **ein** ~**er/eine** ~**e/ein** ~**es** another; **das Kleid gefällt mir nicht, haben Sie noch** ~**e/ein** ~**es?** I don't like that dress, do you have any others/another?; **jemand** ~**er** *od.* ~**es** someone else; (in Fragen) anyone else; **niemand** ~**er** *od.* ~**es** nobody else; **etwas** ~**es** something else; (in Fragen) anything else; **nichts** ~**es** nothing else; not anything else
(b) (verschieden) different
[2] *allein stehend* **ein** ~**r/eine** ~**e:** another [one]; **nicht drängeln, einer nach dem** ~**n** don't push, one after the other; **ein** ~**er/eine** ~**e/ein** ~**es** another [one]; **ein[e]s nach dem** ~**[e]n** first things first; **ich will weder das eine noch das** ~**e** I don't want either

anderen·falls *Adv.* otherwise

anderer·seits *Adv.* on the other hand

ander·mal *Adv.* **ein** ~: another time

ändern [1] *tr. V.* change; alter; alter ⟨garment⟩; change ⟨person⟩
[2] *refl. V.* change

andern·falls *Adv.* otherwise

anders *Adv.* **(a)** (verschieden) ⟨think, act, feel, do⟩ differently (**als** from *or* (esp. Brit) to); ⟨be, look, sound, taste⟩ different (**als** from *or* (esp. Brit.) to); **es war alles ganz** ~: it was all quite different

---

(b) (sonst) else; **niemand** ~: nobody else; **jemand** ~: someone else; (in Fragen) anyone else

anders-, Anders-: ~**artig** *Adj.* different; ~**farbig** *Adj.* different-coloured *attrib.;* of a different colour *postpos.;* ~**gläubige** *der/ die* person of a different religion; ~**herum** *Adv.* the other way round *or* (Amer.) around; ~**herum gehen/fahren** go/drive round *or* (Amer.) around the other way; ~**wo** *Adv.* (ugs.) elsewhere; ~**woher** *Adv.* (ugs.) from somewhere else; ~**wohin** *Adv.* (ugs.) somewhere else

andert·halb *Bruchz.* one and a half; ~ **Stunden** an hour and a half

Änderung *die;* ~, ~**en** change (*Gen.* in); alteration (*Gen.* to)

Änderungs·schneiderei *die* tailor's [that does alterations]

anderweitig [1] *Adj.* other
[2] *adv.* in another way

an|deuten [1] *tr. V.* **(a)** (zu verstehen geben) hint
(b) (nicht vollständig ausführen) outline; (kurz erwähnen) indicate
[2] *refl. V.* be indicated

An·deutung *die* hint

An·drang *der* crowd; (Gedränge) crush

andre... ▸ ANDER...

an|drehen *tr. V.* **(a)** (einschalten) turn on
(b) jmdm. etw. ~ (ugs.) palm sb. off with sth.

andrer·seits *Adv.* on the other hand

an|drohen *tr. V.* **jmdm. etw.** ~: threaten sb. with sth

An·drohung *die* threat

an|drücken *tr. V.* press down

an|ecken *itr. V.; mit sein* **bei jmdm.** ~ (fig. ugs.) rub sb. [up (Brit.)] the wrong way

an|eignen *refl. V.* **(a)** appropriate
(b) (lernen) acquire; learn

an-einander *Adv.* (zusammen) together; (nebeneinander) next to each other; next to one another; ~ **denken** think of each other *or* one another; ~ **vorbeigehen** pass each other *or* one another

***aneinander|binden** *usw.* ▸ ANEINANDER

Anekdote *die;* ~, ~**n** anecdote

an|ekeln *tr. V.* disgust

Anemone *die;* ~, ~**n** anemone

an|erkennen *unr. tr. V.* **(a)** recognize ⟨country, record, verdict, qualification, document⟩; acknowledge ⟨debt⟩; accept ⟨demand, bill, conditions, rules⟩; allow ⟨claim, goal⟩
(b) (nicht leugnen) acknowledge
(c) (würdigen) appreciate; respect ⟨viewpoint, opinion⟩; **ein** ~**der Blick** an appreciative look

anerkennens·wert *Adj.* commendable

Anerkennung *die;* ~, ~**en** ▸ ANERKENNEN:
(a) recognition; acknowledgement; acceptance; allowance
(b) acknowledgement
(c) appreciation; respect (*Gen.* for)

an|fachen *tr. V.* fan; (fig.) arouse ⟨anger, curiosity, enthusiasm⟩; inflame ⟨passion⟩; stir up ⟨hatred⟩; inspire ⟨hope⟩; ferment ⟨discord, war⟩

an|fahren ① *unr. tr. V.* (a) run into; hit
(b) (herbeifahren) deliver
(c) (ansteuern) stop at ⟨village etc.⟩; ⟨ship⟩ put in at ⟨port⟩
(d) (zurechtweisen) shout at
② *unr. itr. V.; mit sein* (a) (starten) start off
(b) angefahren kommen come driving/riding up

An·fahrt *die* (a) (das Anfahren) journey
(b) (Weg) approach

Anfahrts·skizze *die* map showing directions

An·fall *der* attack; (epileptischer ∼, fig.) fit; **einen ∼ bekommen** *od.* (ugs.) **kriegen** have an attack/a fit

an·fallen ① *unr. tr. V.* attack
② *unr. itr V.; mit sein* ⟨costs⟩ be incurred; ⟨interest⟩ accrue; ⟨work⟩ come up

an·fällig *Adj.* ⟨person⟩ with a delicate constitution; ⟨machine⟩ susceptible to faults; **gegen** *od.* **für etw. ∼ sein** be susceptible to sth.

An·fang *der* beginning; start; (erster Abschnitt) beginning; **am** *od.* **zu ∼:** at first; **von ∼ an** from the outset; **∼ 1984/der Woche** *usw.* at the beginning of 1984/of the week *etc.*

an·fangen ① *unr. itr. V.* (a) begin; start; **mit etw. ∼:** start [on] sth.; **∼, etw. zu tun** start to do sth.
(b) (zu sprechen anfangen) begin; **von etw. ∼:** start on about sth.
(c) (eine Stelle antreten) start
② *unr. tr. V.* (a) begin; start; (anbrechen) start
(b) (machen) do

An·fänger *der;* ∼s, ∼, **An·fängerin** *die;* ∼, ∼nen beginner

anfänglich *Adj.* initial

anfangs *Adv.* at first; initially

Anfangs-: ∼**buchstabe** *der* initial [letter]; ∼**stadium** *das* initial stage

an|fassen ① *tr. V.* (a) (fassen, halten) take hold of
(b) (berühren) touch
(c) jmdn. ∼ (an der Hand nehmen) take sb.'s hand
(d) (angehen) tackle ⟨problem, task, etc.⟩
(e) (behandeln) treat ⟨person⟩
② *itr. V.* [mit] ∼: lend a hand

anfechtbar *Adj.:* ▶ ANFECHTEN A: disputable; contestable; challengeable

an|fechten *unr. tr. V.* (a) dispute ⟨statement, contract⟩; contest ⟨will⟩; challenge ⟨decision, law, opinion⟩
(b) (beunruhigen) trouble

an|fertigen *tr. V.* make

an|feuchten *tr. V.* moisten ⟨lips, stamp⟩; dampen ⟨ironing, cloth, etc.⟩

an|feuern *tr. V.* spur on

an|fixen *tr. V.* (Drogenjargon) jmdn. ∼: get sb. shooting up for the first time (sl.); **von etw. angefixt sein** (fig.) be hooked on sth. (coll.)

an|flehen *tr. V.* beseech; implore

an|fliegen ① *unr. itr. V.; mit sein* fly in; **angeflogen kommen** come flying in; **gegen den Wind ∼:** fly into the wind
② *unr. tr. V.* fly to ⟨city, country, airport⟩

An·flug *der* (a) approach
(b) (Hauch) hint
(c) (Anwandlung) fit; **in einem ∼ von Großzügigkeit** in a fit of generosity

an|fordern *tr. V.* ask for; order ⟨goods, materials⟩; send for ⟨ambulance⟩

An·forderung *die* (a) (das Anfordern) request (Gen. for)
(b) (Anspruch) demand

An·frage *die* inquiry; (Parl.) question

an|fragen *itr. V.* inquire; ask

an|freunden *refl. V.* become friends

an|fügen *tr. V.* add

an|fühlen *refl. V.* feel

an|führen *tr. V.* (a) lead
(b) (zitieren) quote
(c) (nennen) give ⟨example, reason, details, proof⟩
(d) (ugs.: hereinlegen) have on (Brit. coll.); dupe

An·führer *der,* **An·führerin** *die* leader; (Rädelsführer) ringleader

An·führung *die* (a) (das Zitieren, Zitat) quotation
(b) (Nennung) giving

Anführungs-: ∼**strich** *der,* ∼**zeichen** *das* quotation mark

An·gabe *die* (a) (das Mitteilen) giving
(b) (Information) piece of information; ∼**n** information *sing.;*
(c) (Ballspiele) service; serve

an|geben ① *unr. tr. V.* (a) give ⟨reason⟩; declare ⟨income, dutiable goods⟩; name ⟨witness⟩
(b) (bestimmen) set ⟨course, direction⟩; **den Takt ∼:** keep time
② *unr. itr. V.* (a) (prahlen) boast; brag; (sich angeberisch benehmen) show off
(b) (Ballspiele) serve

Angeber *der;* ∼s, ∼: braggart

Angeberei *die;* ∼: showing-off

Angeberin *die;* ∼, ∼nen ▶ ANGEBER

angeblich ① *Adj.* alleged
② *adv.* supposedly; allegedly

an-geboren *Adj.* innate ⟨characteristic⟩; congenital ⟨disease⟩

An·gebot *das* (a) offer
(b) (Wirtsch.) supply; (Sortiment) range; **∼ und Nachfrage** supply and demand
(c) (Kaufmannsspr.: Sonder∼) [special] offer; **im ∼:** on [special] offer; **∼ der Woche** bargain of the week

an-gebracht *Adj.* appropriate

an-gegriffen *Adj.* weakened ⟨*health, stomach*⟩; strained ⟨*nerves, voice*⟩

angeheitert *Adj.* tipsy

an|gehen ① *unr. itr. V.; mit sein* **(a)** ⟨*radio, light, heating*⟩ come on; ⟨*fire*⟩ catch **(b)** (anwachsen, wachsen) ⟨*plant*⟩ take root **(c) es mag noch** ∼**:** it's [just about] acceptable **(d) gegen etw./jmdn.** ∼**:** fight sth./sb. ② *unr. tr. V.* **(a)** (angreifen) attack **(b)** (in Angriff nehmen) tackle ⟨*problem, difficulty*⟩; take ⟨*fence, bend*⟩ **(c)** (bitten) ask (**um** for) **(d)** (betreffen) concern; **das geht dich nichts an** it's none of your business

angehend *Adj.* budding; (zukünftig) prospective

an|gehören *itr. V.* **jmdm./einer Sache** ∼**:** belong to sb./sth.; **der Regierung/einer Familie** ∼**:** be a member of the government/a family

an-gehörig *Adj.* belonging (*Dat.* to)

Angehörige *der/die; adj. Dekl.* **(a)** (Verwandte) relative; relation **(b)** (Mitglied) member

Angeklagte *der/die; adj. Dekl.* accused; defendant

Angel *die;* ∼**,** ∼**n (a)** fishing rod **(b)** (Tür∼, Fenster∼ usw.) hinge; **etw. aus den** ∼**n heben** (fig.) turn sth. upside down

An-gelegenheit *die* matter; (Aufgabe, Problem) affair

Angel·haken *der* fish hook

angeln ① *tr. V.* (zu fangen suchen) fish for; (fangen) catch ② *itr. V.* angle; fish

Angel·rute *die* fishing rod

Angel·sachse *der,* **Angel·sächsin** *die* Anglo-Saxon

Angel·schnur *die* fishing line

an-gemessen *Adj.* appropriate; reasonable, fair ⟨*price, fee*⟩

an-genehm ① *Adj.* pleasant; ∼**e Reise/ Ruhe!** [have a] pleasant journey/have a good rest; **[sehr]** ∼**!** delighted to meet you ② *adv.* pleasantly

an-gesehen *Adj.* respected

angesichts *Präp. mit Gen.* (geh.) **(a)** in the face of **(b)** (fig.: in Anbetracht) in view of

angespannt *Adj.* **(a)** close ⟨*attention*⟩; taut ⟨*nerves*⟩ **(b)** tense ⟨*situation*⟩; tight ⟨*market, economic situation*⟩

angestellt *Adj.* **bei jmdm.** ∼ **sein** be employed by sb.; work for sb.

Angestellte *der/die; adj. Dekl.* [salaried] employee

Angestellten·gewerkschaft *die* white-collar union

an-getan *Adj.* **von jmdm./etw.** ∼ **sein** be taken with sb./sth.

an-getrunken *Adj.* [slightly] drunk

an-gewiesen *Adj.* **auf jmdn./etw.** ∼ **sein** have to rely on sb./sth.

an|gewöhnen *tr. V.* **jmdm. etw.** ∼**:** get sb. used to sth.; **jmdm.** ∼**, etw. zu tun** get sb. used to doing sth.; **sich** (*Dat.*) **etw.** ∼**:** get into the habit of sth.; **[es] sich** (*Dat.*) ∼**, etw. zu tun** get into the habit of doing sth.

An·gewohnheit *die* habit

an|gleichen ① *unr. tr. V.* **etw. einer Sache** (*Dat.*) *od.* **an etw.** (*Akk.*) ∼**:** bring sth. into line with sth. ② *unr. refl. V.* **sich jmdm./einer Sache** *od.* **an jmdn./etw.** ∼**:** become like sb./sth.

An-gleichung *die:* **die** ∼ **der Löhne an die Preise** bringing wages into line with prices

Angler *der;* ∼**s,** ∼**, Anglerin** *die;* ∼**,** ∼**nen** angler

Anglikaner *der;* ∼**s,** ∼**, Anglikanerin** *die;* ∼**,** ∼**nen** Anglican

anglikanisch *Adj.* Anglican

Anglistik *die;* ∼**:** English studies *pl., no art.*

Angola *(das);* ∼**s** Angola

Angora-: ∼**katze** *die* angora cat; ∼**wolle** *die* angora [wool]

an|greifen ① *unr. tr. V.* **(a)** (auch fig.) attack **(b)** (schwächen) affect ⟨*health, heart, stomach, intestine, voice*⟩; weaken ⟨*person*⟩ ② *unr. itr. V.* (auch fig.) attack

Angreifer *der;* ∼**s,** ∼**, Angreiferin** *die;* ∼**,** ∼**nen** (auch fig.) attacker

An-griff *der* **(a)** attack; **zum** ∼ **blasen** (auch fig.) sound the attack **(b) etw. in** ∼ **nehmen** tackle sth.

angst *Adj.* **jmdm. ist/wird [es]** ∼ **[und bange]** sb. is/becomes frightened

Angst *die;* ∼**, Ängste (a)** (Furcht) fear; ∼ **bekommen** *od.* (ugs.) **kriegen** become frightened; ∼ **haben** be frightened (**vor** + *Dat.* of) **(b)** (Sorge) anxiety; ∼ **haben** be anxious (**um** about); **keine** ∼**, ich vergesse es schon nicht!** don't worry, I won't forget [it]!

ängstigen ① *tr. V.* frighten; (beunruhigen) worry ② *refl. V.* be frightened; (sich sorgen) worry

ängstlich ① *Adj.* anxious ② *adv.* anxiously

Ängstlichkeit *die;* ∼**:** timidity

an|gucken *tr. V.* (ugs.) look at; **sich** (*Dat.*) **etw./jmdn.** ∼**:** have a look at sth./sb.

an|gurten *tr. V.* strap in; **sich** ∼**:** put on one's seat belt

an|haben *unr. tr. V.* **(a)** (ugs.: am Körper tragen) have on **(b) jmdm./einer Sache etwas** ∼ **können** be able to harm sb./sth.

an|halten ① *unr. tr. V.* **(a)** stop **(b)** (auffordern) urge

2 *unr. itr. V.* **(a)** stop
(b) (andauern) go on; last
anhaltend 1 *Adj.* constant; continuous
2 *adv.* constantly; continuously
An·halter *der* hitch-hiker; **per ~ fahren**
hitch[-hike]
An·halterin *die* hitch-hiker
Anhalts·punkt *der* clue (**für** to); (für eine
Vermutung) grounds *pl.*
an·hand 1 *Präp. mit Gen.* with the help of
2 *Adv.* **~ von** with the help of
An·hang *der* **(a)** (Buchw.) appendix
(b) (Anhängerschaft) following
(c) (Verwandtschaft) family
an|hängen 1 *tr. V.* **(a)** hang up (**an** +
Akk. on)
(b) (ankuppeln) couple on (**an** + *Akk.* to); hitch
up ‹*trailer*› (**an** + *Akk.* to)
(c) (anfügen) add on (**an** + *Akk.* to)
(d) (ugs.: zuschreiben, anlasten) **jmdm. etw. ~**
blame sb. for sth.; blame sth. on sb.; **er will**
mir nur was ~ he just wants to pin
something on me
2 *refl. V.* **(a)** hang on (**an** + *Akk.* to)
(b) (ugs.: sich anschließen) **sich [an jmdn. od.**
bei jmdm.] ~: tag along [with sb.]
An·hänger *der* **(a)** (Mensch) supporter
(b) (Wagen) trailer
(c) (Schmuckstück) pendant
(d) (Schildchen) tag
Anhängerin *die;* **~, ~nen ▶** ANHÄNGER A
Anhängerschaft *die;* **~, ~en** supporters
pl.
anhänglich *Adj.* devoted ‹*dog, friend*›
Anhänglichkeit *die;* **~:** devotion
an|hauchen *tr. V.* breathe on ‹*mirror,*
glasses›; blow on ‹*fingers, hands*›
an|häufen *tr. V.* accumulate
Anhäufung *die* accumulation
an|heben *unr. tr. V.* **(a)** lift [up]
(b) (erhöhen) raise ‹*prices, wages, etc.*›
an|heften *tr. V.* attach ‹*label, list*›; put up
‹*sign, notice*›
anheim (geh.): **[es] jmdm. ~ stellen, etw. zu**
tun leave it to sb. to do sth.
*****anheim|stellen ▶** ANHEIM
An·hieb *der:* **auf ~** (ugs.) straight off
an|himmeln *tr. V.* worship
An·höhe *die* rise
an|hören 1 *tr. V.* listen to; **sich** (*Dat.*)
jmdn./etw. ~: listen to sb./sth.
2 *refl. V.* sound
animieren *tr. V.* encourage
Anis *der;* **~es** aniseed
Ank. *Abk.* = **Ankunft** arr.
An·kauf *der* purchase
an|kaufen *tr. V.* purchase; buy
Anker *der;* **~s, ~** anchor; **vor ~ gehen/**
liegen drop anchor/lie at anchor; **~ werfen**
drop anchor
ankern *itr. V.* **(a)** anchor
(b) (vor Anker liegen) be anchored

Anker·platz *der* anchorage
An·klage *die* **(a)** charge; **unter ~ stehen**
have been charged (**wegen** with)
(b) (~vertretung) prosecution
Anklage·bank *die; Pl.* Anklagebänke
dock; **auf der ~ sitzen** (auch fig.) be in the
dock
an|klagen *tr. V.* **(a)** (Rechtsw.) charge (*Gen.,*
wegen with); accuse
(b) (geh.: beschuldigen) accuse
An·kläger *der,* **An·klägerin** *die*
prosecutor
an|klammern 1 *tr. V.* peg (Brit.), pin
(Amer.) ‹*clothes, washing*›; clip ‹*sheet etc.*›;
(mit Heftklammern) staple ‹*sheet etc.*›
2 *refl. V.* **sich an jmdn./etw. ~:** cling to sb./
sth.
An·klang *der:* **[bei jmdm.] ~ finden** meet
with [sb.'s] approval
an|kleben 1 *tr. V.* stick up ‹*poster, etc.*›
2 *itr. V.; mit sein* stick
an|kleiden *tr. V.* (geh.) dress; **sich ~:** dress
an|klicken *tr. V.* (DV) click on
an|klopfen *itr. V.* knock
an|knüpfen 1 *tr. V.* **(a)** tie on (**an** + *Akk.*
to)
(b) (beginnen) start up ‹*conversation*›;
establish ‹*relations, business links*›; form
‹*relationship*›
2 *itr. V.* **an etw.** (*Akk.*) **~:** take sth. up; **ich**
knüpfe dort an, wo … I'll pick up where …
an|kommen *unr. itr. V.; mit sein* **(a)**
(eintreffen) arrive; **seid ihr gut angekommen?**
did you arrive safely?
(b) [bei jmdm.] [gut] ~ (fig. ugs.) go down
[very] well [with sb.]
(c) **gegen jmdn./etw. ~:** be able to deal with
sb./fight sth.
(d) *unpers.* **es kommt auf jmdn./etw. an**
(jmd./etw. ist ausschlaggebend) it depends on
sb./sth.; **es kommt auf etw.** (*Akk.*) **an** (etw. ist
wichtig) sth. matters (*Dat.* to); **es kommt**
[ganz] darauf od. drauf an (ugs.) it [all]
depends
(e) *unpers.* **es darauf od. drauf ~ lassen**
(ugs.) chance it; **es auf etw.** (*Akk.*) **~ lassen**
[be prepared to] risk sth.
an|koppeln 1 *tr. V.* couple ‹*carriage*› up;
hitch ‹*trailer*› up; dock ‹*spacecraft*›
2 *itr. V.* ‹*spacecraft*› dock
an|kreuzen *tr. V.* mark with a cross
an|kündigen 1 *tr. V.* announce
2 *refl. V.* announce itself
An·kündigung *die* announcement
Ankunft *die;* **~, Ankünfte** arrival; „**~**"
'arrivals'
Ankunfts-: ~halle *die* arrival[s] hall;
~tafel *die* arrivals board
an|kuppeln *tr. V.* **▶** ANKOPPELN 1
an|kurbeln *tr. V.* **(a)** crank [up]
(b) (fig.) boost ‹*economy, production, etc.*›
Anl. *Abk.* = **Anlage** encl.
an|lächeln *tr. V.* smile at

an|lachen ① *tr. V.* smile at
② *refl. V.* sich (*Dat.*) jmdn. ~ (ugs.) get off
with sb. (Brit. coll.); pick sb. up

An·lage *die* (a) (das Anlegen) (einer Kartei)
establishment; (eines Parks, Gartens usw.) laying
out; (eines Parkplatzes, Stausees) construction
(b) (Grünanlage) park; (um ein Schloss usw.
herum) grounds *pl.;*
(c) (Einrichtung) facilities *pl.;* **militärische** ~n
military installations
(d) (Werk) plant
(e) (Musikanlage usw.) system
(f) (Geldanlage) investment
(g) (Konzeption) conception; (Struktur) structure
(h) (Veranlagung) aptitude; (Neigung) tendency
(i) (Beilage zu einem Brief) enclosure

Anlage-: ~**berater** *der,* ~**beraterin**
die investment advisor; ~**kapital** *das*
investment capital

Anlass, *Anlaß *der;* Anlasses, Anlässe (a)
cause (**zu** for); etw. zum ~ nehmen, etw. zu
tun take sth. as an opportunity to do sth.;
aus aktuellem ~: because of current events
(b) (Gelegenheit) occasion

an|lassen ① *unr. tr. V.* (a) leave ⟨light,
radio, heating, etc.⟩ on; leave ⟨engine⟩
running; leave ⟨candle⟩ burning
(b) keep ⟨coat, gloves, etc.⟩ on
(c) (in Gang setzen) start [up]
② *unr. refl. V.* sich gut/schlecht ~: get off to
a good/bad start

Anlasser *der;* ~s, ~: starter

an·lässlich, *an·läßlich *Präp. mit Gen.*
on the occasion of

An·lauf *der* (a) run-up; [mehr] ~ nehmen
take [more of] a run-up
(b) (Versuch) attempt; **beim** *od.* **im ersten/
dritten** ~: at the first/third attempt

an|laufen ① *unr. itr. V.; mit sein* (a)
angelaufen kommen come running along; (auf
einen zu) come running up
(b) **gegen jmdn./etw.** ~: run at sb./sth.
(c) (Anlauf nehmen) take a run-up
(d) (zu laufen beginnen) ⟨engine⟩ start [up]; (fig.)
⟨film⟩ open; ⟨production, campaign, search⟩
start
(e) **rot/dunkel** usw. ~:·go or turn red/dark
etc.;
(f) (beschlagen) mist up
② *unr. tr. V.* put in at ⟨port⟩

an|legen ① *tr. V.* (a) put or lay ⟨domino,
card⟩ [down] (**an** + *Akk.* next to); place,
position ⟨ruler, protractor⟩ (**an** + *Akk.* on);
put ⟨ladder⟩ up (**an** + *Akk.* against)
(b) **die Flügel/Ohren** ~: close its wings/lay
its ears back; **die Arme** ~: put one's arms to
one's sides
(c) (geh.: anziehen, umlegen) don
(d) (schaffen, erstellen) lay out ⟨town, garden,
plantation, street⟩; start ⟨file, album⟩;
compile ⟨statistics, index⟩
(e) (investieren) invest
(f) (ausgeben) spend (**für** on)

(g) **es darauf** ~, etw. **zu tun** be determined to
do sth.
② *itr. V.* (a) (landen) moor
(b) (Kartenspiele) lay a card/cards
(c) (Domino) play [a domino/dominoes]
(d) (zielen) aim (**auf** + *Akk.* at)
③ *refl. V.* sich mit jmdm. ~: pick an
argument with sb

Anlege-: ~**platz** *der* berth; ~**steg** *der*
jetty

an|lehnen ① *tr. V.* (a) lean (**an** + *Akk. od.
Dat.* against)
(b) leave ⟨door, window⟩ slightly open
② *refl. V.* sich [an jmdn. od. jmdm./etw.] ~:
lean [on sb./against sth.]

Anlehnung *die;* in ~ **an** (+ *Akk.*) in
imitation of; following

Anleihe *die;* ~, ~n (Finanzw.) bond

an|leiten *tr. V.* instruct

An·leitung *die* instructions *pl.*

an|lernen *tr. V.* train

an|liegen *unr. itr. V.* (a) ⟨pullover etc.⟩ fit
tightly
(b) (ugs.: vorliegen) be on

An·liegen *das;* ~s, ~ (Bitte) request;
(Angelegenheit) matter

anliegend *Adj.* (a) (angrenzend) adjacent
(b) (beiliegend) enclosed

Anlieger *der;* ~s, ~, **Anliegerin** *die;* ~,
~nen resident; „~ **frei**' 'access only'

an|locken *tr. V.* attract ⟨customers, tourists,
etc.⟩; lure ⟨bird, animal⟩

an|lügen *tr. V.* lie to

an|machen *tr. V.* (a) put ⟨light, radio,
heating⟩ on; light ⟨fire⟩
(b) mix ⟨cement, plaster, paint, etc.⟩; dress
⟨salad⟩
(c) (ugs.: ansprechen) ⟨woman, girl⟩ give ⟨man,
boy⟩ the come-on (coll.); ⟨man, boy⟩ chat
⟨woman, girl⟩ up (Brit. coll.)
(d) (ugs.: begeistern, erregen) get ⟨audience etc.⟩
going; **das macht mich ungeheuer/nicht an** it
really turns me on (coll.)/does nothing for me
(coll.)
(e) (provozieren) **mach mich nicht an!** leave me
alone!

an|malen *tr. V.* paint

an|maßen *refl. V.* sich (*Dat.*) etw. ~: claim
sth. [for oneself]

an·maßend ① *Adj.* presumptuous;
(arrogant) arrogant
② *adv.* presumptuously; (arrogant) arrogantly

Anmaßung *die;* ~, ~en presumption;
(Arroganz) arrogance

Anmelde·formular *das* (a) application
form
(b) (einer Meldebehörde) registration form

an|melden ① *tr. V.* (a) (als Teilnehmer)
enrol (**zu** for); sich ~: enrol (**zu** for)
(b) (melden, anzeigen) license ⟨radio,
television⟩; apply for ⟨patent⟩; register
⟨domicile, change of address, car, trade
mark⟩; sich ~: register one's new address

**old spelling - see note on page xiv

(c) (ankündigen) announce; **sind Sie angemeldet?** do you have an appointment?; **sich beim Arzt ~:** make an appointment to see the doctor
(d) (geltend machen) express ⟨*reservation, doubt, wish*⟩; put forward ⟨*demand*⟩
2 *refl. V.* (DV) log on

An·meldung *die* **(a)** (zur Teilnahme) enrolment
(b) ▶ ANMELDEN B: licensing; application (*Gen.* for); registration
(c) (Ankündigung) announcement; (beim Arzt, Rechtsanwalt usw.) making an appointment

an|merken *tr. V.* **(a)** **jmdm. seinen Ärger/ seine Verlegenheit** *usw.* **~:** notice that sb. is annoyed/embarrassed *etc.;* **man merkt ihm [nicht] an, dass er krank ist** you can[not] tell that he is ill; **sich nichts ~ lassen** not let it show
(b) (geh.: bemerken) note

Anmerkung *die;* ~, ~en **(a)** (Fußnote) note
(b) (geh.: Bemerkung) comment

an|motzen *tr. V.* (ugs.) swear at

Anmut *die;* ~ (geh.) grace

an·mutig (geh.) 1 *Adj.* graceful ⟨*girl, movement, dance*⟩; charming, delightful ⟨*girl, smile, picture, landscape*⟩
2 *adv.* ⟨*move, dance*⟩ gracefully; ⟨*smile, greet*⟩ charmingly

an|nähen *tr. V.* sew on

an|nähern 1 *refl. V.* get closer (*Dat.* to sth)
2 *tr. V.* bring closer (*Dat.* to)

annähernd 1 *Adv.* almost; (ungefähr) approximately
2 *adj.* approximate

Annahme *die;* ~, ~n **(a)** (das Annehmen) acceptance
(b) (Vermutung) assumption; **in der ~, dass ...:** on the assumption that ...

annehmbar 1 *Adj.* **(a)** acceptable
(b) (recht gut) reasonable
2 *adv.* reasonably [well]

an|nehmen *unr. tr. V.* **(a)** accept; take; accept ⟨*alms, invitation, condition, help*⟩; take ⟨*food, telephone call*⟩; accept, take up ⟨*offer, challenge*⟩
(b) (Sport) take ⟨*ball, pass, etc.*⟩
(c) (billigen) approve
(d) (aufnehmen) take on ⟨*worker, patient, pupil*⟩
(e) (hinnehmen) accept ⟨*fate, verdict, punishment*⟩
(f) (adoptieren) adopt
(g) (haften lassen) take ⟨*dye, ink*⟩
(h) (sich aneignen) adopt ⟨*habit, mannerism, name, attitude*⟩
(i) (bekommen) take on ⟨*look, appearance, form, dimension*⟩
(j) (vermuten, voraussetzen) assume; **angenommen, [dass]** ...: assuming [that] ...

Annehmlichkeit *die;* ~, ~en comfort; (Vorteil) advantage

annektieren *tr. V.* annex

Annektierung *die;* ~, ~en, **Annexion** *die;* ~, ~en annexation

Annonce /a'nõːsə/ *die;* ~, ~n advertisement; advert (Brit. coll.)

annoncieren *itr. V.* advertise

annullieren *tr. V.* annul

Annullierung *die;* ~, ~en annulment

anonym 1 *Adj.* anonymous
2 *adv.* anonymously

Anonymität *die;* ~: anonymity

Anorak *der;* ~s, ~s anorak

an|ordnen *tr. V.* **(a)** (arrangieren) arrange
(b) (befehlen) order

An·ordnung *die* ▶ ANORDNEN: **(a)** arrangement
(b) order

anorektisch /anˌoˈrɛktɪʃ/ *Adj.* anorexic

Anorexie /anˌoʀɛˈksiː/ *die;* ~ (Med.) anorexia

an·organisch *Adj.* inorganic

an|packen 1 *tr. V.* **(a)** (ugs.: anfassen) grab hold of
(b) (angehen) tackle
2 *itr. V.* [mit] ~ (ugs.: mithelfen) lend a hand

an|passen 1 *tr. V.* **(a)** (passend machen) fit
(b) (abstimmen) suit (*Dat.* to)
2 *refl. V.* adapt [oneself] (*Dat.* to); ⟨*animal*⟩ adapt

Anpassung *die;* ~, ~en adaptation (an + *Akk.* to)

anpassungs·fähig *Adj.* adaptable

an|pfeifen 1 *unr. tr. V.* **das Spiel/die zweite Halbzeit ~:** blow the whistle to start the game/the second half
2 *unr. itr. V.* blow the whistle

An·pfiff *der* **(a)** (Sport) whistle for the start of play
(b) (salopp: Zurechtweisung) bawling-out (coll.)

an|pflanzen *tr. V.* **(a)** plant
(b) (anbauen) grow

an|pöbeln *tr. V.* (ugs.) abuse

an|prangern *tr. V.* denounce (**als** as)

an|preisen *unr. tr. V.* extol

An·probe *die* fitting

an|probieren *tr. V.* try on

an|rechnen *tr. V.* **(a)** count
(b) **jmdm. etw. ~** (in Rechnung stellen) charge sb. for sth.

An·recht *das* right; **ein ~ auf etw.** (*Akk.*) **haben** be entitled to sth.

An·rede *die* form of address

an|reden *tr. V.* address

an|regen *tr. V.* **(a)** stimulate ⟨*imagination, digestion*⟩; whet ⟨*appetite*⟩
(b) (ermuntern) prompt; (vorschlagen) propose

anregend *Adj.* stimulating

An·regung *die* **(a)** ▶ ANREGEN A: stimulation; whetting
(b) (Denkanstoß) stimulus
(c) (Vorschlag) proposal

an|reichern 1 *tr. V.* enrich ⋯⟩

2 *refl. V.* accumulate

An·reise *die* journey [there/here]

an|reisen *itr. V.; mit sein* travel there/here; **mit der Bahn** ∼: go/come by train

An·reiz *der* incentive

an|rempeln *tr. V.* barge into; (absichtlich) jostle

Anrichte *die;* ∼, ∼n sideboard

an|richten *tr. V.* (a) arrange ⟨*food*⟩; (servieren) serve
(b) cause ⟨*disaster, confusion, devastation, etc.*⟩

anrüchig *Adj.* (a) disreputable
(b) (unanständig) indecent

an|rücken *itr. V.; mit sein* ⟨*troops*⟩ advance; ⟨*firemen, police*⟩ move in

An·ruf *der* call

Anruf·beantworter *der;* ∼s, ∼: [telephone] answering machine

an|rufen *unr. tr. V.* (a) call *or* shout to ⟨*friend, passer-by*⟩; call ⟨*sleeping person*⟩
(b) (geh.: angehen, bitten) appeal to ⟨*person, court*⟩ (um for); call upon ⟨*God*⟩
(c) *auch itr.* (telefonisch ∼) call

Anrufer *der;* ∼s, ∼, **Anruferin** *die;* ∼, ∼nen caller

an|rühren *tr. V.* (a) touch
(b) (bereiten) mix

ans *Präp. + Art.* (a) = an das;
(b) **sich** ∼ **Arbeiten machen** set to work

An·sage *die* announcement

an|sagen *tr. V.* (a) announce
(b) (Kartenspiele) bid

Ansager *der;* ∼s, ∼, **Ansagerin** *die;* ∼, ∼nen (Radio, Fernsehen) announcer

an|sammeln 1 *tr. V.* accumulate; amass ⟨*riches, treasure*⟩
2 *refl. V.* accumulate; (fig.) ⟨*anger, excitement*⟩ build up

An·sammlung *die* (a) collection
(b) (Auflauf) crowd

ansässig *Adj.* resident

An·satz *der* (erstes Zeichen, Beginn) beginnings *pl.*

an|schaffen *tr. V.* [**sich** (*Dat.*)] **etw.** ∼ get [oneself] sth.

An·schaffung *die* purchase

an|schalten *tr. V.* switch on

an|schauen *tr. V.* (bes. südd., österr., schweiz.)
▶ ANSEHEN

anschaulich 1 *Adj.* vivid
2 *adv.* vividly

Anschauung *die;* ∼, ∼en (a) (Wahrnehmung) experience
(b) (Auffassung) view

An·schein *der* appearance; **allem** *od.* **dem** ∼ **nach** to all appearances

an·scheinend *Adv.* apparently

an|schieben *unr. tr. V.* push ⟨*vehicle*⟩

an|schießen *unr. tr. V.* shoot and wound

An·schlag *der* (a) (Bekanntmachung) notice; (Plakat) poster
(b) (Attentat) assassination attempt; (auf ein Gebäude, einen Zug usw.) attack
(c) (Texterfassung) keystroke
(d) **mit dem Gewehr im** ∼: with rifle/rifles levelled

an|schlagen *unr. tr. V.* (a) put up, ⟨*notice, announcement, message*⟩ (an + *Akk.* on)
(b) (beschädigen) chip

an|schließen 1 *unr. tr. V.* (a) connect (an + *Akk. od. Dat.* to); connect up ⟨*electrical device*⟩
(b) (festschließen) lock, secure (an + *Dat. od. Akk.* to)
2 *unr. refl. V.* **sich jmdm./einer Sache** ∼: join sb./sth.

An·schluss, ***An·schluß** *der* connection; **kein** ∼ **unter dieser Nummer** number unobtainable

Anschluss-, ***Anschluß-:** ∼**kabel** *das* connecting cable *or* (esp. Brit.) lead; ∼**zug** *der* connecting train

an|schnallen *tr. V.* put on ⟨*skis, skates*⟩; **sich** ∼ (im Auto) put on one's seat belt; (im Flugzeug) fasten one's seat belt

an|schrauben *tr. V.* screw on (an + *Akk.* to)

An·schreiben *das* covering letter

an|schreien *unr. tr. V.* shout at

An·schrift *die* address

Anschuldigung *die;* ∼, ∼en accusation

an|schwärzen *tr. V.* (ugs.) jmdn. ∼ (in Misskredit bringen) blacken sb.'s name; (schlecht machen) run sb. down (**bei** to); (denunzieren) inform *or* (Brit. sl.) grass on sb. (**bei** to)

an|schwellen *unr. itr. V.; mit sein* (a) swell [up]; (fig.) swell; ⟨*water, river*⟩ rise
(b) (lauter werden) grow louder; ⟨*noise*⟩ rise

an|schwemmen *tr. V.* wash ashore

an|sehen *unr. tr. V.* (a) look at; watch ⟨*television programme*⟩; see ⟨*play, film*⟩; **jmdn. groß/böse** ∼: stare at sb./give sb. an angry look; **hübsch** *usw.* **anzusehen sein** be pretty *etc.* to look at; **sieh [mal] [einer] an!** (ugs.) well, I never! (coll.)
(b) (erkennen) **man sieht ihm sein Alter nicht an** he does not look his age; **man sieht ihr die Strapazen an** she's showing the strain
(c) (zusehen bei) **etw. [mit]** ∼: watch sth.; **das kann man doch nicht [mit]** ∼: I/you can't just stand by and watch that

Ansehen *das;* ∼s [high] standing

an·sehnlich *Adj.* (a) (beträchtlich) considerable
(b) (gut aussehend, stattlich) handsome

***an|sein** ▶ AN 3B

an|setzen *tr. V.* (a) (in die richtige Stellung bringen) position ⟨*ladder, jack, drill, saw*⟩
(b) (anfügen) attach, put on (an + *Akk. od. Dat.* to)
(c) (festlegen) fix ⟨*meeting etc.*⟩ (**für, auf** + *Akk.* for); fix, set ⟨*deadline, date, price*⟩

(d) (veranschlagen) estimate
(e) (anrühren) mix

An·sicht die **(a)** (Meinung) opinion; view;
meiner ∼ nach in my opinion or view
(b) (Bild) view

Ansichts·karte die picture postcard

an|spannen tr. V. **(a)** harness ⟨horse etc.⟩
(an + Akk. to); yoke up ⟨oxen⟩ (an + Akk.
to); hitch up ⟨carriage, cart, etc.⟩ (an + Akk.
to)
(b) (anstrengen) strain

An·spannung die strain

an|spielen itr. V. auf jmdn./etw. ∼: allude
to sb./sth.

Anspielung die; ∼, ∼en allusion (auf +
Akk. to); (verächtlich, böse) insinuation (auf +
Akk. about)

Ansporn der; ∼[e]s, ∼e incentive

an|spornen tr. V. spur on

An·sprache die speech; address

an|sprechen [1] unr. tr. V. **(a)** speak to
(b) (gefallen) appeal to
[2] unr. itr. V. (reagieren) respond (auf + Akk.
to)

ansprechend [1] Adj. attractive;
attractive, appealing ⟨personality⟩
[2] adv. attractively

Ansprech·partner der,
Ansprech·partnerin die contact

an|springen [1] unr. itr. V.; mit sein ⟨car,
engine⟩ start
[2] unr. tr. V. jump up at

An·spruch der **(a)** claim; (Forderung)
demand; [keine] Ansprüche stellen make
[no] demands; in ∼ nehmen take advantage
of ⟨offer⟩; exercise ⟨right⟩; take up ⟨time⟩;
[einen] ∼/keinen ∼ auf etw. (Akk.) haben
be/not be entitled to sth.
(b) (Anrecht) right

an·spruchs·: ∼los [1] Adj. **(a)** (genügsam)
undemanding; **(b)** (schlicht) unpretentious;
[2] adv. **(a)** (genügsam) undemandingly; ⟨live⟩
modestly; **(b)** (schlicht) unpretentiously;
∼voll Adj. discriminating ⟨reader,
audience, gourmet⟩; (schwierig) demanding;
ambitious ⟨subject⟩

an|spucken tr. V. spit at

Anstalt die; ∼, ∼en institution

An·stand der decency

anständig [1] Adj. decent; (ehrbar)
respectable
[2] adv. decently; (ordentlich) properly

an|starren tr. V. stare at

an·statt Konj. ∼ zu arbeiten/∼, dass er
arbeitet instead of working

an|stecken [1] tr. V. **(a)** pin on ⟨badge,
brooch⟩; put on ⟨ring⟩
(b) (infizieren, auch fig.) infect
[2] itr. V. be infectious

ansteckend Adj. infectious; (durch
Berührung) contagious

Ansteckung die; ∼, ∼en infection; (durch
Berührung) contagion

Ansteckungs·gefahr die risk or danger
of infection

an|stehen unr. itr. V. (Schlange stehen)
queue [up], (Amer.) stand in line (nach for)

an·stelle [1] Präp. mit Gen. instead of
[2] Adv. ∼ von instead of

an|stellen [1] refl. V. queue [up], (Amer.)
stand in line (nach for)
[2] tr. V. **(a)** (aufdrehen) turn on
(b) (einschalten) switch on
(c) (einstellen) employ

An·stellung die **(a)** employment
(b) (Stellung) job

Anstieg der; ∼[e]s rise, increase (+ Gen.
in)

an|stiften tr. V. incite

An·stifter der, **An·stifterin** die
instigator

An·stiftung die incitement

an|stimmen tr. V. start singing ⟨song⟩;
start playing ⟨piece of music⟩; ein Geschrei
∼: start shouting

An·stoß der **(a)** stimulus (zu for); den
[ersten] ∼ zu etw. geben initiate sth.
(b) ∼ erregen cause offence (bei to); [keinen]
∼ an etw. (Dat.) nehmen [not] object to sth.

an|stoßen [1] unr. itr. V. **(a)** mit sein an
etw. (Akk.) ∼: bump into sth.
(b) [mit den Gläsern] ∼: clink glasses; auf
jmdn./etw. ∼: drink to sb./sth.
[2] unr. tr. V. jmdn./etw. ∼: give sb./sth. a
push; jmdn. aus Versehen ∼: knock into sb.
inadvertently

anstößig [1] Adj. offensive
[2] adv. offensively

an|strahlen tr. V. **(a)** illuminate; (mit
Scheinwerfer) floodlight
(b) (anblicken) beam at

an|streben tr. V. (geh.) aspire to; (mit großer
Anstrengung) strive for

an|streichen unr. tr. V. **(a)** paint
(b) (markieren) mark

an|strengen [1] refl. V. make an effort;
sich mehr/sehr ∼: make more of an effort/a
great effort
[2] tr. V. strain ⟨eyes, ears, voice⟩; be a strain
on ⟨person⟩; seine Fantasie ∼: exercise one's
imagination

anstrengend Adj. (körperlich) strenuous;
(geistig) demanding

Anstrengung die; ∼, ∼en **(a)** effort;
große ∼en machen, etw. zu tun make every
effort to do sth.
(b) (Strapaze) strain

An·strich der paint

An·sturm der rush (auf + Akk. to); (auf
Banken, Waren) run (auf + Akk. on)

Antarktika (das); ∼s Antarctica

Antarktis die; ∼: Antarctic

antarktisch Adj. Antarctic

An·teil der share (an + Dat. of); ∼ an etw.
(Dat.) nehmen take an interest in sth.

An·teilnahme *die;* ~ (a) interest (an +
Dat. in)
(b) (Mitgefühl) sympathy (an + *Dat.* with)
Antenne *die;* ~, ~n aerial; antenna (Amer.)
Anthrax /'antraks/ *der;* ~ (Med.) anthrax
anti-, Anti- anti-
Anti·alkoholiker *der,*
Anti·alkoholikerin *die* teetotaller
Antibiotikum *das;* ~s, **Antibiotika** (Med.)
antibiotic
anti-, Anti- ~**blockier·system** *das*
(Kfz-W.) anti-lock braking system;
~**faschist** *der,* ~**faschistin** *die* anti-fascist;
~**faschistisch** *Adj.* anti-fascist
antik *Adj.* (a) classical
(b) (aus vergangenen Zeiten) antique ⟨*furniture,
fittings, etc.*⟩
Antike *die;* ~: classical antiquity *no art.*
Antilope *die;* ~, ~n antelope
Antipathie *die;* ~, ~n antipathy
Antiquariat antiquarian bookshop/
department; (mit neueren gebrauchten Büchern)
second-hand bookshop/department
Antiquität *die;* ~, ~en antique
Antiviren·software *die* (DV) anti-virus
software
Antlitz *das;* ~es, ~e (dichter., geh.)
countenance (literary); face
Antrag *der;* ~[e]s, **Anträge** (a) application
(auf + *Akk.* for); **einen** ~ **stellen** make an
application
(b) (Formular) application form
Antrags·formular *das* application form
an|treffen *unr. tr. V.* find; (zufällig) come
across
an|treiben *unr. tr. V.* (a) drive ⟨*animals,
column of prisoners*⟩ on or along; (fig.) urge
(b) (in Bewegung setzen) drive; power ⟨*ship,
aircraft*⟩
an|treten ① *unr. itr. V.; mit sein* (a) form
up; (in Linie) line up; (Milit.) fall in
(b) (sich stellen) meet one's opponent; (als
Mannschaft) line up; **gegen jmdn.** ~: meet sb./
line up against sb.
② *unr. tr. V.* start ⟨*job, apprenticeship*⟩; take
up ⟨*position, appointment*⟩; set out on
⟨*journey*⟩; begin ⟨*prison sentence*⟩; come into
⟨*inheritance*⟩
An·trieb *der* drive
An·tritt *der;* **vor** ~ **Ihres Urlaubs** before you
go on holiday (Brit.) *or* (Amer.) vacation; **vor** ~
der Reise before setting out on the journey
an|tun *unr. tr. V.* (a) **jmdm. ein Leid** ~: hurt
sb.; **jmdm. etwas Böses/ein Unrecht** ~: do sb.
harm/an injustice
(b) **jmd./etw. hat es jmdm. angetan** sb. was
taken with sb./sth.; *s. auch* ANGETAN
Antwort *die;* ~, ~en (a) answer; reply; **er
gab mir keine** ~: he didn't answer [me] *or*
reply
(b) (Reaktion) response

antworten *itr. V.* (a) answer; reply; **auf
etw.** (*Akk.*) ~: answer sth.; reply to sth.;
jmdm. ~: answer sb.; reply to sb.
(b) (reagieren) respond (**auf** + *Akk.* to)
an|vertrauen ① *tr. V.* **jmdm. etw.** ~:
entrust sb. with sth.; (fig.: mitteilen) confide
sth. to sb.
② *refl. V.* **sich jmdm./einer Sache** ~: put
one's trust in sb./sth.; **sich jmdm.** ~ (fig.: sich
jmdm. mitteilen) confide in sb.
an|wachsen *unr. itr. V.; mit sein* (a) grow
on
(b) (Wurzeln schlagen) take root
(c) (zunehmen) grow
Anwalt *der;* ~[e]s, **Anwälte**, **Anwältin**
die; ~, ~nen (a) (Rechtsanwalt, -anwältin)
lawyer; solicitor (Brit.); attorney (Amer.); (vor
Gericht) barrister (Brit.); attorney[-at-law]
(Amer.); advocate (Scot.)
(b) (Fürsprecher) advocate
An·wärter *der,* **An·wärterin** *die*
candidate (auf + *Akk.* for); (Sport) contender
(auf + *Akk.* for)
an|weisen *unr. tr. V.* instruct
An·weisung *die* instruction
an|wenden *unr.* (*auch regelm.*) *tr. V.* use,
employ ⟨*process, trick, method, violence,
force*⟩; use ⟨*medicine, money, time*⟩; apply
⟨*rule, paragraph, proverb, etc.*⟩ (**auf** + *Akk.*
to)
Anwender *der;* ~s, ~ (DV) user
anwender·freundlich *Adj.* (bes. DV)
user-friendly
Anwenderin *die;* ~, ~nen (DV) user
An·wendung *die* (a) ▶ ANWENDEN: use;
employment; application
(b) (DV) application
An·wesen *das* property
anwesend *Adj.* present (bei at); **die
Anwesenden** those present
Anwesenheit *die;* ~: presence
an|widern *tr. V.* nauseate
Anwohner *der;* ~s, ~, **Anwohnerin**
die; ~, ~nen resident; **Parken nur für** ~
residents-only parking
An·zahl *die;* ~: number; **eine ganze** ~: a
whole lot
an|zahlen *tr. V.* put down ⟨*sum*⟩ as a
deposit (auf + *Akk.* on); (bei Ratenzahlung)
make a down payment of ⟨*sum*⟩ (auf + *Akk.*
on)
An·zahlung *die* deposit; (bei Ratenzahlung)
down payment
An·zeichen *das* sign; indication
Anzeige *die;* ~, ~n (a) (Straf~) report
(b) (Inserat) advertisement
(c) (eines Instruments) display
an|zeigen *tr. V.* (a) (Strafanzeige erstatten)
jmdn./etw. ~: report sb./sth. to the police/the
authorities
(b) (zeigen) show; indicate; show ⟨*time, date*⟩
(c) (DV) display

Anzeigen-: ∼**blatt** *das* advertiser; ∼**teil** *der* advertisement section *or* pages *pl.*

an|ziehen *unr. tr. V.* **(a)** (auch fig.) attract **(b)** draw up ⟨*knees, feet, etc.*⟩ **(c)** tighten ⟨*rope, wire, screw, knot, belt, etc.*⟩; put on ⟨*handbrake*⟩ **(d)** (ankleiden) dress; **sich** ∼: get dressed **(e)** (anlegen) put on ⟨*clothes*⟩

anziehend *Adj.* attractive

An·ziehung *die* attraction

Anziehungs·kraft *die* attractive force; (fig.) attraction

An·zug *der* **(a)** suit **(b)** **im** ∼ **sein** ⟨*storm*⟩ be approaching; ⟨*fever, illness*⟩ be coming on; ⟨*enemy*⟩ be advancing

anzüglich ⒈ *Adj.* insinuating ⟨*remark, question*⟩ ⒉ *adv.* in an insinuating way

Anzüglichkeit *die;* ∼, ∼**en (a)** (Art) insinuating nature **(b)** (Bemerkung) insinuating remark

an|zünden *tr. V.* light; set fire to ⟨*building etc.*⟩

an|zweifeln *tr. V.* doubt; question

apart ⒈ *Adj.* individual *attrib.;* ⒉ *adv.* in an individual style

Apartheid *die;* ∼: apartheid *no art.*

Apartheit *die;* ∼: individuality

Apartment *das;* ∼**s,** ∼**s** studio flat (Brit.); studio apartment (Amer.)

Apartment·haus *das* block of studio flats (Brit.) *or* (Amer.) studio apartments

Apathie *die;* ∼, ∼**n** apathy

apathisch ⒈ *Adj.* apathetic ⒉ *adv.* apathetically

Aperitif /aperi'tiːf/ *der;* ∼**s,** ∼**s** aperitif

Apfel *der;* ∼**s,** Äpfel apple

Apfel-: ∼**baum** *der* apple tree; ∼**kuchen** *der* apple cake; (mit Äpfeln belegt) apple flan; ∼**mus** *das* apple purée; ∼**saft** *der* apple juice

Apfelsine *die;* ∼, ∼**n** orange

Apfel-: ∼**strudel** *der* apfelstrudel; ∼**wein** *der* cider

Apostel *der;* ∼**s,** ∼: apostle

Apotheke *die;* ∼, ∼**n (a)** chemist's [shop] (Brit.); drugstore (Amer.) **(b)** (Hausapotheke) medicine cabinet; (Reise-, Bordapotheke) first-aid kit

Apotheker *der;* ∼**s,** ∼, **Apothekerin** *die;* ∼, ∼**nen** [dispensing] chemist (Brit.); druggist

App. *Abk.* = **Apparat** ext.

Apparat *der;* ∼**[e]s,** ∼**e (a)** apparatus *no pl.;* (Haushaltsgerät) appliance; (kleiner) gadget **(b)** (Radio) radio; (Fernseher) television; (Kamera) camera **(c)** (Telefon) telephone; (Nebenstelle) extension; **am** ∼! speaking! **(d)** (Personen und Hilfsmittel) organization; (Verwaltungsapparat) system

Apparate·medizin *die* (oft abwertend) high-technology medicine

Appartement /apartə'mãː, (schweiz. auch:) -'mɛnt/ *das;* ∼**s,** ∼**s** (schweiz. auch: ∼**e) (a)** ▶ APARTMENT; **(b)** (Hotelsuite) suite

Appell *der;* ∼**s,** ∼**e (a)** appeal (zu for, **an** + *Akk.* to) **(b)** (Milit.) muster; (Anwesenheits∼) roll-call

appellieren *itr. V.* appeal (**an** + *Akk.* to)

Appetit *der;* ∼**[e]s,** ∼**e** appetite (**auf** + *Akk.* for); **guten** ∼! enjoy your meal!

appetitlich *Adj.* **(a)** appetizing **(b)** (sauber, ansprechend) attractive and hygienic

Appetit·losigkeit *die;* ∼: lack of appetite

applaudieren *itr. V.* applaud

Applaus *der;* ∼**es,** ∼**e** applause

Aprikose *die;* ∼, ∼**n** apricot

April *der;* ∼**[s],** ∼**e** April; **der** ∼: April

apropos /apro'poː/ *Adv.* apropos; by the way; incidentally

Aquädukt *der od. das;* ∼**[e]s,** ∼**e** aqueduct

Aquarell *das;* ∼**s,** ∼**e** watercolour [painting]

Aquarium *das;* ∼**s,** **Aquarien** aquarium

Äquator *der;* ∼**s** equator

Ar *das od. der;* ∼**s,** ∼**e** are

Ära *die;* ∼, Ären era

Araber *der;* ∼**s,** ∼, **Araberin** *die;* ∼, ∼**nen** Arab

Arabien /a'raːbiən/ *(das);* ∼**s** Arabia

arabisch *Adj.* Arabian; Arabic ⟨*language, numeral, literature, etc.*⟩

Arbeit *die;* ∼, ∼**en (a)** work *no indef. art.;* **vor/nach der** ∼ (ugs.) before/after work **(b)** (Produkt, Werk) work **(c)** (Aufgabe) job **(d)** (Klassenarbeit) test

arbeiten ⒈ *itr. V.* work ⒉ *tr. V.* (herstellen) make

Arbeiter *der;* ∼**s,** ∼, **Arbeiterin** *die;* ∼, ∼**nen** worker; (Bau∼, Land∼) labourer

Arbeiter-: ∼**kind** *das* working-class child; ∼**klasse** *die* working class[es *pl.*]

Arbeiterschaft *die;* ∼: workers *pl.*

Arbeit·geber *der;* ∼**s,** ∼: employer

Arbeitgeber·anteil *der* employer's contribution

Arbeit·geberin *die;* ∼, ∼**nen** employer

Arbeitgeber·verband *der* employers' association *or* organization

Arbeitnehmer *der;* ∼**s,** ∼ employee

Arbeitnehmer·anteil *der* employee's contribution

Arbeitnehmerin *die;* ∼, ∼**nen** employee

arbeits-, Arbeits-: ∼**amt** *das* job centre (Brit.); ∼**anfang** *der* starting time [at work]; ∼**bedingungen** *Pl.* working conditions; ∼**beginn** *der* ▶ ∼ANFANG; ∼**belastung** *die* workload; ⋯⋮

~**beschaffungs·maßnahme** *die* job-creation measure; ~**erlaubnis** *die* work permit; ~**fähig** *Adj.* fit for work *postpos.*; (grundsätzlich) able to work *postpos.*; ~**gang** *der* operation; ~**genehmigung** *die* work permit; ~**gericht** *das* industrial tribunal; ~**kollege** *der*, ~**kollegin** *die* (bei Arbeitern) workmate (Brit.); fellow worker; (bei Angestellten, Beamten) colleague; ~**kraft** *die* (a) capacity for work; (b) (Mensch) worker; ~**last** *die* burden of work; ~**leben** *das* (a) (Berufstätigkeit) working life; (b) (Arbeitswelt) world of work; working life *no art.;* ~**los** *Adj.* unemployed; sich ~los melden sign on [for the dole] (coll.;) ~**lose** *der/die; adj. Dekl.* unemployed person/man/woman *etc.;* die ~**losen** the unemployed; ~**losengeld** *das* (full-rate) earnings-related unemployment benefit; ~**losenhilfe** *die* (a) (Geld) reduced-rate unemployment benefit; (b) (Institution) reduced-rate unemployment benefit system; ~**losigkeit** *die;* ~~: unemployment *no indef. art.;* ~**mangel** *der* lack of work; ~**markt** *der* labour market; ~**platz** *der* (a) (Platz im Betrieb) workplace; am ~platz at one's workplace; (b) (~stätte) place of work; den ~platz wechseln change one's place of work; (c) (~verhältnis) job; ~**scheu** *Adj.* work-shy; ~**suchende** *der/die; adj. Dekl.* person/man/woman looking for work; die ~suchenden those looking for work: ~**tag** *der* working day; ~**teilung** *die* division of labour; ~**unfähig** *Adj.* unfit for work *postpos.;* (grundsätzlich) unable to work *postpos.;* ~**unfähigkeit** *die* ▶ ~UNFÄHIG: inability to work; unfitness for work; ~**unfall** *der* industrial accident; er hatte einen ~unfall he had an accident at work; ~**vermittlung** *die* (a) (Tätigkeit) arranging employment; (b) (Stelle) employment exchange; job centre (Brit.); (Firma) employment agency; ~**vertrag** *der* contract of employment; ~**zeit** *die* working hours *pl.;* die tägliche ~zeit the working day; ~**zeit·konto** *das* flexitime work record; ~**zimmer** *das* study

Archäologe *der;* ~n, ~n archaeologist

Archäologie *die;* ~: archaeology *no art.*

Archäologin *die;* ~, ~nen archaeologist

archäologisch *Adj.* archaeological

Arche *die;* ~, ~n ark; die ~ Noah Noah's Ark

Architekt *der;* ~en, ~en, **Architektin** *die;* ~, ~nen architect

Architektur *die;* ~ architecture

Archiv *das;* ~s, ~e archives *pl.;* archive

Ären ▶ ÄRA

Arena *die;* ~, Arenen arena; (Stierkampf~, Manege) ring

arg, ärger, ärgst... (geh., landsch.) ① *Adj.* (a) (schlimm) bad; im Argen liegen be in a sorry state (b) (unangenehm groß, stark) severe ⟨pain, hunger, shock, disappointment⟩; serious ⟨error, dilemma⟩; extreme ⟨embarrassment⟩; gross ⟨exaggeration, injustice⟩ ② *adv.* (äußerst, sehr) extremely

Ärger *der;* ~s (a) annoyance (b) (Unannehmlichkeiten) trouble; ~ bekommen get into trouble

ärgerlich ① *Adj.* (a) annoyed (b) (Ärger erregend) annoying ② *adv.* (a) with annoyance (b) (Ärger erregend) annoyingly

ärgern ① *tr. V.* (a) annoy (b) (reizen) tease ② *refl. V.* sich [über jmdn./etw.] ~: be/get annoyed [at sb./about sth.]

Ärgernis *das;* ~ses, ~se annoyance; (etw. Anstößiges) nuisance

arg-, Arg-: ~**list** *die* deceit; (Heimtücke) malice; ~**listig** *Adj.* deceitful; (heimtückisch) malicious; ~**los** ① *Adj.* unsuspecting; ② *adv.* unsuspectingly; ~**losigkeit** *die;* ~~: unsuspecting nature

ärgst... ▶ ARG

Argument *das;* ~[e]s, ~e argument

Argumentation *die;* ~, ~en argumentation

argumentieren *itr. V.* argue

Argwohn *der;* ~[e]s suspicion

argwöhnisch (geh.) ① *Adj.* suspicious ② *adv.* suspiciously

Arie /'aːriə/ *die;* ~, ~n aria

arisch *Adj.* (Völkerk., Sprachw., ns.) Aryan

Aristokrat *der;* ~en, ~en aristocrat

Aristokratie *die;* ~, ~n aristocracy

Aristokratin *die;* ~, ~nen aristocrat

aristokratisch ① *Adj.* aristocratic ② *adv.* aristocratically

arithmetisch ① *Adj.* arithmetical ② *adv.* arithmetically

Arkade *die;* ~, ~n arcade

Arktis *die;* ~: Arctic

arktisch *Adj.* Arctic; (fig.) arctic

arm, ärmer, ärmst... *Adj.* poor; Arm und Reich (veralt.) rich and poor [alike]; an Nährstoffen poor in nutrients; der/die Ärmste od. Arme the poor man/boy/woman/girl

Arm *der;* ~[e]s, ~e arm; jmdm. [mit etw.] unter die ~e greifen help sb. out [with sth.]; ein Hemd mit halbem ~: a short-sleeved shirt

Armaturen·brett *das* instrument panel; (im Kfz) dashboard

Arm-: ~**band** *das* bracelet; (Uhr~) strap; ~**band·uhr** *die* wristwatch

Armee *die;* ~, ~n (auch fig.) army

Ärmel *der;* ~s, ~: sleeve; [sich (Dat.)] etw. aus dem ~ schütteln (ugs.) produce sth. just like that

Ärmel·kanal *der;* ~s [English] Channel

ärmer ▶ ARM

ärmlich 1 *Adj.* cheap ⟨*clothing*⟩; shabby ⟨*flat, office*⟩; meagre ⟨*meal*⟩
2 *adv.* cheaply ⟨*furnished, dressed*⟩

arm·selig *Adj.* (a) miserable; pathetic ⟨*result, figure*⟩; meagre ⟨*meal, food*⟩; paltry ⟨*return, salary, sum, fee*⟩
(b) (abwertend: erbärmlich) miserable

ärmst... ▶ ARM

Armut *die;* ∼: poverty

Armuts: ∼**falle** *die* poverty trap; ∼**grenze** *die* poverty line

Aroma *das;* ∼s, Aromen (Duft) aroma; (Geschmack) flavour

aromatisch *Adj.* aromatic; distinctive ⟨*taste*⟩; ∼ **duften** give off an aromatic fragrance

arrangieren /arã'ziːrən/ 1 *tr. V.* (geh., Musik) arrange
2 *refl. V.* sich ∼: adapt; sich mit jmdm. ∼: come to an accommodation with sb.

Arrest *der;* ∼[e]s, ∼e detention

arrogant 1 *Adj.* arrogant
2 *adv.* arrogantly

Arroganz *die;* ∼ arrogance

Arsch *der;* ∼[e]s, Ärsche (derb) (a) arse (Brit. coarse); ass (Amer. sl.); **leck mich am** ∼**!** (fig.) piss off (sl.); **im** ∼ **sein** (fig.) be buggered (coarse)
(b) (widerlicher Mensch) arsehole (Brit. coarse); asshole (Amer. coarse.)

Arsch·loch *das* (derb) ▶ ARSCH B

Art *die;* ∼, ∼en (a) kind; sort; **Bücher aller** ∼: all kinds *or* sorts of books; [**so**] **eine** ∼ ...: a sort of ...; (in einer Familie) be different from all the rest of the family
(b) (Biol.) species
(c) (Wesen) nature; (Verhaltensweise) way; (gutes Benehmen) behaviour; **die feine englische** ∼ (ugs.) the proper way to behave
(d) (Weise) way; **auf diese** ∼: in this way; ∼ **und Weise** way; (Kochk.) **nach** ∼ **des Hauses** à la maison; **nach Schweizer** ∼: Swiss style

arten-, Arten-: ∼**barriere** *die,* ∼**grenze** *die* (Biol.) species barrier; ∼**reich** *Adj.* (Biol.) species-rich; ∼**reichtum** *der* (Biol.) species-richness; ∼**schutz** *der* protection of species; species protection

Arterie /ar'teːriə/ *die;* ∼, ∼n artery

artig *Adj.* well-behaved; **sei** ∼: be a good boy/girl/dog *etc.*

Artikel *der;* ∼s, ∼ (a) article
(b) (Ware) item

Artillerie *die;* ∼, ∼n artillery

Artischocke *die;* ∼, ∼n artichoke

Artist *der;* ∼en, ∼en, **Artistin** *die;* ∼, ∼nen [variety/circus] performer

Arznei *die;* ∼, ∼en (veralt.), **Arznei·mittel** *das* medicine

Arzt *der;* ∼es, Ärzte, **Ärztin** *die;* ∼, ∼nen doctor

Arzthelferin *die* doctor's receptionist

ärztlich 1 *Adj.* medical; **auf** ∼**e Verordnung** on doctor's orders
2 *adv.* **sich** ∼ **behandeln lassen** have medical treatment

***As** ▶ ASS

Asbest *der;* ∼[e]s, ∼e asbestos

Asche *die;* ∼, ∼n ash[es *pl.*]; (sterbliche Reste) ashes *pl.*

Aschen-: ∼**becher** *der* ashtray; ∼**brödel** *das;* ∼∼s, ∼∼ (auch fig.) Cinderella

Ascher·mittwoch *der* Ash Wednesday

Äser ▶ AAS

Asiat *der;* ∼en, ∼en, **Asiatin** *die;* ∼, ∼nen Asian

asiatisch *Adj.* Asian

Asien /'aːzjən/ (*das*); ∼s Asia

Asket *der;* ∼en, ∼en, **Asketin** *die;* ∼, ∼nen ascetic

asketisch 1 *Adj.* ascetic
2 *adv.* ascetically

asozial 1 *Adj.* asocial; (gegen die Gesellschaft gerichtet) antisocial
2 *adv.* asocially

Aspekt *der;* ∼[e]s, ∼e aspect

Asphalt *der;* ∼[e]s, ∼e asphalt

aß *1. u. 3. Pers. Sg. Prät. v.* ESSEN

Ass *das;* ∼es, ∼e ace

Assistent *der;* ∼en, ∼en, **Assistentin** *die;* ∼, ∼nen assistant

Ast *der;* ∼[e]s, Äste branch; **sich** (*Dat.*) **einen** ∼ **lachen** (ugs.) split one's sides [with laughter]

Aster *die;* ∼, ∼n aster; (Herbstaster) Michaelmas daisy

ästhetisch 1 *Adj.* aesthetic
2 *adv.* aesthetically

Asthma *das;* ∼s asthma

ast·rein 1 *Adj.* (ugs.) (in Ordnung) on the level (coll.); (echt) genuine; (salopp: prima, toll) fantastic (coll.); great (coll.)
2 *adv.* (salopp: prima) fantastically (coll.)

Astrologe *der;* ∼n, ∼n astrologer

Astrologie *die;* ∼: astrology *no art.*

Astrologin *die;* ∼, ∼nen astrologer

Astronaut *der;* ∼en, ∼en, **Astronautin** *die;* ∼, ∼nen astronaut

Astronom *der;* ∼en, ∼en astronomer

Astronomie *die;* ∼: astronomy *no art.*

Astronomin *die;* ∼, ∼nen astronomer

astronomisch *Adj.* astronomical

Asyl *das;* ∼s, ∼e (a) asylum
(b) (Obdachlosenheim) hostel

Asylant *der;* ∼en, ∼en, **Asylantin** *die;* ∼, ∼nen asylum seeker

Asylanten·heim *das* asylum seekers' hostel

Asyl-: ∼**antrag** *der* application for asylum; ∼**bewerber** *der,* **bewerberin** ⋯⟩

die person seeking [political] asylum;
~bewerber·heim *das* ▶ ASYLANTENHEIM;
~gesetz *das* asylum law[s *pl.*];
~missbrauch, ***~mißbrauch** *der*
misuse of asylum; **~recht** *das* (Rechtsw.) **(a)**
right of [political] asylum; **(b)** (eines Staates)
right to grant [political] asylum; **~werber**
der; ~~s, ~~, **~werberin** *die; ~~,*
~~nen (österr.) ▶ **~**BEWERBER

Atelier /atə'lje:/ *das; ~s, ~s* studio
Atem *der; ~s* breath; **außer ~ sein/geraten**
be/get out of breath
atem-, Atem-: ~beraubend [1] *Adj.*
breathtaking; [2] *adv.* breathtakingly; **~los**
[1] *Adj.* breathless; [2] *adv.* breathlessly;
~pause *die* breathing space; **~zug** *der*
breath
Atheismus *der; ~:* atheism *no art.*
Atheist *der; ~en, ~en,* **Atheistin** *die; ~,*
~nen atheist
atheistisch [1] *Adj.* atheistic
[2] *adv.* atheistically
Athen *(das); ~s* Athens
Äther *der; ~s, ~:* ether
Äthiopien /ɛ'tjo:pjən/ *(das); ~s* Ethiopia
Athlet *der; ~en, ~en* **(a)** (Sportler) athlete
(b) (ugs.: kräftiger Mann) muscleman
Athletin *die; ~, ~nen* athlete
athletisch *Adj.* athletic
Atlanten ▶ ATLAS[1]
Atlantik *der; ~s* Atlantic
atlantisch *Adj.* Atlantic; **der Atlantische
Ozean** the Atlantic Ocean
Atlas *der; ~ od. ~ses, Atlanten od. ~se*
atlas
atmen *itr., tr. V.* breathe
Atmosphäre /atmo'sfɛ:rə/ *die; ~, ~n* (auch
fig.) atmosphere
Atmung *die; ~:* breathing
Atom *das; ~s, ~e* atom
atomar *Adj.* atomic; (Atomwaffen betreffend)
nuclear
atom-, Atom-: ~ausstieg *der*
abandonment of nuclear power; **~bombe**
die atom bomb; **~energie** *die* nuclear
energy *no indef. art.;* **~kern** *der* atomic
nucleus; **~kraft** *die* nuclear power *no indef.
art.;* **~kraftwerk** *das* nuclear power
station; **~krieg** *der* nuclear war; **~müll**
der nuclear waste; **~physik** *die* nuclear
physics *sing., no art.;* **~pilz** *der* mushroom
cloud; **~reaktor** *der* nuclear reactor;
~strom *der* (ugs.) electricity generated by
nuclear power; **~waffe** *die* nuclear
weapon; **~waffen·frei** *Adj.* nuclear-free;
~waffen·test *der* nuclear [weapons] test;
~zeit·alter *das* nuclear age
Attacke *die; ~, ~n* (auch Med.) attack (**auf** +
Akk. on)

Attentat *das; ~[e]s, ~e* assassination
attempt; (erfolgreich) assassination
Attentäter *der; ~s, ~,* **Attentäterin**
die; ~, ~nen would-be assassin; (erfolgreich)
assassin
Attest *das; ~[e]s, ~e* medical certificate
Attraktion *die; ~, ~en* attraction
attraktiv [1] *Adj.* attractive
[2] *adv.* attractively
Attraktivität *die; ~:* attractiveness
Attrappe *die; ~, ~n* dummy
Attribut *das; ~[e]s, ~e* attribute
ätzen [1] *tr. V.* etch
[2] *itr. V.* corrode
ätzend [1] *Adj.* corrosive; (fig.) caustic ‹wit,
remark, criticism›; pungent ‹smell›
[2] *adv.* caustically ‹ironic, critical›
au *Interj.* **(a)** (bei Schmerz) ouch
(b) (bei Überraschung, Begeisterung) oh
Aubergine /obɛr'ʒi:nə/ *die; ~, ~n*
aubergine (Brit.); eggplant
auch [1] *Adv.* **(a)** as well; too; also; **Klaus
war ~ dabei** Klaus was there as well *or* too;
Klaus was also there; **Ich gehe jetzt. – Ich ~:**
I'm going now – So am I; **Mir ist warm. – Mir
~:** I feel warm – So do I; **das weiß ich ~
nicht** I don't know either
(b) (sogar, selbst) even; **~ wenn, wenn ~:** even
if
[2] *Partikel* **(a)** etwas anderes habe ich ~
nicht erwartet I never expected anything else;
nun hör aber ~ zu! now listen!
**(b) bist du dir ~ im Klaren, was das
bedeutet?** are you sure you understand what
that means?; **bist du ~ glücklich?** are you
truly happy?; **lügst du ~ nicht?** you're not
lying, are you?
(c) wo .../wer .../was ... usw. ~: wherever/
whoever/whatever *etc. ...;* **wie dem ~ sei**
however that may be
(d) mag er ~ noch so klug sein no matter
how clever he is
Audienz *die; ~, ~en* audience
Auditorium *das; ~s, Auditorien* **(a)**
(Hörsaal) auditorium
(b) (Zuhörerschaft) audience
auf [1] *Präp. mit Dat.* **(a)** on; **~ See** at sea;
~ dem Baum in the tree; **~ der Erde** on
earth; **~ der Welt** in the world; **~ der Straße**
in the street
(b) at ‹post office, town, hall, police station›;
~ seinem Zimmer (ugs.) in his room; **Geld ~
der Bank haben** have money in the bank; **~
der Schule/Uni** at school/university
(c) at ‹party, wedding›; on ‹course, trip,
walk, holiday, tour›
[2] *Präp. mit Akk.* **(a)** on; **~ einen Berg
steigen** climb up a mountain; **~ die Straße
gehen** go [out] into the street
(b) ~ die Schule/Uni gehen go to school/
university; **~ einen Lehrgang gehen** go on a
course
(c) ~ 10 km [Entfernung] for [a distance of]

10 km; **wir näherten uns der Hütte [bis]** ~
30 m we approached to within 30m of the
hut
(d) ~ **Jahre [hinaus]** for years [to come];
etw. ~ **nächsten Mittwoch verschieben**
postpone sth. until next Wednesday; **die
Nacht von Sonntag** ~ **Montag** Sunday night;
das fällt ~ **einen Montag** it falls on a
Monday
(e) ~ **diese Art und Weise** in this way; ~
Deutsch in German; ~ **das Sorgfältigste**
(geh.) most carefully
(f) ~ **Wunsch** on request; ~ **meine Bitte** at
my request; ~ **Befehl** on command
(g) ein Teelöffel ~ **einen Liter Wasser** one
teaspoon to one litre of water; ~ **die
Sekunde/den Millimeter [genau]** [precise] to
the second/millimetre; ~ **deine Gesundheit!**
your health; ~ **bald/morgen!** (bes. südd.) see
you soon/tomorrow
3 *Adv.* **(a)** (aufgerichtet, aufgestanden) up; ~!
(steh/steht auf!) up you get!
(b) sie waren längst ~ **und davon** they had
made off long before
(c) ~! (bes. südd.: los) come on; ~ **gehts** off
we go; ~ **ins Schwimmbad!** come on, off to
the swimming pool!
(d) ~ **und ab** (hin und her) up and down; to
and fro
(e) Helm/Hut/Brille ~! helmet/hat/glasses
on!
(f) (ugs.: geöffnet, offen) open; **Fenster/Mund** ~!
open the window/your mouth!

auf|atmen *itr. V.* breathe a sigh of relief

auf|bahren *tr. V.* lay out; **aufgebahrt sein**
lie in state

Auf·bau *der;* ~[e]s, ~ten **(a)** building
(b) (Struktur) structure
(c) *Pl.* (Schiffbau) superstructure *sing.*

auf|bauen *tr. V.* **(a)** erect ⟨*hut, kiosk,
podium*⟩; set up ⟨*equipment, train set*⟩; build
⟨*house, bridge*⟩; put up ⟨*tent*⟩
(b) (hinstellen, arrangieren) lay *or* set out ⟨*food,
presents, etc.*⟩
(c) (fig.: schaffen) build ⟨*state, economy, etc.*⟩;
build up ⟨*business, organization, army, spy
network*⟩
(d) (fig.: strukturieren) structure

auf|bäumen *refl. V.* rear up; **sich gegen**
jmdn./etw. ~ (fig.) rise up against sb./sth.

auf|bessern *tr. V.* improve; increase
⟨*pension, wages, etc.*⟩

auf|bewahren *tr. V.* keep; **etw. kühl** ~:
store sth. in a cool place

Auf·bewahrung *die* keeping

auf|bieten *unr. tr. V.* exert ⟨*strength,
energy, will power, influence, authority*⟩; call
on ⟨*skill, wit, powers of persuasion or
eloquence*⟩

auf|blasen *unr. tr. V.* blow up; inflate

auf|bleiben *unr. itr. V.; mit sein* **(a)**
(geöffnet bleiben) stay open
(b) (nicht zu Bett gehen) stay up

auf|blenden *itr. V.* switch to full beam

auf|blicken *itr. V.* **(a)** look up; (kurz)
glance up
(b) zu jmdm. ~ (fig.) look up to sb.

auf|blühen *itr. V.; mit sein* **(a)** come into
bloom; ⟨*bud*⟩ open
(b) (fig.: aufleben) blossom [out]

auf|brauchen *tr. V.* use up

auf|brechen **1** *unr. tr. V.* break open
⟨*lock, safe, box, crate, etc.*⟩; break into ⟨*car*⟩;
force [open] ⟨*door*⟩
2 *unr. itr. V.; mit sein* **(a)** ⟨*bud*⟩ open; ⟨*ice
[sheet], surface, ground*⟩ break up; ⟨*wound*⟩
open
(b) (losgehen, -fahren) set off

auf|bringen *unr. tr. V.* **(a)** find; raise
⟨*money*⟩; (fig.) summon [up] ⟨*strength, energy,
courage*⟩; find ⟨*patience*⟩
(b) (kreieren) start ⟨*fashion, custom, rumour*⟩;
introduce ⟨*slogan, theory*⟩
(c) jmdn. ~: make sb. angry
(d) jmdn. gegen jmdn./etw. ~: set sb.
against sb./sth.

Auf·bruch *der* departure

auf|brühen *tr. V.* brew [up]

auf|decken *tr. V.* **(a)** uncover
(b) (Kartenspiele) show
(c) (fig.) reveal; uncover; (enthüllen) expose

auf|drängen **1** *tr. V.* **jmdm. etw.** ~: force
sth. on sb.
2 *refl. V.* **sich jmdm.** ~: force oneself on sb.

auf|drehen *tr. V.* **(a)** unscrew ⟨*bottle cap,
nut*⟩; undo ⟨*screw*⟩; turn on ⟨*tap, gas, water*⟩;
open ⟨*valve, bottle, vice*⟩
(b) (ugs.) turn up ⟨*radio, record player, etc.*⟩

auf·dringlich **1** *Adj.* pushy (coll.)
⟨*person*⟩; (fig.) insistent ⟨*music,
advertisement*⟩; pungent ⟨*perfume, smell*⟩;
loud ⟨*colour, wallpaper*⟩
2 *adv.* ⟨*behave*⟩ pushily (coll.)

Aufdringlichkeit *die;* ~ ▶ AUFDRINGLICH:
pushiness (coll.); insistent manner; pungency

auf·einander *Adv.* **(a)** on top of one
another; ~ **prallen** crash into one another;
collide; (fig.) ⟨*opinions*⟩ clash; ~ **treffen** (fig.)
meet
(b) ~ **folgen** follow one another; ~**folgend**
successive

Aufeinander·folge *die* sequence; **in
rascher** ~ in rapid *or* quick succession

***aufeinander|folgen** *usw.*
▶ AUFEINANDER

Aufenthalt *der;* ~[e]s, ~e **(a)** stay
(b) (Fahrtunterbrechung) stop

Aufenthalts-: ~**erlaubnis** *die*
residence permit; ~**raum** *der* (in einer Schule
o. Ä.) common room (Brit.); (in einer
Jugendherberge) day room; (in einem Betrieb o. Ä.)
recreation room

auf|essen *unr. tr. V.* (auch itr.) *V.* eat up

auf|fahren **1** *unr. itr. V.; mit sein* **(a) auf
ein anderes Fahrzeug** ~ (aufprallen) drive into
the back of another vehicle ⋯⋗

(b) **auf den Vordermann zu dicht** ∼: drive too close to the car in front
(c) (vorfahren) drive up
(d) (in Stellung gehen) move up [into position]
② *unr. tr. V.* (a) (in Stellung bringen) move up
(b) (ugs.: auftischen) serve up

Auf·fahrt *die* (a) drive up
(b) (Weg) drive
(c) (Autobahnauffahrt) slip road (Brit.); access road (Amer.)
(d) (schweiz.) ▶ HIMMELFAHRT

Auffahr·unfall *der* rear-end collision

auf|fallen *unr. itr. V.; mit sein* stand out; **jmdm. fällt etw. auf** sb. notices sth.

auffallend ① *Adj.* conspicuous; (eindrucksvoll, bemerkenswert) striking
② *adv.* conspicuously; (eindrucksvoll, bemerkenswert) strikingly

auf·fällig ① *Adj.* conspicuous; garish ⟨colour⟩
② *adv.* conspicuously

auf|fangen *unr. tr. V.* (a) catch
(b) (aufnehmen, sammeln) collect

Auffang·lager *das* reception camp

auf|fassen *tr. V.* grasp; **etw. als etw.** ∼: regard sth. as sth.; **etw. persönlich/falsch** ∼: take sth. personally/misunderstand sth.

Auf·fassung *die* (Ansicht) view; (Begriff) conception; **der** ∼ **sein, dass** ...: take the view that ...

auffindbar *Adj.* findable

auf|finden *unr. tr. V.* find

auf|fordern *tr. V.* **jmdn.** ∼, **etw. zu tun** call upon sb. to do sth.; (einladen, ermuntern) ask sb. to do sth.; **jmdn. [zum Tanz]** ∼: ask sb. to dance

Auf·forderung *die* request; (nachdrücklicher) demand; (Einladung, Ermunterung) invitation

auf|forsten ① *tr. V.* afforest; (wieder ∼) reforest; **einen Wald** ∼: restock a forest
② *itr. V.* establish woods; (wieder ∼) reestablish the woods

Aufforstung *die;* ∼, ∼**en** afforestation; (Wieder∼) reforestation; **die** ∼ **der Wälder** restocking the forests

auf|fressen *unr. tr. V.* (auch fig.) eat up

auf|frischen ① *tr. V.* freshen up; brighten up ⟨colour, paintwork⟩; renovate ⟨polish, furniture⟩; (restaurieren) restore ⟨tapestry, fresco, etc.⟩; (fig.) revive ⟨old memories⟩; renew ⟨acquaintance, friendship⟩; **seine Englischkenntnisse** ∼: brush up one's [knowledge of] English
② *itr. V.; auch mit sein* ⟨wind⟩ freshen

auf|führen ① *tr. V.* (a) put on ⟨film⟩; stage ⟨play, ballet, opera⟩; perform ⟨piece of music⟩
(b) (auflisten) list
② *refl. V.* behave

Auf·führung *die* performance

Auf·gabe *die* (a) task
(b) (fig.: Zweck, Funktion) function

───────────────

*alte Schreibung - vgl. Hinweis auf S. xiv

(c) (Schulw.) (Übung) exercise; (Prüfungs∼) question; (Haus∼) ▶ HAUSAUFGABE
(d) (Rechen∼, Mathematik∼) problem
(e) (Kapitulation) retirement; (im Schach) resignation; **jmdn. zur** ∼ **zwingen** force sb. to retire/resign
(f) (das Aufgeben a) giving up
(g) (einer Postsendung) posting (Brit.); mailing (Amer.); (eines Telegramms) handing in; (einer Bestellung, einer Annonce) placing
(h) (von Gepäck) checking in

Aufgaben-: ∼**bereich** *der,* ∼**gebiet** *das* area of responsibility

Auf·gang *der* (a) (eines Gestirns) rising
(b) (Treppe) stairs *pl.;* staircase; stairway; (in einem Bahnhof, zu einer Galerie, einer Tribüne) steps *pl.*

auf|geben ① *unr. tr. V.* (a) give up; (Sport) retire from ⟨race, competition⟩
(b) (übergeben, übermitteln) post (Brit.), mail ⟨letter, parcel⟩; hand in, (telefonisch) phone in ⟨telegram⟩; place ⟨advertisement, order⟩; check ⟨luggage, baggage⟩ in
(c) (Schulw.: als Hausaufgabe) set (Brit.); assign (Amer.)
(d) **jmdm. ein Rätsel** ∼: set (Brit.) *or* (Amer.) assign sb. a puzzle
② *unr. itr. V.* give up; (im Sport) retire; (im Schach) resign

Auf·gebot *das* (a) contingent; **ein gewaltiges** ∼ **an Polizisten/Fahrzeugen/ Material** a huge force of police/array of vehicles/materials
(b) (zur Heirat) notice of an/the intended marriage; (kirchlich) banns *pl.*

auf|gehen *unr. itr. V.; mit sein* (a) rise
(b) (sich öffnen [lassen]) ⟨door, parachute, wound⟩ open; ⟨stage curtain⟩ go up; ⟨knot, button, zip, bandage, shoelace, stitching⟩ come undone; ⟨boil, pimple, blister⟩ burst; ⟨flower, bud⟩ open [up]
(c) (keimen) come up
(d) (aufgetrieben werden) ⟨dough, cake⟩ rise
(e) (Math.) ⟨calculation⟩ work out; ⟨equation⟩ come out
(f) **etw. geht jmdm. auf** sb. realizes sth.

auf|geilen *refl. V.* (salopp) **jmdn. [mit/durch etw.]** ∼: get sb. randy [with sth.]; **sich [an etw.** *(Dat.)*] ∼: get randy [with sth.]; (fig.) get worked up [about sth.]

aufgeklärt *Adj.* enlightened; ∼ **sein** (sexualkundlich) know the facts of life

auf·gelegt *Adj.* **gut/schlecht** *usw.* ∼ **sein** be in a good/bad *etc.* mood; **zu etw.** ∼ **sein** be in the mood for sth.

auf·gelöst *Adj.* distraught ⟨person⟩

aufgeregt ① *Adj.* excited; (nervös, beunruhigt) agitated
② *adv.* excitedly; (nervös, beunruhigt) agitatedly

auf·geschlossen *Adj.* open-minded (gegenüber as regards, about); (interessiert, empfänglich) receptive (Dat., für to); (zugänglich) approachable

Auf·geschlossenheit *die*
▶ AUFGESCHLOSSEN: open-mindedness;
receptiveness; approachableness
aufgeweckt *Adj.* bright
Aufgewecktheit *die;* ∼: brightness
auf|gießen *unr. tr. V.* make ⟨*coffee, tea*⟩
auf|gliedern *tr. V.* subdivide, break down
(in + *Akk.* into)
Auf·gliederung *die* subdivision;
breakdown
auf|greifen *unr. tr. V.* pick up
aufgrund *Präp. mit Gen.* on the basis *or*
strength of; (wegen) because of
auf|haben (ugs.) 1 *unr. tr. V.* (a) (aufgesetzt
haben) have on
(b) (geöffnet haben) have ⟨*zip*⟩ undone; have
⟨*door, window, jacket, blouse*⟩ open
2 *unr. itr. V.* ⟨*shop, office*⟩ be open
auf|halsen *tr. V.* (ugs.) jmdm./sich etw. ∼:
saddle sb./oneself with sth.; sich (*Dat.*) etw.
∼ **lassen** get oneself saddled with sth.
auf|halten 1 *unr. tr. V.* (a) halt
(b) (stören) hold up
(c) (ugs.: geöffnet halten) hold ⟨*sack, door, etc.*⟩
open; **die Augen [und Ohren]** ∼: keep one's
eyes [and ears] open
2 *unr. refl. V.* (a) stay
(b) **sich mit jmdm./etw.** ∼: spend [a long]
time on sb./sth
auf|hängen 1 *tr. V.* (a) hang up; hang
⟨*picture, curtains*⟩
(b) (erhängen) hang
2 *refl. V.* hang oneself
Aufhänger *der;* ∼s, ∼: loop
auf|heben *unr. tr. V.* (a) pick up
(b) (aufbewahren) keep
(c) (abschaffen) abolish; repeal ⟨*law*⟩; rescind
⟨*order, instruction*⟩; cancel ⟨*contract*⟩; lift
⟨*ban, prohibition*⟩
(d) (ausgleichen) cancel out; neutralize ⟨*effect*⟩
Aufheben *das;* ∼s: viel ∼[s]/kein ∼ von
jmdm./etw. machen make a great fuss/not
make any fuss about sb./sth.
Aufhebungs·vertrag *der* agreement to
terminate a/the contract
auf|heitern 1 *tr. V.* cheer up
2 *refl. V.* ⟨*weather*⟩ brighten up
Aufheiterung *die;* ∼, ∼en (a) (des Wetters)
bright period
(b) (Erheiterung) cheering up
auf|hetzen *tr. V.* incite
auf|holen 1 *tr. V.* make up ⟨*time, delay*⟩;
pull back ⟨*lead*⟩
2 *itr. V.* catch up; ⟨*athlete, competitor*⟩
make up ground
auf|horchen *itr. V.* prick up one's ears
auf|hören *itr. V.* stop; [damit] ∼, etw. zu
tun stop doing sth.
auf|kaufen *tr. V.* buy up
auf|klappen *tr. V.* open, fold open ⟨*chair,
table*⟩; open [up] ⟨*suitcase, trunk*⟩; open
⟨*book, knife*⟩
auf|klären 1 *tr. V.* (a) clear up ⟨*matter,*

*mystery, question, misunderstanding, error,
confusion*⟩; solve ⟨*crime, problem*⟩; explain
⟨*event, incident, cause*⟩; resolve
⟨*contradiction, disagreement*⟩
(b) (unterrichten) enlighten; **ein Kind** ∼
(sexualkundlich) tell a child the facts of life
2 *refl. V.* (a) ⟨*misunderstanding, mystery*⟩
be cleared up
(b) ⟨*weather*⟩ brighten [up]; ⟨*sky*⟩ brighten
Auf·klärung *die* ▶ AUFKLÄREN 1: (a)
clearing up; solution; explanation;
resolution
(b) enlightenment; **die** ∼ **der Kinder** (über
Sexualität) telling the children the facts of life
auf|kleben *tr. V.* stick on; (mit Kleister)
paste on
Auf·kleber *der* sticker
auf|knöpfen *tr. V.* unbutton; undo
auf|kochen 1 *tr. V.* bring to the boil
2 *itr. V.; mit sein* come to the boil
auf|kommen *unr. itr. V.; mit sein* (a)
⟨*wind*⟩ spring up; ⟨*storm, gale*⟩ blow up;
⟨*fog*⟩ come down; ⟨*rumour*⟩ start; ⟨*suspicion,
doubt, feeling*⟩ arise; ⟨*fashion, style,
invention*⟩ come in; ⟨*boredom*⟩ set in; ⟨*mood,
atmosphere*⟩ develop
(b) ∼ **für** (bezahlen) bear ⟨*costs*⟩; pay for
⟨*damage*⟩; pay ⟨*expenses*⟩; be liable for
⟨*debts*⟩; stand ⟨*loss*⟩
(c) ∼ **für** (Verantwortung tragen für) be
responsible for
auf|krempeln *tr. V.* roll up
auf|laden 1 *unr. tr. V.* (a) load (auf +
Akk. on [to])
(b) jmdm. etw. ∼ (ugs.) load sb. with sth.;
(fig.) saddle sb. with sth.
(c) charge [up] ⟨*battery*⟩
2 *unr. refl. V.* ⟨*battery*⟩ charge
Auf·lage *die* (a) (Buchw.) edition
(b) (Verpflichtung) condition
auflagen·stark *Adj.* high-circulation
⟨*newspaper, magazine*⟩
auf|lassen *unr. tr. V.* (ugs.) (a) leave ⟨*door,
window, jacket, etc.*⟩ open
(b) keep on ⟨*hat, glasses, etc.*⟩
auf|lauern *itr. V.* jmdm. ∼: lie in wait for
sb.
Auf·lauf *der* (a) (Menschen∼) crowd
(b) (Speise) soufflé
auf|leben *itr. V.; mit sein* revive; (fig.: wieder
munter werden) come to life
auf|legen 1 *tr. V.* (a) put on; **den Hörer**
∼: put down the receiver
(b) (Buchw.) publish
2 *itr. V.* (den Hörer auflegen) hang up
auf|lehnen *refl. V.* rebel
Auflehnung *die;* ∼, ∼en rebellion
auf|leuchten *itr. V.; auch mit sein* light
up; (für kurze Zeit) flash
auf|lockern *tr. V.* (a) loosen; break up
⟨*soil*⟩
(b) (fig.) introduce some variety into ⋯⊹

⟨landscape, lesson, lecture⟩; relieve ⟨pattern, façade⟩; make ⟨mood, atmosphere, evening⟩ more relaxed

Auf·lockerung die (a) ▶ AUFLOCKERN A: loosening; breaking up
(b) zur ~ der Stimmung/des Abends to make the mood/evening more relaxed

auf|lösen [1] tr. V. dissolve; resolve ⟨difficulty, contradiction⟩; solve ⟨puzzle, equation⟩; break off ⟨engagement⟩; cancel ⟨arrangement, contract, agreement⟩; dissolve ⟨organization⟩
[2] refl. V. dissolve (in + Akk. into); ⟨parliament⟩ dissolve itself; ⟨crowd, demonstration⟩ break up; ⟨fog, mist⟩ lift; (fig.) ⟨empire, social order⟩ disintegrate

Auf·lösung die (a) ▶ AUFLÖSEN 1: dissolving; resolution; solution; breaking off; cancellation; dissolution
(b) ▶ AUFLÖSEN 2: dissolving; breaking up lifting; disintegration

auf|machen [1] tr. V. (a) open; undo ⟨button, knot⟩
(b) (ugs.: eröffnen) open [up] ⟨shop, business, etc.⟩
[2] itr. V. (a) ⟨shop, office, etc.⟩ open
(b) (ugs.: die Tür öffnen) open the door; jmdm. ~: open the door to sb.
(c) (ugs.: eröffnet werden) ⟨shop, business⟩ open [up]

Aufmachung die; ~, ~en presentation; (Kleidung) get-up

Aufmarsch·gebiet das (Milit.) deployment area

auf|marschieren itr. V.; mit sein assemble; (heranmarschieren) march up;
Truppen sind an der Grenze aufmarschiert troops were deployed along the border

aufmerksam [1] Adj. (a) attentive; sharp ⟨eyes⟩; jmdn. auf jmdn./etw. ~ machen draw sb.'s attention to sb./sth.; auf jmdn./etw. ~ werden become aware of sb./sth.; ~ werden notice
(b) (höflich) attentive
[2] adv. attentively

Aufmerksamkeit die; ~, ~en (a) attention
(b) (Höflichkeit) attentiveness
(c) (Geschenk) small gift

auf|motzen tr. V. (ugs.) tart up (Brit. coll.); doll up (coll.)

auf|muntern tr. V. (a) cheer up
(b) (beleben) liven up
(c) (ermutigen) encourage

Aufmunterung die; ~ ▶ AUFMUNTERN: cheering up; livening up; encouragement

Aufnahme die; ~, ~n (a) ▶ AUFNEHMEN B: opening; establishment; taking up
(b) (Empfang) reception
(c) ▶ AUFNEHMEN D: admission (in + Akk. into)
(d) (Einschließung) inclusion

(e) (Finanzw.) raising
(f) (Aufzeichnung) taking down; (von Personalien, eines Diktats) taking [down]
(g) ▶ AUFNEHMEN K: taking: photographing; filming
(h) (Bild) shot
(i) (das Aufnehmen auf Tonträger, das Aufgenommene) recording
(j) (Anklang) reception; response (Gen. to)
(k) (Einverleibung, Absorption) absorption

aufnahme-, Aufnahme-: ~antrag der application for membership; ~fähig Adj. receptive (für to); ich bin nicht mehr ~fähig I can't take any more in; ~fähigkeit die receptivity (für to); ability to take things in; ~land das host country

auf|nehmen unr. tr. V. (a) (aufheben) pick up; (fig.) take up ⟨idea, theme, etc.⟩; es mit jmdm./etw. ~/nicht ~ können (fig.) be a/no match for sb./sth.
(b) (beginnen mit) open ⟨negotiations, talks⟩; establish ⟨relations, contacts⟩; take up ⟨studies, activity, occupation⟩; start ⟨production, investigation⟩
(c) (empfangen) receive; (beherbergen) take in
(d) (beitreten lassen) admit (in + Akk. to)
(e) (einschließen, verzeichnen) include
(f) (erfassen) take in ⟨impressions, information, etc.⟩
(g) (absorbieren) absorb
(h) (Finanzw.) raise ⟨mortgage, money, loan⟩
(i) (reagieren auf) receive
(j) (aufschreiben) take down; take [down] ⟨dictation, particulars⟩
(k) (fotografieren) take ⟨picture⟩; photograph, take a photograph of ⟨scene, subject⟩; (filmen) film
(l) (auf Tonträger) record
(m) (auf Videoband) videotape; video

auf|opfern refl. V. devote oneself sacrificingly (für to)

aufopfernd [1] Adj. self-sacrificing
[2] adv. self-sacrificingly

auf|passen itr. V. (a) watch out; (konzentriert sein) pay attention; pass mal auf! (ugs.: hör mal zu!) now listen
(b) auf jmdn./etw. ~: keep an eye on sb./sth.

auf|platzen itr. V.; mit sein burst open; ⟨seam, cushion⟩ split open; ⟨wound⟩ open up

Auf·prall der; ~[e]s, ~e impact

auf|prallen itr. V.; mit sein auf etw. (Akk.) ~: hit sth.

Auf·preis der additional charge

auf|pumpen tr. V. pump up

auf|putschen tr. V. stimulate; arouse ⟨passions, urge⟩

Aufputsch·mittel das stimulant

auf|räumen tr., itr. V. clear up

Aufräumungs·arbeiten Pl. clearance work sing.

auf·recht [1] Adj. (auch fig.) upright
[2] adv. ⟨walk, sit, hold oneself⟩ straight

aufrecht|erhalten unr. tr. V. maintain; keep up ⟨deception, fiction, contact, custom⟩

auf|regen 1 *tr. V.* excite; (ärgern) annoy; irritate; (beunruhigen) agitate
2 *refl. V.* get worked up (**über** + *Akk.* about)

Auf·regung *die* excitement *no pl.;* (Beunruhigung) agitation *no pl.;* jmdn. **in** ~ **versetzen** make sb. excited/agitated

auf|reißen 1 *unr. tr. V.* (a) (öffnen) tear open; wrench open ⟨drawer⟩; fling open ⟨door, window⟩; **die Augen/den Mund** ~: open one's eyes/mouth wide
(b) (beschädigen) tear open; tear ⟨clothes⟩; break up ⟨road, soil⟩
2 *itr. V.; mit sein* ⟨clothes⟩ tear; ⟨seam⟩ split; ⟨wound⟩ open; ⟨cloud⟩ break up

auf|reizen *tr. V.* excite

auf·reizend 1 *Adj.* provocative
2 *adv.* provocatively

auf|richten 1 *tr. V.* erect; put up; **den Oberkörper** ~: raise one's upper body; jmdn. [**wieder**] ~ (fig.) give fresh heart to sb.
2 *refl. V.* stand up [straight]; **sich an jmdm./ etw. [wieder]** ~ (fig.) take heart from sb./sth.

auf·richtig 1 *Adj.* sincere
2 *adv.* sincerely

Auf·richtigkeit *die* sincerity

auf|rücken *itr. V.; mit sein* move up

Auf·ruf *der* (a) call
(b) (Appell) appeal (**an** + *Akk.* to)

auf|rufen *unr. tr. V.* (a) call
(b) jmdn. ~, **etw. zu tun** call upon sb. to do sth.
(c) (Rechtsw.) appeal for ⟨witnesses⟩

Aufruhr *der;* ~**s,** ~**e** (a) (Widerstand) rebellion
(b) (Erregung) turmoil

aufrührerisch *Adj.* inflammatory

auf|rüsten *tr., itr. V.* (a) arm; **wieder** ~: rearm
(b) (DV) upgrade

Auf·rüstung *die* armament

aufs *Präp. + Art.* = **auf das**

auf|sagen *tr. V.* recite

auf|sammeln *tr. V.* gather up

aufsässig 1 *Adj.* recalcitrant
2 *adv.* recalcitrantly

Aufsässigkeit *die;* ~, ~**en** (a) recalcitrance
(b) (Handlung) piece of recalcitrance

Auf·satz *der* (Text) essay

auf|saugen *unr.* (auch regelm.) *tr. V.* soak up; (fig.) absorb

auf|schieben *unr. tr. V.* postpone

Auf·schlag *der* (a) (Aufprall) impact
(b) (Preis~) surcharge
(c) (Ärmel~) cuff; (Hosen~) turn-up; (Revers) lapel
(d) (Tennis usw.) serve

auf|schlagen 1 *unr. itr. V.* (a) *mit sein* **auf etw.** (*Dat. od. Akk.*) ~: hit sth.
(b) (teurer werden) ⟨price, rent, costs⟩ go up
(c) (Tennis usw.) serve

2 *unr. tr. V.* (a) (öffnen) crack ⟨nut, egg⟩ [open]; knock a hole in ⟨ice⟩; **sich** (*Dat.*) **das Knie/den Kopf** ~: cut one's knee/head
(b) open ⟨book, newspaper, one's eyes⟩; **schlagt Seite 15 auf!** turn to page 15
(c) turn up ⟨collar, sleeve, trouser leg⟩
(d) (aufbauen) set up ⟨camp⟩; pitch ⟨tent⟩; put up ⟨bed, hut, scaffolding⟩
(e) **5 % auf etw.** (*Akk.*) ~: put 5% on sth.

auf|schließen 1 *unr. tr. V.* unlock
2 *unr. itr. V.* [jmdm.] ~: unlock the door/ gate etc. [for sb.]

Auf·schluss, *****Auf·schluß** *der* information *no pl.*

auf|schneiden 1 *unr. tr. V.* (a) cut open
(b) (zerteilen) cut
2 *unr. itr. V.* (ugs.: prahlen) boast (**mit** about)

Auf·schneider *der,* **Auf·schneiderin** *die* (ugs. abwertend) boaster; braggart

Auf·schnitt *der* [assorted] cold meats *pl./* cheeses *pl.*

auf|schnüren *tr. V.* undo

auf|schrauben *tr. V.* unscrew; unscrew the top of ⟨bottle, jar, etc.⟩

Auf·schrei *der* cry; (stärker) yell; (schriller) scream; **ein** ~ **der Empörung** *od.* **Entrüstung** (fig.) an outcry

auf|schreiben *unr. tr. V.* write down; [**sich** (*Dat.*)] **etw.** ~: make a note of sth.

auf|schreien *unr. itr. V.* cry out; (stärker) yell out; (schrill) scream

Auf·schrift *die* inscription

Auf·schub *der* postponement; **die Sache duldet keinen** ~: the matter brooks no delay

Auf·schwung *der* upturn (*Gen.* in)

Aufsehen *das;* ~**s** stir; [**großes**] ~ **erregen** cause a [great] stir

Auf·seher *der,* **Auf·seherin** *die;* ~, ~**nen** (im Gefängnis) warder (Brit.); [prison] guard (Amer.); (im Park) park-keeper; (im Museum, auf dem Parkplatz) attendant; (auf einem Gut, Sklavenaufseher) overseer

*****auf|sein** ▶ AUF 3A, F

auf|setzen 1 *tr. V.* (a) put on
(b) (verfassen) draw up ⟨text⟩
2 *refl. V.* sit up

Auf·sicht *die* supervision; (bei Prüfungen) invigilation (Brit.); proctoring (Amer.)

auf|spielen 1 *refl. V.* (ugs. abwertend: angeben) put on airs; **sich vor jmdm.** ~: show off in front of sb.
2 *itr. V.* (a) (musizieren) play; **zum Tanz** ~: play dance music
(b) (Sport) **groß/eindrucksvoll** ~: give a fine/ impressive display

auf|springen *unr. itr. V.; mit sein* (a) jump up
(b) (hinaufspringen) jump on (**auf** + *Akk.* to)
(c) (rissig werden) crack

auf|stacheln *tr. V.* incite

Auf·stand *der* rebellion

auf·ständisch *Adj.* rebellious

auf|stehen *unr. itr. V.; mit sein* stand up; (aus dem Liegen) get up

auf|steigen *unr. itr. V.; mit sein* (a) (auf ein Fahrzeug) get on; **auf etw.** (*Akk.*) ~: get on [to] sth.
(b) (bergan steigen) climb
(c) (hochsteigen) ⟨*sap, smoke, mist*⟩ rise
(d) (beruflich, gesellschaftlich) rise (**zu** to); **zum Direktor** ~: rise to be manager

auf|stellen ① *tr. V.* (a) put up (auf + *Akk.* on); set up ⟨*skittles*⟩; (postieren) post
(b) (aufrecht hinstellen) stand up
(c) (Sport) select, pick ⟨*team, player*⟩
(d) (bilden) put together ⟨*team of experts*⟩; raise ⟨*army*⟩
(e) (nominieren) nominate; put up
② *refl. V.* position oneself

Auf·stellung *die* (a) ▶ AUFSTELLEN 1A: putting up; setting up; posting
(b) ▶ AUFSTELLEN B: standing up
(c) ▶ AUFSTELLEN C: selection; picking
(d) ▶ AUFSTELLEN D: putting together; raising
(e) (Nominierung) nomination

Aufstieg *der;* ~[e]s, ~e (a) climb
(b) ▶ AUFSTEIGEN D: rise

auf|stoßen ① *unr. tr. V.* push open
② *unr. itr. V.* belch; ⟨*baby*⟩ bring up wind

Auf·strich *der* spread

auf|stützen ① *tr. V.* rest ⟨*one's arms etc.*⟩
② *refl. V.* support oneself; **die Arme auf etw.** (*Akk. od. Dat.*) ~: rest one's arms on sth.

auf|suchen *tr. V.* call on; go to ⟨*doctor*⟩

Auf·takt *der* (a) (fig.) start
(b) (Musik) upbeat

auf|tauchen *itr. V.; mit sein* (a) surface
(b) (sichtbar werden) appear

auf|tauen ① *tr. V.* thaw
② *itr. V.; mit sein* (auch fig.) thaw

auf|teilen *tr. V.* (a) divide [up]
(b) (verteilen) share out

Auftrag *der;* ~[e]s, **Aufträge** (a) instructions *pl.;* **in jmds.** ~ (*Dat.*) on sb.'s instructions; (für jmdn.) on behalf of sb
(b) (Bestellung) order; (bei Künstlern, Architekten usw.) commission
(c) (Mission) task; (Aufgabe) job

auf|tragen *unr. tr. V.* (a) jmdm. ~, etw. zu tun instruct sb. to do sth.
(b) (aufstreichen) put on ⟨*paint, make-up, etc.*⟩

Auftrag·geber *der;* ~s, ~, **Auftrag·geberin** *die;* ~, ~nen client

auftrags-, Auftrags-: ~**buch** *das* (Kaufmannsspr.) order book; ~**killer** *der,* ~**killerin** *die* contract killer

auf|treten *unr. itr. V.; mit sein* (a) tread
(b) (sich benehmen) behave
(c) (eine Vorstellung geben) appear; **als Zeuge/Kläger** ~: appear as a witness/a plaintiff
(d) (auftauchen) ⟨*problem, difficulty, difference of opinion*⟩ arise; ⟨*symptom, danger, pest*⟩ appear

Auftreten *das;* ~s (Benehmen) manner

---

*alte Schreibung - vgl. Hinweis auf S. xiv

Auf·trieb *der* (a) (Physik) (statischer ~) buoyancy; (dynamischer ~) lift
(b) (fig.) impetus; **das hat ihm** ~/**neuen** ~ **gegeben** that has given him a lift/given him new impetus

Auf·tritt *der* (a) (Vorstellung) appearance
(b) (Theater: das Auftreten) entrance; (Szene) scene

auf|tun *unr. refl. V.* (geh.) open; (fig.) open up

auf|wachen *itr. V.; mit sein* wake up, awaken (**aus** from); (aus Ohnmacht, Narkose) come round (**aus** from)

auf|wachsen *unr. itr. V.; mit sein* grow up

Auf·wand *der;* ~[e]s cost; expense

aufwändig ▶ AUFWENDIG

Aufwands·entschädigung *die* expense allowance

auf|wärmen ① *tr. V.* heat or warm up ⟨*food*⟩
② *refl. V.* warm oneself up

aufwärts *Adv.* upwards

Aufwärts·trend *der* upward trend

auf|wecken *tr. V.* wake [up]; waken

auf|weichen ① *tr. V.* soften
② *itr. V.; mit sein* become soft; soften up

auf|wenden *unr.* (*auch regelm.*) *tr. V.* use ⟨*skill, influence*⟩; expend ⟨*energy, resources*⟩; spend ⟨*money, time*⟩; **viel Geld/seine ganze Freizeit für etw.** ~ spend a great deal of money/all one's spare time on sth.

auf·wendig ① *Adj.* lavish; (kostspielig) costly; expensive
② *adv.* lavishly; (kostspielig) expensively

Auf·wendung *die* (a) ▶ AUFWENDEN: using; expenditure; spending; **unter** ~ **von etw.** by using/expending/spending sth.
(b) *Pl.* (Kosten) expenditure *sing.*

auf|wiegeln *tr. V.* incite; stir up

auf|wirbeln *tr. V.* swirl up

auf|wischen *tr. V.* (a) wipe or mop up
(b) (säubern) wipe ⟨*floor*⟩; (mit Wasser) wash ⟨*floor*⟩

auf|zählen *tr. V.* list

Auf·zählung *die* (a) listing
(b) (Liste) list

auf|zeichnen *tr. V.* (a) record
(b) (zeichnen) draw

Auf·zeichnung *die* record; (Film-, Tonaufzeichnung) recording; ~en (Notizen) notes

auf|ziehen ① *unr. tr. V.* (a) pull open ⟨*drawer*⟩; open, draw [back] ⟨*curtains*⟩; undo ⟨*zip*⟩
(b) wind up ⟨*clock, toy, etc.*⟩
② *unr. itr. V.; mit sein* come up; ⟨*clouds, storm*⟩ gather

Auf·zucht *die* raising; rearing

Auf·zug *der* (a) (Lift) lift (Brit.); elevator (Amer.)
(b) (abwertend: Aufmachung) get-up
(c) (Theater: Akt) act

Aug·apfel *der* eyeball

Auge *das;* ~s, ~n eye; **gute/schlechte** ~n

haben have good/poor eyesight; **auf einem** ∼ **blind** blind in one eye; **da wird er** ∼n **machen** (fig. ugs.) his eyes will pop out of his head; **ich traute meinen** ∼n **nicht** (ugs.) I couldn't believe my eyes; **ein** ∼ od. **beide** ∼n **zudrücken** (fig.) turn a blind eye; **jmdn./ etw. nicht aus den** ∼n **lassen** not take one's eyes off sb./sth.; **ins** ∼ **gehen** (fig. ugs.) end in disaster; **unter vier** ∼n (fig.) in private

augen; Augen-: ∼**arzt** der, ∼**ärztin** die eye specialist; ∼**blick** /auch: --'-/ der ▶ MOMENT[1]; ∼**blicklich** /auch: --'--/ ⌐1⌐ Adj. (a) (sofortig) immediate; (b) (gegenwärtig) present; ⌐2⌐ adv. (a) (sofort) at once; (b) (zurzeit) at the moment; ∼**braue** die eyebrow; ∼**farbe** die colour of one's eyes; ∼**klinik** die eye hospital; ∼**lid** das eyelid; ∼**maß** das: **ein gutes/schlechtes** ∼**maß haben** have a good eye/no eye for distances; ∼**merk** das: **sein** ∼**merk auf jmdn./etw. richten** od. **lenken** give one's attention to sb./sth.; ∼**optiker** der, ∼**optikerin** die ophthalmic optician

Augen·schein der (geh.) (a) (Eindruck) appearance; **dem** ∼ **nach** by all appearances (b) (Betrachtung) inspection; **jmdn./etw. in** ∼ **nehmen** have a close look at sb./sth.; give sb./sth. a close inspection

augen·scheinlich (geh.) ⌐1⌐ Adj. (scheinbar) apparent; evident; (sichtbar) obvious; evident ⌐2⌐ adv. (scheinbar) apparently; evidently; (sichtbar) obviously; evidently

augen-, Augen-: ∼**weide** die feast for the eyes; ∼**zeuge** der, ∼**zeugin** die eyewitness; ∼**zwinkernd** ⌐1⌐ Adj. tacit ⟨agreement⟩; ⌐2⌐ adv. with a wink

August der; ∼[e]s od. ∼, ∼e August

Auktion die; ∼, ∼en auction

Aula die; ∼, Aulen od. ∼s hall

aus ⌐1⌐ Präp. mit Dat. (a) (aus dem Inneren von) out of (b) (Herkunft, Quelle, Ausgangspunkt angebend, auch zeitlich) from; ∼ **Spanien/Köln** usw. from Spain/Cologne etc.; (c) ∼ **der Mode/Übung sein** be out of fashion/training (d) (Grund, Ursache angebend) out of; **etw.** ∼ **Erfahrung wissen** know sth. from experience; ∼ **Versehen** by mistake (e) (bestehend ∼) of; (hergestellt ∼) made of; ∼ **etw. bestehen** consist of sth. (f) ∼ **ihm ist ein guter Arzt geworden** he made a good doctor ⌐2⌐ Adv. (a) (ugs.: vorbei) over; **wann ist die Vorstellung** ∼? what time does the performance end?; **die Schule ist** ∼ school is out; ∼ **jetzt!** that's enough (b) (ausgeschaltet) off; (erloschen) out (c) **vom Fenster/obersten Stockwerk** ∼: from the window/top storey; **von mir** ∼ (ugs.) if you like; **von sich** (Dat.) ∼: of one's own accord

aus|atmen itr., tr. V. breathe out

aus|baden tr. V. (ugs.) carry or take the can for (Brit. coll.); take the rap for (coll.)

Aus·bau der; ∼[e]s (a) (Erweiterung) extension (b) (Ausgestaltung) conversion (**zu** into)

aus|bauen tr. V. (a) (demontieren) remove (**aus** from) (b) (erweitern) extend

Aus·beute die yield

aus|beuten tr. V. exploit

Ausbeutung die; ∼, ∼en exploitation

aus|bilden tr. V. (a) train (b) (entwickeln) develop

Aus·bildung die (a) training (b) (Entwicklung) development

Aus·blick der view (**auf** + Akk. of)

aus|brechen unr. itr. V.; mit sein (a) break out (**aus** of); (fig.) break free (**aus** from) (b) **jmdm. bricht der Schweiß aus** sb. breaks into a sweat (c) ⟨volcano⟩ erupt (d) (beginnen) break out; ⟨crisis⟩ break (e) **in Gelächter/Weinen** ∼: burst out laughing/crying; **in Beifall/Tränen** ∼: burst into applause/tears

aus|breiten ⌐1⌐ tr. V. spread; spread [out] ⟨map, cloth, sheet, etc.⟩; open out ⟨fan, newspaper⟩; (nebeneinander legen) spread out ⌐2⌐ refl. V. spread

Aus·bruch der (a) (Flucht) escape (**aus** from) (b) (Beginn) outbreak (c) (Gefühlsausbruch) outburst (d) (eines Vulkans) eruption

aus|brüten tr. V. hatch out; (im Brutkasten) incubate

aus|bürsten tr. V. brush out ⟨dust, dirt⟩ (**aus** of); brush ⟨clothes, upholstery, etc.⟩

Aus·dauer die stamina

aus·dauernd Adj. with stamina postpos.

Ausdauer·training das stamina training

aus|dehnen ⌐1⌐ tr. V. (a) stretch; (fig.) extend (**auf** + Akk. to) (b) (zeitlich) prolong ⌐2⌐ refl. V. expand; (zeitlich) go on

Aus·dehnung die expansion; (fig.) extension; (zeitlich) prolongation

aus|denken unr. refl. V. sich (Dat.) **etw.** ∼: think sth. up

aus|diskutieren tr. V. **etw.** ∼: discuss sth. fully or thoroughly

Aus·druck der; Pl. Ausdrücke expression; (Terminus) term; **etw. zum** ∼ **bringen** express sth.

aus|drucken tr. V. (Nachrichtenw., DV) print out

aus|drücken ⌐1⌐ tr. V. (a) (auspressen) squeeze ⟨juice⟩ out; squeeze [out] ⟨lemon, grape, orange, etc.⟩; squeeze out ⟨sponge⟩; squeeze ⟨boil, pimple⟩ (b) stub out ⟨cigarette⟩ (c) (mitteilen) express ⋯⟩

a

⌐2⌐ *refl. V.* (a) express oneself
(b) (offenbar werden) be expressed
ausdrücklich /*od.* ⸱-⸱-/ ⌐1⌐ *Adj.* express
attrib. ⟨command, wish, etc.⟩; explicit
⟨reservation⟩
⌐2⌐ *adv.* expressly; ⟨mention⟩ explicitly
ausdrucks-: ∼**los** ⌐1⌐ *Adj.* expressionless;
⌐2⌐ *adv.* expressionlessly; ∼**voll** ⌐1⌐ *Adj.*
expressive; ⌐2⌐ *adv.* expressively
aus·einander *Adv.* (a) (voneinander getrennt)
apart; etw. ∼ **schreiben** write sth. as
separate words; ∼ **brechen** break up; etw. ∼
brechen break sth. up; ∼ **gehen** part;
⟨crowd⟩ disperse; ⟨opinions, views⟩ differ;
zwei Dinge ∼ **halten** (unterscheiden) distinguish
between two things; **ich kann die beiden
Brüder nicht** ∼ **halten** I cannot tell the two
brothers apart; etw. ∼ **nehmen** take sth.
apart
(b) jmdm. etw. ∼ **setzen** explain sth. to sb.;
sich mit jmdm. ∼ **setzen** have it out with sb.;
sich mit etw. ∼ **setzen** concern oneself with
sth.
***auseinander|brechen** *usw.*
▶ AUSEINANDER
Auseinandersetzung *die;* ∼, ∼**en** (a)
(Streit) argument
(b) (Kampfhandlung) clash
Aus·fahrt *die* exit
Aus·fall *der* (a) (das Nichtstattfinden)
cancellation
(b) (Einbuße, Verlust) loss
(c) (eines Motors) failure; (einer Maschine, eines
Autos) breakdown
aus|fallen *unr. itr. V.; mit sein* (a) fall out
(b) (nicht stattfinden) be cancelled; etw. ∼
lassen cancel sth.
(c) (ausscheiden) drop out
(d) (nicht mehr funktionieren) ⟨engine, brakes,
signal⟩ fail; ⟨machine, car⟩ break down
(e) (ein bestimmtes Ergebnis zeigen) turn out
ausfallend *Adj.* [gegen jmdn.] ∼ sein/
werden be/become abusive [towards sb.]
Ausfall·straße *die* main road out of the/a
town/city
aus·findig *Adv.* jmdn./etw. ∼ **machen** find
sb./sth.
Aus·flug *der* outing
Ausflügler *der;* ∼**s**, ∼, **Ausflüglerin**
die; ∼, ∼**nen** day tripper; excursionist
(Amer.)
Ausflugs-: ∼**dampfer** *der* pleasure
steamer; ∼**lokal** *das* restaurant/café
catering for [day] trippers; ∼**verkehr** *der*
(am Wochenende) weekend holiday traffic; (an
Feiertagen) holiday traffic
aus|fragen *tr. V.* jmdn. ∼: question sb.,
ask sb. questions (nach, über + *Akk.* about)
aus|fransen *itr. V.; mit sein* fray
Aus·fuhr *die;* ∼, ∼**en** ▶ EXPORT

aus|führen *tr. V.* (a) (ausgehen mit) take
⟨person⟩ out
(b) (spazieren führen) take ⟨person, animal⟩ for
a walk
(c) (exportieren) export
(d) (durchführen) carry out; (Sport) take
⟨penalty, free kick, corner⟩
ausführlich /*auch:* ⸱-⸱-/ ⌐1⌐ *Adj.* detailed;
full
⌐2⌐ *adv.* in detail
Ausfuhr·sperre *die* ▶ AUSFUHRVERBOT
Aus·führung *die* (Durchführung) carrying out;
(Sport) taking
Ausfuhr·verbot *das* (Wirtsch.) export
embargo
aus|füllen *tr. V.* (a) fill; fill in ⟨form,
crossword puzzle⟩
(b) (beanspruchen, einnehmen) take up ⟨space⟩
Aus·gabe *die* (a) giving out; (von Essen)
serving
(b) (Geldausgabe) item of expenditure; ∼**n**
expenditure *sing.* (**für** on)
(c) (Edition) edition
(d) (DV) output
Ausgabe·gerät *das* (DV) output device
Aus·gang *der* (a) (Erlaubnis zum Ausgehen)
time off; (von Soldaten) leave
(b) (Tür ins Freie) exit (*Gen.* from)
(c) (Anat.) outlet
(d) (Ende) end; (eines Romans, Films usw.)
ending
(e) (Ergebnis) outcome; (eines Wettbewerbs)
result; **ein Unfall mit tödlichem** ∼: an
accident with fatal consequences
Ausgangs-: ∼**punkt** *der* starting point;
∼**sperre** *die* (bes. Milit.) (für Zivilisten) curfew;
(für Soldaten) confinement to barracks; [eine]
∼**sperre verhängen** impose a curfew/confine
the soldiers/regiment *etc.* to barracks
aus|geben *unr. tr. V.* (a) give out; serve
⟨food, drinks⟩
(b) (verbrauchen) spend ⟨money⟩ (**für** on)
ausgebucht *Adj.* booked up
ausgedehnt *Adj.* extensive
aus·gefallen *Adj.* unusual
Ausgeflippte *der/die; adj. Dekl.* (salopp)
dropout (coll.)
ausgeglichen *Adj.* balanced; well-
balanced ⟨person⟩; equable ⟨climate⟩
aus|gehen *unr. itr. V.; mit sein* (a) go out
(b) (fast aufgebraucht sein) run out
(c) (enden) end; **gut/schlecht** ∼: turn out
well/badly; ⟨story, film⟩ end happily/
unhappily
(d) von jmdm./etw. ∼: come from sb./sth.
(e) von etw. ∼ (etw. zugrunde legen) take sth. as
one's starting point; (etw. annehmen) assume
sth.
aus·gelassen ⌐1⌐ *Adj.* exuberant ⟨mood,
person⟩; lively ⟨party, celebration⟩; (wild)
boisterous
⌐2⌐ *adv.* exuberantly; (wild) boisterously

---

*old spelling - see note on page xiv

aus·gemacht Adj. (a) (beschlossen) agreed; **es ist [eine]** ~**e Sache, dass ...** it is an accepted fact that ...
(b) (vollkommen) complete; complete, utter ‹nonsense›; **eine** ~**e Dummheit** downright stupidity

aus·genommen Konj. except

ausgeprägt Adj. marked

ausgerechnet Adv. (ugs.) ~ **heute/ morgen** today/tomorrow of all days; ~ **hier** here of all places; ~ **Sie** you of all people

aus·geschlossen Adj. **das ist** ~: that is out of the question

aus·geschnitten Adj. low-cut ‹dress, blouse, etc.›

aus·gesprochen ①Adj. definite, marked ‹preference, inclination, resemblance›; pronounced ‹dislike›; marked ‹contrast›; ~**es Pech/Glück haben** be decidedly unlucky/lucky; **ein** ~**es Talent für etw.** a definite talent for sth.; **ein** ~**er Gegner von etw. sein** be a strong opponent of sth.
② adv. (besonders) decidedly; downright ‹stupid, ridiculous, ugly›

aus·gestorben Adj. [wie] ~: deserted

aus·gewogen Adj. (ausgeglichen) balanced; [well-]balanced ‹personality›

Aus·gewogenheit die; ~: balance

ausgezeichnet /od. '‑·‑‑/ ①Adj. excellent; outstanding ‹expert›
② adv. excellently

ausgiebig ①Adj. substantial ‹meal›
② adv. ‹profit› handsomely; ‹read› extensively; **von etw.** ~ **Gebrauch machen** make full use of sth.

aus|gießen unr. tr. V. (a) pour out (aus of)
(b) (leeren) empty

Ausgleich der; ~[e]s, ~e (a) ▶ AUSGLEICHEN A: evening out; reconciliation
(b) (Schadensersatz) compensation; als od. **zum** ~ **für etw.** to make up for sth.

aus|gleichen unr. tr. V. (a) even out; reconcile ‹differences of opinions, contradictions›
(b) compensate for ‹damage›; make up for ‹misfortune, lack›; **etw. durch etw.** ~: make up for sth. with sth.; **sich** ~: balance out; (sich gegenseitig aufheben) cancel each other out

aus|graben unr. tr. V. dig up; (Archäol.) excavate

Aus·grabung die (Archäol.) excavation

Aus·guss, *Aus·guß der sink

aus|halten unr. tr. V. stand; bear; endure; withstand ‹attack, load, pressure, test, wear and tear›; **er konnte es zu Hause nicht mehr** ~: he couldn't stand it at home any more; **es ist nicht zum Aushalten** it is unbearable

aus|handeln tr. V. negotiate

aus|händigen tr. V. hand over

Aus·hang der notice; **einen** ~ **machen** put up a notice

aus|heben unr. tr. V. dig out ‹earth etc.›; dig ‹trench, grave, etc.›

aus|helfen unr. itr. V. help out; **jmdm.** ~: help sb. out (**mit, bei** with)

Aus·hilfe die (a) (das Aushelfen) help
(b) ▶ AUSHILFSKRAFT

aushilfs-, Aushilfs-: ~**kraft** die temporary worker; (in Läden, Gaststätten) temporary assistant; (Sekretärin) temporary secretary; temp (coll.); ~**lehrer** der, ~**lehrerin,** die supply teacher; ~**weise** adv. on a temporary basis

aus|holen itr. V. [mit dem Arm] ~: draw back one's arm; (zum Schlag) raise one's arm

aus|kennen unr. refl. V. (an einem Ort usw.) know one's way around; (in einem Fach, einer Angelegenheit usw.) know what's what; **sie kennt sich in dieser Stadt aus** she knows her way around the town; **sich [gut] mit/in etw.** (Dat.) ~: know [a lot] about sth.

Aus·klang der (geh.) end; **zum** ~ **des Festes** to end or close the festival

aus|kleiden tr. V. (geh.) undress; **sich** ~: undress

aus|klingen unr. itr. V.; mit sein end

aus|klopfen tr. V. (a) beat out (aus + Dat. of)
(b) (säubern) beat ‹carpet›; knock ‹pipe› out

aus|kochen tr. V. boil; (keimfrei machen) sterilize ‹instruments etc.› [in boiling water]

aus|kommen unr. itr. V.; mit sein (a) manage (mit on)
(b) **mit jmdm. [gut]** ~: get on [well] with sb.

Auskommen das; ~s livelihood

Auskunft die; ~, **Auskünfte** (a) piece of information; **Auskünfte** information sing.; [**jmdm. über etw.** (Akk.)] ~ **geben** give [sb.] information [about sth.]
(b) (Stelle) information desk/counter/office/ centre etc.; (Fernspr.) directory enquiries no art. (Brit.); directory information no art. (Amer.)

Auskunftei die; ~, ~**en** private detective agency; (Kredit~) credit reference agency

Auskunfts-: ~**büro** das information office; enquiry office (Brit.); ~**schalter** der information counter; ~**stelle** die information office

aus|kungeln tr. V. (ugs.) reach by wheeling and dealing

aus|kurieren tr. V. heal ‹wound› [completely]

aus|lachen tr. V. laugh at

aus|laden unr. tr. V. unload ‹goods etc.›

Aus·lage die (a) Pl. (Unkosten) expenses
(b) (ausgestellte Ware) item on display; ~**n** goods on display

aus|lagern tr. V. (a) remove ‹art treasures› for safe-keeping
(b) relocate ‹firm, activity› (**nach** to); (an einen externen Dienstleister) outsource ‹function, activity›

Aus·land *das* foreign countries *pl.;* im/ins ∼: abroad; **aus dem** ∼: from abroad

Ausländer *der;* ∼s, ∼, **Ausländerin** *die;* ∼, ∼nen foreigner

ausländer·feindlich *Adj.* hostile to foreigners *postpos.*

ausländisch *Adj.* foreign

Auslands-: ∼**aufenthalt** *der* stay abroad; ∼**gespräch** *das* (Fernspr.) international call; ∼**korrespondent** *der,* ∼**korrespondentin** *die* foreign correspondent; ∼**reise** *die* trip abroad

aus|lassen *unr. tr. V.* (a) (weglassen) leave out
(b) (versäumen) miss ⟨*opportunity, chance, etc.*⟩

Auslauf *der* (a) keinen/zu wenig ∼ haben have no/too little chance to run around outside
(b) (Raum) space to run around in

aus|laufen *unr. itr. V.; mit sein* (a) run out (aus of)
(b) (leer laufen) empty; ⟨*egg*⟩ run out
(c) (in See stechen) sail (**nach** for)
(d) (erlöschen) ⟨*contract, agreement, etc.*⟩ run out

Aus·läufer *der* (a) (Geogr.) foothill *usu. in pl.;*
(b) (Met.) (eines Hochs) ridge; (eines Tiefs) trough

aus|legen *tr. V.* (a) (hinlegen) lay out; display ⟨*goods, exhibits*⟩
(b) etw. mit Fliesen/Teppichboden ∼: tile/carpet sth.
(c) (leihen) lend
(d) (interpretieren) interpret; etw. falsch ∼: misinterpret sth.

Auslegung *die;* ∼, ∼en interpretation

aus|leihen *unr. tr. V.* ▶ LEIHEN

aus|liefern *tr. V.* (a) jmdm. etw. *od.* etw. an jmdn. ∼: hand sth. over to sb.
(b) *auch itr.* (Kaufmannsspr.: liefern) deliver

Aus·lieferung *die* (a) (Übergabe) handing over; (an ein Land) extradition; jmds. ∼ fordern demand that sb. be handed over/extradited
(b) (Kaufmannsspr.: Lieferung) delivery

Auslieferungs-: ∼**antrag** *der* application for extradition; ∼**lager** *das* (Wirtsch.) distribution centre

aus|loggen *refl. V.* (DV) log off *or* out

aus|löschen *tr. V.* (a) extinguish
(b) (beseitigen) erase ⟨*drawing, writing*⟩

aus|losen *tr. V.* etw. ∼: draw lots for sth.

aus|lösen *tr. V.* (a) trigger ⟨*mechanism, device, alarm, etc.*⟩; release ⟨*camera shutter*⟩
(b) provoke ⟨*discussion, anger, laughter, reaction, outrage, heart attack*⟩; cause ⟨*sorrow, horror, surprise, disappointment, panic, war*⟩; excite, arouse ⟨*interest, enthusiasm*⟩

Auslöser *der;* ∼s, ∼ (Fot.) shutter release

---

*alte Schreibung - vgl. Hinweis auf S. xiv

aus|machen *tr. V.* (a) (ugs.) put out ⟨*light, fire, cigarette, candle*⟩; switch off ⟨*television, radio, hi-fi*⟩; turn off ⟨*gas*⟩
(b) (vereinbaren) agree [on]; ∼, **dass** ...: agree that ...
(c) (auszeichnen, kennzeichnen) make up
(d) wenig/nichts/viel ∼: make little/no/a great difference
(e) das macht mir nichts aus I don't mind

Aus·maß *das* (a) (Größe) size
(b) (Grad) extent

aus|messen *unr. tr. V.* measure up

Aus·nahme *die;* ∼, ∼n exception; mit ∼ von with the exception of; bei jmdm. eine ∼ machen make an exception in sb.'s case

Ausnahme-: ∼**erscheinung** *die* exceptional phenomenon; ∼**zustand** *der* state of emergency

ausnahms-: ∼**los** ① *Adj.* unanimous ⟨*approval, agreement*⟩; ② *adv.* without exception; ∼**weise** *Adv.* by way of an exception; **Dürfen wir mitkommen? – Ausnahmsweise [ja]** May we come too? – Yes, just this once

aus|nehmen *unr. tr. V.* (a) gut ⟨*fish, rabbit, chicken*⟩
(b) (ausschließen von) exclude; (gesondert behandeln) make an exception of

aus|nüchtern *tr., itr., refl. V.* sober up

Ausnüchterung *die;* ∼, ∼en sobering up; jmdn. zur ∼ auf die Wache bringen take sb. to the [police] station to sober up

Ausnüchterungs·zelle *die* drying-out cell

aus|nutzen, (bes. südd., österr.) **aus|nützen** *tr. V.* (a) take advantage of
(b) (ausbeuten) exploit

Aus·nutzung *die,* (bes. südd., österr.) **Ausnützung** *die;* ∼: use; (Ausbeutung) exploitation; unter voller ∼ einer Sache (*Gen.*) making full use of sth.

aus|packen ① *tr., itr. V.* unpack; (auswickeln) unwrap
② *itr. V.* (ugs.) (Geheimnisse verraten) talk (coll.); squeal (sl.)

aus|pressen *tr. V.* squeeze out ⟨*juice*⟩; squeeze ⟨*orange, lemon*⟩; (keltern) press ⟨*grapes etc.*⟩

aus|probieren *tr. V.* try out

Aus·puff *der* exhaust

Auspuffgase *Pl.* exhaust fumes *pl.*

aus|radieren *tr. V.* rub out; erase

aus|rangieren *tr. V.* (ugs.) throw out; discard; scrap ⟨*vehicle, machine*⟩; ausrangierte Fahrzeuge scrap vehicles

aus|rasten *itr. V.; mit sein* (Technik) disengage; er rastete aus, es rastete bei ihm aus (fig. salopp) something snapped in him

aus|rauben *tr. V.* rob

aus|räuchern *tr. V.* (auch fig.) smoke out; fumigate ⟨*room*⟩

aus|räumen ① *tr. V.* (a) clear out (aus of)

(b) (fig.) clear up; dispel ⟨*prejudice, suspicion, misgivings*⟩
☐2 *itr. V.* clear everything out

aus|rechnen *tr. V.* work out; **das kannst du dir leicht ~** (ugs.) you can easily work that out [for yourself]

Aus·rede *die* excuse

aus|reden ☐1 *itr. V.* finish [speaking]
☐2 *tr. V.* **jmdm. etw. ~:** talk sb. out of sth.

aus|reichen *itr. V.* be enough *or* sufficient **(zu for)**

ausreichend ☐1 *Adj.* sufficient; enough; (als Note) fair
☐2 *adv.* sufficiently

Aus·reise *die:* **jmdm. die ~ verweigern** refuse sb. permission to leave [the/a country]; **vor/bei der ~:** before/when leaving the country

Ausreise·antrag *der* application to leave the country; application for an exit visa

aus|reißen ☐1 *unr. tr. V.* tear out; pull out ⟨*plants, weeds*⟩
☐2 *unr. itr. V.; mit sein* **(a)** (sich lösen) come off
(b) (ugs.: weglaufen) run away (*Dat.* from)

aus|renken *tr. V.* dislocate

aus|richten *tr. V.* **(a)** jmdm. etw. ~: tell sb. sth.
(b) (einheitlich anordnen) line up
(c) (erreichen) achieve

aus|rollen *tr. V.* roll out

aus|rotten *tr. V.* eradicate

Aus·ruf *der* cry

aus|rufen *unr. tr. V.* **(a)** call out; „Schön!", **rief er aus** 'Lovely', he exclaimed
(b) (offiziell verkünden) proclaim; declare ⟨*state of emergency*⟩
(c) (zum Kauf anbieten) cry

Ausrufe·zeichen *das* exclamation mark

aus|ruhen *refl., itr. V.* have a rest; **[sich] ein wenig/richtig ~:** rest a little/have a good rest; **ausgeruht sein** be rested

aus|rüsten *tr. V.* equip

Aus·rüstung *die* **(a)** equipping
(b) (Gegenstände) equipment *no pl.*

Ausrüstungs·gegenstand *der* item of equipment

aus|rutschen *itr. V.; mit sein* slip

aus|säen *tr. (auch itr.) V.* (auch fig.) sow

Aus·sage *die* statement

aussage-, Aussage-: **~kraft** *die* meaningfulness; (Ausdruckskraft) expressiveness; **~kräftig** *Adj.* meaningful; (ausdruckskräftig) expressive

aus|sagen ☐1 *tr. V.* **(a)** say
(b) (vor Gericht, vor der Polizei) state; (unter Eid) testify
☐2 *itr. V.* make a statement; (unter Eid) testify

aus|saugen *regelm. (geh. auch unr.) tr. V.* **(a)** suck out **(aus** of); (leer saugen) suck dry

(b) (fig.: ausbeuten) **jmdn./etw. ~:** bleed sb./ sth. [white]; **jmdn. bis aufs Blut** *od.* **Mark ~:** bleed sb. white

aus|schaben *tr. V.* **(a)** scrape out
(b) (Med.) remove; (mit der Kürette) curette

aus|schalten *tr. V.* **(a)** switch *or* turn off
(b) (fig.) eliminate; exclude ⟨*emotion, influence*⟩; dismiss ⟨*doubt, objection*⟩; shut out ⟨*feeling, thought*⟩

Aus·schank *der;* **~[e]s** serving

Aus·schau *die:* **nach jmdm./etw. ~ halten** keep a lookout for sb./sth.

aus|schauen *itr. V.* **nach jmdm./etw. ~:** look out for sb./sth.

aus|scheiden ☐1 *unr. itr. V.; mit sein* **(a)** **aus etw. ~:** leave sth.; **aus dem Amt ~:** leave office
(b) (Sport) be eliminated
(c) **diese Möglichkeit/dieser Kandidat scheidet aus** this possibility/candidate has to be ruled out
☐2 *unr. tr. V.* (Physiol.) excrete ⟨*waste*⟩; eliminate, expel ⟨*poison*⟩; exude ⟨*sweat*⟩

Aus·scheidung *die* **(a)** (Physiol.)
▶ AUSSCHEIDEN 2: excretion; elimination; expulsion; exudation; **~en** (Ausgeschiedenes) excreta
(b) (Sport) qualifier

aus|schenken *tr. V.* serve

aus|scheren *itr. V.; mit sein* pull out

aus|schildern *tr. V.* signpost

aus|schimpfen *tr. V.* jmdn. ~: tell sb. off

aus|schlachten *tr. V.* **(a)** (ugs.: brauchbare Teile ausbauen aus) cannibalize ⟨*machine, vehicle*⟩; break ⟨*vehicle*⟩ for spares
(b) (ugs. abwertend: ausnutzen) exploit; **etw. politisch ~:** make political capital out of sth.

aus|schlafen ☐1 *unr. itr., refl. V.* have a good sleep
☐2 *unr. tr. V.* **seinen Rausch ~:** sleep off the effects of alcohol

Aus·schlag *der* **(a)** (Hautausschlag) rash
(b) (eines Zeigers, einer Waage) deflection; (eines Pendels) swing; **den ~ geben** (fig.) tip the scales (fig.)

aus|schlagen ☐1 *unr. tr. V.* **(a)** knock out
(b) (ablehnen) turn down
☐2 *unr. itr. V.* **(a)** ⟨*horse*⟩ kick
(b) ⟨*needle, pointer*⟩ be deflected, swing
(c) (sprießen) come out [in bud]

ausschlag·gebend *Adj.* decisive

aus|schließen *unr. tr. V.* **(a)** (ausstoßen) expel **(aus** from)
(b) (nicht teilnehmen lassen) exclude **(aus** from)
(c) (fig.) rule out ⟨*possibility*⟩; **jeden Irrtum ~:** rule out all possibility of error
(d) (aussperren) lock out

aus·schließlich *[od.* '-'--, -'--/ ☐1 *Adj.* exclusive
☐2 *Adv.* exclusively
☐3 *Präp. mit Gen.* excluding

Ausschließlichkeit die; ~:
exclusiveness

Aus·schluss, *Aus·schluß der
exclusion (**von** from); (aus einer Gemeinschaft)
expulsion (**aus** from); **unter** ~ **der**
Öffentlichkeit with the public excluded;
(Rechtsw.) in camera

aus|schmücken tr. V. deck out

aus|schneiden unr. tr. V. cut out; (DV)
cut

Aus·schnitt der (a) (Zeitungsausschnitt)
cutting; clipping
(b) (Halsausschnitt) neck; **ein tiefer** ~: a
plunging neckline
(c) (Teil) part; (eines Textes) excerpt; (eines
Films) clip; (Bildausschnitt) detail

aus|schreiben unr. tr. V. (a) (nicht
abgekürzt schreiben) **etw.** ~: write sth. out in
full
(b) (ausstellen) make out ⟨cheque, invoice,
receipt⟩
(c) (bekannt geben) call ⟨election, meeting⟩;
advertise ⟨flat, job⟩; put ⟨supply order etc.⟩
out to tender

Aus·schreibung die ▶ AUSSCHREIBEN C:
calling; advertisement; invitation to tender

Ausschreitungen Pl. acts of violence

Aus·schuss, *Aus·schuß der
committee

aus|schütten tr. V. tip out ⟨water, sand,
coal, etc.⟩; (ausleeren) empty ⟨bucket, bowl,
container⟩

ausschweifend ① Adj. wild
⟨imagination, emotion, hope, desire, orgy⟩;
extravagant ⟨idea⟩; riotous, wild ⟨enjoyment⟩;
dissolute ⟨life, person⟩
② adv. ~ **leben** lead a dissolute life

Ausschweifung die; ~, ~en (im Genießen)
dissolution

aus|sehen unr. itr. V. look (**wie** like); **so
siehst du aus!** (ugs.) that's what you think!

Aussehen das; ~s appearance

*aus|sein unr. itr. V.; mit sein; nur im Inf.
und Part. zusammengeschrieben (a) ⟨play,
film, war⟩ be over; **wann ist die Vorstellung
aus?** what time does the performance end?;
die Schule ist aus school is out
(b) ⟨fire, candle, etc.⟩ be out
(c) ⟨radio, light, etc.⟩ be off

außen Adv. outside; **die Vase ist** ~ **bemalt**
the vase is painted on the outside; **das
Fenster geht nach** ~ **auf** the window opens
outwards; **von** ~: from the outside

außen-, Außen-: ~**dienst** der: **im**
~**dienst sein** od. **arbeiten**, ~**dienst machen**
od. **haben** be working out of the office;
⟨salesman⟩ be on the road; ~**handel** der
foreign trade no art.; ~**handels·bilanz**
die balance of trade; ~**minister** der,
~**ministerin** die Foreign Minister;
~**ministerium** das Foreign Ministry;
~**politik** die foreign politics sing.;

~**politisch** ① Adj. ⟨question⟩ relating to
foreign policy; ② adv. as regards foreign
policy; ~**seite** die outside

Außenseiter der; ~s, ~,
Außenseiterin die; ~, ~nen outsider

Außen-: ~**spiegel** der exterior mirror;
~**stände** Pl. outstanding debts or
accounts; ~**wand** die external or outside
wall; ~**welt** die outside world

außer ① Präp. mit Dat. (a) (abgesehen von)
apart from; aside from (Amer.)
(b) (außerhalb von) out of; ~ **sich sein** be
beside oneself (**vor** + Dat. with)
(c) (zusätzlich zu) in addition to
② Präp. mit Akk. ~ **sich geraten** become
beside oneself (**vor** + Dat. with)
③ Konj. except

äußer... Adj. outer; outside ⟨pocket⟩;
outlying ⟨district, area⟩; external ⟨injury,
form, circumstances, cause, force⟩; outward
⟨appearance, similarity, effect, etc.⟩; foreign
⟨affairs⟩

außer·dem /auch: --'-/ Adv. as well;
(überdies) besides

Äußere das; adj. Dekl. [outward]
appearance

außer-: ~**ehelich** ① Adj. extra-marital;
illegitimate ⟨child, birth⟩; ② adv. outside
marriage; ~**gewöhnlich** ① Adj. (a)
unusual; (b) (das Gewohnte übertreffend)
exceptional; ② adv. (a) unusually; (b) (sehr)
exceptionally; ~**halb** Präp. mit Gen.
outside

äußerlich ① Adj. external ⟨use, injury⟩;
outward ⟨appearance, calm, similarity, etc.⟩
② adv.: s. Adj.: externally; outwardly

Äußerlichkeit die; ~, ~en formality;
(Unwesentliches) minor point

äußern ① tr. V. express, voice ⟨opinion,
view, criticism, reservations, disapproval,
doubt⟩; express ⟨wish⟩; voice ⟨suspicion⟩
② refl. V. **sich über etw.** (Akk.) ~: give
one's view on sth.
(b) ⟨illness⟩ manifest itself (**in** + Dat., **durch**
in)

außer-: ~**ordentlich** ① Adj. (a)
extraordinary; (b) (das Gewohnte übertreffend)
exceptional; ② adv. (sehr) exceptionally;
extremely ⟨pleased, relieved⟩; ~**schulisch**
Adj. outside the school postpos.

äußerst Adv. extremely

äußerst... Adj. (a) extreme
(b) (letztmöglich) latest possible ⟨date,
deadline⟩; (höchst...) highest ⟨price⟩; (niedrigst...)
lowest ⟨price⟩
(c) (schlimmst...) worst

außerstande Adv. ~ **sein, etw. zu tun**
(nicht befähigt) be unable to do sth.; (nicht in der
Lage) not be in a position to do sth.

Äußerung die; ~, ~en comment

aus|setzen ① tr. V. (a) expose (Dat. to);
Belastungen ausgesetzt sein be subject to
strains

43

Aussicht ⋯⟩ ausströmen ⋯⋯

(b) (sich selbst überlassen) abandon ⟨*baby, animal*⟩; (auf einer einsamen Insel) maroon
(c) an jmdn./etw. etwas auszusetzen haben find fault with sb./sth.
2 *itr. V.* **(a)** (aufhören) stop; ⟨*engine, machine*⟩ cut out
(b) (pausieren) ⟨*player*⟩ miss a turn; **mit der Arbeit/dem Training [ein paar Wochen] ~:** stop work/training [for a few weeks]
Aus·sicht *die* **(a)** view (auf + *Akk.* of)
(b) (fig.) prospect; **~ auf etw.** (*Akk.*) **haben, etw. in ~ haben** have the prospect of sth.
aussichts-, Aussichts-: ~los **1** *Adj.* hopeless; **2** *adv.* hopelessly; **~losigkeit** *die; ~~*: hopelessness; **~punkt** *der* vantage point; **~reich** *Adj.* promising; **~turm** *der* lookout tower
Aus·siedler *der* (Auswanderer) emigrant; (Evakuierter) evacuee; (Umsiedler) resettled person
Aussiedler·heim *das* resettlement hostel (*for German nationals and ethnic Germans from Eastern europe*)
Aussiedlerin *die* ▶ AUSSIEDLER
aus|sortieren *tr. V.* sort out
aus|spannen *itr. V.* take *or* have a break
aus|sparen *tr. V.* leave ⟨*line etc.*⟩ blank; (fig.) leave out; omit
Aussparung *die; ~, ~en* **(a)** (das Aussparen) leaving blank
(b) (Stelle) gap
aus|sperren **1** *tr. V.* lock out; shut ⟨*animal*⟩ out
2 *itr. V.* lock the workforce out
Aus·sperrung *die* lockout
aus|spielen *tr. V.* **(a)** *auch itr.* (Kartenspiel) lead
(b) jmdn./etw. gegen jmdn./etw. ~: play sb./sth. off against sb./sth.
Aus·sprache *die* **(a)** pronunciation
(b) (Gespräch) discussion
aus|sprechen **1** *unr. tr. V.* **(a)** pronounce
(b) (ausdrücken) express; voice ⟨*suspicion, request*⟩
2 *unr. refl. V.* **(a)** sich lobend/missbilligend *usw.* über jmdn./etw. ~: speak highly/disapprovingly of *etc.* sb./sth.
(b) (offen sprechen) say what's on one's mind; **sich bei jmdm. ~:** have a heart-to-heart talk with sb.
(c) (Strittiges klären) talk things out (mit with)
3 *unr. itr. V.* (zu Ende sprechen) finish [speaking]
Aus·spruch *der* remark
aus|spucken **1** *itr. V.* spit
2 *tr. V.* spit out
aus|spülen *tr. V.* rinse out
Aus·stand *der* strike
aus|statten /'au:sʃtatn/ *tr. V.* provide (**mit** with); (mit Gerät) equip; (mit Möbeln, Teppichen, Gardinen usw.) furnish

Ausstattung *die; ~, ~en* **(a)** ▶ AUSSTATTEN provision; equipping; furnishing
(b) (Ausrüstung) equipment; (Innenausstattung eines Autos) trim
(c) (Einrichtung) furnishings *pl.*
aus|stehen **1** *unr. itr. V.* **noch ~** ⟨*debt*⟩ be outstanding; ⟨*decision*⟩ be still to be taken; ⟨*solution*⟩ be still to be found
2 *unr. tr. V.* **ich kann ihn/das nicht ~:** I can't stand him/it
aus|steigen *unr. itr. V.;* **(a)** *mit sein* get out; (aus einem Zug, Bus) get off
(b) (ugs.: sich nicht mehr beteiligen) ~ aus opt out of; give up ⟨*show business, job*⟩; leave ⟨*project;*⟩
(c) (ugs.: der Gesellschaft den Rücken kehren) drop out
Aussteiger *der; ~s, ~,* **Aussteigerin** *die; ~, ~nen* (ugs.) dropout (coll.)
aus|stellen *tr. V.* **(a)** put on display; display; (im Museum, auf einer Messe) exhibit
(b) (ausfertigen) make out ⟨*cheque, prescription, receipt, bill*⟩; issue ⟨*visa, passport, certificate*⟩; **einen Scheck auf jmdn. ~:** make out a cheque to sb.
(c) (ugs.: ausschalten) switch off ⟨*cooker, radio, heating, engine*⟩
Aus·stellung *die* **(a)** exhibition
(b) ▶ AUSSTELLEN B: making out; issuing
Ausstellungs-: ~gelände *das* exhibition site; **~katalog** *der* exhibition catalogue
aus|sterben *unr. itr. V.;* *mit sein* die out; ⟨*species*⟩ become extinct; **vom Aussterben bedroht sein** be threatened with extinction
Aus·steuer *die* trousseau (*consisting mainly of household linen*)
Ausstieg *der; ~[e]s, ~e* **(a)** exit
(b) (ugs.) opting out (aus of); **der ~ aus einem Projekt/aus der Atomenergie** leaving a project/abandoning nuclear energy
aus|stopfen *tr. V.* stuff
Aus·stoß *der* (Wirtsch.) output
aus|stoßen *unr. tr. V.* **(a)** expel; give off, emit ⟨*gas, fumes, smoke*⟩
(b) give ⟨*cry, whistle, laugh, sigh, etc.*⟩; let out ⟨*cry, scream, yell*⟩; utter ⟨*curse, threat, etc.*⟩
aus|strahlen **1** *tr. V.* **(a)** (auch fig.) radiate; ⟨*lamp*⟩ give out ⟨*light*⟩
(b) (Rundf., Ferns.) broadcast
2 *itr. V.* **(a)** radiate; ⟨*light*⟩ be given out; (fig.) ⟨*pain*⟩ spread
(b) auf jmdn./etw. ~ (fig.) communicate itself to sb./influence sth.
Aus·strahlung *die* (fig.) charisma
aus|strecken **1** *tr. V.* stretch out; put out ⟨*feelers*⟩
2 *refl. V.* stretch out
aus|streichen *unr. tr. V.* cross out
aus|strömen *itr. V.; mit sein* pour out; ⟨*gas, steam*⟩ escape

aus|suchen tr. V. choose; pick

Aus-tausch der **(a)** exchange; **im ~ für** od. **gegen** in exchange for

(b) (das Ersetzen) replacement **(gegen** with)

aus|tauschen tr. V. **(a)** exchange **(gegen** for)

(b) (ersetzen) replace **(gegen** with)

Austausch-: **~motor** der replacement engine; **~schüler** der, **~schülerin** die exchange pupil or student

aus|teilen tr. V. distribute **(an** + Akk. to); (aushändigen) hand out ⟨books, post, etc.⟩ **(an** + Akk. to); give ⟨orders⟩; deal [out] ⟨cards⟩; give out ⟨marks, grades⟩; serve ⟨food etc.⟩

Auster die; **~,** **~n** oyster

aus|tragen unr. tr. V. **(a)** deliver ⟨newspapers, post⟩

(b) ⟨pregnant woman⟩ carry ⟨child⟩ to full term; (nicht abtreiben) have ⟨child⟩

(c) (ausfechten) settle ⟨conflict, differences⟩; fight out ⟨battle⟩

Australien /auːsˈtraːli̯ən/ (das); **~s** Australia

Australier der; **~s,** **~,** **Australierin** die; **~,** **~nen** Australian

australisch Adj. Australian

aus|treiben unr. tr. V. **(a)** exorcize, cast out ⟨evil spirit, demon⟩

(b) jmdm. etw. **~:** cure sb. of sth.

aus|treten ① unr. tr. V. **(a)** tread out ⟨spark, cigarette end⟩; trample out ⟨fire⟩

(b) (bahnen) tread out ⟨path⟩

(c) wear out ⟨shoes⟩

② unr. itr. V.; mit sein **(a)** (ugs.: zur Toilette gehen) pay a call (coll.)

(b) aus etw. **~** (ausscheiden) leave sth.

aus|trinken tr. V. drink up ⟨drink⟩; finish ⟨glass, cup, etc.⟩

Aus-tritt der leaving

aus|trocknen ① tr. V. dry out; dry up ⟨river bed, marsh⟩

② itr. V.; mit sein dry out; ⟨river bed, pond, etc.⟩ dry up; ⟨skin, hair⟩ become dry

aus|üben tr. V. practise ⟨art, craft⟩; follow ⟨profession⟩; carry on ⟨trade⟩; do ⟨job⟩; hold ⟨office⟩; wield ⟨power, right, control⟩

Aus-verkauf der sale

ausverkauft Adj. sold out

Aus-wahl die **(a)** choice

(b) (Sortiment) range; **viel/wenig ~ haben** have a wide/limited selection **(an** + Dat., **von** of)

aus|wählen tr. V. choose **(aus** from)

Aus-wanderer der, **Aus-wanderin** die emigrant

aus|wandern itr. V.; mit sein emigrate

Aus-wanderung die emigration

auswärtig Adj. **(a)** non-local

(b) (das Ausland betreffend) foreign

auswärts Adv. **(a)** (nach außen) outwards

(b) (nicht zu Hause) ⟨sleep⟩ away from home; **~ essen** eat out

(c) (nicht am Ort) in another town; (Sport) away

Auswärts-spiel das (Sport) away match

aus|waschen unr. tr. V. wash out

aus|wechseln tr. V. **(a)** change **(gegen** + Akk. for)

(b) (ersetzen) replace **(gegen** with); (Sport) substitute ⟨player⟩

Aus-weg der way out **(aus** of)

ausweg-los ① Adj. hopeless

② adv. hopelessly

Ausweglosigkeit die; **~:** hopelessness

aus|weichen unr. tr. V.; mit sein get out of the way **(Dat.** of); (Platz machen) make way **(Dat.** for); **einem Schlag/Angriff ~:** dodge a blow/evade an attack; **dem Feind ~:** avoid [contact with] the enemy; **einer Frage ~:** evade a question; **eine ~de Antwort** an evasive answer

Ausweich-manöver das evasive manœuvre

aus|weinen refl. V. have a good cry; **sie hat sich bei mir darüber ausgeweint** (ugs.) she had a good cry on my shoulder about it

Ausweis der; **~es,** **~e** card; (Personalausweis) identity card

aus|weisen ① unr. tr. V. **(a)** expel **(aus** from)

(b) jmdn. als etw. **~:** show that sb. is/was sth.

② unr. refl. V. prove or establish one's identity [by showing one's papers]; **können Sie sich ~?** do you have any means of identification?

Ausweis-papiere Pl. identity papers

Aus-weisung die expulsion **(aus** from)

aus|weiten tr. V. stretch

aus-wendig Adv. etw. **~ können/lernen** know/learn sth. [off] by heart

aus|werfen unr. tr. V. **(a)** cast ⟨net, anchor, rope, line, etc.⟩

(b) (herausschleudern) throw out ⟨sparks⟩; ⟨volcano⟩ eject, spew out ⟨lava, ash, etc.⟩; eject ⟨cartridge case⟩

aus|werten tr. V. analyse and evaluate

Aus-wertung die analysis and evaluation

aus|wirken refl. V. have an effect **(auf** + Akk. on); **sich günstig ~:** have a favourable effect

Aus-wirkung die effect **(auf** + Akk. on)

Aus-wuchs der **(a)** (Wucherung) growth; excrescence (Med., Bot.)

(b) (fig.) unhealthy product; (Exzess) excess

aus|wuchten tr. V. (Technik) **die Räder ~:** balance the wheels

aus|zahlen ① tr. V. **(a)** pay out ⟨money⟩

(b) pay off ⟨employee, worker⟩; buy out ⟨business partner⟩

② refl. V. pay

aus|zählen tr. V. **(a)** count [up] ⟨votes etc.⟩

(b) (Boxen) count out

---

*alte Schreibung - vgl. Hinweis auf S. xiv

aus|zeichnen *tr. V.* **(a)** (mit einem Preisschild) mark **(b)** (ehren) honour

Aus·zeichnung *die* **(a)** (von Waren) marking **(b)** (Ehrung) honouring; (Orden) decoration; (Preis) award

aus|ziehen ⓵ *unr. tr. V.* **(a)** pull out ⟨*couch*⟩; extend ⟨*table, tripod, etc.*⟩ **(b)** (ablegen) take off ⟨*clothes*⟩ **(c)** (entkleiden) undress; **sich ~**: get undressed
⓶ *unr. itr. V.; mit sein* move out (**aus** of)

Auszubildende *der/die; adj. Dekl.* (bes. Amtsspr.) trainee; (im Handwerk) apprentice

Aus·zug *der* **(a)** (das Ausziehen) move **(b)** (Bankw.) statement **(c)** (Textpassage) extract

auszugs·weise *Adv.* in extracts *or* excerpts; **etw. ~ lesen** read extracts from sth.

authentisch *Adj.* authentic

Autist *der; ~en, ~en,* **Autistin** *die; ~, ~nen* autistic

autistisch *Adj.* (Med.) autistic

Auto *das; ~s, ~s* car; automobile (Amer.); **~ fahren** drive; (mitfahren) go in the car

auto-, Auto-: **~bahn** *die* motorway (Brit.); expressway (Amer.); **~biografie** /-----'-/ *die* autobiography; **~biografisch** /----'--/ *Adj.* autobiographical; **~bombe** *die* car bomb; **~bus** *der* ▶ BUS; **~dieb** *der,* **~diebin** *die* car thief; **~fähre** *die* car ferry; **~fahren** *das; ~~s* driving; motoring; **~fahrer** *der,* **~fahrerin** *die* [car] driver; **~fahrt** *die* drive; **~gramm** /--'-/ *das; ~~s, ~~e* autograph; **~immun·erkrankung** *die* autoimmune disease; **~kino** *das* drive-in cinema

Automat *der; ~en, ~en* **(a)** (Verkaufs~) [vending] machine; (Spiel~) slot machine **(b)** (in der Produktion) robot

Automatik *die; ~, ~en* automatic control mechanism; (Getriebeautomatik) automatic transmission

automatisch (auch fig.) ⓵ *Adj.* automatic ⓶ *adv.* automatically

automatisieren *tr. V.* automate

Automatisierung *die; ~, ~en* automation

auto-, Auto-: **~mobil** /---'-/ *das; ~~s, ~~e* (geh.) motor car; automobile (Amer.); **~nom** /--'-/ ⓵ *Adj.* autonomous; ⓶ *adv.* autonomously; **~nomie** /---'-/ *die; ~~, ~~n* autonomy; **~nummer** *die* [car] registration number; **~pilot** *der* (Flugw.) autopilot

Autopsie /auto'psi:/ *die; ~, ~n* post mortem [examination]

Autor *der; ~s, ~en* author

Auto-: **~radio** *das* car radio; **~reifen** *der* car tyre; **~reise·zug** *der* Motorail train (Brit.); auto train (Amer.); **~reparatur** *die* car repair; repair to the/a car

Autorin *die; ~, ~nen* authoress; author

autoritär *Adj.* authoritarian

Autorität *die; ~, ~en* authority

Auto-: **~schalter** *der* drive-in counter; **~schlange** *die* queue of cars; **~schlüssel** *der* car key; **~skooter** /-sku:tɐ/ *der; ~~s, ~~:* dodgem; bumper car; **~stopp** *der* hitch-hiking; **per ~stopp fahren, ~stopp machen** hitch-hike; **~telefon** *das* car telephone; **~tür** *die* car door; **~unfall** *der* car accident; **~vermietung** *die* car rental firm; **~verwerter** *der,* **~verwerterin** *die* car breaker; **~verwertung** *die* car breaker's [yard]; **~wäsche** *die* car wash; **~werkstatt** *die* garage

Avocado /avo'ka:do/ *die; ~, ~s* avocado [pear]

Axt *die; ~, Äxte* axe

Azalee /atsa'le:ə/ *die; ~, ~n* azalea

Azubi *der; ~s, ~s/die; ~, ~s* (ugs.) ▶ AUSZUBILDENDE

b

Bb

b, B /be:/ *das;* ~, ~ (a) (Buchstabe) b/B
(b) (Musik) [key of] B flat

B *Abk.* = **Bundesstraße** ≈ A (Brit.)

Baby /'be:bi/ *das;* ~s, ~s baby

Baby·sitter /'be:bɪsɪtɐ/ *der;* ~s, ~;
  Baby·sitterin *die;* ~, ~: babysitter

Bach *der;* ~[e]s, **Bäche (a)** stream; brook
(b) (Rinnsal) stream [of water]

Back·blech *das* baking sheet

Back·bord *das* (Seew., Luftf.) port [side]

Backe *die;* ~, ~n cheek

backen [1] *unr. itr. V.* bake
  [2] *unr. tr. V.* (a) bake
  (b) (bes. südd.) ▶ BRATEN

Backen·zahn *der* molar

Bäcker *der;* ~s, ~: baker; **er ist** ~: he is a
baker; **zum/beim** ~: to the/at the baker's

Bäckerei *die;* ~, ~en baker's [shop]

Bäckerin *die;* ~, ~nen baker

Back-: ~**fisch** *der* fried fish (*in
breadcrumbs*); ~**form** *die* baking tin (Brit.);
baking pan (Amer.); ~**hähnchen** *das,*
~**hen** *das* (österr.), ~**huhn** *das* fried
chicken (*in breadcrumbs*); ~**ofen** *der* oven;
~**pulver** *das* baking powder; ~**stein** *der*
brick; ~**waren** *Pl.* bread, cakes, and
pastries

Bad *das;* ~[e]s, **Bäder (a)** bath; (das
Schwimmen) swim; (im Meer usw.) bathe; **ein** ~
nehmen (geh.) take a bath; (schwimmen) go for
a swim; (im Meer usw.) bathe
(b) (Badezimmer) bathroom; **ein Zimmer mit** ~:
a room with [private] bath
(c) (Schwimm~) [swimming] pool
(d) (Heil~) spa; (See~) [seaside] resort

Bade-: ~**anzug** *der* bathing costume;
~**hose** *die* bathing trunks *pl;* ~**mantel**
der dressing gown; bathrobe; ~**meister**
der, ~**meisterin** *die* swimming-pool
attendant; ~**mütze** *die* bathing cap

baden [1] *itr. V.* (a) have a bath
(b) (schwimmen) bathe; ~ **gehen** go for a
bathe
  [2] *tr. V.* bath ⟨child, patient, etc.⟩; bathe
⟨wound, eye, etc.⟩

Baden-Württemberg (*das*); ~s Baden-
Württemberg

Bäder ▶ BAD

Bade-: ~**strand** *der* bathing beach;
~**tuch** *das; Pl.* ~**tücher** bath towel;
~**wanne** *die* bath[tub]; ~**wasser** *das*
bath water; ~**zimmer** *das* bathroom

Badminton *das;* ~s badminton

---

*old spelling - see note on page xiv

Bagatelle *die;* ~, ~n trifle

Bagger *der;* ~s, ~: excavator;
(Schwimmbagger) dredger

Bagger·see *der* flooded gravel pit

Bahn *die;* ~, ~en (a) (Weg) path
(b) (Route) path; (eines Geschosses) trajectory
(c) (Sport) track; (für Pferderennen) course (Brit.);
track (Amer.); (für einzelne Teilnehmer) lane;
(Kegel~) alley; (Bowling~) lane
(d) (Eisen~) railways *pl.;* railroad (Amer.);
(Zug) train; **jmdm. zur** ~ **bringen** take sb. to
the station; **[mit der]** ~ **fahren** go by train
(e) (Straßen~) tram; streetcar (Amer.)

bahn-, Bahn-: ~**beamte** *der,*
~**beamtin** *die* railway or (Amer.) railroad
official; ~**brechend** *Adj.* pioneering;
~**brecher** *der,* ~**brecherin** *die;* ~~,
~~**nen** pioneer; ~**bus** *der* railway bus;
~**damm** *der* railway embankment

bahnen *tr. V.* clear ⟨way, path⟩; **jmdm./einer
Sache einen Weg** ~ (fig.) pave the way for
sb./sth.

Bahn-: ~**fahrt** *die* train journey; ~**hof**
der [railway or (Amer.) railroad] station;
~**reise** *die* train journey; ~**schranke**
die level crossing (Brit.) or (Amer.) grade
crossing barrier/gate; ~**steig** *der;* ~~[e]s,
~~e [station] platform; ~**übergang** *der*
level crossing (Brit.); grade crossing (Amer.);
~**verbindung** *die* train connection

Bahre *die;* ~, ~n (a) (Trage) stretcher
(b) (Totenbahre) bier

Baiser /bɛ'ze:/ *das;* ~s, ~s meringue

Bajonett *das;* ~[e]s, ~e bayonet

Bakterie /bak'te:rjə/ *die;* ~, ~n bacterium

Balance /ba'laŋsə/ *die;* ~, ~n balance

balancieren *itr., tr. V.;* *itr. mit sein*
balance

bald *Adv.* (a) soon; (leicht, rasch) quickly;
easily; **wirds** ~? get a move on, will you; **bis**
~! see you soon
(b) (ugs.: fast) almost

Baldrian /'baldria:n/ *der;* ~s, ~e valerian

Balkan /'balka:n/ *der;* ~s: **der** ~: the
Balkans *pl.;* (Gebirge) the Balkan Mountains
pl. **auf dem** ~: in the Balkans

Balken *der;* ~s, ~: beam

Balkon /bal'kɔŋ, bal'ko:n/ *der;* ~s, ~s
/bal'kɔŋs/ *od.* ~e /bal'ko:nə/ (a) balcony
(b) (im Theater, Kino) circle

Ball *der;* ~[e]s, **Bälle (a)** ball; ~ **spielen** play
ball
(b) (Fest) ball

Ballade *die;* ~, ~n ballad

Ballast *der;* ~[e]s, ~e ballast

Ballast·stoffe Pl. (Med.) roughage sing.
ballen ①tr. V. clench ‹fist›
②refl. V. ‹fist› clench
Ballen der; ~s, ~ (a) (Packen) bale
(b) (Hand-, Fußballen) ball
Ballerina die; ~, Ballerinen ballerina
Ballett das; ~[e]s, ~e ballet
Ballett-: ~schuh der ballet shoe;
~schule die ballet school; ~tänzer der,
~tänzerin die ballet dancer
Ball-: ~junge der ballboy; ~kleid das
ball gown
Ballon /ba'lɔŋ/ der; ~s, ~s balloon
Ball-: ~saal der ballroom; ~spiel das
ball game; ~spielen das; ~~s playing
ball no art.
Ballungs·gebiet das conurbation
Balsam der; ~s, ~e balsam; (fig.) balm
Balte der; ~n, ~n, **Baltin** die; ~, ~nen
Balt
Baltikum das; ~s Baltic States pl.
baltisch Adj. Baltic
Bambus der; ~ od. ~ses, ~se bamboo
banal Adj. (a) banal
(b) (gewöhnlich) commonplace
Banane die; ~, ~n banana
Banause der; ~n, ~n, **Banausin** die; ~,
~nen (abwertend) philistine
band 1. u. 3. Pers. Sg. Prät. v. BINDEN
Band¹ das; ~[e]s, Bänder (a) ribbon;
(Haar~, Hut~) band; (Schürzen~) string
(b) (Klebe~, Isolier~, Ton~ usw.) tape; etw. auf
~ ‹Akk.› aufnehmen tape[-record] sth.
(c) ▶ FÖRDERBAND;
(d) ▶ FLIESSBAND;
(e) am laufenden ~ (ugs.) nonstop
(f) (Anat.) ligament
Band² der; ~[e]s, Bände /'bɛndə/ volume
Band³ /bɛnt/ die; ~, ~s band; (Beat~,
Rock~ usw.) group
Bande¹ die; ~, ~n (a) gang
(b) (ugs.: Gruppe) mob (coll.)
Bande² die; ~, ~n (Sport) [perimeter]
barrier; (mit Reklame) billboards pl.; (Billard)
cushion
Banden-: ~krieg der gang war;
~werbung die: advertising on hoardings
around the perimeter of a football pitch etc.
Bänder ▶ BAND¹
Bänder-: ~riss, *~riß der (Med.) torn
ligament; ~zerrung die (Med.) pulled
ligament
bändigen tr. V. tame ‹animal›; control
‹person, anger, urge›
Bandit der; ~en, ~en bandit
Band·scheibe die [intervertebral] disc
bang, bange; banger, bangst... od.
bänger, bängst...: ①Adj. afraid; scared;
(besorgt) anxious; mir ist/wurde ~ [zumute] I
am/became scared
②adv. anxiously
bangen itr. V. be anxious

Bank¹ die; ~, Bänke bench; (mit Lehne)
bench seat; (Kirchen~) pew; etw. auf die lange
~ schieben (ugs.) put sth. off
Bank² die; ~, ~en bank
Bankett¹ das; ~[e]s, ~e banquet
Bankett² das; ~[e]s, ~e (an Straßen)
shoulder; (unbefestigt) verge
Bank·geheimnis das (Wirtsch.) bankers'
duty to maintain confidentiality
Bankier /baŋ'kje:/ der; ~s, ~s banker
Bank-: ~kauffrau die, ~kaufmann
der [qualified] bank/building society/stock
market clerk; ~konto das bank account;
~leitzahl die [bank] sort code; ~note
die banknote; bill (Amer.); ~raub der bank
robbery; ~räuber der, ~räuberin die
bank robber
bankrott Adj. bankrupt; **Bankrott** od. *~
gehen go bankrupt
Bankrott der; ~[e]s, ~e bankruptcy; ~
machen go bankrupt; s. auch BANKROTT
Bankrott·erklärung die declaration of
bankruptcy; (fig.) declaration of [one's own]
failure
Bank-: ~überfall der bank raid;
~verbindung die particulars of one's
bank account; ~wesen das banking
system
Bann der; ~[e]s (fig. geh.) spell
bar ①Adj. cash
②adv. in cash; etw. [in] ~ bezahlen pay for
sth. in cash; pay cash for sth.
Bar die; ~, ~s bar
Bär der; ~en, ~en bear
Baracke die; ~, ~n hut
Barbar der; ~en, ~en barbarian
Barbarei die; ~, ~en (a) (Rohheit)
barbarity
(b) (Kulturlosigkeit) barbarism no indef. art.
Barbarin die; ~, ~nen barbarian
barbarisch ①Adj. (a) (roh) barbarous
(b) (unzivilisiert) barbaric
②adv. (a) (roh) barbarously
(b) (unzivilisiert) barbarically
Bar·dame die barmaid
bären-, Bären-: ~dienst der: jmdm.
einen ~dienst erweisen do sb. a disservice;
~hunger der (ugs.) einen ~hunger haben/
kriegen be famished (coll.) or starving (coll.)/
get famished (coll.) or ravenous (coll.);
~stark Adj. as strong as an ox postpos.
Barett das; ~[e]s, ~e (eines Geistlichen)
biretta; (eines Richters, Professors) cap;
(Baskenmütze) beret
bar·fuß indekl. Adj.; nicht attr. barefooted;
~ herumlaufen/gehen run about/go barefoot
barg 1. u. 3. Pers. Sg. Prät. v. BERGEN
bar-, Bar-: ~geld das cash; ~geld·los
Adj. cashless; ~hocker der bar stool
Bariton /'baːritɔn/ der; ~s, ~e baritone
Barkasse die; ~, ~n launch
barmherzig (geh.) ①Adj. merciful ⋯⋯▷

b

②*adv.* mercifully

Barmherzigkeit *die;* ~ (geh.) mercy

Barock *das od. der;* ~[s] **(a)** baroque
(b) (Zeit) baroque age

Baro·meter *das* barometer

Baron *der;* ~s, ~e baron; (als Anrede) **[Herr]** ~: ≈ my lord

Baronin *die;* ~, ~nen baroness; (als Anrede) **[Frau]** ~: ≈ my Lady

Barren *der;* ~s, ~ **(a)** (Gold~, Silber~ usw.) bar
(b) (Turngerät) parallel bars *pl.*

Barriere /ba'rie̩ːrə/ *die;* ~, ~n (auch fig.) barrier

Barrikade *die;* ~, ~n barricade

barsch ①*Adj.* curt
②*adv.* curtly

Barsch *der;* ~[e]s, ~e perch

barst *1. u. 3. Pers. Sg. Prät. v.* BERSTEN

Bart *der;* ~[e]s, Bärte **(a)** beard; (Oberlippen~, Schnurr~) moustache
(b) (von Katzen, Mäusen, Robben) whiskers *pl.;*
(c) (am Schlüssel) bit

Barten·wal *der* (Zool.) whalebone whale

bärtig *Adj.* bearded

Bart·wuchs *der* growth of beard

Bar-: ~zahlung *die* cash payment; ~zahlungs·rabatt *der* cash discount

Basalt *der;* ~[e]s, ~e basalt

Basar *der;* ~s, ~e bazaar

Basis *die;* ~, Basen **(a)** (Grundlage) basis
(b) (Math., Archit., Milit.) base

Baske *der;* ~n, ~n Basque

Basken-: ~land *das* Basque region; ~mütze *die* beret

Baskin *die;* ~, ~nen Basque

Basket·ball /'baː(:)skət-/ *der* basketball

Bass, *Baß *der;* Basses, Bässe (Musik) **(a)** bass
(b) (Instrument) double bass

Bassin /ba'sɛ̃ː/ *das;* ~s, ~s (Schwimmbecken) pool; (im Garten) pond

Bassist *der;* ~en, ~en (Musik) **(a)** (Sänger) bass
(b) (Instrumentalist) double-bass player; bassist; (in einer Rockband) bass guitarist

Bassistin *die;* ~, ~nen ▶ BASSIST B

Bast *der;* ~[e]s, ~e bast; (Raffia~) raffia

basta *Interj.* (ugs.) that's enough; **und damit** ~**!** and that's that!

Bastelei *die;* ~, ~en; **(a)** (Gegenstand) piece of handicraft work
(b) (ugs.: das Basteln) handicraft work

basteln ①*tr. V.* make
②*itr. V.* make things [with one's hands]

Bastion *die;* ~, ~en bastion

bat *1. u. 3. Pers. Sg. Prät. v.* BITTEN

Bataillon /batal'joːn/ *das;* ~s, ~e (Milit.) battalion

Batik *der;* ~s, ~en *od. die;* ~, ~en batik

Batist *der;* ~[e]s, ~e batiste

Batterie *die;* ~, ~n battery

batterie-, Batterie-: ~betrieb *der* battery operation; ~betrieben *Adj.* battery-operated; ~huhn *das* battery chicken; (Henne) battery hen

Batzen *der;* ~s, ~ (ugs.) **(a)** (Klumpen) lump
(b) (Menge) pile (coll.)

Bau[1] *der;* ~[e]s, ~ten **(a)** (Errichtung) building; **im** ~ **sein** be under construction
(b) (Gebäude) building
(c) **auf dem** ~ **arbeiten** (Bauarbeiter sein) be in the building trade
(d) (Struktur) structure

Bau[2] *der;* ~[e]s, ~e (Kaninchenbau) burrow; hole; (Fuchsbau) earth

Bau·arbeiten *Pl.* building work *sing.*

Bauch *der;* ~[e]s, Bäuche (auch fig.: von Schiffen, Flugzeugen) belly

bauchig *Adj.* bulbous

Bauch-: ~laden *der* vendor's tray; ~landung *die* belly landing; ~nabel *der* (ugs.) belly button (coll.); ~redner *der,* ~rednerin *die* ventriloquist; ~schmerzen *Pl.* stomach ache *sing.;* ~speichel·drüse *die* pancreas; ~tanz *der* belly dance; ~tänzerin *die* belly dancer; ~weh *das* (ugs.) tummy ache (coll.); stomach ache

Bau·denkmal *das* architectural monument

bauen ①*tr. V.* build
②*itr. V.* **(a)** build; **wir wollen** ~: we want to build a house; (bauen lassen) we want to have a house built
(b) auf jmdn./etw. ~ (fig.) rely on sb./sth.

Bauer[1] *der;* ~n, ~n **(a)** farmer; (mit niedrigem sozialem Status) peasant
(b) (Schachfigur) pawn
(c) (Kartenspiele) ▶ BUBE

Bauer[2] *das od. der;* ~s, ~: [bird]cage

Bäuerin *die;* ~, ~nen **(a)** ▶ BAUER[1] A: [lady] farmer; peasant [woman]
(b) (Frau eines Bauern) farmer's wife

bäuerlich *Adj.* farming *attrib.;* (ländlich) rural

Bauern-: ~haus *das* farmhouse; ~hof *der* farm

bau-, Bau-: ~fällig *Adj.* ramshackle; unsafe ⟨roof, ceiling⟩; ~fälligkeit *die* bad state of dilapidation; badly dilapidated state; ~herr *der,* ~herrin *die* client (*for whom a house etc. is being built*); ~jahr *das* year of construction; (bei Autos) year of manufacture; ~kasten *der* construction set; (mit Holzklötzen) box of bricks; ~kasten·system *das* unit construction system; ~klotz *der* building brick; ~kran *der* construction crane

baulich *Adj.* structural

Baum *der;* ~[e]s, Bäume tree

Bau-: ~markt *der* (Kaufhaus) DIY

---

hypermarket; **~maschine** die piece of construction plant or machinery; **~maschinen** construction plant sing. or machinery

Bäumchen das; ~s, ~ small tree

Bau·meister der (hist.) [architect and] master builder

baumeln itr. V. (ugs.) dangle (an + Dat. from)

Baum-: **~schule** die tree nursery; **~stamm** der tree trunk; **~sterben** das; ~~s, ~~: dying-off of trees; **~stumpf** der tree stump; **~wolle** die cotton

Bau·platz der site for building

bäurisch (abwertend) 1 Adj. boorish 2 adv. boorishly

Bau·satz der kit

Bausch der; ~[e]s, ~e od. Bäusche (a) (Watte~) a wad
(b) etw. in ~ und Bogen verwerfen/ verdammen reject/condemn sth. wholesale

bauschen 1 tr. V. billow ⟨sail, curtains, etc.⟩
2 refl. V. ⟨dress, sleeve⟩ puff out; (ungewollt) bunch up; (im Wind) ⟨curtain, flag, etc.⟩ billow [out]

bauschig Adj. puffed ⟨dress⟩; baggy ⟨trousers⟩

bau-, Bau-: **~sparen** itr. V.; nur Inf. gebr. save with a building society; **~sparkasse** die building society; **~stein** der (a) building stone; (b) (Bestandteil) element; (Elektronik, DV) module; (c) (~klotz) building brick; **~stelle** die building site; (beim Straßenbau) roadworks pl.; **~stoff** der building material; **~teil** das component

Bauten Pl.: ▶ BAU

Bau-: **~unternehmer** der, **~unternehmerin** die building contractor; **~weise** die method of construction; **~werk** das building; (Brücke, Staudamm) structure; **~wirtschaft** die building or construction industry

Bayer der; ~n, ~n **Bayerin** die; ~, ~nen Bavarian

bay[e]risch Adj. Bavarian

Bayern (das); ~s Bavaria

Bazille die; ~, ~n (ugs.) ▶ BAZILLUS A

Bazillus der; ~, Bazillen (a) bacillus
(b) (fig.) cancer

Bd. Abk. = **Band** Vol.

beabsichtigen tr. V. intend

beachten tr. V. (a) follow ⟨rule, regulations, instruction⟩; heed, follow ⟨advice⟩; obey ⟨traffic signs⟩; observe ⟨formalities⟩
(b) (berücksichtigen) take account of; (achten auf) pay attention to

beachtlich 1 Adj. considerable 2 adv. considerably

Beachtung die; ~ (a) ▶ BEACHTEN A: following; heeding; obeying

(b) (Berücksichtigung) consideration
(c) (Aufmerksamkeit) attention

Beamte der; adj. Dekl. official; (Staats~) [permanent] civil servant; (Kommunal~) [established] local government officer; (Polizei~) [police] officer

Beamtin die; ~, ~nen ▶ BEAMTE

beängstigend Adj. worrying

beanspruchen tr. V. (a) claim; etw. ~ können be entitled to expect sth.
(b) (ausnutzen) make use of ⟨person, equipment⟩; take advantage of ⟨hospitality, services⟩
(c) (erfordern) demand ⟨energy, attention, stamina⟩; take up ⟨time, space, etc.⟩

Beanspruchung die; ~, ~en demands pl. (Gen. on); die ~ durch den Beruf the demands of his/her job

beanstanden tr. V. take exception to; (sich beklagen über) complain about

Beanstandung die; ~, ~en complaint

beantragen tr. V. apply for

beantworten tr. V. answer; reply to ⟨letter⟩; return ⟨greeting⟩

bearbeiten tr. V. (a) deal with; handle ⟨case⟩
(b) edit ⟨text, document⟩
(c) (adaptieren) adapt (für for)

Bearbeitung die; ~, ~en (a) die ~ eines Antrags/eines Falles usw. dealing with an application/handling a case etc.;
(b) (Adaption) adaptation

beaufsichtigen tr. V. supervise; look after ⟨child⟩

beauftragen tr. V. entrust

bebauen tr. V. build on; develop

bebaut Adj. ein [dicht] ~es Gebiet a densely built-up area; ein ~es Gelände a developed site

Bebauung die; ~, ~en (a) development
(b) (Gebäude) buildings pl.

beben itr. V. shake

Beben das; ~s, ~ ▶ ERDBEBEN

bebildern tr. V. illustrate

Bebilderung die; ~, ~en illustrations pl.

Becher der; ~s, ~ (Glas~, Porzellan~) glass; tumbler; (Plastik~) beaker; cup; (Eis~) (aus Glas, Metall) sundae dish; (aus Pappe) tub; (Joghurt~) carton

Becken das; ~s, ~ (a) (Wasch~) basin; (Abwasch~) sink; (Toiletten~) pan
(b) (Anat.) pelvis
(c) Pl. (Musik) cymbals

bedacht Adj. auf etw. (Akk.) ~ sein be intent on sth.

bedächtig 1 Adj. (a) deliberate; measured ⟨steps, stride, speech⟩
(b) (besonnen) thoughtful; well-considered ⟨words⟩
2 adv. (a) deliberately
(b) (besonnen) thoughtfully

bedanken *refl. V.* say thank you; **sich bei jmdm. [für etw.]** ∼: thank sb. [for sth.]

Bedarf *der;* ∼[e]s need (**an** + *Dat.* of); requirement (**an** + *Dat.* for); (Bedarfsmenge) needs *pl.;* requirements *pl.;* **bei** ∼: if required

bedauerlich *Adj.* regrettable

bedauerlicher·weise *Adv.* regrettably

bedauern *tr., itr. V.* **(a)** feel sorry for; **sie lässt sich gerne** ∼: she likes being pitied **(b)** (schade finden) regret; **ich bedaure sehr, dass ...**: I am very sorry that ...

Bedauern *das;* ∼s regret; **zu meinem** ∼: to my regret

bedauerns·wert *Adj.* (geh.) unfortunate ⟨*person*⟩

bedecken *tr. V.* cover

bedeckt *Adj.* overcast ⟨*sky*⟩

bedenken *unr. tr. V.* **(a)** consider **(b)** (beachten) take into consideration

Bedenken *das;* ∼s, ∼ reservation (**gegen** about); **ohne** ∼: without hesitation

bedenken·los ⏹1 *Adj.* unhesitating; (skrupellos) unscrupulous ⏹2 *adv.* without hesitation; (skrupellos) unscrupulously

bedenklich ⏹1 *Adj.* **(a)** dubious ⟨*methods, transactions, etc.*⟩ **(b)** (bedrohlich) alarming ⏹2 *adv.* alarmingly

Bedenk·zeit *die* time for reflection

bedeuten *tr. V.* **(a)** mean; **was soll das** ∼? what does that mean? **(b)** (sein) represent; **das bedeutet ein Wagnis** that is being really daring

bedeutend ⏹1 *Adj.* **(a)** significant; important **(b)** (groß) substantial; considerable ⟨*success*⟩ ⏹2 *adv.* considerably

Bedeutung *die;* ∼, ∼en **(a)** meaning **(b)** (Wichtigkeit) importance

bedeutungs·: ∼los *Adj.* insignificant; ∼voll ⏹1 *Adj.* **(a)** significant; **(b)** (viel sagend) meaningful; meaning ⟨*look*⟩; ⏹2 *adv.* meaningfully

bedienen ⏹1 *tr. V.* **(a)** serve; **werden Sie schon bedient?** are you being served? **(b)** (handhaben) operate ⟨*machine*⟩ ⏹2 *itr. V.* serve ⏹3 *refl. V.* help oneself; **sich selbst** ∼ (im Geschäft, Restaurant usw.) serve oneself

Bedienstete *der/die; adj. Dekl.* (Amtsspr.) employee

Bedienung *die;* ∼, ∼en **(a)** (das Bedienen) service; ∼ **inbegriffen** service included **(b)** (das Handhaben) operation **(c)** (Servierer[in]) waiter/waitress

Bedienungs·anleitung *die* operating instructions *pl.*

bedingen *tr. V.* cause

Bedingung *die;* ∼, ∼en condition; **unter der** ∼, **dass ...**: on condition that ...

bedingungs·los *Adj.* unconditional

bedrängen *tr. V.* **(a)** besiege ⟨*town, fortress, person*⟩; put ⟨*opposing player*⟩ under pressure **(b)** (belästigen) pester

Bedrängnis *die;* ∼, ∼se (geh.) (innere Not) distress; (wirtschaftliche Not) [great] difficulties *pl.;* **in** ∼ **geraten/sein** get into/be in great difficulties *pl.*

bedrohen *tr. V.* threaten

bedrohlich ⏹1 *Adj.* (Unheil verkündend) ominous; (gefährlich) dangerous ⏹2 *adv.* (Unheil verkündend) ominously; (gefährlich) dangerously

Bedrohlichkeit *die;* ∼: dangerousness; (einer Krankheit usw.) dangerous nature

Bedrohung *die* threat (*Gen.* to)

bedrucken *tr. V.* print

bedrücken *tr. V.* depress

Beduine *der;* ∼n, ∼n, **Beduinin** *die;* ∼, ∼nen Bed[o]uin

bedürfen *unr. itr. V.* **jmds./einer Sache** ∼ (geh.) require *or* need sb./sth.

Bedürfnis *das;* ∼ses, ∼se need (**nach** for); **das** ∼ **haben, etw. zu tun** feel a need to do sth.

bedürfnislos *Adj.* ⟨*person*⟩ with few [material] needs; modest, simple ⟨*life*⟩; ∼ **sein** have few [material] needs

Bedürfnislosigkeit *die;* ∼: lack of [material] needs

bedürftig *Adj.* needy

Beef·steak /'bi:f-/ *das* [beef]steak; **deutsches** ∼: ≈ beefburger

beehren *tr. V.* (geh.) honour

beeiden *tr. V.* ∼, **dass ...**: swear [on oath] that ...; **eine Aussage** ∼: swear to the truth of a statement

beeilen *refl. V.* hurry [up (coll.)]

beeindrucken *tr. V.* impress

beeindruckend *Adj.* impressive

beeinflussen *tr. V.* influence

Beeinflussung *die;* ∼, ∼en influencing

beeinträchtigen *tr. V.* restrict ⟨*sights, freedom*⟩; detract from ⟨*pleasure, enjoyment, value*⟩; spoil ⟨*appetite, good humour*⟩; impair ⟨*quality, reactions, efficiency, vision, hearing*⟩; damage, harm ⟨*sales, reputation*⟩

Beeinträchtigung *die;* ∼, ∼en ▸ BEEINTRÄCHTIGEN: restriction; detracting (+ *Gen.* from); spoiling; impairment; damage (*Gen.* to)

beenden, beendigen *tr. V.* **(a)** end; finish ⟨*piece of work etc.*⟩; complete ⟨*studies*⟩ **(b)** (DV) quit ⟨*program*⟩

beengen *tr. V.* hinder, restrict ⟨*movements*⟩; (fig.) restrict ⟨*freedom [of action]*⟩; **beengt wohnen** live in cramped surroundings *or* conditions; **sich beengt fühlen** feel cramped

---

*old spelling - see note on page xiv

beerben *tr. V.* jmdn. ~: inherit sb.'s estate

beerdigen *tr. V.* bury

Beerdigung *die;* ~, ~en burial; (Trauerfeier) funeral

Beerdigungs-institut *das* [firm *sing.* of] undertakers *pl.*

Beere *die;* ~, ~n berry

Beet *das;* ~[e]s, ~e (Blumenbeet) bed; (Gemüsebeet) plot

befahrbar *Adj.* passable

befahren *unr. tr. V.* **(a)** drive on ⟨*road*⟩; drive across ⟨*bridge*⟩; use ⟨*railway line*⟩; **die Straße ist stark/wenig ~:** the road is heavily/little used; **eine stark ~e Straße** a busy road
(b) sail ⟨*sea*⟩; navigate, sail up/down ⟨*river, canal*⟩

befallen *unr. tr. V.* **(a)** overcome; ⟨*misfortune*⟩ befall; **von Panik/Angst ~ werden** be seized with panic/fear
(b) ⟨*pests*⟩ attack

befangen ① *Adj.* **(a)** self-conscious ⟨*person*⟩
(b) (voreingenommen) biased
② *adv.* self-consciously

Befangenheit *die;* ~ **(a)** self-consciousness
(b) (Voreingenommenheit) bias

befassen *refl. V.* **sich mit etw. ~:** occupy oneself with sth.; ⟨*article, book*⟩ deal with sth.; (etw. studieren) study sth.

Befehl *der;* ~[e]s, ~e **(a)** order
(b) den ~ über jmdn./etw. haben be in command of sb./sth.

befehlen ① *unr. tr., itr. V.* order; (Milit.) order; **man befahl ihm zu warten** he was told to wait
② *unr. itr. V.* **über jmdn./etw. ~:** have command of *or* be in command of sb./sth.

Befehls-haber *der;* ~s, ~ (Milit.) commander

befestigen *tr. V.* **(a)** fix; **etw. an der Wand ~:** fix sth. to the wall
(b) (haltbar machen) stabilize ⟨*bank, embankment*⟩; make up ⟨*road, path, etc.*⟩
(c) (sichern) fortify ⟨*town etc.*⟩; strengthen ⟨*border*⟩

Befestigung *die;* ~, ~en **(a)** fixing
(b) (Milit.) fortification

befeuchten *tr. V.* moisten; damp ⟨*hair, cloth*⟩

befiehlst, befiehlt 2., 3. *Pers. Sg. Präsens v.* BEFEHLEN

befinden *unr. refl. V.* be

Befinden *das;* ~s health; (eines Patienten) condition

befindlich *Adj.*(a) to be found *postpos.;* **das in der Kasse ~e Geld** the money in the till
(b) (in einem Zustand) **die im Bau ~en Häuser** the houses [which are/were] under construction

Befindlichkeit *die;* ~, ~en (geh.) state

beflecken *tr. V.* stain

befohlen 2. *Part. v.* BEFEHLEN

befolgen *tr. V.* follow, obey ⟨*instruction, grammatical rule*⟩; obey, comply with ⟨*law, regulation*⟩; follow ⟨*advice, suggestion*⟩

Befolgung *die;* ~ ▶ BEFOLGEN: following; obedience (*Gen.* to); compliance (*Gen.* with)

befördern *tr. V.* **(a)** carry; transport
(b) (aufrücken lassen) promote

Beförderung *die;* ~, ~en **(a)** carriage; transport; (von Personen) transport
(b) (das Aufrückenlassen) promotion

befragen *tr. V.* **(a)** question (**über** + *Akk.* about)
(b) (konsultieren) ask

Befragung *die;* ~, ~en **(a)** questioning
(b) (Konsultation) consultation
(c) (Umfrage) opinion poll

befreien ① *tr. V.* **(a)** free; liberate ⟨*country, people*⟩ (**von** from)
(b) (freistellen) exempt (**von** from)
(c) jmdn. von Schmerzen ~: free sb. of pain
② *refl. V.* free oneself (**von** from)

Befreier *der,* **Befreierin** *die;* ~, ~nen liberator

Befreiung *die;* ~ **(a)** ▶ BEFREIEN 1A: freeing; liberation
(b) (Freistellung) exemption
(c) die ~ von Schmerzen release from pain

befremden *tr. V.* jmdn. ~: put sb. off

Befremden *das;* ~s surprise and displeasure

befremdlich (geh.) ① *Adj.* strange; odd
② *adv.* strangely

befreunden *refl. V.* ▶ ANFREUNDEN; [gut *od.* eng] **befreundet sein** be [good *or* close] friends (**mit** with)

befriedigen *tr. V.* **(a)** satisfy; gratify ⟨*lust*⟩
(b) (ausfüllen) ⟨*job, occupation, etc.*⟩ fulfil
(c) (sexuell) satisfy; **sich [selbst] ~:** masturbate

befriedigend ① *Adj.* satisfactory
② *adv.* satisfactorily

Befriedigung *die;* ~ **(a)** ▶ BEFRIEDIGEN A: satisfaction; gratification
(b) (Genugtuung) satisfaction

befristet *Adj.* temporary ⟨*visa*⟩; fixed-term ⟨*ban, contract*⟩

befruchten *tr. V.* fertilize ⟨*egg*⟩; pollinate ⟨*flower*⟩; impregnate ⟨*female*⟩; **ein Tier künstlich ~:** artificially inseminate an animal

Befruchtung *die;* ~, ~en ▶ BEFRUCHTEN: fertilization; pollination; impregnation; **künstliche ~:** artificial insemination

Befugnis *die;* ~, ~se authority

befühlen *tr. V.* feel

Befund *der* (bes. Med.) result[s *pl.*]

befürchten *tr. V.* fear; **ich befürchte, dass ...:** I am afraid that ...

befürworten *tr. V.* support

begabt *Adj.* talented; gifted; **hoch** ~: highly talented *or* gifted

Begabung *die;* ~, ~en talent; gift

begann *1. u. 3. Pers. Sg. Prät. v.* BEGINNEN

begatten *tr. V.* mate with; ‹*man*› copulate with; **sich** ~: mate; ‹*persons*› copulate

Begattung *die;* ~, ~en mating; (bei Menschen) copulation

begeben *unr. refl. V.* (geh.) proceed; make one's way; go; **sich zu Bett** ~: retire to bed; **sich an die Arbeit** ~: commence work

Begebenheit *die;* ~, ~en (geh.) event; occurrence

begegnen *itr. V.; mit sein* jmdm. ~: meet sb.; **sich** *(Dat.)* ~: meet [each other]

Begegnung *die;* ~, ~en (a) meeting (b) (Sport) match

begehen *unr. tr. V.* (a) commit ‹*crime, adultery, indiscretion, sin, suicide, faux-pas, etc.*›; make ‹*mistake*›; **eine [furchtbare] Dummheit** ~: do something [really] stupid (b) (geh.: feiern) celebrate

begehren *tr. V.* desire

begehrens·wert *Adj.* desirable

begehrlich 1 *Adj.* greedy
2 *adv.* greedily

begehrt *Adj.* much sought-after

begeistern 1 *tr. V.* jmdn. [für etw.] ~: fire sb. with enthusiasm [for sth.]
2 *refl. V.* get enthusiastic (**für** about)

begeisternd *Adj.* rousing

begeistert 1 *Adj.* enthusiastic (**von** about)
2 *adv.* enthusiastically

Begeisterung *die;* ~: enthusiasm

begeisterungs-, Begeisterungs-: ~**fähig** *Adj.* ‹*children, people, etc.*› who are able to get enthusiastic *or* are capable of enthusiasm; ~**fähigkeit** *die* capacity for enthusiasm; ~**sturm** *der* storm of enthusiastic applause

Begierde *die;* ~, ~n desire (**nach** for)

begierig 1 *Adj.* eager
2 *adv.* eagerly

begießen *unr. tr. V.* water ‹*plants*›

Beginn *der;* ~[e]s beginning; [**gleich] zu** ~: [right] at the beginning

beginnen 1 *unr. itr. V.* start; begin; **mit dem Bau** ~: start *or* begin building; **dort beginnt der Wald** the forest starts there
2 *unr. tr. V.* start; begin; start ‹*argument*›; ~, **etw. zu tun** start to do sth.

beglaubigen *tr. V.* certify

Beglaubigung *die;* ~, ~en certification

begleichen *unr. tr. V.* settle ‹*bill, debt*›; pay ‹*sum*›

Begleit·brief *der* covering *or* accompanying letter

begleiten *tr. V.* accompany; **jmdn. nach Hause** ~: see sb. home

Begleiter *der;* ~s, ~, **Begleiterin** *die;* ~, ~nen companion; (zum Schutz) escort; (Führer[in]) guide

Begleitung *die;* ~, ~en (a) **er bot uns seine** ~ an he offered to accompany us; **in** ~ **eines Erwachsenen** accompanied by an adult (b) (Musik) accompaniment

beglückwünschen *tr. V.* congratulate (**zu** on)

begnadet *Adj.* (geh.) divinely gifted

begnadigen *tr. V.* pardon; reprieve

Begnadigung *die;* ~, ~en reprieving; (Straferlass) pardon; reprieve

begnügen *refl. V.* content oneself

Begonie /be'go:njə/ *die;* ~, ~n begonia

begonnen *2. Part. v.* BEGINNEN

begraben *unr. tr. V.* bury

Begräbnis *das;* ~ses, ~se burial; (~feier) funeral

begreifen 1 *unr. tr. V.* understand; **er konnte nicht** ~, **was geschehen war** he could not grasp what had happened
2 *itr. V.* understand; **schnell** *od.* **leicht/ langsam** *od.* **schwer** ~: be quick/slow on the uptake

begreiflich *Adj.* understandable

begrenzen *tr. V.* limit, restrict (**auf** + *Akk.* to)

Begriff *der* (a) concept; (Terminus) term (b) (Auffassung) idea; **sich** *(Dat.)* **keinen** ~ **von etw. machen können** not be able to imagine sth.; **ein/kein** ~ **sein** be/not be well known (c) **im** ~ **sein** *od.* **stehen, etw. zu tun** be about to do sth.

begriffs·stutzig *Adj.* (abwertend) obtuse

Begriffsstutzigkeit *die;* ~ (abwertend) obtuseness

begründen *tr. V.* (a) give reasons for (b) (gründen) found; establish ‹*fame, reputation*›

Begründer *der;* ~s, ~, **Begründerin** *die;* ~, ~nen founder

begründet *Adj.* well-founded; reasonable ‹*demand, objection, complaint*›

Begründung *die;* ~, ~en reason[s]; **mit der** ~, **dass** ...: on the grounds that ...

begrüßen *tr. V.* (a) greet; ‹*hostess, host*› welcome (b) (fig.) welcome

Begrüßung *die;* ~, ~en greeting; (von Gästen) welcoming; (Zeremonie) welcome (*Gen.* for)

begünstigen *tr. V.* favour

Begünstigung *die;* ~: favouring

begutachten *tr. V.* (a) examine and report on (b) (ugs.) have a look at

Begutachtung *die;* ~, ~en examination

begütert *Adj.* wealthy

begütigen *tr. V.* placate

behaart *Adj.* hairy; **stark** ~ **sein** be covered with hair; **stark** ~**e Beine** very hairy legs

---

*alte Schreibung – vgl. Hinweis auf S. xiv

behäbig 1 *Adj.* slow and ponderous
2 *adv.* slowly and ponderously

behagen *itr. V.* **etw. behagt jmdm.** sb. likes sth.

Behagen *das;* ~s pleasure

behaglich 1 *Adj.* comfortable
2 *adv.* comfortably

Behaglichkeit *die;* ~: comfortableness

behalten *unr. tr. V.* **(a)** keep; **etw. für sich** ~: keep sth. to oneself
(b) (zurück~) be left with ⟨scar, defect, etc.⟩
(c) (sich merken) remember

Behälter *der;* ~s, ~ container; (für Abfälle) receptacle

behämmert *Adj.* (salopp) ▶ BEKLOPPT

behänd, behände 1 *Adj.* (geschickt) deft; (flink) nimble
2 *adv. s. Adj.:* deftly; nimbly

behandeln *tr. V.* (auch Med.) treat; handle ⟨matter, machine, device⟩; deal with ⟨subject, question etc.⟩

Behandlung *die;* ~, ~en treatment

behängen *tr. V.* hang

beharren *itr. V.* **auf etw.** (*Dat.*) ~ (etw. nicht aufgeben) persist in sth.; (auf etw. bestehen) insist on sth.

beharrlich 1 *Adj.* dogged
2 *adv.* doggedly

Beharrlichkeit *die;* ~: doggedness

behauen *unr. tr. V.* hew

behaupten 1 *tr. V.* **(a)** maintain; assert; ~, jmd. zu sein/etw. zu wissen claim to be sb./know sth.; **man behauptet** *od.* **es wird behauptet, dass …:** it is said *or* claimed that …
(b) (verteidigen) maintain ⟨position⟩; retain ⟨record⟩
2 *refl. V.* **(a)** assert oneself; (nicht untergehen) hold one's ground; (dableiben) survive
(b) (Sport) win through

Behauptung *die;* ~, ~en assertion

Behausung *die;* ~, ~en dwelling

beheben *unr. tr. V.* remove ⟨danger, difficulty⟩; repair ⟨damage⟩; remedy ⟨abuse, defect⟩

Behebung *die;* ~, ~en ▶ BEHEBEN: removal; repair; remedying

beheimatet *Adj.* **an einem Ort/in einem Land** *usw.* ~ **sein** be native to a place/to a country *etc.*

beheizbar *Adj.* heatable; **eine** ~**e Heckscheibe** a heated rear window

beheizen *tr. V.* heat

behelfen *unr. refl. V.* make do

behelfs·mäßig 1 *Adj.* makeshift
2 *adv.* in a makeshift way

behelligen *tr. V.* bother; (zudringlich werden gegen) pester

*behend, *behende ▶ BEHÄND, BEHÄNDE

beherbergen *tr. V.* accommodate

beherrschen 1 *tr. V.* **(a)** control; rule ⟨country, people⟩

(b) (meistern) control ⟨vehicle, animal⟩; be in control of ⟨situation⟩
(c) (bestimmen, dominieren) dominate ⟨townscape, landscape, discussions⟩
(d) (zügeln) control ⟨feelings⟩; control, curb ⟨impatience⟩
(e) (gut können) have mastered ⟨instrument, trade⟩; have a good command of ⟨language⟩
2 *refl. V.* control oneself

beherrscht 1 *Adj.* self-controlled
2 with self-control

Beherrschung *die;* ~ **(a)** control; (eines Volks, Landes usw.) rule
(b) (das Meistern) control
(c) (Beherrschtheit) self-control
(d) (das Können) mastery

beherzigen *tr. V.* take ⟨sth.⟩ to heart

beherzt 1 *Adj.* spirited
2 *adv.* spiritedly

behilflich *Adj.* [jmdm.] ~ **sein** help [sb.] (bei with)

behindern *tr. V.* **(a)** hinder; impede ⟨movement⟩; hold up ⟨traffic⟩
(b) (Sport, Verkehrsw.) obstruct

behindert *Adj.* handicapped

Behinderte *der/die; adj. Dekl.* handicapped person; **die** ~**n** the handicapped; **WC für** ~: toilet for disabled persons

Behinderung *die;* ~, ~en **(a)** hindrance
(b) (Sport, Verkehrsw.) obstruction
(c) (Gebrechen) handicap

Behörde *die;* ~, ~n authority; (Amt, Abteilung) department

behördlich 1 *Adj.* official
2 *adv.* officially

behüten *tr. V.* protect (**vor** + *Dat.* from); (bewachen) guard

behutsam 1 *Adj.* careful
2 *adv.* carefully

bei *Präp. mit Dat.* **(a)** (nahe) near; (dicht an, neben) by; **wer steht da** ~ **ihm?** who is standing there with him?; **etw.** ~ **sich haben** have sth. with *or* on one; **sich** ~ **jmdm. entschuldigen** apologize to sb.
(b) (unter) among; **war heute ein Brief für mich** ~ **der Post?** was there a letter for me in the post today?
(c) (an) by; **jmdn.** ~ **der Hand nehmen** take sb. by the hand
(d) (im Wohn-/Lebens-/Arbeitsbereich von); ~ **uns tut man das nicht** we don't do that; ~ **mir [zu Hause]** at my house; ~ **uns um die Ecke/ gegenüber** round the corner from us/ opposite us; ~ **seinen Eltern leben** live with one's parents; **wir sind** ~ **ihr eingeladen** we have been invited to her house; **wir treffen uns** ~ **uns/Peter** we'll meet at our/Peter's place; ~ **uns in der Firma** in our company; ~ **Schmidt** (auf Briefen) c/o Schmidt; ~ **einer Firma sein** be with a company; ~ **jmdm./ einem Verlag arbeiten** work for sb./a publishing house
(e) (im Bereich eines Vorgangs) at; ~ **einer** ┉┅

b

Hochzeit/einem Empfang *usw.* be at a wedding/reception *etc.;* ~ einem Unfall in an accident
(**f**) (im Werk von) ~ Goethe in Goethe
(**g**) (im Falle von) in the case of; wie ~ den Römern as with the Romans; ~ der Hauskatze in the domestic cat
(**h**) (modal) ~ Tag/Nacht by day/night; ~ Tageslicht by daylight; ~ Nebel in fog
(**i**) (im Falle des Auftretens von) „~ Nässe Schleudergefahr" 'slippery when wet'
(**j**) (angesichts) with; ~ dieser Hitze in this heat; ~ deinen guten Augen/ihrem Talent with your good eyesight/her talent
(**k**) (trotz) ~ all seinem Engagement/seinen Bemühungen in spite of *or* despite *or* for all his commitment/efforts

bei|behalten *unr. tr. V.* keep; retain; keep up ⟨custom, habit⟩; keep to ⟨course, method⟩; preserve, maintain ⟨way of life; attitude⟩

bei|bringen *unr. tr. V.* (**a**) jmdm. etw. ~: teach sb. sth.
(**b**) (ugs.: mitteilen) jmdm. ~, dass ...: break it to sb. that ...
(**c**) (zufügen) jmdm./sich etw. ~: inflict sth. on sb./oneself

Beichte *die;* ~, ~n confession *no def. art.*

beichten **1** *itr. V.* confess
2 *tr. V.* (auch fig.) confess

Beicht-: ~stuhl *der* confessional; ~vater *der* father confessor

beid... *Indefinitpron. u. Zahlw.* **1** *Pl.* ~e both; (der/die/das eine oder der/die/das andere) either *sing.;* die ~en the two; die/seine ~en Brüder the/his two brothers; die ~en ersten Strophen the first two verses; kennst du die ~en? do you know those two?; alle ~e both of us/you/them; ihr/euch ~e you two; ihr/euch ~e nicht neither of you; wir/uns ~e the two of us/both of us; er hat ~e Eltern verloren he has lost both [his] parents; mit ~en Händen with both hands; ich habe ~e gekannt I knew both of them; einer/eins von ~en one of the two; keiner/keins von ~en neither [of them]
2 *Neutr. Sg.;* ~es both *pl.;* (das eine oder das andere) either; ~es ist möglich either is possible; ich glaube ~es/~es nicht I believe both things/neither thing; das ist ~es nicht richtig neither of those is correct

beiderlei *indekl. Adj.* ~ Geschlechts of both sexes

beider·seits **1** *Präp. mit Gen.* on both sides of
2 *Adv.* on both sides

bei·einander *Adv.* together; ~ Trost suchen seek comfort from each other

Bei·fahrer *der,* **Bei·fahrerin** *die* (**a**) passenger
(**b**) (berufsmäßig) co-driver; (im LKW) driver's mate

---

*old spelling - see note on page xiv

Beifahrer·sitz *der* passenger seat; (eines Motorrads) pillion

Bei·fall *der* (**a**) applause
(**b**) (Zustimmung) approval

bei·fällig **1** *Adj.* approving
2 *adv.* approvingly

beige /beːʃ/ *Adj.* beige

Beige /beːʃ/ *das;* ~, ~ *od.* (ugs.) ~s beige

Bei·geschmack *der:* einen bitteren *usw.* ~ haben have a slightly bitter *etc.* taste [to it]

Bei·hilfe *die* (**a**) aid; (Zuschuss) allowance
(**b**) (Rechtsw.: Mithilfe) aiding and abetting

bei|kommen *unr. itr. V.; mit sein* (**a**) (gewachsen sein) jmdm. ~: get the better of sb.
(**b**) (bewältigen) den Schwierigkeiten/der Unruhe/jmds. Sturheit ~: overcome the difficulties/deal with the unrest/cope with sb.'s obstinacy

Beil *das;* ~[e]s, ~e axe; (kleiner) hatchet

Bei·lage *die* (**a**) (Zeitungs~) supplement
(**b**) (zu Speisen) side dish; (Gemüse) vegetables *pl.*

bei·läufig **1** *Adj.* casual
2 *adv.* casually

bei|legen *tr. V.* (**a**) enclose
(**b**) (schlichten) settle ⟨dispute etc.⟩

Bei·leid *das* sympathy; [mein] herzliches *od.* aufrichtiges ~! please accept my sincere condolences

bei|liegen *unr. itr. V.* einem Brief ~: be enclosed with a letter

bei·liegend *Adj.* enclosed; ~ senden wir ...: please find enclosed ...

beim *Präp. + Art.* (**a**) = bei dem;
(**b**) ~ Film sein be in films
(**c**) er will ~ Arbeiten nicht gestört werden he doesn't want to be disturbed when working; ~ Duschen sein be taking a shower

bei|messen *unr. tr. V.* attach

Bein *das;* ~[e]s, ~e leg; jmdm. ein ~ stellen trip sb.; (fig.) put *or* throw a spanner *or* (Amer.) a monkey wrench in sb.'s works; wieder auf den ~en sein be back on one's feet again

bei·nah[e] *Adv.* almost

Bei·name *der* epithet

Bein·bruch *der:* das ist [doch] kein ~ (ugs.) it's not the end of the world

bei|nhalten *tr. V.* (Papierdt.) involve

-beinig *adj.* -legged

bei|pflichten *itr. V.* agree (*Dat.* with)

bei|rren *tr. V.* sich durch nichts/von niemandem ~ lassen not be deterred by anything/anybody

beisammen *Adv.* together

beisammen|haben *unr. tr. V.* (**a**) have got together
(**b**) er hat [sie] nicht alle beisammen (ugs.) he's not all there (coll.)

Beisammen·sein *das* get-together

Bei·schlaf *der* sexual intercourse

Bei·sein *das:* in jmds. ∼: in the presence of sb. *or* in sb.'s presence

bei·seite *Adv.* aside

Beis[e]l *das;* ∼s, ∼ *od.* ∼n (österr.) pub (Brit.); bar (Amer.)

bei|setzen *tr. V.* lay to rest; inter ⟨*ashes*⟩

Bei·setzung *die;* ∼, ∼en funeral; burial

Bei·spiel *das* example (**für** of); **zum** ∼: for example; **mit gutem** ∼ **vorangehen** set a good example

beispielhaft *Adj.* exemplary

beispiel·los *Adj.* unparalleled

beispiels·weise *Adv.* for example

beißen ①︎ *unr. tr., itr. V.* (auch fig.) bite; ②︎ *unr. refl. V.* (ugs.) ⟨*colours, clothes*⟩ clash

beißend *Adj.* biting ⟨*cold*⟩; acrid ⟨*smoke, fumes*⟩; sharp ⟨*frost*⟩

Beiß·zange *die* ▶ KNEIFZANGE

Bei·stand *der* (geh.: Hilfe) aid

bei|stehen *unr. itr. V.* **jmdm.** ∼: aid sb.

bei|steuern *tr. V.* contribute

Beitrag *der;* ∼[e]s, Beiträge contribution; (Versicherungsbeitrag) premium; (Mitgliedsbeitrag) subscription

bei|tragen *unr. tr., itr. V.* contribute (**zu** to)

bei|treten *unr. itr. V.; mit sein* join ⟨*union, club, etc.*⟩; **einem Abkommen/Pakt** accede to ⟨*pact, agreement*⟩

Bei·tritt *der* joining

Bei·wagen *der* sidecar

Bei·werk *das* accessories *pl.*

bei|wohnen *itr. V.* **einer Sache** (*Dat.*) ∼ (geh.) be present at sth.

Beize *die;* ∼, ∼n (Holzbearb.) [wood]stain

beizeiten *Adv.* in good time

beizen *tr. V.* (Holzbearb.) stain

bejahen /bə'jaːən/ *tr. V.* (a) *auch itr.* answer ⟨*sth.*⟩ in the affirmative
(b) (gutheißen) approve of; **das Leben** ∼: have a positive *or* an affirmative attitude to life

Bejahung *die;* ∼, ∼en (a) affirmative reply
(b) (das Gutheißen) approval

bejammern *tr. V.* lament

bejubeln *tr. V.* cheer; acclaim

bekämpfen *tr. V.* (a) fight against
(b) combat ⟨*disease, epidemic, pest, unemployment, crime, etc.*⟩

Bekämpfung *die;* ∼ (a) fight (*Gen.* against)
(b) ▶ BEKÄMPFEN B: combating

bekannt *Adj.* (a) well-known; **etw.** ∼ **geben** announce sth.; **etw.** ∼ **machen** announce sth.; (der Öffentlichkeit) make sth. public; **∼ werden** become known; **es ist nichts davon** ∼: nothing is known concerning it
(b) **jmd./etw. ist jmdm.** ∼: sb. knows sb./sth.; **Darf ich** ∼ **machen? Meine Eltern** may I introduce my parents?

Bekannte *der/die; adj. Dekl.* acquaintance

Bekannt·gabe *die;* ∼: announcement

*bekannt|geben ▶ BEKANNT A

bekanntlich *Adv.* as is well known; **etw. ist** ∼ **der Fall** sth. is known to be the case

*bekannt|machen ▶ BEKANNT A

Bekannt·machung *die;* ∼, ∼en announcement

Bekanntschaft *die;* ∼, ∼en acquaintance

*bekannt|werden ▶ BEKANNT A

bekehren ①︎ *tr. V.* convert
②︎ *refl. V.* become converted

Bekehrung *die;* ∼, ∼en (auch fig.) conversion (**zu** to)

bekennen ①︎ *unr. tr. V.* (a) confess; ∼, **dass ...** admit that ...
(b) (Rel.) profess
②︎ *refl. V.* **sich zum Islam** ∼: profess Islam; **sich zu Buddha** ∼: profess one's faith in Buddha; **sich zu seiner Schuld** ∼: confess one's guilt; **sich schuldig/nicht schuldig** ∼: confess/not confess one's guilt; (vor Gericht) plead guilty/not guilty

Bekenntnis *das;* ∼ses, ∼se (a) confession
(b) (Eintreten) **ein** ∼ **zum Frieden** a declaration for peace
(c) (Konfession) denomination

bekiffen *refl. V.* (ugs.) get stoned (sl.)

bekifft *Adj.* (ugs.) stoned

beklagen ①︎ *tr. V.* (geh.) (a) (betrauern) mourn
(b) (bedauern) lament
②︎ *refl. V.* complain

bekleckern *tr. V.* (ugs.) **etw./sich [mit Soße usw.]** ∼: drop *or* spill sauce *etc.* down sth./oneself

bekleiden *tr. V.* (a) clothe; **mit etw. bekleidet sein** be wearing sth.
(b) (geh.: innehaben) occupy ⟨*office, position*⟩

Bekleidung *die;* ∼, ∼en clothing; clothes *pl.*

beklemmend *Adj.* oppressive

Beklemmung *die;* ∼, ∼en oppressive feeling

beklommen *Adj.* uneasy; (stärker) apprehensive

bekloppt *Adj.* (salopp) barmy (Brit. coll.); loony (coll.)

beknackt *Adj.* (salopp) lousy (coll.); **ein** ∼**er Typ** a berk (Brit. coll.); a jerk (coll.)

beknien *tr. V.* (ugs.) beg

bekommen ①︎ *unr. tr. V.* (a) get; get, receive ⟨*money, letter, reply, news, orders*⟩; (erreichen) catch ⟨*train, bus, flight*⟩; **was** ∼ **Sie?** (im Geschäft) can I help you?; (im Lokal, Restaurant) what would you like?; **was** ∼ **Sie [dafür]?** how much is that?; **Hunger/Durst** ∼: get hungry/thirsty; **Angst/Mut** ∼: become frightened/take heart; **er bekommt einen Bart** he's growing a beard; **sie bekommt eine** ⋯◈

b

Brust her breasts are developing; **Zähne** ~:
⟨*baby*⟩ teethe; **sie bekommt ein Kind** she's
expecting a baby
(b) etw. durch die Tür/ins Auto ~: get sth.
through the door/into the car
2 *unr. V.; in der Funktion eines Hilfsverbs
zur Umschreibung des Passivs* get; **etw.
geschenkt** ~: get [given] sth. *or* be given sth.
as a present
3 *unr. itr. V.; mit sein* **jmdm. gut** ~: do sb.
good; **jmdm. [gut]** ~: ⟨*food, medicine*⟩ agree
with sb.; **wohl bekomms!** your [very good]
health!
bekömmlich *Adj.* easily digestible
beköstigen *tr. V.* cater for
bekräftigen *tr. V.* reinforce ⟨*statement*⟩;
reaffirm ⟨*promise*⟩
bekreuzigen *refl. V.* (kath. Kirche) cross
oneself
bekriegen *tr. V.* wage war on; (fig.) fight;
sich ~: be at war; (fig.) fight
bekümmern *tr. V.* **jmdn.** ~: cause sb.
worry
bekümmert *Adj.* worried; (stärker)
distressed
bekunden *tr. V.* express
belächeln *tr. V.* smile [pityingly/tolerantly
etc.] at
beladen *unr. tr. V.* load ⟨*ship*⟩; load [up]
⟨*car, wagon*⟩; load up ⟨*horse, donkey*⟩
Belag *der;* ~[e]s, **Beläge (a)** coating
(b) (Fußbodenbelag) covering; (Straßenbelag)
surface; (Bremsbelag) lining
(c) (von Kuchen, Scheibe Brot usw.) topping; (von
Sandwiches) filling
belagern *tr. V.* (auch fig.) besiege
Belagerung *die;* ~, ~en siege; (fig.)
besieging
Belang *der;* ~[e]s, ~e **(a) von/ohne** ~ **sein**
be of importance/of no importance
(b) *Pl.* (Interessen) interests
belangen *tr. V.* (Rechtsw.) sue; (strafrechtlich)
prosecute
belang·los *Adj.* (trivial) trivial; (unerheblich) of
no importance (**für** for)
Belanglosigkeit *die;* ~, ~en
unimportance; (Trivialität) triviality
belassen *unr. tr. V.* leave
belastbar *Adj.* tough, resilient ⟨*person*⟩;
seelisch/körperlich ~ **sein** be emotionally/
physically tough *or* resilient; be able to
stand emotional/physical stress; **ein** ~**er
Mitarbeiter** an employee who can work under
pressure
Belastbarkeit *die;* ~, ~n toughness;
resilience; (von Mitarbeitern) ability to work
under pressure
belasten *tr. V.* **(a) etw.** ~: put sth. under
strain; (durch Gewicht) put weight on sth.
(b) (beeinträchtigen) pollute ⟨*atmosphere*⟩; put
pressure on ⟨*environment*⟩

(c) (in Anspruch nehmen) burden (**mit** with)
(d) **jmdn.** ~ ⟨*responsibility, guilt*⟩ weigh
upon sb.; ⟨*thought*⟩ weigh upon sb.'s mind
(e) (Rechtsw.) incriminate
(f) (Geldw.) **jmds. Konto mit 100 Euro** ~: debit
sb.'s account with 100 euros
belästigen *tr. V.* bother; (sehr aufdringlich)
pester; (sexuell) molest
Belästigung *die* ▸ BELÄSTIGEN: bothering;
pestering; molestation
Belastung *die;* ~, ~en **(a)** strain; (das
Belasten) straining; (durch Gewicht) loading;
(Last) load
(b) die ~ **der Atmosphäre/Umwelt durch
Schadstoffe** the pollution of the atmosphere
by harmful substances/the pressure on the
environment caused by harmful substances
(c) (Bürde, Sorge) burden
Belastungs-: ~**-EKG** *das* (Med.)
electrocardiogram after effort; ~**zeuge** *der,*
~**zeugin** *die* (Rechtsw.) witness for the
prosecution
belaufen *unr. refl. V.* **sich auf ...**
(*Akk.*) ~: come to ...
belauschen *tr. V.* eavesdrop on
beleben **1** *tr. V.* enliven; stimulate
⟨*economy*⟩
2 *refl. V.* ⟨*market, economic activity*⟩ revive,
pick up
belebend **1** *Adj.* invigorating
2 *adv.* ~ **wirken** have an invigorating effect
belebt *Adj.* busy ⟨*street, crossing, town, etc.*⟩
Beleg *der;* ~[e]s, ~**e** (Beweisstück) piece of
[supporting] documentary evidence; (Quittung)
receipt
belegen *tr. V.* **(a)** (Milit.: beschießen) bombard;
(mit Bomben) attack
(b) (mit Belag versehen) cover ⟨*floor*⟩ (**mit** with);
fill ⟨*flan base, sandwich*⟩; top ⟨*open
sandwich*⟩; **eine Scheibe Brot mit Käse** ~:
put some cheese on a slice of bread
(c) (in Besitz nehmen) occupy ⟨*seat, room, etc.*⟩
(d) (Hochschulw.) enrol for ⟨*seminar, lecture
course*⟩
(e) den ersten/letzten Platz ~ (Sport) take
first place/come last
(f) (nachweisen) prove; give a reference for
⟨*quotation*⟩
Belegschaft *die;* ~, ~en staff
belegt *Adj.* **(a) ein** ~**es Brot** an open *or*
(Amer.) openface sandwich; (zugeklappt) a
sandwich; **ein** ~**es Brötchen** a roll with
topping; an open-face roll (Amer.); (zugeklappt)
a filled roll; a sandwich roll (Amer.)
(b) (mit Belag bedeckt) furred ⟨*tongue, tonsils*⟩
(c) (heiser) husky ⟨*voice*⟩
(d) (nicht mehr frei) ⟨*room, flat*⟩ occupied
belehren *tr. V.* teach; instruct; (aufklären)
enlighten; (informieren) inform; **ich lasse mich
gern** ~: I'm quite willing to believe
otherwise
Belehrung *die;* ~, ~en instruction;
(Zurechtweisung) lecture
beleibt *Adj.* (geh.) portly

beleidigen *tr. V.* insult
beleidigt *Adj.* insulted; (gekränkt) offended
Beleidigung *die;* ~, ~en (a) insult
  (b) (Rechtsw.) (schriftlich) libel; (mündlich)
  slander
belesen *Adj.* well-read
beleuchten *tr. V.* light up; light ⟨stairs,
  room, street, etc.⟩
Beleuchtung *die;* ~, ~en lighting;
  (Anstrahlung) illumination
beleumdet *Adj.* übel/gut ~ sein have a
  bad/good reputation
Belgien /'bɛlgiən/ (das); ~s Belgium
Belgier *der;* ~s, ~, **Belgierin** *die;* ~,
  ~nen Belgian
belgisch *Adj.* Belgian
belichten *tr. V.* (Fot.) expose; *itr.* richtig/
  falsch/kurz ~: use the right/wrong
  exposure/a short exposure time
Belichtung *die* (Fot.) exposure
Belieben *das;* ~s: nach ~: just as you/
  they *etc.* like
beliebig ① *Adj.* any
  ② *adv.* as you like/he likes *etc.;* ~ lange/
  viele as long/many as you like/he likes *etc.*
beliebt *Adj.* popular; favourite *attrib.*
Beliebtheit *die;* ~: popularity
beliefern *tr. V.* supply
bellen *itr. V.* bark
Belletristik /bɛle'trɪstɪk/ *die;* ~: belles-
  lettres *pl.*
belohnen *tr. V.* reward ⟨person, thing⟩
Belohnung *die;* ~, ~en reward
belüften *tr. V.* ventilate
Belüftung *die* ventilation
belügen *unr. tr. V.* lie to
belustigen *tr. V.* amuse
Belustigung *die;* ~, ~en amusement
bemächtigen *refl. V.* sich jmds./einer
  Sache ~ (geh.) seize sb./sth.
bemalen *tr. V.* paint; (verzieren) decorate
bemängeln *tr. V.* find fault with
bemerkbar *Adj.* sich ~ machen attract
  attention; (erkennbar werden) become apparent;
  (spürbar werden) make itself felt
bemerken *tr. V.* (a) (wahrnehmen) notice;
  ich wurde nicht bemerkt I was unobserved
  (b) (äußern) remark
bemerkenswert ① *Adj.* remarkable
  ② *adv.* remarkably
Bemerkung *die;* ~, ~en (a) (Äußerung)
  remark; comment
  (b) (Notiz) note; (Anmerkung) comment
bemitleiden *tr. V.* pity; feel sorry for
bemitleidens·wert *Adj.* pitiable
bemogeln *tr. V.* (ugs.) cheat; diddle (Brit.
  coll.)
bemühen *refl. V.* make an effort; sich ~,
  etw. zu tun endeavour to do sth.; sich um
  etw. ~: try to obtain sth.; sich um eine
  Stelle ~: try to get a job; sich um jmdn. ~
  (kümmern) seek to help sb.

Bemühung *die;* ~, ~en effort
benachbart *Adj.* neighbouring *attrib.*
benachrichtigen *tr. V.* notify (von of)
Benachrichtigung *die;* ~, ~en
  notification
benachteiligen *tr. V.* put at a
  disadvantage; (diskriminieren) discriminate
  against; die sozial benachteiligten Schichten
  the underprivileged classes
Benachteiligte *der/die; adj. Dekl.*
  disadvantaged person; die ~n the
  disadvantaged; those at a disadvantage; die
  sozial ~n the underprivileged
benehmen *unr. refl. V.* behave
Benehmen *das;* ~s behaviour; kein ~
  haben have no manners *pl.*
beneiden *tr. V.* envy; jmdn. um etw. ~:
  envy sb. sth.
beneidens·wert *Adj.* enviable
Benelux·länder *Pl.* Benelux countries
benennen *unr. tr. V.* name
Bengel *der;* ~s, ~ od. (nordd.) ~s (a)
  (abwertend: junger Bursche) young rascal
  (b) (fam.: kleiner Junge) little lad
benommen *Adj.* dazed; (durch Fieber,
  Alkohol) muzzy
benoten *tr. V.* mark (Brit.); grade (Amer.);
  einen Test mit „gut" ~: mark a test 'good'
  (Brit.); assign a grade of 'good' to a test
  (Amer.)
benötigen *tr. V.* need; require
benutzen *tr. V.* use
Benutzer *der;* ~s, ~: user
benutzer·freundlich *Adj.* user-friendly
Benutzerin *die;* ~, ~nen user
Benutzer·name *der* (DV) user name
Benutzung *die;* ~: use
Benzin *das;* ~s petrol (Brit.); gasoline
  (Amer.); gas (Amer. coll.); (Wasch~) benzine
Benzol *das;* ~s, ~e (Chemie) benzene
beobachten *tr. V.* observe; watch
Beobachter *der;* ~s, ~,
  Beobachterin *die;* ~, ~nen observer
Beobachtung *die;* ~, ~en observation
bepacken *tr. V.* load
bepfanden *tr. V.* charge a deposit on
  ⟨bottle etc.⟩
bepflanzen *tr. V.* plant
bequem ① *Adj.* (a) comfortable
  (b) (abwertend: träge) idle
  ② *adv.* (a) comfortably
  (b) (leicht) easily
bequemen *refl. V.* sich dazu ~, etw. zu
  tun (geh.) condescend to do sth.
Bequemlichkeit *die;* ~ (a) comfort
  (b) (Trägheit) idleness
berappen *tr., itr. V.* (ugs.) ▶ BLECHEN
beraten ① *unr. tr. V.* (a) advise; jmdn.
  gut/schlecht ~: give sb. good/bad advice
  (b) (besprechen) discuss ⟨plan, matter⟩ ⋯❯

b

[2] *unr. itr. V.* über etw. (*Akk.*) ~: discuss sth.

[3] *unr. refl. V.* sich mit jmdm. ~, ob ...: discuss with sb. whether ...

Ber<u>a</u>ter *der;* ~s, ~, **Ber<u>a</u>terin** *die;* ~, ~nen adviser

ber<u>a</u>tschlagen [1] *tr. V.* discuss
[2] *itr. V.* über etw. (*Akk.*) ~: discuss sth.

Ber<u>a</u>tung *die;* ~, ~en (a) advice *no indef. art.;* (durch Arzt, Rechtsanwalt) consultation
(b) (Besprechung) discussion

ber<u>au</u>ben *tr. V.* (auch fig.) rob (*Gen.* of)

ber<u>au</u>schen (geh.) [1] *tr. V.* (auch fig.) intoxicate
[2] *refl. V.* become intoxicated (**an** + *Dat.* with)

Berber *der;* ~s, ~(a) Berber
(b) (Teppich) Berber carpet/rug
(c) (Nichtsesshafter) tramp

B<u>e</u>rberin *die;* ~, ~nen ▶ BERBER A, C

berechenbar *Adj.* calculable; predictable ⟨behaviour⟩

Ber<u>e</u>chenbarkeit *die;* ~: calculability; (des Verhaltens) predictability

ber<u>e</u>chnen *tr. V.* (a) (auch fig.) calculate; predict ⟨behaviour, consequences⟩
(b) (anrechnen) charge; **jmdm. 10 Euro für etw.** *od.* **jmdm. etw. mit 10 Euro ~:** charge sb. 10 euros for sth.; **jmdm. zu viel ~:** overcharge sb.

Ber<u>e</u>chnung *die;* ~, ~en (a) calculation
(b) (Eigennutz) [calculating] self-interest

ber<u>e</u>chtigen *tr. V.* entitle; *itr.* **die Karte berechtigt zum Eintritt** the ticket entitles the bearer to admission

ber<u>e</u>chtigt *Adj.* (a) (gerechtfertigt) justified
(b) (befugt) authorized

Ber<u>e</u>chtigung *die;* ~, ~en (a) (Befugnis) entitlement; (Recht) right
(b) (Rechtmäßigkeit) legitimacy

ber<u>e</u>den *tr. V.* (a) (besprechen) discuss
(b) jmdn. ~, etw. zu tun talk sb. into doing sth.

beredsam *Adj.* eloquent

Ber<u>e</u>dsamkeit *die;* ~: eloquence

beredt *Adj.* (auch fig.) eloquent

Ber<u>ei</u>ch *der;* ~[e]s, ~e area; **im privaten/ staatlichen ~:** in the private/public sector

ber<u>ei</u>chern *refl. V.* get rich

Ber<u>ei</u>cherung *die;* ~, ~en (a) money-making
(b) (Nutzen) valuable acquisition

ber<u>ei</u>fen *tr. V.* put tyres on ⟨car⟩; put a tyre on ⟨wheel⟩

Ber<u>ei</u>fung *die;* ~, ~en [set *sing.* of] tyres *pl.*

ber<u>ei</u>nigen *tr. V.* clear up ⟨misunderstanding⟩; settle, resolve ⟨dispute⟩

ber<u>ei</u>sen *tr. V.* travel around *or* about;

*old spelling - see note on page xiv

travel through ⟨towns⟩; (beruflich) ⟨representative etc.⟩ cover ⟨area⟩; **fremde Länder ~:** travel in foreign countries

ber<u>ei</u>t *Adj.* ready; ~ **sein, etw. zu tun** be ready *or* willing to do sth.

ber<u>ei</u>ten *tr. V.* (a) prepare; make ⟨tea, coffee⟩
(b) (verursachen) cause ⟨trouble, sorrow, difficulty, etc.⟩

ber<u>ei</u>t-: ~|**halten** *unr. tr. V.* have ready; ~|**legen** *tr. V.* lay out ready; ~|**liegen** *unr. itr. V.* be ready

ber<u>ei</u>ts *Adv.* already

Ber<u>ei</u>tschaft *die;* ~: readiness; willingness

Ber<u>ei</u>tschafts-dienst *der;* ~ **haben** ⟨doctor, nurse⟩ be on call; ⟨policeman, fireman⟩ be on standby duty; ⟨chemist's⟩ be on rota duty (*for dispensing outside normal hours*)

ber<u>ei</u>t-: ~|**stehen** *unr. itr. V.* be ready; ~|**stellen** *tr. V.* place ready; get ready ⟨food, drinks⟩; ready, make ⟨money, funds⟩ available; ~**willig** [1] *Adj.* willing. [2] *adv.* readily

Ber<u>ei</u>twilligkeit *die;* ~: willingness

ber<u>eu</u>en [1] *tr. V.* regret
[2] *itr. V.* be sorry; (Rel.) repent

Berg *der;* ~[e]s, ~e (a) hill; (im Hochgebirge) mountain
(b) (Haufen) huge pile; (von Akten, Abfall auch) mountain

berg-, Berg-: ~**ab** /-'-/ *Adv.* downhill; ~**auf** /-'-/ *Adv.* uphill; ~**bahn** *die* mountain railway; (Seilbahn) mountain cableway; ~**bau** *der* mining

bergen *unr. tr. V.* (a) rescue, save ⟨person⟩; salvage ⟨ship, cargo, belongings⟩
(b) (geh.: enthalten) hold

Berg-: ~**führer** *der,* ~**führerin** *die;* ~~, ~~nen mountain guide; ~**hütte** *die* mountain hut

bergig *Adj.* hilly; (mit hohen Bergen) mountainous

Berg-: ~**kette** *die* range *or* chain of mountains; mountain range *or* chain; ~**kristall** *der* rock crystal; ~**land** *das* hilly country *no indef. art;* (mit hohen Bergen) mountainous country *no indef. art.;* ~**mann** *der; Pl.* ~**leute** miner; ~**station** *die* top station; ~**steigen** *das;* ~~s mountaineering *no art.;* ~**steiger** *der,* ~**steigerin** *die;* ~~, ~~nen mountaineer

Bergung *die;* ~, ~en (a) rescue
(b) (von Schiffen, Gut) salvaging

Berg-: ~**wacht** *die* mountain rescue service; ~**werk** *das* mine

Ber<u>i</u>cht *der;* ~[e]s, ~e report

ber<u>i</u>chten *tr., itr. V.* report

Ber<u>i</u>cht-: ~**erstatter** *der;* ~~s, ~~, ~**erstatterin** *die;* ~~, ~~nen reporter; ~**erstattung** *die* reporting *no indef. art.*

ber<u>i</u>chtigen *tr. V.* correct

Berichtigung *die;* ~, ~en correction
berieseln *tr. V.* **(a)** (bewässern) irrigate
(b) sich ständig mit Musik ~ **lassen** (ugs. abwertend) constantly have music on in the background
Berlin *(das);* ~s Berlin
Berliner ☐ *indekl. Adj.* Berlin
☐ *der;* ~s, ~: **(a)** Berliner
(b) (Gebäck) [jam (Brit.) *or* (Amer.) jelly] doughnut
Berlinerin *die;* ~, ~nen Berliner
berlinisch *Adj.* Berlin *attrib.*
Bern *(das)* ~s Bern[e]
Bernhardiner *der;* ~s, ~: St. Bernard [dog]
Bern·stein *der* amber
bersten *unr. itr. V.; mit sein* (geh.) ⟨ice⟩ break up; ⟨glass⟩ shatter [into pieces]; ⟨wall⟩ crack up
berüchtigt *Adj.* notorious **(wegen** for); (verrufen) disreputable
berücksichtigen *tr. V.* take into account; consider ⟨applicant, application, suggestion⟩
Berücksichtigung *die;* ~: **bei** ~ **aller Umstände** taking all the circumstances into account
Beruf *der;* ~[e]s, ~e occupation; (akademischer) profession; (handwerklicher) trade; **was sind Sie von** ~? what do you do for a living?
berufen[1] ☐ *unr. tr. V.* **(a)** (einsetzen) appoint
(b) berufe es nicht! (ugs.) don't speak too soon!
☐ *unr. refl. V.* **sich auf etw.** *(Akk.)* ~: refer to sth.; **sich auf jmdn.** ~: quote *or* mention sb.'s name
berufen[2] *Adj.* **(a)** competent; **aus** ~**em Munde** from somebody qualified to speak
(b) sich dazu ~ **fühlen, etw. zu tun** feel called to do sth.
beruflich ☐ *Adj.* vocational ⟨training etc.⟩; (bei akademischen Berufen) professional ⟨training etc.⟩
☐ *adv.* ~ **erfolgreich sein** be successful in one's career; **sich** ~ **weiterbilden** undertake further job training
berufs-, Berufs-: ~**akademie** *die* vocational college ~**ausbildung** *die* vocational training; ~**aussichten** *Pl.* job prospects ⟨in a particular profession etc.⟩;
~**berater** *der,* ~**beraterin** *die* vocational adviser; ~**beratung** *die* vocational guidance; ~**bild** *das* outline of a/the profession/trade as a career;
~**erfahrung** *die* [professional] experience; ~**geheimnis** *das* professional secret; (Schweigepflicht) professional secrecy;
~**krankheit** *die* occupational disease; ~**leben** *das* working life; ~**schule** *die* vocational school; ~**soldat** *der,*
~**soldatin** *die* regular soldier;

~**sportler** *der* professional sportsman; ~**sportlerin** *die* professional sportswoman; ~**tätig** *Adj.* working *attrib.;*
~**tätige** *der/die; adj. Dekl.* working person; ~**tätige** *Pl.* working people; ~**verkehr** *der* rush hour traffic
Berufung *die;* ~, ~en **(a)** (für ein Amt) offer of an appointment **(auf, in, an** + *Akk.* to)
(b) (innerer Auftrag) vocation
(c) (das Sichberufen) **unter** ~ *(Dat.)* **auf jmdn./ etw.** referring *or* with reference to sb./sth.
(d) (Rechtsw.: Einspruch) appeal; ~ **einlegen** lodge an appeal
beruhen *itr. V.* **auf etw.** *(Dat.)* ~: be based on sth.; **etw. auf sich** ~ **lassen** let sth. rest
beruhigen /bə'ruːɪgn/ ☐ *tr. V.* calm [down]; pacify ⟨child, baby⟩; salve ⟨conscience⟩; (trösten) soothe; (von einer Sorge befreien) reassure
☐ *refl. V.* ⟨person⟩ calm down; ⟨sea⟩ become calm
Beruhigung *die;* ~ ▶ BERUHIGEN 1: calming [down]; pacifying; salving; soothing; reassurance
Beruhigungs·mittel *das* tranquillizer
berühmt *Adj.* famous
berühmt-berüchtigt *Adj.* notorious
Berühmtheit *die;* ~, ~en **(a)** (Ruhm) fame
(b) (Mensch) celebrity
berühren *tr. V.* **(a)** touch; (fig.) touch on ⟨topic, issue. etc.⟩; **sich** ~: touch
(b) (beeindrucken) affect; **das berührt mich nicht** it's a matter of indifference to me
Berührung *die;* ~, ~en touch; **mit jmdm./ etw. in** ~ *(Akk.)* **kommen** (auch fig.) come into contact with sb./sth.
besagen *tr. V.* say; (bedeuten) mean
besänftigen *tr. V.* calm [down]; pacify; calm, soothe ⟨temper⟩
Besatz *der;* ~es, Besätze (Borte) trimming *no indef. art.*
Besatzung *die;* ~, ~en **(a)** (Mannschaft) crew
(b) (Milit.: Verteidigungstruppe) garrison
(c) (Milit.: Okkupationstruppen) occupying forces *pl.*
Besatzungs-: ~**macht** *die* occupying power; ~**zone** *die* occupied zone
besaufen *unr. refl. V.* (salopp) get canned (Brit. sl.) *or* bombed (Amer. sl.)
Besäufnis *das;* ~ses, ~se (salopp) booze-up (Brit. coll.): blast (Amer. coll.)
beschädigen *tr. V.* damage
Beschädigung *die;* ~, ~en **(a)** damaging
(b) (Schaden) damage
beschaffen[1] *tr. V.* obtain, get *(Dat.* for)
beschaffen[2] *Adj.* **so** ~ **sein, dass ...:** be such that ...
Beschaffenheit *die;* ~: properties *pl.*
Beschaffung *die;* ~: ▶ BESCHAFFEN: obtaining; getting
beschäftigen ☐ *refl. V.* occupy oneself; ···⟩

sich viel mit Musik/den Kindern ∼: devote a great deal of one's time to music/the children; **sehr beschäftigt sein** be very busy ☐2 *tr. V.* **(a)** (geistig in Anspruch nehmen) **jmdn.** ∼: preoccupy sb.
(b) (angestellt haben) employ ⟨*workers, staff*⟩
(c) (zu tun geben) occupy; **jmdn. mit etw.** ∼: give sb. sth. to occupy him/her
Beschäftigte *der/die; adj. Dekl.* employee
Beschäftigung *die;* ∼, ∼**en (a)** (Tätigkeit) activity
(b) (Anstellung, Stelle) job
(c) (mit einer Frage, einem Problem) consideration (**mit** of); (Studium) study (**mit** of)
(d) (von Arbeitskräften) employment
beschämen *tr. V.* shame
beschämend ☐1 *Adj.* **(a)** (schändlich) shameful
(b) (demütigend) humiliating
☐2 *adv.* shamefully
beschämt *Adj.* ashamed
Beschämung *die;* ∼: shame
beschatten *tr. V.* **(a)** (geh.) shade
(b) (überwachen) shadow
beschaulich ☐1 *Adj.* peaceful ⟨*life, manner, etc.*⟩
☐2 *adv.* peacefully
Beschaulichkeit *die;* ∼: peacefulness
Bescheid *der;* ∼[e]s, ∼e **(a)** (Auskunft) information; (Antwort) answer; reply; **jmdm.** ∼ **geben** *od.* **sagen[, ob …]** let sb. know or tell sb. [whether …]; **sage bitte im Hotel** ∼, **dass** …: please let the hotel know that …; [**über etw. (*Akk.*)**] ∼ **wissen** know [about sth.]
(b) (Entscheidung) decision
bescheiden¹ ☐1 *unr. tr. V.* **jmdn./etw. abschlägig** ∼: turn sb./sth. down
☐2 *unr. refl. V.* (geh.) be content
bescheiden² ☐1 *Adj.* modest
☐2 *adv.* modestly
Bescheidenheit *die;* ∼: modesty
bescheinigen *tr. V.* confirm ⟨*sth.*⟩ in writing
Bescheinigung *die;* ∼, ∼**en** written confirmation *no indef. art.;* (Schein, Attest) certificate
bescheißen *unr. tr. V.* (derb) **jmdn.** ∼: rip sb. off (coll.); screw sb. (coarse)
beschenken *tr. V.* give ⟨*sb.*⟩ a present/presents
bescheren *tr. V.* **jmdn. [mit etw.]** ∼: give sb. [sth. as] a Christmas present/Christmas presents
Bescherung *die;* ∼, ∼**en (a)** (zu Weihnachten) giving out of the Christmas presents
(b) das ist ja eine schöne ∼ (ugs.) this is a pretty kettle of fish
bescheuert *Adj.* (salopp) **(a)** (verrückt) barmy (Brit. coll.); nuts (coll.)
(b) (unangenehm) stupid ⟨*task, party, etc.*⟩

beschichten *tr. V.* (Technik) coat
Beschichtung *die;* ∼, ∼**en** (Technik) coating
beschießen *unr. tr. V.* fire at; (mit Artillerie) bombard
beschimpfen *tr. V.* abuse; swear at
Beschimpfung *die;* ∼, ∼**en** insult; ∼**en** abuse *sing.;* insults
beschissen *Adj.* (derb) lousy (coll.); shitty (coarse)
Beschlag *der;* ∼[e]s, **Beschläge (a)** fitting
(b) jmdn./etw. mit ∼ **belegen** *od.* **in** ∼ **nehmen** monopolize sb./sth.
beschlagen¹ ☐1 *unr. tr. V.* shoe ⟨*horse*⟩
☐2 *unr. itr. V.; mit sein* ⟨*window*⟩ mist up (Brit.), fog up (Amer.); (durch Dampf) steam up
beschlagen² *Adj.* knowledgeable
Beschlagnahme *die;* ∼, ∼**n** confiscation
beschlagnahmen *tr. V.* confiscate
Beschlagnahmung *die;* ∼, ∼**en**
▶ BESCHLAGNAHME
beschleunigen ☐1 *tr. V.* accelerate; speed up ⟨*work, delivery*⟩; quicken ⟨*pace, step[s], pulse*⟩
☐2 *refl. V.* ⟨*heart rate*⟩ increase; ⟨*pulse*⟩ quicken
☐3 *itr. V.* ⟨*driver, car, etc.*⟩ accelerate
Beschleunigung *die;* ∼, ∼**en**
▶ BESCHLEUNIGEN 1: acceleration; speeding up; quickening
beschließen *unr. tr. V.* **(a)** decide; pass ⟨*law*⟩; ∼, **etw. zu tun** decide *or* resolve to do sth.
(b) (beenden) end
Beschluss, *Beschluß *der;* **Beschlusses, Beschlüsse** decision; (gemeinsam gefasst) resolution; **einen** ∼ **fassen** come to a decision/pass a resolution
beschluss·fähig, *beschluß·fähig *Adj.* quorate
Beschluss·fähigkeit, *Beschluß·fähigkeit *die* presence of a quorum
beschmieren *tr. V.* **etw./sich** ∼: get sth./oneself in a mess
beschmutzen *tr. V.* make ⟨*sth.*⟩ dirty
beschneiden *unr. tr. V.* **(a)** cut ⟨*hedge*⟩; prune ⟨*bush*⟩; cut back ⟨*tree*⟩; **einem Vogel die Flügel** ∼: clip a bird's wings
(b) (Med., Rel.) circumcise
Beschneidung *die;* ∼, ∼**en (a)**
▶ BESCHNEIDEN A: cutting; pruning; cutting back
(b) (Med., Rel.) circumcision
beschnüffeln *tr. V.* sniff at
beschönigen *tr. V.* gloss over
beschränken ☐1 *tr. V.* restrict (**auf** + *Akk.* to)
☐2 *refl. V.* **sich auf etw. (*Akk.*)** ∼: restrict oneself to sth.
beschränkt ☐1 *Adj.* **(a)** (dumm) dull-witted
(b) (engstirnig) narrow-minded

b

2 *adv.* narrow-mindedly

Beschränktheit *die;* ~: **(a)** (Dummheit) lack of intelligence
(b) (Engstimigkeit) narrow-mindedness

Beschränkung *die;* ~, ~en restriction

beschreiben *unr. tr. V.* **(a)** write on; (voll schreiben) write ⟨*page, side, etc.*⟩
(b) (darstellen) describe

Beschreibung *die;* ~, ~en description

beschriften *tr. V.* label; inscribe ⟨*stone*⟩; letter ⟨*sign, label, etc.*⟩; (mit Adresse) address

beschuldigen *tr. V.* accuse (*Gen.* of)

Beschuldigte *der/die; adj. Dekl.* accused

Beschuldigung *die;* ~, ~en accusation

beschummeln *tr. V.* (ugs.) cheat; diddle (Brit. coll.)

Beschuss, *Beschuß *der; Beschusses* fire; [heftig *od.* stark] unter ~ geraten/stehen *od.* liegen (auch fig.) come/be under [heavy] fire

beschützen *tr. V.* protect (**vor** + *Dat.* from)

Beschützer *der;* ~s, ~, **Beschützerin** *die;* ~, ~nen protector

Beschwerde *die;* ~, ~n **(a)** complaint (**gegen, über** + *Akk.* about)
(b) *Pl.* (Schmerz) pain *sing.;* (Leiden) trouble *sing.*

beschweren 1 *refl. V.* complain (**über** + *Akk., wegen* about); **sich bei jmdm.** ~: complain to sb.
2 *tr. V.* weight down

beschwerlich *Adj.* arduous; (ermüdend) exhausting

beschwichtigen *tr. V.* pacify; mollify ⟨*anger etc.*⟩

Beschwichtigung *die;* ~, ~en pacification; (des Zorns usw.) mollification

beschwingt *Adj.* lively

beschwipst *Adj.* (ugs.) tipsy

beschwören *unr. tr. V.* **(a)** swear to; ~, **dass** ...: swear that ...; **eine Aussage** ~: swear a statement on oath
(b) charm ⟨*snake*⟩
(c) (erscheinen lassen) invoke ⟨*spirit*⟩
(d) (bitten) implore

Beschwörung *die;* ~, ~en **(a)** (Zauberspruch) spell; incantation
(b) ▶ BESCHWÖREN c: invoking
(c) (Bitte) entreaty

beseitigen *tr. V.* remove; eliminate ⟨*error, difficulty*⟩; dispose of ⟨*rubbish*⟩

Beseitigung *die;* ~: ▶ BESEITIGEN: removal; elimination; disposal

Besen *der;* ~s, ~ broom; **ich fress einen** ~, **wenn das stimmt** (salopp) I'll eat my hat if that's right (coll.); **neue** ~ **kehren gut** (Spr.) a new broom sweeps clean (prov.)

besessen *Adj.* **(a)** possessed
(b) (fig.) obsessive ⟨*gambler*⟩; **von einer Idee** ~ **sein** be obsessed with an idea

Besessenheit *die;* ~ **(a)** possession

(b) obsessiveness

besetzen *tr. V.* **(a)** (mit Pelz, Spitzen) edge; trim; **mit Perlen besetzt** set with pearls
(b) (belegen; auch Milit.: erobern) occupy
(c) (vergeben) fill ⟨*post, position, role, etc.*⟩

besetzt *Adj.* occupied; ⟨*table, seat*⟩ taken *pred.;* (gefüllt) full; (Fernspr.) engaged; busy (Amer.)

Besetzung *die;* ~, ~en **(a)** (einer Stellung) filling
(b) (Film, Theater usw.) cast
(c) (Eroberung) occupation

besichtigen *tr. V.* see ⟨*sights*⟩; see the sights of ⟨*town*⟩; view ⟨*house etc. for sale*⟩

Besichtigung *die;* ~, ~en: **zur** ~ **der Stadt/des Schlosses/der Wohnung** to see the sights of the town/to see the castle/to view the flat

besiedeln *tr. V.* settle

besiedelt *Adj.* **dicht/dünn** ~: densely/thinly populated

besiegen *tr. V.* defeat

besinnen *unr. refl. V.* **(a)** think it over
(b) **sich [auf jmdn./etw.]** ~: remember [sb./sth.]

Besinnung *die;* ~: consciousness; **die** ~ **verlieren** faint; **[wieder] zur** ~ **kommen** regain consciousness

besinnungs·los 1 *Adj.* unconscious
2 *adv.* mindlessly

Besinnungslosigkeit *die;* ~: unconsciousness *no art.*

Besitz *der* **(a)** property
(b) (das Besitzen) possession; **im** ~ **einer Sache** (*Gen.*) **sein** be in possession of sth.

Besitz·anspruch *der* claim to ownership

besitzen *unr. tr. V.* own; have ⟨*quality, talent, etc.*⟩; (nachdrücklicher) possess

Besitzer *der;* ~s, ~, **Besitzerin** *die;* ~, ~nen owner

besoffen *Adj.* (salopp) canned (Brit. sl.); bombed (Amer. sl.)

Besoffene *der/die; adj. Dekl.* (salopp) drunk

besohlen *tr. V.* sole; **neu** ~: resole

besonder... *Adj.* special; **ein** ~es **Ereignis** an unusual *or* a special event; **keine** ~e **Leistung** no great achievement

Besonderheit *die;* ~, ~en special feature; (Eigenart) peculiarity

besonders 1 *Adv.* particularly
2 *Adj.; nicht attr.; nur verneint* (ugs.) **nicht** ~ **sein** be nothing special

besonnen 1 *Adj.* prudent
2 *adv.* prudently

Besonnenheit *die;* ~: prudence

besorgen *tr. V.* **(a)** get; (kaufen) buy
(b) (erledigen) take care of

Besorgnis *die;* ~, ~se concern

besorgt 1 *Adj.* concerned (**um** about)
2 *adv.* with concern

Besorgung *die;* ~, ~en purchase

b

bespitzeln *tr. V.* spy on

besprechen *unr. tr. V.* discuss; (rezensieren) review

Besprechung *die;* ∼, ∼en discussion; (Konferenz) meeting; (Rezension) review

bespritzen *tr. V.* (a) splash; (mit einem Wasserstrahl) spray (b) (beschmutzen) bespatter

besprühen *tr. V.* spray

besser 1 *Adj.* (a) better; **umso** ∼: so much the better (b) (sozial höher gestellt) superior 2 *adv.* [immer] **alles** ∼ **wissen** always know better; **es** ∼ **haben** be better off; **es geht ihr** ∼: she feels better; ∼ **gesagt** to be [more] precise 3 *Adv.* (lieber) **das lässt du** ∼ **sein** od. (ugs.) **bleiben** you'd better not do that

***besser|gehen** ▸ BESSER 2

bessern 1 *refl. V.* improve; ⟨person⟩ mend one's ways 2 *tr. V.* improve; reform ⟨criminal⟩

Besserung *die;* ∼, ∼en recovery; **gute** ∼! get well soon

best... 1 *Adj.* (a) best; **bei** ∼**er Gesundheit/ Laune sein** be in the best of health/spirits *pl.;* **im** ∼**en Falle** at best; **in den** ∼**en Jahren, im** ∼**en Alter** in one's prime; ∼**e Grüße an ...** (*Akk.*) best wishes to ...; **mit den** ∼**en Grüßen** *od.* **Wünschen** with best wishes; (als Briefschluss) ≈ yours sincerely (b) **es ist** *od.* **wäre das Beste, wenn ...:** it would be best if ...; **der/die/das nächste Beste ...:** the first ... one comes across; **einen Witz zum Besten geben** entertain [those present] with a joke; **das Beste vom Besten** the very best; **sein Bestes tun** do one's best; **zu deinem Besten** for your benefit 2 *adv.* **am** ∼**en** best 3 *Adv.* **am** ∼**en fährst du mit dem Zug** it would be best for you to go by train

Bestand *der;* ∼, **Bestände** (a) existence, (Fort∼) continued existence (b) (Vorrat) stock (**an** + *Dat.* of)

bestanden *Adj.* **von** *od.* **mit etw.** ∼ **sein** have sth. growing on it; **mit Tannen** ∼**e Hügel** fir-covered hills

beständig 1 *Adj.* (a) constant (b) (gleich bleibend) constant; steadfast ⟨person⟩; settled ⟨weather⟩ (c) (widerstandsfähig) resistant (**gegen** to) 2 *adv.* constantly

Beständigkeit *die;* ∼ (a) steadfastness (b) (Widerstandsfähigkeit) resistance (**gegen** to)

Bestand·teil *der* component

bestärken *tr. V.* confirm

bestätigen 1 *tr. V.* confirm; endorse ⟨document⟩; acknowledge ⟨receipt⟩ 2 *refl. V.* be confirmed; ⟨rumour⟩ prove to be true

Bestätigung *die;* ∼, ∼en confirmation; (des Empfangs) acknowledgement; (schriftlich) letter of confirmation

bestatten *tr. V.* (geh.) inter (formal); bury

Bestattung *die;* ∼, ∼en (geh.) interment (formal); burial; (Feierlichkeit) funeral

Bestattungs-: ∼**institut** *das,* ∼**unternehmen** *das* [firm of] undertakers *pl. or* funeral directors *pl.;* funeral parlor (Amer.)

bestäuben *tr. V.* (a) dust (b) (Biol.) pollinate

bestaunen *tr. V.* marvel at

bestechen *unr. tr. V.* bribe

bestechlich *Adj.* corruptible; open to bribery *postpos.*

Bestechung *die;* ∼, ∼en bribery *no indef. art.*

Bestechungs-: ∼**geld** *das* bribe; ∼**versuch** *der* attempted bribery

Besteck *das;* ∼[e]s, ∼e cutlery setting; (ugs.: Gesamtheit der Bestecke) cutlery

bestehen 1 *unr. itr. V.* (a) exist; **es besteht [die] Aussicht/Gefahr, dass ...:** there is a prospect/danger that ...; **noch besteht die Hoffnung, dass ...:** there is still hope that ...; ∼ **bleiben** remain; ⟨regulation⟩ remain in force (b) (fortdauern) survive; last (c) **aus etw.** ∼: consist of sth.; (hergestellt sein) be made of sth. (d) **auf etw.** (*Dat.*) ∼: insist on sth. 2 *unr. tr. V.* pass ⟨test, examination⟩

Bestehen *das;* ∼s existence; **die Firma feiert ihr 10-jähriges** ∼: the firm is celebrating its tenth anniversary

***bestehen|bleiben** ▸ BESTEHEN 1A

bestehend *Adj.* existing; current ⟨conditions⟩

bestehlen *unr. tr. V.* rob

besteigen *unr. tr. V.* (a) climb; mount ⟨horse, bicycle⟩; ascend ⟨throne⟩ (b) board ⟨ship, aircraft⟩; get on ⟨bus, train⟩

Besteigung *die;* ∼, ∼en ascent

bestellen *tr. V.* (a) *auch itr.* order (**bei** from); **würden Sie mir bitte ein Taxi** ∼? would you order me a taxi? (b) (reservieren lassen) reserve ⟨tickets, table⟩ (c) **jmdn. [für 10 Uhr] zu sich** ∼: ask sb. to go/come to see one [at 10 o'clock] (d) (ausrichten) **jmdm. etw.** ∼: tell sb. sth.; **bestell deinem Mann schöne Grüße von mir** give your husband my regards

Bestellung *die;* ∼, ∼en (a) order (b) (Reservierung) reservation

besten·falls *Adv.* at best

bestens *Adv.* extremely well

besteuern *tr. V.* tax

bestialisch 1 *Adj.* (a) bestial (b) (ugs.: schrecklich) ghastly (coll.) 2 *adv.* (a) in a bestial manner (b) (ugs.: schrecklich) awfully (coll.)

Bestialität *die;* ∼: bestiality

---

*old spelling - see note on page xiv

besticken *tr. V.* embroider

Bestie /'bɛstiə/ *die;* ~, ~n beast

bestimmen **1** *tr. V.* (a) (festsetzen) decide on; fix ⟨*price, time, etc.*⟩
(b) (vorsehen) intend; **das ist für dich bestimmt** that is meant for you
(c) (identifizieren) identify; determine ⟨*age, position*⟩; define ⟨*meaning*⟩
(d) (prägen) determine the character of
2 *itr. V.* (a) make the decisions
(b) **über jmdn.** ~: tell sb. what to do; [frei] **über etw.** (*Akk.*) ~: do as one wishes with sth.

bestimmend **1** *Adj.* decisive
2 *adv.* decisively

bestimmt **1** *Adj.* (a) (speziell) particular; (gewiss) certain; (genau) definite
(b) (festgelegt) fixed; given ⟨*quantity*⟩
(c) (Sprachw.) definite ⟨*article etc.*⟩
(d) (entschieden) firm
2 *adv.* (a) (deutlich) clearly; (genau) precisely
(b) (entschieden) firmly
3 *Adv.* for certain; **du weißt es doch [ganz]** ~ **noch** I'm sure you must remember it; **ich habe das** ~ **liegen gelassen** I must have left it behind

Bestimmtheit *die;* ~: firmness; (im Auftreten) decisiveness

Bestimmung *die;* ~, ~en (a) (das Festsetzen) fixing
(b) (Vorschrift) regulation
(c) (Zweck) purpose
(d) ▶ BESTIMMEN 1c: identification; determination; definition
(e) (Sprachw.) modifier; **adverbiale** ~: adverbial qualification

best·möglich *Adj.* best possible

bestrafen *tr. V.* punish (**für, wegen** for); **es wird mit Gefängnis bestraft** it is punishable by imprisonment

Bestrafung *die;* ~, ~en punishment

bestrahlen *tr. V.* (a) illuminate; floodlight ⟨*building*⟩
(b) (Med.) treat ⟨*tumour, part of body*⟩ using radiotherapy

Bestrahlung *die;* ~, ~en (Med.) radiation [treatment] *no indef. art.*

Bestreben *das;* ~s endeavour[s *pl.*]

bestrebt *Adj.:* ~ **sein, etw. zu tun** endeavour to do sth.

Bestrebung *die;* ~, ~en effort; (Versuch) attempt

bestreichen *unr. tr. V.* **A mit B** ~: spread B on A

bestreiten *unr. tr. V.* (a) dispute; (leugnen) deny
(b) (finanzieren) finance ⟨*studies*⟩; pay for ⟨*studies, sb.'s keep*⟩; meet ⟨*costs, expenses*⟩
(c) (gestalten) carry ⟨*programme, conversation, etc.*⟩

bestreuen *tr. V.* sprinkle

Bestseller /'bɛstzɛlɐ/ *der;* ~s, ~: best seller

bestürzend *Adj.* disturbing; (erschreckend) alarming

bestürzt **1** *Adj.* dismayed
2 *adv.* with dismay

Bestürzung *die;* ~: dismay

Besuch *der;* ~[e]s, ~e (a) visit (*Gen.*, **bei** to); **ein** ~ **bei jmdm.** a visit to sb.; (kurz) a call on sb.
(b) (Teilnahme) attendance (*Gen.* at)
(c) (Gast) visitor; (Gäste) visitors *pl.*; ~ **haben** have visitors/a visitor

besuchen *tr. V.* (a) visit; (weniger formell) go to see ⟨*person*⟩; go to ⟨*exhibition, theatre, museum, etc.*⟩; (zur Besichtigung) go to see ⟨*church, exhibition, etc.*⟩
(b) **die Schule/Universität** ~: go to school/university

Besucher *der;* ~s, ~, **Besucherin** *die;* ~, ~nen visitor

Besuchs-: ~**erlaubnis** *die* visiting permit; ~**zeit** *die* visiting time *or* hours *pl.*; **es ist keine** ~**zeit** it is not visiting time

besucht *Adj.* **gut/schlecht** ~: well/poorly attended ⟨*lecture, performance, etc.*⟩; much/little frequented ⟨*restaurant etc.*⟩

Beta·blocker /-blɔkɐ/ *der;* ~s, ~ (Med.) betablocker

betagt *Adj.* (geh.) elderly

betasten *tr. V.* feel [with one's fingers]

betätigen **1** *refl. V.* occupy oneself; **sich politisch/körperlich** ~: engage in political/physical activity
2 *tr. V.* operate ⟨*lever, switch, flush, etc.*⟩; apply ⟨*brake*⟩

Betätigung *die;* ~, ~en: (a) activity
(b) ▶ BETÄTIGEN 2: operation; application

betäuben *tr. V.* (a) (Med.) anaesthetize; deaden ⟨*nerve*⟩; **jmdn. örtlich** ~: give sb. a local anaesthetic
(b) (unterdrücken) deaden ⟨*pain*⟩; still ⟨*unease, fear*⟩
(c) (benommen machen) daze; (mit einem Schlag) stun

Betäubung *die;* ~, ~en: (a) (Med.) anaesthetization; (Narkose) anaesthesia
(b) (Benommenheit) daze

Betäubungs·mittel *das* narcotic; (Med.) anaesthetic

beteiligen **1** *refl. V.* take part (**an** + *Dat.* in)
2 *tr. V.* **jmdn.** [mit 10 %] **an etw.** (*Dat.*) ~: give sb. a [10%] share of sth.

beteiligt *Adj.* (a) involved (**an** + *Dat.* in)
(b) (finanziell) **an einem Unternehmen/am Gewinn** ~ **sein** have a share in a business/in the profit

Beteiligte *der/die; adj. Dekl.* person involved

Beteiligung *die;* ~, ~en (a) participation (**an** + *Dat.* in)
(b) (Anteil) share (**an** + *Dat.* in)

beten **1** *itr. V.* pray (**für, um** for)
2 *tr. V.* say ⟨*prayer*⟩

beteuern *tr. V.* affirm; protest ⟨*one's innocence*⟩

Beteuerung *die;* ~, ~en ▶ BETEUERN: affirmation; protestation

Beton /be'tɔŋ, *bes. österr.:* be'toːn/ *der;* ~s, ~s /-ɔŋs/ *od.* (*bes. österr.:*) ~e /-oːnə/ concrete

betonen *tr. V.* (a) stress ⟨*word, syllable*⟩ (b) (hervorheben) emphasize

betonieren *tr. V.* concrete; surface ⟨*road etc.*⟩ with concrete

betont 1 *Adj.* (a) stressed (b) (bewusst) studied 2 *adv.* studiedly

Betonung *die;* ~, ~en (a) stressing (b) (Akzent) stress; (Intonation) intonation (c) (Hervorhebung) emphasis

betören *tr. V.* (geh.) captivate

betr. *Abk.* = **betreffs, betrifft** re

Betr. *Abk.* = **Betreff** re

Betracht: jmdn./etw. in ~ ziehen consider sb./sth.; jmdn./etw. außer ~ lassen disregard sb./sth.

betrachten *tr. V.* (a) look at (b) jmdn./etw. als etw. ~: regard sb./sth. as sth. (c) (beurteilen) consider

Betrachter *der;* ~s, ~, **Betrachterin** *die;* ~, ~nen observer

beträchtlich 1 *Adj.* considerable 2 *adv.* considerably

Betrachtung *die;* ~, ~en (a) contemplation; (Untersuchung) examination (b) (Überlegung) reflection

Betrachtungs·weise *die* way of looking at things; (Standpunkt) point of view

Betrag *der;* ~[e]s, Beträge amount; „~ dankend erhalten" 'received with thanks'

betragen 1 *unr. itr. V.* be; (bei Geldsummen) come to; amount to 2 *unr. refl. V.* behave

Betragen *das;* ~s behaviour

Betreff *der;* ~[e]s, ~e (im Brief) heading

betreffen *unr. tr. V.* concern; ⟨*new rule, change, etc.*⟩ affect

betreffend *Adj.* concerning; der ~e Sachbearbeiter the person dealing with this matter; in dem ~en Fall in the case in question

betreffs *Präp. mit Gen.* (Amtsspr., Kaufmannsspr.) concerning

betreiben *unr. tr. V.* (a) proceed with, (energisch) press ahead with ⟨*task, case, etc.*⟩; pursue ⟨*policy, studies*⟩; carry on ⟨*trade*⟩; go in for ⟨*sport*⟩ (b) run ⟨*business, shop*⟩ (c) (in Betrieb halten) operate

betreten[1] *unr. tr. V.* (hineintreten in) enter; (treten auf) step on to; (begehen) walk on ⟨*carpet, grass, etc.*⟩; „Betreten verboten" 'Keep off'; (kein Eintritt) 'Keep out'

betreten[2] 1 *Adj.* embarrassed 2 *adv.* with embarrassment

betreuen *tr. V.* look after; care for ⟨*invalid*⟩; supervise ⟨*youth group*⟩; see to the needs of ⟨*tourists, sportsmen*⟩

Betreuung *die;* ~: care *no indef. art.*

Betrieb *der;* ~[e]s, ~e (a) business; (Firma) firm (b) (das In-Funktion-Sein) operation; außer ~ sein not operate; (wegen Störung) be out of order; in/außer ~ setzen start up/stop ⟨*machine etc.*⟩ (c) (ugs.: Treiben) bustle; (Verkehr) traffic; es herrscht großer ~, es ist viel ~: it's very busy

betrieblich *Adj.* firm's; company

Betriebs-: ~angehörige *der/die* employee; ~anleitung *die,* ~anweisung *die* operating instructions *pl.;* ~ausflug *der* staff outing; ~ferien *Pl.* firm's annual close-down *sing.;* „Wegen ~ferien geschlossen" 'closed for annual holidays'; ~klima *das* working atmosphere; ~rat *der* (a) works committee; (b) (Person) member of a/the works committee; ~rätin *die* ▶ BETRIEBSRAT B; ~system *das* (DV) operating system; ~versammlung *die* meeting of the workforce; ~wirt *der,* ~wirtin *die* graduate in business management; ~wirtschaft *die* business management

betrinken *unr. refl. V.* get drunk

betroffen 1 *Adj.* upset; (bestürzt) dismayed 2 *adv.* in dismay

Betroffenheit *die;* ~: dismay

betrüblich *Adj.* gloomy

betrübt 1 *Adj.* sad; gloomy ⟨*face etc.*⟩ 2 sadly; (schwermütig) gloomily

Betrug *der;* ~[e]s deception; (Delikt) fraud

betrügen 1 *unr. tr. V.* deceive; be unfaithful to ⟨*husband, wife*⟩; (Rechtsw.) defraud; (beim Spielen) cheat; jmdn. um 100 Euro ~: cheat *or* (coll.) do sb. out of 100 euros; (arglistig) swindle sb. out of 100 euros 2 *unr. itr. V.* cheat; (bei Geschäften) swindle people

Betrüger *der;* ~s, ~: swindler; (Hochstapler) conman (coll.); (beim Spielen) cheat

Betrügerei *die;* ~, ~en deception; (beim Spielen usw.) cheating; (bei Geschäften) swindling

Betrügerin *die;* ~, ~nen swindler; (beim Spielen) cheat

betrunken *Adj.* drunken *attrib.;* drunk *pred.*

Betrunkene *der/die; adj. Dekl.* drunk

Bett *das;* ~[e]s, ~en (a) bed; ins *od.* zu ~ gehen go to bed; die Kinder ins ~ bringen put the children to bed (b) (Feder~) duvet

Bett-: ~bezug *der* duvet cover; ~decke *die* blanket; (gesteppt) quilt

Bettelei *die;* ~, ~en begging *no art.*

---

*alte Schreibung - vgl. Hinweis auf S. xiv

betteln *itr. V.* beg (um for)
bett·lägerig *Adj.* bedridden
Bett·laken *das* sheet
Bett·lektüre *die* bedtime reading *no indef. art.*
Bettler *der;* ~s, ~, **Bettlerin** *die;* ~, ~nen beggar
bett-, Bett-: ~**reif** *Adj.* (ugs.) ready for bed *pred.;* ~**ruhe** *die* bed rest; ~**schwere** *die:* die nötige *od.* notwendige ~schwere haben (ugs.) be ready for one's bed; ~**tuch** *das; Pl.* ~tücher sheet; ~**wäsche** *die* bedlinen; ~**zeug** *das* (ugs.) bedclothes *pl.*
betucht *Adj.* (ugs.) well-heeled (coll.); well-off
betupfen *tr. V.* dab
Beuge *die;* ~, ~n (Turnen) bend
beugen [1] *tr. V.* (a) bend; bow ⟨head⟩ (b) (Sprachw.: flektieren) inflect ⟨word⟩ [2] *refl. V.* (a) bend over; sich nach vorn/hinten ~: bend forwards/bend over backwards; sich aus dem Fenster ~: lean out of the window (b) (sich fügen) give way
Beugung *die;* ~, ~en (Sprachw.) inflexion
Beule *die;* ~, ~n bump; (Vertiefung) dent
beulen *itr. V.* bulge
beunruhigen *tr., refl. V.* worry
beurlauben *tr. V.* (a) jmdn. [für zwei Tage] ~: give sb. [two days'] leave of absence (b) (suspendieren) suspend
beurteilen *tr. V.* judge; assess ⟨situation etc.⟩
Beurteilung *die;* ~, ~en (a) judgement; (einer Lage usw.) assessment (b) (Gutachten) assessment
Beute *die;* ~, ~n (a) (Gestohlenes) haul; loot *no indef. art.;* (b) (von Raubtieren) prey; (eines Jägers) bag
Beute·kunst *die* looted art
Beutel *der;* ~s, ~ bag; (kleiner, für Tabak usw.) pouch
bevölkern *tr. V.* populate
Bevölkerung *die;* ~, ~en population; (Volk) people
Bevölkerungs-: ~**dichte** *die* population density; ~**explosion** *die* population explosion; ~**zunahme** *die,* ~**zuwachs** *der* increase in population
bevollmächtigen *tr. V.* authorize
Bevollmächtigte *der/die; adj. Dekl.* authorized representative
bevor *Konj.* before; ~ du nicht unterschrieben hast until you have signed
bevor·munden *tr. V.* jmdn. ~: impose one's will on sb.; sie wollen sich nicht länger ~ lassen they do not want to be dictated to any longer
bevor|stehen *unr. itr. V.* be near; unmittelbar ~: be imminent; jmdm. steht etw. bevor sth. is in store for sb.

bevorstehend *Adj.* forthcoming; unmittelbar ~: imminent
bevorzugen *tr. V.* (a) (vorziehen) prefer (vor + *Dat.* to) (b) (begünstigen) favour; give preference or preferenzial treatment to (vor + *Dat.* over)
bevorzugt [1] *Adj.* favoured; (privilegiert) privileged; preferenzial ⟨treatment⟩ [2] *adv.* jmdn. ~ behandeln give sb. preferential treatment
Bevorzugung *die;* ~, ~en (Begünstigung) preferential treatment
bewachen *tr. V.* guard; bewachter Parkplatz car park with an attendant
Bewacher *der;* ~s, ~, **Bewacherin** *die;* ~, ~nen guard
Bewachung *die;* ~, ~en guarding
bewaffnen [1] *tr. V.* arm [2] *refl. V.* (auch fig.) arm oneself (mit with)
bewaffnet *Adj.* armed; bis an die Zähne ~: armed to the teeth
Bewaffnung *die;* ~, ~en (a) arming (b) (Waffen) weapons *pl.*
bewahren *tr. V.* (a) protect (vor + *Dat.* from) (b) (erhalten) seine Fassung ~: retain one's composure; Stillschweigen ~: remain silent
bewähren *refl. V.* prove oneself/itself
bewährt *Adj.* proven ⟨method, design, etc.⟩; well-tried ⟨recipe, cure⟩; reliable ⟨worker⟩
Bewährung *die;* ~, ~en (Rechtsw.) probation
Bewährungs-: ~**frist** *die* (Rechtsw.) period of probation; ~**helfer** *der,* ~**helferin** *die* probation officer; ~**zeit** *die* (Rechtsw.) probation period
bewaldet *Adj.* wooded
bewältigen *tr. V.* cope with; overcome ⟨difficulty, problem⟩; cover ⟨distance⟩
Bewältigung *die;* ~, ~en ▶ BEWÄLTIGEN: coping with; overcoming; covering
bewandert *Adj.* well-versed
Bewandtnis *die;* ~,·~se: mit etw. hat es [s]eine eigene/besondere ~: there's a [special] story behind sth.
bewässern *tr. V.* irrigate
Bewässerung *die;* ~, ~en irrigation
bewegen[1] [1] *tr. V.* (a) move (b) (ergreifen) move (c) (innerlich beschäftigen) preoccupy [2] *refl. V.* move
bewegen[2] *unr. tr. V.* jmdn. dazu ~, etw. zu tun ⟨thing⟩ induce sb. to do sth.; ⟨person⟩ prevail upon sb. to do sth.
Beweg·grund *der* motive
beweglich *Adj.* (a) movable; moving ⟨target⟩ (b) (rege) agile ⟨mind⟩
bewegt *Adj.* eventful; (unruhig) turbulent
Bewegung *die;* ~, ~en (a) movement; (bes. Technik, Physik) motion (b) (körperliche ~) exercise ┄┄❯

(c) (Ergriffenheit) emotion
(d) (Bestreben, Gruppe) movement
Bewegungs·freiheit *die* freedom of movement
bewegungslos *Adj.* motionless
Bewegungslosigkeit *die;* ~: motionlessness
beweiden *tr. V.* (Landw.) **(a)** graze the grass in ⟨*garden etc.*⟩
(b) (als Weide nutzen) use ⟨*meadow etc.*⟩ as pasture
Beweis *der;* ~es, ~e proof (*Gen.,* für of); **belastende** ~e incriminating evidence
beweisbar *Adj.* provable
beweisen *unr. tr. V.* prove
Beweis-: ~**material** *das* evidence; ~**mittel** *das* (Rechtsw.) form of evidence; ~**stück** *das* piece of evidence; ~**stücke** evidence *sing.*
bewenden *unr. V.* es bei *od.* mit etw. ~ lassen content oneself with sth.
bewerben *unr. V. refl.* apply (bei to, um for)
Bewerber *der;* ~s, ~, **Bewerberin** *die;* ~, ~nen applicant
Bewerbung *die* application
Bewerbungs-: ~**bogen** *der* application form; ~**schreiben** *das* letter of application; ~**unterlagen** *Pl.* documents in support of an/the application
bewerfen *unr. tr. V.* jmdn./etw. mit etw. ~: throw sth. at sb./sth.
bewerkstelligen *tr. V.* pull off, manage ⟨*deal, sale, etc.*⟩; es ~, etw. zu tun contrive *or* manage to do sth.
bewerten *tr. V.* assess; rate; (dem Geldwert nach) value (mit at)
Bewertung *die;* ~, ~en assessment; (dem Geldwert nach) valuation
bewilligen *tr. V.* grant
Bewilligung *die;* ~, ~en granting
bewirken *tr. V.* bring about; cause
bewirten *tr. V.* feed; jmdn. mit etw. ~: serve sb. sth.
bewirtschaften *tr. V.* **(a)** manage ⟨*estate, farm, restaurant, business, etc.*⟩
(b) farm ⟨*fields, land*⟩
Bewirtung *die;* ~, ~en provision of food and drink
bewog *1. u. 3. Pers. Sg. Prät. v.* BEWEGEN[2]
bewohnbar *Adj.* habitable
bewohnen *tr. V.* inhabit, live in ⟨*house, area*⟩; live in ⟨*room, flat*⟩
Bewohner *der;* ~s, ~, **Bewohnerin** *die;* ~, ~nen (eines Hauses, einer Wohnung) occupant; (einer Stadt, eines Gebietes) inhabitant
bewohnt *Adj.* occupied ⟨*house etc.*⟩; inhabited ⟨*area*⟩
bewölken *refl. V.* cloud over; become overcast
bewölkt *Adj.* cloudy; overcast
Bewölkung *die;* ~, ~en cloud [cover]

Bewunderer *der;* ~s, ~, **Bewunderin** *die;* ~, ~nen admirer
bewundern *tr. V.* admire (wegen, für for)
bewunderns·wert [1] *Adj.* admirable
[2] *adv.* admirably
Bewunderung *die;* ~: admiration
bewusst, *bewußt [1] *Adj.* conscious ⟨*reaction, behaviour, etc.*⟩; (absichtlich) deliberate ⟨*lie, deception, attack, etc.*⟩; etw. ist/wird jmdm. ~: sb. is/becomes aware of sth.; sb. realizes sth.; sich (*Dat.*) einer Sache (*Gen.*) ~ sein/werden be/become aware of something
[2] *adv.* consciously; (absichtlich) deliberately
bewusst·los, *bewußt·los *Adj.* unconscious
Bewusstlosigkeit, *Bewußtlosigkeit *die;* ~: unconsciousness
Bewusst·sein, *Bewußt·sein *das* **(a)** consciousness; das ~ verlieren/ wiedererlangen lose/regain consciousness; bei vollem ~ sein be fully conscious
(b) (deutliches Wissen) awareness
bewusstseins-, *bewußtseins-, Bewusstseins-, *Bewußtseins-: ~**erweiternd** *Adj.* mind-expanding; psychedelic; ~**erweiterung** *die* expansion of consciousness; ~**trübung** *die* clouding *or* dimming of consciousness; ~**veränderung** *die* change of awareness
bezahlbar *Adj.* affordable
bezahlen [1] *tr. V.* pay ⟨*person, bill, taxes, rent, amount*⟩; pay for ⟨*goods etc.*⟩; das macht sich bezahlt it pays off
[2] *itr. V.* pay; ich möchte ~ *od.* bitte ~: the bill *or* (Amer.) check please
Bezahl·fernsehen *das* pay television; pay TV
Bezahlung *die;* ~, ~en payment; (Lohn, Gehalt) pay
bezaubernd [1] *Adj.* enchanting
[2] *adv.* enchantingly
bezeichnen *tr. V.* **(a)** jmdn./sich/etw. als etw. ~: call sb./oneself/sth. sth.
(b) (Name, Wort sein für) denote
bezeichnend *Adj.* characteristic (für of)
Bezeichnung *die;* ~, ~en **(a)** marking; (Angabe durch Zeichen) indication
(b) (Name) name
bezeugen *tr. V.* testify to
bezichtigen *tr. V.* accuse
beziehen [1] *unr. tr. V.* **(a)** cover ⟨*seat, cushion, etc.*⟩; die Betten frisch ~: put clean sheets on the beds
(b) (einziehen in) move into ⟨*house, office*⟩
(c) (Milit.) take up ⟨*position, post*⟩
(d) (erhalten) obtain ⟨*goods*⟩; take ⟨*newspaper*⟩; draw ⟨*pension, salary*⟩
(e) (in Beziehung setzen) apply (auf + *Akk.* to)
[2] *unr. refl. V.* **(a)** es/der Himmel bezieht sich it/the sky is clouding over *or* becoming overcast

---

(b) sich auf jmdn./etw. ∼ (sich berufen auf) ⟨*person, letter, etc.*⟩ refer to sb./sth.; (betreffen) ⟨*question, statement, etc.*⟩ relate to sb./sth.; **wir** ∼ **uns auf Ihr Schreiben vom 28. 8.** with reference to your letter of 28 August

Beziehung *die;* ∼**,** ∼**en (a)** relation; (Zusammenhang) connection (**zu** with); **zwischen A und B besteht keine/eine** ∼: there is no/a connection between A and B **(b)** (Freundschaft, Liebes∼) relationship **(c)** (Hinsicht) respect; **in mancher** ∼: in many respects

beziehungs·weise *Konj.* and … respectively; (oder) or

beziffern *tr. V.* estimate (**auf** + *Akk.* at); **den Schaden auf 3 000 Euro** ∼: estimate the damage at 3,000 euros

Bezirk *der;* ∼**[e]s,** ∼**e** district

*****bezug** ▸ BEZUG D

Bezug *der* **(a)** (für Kissen usw.) cover; (für Polstermöbel) loose cover; slip cover (Amer.); (für Betten) duvet cover; (für Kopfkissen) pillowcase **(b)** (Erwerb) obtaining; (Kauf) purchase; ∼ **einer Zeitung** taking a newspaper **(c)** *Pl.* salary *sing.* **(d)** (Papierdt.) **mit** *od.* **unter** ∼ **auf etw.** (*Akk.*) with reference to sth.; **in** ∼ **auf jmdn./etw.** regarding sb./sth.; ∼ **nehmend auf unser Telex** with reference to our telex

bezüglich *Präp. mit Gen.* regarding

bezwecken *tr. V.* aim to achieve

bezweifeln *tr. V.* doubt

bezwingen *unr. tr. V.* conquer ⟨*enemy, mountain, pain, etc.*⟩; defeat ⟨*opponent*⟩; capture ⟨*fortress*⟩

BH /beːˈhaː/ *der;* ∼**[s],** ∼**[s]** *Abk.* = **Büstenhalter** bra

Bibel *die;* ∼**,** ∼**n** (auch fig.) Bible

Biber *der;* ∼**s,** ∼: beaver

Bibliographie *die;* ∼**,** ∼**n** bibliography

bibliographisch *Adj.* bibliographical

Bibliothek *die;* ∼**,** ∼**en** library

Bibliothekar *der;* ∼**s,** ∼**e,** **Bibliothekarin** *die;* ∼**,** ∼**nen** librarian

biblisch *Adj.* biblical

Bidet /biˈdeː/ *das;* ∼**s,** ∼**s** bidet

bieder *Adj.* unsophisticated; (langweilig) stolid; (treuherzig) trusting

biegen ① *unr. tr. V.* bend ② *unr. refl. V.* bend; (nachgeben) give ③ *unr. itr. V.; mit sein* turn

biegsam *Adj.* flexible; pliable ⟨*material*⟩

Biegsamkeit *die;* ∼ ▸ BIEGSAM: flexibility; pliability

Biegung *die;* ∼**,** ∼**en** bend

Biene *die;* ∼**,** ∼**n** bee

Bienen-: ∼**honig** *der* bees' honey; ∼**königin** *die* queen bee; ∼**korb** *der* straw hive; ∼**stock** *der* beehive

Bier *das;* ∼**[e]s,** ∼**e** beer

Bier-: ∼**bauch** *der* (ugs. spött.) beer belly;

∼**brauerei** *die* brewery; ∼**deckel** *der* beer mat; ∼**dose** *die* beer can; ∼**fass,** *****∼**faß** *das* beer barrel; ∼**flasche** *die* beer bottle; ∼**garten** *der* beer garden; ∼**glas** *das* beer glass; ∼**kasten** *der* beer crate; ∼**trinker** *der,* ∼**trinkerin** *die* beer drinker; ∼**zelt** *das* beer tent

Biest *das;* ∼**[e]s,** ∼**er** (ugs. abwertend) **(a)** (Tier, Gegenstand) wretched thing **(b)** (Mensch) wretch

bieten ① *unr. tr. V.* **(a)** offer; put on ⟨*programme etc.*⟩; provide ⟨*shelter, guarantee, etc.*⟩ **(b) ein schreckliches Bild** ∼: present a terrible picture; **einen prächtigen Anblick** ∼: be a splendid sight ② *unr. refl. V.* **sich jmdm.** ∼: present itself to sb. ③ *unr. itr. V.* bid

Bigamie *die;* ∼: bigamy *no def. art.*

Bigamist *der;* ∼**en,** ∼**en, Bigamistin** *die;* ∼**,** ∼**nen** bigamist

Bikini *der;* ∼**s,** ∼**s** bikini

Bilanz *die;* ∼**,** ∼**en (a)** balance sheet **(b)** (Ergebnis) outcome; ∼ **ziehen** take stock

Bild *das;* ∼**[e]s,** ∼**er (a)** picture **(b)** (Anblick) sight **(c)** (Metapher) image

bilden ① *tr. V.* **(a)** form (**aus** from); (modellieren) mould (**aus** from); **eine Gasse** ∼: make a path; **sich** (*Dat.*) **ein Urteil** ∼: form an opinion **(b)** (ansammeln) build up ⟨*fund, capital*⟩ **(c)** (darstellen) be ⟨*exception etc.*⟩ **(d)** (erziehen) educate ② *refl. V.* **(a)** form **(b)** (lernen) educate oneself

bildend *Adj.* **(a) die** ∼**e Kunst, die** ∼**en Künste** the plastic arts *pl.* (*including painting and architecture*) **(b)** (belehrend) educational

Bilder-: ∼**buch** *das* picture book (*for children*); ∼**geschichte** *die* picture story; ∼**rahmen** *der* picture frame; ∼**rätsel** *das* picture puzzle; (Rebus) rebus

bild-, Bild-: ∼**hauer** *der* sculptor; ∼**hauerin** *die;* ∼∼**,** ∼∼**nen** sculptress; ∼**hübsch** *Adj.* really lovely; stunningly beautiful ⟨*girl*⟩

bildlich ① *Adj.* pictorial; (übertragen) figurative ② *adv.* pictorially; (übertragen) figuratively

Bildnis /ˈbɪltnɪs/ *das;* ∼**ses,** ∼**se** portrait

Bild-: ∼**qualität** *die* picture quality; ∼**röhre** *die* (Ferns.) picture tube

Bild·schirm *der* (Ferns., Informationst.) screen

Bildschirm-: ∼**gerät** *das* VDU; visual display unit; ∼**schoner** *der;* ∼∼**s,** ∼∼ (DV) screen saver

bild-, Bild-: ∼**schön** *Adj.* really lovely; stunningly beautiful ⟨*girl, woman*⟩; ∼**telefon** *das* video telephone

b

Bildung die; ~, ~en (a) (Erziehung) education; (Kultur) culture
(b) (das Formen) formation
Bildungs-: ~**lücke** die gap in one's education; ~**minister** der, ~**ministerin** die minister of education; ≈ Secretary of State for Education (Brit.); ~**wesen** das education system; das ~**wesen** education
Bild·unterschrift die caption
Billard /'bɪljart, österr.: bi'jaːɐ̯/ das; ~s, ~e billiards
Billard-: ~**kugel** die billiard ball; ~**stock** der billiard cue; ~**tisch** der billiard table
Billett /bɪl'jɛt/ das; ~[e]s, ~e od. ~s (schweiz., veralt.) ticket
Billiarde die; ~, ~n thousand million million; quadrillion (Amer.)
billig ⟨1⟩ Adj. (a) cheap
(b) (abwertend: primitiv) cheap ⟨trick⟩; feeble ⟨excuse⟩
⟨2⟩ adv. cheaply
Billig·angebot das special or cut-price offer
billigen tr. V. approve
Billig-: ~**flug** der cheap flight; ~**flug·linie** die low-cost airline; ~**lohn·land** das low-wage country
Billigung die; ~: approval
Billion die; ~, ~en trillion; million million
bimmeln itr. V. (ugs.) ring
bin 1. Pers. Sg. Präsens v. SEIN¹
binär Adj. binary
Binde die; ~, ~n (a) (Verband) bandage; (Augenbinde) blindfold
(b) (Armbinde) armband
Binde-: ~**gewebe** das (Anat.) connective tissue; ~**haut** die (Anat.) conjunctiva
binden unr. tr. V. (a) (auch fig.) tie; knot ⟨tie⟩; make up ⟨wreath, bouquet⟩; jmdn. an sich (Akk.) ~ (fig.) make sb. dependent on one
(b) (fesseln, festhalten, zusammenhalten, fig.: verpflichten, Buchw.) bind
(c) (Kochk.: legieren) thicken ⟨sauce⟩
Binder der; ~s, ~ tie
Binde·strich der hyphen
Bind·faden der string
Bindung die; ~, ~en (a) (Beziehung) relationship (an + Akk. to)
(b) (Verbundenheit) attachment (an + Akk. to)
(c) (Skibindung) binding
binnen Präp. mit Dat. od. (geh.) Gen. within
Binnenmarkt der (Wirtsch.) domestic or home market; europäischer ~: internal European market
Binsen·weisheit die truism
Bio- (ugs.) organic ⟨farmer, garden, vegetables, etc.⟩
bio-, Bio-: ~**abfall** der biowaste;

~**chemie** die biochemistry; ~**graf** der; ~~en, ~~en biographer; ~**grafie** die; ~~, ~~n biography; ~**grafin** die; ~~, ~~nen biographer; ~**grafisch** Adj. biographical; ~**loge** der; ~~n, ~~n biologist; ~**logie** die; ~~: biology no art.; ~**login** der; ~~, ~~nen biologist; ~**logisch** Adj. (a) biological; (b) (natürlich) natural ⟨medicine, cosmetic, etc.⟩; ~**masse** die biomass; ~**müll** der biowaste; ~**technologie** die biotechnology; ~**terrorismus** der bioterrorism; ~**top** der od. das; ~~s, ~~e (Biol.) biotope; ~**waffe** die biological weapon
Birke die; ~, ~n birch [tree]; (Holz) birch[wood]
Birma (das); ~s Burma
Birn·baum der pear tree
Birne die; ~, ~n (a) pear
(b) (Glühlampe) [light]bulb
(c) (salopp: Kopf) nut (coll.)
bis ⟨1⟩ Präp. mit Akk. (a) (zeitlich) until; till; (die ganze Zeit über und bis zu einem bestimmten Zeitpunkt) up until; up till; (nicht später als) by
(b) (räumlich) to; dieser Zug fährt nur ~ Offenburg this train only goes as far as Offenburg; ~ 5 000 Euro up to 5,000 euros
(c) ~ auf (einschließlich) down to; (mit Ausnahme von) except for
⟨2⟩ Adv. ~ zu 6 Personen up to six people
⟨3⟩ Konj. (a) (nebenordnend) to
(b) (unterordnend) until; till; (österr.: sobald) when
Bischof der; ~s, Bischöfe, **Bischöfin** die; ~, ~nen bishop
bischöflich Adj. episcopal
bi·sexuell ⟨1⟩ Adj. bisexual
⟨2⟩ adv. bisexually
bis·her Adv. up to now; (aber jetzt nicht mehr) until now; till now
bisherig Adj. (vorherig) previous; (momentan) present
Biskuit /bɪs'kviːt/ das od. der; ~[e]s, ~s od. ~e (a) sponge biscuit
(b) (~teig) sponge
bis·lang Adv.; ▶ BISHER
Bison der; ~s, ~s bison
Biss, *Biß der; Bisses, Bisse bite
bisschen, *bißchen indekl. Indefinitpron. (a) adj. ein ~ Geld/Wasser a bit of or a little money/a drop of or a little water; ein/kein ~ Angst haben be a bit/not a bit frightened
(b) adv. ein/kein ~: a bit or a little/not a or one bit
(c) subst. ein ~: a bit; a little; (bei Flüssigkeiten) a drop; a little; das/kein ~: the little [bit]/not a or one bit
Bissen der; ~s, ~: mouthful
bissig ⟨1⟩ Adj. (a) ~ sein ⟨dog⟩ bite; ein ~er Hund a dog that bites; „Vorsicht, ~er Hund" 'beware of the dog'
(b) cutting ⟨remark, tone, etc.⟩
⟨2⟩ adv. ⟨say⟩ cuttingly

---

*alte Schreibung - vgl. Hinweis auf S. xiv

Biss·wunde, *Biß·wunde die bite

bist 2. Pers. Sg. Präsens v. SEIN[1]

Bistum /ˈbɪstuːm/ das; ∼s, Bistümer bishopric; diocese

bis·weilen Adv. (geh.) from time to time

Bit /bɪt/ das; ∼s, ∼[s] (DV) bit

bitte [1] Adv. please
[2] Interj. (a) (Bitte, Aufforderung) please; **zwei Tassen Tee,** ∼: two cups of tea, please; ∼[, **nehmen Sie doch Platz]!** do take a seat; **Noch eine Tasse Tee? – [Ja]** ∼! Another cup of tea? – Yes, please
(b) (Aufforderung, etw. entgegenzunehmen) ∼ [**schön** od. **sehr]!** there you are!
(c) (Ausdruck des Einverständnisses) ∼ [**gern]!** certainly; of course; **Entschuldigung! – Bitte!** [I'm] sorry! – That's all right!
(d) ∼ [**schön** od. **sehr]!** (im Laden, Lokal) yes, please?
(e) [**wie**] ∼? (Nachfrage) sorry
(f) **Vielen Dank! – Bitte [schön** od. **sehr]** Many thanks! – Not at all or you're welcome

Bitte die; ∼, ∼n request; (inständig) plea

bitten unr. tr. V. (a) auch itr. ask (**um** for); **darf ich Sie um Feuer/ein Glas Wasser** ∼? could I ask you for a light/a glass of water, please?
(b) (einladen) ask

bitter [1] Adj. (a) bitter; plain ⟨chocolate⟩
(b) (fig.) (verbittert) bitter
(c) (schmerzlich) bitter, painful, hard ⟨loss⟩; hard ⟨time, fate, etc.⟩; dire ⟨need⟩; desperate ⟨poverty⟩; grievous ⟨injustice, harm⟩
[2] adv. (sehr stark) desperately; ⟨regret⟩ bitterly

bitter-: ∼**böse** [1] Adj. furious; [2] adv. furiously; ∼**kalt** Adj. bitterly cold

bitterlich [1] Adj. slightly bitter ⟨taste⟩
[2] adv. (heftig) ⟨cry, complain, etc.⟩ bitterly

bitter-süß Adj. (auch fig.) bitter-sweet

Bitt·steller der; ∼s, ∼, **Bitt·stellerin** die; ∼, ∼nen petitioner

Biwak das; ∼s, ∼s (bes. Milit., Bergsteigen) bivouac

bizarr [1] Adj. bizarre
[2] adv. bizarrely

Bizeps der; ∼[es], ∼e biceps

Blähung die; ∼, ∼en flatulence no art., no pl.

Blamage /blaˈmaːʒə/ die; ∼, ∼n disgrace

blamieren [1] tr. V. disgrace
[2] refl. V. disgrace oneself; (sich lächerlich machen) make a fool of oneself

blank Adj. shiny

Blanko-: ∼**scheck** der (auch fig.) blank cheque; ∼**vollmacht** die (auch fig.) carte blanche

Bläschen /ˈblɛːsçən/ das; ∼s, ∼ (a) [small] bubble
(b) (in der Haut) [small] blister

Blase die; ∼, ∼n (a) bubble
(b) (in der Haut) blister
(c) (Harn∼) bladder

Blase·balg der; ∼s, Blasebälge bellows pl.

blasen [1] unr. itr. V. blow
[2] unr. tr. V. (a) blow
(b) (spielen) play ⟨musical instrument, tune, melody, etc.⟩

Bläser der; ∼s, ∼, **Bläserin** die; ∼, ∼nen (Musik) wind player

blasiert (abwertend) [1] Adj. blasé
[2] adv. in a blasé way

Blas-: ∼**instrument** das wind instrument; ∼**kapelle** die brass band; ∼**musik** die brass-band music

Blasphemie /blasfeˈmiː/ die; ∼, ∼n blasphemy

Blas·rohr das blowpipe

blass, *blaß [1] Adj. pale
[2] adv. palely

Blässe die; ∼: paleness

Blatt das; ∼[e]s, Blätter (a) (von Pflanzen) leaf
(b) (Papier) sheet
(c) (Buchseite usw.) page; **etw. vom** ∼ **spielen** sight-read sth.
(d) (Zeitung) paper
(e) (Spielkarten) hand
(f) (am Werkzeug, Ruder) blade

Blättchen das; ∼s, ∼ (a) (von Pflanzen) [small] leaf
(b) (Papier) [small] sheet

blättern itr. V. **in einem Buch** ∼: leaf through a book

Blätter·teig der puff pastry

Blatt-: ∼**gold** das gold leaf; ∼**grün** das chlorophyll; ∼**laus** die aphid

blau Adj. blue; **ein** ∼**er Fleck** a bruise; ∼ **sein** (fig. ugs.) be tight (coll.); **das Blaue vom Himmel herunterlügen** (ugs.) lie like anything

Blau das; ∼s, ∼ od. (ugs.:) ∼s blue

blau-, Blau-: ∼**äugig** Adj. (a) blue-eyed;
(b) (naiv) naive; ∼**beere** die bilberry;
∼**grau** Adj. blue-grey; ∼**grün** Adj. blue-green

bläulich Adj. bluish

blau-, Blau-: ∼**licht** das flashing blue light; ∼|**machen** itr. V. (ugs.) skip work;
∼**mann** der; Pl. ∼männer (ugs.) boiler suit;
∼**säure** die (Chemie) prussic acid;
∼**stichig** Adj. (Fot.) with a blue cast postpos., not pred.; ∼**stichig sein** have a blue cast

Blazer /ˈbleːzɐ/ der; ∼s, ∼: blazer

Blech das; ∼[e]s, ∼e (a) sheet metal; (Stück Blech) metal sheet
(b) (Back∼) [baking] tray

Blech-: ∼**bläser** der, ∼**bläserin** die brass player; **die** ∼**bläser** (im Orchester) the brass [section] sing; ∼**büchse** die, ∼**dose** die tin

blechen tr., itr. V. (ugs.) cough up (coll.)

blechern [1] Adj. (metallisch klingend) tinny ⟨sound, voice⟩
[2] adv. tinnily

Blech-: ∼**musik** die (abwertend) brass-band music; ∼**napf** der metal bowl

Blęchner *der;* ~s, ~, **Blęchnerin** *die;* ~, ~nen (südd.) ▶ KLEMPNER

Blech-: ~**schaden** *der* (Kfz-W.) damage *no indef. art.* to the bodywork; ~**trommel** *die* tin drum

blęcken *tr. V.* die Zähne ~: bare one's/its teeth

Blei *das;* ~[e]s, ~e lead

Bleibe *die;* ~, ~n place to stay

bleiben *unr. itr. V.; mit sein* **(a)** stay; remain; ~ Sie bitte am Apparat hold the line please; **wo bleibt er so lange?** where has he got to?; **auf dem Weg** ~: keep to the path; **sitzen** ~: stay *or* remain sitting down *or* seated; **bei etw.** ~ (fig.: an etw. festhalten) keep to sth. **(b)** (übrig bleiben) be left; remain **(c)** etw. ~ **lassen** give sth. a miss

bleibend *Adj.* lasting; permanent ⟨*damage*⟩

*****bleiben|lassen** ▶ BLEIBEN C

bleich *Adj.* pale

bleichen[1] *tr. V.* bleach

bleichen[2] *regelm., veralt. auch unr. itr. V.* become bleached

blei-, Blei-: ~**frei** *Adj.* unleaded ⟨*fuel*⟩; ~**kristall** *das* lead crystal; ~**kugel** *die* lead ball; (Geschoss) lead bullet; ~**schwer** *Adj.* heavy as lead *postpos.;* ~**stift** *der* pencil; **mit** ~**stift** in pencil; ~**stift-spitzer** *der* pencil sharpener

Blende *die;* ~, ~n **(a)** (Lichtschutz) shade; (am Fenster) blind **(b)** (Optik, Film, Fot.) diaphragm; (Blendenzahl) aperture setting

blenden [1] *tr. V.* **(a)** (auch fig.) dazzle **(b)** (blind machen) blind [2] *itr. V.* ⟨*light*⟩ be dazzling

blendend [1] *Adj.* es geht mir ~: I feel wonderfully well [2] *adv.* wir haben uns ~ amüsiert we had a marvellous time

blich *1. u. 3. Pers. Sg. Prät. v.* BLEICHEN[2]

Blick *der;* ~[e]s, ~e **(a)** look; (flüchtig) glance **(b)** (Ausdruck) look in one's eyes; **mit misstrauischem** ~: with a suspicious look in one's eyes **(c)** (Aussicht) view; **ein Zimmer mit** ~ **aufs Meer** a room with a sea view **(d)** (Urteil[skraft]) eye

blicken [1] *itr. V.* look; (flüchtig) glance [2] *tr. V.* sich ~ lassen put in an appearance

Blick-: ~**fang** *der* eye-catcher; **als** ~**fang dienen** serve to catch the eye; ~**feld** *das* field of vision; ~**kontakt** *der* eye contact; ~**punkt** *der* view; ~**winkel** *der* **(a)** angle of vision; **(b)** (fig.) point of view; viewpoint

blieb *1. u. 3. Pers. Sg. Prät. v.* BLEIBEN

blies *1. u. 3. Pers. Sg. Prät. v.* BLASEN

blind [1] *Adj.* **(a)** (auch fig.) blind; ~ **werden** go blind **(b)** (trübe) clouded ⟨*glass*⟩

(c) ein ~**er Passagier** a stowaway **(d)** ~**er Alarm** a false alarm [2] *adv.* **(a)** (ohne hinzusehen) without looking; (wahllos) blindly **(b)** (unkritisch) ⟨*trust*⟩ implicitly; ⟨*obey*⟩ blindly

Blind-: ~**bewerbung** *die* unsolicited application; ~**darm** *der* **(a)** caecum; **(b)** (volkst.: Wurmfortsatz) appendix

Blinde *der/die; adj. Dekl.* blind person; blind man/woman; **die** ~**n** the blind

Blinde·kuh: ~ **spielen** play blind man's buff

Blinden-: ~**hund** *der* guide dog; ~**schrift** *die* Braille

Blindheit *die;* ~ (auch fig.) blindness

blindlings *Adv.* blindly; ⟨*trust*⟩ implicitly

blind-, Blind-: ~**schleiche** *die;* ~, ~n slowworm; ~**wütig** [1] *Adj.* raging ⟨*anger, hatred, fury, etc.*⟩; wild ⟨*rage*⟩; [2] *adv.* in a blind rage

blinken [1] *itr. V.* **(a)** ⟨*light, glass, crystal*⟩ flash; ⟨*star*⟩ twinkle; ⟨*metal, fish*⟩ gleam **(b)** (Verkehrsw.) indicate [2] *tr. V.* flash

Blinker *der;* ~s, ~: indicator [light]

Blink-: ~**licht** *das* **(a)** flashing light; **(b)** ▶ BLINKER; ~**zeichen** *das* flashlight signal

blinzeln *itr. V.* blink; (mit einem Auge, um ein Zeichen zu geben) wink

Blitz *der;* ~es, ~e **(a)** lightning *no indef. art.;* **ein** ~: a flash of lightning; [schnell] **wie der** ~: like lightning **(b)** (Blitzlicht) flash

blitz-, Blitz-: ~**ab·leiter** *der* lightning conductor; ~**artig** [1] *Adj.* lightning; [2] *adv.* like lightning; ⟨*disappear*⟩ in a flash; ~**blank** *Adj.* (ugs.) ~**blank** [geputzt] sparkling clean; brightly polished ⟨*shoes*⟩

blitzeblank ▶ BLITZBLANK

blitzen *itr. V.* **(a)** *unpers.* es blitzte (einmal) there was a flash of lightning; (mehrmals) there was lightning **(b)** (glänzen) ⟨*light, glass, crystal*⟩ flash; ⟨*metal*⟩ gleam

blitz-, Blitz-: ~**gerät** *das* flash [unit]; ~**licht** *das* flash[light]; ~**schnell** [1] *Adj.* lightning *attrib.;* ~**schnell sein** be like lightning; [2] *adv.* like lightning; ⟨*disappear*⟩ in a flash; ~**start** *der* lightning start

Block *der;* ~[e]s, Blöcke *od.* ~s **(a)** *Pl. nur* Blöcke (Brocken) block **(b)** (Wohnblock) block **(c)** *Pl. nur* Blöcke (Gruppierung von politischen Kräften, Staaten) bloc **(d)** (Schreibblock) pad

Blockade *die;* ~, ~n blockade

Block-: ~**flöte** *die* recorder; ~**haus** *das,* ~**hütte** *die* log cabin

blockieren *tr. V.* block; jam ⟨*telephone line*⟩; halt ⟨*traffic*⟩; lock ⟨*wheel, machine, etc.*⟩

Block·schrift *die* block capitals *pl.*

blöd[e] (ugs.) [1] *Adj.* **(a)** (dumm) stupid; idiotic (coll.)

---

*old spelling - see note on page xiv

(b) (unangenehm) stupid
[2] adv. stupidly; idiotically (coll.)
Blödel|ei die; ~, ~en silly joke
blödeln itr. V. make silly jokes
Blödheit die; ~, ~en stupidity
blöd-, Blöd-: ~**mann** der; Pl. ~männer
(salopp) stupid idiot (coll.); ~**sinn** der (ugs.)
nonsense; **mach doch keinen** ~**sinn!** don't be
stupid; ~**sinnig** (ugs.) [1] Adj. idiotic (coll.);
[2] adv. idiotically (coll.)
blöken itr. V. ⟨sheep⟩ bleat; ⟨cattle⟩ low
blond Adj. fair-haired, blond ⟨man, race⟩;
blonde ⟨woman⟩; blond/blonde, fair ⟨hair⟩
Blondine die; ~, ~n blonde
bloß [1] Adj. **(a)** (nackt) naked
(b) (nichts als) mere ⟨words, promises,
triviality, suspicion, etc.⟩; **der** ~**e Gedanke
daran** the mere thought of it
[2] Adv. (ugs.: nur) only
[3] Partikel **was hast du dir** ~ **dabei
gedacht?** what on earth were you thinking
of?
Blöße die; ~: **sich** (Dat.) **eine/keine** ~
geben show a/not show any weakness
bloß|stellen tr. V. show up; expose
⟨swindler, criminal, etc.⟩
Blouson /blu'zõ:/ das od. der; ~s, ~s
blouson
blubbern itr. V. (ugs.) bubble
Bluejeans /'blu:dʒi:ns/ Pl. od. die; ~, ~:
[blue] jeans pl.
Blues /blu:s/ der; ~, ~: blues pl.
Bluff der; ~s, ~s bluff
bluffen tr., itr. V. bluff
blühen itr. V. **(a)** ⟨plant⟩ flower, be in
flower or bloom; ⟨flower⟩ be in bloom, be
out; ⟨tree⟩ be in blossom; ~**de Gärten**
gardens full of flowers
(b) (florieren) thrive
(c) (ugs.: bevorstehen) **jmdm.** ~: be in store for
sb.; **das kann dir auch noch** ~: the same
could happen to you
blühend Adj. **(a)** (frisch, gesund) glowing
⟨colour, complexion, etc.⟩; radiant ⟨health⟩
(b) (übertrieben) vivid ⟨imagination⟩
Blümchen das; ~s, ~: [little] flower
Blume die; ~, ~n **(a)** flower
(b) (des Weines) bouquet
(c) (des Biers) head
blumen-, Blumen-: ~**beet** das flower
bed; ~**erde** die potting compost;
~**geschäft** das florist's;
~**geschmückt** Adj. flower-bedecked;
adorned with flowers postpos.; ~**kasten**
der flower box; (vor einem Fenster) window
box; ~**kohl** der cauliflower; ~**strauß** der;
Pl. ~**sträuße** bunch of flowers; (Bukett)
bouquet of flowers; ~**topf** der flowerpot;
~**vase** die [flower] vase; ~**zwiebel** die
bulb
Bluse die; ~, ~n blouse
Blut das; ~[e]s blood
blut-, Blut-: ~**arm** Adj. (Med.) anaemic;

~**armut** die (Med.) anaemia; ~**bad** das
bloodbath; ~**bahn** die bloodstream;
~**bank** die; Pl. ~~en (Med.) blood bank;
~**befleckt** Adj. bloodstained;
~**beschmiert** Adj. smeared with blood
postpos.; ~**buche** die copper beech;
~**druck** der; Pl. ~**drücke** blood pressure
Blüte die; ~, ~n **(a)** flower; bloom; (eines
Baums) blossom; ~**n treiben** flower; ⟨tree⟩
blossom
(b) (das Blühen) flowering; (Baumblüte)
blossoming
Blut·egel der; ~s, ~: leech
bluten itr. V. bleed (aus from)
blüten-, Blüten-: ~**blatt** das petal;
~**honig** der blossom honey; ~**staub** der
pollen; ~**weiß** Adj. sparkling white
Bluter der; ~s, ~, **Bluterin** die; ~, ~nen
(Med.) haemophiliac
Blut·erguss, *Blut·erguß der
haematoma; (blauer Fleck) bruise
Bluter·krankheit die haemophilia no art.
Blut-: ~**fleck[en]** der bloodstain;
~**gefäß** das (Anat.) blood vessel;
~**gerinnsel** das; ~~s, ~~ blood clot;
~**gruppe** die blood group;
~**hochdruck** der high blood pressure;
~**hund** der bloodhound
blutig (a) bloody; **jmdn.** ~ **schlagen** beat
sb. to a pulp
(b) (fig. ugs.: völlig) complete ⟨beginner,
layman, etc.⟩
blut-, Blut-: ~**jung** Adj. very young;
~**konserve** die container of stored blood;
~konserven stored blood; ~**körperchen**
das; ~~s, ~~: blood corpuscle; **rote/weiße**
~**körperchen** red/white corpuscles;
~**krebs** der leukaemia; ~**kreislauf** der
blood circulation; ~**lache** die pool of
blood; ~**leer** Adj. bloodless; ~**leere** die
restricted blood supply; ~**orange** die
blood orange; ~**plasma** das (Physiol.) blood
plasma; ~**probe** die **(a)** (~entnahme,
~untersuchung) blood test; **(b)** (kleine ~menge)
blood sample; ~**rache** die blood revenge;
~**rot** Adj. blood-red; ~**rünstig** [1] Adj.
bloodthirsty; [2] adv. bloodthirstily;
~**schande** die incest; ~**spende** die (das
Spenden) giving no indef. art. of blood;
(~menge) blood donation; ~**spender** der;
~**spenderin** die blood donor; ~**spur** die
trail of blood; ~**stillend** Adj. styptic
bluts-, Bluts-: ~**tropfen** der drop of
blood; ~**verwandt** Adj. related by blood
postpos.; ~**verwandtschaft** die blood
relationship
Blut-: ~**tat** die (geh.) bloody deed;
~**transfusion** die blood transfusion;
~**übertragung** die blood transfusion
Blutung die; ~, ~en **(a)** bleeding no indef.
art., no pl.;
(b) (Regelblutung) period
blut-, Blut-: ~**unterlaufen** Adj.
suffused with blood postpos.; bloodshot ⋯⁞

⟨*eyes*⟩; ∼**vergießen** *das;* ∼∼s bloodshed; ∼**vergiftung** *die* blood poisoning *no indef. art., no pl.;* ∼**wurst** *die* black pudding; ∼**zucker·spiegel** *der* (Physiol.) blood-sugar level

Bö *die;* ∼, ∼en gust [of wind]

Bob *der;* ∼, ∼s bob[sleigh]

Bob-: ∼**bahn** *die* bob[sleigh] run; ∼**fahrer** *der,* ∼**fahrerin** *die* bobber

Bock¹ *der;* ∼[e]s, Böcke **(a)** (Reh∼, Kaninchen∼) buck; (Ziegen∼) billy goat; he-goat; (Schafs∼) ram; einen/keinen ∼ auf etw. (*Akk.*) haben (ugs.) fancy/not fancy sth.; einen/keinen ∼ haben, etw. zu tun (ugs.) fancy/not fancy doing sth. **(b)** (Gestell) trestle **(c)** (Turngerät) buck

Bock² *das;* ∼s (Bier) bock [beer]

Bock·bier *das* bock [beer]

bocken *itr. V.* refuse to go on; (vor einer Hürde) refuse; (sich aufbäumen) buck

bockig 1 *Adj.* stubborn and awkward 2 *adv.* stubbornly [and awkwardly]

Bocks·horn *das:* sich ins ∼ jagen lassen (ugs.) let oneself be browbeaten

Bock-: ∼**springen** *das;* ∼∼s (Turnen) vaulting [over the buck]; ∼**wurst** *die* bockwurst

Boden *der;* ∼s, Böden **(a)** (Erd∼) ground; (Fuß∼) floor; am ∼ zerstört [sein] (ugs.) [be] shattered (coll.); bleiben wir doch auf dem ∼ der Tatsachen (fig.) let's stick to the facts **(b)** (unterste Fläche) bottom; (Torten∼) base **(c)** (Dach∼, Heu∼) loft

boden-, Boden-: ∼**belag** *der* floor-covering; ∼**ertrag** *der* crop yield; ∼**fläche** *die* land area; ∼**frost** *der* ground frost; ∼**kammer** *die* attic; ∼**los** *Adj.* **(a)** bottomless; **(b)** (ugs.: unerhört) incredible ⟨*foolishness, meanness, etc.*⟩; ∼**nebel** *der* ground fog/mist; ∼**satz** *der* sediment; ∼**schätze** *Pl.* mineral resources

Boden·see *der;* ∼s Lake Constance

boden-, Boden-: ∼**ständig** *Adj.* indigenous ⟨*culture, population, etc.*⟩; ∼**turnen** *das* floor exercises *pl.;* ∼**welle** *die* bump

Bodybuilding /ˈbɔdibɪldɪŋ/ *das;* ∼s bodybuilding *no art.*

Böe *die;* ∼, ∼n ▶ Bö

bog *1. u. 3. Pers. Sg. Prät. v.* BIEGEN

Bogen *der;* ∼s, ∼, (südd., österr.:) Bögen **(a)** curve; (Math.) arc **(b)** (Archit.) arch **(c)** (Waffe, Musik: Geigen∼ usw.) bow **(d)** (Papier∼) sheet

bogen-, Bogen-: ∼**fenster** *das* arched window; ∼**förmig** *Adj.* arched; ∼**schießen** *das;* ∼∼s archery *no art.*

Boheme /boˈeːm/ *die;* ∼: bohemian society

Bohemien /boeˈmĭɛ:/ *der;* ∼s, ∼s bohemian

Bohle *die;* ∼, ∼n [thick] plank

Böhnchen *das;* ∼s, ∼: [small] bean

Bohne *die;* ∼, ∼n bean; nicht die ∼ (ugs.) not one little bit

Bohnen-: ∼**eintopf** *der* bean stew; ∼**kaffee** *der* real coffee; ∼**kraut** *das* savory; ∼**stange** *die* (auch ugs.: Mensch) beanpole; ∼**stroh** *das:* dumm wie ∼stroh (ugs.) as thick as two short planks (coll.); ∼**suppe** *die* bean soup

bohnern *tr., itr. V.* polish

Bohner·wachs *das* floor polish

bohren 1 *tr. V.* **(a)** bore; (mit Bohrer, Bohrmaschine) drill, bore ⟨*hole*⟩; sink ⟨*well, shaft, pole, post etc.*⟩ (in + *Akk.* into) **(b)** (bearbeiten) drill ⟨*wood, concrete, etc.*⟩ **(c)** (drücken in) poke (in + *Akk.* in[to]) 2 *itr. V.* **(a)** drill; in der Nase ∼: pick one's nose; nach Öl/Wasser *usw.* ∼: drill for oil/water *etc.;* **(b)** (ugs.: drängen, fragen) keep on 3 *refl. V.* bore its way

bohrend *Adj.* **(a)** gnawing ⟨*pain, hunger, remorse*⟩ **(b)** (hartnäckig) piercing ⟨*look etc.*⟩; probing ⟨*question*⟩

Bohrer *der;* ∼s, ∼ drill

Bohr-: ∼**insel** *die* drilling rig; ∼**maschine** *die* drill; ∼**schrauber** *der* power drill/screwdriver; ∼**turm** *der* derrick

Bohrung *die;* ∼, ∼en drill hole

böig *Adj.* gusty

Boiler /ˈbɔylɐ/ *der;* ∼s, ∼: water heater

Boje *die;* ∼, ∼n buoy

Bolivien /boˈliːvjən/ (*das*) ∼s Bolivia

Böller·schuss, *Böller·schuß *der* gun salute

Boll·werk *das* bulwark; (fig.) bulwark; bastion; stronghold

Bolschewik *der;* ∼en, ∼i, (abwertend:) ∼en, **Bolschewikin** *die;* ∼, ∼nen Bolshevik

Bolschewismus *der;* ∼: Bolshevism *no art.*

Bolschewist *der;* ∼en, ∼en, **Bolschewistin** *die;* ∼, ∼nen Bolshevist

bolschewistisch *Adj.* Bolshevik

bolzen (ugs.) *itr. V.* kick the ball about

Bolzen *der;* ∼s, ∼: bolt

bombardieren *tr. V.* **(a)** bomb **(b)** (fig. ugs.) bombard

Bombardierung *die;* ∼, ∼en **(a)** (Milit.) bombing **(b)** (fig. ugs.) bombardment

bombastisch 1 *Adj.* bombastic 2 *adv.* bombastically

Bombe *die;* ∼, ∼n bomb

bomben-, Bomben-: ∼**angriff** *der* bomb attack; ∼**anschlag** *der* bomb attack; ∼**attentat** *das* bomb attack; ∼**drohung**

---

die bomb threat; ~**erfolg** *der* (ugs.) smash hit (coll.); ~**fest** *Adj.* (ugs.: unveränderbar) dead certain; ~**fest stehen** be dead certain; be a dead cert (Brit. coll.); ~**form** *die* (ugs.) top form; ~**sicher** *Adj.* (ugs.: gewiss) dead certain; **das ist eine** ~**sichere Sache** that's dead certain; that's a dead cert (Brit. coll.) *or* a sure thing (Amer.); ~**stimmung** *die* (ugs.) tremendous *or* fantastic atmosphere (coll.); ~**trichter** *der* bomb crater

Bomber *der;* ~**s**, ~: bomber

Bon /bɔŋ/ *der;* ~**s**, ~**s** **(a)** voucher; coupon **(b)** (Kassenzettel) receipt

Bonbon /bɔŋ'bɔŋ/ *der od.* (österr. nur) *das;* ~**s**, ~**s** sweet (Brit.); candy (Amer.); (fig.) treat

bongen *tr. V.* (ugs.) ring up; **gebongt sein** (ugs.) be fine; **ist gebongt!** (ugs.) fine!

Bongo *das;* ~**[s]**, ~**s** *od. die;* ~, ~**s** bongo [drum]

Bonmot /bõ'moː/ *das;* ~**s**, ~**s** bon mot

Bonze *der;* ~**n**, ~**n** bigwig (coll.)

Boom /buːm/ *der;* ~**s**, ~**s** boom

Boot *das;* ~**[e]s**, ~**e** boat

Boots-: ~**fahrt** *die* boat trip; ~**haus** *das* boathouse; ~**steg** *der* landing stage; ~**verleih** *der* boat hire

Bord[1] *das;* ~**[e]s**, ~**e** shelf

Bord[2] *der;* ~**[e]s**, ~**e** (eines Schiffes) side; **an** ~: on board; **über** ~: overboard

Bordell *das;* ~**s**, ~**e** brothel

Bord·stein *der* kerb

Bordüre *die;* ~, ~**n** edging

borgen *tr. V.:* ▶ LEIHEN

Borke *die;* ~, ~**n** bark

Borken·käfer *der* bark beetle

borniert [1] *Adj.* bigoted [2] *adv.* in a bigoted way

Börse *die;* ~, ~**n** stock market; (Gebäude) stock exchange

Börsen-: ~**krach** *der* stock market crash; ~**makler** *der* stockbroker

Borste *die;* ~, ~**n** bristle

borstig *Adj.* bristly

Borte *die;* ~, ~**n** braiding *no indef. art.;* edging *no indef. art.*

bös ▶ BÖSE

bös·artig [1] *Adj.* **(a)** (heimtückisch) malicious ⟨*person, remark, etc.*⟩; vicious ⟨*animal*⟩ **(b)** (Med.) malignant [2] *adv.* maliciously

Bös·artigkeit *die;* ~ **(a)** maliciousness; (von Tieren) viciousness **(b)** (Med.) malignancy

Böschung *die;* ~, ~**en** embankment

böse [1] *Adj.* **(a)** wicked; evil **(b)** (übel) bad ⟨*times, illness, dream, etc.*⟩; nasty ⟨*experience, affair, situation, trick, surprise, etc.*⟩ **(c)** (ugs.) (wütend) mad (coll.); (verärgert) cross (coll.) **(d)** (fam.: ungezogen) naughty

(e) (ugs.: arg) terrible (coll.) ⟨*pain, fall, shock, disappointment, storm, etc.*⟩ [2] *adv.* **(a)** (übel) ⟨*end*⟩ badly; **es war doch nicht** ~ **gemeint** I didn't mean it nastily **(b)** (ugs.) (wütend) angrily; (verärgert) crossly (coll.) **(c)** (ugs.: sehr) terribly (coll.)

boshaft [1] *Adj.* malicious [2] *adv.* maliciously

Boshaftigkeit *die;* ~, ~**en (a)** maliciousness **(b)** (Bemerkung) malicious remark

Bosheit *die;* ~, ~**en (a)** malice **(b)** (Bemerkung) malicious remark

Boss, *Boß *der;* **Bosses**, **Bosse** (ugs.) boss (coll.)

bös·willig [1] *Adj.* malicious; wilful ⟨*desertion*⟩ [2] *adv.* maliciously; wilfully ⟨*desert*⟩

Bös·willigkeit *die;* ~: malice; maliciousness

bot *1. u. 3. Pers. Sg. Prät. v.* BIETEN

Botanik *die;* ~: botany *no art.*

botanisch [1] *Adj.* botanical [2] *adv.* botanically

Bötchen *das;* ~**s**, ~: little boat

Bote *der;* ~**n**, ~**n (a)** messenger **(b)** (Laufbursche) errand boy

Botin *die;* ~, ~**nen** ▶ BOTE: **(a)** messenger **(b)** errand girl

Botschaft *die;* ~, ~**en (a)** message **(b)** (diplomatische Vertretung) embassy

Botschafter *der;* ~**s**, ~, **Botschafterin** *die;* ~, ~**nen** ambassador

Böttcher *der;* ~**s**, ~, **Böttcherin** *die;* ~, ~**nen** cooper

Bottich *der;* ~**s**, ~**e** tub

Bouillon /bul'jɔŋ/ *die;* ~, ~**s** bouillon

Boulevard /bulə'vaːɐ̯/ *der;* ~**s**, ~**s** boulevard

Boulevard-: ~**blatt** *das* ▶ BOULEVARDZEITUNG; ~**presse** *die* (abwertend) popular press; ~**stück** *das* (Theater) boulevard drama; ~**zeitung** *die* (abwertend) popular rag (derog.); tabloid

Bourgeoisie /burʒ̩oa'ziː/ *die;* ~, ~**n** bourgeoisie

Boutique /bu'tiːk/ *die;* ~, ~**s** *od.* ~**n** boutique

Bowle /'boːlə/ *die;* ~, ~**n** punch (made of wine, champagne, sugar, and fruit or spices)

bowlen /'boːlən/ *itr. V.* bowl

Bowling /'boːlɪŋ/ *das;* ~**s**, ~**s** [tenpin] bowling

Bowling·bahn *die* bowling alley

Box *die;* ~, ~**en (a)** box **(b)** (Lautsprecher) speaker **(c)** (Pferdebox) [loose] box **(d)** (Motorsport) pit

boxen [1] *itr. V.* box; **gegen jmdn.** ~: fight sb.; box [against] sb. [2] *tr. V.* punch

Bọxer der; ~s, ~ (Sportler, Hund) boxer

Bọxerin die; ~, ~nen boxer

Box-: ~**handschuh** der boxing glove; ~**kampf** der boxing match; (im Streit) fist fight; ~**ring** der boxing ring; ~**sport** der boxing no art.

Boy /bɔy/ der; ~s, ~s servant; (im Hotel) pageboy

Boykott /bɔy'kɔt/ der; ~[e]s, ~s boycott

boykottieren tr. V. boycott

brach¹ 1. u. 3. Pers. Sg. Prät. v. BRECHEN

brach² Adj. fallow; (auf Dauer) uncultivated

Brachial·gewalt die brute force

Brach·land das fallow [land]; (auf Dauer) uncultivated land

brach|liegen unr. itr. V. (auch fig.) lie fallow; (auf Dauer) lie waste

brạchte 1. u. 3. Pers. Sg. Prät. v. BRINGEN

Branche /'brã:ʃə/ die; ~, ~n [branch of] industry

Brạnchen·verzeichnis das classified directory; (Telefonbuch) Yellow Pages ® pl.

Brạnd der; ~[e]s, Brände fire; beim ~ der Scheune when the barn caught fire; etw. in ~ stecken set fire to sth.

Brạnd·anschlag der arson attack (auf + Akk. on)

brạnden itr. V. (geh.) break

Brạnden·burg (das); ~s Brandenburg

brand-, Brạnd-: ~**marken** tr. V. brand ⟨person⟩; denounce ⟨thing⟩; ~**neu** Adj. (ugs.) brand-new; ~**salbe** die ointment for burns; ~**schaden** der fire damage no pl., no indef. art.; ~**stelle** die burn; ~**stifter** der, ~**stifterin** die arsonist; ~**stiftung** die arson

Brạndung die; ~, ~en surf

Brạnd·wunde die burn

brạnnte 1. u. 3. Pers. Sg. Prät. v. BRENNEN

Brạnnt·wein der spirits pl.; (Sorte) spirit

Brasilianer der; ~s, ~, **Brasilianerin** die; ~, ~nen Brazilian

brasilianisch Adj. Brazilian

Brasilien /bra'zi:liən/ (das); ~s Brazil

brät 3. Pers. Sg. Präsens v. BRATEN

Brạt·apfel der baked apple

braten unr. tr., itr. V. fry; (im Backofen) roast

Braten der; ~s, ~ (a) joint (b) roast [meat] no indef. art.

Braten-: ~**saft** der meat juice[s pl.]; ~**soße** die gravy

Brat-: ~**fett** das [cooking] fat; ~**fisch** der fried fish; ~**hähnchen** das, (südd., österr.) ~**hendl** das roast chicken; (gegrillt) broiled chicken; ~**hering** der fried herring; ~**kartoffeln** Pl. fried potatoes; home fries (Amer.); ~**pfanne** die frying pan; ~**spieß** der spit; ~**wurst** die [fried/grilled] sausage

Brauch der; ~[e]s, Bräuche custom

brauchbar Adj. useful; (benutzbar) usable; wearable ⟨clothes⟩

brauchen ⊡ tr. V. (a) (benötigen) need (b) (aufwenden müssen) **mit dem Auto braucht er zehn Minuten** it takes him ten minutes by car; **wie lange brauchst du dafür?** how long will it take you?; (im Allgemeinen) how long does it take you? (c) (benutzen, gebrauchen) use; **ich könnte es gut ~:** I could do with it ⊡ mod. V.; 2. Part **brauchen:** need; **du brauchst nicht zu helfen** there is no need [for you] to help; **du brauchst doch nicht gleich zu weinen** there's no need to start crying

Brauchtum /'braʊxtuːm/ das; ~s, Brauchtümer custom

Braue die; ~, ~n [eye]brow

brauen tr. V. brew

Brauerei die; ~, ~en brewery

braun Adj. brown; ~ **werden** (sonnengebräunt) get a tan; ~ **gebrannt** [sun]-tanned

Braun das; ~s, ~, (ugs.) ~s brown

Braun·bär der brown bear

Bräune die; ~: [sun]tan

bräunen tr. V. (a) tan; **sich** ~: get a tan (b) (Kochk.) brown

braun-, Braun-: *~**gebrannt** ▶ BRAUN; ~**kohle** die brown coal; lignite

bräunlich Adj. brownish

Bräunung die; ~, ~en browning

Braus ▶ SAUS

Brause die; ~, ~n (a) fizzy drink; (~pulver) sherbet (b) (veralt.: Dusche) shower

brausen ⊡ itr. V. (a) ⟨wind, water, etc.⟩ roar (b) (sich schnell bewegen) race (c) auch refl.: ▶ DUSCHEN 1; ⊡ tr. V. ▶ DUSCHEN 2

Brause-: ~**pulver** das sherbet; ~**tablette** die effervescent tablet

Braut die; ~, Bräute bride

Bräutigam der; ~s, ~e [bride]groom

Braut-: ~**jungfer** die bridesmaid; ~**kleid** das wedding dress; ~**paar** das bride and groom

brav ⊡ Adj. (a) (artig) good (b) (redlich) honest ⊡ adv. **nun iss schön ~ deine Suppe** be a good boy/girl and eat up your soup

bravo /'braːvo/ Interj. bravo

Bravo das; ~s, ~s cheer

Bravo·ruf der cheer

BRD Abk. = **Bundesrepublik Deutschland** FRG

Brech-: ~**bohne** die green bean; ~**eisen** das crowbar

brechen ⊡ unr. tr. V. (a) break; **sich** (Dat.) **den Arm/das Genick** ~: break one's arm/ neck (b) (ablenken) break ⟨waves⟩; refract ⟨light⟩

---

*old spelling - see note on page xiv

(c) (bezwingen) overcome ⟨*resistance*⟩; break ⟨*will, silence, record, blockade, etc.*⟩
(d) (nicht einhalten) break ⟨*agreement, contract, promise, the law, etc.*⟩
(e) (ugs.: erbrechen) bring up
2 *unr. itr. V.* **(a)** *mit sein* break; **brechend voll sein** be full to bursting
(b) mit jmdm. ~: break with sb.
(c) *mit sein* **durch etw. ~:** break through sth.
(d) (ugs.: sich erbrechen) throw up
3 *unr. refl. V.* ⟨*waves etc.*⟩ break; ⟨*rays etc.*⟩ be refracted

Brẹcher *der; ~s, ~:* breaker

Brẹch-: **~mittel** *das* emetic; **~reiz** *der* nausea; **~stange** *die* crowbar

Bredouille /bre'dʊljə/ *die; ~, ~n* (ugs.) **in der ~ sein** *od.* **sitzen** be in real trouble; **in die ~ kommen** get into real trouble

Brei *der; ~[e]s, ~e* (Hafer~) porridge (Brit.), oatmeal (Amer.) *no indef. art.;* (Reis~) rice pudding; (Grieß~) semolina *no indef. art.*

breiig *Adj.* mushy

breit **1** *Adj.* **(a)** wide; broad, wide ⟨*hips, face, shoulders, forehead, etc.*⟩; **etw. ~er machen** widen sth.; **die Beine ~ machen** open one's legs; **ein 5 cm ~er Saum** a hem 5 cm wide
(b) (groß) **die ~e Masse** the general public
(c) sich ~ machen take up room; (sich ausbreiten) be spreading
2 *adv.* **~ gebaut** sturdily built

Breit·band *das* (DV) broadband

breit·beinig **1** *Adj.* rolling ⟨*gait*⟩
2 *adv.* with one's legs apart

Breite *die; ~, ~n* **(a)** ▶ BREIT 1A: width; breadth
(b) (Geogr.) latitude

breiten (geh.) *tr., refl. V.* spread

Breiten-: **~grad** *der* degree of latitude; parallel (~kreis); **~kreis** *der* parallel

breit-, Breit-: **~|machen* ▶ BREIT 1C; **~schult[e]rig** *Adj.* broad-shouldered; **~seite** *die* long side; (eines Schiffes) side; *~|treten unr. tr. V.* (ugs. abwertend) go on about; **~wand** *die* (Kino) big screen

Bremen *(das); ~s* Bremen

Brems-: **~backe** *die* brake shoe; **~belag** *der* brake lining

Brẹmse[1] *die; ~, ~n* brake

Brẹmse[2] *die; ~, ~n* (Insekt) horsefly

brẹmsen *tr. V.* **(a)** *auch itr.* brake
(b) (fig.) slow down ⟨*rate, development, production, etc.*⟩; restrict ⟨*imports etc.*⟩

Brẹms-: **~klotz** *der* brake pad; **~licht** *das* brake light; **~pedal** *das* brake pedal; **~spur** *die* skid mark; **~weg** *der* braking distance; **~zug** *der* brake cable

brẹnn·bar *Adj.* combustible

brẹnnen **1** *unr. itr. V.* **(a)** burn; ⟨*house etc.*⟩ be on fire; **schnell/leicht ~:** catch fire quickly/easily; **es brennt!** fire!
(b) (glühen) be alight

(c) (leuchten) be on; **das Licht ~ lassen** leave the light on
(d) die Sonne brannte the sun was burning down
(e) (schmerzen) ⟨*wound etc.*⟩ sting; ⟨*feet etc.*⟩ be sore
(f) darauf ~, etw. zu tun be dying to do sth.
2 *unr. tr. V.* **(a)** burn ⟨*hole, pattern, etc.*⟩; **einem Tier ein Zeichen ins Fell ~:** brand an animal
(b) (mit Hitze behandeln) fire ⟨*porcelain etc.*⟩; distil ⟨*spirits*⟩
(c) (rösten) roast ⟨*coffee beans, almonds, etc.*⟩

brẹnnend **1** *Adj.* (auch fig.) burning; lighted ⟨*cigarette*⟩; urgent ⟨*topic*⟩
2 *adv.* **es interessiert mich ~, ob …:** I'm dying to know whether …

Brẹnner *der; ~s, ~:* burner

Brẹnnerei *die; ~, ~en* distillery

*****Brẹnnnessel** *die; ~, ~n* ▶ BRENNNESSEL

Brẹnn-: **~glas** *das* burning glass; **~holz** *das* firewood; **~material** *das* fuel; **~nessel** *die* stinging nettle; **~ofen** *der* kiln; **~punkt** *der* focus; **~spiritus** *der* methylated spirits *pl.;* **~stoff** *der* fuel; **~weite** *die* (Optik) focal length

brẹnzlig *Adj.* **(a)** ⟨*smell, taste, etc.*⟩ of burning *not pred.;*
(b) (ugs.: gefährlich) dicey (coll.)

Brẹsche *die; ~, ~n* gap; breach; **[für jmdn.] in die ~ springen** stand in [for sb.]

Brẹtt *das; ~[e]s, ~er* board; (lang und dick) plank; (Diele) floorboard; **schwarzes ~:** noticeboard; **ein ~ vor dem Kopf haben** (fig. ugs.) be thick

Brẹtter-: **~wand** *die* wooden partition; **~zaun** *der* wooden fence

Brẹtt·spiel *das* board game

Brẹzel *die; ~, ~n* pretzel

Bridge /brɪtʃ:/ *das; ~:* bridge

Brief *der; ~[e]s, ~e*

Brief-: **~beschwerer** *der; ~~s, ~~:* paperweight; **~block** *der; Pl. ~~s od. ~~blöcke** writing pad; **~bogen** *der* sheet of writing paper; **~freund** *der,* **~freundin** *die* penfriend; pen pal (coll.); **~freundschaft** *die* penfriendship; **~geheimnis** *das* privacy of the post; **~karte** *die* correspondence card; **~kasten** *der* **(a)** postbox; **(b)** (privat) letter box; **~kopf** *der* **(a)** letter heading; **(b)** (aufgedruckt) letterhead; **~kuvert** *das* (veralt.) ▶ ~UMSCHLAG

brieflich **1** *Adj.* written
2 *adv.* by letter

Brief·marke *die* [postage] stamp

Briefmarken-: **~album** *das* stamp album; **~sammler** *der,* **~sammlerin** *die* stamp collector; **~sammlung** *die* stamp collection

Brief-: **~öffner** *der* letter-opener; **~papier** *das* writing paper; **~partner** ⋯⋗

der, ~**partnerin** *die* penfriend;
~**schreiber** *der,* ~**schreiberin** *die*
[letter-]writer; ~**tasche** *die* wallet;
~**taube** *die* carrier pigeon; ~**träger** *der*
postman; letter-carrier (Amer.); ~**trägerin**
die postwoman; [female] letter-carrier (Amer.);
~**umschlag** *der* envelope; ~**waage** *die*
letter scales *pl.;* ~**wahl** *die* postal vote;
~**wechsel** *der* correspondence

Bries *das;* ~**es,** ~**e** (Kochk.) sweetbreads *pl.*

briet *1. u. 3. Pers. Sg. Prät. v.* BRATEN

Brigade *die;* ~, ~**n** (Milit.) brigade

Brikett *das;* ~**s,** ~**s** briquette

brillant /brɪl'jant/ 1 *Adj.* brilliant
2 *adv.* brilliantly

Brillant *der;* ~**en,** ~**en** brilliant

Brillant-: ~**ring** *der* (brilliant-cut) diamond
ring; ~**schmuck** *der* (brilliant-cut) diamond
jewellery

Brillanz /brɪl'jants:/ *die;* ~: brilliance

Brille *die;* ~, ~**n (a)** glasses *pl.;* spectacles
pl.; **eine** ~: a pair of glasses *or* spectacles;
eine ~ **tragen** wear glasses *or* spectacles
(b) (ugs.: Klosettbrille) [lavatory] seat

Brillen-: ~**etui** *das,* ~**futteral** *das*
glasses case; spectacle case; ~**glas** *das*
[spectacle] lens; ~**schlange** *die* spectacled
cobra; ~**träger** *der,* ~**trägerin** *die*
person who wears glasses; ~**träger/-trägerin**
sein wear glasses

Brimborium *das;* ~**s** (ugs. abwertend) hoo-ha
(coll.)

bringen *unr. tr. V.* **(a)** (her~) bring; (hin~)
take; **jmdm. Glück/Unglück** ~: bring sb.
[good] luck/bad luck; **jmdm. eine Nachricht**
~: bring sb. news
(b) (begleiten) take; **jmdn. nach Hause/zum**
Bahnhof ~: take sb. home/to the station
(c) es zu etwas/nichts ~: get somewhere/get
nowhere
(d) jmdn. ins Gefängnis ~ ⟨crime, misdeed⟩
land sb. in gaol; **jmdn. wieder auf den**
rechten Weg ~ (fig.) get sb. back on the
straight and narrow; **jmdn. zum Lachen/zur**
Verzweiflung ~: make sb. laugh/drive sb. to
despair; **jmdn. dazu** ~, **etw. zu tun** get sb. to
do sth.; **etw. hinter sich** ~ (ugs.) get sth. over
and done with
(e) jmdn. um seinen Besitz ~: do sb. out of
his property
(f) (präsentieren) present; (veröffentlichen)
publish; (senden) broadcast
(g) ein Opfer ~: make a sacrifice
(h) einen großen Gewinn/hohe Zinsen ~:
make a large profit/earn high interest
(i) das bringt es mit sich, dass …: that
means that …
(j) (verursachen) cause

brisant *Adj.* explosive

Brisanz *die;* ~: explosiveness

Brise *die;* ~, ~**n** breeze

Britannien (*das*); ~**s** Britain; (hist.)
Britannia

Brite *der;* ~**n,** ~**n** Briton; **die** ~**n** the
British; **er ist [kein]** ~: he is [not] British

Britin *die;* ~, ~**nen** Briton; British girl/
woman

britisch *Adj.* British; **die Britischen Inseln**
the British Isles

bröckelig *Adj.* crumbly

bröckeln 1 *itr. V.* **(a)** crumble
(b) *mit sein* **von der Wand** ~: crumble away
from the wall
2 *tr. V.* crumble

Brocken *der;* ~**s,** ~ (von Brot) hunk; (von
Fleisch) chunk; (von Lehm, Kohle, Erde) lump; **ein**
paar ~ **Englisch** (fig.) a smattering of English

brodeln *itr. V.* bubble

Broiler /'brɔy:lɐ/ *der;* ~**s,** ~ (regional)
▶ BRATHÄHNCHEN

Brokat *der;* ~**[e]s,** ~**e** brocade

Brokkoli *der;* ~**s,** ~**[s]** broccoli

Brom·beere *die* blackberry

Bronchie /'brɔncɪə/ *die;* ~, ~**n** bronchial
tube

Bronchitis *die;* ~, bronchitis

Bronze /'brõːsə/ *die;* ~: bronze

Bronze-: ~**medaille** *die* bronze medal;
~**zeit** *die* Bronze Age

Brosche *die;* ~, ~**n** brooch

Broschüre *die;* ~, ~**n** booklet

Brösel *der;* ~**s,** ~: breadcrumb

bröselig *Adj.* crumbly

bröseln *itr. V.* crumble

Brot *das;* ~**[e]s,** ~**e** bread *no pl., no indef.*
art.; (Laib) loaf [of bread]; (Scheibe) slice [of
bread]

Brot-: ~**aufstrich** *der* spread; ~**belag**
der topping; (im zusammengeklappten Brot) filling

Brötchen *das;* ~**s,** ~: roll

Brot-: ~**erwerb** *der* way to earn a living;
~**korb** *der* bread basket; ~**laib** *der* loaf [of
bread]; ~**messer** *das* bread knife;
~**rinde** *die* [bread] crust; ~**zeit** *die* (südd.)
(a) (Pause) [tea/coffee/lunch] break; **(b)**
(Vesper) snack; (Vesperbrot) sandwiches *pl.*

Browser /'brauzɐ/ *der;* ~**s,** ~ (DV) browser

Bruch *der;* ~**[e]s,** **Brüche (a)** break; **in die**
Brüche gehen (zerbrechen) get broken; (fig.)
break up
(b) (Med.: Knochen~) fracture; break
(c) (Med.: Eingeweide~) hernia
(d) (fig.) (eines Versprechens) breaking; (eines
Abkommens, Gesetzes) violation
(e) (Math.) fraction

brüchig *Adj.* **(a)** brittle ⟨rock, brickwork⟩
(b) (fig.) crumbling ⟨relationship, marriage,
etc.⟩

Bruch-: ~**landung** *die* crash-landing;
~**rechnen** *das* fractions *pl.;* ~**strich** *der*
fraction line; ~**stück** *das* fragment; ~**teil**
der fraction; **im** ~**teil einer Sekunde** in a
split second

Brücke *die;* ~, ~n (a) (auch: Kommandobrücke, Zahnmed., Bodenturnen, Ringen) bridge
(b) (Landungsbrücke) gangway
(c) (Teppich) rug

Brücken-: ~**bogen** *der* arch [of a/the bridge]; ~**geländer** *das* parapet; ~**kopf** *der* (Milit., auch fig.) bridgehead

Bruder *der;* ~s, Brüder brother

Brüderchen *das;* ~s, ~: little brother

brüderlich ⒈ *Adj.* brotherly
⒉ *adv.* in a brotherly way

Brüderlichkeit *die;* ~: brotherliness

Brüderschaft *die;* ~: [mit jmdm.] ~ trinken drink to close friendship [with sb.] (*agreeing to use the familiar 'du' form*)

Brühe *die;* ~, ~n (a) stock; (als Suppe) clear soup
(b) (ugs. abwertend) (Getränk) muck; (verschmutztes Wasser) filthy water

brühen *tr. V.* (a) blanch
(b) (auf~) brew, make ⟨*tea*⟩; make ⟨*coffee*⟩

brüh-, Brüh-: ~**warm** *Adj.* etw. ~warm weitererzählen (ugs.) pass sth. on straight away; ~**würfel** *der* stock cube

brüllen ⒈ *itr. V.* (a) ⟨*bull, cow, etc.*⟩ bellow; ⟨*lion, tiger, etc.*⟩ roar
(b) (ugs.) (schreien) roar; (weinen) howl
⒉ *tr. V.* yell

brummen *tr., itr. V.* (a) ⟨*insect*⟩ buzz; ⟨*bear*⟩ growl; ⟨*engine etc.*⟩ drone
(b) (unmelodisch singen) drone
(c) (mürrisch sprechen) mumble

Brummer *der;* ~s, ~ (ugs.) (a) (Fliege) bluebottle
(b) (LKW) heavy lorry (Brit.) *or* truck

brummig *Adj.* (ugs.) grumpy

Brumm-: ~**kreisel** *der* humming top; ~**schädel** *der* (ugs.) thick head

brünett *Adj.* dark-haired ⟨*person*⟩; dark ⟨*hair*⟩

Brünette *die;* ~, ~n brunette

Brunnen *der;* ~s, ~ (a) well
(b) (Springbrunnen) fountain

Brunnen-kresse *die* watercress

Brunst *die;* ~, Brünste (von männlichen Tieren) rut; (von weiblichen Tieren) heat

Brunst·zeit *die* (bei männlichen Tieren) rutting season; (bei weiblichen Tieren) [season of] heat

brüsk ⒈ *Adj.* brusque
⒉ *adv.* brusquely

brüskieren *tr. V.* offend; (stärker) insult; (schneiden) snub

Brüssel (*das*); ~s Brussels

Brust *die;* ~, Brüste (a) chest
(b) (der Frau) breast
(c) (Hähnchen~) breast; (Rinder~) brisket
(d) (Brustschwimmen) breaststroke

brüsten *refl. V.* sich mit etw. ~: boast about sth.

brust-, Brust-: ~**kasten** (ugs.) chest;
~**korb** *der* (Anat.) thorax (Anat.); ~**krebs** *der* breast cancer; ~**schwimmen** *unr. itr. V.; nur im Inf.* do [the] breaststroke; ~**schwimmen** *das* breaststroke; ~**tasche** *die* breast pocket

Brüstung *die;* ~, ~en parapet; (Balkon~) balustrade

Brust·warze *die* nipple

Brut *die;* ~, ~en (a) brooding
(b) (Jungtiere, auch scherzh.: Kinder) brood

brutal ⒈ *Adj.* brutal; violent ⟨*attack, programme, etc.*⟩; brute ⟨*force, strength*⟩
⒉ *adv.* brutally

Brutalität *die;* ~, ~en (a) brutality
(b) (Handlung) act of brutality

brüten *itr. V.* (a) brood
(b) (grübeln) ponder (über + *Dat.* over); **brütend:** ~ heiß: (ugs.) boiling hot

Brüter *der;* ~s, ~ (Kernphysik) breeder

Brut-: ~**kasten** *der* incubator; ~**reaktor** *der* (Kernphysik) breeder reactor; ~**stätte** *die* (auch fig.) breeding ground

brutto *Adv.* gross

Brutto-: ~**einkommen** *das* gross income; ~**gehalt** *das* gross salary; ~**sozialprodukt** *das* (Wirtsch.) gross national product

brutzeln ⒈ *itr. V.* sizzle
⒉ *tr. V.* (ugs.) fry [up]

BSE /beːsˈeː/ *die;* ~: BSE

Bub *der;* ~en, ~en (südd., österr., schweiz.) boy; lad

Bube *der;* ~n, ~n (Kartenspiele) jack; knave

Bubi *der;* ~s, ~s (a) [little] boy *or* lad
(b) (salopp: Schnösel) young lad

Buch *das;* ~[e]s, Bücher book; (Dreh~) script; über etw. (*Akk.*) ~ führen keep a record of sth.

Buch-: ~**besprechung** *die* book review; ~**binder** *der*, ~**binderin** *die;* ~~, ~~nen bookbinder; ~**druck** *der* letterpress printing

Buche *die;* ~, ~n (a) beech [tree]
(b) (Holz) beech[wood]

Buch·ecker *die;* ~, ~n beech nut

buchen *tr. V.* (a) enter
(b) (vorbestellen) book

Bücher·brett *das* bookshelf

Bücherei *die;* ~, ~en library

Bücher-: ~**regal** *das* bookshelves *pl.;* ~**schrank** *der* bookcase; ~**wurm** *der* (scherzh.) bookworm; ~**verbrennung** *die* burning of books

Buch-: ~**fink** *der* chaffinch; ~**führung** *die* bookkeeping; ~**halter** *der*, ~**halterin** *die* bookkeeper; ~**haltung** *die* (a) accountancy; (b) (Abteilung) accounts department; ~**händler** *der*, ~**händlerin** *die* bookseller; ~**handlung** *die* bookshop; ~**klub** *der* book club; ~**laden** *der; Pl.* ~läden ▸ ~HANDLUNG; ~**messe** *die* book fair; ~**rücken** *der* spine

Buchs·baum /ˈbʊks-/ *der* box [tree]
Buchse /ˈbʊksə/ *die;* ~, ~n **(a)** (Elektrot.) socket
(b) (Technik) bush
Büchse /ˈbʏksə/ *die;* ~, ~n **(a)** tin
(b) (ugs.: Sammel~) [collecting] box
(c) (Gewehr) rifle; (Schrot~) shotgun
Büchsen- ▶ DOSEN-
Buchstabe *der;* ~ns, ~n letter; (Druckw.) character; **ein großer/kleiner** ~: a capital [letter]/small letter
buchstabieren *tr. V.* spell
buchstäblich *Adv.* literally
Bucht *die;* ~, ~en bay
Buchung *die;* ~, ~en **(a)** entry
(b) (Vorbestellung) booking
Buckel *der;* ~s, ~ **(a)** hump; **einen** ~ **machen** ⟨cat⟩ arch its back; ⟨person⟩ hunch one's shoulders
(b) (ugs.: Rücken) back; **rutsch mir den** ~ **runter!** (salopp) get lost! (coll.)
buckeln *itr. V.* (ugs.) bow and scrape; **vor jmdm.** ~: kowtow to sb.
bücken *refl. V.* bend down
bucklig *Adj.* hunchbacked
Bucklige *der/die; adj. Dekl.* hunchback
Bückling¹ *der;* ~s, ~e (ugs. scherzh.: Verbeugung) bow
Bückling² *der;* ~s, ~e (Hering) bloater
buddeln *itr., tr. V.* (ugs.) dig
Buddha /ˈbʊda/ *der;* ~s, ~s Buddha
Buddhismus *der;* ~: Buddhism *no art.*
Buddhist *der;* ~en, ~en, **Buddhistin** *die;* ~, ~nen Buddhist
buddhistisch *Adj.* Buddhist *attrib.*
Bude *die;* ~, ~n **(a)** kiosk; (Markt~) stall; (Jahrmarkts~) booth
(b) (Bau~) hut
(c) (ugs.: Haus) dump (coll.); (Zimmer) room; digs *pl.* (Brit. coll.)
Budget /byˈdʒeː/ *das;* ~s, ~s budget
Büfett *das;* ~[e]s, ~s *od.* ~e **(a)** sideboard
(b) (Schanktisch) bar
(c) (Verkaufstisch) counter
(d) kaltes ~: cold buffet
Büffel *der;* ~s, ~: buffalo
büffeln (ugs.) ⟨1⟩ *itr. V.* swot (Brit. coll.); cram ⟨2⟩ *tr. V.* swot up (Brit. coll.); cram
Buffet /byˈfeː/ *das;* ~s, ~s ▶ BÜFETT
Bug *der;* ~[e]s, ~e *u.* Büge bow
Bügel *der;* ~s, ~ **(a)** (Kleider~) hanger
(b) (Brillen~) earpiece
(c) (an einer Tasche, Geldbörse) frame
bügel-, Bügel-: ~**brett** *das* ironing board; ~**eisen** *das* iron; ~**falte** *die* [trouser] crease; ~**frei** *Adj.* non-iron
bügeln *tr., itr. V.* iron
bugsieren /bʊˈksiːrən/ *tr. V.* (ugs.) shift; manœuvre; steer ⟨person⟩

buh *Interj.* boo
Buh *das;* ~s, ~s (ugs.) boo
buhen *itr. V.* (ugs.) boo
buhlen *itr. V.* (geh. abwertend) **um jmds. Gunst** ~: court sb.'s favour
Buh·mann *der* whipping boy
Buhne /ˈbuːnə/ *die;* ~, ~n groyne
Bühne *die;* ~, ~n **(a)** stage; **ein Stück auf die** ~ **bringen** put on *or* stage a play
(b) (Theater) theatre
bühnen-, Bühnen-: ~**arbeiter** *der,* ~**arbeiterin** *die* stagehand; ~**ausstattung** *die* stage set; ~**bild** *das* [stage] set; ~**bildner** *der;* ~~s, ~~, ~**bildnerin** *die;* ~~, ~~nen stage designer; ~**reif** *Adj.* ⟨play etc.⟩ ready for the stage; ⟨imitation etc.⟩ worthy of the stage; dramatic ⟨entrance etc.⟩
Buh·ruf *der* boo
buk *1. u. 3. Pers. Sg. Prät. v.* BACKEN
Bukett *das;* ~s, ~s *od.* ~e (geh.) bouquet
Bulette *die;* ~, ~n (bes. berl.) rissole
Bulgare *der;* ~n, ~n Bulgarian
Bulgarien /bʊlˈgaːriən/ *(das);* ~s Bulgaria
Bulgarin *die;* ~, ~nen Bulgarian
bulgarisch *Adj.* Bulgarian
Bull-: ~auge *das* circular porthole; ~**dogge** *die* bulldog; ~**dozer** /-doːzɐ/ *der;* ~~s, ~~: bulldozer
Bulle *der;* ~n, ~n **(a)** bull
(b) (salopp: Polizist) cop (coll.)
Bullen·hitze *die* (ugs.) sweltering *or* boiling heat
Bulletin /bylˈtɛ̃ː/ *das;* ~s, ~s bulletin
bullig ⟨1⟩ *Adj.* **(a)** beefy ⟨person, appearance, etc.⟩; chunky ⟨car⟩
(b) (drückend) sweltering ⟨heat⟩
⟨2⟩ *adv.* ~ **heiß** boiling hot
Bull·terrier *der* bull terrier
bum *Interj.* bang
Bumerang *der;* ~s, ~e *od.* ~s boomerang
Bummel *der;* ~s, ~ **(a)** stroll (**durch** around)
(b) (durch Lokale) pub crawl (coll.)
Bummelei *die;* ~, ~en (ugs.) **(a)** dawdling
(b) (Faulenzerei) loafing about
bummelig (ugs.) ⟨1⟩ *Adj.* **(a)** slow
(b) (nachlässig) slipshod
⟨2⟩ *adv.* **(a)** slowly
(b) (nachlässig) in a slipshod way
bummeln *itr. V.* **(a)** mit sein stroll (**durch** around); **durch die Kneipen** ~: go on a pub crawl (Brit. coll.)
(b) (trödeln) dawdle
(c) (faulenzen) laze about
bums *Interj.* bang
Bums *der;* ~es, ~e (ugs.) bang; (dumpfer) thud
bumsen *itr. V.* (ugs.) **(a)** bang; (dumpfer) thump; *unpers.* **es bumste ganz furchtbar** there was a terrible bang/thud
(b) mit sein (stoßen) bang

Bund[1] *der;* ~[e]s, Bünde (a) (Vereinigung) association; (Bündnis, Pakt) alliance
(b) (föderativer Staat) federation
(c) (an Röcken, Hosen) waistband
Bund[2] *das;* ~[e]s, ~e bunch
Bündchen *das;* ~s, ~ band
Bündel *der;* ~s, ~ bundle
bündeln *tr. V.* bundle up ⟨*newspapers, old clothes, rags, etc.*⟩; tie ⟨*banknotes etc.*⟩ into bundles/a bundle; tie ⟨*flowers, radishes, carrots, etc.*⟩ into bunches/a bunch; sheave ⟨*straw, hay, etc.*⟩
Bundes- federal; (in Namen, Titeln) Federal
bundes-, Bundes-: ~**bürger** *der,* ~**bürgerin** *die* (veralt.) West German citizen; ~**deutsch** *Adj.* (veralt.) West German; ~**ebene** *die:* auf ~ebene at federal *or* national level; ~**gerichtshof** *der* Federal Supreme Court; ~**kabinett** *das* Federal Cabinet; ~**kanzler** *der* (a) Federal Chancellor; (b) (schweiz.) Chancellor of the Confederation; ~**land** *das* [federal] state; (österr.) province; ~**liga** *die* national division; ~**minister** *der,* ~**ministerin** *die* Federal Minister; ~**ministerium** *das* Federal Ministry; ~**präsident** *der,* ~**präsidentin** *die* (a) [Federal] President; (b) (schweiz.) President of the Confederation; ~**rat** *der* Bundesrat; ~**regierung** *die* Federal Government; ~**republik** *die* federal republic; die ~**republik Deutschland** The Federal Republic of Germany; ~**straße** *die* federal highway; ≈ A road (Brit.); ~**tag** *der* Bundestag
Bundestags-: ~**abgeordnete** *der/die* member of parliament; member of the Bundestag; ~**präsident** *der,* ~**präsidentin** *die* President of the Bundestag; ~**wahl** *die* parliamentary *or* general election
bundes-, Bundes-: ~**trainer** *der,* ~**trainerin** *die* national team manager; ~**verfassungs-gericht** *das* Federal Constitutional Court; ~**verwaltungs-gericht** *das* Supreme Administrative Court; ~**wehr** *die* [Federal] Armed Forces *pl.;* ~**weit** *Adj., adv.* nationwide
Bund-: ~**falten** *Pl.* pleats; ~**falten-hose** *die* pleat[ed]-front trousers *pl.;* ~**hose** *die* knee breeches
bündig [1] *Adj.* (a) succinct
(b) (schlüssig) conclusive
[2] *adv.* (a) succinctly
(b) (schlüssig) conclusively
Bündnis *das;* ~ses, ~se alliance
Bungalow /ˈbʊŋɡalo/ *der;* ~s, ~s bungalow
Bunker *der;* ~s, ~ (a) bunker
(b) (Luftschutzbunker) air-raid shelter
bunt [1] *Adj.* (a) colourful; (farbig) coloured; ~e **Farben/Kleidung** bright colours/brightly coloured clothes
(b) (fig.) varied ⟨*programme etc.*⟩

[2] *adv.* (a) colourfully; ~ **bemalt** brightly painted
(b) (fig.) **ein ~ gemischtes Programm** a varied programme
bunt-, Bunt-: ***~**bemalt** ▶ BUNT 2A; ~**papier** *das* coloured paper; ~**specht** *der* spotted woodpecker; ~**stift** *der* coloured pencil/crayon
Bürde *die;* ~, ~n (geh.) weight; load
Burg *die;* ~, ~en (a) castle
(b) (Strand~) wall of sand
Bürge *der;* ~n, ~n guarantor
bürgen *itr. V.* (a) für jmdn./etw. ~: vouch for sb./sth.
(b) (fig.) guarantee
Bürger *der;* ~s, ~, **Bürgerin** *die;* ~, ~nen citizen
Bürger-: ~**initiative** *die* citizens' action group; ~**krieg** *der* civil war
bürgerlich *Adj.* (a) (staats~) civil ⟨*rights, marriage, etc.*⟩; civic ⟨*duties*⟩
(b) (dem Bürgertum zugehörig) middle-class; die ~e **Küche** good plain cooking
(c) (Polit.) non-socialist; (nicht marxistisch) non-Marxist
bürger-, Bürger-: ~**meister** *der,* ~**meisterin** *die* mayor; ~**nah** *Adj.* which/who reflects the general public's interests *postpos., not pred.;* ~**pflicht** *die* duty as a citizen; ~**steig** *der;* ~~s, ~~e pavement (Brit.); sidewalk (Amer.)
Bürgertum /ˈ--tuːm/ *das;* ~s (a) middle class
(b) (Großbürgertum) bourgeoisie
Bürgin *die;* ~, ~nen ▶ BÜRGE
Bürgschaft *die;* ~, ~en (a) guarantee
(b) (Betrag) penalty
Büro *das;* ~s, ~s office
Büro-: ~**angestellte** *der/die* office worker; ~**artikel** *der* item of office equipment; ~**haus** *das* office block; ~**klammer** *die* paper clip; ~**kraft** *die* clerical worker
Bürokrat *der;* ~en, ~en bureaucrat
Bürokratie *die;* ~, ~n bureaucracy
Bürokratin *die;* ~, ~nen bureaucrat
bürokratisch [1] *Adj.* bureaucratic
[2] *adv.* bureaucratically
Büro-technik *die* office technology
Bürschchen /ˈbʏrʃçən/ *das;* ~, ~: little fellow
Bursche *der;* ~n, ~n (a) boy; lad
(b) (abwertend: Kerl) guy (coll.)
burschikos [1] *Adj.* (a) sporty ⟨*look, clothes*⟩; [tom]boyish ⟨*behaviour, girl, haircut*⟩
(b) (ungezwungen) casual ⟨*comment, behaviour, etc.*⟩
[2] *adv.* (a) [tom]boyishly
(b) (ungezwungen) in a colloquial way
Bürste *die;* ~, ~n brush
bürsten *tr. V.* brush

Bus *der;* ~ses, ~se bus

Bus-bahnhof *der* bus station

Busch *der;* ~[e]s, Büsche bush; **auf den** ~ **klopfen** (fig. ugs.) sound things out

Büschel *das;* ~s, ~: tuft; (von Heu, Stroh) handful

Busen *der;* ~s, ~ bust

Bus-: ~**fahrer** *der,* ~**fahrerin** *die* bus driver; ~**haltestelle** *die* bus stop; ~**linie** *die* bus route

Bussard *der;* ~s, ~e buzzard

Buße *die;* ~, ~n (Rel.) penance *no art.*

büßen ① *tr. V.* (a) atone for
(b) (fig.) pay for
② *itr. V.* (a) **für etw.** ~: atone for sth.
(b) (fig.) pay

Buß-geld *das* (Rechtsw.) fine

Buß- und Bettag *der* (ev. Kirche) Day of Prayer and Repentance (*Wednesday eleven days before the first Sunday in Advent*)

Büsten-halter *der* bra; brassière (formal)

Butan-gas *das* butane gas

Butt *der;* ~[e]s, ~e flounder; butt

Bütten-papier *das* handmade paper (*with deckle edge*)

Butter *die;* ~: butter; **es ist alles in** ~ (ugs.) everything's fine

butter-, Butter-: ~**berg** *der* (ugs.) butter mountain; ~**blume** *die* (Sumpfdotterblume) marsh marigold; (Hahnenfuß) buttercup; ~**brot** *das* slice of bread and butter; (zugeklappt) sandwich; ~**creme** *die* buttercream; ~**milch** *die* buttermilk; ~**weich** *Adj.* beautifully soft

b. w. *Abk.* = **bitte wenden** p.t.o.

Bypass /'baɪpɑs/ *der;* ~es, Bypässe (Med.) bypass

Byte /baɪt/ *das;* ~s, ~[s] (DV) byte

bzw. *Abk.* = **beziehungsweise**

Cc

c, C /ts̬eː/ *das;* ~, ~: (a) (Buchstabe) c/C
(b) (Musik) [key of] C

C *Abk.* = **Celsius** C

ca. *Abk.* = **cirka** c.

Café *das;* ~s, ~s café

Cafeteria *die;* ~, ~s cafeteria

cal *Abk.* = **[Gramm]kalorie** cal.

Callboy /'kɔːlbɔɪ/ *der;* ~s, ~s call-boy

Callgirl /'kɔːlgəːl/ *das;* ~s, ~s call girl

Camp /kɛmp/ *das;* ~s, ~s camp

campen *itr. V.* camp

Camping *das;* ~s camping

Camping-: ~**bus** *der* motor caravan; camper; ~**kocher** *der* camping stove; ~**platz** *der* campsite; campground (Amer.)

Cannabis /'kanabɪs/ *der;* ~: cannabis

Cantilever-bremse /'kæntɪliːvɐ-/ *die* cantilever brake

Caravan /'ka(ː)ravan/ *der;* ~s, ~s (Wohnwagen) caravan; trailer (Amer.)

Cashflow /kæʃ'floʊ/ *der;* ~s (Wirtsch.) [gross] cash flow

Castor-: ~**behälter** *der* Castor container; Castor cask; ~**transport** *der* Castor transport

Catcher /'kɛtʃɐ/ *der;* ~s, ~, **Catcherin** *die;* ~, ~nen all-in wrestler

Cayenne-pfeffer /ka'jɛn-/ *der* cayenne [pepper]

CD /tseːˈdeː/ *die;* ~, ~s CD

CD-Brenner *der;* ~s, ~ (DV) CD burner; CD writer

CD-ROM /tse̬eːdeːˈrɔm/ *die;* ~, ~[s] (DV) CD-ROM

CD-ROM-Laufwerk *das* (DV) CD-ROM drive

CD-Spieler /tse̬eːˈdeː-/ *der* CD player

CDU *Abk.* = **Christlich-Demokratische Union [Deutschlands]** [German] Christian Democratic Party

C-Dur /'ts̬eː-/ *das* C major

Cellist /tʃɛˈlɪst/ *der;* ~en, ~en, **Cellistin** *die;* ~, ~nen cellist

Cello /'tʃɛlo/ *das;* ~s, ~s *od.* Celli cello

Celsius: 20 Grad ~: 20 degrees Celsius *or* centigrade

Cembalo /'tʃɛmbalo/ *das;* ~s, ~s *od.* Cembali harpsichord

Cent *der;* ~[s], ~[s] cent; **50** ~ 50 cents

Champagner /ʃam'panjɐ/ *der;* ~s, ~ champagne (from Champagne)

Champignon /'ʃampɪnjɔn/ *der;* ~s, ~s mushroom

Chance /'ʃãːsə/ *die;* ~, ~n (a) chance
(b) *Pl.* (Aussichten) prospects; [**bei jmdm**] ~n **haben** stand a chance [with sb.]

Chancen-gleichheit *die* (Soziol.) equality *no art.* of opportunity

---

*alte Schreibung - vgl. Hinweis auf S. xiv

Chaos /'k.../ *das;* ~: chaos *no art.*

Chaot /ka'oːt/ *der;* ~en, ~en, **Chaotin** *die;* ~, ~nen(a) (Politik) anarchist (trying to undermine society)
(b) (salopp: unordentlicher Mensch) **ein [furchtbarer]** ~ **sein** be [terribly] disorganized

chaotisch 1 *Adj.* chaotic
2 *adv.* chaotically; **es geht** ~ **zu** there is chaos

Charakter /ka.../ *der; ~s, ~e* /...'teːrə/ character

charakterisieren *tr. V.* characterize

charakteristisch *Adj.* characteristic (**für** of)

charakterlich 1 *Adj.* character *attrib.;* 2 *adv.* in [respect of] character

charakter·los *Adj.* unprincipled; (niederträchtig) despicable; (labil) spineless

Charisma /'çaˑrɪsma/ *das;* ~s, Charismen charisma

charismatisch /çarɪs'maːtɪʃ/ *Adj.* charismatic

charmant /ʃar'mant/ 1 *Adj.* charming
2 *adv.* charmingly

Charme /ʃarm/ *der;* ~s charm

Charter- /'tʃartɐ-/: ~**flug** *der* charter flight; ~**maschine** *die* chartered aircraft

Charts /tʃarts/ *Pl.* charts

Chassis /ʃa'siː/ *das;* ~ /ʃa'siː(s),/ ~ /ʃa'siːs/ chassis

chatten /'tʃɛtn/ *itr. V.* (DV Jargon) chat

Chauffeur /ʃɔ'føːɐ/ *der;* ~s, ~e, **Chauffeurin** /ʃɔ'føːrɪn/ *die;* ~, ~nen driver; (privat angestellt) chauffeur

checken /'tʃɛkn/ *tr. V.* (a) (bes. Technik: kontrollieren) check; examine
(b) (salopp: begreifen) twig (coll.); (bemerken) spot; **ich habe das noch nicht gecheckt** I haven't got it yet

Check·liste *die* checklist; (Passagierliste) passenger list

Chef /ʃɛf/ *der;* ~s, ~s, **Chefin** /'ʃɛfɪn/ *die;* ~, ~nen (Leiter[in]) head; (der Polizei, des Generalstabs) chief; (einer Partei, Bande) leader; (Vorgesetzte[r]) superior; boss (coll.)

Chef-: ~**koch** *der,* ~**köchin** *die* chef; head cook; ~**sekretärin** *die* director's secretary

Chemie *die;* ~ (a) chemistry *no art.;* (b) (ugs.: Chemikalien) chemicals *pl.*

Chemikalie /çemi'kaːliə/ *die;* ~, ~n chemical

Chemiker *der;* ~s, ~, **Chemikerin** *die;* ~, ~nen (graduate) chemist

chemisch 1 *Adj.* chemical
2 *adv.* chemically

Chemo·therapie *die* (Med.) chemotherapy

Chicorée /'ʃikore/ *der;* ~s *od. die;* ~: chicory

Chiffon /'ʃɪfõ/ *der;* ~s, ~s chiffon

Chiffre /'ʃɪfrə/ *die;* ~, ~n (a) (Zeichen) symbol
(b) (Geheimzeichen) cipher
(c) (in Annoncen) box number

Chile /'tʃiːle, 'çiːlə/ *(das);* ~s Chile

Chilene /tʃi'leːnə, çi'leːnə/ *der;* ~n, ~n, **Chilenin** *die;* ~, ~nen Chilean

chilenisch *Adj.* Chilean

Chili /'tʃiːli/ *der;* ~s, ~es (a) Pl. (Schoten) chillies
(b) (Gewürz) chilli [powder]

China *(das)* ~s China

Chinese *der;* ~n, ~n, **Chinesin** *die;* ~, ~nen Chinese

chinesisch *Adj.* Chinese

Chip /tʃɪp/ *der;* ~s, ~s (a) (Spielmarke) chip
(b) (Kartoffel~) [potato] crisp (Brit.) *or* (Amer.) chip
(c) (Elektronik) [micro]chip

Chip·karte *die* smart card

Chirurg *der;* ~en, ~en surgeon

Chirurgie *die;* ~, ~n (a) surgery *no art.;* (b) (Abteilung) surgical department; (Station) surgical ward

Chirurgin *die;* ~, ~nen surgeon

chirurgisch 1 *Adj.* surgical
2 *adv.* surgically; by surgery

Chlor /k.../ *das;* ~s chlorine

Chloroform /k.../ *das;* ~s chloroform

Chlorophyll /k.../ *das;* ~s chlorophyll

Cholera *die;* ~: cholera

cholerisch *Adj.* irascible; choleric ⟨temperament⟩

Cholesterin *das;* ~s cholesterol

Chor *der;* ~[e]s, Chöre /'køːrə/ (auch Archit.) choir; (in Oper, Sinfonie, Theater; Komposition) chorus; **im** ~ **rufen** shout in chorus

Choral *der;* ~s, Choräle (Kirchenlied) chorale

Choreograph /koreo'graːf/ *der;* ~en, ~en choreographer

Choreographie *die;* ~, ~n choreography

Choreographin *die;* ~, ~nen choreographer

choreographisch *Adj.* choreographic

Chose /'ʃoːzə/ *die;* ~, ~n (ugs.) stuff; **die ganze** ~: the whole lot (coll.) *or* (coll.) shoot

Chow-Chow /tʃaʊ tʃaʊ/ *der;* ~s, ~s chow

Christ /k.../ *der;* ~en, ~en Christian

Christ-: ~**baum** *der* (bes. südd.) Christmas tree; ~**demokrat** *der,* ~**demokratin** *die* (Politik) Christian Democrat

Christenheit *die;* ~: Christendom *no art.*

Christentum *das;* ~s Christianity *no art.;* (Glaube) Christian faith

Christin *die;* ~, ~nen Christian

Christ·kind *das* Christ-child (*as bringer of Christmas gifts*)

christlich 1 *Adj.* Christian
2 *adv.* in a [truly] Christian spirit

Christ-: ~**messe** *die* (kath. Rel.) Christmas ⋯

Mass; ~**mette** *die;* ~~, ~~**n** (kath. Rel.)
Christmas Mass; (ev. Rel.) midnight service
[on Christmas Eve]; ~**rose** *die* Christmas
rose; ~**stollen** *der* stollen; [German]
Christmas loaf (*with candied fruit, almonds,
etc.*)

Christus (*der*); ~ *od.* **Christi** Christ

Chrom /k.../ *das;* ~s chromium

Chromosom /k.../ *das;* ~s, ~en (Biol.)
chromosome

Chromosomen·satz *der* (Biol.)
chromosome set

Chronik /k.../ *die;* ~, ~en chronicle

chronisch *Adj.* chronic

Chrysantheme /k.../ *die;* ~, ~n
chrysanthemum

City /'sɪti/ *die;* ~, ~s city centre

clean /kliːn/ *Adj.* (ugs.) clean (coll.); ~
werden come off drugs

clever /'klɛvɐ/ [1] *Adj.* (raffiniert) shrewd;
(intelligent, geschickt) clever
[2] *adv.: s. Adj.:* shrewdly; cleverly

Clique /'klɪkə/ *die;* ~, ~n (a) (abwertend)
clique
(b) (Freundeskreis) set; (größere Gruppe) crowd
(coll.)

Clown /klaʊn/ *der;* ~s, ~s, **Clownin**
/'klaʊnɪn/ *die;* ~, ~nen clown

Club ▶ KLUB

cm *Abk.* = **Zentimeter** cm.

Co. *Abk.* = **Compagnie** Co.

Coach /koʊtʃ/ *der;* ~s, ~s (Sport) coach;
(bes. Fußball: Trainer) manager

coachen /'koʊtʃn̩/ *tr., itr. V.* (Sport) coach;
(Trainer sein) manage

Cockpit *das;* ~s, ~s cockpit

Cocktail /'kɔkteɪl/ *der;* ~s, ~s cocktail

Cognac (Ⓦ) /'kɔnjak/ *der;* ~s, ~s Cognac

Cola /'koːla/ *das;* ~s, ~s *od.* die; ~, ~s
(ugs.) Coke ®

Color- (Fot.) colour (*film, slide, etc.*)

Colt (Ⓦ) *der;* ~s, ~s Colt ® [revolver]

Comeback /kam'bɛk/ *das;* ~s, ~s
comeback; **ein** ~ **feiern** stage a comeback

Comic·heft *das* comic

Computer /kɔm'pjuːtɐ/ *der;* ~s, ~:
computer

computer·gestützt *Adj.* computer-aided;
computer-assisted

computerisieren *tr. V.* computerize
⟨*data, system*⟩; (aufbereiten) make ⟨*data*⟩
computer-compatible

computer-, Computer-: ~**raum** *der*
computer rooom; ~**spiel** *das* computer
game ~**unterstützt** *Adj.* computer-aided;
computer-assisted

Container /kɔn'teːnɐ/ *der;* ~s, ~:
container; (für Müll) [refuse] skip

cool /kuːl/ (ugs.) [1] *Adj.* cool; ~ **bleiben**
keep one's cool (coll.)
[2] *adv.* coolly (coll.)

Cord *der;* ~[e]s, ~e *od.* ~s cord; (~samt)
corduroy

Corned Beef /'kɔːnd'biːf/ *das;* ~s corned
beef

Couch /kaʊtʃ/ *die,* (schweiz. auch:) *der;* ~,
~es sofa

Coup /kuː/ *der;* ~s, ~s coup

Coupon /ku'pɔː/ *der;* ~s, ~s coupon;
voucher

Courage /ku'raːʒə/ *die;* ~ (ugs.) courage

Cousin /ku'zɛ̃:/ *der;* ~s, ~s, **Cousine** *die;*
~, ~n cousin

Cover /'kavɐ/ *das;* ~s, ~s (a) (von Illustrierten)
cover
(b) (von Schallplatten) sleeve

covern /'kavɐn/ *tr. V.* cover ⟨*song, record*⟩

Cowboy /'kaʊbɔy:/ *der;* ~s, ~s cowboy

Credo ▶ KREDO

Creme /kreːm/ *die;* ~, ~s, (schweiz.:) ~n
cream

CSU *Abk.* = **Christlich-Soziale Union**
CSU

CT (Med.) *Abk.*
= **Computertomographie** CT

Curry /'kœri/ *das;* ~s, ~s curry powder

Curry·wurst *die: sliced fried sausage
sprinkled with curry powder and served with
ketchup*

Cursor /'kɐːsɐ/ *der;* ~s, ~s (DV) cursor

Cyberspace /'saibɐspeɪs/ *der;* ~ (DV)
cyberspace

Dd

d, D /de:/ *das;* ~, ~ **(a)** (Buchstabe) d/D
(b) (Musik) [key of] D

D *Abk.* = **Damen**

da [1] *Adv.* **(a)** (dort) there; **da draußen/
drinnen/drüben/unten** out/in/over/down
there; **da, wo** where
(b) (hier) here
(c) (zeitlich) then; (in dem Augenblick) at that
moment
(d) (deshalb) **der Zug war schon weg, da habe
ich den Bus genommen** the train had
already gone, so I took the bus
(e) (ugs.: in diesem Fall) **da kann man nichts
machen** there's nothing one can do about it
(f) **da sein** (existieren) exist; (übrig sein) be left;
(anwesend sein) be about *or* around; (im Haus,
zu Hause sein) be in; (zu sprechen sein) be
available; (angekommen, eingetroffen sein) have
arrived; (fig.) ⟨*case*⟩ have occurred; ⟨*moment*⟩
have arrived; ⟨*situation*⟩ have arisen; **ich bin
gleich wieder da** I'll be right *or* straight
back
[2] *Konj.* (weil) as; since

da·bei *Adv.* **(a)** with it/him/her/them; **nahe
~:** close by; **~ sein** (anwesend sein) be there;
be present (**bei** at); (teilnehmen) take part (**bei**
in)
(b) (währenddessen) at the same time; (bei
diesem Anlass) then; on that occasion; **die ~
entstehenden Kosten** the expense involved;
[gerade] **~ sein, etw. zu tun** be just doing
sth.
(c) (außerdem) **~** [auch] what is more
(d) (hinsichtlich dessen) about it/them; **was hast
du dir denn ~ gedacht?** what 'were you
thinking of?

dabei-: ~|**bleiben** *unr. itr. V.; mit sein*
stay there; be there; ~|**haben** *unr. tr. V.*
have with one; ***~|**sein** ▶ DABEI A, B;
~|**stehen** *unr. itr. V.* stand there

da|bleiben *unr. itr. V.; mit sein* stay there;
(hier bleiben) stay here

Dach *das;* ~[e]s, **Dächer** roof

Dach-: ~**antenne** *die* roof aerial;
~**boden** *der* loft; **auf dem** ~**boden** in the
loft; ~**decker** /-dɛkɐ/ *der;* ~~s, ~~,
~**deckerin** *die;* ~~, ~~**nen** roofer;
~**fenster** *das* skylight; (~gaube) dormer
window; ~**garten** *der* roof garden;
~**gaube** *die* dormer window;
~**gepäckträger** *der* (Kfz-W.) roof rack;
~**geschoss,** ***~**geschoß** *das* attic
[storey]; ~**kammer** *die* attic [room];
~**luke** *die* skylight; ~**pappe** *die* roofing
felt; ~**rinne** *die* gutter

Dachs /daks/ *der;* ~es, ~e badger

Dach·stuhl *der* roof truss

dachte *1. u. 3. Pers. Sg. Prät. v.* DENKEN

Dach-: ~**terrasse** *die* roof terrace;
~**wohnung** *die* attic flat (Brit.) *or* (Amer.)
apartment; ~**ziegel** *der* roof tile;
~**zimmer** *das* attic room

Dackel *der;* ~s, ~: dachshund

da·durch *Adv.* **(a)** through it/them
(b) (durch diesen Umstand) as a result; (durch
dieses Mittel) by this [means]

da·für *Adv.* **(a)** for it/them; ~, **dass ...** (wenn
man berücksichtigt, dass) considering that ...;
(damit) so that ...; ~ **sorgen** [, **dass ...**] see to
it [that ...]
(b) ~ **sein** be in favour [of it]; **ein Beispiel
~ ist ...:** an example of this is ...
(c) (als Gegenleistung) in return [for it]; (beim
Tausch) in exchange; (stattdessen) instead
(d) **etwas/nichts ~ können** be/not be
responsible

***dafür|können ▶ DAFÜR D

dagegen *Adv.* **(a)** against it/them; **etwas
~ haben** have sth. against it; **ich habe
nichts ~:** I've no objection; ~ **sein** be
against it
(b) (im Vergleich dazu) by *or* in comparison

da·heim *Adv.* (bes. südd., österr., schweiz.) **(a)**
(zu Hause) at home; ⟨*nach Präp.*⟩ home
(b) (in der Heimat) [back] home

da·her *Adv.* **(a)** from there
(b) (durch diesen Umstand) hence
(c) (deshalb) therefore; so

daher|kommen *unr. itr. V.* come along

da·hin (a) there
(b) (fig.) ~ **musste es kommen** it had to
come to that
(c) **bis ~:** to there; (zeitlich) until then
(d) ~ **sein** be *or* have gone
(e) (in diesem Sinne) ~ [gehend], **dass ...:** to
the effect that ...

da·hinten *Adv.* over there

da·hinter *Adv.* behind it/them; ⟨folgend⟩
after it/them

Dahlie /'da:lĭə/ *die;* ~, ~n dahlia

da-: ~|**lassen** *unr. tr. V.* (ugs.) leave
[there]; (hier lassen) leave here; ~|**liegen**
unr. itr. V. lie there

dalli *Adv.* (ugs.) [~] ~! get a move on!

damalig *Adj.* at that *or* the time *postpos.*

damals *Adv.* at that time

Damast *der;* ~[e]s, ~e damask

Dame *die;* ~, ~n **(a)** (Frau) lady
(b) (Schach, Kartenspiele) queen
(c) (Spiel) draughts (Brit.); checkers (Amer.)

Damen-: ~**binde** *die* sanitary towel (Brit.)
or (Amer.) napkin; ~**friseur** *der,* ····⟩

∼**friseurin** *die* ladies' hairdresser; ∼**rad** *das* lady's bicycle; ∼**toilette** *die* ladies' toilet

da·mịt ⑴ *Adv.* (a) with it/them (b) (gleichzeitig) with that (c) (daher) thus ⑵ *Konj.* so that

dämlich (ugs. abwertend) ⑴ *Adj.* stupid ⑵ *adv.* stupidly

Dạmm *der;* ∼[e]s, Dämme embankment; levee (Amer.); (Deich) dike; (Stau∼)

dämmern *itr. V.* es dämmert (morgens) it is getting light; (abends) it is getting dark

Dạ̈mmerung *die;* ∼, ∼en (a) (Abend∼) twilight; dusk (b) (Morgen∼) dawn

Dämon *der;* ∼s, ∼en /dɛ'mo:nən/ demon

dämọnisch *Adj.* demonic

dämonisịeren *tr. V.* demonize; portray as a demon/demons

Dạmpf *der;* ∼[e]s, Dämpfe steam *no pl., no indef. art.*

Dạmpf·bügel·eisen *das* steam iron

dạmpfen *itr. V.* steam (**vor** + *Dat.* with)

dạ̈mpfen *tr. V.* (a) (garen) steam ⟨*fish, vegetables, potatoes*⟩ (b) (mildern) muffle ⟨*sound*⟩; cushion, absorb ⟨*blow, impact, shock*⟩

Dạmpfer *der;* ∼s, ∼: steamer

Dạmpf-: ∼**kochtopf** *der* pressure cooker; ∼**maschine** *die* steam engine; ∼**nudel** *die* (südd., Kochk.) steamed yeast dumpling; ∼**walze** *die* steamroller

da·nạch *Adv.* (a) (zeitlich) after it/that; then (b) (räumlich) after it/them (c) (entsprechend) in accordance with it/them

Däne *der;* ∼n, ∼n Dane

da·nẹben *Adv.* (a) beside him/her/it/them *etc.;* (b) (im Vergleich dazu) in comparison

danẹben-: ∼|**benehmen** *unr. refl. V.* (ugs.) blot one's copybook (coll.); ∼|**gehen** *unr. itr. V.; mit sein* miss [the target]; ∼|**schießen** *unr. itr. V.* miss [the target]

Dänemark *(das);* ∼s Denmark

Dänin *die;* ∼, ∼nen Dane; Danish woman/ girl

dänisch *Adj.* Danish

dạnk *Präp. mit Dat. u. Gen.* thanks to

Dạnk *der;* ∼[e]s thanks *pl.;* **mit** [**vielem** *od.* **bestem**] ∼ **zurück** thanks for the loan; (bes. geschrieben) returned with thanks!; **vielen/ besten/herzlichen** ∼! thank you very much

dạnkbar ⑴ *Adj.* grateful; (anerkennend) appreciative ⟨*child, audience, etc.*⟩; [jmdm.] **für etw.** ∼ **sein** be grateful [to sb.] for sth. ⑵ *adv.* gratefully

Dạnkbarkeit *die;* ∼: gratitude

dạnke *Höflichkeitsformel* thank you; (ablehnend) no, thank you; ∼ **schön/sehr/ vielmals** thank you very much

dạnken ⑴ *itr. V.* (Dank aussprechen) thank; **ich danke Ihnen vielmals** thank you very much; **na, ich danke!** (ugs.) no, 'thank you! ⑵ *tr. V.* [aber bitte,] **nichts zu** ∼: don't mention it

Dạnke·schön *das;* ∼s thank-you

dạnn *Adv.* (a) then; **was** ∼? what happens then?; **noch drei Tage,** ∼ **ist Ostern** another three days and it will be Easter; **bis** ∼: see you then; ∼ **und wann** now and then (b) (in diesem Falle) then; in that case; ∼ **will ich nicht weiter stören** in that case I won't disturb you any further; [**na,**] ∼ **eben nicht!** in that case, forget it!; **nur** ∼, **wenn ...:** only if ...

daran /da'ran/ *Adv.* (a) (an dieser/diese Stelle, an diesem/diesen Gegenstand) on it/them; **dicht** ∼: close to it/them; **nahe** ∼ **sein, etw. zu tun** be on the point of doing sth. (b) (hinsichtlich dieser Sache) about it/them; ∼ **ist nichts zu machen** there's nothing one can do about it; **kein Wort** ∼ **ist wahr** not a word of it is true; **mir liegt viel** ∼**:** it means a lot to me (c) **ich wäre beinahe** ∼ **erstickt** I almost choked on it; **er ist** ∼ **gestorben** he died of it

darạn|setzen *tr. V.* devote ⟨*energy etc.*⟩ to it; summon up ⟨*ambition*⟩ for it; (aufs Spiel setzen) risk ⟨*one's life, one's honour*⟩ for it

darạuf *Adv.* (a) on it/them; (oben ∼) on top of it/them (b) **er hat** ∼ **geschossen** he shot at it/them (c) (danach) after that; **ein Jahr** ∼/**kurz** ∼ **starb er** he died a year later/shortly afterwards; ∼ **folgend** following

darạuf-: *∼**folgend** ▶ DARAUF C; ∼**hin** /-'-'-/ *Adv.* (a) thereupon; (b) (unter diesem Gesichtspunkt) with a view to this/that

darạus *Adv.* (a) from it/them; out of it/ them (b) **mach dir nichts** ∼**:** don't worry about it; **was ist** ∼ **geworden?** what has become of it?

dạr|bieten (geh.) *unr. tr. V.* (aufführen, vortragen) perform; **es wurden Gedichte und Lieder dargeboten** a recital of poems and songs was presented

Dạrbietung *die;* ∼, ∼en (geh.) (a) presentation (b) (Aufführung) performance; (beim Varieté usw.) act

dạrf *1. u. 3. Pers. Sg. Präsens v.* DÜRFEN

dạrfst *2. Pers. Sg. Präsens v.* DÜRFEN

darịn *Adv.* (a) in it/them (b) (in dieser Hinsicht) in that respect

dạr|legen *tr. V.* explain; set forth ⟨*reasons, facts*⟩

Dạrlehen *das;* ∼s, ∼: loan; **ein** ∼ **aufnehmen** get *or* raise a loan; **jmdm. ein** ∼ **gewähren** give *or* grant sb. a loan

Dạrm *der;* ∼[e]s, Dạ̈rme intestines *pl.;* bowels *pl.*

---

dar|stellen *tr. V.* (a) depict; portray; **etw. grafisch ~:** present sth. graphically
(b) (verkörpern) play; act
(c) (schildern) describe ⟨*person, incident, etc.*⟩; present ⟨*matter, argument*⟩
(d) (sein, bedeuten) represent

Darsteller *der; ~s, ~:* actor

Darstellerin *die; ~, ~nen* actress

Darstellung *die* (a) representation; (Schilderung) portrayal; (Bild) picture; **grafische/schematische ~:** diagram; (Graph) graph
(b) (Beschreibung, Bericht) description; account;
(c) (einer Theaterrolle) interpretation; **seine ~ des Mephisto** his portrayal *or* interpretation of Mephisto

darüber *Adv.* (a) over it/them; **~ stehen** (fig.) be above such things
(b) **~ hinaus** in addition [to that]; (noch obendrein) what is more
(c) (über dieser/diese Angelegenheit) about it/them
(d) (über diese Grenze, dieses Maß hinaus) over [that]

*darüber|stehen ▶ DARÜBER A

darum *Adv.* (a) [a]round it/them
(b) (diesbezüglich) **ich sorge mich ~:** I worry about it
(c) /'--/ (deswegen) for that reason

darunter *Adv.* (a) (unter dem Genannten/das Genannte) under it/them
(b) (unter dieser Grenze, diesem Maß) less; **Bewerber im Alter von 40 Jahren und ~:** applicants aged 40 and under

das ⓵ *best. Art. Nom. u. Akk.* the
⓶ *Demonstrativpron.* (a) *attr.* **das Kind war es** it was 'that child
(b) *allein stehend* **das [da]** that one; **das [hier]** this one [here]
⓷ *Relativpron.* (Mensch) who; that; (Sache, Tier) which; that

*da|sein ▶ DA 1F

Da·sein *das* existence

Daseins·berechtigung *die* right to exist; **das findet darin** *od.* **dadurch seine ~:** this justifies its existence

da|sitzen *unr. itr. V.* sit there

dasjenige ▶ DERJENIGE

dass, *daß *Konj.* (a) that; **entschuldigen Sie bitte, ~ ich mich verspätet habe** please forgive me for being late; **ich verstehe nicht, ~ sie ihn geheiratet hat** I don't understand why she married him
(b) (nach Pronominaladverbien o. Ä.) [the fact] that; **das liegt daran, ~ du nicht aufgepasst hast** that comes from your not paying attention
(c) (im Konsekutivsatz) that; **[so]~:** so that
(d) (im Finalsatz) so that
(e) (im Ausruf) **~ mir das passieren musste!** why did it have to [go and] happen to me!

dasselbe ▶ DERSELBE

da|stehen *unr. itr. V.* (a) stand there

(b) (fig.) **gut ~:** be in a good position; **[ganz] allein ~:** be [all] alone in the world

Datei /da'tai:/ *die; ~, ~en* data file

Daten ⓵ ▶ DATUM
⓶ *Pl.* data

Daten-: ~autobahn *die* (DV) data highway; **~bank** *die; Pl. ~~en* data bank; **~erfassung** *die* data collection *or* capture; **~schutz** *der* data protection *no def. art.;* **~träger** *der* data carrier; **~verarbeitung** *die* data processing *no def. art.*

datieren *tr. V.* date

Dativ *der; ~s, ~e* (Sprachw.) dative [case]

Dativ·objekt *das* (Sprachw.) indirect object

Dattel *die; ~, ~n* date

Dattel·palme *die* date palm

Datum *das; ~s,* **Daten** date

Dauer *die; ~* (a) length; **für die ~ eines Jahres** *od.* **von einem Jahr** for a period of one year
(b) (Fortbestehen) **von ~ sein** last [long]; **auf die ~:** in the long run; **auf ~:** permanently

dauer-, Dauer-: ~auftrag *der* (Bankw.) standing order; **~haft** ⓵ *Adj.* (a) [long-]lasting ⟨*peace, friendship, etc.*⟩; (b) (haltbar) durable; ⓶ *adv.* lastingly; **~karte** *die* season ticket; **~lauf** *der* jogging *no art.;* **ein ~lauf** a jog

dauern *itr. V.* last; ⟨*job etc.*⟩ take; **einen Moment, es dauert nicht lange** just a minute, it won't take long

dauernd ⓵ *Adj.* constant ⟨*noise, interruptions, etc.*⟩; permanent ⟨*institution*⟩ ⓶ *adv.* constantly; **er kommt ~ zu spät** he keeps on arriving late

Dauer-: ~regen *der* continuous rain; **~stellung** *die* permanent position; **~welle** *die* perm; **~wurst** *die* smoked sausage ⟨*with good keeping properties, esp. salami*⟩; **~zustand** *der* permanent state [of affairs]; **zum ~zustand werden** become permanent *or* a permanent state

Daumen *der; ~s, ~:* thumb

Daune *die; ~, ~n* down [feather]; **~n** down *sing.*

davon *Adv.* (a) (von dieser Stelle entfernt, weg) from it/them; (von dort) from there; (mit Entfernungsangabe) away [from it/them]
(b) (hinsichtlich dieser Sache) about it/them
(c) (durch diese Angelegenheit verursacht) by it/them; **das kommt ~!** (ugs.) [there you are,] that's what happens
(d) **ich hätte gern ein halbes Pfund ~:** I would like half a pound of that/those
(e) **~ kann man nicht leben** you can't live on that

davon-: ~|fahren *unr. itr. V.; mit sein* leave; (mit dem Auto) drive off; (mit dem Fahrrad, Motorrad) ride off; **~|kommen** *unr. itr. V.; mit sein* get away; **~|laufen** *unr. itr. V.; mit sein* run away; **~|tragen** *unr. tr. V.* (a) ⋯⋮⟩

carry away; take away ⟨*rubbish*⟩; **(b)** (geh.: erringen) gain ⟨*a victory, fame*⟩; **(c)** (geh.: sich zuziehen) receive ⟨*injuries*⟩

da·vor *Adv.* **(a)** in front of it/them; ∼ **liegen/stehen** *usw.* lie/stand *etc.* in front of it/them
(b) (zeitlich) before [it/them]

*davor|liegen *usw.* ▶ DAVOR A

Dax *der;* ∼: Dax [index]

da·zu *Adv.* **(a)** (zusätzlich zu dieser Sache) with it/them; (gleichzeitig) at the same time; (außerdem) what is more
(b) (diesbezüglich) about it/them
(c) (zu diesem Zweck) for it
(d) (zu diesem Ergebnis) to it; ∼ **reicht unser Geld nicht** we haven't enough money for that

dazu-: ∼|**geben** *unr. tr. V.* add; ∼|**gehören** *tr. V.* belong to it/them; ∼|**kommen** *unr. itr. V.; mit sein* **(a)** (hinkommen) arrive; **(b)** (hinzukommen) **kommt noch etwas dazu?** is there anything else [you would like]?; ∼ **kommt, dass ...** (fig.) what's more, ...; on top of that ...; ∼|**rechnen** *tr. V.* add on; ∼|**tun** *unr. tr. V.* (ugs.) add

da·zwischen *Adv.* in between; between them; (darunter) among them

dazwischen-: ∼|**kommen** *unr. itr. V.; mit sein* **(a)** **mit dem Finger** ∼**kommen** get one's finger caught [in it]; **(b)** (es verhindern) prevent it; **es ist mir etwas** ∼**gekommen** I had problems; ∼|**reden** *itr. V.* interrupt

DDR *Abk.* = **Deutsche Demokratische Republik** GDR; East Germany

Deal /diːl/ *der od. das;* ∼s, ∼s (salopp) deal

dealen /'diːlən/ *itr. V.* (ugs.) push drugs; **mit LSD** ∼: push LSD

Dealer *der;* ∼s, ∼, **Dealerin** *die;* ∼, ∼nen (ugs.) pusher

Debatte *die;* ∼, ∼n debate (**über** + *Akk.* on); **zur** ∼ **stehen** be under discussion

Debüt /de'byː/ *das;* ∼s, ∼s debut

Deck *das;* ∼[e]s, ∼s deck

Deck·bett *das* ▶ OBERBETT

Decke *die;* ∼, ∼n **(a)** (Tisch∼) tablecloth
(b) (Woll∼, Pferde∼, fig.) blanket; (Reise∼) rug
(c) (Zimmer∼) ceiling

Deckel *der;* ∼s, ∼ **(a)** lid; (auf Flaschen, Gläsern usw.) top; (Schacht∼, Uhr∼, Buch∼ usw.) cover
(b) (Bier∼) beer mat

decken ① *tr. V.* **(a)** etw. über etw. (*Akk.*) ∼: spread sth. over sth.
(b) roof ⟨*house*⟩; cover ⟨*roof*⟩
(c) **den Tisch** ∼: lay the table
(d) (schützen; Finanzw., Versicherungsw.) cover
(e) (befriedigen) meet ⟨*need, demand*⟩
② *itr. V.* (den Tisch decken) lay the table

Deck·mantel *der* cover

---

*old spelling - see note on page xiv

Deckung *die;* ∼, ∼en **(a)** (Schutz; auch fig.) cover (esp. Mil.); (Boxen) guard; (bes. Fußball) defence; **in** ∼ **gehen** take cover
(b) (Befriedigung) meeting
(c) (Finanzw., Versicherungsw.) cover[ing]

deckungs·gleich *Adj.* (Geom.) congruent

defekt *Adj.* defective; faulty; ∼ **sein** have a defect; be faulty; (nicht funktionieren) not be working

Defekt *der;* ∼[e]s, ∼e defect, fault (**an** + *Dat.* in)

defensiv ① *Adj.* defensive
② *adv.* defensively

Defensive *die;* ∼, ∼n defensive; **in der** ∼: on the defensive; **die** ∼ (Sport) defensive play

definieren *tr. V.* define

Definition *die;* ∼, ∼en definition

definitiv ① *Adj.* definitive
② *adv.* finally

Defizit *das;* ∼s, ∼e **(a)** deficit
(b) (Mangel) deficiency

deformieren *tr. V.* **(a)** (verformen) distort
(b) (entstellen) deform (also fig.)

deftig *Adj.* (ugs.) **(a)** [good] solid *attrib.* ⟨*meal etc.*⟩; [nice] big ⟨*sausage etc.*⟩
(b) (derb) crude, coarse ⟨*joke, speech, etc.*⟩

Degen *der;* ∼s, ∼ **(a)** (Waffe) [light] sword
(b) (Fechtsport) épée

degradieren *tr. V.* demote

Degradierung *die;* ∼, ∼en **(a)** (im Rang) demotion
(b) (Herabwürdigung) degradation; reduction (**zu** to the level of)

dehnbar *Adj.* **(a)** (elastisch) ⟨*material etc.*⟩ that stretches *not pred.;* elastic ⟨*waistband etc.*⟩
(b) (fig.: vage) elastic; **das ist ein** ∼**er Begriff** it's a loose concept

Dehnbarkeit *die;* ∼: elasticity

dehnen *tr., refl. V.* stretch

Deich *der;* ∼[e]s, ∼e dike

Deichsel /'daiksl/ *die;* ∼, ∼n shaft

deichseln *tr. V.* (ugs.) fix

dein *Possessivpron.* your; **viele Grüße von** ∼**em Emil** with best wishes, yours Emil; **das Buch dort, ist das** ∼[e]s? that book over there, is it yours?; **du und die Deinen** (geh.) you and yours

deiner *Gen. des Personalpronomens* du (geh.) of you

deiner·seits *Adv.* (von deiner Seite) on your part; (auf deiner Seite) for your part

deinet·wegen *Adv.* because of you; (für dich) on your behalf; (dir zuliebe) for your sake

Dekade /de'kaːdə/ *die;* ∼, ∼n decade

dekadent *Adj.* decadent

Dekadenz *die;* ∼: decadence

deklamieren *tr., itr. V.* recite

Deklination *die;* ∼, ∼en (Sprachw.) declension

deklinieren *tr. V.* (Sprachw.) decline

dekodieren *tr. V.* (fachspr.) decode

Dekolleté ⋯⋗ denken ⋯ ⋮

Dekolleté /dekɔl'te:/ *das;* ~s, ~s low[-cut] neckline; décolletage

Dekor *das;* ~s, ~s *od.* ~e decoration; (Muster) pattern

Dekorateur /dekora'tøːɐ̯/ *der;* ~s, ~e, **Dekorateurin** *die;* ~, ~nen (Schaufenster~) window dresser; (von Innenräumen) interior designer

Dekoration *die;* ~, ~en decorations *pl.;* (Schaufenster~) window display

dekorativ ① *Adj.* decorative ② *adv.* decoratively

dekorieren *tr. V.* decorate ⟨room etc.⟩; dress ⟨shop window⟩

Deko·stoff *der* furnishing fabric

Dekret *das;* ~[e]s, ~e decree

Delegation *die;* ~, ~en delegation

delegieren *tr. V.* (a) send as a delegate/as delegates

(b) delegate ⟨task etc.⟩ (an + Akk. to)

Delegierte *der/die; adj. Dekl.* delegate

Delfin ▶ DELPHIN

delikat *Adj.* (a) delicious; (fein) delicate ⟨bouquet, aroma⟩

(b) (heikel) delicate

Delikatesse *die;* ~, ~n delicacy

Delikt *das;* ~[e]s, ~e offence

Delinquent *der;* ~en, ~en, **Delinquentin** *die;* ~, ~nen offender

Delirium *das;* ~s, Delirien delirium

Delle *die;* ~, ~n (ugs.) dent

Delphin *der;* ~s, ~e dolphin

dem ① *best. Art., Dat. Sg. v.* DER¹ 1 *u.* DAS 1: to the; (nach Präp.) the ② *Demonstrativpron., Dat. Sg. v.* DER¹ 2 *u.* DAS 2: (a) *attr.* that; **gib es dem Mann** give it to 'that man

(b) *allein stehend* **gib es nicht dem, sondern dem da!** don't give it to him, give it to that man/child *etc.;* ③ *Relativpron., Dat. Sg. v.* DER¹ 3 *u.* DAS 3 (Person) that/whom; (Sache) that/which; **der Mann/das Kind, dem ich das Geld gab** the man/the child I gave the money to

Demagoge *der;* ~n, ~n, **Demagogin** *die;* ~, ~nen demagogue

demagogisch *Adj.* demagogic

Dementi *das;* ~s, ~s denial

dementieren ① *tr. V.* deny ② *itr. V.* deny it

dem-: ~**entsprechend** ① *Adj.* appropriate; ② *adv.* accordingly; (vor Adjektiven) correspondingly; ~**gemäß** *Adv.* (a) (infolgedessen) consequently; (b) (entsprechend) accordingly; ~**jenigen** ▶ DERJENIGE; ~**nach** *Adv.* therefore; ~**nächst** *Adv.* shortly

Demo *die;* ~, ~s (ugs.) demo; **auf der** ~: at the demo

Demokrat *der;* ~en, ~en democrat; (Parteimitglied) Democrat

Demokratie *die;* ~, ~n democracy

Demokratin *die;* ~, ~nen ▶ DEMOKRAT

demokratisch ① *Adj.* democratic ② *adv.* democratically

demokratisieren *tr. V.* democratize

demolieren *tr. V.* wreck; smash up ⟨furniture⟩

Demonstrant *der;* ~en, ~en, **Demonstrantin** *die;* ~, ~nen demonstrator

Demonstration *die;* ~, ~en demonstration (**für** in support of, **gegen** against)

demonstrativ ① *Adj.* (a) pointed (b) (Sprachw.) demonstrative ② *adv.* pointedly

Demonstrativ·pronomen *das* (Sprachw.) demonstrative pronoun

demonstrieren ① *itr. V.* demonstrate (**für** in support of, **gegen** against) ② *tr. V.* demonstrate

dem·selben ▶ DERSELBE

Demut *die;* ~: humility

demütig ① *Adj.* humble ② *adv.* humbly

demütigen ① *tr. V.* humiliate ② *refl. V.* humble oneself

Demütigung *die;* ~, ~en humiliation

dem·zufolge *Adv.* consequently

den¹ ① *best. Art., Akk. Sg. v.* DER¹ 1: the ② *Demonstrativpron., Akk. Sg. v.* DER¹ 2: (a) *attr.* that; **ich meine den Mann** I mean 'that man

(b) *allein stehend* **ich meine den [da]** I mean 'that one ③ *Relativpron., Akk. Sg. v.* DER¹ 3 (Person) that/whom; (Sache) that/which; **der Mann, den ich gesehen habe** the man that I saw

den² ① *best. Art., Dat. Pl. v.* DER¹ 1, DIE¹ 1, DAS 1: the ② *Demonstrativpron. Dat. Pl. v.* DER¹ 2A, DIE¹ 2A, DAS 2A: those

denen ① *Demonstrativpron., Dat. Pl. v.* DER¹ 2B, DIE¹ 2B, DAS 2B them; **gib es** ~, **nicht den anderen** give it to 'them, not to the others ② *Relativpron., Dat. Pl. v.* DER¹ 3, DIE¹ 3, DAS 3 (Personen) that/whom; (Sachen) that/which; **die Menschen,** ~ **wir Geld gegeben haben** the people to whom we gave money; **die Tiere,** ~ **er geholfen hat** the animals that he helped

denjenigen ▶ DERJENIGE

denkbar ① *Adj.* conceivable ② *adv.* (sehr, äußerst) extremely

denken ① *unr. itr. V.* think (**an** + *Akk.* of, **über** + *Akk.* about); **wie denkst du darüber?** what do you think about it?; what's your opinion of it?; **schlecht von jmdm.** ~: think badly of sb.; **denk daran, dass .../zu ...:** don't forget that .../to ...; **ich denke nicht daran!** ⋯⋗

no way!; not on your life!; **ich denke nicht daran, das zu tun** I've no intention of doing that

② *unr. tr. V.* think; **wer hätte das gedacht?** who would have thought it?; **eine gedachte Linie** an imaginary line

③ *unr. refl. V.* **(a)** (sich vorstellen) imagine **(b)** sich *(Dat.)* **bei etw. etwas ∼:** mean something by sth.; **ich habe mir nichts [Böses] dabei gedacht** I didn't mean any harm [by it]

Denken *das;* ∼s thinking; (Denkweise) thought

Denker *der;* ∼s, ∼, **Denkerin** *die;* ∼, ∼nen thinker

denk·faul *Adj.* mentally lazy

Denk-: ∼**fehler** *der* flaw in one's reasoning; ∼**mal** *das; Pl.* ∼mäler *od.* ∼e monument; memorial; **jmdm. ein ∼ errichten** *od.* **setzen** erect *or* put up a memorial to sb.

Denkmal[s]·schutz *der* protection of historic monuments; **unter ∼ stehen/stellen** be/put under a preservation order

denk-, Denk-: ∼**pause** *die* pause for thought; ∼**sport·aufgabe** *die* brain teaser; ∼**vermögen** *das* ability to think [creatively]; ∼**würdig** *Adj.* memorable; ∼**zettel** *der* lesson

denn ① *Konj.* **(a)** (kausal) for; because **(b)** (geh.: als) than ② *Adv.* **es sei ∼, …:** unless … ③ *Partikel* (in Fragesätzen) **wie geht es dir ∼?** tell me, how are you?; **wie heißt du ∼?** tell me your name; **warum ∼ nicht?** why ever not?

dennoch *Adv.* nevertheless

denselben ▶ DERSELBE

Denunziant *der;* ∼en, ∼en, **Denunziantin** *die;* ∼, ∼nen informer; grass (sl.)

denunzieren *tr. V.* denounce; (bei der Polizei) inform against; grass on (sl.) **(bei to)**

Deo *das;* ∼s, ∼s, **Deodorant** *das;* ∼s, ∼s (auch:) ∼e deodorant

Deo·spray *das* deodorant spray

Deponie *die;* ∼, ∼n tip (Brit.); dump

deponieren *tr. V.* put; (im Safe o. Ä.) deposit

Deportation *die;* ∼, ∼en transportation; (ins Ausland) deportation

deportieren *tr. V.* transport; (ins Ausland) deport

Deportierte *der/die; adj. Dekl.* transportee; (ins Ausland) deportee

Depot /de'po:/ *das;* ∼s, ∼s **(a)** depot; (Lagerhaus) warehouse; (für Möbel usw.) depository; (im Freien, für Munition o. Ä.) dump; (in einer Bank) strongroom; safe deposit **(b)** (hinterlegte Wertgegenstände) deposits *pl.*

Depp *der;* ∼en (auch:) ∼s, ∼en (auch:) ∼e (bes. südd., österr., schweiz. abwertend) ▶ DUMMKOPF

*alte Schreibung - vgl. Hinweis auf S. xiv

Depression *die;* ∼, ∼en depression

depressiv ① *Adj.* depressive ② *adv.* **∼ veranlagt sein** have a tendency towards depression

deprimieren *tr. V.* depress

deprimierend *Adj.* depressing

deprimiert ① *Adj.* depressed ② *adv.* dejectedly

der[1] ① *best. Art. Nom.* the; **der Tod** death; **der „Faust"** 'Faust'; **der Bodensee/Mount Everest** Lake Constance/Mount Everest; **der Iran/Sudan** Iran/the Sudan; **der Mensch/ Mann ist …:** man is …/men are …
② *Demonstrativpron.* **(a)** *attr.* that; **der Mann war es** it was 'that man
(b) *allein stehend* he; **der war es** it was 'him; **der [da]** (Person) that man/boy; (Sache) that one; **der [hier]** (Person) this man/boy; (Sache) this one
③ *Relativpron.* (Person) who/that; (Sache) which/that; **der Mann, der da drüben entlanggeht** the man walking along over there
④ *Relativ- u. Demonstrativpron.* the one who

der[2] ① *best. Art.* **(a)** *Gen. Sg. v.* DIE[1] 1: **der Hut der Frau** the woman's hat; **der Henkel der Tasse** the handle of the cup
(b) *Dat. Sg. v.* DIE[1] 1 to the; (nach Präp.) the
(c) *Gen. Pl. v.* DER[1] 1, DIE[1] 1, DAS 1: **das Haus der Freunde** our/their *etc.* friends' house; **das Bellen der Hunde** the barking of the dogs
② *Demonstrativpron.* **(a)** *Gen. Sg. v.* DIE[1] 2: of the; of that
(b) *Dat. Sg. v.* DIE[1] 2 *attr.* **der Frau [da/hier] gehört es** it belongs to that woman there/ this woman here
(c) *Gen. Pl. v.* DER[1] 2A, DIE[1] 2A, DAS 2A: of those
③ *Relativpron.; Dat. Sg. v.* DIE[1] 3: **die Frau, der ich es gegeben habe** the woman I gave it to; **die Katze, der er einen Tritt gab** the cat [that] he kicked

der·art *Adv.* so; **es hat lange nicht mehr ∼ geregnet** it hasn't rained as hard as that for a long time; **sie hat ∼ geschrien, dass …:** she screamed so much that …

der·artig ① *Adj.* such ② *adv.* ▶ DERART

derb ① *Adj.* **(a)** tough ⟨*material*⟩; stout, ⟨*shoes*⟩
(b) (kraftvoll, deftig) earthy ⟨*scenes, humour*⟩ ② *adv.* **(a)** strongly ⟨*made, woven, etc.*⟩
(b) (kraftvoll, deftig) earthily

deren ① *Relativpron.* **(a)** *Gen. Sg. v.* DIE[1] 3 (Personen) whose; (Sachen) of which
(b) *Gen. Pl. v.* DER[1] 3, DIE[1] 3, DAS 3 (Personen) whose; (Sachen) **Maßnahmen, ∼ Folgen wir noch nicht absehen können** measures, the consequences of which we cannot yet foresee ② *Demonstrativpron.* **(a)** *Gen. Sg. v.* DIE[1] 2: **meine Tante, ihre Freundin und ∼ Hund** my aunt, her friend and her dog

(b) *Gen. Pl. v.* DER[1] 2, DIE[1] 2, DAS 2: **meine Verwandten und ~ Kinder** my relatives and their children

der·ent-: ~wegen *Adv.* [1] *relativ* (Personen) because of whom; (Sachen) because of which; [2] *demonstrativ* because of them; **~willen** *Adv.* **um ~willen** (Personen) for whose sake; (Sachen) for the sake of which

derer *Demonstrativpron.; Gen. Pl. v.* DER[1] 2, DIE[1] 2, DAS 2 of those

der·gleichen *indekl. Demonstrativpron.* **(a)** *attr.* such; like that *postpos., not pred.;* **(b)** *allein stehend* that sort of thing

Derivat *das; ~[e]s, ~e* derivative

der·jenige, die·jenige, das·jenige *Demonstrativpron.* **(a)** *attr.* that; *Pl.* those **(b)** *allein stehend* that one; *Pl.* those

derlei *indekl. Demonstrativpron.:* ▶ DERGLEICHEN

der·maßen *Adv.* **~ schön** *usw.,* **dass ...:** so beautiful *etc.* that ...

derselbe, dieselbe, dasselbe *Demonstrativpron.* **(a)** *attr.* the same **(b)** *allein stehend* the same one; *Pl.* the same people; **er sagt immer dasselbe** he always says the same thing; **noch einmal dasselbe, bitte** (ugs.) [the] same again please

der·zeit *Adv.* at present

der·zeitig *Adj.* present; current

des [1] *best. Art.; Gen. Sg. v.* DER[1] 1, DAS 1: **die Mütze des Jungen** the boy's cap; **das Klingeln des Telefons** the ringing of the telephone [2] *Demonstrativpron.; Gen. Sg. v.* DER[1] 2, DAS 2: **er ist der Sohn des Mannes, der ...:** he's the son of the man who ...

Deserteur /dezɛrˈtøːɐ̯/ *der; ~s, ~e,* **Deserteurin** /dezɛrˈtøːrɪn/ *die; ~, ~nen* deserter

desertieren *itr. V.; mit sein* desert

des·gleichen *Adv.* likewise; **er ist Arzt, ~ sein Sohn** he is a doctor, as is his son

des·halb *Adv.* for that reason; **~ bin ich zu dir gekommen** that is why I came to you

Design /diˈzaɪn/ *das; ~s, ~s* design

Designer /diˈzaɪnɐ/ *der; ~s, ~,* **Designerin** *die; ~, ~nen* designer

Designer·droge /-ˈ----/ *die; ~, ~n* designer drug

Desinfektion *die; ~, ~nen* disinfection

Desinfektions·mittel *das* disinfectant

desinfizieren *tr. V.* disinfect

Desinteresse *das; ~s* lack of interest

Despot /dɛsˈpoːt/ *der; ~en, ~en,* **Despotin** *die; ~, ~nen* despot; (fig. abwertend) tyrant

despotisch [1] *Adj.* despotic [2] *adv.* despotically

des·selben ▶ DERSELBE

dessen [1] *Relativpron.; Gen. Sg. v.* DER[1] 3, DAS 3 *attr.* (Person) whose; (Sache) of which

[2] *Demonstrativpron.; Gen. Sg. v.* DER[1] 2, DAS 2: **mein Onkel, sein Sohn und ~ Hund** my uncle, his son, and 'his dog

Dessert /dɛˈseːɐ̯/ *das; ~s, ~s* dessert

Destille *die; ~, ~n* distillery

destillieren *tr. V.* (Chemie) distil

desto *Konj., vor Komp.* **je eher, ~ besser** the sooner the better

des·wegen *Adv.* ▶ DESHALB

Detail /deˈtaɪ/ *das; ~s, ~s* detail

detailliert [1] *Adj.* detailed [2] *adv.* in detail; **sehr ~:** in great detail

Detektiv *der; ~s, ~e,* **Detektivin** *die; ~, ~nen* [private] detective

Detonation *die; ~, ~en* detonation; explosion

detonieren *itr. V.; mit sein* detonate; explode

Deut **keinen ~:** not one bit

deuten [1] *itr. V.* point; **[mit dem Finger] auf jmdn./etw. ~:** point [one's finger] at sb./sth. [2] *tr. V.* interpret

deutlich [1] *Adj.* clear [2] *adv.* clearly

Deutlichkeit *die; ~* **(a)** clarity **(b)** (Eindeutigkeit) clearness

deutsch [1] *Adj.* German; **Deutsche Mark** Deutschmark; German mark [2] *adv.* **Deutsch sprechen/schreiben** speak/write German

Deutsch *das; ~[s]* German; **gutes/fließend ~ sprechen** speak good/fluent German; **auf** *od.* **in ~:** in German; **auf [gut] ~** (ugs.) in plain English

Deutsche[1] *der/die; adj. Dekl.* German; **er ist ~r** he is German

Deutsche[2] *das; adj. Dekl.* **das ~:** German; **aus dem ~n/ins ~ übersetzen** translate from/into German

Deutschland *(das); ~s* Germany

deutsch-, Deutsch-: ~lehrer *der,* **~lehrerin** *die* German teacher; **~sprachig** *Adj.* **(a)** German-speaking; **(b)** German-language *attrib.;* **~unterricht** *der* German teaching; (Unterrichtsstunde) German lesson

Deutung *die; ~, ~en* interpretation

Devise *die; ~, ~n* motto

Devisen *Pl.* foreign currency *sing.*

Devisen-: ~börse *die* foreign exchange market; **~kurs** *der* exchange rate; rate of exchange

Dezember *der; ~s, ~:* December

dezent [1] *Adj.* quiet ⟨colour, pattern, suit⟩; subdued ⟨lighting, music⟩ [2] *adv.* discreetly; ⟨dress⟩ unostentatiously

dezimal *Adj.* decimal

Dezimal-: ~system *das* decimal system; **~zahl** *die* decimal [number]

dezimieren *tr. V.* decimate

dgl. *Abk.* = **dergleichen,**
desgleichen
d. h. *Abk.* = **das heißt** i.e.
Di. *Abk.* = **Dienstag** Tue[s].
Dia *das;* ～s, ～s slide
Diabetes *der;* ～: diabetes
Diabetiker *der;* ～s, ～, **Diabetikerin**
die; ～, ～nen diabetic
Diagnose /dia'gno:zə/ *die;* ～, ～n diagnosis
diagonal ① *Adj.* diagonal
② *adv.* diagonally
Diagonale *die;* ～, ～n diagonal
Diagramm *das* graph; (von Gegenständen)
diagram
Dialekt *der;* ～[e]s, ～e dialect
Dialog *der;* ～[e]s, ～e dialogue
Dialog·fenster *das* (DV) dialogue box
Dialyse /dia'ly:zə/ *die;* ～, ～n (Physik,
Chemie, Med.) dialysis
Diamant *der;* ～en, ～en diamond
**diät ▶ DIÄT
Diät *die;* ～, ～en diet; **eine ～ einhalten** keep
to a diet; **～ essen** be on a diet; **～ kochen**
cook according to a/one's diet
Diäten *Pl.* [parliamentary] allowance *sing.*
dich ① *Akk. von* DU you
② *Akk. des Reflexivpron. der 2. Pers. Sg.*
yourself
dicht ① *Adj.* (a) thick; dense ⟨*forest, hedge,*
crowd⟩; heavy, dense ⟨*traffic*⟩
(b) (undurchlässig) (für Luft) airtight; (für Wasser)
watertight
② *adv.* (a) densely ⟨*populated, wooded*⟩; ～
bebaut heavily built up
(b) (undurchlässig) tightly
(c) *mit Präp.* (nahe) ～ **neben** right next to
**dicht·bebaut ▶ DICHT 2A
Dichte *die;* ～ (Physik, fig.) density
dichten ① *itr. V.* write poetry
② *tr. V.* (verfassen) write; compose
Dichter *der;* ～s, ～: poet; (Schriftsteller)
writer; author
Dichterin *die;* ～, ～nen poet[ess];
(Schriftstellerin) writer; author[ess]
dichterisch *Adj.* poetic; (schriftstellerisch)
literary
dicht|machen *tr., itr. V.* (ugs.) shut;
(endgültig) shut down
Dichtung¹ *die;* ～, ～en seal; (am Hahn usw.)
washer; (am Vergaser, Zylinder usw.) gasket
Dichtung² *die;* ～, ～en (a) work of
literature; (in Versform) poetic work; poem
(b) (Dichtkunst) literature; (in Versform) poetry
dick ① *Adj.* (a) thick; stout ⟨*tree*⟩; fat
⟨*person, legs, etc.*⟩; swollen ⟨*cheek, ankle,*
tonsils, etc.⟩; ～ **werden** get fat; **5 cm ～ sein**
be 5 cm thick
(b) (ugs.) big ⟨*mistake*⟩; hefty ⟨*salary*⟩
② *adv.* thickly; **etw. ～ unterstreichen**
underline sth. heavily; **sich ～ anziehen** wrap

up warm[ly]; **etw. 5 cm ～ schneiden** cut sth.
5 cm. thick; ～ **geschwollen** (ugs.) badly
swollen
Dicke¹ *die;* ～: thickness; (von Menschen,
Körperteilen) fatness
Dicke² *der/die; adj. Dekl.* (ugs.) fatty (coll.)
dick·fellig (ugs.) *Adj.* thick-skinned
Dickfelligkeit *die;* ～ (ugs.) insensitivity
Dickicht /'dɪkɪçt/ *das;* ～[e]s, ～e thicket
dick-, Dick-: ～**kopf** *der* (ugs.) mule (coll.);
ein ～kopf sein be stubborn as a mule; **einen**
～**kopf haben** be pigheaded; ～**köpfig** *Adj.*
(ugs.) pigheaded; ～**macher** *der* (ugs.)
fattening food; ～**milch** *die* sour milk
die¹ ① *best. Art. Nom.* the; **die Helga** (ugs.)
Helga; **die Frau/Menschheit** women *pl.*/
mankind
② *Demonstrativpron.* (a) *attr.* **die Frau war**
es it was 'that woman
(b) *allein stehend* she; **die war es** it was 'her;
die [da] (Person) that woman/girl; (Sache) that
one
③ *Relativpron. Nom.* (Person) who; that;
(Sache, Tier) which; that
④ *Relativ- u. Demonstrativpron.* the one who
die² ① *best. Art.* (a) *Akk. Sg. v.* DIE¹ 1 the;
ich sah die Frau I saw the women
(b) *Nom. u. Akk. Pl. v.* DER¹ 1, DIE¹ 1, DAS 1:
the
② *Demonstrativpron. Nom. u. Akk. Pl. v.*
DER¹ 1, DIE¹ 1, DAS 1: *attr.* **ich meine die**
Männer, die ... I mean those men who ...;
allein stehend **ich meine die [da]** I mean
'them
③ *Relativpron.* (a) *Akk. Sg. v.* DIE¹ 3 (Person)
who; (Sache) that
(b) *Nom. u. Akk. Pl. v.* DER¹ 3, DIE¹ 3, DAS 3
(Personen) whom; (Sachen) which; **die Männer,**
die ich gesehen habe the men I saw
Dieb *der;* ～[e]s, ～e thief
Diebin *die;* ～, ～nen [woman] thief
diebisch ① *Adj.* (a) thieving
(b) (verstohlen) mischievous
② *adv.* mischievously
Diebstahl *der;* ～[e]s, Diebstähle theft
die·jenige ▶ DERJENIGE
Diele *die;* ～, ～n hall[way]
dienen *itr. V.* serve; **womit kann ich ～?**
what can I do for you?
Diener *der;* ～s, ～: servant; **einen ～**
machen (ugs.) bow; make a bow
Dienerin *die;* ～, ～nen maid; servant
dienlich *Adj.* helpful
Dienst *der;* ～[e]s, ～e (a) (Tätigkeit) work;
(von Soldaten, Polizeibeamten, Krankenhauspersonal
usw.) duty; **seinen ～ antreten** start work/go
on duty; **～ haben** be at work/on duty;
⟨*doctor*⟩ be on call; ⟨*chemist*⟩ be open
(b) (Arbeitsverhältnis) post; **Major außer ～:**
retired major
(c) (Tätigkeitsbereich) service; *s. auch*
ÖFFENTLICH;
(d) (Hilfe) service

Diens·tag *der* Tuesday; **am** ∼: on Tuesday; ∼, **der 1. Juni** Tuesday, 1 June; **er kommt** ∼: he is coming on Tuesday; **ab nächsten** ∼: from next Tuesday [onwards]; ∼ **in einer Woche** a week on Tuesday; ∼ **vor einer Woche** a week last Tuesday

diens·tags *Adv.* on Tuesday[s]

dienst-, Dienst-: ∼**bereit** *Adj.* ⟨*chemist*⟩ open *pred.;* ⟨*doctor*⟩ on call; ⟨*dentist*⟩ on duty; ∼**bote** *der,* ∼**botin** *die* servant; ∼**eifrig** *Adj.* zealous; ∼**frei** *Adj.* free ⟨*time*⟩; ∼**geheimnis** *das* (a) professional secret; (im Staatsdienst) official secret; (b) professional secrecy; (im Staatsdienst) official secrecy; ∼**grad** *der* (Milit.) rank; ∼**leister** *der;* ∼∼s, ∼∼, ∼**leisterin** *die;* ∼∼, ∼∼nen (Firma, auch DV) service provider; ∼**leistung** *die* (auch Wirtsch.) service

Dienstleistungs-: ∼**branche** *die* (Wirtsch.) (a) service industry; (b) ▶ ∼sᴇᴋᴛᴏʀ; ∼**sektor** *der* (Wirtsch.) service sector

dienstlich ①*Adj.* business ⟨*call*⟩; (im Staatsdienst) official ⟨*letter, call, etc.*⟩ ②*adv.* on business; (im Staatsdienst) on official business

Dienst-: ∼**reise** *die* business trip; ∼**stelle** *die* office; ∼**wagen** *der* official car; (Geschäftswagen) company car; ∼**weg** *der* official channels *pl.;* ∼**zeit** *die* (a) period of service; (b) (tägliche Arbeitszeit) working hours *pl.*

dies ▶ ᴅɪᴇsᴇʀ

dies·bezüglich *adv.* regarding this

diese ▶ ᴅɪᴇsᴇʀ

Diesel *der;* ∼s, ∼: diesel

die·selbe ▶ ᴅᴇʀsᴇʟʙᴇ

Diesel·motor *der* diesel engine

dieser, diese, dieses, dies *Demonstrativpron.* (a) *attr.* this; *Pl.* these (b) *allein stehend* this one; *Pl.* these; **dies alles** all this; **dies und das,** (geh.) **dieses und jenes** this and that

diesig *Adj.* hazy

dies-: ∼**mal** *Adv.* this time; ∼**seits** ①*Präp. mit Gen.* on this side of; ②*Adv.* ∼seits von on this side of

Dietrich *der;* ∼s, ∼e picklock

diffamieren *tr. V.* defame

Diffamierung *die;* ∼, ∼en defamation

Differential *usw.* ▶ ᴅɪꜰꜰᴇʀᴇɴᴢɪᴀʟ *usw.*

Differenz *die;* ∼, ∼en difference; ⟨Meinungsverschiedenheit⟩ difference [of opinion]

Differenzial /dɪfərən'tsiːaːl/ *das;* ∼s, ∼e (a) (Math.) differential (b) (Technik) differential [gear]

Differenzial·rechnung *die* (Math.) differential calculus

differenziert *Adj.* complex; subtly differentiated ⟨*methods, colours*⟩; sophisticated ⟨*taste*⟩

diffus ①*Adj.* (a) (Physik, Chemie) diffuse

(b) (geh.) vague; vague and confused ⟨*idea, statement, etc.*⟩ ②*adv.* in a vague and confused way

digital (DV) ①*Adj.* digital ②*adv.* digitally

Digital- digital ⟨*clock, display, etc.*⟩

Digital·fernsehen *das* digital television

digitalisieren *tr. V.* (DV) digitalize

Digital·radio *das* digital radio

Diktat *das;* ∼[e]s, ∼e dictation

Diktator *der;* ∼s, ∼en, **Diktatorin** *die;* ∼, ∼nen dictator

diktatorisch ①*Adj.* dictatorial ②*adv.* dictatorially

Diktatur *die;* ∼, ∼en dictatorship

diktieren *tr. V.* dictate

Diktier·gerät *das* dictating machine

Dilemma *das;* ∼s, ∼s dilemma

Dilettant /dile'tant/ *der;* ∼en, ∼en, **Dilettantin** *die;* ∼, ∼nen dilettante

dilettantisch ①*Adj.* dilettante; amateurish ②*adv.* amateurishly

Dimension *die;* ∼, ∼en (Physik, fig.) dimension

DIN /diːn/ *Abk.* = **Deutsche Industrie-Norm[en]** *German Industrial Standard[s];* DIN; **DIN-A4-Format** A4

Ding¹ *das;* ∼[e]s, ∼e (a) thing (b) **nach Lage der** ∼**e** the way things are; **persönliche/private** ∼**e** personal/private matters; **ein** ∼ **der Unmöglichkeit sein** be quite impossible; **vor allen** ∼**en** above all (c) **guter** ∼**e sein** (geh.) be in good spirits

Ding² *das;* ∼[e]s, ∼er (ugs.) thing; **das ist ja ein** ∼! that's really something

Dino *der;* ∼s, ∼s (ugs.) dinosaur

Dino·saurier *der;* ∼s, ∼: dinosaur

Diode *die;* ∼, ∼n (Elektrot.) diode

Dioden·rücklicht *das* LED rear light

Dioxin *das;* ∼s (Chemie) dioxin

Diözese *die;* ∼, ∼n diocese

Dipl.-Ing. *Abk.* = **Diplomingenieur** *academically qualified engineer*

Diplom *das;* ∼s, ∼e ≈ [first] degree (*in a scientific or technical subject*); (für einen Handwerksberuf) diploma

Diplom- qualified

Diplomat *der;* ∼en, ∼en, **Diplomatin** *die;* ∼, ∼nen diplomat

diplomatisch ①*Adj.* diplomatic ②*adv.* diplomatically

dir ①*Dat. von* ᴅᴜ to you; (nach Präp.) you; **Freunde von** ∼: friends of yours ②*Dat. des Reflexivpron. der 2. Pers. Sg.* yourself

direkt ①*Adj.* direct ②*adv.* straight; directly; **etw.** ∼ **übertragen** broadcast sth. live

Direkt·flug *der* direct flight

Direktion *die;* ∼, ∼en management;
(Büroräume) managers' offices *pl.*

Direktor *der;* ∼s, ∼en, **Direktorin** *die;*
∼, ∼nen director; (einer Schule) headmaster/
headmistress; (einer Strafanstalt) governor; (einer
Abteilung) manager

Direkt·übertragung *die* live broadcast

Dirigent *der;* ∼en, ∼en, **Dirigentin** *die;*
∼, ∼nen conductor

dirigieren *tr. V.* (a) *auch itr.* conduct
(b) (führen) steer

Disc·jockey /'dıskdʒɔke/ *der* disc jockey

Disco /'dısko:/ *die;* ∼, ∼s disco

Diskette *die;* ∼, ∼n (DV) floppy disk

Disketten·laufwerk *das* (DV) [floppy-
]disk drive

Diskont·satz *der* (Finanzw.) discount rate

Diskothek *die;* ∼, ∼en discothèque

Diskrepanz *die;* ∼, ∼en discrepancy

diskret ⒈ *Adj.* (vertraulich) confidential;
(taktvoll) discreet; tactful
⒉ *adv.* (vertraulich) confidentially; (taktvoll)
discreetly; tactfully

Diskretion *die;* ∼ (a) (Verschwiegenheit, Takt)
discretion
(b) (Unaufdringlichkeit) discreetness

diskriminieren *tr. V.* discriminate against

Diskriminierung *die;* ∼, ∼en
discrimination

Diskussion *die;* ∼, ∼en discussion; **zur** ∼
stehen be under discussion

Diskussions-: ∼**beitrag** *der*
contribution to a/the discussion; ∼**leiter**
der chair[man] [of the discussion];
∼**leiterin** *die* chair[woman] [of the
discussion]

diskutieren ⒈ *itr. V.* über etw. (*Akk.*) ∼:
discuss sth.
⒉ *tr. V.* discuss

Disqualifikation *die;* ∼, ∼en (auch Sport)
disqualification

disqualifizieren *tr. V.* disqualify

Distanz *die;* ∼, ∼en (auch fig.) distance

distanzieren *refl. V.* sich von jmdm./etw.
∼ (fig.) dissociate oneself from sb./sth.

distanziert *Adj.* reserved

Distel *die;* ∼, ∼n thistle

Distel·fink *der* goldfinch

Disziplin *die;* ∼, ∼en discipline;
(Selbstbeherrschung) [self-]discipline

disziplinieren ⒈ *tr. V.* discipline
⒉ *refl. V.* discipline oneself

diszipliniert ⒈ *Adj.* well-disciplined;
(beherrscht) disciplined
⒉ *adv.* in a well-disciplined way; (beherrscht)
in a disciplined way

divers... /di'vɛrs.../ *Adj.* various; (mehrer...)
several

Dividende /divi'dɛndə/ *die;* ∼, ∼n (Wirtsch.)
dividend

dividieren *tr. V.* divide

Division *die;* ∼, ∼en (auch Milit.) division

DM *Abk.* = **Deutsche Mark** DM

D-Mark /'de:-/ *die* Deutschmark

DNS *Abk.* (Chemie)
= **Desoxyribonukleinsäure** DNA

Do. *Abk.* = **Donnerstag** Thur[s].

doch ⒈ *Konj.* but
⒉ *Adv.* (a) (jedoch) but
(b) (dennoch) all the same; still
(c) (geh.: nämlich) **wusste er** ∼, **dass** ...:
because he knew that ...
(d) (entgegen allen gegenteiligen Behauptungen,
Annahmen) **er war also** ∼ **der Mörder!** so he
'was the murderer!
(e) (ohnehin) in any case
⒊ *Interj.* **Das stimmt nicht. – Doch!** That's
not right. – [Oh] yes it is!; **Hast du keinen
Hunger? – Doch!** Aren't you hungry? – Yes [I
am]!
⒋ *Partikel* (a) (Ungeduld ausdrückend) **pass** ∼
auf! [oh] do be careful!; **das ist** ∼ **nicht zu
glauben** that's just incredible
(b) (Zweifel ausdrückend) **du hast** ∼ **meinen
Brief erhalten?** you did get my letter, didn't
you?
(c) (Überraschung ausdrückend) **das ist** ∼ **Karl!**
there's Karl!
(d) (verstärkt Bejahung/Verneinung ausdrückend)
gewiss/sicher ∼: [why] certainly; of course;
ja ∼: [yes,] all right; **nicht** ∼**!** (abwehrend)
[no,] don't!
(e) (Wunsch verstärkend) **wäre es** ∼ ...: if only
it were ...

Docht *der;* ∼[e]s, ∼e wick

Dock *das;* ∼s, ∼s dock

Dogge *die;* ∼, ∼n: [deutsche] ∼: Great
Dane

Dogma *das;* ∼s, Dogmen (auch fig.) dogma

dogmatisch (Theol., auch fig.) *Adj.* dogmatic

Dohle *die;* ∼, ∼n jackdaw

Doktor *der;* ∼s, ∼en (auch ugs.: Arzt) doctor;
(Titel) Doctor

Doktor·arbeit *die* doctoral thesis

Doktor·grad *der* doctorate; doctor's degree

Doktorin *die;* ∼, ∼nen ▶ DOKTOR

Doktor·titel *der* title of doctor

Doktrin *die;* ∼, ∼en doctrine

Dokument *das;* ∼[e]s, ∼e document

Dokumentar-: ∼**bericht** *der*
documentary report; ∼**film** *der*
documentary [film]

Dokumentation *die;* ∼, ∼en (a)
documentation
(b) (Bericht) documentary report

dokumentieren *tr. V.* (a) document; (fig.)
demonstrate
(b) (festhalten) record

Dolch *der;* ∼[e]s, ∼e dagger

Dolde *die;* ∼, ∼n (Bot.) umbel

doll (bes. norddt., salopp) ⒈ *Adj.* (a)
(ungewöhnlich) incredible

---

*alte Schreibung - vgl. Hinweis auf S. xiv

(b) (großartig) great (coll.)
2 *adv.* **(a)** (großartig) fantastically [well] (coll.)
(b) (sehr) ⟨hurt⟩ dreadfully (coll.), like mad

Dollar *der;* ~s, ~s dollar; **zwei** ~: two dollars

dolmetschen *itr. V.* act as interpreter

Dolmetscher *der;* ~s, ~, **Dolmetscherin** *die;* ~, ~nen interpreter

Dom *der;* ~[e]s, ~e cathedral

dominieren *itr. V.* dominate

dominikanisch *Adj.* Dominican; **die Dominikanische Republik** the Dominican Republic

Domino *das;* ~s, ~s (Spiel) dominoes *sing.*

Domizil *das;* ~s, ~e (geh.) domicile; residence

Dom·pfaff *der;* ~en *od.* ~s, ~en (Zool.) bullfinch

Dompteur /dɔmpˈtøːɐ̯/ *der;* ~s, ~e, **Dompteurin** /dɔmpˈtøːrɪn/ *die;* ~, ~nen, **Dompteuse** /dɔmpˈtøːzə/ *die;* ~, ~nen tamer

Donau *die;* ~: Danube

Donner *der;* ~s, ~: thunder

donnern *itr. V.* **(a)** (*unpers.*) thunder **(b)** (fig.) thunder; ⟨engine⟩ roar

Donners·tag *der* Thursday; *s. auch* DIENSTAG

donnerstags *Adv.* on Thursday[s]; *s. auch* DIENSTAGS

Donner·wetter *das* (ugs.) **(a)** (Krach) row **(b)** /'--'--/ **zum** ~ **[noch einmal]!** damn it!; ~! my word

doof (ugs.) **1** *Adj.* stupid; dumb (coll.) **2** *adv.* stupidly

Doping /'doːpɪŋ/ *das;* ~s (Sport) taking drugs

Doping·kontrolle *die* (Sport) drug[s] test

Doppel *das,* ~s, ~ **(a)** (Kopie) duplicate; copy **(b)** (Sport) doubles *sing. or pl.*

doppel-, Doppel-: ~**bett** *das* double bed; ~**bock** *das* extra-strong bock beer; ~**decker** *der;* ~~s, ~~: biplane; ~**deutig** /-dɔy̯tɪç/ **1** *Adj.* **(a)** (ambiguous; **(b)** (anzüglich) suggestive; **2** *adv.* **(a)** ambiguously; **(b)** (anzüglich) suggestively; ~**fenster** *das* double-glazed window; ~**gänger** *der;* ~~s, ~~, ~**gängerin** *die;* ~~, ~~nen double; ~**haus** *das* pair of semi-detached houses; ~**haus·hälfte** *die* semi[-detached house]; ~**kinn** *das* double chin; ~**klick** *der;* ~~s, ~~s (DV) double click; ~**moral** *die* double standards *pl.;* ~**pass**, **~***paß** *der* (ugs.) der ~**pass** dual nationality *no art.;* ~**punkt** *der* colon; ~**stunde** *die* double period

doppelt **1** *Adj.* double; **die** ~**e Menge** twice the quantity; **mit** ~**er Kraft arbeiten** work with twice as much energy

2 *adv.* ~ **so groß/alt wie …:** twice as large/old as …; **sich** ~ **anstrengen** try twice as hard

Doppelte *das; adj. Dekl.* **das** ~ **bezahlen** pay twice as much; pay double

Doppel-: ~**tür** *die* double door; ~**zentner** *der* 100 kilograms; ~**zimmer** *das* double room

Dorf *das;* ~[e]s, Dörfer village; **auf dem** ~: in the country

Dorf-: ~**bewohner** *der,* ~**bewohnerin** *die* villager; ~**depp** *der* (bes. südd., österr.) village idiot; ~**trottel** *der* village idiot

Dorn *der;* ~[e]s, ~en thorn; **jmdm. ein** ~ **im Auge sein** annoy sb. intensely

dornig *Adj.* thorny

Dorn·röschen (*das*) the Sleeping Beauty

dörren *tr. V.* dry

Dörr-: ~**fleisch** *das* (südd.) lean bacon; ~**obst** *das* dried fruit

Dorsch *der;* ~[e]s, ~e cod

dort *Adv.* there; ~ **bleiben** stay there; *s. auch* DA 1A

dort-: ***~\|**bleiben** ▶ DORT; ~**her** *Adv.* [von] ~**her** from there; ~**hin** *Adv.* there

dortig *Adj.* there

Dose *die;* ~, ~n **(a)** (Blech~) tin; (Pillen~) box; (Zucker~) bowl **(b)** (Konserven~) can; tin (Brit.); (Bier~) can

dösen *itr. V.* (ugs.) doze

Dosen-: ~**bier** *das* canned beer; ~**milch** *die* canned *or* (Brit.) tinned milk; ~**öffner** *der* can-opener; tin-opener (Brit.); ~**pfand** *das* deposit on [drink] cans

dosieren *tr. V.* etw. ~: measure out the required dose of sth.

Dosierung *die;* ~, ~en **(a)** measuring out; (das Zuführen) administering; (fig.) dispensing **(b)** ▶ DOSIS

Dosis *die;* ~, Dosen dose

Dossier /dɔˈsi̯eː/ *das,* (veraltet:) *der;* ~s, ~s dossier

Dotcom /'dɔtkɔm/ *das;* ~s, ~ dot-com [company]

Dotter *der od. das;* ~s, ~: yolk

Dotter·blume *die* marsh marigold

doubeln /'duːbl̩n/ *tr. V.* stand in for ⟨actor⟩; use a stand-in for ⟨scene⟩; **sich** ~ **lassen** use *or* have a stand-in

Dozent *der;* ~en, ~en, **Dozentin** *die;* ~, ~nen lecturer (für in)

dpa *Abk.* = **Deutsche Presse-Agentur** German Press Agency

Dr. *Abk.* = **Doktor** Dr

Drache *der;* ~n, ~n (Myth.) dragon

Drachen *der;* ~s, ~ **(a)** kite **(b)** (Fluggerät) hang-glider

Draht *der;* ~[e]s, Drähte **(a)** wire **(b)** (Leitung) wire; (Telefonleitung) line; wire **(c)** (Telefonverbindung) line

draht-, Draht-: ~**los** (Nachrichtenw.) **1** *Adj.* wireless; **2** *adv.* etw. ~**los** ⋯⟫

telegrafieren/übermitteln radio sth.; ~**seil**
das [steel] cable; ~**seil·bahn** *die* cable
railway; ~**zieher** *der;* ~~s, ~~,
~**zieherin** *die;* ~~, ~~nen (fig.) wire
puller

drall *Adj.* strapping ‹*girl*›; full, rounded
‹*cheeks, face, bottom*›

Drama *das;* ~s, Dramen drama; (fig., ugs.)
disaster

Dramatiker *der;* ~s, ~, **Dramatikerin**
die; ~, ~nen dramatist

dramatisch ① *Adj.* dramatic
② *adv.* dramatically

dramatisieren *tr. V.* dramatize

dramaturgisch *adj.* dramaturgical

dran *Adv.* (ugs.) (a) häng das Schild ~! put
the sign up!
(b) arm ~ sein be in a bad way; gut/schlecht
~ sein be well off/badly off; früh/spät ~ sein
be early/late; **ich bin ~**: it's my turn

dran|bleiben *unr. itr. V.; mit sein* (ugs.) (am
Telefon) hang on (coll.)

drang *1. u. 3. Pers. Sg. Prät. v.* DRINGEN

Drang *der;* ~[e]s, Dränge urge

dränge *1. u. 3. Pers. Sg. Konjunktiv II v.*
DRINGEN

drängeln (ugs.) ① *itr. V.* (a) push [and
shove]
(b) (auf jmdn. einreden) go on (coll.)
② *tr. V.* (a) push; shove
(b) (einreden auf) go on at (coll.)
③ *refl. V.* **sich nach vorn** ~: push one's way
to the front

drängen ① *itr. V.* (a) push
(b) **die Zeit drängt** time is pressing
② *tr. V.* (a) push
(b) (antreiben) press; urge
③ *refl. V.* crowd

drangsalieren *tr. V.* (quälen) torment;
(plagen) plague

dran-: ~|**halten** *unr. refl. V.* (ugs.) get a
move on (coll.); ~|**kommen** *unr. itr. V.; mit
sein* (ugs.) have one's turn; ~|**nehmen** *unr.
tr. V.* (ugs.) (beim Friseur usw.) see to; (beim Arzt)
see

drastisch ① *Adj.* drastic ‹*measure, means*›
② *adv.* drastically; ‹*punish*› severely

drauf *Adv.* (ugs.) on it

drauf-, Drauf-: ~**gänger** *der;* ~~s, ~~,
~**gängerin** *die;* ~~, ~~nen daredevil;
~**gängerisch** *Adj.* daring; ~|**gehen**
unr. itr. V.; mit sein (ugs.) (a) (umkommen) kick
the bucket (coll.); (b) (verbraucht werden) go (**für**
on); ~|**zahlen** (ugs.) ① *tr. V.* noch etwas/50
Euro ~zahlen fork out (coll.) *or* pay a bit
more/an extra 50 euros; ② *itr. V.* (Unkosten
haben) **ich zahle dabei noch** ~: it's costing
me money

draußen *Adv.* outside; **hier/da** ~: out here/
there; **von/nach** ~: from outside/outside

Dreck *der;* ~[e]s (a) (ugs.) dirt; (sehr viel)
filth; (Schlamm) mud
(b) (salopp abwertend: Angelegenheit) **mach
deinen** ~ **allein** do it yourself; **das geht dich
einen [feuchten]** ~ **an** (salopp) none of your
damned business (coll.)
(c) (salopp abwertend: Zeug) junk *no indef. art.*

Dreck·arbeit *die* (auch fig.) dirty work *no
indef. art., no pl.*/dirty job

dreckig ① *Adj.* (a) (ugs., auch fig.) dirty;
(sehr schmutzig) filthy
(b) (salopp: unverschämt) cheeky
② *adv.* (a) **es geht ihm** ~ (ugs.) he's in a bad
way
(b) (salopp: unverschämt) cheekily

Dreck-: ~**sau** *die,* ~**schwein** *das* (derb)
filthy swine

Dreh *der;* ~s, ~s (ugs.) (a) **den** ~
heraushaben have [got] the knack
(b) [so] **um den** ~: about that

Dreh-: ~**arbeiten** *Pl.* (Film) shooting *sing.*
(**zu** *of*); ~**bank** *die; Pl.* ~bänke lathe;
~**buch** *das* screenplay; [film] script

drehen ① *tr. V.* (a) turn
(b) (formen) twist ‹*rope, thread*›; roll
‹*cigarette*›
(c) (Film) shoot ‹*scene*›; film ‹*report*›; make
‹*film*›
② *itr. V.* (a) ‹*car*› turn; ‹*wind*› change
(b) **an etw.** (*Dat.*) ~: turn sth.
(c) (Film) shoot; film
③ *refl. V.* (a) turn
(b) (ugs.: zum Gegenstand haben) **sich um etw.**
~: be about sth.

Dreh-: ~**kreuz** *das* turnstile; ~**orgel** *die*
barrel organ; ~**ort** *der* (Film) location;
~**restaurant** *das* revolving restaurant;
~**stuhl** *der* swivel chair; ~**tür** *die*
revolving door

Drehung *die;* ~, ~en turn; (um einen
Mittelpunkt) revolution

Dreh-: ~**zahl** *die* revolutions *or* (coll.) revs
(*esp. per minute*); ~**zahl·messer** *der;*
~~s, ~~: revolution counter; rev counter
(coll.); tachometer

drei *Kardinalz.* three;

Drei *die;* ~, ~en three; **eine** ~ **schreiben**
(Schulw.) get a C

drei-, Drei-: ~**eck** *das* (Geom.) triangle;
~**eckig** *Adj.* triangular; ~**ein·halb**
Bruchz. three and a half

Dreier *der;* ~s, ~ (ugs.) three

dreierlei *indekl. Adj.* (a) *attr.* three kinds
or sorts of; three different
(b) *subst.* three [different] things

drei-, Drei-: ~**fach** *Vervielfältigungsz.*
triple; **die** ~**fache Menge** three times the
amount; ~**fache** *das; adj. Dekl.* **das**
~**fache kosten** cost three times as much; **das**
~**fache von 3 ist 9** Three times three is nine;
~**faltigkeit** *die;* ~~ (christl. Rel.) Trinity;
~**hundert** *Kardinalz.* three hundred;
~**jährig** *Adj.* (3 Jahre alt) three-year-old
attrib.; (3 Jahre dauernd) three-year *attrib.;*

∼**kampf** *der* (Sport) triathlon; ∼**klang** *der* triad; ∼**köpfig** *Adj.* ⟨*family, crew*⟩ of three; ∼**mal** *Adv.* three times; ∼**malig** *Adj.* eine ∼malige Wiederholung three repeats

drein (ugs.) ▶ DAREIN

drein-: ∼|**blicken,** ∼|**schauen** *itr. V.* look

drei-, Drei-: ∼**rad** *das* tricycle; ∼**satz** *der* rule of three; ∼**seitig** *Adj.* three-sided ⟨*figure*⟩; three-page ⟨*letter, leaflet, etc.*⟩

dreißig *Kardinalz.* thirty; *s. auch* ACHTZIG

dreißigjährig *Adj.* (30 Jahre alt) thirty-year-old *attrib.;* (30 Jahre dauernd) thirty-year *attrib.*

dreißigst... *Ordinalz.* thirtieth

Dreißigstel *das;* ∼s, ∼: thirtieth

dreist ⟨1⟩ *Adj.* brazen; barefaced ⟨*lie*⟩ ⟨2⟩ *adv.* brazenly

drei-stellig *Adj.* three-figure *attrib.*

Dreistigkeit *die;* ∼, ∼en (a) brazenness (b) (Handlung) brazen act

drei-, Drei-: ∼**tausend** *Kardinalz.* three thousand; ∼**teilig** *Adj.* three-part *attrib.;* three-piece *attrib.* ⟨*suit*⟩; ***∼**viertel** ▶ VIERTEL; ∼**viertel-stunde** /···'··/ *die* three-quarters of an hour; ∼**viertel-takt** /·'···/ *der* three-four time; ∼**zehn** *Kardinalz.* thirteen; *s. auch* ACHTZEHN

Dresche *die;* ∼ (salopp) walloping (coll.); thrashing

dreschen ⟨1⟩ *unr. tr. V.* (a) thresh (b) (salopp: schlagen) wallop (coll.); thrash ⟨2⟩ *unr. itr. V.* thresh

dressieren *tr. V.* train ⟨*animal*⟩

Dressur *die;* ∼, ∼en training

Drill *der;* ∼[e]s drilling; (Milit.) drill

drillen *tr. V.* (auch Milit.) drill

Drilling *der;* ∼s, ∼e triplet

drin *Adv.* (ugs.) (a) in it (b) ▶ DRINNEN

dringen *unr. itr. V.* (a) *mit sein* **durch/in** etw. ∼: penetrate etw. (b) *mit sein* **in jmdn.** ∼ (geh.) press sb. (c) **auf etw.** (*Akk.*) ∼: insist upon sth.

dringend ⟨1⟩ *Adj.* urgent; strong ⟨*suspicion, advice*⟩ ⟨2⟩ *adv.* urgently; ⟨*advise, suspect*⟩ strongly; ∼ **erforderlich** essential

dringlich ⟨1⟩ *Adj.* urgent ⟨2⟩ *adv.* urgently

Dringlichkeit *die;* ∼: urgency

drinnen *Adv.* inside; (im Haus) indoors; inside

dritt *in* **wir waren zu** ∼: there were three of us

dritt... *Ordinalz.* third

Drittel *das,* (schweiz. meist *der*); ∼s, ∼: third

dritteln *tr. V.* split *or* divide three ways

drittens *Adv.* thirdly

DRK *Abk.* = **Deutsches Rotes Kreuz** German Red Cross

Dr. med. *Abk.* = **doctor medicinae** MD

droben *Adv.* (südd., österr., sonst geh.) up there

Droge *die;* ∼, ∼n drug

drogen-, Drogen-: ∼**abhängig** *Adj.* addicted to drugs *postpos.;* ∼**abhängige** *der/die; adj. Dekl.* drug addict; ∼**abhängigkeit** *die* drug addiction; ∼**beratungs-stelle** *die* drug advice centre; ∼**gefährdet** *Adj.* at risk from drugs *postpos.;* ∼**handel** *der* drug trafficking; ∼**konsum** *der* drug-taking; ∼**konsument** *der,* ∼**konsumentin** *die* drug user; ∼**missbrauch,** *∼**mißbrauch** *der* drug abuse; ∼**rausch** *der* [state of] drug intoxication; **etw. im** ∼**rausch tun** do sth. while under the influence of drugs *or* while [high (coll.)] on drugs; ∼**süchtig** *Adj.* ▶ ∼ABHÄNGIG; ∼**szene** *die* drug scene

Drogerie *die;* ∼, ∼n chemist's [shop] (Brit.); drugstore (Amer.)

Drogist *der;* ∼en, ∼en, **Drogistin** *die;* ∼, ∼nen chemist (Brit.); druggist (Amer.)

drohen *itr. V., mod. V.* threaten; (bevorstehen) be threatening; **jmdm. droht etw.** sb. is threatened with sth.

drohend *Adj.* threatening; (bevorstehen) impending

Drohne *die;* ∼, ∼n drone

dröhnen *itr. V.* boom; ⟨*machine*⟩ roar

Drohung *die;* ∼, ∼en threat

drollig ⟨1⟩ *Adj.* funny; comical; (niedlich) sweet; cute (Amer.) ⟨2⟩ *adv.: s. Adj.:* comically; sweetly; cutely (Amer.)

Dromedar *das;* ∼s, ∼e dromedary

Drops *der od. das;* ∼, ∼: fruit *or* (Brit.) acid drop

drosch *1. u. 3. Pers. Sg. Prät. v.* DRESCHEN

Drossel *die;* ∼, ∼n thrush

drosseln *tr. V.* (a) turn down ⟨*heating, air conditioning*⟩; throttle back ⟨*engine*⟩ (b) (herabsetzen) reduce

Dr. phil. *Abk.* = **doctor philosophiae** Dr

drüben *Adv.* **dort** *od.* **da** ∼: over there; ∼ **auf der anderen Seite** over on the other side

Druck¹ *der;* ∼[e]s, **Drücke** (a) (auch fig.) pressure (b) **ein** ∼ **auf den Knopf** a touch of the button

Druck² *der;* ∼[e]s, ∼e (a) printing; **in** ∼ **gehen** go to press (b) (Produkt) print

Druck-buchstabe *der* printed letter

drucken *tr., itr. V.* print

drücken ⟨1⟩ *tr. V.* (a) press; press, push ⟨*button*⟩; squeeze ⟨*juice, pus*⟩ (**aus** out of); **jmdm. die Hand** ∼: squeeze sb.'s hand (b) (liebkosen) **jmdn.** ∼: hug [and squeeze] sb. (c) ⟨*shoe etc.*⟩ pinch ···⟩

(d) (herabsetzen) push down ⟨price, rate⟩; depress ⟨sales⟩; bring down ⟨standard⟩ **2** itr. V. **(a)** press; **auf den Knopf** ∼: press or push the button; „**bitte** ∼": 'push' **(b)** (Druck verursachen) ⟨shoe etc.⟩ pinch **3** refl. V. (ugs.: sich entziehen) shirk; **sich vor etw.** (Dat.) ∼: get out of sth.

drückend Adj. **(a)** heavy ⟨debt, taxes⟩; serious ⟨worries⟩; grinding ⟨poverty⟩ **(b)** (schwül) oppressive

Drucker der; ∼s, ∼: printer

Druckerei die; ∼, ∼en printing works; (Firma) printing house; printer's

Druckerin die; ∼, ∼nen printer

druck-, Druck-: ∼**fehler** der misprint; printer's error; ∼**knopf** der press stud (Brit.); snap fastener; ∼**luft** die compressed air; ∼**mittel** das means of bringing pressure to bear (**gegenüber** on); ∼**reif** **1** Adj. ready for publication; (∼fertig) ready for press; **2** adv. ⟨speak⟩ in a polished manner; ∼**sache** die (Postw.) printed matter; ∼**schrift** die **(a)** printed writing; **(b)** (Schriftart) type[face]; **(c)** (Schriftwerk) pamphlet

drum Adv. (ugs.) **(a)** ▶ DARUM; **(b)** [a]round; **alles** od. **das [ganze] Drum und Dran** (bei einer Mahlzeit) all the trimmings; (bei einer Feierlichkeit) all the palaver that goes with it (coll.)

Drum·herum das; ∼s everything that goes/went with it

drunter Adv. (ugs.) underneath; **es** od. **alles geht ∼ und drüber** everything is topsy-turvy

Drüse die; ∼, ∼n gland

Dschungel /'dʒʊŋl̩ / der; ∼s, ∼ (auch fig.) jungle

dt. Abk. = **deutsch** G.

Dtzd. Abk. = **Dutzend** doz.

du Personalpron.; 2. Pers. Sg. Nom. you; **Du zueinander sagen** use the familiar form in addressing one another; s. auch (Gen.) DEINER, (Dat.) DIR, (Akk.) DICH

Dübel der; ∼s, ∼: plug

ducken **1** refl. V. duck **2** itr. V. (fig. abwertend) humble oneself (**vor** + Dat. before)

Duckmäuser der; ∼s, ∼, **Duckmäuserin** die; ∼, ∼nen (abwertend) moral coward

Duckmäusertum das; ∼s (abwertend) moral cowardice

Dudel·sack der bagpipes pl.

Duell das; ∼s, ∼e duel

duellieren refl. V. fight a duel

Duett das; ∼[e]s, ∼e (Musik) duet; **im ∼ singen** sing a duet

Duft der; ∼[e]s, Düfte scent; (von Parfüm, Blumen) scent; fragrance; (von Kaffee usw.) aroma

duften itr. V. smell (**nach** of)

dulden tr. V. tolerate; put up with

duldsam **1** Adj. tolerant (**gegen** towards) **2** adv. tolerantly

Duma die: die ∼: the Duma

dumm, dümmer, dümmst... **1** Adj. **(a)** stupid **(b)** (unvernünftig) foolish **(c)** (ugs.: töricht, albern) idiotic; silly **(d)** (ugs.: unangenehm) nasty ⟨feeling⟩; annoying ⟨habit⟩; **das wird mir jetzt zu ∼** (ugs.) I've had enough of it **2** adv. (ugs.) idiotically

Dumme der/die; adj. Dekl. fool; **der/die ∼ sein** (ugs.) be the loser

dummer·weise Adv. **(a)** unfortunately; (ärgerlicherweise) annoyingly **(b)** (törichterweise) foolishly

Dummheit die; ∼, ∼en **(a)** stupidity **(b)** (unkluge Handlung) stupid thing

Dumm·kopf der (ugs.) nitwit (coll.)

dumpf **1** Adj. **(a)** dull ⟨thud, rumble of thunder⟩; muffled ⟨sound, thump⟩ **(b)** (muffig) musty **(c)** (stumpfsinnig) dull **2** adv. **(a)** ⟨echo⟩ hollowly **(b)** (stumpfsinnig) apathetically

Dumping /'dampɪŋ/ das; ∼s (Wirtsch.) dumping

Dumping·preis der dumping price

Düne die; ∼, ∼n dune

düngen **1** tr. V. fertilize ⟨soil, lawn⟩; spread fertilizer on ⟨field⟩; scatter fertilizer around ⟨plants⟩ **2** itr. V. **gut ∼** ⟨substance⟩ be a good fertilizer

Dünger der; ∼s, ∼: fertilizer

dunkel **1** Adj. (auch fig.) dark; (tief) deep ⟨voice, note⟩; (undeutlich) vague **2** adv. **(a)** (tief) ⟨speak⟩ in a deep voice **(b)** (undeutlich) vaguely

Dünkel der; ∼s (geh.) arrogance; (Einbildung) conceit[edness]

dunkel-: ∼**blond** Adj. light brown ⟨hair⟩; ⟨person⟩ with light brown hair; ∼**häutig** Adj. dark-skinned

Dunkelheit die; ∼: darkness

Dunkel·kammer die darkroom

dunkeln itr. V. (unpers.) **es dunkelt** (geh.) it is growing dark

Dunkel·ziffer die number of unrecorded cases

dünn **1** Adj. thin; slim ⟨book⟩; fine ⟨stocking⟩; watery ⟨coffee, tea, beer⟩ **2** adv. thinly ⟨sliced, populated⟩; lightly ⟨dressed⟩

Dunst der; ∼[e]s, Dünste **(a)** haze; (Nebel) mist **(b)** (Geruch) smell

dünsten tr. V. steam ⟨fish, vegetables⟩; braise ⟨meat⟩; stew ⟨fruit⟩

dunstig Adj. hazy

Duo *das;* ~s, ~s (Musik) duet; (fig. scherzh.) duo; pair

Duplikat *das;* ~[e]s, ~e duplicate

duplizieren *tr. V.* duplicate

Dur *das;* ~ (Musik) major [key]

durch [1] *Präp. mit Akk.* **(a)** (räumlich) through

(b) (modal) by; ~ Boten by courier; zehn [geteilt] ~ zwei ten divided by two

[2] *Adv.* **(a)** (hin~) das ganze Jahr ~: throughout the whole year

(b) (ugs.: vorbei) es war 3 Uhr ~: it was gone 3 o'clock

(c) ~ und ~ nass/überzeugt wet through [and through]/completely *or* totally convinced

(d) [durch etw.] ~ sein be through [sth.]

(e) ~ sein (abgefahren sein) ⟨train, bus, etc.⟩ have gone

(f) ~ sein (fertig sein) have finished; durch etw. ~ sein have got through sth.

(g) ~ sein ⟨cheese⟩ be ripe; ⟨meat⟩ be well done

durch|arbeiten [1] *tr. V.* work through [2] *itr. V.* work through; die Nacht ~: work through the night

durch·aus *Adv.* absolutely; perfectly, quite ⟨correct, possible, understandable⟩; das ist ~ richtig that is entirely right; ~ nicht by no means

durch|beißen *unr. tr. V.* bite through

durch|blättern *tr. V.* leaf through

Durch·blick *der* (ugs.) den [absoluten] ~ haben know [exactly] what's going on

durch|blicken *itr. V.* **(a)** look through; durch etw. ~: look through sth.

(b) ~ lassen, dass .../wie ...: hint that .../at how ...

Durch·blutung *die* flow of blood (+ *Gen.* to); [blood] circulation

Durchblutungs·störung *die* disturbance of the blood supply

durch|bohren¹ *tr. V.* drill through ⟨wall, plank⟩; drill ⟨hole⟩

durch·bohren² *tr. V.* pierce

durch|brechen¹ [1] *unr. tr. V.* etw. ~: break sth. in two

[2] *unr. itr. V.; mit sein* **(a)** break in two

(b) (hervorkommen) ⟨sun⟩ break through

(c) (einbrechen) fall through ⟨ice, floor, etc.⟩

durch·brechen² *unr. tr. V.* break through

durch|brennen *unr. itr. V.; mit sein* **(a)** ⟨heating coil, lightbulb⟩ burn out; ⟨fuse⟩ blow

(b) (ugs.: weglaufen) (von zu Hause) run away; (mit der Kasse, mit dem Geliebten/der Geliebten) run off

durch|bringen *unr. tr. V.* get through; (bei Wahlen) jmdn. ~: get sb. elected; seine Familie/sich ~: support one's family/oneself

Durch·bruch *der* (fig.) breakthrough

durch·dacht *Adj.* ein wenig/gut ~er Plan a badly/well thought-out plan; nicht [genügend] ~ sein not be sufficiently well thought-out

durch|drehen [1] *tr. V.* put ⟨meat⟩ through the mincer *or* (Amer.) grinder

[2] *itr. V. auch mit sein* (ugs.) crack up (coll.)

durch|dringen¹ *unr. tr. V.; mit sein* ⟨rain, sun⟩ come through

durch·dringen² *unr. tr. V.* penetrate; jmdn. ~ ⟨idea⟩ take hold of sb. [completely]

durch·einander *Adv.* ~ bringen (+ *Akk.*) (in Unordnung bringen) get ⟨room, flat⟩ into a mess; get ⟨papers, file⟩ into a muddle; muddle up ⟨papers, file⟩; (verwirren) confuse; (verwechseln) confuse ⟨names, etc⟩; get ⟨names etc.⟩ mixed up; ~ sein ⟨papers, desk, etc.⟩ be in a muddle; (verwirrt sein) be confused; (aufgeregt sein) be flustered

Durcheinander *das;* ~s **(a)** muddle; mess

(b) (Wirrwarr) confusion

*durcheinander|bringen
▶ DURCHEINANDER

durch|exerzieren *tr. V.* (ugs.) go through, practise ⟨rules, multiplication tables⟩; rehearse ⟨situation⟩

durch|fahren *unr. itr. V.; mit sein* **(a)** [durch etw.] ~: drive through [sth.]

(b) (nicht anhalten) go straight through; (mit dem Auto) drive straight through; der Zug fährt [in H.] durch the train doesn't stop [at H.]

Durch·fahrt *die* **(a)** „~ verboten" 'no entry except for access'; auf der ~ sein be passing through

(b) (Weg) thoroughfare; „bitte [die] ~ freihalten" 'please do not obstruct'

Durch·fall *der* diarrhoea *no art.*

durch|fallen *unr. itr. V.; mit sein* **(a)** fall through

(b) (ugs.: nicht bestehen) fail

durch|finden *unr. refl. V.* find one's way through

durchführbar *Adj.* practicable

Durchführbarkeit *die;* ~: practicability;

durch|führen [1] *tr. V.* carry out; put into effect ⟨decision, programme⟩; perform ⟨operation⟩; hold ⟨meeting, election, examination⟩

[2] *itr. V.* durch etw./unter etw. (*Dat.*) ~ ⟨track, road⟩ go through/under sth.

Durch·führung *die* carrying out; (einer Operation) performing; (einer Versammlung, Wahl, Prüfung) holding; (eines Wettbewerbs) staging

Durch·gang *der* **(a)** passage[way]; „kein ~", „ ~ verboten" 'no thoroughfare'

(b) (Phase) stage; (einer Versuchsreihe) run; (Sport, Wahlen) round

Durchgangs-: ~straße *die* through road; ~verkehr *der* through traffic

durch|geben *unr. tr. V.* announce ⟨news⟩; ···⟶

give ⟨*results, weather report*⟩; **eine Meldung im Radio/Fernsehen** ∼: make an announcement on the radio/on television

du̇rch·gefroren *Adj.* frozen stiff; chilled to the bone

du̇rch|gehen ⓵ *unr. itr. V.; mit sein* **(a)** [durch etw.] ∼: go *or* walk through [sth.] **(b)** (hindurchdringen) [durch etw.] ∼: ⟨*rain, water*⟩ come through [sth.] **(c)** (direkt zum Ziel führen) ⟨*train etc.*⟩ go [right] through (**bis** to); ⟨*flight*⟩ go direct **(d)** (andauern) go on (**bis zu** until) **(e)** (hingenommen werden) ⟨*discrepancy*⟩ be tolerated; ⟨*mistake, discourtesy*⟩ be allowed to pass; **jmdm. etw.** ∼ **lassen** let sb. get away with sth. **(f)** ⟨*horse*⟩ bolt ⓶ *unr. tr. V.; mit sein* go through ⟨*newspaper, text*⟩

du̇rch·gehend ⓵ *Adj.* **(a)** continuous ⟨*line, pattern, etc.*⟩; constantly recurring ⟨*motif*⟩ **(b)** (direkt) through *attrib.* ⟨*train, carriage*⟩; direct ⟨*flight, connection*⟩ ⓶ *adv.* ∼ **geöffnet haben/bleiben** be/stay open all day

du̇rchgeknallt *Adj.* (ugs.) crazy

du̇rch·geschwitzt *Adj.* ⟨*person*⟩ soaked *or* bathed in sweat; ⟨*clothes*⟩ soaked with sweat; sweat-soaked *attrib.* ⟨*clothes*⟩

du̇rch|greifen *unr. itr. V.* [hart] ∼: take drastic measures *or* steps

du̇rch|halten ⓵ *unr. itr. V.* hold out; (bei einer schwierigen Aufgabe) see it through ⓶ *unr. tr. V.* stand

du̇rch|hängen *unr. itr. V.* sag

du̇rch|kämmen *tr. V.* **(a)** comb ⟨*hair*⟩ through **(b)** (durchsuchen) comb ⟨*area etc.*⟩

du̇rch|kommen *unr. itr. V.; mit sein* **(a)** come through; (mit Mühe) get through **(b)** (ugs.: beim Telefonieren) get through **(c)** (durchgehen, -fahren usw.) **durch etw.** ∼: come through sth. **(d)** (ugs.: überleben) pull through

du̇rch|kreuzen¹ *tr. V.* cross out

durch·kreuzen² *tr. V.* (vereiteln) frustrate

du̇rch|lassen *unr. tr. V.* **(a)** jmdn. [durch etw.] ∼: let sb. through [sth.] **(b)** (durchlässig sein) let ⟨*light, water, etc.*⟩ through

du̇rchlässig *Adj.* permeable; (porös) porous; (undicht) leaky; ⟨*raincoat, shoe*⟩ that lets in water

Du̇rch·lauf *der* (Sport, DV) run

du̇rch|laufen¹ ⓵ *unr. itr. V.; mit sein* **(a)** [durch etw.] ∼: run through [sth.]; (durchrinnen) trickle through [sth.] **(b)** (passieren) ⟨*runners*⟩ run *or* pass through **(c)** (ohne Pause laufen) run without stopping ⓶ *unr. tr. V.* go through ⟨*soles*⟩

durch·laufen² *unr. tr. V.* go through ⟨*phase, stage*⟩

du̇rchlaufend ⓵ *Adj.* continuous ⓶ *adv.* ⟨*numbered, marked*⟩ in sequence

du̇rch|lesen *unr. tr. V.* etw. [ganz] ∼: read sth. [all the way] through

durch·leuchten *tr. V.* x-ray; (fig.) investigate ⟨*case, matter, problem, etc.*⟩ thoroughly

durch·löchern *tr. V.* make holes in

du̇rch|machen (ugs.) ⓵ *tr. V.* **(a)** undergo ⟨*change*⟩; complete ⟨*training course*⟩; go through ⟨*stage, phase*⟩; serve ⟨*apprenticeship*⟩ **(b)** (erleiden) go through **(c)** (durcharbeiten) work through ⟨*lunch break etc.*⟩ ⓶ *itr. V.* (durcharbeiten) work [right] through; (durchfeiern) celebrate all night/day etc.; keep going all night/day etc.

Du̇rchmesser *der;* ∼s, ∼: diameter

du̇rch|nehmen *unr. tr. V.* (Schulw.: behandeln) do

du̇rch|pauken *tr. V.* (ugs.) force through ⟨*law, regulation, etc.*⟩

du̇rch|peitschen *tr. V.* (ugs. abwertend) railroad ⟨*law, application, etc.*⟩ through

du̇rch|probieren *tr. V.* taste ⟨*wines, cakes, etc.*⟩ one after another

durch·queren *tr. V.* cross; travel across ⟨*country*⟩; ⟨*train*⟩ go through ⟨*country*⟩

du̇rch|rechnen *tr. V.* calculate ⟨*costs etc.*⟩ [down to the last penny]; check ⟨*bill*⟩ thoroughly

Du̇rch·reise *die* journey through

du̇rch|reisen *itr. V.; mit sein* travel through

Du̇rchreise·visum *das* transit visa

du̇rch|reißen ⓵ *unr. tr. V.* etw. ∼: tear sth. in two *or* in half ⓶ *unr. itr. V.; mit sein* ⟨*fabric, garment*⟩ rip, tear; ⟨*thread, rope*⟩ snap [in two]

du̇rch|rosten *itr. V.; mit sein* rust through

du̇rchs *Präp.* + *Art.* = durch das

Du̇rch·sage *die* announcement; (an eine bestimmte Person) message

durchschaubar *Adj.* transparent; **leicht** ∼: easy to see through

durch·schauen *tr. V.* see through ⟨*person, plan, etc.*⟩; see ⟨*situation*⟩ clearly

du̇rch|schlafen *unr. itr. V.* sleep [right] through

Du̇rch·schlag *der* **(a)** (Kopie) carbon [copy] **(b)** (Küchengerät) strainer

du̇rch|schlagen *unr. tr. V.* etw. ∼: chop sth. in two

du̇rchschlagend *Adj.* resounding ⟨*success*⟩; decisive ⟨*effect, measures*⟩; conclusive ⟨*evidence*⟩

du̇rch|schneiden *unr. tr. V.* cut through

⟨thread, cable⟩; cut ⟨ribbon, sheet of paper⟩ in two; cut ⟨throat, umbilical cord⟩; **etw. in der Mitte ∼:** cut sth. in half

Durch·schnitt der average; **im ∼:** on average; **über/unter dem ∼ liegen** be above/below average

durchschnittlich [1] Adj. (a) nicht präd. average ⟨growth, performance, output⟩ (b) (ugs.: nicht außergewöhnlich) ordinary ⟨life, person, etc.⟩ (c) (mittelmäßig) modest; ordinary ⟨appearance⟩ [2] adv. ⟨earn etc.⟩ on [an] average; **∼ groß** of average height

Durchschnitts-: **∼alter** das average age; **∼geschwindigkeit** die average speed; **∼mensch** der average person; (Alltagsmensch) ordinary person; **∼temperatur** die average temperature; **∼wert** der average or mean value

Durch·schrift die carbon [copy]

durch|sehen [1] unr. itr. V. [durch etw.] ∼: look through [sth.] [2] unr. tr. V. look through

***durch|sein ▶ DURCH 2 D–G

durch|setzen [1] tr. V. carry through; achieve ⟨objective⟩; enforce ⟨demand, claim⟩ [2] refl. V. assert oneself; ⟨idea etc.⟩ find or gain acceptance

Durch·sicht die: nach ∼ der Unterlagen after looking or checking through the documents

durchsichtig Adj. (auch fig.) transparent

durch|sprechen unr. tr. V. talk ⟨matter etc.⟩ over; discuss ⟨matter etc.⟩ thoroughly

durch|stehen unr. tr. V. stand ⟨pace, boring job⟩; come through ⟨difficult situation⟩; get over ⟨illness⟩

durch|stellen tr. V. put ⟨call⟩ through (**in** + Akk., **auf** + Akk. to)

durch|streichen unr. tr. V. cross out; (in Formularen) delete

durch·suchen tr. V. search (**nach** for); search, scour ⟨area⟩ (**nach** for)

Durchsuchung die; ∼, ∼en search

durch|treten unr. tr. V. press ⟨clutch pedal, brake pedal⟩ right down

durchtrieben (abwertend) [1] Adj. crafty; sly [2] adv. craftily; slyly

durch·wachsen Adj. **∼er Speck** streaky bacon

Durch·wahl die (a) direct dialling; **mein Apparat hat keine ∼:** I don't have an outside line (b) ▶ DURCHWAHLNUMMER

durch|wählen itr. V. (a) dial direct (b) (bei Nebenstellenanlagen) dial straight through

Durchwahl·nummer die number of the/one's direct line

durch|zählen tr. V. count; count up

durch|ziehen [1] unr. tr. V. jmdn./etw. [durch etw.] ∼: pull sb./sth. through [sth.]; **ein Gummiband [durch etw.] ∼:** draw an elastic through [sth.] [2] unr. itr. V.; mit sein pass through; ⟨soldiers⟩ march through

Durch·zug der draught

dürfen [1] unr. Modalverb; 2. Part. dürfen: (a) etw. tun ∼: be allowed to do sth.; **darf ich rauchen?** may I smoke?; **was darf es sein?** can I help you? (b) Konjunktiv II + Inf. **das dürfte der Grund sein** that is probably the reason [2] unr. tr., itr. V. **er hat nicht gedurft** he was not allowed to

durfte 1. u. 3. Pers. Sg. Prät. v. DÜRFEN

dürfte 1. u. 3. Pers. Sg. Konjunktiv II v. DÜRFEN

dürr Adj. (a) withered; arid, barren ⟨ground, earth⟩ (b) (mager) scrawny

Dürre die; ∼, ∼n drought

Durst der; ∼[e]s thirst; ∼ haben be thirsty; **ich habe ∼ auf ein Bier** I could just drink a beer

durstig Adj. thirsty

durst-, Durst-: **∼löscher** der thirst-quencher; **∼stillend** Adj. thirst-quenching; **∼strecke** die lean period or time

Dusche die; ∼, ∼n shower

duschen itr., refl. V. have a shower

Düse die; ∼, ∼n (Technik) nozzle; (eines Vergasers) jet

Düsen-: **∼flugzeug** das jet aircraft; **∼motor** der jet engine

düster [1] Adj. (a) dark; gloomy; dim ⟨light⟩ (b) (fig.) gloomy; sombre ⟨colour, music⟩ [2] adv. (fig.) gloomily

Dutzend das; ∼s, ∼e dozen; **zwei ∼:** two dozen

dutzend·weise Adv. in [their] dozens (coll.)

duzen tr. V. call ⟨sb.⟩ 'du' (the familiar form of address)

Duz·freund der, **Duz·freundin** die good friend (whom one addresses with 'du')

dynamisch [1] Adj. (auch fig.) dynamic [2] adv. dynamically

Dynamit das; ∼s dynamite

Dynamo der; ∼s, ∼s dynamo

Dynastie die; ∼, ∼n dynasty

D-Zug /'de:-/ der express train

Ee

e, E /e:/ *das;* ~, ~ **(a)** (Buchstabe) e/E
(b) (Musik) [key of] E

Ebbe *die;* ~, ~n ebb tide; (Zustand) low tide;
es ist ~: the tide is out

eben 1 *Adj.* **(a)** flat
(b) (glatt) level
2 *adv.* **(a)** (gerade jetzt) just
(b) (kurz) [for] a moment

Ebene *die,* ~, ~n **(a)** plain; **in der** ~: on
the plain
(b) (Geom., Physik) plane
(c) (fig.) level

eben·falls *Adv.* likewise; as well; **danke,** ~:
thank you, [and] [the] same to you

Eben·holz *das* ebony

eben·so *Adv.* **(a)** *mit Adjektiven, Adverbien*
just as; **ich mag Erdbeeren** ~ **gern [wie...]** I
like strawberries just as much [as ...]; ~
gern würde ich an den Strand gehen I would
just as soon go to the beach; ~ **gut** just as
well
(b) *mit Verben* in exactly the same way

***ebenso·gern** *usw.* ▶ EBENSO A

Eber *der;* ~s, ~: boar

Eber·esche *die* rowan; mountain ash

ebnen *tr. V.* level ⟨*ground*⟩

Echo *das;* ~s, ~s echo

echt 1 *Adj.* **(a)** genuine; real ⟨*love,
friendship*⟩
(b) (typisch) real, typical
2 *adv.* **(a)** (ugs. verstärkend) really
(b) (typisch) typically

Eck *das;* ~s, ~e (südd., österr.:) ~e corner

Eck-: ~**ball** *der* (Sport) corner [kick/hit/
throw]; **einen** ~**ball treten** take a corner;
~**bank** *die; Pl.* ~**bänke** corner seat

Ecke *die;* ~, ~n corner; **an der** ~: on *or* at
the corner; **um die** ~: round the corner

eckig *Adj.* square; angular

Eck·zahn *der* canine tooth

edel *Adj.* **(a)** thoroughbred ⟨*horse*⟩; species
⟨*rose*⟩
(b) (großmütig) noble[-minded], high-minded
⟨*person*⟩; noble ⟨*thought, gesture, feelings,
deed*⟩; honourable ⟨*motive*⟩

Edel-: ~**metall** *das* precious metal;
~**nutte** *die* (salopp) high-class tart (sl.);
~**pilz·käse** *der* blue[-veined] cheese;
~**stahl** *der* stainless steel; ~**stein** *der*
precious stone; gem[stone]

Edition *die;* ~, ~en edition

Edutainment /ɛdju'temmənt/ *das;* ~s
edutainment

EDV *Abk.* = **elektronische
Datenverarbeitung** EDP

EEG *Abk.*
= **Elektroenzephalogramm** EEG; **ein
EEG machen lassen** have an EEG

Efeu *der;* ~s ivy

Effekt *der;* ~[e]s, ~e effect

effekt·voll *Adj.* effective; dramatic ⟨*pause,
gesture, entrance*⟩

EG *Abk.* **(a)** = **Europäische
Gemeinschaft** EC
(b) = **Erdgeschoss**

egal *Adj.* (ugs.: einerlei) **es ist jmdm.** ~: it's all
the same to sb.; **[ganz]** ~, **wie/wer** *usw.* ...:
no matter how/who *etc.* ...

Egge *die;* ~, ~n harrow

E-Gitarre *die* electric guitar

Egoist *der;* ~en, ~en, **Egoistin** *die;* ~,
~nen egoist

egoistisch 1 *Adj.* egoistic[al]
2 *adv.* egoistically

ehe *Konj.* before

Ehe *die;* ~, ~n marriage

Ehe-: ~**bett** *das* marriage bed; (Doppelbett)
double bed; ~**bruch** *der* adultery; ~**frau**
die wife; (verheiratete Frau) married woman;
~**krach** *der* (ugs.) row; ~**leute** *Pl.*
married couple

ehelich *Adj.* marital; matrimonial; conjugal
⟨*rights, duties*⟩; legitimate ⟨*child*⟩

ehemalig *Adj.* former

ehe-, Ehe-: ~**mann** *der; Pl.* ~**männer**
husband; (verheirateter Mann) married man;
~**mündig** *Adj.* (Rechtsspr.) of marriageable
age *postpos.*; ~**mündig sein** be of
marriageable age *or* of an age to marry;
~**mündigkeit** *die* (Rechtsspr.) being of
marriageable age; ~**paar** *das* married
couple

eher *Adv.* **(a)** (früher) earlier; sooner
(b) (lieber) rather; sooner

Ehe-: ~**ring** *der* wedding ring;
~**scheidung** *die* divorce; ~**vertrag** *der*
(Rechtsw.) marriage contract

Ehre *die;* ~, ~n honour; **jmdm.** ~ **antun** pay
tribute to sb.

ehren *tr. V.* **(a)** honour; **Sehr geehrter Herr
Müller!/Sehr geehrte Frau Müller!** Dear Herr
Müller/Dear Frau Müller
(b) (Ehre machen) **deine Hilfsbereitschaft ehrt
dich** your willingness to help does you credit

ehren-, Ehren-: ~**amt** *das* honorary
position *or* post; ~**amtlich** 1 *Adj.*

honorary ⟨*position, membership*⟩; voluntary ⟨*help, worker*⟩; **2** *adv.* in an honorary capacity; (freiwillig) on a voluntary basis

ehrenhaft *Adj.* honourable

ehren-, Ehren-: ~**rührig** *Adj.* defamatory ⟨*allegations*⟩; ~**sache** *die:* das ist ~sache that is a point of honour; ~sache! you can count on me!; ~**voll** *Adj.* honourable; ~**wert** *Adj.* (geh.) worthy; ~**wort** *das; Pl.* ~~e: ~wort [!/?] word of honour [!/?]

ehrerbietig *Adj.* (geh.) respectful

Ehr·furcht *die* reverence (vor + *Dat.* for)

ehrfürchtig *Adj.* reverent

ehr-, Ehr-: ~**gefühl** *das* sense of honour; ~**geiz** *der* ambition; ~**geizig** *Adj.* ambitious

ehrlich *Adj.* honest; genuine ⟨*concern, desire, admiration*⟩; upright ⟨*character*⟩

Ehrlichkeit *die;* ~ ▸ EHRLICH: honesty; genuineness; uprightness

ehr·los *Adj.* dishonourable

Ehrung *die;* ~, ~en: die ~ der Preisträger the prize-giving (Brit.) *or* (Amer.) awards ceremony; bei der ~ der Sieger when the winners were awarded their medals/ trophies

ehr·würdig *Adj.* venerable

Ei *das;* ~[e]s, ~er egg

Eiche *die;* ~, ~n oak [tree]; (Holz) oak [wood]

Eichel *die;* ~, ~n acorn

eichen *tr. V.* calibrate ⟨*measuring instrument, thermometer*⟩; standardize ⟨*weights, measures, containers, products*⟩; adjust ⟨*weighing scales*⟩

Eich·hörnchen *das* squirrel

Eid *der;* ~[e]s, ~e oath

Eidechse /'ai:dɛksə/ *die;* ~, ~n lizard

eides·stattlich *Adj.* (Rechtsw.) eine ~e Erklärung a statutory declaration

Ei·dotter *der od. das* egg yolk

Eier-: ~**becher** *der* eggcup; ~**kuchen** *der* pancake; (Omelett) omelette; ~**likör** *der* egg flip; ~**stock** *der* (Physiol., Zool.) ovary; ~**uhr** *die* egg timer

Eifer *der;* ~s eagerness

Eifer·sucht *die* jealousy (auf + *Akk.* of)

eifer·süchtig *Adj.* jealous (auf + *Akk.* of)

eifrig *Adj.* eager

Ei·gelb *das;* ~[e]s, ~e egg yolk

eigen *Adj.* own; (selbstständig) separate

eigen-, Eigen-: ~**art** *die* (Wesensart) particular nature; (Zug) peculiarity; eine ~art dieser Stadt one of the characteristic features of this city; ~**artig** *Adj.* peculiar; strange; odd; ~**artigerweise** *Adv.* strangely [enough]; oddly [enough]; ~**artigkeit** *die* peculiarity; strangeness; oddness; ~**brötelei** *die;* ~~, ~~en taking an [unduly] independent line; ~**brötler** *der;* ~~s, ~~, ~**brötlerin**

die; ~~, ~~**nen** loner; lone wolf; ~**dynamik** *die* inherent dynamism; ~**händig** **1** *Adj.* personal ⟨*signature*⟩; holographic ⟨*will, document*⟩; **2** *adv.* ⟨*present, sign*⟩ personally; ~**heim** *das* house of one's own

Eigenheit *die;* ~, ~en peculiarity

eigen-, Eigen-: ~**initiative** *die* initiative of one's own; ~**lob** *das* self-praise; ~**mächtig** *Adj.* unauthorized; ~**name** *der* proper name; ~**nützig** *Adj.* self-seeking; selfish ⟨*motive*⟩

eigens *Adv.* specially

Eigenschaft *die;* ~, ~en quality; characteristic; (von Sachen, Stoffen) property

Eigenschafts·wort *das; Pl.* Eigenschaftswörter adjective

eigen-, Eigen-: ~**sinn** *der* obstinacy; ~**sinnig** *Adj.* obstinate; ~**ständig** *Adj.* independent; ~**ständigkeit** *die;* ~~: independence

eigentlich **1** *Adj.* (wirklich) actual; real; (wahr) true; (ursprünglich) original **2** *Adv.* actually **3** *Partikel* wie spät ist es ~? tell me, what time is it?; was willst du ~? what exactly do you want?

Eigen·tor *das* (Ballspiele, fig.) own goal

Eigentum *das;* ~s property; (einschließlich Geld usw.) assets *pl.*

Eigentümer *der;* ~s, ~: owner; (Hotel~, Geschäfts~) proprietor

Eigentümerin *die;* ~, ~nen owner; (Hotel~, Geschäfts~) proprietress; proprietor

Eigentums·wohnung *die* owner-occupied flat (Brit.); condominium apartment (Amer.)

eigen-, Eigen-: ~**vorsorge** private [pension] provision; ~**willig** *Adj.* self-willed

eignen *refl. V.* be suitable

Eigner *der;* ~s, ~, **Eignerin** *die;* ~, ~nen owner

Eignung *die;* ~: suitability; seine ~ zum Fliegen his aptitude for flying

Eignungs-: ~**prüfung** *die,* ~**test** *der* aptitude test

Eil-: ~**bote** *der,* ~**botin** *die* special messenger; „durch *od.* per ~boten" (veralt.) 'express'; ~**brief** *der* express letter

Eile *die;* ~: hurry; in ~ sein be in a hurry

eilen *itr. V.* (a) mit sein hurry; (besonders schnell) rush
(b) (dringend sein) be urgent; „eilt!" 'urgent'

eilig **1** *Adj.* (a) hurried; es ~ haben be in a hurry
(b) (dringend) urgent **2** *adv.* hurriedly

Eil·zug *der* semi-fast train

Eimer *der;* ~s, ~: bucket; (Milch~) pail; (Abfall~) bin; ein ~ [voll] Wasser a bucket of water; im ~ sein (salopp) be up the spout (coll.)

ein¹ ① *Kardinalz.* one; ∼ **für alle Mal,** *∼ **für allemal** once and for all
② *unbest. Art.* a/an
③ *Indefinitpron.* ▶ IRGENDEIN A; *s. auch* EINER

ein² (elliptisch) ∼ – **aus** (an Schaltern) on – off

Ein|akter *der;* ∼**s,** ∼: one-act play

einander *reziprokes Pron.; Dat. u. Akk.* (geh.) each other; one another

ein|arbeiten *tr. V.* train ⟨*employee*⟩

ein·armig *Adj.* one-armed

ein|äschern *tr. V.* cremate

ein|atmen *tr., itr. V.* breathe in

ein·äugig *Adj.* one-eyed

Ein·bahn·straße *die* one-way street

Ein·band *der; Pl.* **Einbände** binding

Ein·bau *der; Pl.* ∼**ten** fitting; (eines Motors) installation

ein|bauen *tr. V.* build in, fit; install ⟨*engine, motor*⟩

Einbau·küche *die* fitted kitchen

ein·beinig *Adj.* one-legged

ein|berufen *unr. tr. V.* summon; call

Ein·berufung *die* (a) (das Einberufen) calling (b) (zur Wehrpflicht) call-up; conscription; draft (Amer.)

Einbett·zimmer *das* single room

ein|beziehen *unr. tr. V.* include

ein|biegen *unr. itr. V.; mit sein* turn

ein|bilden *refl. V.* (a) sich (*Dat.*) etw. ∼: imagine sth.
(b) (ugs.) sich (*Dat.*) etwas ∼: be conceited (auf + *Akk.* about)

Ein·bildung *die* (a) imagination
(b) (falsche Vorstellung) fantasy
(c) (Hochmut) conceitedness

ein|binden *unr. tr. V.* bind ⟨*book*⟩; etw. neu ∼: rebind sth.

ein|blenden *tr. V.* (Rundf., Ferns., Film) insert

Ein·blick *der* (a) view; ∼ **in etw.** (*Akk.*) **haben** be able to see into sth.
(b) (Durchsicht) jmdm. ∼ **in etw.** (*Akk.*) **gewähren** allow sb. to look at *or* examine sth.
(c) (Kenntnis) insight

ein|brechen *unr. itr. V.* (a) *mit haben od. sein* break in; **in eine Bank** ∼: break into a bank; **bei jmdm.** ∼: burgle sb.
(b) *mit sein* (einstürzen) ⟨*roof, ceiling*⟩ cave in
(c) *mit sein* (durchbrechen) fall through

Ein·brecher *der;* ∼**s,** ∼, **Einbrecherin** *die;* ∼, ∼**nen** burglar

ein|bringen *unr. tr. V.* (a) bring in ⟨*harvest*⟩
(b) (verschaffen) Gewinn/Zinsen ∼: yield a profit/bring in interest; jmdm. Ruhm ∼: bring sb. fame
(c) (Parl.: vorlegen) introduce ⟨*bill*⟩
(d) invest ⟨*capital, money*⟩

Ein·bruch *der* (a) burglary; **ein** ∼ **in eine Bank** a break-in at a bank
(b) (das Einstürzen) collapse

einbürgern ① *tr. V.* naturalize
② *refl. V.* ⟨*custom, practice*⟩ become established; ⟨*person, plant, animal*⟩ become naturalized

Einbürgerung *die;* ∼, ∼**en** naturalization

Ein·buße *die* loss

ein|büßen *tr. V.* lose; (durch eigene Schuld) forfeit

ein|checken *tr., itr. V.* (Flugw.) check in

ein|cremen *tr. V.* put cream on ⟨*hands etc.*⟩; **sich** ∼: put cream on

ein|dämmen *tr. V.* (fig.) check; stem

ein|decken ① *refl. V.* stock up
② *tr. V.* (ugs.: überhäufen) jmdn. mit Arbeit ∼: swamp sb. with work

Eindecker *der;* ∼**s,** ∼ (Flugw.) monoplane

eindeutig *Adj.* clear

Eindeutigkeit *die;* ∼, ∼**en** clarity

ein|dringen *unr. itr. V.; mit sein* **in etw.** (*Akk.*) ∼: penetrate into sth.; ⟨*bullet*⟩ pierce sth.; (allmählich) ⟨*water, sand, etc.*⟩ seep into sth.

ein·dringlich *Adj.* urgent; impressive ⟨*voice*⟩; forceful, powerful ⟨*words*⟩

Eindringling *der;* ∼**s,** ∼**e** intruder

Ein·druck *der; Pl.* **Eindrücke** impression

ein|drücken *tr. V.* smash in ⟨*mudguard, bumper*⟩; stave in ⟨*side of ship*⟩; smash ⟨*pier, column, support*⟩; break ⟨*window*⟩; crush ⟨*ribs*⟩; flatten ⟨*nose*⟩

eindrucks·voll ① *Adj.* impressive
② *adv.* impressively

eine ▶ EIN¹

ein|ebnen *tr. V.* level

eineiig /'ai:n|ai:ɪç/ *Adj.* identical ⟨*twins*⟩

ein-ein·halb *Bruchz.* one and a half; ∼ **Stunden** an hour and a half

ein|engen *tr. V.* (a) jmdn. ∼: restrict sb.'s movement[s]
(b) (fig.) restrict

einer, eine, eines, eins *Indefinitpron.* (man) one; (jemand) someone; somebody; (fragend, verneint) anyone; anybody; **kaum einer** hardly anybody; **ein[e]s ist sicher** one thing is for sure

Einer *der;* ∼**s,** ∼ (a) (Math.) unit
(b) (Sport) single sculler; **im** ∼: in the single sculls

einerlei *Adj.* ∼, **ob/wo/wer** *usw.* no matter whether/where/who *etc.*; **es ist** ∼: it makes no difference

Einerlei *das;* ∼**s** monotony

einerseits *Adv.* on the one hand

ein·fach ① *Adj.* (a) simple
(b) (nicht mehrfach) single ⟨*knot, ticket, journey*⟩
② *Partikel* simply; just

Einfachheit *die;* ∼: simplicity

ein|fädeln ① *tr. V.* thread (**in** + *Akk.* into)

---
*old spelling - see note on page xiv

2 *refl. V.* (Verkehrsw.) filter in

ein|fahren **1** *unr. itr. V.; mit sein* come in; ⟨train⟩ pull in; **in den Bahnhof ~:** pull into the station
2 *unr. tr. V.* **(a)** bring in ⟨harvest⟩ **(b)** (beschädigen) knock down ⟨wall⟩; smash in ⟨mudguard⟩

Ein·fahrt *die* **(a)** (das Hineinfahren) entry; **Vorsicht bei der ~ des Zuges!** stand clear [of the edge of the platform], the train is approaching
(b) (Zufahrt) entrance; (Autobahn~) slip road; „**keine ~**" 'no entry'

Ein·fall *der* **(a)** (Idee) idea
(b) (Licht~) incidence (Optics)

ein|fallen *unr. itr. V.; mit sein* **(a)** jmdm. **~:** occur to sb.; **was fällt dir denn ein!** what do you think you're doing?
(b) (in Erinnerung kommen) **ihr Name fällt mir nicht ein** I cannot think of her name; **plötzlich fiel ihr ein, dass ...:** suddenly she remembered that ...
(c) (von Licht) come in

einfalls-, Einfalls-: **~los** *Adj.* unimaginative; lacking in ideas; **~losigkeit** *die;* **~~:** unimaginativeness; lack of ideas; **~reich** *Adj.* imaginative; full of ideas; **~reichtum** *der* imaginativeness; wealth of ideas; **~tor** *das* gateway

Einfalt *die;* **~:** simpleness; simple-mindedness

einfältig *Adj.* simple; naïve; naïve ⟨remarks⟩

Ein·familien·haus *das* house (as opposed to block of flats etc.)

ein|fangen *unr. tr. V.* catch

ein|fassen *tr. V.* border; edge; frame ⟨picture⟩; set ⟨gem⟩; edge ⟨grave, lawn, etc.⟩

Ein·fassung *die* ▶ EINFASSEN: border; edging; frame; setting

ein|fetten *tr. V.* grease; dubbin ⟨leather⟩; **sich** (*Dat.*) **die Haut/Hände ~:** rub cream into one's skin/hands

ein|finden *unr. refl. V.* arrive; (sich treffen) meet; ⟨crowd⟩ gather

ein|fliegen *unr. tr. V.* fly in

ein|flößen *tr. V.* **(a)** jmdm. Tee **~:** pour tea into sb.'s mouth
(b) (fig.) jmdm. Angst **~:** put fear into sb.

Ein·fluss, *Ein·fluß *der* influence

einfluss-, *einfluß-, Einfluss-, *Einfluß-: **~bereich** *der* sphere of influence; **~nahme,** *die;* **~~:** exertion of influence (**auf** + *Akk.* on); **~reich** *Adj.* influential

ein·förmig *Adj.* monotonous

ein|frieren **1** *unr. itr. V.; mit sein* freeze; ⟨pipes⟩ freeze up
2 *unr. tr. V.* **(a)** deep-freeze ⟨food⟩
(b) (fig.) freeze

ein|fügen *tr. V.* **(a)** fit in; **etw. in etw.** (*Akk.*) **~:** fit sth. into sth.
(b) (DV) insert; paste

ein|fühlen *refl. V.* **sich in jmdn. ~:** empathize with sb.

einfühlsam *Adj.* understanding

Ein-fühlung *die;* **~:** empathy (**in** + *Akk.* with)

Ein·fuhr *die;* **~, ~en** ▶ IMPORT

ein|führen *tr. V.* **(a)** (als Neuerung) introduce ⟨fashion, method, technology⟩
(b) (importieren) import

Einfuhr-: **~sperre** *die,* **~stopp** *der* embargo *or* ban on imports

Ein·führung *die* introduction

Einfuhr·verbot *das* ▶ **~SPERRE**

Ein·gabe *die* **(a)** (Gesuch) petition; (Beschwerde) complaint
(b) (DV) input

Eingabe-: **~gerät** *das* (DV) input device; **~taste** *die* (DV) enter key

Ein-gang *der* entrance; „**kein ~**" 'no entry'

ein·gängig *Adj.* catchy

eingangs *Adv.* at the beginning *or* start

Eingangs-: **~halle** *die* entrance hall; (eines Hotels, Theaters) foyer; **~tür** *die* (von Kaufhaus, Hotel usw.) [entrance] door; (von Wohnung, Haus usw.) front door

ein|geben *unr. tr. V.* (DV) input; **etw. in den Computer ~:** input sth. into the computer

ein·gebildet *Adj.* **(a)** imaginary ⟨illness⟩
(b) (arrogant) conceited

Eingeborene *der/die; adj. Dekl.* (veralt.) native

ein·gefahren *Adj.* long-established; deep-rooted ⟨prejudice⟩; **sich auf** *od.* **in ~en Bahnen** *od.* **Gleisen bewegen** go on in the same old way

ein|gehen **1** *unr. itr. V.; mit sein* **(a)** arrive
(b) (fig.) **in die Geschichte ~:** go down in history
(c) (schrumpfen) shrink
(d) **auf eine Frage ~/nicht ~:** go into *or* deal with/ignore a question; **auf jmdn. ~:** be responsive to sb.; **auf jmdn. nicht ~:** ignore sb.'s wishes
2 *unr. tr. V.* enter into ⟨contract, matrimony⟩; take ⟨risk⟩; accept ⟨obligation⟩

eingehend *Adj.* detailed

Ein·gemachte *das; adj. Dekl.* preserved fruit/vegetables

ein|gemeinden *tr. V.* incorporate ⟨village⟩ (**in** + *Akk.,* nach into)

ein·geschnappt *Adj.* (ugs.) huffy

Ein·geständnis *das* admission

ein|gestehen *unr. tr. V.* admit

Eingeweide *das;* **~s, ~:** entrails *pl.;* innards *pl.*

ein|gewöhnen *refl. V.* get used to one's new surroundings

ein|gießen *unr. tr., itr. V.* pour in

ein|gliedern tr. V. integrate (in + Akk. into); incorporate ⟨village, company⟩ (in + Akk. into); (einordnen) include (in + Akk. in)

Ein·gliederung die ▶ EINGLIEDERN: integration; incorporation; inclusion

ein|graben unr. tr. V. bury (in + Akk. in); sink ⟨pile, pipe⟩ (in + Akk. into)

ein|gravieren tr. V. engrave (in + Akk. on)

ein|greifen unr. itr. V. intervene (in + Akk. in)

Ein·griff der (a) intervention (in + Akk. in) (b) (Med.) operation

ein|haken ⓵ tr. V. (a) (mit Haken befestigen) fasten (b) sich ~: link arms ⓶ refl. V. sich bei jmdm. ~: link arms with sb.

Ein·halt der: jmdm./einer Sache ~ gebieten od. tun (geh.) halt sb./sth.

ein|halten ⓵ unr. tr. V. keep ⟨appointment⟩; meet ⟨deadline, commitments⟩; keep to ⟨diet, speed limit, agreement⟩; observe ⟨regulation⟩ ⓶ unr. itr. V. (geh.) stop

ein·heimisch Adj. native; home attrib. ⟨team⟩

Einheimische der/die; adj. Dekl. local

Einheit die; ~, ~en unity

einheitlich ⓵ Adj. unified; (unterschiedslos) uniform ⟨dress⟩; standard ⟨procedure, practice⟩ ⓶ adv. ~ gekleidet sein be dressed the same

einhellig ⓵ Adj. unanimous ⓶ adv. unanimously

ein|holen ⓵ tr. V. (a) catch up with ⟨person, vehicle⟩ (b) make up ⟨arrears, time⟩ ⓶ itr. V. (ugs.) ▶ EINKAUFEN 1

ein·hundert Kardinalz. ▶ HUNDERT

einig Adj. sich (Dat.) ~ sein be agreed; sich (Dat.) ~ werden reach agreement

einig... Indefinitpron. u. unbest. Zahlwort some; ~e wenige a few; ~e Hundert several hundred

einigen ⓵ tr. V. unite ⓶ refl. V. reach an agreement

einigermaßen Adv. somewhat

Einigkeit die; ~ (a) unity (b) (Übereinstimmung) agreement

ein·jährig Adj. (ein Jahr alt) one-year-old attrib.; one year old pred.; (ein Jahr dauernd) one-year attrib.

Ein·kauf der (a) Einkäufe machen do some shopping (b) (eingekaufte Ware) purchase (c) (Abteilung) purchasing department

ein|kaufen ⓵ itr. V. shop; ~ gehen go shopping ⓶ tr. V. buy; purchase

Ein·käufer der, **Ein·käuferin** die buyer

Einkaufs-: ~**bummel** der [leisurely] shopping expedition; ~**liste** die shopping list; ~**preis** der (Kaufmannsspr.) wholesale price; ~**tasche** die shopping bag; ~**tüte** die shopping bag; ~**zentrum** das shopping centre; ~**zettel** der shopping list

ein|kehren itr. V.; mit sein stop; in einem Wirtshaus ~: stop at an inn

ein|klammern tr. V. etw. ~: put sth. in brackets; bracket sth.

Ein·klang der harmony; in od. im ~ stehen accord

ein|kleben tr. V. stick in

ein|kleiden tr. V. clothe

ein|klemmen tr. V. (a) (quetschen) catch (b) (fest einfügen) clamp

ein|kochen tr. V. preserve ⟨fruit etc.⟩

Einkommen das; ~s, ~: income

Einkommen·steuer die income tax

ein|kreisen tr. V. (a) etw. ~: put a circle round sth. (b) (umzingeln) surround

Einkünfte Pl. income sing.; feste ~: a regular income

ein|laden¹ unr. tr. V. load ⟨goods⟩

ein|laden² unr. tr. V. invite ⟨person⟩ (zu for)

einladend Adj. inviting

Ein·ladung die invitation

Ein·lage die (a) (in Brief) enclosure (b) (Kochk.) vegetables, dumplings, etc. added to a clear soup; (c) (Schuh~) arch support (d) (Programm~) interlude

ein|lagern tr. V. store; lay in ⟨stores⟩

Einlass, *Einlaß der; Einlasses, Einlässe admission

ein|lassen unr. tr. V. (a) (hereinlassen) admit; let in (b) (einfüllen) run ⟨water⟩

Ein·lauf der (Med.) enema

ein|laufen ⓵ unr. itr. V.; mit sein (a) ⟨ship⟩ come in (b) (kleiner werden) shrink ⓶ unr. tr. V. wear in ⟨shoes⟩>

ein|leben refl. V. settle down>

ein|legen tr. V. (a) load ⟨film⟩; engage ⟨gear⟩ (b) (Kochk.) pickle

ein|leiten tr. V. (a) introduce (b) induce ⟨birth⟩ (c) lead in; etw. in etw. (Akk.) ~: lead sth. into sth.

Ein·leitung die (a) introduction (b) (einer Geburt) induction

ein|leuchten itr. V. jmdm. ~: be clear to sb.

einleuchtend Adj. plausible

ein|liefern tr. V. take ⟨letter, person⟩ (bei, in + Akk. to)

---

*alte Schreibung - vgl. Hinweis auf S. xiv

Einlieger·wohnung *die* ≈ granny flat

ein|lösen *tr. V.* cash ⟨*cheque*⟩

ein|machen *tr. V.* preserve ⟨*fruit etc.*⟩; (in Gläser) bottle

einmal [1] *Adv.* (a) once; **noch ~ so groß** [wie] twice as big [as]; **etw. noch ~ tun** do sth. again
(b) /'-'-/ (später) one day; (früher) once; **es war ~ ...**: once upon a time there was ...
[2] *Partikel* **nicht ~**: not even; **wieder ~**: yet again

Einmal·eins *das;* **~**: [multiplication] tables *pl.*

einmalig [1] *Adj.* (a) unique; one-off ⟨*payment, purchase*⟩
(b) (ugs.) fantastic (coll.)
[2] *adv.* (ugs.) really fantastically (coll.)

Ein·marsch *der* (a) entry
(b) (Besetzung) invasion (in + *Akk.* of)

ein|marschieren *itr. V.; mit sein* march in

ein|massieren *tr. V.* massage *or* rub in

ein|mauern *tr. V.* (a) immure ⟨*prisoner, traitor*⟩; wall in ⟨*relic, treasure*⟩
(b) (ins Mauerwerk einfügen) **etw. in die Wand usw. ~**: set sth. into the wall *etc.*

ein|mischen *refl. V.* interfere (in + *Akk.* in)

ein|motten *tr. V.* **etw. ~**: put sth. into mothballs; (fig.) mothball

Ein·mündung *die* (von Straßen) junction

einmütig [1] *Adj.* unanimous
[2] *adv.* unanimously

ein|nähen *tr. V.* sew in

Einnahme *die;* **~, ~n** (a) income; (Staats~) revenue; (Kassen~) takings *pl.;*
(b) (von Arzneimitteln) taking
(c) (einer Stadt, Burg) taking

Einnahme·quelle *die* source of income; (des Staates) source of revenue

ein|nehmen *unr. tr. V.* (a) take; (verdienen) earn
(b) (ausfüllen) take up ⟨*amount of room*⟩
(c) (beeinflussen) **jmdn. für sich ~**: win sb. over

einnehmend *Adj.* winning ⟨*manner*⟩; **ein ~es Wesen haben** (scherzh.) take everything one can get

Ein·öde *die* barren waste

ein|ölen *tr. V.* (a) (mit Öl einreiben) **sich/jmdn. ~**: put *or* rub oil on oneself/sb.
(b) (ölen) oil

ein|ordnen [1] *tr. V.* arrange; put in order
[2] *refl. V.* (a) (Verkehrsw.) get into the correct lane; „~" 'get in lane'
(b) (sich einfügen) fit in

ein|packen [1] *tr. V.* pack (in + *Akk.* in); (einwickeln) wrap [up]
[2] *itr. V.* (ugs.) **er kann ~**: he's had it (coll.)

ein|parken *tr., itr. V.* park

ein|pflanzen *tr. V.* plant
(b) (Med., fig.) implant

ein|prägen *tr. V.* (a) stamp (in + *Akk.* into, on)
(b) (fig.) **sich** (*Dat.*) **etw. ~**: memorize sth.; **jmdm. etw. ~**: impress sth. on sb.

einprägsam *Adj.* easily remembered

ein|pudern *tr. V.* powder; **sich** (*Dat.*) **das Gesicht ~**: powder one's face

ein|rahmen *tr. V.* frame

ein|räumen *tr. V.* (a) put away
(b) (füllen) **seinen Schrank ~**: put one's things away in one's cupboard; **ein Zimmer ~**: put the furniture into a room
(c) (zugestehen) admit

ein|reden [1] *tr. V.* **jmdm. etw. ~**: talk sb. into believing sth.; **sich** (*Dat.*) **~, dass ...**: persuade oneself that ...
[2] *itr. V.* **auf jmdn. ~**: talk insistently to sb.

ein|regnen *refl. V.; unpers.* **es hat sich eingeregnet** it's begun to rain steadily

ein|reiben *unr. tr. V.* rub ⟨*substance*⟩ in; **etw. mit Öl ~**: rub oil into sth.

ein|reichen *tr. V.* submit; lodge ⟨*complaint*⟩; tender ⟨*resignation*⟩

ein|reihen [1] *refl. V.* **sich in etw.** (*Akk.*) **~**: join sth.
[2] *tr. V.* **jmdn. in eine Kategorie ~**: place sb. in a category

Einreiher *der;* **~s, ~**: single-breasted suit/jacket

Ein·reise *die* entry

Einreise·erlaubnis *die* entry permit

ein|reisen *itr. V.; mit sein* enter; **nach Schweden ~**: enter Sweden

ein|reißen [1] *unr. tr. V.* (a) pull down ⟨*building*⟩
(b) (einen Riss machen in) tear; rip
[2] *unr. itr. V.; mit sein* tear; rip

ein|renken *tr. V.* (a) (Med.) set
(b) (ugs.: bereinigen) sort out

ein|richten [1] *refl. V.* **sich schön ~**: furnish one's home beautifully; **sich häuslich ~**: make oneself at home
[2] *tr. V.* furnish ⟨*flat, house*⟩; fit out ⟨*shop*⟩; equip ⟨*laboratory*⟩

Ein·richtung *die* (a) furnishing
(b) (Mobiliar) furnishings *pl.*

ein|rollen [1] *tr. V.* roll up ⟨*carpet etc.*⟩; put ⟨*hair*⟩ in curlers
[2] *itr. V.; mit sein* roll in

ein|rosten *itr. V.; mit sein* go rusty

ein|rücken [1] *itr. V.; mit sein* (einmarschieren) move in
[2] *tr. V.* indent ⟨*line, heading, etc.*⟩

eins [1] *Kardinalz.* one; **es ist ~** it is one o'clock; **~ zu null** one-nil; **~ zu ~**: one all; **„~, zwei, drei!"** 'ready, steady, go'
[2] *Adj.* **mir ist alles ~**: it's all the same to me
[3] *Indefinitpron.* ▶ IRGENDEIN A

Eins *die;* **~, ~en** (a) one
(b) (Schulnote) one; A

einsam *Adj.* (a) lonely ⟨*person, decision*⟩
(b) (einzeln) solitary ⟨*tree, wanderer*⟩ ⋯⋮

(c) (abgelegen) isolated
(d) (menschenleer) deserted
Einsamkeit *die;* ∼ **(a)** loneliness
(b) (Alleinsein) solitude
(c) (Abgeschiedenheit) isolation
ein|sammeln *tr. V.* **(a)** (auflesen) pick up;
gather up
(b) (sich aushändigen lassen) collect in; collect
⟨*tickets*⟩
Ein·satz *der* **(a)** (aus Stoff) inset; (in Kochtopf,
Nähkasten usw.) compartment
(b) (Betrag) stake
(c) (Gebrauch) use; (von Truppen) deployment
Einsatz-: ∼**befehl** *der* order to go into
action; **den** ∼**befehl haben** have operational
command; ∼**leiter** *der,* ∼**leiterin** *die*
head of operations; ∼**wagen** *der* (der Polizei)
police car; (der Feuerwehr) fire engine;
(Notarztwagen) ambulance
ein|saugen *unr. (auch regelm.) tr. V.* suck
in; breathe [in] ⟨*fresh air*⟩
ein|schalten ① *tr. V.* **(a)** switch on
⟨*radio, TV, electricity, etc.*⟩
(b) (fig.) call in ⟨*press, police, expert, etc.*⟩
② *refl. V.* **(a)** switch [itself] on
(b) (eingreifen) intervene (**in** + *Akk.* in)
Einschalt·quote *die* (Rundf.) listening
figures *pl.;* (Ferns.) viewing figures *pl.*
ein|schärfen *tr. V.* **jmdm. etw.** ∼: impress
sth. [up]on sb.
ein|schätzen *tr. V.* judge ⟨*person*⟩; assess
⟨*situation, income, damages*⟩; (schätzen)
estimate
Ein·schätzung *die* ▶ EINSCHÄTZEN:
judging; assessment; estimation
ein|schenken *tr., itr. V.* **(a)** (eingießen)
pour [out]; **jmdm. etw.** ∼: pour out sth. for
sb.
(b) (füllen) fill [up] ⟨*glass, cup*⟩
ein|scheren *itr. V.; mit sein* **auf eine
Fahrspur** ∼: get *or* move into a lane
ein|schicken *tr. V.* send in
ein|schieben *unr. tr. V.* **(a)** push in
(b) (einfügen) insert; put on ⟨*trains, buses*⟩
ein|schiffen *tr., refl. V.* embark
einschl. *Abk. =* **einschließlich** incl.
ein|schlafen *unr. itr. V.; mit sein* **(a)** fall
asleep
(b) (verhüll.: sterben) pass away
(c) (gefühllos werden) go to sleep
ein|schläfern *tr. V.* **(a)** **jmdn.** ∼: send sb.
to sleep, (betäuben) put sb. to sleep
(b) (schmerzlos töten) **ein Tier** ∼: put an animal
to sleep
einschläfernd ① *Adj.* soporific
② *adv.* ∼ **wirken** have a soporific effect
ein|schlagen ① *unr. tr. V.* **(a)** knock in
(b) (zertrümmern) smash [in]
(c) (einwickeln) wrap up ⟨*present*⟩; cover
⟨*book*⟩

② *unr. itr. V.* **(a)** ⟨*bomb*⟩ land; ⟨*lightning*⟩
strike
(b) auf jmdn./etw. ∼: rain blows on sb./sth.
einschlägig ① *Adj.* specialist ⟨*journal,
shop*⟩; relevant ⟨*literature, passage*⟩
② *adv.* **er ist** ∼ **vorbestraft** he has previous
convictions for a similar offence/similar
offences
ein|schleichen *unr. refl. V.* steal in
ein|schließen *unr. tr. V.* **(a) etw. in etw.**
(*Dat.*) ∼: lock sth. up [in sth.]; **jmdn./sich** ∼:
lock sb./oneself in
(b) (umgeben) surround
einschließlich ① *Präp. mit Gen.*
including; ∼ **der Unkosten** including
expenses
② *adv.* **bis** ∼ **30. Juni** up to and including 30
June
ein|schmeicheln *refl. V.* **sich bei jmdm.**
∼: ingratiate oneself with sb.
ein|schmuggeln *tr. V.* smuggle in
ein|schneiden *unr. tr. V.* **(a)** make a cut
in
(b) (einritzen) carve
einschneidend *Adj.* drastic
ein|schneien *itr. V.; mit sein* get snowed
in
Ein·schnitt *der* cut
ein|schränken ① *tr. V.* **(a)** reduce, curb
⟨*expenditure, consumption*⟩
(b) (einengen) limit; restrict; **jmdn. in seinen
Rechten** ∼: limit *or* restrict sb.'s rights
② *refl. V.* economize
Einschränkung *die;* ∼, ∼**en** **(a)**
restriction; limitation
(b) (Vorbehalt) reservation
ein|schrauben *tr. V.* screw in
ein|schreiben *unr. tr. V.* **(a)** (Postw.)
register ⟨*letter*⟩
(b) (eintragen) **sich/jmdn.** ∼: enter one's/sb.'s
name
Ein·schreiben *das* (Postw.) registered
letter; **per** ∼: by registered mail
ein|schreiten *unr. itr. V.* intervene
ein|schrumpfen *itr. V.; mit sein* shrivel
up; (fig.) dwindle
ein|schüchtern *tr. V.* intimidate
ein|schulen *tr. V.* **eingeschult werden** start
school
ein|sehen *unr. tr. V.* **(a)** (überblicken) see
into
(b) (prüfend lesen) look at
(c) (erkennen) realize
(d) (begreifen) see
ein|seifen *tr. V.* lather
ein-seitig ① *Adj.* **(a)** on one side *postpos.;*
(b) (tendenziös) one-sided
② *adv.* **(a)** on one side
(b) (tendenziös) one-sidedly
ein|senden *unr. (auch regelm.) tr. V.* send
[in]

---

*old spelling - see note on page xiv

Ein·sender der, **Ein·senderin** die; ∼, ∼nen sender; (bei einem Preisausschreiben) entrant

Einsende·schluss, ***Einsende·schluß** der closing date

ein|setzen 1 tr. V. (a) (hineinsetzen) put in (b) put on ⟨special train etc.⟩ (c) (ernennen) appoint (d) (in Aktion treten lassen) use (e) (aufs Spiel setzen) stake ⟨money⟩ (f) (riskieren) risk 2 itr. V. begin; ⟨storm⟩ break 3 refl. V. (sich engagieren) **ich werde mich dafür** ∼, **dass** ...: I shall do what I can to see that ...; **sich nicht genug** ∼: ⟨pupil⟩ be lacking application; ⟨minister⟩ be lacking in commitment

Ein·sicht die (a) view (in + Akk. into) (b) (Einblick) ∼ **in die Akten nehmen** take or have a look at the files (c) (Erkenntnis) insight

einsichtig Adj. (a) (verständnisvoll) understanding (b) (verständlich) comprehensible

Ein·siedler der, **Ein·siedlerin** die hermit

ein·silbig Adj. (a) monosyllabic ⟨word⟩ (b) (fig.) taciturn ⟨person⟩

Einsilbigkeit die; ∼ (fig.) taciturnity

ein|sinken unr. itr. V. sink in

ein|sitzen unr. itr. V. (Rechtsw.) serve a prison sentence; **er sitzt für drei Jahre ein** he is serving three years or a three-year sentence

Einsitzer der; ∼s, ∼: single-seater

einsitzig Adj. single-seater attrib.

ein|spannen tr. V. harness ⟨horse⟩; put in ⟨paper⟩; fix ⟨fabric⟩; clamp ⟨work⟩

ein|sparen tr. V. save

Einsparung die; ∼, ∼en saving (an + Dat. in); ∼en an Kosten/Energie/Material savings or economies in costs/energy/materials

ein|speichern tr. V. (DV) feed in; input

ein|speisen tr. V. (Technik, DV) feed in

ein|sperren tr. V. lock up

einsprachig Adj. monolingual

ein|springen unr. itr. V.; mit sein stand in; (aushelfen) step in and help out

ein|spritzen tr. V. inject; **jmdm. etw.** ∼: inject sb. with sth.

Einspritz·motor der fuel-injection engine

Ein·spruch der objection (**gegen** to)

einspurig 1 Adj. single-track ⟨road⟩ 2 adv. **die Autobahn ist nur** ∼ **befahrbar** only one lane of the motorway is open

einst Adv. (geh.) once

ein|stampfen tr. V. pulp ⟨books⟩

Ein·stand der: **seinen** ∼ **geben** celebrate starting a new job

ein|stecken tr. V. (a) put in (b) (mitnehmen) put ⟨sth.⟩ in one's pocket/bag etc.

ein|stehen unr. itr. V. **für jmdn.** ∼: vouch for sb.; **für etw.** ∼: take responsibility for sth.

ein|steigen unr. itr. V.; mit sein (a) (in ein Fahrzeug) get in; **in ein Auto** ∼: get into a car; **in den Bus** ∼: get on the bus (b) (eindringen) climb in

einstellbar Adj. adjustable

ein|stellen 1 tr. V. (a) (einordnen) put away ⟨books etc.⟩ (b) (unterstellen) put in ⟨car, bicycle⟩ (c) (beschäftigen) take on ⟨workers⟩ (d) (regulieren) adjust (e) (beenden) stop; call off ⟨search, strike⟩ (f) (Sport) equal ⟨record⟩ 2 refl. V. (a) arrive (b) ⟨pain, worry⟩ begin; ⟨success⟩ come; ⟨symptoms, consequences⟩ appear (c) **sich auf etw.** (Akk.) ∼: prepare oneself for sth.; **sich schnell auf neue Situationen** ∼: adjust quickly to new situations

ein·stellig Adj. single-figure attrib.

Ein·stellung die (a) (von Arbeitskräften) employment (b) (Regulierung) adjustment (c) (Beendigung) stopping (d) (Sport) **die** ∼ **eines Rekordes** the equalling of a record (e) (Ansicht) attitude; **ihre politische/religiöse** ∼: her political/religious views pl.; (f) (Film) take

Ein·stich der (a) insertion (b) (∼stelle) puncture; prick

Ein·stieg der; ∼[e]s, ∼e (Eingang) entrance; (Tür) door/doors; „kein ∼" 'exit only'

Einstiegs·droge die come-on drug

ein|stimmen 1 itr. V. join in 2 tr. V. **jmdn. auf etw.** (Akk.) ∼: get sb. in the [right] mood for sth.

einstimmig 1 Adj. (a) (Musik) for one voice (b) (einmütig) unanimous ⟨decision, vote⟩ 2 adv. (a) (Musik) in unison (b) (einmütig) unanimously

ein·stöckig Adj. single-storey attrib.

ein|stöpseln tr. V. plug in ⟨telephone, electrical device⟩

Ein·strahlung die irradiation; (Sonnen∼) insolation

ein|streichen unr. tr. V. (ugs.: für sich behalten) pocket ⟨money, winnings, etc.⟩; (ugs. abwertend) rake in (coll.) ⟨money, profits, etc.⟩

ein|studieren tr. V. rehearse

ein|stufen tr. V. classify; categorize

ein·stündig Adj. one-hour attrib.

ein|stürmen itr. V. mit sein **mit Fragen auf jmdn.** ∼: besiege sb. with questions

Ein·sturz der collapse

ein|stürzen itr. V.; mit sein collapse

einst·weilen Adv. for the time being

eintägig Adj. one-day attrib.

Eintags·fliege die (Zool.) mayfly; (fig. ugs.) seven-day wonder

ein|tauchen ① *tr. V.* dip; (untertauchen) immerse
② *itr. V.; mit sein* dive in; ‹submarine› dive

ein|tauschen *tr. V.* exchange (**gegen** for)

ein·tausend *Kardinalz.:* ▸ TAUSEND

ein|teilen *tr. V.* (a) divide up; classify ‹plants, species›
(b) (disponieren, verplanen) organize

einteilig *Adj.* one-piece

ein|tippen *tr. V.* (in die Kasse) register; (in einen Rechner) key in

eintönig ① *Adj.* monotonous
② *adv.* monotonously

Eintönigkeit *die;* ∼: monotony

Ein·topf *der* stew

Ein·tracht *die* harmony

ein·trächtig *Adj.* harmonious

Eintrag *der;* ∼[e]s, Einträge entry

ein|tragen *unr. tr. V.* (a) enter
(b) (Amtsspr.) register

einträglich *Adj.* lucrative

ein|treffen *unr. itr. V.; mit sein* (a) arrive
(b) (verwirklicht werden) come true

ein|treiben *unr. tr. V.* collect ‹taxes, debts›; (durch Gerichtsverfahren) recover ‹debts, money›

Eintreibung *die;* ∼, ∼en (von Steuern, Schulden) collection; (durch Gerichtsverfahren) recovery

ein|treten ① *unr. itr. V.; mit sein* (a) enter; **bitte, treten Sie ein!** please come in
(b) (Mitglied werden) **in einen Verein/einen Orden** ∼: join a club/enter a religious order
(c) (Raumfahrt) enter
② *unr. tr. V.* kick in ‹door, window, etc.›

ein|trichtern *tr. V.* (salopp) **jmdm. etw.** ∼: drum sth. into sb.

Ein·tritt *der* (a) entry; entrance; **vor dem** ∼ **in die Verhandlungen** (fig.) before entering into negotiations
(b) (Beitritt) **der** ∼ **in einen Verein/einen Orden** joining a club/entering a religious order
(c) (von Raketen) entry
(d) (Zugang, Eintrittsgeld) admission
(e) (Beginn) onset; ∼ **der Dunkelheit** nightfall

Eintritts-: ∼**geld** *das* admission fee; ∼**karte** *die* admission ticket; ∼**preis** *der* admission charge

ein|trocknen *itr. V.; mit sein* dry; ‹water, toothpaste› dry up; ‹leather› dry out; ‹berry, fruit› shrivel

ein|üben *tr. V.* practise

Ein·vernehmen *das;* ∼s harmony; (Übereinstimmung) agreement

ein·vernehmlich (Amtsspr.) ① *Adv.* conjointly
② *adj.* conjoint

einverstanden *Adj.* ∼ **sein** agree; **mit jmdm./etw.** ∼ **sein** approve of sb./sth.

Ein·verständnis *das* consent (**zu** to)

Ein·waage *die* (Kaufmannsspr.) contents *pl.*

ein|wachsen *unr. itr. V.; mit sein* grow into the flesh; **eingewachsen** ingrown ‹toenail›

Einwand *der;* ∼[e]s, Einwände objection (**gegen** to)

Ein·wanderer *der*, **Ein·wanderin** *die* immigrant

ein|wandern *itr. V.; mit sein* immigrate (**in** + *Akk.* into)

Ein·wanderung *die* immigration

Einwanderungs-: ∼**behörde** *die* immigration authorities *pl.;* ∼**land** *das* country of immigration

einwand·frei ① *Adj.* flawless; impeccable ‹behaviour›; indisputable ‹proof›
② *adv.* flawlessly; ‹behave› impeccably; ‹prove› beyond question

ein|wechseln *tr. V.* (a) change ‹money›
(b) (Sport) substitute ‹player›

ein|wecken *tr. V.* preserve; bottle

Ein·weg-: ∼**flasche** *die* non-returnable bottle; ∼**pfand** *das* deposit on a/the disposable container; ∼**spritze** *die* disposable [hypodermic] syringe; ∼**verpackung** *die* disposable container

ein|weichen *tr. V.* soak

ein|weihen *tr. V.* open [officially] ‹bridge, road›; dedicate ‹monument›

Einweihung *die;* ∼, ∼en ▸ EINWEIHEN: [official] opening; dedication

ein|weisen *unr. tr. V.* (a) (in eine Tätigkeit) introduce
(b) (in ein Amt) install

ein|wenden *unr. (auch regelm.) tr. V.* **dagegen lässt sich vieles** ∼: there is a lot to be said against that

ein|werfen *unr. tr. V.* (a) mail ‹letter›; insert ‹coin›
(b) smash ‹window›
(c) throw in ‹ball›
(d) (bemerken, sagen) throw in ‹remark›

ein|wickeln *tr. V.* wrap [up]

ein|willigen *itr. V.* agree (**in** + *Akk.* to)

Einwilligung *die;* ∼, ∼en agreement

ein|wirken (a) (beeinflussen) **auf jmdn.** ∼: influence sb.
(b) (eine Wirkung ausüben) have an effect (**auf** + *Akk.* on)

Ein·wirkung *die* (Einfluss) influence; (Wirkung) effect

Einwohner *der;* ∼s, ∼, **Einwohnerin** *die;* ∼, ∼nen inhabitant

Einwohner·zahl *die* population

Ein·wurf *der* (a) insertion; (von Briefen) mailing
(b) (Ballspiele) throw-in
(c) (Bemerkung) interjection

Ein·zahl *die* singular

ein|zahlen *tr. V.* pay in; **Geld auf ein Konto** ∼: pay money into an account

Ein·zahlung *die* payment

ein|zäunen *tr. V.* fence in; enclose

Einzäunung *die;* ~, ~en fencing-in

ein|zeichnen *tr. V.* draw *or* mark in

einzeilig *Adj.* one-line *attrib.*

Einzel *das;* ~s, ~ (Sport) singles *pl.*

Einzel-: ~**bett** *das* single bed; ~**fall** *der*
(a) particular case; (b) (Ausnahme) isolated
case; ~**gänger** *der;* ~~s, ~~,
~**gängerin** *die;* ~~, ~~nen loner;
~**haft** *die* solitary confinement;

Einzel·handel *der* retail trade

Einzelhandels·preis *der* retail price

Einzel·händler *der,* ~**händlerin** *die*
retailer

Einzelheit *die;* ~, ~en (a) detail
(b) (einzelner Umstand) particular

Einzel·kind *das* only child

Einzeller *der;* ~s, ~ (Biol.) unicellular
organism

einzeln *Adj.* (a) (für sich allein) individual
(b) (allein stehend) solitary ⟨building, tree⟩;
single ⟨lady, gentleman⟩
(c) ~e (wenige) a few; (einige) some
(d) *substantivisch* **der/jeder Einzelne** the/
each individual; **Einzelnes** (manches) some
things *pl.;* **das Einzelne** the particular

Einzel-: ~**preis** *der* individual price;
~**teil** *das* individual part; ~**zelle** *die*
single cell; ~**zimmer** *das* single room

ein|ziehen ① *unr. tr. V.* (a) put in; thread
in ⟨tape, elastic⟩
(b) (einholen) haul in ⟨net⟩
(c) (einatmen) breathe in ⟨scent, fresh air⟩;
inhale ⟨smoke⟩
(d) (einberufen) call up ⟨recruits⟩
(e) (beitreiben) collect
② *unr. itr. V.; mit sein* (a) ⟨liquid⟩ soak in
(b) (einkehren) enter
(c) (in eine Wohnung) move in

einzig ① *Adj.* only; **kein** ~**es Wort** not a
single word
② *adv.* (a) *intensivierend bei Adj.*
extraordinarily
(b) (ausschließlich) only; **das** ~ **Wahre** the only
thing

einzig·artig ① *Adj.* unique
② *adv.* uniquely

Einzigartigkeit *die,* **Einzigkeit** *die*
uniqueness

Ein·zug *der* (a) entry (**in** + *Akk.* into)
(b) (in eine Wohnung) move

Einzugs·bereich *der* catchment area

Eis *das;* ~es (a) ice; ~ **laufen** ice-skate
(b) (Speise~) ice cream; **ein** ~ **am Stiel** an
ice lolly (Brit.) *or* (Amer.) ice pop

Eis-: ~**bahn** *die* ice rink; ~**bär** *der* polar
bear; ~**becher** *der* ice cream sundae;
~**bein** *das* (Kochk.) knuckle of pork;
~**berg** *der* iceberg; ~**beutel** *der* ice bag;
~**blume** *die* frost flower; ~**bombe** *die*
(Gastr.) bombe glacée; ~**brecher** *der* ice-
breaker; ~**café** *das* ice cream parlour

Eis·schnee *der* stiffly beaten egg white

Eis·diele *die* ice cream parlour

Eisen *das;* ~s, ~: iron

Eisen·bahn *die* (a) railway; railroad
(Amer.); **mit der** ~ **fahren** go by train
(b) (Bahnstrecke) railway line; railroad track
(Amer.)

Eisenbahn·abteil *das* railway *or* (Amer.)
railroad compartment

Eisenbahner *der;* ~s, ~: railwayman;
railway worker; railroader (Amer.)

Eisenbahnerin *die;* ~, ~nen railway
worker

Eisenbahn·unglück *das* train crash

Eisen-: ~**erz** *das* iron ore; ~**kette** *die*
iron chain; ~**ring** *der* iron ring;
~**stange** *die* iron bar; ~**waren** *Pl.*
ironmongery *sing.;* ~**zeit** *die* Iron Age

eisern ① *Adj.* (auch fig.) iron
② *adv.* resolutely; ⟨save, train⟩ with iron
determination; ~ **durchgreifen** take drastic
measures

eis-, Eis-: ~**fach** *das* freezing
compartment; ~**frei** *Adj.* ice-free;
~**gekühlt** *Adj.* iced; ~**glatt** *Adj.* (a) icy
⟨road⟩; (b) /'-'-/ (ugs.) ⟨floor, steps⟩ as
slippery as ice; ~**glätte** *die* black ice;
~**hockey** *das* ice hockey

eisig ① *Adj.* (a) icy ⟨wind, cold⟩; icy [cold]
⟨water⟩
(b) (fig.) frosty
② *adv.* (a) ~ **kalt sein** be icy cold
(b) (fig.) ⟨smile⟩ frostily

****eisig·kalt** *Adj.* ▶ **EISKALT 1A**

eis-, Eis-: ~**kaffee** *der* iced coffee;
~**kalt** ① *Adj.* (a) ice-cold ⟨drink⟩; freezing
cold ⟨weather⟩; (b) (gefühllos) icy; ice-cold
⟨look⟩; ② *adv.* **es lief mir** ~**kalt über den
Rücken** a cold shiver went down my spine;
~**kunst·lauf** *der* figure skating;
~**kunst·läufer** *der,* ~**kunst·läuferin**
die figure skater; ~**lauf** *der* ice skating;
*~**laufen** ▶ **EIS A;** ~**laufen** *das;* ~~s
ice skating; ~**läufer** *der,* ~**läuferin** *die*
ice skater

Ei·sprung *der* (Physiol.) ovulation

Eis-: ~**regen** *der* sleet; ~**schrank** *der*
refrigerator; ~**sport** *der* ice sports *pl.;*
~**tanz** *der* (Sport) ice dancing; ~**waffel**
die [ice cream] wafer; ~**wein** *der:* wine
made from grapes frozen on the vine;
~**würfel** *der* ice cube; ~**zapfen** *der*
icicle; ~**zeit** *die* ice age

eitel *Adj.* vain

Eitelkeit *die;* ~, ~en vanity

Eiter *der;* ~s pus

eitern *itr. V.* suppurate

eitrig *Adj.* suppurating

Ei·weiß *das;* ~es, ~e (a) egg white
(b) (Protein) protein

eiweiß-: ~**arm** *Adj.* low-protein *attrib.;*
low in protein *postpos.;* ~**reich** *Adj.* high-
protein *attrib.;* rich in protein *postpos.*

Ejakulation *die;* ~, ~en (Physiol.)
ejaculation

Ekel¹ *der;* ~s revulsion; [einen] ~ vor etw. (*Dat.*) haben have a revulsion for sth.

Ekel² *das;* ~s, ~ (ugs. abwertend) horror; **er ist ein [altes] ~:** he is quite obnoxious

ekelhaft *Adj.* revolting ⟨*sight*⟩; horrible ⟨*weather, person*⟩

ekeln ① *refl. V.* be disgusted; **sich vor etw.** (*Dat.*) ~: find sth. repulsive
② *tr., itr. V.* (*unpers.*) **es ekelt mich** *od.* **mir ekelt davor** I find it revolting

eklig *Adj.* (a) ▶ EKELHAFT;
(b) (ugs.: gemein) nasty

Ekstase /ɛkˈstaːzə/ *die;* ~, ~n ecstasy

Ekzem *das;* ~s, ~e (Med.) eczema

Elan *der;* ~s zest; vigour

elastisch *Adj.* elasticated ⟨*material*⟩; springy ⟨*surface*⟩; supple ⟨*person, body*⟩

Elastizität *die;* ~: elasticity; (Federkraft) springiness; (Geschmeidigkeit) suppleness

Elch *der;* ~[e]s, ~e elk; (in Nordamerika) moose

Elefant *der;* ~en, ~en elephant

elegant ① *Adj.* elegant
② *adv.* elegantly

Eleganz *die;* ~: elegance

elektrifizieren *tr. V.* electrify

Elektrifizierung *die;* ~, ~en electrification

Elektriker *der;* ~s, ~, **Elektrikerin** *die;* ~, ~nen electrician

elektrisch ① *Adj.* electric; electrical ⟨*resistance, wiring, system*⟩
② *adv.* ~ **kochen** cook with electricity; ~ **geladen sein** be electrically charged

elektrisieren ① *tr. V.* (Med.) treat using electricity
② *refl. V.* get an electric shock

Elektrizität *die;* ~ electricity

Elektrizitäts·werk *das* power station

elektro-, Elektro-: ~**artikel** *der* electrical appliance; ~**auto** *das* electric car; ~**gerät** *das* electrical appliance; ~**geschäft** *das* electrical shop *or* (Amer.) store; ~**herd** *der* electric cooker; ~**magnet** *der* electromagnet; ~**magnetisch** ① *Adj.* electromagnetic; ② *adv.* electromagnetically; ~**mobil** *das;* ~~s, ~~e electric car; ~**motor** *der* electric motor

Elektron *das;* ~s, ~en /-ˈtroːnən/ electron

Elektronen-: ~[**ge**]**hirn** *das* (ugs.) electronic brain (coll.); ~**hülle** *die* electron shell; ~**rechner** *der* electronic computer

Elektronik *die;* ~ (a) electronics *sing., no art.;*
(b) (Teile) electronics *pl.*

Elektronik·schrott *der* scrapped electrical appliances *pl.*

elektronisch ① *Adj.* electronic
② *adv.* electronically

elektro-, Elektro-: ~**rasierer** *der* electric shaver; ~**smog** *der* (Jargon) electronic smog; ~**statisch** ① *Adj.* electrostatic; ② *adv.* electrostatically; ~**technik** *die* electrical engineering *no art.;* ~**techniker** *der,* ~**technikerin** *die* (a) electronics engineer; (b) (Elektriker) electrician

Element *das;* ~[e]s, ~e element

elementar *Adj.* (a) (grundlegend) fundamental
(b) (einfach) elementary ⟨*knowledge*⟩
(c) (naturhaft) elemental ⟨*force*⟩

Elementar·teilchen *das* (Physik) elementary particle

elend *Adj.* wretched; miserable

Elend *das;* ~s misery

Elends-: ~**quartier** *das* slum [dwelling]; ~**viertel** *das* slum area

elf *Kardinalz.* eleven

Elf *die;* ~, ~en (a) eleven
(b) (Sport) team; side

Elfe *die;* ~, ~n fairy

Elfen·bein *das* ivory

Elfenbein-: ~**schnitzerei** *die* ivory carving; ~**turm** *der* (fig.) ivory tower

Elf·meter *der* (Fußball) penalty; **einen** ~ **schießen** take a penalty

Elfmeter·schießen *das;* ~s (Fußball) **durch** ~: by *or* on penalties

eliminieren *tr. V.* eliminate

elitär *adj.* élitist; **ein** ~**es Bewusstsein** an élite-awareness

Elite *die;* ~, ~n élite

Elite·truppe *die* (Milit.) élite *or* crack force

Ell·bogen *der; Pl.* ~: elbow

Elle *die;* ~, ~n (Anat.) ulna

Ellen·bogen *der; Pl.* ~: ▶ ELLBOGEN

Ellipse *die;* ~, ~n ellipse

Elsass, *Elsaß *das;* ~ *od.* **Elsasses** Alsace

Elster *die;* ~, ~n magpie

elterlich *Adj.* parental

Eltern *Pl.* parents *pl.*

eltern-, Eltern-: ~**abend** *der* (Schulw.) parents' evening; ~**bei·rat** *der* (Schulw.) parents' association; ~**haus** *das* home; ~**los** *Adj.* orphaned; ~**teil** *der* parent; ~**zeit** *die* [period of] parental leave

Email /eˈmaɪ̯/ *das;* ~s, ~s, **Emaille** /eˈmaljə/ *die;* ~, ~n enamel

E-Mail /ˈiːmeɪ̯l/ *die;* ~, ~s (DV) e-mail

Emanzipation *die;* ~, ~en emancipation

emanzipieren *refl. V.* emancipate

emanzipiert *Adj.* emancipated; emancipated, liberated ⟨*woman*⟩

Embargo *das;* ~s, ~s embargo

Emblem *das;* ~s, ~e emblem

Embryo *der;* ~s, ~nen /-ˈyoːnən/ *od.* ~s embryo

Embryonen·forschung *die* embryo research

Emigrant *der;* ~en, ~en, **Emigrantin**
die; ~, ~nen emigrant; (Flüchtling) emigré
Emigration *die;* ~, ~en (das Emigrieren)
emigration

emigrieren *itr. V.; mit sein* emigrate

Emission (a) (Physik, Ökologie) emission
(b) (Ausgabe [von Briefmarken, Wertpapieren])
issue

emissions·arm *Adj.* low-emission; ~ sein
be low in emissions

Emotion *die;* ~, ~en emotion

emotional [1] *Adj.* emotional; emotive
⟨topic, question⟩
[2] *adv.* emotionally

Empfang *der;* ~[e]s, Empfänge reception;
(Entgegennahme) receipt

empfangen *unr. tr. V.* receive

Empfänger *der;* ~s, ~ **(a)** recipient; (eines
Briefs) addressee
(b) (Empfangsgerät) receiver

Empfängerin *die;* ~, ~nen ▶ EMPFÄNGER
A

empfänglich *Adj.* **(a)** receptive (für to)
(b) (beeinflussbar) susceptible

Empfänglichkeit *die;* ~ **(a)**
(Zugänglichkeit) receptivity, receptiveness (für
to)
(b) (Beeinflussbarkeit) susceptibility (für to)

Empfängnis *die;* ~: conception

Empfängnis·verhütung *die*
contraception

empfangs-, Empfangs-:
~**berechtigt** *Adj.* authorized to receive
payment/goods *postpos.;* ~**chef** *der* head
receptionist; ~**dame** *die* receptionist;
~**halle** *die* reception lobby

empfehlen [1] *unr. tr. V.* recommend
[2] *unr. refl. V.* **(a)** take one's leave
(b) *unpers.* es empfiehlt sich, ... zu ...: it's
advisable to ...

empfehlens·wert *Adj.* **(a)** to be
recommended *postpos.;* recommendable
(b) (ratsam) advisable

Empfehlung *die;* ~, ~en **(a)**
recommendation
(b) (Empfehlungsschreiben) letter of
recommendation

empfiehl *Imperativ Sg. v.* EMPFEHLEN

empfiehlst *2. Pers. Sg. Präsens v.*
EMPFEHLEN

empfiehlt *3. Pers. Sg. Präsens v.*
EMPFEHLEN

empfinden *unr. tr. V.* **(a)** (wahrnehmen) feel
(b) (auffassen) **etw. als Beleidigung** ~: feel
sth. to be an insult

Empfinden *das;* ~s feeling; **für mein** *od.*
nach meinem ~: to my mind

empfindlich [1] *Adj.* **(a)** sensitive; fast
⟨film⟩
(b) (leicht beleidigt) sensitive
(c) (anfällig) **zart und** ~: delicate
(d) (spürbar) severe ⟨punishment, shortage⟩

[2] *adv.* ~ **auf etw.** (*Akk.*) **reagieren** (sensibel)
be susceptible to sth.; (beleidigt) react
oversensitively to sth.

Empfindlichkeit *die;* ~, ~en
▶ EMPFINDLICH: sensitivity; severity; (eines
Films) speed

empfindsam *Adj.* sensitive ⟨nature⟩

Empfindung *die;* ~, ~en (Gefühl) feeling

empfing *1. u. 3. Pers. Sg. Prät. v.*
EMPFANGEN

empfohlen [1] *2. Part. v.* EMPFEHLEN;
[2] *Adj.* recommended

empirisch [1] *Adj.* empirical
[2] *adv.* empirically

empor *Adv.* (geh.) upwards

empören [1] *tr. V.* fill with indignation;
outrage
[2] *refl. V.* become indignant *or* outraged

empörend *Adj.* outrageous

empört *Adj.* outraged

Empörung *die;* ~, ~en outrage

emsig [1] *Adj.* industrious ⟨person⟩;
bustling ⟨activity⟩
[2] *adv.* industriously

Emu *der;* ~s, ~s (Zool.) emu

Ende *das;* ~s, ~n end; **am** ~ **der Straße/**
Stadt at the end of the road/town; **am/bis/**
gegen ~ **des Monats** at/by/towards the end
of the month; ~ **April** at the end of April; **zu**
~ **sein** ⟨patience, war⟩ be at an end; ⟨school⟩
be over; ⟨film, game⟩ have finished; ~ **gut,**
alles gut all's well that ends well (prov.)

End·effekt *der* **im** ~: in the end; in the
final analysis

enden *itr. V.* **(a)** end; ⟨programme⟩ finish
(b) in der Gosse ~: end up in the gutter;
(dort sterben) die in the gutter

end-, End-: ~**ergebnis** *das* final result;
~**gültig** [1] *Adj.* final ⟨consent, decision⟩;
conclusive ⟨evidence⟩; [2] *adv.* **das ist**
~**gültig vorbei** that's all over and done with;
sich ~**gültig trennen** separate for good;
~**haltestelle** *die* terminus; ~**kampf**
der (Sport) final; (Milit.) final battle; ~**lauf**
der (Sport) final

endlich *Adv.* **(a)** (nach langer Zeit) at last
(b) (schließlich) in the end

end-, End-: ~**los** [1] *Adj.* **(a)** (ohne Ende)
infinite; (ringförmig) continuous; **(b)** (nicht
enden wollend) endless; interminable ⟨speech⟩;
[2] *adv.* ~**los lange dauern** be interminably
long; ~**lösung** *die* (ns. verhüll.) Final
Solution (to the Jewish question);
~**resultat** *das* final result; ~**runde** *die*
(Sport) final; ~**spiel** *das* (Sport) final;
~**spurt** *der* (bes. Leichtathletik) final spurt;
~**stadium** *das* final stage; (Med.) terminal
stage; ~**station** *die* terminus; ~**summe**
die [sum] total

Endung *die;* ~, ~en (Sprachw.) ending

End-: ~**verbraucher** *der,*
~**verbraucherin** *die* (Wirtsch.) consumer; ···⟩

∼**ziffer** *die* final number; **das Los mit der**
∼**ziffer 4** the coupon with a number ending
in 4

Energie *die;* ∼, ∼n energy

energie-, Energie-: ∼**bewusst,**
*∼**bewußt** *Adj.* energy-conscious; ∼**mix**
der mix of energy sources; ∼**politik** *die*
energy policy; ∼**quelle** *die* energy source;
∼**spar·lampe** *die* energy-saving lamp;
∼**verbrauch** *der* energy consumption;
∼**versorgung** *die* energy supply;
∼**wirtschaft** *die* energy sector

energisch ⒈ *Adj.* (a) energetic ⟨*person*⟩;
firm ⟨*action*⟩
(b) forceful ⟨*voice, words*⟩
⒉ *adv.* (a) energetically; ∼ **durchgreifen**
take drastic action
(b) ⟨*reject, say*⟩ forcefully; ⟨*stress*⟩
emphatically; ⟨*deny*⟩ strenuously

eng /ɛŋ/ ⒈ *Adj.* (a) (schmal) narrow
(b) (dicht) close ⟨*writing*⟩
(c) (fest anliegend) close-fitting
(d) (beschränkt) narrow
(e) (nahe) close ⟨*friend*⟩
⒉ *adv.* (a) (dicht) ∼ **[zusammen]sitzen/stehen**
sit/stand close together
(b) (fest anliegend) ∼ **anliegen/sitzen** fit closely
(c) (beschränkt) **etw. zu** ∼ **auslegen** interpret
sth. too narrowly
(d) (nahe) closely

Engagement /ãgaʒə'mã:/ *das;* ∼s, ∼s
(a) (Einsatz) involvement; **sein** ∼ **für etw.** his
commitment to sth.; **sein** ∼ **gegen etw.** his
committed stand against sth.
(b) (eines Künstlers) engagement

engagiert *Adj.* committed ⟨*literature, film,
director*⟩; **politisch/sozial** ∼ **sein** be
politically/socially committed *or* involved

Engagiertheit *die;* ∼: commitment;
involvement

Enge *die;* ∼, ∼n confinement

Engel *der;* ∼s, ∼: angel

eng·herzig *Adj.* petty

England (*das*); ∼s England

Engländer *der;* ∼s, ∼: Englishman/
English boy; **er ist** ∼: he is English; **die** ∼:
the English

Engländerin *die;* ∼, ∼nen Englishwoman/
English girl; **sie ist** ∼: she is English

englisch ⒈ *Adj.* English; **die** ∼**e Sprache/
Literatur** the English language/English
literature
⒉ *adv.* ∼ **sprechen** speak English

Englisch *das;* ∼[s] English

englisch-, Englisch-: ∼**lehrer** *der,*
∼**lehrerin** *die* English teacher;
∼**sprachig** *Adj.* (a) English-language
⟨*book, magazine*⟩; (b) (Englisch sprechend)
English-speaking ⟨*population, country*⟩;
∼**unterricht** *der* English teaching;
(Unterrichtsstunde) English lesson

───────────────
***alte Schreibung - vgl. Hinweis auf S. xiv

Eng·pass, *Eng·paß *der* (a) defile
(b) (fig.) bottleneck

eng·stirnig *Adj.* narrow-minded

Enkel *der;* ∼s, ∼: grandson

Enkelin *die;* ∼, ∼nen granddaughter

Enkel·kind *das* grandchild

enorm ⒈ *Adj.* enormous ⟨*sum, costs*⟩;
tremendous (coll.) ⟨*effort*⟩; immense ⟨*strain*⟩
⒉ *adv.* tremendously (coll.)

Ensemble /ã'sã:bl/ *das;* ∼, ∼s ensemble;
(Theater∼) company

entarten *itr. V.; mit sein* degenerate

entbehren *tr. V.* (verzichten auf) do without

entbehrlich *Adj.* dispensable

Entbehrung *die;* ∼, ∼en privation

entbinden ⒈ *unr. tr. V.* (a) **jmdn. von
einem Versprechen** ∼: release sb. from a
promise; **seines Amtes** *od.* **von seinem Amt
entbunden werden** be relieved of [one's]
office
(b) **jmdn.** ∼ (Med.) deliver sb.'s baby
⒉ *unr. itr. V.* give birth

Entbindung *die* (Med.) delivery

Entbindungs·station *die* maternity
ward

entblößen ⒈ *refl. V.* take one's clothes off;
⟨*exhibitionist*⟩ expose oneself
⒉ *tr. V.* uncover ⟨*one's arm etc.*⟩

entdecken *tr. V.* (a) discover
(b) (ausfindig machen) **jmdn.** ∼: find sb.; **etw.**
∼: find *or* discover sth.

Entdecker *der;* ∼s, ∼, **Entdeckerin**
die; ∼, ∼nen discoverer

Entdeckung *die;* ∼, ∼en discovery

Ente *die;* ∼, ∼n duck

entehren *tr. V.* dishonour; ∼**d** degrading

enteignen *tr. V.* expropriate

Enteignung *die;* ∼, ∼en expropriation

enterben *tr. V.* disinherit

entern *tr., itr. V.* board ⟨*ship*⟩

entfachen *tr. V.* (geh.) (a) kindle, light
⟨*fire*⟩
(b) (fig.) provoke ⟨*quarrel, argument*⟩; arouse
⟨*passion, enthusiasm*⟩

entfallen *unr. itr. V.; mit sein* (a) (aus dem
Gedächtnis) **es ist mir** ∼: it escapes me
(b) (zugeteilt werden) **auf jmdn./etw.** ∼: be
allotted to sb./sth.
(c) (wegfallen) lapse

entfalten ⒈ *tr. V.* (a) open [up]; unfold
⟨*map etc.*⟩
(b) (fig.) display ⟨*ability, talent*⟩
⒉ *refl. V.* (a) open [up]
(b) (fig.) ⟨*personality, talent, etc.*⟩ develop

Entfaltung *die;* ∼, ∼en (fig.) (a) (Entwicklung)
development
(b) ▶ ENTFALTEN 1B: display

entfernen ⒈ *tr. V.* remove; take out
⟨*tonsils etc.*⟩
⒉ *refl. V.* go away

entfernt ⒈ *Adj.* (a) (fern) remote; **das ist**

od. **liegt weit ～ von der Stadt** it is a long way from the town; **10 km/zwei Stunden ～:** 10 km/two hours away
(b) slight ⟨*acquaintance*⟩; distant ⟨*relation*⟩; slight ⟨*resemblance*⟩
2 *adv.* **(a)** (fern) remotely
(b) slightly ⟨*acquainted*⟩; distantly ⟨*related*⟩

Entfernung *die;* ～, ～en **(a)** (Abstand) distance
(b) (das Beseitigen) removal

entfesseln *tr. V.* unleash

entflammen **1** *tr. V.* arouse ⟨*enthusiasm etc*⟩
2 *itr. V.; mit sein* flare up

entfliehen *unr. itr. V.; mit sein* escape; **jmdm. ～:** escape from sb.

entfremden **1** *tr. V.* **(a) etw. seinem Zweck ～:** use sth. for a different purpose
(b) (Philos., Soziol.) entfremdet alienated
2 *refl. V.* **sich jmdm./einer Sache ～:** become estranged from sb./unfamiliar with sth.

Entfremdung *die;* ～, ～en alienation; estrangement

entführen *tr. V.* kidnap ⟨*child etc.*⟩; hijack ⟨*plane, lorry, etc.*⟩

Entführer *der,* **Entführerin** *die* ▶ ENTFÜHREN: kidnapper; hijacker

Entführung *die* ▶ ENTFÜHREN: kidnapping; hijacking

entgegen **1** *Adv.* towards
2 *Präp. mit Dat.* **～ meinem Wunsch** against my wishes; **～ dem Befehl** contrary to orders

entgegen-, Entgegen-: ～|**bringen** *unr. tr. V.* (fig.) show ⟨*love, understanding*⟩; ～|**fahren** *unr. itr. V.; mit sein* jmdm. ～fahren come/go to meet sb.; ～|**gehen** *unr. itr. V.; mit sein* **(a)** jmdm. ～gehen go to meet sb.; **(b)** (fig.) be heading for ⟨*catastrophe, hard times*⟩; ～**gesetzt** **1** *Adj.* **(a)** (umgekehrt) opposite ⟨*end, direction*⟩; **(b)** (gegensätzlich) opposing; **2** *adv.* **genau ～gesetzt handeln/denken** do/think exactly the opposite; ～|**kommen** *unr. itr. V.; mit sein* jmdm. ～kommen come to meet sb.; (Zugeständnisse machen) be accommodating towards sb.; ～**kommen** *das;* ～～s cooperation; (Zugeständnis) concession; ～**kommend** *Adj.* obliging; ～|**nehmen** *unr. itr. V.* receive; ～|**treten** *unr. itr. V.; mit sein* go/come up to; (fig.) stand up to ⟨*difficulties*⟩

entgegnen *tr. V.* retort; reply

entgehen *unr. itr. V.; mit sein* **(a)** (entkommen) escape
(b) jmdm. entgeht etw. sb. misses sth.

entgeistert *Adj.* dumbfounded

Entgelt *das;* ～[e]s, ～e payment; fee

entgiften *tr. V.* decontaminate ⟨*substance etc.*⟩; detoxicate ⟨*body etc.*⟩

entgleisen *itr. V.; mit sein* **(a)** be derailed
(b) (fig.) make a/some faux pas

entgräten *tr. V.* fillet

enthaaren *tr. V.* remove hair from

Enthaarungs·mittel *das* hair remover

enthalten¹ **1** *unr. tr. V.* contain
2 *unr. refl. V.* **sich einer Sache** (*Gen.*) ～: abstain from sth.; **sich der Stimme ～:** abstain

enthalten² *Adj.* **in etw.** (*Dat.*) **～ sein** be contained in sth.; **das ist im Preis ～:** that is included in the price

enthaltsam **1** *Adj.* abstemious; (sexuell) abstinent
2 *adv.* **～ leben** live in abstinence

Enthaltsamkeit *die;* ～: abstinence

Enthaltung *die;* ～, ～en abstention

enthaupten *tr. V.* (geh.) behead

enthäuten *tr. V.* skin

entheben *unr. tr. V.* (geh.) relieve

enthemmt *Adj.* uninhibited

enthüllen *tr. V.* unveil ⟨*monument etc.*⟩; reveal ⟨*face, truth, secret*⟩

Enthüllung *die;* ～, ～en ▶ ENTHÜLLEN: unveiling; revelation

Enthusiasmus /ɛntu'zjasmʊs/ *der;* ～: enthusiasm

Enthusiast *der;* ～en, ～en, **Enthusiastin** *die;* ～, ～nen enthusiast

enthusiastisch **1** *Adj.* enthusiastic
2 *adv.* enthusiastically

entkalken *tr. V.* decalcify

entkleiden *tr. V.* (geh.) **(a)** undress
(b) (berauben) strip

entkommen *unr. itr. V.; mit sein* escape

entkorken *tr. V.* uncork ⟨*bottle*⟩

entkräften *tr. V.* **(a)** weaken; **völlig ～:** exhaust
(b) (fig.) refute ⟨*argument etc.*⟩

Entkräftung *die;* ～, ～en **(a)** debility; **völlige ～:** exhaustion
(b) (fig.) refutation

entladen **1** *unr. tr. V.* unload
2 *unr. refl. V.* **(a)** ⟨*storm*⟩ break
(b) (fig.) ⟨*anger etc.*⟩ erupt; ⟨*aggression etc.*⟩ be released

entlang **1** *Präp. mit Akk. u. Dat.* along
2 *Adv.* along; **hier/dort ～, bitte!** this/that way please!

entlang-: ～|**fahren** *unr. itr. V.; mit sein* **(a)** drive along; **(b)** (streichen) go along; ～|**gehen** *unr. itr. V.; mit sein* ⟨*person*⟩ go or walk along; ～|**laufen** *unr. itr. V.; mit sein* **(a)** walk/run along; **(b)** (verlaufen) go or run along

entlarven *tr. V.* expose

entlassen *unr. tr. V.* **(a)** (aus dem Gefängnis) release; (aus dem Krankenhaus, der Armee) discharge
(b) (aus einem Arbeitsverhältnis) dismiss; (wegen Arbeitsmangels) make redundant (Brit.); lay off

Entlassung *die;* ～, ～en ▶ ENTLASSEN: release; discharge; dismissal; redundancy (Brit.); laying off

entlasten *tr. V.* **(a)** relieve ⋯✦

(b) (Rechtsw.) exonerate ⟨*defendant*⟩

Entlastung *die;* ~, ~en (a) relief
(b) (Rechtsw.) exoneration; defence

entlaufen *unr. itr. V.; mit sein* run away;
ein ~er Sträfling/Sklave an escaped convict/a
runaway slave

entlausen *tr. V.* delouse

entledigen *refl. V.* sich jmds./einer Sache
(*Gen.*) ~ (geh.) rid oneself of sb./sth.

entleeren *tr. V.* empty; evacuate ⟨*bowels,
bladder*⟩

entlegen *Adj.* remote

entleihen *unr. tr. V.* borrow

entlocken *tr. V.* (geh.) jmdm. etw. ~: elicit
sth. from sb.

entlohnen *tr. V.* pay

Entlohnung *die;* ~, ~en payment; (Lohn)
pay

entlüften *tr. V.* ventilate

Entlüfter *der;* ~s, ~: ventilator

entmachten *tr. V.* deprive of power

entmilitarisieren *tr. V.* demilitarize

entmündigen *tr. V.* incapacitate

Entmündigung *die;* ~, ~en
incapacitation

entmutigen *tr. V.* discourage

Entnahme *die;* ~, ~n (von Wasser) drawing;
(von Blut) extraction

Entnazifizierung *die;* ~, ~en
denazification

entnehmen *unr. tr. V.* (a) etw. [einer
Sache (*Dat.*)] ~: take sth. [from sth.]
(b) (ersehen aus) gather (*Dat.* from)

entnervend *Adj.* nerve-racking

entnervt *Adj.* ~ sein be worn down; have
reached *or* be at the end of one's tether; er
gab ~ auf he had reached the end of his
tether and gave up

entpuppen *refl. V.* sich als etw./jmd. ~:
turn out to be sth./sb.

entrahmen *tr. V.* skim ⟨*milk*⟩

entreißen *unr. tr. V.* jmdm. etw. ~: snatch
sth. from sb.

entrichten *tr. V.* (Amtsspr.) pay ⟨*fee*⟩

entrümpeln *tr. V.* clear out

Entrümpelung *die;* ~, ~en clear-out

entrüsten ① *refl. V.* sich [über etw. (*Akk.*)]
~: be indignant [at *or* about sth.]
② *tr. V.* (empören) jmdn. ~: make sb.
indignant

Entrüstung *die;* ~, ~en indignation (über
+ *Akk.* at, about)

Entsafter *der;* ~s, ~: juice extractor

entsagen *itr. V.* einer Sache (*Dat.*) ~ (geh.)
renounce sth.

Entsagung *die;* ~, ~en (geh.) renunciation

entschädigen *tr. V.* compensate (**für** for);
jmdn. für etw. ~ (fig.) make up for sth.

Entschädigung *die;* ~, ~en
compensation

entschärfen *tr. V.* defuse; tone down
⟨*discussion, criticism*⟩

entscheiden ① *unr. refl. V.* (a) decide
(b) (*unpers.*) morgen entscheidet es sich,
ob ...: I/we/you will know tomorrow
whether ...
② *unr. itr. V.* über etw. (*Akk.*) ~: settle sth.
③ *unr. tr. V.* decide on ⟨*dispute*⟩; decide
⟨*outcome, result*⟩

entscheidend ① *Adj.* crucial; decisive
⟨*action*⟩
② *adv.* jmdn./etw. ~ beeinflussen have a
decisive influence on sb./sth.

Entscheidung *die;* ~, ~en decision

entschieden ① *Adj.* (a) (entschlossen)
determined; resolute
(b) (eindeutig) definite
② *adv.* resolutely; das geht ~ zu weit that is
going much too far

Entschiedenheit *die;* ~: decisiveness;
etw. mit ~ behaupten/verneinen state/deny
sth. categorically; etw. mit ~ fordern demand
sth. emphatically

entschlafen *unr. itr. V.; mit sein* pass
away

entschließen *unr. refl. V.* decide

Entschließung *die;* ~, ~en resolution

entschlossen *Adj.* determined

Entschlossenheit *die;* ~: determination

Entschluss, *Entschluß *der;*
Entschlusses, Entschlüsse decision

entschlüsseln *tr. V.* decipher

entschuldigen ① *refl. V.* apologize
② *tr.* (*auch itr.*) *V.* excuse ⟨*person*⟩; sich ~
lassen ask to be excused; ~ Sie [bitte]! (bei
Fragen, Bitten) excuse me; (bedauernd) I'm sorry

Entschuldigung *die;* ~, ~en (a) apology
(b) (Grund) excuse
(c) (Höflichkeitsformel) ~! (bei Fragen, Bitten)
excuse me; (bedauernd) [I'm] sorry

entschwinden *unr. itr. V.; mit sein* (geh.)
disappear; vanish

entsetzen ① *refl. V.* be horrified
② *tr. V.* horrify; über etw. (*Akk.*) entsetzt
sein be horrified by sth.

Entsetzen *das;* ~s horror

entsetzlich ① *Adj.* (a) horrible ⟨*accident,
crime, etc.*⟩
(b) (ugs.: stark) terrible ⟨*thirst, hunger*⟩
② *adv.* terribly (coll.)

entsinnen *unr. refl. V.* sich jmds./einer
Sache ~: remember sb./sth.

entsorgen *tr. V.* (Amtsspr., Wirtsch.) dispose
of ⟨*waste etc.*⟩

Entsorgung *die;* ~, ~en (Amtsspr., Wirtsch.)
waste disposal

entspannen ① *tr. V.* relax
② *refl. V.* (a) ⟨*person*⟩ relax
(b) (fig.) ⟨*situation, tension*⟩ ease

Entspannung *die;* ~ (a) relaxation
(b) (politisch) easing of tension; détente

---

*old spelling - see note on page xiv

Entspạnnungs·politik *die* policy of détente

entsprẹchen *unr. itr. V.* **(a)** (übereinstimmen mit) **einer Sache** *(Dat.)* ~: correspond to sth.; **der Wahrheit/den Tatsachen** ~: be in accordance with the truth/the facts **(b)** (nachkommen) **einem Wunsch** ~: comply with a request; **den Anforderungen** ~: meet the requirements

entsprẹchend ⒈ *Adj.* **(a)** corresponding; (angemessen) appropriate **(b)** (dem~) in accordance *postpos.*; ⒉ *adv.* **(a)** (angemessen) appropriately **(b)** (dem~) accordingly ⒊ *Präp. mit Dat.* in accordance with

entsprịngen *unr. itr. V.; mit sein* **(a)** ‹*river*› rise **(b)** (entstehen aus) **einer Sache** *(Dat.)* ~: spring from sth.

entstẹhen *unr. itr. V.; mit sein* **(a)** originate; ‹*quarrel, friendship, etc.*› arise **(b)** (gebildet werden) be formed (**aus** from, **durch** by) **(c)** (sich ergeben) occur; (als Folge) result

Entstẹhung *die;* ~: origin

entstẹinen *tr. V.* stone

entstẹllen *tr. V.* **(a)** disfigure **(b)** (verfälschen) distort ‹*text, facts*›

Entstẹllung *die;* ~, ~en **(a)** disfigurement **(b)** (Verfälschung) distortion

entstören *tr. V.* (Elektrot.) suppress ‹*engine, electrical appliance*›

Entstörungs·stelle *die* fault repair service

enttạrnen *tr. V.* uncover

enttäuschen *tr. V.* disappoint

enttäuschend *Adj.* disappointing

enttäuscht *Adj.* disappointed; dashed ‹*hopes*›

Enttäuschung *die;* ~, ~en disappointment

entwạchsen *unr. itr. V.; mit sein* **einer Sache** *(Dat.)* ~: grow out of sth.

entwạffnen *tr. V.* (auch fig.) disarm

entwạffnend *Adj.* disarming

entwạrnen *itr. V.* sound the all-clear

Entwạrnung *die;* ~, ~en all-clear

entwässern *tr. V.* drain

Entwässerung *die;* ~, ~en drainage

ẹntweder *Konj.:* ~ ... **oder** either ... or

entweịchen *unr. itr. V.; mit sein* escape

entwẹnden *tr. V.* (geh.) purloin

entwẹrfen *unr. tr. V.* design ‹*furniture, dress*›; draft ‹*novel etc.*›; draw up ‹*plans etc.*›

entwẹrten *tr. V.* **(a)** cancel ‹*ticket, postage stamp*› **(b)** devalue ‹*currency*›

Entwẹrter *der;* ~s, ~: ticket-cancelling machine

entwịckeln ⒈ *refl. V.* develop

⒉ *tr. V.* produce ‹*vapour, smell*›; display ‹*ability, characteristic*›; develop ‹*equipment, photograph, film*›; elaborate ‹*theory, ideas*›

Entwịcklung *die;* ~, ~en **(a)** development; (von Dämpfen usw.) production; **in der** ~ **sein** ‹*young person*› be adolescent **(b)** (Darlegung) elaboration **(c)** (Fot.) developing

Entwịcklungs-: ~**helfer** *der,* ~**helferin** *die* development aid worker; ~**hilfe** *die* [development] aid; ~**land** *das* developing country; ~**politik** *die* development aid policy

entwịrren *tr. V.* disentangle

entwịschen *itr. V.; mit sein* (ugs.) get away

entwöhnen *tr. V.* wean

entwürdigend *Adj.* degrading

Entwụrf *der;* ~, **Entwürfe (a)** design **(b)** (Konzept) draft

entwụrzeln *tr. V.* uproot

entziẹhen ⒈ *unr. tr. V.* **(a)** take away **(b)** (nicht zugestehen) withdraw ⒉ *unr. refl. V.* **sich seinen Pflichten** *(Dat.)* ~: evade one's duty; **das entzieht sich meiner Kontrolle** that is beyond my control

Entziẹhung *die;* ~, ~en **(a)** withdrawal **(b)** (Entziehungskur) withdrawal treatment *no indef. art.*

entzịffern *tr. V.* decipher

entzụ̈ckend *Adj.* delightful

entzụ̈ckt *Adj.* delighted

Entzụg *der;* ~[e]s withdrawal

Entzugs·erscheinung *die* withdrawal symptom

entzụ̈ndbar *Adj.* [in]flammable

entzụ̈nden ⒈ *tr. V.* light ‹*fire*›; strike ‹*match*› ⒉ *refl. V.* **(a)** ignite **(b)** (anschwellen) become inflamed

entzụ̈ndlich *Adj.* **(a)** [in]flammable ‹*substance*› **(b)** (Med.) inflammatory

Entzụ̈ndung *die;* ~, ~en inflammation

entzwei *Adj.* (geh.) in pieces

entzweien *refl. V.* fall out

entzwei|gehen *unr. itr. V.; mit sein* (geh.) break

Ẹnzian *der;* ~s, ~e gentian

Enzyklika *die;* ~, **Enzykliken** encyclical

Enzyklopädie *die;* ~, ~n encyclopaedia

enzyklopädisch *Adj.* encyclopaedic

Epen ▶ EPOS

Epidemie *die;* ~, ~n epidemic

epigonạl *Adj.* (geh.) ▶ EPIGONENHAFT

Epigone *der;* ~n, ~n (geh.) imitator

epigonenhaft *Adj.* (geh.) imitative; unoriginal

Epigonin *die;* ~, ~nen ▶ EPIGONE

Epik /'e:pɪk/ *die;* ~ (Literaturw.) epic poetry

Epilepsie *die;* ~, ~n (Med.) epilepsy *no art.*

Epileptiker *der;* ~s, ~, **Epileptikerin** *die;* ~, ~nen epileptic

epileptisch *Adj.* epileptic

episch *Adj.* epic

Episode *die;* ~, ~n episode

Epoche *die;* ~, ~n epoch

Epos /'e:pɔs/ *das;* ~, Epen epic [poem]; epos

er *Personalpron. 3. Pers. Sg. Nom. Mask.* he; (betont) him; (bei Dingen/Tieren) it; *s. auch* IHM; IHM; SEINER

erachten *tr. V.* (geh.) consider; **etw. als** *od.* **für seine Pflicht** ~: consider sth. [to be] one's duty

erarbeiten *tr. V.* work for

Erb·anlage *die* hereditary disposition

erbarmen *refl. V.* (geh.) take pity (*Gen.* on)

Erbarmen *das;* ~s pity

erbärmlich ⟦1⟧ *Adj.* **(a)** (elend) wretched **(b)** (unzulänglich) pathetic **(c)** (abwertend: gemein) mean; wretched **(d)** (sehr groß) terrible ⟨*hunger, fear, etc.*⟩ ⟦2⟧ *adv.* terribly

erbauen ⟦1⟧ *tr. V.* **(a)** build **(b)** (geh.: erheben) uplift ⟦2⟧ *refl. V.* **sich an etw.** (*Dat.*) ~: be uplifted by sth.

Erbauer *der;* ~s, ~, **Erbauerin** *die;* ~, ~nen architect

Erbe¹ *das;* ~s **(a)** inheritance **(b)** (Vermächtnis) legacy

Erbe² *der;* ~n ~n heir

erben *tr.* (*auch itr.*) *V.* inherit

erbetteln *tr. V.* get by begging

erbeuten *tr. V.* carry off, get away with ⟨*valuables, prey, etc.*⟩; capture ⟨*enemy plane, tank, etc.*⟩

Erb-: ~**faktor** *der* hereditary factor; ~**folge** *die* succession; ~**gut** *das* (Biol.) genetic make-up

Erbin *die;* ~, ~nen heiress

erbitten *unr. tr. V.* (geh.) request

erbittern *tr. V.* enrage

erbittert ⟦1⟧ *Adj.* bitter ⟦2⟧ *adv.* ~ **kämpfen** wage a bitter struggle

Erb·krankheit *die* hereditary disease

erblassen *itr. V.; mit sein* (geh.) turn pale; blanch (literary)

erbleichen *itr. V.; mit sein* (geh.) ▶ ERBLASSEN

erblich *Adj.* hereditary ⟨*title, disease*⟩

erblicken *tr. V.* (geh.) catch sight of; (fig.) see

erblinden *itr. V.; mit sein* lose one's sight

erblühen *itr. V.; mit sein* (geh.) bloom; blossom

Erb·masse *die* (Biol.) genetic make-up

erbost *Adj.* furious

erbrechen ⟦1⟧ *unr. tr. V.* bring up ⟨*food*⟩

⟦2⟧ *unr. itr., refl. V.* vomit

Erbrechen *das;* ~s vomiting

erbringen *unr. tr. V.* produce

Erbschaft *die;* ~, ~en inheritance

Erbschaft[s]·steuer *die* estate *or* death duties *pl.*

Erb-: ~**schleicher** *der;* ~~s, ~~ (abwertend) legacy hunter; ~**schleicherei** *die;* ~~, ~~en (abwertend) legacy hunting; ~**schleicherin** *die;* ~~, ~~nen ▶ ~SCHLEICHER

Erbse *die;* ~, ~n pea

Erb-: ~**stück** *das* heirloom; ~**sünde** *die* original sin; ~**teil** *das* share of an/the inheritance

Erd-: ~**achse** *die* earth's axis; ~**anziehung** *die* earth's gravitational pull; ~**apfel** *der* (bes. österr.) ▶ KARTOFFEL; ~**atmosphäre** *die* earth's atmosphere; ~**beben** *das* earthquake; ~**beere** *die* strawberry; ~**boden** *der* ground; earth; **etw. dem** ~**boden gleichmachen** raze sth. to the ground

Erde *die;* ~, ~n **(a)** (Erdreich) soil; earth **(b)** (fester Boden) ground **(c)** (Welt) earth; world **(d)** (Planet) Earth

erdenklich *Adj.* conceivable

Erd-: ~**gas** *das* natural gas; ~**geschoss**, ***~**geschoß** *das* ground floor; first floor (Amer.); ~**kugel** *die* terrestrial globe; earth; ~**kunde** *die* geography; ~**magnetismus** *der* terrestrial magnetism; ~**nuss**, ***~**nuß** *die* peanut; ~**oberfläche** *die* earth's surface; ~**öl** *das* oil; ~**öl exportierende Länder** oil-exporting countries

erdöl-, Erdöl-: ***~**exportierend** ▶ ERDÖL; ~**gewinnung** *die* oil production; ~**leitung** *die* oil pipeline

erdrosseln *tr. V.* strangle

erdrücken *tr. V.* **(a)** crush **(b)** (fig.: belasten) overwhelm

erdrückend *Adj.* overwhelming; oppressive ⟨*heat, silence*⟩

Erd-: ~**rutsch** *der* landslide; ~**rutsch·sieg** *der* (Politik) landslide victory; ~**teil** *der* continent

erdulden *tr. V.* endure ⟨*sorrow, misfortune*⟩; tolerate ⟨*insults*⟩; (über sich ergehen lassen) undergo

Erd-: ~**umdrehung** *die* rotation of the earth; ~**umlauf·bahn** *die* orbit [of the earth]

ereifern *refl. V.* get excited

ereignen *refl. V.* happen; ⟨*accident, mishap*⟩ occur

Ereignis *das;* ~ses, ~se event; occurrence

ereignis·reich *Adj.* eventful

Eremit *der;* ~en, ~en, **Eremitin** *die;* ~, ~nen hermit

ererbt *Adj.* inherited

---

erf̲ahren[1] *unr. tr. V.* **(a)** find out; learn; (hören) hear
(b) (geh.: erleben) experience; (erleiden) suffer

erf̲ahren[2] *Adj.* experienced

Erf̲ahrung *die;* ~, ~en experience; ~en sammeln gain experience *sing.;* etw. in ~ bringen discover sth.

erf̲ahrungs·gemäß *Adv.* in our/my experience

erf̲assen *tr. V.* **(a)** (mitreißen) catch
(b) (begreifen) grasp *(situation, etc.)*
(c) (registrieren) record

Erf̲assung *die;* ~, ~en registration

erf̲inden *unr. tr. V.* invent; **das ist alles erfunden** it is pure fabrication

Erf̲inder *der;* ~s, ~, **Erf̲inderin** *die;* ~, ~nen **(a)** inventor
(b) (Urheber) creator

erf̲inderisch *Adj.* inventive; (schlau) resourceful

Erf̲indung *die;* ~, ~en invention

erfl̲ehen *tr. V.* (geh.) beg

Erf̲olg *der;* ~[e]s, ~e success; **keinen ~ haben** be unsuccessful

erf̲olgen *itr. V.; mit sein* take place; occur; **es erfolgte keine Reaktion** there was no reaction

erf̲olg-, Erf̲olg-: ~**los** [1] *Adj.* unsuccessful; [2] *adv.* unsuccessfully; ~**losigkeit** *die;* ~~: lack of success; ~**reich** [1] *Adj.* successful; [2] *adv.* successfully

Erf̲olgs·erlebnis *das* feeling of achievement

erf̲olg·versprechend *Adj.* promising

erf̲orderlich *Adj.* required; necessary

erf̲ordern *tr. V.* require; demand

erf̲orschen *tr. V.* discover *(facts, causes, etc.)*; explore *(country)*

Erf̲orschung *die;* ~ research (+ *Gen.* into); (eines Landes usw.) exploration

erfr̲euen [1] *tr. V.* please
[2] *refl. V.* **sich an etw.** *(Dat.)* ~: take pleasure in sth.

erfr̲eulich *Adj.* pleasant

erfr̲eulicherweise *Adv.* happily

erfr̲ieren [1] *unr. itr. V.; mit sein* freeze to death; *(plant, harvest, etc.)* be damaged by frost
[2] *unr. refl. V.* **sich** *(Dat.)* **die Finger** ~: get frostbite in one's fingers

Erfr̲ierung *die;* ~, ~en frostbite *no pl.;* ~en an den Händen/Füßen frostbitten hands/feet

erfr̲ischen [1] *tr. V.* (auch itr.) refresh
[2] *refl. V.* freshen oneself up

erfr̲ischend (auch fig.) *Adj.* refreshing

Erfr̲ischung *die;* ~, ~en (auch fig.) refreshment

Erfr̲ischungs-: ~**getränk** *das* soft drink; ~**raum** *der* refreshment room; ~**tuch** *das; Pl.* ~**tücher** tissue wipe; towelette

erf̲üllen [1] *tr. V.* grant *(wish, request)*; fulfil *(contract)*; carry out *(duty)*; meet *(condition)*
[2] *refl. V.* *(wish)* come true

Erf̲üllung *die;* **in** ~ **gehen** come true

erf̲unden *Adj.* fictional *(story)*

erg̲änzen *tr. V.* **(a)** (vervollständigen) complete; (erweitern) add to
(b) (hinzufügen) add *(remark)*

Erg̲änzung *die;* ~, ~en **(a)** (Vervollständigung) completion; (Erweiterung) enlargement
(b) (Zusatz) addition; (zu einem Gesetz) amendment

erg̲attern *tr. V.* (ugs.) manage to grab

erg̲aunern *tr. V.* get by underhand means

erg̲eben[1] [1] *unr. refl. V.* **(a) sich in etw.** *(Akk.)* ~: submit to sth.
(b) (kapitulieren) surrender *(Dat.* to)
(c) (folgen, entstehen) arise (**aus** from)
[2] *unr. tr. V.* result in

erg̲eben[2] *Adj.* **(a)** (zugeneigt) devoted
(b) (resignierend) **mit** ~**er Miene** with an expression of resignation

Erg̲ebnis *das;* ~ses, ~se result

erg̲ebnis·los *Adj.* fruitless

erg̲ehen *unr. refl. V.* **sich in etw.** *(Dat.)* ~: indulge in sth.

erg̲iebig *Adj.* rich *(deposits, resources)*; fertile *(topic)*

Erg̲iebigkeit *die;* ~ ▶ ERGIEBIG: richness; fertility

ergon̲omisch [1] *Adj.* ergonomic
[2] *adv.* ergonomically

erg̲ötzen (geh.) [1] *tr. V.* enthrall
[2] *refl. V.* **sich an etw.** *(Dat.)* ~: be delighted by sth.

ergr̲auen *itr. V.; mit sein* go grey

ergr̲eifen *unr. tr. V.* **(a)** (greifen) grab
(b) (festnehmen) catch *(thief etc.)*
(c) (fig.: erfassen) seize
(d) (fig.: aufnehmen) take up *(career)*; take *(initiative, opportunity)*
(e) (fig.: bewegen) move

ergr̲eifend *Adj.* moving

ergr̲iffen *Adj.* moved

Ergr̲iffenheit *die;* ~: **voller** ~: deeply moved

ergr̲ünden *tr. V.* ascertain; discover *(cause)*

Erg̲uss, *Erg̲uß *der* (geh. abwertend) outburst; **ein poetischer** ~: a poetic outpouring

erh̲aben *Adj.* solemn *(moment)*; awe-inspiring *(sight)*; sublime *(beauty)*; **über etw.** *(Akk.)* ~ **sein** be above sth.

Erh̲alt *der;* ~ (Amtsdt.) receipt

erhalten *unr. tr. V.* (a) receive ⟨*letter, news, gift*⟩; be given ⟨*order*⟩; get ⟨*good mark, impression*⟩
(b) (bewahren) preserve ⟨*town, building*⟩
erhältlich *Adj.* obtainable
Erhaltung *die;* ~: preservation; (des Friedens) maintenance
erhängen *tr. V.* hang
erhärten *tr. V.* strengthen ⟨*suspicion, assumption*⟩; substantiate ⟨*claim*⟩
erheben ①*unr. tr. V.* (a) raise
(b) (verlangen) levy ⟨*tax*⟩; charge ⟨*fee*⟩
②*unr. refl. V.* (a) rise
(b) (rebellieren) rise up (**gegen** against)
erhebend *Adj.* uplifting
erheblich ①*Adj.* considerable
②*adv.* considerably
Erhebung *die;* ~, ~en (a) (Anhöhe) elevation
(b) (Aufstand) uprising
(c) (Umfrage) survey
(d) (Einziehen) (von Steuern) levying; (von Gebühren) charging
erheitern *tr. V.* jmdn. ~: cheer sb. up
Erheiterung *die;* ~, ~en amusement
erhellen *tr. V.* light up
erhitzen ①*tr. V.* heat ⟨*liquid*⟩; jmdn. ~: make sb. hot
②*refl. V.* heat up; ⟨*person*⟩ become hot
erhoffen *tr. V.* sich (*Dat.*) viel/wenig von etw. ~: expect a lot/little from sth.
erhöhen ①*tr. V.* increase ⟨*prices, productivity, etc.*⟩
②*refl. V.* ⟨*rent, prices*⟩ rise
Erhöhung *die;* ~, ~en increase (*Gen.* in)
erholen *refl. V.* (auch fig.) recover (**von** from); (sich ausruhen) have a rest
erholsam *Adj.* restful
Erholung *die;* ~: ▶ ERHOLEN: recovery; rest; ~ **brauchen** need a rest
erholungs-bedürftig *Adj.* in need of a rest *postpos.*
Erholungs-urlaub *der* holiday for convalescence
erhören *tr. V.* (geh.) hear
Erika *die;* ~, ~s *od.* Eriken (Bot.) erica
erinnern ①*refl. V.* sich an jmdn./etw. ~: remember sb./sth.; sich [daran] ~, dass ...: remember *or* recall that ...
②*tr. V.* jmdn. an etw./jmdn. ~: remind sb. of sth./sb.
Erinnerung *die;* ~, ~en memory (**an** + *Akk.* of); etw. [noch gut] in ~ haben [still] remember sth. [well]; zur ~ an jmdn./etw. in memory of sb./sth.
Erinnerungs-lücke *die* gap in one's memory
erjagen *tr. V.* (a) catch
(b) (gewinnen) win ⟨*fame*⟩; make ⟨*money, fortune*⟩

erkalten *tr. V.; mit sein* cool
erkälten *refl. V.* catch cold
Erkältung *die;* ~, ~en cold
Erkältungs·krankheit *die* cold
erkämpfen *tr. V.* win; **den Sieg** ~: gain a victory
erkaufen *tr. V.* (a) (durch Opfer) win
(b) (durch Geld) buy
erkennbar *Adj.* recognizable; (sichtbar) visible
erkennen *unr. tr. V.* (a) recognize
(b) (deutlich sehen) make out
erkenntlich *Adj.* (a) sich [für etw.] ~ zeigen show one's appreciation for sth.
(b) ▶ ERKENNBAR
Erkenntnis *die;* ~, ~se discovery; **zu der** ~ **kommen, dass ...:** come to the realization that ...
Erkennungs-: ~**melodie** *die* (einer Sendung) theme music; (eines Senders) signature tune; ~**zeichen** *das* sign [to recognize sb. by]
Erker *der;* ~s, ~: bay window
Erker·fenster *das* bay window
erklärbar *Adj.* explicable
erklären ①*tr. V.* (a) explain
(b) (mitteilen) state; declare
(c) jmdn. für tot ~: pronounce someone dead; jmdn. zu etw. ~: name sb. as sth
②*refl. V.* sich einverstanden/bereit ~: declare oneself [to be] in agreement/willing
erklärlich *Adj.* understandable
erklärt *Adj.* declared
Erklärung *die;* ~, ~en (a) (Darlegung) explanation
(b) (Mitteilung) statement
erklimmen *unr. tr. V.* (geh.) climb
erklingen *unr. itr. V.; mit sein* ring out
erkranken *itr. V.; mit sein* become ill (**an** + *Dat.* with); **schwer erkrankt sein** be seriously ill
Erkrankung *die;* ~, ~en illness; (eines Körperteils) disease
erkunden *tr. V.* reconnoitre ⟨*terrain*⟩
erkundigen *refl. V.* sich nach jmdm./etw. ~: ask after sb./enquire about sth.
Erkundigung *die;* ~, ~en enquiry
Erkundung *die;* ~, ~en (meist Milit.) reconnaissance
Erkundungs-: ~**fahrt** *die* exploratory trip; ~**flug** *der* reconnaissance flight
erlahmen *itr. V.; mit sein* tire; ⟨*strength*⟩ flag
erlangen *tr. V.* gain; obtain ⟨*credit, visa*⟩; reach ⟨*age*⟩
Erlass, *Erlaß *der;* Erlasses, Erlasse decree
erlassen *unr. tr. V.* (a) enact ⟨*law*⟩; declare ⟨*amnesty*⟩; issue ⟨*warrant*⟩
(b) (verzichten auf) remit ⟨*sentence*⟩
erlauben ①*tr. V.* (a) allow
(b) (ermöglichen) permit

---

*old spelling - see note on page xiv

2 *refl. V.* **sich** (*Dat.*) **etw. ~:** permit oneself sth

Erlaubnis *die;* ~, ~se permission; (Schriftstück) permit

erläutern *tr. V.* explain; comment on ⟨*picture etc.*⟩; annotate ⟨*text*⟩

Erläuterung *die* explanation

Erle *die;* ~, ~n alder

erleben *tr. V.* experience; etwas Schreckliches ~: have a terrible experience; er wird das nächste Jahr nicht mehr ~: he won't see next year; du kannst was ~! (ugs.) you won't know what's hit you!

Erlebnis *das;* ~ses, ~se experience

erledigen **1** *tr. V.* deal with ⟨*task*⟩; settle ⟨*matter*⟩; ich muss noch einige Dinge erledigen I must see to a few things; sie hat alles pünktlich erledigt she got everything done on time
2 *refl. V.* ⟨*matter, problem*⟩ resolve itself; vieles erledigt sich von selbst a lot of things sort them'selves out

erledigt *Adj.* closed ⟨*case*⟩; (ugs.) worn out ⟨*person*⟩

erlegen *tr. V.* shoot ⟨*animal*⟩

erleichtern *tr. V.* (a) make easier
(b) (befreien) relieve

Erleichterung *die;* ~, ~en (a) zur ~ der Arbeit to make the work easier
(b) (Befreiung) relief
(c) (Verbesserung, Milderung) alleviation

erleiden *unr. tr. V.* suffer

erlernbar *Adj.* learnable

erlernen *tr. V.* learn

erlesen *Adj.* superior ⟨*wine*⟩; choice ⟨*dish*⟩

erleuchten *tr. V.* (a) light
(b) (geh.: mit Klarheit erfüllen) inspire

Erleuchtung *die;* ~, ~en inspiration

erliegen *unr. itr. V.; mit sein* succumb (*Dat.* to); einem Irrtum ~: be misled; einer Krankheit (*Dat.*) ~: die from an illness

erlogen *Adj.* made up

Erlös *der;* ~es, ~e proceeds *pl.*

erlöschen *unr. itr. V.; mit sein* ⟨*fire*⟩ go out; ein erloschener Vulkan an extinct volcano

erlösen *tr. V.* save, rescue (von from)

Erlöser *der;* ~s, ~ (a) saviour
(b) (christl. Rel.) redeemer

Erlöserin *die;* ~, ~nen ▶ ERLÖSER A

Erlösung *die;* ~, ~en release (von from)

ermächtigen *tr. V.* authorize

Ermächtigung *die;* ~, ~en authorization

ermahnen *tr. V.* admonish; tell (coll.); (warnen) warn

Ermahnung *die;* ~, ~en admonition; (Warnung) warning

Ermang[e]lung *die;* ~: in ~ (+ *Gen.*) (geh.) in the absence of

ermäßigen *tr. V.* reduce

Ermäßigung *die;* ~, ~en reduction

ermatten (geh.) **1** *itr. V.; mit sein* become exhausted
2 *tr. V.* exhaust, tire

ermessen *unr. tr. V.* estimate, gauge

Ermessen *das;* ~s estimation

ermitteln **1** *tr. V.* ascertain ⟨*facts*⟩; discover ⟨*culprit, address*⟩; establish ⟨*identity, origin*⟩; decide ⟨*winner*⟩; calculate ⟨*quota, rates, data*⟩
2 *itr. V.* (Rechtsw.) investigate

Ermittlung *die;* ~, ~en (a) (das Ermitteln) ▶ ERMITTELN A: ascertainment; discovery; establishment
(b) (Untersuchung) investigation

ermöglichen *tr. V.* enable

ermorden *tr. V.* murder

Ermordung *die;* ~, ~en murder

ermüden **1** *itr. V.; mit sein* tire
2 *tr. V.* tire; make tired

ermüdend *Adj.* tiring

Ermüdung *die;* ~, ~en tiredness

ermuntern *tr. V.* encourage

ermunternd *Adj.* encouraging

ermutigen *tr. V.* encourage

Ermutigung *die;* ~, ~en encouragement

ernähren **1** *tr. V.* (a) feed ⟨*young, child*⟩
(b) (unterhalten) keep ⟨*family, wife*⟩
2 *refl. V.* feed oneself

Ernährer *der;* ~s, ~, **Ernährerin** *die;* ~, ~nen breadwinner

Ernährung *die;* ~: feeding; (Nahrung) diet

Ernährungs·wissenschaft *die* dietetics *sing., no art.*

ernennen *unr. tr. V.* appoint

Ernennung *die* appointment (zu as)

erneuerbar *Adj.* renewable; ~e Energien renewable sources of energy

erneuern *tr. V.* (a) replace
(b) (wiederherstellen) renovate ⟨*roof, building*⟩; (fig.) thoroughly reform ⟨*system*⟩

Erneuerung *die;* ~, ~en (a) replacement
(b) (Wiederherstellung) renovation

erneut **1** *Adj.* renewed
2 *adv.* once again

erniedrigen *tr. V.* humiliate

Erniedrigung *die;* ~, ~en humiliation

ernst **1** *Adj.* (a) serious
(b) (aufrichtig) genuine ⟨*intention, offer*⟩
(c) (gefahrvoll) serious ⟨*injury*⟩; grave ⟨*situation*⟩
2 *adv.* seriously; jmdn./etw. ~ nehmen take sb./sth. seriously; ~ gemeint serious; sincere ⟨*wish*⟩

Ernst *der;* ~[e]s (a) seriousness; das ist mein [voller] ~: I mean that [quite] seriously; etw. im ~ meinen mean sth. seriously
(b) (Wirklichkeit) daraus wurde [blutiger/bitterer] ~: it became [deadly] serious; der ~ des Lebens the serious side of life

ernst-, Ernst-: ~fall *der:* im ~fall when the real thing happens; ***~gemeint ⋯⋗

▶ ERNST 2; ~**haft** [1] *Adj.* serious; [2] *adv.*
seriously; ~**haftigkeit** *die;* ~~:
seriousness

ernstlich [1] *Adj.* (a) serious
(b) (aufrichtig) genuine ⟨*wish*⟩
[2] *adv.* (a) seriously
(b) (aufrichtig) genuinely ⟨*sorry, repentant*⟩

Ernte *die;* ~, ~n (a) harvest
(b) (Ertrag) crop; **die** ~ **einbringen** bring in
the harvest

Ernte·dank·fest *das* harvest festival

ernten *tr. V.* harvest

ernüchtern *tr. V.* sober up; (fig.) bring
down to earth; ~**d** sobering

Ernüchterung *die;* ~, ~en (fig.)
disillusionment

Eroberer *der;* ~s, ~, **Eroberin** *die;* ~,
~nen conqueror

erobern *tr. V.* (a) conquer; take ⟨*town,
fortress*⟩
(b) seize ⟨*power*⟩

Eroberung *die;* ~, ~en conquest; (einer
Stadt, Festung) taking

eröffnen *tr. V.* (a) open; start ⟨*business,
practice*⟩
(b) (mitteilen) jmdm. etw. ~: reveal sth. to sb.
(c) ein Testament ~: read a will

Eröffnung *die;* ~, ~en (a) opening; (einer
Sitzung) start
(b) (Mitteilung) revelation
(c) (Testaments~) reading

erogen *Adj.* erogenous ⟨*zone*⟩

erörtern *tr. V.* discuss

Erörterung *die;* ~, ~en discussion

Eros·Center *das* [licensed] brothel; eros
centre

Erosion *die;* ~, ~en erosion

Erotik *die;* ~: eroticism

erotisch *Adj.* erotic

Erpel *der;* ~s, ~: drake

erpicht *Adj.* in auf etw. (*Akk.*) ~ sein be
keen on sth.

erpressbar, *erpreßbar *Adj.*
blackmailable; susceptible to blackmail
postpos.

Erpressbarkeit, *Erpreßbarkeit *die;*
~: susceptibility to blackmail

erpressen *tr. V.* (a) (nötigen) blackmail
(b) (erlangen) extort ⟨*money etc.*⟩

Erpresser *der;* ~s, ~, **Erpresserin** *die;*
~, ~nen blackmailer

Erpressung *die;* ~, ~en blackmail *no
indef. art.;* (von Geld, Geständnis) extortion

Erpressungs·versuch *der* blackmail
attempt

erproben *tr. V.* test ⟨*medicine*⟩ (an + *Akk.*
on)

Erprobung *die;* ~, ~en testing

erquickend *Adj.* (geh.) refreshing

erraten *unr. tr. V.* guess

errechnen *tr. V.* calculate

erregen [1] *tr. V.* (a) annoy
(b) (sexuell) arouse
(c) (verursachen) arouse
[2] *refl. V.* get excited

erregend *Adj.* exciting; (sexuell) arousing

Erreger *der;* ~s, ~ (Med.) pathogen

erregt *Adj.* excited; (sexuell) aroused

Erregung *die;* ~, ~en excitement

erreichbar *Adj.* (a) within reach *postpos.;*
(b) **der Ort ist mit dem Zug** ~: the place can
be reached by train

erreichen *tr. V.* (a) reach; **den Zug** ~:
catch the train; **er ist telefonisch zu** ~: he
can be contacted by telephone
(b) (durchsetzen) achieve ⟨*goal, aim*⟩

errichten *tr. V.* (a) build ⟨*house, bridge,
etc.*⟩
(b) (aufstellen) erect

erringen *unr. tr. V.* gain ⟨*victory*⟩; reach
⟨*first etc. place*⟩

erröten *itr. V.; mit sein* blush

Errungenschaft *die;* ~, ~en
achievement

Ersatz *der;* ~es (a) replacement
(b) (Entschädigung) compensation

Ersatz·: ~**frau** *die* replacement; (Sport)
substitute; ~**kasse** *die* private health
insurance company; ~**mann** *der; Pl.*
~**männer** *od.* ~**leute** *die* replacement; (Sport)
substitute; ~**rad** *das* spare wheel; ~**reifen**
der spare tyre; ~**spieler** *der,* ~**spielerin**
die (Sport) substitute [player]; ~**teil** *das* (bes.
Technik) spare part; spare (Brit.)

ersaufen *unr. itr. V.; mit sein* (salopp)
drown

ersäufen *tr. V.* drown

erschaffen *unr. tr. V.* create

Erschaffung *die* creation

erschaudern *itr. V.; mit sein* (geh.)
shudder (**bei** at)

erscheinen *unr. itr. V.; mit sein* ⟨*book*⟩ be
published

Erscheinung *die;* ~, ~en (a) (Vorgang)
phenomenon
(b) (äußere Gestalt) appearance
(c) (Vision) apparition; **eine** ~ **haben** see a
vision

Erscheinungs·: ~**bild** *das* appearance;
~**form** *die* manifestation; ~**weise** *die* **die**
~**weise einer Zeitung** the frequency of
publication of a newspaper; **wöchentliche/
monatliche** ~**weise** weekly/monthly
publication

erschießen *unr. tr. V.* shoot dead

Erschießung *die;* ~, ~en shooting

erschlaffen *itr. V.; mit sein* ⟨*muscle, limb*⟩
become limp; ⟨*skin*⟩ grow slack

erschlagen[1] *unr. tr. V.* strike dead; kill

erschlagen[2] *Adj.* (ugs.) (a) (erschöpft) worn
out

(b) (verblüfft) wie ∼ sein be flabbergasted (coll.) *or* thunderstruck

erschließen *unr. tr. V.* develop ⟨*area, building land*⟩; tap ⟨*resources*⟩

erschöpfen *tr. V.* exhaust

erschöpfend *Adj.* exhaustive

erschöpft *Adj.* exhausted

Erschöpfung *die;* ∼, ∼en exhaustion

Erschöpfungs·zustand *der* state of exhaustion

erschrecken[1] *unr. itr. V.; mit sein* be startled; **vor etw.** *(Dat.) od.* **über etw.** *(Akk.)* ∼: be startled by sth.

erschrecken[2] *tr. V.* frighten; scare

erschrecken[3] *unr. od. regelm. refl. V.* get a fright

erschreckend *Adj.* alarming

erschrocken [1] *2. Part. v.* ERSCHRECKEN[1]; [2] *Adj.* frightened

erschüttern *tr. V.* (auch fig.) shake

erschütternd *Adj.* deeply distressing; deeply shocking ⟨*conditions*⟩

Erschütterung *die;* ∼, ∼en **(a)** vibration; (der Erde) tremor **(b)** (Ergriffenheit) shock; (Trauer) distress

erschweren *tr. V.* etw. ∼: make sth. more difficult

erschwerend [1] *Adj.* complicating ⟨*factor*⟩ [2] *adv.* es kommt ∼ hinzu, dass er ...: to make matters worse he ...

Erschwernis *die;* ∼, ∼se difficulty

erschwinglich *Adj.* reasonable

ersehen *unr. tr. V.* see; aus etw. zu ∼ sein be evident from sth.

ersetzen *tr. V.* **(a)** replace (durch by) **(b)** (erstatten) reimburse ⟨*expenses*⟩; jmdm. einen Schaden ∼: compensate sb. for damages

Ersetzung *die;* ∼, ∼en (von Kosten usw.) reimbursement; die ∼ von Schäden compensation for damage

ersichtlich *Adj.* apparent

ersinnen *unr. tr. V.* (geh.) devise

erspähen *tr. V.* (geh.) espy (literary); catch sight of

ersparen *tr. V.* save

Ersparnis *die;* ∼, ∼se saving

ersprießlich *Adj.* (geh.) fruitful ⟨*contacts, collaboration*⟩

erst [1] *Adv.* **(a)** (zu∼) first; ∼ einmal first [of all] **(b)** (nicht eher als) eben ∼: only just; ∼ nächste Woche not until next week; er war ∼ zufrieden, als ...: he was not satisfied until ... **(c)** (nicht mehr als) only [2] *Partikel* so was lese ich gar nicht ∼: I don't even start reading that sort of stuff

erst... *Ordinalz.* **(a)** first; etw. das ∼e Mal

tun do sth. for the first time; am Ersten [des Monats] on the first [of the month]; als Erster/Erste etw. tun be the first to do sth. **(b)** (best...) das ∼e Hotel the best hotel; der/ die Erste [der Klasse] the top boy/girl [of the class]

erstarren *itr. V.; mit sein* ⟨*jelly, plaster*⟩ set; ⟨*limbs, fingers*⟩ grow stiff

erstatten *tr. V.* **(a)** reimburse ⟨*expenses*⟩ **(b)** Anzeige gegen jmdn. ∼: report sb. [to the police]

Erstattung *die;* ∼, ∼en (von Kosten) reimbursement

Erst·aufführung *die* première

erstaunen *tr. V.* astonish

Erstaunen *das;* ∼s astonishment

erstaunlich [1] *Adj.* astonishing [2] *adv.* astonishingly

erstaunlicher·weise *Adv.* astonishingly *or* amazingly [enough]

erstaunt *Adj.* astonished; amazed

Erst·ausgabe *die* first edition

erstechen *unr. tr. V.* stab [to death]

erstehen (geh.) [1] *unr. tr. V.* (kaufen) purchase [2] *unr. itr. V.; mit sein* ⟨*difficulties, problems*⟩ arise

ersteigen *unr. tr. V.* climb

ersteigern *tr. V.* buy [at an auction]

erstellen *tr. V.* (Papierdt.) **(a)** (bauen) build **(b)** (anfertigen) make ⟨*assessment*⟩; draw up ⟨*plan, report, list*⟩

*erste·mal ▶ MAL[1]

*ersten·mal ▶ MAL[1]

erstens *Adv.* firstly; in the first place

erster... *Adj.* the former

erst·geboren *Adj.* first-born

ersticken [1] *itr. V.; mit sein* suffocate; (sich verschlucken) choke [2] *tr. V.* **(a)** (töten) suffocate **(b)** smother ⟨*flames*⟩

erstklassig [1] *Adj.* first-class [2] *adv.* superbly

erstmals *Adv.* for the first time

erstrangig *Adj.* **(a)** first-class **(b)** (vordringlich) of top priority *postpos.*

erstreben *tr. V.* strive for

erstrebens·wert *Adj.* ⟨*ideals etc.*⟩ worth striving for; desirable ⟨*situation*⟩

erstrecken *refl. V.* **(a)** (sich ausdehnen) stretch **(b)** (dauern) sich über 10 Jahre ∼: carry on for 10 years

Erst·stimme *die* first vote

erstürmen *tr. V.* take by storm

ersuchen *tr. V.* (geh.) ask; jmdn. ∼, etw. zu tun request sb. to do sth.

ertappen *tr. V.* catch ⟨*thief, burglar*⟩

erteilen *tr. V.* give ⟨*advice, information*⟩; give, grant ⟨*permission*⟩

Erteilung *die;* ~, ~en giving; (einer Genehmigung) granting

ertönen *itr. V.; mit sein* sound

Ertrag *der;* ~[e]s, Erträge **(a)** yield
(b) (Gewinn) return

ertragen *unr. tr. V.* bear

erträglich *Adj.* tolerable; bearable ⟨pain⟩

ertrag·reich *Adj.* lucrative ⟨business⟩; productive ⟨land, soil⟩

ertränken *tr. V.* drown

ertrinken *unr. itr. V.; mit sein* be drowned; drown

erübrigen ① *tr. V.* spare ⟨money, time⟩
② *refl. V.* be unnecessary

erwachen *itr. V.; mit sein* (geh.) awake

Erwachen *das;* ~s (auch fig.) awakening

erwachsen¹ *unr. itr. V.; mit sein* **(a)** grow (aus out of); ⟨rumour⟩ spread
(b) (sich ergeben) ⟨difficulties, tasks⟩ arise

erwachsen² *Adj.* grown-up *attrib.;* ~ sein be grown up

Erwachsene *der/die; adj. Dekl.* adult; grown-up

erwägen *unr. tr. V.* consider

Erwägung *die;* ~, ~en consideration; etw. in ~ ziehen take sth. into consideration

erwählen *tr. V.* (geh.) choose

erwähnen *tr. V.* mention

erwähnens·wert *Adj.* worth mentioning *postpos.*

Erwähnung *die;* ~, ~en mention

erwärmen ① *tr. V.* heat
② *refl. V.* (warm werden) ⟨air, water⟩ warm up

Erwärmung *die;* ~: eine ~ der Luft/des Wassers an increase in air/water temperature; bei ~ der Flüssigkeit when the liquid is heated

erwarten *tr. V.* expect; jmdn. am Bahnhof ~: wait for sb. at the station

Erwartung *die;* ~, ~en expectation

erwartungs-: ~gemäß *Adv.* as expected; ~voll *Adj.* expectant

erwecken *tr. V.* **(a)** (auf~) wake
(b) (erregen) arouse ⟨longing, pity⟩

erweichen *tr. V.* soften

erweisen ① *unr. tr. V.* **(a)** prove
(b) (bezeigen) jmdm. Achtung ~: show respect to sb.
② *unr. refl. V.* sich als etw. ~: prove to be sth.

erweitern ① *tr. V.* widen ⟨river, road⟩; expand ⟨library, business⟩; enlarge ⟨collection⟩; dilate ⟨pupil, blood vessel⟩
② *refl. V.* ⟨road, river⟩ widen; ⟨pupil, blood vessel⟩ dilate

Erweiterung *die;* ~, ~en ▶ ERWEITERN: widening; expansion; enlargement; dilation

Erwerb *der;* ~[e]s **(a)** (Aneignung) acquisition
(b) (Kauf) purchase

erwerben *unr. tr. V.* **(a)** (verdienen) earn
(b) (sich aneignen) gain
(c) (kaufen) acquire

erwerbs-, Erwerbs-: ~fähig *Adj.* capable of gainful employment *postpos.;* able to work *postpos.;* ~fähigkeit *die* ability to work; ~los *Adj.:* ▶ ARBEITSLOS; ~lose *der/ die; adj. Dekl.:* ▶ ARBEITSLOSE; ~tätig *Adj.* gainfully employed; ~unfähig *Adj.* incapable of gainful employment *postpos.;* unable to work *postpos.*

Erwerbung *die* acquisition; (Gekauftes) purchase

erwidern *tr. V.* **(a)** reply
(b) (reagieren auf) return ⟨greeting, visit⟩; reciprocate ⟨sb.'s feelings⟩

Erwiderung *die;* ~, ~en **(a)** reply (auf + Akk. to)
(b) ▶ ERWIDERN B: return; reciprocation

erwiesen *Adj.* proved; proven ⟨fact⟩

erwiesener·maßen *Adv.* as has been proved

erwirken *tr. V.* obtain

erwirtschaften *tr. V.* etw. ~: obtain sth. by careful management

erwischen *tr. V.* (ugs.) **(a)** catch ⟨culprit, train, bus⟩
(b) (greifen) grab
(c) (bekommen) manage to get
(d) (unpers.) es hat ihn erwischt (ugs.) (er ist tot) he's bought it (sl.); (er ist krank) he's got it; (er ist verletzt) he's been hurt; (scherzh.: er ist verliebt) he's got it bad (coll.)

erwünscht *Adj.* wanted

erwürgen *tr. V.* strangle

Erz /ɛrts; *od.* eːrts:/ *das;* ~es, ~e ore

erzählen *tr.* (auch itr.) *V.* tell ⟨joke, story⟩; jmdm. etw. ~: tell sb. sth.

Erzähler *der,* **Erzählerin** *die* storyteller; (Autor[in]) writer [of stories]; narrative writer

Erzählung *die;* ~, ~en narration; (Bericht) account; (Literaturw.) story

Erz-: ~bischof *der* archbishop; ~bistum *das,* ~diözese *die* archbishopric; archdiocese; ~engel *der* archangel

erzeugen *tr. V.* produce; generate ⟨electricity⟩

Erzeuger *der;* ~s, ~ (Vater) father

Erzeugnis *das;* ~ses, ~se product

Erzeugung *die;* ~, ~en (von Lebensmitteln usw.) production; (von Industriewaren) manufacture; (Strom~) generation

Erz·feind *der,* **Erz·feindin** *die* arch enemy

erziehen *unr. tr. V.* bring up; (in der Schule) educate; ein Kind zu Sauberkeit und Ordnung ~: bring a child up to be clean and tidy

Erzieher *der;* ~s, ~, **Erzieherin** *die;* ~, ~nen educator; (Pädagoge) educationalist; (Lehrer) teacher

Erziehung *die;* ~, ~en upbringing; (Schul~) education

---

*old spelling - see note on page xiv

Erziehungs-: ~**berechtigte** der/die; adj. Dekl. parent or [legal] guardian; ~**urlaub** der child-rearing leave

erzielen tr. V. reach ⟨agreement, compromise, speed⟩; achieve ⟨result, effect⟩; make ⟨profit⟩; obtain ⟨price⟩

erzürnen (geh.) tr. V. anger; (stärker) incense

erzwingen unr. tr. V. force

es Personalpron.; 3. Pers. Sg. Nom. u. Akk. Neutr. **(a)** (s. auch Gen. seiner; Dat. ihm) (Sache) it; (weibliche Person) she/her; (männliche Person) he/him
(b) ohne Bezug auf ein bestimmtes Subst., mit unpers. konstruierten Verben, als formales Satzglied it; **ich bin es** it's me; **wir sind traurig, ihr seid es auch** we are sad, and so are you; **es sei denn, [dass]** …: unless …; **es ist genug!** that's enough; **es hat geklopft** there was a knock; **es klingelt** someone is ringing; **es wird schöner** the weather is improving; **es geht ihm gut/schlecht** he is well/unwell; **es wird gelacht** there is laughter; **es lässt sich aushalten** it is bearable; **er hat es gut** he has it good; **er meinte es gut** he meant well

Esche die; ~, ~n (Bot.) ash

Esel der; ~s, ~ **(a)** donkey; ass
(b) (ugs.: Dummkopf) ass (coll.)

Esels-: ~**brücke** die (ugs.) mnemonic; ~**ohr** das (ugs.: umgeknickte Stelle) dog-ear

Eskalation die; ~, ~en escalation

eskalieren tr., itr. V. escalate

Eskapade /ɛska'paːdə/ die; ~, ~n escapade; (Seitensprung) amorous adventure

Eskimo der; ~[s], ~[s] Eskimo

Eskimo·frau die Eskimo woman

Eskorte die; ~, ~n escort

eskortieren tr. V. escort

Espe die; ~, ~n aspen

Essay /'ɛsɛ/ der od. das; ~s, ~s essay

essbar, *eßbar Adj. edible; **nicht** ~: inedible

essen unr. tr., itr. V. eat; **etw. gern** ~: like sth.; **sich satt** ~: eat one's fill; **gut** ~: have a good meal; **(immer) eat well**; ~ **gehen** go out for a meal

Essen das; ~s, ~ (Mahlzeit) meal; (Speise) food; **[das]** ~ **machen/kochen** get/cook the meal

Essen[s]-: ~**marke** die meal ticket; ~**zeit** die mealtime

Essenz die; ~, ~en essence

Esser der; ~s, ~, **Esserin** die; ~, ~nen: **er ist ein schlechter Esser** he has a poor appetite

Essig der; ~s, ~e vinegar

Essig·gurke die pickled gherkin

Ess-, *Eß-: ~**kastanie** die sweet chestnut; ~**löffel** der (Suppenlöffel) soup spoon; (für Nach-, Vorspeise) dessert spoon; ~**stäbchen** das chopstick; ~**teller** der

dinner plate; ~**tisch** der dining table; ~**waren** Pl. food sing.; ~**zimmer** das dining room

Establishment /ɪs'tɛblɪʃmənt/ das; ~s, ~s Establishment

Este der; ~n, ~n, **Estin** die; ~, ~nen Estonian

Est·land (das); ~s Estonia

Estragon /'ɛstragɔn/ der; ~s tarragon

Estrich /'ɛstrɪç/ der; ~s, ~e composition floor

Eszett /ɛs'tsɛt/ das; ~, ~ [the letter] ß

etablieren tr. V. establish; set up

etabliert Adj. established

Etablissement /etablɪs(ə)'mãː/ das; ~s, ~s establishment

Etage /e'taːʒə/ die; ~, ~n floor; storey

Etappe die; ~, ~n stage

Etat /e'taː/ der; ~s, ~s budget

etepetete /eːtəpe'teːtə/ Adj. (ugs.) fussy; finicky

Ethik die; ~, ~en **(a)** ethics sing.; **(b)** (sittliche Normen) ethics pl.

ethisch Adj. ethical

ethnisch 1 Adj. ethnic; ~**e Säuberung** ethnic cleansing
2 adv. ethnically

Etikett das; ~[e]s, ~en od. ~e od. ~s label

Etikette die; ~, ~n etiquette

Etiketten·schwindel der (abwertend) playing with names

etikettieren tr. V. label

etlich… Indefinitpron. u. unbest. Zahlwort: Sg. quite a lot of; Pl. quite a few

Etüde die; ~, ~n (Musik) étude

Etui /ɛt'viː/ das; ~s, ~s case

etwa 1 Adv. **(a)** something; approx. (ungefähr) about; ~ **so groß wie** …: about as large as …; ~ **so roughly like this**
(b) (beispielsweise) for example
2 Partikel **störe ich** ~? am I disturbing you at all?

etwaig… /'ɛtva(ː)ɪg…/ Adj. possible

etwas Indefinitpron. **(a)** something; (fragend, verneinend) anything; **irgend**~: something
(b) (Bedeutsames) **aus ihm wird** ~: he'll make something of himself
(c) (ein Teil) some; (fragend, verneinend) any; ~ **von dem Geld** some of the money
(d) (ein wenig) a little; ~ **lauter/besser** a little louder/better

Etymologie die; ~, ~n etymology

EU Abk. = **Europäische Union** EU

euch 1 Dat. u. Akk. Pl. des Personalpron. ihr you
2 Dat. u. Akk. Pl. des Reflexivpron. der 2. Pers. Pl. yourselves

euer¹ Possessivpron. your; **Grüße von eu[e]rer Helga/eu[e]rem Hans** Best wishes, Yours, Helga/Hans

euer² *Gen. des Personalpron.* **ihr** (geh.) **wir werden** ~ **gedenken** we will remember you

Eule *die;* ~, ~n owl; ~n **nach Athen tragen** carry coals to Newcastle

Eunuch *der;* ~en, ~en eunuch

Euphorie *die;* ~, ~n (bes. Med., Psych.) euphoria

euphorisch (bes. Med., Psych.) ☐1 *Adj.* euphoric

☐2 *adv.* euphorically

eure ▸ EUER¹

eurer·seits ▸ DEINERSEITS

euret·wegen *Adv.* ▸ DEINETWEGEN

Euro *der;* ~[s], ~[s] euro; **50** ~ 50 euros

Eurocheque /ˈɔyːroʃɛk/ *der;* ~s, ~s Eurocheque

Europa (*das*) ~s Europe

Europäer *der;* ~s, ~, **Europäerin** *die;* ~, ~nen European

europäisch *Adj.* European; **die Europäische Union** the European Union

Europa-: ~**meister** *der,* ~**meisterin** *die* (Sport) European champion; ~**meisterschaft** *die* (Sport) **(a)** (Wettbewerb) European Championship; **(b)** (Sieg) European title; ~**parlament** *das* European Parliament; ~**pokal** *der* (Sport) European cup; ~**rat** *der* Council of Europe; ~**straße** *die* European long-distance road

Euro-: ~**scheck** *der* ▸ EUROCHEQUE; ~**zone** *die* eurozone

Euter *das od. der;* ~s, ~: udder

ev. *Abk.* = **evangelisch** ev.

e.V., E.V. *Abk.* = **eingetragener Verein**

evakuieren /evakuˈiːrən/ *tr. V.* evacuate

Evakuierung *die;* ~, ~en evacuation

evangelisch /evaŋˈɡeːlɪʃ/ *Adj.* Protestant

Evangelium *das;* ~s, **Evangelien (a)** (auch fig.) gospel

(b) (christl. Rel.) Gospel

Event /iˈvɛnt/ *der od. das;* ~s, ~s event

Eventualität /evɛntu̯aliˈtɛːt/ *die;* ~, ~en eventuality; contingency

eventuell ☐1 *Adj.* possible

☐2 *adv.* possibly; perhaps

Evolution /evoluˈtsi̯oːn/ *die;* ~, ~en evolution

evtl. *Abk.* = **eventuell**

EWG *Abk.* = **Europäische Wirtschaftsgemeinschaft** EEC

ewig ☐1 *Adj.* eternal; (abwertend) never-ending

☐2 *adv.* eternally; for ever

Ewig·gestrige *der/die; adj. Dekl.* (abwertend) **ein** ~**r sein** be an old reactionary

Ewigkeit *die;* ~, ~en **(a)** eternity

(b) (ugs.) **es dauert eine** ~: it takes ages (coll.)

ex *Adv.* (ugs.) **etw. ex trinken** drink sth. down in one (coll.)

---

*alte Schreibung - vgl. Hinweis auf S. xiv

exakt *Adj.* exact; precise

Exaktheit *die;* ~: precision; exactness

Examen *das;* ~s, ~ *od.* **Examina** examination

exekutieren *tr. V.* **(a)** execute

(b) (österr.) ▸ PFÄNDEN

Exekution *die;* ~, ~en **(a)** execution

(b) (österr.) ▸ PFÄNDUNG

Exekutive *die;* ~, ~n (Rechtsw., Politik) executive

Exempel *das;* ~s, ~: example

Exemplar *das;* ~s, ~e specimen; (Buch, Zeitung usw.) copy

exemplarisch *Adj.* exemplary

exerzieren *tr., itr. V.* drill

Exhibitionist *der;* ~en, ~en, **Exhibitionistin** *die;* ~, ~nen (Psych., fig.) exhibitionist

exhibitionistisch (Psych.) ☐1 *Adj.* exhibitionist

☐2 *adv.* **er ist** ~ **veranlagt** he has exhibitionist tendencies

Exil *das;* ~s, ~e exile

exiliert *Adj.* exiled

Exil·regierung *die* government in exile

existentiell ▸ EXISTENZIELL

Existenz *die;* ~, ~en **(a)** existence

(b) (Lebensgrundlage) livelihood

(c) (Mensch) character

Existenz·grundlage *die* basis of one's livelihood

existenziell *Adj.* existential; **in etw.** (*Dat.*) **eine** ~**e Bedrohung sehen** see in sth. a threat to one's existence

Existenz-: ~**kampf** *der* struggle for existence; ~**minimum** *das* subsistence level

existieren *itr. V.* exist

Exitus *der;* ~ (Med.) death

exkl. *Abk.* = **exklusiv[e]** excl.

exklusiv ☐1 *Adj.* exclusive

☐2 *adv.* exclusively

exklusive *Präp.* + *Gen.* exclusive of

Exklusiv·vertrag *der* exclusive contract

Exkommunikation *die;* ~, ~en excommunication

Exkursion *die;* ~, ~en study trip

exotisch ☐1 *Adj.* exotic

☐2 *adv.* exotically

expandieren *tr., itr. V.* expand

Expansion *die;* ~, ~en expansion

Expedition *die;* ~, ~en expedition

Experiment *das;* ~[e]s, ~e experiment

experimentell ☐1 *Adj.* experimental

☐2 *adv.* experimentally

experimentieren *itr. V.* experiment

Experte *der;* ~n, ~n, **Expertin** *die;* ~, ~nen expert (**für** in)

Experten·system *das* (DV) expert system

explizit ☐1 *Adj.* explicit

☐2 *adv.* ⟨describe, define⟩ explicitly

explodieren itr. V.; mit sein (auch fig.) explode; ⟨costs⟩ rocket

Explosion die; ∼, ∼en explosion

explosiv 1 Adj. (auch fig.) explosive 2 adv. explosively

Exponent der; ∼en, ∼en (Math.) exponent

exponiert Adj. exposed

Export¹ der; ∼[e]s, ∼e export

Export² das; ∼s, ∼e (Bier) export; **zwei ∼:** two export

Export-: ∼**artikel** der export; ∼**bier** das export beer

Exporteur /ɛkspɔr'tøːɐ̯/ der; ∼s, ∼e, **Exporteurin** die; ∼, ∼nen (Wirtsch.) exporter

Export-: ∼**firma** die exporter; ∼**handel** der export trade

exportieren tr., itr. V. export

Express-gut, *Expreß-gut das express freight

Expressionismus der; ∼: expressionism no art.

expressionistisch Adj. expressionist

exquisit 1 Adj. exquisite 2 adv. exquisitely

extern Adj. external

extra Adv. (a) (gesondert) ⟨pay⟩ separately (b) (zusätzlich, besonders) extra (c) (eigens) especially

Extra das; ∼s, ∼s extra

Extra-blatt das special edition

Extrakt der; ∼[e]s, ∼e extract

extra-terrestrisch Adj. (Astron.) extraterrestrial

extravagant /-va'gant/ Adj. flamboyant; flamboyantly furnished ⟨flat⟩

Extravaganz /-va'gants:/ die; ∼, ∼en (a) flamboyance (b) Pl. seine ∼en his flamboyance sing.

extravertiert /-vɛr'tiːɐ̯t/ Adj. (Psych.) extrovert[ed]

Extravertiertheit die; ∼ (Psych.) extroversion

Extra-wurst die (fig. ugs.) **eine ∼ bekommen** get special treatment or special favours

extrem Adj. extreme

Extrem das; ∼s, ∼e extreme

Extrem-fall der extreme case

Extremismus der; ∼: extremism

Extremist der; ∼en, ∼en, **Extremistin** die; ∼, ∼nen extremist

extremistisch Adj. extremist

Extremität /ɛkstremi'tɛːt/ die; ∼, ∼en (a) extremity (b) (das Extremsein) extremeness

Extrem-: ∼**sportart** die extreme sport; ∼**wert** der (Math.) extremum

Exzellenz die; ∼, ∼en Excellency

Exzentriker der; ∼s, ∼, **Exzentrikerin** die; ∼, ∼nen eccentric

exzentrisch 1 Adj. eccentric 2 adv. eccentrically

Exzess, *Exzeß der; Exzesses, Exzesse excess

exzessiv /ɛksts:ɛ'siːf/ 1 Adj. excessive 2 adv. excessively

Ff

f, F /ɛf/ das; ∼, ∼ (a) (Buchstabe) f/F (b) (Musik) [key of] F

f. Abk. = **folgend** f.

Fa. Abk. = **Firma**

Fabel die; ∼, ∼n fable; (Kern einer Handlung) plot

fabelhaft 1 Adj. (ugs.: großartig) fantastic (coll.) 2 adv. (ugs.) fantastically (coll.)

Fabrik die; ∼, ∼en factory

Fabrikant der; ∼en, ∼en manufacturer

Fabrikat das; ∼[e]s, ∼e product; (Marke) make

Fabrikation die; ∼: production

Fabrikations-fehler der manufacturing fault; factory fault

Fabrik-: ∼**besitzer** der, ∼**besitzerin** die factory owner; ∼**direktor** der, ∼**direktorin** die works manager

fabrizieren tr. V. (ugs. abwertend) knock together (coll.)

fabulieren itr. V. invent stories; spin yarns

Fach das; ∼[e]s, Fächer (a) compartment; (für Post) pigeonhole (b) (Studien∼, Unterrichts∼) subject; (Wissensgebiet) field; (Berufszweig) trade; **ein Mann vom ∼:** an expert

Fach-: ∼**arbeiter** der, ∼**arbeiterin** die skilled worker; ∼**arzt** der, ∼**ärztin** die specialist (für in); ∼**bereich** der (Hochschulw.) faculty; school; (in der Schule) department

fächer-übergreifend Adj:
▶ FACHÜBERGREIFEND

Fach-: ~**frau** *die* expert; ~**geschäft** *das* specialist shop; ~**hochschule** *die* college (*offering courses in a special subject*)

fachlich *Adj.* specialist ⟨*knowledge, work*⟩; technical ⟨*problem, explanation, experience*⟩

fach-, Fach-: ~**mann** *der; Pl.* ~**männer** *od.* ~**leute** expert; ~**terminus** *der* specialist/technical term; ~**übergreifend** ⓵ *Adj.* interdisciplinary ⟨*teaching*⟩; ⓶ *adv.* ⟨*think, argue*⟩ along interdisciplinary lines; ⟨*teach*⟩ using interdisciplinary methods; ~**werk** *das* (Bauweise) half-timbered construction; ~**werk·haus** *das* half-timbered house; ~**zeitschrift** *die* specialist/technical journal

Fackel *die;* ~, ~**n** torch

fade *Adj.* insipid; **ein** ~**r Beigeschmack** (fig.) a flat aftertaste

Faden *der;* ~**s**, **Fäden** thread; **ein** ~: a piece of thread

faden·scheinig *Adj.* threadbare; flimsy ⟨*excuse*⟩

Fagott *das;* ~**[e]s**, ~**e** bassoon

fähig *Adj.* **(a)** (begabt) able; capable **(b) zu etw.** ~ **sein** be capable of sth.

Fähigkeit *die;* ~, ~**en (a)** ability; capability; **geistige** ~**en** intellectual faculties **(b)** (Imstandesein) ability (**zu** to)

fahl *Adj.* pale; pallid; wan ⟨*light*⟩

fahnden *itr. V.* search (**nach** for)

Fahndung *die;* ~, ~**en** search

Fahne *die;* ~, ~**n** flag

Fahr·bahn *die* carriageway

Fähr·betrieb *der* ferry service; (von mehreren Fähren) ferry services *pl.*

Fähre *die;* ~, ~**n** ferry

fahren ⓵ *unr. itr. V.; mit sein* **(a)** (als Fahrzeuglenker) drive; (mit dem Fahrrad, Motorrad usw.) ride **(b)** (als Mitfahrer; mit öffentlichem Verkehrsmittel) go (**mit** by); (mit dem Aufzug/der Rolltreppe/der Seilbahn) take the lift (Brit.) *or* (Amer.) elevator/escalator/cable car; (per Anhalter) hitch-hike **(c)** (reisen) go; **in Urlaub** ~: go on holiday **(d)** (los~) go; leave **(e)** ⟨*motor vehicle, train, lift, cable car*⟩ go; ⟨*ship*⟩ sail; **mein Auto fährt nicht** my car won't go **(f)** (verkehren) ⟨*train etc.*⟩ run **(g) etw.** ~ **lassen** (loslassen) let sth. go; (fig.: aufgeben) abandon sth. ⓶ *unr. tr. V.* **(a)** (fortbewegen) drive ⟨*car, lorry, train, etc.*⟩; ride ⟨*bicycle, motor cycle*⟩ **(b) 50/80 km/h** ~: do 50/80 k.p.h.; **hier muss man 50 km/h** ~: you've got to keep to 50 k.p.h. here; sail ⟨*boat*⟩; **Auto** ~: drive [a car]; **Kahn** *od.* **Boot/Kanu** ~: go boating/canoeing; **Ski** ~: ski; **U-Bahn** ~: ride on the underground (Brit.) *or* (Amer.) subway **(c)** (befördern) take

---

*old spelling - see note on page xiv

Fahrenheit: 70 Grad ~: 70 degrees Fahrenheit

*****fahren|lassen** ▶ FAHREN 1G

Fahrer *der;* ~**s**, ~: driver

Fahrerflucht *die:* **wegen** ~: for failing to stop after [being involved in] an accident; ~ **begehen** fail to stop after [being involved in] an accident

Fahrerin *die;* ~, ~**nen** driver

Fahr-: ~**gast** *der* passenger; ~**geld** *das* fare

fahrig *Adj.* nervous

fahr-, Fahr-: ~**karte** *die* ticket; ~**karten·automat** *der* ticket machine; ~**karten·schalter** *der* ticket window; ~**lässig** ⓵ *Adj.* negligent ⟨*behaviour*⟩; ~**lässige Tötung/Körperverletzung** (Rechtsw.) causing death/injury through [culpable] negligence; ⓶ *adv.* negligently; ~**lehrer** *der*, ~**lehrerin** *die* driving instructor

Fähr·mann *der; Pl.* **Fährmänner** *od.* **Fährleute** ferryman

fahr-, Fahr-: ~**plan** *der* timetable; schedule (Amer.); ~**plan·mäßig** ⓵ *Adj.* scheduled ⟨*departure, arrival*⟩; ⓶ *adv.* ⟨*depart, arrive*⟩ according to schedule, on time; ~**preis** *der* fare; ~**prüfung** *die* driving test; ~**rad** *das* bicycle; cycle; **mit dem** ~**rad fahren** cycle; ride a bicycle; ~**rad·kurier** *der*, ~**rad·kurierin** *die* bicycle *or* bike messenger; bicycle *or* bike courier; ~**rad·ständer** *der* bicycle rack; ~**schein** *der* ticket; ~**schein·automat** *der* ticket machine; ~**schein·entwerter** *der* ticket cancelling machine; ~**schule** *die* driving school; ~**spur** *die* traffic lane

fährst *2. Pers. Sg. Präsens v.* FAHREN

Fahr-: ~**stuhl** *der* lift (Brit.); elevator (Amer.); (für Lasten) hoist; ~**stunde** *die* driving lesson

Fahrt *die;* ~, ~**en (a)** journey; **freie** ~ **haben** have a clear run; (Schiffsreise) voyage; (kurze Reise, Ausflug) trip **(b)** (Geschwindigkeit) **in voller** ~: at full speed

fährt *3. Pers. Sg. Präsens v.* FAHREN

Fährte *die* trail; **jmds.** ~ **verfolgen** track sb.

Fahrt·kosten *Pl.* (für öffentliche Verkehrsmittel) fare/fares; (für Autoreisen) travel costs

Fahr·treppe *die* escalator

Fahrt·richtung *die* direction; **in** ~ **parken** park in the direction of the traffic; **die** ~ **ändern** change direction

fahr·tüchtig *Adj.* ⟨*driver*⟩ fit to drive; ⟨*vehicle*⟩ roadworthy

Fahrt-: ~**wind** *der* airflow; ~**ziel** *das* destination

Fahr-: ~**wasser** *das* shipping channel; fairway; **in ein gefährliches** ~**wasser geraten** (fig.) get on to dangerous ground; ~**werk** *das* (Flugw.) undercarriage; ~**zeit** *die* travelling time; ~**zeug** *das* vehicle; (Luft~) aircraft; (Wasser~) vessel; ~**zeug·papiere** *Pl.* vehicle documents *pl.*

fair /fɛːɐ̯/ ① *Adj.* fair (**gegen** to)
② *adv.* fairly

Fäkalien /fɛːˈkaːli̯ən/ *Pl.* faeces *pl.*

Fakten ▶ FAKTUM

faktisch ① *Adj.* real; actual
② *adv.* **das bedeutet** ~ ...: it means in
effect ...

Faktor *der;* ~s, ~en (auch Math.) factor

Faktum *das;* ~s, **Fakten** fact

Fakultät *die;* ~, ~en (Hochschulw.) faculty

Falke *der;* ~n, ~n (auch Politik fig.) hawk

Fall *der;* ~[e]s, **Fälle (a)** (Sturz) fall; **zu** ~
kommen have a fall; **jmdn. zu** ~ **bringen** (fig.)
bring about sb.'s downfall
(b) (das Fallen) descent; **der freie** ~: free fall
(c) (Ereignis; Rechtsw., Med., Grammatik) case; (zu
erwartender Umstand) eventuality; **es ist [nicht]
der** ~: it is [not] the case; **gesetzt den** ~:
assuming; **auf jeden** ~, **in jedem** ~, **auf alle
Fälle** in any case; **auf keinen** ~: on no
account

Falle *die;* ~, ~n (auch fig.) trap

fallen *unr. itr. V.; mit sein* **(a)** fall; **jmdn./
etw.** ~ **lassen** drop sb./sth.
(b) (hin~, stürzen) fall [over]; **über einen Stein**
~: trip over a stone
(c) ⟨*prices, light, glance, choice*⟩ fall;
⟨*temperature, water level*⟩ fall, drop; ⟨*fever*⟩
subside; ⟨*shot*⟩ be fired
(d) (im Kampf sterben) die; fall (literary)

fällen *tr. V.* **(a)** fell ⟨*tree, timber*⟩
(b) ein Urteil ~ ⟨*judge*⟩ pass sentence; ⟨*jury*⟩
return a verdict

*****fallen|lassen** ▶ FALLEN A

fällig *Adj.* due

Fall·obst *das* windfalls *pl.*

Fallout /fɔːlˈaʊt/ *der;* ~s, ~s (Kernphysik)
fallout

falls *Konj.* **(a)** (wenn) if
(b) (für den Fall, dass) in case

Fall·schirm *der* parachute; **mit dem** ~
abspringen (im Notfall) parachute out; (als
Sport) make a [parachute] jump

falsch ① *Adj.* **(a)** (unecht, imitiert) false ⟨*teeth,
plait*⟩; imitation ⟨*jewellery*⟩
(b) (gefälscht) forged; assumed ⟨*name*⟩
(c) (irrig, fehlerhaft) wrong
② *adv.* wrongly; **die Uhr geht** ~: the clock
is wrong

fälschen *tr. V.* forge

Fälscher *der;* ~s, ~, **Fälscherin** *die;* ~,
~nen forger

Falschgeld *das* counterfeit money

fälschlich ① *Adj.* false
② *adv.* falsely

Falsch·meldung *die* false report

Fälschung *die;* ~, ~en fake

Falt·blatt *das* leaflet; (in Zeitungen,
Zeitschriften, Büchern) insert

Falte *die;* ~, ~n **(a)** crease
(b) (im Stoff) fold; (mit scharfer Kante) pleat
(c) (Haut~) wrinkle

falten ① *tr. V.* fold; **die Hände** ~: fold one's
hands
② *refl. V.* (auch Geol.) fold; ⟨*skin*⟩ become
wrinkled

Falten-rock *der* pleated skirt

Falter *der;* ~s, ~ (Nacht~) moth; (Tag~)
butterfly

faltig (a) *Adj.* ⟨*clothes*⟩ gathered [in folds];
wrinkled ⟨*skin, hands*⟩
(b) (zerknittert) creased

-fältig *Adj., adv.* -fold

Falt·rad *das* folding bicycle

Falz *der;* ~es, ~e fold

falzen *tr. V.* fold; seam

familiär *Adj.* **(a)** family ⟨*problems, worries*⟩
(b) (zwanglos) familiar; informal

Familie /faˈmiːli̯ə/ *die;* ~, ~n family; ~
Meyer the Meyer family

Familien-: ~**angehörige** *der/die*
member of the family; ~**feier** *die* family
party; ~**grab** *das* family grave; ~**leben**
das family life; ~**name** *der* surname;
~**planung** *die* family planning *no art.;*
~**stand** *der* marital status; ~**vater** *der;*
~vater sein be the father of a family; **ein
guter** ~vater a good husband and father

Fan /fɛn/ *der;* ~s, ~s fan

Fanatiker *der;* ~s, ~, **Fanatikerin** *die;*
~, ~nen fanatic; (religiös) fanatic; zealot

fanatisch ① *Adj.* fanatical
② *adv.* fanatically

fanatisieren *tr. V.* rouse to fanaticism;
der fanatisierte Mob the fanatically excited
mob

fand *1. u. 3. Pers. Sg. Prät. v.* FINDEN

Fanfare *die;* ~, ~n (Signal) fanfare

Fang *der;* ~[e]s, **Fänge (a)** (Tier~) trapping;
(von Fischen) catching
(b) (Beute) bag; (von Fischen) catch

fangen ① *unr. tr. V.* catch; capture
⟨*fugitive etc.*⟩; **jmdn./ein Tier gefangen halten**
hold sb. prisoner/keep an animal in
captivity; **jmdn. gefangen nehmen** take sb.
prisoner
② *unr. refl. V.* **(a)** (in eine Falle geraten) be
caught
(b) (wieder in die normale Lage kommen) **sich
[gerade] noch** ~: [just] manage to steady
oneself

Fang·frage *die* catch question

Fantasie *die;* ~, ~n **(a)** imagination
(b) (Produkt der ~) fantasy

fantasie·los ① *Adj.* unimaginative
② *adv.* unimaginatively

Fantasielosigkeit *die;* ~: lack of
imagination; (Eintönigkeit) dullness

fantasieren *itr. V.* indulge in fantasies,
fantasize (**von** about)

fantasievoll ① *Adj.* imaginative
② *adv.* imaginatively

fantastisch ① *Adj.* **(a)** fantastic; ⟨*idea*⟩
divorced from reality
(b) (ugs.: großartig) fantastically (coll.)

Farb-: ∼**bild** das (Foto) colour photo; ∼**dia** das colour slide; ∼**drucker** der (DV) colour printer

Farbe die; ∼, ∼n (a) colour
(b) (für Textilien) dye; (zum Malen, Anstreichen) paint; ∼n mischen/auftragen mix/apply paint

farb·echt Adj. colour-fast

färben ①tr. V. dye
②refl. V. change colour; **sich schwarz/rot** usw. ∼: turn black/red etc.
③itr. V. (ugs.: ab∼) ⟨material, blouse etc.⟩ run

-farben Adj. coloured

farben-, Farben-: ∼**blind** Adj. colour-blind; ∼**froh** Adj. colourful; ∼**pracht** die colourful splendour; ∼**prächtig** Adj. vibrant with colour postpos.

Farb-: ∼**fernsehen** das colour television; ∼**fernseher** der (ugs.) colour telly (coll.) or television; ∼**film** der colour film; ∼**foto** das colour photo

farbig ①Adj. (a) coloured
(b) (bunt, auch fig.) colourful
②adv. colourfully

-farbig Adj. -coloured

Farbige der/die; adj. Dekl. coloured man/woman; Pl. coloured people

farblich ①Adj. in colour postpos.; as regards colour postpos;
②adv. etw. ∼ abstimmen match sth. in colour

farb-, Farb-: ∼**los** Adj. (auch fig.) colourless; clear ⟨varnish⟩; neutral ⟨shoe polish⟩; ∼**losigkeit** die; ∼∼ (auch fig.) colourlessness; ∼**stift** der coloured pencil; ∼**stoff** der (a) (Med., Biol.) pigment; (b) (für Textilien) dye; (c) (für Lebensmittel) colouring; ∼**ton** der; Pl. ∼**töne** shade; ∼**tupfen, ∼tupfer** der spot of colour

Färbung die; ∼, ∼en colouring

Farn der; ∼[e]s, ∼e, **Farn·kraut** das fern

Fasan der; ∼[e]s, ∼e[n] pheasant

Fasching der; ∼s, ∼e od. ∼s [pre-Lent] carnival

Faschismus der; ∼: fascism no art.

Faschist der; ∼en, ∼en, **Faschistin** die; ∼, ∼nen fascist

faschistisch Adj. fascist

faseln itr. V. (ugs. abwertend) drivel

Faser die; ∼, ∼n fibre

fasern itr. V. fray

Fass, *Faß das; Fasses, Fässer barrel; (Öl∼) drum; (kleines Bier∼) keg; (kleines Sherry∼ usw.) cask; **Bier vom** ∼: draught beer; **ein** ∼ **ohne Boden** an endless drain on sb.'s resources

Fassade die; ∼, ∼n façade

fassbar, *faßbar Adj. (a) tangible ⟨results⟩

(b) (verständlich) comprehensible

Fass·bier, *Faß·bier das draught beer; beer on draught

fassen ①tr. V. (a) (greifen) grasp; take hold of
(b) (festnehmen) catch ⟨thief, culprit⟩
(c) (aufnehmen können) ⟨hall, tank⟩ hold
(d) (begreifen) **ich kann es nicht** ∼: I cannot take it in
(e) **einen Entschluss** ∼: make or take a decision
②itr. V. (greifen) **nach etw.** ∼: reach for sth.; **in etw.** (Akk.) ∼: put one's hand in sth.

fasslich, *faßlich Adj. comprehensible

Fasson /faˈsõː/ die; ∼, ∼s style; shape

Fassung die; ∼, ∼en (a) (Form) version
(b) (Selbstbeherrschung) composure; **die** ∼ **bewahren** keep one's composure; **die** ∼ **verlieren** lose one's self-control; **jmdn. aus der** ∼ **bringen** upset sb.
(c) (für Glühlampen) holder

fassungs·los Adj. stunned

fast Adv. almost; nearly; ∼ **nie** hardly ever

fasten itr. V. fast

Fast·nacht die carnival; ∼ **feiern** celebrate Shrovetide or the carnival

Fastnachts-: ∼**brauch** der Shrovetide custom; ∼**dienstag** der Shrove Tuesday; ∼**zug** der carnival procession

faszinieren tr. V. fascinate

faszinierend ①Adj. fascinating
②adv. fascinatingly

fatal Adj. (a) (peinlich, misslich) awkward
(b) (verhängnisvoll) fatal

fauchen itr. V. ⟨cat⟩ hiss; ⟨tiger, person⟩ snarl

faul Adj. (a) (verdorben) rotten; bad ⟨food, tooth⟩; foul ⟨water, air⟩
(b) (träge) lazy

Fäule die; ∼: foulness

faulen itr. V.; meist mit sein rot; ⟨water⟩ go foul; ⟨meat, fish⟩ go off

faulenzen itr. V. laze about; loaf about (derog.)

Faulenzer der; ∼s, ∼, **Faulenzerin** die; ∼, ∼nen idler; lazybones sing. (coll.)

Faulheit die; ∼: laziness

faulig Adj. stagnating ⟨water⟩; ∼ **schmecken/riechen** taste/smell off

Fäulnis die; ∼: rottenness

Faul-: ∼**pelz** der (fam.) lazybones sing. (coll.); ∼**tier** das (a) (Zool.) sloth; (b) (ugs.: Faulenzer[in]) ▶ ∼PELZ

Fauna die; ∼, Faunen (Zool.) fauna

Faust die; ∼, Fäuste fist; **eine** ∼ **machen** clench one's fist; **das passt wie die** ∼ **aufs Auge** (ugs.) (passt nicht) that clashes horribly; (passt) that matches perfectly; **auf eigene** ∼: on one's own initiative

Fäustchen das; ∼s, ∼: **sich** (Dat.) **ins** ∼ **lachen** laugh up one's sleeve

---

*alte Schreibung - vgl. Hinweis auf S. xiv

faust·dick *Adj.* as thick as a man's fist *postpos.;* (fig.) barefaced ⟨*lie*⟩

Fäustling *der;* ~s, ~e mitten

Faust·regel *die* rule of thumb

Favorit /favo'ri:t/ *der;* ~en, ~en, **Favoritin** *die;* ~, ~nen favourite

Fax *das;* ~, ~[e] fax

Fax·anschluss, *Fax·anschluß *der* fax line

faxen *tr. V.* fax

Faxen *Pl.* (ugs.) fooling around

Fax-: ~**gerät** *das* fax machine; ~**nachricht** *der* fax message; ~**nummer** *die* fax number

Fazit *das;* ~s, ~s *od.* ~e result

FCKW *Abk.* = **Fluorchlorkohlenwasserstoff** CFC

FCKW-frei *Adj* CFC-free

FDP, F.D.P. *Abk.* = **Freie Demokratische Partei**

Feature /'fi:tʃɐ/ *das;* ~s, ~s (Rundf., Ferns., Zeitungsw.) feature

Februar *der;* ~[s], ~e February

fechten *unr. itr., tr. V.* fence

Fechter *der;* ~s, ~, **Fechterin** *die;* ~, ~nen fencer

Feder *die;* ~, ~n (a) (Vogel~) feather (b) (zum Schreiben) nib (c) (Technik) spring

feder-, Feder-: ~**ball** *der* (a) (Spiel) badminton; (b) (Ball) shuttlecock; ~**bett** *das* duvet (Brit.); stuffed quilt (Amer.); ~**führend** *Adj.* in charge *postpos.;* ~**halter** *der* fountain pen; ~**leicht** *Adj.* ⟨*person*⟩ as light as a feather; featherweight ⟨*object*⟩; ~**lesen** *das:* nicht viel ~lesen[s] mit jmdm./etw. machen give sb./sth. short shrift

federn [1] *itr. V.* ⟨*springboard, floor, etc.*⟩ be springy [2] *tr. V.* (mit einer Federung versehen) spring; das Bett ist gut gefedert the bed is well-sprung

Federung *die;* ~, ~en (Kfz-W.) suspension

Fee *die;* ~, ~n fairy

Feedback /'fi:dbæk/ *das;* ~s, ~s feedback

Fege·feuer *das* purgatory

fegen [1] *tr. V.* (a) (bes. nordd.: säubern) sweep (b) (schnell entfernen) brush [2] *itr. V.* sweep up

Fehde *die;* ~, ~n feud

Fehde·hand·schuh *der* jmdm. den ~ hinwerfen throw down the gauntlet to sb.

fehl *Adv.* ~ am Platz[e] sein be out of place

Fehl·anzeige *die;* ~! (ugs.) no chance! (coll.)

fehlen *itr. V.* (a) (nicht vorhanden sein) ihm fehlt das Geld he has no money (b) (ausbleiben) be absent

(d) (verschwunden sein) be missing; in der Kasse fehlt Geld money is missing from the till

(d) (vermisst werden) er/das wird mir ~: I shall miss him/that

(e) (erforderlich sein) be needed; ihm ~ noch zwei Punkte zum Sieg he needs only two points to win; es fehlte nicht viel, und ich wäre eingeschlafen I all but fell asleep

(f) *unpers.* (mangeln) es fehlt an Lehrern there is a lack of teachers

(g) (krank sein) was fehlt Ihnen? what seems to be the matter?; fehlt dir etwas? is there something wrong?

Fehl-: ~**entscheidung** *die* wrong decision; ~**entwicklung** *die* abortive development

Fehler *der;* ~s, ~ (a) (Irrtum) mistake; error; (Sport) fault (b) (schlechte Eigenschaft) fault

fehler·frei *Adj.* faultless

fehlerhaft *Adj.* faulty; defective; imperfect ⟨*pronunciation*⟩

Fehler·quelle *die* source of error

fehl-, Fehl-: ~**geburt** *die* miscarriage; ~**investition** *die* (bes. Wirtsch.) bad investment; ~**planung** *die* [piece of] bad planning *no art.;* ~**schlag** *der* failure; ~|**schlagen** *unr. itr. V.; mit sein* fail; ~**start** *der* (Leichtathletik) false start; ~**tritt** *der* (fig. geh.) slip; ~**urteil** *das* (a) (Rechtsw.) ein ~urteil fällen ⟨*jury*⟩ return a wrong verdict; ⟨*judge*⟩ pass a wrong judgement (b) (falsche Beurteilung) error of judgement; ~**verhalten** *das* (fehlerhaftes Verhalten) incorrect conduct; ~**zündung** *die* (Technik) misfire

Feier *die;* ~, ~n (a) (Veranstaltung) party; (aus festlichem Anlass) celebration (b) (Zeremonie) ceremony

Feier·abend *der* (Arbeitsschluss) finishing time; nach ~: after work; ~ machen finish work

feierlich [1] *Adj.* ceremonial ⟨*act etc.*⟩; solemn ⟨*silence*⟩ [2] *adv.* solemnly; ceremoniously

Feierlichkeit *die;* ~, ~en (a) solemnity (b) (Veranstaltung) celebration

feiern [1] *tr. V.* (a) celebrate ⟨*birthday, wedding, etc.*⟩ (b) acclaim ⟨*artist, sportsman, etc.*⟩ [2] *itr. V.* celebrate

Feier·tag *der* holiday; ein gesetzlicher/ kirchlicher ~: a public holiday/religious festival

feig[e] [1] *Adj.* cowardly [2] *adv.* in a cowardly way

Feige *die;* ~, ~n fig

Feigheit *die;* ~: cowardice

Feigling *der;* ~s, ~e coward

Feile *die;* ~, ~n file

feilen *tr., itr. V.* file

feilschen *itr. V.* haggle (um over)

fein [1] *Adj.* **(a)** fine; finely-ground ⟨*flour*⟩; finely-granulated ⟨*sugar*⟩; **(b)** (hochwertig) high-quality ⟨*fruit, soap, etc.*⟩; fine ⟨*silver, gold*⟩; fancy ⟨*cakes, pastries, etc.*⟩ **(c)** (ugs.: erfreulich) great (coll.) **(d)** sich ∼ machen (ugs.) dress up [2] *adv.* ∼ [he]raus sein (ugs.) be sitting pretty (coll.)

Feind *der;* ∼[e]s, ∼e, **Feindin** *die;* ∼, ∼nen enemy

feindlich [1] *Adj.* **(a)** hostile **(b)** (Milit.) enemy ⟨*attack, activity*⟩ [2] *adv.* in a hostile manner

Feindschaft *die;* ∼, ∼en enmity

feind·selig *Adj.* hostile

Feind·seligkeit *die;* ∼, ∼en hostility; ∼en (Milit.) hostilities

Feinheit *die;* ∼, ∼en **(a)** fineness; delicacy **(b)** (Nuance) subtlety

fein-, Fein-: ∼kost·geschäft *das* delicatessen; ***∼|**machen** ▶ FEIN 1D; ∼**schmecker** *der;* ∼∼s, ∼∼, ∼**schmeckerin** *die;* ∼∼, ∼∼nen gourmet; ∼**sinnig** *Adj.* sensitive and subtle; ∼**waschmittel** *das* mild detergent

feist *Adj.* (meist abwertend) fat

Feld *das;* ∼[e]s, ∼er **(a)** field **(b)** (Sport: Spiel∼) pitch; field **(c)** (auf Formularen) box; space; (auf Brettspielen) space; (auf dem Schachbrett) square **(d)** (Tätigkeitsbereich) field; sphere

Feld-: ∼herr *der* (veralt.) commander; ∼**marschall** *der* Field Marshal; ∼**salat** *der* corn salad; ∼**stecher** *der;* ∼∼s, ∼∼ binoculars *pl.;* ∼**versuch** *der* (Wissensch.) field experiment; ∼**webel** *der;* ∼∼s, ∼∼ (Milit.) sergeant; ∼**weg** *der* path; track; ∼**zug** *der* (Milit., fig.) campaign

Felge *die;* ∼, ∼n [wheel] rim

Fell *das;* ∼[e]s, ∼e **(a)** (Haarkleid) fur; (Pferde∼, Hunde∼, Katzen∼) coat; (Schaf∼) fleece **(b)** (Material) fur **(c)** (abgezogen) hide; ein dickes ∼ haben (ugs.) be thick-skinned

Fels *der;* ∼en, ∼en rock

Felsen *der;* ∼s, ∼: rock; (an der Steilküste) cliff

felsen-, Felsen-: ∼fest *Adj.* firm; unshakeable ⟨*opinion, belief*⟩; ∼**küste** *die* rocky coast or coastline

felsig *Adj.* rocky

Fels-: ∼spalte *die* crevice [in the rock]; ∼**wand** *die* rock face

feminin *Adj.* feminine

Feminismus *der;* ∼: feminism *no art.*

Feminist *der;* ∼en, ∼en, **Feministin** *die;* ∼, ∼nen feminist

Fenchel *der;* ∼s fennel

Fenster *das;* ∼s, ∼: window

Fenster-: ∼bank *die Pl.* ∼bänke window sill; ∼**laden** *der* [window] shutter; ∼**leder** *das* wash leather; ∼**platz** *der* window seat; ∼**putzer** *der;* ∼∼s, ∼∼, ∼**putzerin** *die;* ∼∼, ∼∼nen window cleaner; ∼**rahmen** *der* window frame; ∼**scheibe** *die* window pane

Ferien /'feːriən/ *Pl.* holiday[s *pl.*] (Brit.); vacation (Amer.); in die ∼ fahren go on holiday/vacation; ∼ haben have a or be on holiday/vacation

Ferien-: ∼arbeit *die* vacation work; eine ∼arbeit a vacation job; ∼**haus** *das* holiday house (Brit.); vacation house (Amer.); ∼**job** *der* vacation job; ∼**ort** *der* holiday resort (Brit.); vacation resort (Amer.); ∼**paradies** *das* holiday[maker's] paradise (Brit.); vacationer['s] paradise (Amer.); ∼**wohnung** *die* holiday flat or apartment (Brit.); vacation apartment (Amer.)

Ferkel *das;* ∼s, ∼: piglet

fern [1] *Adj.* distant; jmdn./etw. ∼ halten keep sb./sth. away [2] *adv.* ∼ von der Heimat far from home

fern-, Fern-: ∼bedienung *die* remote control; ∼|**bleiben** *unr. itr. V.; mit sein* (geh.) stay away

Ferne *die;* ∼, ∼n distance

ferner *Adv.* furthermore

fern-, Fern-: ∼fahrer *der*, ∼**fahrerin** *die* long-distance lorry driver (Brit.) or (Amer.) trucker; ∼**flug** *der* long-distance or long-haul flight; ∼**gelenkt** *Adj.* remote-controlled; ∼**gespräch** *das* long-distance call; ∼**gesteuert** *Adj.* ▶ ∼GELENKT; ∼**glas** *das* binoculars *pl.;* ***∼|**halten** ▶ FERN 1; ∼**heizung** *die* district heating system; ∼**lenkung** *die* remote control; ∼**licht** *das* (Kfz-W.) full beam; ∼**melde·amt** *das* telephone exchange; ∼**ost** *in/aus/nach* ∼ost in/from/to the Far East; ∼**rohr** *das* telescope; ∼**ruf** *der* telephone number; ∼**schreiben** *das* telex [message]; ∼**schreiber** *der* telex [machine]

Fernseh-: ∼antenne *die* television aerial (Brit.) or (Amer.) antenna; ∼**apparat** *der* television [set]; ∼**bericht** *der* television report; ∼**bild** *das* television picture

fern|sehen *unr. itr. V.* watch television

Fern·sehen *das;* ∼s television; im ∼: on television

Fern·seher *der;* ∼s, ∼ (ugs.) telly (Brit. coll.); TV

Fernseh-: ∼gebühren *Pl.* television licence fee; ∼**gerät** *das* television [set]; ∼**journalist** *der*, ∼**journalistin** *die* television reporter; ∼**kanal** *der* television channel; ∼**nachrichten** *Pl.* television news; ∼**programm** *das* **(a)** (Sendungen) television programmes *pl.;* **(b)** (Kanal) television channel; **(c)** (Blatt, Programmheft) television [programme] guide; ∼**publikum**

Fernsehsendung ⋯⟶ Fete ⋯

das viewing public**; ~sender** *der* television transmitter**; ~sendung** *die* television programme; **~serie** *die* television series**; ~spiel** *das* television play; **~star** *der* television star; **~studio** *das* television studio, **~zuschauer** *der,* **~zuschauerin** *die* television viewer

Fern·sicht *die* (Aussicht) view; (gute Sicht) visibility

Fern·sprecher *der* telephone

Fernsprech-: **~gebühren** *Pl.* telephone charges; **~teilnehmer** *der,* **~teilnehmerin** *die* telephone subscriber; telephone customer (Amer.)

Fern-: **~steuerung** *die* (Technik) remote control; **~straße** *die* major road; **~studium** *das* correspondence course; ≈ Open University course (Brit.); **~unterricht** *der* correspondence courses *pl.;* **~verkehr** *der* long-distance traffic; **~zug** *der* long-distance train

Ferse *die;* **~, ~n** heel

fertig *Adj.* (a) finished ‹*manuscript, picture, etc.*›; **das Essen ist ~:** lunch/dinner *etc.* is ready; **[mit etw.] ~ sein/werden** have finished/finish [sth.]; **etw. ~ machen** finish sth.
(b) (bereit, verfügbar) ready (**zu, für** for)
(c) (ugs.: erschöpft) shattered (coll.); **jmdn. ~ machen** (erschöpfen) wear sb. out; (schikanieren) wear sb. down; (deprimieren) get sb. down
(d) **etw. ~ bekommen** *od.* **bringen** *od.* (ugs.) **kriegen** manage sth; **etw. ~ stellen** complete sth.

fertig-, Fertig-: **~bau** *der; Pl.* **~~ten** prefabricated building; **~bauweise** *die* prefabricated construction; prefabrication; **~|bringen* ▶ FERTIG D

fertigen *tr. V.* make

Fertig-: **~gericht** *das* ready-to-serve meal; **~haus** *das* prefabricated house

Fertigkeit *die;* **~, ~en** skill

fertig-, Fertig-: **~|machen* ▶ FERTIG A, C; **~|stellen* ▶ FERTIG D; **~stellung** *die* completion

Fertigung *die;* **~:** production; manufacture

Fessel *die;* **~, ~n** fetter; shackle; (Kette) chain

fesseln *tr. V.* (a) tie up; **ans Bett/ans Haus/ an den Rollstuhl gefesselt sein** (fig.) be confined to [one's] bed/tied to the house/ confined to a wheelchair
(b) (faszinieren) ‹*book*› grip; ‹*work, person*› fascinate

fesselnd ① *Adj.* compelling ② *adv.* compellingly

fest ① *Adj.* (a) (nicht flüssig *od.* gasförmig) solid
(b) firm ‹*bandage*›; sound ‹*sleep*›; sturdy ‹*shoes*›; strong ‹*fabric*›; solid ‹*house, shell*›; steady ‹*voice*›; **der ~en Überzeugung sein, dass ...:** be of the firm opinion that ...
(c) (dauernd) permanent ‹*address*›; fixed ‹*income*›
② *adv.* (a) ‹*tie, grip*› tight[ly]

(b) (ugs. auch ~e) ‹*work*› with a will; ‹*eat*› heartily; ‹*sleep*› soundly
(c) ‹*believe, be convinced*› firmly; **sich auf jmdn./etw. ~ verlassen** rely one hundred per cent on sb./sth.
(d) (endgültig) firmly; **etw. ~ vereinbaren** come to a firm arrangement about sth.
(e) (auf Dauer) permanently; **~ befreundet sein** be close friends; (als Paar) be going steady

Fest *das;* **~[e]s, ~e** (a) celebration; (Party) party
(b) (Feiertag) festival; **frohes ~!** happy Christmas/Easter!

fest-, Fest-: **~akt** *der* ceremony; *~|binden* *unr. tr. V.* tie [up]; *~|bleiben* *unr. itr. V.; mit sein* stand firm; **~essen** *das* banquet; *~|fahren* *unr. itr., refl. V.* (itr. V. mit sein) get stuck; (fig.) get bogged down; *~|halten* ① *unr. tr. V.* (a) (halten, packen) hold on to; (b) (nicht weiterleiten) withhold ‹*letter, parcel, etc.*›; (c) (verhaftet haben) hold, detain ‹*suspect*›; ② *unr. refl. V.* **sich an jmdm./etw. ~halten** hold on to sb./sth.

festigen ① *tr. V.* strengthen; consolidate ‹*position*› ② *refl. V.* ‹*friendship, ties*› become stronger

Festival /ˈfɛstivəl/ *das;* **~s, ~s** festival

fest-, Fest-: *~|kleben* *tr., itr. V.; mit sein* stick (**an** + *Dat.* to); **~land** *das* (Kontinent) continent; (im Gegensatz zu den Inseln) mainland; *~|legen* *tr. V.* (a) fix ‹*time, deadline, price*›; arrange ‹*programme*›; (b) (verpflichten) **sich [auf etw. (*Akk.*)] ~legen** [lassen] commit oneself [to sth.]; **jmdn. [auf etw. (*Akk.*)] ~legen** tie sb. down [to sth.]

festlich ① *Adj.* festive ‹*atmosphere*›; formal ‹*dress*› ② *adv.* festively; formally

fest-, Fest-: *~|machen* *tr. V.* (a) (befestigen) fix; (b) (fest vereinbaren) arrange ‹*meeting etc.*›; *~|nageln* *tr. V.* (a) (befestigen) nail (**an** + *Dat.* to); (b) (ugs.: festlegen) **jmdn. [auf etw. (*Akk.*)] ~nageln** tie sb. down [to sth.]; **~nahme** *die;* **~~, ~~n** arrest; **bei seiner ~nahme** when he was/is arrested; *~|nehmen* *unr. tr. V.* arrest; **~platte** *die* (DV) fixed disk; **~rede** *die* speech; *~|schnallen* *tr. V.* tie (**an** + *Dat.* to); *~|sitzen* *unr. itr. V.* be stuck; *~|stehen* *unr. itr. V.* ‹*order, appointment, etc.*› have been fixed; ‹*decision*› be definite; ‹*fact*› be certain; *~|stellen* *tr. V.* (a) establish ‹*identity, age, facts*›; (b) (wahrnehmen) detect; diagnose ‹*illness*›; **~stellung** *die* (a) establishment; (b) (Wahrnehmung) realization; **die ~stellung machen, dass ...:** realize that ...

Fest·tag *der* holiday; (Ehrentag) special day

Festung *die;* **~, ~en** fortress

fest-, Fest-: **~zeit** *die* holiday (Brit.) *or* (Amer.) vacation [period]; **~zelt** *das* marquee; *~|ziehen* *unr. tr. V.* pull tight

Fete *die;* **~, ~n** (ugs.) party

fẹtt $\boxed{1}$ *Adj.* (a) fatty ⟨*food*⟩; ~er Speck fat bacon
(b) (sehr dick) fat
(c) (Druckw.) bold
$\boxed{2}$ *adv.* (a) ~ essen eat fatty foods
(b) ~ gedruckt bold

Fẹtt *das;* ~[e]s, ~e fat; ~ ansetzen ⟨*animal*⟩ fatten up; ⟨*person*⟩ put on weight

fett-, Fẹtt-: ~arm *Adj.* low-fat ⟨*food*⟩; low in fat *pred.;* ~auge *das* speck of fat; ~creme *die* enriched [skim] cream; ~druck *der* bold type; ~fleck[en] *der* grease mark; ***~gedruckt ▶ FETT 2B; ~gehalt *der* fat content

fẹttig *Adj.* greasy

fett-, Fẹtt-: ~leibig *Adj.* obese; ~leibigkeit *die;* ~~: obesity; ~näpfchen *das:* ins ~näpfchen treten (scherzh.) put one's foot in it; ~polster *das* subcutaneous fat *no indef. art.;* fat pad; ~reich *Adj.* high-fat; ~säure *die* (Chemie) fatty acid; ~wanst *der* (salopp abwertend) fatso (coll.)

Fetus *der;* ~ *od.* ~ses, ~se *od.* Feten (Med.) foetus

Fẹtzen *der;* ~s, ~: scrap

feucht *Adj.* damp; humid ⟨*climate*⟩

feucht·fröhlich *Adj.* (ugs. scherzh.) merry ⟨*company*⟩; boozy (coll.) ⟨*evening*⟩

Feuchtigkeit *die* moisture

Feuchtigkeits·creme *die* (Kosmetik) moisturizing cream; moisturizer

feucht-: ~kalt *Adj.* cold and damp; ~warm *Adj.* muggy

feudal *Adj.* (a) feudal ⟨*system*⟩
(b) aristocratic ⟨*regiment etc.*⟩
(c) (ugs.: vornehm) plush ⟨*hotel etc.*⟩

Feuer *das;* ~s, ~ (a) fire; jmdm. ~ geben give sb. a light
(b) (Brand) fire; blaze; ~! fire!
(c) (Milit.) das ~ einstellen cease fire

feuer-, Feuer-: ~alarm *der* fire alarm; ~eifer *der* enthusiasm; zest; ~fest *Adj.* heat-resistant ⟨*dish, plate*⟩; fireproof ⟨*material*⟩; ~gefährlich *Adj.* [in]flammable; ~holz *das* firewood; ~leiter *die* (bei Häusern) fire escape; (beim ~wehrauto) [fireman's] ladder; ~löscher *der;* ~~s, ~~: fire extinguisher; ~melder *der;* ~~s, ~~: fire alarm

feuern $\boxed{1}$ *tr. V.* (a) (ugs.: entlassen) fire (coll.); sack (coll.)
(b) (ugs.: schleudern, werfen) fling
$\boxed{2}$ *itr. V.* (Milit.) fire (auf + *Akk.* at)

feuer-, Feuer-: ~rot *Adj.* fiery red; ~schlucker *der,* ~schluckerin *die;* ~~, ~~nen fire-eater; ~sirene *die* fire siren; ~stein *der* flint; ~versicherung *die* fire insurance; ~waffe *die* firearm; ~wehr *die;* ~~, ~~en fire service; ~wehr·auto *das* fire engine; ~wehr·mann *der; Pl.* ~männer *od.*

~leute fireman; ~wehr·wagen *der* fire engine; ~werk *das* firework display; (~werkskörper) fireworks *pl.;* ~werks·körper *der* firework; ~zeug *das* lighter

Feuilleton /fœjə'tõ:/ *das;* ~s, ~s arts section

feurig *Adj.* fiery

ff. *Abk.* = **folgende [Seiten]** ff.

Ffm. *Abk.* = **Frankfurt am Main**

Fiaker /'fjakɐ/ *der;* ~s, ~ (österr.) cab

Fiasko *das;* ~s, ~s fiasco

Fibel *die;* ~, ~n reader; primer

ficht /fɪçt/ *Imperativ Sg. u. 3. Pers. Sg. Präsens v.* FECHTEN

Fichte *die;* ~, ~n spruce

ficken *tr., itr. V.* (vulg.) fuck (coarse)

fick[e]rig *Adj.* (landsch.: nervös) nervous

fidel *Adj.* (ugs.) jolly

Fieber *das;* ~s [high] temperature; (über 38°C) fever; ~ haben have a [high] temperature/a fever; bei jmdm. ~ messen take sb.'s temperature

fieber·frei *Adj.* ⟨*person*⟩ free from fever

fieberhaft *Adj.* feverish

fieberig *Adj.* feverish

fiebern *itr. V.* have a temperature

Fieber·thermometer *das* [clinical] thermometer

fiebrig *Adj.* feverish

Fiedel *die;* ~, ~n (veralt., scherzh.) fiddle

fiel *1. u. 3. Pers. Sg. Prät. v.* FALLEN

fiepen *itr. V.* ⟨*dog*⟩ whimper; ⟨*bird*⟩ cheep

fies $\boxed{1}$ *Adj.* (ugs.) nasty ⟨*person, character*⟩
$\boxed{2}$ *adv.* in a nasty way

Figur *die;* ~, ~en (a) (einer Frau) figure; (eines Mannes) physique
(b) (Bildwerk) figure
(c) (geometrisches Gebilde) shape
(d) (Spielstein) piece
(e) (Persönlichkeit) figure
(f) (literarische Gestalt) character

fiktiv *Adj.* fictitious

Filet /fi'le:/ *das;* ~s, ~s fillet

Filiale *die;* ~, ~n branch

Filigran *das;* ~s, ~e filigree

Film *der;* ~[e]s, ~e (a) (Fot.) film
(b) (Kino~) film; movie (Amer. coll.)

Filme·macher *der,* **Filme·macherin** *die* film-maker

filmen *tr., itr. V.* film

Film-: ~festival *das* film festival; ~festspiele *Pl.* film festival *sing.;* ~industrie *die* film industry; ~kamera *die* film camera; (Schmalfilmkamera) cine camera; ~kunst *die* cinematic art; ~musik *die* film music; (eines einzelnen ~s) theme music; ~plakat *das* film poster; ~produzent *der,* ~produzentin *die* film producer; ~regisseur *der,* ~regisseurin *die* film director;

∿**schauspieler** der, ∿**schauspielerin** die film actor; ∿**star** der film star

Filter der, ∿**s**, ∿: filter

filtern tr. V. filter

Filter-: ∿**papier** das filter paper; ∿**zigarette** die [filter-]tipped cigarette

Filz der; ∿**es**, ∿**e** felt

filzen tr. V. (ugs.: durchsuchen) search ⟨room, car, etc.⟩; frisk ⟨person⟩

Filz·stift der felt-tip pen

Fimmel der; ∿**s**, ∿: einen ∿ für etw. haben (ugs. abwertend) have a thing about sth. (coll.)

Finale das; ∿**s**, ∿**[s]** (a) (Sport) final (b) finale

Finalist der; ∿**en**, ∿**en**, **Finalistin** die; ∿, ∿**nen** (Sport) finalist

Finanz die; ∿: finance no art.

Finanz-: ∿**amt** das (a) (Behörde) ≈ Inland Revenue; (b) (Gebäude) tax office; ∿**beamte** der, ∿**beamtin** die tax officer

Finanzen Pl. finances

finanziell /finanˈtsi̯ɛl/ Adj. financial

finanzieren tr. V. finance

Finanzierung die; ∿, ∿**en** financing

finanz-, Finanz-: ∿**kraft** die financial strength; ∿**kräftig** Adj. financially powerful; ∿**lage** die financial situation; ∿**minister** der, ∿**ministerin** die minister of finance; ∿**politik** die (des Staates, eines Unternehmens) financial policy; (allgemeine) politics of finance

Findel·kind das foundling

finden unr. tr. V. (a) find (b) Freunde ∿: make friends (c) (einschätzen, beurteilen) etw. gut/richtig ∿: think sth. is good/right; wie ∿ Sie dieses Bild? what do you think of this painting?

Finder der; ∿**s**, ∿: finder

Finder·lohn der reward [for finding sth.]

findig Adj. resourceful

Findling der; ∿**s**, ∿**e** (a) (Findelkind) foundling (b) (Geol.) erratic block

fing 1. u. 3. Pers. Sg. Prät. v. FANGEN

Finger der; ∿**s**, ∿: finger; lange ∿ machen (ugs.) get itchy fingers

Finger-: ∿**abdruck** der fingerprint; ∿**fertigkeit** die dexterity; ∿**handschuh** der glove [with fingers]; ∿**hut** der thimble; ∿**kuppe** die fingertip

fingern itr. V. fiddle; an etw. (Dat.) ∿: fiddle with sth.; nach etw. ∿: fumble [around] for sth.

Finger-: ∿**nagel** der fingernail; ∿**spitze** die fingertip; ∿**spitzen·gefühl** das feeling

fingieren tr. V. fake; ein fingierter Name a false name

Fink der; ∿**en**, ∿**en** finch

Finne der; ∿**n**, ∿**n**, **Finnin** die; ∿, ∿**nen** Finn

finnisch Adj. Finnish

Finnland (das); ∿**s** Finland

finster ① Adj. dark; dimly-lit ⟨pub, district⟩ ② adv. jmdn. ∿ ansehen give sb. a black look

Finsternis die; ∿, ∿**se** darkness; (auch bibl., fig.) dark

Finte die; ∿, ∿**n** trick; jmdn. durch eine ∿ täuschen deceive sb. by trickery

Firlefanz der; ∿**es** (ugs. abwertend) frippery; trumpery

firm Adj. in etw. (Dat.) ∿ sein be well up in sth.

Firma die; ∿, **Firmen** firm; company

Firmen-: ∿**inhaber** der, ∿**inhaberin** die owner of the/a company; ∿**schild** das company's name plate; ∿**zeichen** das trademark

Firmung die; ∿, ∿**en** confirmation

First der; ∿**[e]s**, ∿**e** ridge

Fisch der; ∿**[e]s**, ∿**e** (a) fish; [fünf] ∿**e** fangen catch [five] fish; kleine ∿**e** (fig.) small fry (b) (Astrol.) die ∿**e** Pisces; er ist [ein] ∿: he is a Piscean

fischen ① tr. V. (a) fish for (b) (ugs.) etw. aus etw. ∿: fish sth. out of sth. ② itr. V. fish; nach etw. ∿: fish for sth.

Fischer der; ∿**s**, ∿: fisherman

Fischer-: ∿**boot** das fishing boat; ∿**dorf** das fishing village

Fischerei die; ∿: fishing

Fischerin die; ∿, ∿**nen** fisherwoman

Fisch-: ∿**fang** der: vom ∿**fang** leben make a/one's living by fishing; auf ∿**fang** gehen go fishing; ∿**geschäft** das fishmonger's [shop] (Brit.); fish store (Amer.); ∿**grät[en]·muster** das (Textilw.) herringbone pattern; ∿**industrie** die fishing industry; ∿**konserve** die canned fish; ∿**kutter** der fishing trawler; ∿**stäbchen** das (Kochk.) fish finger; ∿**sterben** das death of the fish

Fiskus der; ∿, **Fisken** od. ∿**se** Government (as managing the State finances)

Fitness-zentrum das fitness centre

Fittich der; ∿**[e]s**, ∿**e** (dichter.) wing

fix ① Adj. (ugs.) quick; ein ∿**er** Bursche a bright lad; ∿ und fertig quite finished; (völlig erschöpft) completely shattered (coll.) ② adv. (ugs.) quickly; mach ∿! hurry up!

fixen itr. V. (Drogenjargon) fix (sl.)

Fixer der; ∿**s**, ∿, **Fixerin** die; ∿, ∿**nen** (Drogenjargon) fixer

fixieren tr. V. (a) fix one's gaze on; jmdn. scharf ∿: gaze sharply at sb. (b) (geh.: schriftlich niederlegen) take down

Fix·stern der (Astron.) fixed star

Fjord /fjɔrt/ der; ∿**[e]s**, ∿**e** fiord

FKK /ɛf kaːˈkaː/ *Abk.*
= **Freikörperkultur** nudism *no art.;* naturism *no art.*

FKK-Strand *der* nudist beach

flach *Adj.* **(a)** flat
(b) (niedrig) low
(c) (nicht tief) shallow ⟨*water, dish*⟩

Fläche *die;* ~, ~n **(a)** area
(b) (Ober~) surface
(c) (Geom.) area; (einer dreidimensionalen Figur) side

Flächen-: ~**inhalt** *der* area; ~**maß** *das* unit of square measure; ~**staat** *der* territorial state

flach, Flach-: ~|**fallen** *itr. V.; mit sein* (ugs.) ⟨*trip*⟩ fall through; ⟨*event*⟩ be cancelled; ~**land** *das* lowland

Flachs *der;* ~es flax

flachsen *itr. V.* mit jmdm. ~ (ugs.) joke with sb.

Flach·zange *die* flat tongs *pl.*

flackern *itr. V.* flicker

Fladen *der;* ~s, ~: *flat, round unleavened cake made with oat or barley flour*

Flagge *die;* ~, ~n flag

flaggen *itr. V.* put out the flags

flambieren *tr. V.* (Kochk.) flambé

Flamme *die;* ~, ~n **(a)** flame
(b) (Brennstelle) burner

Flanell *der;* ~s, ~e flannel

flanieren *itr. V.; mit Richtungsangabe mit sein* stroll

Flanke *die;* ~, ~n **(a)** (Weiche) flank
(b) (Ballspiele: Vorlage) centre
(c) (Teil des Spielfeldes) wing

Flasche *die;* ~, ~n bottle; eine ~ Wein a bottle of wine; dem Kind die ~ geben feed the baby

Flaschen-: ~**bier** *das* bottled beer; ~**öffner** *der* bottle-opener; ~**post** *die* message in a/the bottle; ~**zug** *der* block and tackle

flatterhaft *Adj.* fickle

flattern *itr. V.; mit Richtungsangabe mit sein* flutter

flau *Adj.* **(a)** slack ⟨*breeze*⟩
(b) (leicht übel) queasy ⟨*feeling*⟩

Flaum *der;* ~[e]s fuzz

Flausch *der;* ~[e]s, ~e brushed wool

flauschig *Adj.* fluffy

Flause *die;* ~, ~n; *meist Pl.* (ugs.) er hat nur ~n im Kopf he can never think of anything sensible

Flaute *die;* ~, ~n **(a)** (Seemannsspr.) calm
(b) (Kaufmannsspr.) fall[-off] in trade

Flechte *die;* ~, ~n **(a)** (Bot.) lichen
(b) (Med.) eczema

flechten *unr. tr. V.* plait ⟨*hair*⟩; weave ⟨*basket, mat*⟩

Fleck *der;* ~[e]s, ~e **(a)** stain

(b) (andersfarbige Stelle) patch

flecken *itr. V.* stain

flecken·los ① *Adj.* spotless
② *adv.* spotlessly

Fleck·entferner *der* stain *or* spot remover

fleckig *Adj.* stained; blotchy ⟨*face, skin*⟩

Fleder·maus *die* bat

Flegel *der;* ~s, ~ (abwertend) lout

Flegelei *die;* ~, ~en (abwertend) loutish behaviour

flegelhaft *Adj.* (abwertend) loutish

flegeln *refl. V.* (abwertend) sich auf ein Sofa/in einen Sessel ~: flop on to a sofa/into an armchair

flehen /ˈfleːən/ *itr. V.* plead (um for)

Fleisch *das;* ~[e]s **(a)** flesh; ~ fressend (Biol.) carnivorous
(b) (Nahrungsmittel) meat

Fleisch·brühe *die* bouillon; consommé

Fleischer *der;* ~s, ~: butcher

Fleischerei *die;* ~, ~en butcher's shop

fleisch·fressend *Adj.* carnivorous

Fleisch·fresser *der* (Biol.) carnivore

fleischig *Adj.* plump ⟨*hands, face*⟩; fleshy ⟨*leaf, fruit*⟩

Fleisch-: ~**käse** *der;* ~~s, ~~: meat loaf; ~**klößchen** *das;* ~~s, ~~: small meat ball; ~**pastete** *die* (Kochk.) pâté; ~**salat** *der* (Kochk.) meat salad; ~**vergiftung** *die* food poisoning [from meat]; ~**waren** *Pl.* meat products; ~**wolf** *der* mincer; ~**wunde** *die* flesh wound; ~**wurst** *die* pork sausage

Fleiß *der;* ~es hard work; (Eigenschaft) diligence

fleißig ① *Adj.* hard-working
② *adv.* hard; ~ lernen learn as much as one can

flennen *itr. V.* (ugs.) blubber

fletschen *tr., itr. V.* die Zähne *od.* mit den Zähnen ~: bare one's teeth

Fleurop Ⓦ /ˈflɔyˌrɔp/ *die* Interflora ®

flexibel ① *Adj.* flexible
② *adv.* flexibly

flicht *Imperativ Sg. u. 3. Pers. Sg. Präsens v.* FLECHTEN

flicken *tr. V.* mend; repair ⟨*engine, cable*⟩

Flicken *der;* ~s, ~: patch

Flick-: ~**werk** *das* (abwertend) botched-up job; ~**zeug** *das* repair kit

Flieder *der;* ~s, ~: lilac

Fliege *die;* ~, ~n **(a)** fly
(b) (Schleife) bow tie

fliegen ① *unr. itr. V.; mit sein* **(a)** fly
(b) (ugs.: fallen) vom Pferd/Fahrrad ~: fall off a/the horse/bicycle
(c) (ugs.: entlassen werden) get the sack (coll.); von der Schule ~: be chucked out [of the school] (coll.)
② *unr. tr. V.* fly

Fliegen-: ~**draht** *der* fly screen;
~**fenster** *das* wire-mesh window;
~**gewicht** *das* (Schwerathletik) flyweight;
~**pilz** *der* fly agaric

Flieger *der;* ~s, ~: pilot

Flieger-alarm *der* air-raid warning

Fliegerin *die;* ~, ~nen pilot

fliegerisch *Adj.* aeronautical

fliehen /'fliːən/ *unr. itr. V.; mit sein* flee
(vor + *Dat.* from); (aus dem Gefängnis usw.)
escape (aus from); **ins Ausland/über die
Grenze** ~: flee the country/escape over the
border

Flieh·kraft *die* (Physik) centrifugal force

Fliese *die;* ~, ~n tile

Fließ·band *das* conveyor belt; **am** ~
arbeiten *od.* (ugs.) **stehen** work on the
assembly line

fließen *unr. itr. V.; mit sein* flow; ~**des
Wasser** running water; **eine Sprache** ~**d
sprechen** speak a language fluently

Flimmer·kasten *der,* **Flimmer·kiste**
die (ugs.) telly (coll.); box (coll.)

flimmern *itr. V.* shimmer

flink 1 *Adj.* nimble ⟨*fingers*⟩; sharp ⟨*eyes*⟩;
quick ⟨*hands*⟩
2 *adv.* quickly

Flinkheit *die;* ~ ▶ FLINK 1: nimbleness;
sharpness; quickness

Flinte *die;* ~, ~n shotgun; **die** ~ **ins Korn
werfen** (fig.) throw in the towel

Flirt *der;* ~s, ~s flirtation

flirten *itr. V.* flirt

Flittchen *das;* ~s, ~ (ugs. abwertend)
floozie

Flitter *der;* ~s frippery; trumpery

Flitter·wochen *Pl.* honeymoon *sing.*

flitzen *itr. V.; mit sein* (ugs.) shoot; dart

Flitzer *der;* ~s, ~ (ugs.) sporty job (coll.)

floaten /'floʊtn/ *tr., itr. V.* (Wirtsch.) float

flocht *1. u. 3. Pers. Sg. Prät. v.* FLECHTEN

Flocke *die;* ~, ~n (a) flake
(b) (Staub~) piece of fluff

flockig *Adj.* fluffy

flog *1. u. 3. Pers. Sg. Prät. v.* FLIEGEN

floh *1. u. 3. Pers. Sg. Prät. v.* FLIEHEN

Floh *der;* ~[e]s, Flöhe flea

Floh-: ~**markt** *der* flea market; ~**zirkus**
der flea circus

Flora *die;* ~, Floren flora

Florett *das;* ~[e]s, ~e foil

florieren *itr. V.* flourish

Florist *der;* ~en, ~en, **Floristin** *die;* ~,
~nen [qualified] flower arranger

Floskel *die;* ~, ~n cliché

floss *1. u. 3. Pers. Sg. Prät. v.* FLIESSEN

Floß *das;* ~es, Flöße raft

Flosse *die;* ~, ~n (a) (Zool., Flugw.) fin
(b) (zum Tauchen) flipper

flößen *tr., itr. V.* float

Flößer *der;* ~s, ~: raftsman

Flößerin *die;* ~, ~nen raftswoman

Flöte *die;* ~, ~n flute; (Block~) recorder

flöten 1 *itr. V.* ⟨*bird*⟩ flute; ~ **gehen** (ugs.)
⟨*money*⟩ go down the drain; ⟨*time*⟩ be wasted
2 *tr. V.* whistle

flöten|gehen ▶ FLÖTEN 1

flott 1 *Adj.* (a) (schwungvoll) lively
(b) (schick) smart
2 *adv.* ⟨*work*⟩ quickly; ⟨*dance, write*⟩ in a
lively manner; ⟨*be dressed*⟩ smartly

Flotte *die;* ~, ~n fleet

flott|machen *tr. V.* refloat ⟨*ship*⟩; get
⟨*car*⟩ back on the road

Flöz *das;* ~es, ~e (Bergbau) seam

Fluch *der;* ~[e]s, Flüche curse; oath

fluchen *itr. V.* curse; swear

Flucht *die;* ~: flight

flucht·artig 1 *Adj.* hurried; hasty
2 *adv.* hurriedly; hastily

flüchten 1 *itr. V.; mit sein* **vor jmdm./etw.**
~: flee from sb./sth.; **vor der Polizei** ~: run
away from the police
2 *refl. V.* take refuge

Flucht-: ~**fahrzeug** *das* getaway vehicle;
~**helfer** *der,* ~**helferin** *die* person who
aids/aided an/the escape; ~**hilfe** *die* aiding
an escape

flüchtig 1 *Adj.* (a) fugitive
(b) cursory; superficial ⟨*insight*⟩
2 *adv.* (a) (oberflächlich) cursorily
(b) (eilig) hurriedly

Flüchtigkeit *die;* ~, ~en cursoriness

Flüchtigkeits·fehler *der* slip

Flüchtling *der;* ~s, ~e refugee

Flüchtlings-: ~**elend** *das* hardship
among refugees; ~**hilfe** *die* refugee relief;
(Organisation) refugee relief agency; ~**lager**
das refugee camp; ~**treck** *der* long stream
of refugees

Flucht·weg *der* escape route

Flug *der;* ~[e]s, Flüge flight

Flug-: ~**bahn** *die* trajectory; ~**blatt** *das*
pamphlet; leaflet

Flügel *der;* ~s, ~ (a) wing
(b) (Klavier) grand piano

Flügel·mutter *die; Pl.* ~n wing nut

Flug·gast *der* [air] passenger

flügge *Adj.* fully-fledged

Flug-: ~**gesellschaft** *die* airline;
~**hafen** *der* airport; ~**hafen·steuer** *die*
airport tax; ~**linie** *die* (a) (Strecke) air
route; (b) (Gesellschaft) airline; ~**lotse** *der,*
~**lotsin** *die* air traffic controller; ~**platz**
der airfield; ~**schein** *der* air ticket;
~**schreiber** *der* flight recorder;
~**verbindung** *die* air connection;
~**verkehr** *der* air traffic

Flug·zeug *das* aeroplane (Brit.); airplane
(Amer.); aircraft

Flugzeug-: ~**absturz** *der* plane crash;
~**entführer** *der,* ~**entführerin** *die* ⋯⋗

[aircraft] hijacker; ~**entführung** *die* [aircraft] hijack[ing]; ~**katastrophe** *die* air disaster; ~**träger** *der* aircraft carrier

Flunder *die;* ~, ~n flounder

flunkern *itr. V.* tell stories

Fluor *das;* ~s (Chemie) fluorine

Fluor·chlor·kohlen·wasserstoff *der* (Chemie) chlorofluorocarbon

Flur[1] *der;* ~[e]s, ~e (Korridor) corridor; (Diele) [entrance] hall; **im/auf dem** ~: in the corridor/hall

Flur[2] *die;* ~, ~en farmland *no indef. art.*

Fluss, *Fluß *der;* Flusses, Flüsse river; (fließende Bewegung) flow

fluss-, *fluß-, Fluss-, *Fluß-: ~**ab**[**wärts**] *Adv.* downstream; ~**auf**[**wärts**] *Adv.* upstream; ~**bett** *das* river bed

Flüsschen, *Flüßchen *das;* ~s, ~: small river

Fluss-diagramm *das* (DV, Arbeitswiss.) flow chart

flüssig [1] *Adj.* (a) liquid; (b) (fließend, geläufig) fluent; (c) **einen Betrag** ~ **machen** make a sum of money available; [2] *adv.* ⟨write, speak⟩ fluently

Flüssig·gas *das* liquid gas

Flüssigkeit *die;* ~, ~en (a) liquid; (auch Gas) fluid; (b) (Geläufigkeit) fluency

Flüssig·kristall·anzeige *die* (Technik) liquid crystal display

*flüssig|machen ▶ FLÜSSIG 1c

Fluss·pferd, *Fluß·pferd *das* hippopotamus

flüstern *itr., tr. V.* whisper

Flut *die;* ~, ~en (a) tide; (b) (geh.: Wassermasse) flood

fluten *itr. V.; mit sein* (geh.) flood

Flut·licht *das* floodlight

focht *1. u. 3. Pers. Sg. Prät. v.* FECHTEN

Föderalismus *der;* ~: federalism *no art.*

föderalistisch *Adj.* federalist

Fohlen *das;* ~s, ~: foal

Föhn *der;* ~[e]s, ~e (a) föhn; (b) (Haartrockner) hair-drier

föhnen *tr. V.* blow-dry

Folge *die;* ~, ~n (a) (Auswirkung) consequence; (Ergebnis) consequence; result; (b) (Aufeinander~) succession; (zusammengehörend) sequence; (c) (Fortsetzung) (einer Sendung) episode; (eines Romans) instalment

Folge·erscheinung *die* consequence

folgen *itr. V.; mit sein* follow; **jmdm. im Amt/ in der Regierung** ~: succeed sb. in office/in government; **auf etw.** *(Akk.)* ~: follow sth.; **aus etw.** ~: follow from sth.

folgend *Adj.* following; **der/die/das**

Folgende the next in order; **im Folgenden** *od.* **in Folgendem** in [the course of] the following discussion/passage *etc.*

folgendermaßen *Adv.* as follows; (so) in the following way

folge·richtig [1] *Adj.* logical; consistent ⟨behaviour, action⟩; [2] *adv.* logically; ⟨act, behave⟩ consistently

Folge·richtigkeit *die* (einer Entscheidung, Schlussfolgerung) logicality; (eines Verhaltens, Handlung) consistency

folgern [1] *tr. V.* etw. aus etw. ~: infer sth. from sth. [2] *itr. V.* **richtig** ~: draw a/the correct conclusion

Folgerung *die;* ~, ~en conclusion

Folge·schaden *der* (a) damaging after-effects; (b) (Versicherungsw.) consequential damage

folglich *Adv.* consequently

folgsam [1] *Adj.* obedient; [2] *adv.* obediently

Folgsamkeit *die;* ~: obedience

Folie /'fo:liə/ *die;* ~, ~n (Metall~) foil; (Plastik~) film

Folklore *die;* ~ (a) folklore; (b) (Musik) folk music

folkloristisch [1] *Adj.* folkloric; [2] *adv.* in a folkloric way

Folter *die;* ~, ~n torture; **jmdn. auf die** ~ **spannen** (fig.) keep sb. in an agony of suspense

Folterer *der;* ~s, ~, **Folterin** *die;* ~, ~nen torturer

foltern *tr. V.* torture; (fig.) torment

Folterung *die;* ~, ~en torture

Fön *der;* Ⓦ ~[e]s, ~e hairdrier

Fond /fõ:/ *der;* ~s, ~s (geh.) back

Fonds /fõ:/ *der;* ~ /fõ:(s),/ ~ /fõ:s/ fund

Fondue /fõ'dy:/ *die;* ~, ~s *od. das;* ~s, ~s (Kochk.) fondue

*fönen ▶ FÖHNEN

Fontäne *die;* ~, ~n jet; (Springbrunnen) fountain

forcieren /for'si:rən/ *tr. V.* step up ⟨production⟩; intensify ⟨efforts⟩; push forward ⟨developments⟩

Förderer *der;* ~s, ~: patron

Förderin *die;* ~, ~nen patroness

fordern *tr. V.* (a) demand; (b) (in Anspruch nehmen) make demands on

fördern *tr. V.* (a) promote; patronize; support ⟨artist, art⟩; further ⟨investigation⟩; foster ⟨talent, tendency⟩; improve ⟨appetite⟩; aid ⟨digestion, sleep⟩; (b) (Bergbau, Technik) mine ⟨coal, ore⟩; extract ⟨oil⟩

Forderung *die;* ~, ~en (a) demand; (b) (Kaufmannsspr.) claim (an + Akk. against)

Förderung *die;* ~, ~en (a) ▶ FÖRDERN A: promotion; patronage; support; furthering; fostering; improvement; aiding

---
*alte Schreibung - vgl. Hinweis auf S. xiv

(b) (Bergbau, Technik) output; (das Fördern) mining; (von Erdöl) extraction

Forelle *die;* ~, ~n trout

Form *die;* ~, ~en **(a)** shape; **in** ~ **von Tabletten** in the form of tablets
(b) (bes. Sport: Verfassung) form; **in** ~ **sein** be on form
(c) (vorgeformtes Modell) mould; (Back~) baking tin
(d) (Darstellungs~, Umgangs~) form

formal ⟦1⟧ *Adj.* formal
⟦2⟧ *adv.* formally

formalisieren *tr. V.* formalize

Formalität *die;* ~, ~en formality

Format *das;* ~[e]s, ~e **(a)** size; (Buch~, Papier~, Bild~) format
(b) (Persönlichkeit) stature

formatieren *tr. V.* (DV) format

formbar *Adj.* malleable

Form-: ~**blatt** *das* form; ~**brief** *der* form letter

Formel *die;* ~, ~n formula

formell *Adj.* formal

formen *tr. V.* **(a)** (gestalten) form; shape
(b) (bilden, prägen) mould, form ⟨*character, personality*⟩

Form·fehler *der* irregularity

formieren *tr., refl. V.* form

förmlich ⟦1⟧ *Adj.* **(a)** formal
(b) (regelrecht) positive
⟦2⟧ *adv.* **(a)** formally
(b) (geradezu) **sich** ~ **fürchten** be really afraid

form·los *Adj.* **(a)** informal
(b) (gestaltlos) shapeless

Form·sache *die* formality

Formular *das;* ~s, ~e form

formulieren *tr. V.* formulate

Formulierung *die;* ~, ~en **(a)** (das Formulieren) formulation; (eines Entwurfes, Gesetzes) drafting
(b) (formulierter Text) formulation

form·vollendet ⟦1⟧ *Adj.* perfectly executed ⟨*pirouette, bow, etc.*⟩; ⟨*poem*⟩ perfect in form
⟦2⟧ *adv.* faultlessly

forsch *Adj.* forceful

forschen *itr. V.* **(a)** **nach jmdm./etw.** ~: search *or* look for sb./sth.
(b) (als Wissenschaftler) research

Forscher *der;* ~s, **Forscherin** *die;* ~, ~nen researcher

Forschung *die;* ~, ~en research

Forschungs-: ~**reaktor** *der* research reactor; ~**reisende** *der/die* explorer

Forst *der;* ~[e]s, ~e[n] forest

Förster *der;* ~s, ~, **Försterin** *die;* ~, ~nen forest warden

Forst·wirtschaft *die* forestry

Forsythie /fɔrˈzytsiə/ *die;* ~, ~n forsythia

fort *Adv.* **(a)** ▶ WEG;

(b) (weiter) **und so** ~: and so on

fort-, Fort-: ~**an** /-'-/ *Adv.* from now/then on; ~**bestand** *der* continuation; (eines Staates) continued existence; ~|**bewegen** ⟦1⟧ *tr. V.* move; shift; ⟦2⟧ *refl. V.* move [along]; ~|**bilden** *tr. V.* **sich**/jmdn. ~**bilden** continue one's/sb.'s education; ~**bildung** *die* further education; (beruflich) further training; ~**bildungs·kurs** *der* further education course; (beruflich) training course; ~|**bleiben** *unr. itr. V.;* mit sein fail to come; ~|**bringen** *unr. tr. V.:*
▶ WEGBRINGEN; ~**dauer** *die* continuation; ~|**dauern** *itr. V.* continue; ~|**fahren** ⟦1⟧ *unr. itr. V.* **(a)** mit sein leave; **(b)** auch mit sein (weitermachen) continue; go on; ⟦2⟧ *unr. tr. V.* drive away; ~|**führen** *tr. V.* **(a)** lead away; **(b)** (fortsetzen) continue; ~**gang** *der* **(a)** departure (aus from); **(b)** (Weiterentwicklung) progress; ~|**gehen** *unr. itr. V.;* mit sein leave; geh ~! go away!; ~**geschritten** *Adj.* advanced; ~**geschrittene** *der/die; adj. Dekl.* advanced student/player; ~|**kommen** *unr. itr. V.;* mit sein ▶ WEGKOMMEN A, B; ~|**laufen** *unr. itr. V.;* mit sein **(a)** ▶ WEGLAUFEN; **(b)** (sich ~setzen) continue; ~**laufend** ⟦1⟧ *Adj.* continuous; ⟦2⟧ *adv.* continuously; ~|**pflanzen** *refl. V.* **(a)** reproduce [oneself/itself]; **(b)** (sich verbreiten) ⟨*idea, mood*⟩ spread; ⟨*sound, light*⟩ travel; ~**pflanzung** *die;* ~~: reproduction; ~|**schaffen** *tr. V.* take away; ~|**schreiben** *unr. tr. V.* update; (in die Zukunft) project forward; ~**schreibung** *die* updating; (in die Zukunft) forward projection; ~|**schreiten** *unr. itr. V.;* mit sein ⟨*process*⟩ continue; ⟨*time*⟩ move on; ~**schritt** *der* progress; ~**schritte** progress *sing.;* **ein** ~**schritt** a step forward; ~**schrittlich** ⟦1⟧ *Adj.* progressive; ⟦2⟧ *adv.* progressively; ~**schrittlichkeit** *die;* ~~: progressiveness; ~|**setzen** ⟦1⟧ *tr. V.* continue; ⟦2⟧ *refl. V.* continue; ~**setzung** *die;* ~~, ~~en **(a)** (das ~setzen) continuation; **(b)** (anschließender Teil) instalment; ~**setzungs·roman** *der* serial; serialized novel; ~|**während** ⟦1⟧ *Adj.* continual; ⟦2⟧ *adv.* continually; ~|**werfen** *unr. tr. V.:* ▶ WEGWERFEN

fossil *Adj.* fossilized; fossil *attrib.*

Foto *das;* ~s, ~s photo; ~**s machen** take photos

Foto-: ~**album** *das* photo album; ~**apparat** *der* camera

fotogen *Adj.* photogenic

Foto·graf *der;* ~en, ~en photographer

Fotografie *die;* ~, ~n **(a)** photography no art.
(b) (Lichtbild) photograph

fotografieren *tr. V.* photograph; take a photograph/photographs of

Fotografin *die;* ~, ~nen photographer

foto-, Foto-: ~**kopie** *die* photocopy; ~**kopieren** *tr., itr. V.* photocopy; ~**kopierer** *der* photocopier

Foto-: ~**labor** *das* photographic laboratory; ~**modell** *das* photographic model

Foul /fauːl/ *das;* ~s, ~s (Sport) foul (**an** + *Dat.* on)

Foul-spiel /ˈfauːl-/ *das* foul

Foyer /foaˈjeː/ *das;* ~s, ~s foyer

FPÖ *Abk.* = **Freiheitliche Partei Österreichs**

Fr. *Abk.* (a) = **Franken** SFr.
(b) = **Frau;**
(c) = **Freitag** Fri.

Fracht *die;* ~, ~en (Schiffs~, Luft~) cargo; freight; (Bahn~, LKW~) goods *pl.;* freight

Fracht-brief *der* consignment note; waybill

Frachter *der;* ~s, ~: freighter

Fracht-: ~gut *das* slow freight; slow goods *pl.;* ~**schiff** *das* cargo ship

Frack *der;* ~[e]s, Fräcke tails *pl.;* evening dress

Frage *die;* ~, ~n question; (Angelegenheit) issue; **in** ~: ▶ INFRAGE

Fragebogen *der* questionnaire; (Formular) form

fragen ① *tr., itr. V.* (a) ask
(b) (sich erkundigen) **nach etw.** ~: ask *or* inquire about sth.
(c) (nachfragen) ask for
② *refl. V.* **sich** ~, **ob** …: wonder whether …

Frage-zeichen *das* question mark

fraglich *Adj.* (a) doubtful
(b) (betreffend) in question *postpos.;* relevant

Fragment *das;* ~[e]s, ~e fragment

frag-würdig *Adj.* (a) questionable
(b) (zwielichtig) dubious

Fragwürdigkeit *die;* ~, ~en
(a) questionableness
(b) (Zwielichtigkeit) dubiousness

Fraktion *die;* ~, ~en parliamentary party; (mit zwei Parteien) parliamentary coalition

Fraktions- (Parl.)**:** ~**führer** *der,* ~**führerin** *die* leader of the parliamentary party/coalition; ~**zwang** *der* obligation to vote in accordance with party policy

frank *Adv.* ~ **und frei** frankly and openly; openly and honestly

Franken *der;* ~s ~: [Swiss] franc

Frankfurter *die;* ~, ~ (Wurst) frankfurter

frankieren *tr. V.* frank

Frank-reich *(das);* ~s France

Franse *die;* ~, ~n strand [of a/the fringe]

Franzose *der;* ~n, ~n Frenchman; **er ist** ~: he is French; **die** ~n the French

Französin *die;* ~, ~nen Frenchwoman

französisch *Adj.* French

Französisch *das;* ~[s] French

Fräse *die;* ~, ~n (für Holz) moulding machine; (für Metall) milling machine

fraß *1. u. 3. Pers. Sg. Prät. v.* FRESSEN

Fraß *der;* ~es (derb) muck

Fratze *die;* ~, ~n (a) hideous face
(b) (ugs.: Grimasse) grimace

Frau *die;* ~, ~en (a) woman
(b) (Ehe~) wife
(c) (Titel, Anrede) ~ **Schulze** Mrs Schulze; (in Briefen) **Sehr geehrte** ~ **Schulze** Dear Madam; (bei persönlicher Bekanntschaft) Dear Mrs/Miss/ Ms Schulze

Frauen-: ~**arzt** *der,* ~**ärztin** *die* gynaecologist; ~**bewegung** *die* women's movement; ~**emanzipation** *die* female emancipation; women's emancipation; ~**gefängnis** *das* women's prison; ~**gruppe** *die* women's group; ~**haus** *das* battered wives' refuge; ~**klinik** *die* gynaecological hospital *or* clinic; ~**misshandlung,** *∗*~**mißhandlung** *die* abuse of women; ~**recht** *das* women's right; ~**rechtlerin** *die;* ~~, ~~nen feminist; Women's Libber (coll.); ~**zeitschrift** *die* women's magazine; ~**zimmer** *das* (abwertend) female

Fräulein *das;* ~s, ~ (*ugs.* ~s) (a) (junges ~) young lady; (ältliches ~) spinster
(b) (Titel, Anrede) ~ **Mayer/Schulte** Miss Mayer/Schulte

fraulich ① *Adj.* feminine
② *adv.* in a feminine way

frech ① *Adj.* (a) impertinent; cheeky; barefaced ⟨lie⟩
(b) (keck, kess) saucy
② *adv.* impertinently; cheekily

Frech-dachs *der* (ugs., meist scherzh.) cheeky little thing

Frechheit *die;* ~, ~en (a) impertinence; cheek
(b) (Äußerung) impertinent *or* cheeky remark

frei ① *Adj.* (a) (unabhängig) free
(b) (nicht angestellt) freelance
(c) (ungezwungen) free and easy
(d) (nicht mehr in Haft) free
(e) (offen) open; **im Freien sitzen/übernachten** sit out of doors/spend the night in the open; **ständig im Freien übernachten** sleep rough
(f) (unbesetzt) vacant; free
(g) (kostenlos) free ⟨food, admission⟩
(h) (verfügbar) spare; free ⟨time⟩
② *adv.* freely

frei-, Frei-: ~**bad** *das* open-air swimming pool; ~**bekommen** ① *unr. itr. V.* (ugs.) get time off; ② *unr. tr. V.* **jmdn./etw.** ~**bekommen** get sb./sth. released; ~**beruflich** ① *Adj.* self-employed; freelance; ⟨doctor, lawyer⟩ in private practice; ② *adv.* ~**beruflich tätig sein/ arbeiten** work freelance/practise privately; ~**betrag** *der* (Steuerw.) [tax] allowance; ~**bier** *das* free beer

Freier *der;* ~s, ~ (veralt.) suitor

frei-, Frei-: ~**exemplar** *das* (Buch) free

---

copy; (Zeitung) free issue; ~**frau** *die* baroness; ~**gabe** *die* release; ~|**geben** *unr. tr. V.* release; ~**gebig** *Adj.* generous; open-handed; ~**gebigkeit** *die;* ~~: generosity; open-handedness; ~**gehege** *das* outdoor enclosure; ~**gepäck** *das* baggage allowance; ~**hafen** *der* free port; ~|**halten** *unr. tr. V.* (a) treat; (b) (offen halten) keep ⟨entrance, roadway⟩ clear; Einfahrt ~**halten**! no parking in front of entrance; ~**handels·zone** *die* free-trade zone; ~**händig** *adv.* ⟨cycle⟩ without holding on

Freiheit *die;* ~, ~**en** (a) freedom; ~, Gleichheit, Brüderlichkeit Liberty, Equality, Fraternity
(b) (Vorrecht) freedom; privilege

freiheitlich ⟦1⟧ *Adj.* liberal ⟨philosophy, conscience⟩; ~ **und demokratisch** free and democratic
⟦2⟧ *adv.* liberally

Freiheits-: ~**beraubung** *die* (jur.) wrongful detention; ~**strafe** *die* (Rechtsw.) term of imprisonment; prison sentence

frei-, Frei-: ~**herr** *der* baron; ~**karte** *die* complimentary ticket; ~|**kaufen** *tr. V.* ransom ⟨hostage⟩; buy the freedom of ⟨slave⟩; ~|**kommen** *unr. itr. V.* **aus dem Gefängnis** ~**kommen** be released from prison; ~**körper·kultur** *die* nudism *no art.;* naturism *no art.;* ~|**land** *das* open ground; ~|**lassen** *unr. tr. V.* set free; release; ~|**legen** *tr. V.* uncover

freilich *Adv.* of course

Frei·licht-: ~**bühne** *die,* ~**theater** *das* open-air theatre

frei-, Frei-: ~|**machen** ⟦1⟧ *refl. V.* (ugs.: frei nehmen) take time off; ⟦2⟧ *tr. V.* (Postw.) frank; etw. mit 0,56 Euro ~**machen** put a 0.56 euro stamp on sth.; ~**marke** *die* postage stamp; ~**mütig** ⟦1⟧ *Adj.* candid; frank; ⟦2⟧ *adv.* candidly; frankly; ~**mütigkeit** *die;* ~~: candidness; frankness; ~**schaffend** *Adj.* freelance; ~**schärler** *der;* ~~**s,** ~~, ~**schärlerin** *die;* ~~, ~~**nen** irregular [soldier]; ~|**schwimmen** *unr. refl. V.* sich ~**schwimmen** pass the 15-minute swimming test; ~|**sprechen** *unr. tr. V.* (a) (Rechtsw.) acquit; (b) (für unschuldig erklären) exonerate (von from); ~**spruch** *der* (Rechtsw.) acquittal; ~|**stellen** *tr. V.* (a) jmdm. etw. ~**stellen** leave sth. up to sb.; (b) (befreien) release ⟨person⟩; jmdn. vom Wehrdienst ~**stellen** exempt sb. from military service; ~**stoß** *der* (Fußball) free kick

Frei·tag *der* Friday; *s. auch* DIENSTAG *usw.*

freitags *Adv.* on Friday[s]; *s. auch* DIENSTAGS

frei-, Frei-: ~**tod** *der* (verhüll.) suicide *no art.;* ~**treppe** *die* [flight of] steps; ~**übung** *die; meist Pl.* (Sport) keep-fit exercise; ~**wild** *das* fair game; ~**willig**

⟦1⟧ *Adj.* voluntary ⟨decision⟩; optional ⟨subject⟩; ⟦2⟧ *adv.* voluntarily; sich ~**willig melden** volunteer; ~**willige** *der/die; adj. Dekl.* volunteer; ~**zeichen** *das* ringing tone;

Frei·zeit *die* spare time

Freizeit-: ~**beschäftigung** *die* hobby; leisure pursuit; ~**gestaltung** *die* (Soziol., Päd.) leisure activity; ~**park** *der* amusement park

frei-, Frei-: ~**zügig** *Adj.* (a) generous; (b) (gewagt, unmoralisch) risqué ⟨remark, film, dress⟩; ~**zügigkeit** *die;* ~~ (a) generosity; (b) (freie Wahl des Wohnsitzes) freedom of domicile

fremd *Adj.* (a) foreign
(b) (nicht eigen) other people's; of others *postpos.;*
(c) (unbekannt) strange

fremd-, Fremd-: ~**arbeiter** *der,* ~**arbeiterin** *die* (veralt., schweiz.) foreign worker; ~**artig** *Adj.* strange

Fremde[1] *der/die; adj. Dekl.* (a) stranger
(b) (Ausländer) foreigner

Fremde[2] *die;* ~ (geh.) die ~: foreign parts *pl.*

fremden-, Fremden-: ~**feindlich** *Adj.* xenophobic; hostile to strangers/ foreigners *postpos.;* ~**feindlichkeit** *die* xenophobia; hostility towards foreigners; ~**führer** *der,* ~**führerin** *die* tourist guide; ~**hass,** ***~**haß** *der* xenophobia; hatred of foreigners; ~**verkehr** *der* tourism *no art.;* ~**zimmer** *das* room

fremd-, Fremd-: ~|**gehen** *unr. itr. V.;* mit sein (ugs.) be unfaithful; ~**herrschaft** *die* foreign domination; ~**ländisch** *Adj.* foreign; (exotisch) exotic

Fremdling *der;* ~**s,** ~**e** (veralt.) stranger

fremd-, Fremd-: ~**sprache** *die* foreign language; ~**sprachen·assistent** *der,* ~**sprachen·assistentin** *die* foreign-language assistant; ~**sprachig** *Adj.* bilingual/multilingual ⟨staff, secretary⟩; foreign ⟨literature⟩; foreign-language ⟨edition, teaching⟩; ~**sprachlich** *Adj.* foreign-language ⟨teaching⟩; foreign ⟨word⟩; ~**wort** *das; Pl.* ~**wörter** foreign word

frenetisch ⟦1⟧ *Adj.* frenetic
⟦2⟧ *adv.* frenetically

Frequenz *die;* ~, ~**en** (Physik) frequency; (Med.: Puls~) rate

Fressalien /frɛˈsaljən/ *Pl.* (ugs. scherzh.) grub (coll.)

Fresse *die;* ~, ~**n** (derb) (a) (Mund) gob (sl.)
(b) (Gesicht) mug (coll.)

fressen ⟦1⟧ *unr. tr. V.* (a) ⟨animal⟩ eat; (sich ernähren von) feed on
(b) (ugs.: verschlingen) swallow up ⟨money, time, distance⟩; drink ⟨petrol⟩
(c) (zerstören) eat away
(d) (derb: von Menschen) guzzle
⟦2⟧ *unr. itr. V.* (von Tieren) feed; (derb: von Menschen) stuff one's face (sl.)

Fressen *das;* ∼s **(a)** (für Hunde, Katzen usw.) food; (für Vieh) feed **(b)** (derb: Essen) grub (coll.)

Fresserei *die;* ∼, ∼en (derb) guzzling

Freude *die;* ∼, ∼n joy; (Vergnügen) pleasure; ∼ an etw. (*Dat.*) haben take pleasure in sth.

Freuden-: ∼**fest** *das* celebration; **ein** ∼**fest feiern** hold a celebration; ∼**haus** *das* house of pleasure; ∼**tag** *der* happy day

freudestrahlend *Adj.* beaming with joy;

freudig *Adj.* joyful; joyous ⟨*heart*⟩; delightful ⟨*surprise*⟩;

freud-los *Adj.* joyless;

freuen [1] *refl. V.* be glad (**über** + *Akk.* about); (froh sein) be happy; **sich auf etw.** (*Akk.*) ∼: look forward to sth. [2] *tr. V.* please; **es freut mich, dass** ... I am pleased *or* glad that ...; **das hat ihn sehr gefreut** he was very pleased about it

Freund *der;* ∼es, ∼e **(a)** friend **(b)** (Verehrer, Geliebter) boyfriend

Freundes·kreis *der* circle of friends; **im engen** ∼: among close friends

Freundin *die;* ∼, ∼nen **(a)** friend **(b)** (Geliebte) girlfriend; (älter) lady friend

freundlich [1] *Adj.* **(a)** kind ⟨*face*⟩; friendly ⟨*reception*⟩ **(b)** (angenehm) pleasant **(c)** (freundschaftlich) friendly [2] *adv.* **jmdm.** ∼ **danken** thank sb. kindly

Freundlichkeit *die;* ∼: kindness

Freundschaft *die;* ∼, ∼en friendship; **mit jmdm.** ∼ **schließen** make friends with sb.

freundschaftlich [1] *Adj.* friendly [2] *adv.* in a friendly way

Frevel /ˈfreːfl̩/ *der;* ∼s, ∼ (geh., veralt.) crime; outrage

frevelhaft (geh.) [1] *Adj.* wicked ⟨*deed, rebellion, person*⟩; criminal ⟨*stupidity*⟩ [2] *adv.* wickedly

Friede *der;* ∼ns, ∼n (älter, geh.) ▶ FRIEDEN

Frieden *der;* ∼s, ∼: peace

Friedens-: ∼**abkommen** *das* peace agreement; (Friedensvertrag) peace treaty; ∼**bewegung** *die* peace movement; ∼**bruch** *der* violation of the peace; ∼**forschung** *die* peace studies *pl., no art.;* ∼**konferenz** *die* peace conference; ∼**nobelpreis** *der* Nobel Peace Prize; ∼**pfeife** *die* pipe of peace; ∼**richter** *der,* ∼**richterin** *die: lay magistrate dealing with minor offences;* ≈ Justice of the Peace; ∼**taube** *die* dove of peace; ∼**verhandlungen** *Pl.* peace negotiations; ∼**vertrag** *der* peace treaty; ∼**zeiten** *Pl.* peacetime *sing.*

fried·fertig *Adj.* peaceable ⟨*person, character*⟩

Fried·fertigkeit *die;* ∼: peaceableness

Fried·hof *der* cemetery; (Kirchhof) graveyard

friedlich [1] *Adj.* peaceful

---

*alte Schreibung - vgl. Hinweis auf S. xiv

[2] *adv.* peacefully

Friedlichkeit *die;* ∼: peacefulness

fried·liebend *Adj.* peace-loving

frieren *unr. itr. V.* **(a)** be *or* feel cold **(b)** *mit sein* (gefrieren) freeze

Frikadelle *die;* ∼, ∼n rissole

frisch [1] *Adj.* fresh; new-laid ⟨*egg*⟩; clean ⟨*linen, underwear*⟩; wet ⟨*paint*⟩ [2] *adv.* freshly

Frische *die;* ∼ freshness; **geistige** ∼: mental alertness; **körperliche** ∼: physical fitness

Frisch-: ∼**fleisch** *das* fresh meat; ∼**halte·beutel** *der* airtight bag; ∼**luft** *die* fresh air; ∼**milch** *die* fresh milk

Friseur /friˈzøːɐ̯/ *der;* ∼s, ∼e, **Friseuse** /friˈzøːzə/ *die;* ∼, ∼n hairdresser

frisieren *tr. V.* **jmdn./sich** ∼: do sb.'s/one's hair; **sich** ∼ **lassen** have one's hair done

friss, *friß *Imperativ Sg. v.* FRESSEN

frisst, *frißt *2. u. 3. Pers. Sg. Präsens v.* FRESSEN

Frist *die;* ∼, ∼en **(a)** time; period; **die** ∼ **verlängern** extend the deadline **(b)** (begrenzter Aufschub) extension

frist-: ∼**gemäß,** ∼**gerecht** *Adj., adv.* within the specified time *postpos.;* (bei Anmeldung usw.) before the closing date *postpos.;* ∼**los** [1] *Adj.* instant; [2] *adv.* without notice

Frisur *die;* ∼, ∼en hairstyle

fritieren *tr. V.* deep-fry

frivol /friˈvoːl/ *Adj.* **(a)** (schamlos) suggestive ⟨*remark, picture, etc.*⟩; risqué ⟨*joke*⟩; earthy ⟨*man*⟩; flighty ⟨*woman*⟩ **(b)** (leichtfertig) frivolous

froh *Adj.* **(a)** happy; cheerful ⟨*person, mood*⟩; good ⟨*news*⟩ **(b)** (ugs.: erleichtert) pleased, glad (**über** + *Akk.* about)

fröhlich *Adj.* cheerful; happy

Fröhlichkeit *die;* ∼: cheerfulness; (eines Festes, einer Feier) gaiety

Froh-: ∼**natur** *die* cheerful person; ∼**sinn** *der* cheerfulness; gaiety

fromm; ∼**er** *od.* **frömmer,** ∼**st...** *od.* **frömmst...** [1] *Adj.* pious, devout ⟨*person*⟩; devout ⟨*Christian*⟩ [2] *adv.* piously

Frömmigkeit *die;* ∼: piety; devoutness

Fron·leichnam /froːn-/ (*das*); ∼s [the feast of] Corpus Christi

Front *die;* ∼, ∼en **(a)** (Gebäude∼) front; façade **(b)** (Kampfgebiet) front [line]

frontal [1] *Adj.* head-on ⟨*collision*⟩; frontal ⟨*attack*⟩ [2] *adv.* ⟨*collide*⟩ head-on; ⟨*attack*⟩ from the front

Front·antrieb *der* (Kfz-W.) front-wheel drive

fror *1. u. 3. Pers. Sg. Prät. v.* FRIEREN

Frosch *der;* ~[e]s, Frösche frog
Frosch-: ~**mann** *der; Pl.* ~**männer**
frogman; ~**perspektive** *die* worm's-eye
view; ~**schenkel** *der* frog's leg
Frost *der;* ~[e]s, Fröste frost
Frostbeule *die* chilblain
frösteln *itr. V.* feel chilly
Frost·grenze *die* (Met.) 0° C isotherm;
(Geol.) frost line
frostig ⟨1⟩ *Adj.* (auch fig.) frosty
⟨2⟩ *adv.* frostily
Frostigkeit *die;* ~: frostiness
Frost-: ~**schaden** *der* frost damage;
~**schutz·mittel** *das* (a) frost protection
agent; (b) (Kfz-W.) antifreeze
Frottee *das* u. *der;* ~s, ~s terry towelling
Frottee·handtuch *das* terry towel
frottieren *tr. V.* rub; towel
frotzeln ⟨1⟩ *tr. V.* tease
⟨2⟩ *itr. V.* über jmdn./etw. ~: make fun of
sb./sth.
Frucht *die;* ~, Früchte fruit
frucht·bar *Adj.* fertile; fruitful ⟨*work, idea,*
etc.⟩
Fruchtbarkeit *die;* ~: fertility;
fruitfulness
Frucht·becher *der* fruit sundae
fruchten *tr. V.* nichts ~: be no use
fruchtig *Adj.* fruity
frucht·los *Adj.* fruitless, vain ⟨*efforts*⟩
Frucht·losigkeit *die;* ~~: fruitlessness
Frucht-: ~**saft** *der* fruit juice;
~**wasser** *das; Pl.* ~**wässer** (Anat.)
amniotic fluid; waters *pl.* (coll.)
früh ⟨1⟩ *Adj.* (a) early
(b) (vorzeitig) premature
⟨2⟩ *adv.* early; heute ~: this morning
früh·auf: von ~ from early childhood
on[wards]
Frühaufsteher *der;* ~s, ~,
Frühaufsteherin *die;* ~, ~nen early
riser
Frühe *die;* ~: in aller ~: at the crack of
dawn
früher ⟨1⟩ *Adj., nicht präd.* (a) (vergangen)
earlier; former
(b) (ehemalig) former ⟨*owner, occupant,*
friend⟩
⟨2⟩ *adv.* formerly; ~ war er ganz anders he
used to be quite different
Früh·erkennung *die* (Med.) early
recognition
frühestens *Adv.* at the earliest
Früh·geburt *die* (a) premature birth
(b) (Kind) premature baby
Früh·jahr *das* spring
Frühjahrsmüdigkeit *die* springtime
tiredness
Frühling *der;* ~s, ~e spring
Frühlings·anfang *der* first day of
spring

früh-, Früh-: ~**reif** *Adj.* precocious
⟨*child*⟩; ~**schoppen** *der* morning drink;
(um Mittag) lunchtime drink; ~**sport** *der*
early-morning exercise
Früh·stück *das;* ~s, ~e breakfast
frühstücken *itr. V.* have breakfast
Frühstücks-: ~**fernsehen** *das*
breakfast television; ~**pause** *die* morning
break; coffee break
früh-, Früh-: ~**warn·system** *das* early
warning system; ~**zeitig** ⟨1⟩ *Adj.* early;
(vorzeitig) premature; ⟨2⟩ *adv.* early; (vorzeitig)
prematurely
Frustration *die;* ~, ~en (Psych.)
frustration
frustrieren *tr. V.* frustrate
Fuchs *der;* ~es, Füchse fox
fuchsen *tr. V.* annoy; vex
fuchs·teufels·wild *Adj.* (ugs.) livid (coll.)
Fuchtel *die;* ~: unter jmds. ~ (ugs.) under
sb.'s thumb
fuchteln *itr. V.* (ugs.) mit etw. ~: wave sth.
about
Fuder *das;* ~s, ~: cartload
Fuge[1] *die;* ~, ~n joint; (Zwischenraum) gap
Fuge[2] *die;* ~, ~n (Musik) fugue
fügen ⟨1⟩ *tr. V.* place; set; etw zu etw. ~ (fig.)
add sth. to sth.
⟨2⟩ *refl. V.* (a) (sich ein~) sich in etw. (*Akk.*)
~: fit into sth.
(b) (gehorchen) sich ~: fall into line
fügsam *Adj.* obedient
fühlbar *Adj.* noticeable
fühlen ⟨1⟩ *tr., itr. V.* feel
⟨2⟩ *refl. V.* sich krank ~: feel sick
Fühler *der;* ~s, ~: feeler; antenna
Fühlungnahme *die;* ~: initial contact
fuhr *1. u. 3. Pers. Sg. Prät. v.* FAHREN
Fuhre *die;* ~, ~n load
führen ⟨1⟩ *tr. V.* (a) lead; jmdn. durch ein
Haus/eine Stadt ~: show sb. around a
house/town; durch das Programm führt [Sie]
Klaus Frank Klaus Frank will present the
programme
(b) (verkaufen) stock, sell ⟨*goods*⟩
(c) (durch~) Gespräche/Verhandlungen ~:
hold conversations/negotiations; eine
glückliche Ehe ~: be happily married
(d) (leiten) manage, run ⟨*company, business,*
pub, etc.⟩; lead ⟨*party, country*⟩; command
⟨*regiment*⟩
(e) (Amtsspr.) drive ⟨*train, motor, vehicle*⟩
(f) (als Kennzeichnung, Bezeichnung haben) bear;
einen Titel/Künstlernamen ~: have a title/
use a stage name
(g) (angelegt haben) keep ⟨*diary, list, file*⟩
(h) (registrieren) jmdn. in einer Liste/Kartei ~:
have sb. on a list/on file
(i) (tragen) etw. bei od. mit sich ~: have sth.
on one; eine Waffe/einen Ausweis bei sich
~: carry a weapon/a pass
⟨2⟩ *itr. V.* (a) lead
(b) (an der Spitze liegen) lead; be ahead

führend *Adj.* leading; high-ranking ⟨*official*⟩; prominent ⟨*position*⟩

Führer *der;* ∼s, ∼ (a) (Leiter) leader (b) (Fremdenführer, Buch) guide

Führerin *die;* ∼, ∼nen ▶ FÜHRER

führer-, Führer-: ∼**los** 1 *Adj.* leaderless; (ohne Lenker) driverless ⟨*car*⟩ 2 *adv.* ▶ 1: without a leader; without a driver; ∼**schein** *der* driving licence (Brit.); driver's license (Amer.); ∼**schein-entzug** *der* disqualification from driving; driving ban

Führung *die;* ∼, ∼en (a) ▶ FÜHREN 1D: management; running; leadership; command (b) (Fremdenführung) guided tour (c) (führende Position) lead

Führungs-: ∼**kraft** *die* manager; ∼**spitze** *die* (Politik) top leadership; (im Betrieb) top management; ∼**zeugnis** *das:* document issued by police certifying that holder has no criminal record

Fuhr-: ∼**unternehmer** *der,* ∼**unternehmerin** *die* haulage contractor; ∼**werk** *das* cart

Fülle *die;* ∼ (a) wealth; abundance (b) (Körper∼) corpulence

füllen 1 *tr. V.* (a) fill; (Kochk.) stuff (b) (fig.) fill in ⟨*gap, time*⟩ 2 *refl. V.* (voll werden) fill [up]

Füller *der;* ∼s, ∼ (ugs.) [fountain] pen

Füll-federhalter *der* fountain pen

füllig *Adj.* corpulent, portly ⟨*person*⟩; ample ⟨*figure, bosom*⟩

Füllung *die;* ∼, ∼en stuffing; (Kochk.; Zahnmed.) filling; (in Schokolade) centre

fummeln *itr. V.* (ugs.) (a) (fingern) fiddle (b) (erotisch) pet

Fund *der;* ∼[e]s, ∼e (auch Archäol.) find

Fundament *das;* ∼[e]s, ∼e (a) (Bauw.) foundations *pl.;* (b) (Basis) base; basis

fundamental *Adj.* fundamental

Fundamentalismus *der;* ∼: fundamentalism

Fundamentalist *der;* ∼en, ∼en, **Fundamentalistin** *die;* ∼, ∼nen fundamentalist

Fund-: ∼**büro** *das* lost property office (Brit.); lost and found office (Amer.); ∼**grube** *die* treasure house

fundieren *tr. V.* underpin

fündig *Adj.* ∼ sein yield something; ∼ werden make a find; (bei Bohrungen) make a strike

Fund-ort *der* place *or* site where sth. is/was found

fünf *Kardinalz.* five

Fünf *die;* ∼, ∼en five; (Schulnote) E

fünf-, Fünf-: ∼**eck** *das;* pentagon; ∼**fach** *Vervielfältigungsz.* fivefold; ∼**fache** *das;*

---

adj. Dekl. five times as much; ∼**hundert** *Kardinalz.* five hundred; ∼**kampf** *der* (Sport) pentathlon

Fünfling *der;* ∼s, ∼e quintuplet; quin (coll.)

fünf-: ∼**mal** *Adv.* five times; ∼**stellig** *Adj.* five-figure

fünft... *Ordinalz.* fifth

Fünf-tagewoche *die* five-day [working] week

fünf-tausend *Kardinalz.* five thousand

fünftel *Bruchz.* fifth

Fünftel *das* (schweiz. meist *der*); ∼s, ∼: fifth

fünftens *Adv.* fifthly

fünf-zehn *Kardinalz.* fifteen

fünfzig *Kardinalz.* fifty

Fünfzig *die;* ∼: fifty

fünfziger *indekl. Adj.* **die Fünfzigerjahre** the fifties

Fünfziger *der;* ∼s, ∼ (a) (ugs.) fifty-pfennig piece/fifty-euro note *etc.* (b) (50-Jähriger) fifty-year-old

fünfzig-: ∼**mark-schein** *der* fifty-mark note; ∼**pfennig-stück** *das* fifty-pfennig piece

fünfzigst... *Ordinalz.* fiftieth

fungieren *itr. V.* **als etw.** ∼ ⟨*person*⟩ act as sth.; ⟨*word etc.*⟩ function as sth.

Funk *der;* ∼s radio

Funk-ausstellung *die* radio and television exhibition

Funke *der;* ∼ns, ∼n (auch fig.) spark

funkeln *itr. V.* ⟨*light, star*⟩ twinkle; ⟨*gold, diamonds*⟩ glitter; ⟨*eyes*⟩ blaze

funken *tr. V.* radio; ⟨*transmitter*⟩ broadcast

Funker *der;* ∼s, ∼, **Funkerin** *die;* ∼, ∼nen radio operator

Funk-: ∼**gerät** *das* radio set; (tragbar) walkie-talkie; ∼**haus** *das* broadcasting centre; ∼**kolleg** *das* radio-based [adult education] course; ∼**sprech-gerät** *das* radiophone; (tragbar) walkie-talkie; ∼**spruch** *der* radio signal; (Nachricht) radio message; ∼**station** *die,* ∼**stelle** *die* radio station; ∼**stille** *die* radio silence; ∼**streife** *die* [police] radio patrol; ∼**taxi** *das* radio taxi; ∼**telefon** *das* radio-telephone

Funktion *die;* ∼, ∼en function

Funktionär *der;* ∼s, ∼e official; functionary

funktionieren *itr. V.* work; function

funktions-tüchtig *Adj.* working; sound ⟨*organ*⟩

Funk-: ∼**turm** *der* radio tower; ∼**verbindung** *die* radio contact

Funzel *die;* ∼, ∼n (ugs.) useless light

für *Präp. mit Akk.* for; etw. ∼ ungültig erklären declare sth. invalid; *s. auch* WAS 1

Furche *die;* ∼, ∼n (a) furrow (b) (Wagenspur) rut

---

*old spelling - see note on page xiv

Furcht *die;* ~: fear; ~ **vor jmdm./etw. haben** fear sb./sth.

furchtbar ① *Adj.* **(a)** dreadful **(b)** (ugs.: unangenehm) terrible (coll.)
② *adv.* (ugs.) terribly (coll.)

fürchten ① *refl. V.* **sich [vor jmdm./etw.]** ~: be afraid *or* frightened [of sb./sth.]
② *tr. V.* be afraid of; **ich fürchte, [dass] ...:** I'm afraid [that] ...

fürchterlich *Adj., adv.* ▶ FURCHTBAR

furcht·los ① *Adj.* fearless
② *adv.* fearlessly

furchtsam ① *Adj.* timid
② *adv.* timidly

für·einander *Adv.* for one another; for each other

Furie /ˈfuːri̯ə/ *die;* ~, ~n Fury

Furnier *das;* ~s, ~e veneer

Für·sorge *die;* ~ **(a)** care **(b)** (veralt.: Sozialhilfe) welfare **(c)** (veralt.: Sozialamt) social services *pl.*

für·sorglich ① *Adj.* considerate
② *adv.* considerately

Für·sprache *die* support

Für·sprecher *der,* **Für·sprecherin** *die* advocate

Fürst *der;* ~en, ~en prince

Fürstentum *das;* ~s, Fürstentümer principality

Fürstin *die;* ~, ~nen princess

fürstlich ① *Adj.* **(a)** royal **(b)** (fig.: üppig) lavish
② *adv.* lavishly

Furt *die;* ~, ~en ford

Furunkel *der od. das;* ~s, ~: boil; furuncle

Für·wort *das; Pl.* -wörter pronoun

Furz *der;* ~es, Fürze (derb) fart (coarse); **einen** ~ **lassen** let off a fart; **jeder** ~ (fig.) the slightest thing

furzen *itr. V.* (derb) fart (coarse)

Fusion *die;* ~, ~en amalgamation; (von Konzernen) merger

fusionieren *itr. V.* merge

Fuß *der;* ~es, Füße foot; (einer Lampe, Säule) base; (von Möbeln) leg; **zu** ~ **gehen** go on foot;

walk; **bei** ~**!** heel!; (fig.) **auf freiem** ~ **sein** be at large; **auf großem** ~ **leben** live in great style

Fuß·ball *der* **(a)** (Ballspiel) [Association] football **(b)** (Ball) football

Fußballer *der;* ~s, ~, **Fußballerin** *die;* ~, ~nen footballer

Fußball-: ~**platz** *der* football ground; (Spielfeld) football pitch; ~**spiel** *das* **(a)** football match; **(b)** (Sportart) football *no art.;* ~**spieler** *der,* ~**spielerin** *die* football player

Fuß·boden *der* floor

Fußboden·heizung *die* underfloor heating

fußen *itr. V.* **auf etw.** *(Dat.)* ~: be based on sth.

Fuß·ende *das* foot

Fußgänger *der;* ~s, ~, **Fußgängerin** *die;* ~, ~nen pedestrian

Fußgänger-: ~**brücke** *die* footbridge; ~**übergang** *der,* ~**überweg** *der* pedestrian crossing; ~**unterführung** *die* pedestrian subway; ~**zone** *die* pedestrian precinct

Fuß-: ~**nagel** *der* toenail; ~**note** *die* footnote; ~**stapfen** *der;* ~~s, ~~: footprint; ~**tritt** *der* kick; ~**volk** *das* **(a)** (hist.) footmen *pl.;* **(b)** (abwertend: Untergeordnete) lower ranks *pl.;* ~**weg** *der* footpath

futsch *Adj.* (salopp) ~ **sein** have gone for a burton (Brit. coll.)

Futter¹ *das;* ~s (Tiernahrung) feed; (für Pferde, Kühe) fodder

Futter² *das;* ~s, ~ (von Kleidungsstücken usw.) lining

Futteral *das;* ~s, ~e case

Futter·mittel *das* animal food

füttern¹ *tr. V.* feed

füttern² *tr. V.* (mit Futter² ausstatten) line

Futter·pflanze *die* fodder plant; forage plant

Fütterung *die;* ~, ~en feeding

Futur *das;* ~s, ~e (Sprachw.) future [tense]

Fuzzi *der;* ~s, ~s (salopp) bozo (sl.)

Gg

g, G /geː/ *das;* ~, ~ (a) (Buchstabe) g/G
  (b) (Musik) [key of] G

g *Abk.* (a) = **Gramm** g
  (b) = **Groschen**

gab *1. u. 3. Pers. Sg. Prät. v.* GEBEN

Gabe *die;* ~, ~n (a) (geh.: Geschenk, Talent) gift
  (b) (Almosen, Spende) alms *pl.*

Gabel *die;* ~, ~n fork; (Telefon~) cradle

gabeln *refl. V.* fork

Gabel-: ~**schlüssel** *der* flat spanner; ~**stapler** *der;* ~~s, ~~: forklift truck

Gabelung *die;* ~, ~en fork

Gaben·tisch *der* gift table

gackern *itr. V.* (a) cluck
  (b) (ugs.: lachen) cackle

gaffen *itr. V.* (abwertend) gape; gawp (coll.)

Gaffer *der;* ~s, ~, **Gafferin** *die;* ~, ~nen gaper; starer

Gag /gɛk/ *der;* ~s, ~s (a) (Theater, Film) gag
  (b) (Besonderheit) gimmick

Gage /ˈgaːʒə/ *die;* ~, ~n salary; (für einzelnen Auftritt) fee

gähnen *itr. V.* (auch fig.) yawn

Gala /ˈgaːla, *auch* ˈgala/ *die;* ~: formal dress

galant ① *Adj.* gallant; (amourös) amorous
  ② *adv.* gallantly

Gala·vorstellung *die* gala performance

Galeere *die;* ~, ~n galley

Galerie *die;* ~, ~n gallery

Galgen *der* gallows *sing.*

Galgen-: ~**frist** *die* reprieve; ~**humor** *der* gallows humour

Galle *die;* ~, ~n (a) (Gallenblase) gall [bladder]
  (b) (Sekret) (bei Tieren) gall; (bei Menschen) bile

Galopp *der;* ~s, ~s *od.* ~e gallop

galoppieren *itr. V.; meist mit sein* gallop

galt *1. u. 3. Pers. Sg. Prät. v.* GELTEN

galvanisch /galˈvaːnɪʃ/ *Adj.* galvanic

Gamasche *die;* ~, ~n gaiter; (bis zum Knöchel reichend) spat

Gambe *die;* ~, ~n (Musik) viola da gamba

Gamma·strahlen *Pl.* (Physik, Med.) gamma rays

gammelig *Adj.* (ugs.) (a) bad; rotten
  (b) (unordentlich) scruffy

gammeln *itr. V.* (a) (ugs.) go off
  (b) (nichts tun) loaf around; bum around (Amer. coll.)

Gammler *der;* ~s, ~, **Gammlerin** *die;* ~, ~nen (ugs.) dropout (coll.)

Gämse *die;* ~, ~n chamois

gang: ~ und gäbe sein be quite usual

Gang *der;* ~[e]s, Gänge (a) walk; gait
  (b) (Besorgung) errand
  (c) (Verlauf) course
  (d) (Technik) gear
  (e) (Flur) (in Zügen, Gebäuden usw.) corridor; (Verbindungs~) passage[way]; (im Theater, Kino, Flugzeug) aisle
  (f) (Kochk.) course

gangbar *Adj.* passable; (fig.) practicable

Gängel·band *das:* jmdn. am ~ führen keep sb. in leading reins

gängeln *tr. V.* (ugs.) jmdn. ~: boss sb. around

gang·genau *Adj.* accurate

Gang·genauigkeit *die* accuracy

gängig *Adj.* (a) (üblich) common; (aktuell) current
  (b) (leicht verkäuflich) popular

Gang·schaltung *die* (Technik) gear system; (Art) gear change

Gangway /ˈgænweɪ/ *die;* ~, ~s gangway

Ganove /gaˈnoːvə/ *der;* ~n, ~n (ugs. abwertend) crook (coll.)

Gans *die;* ~, Gänse goose

Gänse-: ~**blümchen** *das* daisy; ~**braten** *der* roast goose; ~**füßchen** *das;* ~~s, ~~ (ugs.) ▶ ANFÜHRUNGSZEICHEN; ~**haut** *die* (fig.) gooseflesh; goose pimples *pl.;* ~**marsch** im ~marsch in single *or* Indian file

Gänserich *der;* ~s, ~e gander

ganz ① *Adj.* (a) (gesamt) whole; entire; **den** ~en Tag/das ~e Jahr all day/year
  (b) (ugs.: alle) **die** ~en Kinder/Leute/Gläser *usw.* all the children/people/glasses *etc.;*
  (c) (vollständig) whole
  (d) (ugs.: ziemlich [groß]) **eine** ~e Menge/ein ~er Haufen quite a lot/quite a pile
  (e) (ugs.: unversehrt) intact; **etw. wieder** ~ **machen** mend sth.
  ② *adv.* quite

Ganze *das; adj. Dekl.* (a) whole
  (b) (alles) **das** ~: the whole thing

gänzlich *Adv.* entirely

ganz-: ~**tägig** ① *Adj.* all-day; **eine** ~tägige Arbeit a full-time job; ② *adv.* all day; ~**tags** *Adv.* arbeiten work full-time

Ganztags-: ~**schule** *die* all-day school; (System) all-day schooling *no art.;* ~**stelle** *die* full-time job

gar¹ *Adj.* cooked; done *pred.*

gar² *Partikel* (a) (überhaupt) ~ nicht [wahr] not [true] at all; ~ nichts nothing at all; ~

---

niemand *od.* **keiner** nobody at all; ~ **keines** not a single one; ~ **kein Geld** no money at all
(b) (südd., österr., schweiz.: verstärkend) ~ **zu** only too
(c) (geh.: sogar) even
Garage /ga'ra:ʒə/ *die;* ~, ~n garage
Garagen-: ~**firma** *die* garage startup; ~**wagen** *der* garaged car
Garant *der;* ~en, ~en guarantor
Garantie *die;* ~, ~n guarantee
Garantie·frist *die* guarantee period
garantieren ① *tr. V.* guarantee
② *itr. V.* **für etw.** ~: guarantee sth.
garantiert *Adv.* (ugs.) **wir kommen** ~ **zu spät** we're dead certain to arrive late (coll.)
Garantie·schein *der* guarantee [certificate]
Garantin *die;* ~, ~nen gúarantor
Garaus /'ga:g|au:s/: **jmdm. den** ~ **machen** do sb. in (coll.)
Garbe *die;* ~, ~n **(a)** sheaf
(b) (Geschoss~) burst of fire
Garde *die;* ~, ~n guard
Garderobe *die;* ~, ~n **(a)** wardrobe; clothes *pl.;*
(b) (Flur~) coat rack
(c) (im Theater usw.) cloakroom; checkroom (Amer.)
Garderoben·frau *die* cloakroom *or* (Amer.) checkroom attendant
Gardine *die;* ~, ~n **(a)** net curtain
(b) (landsch., veralt.) curtain
Gardinen-: ~**predigt** *die* (ugs.) telling-off (coll.); (einer Ehefrau zu ihrem Mann) curtain lecture; ~**stange** *die* curtain rail
garen *tr., itr. V.* cook
gären *regelm.* (*auch unr.*) *itr. V.* ferment; (fig.) seethe
Garn *das;* ~[e]s, ~e **(a)** thread; (Näh~) cotton
(b) (Seew.) yarn
Garnele *die;* ~, ~n shrimp
garnieren *tr. V.* **(a)** decorate
(b) (Gastr.) garnish
Garnison *die;* ~, ~en garrison
Garnitur *die;* ~, ~en **(a)** set; (Wäsche) set of [matching] underwear; (Möbel) suite
(b) (ugs.) **die erste/zweite** ~: the first/second-rate people *pl.*
garstig *Adj.* nasty; bad ⟨*behaviour*⟩
Garstigkeit *die;* ~, ~en **(a)** nastiness
(b) (Handlung) piece of nastiness
Gärtchen *das;* ~s, ~: little garden
Garten *der;* ~s, Gärten garden
Garten-: ~**abfall** *der* garden waste; ~**abfälle** garden waste; ~**arbeit** *die* gardening; ~**bau** *der* horticulture; ~**fest** *das* garden party; ~**haus** *das* summer house; ~**laube** *die* summerhouse; garden house; ~**lokal** *das* beer garden; (Restaurant) open-air café; ~**schau** *die* horticultural

show; ~**wirtschaft** *die* ▶ ~LOKAL;
~**zwerg** *der* **(a)** garden gnome; **(b)** (salopp abwertend) little runt
Gärtner *der;* ~s, ~: gardener
Gärtnerei *die;* ~, ~en nursery
Gärtnerin *die;* ~, ~nen gardener
Gärung *die;* ~, ~en fermentation
Gas *das;* ~es, ~e **(a)** gas
(b) (Treibstoff) petrol (Brit.); gasoline (Amer.); gas (Amer. coll.); ~ **wegnehmen** take one's foot off the accelerator; ~ **geben** accelerate; put one's foot down (coll.)
gas-, Gas-: ~**flasche** *die* gas cylinder; (für einen Herd, Ofen) gas bottle; ~**förmig** *Adj.* gaseous; ~**hahn** *der* gas tap; ~**herd** *der* gas cooker; ~**kammer** *die* gas chamber; ~**leitung** *die* gas pipe; (Hauptrohr) gas main; ~**maske** *die* gas mask; ~**pedal** *das* accelerator [pedal]; gas pedal (Amer.); ~**pistole** *die* pistol that fires gas cartridges
Gasse *die;* ~, ~n lane; (österr.) street
Gassen·junge *der* (abwertend) street urchin
Gast *der;* ~[e]s, Gäste **(a)** guest
(b) (Besucher eines Lokals) patron
(c) (Besucher) visitor
Gast-: ~**arbeiter,** *der,* ~**arbeiterin** *die* immigrant *or* guest worker; ~**dozent** *der,* ~**dozentin** *die* (Hochschulw.) visiting lecturer
Gäste-: ~**buch** *das* guest book; ~**haus** *das* guest house; ~**zimmer** *das* (privat) guest room; spare room; (im Hotel) room
gast-, Gast-: ~**freundlich** *Adj.* hospitable; ~**freundlichkeit** *die,* ~**freundschaft** *die* hospitality; ~**geber** *der* host; ~**geberin** *die* hostess; ~**haus** *das,* ~**hof** *der* inn
gastieren *itr. V.* give a guest performance
gastlich *Adj.* hospitable
Gastlichkeit *die;* ~: hospitality
Gast·professor *der,*
Gast·professorin *die* visiting professor
Gastronom *der;* ~en, ~en restaurateur
Gastronomie *die;* ~: catering no art.; (Gaststättengewerbe) restaurant trade
Gastronomin *die;* ~, ~nen restaurateur
Gast-: ~**spiel** *das* guest performance; ~**stätte** *die* public house; (Speiselokal) restaurant; ~**wirt** *der* publican; landlord; (eines Restaurants) [restaurant] proprietor; (Pächter) restaurant manager; ~**wirtin** *die* ▶ ~WIRT: publican; landlady; [restaurant] proprietress *or* owner; restaurant manageress; ~**wirtschaft** *die* ▶ ~STÄTTE
Gas-: ~**vergiftung** *die* gas poisoning no indef. art.; ~**versorgung** *die* gas supply; ~**werk** *das* gasworks sing.; ~**zähler** *der* gas meter
Gatte *der;* ~n, ~n husband
Gatter *das;* ~s, ~ **(a)** (Zaun) fence; (Lattenzaun) fence; paling ⋯⟶

(b) (Tor) gate

Gạttin die; ~, ~nen (geh.) wife

Gạttung die; ~, ~en (a) kind; sort; (Kunst~) genre; form
(b) (Biol.) genus

GAU der; ~s, ~s Abk. = **größter anzunehmender Unfall** MCA; maximum credible accident

Gaudi das; ~s (bayr., österr.) die; ~ (ugs.) bit of fun

Gaukler der; ~s, ~, **Gauklerin** die; ~, ~nen (a) (veralt.: Taschenspieler[in]) itinerant entertainer
(b) (geh.: Betrüger[in]) charlatan

Gaul der; ~[e]s, **Gäule** nag (derog.)

Gaumen der; ~s, ~: palate

Gauner der; ~s, ~ (abwertend) crook (coll.); rogue

Gaunerei die; ~, ~en swindle

Gaunerin die; ~, ~nen ▶ GAUNER

Gauner·sprache die thieves' cant or Latin

Gaze /'ɡaːzə/ die; ~, ~n gauze

geạchtet Adj. respected

Geạst das; ~[e]s branches pl.

geb. Abk. (a) = **geboren;**
(b) = **geborene**

Gebäck das; ~[e]s, ~e cakes and pastries pl.; (Kekse) biscuits pl.; (Törtchen) tarts pl.

gebạcken 2. Part. v. BACKEN

Gebälk das; ~[e]s, ~e beams pl.; (Dach~) rafters pl.

gebar 1. u. 3. Pers. Sg. Prät. v. GEBÄREN

Gebärde die; ~, ~n gesture

gebärden refl. V. behave

gebären unr. tr. V. bear; give birth to; s. auch GEBOREN

gebär·fähig Adj. Frauen im ~en Alter women of child-bearing age.

Gebär·mutter die; Pl. Gebärmütter womb

Gebäude das; ~s, ~ (a) building
(b) (Gefüge) structure

gebaut Adj. gut ~ sein have a good figure

Gebein das; ~[e]s, ~e Pl. (geh.) bones pl.; (sterbliche Reste) [mortal] remains

Gebell das; ~[e]s barking; (der Jagdhunde) baying

geben ① unr. tr. V. give; jmdm. die Hand ~: shake sb.'s hand; ~ Sie mir bitte Herrn N. please put me through to Mr N.; Unterricht ~: teach; eins plus eins gibt zwei one and one is or makes two; etw. von sich ~: utter sth.
② unr. tr. V. (unpers.) es gibt there is/are; heute gibts Fisch we're having fish today; morgen gibt es Schnee it'll snow tomorrow
③ unr. tr. V. (a) (Karten austeilen) deal
(b) (Sport: aufschlagen) serve
④ unr. refl. V. (a) sich [natürlich/steif] ~: act or behave [naturally/stiffly]

(b) das gibt sich noch it will get better

Gebet das; ~[e]s, ~e prayer

gebeten 2. Part. v. BITTEN

Gebets-: ~mühle die prayer wheel; **~teppich** der (islam. Rel.) prayer mat

gebiert 3. Pers. Sg. Präsens v. GEBÄREN

Gebiet das; ~[e]s, ~e region; area; (Staats~) territory; (Bereich, Fach) field

gebieten (geh.) (a) command; order
(b) (erfordern) demand

Gebieter der; ~s, ~ (veralt.) master

Gebieterin die; ~, ~nen (veralt.) mistress

gebieterisch (geh.) Adj. imperious; (herrisch) domineering; peremptory ⟨tone⟩

Gebiets·anspruch der territorial claim

Gebilde das; ~s, ~: object; (Bauwerk) structure

gebildet Adj. educated

Gebimmel das; ~s (ugs.) ringing; (von kleinen Glocken) tinkling

Gebirge das; ~s, ~: mountain range; im ~: in the mountains

gebirgig Adj. mountainous

Gebiss, *Gebiß das; Gebisses, Gebisse
(a) set of teeth; teeth pl.;
(b) (Zahnersatz) denture; plate (coll.); (für beide Kiefer) dentures pl.

gebissen 2. Part. v. BEISSEN

geblasen 2. Part. v. BLASEN

geblichen 2. Part. v. BLEICHEN

geblümt Adj. flowered

Geblüt das; ~[e]s (geh.) blood

gebogen 2. Part. v. BIEGEN

geboren ① 2. Part. v. GEBÄREN;
② Adj. **blind/taub ~ sein** be born blind/deaf; **Frau Anna Schmitz ~e Meyer** Mrs Anna Schmitz née Meyer

geborgen ① 2. Part. v. BERGEN;
② Adj. safe; secure

Geborgenheit die; ~: security

geborsten 2. Part. v. BERSTEN

gebot 1. u. 3. Pers. Sg. Prät. v. GEBIETEN

Gebot das; ~[e]s, ~e (a) (Grundsatz) precept; **die Zehn ~e** (Rel.) the Ten Commandments
(b) (Vorschrift) regulation

geboten ① 2. Part. v. BIETEN, GEBIETEN;
② Adj. (ratsam) advisable; (notwendig) necessary

Gebr. Abk. = **Gebrüder** Bros.

gebrạcht 2. Part. v. BRINGEN

gebrạnnt 2. Part. v. BRENNEN

gebrạten 2. Part. v. BRATEN

Gebrauch der (a) use
(b) (Brauch) custom

gebrauchen tr. V. use

gebräuchlich Adj. (a) normal; customary
(b) (häufig) common

gebrauchs-, Gebrauchs-: ~anweisung die instructions pl. [for

---

use]; ∼**fertig** *Adj.* ready for use *pred.;*
∼**gegenstand** *der* item of practical use;
∼**wert** *der* utility value

gebraucht *Adj.* second-hand; used ‹*car*›

Gebraucht·wagen *der* used car

Gebrechen *das;* ∼s, ∼ (geh.) affliction

gebrechlich *Adj.* infirm

Gebrechlichkeit *die;* ∼: infirmity

gebrochen [1] *2. Part. v.* BRECHEN;
[2] *Adj.* ∼es Englisch/Deutsch broken
English/German
[3] *adv.* ∼ Deutsch sprechen speak broken
German

Gebrüder *Pl.:* die ∼ Meyer Meyer Brothers

Gebrüll *das;* ∼[e]s roaring

Gebrumm *das;* ∼[e]s (von Bären) growling;
(von Flugzeugen, Bienen) droning; (von Insekten)
buzz[ing]

gebückt *Adj.* in ∼er Haltung bending
forward

Gebühr *die;* ∼, ∼en charge; (Maut) toll;
(Anwalts∼) fee

gebühren (geh.) *itr. V.* jmdm. gebührt
Achtung *usw.* sb. deserves respect *etc.*

Gebühren·anzeiger *der* (Fernspr.)
telephone meter

gebührend [1] *Adj.* fitting
[2] *adv.* fittingly

gebühren-, Gebühren-:
∼**ermäßigung** *die* reduction of charges/
fees; ∼**frei** [1] *Adj.* free of charge *pred.;*
[2] *adv.* free of charge; ∼**pflichtig** *Adj.*
eine ∼pflichtige Verwarnung a fine and a
caution; ∼**vignette** *die* [Swiss] motorway
fee sticker

gebunden [1] *2. Part. v.* BINDEN;
[2] *Adj.* (verpflichtet) bound

Geburt *die;* ∼, ∼en birth

Geburten-: ∼**kontrolle** *die* birth
control; ∼**rate** *die* birth rate; ∼**ziffer** *die*
birth rate

gebürtig *Adj.* ein ∼er Schwabe a Swabian
by birth

Geburts-: ∼**anzeige** *die* birth
announcement; ∼**datum** *das* date of birth;
∼**haus** *das:* das ∼haus Beethovens the
house where Beethoven was born;
Beethoven's birthplace; ∼**helfer** *der,*
∼**helferin** *die* (Arzt, Ärztin) obstetrician;
∼**hilfe** *die* (Med.) obstetrics *sing.;* (von einer
Hebamme) midwifery; ∼**stadt** *die* native
town/city; ∼**ort** *der* place of birth; ∼**tag**
der birthday; jmdm. zum ∼tag gratulieren
wish sb. many happy returns of the day;
∼**ur·kunde** *die* birth certificate

Gebüsch *das;* ∼[e]s, ∼e bushes *pl.*

gedacht *2. Part. v.* DENKEN, GEDENKEN

Gedächtnis *das;* ∼ses, ∼se (a) memory
(b) (Andenken) memory

Gedächtnis-: ∼**lücke** *die* gap in one's
memory; ∼**schwund** *der* loss of memory

gedämpft *Adj.* subdued ‹*mood*›; subdued,
soft ‹*light*›; muffled ‹*sound*›

Gedanke *der;* ∼ns, ∼n (a) thought; der ∼
an etw. (*Akk.*) the thought of sth.
(b) *Pl.* (Meinung) ideas
(c) (Einfall) idea

gedanken-, Gedanken-: ∼**gang** *der*
train of thought; ∼**gut** *das* thought;
christliches ∼gut Christian thought;
staatszersetzendes ∼gut subversive ideas
pl.; ∼**los** [1] *Adj.* unconsidered; (zerstreut)
absent-minded; [2] *adv.* without thinking;
(zerstreut) absent-mindedly; ∼**losigkeit** *die;*
∼∼ (Zerstreutheit) absent-mindedness;
(Unüberlegtheit) lack of thought; ∼**strich** *der*
dash; ∼**verloren** *Adv.* lost in thought;
∼**voll** [1] *Adj.* pensive; [2] *adv.* pensively

gedanklich [1] *Adj.* intellectual
[2] *adv.* intellectually

Gedärm *das;* ∼[e]s, ∼e intestines *pl.;*
bowels *pl.,* (eines Tieres) entrails *pl.*

Gedeck *das;* ∼[e]s, ∼e (a) place setting;
cover
(b) (Menü) set meal
(c) (Getränk) drink [with a cover charge]

gedeihen *unr. itr. V.; mit sein* (a) thrive;
(wirtschaftlich) flourish; prosper
(b) (fortschreiten) progress

gedenken *unr. itr. V.* (a) jmds./einer
Sache ∼ (geh.) remember sb./sth.; (in einer
Feier) commemorate sb./sth.
(b) etw. zu tun ∼: intend to do *or* doing sth.

Gedenk·stätte *die* memorial

Gedicht *das;* ∼[e]s, ∼e poem

gediegen [1] *Adj.* solid ‹*furniture*›; sound
‹*piece of work*›
[2] *adv.* ∼ gebaut/verarbeitet solidly built/
made

gedieh *1. u. 3. Pers. Sg. Prät. v.* GEDEIHEN

gediehen *2. Part. v.* GEDEIHEN

Gedränge *das;* ∼s (a) pushing and
shoving; (Menge) crush; crowd
(b) ins ∼ kommen *od.* geraten get into
difficulties

gedroschen *2. Part. v.* DRESCHEN

gedrungen [1] *2. Part. v.* DRINGEN;
[2] *Adj.* stocky; thickset

Geduld *die;* ∼: patience

gedulden *refl. V.* be patient; ∼ Sie sich
bitte ein paar Minuten please be so good as
to wait a few minutes

geduldig [1] *Adj.* patient
[2] *adv.* patiently

Gedulds-: ∼**probe** *die* trial of one's
patience; ∼**spiel** *das* puzzle

gedurft *2. Part. v.* DÜRFEN

geeignet *Adj.* suitable; (richtig) right

Gefahr *die;* ∼, ∼en (a) danger; (Bedrohung)
danger; threat (für to); bei ∼: in case of
emergency
(b) (Risiko) risk; auf eigene ∼: at one's own
risk

gefährden *tr. V.* endanger; jeopardize
⟨*enterprise, success, position, etc.*⟩
gefährdet *Adj.* ⟨*people, adolescents, etc.*⟩ at
risk *postpos.*
Gefährdung *die;* ~, ~en **(a)** endangering;
(eines Unternehmens, einer Position usw.)
jeopardizing
(b) (Gefahr) threat (+ *Gen.* to)
gefahren *2. Part. v.* FAHREN
gefährlich 1 *Adj.* dangerous; (gewagt)
risky
2 *adv.* dangerously
gefahr·los 1 *Adj.* safe
2 *adv.* safely
Gefährt *das;* ~[e]s, ~e (geh.) vehicle
Gefährte *der;* ~n, ~n, **Gefährtin** *die;* ~,
~nen (geh.) companion; (Ehemann/Ehefrau)
partner in life
Gefälle *das;* ~s, ~: slope; incline; (einer
Straße) gradient
gefallen[1] *unr. itr. V.* **(a)** das gefällt mir
[gut] I like it [a lot]
(b) sich (*Dat.*) etw. ~ lassen put up with sth.
gefallen[2] *2. Part. v.* FALLEN, GEFALLEN
Gefallen[1] *der;* ~s, ~: favour
Gefallen[2] *das;* ~s pleasure
Gefallene *der; adj. Dekl.* soldier killed in
action; **die** ~n the fallen
Gefälle·strecke *die* incline
gefällig 1 *Adj.* **(a)** obliging; helpful
(b) (anziehend) pleasing; agreeable
⟨*programme, behaviour*⟩
2 *adv.* pleasingly; agreeably
Gefälligkeit *die;* ~, ~en favour
gefälligst *Adv.* (ugs.) kindly
gefangen *2. Part. v.* FANGEN
Gefangene *der/die; adj. Dekl.* prisoner
gefangen-: **~|halten, *~|nehmen
▶ FANGEN 1
Gefangenschaft *die;* ~, ~en captivity
Gefängnis *das;* ~ses, ~se **(a)** prison; gaol
(b) (Strafe) imprisonment
Gefängnis-: ~strafe *die* prison
sentence; ~wärter *der,* ~wärterin *die*
[prison] warder
Gefasel *das;* ~s (ugs. abwertend) twaddle
(coll.); drivel (derog.)
Gefäß *das;* ~es, ~e **(a)** vessel; container
(b) (Anat.) vessel
gefasst, *gefaßt *Adj.* **(a)** calm; composed
(b) in auf etw. (*Akk.*) [nicht] ~ sein [not] be
prepared for sth.
Gefecht *das;* ~[e]s, ~e battle
Gefieder *das;* ~s, ~: plumage; feathers *pl.*
gefiedert *Adj.* feathered
geflissentlich 1 *Adj.* deliberate
2 *adv.* deliberately
geflochten *2. Part. v.* FLECHTEN
geflogen *2. Part. v.* FLIEGEN

geflohen *2. Part. v.* FLIEHEN
geflossen *2. Part. v.* FLIESSEN
Geflügel *das;* ~s poultry
Geflügel·schere *die* poultry shears *pl.*
geflügelt *Adj.* winged ⟨*insect, seed*⟩; **ein**
~es Wort (fig.) a standard *or* familiar
quotation
gefochten *2. Part. v.* FECHTEN
Gefolge *das;* ~s, ~: entourage
Gefolgschaft *die;* ~, ~en: jmdm. ~
leisten obey *or* follow sb.; give one's
allegiance to sb.; jmdm. die ~ verweigern
refuse to obey *or* follow sb.; refuse to give
sb. one's allegiance
gefragt *Adj.* in great demand *postpos.;*
sought-after
gefräßig *Adj.* (abwertend) greedy
Gefreite *der; adj. Dekl.* (Milit.) lance
corporal (Brit.); private first class (Amer.);
(Marine) able seaman; (Luftw.) aircraftman first
class (Brit.); airman third class (Amer.)
gefressen *2. Part. v.* FRESSEN
gefrieren *unr. itr. V.; mit sein* freeze
gefrier-, Gefrier-: ~fach *das* freezing
compartment; ~punkt *der* freezing point;
~schrank *der* freezer; ~|trocknen *tr.*
V.; meist im Inf. u. 2. Part. freeze-dry;
~truhe *die* [chest] freezer
gefroren *2. Part. v.* FRIEREN, GEFRIEREN
gefrustet *Adj.* (ugs.) frustrated
Gefüge *das;* ~s, ~: structure
gefügig *Adj.* compliant; docile ⟨*animal*⟩
Gefühl *das;* ~s, ~e **(a)** sensation; feeling
(b) (Gemütsverfassung) feeling
gefühl-los *Adj.* **(a)** numb
(b) (herzlos, kalt) unfeeling
gefühls-, Gefühls-: ~betont *Adj.*
emotional; ~duselei *die;* ~~ (ugs.
abwertend) mawkishness; ~mäßig *Adj.*
emotional ⟨*reaction*⟩; ⟨*action*⟩ based on
emotion; ~regung *die* emotion
gefühl·voll 1 *Adj.* sensitive; (ausdrucksvoll)
expressive
2 *adv.* sensitively; expressively
gefüllt *2. Part. v.* FÜLLEN
gefunden *2. Part. v.* FINDEN; *s. auch*
FRESSEN B
Gegacker *das;* ~s **(a)** (dauerndes Gackern)
cackling
(b) (ugs.: Kichern) giggling
gegangen *2. Part. v.* GEHEN
gegeben *2. Part. v.* GEBEN
gegebenen·falls *Adv.* should the
occasion arise
gegen *Präp. mit Akk.* **(a)** against; ~ etw.
stoßen knock into sth.; **ein Mittel** ~ Krebs a
cure for cancer; ~ die Abmachung contrary
to the agreement
(b) ~ Abend/Morgen towards evening/dawn;
~ vier Uhr around 4 o'clock
(c) (im Vergleich zu) compared with

(d) (im Ausgleich für) for; ~ **Quittung** against a receipt

Gegen-: ~**angriff** der counter-attack; ~**argument** das counter-argument; ~**besuch** der return visit

Gegend die; ~, ~**en (a)** area **(b)** (Körperregion) region

Gegen-: ~**darstellung** die: eine ~darstellung [der Sache] an account [of the matter] from an opposing point of view; ~**druck** der counter pressure

gegen·einander Adv. against each other or one another

gegen-, Gegen-: ~**gewicht** das counterweight; ein ~gewicht zu od. gegen etw. bilden (fig.) counterbalance sth.; ~**gift** das antidote; ~**kandidat** der, ~**kandidatin** die opposing candidate; rival candidate; ~**leistung** die service in return; ~**mittel** das (gegen Gift) antidote; (gegen Krankheit) remedy; ~**partei** die opposing side; other side; (Sport) opposing side or team; ~**probe** die cross-check; ~**satz** der **(a)** (Gegenteil) opposite; **im** ~**satz zu** in contrast to or with; unlike **(b)** (Widerspruch) conflict; ~**sätzlich** Adj. conflicting; ~**schlag** der counterstroke; **zum** ~**schlag ausholen** prepare to counter-attack or strike back; ~**seite** die **(a)** (einer Straße, eines Flusses) other side; far side; **(b)** ▶ ~PARTEI; ~**seitig** ① Adj. (wechselseitig) mutual; ② adv. **sich** ~**seitig helfen/überbieten** help/outdo each other or one another; ~**seitigkeit** die; ~~: reciprocity; **auf** ~**seitigkeit** (Dat.) **beruhen** be mutual; ~**spieler** der, ~**spielerin** die opponent; (Sport) opposite number

Gegen·stand der object; (Thema) subject; topic

gegenständlich Adj. (Kunst) representational; (Philos.) objective

gegenstands·los Adj. **(a)** (hinfällig) invalid **(b)** (grundlos, unbegründet) unfounded ‹accusation, complaint, jealousy›; baseless ‹fear›

gegen-, Gegen-: ~**stimme** die vote against; **ohne** ~**stimme** unanimously; ~**stück** das companion piece; (fig.) counterpart; ~**teil** das opposite; **im** ~**teil** on the contrary; ~**teilig** Adj. opposite; contrary; ~**tor** das (Sport) goal for the other side

gegen·über Präp. mit Dat. **(a)** opposite **(b)** (in Bezug auf) ~ **jmdm.** od. **jmdm.** ~ **freundlich sein** be kind to sb. **(c)** (im Vergleich zu) compared with

gegenüber-, Gegenüber-: ~|**stehen** unr. itr. V. **(a)** jmdm./einer Sache ~stehen stand facing sb./sth.; (fig.) face sb./sth.; **(b)** jmdm./einer Sache feindlich/wohlwollend ~stehen be ill/well disposed towards sb./sth.; ~|**stellen** tr. V. confront; ~**stellung** die **(a)** confrontation; **(b)**

(Vergleich) comparison; **(c)** (zur Identifizierung) identification parade; ~|**treten** unr. itr. V.; **mit sein** jmdm./einer Sache ~treten (auch fig.) face sb./sth.

Gegen·verkehr der oncoming traffic

Gegenwart die; ~ **(a)** present **(b)** (Anwesenheit) presence **(c)** (Grammatik) present [tense]

gegenwärtig ① Adj. present ② adv. at present; at the moment

Gegen-: ~**wehr** die resistance; ~**wert** der equivalent; ~**wind** der head wind; ~**zug** der (Brettspiele, fig.) countermove

gegessen 2. Part. v. ESSEN

geglichen 2. Part. v. GLEICHEN

geglitten 2. Part. v. GLEITEN

Gegner der; ~s, ~, **Gegnerin** die; ~, ~nen **(a)** adversary; opponent **(b)** (Sport) opponent

gegnerisch Adj. opposing; opponents' ‹goal›

Gegnerschaft die; ~ (Einstellung) hostility; antagonism

gegolten 2. Part. v. GELTEN

gegoren 2. Part. v. GÄREN

gegossen 2. Part. v. GIESSEN

gegriffen 2. Part. v. GREIFEN

Gehabe das; ~s (abwertend) affected behaviour; **ihr wichtigtuerisches** ~: her pompous behaviour

gehabt Adj. (ugs.: schon da gewesen) same old (coll.); usual; **wie** ~: as before

Gehalt[1] der; ~[e]s, ~e **(a)** meaning **(b)** (Anteil) content

Gehalt[2] das (österr. auch: der); ~[e]s, **Gehälter** salary

gehalten 2. Part. v. HALTEN

Gehalts-: ~**abrechnung** die salary statement; payslip; ~**empfänger** der, ~**empfängerin** die salary earner; ~**erhöhung** die salary increase; ~**zettel** der salary slip

gehalt·voll Adj. nutritious ‹food›; ‹novel, speech› rich in substance

gehässig Adj. (abwertend) spiteful

Gehässigkeit die; ~, ~en **(a)** (Wesen) spitefulness **(b)** (Äußerung) spiteful remark

gehauen 2. Part. v. HAUEN

gehäuft Adj. **ein** ~**er Teelöffel/Esslöffel** a heaped teaspoon/tablespoon

Gehäuse das; ~s, ~ (einer Maschine) casing; housing; (einer Kamera, Uhr) case

geh·behindert Adj. able to walk only with difficulty postpos.; disabled

Gehege das; ~s, ~ **(a)** (Jägerspr.) preserve; **jmdm. ins** ~ **kommen** (fig.) poach on sb.'s preserve; **sich** (Dat.) **[gegenseitig] ins** ~ **kommen** (fig.) encroach on each other's territory **(b)** (im Zoo) enclosure

geheim ① *Adj.* **(a)** secret; **etw. ~ halten** keep sth. secret
(b) (mysteriös) mysterious
② *adv.* **~ abstimmen** vote by secret ballot
geheim-, Geheim-: **~agent** der, **~agentin** die secret agent; **~dienst** der secret service; **~|halten* ▶ GEHEIM 1A
Geheimnis das; ~ses, ~se secret
Geheimnis·tuerei die; ~ (ugs.) secretiveness
geheimnis·voll Adj. mysterious
Geheim·nummer die **(a)** (Bankw.) personal identification number; PIN
(b) (Telefonnummer) ex-directory number; unlisted number (Amer.)
Geheim·zahl die ▶ GEHEIMNUMMER A
Geheiß das: **auf jmds. ~** (geh.) at sb.'s behest
gehen ① unr. itr. V.; mit sein **(a)** walk; go; **über die Straße ~:** cross the street
(b) (sich irgendwohin begeben) go
(c) (regelmäßig besuchen) attend
(d) (weg~) go; leave
(e) (in Funktion sein) work; **meine Uhr geht falsch** my watch is wrong
(f) (möglich sein) **ja, das geht** yes, I/we can manage that; **das geht nicht** that can't be done
(g) (ugs.: gerade noch angehen) **Hast du gut geschlafen? – Es geht** Did you sleep well? – Not too bad
(h) (sich entwickeln) **der Laden/das Geschäft geht gut/gar nicht** the shop/business is doing well/not doing well at all; **es ist gut gegangen** it turned out well
(i) (unpers.) **wie geht es dir?** How are you?; **jmdm. geht es gut/schlecht** (gesundheitlich) sb. is well/not well; (geschäftlich) sb. is doing well/badly
(j) (unpers.) (sich um etw. handeln); **worum geht es hier?** what is this all about?
(k) sich ~ lassen (sich nicht beherrschen) lose control of oneself; (sich vernachlässigen) let oneself go
(l) (ein Liebespaar sein) **mit jmdm. ~:** go out with sb.
② unr. tr. V. (zurücklegen) **10 km ~:** walk 10 km
*gehen|lassen ▶ GEHEN 1K
geheuer Adj. **(a) in diesem Gebäude ist es nicht ~:** this building is eerie
(b) ihr war doch nicht [ganz] ~: she felt [a little] uneasy
(c) die Sache ist [mir] nicht ganz ~: [I feel] there's something odd about this business
Gehilfe der; ~n, ~n, **Gehilfin** die; ~, ~nen assistant
Gehirn das; ~[e]s, ~e brain
Gehirn-: **~erschütterung** die concussion; **~schlag** der stroke; **~wäsche** die brainwashing no indef. art.
gehoben ① 2. Part. v. HEBEN;

② *Adj.* **(a)** higher; senior ‹position›
(b) (gewählt) elevated, refined
geholfen 2. Part. v. HELFEN
Gehör das; ~[e]s [sense of] hearing; **[etw.] nach dem ~ singen/spielen** sing/play [sth.] by ear; **das absolute ~** (Musik) absolute pitch
gehorchen itr. V. jmdm. ~: obey sb.
gehören ① itr. V. **(a)** jmdm. ~: belong to sb.
(b) (Teil eines Ganzen sein) **zu jmdm. Freunden/Aufgaben ~:** be one of sb.'s friends/part of sb.'s duties
(c) (passend sein) **dein Roller gehört nicht in die Küche!** your scooter does not belong in the kitchen!
(d) (nötig sein) **es hat viel Fleiß dazu gehört** it took a lot of hard work; **dazu gehört sehr viel** that takes a lot
② refl. V. (sich schicken) be fitting; **es gehört sich [nicht], ... zu ...:** it is [not] good manners to ...
gehörig ① *Adj.* **(a)** proper
(b) (ugs.: beträchtlich) **ein ~er Schrecken/eine ~e Portion Mut** a good fright/a good deal of courage
② *adv.* (ugs.: beträchtlich) **~ essen/trinken** eat/drink heartily
gehorsam Adj. obedient
Gehorsam der; ~s obedience
Geh·steig der; ~[e]s, ~e pavement (Brit.); sidewalk (Amer.)
Geht·nicht·mehr das: **bis zum ~** (salopp) ad nauseam
Gehupe das; ~s honking; hooting
Geier der; ~s, ~: vulture
Geige die; ~, ~n violin
Geiger der; ~s, ~, **Geigerin** die; ~, ~nen violin player; violinist
Geiger·zähler der (Physik) Geiger counter
geil Adj. **(a)** (oft abwertend: sexuell erregt) randy; horny (sl.); (lüstern) lecherous
(b) (Jugendspr.) great (coll.); fabulous (coll.)
Geilheit die; ~ ▶ GEIL A randiness; horniness (sl.); lecherousness
Geisel die; ~, ~n hostage
Geisel-: **~nahme** die; ~, ~~n taking of hostages; **~nehmer** der; ~~s, ~~, **~nehmerin** die; ~~, ~~nen terrorist/guerrilla etc. holding the hostages
Geißel die; ~, ~n (hist., auch fig.) scourge
Geist der; ~[e]s, ~er **(a)** (Verstand) mind
(b) (Scharfsinn) wit
(c) (innere Einstellung) spirit
(d) (denkender Mensch) mind; intellect; **ein großer/kleiner ~:** a great mind/a person of limited intellect
(e) (überirdisches Wesen) spirit; **der Heilige ~** (christl. Rel.) the Holy Ghost or Spirit
(f) (Gespenst) ghost
Geister-: **~bahn** die ghost train; **~fahrer** der; **~fahrerin** die: person driving on the wrong side of the road or the wrong carriageway

geisterhaft *Adj.* ghostly; eerie ⟨*atmosphere*⟩

Geister·hand *die;* wie von *od.* durch ~: as if by an invisible hand

geistes-, Geistes-: ~**abwesend** ⓵ *Adj.* absent-minded; ⓶ *adv.* absent-mindedly; ~**blitz** *der* (ugs.) brainwave; ~**gegenwart** *die* presence of mind; ~**gegenwärtig** ⓵ *Adj.* quick-witted; ⓶ *adv.* with great presence of mind; ~**krank** *Adj.* mentally ill; ~**krankheit** *die* mental illness; ~**wissenschaften** *Pl.* arts; humanities; ~**wissenschaftler** *der,* ~**wissenschaftlerin** *die* arts scholar; scholar in the humanities; ~**zustand** *der* mental state

geistig ⓵ *Adj.* (a) intellectual; (Psych.) mental
(b) alcoholic ⟨*drinks*⟩
⓶ *adv.* intellectually; (Psych.) mentally

geistlich *Adj.* sacred ⟨*song, music*⟩; religious ⟨*order, book, writings*⟩

Geistliche *der; adj. Dekl.* clergyman

geist-, Geist-: ~**los** *Adj.* dim-witted; (trivial) trivial; ~**losigkeit** *die;* ~~: dim-wittedness; (Trivialität) triviality; ~**reich** ⓵ *Adj.* witty; (klug) clever; ⓶ *adv.:* wittily; cleverly; ~**tötend** *Adj.* soul-destroying ⟨*work, job*⟩; stupefyingly boring ⟨*chatter, drivel*⟩

Geiz *der;* ~es meanness; (Knauserigkeit) miserliness

geizen *itr. V.* be mean

Geiz·hals *der* (abwertend) skinflint

geizig *Adj.* mean; (knauserig) miserly

gekannt 2. *Part. v.* KENNEN

Gekicher *das;* ~s giggling

geklungen 2. *Part. v.* KLINGEN

geknickt *Adj.* (ugs.) dejected

gekniffen 2. *Part. v.* KNEIFEN

gekommen 2. *Part. v.* KOMMEN

gekonnt ⓵ 2. *Part. v.* KÖNNEN; ⓶ *Adj.* accomplished; (hervorragend ausgeführt) masterly

gekrochen 2. *Part. v.* KRIECHEN

gekünstelt ⓵ *Adj.* artificial
⓶ *adv.* er lächelte ~: he gave a forced smile

Gelächter *das;* ~s, ~: laughter

geladen 2. *Part. v.* LADEN

Gelände *das;* ~s, ~ (a) (Landschaft) ground; terrain
(b) (Grundstück) site; (von Schule, Krankenhaus usw.) grounds *pl.*

Geländer *das;* ~s, ~: banisters *pl.;* handrail; (am Balkon, an einer Brücke) railing[s *pl.*]; (aus Stein) parapet

gelang 3. *Pers. Sg. Prät. v.* GELINGEN

gelangen *itr. V.; mit sein* an etw. (Akk.)/zu etw. ~: reach sth.; (fig.) zu Ansehen ~: gain esteem

gelassen ⓵ 2. *Part. v.* LASSEN; ⓶ *Adj.* calm; (gefasst) composed

Gelassenheit *die;* ~: calmness; (Gefasstheit) composure

Gelatine /ʒelaˈtiːnə/ *die;* ~: gelatine

gelaufen 2. *Part. v.* LAUFEN

geläufig *Adj.* (vertraut) common ⟨*expression, concept*⟩

gelaunt *Adj.* gut ~: cheerful; schlecht ~: bad-tempered; gut/schlecht ~ sein be in a good/bad mood

gelb *Adj.* yellow

Gelb *das;* ~s, ~ *od.* (ugs.) ~s yellow

gelblich *Adj.* yellowish; yellowed ⟨*paper*⟩; sallow ⟨*skin*⟩

Gelb·sucht *die* (Med.) jaundice

Geld *das;* ~es, ~er money; großes ~: large denominations *pl.;* kleines/bares ~: change/cash

geld-, Geld-: ~**automat** *der* cash dispenser; ~**beutel** *der* (bes. südd.) purse; ~**börse** *die* purse; ~**buße** *die* fine; ~**gier** *die* avarice; ~**gierig** *Adj.* avaricious; ~**institut** *das* financial institution; ~**mangel** *der* lack of money; ~**mittel** *Pl.* financial resources; ~**preis** *der* cash prize; ~**rück·gabe** *die* (a) ~rückgabe verlangen ask for one's money back; Anspruch auf ~rückgabe haben be entitled to one's money back; (b) (eines Automaten) coin return; ~**schein** *der* banknote; bill (Amer.); ~**schrank** *der* safe; ~**schwierigkeiten** *Pl.* financial difficulties *or* straits; ~**spende** *die* donation; contribution; ~**strafe** *die* fine; ~**stück** *das* coin; ~**wechsel** *der* exchanging of money; „~wechsel" 'bureau de change'

Gelee /ʒeˈleː/ *der od. das;* ~s, ~s jelly

gelegen ⓵ 2. *Part. v.* LIEGEN; ⓶ *Adj.* (passend) convenient

Gelegenheit *die;* ~, ~en opportunity; (Anlass) occasion

Gelegenheits-: ~**arbeit** *die* casual work; ~**kauf** *der* bargain

gelegentlich ⓵ *Adj.* occasional
⓶ *adv.* occasionally

gelehrig *Adj.* ⟨*child*⟩ who is quick to learn; ⟨*animal*⟩ that is quick to learn

gelehrt *Adj.* learned

Gelehrte *der/die; adj. Dekl.* scholar

Geleit *das;* ~[e]s, ~e (geh.) sie bot uns ihr ~ an she offered to accompany us

geleiten *tr. V.* (geh.) escort

Geleit·schutz *der* (Milit.) escort

Gelenk *das;* ~[e]s, ~e joint

gelenkig ⓵ *Adj.* agile ⟨*person*⟩; supple ⟨*limb*⟩
⓶ *adv.* agilely

Gelenkigkeit *die;* ~: agility; (von Gliedmaßen) suppleness

gelernt *Adj.* qualified

gelesen 2. *Part. v.* LESEN

Geliebte *der/die; adj. Dekl.* lover/mistress

geliefert *Adj.:* ~ **sein** (salopp) have had it (coll.)

geliehen 2. *Part. v.* LEIHEN

gelind[e] ⓵ *Adj.* mild
⓶ *adv.* mildly; ~e **gesagt** to put it mildly

gelingen *unr. itr. V.; mit sein* succeed

Gelingen *das;* ~s success

gelitten 2. *Part. v.* LEIDEN

gellen *itr. V.* (a) (hell schallen) ring out
(b) (nachhallen) ring

geloben *tr. V.* (geh.) vow; **das Gelobte Land** the Promised Land

gelogen 2. *Part. v.* LÜGEN

gelöst *Adj.* relaxed

gelten ⓵ *unr. itr. V.* (a) (gültig sein) be valid; ⟨banknote, coin⟩ be legal tender; ⟨law etc.⟩ be in force
(b) (angesehen werden) **als etw.** ~: be regarded as sth.
(c) (+ *Dat.*) (bestimmt sein für) be directed at
⓶ *unr. tr. V.* (a) (wert sein) **sein Wort gilt viel/ wenig** his word carries a lot of/little weight
(b) *unpers.* **es gilt, etw. zu tun** it is essential to do sth.

geltend: etw. ~ **machen** assert sth.

Geltung *die;* ~ (a) (validity; **für jmdn.** ~ **haben** apply to sb.
(b) (Wirkung) recognition; **zur** ~ **kommen** show to [its best] advantage

Geltungs·bedürfnis *das* need for recognition

gelungen ⓵ 2. *Part. v.* GELINGEN;
⓶ *Adj.* (a) (ugs.: spaßig) priceless
(b) (ansprechend) inspired

gemächlich /ɡəˈmɛ(ː)çlɪç/ ⓵ *Adj.* leisurely
⓶ *adv.* in a leisurely manner

Gemächlichkeit *die;* ~: leisureliness

gemacht: ein ~**er Mann sein** (ugs.) be a made man

Gemahl *der;* ~s, ~e (geh.) consort; husband

Gemahlin *die;* ~, ~nen (geh.) consort; wife

Gemälde *das;* ~s, ~: painting

gemäß *Präp. + Dat.* in accordance with

gemäßigt *Adj.* moderate; qualified ⟨optimism⟩; temperate ⟨climate⟩

Gemecker[e] *das;* ~s (a) (von Schafen, Ziegen) bleating
(b) (ugs. abwertend: Nörgelei) griping (coll.); grousing (coll.); moaning

gemein ⓵ *Adj.* (a) vulgar ⟨joke, expression⟩; nasty ⟨person⟩
(b) (niederträchtig) mean; dirty ⟨lie⟩; mean ⟨trick⟩
⓶ *adv.* in a mean *or* nasty way

Gemeinde *die;* ~, ~n (a) municipality; (Bewohner) community
(b) (Pfarr~) parish
(c) (versammelte Gottesdienstteilnehmer) congregation

Gemeinde-: ~**rat** *der* (a) (Gremium) local council; (b) (Mitglied) local councillor;
~**rätin** *die* local councillor;
~**schwester** *die* district nurse;
~**verwaltung** *die* local administration

gemein·gefährlich *Adj.* dangerous to the public

Gemein·gut *das* (geh.) common property

Gemeinheit *die;* ~, ~en (a) meanness
(b) (Handlung) mean trick

gemein·nützig *Adj.* serving the public good *postpos., not pred.;* (wohltätig) charitable

gemeinsam ⓵ *Adj.* (a) common ⟨interests, characteristics⟩; mutual ⟨acquaintance, friend⟩; joint ⟨property, account⟩; shared ⟨experience⟩; ~**e Interessen/Merkmale haben** have interests/characteristics in common
(b) (miteinander unternommen) joint; **viel Gemeinsames haben** have a lot in common
⓶ *adv.* together

Gemeinsamkeit *die;* ~, ~en common feature

Gemeinschaft *die;* ~, ~en (a) community
(b) (Verbundenheit) coexistence

gemeinschaftlich ▶ GEMEINSAM

gemein·verständlich *Adj.* generally comprehensible

Gemein·wohl *das* public good

gemessen ⓵ 2. *Part. v.* MESSEN;
⓶ *Adj.* (würdevoll) measured ⟨steps, tones, language⟩; deliberate ⟨words, manner of speaking⟩

Gemetzel *das;* ~s, ~: massacre

gemieden 2. *Part. v.* MEIDEN

Gemisch *das;* ~[e]s, ~e mixture (**aus, von** of)

gemocht 2. *Part. v.* MÖGEN

gemolken 2. *Part. v.* MELKEN

***Gemse** ▶ GÄMSE

Gemurmel *das;* ~s murmuring

Gemüse *das;* ~s, ~: vegetables *pl.*

gemusst, * **gemußt** 2. *Part. v.* MÜSSEN

Gemüt *das;* ~[e]s, ~er (a) nature
(b) (Empfindungsvermögen) heart
(c) (Mensch) soul

gemütlich ⓵ *Adj.* snug; cosy; (bequem) comfortable; (ungezwungen) informal
⓶ *adv.* cosily; (bequem) comfortably; ~ **beisammensitzen** sit pleasantly together

Gemütlichkeit *die;* ~: snugness; (Zwanglosigkeit) informality

gemüts-, Gemüts-: ~**krank** *Adj.* (Med., Psych.) emotionally disturbed; ~**mensch** *der* (ugs.) even-tempered person

gemüt·voll *Adj.* warm-hearted; (empfindsam) sentimental

Gen *das;* ~s, ~e (Biol.) gene

genannt 2. *Part. v.* NENNEN

genas 1. *u.* 3. *Pers. Sg. Prät. v.* GENESEN

genau ⓵ *Adj.* (a) (exakt) exact; precise

(b) (sorgfältig, gründlich) meticulous; ⟨person⟩; careful ⟨study⟩
2 *adv.* **(a)** exactly; precisely; ∼ **um 8⁰⁰** at 8 o'clock precisely
(b) (gerade, eben) just
(c) (als Verstärkung) just
(d) (als Zustimmung) exactly; precisely
(e) (sorgfältig) ∼ **arbeiten/etw.** ∼ **durchdenken** work/think sth. out meticulously; ∼ **genommen** strictly speaking

*****genau·genommen** ▶ GENAU 2E
Genauigkeit *die;* ∼ **(a)** (Exaktheit) exactness; precision; (einer Waage) accuracy
(b) (Sorgfalt) meticulousness

genau·so *Adv.* **(a)** *mit Adjektiven* just as
(b) *mit Verben* in exactly the same way; (in demselben Maße) just as much

genaustens *Adv.* etw. ∼ **durchdenken/beachten** think sth. out/observe sth. most meticulously

Gendarm /ʒan'darm/ *der;* ∼**en,** ∼**en** (österr., sonst veralt.) village *or* local policeman *or* constable

Gendarmerie /ʒandarmə'riː/ *die;* ∼**,** ∼**n** (österr., sonst veralt.) village *or* local constabulary

genehm *Adj.* **jmdm.** ∼ **sein** (geh.) (jmdm. passen) be convenient to sb.; (jmdm. angenehm sein) be acceptable to sb.

genehmigen *tr. V.* approve ⟨plan, alterations, application⟩; authorize ⟨stay⟩; grant ⟨request⟩; give permission for ⟨demonstration⟩; **sich** (*Dat.*) **etw.** ∼ (ugs.) treat oneself to sth.

Genehmigung *die;* ∼**,** ∼**en (a)** ▶ GENEHMIGEN; approval; authorization; granting; permission (*Gen.* for)
(b) (Schriftstück) permit; (Lizenz) licence

geneigt *Adj.* **in** ∼ **sein, etw. zu tun** be inclined to do sth.

General *der;* ∼**s,** ∼**e** *od.* **Generäle** general
General-: ∼**direktor** *der* chairman; president (Amer.); ∼**direktorin** *die* chairwoman; president (Amer.)

generalisieren *tr., itr. V.* generalize
Generalisierung *die;* ∼**,** ∼**en** generalization
general-, General-: ∼**probe** *die* (auch fig.) dress rehearsal; ∼**streik** *der* general strike; ∼**überholen** *tr. V.; nur im Inf. und 2. Part. gebr.* (bes. Technik) **etw.** ∼**überholen** give sth. a general overhaul; ∼**vertreter** *der,* ∼**vertreterin** *die* general representative; ∼**vollmacht** *die* (Rechtsw.) full *or* unlimited power of attorney

Generation *die;* ∼**,** ∼**en** generation
Generations·konflikt *der* generation gap
Generator *der;* ∼**s,** ∼**en** generator
generell **1** *Adj.* general
2 *adv.* generally
genervt *Adj.* annoyed
genesen *unr. itr. V.; mit sein* (geh.) recover

Genesung *die;* ∼**,** ∼**en** (geh.) recovery
genetisch (Biol.) *Adj.* genetic
Genf (*das*); ∼**s** Geneva
Genfer **1** *der;* ∼**s,** ∼**:** Genevese
2 *Adj.* Genevese; **der** ∼ See Lake Geneva
Genferin *die;* ∼**,** ∼**nen** Genevese
Gen-forschung *die* (Biol.) genetic research
genial *Adj.* brilliant
Genialität *die;* ∼**:** genius
Genick *das;* ∼**[e]s,** ∼**e** back *or* nape of the neck
Genie /ʒe'niː/ *das;* ∼**s,** ∼**s** genius
genieren /ʒe'niːrən/ *refl. V.* be embarrassed
genießbar *Adj.* (essbar) edible; (trinkbar) drinkable; **er ist heute nicht** ∼ (fig. ugs.) he is unbearable today
genießen *unr. tr. V.* enjoy
Genießer *der;* ∼**s,** ∼**, Genießerin** *die;* ∼**,** ∼**nen: er ist ein richtiger Genießer** he is a regular 'bon viveur'; **sie ist eine stille Genießerin** she enjoys life [to the full] in her own quiet way
genießerisch **1** *Adj.* appreciative
2 *adv.* appreciatively; ⟨drink, eat⟩ with relish
Genitale *das;* ∼**s, Genitalien** /ɡeni'taːliən/, **Genital·organ** *das* genital organ
Genitiv *der;* ∼**s,** ∼**e** (Sprachw.) genitive [case]
Gen·manipulation *die* genetic manipulation
gen·manipuliert *Adj.* genetically engineered; genetically manipulated
Genom /ɡe'noːm/ *das;* ∼**s,** ∼**e** (Biol.) genome
genommen 2. *Part. v.* NEHMEN
genoss, *genoß 1. u. 3. Pers. Sg. Prät. v. GENIESSEN
Genosse *der;* ∼**n,** ∼**n** comrade
genossen 2. *Part. v.* GENIESSEN
Genossenschaft *die;* ∼**,** ∼**en** cooperative
Genossin *die;* ∼**,** ∼**nen** comrade
gen-, Gen-: ∼**technik** *die* genetic engineering *no art.;* ∼**technisch** **1** *Adj.* genetic engineering ⟨techniques, research etc.⟩; ⟨research, developments etc.⟩ in genetic engineering **2** *adv.* by genetic engineering; ∼**technisch verändert** genetically altered *or* modified; altered *or* modified by genetic engineering; ∼**technologie** *die* genetic engineering *no art.*
genug *Adv.* enough
genügen *itr. V.* **(a)** be enough
(b) einer Sache (*Dat.*) ∼**:** satisfy sth.
genügend **1** *Adj.* **(a)** enough
(b) (befriedigend) satisfactory
2 *adv.* enough
genügsam *Adj.* modest
Genugtuung /-tuːʊŋ/ *die;* ∼**,** ∼**en** satisfaction

Gẹnus *das;* ~, Gẹnera (Sprachw.) gender
Genuss, *Genuß *der;* Genụsses, Genụsse
(a) consumption
(b) (Wohlbehagen) **etw. mit** ~ **essen/lesen** eat
sth. with relish/enjoy reading sth.
genüsslich, *genüßlich *Adv. ‹eat,*
drink› with relish
gen·verändert *Adj.* genetically modified
Geograph *der;* ~en, ~en geographer
Geographie *die;* ~: geography *no art.*
Geographin *die;* ~, ~nen geographer
geographisch *Adj.* geographic[al]
Geologe *der;* ~n, ~n geologist
Geologie *die;* ~: geology *no art.*
Geologin *die;* ~, ~nen geologist
geologisch *Adj.* geological
Geometrie *die;* ~: geometry *no art.*
geometrisch *Adj.* geometric[al]
Gepäck *das;* ~[e]s luggage (Brit.); baggage
(Amer.); (am Flughafen) baggage
Gepäck-: ~**annahme** *die* (a) checking
in the luggage/baggage; (b) (Schalter) [in-
counter of the] luggage office (Brit.) *or*
baggage office (Amer.); (zur Aufbewahrung) [in-
counter of the] left-luggage office (Brit.) *or*
checkroom (Amer.); (am Flughafen) baggage
check-in; ~**aufbewahrung** *die* left-
luggage office (Brit.); checkroom (Amer.);
(Schließfächer) luggage lockers (Brit.); baggage
lockers (Amer.); ~**ausgabe** *die* [out-counter
of the] luggage office (Brit.) *or* (Amer.) baggage
office; (zur Aufbewahrung) [out-counter of the]
left-luggage office (Brit.) *or* (Amer.) checkroom;
(am Flughafen) baggage reclaim; ~**kontrolle**
die baggage check; ~**netz** *das* luggage rack
(Brit.); baggage rack (Amer.); ~**schalter** *der*
▶~ANNAHME B; ~**schein** *der* luggage
ticket (Brit.); baggage check (Amer.); ~**träger**
der (a) porter; (b) (am Fahrrad) carrier; rack
Gepard *der;* ~s, ~e cheetah
gepfeffert *Adj.* (ugs.) steep (coll.) *‹price,*
rent, etc.›
Gepfeife *das;* ~s (ugs. abwertend)
[continuous, tuneless] whistling
gepfiffen 2. *Part. v.* PFEIFEN
gepflegt *Adj.* (a) well-groomed; spruce
‹appearance›; neat *‹clothing›*
(b) (hochwertig) choice *‹food, drink›*
Gepflogenheit *die;* ~, ~en (geh.) custom;
(Gewohnheit) habit
Geplapper *das;* ~s (ugs., oft abwertend)
prattling
geplättet *Adj.* (salopp) flabbergasted
Gepolter *das;* ~s clatter
gepriesen 2. *Part. v.* PREISEN
Gequake *das;* ~s (ugs.) croaking; (von
Enten) quacking
Gequäke *das;* ~s (ugs.) bawling
gequält *Adj.* forced *‹smile, gaiety›;* pained
‹expression›

gequollen 2. *Part. v.* QUELLEN
gerade ①*Adj.* (a) straight; **etw.** ~ **biegen**
bend sth. straight; straighten sth. [out]; ~
stehen stand up straight
(b) (nicht schief) upright
(c) (aufrichtig) forthright; direct
(d) (Math.) even *‹number›*
②*Adv.* just; (direkt) right
Gerade *die;* ~, ~n; *auch adj. Dekl.* (Geom.)
straight line
gerade-: ~**aus** *Adv.* straight ahead;
~|**biegen** *unr. tr. V.* (ugs.: bereinigen)
straighten out; ~**heraus** /----'-/ (ugs.) *Adv.*
etw. ~heraus sagen say sth. straight out;
~**so** *Adv.* ~so groß/lang wie ...: just as big/
long as ...; ~|**stehen** *unr. itr. V.* (fig.:
einstehen) **für etw.** ~**stehen** accept
responsibility for sth.; ~**zu** *Adv.* really;
(beinahe) almost
gerad-, Gerad-: ~**linig** ①*Adj.* (a)
straight; direct, lineal *‹descent, descendant›*
(b) (aufrichtig) straightforward; ②*adv.*
(a) ~linig verlaufen run in a straight line
(b) (aufrichtig) ~linig handeln/denken be
straightforward; ~**linigkeit** *die;* ~~
(a) straightness; (b) (Aufrichtigkeit)
straightforwardness
gerammelt *Adv.* ~ **voll** (ugs.) [jam-]packed
(coll.); packed out (coll.)
Geranie /ge'ra:niə/ *die;* ~, ~n geranium
gerann 3. *Pers. Sg. Prät. v.* GERINNEN
gerannt 2. *Part. v.* RENNEN
gerät 3. *Pers. Sg. Präsens v.* GERATEN[1]
Gerät *das;* ~[e]s, ~e (a) piece of
equipment; (Fernseher, Radio) set; (Garten~)
tool
(b) (Turnen) piece of apparatus
geraten[1] *unr. itr. V.; mit sein* (a) (gelangen)
get
(b) (werden) turn out; (gut ~) turn out well
geraten[2] ①2. *Part. v.* RATEN, GERATEN[1]
②*Adj.* advisable
Geratewohl: aufs ~ (ugs.) *‹select›* at
random; **wir fuhren aufs** ~ **los** (ugs.) we went
for a drive just to see where we ended up
geraum *Adj.* (geh.) considerable
geräumig *Adj.* spacious *‹room›;* roomy
‹cupboard etc.›
Geräusch *das;* ~[e]s, ~e sound;
(unerwünscht) noise
geräusch-, Geräusch-: ~**arm** ①*Adj.*
quiet; ②*adv.* quietly; ~**los** ①*Adj.* silent
②*adv.* (a) silently; (b) (fig. ugs.) without
[any] fuss; ~**pegel** *der* noise level; ~**voll**
Adj. noisy
gerben *tr. V.* tan *‹hides, skins›*
gerecht ①*Adj.* just; (unparteiisch) fair
②*adv.* justly
gerechtfertigt *Adj.* justified
Gerechtigkeit *die;* ~: justice
Gerechtigkeits·sinn *der* sense of justice
Gerede *das;* ~s (abwertend) (a) (ugs.) talk
(b) (Klatsch) gossip

geregelt *Adj.* regular, steady ⟨*job*⟩

gereizt *Adj.* irritable

Gericht¹ *das;* ~[e]s, ~e court; (Richter) bench; (Gebäude) court [house]; **das Jüngste** ~ (Rel.) the Last Judgement

Gericht² *das;* ~[e]s, ~e dish

gerichtlich ① *Adj.* judicial; legal ⟨*proceedings*⟩ ② *adv.* jmdn. ~ **verfolgen** take sb. to court

Gerichts-: ~**hof** *der* Court of Justice; ~**kosten** *Pl.* legal costs; ~**saal** *der* courtroom; ~**verfahren** *das* legal proceedings *pl.;* **ein ~verfahren einleiten** institute legal *or* court proceedings; **ohne** ~**verfahren** without trial; ~**vollzieher** *der;* ~~s, ~~, ~**vollzieherin** *die;* ~~, ~~**nen** bailiff

gerieben 2. *Part. v.* REIBEN

geriffelt *Adj.* corrugated ⟨*surface, sheet metal*⟩; fluted ⟨*column*⟩; ribbed ⟨*glass*⟩

gering *Adj.* (a) low; little ⟨*value*⟩; small ⟨*quantity, amount*⟩; short ⟨*distance, time*⟩ (b) (unbedeutend) slight; minor ⟨*role*⟩; **nicht im Geringsten** not in the slightest *or* least; **jmdn./etw.** ~ **achten** *od.* **schätzen** have a low opinion of *or* think very little of sb./sth.; **den Erfolg/Reichtümer** ~ **achten** *od.* **schätzen** set little store by success/riches

geringfügig ① *Adj.* slight; minor ⟨*alteration, injury*⟩; trivial ⟨*amount, detail*⟩ ② *adv.* slightly

Geringfügigkeit *die;* ~, ~**en** triviality

*gering|schätzen ▶ GERING B

geringschätzig *Adj.* disdainful; disparaging ⟨*remark*⟩

gerinnen *unr. itr. V.; mit sein* ⟨*blood*⟩ clot; ⟨*milk*⟩ curdle

Gerippe *das;* ~s, ~: skeleton

gerippt *Adj.* ribbed; fluted ⟨*glass, column*⟩

gerissen ① 2. *Part. v.* REISSEN; ② *Adj.* (ugs.) crafty

geritten 2. *Part. v.* REITEN

geritzt *Adj.* (salopp) etw. **ist** ~: sth. is [all] settled; **ist** ~! will do! (coll.)

Germane *der;* ~n, ~n, **Germanin** *die;* ~, ~**nen** (hist.) ancient German; Teuton

germanisch *Adj.* (auch fig.) Germanic; Teutonic

Germanistik *die;* ~: German studies *pl.,* *no art.*

gern[e]; lieber, am liebsten *Adv.* (a) etw. ~ **tun** like *or* enjoy doing sth.; **er spielt lieber Tennis als Golf** he prefers playing tennis to golf; **etw.** ~/**am liebsten essen** like sth./like sth. best; **ja,** ~/**aber** ~: yes, of course; certainly! (b) (durchaus) **das glaube ich** ~: I can well believe that

gerochen 2. *Part. v.* RIECHEN

Geröll *das;* ~s, ~e debris; (größer) boulders *pl.*

geronnen 2. *Part. v.* RINNEN, GERINNEN

Gerste *die;* ~: barley

Gersten·korn *das* (Med.) sty

Gerte *die;* ~, ~n switch

Geruch *der;* ~[e]s, **Gerüche** smell; (von Blumen) scent

Gerücht *das;* ~[e]s, ~e rumour

gerufen 2. *Part. v.* RUFEN

geruhsam ① *Adj.* peaceful; leisurely ⟨*stroll*⟩ ② *adv.* leisurely; quietly

Geruhsamkeit *die;* ~: peacefulness; (eines Spaziergangs) leisureliness

Gerümpel *das;* ~s junk

gerungen 2. *Part. v.* RINGEN

Gerüst *das;* ~[e]s, ~e scaffolding *no pl., no indef. art.*

gesamt *Adj.* whole; entire

gesamt-, Gesamt-: ~**deutsch** *Adj.* all-German; ~**eindruck** *der* general impression

Gesamtheit *die:* **die** ~ **der Bevölkerung** the entire population

Gesamt-: ~**schule** *die* comprehensive [school]; ~**werk** *das* œuvre; (Bücher) complete works *pl.*

gesandt 2. *Part. v.* SENDEN

Gesandte *der/die; adj. Dekl.* envoy

Gesandtschaft *die;* ~, ~**en** legation

Gesang *der;* ~[e]s, **Gesänge** (a) singing (b) (Lied) song

Gesang-: ~**buch** *das* hymn book; ~**verein** *der* choral society

Gesäß *das;* ~es, ~e backside; buttocks *pl.*

geschaffen 2. *Part. v.* SCHAFFEN 1

Geschäft *das;* ~[e]s, ~e (a) business; (Transaktion) [business] deal; **mit jmdm.** ~**e/ein** ~ **machen** do business with sb./strike a bargain *or* do a deal with sb.; **ein gutes** ~ **machen** make a good profit (b) (Laden) shop; store (Amer.)

Geschäfte·macher *der,* **Geschäfte·macherin** *die* (abwertend) profit-seeker

geschäftig *Adj.* bustling

geschäftlich ① *Adj.* business *attrib.* ② *adv.* on business

geschäfts-, Geschäfts-: ~**bedingungen** *Pl.* terms [and conditions] of trade; ~**brief** *der* business letter; ~**frau** *die* businesswoman; ~**freund** *der,* ~**freundin** *die* business associate; ~**führer** *der* manager; (Vereinswesen) secretary; ~**führerin** *die* ▶ ~FÜHRER: manageress; secretary; ~**führung** *die* management; ~**gebaren** *das* business *no art.;* business practices *pl.;* ~**inhaber** *der,* ~**inhaberin** *die* owner of the/a business; ~**jahr** *das* financial year; ~**kosten** *Pl.* **auf** ~**kosten** on expenses; ~**lage** *die* [business] position; ~**leitung** *die* ▶ ~FÜHRUNG; ~**leute** ▶ ~MANN; ~**mann** *der; Pl.* ~**leute** businessman; ·····⟩

~ordnung die standing orders pl.; (im Parlament) [rules pl. of] procedure; **~partner** der, **~partnerin** die business partner; **~reise** die business trip; **~schluss** der closing time; **~stelle** die branch; (einer Partei, eines Vereins) office; **~straße** die shopping street; **~tüchtig** Adj. able, ⟨businessman, landlord, etc.⟩; **~viertel** das business quarter; (Einkaufszentrum) shopping district; **~wagen** der company car; **~zeit** die business hours pl.; (im Büro) office hours pl.

geschah 3. Pers. Sg. Prät. v. GESCHEHEN

geschehen unr. itr. V.; mit sein happen; occur; (ausgeführt werden) be done; **jmdm. geschieht etw.** sth. happens to sb.

gescheit Adj. (a) (intelligent) clever (b) (ugs.: vernünftig) sensible

Gescheitheit die; ~: cleverness

Geschenk das; ~[e]s, ~e present; gift

Geschenk-: **~artikel** der gift; **~packung** die gift pack

Geschichte die; ~, ~n (a) history (b) (Erzählung) story

geschichtlich Adj. (a) historical (b) (bedeutungsvoll) historic

Geschichts-: **~atlas** der historical atlas; **~buch** das history book

Geschick¹ das; ~[e]s, ~e (geh.) fate

Geschick² das; ~[e]s skill

Geschicklichkeit die; ~: skilfulness; skill

geschickt [1] Adj. (a) skilful (b) (klug) clever; adroit [2] adv. (a) (gewandt) skilfully (b) (klug) cleverly; adroitly

geschieden 2. Part. v. SCHEIDEN

geschienen 2. Part. v. SCHEINEN

Geschirr das; ~[e]s, ~e (a) crockery; (benutzt) dishes pl.; (b) (für Zugtier) harness

Geschirr-: **~spül·maschine** die dishwasher; **~tuch** das; Pl. ~tücher tea towel; dish towel (Amer.)

geschissen 2. Part. v. SCHEISSEN

geschlafen 2. Part. v. SCHLAFEN

geschlagen 2. Part. v. SCHLAGEN

Geschlecht das; ~[e]s, ~er (a) sex (b) (Generation) generation (c) (Sippe) family (d) (Sprachw.) gender

geschlechtlich Adj. sexual

geschlechts-, Geschlechts-: **~akt** der sex[ual] act; **~chromosom** das (Biol.) sex chromosome; **~krank** Adj. ⟨person⟩ suffering from VD; **~krankheit** die venereal disease; **~organ** das sex[ual] organ; genital organ; **~teil** das genitals pl.; **~verkehr** der sexual intercourse; **~wort** das ▶ ARTIKEL A

geschlichen 2. Part. v. SCHLEICHEN

geschliffen [1] 2. Part. v. SCHLEIFEN; [2] Adj. polished

geschlossen [1] 2. Part. v. SCHLIESSEN; [2] Adj. united ⟨action, front⟩; unified ⟨procedure⟩; **eine ~e Ortschaft** a built-up area

Geschlossenheit die; ~: unity

geschlungen 2. Part. v. SCHLINGEN

Geschmack der; ~[e]s, Geschmäcke taste

geschmacklos [1] Adj. tasteless [2] adv. tastelessly

Geschmacklosigkeit die; ~, ~en lack of [good] taste; bad taste; (Äußerung) tasteless remark

Geschmack[s]·sache die **das ist ~:** that is a question or matter of taste

geschmack·voll [1] Adj. tasteful [2] adv. tastefully

Geschmatze das; ~s (ugs. abwertend) smacking one's lips no art.; (beim Essen) noisy eating no art.

Geschmeide das; ~s, ~ (geh.) jewellery no pl.

geschmeidig [1] Adj. (a) sleek ⟨hair, fur⟩; soft ⟨leather, boots, skin⟩ (b) (gelenkig) supple ⟨fingers⟩; lithe ⟨body, movement, person⟩ [2] adv. (gelenkig) agilely

Geschmeidigkeit die; ~: ▶ GESCHMEIDIG 1: sleekness; suppleness; softness; litheness

geschmissen 2. Part. v. SCHMEISSEN

geschmolzen 2. Part. v. SCHMELZEN

Geschmuse das; ~s (ugs.) cuddling; (eines Pärchens) kissing and cuddling

Geschnetzelte das; adj. Dekl.: small, thin slices of meat [cooked in sauce]

geschnitten 2. Part. v. SCHNEIDEN

geschoben 2. Part. v. SCHIEBEN

geschollen 2. Part. v. SCHALLEN

gescholten 2. Part. v. SCHELTEN

Geschöpf das; ~[e]s, ~e creature

geschoren 2. Part. v. SCHEREN

Geschoss¹, *Geschoß das; Geschosses, Geschosse projectile; (Kugel) bullet; (Rakete) missile

Geschoss², *Geschoß das; Geschosses, Geschosse floor; storey

geschossen 2. Part. v. SCHIESSEN

geschraubt Adj. (ugs.) stilted

Geschrei das; ~s (a) shouting; (von Verletzten, Tieren) screaming; screams pl.; (b) (ugs. fig) fuss

geschrieben 2. Part. v. SCHREIBEN

geschrie[e]n 2. Part. v. SCHREIEN

geschritten 2. Part. v. SCHREITEN

geschunden 2. Part. v. SCHINDEN

Geschütz das; ~es, ~e [big] gun

Geschütz·feuer das artillery fire; shell fire

geschützt Adj. (a) sheltered

---

*alte Schreibung - vgl. Hinweis auf S. xiv

(b) (unter Naturschutz) protected
(c) ~er Geschlechtsverkehr sex with a condom
Geschwader das; ~s, ~ (Marine) squadron; (Luftwaffe) wing (Brit.); group (Amer.)
Geschwätz das; ~es (ugs. abwertend) prattling; (Klatsch) gossip
geschwätzig Adj. (abwertend) talkative
geschweige Konj. ~ [denn] let alone; never mind
geschwiegen 2. Part. v. SCHWEIGEN
geschwind (bes. südd.) 1 Adj. swift; quick 2 adv. swiftly; quickly
Geschwindigkeit die; ~, ~en speed
Geschwindigkeits-: ~begrenzung die, ~beschränkung die speed limit
Geschwister Pl. brothers and sisters
geschwollen 1 2. Part. v. SCHWELLEN; 2 Adj. (a) swollen (b) (fig. abwertend) pompous 3 adv. pompously
geschwommen 2. Part. v. SCHWIMMEN
geschworen 2. Part. v. SCHWÖREN
Geschworene der/die; adj. Dekl. juror
Geschwulst die; ~, Geschwülste tumour
geschwunden 2. Part. v. SCHWINDEN
geschwungen 1 2. Part. v. SCHWINGEN; 2 Adj. curved
Geschwür das; ~s, ~e ulcer; (Furunkel) boil
gesehen 2. Part v. SEHEN
Geseire das; ~s (ugs.) drivel
Geselle der; ~n, ~n journeyman; (Kerl) fellow
gesellen refl. V. sich zu jmdm. ~: join sb.
gesellig Adj. sociable; ein ~er Abend/~es Beisammensein a convivial evening/a friendly get-together
Geselligkeit die; ~: die ~ lieben enjoy [good] company
Gesellin die; ~, ~nen journeyman; journeywoman (rare)
Gesellschaft die; ~, ~en (a) society (b) (Veranstaltung) party (c) (Kreis von Menschen) group of people (d) (Wirtschaft) company
Gesellschafter der; ~s, ~ (a) ein guter ~ sein be good company (b) (Wirtsch.) partner; (Teilhaber) shareholder
Gesellschafterin die; ~, ~nen (a) [lady] companion (b) (Wirtsch.) partner; (Teilhaberin) shareholder
gesellschaftlich Adj. social
gesellschafts-, Gesellschafts-: ~fähig Adj. (auch fig.) socially acceptable; ~ordnung die social order; ~reise die group tour; ~schicht die stratum of society; ~spiel das party game
gesessen 2. Part. v. SITZEN
Gesetz das; ~es, ~e (a) law; (geschrieben) statute (b) (Regel) rule

gesetz-, Gesetz-: ~buch das statute book; ~gebend Adj. legislative; ~geber der legislator; (Organ) legislature; ~gebung die; ~: legislation
gesetzlich 1 Adj. legal; statutory ⟨holiday⟩; lawful ⟨heir, claim⟩ 2 adv. legally
gesetz-, Gesetz-: ~los Adj. lawless; ~losigkeit die; ~: lawlessness; ~mäßig 1 Adj. (a) law-governed; ~mäßig sein be governed by or obey a [natural] law/[natural] laws; (b) (gesetzlich) legal; (rechtmäßig) lawful; 2 adv. in accordance with a [natural] law/[natural] laws; ~mäßigkeit die (a) conformity to a [natural] law/[natural] laws; (b) (Gesetzlichkeit) legality; (Rechtmäßigkeit) lawfulness
gesetzt Adj. staid
Gesetztheit die; ~: staidness
gesetz·widrig Adj. illegal; unlawful
Gesetz·widrigkeit die illegality; unlawfulness
Gesicht das; ~[e]s, ~er face; (fig.) das ~ einer Stadt the appearance of a town
Gesichts-: ~ausdruck der expression; look; ~creme die face cream; ~punkt der point of view; ~wasser das face lotion; ~züge Pl. features
Gesindel das; ~s (abwertend) rabble
gesinnt Adj. christlich/sozial ~ [sein] [be] Christian-minded/public-spirited; jmdm. freundlich ~ sein be well-disposed towards sb.
Gesinnung die; ~, ~en [basic] convictions pl.; [fundamental] beliefs pl.
gesinnungs-, Gesinnungs-: ~los (abwertend) Adj. unprincipled; ~wandel der change of attitude
gesittet Adj. well-behaved; well-mannered
gesogen 2. Part. v. SAUGEN
gesondert 1 Adj. separate 2 adv. separately
gesonnen Adj. ~ sein, etw. zu tun feel disposed to do sth.
gesotten 2. Part. v. SIEDEN
Gespann das; ~[e]s, ~e (a) (Zugtiere) team (b) (Wagen) horse and carriage (c) (Menschen) couple; pair
gespannt Adj. (a) eager; rapt ⟨attention⟩; ~ zuhören listen with rapt attention (b) tense ⟨situation, atmosphere⟩; strained ⟨relationships⟩
Gespenst das; ~[e]s, ~er (a) ghost (b) (geh.: Gefahr) spectre
gespenstig, gespenstisch Adj. ghostly; eerie ⟨building, atmosphere⟩
gespie[e]n 2. Part. v. SPEIEN
gesponnen 2. Part. v. SPINNEN
Gespött das; ~[e]s mockery; ridicule
Gespräch das; ~[e]s, ~e conversation; (Diskussion) discussion; (Telefon~) call (mit to)

gesprächig *Adj.* talkative

Gesprächs-: ~**partner** *der*,
~**partnerin** *die:* wer war dein ~partner/
deine ~partnerin? who were you talking to?;
~**stoff** *der* topics *pl.* of conversation;
~**thema** *das* topic of conversation

gesprochen 2. *Part. v.* SPRECHEN

gesprossen 2. *Part. v.* SPRIESSEN

gesprungen 2. *Part. v.* SPRINGEN

Gespür *das;* ~s feel

gest. *Abk.* = **gestorben** d.

Gestalt *die;* ~, ~en (a) build
(b) (Mensch, Persönlichkeit) figure
(c) (in der Dichtung) character
(d) (Form) form

gestalten *tr. V.* fashion; lay out ⟨*public gardens*⟩; shape ⟨*character, personality*⟩; arrange ⟨*party, conference, etc.*⟩

Gestaltung *die;* ~, ~en ▶ GESTALTEN: fashioning; laying out; arranging

gestand 1. *u.* 3. *Pers. Sg. Prät. v.* GESTEHEN

gestanden ① 2. *Part. v.* STEHEN, GESTEHEN;
② *Adj.* ein ~er Mann a grown man; ein ~er Parlamentarier an experienced *or* seasoned parliamentarian

geständig *Adj.:* ~ sein have confessed

Geständnis *das;* ~ses, ~se confession

Gestank *der;* ~[e]s (abwertend) stench; stink

Gestapo *die;* ~ (ns.) Gestapo

gestatten ① *tr., itr. V.* permit; allow; ~ Sie, dass ich ...: may I ...?
② *refl. V.* sich (*Dat.*) etw. ~: allow oneself sth.

Geste /'ɡɛstə, 'ɡeːstə/ *die;* ~, ~n (auch fig.) gesture

Gesteck *das;* ~[e]s, ~e flower arrangement

gestehen *tr., itr. V.* confess

Gestein *das;* ~[e]s, ~e rock

Gestell *das;* ~[e]s, ~e (a) (für Weinflaschen) rack; (zum Wäschetrocknen) horse
(b) (Unterbau) frame

gestern *Adv.* yesterday

gestiegen 2. *Part. v.* STEIGEN

gestikulieren *itr. V.* gesticulate

Gestirn *das;* ~[e]s, ~e star

gestochen ① 2. *Part. v.* STECHEN;
② *Adj.* extremely neat ⟨*handwriting*⟩

gestohlen 2. *Part. v.* STEHLEN

Gestöhne *das;* ~s groaning

gestorben 2. *Part. v.* STERBEN

gestoßen 2. *Part. v.* STOSSEN

Gestrampel *das;* ~s (ugs.) kicking about; (beim Radfahren) pedalling

Gesträuch *das;* ~[e]s, ~e shrubbery; bushes *pl.*

gestreift *Adj.* striped

gestrichen ① 2. *Part. v.* STREICHEN;
② *Adj.* level ⟨*measure*⟩

gestrig *Adj.* yesterday's

gestritten 2. *Part. v.* STREITEN

Gestrüpp *das;* ~[e]s, ~e undergrowth

gestunken 2. *Part. v.* STINKEN

Gestüt *das;* ~[e]s, ~e stud [farm]

Gesuch *das;* ~[e]s, ~e request (um for); (Antrag) application (um for)

gesucht *Adj.* (a) [much] sought-after
(b) (gekünstelt) laboured

gesund; gesünder, *seltener:* ~er, gesündest..., *seltener:* ~est... *Adj.* healthy; wieder ~ werden get better; bleib ~! look after yourself!

gesunden *itr. V.; mit sein* ⟨*person*⟩ recover

Gesundheit *die;* ~: health; ~! (ugs.) bless you!

gesundheitlich ① *Adj.; nicht präd.* ~e Betreuung health care; sein ~er Zustand [the state of] his health
② *adv.* wie geht es Ihnen ~? how are you?

gesundheits-, Gesundheits-: ~**amt** *das* [local] public health department;
~**gefährdend** *Adj.* ~gefährdend sein be a danger to health; ~gefährdende Bakterien/ Produkte bacteria that are a danger to health/products that are a health risk;
~**gefährdung** *die* risk to health;
~**schädlich** *Adj.* detrimental to [one's] health *postpos.*; ~**system** *das* health-care system; ~**vorsorge** *die* health care;
~**zeugnis** *das* certificate of health;
~**zustand** *der* state of health

gesungen 2. *Part. v.* SINGEN

gesunken 2. *Part. v.* SINKEN

getan 2. *Part. v.* TUN

Getöse *das;* ~s [thunderous] roar; (von vielen Menschen) din

getragen 2. *Part. v.* TRAGEN

Getränk *das;* ~[e]s, ~e drink; beverage (formal)

getrauen *refl. V.* dare

Getreide *das;* ~s grain

Getreide-: ~**anbau** *der* growing of cereals; ~**handel** *der* corn trade

getrennt ① *Adj.* separate
② *adv.* ⟨*pay*⟩ separately; ⟨*sleep*⟩ in separate rooms

getreten 2. *Part. v.* TRETEN

getreu ① *Adj.* (geh.) exact; faithful ⟨*image*⟩
② *adv.* (geh.) ⟨*report, describe*⟩ faithfully

Getriebe *das;* ~s, ~: gears *pl.;* (in einer Maschine) gear system

getrieben 2. *Part. v.* TREIBEN

getroffen 2. *Part. v.* TREFFEN, TRIEFEN

getrogen 2. *Part. v.* TRÜGEN

getrost ① *Adj.* confident
② *adv.* confidently; du kannst es mir ~ glauben you can take my word for it

getrunken 2. *Part. v.* TRINKEN

Getto *das;* ~s, ~s ghetto

Getue *das;* ~s (ugs. abwertend) fuss (**um** about)

Getümmel *das;* ~s tumult

geübt *Adj.* accomplished; practised ⟨*eye, ear*⟩

Gewächs *das;* ~es, ~e plant

gewachsen 1 *2. Part. v.* WACHSEN; 2 jmdm./einer Sache ~ sein be a match for sb./be equal to sth.

gewagt *Adj.* daring; (gefährlich) risky; (fast anstößig) risqué ⟨*joke etc.*⟩

gewählt 1 *Adj.* refined 2 *adv.* in a refined manner

Gewähr *die;* ~: guarantee; keine ~ übernehmen be unable to guarantee sth.

gewähren *tr. V.* grant; give ⟨*pleasure, joy*⟩

gewähr·leisten *tr. V.* guarantee

Gewahrsam *der;* ~s (a) (Obhut) safe-keeping
(b) (Haft) custody

Gewährs·mann *der; Pl.* ~männer *od.* ~leute, **Gewährs·person** *die* informant; source

Gewalt *die;* ~, ~en (a) power
(b) (Willkür) force
(c) (körperliche Kraft) force; violence

gewalt-, Gewalt-: ~**akt** *der* act of violence; ~**anwendung** *die* use of force *or* violence ~**bereit** *Adj.* ⟨*person*⟩ prone to violence; ⟨*group, organization*⟩ prepared to resort to *or* use violence; ~**bereitschaft** *die: s.* ~BEREIT: propensity to violence; willingness to resort to *or* use violence

Gewalten·teilung *die* separation of powers

gewaltig 1 *Adj.* (a) (immens) huge
(b) (imponierend) mighty, huge, massive ⟨*building etc*⟩; monumental ⟨*literary work etc.*⟩
2 *adv.* (ugs.) very much

gewalt·los 1 *Adj.* non-violent
2 *adv.* without violence

Gewalt·losigkeit *die;* ~: non-violence

gewaltsam 1 *Adj.* forcible ⟨*expulsion*⟩; enforced ⟨*separation*⟩; violent ⟨*death*⟩
2 *adv.* forcibly

gewalt·tätig *Adj.* violent

Gewalt·tätigkeit *die* (a) (gewalttätige Art) violence
(b) ▶ GEWALTAKT

Gewand *das;* ~[e]s, Gewänder (geh.) robe; gown

gewandt 1 *2. Part. v.* WENDEN;
2 *Adj.* skilful; (körperlich) agile
3 *adv.* skilfully; (körperlich) agilely

Gewandtheit *die;* ~: ▶ GEWANDT 2: skill; skilfulness; agility

gewann *1. u. 3. Pers. Sg. Prät. v.* GEWINNEN

gewaschen *2. Part. v.* WASCHEN

Gewässer *das;* ~s, ~: stretch of water

Gewebe *das;* ~s, ~ (a) (Stoff) fabric
(b) (Med., Biol.) tissue

Gewehr *das;* ~[e]s, ~e rifle; (Schrot~) shotgun

Geweih *das;* ~[e]s, ~e antlers *pl.*

Gewerbe *das;* ~s, ~: business; (Handel, Handwerk) trade

Gewerbe-: ~**freiheit** *die* right to carry on a business *or* trade; ~**ordnung** *die* laws *pl.* governing trade and industry; ~**schein** *der* licence to carry on a business *or* trade; ~**treibende** *der/die; adj. Dekl.* tradesman/tradeswoman; ~**zweig** *der* branch of trade

gewerblich 1 *Adj.* commercial; business *attrib.;* (industriell) industrial
2 *adv.* ~ tätig sein work

gewerbs·mäßig *Adj.* professional

Gewerkschaft *die;* ~, ~en trade union

Gewerkschaft[l]er *der;* ~s, ~, **Gewerkschaft[l]erin** *die;* ~, ~nen trade unionist

gewerkschaftlich 1 *Adj.* [trade] union *attrib.;*
2 *adv.* ~ organisiert sein belong to a [trade] union

Gewerkschafts·funktionär *der,* **Gewerkschafts·funktionärin** *die* [trade] union official

gewesen *2. Part. v.* SEIN[1]

gewichen *2. Part. v.* WEICHEN

Gewicht *das;* ~[e]s, ~e (auch fig.) weight; [nicht] ins ~ fallen be of [no] consequence

Gewicht·heben *das;* ~s weightlifting

gewichtig *Adj.* weighty

Gewichts·klasse *die* (Sport) weight [division *or* class]

gewieft *Adj.* (ugs.) cunning

gewiesen *2. Part. v.* WEISEN

gewillt *Adj.* in [nicht] ~ sein, etw. zu tun be [un]willing to do sth.

Gewimmel *das;* ~s throng; (von Insekten) teeming mass

Gewinde *das;* ~s, ~ (Technik) thread

Gewinn *der;* ~[e]s, ~e (a) profit
(b) (Preis einer Lotterie) prize; (beim Spiel) winnings *pl.;*
(c) (Sieg) win

Gewinn·beteiligung *die* (Wirtsch.) profit sharing; (Betrag) profit-sharing bonus

gewinn·bringend *Adj.* lucrative

gewinnen 1 *unr. tr. V.* win; gain ⟨*time, influence, validity, etc.*⟩
2 *unr. itr. V.* win (**bei** at)

gewinnend *Adj.* winning

Gewinner *der;* ~s, ~, **Gewinnerin** *die;* ~, ~nen winner

Gewinn-: ~**quote** *die* share of prize money; ~**spanne** *die* profit margin; ~**sucht** *die* greed for profit

Gewinnung *die;* ~ (a) (von Kohle, Erz usw.) mining; extraction; (von Öl) recovery; (von Metall aus Erz) extraction
(b) (Erzeugung) production

Gewinn·zahl *die* winning number

Gewirr *das;* ~[e]s (a) tangle   ···⊱

(b) (Durcheinander) ein ∼ von Ästen a maze of branches

gewiss, *gewiß ①*Adj.* certain ②*adv.* certainly

Gewissen *das;* ∼s, ∼: conscience

gewissenhaft ①*Adj.* conscientious ②*adv.* conscientiously

gewissen·los *Adj.* unscrupulous

Gewissens·bisse *Pl.* pangs of conscience

gewissermaßen *Adv.* (sozusagen) as it were; (in gewissem Sinne) to a certain extent

Gewissheit, *Gewißheit *die;* ∼, ∼en certainty

Gewitter *das;* ∼s, ∼: thunderstorm

Gewitter·wolke *die* thundercloud

gewittrig *Adj.* thundery

gewitzt *Adj.* shrewd

gewoben *2. Part. v.* WEBEN

gewogen ①*2. Part. v.* WIEGEN ②*Adj.* (geh.) well disposed (+ *Dat.* towards)

gewöhnen ①*tr. V.* jmdn. an jmdn./etw. ∼: get sb. used to sb./sth.; accustom sb. to sb./sth. ②*refl. V.* sich an jmdn./etw. ∼: get used *or* get *or* become accustomed to sb./sth.; accustom oneself to sb./sth.

Gewohnheit *die;* ∼, ∼en habit

gewohnheits-, Gewohnheits-: ∼mäßig ①*Adj.* habitual ⟨*drinker etc.*⟩; automatic ⟨*reaction etc.*⟩; ②*adv.* (regelmäßig) habitually; ∼mensch *der* creature of habit; ∼tier *das* (scherzh.) creature of habit; ∼trinker *der,* ∼trinkerin *die* habitual drinker; ∼verbrecher *der,* ∼verbrecherin *die* (Rechtsw.) habitual criminal

gewöhnlich ①*Adj.* (a) normal; ordinary **(b)** (gewohnt, üblich) usual **(c)** (abwertend: ordinär) common ②*adv.* (a) [für] ∼: usually; wie ∼: as usual **(b)** (abwertend: ordinär) in a common way

gewohnt *Adj.* (a) usual **(b)** etw. (*Akk.*) ∼ sein be used to sth.

Gewölbe *das;* ∼s, ∼: vault

gewonnen *2. Part. v.* GEWINNEN

geworben *2. Part. v.* WERBEN

geworfen *2. Part. v.* WERFEN

gewrungen *2. Part. v.* WRINGEN

Gewühl *das;* ∼[e]s milling crowd

gewunden *2. Part. v.* WINDEN

Gewürz *das;* ∼es, ∼e spice; (würzende Zutat) seasoning

Gewürz-: ∼gurke *die* pickled gherkin; ∼nelke *die* clove

gewusst, *gewußt *2. Part. v.* WISSEN

gez. *Abk.* = **gezeichnet** sgd.

Gezeit *die;* ∼, ∼en tide

Gezerre *das;* ∼s wrangling

gezielt ①*Adj.* specific ⟨*questions,* measures, etc.⟩; deliberate ⟨*insult, indiscretion*⟩; well-directed ⟨*advertising campaign*⟩ ②*adv.* ⟨*proceed, act*⟩ purposefully

geziemen (geh. veralt.) ①*itr. V.* jmdm. [nicht] ∼: [ill] befit sb ②*refl. V.* be proper; sich für jmdn. ∼: befit sb.

geziert ①*Adj.* (abwertend) affected ②*adv.* (abwertend) affectedly

gezogen *2. Part. v.* ZIEHEN

Gezwitscher *das;* ∼s twittering

gezwungen ①*2. Part. v.* ZWINGEN ②*Adj.* forced

gezwungenermaßen *Adv.* of necessity

gib *Imperativ Sg. Präsens v.* GEBEN

gibst *2. Pers. Sg. Präsens v.* GEBEN

gibt *3. Pers. Sg. Präsens v.* GEBEN

Gicht *die;* ∼: gout

Giebel *der;* ∼s, ∼: gable

Gier *die;* ∼: greed (**nach** for)

gierig ①*Adj.* greedy ②*adv.* greedily

gießen ①*unr. tr. V.* **(a)** pour (**in** + *Akk.* into, **über** + *Akk.* over) **(b)** (verschütten) spill (**über** + *Akk.* over) **(c)** (begießen) water ②*unpers.* (ugs.) pour [with rain]

Gießer *der;* ∼s, ∼: caster

Gießerei *die;* ∼, ∼en foundry

Gießerin *die;* ∼, ∼nen caster

Gift *das;* ∼[e]s, ∼e poison; (Schlangen∼) venom

gift·grün *Adj.* garish green

giftig *Adj.* poisonous; venomous ⟨*snake*⟩; toxic, poisonous ⟨*substance, gas, chemical*⟩; (fig.) venomous

Gift-: ∼mord *der* [murder by] poisoning; ∼mörder *der,* ∼mörderin *die* poisoner; ∼müll *der* toxic waste; ∼pilz *der* poisonous mushroom; [poisonous] toadstool; ∼schlange *die* venomous snake; ∼schrank *der* poison cabinet *or* cupboard; ∼stachel *der* poison sting; ∼zahn *der* poison fang

Gigant *der;* ∼en, ∼en giant

gigantisch *Adj.* gigantic

Gilde *die;* ∼, ∼n (hist.) guild

gilt *3. Pers. Sg. Präsens v.* GELTEN

Gimpel *der;* ∼s, ∼: bullfinch

Gin /dʒɪn/ *der;* ∼s, ∼s gin

ging *1. u. 3. Pers. Sg. Prät. v.* GEHEN

Ginster *der;* ∼s, ∼: broom

Gipfel *der;* ∼s, ∼: peak; (höchster Punkt des Berges) summit; (fig.) height

Gipfel·konferenz *die* summit conference

gipfeln *itr. V.* in etw. (*Dat.*) ∼: culminate in sth.

Gipfel·treffen *das* summit meeting

Gips *der;* ∼es, ∼e plaster; gypsum (Chem.)

Gips·abdruck *der* plaster cast

gipsen *tr. V.* plaster; put ⟨*leg, arm, etc.*⟩ in plaster

Gips·verband *der* plaster cast

Giraffe *die;* ∼, ∼n giraffe

Girlande *die;* ∼, ∼n festoon

Giro /ˈʒiːro/ *das;* ∼s, ∼s, österr. auch **Giri** (Finanzw.) giro

Giro·konto *das* (Finanzw.) current account

gis, Gis *das;* ∼, ∼ (Musik) G sharp

Gischt *der;* ∼[e]s, ∼e *od.* **die;** ∼, ∼en spray

Gitarre *die;* ∼, ∼n guitar

Gitarrist *der;* ∼en, ∼en, **Gitarristin** *die;* ∼, ∼nen guitarist

Gitter *das;* ∼s, ∼: bars *pl.;* (vor Fenster-, Türöffnungen) grille; (in der Straßendecke, im Fußboden) grating; (Geländer) railing[s *pl.*]

Gitter·fenster *das* barred window

Glacé·hand·schuh /glaˈseː.../ *der* kid glove

Gladiole *die;* ∼, ∼n gladiolus

Glanz *der;* ∼es (a) (von Licht, Sternen, Augen) brightness; (von Haar, Metall, Perlen, Leder usw.) lustre; sheen
(b) (der Jugend, Schönheit) radiance; (des Adels usw.) splendour

glänzen *itr. V.* (a) (Glanz ausstrahlen) shine; ⟨*hair, metal, etc.*⟩ gleam; ⟨*elbows, trousers, etc.*⟩ be shiny
(b) (Bewunderung erregen) shine (**bei** at)

glänzend (ugs.) ① *Adj.* (a) shining; gleaming ⟨*hair, metal, etc.*⟩; shiny ⟨*elbows, trousers, etc.*⟩
(b) (bewundernswert) brilliant; splendid ⟨*references, marks, results, etc.*⟩
② *adv.* ∼ **mit jmdm. auskommen** get on very well with sb.; **es geht mir/uns** ∼: I am/ we are very well

glanz-, Glanz-: ∼**leistung** *die* (auch iron.) brilliant performance; ∼**los** *Adj.* dull; lacklustre; ∼**nummer** *die* star turn; ∼**voll** ① *Adj.* brilliant; sparkling ⟨*variety number*⟩; ② *adv.* brilliantly

Glas *das;* ∼es, Gläser (a) glass
(b) (Trinkgefäß) glass; **zwei** ∼ *od.* **Gläser Wein** two glasses of wine
(c) (Behälter) jar

Glas: ∼**bläser** *der,* **Glas·bläserin** *die* glass-blower; ∼**container** *der* bottle bank

Gläschen *das;* ∼s, ∼ (a) [little] glass
(b) (kleines Gefäß) [little] [glass] jar

Glaser *der;* ∼s, ∼, **Glaserin** *die;* ∼, ∼nen glazier

gläsern *Adj.* glass

Glas·faser *die* glass fibre

glasieren *tr. V.* (a) glaze
(b) (Kochk.) ice; glaze ⟨*meat*⟩

glasig *Adj.* (a) glassy
(b) (Kochk.) transparent

Glas·malerei *die* stained glass

Glasur *die;* ∼, ∼en (a) glaze
(b) (Kochk.) icing; (auf Fleisch) glaze

glatt ① *Adj.* (a) smooth; (rutschig) slippery
(b) (ugs.: offensichtlich) downright ⟨*lie*⟩; outright ⟨*deception, fraud*⟩; flat ⟨*refusal*⟩
② *adv.* (a) smoothly; ∼ **gehen** (ugs.) go smoothly
(b) (ugs.: rückhaltlos) jmdm. etw. ∼ **ins Gesicht sagen** tell sb. sth. straight to his/her face; ⟨*reject, deny*⟩ flatly

Glätte *die;* ∼: smoothness; (Rutschigkeit) slipperiness

Glatt·eis *das* glaze; ice; (auf der Straße) black ice

glätten *tr. V.* smooth out ⟨*piece of paper, etc.*⟩; smooth [down] ⟨*feathers, fur, etc.*⟩; plane ⟨*wood etc.*⟩

glatt-: ***∼**|gehen** ▶ GLATT 2A; ∼**weg** *Adv.* (ugs.) etw. ∼**weg ablehnen/ignorieren** turn sth. down flat/simply ignore sth.; **das ist** ∼**weg erlogen/erfunden** that's a downright lie/that's pure invention

Glatze *die;* ∼, ∼n bald head; **eine** ∼ **haben/bekommen** be/go bald

Glaube *der;* ∼ns faith (**an** + *Akk.* in); (Überzeugung, Meinung) belief (**an** + *Akk.* in)

glauben ① *tr. V.* (a) (meinen) think
(b) (für wahr halten) believe; **das glaube ich dir nicht** I don't believe you; **das glaubst du doch selbst nicht!** [surely] you can't be serious; **sie glaubt ihm jedes Wort** she believes every word he says; **ob du es glaubst oder nicht ...** believe it or not ...; **das ist doch kaum zu** ∼ (ugs.) it's incredible
② *itr. V.* believe (**an** + *Akk.* in)

Glaubens-: ∼**bekenntnis** *das* creed; ∼**freiheit** *die* religious freedom; ∼**krieg** *der* religious war; ∼**sache** *die* (ugs.) matter of faith *or* belief

glaubhaft ① *Adj.* credible
② *adv.* convincingly

gläubig ① *Adj.* devout; (vertrauensvoll) trusting
② *adv.* devoutly; (vertrauensvoll) trustingly

Gläubige *der/die; adj. Dekl.* believer

Gläubiger *der;* ∼s, ∼: creditor

glaub·würdig ① *Adj.* credible
② *adv.* convincingly

Glaubwürdigkeit *die;* ∼: credibility

gleich ① *Adj.* (a) (identisch, von derselben Art) same; ∼ **bleiben** remain the same; ⟨*speed, temperature, etc.*⟩ remain constant; ∼ **bleibend** constant, steady ⟨*temperature, speed, etc.*⟩; (∼berechtigt, ∼wertig, Math.) equal
(b) (ugs.: gleichgültig) **es ist mir völlig** *od.* **ganz** ∼: I couldn't care less (coll.); **ganz** ∼, **wer anruft, ...:** no matter who calls, ...
② *adv.* (a) (übereinstimmend) ∼ **groß/alt** *usw.* **sein** be the same height/age *etc.;* ∼ **gut/ schlecht** *usw.* equally good/bad *etc.;*
(b) (in derselben Weise) ∼ **aufgebaut/gekleidet** having the same structure/wearing identical clothes
(c) (sofort) at once; straight away; (bald) in a moment   ···

(d) (räumlich) right; just; ~ **rechts/links**
immediately on the right/left
gleich-, Gleich-: ~**alt[e]rig** /-alt(ə)rıç/
Adj. of the same age (**mit** as); ~**artig**
1 *Adj.* of the same kind *postpos.* (**+** *Dat.* as);
(sehr ähnlich) very similar (**+** *Dat.* to); **2** *adv.*
in the same way; ~**berechtigt** *Adj.*
having equal rights *postpos.;* ~**berechtigte**
Partner equal partners; ~**berechtigung**
die equal rights *pl.;* **~*|**bleiben,**
~**bleibend** ▸ GLEICH 1A
gleichen *unr. itr. V.* jmdm./einer Sache ~:
be like *or* resemble sb./sth.;
gleichermaßen *Adv.* equally
gleich-, Gleich-: ~**falls** *Adv.* (auch) also;
(ebenfalls) likewise; **danke** ~**falls!** thank you,
[and] the same to you; ~**förmig** **1** *Adj.* **(a)**
(einheitlich) uniform; **(b)** (monoton) monotonous;
2 *adv.* **(a)** (einheitlich) uniformly; **(b)** (monoton)
monotonously; ~**geschlechtlich** *Adj.*
homosexual; ~**gewicht** *das* balance;
~**gewichts·störung** *die* disturbance of
one's sense of balance; ~**gültig** **1** *Adj.*
indifferent (**gegenüber** towards); (belanglos)
trivial; **das ist mir** ~**gültig** it's a matter of
indifference to me; **2** *adv.* indifferently;
~**gültigkeit** *die* indifference (**gegenüber**
towards)
Gleichheit *die;* ~, ~**en (a)** identity;
(Ähnlichkeit) similarity
(b) (gleiche Rechte) equality
Gleichheits·zeichen *das* equals sign
gleich-, Gleich-: ~|**kommen** *unr. itr.*
V.; mit sein **(a)** (entsprechen) be tantamount to;
(b) (die gleiche Leistung erreichen) jmdm./einer
Sache [an etw. (*Dat.*)] ~**kommen** equal sb./
sth. [in sth.]; ~|**machen** *tr. V.* make equal;
~**macherei** *die;* ~~, ~~**en** (abwertend)
levelling down (derog.); egalitarianism;
~**mäßig** **1** *Adj.* regular (interval, rhythm);
uniform (acceleration, distribution); even
(heat); **2** *adv.* (breathe) regularly; etw.
~**mäßig verteilen/auftragen** distribute sth.
equally/apply sth. evenly; ~**mut** *der*
equanimity; ~**mütig** **1** *Adj.* calm;
composed; **2** *adv.* with equanimity; calmly;
~**namig** *Adj.***(a)** of the same name *postpos.;*
(b) (Math.) ~**namige Brüche** fractions with a
common denominator; **Brüche** ~**namig**
machen reduce fractions to a common
denominator
Gleichnis *das;* ~**ses,** ~**se** (Allegorie)
allegory; (Parabel) parable
gleichsam *Adv.* (geh.) as it were
gleich-, Gleich-: ~|**schalten** *tr. V.*
force into line; ~**schenk[e]lig** *Adj.* (Math.)
isosceles; ~**schritt** *der* marching in step;
~**seitig** *Adj.* (Math.) equilateral; ~|**setzen**
tr. V. equate; ~|**stellen** *tr. V.* equate;
~**strom** *der* (Elektrot.) direct current
Gleichung *die;* ~, ~**en** equation
gleich-: ~**wertig** *Adj.* of the same value

*old spelling - see note on page xiv

postpos.; ~**wohl** /-'-' od. '--/ *Adv.*
nevertheless; ~**zeitig** **1** *Adj.*
simultaneous; **2** *adv.* at the same time
Gleis *das;* ~**es,** ~**e** track; (Bahnsteig)
platform; (einzelne Schiene) rail
gleiten *unr. itr. V.; mit sein* glide; (hand)
slide
Gleit-: ~**flug** *der* glide; ~**zeit** *die*
flexitime; flexible working hours *Pl.*
Gletscher *der;* ~**s,** ~: glacier
Gletscher·spalte *die* crevasse
glich *1. u. 3. Pers. Sg. Prät. v.* GLEICHEN
Glied *das;* ~**[e]s,** ~**er (a)** limb; (Finger~,
Zehen~) joint
(b) (Ketten~, auch fig.) link
(c) (Teil eines Ganzen) section; (Mitglied) member
gliedern **1** *tr. V.* structure; organize
(thoughts)
2 *refl. V.* **sich in Gruppen/Abschnitte** *usw.*
~: be divided into groups/sections *etc.*
Gliederung *die;* ~, ~**en** structure
Glied-: ~**maße** /-ma:sə/ *die;* ~, ~**n** limb;
~**satz** *der* (Sprachw.) subordinate clause
glimmen *unr. od. regelm. itr. V.* glow
Glimm·stängel, *Glimm·stengel *der*
(ugs. scherzh.) fag (coll.); ciggy (coll.)
glimpflich **1** *Adj.* **(a) der Unfall nahm ein**
~**es Ende** the accident turned out not to be
too serious
(b) (mild) lenient (sentence, punishment)
2 *adv.* **(a)** (ohne Schaden) ~ **davonkommen**
get off lightly
(b) (mild) leniently
glitschig *Adj.* (ugs.) slippery
glitt *1. u. 3. Pers. Sg. Prät. v.* GLEITEN
glitzern *itr. V.* (star) twinkle; (diamond,
decorations) sparkle; (snow, eyes, tears)
glisten
global **1** *Adj.* **(a)** global; worldwide
(b) (umfassend) all-round (education); overall
(control, planning, etc.)
(c) (allgemein) general
2 *adv.* **(a)** worldwide
(b) (umfassend) in overall terms
(c) (allgemein) in general terms
globalisieren *tr. V.* globalize
Globalisierung *die;* ~, ~**en** globalization
Globen ▸ GLOBUS
Globetrotter *der;* ~**s,** ~: globetrotter
Globus *der;* ~ *od.* ~**ses, Globen** globe
Glöckchen *das;* ~**s,** ~: [little] bell
Glocke *die;* ~, ~**n** bell
Glocken-: ~**blume** *die* (Bot.) campanula;
~**rock** *der* widely flared skirt; ~**spiel** *das*
(a) carillon; (mit einer Uhr gekoppelt auch)
chimes *pl.;* **(b)** (Instrument) glockenspiel
glomm *1. u. 3. Pers. Sg. Prät. v.* GLIMMEN
Glorien·schein /'glo:rjən-/ *der* glory; (um
den Kopf, fig.) halo
glorifizieren *tr. V.* glorify
Glorifizierung *die;* ~, ~**en** glorification
glor·reich **1** *Adj.* glorious

163

Glossar ···⫶ Gott ····

2 *adv.* gloriously

Glossar *das;* ~s, ~e glossary

Glosse *die;* ~, ~n commentary; (spöttische Bemerkung) sneering comment

Glotze *die;* ~, ~n (salopp) box (coll.); goggle-box (Brit. coll.)

glotzen *itr. V.* (abwertend) goggle; gawp (coll.)

Glotz·kiste *die* (salopp) box (coll.); goggle-box (Brit. coll.)

Glück *das;* ~[e]s (a) luck; [es ist] ein ~, dass ...: it's lucky that ...; [kein] ~ haben be [un]lucky; viel ~! [the] best of luck!; zum ~ *od.* zu meinem/seinem *usw.* ~: luckily *or* fortunately [for me/him *etc.*] (b) happiness

Glucke *die;* ~, ~n brood hen

glücken *tr. V.; mit sein* succeed; etw. glückt jmdm. sb. is successful with sth.

gluckern *itr. V.* gurgle; glug

glücklich 1 *Adj.* (a) happy (über + *Akk.* about) (b) (erfolgreich) lucky ⟨*winner*⟩; successful ⟨*outcome*⟩; safe ⟨*journey*⟩ (c) (vorteilhaft) fortunate 2 *adv.* (a) (erfolgreich) successfully (b) (vorteilhaft, zufrieden) happily ⟨*chosen, married*⟩

glücklicher·weise *Adv.* fortunately; luckily

glück·selig 1 *Adj.* blissfully happy 2 *adv.* blissfully

Glück·seligkeit *die;* ~: bliss

glucksen *itr. V.* (a) ▶ GLUCKERN; (b) (lachen) chuckle

Glücks-: ~klee *der* four-leaf clover; ~pfennig *der* lucky penny; ~pilz *der* (ugs.) lucky devil (coll.)

Glück[s]·sache *die:* das ist ~: it's a matter of luck

Glücks·spiel *das* game of chance

glück·strahlend *Adj.* radiantly happy

Glücks·zahl *die* lucky number

Glück·wunsch *der* congratulations *pl.;* herzlichen ~ zum Geburtstag! happy birthday!

Glüh·birne *die* lightbulb

glühen *itr. V.* glow

glühend 1 *Adj.* red-hot ⟨*metal etc.*⟩; blazing ⟨*heat*⟩; ardent ⟨*admirer etc.*⟩; passionate ⟨*words, letter, etc.*⟩ 2 *adv.* ⟨*love*⟩ passionately; ⟨*admire*⟩ ardently; ~ heiß blazing hot

Glüh-: ~wein *der* mulled wine; ~würmchen *das;* ~~s, ~~ (ugs.) (weiblich) glow-worm; (männlich) firefly

Glut *die;* ~, ~en (a) embers *pl.;* (b) (geh.: Leidenschaft) passion

glut·rot *Adj.* fiery red

Glyzerin *das;* ~s glycerine

GmbH *Abk.* = **Gesellschaft mit beschränkter Haftung** ≈ plc, PLC

Gnade *die;* ~, ~n (Gunst) favour; (Rel.) grace; (Milde) mercy

gnaden-, Gnaden-: ~brot *das:* jmdm./ einem Tier das ~brot geben keep sb./an animal in his/her/its old age; ~frist *die* reprieve; ~gesuch *das* plea for clemency; ~los (auch fig.) 1 *Adj.* merciless; 2 *adv.* mercilessly; ~losigkeit *die;* ~~: mercilessness; ~schuss, ***~schuß *der* coup de grâce (*by shooting*)

gnädig *Adj.* gracious; (glimpflich) lenient ⟨*sentence etc.*⟩

Gnom *der;* ~en, ~en gnome

Gockel *der;* ~s, ~ (bes. südd., sonst ugs. scherzh.) cock

Gold *das;* ~[e]s gold

Gold·barren *der* gold bar

golden 1 *Adj.* (aus Gold) gold; (herrlich) golden ⟨*days, memories, etc.*⟩ 2 *adv.* like gold

Gold-: ~fisch *der* goldfish; ~füllung *die* gold filling; ~grube *die* (auch fig.) gold mine; ~hamster *der* golden hamster

goldig *Adj.* sweet

gold-, Gold-: ~richtig (ugs.) *Adj.* absolutely right; ~schmied *der,* ~schmiedin *die* goldsmith; ~schnitt *der* gilt; ~währung *die* (Wirtsch.) currency tied to the gold standard

Golf¹ *der;* ~[e]s, ~e gulf

Golf² *das;* ~s (Sport) golf

Golf-: ~platz *der* golf course; ~schläger *der* golf club; ~spieler *der,* ~spielerin *die* golfer; ~strom *der* Gulf Stream

Gondel *die;* ~, ~n gondola

gondeln *itr. V.; mit sein* (ugs.) (a) (mit einem Boot) cruise (b) (reisen) travel around (c) (herumfahren) cruise around

Gong *der;* ~s, ~s gong

gongen *itr. V.* es hat gegongt the gong has sounded

gönnen *tr. V.* jmdm. etw. ~: not begrudge sb. sth.; sich/jmdm. etw. ~: allow oneself/sb. sth.

Gönner *der;* ~s, ~: patron

gönnerhaft (abwertend) *Adj.* patronizing

Gönnerin *die;* ~, ~nen patroness

gor 3. Pers. Sg. Prät. v. GÄREN

Göre *die;* ~, ~n (nordd., oft abwertend) kid (coll.)

Gorilla *der;* ~s, ~s gorilla

goss, *goß 1. u. 3. Pers. Sg. Prät. v. GIESSEN

Gosse *die;* ~, ~n gutter

Gotik *die;* ~ (Stil) Gothic [style]; (Epoche) Gothic period

gotisch *Adj.* Gothic

Gott *der;* ~es, Götter (a) God; grüß [dich] ···⫶

~! (landsch.) hello!; **um** ~**es Willen** (bei Erschrecken) for God's sake; (bei einer Bitte) for heaven's sake
(b) (übermenschliches Wesen) god

Gottes-: ~**dienst** der service; ~**haus** das (geh.) house of God; ~**lästerung** die blasphemy

Gottheit die; ~, ~en deity

Göttin die; ~, ~nen goddess

göttlich ⓵ Adj. (auch fig.) divine
⓶ adv. divinely

gott-, Gott-: ~**lob** adv. thank goodness; ~**los** ⓵ Adj. **(a)** ungodly ‹life etc.›; impious ‹words, speech, etc.›; **(b)** (Gott leugnend) godless ‹theory etc.›; ⓶ adv. (verwerflich) irreverently; ~**vater** der God the Father; ~**verlassen** Adj. (ugs.: abseits) godforsaken; ~**vertrauen** das trust in God

Götze der; ~n, ~n (auch fig.) idol

Götzen-: ~**bild** das idol; ~**diener** der idolater; ~**dienerin** die idolatress

Gouverneur /guvɛrˈnøːɐ̯/ der; ~s, ~e governor

Grab das; ~[e]s, Gräber grave; **das Heilige** ~: the Holy Sepulchre; **das ~ des Unbekannten Soldaten** the tomb of the Unknown Warrior

graben unr. tr., itr. V. dig

Graben der; ~s, Gräben ditch; (Schützen~) trench; (Festungs~) moat

Grab-: ~**hügel** der grave mound; ~**kammer** die burial chamber; ~**mal** das; Pl. ~mäler, geh. ~male monument; ~**schändung** die desecration of a/the grave/of [the] graves

grabschen ⓵ tr. V. grab; snatch
⓶ itr. V. **nach etw.** ~: grab at sth.

gräbst 2. Pers. Sg. Präsens v. GRABEN

gräbt 3. Pers. Sg. Präsens v. GRABEN

Grab-stein der gravestone

Grabung die; ~, ~en (bes. Archäol.) excavation

Gracht die; ~, ~en canal

Grad der; ~[e]s, ~e degree; (Milit.) rank

grade (ugs.) ▶ GERADE

Grad-messer der gauge, yardstick (**für** of)

graduell ⓵ Adj. gradual; slight ‹difference etc.›
⓶ adv. gradually; ‹different› in degree

graduiert Adj. graduate; **ein** ~**er Ingenieur** an engineering graduate

Graf der; ~en, ~en count; (britischer ~) earl

Graffito der od. das; ~[s], Graffitti **(a)** (Kunst) graffito
(b) Pl. (Kritzelei) graffiti

Grafik die; ~, ~en graphic art[s pl.]; (Kunstwerk) graphic; (Druck) print

Grafiker der; ~s, ~, **Grafikerin** die; ~, ~nen [graphic] designer; (Künstler[in]) graphic artist

grafisch ⓵ Adj. graphic
⓶ adv. graphically

Gräfin die; ~, ~nen countess

Grafschaft die; ~, ~en **(a)** count's land; (in Großbritannien) earldom
(b) (Verwaltungsbezirk) county

Gram der; ~[e]s (geh.) grief; sorrow

grämen ⓵ tr. V. grieve
⓶ refl. V. grieve (**über** + Akk., **um** over)

Gramm das; ~s, ~e gram

Grammatik die; ~, ~en grammar

grammatisch ⓵ Adj. grammatical
⓶ adv. grammatically

Grammophon Ⓦ das; ~s, ~e gramophone; phonograph (Amer.)

Granat der; ~[e]s, ~e (Schmuckstein) garnet

Granat-apfel der pomegranate

Granate die; ~, ~n shell; (Hand~) grenade

Granat-feuer das shellfire no pl., no indef. art.

grandios ⓵ Adj. magnificent
⓶ adv. magnificently

Granit der; ~s, ~e granite

grantig (südd., österr. ugs.) ⓵ Adj. bad-tempered
⓶ adv. bad-temperedly

Grapefruit /ˈgreːpfruːt/ die; ~, ~s grapefruit

Graph der; ~en, ~en (Math., Naturw.) graph

Graphik usw.: ▶ GRAFIK usw.

Graphit der; ~s, ~e graphite

Gras das; ~es, Gräser **(a)** grass; **über etw.** (Akk.) ~ **wachsen lassen** (ugs.) let the dust settle on sth.
(b) (Drogenjargon) grass (sl.)

grasen itr. V. graze

Gras-: ~**halm** der blade of grass; ~**land** das grassland; ~**narbe** die turf

grässlich, *gräßlich ⓵ Adj. **(a)** (abscheulich) horrible; terrible ‹accident›
(b) (ugs.: unangenehm) dreadful (coll.)
(c) (ugs.: sehr stark) terrible (coll.)
⓶ adv. **(a)** (abscheulich) horribly; terribly
(b) (ugs.: unangenehm) terribly (coll.)
(c) (ugs.: sehr) terribly (coll.)

Grässlichkeit, *Gräßlichkeit die; ~, ~enz **(a)** (Abscheulichkeit) horribleness; (eines Unfalls) terribleness
(b) (unangenehme Art) dreadfulness (coll.)

Grat der; ~[e]s, ~e ridge

Gräte die; ~, ~n [fish] bone

Gratifikation die; ~, ~en bonus

gratinieren tr. V. (Gastr.) brown [the top of]; **gratinierter Blumenkohl** cauliflower au gratin

gratis Adv. free [of charge]; gratis

Gratis-: ~**aktie** die (Börsenw.) bonus share; ~**muster** das, ~**probe** die free sample

Grätsche die; ~, ~n (Turnen) straddle; (Sprung) straddle vault

---

*alte Schreibung - vgl. Hinweis auf S. xiv

Gratulant *der;* ~en, ~en, **Gratulantin** *die;* ~, ~nen well-wisher

Gratulation *die;* ~, ~en congratulations *pl.*

gratulieren *itr. V.* jmdm. ~: congratulate sb.; jmdm. zum Geburtstag ~: wish sb. many happy returns [of the day]

Grat·wanderung *die* ridge walk; (fig.) balancing act

grau *Adj.* grey; (trostlos) dreary; drab; ~ meliert greying ⟨*hair*⟩

Gräuel *der;* ~s, ~ (a) etw./jmd. ist jmdm. ein ~: sb. loathes *or* detests sth./sb.
(b) (geh.) (~tat) atrocity

Gräuel·tat *die* atrocity

grauen[1] *itr. V.* (geh.) der Morgen/der Tag graut morning/day is breaking

grauen[2] *itr. V.* (*unpers.*) ihm graut [es] davor/vor ihr he dreads [the thought of] it/ he's terrified of her

Grauen *das;* ~s, ~: horror (vor + *Dat.* of)

grauen·haft [1] *Adj.* horrifying; (ugs.: sehr unangenehm) terrible (coll.)
[2] *adv.* horrifyingly; (ugs.: sehr unangenehm) terribly (coll.)

grauhaarig *Adj.* grey-haired

gräulich [1] *Adj.* (a) horrifying
(b) (unangenehm) awful
[2] *adv.* (a) horrifyingly
(b) (unangenehm) terribly

***grau·meliert** ▶ GRAU

Graupe *die;* ~, ~n (a) grain of pearl barley
(b) *Pl.* (Gericht) pearl barley *sing.*

Graupel *die;* ~, ~n soft hail pellet; ~n soft hail; graupel

graupeln *itr. V.* (*unpers.*) es graupelt there's soft hail falling

grausam [1] *Adj.* (a) cruel
(b) (furchtbar) terrible; dreadful
[2] *adv.* (a) cruelly
(b) (furchtbar) terribly, dreadfully

Grausamkeit *die;* ~, ~en (a) cruelty
(b) (Handlung) act of cruelty

grausen [1] *tr., itr. V.* (*unpers.*) es grauste ihm *od.* ihn davor/vor ihr he dreaded it/he was terrified of her
[2] *refl. V.* sich vor etw./jmdm. ~: dread sth./ be terrified of sb.

Grausen *das;* ~s horror

grausig *Adj., adv.* ▶ GRAUENHAFT

gravieren *tr. V.* engrave

gravierend *Adj.* serious, grave

Gravierung *die;* ~, ~en engraving

Gravitation *die;* ~ (Physik, Astron.) gravitation

Gravur /graˈvuːɐ̯/ *die;* ~, ~en engraving

Grazie /ˈɡraːtsiə/ *die;* ~, ~n (a) (Anmut) gracefulness
(b) (Myth.) Grace

greif·bar [1] *Adj.* (a) in ~er Nähe (fig.)

within reach; der Urlaub ist in ~e Nähe gerückt (fig.) the holiday is just coming up [now]
(b) (deutlich) tangible; concrete
(c) (ugs.: verfügbar) available
[2] *adv.* ~ nahe (fig.) within reach

greifen [1] *unr. tr. V.* (a) (ergreifen) take hold of; grasp; (rasch ~) seize
(b) (fangen) catch
[2] *unr. itr. V.* (a) in/unter/hinter etw./sich (*Akk.*) ~: reach into/under/behind sth./one; nach etw. ~: reach for sth.; (hastig) make a grab for sth.
(b) (Technik) grip

Greis *der;* ~es, ~e old man

Greisin *die;* ~, ~nen old woman

grell [1] *Adj.* (a) (hell) glaring, ⟨*light, sun, etc.*⟩
(b) (auffallend) garish ⟨*colour etc.*⟩; loud ⟨*dress, pattern, etc.*⟩
(c) (schrill) shrill, ⟨*cry, voice, etc.*⟩
[2] *adv.* (a) (hell) with glaring brightness
(b) (auffallend) gegen *od.* von etw. ~ abstechen contrast sharply with sth.
(c) (schrill) shrilly

Gremium *das;* ~s, Gremien committee

Grenze *die;* ~, ~n (a) boundary; (Staats~) border; (gedachte Trennungslinie) borderline
(b) (fig.) limit

grenzen *itr. V.* an etw. (*Akk.*) ~: border [on] sth.

grenzen·los [1] *Adj.* boundless; (fig.) boundless, unbounded ⟨*joy, wonder, jealousy, grief, etc.*⟩; unlimited ⟨*wealth, power*⟩; limitless ⟨*patience, ambition*⟩; extreme ⟨*tiredness, anger, foolishness*⟩
[2] *adv.* endlessly; (fig.) beyond all measure

Grenzen·losigkeit *die;* ~: boundlessness

Grenz-: ~gänger *der;* ~~s, ~~, ~~gängerin *die;* ~~, ~~nen [regular] commuter across the border *or* frontier; ~konflikt *der* border *or* frontier conflict; ~land *das* border *or* frontier area; ~posten *der* border *or* frontier guard; ~stein *der* boundary stone; ~übergang *der* border crossing-point; ~übertritt *der* crossing of the border; der ungesetzliche ~übertritt crossing the border illegally; ~verkehr *der* [cross-]border traffic

Gretchen·frage *die* crucial question; sixty-four-thousand-dollar question (coll.)

***Greuel** ▶ GRÄUEL

***Greueltat** ▶ GRÄUELTAT

***greulich** ▶ GRÄULICH

Grieche *der;* ~n, ~n Greek

Griechen·land *(das);* ~s Greece

griechisch [1] *Adj.* Greek
[2] *adv.* ⟨*speak, write*⟩ in Greek

Griechisch *das;* ~[s] Greek *no art.*

Griechin *die;* ~, ~nen Greek

griesgrämig [1] *Adj.* grumpy
[2] *adv.* in a grumpy manner

Grieß *der;* ~es, ~e semolina

Grieß·brei der semolina

griff 1. u. 3. Pers. Sg. Prät. v. GREIFEN

Griff der; ∼[e]s, ∼e **(a)** grip; grasp
(b) (Knauf, Henkel) handle

griff·bereit Adj. ready to hand postpos.

Griffel der; ∼s, ∼: slate pencil

griffig Adj. **(a)** (handlich) handy
(b) (gut greifend) that grips well postpos., not
pred.; non-slip ⟨surface, floor⟩

Grill der; ∼s, ∼s grill; (Rost) barbecue

Grille die; ∼, ∼n **(a)** cricket
(b) (sonderbarer Einfall) whim

grillen 1 tr. V. grill
2 itr. V. im Garten ∼: have a barbecue in
the garden

Grill·platz der barbecue area

Grimasse die; ∼, ∼n grimace

grimmig 1 Adj. furious ⟨person⟩; grim
⟨expression⟩
2 adv. grimly

grinsen itr. V. grin; (höhnisch) smirk

Grippe die; ∼, ∼n **(a)** influenza; flu (coll.)
(b) (volkst.: Erkältung) cold

Grips der; ∼es brains pl.

grob 1 Adj. **(a)** coarse; thick ⟨wire⟩; rough
⟨work⟩
(b) (ungefähr) rough
(c) (schwerwiegend) gross; flagrant ⟨lie⟩
(d) (barsch) rude
2 adv. **(a)** coarsely
(b) (ungefähr) roughly
(c) (schwerwiegend) grossly
(d) (barsch) rudely

Grobheit die; ∼, ∼en **(a)** rudeness
(b) (Äußerung) rude remark

Grobian der; ∼[e]s, ∼e lout

Grog der; ∼s, ∼s grog

groggy Adj. **(a)** (Boxen) groggy
(b) (ugs.: erschöpft) whacked [out] (coll.); all in
(coll.)

grölen 1 tr. V. (ugs. abwertend) bawl [out];
roar, howl ⟨approval⟩
2 itr. V. bawl

Groll der; ∼[e]s (geh.) rancour

grollen itr. V. (geh.) **(a)** [mit] jmdm. ∼: bear
a grudge against sb.
(b) ⟨thunder⟩ rumble

Grönland (das); ∼s Greenland

Gros /groː/ das; ∼ /groːs/, ∼ /groːs/ bulk

Groschen der; ∼s, ∼ **(a)** (österreichische
Münze) groschen
(b) (ugs.: Zehnpfennigstück) ten-pfennig piece;
(fig.) penny; cent (Amer.)

groß; größer, größt... 1 Adj. **(a)** big, large;
great ⟨length, width, height⟩; tall ⟨person⟩;
wide ⟨selection⟩; 1m² ∼: 1m² in area; im
Großen und Ganzen by and large
(b) (älter) big ⟨brother, sister⟩; (erwachsen)
grown-up
(c) (lange dauernd) long, lengthy

(d) intense ⟨heat, cold⟩; high ⟨speed⟩; great,
major ⟨event, artist, work⟩
2 adv. (ugs.: besonders) greatly; ∼
geschrieben werden (ugs.) be stressed; s. auch
GROSSSCHREIBEN

groß-, Groß-: ∼abnehmer der,
∼abnehmerin die bulk buyer or
purchaser; ∼aktionär der,
∼aktionärin die (Wirtsch.) principal or
major shareholder; ∼artig 1 Adj.
magnificent; splendid; 2 adv. magnificently;
splendidly; ∼auftrag der (Wirtsch.) large
order

Großbritannien (das); ∼s the United
Kingdom; [Great] Britain

Groß·buchstabe der capital [letter]

Größe die; ∼, ∼n size; (Höhe, Körper∼)
height; (fig.) greatness; **die ∼ der Katastrophe**
the [full] extent of the catastrophe

Groß·eltern Pl. grandparents

Größen·ordnung die order [of
magnitude]; **in einer ∼ von einer Milliarde
Euro** in the order of a thousand million or a
billion euros

großen·teils Adv. largely; for the most
part

Größen·wahn der delusions pl. of
grandeur

größer ▶ GROSS

Groß-: ∼fahndung die large-scale search;
∼familie die (Soziol.) extended family;
(mehrere Kleinfamilien) composite family;
∼handel der wholesale trade; ∼händler
der, ∼händlerin die wholesaler;
∼industrielle der/die; adj. Dekl. big
industrialist

Grossist der; ∼en, ∼en, **Grossistin** die;
∼, ∼nen (Kaufmannsspr.) wholesaler

groß-, Groß-: ∼macht die great power;
∼maul das (ugs. abwertend) bigmouth (coll.);
∼mut die; ∼∼: generosity; ∼mütig Adj.
generous; ∼mutter die; Pl. ∼mütter
grandmother; ∼rechner der (DV)
mainframe [computer]; ∼reinemachen
das; ∼∼s (ugs.) thorough cleaning;
∼|schreiben unr. tr. V. write ⟨word⟩ with
a capital; s. auch GROSS 2; ∼spurig
(abwertend) 1 Adj. boastful; (hochtrabend)
pretentious; 2 adv. boastfully; (hochtrabend)
pretentiously; ∼stadt die city; large town;
∼städter der, ∼städterin die city-
dweller

größt... ▶ GROSS

Groß·teil der **(a)** (Hauptteil) major part
(b) (nicht unerheblicher Teil) large part

größten·teils Adv. for the most part

größt·möglich Adj. greatest possible

groß-, Groß-: ∼|tun unr. itr. V. boast;
∼unternehmen das (Wirtsch.) large-scale
enterprise; big concern; ∼vater der
grandfather; ∼verbraucher der,
∼verbraucherin die bulk or large
consumer; ∼|ziehen unr. tr. V. bring up;

raise; rear ⟨*animal*⟩; **~zügig** ① *Adj.* generous; grand and spacious ⟨*building, garden, etc.*⟩; ② *adv.* generously; **~zügigkeit** *die;* ~~: generosity

grotesk ① *Adj.* grotesque ② *adv.* grotesquely

Grotte *die;* ~, ~n grotto

grub *1. u. 3. Pers. Sg. Prät. v.* GRABEN

Grübchen *das;* ~s, ~: dimple

Grube *die;* ~, ~n pit; (Bergbau) mine

grübeln *itr. V.* ponder (**über** + *Dat.* on, over)

Gruben·arbeiter *der,* **Gruben·arbeiterin** *die* miner; mineworker

grüezi *Interj.* (schweiz.) hallo

Gruft *die;* ~, Grüfte vault; (in einer Kirche) crypt

grün *Adj.* green

Grün *das;* ~s, ~ *od.* (ugs.) ~s (a) green (b) (Pflanzen) greenery

Grün·anlage *die* green space; (Park) park

Grund *der;* ~[e]s, Gründe (a) ground; (eines Gewässers) bottom; **im ~e [genommen]** basically (b) (Ursache, Veranlassung) reason; **auf ~:** ▶ AUFGRUND

Grund-: ~besitz *der* (a) (Eigentum an Land) ownership of land; (b) (Land) land; **~buch** *das* land register

gründen ① *tr. V.* (a) found; set up, establish ⟨*business*⟩; start [up] ⟨*club*⟩ (b) (aufbauen) base ⟨*plan, theory, etc.*⟩ (**auf** + *Akk.* on) ② *itr. V.* **auf** *od.* **in etw.** (*Dat.*) ~: be based on sth. ③ *refl. V.* **sich auf etw.** (*Akk.*) ~: be based on sth.

Gründer *der;* ~s, ~, **Gründerin** *die;* ~, ~nen founder

Grund·erwerb[s]·steuer *die* (Steuerw.) land transfer tax

Grund·gesetz *das* Basic Law

grundieren *tr. V.* prime

Grundierung *die;* ~, ~en (a) (das Grundieren) priming (b) (erster Anstrich) priming coat

grund-, Grund-: ~kenntnis *die* basic knowledge *no pl.* (**in** + *Dat.* of); **~lage** *die* basis; foundation

Grundlagen·forschung *die* basic research

grund·legend ① *Adj.* fundamental, basic (**für** to); seminal ⟨*idea, work*⟩ ② *adv.* fundamentally

gründlich ① *Adj.* thorough ② *adv.* thoroughly

Gründlichkeit *die;* ~: thoroughness

grund·los ① *Adj.* groundless ② *adv.* **sich ~ aufregen/ängstigen** be needlessly agitated/alarmed

Grund·nahrungsmittel *das* basic food[stuff]

Grün·donnerstag *der* Maundy Thursday

Grund-: ~ordnung *die* basic fundamental [constitutional] order; **~prinzip** *das* fundamental principle; **~recht** *das* basic *or* constitutional right; **~riss**, ***~riß *der* (a) (Bauw.) [ground] plan; (b) (Leitfaden) outline; **~satz** *der* principle

grund·sätzlich ① *Adj.* (a) fundamental ⟨*difference, question, etc.*⟩ (b) (aus Prinzip) ⟨*opponent etc.*⟩ on principle (c) (allgemein) ⟨*agreement etc.*⟩ in principle ② *adv.* (a) fundamentally (b) (aus Prinzip) on principle (c) (allgemein) in principle

Grund-: ~schule *die* primary school; **~stein** *der* foundation stone; **~stein·legung** *die;* ~~, ~~en laying of the foundation stone; **~stück** *das* plot [of land]

Gründung *die;* ~, ~en ▶ GRÜNDEN 1A: foundation; setting up; establishing; starting [up]

Grund-: ~wasser *das* (Geol.) ground water; **~wortschatz** *der* (Sprachw.) basic vocabulary; **~zug** *der* essential feature

Grüne¹ *das; adj. Dekl.* green; **im ~n/ins ~:** [out] in/into the country

Grüne² *der/die; adj. Dekl.* (Politik) member of the Green Party; **die ~n** the Greens

Grün-: ~fläche *die* green space; (im Park) lawn; **~gürtel** *der* green belt; **~land** *das* (Landw.) (Wiese) meadow land; (Weide) pastureland; **~pflanze** *die* foliage plant; **~schnabel** *der* (abwertend) [young] whippersnapper; (Neuling) greenhorn; **~span** *der* verdigris; **~streifen** *der* central reservation (*grassed and often with trees and bushes*)

grunzen *tr., itr. V.* grunt

Gruppe *die;* ~, ~n (a) group (b) (Klassifizierung) class; category

Gruppen-: ~druck *der* group pressure; **~dynamik** *die* (Sozialpsych.) group dynamics *sing., no art.;* **~leiter** *der,* **~leiterin** *die* group leader; **~reise** *die* (Touristik) group travel *no pl., no art.;* **eine ~reise nach London machen** travel to London with a group; **~sieg** *der* (Sport) top place in the group

gruppieren ① *tr. V.* arrange ② *refl. V.* form a group/groups

Gruppierung *die;* ~, ~en grouping

gruselig *Adj.* eerie; creepy

gruseln ① *tr., itr. V.* (*unpers.*) **es gruselt jmdn.** *od.* **jmdm.** sb.'s flesh creeps ② *refl. V.* be frightened

Gruß *der;* ~es, Grüße (a) greeting; (Milit.) salute (b) (im Brief) **mit herzlichen Grüßen** [with] best wishes; **mit bestem ~/freundlichen Grüßen** yours sincerely

grüßen ① *tr. V.* (a) greet; (Milit.) salute
(b) (Grüße senden) **grüße deine Eltern [ganz
herzlich] von mir** please give your parents
my [kindest] regards; **grüß dich!** (ugs.) hello
or (coll.) hi [there]!
② *itr. V.* say hello; (Milit.) salute

Grütze *die;* ~, ~n groats *pl.;* **rote** ~: red
fruit pudding *(made with fruit juice, fruit
and cornflour, etc.)*

gucken *itr. V.* (ugs.) (a) look; (heimlich) peep
(b) (hervorsehen) stick out
(c) (dreinschauen) look

Guck·loch *das* spyhole

Guerilla /ge'rɪlja/ *die;* ~, ~s guerrilla war;
(Einheit) guerrilla unit

Gulasch /'gʊlaʃ, 'guːlaʃ/ *das od. der;*
~[e]s, ~e *od.* ~s goulash

Gulden *der;* ~s, ~: guilder

gültig ① *Adj.* valid; current ⟨note, coin⟩

Gültigkeit *die;* ~: validity; ~ **haben/
erlangen** be/become valid

Gummi *der od. das;* ~s, ~[s] rubber

Gummi-: ~**band** *das* rubber *or* elastic
band; (in Kleidung) elastic *no indef. art.;*
~**bärchen** *das;* ~~s, ~~: jelly baby;
~**baum** *der* rubber plant

gummieren *tr. V.* gum

Gummi-: ~**handschuh** *der* rubber glove;
~**knüppel** *der* [rubber] truncheon;
~**sohle** *die* rubber sole; ~**stiefel** *der*
rubber boot; (für Regenwetter) wellington [boot]
(Brit.)

Gunst *die;* ~ (a) favour; goodwill
(b) **zu** ~**en** ▸ ZUGUNSTEN

günstig ① *Adj.* favourable; propitious
⟨sign⟩; auspicious ⟨moment⟩; beneficial
⟨influence⟩; good
② *adv.* favourably; **etw.** ~ **beeinflussen** have
or exert a beneficial influence on sth.

günstig[st]en·falls *Adv.* at best

Gurgel *die;* ~, ~n throat; **jmdm. die** ~
zudrücken throttle sb.

gurgeln *itr. V.* gargle

Gurke *die;* ~, ~n cucumber; (eingelegt)
gherkin

gurren *itr. V.* (auch fig.) coo

Gurt *der;* ~[e]s, ~e strap; (im Auto, Flugzeug)
[seat] belt

Gürtel *der;* ~s, ~: belt

Gürtel-: ~**linie** *die* waist[line]; **das war ein
Schlag unter die** ~**linie** (fig. ugs.) that was
hitting below the belt (fig. coll.); ~**reifen** *der*
radial[-ply] tyre

Gurt·straffer *der;* ~s, ~ (Kfz.-W.) [seat-]belt
tensioner

Guru *der;* ~s, ~s guru

GUS *Abk.* = **Gemeinschaft
Unabhängiger Staaten** CIS

Guss, *Guß *der;* Gusses, Güsse (a) (das
Gießen) casting

(b) (ugs.: Regenschauer) downpour

Guss·eisen, *Guß·eisen, *das* cast iron
guss·eisern, *guß·eisern *Adj.* cast-
iron

gut; besser, best... ① *Adj.* good; fine ⟨wine⟩;
ein ~**es neues Jahr** a happy new year; ~ **tun**
do good; **mir ist nicht** ~: I'm not feeling well;
~ **aussehend** good-looking; ~**en Appetit!**
enjoy your lunch/dinner *etc.!;* **eine** ~**e
Stunde [von hier]** a good hour [from here]
② *adv.* (a) well; ~ **gemeint** well-meant; **so**
~ **wie nichts** next to nothing
(b) (mühelos) easily; *s. auch* BESSER, BEST...

Gut *das;* ~[e]s, **Güter (a)** property; (Besitztum,
auch fig.) possession
(b) (landwirtschaftlicher Grundbesitz) estate
(c) (Fracht~, Ware) item; **Güter** goods;
(Fracht~) freight *sing.;* goods (Brit.)

gut-, Gut-: ~**achten** *das;* ~~s, ~~:
[expert's] report; ~**artig** *Adj.* (a) good-
natured; (b) (nicht gefährlich) benign;
~**artigkeit** *die* (a) good nature;
goodnaturedness; (b) (Ungefährlichkeit)
benignity; *~**aussehend** ▸ GUT 1;
~**bürgerlich** *Adj.* good middle-class;
~**bürgerliche Küche** good plain cooking;
~**dünken** *das;* ~~s discretion

Güte *die;* ~: goodness; kindness; (Qualität)
quality

Gute·nacht·kuss, *Gute·nacht·kuß
der goodnight kiss

Güter-: ~**abfertigung** *die* (a) (Abfertigung
von Waren) dispatch of freight *or* (Brit.) goods;
(b) (Annahmestelle) freight *or* (Brit.) goods
office; ~**bahnhof** *der* freight depot; goods
station (Brit.); ~**wagen** *der* goods wagon
(Brit.); freight car (Amer.); ~**zug** *der* goods
train (Brit.); freight train (Amer.)

gut-, Gut-: *~|**gehen** ▸ GEHEN H, I;
*~**gelaunt** ▸ GELAUNT; *~**gemeint**
▸ GUT 2A; ~**gläubig** *Adj.* innocently
trusting; ~**haben** *das;* ~~s, ~~: credit
balance; ~|**heißen** *unr. tr. V.* approve of;
~**herzig** *Adj.* kind-hearted

gütig ① *Adj.* kindly
② *adv.* ~ **lächeln** give a kindly smile

gütlich *Adj.* amicable

gut-, Gut-: ~|**machen** *tr. V.* make good
⟨damage⟩; put right ⟨omission, mistake, etc.⟩;
~**mütig** *Adj.* good-natured; ~**mütigkeit**
die; ~~: good nature

Guts·besitzer *der,* **Guts·besitzerin**
die owner of a/the estate; landowner

gut-, Gut-: ~**schein** *der* voucher, coupon
(für, auf + *Akk.* for); ~|**schreiben** *unr. tr.
V.* credit; ~**schrift** *die* credit

Guts·hof *der* estate; manor

gut-: *~|**tun** ▸ GUT 1; ~**willig** ① *Adj.*
willing; (entgegenkommend) obliging; ② *adv.*
etw. ~**willig herausgeben/versprechen** hand
sth. over voluntarily/promise sth. willingly

Gymnasium *das;* ~s, **Gymnasien** ≈
grammar school

Gymnastik *die;* ∼: physical exercises *pl.;*
(Turnen) gymnastics *sing.*

Gynäkologe *der;* ∼n, ∼n,
Gynäkologin *die;* ∼, ∼nen gynaecologist

Hh

h, H /ha:/ *das;* ∼, ∼(a) (Buchstabe) h/H
(b) (Musik) [key of] B

h *Abk.* (a) = **Uhr** hrs
(b) = **Stunde** hr[s]

H *Abk.* (a) = **Herren;**
(b) = **Haltestelle**

ha¹ /ha(:)/ *Interj.* (a) (Überraschung) ah
(b) (Triumph) aha

ha² *Abk.* = **Hektar** ha

Haar *das;* ∼[e]s, ∼e hair; blonde ∼e od.
blondes ∼ haben have fair hair; (fig.) ∼e auf
den Zähnen haben (ugs. scherzh.) be a tough
customer; um ein ∼ (ugs.) very nearly

Haar-: ∼**ausfall** *der* hair loss; ∼**bürste**
die hairbrush; ∼**büschel** *das* tuft of hair

haaren *itr. V.* moult

Haares·breite *die;* um ∼: by a hair's
breadth

haar-, Haar-: ∼**festiger** *der;* ∼s, ∼:
setting lotion; ∼**genau** (ugs.) 1 *Adj.* exact;
2 *adv.* exactly

haarig *Adj.* hairy

haar-, Haar-: ∼**klemme** *die* hairgrip;
∼**nadel** *die* hairpin; ∼**nadel·kurve** *die*
hairpin bend; ∼**schnitt** *der* haircut;
(modisch) hairstyle; ∼**spalterei** *die;* ∼,
∼∼en (abwertend) hair-splitting; das ist doch
∼spalterei that's splitting hairs; ∼**spange**
die hairslide; ∼**sträubend** *Adj.* (a)
(grauenhaft) hair-raising; **(b)** (empörend)
outrageous; shocking; ∼**teil** *das* hairpiece;
∼**waschmittel** *das* shampoo;
∼**wasser** *das* hair lotion

Habe *die;* ∼ (geh.) possessions *pl.*

haben 1 *unr. tr. V.* have; have got; **heute**
∼ **wir schönes Wetter** the weather is fine
today; **es gut/schlecht/schwer** ∼: have it
good (coll.)/have a bad time [of it]/have a
difficult time; **du hast zu gehorchen** you
must obey; **das Jahr hat 12 Monate** there are
12 months in a year
2 *refl. V.* (ugs.: sich aufregen) make a fuss
3 *Hilfsverb* have; **ich habe/hatte ihn eben**
gesehen I've/I'd just seen him; **er hat es**
gewusst he knew it
4 *mod. V.* du hast zu gehorchen you must
obey; **er hat sich nicht einzumischen** he's not
to interfere

Haben *das;* ∼s, ∼ (Kaufmannsspr.) credit

Habe·nichts *der;* ∼, ∼e pauper

Haben-: ∼**seite** *die* (Kaufmannsspr.) credit
side; ∼**zinsen** *Pl.* interest *sing.* on
deposits

Hab·gier *die* (abwertend) greed

hab·gierig 1 *Adj.* (abwertend) greedy
2 *adv.* greedily

Habicht *der;* ∼s, ∼e hawk

Hab-: ∼**seligkeiten** *Pl.* [meagre]
belongings; ∼**sucht** *die;* (abwertend) greed;
avarice

Hachse *die;* ∼, ∼n (südd.) knuckle

Hack *das;* ∼s (ugs., bes. nordd.) mince

Hack·braten *der* meat loaf

Hacke¹ *die;* ∼, ∼n hoe; (Pickel) pick[axe]

Hacke² *die;* ∼, ∼n (bes. nordd. u. md.) heel

hacken 1 *itr. V.* (a) hoe
(b) (picken) peck
2 *tr. V.* (a) hoe ⟨garden, flower bed, etc.⟩
(b) (zerkleinern) chop; chop [up] ⟨meat,
vegetables, etc.⟩

Hacker *der;* ∼s, ∼, **Hackerin** *die;* ∼,
∼nen (DV-Jargon) hacker

hacke·zu *Adj.* (salopp) paralytic [drunk]
(coll.)

Hack·fleisch *das* minced meat; mince

Häcksel *der od. das;* ∼s (Landw.) chaff

hadern *itr. V.* (geh.) mit etw. ∼: be at odds
with sth.

Hafen *der;* ∼s, Häfen harbour; port

Hafen-: ∼**arbeiter** *der,* ∼**arbeiterin**
die dock worker; docker; ∼**kneipe** *die*
dockland pub (Brit.) *or* (Amer.) bar;
∼**rundfahrt** *die* trip round the harbour;
∼**stadt** *die* port; ∼**viertel** *das* dock area

Hafer *der;* ∼s oats *pl.*

Hafer-: ∼**brei** *der* porridge; ∼**flocken**
Pl. porridge oats

Haff *das;* ∼[e]s, ∼s od. ∼e lagoon

-haft *Adj., adv.* -like

Haft *die;* ∼ (a) (Gewahrsam) custody; (aus
politischen Gründen) detention
(b) (Freiheitsstrafe) imprisonment

haftbar *Adj.* (bes. Rechtsspr.) für etw. ∼ sein
be liable for sth.

Haft·befehl *der* (Rechtsw.) warrant [of
arrest]

haften¹ *itr. V.* stick (sich festsetzen) ⟨smell,
dirt, etc.⟩; cling (an + *Dat.* to); ∼ bleiben ⋯⟩

stick; (an/auf + *Dat.* to); ⟨*smell, smoke*⟩ cling (an/auf + *Dat.* to); (ugs.: im Gedächtnis bleiben) stick

haften² *itr. V.* für jmdn./etw. ~: be responsible for sb./liable for sth.; (Rechtsw., Wirtsch.) be liable

haften|bleiben ▶ HAFTEN¹

Häftling *der;* ~s, ~e prisoner

Haft·pflicht *die* liability (für for)

Haftpflicht·versicherung *die* personal liability insurance; (für Autofahrer) third party insurance

Haft-: ~**prüfung** *die* (Rechtsw.) review of a/ the remand in custody; ~**schale** *die* contact lens; ~**strafe** *die* (Rechtsspr. veralt.) prison sentence

Haftung *die;* ~, ~en liability; Gesellschaft mit [un]beschränkter ~: [un]limited [liability] company

Hagebutte *die;* ~, ~n (a) (Frucht) rose hip (b) (ugs.: Heckenrose) dog rose

Hagel *der;* ~s, ~ (auch fig.) hail

hageln *itr., tr. V.* (unpers.) hail

Hagel-: ~**schaden** *der* damage *no pl.* caused by hail; ~**schauer** *der* [short] hailstorm; ~**schlag** *der* hail

hager *Adj.* gaunt

haha /ha'ha(:)/ *Interj.* ha ha

Häher *der;* ~s, ~: jay

Hahn¹ *der;* ~[e]s, Hähne cock; (Wetter~) weathercock

Hahn² *der;* ~[e]s, Hähne, *fachspr.:* ~en (a) tap; faucet (Amer.) (b) (bei Waffen) hammer

Hähnchen *das;* ~s, ~: chicken

Hahnen·fuß *der* buttercup

Hai *der;* ~s, ~e shark

Häkchen *das;* ~s, ~ (a) [small] hook (b) (Zeichen) mark; (beim Abhaken) tick

häkeln *tr., itr. V.* crochet

Häkel·nadel *die* crochet hook

haken ① *tr. V.* hook (an + *Akk.* on to) ② *itr. V.* (klemmen) be stuck

Haken *der;* ~s, ~ (a) hook (b) (Zeichen) tick (c) (ugs.: Schwierigkeit) catch (d) (Boxen) hook

haken-, Haken-: ~**förmig** ① *Adj.* hooked; hook-shaped; ② *adv.* ~**förmig** gebogen hooked; hook-shaped; ~**kreuz** *das* swastika; ~**nase** *die* hooked nose; hook nose

halb ① *Adj. u. Bruchz.* half; eine ~e Stunde/ein ~er Meter half an hour/a metre; zum ~en Preis [at] half price; ~ Europa/die ~e Welt half of Europe/half the world; es ist ~ eins it's half past twelve; die ~e Wahrheit half [of] the truth; [noch] ein ~es Kind sein be hardly more than a child ② *adv.* ~ voll/leer half-full/-empty; ~ offen

half-open; ~ angezogen half dressed; ~ links/rechts (Fußball) ⟨*play*⟩ [at] inside left/ right

Halb·dunkel *das* semi-darkness

Halbe *der od. die od. das; adj. Dekl.* (ugs.) half litre (*of beer etc.*)

Halb·edelstein *der* (veralt.) semi-precious stone

halber *Präp. mit Gen.; nachgestellt* (wegen) on account of; (um ... willen) for the sake of

halb-, Halb-: ~**finale** *das* (Sport) semi-final; ~**gar** *Adj.* half-cooked; ~**gefror[e]ne** *das; adj. Dekl.* soft ice cream

Halbheit *die;* ~, ~en (abwertend) half measure

halbieren *tr. V.* cut/tear ⟨*object*⟩ in half; halve ⟨*amount, number*⟩

halb-, Halb-: ~**insel** *die* peninsula; ~**jahr** *das* six months *pl.;* half year; ~**jährlich** ① *Adj.* six-monthly; ② *adv.* every six months; ~**kreis** *der* semicircle; ~**kugel** *die* hemisphere; ~**lang** *Adj.* mid-length ⟨*hair*⟩; mid-calf length ⟨*coat, dress, etc.*⟩; ~**links** /-'-/ *Adv.* (Fußball) ⟨*play*⟩ [at] inside left; ~**mast** *Adv.* at half-mast; ~**mond** *der* (a) (Mond) half-moon; (b) (Figur) crescent; **~***offen** *Adj.:* ▶ HALB 2; ~**pension** *die* half-board; ~**rechts** /-'-/ *Adv.* (Fußball) ⟨*play*⟩ [at] inside right; ~**schlaf** *der* light sleep; im ~**schlaf** liegen be half asleep; doze; ~**schuh** *der* shoe; ~**starke** *der; adj. Dekl.* (ugs. abwertend) [young] hooligan

halb·tags *Adv.* ⟨*work*⟩ part-time; (morgens/ nachmittags) ⟨*work*⟩ [in the] mornings/ afternoons

Halbtags-: ~**arbeit** *die,* ~**beschäftigung** *die* part-time job; (morgens/nachmittags) morning/afternoon job; ~**schule** *die* half-day school; ~**stelle** *die* part-time job; (morgens/nachmittags) morning/ afternoon job

halb-, Halb-: **~***voll** *Adj.:* ▶ HALB 2; ~**wegs** *Adv.* to some extent; ~**wüchsig** /-vy:ksıç/ *Adj.* adolescent; ~**wüchsige** *der/die; adj. Dekl.* adolescent; ~**zeit** *die* (bes. Fußball) (a) half; (b) (Pause) half-time; ~**zeit·pause** *die* (Sport) half-time

Halde *die;* ~, ~n (Bergbau) slag heap

half *1. u. 3. Pers. Sg. Prät. v.* HELFEN

Hälfte *die;* ~, ~n (a) half (b) (ugs.: Teil) part

Halfter¹ *der od. das;* ~s, ~: halter

Halfter² *die;* ~, ~n; *auch das;* ~s, ~: holster

Hall *der;* ~[e]s, ~e (a) (geh.) reverberation (b) (Echo) echo

Halle *die;* ~, ~n hall; (Fabrik~) shed; (Hotel~, Theater~) foyer

hallen *itr. V.* (a) reverberate; ⟨*shot, bell, cry*⟩ ring out (b) (widerhallen) echo

Hallen- indoor ⟨*swimming pool, handball*⟩
Hallig *die;* ∼, ∼en small low island
⟨*particularly one of those off Schleswig-
Holstein*⟩
hallo *Interj.* hello
Hallo *das;* ∼s, ∼s cheering
Halluzination *die;* ∼, ∼en hallucination
Halm *der;* ∼[e]s, ∼e stalk; stem
Hals *der;* ∼es, Hälse neck; (Kehle) throat; ∼
über Kopf (ugs.) in a rush
hals-, Hals-: ∼**ab·schneider** *der,*
∼**ab·schneiderin** *die* (ugs. abwertend)
shark; ∼**band** *das* (für Tiere) collar;
∼**bruch** *der:* ▶ ∼- UND BEINBRUCH;
∼**entzündung** *die* inflammation of the
throat; ∼**kette** *die* necklace; ∼**-Nasen-
Ohren-Arzt** *der,* ∼**-Nasen-Ohren-
Ärztin** *die* ear, nose, and throat specialist;
∼**schlagader** *die* carotid [artery];
∼**schmerzen** *Pl.* sore throat *sing.;*
∼**starrig** *Adj.* (abwertend) stubborn;
obstinate; ∼**tuch** *das; Pl.* ∼tücher cravat;
(des Cowboys) neckerchief; ∼**- und
Beinbruch** *Interj.* (scherzh.) good luck;
∼**weh** *das* (ugs.) ▶ ∼SCHMERZEN
halt *Interj.* stop
Halt *der;* ∼[e]s, ∼e (a) hold
(b) (Stopp) stop; ∼ machen stop
haltbar *Adj.* (a) ∼ sein ⟨*food*⟩ keep [well];
∼ bis 5. 3. use by 5 March
(b) (nicht verschleißend) hard-wearing
⟨*material, clothes*⟩
(c) (aufrechtzuerhalten) tenable ⟨*hypothesis etc.*⟩
Haltbarkeit *die;* ∼ (Strapazierfähigkeit)
durability
Halte·bucht *die* (Verkehrsw.) lay-by (Brit.);
turnout (Amer.)
halten [1] *unr. tr. V.* (a) (auch Milit.) hold; die
Hand vor den Mund ∼: put one's hand in
front of one's mouth
(b) (Ballspiele) save ⟨*shot, penalty, etc.*⟩
(c) (bewahren) keep; (beibehalten, aufrechterhalten)
keep up ⟨*speed etc.*⟩; maintain ⟨*temperature,
equilibrium*⟩
(d) (erfüllen) keep; **sein Wort/ein Versprechen**
∼: keep one's word/a promise
(e) (besitzen, beschäftigen, beziehen) keep
⟨*chickens etc.*⟩; take ⟨*newspaper, magazine,
etc.*⟩
(f) (einschätzen) **jmdn. für reich/ehrlich** ∼:
think sb. is rich/honest; **viel von jmdm.**
∼: think a lot of sb.
(g) (ab∼, veranstalten) give, ⟨*speech, lecture*⟩
[2] *unr. itr. V.* (a) (stehen bleiben) stop
(b) (unverändert, an seinem Platz bleiben) last
(c) (Sport) save
(d) (beistehen) **zu jmdm.** ∼: stand by sb.
[3] *unr. refl. V.* (a) (sich durchsetzen, behaupten)
**wir werden uns/die Stadt wird sich nicht
länger ∼ können** we/the town won't be able
to hold out much longer
(b) (sich bewähren) **sich gut** ∼: do well
(c) (unverändert bleiben) ⟨*weather, flowers, etc.*⟩
last; ⟨*milk, meat, etc.*⟩ keep

(d) (Körperhaltung haben) **sich schlecht/gerade**
∼: hold oneself badly/straight
(e) (bleiben) **sich auf den Beinen/im Sattel** ∼:
stay on one's feet/in the saddle; **sich links/
rechts** ∼: keep [to the] left/right; **sich an
etw.** (*Akk.*) ∼: keep to sth.
Halte·punkt *der* stop
Halter *der;* ∼s, ∼ (a) (Fahrzeug∼) keeper
(b) (Tier∼) owner
(c) (Vorrichtung) holder
Halterin *die;* ∼, ∼nen (a) ▶ HALTER A:
keeper
(b) ▶ HALTER B: owner
Halterung *die;* ∼, ∼en support
Halte-: ∼**stelle** *die* stop; ∼**verbot** *das*
(a) „∼verbot" 'no stopping'; **hier ist** ∼verbot
this is a no-stopping zone; (b) (Stelle) no-
stopping zone; ∼**verbots·schild** *das* no-
stopping sign
-haltig, (österr.) **-hältig: vitamin**∼**/silber**∼
usw. containing vitamins/silver *etc. postpos.,
not pred.;* **vitamin**∼ **sein** contain vitamins
halt-, Halt-: ∼**los** *Adj.* (a) (labil) ∼**los sein**
be a weak character; **ein** ∼**loser Mensch** a
weak character; (b) (unbegründet) unfounded;
∼**losigkeit** *die;* ∼∼ (a) (Labilität) weakness
of character; (b) (mangelnde Begründung)
unfoundedness; *∼*∼|machen ▶ HALT B
Haltung *die;* ∼, ∼en (a) (Körper∼) posture
(b) (Pose) manner
(c) (Einstellung) attitude
(d) (Fassung) composure
Halunke *der;* ∼n, ∼n scoundrel; villain
Hamburger *der;* ∼s, ∼ (Frikadelle)
hamburger
hämisch [1] *Adj.* malicious
[2] *adv.* maliciously
Hammel *der;* ∼s, ∼ (a) wether
(b) (Fleisch) mutton
Hammel·fleisch *das* mutton
Hammer *der;* ∼s, Hämmer (a) hammer;
(Holz∼) mallet; ∼ **und Sichel** hammer and
sickle
(b) (Technik) ram
hämmern *itr., tr. V.* hammer
Hämorrhoiden /hɛmɔro'i:dn̩/ *Pl.* (Med.)
haemorrhoids; piles
Hampel·mann *der* (a) jumping jack
(b) (ugs. abwertend) puppet
hampeln *itr. V.* (ugs.) jump about
Hamster *der;* ∼s, ∼ hamster
hamstern *tr., itr. V.* (a) (horten) hoard
(b) (Lebensmittel tauschen) barter goods for
[food]
Hand *die;* ∼, Hände hand; **eine** ∼ **voll** a
handful; **jmdm. die** ∼ **geben** shake sb.'s
hand; ∼ **und Fuß/weder** ∼ **noch Fuß haben**
(ugs.) make sense/no sense; **alle** *od.* **beide
Hände damit voll haben, etw. zu tun** (ugs.)
have one's hands full doing sth.; **die Hände
in den Schoß legen** sit back and do nothing;
etw. aus der ∼ **geben** let sth. out of one's
hands; ∼ **in** ∼ **arbeiten** work hand in hand; ⋯⋮⋯

etw. zur ∼ haben have sth. handy; **zu** Händen [von] Herrn Müller attention Herr Müller; **unter der** ∼ (fig.) on the quiet

Hand-: ∼**arbeit** *die* (a) handicraft; **etw. in** ∼**arbeit herstellen** make sth. by hand; **(b)** (Gegenstand) handmade article; **(c)** (Nadelarbeit) [piece of] needlework; ∼**ball** *der* handball; ∼**besen** *der* brush; ∼**betrieb** *der* manual operation; ∼**bewegung** *die* (a) movement of the hand; **(b)** (Geste) gesture; ∼**bremse** *die* handbrake; ∼**buch** *das* handbook; (technisches ∼buch) manual

Händchen *das;* ∼s, ∼: [little] hand

Hände ▸ HAND

Hände-: ∼**druck** *der; Pl.* ∼**drücke** handshake; ∼**klatschen** *das;* ∼∼s clapping

Handel *der;* ∼s trade; ∼ **treiben** trade; ∼ **treibend** trading ⟨*nation*⟩

handeln ⓵ *itr. V.* **(a)** trade; deal **(b)** (feilschen) haggle **(c)** (agieren) act **(d)** (sich verhalten) behave **(e) von etw.** *od.* **über etw.** (*Akk.*) ∼ ⟨*book, film, etc.*⟩ be about *or* deal with sth. ⓶ *refl. V.* (*unpers.*) **es handelt sich um ...:** it is a matter of ...; (es dreht sich um) it's about ...

handels-, Handels-: ∼**abkommen** *das* trade agreement; ∼**bank** *die; Pl.* ∼∼en merchant bank; ∼**bilanz** *die* **(a)** (eines Betriebes) balance sheet; **(b)** (eines Staates) balance of trade; ∼**einig, ∼eins: mit** jmdm. ∼einig *od.* ∼eins werden/sein agree/ have agreed terms with sb.; ∼**flotte** *die* merchant fleet; ∼**gesellschaft** *die* company; ∼**kammer** *die:* ▸ INDUSTRIE- UND HANDELSKAMMER; ∼**klasse** *die* grade; ∼**marine** *die* merchant navy; ∼**partner** *der,* ∼**partnerin** *die* trading partner; ∼**register** *das* register of companies; ∼**schiff** *das* merchant ship; ∼**schule** *die* commercial college; ∼**straße** *die* (hist.) trade route; ∼**üblich** *Adj.* ∼übliche Praktiken/Größen standard business practices/standard [commercial] sizes; ∼**unternehmen** *das* trading concern; ∼**vertreter** *der,* ∼**vertreterin** *die* [sales] representative; travelling salesman/ saleswoman; ∼**vertretung** *die* trade mission; ∼**zentrum** *das* trading centre

hände·ringend *Adv.* (ugs.: dringend) ⟨*need*⟩ urgently; ⟨*search for sb./sth.*⟩ desperately

hand-, Hand-: ∼**feger** *der* brush; ∼**fest** *Adj.* **(a)** robust; sturdy; **(b)** substantial ⟨*meal etc.*⟩; **(c)** solid ⟨*proof*⟩; concrete ⟨*suggestion*⟩; complete ⟨*lie*⟩; well-founded ⟨*argument*⟩; ∼**fläche** *die* palm [of one's/the hand]; flat of one's/the hand; ∼**gas** *das* (Kfz-W.) hand throttle; ∼**gearbeitet** *Adj.* handmade; ∼**gelenk** *das* wrist; ∼**gemenge** *das* fight; ∼**gepäck** *das* hand baggage; ∼**geschrieben** *Adj.* handwritten;

∼**granate** *die* hand grenade; ∼**greiflich** *Adj.* **(a)** (tätlich) ∼greiflich werden start using one's fists; **(b)** tangible ⟨*success, advantage, proof, etc.*⟩; palpable ⟨*contradiction, error*⟩; obvious ⟨*fact*⟩; ∼**griff** *der* **(a) mit einem** ∼griff/wenigen ∼griffen in one movement/ without much trouble; (schnell) in no time at all/next to no time; **(b)** (am Koffer, an einem Werkzeug) handle; ∼**habe** *die;* ∼∼, ∼∼n: **eine [rechtliche]** ∼**habe [gegen jmdn.]** a legal handle [against sb.]; ∼**haben** *tr. V.* **(a)** handle; operate ⟨*device, machine*⟩; **(b)** (praktizieren) implement ⟨*law etc.*⟩; ∼**habung** *die;* ∼∼, ∼∼en **(a)** handling; (eines Gerätes, einer Maschine) operation; **(b)** (Durchführung) implementation

Handikap /'hɛndikɛp/ *das;* ∼s, ∼s (auch Sport) handicap

handikapen /'hɛndikɛpn/ *tr. V.* handicap

Hand-: ∼**käse** *der* (landsch.) small, hand-formed curd cheese; ∼**koffer** *der* [small] suitcase; ∼**kuss, *∼kuß** *der* kiss on sb.'s hand; ∼**langer** *der;* ∼∼s, ∼∼, (ungelernter Arbeiter) labourer; (abwertend) lackey; ∼**lauf** *der* handrail

Händler *der;* ∼s, ∼, **Händlerin** *die;* ∼, ∼**nen** trader

handlich *Adj.* handy; easily carried ⟨*parcel, suitcase*⟩; easily portable ⟨*television, camera*⟩

Handlung *die;* ∼, ∼en **(a)** (Vorgehen) action; (Tat) act **(b)** (Fabel) plot

handlungs-, Handlungs-: ∼**arm** *Adj.* short on action *pred.;* ∼**fähig** *Adj.* able to act *pred.;* working *attrib.* ⟨*majority*⟩; ∼**freiheit** *die* freedom of action; ∼**reisende** *der/die* ▸ HANDELSVERTRETER; ∼**weise** *die* conduct

hand-, Hand-: ∼**puppe** *die* glove *or* hand puppet; ∼**schelle** *die* handcuff; ∼**schlag** *der* handshake; ∼**schrift** *die* handwriting; ∼**schriftlich** ⓵ *Adj.* handwritten; ⓶ *adv.* by hand; ∼**schuh** *der* glove; ∼**schuh·fach** *das* glove compartment; ∼**signiert** *Adj.* signed; ∼**spiegel** *der* hand mirror; ∼**stand** *der* (Turnen) handstand; ∼**tasche** *die* handbag; ∼**tuch** *das; Pl.* -tücher towel; ∼**umdrehen: im** ∼**umdrehen** in no time at all; ∼**verlesen** *Adj.* hand-picked; *∼**voll** ▸ HAND; ∼**wäsche** *die* washing by hand

Hand·werk *das* craft; (als Beruf) trade; **sein** ∼ **kennen/beherrschen** know one's job

Handwerker *der;* ∼s, ∼: tradesman

Handwerkerin *die;* ∼, ∼nen tradeswoman;

handwerklich *Adj.* **ein** ∼**er Beruf** a [skilled] trade

Handwerks·zeug *das* tools *pl.*

Handy /'hɛndi/ *das;* ∼s, ∼s mobile [phone]

Handy·nummer *die* mobile number

Hand·zeichen *das* sign [with one's hand]; (eines Autofahrers) hand signal; (Abstimmung) show of hands

---

*alte Schreibung - vgl. Hinweis auf S. xiv

Hanf *der;* ∼[e]s hemp

Hang *der;* ∼[e]s, **Hänge** slope; (Neigung) tendency

Hänge-: ∼**brücke** *die* suspension bridge; ∼**lampe** *die* pendant light; ∼**matte** *die* hammock

hängen[1] *unr. itr. V.; südd., österr., schweiz. mit sein* hang (an + *Dat.* from); (an einem Fahrzeug) be hitched (**an** + *Dat.* to); [**mit der Ärmel** *usw.* **an/in etw.** (*Dat.*) ∼ **bleiben** get one's sleeve *etc.* caught on/in sth.; ∼ **bleiben** (ugs.: haften) stick (**an/auf** + *Dat.*) to; (ugs.: verweilen) get stuck (coll.)

hängen[2] [1] *tr. V.* (a) hang (**in/über** + (*Akk.*) in/over; **an/auf** + *Akk.* on) (b) (befestigen) hitch up (**an** + *Akk.* to); couple on ⟨*railway carriage, etc.*⟩ (**an** + *Akk.* to) [2] *refl. V.* (a) **sich an etw.** (*Akk.*) ∼: hang on to sth. (b) (sich festsetzen) cling (**an** + *Akk.* to)

***hängen|bleiben** ▶ HÄNGEN[1]

hängend *Adj.* hanging

Hänge·schrank *der* wall cupboard

Hang·lage *die* hillside location

Hansaplast Ⓦ *das;* ∼[e]s sticking plaster; Elastoplast ®

hänseln *tr. V.* tease

Hanse·stadt *die* Hanseatic city

Hantel *die;* ∼, ∼n (Sport) (kurz) dumb-bell; (lang) barbell

hantieren *itr. V.* be busy

Häppchen *das;* ∼s, ∼ (a) [small] morsel (b) (Appetithappen) canapé

Happen *der;* ∼s, ∼: morsel

happig *Adj.* (ugs.) ∼e **Preise** fancy prices (coll.)

Happyend, Happy-End /'hɛpi'|ɛnt/ *das;* ∼[s], ∼s happy ending

Hardware /'ha:dwɛə/ *die;* ∼, ∼s (DV) hardware

Harfe *die;* ∼, ∼n harp

Harke *die;* ∼, ∼n rake

harken *tr. V.* rake

harm·los [1] *Adj.* (a) (ungefährlich) harmless; slight ⟨*injury, cold, etc.*⟩; mild ⟨*illness*⟩; safe ⟨*medicine, bend, road, etc.*⟩ (b) (arglos) innocent; harmless ⟨*fun, pastime, etc.*⟩ [2] *adv.* (a) (ungefährlich) harmlessly (b) (arglos) innocently

Harmlosigkeit *die;* ∼ (a) (Ungefährlichkeit) harmlessness; (einer Krankheit) mildness; (eines Medikamentes) safety (b) (Arglosigkeit, harmloses Verhalten) innocence

Harmonie *die;* ∼, ∼n (auch fig.) harmony

harmonieren *itr. V.* (a) harmonize (b) (miteinander auskommen) get on well

Harmonika *die;* ∼, ∼s *od.* **Harmoniken** harmonica

harmonisch [1] *Adj.* harmonious; (Musik) harmonic [2] *adv.* harmoniously; (Musik) harmonically

harmonisieren *tr. V.* coordinate; **etw. mit etw.** ∼ (Wirtsch.) bring sth. into line with sth.

Harmonisierung *die;* ∼, ∼en (Wirtsch.) harmonization

Harmonium *das;* ∼s, **Harmonien** harmonium

Harn *der;* ∼[e]s, ∼e (Med.) urine

Harn·blase *die* bladder

Harnisch *der;* ∼s, ∼e armour

Harpune *die;* ∼, ∼n harpoon

harpunieren *tr. V.* harpoon

harren *itr. V.* (geh.) **jmds./einer Sache** *od.* **auf jmdn./etw.** ∼: await sb./sth.

harsch [1] *Adj.* (a) (vereist) crusted (b) (barsch) harsh [2] *adv.* harshly

Harsch *der;* ∼[e]s crusted snow

hart; härter, härtest... [1] *Adj.* (a) hard; ∼ **gekocht** hard-boiled ⟨*egg*⟩ (b) tough ⟨*situation, job*⟩; harsh ⟨*reality, truth*⟩ (c) (streng) harsh ⟨*penalty, punishment, judgement*⟩; tough ⟨*measure, law, course*⟩ (d) (rau) rough ⟨*game, opponent*⟩ [2] *adv.* hard chair; (a) (mühevoll) ⟨*work*⟩ hard (b) (streng) harshly (c) (nahe) close (**an** + *Dat.* to)

Härte *die;* ∼, ∼n (a) (auch Physik) hardness (b) (Widerstandsfähigkeit) toughness (c) (schwere Belastung) hardship (d) (Strenge) harshness (e) (Heftigkeit) (eines Aufpralls usw.) force; (eines Streits) violence (f) (Rauheit) roughness

Härte·fall *der* (a) case of hardship (b) (ugs.: Person) hardship case

härten *tr., itr. V.* harden

härter ▶ HART

härtest... ▶ HART

hart-, Hart-: *∼**gekocht** ▶ HART 1A; ∼**geld** *das* coins *pl.*; ∼**gummi** *das* hard rubber; ∼**herzig** [1] *Adj.* hard-hearted [2] *adv.* hard-heartedly; ∼**herzigkeit** *die;* ∼∼: hard-heartedness; ∼**käse** *der* hard cheese; ∼**näckig** [1] *Adj.* (a) (eigensinnig) obstinate; stubborn; (b) (ausdauernd) dogged [2] *adv.* (a) (eigensinnig) obstinately; stubbornly; (b) (ausdauernd) doggedly; ∼**näckigkeit** *die;* ∼∼ (a) (Eigensinn) obstinacy; stubbornness; (b) (Ausdauer) doggedness

Härtung *die;* ∼, ∼en hardening; (von Stahl auch) tempering

Hart·wurst *die* dry sausage

Harz *das;* ∼es, ∼e resin

Harzer Käse *der;* ∼ ∼s, ∼ ∼: Harz [Mountain] cheese

Haschee (Kochk.) *das;* ∼s, ∼s hash

Haschen[1] *tr. V.* (veralt.) catch

haschen[2] *itr. V.* (ugs.) smoke [hash] (coll.)

Häschen /'hɛ:sçən/ *das;* ∼, ∼s bunny

Haschisch *das od. der;* ∼[s] hashish

Haschisch-rausch der [state of] hashish intoxication; **etw. im** od. **bei einem ~rausch tun** do sth. while under the effects of hashish or while [high (coll.)] on hashish

Hase der; ~n, ~n (a) hare
(b) (landsch.) ▶ KANINCHEN

Hasel·nuss, *Hasel·nuß die hazelnut

Hasen-: ~**fuß** der (spöttisch abwertend) coward; chicken (coll.); ~**scharte** die (Med.) harelip

Haspel die; ~, ~n (Technik) (für Garn) reel; (für ein Seil, Kabel) drum

Hass, *Haß der; Hasses hatred (auf + Akk., gegen of, for)

hassen tr., itr. V. hate

hass·erfüllt, *haß·erfüllt Adj. filled with hatred postpos.

hässlich, *häßlich 1 Adj. (a) ugly
(b) (gemein) nasty
(c) (unangenehm) awful ⟨weather, cold, situation, etc.⟩
2 adv. (a) ⟨dress⟩ unattractively
(b) (gemein) nastily

Hässlichkeit, *Häßlichkeit die; ~, ~en (a) (Aussehen) ugliness
(b) (Gesinnung) nastiness

hast 2. Pers. Sg. Präsens v. HABEN

Hast die; ~: haste

hasten itr. V.; mit sein hurry

hastig 1 Adj. hasty; hurried
2 adv. hastily; hurriedly

hat 3. Pers. Sg. Präsens v. HABEN

hätscheln tr. V. caress

hatschi Interj. atishoo

hatte 1. u. 3. Pers. Sg. Prät. v. HABEN

hätte 1. u. 3. Pers. Sg. Konjunktiv II v. HABEN

Haube die; ~, ~n (a) bonnet; (einer Krankenschwester) cap
(b) (Kfz-W.) bonnet (Brit.); hood (Amer.)

Hauch der; ~[e]s, ~e (geh.) (a) (Atem, auch fig.) breath
(b) (Luftzug) breath of wind
(c) (leichter Duft) delicate smell
(d) (dünne Schicht) [gossamer-]thin layer

hauch·dünn Adj. gossamer-thin ⟨material, dress⟩; wafer-thin ⟨layer, slice, majority⟩

hauchen itr. V. breathe (gegen, auf + Akk. on)

Haue die; ~, ~n (a) (südd., österr.: Hacke) hoe
(b) (ugs.: Prügel) a hiding (coll.)

hauen 1 unr. tr. V. (a) (ugs.: schlagen) belt; clobber (coll.)
(b) (ugs.: auf einen Körperteil) belt (coll.); hit
(c) (herstellen) carve ⟨figure, statue, etc.⟩ (in + Akk. in)
2 unr. itr. V. (a) (ugs.: prügeln) **er haut immer gleich** he's quick to hit out
(b) (auf einen Körperteil) belt (coll.); hit
(c) (ugs.: auf/gegen etw. schlagen) thump

*old spelling - see note on page xiv

3 unr. refl. V. (ugs.: sich prügeln) have a punch-up (coll.)

Hauer der; ~s, ~ (Jägerspr.) tusk; (fig.) fang

Haufen der; ~s, ~: heap; pile; (Gruppe) bunch (coll.)

häufen 1 tr. V. heap, pile (auf + Akk. on to); (aufheben) hoard ⟨money, supplies⟩
2 refl. V. (sich mehren) pile up

häufig 1 Adj. frequent
2 adv. frequently; often

Häufigkeit die; ~, ~en frequency

Häufung die; ~, ~en increasing frequency

Haupt das; ~[e]s, Häupter (geh., auch fig.) head

haupt-, Haupt-: ~**bahnhof** der main station; ~**beruflich** 1 Adj. seine ~berufliche Tätigkeit his main occupation; 2 adv. **er ist ~beruflich als Elektriker tätig** his main occupation is that of electrician; ~**darsteller** der (Theater, Film) male lead; ~**darstellerin** die (Theater, Film) female lead; ~**eingang** der main entrance; ~**einschalt·zeit** die peak or prime viewing time; ~**fach** das major; ~**figur** die main character; ~**film** der main feature; ~**gang** der (a) main corridor;
(b) ▶ ~GERICHT; ~**gebäude** das main building; ~**gericht** das main course; ~**gewinn** der first prize

Häuptling der; ~s, ~e chief[tain]

haupt-, Haupt-: ~**mahlzeit** die main meal; ~**mann** der; Pl. ~leute (Milit.) captain; ~**person** die central figure; ~**postamt** das main post office; ~**quartier** das (Milit., auch fig.) headquarters sing. or pl.; ~**reise·zeit** die high season; peak [holiday] season; ~**rolle** die main role; lead; **die ~rolle spielen** (fig.) play the leading role; ~**sache** die main thing; ~**sächlich** 1 Adv. mainly; principally; 2 Adj.; nicht präd. main; principal; ~**saison** die high season; ~**satz** der main clause; (allein stehend) sentence; ~**schalter** der (Elektrot.) mains switch; ~**schlagader** die aorta; ~**schul·abschluss,** *~**schul·abschluß** der ≈ secondary school leaving certificate; ~**schule** die ≈ secondary modern school; ~**schüler** der, ~**schülerin** die ≈ secondary modern school pupil; ~**sitz** der head office; headquarters pl.; ~**stadt** die capital [city]; ~**städtisch** Adj. metropolitan; ~**straße** die main street; ~**thema** das main topic or theme; (Musik) main theme; ~**verkehr** der bulk of the traffic

Hauptverkehrs-: ~**straße** die main road; ~**zeit** die rush hour

Haupt-: ~**versammlung** die (Wirtsch.) shareholders' meeting; ~**wache** die main police station; ~**wort** das (Sprachw.) noun

hau ruck Interj. heave[-ho]

Haus das; ~es, Häuser (a) house; (Amts-,

Firmengebäude usw.) building; (Heim) home;
nach ~e home; **zu** ~**e** at home; **das erste** ~
am Platze the best hotel in the town
(b) ~ **halten** be economical

haus-, Haus-: ~**angestellte** der/die
domestic servant; ~**apotheke** die
medicine cabinet; ~**arbeit** die housework;
(Schulw.) homework; ~**arrest** der house
arrest; ~**arzt** der, ~**ärztin** die family
doctor; ~**aufgabe** die homework;
~**backen** ① Adj. plain; unadventurous
⟨clothes⟩; ② adv. ⟨dress⟩ unadventurously;
~**besetzer** der; ~~s, ~~,
~**besetzerin** die; ~~, ~~nen squatter;
~**besitzer** der houseowner; (Vermieter)
landlord; ~**besitzerin** die houseowner;
(Vermieterin) landlady; ~**besuch** der house
call; ~**boot** das houseboat

Häuschen /ˈhɔyːsçən/ das; ~s, ~: small
house; **aus dem** ~ **sein** (ugs.) be over the
moon (coll.)

hausen itr. V. (a) (ugs. abwertend) live
(b) (Verwüstungen anrichten) [**furchtbar**] ~:
wreak havoc

Häuser·block der block [of houses]

haus-, Haus-: ~**flur** der hall[way]; (im
Obergeschoss) landing; ~**frau** die housewife;
~**freund** der (a) friend of the family; **(b)**
(verhüll.: Liebhaber) man friend (euphem.);
~**freundin** die friend of the family;
~**friedens·bruch** der (Rechtsw.) trespass;
~**gebrauch** der domestic use; **das reicht
für den** ~**gebrauch** (ugs.) it's good enough to
get by (coll.); ~**gehilfin** die [home] help;
~**gemacht** Adj. home-made

Haus·halt der (a) household
(b) (Arbeit im ~) housekeeping; **jmdm. den** ~
führen keep house for sb.
(c) (Politik) budget

*****haus|halten** ▶ HAUS B

Haushälterin die; ~, ~nen housekeeper

Haushalts-: ~**artikel** der household
article; ~**debatte** die (Politik) budget
debate; ~**geld** das housekeeping money;
~**jahr** das financial year; ~**kasse** die
housekeeping money; ~**plan** der budget;
~**waren** Pl. household goods

haus-, Haus-: ~**herr** der (a)
(Familienoberhaupt) head of the household; **(b)**
(als Gastgeber) host; **(c)** (Rechtsspr.) (Eigentümer)
owner; (Mieter) occupier ~**herrin** die (a)
▶ ~HERR A; **(b)** ▶ ~HERR B; ~**hoch** ① Adj.
as high as a house; (fig.) overwhelming;
② adv. (fig.) ~**hoch gewinnen** win hands
down

hausieren itr. V. [**mit etw.**] ~: hawk [sth.];
peddle [sth.]; „**Hausieren verboten**" 'no
hawkers'

Hausierer der; ~s, ~, **Hausiererin** die;
~, ~nen pedlar; hawker

häuslich Adj. (a) domestic
(b) (das Zuhause liebend) home-loving

Hausmacher·art die: **nach** ~: home-
made-style attrib.

Haus·mann der: man who stays at home
and does the housework; (Ehemann)
househusband

Hausmanns·kost die plain cooking

Haus-: ~**marke** die (a) house wine; **(b)**
(ugs.: bevorzugtes Getränk) favourite tipple
(coll.); ~**meister** der, ~**meisterin** die
caretaker; ~**mittel** das household remedy;
~**musik** die music at home; ~**nummer**
die house number; ~**ordnung** die house
rules pl.; ~**putz** der spring-clean;
(regelmäßig) clean-out

Haus·rat der household goods pl.

Hausrat·versicherung die [household
or home] contents insurance

Haus-: ~**schlüssel** der front-door key;
house key; ~**schuh** der slipper; ~**segen**
der: **bei ihnen hängt der** ~**segen schief** (ugs.
scherzh.) they've been having a row

Haussuchung die; ~, ~en house search

Haussuchungs·befehl der search
warrant

Haus-: ~**telefon** das internal telephone;
~**tier** das (a) pet; **(b)** (Nutztier) domestic
animal; ~**tür** die front door; ~**verbot** das
ban on entering the house/pub/restaurant
etc.; ~**verwalter** der, ~**verwalterin**
die manager [of the block]; ~**wirt** der
landlord; ~**wirtin** die landlady;
~**wirtschaft** die domestic science and
home economics; ~**zelt** das ridge tent

Haut die; ~, Häute skin; **aus der** ~ **fahren**
(ugs.) go up the wall (coll.)

Haut-: ~**arzt** der, ~**ärztin** die skin
specialist; ~**ausschlag** der [skin] rash

häuten ① tr. V. skin; flay
② refl. V. shed its skin/their skins

haut-, Haut-: ~**eng** Adj. skintight;
~**farbe** die [skin] colour; ~**krankheit**
die skin disease; ~**krebs** der skin cancer

Häutung die; ~, ~en (a) ▶ HÄUTEN 1:
skinning; flaying
(b) (das Sichhäuten) **eine Eidechse bei der** ~:
a lizard shedding its skin

Haxe die; ~, ~n ▶ HACHSE

he Interj. (ugs.) hey

Heb·amme die midwife

Hebel der; ~s, ~: lever

heben unr. tr. V. (a) lift; raise ⟨baton,
camera, glass⟩
(b) (verbessern) raise ⟨standard, level⟩;
increase ⟨turnover, self-confidence⟩; improve
⟨mood⟩; enhance ⟨standing⟩; boost ⟨morale⟩

hecheln¹ itr. V. (ugs. abwertend) gossip

hecheln² itr. V. pant [for breath]

Hecht der; ~[e]s, ~e pike

Hecht·sprung der (a) (Turnen) Hecht vault
(b) (Schwimmen) racing dive; (vom Sprungturm)
pike-dive

Heck das; ~[e]s, ~e od. ~s stern;
(Flugzeug~) tail; (Auto~) rear

Heck·antrieb der (Kfz-W.) rear-wheel drive

Hecke *die;* ~, ~n (a) hedge
(b) (wild wachsend) thicket

Hecken-: ~**rose** *die* dogrose; ~**schütze**
der, ~**schützin** *die* sniper

Heck·scheibe *die* rear window

Heer *der;* ~[e]s, ~e armed forces *pl.;* (für
den Landkrieg, fig.) army

Hefe *die;* ~, ~n yeast

Hefe·teig *der* yeast dough

Heft¹ *das;* ~[e]s, ~e (geh.) haft; handle

Heft² *das;* ~[e]s, ~e (a) (bes. Schule)
exercise book
(b) (Nummer einer Zeitschrift) issue

Heftchen *das;* ~s, ~: book [of tickets/
stamps *etc.*]

heften ① *tr. V.* (a) (mit einer Nadel) pin; (mit
einer Klammer) clip; (mit Klebstoff) stick
(b) (Schneiderei) tack
(c) (Buchbinderei) stitch; (mit Klammern) staple
② *refl. V.* **sich an jmds. Fersen** (*Akk.*) ~:
stick hard on sb.'s heels

Hefter *der;* ~s, ~: [loose-leaf] file

heftig ① *Adj.* violent; heavy ⟨rain, shower,
blow⟩; severe ⟨pain⟩; ⟨person⟩ with a violent
temper
② *adv.* ⟨rain, snow, breathe⟩ heavily; ⟨hit⟩
hard; ⟨quarrel⟩ violently

Heftigkeit *die;* ~: ▶ HEFTIG 1: violence;
heaviness; severity

Heft-: ~**klammer** staple; ~**pflaster** *das*
sticking plaster; ~**zwecke** *die*
▶ REISSZWECKE

hegen *tr. V.* (a) (bes. Forstw., Jagdw.) look
after, tend
(b) (geh.: umsorgen) look after
(c) (fig.) feel ⟨contempt, hatred, mistrust⟩;
cherish ⟨hope, wish, desire⟩; harbour
⟨grudge, suspicion⟩

Hehl *der od. das:* **kein[en]** ~ **aus etw.
machen** make no secret of sth.

Hehler *der;* ~s, ~: receiver [of stolen
goods]

Hehlerei *die;* ~, ~en (Rechtsw.) receiving
[stolen goods] *no art.*

Hehlerin *die;* ~, ~nen ▶ HEHLER

Heide¹ *der;* ~n, ~n heathen

Heide² *die;* ~, ~n heath; (Landschaft)
heathland

Heide-: ~**kraut** *das* heather; ~**land** *das*
moorland; heathland

Heidel·beere *die* bilberry

Heidin *die;* ~, ~nen heathen

heidnisch *Adj.* heathen

heikel *Adj.* (a) (schwierig) delicate, ticklish
⟨matter, subject⟩; ticklish tricky ⟨problem,
question, situation⟩
(b) (wählerisch) fussy (**in Bezug auf** + *Akk.*
about)

heil *Adj.* (nicht entzwei) in one piece; **wieder** ~
sein ⟨injured part⟩ have healed [up]

Heil *das;* ~s (a) (Wohlergehen) benefit
(b) (Rel.) salvation

Heiland *der;* ~[e]s, ~e Saviour

Heil·anstalt *die* (Anstalt für Kranke od.
Süchtige) sanatorium; (psychiatrische Klinik)
mental hospital

heilbar *Adj.* curable

Heil·butt *der* halibut

heilen ① *tr. V.* cure; heal ⟨wound⟩
② *itr. V.; mit sein* ⟨wound⟩ heal [up];
⟨fracture⟩ mend

heil·froh *Adj.* very glad

heilig *Adj.* (a) holy; **die Heiligen Drei Könige**
the Three Kings *or* Wise Men; the Magi; **die
Heilige Schrift** the Holy Scriptures *pl.;* **der
Heilige Abend** Christmas Eve
(b) (geh.: unantastbar) sacred ⟨right, tradition,
cause, etc.⟩

Heilig·abend *der* Christmas Eve

Heilige *der/die; adj. Dekl.* saint

heiligen *tr. V.* keep ⟨tradition, Sabbath,
etc.⟩; **der Zweck heiligt die Mittel** the end
justifies the means

Heiligen·schein *der* gloriole; (um den
Kopf) halo

Heiligkeit *die;* ~: holiness

Heiligtum *das;* ~s, Heiligtümer shrine

Heil-: ~**kraut** *das* medicinal herb;
~**mittel** *das* (auch fig.) remedy (**gegen** for);
(Medikament) medicament; ~**praktiker** *der,*
~**praktikerin** *die* non-medical
practitioner

heilsam *Adj.* salutary

Heils·armee *die* Salvation Army

Heilung *die;* ~, ~en (einer Wunde) healing;
(von Krankheit, Kranken) curing

Heim *das;* ~[e]s, ~e (a) (Zuhause) home
(b) (Anstalt, Alters~) home; (für Obdachlose)
hostel

Heim·arbeit *die* outwork

Heimat *die;* ~, ~en (a) (Ort) home; home
town/village; (Land) home; homeland
(b) (Ursprungsland) natural habitat

Heimat-: ~**kunde** *die* local history,
geography, and natural history; ~**land** *das*
native land; (fig.) home

heimatlich *Adj.* native ⟨dialect⟩; nostalgic
⟨emotions⟩

heimat-, Heimat-: ~**los** *Adj.* homeless;
~**museum** *das* museum of local history;
~**ort** *der* home town/village; ~**stadt** *die*
home town; ~**vertriebene** *der/die; adj.
Dekl.* expellee [from his/her homeland]

heim-, Heim-: ~**|bringen** *unr. tr. V.* (a)
jmdn. ~: take *or.* see sb. home; (b) bring
home; ~**computer** *der* home computer;
~**|fahren** ① *unr. itr. V.; mit sein* drive
home; ② *unr. tr. V.* drive home; ~**fahrt** *die*
journey home; (mit dem Auto) drive home;
~**|gehen** *unr. itr. V.; mit sein* go home

heimisch *Adj.* (einheimisch) indigenous,

native ⟨*plants, animals, etc.*⟩ (in + *Dat.* to);
domestic ⟨*industry*⟩; **sich ∼ fühlen** feel at
home; **∼ werden** [in (+ *Dat.*)] settle in[to]

heim-, Heim-: ∼kehr *die;* **∼∼:** return
home; homecoming; **∼|kehren** *itr. V.; mit
sein* return home (aus from); **∼|kommen**
unr. itr. V.; mit sein come home

heimlich 1 *Adj.* secret
2 *adv.* secretly

Heimlichkeit *die;* **∼, ∼en** secret

heim-, Heim-: ∼reise *die* journey home;
∼spiel *das* (Sport) home match *or* game;
∼|suchen *tr. V.* ⟨*storm, earthquake,
epidemic*⟩ strike; ⟨*disease*⟩ afflict;
⟨*nightmares, doubts*⟩ plague; **∼suchung**
die; **∼∼, ∼∼en** affliction; visitation;
∼tückisch 1 *Adj.* (bösartig) malicious;
(fig.) insidious ⟨*disease*⟩; 2 *adv.* maliciously;
∼wärts *Adv.* (nach Hause zu) home; (in
Richtung Heimat) homeward[s]; **∼weg** *der*
way home; **∼weh** *das* homesickness;
∼weh haben be homesick (**nach** for);
∼|zahlen *tr. V.* jmdm. etw. **∼zahlen** pay
sb. back for sth.

Heinzel·männchen *das* brownie

Heirat *die;* **∼, ∼en** marriage

heiraten 1 *itr. V.* get married
2 *tr. V.* marry

Heirats-: ∼antrag *der:* jmdm. einen
∼antrag machen propose to sb.; **∼anzeige**
die announcement of a/the forthcoming
marriage; **∼schwindler** *der,*
∼schwindlerin *die: person who makes a
spurious offer of marriage for purposes of
fraud*

heiser 1 *Adj.* hoarse
2 *adv.* in a hoarse voice

Heiserkeit *die;* **∼:** hoarseness

heiß 1 *Adj.* hot; **jmdm. ist ∼:** sb. feels hot;
etw. ∼ machen heat sth. up; heated ⟨*debate,
argument*⟩; fierce ⟨*fight, battle*⟩; ardent
⟨*wish, love*⟩; **ein ∼es Thema** a controversial
subject
2 *adv.* ⟨*fight*⟩ fiercely; ⟨*love*⟩ dearly; ⟨*long*⟩
fervently

heißen *unr. itr. V.* (den Namen tragen) be
called; (bedeuten) mean; (lauten) ⟨*saying*⟩ go;
(*unpers.*) **es heißt, dass …:** they say that …;
in dem Artikel heißt es …: in the article it
says that …

Heiß·luft *die* hot air

Heißluft·backofen *der* fan oven

heiter *Adj.* cheerful, happy ⟨*person,
nature*⟩; happy, merry ⟨*laughter*⟩; fine
⟨*weather, day*⟩

Heiterkeit *die;* **∼** (a) (Frohsinn)
cheerfulness
(b) (Belustigung) merriment

heizbar *Adj.* heated

Heiz·decke *die* electric blanket

heizen 1 *itr. V.* have the heating on
2 *tr. V.* heat ⟨*room etc.*⟩

Heizer *der;* **∼s, ∼, Heizerin** *die;* **∼,
∼nen** stoker

Heiz-: ∼kissen *das* heating pad;
∼körper *der* radiator; **∼ofen** *der* stove;
heater; **∼platte** *die* hotplate

Heizung *die;* **∼, ∼en (a)** [central] heating
no pl., no indef. art.;
(b) (ugs.: Heizkörper) radiator

Hektar *das od. der;* **∼s, ∼e** hectare

Hektik *die;* **∼:** hectic rush; (des Lebens)
hectic pace

hektisch *Adj.* hectic

Held *der;* **∼en, ∼en** hero

heldenhaft 1 *Adj.* heroic
2 *adv.* heroically

Heldentum *das;* **∼s** heroism

Heldin *die;* **∼, ∼nen** heroine

helfen *unr. itr. V.* help; **jmdm. [bei etw.] ∼:**
help sb. [with sth.]; (*unpers.*) **es hilft nichts**
it's no use *or* good

Helfer *der;* **∼s, ∼, Helferin** *die;* **∼, ∼nen**
helper; (Mitarbeiter[in]) assistant; (eines
Verbrechens) accomplice

Helikopter *der;* **∼s, ∼:** helicopter

hell 1 *Adj.* **(a)** (von Licht erfüllt) light; well-lit
⟨*stairs*⟩
(b) (klar) bright ⟨*day, sky, etc.*⟩
(c) (viel Licht spendend) bright ⟨*light, lamp,
star, etc.*⟩
(d) (blass) light ⟨*colour*⟩; fair ⟨*skin, hair*⟩;
light-coloured ⟨*clothes*⟩
(e) (akustisch) high, clear ⟨*sound, voice*⟩;
ringing ⟨*laugh*⟩
(f) (klug) bright
(g) (ugs.: absolut) sheer, utter ⟨*madness,
foolishness, despair*⟩
2 *adv.* brightly

hell-: ∼blau *Adj.* light blue; **∼blond** *Adj.*
very fair; light blonde

Helle *das; adj. Dekl.* ≈ lager

Heller *der;* **∼s, ∼:** heller; **bis auf den
letzten ∼/bis auf ∼ und Pfennig** (ugs.) down
to the last penny *or* (Amer.) cent

hell-: ∼grün *Adj.* light green; **∼häutig**
Adj. fair-skinned

Helligkeit *die;* **∼, ∼en** (auch Physik)
brightness

hell-, Hell-: ∼rot *Adj.* light red;
∼sehen *unr. itr. V.; nur im Inf.* **∼sehen
können** have second sight; **∼seher** *der,*
∼seherin *die* clairvoyant; **∼wach** *Adj.*
wide awake

Helm *der;* **∼[e]s, ∼e** helmet

Hemd *das;* **∼[e]s, ∼en** shirt; (Unterhemd)
[under]vest; undershirt

Hemds·ärmel *der* shirtsleeve

hemmen *tr. V.* **(a)** (verlangsamen) slow
[down]
(b) (aufhalten) check; stem ⟨*flow*⟩
(c) (beeinträchtigen) hinder

Hemmung *die;* **∼, ∼en (a)** (Gehemmtheit)
inhibition
(b) (Bedenken) scruple

hemmungs·los ▯1▯ *Adj.* unrestrained
▯2▯ *adv.* unrestrainedly

Hendl *das;* ~s, ~[n] (bayr., österr.) chicken;
(Brathähnchen) [roast] chicken

Hengst *der;* ~[e]s, ~e (Pferd) stallion

Henkel *der;* ~s, ~: handle

Henker *der;* ~s, ~: hangman; (Scharfrichter,
auch fig.) executioner

Henne *die;* ~, ~n hen

her /heːɐ̯/ *Adv.* ~ damit give it to me; give it
here (coll.); **vom Fenster** ~: from the window;
wo ist er ~? where is he from?; **von ihrer
Kindheit** ~: since childhood; **von der
Konzeption** ~: as far as the basic design is
concerned; **hinter jmdm.** (ugs.)/**etw.** ~ **sein** be
after sb./sth.; **einen Monat/lange** ~ **sein** be a
month/a long time ago; **es ist lange** ~, **dass
wir...**: it is a long time since we...

herab *Adv.* down; **von oben** ~ (fig.)
condescendingly

herab-: ~|**hängen** *unr. itr. V.* hang
[down] (**von** from); ~**hängende Schultern**
drooping shoulders; ~|**lassen** ▯1▯ *unr. tr.
V.* let down; lower; ▯2▯ *unr. refl. V.* (iron.: bereit
sein) **sich** ~**lassen**, **etw. zu tun** condescend to
do sth.; ~**lassend** ▯1▯ *Adj.* condescending;
patronizing (**zu** towards); ▯2▯ *adv.*
condescendingly; patronizingly; ~|**sehen**
unr. itr. V. **auf jmdn.** ~**sehen** look down on
sb.; ~|**setzen** *tr. V.* (a) reduce; (b)
(abwerten) belittle

heran *Adv.* **an etw.** (*Akk.*) ~: right up to
sth.

heran-, Heran-: ~|**bilden** *tr. V.* train
[up]; (auf der Schule, Universität) educate;
~|**bringen** *unr. tr. V.* (a) bring [up] (**an** +
Akk., **zu** to); (b) (vertraut machen) **jmdn. an etw.**
(*Akk.*) ~**bringen** introduce sb. to sth.;
~|**fahren** *unr. itr. V.; mit sein* drive up (**an**
+ *Akk.* to); ~|**kommen** *unr. itr. V.; mit
sein* **an etw.** (*Akk.*) ~**kommen** come near to
sth.; (erreichen) reach sth.; (erwerben) obtain
sth.; ~|**reifen** *itr. V.; mit sein* ⟨fruit, crops⟩
ripen; **zur Frau** ~**reifen** mature into a
woman; ~|**treten** *unr. itr. V.; mit sein* (sich
wenden) **an jmdn.** ~**treten** approach sb.;
~|**wachsen** *unr. itr. V.; mit sein* grow up;
~**wachsende** *der/die; adj. Dekl.* young
person; ~|**ziehen** *unr. tr. V.* pull over; pull
up ⟨chair⟩; **etw. zu sich** ~**ziehen** pull sth.
towards one

herauf *Adv.* up

herauf-: ~|**beschwören** *tr. V.* (a)
(verursachen) cause ⟨disaster, war, crisis⟩; (b)
(erinnern) evoke ⟨memories etc.⟩; ~|**kommen**
unr. itr. V.; mit sein (nach oben kommen) come
up; ~|**setzen** *tr. V.* increase, put up
⟨prices, rents, interest rates, etc.⟩

heraus *Adv.* ~ **aus den Federn!/dem Bett!**
rise and shine!/out of bed!

heraus-, Heraus-: ~|**bekommen** *unr.
tr. V.* (a) (entfernen) get out (**aus** of); (b) (ugs.:

lösen) work out ⟨problem, answer, etc.⟩; solve
⟨puzzle⟩; (c) (ermitteln) find out; (d) (als
Wechselgeld bekommen) **5 Euro** ~**bekommen** get
back 5 euros change; **ich bekomme noch 5
Euro** ~: I still have 5 euros [change] to come;
~|**bringen** *unr. tr. V.* (a) (nach außen bringen)
bring out (**aus** of); (b) (nach draußen begleiten)
show out; (c) (veröffentlichen) bring out;
(aufführen) put on, stage ⟨play⟩; screen ⟨film⟩;
(d) (auf den Markt bringen) bring out; (e) (populär
machen) make widely known; ~|**fahren**
▯1▯ *unr. itr. V.; mit sein* (a) (nach außen fahren)
aus etw. ~**fahren** drive/ride out of sth.; (b)
(fahrend herauskommen) come out; ▯2▯ *unr. tr. V.*
den Wagen [**aus dem Hof**] ~**fahren** drive the
car out [of the yard]; **jmdn.** ~**fahren** drive sb.
out (**zu** to); ~|**finden** ▯1▯ *unr. itr. V.* find out;
trace ⟨fault⟩; ▯2▯ *unr. itr. V.* find one's way
out (**aus** of); ~|**fordern** ▯1▯ *tr. V.* (a) (auch
Sport) challenge; (b) (heraufbeschwören) provoke
⟨person, resistance, etc.⟩; invite ⟨criticism⟩;
court ⟨danger⟩; ▯2▯ *itr. V.* **zu etw.** ~**fordern**
provoke sth.; ~**forderung** *die* (auch Sport)
challenge; (Provokation) provocation;
~|**geben** ▯1▯ *unr. tr. V.* (a) (aushändigen)
hand over ⟨property, person, hostage, etc.⟩;
(zurückgeben) give back; (b) (als Wechselgeld
zurückgeben) **5 Euro/zu viel** ~**geben** give 5
euros/too much change; (c) (veröffentlichen)
publish; (d) issue ⟨stamp, coin, etc.⟩; ▯2▯ *unr.
itr. V.* give change; ~**geber** *der;* ~~s, ~~,
~**geberin** *die;* ~~, ~~nen publisher;
(Redakteur[in]) editor; ~|**gehen** *unr. itr. V.;
mit sein* (a) go out (**aus** of); (b) (sich entfernen
lassen) ⟨stain etc.⟩ come out; ~|**halten** *unr.
refl. V.* keep out; ~|**hängen** *tr. V.* hang out
(**aus** of); ~|**helfen** *unr. itr. V.* **jmdm.**
~**helfen** (auch fig.) help sb. out (**aus** of);
~|**holen** *tr. V.* (a) (nach außen holen) bring
out; (b) (ugs.: erwirken) win ⟨wage increase,
advantage, etc.⟩; ~|**kommen** *unr. itr. V.;
mit sein* (a) come out (**aus** of); (b) (erscheinen;
ugs.: auf den Markt kommen, bekannt werden) come
out; ~|**nehmen** *unr. tr. V.* (a) take out
(**aus** of); (b) (ugs.: entfernen) take out
⟨appendix, tonsils, tooth, etc.⟩; ~|**reden** *refl.
V.* (ugs.) talk one's way out (**aus** of);
~|**reißen** ▯1▯ *unr. tr. V.* (a) tear out (**aus** of);
pull up ⟨plant⟩; (b) (aus der Umgebung, der
Arbeit) tear away (**aus** from); **die Krankheit hat
ihn aus der Arbeit** ~**gerissen** the illness has
interrupted his work; (b) (Mängel ausgleichen)
den zunächst etwas langweiligen Abend
~**reißen** rescue what had been rather a
boring evening; **die Eins im Aufsatz reißt die
Drei im Diktat heraus** the A for the essay
makes up for the C in the dictation;
~|**rutschen** *itr. V.; mit sein* (ugs.) ⟨remark
etc.⟩ slip out; ~|**stellen** *refl. V.* **es stellte
sich** ~, **dass ...**: it turned out that ...;
~|**suchen** *tr. V.* pick out; look out ⟨file⟩

herb *Adj.* [slightly] sharp ⟨taste⟩; dry ⟨wine⟩;
[slightly] sharp ⟨smell, perfume⟩; bitter
⟨disappointment⟩; severe ⟨face, features⟩;
austere ⟨beauty⟩; harsh ⟨words, criticism⟩

herbei-: ~|**eilen** itr. V.; mit sein hurry over; ~|**laufen** unr. itr. V.; mit sein come running up

Herberge die; ~, ~n (veralt.: Gasthaus) inn

Herbergs-: ~**mutter** die; Pl. ~mütter, ~**vater** der warden [of the/a youth hostel]

her|bringen unr. tr. V. etw. ~: bring sth. [here]

Herbst der; ~[e]s, ~e autumn; fall (Amer.); s. auch FRÜHLING

Herbst·anfang der beginning of autumn

herbstlich Adj. autumn attrib.; autumnal

Herd der; ~[e]s, ~e cooker; (fig.) centre (of disturbance/rebellion)

Herde die; ~, ~n herd

Herd·platte die hot-plate

herein-: ~|**bitten** unr. tr. V. jmdn. ~ bitten ask or invite sb. in; ~|**brechen** unr. itr. V.; mit sein (geh.) ⟨night, evening, dusk⟩ fall; ⟨winter⟩ set in; ⟨storm⟩ strike, break; ~|**bringen** unr. tr. V. bring in; ~|**fallen** unr. itr. V.; mit sein (ugs.) be taken for a ride (coll.); be done (coll.); ~|**kommen** unr. itr. V.; mit sein come in; ~|**lassen** unr. tr. V. let in; ~|**legen** tr. V. (ugs.) jmdn. ~legen take sb. for a ride (coll.) (mit, bei with); ~|**platzen** itr. V.; mit sein (ugs.) burst in; ~|**schneien** unr. itr. V.; mit sein (ugs.) turn up out of the blue (coll.)

her-, Her-: ~**fahrt** die journey here; ~|**fallen** unr. itr. V.; mit sein über jmdn. ~fallen attack sb.; (gierig zu essen beginnen) über etw. (Akk.) ~fallen fall upon sth.; ~**gang** der: der ~gang der Ereignisse the sequence of events; ~|**geben** unr. tr. V. hand over; (weggeben) give away; ~|**gehen** unr. itr. V.; mit sein neben/vor/hinter jmdm. ~gehen walk along beside/in front of/behind sb.; ~|**haben** unr. tr. V. (ugs.) wo hat er/sie das ~? where did he/she get that from?; ~|**halten** unr. itr. V. ~halten müssen [für jmdn./etw.] be the one to suffer [for sb./sth.]; ~|**hören** itr. V. listen

Hering der; ~s, ~e (a) herring (b) (Zeltpflock) peg

her-: ~|**kommen** unr. itr. V.; mit sein come here; ~**kömmlich** Adj. conventional; traditional ⟨custom⟩

Herkunft die; ~, Herkünfte origin

Herkunfts·land das country of origin

her-: ~|**laufen** unr. itr. V.; mit sein vor/hinter/neben jmdm. ~laufen run [along] in front of/behind/alongside sb.; (nachlaufen) hinter jmdm. ~laufen run after sb.; (fig.) chase sb. up; ~|**leiten** tr., refl. V. derive (aus, von from); ~|**machen** (ugs.) refl. V. sich über etw. (Akk.) ~machen get stuck into sth. (coll.)

Hermelin der; ~s, ~e (Pelz) ermine

hermetisch 1 Adj. hermetic 2 adv. hermetically

Heroin das; ~s heroin

Heroin·sucht die heroin addiction

heroin·süchtig Adj. addicted to heroin postpos.

Herr der; ~n, ~en (a) (Mann) gentleman (b) (Titel, Anrede) ~ Schulze Mr Schulze; Sehr geehrter ~ Schulze! Dear Sir; (bei persönlicher Bekanntschaft) Dear Mr Schulze; meine ~en gentlemen (c) (Gebieter) master

herren-, Herren-: ~**ausstatter** der [gentle]men's outfitter; ~**los** Adj. abandoned ⟨car, luggage⟩; stray ⟨dog, cat⟩; ~**salon** der men's hairdressing salon; ~**schuh** der man's shoe; ~schuhe men's shoes; ~**toilette** die [gentle]men's toilet

Herr·gott der; ~s: der [liebe]/unser ~: the Lord [God]; God

Herrgotts·frühe die in aller ~: at the crack of dawn

her|richten tr. V. (bereitmachen) get ⟨room, refreshments, etc.⟩ ready; arrange ⟨table⟩; (in Ordnung bringen) renovate

Herrin die; ~, ~en mistress

herrisch 1 Adj. overbearing; imperious 2 adv. imperiously

herrlich 1 Adj. marvellous; magnificent ⟨view, clothes⟩ 2 adv. marvellously

Herrlichkeit die; ~, ~en (a) (Schönheit) magnificence; splendour (b) (herrliche Sache) marvellous thing

Herrschaft die; ~, ~en (a) rule; (Macht) power (b) Pl. (Damen u. Herren) ladies and gentlemen

herrschen itr. V. rule; ⟨monarch⟩ reign, rule; draußen ~ 30° Kälte it's 30° below outside

Herrscher der; ~s, ~, **Herrscherin** die; ~, ~nen ruler

herrsch-, Herrsch-: ~**sucht** die thirst for power; (herrisches Wesen) domineering nature; ~**süchtig** Adj. domineering

her-: ~|**rühren** itr. V. von jmdm./etw. ~rühren come from sb./stem from sth.; *~|**sein** ▶ HER; ~|**stellen** tr. V. produce; manufacture; make

Hersteller der; ~s, ~, **Herstellerin** die; ~, ~nen producer

Her·stellung die production; manufacture

herüber Adv. over

herum Adv. um ... ~ (Richtung) round; (Anordnung) around; um Weihnachten ~: around Christmas; ~ sein (ugs.: vergangen sein, vorüber sein) have passed

herum-: ~|**ärgern** refl. V. (ugs.) sich mit jmdm./etw. ~ärgern keep getting annoyed with sb./sth.; ~|**drehen** 1 tr. V. (ugs.) turn ⟨key⟩; turn over ⟨coin, mattress, hand, etc.⟩ 2 refl. V. turn [a]round; (ugs.) 1 unr. itr. V.; mit sein (sich plötzlich herumdrehen) spin round; 2 unr. tr. V. jmdn. [in der Stadt] ~fahren drive sb. around the town; ~|**führen** 1 tr. V. jmdn. [in der Stadt] ~führen show sb. around the town; ····▷

2 *itr. V.* um etw. ~**führen** ⟨*road etc.*⟩ go round sth.; ~|**gehen** *unr. itr. V.; mit sein* (vergehen) pass; **um etw.** ~**gehen** go round sth.; **etw.** ~**gehen lassen** circulate sth.; pass; ~|**kommandieren** (ugs.) 1 *tr. V.* jmdn. ~**kommandieren** boss (coll.) *or* order sb. around *or* about; 2 *itr. V.* boss (coll.) *or* order people around *or* about; ~|**kommen** *unr. itr. V.; mit sein* (ugs.) (a) (vermeiden können) **um etw.** [**nicht**] ~**kommen** [not] be able to get out of sth.; (b) (viel reisen) get around *or* about; **in der Welt** ~**kommen** see a lot of the world; ~|**laufen** *unr. itr. V.; mit sein* (a) walk/(schneller) run around *or* about; **um etw.** ~**laufen** go round sth.; (b) (gekleidet sein) **wie ein Hippie** ~**laufen** go about looking like a hippie; ~|**lungern** *itr. V.* (salopp) loaf around; ~|**schlagen** *unr. refl. V.* (ugs.) **sich mit Problemen/Einwänden** ~**schlagen** grapple with problems/battle against objections; ***~|**sein** ▶ HERUM; ~|**sitzen** *unr. itr. V.* (ugs.) sit around *or* about; ~|**sprechen** *unr. refl. V.* get around *or* about; ~|**stöbern** *itr. V.* (ugs.) keep rummaging around *or* about (**in** + *Dat.* in); ~|**treiben** *unr. refl. V.* (ugs. abwertend) **sich auf den Straßen/in Discos** ~**treiben** hang around the streets/in discos; **sich in der Welt** ~**treiben** roam about the world

herunter *Adv.* (a) (nach unten) down; [körperlich] ~ **sein** be in poor health (b) (fort) off; ~ **vom Sofa!** [get] off the sofa!

herunter-: ~|**bringen** *unr. tr. V.* bring down; ~|**fallen** *unr. itr. V.; mit sein* fall down; **vom Tisch/Stuhl** ~**fallen** fall off the table/chair; ~|**gehen** *unr. itr. V.; mit sein* (a) come down; (b) (niedriger werden) ⟨*temperature*⟩ drop; ⟨*prices*⟩ come down, fall; ~**gekommen** 1 *2. Part. v.* ~KOMMEN; 2 *Adj.* poor ⟨*health*⟩; dilapidated ⟨*building*⟩; run-down ⟨*area*⟩; down and out ⟨*person*⟩; ~|**handeln** *tr. V.* (ugs.) **einen Preis** ~**handeln** beat down a price; ~|**hängen** *unr. itr. V.* hang down; ~|**hauen** *unr. tr. V.* (ugs.) **jmdm. eine** ~**hauen** give sb. a clout round the ear (coll.); ~|**kommen** *unr. itr. V.; mit sein* (a) come down; (b) (ugs.: verfallen) go to the dogs (coll.); ~|**lassen** *unr. tr. V.* lower; ~|**schlucken** *tr. V.* swallow; ***~|**sein** ▶ HERUNTER A; ~|**spielen** *tr. V.* (ugs.) play down

hervor *Adv.* **aus** ... ~: out of

hervor-: ~|**heben** *unr. tr. V.* stress; ~**ragend** 1 *Adj.* outstanding[ly good]; 2 *adv.* ~**ragend geschult** outstandingly well trained; ~**ragend spielen/arbeiten** play/work outstandingly well; ~|**tun** *unr. refl. V.* distinguish oneself; (wichtig tun) show off

Herz *das;* ~**ens,** ~**en** heart; (Kartenspiel) hearts *pl.;* **von** ~**en kommen** come from the heart; **ein** ~ **für die Armen haben** feel for the poor; **ein** ~ **für Kinder haben** have a love of children; **schweren** ~**ens** with a heavy

heart; **etw. auf dem** ~**en haben** have sth. on one's mind; **es nicht übers** ~ **bringen, etw. zu tun** not have the heart to do sth.; **sich** ⟨*Dat.*⟩ **etw. zu** ~**en nehmen** take sth. to heart

Herz-: ~**an·fall** *der* heart attack; ~**beschwerden** *Pl.* heart trouble *sing.*

herzens-, Herzens-: ~**gut** /'--'-/ *Adj.* kind-hearted; ~**lust** *die:* **nach** ~**lust** to one's heart's content

herzhaft 1 *Adj.* hearty; (nahrhaft) hearty ⟨*meal*⟩; (von kräftigem Geschmack) tasty 2 *adv.* heartily; (nahrhaft) **er isst gern** ~: he likes to have a hearty meal

her|ziehen *unr. itr. V.; mit sein od. haben* (ugs.) **über jmdn./etw.** ~: run sb./sth. down

herzig 1 *Adj.* sweet; delightful 2 *adv.* sweetly; delightfully

herz-, Herz-: ~**infarkt** *der* heart attack; ~**klappen·fehler** *der* (Med.) valvular defect *or* insufficiency; ~**klopfen** *das;* ~~**s:** **jmd. hat** ~**klopfen** sb.'s heart is pounding; ~**krank** *Adj.* ⟨*person*⟩ with a heart condition; ~**kranz·gefäß** *das* coronary vessel

herzlich 1 *Adj.* warm ⟨*smile, reception*⟩; kind ⟨*words, regards*⟩; (ehrlich gemeint) sincere; ~**en Dank** many thanks 2 *adv.* warmly; (ehrlich gemeint) sincerely; ⟨*congratulate*⟩ heartily; ~ **wenig** very *or* (coll.) precious little

Herzlichkeit *die;* ~: warmth; kindness; (Aufrichtigkeit) sincerity

herz·los 1 *Adj.* heartless 2 *adv.* heartlessly

Herzog *der;* ~**s, Herzöge** duke

Herzogin *die;* ~, ~**nen** duchess

Herz·rhythmus·störung *die* (Med.) disturbance of the heart *or* cardiac rhythm

herz-, Herz-: ~**schlag** *der* heartbeat; (Herzversagen) heart failure; ~**schmerz** *der* pain in the region of the heart; ~**schrittmacher** *der* (Anat., Med.) [cardiac] pacemaker; ~**transplantation** *die* (Med.) heart transplantation; ~**zerreißend** 1 *Adj.* heart-rending; 2 *adv.* heart-rendingly

Hessen ⟨*das*⟩; ~**s** Hesse

hetero·sexuell *Adj.* heterosexual

Hetze *die;* ~ (a) [mad] rush (b) (abwertend) smear campaign

hetzen 1 *tr. V.* (a) hunt (b) (antreiben) rush 2 *itr. V.* (a) (in großer Eile sein) rush (b) *mit sein* (hasten) rush; (rennen) dash; race

Hetz-: ~**kampagne** *die* (abwertend) smear campaign; (gegen eine Minderheit) hate campaign; ~**rede** *die* (abwertend) inflammatory speech

Heu *das;* ~[**e**]**s** hay

Heuchelei *die;* ~: hypocrisy

heucheln 1 *itr. V.* be a hypocrite 2 *tr. V.* feign

---

*alte Schreibung - vgl. Hinweis auf S. xiv

Heuchler der; ~s, ~, **Heuchlerin** die; ~, ~nen hypocrite

heuchlerisch 1 Adj. hypocritical 2 adv. hypocritically

heuer Adv. (südd., österr., schweiz.) this year

Heuer die; ~, ~n (Seemannsspr.) pay; wages pl.

Heu·ernte die (a) hay harvest (b) (Ertrag) hay crop

heulen itr. V. (a) howl; ⟨siren etc.⟩ wail (b) (ugs.: weinen) howl; bawl

Heurige der; adj. Dekl. (bes. österr.) (a) (Wein) new wine (b) (Weinlokal) inn with new wine on tap

Heu-: ~**schnupfen** der hay fever; ~**schrecke** die grasshopper

heute Adv. today; ~ früh early this morning; ~ Morgen/Abend this morning/evening; ~ Mittag [at] midday today; ~ Nacht tonight; (letzte Nacht) last night; ~ in einer Woche a week [from] today; today week; ~ vor einer Woche a week ago today

heutig Adj. (a) (von diesem Tag) today's; der ~e Tag today (b) (gegenwärtig) today's; of today postpos.; in der ~en Zeit nowadays

heut·zu·tage Adv. nowadays

Hexe die; ~, ~n witch

hexen itr. V. work magic

Hexen·schuss, *Hexen·schuß der lumbago no indef. art.

Hexerei die; ~, ~en witchcraft; (von Kunststücken usw.) magic

Hickhack das od. der; ~s, ~s (ugs.) squabbling; bickering

hieb 1. u. 3. Pers. Sg. Prät. v. HAUEN

Hieb der; ~[e]s, ~e (a) (Schlag) blow; (mit der Peitsche) lash (b) Pl. (ugs.: Prügel) hiding sing.

hieb·fest Adj.: hieb- und stichfest watertight; cast-iron

hielt 1. u. 3. Pers. Sg. Prät. v. HALTEN

hier Adv. (a) here; [von] ~ oben/unten [from] up/down here (b) (jetzt) now; von ~ an from now on

hieran Adv. here; sich ~ festhalten hold on to this; (fig.) im Anschluss ~: immediately after this

Hierarchie /hi̯erar'çiː/ die; ~, ~n hierarchy

hierauf Adv. (a) on here; (darauf) on this; wir werden ~ zurückkommen we'll come back to this (b) (danach) after that; then (c) (infolgedessen) whereupon

hieraus Adv. out of here; (aus dieser Tatsache, Quelle) from this

hier-: ~|**behalten** unr. tr. V. jmdn./etw. ~behalten keep sb./sth. here; ~**bei** Adv. (a) (bei dieser Gelegenheit) Diese Übung ist sehr schwierig. Man kann sich ~bei leicht verletzen. This exercise is very difficult. You

can easily injure yourself doing it; (b) (bei der erwähnten Sache) here; ~|**bleiben** itr. V.; mit sein stay here; ~**durch** Adv. through here; (aufgrund dieser Sache) because of this; ~**für** Adv. for this

hier·her Adv. here; ich gehe bis ~ und nicht weiter I'm going this far and no further; ~**gehören** belong here; (hierfür wichtig sein) be relevant [here]; ~**kommen** mit sein come here

hier·hin Adv. here; bis ~: up to here

hier-: ~**in** Adv. (a) (räumlich) in here; (b) in this; ~**mit** Adv. with this/these; ~mit ist der Fall erledigt that puts an end to the matter; ~**nach** Adv. (anschließend) after that

Hieroglyphe /hi̯ero.../ die; ~, ~n hieroglyph

hier-: *~**sein** ▸ HIER A; ~**über** Adv. (a) (über dem Erwähnten) above here; (über das Erwähnte) over here; (b) (das Erwähnte betreffend) about this/these; ~**von** Adv. of this/these; ~**zu** Adv. with this; (hinsichtlich dieser Sache) about this; ~**zu** gehört/gehören ...: this includes/these include; ~zu reicht mein Geld nicht I haven't got enough money for that; ~**zu·lande** Adv. [here] in this country

hiesig Adj. local

hieß 1. u. 3. Pers. Sg. Prät. v. HEISSEN

Hi-Fi-Anlage /'hai̯fiː-/ die hi-fi system

high /hai̯/ Adj. (ugs.) high (coll.)

Hightech-, High-Tech- /'hai̯tɛk-/ high-tech

Hilfe die; ~, ~n (a) help; (für Notleidende) aid; relief; zu ~! help! (b) (Hilfskraft) help; (im Geschäft) assistant

Hilfe-: ~**leistung** die help; ~**ruf** der cry for help; ~**stellung** die (Turnen) jmdm. ~stellung geben act as spotter for sb.

hilflos 1 Adj. helpless 2 adv. helplessly

Hilflosigkeit die; ~ helplessness

hilfs-, Hilfs-: ~**bedürftig** Adj. (a) (schwach) in need of help postpos.; (b) (notleidend) in need; needy; ~**bereit** Adj. helpful; ~**bereitschaft** die helpfulness; ~**gelder** Pl. aid money sing.; ~**kraft** die assistant; ~**mittel** das aid; ~**organisation** die aid or relief organization; ~**programm** das aid or relief programme; ~**verb** das, ~**zeitwort** das (Sprachw.) auxiliary [verb]

Himalaja der; ~[s]: der/im ~: the/in the Himalayas pl.

Him·beere die raspberry

Himmel der; ~s, ~ sky; (Rel.) heaven; ~ noch [ein]mal! for Heaven's sake!

himmel-, Himmel-: ~**bett** das four-poster bed; ~**blau** Adj. sky-blue; clear blue ⟨eyes⟩; ~**fahrt** die (Rel.) (a) Christi/Mariä ~fahrt the Ascension of Christ/the Assumption of the Virgin Mary; (b) (Festtag) [Christi] ~: Ascension Day no art.

Himmels-: ~**richtung** *die* point of the compass; ~**schlüsselchen** *das;* ~~s, ~~: cowslip

himmel·weit *Adj.* enormous, vast ⟨*difference*⟩

himmlisch *Adj.* (auch fig.) heavenly

hin *Adv.* (a) (räumlich) **zur Straße** ~ **liegen** face the road (b) (zeitlich) **gegen Mittag** ~: towards midday (c) (in Verbindungen) **nach außen** ~: outwardly; **auf meinen Rat** ~: on my advice; **auf seine Bitte** ~: at his request (d) (in Wortpaaren) ~ **und zurück** there and back; **einmal Köln** ~ **und zurück** a return [ticket] to Cologne; ~ **und her** to and fro; back and forth; ~ **und wieder** [every] now and then (e) ~ **sein** (ugs.: verloren sein); be gone; (ugs.: nicht mehr brauchbar sein); have had it (coll.); ⟨*car*⟩ be a write-off; (salopp: tot sein) have snuffed it (sl.); **von jmdm./etw. ganz** ~ **sein** (ugs.: hingerissen sein) be mad about sb./bowled over by sb.

hinạb *Adv.* ▶ HINUNTER

hinạb|- ▶ HINUNTER-

hinauf *Adv.* up; **bis** ~ **zu** up to

hinauf-: ~**fahren** *unr. itr. V.; mit sein* go up; (im Auto) drive up; (mit einem Motorrad) ride up; ~**gehen** *unr. itr. V.; mit sein* (a) (nach oben gehen) go up; (b) (nach oben führen) lead up; (c) (ugs.: steigen) ⟨*prices, taxes, etc.*⟩ go up; rise; ~**klettern** *itr. V.; mit sein* climb up; ~**steigen** *unr. itr. V.; mit sein* climb up; ~**ziehen** ① *unr. tr. V.* pull up; ② *unr. itr. V.; mit sein* move up; ③ *unr. refl. V.* (sich erstrecken) stretch up

hinaus *Adv.* (a) (räumlich) out (b) (zeitlich) **auf Jahre** ~: for years to come (c) (etw. überschreitend) **über etw.** (*Akk.*) ~: in addition to (d) **über etw.** (*Akk.*) ~ **sein** be past sth.

hinaus-: ~**bringen** *unr. tr. V.* **jmdn./etw.** ~**bringen** see sb. out/take sth. out (**aus** of); ~**fahren** ① *unr. itr. V.; mit sein* **aus etw.** ~**fahren** (mit dem Auto) drive out of sth.; (mit dem Zweirad) ride out of sth.; ⟨*car, bus*⟩ go out of sth.; ⟨*train*⟩ pull out of sth.; **zum Flugplatz** ~**fahren** drive out to the airport; ② *unr. tr. V.* **jmdn./etw.** ~**fahren** drive sb./take sth. out; ~**fallen** *unr. itr. V.; mit sein* fall out (**aus** of); ~**finden** *unr. itr. V.* find one's way out (**aus** of); ~**gehen** *unr. itr. V.; mit sein* (a) go out (**aus** of); (b) (gerichtet sein) **das Zimmer geht zum Garten/nach Westen** ~: the room looks out on to the garden/faces west; ~**kommen** *unr. itr. V.; mit sein* come out (**aus** of); ~**laufen** *unr. itr. V.; mit sein* (a) run out (**aus** of); (b) (als Ergebnis haben) **auf etw.** (*Akk.*) ~**laufen** lead to sth.; ~**sehen** *unr. itr. V.* look out; **zum Fenster** ~**sehen** look out of the window; **~*|**sein** ▶ HINAUS D; ~|**tragen** *unr. tr. V.* **jmdn./etw.** ~**tragen** carry sb./sth. out; ~|**werfen** *unr. tr. V.*

(auch ugs. fig.) throw out (**aus** of); ~|**ziehen** ① *unr. tr. V.* (a) (nach draußen ziehen) **jmdn./etw.** ~**ziehen** pull sb./sth. out (**aus** of); tow ⟨*ship*⟩ out; (b) (verzögern) put off; delay; ② *unr. refl. V.* be delayed; ~|**zögern** ① *tr. V.* delay; ② *refl. V.* be delayed

hin-, Hịn-: ~**blick** *der:* **im** ~od. **in** ~**blick auf etw.** (*Akk.*) (wegen) in view of; (hinsichtlich) with regard to; ~|**bringen** *unr. tr. V.* **jmdn./etw.** ~**bringen** take sb./sth. [there]; ~|**denken** *unr. itr. V.* **wo denkst du hin?** (ugs.) whatever are you thinking of?

hinderlich *Adj.* ~ **sein** get in the way

hindern *tr. V.* (a) (abhalten) **jmdn.** ~: stop sb. (**an** + *Dat.* from) (b) (behindern) hinder

Hindernis *das;* ~**ses,** ~**se** obstacle

hin|deuten *itr. V.* (a) **auf jmdn./etw.** od. **zu jmdm./etw.** ~: point to sb./sth. (b) **auf etw.** (*Akk.*) ~ (fig.) point to sth.

Hịndu *der;* ~[**s**], ~[**s**] Hindu

Hinduịsmus *der;* ~ Hinduism *no art.*

hin-dụrch *Adv.* (a) (räumlich) **durch den Wald** ~: through the wood (b) (zeitlich) **das ganze Jahr** ~: throughout the year

hinein *Adv.* (a) (räumlich) in; **in etw.** (*Akk.*) ~: into sth. (b) (zeitlich) **bis in den Morgen/tief in die Nacht** ~: till morning/far into the night

hinein-: ~|**bringen** *unr. tr. V.* take in; ~|**fahren** (mit dem Auto) drive in; (mit dem Zweirad) ride in; **in etw.** (*Akk.*) ~**fahren** drive/ ride into sth.; ~|**fallen** *unr. itr. V.; mit sein* fall in; **in etw.** (*Akk.*) ~**fallen** fall into sth.; ~|**gehen** *unr. itr. V.; mit sein* go in; **in etw.** (*Akk.*) ~**gehen** go into sth.; ~|**gucken** *itr. V.* (ugs.) look in; **in etw.** (*Akk.*) ~**gucken** look in[to] sth.; ~|**kommen** *unr. itr. V.; mit sein* (a) come in; **in etw.** (*Akk.*) ~**kommen** come into sth.; (b) (gelangen, auch fig.) get in; **in etw.** (*Akk.*) ~**kommen** get into sth.; ~|**reden** *itr. V.* **jmdm. in seine Angelegenheiten/ Entscheidungen** *usw.* ~**reden** interfere in sb.'s affairs/decisions *etc.;* ~|**sehen** *unr. itr. V.* look in; **in etw.** (*Akk.*) ~**sehen** look into sth.; ~|**versetzen** *refl. V.* **sich in jmdn.** od. **jmds. Lage** ~**versetzen** put oneself in sb.'s position; ~|**ziehen** *unr. tr. V.* (a) pull *or* draw in; **etw./jmdn. in etw.** (*Akk.*) ~**ziehen** pull *or* draw sth./sb. into sth.; (b) (verwickeln) **jmdn. in eine Angelegenheit/ einen Streit/Skandal** ~**ziehen** drag sb. into an affair/a dispute/scandal

hin-, Hịn-: ~|**fahren** ① *unr. itr. V.; mit sein* go there; ② *unr. tr. V.* **jmdn.** ~**fahren** drive sb. there; ~**fahrt** *die* journey there; (Seereise) voyage out; ~|**fallen** *unr. itr. V.; mit sein* (a) fall over; (b) jmdm. fällt etw. ~: sb. drops sth.; **etw.** ~**fallen lassen** drop sth.; ~**fällig** *Adj.* (a) infirm; frail; (b) (ungültig) invalid; ~|**fliegen** *unr. itr. V.; mit sein* fly there; ~**flug** *der* outward flight

hịng *1. u. 3. Pers. Sg. Prät. v.* HÄNGEN

Hin·gabe *die; ~:* devotion; (Eifer) dedication

Hingebung *die; ~:* devotion

hingebungs·voll [1] *Adj.* devoted [2] *adv.* devotedly; with devotion; ⟨*listen*⟩ with rapt attention; ⟨*dance, play*⟩ with abandon

hin·gegen *Konj., Adv.* (jedoch) however; (andererseits) on the other hand

hin-, Hin-: ~|**gehen** *unr. itr. V.; mit sein* (a) go [there]; **zu jmdm./etw.** ~**gehen** go to sb./sth.; (b) (verstreichen) ⟨*time*⟩ go by; ~|**halten** *unr. tr. V.* (a) hold out; (b) (warten lassen) jmdn. ~**halten** keep sb. waiting; ~**halte·taktik** *die* delaying tactics *pl.;* ~|**hören** *itr. V.* listen

hinken /'hɪŋkn̩/ *itr. V.* (a) walk with a limp (b) *mit sein* (hinkend gehen) limp

hin-, Hin-: ~|**kommen** *unr. itr. V.; mit sein* (a) get there; (b) (an einen Ort gehören) go; belong; (c) (ugs.: stimmen) be right; ~**länglich** [1] *Adj.* sufficient; (angemessen) adequate; [2] *adv.* sufficiently; (angemessen) adequately; ~|**legen** [1] *tr. V.* put; (weglegen) put down; [2] *refl. V.* lie down; ~**reichend** [1] *Adj.* sufficient; (angemessen) adequate; [2] *adv.* sufficiently; (angemessen) adequately; ~**reise** *die* journey there; (mit dem Schiff) voyage out; ~**reißend** *Adj.* enchanting ⟨*person, picture, view*⟩; captivating ⟨*speaker, play*⟩; ~|**richten** *tr. V.* execute; ~**richtung** *die* execution

Hinrichtungs·kommando *das* firing squad

hin-, Hin-: ~|**sehen** *unr. itr. V.* look; **~*|**sein** ▶ HIN E; ~|**setzen** [1] *tr. V.* put; [2] *refl. V.* sit down; ~**sicht** *die* in gewisser ~**sicht** in a way/in some respects *or* ways; **in jeder** ~**sicht** in every respect; **in finanzieller** ~**sicht** financially; ~**sichtlich** *Präp. mit Gen.* (Amtsspr.) with regard to; (in Anbetracht) in view of; ~|**stellen** [1] *tr. V.* put; put up ⟨*building*⟩; (absetzen) put down; [2] *refl. V.* stand

hinten *Adv.* at the back; **sich** ~ **anstellen** join the back of the queue (Brit.) *or* (Amer.) line; **weiter** ~: further back; (im einem Buch) further on; **die Adresse steht** ~ **auf dem Brief** the address is on the back of the envelope; **nach** ~ **hinaus liegen/gehen** be at the back; **die anderen sind ganz weit** ~: the others are a long way back

hinter [1] *Präp. mit Dat.* behind; (nach) after; **3 km** ~ **der Grenze** 3 km beyond the frontier; **eine Prüfung** ~ **sich haben** (fig.) have got an examination over [and done] with; **viele Enttäuschungen/eine Krankheit** ~ **sich haben** have experienced many disappointments/have got over an illness [2] *Präp. mit Akk.* behind

hinter... *Adj.; nicht präd.* back

hinter-, Hinter-: ~**einander** *Adv.* (a) (räumlich) one behind the other; (b) (zeitlich)

one after another *or* the other; ~**gedanke** *der* ulterior motive; ~**gehen** /-'--/ *unr. tr. V.* deceive; ~**grund** *der* background; ~**grund·bericht** *der* background report; ~**gründig** [1] *Adj.* enigmatic; [2] *adv.* enigmatically; ~**grund·information** *die* item *or* piece of background information; ~**grundinformationen** [items *or* pieces of] background information *sing.;* ~**halt** *der* ambush; ~**hältig** [1] *Adj.* underhand; [2] *adv.* in an underhand manner; ~**her** *Adv.* (räumlich) behind; (nachher) afterwards; ~**hof** *der* courtyard; ~**land** *das* hinterland; (Milit.) back area; ~**lassen** /-'--/ *unr. tr. V.* leave; ~**legen** /-'--/ *tr. V.* deposit (bei with); ~**list** *die* guile; deceit; ~**listig** *Adj.* deceitful; ~**mann** *der* (a) person behind; (b) (Gewährsmann) [secret] informant

Hintern *der; ~s, ~* (ugs.) backside; bottom

hinter-, Hinter-: ~**rad** *das* rear wheel; ~**sinn** *der* deeper meaning; ~**sinnig** *Adj.* ⟨*remark, story, etc.*⟩ with a deeper meaning; ~**teil** *das* backside; behind; ~**treffen** *das* (ugs.): **ins** ~**treffen geraten** *od.* **kommen** fall behind; ~**treiben** /-'--/ *unr. tr. V.* foil ⟨*plan*⟩; prevent ⟨*marriage, promotion*⟩; block ⟨*law, investigation, reform*⟩; ~**treppe** *die* back stairs *pl.;* ~**tür** *die* back door; ~**wäldler** *der; ~s, ~~* (spött.) backwoodsman; ~**wäldlerin** *die; ~~, ~~nen** backwoodswoman; ~**wäldlerisch** *Adj.* (spött.) backwoods *attrib.* ⟨*views, attitudes, manners, etc.*⟩

hinüber *Adv.* over; across

Hin- und Rück·fahrt *die* journey there and back; round trip (Amer.)

hinunter *Adv.* down

hinunter-: ~|**fahren** [1] *unr. itr. V.; mit sein* go down; (mit dem Auto) drive down; (mit dem Fahrrad) ride down; [2] *unr. tr. V.* jmdn./ **ein Auto/eine Ladung** ~**fahren** drive sb. down/drive a car down/take a load down; ~|**gehen** *unr. itr. V.; mit sein* go down; ⟨*aircraft*⟩ descend; ~|**klettern** *itr. V.; mit sein* climb down; ~|**reichen** [1] *tr. V.* hand down; [2] *itr. V.* (sich bis hinunter erstrecken) reach down (**bis auf** + *Akk.* to)

hin·weg *Adv.* (a) (geh.) ~ **mit dir!** away with you! (b) **über etw.** ~: over sth.

Hin·weg *der* way there

hinweg-: ~|**gehen** *unr. itr. V.; mit sein* **über etw.** (*Akk.*) ~**gehen** pass over sth.; ~|**kommen** *unr. itr. V.; mit sein* **über etw.** (*Akk.*) ~**kommen** get over sth.; ~|**setzen** *refl. V.* **sich über etw.** (*Akk.*) ~**setzen** ignore sth.

Hinweis /'hɪnvaɪs/ *der; ~es, ~e* hint; **unter** ~ **auf** (+ *Akk.*) with reference to

hin-: ~|**weisen** [1] *unr. itr. V.* **auf jmdn./ etw.** ~**weisen** point to sb./sth.; [2] *unr. tr. V.* **jmdn. auf etw.** (*Akk.*) ~**weisen** point sth. out to sb.; ~**weisend** *Adj.* (Grammatik) demonstrative; ~|**werfen** *unr. tr. V.* throw ⋯✣

down; ~|**ziehen** ① *unr. tr. V.* pull, draw (zu to, towards); ② *unr. itr. V.; mit sein* (umziehen) move there; **wo ist sie ~gezogen?** where did she move to?; ③ *unr. refl. V.* **(a)** (sich erstrecken) drag on (über + *Akk.* for); **(b)** (sich verzögern) be delayed

hinzu-: ~|**fügen** *tr. V.* add; ~|**kommen** *unr. itr. V.; mit sein* **(a)** come along; **(b)** (hinzugefügt werden) **zu etw.** ~**kommen** be added to sth.; **es kommt noch** ~**, dass** ... (fig.) there is also the fact that ...; ~|**tun** *unr. tr. V.* (ugs.) add

Hiobs·botschaft *die* bad news

Hirn *das;* ~[e]s, ~e **(a)** brain **(b)** (Speise; ugs.: Verstand) brains *pl.*

Hirsch *der;* ~[e]s, ~e deer; (Rothirsch) red deer; (männlicher Rothirsch) stag; (Speise) venison

Hirse *die;* ~, ~n millet

Hirt *der;* ~en, ~en, **Hirte** *der;* ~n, ~n herdsman; (Schaf~) shepherd

Hirtin *die;* ~, ~nen shepherdess

hissen *tr. V.* hoist

historisch *Adj.* **(a)** historical **(b)** (geschichtlich bedeutungsvoll) historic

Hit *der;* ~[s], ~s (ugs.) hit

Hitler·jugend *die* Hitler Youth

Hit·parade *die* hit parade

Hitze *die;* ~: heat

hitze-, Hitze-: ~**beständig** *Adj.* heat-resistant; ~**frei** *Adj.* ~**frei haben** have the rest of the day off [school/work] because of excessively hot weather; ~**periode** *die* hot spell; spell *or* period of hot weather; ~**welle** *die* heat wave

hitzig *Adj.* **(a)** hot-tempered **(b)** (erregt) heated ⟨discussion etc.⟩

hitz-, Hitz-: ~**kopf** *der* hothead; ~**köpfig** *Adj.* hot-headed; ~**schlag** *der* heatstroke

HIV-: ~**-Anti·körper** *der* HIV antibody; ~**-Infektion** *die* HIV infection; ~**-infiziert** *Adj.* HIV-infected; ~**-kontaminiert** *Adj.* HIV-contaminated; ~**-positiv** *Adj.* HIV-positive; ~**-Test** *der* HIV test; ~**-verseucht** *Adj.* HIV-contaminated

hl *Abk.* = **Hektoliter** hl

H-Milch *die;* ~ long-life *or* UHT milk

HNO-Arzt *der,* **HNO-Ärztin** *die* ENT specialist

hob *1. u. 3. Pers. Sg. Prät. v.* HEBEN

Hobby *das;* ~s, ~s hobby

Hobel *der;* ~s, ~ **(a)** plane **(b)** (Küchengerät) [vegetable] slicer

Hobel·bank *die; Pl.* Hobel·bänke woodworker's bench

hobeln *tr., itr. V.* **(a)** plane **(b)** (schneiden) slice

hoch; höher, höchst... ① *Adj.* high; tall

⟨tree, mast⟩; long ⟨grass⟩; deep ⟨snow, water⟩; heavy ⟨fine⟩; large ⟨sum, amount⟩; severe, extensive ⟨damage⟩; senior ⟨official, officer, post⟩; high-level ⟨diplomacy, politics⟩; **höchste Gefahr** extreme danger; **es ist höchste Zeit, dass ...:** it is high time that ...; **das hohe C** top C; **vier ~ zwei** (Math.) four to the power [of] two; four squared ② *adv.* (in großer Höhe) high; (nach oben) up; (zahlenmäßig viel, sehr) highly; ~ **begabt** highly gifted; ~ **empfindlich** highly sensitive ⟨instrument, device, material, etc.⟩; fast ⟨film⟩; extremely delicate ⟨fabric⟩; ~ **gestellt** ⟨person⟩ in a high position; important ⟨person⟩; ~ **verschuldet/versichert** heavily in debt/insured for a large sum [of money]; **etw.** ~ **und heilig versprechen** promise sth. faithfully

Hoch *das;* ~s, ~s **(a)** (Hochruf) **ein** [dreifaches] ~ **auf jmdn. ausbringen** give three cheers for sb. **(b)** (Met.) high

Hoch·achtung *die* great respect

hochachtungs·voll *Adv.* (Briefschluss) yours faithfully

hoch-, Hoch-: ~**aktuell** *Adj.* highly topical; ~**amt** *das* (kath. Rel.) high mass; ~|**arbeiten** *refl. V.* work one's way up; ~**begabt** *Adj.* highly gifted; ~**betagt** *Adj.* aged; ~**betrieb** *der* (ugs.) **es herrschte** ~**betrieb im Geschäft** the shop was at its busiest; ~**blüte** *die* golden age; ~**burg** *die* stronghold; ~**deutsch** *Adj.* High German; ~**deutsch** *das,* ~**deutsche** *das* High German; ~**druck** *der; Pl.* ~**drücke** (Physik, Met.) high pressure; ***~**empfindlich** ▶ HOCH 2; ~|**fahren** *unr. itr. V.; mit sein* **(a)** (ugs.) go up; (mit dem Auto) drive up; (mit dem Fahrrad, Motorrad) ride up; **(b)** (auffahren) start up; **aus dem Sessel** ~**fahren** start [up] from one's chair; **(c)** (aufbrausen) flare up; ~**finanz** *die* high finance; ~**fliegend** *Adj.* ambitious; ~**form** *die* top form; ~**gebirge** *das* [high] mountains *pl.;* ~**gefühl** *das* [feeling of] elation; ~|**gehen** *unr. itr. V.; mit sein* (ugs.) go up; (zornig werden) blow one's top (coll.); explode; (explodieren) ⟨bomb, mine⟩ go off; ~**genuss,** ***~**genuß** *der:* **ein** ~**genuss sein** be a real delight; ~**geschlossen** *Adj.* high-necked ⟨dress⟩; ***~**gestellt** ▶ HOCH 2; ~**glanz** *der:* **etw. auf** ~**glanz bringen** give sth. a high polish; (fig.) make sth. spick and span; ~**gradig** ① *Adj.* extreme; ② *adv.* extremely; ~|**halten** *unr. tr. V.* hold up; ~**haus** *das* high-rise building; ~|**heben** *unr. tr. V.* lift up; raise ⟨arm, leg, hand⟩; ~**interessant** *Adj.* extremely interesting; ~**kant** *Adv.* (ugs.): **jmdn.** ~**kant hinauswerfen** chuck sb. out (coll.); throw sb. out on his/her ear (coll.); ~|**kommen** *unr. itr. V.; mit sein* (ugs.) come up; (vorwärts kommen) get on; ~**konjunktur** *die* (Wirtsch.) boom; **auf dem Automarkt herrscht** ~**konjunktur** the car market is booming;

**alte Schreibung - vgl. Hinweis auf S. xiv

∼|**krempeln** tr. V. roll up; ∼**land** das highlands Pl.; ∼|**leben** itr. V. jmdn./etw. ∼**leben lassen** cheer sb./sth.; **er lebe ∼!** three cheers for him; ∼**leistungs·sport** der top-level sport; ∼**modern** Adj. ultramodern; ∼**mut** der arrogance; ∼**mütig** Adj. arrogant; ∼**näsig** Adj. (abwertend) stuck-up; ∼|**nehmen** unr. tr. V. (ugs.: verspotten) jmdn. ∼**nehmen** pull sb.'s leg; ∼**ofen** der blast furnace; ∼**prozentig** Adj. high-proof ⟨spirits⟩; ∼|**rechnen** project; ∼**rechnung** die (Statistik) projection; ∼**ruf** der cheer; ∼**saison** die high season; ∼|**schlagen** ①unr. tr. V. turn up ⟨collar, brim⟩; ②unr. itr. V.; mit sein ⟨water, waves⟩ surge up; ⟨flames⟩ leap up; ∼**schule** die college; (Universität) university; ∼|**scrollen** (DV) itr. u. tr. V. scroll up

Hochsee·fischerei die deep-sea fishing no art.

hoch-, Hoch-: ∼**sitz** der (Jägerspr.) raised hide; ∼**sommer** der high summer; ∼**spannung** die (Elektrot.) high voltage; ∼|**spielen** tr. V. blow up

höchst Adv. extremely; most

höchst... ▶ HOCH

Hoch·stapler /-ʃtaːplɐ/ der; ∼s, ∼: confidence trickster; conman (coll.); (Aufschneider) fraud

höchsten·falls Adv. at [the] most or the outside; at the very most

höchstens Adv. at most; (bestenfalls) at best

Höchst-: ∼**fall** der: **im** ∼**fall** at [the] most; ∼**form** die (bes. Sport) peak form; ∼**geschwindigkeit** die top speed; (Geschwindigkeitsbegrenzung) speed limit

Hoch·stimmung die high spirits pl.

höchst-, Höchst-: ∼**leistung** die supreme performance; (Ergebnis) supreme achievement; ∼**maß** das: **ein** ∼**maß an etw.** (Dat.) a very high degree of sth.; ∼**persönlich** ①Adj. personal; ②adv. in person; ∼**temperatur** die maximum or highest temperature; ∼**wahrscheinlich** Adv. very probably; ∼**wert** der maximum value

hoch-, Hoch-: ∼**tour** die: **auf** ∼**touren laufen** run at full speed; (intensiv betrieben werden) be in full swing; ∼**trabend** (abwertend) ①Adj. high-flown; ②adv. in a high-flown manner; ∼|**treiben** unr. tr. V. force up ⟨prices etc.⟩; ∼**verrat** der high treason; ∼**wasser** das (Flut) high tide; (Überschwemmung) flood; ∼**wertig** Adj. high-quality ⟨goods⟩; highly nutritious ⟨food⟩; ∼**würden** der; ∼∼[s] (veralt.) Reverend Father

Hoch·zeit die; ∼, ∼en wedding

Hochzeits-: ∼**feier** die wedding; ∼**nacht** die wedding night; ∼**reise** die honeymoon [trip]

Hocke die; ∼, ∼n (a) (Körperhaltung) squat; crouch

(b) (Turnen) squat vault

hocken ①itr. V. (a) mit haben od. (südd.) sein squat; crouch

(b) mit haben od. (südd.) sein (ugs.: sich aufhalten) sit around

②refl. V. crouch down

Hocker der; ∼s, ∼: stool

Höcker der; ∼s, ∼: hump; (auf der Nase) bump; (auf dem Schnabel) knob

Hockey /ˈhɔki/ das; ∼s hockey

Hoden der; ∼s, ∼: testicle

Hoden·bruch der (Med.) scrotal hernia

Hof der; ∼[e]s, Höfe (a) courtyard; (Schul∼) playground; (Gefängnis∼) [prison] yard

(b) (Bauern∼) farm

(c) (Herrscher, Hofstaat) court

Hof·dame die lady of the court; (Begleiterin der Königin) lady-in-waiting

hof·fähig Adj. presentable at court pred.

hoffen ①tr. V. hope

②itr. V. hope; **auf etw.** (Akk.) ∼: hope for sth.; (Vertrauen setzen auf) **auf jmdn./etw.** ∼: put one's faith in sb./sth.

hoffentlich Adv. hopefully; ∼! let's hope so

Hoffnung die; ∼, ∼en hope

hoffnungs-, Hoffnungs-: ∼**los** ①Adj. hopeless; despairing ⟨person⟩; ②adv. hopelessly; ∼**losigkeit** die; ∼∼: despair; (der Lage) hopelessness; ∼**voll** ①Adj. (a) hopeful; full of hope pred.; (b) (erfolgversprechend) promising; ②adv. (a) full of hope; (b) (erfolgversprechend) promisingly

höflich ①Adj. polite

②adv. politely

Höflichkeit die; ∼: politeness

hoh... ▶ HOCH

Höhe /ˈhøːə/ die; ∼, ∼n height; **etw. in die** ∼ **heben** lift sth. up; **das ist ja die** ∼**!** (fig. ugs.) that's the limit!

Hoheit die; ∼, ∼en sovereignty (über + Akk. over); **Seine/Ihre** ∼: His/Your Highness

Hoheits-: ∼**gebiet** das [sovereign] territory; ∼**gewässer** das territorial waters

Höhen-: ∼**angst** die fear of heights; ∼**flug** der (fig.) flight; ∼**lage** die altitude; ∼**luft** die mountain air; ∼**messer** der altimeter; ∼**sonne** die (Med.) sun lamp; ∼**unterschied** der difference in altitude; ∼**zug** der (Geogr.) range of hills; (Bergkette) range of mountains; mountain range

Höhe·punkt der high point; (einer Veranstaltung) high spot; highlight; (einer Laufbahn, des Ruhms) peak; pinnacle; (Orgasmus; eines Stückes) climax

höher /ˈhøːɐ/ ▶ HOCH

hohl Adj. hollow

Höhle die; ∼, ∼n (a) cave; (größer) cavern (b) (Tierbau) lair

Hohl-: ~**maß** *das* measure of capacity; ~**raum** *der* cavity; [hollow] space; ~**spiegel** *der* concave mirror

Hohn *der;* ~[e]s scorn; derision

höhnen (geh.) *itr. V.* jeer

höhnisch ① *Adj.* scornful
② *adv.* scornfully

Hokuspokus *der;* ~: hocus-pocus; (abwertend: Drum und Dran) fuss

hold *Adj.* (dichter. veralt.) fair; lovely; lovely ⟨sight, smile⟩

holen ① *tr. V.* (a) fetch; get (b) (ab~) fetch (c) (ugs.: erlangen) get ⟨prize etc.⟩; carry off ⟨medal, trophy, etc.⟩
② *refl. V.* (ugs.: sich zuziehen) catch; **sich** (*Dat.*) [beim Baden] einen Schnupfen ~: catch a cold [swimming]

Holland (*das*)*;* ~s Holland

Holländer *der;* ~s, ~: Dutchman

Holländerin *die;* ~, ~nen Dutchwoman

holländisch *Adj.* Dutch

Hölle *die;* ~, ~n hell *no art.*

Höllen-lärm *der* (ugs.) diabolical noise *or* row (coll.)

höllisch ① *Adj.* (a) infernal; ⟨spirits, torments⟩ of hell (b) (ugs.: sehr groß) tremendous (coll.)
② *adv.* (ugs.: sehr) hellishly (coll.)

Holm *der;* ~[e]s, ~e (Turnen) bar

Holocaust *der;* ~[s] Holocaust

holpern *itr. V. mit sein* (fahren) jolt; bump

holprig *Adj.* (a) bumpy; rough (b) (stockend) halting ⟨speech⟩; clumsy ⟨verses, style, language, etc.⟩

Holunder *der;* ~s, ~: elder

Holz *das;* ~es, **Hölzer** wood; (Bau~, Tischler~) timber; wood

Holz-: ~**bein** *das* wooden leg; ~**bläser** *der*, **Holz·bläserin** *die* woodwind player

hölzern *Adj.* (auch fig.) wooden

holz-, Holz-: ~**fäller** *der;* ~~s, ~~: woodcutter; lumberjack (Amer.); ~**frei** *Adj.* wood-free ⟨paper⟩

holzig *Adj.* woody

Holz-: ~**klotz** *der* block of wood; (als Spielzeug) wooden block; ~**kohle** *die* charcoal; ~**kopf** *der* (salopp abwertend) blockhead; ~**pantoffel** *der* clog; ~**scheit** *das* piece of wood; (Brenn~) piece of firewood; ~**schnitt** *der* (a) (Technik) woodcutting *no art.;* (b) (Blatt) woodcut; ~**schuh** *der* clog; ~**stoß** *der* pile of wood; ~**weg** *der:* auf dem ~weg sein be on the wrong track (fig.); ~**wolle** *die* wood wool; ~**wurm** *der* woodworm

homogen *Adj.* homogeneous

homöopathisch *Adj.* homoeopathic

Homo·sexualität *die;* ~: homosexuality

homo·sexuell ① *Adj.* homosexual

② *adv.* ~ **veranlagt sein** have homosexual tendencies

Honig *der;* ~s, ~e honey

Honig·kuchen *der* honey cake

Honig·wabe *die* honeycomb

Honorar *das;* ~s, ~e fee; (Autoren~) royalty

Honoratioren /honoraˈtsːioˑrən/ *Pl.* notabilities

honorieren *tr. V.* (a) jmdn. ~: pay sb. [a/ his/her fee] (b) (würdigen) appreciate; (belohnen) reward

Hopfen *der;* ~s, ~: hop; **bei ihm ist ~ und Malz verloren** (ugs.) he's a hopeless case

hopp *Interj.* quick; look sharp

hoppeln *itr. V.; mit sein* hop; (über + *Akk.* across, over)

hoppla *Interj.* oops; whoops

hopsen *itr. V.; mit sein* (ugs.) (springen) jump; (hüpfen) ⟨animal⟩ hop; ⟨child⟩ skip; ⟨ball⟩ bounce

Hopser *der;* ~s, ~ (ugs.) [little] jump

Hör·apparat *der* hearing aid

hörbar ① *Adj.* audible
② *adv.* audibly; (geräuschvoll) noisily

Hör·buch *das* audiobook

horchen *itr. V.* listen (**auf** + *Akk.* to); (heimlich zuhören) eavesdrop

Horde *die;* ~, ~n horde; (von Halbstarken) mob

hören ① *tr. V.* hear; (anhören) listen to
② *itr. V.* hear; (zuhören) listen; **auf jmdn./ jmds. Rat ~:** listen to sb./sb.'s advice

Hören-sagen *das:* vom ~: from hearsay

Hörer *der;* ~s, ~ (a) listener (b) (Telefon~) receiver

Hörerin *die;* ~, ~nen listener

Hörerschaft *die;* ~, ~en audience

Hör-: ~**fehler** *der* (a) das war ein ~fehler he/she *etc.* misheard; (b) (Schwerhörigkeit) hearing defect; ~**funk** *der* radio; im ~funk on the radio; ~**funk·sendung** *die* radio programme; ~**gerät** *das* hearing aid

hörig *Adj.:* jmdm. ~ sein be submissively dependent on sb.; (sexuell) be sexually enslaved to sb.

Horizont *der;* ~[e]s, ~e (auch Geol., fig.) horizon

horizontal ① *Adj.* horizontal
② *adv.* horizontally

Horizontale *die;* ~, ~n (a) (Linie) horizontal line (b) (Lage) die ~: the horizontal

Hormon *das;* ~s, ~e hormone

Horn *das;* ~[e]s, **Hörner** horn

Hörnchen *das;* ~s, ~ (Gebäck) croissant

Horn·haut *die* (a) callus; hard skin *no indef. art.;* (b) (am Auge) cornea

Hornisse *die;* ~, ~n hornet

Horoskop *das;* ~s, ~e horoscope

---

*old spelling - see note on page xiv

horrend *Adj.* shocking (coll.), horrendous (coll.) ‹*price*›; colossal (coll.) ‹*sum, amount, rent*›

Hör·rohr *das* stethoscope

Horror *der;* ~s horror

Horror-: ~**film** *der* horror film; ~**roman** *der* horror novel

Hör-: ~**saal** *der* lecture theatre *or* hall; ~**spiel** *das* radio play

Horst *der;* ~[e]s, ~e eyrie

Hort *der;* ~[e]s, ~e ▶ KINDERHORT

horten *tr. V.* hoard; stockpile ‹*raw materials*›

Hortensie /hɔr'tɛnziə/ *die;* ~, ~n hydrangea

Hör·weite *die;* in/außer ~weite in/out of earshot

Höschen /'høːsçən/ *das;* ~s, ~: trousers *pl.;* pair of trousers; (kurzes ~) shorts *pl.;* pair of shorts

Hose *die;* ~, ~n (a) trousers *pl.;* pants *pl.* (Amer.); (Unter~) pants *pl.;* (Freizeit~) slacks *pl.;* (Bund~) breeches *pl.;* (Reit~) riding breeches *pl.;* eine ~: a pair of trousers/pants/slacks *etc.;*
(b) (fig.) die ~n anhaben (ugs.) wear the trousers; die ~n runterlassen (salopp) come clean (coll.); in die ~[n] gehen (salopp) be a [complete] flop (coll.); es ist tote ~ (Jugendspr.) there's nothing doing (coll.)

Hosen-: ~**anzug** *der* trouser suit (Brit.); pant suit; ~**matz** *der;* ~~es, ~~e *od.* ~**mätze** (ugs. scherzh.) toddler; ~**rock** *der* culottes *pl.;* ~**tasche** *die* trouser pocket; pants pocket (Amer.); ~**träger** *Pl.* braces; suspenders (Amer.); pair of braces/suspenders

Hospital *das;* ~s, ~e *od.* **Hospitäler** hospital

Hospiz *das;* ~es, ~e hospice

Hostie /'hɔstiə/ *die;* ~, ~n (christl. Rel.) host

Hotel *das;* ~s, ~s hotel

Hotel·bar *die* hotel bar

Hotel garni /- gar'niː/ *das;* ~ ~, ~s ~s /- gar'niː/ bed-and-breakfast hotel

Hotelier /hotɛ'liə:/ *der;* ~s, ~s hotelier

Hotline /'hɔtlaɪn/ *die;* ~, ~s hotline

hüben *Adv.* over here

hübsch ⓵ *Adj.* pretty; nice ‹*area, flat, voice, tune, etc.*›; nice-looking ‹*boy, person*›; ein ~es Sümmchen (ugs.) a tidy sum (coll.); a nice little sum; das ist eine ~e Geschichte (ugs. iron.) this is a fine *or* pretty kettle of fish (coll.)
⓶ *adv.* prettily; (ugs.: sehr) ~ kalt perishing cold

Hub·schrauber *der;* ~s, ~: helicopter

Hubschrauber·lande·platz *der* heliport; (kleiner) helicopter pad; landing pad

huckepack *Adv.* jmdn. ~ tragen (ugs.) give sb. a piggyback

hudeln *itr. V.* (bes. südd., österr.) be sloppy (bei in)

Huf *der;* ~[e]s, ~e hoof

huf-, Huf-: ~**eisen** *das* horseshoe; ~**eisen·förmig** ⓵ *Adj.* horseshoe-shaped; ⓶ *adv.* in [the shape of] a horseshoe; ~**schmied** *der* farrier

Hüfte *die;* ~, ~n hip

Hüft-: ~**gelenk** *das* (Anat.) hip joint; ~**gürtel** *der* girdle

Hügel *der;* ~s, ~ hill

hügelig *Adj.* hilly

Huhn *das;* ~[e]s, **Hühner** chicken; (Henne) chicken; hen

Hühnchen *das;* ~s, ~: small chicken; mit jmdm. [noch] ein ~ zu rupfen haben (ugs.) [still] have a bone to pick with sb.

Hühner-: ~**auge** *das* (am Fuß) corn; ~**brühe** *die* chicken broth

hui /hui:/ *Interj.* whoosh

huldigen *itr. V.* jmdm. ~: pay tribute to sb.

Huldigung *die;* ~, ~en tribute

Hülle *die;* ~, ~n cover

hüllen *tr. V.* (geh.) wrap

Hülse *die;* ~, ~n (a) case
(b) (Bot.) pod

Hülsen·frucht *die* (a) (Frucht) fruit of a leguminous plant; **Hülsenfrüchte** pulse *sing.;*
(b) (Pflanze) legume; leguminous plant

human *Adj.* humane

Humanismus *der;* ~: humanism; (Epoche) Humanism *no art.*

humanitär *Adj.* humanitarian

Humbug *der;* ~s (ugs.) humbug

Hummel *die;* ~, ~n bumble-bee

Hummer *der;* ~s, ~: lobster

Humor *der;* ~s humour; (Sinn für ~) sense of humour; den ~ nicht verlieren remain good-humoured

Humorist *der;* ~en, ~en, **Humoristin** *die;* ~, ~nen (a) (Autor[in]) humorist
(b) (Vortragskünstler[in]) comedian

humoristisch *Adj.* humorous

humor-: ~**los** *Adj.* humourless; ~**losigkeit** *die;* ~~: humourlessness; lack of humour; ~**voll** *Adj.* humorous

humpeln *itr. V.* (a) auch mit sein walk with a limp
(b) mit sein (sich ~d fortbewegen) limp

Hund *der;* ~es, ~e (a) dog; auf den ~ kommen (ugs.) go to the dogs (coll.); vor die ~e gehen (ugs.) go to the dogs (coll.); (sterben) kick the bucket (coll.)
(b) (abwertend) bastard (sl.)

hunde-, Hunde-: ~**elend** *Adj.* (ugs.) [really] wretched *or* awful; ~**hütte** *die* [dog] kennel; ~**kuchen** *der* dog biscuit; ~**müde** *Adj.* (ugs.) dog-tired; ~**rasse** *die* breed of dog

hundert *Kardinalz.* (a) a *or* one hundred
(b) (ugs.: viele) hundreds of

Hundert¹ *das;* ~s, ~e hundred

Hundert² *die;* ~, ~**en** hundred
Hunderter *der;* ~**s**, ~ (ugs.) hundred-euro/ -mark/-dollar *etc.* note
hundert·mal *Adv.* a hundred times; **auch wenn du dich** ~ **beschwerst** (ugs.) however much you complain
Hundert-: ~**mark·schein** *der* hundred-mark note; ~**meter·lauf** *der* (Leichtathletik) hundred metres *sing.*
hundert·prozentig 1 *Adj.* (a) [one-]hundred per cent *attrib.;* (b) (ugs.: völlig) a hundred per cent (c) (ugs.: ganz sicher) absolutely reliable 2 *adv.* (ugs.) **ich bin nicht** ~ **sicher** I'm not a hundred per cent sure
hundertst... /'hʊndɐtst.../ *Ordinalz.* hundredth
hundertstel /'hʊndɐtstl̩/ *Bruchz.* hundredth
Hundertstel *das* (schweiz. meist *der*); ~**s**, ~: hundredth
hundert·tausend *Kardinalz.* a *or* one hundred thousand
Hunde-: ~**scheiße** *die* (derb) dog shit (coarse); ~**steuer** *die* dog licence fee; ~**zwinger** *der* dog run
Hündin *die;* ~, ~**nen** bitch
Hüne *der;* ~**n**, ~**n** giant
Hünen·grab *das* megalithic tomb; (Hügelgrab) barrow
Hunger *der;* ~**s** (a) ~ **bekommen/haben** get/be hungry (b) (geh.: Verlangen) hunger; (nach Ruhm, Macht) craving
Hunger·kur *die* starvation diet
hungern *itr. V.* go hungry; starve; **nach etw.** ~: (fig.) hunger for sth.
Hungers·not *die* famine
Hunger-: ~**streik** *der* hunger strike; ~**tuch** *das:* **am** ~**tuch nagen** (ugs. scherzh.) be on the breadline
hungrig *Adj.* (auch geh. fig.) hungry (**nach** for)
Hupe *die;* ~, ~**n** horn
hupen *itr. V.* sound one's horn; **dreimal** ~: hoot three times
hüpfen *itr. V.; mit sein* hop; ‹*ball*› bounce
Hürde *die;* ~, ~**n** hurdle
Hürden·lauf *der* (Leichtathletik) hurdling; (Wettbewerb) hurdles *pl.*
Hure *die;* ~, ~**n** (abwertend) whore
huren *itr. V.* (abwertend) whore
hurra *Interj.* hurray; hurrah; ~**/Hurra schreien** cheer
Hurra *das;* ~**s**, ~**s** cheer
hurtig 1 *Adj.* rapid 2 *adv.* quickly
huschen *itr. V.; mit sein* (lautlos u. leichtfüßig)

‹*person*› steal; (lautlos u. schnell) dart; ‹*mouse, lizard, etc.*› dart; ‹*smile*› flit; ‹*light*› flash; ‹*shadow*› slide quickly
hüsteln *itr. V.* give a slight cough
husten 1 *itr. V.* cough; (Husten haben) have a cough 2 *tr. V.* cough up ‹*blood, phlegm*›
Husten *der;* ~**s**, ~: cough
Husten-: ~**anfall** *der* coughing fit; fit of coughing; ~**bonbon** *das* cough drop; ~**reiz** *der* tickling in the throat; ~**saft** *der* cough mixture; ~**tropfen** *Pl.* cough drops
Hut¹ *der;* ~**es**, Hüte hat; (fig.) **da geht einem/mir der** ~ **hoch** (ugs.) it makes you/me mad (coll.); **das kann er sich** (*Dat.*) **an den** ~ **stecken** (ugs. abwertend) he can keep it (coll.)
Hut² *die;* ~ (geh.) keeping; care; **auf der** ~ **sein** be on one's guard
hüten 1 *tr. V.* look after; tend ‹*sheep, cattle*› 2 *refl. V.* be on one's guard
Hut·schnur *die:* **das geht mir über die** ~ (ugs.) that's going too far
Hütte *die;* ~, ~**n** (a) hut; (ärmliches Haus) shack; hut (b) (Eisen~) iron [and steel] works *sing. or pl.;* (c) (Jagd~) [hunting] lodge
Hütten-: ~**käse** *der* cottage cheese; ~**schuh** *der* slipper sock
Hyäne *die;* ~, ~**n** hyena
Hyazinthe *die;* ~, ~**n** hyacinth
Hydrant *der;* ~**en**, ~**en** hydrant
Hydrat *das;* ~[**e**]**s**, ~**e** (Chemie) hydrate
Hydraulik *die;* ~ (Technik) (a) (Theorie) hydraulics *sing., no art.;* (b) (Vorrichtungen) hydraulics *pl.*
hydraulisch (Technik) 1 *Adj.* hydraulic 2 *adv.* hydraulically
Hydro·kultur *die* (Gartenbau) hydroponics *sing.*
Hygiene *die;* ~ (a) (Gesundheitspflege) health care (b) (Sauberkeit) hygiene
hygienisch 1 *Adj.* hygienic 2 *adv.* hygienically
Hymne /'hʏmnə/ *die;* ~, ~**n** hymn; (National~) national anthem
Hypnose *die;* ~, ~**n** hypnosis
hypnotisieren *tr. V.* hypnotize
Hypochonder /hypo'xɔndɐ/ *der;* ~**s**, ~, **Hypochonderin** *die;* ~, ~**nen** hypochondriac
hypochondrisch *Adj.* hypochondriac
Hypotenuse *die;* ~, ~**n** (Math.) hypotenuse
Hypothek *die;* ~, ~**en** (Bankw.) mortgage; (fig.) burden
Hypothese *die;* ~, ~**n** hypothesis
hypothetisch 1 *Adj.* hypothetical 2 *adv.* hypothetically
Hysterie *die;* ~, ~**n** hysteria
hysterisch 1 *Adj.* hysterical 2 *adv.* hysterically

I i

i, I /iː/ *das;* ~, ~ i/I; **das Tüpfelchen** *od.* **der Punkt auf dem** ~ (fig.) the final touch
i *Interj.* ugh; **i bewahre, i wo** (ugs.) [good] heavens, no!
i.A. *Abk.* = **im Auftrag[e]** p.p.
IC *Abk.* = **Intercity** IC
ICE *Abk.* = **Intercityexpress[zug]** ICE
ich *Personalpron.; 1. Pers. Sg. Nom.* I; **immer** ~ (ugs.) [it's] always me; ~ **nicht** not me; **Menschen wie du und** ~: people like you and me; *s. auch* (*Gen.*) MEINER, (*Dat.*) MIR, (*Akk.*) MICH
Ich *das;* ~[s], ~[s] (a) self
(b) (Psych.) ego
Ichform *die* first person
Icon /ˈaɪkən/ *das;* ~s, ~s (DV) icon
ideal 1 *Adj.* ideal
2 *adv.* ideally
Ideal *das;* ~s, ~e ideal
Ideal-: ~**bild** *das* ideal; ~**fall** *der* ideal case; ~**gewicht** *das* ideal weight
idealisieren *tr. V.* idealize
Idealismus *der;* ~ (auch Philos.) idealism
Idealist *der;* ~en, ~en, **Idealistin** *die;* ~, ~nen idealist
idealistisch (auch Philos.) 1 *Adj.* idealistic
2 *adv.* idealistically
Idee *die;* ~, ~n (a) idea
(b) (ein bisschen) **eine** ~: a shade; **eine** ~ [Salz/Pfeffer] a touch [of salt/pepper]
ideell *Adj.* non-material; (geistig-seelisch) spiritual
ideen·los *Adj.* [completely] lacking in ideas *postpos.*
Identifikation /idɛntifikaˈtsi̯oːn/ *die;* ~, ~en (auch Psych.) identification
identifizieren 1 *tr. V.* identify
2 *refl. V.* (auch Psych.) **sich mit jmdm./etw.** ~: identify with sb./sth.
identisch *Adj.* identical
Identität *die;* ~: identity
Ideologe *der;* ~n, ~n ideologue
Ideologie *die;* ~, ~n /-i̯ən/ ideology
Ideologin *die;* ~, ~nen ideologue
ideologisch 1 *Adj.* ideological
2 *adv.* ideologically
Idiot *der;* ~en, ~en (auch ugs. abwertend) idiot
idioten-, Idioten-: ~**hügel** *der* (ugs. scherzh.) nursery slope; ~**sicher** *Adj.* (ugs. scherzh.) foolproof
Idiotie *die;* ~, ~n /-i̯ən/ (a) idiocy
(b) (ugs. abwertend: Dummheit) madness
Idiotin *die;* ~, ~nen (auch ugs. abwertend) idiot

idiotisch 1 *Adj.* (a) (Psych.) severely subnormal
(b) (ugs. abwertend) idiotic
2 *adv.* (auch ugs. abwertend) idiotically
Idol *das;* ~s, ~e (auch bild. Kunst) idol
Idyll *das;* ~s, ~e idyll
Idylle *die;* ~, ~n idyll
idyllisch *Adj.* idyllic
Igel *der;* ~s, ~: hedgehog
Iglu *der od. das;* ~s, ~s igloo
Ignoranz /ɪgnoˈrants/ *die;* ~: ignorance
ignorieren *tr. V.* ignore
ihm *Dat. von* ER, ES: (bei männlichen Personen) him; (bei weiblichen Personen) her; (bei Dingen, Tieren) it; **gib es** ~: give it to him; give him it; **Freunde von** ~: friends of his
ihn *Akk. von* ER (bei männlichen Personen) him; (bei Dingen, Tieren) it
ihnen *Dat. von* SIE, *Pl.* them; **gib es** ~: give it to them; give them it; **Freunde von** ~: friends of theirs
Ihnen *Dat. von* SIE you; **ich habe es** ~ **gegeben** I gave it to you; **Freunde von** ~: friends of yours
ihr¹ /iːɐ̯/ *Dat. von* SIE, *Sg.* (bei Personen) her; (bei Dingen, Tieren) it
ihr², *Personalpron.; 2. Pers. Pl. Nom.* you
ihr³ *Possessivpron.* (a) *Sg.* (einer Person) her; (eines Tieres, einer Sache) its
(b) *Pl.* their
Ihr *Possessivpron.* (Anrede) your; ~ **Hans Meier** (Briefschluss) yours, Hans Meier; **welcher Mantel ist** ~**er?** which coat is yours?
ihrer (a) *Gen. von* SIE, *Sg.* (geh.) **wir gedachten** ~: we remembered her
(b) *Gen. von* SIE, *Pl.* (geh.) **wir werden** ~ **gedenken** we will remember them; **es waren** ~ **zwölf** there were twelve of them
Ihrer *Gen. von* SIE (geh.) **wir werden** ~ **gedenken** we will remember you
ihrerseits *Adv.* for her/their part; (von ihr/ihnen) on her/their part
Ihrerseits *Adv.:* ▶ DEINERSEITS
ihres·gleichen *indekl. Pron.* people *pl.* like her/them; (abwertend) the likes of her/them
Ihres·gleichen *indekl. Pron.* people *pl.* like you; (abwertend) the likes of you
ihret·wegen *Adv.:* ▶ MEINETWEGEN: because of her/them; for her/their sake; about her/them; as far as she is/they are concerned
Ihret·wegen *Adv.:* ▶ DEINETWEGEN
Ikone *die;* ~, ~n icon

illegal ① *Adj.* illegal
② *adv.* illegally
Illegalität *die;* ~, ~en illegality
illegitim *Adj.* (geh.) illegitimate
illuminieren *tr. V.* illuminate
Illusion *die;* ~, ~en illusion
illusorisch *Adj.* illusory; (zwecklos) pointless
Illustration *die;* ~, ~en illustration
illustrieren *tr. V.* illustrate
Illustrierte *die; adj. Dekl.* magazine
Iltis *der;* ~ses, ~se polecat; (Pelz) fitch
im *Präp. + Art.* (a) = in dem;
  (b) (räumlich) in the; **im Theater** at the theatre; **im Fernsehen** on television; **im Bett** in bed
  (c) (zeitlich) **im Mai** in May; **im letzten Jahr** last year; **im Alter von ...** at the age of ...
  (d) (Verlauf) **etw. im Sitzen tun** do sth. [while] sitting down; **im Gehen sein** be going
Image /'ɪmɪtʃ/ *das;* ~[s], ~s image
imaginär *Adj.* (geh., Math.) imaginary
Imbiss, *Imbiß *der;* Imbisses, Imbisse (a) (kleine Mahlzeit) snack
  (b) ▶ IMBISSSTUBE
Imbiss·stube, *Imbiß·stube *die* café
Imitation *die;* ~, ~en imitation
imitieren *tr. V.* imitate
Imker *der;* ~s, ~, **Imkerin** *die;* ~, ~nen bee-keeper
Immatrikulation *die;* ~, ~en (Hochschulw.) registration
immatrikulieren *tr., refl. V.* (Hochschulw.) register
immer *Adv.* (a) always; **schon** ~: always; ~ **wieder** time and time again; ~, **wenn** every time that
  (b) immer + *Komp.:* ~ **dunkler** darker and darker; ~ **mehr** more and more
  (c) (ugs.: jeweils) ~ **drei Stufen auf einmal** three steps at a time
  (d) (auch) **wo/wer/wann/wie** [auch] ~: wherever/whoever/whenever/however
  (e) (verstärkend) ~ **noch, noch** ~: still
  (f) (ugs.: bei Aufforderung) ~ **geradeaus!** keep [going] straight on
immer-, Immer-: ~**fort** *Adv.* all the time; ~**grün** *Adj.* evergreen; ~**grün** *das* periwinkle; ~**hin** *Adv.* (a) (wenigstens) at any rate; (b) (trotz allem) all the same; (c) (schließlich) after all; ~**zu** *Adv.* (ugs.) the whole time
Immigrant *der;* ~en, ~en, **Immigrantin** *die;* ~, ~nen immigrant
Immigration *die;* ~, ~en immigration
immigrieren *itr. V.; mit sein* immigrate
Immobilien *Pl.* property *sing.*; real estate *sing.*
immun (a) (Med., fig.) immune (**gegen** to)
  (b) (Rechtsspr.) ~ **sein** have immunity

Immunität *die;* ~, ~en (a) (Med.) immunity (**gegen** to)
  (b) (Rechtsspr.) immunity (**gegen** from)
Immun-: ~**schwäche** *die* (Med.) immunodeficiency; immune deficiency; ~**therapie** *die* (Med.) immunotherapy; immune therapy
Imperativ *der;* ~s, ~e (a) (Sprachw.) imperative
  (b) (Philos.) [**kategorischer**] ~: [categorical] imperative
Imperfekt *das;* ~s, ~e (Sprachw.) imperfect [tense]
Imperialismus *der;* ~: imperialism
imperialistisch *Adj.* imperialistic
Imperium *das;* ~s, Imperien (hist., fig.) empire
impfen *tr. V.* vaccinate; inoculate
Impf-: ~**pass, *~paß** *der* vaccination certificate; ~**stoff** *der* vaccine
Impfung *die;* ~, ~en vaccination
implantieren *tr. V.* (Med.) implant
imponieren *itr. V.* impress
imponierend ① *Adj.* impressive
② *adv.* impressively
Imponier·gehabe *das* (Verhaltensf.) display; (fig.) showing off
Import *der;* ~[e]s, ~e import
Importeur /ɪmpɔr'tø:ɐ̯/ *der;* ~s, ~e, **Importeurin** *die;* ~, ~nen importer
importieren *tr., itr. V.* import
imposant ① *Adj.* imposing; impressive ⟨achievement⟩
② *adv.* imposingly
impotent *Adj.* impotent
Impotenz *die;* ~: impotence
imprägnieren *tr. V.* impregnate; (wasserdicht machen) waterproof
Improvisation *die;* ~, ~en improvisation
improvisieren *tr., itr. V.* improvise
Impuls *der;* ~es, ~e stimulus; (innere Regung) impulse
impulsiv ① *Adj.* impulsive
② *adv.* impulsively
imstande *Adv.* ~ **sein, etw. zu tun** be able to do sth.
in¹ ① *Präp. mit Dat.* (auf die Frage: wo?/wann?/wie?) in; **er hat** ~ **Tübingen studiert** he studied at Tübingen; *s. auch* IM;
② *Präp. mit Akk.* (auf die Frage: wohin?) into; *s. auch* INS
in² *Adj.:* ~ **sein** (ugs.) be in
In·anspruchnahme *die;* ~, ~n (starke Belastung) demands *pl.*
In·begriff *der* quintessence
inbegriffen *Adj.* included
In·betrieb·nahme *die;* ~, ~n, **In·betrieb·setzung** *die;* ~, ~n bringing into service
In·brunst *die;* ~ (geh.) fervour; (der Liebe) ardour

in·brünstig (geh.) ① *Adj.* fervent; ardent
⟨*love*⟩
② *adv.* fervently; ⟨*love*⟩ ardently

in·dem *Konj.* (a) (während) while; (gerade als)
as
(b) (dadurch, dass) ∼ **man etw. tut** by doing
sth.

Inder *der;* ∼s, ∼, **Inderin** *die;* ∼, ∼nen
Indian

in·dessen ① *Konj.* (geh.) (a) (während)
while
(b) (wohingegen) whereas
② *Adv.* (a) (inzwischen) meanwhile; in the
mean time
(b) (jedoch) however

Index *der;* ∼ *od.* ∼es, ∼e *od.* **Indizes** (a) *Pl.*
∼e *od.* **Indizes** (Register) index
(b) *Pl.* ∼e (kath. Kirche) Index

Indianer *der;* ∼s, ∼: [American] Indian

Indianer·häuptling *der* Indian chief

Indianerin *die;* ∼, ∼nen [American]
Indian

indianisch *Adj.* Indian

Indien /'ɪndjən/ (*das*); ∼s India

in·different *Adj.* indifferent

Indikativ *der;* ∼s, ∼e /-iːvə/ (Sprachw.)
indicative [mood]

Indikator *der;* ∼s, ∼en (auch Chemie,
Technik) indicator

in·direkt ① *Adj.* indirect
② *adv.* indirectly

indisch *Adj.* Indian

in·diskret *Adj.* indiscreet

In·diskretion *die;* ∼, ∼en indiscretion

Individualist *der;* ∼en, ∼en,
Individualistin *die;* ∼, ∼nen (geh.)
individualist

Individualität *die;* ∼, ∼en (geh.) (a)
individuality
(b) (Persönlichkeit) personality

individuell ① *Adj.* individual; private
⟨*property, vehicle, etc.*⟩
② *adv.* individually

Individuum *das;* ∼s, **Individuen** (auch
Chemie, Biol.) individual

Indiz *das;* ∼es, ∼ien (a) (Rechtsw.) piece of
circumstantial evidence; ∼ien
circumstantial evidence *sing.;*
(b) (Anzeichen) sign (**für** of)

Indizes ▶ INDEX

Indizien·beweis *der* (Rechtsw.) piece of
circumstantial evidence; ∼e circumstantial
evidence *sing.*

indoktrinieren *tr. V.* indoctrinate

Indonesien /ɪndo'neːzjən/ (*das*); ∼s
Indonesia

Indonesier *der;* ∼s, ∼, **Indonesierin**
die; ∼, ∼nen Indonesian

indonesisch *Adj.* Indonesian

industrialisieren *tr. V.* industrialize

Industrialisierung *die;* ∼:
industrialization

Industrie *die;* ∼, ∼n industry

Industrie-: ∼**betrieb** *der* industrial
firm; ∼**gebiet** *das* industrial area;
∼**kauffrau** *die,* ∼**kaufmann** *der: person
with three years' business training employed
on the business side of an industrial
company*

industriell ① *Adj.* industrial
② *adv.* industrially

Industrielle *der/die; adj. Dekl.*
industrialist

Industrie-: ∼**staat** *der* industrial nation;
∼**stadt** *die* industrial town

Industrie- und Handels·kammer *die*
Chamber of Industry and Commerce

Industriezweig *der* branch of industry

in·einander *Adv.* ∼ **greifen** mesh together
(lit. or fig); ∼ **verliebt sein** be in love with
each other *or* one another; ∼ **verschlungene**
Ornamente intertwined decorations

***ineinander|greifen** ▶ INEINANDER

infam ① *Adj.* disgraceful
② *adv.* disgracefully

Infanterie *die;* ∼, ∼n (Milit.) infantry

infantil (Psych., Med., sonst abwertend) ① *Adj.*
infantile
② *adv.* in an infantile way

Infarkt *der;* ∼[e]s, ∼e (Med.) infarction

Infekt *der;* ∼[e]s, ∼e (Med.) infection

Infektion *die;* ∼, ∼en (Med.) (a) (Ansteckung)
infection
(b) (ugs.: Entzündung) inflammation

Infektions-: ∼**gefahr** *die* (Med.) risk of
infection; ∼**herd** *der* (Med.) seat of the/an
infection; ∼**krankheit** *die* (Med.)
infectious disease

Inferno *das;* ∼s (geh.) inferno

Infinitiv *der;* ∼s, ∼e (Sprachw.) infinitive

infizieren ① *tr. V.* infect
② *refl. V.* become infected; **sich bei jmdm.**
∼: be infected by sb.

in flagranti *Adv.* (geh.) in flagrante
[delicto]

Inflation *die;* ∼, ∼en (Wirtsch.) inflation;
(Zeit der ∼) period of inflation

inflationär *Adj.* inflationary

Inflations·rate *die* inflation rate; rate of
inflation

in·folge ① *Präp. + Gen.* as a result of
② *Adv.* ∼ **von etw.** (*Dat.*) as a result of sth.

infolge·dessen *Adv.* consequently

Informatik *die;* ∼: computer science *no
art.*

Informatiker *der;* ∼s, ∼,
Informatikerin *die;* ∼, ∼nen computer
scientist

Information *die;* ∼, ∼en (a) information
no pl., no indef. art. (**über** + *Akk.* about, on);
eine ∼: [a piece of] information
(b) (Büro) information bureau; (Stand)
information desk

Informations-: ∼**büro** *das* information ⋯⟩

bureau *or* office; ~**freiheit** *die* freedom of information; ~**gesellschaft** *die* (Soziol.) information society; ~**material** *das* informational literature; ~**quelle** *die* source of information; ~**vielfalt** *die* variety of information

informativ *Adj.* informative

informieren ① *tr. V.* inform (über + *Akk.* about)
② *refl. V.* inform oneself, find out (über + *Akk.* about)

in·frage: ~ kommen be possible; **das kommt nicht** ~ (ugs.) that is out of the question

Infra·rot *das* (Physik) infra-red radiation

Infra·struktur *die* infrastructure

Infusion *die;* ~, ~en (Med.) infusion

Ing. *Abk.* = **Ingenieur**

In·gebrauch·nahme *die;* ~, ~n: vor ~ des Geräts before operating the appliance

Ingenieur /ɪnʒeˈnjøːɐ̯/ *der;* ~s, ~e, **Ingenieurin** *die;* ~, ~nen [qualified] engineer

Ingwer *der;* ~s, ~: ginger

Inhaber *der;* ~s, ~, **Inhaberin** *die;* ~, ~nen (a) holder
(b) (Besitzer) owner

inhaftieren *tr. V.* take into custody; detain

Inhaftierung *die;* ~, ~en detention

inhalieren *tr. V.* inhale

Inhalt *der;* ~[e]s, ~e (a) contents *pl.;*
(b) (einer Geschichte usw.) content
(c) (Flächen~) area; (Raum~) volume

inhaltlich ① *Adj.* an ~en Gesichtspunkten gemessen from the point of view of content
② *adv.* ~ ist der Aufsatz gut the essay is good as regards content; ~ übereinstimmen be the same in content

Inhalts-: ~**angabe** *die* summary [of contents]; synopsis; (eines Films, Dramas) synopsis; ~**verzeichnis** *das* table of contents; (auf einem Paket) list of contents

in·human *Adj.* (a) (unmenschlich) inhuman
(b) (rücksichtslos) inhumane

Initiale *die;* ~, ~n initial [letter]

Initiative *die;* ~, ~n initiative

Initiator *der;* ~s, ~en, **Initiatorin** *die;* ~, ~nen initiator; (einer Organisation) founder

Injektion *die;* ~, ~en (Med.) injection

injizieren *tr. V.* (Med.) inject

Inkarnation *die;* ~, ~en incarnation

inkl. *Abk.* = **inklusive** incl.

inklusive /ɪnkluˈziːvə/ ① *Präp.* + *Gen.* (bes. Kaufmannsspr.) including
② *Adv.* inclusive

inkognito *Adv.* (geh.) incognito

in·kompetent *Adj.* incompetent

in·kompetenz *die* incompetence

in·konsequent ① *Adj.* inconsistent
② *adv.* inconsistently

In·konsequenz *die* inconsistency

in·korrekt ① *Adj.* incorrect
② *adv.* incorrectly

In·korrektheit *die;* ~, ~en
(a) (Fehlerhaftigkeit) incorrectness
(b) (Fehler) mistake

In·kraft·treten *das;* ~s: mit [dem] ~ des Gesetzes when the law comes/came into force

Inkubations·zeit *die;* ~, ~en (Med.) incubation period

In·land *das* (a) im ~: at home
(b) (Binnenland) interior; inland; **im/ins** ~: inland

inländisch *Adj.* domestic; home-produced ⟨goods⟩

Inlands-: ~**markt** *der* domestic market; ~**porto** *das* inland postage

in·mitten ① *Präp.* + *Gen.* (geh.) in the midst of
② *Adv.* ~ von in the midst of

inne|haben *unr. tr. V.* hold, occupy ⟨position⟩; hold ⟨office⟩

innen *Adv.* inside; (auf/an der Innenseite) on the inside

innen-, Innen-: ~**architekt** *der,* ~**architektin** *die* interior designer; ~**aufnahme** *die* (Fot.) indoor photo[graph]; (Film) interior shot; ~**einrichtung** *die* furnishings *pl.;* ~**hof** *der* inner courtyard; ~**leben** *das* (a) [inner] thoughts and feelings *pl.;* (b) (oft scherzh.: Ausstattung) inside; ~**minister** *der,* ~**ministerin** *die* Minister of the Interior; ≈ Home Secretary (Brit.); ≈ Secretary of the Interior (Amer.); ~**ministerium** *das* Ministry of the Interior; ≈ Home Office (Brit.); ≈ Department of the Interior (Amer.); ~**politik** *die* (eines Staates) home affairs *pl.;* (einer Regierung) domestic policy/policies *pl.;* ~**politisch** ▶ POLITIK: ① *Adj.* ~politische Fragen matters of domestic policy; ② *adv.* as regards home affairs/domestic policy; ~**stadt** *die* town centre; downtown (Amer.); (einer Großstadt) city centre

inner... *Adj.* inner; (inländisch; Med.) internal; inside ⟨pocket, lane⟩

Innere *das; adj. Dekl.* inside; (eines Gebäudes, Wagens, Schiffes) interior; inside; (eines Landes) interior

Innereien *Pl.* entrails; (Kochk.) offal *sing.*

inner·halb ① *Präp.* + *Gen.* (a) within; ~ der Familie/Partei (fig.) within the family/party
(b) (binnen) within; ~ **einer Woche** within a week
② *Adv.* (a) ~ von within
(b) (im Verlauf) ~ von zwei Jahren within two years

innerlich ① *Adj.* inner
② *adv.* inwardly

innerst... *Adj.* innermost

Innerste *das; adj. Dekl.* innermost being

---

inne|wohnen itr. V. (geh.) etw. wohnt jmdm./einer Sache ~: sb./sth. possesses sth.

innig [1] Adj. deep ⟨affection, sympathy⟩; fervent ⟨wish⟩; intimate ⟨friendship⟩; **mein ~ster Dank** my sincerest thanks
[2] adv. ⟨love⟩ with all one's heart

Innigkeit die; ~: depth; (einer Beziehung) intimacy

innovativ Adj. innovative

Innung /'mʊŋ/ die; ~, ~en [trade] guild

in·offiziell [1] Adj. unofficial
[2] adv. unofficially

in puncto as regards

ins Präp. + Art. **(a)** = in das
(b) (räumlich) to the; ~ **Bett gehen** go to bed
(c) ~ **Schlendern geraten** go into a skid

Insasse der; ~n, ~n, **Insassin** die; ~, ~nen **(a)** (Fahrgast) passenger
(b) (Bewohner[in]) inmate

ins·besond[e]re Adv. particularly; in particular

In·schrift die inscription

Insekt /ɪn'zɛkt/ das; ~s, ~en insect

Insel die; ~, ~n island

Insel-: ~**bewohner** der, ~**bewohnerin** die islander; ~**gruppe** die group of islands; ~**staat** die island state; ~**welt** die islands pl.

Inserat das; ~[e]s, ~e advertisement (in a newspaper)

Inserent der; ~en, ~en, **Inserentin** die; ~, ~nen advertiser

inserieren itr. V. advertise

ins·geheim Adv. secretly

ins·gesamt Adv. in all; altogether; (alles in allem) all in all

insofern [1] Adv. /ɪn'zo:fɛrn/ (in dieser Hinsicht) to this extent; ~ **als** in so far as
[2] Konj. /ɪnzo'fɛrn/ (falls) provided [that]

Insolvenz·verfahren das insolvency proceedings pl.

insoweit [1] adv. /ɪn'zo:vai:t/ ▶ INSOFERN 1;
[2] Konj. /ɪnzo'vai:t/ ▶ INSOFERN 2

in spe /ɪn 'spe:/ future attrib.; **mein Schwiegersohn ~** ~: my future son-in-law

Inspektion die; ~, ~en inspection; (Kfz-W.) service

Inspiration die; ~, ~en inspiration

inspirieren tr. V. inspire

inspizieren tr. V. inspect

Installateur /ɪnstala'tøːɐ̯/ der; ~s, ~e, **Installateurin** die; ~, ~nen plumber; (Gas~) [gas] fitter; (Heizungs~) heating engineer; (Elektro~) electrician

Installation die; ~, ~en installation; (Rohre) plumbing no pl.

installieren tr. V. install

in·stand Adv. etw. **ist gut/schlecht ~:** sth. is in good/poor condition; etw. ~ **halten** keep sth. in good condition; etw. ~ **setzen/bringen** repair sth.

Instand·haltung die maintenance

in·ständig [1] Adj. urgent
[2] adv. urgently

Instand·setzung die; ~, ~en repair; (Renovierung) renovation

Instanz /ɪn'stants:/ die; ~, ~en **(a)** authority
(b) (Rechtsw.) [die] **erste/zweite/dritte ~:** the court of original jurisdiction/the appeal court/the court of final appeal; **durch alle ~en gehen** go through all the courts

Instinkt /ɪn'stɪŋkt/ der; ~[e]s, ~e instinct

instinktiv [1] Adj. instinctive
[2] adv. instinctively

Institut /ɪnstɪ'tuːt/ das; ~[e]s, ~e institute

Institution die; ~, ~en (auch fig.) institution

Instruktion /ɪnstrʊk'tsǐoːn/ die; ~, ~en instruction

Instrument /ɪnstru'mɛnt/ das; ~[e]s, ~e instrument

instrumental (Musik) [1] Adj. instrumental
[2] adv. instrumentally

Insulin das; ~s insulin

inszenieren tr. V. stage; put on; (Regie führen bei) direct; (fig.) (einfädeln) engineer; (organisieren) stage

Inszenierung die; ~, ~en staging; (Regie) direction; (Aufführung) production

intakt Adj. **(a)** (unbeschädigt) intact
(b) (funktionsfähig) in [proper] working order postpos.; healthy ⟨economy⟩

integer Adj. **eine integre Persönlichkeit** a person of integrity; ~ **sein** be a person of integrity

Integral das; ~s, ~e (Math.) integral

Integration die; ~, ~en (auch Math.) integration

integrieren tr. V. integrate

Intellekt der; ~[e]s intellect

intellektuell Adj. intellectual

Intellektuelle der/die; adj. Dekl. intellectual

intelligent [1] Adj. intelligent
[2] adv. intelligently

Intelligenz die; ~, ~en **(a)** intelligence
(b) (Gesamtheit der Intellektuellen) intelligentsia

Intelligenz·quotient der intelligence quotient

Intendant der; ~en, ~en, **Intendantin** die; ~, ~nen (Theater) manager and artistic director; (Fernseh~, Rundfunk~) director general

Intensität die; ~: intensity

intensiv [1] Adj. (gründlich) intensive (kräftig) intense
[2] adv. intensively

intensivieren tr. V. intensify; increase ⟨exports⟩; strengthen ⟨connections⟩

Intensiv·station die intensive-care unit

interaktiv Adj. interactive

Intercityzug der inter-city train

interessant [1] Adj. interesting
[2] adv. ~ **schreiben** write in an interesting way ⋯⋗

interessanterweise *Adv.* interestingly enough

Interesse *das;* ~s, ~n interest; ~ an jmdm./etw. haben be interested in sb./sth.

interesse-halber *Adv.* out of interest

Interessen-gebiet *das* field of interest

Interessent *der;* ~en, ~en,
Interessentin *die;* ~, ~nen interested person; (möglicher Käufer/mögliche Käuferin) potential buyer

Interessen-verband *der* [organized] interest group

Interessen-vertretung *die* **(a)** representation
(b) (Vertreter von Interessen) representative body

interessieren [1] *refl. V.* sich für jmdn./ etw. ~: be interested in sb./sth.
[2] *tr. V.* interest; das interessiert mich nicht I'm not interested [in it]

interessiert *Adj.* interested (**an** + *Dat.* in)

Interjektion *die;* ~, ~en interjection

Inter-: ~**kontinental-rakete** *die* (Milit.) intercontinental ballistic missile; ~**mezzo** *das;* ~~s, ~~s *od.* ~mezzi (Theat., Musik) intermezzo; (fig.) interlude; intermezzo

intern [1] *Adj.* internal
[2] *adv.* internally

Internat *das;* ~[e]s, ~e boarding school

inter-, Inter-: ~**national** [1] *Adj.* international; [2] *adv.* internationally; ~**nationale** *die;* ~, ~n **(a)** International; Internationale; **(b)** (Lied) Internationale

Internats-: ~**schule** *die* boarding school; ~**schüler** *der,* ~**schülerin** *die* boarding school pupil; boarder

Internet /'ɪntɛnɛt/ *das;* ~s Internet; im ~: on the Internet

internet-, Internet: ~**anbeiter** *der,* ~**anbeiterin** *die* (DV) Internet provider; ~**anschluss** *der,* ***~**anschluß** *der* Internet connection; connection to the Internet; einen ~anschluss haben be connected to the Internet; ~**fähig** *Adj.* (DV) Internet-capable; Internet-enabled; ~**seite** *die* (DV) Internet page; Web page

internieren *tr. V.* (Milit.) intern

Internierung *die;* ~, ~en internment

Internist *der;* ~en, ~en, **Internistin** *die;* ~, ~nen (Med.) internist

Interpol *die;* ~: Interpol *no art.*

Interpret *der;* ~en, ~en interpreter (*of music, text, events, etc.*)

Interpretation *die;* ~, ~en interpretation (*of music, text, events, etc.*)

interpretieren *tr. V.* interpret (*music, texts, events, etc.*)

Interpretin *die;* ~, ~nen ▶ INTERPRET

Interpunktion *die;* ~ (Sprachw.) punctuation

Intervall /ɪntɐ'val/ *das;* ~s, ~e (Musik, Math.) interval

intervenieren *itr. V.* (geh., Politik) intervene

Intervention *die;* ~, ~en (geh., Politik) intervention; (Protest) representations *pl.*

Interview /'ɪntɐ'vjuː/ *das;* ~s, ~s interview

interviewen /ɪntɐ'vjuːən/ *tr. V.* interview

Interviewer *der;* ~s, ~, **Interviewerin** *die;* ~, ~nen interviewer

intialisieren *tr. V.* (DV) initialize

intim *Adj.* intimate

Intimität *die;* ~, ~en intimacy

Intim-: ~**partner** *der,* ~**partnerin** *die* intimate partner; sexual partner; ~**sphäre** *die* private life

in-tolerant *Adj.* intolerant

In-toleranz *die* intolerance (**gegenüber** of)

Intonation *die;* ~, ~en intonation

Intranet *das* ~s, ~s (DV) Intranet

in-transitiv [1] *Adj.* (Sprachw.) intransitive
[2] *adv.* intransitively

intravenös (Med.) [1] *Adj.* intravenous
[2] *adv.* intravenously

Intrige *die;* ~, ~n intrigue

Intuition *die;* ~, ~en intuition

intuitiv [1] *Adj.* intuitive
[2] *adv.* intuitively

intus: etw. ~ haben (ugs.) (begriffen haben) have got sth. into one's head; (gegessen od. getrunken haben) have put sth. away (coll.)

Invalide *der; adj. Dekl.* invalid

Invasion *die;* ~, ~en invasion

Inventar *das;* ~s, ~e (einer Firma) fittings and equipment *pl.;* (eines Hauses, Büros) furnishings and fittings *pl.*

inventarisieren *tr. V.* inventory; draw up or make an inventory of

Inventur *die;* ~, ~en stock-taking

investieren *tr., itr. V.* (auch fig.) invest (**in** + *Akk.* in)

Investition *die;* ~, ~en investment

Investitions-güter *Pl.* (Wirtsch.) capital goods

Investor *der;* ~s, ~en /-'toːrən/, **Investorin** *die;* ~, ~nen (Wirtsch.) investor

in-wie-fern *Adv.* in what way; (bis zu welchem Grade) to what extent

in-wie-weit *Adv.* to what extent

In-zahlung-nahme *die;* ~, ~n part exchange; trade in (Amer.)

Inzest *der;* ~[e]s, ~e incest

In-zucht *die;* ~: inbreeding

in-zwischen *Adv.* **(a)** (seither) in the meantime; since [then]
(b) (bis zu einem Zeitpunkt) (in der Gegenwart) by now; (in der Vergangenheit/Zukunft) by then
(c) (währenddessen) meanwhile

IOK *Abk.* **Internationales Olympisches Komitee** IOC

Ion /iːn/ *das;* ~s, ~en (Physik, Chemie) ion

ionisieren *tr. V.* (Physik, Chemie) ionize

Iono·sphäre *die* ionosphere

Irak *(das); ~s od. der; ~*[s] Iraq

Iraker *der; ~s, ~,* **Irakerin** *die; ~, ~nen* Iraqi

irakisch Iraqi

Irak·krieg *der* Iraq War

Iran *(das); ~s od. der; ~*[s] Iran

Iraner *der; ~s, ~,* **Iranerin** *die; ~, ~nen* Iranian

iranisch *Adj.* Iranian

irden *Adj.* earthen[ware]

irdisch *Adj.* **(a)** earthly; worldly ⟨goods, pleasures, possessions⟩ **(b)** (zur Erde gehörig) terrestrial; *das ~e* Leben life on earth

Ire *der; ~n, ~n* Irishman

irgend *Adv.* **(a)** *~ so ein Politiker* (ugs.) some politician [or other]; *~ so etwas* something like that **(b)** (irgendwie) *wenn ~ möglich* if at all possible

irgend-: *~ein Indefinitpron.* **(a)** *attr.* some; (fragend, verneinend) any; **(b)** *subst.* *~einer/~eine* someone; somebody; (fragend, verneinend) anyone; anybody; *~eines od.* (ugs.) *~eins* any one; *~einmal Adv.* sometime; (fragend, verneinend) anytime; *~etwas* something; (fragend, verneinend) anything; *~jemand Indefinitpron.* someone; somebody; (fragend, verneinend) anyone; anybody; *~wann Adv.* [at] some time [or other]; (zu jeder beliebigen Zeit) [at] any time; *~was Indefinitpron.* (ugs.) something [or other]; (fragend, verneinend) anything; *~welch Indefinitpron.* some; (fragend, verneinend) any; *~wer Indefinitpron.* (ugs.) somebody or other (coll.); (fragend, verneinend) anyone; anybody; *~wie Adv.* somehow; *~wo Adv.* somewhere; (fragend, verneinend) anywhere; *~woher Adv.* from somewhere; (fragend, verneinend) from anywhere; *~wohin Adv.* somewhere; (fragend, verneinend) anywhere

Irin *die; ~, ~nen* Irishwoman

Iris *die; ~, ~* (Bot., Anat.) iris

irisch *Adj.* Irish

Irland *(das); ~s* Ireland

Ironie *die; ~, ~n* irony

ironisch ⟨1⟩ *Adj.* ironic; ironical ⟨2⟩ *adv.* ironically

ir·rational ⟨1⟩ *Adj.* irrational ⟨2⟩ *adv.* irrationally

irre ⟨1⟩ *Adj.* **(a)** insane **(b)** (salopp: faszinierend) amazing (coll.) ⟨2⟩ *adv.* (salopp) terribly (coll.)

Irre *der/die; adj. Dekl.* madman/madwoman; lunatic; (fig.) lunatic

irre-, Irre-: *~|führen tr. V.* mislead; (täuschen) deceive; *~führung die: eine bewusste ~führung* a deliberate attempt to mislead; *~führung der Öffentlichkeit* misleading the public

ir·relevant *Adj.* irrelevant (für to)

irre|machen *tr. V.* disconcert; put off

irren ⟨1⟩ *refl. V.* be mistaken; *Sie haben sich in der Nummer geirrt* you've got the wrong number ⟨2⟩ *itr. V.* **(a)** *da ~ Sie* you are wrong there **(b)** *mit sein* (ziellos umherstreifen) wander

Irren-: *~anstalt die* (veralt. abwertend) mental home; *~haus das* (abwertend) [lunatic] asylum

ir·reparabel *Adj.* irreparable

Irr·fahrt *die* wandering

irriger·weise *Adv.* mistakenly

Irritation *die; ~, ~en* irritation

irritieren *tr., itr. V.* **(a)** (verwirren) put off **(b)** (stören) disturb

irr-, Irr-: *~licht das* will o' the wisp; *~sinn der* **(a)** insanity; madness; **(b)** (ugs. abwertend) lunacy; *~sinnig* ⟨1⟩ *Adj.* **(a)** (geistig gestört) insane; mad; (absurd) idiotic; **(b)** (ugs.: extrem) terrible (coll.); terrific (coll.) ⟨speed, heat⟩; ⟨2⟩ *adv.* (ugs.) terribly (coll.)

Irrtum *der; ~s, Irrtümer* mistake; *~!* wrong!; *im ~ sein* be wrong *or* mistaken

irrtümlich ⟨1⟩ *Adj.* incorrect ⟨2⟩ *adv.* by mistake

Irr·weg *der* error; *diese Methode hat sich als ~ erwiesen* this method has proved to be wrong

Ischias *der od. das od.* (Med.) *die; ~*: sciatica

Islam /ɪsˈlaːm *od.* ˈɪslam/ *der; ~*[s] Islam

islamisch *Adj.* Islamic

Islamismus *der; ~*: Islamic fundamentalism; Islamism

Islamist *der; ~en, ~en,* **Islamistin** *die; ~, ~nen* Islamic fundamentalist; Islamist

islamistisch *Adj.* Islamic fundamentalist; Islamist

Island *(das); ~s* Iceland

Isländer *der; ~s, ~,* **Isländerin** *die; ~, ~nen* Icelander

isländisch *Adj.* Icelandic

Isolation *die; ~, ~en* ▶ ISOLIERUNG

Isolator *der; ~s, ~en* insulator

Isolier·band *das* insulating tape

isolieren *tr. V.* **(a)** isolate **(b)** (Technik) insulate ⟨wiring, wall, etc.⟩; lag ⟨boilers, pipes, etc.⟩

Isolier·station *die* (Med.) isolation ward

Isolierung *die; ~, ~en* **(a)** isolation **(b)** (Technik) ▶ ISOLIEREN B: insulation; lagging

Isotop *das; ~s, ~e* isotope

Israel /ˈɪsraeːl/ *(das); ~s* Israel

Israeli *der; ~*[s], *~*[s]/*die; ~, ~*[s] Israeli

israelisch *Adj.* Israeli

Israelit *der; ~en, ~en,* **Israelitin** *die; ~, ~nen* Israelite

israelitisch *Adj.* Israelite

iss, *iß *Imperativ Sg. v.* ESSEN

isst, *ißt *2. u. 3. Pers. Sg. Präsens v.* ESSEN

ist 3. Pers. Sg. Präsens v. SEIN
Italien /i'ta:li̯ən/ (das); ∼s Italy
Italiener der; ∼s, ∼, **Italienerin** die; ∼,
∼nen Italian

italienisch Adj. Italian
I-Tüpfel[chen] das; ∼s, ∼: final touch;
bis aufs [letzte] ∼: down to the last detail
i.V. Abk. = **in Vertretung**

Jj

j, J /jɔt, österr.: je:/ das; ∼, ∼: j/J
ja ⓵ Interj. yes; (nachgestellt: nicht wahr?) won't
you/doesn't it etc.?
⓶ Partikel **Sie wissen ja, dass ...**: you know,
of course, that ...; **da seid ihr ja!** there you
are!
Ja das; ∼[s], ∼[s] yes; **mit ∼ stimmen** vote
yes
Jacht die; ∼, ∼en yacht
Jacke die; ∼, ∼n jacket; (gestrickt) cardigan
Jacken-kleid das dress and jacket
combination
Jacket-krone /'dʒɛkɪt-/ die (Zahnmed.)
jacket crown
Jackett /ʒa'kɛt/ das; ∼s, ∼s jacket
Jade die; ∼: jade
Jagd die; ∼, ∼en (a) die ∼: shooting;
hunting; **auf die ∼ gehen** go hunting/
shooting
(b) (Veranstaltung) shoot; (Hetzjagd) hunt
(c) (Verfolgung) hunt; (Verfolgungsjagd) chase; **auf
jmdn./etw. ∼ machen** hunt for sb./sth.
Jagd-: ∼**beute** die bag; kill; ∼**bomber**
der (Luftwaffe) fighter-bomber; ∼**flieger** der,
∼**fliegerin** die (Luftwaffe) fighter pilot;
∼**flugzeug** das (Luftwaffe) fighter aircraft;
∼**gewehr** das sporting gun; ∼**horn** das
hunting horn; ∼**hund** der gun dog;
∼**hütte** die shooting box; ∼**revier** das
preserve; shoot; ∼**schein** der game
licence; ∼**wurst** die chasseur sausage;
∼**zeit** die open season
jagen ⓵ tr. V. (a) hunt ⟨game, fugitive,
criminal, etc.⟩; shoot ⟨game, game birds⟩;
(hetzen) chase ⟨fugitive, criminal, etc.⟩
(b) (treiben) drive; **jmdn. aus dem Haus ∼**:
throw sb. out of the house
⓶ itr. V. (die Jagd ausüben) go shooting or
hunting
Jäger der; ∼s, ∼: (a) hunter
(b) (Milit.) rifleman
(c) (Soldatenspr.: Jagdflugzeug) fighter
Jäger-hut der huntsman's hat
Jägerin die; ∼, ∼nen huntress
Jäger-: ∼**latein** das (scherzh.) [hunter's]
tall story/stories; **das ist das reinste ∼latein**

that's all wild exaggeration; ∼**rock** der
hunting jacket; ∼**schnitzel** das (Kochk.)
escalope chasseur
Jaguar der; ∼s, ∼e jaguar
jäh ⓵ Adj. (geh.) (a) sudden; abrupt ⟨change,
movement, stop⟩; sudden, sharp ⟨pain⟩
(b) (steil) steep; precipitous
⓶ adv. (a) ⟨change⟩ abruptly
(b) (steil) ⟨fall, drop⟩ steeply
jählings Adv. (geh.) (a) (plötzlich) ⟨change,
end, stop⟩ suddenly, abruptly; ⟨die⟩ suddenly
(b) (steil) steeply
Jahr das; ∼[e]s, ∼e year; **ein halbes ∼**: six
months; **im ∼[e] 1908** in [the year] 1908; **er
ist zwanzig ∼e [alt]** he is twenty years old;
Kinder bis zu zwölf ∼en children up to the
age of twelve; **zwischen den ∼en** between
Christmas and the New Year
jahr-aus Adv. ∼, **jahrein** year in, year out
jahre-lang ⓵ Adj. [many] years of; long-
standing ⟨feud, friendship⟩
⓶ adv. for [many] years
jähren refl. V. **heute jährt sich zum zehnten
Mal, dass ...**: it is ten years ago today that ...
Jahres-: ∼**bilanz** die (Wirtsch.,
Kaufmannsspr.) annual balance [of accounts];
(Dokument) annual balance sheet;
∼**einkommen** das annual income;
∼**ende** das end of the year; ∼**frist: in** od.
innerhalb od. **binnen ∼frist** within [a period
of] a or one year; ∼**hälfte** die: **die erste/
zweite ∼hälfte** the first/second half or six
months of the year; ∼**karte** die yearly
season ticket; ∼**tag** der anniversary;
∼**umsatz** der annual turnover; ∼**urlaub**
der annual holiday or (formal) leave or (Amer.)
vacation; ∼**wechsel** der turn of the year;
zum ∼wechsel die besten Wünsche best
wishes for the New Year; ∼**zahl** die date;
∼**zeit** die season
Jahr-gang der (a) (Altersklasse) year; **der ∼
1900** those born in 1900
(b) (eines Weines) vintage
(c) (einer Zeitschrift) set [of issues] for a/the
year
Jahr-hundert das century
Jahrhundert-wende die turn of the
century
-jährig (a) (... Jahre alt) **ein elfjähriges Kind**
an eleven-year-old child

(b) (... Jahre dauernd) ... year's/years'; **nach vierjähriger Vorbereitung** after four years' preparation; **mit dreijähriger Verspätung** three years late

jährlich ☐1 *Adj.;* annual; yearly
☐2 *adv.* annually; yearly; **zweimal** ~: twice a year

Jahr-: ~**markt** *der* fair; funfair; ~**tausend** *das* thousand years; millennium; ~**tausend·wende** *die* turn of the millennium; ~**zehnt** *das* decade

jahrzehnte·lang ☐1 *Adj.; nicht präd.* decades of ⟨practice, experience, etc.⟩
☐2 *adv.* for decades

Jäh·zorn *der* violent anger

jäh·zornig ☐1 *Adj.* violent-tempered
☐2 *adv.* in a blind rage

ja·ja *Part.* (ugs.) **(a)** (seufzend) ~[, **so ist das Leben]** oh well[, that's life]
(b) (ungeduldig) ~[, **ich komme schon]**! all right, all right[, I'm coming]!

Jalousie /ʒalu'ziː/ *die;* ~, ~n Venetian blind

Jamaika (*das*)*; -s* Jamaica

Jamaikaner *der;* ~s, ~, **Jamaikanerin** *die;* ~, ~**nen** Jamaican

Jammer *der;* ~s [mournful] wailing; (Elend) misery

jämmerlich ☐1 *Adj.* **(a)** pitiful
(b) wretched ⟨appearance, existence, etc.⟩; paltry, meagre ⟨quantity⟩
☐2 *adv.* pitifully

jammern *itr. V.* wail; (sich beklagen) moan

jammer·schade *Adj.* (ugs.) **es ist** ~, **dass** ...: it's a crying shame that ...; **es ist** ~ **um ihn** it's a great pity about him

Janker *der;* ~s, ~ (südd., österr.) Alpine jacket

Januar *der;* ~[s], ~e January

Japan (*das*)*;* ~s Japan

Japaner *der;* ~s, ~, **Japanerin** *die;* ~, ~**nen** Japanese

japanisch *Adj.* Japanese

japsen *itr. V.* (ugs.) pant

Jargon /jar'gõ:/ *der;* ~s, ~s jargon

Jasmin *der;* ~s, ~e jasmine

Ja·stimme *die* yes-vote

jäten *tr., itr. V.* weed; **Unkraut** ~: weed

Jauche *die;* ~, ~n liquid manure

Jauche·grube *die* liquid-manure reservoir

jauchzen *itr. V.* cheer; **vor Freude** ~: shout for joy

Jauchzer *der;* ~s, ~: cry of delight

jaulen *itr. V.* howl

Jause *die;* ~, ~n (österr.) **(a)** snack; **eine** ~ **machen** have a snack
(b) (Nachmittagskaffee) [afternoon] tea

ja·wohl *Part.* certainly

Ja·wort *das* consent; **jmdm. das** ~ **geben** consent to marry sb.

Jazz /dʒæz *od.* dʒɛs *od.* jats:/ *der;* ~: jazz

jazzen /'dʒɛsn̩/ *od.* 'jatsn̩/ *itr. V.* play jazz

Jazzer /'dʒɛsɐ *od.* 'jats:ɐ/ *der;* ~s, ~, **Jazzerin** *die;* ~, ~**nen** jazz musician

Jazz-: ~**keller** *der* jazz cellar; ~**tanz** *der* jazz dance

je[1] ☐1 *Adv.* **(a)** (jemals) ever; **mehr/besser denn je** more/better than ever
(b) (jeweils) **je zehn Personen** ten people at a time; **sie kosten je 30 Euro** they cost 30 euros each
(c) (entsprechend) **je nach Gewicht** according to weight
☐2 *Präp. mit Akk.* per; for each
☐3 *Konj.* **je länger, je lieber** the longer the better; **je nachdem** it all depends

je[2] *Interj.* **ach je, wie schade!** oh dear, what a shame!

Jeans /dʒiːnz/ *Pl. od. die;* ~, ~: jeans *pl.;* denims *pl.*

jede ▸ JEDER

jeden·falls *Adv.* **(a)** in any case
(b) (zumindest) at any rate

jeder, jede, jedes *Indefinitpron. u. unbest. Zahlwort* ☐1 *attr.* **(a)** (alle) every
(b) (alle einzeln) each
(c) (jeglicher) all
☐2 *allein stehend* **(a)** (alle) everyone; everybody
(b) (alle einzeln) **jedes der Kinder** each of the children

jeder-: ~**mann** *Indefinitpron.* everyone; everybody; ~**zeit** *Adv.* [at] any time

jedes ▸ JEDER

*****jedes·mal** ▸ MAL[1]

je·doch *Konj., Adv.* however

je·her /*od.* '·'·/ *Adv.* **seit** *od.* **von** ~: always; since time immemorial

jemals *Adv.* ever

jemand *Indefinitpron.* someone; somebody; (fragend, verneinend) anyone; anybody

Jemen (*das*)*;* ~s *od.* **der;** ~[s] Yemen

jener, jene, jenes *Demonstrativpron.* (geh.) ☐1 *attr.* that; (im Pl.) those
☐2 *allein stehend* that one; (im Pl.) those

jenseits ☐1 *Präp. mit Gen.* on the other side of; (in größerer Entfernung) beyond
☐2 *Adv.* on the other side; ~ **von** on the other side of

Jenseits *das;* ~: hereafter; beyond

Jersey[1] /'dʒøːɐ̯zi/ *der;* ~[s], ~s (Textilind.) jersey

Jersey[2] *das;* ~s, ~s (Sport: Trikot) jersey

Jesus (*der*)*;* Jesu Jesus

Jet /dʒɛt/ *der;* ~[s], ~s jet; **mit einem** ~ **fliegen/reisen** fly/travel by jet

jetzig *Adj.* current

jetzt *Adv.* **(a)** just now; **bis** ~: up to now; **bis** ~ **noch nicht** not yet; **von** ~ **an** *od.* **ab** from now on[wards]; **erst** ~ *od.* ~ **erst** only just; **schon** ~: already
(b) (heutzutage) now; nowadays

jeweilig *Adj.* (a) (in einem bestimmten Fall) particular
(b) (zu einer bestimmten Zeit) current; of the time *postpos., not pred.*;
(c) (zugehörig, zugewiesen) respective

jeweils *Adv.* (a) (jedesmal) ~ **am ersten/ letzten Mittwoch des Monats** on the first/last Wednesday of each month
(b) (zur Zeit) at the time

Jg. *Abk.* = **Jahrgang**

Jh. *Abk.* = **Jahrhundert** c.

JH *Abk.* = **Jugendherberge**

jiddisch /ˈjɪdɪʃ/ *Adj.* Yiddish

Job /dʒɔp/ *der;* ~s, ~s (ugs.; auch DV) job

jobben /dʒɔbn̩/ *itr. V.* (ugs.) do a job/jobs

Job-: ~**killer** *der* destroyer of jobs; ~**sharing** /ˈ-ʃɛərɪŋ/ *das;* ~~s jobsharing

Joch *das;* ~[e]s, ~e yoke

Jockei, Jockey /ˈdʒɔke od. ˈdʒɔki/ *der;* ~s, ~s jockey

Jod *das;* ~[e]s iodine

jodeln *itr., tr. V.* yodel

jod·haltig *Adj.* iodiferous

Joga *der od. das;* ~[s] yoga

joggen /ˈdʒɔgn̩/ *itr. V.; mit Richtungsangabe mit sein* jog

Jogging·anzug *der* jogging suit

Joghurt /ˈjoːgʊrt/ *der od. das;* ~[s], ~[s] yoghurt

Joghurt·becher *der* yoghurt pot (Brit.) *or* (Amer.) container

Johannis·beere *die* currant; **rote/weiße/ schwarze** ~**n** redcurrants/white currants/ blackcurrants

johlen *itr. V.* yell; (vor Wut) howl

Joint /dʒɔɪnt/ *der;* ~s, ~s (ugs.) joint (sl.)

Jolle *die;* ~, ~n keel-centreboard yawl

Jongleur /ʒɔŋˈløːɐ̯/ *der;* ~s, ~e, **Jongleurin** *die;* ~, ~nen juggler

jonglieren *tr., itr. V.* juggle

Joppe *die;* ~, ~n heavy jacket

Jordanien (*das*); ~s Jordan

Jordanier *der;* ~s, ~, **Jordanierin** *die;* ~, ~nen Jordanian

jordanisch *Adj.* Jordanian

Jot *das;* ~, ~: j, J

Journalismus /ʒʊr.../ *der;* ~: journalism *no art.*

Journalist *der;* ~en, ~en, **Journalistin** *die;* ~, ~nen journalist

journalistisch ① *Adj.* journalistic; **eine** ~**e Ausbildung** a training in journalism ② *adv.* journalistically; ~ **tätig sein** be a journalist

Joystick/ˈdʒɔystɪk/ *der;* ~s, ~s (DV) joystick

jr. *Abk.* = **junior** Jr.

Jubel *der;* ~s rejoicing; jubilation; (laut) cheering

Jubel·jahr *das* jubilee; **alle** ~**e [einmal]** once in a blue moon

jubeln *itr. V.* cheer; **über etw.** (*Akk.*) ~: rejoice over sth.

Jubilar *der;* ~s, ~e man celebrating his anniversary/birthday

Jubilarin *die;* ~, ~nen woman celebrating her anniversary/birthday

Jubiläum *das;* ~s, Jubiläen anniversary; (eines Monarchen) jubilee

jubilieren *itr. V.* (geh.) jubilate (literary); rejoice

juchzen *itr. V.* (ugs.) shout with glee

jucken ① *tr., itr. V.* (a) **mir juckt die Haut** I itch; **es juckt mich hier** I've got an itch here
(b) (Juckreiz verursachen) irritate
② *tr. V.* (reizen, verlocken) **es juckt mich, das zu tun** I am itching to do it
③ *refl. V.* (ugs.: sich kratzen) scratch

Juck·reiz *der* itch

Jude *der;* ~n, ~n Jew

Juden: ~**hass**, ***~**haß** *der* anti-Semitism; hatred of [the] Jews; ~**stern** *der* (ns.) Star of David

Judentum *das;* ~s (a) (Volk) Jewry; Jews *pl.*;
(b) (Kultur u. Religion) Judaism

Juden·verfolgung *die* persecution of [the] Jews

Jüdin *die;* ~, ~nen Jewess

jüdisch *Adj.* Jewish

Judo *das;* ~[s] judo *no art.*

Jugend *die;* ~ (a) youth
(b) (Jugendliche) young people

jugend-, Jugend-: ~**amt** *das* youth office (*agency responsible for education and welfare of young people*); ~**arbeitslosigkeit** *die* youth unemployment; ~**arrest** *der* detention in a community home; ~**bewegung** *die* (hist.) [German] youth Movement; ~**buch** *das* book for young people; ~**frei** *Adj.* ⟨film, book, etc.⟩ suitable for persons under 18; **nicht** ~**frei** ⟨film⟩ not U-certificate *pred.*; ~**gefährdend** *Adj.* liable to have an undesirable influence on the moral development of young people *postpos.*; ~**heim** *das* youth centre; ~**herberge** *die* youth hostel; ~**klub** *der* youth club; ~**kriminalität** *die* juvenile delinquency

jugendlich *Adj.* (a) young ⟨offender, customer, etc.⟩
(b) (für Jugendliche charakteristisch) youthful

Jugendliche *der/die; adj. Dekl.* young person; **die** ~**n** the young people

Jugend-: ~**liebe** *die* sweetheart of one's youth; ~**schutz** *der* protection of young people; ~**schutz·gesetz** *das* laws *pl.* protecting young people; ~**sprache** *die* young people's language *no art.*; ~**stil** *der* art nouveau; (in Deutschland) Jugendstil; ~**strafanstalt** *die* detention centre;

**old spelling - see note on page xiv

~**strafe** *die* youth custody sentence; ~**sünde** *die* youthful folly; ~**zeit** *die* youth; ~**zentrum** *das* youth centre

Jugo·slawe *der* Yugoslav

Jugo·slawien *(das);* ~s Yugoslavia

Jugo·slawin *die* Yugoslav

jugo·slawisch *Adj.* Yugoslav[ian]

Julei *der;* ~[s], ~s ▸ JULI

Juli *der;* ~[s], ~s July; *s. auch* APRIL

jung *Adj.;* jünger, jüngst... (a) young; new ⟨project, undertaking, sport, marriage, etc.⟩ (b) (letzt...) recent; **in jüngster Zeit** recently

Junge¹ *der;* ~n, ~n *od.* (ugs.) Jung[en]s boy

Junge² *das; adj. Dekl.* **ein** ~s one of the young; ~ **kriegen** give birth to young

jungen *itr. V.* give birth; ⟨cat⟩ have kittens; ⟨dog⟩ have pups

jungenhaft *Adj.* boyish

jünger *Adj.* youngish; **sie ist noch** ~: she is still quite young; *s. auch* JUNG

Jünger *der;* ~s, ~, **Jüngerin** *die;* ~, ~nen follower

Jungfer *die;* ~, ~n (abwertend: ältere ledige Frau) spinster

Jungfern·fahrt *die* maiden voyage

Jungfern·häutchen *das;* ~s, ~: hymen

Jung·frau *die* (a) virgin (b) (Astrol.) Virgo

jung·fräulich *Adj.* (geh., auch fig.) virgin

Jung·geselle *der* bachelor

Jung·gesellin *die* bachelor girl

Jüngling *der;* ~s, ~e (geh., spött.) youth; boy

jüngst *Adv.* (geh.) recently

jüngst... ▸ JUNG

Jüngste *der/die; adj. Dekl.* youngest [one]

Jung-: ~**verheiratete** *der/die; adj.*
Dekl., young married man/woman; **die** ~**verheirateten** the newly-weds; ~**wähler** *der,* ~**wählerin** *die* first-time voter

Juni *der;* ~[s], ~s June; *s. auch* APRIL

junior *indekl. Adj.; nach Personennamen* junior

Junior *der;* ~s, ~en (a) (oft scherzh.) junior (joc.) (b) (Kaufmannsspr.) junior partner

Junior-: ~**chef** *der* owner's *or* (coll.) boss's son; ~**chefin** *die* owner's *or* (coll.) boss's daughter

Juno *der;* ~[s], ~s ▸ JUNI

Junta /'xʊnta/ *die;* ~, Junten junta

Jura law *sing.;* ~ **studieren** read Law

Jurist *der;* ~en, ~en, **Juristin** *die;* ~, ~nen lawyer; jurist

juristisch *Adj.* legal

Jury /ʒy'ri:/ *die;* ~, ~s (a) (Preisrichter) panel [of judges]; jury (b) (Sachverständige) panel [of experts]

just *Adv.* (veralt., noch scherzh.) just; ~ **in diesem Augenblick** just at that moment; at that very moment

justieren *tr. V.* adjust

Justierung *die;* ~, ~en adjustment

Justiz *die;* ~: justice; (Behörden) judiciary

Justiz-: ~**irrtum** *der* miscarriage of justice; ~**minister** *der,* ~**ministerin** *die* Minister of Justice; ~**ministerium** *das* Ministry of Justice; ~**mord** *der* judicial murder; ~**vollzugs·anstalt** *die* (Amtsspr.) penal institution (formal); prison

Jute *die;* ~: jute

Jütland *(das);* ~s Jutland

Juwel *das od. der;* ~s, ~en piece of jewellery; (Edelstein) jewel

Juwelier /juva'liːɐ̯/ *der;* ~s jeweller

Juwelier·geschäft *das* jeweller's shop

Jux *der;* ~es, ~e (ugs.) joke

Kk

k, K /ka:/ *das;* ~, ~: k/K
Kabarẹtt *das;* ~s, ~s *od.* ~e (a) satirical
revue
(b) (Ensemble) cabaret act
Kabarettịst *der;* ~en, ~en,
Kabarettịstin *die;* ~, ~nen revue
performer
kabarettịstisch *Adj.* [satirical] revue
attrib.; ~e Szenen scenes in the style of a
[satirical] revue
kạbbeln *refl. V.* (ugs.) bicker (**mit** with)
Kabel *das;* ~s, ~: cable; (für kleineres Gerät)
flex
Kabel·fernsehen *das* cable television
Kabeljau *der;* ~s, ~e *od.* ~s cod
kabellos ① *Adj.* wireless
② *adv.* ‹*communicate*› in wireless format;
‹*install*› without wires
Kabịne *die;* ~, ~n (a) cabin
(b) (Umkleideraum, abgeteilter Raum) cubicle
(c) (einer Seilbahn) [cable] car
Kabinẹtt *das;* ~s, ~e Cabinet
Kabrio *das;* ~s, ~s, **Kabriolẹtt** *das;* ~s,
~s convertible
Kạchel *die;* ~, ~n [glazed] tile
kạcheln *tr. V.* tile
Kạchel·ofen *der* tiled stove
Kạcke *die;* ~ (derb; auch fig.) shit (coarse);
crap (coarse)
kạcken *itr. V.* (derb) shit (coarse); crap
(coarse)
Kadạver *der;* ~s, ~: carcass
Kader *der od.* (schweiz.) *das;* ~s, ~ (a) cadre
(b) (Sport) squad
Käfer *der;* ~s, ~: beetle
Kạff *das;* ~s, ~s *od.* Käffer (ugs. abwertend)
dump (coll.)
Kaffee /'kafe *od.* (österr.) ka'fe:/ *der;* ~s, ~s
(a) coffee
(b) (Nachmittags~) afternoon coffee; ~ **trinken**
have afternoon coffee
Kaffee-: ~**kanne** *die* coffee pot;
~**kränzchen** *das* (veralt.) (a)
(Zusammentreffen) coffee afternoon; (b) (Gruppe)
coffee circle; ~**maschine** *die* coffee
maker; ~**mühle** *die* coffee grinder; ~**satz**
der coffee grounds *pl.;* ~**tante** *die* (ugs.
scherzh.) coffee addict
Käfig *der;* ~s, ~e cage
kahl *Adj.* (a) (ohne Haare) bald; **jmdn.** ~
scheren shave sb.'s head
(b) (ohne Grün, schmucklos) bare; **etw.** ~
fressen strip sth. bare

kahl-, Kahl-: **~|**fressen** ▶ KAHL B;
~**köpfig** *Adj.* bald[-headed]; **~|**scheren**
▶ KAHL A; ~**schlag** *der* (a) clear-felling *no
indef. art.;* (b) (Waldfläche) clear-felled area
Kahn *der;* ~[e]s, Kähne (a) (Ruder~) rowing
boat; (Stech~) punt
(b) (Lastschiff) barge
Kai *der;* ~s, ~s quay
Kaiser *der;* ~s, ~: emperor
Kaiserin *die;* ~, ~nen empress
Kaiser-: ~**krone** *die* imperial crown;
~**reich** *das* empire; ~**schnitt** *der*
Caesarean section; ~**wetter** *das* (scherzh.)
glorious, sunny weather (*for an event*)
Kajüte *die;* ~, ~n (Seemannsspr.) cabin
Kakao /ka'kau:/ *der;* ~s, ~s cocoa; jmdn./
etw. durch den ~ ziehen (ugs.) make fun of
sb./sth.
Kakerlak *der;* ~s *od.* ~en, ~en cockroach
Kạktus *der;* ~, Kaktẹen cactus
Kalauer *der;* ~s, ~: corny joke (coll.);
(Wortspiel) atrocious *or* (coll.) corny pun
Kạlb *das;* ~[e]s, Kälber (a) calf
(b) (ugs.: ~fleisch) veal
kạlben *itr. V.* calve
Kạlb·fleisch *das* veal
Kạlbs-: ~**braten** *der* (Kochk.) roast veal *no
indef. art.;* (Gericht) roast of veal; ~**leder**
das calfskin; ~**schnitzel** *das* veal cutlet
Kalẹnder *der;* ~s, ~: calendar; (Taschen~)
diary
Kalẹnder-: ~**jahr** *das* calendar year;
~**monat** *der* calendar month
Kali *das;* ~s, ~s potash
Kaliber *das;* ~s, ~: (a) (Technik, Waffenkunde)
calibre
(b) (ugs., oft abwertend) sort; kind
Kalifornien /kali'fɔrnjən/ (*das*); ~s
California
Kalium (Chemie) *das;* ~s potassium
Kạlk *der;* ~[e]s, ~e calcium carbonate;
(Baustoff) lime; quicklime
kạlken *tr. V.* whitewash
Kạlk-: ~**mangel** *der* calcium deficiency;
~**stein** *der* limestone
Kalkül *das od.* der; ~s, ~e (geh.)
calculation
Kalkulation *die;* ~, ~en (auch Wirtsch.)
calculation
kalkulieren *tr. V.* calculate ‹*cost, price*›;
cost ‹*product, article*›
Kalorie *die;* ~, ~n calorie
kalorien-, Kalorien-: ~**arm** ① *Adj.*

low-calorie *attrib.;* ~arm sein be low in calories; ⟨2⟩ *adv.* ~arm kochen cook low-calorie meals; ~gehalt *der* calorie content

kalt; kälter, kältest... ⟨1⟩ *Adj.* cold; frosty ⟨atmosphere, smile⟩; ~ lassen (fig.) remain unmoved; jmdn. ~ lassen (ugs.) leave sb. unmoved; (nicht interessieren) leave sb. cold (coll.)

⟨2⟩ *adv.* (a) ~ duschen have a cold shower Getränke/Sekt ~ stellen cool drinks/chill champagne

(b) (nüchtern) coldly

(c) (abweisend, unfreundlich) frostily

kalt-, Kalt-: *~|bleiben ▶ KALT 1; ~blütig ⟨1⟩ *Adj.* (a) cool-headed; (b) (abwertend: skrupellos) cold-blooded; ⟨2⟩ *adv.* (a) coolly; (b) (abwertend: skrupellos) cold-bloodedly; ~blütigkeit *die;* ~~: ▶ ~BLÜTIG A, B: cool-headedness; cold-bloodedness

Kälte *die;* ~ cold; (fig.) coldness

Kälte-: ~einbruch *der* (Met.) sudden onset of cold weather; ~grad *der* degree of frost

kälter ▶ KALT

kältest... ▶ KALT

Kälte-welle *die* cold spell

kalt-, Kalt-: ~gepresst, *~gepreßt *Adj.* cold-pressed; ~herzig *Adj.* cold-hearted; *~lächelnd *Adv.* (ugs. abwertend) etw. ~lächelnd tun take callous pleasure in doing sth.; *~|lassen ▶ KALT 1; ~|machen *tr. V.* (salopp) jmdn. ~machen do sb. in (sl.); ~miete *die* rent exclusive of heating; ~schale *die: cold sweet soup made with fruit, beer, wine, or milk;* ~schnäuzig (ugs.) ⟨1⟩ *Adj.* cold and insensitive; (frech) insolent; ⟨2⟩ *adv.* coldly and insensitively; (frech) insolently; ~stellen *tr. V.* (ugs.) jmdn. ~stellen put sb. out of the way (coll. joc.)

kam *1. u. 3. Pers. Prät. v.* KOMMEN

Kambodscha (*das*); ~s Cambodia

käme *1. u. 3. Pers. Konjunktiv II v.* KOMMEN

Kamel *das;* ~s, ~e camel

Kamera *die;* ~, ~s camera

Kamerad *der;* ~en, ~en, **Kameradin** *die;* ~, ~nen companion; (Freund[in]) friend; (Mitschüler[in]) mate; (Soldat[in]) comrade; (Sport) teammate

Kameradschaft *die;* ~: comradeship

kameradschaftlich ⟨1⟩ *Adj.* comradely ⟨2⟩ *adv.* in a comradely way

Kamera-: ~frau *die* camerawoman; ~mann *der Pl.;* ~männer *od.* ~leute cameraman; ~team *das* camera crew

Kamerun /'kaməru:n/ (*das*); ~s Cameroon; the Cameroons *pl.*

Kamille *die;* ~, ~n camomile

Kamin *der, schweiz.: das;* ~s, ~e fireplace

Kamin-feger, Kamin-fegerin *die* (bes. südd.) ▶ SCHORNSTEINFEGER

Kamm *der;* ~[e]s, Kämme (a) comb

(b) (bei Hühnern usw.) comb

(c) (Gebirgs~) ridge

kämmen *tr. V.* comb

Kammer *die;* ~, ~n (a) storeroom

(b) (Biol., Med., Technik, Waffenkunde) chamber

(c) (Parl.) chamber

Kammer-: ~diener *der* (veralt.) valet; ~jäger *der,* ~jägerin *die* pest controller; ~musik *die* chamber music; ~sänger *der,* ~sängerin *die: title awarded to singer of outstanding merit;* ~zofe *die* (veralt.) lady's maid

Kamm-garn *das* worsted

Kampagne /kam'panjə/ *die;* ~, ~n campaign

Kampf *der;* ~[e]s, Kämpfe (a) (militärisch) battle (um for)

(b) (zwischen persönlichen Gegnern) fight; (fig.) struggle

(c) (Wett~) contest; (Boxen) contest; bout

(d) (Einsatz aller Mittel) fight (um, für for; gegen against)

kampf-, Kampf-: ~abstimmung *die* (Politik) crucial vote; ~bereit *Adj.* ready to fight *postpos.;* ⟨army, troops⟩ ready for battle

kämpfen *itr. V.* (a) fight

(b) (Sport: sich messen) ⟨team⟩ play; ⟨wrestler, boxer⟩ fight

Kämpfer *der;* ~s camphor

Kämpfer *der;* ~s, ~, **Kämpferin** *die;* ~, ~nen fighter

kampf-, Kampf-: ~fähig *Adj.* ⟨troops⟩ fit for action; ⟨boxer etc.⟩ fit to fight; ~handlungen *Pl.* fighting *sing.;* ~preis *der* (Wirtsch.) cut price; ~richter *der,* ~richterin *die* (Sport) judge; ~unfähig *Adj.* ⟨troops⟩ unfit for action; ⟨boxer etc.⟩ unfit to fight

kampieren *itr. V.* camp

Kanada (*das*); ~s Canada

Kanadier /ka'na:diɐ/ *der;* ~s, ~, **Kanadierin** *die;* ~, ~nen Canadian

kanadisch *Adj.* Canadian

Kanal *der;* ~s, Kanäle (a) canal

(b) (Geogr.) der ~: the [English] Channel

(c) (für Abwässer) sewer

(d) (zur Entwässerung, Bewässerung) channel; (Graben) ditch

(e) (Rundf., Ferns., Weg der Information) channel

Kanalisation *die;* ~, ~en sewerage system; sewers *pl.*

kanalisieren *tr. V.* (a) (lenken) channel ⟨energies, goods, etc.⟩

(b) (schiffbar machen) canalize

Kanal-tunnel *der* Channel Tunnel

Kanaren *Pl.* Canaries

Kanarien-vogel /ka'na:riən-/ *der* canary

Kanarische Inseln *Pl.* Canary Islands

Kandare *die;* ~, ~n curb bit; jmdn. an die ~ nehmen (fig.) take sb. in hand

Kandidat *der;* ~en, ~en, **Kandidatin** *die;* ~, ~nen (a) candidate

(b) (beim Quiz usw.) contestant

Kandidatur *die;* ~, ~en candidature (auf + *Akk.* for)

kandidieren *itr. V.* stand [as a candidate] (für for)

kandieren *tr. V.* candy; **kandiert** crystallized ⟨*orange, petal*⟩; glacé ⟨*cherry, pear*⟩; candied ⟨*peel*⟩

Kandis *der;* ~, **Kandis·zucker** *der* rock candy

Känguru, *Känguruh *das;* ~s, ~s kangaroo

Kaninchen *das;* ~s, ~: rabbit

Kanister *der;* ~s, ~: can; [metal/plastic] container

kann *1. u. 3. Pers. Sg. Präsens v.* KÖNNEN

Kännchen *das;* ~s, ~: [small] pot; (für Milch) [small] jug

Kanne *die;* ~, ~n (a) pot; (für Milch, Wein, Wasser) jug
(b) (Henkel~) can; (für Milch) pail; (beim Melken) churn

kannst *2. Pers. Sg. Präsens v.* KÖNNEN

kannte *1. u. 3. Pers. Sg. Prät. v.* KENNEN

Kanon *der;* ~s, ~s canon

Kanone *die;* ~, ~n cannon; (fig. ugs.: Könner) ace

Kantate *die;* ~, ~n (Musik) cantata

Kante *die;* ~, ~n edge

kantig *Adj.* square-cut ⟨*timber, stone*⟩; rough-edged ⟨*rock*⟩; angular ⟨*face*⟩; square ⟨*chin*⟩

Kantine *die;* ~, ~n canteen

Kanton *der;* ~s, ~e canton

kantonal [1] *Adj.* cantonal
[2] *adv.* on a cantonal basis

Kantor *der;* ~s, ~en choirmaster and organist

Kantorin *die;* ~, ~nen choirmistress and organist

Kanu *das;* ~s, ~s canoe

Kanüle *die;* ~, ~n (Med.) cannula

Kanzel *die;* ~, ~n (a) pulpit
(b) (Flugw.) cockpit

Kanzlei *die;* ~, ~en (a) (veralt.: Büro) office
(b) (Anwalts~) chambers *pl.* (*of barrister*); office (*of lawyer*)

Kanzler *der;* ~s, ~ chancellor

Kap *das;* ~s, ~s cape

Kapazität *die;* ~, ~en (a) capacity
(b) (Experte) expert

Kapelle *die;* ~, ~n (a) (Archit.) chapel
(b) (Musik~) band; [light] orchestra

Kapell·meister *der,*
Kapell·meisterin *die* bandmaster/-mistress; (im Orchester) conductor; (im Theater usw.) musical director

Kaper *die;* ~, ~n caper *usu. in pl.*

kapern *tr. V.* (a) (hist.) capture

(b) (ugs.) jmdn. [für etw.] ~: rope sb. in[to sth.]

kapieren (ugs.) [1] *tr. V.* (ugs.) get (coll.)
[2] *itr. V.* kapiert? got it? (coll.)

Kapital *das;* ~s, ~e *od.* ~ien (a) capital
(b) (fig.) asset

Kapital·anlage *die* (Wirtsch.) capital investment

Kapitalismus *der;* ~: capitalism *no art.*

Kapitalist *der;* ~en, ~en, **Kapitalistin** *die;* ~, ~nen capitalist

kapitalistisch *Adj.* capitalistic

Kapital·verbrechen *das* serious offence; (mit Todesstrafe bedroht) capital offence

Kapitän *der;* ~s, ~e, **Kapitänin** *die;* ~, ~nen captain

Kapitel *das;* ~s, ~: chapter

Kapitulation *die;* ~, ~en surrender; capitulation; **seine** ~ **erklären** admit defeat

kapitulieren *itr. V.* (a) surrender; capitulate
(b) (fig.: aufgeben) give up; **vor etw.** (*Dat.*) ~: give up in the face of sth.

Kaplan *der;* ~s, Kapläne (kath. Kirche) chaplain; (Hilfsgeistlicher) curate

Kappe *die;* ~, ~n cap

kappen *tr. V.* (a) (Seemannsspr.) cut
(b) (beschneiden) cut back ⟨*hedge etc.*⟩; (abschneiden) cut off ⟨*branches etc.*⟩

Käppi *das;* ~s, ~s garrison cap

Kapsel *die;* ~, ~n capsule

Kapstadt (*das*)*;* ~s Cape Town

kaputt *Adj.* (a) broken; **das Telefon ist** ~: the phone is not working
(b) (ugs.: erschöpft) shattered (coll.)

kaputt-: ~|**gehen** *unr. itr. V.; mit sein* (ugs.) (entzweigehen) break; ⟨*machine*⟩ break down, (coll.) pack up; ⟨*lightbulb*⟩ go; (zerbrechen) be smashed; ~|**lachen** *refl. V.* (ugs.) kill oneself [laughing] (coll.); ~|**machen** (ugs.) [1] *tr. V.* break; spoil ⟨*sth. made with effort*⟩; ruin ⟨*clothes, furniture, etc.*⟩; finish ⟨*person*⟩ off; [2] *refl. V.* wear oneself out

Kapuze *die;* ~, ~n hood; (bei Mönchen) cowl; hood

Kapuziner *der;* ~s, ~: Capuchin [friar]

Karabiner *der;* ~s, ~: carbine

Karaffe *die;* ~, ~n carafe; (mit Glasstöpsel) decanter

Karambolage /karambo'la:ʒə/ *die;* ~, ~n (ugs.) crash; collision

*Karamel *usw.* ▶ KARAMELL *usw.*

Karamell *der* (schweiz.: das); ~s caramel

Karamell·bonbon *der od. das* caramel [toffee]

Karat *das;* ~[e]s, ~e carat

Karate *das;* ~[s] karate

Karawane *die;* ~, ~n caravan

Kardinal *der;* ~s, Kardinäle (kath. Kirche) cardinal

203

Kardinalfehler ⋯⋮ Kasse ⋯

Kardinal-: ∼**fehler** der cardinal error; ∼**tugend** die cardinal virtue; ∼**zahl** die cardinal [number]

Karenz die; ∼, ∼en, **Karenz·zeit** die waiting period

Kar·freitag der Good Friday

karg [1] Adj. meagre ⟨wages etc.⟩; frugal ⟨meal etc.⟩; poor ⟨light, accommodation⟩; (wenig fruchtbar) barren
[2] adv. ∼ bemessen sein ⟨helping⟩ be mingy (Brit. coll.); ⟨supply⟩ be scanty; ∼ leben live frugally

kärglich [1] Adj. meagre, poor ⟨wages etc.⟩; poor ⟨light⟩; frugal ⟨meal⟩; scanty ⟨supply⟩
[2] adv. poorly ⟨lit, paid, rewarded⟩

karibisch Adj. Caribbean

kariert Adj. check, checked ⟨material, pattern⟩; check ⟨jacket etc.⟩; squared ⟨paper⟩

Karies /'ka:ri̯ɛs/ die; ∼: caries

Karikatur die; ∼, ∼en cartoon; (Porträt) caricature

Karikaturist der; ∼en, ∼en, **Karikaturistin** die; ∼, ∼nen cartoonist; (Porträtist) caricaturist

karikieren tr. V. caricature

kariös Adj. (Zahnmed.) carious

karitativ Adj. charitable

Karl /karl/ (der) Charles; ∼ der Große Charlemagne

Karneval /'karnəval/ der; ∼s, ∼e od. ∼s carnival; ∼ feiern join in the carnival festivities

karnevalistisch Adj. carnival attrib.

Karnevals-: ∼**kostüm** das carnival costume; ∼**verein** der carnival society; ∼**zug** der carnival procession

Karnickel das; ∼s, ∼ (landsch.) rabbit

Kärnten (das); ∼s Carinthia

Karo das; ∼s, ∼s (a) square; (auf der Spitze stehend) diamond
(b) (Karomuster) check
(c) (Kartenspiel: Farbe) diamonds pl.;
(d) (Kartenspiel: Karte) diamond

Karosse die; ∼, ∼n [state] coach

Karosserie die; ∼, ∼n bodywork

Karotte die; ∼, ∼n small carrot

Karpaten Pl. Carpathians; Carpathian Mountains

Karpfen der; ∼s, ∼: carp

Karre die; ∼, ∼n (bes. nordd.) (a) ▶ KARREN;
(b) (abwertend: Fahrzeug) [old] heap (coll.)

Karree das; ∼s, ∼s: ums ∼ gehen/fahren walk/drive round the block

karren tr. V. (a) cart
(b) (salopp: mit einem Auto) run (coll.)

Karren der; ∼s, ∼ (bes. südd., österr.) cart; (zweirädrig) barrow

Karriere /ka'ri̯e:rə/ die; ∼, ∼n career; ∼ machen make a [successful] career for oneself

Kärrner·arbeit die donkey work

Kar·samstag der Easter Saturday

Karte die; ∼, ∼n card; (Speise∼) menu; (Fahr∼, Flug∼, Eintritts∼) ticket; (Land∼) map; alles auf eine ∼ setzen stake everything on one chance

Kartei die; ∼, ∼en card file

Kartei-: ∼**karte** die file card; ∼**kasten** der file-card box

Kartell das; ∼s, ∼e (Wirtsch., Politik) cartel

Kartell-: ∼**amt** das: government body concerned with the control and supervision of cartels; ≈ Monopolies and Mergers Commission (Brit.); ∼**gesetz** das law relating to cartels; ≈ monopolies law (Brit.)

Karten-: ∼**haus** das house of cards; ∼**spiel** das (a) (Spiel mit Karten) card game; (b) (Satz Spielkarten) pack or (Amer.) deck [of cards]; ∼**telefon** das cardphone; ∼**vorverkauf** der advance booking

Kartoffel die; ∼, ∼n potato

Kartoffel-: ∼**brei** der mashed potatoes pl.; mash (coll.); ∼**chips** Pl. [potato] crisps (Brit.) or (Amer.) chips; ∼**käfer** der Colorado beetle; ∼**kloß** der potato dumpling; ∼**puffer** der potato pancake (made from grated raw potatoes); ∼**püree** das: ▶ ∼BREI

Karton /kar'tɔŋ/ der; ∼s, ∼s (a) (Pappe) card[board]
(b) (Schachtel) cardboard box

Karussell das; ∼s, ∼s od. ∼e merry-go-round; carousel (Amer.); (kleineres) roundabout

Kar·woche die Holy Week

karzinogen Adj. (Med.) carcinogenic

Karzinom das; ∼s, ∼e (Med.) carcinoma

kaschieren tr. V. conceal; hide; disguise ⟨fault⟩

Kaschmir¹ (das); ∼s Kashmir

Kaschmir² der; ∼s, ∼e (Textilw.) cashmere

Käse der; ∼s, ∼: cheese; (ugs. abwertend: Unsinn) rubbish

Käse-: ∼**blatt** das (salopp abwertend) rag; ∼**glocke** die cheese dome

Kaserne die; ∼, ∼n barracks sing. or pl.

käse·weiß Adj. (ugs.) [as] white as a sheet

käsig Adj. (ugs.) pasty; pale

Kasino das; ∼s, ∼s (a) (Spiel∼) casino
(b) (Offiziers∼) [officers'] mess
(c) (Speiseraum) canteen

Kasko·versicherung die (Voll∼) comprehensive insurance; (Teil∼) insurance against theft, fire, or act of God

Kasper der; ∼s, ∼: ≈ Punch; (fig. ugs.) clown

Kasperl das; ∼s, ∼[n] (österr.), **Kasperle** das od. der; ∼s, ∼: ▶ KASPER

Kasper-: ∼**puppe** die ≈ Punch and Judy puppet; ∼**theater** das ≈ Punch and Judy show; (Puppenbühne) ≈ Punch and Judy theatre

Kasse die; ∼, ∼n (a) cash box; (Registrier∼) till ⋯⋮

(b) (Ort zum Bezahlen) cash desk; (im Supermarkt) checkout; (in einer Bank) counter **(c)** (Kassenraum) cashier's office **(d)** (Theater~, Kino~) box office

Kasseler *das;* ~s smoked loin of pork

Kassen-: ~**arzt** *der,* ~**ärztin** *die: doctor who treats members of health insurance schemes;* ~**bon** *der* sales slip; receipt; ~**lage** *die* financial situation; **die** ~**lage der Firma** the state of the company's finances; **nach** ~**lage** as finances allow/allowed; **eine Rentenpolitik nach** ~**lage** a pensions policy dependent on what finances will allow; ~**patient** *der,* ~**patientin** *die: patient who is a member of a health insurance scheme;* ~**wart** *der;* ~~s, ~~e, ~**wartin** *die;* ~~, ~~nen treasurer; ~**zettel** *der:* ▶ ~BON

Kassette *die;* ~, ~n **(a)** box; case **(b)** (mit Büchern, Schallplatten) boxed set; (Tonband~, Film~) cassette

Kassetten-: ~**deck** *das* cassette deck; ~**recorder,** ~**rekorder** *der;* ~~s, ~~: cassette recorder

kassieren 1 *tr. V.* **(a)** collect **(b)** (ugs.: wegnehmen) confiscate; take away ⟨driving licence⟩ 2 *itr. V.* **bei jmdm.** ~: give sb. his/her bill *or* (Amer.) check; (ohne Rechnung) settle up with sb.; **darf ich bei Ihnen** ~? would you like your bill?/can I settle up with you?

Kassierer *der;* ~s, ~, **Kassiererin** *die;* ~, ~nen cashier; (bei einem Verein) treasurer

Kastanie /kas'taːni̯ə/ *die;* ~, ~n chestnut

kastanien·braun *Adj.* chestnut

Kästchen *das;* ~s, ~ **(a)** small box **(b)** (vorgedrucktes Quadrat) square; (auf Fragebögen) box

Kaste *die;* ~, ~n caste

kasteien *refl. V.* **(a)** (als Bußübung) chastise oneself **(b)** (sich Entbehrungen auferlegen) deny oneself

Kasteiung *die;* ~, ~en **(a)** (als Bußübung) self-chastisement **(b)** (Auferlegung von Entbehrungen) self-denial

Kastell *das;* ~s, ~e **(a)** (hist.: röm. Lager) fort **(b)** (Burg) castle

Kasten *der;* ~s, Kästen **(a)** box; (für Flaschen) crate **(b)** (ugs.: Briefkasten) postbox **(c)** (ugs. abwertend) (Gebäude) barracks *sing. or pl.;* (Auto) heap (coll.); (fig. ugs.) **etw. auf dem** ~ **haben** have got it up top (coll.)

Kasten·brot *das* tin [loaf]

Kastration /kastra'tsjoːn/ *die;* ~, ~en castration

kastrieren *tr. V.* castrate

Kat *der;* ~s, ~s (ugs.) ▶ KATALYSATOR B

Katalog *der;* ~[e]s, ~e (auch fig.) catalogue

katalogisieren *tr. V.* catalogue

Katalysator *der;* ~s, ~en **(a)** (Chemie, fig.) catalyst **(b)** (Kfz-W.) catalytic converter

Katamaran *der od. das;* ~s, ~e catamaran

katapultieren *tr. V.* (auch fig.) catapult; eject ⟨pilot⟩

Katarrh /ka'tar/ *der;* ~s, ~e (Med.) catarrh

katastrophal /katastroˈfaːl/ 1 *Adj.* disastrous; (stärker) catastrophic 2 *adv.* disastrously; (stärker) catastrophically

Katastrophe /katas'troːfə/ *die;* ~, ~n (Unglück) disaster; (stärker, auch Literaturw.) catastrophe

Katastrophen-: ~**alarm** *der* disaster alert; ~**gebiet** *das* disaster area; ~**schutz** *der* (Organisation) emergency services *pl.;* (Maßnahmen) disaster procedures *pl.*

Kategorie *die;* ~, ~n category

kategorisch 1 *Adj.* categorical 2 *adv.* categorically

Kater *der;* ~s, ~ **(a)** tomcat **(b)** (ugs.) hangover

Kathedrale *die;* ~, ~n cathedral

Katholik *der;* ~en, ~en, **Katholikin** *die;* ~, ~nen [Roman] Catholic

katholisch *Adj.* [Roman] Catholic

Katholizismus *der;* ~: [Roman] Catholicism *no art.*

Katz ~ **und Maus [mit jmdm.] spielen** (ugs.) play cat and mouse [with sb.]; **für die** ~ **sein** (salopp) be a waste of time

Kätzchen *das;* ~s, ~ **(a)** little cat; pussy; (junge Katze) kitten **(b)** *meist Pl.* catkin

Katze *die;* ~, ~n cat

katzen-, Katzen-: ~**auge** *das* reflector; Cat's-eye ®; ~**jammer** *der* **(a)** (Kater) hangover; **(b)** (fig.) mood of depression; ~**musik** *die* (ugs. abwertend) terrible row (coll.); ~**sprung** *der* stone's throw; ~**wäsche** *die* (ugs.) ~**wäsche machen** have a lick and a promise (coll.)

Kauderwelsch *das;* ~[s] gibberish *no indef. art.*

kauen *tr., itr. V.* chew; **[die] Nägel** ~: bite one's nails

kauern *itr., refl. V.* crouch [down]; (ängstlich) cower

Kauf *der;* ~[e]s, Käufe **(a)** (das Kaufen) buying; purchasing (formal) **(b)** (das Gekaufte) purchase

kaufen 1 *tr. V.* buy; purchase 2 *itr. V.* (einkaufen) shop

Käufer *der;* ~s, ~, **Käuferin** *die;* ~, ~nen buyer; purchaser (formal)

Kauf-: ~**frau** *die* (Geschäftsfrau) businesswoman; (Händlerin) trader; ~**haus** *das* department store; ~**kraft** *die* (Wirtsch.) **(a)** (Wert des Geldes) purchasing power; **(b)** (Zahlungsfähigkeit) spending power

käuflich ① *Adj.* (a) for sale *postpos.;* (b) (bestechlich) venal; ~ **sein** be easily bought
② *adv.* etw. ~ **erwerben/erstehen** purchase sth.

Kauf·mann *der; Pl.* **Kaufleute (a)** (Geschäftsmann) businessman; (Händler) trader (b) (Besitzer) shopkeeper; (eines Lebensmittelladens) grocer

kaufmännisch *Adj.* commercial; business *attrib.*

Kauf-: ~**preis** *der* purchase price; ~**vertrag** *der* contract of sale; (beim Hauskauf) title deed

Kau·gummi *der od. das;* ~**s,** ~**s** chewing gum

Kaukasus *der;* ~: the Caucasus

Kaulquappe *die;* ~, ~**n** tadpole

kaum *Adv.* hardly; scarcely; ~ **hatte er Platz genommen, als ...:** no sooner had he sat down than ...

kausal *Adj.* (geh., Sprachw.) causal

Kau·tabak *der* chewing tobacco

Kaution *die;* ~, ~**en (a)** (bei Freilassung eines Gefangenen) bail (b) (beim Mieten einer Wohnung) deposit

Kautschuk *der;* ~**s,** ~**e** rubber

Kauz *der;* ~**es, Käuze (a)** (Wald~) tawny owl; (Stein~) little owl (b) (Sonderling) strange fellow; oddball (coll.)

Kavalier /kava'liːɐ̯/ *der;* ~**s,** ~**e** gentleman

Kavaliers·delikt *das* trifling offence

Kavallerie /kavalə'riː/ *die;* ~, ~**n** (Milit. hist.) cavalry

Kavallerist *der;* ~**en,** ~**en** cavalryman

Kaviar /'kaːvi̯ar/ *der;* ~**s,** ~**e** caviare

kcal *Abk.* = **Kilo[gramm]kalorie** kcal

keck ① *Adj.* (a) cheeky; saucy (Brit.) (b) (veralt.: verwegen) bold (c) (flott) jaunty, pert *〈hat etc.〉* ② *adv.* (a) cheekily; saucily (Brit.) (b) (veralt.: verwegen) boldly (c) (flott) jauntily

Keckheit *die;* ~, ~**en (a)** cheek; sauce (Brit.) (b) (veralt.: Kühnheit) boldness

Kegel *der;* ~**s,** ~ **(a)** cone (b) (Spielfigur) skittle; (beim Bowling) pin

Kegel-: ~**bahn** *die* skittle alley; ~**förmig** *Adj.* conical

kegeln ① *itr. V.* play skittles *or* ninepins ② *tr. V.* **eine Partie** ~: play a game of skittles *or* ninepins; **eine Neun** ~: score a nine

Kehle *die;* ~, ~**n** throat

Kehl·kopf *der* (Anat.) larynx

Kehlkopf·krebs *der* (Med.) cancer of the larynx

Kehre *die;* ~, ~**n** sharp bend

kehren¹ ① *tr. V.* turn ② *refl. V.* turn

kehren² ① *itr. V.* (bes. südd.) sweep; do the sweeping ② *tr. V.* sweep; (mit einem Handfeger) brush

Kehricht *der od. das;* ~**s** (schweiz.: Müll) refuse; garbage (Amer.)

Kehr·seite *die* **(a)** back; (einer Münze, Medaille) reverse; (scherzh.) (Gesäß) backside (b) (nachteiliger Aspekt) drawback; disadvantage

kehrt|machen *itr. V.* (ugs.) turn [round and go] back

keifen *itr. V.* (abwertend) nag

Keil *der;* ~**[e]s,** ~**e (a)** (zum Spalten) wedge (b) (zum Festklemmen) chock; (unter einer Tür) wedge

keilen *refl. V.* (ugs.: sich prügeln) fight; scrap

Keiler *der;* ~**s,** ~ (Jägerspr.) wild boar

Keilerei *die;* ~, ~**en** (ugs.) punch-up (coll.); fight

Keil-: ~**riemen** *der* (Technik) V-belt; ~**schrift** *die* cuneiform script

Keim *der;* ~**[e]s,** ~**e** (Bot.) shoot; (Biol.) embryo

Keim-: ~**bahn** *die* (Biol.) germ line; ~**drüse** *die* (Zool., Med.) gonad

keimen *itr. V.* germinate; (fig.) 〈hope〉 stir

keim-, Keim-: ~**frei** *Adj.* germ-free; sterile; ~**zelle** *die* nucleus

kein *Indefinitpron.* **(a)** no (b) (ugs.: nicht ganz, nicht einmal) less than

kein... *Indefinitpron.* ~**er/**~**e** nobody; no one; ~**s von beiden** neither [of them]

keinerlei *indekl. Adj.* no ... what[so]ever

keines-: ~**falls** *Adv.* on no account; ~**wegs** *Adv.* by no means

kein·mal *Adv.* not [even] once

Keks *der;* ~ *od.* ~**es,** ~ *od.* ~**e** biscuit (Brit.); cookie (Amer.)

Kelch *der;* ~**[e]s,** ~**e** goblet; (Rel.) chalice

Kelle *die;* ~, ~**n (a)** ladle (b) (Signalstab) signalling disc (c) (Maurer~) trowel

Keller *der;* ~**s,** ~: cellar; (~geschoss) basement

Keller·assel *die;* ~, ~**n** woodlouse

Kellerei *die;* ~, ~**en** winery; (Kellerräume) [wine] cellars *pl.*

Keller: ~**geschoss,** **~**geschoß** *das* basement; ~**wohnung** *die* basement flat (Brit.) *or* (Amer.) apartment

Kellner *der;* ~**s,** ~: waiter

Kellnerin *die;* ~, ~**nen** waitress

kellnern *itr. V.* (ugs.) work as a waiter/ waitress

Kelte *der;* ~**n,** ~**n** Celt

Kelter *die;* ~, ~**n** winepress

keltern *tr. V.* press 〈grapes etc.〉

Keltin *die;* ~, ~**nen** Celt

keltisch *Adj.* Celtic

Kenia (*das*); ~**s** Kenya

Kenianer *der;* ∼s, ∼, **Kenianerin** *die;* ∼, ∼nen Kenyan

kennen *unr. tr. V.* know; jmdn./etw. ∼ lernen get to know sb./sth.; jmdn. ∼ lernen (jmdm. erstmals begegnen) meet sb.; jmdn. als etw. ∼ lernen come to know sb. as sth.

Kenner *der;* ∼s, ∼: expert (+ *Gen.* on); (von Wein, Speisen) connoisseur

Kenner·blick *der* expert eye; mit ∼: with an expert eye

Kennerin *die;* ∼, ∼nen ▸ KENNER

Kenn·marke *die* [police] identification badge; ≈ [police] warrant card *or* (Amer.) ID card

kenntlich *Adj.:* ∼ sein be recognizable (an by); etw./jmdn. ∼ machen mark sth./make sb. [easily] identifiable

Kenntnis *die;* ∼, ∼se knowledge

*kennen|lernen ▸ KENNEN

Kenntnisnahme *die;* ∼ (Papierdt.) nach ∼ der Akten after giving the documents my/his *etc.* attention

kenntnis·reich *Adj.* well-informed; knowledgeable

kenn-, Kenn-: ∼**wort** *das; Pl.* ∼wörter code word; (Parole) password; code word; ∼**zahl** *die* index; ∼**zeichen** *das* (a) sign; (b) (Erkennungszeichen) badge; (auf einem Behälter, einer Ware usw.) label; (am Fahrzeug) registration number; ∼**zeichnen** *tr. V.* (a) mark; label; mark ⟨*way*⟩; (b) (charakterisieren) characterize; ∼**zeichnend** *Adj.* typical, characteristic (**für** of)

kentern *itr. V. mit sein* capsize

Keramik *die;* ∼, ∼en ceramics *pl.;* pottery; (Gegenstand) piece of pottery

Kerbe *die;* ∼, ∼n notch

Kerbel *der;* ∼s chervil

Kerb·holz *das:* etwas auf dem ∼ haben (ugs.) have done a job (sl.)

Kerker *der;* ∼s, ∼ (hist.) dungeons *pl.;* (einzelne Zelle) dungeon

Kerl *der;* ∼s, ∼e (*nordd., md. auch:* ∼s) (ugs.) fellow (coll.); bloke (Brit. coll.)

Kern *der;* ∼[e]s, ∼e pip; (von Steinobst) stone; (von Nüssen usw.) kernel; (Atom∼) nucleus; (fig.) der ∼ einer Sache the heart of a matter; der harte ∼: the hard core

kern-, Kern-: ∼**energie** *die* nuclear energy *no art.;* ∼**gehäuse** *das* core; ∼**geschäft** *das* core business; ∼**gesund** *Adj.* fit as a fiddle *pred.*

kernig *Adj.* earthy ⟨*language*⟩; forceful ⟨*speech*⟩; pithy ⟨*saying*⟩

kern-, Kern-: ∼**kraft** *die* nuclear power; ∼**kraftwerk** *das* nuclear power station *or* plant; ∼**los** *Adj.* seedless; ∼**obst** *das* pomaceous fruit; ∼**physik** *die* nuclear physics *sing., no art.;* ∼**reaktor** *der* nuclear reactor; ∼**seife** *die* washing soap; ∼**spaltung** *die* (Physik) nuclear fission *no*

art.; ∼**spin·tomographie** /ˈkɛrnspɪntomoɡrafiː/ *die;* ∼∼ (Med.) [nuclear] magnetic resonance imaging; ∼**waffe** *die* nuclear weapon; ∼**zeit** *die* core time

Kerze *die;* ∼, ∼n candle

kerzen-, Kerzen-: ∼**gerade,** (ugs.) ∼**grade** ① *Adj.* dead straight; ② *adv.* bolt upright; ∼**halter** *der* candle holder; ∼**leuchter** *der* candlestick; ∼**licht** *das* the light of a candle/of candles; bei ∼licht by candlelight

kess, *keß ① *Adj.* (a) pert; jaunty ⟨hat, dress, etc.⟩
(b) (frech) cheeky
② *adv.* (a) (flott) jauntily
(b) (frech) cheekily

Kessel *der;* ∼s, ∼ (a) kettle; (zum Kochen) pot; (Wasch∼) copper
(b) (Berg∼) basin-shaped valley
(c) (Milit.) encircled area

Kessel-: ∼**stein** *der* scale; ∼**treiben** *das* (Hetzkampagne) witch-hunt

Kette *die;* ∼, ∼n chain; (Hals∼) necklace; (von Ereignissen) string

ketten *tr. V.* chain (an + *Akk.* to)

Ketten-: ∼**hund** *der* guard dog (*kept on a chain*); ∼**raucher** *das;* ∼∼s chain-smoking *no art.;* ∼**raucher** *der,* ∼**raucherin** *die* chain-smoker; ∼**säge** *die* chain saw; ∼**schaltung** *die* derailleur gears *pl.*

Ketzer *der;* ∼s, ∼ (auch fig.) heretic

Ketzerei *die;* ∼, ∼en (auch fig.) heresy

Ketzerin *die;* ∼, ∼nen ▸ KETZER

keuchen *itr. V.* gasp for breath

Keuch·husten *der* whooping cough *no art.*

Keule *die;* ∼, ∼n (a) club
(b) (Kochk.) leg

keusch ① *Adj.* chaste
② *adv.* ∼ leben lead a chaste life

Keuschheit *die;* ∼: chastity

Kfz *Abk.* = **Kraftfahrzeug**

kg *Abk.* = **Kilogramm** kg

KG *Abk.* = **Kommanditgesellschaft**

kichern *itr. V.* giggle

kicken (ugs.) ① *itr. V.* play football
② *tr. V.* kick

kidnappen /ˈkɪtnɛpn̩/ *tr. V.* kidnap

Kidnapper *der;* ∼s, ∼, **Kidnapperin** *die;* ∼, ∼nen kidnapper

Kiebitz *der;* ∼es, ∼e lapwing; peewit

Kiefer¹ *der;* ∼s, ∼: jaw; (∼knochen) jawbone

Kiefer² *die;* ∼, ∼n pine[tree]

Kiefer·höhle *die* (Anat.) maxillary sinus

Kiefern·holz *das* pine [wood]

Kiel *der;* ∼[e]s, ∼e keel

kiel·holen *tr. V.* (Seemannsspr.) keelhaul ⟨*person*⟩

Kiel·wasser *das* wake

---

k

Kieme die; ~, ~n gill
Kien der; ~[e]s resinous wood
Kies der; ~es, ~e gravel; (auf dem Strand) shingle
Kiesel der; ~s, ~: pebble
Kiesel·stein der pebble
Kies-: ~**grube** die gravel pit; ~**weg** der gravel path
kiffen itr. V. (ugs.) smoke pot (sl.) or grass (sl.)
Kiffer der; ~s, ~, **Kifferin** die; ~, ~nen (ugs.) pothead (sl.)
kikeriki /kikəri'ki:/ Interj. (Kinderspr.) cock-a-doodle-doo
Killer der; ~s, ~, **Killerin** die; ~, ~nen (salopp) killer; (gegen Bezahlung) hit man
Kilo das; ~s, ~[s] kilo
Kilo·gramm das kilogram
Kilometer der; ~s, ~: kilometre
kilometer-, Kilometer-: ~**lang** ① Adj. miles long pred.; ② adv. for miles [and miles]; ~**stand** der mileage reading
Kilowatt·stunde die (Physik; bes. Elektrot.) kilowatt-hour
Kimme die; ~, ~n sighting notch
Kimono der; ~s, ~s kimono
Kind das; ~[e]s, ~er (a) child; ein ~ erwarten be expecting
(b) [~er,] ~er! my goodness!
Kinder-: ~**arzt** der, ~**ärztin** die paediatrician; ~**betreuung** die child care; ~**bett** das cot; (für größeres Kind) child's bed; ~**dorf** das children's village
Kinderei die; ~, ~en childishness no indef. art., no pl.
kinder-, Kinder-: ~**erziehung** die bringing up of children; ~**feindlich** Adj. hostile to children pred.; ~**freundlich** Adj. fond of children pred.; ⟨town, resort⟩ which caters for children; ⟨planning, policy⟩ which caters for the needs of children; ~**garten** der nursery school; ~**gärtnerin** die nusery-school teacher; ~**geld** das child benefit; ~**heilkunde** die paediatrics sing., no art.; ~**hort** der day home for schoolchildren; ~**krankheit** die (a) (Infektionskrankheit) children's disease or illness; (b) Pl. (fig.): Anfangsschwierigkeiten) teething troubles; ~**krippe** die crèche; day nursery; ~**lähmung** die poliomyelitis; ~**leicht** (ugs.) Adj. childishly simple; dead easy; **das ist** ~**leicht** it's kid's stuff (coll.); it's child's play; ~**lieb** Adj. fond of children pred.; ~**los** Adj. childless; ~**reich** Adj. with many children postpos., not pred.; ~**sterblichkeit** die child mortality; ~**stube** die eine gute/schlechte ~**stube** gehabt haben have been well/badly brought up; ~**tages·heim** das, ~**tages·stätte** die day nursery; crèche ~**teller** der (auf der Speisekarte) children's menu; ~**wagen** der pram (Brit.); baby carriage (Amer.); (Sportwagen) pushchair (Brit.); stroller (Amer.)

Kindes-: ~**alter** das childhood; ~**misshandlung**, *~**mißhandlung** die (Rechtsw.) child abuse
Kindheit die; ~: childhood
kindisch ① Adj. childish, infantile; naïve ⟨ideas⟩
② adv. childishly
kindlich ① Adj. childlike
② adv. ⟨behave⟩ in a childlike way
Kinkerlitzchen Pl. (ugs.) trifles
Kinn das; ~[e]s, ~e chin
Kinn-: ~**haken** der hook to the chin; ~**lade** die jaw
Kino das; ~s, ~s cinema (Brit.); movie theater (Amer.)
Kino-: ~**gänger** der; ~~s, ~~, ~**gängerin** die; ~~, ~~nen cinema-goer (Brit.); movie-goer (Amer.); ~**karte** die cinema ticket (Brit.); movie ticket (Amer.)
Kiosk der; ~[e]s, ~e kiosk
Kippe[1] die; ~, ~n (ugs.) cigarette end; dog-end (coll.)
Kippe[2] die; ~, ~n (a) (Bergmannsspr.) slag heap
(b) etw. steht auf der ~ (fig.) it's touch and go with sth.; (etw. ist noch nicht entschieden) sth. hangs in the balance
kippen ① tr. V. (a) tip [up]
(b) (ausschütten) tip [out]
(c) (ugs.: trinken) knock back (coll.); **einen** ~: have a quick one (coll.) or a drink
② itr. V.; mit sein tip over; ⟨top-heavy object⟩ topple over; ⟨person⟩ topple; ⟨boat⟩ overturn; ⟨car⟩ roll over
Kipp-: ~**fenster** das horizontally pivoted window; ~**schalter** der tumbler switch
Kirche die; ~, ~n church; in die ~ gehen go to church
Kirchen-: ~**fest** das church festival; ~**lied** das hymn; ~**musik** die church music; ~**steuer** die church tax
Kirch-: ~**gänger** der; ~~s, ~~, ~**gängerin** die; ~~, ~~nen churchgoer; ~**hof** der (veralt.) churchyard
kirchlich ① Adj. ecclesiastical; church attrib. ⟨wedding, funeral⟩
② adv. ~ getraut/begraben werden have a church wedding/funeral
Kirch-: ~**turm** der [church] steeple; (ohne Turmspitze) church tower; ~**weih** die; ~~, ~~en fair (held on the anniversary of the consecration of a church)
Kirmes die; ~, **Kirmessen** (bes. md., niederd.)
▶ KIRCHWEIH
Kirsch·baum der cherry [tree]
Kirsche die; ~, ~n cherry
Kirsch-: ~**torte** die cherry gateau; (mit Tortenboden) cherry flan; ~**wasser** das; Pl. ~**wässer** kirsch
Kissen das; ~s, ~: cushion; (Kopf~) pillow

Kiste die; ∼, ∼n box; (Truhe) chest; (Latten∼) crate

Kita die; ∼, ∼s day nursery; crèche

Kitsch der; ∼[e]s kitsch

kitschig Adj. kitschy

Kitt der; ∼[e]s, ∼e putty; (für Porzellan, Kacheln usw.) cement

Kittchen das; ∼s, ∼ (ugs.) clink (sl.)

Kittel der; ∼s, ∼ (a) overall; (eines Arztes usw.) white coat
(b) (hemdartige Bluse) smock

kitten tr. V. cement [together]

Kitz das; ∼es, ∼e (Reh∼) fawn; (Ziegen∼, Gämsen∼) kid

kitzeln tr., itr. V. tickle

kitzlig Adj. (auch fig.) ticklish

KKW Abk. = **Kernkraftwerk**

Klacks der; ∼es, ∼e (ugs.) dollop (coll.); (∼ Senf) dab; **etw. ist nur ein ∼ [für jmdn.]** (fig.) sth. is no trouble at all [for sb.]

Kladde die; ∼, ∼n rough book

Kladderadatsch der; ∼[e]s, ∼e (ugs.) unholy mess (coll.)

klaffen itr. V. yawn; ⟨hole, wound⟩ gape

kläffen itr. V. (abwertend) yap

Kläffer der; ∼s, ∼ (ugs. abwertend) yapping dog; yapper

Klafter der od. das; ∼s, ∼ (Raummaß für Holz) cord

Klage die; ∼, ∼n (a) (Äußerung der Trauer) lament
(b) (Beschwerde) complaint
(c) (Rechtsspr.) action; (im Strafrecht) charge

klagen [1] itr. V. (a) (geh.: jammern) wail; (stöhnend) moan
(b) (sich beschweren) complain (**über** + Akk. about)
(c) (bei Gericht) take legal action
[2] tr. V. **jmdm. sein Leid/seine Not ∼:** pour out one's sorrows pl./troubles pl.

Kläger der; ∼s, ∼, **Klägerin** die; ∼, ∼nen (im Zivilrecht) plaintiff; (im Strafrecht) prosecuting party; (bei einer Scheidung) petitioner

kläglich Adj. (a) (Mitleid erregend) pitiful
(b) (minderwertig) pathetic
(c) (erbärmlich) despicable ⟨behaviour, role, compromise⟩; pathetic ⟨result, defeat⟩

Klamauk der; ∼s (ugs. abwertend) fuss; (Lärm, Krach) row (coll.)

klamm Adj. (a) (feucht) cold and damp
(b) (steif) numb

Klammer die; ∼, ∼n (Wäsche∼) peg; (Haar∼) [hair]grip; (Zahn∼) brace; (Büro∼) paper clip; (Heft∼) staple; (Schriftzeichen) bracket

klammern [1] refl. V. **sich an jmdn./etw. ∼** (auch fig.) cling to sb./sth.
[2] tr. V. (a) **eine Wunde ∼:** close a wound with a clip/clips

*alte Schreibung - vgl. Hinweis auf S. xiv

(b) (mit einer Büroklammer) clip; (mit einer Heftmaschine) staple; (mit Wäscheklammern) peg

Klamotten Pl. (salopp) (Kleidung) gear sing. (coll.); (Kram) stuff sing.

Klampfe die; ∼, ∼n (volkst.: Gitarre) guitar

klang 1. u. 3. Pers. Sg. Prät. v. **KLINGEN**

Klang der; ∼[e]s, **Klänge** (a) (Ton) sound
(b) (∼farbe) tone

Klapp·bett das folding bed

Klappe die; ∼, ∼n (a) [hinged] lid; (am LKW) tailgate; (seitlich) side gate; (am Kombiwagen) back; (am Ofen) [drop-]door
(b) (an Musikinstrumenten) key; (an einer Trompete) valve
(c) (Filmjargon) clapperboard
(d) (salopp: Mund) trap (sl.)

klappen [1] tr. V. **nach oben/unten ∼:** turn up/down ⟨collar, hat brim⟩; lift up/put down ⟨lid⟩; **nach vorne/hinten ∼:** tilt forward/back ⟨seat⟩
[2] itr. V. (a) ⟨door, shutter⟩ bang
(b) (stoßen) bang
(c) (ugs.: gelingen) work out all right

klapperig Adj. rickety

klappern itr. V. (a) rattle
(b) (ein Klappern erzeugen) make a clatter

Klapper·schlange die rattlesnake

Klapp·fahrrad das folding bicycle

klapprig Adj. rickety

Klapp-: ∼**sitz** der tip-up seat; ∼**stuhl** der folding chair

Klaps der; ∼es, ∼e (ugs.) smack; slap

Klaps·mühle die (salopp) loony bin (sl.)

klar [1] Adj. (a) (klar; straight ⟨question, answer⟩; **sich** (Dat.) **über etw.** (Akk.) ∼ **werden** realize sth.; **jmdm. ∼ werden** become clear to sb.; **sich** (Dat.) **über etw.** (Akk.) **im Klaren sein** realize sth.; **etw. ∼ machen** (ugs.) make sth. clear
(b) (fertig) ready
[2] adv. clearly; ∼ **sehen** understand the matter

Klär·anlage die sewage treatment plant

Klare der; ∼n, ∼n schnapps

klären [1] tr. V. (a) settle ⟨question, issue, matter⟩; clarify ⟨situation⟩; clear up ⟨case, affair, misunderstanding⟩
(b) (reinigen) purify; treat ⟨effluent, sewage⟩
[2] refl. V. (a) ⟨situation⟩ become clear; ⟨question, issue, matter⟩ be settled
(b) (rein werden) ⟨liquid, sky⟩ clear; ⟨weather⟩ clear [up]

klar|gehen unr. itr. V.; mit sein (ugs.) go OK (coll.)

Klarheit die; ∼: clarity; **sich** (Dat.) **über etw.** (Akk.) ∼ **verschaffen** clarify sth.

Klarinette die; ∼, ∼n clarinet

klar-: ∼**|machen** tr. V. (Seemannsspr.) get ready; *∼**|sehen** ▶ KLAR 2

klaro Adj., Interj. (ugs.) of course; it goes without saying; ∼, **dass** ...: it goes without saying that ...

Klarsicht·folie *die* transparent film
klar|stellen *tr. V.* clear up; clarify
Klar·text *der* (auch DV) clear text; **im ~text** (fig.) in plain language
Klärung *die;* ~, ~en **(a)** clarification **(b)** (Reinigung) purification; (von Abwässern) treatment
*klar|werden ▶ KLAR 1A
Klär·werk *das* sewage works *sing. or pl.*
klasse (ugs.) [1] *indekl. Adj.* great (coll.) [2] *adv.* marvellously
Klasse *die;* ~, ~n **(a)** (Schul~) class; (Raum) classroom; (Stufe) year; grade (Amer.) **(b)** (Sport) league; (Boxen) division **(c)** (Fahrzeug~, Boots~, Qualitätsstufe) class; **das ist einsame** *od.* **ganz große ~!** (ugs.) that's [just] great (coll.) *or* marvellous!
klassen-, Klassen-: ~**arbeit** *die* (Schulw.) [written] class test; ~**buch** *das* (Schulw.) book recording details of pupils' attendance, behaviour, and of topics covered in each lesson; ≈ [class] register; ~**fahrt** *die* (Schulw.) class outing; ~**gesellschaft** *die* (Soziol.) class society; ~**kampf** *der* (marx.) class struggle; ~**lehrer** *der,* ~**lehrerin** *die* (Schulw.) class teacher; ~**los** *Adj.* (Soziol.) classless; ~**sprecher** *der,* ~**sprecherin** *die* (Schulw.) class spokesman; ~**treffen** *das* (Schulw.) class reunion; ~**ziel** *das* (Schulw.) required standard *(for pupils in a particular class)*; ~**zimmer** *das* (Schulw.) classroom
klassifizieren *tr. V.* classify (**als** as)
Klassifizierung *die;* ~, ~en classification
Klassik *die;* ~ **(a)** (Antike) classical antiquity *no art.;* **(b)** (Zeit kultureller Höchstleistung) classical period
Klassiker *der;* ~s, ~, **Klassikerin** *die;* ~, ~nen classical writer/composer
klassisch *Adj.* classical; (vollendet, zeitlos; auch iron.) classic
Klassizismus *der;* ~: classicism
Klatsch *der;* ~[e]s, ~e **(a)** (ugs. abwertend) gossip **(b)** (Geräusch) smack
Klatsch·base *die* (ugs. abwertend) gossip
klatschen *itr. V.* **(a)** *auch mit sein ⟨waves, wet sails⟩* slap **(b)** (mit den Händen; applaudieren) clap **(c)** (schlagen) slap **(d)** (ugs. abwertend: reden) gossip (**über** + *Akk.* about)
klatschhaft *Adj.* gossipy; fond of gossip *pred.*
klatsch-, Klatsch-: ~**mohn** *der* corn poppy; ~**nass, *~naß** *Adj.* (ugs.) sopping wet; dripping wet ⟨*hair*⟩; ~**spalte** *die* (ugs. abwertend) gossip column
Klaue *die;* ~, ~n **(a)** claw; (von Raubvögeln) talon; (salopp: Hand) mitt (coll.) **(b)** (salopp abwertend: Schrift) scrawl

klauen (ugs.) [1] *tr. V.* pinch (coll.); **jmdm. etw. ~:** pinch sth. from sb. [2] *itr. V.* pinch (coll.) things
Klause *die;* ~, ~n hermitage; (Klosterzelle) cell
Klausel *die;* ~, ~n clause; (Bedingung) condition; (Vorbehalt) proviso
Klausur *die;* ~, ~en [examination] paper; (Examen) examination; **eine ~ schreiben** take a[n examination] paper/an examination
Klausur-: ~**arbeit** *die* [examination] paper; ~**tagung** *die* private meeting
Klavier /kla'viːɐ̯/ *das;* ~s, ~e piano
Klebe·folie *die* adhesive film
kleben [1] *itr. V.* **(a)** stick (**an** + *Dat.* to) **(b)** (ugs.: klebrig sein) be sticky (**von, vor** + *Dat.* with) [2] *tr. V.* **(a)** (befestigen) stick; (mit Klebstoff) glue; **jmdm. eine ~** (salopp) belt sb. one (coll.) **(b)** (reparieren) stick *or* glue ⟨*vase etc.*⟩ back together
Kleber *der;* ~s, ~: adhesive; glue
klebrig *Adj.* sticky
Kleb-: ~**stoff** *der* adhesive; glue; ~**streifen** *der* adhesive *or* sticky tape
kleckern (ugs.) *itr. V.* make a mess
Klecks *der;* ~es, ~e **(a)** stain; (nicht aufgesogen) blob; (Tintenfleck) [ink] blot **(b)** (ugs.: kleine Menge) spot; (von Senf, Mayonnaise) dab
klecksen *itr. V.* **(a)** make a stain/stains; (mit Tinte) make a blot/blots; ⟨*pen*⟩ blot **(b)** (ugs. abwertend: schlecht malen) daub
Klee *der;* ~s clover
Klee·blatt *das* cloverleaf
Kleid *das;* ~es, ~er **(a)** dress **(b)** *Pl.* (Kleidung) clothes
kleiden [1] *refl. V.* dress [2] *tr. V.* **(a)** dress **(b)** (jmdm. stehen) suit
Kleider-: ~**bügel** *der* clothes hanger; coat hanger; ~**bürste** *die* clothes brush; ~**haken** *der* coat hook; ~**schrank** *der* wardrobe; ~**spende** *die* donation of [second-hand] clothes *or* clothing; ~**ständer** *der* coat stand
kleidsam *Adj.* becoming
Kleidung *die;* ~: clothes *pl.*
Kleidungs·stück *das* garment
klein [1] *Adj.* **(a)** little; small; **er ist ~er als ich** he is shorter than me; **etw. ~ schneiden** cut sth. into small pieces; **Zwiebeln ~ schneiden/hacken** chop up onions [small] **(b)** (jung) little; **von ~ auf** from an early age **(c)** (von kurzer Dauer) little; short ⟨*while*⟩; short ⟨*walk, break, holiday*⟩; brief ⟨*moment*⟩ **(d)** (von geringer Menge) small; low ⟨*price*⟩; **~es Geld haben** have some [small] change **(e)** (von geringem Ausmaß) small ⟨*party, gift*⟩; scant ⟨*attention*⟩; slight ⟨*cold, indisposition, mistake, irregularity*⟩; minor ⟨*event, error*⟩ ···⬧

(f) (unbedeutend) lowly ⟨*employee*⟩; minor ⟨*official*⟩; ~ **anfangen** (ugs.) start off in a small way

2 *adv.* **die Heizung ~/~er einstellen** turn the heating down low/lower; **ein Wort ~ schreiben** write a word with a small initial letter

klein-, Klein-: ~**aktionär** *der,* ~**aktionärin** *die* (Wirtsch.) small shareholder; ~**anzeige** *die* (Zeitungsw.) small *or* classified advertisement; ~**asien** (*das*) Asia Minor; ~**buchstabe** *der* small letter; ~**bürger** *der,* ~**bürgerin** *die* lower middle-class person; (abwertend: Spießbürger) petit bourgeois; ~**bürgerlich** *Adj.* **(a)** (das Kleinbürgertum betreffend) lower middle-class; **(b)** (abwertend: spießbürgerlich) petit bourgeois

Kleine¹ *der; adj. Dekl.* **(a)** (kleiner Junge) little boy

(b) (ugs. Anrede) little man

Kleine² *die; adj. Dekl.* **(a)** (kleines Mädchen) little girl

(b) (ugs. Anrede) love; (abwertend) little madam

klein-, Klein-: ~**familie** *die* (Soziol.) nuclear family; ~**geld** *das* [small] change; ~**gläubig** *Adj.* sceptical

Kleinigkeit *die;* ~, ~**en** small thing; (Einzelheit) [small] detail; **ich habe noch eine** ~ **zu erledigen** I still have a small matter to attend to; **eine** ~ **essen** have a bite to eat; **eine** ~ **für jmdn. sein** be no trouble for sb.

klein-, Klein-: ~**kind** *das* small child; ~**kram** *der* (ugs.) odds and ends *pl.;* (unbedeutende Dinge) trivial matters *pl.;* ~**kredit** *der* (Bankw.) personal loan *(repayable within two years);* ~|**kriegen** *tr. V.* (ugs.) **(a)** (zerkleinern) crush [to pieces]; **(b)** (zerstören) smash; break; **(c)** (aufbrauchen) get through; **(d) jmdn.** ~**kriegen** get sb. down (coll.); (durch Drohungen) intimidate sb.; (gefügig machen) bring sb. into line; ~**kunst** *die* cabaret; ~**laut** **1** *Adj.* subdued; (verlegen) sheepish; **2** *adv.* in a subdued fashion; (verlegen) sheepishly

kleinlich (abwertend) **1** *Adj.* pernickety; (ohne Großzügigkeit) mean; (engstirnig) small-minded; petty

2 *adv.* meticulously

Kleinod *das;* ~[e]s, ~e *od.* ~**ien** (geh.) **(a)** (Schmuckstück) piece of jewellery; (Edelstein) jewel

(b) (Kostbarkeit) gem

klein-, Klein-: ~|**rechnen** *tr. V.* undercalculate; *~|**schneiden** ▶ KLEIN 1A; ~**stadt** *die* small town; ~**städter** *der,* ~**städterin** *die* small-town dweller

Kleinste *der/die/das; adj. Dekl.* youngest boy/girl/child

klein|stellen *tr. V.* turn down [low]

Klein·wagen *der* small car

Kleister *der;* ~s, ~: paste

Klementine *die;* ~, ~**n** clementine

Klemme *die;* ~, ~**n** clip; **in der** ~ **sein** *od.* **sitzen** (ugs.) be in a fix (coll.)

klemmen **1** *tr. V.* **(a)** (befestigen) tuck **(b)** (quetschen) **sich** (*Dat.*) **den Fuß/die Hand** ~: get one's foot/hand caught *or* trapped **2** *refl. V.* **sich hinter etw.** (*Akk.*) ~ (fig. ugs.) put some hard work into sth. **3** *itr. V.* ⟨*door, drawer, etc.*⟩ stick

Klempner *der;* ~s, ~, **Klempnerin** *die;* ~, ~**nen** tinsmith; (Installateur[in]) plumber

Kleptomanie *die;* ~ (Psych.) kleptomania *no art.*

klerikal *Adj.* (auch abwertend) clerical; church ⟨*property*⟩

Klerus *der;* ~: clergy

Klette *die;* ~, ~**n** bur; (Pflanze) burdock

klettern *itr. V.; mit sein* (auch fig.) climb; **auf einen Baum** ~: climb a tree

Kletter·pflanze *die* creeper; (Bot.) climbing plant; climber

Klett·verschluss, *Klett·verschluß *der* Velcro ® fastening

klicken *itr. V.* click

Klient *der;* ~**en**, ~**en**, **Klientin** *die;* ~, ~**nen** client

Klima *das;* ~s, ~s *od.* **Klimate** climate

Klima·anlage *die* air conditioning *no indef. art.*

klimatisch *Adj.* climatic

klimatisieren *tr. V.* air-condition

Klima-: ~**wandel** *der* climate change; ~**wechsel** *der* climate change; (Med.) change of climate

Klimm·zug *der* (Turnen) pull-up

klimpern **1** *itr. V.* jingle **2** *tr. V.* (ugs. abwertend) plunk out ⟨*tune etc.*⟩

Klinge *die;* ~, ~**n** blade

Klingel *die;* ~, ~**n** bell

Klingel-: ~**beutel** *der* offertory bag; collection bag; ~**knopf** *der* bell push

klingeln *itr. V.* ring; ⟨*alarm clock*⟩ go off; **es klingelt** (an der Tür) there is a ring at the door; (Telefon) the telephone is ringing

Klingel·ton *der* ringtone

klingen *unr. itr. V.* sound; **die Glocken klangen** the bells were ringing

Klinik *die;* ~, ~**en** hospital; (spezialisiert) clinic

Klinke *die;* ~, ~**n** door handle

klipp *Adv.* ~ **und klar** (ugs.) quite plainly

Klippe *die;* ~, ~**n** rock

klirren *itr. V.* clink ⟨*weapons in fight*⟩ clash; ⟨*window pane*⟩ rattle; ⟨*chains, spurs*⟩ rattle; ⟨*harness*⟩ jingle

Klischee *das;* ~s, ~s cliché

klitsch·nass, *klitsch·naß *Adj.* (ugs.) sopping wet; (tropfnass) dripping wet

klitze·klein *Adj.* (ugs.) teeny[-weeny] (coll.)

Klo *das;* ~s, ~s (ugs.) loo (Brit. coll.); john (Amer. coll.)

Kloake *die;* ~, ~n cesspit; (Kanal) sewer

klobig *Adj.* heavy and clumsy[-looking] ⟨*shoes, furniture*⟩; bulky ⟨*figure*⟩; (plump) clumsy

Klon *der;* ~s, ~e (Biol.) clone

klonen *tr. V.* clone

Klo-papier *das* (ugs.) loo paper (Brit. coll.); toilet paper

klopfen ⟦1⟧ *itr. V.* (a) (schlagen) knock
(b) (pulsieren) ⟨*heart*⟩ beat; ⟨*pulse*⟩ throb
⟦2⟧ *tr. V.* beat ⟨*carpet*⟩

Klöppel *der;* ~s, ~ (Glocken~) clapper

klöppeln *tr., itr. V.* [etw.] ~: make [sth. in] pillow lace

Klops *der;* ~es, ~e (nordostd.) meat ball

Klosett *das;* ~s, ~s *od.* ~e lavatory

Kloß *der;* ~es, Klöße dumpling; (Fleisch~) meat ball

Kloster *das;* ~s, Klöster (Mönchs~) monastery; (Nonnen~) convent

Klotz *der;* ~es, Klötze block [of wood]; (Stück eines Baumstamms) log

Klub *der;* ~s, ~s club

Klub-sessel *der* club chair

Kluft¹ *die;* ~, ~en (ugs.) gear (coll.); (Uniform) garb

Kluft² *die;* ~, Klüfte (veralt.) (Spalte) cleft; (im Gletscher, Abgrund) chasm; (fig.) gulf

klug; klüger, klügst... *Adj.* clever; bright ⟨*child, pupil*⟩; intelligent ⟨*eyes*⟩; (vernünftig) wise; sound ⟨*advice*⟩; (geschickt) shrewd ⟨*politician, negotiator, question*⟩; astute ⟨*businessman*⟩

Klugheit *die;* ~ ▸ KLUG: cleverness; brightness; intelligence; wisdom; soundness; shrewdness; astuteness

klumpen *itr. V.* go lumpy

Klumpen *der;* ~s, ~: lump; ein ~ Gold a gold nugget

km *Abk.* = **Kilometer** km.

knabbern ⟦1⟧ *tr. V.* nibble
⟦2⟧ *itr. V.* an etw. (*Dat.*) ~: nibble [at] sth.

Knabe *der;* ~n, ~n (geh. veralt./südd., österr., schweiz.) boy; (ugs.: Bursche) chap (coll.)

knabenhaft ⟦1⟧ *Adj.* boyish
⟦2⟧ *adv.* boyishly

Knäcke-brot *das* crispbread; (Scheibe) slice of crispbread

knacken ⟦1⟧ *itr. V.* (a) ⟨*bed, floor, etc.*⟩ creak
(b) *mit sein* (ugs.: zerbrechen) snap; ⟨*window*⟩ crack
⟦2⟧ *tr. V.* (a) crack ⟨*nut, shell*⟩
(b) (salopp: aufbrechen) crack ⟨*safe*⟩ [open]; break into ⟨*car, bank, etc.*⟩

knackig *Adj.* (a) crisp
(b) (ugs.: attraktiv) delectable

Knacks *der;* ~es, ~e (ugs.) crack; (fig.: Defekt) **einen ~ bekommen** ⟨*person*⟩ have a breakdown; ⟨*health*⟩ suffer

Knall *der;* ~[e]s, ~e bang

knallen ⟦1⟧ *itr. V.* (a) ⟨*shot*⟩ ring out; ⟨*firework*⟩ go bang; ⟨*cork*⟩ pop; ⟨*door*⟩ slam; ⟨*whip, rifle*⟩ crack; **mit der Tür ~:** slam the door
(b) (ugs.: schießen) shoot, fire (**auf** + *Akk.* at)
(c) (Ballspiele ugs.) **aufs Tor ~:** belt the ball/puck at the goal (coll.)
⟦2⟧ *tr. V.* (a) (ugs.) slam down; (werfen) sling (coll.)
(b) (ugs.: schlagen) **jmdm. eine ~** (salopp) belt sb. one (coll.)

knall-: ~**hart** (ugs.) ⟦1⟧ *Adj.* very tough ⟨*demands, measures, etc.*⟩; ⟨*person*⟩ as hard as nails; ⟦2⟧ *adv.* brutally; **gegen etw. ~hart vorgehen** take very tough action against sth.; ~**rot** *Adj.* bright *or* vivid red; **sie wurde ~rot** she turned as red as a beetroot

knapp ⟦1⟧ *Adj.* (a) meagre; narrow ⟨*victory, lead*⟩; narrow, bare ⟨*majority*⟩; **die Vorräte wurden ~:** supplies ran short; **vor einer ~en Stunde** just under an hour ago
(b) (eng) tight-fitting ⟨*garment*⟩; (zu eng) tight ⟨*garment*⟩
(c) (kurz) terse ⟨*reply, greeting*⟩; succinct ⟨*description, account, report*⟩
⟦2⟧ *adv.* (a) ~ **bemessen sein** be meagre, ⟨*time*⟩ be limited; ~ **gewinnen/verlieren** win/lose narrowly; **er ist ~ fünfzig** he is just this side of fifty
(b) (eng) ~ **sitzen** fit tightly; (zu eng) be a tight fit
(c) (kurz) ⟨*reply*⟩ tersely; ⟨*describe, summarize*⟩ succinctly

Knappheit *die;* ~ (a) (Mangel) shortage (**an** + *Dat.* of)
(b) (Kürze) (einer Antwort, eines Grußes) terseness; (einer Beschreibung, eines Berichts) succinctness

Knarre *die;* ~, ~n (salopp: Gewehr) shooting iron (coll.)

knarren *itr. V.* creak

Knast *der;* ~[e]s, Knäste *od.* ~e (ugs.) (a) (Strafe) bird (sl.); time
(b) (Gefängnis) clink (sl.); prison

Knatsch *der;* ~[e]s (ugs.) Ärger) trouble

knattern *itr. V.* clatter; ⟨*sail*⟩ flap; ⟨*radio*⟩ crackle

Knäuel *der od. das;* ~s, ~ ball; (wirres ~) tangle

Knauf *der;* ~[e]s, Knäufe knob; (eines Schwertes, Dolches) pommel

knauserig *Adj.* (ugs. abwertend) stingy; tight-fisted

knausern *itr. V.* (ugs. abwertend) be stingy; skimp

knautschen (ugs.) ⟦1⟧ *tr. V.* crumple; crease ⟨*dress*⟩
⟦2⟧ *itr. V.* ⟨*dress, material*⟩ crease

Knebel *der;* ~s, ~ (a) gag
(b) (Griff) toggle

knebeln *tr. V.* gag

Knecht *der;* ~[e]s, ~e farm labourer

k

knechten tr. V. (geh.) reduce to slavery; enslave; (unterdrücken) oppress

Knechtschaft die; ~, ~en (geh.) bondage; slavery

kneifen [1] unr. tr., itr. V. pinch
[2] unr. itr. V. (a) ⟨clothes⟩ be too tight
(b) (ugs.: sich drücken) chicken (coll.) out (vor + Dat. of)

Kneif·zange die pincers pl.

Kneipe die; ~, ~n (ugs.) pub (Brit. coll.); bar (Amer.)

Kneipen·tour die (ugs.) pub crawl

kneippen itr. V. (ugs.) take a Kneipp cure

Kneipp·kur die Kneipp cure

kneten tr. V. (a) (bearbeiten) knead ⟨dough, muscles⟩; work ⟨clay⟩
(b) (formen) model ⟨figure⟩

Knet·masse die Plasticine ®

Knick der; ~[e]s, ~e sharp bend; (Falz) crease

knicken [1] tr. V. (a) (brechen) snap
(b) (falten) crease ⟨page, paper, etc.⟩
[2] itr. V.; mit sein snap

knick[e]rig Adj. (ugs. abwertend) stingy

Knick[e]rigkeit die; ~ (ugs. abwertend) stinginess

Knicks der; ~es, ~e curtsy

knicksen itr. V. curtsy (vor + Dat. to)

Knie das; ~s, ~ /'kni:(ə)/ (a) knee
(b) (Biegung) sharp bend

knie-, Knie-: ~beuge die knee bend; ~bund·hose die knee breeches pl.; ~fall der: einen ~fall tun od. machen (auch fig.) go down on one's knees (vor + Dat. before); ~kehle die hollow of the knee

knien /'kni:(ə)n/ [1] itr. V. kneel
[2] refl. V. kneel [down]

Knie-: ~scheibe die kneecap; ~strumpf der knee-length sock

Kniff der; ~[e]s, ~e (a) pinch
(b) (Falte) crease
(c) (Kunstgriff) trick

knipsen tr. V. (a) (entwerten) clip; punch
(b) (fotografieren) take a snap[shot] of

Knirps der; ~es, ~e (a) (Ⓦ Taschenschirm) telescopic umbrella
(b) (ugs.: Junge) nipper (coll.)

knirschen itr. V. crunch; **mit den Zähnen ~:** grind one's teeth

knistern itr. V. rustle; ⟨wood, fire⟩ crackle

knittern tr., itr. V. crease; crumple

knobeln itr. V. (mit Würfeln) play dice

Knob·lauch der garlic

Knoblauch·zehe die clove of garlic

Knöchel der; ~s, ~: ankle; (am Finger) knuckle

Knochen der; ~s, ~: bone

knochen-, Knochen-: ~bau der bone

---

structure; ~bruch der fracture; ~hart Adj. (ugs.) rock-hard; ~mark das bone marrow

knochig Adj. bony

Knödel der; ~s, ~ (bes. südd., österr.) dumpling

Knöllchen das; ~s, ~ (ugs.: Strafzettel) [parking] ticket

Knolle die; ~, ~n tuber

Knopf der; ~[e]s, Knöpfe button; (Knauf) knob

knöpfen tr. V. button [up]

Knopf·loch das buttonhole

Knorpel der; ~s, ~ (Anat.) cartilage; (im Steak o. Ä.) gristle

knorrig Adj. gnarled

Knospe die; ~, ~n bud

knospen itr. V. bud

knoten tr. V. knot

Knoten der; ~s, ~: knot; (Haartracht) bun; knot; (Med.) lump

Knoten·punkt der junction; intersection

Know-how /nou'hau:/ das; ~[s] know-how

knuffen tr. V. poke

Knüller der; ~s, ~ (ugs.) sensation; (Angebot, Verkaufsartikel) sensational offer

knüpfen tr. V. (a) tie (an + Akk. to); **Bedingungen an etw.** (Akk.) ~: attach conditions to sth.
(b) (durch Knoten herstellen) knot; make ⟨net⟩

Knüppel der; ~s, ~ cudgel; (Polizei~) truncheon

knüppel-, Knüppel-: ~dick Adv. (ugs.) **es kam ~dick** it was one disaster after the other; ~schaltung die (Kfz-W.) floor[-type] gear change

knurren itr. V. (a) ⟨animal⟩ growl; (wütend) snarl; (fig.) ⟨stomach⟩ rumble
(b) (murren) grumble (über + Akk. about)

knusprig Adj. crisp; crusty ⟨bread, roll⟩

knutschen (ugs.) [1] tr. V. smooch with (coll.); (sexuell berühren) pet; **sich ~:** smooch (coll.)/pet
[2] itr. V. smooch (coll.); (sich sexuell berühren) pet

k. o. /ka:'|o:/ Adj. (a) (Boxen) **jmdn. k. o. schlagen** knock sb. out
(b) (ugs.: übermüdet) all in (coll.)

koalieren itr. V. (Politik) form a coalition (mit with)

Koalition die; ~, ~en coalition

Koax·kabel das (Technik Jargon) coax [cable]; coaxial cable

Kobalt das; ~s (Chemie) cobalt

Kobold der; ~[e]s, ~e goblin

Kobra die; ~, ~s cobra

Koch der; ~[e]s, Köche cook; (Küchenchef) chef

Koch·buch das cookery book (Brit.); cookbook (Amer.)

---

kochen [1] *tr. V.* **(a)** boil; (zubereiten) cook ⟨*meal*⟩; make ⟨*purée, jam*⟩; **Tee** ~: make some tea
(b) (waschen) boil
[2] *itr. V.* **(a)** (Speisen zubereiten) cook
(b) (sieden) ⟨*water, milk, etc.*⟩ boil
Kocher *der;* ~s, ~ [small] stove; (Kochplatte) hotplate
Köcher *der;* ~s, ~ (für Pfeile) quiver
Koch·feld *das* ceramic hob
Köchin *die;* ~, ~nen cook
Koch-: ~**löffel** *der* wooden spoon; ~**nische** *die* kitchenette; ~**salz** *das* common salt; ~**topf** *der* [cooking] pot; ~**wäsche** *die* washing that is to be boiled
Köder *der;* ~s, ~: bait
ködern *tr. V.* lure
Koffein *das;* ~s caffeine
koffein·frei *Adj.* decaffeinated
Koffer *der;* ~s, ~: [suit]case
Koffer-: ~**kuli** *der* luggage trolley; ~**radio** *das* portable radio; ~**raum** *der* boot (Brit.); trunk (Amer.)
Kognak /ˈkɔnjak/ *der;* ~s, ~s brandy; *s. auch* COGNAC
Kohl *der;* ~[e]s **(a)** cabbage
(b) (ugs. abwertend: Unsinn) rubbish; rot (coll.)
Kohl·dampf *der* (salopp) ~ **haben** be ravenously hungry
Kohle *die;* ~, ~n **(a)** coal
(b) (salopp: Geld) dough (coll.)
Kohle·hydrat ▶ KOHLENHYDRAT
kohlen¹ *itr. V.* smoulder; ⟨*wick*⟩ smoke
kohlen² *itr. V.* (fam.) (lügen) tell fibs; (übertreiben) exaggerate
Kohlen-: ~**dioxid**, ~**dioxyd** /--'---/ *das* (Chemie) carbon dioxide; ~**grube** *die* coal mine; ~**händler** *der*, ~**händlerin** *die* coal merchant; ~**hydrat** *das* (Chemie) carbohydrate; ~**monoxid**, ~**monoxyd** /--'---/ *das* (Chemie) carbon monoxide; ~**säure** *die* carbonic acid; ~**stoff** *der* carbon
Kohle·papier *das* carbon paper
Köhler *der;* ~s, ~: charcoal burner
Kohle·zeichnung *die* charcoal drawing
Kohl-: ~**kopf** *der* [head of] cabbage; ~**rübe** *die* swede
Koitus *der;* ~, Koitus (geh.) sexual intercourse; coitus (formal)
Koje *die;* ~, ~n **(a)** (Seemannsspr.) bunk; berth
(b) (Ausstellungsstand) stand
(c) (ugs. scherzh.: Bett) bed
Kokain *das;* ~s cocaine
kokett [1] *Adj.* coquettish
[2] *adv.* coquettishly
kokettieren *itr. V.* mit etw. ~: make much play with sth.
Kokos·nuss, *Kokos·nuß *die* coconut
Koks *der;* ~es coke
Kolben *der;* ~s, ~ **(a)** (Technik) piston

(b) (Chemie: Glas~) flask
(c) (Teil des Gewehrs) butt
Kolchose /kɔlˈçoːzə/ *die;* ~, ~n kolkhoz; Soviet collective farm
Kolibri *der;* ~s, ~s hummingbird
Kolik *die;* ~, ~en colic
Kollaborateur /kolaboraˈtøːɐ̯/ *der;* ~s, ~e, **Kollaborateurin** *die;* ~, ~nen collaborator
Kollaps *der;* ~es, ~e collapse
Kolleg *das;* ~s, ~s lecture
Kollege *der;* ~n, ~n colleague
kollegial [1] *Adj.* helpful and considerate
[2] *adv.* ⟨*act etc.*⟩ like a good colleague/good colleagues
Kollegin *die;* ~, ~nen colleague
Kollegium *das;* ~s, Kollegien **(a)** (Gruppe) group; (unmittelbar zusammenarbeitend) team
(b) (Lehrkörper) [teaching] staff
Kollekte *die;* ~, ~n collection
Kollektion *die;* ~, ~en collection; (Sortiment) range
kollektiv [1] *Adj.* collective
[2] *adv.* collectively
kollidieren *itr. V.* **(a)** mit sein collide
(b) (fig.) conflict
Kollier /kɔˈli̯eː/ *das;* ~s, ~s necklace
Kollision *die;* ~, ~en collision
Köln (*das*); ~s Cologne
Kölner [1] *indekl. Adj.* Cologne *attrib.;* (in Köln) in Cologne *postpos., not pred;* ⟨*suburb, archbishop, mayor, speciality*⟩ of Cologne
[2] *der;* ~s, ~: inhabitant of Cologne; (von Geburt) native of Cologne
Kölnerin *die;* ~, ~nen ▶ KÖLNER 2
Kolonialisierung *die;* ~, ~en colonialization
Kolonialismus *der;* ~: colonialism *no art.*
Kolonie *die;* ~, ~n colony
kolonisieren *tr. V.* colonize
Kolonisierung *die;* ~, ~en colonization
Kolonne *die;* ~, ~n column
Koloss, *Koloß *der;* Kolosses, **Kolosse** (auch fig. ugs.) giant
kolossal [1] *Adj.* **(a)** colossal; gigantic
(b) (ugs.: sehr groß) tremendous (coll.); incredible (coll.) ⟨*rubbish, nonsense*⟩
[2] *adv.* (ugs.) tremendously (coll.)
Kolumbianer *der;* ~s, ~, **Kolumbianerin** *die;* ~, ~nen Colombian
Kolumbien /koˈlʊmbi̯ən/ (*das*); ~s Colombia
Kombination *die;* ~, ~en **(a)** combination
(b) (gedankliche Verknüpfung) deduction; piece of reasoning
(c) (Kleidungsstücke) ensemble; suit; (Herren~) suit
kombinieren [1] *tr. V.* combine
[2] *itr. V.* deduce; reason

Kombi-: ∼**wagen** der estate [car]; station wagon (Amer.); ∼**zange** die combination pliers pl.

Komet der; ∼en, ∼en comet

Komfort /kɔm'foːɐ̯/ der; ∼s comfort

komfortabel ①　Adj. comfortable
② adv. comfortably

Komik die; ∼: comic effect; (komisches Element) comic element

Komiker der; ∼s, ∼, **Komikerin** die ∼, ∼en (a) (Vortragskünstler[in]) comedian
(b) (Darsteller[in]) comic actor

komisch Adj. (a) comical; funny
(b) (seltsam) funny

Komitee das; ∼s, ∼s committee

Komma das; ∼s, ∼s od. ∼ta comma; (Math.) decimal point; **zwei** ∼ **acht** two point eight

Kommandant der; ∼en, ∼en (Milit.) commanding officer

Kommandeur /kɔman'døːɐ̯/ der; ∼s, ∼e (Milit.) ▶ KOMMANDANT

kommandieren ①　tr. V. (a) command; be in command of; order ⟨retreat, advance⟩
(b) (ugs.) jmdn. ∼: boss sb. about (coll.)
② itr. V. (ugs.) boss people about (coll.)

Kommanditgesellschaft die (Wirtsch.) limited partnership

Kommando das; ∼s, ∼s command

Komma-stelle die decimal place; **auf die** ∼ **[genau]** [correct] to the last decimal place; (fig.) ⟨know, calculate⟩ with complete accuracy

kommen unr. itr. V.; mit sein (a) come; **angelaufen** ∼: come running along; (auf jmdn. zu) come running up
(b) (gelangen, geraten) get; **unter ein Auto** ∼: be knocked down by a car; **wie kommst du darauf?** what gives you that idea?
(c) ∼ **lassen** (bestellen) order ⟨taxi⟩; **den Arzt/ die Polizei** ∼ **lassen** send for a doctor/the police
(d) (aufgenommen werden) **zur Schule/aufs Gymnasium** ∼: start school/grammar school
(e) (auftauchen) ⟨seeds, plants⟩ come up; ⟨buds, flowers⟩ come out; ⟨teeth⟩ come through
(f) (seinen festen Platz haben) go; belong; **in die Schublade** ∼: go or belong in the drawer; (seinen Platz erhalten) **in die Mannschaft** ∼: get into the team; **auf den ersten Platz** ∼: go into first place
(g) (Gelegenheit haben) **dazu** ∼, **etw. zu tun** get round to doing sth.
(h) (sich ereignen) come about; **wie kommt es, dass ...:** how is it that ...
(i) (etw. erlangen) **zu Geld** ∼: become wealthy; **zu Erfolg/Ruhm** ∼: gain success/fame

kommend Adj. (a) (folgend) next; **in den** ∼**en Jahren** in years to come
(b) (mit großer Zukunft) **der** ∼**e Mann/Meister** the coming man/future champion

Kommentar der; ∼s, ∼e commentary; (Stellungnahme) comment; **kein** ∼! no comment!

Kommentator der; ∼s, ∼en, **Kommentatorin** die; ∼, ∼nen commentator

kommentieren tr. V. (a) (erläutern) furnish with a commentary ⟨text, work⟩
(b) (Stellung nehmen zu) comment on

kommerziell ①　Adj. commercial
② adv. commercially

Kommiss, *Kommiß der; Kommisses (Soldatenspr.) army

Kommissar der; ∼s, ∼e, **Kommissarin** die; ∼, ∼nen (a) (Beamter/ Beamtin der Polizei) detective superintendent
(b) (staatlicher Beauftragter/staatliche Beauftragte) commissioner

Kommission die; ∼, ∼en (a) (Gremium) committee; (Prüfungs∼) commission
(b) **etw. in** ∼ **nehmen/haben/geben** (Wirtsch.) take/have sth. on commission/give sth. to a dealer for sale on commission

Kommode die; ∼, ∼n chest of drawers

kommunal Adj. local; (bei einer städtischen Gemeinde) municipal; local

Kommunal-wahl die local [government] elections pl.

Kommunikation die; ∼, ∼en (Sprachw., Soziol.) communication

Kommunion die; ∼, ∼en (kath. Kirche) [Holy] Communion

Kommuniqué /kɔmyni'keː/ das; ∼s, ∼s communiqué

Kommunismus der; ∼: communism

Kommunist der; ∼en, ∼en, **Kommunistin** die; ∼, ∼nen communist

kommunistisch ①　Adj. communist
② adv. Communist-⟨influenced, led, ruled, etc.⟩

kommunizieren itr. V. (a) (geh.) communicate
(b) (kath. Kirche) receive [Holy] Communion

Komödiant der; ∼en, ∼en, **Komödiantin** die; ∼, ∼nen (veralt.) actor/ actress; player; (abwertend: Heuchler[in]) play-actor

Komödie /ko'møːdi̯ə/ die; ∼, ∼n comedy; (Theater) comedy theatre

Kompagnon /kɔmpan'jõː/ der; ∼s, ∼s (Wirtsch.) partner; associate

kompakt Adj. solid

Kompanie die; ∼, ∼n company

Komparativ der; ∼s, ∼e (Sprachw.) comparative

Kompass, *Kompaß der; Kompasses, Kompasse compass

kompatibel Adj. (Nachrichtenw., Sprachw.) compatible

Kompatibilität die; ∼, ∼en compatibility

Kompensation die; ∼, ∼en (Wirtsch., Physik, geh.) compensation

kompensieren tr. V. etw. mit etw. od. durch etw. ∼: compensate for sth. by sth.

kompetent Adj. competent

Kompetenz *die;* ~, ~en competence; (bes. Rechtsw.) authority

komplett [1] *Adj.* complete
[2] *adv.* fully ⟨*furnished, equipped*⟩; (ugs.: ganz und gar) completely

komplettieren *tr. V.* complete

Komplett·preis *der* all-inclusive price

komplex *Adj.* complex

Komplex *der;* ~es, ~e (auch Psych.) complex

Komplexität *die;* ~: complexity

Komplikation *die;* ~, ~en (auch Med.) complication

Kompliment *das;* ~[e]s, ~e compliment

Komplize *der;* ~n, ~n (abwertend) accomplice

komplizieren *tr. V.* complicate

kompliziert [1] *Adj.* complicated
[2] *adv.* ~ aufgebaut sein have a complicated *or* complex structure

Kompliziertheit *die;* ~: complexity; complicatedness

Komplizin *die;* ~, ~nen ▶ KOMPLIZE

Komplott *das;* ~[e]s, ~e plot; conspiracy

komponieren *tr., itr. V.* compose

Komponist *der;* ~en, ~en,
  Komponistin *die;* ~, ~nen composer

Komposition *die;* ~, ~en composition

Kompost *der;* ~[e]s, ~e, compost

Kompost·haufen *der* compost heap

kompostierbar *Adj.* compostable

kompostieren *tr. V.* compost

Kompott *das;* ~[e]s, ~e stewed fruit; compote

Kompresse *die;* ~, ~n (Med.) **(a)** (Umschlag) [wet] compress
(b) (Mull) [gauze] pad

Kompression *die;* ~, ~en (Physik, Technik, Med., DV) compression

Kompressor *der;* ~s, ~en (Technik) compressor

komprimieren *tr. V.* (auch Physik, Technik, DV) compress

Kompromiss, *Kompromiß *der;* Kompromisses, Kompromisse compromise

**kompromiss-, *kompromiß-,
Kompromiss-, *Kompromiß-:**
~**bereit** *Adj.* willing to compromise *pred.;*
~**los** [1] *Adj.* uncompromising; [2] *adv.* uncompromisingly; ~**vorschlag** *der* compromise proposal

kompromittieren *tr. V.* compromise

Kondensation *die;* ~, ~en (Physik, Chemie) condensation

Kondensator *der;* ~s, ~en (Elektrot.) capacitor

kondensieren *tr., itr. V.* (*itr. auch mit sein*) (Physik, Chemie) condense

Kondens-: ~**milch** *die* condensed milk;
~**streifen** *der* condensation trail;
~**wasser** *das* condensation

Kondition *die;* ~, ~en condition; **eine gute/schlechte ~ haben** be/not be in good condition *or* shape; **keine ~ haben** be out of condition; (fig.) have no stamina

Konditional·satz *der* (Sprachw.) conditional clause

Konditions·training *das* fitness training

Konditor *der;* ~s, ~en pastry cook

Konditorei *die;* ~, ~en cake shop; (Lokal) café

kondolieren *itr. V.* offer one's condolences; jmdm. [zu jmds. Tod] ~: offer one's condolences to sb. [on sb.'s death]

Kondom *das od. der;* ~s, ~e condom

Konfekt *das;* ~[e]s **(a)** confectionery; sweets *pl.* (Brit.); candies *pl.* (Amer.)
(b) (bes. südd., österr., schweiz.: Teegebäck) [small] fancy biscuits *pl.* (Brit.) *or* (Amer.) cookies *pl.*

Konfektion *die;* ~, ~en ready-made garments *pl.*

Konferenz *die;* ~, ~en conference; (Besprechung) meeting

konferieren *itr. V.* confer (**über** + *Akk.* on, about)

Konfession *die;* ~, ~en denomination

konfessionell [1] *Adj.* denominational
[2] *adv.* as regards denomination; ~ [un]gebunden sein have [no] denominational ties

Konfetti *das;* ~[s] confetti

Konfirmand *der;* ~en, ~en,
  Konfirmandin *die;* ~, ~nen (ev. Rel.) confirmand

Konfirmation *die;* ~, ~en (ev. Rel.) confirmation

konfirmieren *tr. V.* (ev. Rel.) confirm

konfiszieren *tr. V.* (bes. Rechtsw.) confiscate

Konfitüre *die;* ~, ~n jam

Konflikt *der;* ~[e]s, ~e conflict

Konföderation *die;* ~, ~en confederation

konform *Adj.* concurring *attrib.;* ~ **gehen** be in agreement

Konformismus *der;* ~: conformism

Konformist *der;* ~en, ~en,
  Konformistin *die;* ~, ~: conformist

konformistisch [1] *Adj.* conformist
[2] *adv.* in a conformist way

Konfrontation *die;* ~, ~en confrontation

konfrontieren *tr. V.* confront

konfus [1] *Adj.* confused
[2] *adv.* in a confused fashion

Kongo[1] *der;* ~[s] (Fluss) Congo

Kongo[2] (*das*); ~s *od.* der; ~[s] (Staat) the Congo

Kongress, *Kongreß *der;* Kongresses, Kongresse congress; conference; **der ~** (USA) Congress

Kongress·halle, *Kongreß·halle *die* conference hall

König *der;* ~s, ~e king
Königin *die;* ~, ~nen queen
königlich ⟨1⟩ *Adj.* (a) royal
 (b) (vornehm) regal
 (c) (reichlich) princely ⟨*gift, salary, wage*⟩
 ⟨2⟩ *adv.* ⟨*pay*⟩ handsomely; (ugs.:
 außerordentlich) ⟨*enjoy oneself*⟩ immensely (coll.)
König·reich *das* kingdom
Königs·haus *das* royal house
Königtum *das;* ~s, Königtümer (a)
 (Monarchie) monarchy
 (b) (veralt.: Reich) kingdom
Konjugation *die;* ~, ~en (Sprachw.)
 conjugation
konjugieren *tr. V.* (Sprachw.) conjugate
Konjunktion *die;* ~, ~en (Sprachw.)
 conjunction
Konjunktiv *der;* ~s, ~e (Sprachw.)
 subjunctive
Konjunktur *die;* ~, ~en (Wirtsch.) (a)
 (wirtschaftliche Lage) [level of] economic
 activity; economy; (Tendenz) economic trend
 (b) (Hoch~) boom; (Aufschwung) upturn [in the
 economy]
konjunkturell *Adj.* economic
Konjunktur·politik *die* (Wirtsch.) measures
 pl. aimed at avoiding violent fluctuations in
 the economy
konkav (Optik) ⟨1⟩ *Adj.* concave
 ⟨2⟩ *adv.* concavely
konkret ⟨1⟩ *Adj.* concrete
 ⟨2⟩ *adv.* in concrete terms
konkretisieren *tr. V.* etw. ~: put sth. in
 concrete terms
Konkurrent *der;* ~en, ~en,
 Konkurrentin *die;* ~, ~nen (Sport,
 Wirtsch.) competitor
Konkurrenz *die;* ~, ~en (Sport, Wirtsch.)
 competition
konkurrenz-, Konkurrenz-: ~**fähig**
 Adj. competitive; ~**kampf** *der* competition;
 (zwischen zwei Menschen) rivalry
konkurrieren *itr. V.* compete
Konkurs *der;* ~es, ~e (a) (Bankrott)
 bankruptcy; ~ machen *od.* in ~ gehen go
 bankrupt
 (b) (gerichtliches Verfahren) bankruptcy
 proceedings *pl.*
können ⟨1⟩ *unr. Modalverb; 2. Part.* können:
 (a) be able to; er kann gut reden/tanzen he is
 a good talker/dancer; ich kann nicht schlafen
 I cannot *or* (coll.) can't sleep; kann das
 explodieren? could it explode?; man kann nie
 wissen you never know; es kann sein, dass
 ...: it could be that ...; kann ich Ihnen helfen?
 can I help you?
 (b) (Grund haben) du kannst ganz ruhig sein
 you don't have to worry; das kann man wohl
 sagen! you could well say that
 (c) (dürfen) kann ich gehen? can I go?; ~ wir
 mit[kommen]? can we come too?

 ⟨2⟩ *unr. tr. V.* (beherrschen) know ⟨*language*⟩;
 be able to play ⟨*game*⟩; sie kann das [gut]
 she can do that [well]; etw./nichts für etw. ~:
 be/not be responsible for sth.
 ⟨3⟩ *unr. itr. V.* (a) (fähig sein) er kann nicht
 anders there's nothing else he can do; (es ist
 seine Art) he can't help it (coll.)
 (b) (Zeit haben) ich kann heute nicht I can't
 today (coll.)
 (c) (ugs.: Kraft haben) kannst du noch [weiter]?
 can you go on?
 (d) (ugs.: umgehen ~) [gut] mit jmdm. ~: get
 on [well] with sb.
Können *das;* ~s ability
Könner *der;* ~s, ~, **Könnerin** *die;* ~,
 ~nen expert
konnte *1. u. 3. Pers. Sg. Prät. v.* KÖNNEN
könnte *1. u. 3. Pers. Sg. Konjunktiv II v.*
 KÖNNEN
Konsens·gespräch *das* (Politik)
 discussion aimed at reaching a consensus
konsequent ⟨1⟩ *Adj.* consistent; (folgerichtig)
 logical
 ⟨2⟩ *adv.* consistently; (folgerichtig) logically
Konsequenz *die;* ~, ~en (a) (Folge)
 consequence
 (b) (Unbeirrbarkeit) determination
konservativ ⟨1⟩ *Adj.* conservative
 ⟨2⟩ *adv.* conservatively
Konservative *der/die; adj. Dekl.*
 conservative
Konservatorium *das;* ~s, Konservatorien
 conservatoire; conservatory (Amer.)
Konserve *die;* ~, ~n (a) (Büchse) can; tin
 (Brit.)
 (b) (konservierte Lebensmittel) preserved food; (in
 Dosen) canned *or* (Brit.) tinned food
Konserven-: ~**büchse** *die,* ~**dose** *die*
 can; tin (Brit.)
konservieren *tr. V.* preserve; conserve
 ⟨*work of art*⟩
Konservierung *die;* ~, ~en preservation
Konservierungs·mittel *das*
 preservative
konsolidieren *tr. V.* consolidate
Konsolidierung *die;* ~, ~en (Festigung)
 consolidation
Konsonant *der;* ~en, ~en consonant
Konsortium *das;* ~s, Konsortien (Wirtsch.)
 consortium
konspirativ /kɔnspira'tiːf/ *Adj.*
 conspiratorial
konstant /kɔn'stant/ ⟨1⟩ *Adj.* (a) constant
 (b) (beharrlich) persistent
 ⟨2⟩ *adv.* (a) constantly
 (b) (beharrlich) persistently
Konstellation /kɔnstɛla'tsi̯oːn/ *die;* ~,
 ~en (a) (von Parteien usw.) grouping; (von
 Umständen) combination
 (b) (Astron., Astrol.) constellation
konstituieren /kɔnstitu'iːrən/ ⟨1⟩ *tr. V.*
 (gründen) constitute; set up
 ⟨2⟩ *refl. V.* be constituted

Konstitution /kɔnstitu'tsi̯oːn/ *die;* ~, ~en constitution

konstruieren /kɔnstru'iːrən/ *tr. V.* **(a)** (entwerfen) design
(b) (aufbauen, Geom. Sprachw.) construct
(c) (abwertend) fabricate

Konstrukteur /kɔnstrʊk'tøːɐ̯/ *der;* ~s, ~e, **Konstrukteurin** *die;* ~, ~nen designer; design engineer

Konstruktion /kɔnstrʊk'tsi̯oːn/ *die;* ~, ~en **(a)** (Aufbau, Geom., Sprachw.) construction; (das Entwerfen) designing
(b) (Entwurf) design; (Bau) construction

konstruktiv ① *Adj.* constructive
② *adv.* constructively

Konsul *der;* ~s, ~n (Dipl., hist.) consul

Konsulat *das;* ~[e]s, ~e (Dipl., hist.) consulate

Konsulin *die;* ~, ~nen ▶ KONSUL

konsultieren *tr. V.* (auch fig.) consult

Konsum *der;* ~s consumption

Konsument *der;* ~en, ~en, **Konsumentin** *die;* ~, ~nen consumer

Konsum-gesellschaft *die* consumer society

konsumieren *tr. V.* consume

Kontakt *der;* ~[e]s, ~e contact; mit *od.* zu jmdm. ~ haben/halten be/remain in contact with sb.

kontakt-, Kontakt-: ~**freudig** *Adj.* sociable; ~**linse** *die* contact lens; ~**mann** *der; Pl.:* ~männer *od.* ~leute (Agent) contact; ~**person** *die* (Med.) contact

Kontamination *die;* ~, ~en contamination

kontaminieren *tr. V.* contaminate

Konten ▶ KONTO

kontern *tr., itr. V.* (Boxen, auch fig.) counter; (Ballspiele) counter-attack

Konter·revolution *die* counter-revolution

Kontinent *der;* ~[e]s, ~e continent

kontinental *Adj.* continental

Kontingent *das;* ~[e]s, ~e quota

kontinuierlich ① *Adj.* steady
② *adv.* steadily

Kontinuität *die;* ~: continuity

Konto *das;* ~s, Konten *od.* Konti account; ein laufendes ~: a current account

Konto-: ~**auszug** *der* (Bankw.) [bank] statement; ~**bewegung** *die* transaction; ~**nummer** *die* account number

Kontor *das;* ~s, ~e branch; (einer Reederei) office

Konto·stand *der* (Bankw.) balance; state of an/one's account

kontra ① *Präp. mit Akk.* (Rechtsspr., auch fig.) versus
② *Adv.* against

Kontra *das;* ~s, ~s (Kartenspiele) double; jmdm. ~ geben (fig. ugs.) flatly contradict sb.

Kontrahent *der;* ~en, ~en, **Kontrahentin** *die;* ~, ~nen adversary; opponent

konträr *Adj.* contrary; opposite

Kontrast *der;* ~[e]s, ~e contrast

Kontroll·abschnitt *der* stub

Kontrolle *die;* ~, ~n **(a)** (Überwachung) surveillance
(b) (Überprüfung) check; (bei Waren, bei Lebensmitteln) inspection
(c) (Herrschaft) control; die ~ über etw. (*Akk.*) verlieren lose control of sth.

Kontrolleur /kɔntrɔ'løːɐ̯/ *der;* ~s, ~e, **Kontrolleurin** *die;* ~, ~nen inspector

Kontroll·gang *der* tour of inspection; (eines Nachtwächters) round; (eines Polizisten) patrol

kontrollieren *tr. V.* **(a)** (überwachen) check; monitor
(b) (überprüfen) check; inspect ⟨goods, food⟩
(c) (beherrschen) control

Kontroll·turm *der* control tower

kontrovers ① *Adj.* conflicting; (strittig) controversial
② *adv.* sich ~ zu etw. äußern express conflicting opinions on sth.

Kontroverse /kɔntro'vɛrzə/ *die;* ~, ~n controversy (um, über + *Akk.* about)

Kontur *die;* ~, ~en contour; outline

Konvention /kɔnvɛn'tsi̯oːn/ *die;* ~, ~en convention

konventionell ① *Adj.* **(a)** conventional
(b) (förmlich) formal
② *adv.* **(a)** conventionally
(b) (förmlich) formally

Konversation /kɔnvɛrza'tsi̯oːn/ *die;* ~, ~en conversation

Konversations·lexikon *das* encyclopaedia

konvertieren ① *itr. V.; auch mit sein* (Rel.) be converted
② *tr. V.* (Wirtsch., DV) convert

konvex /kɔn'vɛks/ (Optik) ① *Adj.* convex
② *adv.* convexly

Konvoi /kɔn'vɔy̯ / *der;* ~s, ~s (bes. Milit.) convoy

Konzentration *die;* ~, ~en concentration

Konzentrations-: ~**fähigkeit** *die* ability to concentrate; ~**lager** *das* (bes. ns.) concentration camp

konzentrieren *refl., tr. V.* concentrate; sich auf etw. (*Akk.*) ~: concentrate on sth.

konzentriert ① *Adj.* concentrated
② *adv.* with concentration

Konzept *das;* ~[e]s, ~e **(a)** [rough] draft
(b) (Programm) programme; (Plan) plan

Konzern *der;* ~[e]s, ~e (Wirtsch.) group [of companies]

Konzert *das;* ~[e]s, ~e **(a)** (Komposition) concerto
(b) (Veranstaltung) concert

k

Konzert·saal *der* concert hall

Konzession *die;* ~, ~en **(a)** (Amtsspr.) licence

(b) (Zugeständnis) concession

Konzil *das;* ~s, ~e *od.* ~ien (kath. Kirche) council

konzipieren *tr. V.* draft; design ⟨*device, car, etc.*⟩

Kooperation *die;* ~, ~en cooperation *no indef. art.*

kooperativ ① *Adj.* cooperative ② *adv.* cooperatively

kooperieren *tr. V.* cooperate

Koordinate *die;* ~, ~n coordinate

Koordinaten·system *das* (Math.) system of coordinates

koordinieren *tr. V.* coordinate

Kopenhagen *(das);* ~s Copenhagen

Kopf *der;* ~[e]s, Köpfe **(a)** head; **ein** ~ **Salat** a lettuce; ~ **an** ~: shoulder to shoulder; (im Wettlauf) neck and neck; (fig.) ~ **stehen** (ugs.: überrascht sein) be bowled over; **nicht wissen, wo einem der** ~ **steht** not know whether one is coming or going; ~ **hoch!** chin up!; **den** ~ **hängen lassen** become disheartened **(b)** (Person) person; **ein kluger/fähiger** ~ **sein** be a clever/able man/woman; **pro** ~: per head; **die führenden Köpfe der Wirtschaft** the leading minds in the field of economics **(c)** (Wille) **seinen** ~ **durchsetzen** make sb. do what one wants **(d)** (Verstand) mind; head; **sich** (*Dat.*) **den** ~ **zerbrechen** (ugs.) rack one's brains (**über** + *Akk.* over)

Kopf-: ~**bahnhof** *der* terminal station; ~**bedeckung** *die* headgear; **ohne** ~**bedeckung** without anything on one's head

Köpfchen *das;* ~s, ~: brains *pl.;* ~ **muss man haben** you've got to have it up here (coll.)

köpfen *tr. V.* **(a)** decapitate; (hinrichten) behead **(b)** (Fußball) head

kopf-, Kopf-: ~**ende** *das* head end; ~**haut** *die* [skin of the] scalp; ~**hörer** *der* headphones *pl.;* ~**kissen** *das* pillow; ~**lastig** *Adj.* down by the head *pred.;* ~**los** ① *Adj.* rash; (in Panik) panic-stricken; ② *adv.* rashly; ~**los davonrennen** flee in panic; ~**rechnen** *itr. V.; nur im Inf. gebr.* do mental arithmetic; ~**rechnen** *das* mental arithmetic; ~**salat** *der* head lettuce; ~**schmerz** *der* headache; ~**schmerzen haben** have a headache *sing.;* ~**sprung** *der* header; ~**stand** *der* headstand; ***~|**stehen** ▶ KOPF A; ~**stein·pflaster** *das* cobblestones *pl.;* ~**tuch** *das; Pl.* ~**tücher** headscarf; ~**weh** *das* (ugs.) headache; ~**weh haben** have a headache; ~**zerbrechen** *das;* ~s: etw. bereitet *od.*

macht jmdm. ~**zerbrechen** sb. has to rack his/her brains about sth.; (etw. macht jmdm. Sorgen) sth. is a worry to sb.

Kopie *die;* ~, ~n copy; (Durchschrift) carbon copy; (Fotokopie) photocopy; (Fot., Film) print

kopieren *tr. V.* copy; (fotokopieren) photocopy; (Fot., Film) print

Kopierer *der;* ~s, ~: [photo]copier

Kopier·gerät *das* photocopier

Kopilot *der;* ~en, ~en, **Kopilotin** *die;* ~, ~nen (Flugw.) co-pilot

Koppel[1] *das;* ~s, ~, *österr.: die;* ~, ~n (Gürtel) [leather] belt (*as part of a uniform*)

Koppel[2] *die;* ~, ~n paddock

koppeln *tr. V.* couple (**an** + *Akk.* to); dock ⟨*spacecraft*⟩

Koppelung ▶ KOPPLUNG

Kopplung *die;* ~, ~en coupling; (Raumf.) docking

kopulieren *itr. V.* copulate

Koralle *die;* ~, ~n coral

Koran *der;* ~s, ~e Koran

Korb *der;* ~es, Körbe **(a)** basket **(b)** jmdm. einen ~ **geben** turn sb. down

Korb·ball *der* netball

Kord *der;* ~[e]s **(a)** corduroy; cord **(b)** ▶ KORDSAMT

Kordel *die;* ~, ~n cord

Kord·samt *der* cord velvet

Korea *(das);* ~s Korea

Koreaner *der;* ~s, ~, **Koreanerin** *die;* ~, ~nen Korean

koreanisch *Adj.* Korean

Korinthe *die;* ~, ~n currant

Kork *der;* ~s, ~e cork

Korken *der;* ~s, ~: cork

Korken·zieher *der;* ~s, ~: corkscrew

Korn[1] *das;* ~[e]s, Körner **(a)** (Frucht) grain; (Getreide~) grain [of corn]; (Pfeffer~) corn **(b)** *o. Pl.* (Getreide) corn; grain **(c)** (Salz~, Sand~) grain; (Hagel~) stone

Korn[2] *der;* ~[e]s, ~ (ugs.) corn schnapps; corn liquor (Amer.)

Korn·blume *die* cornflower

Körnchen *das;* ~s, ~: tiny grain; (von Sand usw.) [tiny] grain; granule

Körner ▶ KORN

Korn·feld *das* cornfield

körnig *Adj.* granular

Korona *die;* ~, Koronen crowd (coll.)

Körper *der;* ~s, ~: body

körper-, Körper-: ~**bau** *der* physique; ~**behindert** *Adj.* physically handicapped; ~**behinderte** *der/die* physically handicapped person; ~**behinderte** *Pl.* physically handicapped people; ~**geruch** *der* body odour; BO (coll.); ~**größe** *die* height

körperlich ① *Adj.* physical ② *adv.* physically

Körper·pflege *die* body care *no art.*

**old spelling - see note on page xiv

Körperschaft[s]·steuer *die* (Steuerw.) corporation tax

Körper-: ~**spray** *der od. das* deodorant spray; ~**teil** *der* part of the/one's body; ~**verletzung** *die* (Rechtsw.) bodily harm *no indef. art.*

Korps /koːɐ̯/ *das;* ~ /koːɐ̯(s),/ ~ /koːɐ̯s/ **(a)** (Milit.) corps
(b) (Studentenverbindung) student duelling society

korpulent *Adj.* corpulent

korrekt [1] *Adj.* correct
[2] *adv.* correctly

korrekter·weise *Adv.* to be [strictly] correct

Korrektheit *die;* ~: correctness

Korrektor *der;* ~s, ~en /-ˈtoːrən/, **Korrektorin** *die;* ~, ~nen proof-reader

Korrektur *die;* ~, ~en correction

Korrespondent *der;* ~en, ~en, **Korrespondentin** *die;* ~, ~nen correspondent

Korrespondenz *die;* ~, ~en correspondence

korrespondieren *itr. V.* correspond (mit with)

Korridor *der;* ~s, ~e corridor

korrigieren *tr. V.* correct; revise ⟨opinion, view⟩

korrodieren *tr., itr. V.* (*itr. mit sein*) (bes. Chemie, Geol.) corrode

Korrosion *die;* ~, ~en (auch Geol., Med.) corrosion

korrosions-, Korrosions-: ~**beständig** *Adj.,* ~**fest** *Adj.* corrosion-resistant; ~**schutz** *der* protection against corrosion

korrupt *Adj.* corrupt

Korruption *die;* ~, ~en corruption

Korsett *das;* ~s, ~s *od.* ~e corset

Korsika (*das*) ~s Corsica

Kortison *das;* ~s (Med.) cortisone

koscher *Adj.* kosher

Kose-: ~**form** *die* familiar form; ~**name** *der* pet name

Kosinus *der;* ~, ~ *od.* ~se (Math.) cosine

Kosmetik *die;* ~ **(a)** beauty culture *no art.;*
(b) (fig.) cosmetic procedures *pl.*

Kosmetikerin *die;* ~, ~nen cosmetician; beautician

Kosmetikum *das;* ~s, Kosmetika cosmetic

kosmetisch [1] *Adj.* (auch fig.) cosmetic
[2] *adv.* jmdn. ~ beraten give sb. advice on beauty care; **sich** ~ **behandeln lassen** have beauty treatment

kosmisch *Adj.* cosmic ⟨ray, dust, etc.⟩; space ⟨age, station, research, etc.⟩; meteoric ⟨iron⟩

Kosmos *der;* ~: cosmos

Kost *die;* ~: food; ~ **und Logis** board and lodging

kostbar [1] *Adj.* valuable; precious ⟨time⟩
[2] *adv.* expensively ⟨dressed⟩; luxuriously ⟨decorated⟩

Kostbarkeit *die;* ~, ~en **(a)** (Sache) treasure
(b) (Eigenschaft) value

kosten¹ [1] *tr. V.* taste; try
[2] *itr. V.* (probieren) have a taste

kosten² *tr. V.* **(a)** cost
(b) (erfordern) take; cost ⟨lives⟩

Kosten *Pl.* cost *sing.;* costs; (Auslagen) expenses; (Rechtsw.) costs; **auf jmds.** ~: at sb.'s expense

kosten-, Kosten-: ~**deckend** *Adj.* that covers/cover [one's] costs *postpos., not pred.;* ~**erstattung** *die* reimbursement of costs; ~**los** [1] *Adj.* free; [2] *adv.* free of charge; ~**pflichtig** (Rechtsw.) [1] *Adj.* eine ~pflichtige Verwarnung a fine and a caution; [2] *adv.* eine Klage ~pflichtig abweisen dismiss a case with costs; **ein Auto** ~pflichtig abschleppen tow a car away at the owner's expense; ~**punkt** *der* (ugs.) ~punkt? how much is it/are they?; ~punkt 25 Euro it costs/they cost 25 euros; ~**stelle** *die* (Wirtsch.) cost centre; ~**vor·anschlag** *der* estimate

Kost·gänger *der;* ~s, ~, **Kost·gängerin** *die;* ~, ~nen (veralt.) boarder

köstlich [1] *Adj.* delicious; (unterhaltsam) delightful
[2] *adv.* ⟨taste⟩ delicious; **sich** ~ amüsieren/unterhalten enjoy oneself enormously (coll.)

Köstlichkeit *die;* ~, ~en (Sache) delicacy

Kost·probe *die;* ~, ~n taste

kost·spielig *Adj.* costly

Kostüm *das;* ~s, ~e **(a)** suit
(b) (Theater~, Verkleidung) costume

kostümieren *tr. V.* dress up

Kot *der;* ~[e]s, ~e excrement

Kotangens *der;* ~, ~ (Math.) cotangent

Kotelett /kɔtˈlɛt/ *das;* ~s, ~s chop; (vom Nacken) cutlet

Koteletten *Pl.* side whiskers

Köter *der;* ~s, ~ (abwertend) cur

Kot·flügel *der* (Kfz-W.) wing

kotzen *itr. V.* (derb) puke (coarse)

KP *Abk.* = **Kommunistische Partei** CP

Krabbe *die;* ~, ~n **(a)** (Zool.) crab
(b) (ugs.: Garnele) shrimp; (größer) prawn

krabbeln [1] *itr. V.; mit sein* crawl
[2] *tr. V.* (ugs.: kraulen) tickle

Krach *der;* ~[e]s, Kräche **(a)** (Lärm) noise; row
(b) (lautes Geräusch) crash
(c) (ugs.: Streit) row

krachen [1] *itr. V.* **(a)** (Krach auslösen) ⟨thunder⟩ crash; ⟨shot⟩ ring out ⋯

(b) *mit sein* (ugs.: bersten) ⟨ice⟩ crack; ⟨bed⟩ collapse
(c) *mit sein* (ugs.: mit Krach auftreffen) crash
[2] *refl. V.* (ugs.) row (coll.)
krächzen *itr. V.* ⟨raven, crow⟩ caw; ⟨parrot⟩ squawk; ⟨person⟩ croak
kraft *Präp. + Gen.* (Amtsspr.) ~ [meines] Amtes by virtue of my office; ~ **Gesetzes** by law
Kraft *die;* ~, **Kräfte** strength; (Wirksamkeit) power; (Physik) force; (Arbeits~) employee; **mit letzter** ~: with one's last ounce of strength; **aus eigener** ~: by one's own efforts; **mit vereinten Kräften werden wir ...**: if we join forces *or* combine our efforts we will ...; **außer** ~ **setzen** repeal ⟨law⟩; countermand ⟨order⟩; **außer** ~ **sein/treten** no longer be/ cease to be in force; **in** ~ **treten/sein/bleiben** come into/be in/remain in force
Kraft-: ~**aufwand** *der* effort; ~**brühe** *die* strong meat broth; ~**fahrer** *der*, ~**fahrerin** *die* driver; motorist;
Kraft·fahrzeug *das* motor vehicle
Kraftfahrzeug-: ~**brief** *der* vehicle registration document; logbook (Brit.); ~**schein** *der* vehicle registration document; ~**steuer** *die* vehicle tax
kräftig [1] *Adj.* strong, vigorous ⟨plant, shoot⟩; powerful, hefty ⟨blow, kick, etc.⟩; nourishing ⟨soup, bread, meal, etc.⟩ [2] *adv.* powerfully ⟨built⟩; ⟨rain, snow⟩ heavily; ⟨eat⟩ heartily
kräftigen *tr. V.* ⟨holiday, air, etc.⟩ invigorate; ⟨food etc.⟩ fortify
kraft-, Kraft-: ~**meier** *der;* ~~s, ~~ (ugs.: abwertend) muscleman; ~**probe** *die* trial of strength; ~**rad** *das* (Amtsspr.) motorcycle; ~**stoff** *der* (Kfz-W.) fuel; ~**stoff·verbrauch** *der* fuel consumption; ~**voll** [1] *Adj.* powerful; [2] *adv.* powerfully; ~**wagen** *der* motor vehicle; ~**werk** *das* power station
Kragen *der;* ~s, ~, (südd., österr. u. schweiz. auch:) **Krägen** collar
Kragen·weite *die* collar size
Krähe /ˈkrɛːə/ *die;* ~, ~n crow
krähen *itr. V.* (auch fig.) crow
Krähen·füße *Pl.* (ugs.) crow's feet
krakeelen *itr. V.* (ugs.) kick up a row (coll.)
krakeln *tr., itr. V.* (ugs.) scrawl
kraklig *Adj.* (ugs. abwertend) scrawly
Kralle *die;* ~, ~n claw
krallen [1] *refl. V.* **sich an etw.** (Akk.) ~ ⟨cat⟩ dig its claws into sth.; ⟨person⟩ clutch sth. [tightly] [2] *tr. V.* (fest greifen) **die Finger in/um etw.** (Akk.) ~: dig one's fingers into sth./clutch sth. [tightly] with one's fingers
Kram *der;* ~[e]s (ugs.) **(a)** stuff; (Gerümpel) junk **(b)** ⟨Angelegenheit⟩ affair

kramen [1] *itr. V.* **in etw.** (Dat.) ~: rummage about in sth. [2] *tr. V.* (ugs.) **etw. aus etw.** ~: fish (coll.) sth. out of sth.
Krämer *der;* ~s, ~, **Krämerin** *die;* ~, ~nen grocer
Kram·laden *der* (ugs. abwertend) junk shop
Krampf *der;* ~[e]s, **Krämpfe (a)** cramp; (Zuckung) spasm **(b)** (painful strain; (sinnloses Tun) senseless waste of effort
Krampf·ader *die* varicose vein
krampfhaft [1] *Adj.* convulsive; (verbissen) desperate [2] *adv.* convulsively; (verbissen) desperately
Kran *der;* ~[e]s, **Kräne (a)** crane **(b)** (südwestd.: Wasserhahn) tap; faucet (Amer.)
Kranich *der;* ~s, ~e crane
krank; **kränker, kränkst...** *Adj.* ill *usu. pred.*; sick; bad ⟨leg, tooth⟩; diseased ⟨plant, organ⟩; (fig.) ailing ⟨economy, business⟩; ~ **werden** be taken ill
Kranke *der/die; adj. Dekl.* sick man/woman; (Patient) patient
kränkeln *itr. V.* be in poor health
kränken *tr. V.* **jmdn.** ~: hurt sb. *or* sb.'s feelings
Kranken-: ~**geld** *das* sickness benefit; ~**gymnastik** *die* remedial *or* medical gymnastics *sing.*; physiotherapy; ~**gymnastin** *die;* ~~, ~~nen remedial gymnast; medical gymnast; physiotherapist; ~**haus** *das* hospital; ~**kasse** *die* health insurance scheme; (Körperschaft) health insurance institution; (privat) health insurance company; ~**pfleger** *der* male nurse; ~**schein** *der* health insurance certificate; ~**schwester** *die* nurse; ~**versicherung** *die* **(a)** (Versicherung) health insurance; **(b)** (Unternehmen) health insurance company; ~**wagen** *der* ambulance
kränker ▸ KRANK
krank|feiern *itr. V.* (ugs.) skive off work (coll.) [pretending to be ill]
krankhaft [1] *Adj.* pathological; morbid ⟨growth, state, swelling, etc.⟩ [2] *adv.* pathologically; morbidly ⟨swollen, sensitive⟩
Krankheit *die;* ~, ~en **(a)** illness; (bestimmte Art, von Pflanzen, Organen) disease **(b)** (Zeit des Krankseins) illness
Krankheits·erreger *der* pathogen
kränklich *Adj.* ailing
krank|schreiben *tr. V.* give ⟨person⟩ a medical certificate
kränkst... ▸ KRANK
Kränkung *die;* ~, ~en: **eine** ~: an injury to one's/sb.'s feelings
Kranz *der;* ~es, **Kränze** wreath; garland; (auf einem Grab usw.) wreath
Kränzchen *das;* ~s, ~: coffee circle; coffee klatch (Amer.)

Krapfen *der;* ~s, ~: doughnut

krass, *****kraß** [1] *Adj.* blatant ⟨*case*⟩;
flagrant ⟨*injustice*⟩; stark ⟨*contrast*⟩;
complete ⟨*contradiction*⟩; sharp ⟨*difference*⟩;
out-and-out ⟨*egoist*⟩
[2] *adv.* sich ~ ausdrücken put sth. bluntly;
sich von etw. ~ unterscheiden be in stark
contrast to sth

Krater *der;* ~s, ~: crater

Kratz·bürste *die* (ugs. scherzh.) prickly so-
and-so

kratzen [1] *tr. V.* scratch; (entfernen) scrape
[2] *itr. V.* (a) scratch
(b) (jucken) itch

Kratzer *der;* ~s, ~ (ugs.) scratch

kratzig *Adj.* itchy ⟨*material*⟩

Kraul *das;* ~s (Sport) crawl

kraulen[1] [1] *itr. V.* do the crawl
[2] *tr. V.; auch mit sein* eine Strecke ~: cover
a distance using the crawl

kraulen[2] *tr. V.* jmdm. das Kinn ~: tickle
sb. under the chin; jmdn. in den Haaren ~:
run one's fingers through sb.'s hair

kraus *Adj.* creased ⟨*skirt etc.*⟩; frizzy ⟨*hair*⟩

Krause *die;* ~, ~n (Kragen) ruff; (am Ärmel)
ruffle

kräuseln [1] *tr. V.* ruffle ⟨*water, surface*⟩;
gather ⟨*material etc.*⟩; frizz ⟨*hair*⟩
[2] *refl. V.* ⟨*hair*⟩ go frizzy; ⟨*water*⟩ ripple;
⟨*smoke*⟩ curl up

Kraut *das;* ~[e]s, **Kräuter (a)** herb
(b) (bes. südd., österr.: Kohl) cabbage

Kraut·salat *der* coleslaw

Krawall *der;* ~s, ~e (a) riot
(b) (ugs.: Lärm) row (coll.)

Krawatte *die;* ~, ~n tie

kraxeln *itr. V.; mit sein* (bes. südd., österr.
ugs.) climb; (mit Mühe) clamber

kreativ [1] *Adj.* creative
[2] *adv.* ~ veranlagt sein have a creative
bent

Kreativität *die;* ~: creativity

Kreatur *die;* ~, ~en creature

Krebs *der;* ~es, ~e (a) crustacean; (Fluss~)
crayfish; (Krabbe) crab
(b) (Krankheit) cancer
(c) (Astrol.) Cancer; the Crab

krebs-, Krebs-: ~ **erregend**,
~**erzeugend** *Adj.* carcinogenic;
~**forschung** *die* cancer research;
~**geschwulst** *die* cancerous growth *or*
tumour; ~**geschwür** *das* (volkst.)
cancerous ulcer; (fig. geh.) cancer; ~**krank**
Adj. ~krank sein have cancer; ~**rot** *Adj.* as
red as a lobster *postpos.*

Kredit *der;* ~[e]s, ~e credit; (Darlehen) loan

kredit-, Kredit-: ~**institut** *das* credit
institution; ~**karte** *die* credit card; mit
~karte bezahlen pay by credit card;
~**nehmer** *der;* ~s, ~, ~, ~**nehmerin**
die; ~~, ~~nen borrower; ~**würdig** *Adj.*
(Finanzw.) creditworthy

Kreide *die;* ~, ~n chalk

kreide·bleich *Adj.* as white as a sheet
postpos.

Kreide·felsen *der* chalk cliff

kreieren /kre'i:rən/ *tr. V.* create

Kreis *der;* ~es, ~e circle; (Verwaltungsbezirk)
district; (Wahl~) ward

Kreis·bahn *die* orbit

kreischen *itr. V.* screech; ⟨*door*⟩ creak

Kreisel *der;* ~s, ~ (Kinderspielzeug) top; (ugs.:
Kreisverkehr) roundabout

kreisen *itr. V.; auch mit sein* ⟨*planet*⟩
revolve (um around); ⟨*satellite etc.*⟩ orbit;
⟨*aircraft, bird*⟩ circle

kreis-, Kreis-: ~**förmig** *Adj.* circular;
~**lauf** *der* (Physiol.) circulation; (der Natur, des
Lebens usw.) cycle; ~**lauf·störungen** *Pl.*
(Med.) circulatory trouble *sing.;* ~**rund** *Adj.*
[perfectly] round; ~**säge** *die* circular
saw

Kreiß·saal *der* (Med.) delivery room

Kreis-: ~**stadt** *die* chief town of a/the
district; ~**verkehr** *der* roundabout

Krem *die;* ~, ~s ▶ CREME

Krematorium *das;* ~s, **Krematorien**
crematorium

Krempe *die;* ~, ~n brim

Krempel *der;* ~s (ugs. abwertend) stuff;
(Gerümpel) junk

krepieren *itr. V.; mit sein* (salopp) ⟨*person*⟩
snuff it (sl.)

Krepp *der;* ~s, ~s *od.* ~e crêpe

*****Kreppapier** *das,* **Krepp·papier** *das*
crêpe paper

Kresse *die;* ~, ~n (Bot.) cress

Kreta (*das*) ~s Crete

Kreuz *das;* ~es, ~e (a) cross; (Kreuzzeichen)
sign of the cross
(b) (Teil des Rückens) small of the back; jmdn.
aufs ~ legen (salopp) take sb. for a ride (coll.)
(c) (Kartenspiel) (Farbe) clubs *pl.;* (Karte) club
(d) (Autobahn) interchange
(e) (Musik) sharp

kreuzen [1] *tr. V.* (auch Biol.) cross
[2] *refl. V.* (a) (überschneiden) cross
(b) (zuwiderlaufen) clash (mit with)
[3] *itr. V.; mit haben od. sein* (fahren) cruise

Kreuz-: ~**fahrer** *der* (hist.) crusader;
~**fahrt** *die* cruise; ~**feuer** *das* (Milit., auch
fig.) crossfire; ~**gang** *der* cloister

kreuzigen *tr. V.* crucify

Kreuzigung *die;* ~, ~en crucifixion

Kreuz-: ~**otter** *die* adder; [common]
viper; ~**ritter** *der* (hist.) crusader;
~**schlitz·schraube** *die* Phillips
screw ®; ~**schmerzen** *Pl.* pain *sing.* in
the small of the back; ~**spinne** *die* cross
spider; garden spider

Kreuzung *die;* ~, ~en (a) crossroads *sing.*
(b) (Biol.) crossing; cross-breeding; (Ergebnis)
cross

kreuz-, Kreuz-: ~**verhör** *das* cross- ⋯✦

examination; ~**weise** *Adv.* crosswise;
~**wort·rätsel** *das* crossword [puzzle];
~**zug** *der* (hist., fig.) crusade

kribbelig *Adj.* (ugs.) (vor Ungeduld) fidgety;
(nervös) edgy

kribbeln *itr. V.* (jucken) tickle; (prickeln)
tingle

kriechen *unr. itr. V.* **(a)** *mit sein* ⟨insect,
baby⟩ crawl; ⟨plant⟩ creep; ⟨person, animal⟩
creep, crawl
(b) *auch mit sein* (fig. abwertend) crawl (**vor** +
Dat. to)

Kriecher *der;* ~s, ~, **Kriecherin** *die;* ~,
~nen (abwertend) crawler

Kriech·spur *die* (Verkehrsw.) crawler lane

Krieg *der;* ~[e]s, ~e war; ~ **führend**
warring; belligerent

kriegen *tr. V.* (ugs.) get; (erreichen) catch
⟨train, bus, etc.⟩

Krieger *der;* ~s, ~, **Kriegerin** *die;* ~,
~nen warrior

kriegerisch *Adj.* **(a)** (kampflustig) warlike
(b) (militärisch) military; **eine** ~**e**
Auseinandersetzung an armed conflict

****krieg·führend** ▶ KRIEG

kriegs-, Kriegs-: ~**beil** *das* tomahawk;
das ~**beil begraben** (scherzh.) bury the
hatchet; ~**bemalung** *die* (Völkerk.)
warpaint; ~**beschädigt** *Adj.* war-
disabled; ~**beschädigte** *der/die; adj.*
Dekl. war invalid; ~**dienst** *der* **(a)** (im
Krieg) active service; **(b)** (Wehrdienst) military
service; **den** ~**dienst verweigern** be a
conscientious objector;
~**dienst·verweigerer** *der* conscientious
objector; ~**ende** *das* end of the war; **bei/**
vor ~**ende** at/before the end of the war;
~**erklärung** *die* declaration of war;
~**gefangene** *der* prisoner of war; POW;
~**gefangenschaft** *die* captivity;
~**opfer** *das* war victim; ~**schiff** *das*
warship; ~**verbrechen** *das* (Rechtsw.) war
crime; ~**verbrecher** *der,*
~**verbrecherin** *die* war criminal;
~**waise** *die* war orphan

Krimi *der;* ~[s], ~[s] (ugs.) crime thriller

Kriminal·beamte *der,*
Kriminal·beamtin *die* [plain-clothes]
detective

kriminalisieren *tr. V.* jmdn. ~: make sb.
turn to crime

kriminalistisch ① *Adj.* ⟨methods,
practice⟩ of criminalistics; ⟨abilities⟩ in the
field of criminalistics
② *adv.* ⟨proceed etc.⟩ using the methods of
criminalistics

Kriminalität *die;* ~: crime *no art.*

Kriminal-: ~**polizei** *die* criminal
investigation department; ~**roman** *der*
crime novel; (mit Detektiv als Held) detective
novel

kriminell ① *Adj.* criminal
② *adv.* ~ **veranlagt sein** have criminal
tendencies; ~ **handeln** act illegally

Kriminelle *der/die; adj. Dekl.* criminal

Krimskrams *der;* ~[es] (ugs.) stuff

Kringel *der;* ~s, ~ (Kreis) [small] ring;
(Kritzelei) round squiggle; (Gebäck) [ring-
shaped] biscuit

kringeln *refl. V.* curl [up]; ⟨hair⟩ go curly;
sich ~ [**vor Lachen**] (ugs.) kill oneself
[laughing] (coll.)

Kripo *die;* ~ (ugs.) **die** ~: ≈ the CID

Krippe *die;* ~, ~n **(a)** (Futtertrog) manger;
crib
(b) (Weihnachts~) model of a nativity scene
(c) (Kinder~) crèche

Krise *die;* ~, ~n (auch Med.) crisis

kriseln *itr. V.* (unpers.) **es kriselt in ihrer**
Ehe/in der Partei their marriage is in
trouble/the party is in a state of crisis

Krisen-: ~**gebiet** *das* crisis area; ~**herd**
der trouble spot

Kristall[1] /krɪs'tal/ *der;* ~s, ~e crystal

Kristall[2] *das;* ~s crystal *no indef. art.*

Kristallisation *die;* ~, ~en (bes. Chemie)
crystallization

kristallisieren *itr. V.* (bes. Chemie)
crystallize

Kriterium *das;* ~s, Kriterien criterion

Kritik *die;* ~, ~en **(a)** criticism *no indef.*
art. (**an** + *Dat.* of); **an jmdm./etw.** ~ **üben**
criticize sb./sth.
(b) (Besprechung) review

Kritiker *der;* ~s, ~, **Kritikerin** *die;* ~,
~nen critic

kritik·los ① *Adj.* uncritical
② *adv.* uncritically

kritisch ① *Adj.* critical
② *adv.* critically

kritisieren *tr. V.* criticize; review ⟨book,
play, etc.⟩

kritzeln ① *itr. V.* (schreiben) scribble;
(zeichnen) doodle
② *tr. V.* scribble

Kroatien /kro'a:tsjən/ (das); ~s Croatia

kroatisch *Adj.* Croatian

kroch *1. u. 3. Pers. Sg. Prät. v.* KRIECHEN

Krokant *der;* ~s praline

Krokette *die;* ~, ~n (Kochk.) croquette

Krokodil *das;* ~s, ~e crocodile

Krokodils·tränen *Pl.* (ugs.) crocodile
tears

Krokus *der;* ~, ~ *od.* ~se crocus

Krone *die;* ~, ~n crown; (eines Baumes) top;
crown; (einer Welle) crest; **die** ~ **der**
Schöpfung the pride of creation

krönen *tr. V.* (auch fig.) crown

Kronen·korken *der* crown cork

Kron-: ~**juwelen** *Pl.* Crown jewels;

**old spelling - see note on page xiv

~**leuchter** der chandelier; ~**prinz** der crown prince; ~**prinzessin** die crown princess

Krönung die; ~, ~en coronation; (fig.) culmination

Kron·zeuge der, **Kron·zeugin** die (Rechtsw.) person who turns Queen's/King's evidence; **als** ~ **auftreten** turn Queen's/ King's evidence

Kropf der; ~[e]s, Kröpfe (Med.) goitre

Kröte die; ~, ~n (a) toad
(b) Pl. (salopp: Geld) **ein paar/eine ganze Menge** ~**n verdienen** earn a few bob (Brit. coll.)/a fair old whack (coll.)

Krücke die; ~, ~n crutch

Krück·stock der walking stick

Krug der; ~[e]s, Krüge jug; (größer) pitcher; (Bier~) mug

Krume die; ~, ~n crumb

Krümel der; ~s, ~: crumb

krümeln itr. V. (a) crumble
(b) (Krümel machen) make crumbs

krumm ① Adj. (a) bent ⟨nail, back⟩; crooked ⟨stick, branch, etc.⟩; bandy ⟨legs⟩; **sich über etw.** (Akk.) ~ **lachen** (ugs.) fall about laughing over sth.
(b) (ugs.: unrechtmäßig) crooked
(c) etw. ~ **nehmen** (ugs.) take sth. the wrong way
② adv. crookedly

krümmen ① tr. V. bend
② refl. V. (a) (sich winden) writhe
(b) (krumm verlaufen) ⟨road, path, river⟩ bend

krumm-: *~|**lachen** ▶ KRUMM 1A; *~|**nehmen** ▶ KRUMM 1C

Krümmung die; ~, ~en bend

Krüppel der; ~s, ~: cripple

Kruste die; ~, ~n crust; (vom Braten) crisp

Kruzifix das; ~es, ~e crucifix

Krypta die; ~, Krypten (Archit.) crypt

Kuba (das); ~s Cuba

Kubaner der; ~s, ~, **Kubanerin** die; ~, ~nen Cuban

Kübel der; ~s, ~: pail

Kubik- cubic ⟨metre, foot, etc.⟩

Küche die; ~, ~n kitchen; (Einrichtung) kitchen furniture no indef. art.; (Kochk.) cooking; cuisine; **kalte/warme** ~: cold/hot food

Kuchen der; ~s, ~: cake; (Obst~) flan; (Torte) gateau

Küchen-: ~**abfälle** Pl. kitchen scraps; ~**chef** der, ~**chefin** die chef

Kuchen-: ~**form** die cake tin; ~**gabel** die pastry fork

Küchen-: ~**gerät** das kitchen utensil; (als Kollektivum) kitchen utensils pl.; ~**maschine** die food processor; ~**meister** der, ~**meisterin** die chef; ~**messer** das kitchen knife; ~**schabe** die cockroach; ~**schrank** der kitchen cupboard; ~**tisch** der kitchen table

Kuckuck der; ~s, ~e (a) cuckoo; **zum** ~ [noch mal]! (salopp) for crying out loud! (coll.)
(b) (scherzh.: Pfandsiegel) bailiff's seal (placed on distrained goods)

Kuckucks·uhr die cuckoo clock

Kufe die; ~, ~n runner; (von Flugzeugen, Hubschraubern) skid

Kugel die; ~, ~n (a) ball; (Geom.) sphere; (Kegeln) bowl; (beim Kugelstoßen) shot
(b) (ugs.: Geschoss) bullet

Kugel·lager das (Technik) ball bearing

kugeln ① tr. V. roll
② refl. V. sich [vor Lachen] ~ (ugs.) double or roll up [laughing]

kugel-, Kugel-: ~**rund** /-'-'/ Adj. round as a ball postpos.; (scherzh.: dick) rotund; tubby; ~**schreiber** der ball pen; Biro ®; ~**sicher** Adj. bulletproof; ~**stoßen** das; ~~s shot[-put]; (Disziplin) putting the shot no art.

Kuh die; ~, Kühe cow

Kuh-: ~**fladen** der cowpat; ~**handel** der (ugs. abwertend) shady horse-trading no indef. art.; **ein** ~**handel** a bit of shady horse-trading; ~**haut** die: **das geht auf keine** ~**haut** (fig. salopp) it's absolutely staggering

kühl ① Adj. cool; etw. ~ **lagern** keep sth. in a cool place
② adv. coolly

Kuhle die; ~, ~n (ugs.) hollow

Kühle die; ~: coolness

kühlen ① tr. V. cool; chill ⟨wine⟩; refrigerate ⟨food⟩
② itr. V. ⟨cold compress, ointment, breeze, etc.⟩ have a cooling effect

Kühler der; ~s, ~e (a) (am Auto) radiator; (Kühlerhaube) bonnet (Brit.); hood (Amer.)
(b) (Sekt~) ice bucket

Kühler·haube die bonnet (Brit.); hood (Amer.)

Kühl-: ~**fach** das frozen food compartment; ~**haus** das cold store; ~**raum** der cold store; cold-storage room; ~**schrank** der refrigerator; fridge (Brit. coll.); icebox (Amer.); ~**truhe** die [chest] freezer; (im Lebensmittelgeschäft) freezer [cabinet]

Kühlung die; ~, ~en cooling; (Vorrichtung) cooling system; (für Lebensmittel) refrigeration system

Kühl·wasser das cooling water

kühn ① Adj. bold; (dreist) audacious
② adv. boldly; (gewagt) daringly; (dreist) audaciously

Kühnheit die; ~: boldness; (Gewagtheit) daringness; (Dreistigkeit) audacity

Kuh·stall der cowshed

Küken das; ~s, ~: chick

kulant Adj. obliging; fair ⟨terms⟩

Kulanz die; ~: willingness to oblige

Kuli der; ~s, ~s (a) coolie
(b) (ugs.) ballpoint; Biro ®

k

kulinarisch *Adj.* culinary

Kulisse *die;* ~, ~n piece of scenery; flat; (Hintergrund) backdrop; **die** ~n the scenery *sing.;* **hinter den** ~n (fig.) behind the scenes

kullern (ugs.) *itr. V. mit sein* roll

Kult *der;* ~[e]s, ~e (auch fig.) cult

Kult·film *der* cult film

kultivieren *tr. V.* (auch fig.) cultivate

kultiviert [1] *Adj.* cultured; (vornehm) refined
[2] *adv.* in a cultured manner; (vornehm) in a refined manner

Kultur *die;* ~, ~en **(a)** culture; (kultivierte Lebensart) refinement; **ein Mensch von** ~: a cultured person
(b) (Zivilisation, Lebensform) civilization

Kultur-: ~**abkommen** *das* cultural agreement; ~**austausch** *der* cultural exchange; ~**beutel** *der* sponge bag (Brit.); toilet bag

kulturell [1] *Adj.* cultural
[2] *adv.* culturally

Kultur-: ~**film** *der* documentary film; ~**geschichte** *die* history of civilization; (einer bestimmten Kultur) cultural history; ~**politik** *die* cultural and educational policy

Kultus·minister *der,*
Kultus·ministerin *die* minister for education and cultural affairs

Kümmel *der;* ~s, ~: caraway [seed]; (Branntwein) kümmel

Kummer *der;* ~s sorrow; grief; (Ärger, Sorgen) trouble; ~ **um** *od.* **über jmdn.** grief for sb.; **jmdm.** ~ **machen** give sb. trouble

kümmerlich *Adj.* **(a)** (schwächlich) puny; stunted ⟨*vegetation, plants*⟩
(b) (ärmlich) wretched; miserable
(c) (abwertend: gering) miserable; meagre ⟨*knowledge, leftovers*⟩

kümmern [1] *refl. V.* **(a)** sich um jmdn./etw. ~: take care of sb./sth.
(b) (sich befassen mit) **sich nicht um Politik** ~: not be interested in politics
[2] *tr. V.* concern

Kumpan *der;* ~s, ~e, **Kumpanin** *die;* ~, ~nen (ugs.) **(a)** pal (coll.); buddy (coll.)
(b) (abwertend: Mittäter[in]) accomplice

Kumpel *der;* ~s, ~ **(a)** (Bergmannsspr.) miner
(b) (salopp: Kamerad) pal (coll.); buddy (coll.)

Kumulus·wolke *die* (Met.) cumulus cloud

kündbar *Adj.* terminable ⟨*contract*⟩; redeemable ⟨*loan, mortgage*⟩

Kunde[1] *der;* ~n, ~n customer; (eines Architekten-, Anwaltbüros, einer Versicherung usw.) client

Kunde[2] *die;* ~ (geh.) tidings *pl.* (literary)

Kunden-dienst *der* service to customers; (Wartung) after-sales service

Kundgebung *die;* ~, ~en rally

kundig *Adj.* (kenntnisreich) knowledgeable; (sachverständig) expert

kündigen [1] *tr. V.* cancel ⟨*subscription, membership*⟩; terminate ⟨*contract, agreement*⟩; **seine Stellung** ~: hand in one's notice (**bei** to)
[2] *unr. itr. V.* **(a)** (ein Mietverhältnis beenden) ⟨*tenant*⟩ give notice; **jmdm.** ~ ⟨*landlord*⟩ give sb. notice to quit; **zum 1. Juli** ~: give notice for 1 July
(b) (ein Arbeitsverhältnis beenden) ⟨*employee*⟩ hand in one's notice (**bei** to); **jmdm.** ~ ⟨*employer*⟩ give sb. his/her notice

Kündigung *die;* ~, ~en **(a)** (der Mitgliedschaft, eines Abonnements) cancellation; (eines Vertrags) termination
(b) (eines Arbeitsverhältnisses) **jmdm. die** ~ **aussprechen** give sb. his/her notice

Kündigungs-: ~**frist** *die* period of notice; ~**schutz** *der* protection against wrongful dismissal

Kundin *die;* ~, ~nen customer/client

Kundschaft *die;* ~, ~en ▶ KUNDE[1]: customers *pl.;* clientele

Kundschafter *der;* ~s, ~, **Kundschafterin** *die;* ~, ~nen scout

kund|tun (geh.) *unr. tr. V.* announce

künftig [1] *Adj.* future
[2] *adv.* in future

Kunst *die;* ~, Künste **(a)** art; **die bildende** ~, **die bildenden Künste** the plastic arts *pl.;* **die schönen Künste** [the] fine arts
(b) (das Können) skill; **die ärztliche** ~: medical skill; **das ist keine** ~! (ugs.) there's nothing to it

kunst-, Kunst-: ~**ausstellung** *die* art exhibition; ~**buch** *das* art book; ~**druck** *der; Pl.* ~~e **(a)** [fine] art print; **(b)** (Druckw.) fine-art printing; ~**erzieher** *der,* ~**erzieherin** *die* art teacher; ~**faser** *die* synthetic fibre; ~**führer** *der* guide to cultural and artistic monuments [of an/the area]; ~**genuss**, ***~**genuß** *der* enjoyment of art; (Ereignis) artistic treat; ~**gerecht** [1] *Adj.* expert; [2] *adv.* expertly; ~**geschichte** *die* art history; ~**geschichtlich** [1] *Adj.* art historical ⟨*studies, evidence, expertise*⟩; ⟨*work*⟩ on art history; [2] *adv.* ~ **geschichtlich interessiert/versiert** interested/well versed in art history; ~**gewerbe** *das* arts and crafts *pl.;* ~**griff** *der* trick; dodge; ~**halle** *die* art gallery; ~**händler** *der,* ~**händlerin** *die* [fine-]art dealer; ~**handwerk** *das* craftwork; ~**kritiker** *der,* ~**kritikerin** *die* art critic; ~**leder** imitation leather

Künstler *der;* ~s, ~, **Künstlerin** *die;* ~, ~nen **(a)** artist; (Zirkus~, Varietee~) artiste
(b) (Könner) genius (**in** + *Dat.* at)

künstlerisch [1] *Adj.* artistic
[2] *adv.* artistically

Künstler·name *der* stage name

künstlich [1] *Adj.* **(a)** artificial

(b) (gezwungen) forced ⟨*laugh, cheerfulness, etc.*⟩
[2] *adv.* artificially

kunst-, Kunst-: ~**licht** *das* artificial light; ~**los** *Adj.* plain; ~**postkarte** *die* art postcard; ~**saal** *der* art room; ~**sammler** *der*, ~**sammlerin** *die* art collector; ~**sammlung** *die* art collection; ~**schatz** *der* art treasure; ~**stoff** *der* synthetic material; plastic; ~**stück** *das* trick; **das ist kein** ~**stück** (ugs.) it's no great feat; ~**turnen** *das* gymnastics *sing.;* ~**voll** [1] *Adj.* ornate and artistic; (kompliziert) elaborate; [2] *adv.* **(a)** ornately *or* elaborately and artistically; **(b)** (geschickt) skilfully; ~**werk** *das* work of art

kunter·bunt [1] *Adj.* multi-coloured; (abwechslungsreich) varied; (ungeordnet) jumbled ⟨*confusion, muddle, etc.*⟩
[2] *adv.* ⟨*painted, printed*⟩ in many colours; ~ **durcheinander sein** be higgledy-piggledy

Kupfer *das;* ~s **(a)** copper
(b) (~geschirr) copperware; (~geld) coppers *pl.*

Kupfer-: ~**geld** *das* coppers *pl.;* ~**stich** *der* **(a)** copperplate engraving *no art.;* **(b)** (Blatt) copperplate print *or* engraving

Kuppe *die;* ~, ~n **(a)** [rounded] hilltop
(b) (Finger~) tip; end

Kuppel *die;* ~, ~n dome; (kleiner) cupola

Kuppelei *die;* ~: procuring

kuppeln *itr. V.* operate the clutch

Kuppelung ▶ KUPPLUNG

Kuppler *der;* ~s, ~: procurer

Kupplerin *die;* ~, ~nen procuress

Kupplung *die;* ~, ~en **(a)** (Kfz-W.) clutch
(b) (Technik: Vorrichtung zum Verbinden) coupling

Kur *die;* ~, ~en [health] cure; (ohne Aufenthalt im Badeort) course of treatment

Kür *die;* ~, ~en (Eiskunstlauf) free programme; (Turnen) optional exercises *pl.*

Kurbel *die;* ~, ~n crank [handle]; (an Spieldosen, Grammophonen) winder; (an einem Brunnen) [winding] handle

kurbeln *tr. V.* etw. nach oben/unten ~: wind sth. up/down

Kurbel·welle *die* (Technik) crankshaft

Kürbis *der;* ~ses, ~se pumpkin

Kurde *der;* ~n, ~n, **Kurdin** *die;* ~, ~nen Kurd

kurdisch *Adj.* Kurdish

Kur-: ~**fürst** *der* (hist.) Elector; ~**gast** *der* visitor to a/the spa; (Patient) patient at a/the spa

Kurier *der;* ~s, ~e courier

kurieren *tr. V.* (auch fig.) cure **(von** of)

Kurierin *die;* ~, ~nen ▶ KURIER

kurios [1] *Adj.* curious
[2] *adv.* curiously; strangely; oddly

Kuriosität *die;* ~, ~en **(a)** strangeness
(b) (Gegenstand) curiosity; curio

Kur-: ~**konzert** *das* concert [at a spa]; ~**ort** *der* spa; ~**pfuscher** *der*, ~**pfuscherin** *die* (ugs. abwertend) quack

Kurs *der;* ~es, ~e **(a)** (Richtung) course; **ein harter/weicher** ~ (fig.) a hard/soft line
(b) (von Wertpapieren) price; (von Devisen) exchange rate; **der** ~ **des Dollars** the dollar rate
(c) (Lehrgang) course; (Teilnehmer) class

Kürschner *der;* ~s, ~, **Kürschnerin** *die;* ~, ~nen furrier

kursieren *itr. V.; auch mit sein* circulate

Kurs·teilnehmer *der*, **Kurs·teilnehmerin** *die* course participant

Kursus *der;* ~, Kurse ▶ KURS

Kurs·wagen *der* (Eisenb.) through carriage

Kur·taxe *die;* visitors' tax (*at a spa*)

Kurve *die;* ~, ~n **(a)** (einer Straße) bend
(b) (Geom.) curve
(c) (in der Statistik, Temperatur~ usw.) graph

kurven *itr. V.; mit sein* **(a)** ⟨*aircraft*⟩ circle; ⟨*tanks etc.*⟩ circle [round]
(b) (ugs.: fahren) drive around

kurven·reich *Adj.* winding; twisting

kurz; kürzer, kürzest... [1] *Adj.* short; (zeitlich; knapp) short, brief; quick ⟨*look*⟩
[2] *adv.* **(a)** (zeitlich) briefly; (knapp) ~ **gesagt** in a word
(b) (wenig) just; ~ **vor/hinter der Kreuzung** just before/past the crossroads; ~ **vor/nach Pfingsten** just before/after Whitsun

kurz-, Kurz-: ~**arbeit** *die* short-time working; ~**ärm[e]lig** *Adj.* short-sleeved

Kürze *die;* ~ **(a)** shortness
(b) (geringe Dauer) shortness; brevity; **in** ~: shortly
(c) (Knappheit) brevity

Kürzel *das;* ~s, ~: shorthand symbol

kürzen *tr. V.* shorten; abridge ⟨*article, book*⟩; cut ⟨*pension, budget*⟩

kürzer ▶ KURZ

kurzer·hand *Adv.* without more ado

kürzest... ▶ KURZ

kurz-, Kurz-: ~**fristig** [1] *Adj.* **(a)** ⟨*refusal, resignation, etc.*⟩ at short notice; **(b)** (für kurze Zeit) short-term; [2] *adv.* **(a)** at short notice; **(b)** (für kurze Zeit) for a short time; (auf kurze Sicht) in the short term; (in kurzer Zeit) without delay; ~**geschichte** *die* short story; ~**haar-frisur** *die* bob; bobbed hairstyle; ~**lebig** *Adj.* (auch fig.) short-lived; ~**lebigkeit** *die;* ~~: short-livedness

kürzlich *Adv.* recently; not long ago

kurz-, Kurz-: ~**meldung** *die* brief report; (während einer anderen Sendung) news flash; ~**parker** *der;* ~~s, ~~, ~**parkerin** *die;* ~~, ~~nen short-stay (Brit.) *or* short-term parker; ~**schluss,** ***~**schluß** *der* (Elektrot.) short circuit; ~**sichtig** (auch fig.) [1] *Adj.* short-sighted; [2] *adv.* short-sightedly; ~**sichtigkeit** *die;* ~~ (auch fig.) short-sightedness

Kụrzstrecken·rakete *die* short-range missile

Kụ̈rzung *die;* ∼, ∼en cut

kụrz-, Kụrz-: ∼**waren** *Pl.* haberdashery *sing.* (Brit.); notions (Amer.); ∼**welle** *die* (Physik, Rundf.) short wave; ∼**weilig** *Adj.* entertaining; ∼**zeitig** 1 *Adj.* brief; 2 *adv.* briefly

kụschelig *Adj.* cosy

kụscheln *refl. V.* sich an jmdn. ∼: snuggle up to sb.

Kụschel·tier *das* cuddly toy

kụschen *itr. V.* knuckle under (vor + *Dat.* to)

Kusịne *die;* ∼, ∼n ▶ COUSINE

Kụss, *Kụß *der;* Kụsses, Kụ̈sse kiss

kụss·echt, *kụß·echt *Adj.* kissproof

kụ̈ssen *tr., itr. V.* kiss

Kụss·hand, *Kụß·hand *die:* jmdm. eine ∼ zuwerfen blow sb. a kiss; mit ∼ (ugs.) gladly

Kụ̈ste *die;* ∼, ∼n coast

Kụ̈sten-: ∼**linie** *die* coastline; ∼**wache** *die* coastguard [service]

Kụ̈ster *der;* ∼s, ∼, **Kụ̈sterin** *die;* ∼, ∼nen sexton

Kụtsche *die;* ∼, ∼n coach

Kụtscher *der;* ∼s, ∼, **Kụtscherin** *die;* ∼, ∼nen coach driver

kutschịeren 1 *itr. V.; mit sein* drive, ride [in a coach]
2 *tr. V.* jmdn. ∼: drive sb. [in a coach]

Kụtte *die;* ∼, ∼n [monk's/nun's] habit

Kụtter *der;* ∼s, ∼: cutter

Kuvert /ku'veːɐ̯/ *das;* ∼s, ∼s envelope; (geh.: Gedeck) cover

Kuwait /ku'vaiːt/ *(das);* ∼s Kuwait

Kybernetik *die;* ∼: cybernetics *sing.*

Kybernetiker *der;* ∼s, ∼, **Kybernetikerin** *die;* ∼, ∼nen cybernetician; cyberneticist

kybernetisch *Adj.* cybernetic

KZ *Abk.* = **Konzentrationslager**

KZ-Häftling *der,* **KZler** *der;* ∼s, ∼, **KZlerin** *die;* ∼, ∼nen concentration-camp prisoner

Ll

l, L /ɛl/ *das;* ∼, ∼: l/L

l *Abk.* = **Liter** l.

Lab *das;* ∼[e]s, ∼e rennet

lạbberig *Adj.* (ugs. abwertend) (a) (fade) wishy-washy; ∼ schmecken taste of nothing
(b) (weich) floppy, limp ⟨*material*⟩; floppy ⟨*trousers, dress, etc.*⟩

laben (geh.) 1 *tr. V.* jmdn. ∼: give sb. refreshment
2 *refl. V.* refresh oneself (an + *Dat.,* mit with)

labern *itr. V.* (ugs. abwertend) rabbit (Brit. coll.) or babble on

labịl *Adj.* (a) (Med.) delicate ⟨*constitution, health*⟩; poor ⟨*circulation*⟩
(b) (auch Psych.) unstable ⟨*person, character, situation, etc.*⟩

Labor *das;* ∼s, ∼s, *auch:* ∼e laboratory

Laboratorium *das;* ∼s, Laboratorien laboratory

Labor·test *der* laboratory test (an + *Dat.* of; auf + *Akk.* for)

Labyrịnth *das;* ∼[e]s, ∼e maze; labyrinth

Lạche¹ *die;* ∼, ∼n (ugs.) laugh

Lạche² /'laː(ː)xə/ *die;* ∼, ∼n puddle; (von Blut, Öl) pool

lạ̈cheln *itr. V.* smile (über + *Akk.* at)

Lạ̈cheln *das;* ∼s smile

lạchen 1 *itr. V.* laugh (über + *Akk.* at)
2 *tr. V.* was gibt es denn zu ∼? what's so funny?

Lạchen *das;* ∼s laughter; ein lautes ∼: a loud laugh

lạ̈cherlich 1 *Adj.* ridiculous; ludicrous ⟨*argument, statement*⟩
2 *adv.* ridiculously

Lạ̈cherlichkeit *die;* ∼: ridiculousness; (von Argumenten, Behauptungen usw.) ludicrousness

lạchhaft *Adj.* ridiculous

Lạchs *der;* ∼es, ∼e salmon

Lạck *der;* ∼[e]s, ∼e varnish; (für Metall, Lackarbeiten) lacquer

lackịeren *tr. V.* varnish; spray ⟨*car*⟩

Lạck·leder *das* patent leather

laden¹ 1 *unr. tr. V.* load; (Physik) charge
2 *unr. itr. V.* load [up]

laden² *unr. tr. V.* (a) (Rechtsspr.) summon
(b) (geh.: einladen) invite

Laden *der;* ∼s, Lạ̈den (a) shop; store (Amer.); der ∼ läuft (ugs.) business is good
(b) (Fensterladen) shutter

Laden-: ∼**dieb** *der,* ∼**diebin** *die* shoplifter; ∼**diebstahl** *der* shoplifting;

---

*old spelling - see note on page xiv

∼schluss, *∗*∼**schluß** *der* shop *or* (Amer.) store closing time; ∼**tisch** *der* [shop] counter

Lade-: ∼**rampe** *die* loading ramp; ∼**raum** *der* (beim Auto) luggage space; (beim Flugzeug, Schiff) hold; (bei LKWs) payload space

lädieren *tr. V.* damage

lädst *2. Pers. Sg. Präsens v.* LADEN

lädt *3. Pers. Sg. Präsens v.* LADEN

Ladung *die;* ∼, ∼**en (a)** (Schiffs∼, Flugzeug∼) cargo; (eines LKW) load **(b)** (beim Sprengen, Schießen; Physik) charge **(c)** (Rechtsspr.: Vor∼) summons *sing.*

lag *1. u. 3. Pers. Sg. Prät. v.* LIEGEN

Lage *die;* ∼, ∼**n (a)** situation; **eine gute** ∼ **haben** be well situated **(b)** (Art des Liegens) position **(c)** (Situation) situation

Lage·plan *der* map of the area

Lager *das;* ∼**s,** ∼ **(a)** camp **(b)** storeroom; (in Geschäften, Betrieben) stockroom **(c)** (Warenbestand) stock

Lager-: ∼**bestand** *der* (Wirtsch.) stock; **den** ∼**bestand aufnehmen** do a stocktake; ∼**feuer** *das* campfire; ∼**halle** *die* warehouse

lagern ⏐1⏐ *tr. V.* **(a)** store **(b)** (hinlegen) lay down ⏐2⏐ *itr. V.* **(a)** camp **(b)** (liegen) lie; ⟨*foodstuffs, medicines, etc.*⟩ be kept

Lager-: ∼**platz** *der* campsite; ∼**raum** storeroom; (im Geschäft, Betrieb) stockroom

Lagerung *die;* ∼, ∼**en** storage

Lagune *die;* ∼, ∼**n** lagoon

lahm *Adj.* **(a)** (gelähmt) lame; (ugs.: unbeweglich) stiff **(b)** (ugs.: unzureichend) lame ⟨*excuse, explanation, etc.*⟩ **(c)** (ugs. abwertend: matt) dreary

lahmen *itr. V.* be lame

lähmen *tr. V.* paralyse; (fig.) paralyse ⟨*economy, industry*⟩; bring ⟨*traffic*⟩ to a standstill

Lähmung *die;* ∼, ∼**en** paralysis; (fig.) (der Wirtschaft, Industrie) paralysis; **zu einer** ∼ **des Verkehrs führen** bring traffic to a standstill

Laib *der;* ∼**[e]s,** ∼**e** loaf; **ein [halber]** ∼ **Brot** [half] a loaf of bread

Laich *der;* ∼**[e]s,** ∼**e** spawn

laichen *itr. V.* spawn

Laie *der;* ∼**n,** ∼**n** (Mann) layman; (Frau) laywoman

Lakai *der;* ∼**en,** ∼**en** lackey; liveried footman

Lake *die;* ∼, ∼**n** brine

Laken *das;* ∼**s,** ∼ (bes. nordd.) sheet

Lakritze *die;* ∼, ∼**n** liquorice

lallen *tr., itr. V.* ⟨*baby*⟩ babble; ⟨*drunk/ drowsy person*⟩ mumble

Lamelle *die;* ∼, ∼**n** (einer Jalousie) slat; (eines Heizkörpers) rib

lamentieren *itr. V.* (ugs.) moan (**über** + *Akk.* about)

Lametta *das;* ∼**s** lametta

Lamm *das;* ∼**[e]s, Lämmer** lamb

lamm-, Lamm-: ∼**fell** *das* lambskin; ∼**fleisch** *das* lamb; ∼**fromm** ⏐1⏐ *Adj.* ⟨person⟩ as meek as a [little] lamb; ⏐2⏐ *adv.* ⟨answer⟩ like a lamb

Lämpchen *das;* ∼**s,** ∼: small *or* little light; **ein rotes** ∼: a little red light

Lampe *die;* ∼, ∼**n** light; (Tisch∼, Öl∼, Signal∼) lamp

Lampen-: ∼**fieber** *das* stage fright; ∼**schirm** *der* [lamp]shade

Lampion /lamˈpi̯ɔŋ/ *der;* ∼**s,** ∼**s** Chinese lantern

Land *das;* ∼**es, Länder** *od.* (veralt.) ∼**e (a)** land *no indef. art.;* (dörfliche Gegend) country *no indef. art.;* **an** ∼: ashore; **auf dem** ∼ **wohnen** live in the country **(b)** (Staat) country; **hier zu** ∼**e** [here] in this country **(c)** (Bundesland) Land; state; (österr.) province

Land-: ∼**arbeiter** *der,* ∼**arbeiterin** *die* agricultural worker; farm worker; ∼**bevölkerung** *die* rural population

Lande-: ∼**anflug** *der* (Flugw.) [landing] approach; ∼**bahn** *die* (Flugw.) [landing] runway; ∼**erlaubnis** *die* (Flugw.) permission to land *no art.*

landen ⏐1⏐ *itr. V.; mit sein* **(a)** land; (ankommen) arrive **(b)** (ugs.: gelangen) land up ⏐2⏐ *tr. V.* **(a)** land ⟨*aircraft, troops, passengers, fish, etc.*⟩ **(b)** (ugs.: zustande bringen) pull off ⟨*victory, coup*⟩; have ⟨*smash hit*⟩

Ländereien *Pl.* estates

Länder-: ∼**kampf** *der* (Sport) international match; ∼**spiel** *das* (Sport) international [match]

Landes-: ∼**innere** *das* interior [of the country]; ∼**kunde** *die* regional studies *pl.,* *no art.;* ∼**regierung** *die* government of a/ the Land/province; ∼**sprache** *die* language of the country

Lande·steg *der* landing stage; jetty

Landes-: ∼**tracht** *die* national costume *or* dress; ∼**verrat** *der* (Rechtsw.) treason; ∼**währung** *die* currency of a/the country

land-, Land-: ∼**flucht** *die* migration from the land *or* countryside [to the towns]; ∼**friedens·bruch** *der* (Rechtsw.) breach of the peace; ∼**gewinnung** *die* reclamation of land; ∼**haus** *das* country house; ∼**karte** *die* map; ∼**kreis** *der* district; ∼**läufig** *Adj.* widely accepted

ländlich *Adj.* rural; country *attrib.* ⟨life⟩

Land-: ∼**luft** *die* country air; ∼**mine** *die* landmine; ∼**plage** *die* (fig.) pest; nuisance; ∼**ratte** *die* (ugs.) landlubber

Landschaft *die;* ~, ~en landscape; (ländliche Gegend) countryside

landschaftlich 1 *Adj.* regional 2 *adv.* ~ **herrlich gelegen sein** be in a glorious natural setting; **die Umgebung der Stadt ist** ~ **sehr schön** the town is in *or* has a beautiful natural setting

Land·schul·heim *das* ▶ SCHULLANDHEIM

Lands-: ~**mann** *der; Pl.* ~**leute** fellow countryman; compatriot; ~**männin** *die;* ~~, ~~**nen** fellow countrywoman; compatriot

Land-: ~**straße** *die* country road; (im Gegensatz zur Autobahn) ordinary road; ~**streicher** *der;* ~~**s,** ~~, ~**streicherin** *die;* ~~, ~~~**nen** tramp; ~**strich** *der* area; ~**tag** *der* Landtag; state parliament; (österr.) provincial parliament

Landung *die;* ~, ~en landing

Landungs·brücke *die* [floating] landing stage

land-, Land-: ~**weg** *der* overland route; **auf dem** ~**weg** overland; ~**wirt** *der,* ~**wirtin** *die* farmer; ~**wirtschaft** *die* agriculture *no art.;* farming *no art.;* ~**wirtschaftlich** 1 *Adj.* agricultural; 2 *adv.* ~**wirtschaftlich genutzt werden** be used for agricultural purposes; ~**zunge** *die* (Geogr.) tongue of land

lang; länger, längst... 1 *Adj.* long; (ugs.: groß) tall 2 *adv.* [for] a long time; **eine Sekunde/ mehrere Stunden** ~: for a second/several hours

lang-: ~**ärm[e]lig** *Adj.* long-sleeved; ~**atmig** 1 *Adj.* long-winded; 2 *adv.* long-windedly; ⟨relate⟩ at great length

lange; länger, am längsten *Adv.* **(a)** a long time; **bist du schon** ~ **hier?** have you been here long? **(b)** (bei weitem) **ich bin noch** ~ **nicht fertig** I'm nowhere near finished; **hier is es** ~ **nicht so schön** it isn't nearly as nice here

Länge *die;* ~, ~n length; (Geogr.) longitude

langen (ugs.) 1 *itr. V.* **(a)** be enough **(b)** (greifen) reach (**in** + *Akk.* into; **auf** + *Akk.* on to; **nach** for) 2 *tr. V.* **jmdm. eine** ~ (ugs.) give sb. a clout [around the ear] (coll.)

Längen·grad *der* (Geogr.) degree of longitude

länger 1 ▶ LANG, LANGE; 2 *Adj.* **seit** ~**er Zeit** for quite some time

Lange·weile *die;* ~ *od.* **Langenweile** boredom; ~ **haben** be bored

lang-, Lang-: ~**fristig** 1 *Adj.* long-term; long-dated ⟨loan⟩; 2 *adv.* on a long-term basis; ~**jährig** *Adj.* ⟨customer, friend⟩ of many years' standing; long-standing ⟨friendship⟩; ~**jährige Erfahrung** many years

of experience; ~**lauf** *der* (Skisport) cross-country; ~**lebig** *Adj.* long-lived ⟨animals, organisms⟩; durable ⟨goods, materials⟩

länglich *Adj.* oblong

lang-, Lang-: ~**mut** *die;* ~~: forbearance; ~**mütig** *Adj.* forbearing; ~**mütigkeit** *die;* ~~: forbearance

längs 1 *Präp.* + *Gen. od.* (selten) *Dat.* along 2 *Adv.* lengthways

Längs·achse *die* longitudinal axis

langsam 1 *Adj.* slow 2 *adv.* **(a)** slowly; ~, **aber sicher** (ugs.) slowly but surely **(b)** (allmählich) gradually

Lang-: ~**schläfer** *der,* ~**schläferin** *die* late riser; ~**spiel·platte** *die* long-playing record; LP

Längs·schnitt *der* longitudinal section

längst *Adv.* **(a)** (schon lange) a long time ago **(b)** (bei weitem) **hier ist es** ~ **nicht so schön** it isn't nearly as nice here

längst... ▶ LANG

längstens *Adv.* (ugs.) (höchstens) at [the] most; (spätestens) at the latest

Languste *die;* ~, ~n spiny lobster

lang-, Lang-: ~**weilen** 1 *tr. V.* bore; 2 *refl. V.* be bored; ~**weilig** 1 *Adj.* boring; dull ⟨place⟩; 2 *adv.* boringly; ~**welle** *die* (Physik, Rundf.) long wave; ~**wierig** *Adj.* lengthy; prolonged ⟨search⟩

Lanze *die;* ~, ~n lance; (zum Werfen) spear

Laos ⟨das⟩; Laos' Laos

Laote *der;* ~n, ~n, **Laotin** *die;* ~, ~nen Laotian

lapidar 1 *Adj.* (kurz, aber wirkungsvoll) succinct; (knapp) terse 2 *adv.* succinctly/tersely

Lappalie /la'pa:li̯ə/ *die;* ~, ~n trifle

Lappe *der;* ~n, ~n Lapp

Lappen *der;* ~s, ~: cloth; (Fetzen) rag; (Wasch~) flannel

Lappin *die;* ~, ~nen Lapp

läppisch *Adj.* silly

Lapp·land ⟨das⟩; ~s Lapland

Laptop *der;* ~s, ~s (DV) laptop

Lärche *die;* ~, ~n larch

Lärm *der;* ~[e]s noise; (Krach) din; row (coll.)

Lärm·belästigung *die* disturbance caused by noise

lärmen *itr. V.* make a noise *or* (coll.) row

Lärm-: ~**pegel** *der* noise level; ~**schutz** *der* **(a)** protection against noise; **(b)** (Vorrichtung) noise barrier; noise *or* sound insulation *no indef. art.;* ~**schutz·wand** *die* sound-insulating wall

Larve *die;* ~, ~n grub; larva

las 1. *u.* 3. *Pers. Sg. Prät. v.* LESEN

lasch 1 *Adj.* limp ⟨handshake⟩; feeble ⟨action, measure⟩; lax ⟨upbringing⟩ 2 *adv. s. Adj.:* limply; feebly; laxly

---

*alte Schreibung - vgl. Hinweis auf S. xiv

Lạsche *die;* ∼, ∼n (Gürtel∼) loop; (eines Briefumschlags) flap; (Schuh∼) tongue

Laser /'leɪzɐ/ *der;* ∼s, ∼ (Physik) laser

Lạser-: ∼**drucker** *der* (DV) laser printer; ∼**pointer** *der* (DV) laser pointer

lạss, *laß *Imperativ Sg. v.* LASSEN

lạssen ☐1 *unr. tr. V.* **(a)** *mit Inf. + Akk.* (2. *Part.* lassen) (veranlassen) etw. tun/machen/ bauen/waschen ∼: have *or* get sth. done/ made/built/washed; **jmdn. warten** ∼: keep sb. waiting; **jmdn. grüßen** ∼: send one's regards to sb.; **jmdn. kommen/rufen** ∼: send for sb.
(b) *mit Inf. + Akk.* (2.*Part.* lassen) (erlauben) **jmdn. etw. tun** ∼: let sb. do sth.; allow sb. to do sth.
(c) (belassen) **jmdn. in Frieden** ∼: leave sb. in peace
(d) (hinein∼/heraus∼) let *or* allow (**in** + *Akk.* into, **aus** out of)
(e) (unterlassen) stop
(f) (zurück∼; bleiben ∼) leave
(g) (überlassen) **jmdn. etw.** ∼: let sb. have sth.
(h) (als Aufforderung) **lass/lasst uns gehen/ fahren!** let's go!
(i) (verlieren) lose; (ausgeben) spend
☐2 *unr. refl. V.* **die Tür lässt sich leicht öffnen** the door opens easily; **das lässt sich nicht beweisen** it can't be proved
☐3 *unr. itr. V.* **(a)** (ugs.) **Lass mal. Ich mache das schon** Leave it. I'll do it
(b) (veranlassen) **ich lasse bitten** would you ask him/her/them to come in

lässig ☐1 *Adj.* casual
☐2 *adv.* casually

lässt, *läßt *3. Pers. Sg. Präsens v.* LASSEN

Lạst *die;* ∼, ∼en load; (Gewicht) weight; (Bürde) burden

lạsten *itr. V.* be a burden; **auf jmdm./etw.** ∼: weigh heavily [up]on sb./sth.

Lạster¹ *der;* ∼s, ∼ (ugs.) Lkw) truck; lorry (Brit.)

Lạster² *das;* ∼s, ∼: vice

lạsterhaft *Adj.* (abwertend) depraved

lästern ☐1 *itr. V.* (abwertend) **über jmdn./etw.** ∼: make malicious remarks about sb./sth.
☐2 *tr. V.* (veralt.) blaspheme against

lästig *Adj.* tiresome; troublesome ⟨*illness, cough, etc.*⟩

Lạst-: ∼**schrift** *die* debit; ∼**wagen** *der* truck; lorry (Brit.)

Lasụr *die;* ∼, ∼en varnish; (farbig) glaze

Latein *das;* ∼s Latin

Latein·amerika ⟨*das*⟩ Latin America

lateinisch *Adj.* Latin

latẹnt *Adj.* latent

Latẹrne *die;* ∼, ∼n **(a)** (Leuchte) lamp; lantern (Naut.)
(b) (Straßen∼) street light

Latẹrnen·pfahl *der* lamp post

Latrịne *die;* ∼, ∼n latrine

lạtschen *itr. V.; mit sein* (salopp) trudge; (schlurfend) slouch

Lạtschen *der;* ∼s, ∼ (ugs.) old worn-out shoe/slipper

Lạtte *die;* ∼, ∼n **(a)** lath; (Zaun∼) pale
(b) (Sport: Quer∼ des Tores) [cross]bar
(c) (Leichtathletik) bar

Lạtten-: ∼**rost** *der* (auf dem Boden) duckboards *pl.;* (eines Bettes) slatted frame ∼**zaun** *der* paling fence

Lạtz *der;* ∼es, Lätze bib

Lạtzchen *das;* ∼s, ∼: bib

lau *Adj.* tepid, lukewarm ⟨*water etc.*⟩; mild ⟨*wind, air, evening, etc.*⟩

Laub *das;* ∼[e]s leaves *pl.;* **dichtes** ∼: thick foliage

Laub·baum *der* broad-leaved tree

Laube *die;* ∼, ∼n summer house; (überdeckter Sitzplatz) bower; arbour

Laub-: ∼**frosch** *der* tree frog; ∼**säge** *die* fretsaw; ∼**wald** *der* deciduous wood/forest

Lauch *der;* ∼[e]s (Porree) leek

Lauer *die;* ∼: **auf der** ∼ **liegen** *od.* **sein** (ugs.) (jmdm. auflauern) lie in wait

lauern *itr. V.* (auch fig.) lurk

Lauf *der;* ∼[e]s, Läufe **(a)** running
(b) (Sport: Wettrennen) heat
(c) (Ver∼) course; **im** ∼[e] **der Zeit** in the course of time; **im** ∼[e] **der Jahre/des Tages** over the years/during the day
(d) (von Schusswaffen) barrel

Lauf·bahn *die* **(a)** (Werdegang) career
(b) (Leichtathletik) running track

laufen ☐1 *unr. itr. V.; mit sein* **(a)** run; (beim Eislauf) skate; (beim Ski∼) ski; (gehen) go; (zu Fuß gehen) walk; **in** ⟨*Akk.*⟩/**gegen etw.** ∼: walk into sth.; **dauernd zum Arzt** ∼ (ugs.) keep running to the doctor
(b) (im Gang sein) ⟨*machine*⟩ be running; ⟨*radio, television, etc.*⟩ be on; (funktionieren) ⟨*machine*⟩ run; ⟨*radio, television, etc.*⟩ work
(c) (gelten) ⟨*contract, agreement, engagement, etc.*⟩ run
(d) (gespielt werden) ⟨*programme, play, etc.*⟩ be on
☐2 *unr. tr. u. itr. V.* **(a)** *mit sein* (zurücklegen) (zu Fuß) walk; (rennen) run
(b) *mit sein* (erzielen) **einen Rekord** ∼: set up a record
(c) *mit haben od. sein* **Ski/Schlittschuh/ Rollschuh** ∼: ski/skate/roller-skate

laufend ☐1 *Adj.* **(a)** (ständig) regular ⟨*interest, income*⟩; recurring ⟨*costs*⟩
(b) (gegenwärtig) current ⟨*issue, year, month, etc.*⟩
☐2 *adv.* constantly; ⟨*increase*⟩ steadily

Läufer *der;* ∼s, ∼ **(a)** (Sport) runner; (Handball; Fußball veralt.) halfback
(b) (Teppich) ⟨*long narrow*⟩ carpet

Läuferin *die;* ∼, ∼nen ▶ LÄUFER A

Lauf·feuer *das* brush fire; **wie ein** ∼: like wildfire

Lauf-: ∼**masche** *die* ladder; ∼**pass,** ⋯⋟

*~paß der: er hat seiner Freundin den ~pass gegeben (ugs.) he finished with his girlfriend (coll.); **~schritt** der: im ~schritt, marsch, marsch! at the double, quick march!

läufst 2. Pers. Sg. Präsens v. LAUFEN

Lauf·stall der playpen

läuft 3. Pers. Sg. Präsens v. LAUFEN

Laufwerk das (Technik) mechanism; (DV) drive

Lauge die; ~, ~n (a) soapy water (b) (Chemie) alkaline solution

Laugen·brezel die (südd.) pretzel

Laune die; ~, ~n mood

launenhaft Adj. temperamental; (unberechenbar) capricious

launig witty

launisch Adj.: ▶ LAUNENHAFT

Laus die; ~, Läuse louse

Laus·bub der little rascal

Lausch·aktion die, **Lausch·angriff** der bugging operation (coll.)

lauschen itr. V. (a) (horchen) listen (b) (zuhören) listen [attentively]

Lauscher der; ~s, ~, **Lauscherin** die; ~, ~nen eavesdropper

lauschig Adj. cosy, snug ⟨corner⟩

lausig [1] Adj. (ugs.) (a) (abwertend: unangenehm, schäbig) lousy (coll.); rotten (coll.) (b) (sehr groß) perishing (Brit. coll.), freezing ⟨cold⟩; terrible (coll.) ⟨heat⟩ [2] adv. terribly (coll.)

laut[1] [1] Adj. loud; (geräuschvoll) noisy [2] adv. loudly; (geräuschvoll) noisily

laut[2] Präp. + Gen. od. Dat. (Amtsspr.) according to

Laut der; ~[e]s, ~e sound

Laute die; ~, ~n lute

lauten itr. V. ⟨answer, instruction, slogan⟩ be, run; ⟨letter, passage, etc.⟩ read, go; ⟨law⟩ state

läuten [1] tr., itr. V. ring; ⟨alarm clock⟩ go off [2] itr. V. (bes. südd.: klingeln) ring; es läutete the bell rang or went (zu for)

lauter[1] Adj. (geh.) honourable ⟨person, intentions, etc.⟩; honest ⟨truth⟩

lauter[2] indekl. Adj. nothing but; sheer ⟨nonsense, joy, etc.⟩

läutern tr. V. (geh.) reform ⟨character⟩; purify ⟨soul⟩

Läuterung die; ~, ~en (geh.) reformation; (der Seele) purification

laut·hals Adv. at the top of one's voice; ~ lachen roar with laughter

lautlich [1] Adj. phonetic [2] adv. phonetically

laut-, Laut-: **~los** [1] Adj. silent; soundless; (wortlos) silent; [2] adv. silently; soundlessly; **~schrift** die (Phon.) phonetic alphabet; (Umschrift) phonetic transcription;

~sprecher der loudspeaker; (einer Stereoanlage usw.) speaker; **~stark** [1] Adj. loud; vociferous, loud ⟨protest⟩; [2] adv. loudly; ⟨protest⟩ vociferously; **~stärke** die volume

lau·warm Adj. lukewarm

Lava die; ~, Laven (Geol.) lava

Lavendel der; ~s, ~: lavender

Lawine die; ~, ~n (auch fig.) avalanche; eine ~ von Protesten (fig.) a storm of protest

Lawinen·gefahr die danger of avalanches

lax [1] Adj. lax [2] adv. laxly

Laxheit die; ~: laxness; laxity

Layout /ˈleːrˈaʊt/ das; ~s, ~s (Druckw., Elektronik) layout

Lazarett das; ~[e]s, ~e military hospital

Lead·sänger /ˈliːt-/ der, **Lead·sängerin** die lead singer

leasen /ˈliːzn̩/ tr. V. rent; (für längere Zeit mieten) lease ⟨car etc.⟩

leben itr. V. live; (lebendig sein) be alive; **leb[e] wohl!** farewell!!; **von seiner Rente/seinem Gehalt ~:** live on one's pension/salary

Leben das; ~s, ~ (a) life; das ~: life; sich (Dat.) das ~ nehmen take one's [own] life; am ~ sein/bleiben be/stay alive; ums ~ kommen lose one's life (b) (Betriebsamkeit) auf dem Markt herrschte ein reges ~: the market was bustling with activity; das ~ auf der Straße the comings and goings in the street

lebend Adj. living; live ⟨animal⟩

lebendig [1] Adj. living; (lebhaft) lively [2] adv. (lebhaft) in a lively way

Lebendigkeit die; ~: liveliness

lebens-, Lebens-: **~abend** der (geh.) evening of one's life (literary); **~art** die (a) way of life; (b) (Umgangsformen) manners pl.; **~aufgabe** die life's work; **~bejahend** Adj. ⟨person⟩ with a positive attitude to life; **~bereich** der area of life; **~dauer** die lifespan; **~ende** das end [of one's life]; **~erinnerungen** Pl. memories of one's life; (aufgezeichnet) memoirs; **~erwartung** die life expectancy; **~fähig** Adj. (auch fig.) viable; **~freude** die zest for life; **~froh** Adj. full of zest for life postpos.; **~gefahr** die mortal danger; „Achtung, ~gefahr!" 'danger'; **~gefährlich** [1] Adj. highly dangerous; critical ⟨injury⟩; [2] adv. critically ⟨injured, ill⟩; **~gefährte** der, **~gefährtin** die (geh.) companion through life (literary); **~geister** Pl. jmds. [wieder] wecken put new life into sb.; **~groß** Adj. life-size; **~größe** die: eine Statue in ~größe a life-size statue

Lebens·haltung die cost of living

Lebenshaltungs-: **~index** der (Wirtsch.) cost-of-living index; **~kosten** Pl. cost of living sing.

lebens-, Lebens-: **~jahr** das year of [one's] life; **~kraft** die vitality;

~**künstler** der, ~**künstlerin** die: ein [echter/wahrer] ~künstler a person who always knows how to make the best of things; ~**lage** die situation [in life]; ~**lang** ①Adj. lifelong; ②adv. all one's life; ~**länglich** ①Adj. ~länglicher Freiheitsentzug life imprisonment; ②adv. jmdn. ~länglich gefangen halten keep sb. imprisoned for life; ~**lauf** der curriculum vitae; c.v.; ~**licht** das (geh.) flame of life (literary); jmdm. das ~licht ausblasen od. auspusten (ugs.) send sb. to kingdom come (coll.); ~**lustig** Adj. ⟨person⟩ full of the joys of life

Lebens·mittel das food[stuff]; ~ Pl. food sing.

Lebensmittel-: ~**abteilung** die food department; ~**geschäft** das food shop; ~**vergiftung** die food poisoning

lebens-, Lebens-: ~**müde** Adj. weary of life pred.; ~**notwendig** Adj. essential; ~**raum** der (a) (Umkreis) lebensraum; (b) (Biol.) ▶ BIOTOP; ~**retter** der, ~**retterin** die rescuer; ~**standard** der standard of living; ~**unterhalt** der: seinen ~unterhalt verdienen/bestreiten earn one's living/ support oneself; ~**versicherung** die life insurance; ~**wandel** der way of life; ~**weg** der [journey through] life; ~**weise** die way of life; ~**zeichen** das sign of life; ~**zeit** die life[span]; auf ~zeit for life

Leber die; ~, ~n liver

Leber-: ~**fleck** der liver spot; ~**käse** der: meat loaf made with mincemeat, [minced liver,] eggs, and spices; ~**tran** der fish-liver oil; (des Kabeljaus) cod-liver oil; ~**wurst** die liver sausage; ~**zirrhose** die (Med.) cirrhosis of the liver

Lebe-: ~**wesen** das living being; ~**wohl** /--'--/ das; ~~[e]s, ~~ od. ~~e (geh.) farewell

lebhaft ①Adj. (a) lively; busy ⟨traffic⟩; brisk ⟨business⟩
(b) (deutlich) vivid ⟨idea, picture, etc.⟩
(c) (kräftig) bright ⟨colour⟩; vigorous ⟨applause, opposition⟩
②adv. (a) in a lively way
(b) (deutlich) vividly
(c) (kräftig) brightly ⟨coloured⟩

leb-, Leb-: ~**kuchen** der ≈ gingerbread; ~**los** Adj. lifeless; ~**zeiten:** ~zeiten Pl. bei od. zu jmds. ~zeiten during sb.'s lifetime

lechzen itr. V. (geh.) nach einem Trunk ~: long for a drink; nach Rache usw. ~: thirst for revenge etc.

leck Adj. leaky; ~ sein leak

Leck das; ~[e]s, ~s leak

lecken¹ ①tr. V. lick
②itr. V. an etw. (Dat.) ~: lick sth.

lecken² itr. V. (leck sein) leak

lecker Adj. tasty ⟨meal⟩; delicious ⟨cake etc.⟩; good ⟨smell, taste⟩

Lecker·bissen der delicacy; ein musikalischer ~ (fig.) a musical treat

Leckerei die; ~, ~en (ugs.) dainty; (Süßigkeit) sweet [meat]

led. Abk. = **ledig**

Leder das; ~s, ~: leather

Leder-: ~**handschuh** der leather glove; ~**hose** die leather shorts pl.; lederhosen pl.; (lang) leather trousers; ~**jacke** die leather jacket; ~**riemen** der [leather] strap; ~**waren** Pl. leather goods

ledig Adj. single; eine ~e Mutter an unmarried mother

Ledige der/die; adj. Dekl. single person

lediglich Adj. merely

leer Adj. empty; clean ⟨sheet of paper⟩; ~ stehend empty, unoccupied

Leere die; ~ (auch fig.) emptiness

leeren tr., refl. V. empty

leer-, Leer-: ~**gefegt** Adj. deserted ⟨street, town⟩; wie ~gefegt deserted; ~**lauf** der im ~lauf den Berg hinunterfahren ⟨driver⟩ coast down the hill in neutral; ⟨cyclist⟩ freewheel down the hill; *~**stehend** ▶ LEER; ~**taste** die space bar

Leerung die; ~, ~en emptying; (von Briefkästen) collection

Lefze die; ~, ~n lip

legal ①Adj. legal
②adv. legally

legalisieren tr. V. legalize

Legalisierung die; ~, ~en legalization

Legalität die; ~: legality

legen ①tr. V. (a) lay [down]
(b) (verlegen) lay ⟨pipe, cable, carpet, tiles, etc.⟩
②tr., itr. V. ⟨hen⟩ lay
③refl. V. (a) lie down
(b) (nachlassen) die down; abate; ⟨enthusiasm⟩ wear off, subside

legendär Adj. legendary

Legende die; ~, ~n legend

leger /le'ʒeːɐ̯/ ①Adj. casual
②adv. casually

legieren tr. V. alloy

Legierung die; ~, ~en alloy

Legislative die; ~, ~n (Politik) legislature

Legislatur·periode die legislative period

legitim Adj. legitimate

Legitimation die; ~, ~en (a) legitimation
(b) (Ausweis) proof of identity

legitimieren ①tr. V. (a) (rechtfertigen) justify
(b) (bevollmächtigen) authorize
(c) (für legitim erklären) legitimize ⟨child, relationship⟩
②refl. V. show proof of one's identity

Legitimität die; ~: legitimacy

Lehm der; ~s loam; (Ton) clay

Lehne die; ~, ~n (Rücken~) back; (Arm~) arm

lehnen 1 tr., refl. V. lean (**an** + Akk., **gegen** against)
2 itr. V. be leaning (**an** + Dat. against)

Lehn-: ~**stuhl** der armchair; ~**wort** das; Pl. ~**wörter** loanword

Lehr-: ~**auftrag** der lectureship; ~**buch** das textbook

Lehre die; ~, ~n (a) apprenticeship
(b) (Weltanschauung) doctrine
(c) (Theorie, Wissenschaft) theory
(d) (Erfahrung) lesson

lehren tr., itr. V. teach

Lehrer der; ~s, ~ (auch fig.) teacher; (Ausbilder) instructor

Lehrer-: ~**ausbildung** die teacher training no art.; ~**ausflug** die staff outing

Lehrerin die; ~, ~nen teacher

Lehrer-: ~**kollegium** das teaching staff; faculty (Amer.); ~**konferenz** das staff meeting; ~**zimmer** das staffroom

Lehr-: ~**gang** der course (**für, in** + Dat. in); ~**jahr** das year as an apprentice; ~**körper** der (Amtsspr.) teaching staff; faculty (Amer.)

Lehrling der; ~s, ~e apprentice; (in kaufmännischen Berufen) trainee

lehr-, Lehr-: ~**plan** der (Schulw.) syllabus; (Gesamtlehrgang) curriculum; ~**reich** Adj. informative; ~**stelle** die apprenticeship; (in kaufmännischen Berufen) trainee post; ~**stoff** der (Schulw.) syllabus

Leib der; ~[e]s, ~er (geh.) body; **mit ~ und Seele** Arzt/Krankenschwester usw. sein be a dedicated doctor/nurse etc.; **mit ~ und Seele dabei sein** put one's whole heart into it

Leibes-: ~**übungen** Pl. (Schulw.) physical education sing.; PE; ~**visitation** die; ~~, ~~en body search

Leib·gericht das favourite dish

leibhaftig Adj. in person postpos.; (echt) real

leiblich Adj. physical ⟨well-being⟩; (blutsverwandt) real

Leib-: ~**schmerzen** Pl. abdominal pain sing.; ~**wächter** der, ~**wächterin** die bodyguard

Leiche die; ~, ~n [dead] body; corpse

Leichen der hearse

leichen-, Leichen-: ~**blass**, *~**blaß** Adj. deathly pale; ~**schau·haus** das morgue; ~**wagen** der hearse

Leichnam der; ~s, ~e (geh.) body

leicht 1 Adj. light; lightweight ⟨suit, material⟩; easy ⟨task, question, job, etc.⟩; slight ⟨accent, illness, wound, doubt, etc.⟩; mild ⟨cigar, cigarette⟩; ~ **fallen** be easy; **das fällt mir ~:** it's easy for me; **jmdm./sich etw. ~ machen** make sth. easy for sb./oneself; **etw. ~ nehmen** make light of sth.

2 adv. lightly ⟨built⟩; (einfach, schnell, spielend) easily; (geringfügig) slightly; ~ **verletzt** slightly injured

leicht-, Leicht-: ~**athletik** die [track and field] athletics sing.; *~**fallen** ▶ LEICHT 1; ~**fertig** 1 Adj. careless ⟨behaviour, person⟩; rash ⟨promise⟩; ill-considered, slapdash ⟨plan⟩; 2 adv. carelessly; ~**gläubig** Adj. gullible

Leichtigkeit die; ~ (geringes Gewicht) lightness; (Mühelosigkeit) ease

leicht-, Leicht-: *~**|machen** ▶ LEICHT 1; *~**|nehmen** ▶ LEICHT 1; ~**sinn** der carelessness no indef. art.; (mit Gefahr verbunden) recklessness no indef. art.; ~**sinnig** 1 Adj. careless; (sich, andere gefährdend) reckless; (fahrlässig) negligent; 2 adv. carelessly; (gefährlich) recklessly; ⟨promise⟩ rashly; ~**sinniger·weise** Adv. carelessly; (gefährlicherweise) recklessly; ⟨promise⟩ rashly; *~**verletzt** ▶ LEICHT 2

leid Adj. **etw./jmdn. ~ sein/werden** (ugs.) be/get fed up with sth./sb. (coll.); s. auch LEID[2]

Leid[1] das; ~[e]s (a) (Schmerz) suffering; (Kummer) grief; sorrow
(b) (Unrecht) wrong; (Böses) harm

Leid[2]: **es tut mir ~, [dass]...:** I'm sorry [that]...; **er tut mir ~:** I feel sorry for him

leiden 1 unr. itr. V. suffer (**an, unter** + Dat. from)
2 unr. tr. V. (a) **jmdn. [gut] ~ können** od. **mögen** like sb.
(b) (geh.: ertragen müssen) suffer ⟨hunger, thirst, etc.⟩

Leiden das; ~s, ~ (a) (Krankheit) illness; (Gebrechen) complaint
(b) (Qual) suffering

leidend Adj. (a) (krank) ailing
(b) (schmerzvoll) strained ⟨voice⟩; martyred ⟨expression⟩

Leidenschaft die; ~, ~en passion (**zu, für** for)

leidenschaftlich 1 Adj. passionate; vehement ⟨protest⟩
2 adv. passionately; (eifrig) dedicatedly; **etw. ~ gern tun** adore doing sth.

Leidens·genosse der,
Leidens·genossin die fellow sufferer

leider Adv. unfortunately

leidig Adj. tiresome

leidlich Adj. reasonable

Leid·tragende der/die; adj. Dekl. victim

Leier die; ~, ~n lyre

leihen unr. tr. V. (a) **jmdm. etw. ~:** lend sb. sth.
(b) (entleihen) borrow

Leih-: ~**gabe** die loan (Gen. from); ~**gebühr** die hire or (Amer.) rental charge; (bei Büchern) borrowing fee; ~**haus** das pawnbroker's; pawnshop; ~**mutter** die; Pl. ~**mütter** surrogate mother; ~**wagen** der hire or (Amer.) rental car

Leim der; ~[e]s glue

---

leimen *tr. V.* glue (**an** + *Akk.* to)

Leine *die;* ∼, ∼n rope; (Wäsche∼, Angel∼) line; (Hunde∼) lead (esp. Brit.); leash; ∼ **ziehen** (ugs.) clear off

leinen *Adj.* linen ⟨*tablecloth, sheet, etc.*⟩

Leinen *das;* ∼s (a) (Gewebe) linen (b) (Buchw.) cloth

Leinen·band *der* cloth-bound volume

Lein·wand *die* (a) linen; (grob) canvas (b) (des Malers) canvas (c) (für Filme und Dias) screen

leise 1 *Adj.* (a) quiet; soft ⟨*steps, music, etc.*⟩ (b) (leicht) faint; slight; slight, gentle ⟨*touch*⟩ 2 *adv.* (a) quietly (b) (leicht; kaum merklich) slightly; ⟨*touch, rain*⟩ gently

Leiste *die;* ∼, ∼n strip; (Holz∼) batten; (profiliert) moulding

leisten 1 *tr. V.* do ⟨*work*⟩; (schaffen) achieve ⟨*a lot, nothing*⟩; **jmdm. Hilfe** ∼: help sb. 2 *refl. V.* (ugs.) **sich** (*Dat.*) **etw.** ∼: treat oneself to sth.; **sich** (*Dat.*) **etw. [nicht]** ∼ **können** [not] be able to afford sth.

Leisten·bruch *der* rupture

Leistung *die;* ∼, ∼en (a) (Qualität bzw. Quantität der Arbeit) performance (b) (Errungenschaft) achievement; (im Sport) performance (c) (Leistungsvermögen, Physik: Arbeits∼) power (d) (Zahlung, Zuwendung) payment; (Versicherungsw.) benefit (e) (Dienst∼) service

leistungs-, Leistungs-: ∼**druck** *der* (bei Arbeitnehmern) pressure to work harder; (bei Sportlern, Schülern) pressure to achieve *or* to do well; ∼**fähig** *Adj.* capable ⟨*person*⟩; (körperlich) able-bodied; ∼**gesellschaft** *die* competitive society; ∼**prinzip** *das* competitive principle; ∼**sport** *der* competitive sport *no art.*

Leit·artikel *der* (Zeitungsw.) leading article; leader

leiten *tr. V.* (a) (anführen) lead; head; be head of ⟨*school*⟩; (verantwortlich sein für) be in charge of ⟨*project, expedition, etc.*⟩; manage ⟨*factory, enterprise*⟩; (den Vorsitz führen bei) chair; conduct ⟨*orchestra, choir*⟩; ∼**der Angestellter** manager (b) (begleiten, führen) lead (c) (lenken) direct; route ⟨*traffic*⟩; (um∼) divert

Leiter¹ *der;* ∼s, ∼: leader; (einer Abteilung) head; (eines Instituts) director; (einer Schule) head teacher; headmaster (Brit.); principal (esp. Amer.); chair[man]

Leiter² *die;* ∼, ∼n ladder

Leiterin *die;* ∼, ∼nen ▶ LEITER¹; (einer Schule) head teacher; headmistress (Brit.); principal (esp. Amer.)

Leit-: ∼**motiv** *das* (Musik, Literaturw., fig.) (a) leitmotiv; (b) (Leitgedanke) dominant *or*

central theme; ∼**planke** *die* crash barrier; guardrail (Amer.)

Leitung *die;* ∼, ∼en (a) ▶ LEITEN A: leading; heading; being in charge; management; chairing (b) (einer Expedition usw.) leadership; (Verantwortung) responsibility (*Gen.* for); (eines Betriebes, Unternehmens) management; (einer Sitzung, Diskussion) chairmanship (c) (leitende Personen) management; (einer Schule) head and senior staff (d) (Rohr∼) pipe; (Haupt∼) main (e) (Draht, Kabel) cable; (für ein Gerät) lead (f) (Telefon∼) line

Leitungs·wasser *das* tap water

Leit·zins[satz] *der* (Finanzw.) discount rate; ≈ base rate

Lektion /lɛkˈtsi̯oːn/ *die;* ∼, ∼en lesson

Lektor *der;* ∼s, ∼en (a) (Hochschulw.) *junior university teacher in charge of practical or supplementary classes etc.;* (b) (im Verlag) [publisher's] editor

Lektüre *die;* ∼, ∼n (a) reading (b) (Lesestoff) reading [matter]

Lende *die;* ∼, ∼n loin

Lenden-: ∼**gegend** *die* loins *pl.;* lumbar region (Anat.); ∼**schurz** *der* loincloth; ∼**wirbel** *der* (Anat.) lumbar vertebra

lenken *tr. V.* (a) *auch itr.* steer; be at the controls of ⟨*aircraft*⟩; guide ⟨*missile*⟩; (fahren) drive ⟨*car etc.*⟩ (b) direct ⟨*thoughts etc.*⟩ (**auf** + *Akk.* to); turn ⟨*attention*⟩ (**auf** + *Akk.* to) (c) (kontrollieren) control ⟨*person, press, economy*⟩; govern ⟨*state*⟩

Lenker *der;* ∼s, ∼ (a) handlebars *pl.;* (b) (Fahrer) driver

Lenkerin *die;* ∼, ∼nen ▶ LENKER B

Lenk-: ∼**rad** *das* steering wheel; ∼**rad·schloss,** *∼**rad·schloß** das (Kfz-W.) steering [wheel] lock; ∼**stange** *die* handlebars *pl.*

Lenz *der;* ∼es, ∼e (dichter. veralt.) spring

Leopard *der;* ∼en, ∼en leopard

Lepra *die;* ∼: leprosy *no art.*

Lerche *die;* ∼, ∼n lark

lernen 1 *itr. V.* study; (als Lehrling) train 2 *tr. V.* learn (**aus** from)

lesbar *Adj.* legible; (klar) lucid ⟨*style*⟩; (verständlich) comprehensible

Lesbe *die;* ∼, ∼n (ugs.) lesbian

Lesbierin /ˈlɛsbi̯ərɪn/ *die;* ∼, ∼nen lesbian

lesbisch *Adj.* Lesbian

Lese-: ∼**brille** *die* reading glasses *pl.;* ∼**buch** *das* reader

lesen¹ *unr. tr., itr. V.* read

lesen² *unr. tr. V.* (a) pick ⟨*grapes, berries, fruit*⟩; gather ⟨*firewood*⟩; **Ähren** ∼: glean [ears of corn] (b) (aussondern) pick over

Leser *der;* ∼s, ∼: reader

Leserbrief *der* reader's letter; ~e readers' letters; „~e" (Zeitungsrubrik) 'Letters to the editor'

Leserin *die;* ~, ~nen reader

Leserkreis *der* readership

leserlich [1] *Adj.* legible
[2] *adv.* legibly

Lese-zeichen *das* bookmark

Lesung *die;* ~, ~en reading

Lette *der;* ~n, ~n, **Lettin** *die;* ~, ~nen Latvian

lettisch *Adj.* Latvian; Lettish ‹*language*›

Lett·land *(das);* ~s Latvia

Letzt: zu guter ~: in the end

letzt... *Adj.* last; ~en Endes in the end; (äußerst...) ultimate; (neuest...) latest ‹*news*›

*****letzte·mal**: ▶ MAL[1]

*****letzen·mal**: ▶ MAL[1]

letzter... *Adj.* latter

letztlich *Adv.* ultimately; in the end

Leucht·diode *die* light-emitting diode; LED

Leuchte *die;* ~, ~n light

leuchten *itr. V.* (a) ‹*moon, sun, star, etc.*› be shining; ‹*fire, face*› glow
(b) shine a/the light; jmdm. ~: light the way for sb.

leuchtend *Adj.* (a) shining ‹*eyes*›; brilliant ‹*colours*›; bright ‹*blue, red, etc.*›
(b) (großartig) shining ‹*example*›

Leuchter *der;* ~s, ~: candelabrum; (für eine Kerze) candlestick

Leucht-: ~farbe *die* luminous paint; ~kugel *die* flare; ~reklame *die* neon sign; ~stoff·lampe *die* fluorescent light *or* lamp; ~turm *der* lighthouse; ~ziffer·blatt *das* luminous dial

leugnen [1] *tr. V.* deny
[2] *itr. V.* deny it

Leukämie *die;* ~, ~n (Med.) leukaemia

Leumund *der;* ~[e]s (geh.) reputation

Leute *Pl.* people; die reichen/alten ~: the rich/the old

Leutnant *der;* ~s, ~s second lieutenant

leut·selig [1] *Adj.* affable
[2] *adv.* affably

Lexikon *das;* ~s, Lexika *od.* Lexiken encyclopaedia (*Gen.,* für of)

Libanese *der;* ~n, ~n, **Libanesin** *die;* ~, ~nen Lebanese

Libanon *(das) od. der;* ~s Lebanon

Libelle *die;* ~, ~n dragonfly

liberal [1] *Adj.* liberal
[2] *adv.* liberally

Liberale *der/die; adj. Dekl.* liberal

liberalisieren *tr. V.* liberalize; relax ‹*import controls*›

Libero *der;* ~s, ~s (Fußball) sweeper

Libyen *(das);* ~s Libya

libysch *Adj.* Libyan

licht *Adj.* (a) light
(b) (dünn bewachsen) sparse; thin

Licht *das;* ~[e]s, ~er (a) light
(b) (elektrisches) light
(c) *Pl. auch* ~e (Kerze) candle

licht-, Licht-: ~bild *das* [small] photograph (*for passport etc.*); ~empfindlich *Adj.* sensitive to light

lichten[1] [1] *tr. V.* thin out ‹*trees etc.*›
[2] *refl. V.* ‹*trees*› thin out; ‹*hair*› grow thin; ‹*fog, mist*› lift

lichten[2] *tr. V.* (Seemannsspr.) den/die Anker ~: weigh anchor

lichterloh [1] *Adj.* blazing ‹*fire*›; leaping ‹*flames*›
[2] *adv.* ~ brennen be blazing fiercely

Lichter·meer *das* sea of lights

Licht-: ~hupe *die* headlight flasher; ~jahr *das* (Astron.) light year; ~kegel *der* beam; ~maschine *die* (Kfz-W.) (mit Gleichstrom) dynamo; (mit Wechselstrom) alternator; generator (esp. Amer.); ~reklame *die* neon sign; ~schalter *der* light switch; ~schranke *die* photoelectric beam; ~schutz·faktor *der* protection factor (*against sunburn*)

Lichtung *die;* ~, ~en clearing

Lid *das;* ~[e]s, ~er eyelid

lieb [1] *Adj.* (a) (liebevoll) kind ‹*words, gesture*›
(b) (liebenswert) likeable; nice; (stärker) lovable ‹*child, girl, pet*›; ~ aussehen look sweet *or* (Amer.) cute
(c) (artig) good ‹*child, dog*›
(d) (geschätzt) dear; sein liebstes Spielzeug his favourite toy; ~er Hans/~e Else! (am Briefanfang) dear Hans/Else
(e) (angenehm) welcome; es wäre mir ~/~er, wenn ...: I should be glad/should prefer it if ...
(f) jmdn. ~ haben love sb.; (gern haben) be fond of sb.
[2] *adv.* (a) (liebenswert) kindly
(b) (artig) nicely

Liebe *die;* ~, ~n (a) love; ~ zu jmdm./zu etw. love for sb./of sth.; aus ~ [zu jmdm.] for love [of sb.]; tu mir die ~ und ...: do me a favour and ...; mit ~: lovingly; with loving care
(b) (ugs.: geliebter Mensch) love

Liebelei *die;* ~, ~en flirtation

lieben [1] *tr. V.* (a) love; ~: love sb.; (sexuell) make love to sb.; sich ~: be in love; (sexuell) make love
(b) etw. ~: be fond of sth.; (stärker) love sth.
[2] *itr. V.* be in love

liebend *Adv.* etw. ~ gern tun [simply] love doing sth.

liebens·würdig *Adj.* kind; charming ‹*smile*›

lieber *Adv.* (a) ▶ GERN;

---

*old spelling - see note on page xiv

(b) better; **lass das ~:** better not do that

Liebes-: ~brief der love letter; **~paar** das courting couple; **~roman** der romantic novel

liebe·voll 1 Adj. loving attrib. ⟨care⟩; affectionate ⟨embrace, gesture, person⟩ 2 adv. lovingly; affectionately; (mit Sorgfalt) lovingly

***lieb|haben** ▶ LIEB 1F

Liebhaber der; ~s, ~ (a) lover **(b)** (Interessierter, Anhänger) enthusiast (Gen. for); (Sammler) collector

Liebhaberei die; ~, ~: hobby

Liebhaberin die; ~, ~nen ▶ LIEBHABER

lieblich 1 Adj. charming; (angenehm) sweet ⟨scent, sound⟩ 2 adv. sweetly; (angenehm) pleasingly

Liebling der; ~s, ~e (bes. als Anrede) darling; (bevorzugte Person) favourite

Lieblings- favourite

lieb·los 1 Adj. loveless 2 adv. **(a)** without affection **(b)** (ohne Sorgfalt) without proper care

liebsten: am ~: ▶ GERN

Liechtenstein (das); ~s Liechtenstein

Lied das; ~[e]s, ~er song

liederlich Adj. slovenly; messy ⟨hairstyle, person⟩

Lieder-: ~macher der; ~~s, ~~, **~macherin** die; ~~, ~~nen singer-songwriter

lief 1. u. 3. Pers. Sg. Prät. v. LAUFEN

Lieferant der; ~en, ~en, **Lieferantin** die; ~, ~nen supplier

lieferbar Adj. available; (vorrätig) in stock

Liefer·bedingungen Pl. terms of delivery

liefern tr. V. **(a)** (bringen) deliver (an + Akk. to); (zur Verfügung stellen) supply **(b)** (hervorbringen) produce; provide ⟨eggs, honey, examples, raw material, etc.⟩

Liefer-: ~schein der delivery note; **~termin** der delivery date

Lieferung die; ~, ~en delivery

Liefer-: ~wagen der [delivery] van; **~zeit** die delivery time

Liege die; ~, ~n daybed; (zum Ausklappen) bed settee; (als Gartenmöbel) sunlounger

liegen unr. itr. V. lie; ⟨person⟩ be lying down; (sich befinden) be; ⟨object⟩ be [lying]; ⟨town, house, etc.⟩ be [situated]; ⟨in Bett ~: lie in bed; ~ bleiben (liegen gelassen werden) stay; be left; (vergessen werden) be left behind; (unerledigt bleiben) be left undone; (nicht aufstehen) stay [lying]; [im Bett] ~ bleiben stay in bed; etw. ~ lassen leave sth.; (vergessen) leave sth. [behind]; (unerledigt lassen) leave sth. undone; einen Brief ~ lassen (nicht abschicken) leave a letter unposted; (nicht öffnen) leave a letter unopened; das liegt an ihm od. bei ihm it is up to him; (ist seine Schuld) it is his fault; es

liegt mir nicht it doesn't suit me; (es spricht mich nicht an) it doesn't appeal to me; (ich mag es nicht) I don't like it; **daran liegt ihm viel/wenig/nichts** he sets great/little/no store by that

liegen-: *~|bleiben ▶ LIEGEN; *~|lassen** ▶ LIEGEN

Liege-: ~stuhl der deckchair; **~stütz** der; ~~es, ~~e press-up; **~wagen** der couchette car; **~wiese** die sunbathing lawn

lieh 1. u. 3. Pers. Sg. Prät. v. LEIHEN

lies Imperativ Sg. v. LESEN

ließ 1. u. 3. Pers. Sg. Prät. v. LASSEN

liest 3. Pers. Sg. Präsens v. LESEN

Lift der; ~[e]s, ~e od. ~s **(a)** lift (Brit.); elevator (Amer.) **(b)** Pl.: ~e (Ski~, Sessel~) lift

Liga die; ~, Ligen league; (Sport) division

Likör der; ~s, ~e liqueur

lila indekl. Adj. mauve; (dunkel~) purple

Lila das; ~s, ~ od. (ugs.) ~s mauve; (Dunkel~) purple

Lilie /ˈliːljə/ die; ~, ~n lily

Liliputaner der; ~s, ~, **Liliputanerin** die; ~, ~nen dwarf

Limit das; ~s, ~s limit

Limo die, auch: das; ~, ~[s] (ugs.) fizzy drink

Limonade die; ~, ~n fizzy drink; (Zitronen~) lemonade

Limousine die; ~, ~n [large] saloon (Brit.) or (Amer.) sedan

Linde die; ~, ~n lime [tree]

lindern tr. V. relieve ⟨suffering, pain⟩; slake ⟨thirst⟩

Lineal das; ~s, ~e ruler

Linie /ˈliːnjə/ die; ~, ~n line; (Verkehrsstrecke) route; **die ~ 12** (Verkehrsw.) the number 12; **auf die [schlanke] ~ achten** (ugs. scherzh.) watch one's figure; **auf der ganzen ~** (fig.) all along the line

linien-, Linien-: ~bus der regular bus; **~flug** der scheduled flight; **~richter** der, **~richterin** die (Fußball usw.) linesman; (Tennis) line judge; (Rugby) touch judge; **~treu** 1 Adj. loyal to the party line postpos.; 2 adv. ⟨act⟩ in accordance with the party line

linieren, liniieren tr. V. rule

link... Adj. **(a)** left **(b)** (innen, nicht sichtbar) wrong, reverse ⟨side⟩ **(c)** (in der Politik) left-wing

linkisch 1 Adj. awkward 2 adv. awkwardly

links Adv. on the left; (Politik) on the left wing

links-, Links-: ~abbieger der, **~abbiegerin** die (Verkehrsw.) motorist/ cyclist/car etc. turning left; **~außen** der; ~~, ~~ (Ballspiele) left wing; outside left; **~extremist** der, **~extremistin** die ···⫶

(Politik) left-wing extremist; ~**händer** der;
~~s, ~~, ~**händerin** die; ~~, ~~nen
left-hander; ~**kurve** die left-hand bend;
~**radikal** (Politik) [1] Adj. radical left-
wing; [2] adv. eine ~radikal orientierte Gruppe
a group with a radical left-wing orientation;
~**radikale** der/die left-wing radical;
~**radikalismus** der left-wing radicalism;
~**verkehr** der driving no art. on the left
Linoleum das; ~s linoleum; lino
Linse die; ~, ~n (a) (Bot., Kochk.) lentil
(b) (Med., Optik) lens
Lippe die; ~, ~n lip
Lippen·stift der lipstick
liquid Adj. (Wirtsch.) liquid (funds, resources);
solvent (business)
liquidieren (verhüll.: töten; Wirtsch.) liquidate
lispeln itr. V. lisp
Lissabon (das); ~s Lisbon
List die; ~, ~en (a) [cunning] trick
(b) (listige Art) cunning
Liste die; ~, ~n list; schwarze ~: blacklist
listig [1] Adj. cunning; crafty
[2] adv. cunningly; craftily
Litauen (das); ~s Lithuania
Litauer der; ~s, ~, **Litauerin** die; ~,
~nen Lithuanian
litauisch Adj. Lithuanian
Liter der, auch: das; ~s, ~: litre
literarisch Adj. literary
Literatur die; ~, ~en literature
Literatur-: ~**geschichte** die literary
history; history of literature;
~**verzeichnis** das list of references
liter·weise Adv. by the litre; in litres
Litfaß·säule die advertising column
Lithografie, Lithographie die; ~, ~n
(Druck) lithograph
litt 1. u. 3. Pers. Sg. Prät. v. LEIDEN
Litze die; ~, ~n braid
live /laiːf/ (Rundf., Ferns.); [1] Adj. live
[2] adv. live; in dieser Sendung wird nur ~
gesungen in this programme all the singing
is live
Live-: ~**sendung**, *~**-Sendung** die
(Rundf., Ferns.) live programme;
~**übertragung** die (Rundf., Ferns.) live
broadcast
Lizenz die; ~, ~en licence
Lizenz·gebühr die licence fee; (Verlagsw.)
royalty
Lkw, LKW /ɛlkaːˈveː/ der; ~[s], ~[s] Abk.
= **Lastkraftwagen** truck; lorry (Brit.)
Lob das; ~[e]s, ~e praise no indef. art.
Lobby /ˈlɔbi/ die; ~, ~s od. **Lobbies** lobby
loben tr. V. praise
lobens·wert [1] Adj. praiseworthy;
laudable; commendable
[2] adv. laudably; commendably

löblich Adj. commendable
Lob·lied das song of praise
Loch das; ~[e]s, **Löcher** hole
lochen tr. V. punch holes/a hole in; punch
⟨ticket⟩
Locher der; ~s, ~: punch
löcherig Adj. full of holes pred.
Locke die; ~, ~n curl
locken tr. V. (a) lure
(b) (reizen) tempt
Locken·wickler der [hair] curler
locker [1] Adj. loose; (entspannt) relaxed
⟨position, muscles⟩; slack ⟨rope, rein⟩; (fig.)
relax ⟨regulation, law, etc.⟩
[2] adv. ~ sitzen ⟨tooth, screw, nail⟩ be loose;
(entspannt, ungezwungen) loosely
locker|lassen unr. itr. V. (ugs.) nicht ~:
not give up
lockern [1] tr. V. loosen; slacken [off] ⟨rope
etc.⟩; relax ⟨muscles, limbs⟩
[2] refl. V. ⟨brick, tooth, etc.⟩ work itself loose;
⟨person⟩ loosen up
Lockerung die; ~, ~en (a) loosening; (fig.:
von Bestimmung, Gesetz usw.) relaxation
(b) (Entspannung) loosening up; relaxation
lockig Adj. curly
Lock·vogel der decoy
Loden·mantel der loden coat
Löffel der; ~s, ~: spoon; (als Maßangabe)
spoonful; (Jägerspr.) ear
löffeln tr. V. spoon [up]
log 1. u. 3. Pers. Sg. Prät. v. LÜGEN
Logarithmus der; ~, **Logarithmen** (Math.)
logarithm; log
Loge /ˈloːʒə/ die; ~, ~n box
logieren itr. V. (veralt.) stay
Logik die; ~: logic
logisch [1] Adj. logical
[2] adv. logically
logischer·weise Adv. logically;
(selbstverständlich) naturally
logo Adj. (salopp) [ist doch] ~! you bet! (coll.);
of course!
Lohn der; ~[e]s, **Löhne** (a) wage[s pl.]; pay
no indef. art., no pl.
(b) (Belohnung) reward
Lohn·büro das payroll office
lohnen [1] refl., itr. V. be worth it
[2] tr. V. be worth
lohnend Adj. rewarding
Lohn·steuer die income tax
Lohn-: ~**steuer·karte** die income-tax
card; ~**streifen** der payslip; ~**tüte** die
pay packet (Brit.); wage packet
lokal Adj. local
Lokal das; ~s, ~e pub (Brit. coll.); bar (Amer.);
(Speise~) restaurant
Lokalität die; ~, ~en locality
Lokal-: ~**blatt** das local paper;
~**patriotismus** der local patriotism;

~**teil** der (Zeitungsw.) local section;
~**termi⬛n** der (Rechtsspr.) visit to the scene [of the ⬛ime]

Lok·führer der, **Lok·führerin** die:
▶ LOKOMOTIVFÜHRER

Lokomotive /lokomo'ti:və/ die; ~, ~n locomotive

Lokomotiv·führer der,
Lokomotiv·führerin die engine driver (Brit.); engineer (Amer.)

Lokus der; ~ od. ~ses, ~ od. ~se (salopp) loo (Brit. coll.); john (Amer. coll.)

London (das); ~s London

Londoner ⓵ indekl. Adj. London
⓶ der; ~s, ~: Londoner

Londonerin die; ~, ~nen Londoner

Lorbeer der; ~s, ~en (a) laurel
(b) (Gewürz) bayleaf

Lore die; ~, ~n car; (kleiner) tub

los ⓵ Adj. (a) (gelöst, ab) off
(b) es ist etwas ~: there is something going on
(c) jmdn./etw. ~ sein be rid of sb./sth.
⓶ Adv. (als Aufforderung) come on!

Los das; ~es, ~e (a) lot
(b) (Lotterie~) ticket

Lösch·blatt das piece of blotting paper

löschen tr. V. (a) put out; extinguish; seinen Durst ~ (fig.) quench one's thirst
(b) (tilgen) delete ⟨entry⟩; erase ⟨recording, memory, etc.⟩

Lösch-: ~**fahrzeug** das fire engine; ~**papier** das blotting paper

lose ⓵ Adj. loose
⓶ adv. loosely

Löse·geld das ransom

losen itr. V. draw lots (um for)

lösen ⓵ tr. V. (a) remove ⟨stamp, wallpaper⟩; etw. von etw. ~: remove sth. from sth.
(b) (lockern) undo ⟨screw, belt, tie⟩
(c) (klären) solve; resolve ⟨contradiction, conflict⟩
(d) (annullieren) break off ⟨engagement⟩; cancel ⟨contract⟩; sever ⟨relationship⟩
(e) (kaufen) buy, obtain ⟨ticket⟩
⓶ refl. V. (a) (lose werden) come off; (sich lockern) ⟨wallpaper, plaster⟩ come off; ⟨packing, screw⟩ come loose
(b) (sich klären) ⟨puzzle, problem⟩ be solved
(c) (sich auflösen) dissolve

los-: ~|**fahren** unr. itr. V.; mit sein set off; (wegfahren) move off; ~|**gehen** unr. itr. V.; mit sein (a) (aufbrechen) set off; (b) (ugs.: beginnen) start; (c) (ugs.: abgehen) ⟨button, handle, etc.⟩ come off; ~|**kommen** unr. itr. V.; mit sein (a) (ugs.) get away; (b) (freikommen) get free; ~|**lassen** unr. tr. V. (a) (nicht festhalten) let go of; (b) (freilassen) let ⟨person, animal⟩ go; ~|**legen** itr. V. (ugs.) get going

löslich Adj. soluble

Löslichkeit die; ~: solubility

los|machen tr. V. (ugs.) let ⟨animal⟩ loose; untie ⟨string, line, rope⟩; unhitch ⟨trailer⟩

Los·nummer die [lottery-]ticket number

los-: ~|**reißen** unr. refl. V. break free or loose; ~|**sagen** refl. V. sich von jmdm./etw. ~sagen break with sb./sth.; ~|**schlagen** unr. itr. V. (bes. Milit.) attack; launch one's attack

Löss, *Löß der; Lösses, Lösse (Geol.) loess

Losung die; ~, ~en slogan; (Milit.: Kennwort) password

Lösung die; ~, ~en (a) solution ⟨Gen., für to⟩
(b) ▶ LÖSEN 1D: breaking off; cancellation; severing

los|werden unr. tr. V.; mit sein get rid of

Lot das; ~[e]s, ~e plumb [bob]; [nicht] im ~ sein be [out of] plumb

löten tr. V. solder

Lotion die; ~, ~en lotion

Löt·kolben der soldering iron

lot·recht ⓵ Adj. perpendicular; vertical
⓶ adv. perpendicularly; vertically

Lotse der; ~n, ~n (Seew.) pilot

lotsen tr. V. guide

Lotsin die ▶ LOTSE

Lotterie die; ~, ~n lottery

Lotto das; ~s, ~s national lottery

Lotto-: ~**schein** der national-lottery coupon; ~**zahlen** Pl. winning national-lottery numbers

Löt·zinn das [tin-lead] solder

Löwe der; ~n, ~n (a) lion
(b) (Astrol.) Leo; the Lion

Löwen-: ~**anteil** der lion's share; ~**mäulchen** das; ~~s, ~~: snapdragon; ~**zahn** der dandelion

Löwin die; ~, ~nen lioness

loyal /loa'ja:l/ ⓵ Adj. loyal
⓶ adv. loyally

Loyalität die; ~: loyalty

LP /ɛl'pe:/ die; ~, ~[s] Abk.
= Langspielplatte LP

LSD /ɛl|ɛs'de:/ das; ~[s] LSD

Luchs der; ~es, ~e lynx

Lücke die; ~, ~n gap

lücken-, Lücken-: ~**büßer** der, ~~s, ~~, ~**büßerin** die; ~~, ~~nen (ugs.) stopgap; ~**haft** Adj. sketchy; ~**los** Adj. complete

lud 1. u. 3. Pers. Sg. Prät. v. LADEN

Luder das; ~s, ~ (salopp) so-and-so (coll.)

Luft die; ~, Lüfte air; an die frische ~ gehen get out in[to] the fresh air; die ~ anhalten hold one's breath; tief ~ holen take a deep breath; in die ~ gehen (fig. ugs.) blow one's top (coll.)

luft-, Luft-: ~**angriff** der (Milit.) air raid; ~**ballon** der balloon; ~**brücke** der airlift; ~**dicht** Adj. airtight; ~**druck** der (a) (Physik) air pressure; (b) (Druckwelle) blast

lüften [1] *tr. V.* (a) air ⟨*room, clothes, etc.*⟩
(b) raise ⟨*hat*⟩
(c) disclose ⟨*secret*⟩
[2] *itr. V.* air the room/house *etc*

luft-, Luft-: ∼**fahrt** *die* aviation *no art.;*
∼**feuchtigkeit** *die* [atmospheric]
humidity; ∼**gekühlt** *Adj.* air-cooled;
∼**getrocknet** *Adj.* air-dried; ∼**gewehr**
das air rifle; airgun

luftig *Adj.* airy ⟨*room, building, etc.*⟩; light
⟨*clothes*⟩

Luft·kissen·boot *das* hovercraft

luft-, Luft-: ∼**leer** *Adj.* ein ∼leerer Raum
a vacuum; ∼**linie** *die* 1000 km ∼linie 1,000
km. as the crow flies; ∼**loch** *das* air hole;
∼**matratze** *die* airbed; air mattress; Lilo
®; ∼**pirat** *der,* ∼**piratin** *die* [aircraft]
hijacker; ∼**post** *die* airmail; etw. per *od.*
mit ∼post schicken send sth. [by] airmail;
∼**pumpe** *die* air pump; (für Fahrrad) [bicycle]
pump; ∼**röhre** *die* (Anat.) windpipe;
∼**schiff** *das* airship; ∼**schloss,**
*∼**schloß** *das* castle in the air; ∼**schutz**
der air-raid protection *no art.;*
∼**schutz·bunker,** ∼**schutz·keller,**
∼**schutz·raum** *der* air-raid shelter;
∼**verschmutzung** *die* air pollution;
∼**waffe** *die* air force; ∼**zug** *der* [gentle]
breeze; (in Zimmern, Gebäuden) draught

Lüge *die;* ∼, ∼n lie

lügen *itr., tr. V.* lie; **das ist gelogen!** that's a
lie!

Lügner *der;* ∼s, ∼, **Lügnerin** *die;* ∼,
∼nen liar

Luke *die;* ∼, ∼n (Dach∼) skylight; (bei
Schiffen) hatch; (Keller∼) trapdoor

lukrativ [1] *Adj.* lucrative
[2] *adv.* lucratively

Lümmel *der;* ∼s, ∼: lout; (ugs., fam.: Bengel)
rascal

Lump *der;* ∼en, ∼en scoundrel

lumpen (ugs.) *tr. V.* sich nicht ∼ lassen
splash out (coll.)

Lumpen *der;* ∼s, ∼ rag

Lumpen-: ∼**sammler** *die* rag-and-bone
man; ∼**sammlerin** *die* rag-and-bone
woman

Lunge *die;* ∼, ∼n lungs *pl.*

Lungen-: ∼**entzündung** *die* pneumonia
no indef. art.; ∼**krebs** *der* lung cancer;
∼**zug** *der* inhalation

Lunte *die;* ∼, ∼n fuse; match

Lupe *die;* ∼, ∼n magnifying glass

Lurch *der;* ∼[e]s, ∼e amphibian

Lust *die;* ∼ (a) ∼ haben, etw. zu tun feel
like doing sth.
(b) (Vergnügen) pleasure; joy

lustig [1] *Adj.* (a) merry; jolly; enjoyable
⟨*time*⟩
(b) (komisch) funny
[2] *adv.* (a) merrily
(b) (komisch) funnily

lust-, Lust-: ∼**los** [1] *Adj.* listless; [2] *adv.*
listlessly; ∼**spiel** *das* comedy

lutherisch *Adj.* Lutheran

lutschen [1] *tr. V.* suck
[2] *itr. V.* suck; an etw. (*Dat.*) ∼: suck sth.

Luxemburg (*das*) ∼s Luxembourg

luxuriös [1] *Adj.* luxurious
[2] *adv.* luxuriously

Luxus *der;* ∼: luxury

Lymphe *die;* ∼, ∼n lymph

Lymph·knoten *der* lymph node

lynchen *tr. V.* lynch

Lyrik *die;* ∼: lyric poetry

Lyriker *der;* ∼s, ∼, **Lyrikerin** *die;* ∼,
∼nen lyric poet; lyricist

lyrisch *Adj.* lyrical; lyric ⟨*poetry*⟩

Lyzeum *das;* ∼s, Lyzeen girls' high school

M m

m, M /ɛm/ *das;* ∼, ∼ m/M

m *Abk.* = **Meter** m

Mach·art *die* style; (Schnitt) cut

machbar *Adj.* feasible

machen [1] *tr. V.* (a) make; aus Plastik/Holz
usw. gemacht made of plastic/wood *etc.;* sich
(*Dat.*) etw. ∼ lassen have sth. made; etw. aus
jmdm. ∼: make sb. into sth.; jmdn. zum
Präsidenten *usw.* ∼: make sb. president *etc.;*

jmdm./sich [einen] Kaffee ∼: make [some]
coffee for sb./oneself
(b) (verursachen) jmdm. Arbeit ∼: make [extra]
work for sb.; **das macht das Wetter** that's
[because of] the weather
(c) (ausführen) do ⟨*job, repair, etc.*⟩; **einen
Spaziergang** ∼: go for a walk; **eine Reise** ∼:
go on a journey; **einen Besuch [bei jmdm.]**
∼: pay [sb.] a visit
(d) (tun) do; **was machst du da?** what are you
doing?; **so etwas macht man nicht** that [just]
isn't done
(e) **was macht ...?** (wie ist es um ... bestellt?)

*old spelling - see note on page xiv

how is …?; **was macht die Gesundheit/ Arbeit?** how are you keeping/how is the job [getting on]?
(f) (ergeben) (beim Rechnen) be; (bei Geldbeträgen) come to; **zwei mal zwei macht vier** two times two is four; **das macht 12 Euro** that is 12 euros; (Endsumme) that comes to 12 euros
(g) (schaden) **was macht das schon?** what does it matter?; **macht nichts!** (ugs.) it doesn't matter
(h) (teilnehmen an) **einen Kursus** od. **Lehrgang** ∼: take a course
(i) mach's gut! (ugs.) look after yourself!; (auf Wiedersehen) so long!
2 *refl. V.* **(a) sich an etw.** (*Akk.*) ∼: get down to sth.
(b) (ugs.: sich entwickeln) do well
(c) mach dir nichts daraus! (ugs.) don't let it bother you
3 *itr. V.* **(a) mach schon!** (ugs.) get a move on! (coll.)
(b) das macht hungrig/durstig it makes you hungry/thirsty; **das macht dick** it's fattening
Machenschaften *Pl.* (abwertend) wheeling and dealing *sing.*
Macher *der;* ∼s, ∼, **Macherin** *die;* ∼, ∼nen (ugs.) doer; **der Typ des Machers** the dynamic type who just gets on with things
Macho /'matʃ:o/ *der;* ∼s, ∼s (abwertend) macho
Macht *die;* ∼, Mächte power; **an die** ∼ **kommen** come to power
Macht-: ∼**bereich** *der* sphere of influence; ∼**haber** *der;* ∼∼s, ∼∼, ∼**haberin** *die;* ∼∼, ∼∼nen ruler
mächtig 1 *Adj.* **(a)** powerful
(b) (beeindruckend groß) mighty
2 *adv.* (ugs.) terribly (coll.)
macht-, Macht-: ∼**kampf** *der* power struggle; ∼**los** *Adj.* powerless; **gegen etw.** ∼**los sein** be powerless in the face of sth.; ∼**probe** *die* trial of strength
Mach·werk *das* (abwertend) shoddy effort
Macke *die;* ∼, ∼n **(a)** (salopp: Tick) fad
(b) (ugs.: Defekt) defect
Mädchen *das;* ∼s, ∼ **(a)** girl
(b) (Haus∼) maid
mädchenhaft *Adj.* girlish
Mädchen·name *der* **(a)** girl's name
(b) (Name vor der Ehe) maiden name
Made *die;* ∼, ∼n maggot
madig *Adj.* maggoty; **jmdn./etw.** ∼ **machen** (ugs.) run sb./sth. down
Madonna *die;* ∼, Madonnen madonna
mag *1. u. 3. Pers. Sg. Präsens v.* MÖGEN
Magazin *das;* ∼s, ∼e **(a)** (Lager) store; (für Waren) stockroom
(b) (für Patronen, Dias, Film usw.; Zeitschrift) magazine
Magazin·sendung *die* magazine programme
Magen *der;* ∼s, Mägen od. ∼: stomach

magen-, Magen-: ∼**bitter** *der;* ∼∼s, ∼∼: bitters *pl.;* ∼**geschwür** *das* stomach ulcer; ∼**krebs** *der* cancer of the stomach; ∼**schmerzen** *Pl.* stomach ache *sing.*
mager *Adj.* **(a)** thin
(b) (fettarm) low-fat; low in fat *pred.;* lean ⟨meat⟩
(c) (fig.) poor ⟨soil, harvest⟩; meagre ⟨profit, increase, success, report, etc.⟩; thin ⟨programme⟩
Mager-: ∼**milch** *die* skim[med] milk; ∼**quark** *der* low-fat curd cheese; ∼**sucht** *die* (Med.) wasting disease; (Anorexie) anorexia
Magie *die;* ∼: magic
Magier /'ma:giɐ/ *der;* ∼s, ∼, **Magierin** *die;* ∼, ∼nen (auch fig.) magician
magisch *Adj.* magic ⟨powers⟩; (geheimnisvoll) magical
Magistrat *der;* ∼[e]s, ∼e City Council
Magnat *der;* ∼en, ∼en magnate
Magnet *der;* ∼en od. ∼[e]s, ∼e magnet
Magnet·band *das; Pl.* Magnet·bänder magnetic tape
magnetisch 1 *Adj.* magnetic
2 *adv.* magnetically
magnetisieren *tr. V.* magnetize
Magnetismus *der;* ∼: magnetism
Magnet·nadel *die* [compass] needle
Mahagoni *das;* ∼s mahogany
Mäh·drescher *der* combine harvester
mähen 1 *tr. V.* mow; cut ⟨corn⟩
2 *itr. V.* mow; (Getreide ∼) reap
Mahl *das;* ∼[e]s, Mähler (geh.) meal; repast (formal)
mahlen *unr. tr., itr. V.* grind
Mahl·zeit meal
Mähne *die;* ∼, ∼n mane
mahnen *tr. V.* urge; remind ⟨debtor⟩
Mahn-: ∼**mal** *das; Pl.* ∼∼e od. ∼**mäler** memorial (erected as a warning to future generations); ∼**schreiben** *das* reminder
Mahnung *die;* ∼, ∼en **(a)** exhortation; (Warnung) admonition
(b) ▶ MAHNSCHREIBEN
Mai *der;* ∼[e]s od. ∼: May
Mai-: ∼**baum** *der* maypole; ∼**feiertag** *der* May Day *no def. art.;* ∼**glöckchen** *das* lily of the valley; ∼**käfer** *der* May bug
Mais *der;* ∼es maize; corn (esp. Amer.); (als Gericht) sweet corn
Mais·kolben *der* corn cob; (als Gericht) corn on the cob
Majestät *die;* ∼, ∼en **(a)** (Titel) Majesty; **Eure** ∼: Your Majesty
(b) (geh.) majesty
majestätisch 1 *Adj.* majestic
2 *adv.* majestically
Majonäse *die;* ∼, ∼n mayonnaise
Major *der;* ∼s, ∼e (Milit.) major
Majoran *der;* ∼s, ∼e marjoram
makaber *Adj.* macabre

m

Makedonien /makeˈdoːni̯ən/ (das); ~s
Macedonia

Makel der; ~s, ~ (geh.) (a) (Schmach) stigma
(b) (Fehler) blemish

makel·los [1] Adj. flawless; spotless ⟨white,
cleanness⟩
[2] adv. immaculately; spotlessly ⟨clean⟩

Make-up /meːkˈʔap/ das; ~s, ~s make-up

Makkaroni Pl. macaroni sing.

Makler der; ~s, ~, **Maklerin** die; ~,
~nen (a) (Häusermakler) estate agent (Brit.);
realtor (Amer.)
(b) (Börsenmakler) broker

Makrele die; ~, ~n mackerel

Makro der od. das; ~s, ~s (DV) macro

Makrone die; ~, ~n macaroon

mal [1] Adv. times; (bei Flächen) by
[2] Partikel komm ~ her! come here!

Mal[1] das; ~[e]s, ~e time; das erste/zweite
~, zum ersten/zweiten ~: for the first/
second time; beim ersten/zweiten ~: the
first/second time; das letzte, zum letzten ~:
for the last time; letztes, beim letzten ~: last
time; jedes ~: every time; mit einem ~[e] all
at once

Mal[2] das; ~[e]s, ~e od. Mäler mark;
(Muttermal) birthmark; (braun) mole

Malaie der; ~n, ~n, **Malaiin** die; ~,
~nen Malay

Malaria die; ~: malaria

Malaysia (das); ~s Malaysia

Mal·buch das colouring book

malen tr., itr. V. paint; decorate ⟨flat, room,
walls⟩

Maler der; ~s, ~: painter

Malerei die; ~, ~en painting

Malerin der; ~, ~nen painter

malerisch [1] Adj. picturesque
[2] adv. picturesquely

mal|nehmen unr. tr., itr. V. multiply (mit
by)

malträtieren tr. V. maltreat; ill-treat

Malz·bier das malt beer

Mama die; ~, ~s (fam.) mamma

Mami die; ~, ~s (fam.) mummy (Brit. coll.);
mommy (Amer. coll.)

Mammut das; ~s, ~e od. ~s mammoth

mampfen tr., itr. V. (salopp) munch; nosh
(coll.)

man Indefinitpron. im Nom. one; you 2nd
person; (irgendjemand) somebody; (die Behörden;
die Leute dort) they pl.; (die Menschen im
Allgemeinen) people pl; ~ hat mir gesagt ...: I
was told ...

Management /ˈmɛnɪdʒmənt/ das; ~s, ~s
management

managen /ˈmɛnɪdʒn̩/ tr. V. (a) (ugs.) fix;
organize
(b) (betreuen) manage ⟨singer, artist, player⟩

Manager /ˈmɛnɪdʒɐ/ der; ~s, ~,
Managerin die; ~, ~nen manager; (eines
Fußballvereins) club secretary

manch Indefinitpron. (a) attr. many a; in
[so] ~er Beziehung in many respects
(b) allein stehend ~er many a person/man;
~e Pl. some; (viele) many; [so] ~es a number
of things; (allerhand Verschiedenes) all kinds of
things

mancherlei indekl. Adj. (a) attr. various;
a number of
(b) allein stehend various things

manch·mal Adv. sometimes

Mandant der; ~en, ~en, **Mandantin** die;
~, ~nen client

Mandarine die; ~, ~n mandarin [orange]

Mandel die; ~, ~n (a) almond
(b) (Anat.) tonsil

Mandel·entzündung die tonsillitis no
indef. art.

Manege /maˈneːʒə/ die; ~, ~n (im Zirkus)
ring; (in der Reitschule) arena

Mangel[1] der; ~s, Mängel (a) (Fehlen) lack
(an + Dat. of); (Knappheit) shortage, lack (an +
Dat. of)
(b) (Fehler) defect

Mangel[2] die; ~, ~n [large] mangle

mangelhaft [1] Adj. faulty ⟨goods,
German, English, etc.⟩; (unzulänglich)
inadequate ⟨knowledge, lighting⟩; (Schulw.) die
Note „~" the mark 'unsatisfactory'; (bei
Prüfungen) the fail mark
[2] adv. faultily; (unzulänglich) inadequately

mangeln[1] itr. V.; unpers. es mangelt an
etw. (Dat.) (etw. fehlt) there is a lack of sth.;
(etw. ist unzureichend vorhanden) there is a
shortage of sth.; jmdm./einer Sache mangelt
es an etw. (Dat.) sb./sth. lacks sth.

mangeln[2] tr. V. mangle

mangels Präp. mit Gen. in the absence of

Mango die; ~, ~s mango

Mangold der; ~[e]s [Swiss] chard

Manie die; ~, ~n mania

Manier die; ~, ~en (a) manner
(b) Pl. (Umgangsformen) manners

manierlich [1] Adj. (a) (fam.) well-
mannered; well-behaved ⟨child⟩
(b) (ugs.: einigermaßen gut) decent
[2] adv. (a) (fam.) nicely
(b) (ugs.: einigermaßen gut) ganz/recht ~: quite/
really nicely

Manifest das; ~[e]s, ~e manifesto

Maniküre die; ~: manicure

maniküren tr. V. manicure

Manipulation die; ~, ~en (geh.)
manipulation

manipulieren tr. V. manipulate; rig
⟨election result etc.⟩

Manko das; ~s, ~s shortcoming; deficiency

Mann der; ~[e]s, Männer (a) man
(b) (Ehemann) husband

Männchen das; ~s, ~ (a) little man

(b) (Tier∼) male; ∼ **machen** ⟨animal⟩ sit up and beg

Mannequin /'manəkɛ̃/ das; ∼s, ∼s mannequin; [fashion] model

männer-, Männer-: ∼**beruf** der all-male profession; (überwiegend von Männern ausgeübt) male-dominated profession; ∼**mordend** Adj. (ugs. scherzh.) man-eating (fig.); ∼**sache** die: das ist ∼**sache** that's men's business; ∼**überschuss**, *∼**überschuß** der surplus of men

mannig·fach Adj. multifarious

männlich ☐ Adj. (a) male **(b)** ▶ MASKULIN 1; ☑ adv. in a masculine way

Mannschaft die; ∼, ∼en (Sport, auch fig.) team; (Schiffs-, Flugzeugbesatzung) crew; (Milit.) unit

Mannschafts-: ∼**führer** der, ∼**führerin** die (Sport) team captain; ∼**kapitän** der, ∼**kapitänin** die (Sport) team captain; ∼**spiel** das (Sport) team game

Manöver das; ∼s, ∼ (a) (Milit.) exercise; ∼ Pl. manœuvres **(b)** (Bewegung; fig. abwertend: Trick) manœuvre

manövrieren itr., tr. V. manœuvre

Mansarde die; ∼, ∼n attic; (Zimmer) attic room

Manschette die; ∼, ∼n cuff

Manschetten·knopf der cuff link

Mantel der; ∼s, Mäntel coat

Manteltarif·vertrag der (Wirtsch.) framework collective agreement [on working conditions]

Manuskript das; ∼[e]s, ∼e (a) manuscript; (Typoskript) typescript **(b)** (Notizen) notes pl.

Mappe die; ∼, ∼n (a) folder **(b)** (Aktentasche) briefcase; (Schul∼) schoolbag

Marathon·lauf /...tɔn.../ der marathon

Märchen das; ∼s, ∼: fairy story; fairy tale; (ugs.: Lüge) [tall] story (coll.)

Märchen·buch das book of fairy stories

märchenhaft ☐ Adj. magical ☑ adv. magically; (ugs.) fantastically (coll.)

Margarine die; ∼: margarine

Margerite die; ∼, ∼n ox-eye daisy

Maria (die); ∼s od. (Rel.) Mariä Mary

Marien·käfer der ladybird

Marihuana das; ∼s marijuana

Marinade die; ∼, ∼n (Kochk.) marinade; (Salatsoße) [marinade] dressing

Marine die; ∼, ∼n fleet; (Kriegs∼) navy

marinieren tr. V. marinade; **marinierte Heringe** soused herrings

Marionette die; ∼, ∼n puppet; marionette

Marionetten·theater das puppet theatre

Mark¹ die; ∼, ∼: mark; **Deutsche** ∼: Deutschmark

Mark² das; ∼[e]s (a) (Knochen∼) marrow **(b)** (Frucht∼) pulp

markant Adj. striking; prominent ⟨figure, nose, chin⟩; clear-cut ⟨features, profile⟩

Marke die; ∼, ∼n (a) (Waren∼) brand; (Fabrikat) make **(b)** (Brief∼, Rabatt∼, Beitrags∼) stamp **(c)** (Essen∼) meal ticket **(d)** (Erkennungs∼) [identification] disc; (Dienst∼) [police] identification badge; ≈ warrant card (Brit.) or (Amer.) ID card

Marken-: ∼**artikel** der proprietary or (Brit.) branded article; ∼**zeichen** das trade mark

Marketing das; ∼s (Wirtsch.) marketing

markieren ☐ tr. V. (a) mark **(b)** (ugs.: vortäuschen) sham ⟨illness, breakdown, etc.⟩ ☑ itr. V. (ugs.: simulieren) put it on (coll.)

Markierung die; ∼, ∼en marking

Markt der; ∼[e]s, Märkte market; (∼platz) market place or square; **freitags ist** ∼: Friday is market day

markt-, Markt-: ∼**anteil** der share of the market; ∼**beherrschend** Adj. market-dominating attrib.; ∼**einführung** die launch; ∼**forschung** die market research no def. art.; ∼**frau** die market woman; ∼**führer** der, ∼**führerin** die market leader; ∼**halle** die covered market; ∼**lücke** die gap in the market; ∼**platz** der market place; ∼**stand** der market stall; ∼**wirtschaft** die market economy

Marmelade die; ∼, ∼n jam; (Orangen∼) marmalade

Marmor der; ∼s marble

Marokkaner der; ∼s, ∼, **Marokkanerin** die; ∼, ∼nen Moroccan

marokkanisch Adj. Moroccan

Marokko (das); ∼s Morocco

Marone die; ∼, ∼n [sweet] chestnut

Mars der; ∼: Mars no def. art.

Marsch¹ der; ∼[e]s, Märsche march; (Wanderung) [long] walk

Marsch² die; ∼, ∼en fertile marshland

Marsch·flug·körper der cruise missile

marschieren itr. V.; mit sein march; (wandern) walk

Marsch-: ∼**musik** die march music; ∼**verpflegung** die (Milit.) marching rations pl.;

Mars-: ∼**mensch** der Martian; ∼**sonde** die (Raumfahrt) Mars probe

Marter die; ∼, ∼n (geh.) torture; (seelisch) torment

martern tr. V. (geh.) torture

Märtyrer der; ∼s, ∼, **Märtyrerin** die; ∼, ∼nen martyr

Martyrium das; ∼s, Martyrien martyrdom

Marxismus der; ∼: Marxism no art.

Marxist der; ∼en, ∼en, **Marxistin** die; ∼, ∼nen Marxist

marxistisch Adj. Marxist

März der; ∼[es] March

m

Marzip<u>a</u>n *das;* ~s marzipan

M<u>a</u>sche *die;* ~, ~n stitch; (Lauf~) run; ladder (Brit.); (beim Netz) mesh

M<u>a</u>schen-draht *der* wire netting

Masch<u>i</u>ne *die;* ~, ~n (a) (auch ugs.: Motorrad) machine

(b) (ugs.: Automotor) engine

(c) (Flugzeug) [aero]plane

(d) (Schreib~) typewriter; ~ **schreiben** type

masch<u>i</u>ne-geschrieben *Adj.* typewritten

maschin<u>e</u>ll 1 *Adj.* machine *attrib.;* by machine *postpos.;*
2 *adv.* by machine; ~ **hergestellt** machine-made

Masch<u>i</u>nen-: ~**gewehr** *das* machine gun; ~**pistole** *die* sub-machine gun; ~**schlosser** *der,* ~**schlosserin** *die* fitter

*masch<u>i</u>ne|schreiben ▶ MASCHINE D

M<u>a</u>sern *Pl.* measles *sing. or pl.*

M<u>a</u>serung *die;* ~, ~en [wavy] grain

M<u>a</u>ske *die;* ~, ~n mask

M<u>a</u>sken-: ~**ball** *der* masked ball; ~**bildner** *der;* ~~s, ~~, ~**bildnerin** *die;* ~~, ~~nen make-up artist

Masker<u>a</u>de *die;* ~, ~n [fancy-dress] costume

mask<u>ie</u>ren 1 *tr. V.* mask
2 *refl. V.* put on a mask/masks

Mask<u>o</u>ttchen *das;* ~s, ~: [lucky] mascot

maskul<u>i</u>n */auch:* '---/ 1 *Adj.* (auch Sprachw.) masculine
2 *adv.* in a masculine way

Masoch<u>i</u>smus *der;* ~ (Psych.) masochism *no art.*

Masoch<u>i</u>st *der;* ~en, ~en, **Masoch<u>i</u>stin** *die;* ~, ~nen (Psych.) masochist

masoch<u>i</u>stisch (Psych.) 1 *Adj.* masochistic
2 *adv.* masochistically; ~ **veranlagt sein** have masochistic tendencies

ma<u>ß</u> *1. u. 3. Pers. Sg. Prät. v.* MESSEN

Ma<u>ß</u>1 *das;* ~es, ~e (a) measure (für of); (fig.) **das** ~ **ist voll** enough is enough
(b) (Größe) measurement
(c) (Grad) degree (**an** + *Dat.* of); **in großem/ gewissem** ~**e** to a great/certain extent
(d) ~ **halten** exercise moderation

Ma<u>ß</u>2 *die;* ~, ~[e] (bayr., österr.) litre [of beer]

Massage /ma'saːʒə/ *die;* ~, ~n massage

Mass<u>a</u>ker *das;* ~s, ~: massacre

Ma<u>ß</u>-: ~**anzug** *der* made-to-measure suit; ~**arbeit** *die* (a) custom-made item; (Kleidungsstück) made-to-measure item; (b) (genaue Arbeit) neat work

M<u>a</u>sse *die;* ~, ~n (a) mass
(b) (Gemisch) mixture

Ma<u>ß</u>-einheit *die* unit of measurement

M<u>a</u>ssen-: ~**arbeitslosigkeit** *die* mass unemployment; ~**entlassungen** *Pl.* mass redundancies *pl.;* ~**grab** *das* mass grave

m<u>a</u>ssenhaft 1 *Adj.* in huge numbers *postpos.;*
2 *adv.* on a huge scale

m<u>a</u>ssen-, M<u>a</u>ssen-: ~**karambolage** *die* multiple crash; ~**kommunikations-mittel** *das* medium of mass communication; mass medium; ~**medium** *das* mass medium; ~**mörder** *der,* ~**mörderin** *die* mass murderer; ~**produktion** *die* mass production; ~**vernichtung** *die* mass extermination; ~**vernichtungs-waffen** *Pl.* weapons of mass destruction; ~**weise** *Adv.* in huge numbers

Mass<u>eu</u>r /ma'søːɐ̯/ *der;* ~s, ~e masseur

Mass<u>eu</u>rin *die;* ~, ~nen, **Masseuse** /ma'søːzə/ *die;* ~, ~n masseuse

ma<u>ß</u>-gebend, ma<u>ß</u>-geblich 1 *Adj.* authoritative ⟨book, expert, opinion⟩; definitive ⟨text⟩; influential ⟨person, circles, etc.⟩; decisive ⟨factor, influence, etc.⟩
2 *adv.* ⟨influence⟩ to a considerable extent; (entscheidend) decisively

*ma<u>ß</u>|halten ▶ MAß1 D

mass<u>ie</u>ren *tr. V.* massage

m<u>ä</u>ßig 1 *Adj.* moderate; (mittel~) mediocre
2 *adv.* in moderation; moderately ⟨gifted, talented⟩; (mittel~) indifferently

m<u>ä</u>ßigen *refl. V.* (geh.) (a) practise *or* exercise moderation
(b) (sich beherrschen) control *or* restrain oneself

M<u>ä</u>ßigkeit *die;* ~: moderation

M<u>ä</u>ßigung *die;* ~: moderation

mass<u>i</u>v 1 *Adj.* (a) solid
(b) (heftig) massive ⟨demand⟩; crude ⟨accusation, threat⟩; strong ⟨attack, criticism, pressure⟩
2 *adv.* ⟨attack⟩ strongly; ⟨accuse, threaten⟩ crudely

ma<u>ß</u>-, Ma<u>ß</u>-: ~**krug** *der* (südd., österr.) litre beer mug; (aus Steingut) stein; ~**los** 1 *Adj.* extreme; gross ⟨exaggeration, insult⟩; excessive ⟨demand, claim⟩; boundless ⟨ambition, greed, sorrow, joy⟩; 2 *adv.* extremely; ⟨exaggerate⟩ grossly; ~**nahme** *die;* ~~, ~~n measure; ~**regel** *die* regulation; (Maßnahme) measure; ~**regeln** *tr. V.* (zurechtweisen) reprimand; (bestrafen) discipline; ~**stab** *der* (a) standard; (b) (einer Karte, eines Modells usw.) scale; ~**voll** 1 *Adj.* moderate; 2 *adv.* in moderation

Mast *der;* ~[e]s, ~en, *auch:* ~e (Schiffs~, Antennen~) mast; (Stange, Fahnen~) pole; (Hochspannungs~) pylon

m<u>ä</u>sten *tr. V.* fatten

Masturbati<u>o</u>n *die;* ~, ~en masturbation

masturb<u>ie</u>ren *itr., tr. V.* masturbate

Match /mɛtʃ/ *das od.* der; ~[e]s, ~s *od.* ~e
match

Material *das;* ~s, ~ien material; (Bau~;
Hilfsmittel) materials *pl.*

Materialismus *der;* ~: materialism

Materialist *der;* ~en, ~en,
Materialistin *die;* ~, ~nen materialist

materialistisch ① *Adj.* materialistic
② *adv.* materialistically

Materie *die;* ~, ~n (a) matter
(b) (geh.: Thema, Gegenstand) subject matter

materiell ① *Adj.* (finanziell) financial
② *adv.* materially; (finanziell) financially

Mathe *die;* ~ (ugs.) maths *sing.* (Brit. coll.);
math (Amer. coll.)

Mathematik *die;* ~: mathematics *sing.,
no art.*

mathematisch ① *Adj.* mathematical
② *adv.* mathematically

Matjes *der;* ~, ~: matie [herring]

Matratze *die;* ~, ~n mattress

Matrose *der;* ~n, ~n sailor; seaman

Matsch *der;* ~[e]s (ugs.) mud; (breiiger
Schmutz) sludge; (Schnee~) slush

matschig *Adj.* (ugs.) (a) muddy; slushy
⟨snow⟩
(b) (weich) mushy; squashy ⟨fruit⟩

matt ① *Adj.* (a) weak; feeble ⟨applause,
reaction⟩
(b) (glanzlos) matt; dull ⟨metal, mirror, etc.⟩
(c) (undurchsichtig) frosted ⟨glass⟩; pearl
⟨lightbulb⟩
(d) subdued; (Schach) checkmated; ~!
checkmate!
② *adv.* (a) (kraftlos) weakly
(b) (mäßig) ⟨protest, contradict⟩ feebly

Matte *die;* ~, ~n mat

Matt·scheibe *die* (ugs.) telly (Brit. coll.); box
(coll.)

Matur *die;* ~ (schweiz.), **Matura** *die;* ~a
(österr., schweiz.) ▶ ABITUR

Mätzchen *das;* ~s, ~: ~ machen (ugs.)
fool about *or* around

Mauer *die;* ~, ~n wall

mauern ① *tr. V.* build
② *itr. V.* lay bricks

Mauer-: ~segler *der* swift; ~werk *das*
(a) masonry; (aus Ziegeln) brickwork; (b)
(Mauern) walls *pl.*

Maul *das;* ~[e]s, Mäuler (von Tieren) mouth;
(derb: Mund) gob (sl.)

Maul-: ~esel *der* mule; ~korb *der* (auch
fig.) muzzle; ~tier *das* mule

Maul·wurf *der* mole

Maulwurfs-: ~haufen *der,* ~hügel *der*
molehill

Maurer *der;* ~s, ~, **Maurerin** *die;* ~,
~nen bricklayer

Maus *die;* ~, Mäuse mouse

Mauschelei *die;* ~, ~en (ugs. abwertend)
shady wheeling and dealing *no indef. art.*

mauscheln *itr. V.* (ugs. abwertend) engage
in shady wheeling and dealing

Mäuschen *das;* ~s, ~: little mouse

mäuschen·still *Adj.* ~ sein be as quiet
as a mouse

Mause·falle *die* mousetrap

mausern *refl. V.* moult

Maus: ~klick *der;* ~~s, ~~s (DV) mouse
click; ~taste *die* (DV) mouse button;
~zeiger *der* (DV) mouse pointer

Maut *die;* ~, ~en toll

maximal ① *Adj.* maximum
② *adv.* ~ zulässige Geschwindigkeit
maximum permitted speed

Maxime *die;* ~, ~n maxim

maximieren *tr. V.* maximize

Maximum *das;* ~s, Maxima maximum (an
+ *Dat.* of)

Maxi·single *die* maxi-single

Mayonnaise /majoˈnɛːzə/ *die;* ~, ~n
mayonnaise

Mäzen *der;* ~s, ~e (geh.) patron

Mäzenin *die;* ~, ~nen patroness

MdB, M.d.B. *Abk.* = **Mitglied des
Bundestages** Member of the Bundestag

m. E. *Abk.* = **meines Erachtens** in my
opinion *or* view

Mechanik *die;* ~: mechanics *sing., no art.*

Mechaniker *der;* ~s, ~,
Mechanikerin *die;* ~, ~nen mechanic

mechanisch ① *Adj.* mechanical; power
attrib. ⟨loom, press⟩
② *adv.* mechanically

Mechanismus *der;* ~, Mechanismen
mechanism

meckern *itr. V.* (a) (auch fig.) bleat
(b) (ugs.: nörgeln) grumble; moan

Mecklenburg-Vorpommern (*das*); ~s
Mecklenburg-Western Pomerania

Medaille /meˈdaljə/ *die;* ~, ~n medal

Medaillen·gewinner *der,*
Medaillen·gewinnerin *die* medallist;
medal winner

Medaillon /medalˈjõ:/ *das;* ~s, ~s (a)
locket
(b) (Kochk., bild. Kunst) medallion

medial *Adj.* (in den Medien) in the media
postpos.; (von den Medien) by the media
postpos.; eine ~e Präsenz a media presence;
ein ~es Spektakel a media spectacle

Medien-: ~angebot *das* range of media;
~konzern *der* media concern;
~landschaft *die* media scene; ~politik
die media policy; ~präsenz *die* media
presence

Medikament *das;* ~[e]s, ~e medicine;
(Droge) drug

Meditation *die;* ~, ~en meditation

meditieren *itr. V.* meditate (über + *Akk.*
[up]on)

Medium *das;* ~s, Medien medium

m

Medizin *die;* ~, ~en medicine
Mediziner *der;* ~s, ~, **Medizinerin** *die;*
~, ~nen doctor; (Student[in]) medical student
medizinisch ① *Adj.* medical; medicinal
⟨*bath etc.*⟩; medicated ⟨*toothpaste, soap, etc.*⟩
② *adv.* medically
Meer *das;* ~[e]s, ~e (auch fig.) sea; **am** ~: by
the sea
Meer·enge *die* straits *pl.;* strait
Meeres-: ~**boden** *der* sea bed *or* bottom
or floor; ~**bucht** *die* bay; ~**früchte** *Pl.*
(Kochk.) seafood *sing.;* ~**kunde** *die*
oceanography *no art.;* ~**spiegel** *der* sea
level
Meer-: ~**jungfrau** *die* mermaid; ~**katze**
die guenon; ~**rettich** *der* horseradish;
~**schweinchen** *das;* ~~s, ~~: guinea
pig; ~**wasser** *das* sea water
Meeting /'mi:tɪŋ/ *das;* ~s, ~s meeting
mega-, Mega- mega-
Mega·byte *das* (DV) megabyte
Megaphon *das;* ~s, ~e megaphone; loud
hailer
Mehl *das;* ~[e]s flour
mehlig *Adj.* (a) floury
(b) mealy ⟨*potato, apple, etc.*⟩
Mehl-: ~**sack** *der* flour sack; (Sack voll
Mehl) sack of flour; ~**tau** *der* mildew;
~**wurm** *der* mealworm
mehr ① *Indefinitpron.* more
② *Adv.* (a) more
(b) nicht ~: not … any more; no longer; **es
war niemand** ~ **da** there was no one left; **das
wird nie** ~ **vorkommen** it will never happen
again; **da ist nichts** ~ **zu machen** there is
nothing more to be done
mehr-, Mehr-: ~**bändig** *Adj.* in several
volumes *postpos.;* ~**bereichs-öl** *das*
(Technik) multi-purpose oil; ~**deutig** ① *Adj.*
ambiguous; ② *adv.* ambiguously
mehren (geh.) *refl. V.* increase
mehrer... *Indefinitpron. u. unbest. Zahlwort*
(a) *attr.* several
(b) *allein stehend* ~e several people; ~es
several things *pl.*
mehr·fach ① *Adj.* multiple; (wiederholt)
repeated
② *adv.* several times; (wiederholt) repeatedly
Mehrheit *die;* ~, ~en majority
Mehrheits-: ~**beschluss,**
*∗~**beschluß** der,* ~**entscheidung** *die*
majority decision
mehr-, Mehr-: ~**jährig** *Adj.* lasting
several years *postpos.;* ~**malig** *Adj.; nicht
präd.* repeated; ~**mals** *Adv.* several times;
(wiederholt) repeatedly;
~**parteien·system** *das* multi-party
system; ~**sprachig** *Adj.* multilingual;
~**stimmig** (Musik) ① *Adj.* for several
voices *postpos.;* **ein** ~**stimmiges Lied** a part-

song; ② *adv.* ~**stimmig singen** sing in
harmony; ~**teilig** *Adj.* in several parts
postpos.
Mehrweg-: ~**flasche** *die* returnable *or*
reusable bottle; ~**verpackung** *die*
reusable packaging
Mehr-: ~**wert** *der* (Wirtsch.) surplus value;
~**wert·steuer** *die* (Wirtsch.) value added
tax (Brit.); VAT (Brit.); sales tax (Amer.); ~**zahl**
die **(a)** (Sprachw.) plural; **(b)** (Mehrheit)
majority
meiden *unr. tr. V.* (geh.) avoid
Meile *die;* ~, ~n mile
mein *Possessivpron.* my; ~**e Damen und
Herren** ladies and gentlemen; **das Buch dort,
ist das** ~[e]s? that book over there, is it
mine?
Mein·eid *der* perjury *no indef. art.;* **einen** ~
schwören commit perjury
meinen ① *itr. V.* think
② *tr. V.* **(a)** think
(b) (sagen wollen, im Sinn haben) mean
(c) (beabsichtigen) mean; intend; **es gut mit
jmdm.** ~: mean well by sb.
(d) (sagen) say
meiner *Gen. von* ICH (geh.) **gedenkt** ~:
remember me; **erbarme dich** ~: have mercy
upon me
meinerseits *Adv.* for my part; **ganz** ~:
the pleasure is [all] mine
meinetwegen *Adv.* **(a)** because of me; (mir
zuliebe) for my sake; (um mich) about me
(b) /*auch:* --'--/ (von mir aus) as far as I'm
concerned; ~! if you like
Meinung *die;* ~, ~en opinion (**zu** on, **über**
+ *Akk.* about); **er ist der** ~, **dass …** he is of
the opinion *or* takes the view that …; **meiner**
~ **nach** in my opinion; **ganz meine** ~: I
agree entirely; **einer** ~ **sein** be of the same
opinion
Meinungs-: ~**forschung** *die* opinion
research; ~**freiheit** *die* freedom to form
and express one's own opinions; (Redefreiheit)
freedom of speech; ~**umfrage** *die* [public]
opinion poll; ~**verschiedenheit** *die*
difference of opinion
Meise *die;* ~, ~n tit[mouse]
Meißel *der;* ~s, ~: chisel
meißeln *tr. V.* chisel; carve ⟨*statue,
sculpture*⟩ with a chisel
meist *Adv.* mostly
meist... *Indefinitpron. u. unbest. Zahlw.*
most; **die** ~**en Leute …:** most people …; **am**
~**en** most
meistens *Adv.* ▶ MEIST
Meister *der;* ~s, ~ **(a)** master
(b) (Werk~, Polier~) foreman
(c) (Sport) champion
Meister·brief *der* master craftsman's
diploma *or* certificate
meisterhaft ① *Adj.* masterly
② *adv.* in a masterly manner
Meisterin *die;* ~, ~nen ▶ MEISTER A,C

---

meistern *tr. V.* master

Meister·prüfung *die* examination for the/one's master craftsman's diploma *or* certificate

Meisterschaft *die;* ~, ~en (a) mastery **(b)** (Sport) championship

Meister-: ~**stück** *das* masterpiece (**an** + *Dat.* of); ~**titel** *der* (Sport) championship [title]; ~**werk** *das* masterpiece (**an** + *Dat.* of)

Melancholie /melaŋko:'li:/ *die;* ~ melancholy

melancholisch 1 *Adj.* melancholy; melancholy, melancholic ⟨*person, temperament*⟩
2 *adv.* melancholically

melden 1 *tr. V.* report; (registrieren lassen) register ⟨*birth, death, etc.*⟩ (*Dat.* with)
2 *refl. V.* **(a)** report
(b) (am Telefon) answer
(c) (ums Wort bitten) put one's hand up
(d) (von sich hören lassen) get in touch (**bei** with)

Meldung *die;* ~, ~en (a) report; (Nachricht) piece of news
(b) (Wort~) request to speak

meliert *Adj.* mottled; [grau] ~**es Haar** hair streaked with grey

melken *regelm.* (*auch unr.*) *tr. V.* milk

Melodie *die;* ~, ~n melody; (Weise) tune

melodisch 1 *Adj.* melodic
2 *adv.* melodically

Melone *die;* ~, ~n **(a)** melon
(b) (ugs.: Hut) bowler [hat]

Membran *die;* ~, ~en (a) (Technik) diaphragm
(b) (Biol., Chemie) membrane

Memoiren /me'mŏa:rən/ *Pl.* memoirs

Menge *die;* ~, ~n (a) quantity; amount
(b) (große) lot (coll.); **eine** ~ (ugs.) lots [of it/them] (coll.)
(c) (Menschen~) crowd
(d) (Math.) set

Mengen-: ~**lehre** *die* set theory *no art.;* ~**rabatt** *der* bulk discount

Meniskus *der;* ~, Menisken (Anat., Optik) meniscus

Menopause *die;* ~, ~n (Physiol.) menopause

Mensa *die;* ~, ~s *od.* Mensen refectory, canteen (*of university, college*)

Mensch *der;* ~en, ~en (a) (Gattung) der ~: man; die ~en man *sing.;* human beings; mankind *sing.;*
(b) (Person) person; man/woman; ~en people

menschen-, Menschen-: ~**affe** *der* anthropoid [ape]; ~**auflauf** *der* crowd [of people]; ~**feind** *der,* ~**feindin** *die* misanthropist; ~**fresser** *der* (ugs.) cannibal; ~**freund** *der,* ~**freundin** *die* philanthropist; ~**handel** *der* trade or traffic in human beings; ~**kenner** *der,* ~**kennerin** *die* judge of human nature;

~**kenntnis** *die;* ability to judge human nature; ~**leben** *das* life; ~**leer** *Adj.* deserted; ~**menge** *die* crowd [of people]; ~**recht** *das* human right; ~**rechtler** *der;* ~~s, ~~, ~**rechtlerin** *die;* ~~, ~nen human rights campaigner; ~**schlag** *der* breed [of people]; ~**seele** *die:* keine ~seele not a [living] soul

Menschens·kind: ~! (salopp) (erstaunt) good heavens; good grief; (vorwurfsvoll) for heaven's sake

menschen-, Menschen-: ~**unwürdig** 1 *Adj.* ⟨*accommodation*⟩ unfit for human habitation; ⟨*conditions*⟩ unfit for human beings; ⟨*behaviour*⟩ unworthy of a human being; 2 *adv.* ⟨*treat*⟩ in a degrading and inhumane way; ⟨*live, be housed*⟩ in conditions unfit for human beings; ~**verstand** *der* human intellect; ~**würde** *die* human dignity *no art.*

Menschheit *die;* ~: mankind *no art.;* humanity *no art.;* human race

menschlich 1 *Adj.* **(a)** human
(b) (annehmbar) civilized
(c) (human) humane ⟨*person, treatment, etc.*⟩
2 *adv.* **(a)** er ist mir ~ sympathisch I like him as a person
(b) (human) humanely

Menschlichkeit *die;* ~: humanity *no art.*

Mensen ▸ MENSA

Menstruation *die;* ~, ~en (Physiol.) menstruation; (Periode) [menstrual] period

Mentalität *die;* ~, ~en mentality

Menü *das;* ~s, ~s (auch DV) menu

Menü·leiste *die* (DV) menu bar

merkbar 1 *Adj.* noticeable
2 *adv.* noticeably

Merk·blatt *das* leaflet

merken 1 *tr. V.* notice
2 *refl. V.* sich (*Dat.*) etw. ~: remember sth.

merklich ▸ MERKBAR

Merkmal *das;* ~s, ~e feature

Merkur *der;* ~s Mercury

merkwürdig 1 *Adj.* strange; odd
2 *adv.* strangely; oddly

messbar, *meßbar *Adj.* measurable

Messe¹ *die;* ~, ~n (Gottesdienst, Musik) mass

Messe² *die;* ~, ~n (Ausstellung) [trade] fair

messen 1 *unr. tr. V.* **(a)** *auch itr.* measure
(b) (beurteilen) judge (**nach** by)
2 *unr. refl. V.* (geh.) compete (**mit** with)

Messer *das;* ~s, ~: knife

messer-, Messer-: ~**scharf** 1 *Adj.* razor-sharp; (fig.) incisive ⟨*logic*⟩; razor-sharp ⟨*wit, intellect*⟩; 2 *adv.* (fig. ugs.) ⟨*argue*⟩ incisively; ~**stecherei** *die;* ~~, ~~en knife fight; ~**stich** *der* knife thrust; (Wunde) knife wound

Mess·gerät, *Meß·gerät *das* measuring device; (Zähler) meter

Messias *der;* ~, ~se Messiah

Messing *das;* ~s brass

Mess·instrument, *Meß·instrument *das* measuring instrument

Messung *die;* ~, ~en measurement

Metall *das;* ~s, ~e metal

metallic *indekl. Adj.* metallic [grey/blue/ etc.]

Metall·industrie *die* metal-processing and metal-working industries *pl.*

metallisch *Adj.* metallic; metal *attrib.*, metallic ⟨*conductor*⟩

Metapher *die;* ~, ~n metaphor

metaphorisch (Stilk.) ⓵ *Adj.* metaphorical ⓶ *adv.* metaphorically

Meta·physik *die;* ~: metaphysics *sing., no art.*

Metastase *die;* ~, ~n (Med.) metastasis

Meteor *der;* ~s, ~e meteor

Meteorit *der;* ~en *od.* ~s, ~e[n] meteorite

Meteorologe *der;* ~n, ~n meteorologist

Meteorologie *die;* ~: meteorology *no art.*

Meteorologin *die;* ~, ~nen meteorologist

meteorologisch ⓵ *Adj.* meteorological ⓶ *adv.* meteorologically

Meter *der od. das;* ~s, ~: metre

meter-, Meter-: ~**dick** *Adj.* (sehr dick) metres thick *postpos.;* ~**hoch** *Adj.* metres high *postpos.;* ⟨*snow*⟩ metres deep; ~**maß** *das* tape measure; (Stab) [metre] rule

Methan *das;* ~s methane

Methode *die;* ~, ~n method

methodisch ⓵ *Adj.* methodological; (nach einer Methode vorgehend) methodical ⓶ *adv.* methodologically; (nach einer Methode) methodically

Metier /me'tje:/ *das;* ~s, ~s profession

Metrik *die;* ~, ~en metrics

metrisch ⓵ *Adj.* **(a)** (Verslehre, Musik) metrical **(b)** (auf den Meter bezogen) metric ⓶ *adv.* metrically

Metropole *die;* ~, ~n metropolis

Mett·wurst *die: soft smoked sausage made of minced pork and beef*

Metzger *der;* ~s, ~ (bes. westmd., südd., schweiz.) butcher

Metzgerei *die;* ~, ~en (bes. westmd., südd., schweiz.) butcher's [shop]

Meute *die;* ~, ~n **(a)** (Jägerspr.) pack **(b)** (ugs. abwertend) mob

Meuterei *die;* ~, ~en mutiny

meutern *itr. V.* **(a)** mutiny; ⟨*prisoners*⟩ riot **(b)** (ugs.: Unwillen äußern) moan

Mexikaner *der;* ~s, ~, **Mexikanerin** *die;* ~, ~ Mexican

mexikanisch *Adj.* Mexican

Mexiko ⟨*das*⟩ ~s Mexico

MEZ *Abk.* = **mitteleuropäische Zeit** CET

mg *Abk.* = **Milligramm** mg

MG /ɛm'ge:/ *das;* ~s, ~s *Abk.* = **Maschinengewehr**

Mi. *Abk.* = **Mittwoch** Wed.

miau *Interj.* miaow

miauen *itr. V.* miaow

mich ⓵ *Akk. von* ICH me ⓶ *Akk. des Reflexivpron. der 1.Pers. Sg.* myself

mick[e]rig *Adj.* (ugs.) miserable; measly (coll.); puny ⟨*person*⟩

mied *1. u. 3. Pers. Sg. Prät. v.* MEIDEN

Mieder·waren *Pl.* corsetry *sing.*

Miene *die;* ~, ~n expression

mies (ugs.) ⓵ *Adj.* lousy (coll.) ⓶ *adv.* lousily (coll.)

Mies-: ~**macher** *der,* ~**macherin** *die* (ugs. abwertend) carping critic; (Spielverderber) killjoy; ~**muschel** *die* [common] mussel

Miete *die;* ~, ~n rent; (für ein Auto, Boot) hire charge; **zur** ~ **wohnen** live in rented accommodation

mieten *tr. V.* rent; (für kürzere Zeit) hire

Mieter *der;* ~s, ~, **Mieterin** *die;* ~, ~nen tenant

Miets·haus *das* block of rented flats (Brit.) *or* (Amer.) apartments

Miet-: ~**erhöhung** *die* rent increase; ~**vertrag** *der* tenancy agreement; ~**wagen** *der* hire car

Migräne *die;* ~, ~n migraine

Migrant *der;* ~en, ~en, **Migrantin** *die;* ~, ~nen migrant

mikro-, Mikro- micro-

Mikrobe *die;* ~, ~n microbe

mikro-, Mikro-: ~**film** *der* microfilm; ~**phon** /-·'-/ *das;* ~s, ~e microphone; ~**skop** /-·'-/ *das;* ~s, ~e microscope; ~**skopisch** /-·'-/ ⓵ *Adj.* microscopic; ⓶ *adv.* microscopically; ~**welle** *die* (ugs.) microwave [oven]

Milbe *die;* ~, ~n mite

Milch *die;* ~: milk

Milch·flasche *die* milk bottle

milchig ⓵ *Adj.* milky ⓶ *adv.* ~ **weiß** milky-white

Milch-: ~**kaffee** *der* coffee with plenty of milk; ~**kännchen** *das;* ~~s, ~~: milk jug; ~**reis** *der* rice pudding; ~**straße** *die* Milky Way; Galaxy; ~**zahn** *der* milk tooth

mild, milde ⓵ *Adj.* mild; lenient ⟨*judge, judgement*⟩; soft ⟨*light*⟩; smooth ⟨*brandy*⟩ ⓶ *adv.* (gütig) leniently; (gelinde) mildly

Milde *die;* ~: mildness; (Güte) leniency

mildern *tr. V.* moderate; mitigate ⟨*punishment*⟩

Milderung *die;* ~: ▶ MILDERN: moderation; mitigation

Milieu /mi'liø:/ *das;* ~s, ~s environment

militant *Adj.* militant

Militär¹ *das;* ~s armed forces *pl.;* military; (Soldaten) soldiers *pl.*

Militär² *der;* ~s, ~s [high-ranking military] officer

Militär-: ~**dienst** *der* military service; ~**diktatur** *die* military dictatorship

militärisch *Adj.* military

militarisieren *tr. V.* militarize

Militarismus *der;* ~ (abwertend) militarism

Militarist *der;* ~en, ~en (abwertend) militarist

Militär-: ~**macht** *die* military power; ~**putsch** *der* military putsch

Military /'mɪlɪtərɪ/ *die;* ~, ~s (Reiten) three-day event

Miliz *die;* ~, ~en militia; (Polizei) police

Mill. *Abk.* = **Million** m.

milli-, Milli- milli-

Milliarde *die;* ~, ~n billion

Milli-: ~**gramm** *das* milligram; ~**meter** *der od. das* millimetre; ~**meter·papier** *das* [graph] paper ruled in millimetre squares

Million *die;* ~, ~en million

Millionär *der;* ~s, ~e millionaire

Millionen-: ~**schaden** *der* damage *no pl., no indef. art.* running into millions; ~**stadt** *die* town with over a million inhabitants

millionst... *Ordinalz.* millionth

Milz *die;* ~: spleen

Mimik *die;* ~: gestures and facial expressions *pl.*

Mimose *die;* ~, ~n (a) mimosa (b) (fig.) oversensitive person

mimosenhaft [1] *Adj.* oversensitive [2] *adv.* oversensitively

minder *Adv.* (geh.) less

minder... *Adj.* inferior ⟨goods, brand⟩

minder·bemittelt *Adj.* without much money *postpos., not pred.;* ~ sein not have much money; **geistig** ~ (fig. salopp abwertend) not all that bright (coll.)

Minderheit *die;* ~, ~en minority

minder·jährig *Adj.* ⟨child etc.⟩ who is/was a minor

Minder·jährige *der/die; adj. Dekl.* minor

mindern *tr. V.* (geh.) reduce

Minderung *die;* ~, ~en reduction (Gen. in)

minder·wertig *Adj.* inferior

mindest... *Adj.* least; (geringst...) slightest; **das ist das Mindeste** *od.* ~**e, was du tun kannst** it is the least you can do

mindestens *Adv.* at least

Mindest·haltbarkeits·datum *das* best-before date

Mine *die;* ~, ~n (a) (Bergwerk, Sprengkörper) mine (b) (Bleistift~) lead; (Kugelschreiber~, Filzschreiber~) refill

Mineral *das;* ~s, ~e *od.* **Mineralien** mineral

Mineralogie *die;* ~: mineralogy *no art.*

Mineral-: ~**öl** *das* mineral oil; ~**wasser** *das* mineral water

Mini *das;* ~s, ~s (Mode) mini

Mini- mini-

Miniatur *die;* ~, ~en miniature

minimal [1] *Adj.* minimal; marginal ⟨advantage, lead⟩; very slight ⟨benefit, profit⟩ [2] *adv.* minimally

Minimum *das;* ~s, **Minima** minimum (an + Dat. of)

minimieren *tr. V.* (bes. Math.) minimize

Minister *der;* ~s, ~, **Ministerin** *die;* ~, ~nen minister (für for); (eines britischen Hauptministeriums) Secretary of State (für for); (eines amerikanischen Hauptministeriums) Secretary (für of)

Ministerium *das;* ~s, **Ministerien** Ministry; Department (Amer.)

Minister·präsident *der,* **Minister·präsidentin** *die* (a) (eines deutschen Bundeslandes) minister-president (b) (Premierminister[in]) Prime Minister

Minister·rat *der* Council of Ministers

Ministrant *der;* ~en, ~en, **Ministrantin** *die;* ~, ~nen (kath. Kirche) server

Minorität *die;* ~, ~en ▶ MINDERHEIT

minus *Konj., Adv.* (bes. Math.) minus

Minus *das;* ~: deficit

Minus·zeichen *das* minus sign

Minute *die;* ~, ~n minute

minuten·lang [1] *Adj.* lasting [for] several minutes *postpos.;* [2] *adv.* for several minutes

Minuten·zeiger *der* minute hand

Mio. *Abk.* = **Million[en]** m.

mir [1] *Dat. von* ICH to me; (nach Präpositionen) me; **Freunde von** ~: friends of mine; **gehen wir zu** ~: let's go to my place; **von** ~ **aus** as far as I'm concerned [2] *Dat. des Reflexivpron. der 1. Pers. Sg.* myself

Mirabelle *die;* ~, ~n mirabelle

Misch-: ~**brot** *das* bread made from wheat and rye flour; ~**ehe** *die* mixed marriage

mischen [1] *tr. V.* mix [2] *refl. V.* (a) (sich ver~) mix (mit with); ⟨smell, scent⟩ blend (mit with) (b) (sich ein~) **sich in etw.** (Akk.) ~: interfere in sth.

Misch·farbe *die* non-primary colour

Mischling *der;* ~s, ~e half-caste

Mischmasch *der;* ~[e]s, ~e (ugs., meist abwertend) hotchpotch; mishmash

Misch·pult *das* (Film, Rundf., Ferns.) mixing desk *or* console

Mischung *die;* ~, ~en mixture; (Tee~, Kaffee~, Tabak~) blend; (Pralinen~) assortment

m

Mịsch·wald *der* mixed [deciduous and coniferous] forest

miserabel (ugs.) [1] *Adj.* dreadful (coll.)
[2] *adv.* dreadfully (coll.); **ihm geht es gesundheitlich** ∼: he's in a bad way

Misère *die;* ∼, ∼n (geh.) wretched *or* dreadful state; (Elend) misery; (Not) distress

mịss, *mịß* *Imperativ Sg. v.* MESSEN

mịss·ạchten, *mịß·ạchten* *tr. V.* (a) (ignorieren) disregard; ignore
(b) (geringschätzen) be contemptuous of

mịss·bịlligen, *mịß·bịlligen* *tr. V.* disapprove of

Mịss·bịlligung, *Mịß·bịlligung* *die* disapproval

Mịss·brauch, *Mịß·brauch* *der:*
▸ MISSBRAUCHEN: abuse; misuse

mịss·brauchen, *mịß·brauchen* *tr. V.* abuse; misuse; abuse ⟨*trust*⟩

mịssen *tr. V.* (geh.) jmdn./etw. nicht ∼ mögen not want to be without sb./sth.

Mịss·erfolg, *Mịß·erfolg* *der* failure

Mịsse·tat *die* (geh. veralt.) misdeed

mịss·fạllen, *mịß·fạllen* *unr. itr. V.* etw. missfällt jmdm. sb. dislikes sth.

Mịssfallen, *Mịßfallen* *das;* ∼s displeasure; (Missbilligung) disapproval

Mịss·geschick, *Mịß·geschick* *das* mishap

mịss·glụ̈cken, *mịß·glụ̈cken* *itr. V.; mit sein* fail

mịss·gönnen, *mịß·gönnen* *tr. V.* jmdm. etw. ∼: begrudge sb. sth.

Mịss·griff, *Mịß·griff* *der* error of judgement

mịss·hạndeln, *mịß·hạndeln* *tr. V.* maltreat

Mịss·hạndlung, *Mịß·hạndlung* *die* maltreatment

Missiọn *die;* ∼, ∼en mission

Missionạr *der;* ∼s, ∼e, **Missionạrin** *die;* ∼, ∼nen missionary

Mịss·kredit, *Mịß·kredit* *der:* jmdn./etw. in ∼ bringen bring sb./sth. into discredit

misslạng, *mißlạng* *1. u. 3. Pers. Sg. Prät. v.* MISSLINGEN

mịssliebig, *mịßliebig* *Adj.* unpopular

misslịngen, *mißlịngen* *unr. itr. V.; mit sein* fail

Misslịngen, *Mißlịngen* *das;* ∼s failure

misslụngen, *mißlụngen* *2. Part. v.* MISSLINGEN

Mịss·mut, *Mịß·mut* *der* ill humour *no indef. art.*

mịß·mutig, *mịss·mutig* [1] *Adj.* bad-tempered; sullen ⟨*face*⟩
[2] *adv.* bad-temperedly

Mịss·stand, *Mịß·stand* *der* deplorable state of affairs *no pl.*

---

*alte Schreibung - vgl. Hinweis auf S. xiv

mịsst, *mịßt* *2. u. 3. Pers. Sg. Präsens v.* MESSEN

mịss·trauen, *mịß·trauen* *itr. V.* jmdm./einer Sache ∼: mistrust *or* distrust sb./sth.

Mịsstrauen, *Mịß·trauen* *das;* ∼s mistrust, distrust (**gegen** of)

mịsstrauisch, *mịß·trauisch* [1] *Adj.* mistrustful; distrustful
[2] *adv.* mistrustfully; distrustfully

mịss·verständlich, *mịß·verständlich* [1] *Adj.* unclear; ⟨*formulation, concept, etc.*⟩ that could be misunderstood
[2] *adv.* ⟨*express oneself, describe*⟩ in a way that could be misunderstood

Mịss·verständnis, *Mịß·verständnis* *das* misunderstanding

mịss·verstehen, *mịß·verstehen* *unr. tr. V.* ich missverstehe, missverstanden, misszuverstehen misunderstand

Mịss·wirtschaft, *Mịß·wirtschaft* *die* mismanagement

Mịst *der;* ∼[e]s (a) dung; (Dünger) manure; (mit Stroh usw. gemischt) muck
(b) (Misthaufen) dung/manure/muck heap
(c) (ugs. abwertend) (Unsinn) rubbish *no indef. art.;* (Minderwertiges) junk *no indef. art.*

Mịstel *die;* ∼, ∼n mistletoe

Mịst·haufen *der* dung/manure/muck heap

mịt [1] *Präp. mit Dat.* with; **ein Zimmer** ∼ **Frühstück** a room with breakfast included; ∼ **50 [km/h] fahren** drive at 50 [k.p.h]; ∼ **der Bahn/dem Auto fahren** go by train/car; ∼ **20 [Jahren]** at [the age of] twenty
[2] *adv.* (a) too; as well
(b) **seine Arbeit war** ∼ **am besten** (ugs.) his work was among the best

Mịt·arbeit *die* collaboration (**bei/an** + *Dat.* on); (Mithilfe) assistance (**bei, in** + *Dat.* in); (Beteiligung) participation (**in** + *Dat.* in)

mịt|arbeiten *itr. V.* collaborate (**bei/an** + *Dat.* on); (sich beteiligen) participate (**in** + *Dat.* in)

Mịt·arbeiter *der,* **Mịt·arbeiterin** *die* (a) collaborator; **freier** ∼: freelance worker
(b) (Angestellter) employee

mịt|bekommen *unr. tr. V.* (a) etw. ∼: be given sth. to take with one
(b) (wahrnehmen) be aware of; (durch Hören, Sehen) hear/see

mịt|bestimmen [1] *itr. V.* have a say
[2] *tr. V.* have an influence on

Mịt·bestimmung *die* participation (**bei** in); (der Arbeitnehmer) co-determination

mịt|bringen *unr. tr. V.* (a) etw. ∼: bring sth. with one; jmdm./sich etw. ∼: bring sth. with one for sb./bring sth. back for oneself
(b) (haben) have ⟨*ability, gift, etc.*⟩

Mịtbringsel *das;* ∼s, ∼: [small] present; (Andenken) [small] souvenir

Mit·bürger der, **Mit·bürgerin** die fellow citizen; **ältere Mitbürger** (Amtsspr.) senior citizens

mit·einander Adv. (a) with each other or one another; ∼ **sprechen** talk to each other or one another (b) (gemeinsam) together

mit|erleben tr. V. (a) witness ⟨events etc.⟩ (b) (mitmachen) be alive during

mit|fahren unr. itr. V.; mit sein bei jmdm. [im Auto] ∼: go/travel with sb. [in his/her car]; (mitgenommen werden) get a lift with sb. [in his/her car]

mit·fühlend ⓵ Adj. sympathetic ⓶ adv. sympathetically

mit|führen tr. V. (a) (Amtsspr.: bei sich tragen) etw. ∼: carry sth. [with one] (b) (transportieren) ⟨river, stream⟩ carry along

mit|geben unr. tr. V. jmdm. etw. ∼: give sb. sth. to take with him/her; (fig.) provide sb. with sth.

Mit·gefühl das sympathy

mit|gehen unr. itr. V.; mit sein (a) go too; mit jmdm. ∼: go with sb. (b) (sich mitreißen lassen) begeistert ∼: respond enthusiastically

Mit·gift die; ∼, ∼en (veralt.) dowry

Mit·glied das member (Gen., in + Dat. of)

Mitglieder·versammlung die general meeting

Mitglieds-: ∼**ausweis** der membership card; ∼**beitrag** der membership subscription

Mitgliedschaft die; ∼: membership (+ Gen., in + Dat.) of

Mitglied[s]·staat der member state or country

mit|halten unr. itr. V. keep up (**bei** in, **mit** with)

mit|helfen unr. itr. V. help (**bei, in** + Dat. with)

mit·hilfe ⓵ Präp. mit Gen. with the help or aid of ⓶ Adv. ∼ **von** with the help or aid of

Mit·hilfe die help; assistance

mit|hören ⓵ tr. V. listen to; (zufällig) overhear ⟨conversation, argument, etc.⟩; (abhören) listen in on ⓶ itr. V. listen; (zufällig) overhear

mit|kommen unr. itr. V.; mit sein (a) come too; **kommst du mit?** are you coming [with me/us]? (b) (Schritt halten) keep up

Mit·läufer der, **Mit·läuferin** die (abwertend) [mere] supporter

Mit·laut der consonant

Mit·leid das pity, compassion (**mit** for); (Mitgefühl) sympathy (**mit** for)

Mit·leidenschaft die: jmdn./etw. in ∼ ziehen affect sb./sth.

mit·leidig ⓵ Adj. compassionate; (mitfühlend) sympathetic

⓶ adv. compassionately; (mitfühlend) sympathetically

mit|machen ⓵ tr. V. (a) (teilnehmen an) go on ⟨trip⟩; join in ⟨joke⟩; follow ⟨fashion⟩; fight in ⟨war⟩; do ⟨course, seminar⟩; **das mache ich nicht mit** (ugs.) I can't go along with it (b) (ugs.: erleiden) **zwei Weltkriege/viele Bombenangriffe mitgemacht haben** have been through two world wars/many bomb attacks ⓶ itr. V. (a) (sich beteiligen) join in (b) (ugs.: funktionieren) **mein Herz/Kreislauf macht nicht mit** my heart/circulation can't take it

Mit·mensch der fellow human being

mit|nehmen unr. tr. V. (a) jmdn. ∼: take sb. with one; etw. ∼: take sth. with one; (verhüll.: stehlen) walk off with sth. (coll.); (kaufen) take sth.; **Essen/Getränke zum Mitnehmen** food/drinks to take away or (Amer.) to go (b) (in Mitleidenschaft ziehen) jmdn. ∼: take it out of sb.

mit|reden itr. V. (a) join in the conversation (b) (mitbestimmen) have a say

Mit·reisende der/die fellow passenger

mit|reißen unr. tr. V. die Begeisterung/ seine Rede hat alle Zuhörer mitgerissen the audience was carried away with enthusiasm/by his speech

mit·samt Präp. mit Dat. together with

mit|schneiden unr. tr. V. (Rundf., Ferns.) record [live]

Mit·schuld die share of the blame or responsibility (**an** + Dat. for)

Mit·schüler der, **Mit·schülerin** die schoolfellow

mit|spielen itr. V. (a) join in the game (b) **in einem Film** ∼: be in a film; **in einem Orchester/in** od. **bei einem Fußballverein** ∼: play in an orchestra/for a football club

Mit·spieler der, **Mit·spielerin** die player; (in derselben Mannschaft) teammate

***mittag** ▶ MITTAG

Mittag der; ∼s, ∼e (a) midday no art.; **gegen** ∼: around midday; **zu** ∼ **essen** have lunch; **heute/Montag** ∼: at midday today/on Monday (b) (ugs.: Mittagspause) lunch hour

Mittag·essen das lunch

mittags Adv. at midday; **12 Uhr** ∼: 12 noon

Mittags-: ∼**pause** die lunch hour; ∼**ruhe** die period of quiet after lunch; ∼**zeit** die (a) (Zeit gegen 12 Uhr) lunchtime no art.; (b) (Mittagspause) lunch hour

Mitte die; ∼, ∼n middle; (eines Kreises, einer Kugel, Stadt) centre; ∼ **des Monats/Jahres** in the middle of the month/year

mit|teilen tr. V. jmdm. etw. ∼: tell sb. sth.; (informieren) inform sb. of sth.

mitteilsam *Adj.* communicative; (gesprächig) talkative

Mit·teilung *die* communication; (Bekanntgabe) announcement

Mittel *das;* ~s, ~ (a) means; (Methode) way; method; (Werbe~, Propaganda~ *usw.*) device *(Gen.* for); **mit allen ~n versuchen, etw. zu tun** try by every means to do sth.
(b) (Arznei) **ein ~ gegen Husten** *usw.* a cure for coughs *etc.;*
(c) *Pl.* (Geldmittel) funds; [financial] resources; (Privatmittel) means

Mittel·alter *das* Middle Ages *pl.*

mittel·alterlich *Adj.* medieval

mittelbar ① *Adj.* indirect
② *adv.* indirectly

mittel-, Mittel-: ~**ding** *das* **ein ~ding sein** be something in between; ~**europa** *(das)* Central Europe; ~**finger** *der* middle finger; ~**gebirge** *das* low mountains *pl.;* ~**groß** *Adj.* medium-sized; *(person)* of medium height; ~**klasse·wagen** *der* medium-sized car; ~**linie** *die* centre line; (Fußball) half-way line; ~**los** *Adj.* without means *postpos.;* ~**mäßig** *Adj.* mediocre; ~**meer** *das* Mediterranean [Sea]; ~**punkt** *der* (a) (Geom.) centre; (einer Strecke) midpoint; (b) (Mensch/Sache im Zentrum) centre of attention; ~**scheitel** *der* centre parting; ~**schule** *die.*▶ REALSCHULE; ~**stand** *der* middle class; ~**strecken·rakete** *die* medium-range missile; ~**streifen** *der* central reservation; median strip (Amer.); ~**weg** *der* middle course; ~**welle** *die* (Physik, Rundf.) medium wave

mitten *Adv.* ~ **an/auf etw.** *(Akk./Dat.)* in the middle of sth.; ~ **durch die Stadt** right through the town

mitten-: ~**drin** *Adv.* [right] in the middle; ~**durch** *Adv.* [right] through the middle

Mitter·nacht *die* midnight *no art.*

Mitternachts·sonne *die* midnight sun

Mittler *der;* ~s, ~ mediator

mittler... *Adj.* middle; moderate *(speed);* medium-sized *(company, town);* medium *(quality, size);* (durchschnittlich) average; **die ~e Reife** (Schulw.) *standard of achievement for school-leaving certificate at a Realschule or for entry to the sixth form in a Gymnasium*

Mittlerin *die;* ~, ~nen mediator

Mittler·rolle *die* mediating role

mittler·weile *Adv.* since then; (bis jetzt) by now; (unterdessen) in the meantime

Mittwoch *der;* ~[e]s, ~e Wednesday; *s. auch* DIENSTAG

mittwochs *Adv.* on Wednesday[s]

mit·unter *Adv.* from time to time

mit·wirken *itr. V.* **an etw.** *(Dat.)/***bei etw.** ~: collaborate on/be involved in sth.; **in einem Orchester/Theaterstück** ~: play in an orchestra/act *or* appear in a play

Mitwirkende *der/die adj. Dekl.* (an einer Sendung) participant; (in einer Show) performer; (in einem Theaterstück) actor

Mit·wisser *der;* ~s ~, **Mit·wisserin** *die;* ~, ~nen: ~ **einer Sache** *(Gen.)* **sein** be an accessory to sth.

mixen *tr. V.* mix; **sich** *(Dat.)* **einen Drink** ~: fix oneself a drink

Mixer *der;* ~s, ~, (a) (Bar~) barman; bartender (Amer.)
(b) (Gerät) blender and liquidizer

Mixerin *die;* ~, ~nen barmaid

mm *Abk.* = **Millimeter** mm.

Mo. *Abk.* = **Montag** Mon.

Mob *der;* ~s (abwertend) mob

Möbel *das;* ~s, ~ (a) *Pl.* furniture *sing., no indef. art.;*
(b) piece of furniture

Möbel·wagen *der* furniture van; removal van

mobil *Adj.* (a) mobile; *s. auch* MOBILMACHEN;
(b) (ugs.) (lebendig) lively

Mobiliar *das;* ~s furnishings *pl.*

mobilisieren *tr. V.* (a) (Milit., fig.) mobilize
(b) (aktivieren) activate

mobil|machen *itr. V.* mobilize

Mobilmachung *die;* ~, ~en mobilization

Mobil·telefon *das* cellular phone

möblieren *tr. V.* furnish

mochte *1. u. 3. Pers. Sg. Prät. v.* MÖGEN

möchte *1. u. 3. Pers. Sg. Konjunktiv II v.* MÖGEN

Mode *die;* ~, ~n fashion

Mode·farbe *die* fashionable colour

Modell *das;* ~s, ~e (auch fig.) model; **jmdm.** ~ **sitzen** *od.* **stehen** sit for sb.

modellieren *tr. V.* model, mould *(figures, objects);* mould *(clay, wax)*

Modell·kleid *das* model dress

Modem *der od. das;* ~s, ~s (DV) modem

Moden·schau *die* fashion show

Moder *der;* ~s mould; (~geruch) mustiness

Moderation *die;* ~, ~en (Rundf., Ferns.) presentation

Moderator *der;* ~s, ~en, **Moderatorin** *die;* ~, ~nen (Rundf., Ferns.) presenter

moderieren *tr. V.* (Rundf., Ferns.) present *(programme)*

modern¹ *itr. V.; auch mit sein* go mouldy

modern² ① *Adj.* modern; (modisch) fashionable
② *adv.* in a modern manner; (modisch) fashionably

modernisieren *tr. V.* modernize

Mode-: ~**schöpfer** *der* couturier; ~**schöpferin** *die* couturière; ~**wort** *das; Pl.* ~**wörter** vogue word; ~**zeitschrift** *die* fashion magazine

modifizieren *tr. V.* (geh.) modify

modisch ① *Adj.* fashionable
② *adv.* fashionably

---

*old spelling - see note on page xiv

Mofa *das;* ~s, ~s [low-powered] moped
Mogelei *die;* ~, ~en (ugs.) cheating *no pl.*
mogeln *itr. V.* cheat
Mogel·packung *die* (abwertend) deceptive
packaging
mögen ⟨1⟩ *unr. Modalverb; 2.Part.* mögen:
(a) (wollen) want to; **das hätte ich sehen** ~: I
would have liked to see that
(b) (geh.: sollen) **das mag genügen** that
should be enough
(c) (Vermutung, Möglichkeit) **sie mag/mochte
vierzig sein** she must be/must have been
[about] forty; **[das] mag sein** maybe
(d) *Konjunktiv II* (den Wunsch haben) **ich/sie
möchte gern wissen …:** I would/she would
like to know …
⟨2⟩ *unr. tr. V.* like; **sie mag keine Rosen** she
does not like roses; **sie** ~ **sich** they're fond
of one another; **möchten Sie ein Glas Wein?**
would you like a glass of wine?; **ich möchte
lieber Tee** I would prefer tea
⟨3⟩ *unr. itr. V.* (a) (es wollen) like to
(b) **ich möchte nach Hause** I want to go
home; **er möchte zu Herrn A** he would like to
see Mr A
möglich *Adj.* possible; **es war ihm nicht** ~
[**zu kommen**] he was unable [to come]; **alles
Mögliche** (ugs.) all sorts of things; **[das ist
doch] nicht** ~**!** impossible!; **sein Möglichstes
tun** do one's utmost
möglicher·weise *Adv.* possibly
Möglichkeit *die;* ~, ~en (a) possibility;
(Methode) way; **es besteht die** ~, **dass …:**
there is a possibility that …
(b) (Gelegenheit) opportunity; chance
möglichst *Adv.* (a) if [at all] possible
(b) ~ **schnell** as fast as possible
Mohammed (*der*) Muhammad
Mohammedaner *der;* ~s, ~,
Mohammedanerin *die;* ~, ~nen
Muslim; Muhammadan
mohammedanisch *Adj.* Muslim;
Muhammadan
Mohn *der;* ~s poppy; (Samen) poppy seed;
(auf Brot, Kuchen) poppy seeds *pl.*
Mohn-: ~**blume** *die* poppy; ~**brötchen**
das poppy-seed roll; ~**kuchen** *der* poppy-
seed cake
Möhre *die;* ~, ~n carrot
Mohren·kopf *der* chocolate marshmallow
Mohr·rübe *die* carrot
mokieren *refl. V.* (geh.) **sich über etw.**
(*Akk.*) ~: scoff at sth.; **sich über jmdn.** ~:
mock sb.
Mokka *der;* ~s strong black coffee
Molch *der;* ~[e]s, ~e newt
Mole *die;* ~, ~n [harbour] mole
Molekül *das;* ~s, ~e molecule
molekular *Adj.* molecular
molk *1. u. 3. Pers. Sg. Prät. v.* MELKEN
Molkerei *die;* ~, ~en dairy
Moll *das;* ~ (Musik) minor [key]

mollig ⟨1⟩ *Adj.* (a) (rundlich) plump
(b) (warm) snug
⟨2⟩ *adv.* snugly; ~ **warm** warm and snug
Moment¹ *der;* ~[e]s, ~e moment; **jeden** ~
(ugs.) [at] any moment; **im** ~: at the moment
Moment² *das;* ~[e]s, ~e factor, element
(für in)
momentan ⟨1⟩ *Adj.* (a) present
(b) (vorübergehend) temporary; (flüchtig)
momentary
⟨2⟩ *adv.* (a) at present
(b) (vorübergehend) temporarily
Monaco (*das*) ~s Monaco
Monarch *der;* ~en, ~en monarch
Monarchie *die;* ~, ~n monarchy
Monarchin *die;* ~, ~nen monarch
Monat *der;* ~s, ~e month; **im** ~ **April** in
the month of April
monatelang ⟨1⟩ *Adj.* lasting for months
postpos., not pred.;
⟨2⟩ *adv.* for months [on end]
monatlich ⟨1⟩ *Adj.* monthly
⟨2⟩ *adv.* every month; (pro Monat) per month
Monats-: ~**ende** *das* end of the month;
~**erste** *der; adj. Dekl.* first [day] of the
month; ~**hälfte** *die* half of the month;
~**karte** *die* monthly season ticket;
~**letzte** *der; adj. Dekl.* last day of the
month
Mönch *der;* ~[e]s, ~e monk
Mond *der;* ~[e]s, ~e moon; **auf** od. **hinter
dem** ~ **leben** (fig. ugs.) be a bit behind the
times; **nach jmdm.** ~ **gehen** (ugs.) ⟨*clock,
watch*⟩ be hopelessly wrong
Mond-: ~**fähre** *die* (Raumf.) lunar module;
~**finsternis** *die* eclipse of the moon;
~**landung** *die* moon landing; ~**licht** *das*
moonlight; ~**phase** *die* moon's phase
Mongole *der;* ~n, ~n (a) Mongol
(b) (Bewohner der Mongolei) Mongolian
Mongolei *die;* ~: Mongolia
Mongolin *die;* ~, ~nen ▶ MONGOLE
Monitor *der;* ~s, ~en monitor
mono-, Mono-: mono-
Mono·gramm *das;* ~s, ~e monogram
Monographie *die;* ~, ~n monograph
Monolog *der;* ~s, ~e monologue
Monopol *das;* ~s, ~e monopoly (**auf** +
Akk., **für** in, of)
monoton ⟨1⟩ *Adj.* monotonous
⟨2⟩ *adv.* monotonously
Monotonie *die;* ~, ~n monotony
Monster *das;* ~s, ~: monster; (hässlich)
[hideous] brute
Monstren ▶ MONSTRUM
monströs *Adj.* monstrous
Monstrum *das;* ~s, Monstren (a) monster
(b) (Sache) hulking great thing (coll.)
Monsun *der;* ~s, ~e (Geogr.) monsoon
Mon·tag *der* Monday; *s. auch* DIENSTAG
Montage /mɔn'taːʒə/ *die;* ~, ~n (a)   ⋯⋗

(Zusammenbau) assembly; (Einbau) installation; (Aufstellen) erection; (Anbringen) fitting (**an** + *Akk. od. Dat.* to); mounting (**auf** + *Akk. od. Dat.* on)
(b) (Film, bild. Kunst, Literaturw.) montage

montags *Adv.* on Monday[s]

montieren *tr. V.* **(a)** (zusammenbauen) assemble (**aus** from); erect ‹*building*›
(b) (anbringen) fit (**an** + *Akk. od. Dat.* to; **auf** + *Akk. od. Dat.* on); (einbauen) install (**in** + *Akk.* in); (befestigen) fix (**an** + *Akk. od. Dat.* to)

Monument *das;* ∼[e]s, ∼e monument

monumental *Adj.* monumental

Moor *das;* ∼[e]s, ∼e bog; (Bruch) marsh

Moos *das;* ∼es, ∼e moss

Moped /'mo:pɛt/ *das;* ∼s, ∼s moped

Mops *der;* ∼es, Möpse pug [dog]; (salopp: dicke Person) podge (coll.)

Moral *die;* ∼ **(a)** (Norm) morality
(b) (Sittlichkeit) morals *pl.;*
(c) (Selbstvertrauen) morale
(d) (Lehre) moral

moralisch ① *Adj.* **(a)** moral
(b) (tugendhaft) virtuous
② *adv.* **(a)** morally
(b) (tugendhaft) virtuously

moralisieren *itr. V.* (geh.) moralize

Moralist *der;* ∼en, ∼en, **Moralistin** *die;* ∼, ∼nen moralist

Moral·predigt *die* (abwertend) [moralizing] lecture; homily

Morast *der;* ∼[e]s, ∼e *od.* Moräste (a) bog; swamp
(b) (Schlamm) mud

Mord *der;* ∼[e]s, ∼e murder (**an** + *Dat.* of); (durch ein Attentat) assassination; **einen** ∼ **begehen** commit murder

Mord-: ∼**anschlag** *der* attempted murder (**auf** + *Akk.* of); (Attentat) assassination attempt (**auf** + *Akk.* on); ∼**drohung** *die* murder threat

morden *tr., itr. V.* murder

Mörder *der;* ∼s, ∼: murderer (esp. Law); killer; (politischer) assassin

Mörderin *die;* ∼, ∼nen murderer; murderess; (politische) assassin

mörderisch ① *Adj.* murderous
② *adv.* (ugs.) dreadfully (coll.)

Mord·fall *der* murder case

mords-, Mords- (ugs.) terrific (coll.)

mords·mäßig *Adj.* terrific (coll.); tremendous (coll.); (entsetzlich) terrible (coll.)

Mord-: ∼**verdacht** *der* suspicion of murder; ∼**versuch** *der* attempted murder; (Attentat) assassination attempt; ∼**waffe** *die* murder weapon

morgen *Adv.* tomorrow; ∼ **in einer Woche** tomorrow week; a week tomorrow; ∼ **um diese Zeit** this time tomorrow; **bis** ∼! until tomorrow!; see you tomorrow!

Morgen *der;* ∼s, ∼: morning; **am** ∼: in the morning; **am folgenden** *od.* **nächsten** ∼: next morning; **früh am** ∼, **am frühen** ∼: early in the morning; **heute** ∼: this morning; **guten** ∼! good morning!

morgendlich *Adj.* morning

Morgen-: ∼**grauen** *das* daybreak; ∼**mantel** *der* dressing gown; ∼**rot** *das* (geh.) rosy dawn

morgens *Adv.* in the morning; (jeden Morgen) every morning; **Dienstag** *od.* **dienstags** ∼: on Tuesday morning[s]; **von** ∼ **bis abends** from morning to evening

morgig *Adj.* tomorrow's

Morphium *das;* ∼s morphine

morphium·süchtig *Adj.* addicted to morphine *pred.*

morsch *Adj.* (auch fig.) rotten

Mörser *der;* ∼s, ∼ (Gefäß, Geschütz) mortar

Mörtel *der;* ∼s mortar

Mosaik *das;* ∼s, ∼en *od.* ∼e mosaic

Mosambik *(das);* ∼s Mozambique

Moschee *die;* ∼, ∼n mosque

Moschus *der;* ∼: musk

Mosel *die;* ∼: Moselle

Mosel·wein *der* Moselle [wine]

mosern *itr. V.* (ugs.) gripe (coll.) (**über** + *Akk.*)

Moskau *(das);* ∼s Moscow

Moskauer ① *indekl. Adj.* Moscow *attrib.;*
② *der;* ∼s, ∼: Muscovite

Moskauerin *die;* ∼, ∼nen Muscovite

Moskito *der;* ∼s, ∼s mosquito

Moslem *der;* ∼s, ∼s ▶ MUSLIM

Moslemin *die;* ∼, ∼nen ▶ MUSLIMIN

moslemisch ▶ MUSLIMISCH

Most *der;* ∼[e]s, ∼e (a) [cloudy fermented] fruit juice
(b) (landsch.: neuer Wein) new wine

Mostrich *der;* ∼s (nordostd.) mustard

Motel *das;* ∼s, ∼s motel

Motiv *das;* ∼s, ∼e (a) motive
(b) (fachspr.: Thema) motif; theme; (Kunst) subject

Motor *der;* ∼s, ∼en engine; (Elektro∼) motor

Motor·haube *die* (Kfz-W.) bonnet (Brit.); hood (Amer.)

motorisieren *tr. V.* motorize

Motor-: ∼**rad** *das* motor cycle; ∼**rad·fahrer** *der,* ∼**rad·fahrerin** *die* motorcyclist; ∼**roller** *der* motor scooter; ∼**schaden** *der* engine trouble *no indef. art.*

Motte *die;* ∼, ∼n moth

Motten·kugel *die* mothball

Motto *das;* ∼s, ∼s motto; (Schlagwort) slogan

Möwe *die;* ∼, ∼n gull

Mrd. *Abk.* = **Milliarde** bn.

Mücke *die;* ∼, ∼n midge; (größer) mosquito

Mücken·stich *der* midge/mosquito bite

---

*alte Schreibung - vgl. Hinweis auf S. xiv

Mucks *der;* ∼es, ∼e (ugs.) murmur [of protest]; **keinen** ∼ **sagen** not utter a [single] word

müde [1] *Adj.* tired; (ermattet) weary; (schläfrig) sleepy; **jmdn./etw.** *od.* **jmds./einer Sache** ∼ **sein** (geh.) be tired of sb./sth.
[2] *adv.* wearily; (schläfrig) sleepily

Müdigkeit *die;* ∼: tiredness

muffelig (ugs.) [1] *Adj.* grumpy
[2] *adv.* grumpily

muffig *Adj.* musty

Mühe *die;* ∼, ∼n trouble; **sich** (*Dat.*) **mit jmdm./etw.** ∼ **geben** take [great] pains over sb./sth.; **mit Müh und Not** with great difficulty

mühelos [1] *Adj.* effortless
[2] *adv.* effortlessly

mühe·voll *Adj.* laborious; painstaking ⟨*work*⟩

Mühle *die;* ∼, ∼n (a) mill; (Kaffee∼) [coffee] grinder
(b) (Spiel) nine men's morris

Mühsal *die;* ∼, ∼e (geh.) tribulation; (Strapaze) hardship

mühsam [1] *Adj.* laborious
[2] *adv.* laboriously

müh·selig (geh.) [1] *Adj.* laborious; arduous ⟨*journey, life*⟩
[2] *adv.* with [great] difficulty

Mulde *die;* ∼, ∼n hollow

Mull *der;* ∼[e]s (Stoff) mull; (Verband∼) gauze

Müll *der;* ∼s refuse; rubbish; garbage (Amer.); trash (Amer.); (Industrie∼) [industrial] waste

Müll-: ∼**abfuhr** *die* refuse *or* (Amer.) garbage collection; ∼**ablade·platz** *der* [refuse] dump *or* (Brit.) tip

Müll·binde *die* gauze bandage

Müll·deponie *die* (Amtsspr.) refuse disposal site

Müller *der;* ∼s, ∼: miller

Müll-: ∼**halde** *die* refuse dump; ∼**kippe** *die* ▶ MÜLLABLADEPLATZ; ∼**mann** *der;* (ugs.) dustman (Brit.); garbage man (Amer.); ∼**sack** *der* refuse bag; ∼**schlucker** *der* rubbish *or* (Amer.) garbage chute; ∼**tonne** *die* dustbin (Brit.); garbage *or* trash can (Amer.); ∼**tüte** *die* bin bag; ∼**wagen** *der* dustcart (Brit.); garbage truck (Amer.)

mulmig *Adj.* (ugs.) uneasy

Multimedia·technik *die* (DV) multimedia technology

Multiplex *das;* ∼es, ∼e multiplex

Multiplikation *die;* ∼, ∼en (Math.) multiplication

multiplizieren *tr. V.* multiply (**mit** by)

Mumie /'muːmiə/ *die;* ∼, ∼n mummy

Mumm *der;* ∼s (ugs.) (Mut) guts *pl.* (coll.); (Tatkraft) drive; zap (coll.); (Kraft) muscle power

Mumps *der od. die;* ∼: mumps *sing.*

München ⟨*das*⟩; ∼s Munich

Münch[e]ner [1] *indekl. Adj.* Munich *attrib*
[2] *der;* ∼s, ∼: inhabitant/native of Munich

Münch[e]nerin *die;* ∼, ∼nen
▶ MÜNCH[E]NER 2

Mund *der;* ∼[e]s, Münder mouth; **er küsste sie auf den** ∼: he kissed her on the lips; **mit vollem** ∼ **sprechen** speak with one's mouth full; **den** ∼ **nicht aufmachen** (fig. ugs.) not say anything; **den** *od.* **seinen** ∼ **halten** (ugs.) (zu sprechen aufhören) shut up (coll.); (nichts sagen) not say anything; (nichts verraten) keep quiet (**über** + *Akk.* about); **sie ist nicht auf den** ∼ **gefallen** (fig. ugs.) she's never at a loss for words

Mund·art *die* dialect

münden *itr. V.; mit sein* **in etw.** (*Akk.*) ∼: ⟨*river*⟩ flow into sth.; ⟨*corridor, street*⟩ lead into sth.

Mund-, Mund-: ∼**faul** *Adj.* (ugs.) uncommunicative; ∼**gerecht** *Adj.* bite-sized; ∼**geruch** *der* bad breath *no indef. art.;* ∼**harmonika** *die* mouth organ

mündig *Adj.* of age *pred.;* ∼ **werden** come of age

mündlich [1] *Adj.* oral
[2] *adv.* orally

Mund·stück *das* mouthpiece; (bei Zigaretten) tip

mund·tot *Adj.* **jmdn.** ∼ **machen** silence sb.

Mündung *die;* ∼, ∼en (a) mouth; (größere Trichter∼) estuary
(b) (bei Feuerwaffen) muzzle

Mund·wasser *das; Pl.* ∼wässer mouthwash

Mund-zu-Mund-Beatmung *die* mouth-to-mouth resuscitation

Munition *die;* ∼: ammunition

munkeln *tr., itr. V.* (ugs.) **man munkelt, dass …:** there is a rumour that …

Münster *das;* ∼s, ∼: minster; (Dom) cathedral

munter [1] *Adj.* (a) cheerful; (lebhaft) lively ⟨*eyes, game*⟩
(b) (wach) awake
[2] *adv.* cheerfully

Munterkeit *die;* ∼: cheerfulness

Münz·automat *der* slot machine

Münze *die;* ∼, ∼n coin

Münz-: ∼**fernsprecher** *der* payphone; pay station (Amer.); ∼**tankstelle** *die* coin-in-the-slot petrol (Brit.) *or* (Amer.) gas station; ∼**wechsler** *der* change machine

mürbe *Adj.* crumbly ⟨*biscuit, cake, etc.*⟩; tender ⟨*meat*⟩; soft ⟨*fruit*⟩; **jmdn.** ∼ **machen** (fig.) wear sb. down

Murmel *die;* ∼, ∼n marble

murmeln *tr., itr. V.* mumble; mutter; (sehr leise) murmur

Murmel·tier *das* marmot

murren *itr. V.* grumble

mürrisch [1] *Adj.* grumpy   ⋯⁚

2 *adv.* grumpily

Mus *das od. der;* ~es, ~e purée

Muschel *die;* ~, ~n (a) mussel; (Schale) [mussel] shell
(b) (am Telefon) (Hör~) earpiece; (Sprech~) mouthpiece

Muse *die;* ~, ~n muse

Museum *das;* ~s, Museen museum

Musik *die;* ~, ~en music

musikalisch 1 *Adj.* musical
2 *adv.* musically

Musikant *der;* ~en, ~en, **Musikantin** *die;* ~, ~nen musician

Musik·box *die* jukebox

Musiker *der;* ~s, ~, **Musikerin** *die;* ~, ~nen musician

Musik-: ~**hochschule** *die* college of music; ~**instrument** *das* musical instrument; ~**saal** *der* (in der Schule) music room; ~**sender** *der* music station; ~**stück** *das* piece of music; **ein** ~**stück** Chopins/von Chopin a piece by Chopin; ~**stunde** *die* music lesson; ~**szene** *die* music scene

musisch 1 *Adj.* artistic; ‹education› in the arts
2 *adv.* artistically

musizieren *itr. V.* play music; (bes. unter Laien) make music

Muskat *der;* ~[e]s, ~e nutmeg

Muskat·nuss, *Muskat·nuß *die* nutmeg

Muskel *der;* ~s, ~n muscle

Muskel-: ~**kater** *der* stiff muscles *pl.;* ~**kraft** *die* muscle power; ~**krampf** *der* cramp; ~**pille** *die* (scherzh.) muscle-building pill; muscle builder ~**protz** *der* (ugs.) muscleman; ~**zerrung** *die* (Med.) pulled muscle; **sich** (*Dat.*) **eine** ~**zerrung zuziehen** pull a muscle

Muskulatur *die;* ~, ~en musculature; muscular system

muskulös *Adj.* muscular

Müsli *das;* ~s, ~s muesli

Muslim *der;* ~s, ~e *od.* ~s Muslim

Muslimin *die;* ~, ~nen Muslim [woman]

muslimisch 1 *Adj.* Muslim
2 *adv.* on Muslim principles; ~ **erzogen werden** be brought up in the Muslim faith

muss, *muß 1. u. 3.Pers. Sg. Präsens v. MÜSSEN

Muss, *Muß *das;* ~: necessity; must (coll.)

Muße *die;* ~: leisure

müssen 1 *unr. Modalverb; 2.Part.* müssen:
(a) have to; **er muss es tun** he has to or (coll.) has got to do it; **das muss 1968 gewesen sein** it must have been in 1968; **er muss gleich hier sein** he will be here at any moment

(b) *Konjunktiv II* **es müsste doch möglich sein** it ought to be possible; **reich müsste man sein!** how nice it would be to be rich!
2 *unr. itr. V.* **ich muss nach Hause** I have to or must go home; **ich muss mal** (fam.) I need to spend a penny (Brit. coll.) *or* (Amer. coll.) go to the john

müßig 1 *Adj.* idle ‹person›; ‹hours, weeks, life› of leisure
2 *adv.* idly

Müßig-: ~**gang** *der* leisure; (Untätigkeit) idleness ~**gänger** *der;* ~s, ~, ~**gängerin** *die;* ~, ~nen idler; ~**gänger** *Pl.* people with time on their hands

musste, *mußte 1. u. 3. Pers. Sg. Prät. v. MÜSSEN

Muster *das;* ~s, ~ (a) (Vorlage) pattern
(b) (Vorbild) model (**an** + *Dat.* of)
(c) (Verzierung) pattern
(d) (Warenprobe) sample

muster-, Muster-: ~**beispiel** *das* perfect example; ~**gültig** 1 *Adj.* exemplary; impeccable ‹order›; 2 *adv.* in an exemplary fashion; ~**prozess, *~prozeß** *der* test case

mustern *tr. V.* (a) eye
(b) (Milit.: ärztlich untersuchen) **jmdn.** ~: give sb. his medical

Musterung *die;* ~, ~en (a) scrutiny
(b) (Milit.: von Wehrpflichtigen) medical examination; medical

Mut *der;* ~[e]s courage

mutig 1 *Adj.* brave
2 *adv.* bravely

mut·los *Adj.* dejected; (entmutigt) disheartened

Mut·losigkeit *die;* ~: dejection

mutmaßen *tr., itr. V.* conjecture

mutmaßlich *Adj.* supposed; suspected ‹murderer etc.›

Mutmaßung *die;* ~, ~en conjecture

Mut·probe *die* test of courage

Mutter¹ *die;* ~, Mütter mother

Mutter² *die;* ~, ~n nut

mütterlich 1 *Adj.* (a) maternal ‹line, love, instincts, etc.›
(b) (fürsorglich) motherly ‹woman, care›
2 *adv.* in a motherly way

mütterlicher·seits *Adv.* on the/his/her etc. mother's side

Mütterlichkeit *die;* ~: motherliness; (mütterliche Gefühle) motherly feeling

Mutter-: ~**liebe** *die* motherly love *no art.;* ~**mal** *das;* ~~e birthmark

Mutterschaft *die;* ~: motherhood

Mutterschafts·urlaub *der* maternity leave

mutter-, Mutter-: ~**seelen·allein** *Adj.* all alone; ~**söhnchen** *das* mummy's *or* (Amer.) mama's boy; ~**sprache** *die* mother tongue; ~**tag** *der* Mother's Day *no def. art.*

Mutti *die;* ~, ~s mummy (Brit. coll.); mum (Brit. coll.); mommy (Amer. coll.); mom (Amer. coll.)

mut·willig [1] *Adj.* wilful; wanton ⟨*destruction*⟩
[2] *adv.* wilfully

Mütze *die;* ~, ~n cap

MW *Abk.* (Rundf.) = **Mittelwelle** MW

Mw.-St., MwSt. *Abk.* Mehrwertsteuer VAT

mysteriös [1] *Adj.* mysterious
[2] *adv.* mysteriously

Mystik *die;* ~: mysticism

Mystery- /ˈmɪstəri/ mystery *attrib.*

Mythologie *die;* ~, ~n mythology

mythologisch *Adj.* mythology

Mythos *der;* ~, **Mythen** myth

Nn

n, N /ɛn/ *das;* ~, ~: n/N

N *Abk.* = **Nord[en]** N

na *Interj.* (ugs.) well; **na so [et]was!** well I never!; **na und?** (wennschon) so what?; (beschwichtigend) **na, na, na!** now, now, come along; (triumphierend) **na also!** there you are!; (unsicher) **na, ich weiß nicht** hmm, I'm not sure; (ärgerlich) **na, was soll das denn?** now what's all this about?; (drohend) **na warte!** just [you] wait!

Nabe *die;* ~, ~n hub

Nabel *der;* ~s, ~: navel

Nabel-: ~**bruch** *der* (Med.) umbilical hernia; ~**schnur** *die* umbilical cord

Naben·schaltung *die* hub gear

nach [1] *Präp. mit Dat.* (a) (räumlich) to; **der Zug ~ München** the train for Munich *or* the Munich train; **~ Hause gehen** go home; **~ Osten [zu]** eastwards; [towards the] east
(b) (zeitlich) after; **zehn [Minuten] ~ zwei** ten [minutes] past two
(c) (mit bestimmten Verben, bezeichnet das Ziel der Handlung) for
(d) (bezeichnet [räumliche und zeitliche] Reihenfolge) after; **~ Ihnen/dir!** after you
(e) (gemäß) according to; **~ meiner Ansicht** *od.* **Meinung, meiner Ansicht** *od.* **Meinung ~:** in my view *or* opinion; **~ der neusten Mode gekleidet** dressed in [accordance with] the latest fashion; **dem Gesetz ~:** in accordance with the law; by law; **~ etw. schmecken/riechen** taste/smell of sth.
[2] *Adv.* (a) (räumlich) **[alle] mir ~!** [everybody] follow me!
(b) (zeitlich) **~ und ~:** little by little; gradually; **~ wie vor** still

nach|ahmen *tr. V.* imitate

Nachahmung *die;* ~, ~en imitation

Nachbar *der;* ~n, ~n neighbour

Nachbar·haus *das* house next door

Nachbarin *die;* ~, ~nen neighbour

Nachbar·land *das* neighbouring country

Nachbarschaft *die;* ~, ~en (a) the whole neighbourhood
(b) (Beziehungen) **gute ~:** good neighbourliness
(c) (Gegend) neighbourhood; (Nähe) vicinity

Nach·beben *das* aftershock

nach|bestellen *tr. V.* [noch] etw. ~: order more of sth.; ⟨*shop*⟩ reorder sth.

Nach·bildung *die* (a) copying
(b) (Gegenstand) copy

nach|blicken *tr. V.* (geh.) **jmdm./einer Sache ~:** gaze after sb./sth.

nach|datieren *tr. V.* backdate

nach·dem *Konj.* (a) after
(b) ▶ ᴊᴇ¹ 3

nach|denken *unr. itr. V.* think; **denk mal [gut** *od.* **scharf] nach** have a [good] think

Nach·denken *das* thought

nachdenklich [1] *Adj.* thoughtful
[2] *adv.* thoughtfully

Nach·druck *der; Pl.* ~e (a) **mit ~:** emphatically
(b) (Druckw.) reprint

nachdrücklich [1] *Adj.* emphatic
[2] *adv.* emphatically

Nachdrücklichkeit *die;* ~: emphatic nature

nach|dunkeln *itr. V.; mit sein* get darker

Nach·durst *der* morning-after thirst

nach|eifern *itr. V.* jmdm. ~: emulate sb.

nach·einander *Adv.* one after the other

nach|empfinden *unr. tr. V.* empathize with ⟨*feeling*⟩; share ⟨*delight, sorrow*⟩

Nach·erzählung *die* retelling [of a story]; (Schulw.) reproduction

Nachfahr *der;* ~en, ~en, **Nachfahrin** *die;* ~, ~nen (geh.) descendant

nach|fahren *unr. itr. V.; mit sein* follow [on]; jmdm. ~: follow sb.

Nach·folge *die* succession

Nachfolger *der;* ~s, ~, **Nachfolgerin** *die;* ~, ~nen successor

n

Nach·forschung *die* investigation

Nach·frage *die* demand (**nach** for)

nach|fragen *itr. V.* ask; inquire; **bei jmdm. ~**: ask sb.; **ob ich mal ~ soll?** should I ask about it *or* make inquiries?

nach|fühlen *tr. V.* empathize with; **das kann ich dir ~!** I know how you feel!

nach|füllen *tr. V.* top up; **Salz/Wein ~**: put [some] more salt/wine in

nach|geben *unr. itr. V.* give way

Nach·gebühr *die* excess postage

nach|gehen *unr. itr. V.; mit sein* (a) **jmdm./einer Sache ~**: follow sb./sth.; **einer Sache ~** (fig.) look into a matter; **einem Beruf ~**: practise a profession (b) (nicht aus dem Kopf gehen) **jmdm. ~**: remain on sb.'s mind (c) ⟨clock, watch⟩ be slow; **[um] eine Stunde ~**: be an hour slow

Nach·geschmack *der* aftertaste

nach·giebig *Adj.* indulgent

Nachgiebigkeit *die; ~*: indulgence

nach·haltig ① *Adj.* (a) lasting (b) (Ökologie) sustainable ② *adv.* (a) (auf längere Zeit) for a long time (b) (Ökologie) sustainably

Nach·hause·weg *der* way home

nach|helfen *unr. itr. V.* help

nach·her /auch: '-–/ *Adv.* afterwards; (später) later [on]; **bis ~!** see you later!

Nach·hilfe *die* coaching

Nachhilfe·unterricht *der* coaching

***nach·hinein, Nachhinein: im ~** (nachträglich) afterwards; later; (zurückblickend) with hindsight

nach|holen *tr. V.* (nachträglich erledigen) catch up on ⟨work, sleep⟩; make up for ⟨working hours missed⟩

nach|jagen *itr. V.; mit sein* **jmdm./einer Sache ~**: chase after sb./sth.

Nachkomme *der; ~n, ~n* descendant

nach|kommen *unr. itr. V.; mit sein* follow [later]; come [on] later

Nachkommenschaft *die; ~*: descendants *pl.*

Nachkömmling *der; ~s, ~e* much younger child (*than the rest*)

Nach·kriegs- post-war ⟨generation, period, etc.⟩

Nach·lass, *Nach·laß *der; Nachlasses, Nachlasse od. Nachlässe* (a) estate (b) (Kaufmannsspr.: Rabatt) discount

nach|lassen ① *unr. itr. V.* let up; ⟨pain, stress, pressure⟩ ease; ⟨effect⟩ wear off; ⟨interest, enthusiasm, strength, courage⟩ wane; ⟨health, hearing, memory⟩ deteriorate; ⟨business⟩ drop off ② *unr. tr. V.* (Kaufmannsspr.) give a discount of

nach·lässig ① *Adj.* careless

② *adv.* carelessly

Nach·lässigkeit *die; ~, ~en* carelessness

Nachlass·verwalter *der,* **Nachlass·verwalterin**, *die* (Rechtsw.) executor

nach|laufen *unr. itr. V.; mit sein* **jmdm./einer Sache ~**: run after sb./sth.

nach|lesen *unr. tr. V.* look up

nach|lösen ① *tr. V.* **eine Fahrkarte ~**: buy a ticket [on the train, bus, etc.] ② *itr.* pay the excess [fare]

nach|machen *tr. V.* (auch tun) copy; (imitieren) imitate; (genauso herstellen) reproduce ⟨period furniture etc.⟩; forge ⟨signature⟩

***nach·mittag** ▶ NACHMITTAG

Nach·mittag *der* afternoon; **am ~**: in the afternoon; **am späten ~**: late in the afternoon; **heute ~**: this afternoon

nach·mittags *Adv.* in the afternoon; **dienstags od. Dienstag ~**: on Tuesday afternoons; **um vier Uhr ~**: at four in the afternoon; at 4 p.m.

Nachnahme *die; ~, ~n*: **per ~**: cash on delivery; COD

Nach·name *der* surname

Nach·porto *das* excess postage

nachprüfbar *Adj.* verifiable

nach|prüfen *tr., itr. V.* check

nach|rechnen *tr. V.* check ⟨figures⟩

Nach·rede *die*: **üble ~**: malicious gossip; (Rechtsw.) defamation [of character]

nach|rennen *unr. itr. V.:* ▶ NACHLAUFEN

Nachricht *die; ~, ~en* (a) news *no pl.; das ist eine gute ~*: that is [a piece of] good news; **eine ~ hinterlassen** leave a message (b) *Pl.* (Ferns., Rundf.) news *sing.;* **~en hören** listen to the news

Nachrichten-: ~sprecher *der,* **~sprecherin** *die* newsreader

nach|rücken *itr. V.; mit sein* move up

Nach·ruf *der* obituary (**auf** + *Akk.* of)

nach|rufen *unr. tr., itr. V.* **jmdm. [etw.] ~**: call [sth.] after sb.

nach|rüsten ① *itr. V.* counter-arm ② *tr. V.* (Technik: zusätzlich ausstatten) **mit etw. ~** (+ *Akk.*) equip additionally with sth.; upgrade ⟨television, hi-fi, etc.⟩ with sth.

nach|sagen *tr. V.* (a) (wiederholen) repeat (b) **man sagt ihm nach, er sei ...**: he is said to be ...; **jmdm. Schlechtes ~**: speak ill of sb.

Nach·saison *die* late season

nach|schicken *tr. V.* (a) (durch die Post o. Ä.) forward (b) **jmdm. jmdn. ~**: send sb. after sb.

Nach·schlag *der* (ugs.: zusätzliche Portion) second helping; seconds *pl.*

nach|schlagen ① *unr. itr. V.* look up ② *unr. itr. V.* **im Lexikon/Wörterbuch ~**: consult the encyclopaedia/dictionary

Nachschlage·werk *das* work of reference

Nach·schlüssel *der* duplicate key

---

*alte Schreibung - vgl. Hinweis auf S. xiv

nach|schmeißen *unr. tr. V.* (ugs.) **man kriegt sie nachgeschmissen** you get them for next to nothing

Nach·schub *der* (Milit.) (a) supply (an + *Dat.* of)
(b) (∼material) supplies *pl.* (an + *Dat.* of)

nach|sehen ① *unr. itr. V.* (a) jmdm./einer Sache ∼: gaze after sb./sth.
(b) (kontrollieren) check
(c) (nachschlagen) have a look
② *unr. tr. V.* (a) (nachlesen) look up
(b) (überprüfen) check [over]

Nach·sehen *das:* **das ∼ haben** not get a look-in; (nichts abbekommen) be left with nothing

nach|senden *unr. od. regelm. tr. V.* forward

Nach·sicht *die* leniency

nachsichtig ① *Adj.* lenient (gegen, mit towards)
② *adv.* leniently

Nachsichtigkeit *die;* ∼: leniency

Nach·silbe *die* (Sprachw.) suffix

nach|sitzen *unr. itr. V.* be in detention; [eine Stunde] ∼ müssen have [an hour's] detention

Nach·spann *der;* ∼[e]s, ∼e (Film, Ferns.) [final] credits *pl.*

Nach·speise *die* dessert; sweet

Nach·spiel *das:* **die Sache wird noch ein ∼ haben** this affair will have repercussions; **ein gerichtliches ∼ haben** result in court proceedings

nach|spionieren *itr. V.* jmdm. ∼: spy on sb.

nach|sprechen *unr. tr. V.* [jmdm.] etw. ∼: repeat sth. [after sb.]

nächst... *Sup. zu* NAH: *Adj.* next; (kürzest) shortest ⟨way⟩; **am ∼en Tag** the next day; **beim ∼en Mal, das ∼e Mal** the next time; **der ∼e bitte!** next [one], please; **wer kommt als ∼er dran?** whose turn is it next?

Nächste *der; adj. Dekl.* (geh.) neighbour

nach|stehen *unr. itr. V.* jmdm. an etw. (*Dat.*) nicht ∼: be sb.'s match in sth.; **jmdm./einer Sache in nichts ∼:** be in no way inferior to sb./sth.

nach·stehend ① *Adj.* following
② *adv.* below

Nächsten·liebe *die* charity [to one's neighbour]

nächstens *Adv.* (a) shortly
(b) (ugs.; wenn es so weitergeht) if it goes on like this

nächst-: ∼**liegend** *Adj.* first, immediate ⟨problem⟩; [most] obvious ⟨explanation etc.⟩; ∼**möglich** *Adj.* earliest possible

nach|suchen *itr. V.* (geh.) um etw. ∼: request sth.; (bes. schriftlich) apply for sth.

*nacht ▸ NACHT

Nacht *die;* ∼, **Nächte** night; **gestern/morgen/Dienstag ∼:** last night/tomorrow

night/on Tuesday night; **heute ∼:** tonight; **bei ∼, in der ∼:** at night[-time]; **über ∼ bleiben** stay overnight; **gute ∼!** good night!

nacht-, Nacht-: ∼**arbeit** *die* night work *no art.;* ∼**blind** *Adj.* night-blind; ∼**blindheit** *die* night blindness; ∼**creme** *die* night cream; ∼**dienst** *der* night duty; ∼**dienst haben** be on night duty; ⟨chemist's shop⟩ be open late

Nach·teil *der* disadvantage

nachteilig ① *Adj.* detrimental; harmful
② *adv.* detrimentally; harmfully

Nacht-: ∼**essen** *das* (bes. südd., schweiz.) ▸ ABENDESSEN; ∼**hemd** *das* nightshirt

Nachtigall *die;* ∼, ∼**en** nightingale

nächtigen *itr. V.* (österr., sonst geh.) spend the night

Nach·tisch *der* dessert; sweet

nächtlich *Adj.* nocturnal; night ⟨sky⟩; ⟨darkness, stillness⟩ of the night

Nacht·lokal *das* night spot (coll.)

nach|tragen *unr. tr. V.* (schriftlich ergänzen) insert; add

nach·tragend *Adj.* unforgiving; (rachsüchtig) vindictive

nachträglich ① *Adj.* later; subsequent ⟨apology⟩; (verspätet) belated ⟨greetings, apology⟩
② *adv.* afterwards; subsequently; (verspätet) belatedly

nach|trauern *itr. V.* jmdm./einer Sache ∼: bemoan the passing of sb./sth.

Nacht·ruhe *die* night's sleep

nachts *Adv.* at night; **Montag od. montags ∼:** on Monday nights; **um 3 Uhr ∼:** at 3 o'clock in the morning

Nacht-: ∼**schicht** *die* night shift; ∼**schwester** *die* night nurse; ∼**tisch** *der* bedside table; ∼**tisch·lampe** *die* bedside light; ∼**topf** *der* chamber pot; ∼**wächter** *der,* ∼**wächterin** *die* nightwatchman

Nach·untersuchung *die* follow-up examination; check-up

nach|vollziehen *unr. tr. V.* reconstruct; (begreifen) comprehend

nach|wachsen *unr. itr. V.; mit sein* [wieder] ∼: grow again

Nach·wehen *Pl.* (Med.) afterpains; (fig. geh.) unpleasant after-effects

Nachweis *der;* ∼**es,** ∼**e** proof *no indef. art.* (Gen., über + Akk. of); (Zeugnis) certificate (über + Akk. of)

nachweisbar ① *Adj.* demonstrable ⟨fact, truth, error, defect, guilt⟩; detectable ⟨substance, chemical⟩
② *adv.* demonstrably

nach|weisen *unr. tr. V.* prove

nachweislich *Adv.* as can be proved

Nach·welt *die* posterity *no art.;* future generations *pl., no art.*

n

n<u>a</u>ch|winken *itr. V.* jmdm./einer Sache ~: wave after sb./sth.

N<u>a</u>ch·wirkung *die* after-effect

N<u>a</u>ch·wort *das; Pl.* ~e afterword

N<u>a</u>ch·wuchs *der* **(a)** (fam.: Kind[er]) offspring
(b) (junge Kräfte) new blood; (für eine Branche usw.) new recruits *pl.;* (in der Ausbildung) trainees *pl.*

n<u>a</u>ch|zahlen *tr., itr. V.* **(a)** pay later **(b)** (zusätzlich zahlen) **25 Euro** ~: pay another 25 euros

n<u>a</u>ch|zählen *tr., itr. V.* [re]count

N<u>a</u>ch·zahlung *die* additional payment

n<u>a</u>ch|ziehen *unr. itr. V.* **(a)** (ugs.: ebenso handeln) do likewise; follow suit
(b) *mit sein* (nachträglich übersiedeln) **jmdm.** ~: [go to] join sb.

N<u>a</u>chzügler *der;* ~s, ~, **N<u>a</u>chzüglerin** *die;* ~, ~nen straggler; (spät Ankommende[r]) latecomer

N<u>a</u>ckedei *der;* ~s, ~s (fam. scherzh.) [kleiner] ~: naked little thing

N<u>a</u>cken *der;* ~s, ~: back *or* nape of the neck; (Hals) neck

n<u>a</u>ckt *Adj.* naked; bare ⟨feet, legs, arms, skin, fists⟩; (fig.) plain ⟨truth, fact⟩; bare ⟨existence⟩

N<u>a</u>ckt·bade·strand *der* nudist beach

N<u>a</u>ckte *der/die; adj. Dekl.* naked man/ woman

N<u>a</u>ckt·foto *das* nude photo

N<u>a</u>del *die;* ~, ~n needle; (Steck~, Hut~, Haar~) pin; **an der ~ hängen** (fig. ugs.) be on the needle (sl.)

N<u>a</u>del·baum *der* conifer

N<u>a</u>deldrucker *der* (DV) dot-matrix printer

n<u>a</u>deln *itr. V.* ⟨tree⟩ shed its needles

N<u>a</u>del·wald *der* coniferous forest

N<u>a</u>gel *der;* ~s, Nägel nail; **den ~ auf den Kopf treffen** (fig. ugs.) hit the nail on the head

N<u>a</u>gel-: ~**bürste** *die* nailbrush; ~**feile** *die* nail file; ~**lack** *der* nail varnish (Brit.); nail polish

n<u>a</u>geln *tr. V.* nail (**an** + *Akk.* to, **auf** + *Akk.* on); (Med.) pin

n<u>a</u>gel·neu *Adj.* (ugs.) brand-new

N<u>a</u>gel·schere *die* nail scissors *pl.*

n<u>a</u>gen ① *itr. V.* gnaw; **an etw.** (*Dat.*) ~: gnaw [at] sth.
② *tr. V.* gnaw off; **ein Loch ins Holz** ~: gnaw a hole in the wood

N<u>a</u>ge·tier *das* rodent

n<u>a</u>h ▶ NAHE

N<u>a</u>h·aufnahme *die* (Fot.) close-up [photograph]

n<u>a</u>he /'naːə,/ näher /'nɛːɐ,/ nächst... ① *Adj.* **(a)** (räumlich) near *pred.;* close *pred.;* nearby *attrib.;*
(b) (zeitlich) imminent; near *pred.*

(c) (eng) close ⟨relationship etc.⟩
② *adv.* **(a)** (räumlich) ~ **an** (+ *Dat./Akk.*), ~ **bei** close to; ~ **gelegen** nearby; **von** ~**m** from close up; **jmdm.** ~ **gehen** affect sb. deeply; **eine Sache** (*Dat.*) ~ **kommen** come close to sth.; ⟨amount⟩ approximate to sth.; **jmdm/ sich** [menschlich] ~ **kommen** get to know sb./one another well; **jmdm/sich** [menschlich] **näher kommen** get on closer terms with sb.; **jmdm.** ~ **stehen** be on intimate terms with sb.; **jmdm. etw.** ~ **legen** (fig.) suggest sth. to sb.; **einen Verdacht/einen Gedanken** usw. ~ **legen** give rise to a suspicion/thought *etc.*; ~ **liegen** (fig.) ⟨thought⟩ suggest itself; ⟨suspicion, question⟩ arise
(b) (zeitlich) ~ **an die achtzig** (ugs.) pushing eighty (coll.)
(c) (eng) closely
③ *Präp. mit Dat.* (geh.) near; close to

N<u>ä</u>he *die;* ~: closeness

nahe-: ~**bei** *Adv.* nearby; close by; ~|**gehen** *usw.* ▶ NAHE 2A; ~**liegend** *Adj.* obvious ⟨reason, solution⟩

n<u>a</u>hen *itr. V.; mit sein* (geh.) draw near; **sein/ ihr** *usw.* **Ende nahte** the end was near

n<u>ä</u>hen ① *itr. V.* sew; (Kleider machen) make clothes
② *tr. V.* **(a)** sew ⟨seam, hem⟩; make ⟨dress etc.⟩
(b) (Med.) stitch

n<u>ä</u>her ① *Komp. zu* nahe;
② *Adj.* **(a)** (kürzer) shorter ⟨way, road⟩
(b) (genauer) more precise ⟨information⟩; closer ⟨investigation, inspection⟩
③ *adv.* **(a)** bitte treten Sie ~! please come in/nearer/this way
(b) (genauer) more closely; (im Einzelnen) in [more] detail

*n<u>ä</u>her|kommen ▶ NAHE 2A

n<u>ä</u>hern *refl. V.* approach; **sich jmdm./einer Sache** ~: approach sb./sth.

nahe-: *~|stehen ▶ NAHE 2A; ~**zu** *Adv.* almost; nearly; (mit Zahlenangabe) close on

N<u>ä</u>h-: ~**garn** *das* [sewing] cotton; ~**kasten** *der* sewing box

nahm *1. u. 3. Pers. Sg. Prät. v.* NEHMEN

N<u>ä</u>h-: ~**maschine** *die* sewing machine; ~**nadel** *die* sewing needle

nah-östlich *Adj.* Middle Eastern

N<u>ä</u>hr·boden *der* culture medium; (fig.) breeding ground

n<u>ä</u>hren ① *tr. V.* feed (mit on)
② *refl. V.* (geh.) **sich von etw.** ~: live on sth.; ⟨animal⟩ feed on sth.

n<u>a</u>hrhaft *Adj.* nourishing

N<u>a</u>hrung *die;* ~: food

N<u>a</u>hrungs-mittel *das* food [item]; ~ *Pl.* foodstuffs

N<u>ä</u>hr·wert *der* nutritional value

N<u>ä</u>h·seide *die* sewing silk

Naht *die;* ~, Nähte seam

naht·los ① *Adj.* seamless; (fig.) perfectly smooth ⟨transition⟩

2 *adv.* Studium und Beruf gehen nicht ∼ ineinander über there is not a perfectly smooth transition from study to work

Nah-: ∼**verkehr** *der* local traffic; ∼**verkehrs·zug** *der* local train

Näh·zeug *das* sewing things *pl.*

naiv **1** *Adj.* naïve
2 *adv.* naïvely

Naivität *die;* ∼: naïvety

Name *der;* ∼ns, ∼n name

namens *Adv.* by the name of

Namens-: ∼**schild** *das* (a) (an Türen usw.) nameplate; (b) (zum Anstecken) name badge; ∼**tag** *der* name day

namentlich **1** *Adj.* by name *postpos.;*
2 *adv.* by name
3 *Adv.* (besonders) particularly

namhaft *Adj.* (a) (berühmt) noted (b) (ansehnlich) noteworthy ⟨*sum, difference*⟩; notable ⟨*contribution, opportunity*⟩

nämlich *Adv.* (a) er kann nicht kommen, er ist ∼ krank he cannot come, as he is ill (b) (und zwar) namely

nannte *1. u. 3. Pers. Sg. Prät. v.* NENNEN

nanu *Interj.* ∼, was machst du denn hier? hello, what are you doing here?; ∼, Sie gehen schon? what, you're going already?

Napf *der;* ∼[e]s, Näpfe bowl (esp. for animal's food)

Narbe *die;* ∼, ∼n scar

narbig *Adj.* scarred

Narkose *die;* ∼, ∼n (Med.) narcosis

narkotisieren *tr. V.* (Med.) anaesthetize ⟨*patient*⟩; put ⟨*patient*⟩ under a general anaesthetic

Narr *der;* ∼en, ∼en fool

Narren·freiheit *die* freedom to do as one pleases

Närrin *die;* ∼, ∼nen fool

närrisch **1** *Adj.* crazy; carnival-crazy ⟨*season*⟩
2 *adv.* crazily

Narzisse *die;* ∼, ∼n narcissus

naschen **1** *itr. V.* (Süßes essen) eat sweet things; (heimlich essen) have a nibble
2 *tr. V.* eat ⟨*sweets, chocolate, etc.*⟩; er hat Milch genascht he has been at the milk

Näscherei *die;* ∼, ∼en (a) [continually] eating sweet things; hör auf mit der ∼! don't keep eating sweet things all the time! (b) (Süßigkeit) ∼en sweets

naschhaft *Adj.* sweet-toothed; ∼ sein have a sweet tooth

Nase *die;* ∼, ∼n nose; die ∼ voll haben (ugs.) have had enough

Nasen-: ∼**bluten** *das;* ∼∼s bleeding from the nose; ∼**loch** *das* nostril; ∼**spitze** *die* tip of the/one's nose; jmdm. etw. an der ∼spitze ansehen (fig. ugs.) tell sth. by sb.'s face; ∼**tropfen** *Pl.* nose drops; ∼**wurzel** *die* root of the nose

nase-: ∼**rümpfend** **1** *Adj.* disapproving

2 *adv.* disdainfully; ∼**weis** **1** *Adj.* precocious; pert ⟨*remark, reply*⟩; **2** *adv.* precociously

Nas·horn *das* rhinoceros

nass, *naß *Adj.* nasser *od.* nässer, nassest... *od.* nässest...: *Adj.* wet; sich/das Bett ∼ machen wet oneself/one's bed

Nässe *die;* ∼: wetness

nass·kalt, *naß·kalt *Adj.* cold and wet

Nass·rasur, *Naß·rasur *die* wet shaving *no art.*

Nation *die;* ∼, ∼en nation

national **1** *Adj.* national
2 *adv.* nationally

National-: ∼**elf** *die* (Fußball) national side; ∼**hymne** *die* national anthem

Nationalisierung *die;* ∼, ∼en nationalization

Nationalismus *der;* ∼: nationalism *usu.* no art.

nationalistisch **1** *Adj.* nationalist; nationalistic
2 *adv.* nationalistically

Nationalität *die;* ∼, ∼en nationality

national-, **National-:** ∼**mannschaft** *die* national team; ∼**sozialismus** *der* National Socialism; ∼**sozialist** *der,* ∼**sozialistin** *die* National Socialist; ∼**sozialistisch** *Adj.* National Socialist; ∼**spieler** *der,* ∼**spielerin** *die* (Sport) national player; international; ∼**staat** *der* nation state; ∼**stolz** *der* national pride; ∼**versammlung** *die* National Assembly

NATO, Nato *die;* ∼: NATO, Nato *no art.*

Natron *das;* ∼s [doppeltkohlensaures] ∼: sodium bicarbonate; [kohlensaures] ∼: sodium carbonate

Natter *die;* ∼, ∼n colubrid

Natur *die;* ∼, ∼en nature; die freie ∼: [the] open countryside

Naturalien /natuˈraːli̯ən/ *Pl.* natural produce *sing.* (used as payment); in ∼ (*Dat.*) bezahlen pay in kind

Naturalismus *der;* ∼: naturalism

naturalistisch **1** *Adj.* naturalistic
2 *adv.* naturalistically

Naturell *das;* ∼s, ∼e temperament

natur-, Natur-: ∼**erscheinung** *die* natural phenomenon; ∼**farben** *Adj.* natural-coloured; ∼**freund** *der,* ∼**freundin** *die* nature lover; ∼**gemäß** *Adv.* naturally; ∼**geschichte** *die* natural history; ∼**gesetz** *das* law of nature; ∼**getreu** **1** *Adj.* lifelike ⟨*portrait, imitation*⟩; faithful ⟨*reproduction*⟩; **2** *adv.* ⟨*draw*⟩ true to life; ⟨*reproduce*⟩ faithfully; ∼**heilkunde** *die* naturopathy *no art.;* ∼**katastrophe** *die* natural disaster

natürlich **1** *Adj.* natural
2 *adv.* ⟨*laugh, behave*⟩ naturally
3 *Adv.* (a) (selbstverständlich, wie erwartet) naturally; of course
(b) (zwar) of course

n

Natürlichkeit *die;* ~: naturalness

natur-, Natur-: ~**park** *der* ≈ national park; ~**produkt** *das* natural product; ~**schutz** *der* [nature] conservation; **unter** ~**schutz** *(Dat.)* **stehen** be protected by law; be a protected species/variety/area *etc.*; ~**schutz-gebiet** *das* nature reserve; ~**talent** *das* [great] natural talent *or* gift; (begabter Mensch) naturally talented *or* gifted person; ~**verbunden** *Adj.* ⟨person⟩ in tune with nature; ~**volk** *das* primitive people; ~**wissenschaft** *die* natural science *no art.;* ~**wissenschaftler** *der,* ~**wissenschaftlerin** *die* [natural] scientist; [2] *adv.* scientifically; ~**wunder** *das* miracle *or* wonder of nature

Navigation *die;* ~: navigation *no art.*

navigieren *tr., itr. V.* navigate

n. Chr. *Abk.* = **nach Christus** AD

Neandertaler *der;* ~s, ~: Neanderthal man

Nebel *der;* ~s, ~: fog; (weniger dicht) mist

nebelig ▶ NEBLIG

Nebel-: ~**scheinwerfer** *der* fog lamp; ~**schluss-leuchte**, ***~**schluß-leuchte** *die* rear fog lamp; ~**schwaden** *Pl.* swathes of mist; ~**wand** *die* wall of fog

neben [1] *Präp. mit Dat.* **(a)** (Lage) next to; beside **(b)** (außer) apart from; aside from (Amer.) **(c)** (verglichen mit) beside [2] *Präp. mit Akk.* (Richtung) next to; beside

neben-, Neben-: ~**an** *Adv.* next door; ~**bei** *Adv.* **(a)** ⟨work⟩ on the side; (zusätzlich) as well; **(b)** (beiläufig) ⟨remark, ask⟩ by the way; ⟨mention⟩ in passing; ~**beruf** *der* second job; sideline; ~**beruflich** [1] *Adj.* eine ~berufliche Tätigkeit a second job; [2] *adv.* on the side; **er arbeitet** ~**beruflich als Übersetzer** he translates as a sideline; ~**beschäftigung** *die* second job; sideline; ~**buhler** *der,* ~**buhlerin** *die* rival

neben-einander *Adv.* **(a)** next to each other; ⟨be sitting, standing⟩ next to one another, side by side; (fig.: zusammen) ⟨live, exist⟩ side by side; ~ **wohnen** live next door to each other; ~ **legen** (+ *Akk.*) lay *or* place ⟨objects⟩ next to each other *or* side by side **(b)** (gleichzeitig) together

*****nebeneinander|legen** *usw.* ▶ NEBENEINANDER A

Neben-: ~**erwerb** *der* secondary occupation; ~**fach** *das* subsidiary subject; minor (Amer.); ~**fluss**, ***~**fluß** *der* tributary; ~**gebäude** *das* **(a)** annexe; outbuilding **(b)** (Nachbargebäude) neighbouring building; ~**geräusch** *das* background noise; ~**haus** *das* house next door

neben-her *Adv.* ▶ NEBENBEI

nebenher-: ~|**fahren** *unr. itr. V.; mit sein* drive/ride alongside; ~|**gehen** *unr. itr. V.; mit sein* walk alongside

neben-, Neben-: ~**höhle** *die* (Anat.) paranasal sinus; ~**kläger** *der,* ~**klägerin** *die* (Rechtsw.) accessory prosecutor; ~**kosten** *Pl.* **(a)** additional costs; **(b)** (bei Mieten) heating, lighting, and services; ~**produkt** *das* by-product; ~**rolle** *die* supporting role; ~**sache** *die* minor matter; ~**sachen** inessentials; ~**sächlich** *Adj.* of minor importance *postpos.;* unimportant; minor ⟨detail⟩; ~**sächlichkeit** *die;* ~~, ~~**en** (Unwichtiges) matter of minor importance; unimportant matter; ~**satz** *der* (Sprachw.) subordinate clause; ~**stelle** *die* extension; ~**straße** *die* side street; ~**tätigkeit** *die* second job; sideline; ~**tisch** *der* next table; ~**verdienst** *der* additional income; ~**wirkung** *die* side effect; ~**zimmer** *das* next room

neblig *Adj.* foggy; (weniger dicht) misty

Necessaire /nesεˈsɛːɐ̯/ *das;* ~s, ~s sponge bag (Brit.); toilet bag (Amer.)

necken *tr. V.* tease

Neckerei *die;* ~: teasing

nee (ugs.) no; nope (Amer. coll.)

Neffe *der;* ~n, ~n nephew

negativ [1] *Adj.* negative [2] *adv.* ⟨answer⟩ in the negative

Negativ *das;* ~s, ~e (Fot.) negative

Neger *der;* ~s, ~: Negro

Negerin *die;* ~, ~nen Negress

nehmen *unr. tr. V.* take; **sich** *(Dat.)* **etw.** ~: take sth.; (sich bedienen) help oneself to sth.; **auf sich** *(Akk.)* ~: take on ⟨responsibility, burden⟩; **jmdm./einer Sache etw.** ~: deprive sb./sth. of sth.; **was nehmen Sie dafür?** how much do you charge for it?

Neid *der;* ~[e]s envy; jealousy

neiden *tr. V.* (geh.) **jmdm. etw.** ~: envy sb. [for] sth.

Neid-hammel *der* (salopp abwertend) envious sod (sl.)

neidisch [1] *Adj.* envious [2] *adv.* enviously

neigen [1] *tr. V.* tip; tilt; incline ⟨head, upper part of body⟩ [2] *refl. V.:* ⟨person⟩ lean; ⟨ship⟩ heel over, list; ⟨scales⟩ tip [3] *itr. V.* **(a) zu Erkältungen/Krankheiten** ~: be prone to colds/illnesses **(b)** (tendieren) tend

Neigung *die;* ~, ~en **(a)** (Vorliebe) inclination **(b)** (Tendenz) tendency

nein *Interj.* no

Nein *das;* ~[s], ~[s] no

Nein-stimme *die* no-vote

Nektar *der;* ~s, ~e (Bot.) nectar

Nektarine *die;* ~, ~n nectarine

**alte Schreibung - vgl. Hinweis auf S. xiv

Nelke *die;* ∼, ∼n (a) pink; (Dianthus caryophyllus) carnation
(b) (Gewürz) clove
nennen ①*unr. tr. V.* (a) call
(b) (angeben) give ⟨*name, date of birth, address, reason, price, etc.*⟩
(c) (anführen) give ⟨*example*⟩; (erwähnen) mention ⟨*person, name*⟩
②*unr. refl. V.* ⟨*person, thing*⟩ be called
nennens·wert *Adj.* considerable ⟨*influence, changes, delays, damage*⟩; kaum ∼e Veränderungen changes scarcely worth mentioning
Nenner *der;* ∼s, ∼ (Math.) denominator
neo-, Neo- neo-
neo-: ∼**konservativ** *Adj.* neo-conservative; neo-con (coll.); ∼**liberal** *Adj.* neo-liberal
Neon *das;* ∼s neon
Neon-: ∼**licht** *das* neon light; ∼**röhre** *die* neon tube
Nepal (*das*) ∼s Nepal
Nepp *der;* ∼s (ugs. abwertend) daylight robbery *no art.;* rip-off (coll.)
neppen *tr. V.* (ugs. abwertend) rook; rip ⟨*tourist, customer, etc.*⟩ off (sl.)
Nepper *der;* ∼s, ∼, **Nepperin** *die;* ∼, ∼nen (ugs.) shark; rip-off merchant (coll.)
Nepp·lokal *das* (ugs.) clip joint (coll.)
Nerv *der;* ∼s, ∼en nerve; die ∼en verlieren lose control [of oneself]; jmdm. auf die ∼en gehen *od.* fallen get on sb.'s nerves
nerven (salopp)① *tr. V.* jmdn. ∼: get on sb.'s nerves
②*itr. V.* be wearing on the nerves
nerven-, Nerven-: ∼**aufreibend** *Adj.* nerve-racking; ∼**bündel** *das* (ugs.) bundle of nerves (coll.); ∼**gift** *das* neurotoxin; ∼**heil·anstalt** *die* (veralt.) psychiatric hospital; ∼**krank** *Adj.* ⟨*person*⟩ suffering from a nervous disease; ∼**probe** *die* mental trial; ∼**säge** *die* (salopp) pain in the neck (coll.); ∼**zusammen·bruch** *der* nervous breakdown
nervig *Adj.* (auch fig.) sinewy
nervlich *Adj.* nervous ⟨*strain*⟩
nervös ①*Adj.* (auch Med.) nervous; jittery ⟨*person*⟩
②*adv.* nervously
Nervosität *die;* ∼ nervousness
nerv·tötend *Adj.* nerve-racking ⟨*wait*⟩; soul-destroying ⟨*activity, work*⟩
Nerz *der;* ∼es, ∼e mink
Nerz·mantel *der* mink coat
Nessel *die;* ∼, ∼n nettle
Nest *das;* ∼[e]s, ∼er (a) nest
(b) (fam.: Bett) bed
(c) (ugs. abwertend: kleiner Ort) little place
nett ①*Adj.* nice; (freundlich) kind
②*adv.* nicely; (freundlich) nicely; kindly
netter·weise *Adv.* kindly
netto *Adv.* ⟨*weigh, earn, etc.*⟩ net

Netto-: ∼**einkommen** *das* net income; ∼**gehalt** *das* net salary; ∼**preis** *der* net price
Netz *das;* ∼es, ∼e (a) net; (Einkaufs∼) string bag; (Gepäck∼) [luggage] rack
(b) (Spinnen∼) web
(c) (Netzwerk) network; (für Strom, Wasser, Gas) mains *pl.*
Netz-: ∼**haut** *die* (Anat.) retina; ∼**werk** *das* (auch Elektrot.) network
neu ①*Adj.* new; die ∼este Mode the latest fashion; das ist mir ∼: that is news to me; der/die Neue the new man/woman/boy/girl
②*adv.* (a) ∼ tapeziert/gestrichen repapered/repainted; sich ∼ einrichten refurnish one's home
(b) (gerade erst) diese Ware ist ∼ eingetroffen this item has just come in; ∼ eröffnet newly-opened; (wieder eröffnet) reopened
neu·artig *Adj.* new; ∼e Lebensmittel novel foods
Neu·artigkeit *die;* ∼∼: novelty
neu-, Neu-: ∼**bau** *der; Pl.* ∼∼ten new house/building; ∼**bau·wohnung** *die* flat (Brit.) *or* (Amer.) apartment in a new block/house; ∼**beginn** *der* new beginning
neuerdings *Adv.* er trägt ∼ eine Brille he has recently started wearing glasses
**neu·eröffnet ▶ NEU 2B
Neu·eröffnung *die* (a) opening
(b) (Wiedereröffnung) reopening
Neuerung *die;* ∼, ∼en innovation
neu·geboren *Adj.* newborn
Neu·gier, Neugierde *die;* ∼: curiosity; (Wissbegierde) inquisitiveness
neu·gierig ①*Adj.* curious; inquisitive; inquisitive ⟨*person*⟩; ich bin ∼, was er dazu sagt I'm curious to know what he'll say about it
②*adv.* ⟨*ask*⟩ inquisitively; ⟨*peer*⟩ nosily (coll. derog.)
Neuheit *die;* ∼, ∼en (a) novelty
(b) (Neues) new product/gadget/article *etc.*
Neuigkeit *die;* ∼, ∼en piece of news; ∼en news *sing.*
Neu: ∼**jahr** *das* New Year's Day; ∼**land** *das* (fig.) new ground
neulich *Adv.* recently; ∼ morgens the other morning
Neuling *der;* ∼s, ∼e newcomer; (auf einem Gebiet) novice
Neu·mond *der* new moon
neun *Kardinalz.* nine
Neun *die;* ∼, ∼en nine
neun-: ∼**hundert** *Kardinalz.* nine hundred; ∼**jährig** *Adj.* (9 Jahre alt) nine-year-old *attrib.;* (9 Jahre dauernd) nine-year *attrib.;* ∼**mal** *Adv.* nine times
neunt... *Ordinalz.* ninth
neun·tausend *Kardinalz.* nine thousand
Neuntel *das* (schweiz. meist *der*); ∼s, ∼: ninth

neuntens *Adv.* ninthly
neun·zehn *Kardinalz.* nineteen
neunzig *Kardinalz.* ninety
neunziger *indekl. Adj.* die ~ Jahre the nineties
neunzigst... *Ordinalz.* ninetieth
neuralgisch *Adj.* (Med.) neuralgic
neu·reich *Adj.* nouveau riche
Neurodermitis *die;* ~, Neurodermitiden (Med.) neurodermatitis
Neurologe *der;* ~n, ~n neurologist
Neurologie *die;* ~: neurology
Neurologin *die;* ~, ~nen neurologist
neurologisch *Adj.* neurological
Neurose *die;* ~, ~n (Med., Psych.) neurosis
Neurotiker *der;* ~s, ~, **Neurotikerin** *die;* ~, ~nen (Med., Psych., auch ugs.) neurotic
neurotisch *Adj.* (Med., Psych., auch ugs.) neurotic
Neu·see·land (*das*) ~s New Zealand
Neuseeländer *der;* ~s, ~, **Neuseeländerin** *die;* ~, ~nen New Zealander
neutral [1] *Adj.* neutral
[2] *adv.* sich ~ verhalten remain neutral
Neutralität *die;* ~, ~en neutrality
Neutron *das;* ~s, ~en neutron
Neutrum *das;* ~s, Neutra (österr. nur so) *od.* Neutren (Sprachw.) neuter
neu-, Neu-: ~wert *der* value when new; ~wertig *Adj.* as new; ~zeit *die* modern age; ~zeitlich *Adj.* modern
nicht *Adv.* not; ~! [no,] don't!; ~ rostend non-rusting ⟨blade⟩; stainless ⟨steel⟩; ~ [wahr]? isn't it/he/she *etc.;* don't you/we/they *etc.;* du magst das, ~ [wahr]? you like that, don't you?; was du ~ sagst! you don't say!
nicht-, Nicht- non-
Nicht·angriffs·pakt *der* nonaggression pact
Nichte *die;* ~, ~n niece
nichtig *Adj.* (a) (geh.) vain ⟨things, pleasures, etc.⟩; trivial ⟨reason⟩ (b) (Rechtsspr.) void
Nicht·raucher *der* non-smoker; „~raucher" 'no smoking'
*****nicht·rostend** ▸ NICHT
nichts *Indefinitpron.* nothing; ich möchte ~: I don't want anything; ~ sagend (fig.) empty; (ausdruckslos) expressionless ⟨face⟩
nichts·desto·weniger *Adv.* nevertheless; none the less
nichts-, Nichts-: ~nutz *der;* ~~es, ~~e (veralt.) good-for-nothing; ~nutzig *Adj.* (veralt.) good-for-nothing ⟨attrib.;⟩ worthless ⟨existence⟩; *****~sagend** ▸ NICHTS; ~tun *das* idleness *no art.*
Nicht·wähler *der,* **Nicht·wählerin** *die* non-voter; abstainer

Nickel *das;* ~s nickel
nicken *itr. V.* nod
nie *Adv.* never
nieder [1] *Adj.; nicht präd.* lower ⟨class, intelligence⟩; minor ⟨official⟩; lowly ⟨family, origins, birth⟩; menial ⟨task⟩
[2] *Adv.* down
nieder-, Nieder-: ~gang *der* fall; decline; ~|gehen *unr. itr. V.; mit sein* ⟨plane etc., rain, avalanche⟩ come down; ~geschlagen *Adj.* dejected; ~geschlagenheit *die;* ~: dejection; ~lage *die* defeat
Nieder·lande *Pl.:* die ~: the Netherlands
Niederländer *der;* ~s, ~: Dutchman
Niederländerin *die;* ~, ~nen Dutchwoman
niederländisch *Adj.* Dutch; Netherlands *attrib.* ⟨government, embassy, etc.⟩
nieder-, Nieder-: ~|lassen *unr. refl. V.* (a) set up in business; ⟨doctor, lawyer⟩ set up in practice; (b) (seinen Wohnsitz nehmen) settle; ~lassung *die;* ~~, ~~en (Wirtsch.) branch; ~|legen *tr. V.* (a) (geh.: hinlegen) lay or put down; lay ⟨wreath⟩; (b) (fig.) resign [from] ⟨office⟩; relinquish ⟨command⟩
Nieder·sachsen (*das*) Lower Saxony
nieder-, Nieder-: ~schlag *der* precipitation; ~|schlagen *unr. tr. V.* (a) jmdn. ~schlagen knock sb. down; (b) (beenden) suppress, put down ⟨revolt, uprising, etc.⟩; (c) (senken) lower ⟨eyes, eyelids⟩; ~schmetternd *Adj.* shattering ⟨experience, news⟩; devastating ⟨result, review⟩; ~trächtig [1] *Adj.* malicious ⟨person, slander, lie, etc.⟩; (verachtenswert) despicable ⟨person⟩; base ⟨misrepresentation, slander, lie⟩; [2] *adv.* ⟨betray, lie, treat⟩ in a despicable way; ~trächtigkeit *die;* ~~, ~~en (a) ▸ ~TRÄCHTIG 1: maliciousness; despicableness; baseness; (b) (gemeine Handlung) despicable act
Niederung *die;* ~, ~en low-lying area; (an Flussläufen, Küsten) flats *pl.;* (Tal) valley
niedlich [1] *Adj.* sweet; cute (Amer. coll.)
[2] *adv.* sweetly
niedrig [1] *Adj.* low; lowly ⟨origins, birth⟩; base ⟨instinct, desire, emotion⟩; vile ⟨motive⟩
[2] *adv.* ⟨hang, fly⟩ low
Niedrig-: ~lohn·land *das* country with a low-wage country; ~wasser *das* (a) (von Seen/Flüssen) bei ~wasser when the [level of the] lake/river is low; (b) (bei Ebbe) low tide; low water; bei ~wasser at low tide *or* low water
niemals *Adv.* never
niemand *Indefinitpron.* nobody; no one
Niemands·land *das* (auch fig.) no man's land
Niere *die;* ~, ~n kidney
Nieren-: ~entzündung *die* nephritis; ~stein *der* kidney stone
nieseln *unpers. itr. V.* drizzle

─────────────────────────────

*****old spelling - see note on page xiv

Niesel·regen *der* drizzle
niesen *itr. V.* sneeze
Niete[1] *die;* ~, ~n (a) (Los) blank
(b) (ugs.: Mensch) dead loss (coll.) (**in** + *Dat.* at)
Niete[2] *die;* ~, ~n rivet
nieten *tr. V.* rivet
niet- und nagelfest: [alles] was nicht ~
ist (ugs.) [everything] that's not nailed *or*
screwed down
Nikolaus /'nɪkolaʊs/ *der;* ~, ~e (ugs.)
Nikoläuse (a) St Nicholas
(b) (Tag) St Nicholas' Day
Nikotin *das;* ~s nicotine
nikotin·arm *Adj.* low-nicotine *attrib.;* low
in nicotine *pred.*
Nikotin·sucht *die* nicotine addiction
Nil *der;* ~[s] Nile
Nil·pferd *das* hippopotamus
nimm *Imperativ Sg. v.* NEHMEN
nippen *itr. V.* sip
nirgends, nirgend·wo *Adv.* nowhere
Nische *die;* ~, ~n niche; (Erweiterung eines
Raumes) recess
nisten *itr. V.* nest
Nitrat *das;* ~[e]s, ~e nitrate
Niveau /ni'vo:/ *das;* ~s, ~s level;
(Qualitäts~) standard
Nixe *die;* ~, ~n nixie; (mit Fischschwanz)
mermaid
nobel *Adj.* (a) (geh.) noble; noble[-minded]
⟨person⟩
(b) (oft spött.: luxuriös) elegant; posh (coll.)
Nobel·preis *der* Nobel prize
noch [1] *Adv.* (a) ([wie] bisher) still; ~ nicht
not yet; sie sind immer ~ nicht da they're
still not here; ich habe Großvater ~ gekannt
I'm old enough to have known grandfather;
er hat ~ Glück gehabt he was lucky; das
geht ~: that's [still] all right
(b) (als Rest einer Menge) ich habe [nur] ~
zehn Euro I've [only] ten euros left; es sind
~ 10 km bis zur Grenze it's another 10 km.
to the border
(c) (bevor etw. anderes geschieht) just; ich will ~
[schnell] duschen I just want to have a
[quick] shower
(d) (irgendwann einmal) some time; one day; er
wird ~ anrufen/kommen he will still call/
come
(e) (womöglich) if you're/he's *etc.* not careful;
du kommst ~ zu spät! you'll be late if
you're not careful
(f) (drückt eine geringe zeitliche Distanz aus) only;
gestern habe ich ihn ~ gesehen I saw him
only yesterday
(g) (nicht später als) ~ am selben Abend the
[very] same evening
(h) (außerdem, zusätzlich) wer war ~ da? who
else was there?; ~ etwas Kaffee? [would you
like] some more coffee?; Geld/Kleider *usw.* ~
und ~ heaps and heaps of money/clothes
etc. (coll.)
(i) er ist ~ größer [als Karl] he is even taller

[than Karl]; er will ~ mehr haben he wants
even more; jeder ~ so dumme Mensch
versteht das anyone, however stupid, can
understand that
(j) wie heißt sie [doch] ~? [now] what's her
name again?
[2] *Partikel* das ist ~ Qualität! that's what I
call quality; der wird sich ~ wundern (ugs.)
he's in for a surprise; er kann ~ nicht
einmal lesen he can't even read
[3] *Konj.* (und auch nicht) nor; weder ... noch
neither ... nor
noch·mals *Adv.* again
Nominativ *der;* ~s, ~e (Sprachw.)
nominative [case]
nominieren *tr. V.* nominate
Nominierung *die;* ~, ~en nomination
Nonne *die;* ~, ~n nun
Nord (bes. Seemannsspr., Met.) ▶ NORDEN
nord-, Nord-: ~afrika (*das*) North
Africa; ~amerika (*das*) North America;
~deutsch *Adj.* North German
Norden *der;* ~s north; der ~: the North;
nach ~: northwards
Nord·irland (*das*) Northern Ireland
nordisch *Adj.* Nordic
Nord·kap *das* North Cape
nördlich [1] *Adj.* (a) (im Norden gelegen)
northern
(b) (nach, aus dem Norden) northerly
(c) (aus dem Norden kommend, für den Norden
typisch) northern
[2] *adv.* northwards; ~ von ...: [to the] north
of ...
[3] *Präp. mit Gen.* [to the] north of
Nord-: ~licht *das* northern lights *pl.;*
aurora borealis; ein ~licht/~lichter the
northern lights; ~pol *der* North Pole
Nordrhein-Westfalen (*das*); ~s North
Rhine-Westphalia
Nord·see *die;* ~: North Sea
nord·wärts *Adv.* northwards
Nord·wind *der* northerly wind
Nörgelei *die;* ~ (abwertend) grumbling
nörgeln *itr. V.* (abwertend) moan, grumble
(**an** + *Dat.* about)
Norm *die;* ~, ~en (a) norm
(b) (geforderte Arbeitsleistung) quota
(c) (Sport) qualifying standard
(d) (technische, industrielle ~) standard
normal [1] *Adj.* normal
[2] *adv.* normally
Normal·benzin *das* ≈ two-star petrol
(Brit.); regular (Amer.)
normalerweise *Adv.* normally
normalisieren [1] *tr. V.* normalize
[2] *refl. V.* return to normal
Normalität *die;* ~: normality *no def. art.*
Normal·zustand *der* normal state
Normandie *die;* ~: Normandy
normen *tr. V.*, **normieren** *tr. V.*
standardize

Norwegen (das); ~s Norway
Norweger der; ~s, ~, **Norwegerin** die;
~, ~nen Norwegian
norwegisch Adj. Norwegian
Nostalgie die; ~: nostalgia
Not die; ~, **Nöte (a)** (Gefahr) **in** ~ **sein** be in
desperate straits
(b) (Mangel, Armut) need; poverty [and
hardship]; ~ **leiden** suffer poverty [and
hardship]; **in** ~ **geraten/sein** encounter hard
times/be suffering want [and deprivation]
(c) (Verzweiflung) distress
(d) (Sorge, Mühe) trouble; **mit knapper** ~: by
the skin of one's teeth
(e) (veralt.: Notwendigkeit) necessity; **zur** ~: if
need be
Notar der; ~s, ~e notary
Notariat das; ~[e]s, ~e **(a)** (Amt)
notaryship
(b) (Kanzlei) notary's office
not-, Not-: ~**arzt** der doctor on
[emergency] call; ~**aufnahme** die
casualty department; casualty no art.;
~**ausgang** der emergency exit;
~**bremse** die emergency brake; ~**dienst**
der ▶ BEREITSCHAFTSDIENST; ~**durft** die; ~
(geh.) **seine [große/kleine]** ~**durft verrichten**
relieve oneself; ~**dürftig** ① Adj. makeshift
⟨shelter, repair⟩; scanty ⟨cover, clothing⟩;
② adv. scantily ⟨clothed⟩
Note die; ~, ~**n (a)** (Zeichen) note
(b) Pl. (Text) music sing.;
(c) (Schul~) mark
(d) (Eislauf, Turnen) score
Notebook /'nɔʊtbʊk/ das; ~s, ~s (DV)
notebook [computer]
not-, Not-: ~**fall** der **(a)** emergency; **(b) im**
~**fall** (nötigenfalls) if need be; ~**falls** Adv. if
need be; ~**gedrungen** Adv. of necessity
notieren ① tr. V. **[sich** (Dat.)] **etw.** ~:
make a note of sth.
② itr. V. (Börsenw., Wirtsch.) be quoted (**mit** at)
Notierung die; ~, ~en (Börsenw., Wirtsch.)
quotation; (Preis) quoted [price] (**für** of); (von
Devisen) rate (**für** for)
nötig ① Adj. necessary; **etw./jmdn.** ~ **haben**
need sth./sb.
② adv. **er braucht** ~ **Hilfe** he is in urgent
need of help
nötigen tr. V. compel; force; (Rechtsspr.)
coerce
Nötigung die; ~, ~en (bes. Rechtsspr.)
intimidation; coercion
Notiz die; ~, ~en note; (Zeitungs~) brief
report; **von jmdm./etw. [keine]** ~ **nehmen**
take [no] notice of sb./sth.
Notiz-: ~**block** der; Pl. ~**blocks**, schweiz.:
~**blöcke** notepad; ~**buch** das notebook
not-, Not-: ~**lage** die serious difficulties
pl.; ~**landen** itr. V.; mit sein; **ich notlande,**
notgelandet, notzulanden do an emergency

landing; ~**landung** die emergency landing;
~**leidend** Adj. needy; ~**lösung** die
stopgap; ~**lüge** die evasive lie; (aus
Rücksichtnahme) white lie
notorisch ① Adj. notorious
② adv. notoriously
Not-: ~**ruf** der **(a)** (Hilferuf) emergency call;
(eines Schiffes) Mayday call; **(b)** (Nummer)
emergency number; ~**ruf·nummer** die
emergency number; ~**ruf·säule** die
emergency telephone (mounted in a pillar);
~**stand** der crisis; (Staatsrecht) state of
emergency; ~**unterkunft** die emergency
accommodation no pl., no indef. art.;
~**wehr** die self-defence
not·wendig Adj. necessary
Notwendigkeit die; ~, ~en necessity
Not·zucht die (Rechtsw. veralt.) rape; ~ **[an**
jmdm.] begehen od. **verüben** commit rape [on
sb.]
Novelle die; ~, ~n (Literaturw.) novella
November der; ~[s], ~: November
Novität die; ~, ~en novelty; (neue Erfindung)
innovation; (neue Schallplatte) new release;
(neues Buch) new publication
Nr. Abk. = **Nummer** No
Nu der: **im Nu** in no time
Nuance /'nỹã:sə/ die; ~, ~n nuance; (Grad)
shade
nüchtern ① Adj. (nicht betrunken; realistisch)
sober; (ungeschminkt) bare, plain ⟨fact⟩; **der**
Patient muss ~ **sein** the patient's stomach
must be empty
② adv. soberly
Nüchternheit die; ~: sobriety
nuckeln (ugs.) itr. V. suck (**an** + Dat. at)
Nudel die; ~, ~n piece of spaghetti/
vermicelli/tortellini etc.; (als Suppeneinlage)
noodle; ~**n** (Teigwaren) pasta sing.; (als
Suppeneinlage) noodles
Nugat /'nu:gat/ der; auch das; ~s nougat
nuklear ① Adj. nuclear
② adv. ~ **angetrieben** nuclear-powered
Nuklear-: ~**medizin** die nuclear
medicine no art.; ~**waffe** die nuclear
weapon
null Kardinalz. nought; ~ **Komma sechs**
[nought] point six; **gegen** ~ **Uhr** around
twelve midnight
Null die; ~, ~en **(a)** nought; zero; **in** ~
Komma nichts (ugs.) in less than no time;
gleich ~ **sein** (fig.) be practically zero; **auf** ~
stehen ⟨indicator, needle, etc.⟩ be at zero
(b) (ugs.: Versager) failure; dead loss (coll.)
Null-: ~**punkt** der zero;
~**summen·spiel** das zero-sum game
*****numerieren** tr. V. number
*****Numerierung** die; ~, ~en numbering
Numerus clausus der; ~: fixed number
of students admissible to a university to study
a particular subject; numerus clausus
Nummer die; ~, ~n **(a)** number; **ein Wagen**

---

mit [einer] Münchner ∼: a car with a Munich registration; **ich bin unter der** ∼ **242679 zu erreichen** I can be reached on 242679
(b) (Ausgabe) issue
(c) (Größe) size
Nummern·schild das number plate; license plate (Amer.)
nummerieren tr. V. number
Nummerierung die; ∼, ∼en numbering
nun [1] adv. now
[2] Partikel now; **das hast du** ∼ **davon!** it serves you right!; **kommst du** ∼ **mit oder nicht?** now are you coming or not?; ∼ **gut** [well,] all right; ∼, ∼! now, come on; ∼ **ja** …: well, yes …
nur [1] adv. (a) (nicht mehr als) only; just
(b) (ausschließlich) only; **nicht** ∼ …, **sondern auch** …: not only …, but also …; ∼ **so zum Spaß** just for fun
[2] Konj. but; **ich kann dir das Buch leihen,** ∼ **nicht heute** I can lend you the book, only not today
[3] Partikel **wenn er** ∼ **hier wäre** if only he were here; ∼ **zu!** go ahead; **lass dich** ∼ **nicht erwischen** just don't let me/them etc. catch you; **was sollen wir** ∼ **tun?** what on earth are we going to do?; **so schnell er** ∼ **konnte** just as fast as he could
Nürnberg (das); ∼s Nuremberg
nuscheln tr., itr. V. (ugs.) mumble
Nuss, *Nuß die; ∼, Nüsse nut
Nuss-, *Nuß-: ∼**baum,** der walnut tree; ∼**knacker** der nutcrackers pl.; ∼**schale** die nutshell
Nüster die; ∼, ∼n nostril
Nut die; ∼, ∼en (Technik) groove

Nutte die; ∼, ∼n (derb) tart (sl.); hooker (Amer. sl.)
nutz-: ∼**bar** Adj. usable; exploitable, utilizable ⟨mineral resources, invention⟩; cultivatable ⟨land, soil⟩; ∼**bringend**
[1] Adj. useful; (gewinnbringend) profitable
[2] adv. profitably
nutzen [1] tr. V. (a) use; exploit, utilize ⟨natural resources⟩; cultivate ⟨land, soil⟩; harness ⟨energy source⟩; exploit ⟨advantage⟩
(b) (be-, ausnutzen) use; make use of
[2] itr. V. ▶ NÜTZEN 1
Nutzen der; ∼s (a) benefit; [jmdm.] **von** ∼ **sein** be of use [to sb.]
(b) (Profit) profit
nützen [1] itr. V. be of use (Dat. to); **nichts** ∼: be no use
[2] tr. V. ▶ NUTZEN 1
nützlich Adj. useful
Nützlichkeit die; ∼: usefulness
nutzlos [1] Adj. useless; (vergeblich) vain attrib.; in vain pred.;
[2] adv. uselessly; (vergeblich) in vain
Nutz·losigkeit die; ∼: uselessness; (Vergeblichkeit) futility
Nutznießer der; ∼s, ∼, **Nutznießerin** die; ∼, ∼nen beneficiary
Nutzung die; ∼, ∼en use; (des Landes, des Bodens) cultivation; (von Bodenschätzen) exploitation; utilization; (einer Energiequelle) harnessing
Nylon ⓦ /'naɪlɔn/ das; ∼s nylon
Nymphe die; ∼, ∼n (Myth., Zool.) nymph
Nymphomanin die; ∼, ∼nen (Psych.) nymphomaniac

Oo

o, O das; ∼, ∼: o/O
ö, Ö das; ∼, ∼: o/O umlaut
O Abk. = **Ost[en]** E
Oase die; ∼, ∼n (auch fig.) oasis
ob Konj. (a) whether
(b) **und ob!** of course!
OB Abk. = **Oberbürgermeister[in]**
Obacht die; ∼ (bes. südd.) caution; ∼ **auf jmdn./etw. geben** take care of sb./sth.; (aufmerksam sein) pay attention to sb./sth.
Obdach das; ∼[e]s (geh.) shelter
obdach·los Adj. homeless
Obdachlose der/die; adj. Dekl. homeless person/man/woman; **die** ∼**n** the homeless
Obdachlosen-: ∼**heim** das hostel for the homeless; ∼**siedlung** die estate of houses for the homeless

Obdachlosigkeit die; ∼: homelessness
Obduktion die; ∼, ∼en (Med., Rechtsw.) post mortem [examination]; autopsy
obduzieren tr. V. carry out or perform a/ the postmortem [examination] or autopsy on
O-Beine Pl. bandy legs; bow legs
oben Adv. (a) **hier/dort** ∼: up here/there; **weiter** ∼: further up; **nach** ∼: upwards; **von** ∼: from above; **von** ∼ **herab** (fig.) condescendingly
(b) (im Gebäude) upstairs; **nach** ∼: upstairs
(c) (am oberen Ende, zum oberen Ende hin) at the top; **nach** ∼ **[hin]** towards the top; **von** ∼: from the top; ∼ **ohne** topless
(d) (an der Oberseite) on top
(e) (in einer Hierarchie, Rangfolge) at the top
(f) ([weiter] vorn im Text) above; ∼ **genannt** above-mentioned

0

***oben·genannt** ▶ OBEN F

Ober *der;* ~s, ~: waiter; **Herr** ~! waiter!

ober... *Adj.* upper *attrib.;* top *attrib.*

Ober-: ~**arm** *der* upper arm;
~**bekleidung** *die* outer clothing;
~**bürgermeister** *der* mayor; ~**fläche**
die surface; (Flächeninhalt) surface area

oberflächlich ⓵ *Adj.* superficial
⓶ *adv.* superficially

Ober·geschoss, *Ober·geschoß *das*
upper storey; **im fünften** ~: on the fifth floor
(Brit.) *or* (Amer.) the sixth floor

ober·halb ⓵ *Adv.* above; ~ **von** above
⓶ *Präp. mit Gen.* above

Ober-: ~**hand** *die* die ~hand [über jmdn./
etw.] haben have the upper hand [over sb./
sth.]; **die** ~**hand [über jmdn./etw.] gewinnen/
bekommen** gain *or* get the upper hand [over
sb./sth.]; ~**haupt** *das* head; (einer
Verschwörung) leader; ~**hemd** *das* shirt;
~**kiefer** *der* upper jaw; ~**körper** *der*
upper part of the body; ~**lippen·bart** *der*
moustache; ~**schenkel** *der* thigh;
~**schicht** *die* (Soziol.) upper class;
~**schule** *die* secondary school; ~**seite**
die top

oberst... ▶ OBER...

Ober-: ~**stufe** *die* (Schulw.) upper school;
~**teil** *das od. der* top [part]; (eines Bikinis,
Anzugs, Kleids usw.) top [half]; ~**wasser** *das*
headwater; (fig.) ~**wasser haben** feel in a
strong position; ~**wasser bekommen/kriegen**
have one's hand strengthened

ob·gleich *Konj.* ▶ OBWOHL

obig *Adj.* above

Objekt *das;* ~s, ~e object; (Kaufmannsspr.:
Immobilie) property

objektiv ⓵ *Adj.* objective
⓶ *adv.* objectively

Objektiv *das;* ~s, ~e lens

Objektivität *die;* ~: objectivity

Obrigkeit *die;* ~, ~en authorities *pl.*

ob·schon *Konj.* (geh.) although

Obst *das;* ~[e]s fruit

Obst-: ~**baum** *der* fruit tree; ~**garten**
der orchard; ~**kuchen** *der* fruit flan

Obstler *der;* ~s, ~ (bes. südd.) fruit brandy

Obst-: ~**saft** *der* fruit juice; ~**salat** *der*
fruit salad; ~**wein** *der* fruit wine

obszön ⓵ *Adj.* obscene
⓶ *adv.* obscenely

Obszönität *die;* ~, ~en obscenity

ob·wohl *Konj.* although; though

Ochse /ˈɔksə/ *der;* ~n, ~n (a) ox; bullock
(b) (salopp) numskull (coll.)

Ochsen·schwanz·suppe *die* oxtail
soup

od. *Abk.* = **oder**

öde *Adj.* (a) deserted; desolate ⟨area,
landscape⟩

(b) (unfruchtbar) barren
(c) (langweilig) tedious; dreary ⟨life, time,
existence⟩

Öde *die;* ~ ▶ ÖDE A–C: desertedness;
desolateness; barrenness; tediousness;
dreariness

oder *Konj.* or; (in Fragen) **er ist doch hier,** ~?
he is here, isn't he? (zweifelnd) he is here – or
isn't he?

Öd·land *das* uncultivated land

Oeuvre /ˈøːvrə/ *das;* ~, ~s (geh.) œuvre

OEZ *Abk.* = **osteuropäische Zeit** EET

Ofen *der;* ~s, Öfen heater; (Kohle~) stove;
(Back~) oven; (Brenn~, Trocken~) kiln

Ofen·rohr *das* [stove] flue

offen ⓵ *Adj.* (a) open; ~ **bleiben** stay open;
etw. ~ **lassen** leave sth. open; ~ **stehen** be
open; **ein** ~**es Hemd** a shirt with the collar
unfastened; ~ **haben** *od.* **sein** be open; ~**es
Licht** a naked light
(b) (frei) vacant ⟨job, post⟩
(c) (ungewiss, ungeklärt) open ⟨question⟩;
uncertain ⟨result⟩; ~ **bleiben** remain open;
⟨decision⟩ be left open
(d) (noch nicht bezahlt) outstanding ⟨bill⟩
(e) (freimütig, aufrichtig) frank [and open]
⟨person⟩; frank, candid ⟨look, opinion, reply⟩
⓶ *adv.* openly; ~ **gesagt** frankly; to be
frank

offen·bar ⓵ *Adj.* obvious
⓶ *adv.* obviously

Offenbarung *die;* ~, ~en revelation

***offen|bleiben** ▶ OFFEN 1A, C

Offen·heit *die;* ~ ▶ OFFEN E: frankness
[and openness]; candour

offen-: ~**kundig** ⓵ *Adj.* obvious; ⓶ *adv.*
obviously; *~|lassen** ▶ OFFEN 1A;
~**sichtlich** ⓵ *Adj.* obvious; ⓶ *adv.*
obviously

offensiv ⓵ *Adj.* (a) offensive
(b) (Sport) attacking
⓶ *adv.* (a) offensively
(b) (Sport) ~ **spielen** play an attacking game

Offensive *die;* ~, ~n (auch Sport) offensive

***offen|stehen** ▶ OFFEN 1A

öffentlich ⓵ *Adj.* public; state *attrib.*,
[state-]maintained ⟨school⟩; **der** ~**e Dienst**
the civil service
⓶ *adv.* publicly; ⟨perform, appear⟩ in public

Öffentlichkeit *die;* ~: public

offiziell ⓵ *Adj.* official
⓶ *adv.* officially

Offizier *der;* ~s, ~e, **Offizierin** *die;* ~,
~nen officer

öffnen ⓵ *tr. V.* open; turn on ⟨tap⟩; undo
⟨coat, blouse, button, zip⟩
⓶ *itr. V.* (a) [jmdm.] ~: open the door [to
sb.]
(b) (geöffnet werden) ⟨shop, bank, etc.⟩ open
⓷ *refl. V.* open

Öffner *der;* ~s, ~: opener

Öffnung *die;* ~, ~en opening

Öffnungs·zeiten *Pl.* opening times

Offroader /ɔfˈrəʊdɐ/ *der;* ∼s, ∼: offroader

oft *Adv.* öfter, am öftesten often; **wie oft soll ich dir noch sagen, dass …?** how many [more] times do I have to tell you that …?

öfter *Adv.* now and then

oftmals *Adv.* often; frequently

ohne ⟨1⟩ *Präp. mit Akk.* without; ∼ **mich!** [you can] count me out!; ∼ **weiteres** (leicht, einfach) easily; (ohne Einwand) readily ⟨2⟩ *Konj.* ∼ **zu zögern** without hesitation

ohne·hin *Adv.* anyway

Ohnmacht *die;* ∼, ∼en (a) faint; **in** ∼ **fallen** faint (b) (Machtlosigkeit) powerlessness; impotence

ohnmächtig ⟨1⟩ *Adj.* (a) unconscious; ∼ **werden** faint; ∼ **sein** have fainted (b) (machtlos) powerless; impotent ⟨2⟩ *adv.* impotently; ∼ **zusehen** watch helplessly

Ohr *das;* ∼[e]s, ∼en ear; **gute/schlechte** ∼**en haben** have good/poor hearing *sing.;* **jmdn. übers** ∼ **hauen** (fig. ugs.) put one over on sb. (coll.)

Öhr *das,* ∼[e]s, ∼e eye

ohren-, Ohren-: ∼**arzt,** *der,* ∼**ärztin,** *die* otologist; ear specialist; ∼**betäubend** ⟨1⟩ *Adj.* ear-splitting; deafening; deafening ⟨applause⟩; ⟨2⟩ *adv.* deafeningly; ∼**sausen** *das;* ∼∼s ringing in the *or* one's ears; tinnitus (Med.); ∼**schmerz** *der* earache; ∼**schmerzen haben** have [an] earache *sing.*

ohr-, Ohr-: ∼**feige** *die* box on the ears; ∼**feigen** *tr. V.* jmdn. ∼feigen box sb.'s ears; **ich könnte mich** ∼**feigen!** (ugs.) I could kick myself!; ∼**läppchen** *das* ear lobe; ∼**ring** *der* earring; ∼**wurm** *der* (a) earwig; (b) (ugs.: Melodie) catchy tune; **ein** ∼**wurm sein** be really catchy

okay /oˈke/ (ugs.) *Interj., Adj., adv.* OK (coll.); okay (coll.)

öko-, Öko- eco-

Ökologie *die;* ∼: ecology

ökologisch ⟨1⟩ *Adj.* ecological ⟨2⟩ *adv.* ecologically

ökonomisch ⟨1⟩ *Adj.* (a) economic (b) (sparsam) economical ⟨2⟩ *adv.* economically

Öko-: ∼**produkt** *das* ecoproduct; environmentally friendly *or* safe product; ∼**steuer** *die* eco-tax; ∼**system** *das* ecosystem; ∼**tourismus** *der* ecotourism

Oktober *der;* ∼[s], ∼: October

ökumenisch *Adj.* (christl. Rel.) ecumenical

Öl *das;* ∼[e]s, ∼e oil; **in Öl malen** paint in oils

ölen *tr. V.* oil

Öl-: ∼**embargo** *das* oil embargo; ∼**farbe** *die* (a) oil-based paint; (b) (zum Malen) oil paint; ∼**gemälde** *das* oil painting

ölig *Adj.* oily

Olive *die;* ∼, ∼n olive

Oliven-: ∼**baum** *der* olive tree; ∼**öl** *das* olive oil

Öl-: ∼**ofen** *der* oil heater; ∼**pest** *die* oil pollution *no indef. art.;* ∼**quelle** *die* oil well; ∼**sardine** *die* sardine in oil; **eine Dose** ∼**sardinen** a tin of sardines; ∼**teppich** *der* oil slick; ∼**wechsel** *der* (bes. Kfz-W.) oil change

Olympiade *die;* ∼, ∼n Olympic Games *pl.;* Olympics *pl.*

Olympia-: ∼**sieger** *der,* ∼**siegerin** *die* Olympic champion; ∼**stadion** *das* Olympic stadium

olympisch *Adj.* Olympic; **die Olympischen Spiele** the Olympic Games; the Olympics

Oma *die;* ∼, ∼s (fam.) granny (coll./child lang.)

Omelett /ɔm(ə)ˈlɛt/ *das;* ∼[e]s, ∼e *od.* ∼s omelette

Omi *die;* ∼, ∼s ▶ OMA

Omnibus *der;* ∼ses, ∼se omnibus (formal); (Privat- und Reisebus auch) coach

Onanie *die;* ∼: onanism *no art.;* masturbation *no art.*

onanieren *itr. V.* masturbate

Onkel *der;* ∼s, ∼ *od.* (ugs.) ∼s uncle

online /ˈɔnlaɪn/ ⟨1⟩ *Adj.* online; ∼ **gehen** go online ⟨2⟩ *Adv.* online

Online-shopping *das* online shopping

OP /oːˈpeː/ *der;* ∼[s], ∼[s] *Abk.* = **Operationssaal**

Opa *der;* ∼s, ∼s (fam.) grandad (coll./child lang.)

Opal *der;* ∼s, ∼e opal

OPEC /ˈoːpɛk/ *die;* ∼: *Abk.* OPEC

Oper *die;* ∼, ∼n opera; (Opernhaus) Opera; opera house

Operation *die;* ∼, ∼en operation

Operations·saal *der* operating theatre (Brit.) *or* room

operativ ⟨1⟩ *Adj.*(Med.) operative ⟨2⟩ *adv.* (Med.) by operative surgery; **etw.** ∼ **entfernen** operate to remove sth.

Operette *die;* ∼, ∼n operetta

operieren ⟨1⟩ *tr. V.* operate on ⟨patient⟩ ⟨2⟩ *itr. V.* operate

Opern·glas *das* opera glass[es *pl.*]

Opfer *das;* ∼s, ∼ (a) sacrifice (b) (Geschädigter) victim

opfern *tr. V.* (auch fig.) sacrifice; offer up ⟨fruit, produce, etc.⟩

Opi *der* ∼s, ∼s ▶ OPA

Opium *das;* ∼s opium

opponieren *itr. V.* gegen jmdn./etw. ∼: oppose sb./sth.

Opposition *die;* ∼, ∼en opposition

oppositionell *Adj.* opposition *attrib.* ⟨group, movement, etc.⟩; ⟨newspaper, writer, artist, etc.⟩ opposed to the government

Optik *die;* ∼: optics *sing., no art.*

Optiker *der;* ~s, ~, **Optikerin** *die;* ~,
~nen optician

optimal [1] *Adj.* optimal; optimum *attrib.;*
[2] *adv.* jmdn. ~ beraten give sb. the best
possible advice

optimieren *tr. V.* optimize

Optimierung *die;* ~, ~en optimization

Optimismus *der;* ~: optimism

Optimist *der;* ~en, ~en, **Optimistin** *die;*
~, ~nen optimist

optimistisch [1] *Adj.* optimistic
[2] *adv.* optimistically

optisch [1] *Adj.* optical; visual ‹*impression*›;
eine ~e Täuschung an optical illusion
[2] *adv.* optically; visually ‹*impressive,
effective*›

orange /oˈrãː(ə)/ *indekl. Adj.* orange

Orange *die;* ~, ~n orange

Orangen-: ~marmelade *die* orange
marmalade; **~saft** *der* orange juice

Orchester /ɔrˈkɛstɐ/ *das;* ~s, ~: orchestra

Orden *der;* ~s, ~ **(a)** order
(b) (Ehrenzeichen) decoration

ordentlich [1] *Adj.* **(a)** [neat and] tidy; neat
‹*handwriting, clothes*›
(b) (anständig) respectable; proper ‹*manners*›
(c) (planmäßig) ordinary ‹*meeting*›; ~es
Mitglied full member
(d) (ugs.: richtig) proper; real; ein ~es Stück
Kuchen a nice big piece of cake
(e) (ugs.: recht gut) decent ‹*wine, flat, marks,
etc.*›; ganz ~: pretty good
[2] *adv.* **(a)** tidily; neatly; ‹*write*› neatly
(b) (anständig) properly
(c) (ugs.: gehörig) ~ feiern have a real good
celebration (coll.)
(d) (ugs.: recht gut) ‹*ski, speak, etc.*› really well

ordern *tr., itr. V.* (Kaufmannsspr.) order

Ordinal·zahl *die* ordinal [number]

ordinär [1] *Adj.* vulgar
[2] *adv.* vulgarly

Ordinate *die;* ~, ~n (Math.) ordinate

ordnen *tr. V.* arrange; **sein Leben/seine
Finanzen** ~: straighten out one's life/put
one's finances in order

Ordner *der;* ~s, ~ (Hefter) file

Ordnung *die;* ~, ~en order; (geregelter
Ablauf) routine; ~ halten keep things tidy; in
~ sein (ugs.) be OK (coll.) *or* all right; hier ist
etw. nicht in ~: there's something wrong
here; sie ist in ~ (ugs.) she's OK (coll.); in ~!
(ugs.) OK! (coll.); all right!

ordnungs-, Ordnungs-: ~gemäß
[1] *Adj.* ‹*conduct etc.*› in accordance with the
regulations; [2] *adv.* in accordance with the
regulations; **~halber** *Adv.* as a matter of
form; **~widrig** (Rechtsw.) [1] *Adj.* ‹*actions,
behaviour, etc.*› contravening the regulations;
illegal ‹*parking*›; [2] *adv.* **~widrig parken**

park illegally; **~widrigkeit** *die* (Rechtsw.)
infringement of the regulations; **~zahl** *die*
ordinal [number]

Organ *das;* ~s, ~e organ; (ugs.: Stimme)
voice

Organisation *die;* ~, ~en organization

Organisator *der;* ~s, ~en,
Organisatorin *die;* ~, ~nen organizer

organisatorisch *Adj.* organizational

organisch [1] *Adj.* organic
[2] *adv.* organically

organisieren [1] *tr. V.* organize
[2] *itr. V.* gut ~ können be a good organizer
[3] *refl. V.* organize

Organismus *der;* ~, Organismen organism

Organist *der;* ~en, ~en, **Organistin** *die;*
~, ~nen organist

Organ·spender *der,*
Organ·spenderin *die* organ donor

Orgasmus *der;* ~, Orgasmen orgasm

Orgel *die;* ~, ~n organ

Orgie /ˈɔrgiə/ *die;* ~, ~n (auch fig.) orgy

Orient /ˈoːriɛnt/ *der;* ~s Middle East and
south-western Asia (*including Afghanistan
and Nepal*); **der Vordere** ~: the Middle East

orientalisch *Adj.* oriental

orientieren [1] *refl. V.* **(a)** get one's
bearings
(b) sich über etw. (*Akk.*) ~ (fig.) inform
oneself about sth.
(c) sich an etw. (*Dat.*) ~ (fig.) be oriented
towards sth.; ‹*policy, advertising*› be geared
towards sth.
[2] *tr. V.* (unterrichten) inform (über + *Akk.*
about)

Orientierung *die;* ~ **(a)** die ~ verlieren
lose one's bearings
(b) (Unterrichtung) zu Ihrer ~: for your
information

Orientierungs·sinn *der* sense of
direction

original [1] *Adj.* original
[2] *adv.* ~ italienischer Espresso genuine
Italian espresso coffee; etw. ~ übertragen
broadcast sth. live

Original *das;* ~s, ~e original

Original-: ~fassung *die* original version;
~gemälde *das* original painting

Originalität *die;* ~: originality

Original·ton *der; Pl.* Original·töne (Film,
Ferns.) direct sound; original sound

originell [1] *Adj.* original
[2] *adv.* with originality

Orkan *der;* ~[e]s, ~e hurricane

Ornament *das;* ~[e]s, ~e ornament

Ort¹ /ɔrt/ *der;* ~[e]s, ~e place; (Dorf) village;
(Stadt) town; **an ~ und Stelle** there and then

Ort² vor ~ (fig.) on the spot

orthodox *Adj.* orthodox

Orthographie *die;* ~, ~n orthography

orthographisch [1] *Adj.* orthographic; ~e
Fehler spelling mistakes

---

*alte Schreibung - vgl. Hinweis auf S. xiv

2 *adv.* orthographically

Orthopäde *der;* ~n, ~n orthopaedic specialist

orthopädisch 1 *Adj.* orthopaedic
2 *adv.* orthopaedically

örtlich 1 *Adj.* (auch Med.) local
2 *adv.* (auch Med.) locally; ~ **betäubt werden** be given a local anaesthetic

Ortschaft *die;* ~, ~en (Dorf) village; (Stadt) town

Orts-: ~**gespräch** *das* (Fernspr.) local call; ~**name** *der* place name; ~**netz·kennzahl** *die* (Fernspr.) dialling code; area code (Amer.)

Öse *die;* ~, ~n eye

Ossi *der;* ~s, ~s (salopp) East German

Ost (bes. Seemannsspr., Met.) ▶ OSTEN

ost-, Ost-: ~**block** *der* Eastern bloc; ~**deutsch** *Adj.* Eastern German; (hist.: auf die DDR bezogen) East German; ~**deutschland** (*das*) Eastern Germany; (hist.: DDR) East Germany

Osten *der;* ~s east; **der** ~: the East; **der Ferne** ~: the Far East; **der Nahe** ~: the Middle East

Oster-: ~**ei** *das* Easter egg; ~**glocke** *die* daffodil; ~**hase** *der* Easter hare (*said to bring children their Easter Eggs*); ~**montag** *der* Easter Monday *no def. art.*

Ostern *das;* ~, ~: Easter; **Frohe** od. **Fröhliche** ~: Happy Easter!; **zu** ~: at Easter

Österreich (*das*); ~s Austria

Österreicher *der;* ~s, **Österreicherin** *die* ~, ~nen Austrian

österreichisch *Adj.* Austrian

Oster·sonntag *der* Easter Sunday *no def. art.*

Ost·europa (*das*) Eastern Europe

Ostler *der;* ~s, ~, **Ostlerin** *die;* ~, ~nen (ugs.) East German

östlich 1 *Adj.* (a) (im Osten gelegen) eastern (b) (nach, aus dem Osten) easterly (c) (aus dem Osten kommend, für den Osten typisch; Politik) Eastern; ⟨influence, policies⟩ of the East
2 *adv.* eastwards; ~ **von** ...: [to the] east of ...
3 *Präp. mit Gen.* [to the] east of

Ost·see *die;* ~: Baltic [Sea]

ost·wärts *Adv.* eastwards

Ost·wind *der* easterly wind

Otter¹ *der;* ~s, ~ (Fisch~) otter

Otter² *die;* ~, ~n (Viper) adder; viper

Otto·motor *der* Otto engine

out /aʊt/ *Adj.* ~ **sein** (ugs.) be out

Outfit /'aʊtfɪt/ *das;* ~[s], ~s outfit

Ouvertüre /uvɛr'tyːrə/ *die;* ~, ~n (auch fig.) overture (*Gen.* to)

oval *Adj.* oval

Ovation *die;* ~, ~en ovation; **jmdm.** ~**en darbringen** give sb. an ovation

Ozean *der;* ~s, ~e ocean

Ozean·dampfer *der* ocean liner

Ozon *der* od. *das;* ~s ozone

Ozon-: ~**alarm** *der* ozone alert; ~**loch** *das* hole in the ozone layer; ~**schicht** *die* ozone layer; ~**zerstörung** *die* ozone destruction

P p

p, P /peː/ *das;* ~, ~: p/P

paar *indekl. Indefinitpron.* **ein** ~ ...: a few ...; (zwei od. drei) a couple of ...

Paar *das;* ~[e]s, ~e pair; (Mann und Frau) couple; **ein** ~ **Würstchen** two sausages

paaren *refl. V.* ⟨animals⟩ mate; ⟨people⟩ copulate

Paar·lauf *der* pairs *pl.*

paar·mal *Adv.* **ein** ~ a few times; (zwei- oder dreimal) a couple of times

Paarung *die;* ~, ~en (Zool.) mating

paar·weise *Adv.* in pairs

Pacht *die;* ~, ~en lease; **etw. in** ~ **nehmen** lease sth.; **etw. in** ~ **haben** have sth. on lease; **etw. in** ~ **geben** lease sth.

pachten *tr. V.* lease

Pächter *der;* ~s, ~, **Pächterin** *die;* ~, ~nen leaseholder; (eines Hofes) tenant

Pacht-: ~**vertrag** *der* lease; ~**zins** *der; Pl.* ~~e rent

Pack¹ *der;* ~[e]s, ~e od. **Päcke** (a) pack (b) ▶ PACKEN

Pack² *das;* ~[e]s (ugs. abwertend) rabble

Päckchen *das;* ~s, ~ (a) package; (auch Postw.) small parcel; (Bündel) packet (b) ▶ PACKUNG A

packen 1 *tr. V.* (a) pack (b) (fassen) grab [hold of]; (fig.) **Furcht packte ihn/er wurde von Furcht gepackt** he was seized with fear
2 *itr. V.* (Koffer usw. ~) pack

Packen *der;* ~s, ~: pile; (zusammengeschnürt) bundle; (von Geldscheinen) wad

packend [1] *Adj.* gripping
[2] *adv.* grippingly

Pack-papier *das* [stout] wrapping paper

Packung *die;* ~, ~en (a) packet; pack (esp. Amer.)
(b) (Med., Kosmetik) pack

Pädagoge *der;* ~n, ~n (Erzieher, Lehrer) teacher; (Wissenschaftler) educationalist

Pädagogik *die;* ~: [theory and methodology of] education

Pädagogin *die;* ~, ~nen ▶ PÄDAGOGE

pädagogisch [1] *Adj.* educational; seine ~en Fähigkeiten his teaching ability *sing.;*
[2] *adv.* educationally ⟨sound, wrong⟩

Paddel *das;* ~s, ~: paddle

Paddel-boot *das* canoe

paddeln *itr. V.; mit sein* paddle; (als Sport) canoe

Päderast *der;* ~en, ~en pederast

pädophil *Adj.* paedophile

Pädophile *der; adj. Dekl.* paedophile

paffen [1] *tr. V.* puff at ⟨pipe etc.⟩
[2] *itr. V.* puff away

Page /'pa:ʒə/ *der;* ~n, ~n bellboy

Paket *das;* ~[e]s, ~e pile; (zusammengeschnürt) bundle; (Eingepacktes, Post~) parcel; (Packung) packet; pack (esp. Amer.)

Paket-: ~**karte** *die* parcel dispatch form; ~**schalter** *der* parcels counter

Pakistan (*das*) ~s Pakistan

Pakistaner *der;* ~s, ~, **Pakistanerin** *die;* ~, ~nen, **Pakistani** *der;* ~[s], ~[s] Pakistani

pakistanisch *Adj.* Pakistani

Pakt *der;* ~[e]s, ~e pact

paktieren *itr. V.* make *or* do a deal/deals

Palast *der;* ~[e]s, Paläste palace

Palästina (*das*) ~s Palestine

Palästinenser *der;* ~s, ~, **Palästinenserin** *die;* ~, ~nen Palestinian

palästinensisch *Adj.* Palestinian

Palaver /pa'la:vɐ/ *das;* ~s, ~ (ugs. abwertend) palaver

palavern *itr. V.* (ugs. abwertend) palaver

Palette *die;* ~, ~n (a) palette
(b) (bes. Werbespr.: Vielfalt) diverse range; die ganze ~: the whole range
(c) (Technik, Wirtsch.: Untersatz) pallet

paletti *Adj.* alles ~ (ugs.) everything's OK (coll.) *or* all right

Palme *die;* ~, ~n palm [tree]

Pampelmuse *die;* ~, ~n grapefruit

Panade *die;* ~, ~n (Kochk.) breadcrumb coating

Panama (*das*) ~s Panama

Panama-kanal *der;* ~s Panama Canal

Panel /'pɛnl/ *das;* ~s, ~s panel

Pan-flöte *die* pan pipes *pl.*

panieren *tr. V.* bread; coat ⟨sth.⟩ with breadcrumbs

Panier-mehl *das* breadcrumbs *pl.*

Panik *die;* ~, ~en panic

Panik-: ~**mache** *die;* ~~ (abwertend) panicmongering; ~**macher** *der,* ~**macherin** *die* (abwertend) panicmonger

Panne *die;* ~, ~n (a) breakdown; (Reifen~) puncture; flat [tyre]
(b) (Missgeschick) mishap

Pannen-dienst *der* breakdown service

Panorama *das;* ~s, Panoramen panorama

Panter, ***Panther** *der;* ~s, ~: panther

Pantoffel *der;* ~s, ~n backless slipper

Pantomime *die;* ~, ~n mime

Panzer *der;* ~s, ~ (a) (Milit.) tank
(b) (Zool.) armour *no indef. art.;* (von Schildkröten, Krebsen) shell

Panzer-glas *das* bulletproof glass

panzern *tr. V.* armour[-plate]

Panzer-schrank *der* safe

Papa *der;* ~s, ~s (ugs.) daddy (coll.)

Papagei *der;* ~en *od.* ~s, ~e[n] parrot

Paparazzo *der;* ~s, Paparazzi paparazzo

Paperback /'peɪpəbæk/ *das;* ~s, ~s paperback

Papi *der;* ~s, ~s (ugs.) daddy (coll.)

Papier *das;* ~s, ~e (a) paper
(b) *Pl.* (Ausweis[e]) [identity] papers
(c) (Finanzw.: Wert~) security

Papier-: ~**geld** *das* paper money; ~**korb** *der* waste-paper basket

Pappe *die;* ~, ~n cardboard

Pappel *die;* ~, ~n poplar

päppeln *tr. V.* feed up

Papp-karton *der* cardboard box

Paprika *der;* ~s, ~[s] (a) pepper
(b) (Gewürz) paprika

Papst *der;* ~[e]s, Päpste, **Päpstin** *die;* ~, ~nen pope

päpstlich *Adj.* papal

Para *der;* ~s, ~s para (coll.)

Parabel *die;* ~, ~n (a) (bes. Literaturw.) parable
(b) (Math.) parabola

Parade *die;* ~, ~n parade

Parade-beispiel *das* perfect example

Paradeiser *der;* ~s, ~ (österr.) tomato

Paradies *das;* ~es, ~e paradise

paradiesisch *Adj.* paradisical; (herrlich) heavenly

Paradigma *das;* ~s, Paradigmen paradigm

paradox *Adj.* paradoxical

Para-gleiten *das;* ~s, **Para-gliding** /'paraglaːdɪŋ/ *das;* ~s paragliding

Paragraph *der;* ~en, ~en section; (in Vertrag) clause

parallel [1] *Adj.* parallel
[2] *adv.* ~ **verlaufen** run parallel (**mit, zu** to)

Parallele *die;* ~, ~n parallel
Parallelogramm *das;* ~s, ~e
parallelogram
Parallel·straße *die* street running
parallel (*Gen.* to)
Para·nuss, ***Para·nuß** *die* Brazil nut
Parasit *der;* ~en, ~en (auch fig.) parasite
parat *Adj.* ready
Pardon /par'dõ/ *der od. das;* ~s pardon; ~!
I beg your pardon
Parfum /par'fœ:/, **Parfüm** *das;* ~s, ~s
perfume
Parfümerie *die;* ~, ~en perfumery
parfümieren *tr. V.* perfume
Pariser 1 *indekl. Adj.* Parisian; Paris
attrib.;
2 *der;* ~s, ~ (a) (Einwohner) Parisian
(b) (ugs.: Kondom) French letter (coll.)
Pariserin *die;* ~, ~nen Parisian
Parität *die;* ~, ~en parity
Park /park/ *der;* ~s, ~s park; (Schloss~
usw.) grounds *pl.*
Parka *der;* ~s, ~s parka
parken *tr., itr. V.* park; „Parken verboten!"
'No Parking'
Parkett *das;* ~[e]s, ~e (a) parquet floor
(b) (Theater) [front] stalls *pl.;* parquet (Amer.)
Parkett-: ~[fuß]boden *der* parquet
floor; ~handel *der* (Börsenw.) floor trading
Park-: ~gebühr *die* parking fee; ~haus
das multi-storey car park
parkieren *tr., itr. V.* (schweiz.) ▶ PARKEN
Park-: ~lücke *die* parking space; ~platz
der car park; parking lot (Amer.); (für ein
einzelnes Fahrzeug) parking space;
~scheibe *die* parking disc; ~schein
der car park ticket; ~uhr *die* parking
meter; ~verbot *das* ban on parking; im
~verbot stehen be parked illegally;
~verbots·schild *das* no-parking sign
Parlament *das;* ~[e]s, ~e parliament
Parlamentarier *der;* ~s, ~,
Parlamentarierin *die;* ~, ~nen
member of parliament
parlamentarisch *Adj.* parliamentary
Parodie *die;* ~, ~n parody (auf + *Akk.* of)
Parole *die;* ~, ~n (a) (Wahlspruch) motto;
(Schlagwort) slogan
(b) (bes. Milit.: Kennwort) password
Partei *die;* ~, ~en (a) (Politik, Rechtsw.) party
(b) (Gruppe, Mannschaft) side; für jmdn. ~
ergreifen *od.* nehmen side with sb.
Partei·gänger *der;* ~~s, ~~,
Partei·gängerin *die;* ~~, ~~nen (oft
abwertend) [loyal] party supporter
parteiisch 1 *Adj.* biased
2 *adv.* in a biased manner
parteilich 1 *Adj.* (parteiisch) biased
2 *adv.* in a biased manner
Parteilichkeit *die;* ~ (einseitige Parteinahme)
bias; partiality
partei-, Partei-: ~los *Adj.* (Politik)

independent ⟨MP⟩; ~lose *der/die; adj.*
Dekl. (Politik) independent; person not
attached to a party; ~nahme *die;* ~~,
~~n partisanship; taking sides *no art.;*
~politik *die* party politics *sing.;*
~politisch 1 *Adj.* party political;
2 *adv.* from a party political point of view;
~tag *der* party conference *or* (Amer.)
convention
Parterre *das;* ~s, ~s ground floor; first
floor (Amer.)
Partie *die;* ~, ~n (a) part
(b) (Spiel, Sport: Runde) game; (Golf) round
(c) eine gute ~ [für jmdn.] sein be a good
match [for sb.]
Partisan *der;* ~s *od.* ~en, ~en,
Partisanin *die;* ~, ~nen guerrilla; (gegen
Besatzungstruppen im Krieg) partisan
Partitur *die;* ~, ~en (Musik) score
Partizip *das;* ~s, ~ien /-'ts:i:pi̯ən/ (Sprachw.)
participle
Partner *der;* ~s, ~, **Partnerin** *die;* ~,
~nen partner
Partnerschaft *die;* ~, ~en partnership
partnerschaftlich 1 *Adj.* ⟨cooperation
etc.⟩ on a partnership basis
2 *adv.* in a spirit of partnership
Partner-: ~schule *die* partner school;
~stadt *die* twin town (Brit.); sister city *or*
town (Amer.); ~vermittlung *die* (a)
matchmaking; (b) (Agentur) [introduction
and] matchmaking agency;
~vermittlungs·büro *das;* ▶
PARTNERVERMITTLUNG B
Party /'pa:ɐ̯ti/ *die;* ~, ~s party
Parzelle *die;* ~, ~n [small] plot [of land]
Pass, ***Paß** *der;* Passes, Pässe (a)
(Reisepass) passport
(b) (Gebirgspass; Ballspiele) pass
passabel 1 *Adj.* reasonable; presentable
⟨appearance⟩
2 *adv.* reasonably well
Passage /pa'sa:ʒə/ *die;* ~, ~n (a)
[shopping] arcade
(b) (Abschnitt) passage
Passagier /pasa'ʒi:ɐ̯/ *der;* ~s, ~e
passenger; blinder ~: stowaway
Passagier-: ~dampfer *der* passenger
steamer; ~flugzeug *das* passenger
aircraft
Passagierin *die;* ~, ~nen passenger
Passagier·liste *die* passenger list
Pass·amt, ***Paß·amt** *das* passport office
Passant *der;* ~en, ~en, **Passantin** *die;*
~, ~nen passer-by
Pass·bild, ***Paß·bild** *das* passport
photograph
Pässe ▶ PASS
passen *itr. V.* (a) (die richtige Größe/Form
haben) fit
(b) (geeignet sein) be suitable (auf + *Akk.*, zu
for); (harmonieren) ⟨colour etc.⟩ match; zu etw./ ⋯⋗

p

jmdm. ~: go well with sth./be well suited to
sb.; **zueinander** ~ ⟨*things*⟩ go well together;
⟨*two people*⟩ be suited to each other
(c) (genehm sein) **jmdm.** ~ ⟨*time*⟩ suit sb.
(d) (Kartenspiel) pass

passend *Adj.* **(a)** (geeignet) suitable ⟨*dress,
present, etc.*⟩; right ⟨*words, expression,
moment*⟩
(b) (harmonierend) matching ⟨*shoes etc.*⟩

Pass·foto, **Paß·foto** *das* ▶ PASSBILD

passierbar *Adj.* passable ⟨*road*⟩; navigable
⟨*river*⟩; negotiable ⟨*path*⟩

passieren ⟦1⟧ *tr. V.* pass; **die Grenze** ~:
cross the border
⟦2⟧ *itr. V.; mit sein* happen

Passion *die;* ~, ~**en (a)** passion
(b) (christl. Rel.) Passion

passioniert *Adj.* passionate ⟨*collector, card
player, huntsman*⟩

passiv ⟦1⟧ *Adj.* passive
⟦2⟧ *adv.* passively

Passiv *das;* ~**s**, ~**e** (Sprachw.) passive

Passivität *die;* ~: passivity

Passivraucher *der,* **Passivraucherin**
die passive smoker

pass‑, **paß**, **Pass‑**, **Paß‑:
~**kontrolle** *die* passport check; ~**straße**
die [mountain] pass road; ~**wort** *das; Pl.*
~**wörter** (DV) password;
~**wort‑geschützt** (DV) ⟦1⟧ *Adj.*
password-protected; ⟦2⟧ *adv.* with password
protection; ~**zwang** *der* obligation to
carry a passport

Paste *die;* ~, ~**n** paste

Pastell *das;* ~**[e]s**, ~**e (a)** (Farbton) pastel
shade
(b) (Maltechnik) pastel *no art.*

Pastell‑: ~**farbe** *die* pastel colour; ~**ton**
der pastel shade

Pastete *die;* ~, ~**n (a)** (gefüllte) vol-au-vent
(b) (in einer Schüssel o. Ä. gegart) pâté; (in einer
Hülle aus Teig gebacken) pie

pasteurisieren *tr. V.* pasteurize

Pastille *die;* ~, ~**n** pastille

Pastor *der;* ~**s**, ~**en**, **Pastorin** *die;* ~,
~**nen** pastor

Pate *der;* ~**n**, ~**n** godfather; (männlich od.
weiblich) godparent

Paten‑: ~**kind** *das* godchild; ~**onkel** *der*
godfather; ~**stadt** *die* ▶ PARTNERSTADT

patent (ugs.) ⟦1⟧ *Adj.* **(a)** (tüchtig) capable
(b) (zweckmäßig) ingenious
⟦2⟧ *adv.* ingeniously; neatly ⟨*solved*⟩

Patent *das;* ~**[e]s**, ~**e (a)** (Schutz) patent;
etw. zum od. als ~ **anmelden** apply for a
patent for sth.
(b) (Erfindung) [patented] invention

Patent·amt *das* Patent Office

Paten·tante *die* godmother

patentieren *tr. V.* patent

*alte Schreibung - vgl. Hinweis auf S. xiv

Patent‑: ~**lösung** *die* patent remedy (**für,
zu** for); ~**rezept** *das* patent remedy
(**gegen, für** for)

Pater *der;* ~**s**, ~ *od.* **Patres** (kath. Kirche)
Father

pathetisch ⟦1⟧ *Adj.* emotional ⟨*speech,
manner*⟩; melodramatic ⟨*gesture*⟩
⟦2⟧ *adv.* emotionally; (dramatisch)
[melo]dramatically

Pathos *das;* ~: emotionalism

Patience /pa'si̯ã:s/ *die;* ~, ~**n** [game of]
patience; ~**n/eine** ~ **legen** play patience/a
game of patience

Patient /pa'ts:i̯ɛnt/ *der;* ~**en**, ~**en**,
Patientin *die;* ~, ~**nen** patient

Patin *die;* ~, ~**nen** godmother

Patres ▶ PATER

Patriot *der;* ~**en**, ~**en**, **Patriotin** *die;* ~,
~**nen** patriot

patriotisch ⟦1⟧ *Adj.* patriotic
⟦2⟧ *adv.* patriotically

Patriotismus *der;* ~: patriotism

Patrone *die;* ~, ~**n** cartridge

Patrouille /pa'trʊljə/ *die;* ~, ~**n** patrol

patrouillieren /patrʊl'ji:rən/ *itr. V.; auch
mit sein* be on patrol

Patsche *die;* ~, ~**n** (ugs.) ▶ KLEMME

patschen *itr. V., mit sein* (ugs.) splash

patsch·nass, **patsch·naß** *Adj.* (ugs.)
sopping wet

patt *Adj.* (Schach) stalemated

Patt *das;* ~**s**, ~**s** (Schach; auch fig.) stalemate

Patt·situation *die* [position of] stalemate

Patzer *der;* ~**s**, ~ (ugs.) slip (coll.); boob
(coll.)

patzig (ugs.) ⟦1⟧ *Adj.* snotty (coll.); (frech)
cheeky
⟦2⟧ *adv.* snottily (coll.); (frech) cheekily

Pauke *die;* ~, ~**n** kettledrum; **auf die** ~
hauen (ugs.) (feiern) paint the town red (coll.);
(sich lautstark äußern) come right out with it

pauken (ugs.) ⟦1⟧ *tr. V.* swot up (Brit. sl.),
bone up on (Amer. coll.) ⟨*facts, figures, etc.*⟩;
Latein/Mathe ~: swot up one's Latin/maths
⟦2⟧ *itr. V.* swot (Brit. sl.); (fürs Examen) cram
(coll.)

pausbäckig *Adj.* chubby-faced; chubby
⟨*face*⟩

pauschal ⟦1⟧ *Adj.* **(a)** all-inclusive ⟨*price,
settlement*⟩
(b) (verallgemeinernd) sweeping ⟨*judgement,
criticism, statement*⟩; indiscriminate
⟨*prejudice*⟩; wholesale ⟨*discrimination*⟩
⟦2⟧ *adv.* **(a)** ⟨*cost*⟩ all in all; ⟨*pay*⟩ in a lump
sum
(b) (ohne zu differenzieren) wholesale

Pauschale *die;* ~, ~**n** flat-rate payment

Pauschal‑: ~**preis** *der* flat rate;
(Inklusivpreis) all-in price; ~**reise** *die* package
holiday; (mit mehreren Reisezielen) package tour

Pause *die;* ~, ~**n** break; (Ruhe~) rest;
(Theater) interval (Brit.); intermission (Amer.)

pausen *tr. V.* trace; (eine Lichtpause machen)
Photostat (*Brit.* ®)

pausen-, Pausen-: ∼**brot** *das*
sandwich *(eaten during break)*; ∼**hof** *der*
school yard; ∼**los** [1] *Adj.* incessant *(noise,
moaning, questioning)*; continous *(work,
operation)*
[2] *adv.* incessantly; *(work)* non-stop

Pavian /ˈpaːviaːn/ *der;* ∼**s,** ∼**e** baboon

Pavillon /ˈpavɪljɔn/ *der;* ∼**s,** ∼**s** pavilion

Pazifik *der;* ∼**s** Pacific

pazifisch *Adj.* Pacific *(area)*; **der Pazifische
Ozean** the Pacific Ocean

Pazifismus *der;* ∼: pacifism *no art.*

Pazifist *der;* ∼**en,** ∼**en, Pazifistin** *die;*
∼, ∼**nen** pacifist

pazifistisch [1] *Adj.* pacifist
[2] *adv.* in a pacifist way

PC *der;* ∼**[s],** ∼**[s]** (DV) PC

PDS *Abk.* = **Partei des
Demokratischen Sozialismus**
Party of Democratic Socialism

Peanuts /ˈpiːnʌts/ *Pl.* peanuts (coll.)

Pech *das;* ∼**[e]s,** ∼**e (a)** pitch
(b) (Missgeschick) bad luck

pech·schwarz *Adj.* (ugs.) jet-black

Pedal *das;* ∼**s,** ∼**e** pedal

Pedant *der;* ∼**en,** ∼**en, Pedantin** *die;* ∼,
∼**nen** pedant

pedantisch [1] *Adj.* pedantic
[2] *adv.* pedantically

Pediküre *die;* ∼, ∼**n** pedicure

pediküren *tr. V.* pedicure

Pegel *der;* ∼**s,** ∼ **(a)** water level indicator;
(Tide∼) tide gauge
(b) (Wasserstand) water level

peilen *tr. V.* take a bearing on *(transmitter,
fixed point)*

Pein *die;* ∼ (geh.) torment

peinigen *tr. V.* (geh.) torment; (foltern)
torture

peinlich [1] *Adj.* **(a)** embarrassing;
awkward *(question, position, pause)*; **es ist
mir sehr** ∼: I feel very bad (coll.) *or*
embarrassed about it
[2] *adv.* **(a)** unpleasantly *(surprised)*
(b) (überaus [genau]) meticulously

Peinlichkeit *die;* ∼, ∼**en (a)**
embarrassment; **die** ∼ **der Situation** the
awkwardness of the situation
(b) (Genauigkeit) meticulousness
(c) (peinliche Situation) embarrassing situation

Peitsche *die;* ∼, ∼**n** whip

peitschen *tr. V.* whip; (fig.) *(storm, waves,
rain)* lash

Pelikan *der;* ∼**s,** ∼**e** pelican

Pelle *die;* ∼, ∼**n** (bes. nordd.) skin; (abgeschält)
peel

pellen (bes. nordd.) *tr., refl. V.* peel

Pell·kartoffel *die* potato boiled in its skin

Pelz *der;* ∼**es,** ∼**e (a)** fur; coat; (des toten
Tieres) skin; pelt
(b) (Material) fur; (∼mantel) fur coat

Pelz·mantel *der* fur coat

Pendel *das;* ∼**s,** ∼: pendulum

pendeln *itr. V.* **(a)** swing [to and fro]; (mit
weniger Bewegung) dangle
(b) *mit sein (bus, ferry, etc.)* operate a
shuttle service; *(person)* commute

Pendler *der;* ∼**s,** ∼, **Pendlerin** *die;* ∼,
∼**nen** commuter

penetrant [1] *Adj.* **(a)** penetrating *(smell,
taste)*; overpowering *(stink, perfume)*
(b) (aufdringlich) pushing, (coll.) pushy
(person); overbearing *(tone, manner)*;
aggressive *(question)*
[2] *adv.* **(a)** overpoweringly
(b) (aufdringlich) overbearingly

penibel [1] *Adj.* over-meticulous *(person)*;
(pedantisch) pedantic
[2] *adv.* painstakingly; over-meticulously
(dressed)

Penis *der;* ∼, ∼**se** penis

pennen *itr. V.* (salopp) **(a)** (schlafen) kip (coll.)
(b) (fig.: nicht aufpassen) be half asleep
(c) (koitieren) **mit jmdm.** ∼: sleep with sb.

Penner *der;* ∼**s,** ∼, **Pennerin** *die;* ∼,
∼**nen** (salopp) tramp (Brit.); hobo (Amer.)

Pensen ▶ PENSUM

Pension /pãˈzjoːn/ *die;* ∼, ∼**en (a)**
(Ruhestand) **in** ∼ **gehen** retire; **in** ∼ **sein** be
retired
(b) (Ruhegehalt) [retirement] pension
(c) (Haus für [Ferien]gäste) guest house
(d) (Unterkunft u. Verpflegung) board

Pensionär /pãzjoˈnɛːɐ̯/ *der;* ∼**s,** ∼**e,
Pensionärin** *die;* ∼, ∼**nen** retired civil
servant

pensionieren *tr. V.* pension off; retire;
sich [vorzeitig] ∼ **lassen** take [early]
retirement; **ein pensionierter Schulmeister/
Politiker** a retired schoolmaster/politician

Pensionierung *die;* ∼, ∼**en** retirement

Pensions-: ∼**alter** *das* retirement age;
∼**anspruch** *der* pension entitlement

Pensum *das;* ∼**s, Pensen** work quota

per *Präp. mit Akk.* **(a)** (mittels) by; ∼ **Adresse
X** care of X; c/o X
(b) (Kaufmannsspr.: [bis] zum) by; (am) on
(c) (Kaufmannsspr.: pro) per

perfekt [1] *Adj.* **(a)** perfect *(crime, host)*;
faultless *(English, French, etc.)*
(b) ∼ **sein** (ugs.: abgeschlossen, fertig sein) be
finalized
[2] *adv.* perfectly

Perfekt *das;* ∼**s** (Sprachw.) perfect

Perfektion *die;* ∼: perfection

perfektionieren *tr. V.* perfect

Perfektionismus *der;* ∼: perfectionism

Perfektionist *der;* ∼**en,** ∼**en,
Perfektionistin** *die;* ∼, ∼**nen**
perfectionist

perfektionistisch [1] *Adj.* perfectionist
(standards etc.)
[2] *adv.* in a perfectionist manner

p

Pergament·papier *das* greaseproof paper

Periode *die;* ~, ~n period

Perle *die;* ~, ~n **(a)** (auch fig.) pearl **(b)** (aus Holz, Glas o. Ä.) bead

Perlmutt *das;* ~s mother-of-pearl

Perlon Ⓦ⒵ *das;* ~s ≈ nylon

Perser *der;* ~s, ~ **(a)** Persian **(b)** ▶ PERSERTEPPICH

Perserin *die;* ~, ~nen Persian

Perser·teppich *der* Persian carpet

Persianer *der;* ~s, ~ (Mantel) Persian lamb coat

Persien (*das*)*;* ~s Persia

persisch *Adj.* Persian

Person *die;* ~, ~en person; (in der Dichtung, im Film) character

Personal *das;* ~s (in einem Betrieb o. Ä.) staff; (im Haushalt) domestic staff *pl.*

Personal-: ~**abbau** *der* reduction in staff; (in mehreren Abteilungen/Betrieben) staff cuts *pl.;* ~**abteilung** *die* personnel department; ~**ausweis** *der* identity card; ~**büro** *das* personnel office; ~**chef** *der*, ~**chefin** *die* personnel manager

Personalien *Pl.* personal particulars

Personal-: ~**kosten** *Pl.* (Wirtsch., Verwaltung) staff costs; ~**mangel** *der* staff shortage; ~**pronomen** *das* (Sprachw.) personal pronoun; ~**rat** *der* **(a)** (Ausschuss) staff council *(for civil servants)*; **(b)** (Mitglied) staff council representative; ~**rätin** *die;* ▶ ~RAT B

Personen-: ~**kraftwagen** *der* (bes. Amtsspr.) private car *or* (Amer.) automobile; ~**name** *der* personal name; ~**wagen** *der* (Auto) [private] car; automobile (Amer.); (im Unterschied zum Lastwagen) passenger car *or* (Amer.) automobile; ~**zug** *der* stopping train

Personifikation *die;* ~, ~en personification

personifizieren *tr. V.* personify

Personifizierung *die;* ~, ~en personification

persönlich ① *Adj.* personal; ~ werden get personal ② *adv.* personally; (auf Briefen) 'private [and confidential]'

Persönlichkeit *die;* ~, ~en **(a)** personality **(b)** (Mensch) person of character; eine ~ sein have a strong personality; ~en des öffentlichen Lebens public figures

Perspektive *die;* ~, ~n perspective; (Blickwinkel) angle; (Zukunftsaussicht) prospect

Peru (*das*)*;* ~s Peru

Peruaner *der;* ~s, ~, **Peruanerin** *die;* ~, ~nen Peruvian

peruanisch *Adj.* Peruvian

Perücke *die;* ~, ~n wig

pervers *Adj.* perverted

*old spelling - see note on page xiv

Perversion *die;* ~, ~en perversion

Pessimismus *der;* ~: pessimism

Pessimist *der;* ~en, ~en, **Pessimistin** *die;* ~, ~nen pessimist

pessimistisch ① *Adj.* pessimistic ② *adv.* pessimistically

Pest *die;* ~: plague

Pestizid *das;* ~s, ~e pesticide

Petersilie /petɐˈziːljə/ *die;* ~: parsley

Petition *die;* ~, ~en (Amtsspr.) petition

Petroleum /peˈtroːleʊm/ *das;* ~s paraffin (Brit.); kerosene (Amer.)

Petrus (*der*)*;* Petri (christl. Rel.: Apostel) St Peter

petzen (Schülerspr.) ① *itr. V.* tell tales; sneak (Brit. school coll.) ② *tr. V.* ~, dass ...: tell teacher/sb.'s parents that ...

Pf *Abk.* = **Pfennig**

Pfad *der;* ~[e]s, ~e path

Pfad-: ~**finder** *der* Scout; ~**finderin** *die;* ~, ~nen Guide (Brit.); girl scout (Amer.)

Pfaffe *der;* ~n, ~n (abwertend) cleric; Holy Joe (derog.)

Pfahl *der;* ~[e]s, Pfähle post; stake

Pfand *das;* ~[e]s, Pfänder **(a)** security; pledge (esp. fig.) **(b)** (für Flaschen usw.) deposit (**auf** + *Dat.* on)

pfänden *tr. V.* seize [under distress] (Law) ⟨goods, chattels⟩; attach ⟨wages etc.⟩ (Law)

Pfand·flasche *die* returnable bottle (*on which a deposit is payable*)

Pfändung *die;* ~, ~en seizure; distraint (Law); (von Geldsummen, Vermögensrechten) attachment (Law)

Pfanne *die;* ~, ~n [frying] pan

Pfann·kuchen *der* **(a)** pancake **(b)** (Berliner) doughnut

Pfarrei *die;* ~, ~en **(a)** (Bezirk) parish **(b)** (Dienststelle) parish office **(c)** ▶ PFARRHAUS

Pfarrer *der;* ~s, ~ pastor; (anglikanisch) vicar; (von Freikirchen) minister

Pfarrerin *die;* ~, ~nen [woman] pastor; (in Freikirchen) [woman] minister

Pfarr·haus *das* vicarage; (katholisch) presbytery; (in Schottland) manse

Pfau *der;* ~[e]s, ~en peacock

Pfauen·auge *das* peacock butterfly

Pfd. *Abk.* = **Pfund** lb.

Pfeffer *der;* ~s, ~: pepper

Pfeffer-: ~**kuchen** *der* ≈ gingerbread; ~**minze** *die* peppermint [plant]; ~**minz·tee** *der* peppermint tea; ~**mühle** *die* pepper mill

pfeffern *tr. V.* season with pepper

Pfeffer·streuer *der;* ~s, ~: pepper pot

Pfeife *die;* ~, ~n pipe; (Triller~) whistle

pfeifen ① *unr. itr. V.* whistle; ⟨bird⟩ sing;

(auf einer Trillerpfeife o. Ä.) ⟨*policeman, referee, etc.*⟩ blow one's whistle; **auf jmdn./etw.** ~ (ugs.) not give a damn about sb./sth. ② *unr. tr. V.* whistle ⟨*tune etc.*⟩; ⟨*bird*⟩ sing ⟨*song*⟩; (auf einer Pfeife) pipe, play ⟨*tune etc.*⟩

Pfeil *der;* ~[e]s, ~e arrow

Pfeiler *der;* ~s, ~: pillar; (Brücken~) pier

Pfennig *der;* ~s, ~e pfennig; **es kostete damals 20** ~: it cost 20 pfennig[s] at that time

pferchen *tr. V.* cram; pack

Pferd *das;* ~[e]s, ~e horse; (Schachfigur) knight; **mit ihr kann man** ~**e stehlen** (ugs.) she's game for anything

Pferde-: ~**rennen** *das* horse race; (Sportart) horseracing; ~**schwanz** *der* (Frisur) ponytail; ~**stall** *der* stable

pfiff *1. u. 3. Pers. Sg. Prät. v.* PFEIFEN

Pfiff *der;* ~[e]s, ~e **(a)** whistle **(b)** (ugs.: besonderer Reiz) style

Pfifferling *der;* ~s, ~e chanterelle; **keinen** *od.* **nicht einen** ~ **wert sein** (ugs.) be not worth a bean (coll.)

pfiffig ① *Adj.* smart; bright ⟨*idea*⟩; artful ⟨*smile, expression*⟩ ② *adv.* artfully

Pfingsten *das;* ~, ~: Whitsun

Pfingst-: ~**montag** *der* Whit Monday *no def. art.;* ~**sonntag** *der* Whit Sunday *no def. art.*

Pfirsich *der;* ~s, ~e peach

Pflanze *die;* ~, ~n plant

pflanzen *tr. V.* plant

Pflanzen-öl *das* vegetable oil

pflanzlich *Adj.* plant *attrib.* ⟨*life, motif*⟩; vegetable ⟨*dye, fat*⟩

Pflaster *das;* ~s, ~ **(a)** (Straßen~) road surface; (auf dem Gehsteig) pavement; **ein teures/gefährliches** ~ (ugs.) an expensive/dangerous place *or* spot to be **(b)** (Wund~) sticking plaster

pflastern *tr.* (*auch itr.*) *V.* surface; (mit Kopfsteinpflaster, Steinplatten) pave

Pflaster-stein *der* paving stone; (Kopfstein) cobblestone

Pflaume *die;* ~, ~n plum; **getrocknete** ~**n** [dried] prunes

Pflege *die;* ~: care; (Maschinen~, Fahrzeug~) maintenance; (fig.: von Beziehungen, Kunst, Sprache) cultivation; **jmdn./etw. in** ~ (*Akk.*) **nehmen** look after sb./sth.

pflege-, Pflege-: ~**bedürftig** *Adj.* needing care *or* attention *postpos.;* ⟨*person*⟩ in need of care; ~**bedürftig sein** need looking after; need attention; ~**eltern** *Pl.* foster-parents; ~**fall** *der;* **ein** ~**fall sein** be in [permanent] need of nursing; ~**heim** *das* nursing home (esp. Brit.); ~**kind** *das* foster-child; ~**leicht** *Adj.* easy-care *attrib.* ⟨*textiles, flooring*⟩

pflegen ① *tr. V.* look after; care for; take care of ⟨*skin, teeth, floor*⟩; look after ⟨*bicycle,*

car, machine⟩; look after, tend ⟨*garden, plants*⟩; cultivate ⟨*relations, arts, interests*⟩; foster ⟨*contacts, cooperation*⟩; pursue ⟨*hobby*⟩ ② *mod. V.* etw. zu tun ~: usually do sth.

Pflege-personal *das* nursing staff

Pfleger *der;* ~s, ~ **(a)** (Krankenpfleger) [male] nurse **(b)** (Tierpfleger) keeper

Pflegerin *die;* ~, ~nen **(a)** (Krankenpflegerin) nurse **(b)** (Tierpflegerin) keeper

Pflege-versicherung *die* (long-term) [nursing-]care insurance

Pflicht *die;* ~, ~en duty

pflicht-, Pflicht-: ~**bewusst,** ***~**bewußt** ① *Adj.* conscientious; ② *adv.* with a sense of duty; ~**bewusstsein,** ***~**bewußtsein** *das,* sense of duty; ~**fach** *das* compulsory subject; ~**gefühl** *das* sense of duty; ~**übung** *die* (fig.) ritual exercise; ~**verteidiger** *der,* ~**verteidigerin** *die* (Rechtsw.) *defense counsel appointed by the court;* assigned counsel

Pflock *der;* ~[e]s, Pflöcke peg

pflücken *tr. V.* pick

Pflug *der;* ~[e]s, Pflüge plough

pflügen *tr., itr. V.* plough

Pforte *die;* ~, ~n (Tor) gate; (Tür) door; (Eingang) entrance

Pförtner *der;* ~s, ~, **Pförtnerin** *die;* ~, ~nen porter; (eines Wohnblocks, Büros) doorkeeper; (am Tor) gatekeeper

Pförtner-loge *die* porter's lodge

Pfosten *der;* ~s, ~: post

Pfote *die;* ~, ~n paw

Pfropf *der;* ~[e]s, ~e blockage

pfropfen *tr. V.* (ugs.) cram; stuff; **gepfropft voll** crammed [full]; packed

Pfropfen *der;* ~s, ~: stopper; (Korken) cork; (für Fässer) bung

pfui *Interj.* ugh; ~ **rufen** boo

Pfund *das;* ~[e]s, ~e pound

Pfusch *der;* ~[e]s **(a)** (ugs. abwertend) **das ist** ~: it's a botch-up **(b)** (österr.: Schwarzarbeit) work done on the side (*and not declared for tax*); (nach Feierabend) moonlighting (coll.)

pfuschen *itr. V.* **(a)** (ugs. abwertend) botch it; do a botched-up job **(b)** (österr.: schwarzarbeiten) do work on the side (*not declared for tax*); (nach Feierabend) moonlight (coll.)

Pfütze *die;* ~, ~n puddle

Phänomen *das;* ~s, ~e phenomenon

Phantasie *usw.:* ▶ FANTASIE *usw.*

Pharma-: ~**berater** *der,* ~**beraterin** *die:* ▶ ~REFERENT *usw.;* ~**industrie** *die* pharmaceutical industry

Pharmakologie *die;* ~: pharmacology *no art.*

Pharma·referent der,
Pharma·referentin die pharmaceutical
representative
pharmazeutisch Adj. pharmaceutical
Phase die; ~, ~n phase
Philosoph der; ~en, ~en philosopher
Philosophie die; ~, ~n philosophy
philosophieren itr. (auch tr.) V.
philosophize
Philosophin die; ~, ~nen philosopher
philosophisch ① Adj. philosophical;
⟨dictionary, principles⟩ of philosophy
② adv. philosophically
Phosphat das; ~[e]s, ~e (Chemie)
phosphate
Photo das; ~s, ~s ▶ FOTO
Phrase die; ~, ~n (abwertend) [empty]
phrase; cliché
Physik die; ~: physics sing., no art.
physikalisch Adj. physics attrib.
⟨experiment, formula, research, institute⟩;
physical ⟨map, process⟩
Physiker der; ~s, ~, **Physikerin** die; ~,
~nen physicist
physisch ① Adj. physical
② adv. physically
Pianist der; ~en, ~en, **Pianistin** die; ~,
~nen pianist
Pickel der; ~s, ~: pimple
picken ① itr. V. peck (nach at; an + Akk.,
gegen on, against)
② tr. V. ⟨bird⟩ peck; (ugs.) ⟨person⟩ pick
Picknick das; ~s, ~e od. ~s picnic
piek·fein (ugs.) ① Adj. posh (coll.)
② adv. poshly (coll.)
piepe, piep·egal Adj. [jmdm.] ~ sein
(ugs.) not matter at all [to sb.]; **es ist mir ~**
(ugs.) I don't give a damn
Piepen Pl. (salopp: Geld) dough sing. (coll.)
piep[s]en itr. V. (ugs.) squeak; ⟨small bird⟩
cheep; **bei dir piept's wohl!** (salopp) you must
be off your rocker (coll.); **zum Piepen sein**
(ugs.) be a hoot or a scream (coll.)
Pietät /pie'tɛ:t/ die; ~: respect; (Ehrfurcht)
reverence
Pik das; ~[s], ~[s] (Kartenspiel) (a) (Farbe)
spades pl.;
(b) (Karte) spade
pikant ① Adj. (a) piquant
(b) (fig.: witzig) ironical
(c) (verhüll.: schlüpfrig) racy ⟨joke, story⟩
② adv. piquantly ⟨seasoned⟩
pikiert ① Adj. piqued
② adv. ⟨reply, say⟩ in an aggrieved tone
Pilger der; ~s, ~, **Pilgerin** die; ~, ~nen
pilgrim
pilgern itr. V. go on a pilgrimage
Pille die; ~, ~n pill
Pilot der; ~en, ~en, **Pilotin** die; ~, ~nen
pilot

Pils das; ~, ~: Pils
Pilz der; ~es, ~e fungus; (Speise~, auch fig.)
mushroom
Pinguin der; ~s, ~e penguin
Pinie /'pi:niə/ die; ~, ~n [stone or
umbrella] pine
pinkeln itr. V. (salopp) pee (coll.)
Pinsel der; ~s, ~: brush; (Mal~) paintbrush
Pinzette die; ~, ~n tweezers pl.
Pionier der; ~s, ~e (Milit.) sapper; (fig.:
Wegbereiter) pioneer
Pionierin die; ~, ~nen pioneer
Pionier·arbeit die pioneering work
Pipi das; ~s (Kinderspr.) ~ **machen** do wee-
wees (sl.); ~ **müssen** have to do wee-wees or
have a wee (sl.)
Pirat der; ~en, ~en, **Piratin** die; ~, ~nen
pirate
pissen itr. V. (derb) piss (coarse)
Pistazie /pɪs'ta:tsiə/ die; ~, ~n pistachio
Piste die; ~, ~n (Ski~) piste; (Renn~)
course; (Flugw.) runway
Pistole die; ~, ~n pistol
Pizza die; ~, ~s od. Pizzen pizza
Pkw, PKW /'pe:ka:ve:/ der; ~[s], ~[s]
[private] car; automobile (Amer.)
plädieren itr. V. (Rechtsspr.) plead (auf + Akk.
for); (fig.) argue
Plädoyer /plɛdoa'je:/ das; ~s, ~s (Rechtsspr.)
summing up (for the defence/prosecution);
(fig.) plea
Plage die; ~, ~n (a) nuisance
(b) (ugs.: Mühe) bother; trouble
plagen ① tr. V. (a) torment
(b) (ugs.: bedrängen) harass; (mit Bitten, Fragen)
pester
② refl. V. (a) (sich abmühen) slave away
(b) (leiden) **sich mit etw. ~:** be bothered by
sth.
Plagiat das; ~[e]s, ~e plagiarism no art.
Plakat das; ~[e]s, ~e poster
Plakette die; ~, ~n badge
Plan der; ~[e]s, **Pläne** (a) plan
(b) (Karte) map; plan
Plane die; ~, ~n tarpaulin
planen tr., itr. V. plan
Planet der; ~en, ~en planet
planieren tr. V. level; grade
Planier·raupe die bulldozer
Planke die; ~, ~n plank
plan-: ~**los** ① Adj. aimless; (ohne System)
unsystematic; ② adv. ▶ 1: aimlessly;
unsystematically; ~**mäßig** ① Adj. (a)
scheduled ⟨service, steamer⟩; ~**mäßige**
Ankunft/Abfahrt scheduled time of arrival/
departure; (b) (systematisch) systematic
② adv. (a) (wie geplant) according to plan;
(pünktlich) on schedule; (b) (systematisch)
systematically
Plansch·becken das paddling pool
planschen itr. V. splash [about]

Plantage /plan'ta:ʒə/ *die;* ~, ~n plantation

Planung *die;* ~, ~en planning

Plan·wirtschaft *die* planned economy

Plastik¹ *die;* ~, ~en sculpture

Plastik² *das;* ~s (ugs.) plastic

Plastik·beutel *der,* **Plastik·tüte** *die* plastic bag

Platane *die;* ~, ~n plane tree

Platin *das;* ~s platinum

platschen *itr. V.* **(a)** splash
(b) *mit sein* (~d auftreffen) splash (**an** + *Akk.,* **gegen** against)

plätschern *itr. V.* **(a)** splash; ⟨*rain*⟩ patter; ⟨*stream*⟩ burble
(b) *mit sein* ⟨*stream*⟩ burble along

platt *Adj.* flat; **ein Platter** (ugs.) a flat (coll.); **etw.** ~ **machen** (salopp abwertend) close sth. down

Platt *das;* ~[s] [local] Low German dialect

Plättchen *das;* ~s, ~: small plate *or* disc

platt·deutsch *Adj.* Low German

Platte *die;* ~, ~n **(a)** (Stein~) slab; (Metall~) plate; sheet; (Span~, Hartfaser~ usw.) board; (Tisch~) [table] top; (Grab~) [memorial] slab
(b) (Koch~) hotplate
(c) (Schall~) [gramophone] record
(d) (Teller) plate; (zum Servieren, aus Metall) dish; **kalte** ~: selection of cold meats [and cheese]

Platten·spieler *der* record player

Platt·fuß *der* **(a)** flat foot
(b) (ugs.: Reifenpanne) flat (coll.)

Platz *der;* ~es, **Plätze (a)** square
(b) (Sport~) ground; (Spielfeld) field; (Tennis~, Volleyball~ usw.) court; (Golf~) course
(c) (Stelle, wo jmd., etw. hingehört) place; **nicht** *od.* **fehl am** ~[e] **sein** (fig.) be out of place
(d) (Sitz~) seat; (am Tisch, Steh~ usw.) place; ~ **nehmen** sit down
(e) (bes. Sport: Platzierung) place
(f) (Ort) place; **am** ~: in the town/village
(g) (Raum) space; room; ~ **machen** make room (*Dat.* for)

Platz·angst *die* (volkst.: Klaustrophobie) claustrophobia

Plätzchen *das;* ~s, ~ **(a)** little place
(b) (Keks) biscuit (Brit.); cookie (Amer.)

platzen *itr. V.; mit sein* **(a)** burst; (explodieren) explode
(b) (ugs.: scheitern) fall through; **der Wechsel/ das Treffen ist geplatzt** the bill has bounced (coll.)/the meeting is off
(c) **in eine Versammlung** ~ (ugs.) burst into a meeting

Platz-: ~**karte** *die* reserved-seat ticket; ~**konzert** *das* open-air concert (*by a military or brass band*); ~**mangel** *der* lack of space; ~**not** *die* [acute] lack of space; ~**regen** *der* cloudburst; ~**wunde** *die* lacerated wound

Plauderei *die;* ~, ~en chat

plaudern *itr. V.* chat

plausibel *Adj.* plausible

Play·boy /'pleɪbɔɪ/ *der* playboy

Player /'pleɪɐ/ *der:* ~, ~: player

pleite (ugs.) ~ **sein** ⟨*person*⟩ be broke (coll.); ⟨*company*⟩ have gone bust (coll.); *s. auch* PLEITE A

Pleite *die;* ~, ~n (ugs.) **(a)** (Bankrott) bankruptcy *no def. art.;* ~ **gehen/machen** go bust (coll.)
(b) (Misserfolg) washout (coll.)

Pleite-: ~**geier** *der* (ugs.) spectre of bankruptcy; ~**wirtschaft** *die* (ugs.) bankrupt economy

Plissee *das;* ~s, ~s accordion pleats *pl.*

Plombe *die;* ~, ~n **(a)** (Siegel) [lead] seal
(b) (veralt.: Zahnfüllung) filling

plombieren *tr. V.* **(a)** (versiegeln) seal
(b) (veralt.) fill ⟨*tooth*⟩

plötzlich ⓵ *Adj.* sudden
⓶ *adv.* suddenly

Plötzlichkeit *die;²* ~: suddenness

plump ⓵ *Adj.* **(a)** (dick) plump; (unförmig) ungainly ⟨*shape*⟩; (rundlich) bulbous
(b) (schwerfällig) clumsy ⟨*movements, style*⟩
(c) (fig.) (dreist) crude ⟨*lie, deception, trick*⟩; (leicht durchschaubar) blatantly obvious; (unbeholfen) clumsy ⟨*excuse, advances*⟩; crude ⟨*joke, forgery*⟩
⓶ *adv.* **(a)** (schwerfällig) clumsily
(b) (fig.) in a blatantly obvious manner

Plumpheit *die;* ~ **(a)** (Dicke) plumpness; (Unförmigkeit) ungainliness; (Rundlichkeit) bulbousness
(b) (Schwerfälligkeit) clumsiness
(c) (abwertend: Dreistigkeit) blatant nature

plumps *Interj.* bump; thud; (ins Wasser) splash; ~ **machen** go bump

Plumps *der;* ~es, ~e (ugs.) bump; thud; (ins Wasser) splash

plumpsen *itr. V.* fall with a bump; thud; (ins Wasser) splash

Plünderer *der;* ~s, ~, **Plünderin** *die;* ~, ~nen looter

plündern *itr., tr. V.* **(a)** loot; plunder ⟨*town*⟩
(b) (scherzh.) raid ⟨*larder, fridge, account*⟩

Plünderung *die;* ~, ~en looting; (einer Stadt) plundering; ~en cases of looting/ plundering

Plural *der;* ~s, ~e plural

Pluralismus *der;* ~: pluralism

pluralistisch ⓵ *Adj.* pluralistic
⓶ *adv.* pluralistically; along pluralistic lines

plus *Konj., Adv.* plus

Plus *das;* ~: surplus; (Vorteil) advantage

Plüsch *der;* ~[e]s, ~e plush

Plusquam·perfekt *das* pluperfect [tense]

PLZ *Abk.* = **Postleitzahl**

Po *der;* ~s, ~s (ugs.) bottom

Pöbel *der;* ~s rabble

pöbeln *itr. V.* make rude *or* coarse remarks

pochen *itr. V.* (klopfen) knock (**gegen/an** + *Akk.* at, on); (geh.: pulsieren) ⟨*heart*⟩ pound

Pocken *Pl.* smallpox *sing.*

Podest *das od. der;* ~[e]s, ~e rostrum

Podium *das;* ~s, Podien (Plattform) platform; (Bühne) stage; (trittartige Erhöhung) rostrum

Poesie *die;* ~: poetry

Poet *der;* ~en, ~en (veralt.) poet; bard (literary)

poetisch ①*Adj.* poetic[al] ②*adv.* poetically

Pogrom *das od. der;* ~s, ~e pogrom

Pointe /'po̯ɛ̃:tə/ *die;* ~, ~n (eines Witzes) punch line; (einer Geschichte) point; (eines Sketches) curtain line

pointiert /po̯ɛ̃'ti:ɐt/ ①*Adj.* pointed ⟨*remark*⟩ ②*adv.* pointedly

Pokal *der;* ~s, ~e (a) (Trinkgefäß) goblet (b) (Siegestrophäe, ~wettbewerb) cup

Pökel·fleisch *das* salt meat

pökeln *tr. V.* salt

Poker *das od. der;* ~s poker

Poker·gesicht *das* poker face

pokern *itr. V.* play poker

Pol *der;* ~s, ~e pole

Polar·licht *das* aurora; polar lights *pl.*

Polaroid·kamera Ⓦ *die* Polaroid camera ®

Pole *der;* ~n, ~n Pole

polemisch ①*Adj.* polemic[al] ②*adv.* polemically

Polen *das;* ~s Poland

Polente *die;* ~ (salopp) cops *pl.* (coll.)

Police /po'li:sə/ *die;* ~, ~n (Versicherungsw.) policy

polieren *tr. V.* polish

Poli·klinik *die* outpatients' clinic

Polin *die;* ~n, ~nen Pole

Polit·büro *das* politburo

Politik *die;* ~, ~en (a) politics *sing., no art.* (b) (eine spezielle ~) policy

Politiker *der;* ~s, ~, **Politikerin** *die;* ~, ~nen politician

politisch ①*Adj.* political ②*adv.* politically

politisieren ①*itr. V.* talk politics ②*tr. V.* make politically active

Politur *die;* ~, ~en polish

Polizei *die;* ~, ~en police *pl.*

Polizei-: ~**auto** *das* police car; ~**beamte** *der* police officer; ~**kontrolle** *die* police check

polizeilich ①*Adj.* police; ~e Meldepflicht obligation to register with the police ②*adv.* by the police

Polizei-: ~**präsidium** *das* police headquarters *sing. or pl.;* ~**revier** *das*

police station; ~**streife** *die* police patrol; ~**stunde** *die* closing time; ~**wache** *die* police station

Polizist *der;* ~en, ~en policeman

Polizistin *die;* ~, ~nen policewoman

Pollen *der;* ~s, ~ (Bot.) pollen

Poller *der;* ~s, ~: bollard

polnisch *Adj.* Polish

Polster *das;* ~s, ~: upholstery *no pl., no indef. art.*

Polster·möbel *Pl.* upholstered furniture *sing.*

polstern *tr. V.* upholster ⟨*furniture*⟩

poltern *itr. V.* (a) crash about (b) *mit sein* der Karren polterte über das Pflaster the cart clattered over the cobblestones

Polyp *der;* ~en, ~en (Zool., Med.) polyp

Pommern (*das*)*;* ~s Pomerania

Pommes frites /pɔm'frit/ *Pl.* chips (Brit.); French fries (Amer.)

pompös ①*Adj.* grandiose ②*adv.* grandiosely

Pony[1] /'pɔni/ *das;* ~s, ~s pony

Pony[2] *der;* ~s, ~s (Frisur) fringe

Popel *der;* ~s, ~ (ugs.) bogy (sl.)

popelig (ugs. abwertend) ①*Adj.* crummy (coll.); lousy (coll.); (durchschnittlich) second-rate ②*adv.* crummily (sl.)

Popeline·mantel *der* poplin coat

popeln *itr. V.* (ugs.) [in der Nase] ~: pick one's nose

Pop-: ~**musik** *die* pop music; ~**star** *der* pop star

populär ①*Adj.* popular (**bei** with) ②*adv.* popularly

popularisieren *tr. V.* popularize

Popularität *die;* ~: popularity

Pore *die;* ~, ~n pore

Porno *der;* ~s, ~s (ugs.) porn[o] film/ magazine *etc.*

Pornographie *die;* ~: pornography

pornographisch ①*Adj.* pornographic ②*adv.* pornographically

Porree *der;* ~s leek

Portal *das;* ~s, ~e portal

Portemonnaie /pɔrtmɔ'ne:/ *das;* ~s, ~s purse

Porti *Pl.* ▶ PORTO

Portier /pɔr'tie:/ *der;* ~s, ~s, österr.: /pɔr'ti:ɐ/ *der;* ~s, ~e porter

Portion /pɔr'ts:jo:n/ *die;* ~, ~en (a) (beim Essen) portion; helping (b) (ugs.: Anteil) amount

Porto *das;* ~s, ~s od. Porti postage (**für** on, for)

Portugal (*das*)*;* ~s Portugal

Portugiese *der;* ~n, ~n, **Portugiesin** *die;* ~, ~nen Portuguese

portugiesisch *Adj.* Portuguese

Portwein *der* port

Porzellan *das;* ~s porcelain; china

Posaune *die;* ~, ~n trombone

Position /poziˈtsi̯oːn/ *die;* ~, ~en position

positiv ① *Adj.* positive
② *adv.* positively

Positiv *das;* ~s, ~e (Fot.) positive

Possessiv·pronomen *das* (Sprachw.) possessive pronoun

Post *die;* ~, ~en (a) post (Brit.); mail; **etw. mit der** *od.* **per** ~ **schicken** send sth. by post *or* mail; **die** ~ **geht ab** (fig. ugs.) it's all happening; **ab 20 Uhr geht die** ~ **ab** (fig. ugs.) it'll all be happening from 8 o'clock; **auch beim Publikum geht die** ~ **ab** (fig. ugs.) the audience is having a ball too (coll.)
(b) (Postamt) post office

Post-: ~**amt** *das* post office; ~**anweisung** *die* postal remittance form; ~**auto** *das* mail van; ~**bote** *der* (ugs.) postman (Brit.); mailman (Amer.); ~**botin** *die* (ugs.) postwoman (Brit.); mailwoman (Amer.)

Posten *der;* ~s, ~ (a) post
(b) (bes. Milit.: Wachmann) sentry

post-, Post-: ~**fach** *das* post office *or* PO box; (im Büro, Hotel usw.) pigeonhole; ~**karte** *die* postcard; ~**lagernd** *Adj., adv.* poste restante; general delivery (Amer.); ~**leit·zahl** *die* postcode; Zip code (Amer.); ~**stempel** *der* (Abdruck) postmark; ~**wendend** *Adv.* by return [of post]

potent *Adj.* potent

Potenz *die;* ~, ~en (a) potency
(b) (Math.) power

potenzieren *tr. V.* (Math.) **mit 5** ~: raise to the power [of] 5

Pracht *die;* ~: splendour

prächtig, pracht·voll ① *Adj.* splendid
② *adv.* splendidly

prädestiniert *Adj.* predestined

Prädikat *das;* ~[e]s, ~e (a) (Auszeichnung) rating
(b) (Sprachw.) predicate

Prag *(das);* ~s Prague

prägen *tr. V.* (a) emboss
(b) mint ⟨coin⟩
(c) (fig.: beeinflussen) shape

prägnant ① *Adj.* concise; succinct
② *adv.* concisely; succinctly

Prägung *die;* ~, ~en embossing; (von Münzen) minting

prahlen *itr. V.* boast, brag (**mit** about)

Prahler *der;* ~s, ~: boaster; braggart

Prahlerei *die;* ~, ~en (abwertend) boasting; bragging; ~**en** boasts

Prahlerin *die;* ~, ~nen boaster; braggart

Praktik *die;* ~, ~en practice

Praktika ▶ PRAKTIKUM

praktikabel *Adj.* practicable; practical

Praktikant *der;* ~en, ~en,
Praktikantin *die;* ~, ~nen (a) (in einem Betrieb) student trainee

(b) (an der Hochschule) physics/chemistry student (*doing a period of practical training*)

Praktikum *das;* ~s, **Praktika** period of practical training

praktisch ① *Adj.* practical; ~**er Arzt** general practitioner
② *adv.* practically; (auf die Praxis bezogen; wirklich) in practice

praktizieren *tr. V.* practise

Praline *die;* ~, ~n [filled] chocolate

prall *Adj.* (a) hard ⟨ball⟩; bulging ⟨sack, wallet, bag⟩; big strong *attrib.* ⟨thighs, muscles, calves⟩; well-rounded ⟨breasts⟩
(b) (intensiv) blazing ⟨sun⟩

prallen *itr. V.; mit sein* crash (**gegen/auf/an** + *Akk.* into); collide (**gegen/auf/an** + *Akk.* with)

Prämie /ˈprɛːmi̯ə/ *die;* ~, ~n (a) (Leistungs~; Wirtschaft) bonus; (Belohnung) reward; (Spar~, Versicherungs~) premium
(b) (einer Lotterie) [extra] prize

prämieren *tr. V.* award a prize to ⟨person, film⟩; give an award for ⟨best essay etc.⟩

Pranger *der;* ~s, ~ (hist.) pillory

Pranke *die;* ~, ~n paw

Präparat *das;* ~[e]s, ~e preparation

präparieren ① *tr. V.* prepare
② *refl. V.* (geh.: sich vorbereiten) prepare oneself

Präposition *die;* ~, ~en (Sprachw.) preposition

Prärie *die;* ~, ~n prairie

Präsens /ˈprɛːzɛns/ *das;* ~ (Sprachw.) present [tense]

präsentieren *tr. V.* present

Präservativ *das;* ~s, ~e condom

Präsident *der;* ~en, ~en, **Präsidentin** *die;* ~, ~nen president

Präsidium *das;* ~s, **Präsidien** (a) committee
(b) (Vorsitz) chairmanship
(c) (Polizei~) police headquarters *sing. or pl.*

prasseln *itr. V.* pelt down; ⟨shots⟩ clatter; ⟨fire⟩ crackle

prassen *itr. V.* live extravagantly; (schlemmen) feast

Präteritum *das;* ~s (Sprachw.) preterite [tense]

Prävention *die;* ~, ~en prevention

Praxis *die;* ~, **Praxen** (a) (im Unterschied zur Theorie) practice *no art.;* (Erfahrung) [practical] experience
(b) (eines Arztes, Anwalts usw.) practice; (Räume) (eines Arztes) surgery (Brit.); office (Amer.); (eines Anwalts usw.) office

präzise ① *Adj.* precise
② *adv.* precisely

Präzision *die;* ~: precision

predigen ① *itr. V.* deliver a/the sermon
② *tr. V.* preach

Prediger *der;* ~s, ~, **Predigerin** *die;* ~, ~nen preacher

Predigt die; ~, ~en sermon

Preis der; ~es, ~e: (a) (Kaufpreis) price (**für** of)
(b) (Belohnung) prize

Preis-: ~anstieg der rise or increase in prices; ~aus·schreiben das [prize] competition; ~bindung die (Wirtsch.) price-fixing

Preisel·beere die cranberry

preisen unr. tr. V. (geh.) praise

preis-, Preis-: ~erhöhung die price increase or rise; ~geld das prize money; ~günstig 1 Adj. ⟨goods⟩ available at unusually low prices; ⟨purchases⟩ at favourable prices; inexpensive ⟨holiday⟩; das ~günstigste Angebot the best bargain or value; das ist [sehr] ~günstig that is [very] good value; 2 adv. at a low price; etw. ~günstig herstellen/verkaufen/bekommen produce/sell/get sth. at a low price; ~kampf der price war; ~liste die price list; ~nachlass, *~nachlaß der price reduction; ~richter der, ~richterin die judge; ~schild das price tag; ~senkung die price reduction or cut; ~steigerung die rise or increase in prices; ~tafel die price list; ~träger der, ~trägerin die prizewinner; ~verleihung die presentation [of prizes/awards]; ~wert 1 Adj. good value pred.; 2 adv. ⟨eat⟩ at a reasonable price; dort kann man ~wert einkaufen you get good value for money there

prellen tr. V. (a) (betrügen) cheat (**um** out of); die Zeche ~: avoid paying the bill
(b) (verletzen) bash; bruise

Prellung die; ~, ~en bruise

Premiere /prə'mi̯eːrə/ die; ~, ~n opening night

Presse die; ~, ~n (a) press; (Zitronen~) squeezer
(b) (Zeitungen) press

Presse-: ~erklärung die press statement; ~freiheit die freedom of the press; ~information die press release; ~konferenz die press conference; ~meldung die press report

pressen tr. V. press

Presse·sprecher der, ~sprecherin die spokesman; press officer

Press·luft-, *Preß·luft-: ~bohrer der pneumatic drill; ~hammer der pneumatic hammer

Prestige /prɛs'tiːʒə/ das; ~s prestige

prickeln itr. V. tingle

pries 1. u. 3. Pers. Sg. Prät. v. PREISEN

Priester der; ~s, ~: priest

Priesterin die; ~, ~nen priestess

prima (ugs.) 1 indekl. Adj. great (coll.)
2 adv. ⟨taste⟩ great (coll.); ⟨sleep⟩ fantastically well (coll.)

primär 1 Adj. primary
2 adv. primarily

Primel die; ~, ~n primula; (Schlüsselblume) cowslip

primitiv 1 Adj. primitive; (einfach, schlicht) simple
2 adv. primitively; (einfach, schlicht) in a simple manner

Prim·zahl die (Math.) prime [number]

Prinz der; ~en, ~en prince

Prinzessin die; ~, ~nen princess

Prinzip das; ~s, ~ien /-'tsiːpi̯ən/ principle; **aus** ~: on principle; **im** ~: in principle

prinzipiell 1 Adj. in principle postpos., not pred.; ⟨rejection⟩ on principle
2 adv. (im Prinzip) in principle; (aus Prinzip) on principle

Prion das; ~s, ~en (Biol.) prion

Prise die; ~, ~n pinch

privat 1 Adj. private; (persönlich) personal
2 adv. privately

Privat-: ~adresse die private or home address; ~angelegenheit die private matter; ~besitz der private property; ~eigentum das private property

privatisieren tr. V. (Wirtsch.) privatize; transfer into private ownership

Privatisierung die; ~, ~en (Wirtsch.) privatization; transfer into private ownership

Privat-: ~leben das private life; ~lehrer der, ~lehrerin die private tutor; ~patient der, ~patientin die private patient; ~schule die private school; (Eliteschule in Großbritannien) public school; ~unterricht der private tuition; ~vermögen das private fortune; ~versicherung die private insurance; ~weg der private way; ~wirtschaftlich Adj. private-sector attrib.

privilegiert Adj. privileged

pro Präp. mit Akk. per; ~ **Stück** each; a piece

pro- pro-; ~westlich/~kommunistisch pro-western/pro-communist

Probe die; ~, ~n (a) test
(b) (Muster, Teststück) sample
(c) (Theater~, Orchester~) rehearsal

Probe-: ~fahrt die trial run; (vor dem Kauf, nach einer Reparatur) test drive; ~jahr das probationary year

proben tr., itr. V. rehearse

probe·weise Adv. ⟨employ⟩ on a trial basis

Probe·zeit die probationary period

probieren 1 tr. V. (a) try; have a go at
(b) (kosten) taste; try
(c) (aus~) try out; (an~) try on ⟨clothes, shoes⟩
2 itr. V. (a) (versuchen) try
(b) (kosten) have a taste

Problem das; ~s, ~e problem

---

problematisch Adj. problematic[al]
problematisieren tr. V. etw. ~: expound
the problems of sth.
problem·los ①Adj. problem-free
②adv. without any problems
Product-placement
/'prɔdaktpleɪsmənt/ das; ~s, ~ product
placement
Produkt das; ~[e]s, ~e (auch Math., fig.)
product
Produktion die; ~, ~en production
produktiv ① productive; prolific ⟨writer,
artist, etc.⟩
②adv. ⟨work, cooperate⟩ productively
Produktivität die; ~: productivity
Produzent der; ~en, ~en,
Produzentin die; ~, ~nen producer
produzieren tr. V. produce
Prof. Abk. = **Professor** Prof.
professionell ①Adj. professional
②adv. professionally
Professor der; ~s, ~en, **Professorin**
die; ~, ~nen professor
Professur die; ~, ~en professorship,
chair (für in)
Profi der; ~s, ~s (ugs.) pro (coll.)
Profil das; ~s, ~e (a) (Seitenansicht) profile;
im ~: in profile
(b) (von Reifen, Schuhsohlen) tread
Profit der; ~[e]s, ~e profit
profitieren itr. V. profit (von, bei by)
profund Adj. (geh.) profound; deep
Prognose die; ~, ~n prognosis; (Wetter~,
Wirtschafts~) forecast
prognostizieren tr. V. (geh.) forecast;
predict
Programm das; ~s, ~e programme;
program (Amer., Computing); (Ferns.: Sender)
channel
Programm-: ~**fehler** der (DV) program
error; error in the/a program; ~**heft** das
programme; ~**hinweis** der programme
announcement
programmieren tr. V. (a) (DV) program
(b) (auf etw. festlegen) programme
Programmierer der; ~s, ~,
Programmiererin die; ~, ~nen (DV)
programmer
Programm-: ~**vorschau** die (im
Fernsehen) preview [of the week's/evening's
etc. viewing]; (im Kino) trailers pl.;
~**zeitschrift** die radio and television
magazine
progressiv ①Adj. progressive
②adv. progressively
Projekt das; ~[e]s, ~e project
Projekt·management das project
management
Projektor /pro'jɛktɔr/ der; ~s, ~en
/-'toːrən/ projector
Projekt·tage Pl. (Schulw.) project[-work]
days

projizieren /proji'tsiːrən/ tr. V. (Optik)
project
proklamieren tr. V. proclaim
Prolet der; ~en, ~en (abwertend) peasant
Proletariat das; ~[e]s proletariat
Proletarier /prole'taːrɪɐ/ der; ~s, ~:
proletarian
proletarisch Adj. proletarian
prollig Adj. (salopp) boorish
Promenade die; ~, ~n promenade
Promille das; ~s, ~: [part] per thousand;
er fährt nur ohne ~ (ugs.) he never drinks
and drives; er hatte 1,8 ~: he had a blood
alcohol level of 1.8 per thousand
Promille·grenze die (ugs.) legal [alcohol]
limit
prominent Adj. prominent
Prominente der/die; adj. Dekl. prominent
figure
Prominenz die; ~: prominent figures pl.
Promotion /promo'tsioːn/ die; ~ (Wirtsch.)
promotion; für etw. ~ machen promote sth.
promovieren ① itr. V. (a) (die Doktorwürde
erlangen) gain or obtain a/one's doctorate
(b) (eine Dissertation schreiben) do a doctorate
(über + Akk. on)
② tr. V. confer a doctorate or the degree of
doctor on
prompt ①Adj. prompt
②adv. (a) promptly
(b) (ugs., meist iron.: wie erwartet) [and] sure
enough
Promptheit die; ~: promptness
Pronomen das; ~s, ~ od. **Pronomina**
(Sprachw.) pronoun
Propaganda die; ~: propaganda
propagieren tr. V. propagate
Propan·gas das propane
Propeller der; ~s, ~ propeller
Prophet der; ~en, ~en, **Prophetin** die;
~, ~nen prophet
prophezeien tr. V. prophesy (Dat. for);
predict ⟨result, weather⟩
Proportion die; ~, ~en proportion
Prosa die; ~: prose
Prosa·literatur die prose writing
prosit Interj. your [very good] health; ~
Neujahr! happy New Year!
Prospekt der od. (bes. österr.) das; ~[e]s,
~e (Werbeschrift) brochure; (Werbezettel) leaflet
prost Interj. (ugs.) cheers (Brit. coll.)
Prostituierte die/der; adj. Dekl. prostitute
Prostitution die; ~: prostitution no art.
Protagonist der; ~en, ~en,
Protagonistin die; ~, ~nen (geh.)
protagonist
Protest der; ~[e]s, ~e protest
Protestant der; ~en, ~en,
Protestantin die; ~, ~nen Protestant
protestantisch Adj. Protestant

p

Protestantismus *der;* ~: Protestantism *no art.*

protestieren *itr. V.* protest, make a protest (**gegen** against, about)

Protest·kundgebung *die* protest rally

Prothese *die;* ~, ~n artificial limb; prosthesis (Med.); (Zahn~) set of dentures; dentures *pl.*

Protokoll *das;* ~s, ~e (a) (wörtlich mitgeschrieben) transcript; (Ergebnis~) minutes *pl.;* (bei Gericht) record; **etw. zu ~ geben** make a statement about sth.
(b) (diplomatisches Zeremoniell) protocol

protokollieren 1 *tr. V.* take down; take the minutes of ⟨*meeting*⟩; minute ⟨*remark*⟩
2 *itr. V.* take the minutes; (bei Gericht) keep the record

protzen *itr. V.* (ugs.) swank (coll.); show off; **mit etw.** ~: show sth. off

protzig (ugs. abwertend) 1 *Adj.* swanky (coll.); showy
2 *adv.* swankily (coll.)

Proviant *der;* ~s, ~e provisions *pl.*

Provinz *die;* ~, ~en province

provinziell 1 *Adj.* provincial
2 *adv.* provincially

Provision *die;* ~, ~en (Kaufmannsspr.) commission

provisorisch 1 *Adj.* provisional; temporary
2 *adv.* temporarily

Pro·vitamin *das* provitamin

Provokation *die;* ~, ~en provocation

provozieren *tr. V.* provoke

Prozedur *die;* ~, ~en procedure

Prozent *das;* ~[e]s, ~e (a) *nach Zahlenangaben Pl. ungebeugt* per cent *sing.;* **fünf** ~: five per cent
(b) *Pl.* (ugs.) (Gewinnanteil) share *sing.* of the profits; (Rabatt) discount *sing.;* **auf etw.** (*Akk.*) ~e **bekommen** get a discount on sth.

-prozentig *adj.* -per-cent

Prozent-: ~**punkt** *der* percentage point; ~**rechnung** *die* percentage calculation; ~**satz** *der* percentage

prozentual 1 *Adj.* percentage
2 *adv.* ~ **am Gewinn beteiligt sein** have a percentage share in the profits

Prozess, *Prozeß *der;* Prozesses, Prozesse (a) trial; (Fall) [court] case; **einen** ~ **gewinnen/verlieren** win/lose a case
(b) (Vorgang) process

prozessieren *itr. V.* go to court; **gegen jmdn.** ~: bring an action against sb.

Prozess·kosten, *Prozeß·kosten *Pl.* legal costs

Prozessor *der;* ~s, ~en (DV) [central] processor

prüde (abwertend) 1 *Adj.* prudish
2 prudishly

Prüderie *die;* ~ (abwertend) prudery; prudishness

prüfen *tr. V.* (a) *auch itr.* examine ⟨*pupil, student, etc.*⟩; **mündlich/schriftlich geprüft werden** have an oral/a written examination
(b) (untersuchen) examine (**auf** + *Akk.* for); check ⟨*device, machine, calculation*⟩ (**auf** + *Akk.* for); investigate ⟨*complaint*⟩; (testen) test (**auf** + *Akk.* for)
(c) (kontrollieren) check; examine ⟨*accounts, books*⟩
(d) (vor einer Entscheidung) check ⟨*price*⟩; examine ⟨*offer*⟩; consider ⟨*application*⟩

Prüfer *der;* ~s, ~, **Prüferin** *die;* ~, ~nen (a) inspector; (Buch~) auditor
(b) (im Examen) examiner

Prüfling *der;* ~s, ~e examinee; [examination] candidate

Prüfung *die;* ~, ~en (a) examination; exam (coll.); **eine** ~ **machen** *od.* **ablegen** take an examination
(b) ▶ PRÜFEN B–D: examination; check; investigation; test; consideration

Prügel *Pl.* (Schläge) beating *sing.;* (als Strafe für Kinder) hiding (coll.)

Prügelei *die;* ~, ~en (ugs.) punch-up (coll.); fight

Prügel·knabe *der* whipping boy

prügeln 1 *tr.* (*auch itr.*) *V.* beat
2 *refl. V.* **sich** ~: fight; **sich mit jmdm.** [**um etw.**] ~: fight sb. [over *or* for sth.]

Prunk *der;* ~[e]s splendour; magnificence

Prunk-: ~**bau** *der; Pl.* ~~ten magnificent building; ~**stück** *das* showpiece

PS /peː'|ɛs/ *das,* ~, ~: *Abk.*
= **Pferdestärke** h.p.

Psalm *der;* ~s, ~en psalm

Psychiater *der;* ~s, ~, **Psychiaterin** *die;* ~, ~nen psychiatrist

Psychiatrie *die;* ~: psychiatry *no art.*

psychisch 1 *Adj.* psychological; mental ⟨*process, illness*⟩
2 *adv.* psychologically; ~ **gesund/krank sein** be mentally fit/ill

psycho-: Psycho- /psyˈçoː-/: ~**loge** *der;* ~~n, ~~n psychologist; ~**logie** *die;* ~~: psychology; ~**login** *die;* ~~, ~~nen psychologist; ~**logisch** 1 *Adj.* psychological; 2 *adv.* psychologically; ~**path** *der;* ~~en, ~~en, ~**pathin** *die;* ~~, ~~nen psychopath

Psychose *die;* ~, ~n psychosis

psychotisch *Adj.* psychotic

pubertär *Adj.* pubertal

Pubertät *die;* ~: puberty

pubertieren *itr. V.* reach puberty; ~d pubescent

publik *Adj.* ~ **sein/werden** be/become public knowledge

Publikum *das;* ~s (a) (Zuschauer, Zuhörer) audience; (bei Sportveranstaltungen) crowd
(b) (Kreis von Interessierten) public; (eines Schriftstellers) readership

---

*old spelling - see note on page xiv

(c) (Besucher) clientele

Publikums-: ~erfolg der success with the public; **~liebling** der idol of the public; **~sport** der spectator sport

publizieren tr. (auch itr.) V. publish

Publizität die; ~: publicity

Pudding der; ~s, ~e od. ~s thick, usually flavoured, milk-based dessert; ≈ blancmange

Pudel der; ~s, ~: poodle

Puder der; ~s, ~: powder

Puder·dose die powder compact

pudern tr. V. powder

Puder·zucker der icing sugar (Brit.); confectioners' sugar (Amer.)

Puff¹ der; ~[e]s, Püffe (ugs.) **(a)** (Stoß) thump; (leichter/kräftiger Stoß mit dem Ellenbogen) nudge/dig
(b) (Knall) bang

Puff² der od. das; ~s, ~s (salopp: Bordell) knocking shop (Brit. sl.); brothel

puffen (ugs.) tr. V.: ▶ PUFF¹ A: thump; nudge; dig

Puff·reis der puffed rice

Pulli der; ~s, ~s (ugs.), **Pullover** der; ~s, ~: pullover; sweater

Pullunder der; ~s, ~: slipover

Puls der; ~es, ~e pulse

Puls·ader die artery

Pult das; ~[e]s, ~e desk; (Lese~) lectern

Pulver das; ~s, ~: powder

pulverisieren tr. V. pulverize; powder

Pulver·kaffee der instant coffee

pumm[e]lig Adj. (ugs.) chubby

Pumpe die; ~, ~n pump

pumpen tr., itr. V. (a) (auch fig.) pump
(b) (salopp) ▶ LEIHEN A, B

Pump-: ~spray das pump spray; **~zerstäuber** der pump-action atomizer

Punkt der; ~[e]s, ~e **(a)** (Tupfen) dot; (größer) spot
(b) (Satzzeichen) full stop
(c) (I-Punkt) dot
(d) (Stelle) point; **ein schwacher/wunder ~** (fig.) a weak/sore point
(e) (Gegenstand, Thema, Abschnitt) point; (einer Tagesordnung) item
(f) (Bewertungs~) point; (bei einer Prüfung) mark
(g) ~ 12 Uhr at 12 o'clock on the dot

pünktlich 1 Adj. punctual
2 adv. punctually; on time

Pünktlichkeit die; ~: punctuality

Punsch der; ~[e]s, ~e od. Pünsche punch

Pupille die; ~, ~n pupil

Puppe die; ~, ~n **(a)** doll[y]
(b) (Marionette) puppet; marionette

Puppen-: ~stube die doll's house; dollhouse (Amer.); **~wagen** der doll's pram

pur Adj. **(a)** (rein) pure
(b) (unvermischt) neat ‹whisky etc.›; straight

Püree das; ~s, ~s **(a)** purée
(b) ▶ KARTOFFELBREI

pürieren tr. V. (Kochk.) purée ‹potatoes, apples, etc.›; (zerstampfen) mash

Purpur der; ~s crimson

purzeln itr. V.; mit sein (fam.) tumble

pushen tr. V. **(a)** (Drogenjargon) push
(b) (Journalistenjargon) push

Puste die; ~ (salopp) puff; breath

Pustel die; ~, ~n pimple; pustule (Med.)

pusten (ugs.) tr., itr. V. blow

Pute die; ~, ~n turkey hen; (als Braten) turkey

Puter der; ~s, ~: turkeycock; (als Braten) turkey

Putsch der; ~[e]s, ~e putsch; coup [d'état]

putschen itr. V. organize a putsch or coup

Putsch·versuch der attempted putsch or coup

Putz der; ~es plaster; (für Außenmauern) rendering

putzen tr. V. **(a)** (blank reiben) polish
(b) (säubern) clean; groom ‹horse›; [sich (Dat.)] die Zähne/die Nase ~: clean or brush one's teeth/blow one's nose
(c) auch itr. (sauber machen) clean ‹room, shop, etc.›; **~ gehen** work as a cleaner
(d) (vorbereiten) wash and prepare ‹vegetables›

Putz-: ~fimmel der (ugs. abwertend) mania for cleaning; **~frau** die cleaner

putzig Adj. (ugs.) (entzückend) sweet; cute (Amer.); (possierlich) funny; comical

Putz-: ~lappen der [cleaning] rag; cloth; **~leute** Pl. cleaners; **~mann** der cleaner; **~mittel** das cleaning agent; **~tuch** das; Pl. **~tücher** cloth; (Lappen) [cleaning] rag

puzzeln /'pʊzln/ itr. V. do jigsaw puzzles/a jigsaw [puzzle]

Puzzle /'pʊzl/ das; ~s, ~s, **Puzzlespiel** das jigsaw [puzzle]

Pyjama /py'dʒaːma/ der (österr., schweiz. auch: das); ~s, ~s pyjamas pl.

Pyramide die; ~, ~n pyramid

pyramiden·förmig Adj. pyramidal; pyramid-shaped

Python der; ~s, ~s od. ~en, **Python·schlange** die python

p

Qq

q, Q /kuː/ *das;* ~, ~: q/Q
Quacksalber *der;* ~s, ~,
  Quacksalberin *die;* ~, ~nen (abwertend)
  quack [doctor]
Quader *der;* ~s, ~ *od.* (österr.:) ~n **(a)**
  (Steinblock) ashlar block; [rectangular] block
  of stone
  (b) (Geom.) rectangular parallelepiped;
  cuboid
Quadrat *das;* ~[e]s, ~e square
quadratisch *Adj.* square
Quadrat-: ~**meter** *der od. das* square
  metre; ~**wurzel** *die* (Math.) square root (**aus**
  of); ~**zahl** *die* square number
quaken *itr. V.* ‹*duck*› quack; ‹*frog*› croak
Qual *die;* ~, ~en **(a)** torment
  (b) (Schmerzen) agony; ~en pain *sing.;* agony
  sing.; (seelisch) torment *sing.*
quälen *tr. V.* **(a)** torment ‹*person, animal*›;
  be cruel to ‹*animal*›; (foltern) torture
  (b) (plagen) ‹*cough etc.*› plague; (belästigen)
  pester
Quälerei *die;* ~, ~en **(a)** torment; (Folter)
  torture; (Grausamkeit) cruelty
  (b) (das Belästigen) pestering
Qualifikation *die;* ~, ~en **(a)** (Ausbildung)
  qualifications *pl.*
  (b) (Sport) qualification
qualifizieren *refl. V.* **(a)** gain
  qualifications
  (b) (Sport) qualify
qualifiziert *Adj.* **(a)** ‹*work, post*› requiring
  particular qualifications
  (b) (sachkundig) competent; skilled ‹*work*›
Qualität *die;* ~, ~en quality
qualitativ ① *Adj.* qualitative; ‹*difference,
  change*› in quality
  ② *adv.* with regard to quality
Qualitäts·erzeugnis *das* quality product
Qualle *die;* ~, ~n jellyfish
Qualm *der;* ~[e]s [thick] smoke
qualmen *itr. V.* **(a)** give off clouds of [thick]
  smoke
  (b) (ugs.: rauchen) puff away
qualmig *Adj.* (ugs.) thick with smoke
  postpos.; smoke-filled
qual·voll ① *Adj.* agonizing
  ② *adv.* agonizingly
Quantität *die;* ~, ~en quantity
quantitativ ① *Adj.* quantitative
  ② *adv.* quantitatively
Quantum *das;* ~s, **Quanten** quota (**an** +
  Dat. of); (Dosis) dose

Quarantäne /karan'tɛːnə/ *die;* ~, ~n
  quarantine
Quark *der;* ~s quark
Quark·speise *die* quark dish
Quartal *das;* ~s, ~e quarter [of the year]
Quartett *das;* ~[e]s, ~e **(a)** quartet
  (b) (Spiel) ≈ Happy Families; (Satz von vier
  Karten) set [of four]
Quartier *das;* ~s, ~e accommodation *no
  indef. art.;* accommodations *pl.* (Amer.); place
  to stay; (Mil.) quarters *pl.*
Quarz *der;* ~es, ~e quartz
Quarz·uhr *die* quartz clock; (Armbanduhr)
  quartz watch
quasi *Adv.* [so] ~: more or less; (so gut wie)
  as good as
quasseln (ugs.) ① *itr. V.* chatter; rabbit on
  (Brit. sl.) (**von** about)
  ② *tr. V.* spout, babble ‹*nonsense*›
Quaste *die;* ~, ~n tassel
Quatsch *der;* ~[e]s (ugs.) **(a)** (Äußerung)
  rubbish
  (b) (Handlung) nonsense; (Unfug) messing
  about; **lass den** ~: stop that nonsense
quatschen (ugs.) ① *itr. V.* **(a)** (dumm reden)
  rabbit on (Brit. coll.)
  (b) (klatschen) gossip; **es wird so viel
  gequatscht** there is so much gossip
  (c) (sich unterhalten) [have a] chat *or* (coll.)
  natter
  ② *tr. V.* (äußern) spout ‹*nonsense, rubbish*›
Quatsch·kopf *der* (salopp) stupid
  chatterbox; (Schwätzer, Schwafler) windbag
Queck·silber *das* mercury
Quell·bewölkung *die* (Met.) cumulus
  clouds *pl.*
Quelle *die;* ~, ~n spring; (eines Flusses) fig.)
  source
quellen *unr. itr. V.; mit sein* **(a)** ‹*liquid*›
  gush, stream; (aus der Erde) well up; ‹*smoke*›
  billow
  (b) (sich ausdehnen) swell [up]
Quell·wasser *das; Pl.* ~ *od.* Quell·wässer
  spring water
quengeln *itr. V.* (*auch tr.*) *V.* (ugs.) **(a)** (weinen)
  ‹*baby*› whimper, (coll.) grizzle
  (b) (drängen) nag
  (c) (nörgeln) carp
quer *Adv.* sideways; (schräg) diagonally;
  (rechtwinklig) at right angles; ~ **durch/über**
  (+ *Akk.*) straight through/across
Quer-: ~**achse** *die* transverse axis;
  ~**denker** *der,* ~**denkerin** *die* lateral
  thinker

---
*alte Schreibung - vgl. Hinweis auf S. xiv

Quere *die* jmdm. in die ~ kommen bump into sb. (coll.); (fig.: jmdn. behindern) get in sb.'s way (coll.)

quer-, Quer-: ~**flöte** *die* transverse flute; ~**format** *das* landscape format; ~**kopf** *der* (ugs.) awkward cuss (coll.); (komischer Kauz) oddball (coll.); ~**köpfig** *Adj.* awkward; perverse; ~**schläger** *der* deflected shot; ricochet; ~**schnitt** *der* (auch fig.) cross section; ~**schnitt[s]·gelähmt** *Adj.* (Med.) paraplegic; ~**straße** *die* intersecting road; ~**treiber** *der;* ~~s, ~~, ~**treiberin** *die;* ~~, ~~**nen** (ugs. abwertend) troublemaker

Querulant *der;* ~en, ~en, **Querulantin** *die;* ~, ~**nen** (abwertend) malcontent

quetschen *tr. V.* crush; sich (*Dat.*) die Hand ~: get one's hand caught

Quetschung *die;* ~, ~en bruise; contusion (Med.)

quietschen *itr. V.* squeak; ⟨brakes, tyres⟩ squeal, screech; (ugs.) ⟨person⟩ squeal, shriek

Quirl *der;* ~[e]s, ~e *long-handled blender with a star-shaped head*

quirlig *Adj.* lively; (flink) nimble

quitt *Adj.* (ugs.) quits

Quitte *die;* ~, ~n quince

quittieren *tr. V.* (a) *auch itr.* acknowledge, confirm ⟨receipt, condition⟩; give a receipt for ⟨sum, invoice⟩
(b) etw. mit etw. ~: react *or* respond to sth. with sth.

Quittung *die;* ~, ~en (a) receipt
(b) (fig.) come-uppance (coll.)

Quiz /kvɪs/ *das;* ~, ~: quiz

quoll *1. u. 3. Pers. Sg. Prät. v.* QUELLEN

Quote *die;* ~, ~n proportion

Quoten·regelung *die: requirement that women should be adequately represented*

Quotient *der;* ~en, ~en (Math.) quotient (aus of)

∙ ∙

Rr

∙ ∙

r, R /ɛr/ *das;* ~, ~: r/R

Rabatt *der;* ~[e]s, ~e discount

Rabatte *die;* ~, ~n border

Rabbi *der;* ~[s], ~nen *od.* ~s (a) (Titel) Rabbi
(b) (Person) rabbi

Rabbiner *der;* ~s, ~: rabbi

Rabe *der;* ~n, ~n raven

Rabenmutter *die; Pl.* Rabenmütter (abwertend) uncaring [brute of a] mother

rabiat ⊡ *Adj.* violent; brutal; ruthless ⟨methods⟩
⊡ *adv.* (gewalttätig) violently; brutally

Rache *die;* ~: revenge; [an jmdm.] ~ nehmen take revenge [on sb.]

Rache·akt *der* (geh.) act of revenge, reprisal (*Gen.* by, on the part of)

Rachen *der;* ~s, ~ (a) (Schlund) pharynx (Anat.)
(b) (Maul) mouth; maw (literary); (fig.) jaws *pl.*

rächen ⊡ *tr. V.* avenge ⟨person, crime⟩; take revenge for ⟨insult, crime⟩
⊡ *refl. V.* (a) take one's revenge
(b) ⟨mistake etc.⟩ take its/their toll

Rachitis *die;* ~ (Med.) rickets *sing.*

Rach·sucht *die* (geh.) lust for revenge

rach·süchtig (geh.) ⊡ *Adj.* vengeful
⊡ *adv.* vengefully

Rad *das;* ~es, Räder (a) wheel; das fünfte ~ am Wagen sein (fig. ugs.) be superfluous; ein ~ abhaben (fig. ugs.) have a screw loose (coll.)
(b) (Fahrrad) bicycle; bike (coll.); ~ fahren cycle; ride a bicycle *or* (coll.) bike

Radar *der od. das;* ~s radar

Radar-: ~**falle** *die* (ugs.) [radar] speed trap; ~**kontrolle** *die* [radar] speed check; ~**schirm** *der* radar screen

Rad·dampfer *der* paddle steamer

radeln *itr. V.; mit sein* (ugs., bes. südd.) cycle

Rädels·führer *der,* **Rädels·führerin** *die* (abwertend) ringleader

rad-, Rad-: *~|**fahren** ▶ RAD B; ~**fahrer** *der,* ~**fahrerin** *die* cyclist

Radien ▶ RADIUS

radieren *tr. V.* (auch itr.) V. erase

Radier·gummi *der* rubber [eraser]

Radierung *die;* ~, ~en (Grafik) etching

Radieschen *das;* ~s, ~: radish

radikal ⊡ *Adj.* radical; drastic ⟨measure, method, cure⟩
⊡ *adv.* radically; (vollständig) totally

Radikalismus *der;* ~: radicalism

Radikalität *die;* ~: radicalness; radical nature

Radio *das* (südd., schweiz. auch: *der*); ~s, ~s radio; ~ hören listen to the radio

radio-, Radio-: ~**aktiv** /----'-/ ⊡ *Adj.* radioactive; ⊡ *adv.* radioactively; ~**aktivität** /-----'-/ *die* radioactivity; ~**sender** *der* radio station; ~**wecker** *der* radio alarm clock

Radius *der;* ~, Radien radius

Rad-: ~**kappe** *die* hubcap; ~**lager** *das* wheel bearing

Radler *der;* ~s, ~: (a) cyclist
(b) (bes. südd.: Getränk) shandy

Radlerin *die;* ~, ~nen cyclist

Rad-: ~**rennbahn** *die* cycle racing track; ~**rennen** *das* cycle race; (Sport) cycle racing; ~**sport** *der* cycling *no def. art.;* ~**tour** *die* cycling tour; ~**weg** *der* cycle path *or* track

raffen *tr. V.* (a) snatch; rake in (coll.) ⟨money⟩; etw. [an sich] ~: seize sth.; (eilig) snatch sth.
(b) gather ⟨material, curtain⟩

Raffinerie *die;* ~, ~n refinery

Raffinesse *die;* ~, ~n (a) (Schlauheit) guile; ingenuity
(b) (Finesse) refinement

raffiniert ⓵ *Adj.* (a) ingenious ⟨plan, design⟩; (verfeinert) refined, subtle ⟨colour, scheme, effect⟩; sophisticated ⟨dish, cut (of clothes)⟩
(b) (gerissen) cunning ⟨person, trick⟩
⓶ *adv.* (a) ingeniously; (verfeinert) with great refinement/sophistication
(b) (gerissen) cunningly

Raffiniertheit *die;* ~ (a) (Klugheit) ingenuity; (Verfeinerung) refinement; sophistication
(b) (Gerissenheit) cunning

Raft *das;* ~s, ~s raft

raften *itr. V.* raft

Rafting *das;* ~s rafting

Rage /'ra:ʒə/ *die;* ~ (ugs.) fury

ragen *itr. V.* (a) (vertikal) rise [up]; ⟨mountains⟩ tower up
(b) (horizontal) project, stick out (in + Akk. into; über + Akk. over)

Ragout /ra'gu:/ *das;* ~s, ~s ragout

Rahm *der;* ~[e]s cream

rahmen *tr. V.* frame

Rahmen *der;* ~s, ~ (a) frame; (Fahrgestell) chassis
(b) (fig.) framework

Rakete *die;* ~, ~n rocket; (Lenkflugkörper) missile

rammen *tr. V.* ram

Rampe *die;* ~, ~n (a) (Lade~) [loading] platform
(b) (schiefe Fläche) ramp

Rampen·licht *das;* im ~ [der Öffentlichkeit] stehen be in the limelight

Ramsch *der;* ~[e]s, ~e (ugs.) (a) (Ware) trashy goods *pl.;*
(b) (Kram) junk

ran *Adv.* (ugs.) (a) ▶ HERAN;
(b) (fang[t] an) off you go; (fangen wir an) let's go
(c) (greif[t] an) go at him/them!

Rand *der;* ~[e]s, Ränder (a) edge; (Einfassung) border; (Hut~) brim; (Brillen~, Gefäß~, Krater~) rim; (eines Abgrunds) brink; (auf einem Schriftstück) margin; (Weg~) verge; (Stadt~) outskirts *pl.;*
(b) (Schmutz~) mark; (rund) ring

randalieren *itr. V.* riot

Randalierer *der;* ~s, ~,
Randaliererin *die;* ~, ~nen hooligan

rand-, Rand-: ~**bemerkung** *die* marginal note *or* comment; ~**gruppe** *die* (Soziol.) fringe *or* marginal group; ~**stein** *der* kerb; ~**voll** *Adj.* ⟨glass etc.⟩ full to the brim

rang *1. u. 3. Pers. Sg. Prät. v.* RINGEN

Rang *der;* ~[e]s, Ränge (a) rank; (in der Gesellschaft) status
(b) (im Theater) circle; **erster** ~: dress circle; **zweiter** ~: upper circle; **dritter** ~: gallery

rangieren /raŋ'ʒi:rən/ *tr. V.* shunt ⟨trucks etc.⟩; switch ⟨cars⟩ (Amer.)

Rang-: ~**liste** *die* ranking list; **Nummer eins der internationalen** ~**liste** number one in the world rankings; ~**ordnung** *die* order of precedence; (Verhaltensf.) pecking order

Ranke *die;* ~, ~n (Bot.) tendril

ranken *refl. V.* climb, grow (an + Dat. up, über + Akk. over)

Ranking /'ræŋkɪŋ/ *das;* ~s ranking

rann *1. u. 3. Pers. Sg. Prät. v.* RINNEN

rannte *1. u. 3. Pers. Sg. Prät. v.* RENNEN

Ranzen *der;* ~s, ~: satchel

ranzig *Adj.* rancid

Rap /ræp/ *der;* ~[s], ~s rap

Rappe *der;* ~n, ~n black horse

rappen /'ræpn̩/ *itr. V.* rap

Rappen *der;* ~s, ~: [Swiss] centime

Rapper /'ræpɐ/ *der;* ~s, ~, **Rapperin** *die;* ~, ~nen rapper

Raps *der;* ~es (Bot.) rape

rar *Adj.* scarce; (selten) rare

Rarität *die;* ~, ~en rarity

rasant (ugs.) ⓵ *Adj.* tremendously fast (coll.) ⟨car, horse, etc.⟩
⓶ *adv.* at terrific speed (coll.)

rasch ⓵ *Adj.* quick; speedy, swift ⟨end, action, decision, progress⟩
⓶ *adv.* quickly; ⟨decide, end, proceed⟩ swiftly, rapidly

rascheln *itr. V.* rustle; ⟨mouse etc.⟩ make a rustling noise

rasen *itr. V.* (a) *mit sein* (ugs.: eilen) dash *or* rush [along]; (fahren) tear *or* race along; (fig.) ⟨pulse⟩ race
(b) (toben) ⟨person⟩ rage

Rasen *der;* ~s, ~: grass *no indef. art.;* (gepflegte Rasenfläche) lawn

rasend ⓵ *Adj.* (a) (sehr schnell) breakneck *attrib.* ⟨speed⟩
(b) (tobend) raging
(c) (heftig) violent
⓶ *adv.* (ugs.) incredibly (coll.)

Rasen·mäher *der;* ~s, ~: lawn-mower

Raser *der;* ~s, ~ (ugs. abwertend) speed merchant (coll.); (rücksichtslos) road hog

Raserei *die;* ~, ~en (ugs.) tearing along *no art.*

Raserin *die*; ~, ~nen ▶ RASER

Rasier·apparat *der* [safety] razor; (elektrisch) electric shaver

rasieren *tr. V.* shave; **sich** ~: shave; **sich nass/trocken/elektrisch** ~: have a wet shave/have a dry shave/use an electric shaver

Rasierer *der;* ~s, ~ (ugs.) [electric] shaver

Rasier·: ~**klinge** *die* razor blade; ~**messer** *das* cutthroat razor; ~**pinsel** *der* shaving brush; ~**schaum** *der* shaving foam; ~**seife** *die* shaving soap; ~**wasser** *das* aftershave; (vor der Rasur) pre-shave lotion

Räson /rɛˈzɔŋ/ *die* **zur** ~ **kommen** come to one's senses; **jmdn. zur** ~ **bringen** make sb. see reason

Rasse *die;* ~, ~n (a) breed
(b) (Menschen~) race

Rassel *die;* ~, ~n rattle

rasseln *itr. V.* rattle

Rassen·: ~**hass**, *~**haß** *der* racial hatred *no art.;* ~**krawall** *der* race riot; ~**trennung** *die* racial segregation *no art.*

Rassismus *der;* ~: racism; racialism

Rassist *der;* ~en, ~en, **Rassistin** *die;* ~, ~nen racist; racialist

rassistisch *Adj.* racist; racialist

Rast *die;* ~, ~en rest; ~ **machen** stop for a break

rasten *itr. V.* rest; take a rest *or* break

Raster *der;* ~s, ~ (a) (Druckw.) screen
(b) (fig.) [conceptual] framework; set pattern

Rast·: ~**haus** *das* roadside café; (an der Autobahn) motorway restaurant; ~**hof** *der* [motorway] motel [and service area]; ~**platz** *der* (a) place to rest; (b) (an Autobahnen) parking place (*with benches and WCs*); picnic area; ~**stätte** *die* service area

Rasur *die;* ~, ~en shave

Rat *der;* ~[e]s, **Räte** (a) advice; **ein** ~: a word of advice
(b) (Gremium) council

rät *3. Pers. Sg. Präsens v.* RATEN

Rate *die;* ~, ~n (a) (Teilbetrag) instalment; **etw. auf** ~n **kaufen** buy sth. by instalments *or* (Brit.) on hire purchase *or* (Amer.) on the installment plan
(b) (Statistik) rate

raten ① *unr. itr. V.* (a) **jmdm.** ~: advise sb.
(b) (schätzen) guess
② *tr. V.* (a) **jmdm.** ~, **etw. zu tun** advise sb. to do sth.
(b) (erraten) guess

Raten·zahlung *die* payment by instalments

Rat·haus *das* town hall

Ratifizierung *die;* ~, ~en ratification

Rätin *die;* ~, ~nen councillor

Ration *die;* ~, ~en ration

rational *Adj.* rational

rationalisieren *tr., itr. V.* rationalize

rationell ① *Adj.* efficient; (wirtschaftlich) economic
② *adv.* efficiently; (wirtschaftlich) economically

rationieren *tr. V.* ration

rat·los ① *Adj.* baffled; helpless ⟨look⟩
② *adv.* helplessly

Rat·losigkeit *die;* ~: helplessness

ratsam *Adj.* advisable

Ratschlag *der* [piece of] advice

Rätsel *das;* ~s, ~ (a) riddle; (Bilder~, Kreuzwort~ usw.) puzzle
(b) (Geheimnis) mystery

rätselhaft ① *Adj.* mysterious; (unergründlich) enigmatic
② *adv.* mysteriously; (unergründlich) enigmatically

rätseln *itr. V.* puzzle, rack one's brains (**über** + *Akk.* over); ~, **wer** .../**ob** ...: try to work out who .../whether ...

Ratte *die;* ~, ~n (auch fig.) rat

rau ① *Adj.* (a) (nicht glatt) rough
(b) (nicht mild) harsh, raw ⟨climate, winter⟩; raw ⟨wind⟩
(c) (kratzig) husky, hoarse ⟨voice⟩
(d) (entzündet) sore ⟨throat⟩
(e) (nicht feinfühlig) rough; harsh ⟨words, tone⟩
② *adv.* (a) (kratzig) ⟨speak etc.⟩ huskily, hoarsely
(b) (nicht feinfühlig) roughly

Raub *der;* ~[e]s (a) robbery
(b) (Beute) stolen goods *pl.*

Raub·bau *der* overexploitation (**an** + *Dat.* of); ~ **an etw.** (*Dat.*) **treiben** over-exploit sth.

rauben *tr. V.* steal; kidnap ⟨person⟩; **jmdm. etw.** ~: rob sb. of sth.; (geh.: wegnehmen) deprive sb. of sth.

Räuber *der;* ~s, ~, **Räuberin** *die;* ~, ~nen robber

Raub·: ~**fisch** *der* predatory fish; ~**kopie** *die* pirated copy; ~**mord** *der* (Rechtsw.) murder (**an** + *Dat.* of) in the course of a robbery *or* with robbery as motive; ~**tier** *das* predator; ~**überfall** *der* robbery (**auf** + *Akk.* of); ~**vogel** *der* bird of prey

Rauch *der;* ~[e]s smoke

rauchen ① *itr. V.* smoke
② *tr. (auch itr.)* *V.* smoke ⟨cigarette, pipe, etc.⟩; „Rauchen verboten" 'No smoking'

Raucher *der;* ~s, ~: smoker

Raucher·: ~**abteil** *das* smoking compartment; smoker; ~**husten** *der* smoker's cough

Raucherin *die;* ~, ~nen smoker

räuchern *tr. V.* smoke ⟨meat, fish⟩

rauch·frei *Adj.* smoke-free ⋯⟶

rauchig *Adj.* smoky; husky ‹*voice*›
Rauch-: ∼**melder** *der* smoke detector;
∼**schwaden** *der* cloud of smoke;
∼**verbot** *das* ban on smoking; ∼**wolke**
die cloud of smoke
räudig *Adj.* mangy
rauf *Adv.* (ugs.) up; ∼ **mit euch!** up you go!;
s. auch HERAUF; HINAUF
Rau·faser·tapete *die* woodchip wallpaper
raufen ① *itr., refl. V.* fight
② *tr. V.* **sich** (*Dat.*) **die Haare/den Bart** ∼:
tear one's hair/at one's beard
Rauferei *die;* ∼, ∼**en** fight
****rauh** *usw.* ▶ RAU *usw.*
Raum *der;* ∼**[e]s, Räume (a)** (Wohn∼, Nutz∼)
room
(b) (Gebiet) area; region
(c) (Platz) room; space
räumen *tr. V.* **(a)** clear [away]; clear ‹*snow*›
(b) (an einen Ort) clear; move
(c) (freimachen) clear ‹*street, building,
warehouse, stocks, etc.*›
(d) (verlassen) vacate
Raum·fahrt *die;* ∼: space travel
räumlich ① *Adj.* **(a)** spatial; **aus** ∼**en**
Gründen for reasons of space
(b) (dreidimensional) three-dimensional;
stereoscopic ‹*vision*›
② *adv.* **(a)** spatially
(b) (dreidimensional) three-dimensionally
Räumlichkeit *die;* ∼, ∼**en (a)** *Pl.* rooms
(b) (räumliche Wirkung) three-dimensionality
Raum-: ∼**schiff** *das* spaceship; ∼**sonde**
die space probe
Räumung *die;* ∼, ∼**en (a)** clearing
(b) (das Verlassen) vacation; vacating
(c) (wegen Gefahr) evacuation
(d) (eines Lagers) clearance
Räumungs·verkauf *der* (Kaufmannsspr.)
clearance sale
raunen *tr., itr. V.* (geh.) whisper
Raupe *die;* ∼, ∼**n** caterpillar
Rau·reif *der* hoar frost
raus *Adv.* (ugs.) out; ∼ **mit euch!** out you go!;
s. auch HERAUS; HINAUS
Rausch *der;* ∼**[e]s, Räusche (a)** state of
drunkenness
(b) (starkes Gefühl) transport; **der** ∼ **der
Geschwindigkeit** the exhilaration *or* thrill of
speed
rauschen *itr. V.* ‹*water, wind, torrent*›
rush; ‹*trees, leaves*› rustle; ‹*skirt, curtains,
silk*› swish; ‹*waterfall, strong wind*› roar;
‹*rain*› pour down
Rausch·gift *das* drug; narcotic; ∼ **nehmen**
take drugs; be on drugs
Rauschgift-: ∼**händler** *der,*
∼**händlerin** *die* drug trafficker; ∼**sucht**
die drug addiction

raus|fliegen *unr. itr. V.; mit sein* (ugs.) be
fired (coll.)
räuspern *refl. V.* clear one's throat
raus|schmeißen *unr. tr. V.* (ugs.) chuck
(coll.) ‹*objects*› out *or* away; give ‹*employee*›
the push (coll.) *or* sack (coll.); chuck (coll.) *or*
throw ‹*customer, drunk, tenant*› out (**aus** of)
Raute *die;* ∼, ∼**n** (Geom.) rhombus
Rave /reɪv/ *der;* ∼**s,** ∼**s** rave
Raver /'reɪvɐ/ *der;* ∼**s,** ∼, **Raverin** *die;* ∼,
∼**nen** raver
Razzia *die;* ∼, **Razzien** raid
reagieren *itr. V.* react (**auf** + *Akk.* to)
Reaktion *die;* ∼, ∼**en** reaction (**auf** + *Akk.*
to)
reaktionär *Adj.* reactionary
Reaktionär *der;* ∼**s,** ∼**e** reactionary
Reaktor *der;* ∼**s,** ∼**en** /-'to:rən/ reactor
real ① *Adj.* real
② *adv.* actually
realisieren *tr. V.* (geh.) realize
Realismus *der;* ∼: realism
Realist *der;* ∼**en,** ∼**en, Realistin** *die;* ∼,
∼**nen** realist
realistisch ① *Adj.* realistic
② *adv.* realistically
Realität *die;* ∼, ∼**en** reality
Real·schule *die* ≈ secondary modern
school (Brit. Hist.)
Rebe *die;* ∼, ∼**n (a)** vine shoot
(b) (Weinstock) [grape] vine
Rebell *der;* ∼**en,** ∼**en, Rebellin** *die;* ∼,
∼**nen** rebel
rebellieren *itr. V.* rebel (**gegen** against)
Rebellion *die;* ∼, ∼**en** rebellion
rebellisch *Adj.* rebellious
Reb-: ∼**huhn** *das* partridge; ∼**stock** *der*
vine
rechen *tr. V.* (bes. südd.) rake
Rechen *der;* ∼**s,** ∼ (bes. südd.) rake
Rechen-: ∼**fehler** *der* arithmetical error;
∼**maschine** *die* calculator
Rechenschaft *die;* ∼: account; **jmdn. für
etw. zur** ∼ **ziehen** call *or* bring sb. to account
for sth.
Rechenschafts·bericht *der* report
Recherche /re'ʃɛrʃə/ *die;* ∼, ∼**n (a)** (geh.)
investigation; enquiry
(b) (DV) search
recherchieren *itr., tr. V.* (geh.) investigate
rechnen ① *tr. V.* **(a) eine Aufgabe** ∼: work
out a problem
(b) (veranschlagen) reckon; estimate; **gut/rund
gerechnet** at a generous/rough estimate
(c) (berücksichtigen) take into account
(d) (einbeziehen) count
② *itr. V.* **(a)** do *or* make a calculation/
calculations; **gut/schlecht** ∼ **können** be good/
bad at figures
(b) (zählen) reckon
(c) (ugs.: berechnen) calculate; estimate

**alte Schreibung - vgl. Hinweis auf S. xiv

(d) (wirtschaften) budget carefully
(e) auf jmdn./etw. *od.* **mit jmdm./etw.** ∼: count on sb./sth.
(f) mit etw. ∼ (etw. einkalkulieren) reckon with sth.; (etw. erwarten) expect sth.

Rechnen *das;* ∼**s** arithmetic

Rechner *der;* ∼**s,** ∼: calculator; (Computer) computer

rechnerisch *Adj.* arithmetical

Rechnung *die;* ∼, ∼**en** **(a)** calculation
(b) (schriftliche Kosten∼) bill; invoice (Commerc.); **[jmdm.] etw. in** ∼ **stellen** charge [sb.] for sth.

recht ⟦1⟧ *Adj.* **(a)** (geeignet, richtig) right
(b) (gesetzmäßig, anständig) right; proper; ∼ **und billig** right and proper
(c) (wunschgemäß) **jmdm.** ∼ **sein** be all right with sb.
(d) (wirklich, echt) real
⟦2⟧ *adv.* **(a)** (geeignet) **du kommst gerade** ∼: you are just in time
(b) (richtig) correctly
(c) (gesetzmäßig, anständig) properly
(d) (wunschgemäß) **es jmdm.** ∼ **machen** please sb.
(e) (wirklich, echt) really
(f) (ziemlich) quite; rather; *s. auch* RECHT D

Recht *das;* ∼**[e]s,** ∼**e (a)** (Rechtsordnung) law
(b) (Rechtsanspruch) right; **sein** ∼ **fordern** *od.* **verlangen** demand one's rights
(c) (Berechtigung) right **(auf +** *Akk.* to); **gleiches** ∼ **für alle!** equal rights for all!; **im** ∼ **sein** be in the right; **zu** ∼: rightly
(d) ∼ **haben** be right; **jmdm.** ∼ **geben** admit that sb. is right

recht... *Adj.* **(a)** right; right[-hand] ⟨*edge*⟩
(b) (außen, sichtbar) right ⟨*side*⟩
(c) (in der Politik) right-wing

recht·fertigen *tr. V.* justify **(vor +** *Dat.* to)

Recht·fertigung *die* justification

rechtlich ⟦1⟧ *Adj.* legal
⟦2⟧ *adv.* legally

Rechtlichkeit *die;* ∼ *s.:* RECHTMÄSSIGKEIT

recht·los *Adj.* without rights *postpos.*

Rechtlosigkeit *die;* ∼: lack of rights

rechtmäßig ⟦1⟧ *Adj.* lawful; rightful; legitimate ⟨*claim*⟩
⟦2⟧ *adv.* lawfully; rightfully

Rechtmäßigkeit *die;* ∼: legality; (eines Anspruchs) legitimacy

rechts *Adv.* **(a)** on the right; **von** ∼: from the right
(b) (Politik) on the right wing

Rechts-: ∼**abbieger** *der,* ∼**abbiegerin** *die* (Verkehrsw.) motorist/cyclist/car *etc.* turning right; ∼**anwalt** *der,* ∼**anwältin** *die* lawyer; solicitor (Brit.); attorney (Amer.); (vor Gericht) barrister (Brit.); attorney[-at-law] (Amer.); advocate (Scot.); ∼**außen** /-'--/ *der;* ∼, ∼ (Ballspiele) right wing; outside right

recht-, Recht-: ∼**schaffen** ⟦1⟧ *Adj.*

honest; ⟦2⟧ *adv.* honestly;
∼**schreib·fehler** *der* spelling mistake;
∼**schreibung** *die* orthography

rechts-, Rechts-: ∼**empfinden** *das* sense of [what is] right and wrong;
∼**extremist** *der,* ∼**extremistin** *die* (Politik) right-wing extremist; ∼**händer** *der;* ∼∼**s,** ∼∼, ∼**händerin** *die;* ∼∼, ∼∼**nen** right-hander; ∼**kräftig** (Rechtsw.) ⟦1⟧ *Adj.* final [and absolute] ⟨*decision, verdict, etc.*⟩; ⟦2⟧ *adv.* **jmdn.** ∼**kräftig verurteilen** pass a final sentence on sb.; ∼**kurve** *die* right-hand bend

Recht·sprechung *die;* ∼, ∼**en** administration of justice; (eines Gerichts) jurisdiction

rechts-, Rechts-: ∼**radikal** (Politik) ⟦1⟧ *Adj.* radical right-wing; ⟦2⟧ *adv.* **eine** ∼**radikal orientierte Gruppe** a group with a radical right-wing orientation; ∼**radikale** *der/die* right-wing radical;
∼**radikalismus** *der* right-wing radicalism; ∼**staat** *der* [constitutional] state founded on the rule of law;
∼**staatlich** *Adj.* founded on the rule of law *postpos.;* ∼**verkehr** *der* driving *no art.* on the right; ∼**verletzung** *die* (Rechtsw.) infringement *or* violation of the law;
∼**widrig** ⟦1⟧ *Adj.* unlawful; ⟦2⟧ *adv.* unlawfully; ∼**widrigkeit** *die* **(a)** unlawfulness; **(b)** (Handlung) unlawful act

recht-: ∼**wink[e]lig** *Adj.* right-angled; ∼**zeitig** ⟦1⟧ *Adj.* timely; (pünktlich) punctual; ⟦2⟧ *adv.* in time; (pünktlich) on time

Reck *das;* ∼**[e]s,** ∼**e** *od.* ∼**s** horizontal bar

recken ⟦1⟧ *tr. V.* stretch
⟦2⟧ *refl. V.* stretch oneself

recyceln /ri'saɪ:kl̩n/ *tr. V.; 2. Part.* **recycelt** recycle

Recycling /ri'saɪ:klɪŋ/ *das;* ∼**s** recycling

Recycling·papier /ri'saɪ:klɪŋ-/ *das* recycled paper

Redakteur /redak'tø:ɐ̯/ *der;* ∼**s,** ∼**e,** **Redakteurin** *die;* ∼, ∼**nen** editor

Redaktion *die;* ∼, ∼**en (a)** (Redakteure) editorial staff
(b) (Büro) editorial department *or* office/offices *pl.*

redaktionell ⟦1⟧ *Adj.* editorial
⟦2⟧ *adv.* editorially

Rede *die;* ∼, ∼**n (a)** (Ansprache) address; speech; **eine** ∼ **halten** give *or* make a speech
(b) (Vortrag) rhetoric
(c) (Äußerung, Ansicht) **nicht der** ∼ **wert sein** be not worth mentioning; **jmdn. zur** ∼ **stellen** make someone explain himself/herself; **von jmdm./etw. ist die** ∼: there is some talk about sb./sth.; **es ist die** ∼ **davon, dass ...:** it is being said *or* people are saying that ...; **davon kann keine** ∼ **sein** it's out of the question

reden ⟦1⟧ *tr. V.* talk; **Unsinn** ∼: talk nonsense; **kein Wort** ∼: not say *or* speak a word ⋯⟶

2 *itr. V.* **(a)** (sprechen) talk; speak; **viel/wenig** ~: talk a lot (coll.)/not talk much
(b) (sich äußern, eine Rede halten) speak; **gut ~ können** be a good speaker
(c) (sich unterhalten) talk; **mit jmdm./über jmdn.** ~: talk to/about sb.

Redens·art *die* **(a)** *expression;* (Sprichwort) saying
(b) *Pl.* (Phrase) empty *or* meaningless words

Rede·wendung *die* (Sprachw.) idiom

redlich **1** *Adj.* honest
2 *adv.* honestly

Redlichkeit *die;* ~: honesty

Redner *der;* ~s, ~, **Rednerin** *die* ~, ~nen **(a)** speaker
(b) (Rhetoriker) orator

red·selig *Adj.* talkative

reduzieren **1** *tr. V.* reduce (**auf** + *Akk.* to)
2 *refl. V.* decrease; diminish

Reeder *der;* ~s, ~: shipowner

Reederei *die;* ~, ~en shipping firm

Reederin *die;* ~, ~nen shipowner

reell **1** *Adj.* honest, straight ⟨*person, deal, etc.*⟩; sound, solid ⟨*business, firm, etc.*⟩; straight ⟨*offer*⟩
2 *adv.* honestly

Reet *das;* ~s (nordd.) reeds *pl.*

Referat *das;* ~[e]s, ~e **(a)** paper
(b) (kurzer schriftlicher Bericht) report

Referendar *der;* ~s, ~e, **Referendarin** *die;* ~, ~nen *candidate for a higher civil-service post who has passed the first state examination and is undergoing in-service training*

Referenz *die;* ~, ~en (Person, Stelle) referee; **jmdn. als** ~ **angeben** give sb.'s name *or* give sb. as a reference

referieren *itr. V.* **über etw.** (*Akk.*) ~: present a paper on sth.; (zusammenfassend) give a report on sth.

reflektieren *tr. V.* reflect

Reflex *der;* ~es, ~e reflex

Reflexion *die;* ~, ~en reflection

Reflexiv·pronomen *das* (Sprachw.) reflexive pronoun

Reform *die;* ~, ~en reform

Reformation *die;* ~ (hist.) Reformation

Reformations·fest *das* Reformation Day

Reform·haus *das* health food shop

reformieren *tr. V.* reform

Refrain /rə'frɛː/ *der;* ~s, ~s chorus

Regal *das;* ~s, ~e [set *sing.* of] shelves *pl.*

rege **1** *Adj.* **(a)** (betriebsam) busy ⟨*traffic*⟩; brisk ⟨*demand, trade, business, etc.*⟩
(b) (lebhaft) lively; keen ⟨*interest*⟩
2 *adv.* **(a)** (betriebsam) actively
(b) (lebhaft) actively

Regel *die;* ~, ~n **(a)** rule; **nach allen** ~n **der Kunst** (fig.) well and truly

(b) rule; custom; **die** ~ **sein** be the rule; **in der** *od.* **aller** ~: as a rule
(c) (Menstruation) period

regel·mäßig **1** *Adj.* regular
2 *adv.* regularly

Regel·mäßigkeit *die* regularity

regeln **1** *tr. V.* **(a)** settle ⟨*matter, question, etc.*⟩; put ⟨*finances, affairs, etc.*⟩ in order
(b) (einstellen, regulieren) regulate; (steuern) control
2 *refl. V.* take care of itself

regelrecht **1** *Adj.* (ugs.: richtiggehend) proper (coll.); real; real ⟨*shock*⟩; real, absolute ⟨*scandal*⟩; complete, utter ⟨*flop, disaster*⟩; **ich hatte** ~e **Angst** I was really afraid
2 *adv.* (ugs.: richtiggehend) really

Regelung *die;* ~, ~en **(a)** ▶ REGELN 1A, B: settlement; putting in order; regulation; control
(b) (Vorschrift) regulation

regen **1** *tr. V.* (geh.) move
2 *refl. V.* **(a)** (sich bewegen) move
(b) (geh.) ⟨*hope, doubt, desire, conscience*⟩ stir

Regen *der;* ~s, ~ **(a)** rain; **vom** *od.* **aus dem** ~ **in die Traufe kommen** (fig.) jump out of the frying pan into the fire
(b) (fig.) shower

Regen-: ~**bogen** *der* rainbow; ~**mantel** *der* raincoat; mackintosh; ~**schirm** *der* umbrella; ~**tag** *der* rainy day; ~**wald** *der* (Geogr.) rainforest; ~**wasser** *das* rainwater; ~**wetter** *das* wet weather; ~**wolke** *die* rain cloud; ~**wurm** *der* earthworm; ~**zeit** *die* rainy season

Regie /re'ʒiː/ *die;* ~ **(a)** (Theater, Film, Ferns., Rundf.) direction; **die** ~ **bei etw. haben** *od.* **führen** direct sth.
(b) (Leitung, Verwaltung) management

regieren **1** *itr. V.* rule (**über** + *Akk.* over); ⟨*party, administration*⟩ govern
2 *tr. V.* rule; govern; ⟨*monarch*⟩ reign over

Regierung *die;* ~, ~en **(a)** (Herrschaft) rule; (eines Monarchen) reign
(b) (Kabinett) government

Regierungs·sitz *der* seat of government

Regiment *das;* ~[e]s, ~e *od.* ~er **(a)** *Pl.* ~e (Herrschaft) rule
(b) *Pl.* ~er (Milit.) regiment

Region *die;* ~, ~en region

regional **1** *Adj.* regional
2 *adv.* regionally

Regisseur /reʒɪ'søːɐ̯/ *der;* ~s, ~e, **Regisseurin** *die;* ~, ~nen director

Register *das;* ~s, ~ **(a)** index
(b) (amtliche Liste) register
(c) (Musik) (bei Instrumenten) register; (Orgel~) stop

registrieren *tr. V.* **(a)** register
(b) (bewusst wahrnehmen) note; register

Regler *der;* ~s, ~ (Technik) regulator; (Kybernetik) control

reg·los *Adj.* motionless

---

*old spelling - see note on page xiv

regnen 1 *itr., tr. V. (unpers.)* rain; **es regnet** it is raining
2 *itr. V.; mit sein* (fig.) rain down
regnerisch *Adj.* rainy
regulär *Adj.* **(a)** proper; normal ⟨*working hours*⟩
(b) (normal, üblich) normal
regulieren *tr. V.* regulate
Regulierung *die; ~, ~en* regulation
Regung *die; ~, ~en* (geh.: Gefühl) stirring
regungs·los *Adj.* motionless
Reh *das; ~[e]s, ~e* roe deer
Rehabilitation *die; ~, ~en* rehabilitation
rehabilitieren *tr. V.* rehabilitate
Reh-: ~**bock** *der* roebuck; ~**kitz** *das* fawn [of a/the roe deer]
Reibach *der; ~s* (ugs.) profits *pl.;* **einen [kräftigen] ~ machen** make a killing (coll.)
Reibe *die; ~, ~n,* **Reib·eisen** *das* grater
reiben 1 *unr. tr. V.* **(a)** rub
(b) (zerkleinern) grate
2 *unr. itr. V.* rub **(an +** *Dat.* on)
Reib·fläche *die* striking surface (*of matchbox*)
Reibung *die; ~, ~en* (Physik, fig.) friction
reibungs·los 1 *Adj.* smooth
2 *adv.* smoothly
reich 1 *Adj.* **(a)** (vermögend) rich
(b) (prächtig) costly ⟨*goods, gifts*⟩; rich ⟨*décor, finery*⟩
(c) (üppig) rich; abundant ⟨*harvest*⟩; abundant ⟨*mineral resources*⟩; **~ an etw.** (*Dat.*) **sein** be rich in sth.
(d) (vielfältig) rich ⟨*collection, possibilities*⟩; wide, large ⟨*selection, choice*⟩; wide ⟨*knowledge, experience*⟩
2 *adv.* richly
Reich *das; ~[e]s, ~e* **(a)** empire; (König~) kingdom; realm; **das [Deutsche] ~** (hist.) the German Reich *or* Empire; **das Dritte ~** (hist.) the Third Reich
(b) (fig.) realm
reichen 1 *itr. V.* **(a)** (ausreichen) be enough; **das Geld reicht nicht** I/we *etc.* haven't got enough money; **jetzt reichts mir aber!** now I've had enough!; **danke, es reicht** that's enough, thank you
(b) (sich erstrecken) reach; ⟨*forest, fields, etc.*⟩ extend
2 *tr. V.* **(a)** pass; hand; **jmdm. die Hand ~:** hold out one's hand to sb.; **sich** (*Dat.*) **die Hand ~:** shake hands
(b) (servieren) serve ⟨*food, drink*⟩
reich·haltig *Adj.* extensive; varied ⟨*programme*⟩; substantial ⟨*meal*⟩
Reich·haltigkeit *die; ~~:* extensiveness; (eines Programms) varied content; (einer Mahlzeit) substantialness
reichlich 1 *Adj.* large; ample ⟨*space, time*⟩; good ⟨*hour, year*⟩
2 *adv.* **(a)** amply
(b) (mehr als) over; more than

(c) (ugs.: ziemlich, sehr) a bit too ⟨*cheeky, dear, late*⟩
Reichtum *der; ~s,* **Reichtümer (a)** wealth **(an +** *Dat.* of)
(b) *Pl.* (Vermögenswerte) riches
Reich·weite *die* reach; (eines Geschützes, Senders, Flugzeugs) range
reif *Adj.* **(a)** ripe ⟨*fruit, grain, cheese*⟩; mature ⟨*brandy, cheese*⟩; **~ für etw. sein** (ugs.) be ready for sth.
(b) (erwachsen, ausgewogen) mature
Reif[1] *der; ~[e]s* hoar frost
Reif[2] *der; ~[e]s, ~e* (geh.) ring; (Arm~) bracelet; (Diadem) circlet
Reife *die; ~* **(a)** ripeness; (von Menschen, Gedanken, Produkten) maturity
(b) (Reifung) ripening
(c) mittlere ~ (Schulw.) *school-leaving certificate usually taken after the fifth year of secondary school*
reifen 1 *itr. V.; mit sein* **(a)** ⟨*fruit, cereal, cheese*⟩ ripen
(b) (geh.: älter, reifer werden) mature (**zu** into)
(c) ⟨*idea, plan, decision*⟩ mature
2 *tr. V.* ripen ⟨*fruit, cereal*⟩
Reifen *der; ~s, ~* **(a)** hoop
(b) (Gummi~) tyre
(c) ▶ REIF[2]
Reifen-: ~**druck** *der; Pl.* ~**drücke** tyre pressure; ~**panne** *die* puncture; ~**wechsel** *der* tyre change
Reif·glätte *die* ice on the roads
reiflich 1 *Adj.* [very] careful
2 *adv.* [very] carefully
Reifung *die; ~:* ▶ REIFEN 1: ripening; maturing; maturation
Reigen *der; ~s, ~* **(a)** round dance
(b) (fig.) **den ~ eröffnen** start off
Reihe *die; ~, ~n* **(a)** row; **in Reih und Glied** (Milit.) in rank and file; **aus der ~ tanzen** (fig. ugs.) be different
(b) (Reihenfolge) series; **er/sie** *usw.* **ist an der ~:** it's his/her *etc.* turn; **der ~ nach, nach der ~:** in turn
(c) (größere Anzahl) number
reihen (geh.) *tr. V.* string; thread
Reihen-: ~**folge** *die* order; ~**haus** *das* terraced house
Reiher *der; ~s, ~:* heron
Reim *der; ~[e]s, ~e* rhyme
reimen 1 *itr. V.* make up rhymes
2 *tr., refl. V.* rhyme (**auf +** *Akk.* with)
rein[1] *Adv.* (ugs.) **~ mit dir!** in you go/come!
rein[2] 1 *Adj.* **(a)** (unvermischt) pure
(b) (nichts anderes als) pure; sheer; plain, unvarnished ⟨*truth*⟩
(c) (frisch, sauber) clean; fresh ⟨*clothes, sheet of paper, etc.*⟩; pure, clean ⟨*water, air*⟩; clear ⟨*complexion*⟩; **etw. ins Reine schreiben** make a fair copy of sth.; **etw. ins Reine bringen** clear sth. up
2 *Adv.* purely; **~ gar nichts** (ugs.) absolutely nothing

Rein·fall der (ugs.) let-down
rein|fallen unr. itr. V.; mit sein (ugs.)
▶ HEREINFALLEN
Rein·gewinn der net profit
Reinheit die; ~ (a) purity
  (b) (Sauberkeit) cleanness; (des Wassers, der Luft)
  purity; (der Haut) clearness
reinigen tr. V. clean; purify ⟨effluents, air,
  water, etc.⟩; **Kleider [chemisch] ~ lassen**
  have clothes [dry-]cleaned
Reinigung die; ~, ~en (a) ▶ REINIGEN:
  cleaning; purification; dry-cleaning
  (b) (Betrieb) [dry-]cleaner's
reinlich Adj. cleanly
Reinlichkeit die; ~: cleanliness
rein, Rein-: ~**rassig** Adj. thoroughbred
  ⟨animal⟩; ~|**reiten** tr. V. (ugs.) jmdn.
  ~reiten drag sb. in (fig.); ~**schrift** die fair
  copy
rein|ziehen unr. tr. V. (a) ▶ HINEINZIEHEN;
  (b) sich (Dat.) etw. ~ziehen (salopp) take
  ⟨drug⟩; watch ⟨film, show, video⟩
Reis der; ~es rice
Reis·brei der rice pudding
Reise die; ~, ~n journey; (kürzere Fahrt,
  Geschäfts~) trip; (Ausflug) outing; trip;
  (Schiffs~) voyage; **eine ~ machen** go on a
  trip/an outing; **auf ~n sein** travel; (nicht zu
  Hause sein) be away; **glückliche od. gute ~!**
  have a good journey
reise-, Reise-: ~**andenken** das
  souvenir; ~**boom** das tourist boom;
  ~**büro** das travel agent's; travel agency;
  ~**bus** der coach; ~**freiheit** die freedom of
  travel; ~**führer** der (a) (Reiseleiter) courier;
  (b) (Buch) guidebook; ~**führerin** die
  courier; ~**gepäck** das luggage (Brit.);
  baggage (Amer.); (am Flughafen) baggage;
  ~**gesellschaft** die (a) (Reisegruppe) party
  of tourists; (b) (ugs.: Reiseveranstalter) tour
  operator; ~**kosten** Pl. travel expenses;
  ~**krank** Adj. travel-sick; ~**krankheit** die
  travel sickness no pl.; ~**leiter** der,
  ~**leiterin** die courier
reisen itr. V.; mit sein (a) travel
  (b) (abreisen) leave; set off
Reisende der/die; adj. Dekl. traveller;
  (Fahrgast) passenger
Reise-: ~**pass**, *~**paß** der passport;
  ~**planung** die travel planning; **die**
  ~**planung umstellen** change one's travel
  plans; ~**prospekt** der travel brochure;
  ~**route** die route; ~**scheck** der
  traveller's cheque; ~**tasche** die holdall;
  ~**verkehr** der holiday traffic;
  ~**wetterbericht** der holiday weather
  forecast; ~**ziel** das destination
Reisig das; ~s brushwood
Reiß·brett das drawing board
reißen [1] unr. tr. V. (a) tear; (in Stücke) tear
  up

  (b) (ziehen an) pull; (heftig) yank (coll.)
  (c) (werfen, ziehen) **jmdn. zu Boden/in die Tiefe
  ~:** knock sb. to the ground/drag sb. down
  into the depths
  (d) (töten) ⟨wolf, lion, etc.⟩ kill ⟨prey⟩
  (e) **etw. an sich ~** (fig.) seize sth.
  [2] unr. itr. V. (a) mit sein ⟨paper, fabric⟩
  tear, rip; ⟨rope, thread⟩ break, snap; ⟨film⟩
  break; ⟨muscle⟩ tear
  (b) (ziehen) **an etw.** (Dat.) ~**:** pull at sth.
  [3] unr. refl. V. (ugs.: sich bemühen um) **sie ~
  sich um die Eintrittskarten** they are fighting
  each other to get tickets
reißend Adj. rapacious ⟨animal⟩; raging
  ⟨torrent⟩; ~**en Absatz finden** sell like hot
  cakes
reißerisch (abwertend) [1] Adj. sensational;
  lurid ⟨headline⟩; garish, lurid ⟨colour⟩
  [2] adv. sensationally
Reiß-: ~**leine** die (Flugw.) ripcord;
  ~**nagel** der; ▶ ~ZWECKE; ~**verschluss**,
  *~**verschluß** der zip [fastener];
  ~**zwecke** die drawing pin (Brit.);
  thumbtack (Amer.)
reiten [1] unr. itr. V.; meist mit sein ride
  [2] unr. tr. V.; auch mit sein ride; **Schritt/
  Trab/Galopp ~:** ride at a walk/trot/gallop
Reiten das; ~s riding no art.
Reiter der; ~s, ~, **Reiterin** die; ~, ~nen
  rider
Reit-: ~**hose** die riding breeches pl.;
  ~**pferd** das saddle horse; ~**stiefel** der
  riding boot
Reiz der; ~es, ~e (a) (Physiol.) stimulus
  (b) (Anziehungskraft) attraction; appeal no pl.;
  (des Verbotenen, der Ferne usw.) lure
  (c) (Zauber) charm
reizbar Adj. irritable
Reizbarkeit die; ~: irritability
reizen [1] tr. V. (a) annoy; tease ⟨animal⟩;
  (herausfordern, provozieren) provoke; s. auch
  GEREIZT
  (b) (Physiol.) irritate
  (c) (Interesse erregen bei) **jmdn. ~:** attract sb.;
  appeal to sb.
  (d) (Kartenspiele) bid
  [2] itr. V. (Kartenspiele) bid
reizend [1] Adj. charming; delightful, lovely
  ⟨child⟩
  [2] adv. charmingly
reizlos Adj. unattractive; ⟨landscape,
  scenery⟩ lacking in charm
reizvoll Adj. (a) (hübsch) charming
  (b) (interessant) attractive
rekeln refl. V. (ugs.) stretch
Reklamation /reklama'tsɪo:n/ die; ~,
  ~en complaint (wegen about)
Reklame die; ~, ~n (a) advertising no
  indef. art.; **~ für jmdn./etw. machen** promote
  sb./advertise or promote sth.
  (b) (ugs.: Werbemittel) advert (Brit. coll.); ad (coll.);
  (im Fernsehen, Radio auch) commercial

---

*alte Schreibung - vgl. Hinweis auf S. xiv

Reklame-: ~**schild** *das* advertising sign; ~**tafel** *die* advertising hoarding; (klein) advertising board

reklamieren ⒈ *itr. V.* complain ⒉ *tr. V.* **(a)** complain about (**bei** to, **wegen** on account of) **(b)** (beanspruchen) claim

rekonstruieren *tr. V.* reconstruct

Rekord *der;* ~[e]s, ~e record

Rekord·halter *der*, **Rekord·halterin** *die*, **Rekord·inhaber** *der*, **Rekord·inhaberin** *die* record holder

Rekrut *der;* ~en, ~en (Milit.) recruit

Rektor *der;* ~s, ~en **(a)** (einer Schule) head[master] **(b)** (Universitäts~) Rector; ≈ Vice-Chancellor (Brit.); (einer Fachhochschule) principal

Rektorin *die;* ~, ~nen **(a)** (einer Schule) head[mistress] **(b)** ▸ REKTOR B

Relation *die;* ~, ~en relation

relativ ⒈ *Adj.* relative ⒉ *adv.* relatively

relativieren *tr. V.* relativize

Relativierung *die;* ~, ~en relativization

Relativ-: ~**pronomen** *das* (Sprachw.) relative pronoun; ~**satz** *der* (Sprachw.) relative clause

relaxed /ri'lɛkst/ *Adj.* (salopp) laid-back (coll.)

relevant /rele'vant/ *Adj.* relevant (**für** to)

Relevanz *die;* ~: relevance (**für** to)

Relief *das;* ~s, ~s *od.* ~e relief

Religion *die;* ~, ~en religion

religiös ⒈ *Adj.* religious ⒉ *adv.* in a religious manner

Religiosität *die;* ~: religiousness

Relikt *das;* ~[e], ~e relic

Reling *die;* ~, ~s *od.* ~e [deck] rail

Reliquie /re'li:kvjə/ *die;* ~, ~n relic

Remis *das;* ~ /rə'mi:(s)/, ~ /rə'mi:s/ (bes. Schach) draw

Ren *das;* ~s, ~s *od.* ~e reindeer

Renaissance /rənɛ'sã:s/ *die;* ~, ~n **(a)** Renaissance **(b)** (Wiederaufleben) revival

Rendezvous /rãde'vu:/ *das;* ~ /...'vu:(s)/, ~ /'rãde'vu:s/ rendezvous

Renn·bahn *die* (Sport) racetrack; (für Pferde) racecourse

rennen *unr. itr. V.; mit sein* run; **an/gegen jmdn./etw.** ~: run *or* bang into sb./sth.

Rennen *das;* ~s, ~: running; (Pferde~, Auto~) racing; (Wettbewerb) race

Renner *der;* ~s, ~ (ugs.: Verkaufserfolg) big seller

Renn-: ~**fahrer** *der*, ~**fahrerin** *die* racing driver; ~**pferd** *das* racehorse; ~**rad** *das* racing cycle; ~**wagen** *der* racing car

renommiert *Adj.* renowned

renovieren *tr. V.* renovate; redecorate ⟨*room, flat*⟩

Renovierung *die;* ~, ~en renovation; (eines Zimmers, einer Wohnung) redecoration

rentabel ⒈ *Adj.* profitable ⒉ *adv.* profitably

Rentabilität *die;* ~ (bes. Wirtsch.) profitability

Rente *die;* ~, ~n **(a)** pension **(b)** (Kapitalertrag) annuity

Renten-: ~**alter** *das* pensionable age *no art.;* ~**empfänger** *der*, ~**empfängerin** *die* pensioner; ~**versicherung** *die* pension scheme

Ren·tier *das* reindeer

rentieren *refl. V.* be profitable; ⟨*equipment, machinery*⟩ pay its way

Rentner *der;* ~s, ~, **Rentnerin** *die;* ~, ~nen pensioner

Reparatur *die;* ~, ~en repair (**an** + *Dat.* to)

Reparatur·werkstatt *die* repair [work]shop; (für Autos) garage

reparieren *tr. V.* repair; mend

Repertoire /repɛ'toa:ɐ/ *das;* ~s, ~s repertoire

Report *der;* ~[e]s, ~e, **Reportage** /repɔr'ta:ʒə/ *die;* ~, ~n report

Reporter *der;* ~s, ~, **Reporterin** *die;* ~, ~nen reporter

Repräsentant *der;* ~en, ~en, **Repräsentantin** *die;* ~, ~nen representative

repräsentativ *Adj.* representative

repräsentieren *tr. V.* represent

Repressalie /reprɛ'sa:liə/ *die;* ~, ~n repressive measure

Reproduktion *die* reproduction

reproduzieren *tr. V.* reproduce

Reptil *das;* ~s, ~ien reptile

Republik *die;* ~, ~en republic

republikanisch *Adj.* republican

Reservat *das;* ~[e]s, ~e **(a)** reservation **(b)** (Naturschutzgebiet) reserve

Reserve *die;* ~, ~n reserve

Reserve-: ~**rad** *das* spare wheel; ~**reifen** *der* spare tyre

reservieren *tr. V.* reserve

reserviert ⒈ *Adj.* reserved ⒉ *adv.* in a reserved way

Reserviertheit *die;* ~: reserve

Reservierung *die;* ~, ~en reservation

Reservoir /rezɛr'voa:ɐ/ *das;* ~s, ~e (auch fig.) reservoir (**an** + *Dat.* of)

Residenz *die;* ~, ~en **(a)** residence **(b)** (Hauptstadt) [royal] capital

Resignation *die;* ~, ~en resignation

resignieren *itr. V.* give up

resigniert ⒈ *Adj.* resigned ⒉ *adv.* resignedly

resolut ⒈ *Adj.* resolute ⋯⋗

r

2 *adv.* resolutely

Resolution *die;* ~, ~en resolution

Resonanz *die;* ~, ~en resonance

resozialisieren *tr. V.* (bes. Rechtsspr.)
reintegrate into society

Resozialisierung *die;* ~, ~en (bes.
Rechtsspr.) reintegration into society

Respekt *der;* ~[e]s **(a)** (Achtung) respect
(**vor** + *Dat.* for)
(b) (Furcht) jmdm. ~ **einflößen** intimidate sb.

respektabel 1 *Adj.* respectable
2 *adv.* respectably

respektieren *tr. V.* respect

respekt·los 1 *Adj.* disrespectful
2 *adv.* disrespectfully

Respekt·losigkeit *die;* ~:
disrespectfulness

respekt·voll 1 *Adj.* respectful
2 *adv.* respectfully

Ressort /rɛ'soːɐ̯/ *das;* ~s, ~s area of
responsibility; (Abteilung) department

Ressource /rɛ'sʊrsə/ *die;* ~, ~n resource

Rest *der;* ~[e]s, ~e **(a)** rest; **ein** ~ **von** a
little bit of
(b) (Endstück) remnant
(c) (Math.) remainder

Rest·alkohol *der* residual alcohol

Restaurant /rɛsto'rãː/ *das;* ~s, ~s
restaurant

restaurieren *tr. V.* restore

restlich *Adj.* remaining

rest·los 1 *Adj.* complete
2 *adv.* completely

Rest·müll *der* general waste; non-
recyclable waste

Resultat *das;* ~[e]s, ~e result

resultieren *itr. V.* result

Retorte *die;* ~, ~n retort

Retorten·baby *das* (ugs.) test tube baby

Retrospektive *die;* ~, ~n **(a)** (Rückblick)
retrospective view; **in der** ~: in retrospect
(b) (Ausstellung) retrospective

retten 1 *tr. V.* save; (vor Gefahr) save;
rescue; (befreien) rescue; **jmdm. das Leben** ~:
save sb.'s life
2 *refl. V.* (fliehen) escape (**aus** from)

Retter *der;* ~s, ~, **Retterin** *die;* ~, ~nen
rescuer

Rettich *der;* ~s, ~e radish

Rettung *die* rescue; (vor Zerstörung) saving

rettungs-, Rettungs-: ~**aktion** *die*
rescue operation; ~**boot** *das* lifeboat;
~**hubschrauber** *der* rescue helicopter;
~**los** 1 *Adj.* hopeless; inevitable ‹*disaster*›;
2 *adv.* hopelessly; ~**ring** *der* lifebelt

Reue *die;* ~: remorse (**über** + *Akk.* for); (Rel.)
repentance

reuen *tr. V.* etw. reut jmdn. sb. regrets sth.

reu·mütig *Adj.* remorseful; repentant
‹*sinner*›

Reuse *die;* ~, ~n fish trap

Revanche /re'vãːʃ(ə)/ *die;* ~, ~n revenge;
(Sport) return match/fight/game

revanchieren *refl. V.* **(a)** get one's
revenge, (coll.) get one's own back (**bei** on)
(b) sich bei jmdm. für eine Einladung ~ (ugs.)
return sb.'s invitation

Revers /rə'veːɐ̯/ *das od.* (österr.) *der;* ~
/rə'veːɐ̯(s)/, ~ /rə'veːɐ̯s/ lapel

reversibel /rever'ziːbl̩/ *Adj.* (Technik, Med.)
reversible

revidieren /revi'diːrən/ *tr. V.* (abändern)
revise; amend ‹*law, contract*›

Revier /re'viːɐ̯/ *das;* ~s, ~e **(a)**
(Aufgabenbereich) province
(b) (Zool.) territory
(c) (Polizei~) (Dienststelle) [police] station;
(Bereich) district; (des einzelnen Polizisten) beat

Revision /revi'zjoːn/ *die;* ~, ~en **(a)**
revision; (Änderung) amendment
(b) (Rechtsw.) appeal [on a point/points of
law]; ~ **einlegen, in die** ~ **gehen** lodge an
appeal [on a point/points of law]

Revolte /re'vɔltə/ *die;* ~, ~n revolt

revoltieren /revɔl'tiːrən/ *itr. V.* revolt,
rebel (**gegen** against); (fig.) ‹*stomach*› rebel

Revolution /revolu'tsi̯oːn/ *die;* ~, ~en
(auch fig.) revolution

revolutionär 1 *Adj.* revolutionary
2 *adv.* in a revolutionary way

Revolutionär *der;* ~s, ~e,
Revolutionärin *die;* ~, ~nen
revolutionary

Revolver /re'vɔlvɐ/ *der;* ~s, ~: revolver

Rezept *das;* ~[e]s, ~e **(a)** (Med.)
prescription
(b) (Anleitung) recipe

rezept·frei 1 *Adj.* ~e Mittel medicines
obtainable without a prescription
2 *adv.* etw. ~ **verkaufen/erhalten** sell/obtain
sth. without a prescription *or* over the
counter

Rezeption *die;* ~, ~en reception *no art.*

rezept·pflichtig *Adj.* ‹*drug etc.*›
obtainable only on prescription

Rezession *die;* ~, ~en (Wirtsch.) recession

R-Gespräch /'ɛr-/ *das* (Fernspr.) reverse-
charge call (Brit.); collect call (Amer.)

Rhabarber *der;* ~s rhubarb

Rhein *der;* ~[e]s Rhine

rheinisch *Adj.* Rhenish; ‹*speciality etc.*› of
the Rhine region

Rhein·land *das;* ~[e]s Rhineland

Rheinland-Pfalz (*das*); ~: the Rhineland-
Palatinate

Rhetorik *die;* ~, ~en rhetoric

Rheuma *das;* ~s (ugs.) rheumatism

rheumatisch (Med.) 1 *Adj.* rheumatic
2 *adv.* rheumatically

---

*old spelling - see note on page xiv

Rheumatịsmus *der;* ~, **Rheumatịsmen** (Med.) rheumatism

Rhinọzeros *das;* ~[ses], ~se rhinoceros; rhino (coll.)

Rhododẹndron *der od. das;* ~s, **Rhododẹndren** rhododendron

rhythmisch 1 *Adj.* rhythmical; rhythmic 2 *adv.* rhythmically

Rhythmus *der;* ~, **Rhythmen** (auch fig.) rhythm

rịchten 1 *tr. V.* (a) direct ⟨*gaze*⟩ (auf + *Akk.* at, towards); turn ⟨*eyes, gaze*⟩ (auf + *Akk.* towards); point ⟨*torch, telescope, gun*⟩ (auf + *Akk.* at); aim ⟨*gun, missile, telescope, searchlight*⟩ (auf + *Akk.* on); (fig.) direct ⟨*activity, attention*⟩ (auf + *Akk.* towards); address ⟨*letter, remarks, words*⟩ (an + *Akk.* to); level ⟨*criticism*⟩ (an + *Akk.* at)
(b) (geraderichten) straighten
(c) (aburteilen) judge; (verurteilen) condemn; *s. auch* ZUGRUNDE A;
2 *refl. V.* (a) (sich hinwenden) **sich auf jmdn./ etw.** ~ (auch fig.) be directed towards sth./sb.
(b) **sich an jmdn./etw.** ~ ⟨*person*⟩ turn on sb./sth.; ⟨*appeal, explanation*⟩ be directed at sb./sth.; **sich gegen jmdn./etw.** ~ ⟨*person*⟩ criticize sb./sth.; ⟨*criticism, accusations, etc.*⟩ be aimed *or* levelled at sb./sth.
(c) (sich orientieren) **sich nach jmdm./jmds. Wünschen** ~: fit in with sb./sb.'s wishes
(d) (abhängen) **sich nach jmdm./etw.** ~: depend on sb./sth.
3 *itr. V.* (urteilen) judge

Rịchter *der;* ~s, ~, **Rịchterin** *die;* ~, ~nen judge

Rịcht·geschwindigkeit *die* recommended maximum speed

rịchtig 1 *Adj.* (a) right; (zutreffend) right; correct; accurate ⟨*prophecy, premonition*⟩; **etw.** ~ **stellen** correct sth.
(b) (ordentlich) proper
(c) (wirklich, echt) real
2 *adv.* (a) right; correctly
(b) (ordentlich) properly
(c) (richtiggehend) really

rịchtig-gehend 1 *Adj.* real; proper (coll.) 2 *adv.* really

Rịchtigkeit *die;* ~: correctness; **etw. hat seine** ~, **mit etw. hat es seine** ~: sth. is right; **das wird schon seine** ~ **haben** I'm sure it's all right *or* (coll.) OK

*rịchtig|stellen ▶ RICHTIG 1A

Rịcht-: ~**linie** *die* guideline; ~**schnur** *die; Pl.* ~~en (fig.) guiding principle

Rịchtung *die;* ~, ~en (a) direction; **in** ~ **Ulm** in the direction of Ulm
(b) (fig.: Tendenz) movement; trend

rịchtung-weisend *Adj.* ⟨*idea, resolution, paper, speech*⟩ that points the way ahead

rieb *1. u. 3. Pers. Sg. Prät. v.* REIBEN

riechen 1 *unr. tr. V.* (a) smell
(b) (wittern) ⟨*dog etc.*⟩ pick up the scent of
2 *unr. itr. V.* (a) smell; **an jmdm./etw.** ~: smell sb./sth.

(b) (einen Geruch haben) smell (**nach** of)

rief *1. u. 3. Pers. Sg. Prät. v.* RUFEN

Riegel *der;* ~s, ~ (a) bolt
(b) **ein** ~ **Schokolade** a bar of chocolate

Riemen *der;* ~s, ~ (a) strap; (Treib~, Gürtel) belt; **sich am** ~ **reißen** (ugs.) pull oneself together; get a grip on oneself
(b) (Ruder) [long] oar

Riese *der;* ~n, ~n giant

rieseln *itr. V.; mit Richtungsangabe mit sein* trickle [down]; ⟨*snow*⟩ fall gently

Riesen- giant; enormous ⟨*selection, profit, portion*⟩; tremendous (coll.) ⟨*effort, rejoicing, success*⟩; terrific (coll.), terrible (coll.) ⟨*stupidity, scandal, fuss*⟩

riesen-, Riesen-: ~**groß** *Adj.* enormous; huge; terrific (coll.) ⟨*surprise*⟩; ~**schritt** *der* giant stride; ~**welle** *die* giant wave

riesig 1 *Adj.* enormous; huge; vast ⟨*country*⟩; tremendous ⟨*effort, progress*⟩ 2 *adv.* (ugs.) tremendously (coll.)

Riesin *die;* ~, ~nen giantess

Riesling *der;* ~s, ~e Riesling

riet *1. u. 3. Pers. Sg. Prät. v.* RATEN

Riff *das;* ~[e]s, ~e reef

rigoros 1 *Adj.* rigorous 2 *adv.* rigorously

Rille *die;* ~, ~n groove

Rịnd *das;* ~[e]s, ~er (a) cow; (Stier) bull; ~**er** cattle *pl.;*
(b) (~fleisch) beef

Rịnde *die;* ~, ~n (a) (Baum~) bark
(b) (Brot~) crust; (Käse~) rind

Rịnder·braten *der* roast beef *no indef. art.;* (roh) roasting beef *no indef. art.*

Rịnder·wahnsinn *der* mad cow disease

Rịnd-: ~**fleisch** *das* beef; ~**vieh** *das* (a) cattle *pl.;* (b) (ugs. abwertend) ass; [stupid] fool

Rịng *der;* ~[e]s, ~e ring

Rịngel·natter *die* ring snake

rịngen 1 *unr. tr. V.* (Sport, fig.) wrestle; (fig.: kämpfen) struggle, fight (**um** for; **gegen, mit** with); **nach Luft** ~: struggle for breath
2 *unr. tr. V.* **die Hände** ~: wring one's hands

Rịngen *das;* ~s (Sport) wrestling *no art.*

Rịng-: ~**finger** *der* ring finger; ~**kampf** *der* (a) [stand-up] fight; (b) (Sport) wrestling bout

rịngs *Adv.* all around

rịngs·herum *Adv.* all around [it/them *etc.*]

Rịng·straße *die* ring road

rịngs-: ~**um**, ~**umher** *Adv.* all around

Rịnne *die;* ~, ~n channel; (Dach~, Rinnstein) gutter; (Abfluss) drainpipe

rịnnen *unr. itr. V.; mit sein* run

Rịnn·stein *der* gutter

Rịppchen *das;* ~s, ~ (Kochk. südd.) rib [of pork]

Rịppe *die;* ~, ~n rib

r

Rippen-bruch der (Med.) rib fracture
Risiko das; ~s, **Risiken** risk
Risiko-: ~**faktor** der risk factor;
~**gruppe** die risk group
riskant ① Adj. risky
  ② adv. riskily
riskieren tr. V. risk
riss, *riß 1. u. 3. Pers. Sg. Prät. v. REISSEN
Riss, *Riß der; **Risses, Risse** tear; (Spalt,
  Sprung) crack
rissig Adj. cracked; chapped ⟨lips⟩
ritt 1. u. 3. Pers. Sg. Prät. v. REITEN
Ritt der; ~[e]s, ~e ride
Ritter der; ~s, ~: knight
Ritter-sporn der delphinium
rittlings Adv. astride
Ritze die; ~, ~n crack; [narrow] gap
ritzen tr. V. scratch
Rivale der; ~n, ~n, **Rivalin** die; ~, ~nen
  rival
Rivalität die; ~, ~en rivalry no indef. art.
Roastbeef /'ro:stbi:f/ das; ~s, ~s roast
  [sirloin (Brit.) of] beef
Robbe die; ~, ~n seal
Robe die; ~, ~n robe; (schwarz) gown
Roboter der; ~s, ~: robot
robust Adj. robust
roch 1. u. 3. Pers. Sg. Prät. v. RIECHEN
Rochade die; ~, ~n (Schach) castling
röcheln itr. V. give the death rattle
Rock¹ der; ~[e]s, **Röcke** skirt
Rock² der; ~[s] (Musik) rock [music]
Rock and Roll /'rɔk ɛnt 'rɔl/ der; ~[s],
  ~[s] rock and roll no pl.
Rock-band die rock band
rocken itr. V. rock
Rocker der; ~s, ~: rocker
rockig Adj. rock ⟨music⟩; rock-like ⟨jazz
  etc.⟩
Rock-musik die rock music
Rodel-bahn die toboggan run; (Sport) luge
  run
rodeln itr. V.; mit sein sledge; toboggan
roden tr. V. clear ⟨wood, land⟩; (ausgraben)
  grub up ⟨tree⟩
Rogen der; ~s, ~: roe
Roggen der; ~s rye
Roggen-: ~**brot** das rye bread; **ein** ~**brot**
  a loaf of rye bread; ~**brötchen** das rye-
  bread roll
roh ① Adj. (a) raw ⟨food⟩; unboiled ⟨milk⟩;
  unfinished ⟨wood⟩
  (b) (ungenau) rough
  (c) (brutal) brutish; brute attrib. ⟨force⟩
  ② adv. (a) (ungenau) roughly
  (b) (brutal) brutishly; (grausam) callously; (grob)
  coarsely
Roh-: ~**bau** der shell [of a/the building];

~**kost** die raw fruit and vegetables pl.;
~**material** das raw material; ~**öl** das
  crude oil
Rohr das; ~[e]s, ~e (a) (Leitungs~) pipe; (als
  Bauteil) tube
  (b) o. Pl. (Röhricht) reeds pl.;
  (c) o. Pl. (Werkstoff) reed
Röhre die; ~, ~n tube; (Elektronen~) valve
  (Brit.); tube (Amer.)
Roh-stoff der raw material
Rokoko das; ~[s] rococo
***Rolladen** ▶ ROLLLADEN
Roll-bahn die (Flugw.) taxiway
Rolle die; ~, ~n (a) (Spule) reel
  (b) (zylindrischer [Hohl]körper; Zusammengerolltes)
  roll
  (c) (Walze) roller
  (d) (Rad) [small] wheel; (an Möbeln usw.)
  castor; (für Gardine, Schiebetür usw.) runner
  (e) (Turnen, Kunstflug) roll
  (f) (Theater, Film usw., fig.) role; part; (Soziol.)
  role; **es spielt keine** ~: it is of no
  importance; (es macht nichts aus) it doesn't
  matter
rollen ① tr. V. roll
  ② itr. V. mit sein ⟨ball, wheel, etc.⟩ roll;
  ⟨vehicle⟩ move; ⟨aircraft⟩ taxi
Roller der; ~s, ~: scooter
Roll-: ~**feld** das runway[s] and taxiway[s];
~**kragen** der polo neck; ~**laden** der
  [roller] shutter; ~**mops** der rollmops;
~**schuh** der roller skate; ~**schuh laufen**
  roller-skate; ~**splitt** der loose chippings pl.;
~**stuhl** der wheelchair; ~**treppe** die
  escalator
Rom (das); ~s Rome
Roman der; ~s, ~e novel
Romantik die; ~: romanticism; **die** ~:
  Romanticism
romantisch ① Adj. romantic
  ② adv. romantically
Romanze die; ~, ~n romance
Römer der; ~s, ~, **Römerin** die; ~, ~nen
  Roman
römisch-katholisch Adj. Roman
  Catholic
röntgen tr. V. X-ray
Röntgen-: ~**aufnahme** die, ~**bild** das
  X-ray [image/photograph or picture];
~**strahlen** Pl. X-rays
rosa ① indekl. Adj. pink
  ② adv. pink
Rosa das; ~s, ~ od. ~s pink
Rose die; ~, ~n rose
rosé indekl. Adj. pale pink
Rosé der; ~s, ~s rosé [wine]
Rosen-: ~**kohl** der [Brussels] sprouts pl.;
~**kranz** der (kath. Kirche) rosary; **einen**
~**kranz beten** say a rosary; ~**montag** der
  the day before Shrove Tuesday
rosig Adj. (a) rosy; pink ⟨piglet etc.⟩
  (b) (fig.) rosy; optimistic ⟨mood⟩

---

*alte Schreibung - vgl. Hinweis auf S. xiv

Rosine *die;* ~, ~n raisin
Rosmarin *der;* ~s rosemary
Ross, *Roß *das;* Rosses, Rosse *od.* Rösser
horse; steed (poet./joc.); **hoch zu** ~: on
horseback; **auf dem** *od.* **seinem hohen** ~
sitzen (fig.) be on one's high horse
Ross-, *Roß-: ~**haar** *das* horsehair;
~**kastanie** *die* horse chestnut
Rost¹ *der;* ~[e]s, ~e **(a)** (Gitter) grating;
(eines Ofens, einer Feuerstelle) grate; (Brat~) grill
(b) (Bett~) base
Rost² *der;* ~[e]s rust
Rost-: ~**braten** *der* grilled steak;
~**bratwurst** *die* grilled sausage
rosten *itr. V.; auch mit* sein rust
rösten /'rœstn̩, 'rø:stn̩/ *tr. V.* roast; toast
⟨bread⟩
rost·frei *Adj.* stainless ⟨steel⟩
Rösti *die;* ~ (schweiz. Kochk.) thinly sliced
fried potatoes *pl.*
rostig *Adj.* rusty
rot ① *Adj.* red; ~ **werden** turn red; ⟨person⟩
blush; ⟨traffic light⟩ change to red
② *adv.* red
Rot *das;* ~s, ~ *od.* ~s red
Rot·barsch *der* rosefish
Röte *die;* ~: red[ness]
röten ① *tr. V.* redden
② *refl. V.* go *or* turn red
rot·haarig *Adj.* red-haired
Rot·hirsch *der* red deer
rotieren *itr. V.* **(a)** rotate
(b) (ugs.: hektisch sein) get into a flap (coll.)
Rot-: ~**käppchen** *das;* ~s Little Red
Riding Hood; ~**kehlchen** *das;* ~~s, ~~:
robin [redbreast]; ~**kohl** *der,* (bes. südd.,
öster.) ~**kraut** *das* red cabbage
rötlich *Adj.* reddish
Rot-: ~**licht** *das* red light; **bei** ~**licht**
under a red light; ~**stift** *der* red pencil
Rötung *die;* ~, ~en reddening
Rot·wein *der* red wine
Rotz *der;* ~es (salopp) snot (sl.)
rotzen (derb) ① *itr. V.* **(a)** blow one's nose
loudly
(b) (Schleim in den Mund ziehen) sniff back
one's snot (sl.)
(c) (ausspucken) gob (sl.)
② *tr. V.* spit
rotz·frech (salopp) ① *Adj.* insolent; snotty
(sl.)
② *adv.* insolently; snottily (sl.)
Rouge /ruːʒ/ *das;* ~s, ~s rouge
Roulade /ruˈlaːdə/ *die;* ~, ~n (Kochk.)
[beef/veal/pork] olive
Route /'ruːtə/ *die;* ~, ~n route
Routine /ruˈtiːnə/ *die;* ~ **(a)** (Erfahrung)
experience; (Übung) practice
(b) (Gewohnheit) routine *no def. art.*
routiniert /rutiˈniːɐ̯t/ ① *Adj.* (gewandt)
expert; skilled; (erfahren) experienced

② *adv.* expertly; skilfully
Rowdy /'rauːdi/ *der;* ~s, ~s (abwertend)
hooligan
Rübe *die;* ~, ~n turnip; **Rote** ~: beetroot;
Gelbe ~ (südd.) carrot
rüber *Adv.* (ugs.) over
Rubin *der;* ~s, ~e ruby
Rubrik *die;* ~, ~en column; (fig.: Kategorie)
category
Ruck *der;* ~[e]s, ~e jerk
Rück·blick *der* look back (**auf** + *Akk.* at);
retrospective view (**auf** + *Akk.* of)
rücken *itr., tr. V.* move
Rücken *der;* ~s, ~: back; (Buch~) spine
Rücken-: ~**deckung** *die* **(a)** (bes. Milit.)
rear cover; **(b)** (fig.) backing; ~**lehne** *die*
[chair/seat] back; ~**mark** *das* (Anat.) spinal
cord; ~**schmerzen** *Pl.* backache *sing.;*
~**schwimmen** *das* backstroke; ~**wind**
der tail wind
rück-, Rück-: ~**|erstatten** *tr. V.; nur*
im Inf. u. 2. Part. repay; ~**erstattung** *die*
repayment; ~**fahr·karte** *die,*
~**fahr·schein** *der* return [ticket];
~**fahrt** *die* return journey; ~**fall** *der* (Med.,
auch fig.) relapse; ~**fällig** *Adj.* (Med., auch fig.)
relapsed ⟨patient, alcoholic, etc.⟩; ~**fällig**
werden have a relapse; ⟨alcoholic etc.⟩ go
back to one's old ways; ⟨criminal⟩ commit a
second offence; ~**flug** *der* return flight;
~**frage** *die* query; ~**gabe** *der* return;
~**gang** *der* drop, fall (Gen. in); ~**gängig**
Adj. ~**gängig machen** cancel ⟨agreement,
decision, etc.⟩; ~**grat** *das;* ~[e]s, ~~e
spine; (bes. fig.) backbone; ~**halt** *der*
support; backing; ~**halt·los** ① *Adj.*
unreserved, unqualified ⟨support⟩; ② *adv.*
unreservedly; ~**kehr** *die;* ~~: return;
~**kopp[e]lung** *die* (Elektrot.) feedback;
~**lage** *die* savings *pl.;* ~**läufig** *Adj.*
decreasing ⟨number⟩; declining ⟨economic
growth etc.⟩; falling ⟨rate, production, etc.⟩;
~**licht** *das* rear *or* tail light
rücklings *Adv.* on one's back
Rück-: ~**nahme** *die;* ~~: taking back;
~**reise** *die* return journey; ~**ruf** *der*
(Fernspr.) return call
Ruck·sack *der* rucksack; (Touren~)
backpack
Rucksack·urlaub *der* backpacking
holiday
rück-, Rück-: ~**schlag** *der* setback;
~**schritt** *der* retrograde step; ~**seite** *die*
back; (einer Münze usw.) reverse; far side;
~**sicht** *die* consideration; ~**sicht auf jmdn.**
nehmen show consideration for *or* towards
sb.; ~**sicht·nahme** *die;* ~~:
consideration; ~**sichts·los** ① *Adj.*
inconsiderate; thoughtless; (verantwortungslos)
reckless ⟨driver⟩; (schonungslos) ruthless;
② *adv. s. Adj:* inconsiderately; recklessly;
ruthlessly; ~**sichtslosigkeit** *die;* ~~,
~~en ▸ RÜCKSICHTSLOS: lack of
consideration; recklessness; ruthlessness; ⋯⋗

r

~**sichts·voll** ① *Adj.* considerate; ② *adv.*
considerately; ~**sitz** *der* back seat;
~**spiegel** *der* rear-view mirror;
~**sprache** *die* consultation; ~**stand** *der*
(a) (Rest) residue; (b) (ausstehende Zahlung)
arrears *pl.*; (c) (Zurückbleiben hinter dem gesetzten
Ziel) backlog; (bes. Sport: hinter dem Gegner)
deficit; [mit etw.] im ~**stand sein/in** ~**stand**
(*Akk.*) **geraten** be/get behind [with sth.];
~**ständig** *Adj.* (a) backward; (b) (schon
länger fällig) outstanding ⟨payment, amount⟩;
⟨wages⟩ still owing; ~**strahler** *der*
reflector; ~**tritt** *der* resignation (**von** from);
(von einer Kandidatur, einem Vertrag usw.)
withdrawal (**von** from)

rückwärts *Adv.* backwards

Rückwärts·gang *der* reverse [gear]

rück-, Rück-: ~**weg** *der* return journey;
~**wirkend** ① *Adj.* retrospective; ② *adv.*
backdated ⟨pay increase⟩; retrospectively);
~**zahlung** *die* repayment; ~**zug** *der*
retreat

Rüde *der;* ~**n**, ~**n** [male] dog

Rudel *das;* ~**s**, ~: herd; (von Wölfen, Hunden)
pack

Ruder *das;* ~**s**, ~ (a) (Riemen) oar
(b) (Steuer~) rudder

Ruder·boot *das* rowboat; rowing boat (Brit.)

Rudergänger *der;* ~~**s**, ~~, ~**gast** *der*
(Seemannsspr.) helmsman

rudern ① *itr. V.; mit sein* row
② *tr. V.* row

Ruder·regatta *die* rowing regatta

Ruf *der;* ~**[e]s**, ~**e** (a) call; (Schrei) shout;
cry; (Tierlaut) call
(b) (fig.: Forderung) call (**nach** for)
(c) (Telefonnummer) telephone [number]
(d) (Leumund) reputation

rufen ① *unr. itr. V.* call (**nach** for); (schreien)
shout (**nach** for); ⟨animal⟩ call
② *unr. tr. V.* (a) (ausrufen) call; (schreien)
shout
(b) (herbeirufen, anrufen) **jmdn.** ~: call sb.;
jmdn. zu Hilfe ~: call to sb. to help

Ruf-: ~**mord** *der* character assassination;
~**mord·kampagne** *die* smear campaign;
~**name** *der* first name (by which one is
generally known); ~**nummer** *die* telephone
number

Rüge *die;* ~, ~**n** reprimand

rügen *tr. V.* reprimand ⟨person⟩ (**wegen** for);
censure ⟨carelessness etc.⟩

Ruhe *die;* ~ (a) (Stille) silence; ~ [**bitte**]!
quiet *or* silence [please]!
(b) (Ungestörtheit) peace; **jmdn. mit etw. in** ~
lassen stop bothering sb. with sth.
(c) (Unbewegtheit) rest
(d) (Erholung) rest *no def. art.;*
(e) (Gelassenheit) calm[ness]; composure; [**die**]
~ **bewahren/die** ~ **verlieren** keep calm/lose
one's composure; **in** [**aller**] ~: [really] calmly

ruhe·los ① *Adj.* restless
② *adv.* restlessly

ruhen *itr. V.* (a) (ausruhen) rest
(b) (geh.: schlafen) sleep
(c) (stillstehen) ⟨work, business⟩ have stopped;
⟨production, firm⟩ be at a standstill

Ruhe-: ~**pause** *die* break; ~**stand** *der*
retirement; **in den** ~**stand gehen/versetzt**
werden go into retirement/be retired;
~**störung** *die* disturbance; (Rechtsw.)
disturbance of the peace; ~**tag** *der* closing
day; „Dienstag ~**tag**" 'closed on Tuesdays'

ruhig ① *Adj.* (a) (still, leise) quiet
(b) (friedlich, ungestört) peaceful ⟨times, life,
valley, etc.⟩; quiet ⟨talk, reflection, life⟩
(c) (unbewegt) calm ⟨sea, weather⟩; still ⟨air⟩;
(fig.) peaceful ⟨melody⟩; (gleichmäßig) steady
⟨breathing, hand, steps⟩; smooth ⟨flight,
crossing⟩
(d) (gelassen) calm ⟨voice etc.⟩; quiet, calm
⟨person⟩
② *adv.* (a) (still, leise) quietly; **sich** ~
verhalten keep quiet
(b) (friedlich, ohne Störungen) peacefully; (ohne
Zwischenfälle) uneventfully; ⟨work, think⟩ in
peace
(c) (unbewegt) ⟨sit, lie, stand⟩ still; (gleichmäßig)
⟨burn, breathe⟩ steadily; ⟨run, fly⟩ smoothly
(d) (gelassen) ⟨speak, watch, sit⟩ calmly
③ *Adv.* by all means

Ruhm *der;* ~**[e]s** fame

rühmen ① *tr. V.* praise
② *refl. V.* boast (+ *Gen.* about)

ruhm·reich *Adj.* glorious ⟨victory, history⟩;
celebrated ⟨general, army, victory⟩

Ruhr *die;* ~, ~**en** dysentery *no art.*

Rühr·ei *das* scrambled egg[s *pl.*]

rühren ① *tr. V.* (a) (umrühren) stir; (einrühren)
stir ⟨egg, powder, etc.⟩ (**an**, **in** + *Akk.* into)
(b) (bewegen) move ⟨limb, fingers, etc.⟩
(c) (fig.) move; touch
② *itr. V.* (a) (umrühren) stir
(b) (geh.: herrühren) **das rührt daher, dass ...:**
that stems from the fact that ...
③ *refl. V.* (a) (sich bewegen) move
(b) (Milit.) **rührt euch!** at ease!

rührend ① *Adj.* touching
② *adv.* touchingly

rühr·selig ① *Adj.* (a) emotional ⟨person⟩
(b) (allzu gefühlvoll) over-sentimental; ⟨manner,
mood, etc.⟩; maudlin, (coll.) tear-jerking ⟨play,
song, etc.⟩
② *adv.* (allzu gefühlvoll) in an over-sentimental
manner

Rühr·seligkeit *die* sentimentality

Rührung *die;* ~: emotion

Ruine *die;* ~, ~**n** ruin

ruinieren *tr. V.* ruin

rülpsen *itr. V.* (ugs.) burp

rum *Adv.* (ugs.) ▶ HERUM

Rum *der;* ~**s**, ~**s** rum

Rumäne *der;* ~**n**, ~**n** Romanian

Rumänien (*das*); ~**s** Romania

---
*old spelling - see note on page xiv

Rumänin *die;* ~, ~nen Romanian
rumänisch *Adj.* Romanian
Rummel *der;* ~s (ugs.) **(a)** commotion;
(Aufhebens) fuss (**um** about)
(b) (Jahrmarkt) fair
Rummel·platz *der* (bes. nordd.) fairground
Rumpel·kammer *die* (ugs.) boxroom
(Brit.); junk room
rumpeln *itr. V.* (ugs.) bump and bang about
Rumpf *der;* ~[e]s, Rümpfe **(a)** trunk [of the body]
(b) (beim Schiff) hull
(c) (beim Flugzeug) fuselage
rümpfen *tr. V.* **die Nase [bei etw.]** ~:
wrinkle one's nose [at sth.]; **über jmdn./etw.
die Nase rümpfen** (fig.) look down one's nose
at sb./turn up one's nose at sth.
Rumpsteak /ˈrʊmpsteːk/ *das;* ~s, ~s
rump steak
rum|treiben *unr. refl. V.* (ugs.)
▶ HERUMTREIBEN
rund ① *Adj.* **(a)** round
(b) (dicklich) plump ⟨*arms etc.*⟩; chubby
⟨*cheeks*⟩; fat ⟨*stomach*⟩
(c) (ugs.: ganz) round ⟨*dozen, number, etc.*⟩
② *Adv.* **(a)** (ugs.: etwa) about
(b) ~ **um jmdn./etw.** [all] around sb./sth.
Rund-: ~**blick** *der* panorama; view in all
directions; ~**brief** *der* circular [letter]
Runde *die;* ~, ~n **(a)** (Sport: Strecke) lap
(b) (Sport: Durchgang usw.) round; **über die** ~**n
kommen** (fig. ugs.) get by; manage
(c) (Personenkreis) circle; (Gesellschaft)
company
(d) (Rundgang) round
(e) (Lage) round
rund-, Rund-: ~**erneuern** *tr. V.; ich
runderneuere, runderneuert, rundzuerneuern*
(Kfz-W.) remould; ~**funk** *der* **(a)** radio; **(b)** (Einrichtung,
Gebäude) radio station
Rundfunk-: ~**anstalt** *die* broadcasting
corporation; ~**gebühren** *Pl.* radio licence
fees; ~**gerät** *das* radio set; ~**sendung**
die radio programme; ~**sprecher** *der,*
~**sprecherin** *die* radio announcer
rund-, Rund-: ~**gang** *der* round (**durch**
of); ~**herum** *Adv.* **(a)** (ringsum) all around;
(b) (völlig) completely
rundlich *Adj.* **(a)** roundish
(b) (mollig) plump

Rund-: ~**reise** *die* [circular] tour (**durch**
of); ~**schreiben** *das:* ▶ ~BRIEF; ~**weg**
der circular path *or* walk
runter *Adv.* (ugs.) ~ **[da]!** get off [there]; *s.
auch* HERUNTER; HINUNTER
runter|scrollen *tr., auch itr. V.* (DV)
scroll down
Runzel *die;* ~, ~n wrinkle
runz[e]lig *Adj.* wrinkled
runzeln *tr. V.* **die Stirn/die Brauen** ~:
wrinkle one's brow/knit one's brows;
(ärgerlich) frown
rupfen *tr. V.* **(a)** pluck ⟨*goose, hen, etc.*⟩
(b) (abreißen) pull up ⟨*weeds, grass*⟩; pull off
⟨*leaves etc.*⟩
ruppig *Adj.* (abwertend) gruff ⟨*person,
behaviour*⟩; sharp ⟨*tone*⟩; **er war** ~ **zu ihr** he
was short with her; he snapped at her
Rüsche *die;* ~, ~n ruche; frill
Ruß *der;* ~es soot
Russe *der;* ~n, ~n Russian
Rüssel *der;* ~s, ~ (des Elefanten) trunk; (des
Schweins) snout; (bei Insekten u. Ä.) proboscis
rußen *itr. V.* give off sooty smoke
Russin *die;* ~, ~nen Russian
russisch ① *Adj.* Russian
② *adv.* (auf ~) in Russian
Russisch *das;* ~[s] Russian
Russ·land, *Ruß·land (das)* ~s Russia
rüsten *itr. V.* arm
rüstig *Adj.* sprightly; active
rustikal *Adj.* country-style ⟨*food, inn,
clothes, etc.*⟩; rustic ⟨*furniture*⟩
Rüstung *die;* ~, ~en **(a)** armament *no
art.;* (Waffen) arms *pl.;* weapons *pl.*
(b) (hist.) suit of armour
Rüstungs-: ~**industrie** *die* armaments
or arms industry; ~**kontrolle** *die* arms
control; ~**stopp** *der* arms freeze;
~**wettlauf** *der* arms race
Rute *die;* ~, ~n switch; (Birken~, Angel~,
Wünschel~) rod
Rutsch *der* **guten** ~ **[ins neue Jahr]!** (ugs.)
happy New Year!
Rutsch·bahn *die* slide
Rutsche *die;* ~, ~n chute
rutschen *itr. V.; mit sein* slide; ⟨*clutch,
carpet*⟩ slip
rutschig *Adj.* slippery
rütteln *tr., itr. V.* shake

r

Ss

s, S /ɛs/ *das;* ∼, ∼ s/S

s *Abk.* = **Sekunde** sec.; s.

s. *Abk.* = **siehe**

S *Abk.* **(a)** = **Süden** S.
 (b) (österr.) = **Schilling** Sch.

S. *Abk.* = **Seite** p.

Sa. *Abk.* = **Samstag** Sat.

Saal *der;* ∼[e]s, **Säle (a)** hall; (Ballsaal) ballroom
 (b) (Publikum) audience

Saar·land *das;* ∼[e]s Saarland; Saar (esp. Hist.)

Saat *die;* ∼, ∼en **(a)** (das Gesäte) [young] crops *pl.*
 (b) (das Säen) sowing
 (c) (Samenkörner) seed[s *pl.*]

Säbel *der;* ∼s, ∼: sabre

Sabotage /zaboˈtaːʒə/ *die;* ∼, ∼n sabotage *no art.*

Sabotage·akt *der* act of sabotage

sabotieren *tr. V.* sabotage

Sach-: ∼**bearbeiter** *der,*
 ∼**bearbeiterin** *die* person responsible (für for); (Experte) specialist, expert (für on);
 ∼**beschädigung** *die* (Rechtsw.) wilful damage to property; ∼**buch** *das* [popular] non-fiction book; ∼**bücher lesen** read non-fiction *sing.*

sach·dienlich *Adj.* useful

Sache *die;* ∼, ∼n **(a)** things
 (b) (Angelegenheit) matter; business (esp. derog.); **zur** ∼ **kommen** come to the point
 (c) (Rechtssache) case
 (d) (Anliegen) cause

sach-, Sach-: ∼**gebiet** *das* subject [area]; field; ∼**gemäß,** ∼**gerecht** [1] *Adj.* proper; correct; [2] *adv.* properly; correctly; ∼**kenntnis** *die* expertise; knowledge of the subject; ∼**kundig** [1] *Adj.* with a knowledge of the subject *postpos., not pred.;* [2] *adv.* expertly

sachlich [1] *Adj.* **(a)** (objektiv) objective; (nüchtern) functional ⟨*building, style, etc.*⟩; matter-of-fact ⟨*letter etc.*⟩
 (b) (sachbezogen) factual ⟨*error*⟩
 [2] *adv.* **(a)** (objektiv) objectively; ⟨*state*⟩ as a matter of fact; (nüchtern) ⟨*furnished*⟩ in a functional style; ⟨*written*⟩ in a matter-of-fact way
 (b) (sachbezogen) factually ⟨*wrong*⟩

sächlich *Adj.* (Sprachw.) neuter

Sachlichkeit *die;* ∼: objectivity; (Nüchternheit) functionalism

Sach-: ∼**register** *das* [subject] index; ∼**schaden** *der* damage [to property] *no indef. art.*

Sachse *der;* ∼n, ∼n Saxon

Sachsen (*das*); ∼s Saxony

Sachsen-Anhalt (*das*); ∼s Saxony-Anhalt

Sächsin *die;* ∼, ∼nen Saxon

sacht, sachte [1] *Adj.* **(a)** (behutsam) gentle
 (b) (leise) quiet
 [2] *adv.* **(a)** gently
 (b) (leise) quietly

Sach-: ∼**verhalt** *der;* ∼∼[e]s, ∼∼e facts *pl.* [of the matter]; ∼**verstand** *der* expertise; grasp of the subject; ∼**verständige** *der/die; adj. Dekl.* expert

Sack *der;* ∼[e]s, **Säcke** sack; (aus Papier, Kunststoff) bag

Sack-: ∼**gasse** *die* cul-de-sac; ∼**hüpfen** *das;* ∼∼s sack race

Sadismus *der;* ∼: sadism *no art.*

Sadist *der;* ∼en, ∼en, **Sadistin** *die;* ∼, ∼nen sadist

sadistisch [1] *Adj.* sadistic
 [2] *adv.* sadistically

säen *tr.* (*auch itr.*) *V.* sow

Saft *der;* ∼[e]s, **Säfte (a)** juice
 (b) (in Pflanzen) sap

saftig *Adj.* **(a)** juicy; sappy ⟨*stem*⟩; lush ⟨*meadow, green*⟩
 (b) (ugs.) hefty ⟨*slap, blow*⟩; steep (coll.) ⟨*prices, bill*⟩; crude ⟨*joke, song, etc.*⟩; strongly-worded ⟨*letter etc.*⟩

saft-, Saft-: ∼**laden** *der* (salopp abwertend) lousy outfit (coll.); ∼**los** *Adj.* **(a)** juiceless
 (b) (fig.) feeble, anodyne ⟨*language*⟩; ∼ **und kraftlos** feeble, wishy-washy; (*adv.*) without any zest; ∼**sack** *der* (derb abwertend) bastard (coll.)

Sage *die;* ∼, ∼n legend; (bes. nordische) saga

Säge *die;* ∼, ∼n saw

Säge-: ∼**blatt** *das* saw blade; ∼**mehl** sawdust

sagen [1] *tr. V.* **(a)** say; **was ich noch** ∼ **wollte** [oh] by the way; **unter uns gesagt** between you and me
 (b) (mitteilen) **jmdm. etw.** ∼: say sth. to sb.; (zur Information) tell sb. sth.
 (c) (nennen) **zu jmdm./etw. X** ∼: call sb./sth. X
 (d) (anordnen, befehlen) tell
 [2] *refl. V.* **sich** (*Dat.*) **etw.** ∼: say sth. to oneself

sägen *tr., itr. V.* saw

---

*alte Schreibung - vgl. Hinweis auf S. xiv

301

Sägespäne ⋯⟶ sanieren ⋯⋯

Säge-: ∼**späne** Pl. wood shavings; ∼**werk** das sawmill

sah 1. u. 3. Pers. Sg. Prät. v. SEHEN

Sahne die; ∼: cream

Saison /zɛˈzõː/ die; ∼, ∼s season

saisonal /zɛzoˈnaːl/ ① Adj. seasonal ② adv. ⟨fluctuate⟩ according to the season

Saite die; ∼, ∼n string

Saiten·instrument das stringed instrument

Sakko der od. das; ∼s, ∼s jacket

Sakrament das; ∼[e]s, ∼e sacrament

Sakristei die; ∼, ∼en sacristy

säkularisieren tr. V. secularize ⟨property, art, etc.⟩; deconsecrate ⟨church⟩

Salami die; ∼, ∼[s] salami

Salami·taktik die step-by-step policy

Salat der; ∼[e]s, ∼e (a) salad (b) [grüner] ∼: lettuce; ein Kopf ∼: a [head of] lettuce

Salat-: ∼**besteck** das salad servers pl.; ∼**soße** die salad dressing

Salbe die; ∼, ∼n ointment

Salbei der od. die; ∼: sage

Saldo der; ∼s, ∼s od. Saldi (Buchf., Finanzw.) balance

Säle ▶ SAAL

Salmiak der od. das; ∼: sal ammoniac

Salmonelle die; ∼, ∼n salmonella

Salon /zaˈlõː/ der; ∼s, ∼s (a) (Raum) drawing room (b) (Geschäft) [hair etc.] salon

salopp ① Adj. casual ⟨clothes⟩; informal ⟨behaviour⟩ ② adv. ⟨dress⟩ casually

Salto der; ∼s, ∼s od. Salti somersault

Salut der; ∼[e]s, ∼e (Milit.) salute; ∼ schießen fire a salute

salutieren itr. V. (bes. Milit.) salute

Salut·schuss, *Salut·schuß der (Milit.) gun salute

Salve die; ∼, ∼n (Milit.) salvo; (aus Gewehren) volley

Salz das; ∼es, ∼e salt

salzen tr. V. salt

salzig Adj. salty

Salz-: ∼**kartoffel** die boiled potato; ∼**säure** die (Chemie) hydrochloric acid; ∼**stange** die salt stick; ∼**streuer** der; ∼∼s, ∼∼: salt sprinkler; salt shaker (Amer.); ∼**wasser** das (a) (zum Kochen) salted water; (b) (Meerwasser) salt water

Sambia (das); ∼s Zambia

Samen der; ∼s, ∼ (a) (Samenkorn) seed (b) (Samenkörner) seed[s pl.] (c) (Sperma) sperm; semen

Samen-: ∼**bank** die; Pl. ∼∼en (Med., Tiermed.) sperm bank; ∼**erguss, *∼erguß** der ejaculation; ∼**korn** das seed; ∼**spender** der (Med.) sperm donor

Sammel-: ∼**büchse** die collecting box; ∼**mappe** die folder; file

sammeln ① tr. (auch itr.) V. (a) collect; gather ⟨honey, firewood, fig.: experiences, impressions, etc.⟩; gather, pick ⟨berries etc.⟩ (b) (zusammenkommen lassen) gather ⟨people⟩ [together]; assemble ⟨people⟩; cause ⟨light rays⟩ to converge ② refl. V. gather [together]

Sammler der; ∼s, ∼: collector

Sammlung die; ∼, ∼en (a) collection (b) [innere] ∼: composure

Samstag der; ∼[e]s, ∼e Saturday; s. auch DIENSTAG

samstags Adv. on Saturdays

samt ① Präp. mit Dat. together with ② Adv. ∼ und sonders one and all

Samt der; ∼[e]s, ∼e velvet

samten Adj. velvet

Samt·handschuh der velvet glove; jmdn. mit ∼en anfassen (fig.) handle sb. with kid gloves

samtig Adj. velvety

sämtlich Indefinitpron. u. unbest. Zahlwort all the

Sand der; ∼[e]s sand

Sandale die; ∼, ∼n sandal

Sand-: ∼**bank** die; Pl. ∼bänke sandbank; ∼**dorn** der; Pl. ∼∼e (Bot.) hippopha; [Echter] ∼dorn sea buckthorn ∼**düne** die sand dune

sandig Adj. sandy

sand-, Sand-: ∼**kasten** der [child's] sandpit; sandbox (Amer.); ∼**kuchen** der Madeira cake; ∼**mann** der, ∼**männchen** das sandman; ∼**stein** der sandstone; ∼**strahlen** tr. V. (Technik) sandblast; ∼**strand** der sandy beach

sandte 1. u. 3. Pers. Sg. Prät. v. SENDEN

sanft ① Adj. gentle; (leise) soft; (friedlich) peaceful ② adv. gently; (leise) softly; (friedlich) peacefully

Sänfte die; ∼, ∼n litter; (geschlossen) sedan chair

Sanftheit die; ∼: gentleness; (von Klängen, Licht, Farben) softness

Sanftmut die; ∼: gentleness; mit ∼: gently; (nachsichtig) leniently

sanftmütig ① Adj. gentle; docile ⟨horse⟩ ② adv. gently

Sanftmütigkeit die; ∼: gentleness; (Fügsamkeit) docility

sang 1. u. 3. Pers. Sg. Prät. v. SINGEN

Sänger der; ∼s, ∼, **Sängerin** die; ∼, ∼nen singer

sanieren ① tr. V. (a) redevelop ⟨area⟩; rehabilitate ⟨building⟩; (renovieren) renovate [and improve] ⟨flat etc.⟩ (b) (Wirtsch.) restore ⟨firm⟩ to profitability ⋯⟶

S

2 *refl. V. ⟨company etc.⟩* restore itself to profitability; ⟨*person*⟩ get oneself out of the red

Sanierung *die;* ~, ~en (a) ▶ SANIEREN A: redevelopment; rehabilitation; renovation
(b) ▶ SANIEREN B: restoration to profitability

sanitär *Adj.* sanitary

Sanitäter *der;* ~s, ~, **Sanitäterin** *die;* ~, ~nen first-aid worker; (im Krankenwagen) ambulance worker

sank *1. u. 3. Pers. Sg. Prät. v.* SINKEN

Sanktion *die;* ~, ~en sanction

sanktionieren *tr. V.* sanction

Sanktionierung *die;* ~, ~en sanctioning

sann *1. u. 3. Pers. Sg. Prät. v.* SINNEN

Saphir *der;* ~s, ~e sapphire

Sardelle *die;* ~, ~n anchovy

Sardine *die;* ~, ~n sardine

Sarg *der;* ~[e]s, **Särge** coffin

Sarkasmus *der;* ~: sarcasm

sarkastisch **1** *Adj.* sarcastic
2 *adv.* sarcastically

SARS, Sars /zars/ *das;* ~: SARS

saß *1. u. 3. Pers. Sg. Prät. v.* SITZEN

Satan *der* (bibl.) Satan *no def. art.*

Satellit *der;* ~en, ~en satellite

Satelliten-: ~**fernsehen** *das* satellite television; ~**navigation** *die* satellite navigation; ~**schüssel** *die* (ugs.) satellite dish; ~**technologie** *die* satellite technology

Satire *die;* ~, ~n satire

satirisch **1** *Adj.* satirical
2 *adv.* satirically; with a satirical touch

satt *Adj.* (a) full [up] *pred.*; well-fed; **sich** ~ **essen/trinken** eat/drink as much as one wants; eat/drink one's fill
(b) *jmdn./etw.* ~ **haben** (ugs.) be fed up with sb./sth. (coll.)

Sattel *der;* ~s, **Sättel** saddle

satteln **1** *tr. V.* saddle
2 *itr. V.* saddle the/one's horse

sättigen *itr. V.* be filling

Sattler *der;* ~s, ~, **Sattlerin** *die;* ~, ~nen saddler; (allgemein) leather worker

Satz *der;* ~es, **Sätze** (a) (sprachliche Einheit) sentence
(b) (Musik) movement
(c) (Tennis, Volleyball) set; ⟨Tischtennis, Badminton⟩ game
(d) (Sprung) leap; jump
(e) (Amtsspr.: Tarif) rate
(f) (Set) set
(g) (Bodensatz) sediment; (von Kaffee) grounds *pl.*

Satz·glied *das,* **Satz·teil** *der* (Sprachw.) component part [of a/the sentence]

Satzung *die;* ~, ~en articles of association *pl.;* statutes *pl.*

Satz·zeichen *das* punctuation mark

Sau *die;* ~, **Säue (a)** (weibliches Schwein) sow
(b) (bes. südd.: Schwein) pig
(c) die ~ rauslassen (fig. ugs.) let one's hair down

sau-, Sau- (salopp) bloody ... (Brit. sl.); damn ... (coll.)

sauber **1** *Adj.* (a) clean; **etw.** ~ **machen** clean sth.; ~ **machen** (putzen) clean; do the cleaning
(b) (sorgfältig) neat
2 *adv.* (a) (sorgfältig) neatly
(b) (fehlerlos) [sehr] ~: [quite] perfectly

Sauberkeit *die;* ~: cleanness

säuberlich **1** *Adj.* neat
2 *adv.* neatly; **fein** ~ **geordnet/verpackt** *usw.* neatly arranged/packed *etc.*

*sauber|machen ▶ SAUBER 1A

säubern *tr. V.* (a) clean
(b) (befreien) clear, rid (von of); purge ⟨party, government, etc.⟩ (von of)

Säuberung *die;* ~, ~en (a) cleaning
(b) (Entfernung) purging
(c) (Politik) purge; **ethnische** ~ (verhüll.) ethnic cleansing

Säuberungs·aktion *die* (Politik) purge; clean-up operation

Sauce ▶ SOSSE

Saudi *der;* ~s, ~s Saudi

Saudi-Arabien (*das*) Saudi Arabia

sauer *Adj.* (a) sour; pickled ⟨herring, gherkin, etc.⟩; acid[ic] ⟨wine, vinegar⟩; **saurer Regen** acid rain
(b) (ugs.: verärgert) cross, annoyed (**auf** + *Akk.* with)

Sauer·braten *der:* braised beef marinated in vinegar and herbs; sauerbraten (Amer.)

Sauerei *die;* ~, ~en (salopp abwertend) (a) (Unflätigkeit) obscenity
(b) (Gemeinheit) bloody scandal (coll.)

Sauer-: ~**kirsche** *die* sour cherry; ~**kraut** *das* sauerkraut

säuerlich *Adj.* [leicht] ~: slightly sour; slightly sharp ⟨sauce⟩

Sauer-: ~**stoff** *der* oxygen; ~**stoff·gerät** *das* oxygen apparatus; ~**stoff·mangel** *der* lack of oxygen; ~**teig** *der* leaven

saufen **1** *unr. itr. V.* (salopp: trinken) drink; swig (coll.); (Alkohol trinken) drink; booze (coll.)
2 *unr. tr. V.* (salopp: trinken) drink

Säufer *der;* ~s, ~ (salopp) boozer (coll.)

säuft *3. Pers. Sg. Präsens v.* SAUFEN

saugen **1** *tr. V.* (a) *auch unr.* suck
(b) *auch itr.* (staubsaugen) vacuum; hoover (coll.)
2 *regelm.* (*auch unr.*) *itr. V.* **an etw.** (*Dat.*) ~: suck [at] sth.
3 *unr.* (*auch regelm.*) *refl. V.* **sich voll etw.** ~: become soaked with sth.

säugen *tr. V.* suckle

Säuge·tier *das* (Zool.) mammal

Säugling *der;* ~s, ~e baby

Säuglings-: ∼**alter** das infancy; babyhood; ∼**pflege** die baby care

Säule die; ∼, ∼n column; (nur als Stütze, auch fig.) pillar

Saum der; ∼[e]s, Säume hem

säumen tr. V. hem; (fig. geh.) line

säumig (geh.) Adj. tardy

Sauna die; ∼, ∼s od. Saunen sauna

Säure die; ∼, ∼n (a) (von Früchten) sourness; (von Wein, Essig) acidity; (von Soßen) sharpness (b) (Chemie) acid

säure-: ∼**beständig** Adj. acid-resistant; ∼**frei** Adj. acid-free

Saure-gurken-zeit, Saure-Gurken-Zeit die (ugs.) silly season (Brit.)

Saurier /'zauːriɐ̯/ der; ∼s, ∼: large prehistoric reptile

Saus: in ∼ und Braus leben live the high life

säuseln 1 itr. V. ‹leaves, branches, etc.› rustle; ‹wind› murmur
2 tr. V. (iron.: sagen) whisper

sausen itr. V. (a) ‹wind› whistle; ‹storm› roar; ‹head, ears› buzz
(b) mit sein ‹person› rush; ‹vehicle› roar
(c) mit sein ‹whip, bullet, etc.› whistle

sau-, Sau-: ∼**stall** der (fig. salopp abwertend) hole (coll.); dump (coll.); ∼**stark** Adj. (salopp) bloody brilliant (sl.); ∼**wetter** das (salopp abwertend) lousy weather (coll.); ∼**wohl** Adj. sich ∼wohl fühlen (salopp) feel bloody (Brit. sl.) or (coll.) damn good or great

Savanne /za'vanə/ die; ∼, ∼n savannah

Saxophon das; ∼s, ∼e saxophone

SB- /ɛsˈbeː-/ self-service attrib.

S-Bahn /'ɛs-/ die city and suburban railway

Scanner /'skænɐ/ der; ∼s, ∼ (DV, Med., graf. Technik) scanner

Schabe die; ∼, ∼n cockroach

schaben tr., itr. V. scrape

Schaber der; ∼s, ∼: scraper

schäbig 1 Adj. (a) (abgenutzt) shabby
(b) (jämmerlich, gering) pathetic
(c) (gemein) shabby
2 adv. (a) (abgenutzt) shabbily
(b) (jämmerlich) miserably
(c) (gemein) meanly

Schablone die; ∼, ∼n pattern

Schach das; ∼s, ∼s (a) (Spiel) chess
(b) (Stellung) check; jmdn./etw. in ∼ halten (ugs. fig.) keep sb./sth. in check

Schach-: ∼**brett** das chessboard; ∼**figur** die chess piece; ∼**spiel** das (a) (Spiel) chess; (das Spielen) chess-playing; (b) (Brett und Figuren) chess set

Schacht der; ∼[e]s, Schächte shaft

Schachtel die; ∼, ∼n (a) box; eine ∼ Zigaretten a packet or (Amer.) pack of cigarettes
(b) alte ∼ (salopp abwertend) old bag (sl.)

schade Adj. [ach, wie] ∼! [what a] pity or

shame; [es ist] ∼ um jmdn./etw. it's a pity or shame about sb./sth.; für jmdn./für od. zu etw. zu ∼ sein be too good for sb./sth.

Schädel der; ∼s, ∼: skull; (Kopf) head

Schädel-basis-bruch der (Med.) basal skull fracture

Schädel-bruch der (Med.) skull fracture

schaden itr. V. jmdm./einer Sache ∼: damage or harm sb./sth.

Schaden der; ∼s, Schäden (a) damage no pl., no indef. art.; ein kleiner/großer ∼: little/ major damage
(b) (Nachteil) disadvantage

schaden-, Schaden-: ∼**ersatz** der (Rechtsw.) damages pl.; ∼**freude** die malicious pleasure; ∼**froh** 1 Adj. gloating; ∼froh sein gloat; 2 adv. with malicious pleasure

schadhaft Adj. defective

Schadhaftigkeit die; ∼: defectiveness

schädigen tr. V. damage ‹health, reputation, interests›; harm, hurt ‹person›; cause losses to ‹firm, industry, etc.›

Schädigung die; ∼, ∼en damage no pl., no indef. art. (Gen. to)

schädlich Adj. harmful

Schädling der; ∼s, ∼e pest

Schad-stoff der harmful chemical

schadstoff-arm Adj. (bes. Kfz-W.) low in harmful substances postpos.; clean-exhaust attrib. ‹vehicle›

Schaf das; ∼[e]s, ∼e (a) sheep
(b) (ugs.: Dummkopf) twit (Brit. coll.)

Schaf-bock der ram

Schäfchen das; ∼s, ∼: [little] sheep; (Lamm) lamb

Schäfchen-wolke die fleecy cloud

Schäfer der; ∼s, ∼: shepherd

Schäfer-hund der sheepdog; [deutscher] ∼: Alsatian

Schäferin die; ∼, ∼nen shepherdess

Schaf-fell das sheepskin

schaffen 1 unr. tr. V. (a) create
(b) auch regelm. (herstellen) create ‹conditions, jobs, situation, etc.›; make ‹room, space, fortune›
2 tr. V. (a) (bewältigen) manage; es ∼, etw. zu tun manage to do sth.
(b) (ugs.: erschöpfen) wear out
(c) etw. aus etw./in etw. (Akk.) ∼: get sth. out of/into sth.
3 itr. V. (a) (südd.: arbeiten) work
(b) sich (Dat.) zu ∼ machen busy oneself; jmdm. zu ∼ machen cause sb. trouble

Schaffner der; ∼s ∼ (im Bus) conductor; (im Zug) guard (Brit.); conductor (Amer.)

Schaffnerin die; ∼, ∼nen (im Bus) conductress (Brit.); (im Zug) guard (Brit.); conductress (Amer.)

Schaffung die; ∼: creation

Schafott das; ∼[e]s, ∼e scaffold

Schafs-käse der sheep's milk cheese

S

Schaf·wolle *die* sheep's wool

Schakal *der;* ~s, ~e jackal

schal *Adj.* stale ⟨*drink, taste, smell, joke*⟩; empty ⟨*words, feeling*⟩

Schal *der;* ~s, ~s *od.* ~e scarf

Schale *die;* ~, ~n (a) (Obstschale) skin; (abgeschälte ~) peel *no pl.;*
(b) (Nussschale, Eierschale) shell
(c) (Schüssel) bowl; (flacher) dish
(d) sich in ~ werfen *od.* schmeißen (ugs.) get dressed [up] to the nines

schälen ① *tr. V.* peel ⟨*fruit, vegetable*⟩; shell ⟨*egg, nut, pea*⟩
② *refl. V.* peel

Schall *der;* ~[e]s, ~e *od.* Schälle sound

Schall·dämpfer *der* (a) silencer
(b) (Musik) mute

schall·dicht *Adj.* soundproof

schallen *regelm.* (*auch unr.*) *itr. V.* ring out; ~des Gelächter ringing laughter

Schall-: ~geschwindigkeit *die* speed *or* velocity of sound; ~mauer *die* sound *or* sonic barrier; ~platte *die* record

Schalotte *die;* ~, ~n shallot

schalt *1. u. 3. Pers. Sg. Prät. v.* SCHELTEN

schalten ① *tr. V.* switch
② *itr. V.* (a) (Schalter betätigen) switch, turn (auf + *Akk.* to)
(b) ⟨*machine*⟩ switch (auf + *Akk.* to)
(c) (im Auto) change [gear]
(d) ~ und walten manage one's affairs
(e) (ugs.: begreifen) twig (coll.); catch on (coll.)

Schalter *der;* ~s, ~ (a) switch
(b) (Post-, Bankschalter usw.) counter

Schalter-: ~beamte *der,* ~beamtin *die* counter clerk; (im Bahnhof) ticket clerk; ~halle *die* hall; (im Bahnhof) booking hall (Brit.); ticket office

Schalt·jahr *das* leap year

Schaltung *die;* ~, ~en (Elektrot.) circuit; wiring system

Scham *die;* ~: shame

schämen *refl. V.* be ashamed (*Gen.,* für, wegen of)

Scham·gefühl *das* sense of shame

schamhaft ① *Adj.* bashful
② *adv.* bashfully

scham·los ① *Adj.* (a) (skrupellos, dreist) shameless
(b) (unanständig) indecent; shameless ⟨*person*⟩
② *adv.* (a) (skrupellos, dreist) shamelessly
(b) (unanständig) indecently

Schampon *das;* ~s, ~s ▶ SHAMPOO

schamponieren *tr. V.* shampoo

Schande *die;* ~: disgrace

schändlich ① *Adj.* disgraceful
② *adv.* disgracefully

Schändlichkeit *die;* ~: disgracefulness

Schar *die;* ~, ~en crowd; horde

scharen·weise *Adv.* in swarms *or* hordes

scharf; schärfer, schärfst... ① *Adj.* (a) sharp
(b) (stark gewürzt, brennend, stechend) hot; strong ⟨*drink, vinegar, etc.*⟩; caustic ⟨*chemical*⟩; pungent ⟨*smell*⟩
(c) (durchdringend) shrill; (hell) harsh; (kalt) biting ⟨*cold, wind, etc.*⟩; sharp ⟨*frost*⟩
(d) (deutlich wahrnehmend) keen
(e) (schnell) fast; hard ⟨*ride, gallop, etc.*⟩
(f) (explosiv) live; (Ballspiele) powerful ⟨*shot*⟩
(g) das ~e S (bes. österr.) the letter 'ß'
(h) ~ auf jmdn./etw. sein (ugs.) really fancy sb. (coll.)/be really keen on sth.
② *adv.* (a) ~ würzen/abschmecken season/flavour highly; ~ riechen smell pungent
(b) (durchdringend) shrilly; (hell) harshly; (kalt) bitingly
(c) (deutlich wahrnehmend) ⟨*listen, watch, etc.*⟩ closely, intently; ⟨*think, consider, etc.*⟩ hard
(d) (deutlich hervortretend) sharply
(e) (schonungslos) ⟨*attack, criticize, etc.*⟩ sharply, strongly; ⟨*watch, observe, etc.*⟩ closely
(f) (schnell) fast; ~ bremsen brake hard *or* sharply

Schärfe *die;* ~ (a) sharpness
(b) (von Geschmack) hotness; (von Chemikalien) causticity; (von Geruch) pungency
(c) (Intensität) shrillness; (des Frostes) sharpness

schärfen ① *tr. V.* (auch fig.) sharpen
② *refl. V.* become sharper *or* keener

scharf-, Scharf-: ~kantig *Adj.* sharp-edged; ~macher *der* (ugs.) rabble-rouser; ~macherei *die;* ~~, ~~en (ugs.) rabble-rousing; ~macherin *die;* ▶ ~MACHER; ~sichtig *Adj.* sharp-sighted; perspicacious; ~sinn *der* astuteness; ~sinnig ① *Adj.* astute; ② *adv.* astutely

Scharlach *der;* ~s (Med.) scarlet fever

Scharlatan *der;* ~s, ~e (abwertend) charlatan

Scharnier *das;* ~s, ~e hinge

scharren ① *itr. V.* (a) scrape
(b) (wühlen) scratch
② *tr. V.* scrape, scratch out ⟨*hole, hollow, etc.*⟩

Schaschlik *der od. das;* ~s, ~s (Kochk.) shashlik

Schatten *der;* ~s, ~ (a) shadow
(b) (schattiger Bereich) shade

Schatten-: ~kabinett *das* (Politik) shadow cabinet; ~riss, **~riß der* silhouette; ~seite *die* shady side; die ~seiten des Lebens kennen lernen (fig.) get to know the dark side of life

schattig *Adj.* shady

Schatz *der;* ~es, Schätze treasure *no indef. art.*

schätzen ① *tr. V.* (a) estimate; sich glücklich ~: deem oneself lucky
(b) (ugs.: annehmen) reckon
(c) (würdigen, hoch achten) jmdn. ~: hold sb. in high esteem

**alte Schreibung - vgl. Hinweis auf S. xiv

② *itr. V.* guess

Schätzung *die;* ~, ~en estimate

Schätz·wert *der* estimated value

Schau *die;* ~, ~en (a) (Ausstellung) exhibition
(b) (Vorführung) show
(c) zur ~ **stellen** (ausstellen) exhibit; display; (offen zeigen) display

Schauder *der;* ~s, ~: shiver

schauderhaft ① *Adj.* terrible
② *adv.* terribly

schaudern *itr. V.* (a) (vor Kälte) shiver
(b) (vor Angst) shudder

schauen (bes. südd., österr., schweiz.)
① *itr. V.* (a) look
(b) (sich kümmern um) **nach jmdm./etw.** ~: take *or* have a look at sb./sth.
(c) (achten) **auf etw.** (*Akk.*) ~: set store by sth.
(d) (ugs.: sich bemühen) **schau, dass du** ...: see *or* mind that you ...
(e) (nachsehen) have a look
② *tr. V.* **Fernsehen** ~: watch television

Schauer *der;* ~s, ~: shower

Schauer·geschichte *die* horror story

schauerlich ① *Adj.* (a) horrifying
(b) (ugs.: fürchterlich) terrible (coll.)
② (ugs.: fürchterlich) terribly (coll.)

Schaufel *die;* ~, ~n shovel; (Kehr~) dustpan

schaufeln *tr. V.* shovel; (graben) dig

Schau·fenster *das* shop window

Schaufenster-: ~**bummel** *der:* einen ~**bummel machen** go window shopping; ~**einbruch** *der* raid on a shop window

Schaukel *die;* ~, ~n (a) swing
(b) (Wippe) see-saw

schaukeln ① *itr. V.* (a) swing; (im Schaukelstuhl) rock
(b) (sich hin und her bewegen) sway [to and fro]; (sich auf und ab bewegen) ⟨*ship, boat*⟩ pitch and toss; ⟨*vehicle*⟩ bump [up and down]
② *tr. V.* rock

Schaukel-: ~**pferd** *das* rocking horse; ~**stuhl** *der* rocking chair

Schau·lustige *der/die; adj. Dekl.* curious onlooker

Schaum *der;* ~s, Schäume (a) foam; (von Seife usw.) lather; (von Getränken, Suppen usw.) froth
(b) (Geifer) foam; froth

schäumen *itr. V.* foam; froth; ⟨*soap etc.*⟩ lather; ⟨*beer, fizzy drink, etc.*⟩ froth [up]

Schaum·gummi *der* foam rubber

schaumig *Adj.* frothy; **Butter und Zucker** ~ **rühren** beat butter and sugar until fluffy

Schaum-: ~**schläger** *der* (abwertend) boaster; ~**schlägerei** *die* (abwertend) boasting; ~**schlägerin** *die:* ▶ ~SCHLÄGER; ~**stoff** *der* [plastic] foam; ~**wein** *der* sparkling wine

Schau·platz *der* scene

schaurig *Adj.* (furchtbar) dreadful; frightful; (unheimlich) eerie

Schau-: ~**spiel** *das* (a) (Drama) drama *no art.;* (b) (ernstes Stück) play; (c) (geh.: Anblick) spectacle; ~**spieler** *der* actor; ~**spielerin** *die* actress; ~**steller** *der;* ~~s, ~~: showman; ~**stellerin** *die;* ~~, ~~nen showwoman

Scheck *der;* ~s, ~s cheque

Scheck-: ~**heft** *das* chequebook; ~**karte** *die* cheque card

scheel (ugs.) ① *Adj.* disapproving; (neidisch) envious; jealous
② *adv.* disapprovingly; (neidisch) enviously; jealously

scheffeln *tr. V.* (ugs.) rake in (coll.)

Scheibe *die;* ~, ~n (a) disc
(b) (abgeschnittene) slice
(c) (Glasscheibe) pane [of glass]; (Fensterscheibe) [window] pane

Scheiben-: ~**bremse** *die* disc brake; ~**wasch·anlage** *die* (Kfz-W.) windscreen washer system *or* unit; ~**wischer** *der* windscreen wiper

Scheide *die;* ~, ~n (a) sheath
(b) (Anat.) vagina

scheiden *unr. tr. V.* dissolve ⟨*marriage*⟩; divorce ⟨*married couple*⟩; **sich** ~ **lassen** get divorced *or* get a divorce

Scheidung *die;* ~, ~en divorce

Schein *der;* ~[e]s, ~e (a) (Lichtschein) light
(b) (Anschein) appearances *pl., no art.;* (Täuschung) pretence; **etw. nur zum** ~ **tun** [only] pretend to do sth.; make a show of doing sth.
(c) (Geldschein) note

scheinbar ① *Adj.* apparent; seeming
② *adv.* seemingly

scheinen *unr. itr. V.* (a) shine
(b) (den Eindruck erwecken) seem; appear; **mir scheint, [dass]** ...: it seems *or* appears to me that ...

schein-, Schein-: ~**heilig** ① *Adj.* hypocritical; ② *adv.* hypocritically; ~**heiligkeit** *die* hypocrisy; ~**tot** *Adj.* (a) (Med.) apparently *or* seemingly dead; (b) (salopp: sehr alt) with one foot in the grave *postpos.;* ~**werfer** *der* floodlight; (am Auto) headlight; ~**werfer·licht** *das* floodlight; (des Autos) headlights *pl.;* (im Theater, Museum usw.) spotlight [beam]

Scheiße *die;* ~ (derb) shit (coarse); crap (coarse)

scheiß·egal *Adj.* (derb) ~ **sein** not matter a damn (sl.); **das ist mir** ~: I don't give a damn (sl.) *or* (coarse) shit

scheißen *unr. itr. V.* (derb) [have *or* (Amer.) take a] shit (coarse); crap (coarse); have a crap (coarse)

Scheiß·kerl *der* (derb) bastard (coll.)

Scheitel *der;* ~s, ~: parting

scheiteln *tr. V.* part ⟨*hair*⟩

scheitern itr. V.; mit sein fail; ⟨talks, marriage⟩ break down; ⟨plan, project⟩ fail, fall through

Schelle die; ~, ~n bell

schellen itr. V. (westd.) ▶ KLINGELN

Schell·fisch der haddock

Schelm der; ~[e]s, ~e rascal; rogue

schelmisch ① Adj. roguish
② adv. roguishly

Schelte die; ~, ~n (geh.) scolding

schelten (südd., geh.) ① unr. itr. V. auf od. über jmdn./etw. ~: moan about sb./sth.
② unr. tr. V. scold

Schema das; ~s, ~s od. ~ta od. Schemen pattern

schematisch ① Adj. (a) diagrammatic
(b) (mechanisch) mechanical
② adv. (a) in diagram form
(b) (mechanisch) mechanically

Schemel der; ~s, ~ (a) stool
(b) (südd.: Fußbank) footstool

Schenkel der; ~s, ~: thigh

schenken tr. V. (a) give; jmdm. etw. [zum Geburtstag] ~: give sb. sth. or sth. to sb. [as a birthday present or for his/her birthday]
(b) (ugs.: erlassen) jmdm./sich etw. ~: spare sb./oneself sth.

scheppern itr. V. (ugs.) clank

Scherbe die; ~, ~n fragment

Schere die; ~, ~n (a) scissors pl.; eine ~: a pair of scissors
(b) (Zool.) claw

scheren¹ unr. tr. V. crop; (von Haar befreien) shear, clip ⟨sheep⟩

scheren² tr., refl. V. sich um jmdn./etw. nicht ~: not care about sb./sth.

Schererei̯en Pl. (ugs.) trouble no pl.

Scherz der; ~es, ~e joke

scherzen itr. V. joke

scherzhaft ① Adj. jocular
② adv. jocularly

scheu ① Adj. shy; timid ⟨animal⟩; (ehrfürchtig) awed
② adv. shyly; (von Tieren) timidly

Scheu die; ~ (a) shyness; (Ehrfurcht) awe
(b) (von Tieren) timidity

scheuchen tr. V. shoo; drive

scheuen ① tr. V. shrink from; shun ⟨people, light, company, etc.⟩
② refl. V. sich vor etw. (Dat.) ~: be afraid of or shrink from sth.
③ itr. V. ⟨horse⟩ shy (vor + Dat. at)

scheuern ① tr., itr. V. (a) (reinigen) scour; scrub
(b) (reiben) rub; chafe
② tr. V. (reiben an) rub

Scheuer-: ~pulver das scouring powder; ~tuch das; Pl. ~tücher scouring cloth

Scheune die; ~, ~n barn

Scheusal das; ~s, ~e monster

scheußlich ① Adj. (a) dreadful
(b) (ugs.: äußerst unangenehm) dreadful (coll.); ghastly (coll.) ⟨weather, taste, smell⟩
② adv. (a) dreadfully
(b) (ugs.: sehr) dreadfully (coll.)

Scheußlichkeit die; ~, ~en (a) dreadfulness
(b) (etw. Scheußliches) dreadful thing

Schi usw. ▶ SKI usw.

Schicht die; ~, ~en (a) (Lage) layer; (Geol.) stratum; (von Farbe) coat; (sehr dünn) film
(b) (Gesellschaftsschicht) stratum
(c) (Arbeitsschicht) shift; ~ arbeiten work shifts; be on shift work

Schicht·arbeit die shift work

schichten tr. V. stack

schick ① Adj. (a) stylish; chic ⟨clothes, fashions⟩; smart ⟨woman, girl, man⟩
(b) (ugs.: großartig, toll) great (coll.); fantastic (coll.)
② adv. stylishly; smartly ⟨furnished, decorated⟩

schicken ① tr. V. send; jmdm. etw. ~, etw. an jmdn. ~: send sth. to sb.; send sth. to sb.
② itr. V. nach jmdm. ~: send for sb.
③ refl. V. (veralt.: sich ziemen) be proper or fitting

Schickeria die; ~ (ugs.) smart set

Schicksal das; ~s, ~e: [das] ~: fate; destiny; (schweres Los) fate

Schicksals·schlag der stroke of fate

Schiebe·dach das sunroof

schieben ① unr. tr. V. (a) push
(b) (stecken) put
(c) etw. auf jmdn./etw. ~: blame sb./sth. for sth.
② unr. refl. V. sich durch die Menge ~: push one's way through the crowd
③ unr. itr. V. push; (heftig) shove

Schiebe·tür die sliding door

Schiebung die; ~, ~en (ugs.) (a) shady deal
(b) (Begünstigung) pulling strings

schied 1. u. 3. Pers. Sg. Prät. v. SCHEIDEN

Schieds·richter der,
Schieds·richterin die referee; (Tennis, Hockey, Kricket) umpire

schief ① Adj. (a) (schräg) leaning ⟨wall, fence, post⟩; (nicht parallel) crooked; sloping ⟨surface⟩; worn[-down] ⟨heels⟩
(b) (fig.: verzerrt) distorted ⟨picture, presentation, view, impression⟩; false ⟨comparison⟩
② adv. (a) (schräg) das Bild hängt/der Teppich liegt ~: the picture/carpet is crooked; der Tisch steht ~: the table isn't level
(b) (fig.: verzerrt) etw. ~ darstellen give a distorted account of sth.
(c) ~ gehen od. laufen (ugs.) go wrong

Schiefer der; ~s (Gestein) slate

***schief-:** ~|gehen, ~|laufen ▶ SCHIEF 2c

---

schielen *itr. V.* **(a)** squint; **auf dem rechten Auge** ∼: have a squint in one's right eye **(b)** (ugs.: blicken) look out of the corner of one's eye

schien *1. u. 3. Pers. Sg. Prät. v.* SCHEINEN

Schien·bein *das* shinbone

Schiene *die;* ∼, ∼n **(a)** rail **(b)** (Gleitschiene) runner **(c)** (Med.: Stütze) splint

schienen *tr. V.* jmds. Arm/Bein ∼: put sb.'s arm/leg in a splint/splints

schießen ⟦1⟧ *unr. itr. V.* **(a)** shoot; **auf jmdn./etw.** ∼: shoot/fire at sb./sth. **(b)** *mit sein* (strömen) gush; (spritzen) spurt **(c)** *mit sein* (schnell wachsen) shoot up ⟦2⟧ *unr. tr. V.* **(a)** shoot; fire ⟨*bullet, missile, rocket*⟩ **(b)** (Fußball) score ⟨*goal*⟩ **(c)** (ugs.: fotografieren) **einige Aufnahmen** ∼: take a few snaps

Schießerei *die;* ∼, ∼en **(a)** shooting *no indef. art., no pl.;* **(b)** (Schusswechsel) gun battle

Schiff *das;* ∼[e]s, ∼e **(a)** ship; **mit dem** ∼: by ship *or* sea **(b)** (Archit.) (Mittelschiff) nave; (Querschiff) transept; (Seitenschiff) aisle

*Schiffahrt ▶ SCHIFFFAHRT

schiffbar *Adj.* navigable

Schiff-: ∼**bau** *der* shipbuilding *no art.;* ∼**bruch** *der* (veralt.) shipwreck; **[mit etw.]** ∼**bruch erleiden** (fig.) fail [in sth.]; ∼**brüchige** *der/die; adj. Dekl.* shipwrecked man/woman

Schiffer *der;* ∼s, ∼, **Schifferin** *die;* ∼, ∼nen boatman/boatwoman; (eines Lastkahns) bargee; (Kapitän[in]) skipper

Schiff·fahrt *die* shipping *no indef. art.;* (Schifffahrtskunde) navigation

Schiffs-: ∼**arzt** *der* ship's doctor; ∼**brücke** *die* pontoon bridge; ∼**junge** *der* ship's boy; ∼**reise** *die* voyage; (Vergnügungsreise) cruise; ∼**verkehr** *der* shipping traffic

Schikane *die;* ∼, ∼n **(a)** harassment *no indef. art.* **(b)** **mit allen** ∼n (ugs.) ⟨*kitchen, house*⟩ with all mod cons (Brit. coll.); ⟨*car, bicycle, stereo*⟩ with all the extras

schikanieren *tr. V.* harass

Schild¹ *der;* ∼[e]s, ∼e shield

Schild² *das;* ∼[e]s, ∼er sign; (Nummernschild) number plate; (Namensschild) nameplate; (auf Denkmälern, Gebäuden usw.) plaque; (Etikett) label

Schild·drüse *die* (Med.) thyroid [gland]

schildern *tr. V.* describe

Schild·kröte *die* tortoise; (Meeresschildkröte) turtle

Schilf *das;* ∼[e]s **(a)** reed **(b)** (Röhricht) reeds *pl.*

schillern *itr. V.* shimmer

Schilling *der;* ∼s, ∼e schilling

schilt *3. Pers. Sg. Präsens v.* SCHELTEN

Schimmel *der;* ∼s, ∼ **(a)** mould; (auf Leder, Papier) mildew **(b)** (Pferd) white horse

schimmelig *Adj.* mouldy; mildewy ⟨*paper, leather*⟩

schimmeln *itr. V.; auch mit sein* go mouldy; ⟨*leather, paper*⟩ get covered with mildew

Schimmel·pilz *der* mould

Schimmer *der;* ∼s (Schein) gleam; (von Seide) shimmer; sheen; **keinen** ∼ **[von etw.] haben** (ugs.) not have the faintest idea [about sth.] (coll.)

schimmern *itr. V.* gleam; ⟨*water, sea*⟩ glisten, shimmer; ⟨*metal*⟩ glint, gleam; ⟨*silk etc.*⟩ shimmer

schimmlig ▶ SCHIMMELIG

Schimpanse *der;* ∼n, ∼n chimpanzee

schimpfen ⟦1⟧ *itr. V.* **(a)** carry on (coll.) (**auf, über** + *Akk.* about); (meckern) grumble, moan (**auf, über** + *Akk.* at) **(b)** **mit jmdm.** ∼: tell sb. off; scold sb. ⟦2⟧ *tr. V.* jmdn. ∼: tell sb. off

Schimpf·wort *das; Pl.* **Schimpf·wörter** (Beleidigung) insult; (derbes Wort) swear word

schinden *unr. tr. V.* maltreat; ill-treat; **Zeit** ∼ (ugs.) play for time

Schinderei *die;* ∼, ∼en (Strapaze, Qual) struggle; (Arbeit) toil

Schinken *der;* ∼s, ∼: ham

Schinken·speck *der* bacon

Schippe *die;* ∼, ∼n (Schaufel) shovel

Schirm *der;* ∼[e]s, ∼e umbrella; brolly (Brit. coll.); (Sonnenschirm) sunshade

Schirm-: ∼**herr** *der* patron; ∼**herrin** *die* patroness; ∼**herrschaft** *die* patronage; ∼**ständer** *der* umbrella stand

schiss, *schiß *1. u. 3. Pers. Sg. Prät. v.* SCHEISSEN

Schlacht *die;* ∼, ∼en battle

schlachten *tr. (auch itr.) V.* slaughter; kill ⟨*rabbit, chicken, etc.*⟩

Schlachter *der;* ∼s, ∼ (nordd.) butcher

Schlachterei *die;* ∼, ∼en (nordd.) butcher's [shop]

Schlacht-: ∼**feld** *das* battlefield; ∼**hof** *der* abattoir; ∼**tier** *das* animal kept for meat; (kurz vor der Schlachtung) animal for slaughter

Schlachtung *die;* ∼, ∼en slaughter[ing]

Schlacht·vieh *das* animals *pl.* kept for meat; (kurz vor der Schlachtung) animals *pl.* for slaughter

Schlacke *die;* ∼, ∼n cinders *pl.;* (Hochofen∼) slag

Schlaf *der;* ∼[e]s sleep; **einen leichten/ festen/gesunden** ∼ **haben** be a light/heavy/ good sleeper

Schlaf·anzug *der* pyjamas *pl.*

Schläfchen *das;* ∼s, ∼: nap; snooze (coll.)

Schläfe *die;* ∼, ∼n temple

schlafen *unr. itr. V.* **(a)** (auch fig.) sleep; **tief od. fest** ~: be sound asleep; **lange** ~: sleep for a long time; (am Morgen) sleep in; ~ **gehen** go to bed

(b) (ugs.: nicht aufpassen) be asleep

Schläfer *der;* ~**s**, ~, **Schläferin** *die;* ~, ~**nen** sleeper

schlaff ① *Adj.* **(a)** slack; flabby ⟨*stomach, muscles*⟩

(b) (schlapp, matt) limp ⟨*body, hand, handshake*⟩; shaky ⟨*knees*⟩

② *adv.* **(a)** slackly

(b) (schlapp, matt) limply

Schlaf-: ~**gelegenheit** *die* place to sleep; ~**mittel** *das* sleep-inducing drug

schläfrig ① *Adj.* sleepy

② *adv.* sleepily

Schläfrigkeit *die;* ~: sleepiness

Schlaf-: ~**saal** *der* dormitory; ~**sack** sleeping bag

schläft *3. Pers. Sg. Präsens v.* SCHLAFEN

Schlaf-: ~**tablette** *die* sleeping pill; ~**wagen** *der* sleeping car; sleeper; ~**zimmer** *das* bedroom

Schlag *der;* ~**[e]s**, **Schläge** **(a)** blow; (Faust~) punch; (Klaps) slap; (Tennis, Golf) stroke; shot; ~ **auf** ~ (fig.) in quick succession

(b) (Aufprall) bang; (dumpf) thud; (Klopfen) knock

(c) (des Herzens, Pulses) beating; (eines Pendels) swinging

(d) (einzelne rhythmische Bewegung) beat; (eines Pendels) swing

(e) (Töne) (einer Uhr) striking; (einer Glocke) ringing

(f) (einzelner Ton) (Stundenschlag) stroke; (Glockenschlag) ring; ~ **acht Uhr** on the stroke of eight

schlag-, Schlag-: ~**ader** *die* artery; ~**anfall** *der* stroke; ~**artig** ① *Adj.* very sudden; ② *adv.* quite suddenly; ~**baum** *der* barrier; ~**bohrer** *der,* ~**bohr·maschine** *die* percussion drill; hammer drill

schlagen ① *unr. tr. V.* **(a)** hit; beat; strike; (mit der Faust) punch; hit; (mit der flachen Hand) slap

(b) (mit Richtungsangabe) hit ⟨*ball*⟩; **einen Nagel in etw.** (*Akk.*) ~: knock a nail into sth.

(c) (rühren) beat ⟨*mixture*⟩; whip ⟨*cream*⟩; (mit einem Schneebesen) whisk

(d) (läuten) ⟨*clock*⟩ strike; ⟨*bell*⟩ ring

(e) (legen) throw

(f) (einwickeln) wrap (**in** + *Akk.* in)

(g) (besiegen, übertreffen) beat

② *unr. itr. V.* **(a)** **er schlug mit der Faust auf den Tisch** he beat the table with his fist

(b) **mit den Flügeln** ~ ⟨*bird*⟩ beat or flap its wings

(c) *mit sein* (prallen) bang; **mit dem Kopf auf etw.** (*Akk.*)/**gegen etw.** ~: bang one's head on/against sth.

(d) *mit sein* jmdm. **auf den Magen** ~: affect sb.'s stomach

(e) (pulsieren) ⟨*heart, pulse*⟩ beat; (heftig) ⟨*heart*⟩ pound; ⟨*pulse*⟩ throb

(f) (läuten) ⟨*clock*⟩ strike; ⟨*bell*⟩ ring

③ *unr. refl. V.* fight; **sich mit jmdm.** ~: fight with sb.

Schlager *der;* ~**s**, ~ **(a)** pop song

(b) (Erfolg) (Buch) best seller; (Ware) best-selling line; (Film, Stück, Lied) hit

Schläger *der;* ~**s**, ~ **(a)** (Raufbold) tough; thug

(b) (Tennis, Federball, Squash) racket; (Tischtennis, Kricket) bat; ([Eis]hockey, Polo) stick; (Golf) club

Schlägerei *die;* ~, ~**en** brawl; fight

Schlägerin *die;* ~, ~**nen** ▶ SCHLÄGER A

Schlager·sänger *der,* **Schlager·sängerin** *die* pop singer

schlag-, Schlag-: ~**fertig** *Adj.* quick-witted ⟨*reply*⟩; ⟨*person*⟩ who is quick at repartee; ~**fertigkeit** *die* quickness at repartee; ~**licht** *das* (Kunst, Fot.) shaft of light; **ein** ~**licht auf etw. werfen** highlight sth.; ~**loch** *das* pothole; ~**obers** *das;* ~~ (österr.), ~**rahm** *der* (bes. südd., österr., schweiz.), ~**sahne** *die* whipping cream; (geschlagen) whipped cream; ~**seite** *die* list; [**starke** *od.* **schwere**] ~**seite haben/bekommen** be listing [heavily] *or* have a [heavy] list/ develop a [heavy] list; ~**stock** *der* cudgel; (für Polizei) truncheon; ~**wort** *das* **(a)** *Pl.* meist ~~**e** (Parole) slogan; catchphrase; **(b)** *Pl.* ~**wörter** (Buchw.: Stichwort) headword; ~**zeile** *die* headline; ~**zeug** *das* drums *pl.*

schlaksig (ugs.) *Adj.* gangling; lanky

Schlamassel *der od. das.* ~**s** (ugs.) mess

Schlamm *der;* ~**[e]s**, ~**e** *od.* **Schlämme** **(a)** mud

(b) (Schlick) sludge

schlammig *Adj.* **(a)** muddy

(b) (schlickig) sludgy; muddy

Schlamperei *die;* ~, ~**en** (ugs. abwertend) sloppiness

schlampig (ugs. abwertend) ① *Adj.* **(a)** (liederlich) slovenly

(b) (nachlässig) sloppy, slipshod ⟨*work*⟩

② *adv.* **(a)** (liederlich) in a slovenly way

(b) (nachlässig) sloppily

schlang *1. u. 3. Pers. Sg. Prät. v.* SCHLINGEN

Schlange *die;* ~, ~**n** **(a)** snake

(b) (Warteschlange) queue; line (Amer.); ~ **stehen** queue; stand in line (Amer.)

(c) (Autoschlange) tailback (Brit.); backup (Amer.)

schlängeln *refl. V.* ⟨*snake*⟩ wind [its way]; ⟨*road*⟩ wind, snake [its way]

Schlangen·linie *die* wavy line

schlank *Adj.* slim ⟨*person*⟩; slim, slender ⟨*build, figure*⟩

---

*alte Schreibung - vgl. Hinweis auf S. xiv

Schlankheit *die;* ~ ▶ SCHLANK: slimness; slenderness

Schlankheits·kur *die* slimming diet

schlapp *Adj.* (a) worn out; tired out; (wegen Schwüle) listless; (wegen Krankheit) run-down
(b) (ugs.: ohne Schwung) wet (coll.); feeble
(c) slack ⟨*rope, cable*⟩; loose ⟨*skin*⟩; flabby ⟨*stomach, muscles*⟩

Schlappe *die;* ~, ~n setback

schlapp|machen *itr. V.* (ugs.) flag; (zusammenbrechen) flake out (coll.); (aufgeben) give up

Schlaraffen·land *das;* ~[e]s Cockaigne

schlau ① *Adj.* (a) shrewd; astute; (gerissen) wily; crafty; cunning
(b) (ugs.: gescheit) clever; bright; smart; **aus jmdm. nicht** ~ **werden** (ugs.) not be able to make sb. out
② *adv.* shrewdly; astutely; (gerissen) craftily; cunningly

Schlauch *der;* ~[e]s, Schläuche (a) hose
(b) (im Reifen) tube

Schlauch·boot *das* rubber dinghy; inflatable [dinghy]

schlauchen (ugs.) *tr., auch itr. V.* jmdn. ~: take it out of sb.

schlauch·los *Adj.* tubeless ⟨*tyre*⟩

Schläue *die;* ~: shrewdness; astuteness; (Gerissenheit) wiliness; craftiness; cunning

Schlaufe *die;* ~, ~n loop

schlecht ① *Adj.* (a) bad; poor, bad ⟨*food, quality, style, harvest, health, circulation*⟩; poor ⟨*salary, eater, appetite*⟩; poor-quality ⟨*goods*⟩; bad, weak ⟨*eyes*⟩; **um jmdn./mit etw. steht es** ~: sb./sth. is in a bad way; **jmdn.** ~ **machen** run sb. down; disparage sb.
(b) (böse) bad; wicked
(c) (ungenießbar) off; **das Fleisch ist** ~ **geworden** the meat has gone off
② *adv.* (a) badly; **er sieht/hört** ~: his sight is poor/he has poor hearing; **über jmdn. od. von jmdn.** ~ **sprechen** speak ill of sb.; ~ **bezahlt** badly *or* poorly paid
(b) (schwer) **heute geht es** ~: today is difficult
(c) ~ **und recht, mehr** ~ **als recht** after a fashion

schlecht·: *~**bezahlt** ▶ SCHLECHT 2A;
*~**|gehen** ▶ GEHEN I; *~**gelaunt** ▶ GELAUNT

Schlechtigkeit *die;* ~: badness; wickedness

*****schlecht|machen** ▶ SCHLECHT 1A

schlecken (bes. südd., österr.) *tr. V.* lap up

schleichen ① *unr. itr. V.; mit sein* creep; (heimlich) creep; sneak; ⟨*cat*⟩ slink, creep; (langsam fahren) crawl along
② *unr. refl. V.* creep; sneak; ⟨*cat*⟩ slink, creep

schleichend *Adj.* insidious ⟨*disease*⟩; slow[-acting] ⟨*poison*⟩; creeping ⟨*inflation*⟩; gradual ⟨*crisis*⟩

Schleich·werbung *die* surreptitious advertising

Schleier *der;* ~s, ~: veil

schleier·haft *Adj.* jmdm. ~ **sein/bleiben** be/remain a mystery to sb.

Schleife *die;* ~, ~n (a) bow; (Fliege) bow tie
(b) (starke Biegung) loop

schleifen[1] *unr. tr. V.* grind; cut ⟨*diamond, glass*⟩; (mit Schleifpapier usw.) sand; (schärfen) sharpen

schleifen[2] ① *tr. V.* (a) (auch fig.) drag
(b) (niederreißen) raze ⟨*sth.*⟩ [to the ground]
② *tr. V.; auch mit sein* drag; **die Kupplung** ~ **lassen** (Kfz-W.) slip the clutch

Schleim *der;* ~[e]s, ~e mucus; (im Hals) phlegm; (von Schnecken) slime

schleimig *Adj.* (auch fig.) slimy; (Physiol., Zool.) mucous

schlemmen *itr. V.* have a feast

Schlemmer *der;* ~s, ~: gourmet

schlendern *itr. V.; mit sein* stroll

Schlenker *der;* ~s, ~ (ugs.) swerve; **einen** ~ **machen** swerve

schlenkern *tr., itr. V.* swing; **mit den Armen** ~: swing one's arms

Schleppe *die;* ~, ~n train

schleppen ① *tr. V.* (a) (ziehen) tow ⟨*vehicle, ship*⟩
(b) (tragen) carry; lug
(c) (ugs.: mitnehmen) drag
② *refl. V.* drag *or* haul oneself

schleppend *Adj.* (nicht zügig) slow

Schlepper *der;* ~s, ~ (a) (Schiff) tug
(b) (Traktor) tractor

Schlepper·organisation *die:* organization smuggling illegal immigrants and emigrants

Schlepp·: ~**lift** *der* T-bar [lift]; ~**tau** *das* towline; **in jmds.** ~**tau** (fig.) in sb.'s wake

Schleswig-Holstein ⟨*das*⟩; ~s Schleswig-Holstein

Schleuder *die;* ~, ~n sling; (mit Gummiband) catapult (Brit.); slingshot (Amer.)

schleudern ① *tr. V.* hurl
② *itr. V.; mit sein* ⟨*vehicle*⟩ skid

schleunigst *Adv.* (a) (auf der Stelle) at once; immediately; straight away
(b) (eilends) hastily; with all haste

Schleuse *die;* ~, ~n lock

schlich *1. u. 3. Pers. Sg. Prät. v.* SCHLEICHEN

schlicht ① *Adj.* (a) simple; plain ⟨*pattern, furniture*⟩
(b) (unkompliziert) simple, unsophisticated ⟨*person, view, etc.*⟩
② *adv.* simply; simply, plainly ⟨*dressed, furnished*⟩

schlichten ① *tr. V.* settle ⟨*argument etc.*⟩; settle ⟨*industrial dispute etc.*⟩ by mediation
② *itr. V.* mediate

S

Schlichtheit *die;* ∼ ▶ SCHLICHT A, B: simplicity; plainness; unsophisticatedness

Schlick *der;* ∼[e]s, ∼e silt

schlief *1. u. 3. Pers. Sg. Prät. v.* SCHLAFEN

Schließe *die;* ∼, ∼n clasp; (Schnalle) buckle

schließen ① *unr. tr. V.* (a) close; shut; turn off ⟨*tap*⟩; fasten ⟨*belt, bracelet*⟩; do up ⟨*button, zip*⟩; close ⟨*street, route, border, electrical circuit*⟩; fill, close ⟨*gap*⟩
(b) (außer Betrieb setzen) close [down] ⟨*shop, school*⟩
(c) etw./jmdn./sich in etw. (*Akk.*) ∼: lock sth./sb./oneself in sth.
(d) (beenden) close ⟨*meeting, proceedings, debate*⟩; end, conclude ⟨*letter, speech, lecture*⟩
(e) (eingehen, vereinbaren) conclude ⟨*treaty, pact, ceasefire, agreement*⟩; reach ⟨*settlement, compromise*⟩; enter into ⟨*contract*⟩
(f) (folgern) infer (aus from)
② *unr. itr. V.* (a) close, shut
(b) (enden) end; conclude
(c) [aus etw.] auf etw. (*Akk.*) ∼: infer sth. [from sth.]
③ *unr. refl. V.* ⟨*door, window*⟩ close, shut; ⟨*wound, circle*⟩ close

Schließ·fach *das* locker; (bei der Post) PO box; (bei der Bank) safe-deposit box

schließlich *Adv.* (a) finally; in the end
(b) (immerhin, doch) after all

schliff *1. u. 3. Pers. Sg. Prät. v.* SCHLEIFEN

Schliff *der;* ∼[e]s, ∼e (a) cutting; (von Messern, Sensen usw.) sharpening
(b) (Art, wie etw. geschliffen wird) cut; (von Messern, Scheren usw.) edge
(c) einem Brief/Text *usw.* den letzten ∼ geben put the finishing touches *pl.* to a letter/text *etc.*

schlimm ① *Adj.* (a) grave, serious ⟨*error, mistake, accusation, offence*⟩; bad, serious ⟨*error, mistake*⟩
(b) (übel) bad; nasty, bad ⟨*experience*⟩; [das ist alles] halb so ∼: it's not as bad as all that; ist nicht ∼! [it] doesn't matter
② *adv.* ∼ dran sein be in a bad way; (in einer Notlage) be in dire straits

schlimmsten·falls *Adv.* if the worst comes to the worst

Schlinge *die;* ∼, ∼n (a) loop; (für den Arm) sling; (zum Erhängen) noose
(b) (Fanggerät) snare

Schlingel *der;* ∼s, ∼: rascal; rogue

schlingen ① *unr. tr. V.* etw. um etw. ∼: loop sth. round sth.
② *unr. refl. V.* sich um etw. ∼: wind itself round sth.
③ *unr. itr. V.* bolt one's food

schlingern *itr. V.; mit sein* ⟨*ship, boat*⟩ roll; ⟨*train, vehicle*⟩ lurch from side to side

Schlips *der;* ∼es, ∼e tie

Schlitten *der;* ∼s, ∼: sledge; sled; (Pferdeschlitten) sleigh; (Rodelschlitten) toboggan; ∼ fahren go tobogganing

schlittern *itr. V.* slide

Schlitt-: ∼schuh *der* [ice] skate; ∼schuh laufen *od.* fahren [ice-]skate;
∼schuh·laufen *das* [ice] skating *no art.;*
∼schuh·läufer *der,* ∼schuh·läuferin *die* [ice] skater

Schlitz *der;* ∼es, ∼e (a) slit; (am Briefkasten, Automaten) slot
(b) (Hosenschlitz) flies *pl.;* fly

schlitz-, Schlitz-: ∼auge *das* slit eye; ∼äugig *Adj.* slit-eyed; ∼ohr *das* (ugs.) wily *or* crafty devil; ∼ohrig (ugs.) ① *Adj.* wily; crafty; ② *adv.* craftily

schloss, *schloß *1. u. 3. Pers. Sg. Prät. v.* SCHLIESSEN

Schloss, *Schloß *das;* Schlosses, Schlösser (a) lock; (Vorhänge∼) padlock; hinter ∼ und Riegel (ugs.) behind bars
(b) (Verschluss) clasp
(c) (Wohngebäude) castle; (Palast) palace; (Herrschaftshaus) mansion

Schlosser *der;* ∼s, ∼, **Schlosserin** *die;* ∼, ∼nen metalworker; (Maschinenschlosser) fitter; (für Schlösser) locksmith

Schlot *der;* ∼[e]s, ∼e *od.* **Schlöte** chimney [stack]; (eines Schiffes) funnel

schlottern *itr. V.* (a) shake
(b) ⟨*clothes*⟩ hang loose

Schlucht *die;* ∼, ∼en ravine

schluchzen *itr. V.* sob

Schluck *der;* ∼[e]s, ∼e *od.* **Schlücke** swallow; mouthful; (großer ∼) gulp; (kleiner ∼) sip

Schluck·auf *der;* ∼s hiccups *pl.*

Schlückchen *das;* ∼s, ∼: sip

schlucken ① *tr. V.* swallow; etw. hastig ∼: gulp sth. down
② *itr. V.* swallow

Schlucker *der;* ∼s, ∼: armer ∼ (ugs.) poor devil *or* (Brit. coll.) blighter

schluderig ▶ SCHLUDRIG

schludern *itr. V.* (ugs.) work sloppily

schludrig (ugs.) ① *Adj.* (a) slipshod ⟨*work, examination*⟩; botched ⟨*job*⟩; slapdash ⟨*person, work*⟩
(b) (schlampig [aussehend]) scruffy
② *adv.* (a) in a slipshod *or* slapdash way
(b) (schlampig) scruffily

schlug *1. u. 3. Pers. Sg. Prät. v.* SCHLAGEN

Schlummer *der;* ∼s (geh.) slumber (poet./ rhet.)

schlummern *itr. V.* (geh.) slumber (poet./ rhet.)

Schlund *der;* ∼[e]s, **Schlünde** [back of the] throat; pharynx (Anat.)

schlüpfen *itr. V.; mit sein* slip; [aus dem Ei] ∼ ⟨*chick*⟩ hatch out

Schlüpfer *der;* ∼s, ∼ (für Damen) knickers *pl.* (Brit.); panties *pl.;* (für Herren) [under]pants *pl.* or trunks *pl.*

schlüpfrig *Adj.* (a) slippery
(b) (anstößig) lewd

Schlüpfrigkeit *die;* ~, ~en (a) (feuchte Glätte) slipperiness
(b) (Anstößigkeit) lewdness
schlurfen *itr. V.; mit sein* shuffle
schlürfen ① *tr. V.* slurp [up] (coll.)
② *itr. V.* slurp (coll.)
Schluss, *Schluß *der;* Schlusses, Schlüsse (a) end; (eines Vortrags o. Ä.) conclusion; (eines Buchs, Schauspiels usw.) ending; **am** *od.* **zum** ~: at the end; (schließlich) in the end
(b) (Folgerung) conclusion
Schlüssel *der;* ~s, ~: key
Schlüssel-: ~**bein** *das* collarbone; clavicle (Anat.); ~**blume** *die* cowslip; (Primel) primula; ~**bund** *der od. das* bunch of keys; ~**figur** *die* key figure; ~**loch** *das* keyhole; ~**stellung** *die* key position
schluss·folgern, *schluß folgern *tr. V.* conclude (aus from)
Schluss·folgerung, *Schluß·folgerung *die* conclusion, inference (aus from); ~**en ziehen** draw conclusions
schlüssig ① *Adj.* (a) conclusive ⟨*proof, evidence*⟩; convincing, logical ⟨*argument, conclusion*⟩
(b) **sich** (*Dat.*) ~ **werden** make up one's mind
② *adv.* conclusively
Schlüssigkeit *die;* ~: conclusiveness
Schluss-, *Schluß-: ~**licht** *das* tail *or* rear light; ~**strich** *der* [bottom] line; ~**verkauf** *der* [end-of-season] sale[s *pl.*]
schmächtig *Adj.* slight
schmackhaft *Adj.* tasty
Schmähung *die;* ~, ~en diatribe; ~**en** abuse *sing.*; invective *sing.*
schmal; ~**er** *od.* schmäler, ~**st**... *od.* schmälst... *Adj.* narrow; slim, slender ⟨*hips, hands, figure, etc.*⟩; thin ⟨*lips, face, nose, etc.*⟩
schmälern *tr. V.* diminish; restrict ⟨*rights*⟩
Schmalz¹ *das;* ~**es** dripping; (Schweineschmalz) lard
Schmalz² *der;* ~**es** (abwertend) schmaltz (coll.)
Schmalz·brot *das* slice of bread and dripping
schmalzig (abwertend) ① *Adj.* schmaltzy (coll.)
② *adv.* with slushy sentimentality
schmarotzen *itr. V.* (fig.) sponge; freeload (coll.)
Schmarren *der;* ~**s**, ~ (österr., auch südd.) *pancake broken up with a fork after frying*
schmatzen *itr. V.* smack one's lips; (geräuschvoll essen) eat noisily
Schmaus *der;* ~**es**, Schmäuse (veralt., scherzh.) [good] spread (coll.)
schmecken ① *itr. V.* taste (**nach** of); [**gut**] ~: taste good; **schmeckt es** [**dir**]**?** are you enjoying it *or* your meal?

② *tr. V.* taste; (kosten) sample
schmeicheln *itr. V.* jmdm. ~: flatter sb.
Schmeichler *der;* ~**s**, ~,
Schmeichlerin *die;* ~, ~nen flatterer
schmeißen (ugs.) ① *unr. tr. V.* chuck (coll.); sling (coll.); (schleudern) fling; hurl
② *unr. refl. V.* throw oneself; (mit Wucht) hurl oneself
③ *unr. itr. V.* **mit etw. [nach jmdm.]** ~: chuck sth. [at sb.] (coll.)
Schmeiß·fliege *die* blowfly; (blaue) bluebottle
schmelzen ① *unr. itr. V.; mit sein* melt; (fig.) ⟨*doubts, apprehension, etc.*⟩ dissolve, fade away
② *unr. tr. V.* melt; smelt ⟨*ore*⟩; render ⟨*fat*⟩
Schmelz-: ~**käse** *der* processed cheese; ~**wasser** *das* melted snow and ice; meltwater (Geol.)
Schmerz *der;* ~**es**, ~**en** (a) (physisch) pain; (dumpf u. anhaltend) ache; **wo haben Sie** ~**en?** where does it hurt?; ~**en haben** be in pain
(b) (psychisch) pain; (Kummer) grief
schmerz·empfindlich *Adj.* sensitive to pain *pred.*
Schmerz·empfindlichkeit *die;* ~: sensitivity to pain
schmerzen ① *tr. V.* jmdn. ~: hurt sb.; (jmdm. Kummer bereiten) grieve sb.; cause sb. sorrow
② *itr. V.* hurt
schmerz·frei *Adj.* free of pain *pred.*; painless ⟨*operation*⟩
Schmerz·grenze *die* (fig.) **jetzt/dann ist die** ~ **erreicht** this/that is the absolute limit
schmerzhaft *Adj.* painful
schmerzlich ① *Adj.* painful; distressing
② *adv.* painfully
schmerz-, Schmerz-: ~**lindernd** *Adj.* pain-relieving; ~**los** ① *Adj.* painless; ② *adv.* painlessly; ~**stillend** *Adj.* pain-killing; ~**tablette** *die* pain-killing tablet
Schmetterling *der;* ~**s**, ~**e** butterfly
schmettern ① *tr. V.* (a) hurl (**an** + *Akk.* at, **gegen** against)
(b) (laut spielen, singen usw.) blare out ⟨*march, music*⟩; ⟨*person*⟩ sing lustily ⟨*song*⟩
(c) (Tennis usw.) smash ⟨*ball*⟩
② *itr. V.* ⟨*trumpet, music, etc.*⟩ blare out
Schmied *der;* ~**[e]s**, ~**e** blacksmith
Schmiede *die;* ~, ~**n** smithy; forge
schmieden *tr. V.* (auch fig.) forge
Schmiedin *die;* ~, ~nen ▶ SCHMIED
schmiegen ① *refl. V.* snuggle, nestle (**in** + *Akk.* in); **sich an jmdn.** ~: snuggle [close] up to sb.
② *tr. V.* press (**an** + *Akk.* against)
schmieren ① *tr. V.* (a) lubricate
(b) (streichen) spread ⟨*butter, jam, etc.*⟩ (**auf** + *Akk.* on); **Brote** ~: spread slices of bread
② *tr. V.* (a) ⟨*oil, grease*⟩ lubricate
(b) (ugs: unsauber schreiben) ⟨*person*⟩ scrawl, scribble; ⟨*pen, ink*⟩ smudge, make smudges

schmierig *Adj.* greasy

Schmier-: ~**mittel** *das* lubricant; ~**seife** *die* soft soap

schmilzt *2. u. 3. Pers. Sg. Präsens v.* SCHMELZEN

Schminke *die;* ~, ~n make-up

schminken [1] *tr. V.* make up ⟨*face, eyes*⟩ [2] *refl. V.* make oneself up

schmirgeln *tr. V.* rub down; (bes. mit Sandpapier) sand

Schmirgel·papier *das* emery paper; (Sandpapier) sandpaper

schmiss, *schmiß *1. u. 3. Pers. Sg. Prät. v.* SCHMEISSEN

Schmöker *der;* ~s, ~ (ugs.) lightweight adventure story/romance

schmökern (ugs.) [1] *itr. V.* bury oneself in a book [2] *tr. V.* bury oneself in ⟨*book*⟩

schmollen *itr. V.* sulk

Schmoll·mund *der* pouting mouth

schmolz *1. u. 3. Pers. Sg. Prät. v.* SCHMELZEN

Schmor·braten *der* braised beef

schmoren [1] *tr. V.* braise [2] *itr. V.* **(a)** braise **(b)** (ugs.: schwitzen) swelter

schmuck *Adj.* attractive

Schmuck *der;* ~[e]s **(a)** jewelry; jewellery (esp. Brit.) **(b)** ▶ SCHMUCKSTÜCK **(c)** (Zierde) decoration

schmücken *tr. V.* decorate; embellish ⟨*writings, speech*⟩

schmuck-, Schmuck-: ~**kästchen** *das,* ~**kasten** *der* jewelry or (esp. Brit.) jewellery box; ~**los** *Adj.* plain; bare ⟨*room*⟩; ~**losigkeit** *die;* ~~: plainness; (eines Zimmers) bareness; ~**stück** *das* piece of jewelry or (esp. Brit.) jewellery

schmuddelig *Adj.* (ugs.) grubby; mucky (coll.); (schmutzig u. unordentlich) messy; grotty (Brit. coll.)

Schmuggel *der;* ~s smuggling *no art.*

schmuggeln *tr., itr. V.* smuggle (**in** + *Akk.* into; **aus** out of)

Schmuggler *der;* ~s, ~, **Schmugglerin** *die;* ~, ~nen smuggler

schmunzeln *itr. V.* smile to oneself

schmusen *itr. V.* (ugs.) cuddle; ⟨*couple*⟩ kiss and cuddle

Schmutz *der;* ~es dirt; (Schlamm) mud

schmutzen *itr. V.* get dirty

schmutzig *Adj.* dirty

Schmutz·wasser *das* dirty water; (Abwasser) sewage

Schnabel *der;* ~s, **Schnäbel (a)** beak **(b)** (ugs.: Mund) gob (sl.)

Schnake *die;* ~, ~n **(a)** daddy-long-legs **(b)** (bes. südd.: Stechmücke) mosquito

Schnalle *die;* ~, ~n buckle

schnallen *tr. V.* **(a)** (mit einer Schnalle festziehen) buckle ⟨*shoe, belt*⟩; fasten ⟨*strap*⟩ **(b)** (mit Riemen/Gurten befestigen) strap (**auf** + *Akk.* on to)

schnalzen *itr. V.* [mit der Zunge/den Fingern] ~: click one's tongue/snap one's fingers

Schnäppchen *das;* ~s, ~ (ugs.) snip (Brit. coll.); [real] bargain; **ein** ~ **machen** get a [real] bargain

schnappen [1] *itr. V.* **nach jmdm./etw.** ~ ⟨*animal*⟩ snap at sb./sth.; **nach Luft** ~: gasp for breath [2] *tr. V.* ⟨*dog, bird, etc.*⟩ snatch; [**sich** ⟨*Dat.*⟩] **jmdn./etw.** ~ (ugs.) ⟨*person*⟩ grab sb./sth.; (mit raschem Zugriff) snatch sb./sth

Schnapp·schuss, *Schnapp·schuß *der* snapshot

Schnaps *der;* ~es, **Schnäpse (a)** spirit; (Klarer) schnapps **(b)** (Spirituosen) spirits *pl.*

schnarchen *itr. V.* snore

schnattern *itr. V.* **(a)** ⟨*goose etc.*⟩ cackle, gaggle **(b)** (ugs.: eifrig schwatzen) jabber [away]; chatter

schnauben *itr. V.* snort (**vor** with)

schnaufen *itr. V.* puff (**vor** with)

Schnauze *die;* ~, ~n **(a)** (von Tieren) muzzle; (der Maus usw.) snout; (Maul) mouth **(b)** (derb: Mund) gob (sl.); [**halt die**] ~! shut your trap! (sl.)

schnauzen *tr., itr. V.* (ugs.) bark; (ärgerlich) snap; snarl

Schnecke *die* snail; (Nacktschnecke) slug

Schnecken·haus *das* snail shell

Schnee *der;* ~s snow

schnee-, Schnee-: ~**ball** *der* snowball; ~**besen** *der* whisk; ~**flocke** *die* snowflake; ~**gestöber** *das* snow flurry; ~**glöckchen** *das* snowdrop; ~**kette** *die* snow chain; ~**matsch** *der* slush; ~**pflug** *der* snowplough; ~**schmelze** *die;* ~~, ~~**n** melting of the snow; thaw; ~**sturm** *der* snowstorm; ~**treiben** *das* driving snow; ~**wehe** *die* snowdrift; ~**weiß** *Adj.* snow-white; as white as snow *postpos.*

Schneewittchen *das;* ~s Snow White

Schneid·brenner *der* (Technik) cutting torch; oxyacetylene cutter

Schneide *die;* ~, ~n [cutting] edge

schneiden [1] *unr. itr. V.* cut (**in** + *Akk.* into) [2] *unr. tr. V.* **(a)** cut; (in Scheiben) slice ⟨*bread, sausage, etc.*⟩; (klein ~) cut up, chop ⟨*wood, vegetables*⟩; (stutzen) prune ⟨*tree, bush*⟩; trim ⟨*beard*⟩; cut, mow ⟨*grass*⟩; **sich** ⟨*Dat.*⟩ **die Haare** ~ **lassen** have one's hair cut **(b)** **eine Kurve** ~: cut a corner

Schneider *der;* ~s, ~: tailor; (Damenschneider) dressmaker

---

*alte Schreibung - vgl. Hinweis auf S. xiv

Schneiderei *die;* ~, ~en tailor's shop; (Damenschneider) dressmaker's shop

Schneiderin *die;* ~, ~nen ▶ SCHNEIDER

schneidern *tr. V.* make; make, tailor ⟨suit⟩

Schneide·zahn *der* incisor

schneien ① *itr., tr. V.* (*unpers.*) snow; **es schneit** it is snowing
② *itr. V.; mit sein* (fig.) rain down; fall like snow

Schneise *die;* ~, ~n (Wald~) aisle; (als Feuerschutz) firebreak

schnell ① *Adj.* quick ⟨journey, decision, service, etc.⟩; fast ⟨car, skis, road, track, etc.⟩; quick, swift ⟨progress, movement, blow, action⟩
② *adv.* quickly; ⟨drive, move, etc.⟩ fast, quickly; ⟨spread⟩ quickly, rapidly; (bald) soon ⟨sold, past, etc.⟩; **mach** ~! (ugs.) move it! (coll.)

schnellen *itr. V.; mit sein* shoot (**aus** + *Dat.* out of; **in** + *Akk.* into)

Schnelligkeit *die;* ~, ~en speed

Schnell-: ~**imbiss,** *~*~**imbiß** *der* snackbar; ~**koch·topf** *der* pressure cooker

schnellstens *Adv.* as quickly as possible

Schnell-: ~**straße** *die* expressway; ~**zug** *der* express [train]

Schnepfe *die;* ~, ~n snipe

schneuzen ① *tr. V.* **sich/einem Kind die Nase** ~: blow one's/a child's nose
② *refl. V.* blow one's nose

schnippeln (ugs.) ① *itr. V.* snip [away] (**an** + *Dat.* at)
② *tr. V.* shred ⟨vegetables⟩; chop ⟨beans etc.⟩ [finely]

schnippen ① *itr. V.* snap one's fingers (**nach** at)
② *tr. V.* flick (**von** off, from)

schnippisch ① *Adj.* pert ⟨reply, tone, etc.⟩
② *adv.* pertly

Schnipsel *der od. das;* ~s, ~: scrap; (aus Papier, Stoff) snippet; shred

schnipseln ▶ SCHNIPPELN

schnitt *1. u. 3. Pers. Sg. Prät. v.* SCHNEIDEN

Schnitt *der;* ~[e]s, ~e **(a)** cut
(b) (das Mähen) (von Gras) mowing; (von Getreide) harvest

Schnitt-: ~**blume** *die* cut flower; ~**bohne** *die* French bean

Schnittchen *das;* ~s, ~: canapé; [small] open sandwich

Schnitte *die;* ~, ~n slice; **eine** ~ **[Brot]** a slice of bread

Schnitt·fläche *die* cut surface

schnittig ① *Adj.* stylish, smart ⟨suit, appearance, etc.⟩; (sportlich) racy ⟨car, yacht, etc.⟩
② *adv.* stylishly; (sportlich) racily

Schnitt-: ~**lauch** *der* chives *pl.;*
~**menge** *die* (Math.) intersection; ~**punkt**

der. intersection; (Geom.) point of intersection; ~**stelle** *die* (DV) interface; ~**wunde** *die* cut; (lang u. tief) gash

Schnitzel *das;* ~s, ~ **(a)** (Fleisch) [veal/pork] escalope
(b) (von Papier) scrap; (von Holz) shaving

schnitzeln *tr. V.* chop up ⟨vegetables⟩ [into small pieces]; shred ⟨cabbage⟩

schnitzen *tr., itr. V.* carve

schnodderig (ugs.) ① *Adj.* brash
② *adv.* brashly

schnöde (geh.) ① *Adj.* **(a)** (verachtenswert) contemptible
(b) (gemein) contemptuous, scornful ⟨glance, reply, etc.⟩
② *adv.* (gemein) contemptuously; ⟨exploit, misuse⟩ flagrantly

Schnorchel *der;* ~s, ~: snorkel

Schnörkel *der;* ~s, ~: scroll; (der Handschrift, in der Rede) flourish

schnorren *tr., itr. V.* (ugs.) scrounge (coll.) (**bei, von** + *Dat.* off)

Schnorrer *der;* ~s, ~, **Schnorrerin** *die;* ~, ~nen (ugs.) scrounger (coll.)

Schnösel *der;* ~s, ~ (ugs. abwertend) young whippersnapper

schnüffeln *itr. V.* **(a)** sniff
(b) (ugs.: spionieren) snoop [about] (coll.)
(c) (Drogenjargon: Dämpfe ~) sniff [glue/paint etc.]

Schnüffler *der;* ~s, ~, **Schnüfflerin** *die;* ~, ~nen **(a)** (ugs.) Nosey Parker; (Spion) snooper (coll.)
(b) (Drogenjargon) [glue-, paint-, *etc.*]sniffer

Schnulze *die;* ~, ~n (ugs. abwertend) (Lied/Melodie) slushy song/tune; (Theaterstück, Film, Fernsehspiel) tear jerker (coll.); slushy play

schnupfen ① *tr. V.* sniff; **Tabak** ~: take snuff
② *itr. V.* take snuff

Schnupfen *der;* ~s, ~: [head] cold; [den od. einen] ~ **haben** have a [head] cold

Schnupf·tabak *der* snuff

schnuppe: das/er ist mir ~/**mir völlig** ~ (ugs.) I don't care/I couldn't care less about it/him (coll.)

schnuppern *itr. V.* sniff; **an etw.** (*Dat.*) ~: sniff sth.

Schnur *die;* ~, **Schnüre (a)** (Bindfaden) piece of string; (Kordel) piece of cord
(b) (ugs.: Kabel) flex (Brit.); lead; cord (Amer.)

schnüren *tr. V.* tie ⟨bundle, string, etc.⟩; tie, lace up ⟨shoe, corset, etc.⟩

schnur·los *Adj.* cordless

Schnurr·bart *der* moustache

schnurren *itr. V.* ⟨cat⟩ purr; ⟨machine⟩ hum

Schnür-: ~**schuh** *der* lace-up shoe; ~**senkel** *der;* ~~s, ~ (bes. nordd.) [shoe]lace; (für Stiefel) bootlace

schnur·stracks *Adv.* (ugs.) straight

schob *1. u. 3. Pers. Prät. v.* SCHIESSEN

Schock *der;* ~[e]s, ~s shock
schockieren *tr. V.* shock; **über etw.** (*Akk.*) **schockiert sein** be shocked at sth.
Schöffe *der;* ~n, ~n lay judge (*acting together with another lay judge and a professional judge*)
Schöffen·gericht *das: court presided over by a professional judge and two lay judges*
Schöffin *die;* ~, ~nen ▶ SCHÖFFE
Schokolade *die;* ~, ~n (a) chocolate
(b) (Getränk) [drinking] chocolate
Schokolade[n]-: ~**eis** *das* chocolate ice cream; ~**guss**, ***~**guß** *der* chocolate icing; ~**pudding** *der* chocolate blancmange; ~**torte** *die* chocolate cake *or* gateau
scholl *1. u. 3. Pers. Sg. Prät. v.* SCHALLEN
Scholle *die;* ~, ~n (a) (Erdscholle) clod [of earth]
(b) (Eisscholle) [ice] floe
(c) (Fisch) plaice
schon ⓵ *Adv.* (a) (bereits) (oft nicht übersetzt) already; (in Fragen) yet; **wie lange bist du** ~ **hier?** how long have you been here?
(b) (fast gleichzeitig) there and then
(c) (jetzt) ~ [**mal**] now; (inzwischen) meanwhile
(d) (selbst, sogar) even; (nur) only
(e) (ohne Ergänzung, ohne weiteren Zusatz) on its own; [**allein**] ~ **der Gedanke daran** the mere thought of it; ~ **deshalb** for this reason alone
(f) (wohl) really; **Lust hätte ich** ~, **aber** ...: I'd certainly like to, but ...
⓶ *Partikel* (a) (ugs. ungeduldig: endlich) **nun komm** ~! come on!; hurry up!
(b) (beruhigend: bestimmt) all right
(c) (durchaus) **das ist** ~ **möglich** that is quite possible
schön ⓵ *Adj.* (a) beautiful; handsome (*youth, man*)
(b) (angenehm) pleasant, nice (*day, holiday, dream, relaxation, etc.*); fine (*weather*); (nett) nice; **das war eine** ~**e Zeit** those were wonderful days
(c) (gut) good
(d) (in Höflichkeitsformeln) ~**e Grüße** best wishes; **recht** ~**en Dank für** ...: thank you very much for ...
(e) ~! (ugs.: einverstanden) OK (coll.); all right
(f) (iron.: leer) ~**e Worte** fine[-sounding] words; (schmeichlerisch) honeyed words
(g) (ugs.: beträchtlich) handsome, (coll.) tidy (*sum, fortune, profit*); considerable (*quantity, distance*); pretty good (*pension*)
(h) (iron.: unerfreulich) nice (coll. iron.); **das sind ja** ~**e Aussichten!** this is a fine lookout *sing.* (iron.)
(i) **sich** ~ **machen** smarten oneself up
⓶ *adv.* (a) beautifully
(b) (angenehm, erfreulich) nicely; ~ **warm/weich/langsam** nice and warm/soft/slow
(c) (gut) well

*old spelling - see note on page xiv

(d) (in Höflichkeitsformeln) **bitte** ~, **können Sie mir sagen, ...: excuse me, could you tell me ...
(e) (iron.) **wie es so** ~ **heißt, wie man so** ~ **sagt** as they say
(f) (ugs.: beträchtlich) really; (vor einem Adjektiv) pretty; **ganz** ~ **arbeiten müssen** have to work jolly hard (Brit. coll.)
⓷ *Partikel* (ugs.) **bleib** ~ **liegen!** lie there and be good
schonen ⓵ *tr. V.* treat (*clothes, books, furniture, etc.*) with care; (schützen) protect (*hands, furniture*); (nicht strapazieren) spare (*voice, eyes, etc.*); conserve (*strength*)
⓶ *refl. V.* take things easy
Schönheit *die;* ~, ~en beauty
Schönheits-: ~**chirurgie** *die* cosmetic surgery *no art.;* ~**pflege** *die* beauty care *no art.*
Schon·kost *die* light food
***schön|machen** (ugs.) ▶ SCHÖN 1i
Schonung *die;* ~, ~en (a) (Nachsicht) consideration; (nachsichtige Behandlung) considerate treatment; (nach Krankheit/Operation) [period of] rest; (von Gegenständen) careful treatment
(b) (Jungwald) [young] plantation
schonungs·los ⓵ *Adj.* unsparing, ruthless (*criticism etc.*); blunt (*frankness*)
⓶ *adv.* unsparingly; (*say*) without mincing one's words
Schonungslosigkeit *die;* ~: ruthlessness; (Strenge) rigour
Schopf *der;* ~[e]s, Schöpfe shock of hair
schöpfen *tr. V.* (a) scoop [up] (*water, liquid*); (mit einer Kelle) ladle (*soup*)
(b) (geh.: einatmen) draw, take (*breath*)
Schöpfer *der;* ~s, ~: creator; (Gott) Creator
Schöpferin *die;* ~, ~nen creator
schöpferisch ⓵ *Adj.* creative
⓶ *adv.* creatively
Schöpf-: ~**kelle** *die,* ~**löffel** *der* ladle
Schöpfung *die;* ~, ~en (geh.) creation; **die** ~ (die Welt) Creation
Schoppen *der;* ~s, ~: [quarter-litre/half-litre] glass of wine/beer
schor *1. u. 3. Pers. Sg. Prät. v.* SCHEREN
Schorf *der;* ~[e]s, ~e scab
Schorle *die;* ~, ~n wine with mineral water; ≈ spritzer
Schorn·stein *der* chimney; (Lokomotive, Schiff usw.) funnel
Schornstein·feger *der;* ~s, ~, **Schornstein·fegerin** *die;* ~, ~nen chimney sweep
schoss, ***schoß** *1. u. 3. Pers. Sg. Prät. v.* SCHIESSEN
Schoß *der;* ~es, Schöße lap
Schote *die;* ~, ~n pod
Schotte *der;* ~n, ~n Scot; Scotsman; **die** ~n the Scots; the Scottish

Schotten·rock der tartan skirt; (Kilt) kilt

Schottin die; ~, ~nen Scot; Scotswoman

schottisch Adj. Scottish; ~er Whisky Scotch whisky

Schottland (das); ~s Scotland

schräg [1] Adj. diagonal ⟨line, beam, cut, etc.⟩; sloping ⟨surface, roof, wall, side, etc.⟩; slanting, slanted ⟨writing, eyes, etc.⟩; tilted ⟨position of the head etc., axis⟩
[2] adv. at an angle; (diagonal) diagonally

Schräge die; ~, ~n (a) (schräge Fläche) sloping surface
(b) (Neigung) slope

Schräg·strich der oblique stroke

schrak 1. u. 3. Pers. Sg. Prät. v. SCHRECKEN

Schramme die; ~, ~n scratch

schrammen tr. V. scratch

Schrank der; ~[e]s, Schränke cupboard; closet (Amer.); (Glas~; kleiner Wand~) cabinet; (Kleiderschrank) wardrobe; (Bücher~) bookcase

Schränkchen das; ~s, ~: cabinet

Schranke die; ~, ~n (a) (auch fig.) barrier
(b) (fig.: Grenze) limit

Schraube die; ~, ~n bolt; (Holz-, Blechschraube) screw

schrauben tr. V. (a) ▶ SCHRAUBE: bolt/ screw (an, auf + Akk. on to)
(b) (drehen) screw ⟨nut, hook, lightbulb, etc.⟩ (auf + Akk. on to; in + Akk. into)

Schrauben-: ~schlüssel der spanner; ~zieher der; ~s, ~: screwdriver

Schraub·verschluss,
***Schraub·verschluß** der screw top

Schreber·garten der ≈ allotment (cultivated primarily as a garden)

Schreck der; ~[e]s, ~e fright; scare; (Schock) shock; jmdm. einen ~ einjagen give sb. a fright

schrecken regelm. (auch unr.) itr. V. start [up]; aus dem Schlaf ~: awake with a start; start from one's sleep

Schrecken der; ~s, ~: fright; scare; (Entsetzen) horror; (große Angst) terror; jmdm. einen ~ einjagen give sb. a fright

schreckhaft Adj. easily scared

Schreckhaftigkeit die; ~: easily scared nature; tendency to take fright

schrecklich [1] Adj. terrible
[2] adv. terribly

Schredder der; ~s, ~: shredder

schreddern tr. V. shred

Schrei der; ~[e]s, ~e cry; (lauter Ruf) shout; (durchdringend) yell; (gellend) scream; (kreischend) shriek

Schreib·block der; Pl. ~s od. Schreib·blöcke writing pad

schreiben [1] unr. itr. V. write; (mit der Schreibmaschine) type; an einem Roman usw. ~: be writing a novel etc.; jmdm. od. an jmdn. ~: write to sb.

[2] unr. tr. V. write; (mit der Schreibmaschine) type; wie schreibt man dieses Wort? how is this word spelt?
[3] unr. refl. V. be spelt

Schreiben das; ~s, ~ (a) writing no def. art.;
(b) (Brief) letter

Schreiber der; ~s, ~: writer; (Verfasser) author

Schreiberin die; ~, ~en writer; (Verfasserin) authoress

Schreib-: ~marke die (DV) cursor; ~maschine die typewriter; ~maschinen·papier das typing paper; ~papier das writing paper; ~schutz der (DV) write protection; ~tisch der desk

Schreibung die; ~, ~en spelling

Schreib-: ~waren Pl. stationery sing.; ~waren·geschäft das stationer's

schreien unr. itr. V. ⟨person⟩ cry [out]; (laut rufen/sprechen) shout; (durchdringend) yell; (gellend) scream; ⟨baby⟩ yell, bawl; zum Schreien sein (ugs.) be a scream (coll.)

Schrei·hals der (ugs.) (a) (Kind) bawler
(b) (abwertend: Randalierer) rowdy

Schreiner der; ~s, ~, (bes. südd.)
▶ TISCHLER

Schreinerei die; ~, ~en (bes. südd.)
▶ TISCHLEREI

Schreinerin die; ~, ~nen (bes. südd.)
▶ TISCHLERIN

schreiten unr. itr. V.; mit sein (geh.) walk; (mit großen Schritten) stride

schrickst 2. Pers. Sg. Präsens v.
SCHRECKEN

schrickt 3. Pers. Sg. Präsens v. SCHRECKEN

schrie 1. u. 3. Pers. Sg. Prät. v. SCHREIEN

schrieb 1. u. 3. Pers. Sg. Prät. v. SCHREIBEN

Schrieb der; ~[e]s, ~e (ugs.) missive (coll.)

Schrift die; ~, ~en (a) (System) script; (Alphabet) alphabet
(b) (Handschrift) [hand]writing
(c) (Werk) work

Schrift·art die (Druckw.) [type]face

schriftlich [1] Adj. written
[2] adv. in writing

Schrift-: ~steller der; ~~s, ~~, ~stellerin die; ~~, ~~nen writer; ~stück das (offiziell) document; ~wechsel der correspondence; ~zeichen das character; ~zug der (Namenszug) lettering; (als Firmenzeichen) logo

schrill [1] Adj. shrill
[2] adv. shrilly

schrillen itr. V. shrill; sound shrilly

schritt 1. u. 3. Pers. Sg. Prät. v. SCHREITEN

Schritt der; ~[e]s, ~e (a) step; einen ~ machen od. tun take a step
(b) Pl. (Geräusch) footsteps
(c) (Entfernung) pace
(d) (Gleich~) aus dem ~ kommen get out of step ⋯⋗

S

(e) (Gangart) walk; **seinen ~ verlangsamen/ beschleunigen** slow/quicken one's pace; **[mit jmdm./etw.] ~ halten** (auch fig.) keep up or keep pace [with sb./sth.]

(f) (Schrittgeschwindigkeit) walking pace; „**~ fahren**' 'dead slow'

(g) (fig.: Maßnahme) step; measure

Schritt-: ~**geschwindigkeit** die walking pace; ~**macher** der, ~**macherin** die pacemaker

schroff [1] Adj. **(a)** precipitous ‹rock etc.›

(b) (plötzlich) sudden ‹transition, change›; (krass) stark ‹contrast›

(c) (barsch) curt ‹refusal, manner›; brusque ‹manner, behaviour, tone›

[2] adv. **(a)** ‹rise, drop› sheer; ‹fall away› precipitously

(b) (plötzlich, unvermittelt) suddenly

(c) (barsch) curtly; ‹interrupt› abruptly; ‹treat› brusquely

schröpfen tr. V. (ugs.) fleece

Schrot der od. das; ~[e]s, ~e **(a)** coarse meal; (aus Getreide) whole meal (Brit.); whole grain

(b) (Munition) shot

schroten tr. V. grind ‹grain etc.› [coarsely]; crush ‹malt› [coarsely]

Schrot-: ~**flinte** die shotgun; ~**kugel** die pellet

Schrott der; ~[e]s, ~e **(a)** scrap [metal]; **ein Auto zu ~ fahren** (ugs.) write a car off

(b) (salopp fig.) rubbish

schrott·reif Adj. ready for the scrap heap postpos.

schrubben tr. (auch itr.) V. scrub

Schrubber der; ~s, ~: [long-handled] scrubbing brush

Schrulle die; ~, ~n cranky idea; (Marotte) quirk

schrumpelig Adj. (ugs.) wrinkly

schrumpeln itr. V.; mit sein (ugs.) ‹skin› go wrinkled; ‹apple etc.› shrivel

schrumpfen itr. V.; mit sein shrink; ‹metal, rock› contract; ‹apple etc.› shrivel; ‹skin› go wrinkled; (abnehmen) decrease; ‹supplies, capital, hopes› dwindle

Schrumpf-: ~**leber** die cirrhotic liver; ~**niere** die cirrhotic kidney

Schub der; ~[e]s, **Schübe (a)** (Physik) thrust

(b) (Med.: Phase) phase; stage

(c) (Gruppe, Anzahl) batch

Schuber der; ~s, ~: slip case

Schub-: ~**fach** das drawer; ~**karre** die, ~**karren** der wheelbarrow; ~**lade** die drawer

Schubs der; ~es, ~e (ugs.) shove

schubsen tr. (auch itr.) V. (ugs.) push; shove

schub·weise Adv. (Med.) in phases or stages

schüchtern [1] Adj. **(a)** shy ‹person, smile, etc.›; shy, timid ‹voice, knock, etc.›

(b) (fig.: zaghaft) tentative, cautious ‹attempt, beginnings, etc.›

[2] adv. shyly; ‹knock, ask, etc.› timidly

Schüchternheit die; ~: shyness

Schuft der; ~[e]s, ~e scoundrel

schuften (ugs.) itr. V. slave away

Schufterei die; ~ (ugs.) slaving away no indef. art.; slog

Schuh der; ~[e]s, ~e shoe; (hoher ~, Stiefel) boot; **jmdm. etw. in die ~e schieben** (fig. ugs.) pin the blame for sth. on sb.

Schuh-: ~**anzieher** der; ~~s, ~~: shoehorn; ~**band** das; Pl. ~**bänder** (bes. südd.) shoelace; ~**creme** die shoe polish; ~**größe** die shoe size; **welche ~größe hast du?** what size shoe[s] do you take?; ~**löffel** der shoehorn; ~**macher** der, ~**macherin** die shoemaker; ~**sohle** die sole [of a/one's shoe]

Schul-: ~**abschluss**, *~**abschluß** der school-leaving qualification; ~**arbeit** die **(a)** ▶ ~**AUFGABE**; **(b)** (österr.: Klassenarbeit) [written] class test; ~**aufgabe** die item of homework; ~**aufgaben** homework sing.; ~**beirat** der school advisory board; ~**buch** das school book; ~**bus** der school bus

schuld ▶ SCHULD B

Schuld die; ~, ~en **(a)** guilt; **er ist sich** (Dat.) **keiner ~ bewusst** he is not conscious of having done any wrong

(b) (Verantwortlichkeit) blame; **es ist [nicht] seine ~:** it is [not] his fault; **[an etw.** (Dat.)] **~ haben** od. **schuld sein** be to blame [for sth.]

(c) (Verpflichtung zur Rückzahlung) debt; **5 000 Euro ~en haben** have debts of 5,000 euros; owe 5,000 euros

schuld·bewusst, *schuld·bewußt**
[1] Adj. guilty ‹look, face, etc.›
[2] adv. guiltily

schulden tr. V. owe; **was schulde ich Ihnen?** how much do I owe you?

Schuld·gefühl das feeling of guilt

schuldig Adj. **(a)** guilty; **der [an dem Unfall] ~e Autofahrer** the driver to blame [for the accident]

(b) jmdm. etw. ~ sein/bleiben owe sb. sth.

(c) (gebührend) proper

Schuldige der/die; adj. Dekl. guilty person; (im Strafprozess) guilty party

Schuldigkeit die; ~, ~en duty; **meine [verdammte] Pflicht und ~:** my bounden duty; **seine ~ getan haben** (fig.) have served its/his purpose

Schul·direktor der, **Schul·direktorin** die head teacher; headmaster/headmistress

schuld-, Schuld-: ~**los** Adj. innocent (an + Dat. of); ~**spruch** der verdict of guilty

---

Schule *die;* ~, ~n school; **zur** *od.* **in die** ~ **gehen, die** ~ **besuchen** go to school; **auf** *od.* **in der** ~: at school

schulen *tr. V.* train

Schüler *der;* ~s, ~: pupil; (Schuljunge) schoolboy

Schüler·austausch *der* school exchange

Schülerin *die;* ~, ~nen pupil; (Schulmädchen) schoolgirl

Schüler·mit·verwaltung *die* pupil participation *no art.* in school administration

schul-, Schul-: ~**ferien** *Pl.* school holidays *or* (Amer.) vacation *sing.;* ~**fernsehen** *das* educational television; television for schools; ~**fest** *das* school open day; ~**frei** *(day)* off school; **morgen ist/haben wir** ~**frei** there is/we have no school tomorrow; ~**frei bekommen** be let off school; ~**hof** *der* school yard; ~**jahr** *das* **(a)** school year; **(b)** (Klasse) year; ~**junge** *der* schoolboy; ~**kind** *das* schoolchild; ~**klasse** *die* [school] class; ~**land·heim** *das* [school's] country hostel (*visited by school classes*); ~**mädchen** *das* schoolgirl; ~**ordnung** *die* school rules *pl.;* ~**pflicht** the obligation to attend school; **die Einführung der [allgemeinen]** ~**pflicht** the introduction of compulsory school attendance [for all children]; ~**pflichtig** *Adj.* required to attend school *postpos.;* ~**pflichtig sein** have to attend school; **im** ~**pflichtigen Alter** of school age; ~**ranzen** *der* [school] satchel; ~**sportfest** *das* inter-school sports day; ~**sprecher** *der* pupils' representative; ≈ head boy; ~**sprecherin** *die* pupils' representative; ≈ head girl; ~**tag** *der* school day; ~**tasche** *die* schoolbag; (Ranzen) [school] satchel; ~**uniform** *die* school uniform

Schulter *die;* ~, ~n shoulder; **jmdm. auf die** ~ **klopfen** pat sb. on the shoulder *or* (fig.) back

Schulter·blatt *das* (Anat.) shoulder blade

schultern *tr. V.* shoulder; **das Gewehr** ~: shoulder arms

Schul-: ~**weg** *der* way to school; ~**zeit** *die* schooldays *pl.*

Schummelei *die;* ~, ~en (ugs.) ▶ MOGELEI

schummeln *itr., tr., refl. V.* (ugs.) ▶ MOGELN

schummerig *Adj.* dim ⟨light etc.⟩; dimly lit ⟨room etc.⟩

Schummler *der;* ~s, ~, **Schummlerin** *die;* ~, ~nen (ugs.) cheat

Schund *der;* ~[e]s trash

Schuppe *die;* ~, ~n **(a)** scale **(b)** *Pl.* (auf dem Kopf) dandruff *sing.;* (auf der Haut) flaking skin *sing.*

schuppen ⚀ *tr. V.* scale ⟨fish⟩ ⚁ *refl. V.* ⟨skin⟩ flake; ⟨person⟩ have flaking skin

Schuppen *der;* ~s, ~ **(a)** shed

(b) (ugs.: Lokal) joint (coll.)

schüren *tr. V.* **(a)** poke ⟨fire⟩ **(b)** (fig.) stir up ⟨hatred, envy, etc.⟩

schürfen ⚀ *itr. V.* scrape ⚁ *tr. V.* **(a)** **sich** (*Dat.*) **das Knie** *usw.* ~: graze one's knee *etc.;* **(b)** (Bergbau) mine ⟨ore etc.⟩ open-cast *or* (Amer.) opencut

Schürf·wunde *die* graze; abrasion

Schurke *der;* ~n, ~n, **Schurkin** *die;* ~, ~nen rogue

Schur·wolle *die* new wool

Schürze *die;* ~, ~n apron; (Latzschürze) pinafore

Schuss, *Schuß *der;* Schusses, Schüsse **(a)** shot (**auf** + *Akk.* at); **weit** *od.* **weitab vom** ~ (fig. ugs.) well away from the action **(b)** (Menge Munition/Schießpulver) round; **drei** ~ **Munition** three rounds of ammunition **(c)** (Schusswunde) gunshot wound **(d)** (kleine Menge) dash **(e)** (Drogenjargon) shot; fix (sl.) **(f)** (Skisport) schuss; ~ **fahren** schuss **(g)** (ugs.) **etw. in** ~ **bringen/halten** get sth. into/keep sth. in [good] shape

Schüssel *die;* ~, ~n bowl; (flacher) dish

schusselig (ugs.) ⚀ *Adj.* scatterbrained ⚁ *adv.* in a scatterbrained way

Schusseligkeit *die;* ~ (ugs.) scatterbrained way

Schuss-, *Schuß-: ~**linie** *die* line of fire; **in die/jmds.** ~**linie geraten** *od.* **kommen** (auch fig.) come under fire/come under fire from sb.; ~**verletzung** *die* gunshot wound; ~**waffe** *die* weapon (*firing a projectile*); (Gewehr usw.) firearm; ~**wechsel** *der* exchange of shots

Schuster *der;* ~s, ~, **Schusterin** *die;* ~, ~nen (ugs.) shoemaker; (jmd., der Schuhe repariert) shoe repairer

Schutt *der;* ~[e]s rubble; „~ **abladen verboten"** 'no tipping'; 'no dumping'

Schüttel·frost *der* [violent] shivering fit

schütteln ⚀ *tr. V.* **(a)** shake; **den Kopf [über etw.** (*Akk.*)**]** ~: shake one's head [over sth.]; **jmdm. die Hand** ~: shake sb.'s hand; shake sb. by the hand **(b)** (*unpers.*) **es schüttelte ihn [vor Kälte]** he was shaking [with *or* from cold] ⚁ *refl. V.* shake oneself/itself ⚂ *itr. V.* **mit dem Kopf** ~: shake one's head

schütten ⚀ *tr. V.* pour ⟨liquid, flour, etc.⟩; (unabsichtlich) spill ⟨liquid, flour, etc.⟩; tip ⟨rubbish, coal, etc.⟩ ⚁ *itr. V.* (*unpers.*) (ugs.: regnen) pour [down]

schütter *Adj.* sparse; thin

Schutt-: ~**halde** *die* pile *or* heap of rubble; ~**haufen** *der* pile of rubble; (Abfallhaufen) rubbish heap

Schutz *der;* ~es protection (**vor** + *Dat.*, **gegen** against); (Zuflucht) refuge; ~ **suchend** seeking protection *postpos.*

schutz-, Schutz-: ~**bedürftig** *Adj.* in ···❖

need of protection *postpos.;*
~**behauptung** *die* (bes. Rechtsw.) attempt
to justify one's behaviour; ~**blech** *das*
mudguard; ~**brief** *der* (Kfz-W.) travel
insurance; (Dokument) travel insurance
certificate

Schütze *der;* ~n, ~n (a) marksman
(b) (Fußball usw.) scorer
(c) (Milit.: einfacher Soldat) private
(d) (Astrol.) Sagittarius

schützen ⸤1⸥ *tr. V.* protect (**vor** + *Dat.* from,
gegen against); safeguard ⟨interest, property,
etc.⟩ (**vor** + *Dat.* from); **gesetzlich geschützt**
registered [as a trade mark]
⸤2⸥ *itr. V.* provide *or* give protection (**vor** +
Dat. from, **gegen** against); (vor Wind, Regen)
give shelter (**vor** + *Dat.* from)

Schützen·fest *das: shooting competition
with fair*

Schutz·engel *der* guardian angel

Schützen-: ~**graben** *der* trench;
~**panzer** *der* armoured personnel carrier;
~**verein** *der* rifle club

Schutz-: ~**helm** *der* helmet; (bei
Motorradfahrern usw.) crash helmet; (bei
Bauarbeitern usw.) safety helmet; ~**hütte** *die*
(a) (Unterstand) shelter; (b) (Berghütte)
mountain hut; ~**impfung** *die* vaccination

Schützin *die;* ~, ~nen (a) markswoman
(b) (Fußball usw.) scorer

Schützling *der;* ~s, ~e protégé;
(Anvertrauter) charge

schutz-, Schutz-: ~**los** *Adj.* defenceless;
~**mann** *der; Pl.* ~männer *od.* ~leute (ugs.
veralt.) [police] constable; copper (Brit. coll.);
~**patron** *der,* ~**patronin** *die* patron
saint; ~**schicht** *die* protective layer (**aus**
of); (flüssig aufgetragen) protective coating;
*~**suchend** ▶ SCHUTZ; ~**umschlag** *der*
dust jacket

schwabbelig *Adj.* flabby ⟨stomach,
person, etc.⟩; wobbly ⟨jelly etc.⟩

schwabbeln *itr. V.* (ugs.) wobble

Schwabe *der;* ~n, ~n Swabian

Schwaben *(das),* ~s Swabia

Schwäbin *die;* ~, ~nen Swabian

schwäbisch *Adj.* Swabian

schwach; schwächer, schwächst... ⸤1⸥ *Adj.*
(a) weak; weak, delicate ⟨child, woman⟩;
frail ⟨invalid, old person⟩; low-powered
⟨engine, bulb, amplifier, etc.⟩; weak, poor
⟨eyesight, memory, etc.⟩; poor ⟨hearing⟩;
delicate ⟨health, constitution⟩; ~ **werden**
grow weak; (fig.: schwanken) weaken; (fig.:
nachgeben) give in
(b) (nicht gut) poor ⟨pupil, player,
performance, result, etc.⟩; weak ⟨argument,
opponent, play, film, etc.⟩
(c) (gering, niedrig) poor, low ⟨attendance etc.⟩;
slight ⟨effect, resistance, gradient, etc.⟩; light

⟨wind, rain, current⟩; faint ⟨voice, pressure,
hope, smile, smell⟩; weak, faint ⟨pulse⟩; faint,
dim ⟨light⟩; pale ⟨colour⟩
(d) (wenig konzentriert) weak ⟨solution, coffee,
poison, etc.⟩
(e) (Sprachw.) weak
⸤2⸥ *adv.* (a) weakly
(b) (nicht gut) poorly
(c) (in geringem Maße) poorly ⟨attended,
developed⟩; slightly ⟨poisonous, sweetened,
inclined⟩; ⟨rain⟩ slightly; ⟨remember, glow,
smile⟩ faintly
(d) (Sprachw.) ~ **gebeugt** weak

Schwäche *die;* ~, ~n weakness; **eine** ~
für jmdn./etw. haben have a soft spot for sb./
a weakness for sth.

Schwäche·anfall *der* sudden feeling of
faintness

schwächen *tr. V.* weaken

schwächlich *Adj.* weakly ⟨person⟩; frail
⟨old person, constitution⟩

Schwächling *der;* ~s, ~e weakling

schwach-, Schwach-: ~**punkt** *der*
weak point; ~**sinn** *der* (a) (Med.) mental
deficiency; (b) (ugs.) [idiotic (coll.)] rubbish;
~**sinnig** ⸤1⸥ *Adj.* (a) (Med.) mentally
deficient; (b) (ugs.) idiotic (coll.), nonsensical
⟨measure, policy, etc.⟩; rubbishy ⟨film etc.⟩;
⸤2⸥ *adv.* (ugs.) idiotically (coll.); stupidly

Schwächung *die;* ~, ~en weakening

Schwaden *der;* ~s, ~: [thick] cloud

schwafeln (ugs.) ⸤1⸥ *itr. V.* rabbit on (Brit.
coll.), waffle (**von** about)
⸤2⸥ *tr. V.* blether ⟨nonsense⟩

Schwager *der;* ~s, Schwäger brother-in-
law

Schwägerin *die;* ~, ~nen sister-in-law

Schwalbe *die;* ~, ~n swallow

Schwall *der;* ~[e]s, ~e torrent

schwamm *1. u. 3. Pers. Sg. Prät. v.*
SCHWIMMEN

Schwamm *der;* ~[e]s, Schwämme (a)
sponge; ~ **drüber!** (ugs.) [let's] forget it
(b) (südd., österr.: Pilz) mushroom

Schwammerl *das;* ~s, ~[n] (bayr., österr.)
mushroom

schwammig ⸤1⸥ *Adj.* (a) spongy
(b) (aufgedunsen) flabby, bloated ⟨face, body,
etc.⟩
(c) (abwertend: unpräzise) woolly ⟨concept,
manner of expression, etc.⟩
⸤2⸥ *adv.* (unpräzise) vaguely

Schwammigkeit *die;* ~ (a) sponginess
(b) (abwertend: Aufgedunsenheit) flabbiness;
bloated appearence
(c) (abwertend: Vagheit) woolliness

Schwan *der;* ~[e]s, Schwäne swan

schwand *1. u. 3. Pers. Sg. Prät. v.*
SCHWINDEN

schwang *1. u. 3. Pers. Sg. Prät. v.*
SCHWINGEN

schwanger *Adj.* pregnant (**von** by)

---

*old spelling - see note on page xiv

Schwangere *die; adj. Dekl.* expectant mother; pregnant woman

schwängern *tr. V.* make ‹*woman*› pregnant

Schwangerschaft *die;* ~, ~en pregnancy

Schwangerschafts-: ~**abbruch** *der* termination of pregnancy; abortion; ~**verhütung** *die* contraception; ~**vertretung** *die* (a) maternity[-leave] cover; **die** ~**vertretung für jmdn. machen** cover for sb. while she is on maternity leave; **(b)** (Person) person covering [a period of] maternity leave

Schwank *der;* ~[e]s, **Schwänke** comic tale; (auf der Bühne) farce

schwanken *itr. V.; mit Richtungsangabe mit sein* **(a)** sway; ‹*boat*› rock; (heftiger) roll; ‹*ground, floor*› shake **(b)** (fig.: unbeständig sein) ‹*prices, temperature, etc.*› fluctuate; ‹*number, usage, etc.*› vary **(c)** (fig.: unentschieden sein) waver; (zögern) hesitate

Schwankung *die;* ~, ~en variation; (der Kurse usw.) fluctuation

Schwanz *der;* ~es, **Schwänze (a)** tail **(b)** (salopp: Penis) prick (coarse); cock (coarse)

Schwänzchen *das;* ~s, ~(a) [little] tail **(b)** (fam.: Penis) willy (coll.)

schwänzeln *itr. V.* wag its tail/their tails

schwänzen *tr., itr. V.* (ugs.) skip, cut ‹*lesson etc.*›; **[die Schule]** ~: play truant *or* (Amer.) hookey

schwappen *itr. V.* slosh

Schwarm *der;* ~[e]s, **Schwärme (a)** swarm **(b)** (fam.: Angebetete[r]) idol; heart-throb

schwärmen *itr. V.* **(a)** *mit Richtungsangabe mit sein* swarm **(b)** (begeistert sein) **für jmdn./etw.** ~: be mad about *or* really keen on sb./sth.; **von etw.** ~: go into raptures about sth.

schwärmerisch ⬚1 *Adj.* rapturous ⬚2 *adv.* rapturously

Schwarte *die;* ~, ~n (a) rind **(b)** (ugs.: dickes Buch) tome

schwarz; schwärzer, schwärzest... ⬚1 *Adj.* **(a)** black; Black ‹*person*›; filthy[-black] ‹*hands, fingernails, etc.*›; **mir wurde Schwarz vor den Augen** everything went black **der** ~**e Erdteil** *od.* **Kontinent** the Dark Continent; **das Schwarze Meer** the Black Sea; **ins Schwarze treffen** (fig.) hit the nail on the head **(b)** (illegal) illicit ‹*deal, exchange, etc.*›; **der** ~**e Markt** the black market **(c)** ~ **sehen** look on the black side; be pessimistic (**für** about) ⬚2 *adv.* (illegal) illegally

Schwarz *das;* ~[es], ~: black

Schwarz·brot *das* black bread

Schwarze *der/die; adj. Dekl.* Black

schwärzen *tr. V.* blacken

schwarz-, Schwarz-: ~|**fahren** *unr.*

itr. V.; mit sein dodge paying the fare; ~**fahrer** *der,* ~**fahrerin** *die* fare dodger; ~**haarig** *Adj.* black-haired; ~**handel** *der* black market (**mit** in); (Tätigkeit) black marketeering (**mit** in); ~**markt** *der* black market; ~|**sehen** *unr. itr. V.* watch television without a licence; *s. auch* SCHWARZ 1C; ~**seher** *der,* ~**seherin** *die* **(a)** (ugs.) pessimist; **(b)** (jmd, der schwarz fernsieht) [television] licence dodger

Schwärzung *die;* ~, ~en blackening

schwarz-, Schwarz-: ~**wald** *der;* ~[**e**]**s** Black Forest; ~**weiß** *Adj.* black and white; ~**weiß·film** *der* black and white film; ~**weiß·foto** *das* black and white photo; ~**wurzel** *die* black salsify

schwatzen, (bes. südd.) **schwätzen** ⬚1 *itr. V.* chat; (über belanglose Dinge) chatter; natter (coll.) ⬚2 *tr. V.* say; talk ‹*nonsense, rubbish*›

Schwätzer *der;* ~s, ~, **Schwätzerin** *die;* ~, ~nen chatterbox; (klatschhafter Mensch) gossip

schwatzhaft *Adj.* talkative; (klatschhaft) gossipy

Schwatzhaftigkeit *die;* ~: talkativeness; (Klatschsucht) gossipiness

Schwebe *die;* **in der** ~ **sein/bleiben** (fig.) be/remain in the balance

Schwebe-: ~**bahn** *die* cableway; ~**balken** *der* (Turnen) [balance] beam

schweben *itr. V.* **(a)** ‹*bird, balloon, etc.*› hover; ‹*cloud, balloon, mist*› hang; **in Gefahr** ~ (fig.) be in danger **(b)** *mit sein* (durch die Luft) float

Schwede *der;* ~n, ~n Swede

Schweden (*das*) ~s Sweden

Schwedin *die;* ~, ~nen Swede

schwedisch *Adj.* Swedish

Schwefel *der;* ~s sulphur

Schwefel-: ~**dioxid,** ~**dioxyd** *das* (Chemie) sulphur dioxide; ~**säure** *die* (Chemie) sulphuric acid; ~**wasserstoff** *der* (Chemie) hydrogen sulphide

Schweif *der;* ~[e]s, ~e tail

schweifen *itr. V.; mit sein* (geh.; auch fig.) wander

Schweige-geld *das* hush money

schweigen *unr. itr. V.* remain *or* stay silent; say nothing; **ganz zu** ~ **von ...**: not to mention ...

Schweigen *das;* ~s silence

schweigsam *Adj.* silent; quiet

Schweigsamkeit *die;* ~: silence; quietness

Schwein *das;* ~[e]s, ~e (a) pig **(b)** (Fleisch) pork **(c)** (salopp: gemeiner Mensch) swine; (Schmutzfink) mucky devil (coll.); mucky pig (coll.) **(d)** (salopp: Mensch) **ein armes** ~: a poor devil; **kein** ~ **war da** there wasn't a bloody (Brit. sl.) *or* (coll.) damn soul there ···⟫

(e) (ugs.: Glück) [großes] ∼ haben have a [big] stroke of luck; (davonkommen) get away with it (coll.)

Schweine-: ∼**braten** *der* roast pork *no indef. art.;* ∼**fleisch** *das* pork; ∼**kotelett** *das* (Kochk.) pork chop

Schweinerei *die;* ∼, ∼en (ugs.) **(a)** (Schmutz) mess **(b)** (Gemeinheit) mean *or* dirty trick

Schweine-: ∼**schnitzel** *das* escalope of pork; ∼**stall** *der* (auch fig.) pigsty; pigpen (Amer.); ∼**steak** *das* pork steak;

schweinisch (ugs.) *Adj.* **(a)** (schmutzig) filthy **(b)** (unanständig) dirty; smutty

Schweins·leder *das* pigskin

Schweiß *der;* ∼es sweat; **mir brach der** ∼ **aus** I broke out in a sweat

Schweiß-: ∼**ausbruch** *der* sweat; ∼**brenner** *der* welding torch; ∼**drüse** *die* (Anat.) sweat gland

schweißen *tr., itr. V.* weld

Schweißer *der;* ∼s, ∼, **Schweißerin** *die;* ∼, ∼nen welder

schweiß-, Schweiß-: ∼**fuß** sweaty foot; ∼**gebadet** *Adj.* bathed in sweat *postpos.;* ∼**nass,** *∗*∼**naß** *Adj.* sweaty; damp with sweat *pred.;* ∼**perle** *die* bead of sweat

Schweiz *die;* ∼: Switzerland *no art.*

Schweizer *der;* ∼s, ∼: Swiss

schweizer·deutsch *Adj.* Swiss German

Schweizerin *die;* ∼, ∼nen Swiss

schweizerisch *Adj.* Swiss

schwelen (auch fig.) smoulder

schwelgen *itr. V.* feast

Schwelle *die;* ∼, ∼n **(a)** threshold **(b)** (Eisenbahnschwelle) sleeper (Brit.); [cross] tie (Amer.)

schwellen *unr. itr. V.; mit sein* swell ⟨limb, face, cheek, etc.⟩ swell [up]

Schwellen·land *das:* country at the stage of economic take-off

Schwellung *die;* ∼, ∼en (Med.) swelling

Schwemme *die;* ∼, ∼n glut (an + *Dat.* of)

Schwemm·land *das* alluvial land

Schwengel *der;* ∼s, ∼ **(a)** (der Glocke) clapper **(b)** (der Pumpe) handle

Schwenk *der;* ∼s, ∼s **(a)** (Drehung) swing **(b)** (Film, Ferns.) pan

schwenken ① *tr. V.* **(a)** swing; wave ⟨flag, handkerchief⟩ **(b)** (spülen) rinse ② *itr. V.; mit sein* ⟨marching column⟩ swing, wheel; ⟨camera⟩ pan; ⟨path, road, car⟩ swing

schwer ① *Adj.* **(a)** heavy; **2 Kilo** ∼ **sein** weigh two kilos **(b)** (mühevoll) heavy ⟨work⟩; hard, tough ⟨job⟩; hard ⟨day⟩; difficult ⟨birth⟩; **es** ∼/**nicht** ∼

haben have it hard/easy; **sich mit** *od.* **bei etw.** ∼ **tun** (ugs.) have trouble with sth.; **jmdm. fällt etw.** ∼: sb. finds sth. difficult; **jmdm./ sich etw.** ∼ **machen** make sth. difficult for sb./oneself **(c)** (schlimm) severe ⟨shock, disappointment, strain, storm⟩; serious, grave ⟨wrong, injustice, error, illness, blow, reservation⟩; serious ⟨accident, injury⟩; heavy ⟨punishment, strain, loss, blow⟩; **etw.** ∼ **nehmen** take sth. seriously ② *adv.* **(a)** heavily ⟨built, laden, armed⟩; ∼ **tragen** be carrying sth. heavy [with difficulty] **(b)** ⟨work⟩ hard; ⟨breathe⟩ heavily; ∼ **hören** be hard of hearing **(c)** (schwierig) with difficulty; ∼ **verdaulich** (auch fig.) hard to digest *pred.* **(d)** (sehr) seriously ⟨injured, ill⟩; greatly, deeply ⟨disappointed⟩; ⟨punish⟩ severely, heavily; ∼ **verunglücken** have a serious accident

Schwer-: ∼**arbeiter** *der* worker engaged in heavy physical work; ∼**behinderte** *der/die* severely handicapped person; (körperlich auch) severely disabled person; **die** ∼**behinderten** the severely handicapped/ disabled; ∼**beschädigte** *der/die; adj. Dekl.* severely disabled person

Schwere *die;* ∼ **(a)** weight **(b)** (Schwerkraft) gravity **(c)** ▶ SCHWER 1C: severity; seriousness; gravity; heaviness

schwere·los *Adj.* weightless

Schwerelosigkeit *die;* ∼: weightlessness

schwer-, Schwer-: *∗*∼|**fallen** ▶ SCHWER 1B; ∼**fällig** ① *Adj.* (auch fig.) ponderous; cumbersome ⟨bureaucracy, procedure⟩; ② *adv.* ponderously; ∼**fälligkeit** *die:* ▶ ∼FÄLLIG: ponderousness; cumbersomeness; ∼**gewicht** *das* **(a)** (Sport) heavyweight; **(b)** (Schwerpunkt) main focus; ∼**hörig** *Adj.* hard of hearing *pred.;* ∼**hörigkeit** *die;* ∼∼: hardness of hearing; ∼**industrie** *die* heavy industry; ∼**kraft** *die* gravity; *∗*∼**krank** ▶ SCHWER 2D

schwerlich *Adv.* hardly

schwer-, Schwer-: *∗*∼|**machen** ▶ SCHWER 1B; ∼**metall** *das* heavy metal; ∼**mütig** ① *Adj.* melancholic; ② *adv.* melancholically; *∗*∼|**nehmen** ▶ SCHWER 1C; ∼**punkt** *der* centre of gravity; (fig.) main focus; (Hauptgewicht) main stress

Schwert *das;* ∼[e]s, ∼er sword

Schwert-: ∼**fisch** *der* swordfish; ∼**lilie** *die* iris

schwer|tun ▶ SCHWER 1B

Schwert·wal *der* (Orka) killer whale

schwer-, Schwer-: ∼**verbrecher** *der,* ∼**verbrecherin** *die* serious offender; *∗*∼**verdaulich** ▶ SCHWER 2C; *∗*∼**verletzt** ▶ SCHWER 2D; ∼**wiegend** *Adj.* serious; momentous ⟨decision⟩

Schwester *die;* ∼, ∼n **(a)** sister

∗alte Schreibung - vgl. Hinweis auf S. xiv

(b) (Krankenschwester) nurse
schwesterlich **1** *Adj.* sisterly
  2 *adv.* ~ **handeln** act in a sisterly way
schwieg *1. u. 3. Pers. Prät. v.* SCHWEIGEN
Schwieger-: ~**eltern** *Pl.* parents-in-law;
  ~**mutter** *die; Pl.* ~**mütter** mother-in-law;
  ~**sohn** *der* son-in-law; ~**tochter** *die*
  daughter-in-law; ~**vater** *der* father-in-law
Schwiele *die;* ~, ~n callus; ~n an den
  Händen horny hands
schwielig *Adj.* callused; ~e Hände horny
  hands
schwierig *Adj.* difficult
Schwierigkeit *die;* ~, ~en difficulty
Schwierigkeits·grad *der* degree of
  difficulty; (von Lehrmaterial usw.) level of
  difficulty
Schwimm-: ~**bad** *das* swimming baths
  pl. (Brit.); swimming pool; ~**becken** *das*
  swimming pool
schwimmen **1** *unr. itr. V.* **(a)** *meist mit*
  sein swim
  (b) *meist mit sein* (treiben, nicht untergehen)
  float
  (c) (ugs.: unsicher sein) be all at sea; **ins**
  Schwimmen geraten start to flounder
  2 *unr. tr. V.; auch mit sein* swim
Schwimmen *das;* ~s: swimming *no art.*
Schwimmer *der;* ~s, ~ **(a)** swimmer
  (b) (Technik) float
Schwimmerin *die;* ~, ~nen swimmer
Schwimm-: ~**flosse** *die* flipper;
  ~**lehrer** *der,* ~**lehrerin** *die* swimming
  instructor; ~**weste** *die* life jacket
Schwindel *der;* ~s **(a)** dizziness;
  giddiness
  (b) (Betrug) swindle; (Lüge) lie
schwindel·frei *Adj.* ~ **sein** have a head
  for heights
schwindelig ▶ SCHWINDLIG
schwindeln *itr. V.* **(a)** (unpers.) mich od.
  mir schwindelt I feel dizzy *or* giddy
  (b) (lügen) tell fibs
schwinden *unr. itr. V.; mit sein* fade;
  ⟨supplies, money⟩ run out; ⟨effect⟩ wear off;
  ⟨fear, mistrust⟩ lessen; ⟨powers, influence⟩
  wane
Schwindler *der;* ~s, ~, **Schwindlerin**
  die; ~, ~nen (Lügner[in]) liar; (Betrüger[in])
  swindler; (Hochstapler[in]) confidence trickster
schwindlig *Adj.* dizzy; giddy; **jmdm. wird**
  es ~: sb. gets dizzy *or* giddy
schwingen **1** *unr. itr. V.* **(a)** *mit sein*
  swing
  (b) (vibrieren) vibrate
  2 *unr. tr. V.* swing; wave ⟨flag, wand⟩;
  brandish ⟨sword, axe, etc.⟩
  3 *unr. refl. V.* sich aufs Pferd/Fahrrad ~:
  leap on to one's horse/bicycle
Schwingung *die;* ~, ~en **(a)** swinging;
  (Vibration) vibration
  (b) (Physik) oscillation

Schwips *der;* ~es, ~e (ugs.) **einen** ~
  haben be tipsy
schwirren *itr. V. mit sein* ⟨arrow, bullet,
  etc.⟩ whiz; ⟨bird⟩ whirl; ⟨insect⟩ buzz
schwitzen *itr. V.* (auch fig.) sweat
schwor *1. u. 3. Pers. Sg. Prät. v.* SCHWÖREN
schwören **1** *unr. tr., itr. V.* swear
  ⟨fidelity, friendship⟩; swear, take ⟨oath⟩
  2 *unr. itr. V.* swear an/the oath
Schwuchtel *die;* ~, ~n (salopp) queen (sl.)
schwul *Adj.* (ugs.) gay (coll.)
schwül *Adj.* sultry; close
Schwule *der; adj. Dekl.* (ugs.) gay (coll.);
  (abwertend) queer (sl.)
Schwüle *die;* ~: sultriness
schwülstig *Adj.* bombastic; pompous;
  over-ornate ⟨art, architecture⟩
Schwund *der;* ~[e]s decrease, drop (Gen.
  in); (an Interesse) waning; falling off
Schwung *der;* ~[e]s, Schwünge **(a)**
  (Bewegung) swing
  (b) (Linie) sweep
  (c) (Geschwindigkeit) momentum; ~ **holen**
  build *or* get up momentum
  (d) (Antrieb) drive; energy
  (e) (mitreißende Wirkung) sparkle
schwung·haft *Adj.* thriving; brisk,
  flourishing ⟨trade, business⟩
schwung·voll **1** *Adj.* **(a)** lively
  (b) (kraftvoll) vigorous; sweeping ⟨movement,
  gesture⟩; bold ⟨handwriting, line, stroke⟩
  2 *adv.* spiritedly; (kraftvoll) with great vigour
Schwur *der;* ~[e]s, Schwüre **(a)** (Gelöbnis)
  vow
  (b) (Eid) oath
Schwur·gericht *das:* court with a jury
scrollen /ˈskrɔlən/ *itr., tr. V.* (DV) scroll
sechs *Kardinalz.* six
Sechs *die;* ~, ~en six
sechs-, Sechs-: ~**eck** *das* hexagon;
  ~**eckig** *Adj.* hexagonal; ~**fach**
  Vervielfältigungsz. sixfold; ~**hundert**
  Kardinalz. six hundred; ~**mal** *Adv.* six
  times
sechst... *Ordinalz.* sixth
sechs·tausend *Kardinalz.* six thousand
sechstel *Bruchz.* sixth
Sechstel *das,* (schweiz. meist *der*); ~s, ~:
  sixth
sechstens *Adv.* sixthly
sechzehn *Kardinalz.* sixteen
sechzig *Kardinalz.* sixty
sechzigst... *Ordinalz.* sixtieth
SED *Abk.* (DDR) = **Sozialistische**
  Einheitspartei Deutschlands
  Socialist Unity Party of Germany (*state*
  party of the former DDR)
See¹ *der;* ~s, ~n lake
See² *die;* ~: **die** ~: the sea; **an die** ~ **fahren**
  go to the seaside; **auf hoher** ~: on the high
  seas
see-, See-: ~**bad** *das* seaside health   ⋯⟶

S

resort; ~**fahrt** die séafaring no art.; sea travel no art.; ~**gang** der leichter/starker od. hoher od. schwerer ~gang light/heavy or rough sea; ~**hund** der [common] seal; (Pelz)seal[skin]; ~**igel** der sea urchin; ~**krank** Adj. seasick; ~**krankheit** die seasickness; ~**lachs** der pollack

Seele die; ~, ~n soul; (Psyche) mind

Seelen·leben das (geh.) inner life

seelen·ruhig ⨵1⨵ Adj. calm; unruffled ⨵2⨵ adv. calmly

seelisch ⨵1⨵ Adj. psychological ⟨cause, damage, tension⟩; mental ⟨equilibrium, breakdown, illness, health⟩ ⨵2⨵ adv. ~ bedingt sein have psychological causes; ~ krank mentally ill

Seel·sorge die pastoral care

Seelsorger der; ~s, ~, **Seelsorgerin** die; ~, ~nen pastoral worker; (Geistliche[r]) pastor

see-, See-: ~**macht** die sea power; ~**mann** der; Pl. ~leute seaman; sailor; ~**meile** die nautical mile; ~**not** die distress [at sea]; in ~not geraten get into difficulties pl.; ~**pferd[chen]** das sea horse; ~**räuber** der, ~**räuberin** die pirate; ~**reise** die voyage; (Kreuzfahrt) cruise; ~**rose** die waterlily; ~**stern** der starfish; ~**tüchtig** Adj. seaworthy; ~**zunge** die sole

Segel das; ~s, ~: sail

Segel-: ~**boot** das sailing boat; ~**flieger** der, ~**fliegerin** die glider pilot; ~**flugzeug** das glider

segeln itr. V.; mit sein sail

Segel-: ~**schiff** das sailing ship; ~**tuch** das; Pl. ~e sailcloth

Segen der; ~s, ~: blessing; (Gebet in der Messe) benediction

Segler der; ~s, ~: yachtsman

Seglerin die; ~, ~nen yachtswoman

segnen tr. V. bless

seh·behindert Adj. partially sighted; visually handicapped

sehen ⨵1⨵ unr. itr. V. (a) see; schlecht/gut ~: have bad/good eyesight; mal ~, wir wollen od. werden ~ (ugs.) we'll see; siehste! (ugs.) there, you see! (b) (hinsehen) look (auf + Akk. at); sieh mal od. doch! siehe da! lo and behold! ⨵2⨵ unr. tr. V. (a) (auch fig.) see; jmdn./etw. [nicht] zu ~ bekommen [not] get to see sb./sth.; ich habe ihn kommen [ge]~: I saw him coming (b) (ansehen) watch ⟨television programme⟩

sehens·wert Adj. worth seeing postpos.

Sehens·würdigkeit die; ~, ~en sight

Seher der; ~s, ~, **Seherin** die; ~, ~nen seer; prophet/prophetess

Seh-: ~**fehler** der sight defect; defect of vision; ~**kraft** die sight

Sehne die; ~, ~n (a) tendon (b) (Bogen~) string

sehnen refl. V. sich nach jmdm./etw. ~: long or yearn for sb./sth.

sehnig Adj. (a) stringy ⟨meat⟩ (b) (kräftig) sinewy ⟨figure, legs, etc.⟩

sehnlichst ⨵1⨵ Adj. das ist mein ~es Verlangen/mein ~er Wunsch that's what I long for most/that's my dearest wish ⨵2⨵ adv. etw. ~ herbeiwünschen look forward longingly to sth.

Sehn·sucht die longing; ~ nach jmdm. haben long to see sb.

sehn·süchtig Adj. longing attrib., yearning attrib. ⟨desire, look, gaze, etc.⟩

sehr Adv. (a) mit Adj. u. Adv. very; ~ viel a great deal; jmdn. ~ gern haben like sb. a lot (coll.) or a great deal (b) mit Verben very much; greatly; danke ~! thank you or thanks [very much]; bitte ~, Ihr Steak! here's your steak, sir/madam

Seh-: ~**schärfe** die visual acuity; ~**test** der eye test; ~**vermögen** das sight

sei 1. u. 3. Pers. Sg. Präsens Konjunktiv u. Imperativ Sg. v. SEIN

seicht ⨵1⨵ Adj. (auch fig.) shallow ⨵2⨵ adv. (fig.) shallowly

Seichtheit die; ~ (auch fig.) shallowness

seid 2. Pers. Pl. Präsens u. Imperativ Pl. v. SEIN

Seide die; ~, ~n silk

Seidel das; ~s, ~: beer mug

seiden Adj. silk

Seiden·papier das tissue paper

seidig ⨵1⨵ Adj. silky ⨵2⨵ adv. silkily

Seife die; ~, ~n soap

Seifen-: ~**blase** die soap bubble; ~**oper** die (ugs.) soap opera; ~**schale** die soap dish; ~**schaum** der lather

Seil das; ~s, ~e rope; (Drahtseil) cable

Seil·bahn die cableway

seil|hüpfen itr. V.; nur im Inf. u. 2. Part.; mit sein ▶ SEILSPRINGEN

Seilschaft die; ~, ~en (Bergsteigen) rope; (fig.) followers pl.

seil-, Seil-: ~|**springen** unr. itr. V.; nur im Inf. u. 2. Part.; mit sein skip; ~**tänzer** der, ~**tänzerin** die tightrope walker; ~**winde** die cable winch

sein¹ ⨵1⨵ unr. itr. V. be; (existieren) be; exist; (sich ereignen) be; happen; wie dem auch sei that as it may; er ist Schwede/Lehrer he is Swedish or a Swede/a teacher; bist du es? is that you?; mir ist kalt/besser I am or feel cold/better; mir ist schlecht I feel sick; drei und vier ist od. (ugs.) sind sieben three and four is or makes seven; es ist drei Uhr/Mai/Winter it is three o'clock/May/winter; er ist aus Berlin he is or comes from Berlin; was darf es ~? (im Geschäft) what can I get you?; es war einmal ein Prinz once upon a time there was a prince

---

*old spelling - see note on page xiv

2 *mod. V.* (in der Funktion von können/müssen + *Passiv*) **es ist niemand zu sehen** there's no one to be seen; **das war zu erwarten** that was to be expected; **die Schmerzen sind kaum zu ertragen** the pain is hardly bearable; **die Richtlinien sind strengstens zu beachten** the guidelines are to be strictly followed **3** *Hilfsverb* **(a)** (zur Perfektumschreibung) have; **er ist gestorben** he has died **(b)** (zur Bildung des Zustandspassivs) be; **wir sind gerettet worden/wir waren gerettet** we were saved

sein[2] *Possessivpron.* (einer männlichen Person) his; (einer weiblichen Person) her; (einer Sache, eines Tiers) its; (nach man) one's; his (Amer.)

Sein *das;* ~s (Philos.) being; (Dasein) existence; ~ **und Schein** appearance and reality

seiner (geh.) *Gen. von* ER: **sich** ~ **erbarmen** have pity on him; ~ **gedenken** remember him

seiner-: ~**seits** *Adv.* for his part; (von ihm) on his part; ~**zeit** *Adv.* at that time

seines·gleichen *indekl. Pron.* his own kind

seinet·wegen *Adv.* ▶ MEINETWEGEN: because of him; for his sake; about him; as far as he is concerned

seismo-, Seismo-: ~**graph** *der;* ~~ en, ~~en seismograph; ~**loge** *der;* ~~n, ~~n seismologist; ~**logie** *die;* ~~: seismology *no art.;* ~**login** *die;* ~~, ~~nen seismologist; ~**logisch** [1] *Adj.* seismological; [2] *adv.* seismologically

seit [1] *Präp. mit Dat.* (Zeitpunkt) since; (Zeitspanne) for; **ich bin** ~ **zwei Wochen hier** I've been here [for] two weeks [2] *Konj.* since; ~ **du hier wohnst** since you have been living here

seit·dem [1] *Adv.* since then [2] *Konj.* ▶ SEIT 2

Seite *die;* ~, ~n **(a)** side; **zur od. auf die** ~ **gehen** move aside *or* to one side; ~ **an** ~: side by side; **jmdm. zur** ~ **stehen** stand by sb.; **von allen** ~**n** (auch fig.) from all sides; **nach allen** ~**n** in all directions; (fig.) on all sides **(b)** (Buch-, Zeitungsseite) page

Seiten-: ~**ansicht** *die* side view; ~**aufprall·schutz** *der* side impact protection; ~**hieb** *der* (fig.) sideswipe (**auf** + *Akk.* at); ~**ruder** *das* (Flugw.) rudder

seitens *Präp. mit Gen.* (Papierdt.) on the part of

Seiten-: ~**sprung** *der* infidelity; ~**straße** *die* side street; ~**wind** *der* side wind; crosswind; ~**zahl** *die* **(a)** page number; **(b)** (Anzahl der Seiten) number of pages

seit·her *Adv.* since then

seitlich [1] *Adj.* at the side (postpos.) [2] *adv.* (an der Seite) at the side; (von der Seite) from the side; (nach der Seite) to the side

seit·wärts *Adv.* sideways

Sekretär *der;* ~s, ~e **(a)** secretary **(b)** (Schreibschrank) bureau (Brit.)

Sekretariat *das;* ~[e]s, ~e [secretary's/ secretaries'] office

Sekretärin *die;* ~, ~nen secretary

Sekt *der;* ~[e]s, ~e high-quality sparkling wine; ≈ champagne

Sekte *die;* ~, ~n sect

Sektor *der;* ~s, ~en **(a)** (Fachgebiet) field; sphere; **industrieller/wirtschaftlicher** ~: industrial/economic sector **(b)** (Geom.; Besatzungszone) sector

sekundär [1] *Adj.* secondary [2] *adv.* secondarily

Sekundar-: ~**schule** *die* (schweiz.) secondary school; ~**stufe** *die* secondary stage (*of education*)

Sekunde *die;* ~, ~n **(a)** (auch Math., Musik) second **(b)** (ugs.: Augenblick) second; moment

Sekunden·zeiger *der* second hand

selb... *Demonstrativpron.* same;

selber *indekl. Demonstrativpron.* ▶ SELBST 1

selbst [1] *indekl. Demonstrativpron.* myself/ yourself/himself/herself/itself/ourselves/ yourselves/themselves; **von** ~: automatically; ~ **gemacht** home-made [2] *Adv.* even

Selbst·achtung *die* self-respect; self-esteem

selb·ständig [1] *Adj.* independent; self-employed ⟨*business man, tradesman, etc.*⟩; **sich** ~ **machen** set up on one's own [2] *adv.* independently; ~ **denken** think for oneself

Selbständigkeit *die;* ~: independence

selbst-, Selbst-: ~**auslöser** *der* (Fot.) delayed-action shutter release; ~**bedienung** *die* self-service *no art.;* ~**befriedigung** *die* masturbation *no art.;* ~**beherrschung** *die* self-control *no art.;* ~**bestätigung** *die* (Psych.) self-affirmation *no art.;* ~**bewusst**, ***~**bewußt** [1] *Adj.* self-confident; [2] *adv.* self-confidently; ~**bewusstsein**, ***~**bewußtsein** *das* self-confidence *no art.;* ~**erkenntnis** *die* self-knowledge *no art.;* ~**gefällig** [1] *Adj.* self-satisfied; smug; [2] *adv.* smugly; ~**gefälligkeit** *die* self-satisfaction; smugness; ***~**gemacht** ▶ SELBST 1; ~**gespräch** *das* conversation with oneself; ~**hilfe** *die* self-help *no art.;* **Hilfe zur** ~**hilfe leisten** help people to help themselves; ~**hilfe·gruppe** *die* self-help group; ~**los** [1] *Adj.* selfless; [2] *adv.* selflessly; unselfishly; ~**mord** *der* suicide *no art.;* ~**mörder** *der,* ~**mörderin** *die* suicide; ~**sicher** [1] *Adj.* self-confident; [2] *adv.* in a self-confident manner; ~**ständig** *usw.* ▶ SELBSTÄNDIG *usw.;* ~**süchtig** [1] *Adj.* selfish; [2] *adv.* selfishly; ~**tätig** [1] *Adj.* automatic; ⋯⋗

S

2 *adv.* automatically; ~**verständlich**
1 *Adj.* natural; etw. für ~verständlich
halten regard sth. as a matter of course; (für
gegeben hinnehmen) take sth. for granted; **2** *adv.*
naturally; of course; ~**verständlichkeit**
die matter of course; etw. mit der größten
~verständlichkeit tun do sth. as if it were the
most natural thing in the world;
~**vertrauen** *das* self-confidence;
~**verwaltung** *die* self-government *no art.;*
~**zweck** *der* end in itself
selektieren *tr. V.* select; pick out
Selektion *die;* ~, ~en selection
selektiv **1** *Adj.* selective
2 *adv.* selectively
selig **1** *Adj.* (a) (Rel.) blessed
(b) (tot) late [lamented]
(c) (glücklich) blissful ⟨*idleness, slumber, etc.*⟩;
blissfully happy ⟨*person*⟩
2 *adv.* blissfully
Seligkeit *die;* ~, ~en bliss *no pl.;* [blissful]
happiness *no pl.*
Sellerie *der;* ~s, ~[s] *od.* die; ~, ~:
celeriac; (Stangen~) celery
selten **1** *Adj.* rare; infrequent ⟨*visit,*
visitor⟩
2 *adv.* (a) rarely
(b) (sehr) exceptionally; uncommonly
Seltenheit *die;* ~, ~en rarity
Seltenheits·wert *der;* ~[es] rarity value
Selters·wasser *das* seltzer [water]
seltsam **1** *Adj.* strange; odd
2 *adv.* strangely
Semester *das;* ~s, ~: semester
Semester·ferien *Pl.* [university] vacation
sing.
Semi·finale *das* (Sport) semi-final
Semi·kolon *das;* ~s, ~s semicolon
Seminar *das;* ~s, ~e (a) seminar (über +
Akk. on)
(b) (Institut) department
Semit *der;* ~en, ~en, **Semitin** *die;* ~,
~nen Semite
semitisch *Adj.* Semitic
Semmel *die;* ~, ~n (bes. österr., bayr., ostmd.)
[bread] roll
Semmel·knödel *der* (bayr., österr.) bread
dumpling
Senat *der;* ~[e]s, ~e senate
Senator *der;* ~s, ~en, **Senatorin** *die;* ~,
~nen senator
senden[1] *unr.* (*auch regelm.*) *tr. V.* (geh.)
send
senden[2] *regelm.* (*schweiz. unr.*) *tr., itr. V.*
broadcast ⟨*programme, play, etc.*⟩; transmit
⟨*signals, Morse, etc.*⟩
Sender *der;* ~s, ~: [broadcasting] station;
(Anlage) transmitter
Sende·reihe *die* series [of programmes]

Sender·such·lauf *der* (Rundf., Ferns.)
[automatic] station search
Sende·schluss, *Sende·schluß *der*
close down
Sende·zeit *die* (Rundf., Ferns.) broadcasting
time; die ~ um zehn Minuten überschreiten
overrun by ten minutes
Sendung *die;* ~, ~en (a) consignment
(b) (Rundf., Ferns.) programme
Senf *der;* ~[e]s, ~e mustard
senil **1** *Adj.* (Med., auch abwertend) senile
2 *adv.* in a senile manner
senior *nach Personennamen* senior
Senior *der;* ~s, ~en (a) (Kaufmannsspr.)
senior partner
(b) (Sport) senior [player]
(c) (Rentner) senior citizen
Senioren·heim *das* home for the elderly
Seniorin *die;* ~, ~nen ▶ SENIOR
Senke *die;* ~, ~n hollow
senken **1** *tr. V.* lower
2 *refl. V.* ⟨*curtain, barrier, etc.*⟩ fall, come
down; ⟨*ground, building, road*⟩ subside, sink;
⟨*water level*⟩ fall, sink
senk-, Senk-: ~**fuß** *der* flat foot;
~**recht** **1** *Adj.* vertical; ~recht zu etw.
perpendicular to sth.; **2** *adv.* vertically;
~**rechte** *die;* ~~, ~~n; *auch adj. Dekl.*
vertical; (Geom.: Gerade) perpendicular
Sensation *die;* ~, ~en sensation
sensationell **1** *Adj.* sensational
2 *adv.* sensationally
Sense *die;* ~, ~n scythe
sensibel **1** *Adj.* sensitive
2 *adv.* sensitively
sensibilisieren *tr. V.* (geh.) make ⟨*person*⟩
more sensitive (für to)
Sensibilität *die;* ~ sensitivity
sentimental **1** *Adj.* sentimental
2 *adv.* sentimentally
Sentimentalität *die;* ~, ~en
sentimentality
separat **1** *Adj.* separate; self-contained
⟨*flat etc.*⟩
2 *adv.* separately
September *der;* ~[s], ~: September
Serbe *der;* ~n, ~n Serb; Serbian
Serbien (*das*); ~s Serbia
Serbin *die;* ~, ~nen ▶ SERBE
serbisch *Adj.* Serbian
Serenade *die;* ~, ~n serenade
Serie /'ze:rjə/ *die;* ~, ~n series
serien·mäßig **1** *Adj.* standard ⟨*product,*
model, etc.⟩
2 *adv.* (a) ~ gefertigt *od.* gebaut produced
in series
(b) (nicht als Sonderausstattung) ⟨*fitted, supplied,*
etc.⟩ as standard
seriös *Adj.* respectable ⟨*person, hotel, etc.*⟩;
trustworthy ⟨*firm, partner, etc.*⟩; serious
⟨*offer, applicant, artist, etc.*⟩

Seriosität *die;* ~ (geh.) **(a)** (Solidität) respectability; (Vertrauenswürdigkeit) trustworthiness
(b) (Ernsthaftigkeit) seriousness

Serpentine *die;* ~, ~n hairpin bend

Serum *das;* ~s, S**e**ren serum

Service¹ /'zɛr'viːs/ *das;* ~, ~: [dinner *etc.*] service

Service² /'zøːɐ̯vɪs/ *der;* ~, ~s /'zøːɐ̯vɪsɪs/ (Bedienung, Kundendienst) service

servieren *tr. V.* serve

Serviererin *die;* ~, ~nen waitress

Serviette /zɛr'vi̯ɛta/ *die;* ~, ~n napkin; serviette (Brit.)

Servo-: ~**bremse** *die* servo[-assisted] brake; ~**lenkung** *die* power[-assisted] steering *no indef. art.*

Servus /'zɛrvʊs/ *Interj.* (bes. südd., österr.) (beim Abschied) goodbye; so long (coll.); (zur Begrüßung) hello

Sesam *der;* ~s sesame seeds *pl.*

Sessel *der;* ~s, ~ **(a)** armchair
(b) (österr.: Stuhl) chair

Sessel-lift *der* chairlift

sesshaft, *seßhaft *Adj.* settled; ~ werden settle down

Sesshaftigkeit, *Seßhaftigkeit *die;* ~: settled way of life

Set *das od. der;* ~[s], ~s **(a)** set, combination (aus of)
(b) (Deckchen) table- *or* place mat

setzen ① *refl. V.* **(a)** sit [down]; setzen Sie sich sit down; take a seat; sich aufs Sofa *usw.* ~: sit on the sofa *etc.;*
(b) ⟨coffee, froth, *etc.*⟩ settle; ⟨sediment⟩ sink to the bottom
② *tr. V.* **(a)** put
(b) (einpflanzen) plant ⟨tomatoes, potatoes, *etc.*⟩
(c) (aufziehen) hoist ⟨flag *etc.*⟩; set ⟨sails, navigation lights⟩
(d) (Druckw.) set ⟨manuscript *etc.*⟩
③ *itr. V.* **(a)** *meist mit sein* (springen) leap; jump
(b) über einen Fluss ~ (mit einer Fähre o. Ä.) cross a river
(c) (beim Wetten) bet; auf ein Pferd/auf Rot ~: back a horse/put one's money on red

Setzer *der;* ~s, ~, **Setzerin** *die;* ~, ~nen (Druckw.) [type]setter

Setzling *der;* ~s, ~e seedling

Seuche *die;* ~, ~n epidemic

Seuchen-gefahr *die* danger of an epidemic

seufzen *itr., tr. V.* sigh

Seufzer *der;* ~s, ~: sigh

Sex *der;* ~[es] sex *no art.*

Sexismus *der;* ~: sexism *no art.*

sexistisch ① *Adj.* sexist
② *adv.* ⟨behave, think, *etc.*⟩ in a sexist manner

Sexualität *die;* ~: sexuality *no art.*

Sexual-: ~**kunde** *die* (Schulw.) sex

education *no art.;* ~**leben** *das* sex life;
~**partner** *der,* ~**partnerin** *die* sexual partner; ~**trieb** *der* sex[ual] drive *or* urge;
~**verbrechen** *das* sex crime;
~**verbrecher** *der* sex offender

sexuell ① *Adj.* sexual
② *adv.* sexually

sezieren *tr. V.* dissect ⟨corpse⟩

sfr., sFr. *Abk.* **Schweizer Franken**

Shampoo /ʃam'puː/, **Shampoon** /ʃam'poːn/ *das;* ~s, ~s shampoo

Shareholdervalue /'ʃeəhoʊldəvælju:/ *der;* ~s, ~s shareholder value

Sherry /'ʃɛrɪ/ *der;* ~s, ~s sherry

Show /ʃoʊ/ *die;* ~, ~s show

siamesisch *Adj.* Siamese

Siam-katze *die* Siamese cat

Sibirien (das); ~s Siberia

sich *Reflexivpron. der 3. Pers. Sg. und Pl. Akk. und Dat.* **(a)** himself/herself/itself/ themselves; (auf man bezogen) oneself; (auf das Anredepronomen Sie bezogen) yourself/ yourselves; ~ freuen/wundern/schämen/ täuschen be pleased/surprised/ashamed/ mistaken; ~ sorgen worry
(b) (reziprok) one another, each other

Sichel *die;* ~, ~n sickle

sicher ① *Adj.* **(a)** safe ⟨road, procedure, *etc.*⟩; secure ⟨job, investment, *etc.*⟩
(b) reliable ⟨evidence, source⟩; certain ⟨proof⟩; reliable, sure ⟨judgment, taste, *etc.*⟩
(c) (selbstbewusst) [self-]assured ⟨person, manner⟩
(d) (gewiss) certain; sure
② *adv.* **(a)** safely
(b) (zuverlässig) reliably; ~ [Auto] fahren be a safe driver
(c) (selbstbewusst) [self-]confidently
③ *Adv.* certainly

sicher|gehen *unr. itr. V.; mit sein* play safe

Sicherheit *die;* ~, ~en **(a)** safety; (der Öffentlichkeit) security; jmdn./etw. in ~ [vor etw. (*Dat.*)] bringen save *or* rescue sb./sth. [from sth.]
(b) (Gewissheit) certainty
(c) (Wirtsch.: Bürgschaft) security

sicherheits-, Sicherheits-:
~**abstand** *der* (Verkehrsw.) safe distance between vehicles; ~**gurt** *der* seat belt;
~**halber** *Adv.* to be on the safe side;
~**nadel** *die* safety pin; ~**schloss,**
*~**schloß** *das* safety lock

sicherlich *Adv.* certainly

sichern *tr. V.* **(a)** make ⟨door *etc.*⟩ secure; (garantieren) safeguard ⟨rights, peace⟩; (schützen) protect ⟨rights *etc.*⟩; sich (*Dat.*) etw. ~: secure sth.
(b) (DV) back up

sicher|stellen *tr. V.* **(a)** impound ⟨goods, vehicle⟩
(b) guarantee ⟨supply, freedom, *etc.*⟩

S

Sicher·stellung *die* (a) ▶ SICHERSTELLEN
A: impounding
(b) (Gewährleistung) guarantee

Sicherung *die;* ~, ~en (a) safeguarding;
(das Schützen) protection
(b) (Elektrot.) fuse
(c) (techn. Vorrichtung) safety catch

Sicherungs·kopie *die* (DV) back-up
[copy]

Sicht *die;* ~: view (**auf** + *Akk.*, **in** + *Akk.* of);
gute *od.* **klare/schlechte** ~: good/poor
visibility; **in** ~ **kommen** come into sight;
außer ~ **sein** be out of sight

sichtbar [1] *Adj.* visible; (fig.) apparent
⟨*reason*⟩
[2] *adv.* visibly

sichten *tr. V.* sight

sichtlich [1] *Adj.* obvious; evident
[2] *adv.* obviously; evidently; visibly
⟨*impressed*⟩

Sichtung *die;* ~, ~en sighting

Sicht-: ~**verhältnisse** *Pl.* visibility
sing.; ~**vermerk** *der* visa; ~**weite** *die*
visibility *no art.;* **außer/in** ~**weite sein** be out
of/in sight

sickern *itr. V.; mit sein* seep; (spärlich fließen)
trickle

sie [1] *Personalpron.; 3. Pers. Sg. Nom. Fem.*
she; (betont) her; (bei Dingen, Tieren) it; *s. auch*
IHR[1], IHRER A
[2] *Personalpron.; 3. Pers. Pl. Nom.* they;
(betont) them; *s. auch* IHNEN; IHRER B;
[3] *Akk. von* SIE 1: her; (bei Dingen, Tieren) it
[4] *Akk. von* SIE 2A: them

Sie *Personalpron.; 3. Pers. Pl. Nom. u. Akk;*
Anrede an eine od. mehrere Personen you; *s.*
auch IHNEN; IHRER

Sieb *das;* ~[e]s, ~e sieve; (für Tee) strainer

sieben[1] *tr. V.* (a) sieve ⟨*flour etc.*⟩; riddle
⟨*sand, gravel, etc.*⟩
(b) (auswählen) screen ⟨*candidates*⟩

sieben[2] *Kardinalz.* seven

Sieben *die;* ~, ~en seven

sieben-, Sieben-: ~**fach**
Vervielfältigungsz. sevenfold; ~**mal** *Adj.*
seven times; ~**sachen** *Pl.* (ugs.) **meine/**
deine *usw.* ~**sachen** my/your *etc.* belongings
or (coll.) bits and pieces

siebt... *Ordinalz.* seventh

siebtel *Bruchz.* seventh

Siebtel *das,* (schweiz. meist *der*); ~**s**, ~:
seventh

siebtens *Adv.* seventhly

sieb·zehn *Kardinalz.* seventeen

siebzig *Kardinalz.* seventy

siebzigst... *Ordinalz.* seventieth

siedeln *itr. V.* settle

sieden *unr. od. regelm. itr. V.* boil

Siede·punkt *der* (auch fig.) boiling point

Siedler *der;* ~**s**, ~: settler

Siedlung *die;* ~, ~en (a) (Wohngebiet)
[housing] estate
(b) (Niederlassung) settlement

Sieg *der;* ~[e]s, ~e victory, (bes. Sport) win
(**über** + *Akk.* over)

Siegel *das;* ~s, ~: seal; (von Behörden) stamp

siegen *itr. V.* win; **über jmdn.** ~: gain *or*
win a victory over sb.; (bes. Sport) win
against sb.; beat sb.

Sieger *der;* ~s, ~: winner; (Mannschaft)
winners *pl.;* (einer Schlacht) victor

Sieger·ehrung *die* presentation ceremony;
awards ceremony

Siegerin *die;* ~, ~nen winner

sieges·sicher *Adj., adv.* confident of
victory

sieg·gewohnt *Adj.* ⟨*army*⟩ accustomed to
victory; ⟨*team*⟩ used to winning

sieh, siehe *Imperativ Sg. v.* SEHEN

siehst *2. Pers. Sg. Präsens v.* SEHEN

sieht *3. Pers. Sg. Präsens v.* SEHEN

siezen *tr. V.* call ⟨*sb.*⟩ 'Sie' (*the polite form*
of address)

Signal *das;* ~s, ~e signal

signalisieren *tr. V.* indicate ⟨*danger,*
change, etc.⟩

Signatur *die;* ~, ~en (a) initials *pl.;* (Kürzel)
abbreviated signature; (des Künstlers)
autograph
(b) (Unterschrift) signature
(c) (in einer Bibliothek) shelf mark

signieren *tr. V.* sign; autograph ⟨*one's own*
work⟩

Silbe *die;* ~, ~n syllable

Silber *das;* ~s (a) silver
(b) (silbernes Gerät) silver[ware]

Silber·medaille *die* silver medal

silbern [1] *Adj.* silver; silvery ⟨*moonlight,*
shade, gleam, etc.⟩
[2] *adv.* ⟨*shine, shimmer, etc.*⟩ with a silvery
lustre

Silber·papier *das* silver paper

Silhouette /zi'lụɛtə/ *die;* ~, ~n silhouette

Silicium *das;* ~s silicon

Silikon *das;* ~s, ~e (Chemie) silicone

Silo *der od. das;* ~s, ~s silo

Silvester *der od. das;* ~s, ~: New Year's
Eve

Silvester·nacht *die* night of New Year's
Eve

Simbabwe *(das);* ~s Zimbabwe

Sim-Karte, SIM-Karte /'zɪm-/ *die* SIM
card

simpel [1] *Adj.* (a) simple ⟨*question, task*⟩
(b) (beschränkt) simple-minded ⟨*person*⟩;
simple ⟨*mind*⟩
[2] *adv.* (a) simply
(b) (beschränkt) in a simple-minded manner

Simpel *der;* ~s, ~ (bes. südd. ugs.)
simpleton; fool

Sims *der od. das;* ~es, ~e ledge; sill;
(Kamin~) mantelpiece

simsen /'zɪmzn̩/ *itr. V.* (ugs.) send a text message/text messages

Simulant *der;* ~en, ~en **Simulantin** *die;* ~, ~nen malingerer

Simulation *die;* ~, ~en simulation

simulieren [1] *tr. V.* feign, sham ⟨*illness, emotion, etc.*⟩; simulate ⟨*situation, condition*⟩ [2] *itr. V.* feign illness

simultan [1] *Adj.* simultaneous [2] *adv.* simultaneously

sind *1. u. 3. Pers. Pl. Präsens v.* SEIN[1]

Sinfonie *die;* ~, ~n symphony

Sinfonie·orchester *das* symphony orchestra

singen *unr. tr., itr. V.* sing

Single[1] /'zɪŋl̩/ *die;* ~, ~s (Schallplatte) single

Single[2] *der;* ~s, ~s single person; ~s single people *no art.*

Single[3] *das;* ~s, ~s (Badminton, Tennis) singles *sing. or pl.*

Singular *der;* ~s singular

Sing·vogel *der* songbird

sinken *unr. itr. V.; mit sein* (a) ⟨*ship, sun*⟩ sink, go down; ⟨*plane, balloon*⟩ descend, go down
(b) (niedersinken) fall
(c) (niedriger werden) ⟨*temperature, level*⟩ fall, drop
(d) (an Wert verlieren; nachlassen; abnehmen) fall, go down

Sinn *der;* ~[e]s, ~e (a) sense
(b) *Pl.* (geh.: Bewusstsein) senses; mind *sing.;* **nicht bei ~en sein** be out of one's senses
(c) (Gefühl, Verständnis) feeling
(d) (Bedeutung) meaning
(e) (Ziel u. Zweck) point

Sinn·bild *das* symbol

Sinnes-: ~**organ** *das* sense organ; sensory organ; ~**täuschung** *die* trick of the senses

sinn·gemäß [1] *Adj.* eine ~e Übersetzung a translation which conveys the general sense [2] *adv.* etw. ~ übersetzen/wiedergeben translate the general sense of sth./give the gist of sth.

sinnlich *Adj.* sensory ⟨*impression, perception, stimulus*⟩; sensual ⟨*love, mouth*⟩; sensuous ⟨*pleasure, passion*⟩

Sinnlichkeit *die;* ~: sensuality

sinn·los [1] *Adj.* (a) senseless
(b) (zwecklos) pointless [2] *adv.* (a) senselessly
(b) (zwecklos) pointlessly

Sinnlosigkeit *die;* ~ (a) senselessness
(b) (Zwecklosigkeit) pointlessness

sinn·voll [1] *Adj.* (a) (vernünftig) sensible
(b) (einen Sinn ergebend) meaningful [2] *adv.* (a) (vernünftig) sensibly
(b) (einen Sinn ergebend) meaningfully

Sint·flut *die* Flood; Deluge

sintflut·artig [1] *Adj.* torrential [2] *adv.* in torrents

Sinto *der;* ~, **Sinti** Sinte

Sippe *die;* ~, ~n (a) (Völkerk.) sib
(b) (ugs.: Verwandtschaft) clan

Sippschaft *die;* ~, ~en (ugs.) ▸ SIPPE B

Sirene *die;* ~, ~n siren

Sirup *der;* ~s, ~e syrup

Sitte *die;* ~, ~n (a) (Brauch) custom; tradition
(b) (moralische Norm) common decency
(c) *Pl.* (Benehmen) manners

sitten·widrig *Adj.* (a) (Rechtsw.) illegal ⟨*methods, advertising, etc.*⟩
(b) (unmoralisch) immoral ⟨*behaviour*⟩

sittlich [1] *Adj.* moral [2] *adv.* morally

Sittlichkeit *die;* ~: morality

Sittlichkeits-: ~**verbrechen** *das* sexual crime; ~**verbrecher** *der,* ~**verbrecherin** *die* sex offender

Situation *die;* ~, ~en situation

situiert *Adj.* gut/schlechter (usw.) ~ well off/worse off *etc.*

Sitz *der;* ~es, ~e (a) seat
(b) (Verwaltungssitz) headquarters *sing. or pl.;*
(c) (von Kleidungsstücken) fit

Sitz·bank *die; Pl.* Sitzbänke bench

sitzen *unr. itr. V.; südd., österr., schweiz. mit sein* (a) sit
(b) (sein) be
(c) ([gut] passen) fit
(d) ~ **bleiben** (nicht versetzt werden) stay down [a year]; (unverheiratet bleiben) be left on the shelf; **auf etw.** (*Dat.*) ~ **bleiben** (für etw. keinen Käufer finden) be left *or* (coll.) stuck with sth.; **jmdn.** ~ **lassen** (ugs.) (nicht heiraten) jilt sb.; (im Stich lassen) leave sb. in the lurch; **etw. nicht auf sich** (*Dat.*) ~**lassen** not take sth.

sitzen-: *~|**bleiben** ▸ SITZEN D; *~|**lassen** ▸ SITZEN D

Sitz·platz *der* seat

Sitzplatz·stadion *das* all-seater stadium

Sitzung *die;* ~, ~en meeting; (eines Parlaments) sitting; session

Sitzungs·saal *der* conference hall

Skala *die;* ~, Skalen scale

Skalp *der;* ~s, ~e scalp

Skalpell *das;* ~s, ~e scalpel

skalpieren *tr. V.* scalp

Skandal *der;* ~s, ~e scandal

skandalös *Adj.* scandalous

Skandinavien (*das*)*;* ~s Scandinavia

Skandinavier *der;* ~s, ~: Scandinavian

skandinavisch *Adj.* Scandinavian

Skat *der;* ~[e]s, ~e *od.* ~s skat

Skateboard /'skeɪtbɔːd/ *das;* ~s, ~s skateboard

Skateboarder /'skeɪtbɔːdɐ/ *der;* ~s, ~, **Skateboarderin** *die;* ~, ~nen skateboarder

Skelett *das;* ~[e]s, ~e skeleton

Skepsis *die;* ~: scepticism

S

skeptisch ① *Adj.* sceptical
② *adv.* sceptically

Ski /ʃiː/ *der;* ~s, ~er *od.* ~: ski; ~ **laufen** *od.* **fahren** ski

Ski-: ~**läufer** *der,* ~**läuferin** *die* skier; ~**lehrer** *der,* ~**lehrerin** *die* ski instructor; ~**lift** *der* ski lift; ~**springen** *das;* ~~s ski jumping *no art.*

Skinhead /'skɪnhɛd/ *der;* ~s, ~s skinhead

Skizze *die;* ~, ~n sketch

Skizzen·block *der* sketch pad

skizzieren *tr. V.* sketch

Sklave *der;* ~n, ~n slave

Sklaven·händler *der,* **Sklaven·händlerin** *die* slave trader

Sklaverei *die;* ~: slavery *no art.*

Sklavin *die;* ~, ~nen slave

sklavisch ① *Adj.* slavish
② *adv.* slavishly

Skonto *der od. das;* ~s, ~s (Kaufmannsspr.) [cash] discount

Skorbut *der;* ~[e]s scurvy *no art.*

Skorpion *der;* ~s, ~e scorpion; (Astrol.) Scorpio

Skrupel *der;* ~s, ~: scruple

skrupel·los ① *Adj.* unscrupulous
② *adv.* unscrupulously

Skrupellosigkeit *die;* ~: unscrupulousness

Skulptur *die;* ~, ~en sculpture

skurril ① *Adj.* absurd; droll ⟨*person*⟩
② *adv.* absurdly

Skurrilität *die;* ~, ~en absurdity

Slalom *der;* ~s, ~s slalom

Slawe *der;* ~n, ~n, **Slawin** *die;* ~, ~nen Slav

slawisch *Adj.* Slav[ic]; Slavonic

Slip *der;* ~s, ~s briefs *pl.*

Slogan /'sloːgn̩/ *der;* ~s, ~s slogan

Slowake *der;* ~n, ~n Slovak

Slowakei *die;* ~: Slovakia *no art.*

Slowakin *die;* ~, ~nen Slovak

Slowene *der;* ~n, ~n Slovene; Slovenian

Slowenien /sloˈveːni̯ən/ (*das*); ~s Slovenia

Slowenin *die;* ~, ~nen Slovene; Slovenian

Slum /slam/ *der;* ~s, ~s slum

Smaragd *der;* ~[e]s, ~e emerald

Smog *der;* ~[s], ~s smog

Smoking *der;* ~s, ~s dinner jacket *or* (Amer.) tuxedo and dark trousers

Snowboard /'snoʊbɔːd/ *das;* ~s, ~s snowboard

Snowboarder /'snoʊbɔːdɐ/ *der;* ~s, ~, **Snowboarderin** *die;* ~, ~nen snowboarder

so ① *Adv.* **(a)** (auf diese Weise; in, von dieser Art) like this/that; this/that way; **weiter so!** carry on in the same way!; **so gennant** so-called
(b) (dermaßen, überaus) so

(c) (genauso) as; **so wenig/viel wie** *od.* **als** as little/much as; **halb/doppelt so viel** half/twice as much; **so weit wie möglich** as far as possible; **so weit** (im großen Ganzen) by and large; (bis jetzt) up to now; **so weit sein** (ugs.) be ready; **so gut ich konnte** as best I could
(d) (ugs.: solch) such; **so ein Idiot!** what an idiot!; **so einer/eine/eins** one like that
(e) *betont* (eine Zäsur ausdrückend) right; OK (coll.)
(f) (ugs.: schätzungsweise) about
② *Partikel* **(a)** just; **ach, das hab' ich nur so gesagt** oh, I didn't mean anything by that
(b) (in Aufforderungssätzen verstärkend) **so komm doch** come on now

s. o. *Abk.* = **siehe oben**

So. *Abk.* = **Sonntag** Sun.

Soap /soʊp/ *die;* ~, ~s soap [opera]

sobald *Konj.* as soon as

Socke *die;* ~, ~n sock

Sockel *der;* ~s, ~ **(a)** (einer Säule, Statue) plinth
(b) (unterer Teil eines Hauses, Schrankes) base

so·dass, *sodaß *Konj.* **(a)** (damit) so that
(b) (und deshalb) and so

Soda·wasser *das* soda; soda water

Sod·brennen *das;* ~s heartburn

so·eben *Adv.* just

Sofa *das;* ~s, ~s sofa; settee

so·fern *Konj.* provided [that]

soff *1. u. 3. Pers. Sg. Prät. v.* SAUFEN

so·fort *Adv.* immediately; at once

sofortig *Adj.* (unmittelbar) immediate

Sofort·maßnahme *die* immediate measure

Software /'sɔftvɛːɐ̯/ *die;* ~, ~s (DV) software

sog *1. u. 3. Pers. Sg. Prät. v.* SAUGEN

Sog *der;* ~[e]s, ~e suction; (bei Schiffen) wake; (bei Fahr-, Flugzeugen) slipstream; (von Wasser, auch fig.) current

so·gar *Adv.* even

*so·genannt ▶ so 1A

so·gleich *Adv.* immediately; at once

Sohle *die;* ~, ~n **(a)** (Schuh~) sole; (Einlege~) insole
(b) (Fuß~) sole [of the foot]

Sohn *der;* ~es, Söhne son

Soja-: ~**bohne** *die* soy[a] bean; ~**soße** *die* soy[a] sauce

so·lang[e] *Konj.* so or as long as

solar *Adj.* solar

Solar·energie *die* (Physik.) solar energy

Solarium *das;* ~s, Solarien solarium

Solar-: ~**kraftwerk** *das:*
▶ SONNENKRAFTWERK; ~**technik** *die* (Energietechnik) solar technology *no art.*; ~**zelle** *die* (Physik, Elektrot.) solar cell

solch *Demonstrativpron.* **(a)** *attr.* such; **das macht** ~**en Spaß!** it's so much fun!
(b) *allein stehend* ~**e wie die** people like that

*alte Schreibung - vgl. Hinweis auf S. xiv

Sold *der;* ~[e]s, ~e [military] pay

Soldat *der;* ~en, ~en soldier

Soldaten·friedhof *der* military *or* war cemetery

Soldatin *die;* ~, ~nen [female *or* woman] soldier

soldatisch ⓵ *Adj.* military ⟨discipline, expression, etc.⟩; soldierly ⟨figure, virtue⟩
⓶ *adv.* in a military manner

Söldner *der;* ~s, ~, **Söldnerin** *die;* ~, ~nen mercenary

solidarisch ⓵ *Adj.* ~es Verhalten zeigen show one's solidarity
⓶ *adv.* ~ handeln/sich ~ verhalten act in/ show solidarity

solidarisieren *refl. V.* show [one's] solidarity

Solidarität *die;* ~: solidarity

solide ⓵ *Adj.* (a) solid; sturdy ⟨shoes, material⟩; [good-]quality ⟨goods⟩
(b) (gut fundiert) sound ⟨work, education, knowledge⟩; solid ⟨firm⟩
(c) (anständig) respectable ⟨person, life, profession⟩
⓶ *adv.* (a) solidly ⟨built⟩; sturdily ⟨made⟩
(b) (gut fundiert) soundly ⟨educated, constructed⟩
(c) (anständig) ⟨live⟩ respectably, steadily

Solidität *die;* ~: ▶ SOLIDE 1 A-C: solidness; sturdiness; soundness; respectability

Solist *der;* ~en, ~en, **Solistin** *die;* ~, ~nen soloist

Soll *das;* ~[s], ~[s] (a) (Bankw.) debit
(b) (Arbeits~) quota; sein ~ erfüllen *od.* erreichen achieve one's target

sollen ⓵ *unr. Modalverb; 2. Part.* sollen:
(a) (bei Aufforderung, Anweisung, Auftrag) was soll ich als Nächstes tun? what should I do next?; [sagen Sie ihm,] er soll hereinkommen tell him to come in
(b) (bei Wunsch, Absicht, Vorhaben) das sollte ein Witz sein that was meant to be a joke; was soll denn das heißen? what is that supposed to mean?
(c) (bei Ratlosigkeit) was soll ich nur machen? what am I to do?
(d) (Notwendigkeit ausdrückend) man soll so etwas nicht unterschätzen it shouldn't be taken so lightly
(e) *häufig im Konjunktiv II* (Erwartung, Wünschenswertes ausdrückend) du solltest dich schämen you ought to be ashamed of yourself; das hättest du besser nicht tun ~: it would have been better if you hadn't done that
(f) (jmdm. beschieden sein) er sollte seine Heimat nicht wieder sehen he was never to see his homeland again
(g) *im Konjunktiv II* (eine Möglichkeit ausdrückend) wenn du ihn sehen solltest, sage ihm bitte …: if you should see him, please tell him …
(h) *im Präsens* (sich für die Wahrheit nicht verbürgend) das Restaurant soll sehr teuer sein the restaurant is supposed *or* said to be very expensive
(i) *im Konjunktiv II* (Zweifel ausdrückend) sollte das sein Ernst sein? is he really being serious?
(j) (können) mir soll es gleich sein it's all the same to me
⓶ *tr., itr. V.* was soll das? what's the idea?; was soll ich dort? what would I do there?

Solo *das;* ~s, ~s *od.* Soli solo

so·mit /*auch:* '--/ *Adv.* consequently; therefore

Sommer *der;* ~s, ~: summer

Sommer·ferien *Pl.* summer holidays

sommerlich ⓵ *Adj.* summer; summery ⟨warmth, weather⟩; summer's *attrib.* ⟨day, evening⟩
⓶ *adv.* es war ~ warm it was as warm as summer

sommer-, Sommer-: ~reifen *der* standard tyre; ~schluss·verkauf, *~schluß·verkauf *der* summer sale/ sales; ~sprosse *die* freckle; ~sprossig *Adj.* freckled; ~zeit *die* (Uhrzeit) summer time

Sonate *die;* ~, ~n (Musik) sonata

Sonde *die;* ~, ~n probe; (zur Ernährung) tube

Sonder-: ~angebot *das* special offer; ~ausgabe *die* (a) special edition; (b) (Steuerw.: private Aufwendung) tax-deductible expenditure; (c) (Extraausgabe) extra expense

sonderbar ⓵ *Adj.* strange; odd
⓶ *adv.* strangely; oddly

sonderbarer·weise *Adv.* strangely *or* oddly enough

Sonder-: ~fall *der* special case; ~genehmigung *die* special permit

sonder·gleichen *Adv., nachgestellt* eine Frechheit/Unverschämtheit ~: the height of cheek/impudence

sonderlich *Adv.* particularly

Sonderling *der;* ~s, ~e strange *or* odd person

Sonder-: ~marke *die* special issue [stamp]; ~müll *der* hazardous waste

sondern[1] *tr. V.* (geh.) separate (von from)

sondern[2] *Konj.* but; nicht nur …, ~ [auch] …: not only … but also …

Sonder-: ~nummer *die* special edition *or* issue; ~preis *der* special *or* reduced price; ~schule *die* special school; ~schul·lehrer *der*, ~schul·lehrerin *die* teacher at a special school; ~wunsch *der* special request *or* wish; ~zug *der* special train

sondieren *tr. V.* sound out

Sonett *das;* ~[e]s, ~e sonnet

Sonn·abend *der* (bes. nordd.) Saturday; s. *auch* DIENSTAG

sonn·abends *Adv.* on Saturday[s]

Sonne *die;* ~, ~n sun; (Licht der ~) sun[light]

sonnen *refl. V.* sun oneself

sonnen-, Sonnen-: ∼**aufgang** *der* sunrise; ∼**baden** *itr. V.* sunbathe; ∼**blume** *die* sunflower; ∼**brand** *der* sunburn *no indef. art.;* ∼**brille** *die* sunglasses *pl.;* ∼**energie** *die* solar energy; ∼**finsternis** *die* solar eclipse; ∼**hut** *der* sun hat; ∼**kollektor** *der* (Energietechnik) solar collector; ∼**kraftwerk** *das* solar power station; ∼**licht** *das* sunlight; ∼**milch** *die* suntan lotion; ∼**öl** *das* sun oil; ∼**schein** *der* sunshine; ∼**schirm** *der* sunshade; ∼**schutz-creme** *die* suntan lotion; ∼**stich** *der* sunstroke *no indef. art.;* ∼**strahl** *der* ray of sun[shine]; ∼**uhr** *die* sundial; ∼**untergang** *der* sunset

sonnig *Adj.* sunny

Sonn·tag *der* Sunday; *s. auch* DIENSTAG

sonn·täglich ① *Adj.* Sunday *attrib.;* ② *adv.* ∼ **gekleidet** dressed in one's Sunday best

sonntags *Adv.* on Sunday[s]

sonst *Adv.* (a) der ∼ so freundliche Mann …: the man, who is/was usually so friendly, …; alles war wie ∼: everything was [the same] as usual; ∼ **was** (ugs.) something else; (fragend, verneint) anything else; ∼ **wer** (ugs.) somebody else; (fragend, verneint) anybody else; ∼ **wo** (ugs.) somewhere else; (fragend, verneint) anywhere else; ∼ **noch was?** (ugs., auch iron.) anything else?; **wer/was/wie/wo [denn]** ∼? who/what/how/where else? (b) (andernfalls) otherwise; or

sonstig… *Adj.* other; further

***sonst·was** *usw.* ▶ SONST A

so·oft *Konj.* whenever

sophistisch ① *Adj.* sophistic[al] ② *adv.* sophistically

Sopran *der;* ∼**s,** ∼**e** (Musik) soprano; (im Chor) sopranos *pl.*

Sopranistin *die;* ∼, ∼**nen** soprano

Sorge *die;* ∼, ∼**n** worry; keine ∼! don't [you] worry!

sorgen ① *refl. V.* worry (um about) ② *itr. V.* für jmdn./etw. ∼: take care of sb./ sth.

sorgen-, Sorgen-: ∼**frei** ① *Adj.* carefree; ② *adv.* ∼**frei leben** live in a carefree manner; ∼**kind** *das* (auch fig.) problem child; ∼**voll** ① *Adj.* worried; ② *adv.* worriedly

Sorg·falt *die;* ∼: care

sorg·fältig ① *Adj.* careful ② *adv.* carefully

sorg·los ① *Adj.* (a) (ohne Sorgfalt) careless (b) (unbekümmert) carefree ② *adv.* ∼ **mit etw. umgehen** treat sth. carelessly

Sorglosigkeit *die;* ∼ (a) (Mangel an Sorgfalt) carelessness (b) (Unbekümmertheit) carefreeness

---

*old spelling - see note on page xiv

sorgsam ① *Adj.* careful ② *adv.* carefully

Sorte *die;* ∼, ∼**n** (a) sort; type; kind (b) *Pl.* (Devisen) foreign currency *sing.*

Sorten·kurs *der* (Bankw.) exchange rate

sortieren *tr. V.* sort [out] ⟨pictures, letters, washing, etc.⟩; grade ⟨goods etc.⟩

Sortiment *das;* ∼[e]s, ∼e range (an + *Dat.* of)

so·sehr *Konj.* however much

Soße *die;* ∼, ∼**n** sauce; (Bratensoße) gravy; sauce; (Salatsoße) dressing

sott *1. u. 3. Pers. Sg. Prät. v.* SIEDEN

Souffleur /zuˈfløːɐ̯/ *der;* ∼**s,** ∼**e,** **Souffleuse** /zuˈfløːzə/ *die;* ∼, ∼**n** prompter

soufflieren /zuˈfliːrən/ *tr. V.* prompt

Sound-: ∼**check** /ˈsaʊndʃɛk/ *der;* ∼**s,** ∼∼**s** sound check; ∼**karte** *die* (DV) sound card

Souvenir /suvəˈniːɐ̯/ *das;* ∼**s,** ∼**s** souvenir

souverän /zuvəˈrɛːn/ *Adj.* sovereign

Souveränität *die;* ∼: sovereignty

so·viel *Konj.* as *or* so far as; *s. auch* SO 1B

so·weit *Konj.* (a) as *or* so far as; *s. auch* SO 1B; (b) (in dem Maße, wie) [in] so far as; *s. auch* SO 1B

***so·wenig** ▶ SO 1B

so·wie *Konj.* (a) (und) as well as (b) (sobald) as soon as

so·wie·so *Adv.* anyway

sowjetisch *Adj.* Soviet

Sowjet·union *die* (1922–1991) Soviet Union

so·wohl *Konj.* ∼ … als *od.* wie [auch] …: both … and …; … as well as …

sozial ① *Adj.* social ② *adv.* socially

sozial-, Sozial-: ∼**abgaben** *Pl.* social welfare contributions; ∼**arbeiter** *der,* ∼**arbeiterin** *die* social worker; ∼**demokrat** *der,* ∼**demokratin** *die* Social Democrat; ∼**demokratisch** *Adj.* social democratic; ∼**dienst** *der* community services department; ∼**hilfe** *die* social welfare; ∼**hilfe·empfänger** *der,* ∼**hilfe·empfängerin** *die* welfare recipient

Sozialismus *der;* ∼: socialism *no art.;*

Sozialist *der;* ∼**en,** ∼**en, Sozialistin** *die;* ∼, ∼**nen** socialist

sozialistisch ① *Adj.* socialist ② ∼ **regierte Länder** countries with socialist governments

Sozial-: ∼**kunde** *die* social studies *sing., no art.;* ∼**politik** *die* social policy; ∼**produkt** *das* (Wirtsch.) national product; ∼**staat** *der* welfare state

Soziologe *der;* ∼**n,** ∼**n** sociologist

Soziologie *die;* ∼: sociology

Soziologin *die;* ∼, ∼**nen** sociologist

soziologisch ① *Adj.* sociological

2 *adv.* sociologically

Sozius *der;* ~s, ~se (a) *Pl. auch:* **So**zii
(Wirtsch.: Teilhaber) partner
(b) (beim Motorrad) pillion

so·zu·sagen *Adv.* as it were

Spachtel *der;* ~s, ~ *od. die;* ~, ~n putty
knife; (zum Malen) palette knife

Spachtel·masse *die* filler

spachteln *tr. V.* (a) stop, fill ⟨*hole, crack,
etc.*⟩; smooth over ⟨*wall, panel, surface, etc.*⟩
(b) (ugs.: essen) put away (coll.) ⟨*food, meal*⟩

Spagat *der od. das;* ~[e]s, ~e splits *pl.;*
[einen] ~ **machen** do the splits

Spaghetti *Pl.* spaghetti *sing.*

spähen *itr. V.* peer; (durch ein Loch, eine Ritze
usw.) peep

Späher *der;* ~s, ~, **Späherin** *die;* ~,
~nen (Milit.) scout; (Posten) lookout; (Spitzel)
informer

Spalier *das;* ~s, ~e (a) trellis
(b) (Ehren~) guard of honour; ~ **stehen** line
the route; ⟨*soldiers*⟩ form a guard of honour

Spalt *der;* ~[e]s, ~e opening; (im Fels)
fissure; crevice; (zwischen Vorhängen) chink;
gap; (langer Riss) crack

Spalte *die;* ~, ~n (a) crack; (Felsspalte)
crevice
(b) (Druckw.) column

spalten *unr.* (*auch regelm.*) *tr., refl. V.* split

Spaltung *die;* ~, ~en (auch fig.) splitting;
(fig.: das Gespaltensein) split

Span *der;* ~[e]s, Späne (Hobelspan) shaving

Span·ferkel *das* suckling pig

Spange *die;* ~, ~n clasp; (Haarspange)
hairslide (Brit.); barrette (Amer.); (Armspange)
bracelet; bangle

Spaniel /ˈʃpaːni̯əl/ *der;* ~s, ~s spaniel

Spanien /ˈʃpaːni̯ən/ (*das*) ~s Spain

Spanier /ˈʃpaːni̯ɐ/ *der;* ~s, ~, **Spanierin**
die; ~, ~nen Spaniard

spanisch *Adj.* Spanish

Span·korb *der* chip basket; chip

spann *1. u. 3. P. Sing. Prät. v.* SPINNEN

spannen 1 *tr. V.* (a) tighten ⟨*violin string,
violin bow, etc.*⟩; draw ⟨*bow*⟩; tension
⟨*spring, tennis net, drumhead, saw blade*⟩;
stretch ⟨*fabric, shoe, etc.*⟩; draw *or* pull ⟨*line*⟩
tight *or* taut; flex ⟨*muscle*⟩; cock ⟨*gun,
camera shutter*⟩
(b) (befestigen) put up ⟨*washing line*⟩; stretch
⟨*net, wire, tarpaulin, etc.*⟩ (über + *Akk.* over)
(c) (schirren) harness (vor, an + *Akk.* to)
2 *refl. V.* (a) become *or* go taut; ⟨*muscles*⟩
tense
(b) (geh.: sich wölben) sich über etw. (*Akk.*) ~:
span sth.
3 *itr. V.* ⟨*clothing*⟩ be [too] tight; ⟨*skin*⟩ be
taut

spannend 1 *Adj.* exciting; (stärker)
thrilling
2 *adv.* excitingly; (stärker) thrillingly

Spannung *die;* ~, ~en (a) excitement;
(Neugier) suspense
(b) (eines Romans, Films usw.) suspense
(c) (Zwistigkeit, Nervosität) tension
(d) (Elektrot.) voltage

Spannungs·gebiet *das* (Politik.) area of
tension

Spann·weite *die* [wing]span

Span·platte *die* chipboard

Spar-: ~**buch** *das* savings book;
~**büchse** *die* money box

sparen 1 *tr. V.* save
2 *itr. V.* (a) save; **für** *od.* **auf etw.** (*Akk.*) ~:
save up for sth.
(b) (sparsam wirtschaften) economize (mit on);
an etw. (*Dat.*) ~: be sparing with sth.; (beim
Einkauf) economize on sth.

Sparer *der;* ~s, ~, **Sparerin** *die;* ~,
~nen saver

Spargel *der;* ~s, ~, (schweiz. auch) *die;* ~,
~n asparagus *no pl., no indef. art.*

Spar-: ~**groschen** *der* (ugs.) nest egg;
savings *pl.;* ~**kasse** *die* savings bank;
~**konto** *das* savings *or* deposit account

spärlich 1 *Adj.* sparse ⟨*vegetation, beard,
growth*⟩; thin ⟨*hair, applause*⟩; scanty
⟨*leftovers, knowledge, news, evidence,
clothing*⟩; poor ⟨*lighting*⟩
2 *adv.* sparsely, thinly ⟨*populated, covered*⟩;
poorly ⟨*lit, attended*⟩; scantily ⟨*dressed*⟩

sparsam 1 *Adj.* thrifty ⟨*person*⟩;
(wirtschaftlich) economical; **mit etw.** ~ **sein** be
economical with sth.
2 *adv.* ~ **mit der Butter/dem Papier
umgehen** use butter/paper sparingly;
economize on butter/paper

Sparsamkeit *die;* ~: thrift[iness];
(Wirtschaftlichkeit) economicalness

Sparte *die;* ~, ~n (a) (Teilbereich) area; (eines
Geschäfts) line [of business]
(b) (Rubrik) section

Sparten·kanal *der* special-interest
channel

Spar-: ~**vertrag** *der* savings agreement;
~**zins** *der; Pl.* ~~en interest *no pl.* on a
savings account

Spaß *der;* ~es, Späße (a) (Vergnügen) fun; ~
an etw. (*Dat.*) **haben** enjoy sth.; [jmdm.] ~
machen be fun [for sb.]; **viel** ~! have a good
time!
(b) (Scherz) joke; (Streich) prank; **er macht nur**
~: he's only joking; ~ **beiseite!** joking
aside; ~ **muss sein!** there's no harm in a
joke; ~ **verstehen** be able to take a joke; **im**
od. **zum** *od.* **aus** ~: as a joke; for fun

spaßen *itr. V.* (a) (Spaß machen) joke
(b) **er lässt nicht mit sich** ~: he won't stand
for any nonsense; **mit ihm/damit ist nicht zu**
~: he/it is not to be trifled with

spaßes·halber *Adv.* for the fun of it; for
fun

spaßig *Adj.* funny; comical; amusing

Spaß·macher *der,* **Spaß·macherin**
die joker

S

spät ⓵ *Adj.* late; **wie** ~ **ist es?** what time is it?

⓶ *adv.* late; ~ **am Abend** late in the evening

Spaten *der;* ~s, ~: spade

später ⓵ *Adj.* (a) later ⟨*years, generations, etc.*⟩

(b) (zukünftig) future ⟨*owner, wife, etc.*⟩

⓶ *Adv.* later; **bis** ~! see you later!

spätestens *Adv.* at the latest

Spatz *der;* ~en, ~en (a) sparrow

(b) (fam.: Liebling) pet

Spätzle *Pl.* spaetzle; *kind of noodles*

spazieren *itr. V.; mit sein* stroll; ~ **gehen** go for a walk; ~ **fahren** go for a ride; **ein Kind [im Kinderwagen]** ~ **fahren** take a baby for a walk [in a pram]

*spazieren|fahren *usw.* ▶ SPAZIEREN

Spazier-: ~**gang** *der* walk; ~**gänger** *der;* ~s, ~~, ~**gängerin** *die;* ~~, ~~nen person out for a walk

SPD ~ *Abk.* = **Sozialdemokratische Partei Deutschlands** SPD

Specht *der;* ~[e]s, ~e woodpecker

Speck *der;* ~[e]s, ~e (a) bacon fat; (Schinkenspeck) bacon

(b) (ugs. scherzh.: Fettpolster) fat; flab (coll.)

speckig *Adj.* greasy

Spediteur /ʃpedi'tøːɐ̯/ *der;* ~s, ~e, **Spediteurin** *die;* ~, ~nen carrier; haulage contractor; (Möbelspediteur) furniture remover

Spedition *die;* ~, ~en ▶ SPEDITIONSFIRMA

Speditions·firma *die* forwarding agency; (per Schiff) shipping agency; (Transportunternehmen) haulage firm; firm of hauliers; (per Schiff) firm of carriers; (Möbelspedition) removal firm

Speer *der;* ~[e]s, ~e (a) spear

(b) (Sportgerät) javelin

Speichel *der;* ~s saliva

Speicher *der;* ~s, ~ (a) storehouse; (Lagerhaus) warehouse

(b) (südd.: Dachboden) loft

(c) (Elektronik) memory

Speicher·kapazität *die* storage capacity; (DV) memory *or* storage capacity

speichern *tr. V.* store

speien (geh.) *unr. tr., itr. V.* spit

Speise *die;* ~, ~n (a) (Gericht) dish

(b) (geh.: Nahrung) food

Speise-: ~**eis** *das* ice cream; ~**fisch** *der* food fish; ~**gaststätte** *die* restaurant; ~**kammer** *die* larder; ~**karte** *die* menu; ~**lokal** *das* restaurant

speisen (geh.) ⓵ *itr. V.* eat; (dinieren) dine

⓶ *tr. V.* eat; (dinieren) dine on

Speise-: ~**saal** *der* dining hall; (im Hotel, in einer Villa usw.) dining room; ~**wagen** *der* restaurant car (Brit.); ~**zettel** *der* menu

---

*alte Schreibung - vgl. Hinweis auf S. xiv

Spektakel *der;* ~s, ~ (ugs.) (Lärm) row (coll.); rumpus (coll.)

spektakulär ⓵ *Adj.* spectacular

⓶ *adv.* spectacularly

Spekulation *die;* ~, ~en speculation

spekulieren *itr. V.* (a) (ugs.) **darauf** ~, **etw. tun zu können** count on being able to do sth.

(b) (Wirtsch.) speculate (**mit** in)

Spelunke *die;* ~, ~n (ugs. abwertend) dive (coll.)

Spelze *die;* ~, ~n husk

Spende *die;* ~, ~n donation; contribution

spenden *tr., itr. V.* (a) donate; give

(b) (fig. geh.) give ⟨*light*⟩; afford, give ⟨*shade*⟩; give off ⟨*heat*⟩

Spenden·aktion *die* campaign for donations

Spender *der;* ~s, ~, **Spenderin** *die;* ~, ~nen donor; donator; (Organspender, Blutspender) donor

Spender·organ *das* donar organ

spendieren *tr. V.* (ugs.) get, buy ⟨*drink, meal, etc.*⟩; stand ⟨*round*⟩

Spengler *der;* ~s, ~, **Spenglerin** *die;* ~, ~nen (südd., österr., schweiz.) ▶ KLEMPNER

Sperling *der;* ~s, ~e sparrow

Sperma *das;* ~s, Spermen sperm; semen

Sperma·bank *die; Pl.* ~en sperm bank

sperr-, Sperr-: ~**angel·weit** *Adv.* (ugs.) ~**angel-weit offen** *od.* **geöffnet** wide open; ~**bezirk** *der* (a) restricted *or* prohibited area; (b) (für Prostituierte) *area in which prostitution is prohibited;* (c) (Gesundheitswesen) infected area

Sperre *die;* ~, ~n (a) barrier; (Straßensperre) roadblock; (Milit.) obstacle

(b) (fig.) ban; (Handelssperre) embargo; (Import-, Exportsperre) blockade; (Nachrichten~) [news] blackout

sperren ⓵ *tr. V.* (a) close; close off ⟨*area*⟩; block ⟨*entrance, access, etc.*⟩; lock ⟨*mechanism etc.*⟩

(b) cut off ⟨*water, gas, electricity, etc.*⟩

(c) (Bankw.) stop ⟨*cheque, overdraft facility*⟩; freeze ⟨*bank account*⟩

(d) (einsperren) **ein Tier/jmdn. in etw.** (*Akk.*) ~: shut an animal/sb. in sth.

(e) (Sport: von der Teilnahme ausschließen) ban

(f) (Druckw.: spationieren) print ⟨*word, text*⟩ with the letters spaced

⓶ *refl. V.* **sich [gegen etw.]** ~: balk [at sth.]

Sperr·holz *das* plywood

sperrig *Adj.* unwieldy

Sperr-: ~**müll** *der* bulky refuse (*for which there is a separate collection service*); ~**sitz** *der* (im Kino) seat in the back stalls; (im Zirkus) front seat; (im Theater) seat in the front stalls; ~**stunde** *die* closing time

Sperrung *die;* ~, ~en ▶ SPERREN A-C, E: closing; closing off; cutting off; stopping; freezing; banning

Spesen *Pl.* expenses; **auf** ~: on expenses

Spezi *der;* ~s, ~[s] (südd., österr., schweiz. ugs.) [bosom] pal (coll.); chum (coll.)

spezialisieren *refl. V.* specialize (auf + Akk. in)

Spezialist *der;* ~en, ~en, **Spezialistin** *die;* ~, ~nen specialist

Spezialität *die;* ~, ~en speciality

speziell [1] *Adj.* special; specific ⟨question, problem, etc.⟩
[2] *Adv.* especially; (eigens) specially

spezifisch [1] *Adj.* specific; characteristic ⟨smell, style⟩
[2] *adv.* specifically

Sphäre *die;* ~, ~n (auch fig.) sphere

spicken *tr. V.* lard

spie *1. u. 3. Pers. Sg. Prät. v.* SPEIEN

Spiegel *der;* ~s, ~ (a) mirror
(b) (Wasserspiegel, fig.: Konzentration) level

spiegel-, Spiegel-: ~**bild** *das* reflection; ~**blank** *Adj.* shining; ~**ei** *das* fried egg; ~**glatt** *Adj.* like glass *postpos.;* as smooth as glass *postpos.*

spiegeln [1] *itr. V.* (a) (glänzen) shine; gleam
(b) (als Spiegel wirken) reflect the light
[2] *tr. V.* reflect; mirror
[3] *refl. V.* be mirrored *or* reflected

Spiegel·reflex·kamera *die* reflex camera

Spiegelung *die;* ~, ~en (a) (auch fig., Math.) reflection
(b) (Med.) speculum examination

spiegel·verkehrt [1] *Adj.* back-to-front ⟨lettering⟩; eine ~e Abbildung a mirror image
[2] *adv.* etw. ~ abbilden reproduce sth. as a *or* in mirror image

Spiel *das;* ~[e]s, ~e (a) play
(b) (Glücks, Gesellschaftsspiel) game; (Wettspiel) game; match; auf dem ~ stehen be at stake; etw. aufs ~ setzen put sth. at stake; risk sth.

Spiel·bank *die; Pl.* ~en casino

spielen [1] *itr. V.* (a) play; auf der Gitarre ~: play the guitar; um Geld ~: play for money
(b) (als Schauspieler) act; perform
(c) der Roman/Film spielt im 17. Jahrhundert/in Berlin the novel/film is set in the 17th century/in Berlin
(d) (fig.) das Blau spielt ins Violette the blue is tinged with purple
[2] *tr. V.* (a) play; Cowboy ~: play at being a cowboy; Geige usw. ~: play the violin *etc.;*
(b) (aufführen, vorführen) put on ⟨play⟩; show ⟨film⟩; perform ⟨piece of music⟩; play ⟨record⟩; den Beleidigten/Unschuldigen ~ (fig.) act offended/play the innocent

spielend *Adv.* easily

Spieler *der;* ~s, ~: player; (Glücksspieler) gambler

Spielerei *die;* ~, ~en (a) playing *no art.;* (im Glücksspiel) gambling *no art.;*

(b) eine ~ mit Worten/Zahlen playing [around] with words/numbers

Spiel·ergebnis *das* match result

Spielerin *die;* ~, ~nen ▶ SPIELER

spielerisch *Adj.* playful

Spiel-: ~**feld** *das* field; pitch (Brit.); (Tennis, Squash, Volleyball usw.) court; ~**film** *der* feature film; ~**kamerad** *der* playmate; ~**karte** *die* playing card; ~**leitung** *die* (a) (Sport) control of the match; (b) ▶ REGIE; ~**plan** *der* programme; ~**platz** *der* playground; ~**raum** *der* room to move (fig.); scope; latitude; ~**regel** *die* (auch fig.) rule of the game; gegen die ~regeln verstoßen (auch fig.) break the rules; ~**sachen** *Pl.* toys; ~**verderber** *der;* ~~s, ~~, ~**verderberin** *die;* ~~, ~~nen spoilsport; ~**waren** *Pl.* toys; ~**zeit** *die* (a) (Theater: Saison) season; (b) (Sport) playing time; die normale ~zeit normal time; ~**zeug** *das* (a) toy; (fig.) toy; plaything; (b) (Gesamtheit) toys *pl.*

Spieß *der;* ~es, ~e (a) (Waffe) spear; den ~ umdrehen *od.* umkehren (ugs.) turn the tables
(b) (Bratspieß) spit
(c) (Fleischspieß) kebab
(d) (Soldatenspr.) [company] sergeant major

Spieß·bürger *der,* **Spießbürgerin** *die* (abwertend) [petit] bourgeois

Spießer *der;* ~s, ~, **Spießerin** *die;* ~, ~nen (abwertend) [petit] bourgeois

spießig (abwertend) [1] *Adj.* [petit] bourgeois
[2] *adv.* ⟨think, behave, etc.⟩ in a [petit] bourgeois way

Spinat *der;* ~[e]s, ~e spinach

Spind *der od. das;* ~[e]s, ~e locker

Spindel *die;* ~, ~n spindle

Spinne *die;* ~, ~n spider

spinnen [1] *unr. tr. V.* spin (fig.); plot ⟨intrigue⟩; think up ⟨idea⟩; hatch ⟨plot⟩
[2] *unr. itr. V.* (a) spin
(b) (ugs.: verrückt sein) be crazy *or* (coll.) nuts

Spinnen·netz *das* spider's web

Spinner *der;* ~s, ~ (a) (Beruf) spinner
(b) (ugs. abwertend) nutcase (coll.); idiot

Spinnerei *die;* ~, ~en spinning mill

Spinnerin *die;* ~, ~nen ▶ SPINNER

Spinn-: ~**rad** *das* spinning wheel; ~**webe** *die;* ~~, ~~n cobweb

Spion *der;* ~s, ~e (a) spy
(b) (Guckloch) spyhole

Spionage /ʃpio'na:ʒə/ *die;* ~: spying; espionage

spionieren *itr. V.* spy

Spionin *die;* ~, ~nen spy

Spirale *die;* ~, ~n spiral

Spiral·feder *die* coil spring

Spirituose *die;* ~, ~n spirit *usu. in pl.*

Spiritus *der;* ~, ~se spirit; ethyl alcohol

Spiritus·kocher *der* spirit stove

S

Spital *das;* ~s, **Spitäler** (bes. österr., schweiz.) hospital

spitz ①*Adj.* **(a)** pointed; sharp 〈*pencil, needle, stone, etc.*〉; fine 〈*pen nib*〉; (Geom.) acute 〈*angle*〉
(b) (schrill) shrill 〈*cry etc.*〉
(c) (boshaft) cutting 〈*remark etc.*〉
②*adv.* **(a)** ~ **zulaufen** taper to a point; ~ **zulaufend** pointed
(b) (boshaft) cuttingly

Spitz *der;* ~es, ~e spitz

spitz-, Spitz-: ~**bart** *der* goatee; ~**bube** *der* (scherzh.: Schlingel) rascal; ~**bübisch** ①*Adj.* mischievous; ②*adv.* mischievously

spitze *indekl. Adj.* (ugs.) ▶ KLASSE

Spitze *die;* ~, ~n **(a)** point; (Pfeil~, Horn~ usw.) tip
(b) (oberes Ende) top; (eines Berges) summit
(c) (Zigarren-, Haar-, Zweigspitze) end; (Schuhspitze) toe; (Finger-, Nasenspitze) tip
(d) (vorderes Ende) front; **an der** ~ **liegen** (Sport) be in the lead *or* in front
(e) (führende Position) top
(f) (einer Firma, Organisation usw.) head; (einer Hierarchie) top; (leitende Gruppe) management
(g) (Höchstwert) maximum; peak
(h) [**absolute/einsame**] ~ **sein** (ugs.) be [absolutely] great (coll.)
(i) (fig.: Angriff) dig (**gegen** at)
(j) (Textilwesen) lace

Spitzel *der;* ~s, ~: informer

spitzen *tr. V.* sharpen 〈*pencil*〉; purse 〈*lips, mouth*〉; prick up 〈*ears*〉

Spitzen-: ~**erzeugnis** *das* top-quality product; ~**kandidat** *der,* ~**kandidatin** *die* leading *or* top candidate; ~**klasse** *die* top class; ~**qualität** *die* top quality; ~**reiter** *der* **(a)** top rider; (fig.) leader; **(b)** (Mannschaft) top team; **(c)** (Ware) top *or* best seller; ~**reiterin** *die:* ▶ ~REITER A; ~**sportler** *der* top sportsman; ~**sportlerin** *die* top sportswoman

Spitzer *der;* ~s, ~: [pencil] sharpener

spitz-, Spitz-: ~**findig** *Adj.* hair-splitting; ~**findigkeit** *die;* ~~, ~~en **(a)** hair-splitting; **(b)** (etwas Spitzfindiges) nicety; ~**hacke** *die* pick; ~|**kriegen** *tr. V.* (ugs.) tumble to (coll.); ~**maus** *die* shrew; ~**name** *der* nickname

Spleen /ʃpliːn/ *der;* ~s, ~e *od.* ~s strange habit; eccentricity

Splitt *der;* ~[e]s, ~e [stone] chippings *pl.;* (zum Streuen) grit

Splitter *der;* ~s, ~: splinter; (Granat-, Bombensplitter) splinter

splitter·faser·nackt *Adj.* (ugs.) absolutely stark naked; completely starkers *pred.* (Brit. coll.)

splittern *itr. V.* **(a)** (Splitter bilden) splinter
(b) *mit sein* (in Splitter zerbrechen) 〈*glass, windscreen, etc.*〉 shatter

*old spelling - see note on page xiv

splitter·nackt *Adj.* (ugs.) stark naked; starkers *pred.* (Brit. coll.)

Splitter·partei *die* splinter party

SPÖ *Abk.* = **Sozialistische Partei Österreichs** Austrian Socialist Party

sponsern *tr. V.* sponsor

Sponsor *der;* ~s, ~en sponsor

spontan ①*Adj.* spontaneous ②*adv.* spontaneously

Spontaneität /ʃpontanei'tɛːt/ *die;* ~: spontaneity

sporadisch ①*Adj.* sporadic ②*adv.* sporadically

Spore *die;* ~, ~n spore

Sporn *der;* ~[e]s, **Sporen** (des Reiters) spur; **einem Pferd die Sporen geben** spur a horse

Sport *der;* ~[e]s **(a)** sport; (als Unterrichtsfach) sport; PE; ~ **treiben** do sport
(b) (Hobby, Zeitvertreib) hobby; pastime

Sport-: ~**art** *die* [form of] sport; ~**fest** *das* sports festival; (einer Schule) sports day; ~**flugzeug** *das* sports plane; ~**geist** *der* sportsmanship; ~**halle** *die* sports hall; ~**journalist** *der,* ~**journalistin** *die* sports journalist; ~**kleidung** *die* sportswear

Sportler *der;* ~s, ~: sportsman

Sportlerin *die;* ~, ~nen sportswoman

sportlich ①*Adj.* **(a)** sporting *attrib.;*
(b) (fair) sportsmanlike; sporting
(c) (fig.: flott, rasant) sporty 〈*car, driving, etc.*〉
(d) (zu sportlicher Leistung fähig) sporty, athletic 〈*person*〉
(e) (jugendlich wirkend) sporty, smart but casual 〈*clothes*〉; smart but practical 〈*hairstyle*〉
②*adv.* **(a)** as far as sport is concerned
(b) (fair) sportingly
(c) (fig.: flott, rasant) in a sporty manner

Sport-: ~**platz** *der* sports field; (einer Schule) playing field/fields *pl.;* ~**schuh** *der* sports shoe; ~**stadion** *das* [sports] stadium; ~**teil** *der* sport[s] section; ~**verein** *der* sports club; ~**wagen** *der* **(a)** (Auto) sports car; **(b)** (Kinderwagen) pushchair (Brit.); stroller (Amer.); ~**zentrum** *das* sports centre

Spot /spɔt/ *der;* ~s, ~s **(a)** (Werbespot) commercial; advertisement; ad (coll.)
(b) (Leuchte) spotlight; spotlamp

Spott *der;* ~[e]s mockery; (höhnischer) ridicule; derision

spott·billig *Adj., adv.* (ugs.) dirt cheap

spötteln *itr. V.* mock [gently]; poke *or* make [gentle] fun

spotten *itr. V.* **(a)** mock; poke *or* make fun; (höhnischer) ridicule; be derisive
(b) **einer Sache** (*Gen.*) ~: be contemptuous of *or* scorn sth.

Spötter *der;* ~s, ~, **Spötterin** *die;* ~, ~nen mocker

spöttisch ①*Adj.* mocking; (höhnischer) derisive ②*adv.* mockingly

Spott·preis der (ugs.) ridiculously low price

sprach 1. u. 3. Pers. Sg. Prät. v. SPRECHEN

Sprache die; ~, ~n (a) language; **in englischer** ~: in English
(b) (Sprechweise) way of speaking; speech; (Stil) style
(c) etw. zur ~ bringen bring sth. up; raise sth.; **heraus mit der** ~! come on, out with it!

Sprachen·schule die language school

Sprach-: ~**fehler** der speech impediment or defect; ~**führer** der phrase book; ~**grenze** die language boundary; ~**kenntnisse** Pl. knowledge sing. of a language/languages; ~**kurs** der language course; ~**labor** das language laboratory or (coll.) lab

sprachlich ⃞1 Adj. linguistic ⃞2 adv. linguistically

sprach-, Sprach-: ~**los** Adj. (überrascht) speechless; ~**problem** das language problem; ~**rohr** das (Repräsentant) spokesman; (Propagandist) mouthpiece; ~**schule** die language school; ~**unterricht** der language teaching

sprang 1. u. 3. Pers. Sg. Prät. v. SPRINGEN

Spray /ʃpreː/ das od. der; ~s, ~s spray

Spray·dose die aerosol [can]

sprayen tr., itr. V. spray

Sprech-: ~**anlage** die intercom (coll.); ~**chor** der chorus

sprechen ⃞1 unr. itr. V. speak (**über** + Akk. about; **von** about, of); (sich unterhalten, sich besprechen auch) talk (**über** + Akk., **von** about); ⟨parrot etc.⟩ talk; **deutsch/flüsternd** ~: speak German/in a whisper; **für/gegen etw.** ~: speak in favour of/against sth.; **mit jmdm.** ~: speak or talk with or to sb.; **mit wem spreche ich?** who is speaking please? ⃞2 unr. tr. V. (a) speak ⟨language, dialect⟩; say ⟨word, sentence⟩; „**Hier spricht man Deutsch**" 'German spoken'
(b) (rezitieren) say, recite ⟨poem, text⟩; say ⟨prayer⟩
(c) jmdn. ~: speak to sb.
(d) (aussprechen) pronounce ⟨name, word, etc.⟩

Sprecher der; ~s, ~, **Sprecherin** die; ~, ~nen (a) spokesman/spokeswoman
(b) (Ansager[in]) announcer; (Nachrichtensprecher[in]) newscaster; newsreader
(c) (Kommentator[in], Erzähler[in]) narrator

Sprech-: ~**funk·gerät** das radio-telephone; (Walkie-talkie) walkie-talkie; ~**stunde** die consultation hours pl.; (eines Arztes) surgery; ~**stunden·hilfe** die (eines Arztes) receptionist; (eines Zahnarztes) assistant; ~**zimmer** das consulting room

spreizen tr. V. spread ⟨fingers, toes, etc.⟩; **die Beine** ~: spread one's legs apart; open one's legs

Spreiz·fuß der (Med.) spread foot

sprengen tr. V. (a) blow up; blast ⟨rock⟩; **etw. in die Luft** ~: blow sth. up
(b) (gewaltsam öffnen, aufbrechen) force [open] ⟨door⟩; force ⟨lock⟩; burst, break ⟨bonds, chains⟩; (fig.) break up ⟨meeting, demonstration⟩
(c) (besprengen) water ⟨flower bed, lawn⟩; sprinkle ⟨street, washing⟩ with water; (verspritzen) sprinkle; (mit dem Schlauch) spray

Spreng-: ~**stoff** der explosive; ~**stoff·anschlag** der bomb attack

Sprenkel der; ~s, ~: spot; dot; speckle

sprenkeln tr. V. sprinkle spots of ⟨colour⟩; sprinkle ⟨water⟩

Spreu die; ~: chaff

sprich Imperativ Sg. v. SPRECHEN

sprichst 2. Pers. Sg. Präsens v. SPRECHEN

spricht 3. Pers. Sg. Präsens v. SPRECHEN

Sprich·wort das; Pl. Sprichwörter proverb

sprießen unr. itr. V.; meist mit sein ⟨leaf, bud⟩ shoot, sprout; ⟨seedlings⟩ come or spring up; ⟨beard⟩ sprout

Spring·brunnen der fountain

springen ⃞1 unr. itr. V. (a) mit sein (auch Sport) jump; (mit Schwung) leap; spring; jump; ⟨frog, flea⟩ hop, jump; (sich in Sprüngen fortbewegen) bound
(b) mit sein (fig.) ⟨pointer, milometer, etc.⟩ jump (**auf** + Akk. to); ⟨traffic lights⟩ change (**auf** + Akk. to); ⟨spark⟩ leap; ⟨ball⟩ bounce
(c) mit sein ⟨string, glass, porcelain, etc.⟩ break; (Risse, Sprünge bekommen) crack ⃞2 unr. tr. V.; auch mit sein (Sport) perform ⟨somersault, twist dive, etc.⟩

Springer der; ~s, ~ (a) (Sport) jumper
(b) (Schachfigur) knight

Springerin die; ~, ~nen (Sport) jumper

spring·lebendig Adj. extremely lively; full of beans pred. (coll.)

Spring·reiten das showjumping no art.

Sprinkler der; ~s, ~: sprinkler

sprinten itr. (auch tr.) V.; mit sein sprint

Sprinter der; ~s, ~, **Sprinterin** die; ~, ~nen (Sport) sprinter

Sprit der; ~[e]s, ~e (a) (ugs.: Treibstoff) gas (Amer. coll.); juice (sl.); petrol (Brit.)
(b) (ugs.: Schnaps) shorts pl.

Spritze die; ~, ~n (a) syringe
(b) (Injektion) injection
(c) (der Feuerwehr) hose; (Löschfahrzeug) fire engine

spritzen ⃞1 tr. V. (a) (versprühen) spray; (verspritzen) splash; (in Form eines Strahls) spray, squirt ⟨water, foam, etc.⟩; pipe ⟨cream etc.⟩
(b) (bespritzen, besprühen) water ⟨lawn, tennis court⟩; water, spray ⟨street, yard⟩; spray ⟨plants, crops, etc.⟩; (mit Lack) spray ⟨car etc.⟩; **jmdn. nass** ~: splash sb.; (mit Wasserpistole, Schlauch) spray sb.
(c) (injizieren) inject ⟨drug etc.⟩; (ugs.: einer Injektion unterziehen) **jmdn./sich** ~: give sb. an injection/inject oneself ⋯⃗

⟨2⟩ *itr. V.; mit Richtungsangabe mit sein* ⟨*hot fat*⟩ spit; ⟨*mud etc.*⟩ spatter, splash; ⟨*blood, water*⟩ spurt

Spritzer *der;* ~s, ~ (kleiner Tropfen) splash; (von Farbe) splash; spot

spritzig ⟨1⟩ *Adj.* (a) sparkling ⟨*wine*⟩; tangy ⟨*fragrance, perfume*⟩
(b) lively ⟨*show, music, article*⟩; sparkling ⟨*performance*⟩; racy ⟨*style*⟩; nippy (coll.); zippy ⟨*car, engine*⟩; agile ⟨*person*⟩
⟨2⟩ *adv.* sparklingly ⟨*produced, performed, etc.*⟩; racily ⟨*written*⟩

Spritz·tour *die* (ugs.) spin

spröd, spröde *Adj.* (a) brittle ⟨*glass, plastic, etc.*⟩; dry ⟨*hair, lips, etc.*⟩; (rissig) chapped ⟨*lips, skin*⟩; (rauh) rough ⟨*skin*⟩
(b) (fig.: abweisend) aloof ⟨*person, manner, nature*⟩

Sprödheit, Sprödigkeit *die;* ~ (a)
▶ SPRÖDE A: brittleness; dryness; roughness
(b) (fig.: abweisendes Wesen) aloofness

spross, *sproß *1. u. 3. Pers. Sg. Prät. v.* SPRIESSEN

Spross, *Sproß *der;* Sprosses, Sprosse (Bot.) shoot

Sprosse *die;* ~, ~n (a) (auch fig.) rung
(b) (eines Fensters) glazing bar

Sprössling, *Sprößling *der;* ~s, ~e (ugs. scherzh.) offspring; **seine** ~e his offspring *pl.*

Sprotte *die;* ~, ~n sprat

Spruch *der;* ~[e]s, Sprüche (Wahlspruch) motto; (Sinnspruch) maxim; (Ausspruch) saying; aphorism; (Zitat) quotation

spruch·reif *Adj.* das ist noch nicht ~: that's not definite, so people mustn't start talking about it yet

Sprudel *der;* ~s, ~ (a) sparkling mineral water
(b) (österr.) fizzy drink

sprudeln *itr. V.; mit sein* bubble; ⟨*lemonade, champagne, etc.*⟩ fizz, effervesce

Sprudel·wasser *das* sparkling mineral water

Sprüh·dose *die* aerosol [can]

sprühen ⟨1⟩ *tr. V.* spray
⟨2⟩ *itr. V.; mit Richtungsangabe mit sein* ⟨*sparks, spray*⟩ fly; (fig.) ⟨*eyes*⟩ sparkle (vor + *Dat.* with); ⟨*intellect, wit*⟩ sparkle

Sprüh·regen *der* drizzle; fine rain

Sprung *der;* ~[e]s, Sprünge (a) (auch Sport) jump; (schwungvoll) leap; (Satz) bound; (fig.) leap; **keine großen Sprünge machen können** (fig. ugs.) not be able to afford many luxuries; **auf dem** ~[e] **sein** (fig. ugs.) be in a rush
(b) (ugs.: kurze Entfernung) stone's throw
(c) (Riss) crack

Sprung·brett *das* (auch fig.) springboard

sprunghaft ⟨1⟩ *Adj.* (a) erratic ⟨*person, character, manner*⟩; disjointed ⟨*conversation, thoughts*⟩

(b) (unvermittelt) sudden
(c) (ruckartig) rapid ⟨*change*⟩; sharp ⟨*increase*⟩
⟨2⟩ *adv.* ▶ 1B–C: disjointedly; suddenly; rapidly; sharply

Sprunghaftigkeit *die;* ~: ▶ SPRUNGHAFT 1A: erraticness; disjointedness

Sprung·tuch *das; Pl.* Sprungtücher safety blanket

Spucke *die;* ~: spit

spucken ⟨1⟩ *itr. V.* spit; **in die Hände** ~ (fig.: an die Arbeit gehen) go to work with a will
⟨2⟩ *tr. V.* spit; cough up ⟨*blood, phlegm*⟩

Spuk *der;* ~[e]s, ~e [ghostly *or* supernatural] manifestation

spuken *itr. V.; unpers.* **hier/in dem Haus spukt es** this place/the house is haunted

Spül·bürste *die* washing-up brush

Spule *die;* ~, ~n spool; (für Tonband, Film) spool; reel

Spüle *die;* ~, ~n sink unit; (Becken) sink

spulen *tr., itr. V.* spool; (am Tonbandgerät) wind

spülen ⟨1⟩ *tr. V.* (a) rinse; bathe ⟨*wound*⟩
(b) (landsch.: abwaschen) wash up ⟨*dishes, glasses, etc.*⟩; **Geschirr** ~: wash up
⟨2⟩ *itr. V.* (a) (beim WC) flush [the toilet]
(b) (den Mund ausspülen) rinse out [one's mouth]
(c) (landsch.) ▶ ABWASCHEN 2

Spül-: ~**maschine** *die* dishwasher; ~**mittel** *das* washing-up liquid; ~**tuch** *das; Pl.* ~tücher dish cloth; ~**wasser** *das* (a) rinse water; (b) (Abwaschwasser) dishwater

Spund *der;* ~[e]s, ~e/Spünde (a) *Pl.* Spünde (Zapfen) bung
(b) *Pl.* ~e (ugs.) [junger *od.* grüner] ~ young greenhorn *or* tiro

Spur *die;* ~, ~en (a) (Abdruck im Boden) track; (Folge von Abdrücken) tracks *pl.*; **eine heiße** ~ (fig.) a hot trail; **jmdm./einer Sache auf der** ~ **sein** be on to the track *or* trail of sb./sth.
(b) (Anzeichen) trace; (eines Verbrechens) clue (*Gen.* to)
(c) (sehr kleine Menge; auch fig.) trace
(d) (Verkehrsw.: Fahrspur) lane; **die** ~ **wechseln** change lanes

spürbar ⟨1⟩ *Adj.* noticeable; distinct, perceptible ⟨*improvement*⟩; evident ⟨*relief, embarrassment*⟩
⟨2⟩ *adv.* noticeably; perceptibly; (sichtlich) clearly ⟨*relieved, on edge*⟩

spüren *tr. V.* feel; (instinktiv) sense

spur·los ⟨1⟩ *Adj.* total, complete ⟨*disappearance*⟩
⟨2⟩ *adv.* ⟨*disappear*⟩ completely *or* without trace

Spür·sinn *der* (feiner Instinkt) intuition

Spurt *der;* ~[e]s, ~s *od.* ~e spurt

spurten *itr. V.* (a) *mit Richtungsangabe mit sein* spurt
(b) *mit sein* (ugs.: schnell laufen) sprint

sputen *refl. V.* (veralt.) make haste

---

*alte Schreibung - vgl. Hinweis auf S. xiv

St. *Abk.* **(a)** = **Sankt** St.
(b) = **Stück**

Staat *der;* ~[e]s, ~en state

staatlich ⒈ *Adj.* state *attrib.; ‹power, unity, etc.›* of the state; state-owned *‹factory etc.›*
⒉ *adv.* by the state; ~ anerkannt/geprüft state-approved/-certified

staats-, Staats-: ~**angehörige** *der/ die* national; ~**angehörigkeit** *die* nationality; ~**anwalt** *der,* ~**anwältin** *die* public prosecutor; ~**bürger** *der,* ~**bürgerin** *die* citizen; **er ist deutscher** ~**bürger** he is a German citizen *or* national; ~**bürgerlich** *Adj.* civil *‹rights›*; civic *‹duties, loyalty›*; *‹education, attitude›* as a citizen; ~**bürgerschaft** *die*
▶ ~ANGEHÖRIGKEIT; ~**gewalt** *die* authority of the state; (Exekutive) executive power; ~**grenze** *die* state frontier *or* border; ~**mann** *der; Pl.* -männer statesman; ~**oberhaupt** *das* head of state; ~**präsident** *der,* ~**präsidentin** *die* [state] president; ~**sicherheit** *die* **(a)** state security; **(b)** (DDR ugs.)
▶ ~SICHERHEITSDIENST;
~**sicherheits·dienst** *der* (DDR) State Security Service

Stab *der;* ~[e]s, Stäbe **(a)** rod; (länger) pole; (eines Käfigs, Gitters, Geländers) bar
(b) (Milit.) staff
(c) (Team) team

Stäbchen *das;* ~s, ~ **(a)** (kleiner Stab) little rod; [small] stick
(b) (Essstäbchen) chopstick

stabil ⒈ *Adj.* sturdy *‹chair, cupboard›*; robust, sound *‹health›*; stable *‹prices, government, economy, etc.›*
⒉ *adv.* ~ gebaut solidly built

stabilisieren ⒈ *tr. V.* stabilize
⒉ *refl. V.* **(a)** stabilize
(b) *‹health, circulation, etc.›* become stronger

Stabilität *die;* ~ **(a)** (einer Konstruktion) sturdiness; (von Gesundheit, Konstitution usw.) robustness; soundness
(b) (das Beständigsein) stability

Stab·lampe *die* torch (Brit.); flashlight (Amer.)

Stabs·arzt *der,* **Stabs·ärztin** *die* (Milit.) medical officer, MO *(with the rank of captain)*

stach *1. u. 3. Pers. Sg. Prät. v.* STECHEN

Stachel *der;* ~s, ~n **(a)** spine; (Dorn) thorn
(b) (Giftstachel) sting
(c) (Spitze) spike; (an Stacheldraht) barb

Stachel-: ~**beere** *die* gooseberry; ~**draht** *der* barbed wire

stachelig *Adj.* prickly

Stadion *das;* ~s, Stadien stadium

Stadium *das;* ~s, Stadien stage

Stadt *die;* ~, Städte **(a)** town; (Großstadt) city; **die** ~ **Basel** the city of Basel; **in die** ~ **gehen** go into town; go downtown (Amer.)
(b) (Verwaltung) town council; (in der Großstadt) city council; city hall *no art.* (Amer.)

Stadt-: ~**bahn** *die* urban railway;
~**bummel** *der* (ugs.) **einen** ~**bummel machen** take a stroll through the town/city centre

Städter *der;* ~s, ~, **Städterin** *die;* ~, ~nen **(a)** town-dweller; (Großstädter, -städterin) city-dweller
(b) (Stadtmensch) townie (coll.)

Städte·tour *die* city tour

Stadt-: ~**führer** *der* town/city guidebook; ~**führung** *die* guided tour of the town/ city; ~**gespräch** *das:* ~**gespräch sein** be the talk of the town

städtisch ⒈ *Adj.* **(a)** (kommunal) municipal
(b) (urban) urban *‹life, way of life, etc.›*
⒉ *adv.* (kommunal) municipally

Stadt-: ~**mauer** *die* town/city wall;
~**mitte** *die* town centre; (einer Großstadt) city centre; downtown area (Amer.); ~**park** *der* municipal park; ~**plan** *der* [town/city] street plan *or* map; ~**rand** *der* outskirts *pl.* of the town/city; **am** ~**rand** on the outskirts of the town/city; ~**rundfahrt** *die* sightseeing tour round a/the town/city; ~**teil** *der* district; part [of a/the town]; ~**tor** *das* town/city gate; ~**viertel** *das* district

Staffel *die;* ~, ~n **(a)** (Sport: Mannschaft) relay team
(b) (Sport: Staffellauf) relay race
(c) (Luftwaffe: Einheit) flight
(d) (Eskorte) escort formation

Staffelei *die;* ~, ~en easel

staffeln *tr. V.* **(a)** (aufstellen, formieren) arrange in a stagger *or* in an echelon
(b) (einteilen, abstufen) grade *‹salaries, fees, prices›*; stagger *‹times, arrivals, starting places›*

stahl *1. u. 3. Pers. Sg. Prät. v.* STEHLEN

Stahl *der;* ~[e]s, Stähle *od.* ~e steel

Stahl-: ~**beton** *der* reinforced concrete;
~**blech** *das* sheet steel

stählern *Adj.* steel

stak *1. u. 3. Pers. Sg. Prät. v.* STECKEN

Stall *der;* ~[e]s, Ställe (Pferde-, Rennstall) stable; (Kuhstall) cowshed; (Hühnerstall) [chicken] coop; (Schweinestall) [pig]sty; (für Kaninchen, Kleintiere) hutch; (für Schafe) pen

Stallung *die;* ~, ~en (Pferdestall) stable; (Kuhstall) cowshed; (Schweinestall) [pig]sty

Stamm *der;* ~[e]s, Stämme **(a)** (Baumstamm) trunk
(b) (Volksstamm) tribe

Stamm-: ~**aktie** *die* (Wirtsch.) ordinary share; ~**baum** *der* family tree; (eines Tieres) pedigree

stammeln *tr., itr. V.* stammer

stammen *itr. V.* come (**aus, von** from); (datieren) date (**aus, von** from)

Stamm-: ∼**gast** *der* (im Lokal/Hotel) regular customer/visitor; regular (coll.); ∼**tisch** *der* (a) (Tisch) regulars' table (coll.); (b) (Runde) group of regulars (coll.); (c) (Treffen) get-together with the regulars (coll.)

stampfen [1] *itr. V.* (a) (laut auftreten) stamp (b) *mit sein* (sich fortbewegen) tramp; (mit schweren Schritten) trudge
[2] *tr. V.* (a) mit den Füßen den Rhythmus ∼: tap the rhythm with one's feet (b) (feststampfen) compress (c) (zerkleinern) mash ⟨*potatoes*⟩

stand *1. u. 3. Pers. Sg. Prät. v.* STEHEN

Stand *der;* ∼[e]s, Stände (a) (das Stehen) standing position; [bei jmdm. *od.* gegen jmdn.] einen schweren ∼ haben (fig.) have a tough time [of it] [with sb.]
(b) (Standort) position
(c) (Verkaufsstand; Box für ein Pferd) stall; (Messestand, Informationsstand) stand; (Zeitungsstand) [newspaper] kiosk
(d) (erreichte Stufe; Zustand) state; etw. auf den neu[e]sten ∼ bringen bring sth. up to date; außer ∼[e] ▶ AUSSERSTANDE; im ∼[e] ▶ IMSTANDE;
(e) (des Wassers, Flusses) level; (des Thermometers, Zählers, Barometers) reading; (der Kasse, Finanzen) state; (eines Himmelskörpers) position
(f) (Familienstand) status
(g) (Gesellschaftsschicht) class; (Berufsstand) trade; (Ärzte, Rechtsanwälte) [professional] group

Standard *der;* ∼s, ∼s standard

standardisieren *tr. V.* standardize

Standardisierung *die;* ∼, ∼en standardization

Ständchen *das;* ∼s, ∼: serenade; jmdm. ein ∼ bringen serenade sb.

Ständer *der;* ∼s, ∼: stand; (Kleider∼) coat stand; (Wäsche∼) clothes horse

standes-, Standes-: ∼**amt** *das* registry office; ∼**amtlich** [1] *Adj.* registry office ⟨*wedding, document*⟩; [2] *adv.* ∼amtlich heiraten get married in a registry office; ∼**beamte** *der,* ∼**beamtin** *die* registrar

stand-, Stand-: ∼**fest** *Adj.* steady; stable; strong ⟨*stalk, stem*⟩; ∼**haft** [1] *Adj.* steadfast; [2] *adv.* steadfastly; ∼**haftigkeit** *die;* ∼∼: steadfastness; ∼|**halten** *unr. itr. V.* stand firm; **einer Sache** (*Dat.*) ∼halten withstand sth.

ständig [1] *Adj.* constant ⟨*noise, worry, pressure, etc.*⟩; permanent ⟨*residence, correspondent, staff, member, etc.*⟩; standing ⟨*committee*⟩; regular ⟨*income*⟩
[2] *adv.* constantly

Stand-: ∼**licht** *das* (Kfz-W.) sidelights *pl.;* ∼**ort** *der* (a) position; (eines Betriebes usw.) location; site; (b) (Milit.: Garnison) garrison;

base; ∼**punkt** *der* (fig.) point of view; viewpoint; auf dem ∼punkt stehen, dass ...: take the view that ...; ∼**spur** *die* (Verkehrsw.) hard shoulder; ∼**uhr** *die* grandfather clock

Stange *die;* ∼, ∼n pole; (aus Metall) bar; (dünner) rod; (Kleiderstange) rail; (Vogelstange) perch; ein Anzug von der ∼ (ugs.) an off-the-peg-suit

Stängel *der;* ∼s, ∼: stem; stalk

Stangen-: ∼**brot** *das* French bread; ∼**spargel** *der* asparagus spears *pl.*

stank *1. u. 3. Pers. Sg. Prät. v.* STINKEN

Stapel *der;* ∼s, ∼: pile; ein ∼ Holz a pile *or* stack of wood

stapeln [1] *tr. V.* pile up; stack
[2] *refl. V.* pile up

stapfen *itr. V.; mit sein* tramp

Star¹ *der;* ∼[e]s, ∼e *od.* (schweiz.) ∼en (Vogel) starling

Star² *der;* ∼s, ∼s (berühmte Persönlichkeit) star

Star³ *der;* ∼[e]s (Med.) grauer ∼: cataract; grüner ∼: glaucoma

starb *1. u. 3. Pers. Sg. Prät. v.* STERBEN

stark; stärker, stärkst... [1] *Adj.* (a) strong; potent ⟨*drink, medicine, etc.*⟩; powerful ⟨*engine, lens, voice, etc.*⟩; (ausgezeichnet) excellent; *s. auch* STÜCK c;
(b) (dick) thick; stout ⟨*rope, string*⟩; (verhüll.: korpulent) well-built (euphem.)
(c) (zahlenmäßig groß, umfangreich) sizeable, large; big ⟨*demand*⟩; eine 100 Mann ∼e Truppe a 100-strong unit
(d) (heftig, intensiv) heavy; severe ⟨*frost, pain*⟩; strong ⟨*impression, current, resistance, dislike*⟩; grave ⟨*doubt, reservations*⟩; great ⟨*exaggeration, interest*⟩; loud ⟨*applause*⟩
(e) (Jugendspr.: großartig) great (coll.); fantastic (coll.)
[2] *adv.* (a) (sehr, überaus, intensiv) (mit Adj.) very; heavily ⟨*indebted, stressed*⟩; greatly ⟨*increased, reduced, enlarged*⟩; strongly ⟨*emphasized, characterized*⟩; badly ⟨*damaged, worn, affected*⟩; (mit Verb) heavily; ⟨*exaggerate, impress*⟩ greatly; ⟨*enlarge, reduce, increase*⟩ considerably; ⟨*support, oppose, suspect*⟩ strongly; ⟨*remind*⟩ very much; ∼ **erkältet sein** have a heavy *or* bad cold
(b) (Jugendspr.: großartig) fantastically (coll.)

Stark·bier *das* strong beer

Stärke *die;* ∼, ∼n (a) strength; (eines Motors) power; (einer Glühbirne) wattage
(b) (Dicke) thickness; (Technik) gauge
(c) (zahlenmäßige Größe) strength
(d) (besondere Fähigkeit, Vorteil) strength; jmds. ∼/nicht jmds. ∼ sein be sb.'s forte/not be sb.'s strong point
(e) (Intensität) strength; (von Sturm, Schmerzen, Abneigung) intensity; (von Frost) severity; (von Lärm, Verkehr) volume
(f) (organischer Stoff) starch

stärken [1] *tr. V.* (a) strengthen; boost ⟨*power, prestige*⟩; ⟨*drink, food, etc.*⟩ fortify ⟨*person*⟩
(b) (steif machen) starch ⟨*washing etc.*⟩

---
*old spelling - see note on page xiv

2 *refl. V.* refresh oneself

Stärkung *die;* ~, ~**en (a)** strengthening (b) (Erfrischung) refreshment

starr **1** *Adj.* (a) rigid; (steif) stiff (vor + *Dat.* with); fixed ⟨*expression, smile, stare*⟩ (b) (nicht abwandelbar) inflexible, rigid ⟨*law, rule, principle*⟩ (c) (unnachgiebig) inflexible ⟨*person, attitude, etc.*⟩ **2** *adv.* rigidly; (steif) stiffly

starren *itr. V.* (a) stare (in + *Akk.* into, auf, an, gegen + *Akk.* at); jmdm. ins Gesicht ~: stare sb. in the face (b) vor/von Schmutz ~: be filthy

starr-, Starr-: ~**sinn** *der* pigheadedness; ~**sinnig** *Adj.* pigheaded; ~**sinnigkeit** *die* pigheadedness

Start *der;* ~**[e]s,** ~**s** start; (eines Flugzeugs) take-off; (einer Rakete) launch

Start·bahn *die* [take-off] runway

start·bereit *Adj.* ready to start *postpos.;* ⟨*aircraft*⟩ ready for take-off

starten **1** *itr. V.; mit sein* (a) start; ⟨*aircraft*⟩ take off; ⟨*rocket*⟩ blast off, be launched (b) (den Motor anlassen) start the engine **2** *tr. V.* start; launch ⟨*rocket, satellite, attack*⟩; start [up] ⟨*engine, machine, car*⟩

Stasi *die;* ~: *Abk.* (DDR ugs.) **Staatssicherheit**

Stasi·akte *die* Stasi file

Station *die;* ~, ~**en (a)** station (b) (Haltestelle) stop (c) (Zwischenhalt, Aufenthalt) stopover; ~ **machen** stop over or off (d) (im Krankenhaus) ward

stationär **1** *Adj.* (Med.) ⟨*treatment*⟩ in hospital, as an inpatient **2** *adv.* (Med.) in hospital; jmdn. ~ **behandeln** treat sb. as an inpatient

stationieren *tr. V.* station ⟨*troops*⟩; deploy ⟨*weapons, bombers, etc.*⟩

Stationierung *die;* ~, ~**en** stationing; (von Waffen, Raketen usw.) deployment

Stations-: ~**arzt** *der,* ~**ärztin** *die* ward doctor; ~**schwester** *die* ward sister; ~**taste** *die* (Rundf.) preset [tuning] button; preset

statisch *Adj.* static

Statistik *die;* ~: statistics *sing., no art.*

statistisch **1** *Adj.* statistical **2** *adv.* statistically

statt **1** *Präp. mit Gen.* instead of; s. *auch* STATTDESSEN; **2** *Konj.* ▶ ANSTATT

statt·dessen *Adv.* instead [of this]

statt|finden *unr. itr. V.* take place; ⟨*process, development*⟩ occur

statthaft *Adj.* permissible

stattlich **1** *Adj.* (a) well-built; imposing ⟨*figure, stature, building, etc.*⟩; fine ⟨*farm, estate*⟩; impressive ⟨*trousseau, collection*⟩ (b) (beträchtlich) considerable

2 *adv.* impressively

Statue *die;* ~, ~**n** statue

Statur *die;* ~, ~**en** build

Status *der;* ~, ~ /'ʃtaːtuːs/ status

Status quo *der;* ~ (geh.) status quo

Statut *das;* ~**[e]s,** ~**en** statute

Stau *der;* ~**[e]s,** ~**s** od. ~**e (a)** build-up (b) (von Fahrzeugen) tailback (Brit.); backup (Amer.)

Staub *der;* ~**[e]s** dust; ~ **wischen** dust; ~ **saugen** vacuum; or (Brit. coll.) hoover; **sich aus dem** ~**[e] machen** (fig. ugs.) make oneself scarce (coll.)

stauben *itr. V.* cause dust

staubig *Adj.* dusty

staub-, Staub-: ~**saugen** *itr., tr. V.* ich staubsauge, staubgesaugt, staubzusaugen vacuum; (Brit. coll.) hoover; ~**sauger** *der* vacuum cleaner; Hoover (*Brit.* ®); ~**tuch** *das; Pl.* ~**tücher** duster

Stau·damm *der* dam

Staude *die;* ~, ~**n** (Bot.) herbaceous perennial

stauen **1** *tr. V.* dam [up] ⟨*stream, river*⟩; staunch ⟨*blood*⟩ **2** *refl. V.* ⟨*water, blood, etc.*⟩ accumulate, build up; ⟨*people*⟩ form a crowd; ⟨*traffic*⟩ form a tailback/tailbacks (Brit.) or (Amer.) backup/backups

staunen *itr. V.* be amazed or astonished (über + *Akk.* at); (beeindruckt sein) marvel (über + *Akk.* at); ~**d** with or in amazement

Staunen *das;* ~**s** amazement (über + *Akk.* at); (Bewunderung) wonderment

Stau-: ~**see** *der* reservoir; ~**stufe** *die* barrage

Stauung *die;* ~, ~**en (a)** (eines Bachs, Flusses) damming; (des Blutes, Wassers) stemming the flow; (das Sichstauen) build-up (b) (Verkehrsstau) tailback (Brit.); backup (Amer.); jam

Std. *Abk.* = **Stunde** hr.

Steak /steːk/ *das;* ~**s,** ~**s** steak

stechen **1** *unr. itr. V.* (a) prick; ⟨*wasp, bee*⟩ sting; ⟨*mosquito*⟩ bite (b) (hineinstechen) **mit etw. in etw.** (*Akk.*) ~: stick or jab sth. into sth. **2** *unr. tr. V.* (mit dem Messer, Schwert) stab; (mit der Nadel, mit einem Dorn usw.) prick; ⟨*bee, wasp*⟩ sting; ⟨*mosquito*⟩ bite; **sich in den Finger** ~: prick one's finger

stechend *Adj.* penetrating, pungent ⟨*smell*⟩; penetrating ⟨*glance, eyes*⟩

Stech-: ~**mücke** *die* mosquito; gnat; ~**uhr** *die* time clock

Steck-: ~**brief** *der* description [of a/the wanted person]; (Plakat) 'wanted' poster; ~**dose** *die* socket; power point

stecken **1** *tr. V.* (a) put (b) (mit Nadeln) pin ⟨*hem, lining, etc.*⟩; pin [on] ⟨*badge*⟩; pin up ⟨*hair*⟩ **2** *itr. V.* be; ~ **bleiben** get stuck; **den Schlüssel [im Schloss]** ~ **lassen** leave the   ···❖

key in the lock; **wo steckt meine Brille?** (ugs.)
where have my glasses got to *or* gone?;
hinter etw. (*Dat.*) ~ (fig. ugs.) be behind sth.

stecken-, Stecken-: *~|**bleiben**
▸ STECKEN 2; *~|**lassen** ▸ STECKEN 2;
~**pferd** *das* (a) (Spielzeug) hobby horse; (b)
(Liebhaberei) hobby

Stecker *der;* ~s, ~: plug

Steck·nadel *die* pin

Steg *der;* ~[e]s, ~e (Brücke) [narrow] bridge;
(Laufbrett) gangplank; (Boots~) landing stage

Steg·reif *der:* aus dem ~: impromptu

Steh·auf·männchen *das* tumbling
figure; tumbler

stehen *unr. itr. V.; südd., österr., schweiz.*
mit sein (a) stand
(b) (sich befinden) be; ⟨upright object, building⟩
stand
(c) (einen bestimmten Stand haben) **auf etw.** (*Dat.*)
~ ⟨needle, hand⟩ point to sth.; **das Barometer
steht tief/auf Regen** the barometer is reading
low/indicating rain; **das Spiel/es steht 1:1**
(Sport) the score is one all; **die Sache steht
gut/schlecht** things are going well/badly
(d) (einen bestimmten Kurs, Wert haben)
⟨currency⟩ stand (**bei** at); **wie steht das
Pfund?** what is the rate for the pound?
(e) (nicht in Bewegung sein) be stationary;
⟨machine etc.⟩ be at a standstill; **meine Uhr
steht** my watch has stopped; ~ **bleiben**
(anhalten) stop; ⟨traffic⟩ come to a standstill;
(stehen gelassen werden) stay; be left;
(zurückgelassen werden) be left behind; (der
Zerstörung entgehen) ⟨building⟩ be left standing;
etw. ~ **lassen** (nicht entfernen) leave sth.;
(vergessen) leave sth. [behind]
(f) (geschrieben, gedruckt sein) be; **in der Zeitung
steht, dass …:** it says in the paper that …
(g) (Sprachw.: gebraucht werden) ⟨subjunctive
etc.⟩ occur; be found
(h) jmdm. [gut] ~ ⟨dress etc.⟩ suit sb. [well]
(i) **auf etw.** (*Akk.*) ~ (ugs., bes. Jugendspr.:
mögen) be into sth. (coll.); **sie steht total auf
ihn** she's nuts about him

***stehen|bleiben,** ***stehen|lassen**
▸ STEHEN E

Steh·lampe *die* standard lamp (Brit.); floor
lamp (Amer.)

stehlen *unr. tr., itr. V.* steal; *s. auch*
GESTOHLEN 2

Steh·platz *der* (im Theater usw.) standing
place; (im Bus) space to stand

Steiermark *die;* ~: Styria *no art.*

steif ①*Adj.* (a) stiff; (ugs.: erigiert) erect
⟨penis⟩
(b) (Seemannsspr.: stark) stiff ⟨wind, breeze⟩
(c) (förmlich) stiff; formal
②*adv.* stiffly

Steifheit *die;* (a) ~ stiffness
(b) (Förmlichkeit) formality; stiffness

steigen ①*unr. itr. V.; mit sein* (a) climb;
⟨mist, smoke, sun⟩ rise; ⟨balloon⟩ climb, rise;

auf die Leiter ~: get on to the ladder; **in den/
aus dem Bus/Zug** ~: board *or* get on/get off
or out of the bus/train
(b) (ansteigen, zunehmen) rise; ⟨price, cost,
salary, output⟩ increase, rise; ⟨debts, tension⟩
increase, mount; ⟨chances⟩ improve
②*unr. tr. V.; mit sein* climb ⟨stairs, steps⟩

Steiger *der;* ~s, ~ (Bergbau) overman

steigern ①*tr. V.* (a) increase ⟨speed, value,
sales, consumption, etc.⟩ (**auf** + *Akk.* to); step
up ⟨demands, production, etc.⟩; raise
⟨standards, requirements⟩; (verstärken)
intensify ⟨fear, tension⟩; heighten ⟨effect⟩
(b) (Sprachw.) compare ⟨adjective⟩
②*refl. V.* ⟨confusion, speed, profit, etc.⟩
increase; ⟨pain, excitement, tension, etc.⟩
become more intense; ⟨costs⟩ escalate; ⟨effect⟩
be heightened

Steigerung *die;* ~, ~en (a) increase (*Gen.*
in); (Verstärkung) intensification; (einer Wirkung)
heightening; (Verbesserung) improvement
(*Gen.* in); (bes. Sport: Leistungssteigerung)
improvement [in performance]
(b) (Sprachw.) comparison

Steigung *die;* ~, ~en gradient

steil ①*Adj.* steep; meteoric ⟨career⟩; rapid
⟨rise⟩
②*adv.* steeply

Steil-: ~**hang** *der* steep escarpment;
~**küste** *die* (Geogr.) cliffs *pl.*

Stein *der;* ~[e]s, ~e stone; (Fels) rock;
(Baustein) [stone]block; **mir fällt ein** ~ **vom
Herzen** that's a weight off my mind

Stein-: ~**bock** *der* (a) ibex; (b) (Astrol.)
Capricorn; the Goat; ~**bruch** *der* quarry

steinern *Adj.* stone

Stein·gut *das* earthenware

stein·hart *Adj.* rock-hard

steinig *Adj.* stony

steinigen *tr. V.* stone ⟨person⟩

Stein-: ~**kohle** *die* [hard] coal; ~**metz**
der; ~~en, ~~en, ~**metzin** *die;* ~~,
~~nen stonemason; ~**obst** *das* stone fruit;
~**pilz** *der* cep; ~**schlag** *der* rock fall;
„**Achtung** ~**schlag**" 'beware falling rocks';
~**zeit** *die* (Hist.) stone age

Steiß·bein *das* (Anat.) coccyx

Stelle *die;* ~, ~n (a) place; **an jmds.** ~
treten take sb.'s place; **ich an deiner** ~ …: …
if I were you; **an achter** ~ **liegen** be in
eighth place; **die erste** ~ **hinter** *od.* **nach dem
Komma** (Math.) the first decimal place; **an** ~
(+ *Gen.*) instead of; **auf der** ~: immediately
(b) (begrenzter Bereich) patch; (am Körper) spot
(c) (Passage) passage; (Punkt im Ablauf einer Rede
usw.) point
(d) (Arbeitsstelle) job; post; **eine freie** ~: a
vacancy
(e) (Dienststelle) office; (Behörde) authority

stellen ①*tr. V.* (a) (hinstellen) put; (mit Sorgfalt) place;
(aufrecht hin~) stand
(b) (ein~) set ⟨points, clock, scales⟩; **den**

S

Wecker auf 6 Uhr ∼: set the alarm for 6 o'clock; **die Heizung höher/niedriger** ∼: turn the heating up/down
(c) (bereitstellen) provide
(d) jmdn. **besser** ∼: ⟨firm⟩ improve sb.'s pay; **gut/schlecht/besser gestellt** comfortably/badly/better off
(e) verblasst put ⟨question⟩; set ⟨task, topic, condition⟩; make ⟨application, demand, request⟩; jmdm. **eine Frage** ∼: ask sb. a question
[2] refl. V. **(a)** place oneself; **sich auf die Zehenspitzen** ∼: stand on tiptoe
(b) sich schlafend/taub/tot usw. ∼: feign sleep/deafness/death etc.; pretend to be asleep/deaf/dead etc.

stellen-, Stellen-: ∼**angebot** das offer of a job; (Inserat) job advertisement; „∼**angebote**" 'situations vacant'; ∼**anzeige** die job advertisement; ∼**gesuch** das 'situation wanted' advertisement; ∼**markt** der job market; ∼**profil** das job profile; ∼**suche** die job-hunting no art.; search for a job; ∼**weise** Adv. in places; ∼**wert** der **(a)** (Math.) place value; **(b)** (fig.: Bedeutung) standing; status

Stellung die; ∼, ∼en position; **zu etw.** ∼ **nehmen** express one's opinion on sth.

Stellungnahme die; ∼, ∼n opinion; (kurze Äußerung) statement

stell-, Stell-: ∼**vertretend** [1] Adj. acting; (von Amts wegen) deputy ⟨minister, director, etc.⟩; [2] adv. as a deputy; ∼**vertreter** der, ∼**vertreterin** die deputy

Stelze die; ∼, ∼n stilt

stelzen itr. V.; mit sein strut; stalk

stemmen [1] tr. V. **(a)** (hochstemmen) lift [above one's head]
(b) (drücken) brace ⟨feet, knees⟩ (**gegen** against)
[2] refl. V. **sich gegen etw.** ∼: brace oneself against sth.

Stempel der; ∼s, ∼: stamp; (Poststempel) postmark

stempeln tr. V. stamp ⟨passport, form⟩; postmark ⟨letter⟩; cancel ⟨postage stamp⟩

***Stengel** ▶ STÄNGEL

steno-, Steno-: ∼**gramm** das shorthand text; ∼**graph** der; ∼**en**, ∼∼**en** stenographer; ∼**graphie** die; ∼∼, ∼∼**n** stenography no art.; shorthand no art.; ∼**graphieren** itr. V. do shorthand; ∼**graphin** die; ∼∼, ∼∼**nen** stenographer; ∼**typistin** die; ∼∼, ∼∼**nen** shorthand typist

Stepp·decke die quilt

Steppe die; ∼, ∼n steppe

steppen[1] tr. (auch itr.) V. backstitch

steppen[2] itr. V. (tanzen) tap dance

Steppke der; ∼s, ∼s (ugs., bes. berlin.) lad; nipper (coll.)

sterben unr. itr. V.; mit sein die; **im Sterben liegen** lie dying

sterbens·krank Adj. mortally ill

sterblich Adj. mortal

Sterbliche der/die; adj. Dekl. mortal; **ein gewöhnlicher** ∼**r** an ordinary mortal or person

Sterblichkeit die; ∼: mortality

stereo Adv. in stereo

Stereo das; ∼s stereo

Stereo-: ∼**anlage** die stereo [system]; ∼**aufnahme** die stereo recording

steril Adj. sterile

Sterling /'stɛːlɪŋ/: **Pfund** ∼: pound/pounds sterling

Stern der; ∼[e]s, ∼e star

Sternchen das; ∼s, ∼ (Druckw.) asterisk

Stern·schnuppe die; ∼, ∼n shooting star

Stethoskop das; ∼s, ∼e (Med.) stethoscope

Steuer[1] das; ∼s, ∼: [steering] wheel; (von Schiffen) helm

Steuer[2] die; ∼, ∼n tax

steuer-, Steuer-: ∼**belastung** die tax burden; ∼**berater** der, ∼**beraterin** die tax consultant or adviser; ∼**bord** das od. (österr.) der (Seew., Flugw.) starboard; ∼**erhöhung** die tax increase; ∼**erklärung** die tax return; ∼**ermäßigung** die tax relief; ∼**frau** die (Rudersport) cox; ∼**frei** Adj. tax-free

steuerlich [1] Adj. tax ⟨advantages, benefits, etc.⟩
[2] adv. ∼ **absetzbar** tax-deductible

Steuer·mann der; Pl. ∼**leute** od. ∼**männer** (Rudersport) cox

steuern [1] tr. V. (fahren) steer; (fliegen) pilot, fly ⟨aircraft⟩; fly ⟨course⟩
[2] itr. V. **(a)** be at the wheel; (auf dem Schiff) be at the helm
(b) mit sein (Kurs nehmen; ugs.: sich hinbewegen; auch fig.) head

Steuer-: ∼**oase** die (ugs.) tax haven; ∼**senkung** die (Steuerw.) tax cut; reduction in taxation

Steuerung die; ∼, ∼en **(a)** (System) controls pl.;
(b) ▶ STEUERN 1: steering; piloting; flying

Steward /'stjuːɐt/ der; ∼s, ∼s steward

Stewardess, *Stewardeß /'stjuːɐdɛs/ die; ∼, **Stewardessen** stewardess

stich Imper. Sg. v. STECHEN

Stich der; ∼[e]s, ∼e **(a)** (mit einer Waffe) stab
(b) (mit einem Dorn, einer Nadel) prick; (von Wespe, Biene usw.) sting; (Mückenstich usw.) bite
(c) (Stichwunde) stab wound
(d) (beim Nähen) stitch
(e) (Schmerz) stabbing or shooting pain
(f) (Kartenspiel) trick

⋯⟶

(g) jmdn./etw. im ~ **lassen** leave sb. in the lurch/abandon sth.

Stichelei *die;* ~, ~en (ugs. abwertend) **(a)** (Bemerkung) dig; gibe

(b) hör auf mit deiner ~: stop getting at me/ him *etc.* (coll.)

sticheln *itr. V.* make snide remarks (coll.) **(gegen** about)

stich-, Stich-: ~**flamme** *die* tongue of flame; ~**haltig** *Adj.* sound ⟨*argument, reason*⟩; valid ⟨*assertion, reply*⟩; conclusive ⟨*evidence*⟩; ~**haltigkeit** *die;* ~~: ▶ ~HALTIG: soundness; validity; conclusiveness

Stichling *der;* ~s, ~e stickleback

Stich·probe *die* [random] sample; (bei Kontrollen) spot check

stichst 2. *Pers. Sg. Präsens v.* STECHEN

sticht 3. *Pers. Sg. Präsens v.* STECHEN

Stich-: ~**tag** *der* set date; deadline; ~**wunde** *die* stab wound

sticken ① *itr. V.* do embroidery ② *tr. V.* embroider

Stickerei *die;* ~, ~en embroidery *no pl.;* (gestickte Arbeit) piece of embroidery

Stick·garn *das* embroidery thread

stickig *Adj.* stuffy; stale ⟨*air*⟩

Stick-: ~**oxid,** ~**oxyd** *das* nitrogen oxide; ~**oxid·emission,** ~**oxyd·emission** *die* nitrogen oxide emission; ~**stoff** *der* nitrogen; ~**stoff·oxid,** ~**stoff·oxyd** *das* nitrogen oxide

Stief- step ⟨*brother, child, mother, etc.*⟩

Stiefel *der;* ~s, ~ boot

stief-, Stief-: ~**mutter** *die; Pl.* ~**mütter** stepmother; ~**mütterchen** *das;* ~~s, ~~ (Bot.) pansy; ~**mütterlich** ① *Adj.* poor, shabby ⟨*treatment*⟩; ② *adv.* ~**mütterlich behandeln** treat ⟨*person*⟩ poorly or shabbily; neglect ⟨*pet, flowers, doll, problem*⟩; ~**vater** *der* stepfather

stieg 1. u. 3. *Pers. Sg. Prät. v.* STEIGEN

Stieglitz *der;* ~es, ~e goldfinch

stiehl *Imp. Sg. v.* STEHLEN

stiehlst 2. *Pers. Sg. Präsens v.* STEHLEN

stiehlt 3. *Pers. Sg. Präsens v.* STEHLEN

Stiel *der;* ~[e]s, ~e (Griff) handle; (Besenstiel) [broom]stick; (für Süßigkeiten) stick; (bei Gläsern) stem; (bei Blumen) stem; (an Obst usw.) stalk

Stier *der;* ~[e]s, ~e bull; (Astrol.) Taurus; the Bull

stieren *itr. V.* stare [vacantly] (**auf** + *Akk.* at)

Stier·kampf *der* bullfight

stieß 1. u. 3. *Pers. Sg. Prät. v.* STOßEN

Stift *der;* ~[e]s, ~e **(a)** (aus Metall) pin; (aus Holz) peg

(b) (Bleistift) pencil; (Malstift) crayon; (Schreibstift) pen

stiften *tr. V.* **(a)** found, establish ⟨*monastery, hospital, etc.*⟩; endow ⟨*prize, scholarship*⟩; (als Spende) donate, give (**für** to)

(b) (herbeiführen) cause, create ⟨*unrest, confusion, strife, etc.*⟩; bring about ⟨*peace, order, etc.*⟩; arrange ⟨*marriage*⟩

Stifter *der;* ~s, ~, **Stifterin** *die;* ~, ~nen founder; (Spender) donor

Stiftung *die;* ~, ~en (Rechtsspr.) foundation; endowment

Stift·zahn *der* (Zahnmed.) post crown

stigmatisieren *tr. V.* stigmatize

Stil *der;* ~[e]s, ~e style

Stil·bruch *der* inconsistency of style

stilistisch ① *Adj.* stylistic ② *adv.* stylistically

still ① *Adj.* quiet; (ohne Geräusche) silent; still; (reglos) still; (wortlos) silent; (heimlich) secret; **der Stille Ozean** the Pacific [Ocean] ② *adv.* quietly; (geräuschlos) silently; (wortlos) in silence

Stille *die;* ~: quiet; (Geräuschlosigkeit) silence; stillness

***stilllegen** ▶ STILLLEGEN

stillen ① *tr. V.* **(a) ein Kind** ~: breastfeed a baby

(b) (befriedigen) satisfy; quench ⟨*thirst*⟩

(c) (eindämmen) stop ⟨*bleeding, tears, pain*⟩ ② *itr. V.* breastfeed

still-, Still-: ~|**halten** *unr. itr. V.* keep or stay still; ~|**legen** *tr. V.* close or shut down; close ⟨*railway line*⟩; ~**schweigen** *das* silence; ~**schweigen bewahren** maintain silence; keep silent; ~**schweigend** ① *Adj.* silent; (ohne Abmachung) tacit ⟨*assumption, agreement*⟩; ② *adv.* in silence; (ohne Abmachung) tacitly; ~|**sitzen** *unr. itr. V.* sit still; ~**stand** *der* standstill; ~|**stehen** *unr. itr. V.* **(a)** ⟨*factory, machine*⟩ stand idle; ⟨*traffic*⟩ be at a standstill; ⟨*heart etc.*⟩ stop; **(b)** (Milit.) stand to attention

Stimm·bruch *der:* **er ist im** ~: his voice is breaking

Stimme *die;* ~, ~n **(a)** voice

(b) (bei Wahlen) vote

stimmen ① *itr. V.* **(a)** be right or correct; **stimmt es, dass ...?** is it true that ...?

(b) (seine Stimme geben) vote; **mit Ja** ~: vote yes or in favour ② *tr. V.* **(a)** (in eine Stimmung versetzen) make **(b)** (Musik) tune ⟨*instrument*⟩

Stimm-: ~**enthaltung** *die* abstention; ~**gabel** *die* (Musik) tuning fork

stimmig *Adj.* harmonious; **die Argumentation ist [in sich** (*Dat.*)] ~: the argument is consistent

Stimm-: ~**lage** *die* **(a)** voice; **(b)** (Musik) voice; register; ~**recht** *das* right to vote

Stimmung *die;* ~, ~en **(a)** mood **(b)** (Atmosphäre) atmosphere

stimmungs·voll ① *Adj.* atmospheric ② *adv.* ⟨*describe, light*⟩ atmospherically; ⟨*sing, recite*⟩ with great feeling

---

*old spelling - see note on page xiv

Stimm·zettel der ballot paper

stimulieren tr. V. stimulate

Stink·bombe die stink bomb

stinken unr. itr. V. stink (**nach** of)

stink·faul Adj. (salopp abwertend) bone idle (coll.)

stinkig Adj. (salopp abwertend) stinking; smelly

stink-: ~**normal** (salopp) [1] Adj. dead (coll.) or boringly ordinary; [2] adv. in a dead ordinary way (coll.); ~**reich** Adj. (salopp) stinking rich (coll.)

Stipendium das; ~**s**, Stipendien (als Auszeichnung) scholarship; (als finanzielle Unterstützung) grant

stirb Imp. Sg. v. STERBEN

stirbst 2. Pers. Sg. Präsens v. STERBEN

stirbt 3. Pers. Sg. Präsens v. STERBEN

Stirn die; ~, ~**en** forehead; brow

Stirn-: ~**höhle** die (Anat.) frontal sinus; ~**runzeln** das; ~~**s** frown; ~**seite** die front [side]

stöbern itr. V. (ugs.) rummage

stochern itr. V. poke

Stock[1] der; ~**[e]s**, Stöcke (a) stick; (Zeigestock) pointer; stick; (Taktstock) baton; (Skistock) pole; stick
  (b) (Pflanze) (Rosenstock) [rose] bush; (Rebstock) vine

Stock[2] der; ~**[e]s**, ~ (Etage) floor; storey; **in welchem** ~? on which floor?

stock·dunkel Adj. (ugs.) pitch-dark

stocken itr. V. (a) ⟨traffic⟩ be held up; ⟨conversation, production⟩ stop; ⟨business⟩ slacken; ⟨journey⟩ be interrupted
  (b) (innehalten) falter

stock·finster Adj. (ugs.) pitch-dark

Stöckel·schuhe Pl. high heels

-stöckig -storey attr.; -storeyed

stock·nüchtern Adj. (ugs.) stone-cold sober

Stockung die; ~, ~**en** hold-up (Gen. in)

Stockwerk das floor; storey

Stoff der; ~**[e]s**, ~**e** (a) material; fabric
  (b) (Materie) substance
  (c) (Philos.) matter
  (d) (Thema) subject [matter]; (Gesprächsthema) topic
  (e) (salopp: Rauschgift) stuff (sl.); dope (sl.)

stofflich Adj. material

Stofflichkeit die; ~: materiality

Stoff·wechsel der metabolism

stöhnen itr. V. moan; (vor Schmerz) groan

Stola die; ~, Stolen shawl; (Pelzstola) stole

Stollen der; ~**s**, ~ (a) (Kuchen) Stollen
  (b) (Bergbau) gallery
  (c) (bei Sportschuhen) stud

stolpern itr. V.; mit sein stumble; trip

stolz [1] Adj. proud (**auf** + Akk. of); **eine** ~**e Summe** (ugs.) a tidy sum
  [2] adv. proudly

Stolz der; ~**es** pride (**auf** + Akk. in)

stolzieren itr. V.; mit sein strut

stop /stɔp/ Interj. stop; (Verkehrsw.) halt

stopfen tr. V. (a) darn
  (b) (hineintun) stuff
  (c) (füllen) stuff ⟨cushion, quilt, etc.⟩; fill ⟨pipe⟩; plug, stop [up] ⟨hole, leak⟩

Stopf-: ~**garn** das darning cotton; ~**nadel** die darning needle

Stopp der; ~**s**, ~**s** stop; (Einstellung) freeze (Gen. on)

Stoppel die; ~, ~**n** stubble no pl.

stoppelig Adj. stubbly

stoppen tr., itr. V. stop

Stopp-: ~**licht** das stop light; ~**schild** das stop sign; ~**uhr** die stopwatch

Stöpsel der; ~**s**, ~: plug

Stör der; ~**s**, ~**e** sturgeon

Storch der; ~**[e]s**, Störche stork

stören [1] tr. V. (a) disturb; disrupt ⟨court proceedings, lecture, church service, etc.⟩; interfere with ⟨transmitter, reception⟩
  (b) (missfallen) bother
  [2] itr. V. (a) disturb
  (b) (Unruhe stiften) make or cause trouble
  [3] refl. V. **sich an jmdm./etw.** ~: take exception to sb./sth.

Störenfried der; ~**[e]s**, ~**e** troublemaker

Stör·fall der (Technik) fault

störrisch [1] Adj. stubborn
  [2] adv. stubbornly

Störung die; ~, ~**en** (a) disturbance; (einer Gerichtsverhandlung, Vorlesung, eines Gottesdienstes usw.) disruption; **bitte entschuldigen Sie die** ~**, aber** ...: I'm sorry to bother you, but ...
  (b) **eine technische** ~: a technical fault

Stoß der; ~**es**, Stöße (a) (mit der Faust) punch; (mit dem Fuß) kick; (mit dem Kopf, den Hörnern) butt; (mit dem Ellbogen) dig
  (b) (mit einer Waffe) (Stich) thrust; (Schlag) blow
  (c) (beim Schwimmen, Rudern) stroke
  (d) (Stapel) pile; stack

stoßen [1] unr. tr. V. (a) auch itr. (mit der Faust) punch; (mit dem Fuß) kick; (mit dem Kopf, den Hörnern) butt; (mit dem Ellbogen) dig
  (b) (hineintreiben) plunge, thrust ⟨dagger, knife⟩; push ⟨stick, pole⟩
  (c) (schleudern) push; **die Kugel** ~: put the shot
  [2] unr. itr. V. (a) mit sein (auftreffen) bump (**gegen** into); **mit dem Kopf gegen etw.** ~: bump one's head on sth.
  (b) mit sein (fig.) **auf etw.** (Akk.) ~ ⟨etw. entdecken⟩ come upon sth.; **auf Ablehnung** ~ (abgelehnt werden) meet with disapproval
  (c) (grenzen) **an etw.** (Akk.) ~ ⟨room, property, etc.⟩ be [right] next to sth.
  [3] unr. refl. V. bump or knock oneself; **sich an etw.** (Dat.) ~ (fig.) object to sth.

Stoß-: ~**seufzer** der heartfelt groan; ~**stange** die bumper

stößt 3. Pers. Sg. Präsens v. STOSSEN

stoß-, Stoß-: ~**weise** Adv. (a) ⸱⸱⸱⟫

S

spasmodically; **(b)** (in Stapeln) by the pile; in piles; **~zahn** der tusk; **~zeit** die peak time; (Hauptverkehrszeit) rush hour

Stotterer der; ~s, ~, **Stotterin** die; ~, ~nen stutterer

stottern ⟦1⟧ itr. V. stutter
⟦2⟧ tr. V. stutter [out]

Str. Abk. **Straße** St./Rd.

stracks Adv. **(a)** (direkt) straight
(b) (sofort) straight away

straf·bar Adj. punishable

Strafe die; ~, ~n punishment; (Rechtsspr.) penalty; (Freiheitsstrafe) sentence; (Geldstrafe) fine

strafen tr. V. punish

straff ⟦1⟧ Adj. **(a)** tight, taut ⟨rope, lines, etc.⟩; firm ⟨breasts, skin⟩
(b) (energisch) tight ⟨organization, planning, etc.⟩; strict ⟨discipline, leadership, etc.⟩
⟦2⟧ adv. **(a)** [zu] ~ sitzen ⟨clothes⟩ be [too] tight
(b) (energisch) tightly, strictly

straf·fällig Adj. ~ werden commit a criminal offence

straffen tr. V. **(a)** tighten; firm ⟨skin⟩
(b) (fig.) tighten up ⟨text, procedure, organization, etc.⟩

straf-, Straf-: ~frei Adj. ~frei ausgehen go unpunished; **~freiheit** die exemption from punishment; **~gefangene** der/die prisoner; **~gericht** das (fig.) judgement; **ein ~gericht des Himmels** divine judgement; **~gesetz·buch** das penal code

sträflich ⟦1⟧ Adj. criminal
⟦2⟧ adv. criminally

Sträfling der; ~s, ~e prisoner

straf-, Straf-: ~los Adj. unpunished;
~rechtlich ⟦1⟧ Adj. criminal attrib. ⟨case, investigation, responsibility⟩; ⟦2⟧ adv. under criminal law; **etw. ~rechtlich verfolgen** prosecute sth.; **~tat** die criminal offence;
~täter der, **~täterin** die offender;
~verfahren das criminal proceedings pl.;
~vollzug der (System) penal system;
~zettel der (ugs.) [parking, speeding, etc.] ticket

Strahl der; ~[e]s, ~en (auch Phys., Math., fig.) ray; (von Scheinwerfern, Taschenlampen) beam; (von Flüssigkeit) jet

Strahle·mann der (ugs.) man/boy with the smiling face

strahlen itr. V. **(a)** shine; **bei ~dem Wetter/Sonnenschein** in glorious sunny weather/in glorious sunshine; **~d weiß** sparkling white
(b) (glänzen) sparkle
(c) (lächeln) beam ⟨vor + Dat. with⟩

Strahler der; ~s, ~ **(a)** radiator
(b) (Heizstrahler) radiant heater

Strahlung die; ~, ~en radiation

Strähne die; ~, ~n strand; **eine graue ~:** a grey streak

strähnig ⟦1⟧ Adj. straggly ⟨hair⟩
⟦2⟧ adv. in strands

stramm ⟦1⟧ Adj. **(a)** (straff) tight, taut ⟨rope, line, etc.⟩; tight ⟨clothes⟩
(b) (kräftig) strapping ⟨girl, boy⟩; sturdy ⟨legs, body⟩
(c) (gerade) upright, erect ⟨posture, etc.⟩
⟦2⟧ adv. **(a)** (straff) tightly
(b) (kräftig) sturdily ⟨built⟩

strampeln itr. V. ⟨baby⟩ kick [his/her feet]

Strand der; ~[e]s, Strände beach; **am ~:** on the beach

Strand-: ~bad das bathing beach (on river, lake); **~burg** die sand den (built as a windbreak)

stranden itr. V.; mit sein ⟨ship⟩ run aground

Strand-: ~korb der basket chair;
~urlaub der beach holiday; beach vacation (Amer.)

Strang der; ~[e]s, Stränge rope

Strapaze die; ~, ~n strain no pl.

strapazieren tr. V. be a strain on ⟨person, nerves⟩

strapazier·fähig Adj. hard-wearing ⟨clothes, shoes⟩; durable ⟨material⟩

Straße die; ~, ~n (in Ortschaften) street; road; (außerhalb) road

Straßen-: ~bahn die tram (Brit.); streetcar (Amer.); **~bahn·haltestelle** die tram stop (Brit.); **~bau·arbeiten** Pl. roadworks;
~café das pavement café; street café;
~ecke die street corner; **~feger** der, **~fegerin** die; ~~, ~~nen (bes. nordd.) road sweeper; **~graben** der ditch [at the side of the road]; **~karte** die road map;
~kehrer der; ~~s, ~~, **~kehrerin** die; ~~, ~~nen (bes. südd.) road sweeper;
~kriminalität die street crime;
~musikant der, **~musikantin** die street musician; busker; **~raub** der street robbery; (gewalttätig) mugging; **~räuber** der, **~räuberin** die street robber; (gewalttätig) mugger; **~schild** das street name sign;
~sperre die roadblock; **~verkehr** der traffic

Strategie die; ~, ~n strategy

strategisch ⟦1⟧ Adj. strategic
⟦2⟧ adv. strategically

Strato·sphäre die stratosphere

sträuben ⟦1⟧ tr. V. ruffle [up] ⟨feathers⟩; bristle ⟨fur, hair⟩
⟦2⟧ refl. V. **(a)** ⟨hair, fur⟩ bristle, stand on end; ⟨feathers⟩ become ruffled
(b) (sich widersetzen) resist

Strauch der; ~[e]s, Sträucher shrub

straucheln itr. V.; mit sein (geh.) stumble

Strauß¹ der; ~es, Sträuße bunch of flowers; bouquet [of flowers]

Strauß² der; ~es, ~e (Vogel) ostrich

Sträußchen das; ~s, ~ posy

streben itr. V. **(a)** mit sein make one's way briskly

---
*alte Schreibung - vgl. Hinweis auf S. xiv

(b) (trachten) strive (**nach** for)

Streber *der;* ~s; ~ (abwertend) pushy person (coll.); (in der Schule) swot (Brit. coll.); grind (Amer. coll.)

strebsam *Adj.* ambitious and industrious

Strecke *die;* ~, ~n distance; (Abschnitt, Route) route; (Eisenbahn~) line

strecken ① *tr. V.* (gerade machen) stretch ‹*arms, legs*›; (dehnen) stretch [out] ‹*arms, legs, etc.*›; **den Kopf aus dem Fenster** ~: stick one's head out of the window (coll.) ② *refl. V.* stretch out

strecken·weise *Adv.* in places; (fig.: zeitweise) at times

Streich *der;* ~[e]s, ~e trick; prank; **jmdm. einen** ~ **spielen** play a trick on sb.

streicheln *tr. V.* stroke

streichen ① *unr. tr. V.* **(a)** stroke
(b) (anstreichen) paint; „**frisch gestrichen**" 'wet paint'
(c) (auftragen) spread ‹*butter, jam, ointment, etc.*›; (bestreichen) **ein Brötchen mit Butter/mit Honig** ~: butter a roll/spread honey on a roll
(d) (tilgen) delete; cancel ‹*train, flight*› ② *unr. itr. V.* **(a)** stroke; **jmdm. über den Kopf** ~: stroke sb.'s head
(b) (anstreichen) paint

Streicher *der;* ~s, ~, **Streicherin** *die;* ~, ~nen (Musik) string player; **die Streicher:** the strings

Streich-: ~**holz** *das* match; ~**instrument** *das* string[ed] instrument; ~**käse** *der* cheese spread; ~**wurst** *die* [soft] sausage for spreading; ≈ meat spread

Streife *die;* ~, ~n **(a)** (Personen) patrol
(b) (Streifengang) patrol

streifen ① *tr. V.* **(a)** (leicht berühren) touch; ‹*shot*› graze
(b) (kurz behandeln) touch [up]on ‹*problem, subject, etc.*›
(c) **den Ring vom Finger** ~: slip the ring off one's finger; **die Ärmel nach oben** ~: pull/ push up one's sleeves ② *itr. V. mit sein* roam

Streifen *der;* ~s, ~ **(a)** stripe
(b) (Stück, Abschnitt) strip

Streifen·wagen *der* patrol car

streifig *Adj.* streaky

Streif·licht *das* streak of light; **ein** ~**licht auf etw.** (*Akk.*) **werfen** (fig.) highlight sth.

Streik *der;* ~[e]s, ~s strike; **in den** ~ **treten** come out or go on strike

Streik·brecher *der,* **Streik·brecherin** *die;* ~, ~nen strike-breaker; blackleg (derog.)

streiken *itr. V.* **(a)** strike; be on strike; (in den Streik treten) come out or go on strike; strike
(b) (ugs.: nicht mitmachen) go on strike
(c) (ugs.: nicht funktionieren) pack up (coll.)

Streikende *der/die; adj. Dekl.* striker

Streik·posten *der* picket

Streit *der;* ~[e]s, ~e (Zank) quarrel; (Auseinandersetzung) dispute; argument

streiten *unr. itr., refl. V.* quarrel; argue; (sich zanken) quarrel

Streiterei *die;* ~, ~en arguing *no pl., no indef. art.;* (Gezänk) quarrelling *no pl.*

Streitigkeit *die;* ~, ~en *meist Pl.* **(a)** quarrel; argument
(b) (Streitfall) dispute

Streit·kräfte *Pl.* armed forces

streng ① *Adj.* **(a)** strict; severe ‹*punishment*›; stringent, strict ‹*rule, regulation, etc.*›; stringent ‹*measure*›; rigorous ‹*examination, check, test, etc.*›; stern ‹*reprimand, look*›; absolute ‹*discretion*›; complete ‹*rest*›
(b) (schmucklos, herb) austere, severe ‹*cut, collar, style, etc.*›; severe ‹*face, features, hairstyle, etc.*›
(c) (durchdringend) pungent, sharp ‹*taste, smell*›
(d) (rau) severe ‹*winter*›; sharp, severe ‹*frost*› ② *adv.* ‹*mark, judge, etc.*› strictly, severely; ‹*punish*› severely; ‹*look, reprimand*› sternly; ‹*smell*› strongly

Strenge *die;* ~ **(a)** ▶ STRENG A: strictness; severity; stringency; rigour; sternness
(b) (von [Gesichts]zügen) severity
(c) (von Geruch, Geschmack) pungency; sharpness
(d) ▶ STRENG D: severity; sharpness

strengstens *Adv.* [most] strictly

Stress, *Streß *der;* Stresses stress

stressen (ugs.) ① *tr. V.* **jmdn.** ~: put sb. under stress; **vollkommen gestresst sein** be under an enormous amount of stress; **die gestressten Großstädter** the stressed city-dwellers ② *itr. V.* be stressful

Streu *die;* ~, ~en straw

streuen *tr. V.* **(a)** spread ‹*manure, sand, grit*›; sprinkle ‹*salt, herbs, etc.*›; strew, scatter ‹*flowers*›
(b) *auch itr.* **die Straßen [mit Sand/Salz]** ~: grit/salt the roads

streunen *itr. V.; meist mit sein* wander or roam about or around; ~**de Katzen/Hunde** stray cats/dogs

Streusel·kuchen *der* streusel cake

strich *1. u. 3. Pers. Sg. Prät. v.* STREICHEN

Strich *der;* ~[e]s, ~e (Linie) line; (Gedankenstrich) dash; (Schrägstrich) diagonal; (Binde-, Trennungsstrich) hyphen; **auf den** ~ **gehen** (salopp) walk the streets

stricheln *tr. V.* **(a)** sketch in [with short lines]
(b) (schraffieren) hatch

Strich-: ~**junge** *der* (salopp) [young] male prostitute; ~**mädchen** *das* (salopp) streetwalker; hooker (Amer. sl.); ~**punkt** *der* semicolon

Strick *der;* ~[e]s, ~e cord; (Seil) rope; **jmdm. aus etw. einen** ~ **drehen** (fig.) use sth. against sb.

stricken *tr., itr. V.* knit

Strick-: ~**jacke** *die* cardigan; ~**nadel** *die* knitting needle; ~**zeug** *das* knitting

striegeln *tr. V.* groom ⟨*horse*⟩

strikt ① *Adj.* strict
② *adv.* strictly

Strip *der;* ~**s,** ~**s** strip[tease]

Strippe *die;* ~, ~**n** (ugs.) string; **an der** ~ **hängen** (fig.) be on the phone (coll.); (dauernd) hog the phone (coll.)

Stripper *der;* ~**s,** ~, **Stripperin** *die;* ~, ~**nen** (ugs.) stripper

Striptease /ˈʃtrɪptiːs/ *der od. das;* ~: striptease

stritt *1. u. 3. Pers. Sg. Prät. v.* STREITEN

strittig *Adj.* contentious ⟨*point, problem*⟩; disputed ⟨*territory*⟩; ⟨*question*⟩ in dispute, at issue

Stroh *das;* ~[e]s straw

Stroh-: ~**blume** *die* (a) (Immortelle) immortelle; (b) (Korbblütler) strawflower; ~**halm** *der* straw; ~**witwe** *die* (ugs. scherzh.) grass widow; ~**witwer** *der* (ugs. scherzh.) grass widower

Strolch *der;* ~[e]s, ~e (fam. scherzh.: Junge) rascal

Strom *der;* ~[e]s, Ströme river; (fig.) stream; (Strömung; Elektrizität) current; (~versorgung) electricity; **unter** ~ **stehen** be live

strom-: ~**abwärts** *Adv.* downstream; ~**auf**[wärts] *Adv.* upstream

strömen *itr. V.; mit sein* stream

Strömung *die;* ~, ~**en** current; (Met.) airstream; (fig.) trend

Strophe *die;* ~, ~**n** verse; (einer Ode) strophe

strotzen *itr. V.* von *od.* vor etw. (*Dat.*) ~: be full of sth.; **von** *od.* **vor Gesundheit** ~: be bursting with health

strubbelig *Adj.* tousled

Strudel *der;* ~**s,** ~ (a) whirlpool
(b) (bes. südd., österr.: Gebäck) strudel

Struktur *die;* ~, ~**en** structure

strukturieren *tr. V.* structure; **neu** ~: restructure

Strumpf *der;* ~[e]s, Strümpfe stocking; (Socke, Knie~) sock

Strumpf-: ~**band** *das* garter; (Straps) suspender (Brit.); garter (Amer.); ~**hose** *die* tights *pl.* (Brit.); pantyhose (esp. Amer.)

Strunk *der;* ~[e]s, Strünke stem; stalk; (Baumstrunk) stump

struppig *Adj.* shaggy; tangled, tousled ⟨*hair*⟩

Stube *die;* ~, ~**n** (a) (veralt.: Wohnraum) [living] room; parlour (dated)
(b) (Milit.) [barrack] room

Stuben·fliege *die* [common] housefly

Stück *das;* ~[e]s, ~e (a) piece; (kleines) bit; (Teil, Abschnitt) part; **ein** ~ **Kuchen** a piece *or*

slice of cake; **ein** ~ **Zucker/Seife** a lump of sugar/a piece *or* bar of soap; **im** *od.* **am** ~: unsliced ⟨*sausage, cheese, etc.*⟩
(b) (Einzelstück) item; (Exemplar) specimen; **ich nehme 5** ~: I'll take five [of them]; **30 Cent das** ~: thirty cents each; ~ **für** ~: piece by piece; (eins nach dem andern) one by one; **das ist** [ja] **ein starkes** ~ (ugs.) that's a bit much; **ein faules/freches** ~ (salopp) a lazy/cheeky thing *or* devil
(c) (Bühnenstück) play; (Musikstück) piece

Stückchen *das;* ~**s,** ~: [little] piece; bit

stückeln *tr. V.* put together ⟨*sleeve, curtain*⟩ with patches

Student *der;* ~**en,** ~**en** (a) student
(b) (österr.: Schüler) [secondary-school] pupil

Studenten·wohnheim *das* student hostel; hall of residence

Studentin *die;* ~, ~**nen** ▶ STUDENT

Studie /ˈʃtuːdjə/ *die;* ~, ~**n** study

Studien-: ~**aufenthalt** *der* study visit (in + *Dat.* to); ~**dauer** *die* length of study; **eine neunsemestrige** ~**dauer** nine semesters of study; ~**freund** *der,* ~**freundin** *die* university/college friend; ~**gebühr** *die* tuition fee; ~**platz** *der* university/college place; ~**reise** *die* study trip

studieren *tr., itr. V.* study

Studierende *der/die; adj. Dekl.* student

Studio *das;* ~**s,** ~**s** studio

Studium *das;* ~**s,** Studien study; (Studiengang) course of study

Stufe *die;* ~, ~**n** (a) step; (einer Treppe) stair; „**Vorsicht,** ~!" 'mind the step'
(b) (Raketenstufe, Geol., fig.: Stadium) stage; (Niveau: level; (Grad) degree; (Rang) grade

Stuhl *der;* ~[e]s, Stühle chair

Stuhl-: ~**gang** *der* bowel movement[s]; (Kot) stool; ~**lehne** *die* (Rückenlehne) chair back; (Armlehne) chair arm

stülpen *tr. V.* etw. auf *od.* über etw. (*Akk.*) ~: pull/put sth. on to *or* over sth.

stumm *Adj.* dumb ⟨*person*⟩; (schweigsam) silent; (wortlos) wordless; mute ⟨*glance, gesture*⟩

Stumme *der/die; adj. Dekl.* mute; **die** ~**n** the dumb

Stummel *der;* ~**s,** ~: stump; (Bleistiftstummel) stub; (Zigaretten-/Zigarrenstummel) [cigarette/ cigar] butt

Stumm·film *der* silent film

Stümper *der;* ~**s,** ~: botcher; bungler

stümperhaft ① *Adj.* incompetent; botched ⟨*job*⟩; (laienhaft) amateurish ⟨*attempt, drawing*⟩
② *adv.* incompetently; (laienhaft) amateurishly

Stümperin *die;* ~, ~**nen** botcher; bungler

stümpern *itr. V.* work incompetently; (pfuschen) bungle

stumpf *Adj.* (a) blunt ⟨*pin, needle, knife, etc.*⟩

Stumpf ···⟶ substanziell ····

(b) (glanzlos, matt) dull ⟨*paint, hair, metal, colour, etc.*⟩

Stumpf *der;* ∼[e]s, Stümpfe stump

Stumpf·sinn *der* **(a)** apathy

(b) (Monotonie) monotony; tedium

stumpf·sinnig ☐1 *Adj.* **(a)** apathetic; vacant ⟨*look*⟩

(b) (monoton) tedious; soul-destroying ⟨*job, work*⟩

☐2 *adv.* **(a)** apathetically; ⟨*stare*⟩ vacantly

(b) (monoton) tediously

Stunde *die;* ∼, ∼n hour; (Unterrichts∼) lesson; eine ∼ Aufenthalt/Pause an hour's stop/break; a stop/break of an hour

stünde *1. u. 3. Pers. Sg. Konjunktiv II v.* STEHEN

stunden *tr. V.* jmdm. einen Betrag *usw.* ∼: allow sb. to defer payment of a sum *etc.*

stunden-, Stunden-: ∼**kilometer** *der* kilometre per hour; k.p.h.; ∼**lang** ☐1 *Adj.* lasting hours *postpos.;* ☐2 *adv.* for hours; ∼**lohn** *der* hourly wage; ∼**plan** *der* timetable; ∼**zeiger** *der* hour hand

-stündig *adj.* -hour

stündlich *Adj., adv.* hourly

-stündlich *adj.* -hourly; zwei∼/halb∼: two-hourly/half-hourly; *adv.* every two hours/half an hour

Stundung *die;* ∼, ∼en deferment of payment

Stups *der;* ∼es, ∼e (ugs.) push; shove; (leicht) nudge

stupsen *tr. V.* (ugs.) push; shove; (leicht) nudge

Stups-nase *die* snub nose

stur (ugs.) ☐1 *Adj.* **(a)** obstinate; dogged ⟨*insistence*⟩; (phlegmatisch) dour

(b) (unbeirrbar) dogged; persistent

(c) (stumpfsinnig) tedious

☐2 *adv.* **(a)** obstinately

(b) (unbeirrbar) doggedly

(c) (stumpfsinnig) tediously; ⟨*learn, copy*⟩ mechanically

stürbe *1. u. 3. Pers. Sg. Konjunktiv II v.* STERBEN

Sturheit *die;* ∼ (ugs.) **(a)** obstinacy; pigheadedness; (phlegmatisches Wesen) dourness

(b) (Stumpfsinnigkeit) deadly monotony

Sturm *der;* ∼[e]s, Stürme **(a)** storm; (heftiger Wind) gale

(b) (Milit.) assault (auf + *Akk.* on); ∼ klingeln ring the [door]bell like mad

stürmen ☐1 *itr. V.* **(a)** unpers. es stürmt [heftig] it's blowing a gale

(b) *mit sein* (rennen) rush; (verärgert) storm

☐2 *tr. V.* (Milit.) storm ⟨*town, position, etc.*⟩; (fig.) besiege ⟨*booking office, shop, etc.*⟩

Stürmer *der;* ∼s, ∼ (Sport) striker; forward

stürmisch ☐1 *Adj.* **(a)** stormy; (fig.) tempestuous, turbulent

(b) (ungestüm) tumultuous ⟨*applause,*

welcome, reception⟩; wild ⟨*enthusiasm*⟩; passionate ⟨*lover, embrace, temperament*⟩; vehement ⟨*protest*⟩

☐2 *adv.* ⟨*protest*⟩ vehemently; ⟨*embrace*⟩ impetuously, passionately; ⟨*demand*⟩ clamorously; ⟨*applaud*⟩ wildly

Sturz *der;* -es, Stürze **(a)** fall; (Unfall) accident

(b) (fig.: von Preis, Temperatur usw.) [sharp] fall, drop (*Gen.* in)

(c) (Verlust des Amtes, der Macht) fall; (Absetzung) overthrow; (Amtsenthebung) removal from office

Sturz·bach *der* [mountain] torrent; (fig.: von Fragen usw.) torrent

sturz·besoffen *Adj* (ugs.) paralytic [drunk] (coll.)

stürzen ☐1 *itr. V.; mit sein* **(a)** fall; (fig.) ⟨*temperature, exchange rate, etc.*⟩ drop [sharply]; ⟨*prices*⟩ tumble; ⟨*government*⟩ fall, collapse

(b) (laufen) rush; dash

(c) (fließen) stream; pour

☐2 *refl. V.* sich auf jmdn./etw. ∼ (auch fig.) pounce on sb./sth.; sich in etw. (*Akk.*) ∼: throw oneself into sth.

☐3 *tr. V.* **(a)** throw; (mit Wucht) hurl

(b) (umdrehen) upturn ⟨*mould*⟩; turn out ⟨*pudding, cake, etc.*⟩

(c) (des Amtes entheben) oust ⟨*person*⟩ [from office]; (gewaltsam) overthrow ⟨*leader, government*⟩

Sturz-: ∼**flug** *der* (Flugw.) [nose]dive; im ∼**flug** in a [nose]dive; ∼**helm** *der* crash helmet

Stuss, *Stuß *der;* Stusses (ugs. abwertend) rubbish; twaddle (coll.)

Stute *die;* ∼, ∼n mare

Stütze *die;* ∼, ∼n (auch fig.) support

stutzen[1] *itr. V.* stop short

stutzen[2] *tr. V.* trim; dock ⟨*tail*⟩; clip ⟨*ear, hedge, wing*⟩; prune ⟨*tree, bush*⟩

stützen ☐1 *tr. V.* support; (mit Pfosten o. Ä.) prop up; (aufstützen) rest ⟨*head, hands, arms, etc.*⟩

☐2 *refl. V.* sich auf jmdn./etw. ∼: lean *or* support oneself on sb./sth.

stutzig *Adj.* ∼ werden begin to wonder; jmdn. ∼ machen make sb. wonder

Styropor Ⓦⓩ *das;* ∼s polystyrene [foam]

s. u. *Abk.* = **siehe unten** see below

Subjekt *das;* ∼[e]s, ∼e **(a)** subject

(b) (abwertend: Mensch) creature

subjektiv ☐1 *Adj.* subjective

☐2 *adv.* subjectively

Subjektivität *die;* ∼: subjectivity

***substantiell** ▶ SUBSTANZIELL

Substantiv *das;* ∼s, ∼e (Sprachw.) noun

Substanz *die;* ∼, ∼en **(a)** (auch fig.) substance

(b) (Grundbestand) die ∼: the reserves *pl.*

substanziell ☐1 *Adj.* substantial

☐2 *adv.* substantially

subtil [1] *Adj.* subtle
[2] *adv.* subtly
Subtilität *die;* ~, ~en subtlety
sub·tropisch *Adj.* subtropical
Subvention *die;* ~, ~en (Wirtsch.) subsidy
Suche *die;* ~, ~n search (nach for); **auf der** ~ **[nach jmdm./etw.] sein** be looking/ (intensiver) searching [for sb./sth.]
suchen [1] *tr. V.* **(a)** look for; (intensiver) search for; „**Leerzimmer gesucht**" 'unfurnished room wanted'
(b) (bedacht sein auf, sich wünschen) seek ⟨protection, advice, company, warmth, etc.⟩; look for ⟨adventure⟩
[2] *itr. V.* search; **nach jmdm./etw.** ~: look/ search for sb./sth.
Sucherei *die;* ~, ~en (ugs., oft abwertend) [endless] searching *no pl.*
Sucht *die;* ~, Süchte *od.* ~en **(a)** addiction (nach to); **[bei jmdm.] zur** ~ **werden** (auch fig.) become addictive [in sb.'s case]
(b) *Pl.* Süchte (übermäßiges Verlangen) craving (nach for)
süchtig *Adj.* **(a)** addicted
(b) (fig.) **nach etw.** ~ **sein** be obsessed with sth.
Sucht·kranke *die/der* addict
Süd (bes. Seemannsspr., Met.) ▶ SÜDEN
Süd-: ~**afrika** *(das)* South Africa; ~**amerika** *(das)* South America
Sudan *(das);* ~s *od. der;* ~s Sudan
Süden *der;* ~s south; **der** ~: the South;
Süd·frucht *die* tropical [or sub-tropical] fruit
Südländer *der;* ~s, ~, **Südländerin** *die;* ~, ~nen Southern European
südländisch *Adj.* Southern [European]; Latin ⟨temperament⟩; ~ **aussehen** have Latin looks
südlich [1] *Adj.* **(a)** southern
(b) (nach, von Süden) southerly
(c) (aus dem Süden) Southern
[2] *adv.* southwards
[3] *Präp. mit Gen.* [to the] south of
süd-, Süd-: ~**licht** *das* southern lights *pl.;* (einzelne Erscheinung) display of the southern lights; ~**pol** *der* South Pole; ~**see** *die;* ~~: **die** ~**see:** the South Seas *pl.;* ~**see·insel** *die* South Sea island; ~**tirol** *(das)* South Tyrol; ~**wärts** *Adv.* southwards; ~**wind** *der* south *or* southerly wind
Sues·kanal *der;* ~s Suez Canal
Sühne *die;* ~, ~n (geh.) atonement; expiation
sühnen *tr., itr. V.* [für] etw. ~: atone for *or* pay the penalty for sth.
Sultanine *die;* ~, ~n sultana
Sülze *die;* ~, ~n **(a)** diced meat/fish in aspic; (vom Schweinskopf) brawn
(b) (Aspik) aspic

sülzen *tr., itr. V.* (salopp) ▶ QUATSCHEN 1A, 2
Summe *die;* ~, ~n sum
summen [1] *itr. V.* hum; (lauter, heller) buzz
[2] *tr. V.* hum ⟨tune, song, etc.⟩
summieren *refl. V.* add up (**auf** + *Akk.* to)
Sumpf *der;* ~[e]s, Sümpfe marsh; (bes. in den Tropen) swamp
sumpfig *Adj.* marshy
Sund *der;* ~[e]s, ~e (Geogr.) sound
Sünde *die;* ~, ~n sin; (fig.) misdeed; transgression
Sünden·bock *der* (ugs.) scapegoat
Sünder *der;* ~s, ~, **Sünderin** *die;* ~, ~nen sinner
sündigen *itr. V.* sin
Super *das;* ~s, ~: four star (Brit.); premium (Amer.)
super- ultra- ⟨long, high, fast, modern, masculine, etc.⟩
Super- super⟨hero, car, group, etc.⟩; terrific (coll.), tremendous (coll.) ⟨success, offer, chance, idea, etc.⟩
Super·benzin *das* four-star petrol (Brit.); premium (Amer.)
Superlativ *der;* ~s, ~e (Sprachw.) superlative
Super-: ~**macht** *die* super power; ~**markt** *der* supermarket
Suppe *die;* ~; ~n soup
Suppen·löffel *der* soup spoon
Surf·brett /ˈsɜːf-/ *das* surfboard
surfen /ˈsɜːfn/ *itr. V.* surf
Surfer /ˈsɜːfɐ/ *der;* ~s, ~, **Surferin** *die;* ~, ~nen surfer
surren *itr. V.* **(a)** (summen) hum; ⟨camera, fan⟩ whirr
(b) *mit sein* (schwirren) whirr
suspekt [1] *Adj.* suspicious; **jmdm.** ~ **sein** arouse sb.'s suspicions
[2] *adv.* suspiciously
süß [1] *Adj.* sweet
[2] *adv.* sweetly
süßen *tr. V.* sweeten
Süßigkeit *die;* ~, ~en sweet (Brit.); candy (Amer.); ~en sweets (Brit.); candy *sing.* (Amer.); (als Ware) confectionery *sing.*
süßlich [1] *Adj.* **(a)** [slightly] sweet; on the sweet side *pred.;*
(b) (sentimental) mawkish
[2] *adv.* ⟨write, paint⟩ mawkishly
süß-, Süß-: ~**most** *der* unfermented fruit juice; ~**sauer** [1] *Adj.* sweet-and-sour; (fig.) wry ⟨smile, face⟩; [2] *adv.* **(a) etw.** ~**sauer** **zubereiten** give sth. a sweet-and-sour flavour; **(b)** (fig.) ⟨smile⟩ wryly; ~**speise** *die* sweet; dessert; ~**stoff** *der* sweetener; ~**wasser** *das* fresh water
Symbol *das;* ~s, ~e symbol
symbolisch [1] *Adj.* symbolic
[2] *adv.* symbolically
Sympathie *die;* ~, ~n sympathy (**für** with)

---

*alte Schreibung - vgl. Hinweis auf S. xiv

sympathisch ☐1 *Adj.* congenial, likeable 〈*person, manner*〉; appealing 〈*voice, appearance, material*〉
☐2 *adv.* in an appealing way; (angenehm) agreeably

Symphonie *usw.* ▶ SINFONIE *usw.*

Symptom *das;* ~s, ~e (Med., geh.) symptom (*Gen.,* **für, von** of)

symptomatisch (Med., geh.) *Adj.* symptomatic (**für** of)

Synagoge *die;* ~, ~n synagogue

synchron ☐1 *Adj.* **(a)** synchronous
(b) (Sprachw.) synchronic
☐2 *adv.* **(a)** synchronously
(b) (Sprachw.) synchronically

Synchronisation *die;* ~, ~en
▶ SYNCHRONISIERUNG

synchronisieren *tr. V.* **(a)** (Film) dub 〈*film*〉
(b) (Technik, fig.) synchronize 〈*watches, operations, etc.*〉; **synchronisiertes Getriebe** synchromesh [gearbox]

Synchronisierung *die;* ~, ~en **(a)** (Film) dubbing
(b) (Technik, fig.) synchronization

Synthese *die;* ~, ~n synthesis (*Gen.,* **von, aus** of)

Synthesizer /'sɪntəsaɪːzɐ/ *der;* ~s, ~ (Musik) synthesizer

synthetisch ☐1 *Adj.* synthetic
☐2 *adv.* synthetically

Syrer *der;* ~s, ~, **Syrerin** *die;* ~, ~nen Syrian

Syrien /'zyːriən/ (*das*); ~s Syria

syrisch *Adj.* Syrian

System *das;* ~, ~e system

systematisch ☐1 *Adj.* systematic
☐2 *adv.* systematically

System·fehler *der* fault in the system

Szenario *das;* ~s, ~s scenario

Szene /'stsːeːnə/ *die;* ~, ~n (auch fig.) scene

Szenen·wechsel *der* (Theater) scene change

Tt

---

t, T /teː/ *das;* ~, ~: t/T

t *Abk.* = **Tonne** t

Tab. *Abk.* = **Tabelle**

Tabak *der;* ~s, ~e tobacco

Tabaks·pfeife *die* [tobacco] pipe

tabellarisch *Adj.* tabular; **ein ~er Lebenslauf** a curriculum vitae in tabular form

Tabelle *die;* ~, ~n table

Tabellen·kalkulation *die* (DV) performing calculations using a spreadsheet; (Program) spreadsheet program

Tabernakel *das od. der;* ~s, ~: tabernacle

Tablett *das;* ~[e]s, ~s *od.* ~e tray

Tablette *die;* ~, ~n tablet

tabletten·süchtig *Adj.* addicted to pills *postpos.*

tabu *Adj.* taboo

Tabu *das;* ~s, ~s taboo

tabuisieren *tr. V.* etw. ~: taboo sth.; make sth. taboo

Ta·cheles [mit jmdm.] ~ **reden** (ugs.) do some straight talking [to sb.]

Tacho *der;* ~s, ~s (ugs.) speedo (coll.)

Tacho-: ~**meter** *der od. das* speedometer;
~**stand** *der* (ugs.: Kilometerstand) mileometer *or* odometer reading

Tadel *der;* ~s, ~ **(a)** censure
(b) (im Klassenbuch) black mark

tadel·los ☐1 *Adj.* impeccable; immaculate 〈*hair, clothing, suit, etc.*〉; perfect 〈*condition, teeth, pronunciation, German, etc.*〉
☐2 *adv.* 〈*dress*〉 impeccably; 〈*fit, speak, etc.*〉 perfectly; 〈*live, behave, etc.*〉 irreproachably

tadeln *tr. V.* jmdn. [**für** *od.* **wegen etw.**] ~: rebuke sb. [for sth.]

Tafel *die;* ~, ~n **(a)** (Schiefertafel) slate; (Wandtafel) blackboard
(b) (plattenförmiges Stück) slab; **eine ~ Schokolade** a bar of chocolate
(c) (Gedenktafel) plaque
(d) (geh.: festlicher Tisch) table

Täfelchen *das;* ~s, ~: ▶ TAFEL B: [small] slab; [small] bar

tafeln *itr. V.* (geh.) feast

täfeln *tr. V.* panel

Tafel-: ~**spitz** *der* (österr.) boiled fillet of beef; ~**wasser** *das* [bottled] mineral water; ~**wein** *der* table wine

taff *Adj.* (ugs.) tough

Taft *der;* ~[e]s, ~e taffeta

Tag *der;* ~[e]s, ~e day; **am ~[e]** during the day[time]; **guten ~!** hello; (bei Vorstellung) how do you do?; **an diesem ~:** on this day; **dreimal am ~:** three times a day; **am folgenden ~:** the next day; **eines ~es** one day; some day

tag·aus *Adv.* ~, **tagein** day in, day out; day after day

Tage·buch *das* diary

tag·ein *Adv.* ▶ TAGAUS

tage·lang [1] *Adj.* lasting for days *postpos.;* nach ∼em Regen after days of rain [2] *adv.* for days [on end]

tagen *itr. V.* meet; das Gericht/Parlament tagt the court/parliament is in session

tages-, Tages-: ∼**aktuell** *Adj.* die ∼aktuellen Nachrichten the [current] news of the day; die ∼aktuellen Kurse the rates of exchange current on the day; ∼**anbruch** *der* daybreak; dawn; ∼**ausflug** *der* day's outing; ∼**karte** *die* (a) (Gastron.) menu of the day; (b) (Fahr-, Eintrittskarte) day ticket; ∼**kasse** *die* (a) box office (*open during the day*); (b) (Tageseinnahme) day's takings *pl.;* ∼**licht** *das* daylight; ∼**licht·projektor** *der* overhead projector; ∼**zeit** *die* time of day; ∼**zeitung** *die* daily newspaper; daily

-tägig (a) (... Tage alt) ein sechstägiges Küken a six-day-old chick (b) (... Tage dauernd) nach dreitägiger Vorbereitung after three days' preparation

täglich [1] *Adj.* daily [2] *adv.* every day; zweimal ∼: twice a day; ∼ drei Tabletten einnehmen take three tablets daily

tags *Adv.* (a) by day; in the daytime (b) ∼ zuvor/davor the day before; ∼ darauf the next *or* following day; the day after

tags·über *Adv.* during the day

tag·täglich (intensivierend) [1] *Adj.* day-to-day; daily [2] *adv.* every single day

Tagung *die;* ∼, ∼en conference

Taifun *der;* ∼s, ∼e typhoon

Taille /'taljə/ *die;* ∼, ∼n waist

Taiwan (*das*); ∼s Taiwan

Takt *der;* ∼[e]s, ∼e (a) (Musik) time; (Einheit) bar; measure (Amer.); aus dem ∼ kommen lose the beat (b) (rhythmischer Bewegungsablauf) rhythm (c) (Feingefühl) tact

Takt·gefühl *das* sense of tact

taktieren *itr. V.* proceed tactically; vorsichtig/klug ∼: use caution/clever tactics

Taktik *die;* ∼, ∼en: [eine] ∼: tactics *pl.*

taktisch [1] *Adj.* tactical [2] *adv.* tactically

taktlos [1] *Adj.* tactless [2] *adv.* tactlessly ·

Taktlosigkeit *die;* ∼, ∼en (a) (taktlose Art) tactlessness (b) (taktlose Handlung) piece of tactlessness

taktvoll [1] *Adj.* tactful [2] *adv.* tactfully

Tal *das;* ∼[e]s, Täler valley

Talent *das;* ∼[e]s, ∼e talent (zu, für for); (Mensch) talented person

talentiert *Adj.* talented

Talg *der;* ∼[e]s, ∼e suet; (zur Herstellung von Seife, Kerzen usw.) tallow

Talisman *der;* ∼s, ∼e talisman

Tampon *der;* ∼s, ∼s tampon

Tamtam *das;* ∼s (ugs. abwertend) [großes] ∼: [a big] fuss

Tang *der;* ∼[e]s, ∼e seaweed

Tangente *die;* ∼, ∼n (Math.) tangent

Tank *der;* ∼s, ∼s tank

tanken *tr., itr. V.* fill up; Öl ∼: fill up with oil

Tanker *der;* ∼s, ∼: tanker

Tank-: ∼**säule** *die* petrol pump (Brit.); gasoline pump (Amer.); ∼**stelle** *die* petrol station (Brit.); gas station (Amer.); ∼**wagen** *der* tanker; ∼**wart** *der;* ∼∼s, ∼∼e, ∼**wartin** *die;* ∼∼, ∼∼nen petrol pump attendant (Brit.); gas station attendant (Amer.)

Tanne *die;* ∼, ∼n fir [tree]

Tannen-: ∼**baum** *der* (ugs.) fir tree; (Weihnachtsbaum) Christmas tree; ∼**grün** *das* fir sprigs *pl.;* ∼**zapfen** *der* fir cone; ∼**zweig** *der* fir branch

Tansania (*das*); ∼s Tanzania

Tante *die;* ∼, ∼n (a) aunt (b) (Kinderspr.: Frau) lady (c) (ugs.: Frau) woman

Tanz *der;* ∼es, Tänze dance

Tanz-: ∼**abend** *der* evening dance; ∼**bar** *die* night spot (coll.) with dancing; ∼**café** *das* coffee house with dancing

tanzen *itr., tr. V.* dance

Tänzer *der;* ∼s, ∼, **Tänzerin** *die;* ∼, ∼nen dancer; (Balletttänzer[in]) ballet dancer

Tanz-: ∼**fläche** *die* dance floor; ∼**lokal** *das* café/restaurant with dancing; ∼**orchester** *das* dance band; ∼**stunde** *die* (a) (∼kurs) dancing class; (b) (einzelne Stunde) dancing lesson

Tapete *die;* ∼, ∼n wallpaper

Tapeten·wechsel *der* (ugs.) change of scene

tapezieren *tr. V.* [wall]paper

tapfer [1] *Adj.* brave [2] *adv.* bravely

Tapferkeit *die;* ∼: courage; bravery

tappen *itr. V.* (a) *mit sein* patter (b) (tastend greifen) grope (nach for)

Taps *der;* ∼es, ∼e (ugs. abwertend) clumsy oaf

Tarif *der;* ∼s, ∼e charge; (Post-, Wassertarif) rate; (Verkehrstarif) fares *pl.;* (Zolltarif) tariff; (Lohntarif) [wage] rate; (Gehaltstarif) [salary] scale

tarnen [1] *tr., itr. V.* camouflage [2] *refl. V.* camouflage oneself

Tasche *die;* ∼, ∼n bag; (in Kleidung, Rucksack usw.) pocket; jmdm. auf der ∼ liegen (fig. ugs.) live off sb.

Taschen-: ∼**buch** *das* paperback; ∼**dieb** *der,* ∼**diebin** *die* pickpocket; ∼**geld** *das* pocket money; ∼**lampe** *die* [pocket] torch (Brit.) *or* (Amer.) flashlight;

---

*old spelling - see note on page xiv

~**messer** *das* penknife; ~**rechner** *der* pocket calculator; ~**tuch** *das; Pl.* ~**tücher** handkerchief; ~**uhr** *die* pocket watch

Tasse *die;* ~, ~**n** cup

Tastatur *die;* ~, ~**en** keyboard

Taste *die;* ~, ~**n (a)** (eines Musikinstruments, einer Schreibmaschine) key
(b) (Pedal) pedal [key]
(c) (am Telefon, Radio, Fernsehgerät, Taschenrechner usw.) button

tasten [1] *itr. V.* (fühlend suchen) grope, feel (nach for)
[2] *refl. V.* (sich tastend bewegen) grope *or* feel one's way

Tasten-: ~**feld** *das* (Elektrot.) keypad; ~**telefon** *das* push-button telephone

tat *1. u. 3. Pers. Sg. Prät. v.* TUN

Tat *die;* ~, ~**en** act; (das Tun) action; **eine gute** ~: a good deed; **in der** ~ (verstärkend) actually; (zustimmend) indeed

Tatar *das;* ~[s] steak tartare

Tat·bestand *der* **(a)** facts *pl.* [of the matter *or* case]
(b) (Rechtsw.) elements *pl.* of an offence

Täter *der;* ~s, ~, **Täterin** *die;* ~, ~**nen** culprit

tätig *Adj.* **(a)** ~ sein work
(b) (rührig, aktiv) active

tätigen *tr. V.* (Kaufmannsspr., Papierdt.) transact ⟨*business, deal, etc.*⟩

Tätigkeit *die;* ~, ~**en** activity; (Arbeit) job

tat-, Tat-: ~**kraft** *die* energy; drive; ~**kräftig** [1] *Adj.* energetic ⟨*person*⟩;
[2] *adv.* energetically

tätlich [1] *Adj.* physical ⟨*clash, attack, resistance, etc.*⟩; **gegen jmdn.** ~ **werden** become violent towards sb.
[2] *adv.* physically; **jmdn.** ~ **angreifen** attack sb. physically; assault sb.

Tat·ort *der* scene of a/the crime

tätowieren *tr. V.* tattoo

Tätowierung *die;* ~, ~**en** tattoo

Tat·sache *die* fact

tatsächlich [1] *Adj.* actual; real
[2] *adv.* actually; really

tätscheln *tr. V.* pat

Tattoo /tɛ'tu:/ *das;* ~s, ~s tattoo

tat·verdächtig *Adj.* suspected

Tat·waffe *die* weapon [used in the crime]

Tatze *die;* ~, ~**n** paw

Tat·zeit *die* time of the crime

Tau¹ *der;* ~[e]s dew

Tau² *das;* ~[e]s, ~e (Seil) rope

taub *Adj.* **(a)** deaf
(b) (wie abgestorben) numb
(c) empty ⟨*nut*⟩

Taube¹ *die;* ~, ~**n** pigeon; (Turteltaube; auch Politik fig.) dove

Taube² *der/die; adj. Dekl.* deaf person; deaf man/woman; **die** ~**n** the deaf

Taubheit *die;* ~: deafness

taub·stumm *Adj.* deaf and dumb

Taub·stumme *der/die; adj. Dekl.* deaf mute

tauchen [1] *itr. V.* **(a)** auch mit sein dive (nach for)
(b) mit sein (eintauchen) dive; (auftauchen) rise; emerge
[2] *tr. V.* **(a)** (eintauchen) dip
(b) (untertauchen) duck

Taucher *der;* ~s, ~: diver; (mit Flossen und Atemgerät) skin diver

Taucher-: ~**anzug** *der* diving suit; ~**brille** *die* diving goggles *pl.*

Taucherin *die;* ~, ~**nen** ▶ TAUCHER

Tauch·sieder *der;* ~s, ~: portable immersion heater

tauen [1] *itr. V.* **(a)** unpers. es taut it's thawing
(b) mit sein (schmelzen) melt
[2] *tr. V.* melt; thaw

Taufe *die;* ~, ~**n** (christl. Rel.) **(a)** (Sakrament) baptism
(b) (Zeremonie) christening; baptism

taufen *tr. V.* **(a)** baptize
(b) (einen Namen geben) christen

taugen *itr. V.* nichts/nicht viel/etwas ~: be no/not much/some good *or* use

tauglich *Adj.* [nicht] ~: [un]suitable; (für Militärdienst) fit [for service]

Taumel *der;* ~s **(a)** [feeling of] dizziness
(b) (Rausch) frenzy; fever

taumelig *Adj.* dizzy; giddy

taumeln *itr. V.* **(a)** auch mit sein (wanken) reel, sway (vor + *Dat.* with)
(b) mit sein (taumelnd gehen) stagger

Tausch *der;* ~[e]s, ~e exchange; **ein guter/ schlechter** ~: a good/bad deal

tauschen [1] *tr. V.* exchange (gegen for); **sie tauschten die Plätze** they changed places
[2] *itr. V.* mit jmdm. ~ (fig.) change places with sb.

täuschen [1] *tr. V.* deceive; **wenn mich nicht alles täuscht** unless I'm completely mistaken
[2] *itr. V.* be deceptive
[3] *refl. V.* be mistaken (in + *Dat.* about)

täuschend [1] *Adj.* remarkable, striking ⟨*similarity, imitation*⟩
[2] *adv.* remarkably

Täuschung *die;* ~, ~**en** deception; (Selbst~) delusion

tausend *Kardinalz.* **(a)** a *or* one thousand
(b) (ugs.: sehr viele) thousands of; ~ **Dank/ Küsse** a thousand thanks/kisses

Tausend *das;* ~s, ~e thousand

tausend-ein[s] *Kardinalz.* a *or* one thousand and one

Tausender *der;* ~s, ~ (ugs.) (Tausendmarkschein usw.) thousand-mark/-dollar *etc.* note; (Betrag) thousand marks/dollars *etc.*

t͟a͟usenderl͟ei *indekl. Adj.* (ugs.) a thousand and one different ⟨answers, kinds, etc.⟩

t͟ausend·mal *Adv.* a thousand times

t͟ausendst... *Ordinalz.* thousandth; *s. auch* ACHT...

t͟ausendstel *Bruchz.* thousandth

T͟ausendstel *das* (schweiz. meist *der*); ~s, ~: thousandth

T͟au-: ~**wasser** *das* meltwater; ~**wetter** *das* thaw; ~**ziehen** *das;* ~~s (auch fig.) tug-of-war

T͟axe *die;* ~, ~**n (a)** (Taxi) taxi **(b)** (Gebühr) charge

T͟axi *das;* ~s, ~s taxi

tax͟ieren *tr. V.* estimate

T͟axi-: ~**fahrer** *der,* ~**fahrerin** *die* taxi driver; ~**stand** *der* taxi rank (Brit.); taxi stand

Tb /te:'be:/, **Tbc** /te:be:'ts:e:/ *die;* ~: *Abk.* = Tuberkulose TB

Team /ti:m/ *das;* ~s, ~s team

Team·arbeit *die* teamwork

T͟echnik *die;* ~, ~**en (a)** technology; (Studienfach) engineering *no art.;* **(b)** (technische Ausrüstung) equipment **(c)** (Arbeitsweise, Verfahren) technique

T͟echniker *der;* ~s, ~, **T͟echnikerin** *die;* ~, ~**nen** technical expert

t͟echnisch ☐1 *Adj.* technical; technological ⟨progress, age⟩ ☐2 *adv.* technically; technologically ⟨advanced⟩

T͟echno /'tɛkno/ *das od. der;* ~s techno

Technolog͟ie *die;* ~, ~**n** technology

technolog͟isch ☐1 *Adj.* technological ☐2 *adv.* technologically

T͟echno·party *die* techno party

Tee *der;* ~s, ~s tea

TEE /te:|e:'|e:/ *der;* ~[s], ~[s] *Abk.* = Trans-Europ-Express TEE

Tee-: ~**beutel** *der* tea bag; ~**kanne** *die* teapot; ~**löffel** *der* teaspoon

T͟eenie /'ti:ni/ *der;* ~s, ~s (ugs.) young teenager

Tee-: sieb *das* tea strainer; ~**tasse** *die* teacup

T͟eich *der;* ~[e]s, ~e pond

T͟eig *der;* ~[e]s, ~e dough; (Kuchen-, Biskuitteig) pastry; (Pfannkuchen-, Waffelteig) batter

T͟eig·waren *Pl.* pasta *sing.*

T͟eil (a) *der;* ~[e]s, ~e part; **fünfter** ~: fifth **(b)** *der od. das;* ~[e]s, ~e (Anteil; Beitrag) share **(c)** *der;* ~[e]s, ~e (beteiligte Person[en]; Rechtsw.: Partei) party **(d)** *das;* ~[e]s, ~e (Einzelteil) part

t͟eil·bar *Adj.* divisible (**durch** by)

T͟eilbarkeit *die;* ~: divisibility

T͟eilchen *das;* ~s, ~ **(a)** (kleines Stück) [small] part **(b)** (Partikel) particle

t͟eilen ☐1 *tr. V.* **(a)** divide (**durch** by) **(b)** (aufteilen) share (**unter** + *Dat.* among) ☐2 *refl. V.* sich (*Dat.*) etw. [mit jmdm.] ~: share sth. [with sb.]

T͟eiler *der;* ~s, ~ (Math.) factor

t͟eil|haben *unr. itr. V.* share (an + *Dat.* in)

T͟eilhaber *der;* ~s, ~, **T͟eilhaberin** *die;* ~, ~**nen** partner

T͟eil·kasko·versicherung *die:* insurance giving limited cover

T͟eilnahme *die;* ~, ~**n (a)** participation (an + *Dat.* in); ~ **an einem Kurs** attendance at a course **(b)** (Interesse) interest (an + *Dat.* in) **(c)** (geh.: Mitgefühl) sympathy

t͟eilnahms·los *Adj.* indifferent

T͟eilnahmslosigkeit *die;* ~: indifference

t͟eilnahms·voll ☐1 *Adj.* compassionate ☐2 *adv.* compassionately

t͟eil|nehmen *unr. itr. V.* [an etw. (*Dat.*)] ~: take part [in sth.]; [an einem Lehrgang] ~: attend [a course]

T͟eilnehmer *der;* ~s, ~, **T͟eilnehmerin** *die;* ~, ~**nen (a)** participant (*Gen.*, an + *Dat.* in); (bei Wettbewerb auch) competitor, contestant (an + *Dat.* in) **(b)** (Fernspr.) subscriber

t͟eils *Adv.* partly

T͟eilung *die;* ~, ~**en** division

t͟eil·weise ☐1 *Adv.* partly ☐2 *adj.* partial

T͟eilzeit-: ~**arbeit** *die* part-time work *no indef. art.;* ~**beschäftigt** *Adj.* ⟨person⟩ in part-time work; ~**beschäftigt sein** work part-time; ~**beschäftigte** *der/die; adj. Dekl.* part-time employee; ~**job** *der* part-time job

T͟eint /tɛ̃:/ *der;* ~s, ~s complexion

Telef͟on /'te:lefo:n, auch tele'fo:n/ *das;* ~s, ~e telephone; phone; **ans** ~ **gehen** answer the [tele]phone

Telef͟on-: ~**anruf** *der* [tele]phone call; ~**anschluss**, *⃰*~**anschluß** *der* telephone; line; ~**apparat** *der* telephone

Telefon͟at *das;* ~[e]s, ~e telephone call

Telef͟on-: ~**buch** *das* [tele]phone book *or* directory; ~**gespräch** *das* telephone conversation

telefon͟ieren *itr. V.* make a [tele]phone call; **mit jmdm.** ~: talk to sb. [on the telephone]

telef͟onisch ☐1 *Adj.* telephone *attrib.* ☐2 *adv.* by telephone

Telefon͟ist *der;* ~en, ~en, **Telefon͟istin** *die;* ~, ~**nen** telephonist; (in einer Firma) switchboard operator

Telef͟on-: ~**karte** *die* phonecard; ~**nummer** *die* [tele]phone number; ~**rechnung** *die* [tele]phone bill; ~**verzeichnis** *das* [tele]phone list; ~**zelle** *die* [tele]phone booth *or* (Brit.) box; call box (Brit.); ~**zentrale** *die* telephone exchange

---

*⃰*alte Schreibung - vgl. Hinweis auf S. xiv

Telegraf *der;* ~en, ~en telegraph
Telegrafie *die;* ~: telegraphy *no art.*
telegrafieren *itr., tr. V.* telegraph
telegrafisch [1] *Adj.* telegraphic
  [2] *adv.* by telegraph *or* telegram
Telegramm *das* telegram
Tele·objektiv *das* (Fot.) telephoto lens
Tele·text *der* teletext *no art.*
Teller *der;* ~s, ~: plate
Tempel *der;* ~s, ~: temple
Temperament *das;* ~[e]s, ~e (a)
  (Wesensart) temperament
  (b) (Schwung) eine Frau mit ~: a woman with
  spirit
temperament·voll *Adj.* spirited ⟨*person,
speech, dance, etc.*⟩
Temperatur *die;* ~, ~en temperature
Temperatur-: ~anstieg *der* rise in
  temperature; ~rückgang *der* drop *or* fall
  in temperature
Tempo *das;* ~s, ~s *od.* Tempi (a) *Pl.* ~s
  speed
  (b) (Musik) tempo; time
Tempo·limit *das* (Verkehrsw.) speed limit
Tempus *das;* ~, Tempora (Sprachw.) tense
Tendenz *die;* ~, ~en trend
tendieren *itr. V.* tend (zu towards)
Teneriffa (*das*)*;* ~s Tenerife
Tennis *das;* ~: tennis *no art.*
Tennis-: ~ball *der* tennis ball; ~platz
  der tennis court; ~schläger *der* tennis
  racket; ~schuh *der* tennis shoe;
  ~schule *die* tennis school; ~spieler
  der, ~spielerin *die* tennis player
Tenor *der;* ~s, Tenöre, (österr. auch:) ~e
  (Musik) tenor; (im Chor) tenors *pl.*
Teppich *der;* ~s, ~e carpet; (kleiner) rug
Teppich·boden *der* fitted carpet
Termin *der;* ~s, ~e date; (Anmeldung)
  appointment; (Verabredung) engagement;
  (Rechtsw.) hearing
Terminal /'tø:gminəl/ *das;* ~s, ~s
  terminal
Termin-: ~geschäft *das* (Börsenw.)
  forward transaction *or* operation;
  ~kalender *der* appointments book
Terminus *der;* ~, Termini term
Terpentin *das,* (österr. meist:) *der;* ~s (a)
  (Harz) turpentine
  (b) (ugs.: Terpentinöl) turps *sing.* (coll.)
Terrain /tɛ'rɛ̃:/ *das;* ~s, ~s terrain
Terrasse *die;* ~, ~n terrace
Terrier /'tɛrɪɐ/ *der;* ~s, ~: terrier
Terrine *die;* ~, ~n tureen
Territorium *das;* ~s, Territorien territory
Terror *der;* ~s terrorism *no art.*
Terror-: ~angriff *der* terrorist attack;
  ~anschlag *der* terrorist attack;
  ~gruppe *die* terrorist group
terrorisieren *tr. V.* (a) terrorize
  (b) (ugs.: belästigen) pester

Terrorismus *der;* ~: terrorism *no art.*
Terrorist *der;* ~en, ~en, **Terroristin**
  die; ~, ~nen terrorist
Terror-: ~verdächtige *der/die* terrorist
  suspect; ~zelle *die* terrorist cell
Test *der;* ~[e]s, ~s *od.* ~e test
Testament *das;* ~[e]s, ~e (a) will
  (b) (christl. Rel.) Testament
Test·bogen *der* test paper
testen *tr. V.* test (auf + *Akk.* for)
teuer [1] *Adj.* expensive; dear *usu. pred.;*
  wie ~ war das? how much did that cost?
  [2] *adv.* expensively; dearly; etw. ~ kaufen/
  verkaufen pay a great deal for sth./sell sth.
  at a high price
Teuerung *die;* ~, ~en rise in prices
Teuerungs·rate *die* rate of price
  increases
Teufel *der;* ~s, ~: devil
Teufels·zeug *das* (ugs.) terrible stuff (coll.)
teuflisch [1] *Adj.* (a) devilish, fiendish
  ⟨*plan, trick, etc.*⟩; diabolical ⟨*laughter,
pleasure, etc.*⟩
  (b) (ugs.: groß, intensiv) terrible (coll.); dreadful
  (coll.)
  [2] *adv.* (a) diabolically
  (b) (ugs.) terribly (coll.)
Text *der;* ~[e]s, ~e text; (Wortlaut) wording;
  (eines Theaterstücks) script; (einer Oper) libretto;
  (eines Liedes, Chansons usw.) words *pl.;* (eines
  Schlagers) words *pl.;* lyrics *pl.;* (zu einer
  Abbildung) caption
texten *tr. V.* write ⟨*song, advertisement,
etc.*⟩
Textilien *Pl.* (a) textiles
  (b) (Fertigwaren) textile goods
Textil·industrie *die* textile industry
Text·verarbeitung *die* text processing;
  word processing
Thailand (*das*)*;* ~s Thailand
Theater *das;* ~s, ~ (a) theatre; ins ~
  gehen go to the theatre; im ~: at the
  theatre; ~ spielen act; (fig.) play-act; pretend
  (b) (fig. ugs.) fuss
Theater-: ~abonnement *das* theatre
  subscription [ticket]; ~stück *das* [stage]
  play
Theke *die;* ~, ~n (a) (Schanktisch) bar
  (b) (Ladentisch) counter
Thema *das;* ~s, Themen subject; topic;
  (einer Abhandlung) subject; theme; (Leitgedanke)
  theme
Themse *die;* ~: Thames
Theologe *der;* ~n, ~n theologian
Theologie *die;* ~, ~n theology *no art.*
Theologin *die;* ~, ~: theologian
theologisch [1] *Adj.* theological
  [2] *adv.* theologically
theoretisch [1] *Adj.* theoretical
  [2] *adv.* theoretically
Theorie *die;* ~, ~n theory

t

Therap<u>eu</u>t der; ~en, ~en,
  Therap<u>eu</u>tin die; ~, ~nen therapeutist
therap<u>eu</u>tisch [1] Adj. therapeutic
  [2] adv. therapeutically
Therap<u>ie</u> die; ~, ~n therapy (**gegen** for)
therap<u>ie</u>ren tr. V. treat
Therm<u>o</u>·m<u>e</u>ter das (österr. u. schweiz. der
  od. das) thermometer
Th<u>e</u>rmos·flasche (W₂) die Thermos flask
  ®; vacuum flask
Thermost<u>a</u>t der; ~[e]s od. ~en, ~e od.
  ~en thermostat
Th<u>e</u>se die; ~, ~n thesis
Thr<u>o</u>n der; ~[e]s, ~e throne
Th<u>u</u>n·fisch der tuna
Th<u>ü</u>ringen (das); ~s Thuringia
Th<u>y</u>mian der; ~s, ~e thyme
T<u>i</u>ck der; ~[e]s, ~s (a) (ugs.: Schrulle) quirk;
  thing (coll.)
  (b) (ugs.: Nuance) tiny bit; shade
t<u>i</u>cken itr. V. tick; **du tickst wohl nicht
  richtig** (salopp) you must be off your rocker
  (coll.)
T<u>i</u>cket das; ~s, ~s ticket
t<u>ie</u>f [1] Adj. (auch fig.) deep; (niedrig) low; low
  ⟨neckline, bow⟩; deep; intense ⟨pain,
  suffering⟩
  [2] adv. deep; (niedrig) low; (intensiv) deeply;
  ⟨stoop, bow⟩ low; ⟨breathe, inhale⟩ deeply
T<u>ie</u>f das; ~s, ~s (Met.) low
t<u>ie</u>f·blau Adj. deep blue
T<u>ie</u>f·druck der (Met.) low pressure
T<u>ie</u>fe die; ~, ~n depth; **in die ~ stürzen**
  plunge into the depths
tief-, Tief-: ~**garage** die underground
  car park; ~**greifend** [1] Adj. profound;
  profound, deep ⟨crisis⟩; far-reaching
  ⟨improvement⟩; [2] adv. profoundly;
  ~**gründig** Adj. profound; ~|**kühlen** tr. V.
  [deep-]freeze
T<u>ie</u>f·kühl-: ~**fach** das freezer
  [compartment]; ~**kost** die frozen food
tief-, Tief-: ~**punkt** der low [point];
  ~**schlag** der (Boxen) low punch; punch
  below the belt (lit. or fig.); ~**see** die (Geogr.)
  deep sea; ~**sinnig** [1] Adj. profound;
  [2] adv. profoundly
T<u>ie</u>fst·temperatur die minimum or
  lowest temperature
T<u>ie</u>gel der; ~s, ~ (zum Kochen) pan;
  (Schmelztiegel) crucible; (Behälter) pot
T<u>ie</u>r das; ~[e]s, ~e animal
T<u>ie</u>r-: ~**arzt** der, ~**ärztin** die veterinary
  surgeon; vet; ~**garten** der zoo; zoological
  garden; ~**heim** das animal home
t<u>ie</u>risch [1] Adj. (a) animal attrib.; savage
  ⟨cruelty, crime⟩
  (b) (ugs.: unerträglich groß) terrible (coll.); ~**er
  Ernst** deadly seriousness

[2] adv. (a) ⟨roar⟩ like an animal; savagely
  ⟨cruel⟩
  (b) (ugs.: unerträglich) terribly (coll.)
tier-, Tier-: ~**kreis** der (Astron., Astrol.)
  zodiac; ~**kreis·zeichen** das (Astron.,
  Astrol.) sign of the zodiac; ~**lieb** Adj. animal-
  loving attrib.; fond of animals postpos.;
  ~**park** der zoo; ~**pfleger** der,
  ~**pflegerin** die animal keeper;
  ~**quälerei** /-‑'‑/ die cruelty to animals;
  ~**rechtler** der; ~~s, ~~, ~**rechtlerin**
  die; ~~, ~~nen animal rights campaigner;
  ~**reich** das animal kingdom
T<u>i</u>ger der; ~s, ~: tiger
t<u>i</u>lgen tr. V. (a) (geh.) delete ⟨word, letter,
  error⟩; erase ⟨record, endorsement⟩; (fig.) wipe
  out ⟨shame, guilt, traces⟩
  (b) (Wirtsch., Bankw.) repay; pay off
T<u>i</u>lgung die; ~, ~en (a) (geh.) ▶ TILGEN A:
  deletion; erasure; wiping out
  (b) (Wirtsch., Bankw.) repayment
T<u>i</u>lsiter der; ~s, ~: Tilsit [cheese]
T<u>i</u>nte die; ~, ~n ink; **in der ~ sitzen** (ugs.)
  be in the soup (coll.)
T<u>i</u>nten-: ~**fisch** der cuttlefish; (Krake)
  octopus; ~**strahl·drucker** der (DV) ink-jet
  printer
****T<u>i</u>p, T<u>i</u>pp** der; ~s, ~s (a) (ugs.) tip
  (b) (bei Toto, Lotto usw.) [row of] numbers
t<u>i</u>ppen [1] itr. V. (a) an/gegen etw. (Akk.) ~:
  tap sth.
  (b) (ugs.: Maschine schreiben) type
  (c) (wetten) do the pools/lottery etc.; **im Lotto
  ~:** do the lottery
  [2] tr. V. (a) tap
  (b) (ugs.: mit der Maschine schreiben) type
  (c) (setzen auf) choose; **sechs Richtige ~:**
  make six correct selections
T<u>i</u>pp-: ~**fehler** der typing error or
  mistake; ~**gemeinschaft** die pools/
  lottery etc. syndicate
t<u>i</u>pp·t<u>o</u>pp (ugs.) [1] Adj. (tadellos)
  immaculate; (erstklassig) tip-top
  [2] adv. immaculately
Tir<u>o</u>l (das); ~s [the] Tyrol
Tir<u>o</u>ler der; ~s, ~, **Tir<u>o</u>lerin** die; ~,
  ~nen Tyrolese; Tyrolean
T<u>i</u>sch der; ~[e]s, ~e table; **reinen ~
  machen** (ugs.) sort things out
T<u>i</u>sch-: ~**dame** die dinner partner;
  ~**decke** die tablecloth; ~**gebet** das grace
  no pl.; ~**herr** der dinner partner; ~**lampe**
  die table lamp
T<u>i</u>schler der; ~s, ~: joiner; (bes. Kunst~)
  cabinetmaker
T<u>i</u>schlerei die; ~, ~en ▶ TISCHLER: (a)
  (Werkstatt) joiner's/cabinetmaker's [workshop]
  (b) (Handwerk) joinery/cabinetmaking
T<u>i</u>schlerin die; ~, ~nen ▶ TISCHLER
T<u>i</u>sch-: ~**nachbar** der person next to one
  [at table]; ~**platte** die table top; ~**tennis**
  das table tennis; ~**tuch** das; Pl. ~tücher

---

*old spelling - see note on page xiv

tablecloth; ~**wäsche** *die* table linen;
~**wein** *der* table wine; ~**zeit** *die*
lunchtime

Titel *der;* ~s, ~ (a) title
(b) (ugs.: Musikstück, Song usw.) number

Titel-: ~**bild** *das* cover picture; ~**blatt**
das title page; ~**rolle** *die* title role;
~**seite** *die* (a) (einer Zeitung, Zeitschrift) [front]
cover; (b) (eines Buchs) title page

Titte *die;* ~, ~n (derb) tit (coarse)

titulieren *tr. V.* call

tja /tja(:)/ *Interj.* [yes] well; (Resignation
ausdrückend) oh, well

Toast /to:st/ *der;* ~[e]s, ~e *od.* ~s toast

Toast-brot *das* [sliced white] bread for
toasting

toasten *tr. V.* toast

Toaster *der;* ~s, ~: toaster

toben *itr. V.* (a) go wild (**vor** + *Dat.* with);
(fig.) 〈storm, sea, battle〉 rage
(b) (tollen) romp *or* charge about
(c) *mit sein* (laufen) charge

Tochter *die;* ~, Töchter (a) daughter
(b) (Wirtsch.) subsidiary

Tochter-gesellschaft *die* (Wirtsch.)
subsidiary [company]

Tod *der;* ~[e]s, ~e death; **eines natürlichen/**
gewaltsamen ~es sterben die a natural/
violent death; **jmdn. zum ~e verurteilen**
sentence sb. to death

tod-ernst [1] *Adj.* deadly serious
[2] *adv.* deadly seriously

Todes-: ~**anzeige** *die* (a) (in einer Zeitung)
death notice; (b) (Karte) *card announcing a*
person's death; ~**fall** *der* death; (in der
Familie) bereavement; ~**nachricht** *die*
news of his/her/their *etc.* death; ~**opfer**
das death; fatality; ~**strafe** *die* death
penalty; ~**ursache** *die* cause of death;
~**urteil** *das* death sentence;
~**verachtung** *die* [utter] fearlessness in
the face of death; **etw. mit ~verachtung**
essen/trinken (ugs.) force sth. down [without
showing one's distaste]

Tod·feind *der,* Tod·feindin *die* deadly
enemy

tod-krank *Adj.* critically ill

tödlich [1] *Adj.* (a) fatal 〈accident, illness,
outcome, etc.〉; lethal, deadly 〈poison, bite,
shot, trap, etc.〉; lethal 〈dose〉
(b) (sehr groß, ausgeprägt) deadly 〈hatred,
seriousness, certainty, boredom〉
[2] *adv.* (a) fatally
(b) (sehr) terribly (coll.)

tod-, Tod-: ~**müde** *Adj.* dead tired;
~**schick** (ugs.) [1] *Adj.* dead smart (coll.);
[2] *adv.* dead smartly (coll.); ~**sicher** (ugs.)
[1] *Adj.* sure-fire (coll.); [2] *adv.* for certain *or*
sure; ~**sünde** *die* (auch fig.) deadly *or*
mortal sin; ~**unglücklich** *Adj.* (ugs.)
extremely *or* desperately unhappy

Toilette /tɔaˈlɛtə/ *die;* ~, ~n toilet

Toiletten-papier *das* toilet paper

toi, toi, toi /ˈtɔy: ˈtɔy: ˈtɔy/ *Interj.* good
luck!; (unberufen!) touch wood!

Tokio (*das*)*;* ~s Tokyo

tolerant [1] *Adj.* tolerant (**gegen** of)
[2] *adv.* tolerantly

Toleranz *die;* ~: tolerance

tolerierbar *Adj.* tolerable

tolerieren *tr. V.* tolerate

toll [1] *Adj.* (a) (ugs.) (großartig) great (coll.);
fantastic (coll.); (erstaunlich) amazing; (heftig,
groß) enormous 〈respect〉; terrific (coll.) 〈noise,
storm〉
(b) (wild) wild
[2] *adv.* (a) (ugs.: großartig) terrifically well
(coll.)
(b) (ugs.: heftig) 〈rain, snow〉 like billy-o (coll.)
(c) (wild) **bei dem Fest ging es ~ zu** it was a
wild party

Tolle *die;* ~, ~n quiff

tollen *itr. V.* (a) romp about
(b) *mit sein* romp

toll-, Toll-: ~**kühn** [1] *Adj.* daredevil
attrib.; daring; [2] *adv.* daringly; ~**wut** *die*
rabies *sing.;* ~**wütig** *Adj.* rabid

Tollpatsch *der;* ~[e]s, ~e (ugs.) clumsy *or*
awkward creature

tollpatschig (ugs.) [1] *Adj.* clumsy;
awkward
[2] *adv.* clumsily; awkwardly

***Tolpatsch** *usw.* ▶ TOLLPATSCH *usw.*

Tölpel *der;* ~s, ~: fool

tölpelhaft [1] *Adj.* foolish
[2] *adv.* foolishly

Tomate *die;* ~, ~n tomato

Tomaten-mark *das* tomato purée

Tombola *die;* ~, ~s raffle

Ton[1] *der;* ~[e]s, ~e clay

Ton[2] *der;* ~[e]s, Töne (a) (auch Physik, Musik;
beim Telefon) tone; (Klang) note
(b) (Film, Ferns. usw., Tonwiedergabe) sound
(c) (ugs.: Äußerung) word
(d) (Farb~) shade
(e) (Akzent) stress

ton-, Ton-: ~**angebend** *Adj.*
predominant; ~**art** *die* (a) (Musik) key; (b)
(fig.) tone; ~**band** *das; Pl.* ~bänder tape;
~**band-gerät** *das* tape recorder;
~**effekt** *der* sound effect

tönen [1] *itr. V.* (geh.) sound; 〈bell〉 sound,
ring; (schallen, widerhallen) resound
[2] *tr. V.* (färben) tint

Ton-: ~**fall** *der* tone; (Intonation) intonation;
~**höhe** *die* pitch; ~**leiter** *die* (Musik) scale

Tonne *die;* ~, ~n (a) (Behälter) drum;
(Mülltonne) bin; (Regentonne) water butt
(b) (Gewicht) tonne

tonnen·weise *Adv., adj.* by the ton

Ton-qualität *die* sound quality

Tönung *die;* ~, ~en tint; shade

Tool /tu:l/ *das;* ~s, ~s (DV) tool

Topf *der;* ~es, Töpfe (a) pot; (Braten~,
Schmor~) casserole; (Stielkasserolle) saucepan　···❯

(b) (zur Aufbewahrung) pot
(c) (Krug) jug
(d) (Nachttopf) chamber pot; (für Kinder) potty (Brit. coll.)
(e) (Blumentopf) [flower]pot

Topf·blume die [flowering] pot plant

Töpfchen das; ~s, ~: potty (Brit. coll.)

Töpfer der; ~s, ~ potter

Töpferei die; ~, ~en **(a)** (Handwerk) pottery no art.;
(b) (Werkstatt) pottery; potter's workshop
(c) (Erzeugnis) piece of pottery; ~en pottery sing.

Töpferin die; ~, ~nen ▶ TÖPFER

Topf-: ~**lappen** der oven cloth; ~**pflanze** die pot plant

Tor¹ das; ~[e]s, ~e **(a)** gate; (einer Garage, Scheune) door; (fig.) gateway
(b) (Ballspiele) goal
(c) (Ski) gate

Tor² der; ~en, ~en (geh.: Narr) fool

Torf der; ~[e]s, ~e peat

Torheit die; ~, ~en (geh.) **(a)** foolishness
(b) (Handlung) foolish act

Tor·hüter der, **Tor·hüterin** die (Ballspiele) goalkeeper

töricht (geh.) [1] Adj. foolish
[2] adv. foolishly

torkeln itr. V.; mit sein stagger

Tor·mann der; Pl. **Tormänner** od. **Torleute** (Ballspiele) goalkeeper

Tornister /tɔr'nɪstɐ/ der; ~s, ~: knapsack; (Schulranzen) satchel

torpedieren tr. V. (Milit., fig.) torpedo

Torpedo der; ~s, ~s torpedo

Törtchen das; ~s, ~: tartlet

Torte die; ~, ~n (Creme-, Sahnetorte) gateau; (Obsttorte) [fruit] flan

Torten-: ~**boden** der flan case; (ohne Rand) flan base; ~**guss**, *~**guß** der glaze; ~**heber** der; ~s, ~~: cake slice

Tortur die; ~, ~en **(a)** ordeal
(b) (veralt.: Folter) torture

Tor-: ~**wart** der; ~~[e]s, ~~e, ~**wartin** die; ~~, ~~nen (Ballspiele) goalkeeper; ~**weg** der gateway

tosen itr. V. roar; ⟨storm⟩ rage

tot Adj. dead; ~ umfallen drop dead; **sich** ~ **stellen** pretend to be dead; play dead; ~ **geboren** stillborn

total [1] Adj. total
[2] adv. totally

Total·ausverkauf der clearance sale

totalitär (Politik) [1] Adj. totalitarian
[2] adv. in a totalitarian way; ⟨organized, run⟩ along totalitarian lines

Total·schaden der (Versicherungsw.) **an beiden Fahrzeugen entstand** ~: both vehicles were a write-off

tot|ärgern refl. V. (ugs.) get livid (coll.)

Tote der/die; adj. Dekl. dead person; **die** ~**n** the dead

töten tr., itr. V. kill; deaden ⟨nerve etc.⟩

toten-, Toten-: ~**blass**, *~**blaß**, ~**bleich** Adj. deathly pale; ~**gräber** der; ~~s, ~~, ~**gräberin** die; ~~, ~~nen gravedigger; ~**kopf** der **(a)** skull; **(b)** (als Symbol) death's head; (mit gekreuzten Knochen) skull and crossbones; ~**schädel** der skull; ~**sonntag** der (ev. Kirche) Sunday before Advent on which the dead are commemorated; ~**still** Adj. deathly quiet; ~**stille** die deathly silence; ~**wache** die vigil by the body

tot-, Tot-: ~|**fahren** unr. tr. V. [run over and] kill; *~|**geboren** ▶ TOT; ~**geburt** die still birth; ~|**lachen** refl. V. (ugs.) kill oneself laughing; **zum Totlachen sein** be killing (coll.)

Toto das od. der; ~s, ~s **(a)** (Pferdetoto) tote (coll.); **im** ~: on the tote
(b) (Fußballtoto) [football] pools pl.; **[im]** ~ **spielen** do the pools

Toto·schein der; ▶ TOTO: pools coupon/ (coll.) tote ticket

tot-, Tot-: ~|**schießen** unr. tr. V. (ugs.) jmdn. ~**schießen** shoot sb. dead; ~**schlag** der (Rechtsw.) manslaughter no indef. art.; ~|**schlagen** unr. tr. V. beat to death; *~|**stellen** ▶ TOT; ~|**treten** unr. tr. V. trample ⟨person⟩ to death; step on and kill ⟨insect⟩

Tötung die; ~, ~en killing; **fahrlässige** ~ (Rechtsspr.) manslaughter by culpable negligence

Touch /tatʃ/ der; ~s, ~s (ugs.) touch

tough /taf/ Adj. (ugs.) tough

Toupet /tu'pe:/ das; ~s, ~s toupee

toupieren /tu'pi:rən/ tr. V. backcomb

Tour /tu:r/ die; ~, ~en tour (durch of); (kürzere Fahrt, Ausflug) trip; (mit dem Auto) drive; (mit dem Fahrrad) ride; (feste Strecke) route; **in einer** ~ (ugs.) the whole time

touren /'tu:rən/ itr. V.; mit sein tour

Tourismus /tu'rɪsmʊs/ der; ~: tourism

Tourismus·branche die tourism industry; tourist industry;

Tourist der; ~en, ~en tourist

Touristen-: ~**klasse** die tourist class; ~**paradies** das tourist paradise; ~**zentrum** das tourist centre

Touristin die; ~, ~nen tourist

Tournee /tʊr'ne:/ die; ~, ~s od. ~n tour; **auf** ~ **sein/gehen** be/go on tour

Trab der; ~[e]s trot; **im** ~: at a trot; **im** ~ **reiten** trot

traben itr. V.; mit sein (auch ugs.: laufen) trot

Tracht die; ~, ~en **(a)** (Volkstracht) national costume; (Berufstracht) uniform
(b) **eine** ~ **Prügel** a thrashing; (als Strafe) a hiding

trachten itr. V. (geh.) strive (nach for, after)

Tradition die; ~, ~en tradition

---

traditionẹll ⟦1⟧ *Adj.* traditional
⟦2⟧ *adv.* traditionally

traf *1. u. 3. Pers. Sg. Prät. v.* TREFFEN

träfe *1. u. 3. Pers. Sg. Konjunktiv II v.* TREFFEN

Trafịk *die;* ~, ~en (österr.) tobacconist's [shop]

Trag·bahre *die* stretcher

trạgbar *Adj.* (a) portable
(b) wearable ⟨clothes⟩
(c) (finanziell) supportable ⟨cost, debt, etc.⟩
(d) (erträglich) bearable; tolerable

trạge ⟦1⟧ *Adj.* sluggish
⟦2⟧ *adv.* sluggishly

Trạge *die;* ~, ~n (a) (Bahre) stretcher
(b) (Traggestell) pannier

trạgen ⟦1⟧ *unr. tr. V.* (a) carry
(b) (bringen) take
(c) (ertragen) bear ⟨fate, destiny⟩; bear, endure ⟨suffering⟩
(d) (halten) hold; **einen/den linken Arm in der Schlinge** ~: have one's arm/one's left arm in a sling
(e) (von unten stützen) support
(f) (belastbar sein durch) be able to carry *or* take ⟨weight⟩
(g) (übernehmen, aufkommen für) bear, carry ⟨costs etc.⟩; take ⟨blame, responsibility, consequences⟩
(h) (am Körper) wear ⟨clothes, wig, glasses, jewellery, etc.⟩
(i) have ⟨false teeth, beard, etc.⟩
(j) (hervorbringen) ⟨tree⟩ bear ⟨fruit⟩; ⟨field⟩ produce ⟨crops⟩
⟦2⟧ *unr. itr. V.* (a) carry
(b) (am Körper) **man trägt [wieder] kurz/lang** short/long skirts are in fashion [again]
(c) **der Baum trägt gut** the tree produces a good crop

trạgend *Adj.* (Stabilität gebend) load-bearing; supporting ⟨wall, column, function, etc.⟩

Träger *der;* ~s, ~ (a) porter
(b) (Austräger) paper boy/girl; delivery boy/girl
(c) (Bauw.) girder; [supporting] beam
(d) (an Kleidung) strap; (Hosenträger) braces *pl.;*
(e) (Inhaber) (eines Amts) holder; (eines Namens, Titels) bearer; (eines Preises) winner

Trägerin *die;* ~, ~nen ▶ TRÄGER A, B, E

Trage·tasche *die* carrier bag

Trag-: ~**fähigkeit** *die* load-bearing capacity; ~**fläche** *die* wing; ~**flügel·boot** *das* hydrofoil

Trägheit *die;* ~, ~en sluggishness

Tragik *die;* ~: tragedy

tragi·kọmisch ⟦1⟧ *Adj.* tragicomic
⟦2⟧ *adv.* tragicomically

trạgisch ⟦1⟧ *Adj.* tragic; **das ist nicht [so]** ~ (ugs.) it's not the end of the world (coll.)
⟦2⟧ *adv.* tragically

Tragödie /tra'gøːdiə/ *die;* ~, ~n tragedy

Trag·weite *die* consequences *pl.*

Trainer /'trɛːnɐ/ *der;* ~s, ~, **Trainerin** *die;* ~, ~nen coach; trainer; (einer Fußballmannschaft) manager

trainieren ⟦1⟧ *tr. V.* (a) train; coach ⟨swimmer, tennis player⟩; manage ⟨football team⟩; exercise ⟨muscles etc.⟩
(b) (üben, einüben) practise ⟨exercise, jump, etc.⟩; **Fußball** ~: do football training
⟦2⟧ *itr. V.* train

Training /'trɛːnɪŋ/ *das;* ~s, ~s training *no indef. art.*

Trainings-: ~**anzug** *der* track suit; ~**hose** *die* track-suit bottoms *pl.* ~**lager** *das* training camp

Trạkt *der;* ~[e]s, ~e section; (Flügel) wing

Traktor *der;* ~s, ~en tractor

trạllern *itr., tr. V.* warble

trạmpeln ⟦1⟧ *itr. V.* (a) [mit den Füßen] ~: stamp one's feet
(b) *mit sein* (treten) trample (**auf** + *Akk.* on)
⟦2⟧ *tr. V.* trample

Trạmpel·pfad *der* [beaten] path

trạmpen /'trɛmpn̩/ *itr. V. mit sein* hitch-hike

Trạmper *der;* ~s, ~, **Trạmperin** *die;* ~, ~nen hitch-hiker

Trampolịn *das;* ~s, ~e trampoline

Tramway /'tramveː/ *die;* ~, ~s (österr.) tram (Brit.); streetcar (Amer.)

Trạn *der;* ~[e]s train-oil

Trance /'trãːs(ə)/ *die;* ~, ~n trance; **in** ~: in a trance

tranchieren /trã'ʃiːrən/ *tr. V.* carve

Träne *die;* ~, ~n tear; ~**n lachen** laugh till one cries

tränen *itr. V.* ⟨eyes⟩ water

trạnig *Adj.* (ugs. abwertend: langsam) sluggish; slow

trạnk *1. u. 3. Pers. Sg. Prät. v.* TRINKEN

Tränke *die;* ~, ~n watering place

tränken *tr. V.* (a) water
(b) (sich voll saugen lassen) soak

Transfẹr *der;* ~s, ~s (bes. Wirtsch., Sport) transfer

Transfer·summe *die* transfer fee

Trans·formạtor *der;* ~s, ~en transformer

Transịstor *der;* ~s, ~en transistor

Transịt /tran'ziːt, *auch:* 'tranzɪt/ *das;* ~s, ~s transit visa

transitịv (Sprachw.) ⟦1⟧ *Adj.* transitive
⟦2⟧ *adv.* transitively

Transịt·verkehr *der* transit traffic

transparẹnt *Adj.* transparent; (Licht durchlassend) translucent

Transparẹnt *das;* ~[e]s, ~e (Spruchband) banner; (Bild) transparency

Transparẹnz *die;* ~ transparency

Transpọrt *der;* ~[e]s, ~e (a) transportation ⋯⋯⟶

(b) (beförderte Lebewesen od. Sachen) (mit dem Zug) trainload; (mit mehreren Fahrzeugen) convoy; (Fracht) consignment

transportabel *Adj.* transportable; (tragbar) portable

Transporteur /...'tøːɐ̯/ *der;* ~s, ~e, **Transporteurin** *die;* ~, ~nen carrier

transport·fähig *Adj.* moveable

transportieren *tr. V.* transport ⟨goods, people⟩; move ⟨patient⟩

Transport·kosten *Pl.* carriage *sing.;* transport costs

Transvestit *der;* ~en, ~en transvestite

Trapez *das;* ~es, ~e **(a)** (Geom.) trapezium (Brit.); trapezoid (Amer.)
(b) (im Zirkus) trapeze

trappeln *itr. V.; mit sein* patter [along]; ⟨feet⟩ patter; ⟨hoofs⟩ go clip-clop

Trara *das;* ~s (ugs.) razzmatazz (coll.)

Trasse *die;* ~, ~n (Verkehrsweg) [marked-out] route *or* line

trat *1. u. 3. Pers. Sg. Prät. v.* TRETEN

Tratsch *der;* ~[e]s (ugs.) gossip; tittle-tattle

tratschen *itr. V.* (ugs.) gossip; (schwatzen) chatter

Traube *die;* ~, ~n **(a)** bunch; (von Johannisbeeren usw.) cluster
(b) (Weinbeere~) grape
(c) (Menschenmenge) bunch; cluster

trauen [1] *itr. V.* jmdm./einer Sache ~: trust sb./sth.
[2] *refl. V.* dare
[3] *tr. V.* (verheiraten) ⟨vicar, registrar, etc.⟩ marry

Trauer *die;* ~ **(a)** grief (über + *Akk.* over); (um einen Toten) mourning (um + *Akk.* for);
(b) (Trauerzeit) [period of] mourning
(c) ~ tragen be in mourning

Trauer-: ~fall *der* bereavement; ~feier *die* memorial ceremony; (beim Begräbnis) funeral ceremony; ~karte *die* [pre-printed] card of condolence; ~kleidung *die* mourning clothes *pl.*

trauern *itr. V.* mourn; um jmdn. ~: mourn for sb.

Trauer-: ~spiel *das* tragedy; (fig. ugs.) deplorable business; ~weide *die* weeping willow

träufeln *tr. V.* [let] trickle (in + *Akk.* into); drip ⟨ear drops etc.⟩

Traum *der;* ~[e]s, Träume /'trɔy:mə/ dream

Trauma *das;* ~s, Traumen *od.* ~ta (Psych., Med.) trauma

traumatisch (Psych., Med.) [1] *Adj.* traumatic
[2] *adv.* traumatically

träumen [1] *itr. V.* dream (von of, about); (unaufmerksam sein) [day]dream
[2] *tr. V.* dream

Träumer *der;* ~s, ~, **Träumerin** *die;* ~, ~nen dreamer

träumerisch [1] *Adj.* dreamy
[2] *adv.* dreamily

traumhaft (ugs.) [1] *Adj.* marvellous; fabulous (coll.)
[2] *adv.* fabulously (coll.)

Traum·urlaub *der* dream holiday

traurig [1] *Adj.* **(a)** sad; unhappy ⟨childhood, youth⟩; painful ⟨duty⟩
(b) (kümmerlich) sorry ⟨state etc.⟩; miserable ⟨result⟩
[2] *adv.* sadly

Traurigkeit *die;* ~: sadness; sorrow

Trau-: ~ring *der* wedding ring; ~schein *der* marriage certificate

Trauung *die;* ~, ~en wedding [ceremony]

Trau·zeuge *der,* **Trau·zeugin** *die* witness (at wedding ceremony)

Trecker *der;* ~s, ~: tractor

Treff *der;* ~s, ~s (ugs.) rendezvous; (Ort) meeting place

treffen [1] *unr. tr. V.* **(a)** hit; ⟨punch, blow, object⟩ strike; **ihn trifft keine Schuld** he is in no way to blame
(b) (erschüttern) affect [deeply]; (verletzen) hurt
(c) (begegnen) meet
(d) (vorfinden) come upon, find ⟨anomalies etc.⟩; **es gut/schlecht** ~: be *or* strike lucky/be unlucky
(e) (als Funktionsverb) make ⟨arrangements, choice, preparations, decision, etc.⟩
[2] *unr. itr. V.* **(a)** ⟨person, shot, etc.⟩ hit the target; **nicht** ~: miss [the target]
(b) *mit sein* auf etw. (*Akk.*) ~: come upon sth.; **auf Widerstand/Ablehnung/Schwierigkeiten** ~: meet with resistance/rejection/difficulties
[3] *unr. refl. V.* **(a)** sich mit jmdm. ~: meet sb.
(b) *unpers.* **es trifft sich gut/schlecht** it is convenient/inconvenient

Treffen *das;* ~s, ~: meeting

treffend [1] *Adj.* apt
[2] *adv.* aptly

Treffer *der;* ~s, ~ **(a)** (Milit., Boxen, Fechten usw.) hit; (Schlag) blow; (Ballspiele) goal
(b) (Gewinn) win; (Los) winner

trefflich (geh.) [1] *Adj.* excellent; splendid ⟨person⟩
[2] *adv.* excellently; splendidly

treff-, Treff-: ~punkt *der* meeting place; ~sicher [1] *Adj.* accurate ⟨language, mode of expression⟩; unerring ⟨judgement⟩; [2] *adv.* accurately; ~sicherheit *die* accuracy

Treib·eis *das* drift-ice

treiben [1] *unr. tr. V.* **(a)** drive
(b) (sich beschäftigen mit) go in for ⟨farming, cattle breeding, etc.⟩; study ⟨French etc.⟩; carry on, pursue ⟨studies, trade, craft⟩; **viel Sport** ~: do a lot of sport; **es wüst/übel/toll** ~ (ugs.) lead a dissolute/bad life/live it up

2 *unr. itr. V. meist, mit Richtungsangabe nur, mit sein* drift

Treiben *das;* ~s **(a)** (Durcheinander) bustle **(b)** (Tun) activities *pl.;* doings *pl.*

Treib-: ~**gas** *das* propellant; ~**haus** *das* hothouse; ~**haus·effekt** *der* greenhouse effect; ~**haus·gas** *das* greenhouse gas; ~**stoff** *der* fuel

trekken /'trɛkn̩/ *itr. V.; mit sein* trek

Trekking *das;* ~s trekking

Trenchcoat /'trɛntʃkoʊt/ *der;* ~s, ~s trench coat

Trend *der;* ~s, ~s trend (**zu** + *Dat.* towards); (Mode) vogue

trendig *Adj.* (ugs.) modern and fashionable

trennen **1** *tr. V.* **(a)** separate (**von** from); sever ⟨*head, arm*⟩ **(b)** (auftrennen) unpick ⟨*dress, seam*⟩ **(c)** (teilen) divide ⟨*word, parts of a room etc., fig.: people*⟩ **2** *refl. V.* **(a)** (voneinander weggehen) part [company] **(b)** (eine Partnerschaft auflösen) ⟨*couple, partners*⟩ split up **(c) sich von etw.** ~: part with sth.

Trennung *die;* ~, ~en (von Menschen) separation (**von** from); (von Gegenständen) parting; (von Wörtern) division

trepp-: ~**ab** *Adv.* down the stairs; ~**auf** *Adv.* up the stairs

Treppe *die;* ~, ~n staircase; [flight *sing.* of] stairs *pl.;* (im Freien, auf der Bühne) [flight *sing.* of] steps *pl.*

Treppen-: ~**absatz** *der* half-landing; ~**geländer** *das* banisters *pl.;* ~**haus** *das* stairwell; ~**stufe** *die* stair; (im Freien) step

Tresen *der;* ~s, ~ (bes. nordd.) bar; (Ladentisch) counter

Tresor *der;* ~s, ~e safe

Tret·boot *das* pedalo

treten **1** *unr. itr. V.* **(a)** *mit sein* step (**in** + *Akk.* into, **auf** + *Akk.* on to) **(b)** (seinen Fuß setzen) **auf etw.** (*Akk.*) ~ tread on sth. **(c)** (ausschlagen) kick **2** *unr. tr. V.* **(a)** (Tritt versetzen) kick ⟨*person, ball, etc.*⟩ **(b)** (trampeln) trample ⟨*path*⟩ **(c)** (mit dem Fuß niederdrücken) step on ⟨*brake, pedal*⟩; operate ⟨*bellows, clutch*⟩

treu **1** *Adj.* faithful; loyal; faithful ⟨*husband, wife*⟩; loyal ⟨*ally, subject*⟩; **jmdm.** ~ **sein** be true to sb.; **sich selbst** (*Dat.*)/ **seinem Glauben** ~ **bleiben** be true to oneself/one's faith **2** *adv.* faithfully; loyally

Treue *die;* ~ **(a)** loyalty; (von [Ehe]partnern) fidelity **(b)** (Genauigkeit) accuracy

treu-, Treu-: ~**hand[anstalt]** *die* (Wirtschaft) German privatization agency; ~**herzig** **1** *Adj.* ingenuous; (naiv) naïve; (unschuldig) innocent; **2** *adv.* ingenuously;

(naiv) naïvely; (unschuldig) innocently; ~**herzigkeit** *die;* ~~: ingenuousness; (Naivität) naivety; (Unschuld) innocence; ~**los** *Adj.* disloyal, faithless ⟨*friend, person*⟩; unfaithful ⟨*husband, wife, lover*⟩

Tribunal *das;* ~s, ~e tribunal

Tribüne *die;* ~, ~n [grand]stand

Tribut *der;* ~[e]s, ~e (fig.) due; **einer Sache** (*Dat.*) ~ **zollen** pay the price for sth.

Trichter *der;* ~s, ~ funnel

Trick *der;* ~s, ~s trick; (fig.: List) ploy

Trick·film *der* animated cartoon [film]

trieb *1. u. 3. Pers. Sg. Prät. v.* TREIBEN

Trieb *der;* ~[e]s, ~e **(a)** (innerer Antrieb) impulse; (Drang) urge; (Verlangen) [compulsive] desire **(b)** (Spross) shoot

trieb-, Trieb-: ~**feder** *die* mainspring; (fig.) driving *or* motivating force; ~**haft** **1** *Adj.* compulsive; carnal ⟨*sensuality*⟩; **2** *adv.* compulsively; ~**täter** *der,* ~**täterin** *die,* ~**verbrecher** *der,* ~**verbrecherin** *die: offender committing a crime in gratifying a compulsive desire;* (Sexualtäter) sexual offender; ~**wagen** *der* (Eisenb.) railcar; ~**werk** *das* engine

triefen *unr. od. regelm. itr. V.* **(a)** *mit sein* (fließen) (in Tropfen) drip; (in kleinen Rinnsalen) trickle **(b)** (nass sein) be dripping wet; ⟨*nose*⟩ run

triff *Imperativ Sg. v.* TREFFEN

trifft *3. Pers. Sg. Präsens v.* TREFFEN

triftig *Adj.* good ⟨*reason, excuse*⟩; valid, convincing ⟨*motive, argument*⟩

Trikot[1] /tri'ko:/ *der od. das;* ~s, ~s (Stoff) cotton jersey

Trikot[2] /tri'ko:/ *das;* ~s, ~ (ärmellos) singlet; (eines Tänzers) leotard; (eines Fußballspielers) shirt

Triller *der;* ~s, ~: trill

trillern **1** *itr. V.* trill **2** *tr. V.* warble ⟨*song*⟩

Triller·pfeife *die* police/referee's whistle

Trillion *die;* ~, ~en quintillion

Trimm-dich-Pfad *der* keep-fit trail

trimmen *tr. V.* (durch Sport) get ⟨*person*⟩ into shape

trinken **1** *unr. itr. V.* drink; **auf jmdn./etw.** ~: drink to sb./sth. **2** *unr. tr. V.* drink; **einen Kaffee/ein Bier** ~: have a coffee/beer

Trinker *der;* ~s, ~: alcoholic

Trinkerei *die;* ~, ~en drinking *no art.*

Trinkerin *die;* ~, ~nen alcoholic

Trink-: ~**geld** *das* tip; ~**halle** *die* **(a)** (in einem Heilbad) pump room; **(b)** (Kiosk) refreshment kiosk; (größer) refreshment stall; ~**wasser** *das* drinking water; „**kein** ~**wasser**" 'not for drinking'

Trio *das;* ~s, ~s (Musik, fig.) trio

Trip *der;* ~s, ~s **(a)** (ugs.: Ausflug) trip; jaunt **(b)** (Drogenjargon: Rausch) trip (coll.) ⋯⁝

(c) (Drogenjargon: Dosis) fix (sl.)

trippeln *itr. V.; mit sein* trip; ⟨*child*⟩ patter

trist *Adj.* dreary; dismal

tritt *Imperativ Sg. u. 3. Pers. Sg. Präsens v.*
TRETEN

Tritt *der;* ~[e]s, ~e (Schritt; Trittbrett) step;
(Fußtritt) kick

Tritt-: ~**brett** *das* step; ~**brett·fahrer**
der, ~**brett·fahrerin** *die* (fig. abwertend) ≈
free rider (Amer.); *person who profits from
another's work*

Triumph *der;* ~[e]s, ~e triumph

triumphieren *itr. V.* **(a)** exult
(b) (siegen) be triumphant; triumph (lit. or fig.)
(über + *Akk.* over)

trivial 1 *Adj.* **(a)** (platt) banal; trite;
(unbedeutend) trivial
(b) (alltäglich) humdrum ⟨*life, career*⟩
2 *adv.* (platt) banally; ⟨*say etc.*⟩ tritely

trocken 1 *Adj.* (auch fig.) dry
2 *adv.* drily

Trocken·haube *die* [hood-type] hairdrier

Trockenheit *die;* ~, ~en **(a)** dryness
(b) (Dürreperiode) drought

trocken-, Trocken-: ~**legen** *tr. V.* **(a)**
ein Baby ~legen change a baby's nappies
(Brit.) *or* (Amer.) diapers; **(b)** (entwässern) drain
⟨*marsh, pond, etc.*⟩; ~**milch** *die* dried milk;
~|**reiben** *unr. tr. V.* rub ⟨*hair, child, etc.*⟩
dry; wipe ⟨*crockery, window, etc.*⟩ dry

trocknen 1 *itr. V.; meist mit sein* dry
2 *tr. V.* dry

Troddel *die;* ~, ~n tassel

Trödel *der;* ~s (ugs.) junk; (für den Flohmarkt)
jumble

trödeln *itr. V.* **(a)** (ugs.) dawdle (**mit** over)
(b) *mit sein* (ugs.: schlendern) saunter

Trödler *der;* ~s, ~, **Trödlerin** *die;* ~,
~**nen** (ugs.) junk dealer

troff *1. u. 3. Pers. Sg. Prät. v.* TRIEFEN

trog *1. u. 3. Pers. Sg. Prät. v.* TRÜGEN

Trog *der;* ~[e]s, Tröge trough

trollen (ugs.) *refl. V.* push off (coll.)

Trommel *die;* ~, ~n drum

Trommel·bremse *die* drum brake

trommeln *itr. V.* **(a)** beat the drum; (als
Beruf, Hobby usw.) play the drums
(b) ([auf etw.] schlagen, auftreffen) drum (**auf** +
Akk. on, **an** + *Akk.* against)

Trommel·wirbel *der* drum roll

Trommler *der;* ~s, ~ drummer

Trompete *die;* ~, ~n trumpet

trompeten 1 *itr. V.* play the trumpet; (fig.)
⟨*elephant*⟩ trumpet
2 *tr. V.* play ⟨*piece*⟩ on the trumpet

Trompeter *der;* ~s, ~, **Trompeterin**
die; ~, ~**nen** trumpeter

Tropen *Pl.* tropics

Tropen- tropical

---

*alte Schreibung - vgl. Hinweis auf S. xiv

Tropen·helm *der* sun helmet

Tropf *der;* ~[e]s, ~e (Med.) drip

Tröpfchen *das;* ~s, ~: droplet; (kleine
Menge) drop

tröpfeln 1 *itr. V.* **(a)** *mit sein* drip (**auf** +
Akk. on to, **aus, von** from)
(b) *unpers.* (ugs.: leicht regnen) **es tröpfelt** it's
spitting [with rain]
2 *tr. V.* let ⟨*sth.*⟩ drip (**in** + *Akk.* into, **auf** +
Akk. on to)

tropfen 1 *itr. V.; mit Richtungsangabe mit
sein* drip; ⟨*tears*⟩ fall; *unpers.* **es tropft [vom
Dach** *usw.*] water is dripping from the roof
etc.;
2 *tr. V.* let ⟨*sth.*⟩ drip (**in** + *Akk.* into, **auf** +
Akk. on to)

Tropfen *der;* ~s, ~ drop; **ein guter/edler** ~:
a good/fine vintage

Tropf·stein·höhle *die* limestone cave
with stalactites and/or stalagmites

Trophäe *die;* ~, ~n (hist., Jagd, Sport) trophy

tropisch *Adj.* tropical

Tross, *Troß *der;* Trosses, Trosse
(a) (Milit.) baggage train
(b) (Gefolge) retinue; (fig.: Zug) procession [of
hangers-on]

Trost *der;* ~[e]s consolation; (bes. geistlich)
comfort; **nicht [ganz** *od.* **recht] bei** ~ **sein**
(ugs.) be out of one's mind

trösten 1 *tr. V.* comfort, console (**mit** with)
2 *refl. V.* console oneself

tröstlich *Adj.* comforting

trost·los *Adj.* **(a)** hopeless; (verzweifelt) in
despair *postpos.;*
(b) (deprimierend, öde) miserable; dreary;
hopeless ⟨*situation*⟩

Trostlosigkeit *die;* ~ **(a)** (einer Person, der
Lage usw.) hopelessness; (Verzweiflung)
despair
(b) (Öde) dreariness

Trost·preis *der* consolation prize

Tröstung *die;* ~, ~en comfort *no indef. art.*

Trott *der;* ~[e]s, ~e trot; (fig.) routine

Trottel *der;* ~s, ~ (ugs.) fool

trottelig (ugs.) 1 *Adj.* doddery
2 *adv.* in a feeble-minded way

trotten *itr. V.; mit sein* trot [along]

trotz *Präp. mit Gen., seltener mit Dat.* in
spite of; despite

Trotz *der;* ~es defiance

trotz·dem /*auch:* '-'-/ *Adv.* nevertheless

trotzen *itr. V.* **(a)** (geh.: widerstehen) jmdm./
einer Sache ~ (auch fig.) defy sb./sth.
(b) (trotzig sein) be contrary

trotzig 1 *Adj.* defiant; (widerspenstig)
contrary; difficult ⟨*child*⟩
2 *adv.* defiantly

trüb[e] 1 *Adj.* **(a)** (nicht klar) murky ⟨*stream,
water*⟩; cloudy ⟨*liquid, wine, juice*⟩;
(schlammig) muddy ⟨*puddle*⟩; (schmutzig) dirty
⟨*glass, window pane*⟩; dull ⟨*eyes*⟩

(b) (nicht hell) dim ⟨*light*⟩; dull, dismal ⟨*day, weather*⟩; grey, overcast ⟨*sky*⟩
2 *adv.* ⟨*shine, light*⟩ dimly

Trubel *der;* ~s [hustle and] bustle; **sie stürzten sich in den dicksten ~:** they plunged into the thick of the hurly-burly

trüben 1 *tr. V.* **(a)** make ⟨*liquid*⟩ cloudy; cloud ⟨*liquid*⟩
(b) (beeinträchtigen) dampen ⟨*mood*⟩; mar ⟨*relationship*⟩; cloud ⟨*judgement*⟩
2 *refl. V.* ⟨*liquid*⟩ become cloudy; ⟨*eyes*⟩ become dull; ⟨*sky*⟩ darken

Trübsal *die;* ~, ~e (geh.) **(a)** (Leiden) affliction
(b) (Kummer) grief; ~ **blasen** (ugs.) mope (**wegen** over, about)

trüb-, Trüb-: ~**selig** 1 *Adj.* **(a)** (öde) dreary, depressing ⟨*place, area, colour*⟩; **(b)** (traurig) gloomy; 2 *adv.* (traurig) gloomily;
~**seligkeit** *die:* **(a)** (Ödheit) dreariness; **(b)** (Traurigkeit) gloom; ~**sinn** *der* melancholy; ~**sinnig** 1 *Adj.* melancholy; 2 *adv.* gloomily

Trübung *die;* ~, ~en **(a)** clouding; (des Auges) dimming
(b) (Beeinträchtigung) deterioration; (der Stimmung) dampening

trudeln *itr. V. mit sein* roll

Trüffel *die;* ~, ~n truffle

trug *1. u. 3. Pers. Prät. v.* TRAGEN

trüge *1. u. 3. Pers. Sg. Konjunktiv II v.* TRAGEN

trügen 1 *unr. tr. V.* deceive
2 *unr. itr. V.* be deceptive; ⟨*feeling, deception*⟩ be a delusion

trügerisch 1 *Adj.* deceptive; false ⟨*hope, sign, etc.*⟩; treacherous ⟨*ice*⟩
2 *adv.* deceptively

Truhe *die;* ~, ~n chest

Trümmer *Pl.* (eines Gebäudes) rubble *sing.;* (Ruinen) ruins; (eines Flugzeugs usw.) wreckage *sing.;* (kleinere Teile) debris *sing.*

Trümmer·haufen *der* pile *or* heap of rubble

Trumpf *der;* ~[e]s, Trümpfe (auch fig.) trump [card]; (Farbe) trumps *pl.;* ~ **sein** (fig.: Mode sein) be the in thing

trumpfen *itr. V.* play a trump

Trunk *der;* ~[e]s, Trünke (geh.) (Getränk) drink; beverage (formal)

Trunkenheit *die;* ~: drunkenness; ~ **am Steuer** drink-driving

Trunk·sucht *die* alcoholism *no art.*

trunk·süchtig *Adj.* alcoholic; ~ **sein** be an alcoholic

Trupp *der;* ~s, ~s troop; (von Arbeitern, Gefangenen) gang; (von Soldaten, Polizisten) squad

Truppe *die;* ~, ~n **(a)** (Einheit der Streitkräfte) unit
(b) *Pl.* (Soldaten) troops
(c) (Streitkräfte) [armed] forces *pl.;* (Heer) army
(d) (Gruppe von Schauspielern, Artisten) troupe; (von Sportlern) squad

Trut·hahn *der* turkey [cock]

tschau *Interj.* (ugs.) ciao (coll.)

Tscheche *der;* ~n, ~n Czech

Tschechien (*das*)*;* ~s Czech Republic

Tschechin *die;* ~, ~nen Czech

tschechisch *Adj.* Czech

Tschechoslowakei *die;* ~ (hist.) Czechoslovakia *no art.*

tschechoslowakisch *Adj.* (hist.) Czechoslovak[ian]

tschüs *Interj.* (ugs.) bye (coll.)

Tsd. *Abk.* = **Tausend**

T-Shirt /'ti:ʃə:t/ *das;* ~s, ~s T-shirt

Tube *die;* ~, ~n tube

Tuberkulose *die;* ~, ~n (Med.) tuberculosis *no art.*

Tuch *das;* ~[e]s, Tücher *od.* ~e **(a)** *Pl.* Tücher cloth; (Kopf-, Halstuch) scarf
(b) *Pl.* ~e (Gewebe) cloth

Tuch·fühlung *die* (scherzh.) physical contact

tüchtig 1 *Adj.* **(a)** efficient; (fähig) capable, competent (**in** + *Dat.* at)
(b) (ugs.: beträchtlich) sizeable ⟨*piece, portion*⟩; big ⟨*gulp*⟩; hearty ⟨*eater, appetite*⟩
2 *adv.* **(a)** efficiently; (fähig) competently
(b) (ugs.: sehr) really ⟨*cold, warm*⟩; ⟨*snow, rain*⟩ good and proper (coll.); ⟨*eat*⟩ heartily

Tüchtigkeit *die;* ~: efficiency; (Fähigkeit) ability; competence; (Fleiß) industry

Tücke *die;* ~, ~n **(a)** (Hinterhältigkeit) deceit[fulness]; (List) guile
(b) ([verborgene] Gefahr/Schwierigkeit) [hidden] danger/difficulty

tuckern *itr. V.; mit Richtungsangabe mit sein* chug

tückisch 1 *Adj.* **(a)** (hinterhältig) wily; (betrügerisch) deceitful
(b) (gefährlich) treacherous ⟨*bend, slope, spot, etc.*⟩
2 *adv.* craftily

tüfteln *itr. V.* (ugs.) fiddle (**an** + *Dat.* with); do finicky work (**an** + *Dat.* on); (geistig) rack one's brains (**an** + *Dat.* over)

Tugend *die;* ~, ~en virtue

tugendhaft 1 *Adj.* virtuous
2 *adv.* virtuously

Tüll *der;* ~s, ~e tulle

Tülle *die;* ~, ~n (bes. nordd.) spout

Tulpe *die;* ~, ~n tulip

tummeln *refl. V.* romp (about)

Tummel·platz *der* (auch fig.) playground

Tumor *der;* ~s, ~en (Med.) tumour

Tümpel *der;* ~s, ~: pond

Tumult *der;* ~[e]s, ~e tumult; commotion; (Protest) uproar

tun 1 *unr. tr. V.* **(a)** do; **so etwas tut man nicht** that is just not done; [**etwas**] **mit etw./jmdm. zu ~ haben** be concerned with sth./ have dealings with sb.
(b) als *Funktionsverb* make ⟨*remark, catch, etc.*⟩; take ⟨*step, jump*⟩; do ⟨*deed*⟩   ···⋄

(c) (bewirken) work, perform ‹miracle›
(d) (antun) jmdm. etw. ~: do sth. to sb.
(e) es ~ (ugs.: genügen) be good enough
(f) (ugs.: irgendwohin bringen) put
[2] *unr. itr. V.* **(a)** (ugs.: funktionieren) work
(b) freundlich/geheimnisvoll ~: pretend to be or (coll.) act friendly/act mysteriously
[3] *unr. refl. V.; unpers.* **es hat sich einiges getan** quite a bit has happened
Tünche *die;* ~, ~n distemper; wash; [weiße] ~: whitewash
tünchen *tr. (auch itr.) V.* distemper; weiß ~: whitewash
Tunell *das;* ~s, ~s (südd., österr., schweiz.) ▶ TUNNEL
tunen /'tjuːnən/ *tr. V.* (Kfz-W.) tune
Tuner /'tjuːnɐ/ *der;* ~s, ~(a) (Elektronik) tuner
(b) (Kfz-W.) tuner; tuning expert
Tunesien /tu'neːzjən/ *(das);* ~s Tunisia
tunesisch *Adj.* Tunisian
Tunke *die;* ~, ~n (bes. ostmd.) sauce; (Bratensoße) gravy
tunken *tr. V.* (bes. ostmd.) dip
tunlichst *Adv.* (geh.) **(a)** (möglichst) as far as possible
(b) (unbedingt) at all costs
Tunnel *der;* ~s, ~ *od.* ~s tunnel
tupfen *tr. V.* **(a)** dab
(b) (mit Tupfen versehen) dot
Tupfen *der;* ~s, ~: dot; (größer) spot
Tupfer *der;* ~s, ~ (Med.) swab
Tür *die;* ~, ~en door; (Garten~) gate; **an die** ~ **gehen** (öffnen) [go and] answer the door; **vor die** ~ **gehen** go outside
Turban *der;* ~s, ~e turban
Turbine *die;* ~, ~n turbine
turbulent [1] *Adj.* (auch fachspr.) turbulent
[2] *adv.* (auch fachspr.) turbulently
Turbulenz *die;* ~, ~en (auch Physik, Astron., Met.) turbulence *no pl.*
Tür-griff *der* door handle
Türke *der;* ~n, ~n Turk
Türkei *die;* ~: Turkey *no art.*
türken *tr. V.* (ugs.) fake ‹scene, letter, document, etc.›; make up ‹story, report›
Türkin *die;* ~, ~nen Turk
türkis *indekl. Adj.* turquoise
Türkis *der;* ~es, ~e turquoise
türkisch *Adj.* Turkish
Tür-klinke *die* door handle
Turm *der;* ~[e]s, Türme **(a)** tower; (spitzer Kirchturm) spire; steeple
(b) (Schach) rook
(c) (Sprungturm) diving platform
Türmchen *das;* ~s, ~: turret

türmen[1] [1] *tr. V.* (stapeln) stack up; (häufen) pile up
[2] *refl. V.* be piled up; ‹clouds› gather
türmen[2] *itr. V.; mit sein* (salopp) scarper (Brit. coll.)
Turm-falke *der* kestrel
turnen [1] *itr. V.* do gymnastics; (Schulw.) do gym
[2] *tr. V.* do, perform ‹exercise, routine›
Turnen *das;* ~s gymnastics *sing., no art.;* (Schulw.) gym *no art.;* PE *no art.*
Turner *der;* ~s, ~, **Turnerin** *die;* ~, ~nen gymnast
Turn-: ~**halle** *die* gymnasium; ~**hemd** *das* [gym] singlet; ~**hose** *die* gym shorts *pl.*
Turnier *das;* ~s, ~e (auch hist.) tournament; (Reitturnier) show; (Tanzturnier) competition
Turn-schuh *der* gym shoe
Turnus *der;* ~, ~se regular cycle
Turn-verein *der* gymnastics club
Tür-: ~**öffner** *der* door-opener; ~**rahmen** *der* doorframe
turteln *itr. V.* (scherzh.: zärtlich sein) bill and coo
Tusch *der;* ~[e]s, ~e fanfare
Tusche *die;* ~, ~n Indian (Brit.) *or* (Amer.) India ink
Tuschelei *die;* ~, ~en **(a)** (das Tuscheln) whispering
(b) (Äußerung) whisper
tuscheln *itr., tr. V.* whisper
Tussi *die;* ~, ~s (salopp) female (derog.)
Tüte *die;* ~, ~n bag
tuten *itr. V.* hoot; ‹siren, [fog]horn› sound
Tutor *der;* ~s, ~en, **Tutorin** *die;* ~, ~nen (Päd.) tutor
Tycoon /tai'kuːn/ *der;* ~s, ~s tycoon
Typ *der;* ~s, ~en **(a)** type
(b) *Gen. auch* ~en (ugs.: Mann) bloke (Brit. coll.)
Type *die;* ~, ~n (Druck-, Schreibmaschinentype) type
Typhus *der;* ~: typhoid [fever]
typisch [1] *Adj.* typical (**für** of)
[2] *adv.* typically
Typographie *die;* ~, ~n (Druckw.) typography
typographisch (Druckw.) [1] *Adj.* typographical
[2] *adv.* typographically
Tyrann *der;* ~en, ~en (auch fig.) tyrant
Tyrannei *die;* ~, ~en (auch fig.) tyranny
Tyrannin *die;* ~, ~nen ▶ TYRANN
tyrannisch [1] *Adj.* tyrannical
[2] *adv.* tyrannically
tyrannisieren *tr. V.* tyrannize

---

*old spelling - see note on page xiv

U u

u, U /uː/ *das;* ~, ~: u/U

u. *Abk.* = **und**

ü, Ü /yː/ *das;* ~, ~: u umlaut

U-Bahn *die* underground (Brit.); subway (Amer.); (bes. in London) tube

U-Bahnhof *der;* U-Bahn-Station *die* underground station (Brit.); subway station (Amer.); (bes. in London) tube station

übel *Adj.* **(a)** foul, nasty ⟨*smell, weather*⟩; bad, nasty ⟨*headache, cold, taste*⟩; nasty ⟨*consequences, situation*⟩; sorry ⟨*state, affair*⟩; foul, (coll.) filthy ⟨*mood*⟩; **nicht** ~ (ugs.) not bad at all

(b) (unwohl) **jmdm. ist/wird** ~: sb. feels sick

(c) (verwerflich) bad; wicked; nasty, dirty ⟨*trick*⟩

(d) jmdm. etw. ~ **nehmen** hold sth. against sb.; **etw.** ~ **nehmen** take offence at sth.

Übel *das;* ~s, ~: evil

Übelkeit *die;* ~, ~en nausea

*übel|nehmen ▶ ÜBEL D

Übel·täter *der,* **Übel·täterin** *die* wrongdoer

üben *tr. V.* **(a)** (*auch itr.*) practise; rehearse ⟨*scene, play*⟩; practise on ⟨*musical instrument*⟩

(b) (trainieren, schulen) exercise ⟨*fingers*⟩; train ⟨*memory*⟩

über [1] *Präp. mit Dat.* **(a)** (Lage, Standort) over; above; (in einer Rangfolge) above; ~ **jmdm. wohnen** live above sb.; **zehn Grad** ~ **Null** ten degrees above zero; **sie trug eine Jacke** ~ **dem Kleid** she wore a jacket over her dress

(b) (während) during; ~ **dem Lesen/der Arbeit einschlafen** fall asleep over one's book/ magazine *etc.*/over one's work

[2] *Präp. mit Akk.* **(a)** (Richtung) over; (quer hinüber) across; ~ **Ulm nach Stuttgart** via Ulm to Stuttgart

(b) (während) over; (für die Dauer von) for

(c) (betreffend) about; ~ **etw. reden/schreiben** talk/write about sth.; **ein Scheck/eine Rechnung** ~ **100 Euro** a cheque/bill for 100 euros

(d) Kinder ~ **10 Jahre** children over ten [years of age]

[3] *Adv.* **(a)** (mehr als) over

(b) ~ **und** ~: all over

über·all /*od.* -'-/ *Adv.* **(a)** everywhere

(b) (bei jeder Gelegenheit) always

überall-: ~**her** *Adv.* from all over the place; ~**hin** *Adv.* everywhere

Über·angebot *das* surplus (an + *Dat.* of); (Schwemme) glut (an + *Dat.* of)

über·anstrengen *tr. V.; ich*

überanstrenge, überanstrengt, zu überanstrengen overtax ⟨*person, energy*⟩; strain ⟨*eyes, nerves, heart*⟩; **sich** ~: overexert oneself

über·arbeiten [1] *tr. V.* rework; revise ⟨*text, edition*⟩

[2] *refl. V.* overwork

über·aus *Adv.* (geh.) extremely

über·backen *unr. tr. V.* **etw. mit Käse** *usw.* ~: top sth. with cheese *etc.* and brown it lightly [under the grill/in a hot oven]

Über·bein *das* (Med.) ganglion

überbelichten *tr. V.; ich* überbelichte, überbelichtet, überzubelichten (Fot.) overexpose

über·bieten *unr. tr. V.* **(a)** outbid (um by)

(b) (übertreffen) surpass; outdo ⟨*rival*⟩; break ⟨*record*⟩ (um by); exceed ⟨*target*⟩ (um by)

Über·blick *der* **(a)** view; **einen guten** ~ **über etw.** (*Akk.*) **haben** have a good view over sth.

(b) (Abriss) survey

(c) (Einblick) overall view

über·blicken *tr. V.* ▶ ÜBERSEHEN A, B

über·bringen *unr. tr. V.* deliver; convey ⟨*greetings, congratulations*⟩

über·brücken *tr. V.* bridge ⟨*gap, gulf*⟩; reconcile ⟨*difference*⟩

Über·brückung *die;* ~, ~en (fig.) bridging; (von Gegensätzen) reconciliation

über·buchen *tr. V.* overbook

überdacht *Adj.* covered ⟨*terrace, station platform, etc.*⟩

über·dauern *tr. V.* survive ⟨*war, separation, hardship*⟩

über·dehnen *tr. V.* overstretch; strain ⟨*muscle*⟩

über·dies *Adv.* moreover

Über·dosis *die* overdose

Über·druck *der; Pl.* Überdrücke excess pressure

Überdruss, *Überdruß *der;* Überdrusses surfeit (an + *Dat.* of)

überdrüssig *Adj.* **jmds./einer Sache** ~ **sein/werden** be/grow tired of sb./sth.

über·eignen *tr. V.* **jmdm. etw.** ~: transfer sth. *or* make sth. over to sb.

Über·eignung *die* transfer (an + *Akk.* to)

über·eilen *tr. V.* rush; **übereilt** overhasty

über·einander *Adv.* **(a)** one on top of the other; **Holzscheite** *usw.*: ~ **legen** lay pieces of wood *etc.* one on top of the other; **Arme/ Beine** ~ **schlagen** fold one's arms/cross one's legs

(b) ⟨*talk etc.*⟩ about each other

*übereinạnder|legen *usw.*
▶ ÜBEREINANDER A

überein|kommen *unr. itr. V.; mit sein*
agree; come to an agreement

Überein·kommen *das; ~s, ~,*

Übereinkunft *die; ~,* Übereinkünfte
agreement

überein|stimmen *itr. V.* (a) (einer Meinung sein) agree (in + *Dat.* on)
(b) (sich gleichen) ⟨*colours, styles*⟩ match; ⟨*figures, statements, reports, results*⟩ tally, agree; ⟨*views, opinions*⟩ coincide

Überein·stimmung *die* agreement (in + *Dat.* on; *Gen.* between)

über·empfindlich ⒈ *Adj.* oversensitive (gegen to); (Med.) hypersensitive (gegen to)
⒉ *adv.* oversensitively; (Med.) hypersensitively

Über·empfindlichkeit *die*
oversensitivity (gegen to); (Med.)
hypersensitivity (gegen to)

über|fahren¹ ⒈ *unr. tr. V.* jmdn. ~: ferry *or* take sb. over
⒉ *unr. itr. V.; mit sein* cross over

über·fahren² *unr. tr. V.* (a) run over
(b) (hinwegfahren über) cross; go over ⟨*crossroads*⟩

Über·fahrt *die* crossing (über + *Akk.* of)

Über·fall *der* attack (auf + *Akk.* on); (aus dem Hinterhalt) ambush (auf + *Akk.* on); (mit vorgehaltener Waffe) hold-up; (auf eine Bank o. Ä.) raid (auf + *Akk.* on)

über·fallen *unr. tr. V.* (a) attack; raid ⟨*bank, enemy position, village, etc.*⟩; (hinterrücks) ambush; (mit vorgehaltener Waffe) hold up
(b) (überkommen) ⟨*tiredness, homesickness, fear*⟩ come over

über·fällig *Adj.* overdue

über·fischen *tr. V.* overfish

über·fliegen *unr. tr. V.* (a) fly over; overfly (formal)
(b) (flüchtig lesen) skim [through]

über·flügeln *tr. V.* outshine; outstrip

Über·fluss, *****Über·fluß** *der* abundance (an + *Dat.* of); (Wohlstand) affluence

über·flüssig *Adj.* superfluous; unnecessary ⟨*purchase, words, work*⟩

über·fluten *tr. V.* (auch fig.) flood

Über|flutung *die; ~, ~en* (auch fig.) flooding

über·fordern *tr. V.* jmdn. [mit etw.] ~: overtax sb. [with sth.]; ask *or* demand too much of sb. [with sth.]

über·fragen *tr. V.* da bin ich überfragt
I don't know the answer to that

über·fremden *tr. V.* überfremdet werden/ sein ⟨*country*⟩ be dominated [by foreign influences]

Über·fremdung *die; ~, ~en* domination [by foreign influences]

über·frieren *unr. itr. V.; mit sein* freeze over; ~de Nässe black ice

über|führen¹ *tr. V.* transfer

über·führen² *tr. V.* (a) ▶ ÜBERFÜHREN¹;
(b) jmdn. [eines Verbrechens] ~: convict sb. [of a crime]

Über·führung *die* (a) transfer
(b) (eines Verdächtigen) conviction
(c) (Brücke) bridge; (Hochstraße) overpass; (für Fußgänger) [foot]bridge

über·füllt *Adj.* crammed full (von with); (mit Menschen) overcrowded (von with); oversubscribed ⟨*course*⟩

Über·gabe *die* (a) handing over (an + *Akk.* to); (von Macht) handing over
(b) (Auslieferung an den Gegner) surrender (an + *Akk.* to)

Über·gang *der* (a) crossing
(b) (Stelle zum Überqueren) crossing; (Bahnübergang) level crossing (Brit.); grade crossing (Amer.); (Grenzübergang) crossing point
(c) (Wechsel, Überleitung) transition (zu, auf + *Akk.* to)

über·geben ⒈ *unr. tr. V.* (a) hand over; pass ⟨*baton*⟩
(b) (übereignen) transfer, make over (*Dat.* to)
(c) (ausliefern) surrender (*Dat.*, an + *Akk.* to)
(d) eine Straße dem Verkehr ~: open a road to traffic
⒉ *unr. refl. V.* (sich erbrechen) vomit

über|gehen¹ *unr. itr. V.; mit sein* (a) pass
(b) zu etw. ~: go over to sth.
(c) in etw. (*Akk.*) ~ (zu etw. werden) turn into sth.

über·gehen² *unr. tr. V.* (a) (nicht beachten) ignore
(b) (auslassen, überspringen) skip [over]
(c) (nicht berücksichtigen) pass over

über·geordnet *Adj.* higher ⟨*court, authority, position*⟩; greater ⟨*significance*⟩; superordinate ⟨*concept*⟩

Über·gewicht *das* (a) excess weight
(b) (fig.) predominance

über·gewichtig *Adj.* overweight

über·glücklich *Adj.* blissfully happy; (hocherfreut) overjoyed

über|greifen *unr. itr. V.* auf etw. (*Akk.*) ~: spread to sth.

Über·griff *der* (unrechtmäßiger Eingriff) encroachment (auf + *Akk.* on); infringement (auf + *Akk.* of); (Angriff) attack (auf + *Akk.* on)

Über·größe *die* outsize

überhand: ~ nehmen get out of hand; ⟨*attacks, muggings, etc.*⟩ increase alarmingly

über|hängen *tr. V.* sich (*Dat.*) eine Jacke ~: put a jacket round one's shoulders; sich (*Dat.*) das Gewehr/die Tasche ~: hang the rifle/bag over one's shoulder

über·häufen *tr. V.* jmdn. mit etw. ~: heap *or* shower sth. on sb.

---

u

überhaupt *Adv.* **(a)** in general
(b) ~ nicht not at all; ~ keine Zeit haben
have no time at all; ~ nichts nothing at all
überheblich ⟨1⟩ *Adj.* arrogant;
supercilious ⟨*grin*⟩
   ⟨2⟩ *adv.* arrogantly; ⟨*grin*⟩ superciliously
Überheblichkeit *die;* ~: arrogance
über·holen ⟨1⟩ *tr. V.* **(a)** overtake (esp. Brit.);
pass (esp. Amer.)
(b) (übertreffen) outstrip
(c) (wieder instand setzen) overhaul
   ⟨2⟩ *itr. V.* overtake (esp. Brit.); pass (esp. Amer.)
Überholspur *die* overtaking lane (esp.
Brit.); pass lane (esp. Amer.)
überholt *Adj.* (veraltet) outdated
Überholung *die;* ~, ~en overhaul
Überhol·verbot *das* ban on overtaking
über·hören *tr. V.* not hear
über·irdisch ⟨1⟩ *Adj.* celestial; heavenly;
(übernatürlich) supernatural
   ⟨2⟩ *adv.* celestially; (übernatürlich)
supernaturally
über|kochen *itr. V.; mit sein* (auch fig. ugs.)
boil over
über·kommen *unr. tr. V.* Mitleid/Ekel/
Furcht überkam mich I was overcome by
pity/revulsion/fear
über·laden *unr. tr. V.* (auch fig.) overload
über·lassen *unr. tr. V.* **(a)** jmdm. etw. ~:
let sb. have sth.
(b) sich (*Dat.*) selbst ~ sein be left to one's
own devices
(c) etw. jmdm. ~ (etw. jmdn. entscheiden/tun
lassen) leave sth. to sb.
über·lasten *tr. V.* overload; overtax
⟨*person*⟩; (mit Arbeit) overwork ⟨*person*⟩
Über·lauf *der* overflow
über|laufen[1] *unr. itr. V.; mit sein* **(a)**
overflow
(b) (auf die gegnerische Seite überwechseln)
defect; ⟨*partisan*⟩ go over to the other side
über·laufen[2] *unr. tr. V.* seize; ein
Frösteln/Schauer überlief mich, es überlief
mich [eis]kalt a cold shiver ran down my
spine
überlaufen[3] *Adj.* overcrowded
Über·läufer *der,* **Über·läuferin** *die*
(auch fig.) defector
über·leben *tr. V.* survive
Über·lebende *der/die; adj. Dekl.* survivor
über|legen[1] *tr. V.* jmdm. etw. ~: put sth.
over sb.
über·legen[2] ⟨1⟩ *tr. V.* consider; think
about; es sich anders ~: change one's mind
   ⟨2⟩ *itr. V.* think
überlegen[3] ⟨1⟩ *Adj.* **(a)** superior; clear,
convincing ⟨*win, victory*⟩; jmdm. ~ sein be
superior to sb. (an + *Dat.* in)
(b) (herablassend) supercilious
   ⟨2⟩ *adv.* **(a)** in a superior manner; ⟨*play*⟩
much the better: ⟨*win, argue*⟩ convincingly
(b) (herablassend) superciliously

Überlegenheit *die;* ~: superiority
überlegt ⟨1⟩ *Adj.* carefully considered
   ⟨2⟩ *adv.* in a carefully considered way
Überlegung *die;* ~, ~en **(a)** thought
(b) (Gedanke) idea; ~en (Gedankengang)
thoughts
über·liefern *tr. V.* hand down
Über·lieferung *die* tradition
überlisten *tr. V.* outwit
überm *Präp. + Art.* = über dem
Über·macht *die* superior strength;
(zahlenmäßig) superior numbers *pl.*
über·mannen *tr. V.* overcome
Über·maß *das* excessive amount, excess
(an + *Dat.* of)
über·mäßig ⟨1⟩ *Adj.* excessive
   ⟨2⟩ *adv.* excessively
über·menschlich *Adj.* superhuman
über·mitteln *tr. V.* send; (als Mittler
weitergeben) pass on, convey ⟨*greetings,
regards, etc.*⟩
über·morgen *Adv.* the day after
tomorrow
über·müden *tr. V.* overtire; übermüdet
overtired; exhausted
Übermüdung *die;* ~: overtiredness;
exhaustion
Über·mut *der* high spirits *pl.*
übermütig ⟨1⟩ *Adj.* high-spirited
   ⟨2⟩ *adv.* high-spiritedly
über·nächst... *Adj.* im ~en Jahr, ~es
Jahr the year after next; am ~en Tag two
days later
über·nachten *itr. V.* stay overnight
übernächtigt *Adj.* ⟨*person*⟩ tired *or* worn
out [through lack of sleep]; tired ⟨*face, look,
etc.*⟩
Übernachtung *die;* ~, ~en overnight
stay; ~ und Frühstück bed and breakfast
Übernahme *die;* ~ (von Waren, einer
Sendung) taking delivery *no art.;* (einer Idee
usw.) adoption, taking over *no indef. art.;* (der
Macht, einer Praxis usw.) take over
über·natürlich *Adj.* supernatural
über·nehmen ⟨1⟩ *unr. tr. V.* **(a)** take
delivery of ⟨*goods, consignment*⟩; take over
⟨*power, practice, business, etc.*⟩; take on ⟨*job,
position, etc.*⟩; undertake to pay ⟨*costs*⟩
(b) (sich zu Eigen machen) adopt ⟨*ideas,
methods, subject, etc.*⟩ **(von** from); borrow
⟨*word, phrase*⟩ **(von** from)
   ⟨2⟩ *unr. refl. V.* overdo things *or* it; sich mit
etw. ~: take on too much with sth.
Über·produktion *die* (Wirtsch., Med.)
overproduction
über·prüfen *tr. V.* check (auf + *Akk.* for);
review ⟨*issue, situation, results*⟩
Über·prüfung *die* **(a)** checking *no indef.
art.* (auf + *Akk.* for)
(b) (Kontrolle) check; (einer Lage, Frage usw.)
review
über·queren *tr. V.* cross

u

über·ragen tr. V. (a) jmdn./etw. ~: tower above sb./sth.
(b) (übertreffen) jmdn. an etw. (Dat.) ~: be head and shoulders above sb. in sth.
überragend ① Adj. outstanding ② adv. outstandingly
über·raschen tr. V. surprise
Überraschung die; ~, ~en surprise
über·reden tr. V. persuade
Überredung die; ~: persuasion
über·regional ① Adj. national ⟨newspaper, radio station⟩ ② adv. nationally
über·reichen tr. V. [jmdm.] etw. ~: present sth. [to sb.]
Überreichung die; ~: presentation
über·reif Adj. over-ripe
über·rumpeln tr. V. jmdn. ~: take sb. by surprise
über·runden tr. V. (a) (Sport) lap (b) (übertreffen) outstrip
übers Präp. + Art. = über das
über·sättigen tr. V. supersaturate ⟨solution⟩; glut ⟨market⟩; satiate ⟨public⟩
Überschall-: ~flugzeug das supersonic aircraft; ~geschwindigkeit die supersonic speed
über·schatten tr. V. overshadow; cast its/their shadow over; (fig.) cast a shadow over
über·schätzen tr. V. overestimate; overrate ⟨artist, talent, etc.⟩
Überschätzung die ▶ ÜBERSCHÄTZEN: overestimation; overrating
überschaubar Adj. eine ~e Menge/Zahl a manageable quantity/number
über·schauen tr. V. ▶ ÜBERSEHEN A, B
Über·schlag der (a) rough calculation or estimate
(b) (Turnen) handspring
(c) ▶ LOOPING
über|schlagen¹ ① unr. tr. V. die Beine ~: cross one's legs
② unr. itr. V.; mit sein ⟨wave⟩ break
über·schlagen² ① unr. tr. V. (a) skip ⟨chapter, page, etc.⟩
(b) (ungefähr berechnen) calculate or estimate roughly
② unr. refl. V. go head over heels; ⟨car⟩ turn over
über|schnappen itr. V.; mit sein (ugs.) go crazy
über·schneiden unr. refl. V. cross, intersect; (fig.) overlap
über·schreiben unr. tr. V. (a) entitle; head ⟨chapter, section⟩
(b) etw. jmdm. od. auf jmdn. ~: transfer sth. to sb.
über·schreiten unr. itr. V. cross; (fig.) exceed

Über·schrift die heading; (in einer Zeitung) headline; (Titel) title
Über·schuss, *Über·schuß der surplus (an + Dat. of)
überschüssig Adj. surplus
über·schütten tr. V. cover
Überschwang der; ~[e]s exuberance
über·schwänglich ① Adj. effusive ⟨words etc.⟩; wild ⟨joy, enthusiasm⟩ ② adv. effusively
über·schwemmen tr. V. (auch fig.) flood
Überschwemmung die; ~, ~en flood; (das Überschwemmen) flooding no pl.
*über·schwenglich ▶ ÜBERSCHWÄNGLICH
Über·see: aus od. von ~: from overseas; in/nach ~: overseas
über·sehen unr. tr. V. (a) look out over
(b) (abschätzen) assess ⟨damage, situation, consequences, etc.⟩
(c) (nicht sehen) overlook; miss; miss ⟨turning, signpost⟩
(d) (ignorieren) ignore
über·senden unr. (auch regelm.) tr. V. send
über|setzen¹ ① tr. V. ferry over ② itr. V.; auch mit sein cross [over]
über·setzen² tr., itr. V. (auch fig.) translate
Über·setzer der, **Übersetzerin** die; ~, ~nen translator
Übersetzung die; ~, ~en translation
Über·sicht die (a) overall view, overview (über + Akk. of)
(b) (Darstellung) survey; (Tabelle) summary
über·sichtlich ① Adj. clear; ⟨crossroads⟩ which allows a clear view ② adv. clearly
Übersichtlichkeit die; ~: clarity; (einer Kreuzung) clear layout
über|siedeln¹, über·siedeln² itr. V.; mit sein move (nach to)
Über·siedler der, **Über·siedlerin** die migrant
überspannt Adj. exaggerated ⟨ideas, behaviour, gestures⟩; extreme ⟨views⟩; inflated ⟨demands, expectations⟩
über·spielen tr. V. (a) (hinweggehen über) cover up; smooth over ⟨difficult situation⟩
(b) (aufnehmen) [auf ein Tonband] ~: transfer ⟨record⟩ to tape; put ⟨record⟩ on tape
über·spitzen tr. V. etw. ~: push or carry sth. too far
über·springen unr. tr. V. (a) jump ⟨obstacle⟩
(b) (auslassen) miss out
über|stehen¹ unr. itr. V.; südd., österr., schweiz. mit sein jut out
über·stehen² unr. tr. V. come through ⟨danger, war, operation⟩; get over ⟨illness⟩
über·steigen unr. tr. V. (a) climb over
(b) (fig.) exceed
über·stimmen tr. V. outvote

---

*old spelling - see note on page xiv

über|streifen *tr. V.* [sich (*Dat.*)] etw. ∼:
slip sth. on

über|stülpen *tr. V.* pull on 〈*hat etc.*〉

Über·stunde *die:* ∼n machen do overtime

über·stürzen [1] *tr. V.* rush
[2] *refl. V.* rush; (rasch aufeinander folgen)
〈*events, news, etc.*〉 come thick and fast

überstürzt [1] *Adj.* hurried 〈*escape,
departure*〉; overhasty 〈*decision*〉
[2] *adv.* 〈*decide, act*〉 overhastily; 〈*depart*〉
hurriedly

über·tölpeln *tr. V.* dupe; con (coll.)

über·tönen *tr. V.* drown out

Über·trag *der;* ∼[e]s, Überträge (bes. Buchf.)
carry-over

über·tragbar *Adj.* transferable (auf + Akk.
to); (auf etw. anderes anwendbar) applicable (auf
+ Akk. to); (übersetzbar) translatable;
(ansteckend) infectious 〈*disease*〉

über·tragen *unr. tr. V.* (a) transfer (auf +
Akk. to); transmit 〈*power, torque, etc.*〉 (auf +
Akk. to); communicate 〈*disease, illness*〉 (auf
+ Akk. to); carry over 〈*subtotal*〉; (auf etw.
anderes anwenden) apply (auf + Akk. to);
(übersetzen) translate
(b) (senden) broadcast 〈*concert, event, match,
etc.*〉; (im Fernsehen) televise
(c) (geben) jmdm. Aufgaben/Pflichten *usw.* ∼:
hand over tasks/duties *etc.* to sb.;
(anvertrauen) entrust sb. with tasks/duties *etc.*

Übertragung *die;* ∼, ∼en (a)
▶ ÜBERTRAGEN A: transference; transmission;
communication; carrying over; application;
translation
(b) (das Senden) broadcasting; (Sendung)
broadcast; (im Fernsehen) televising/television
broadcast

über·treffen *unr. tr. V.* (a) surpass, outdo
(an + Dat. in); break 〈*record*〉
(b) (übersteigen) exceed

über·treiben *unr. tr. V.* (a) *auch itr.*
exaggerate
(b) (zu weit treiben) overdo

Übertreibung *die;* ∼, ∼en exaggeration

über|treten¹ *unr. itr. V.; mit sein* change
sides; zum Katholizismus/Islam ∼: convert
to Catholicism/Islam

über·treten² *unr. tr. V.* contravene 〈*law*〉;
violate 〈*regulation, prohibition*〉

Übertretung *die;* ∼, ∼en (a)
▶ ÜBERTRETEN²: contravention; violation
(b) (Vergehen) misdemeanour

übertrieben *Adj.* [1] exaggerated;
(übermäßig) excessive 〈*care, thrift, etc.*〉
[2] *adv.* excessively

Über·tritt *der* change of allegiance, switch
(zu to); (Rel.) conversion (zu to)

über·trumpfen *tr. V.* outdo

über·tünchen *tr. V.* cover with
whitewash; (fig.) cover up

über·vorteilen *tr. V.* cheat

über·wachen *tr. V.* keep under
surveillance 〈*suspect, agent, area, etc.*〉;
supervise 〈*factory, workers, process*〉; control
〈*traffic*〉; monitor 〈*progress, production
process, experiment, patient*〉

Überwachung *die;* ∼, ∼en
▶ ÜBERWACHEN: surveillance; supervision;
controlling; monitoring

über·wältigen *tr. V.* (a) overpower
(b) (fig.) 〈*sleep, emotion, fear, etc.*〉 overcome
〈*sight, impressions, beauty, etc.*〉 overwhelm

überwältigend [1] *Adj.* overwhelming
〈*sight, impression, victory, majority, etc.*〉;
overpowering 〈*smell*〉; stunning 〈*beauty*〉
[2] *adv.* stunningly 〈*beautiful*〉

über·weisen *unr. tr. V.* (a) transfer
〈*money*〉 (an, auf + Akk. to)
(b) refer 〈*patient*〉 (an + Akk. to)

Über·weisung *die* (a) transfer (an, auf +
Akk. to)
(b) (Summe) remittance
(c) (eines Patienten) referral (an + Akk. to)

überwiegend [1] /auch -'--/ *Adj.*
overwhelming
[2] *adv.* mainly

über·winden [1] *unr. tr. V.* overcome; get
past 〈*stage*〉
[2] *unr. refl. V.* overcome one's reluctance;
sich [dazu] ∼, etw. zu tun bring oneself to
do sth.

Über·windung *die* (a) ▶ ÜBERWINDEN 1:
overcoming; getting past
(b) (das Sichüberwinden) es war eine große ∼
für ihn it cost him a great effort

über·wuchern *tr. V.* overgrow

Über·zahl *die* majority

überzählig *Adj.* surplus

über·zeugen [1] *tr. V.* convince
[2] *itr. V.* be convincing

überzeugend [1] *Adj.* convincing
[2] *adv.* convincingly

überzeugt *Adj.* convinced

Über·zeugung *die* (feste Meinung)
conviction

über|ziehen¹ *unr. tr. V.* pull on

über·ziehen² *unr. tr. V.* (a) etw. mit etw.
∼: cover sth. with sth.
(b) overdraw 〈*account*〉 (um by)

Überziehungs·kredit *der* (Finanzw.)
overdraft facility

überzüchtet *Adj.* overbred; over-
sophisticated 〈*engines, systems*〉

Über·zug *der* (a) (Beschichtung) coating
(b) (Bezug) cover

üblich *Adj.* usual; (normal) normal;
(gebräuchlich) customary

üblicher·weise *Adv.* usually

U-Boot *das* submarine; sub (coll.)

übrig *Adj.* remaining *attrib.*; (ander...) other;
alle ∼en Gäste ...: all the other guests ...; im
Übrigen besides; es ist etwas ∼: there is
some left; ∼ bleiben be left; 〈*food, drink*〉 be
left over; ∼ lassen (+ Akk.) leave; leave
〈*food, drink*〉 over

*übrig|bleiben ▶ ÜBRIG

übrigens *Adv.* by the way

*übrig|lassen ▶ ÜBRIG

Übung *die;* ∼, ∼en (a) exercise
(b) (das Üben, Geübtsein) practice

UdSSR *Abk. die;* ∼ (1922–1991) = **Union
der Sozialistischen
Sowjetrepubliken** USSR

Ufer *das;* ∼s, ∼: bank; (des Meers) shore

UG *Abk.* = **Untergeschoss**

Uganda (*das*); ∼s Uganda

Uhr *die;* ∼, ∼en (a) clock; (Armband-,
Taschenuhr) watch; (Wasser-, Gasuhr) meter; (an
Messinstrumenten) dial; gauge; **auf die** *od.* **nach
der** ∼ **sehen** look at the time; **rund um die** ∼
(ugs.) round the clock
(b) acht ∼: eight o'clock; **wie viel** ∼ **ist es?**
what's the time?; what time is it?

Uhr-: ∼**armband** *das* watch strap;
∼**kette** *die* watch chain; ∼**macher** *der*,
∼**macherin** *die* watchmaker/clockmaker;
∼**werk** *das* clock/watch mechanism;
∼**zeiger** *der* clock/watch hand;
∼**zeiger·sinn** *der:* im/entgegen dem
∼zeigersinn clockwise/anticlockwise; ∼**zeit**
die time; jmdn. nach der ∼zeit fragen ask sb.
the time

Uhu *der;* ∼s, ∼s eagle owl

Ukraine *die;* ∼: Ukraine

Ukrainer *der;* ∼s, ∼, **Ukrainerin** *die;* ∼,
∼nen Ukrainian

UKW *Abk.* = **Ultrakurzwelle** VHF

UKW-Sender *der* VHF station; ≈ FM
station

Ulk *der;* ∼s, ∼e lark (coll.); (Streich) trick;
[practical] joke

ulkig (ugs.) ① *Adj.* funny
② *adv.* in a funny way

Ulme *die;* ∼, ∼n elm

Ultimatum *das;* ∼s, Ultimaten ultimatum

Ultra-kurz-welle *die* ultra-short wave;
(Rundf.: Wellenbereich) very high frequency;
VHF

Ultra·schall *der* (Physik, Med.) ultrasound

Ultraschall·untersuchung *die* (Med.)
ultrasound examination

ultra·violett *Adj.* ultraviolet

um ① *Präp. mit Akk.* (a) (räumlich) [a]round;
um die Ecke round the corner
(b) (zeitlich) (genau) at; (etwa) around [about]
(c) **Tag um Tag/Stunde um Stunde** day after
day/hour after hour
(d) (bei Maß- u. Mengenangaben) by
② *Adv.* around; about; **um [die] 10 Euro/50
Personen [herum]** around *or* about 10 euros/
50 people
③ *Konj.* (a) (final) **um … zu** [in order] to
(b) (konsekutiv) **er ist groß genug/ist noch zu
klein, um … zu …:** he is big enough/is still
too young to …

um|ändern *tr. V.* change; revise ⟨*text,
novel*⟩; alter ⟨*garment*⟩

um·armen *tr. V.* embrace; (an sich drücken)
hug

Umarmung *die;* ∼, ∼en embrace; hug

Um·bau *der;* ∼[e]s, ∼ten ▶ UMBAUEN:
rebuilding; alteration; conversion; (fig.)
reorganization

um|bauen *tr., auch itr. V.* rebuild; (leicht
ändern) alter; (zu etw. anderem) convert (zu
into); (fig.) reorganize ⟨*system,
administration, etc.*⟩

um|benennen *unr. tr. V.* change the name
of; rename

um|biegen ① *unr. tr. V.* bend
② *unr. itr. V.; mit sein* turn

um|binden *unr. tr. V.* put on

um|blättern ① *tr. V.* turn [over]
② *itr. V.* turn the page/pages

um|blicken *refl. V.* (a) look around
(b) (zurückblicken) [turn to] look back (**nach** at)

um|bringen *unr. tr. V.* kill

Um·bruch *der* (a) radical change;
(Umwälzung) upheaval
(b) (Druckw.) make-up; (Ergebnis) page proofs
pl.

um|buchen ① *tr. V.* change (auf + Akk. to)
② *itr. V.* change one's booking (auf + Akk.
to)

Um·buchung *die* change of booking

um|datieren *tr. V.* change the date of;
redate ⟨*contract, letter, etc.*⟩

um|denken *unr. itr. V.* revise one's
thinking; rethink; **ein Prozess des
Umdenkens** a process of rethinking

um|drehen ① *tr. V.* turn round; turn over
⟨*coin, hand, etc.*⟩; turn ⟨*key*⟩
② *refl. V.* turn round; (den Kopf wenden) turn
one's head
③ *itr. V.; auch mit sein* (ugs.: umkehren) turn
back; (ugs.: wenden) turn round

Um·drehung *die* turn; (eines Motors usw.)
revolution; rev (coll.)

um·einander *Adv.* sich ∼ kümmern/
sorgen take care of/worry about each other
or one another

um|fahren¹ *unr. tr. V.* knock down

um·fahren² *unr. tr. V.* go round; make a
detour round ⟨*obstruction etc.*⟩; (im Auto)
drive round; (im Schiff) sail round; (auf einer
Umgehungsstraße) bypass ⟨*town, village, etc.*⟩

um|fallen *unr. itr. V.; mit sein* (a) fall over
(b) (zusammenbrechen) collapse; **tot** ∼: fall
down dead

Um·fang *der* (a) circumference; (eines
Quadrats usw.) perimeter; (eines Baums, Menschen
usw.) girth
(b) (Größe) size
(c) (Ausmaß) extent

umfang·reich *Adj.* extensive; substantial
⟨*book*⟩

um·fassen *tr. V.* (a) grasp; (umarmen)
embrace

(b) (enthalten) contain; (einschließen) include; span, cover ⟨*period*⟩

umfassend ①*Adj.* full ⟨*reply, information, survey, confession*⟩; extensive, wide ⟨*knowledge, powers*⟩ ②*adv.* ⟨*inform*⟩ fully

Um·feld *das* (Psych., Soziol.) milieu

um|formen *tr. V.* reshape; revise ⟨*poem, novel*⟩; transform ⟨*person*⟩

Um·frage *die* survey; (Politik) opinion poll

um|füllen *tr. V.* etw. in etw. (*Akk.*) ∼: transfer sth. into sth.

um|funktionieren *tr. V.* change the function of; etw. zu etw. ∼: turn sth. into sth.

Um·gang *der* **(a)** (gesellschaftlicher Verkehr) contact **(b)** (das Umgehen) den ∼ mit Pferden lernen learn how to handle horses

umgänglich *Adj.* affable; (gesellig) sociable

Umgangs-: ∼form *die* gute/schlechte/. keine ∼formen haben have good/bad/no manners; ∼sprache *die* colloquial language

um·garnen *tr. V.* beguile

um·geben *unr. tr. V.* **(a)** surround; ⟨*hedge, fence, wall, etc.*⟩ enclose **(b)** etw. mit etw. ∼: surround sth. with sth.; (einfrieden) enclose sth. with sth.

Umgebung *die;* ∼, ∼en surroundings *pl.;* (Nachbarschaft) neighbourhood; (eines Ortes) surrounding area

um|gehen¹ *unr. itr. V.; mit sein* **(a)** (im Umlauf sein) ⟨*list, rumour, etc.*⟩ go round, circulate; ⟨*illness, infection*⟩ go round **(b)** (spuken) hier geht ein Gespenst um this place is haunted **(c)** (behandeln) mit jmdm. freundlich/liebevoll usw. ∼: treat sb. kindly/lovingly *etc.;* er kann mit Geld nicht ∼: he can't handle money

um·gehen² *unr. tr. V.* **(a)** go round; make a detour round; (auf einer Umgehungsstraße) bypass ⟨*town etc.*⟩ **(b)** (vermeiden) avoid; evade ⟨*question, issue*⟩ **(c)** (nicht befolgen) circumvent ⟨*law, restriction, etc.*⟩; evade ⟨*obligation, duty*⟩

umgehend ①*Adj.* immediate ②*adv.* immediately

Umgehung *die;* ∼, ∼en **(a)** durch ∼ der Innenstadt by bypassing *or* avoiding the town centre **(b)** ▶ UMGEHEN² C: circumvention; evasion

Umgehungs·straße *die* bypass

umgekehrt ①*Adj.* inverse ⟨*ratio, proportion*⟩; reverse ⟨*order*⟩; opposite ⟨*sign*⟩ ②*adv.* inversely ⟨*proportional*⟩; vom Englischen ins Deutsche und ∼ übersetzen translate from English into German and vice versa

um|gestalten *tr. V.* reshape; remodel; redesign ⟨*square, park, room, etc.*⟩

um|graben *unr. tr. V.* dig over

Um·hang *der* cape

um|hängen *tr. V.* **(a)** etw. ∼: hang sth. somewhere else **(b)** jmdm./sich einen Mantel/eine Decke ∼: drape a coat/blanket round sb.'s/one's shoulders

um|hauen *unr. tr. V.* fell; (fig.) knock down

um·her *Adv.* around

umher- ▶ HERUM-

um|hören *refl. V.* keep one's ears open; (direkt fragen) ask around

um|jubeln *tr. V.* cheer

um|kehren ①*itr. V.; mit sein* turn back ②*tr. V.* turn upside down; turn over ⟨*sheet of paper*⟩; (nach links drehen) turn ⟨*garment etc.*⟩ inside out; (nach rechts drehen) turn ⟨*garment etc.*⟩ right side out

um|kippen ①*itr. V.; mit sein* **(a)** fall over; ⟨*boat*⟩ capsize, turn over; ⟨*vehicle*⟩ overturn **(b)** (ugs.: ohnmächtig werden) keel over **(c)** (Ökologie) ⟨*river, lake*⟩ reach the stage of biological collapse ②*tr. V.* tip over; knock over ⟨*lamp, vase, glass, cup*⟩; capsize ⟨*boat*⟩; turn ⟨*boat*⟩ over; overturn ⟨*vehicle*⟩

um|klappen *tr. V.* fold down

Umkleide·kabine *die* changing cubicle

um|knicken *itr. V.; mit sein* **(a)** [mit dem Fuß] ∼: go over on one's ankle **(b)** bend; ⟨*branch*⟩ bend and snap

um|kommen *unr. itr. V.; mit sein* die; (bei einem Unglück, durch Gewalt) get killed; die; ⟨*food*⟩ go off

Um·kreis *der* surrounding area; im ∼ von 5 km within a radius of 5 km.

um·kreisen *tr. V.* circle; ⟨*spacecraft, satellite*⟩ orbit; ⟨*planet*⟩ revolve [a]round

Um·lauf *der* **(a)** (von Planeten) revolution **(b)** (Zirkulation) circulation; in *od.* im ∼ sein be circulating; ⟨*coin, banknote*⟩ be in circulation; in ∼ bringen circulate; bring ⟨*coin, banknote*⟩ into circulation

Umlauf·bahn *die* (Astron., Raumf.) orbit

Um·laut *der* (Sprachw.) umlaut

um|legen *tr. V.* **(a)** (um einen Körperteil) put on **(b)** (verlegen) transfer ⟨*patient, telephone call*⟩ **(c)** (salopp: ermorden) jmdn. ∼: bump sb. off (coll.)

um|leiten *tr. V.* divert

Um·leitung *die* diversion

umliegend *Adj.* surrounding ⟨*area*⟩; (nahe) nearby ⟨*building*⟩

um|modeln *tr. V.* (ugs.) change ⟨*house, flat*⟩ round; refashion, alter ⟨*jacket etc.*⟩

um·nachtet *Adj.* (geh.) deranged

Umnachtung *die;* ∼, ∼en (geh.) derangement

um|pflanzen *tr. V.* transplant

um|pflügen *tr. V.* plough up

um|räumen ①*tr. V.* rearrange ②*itr. V.* rearrange things

u

um|rechnen *tr. V.* convert (**in** + *Akk.* into)

Um·rechnung *die* conversion (**in** + *Akk.* into)

Umrechnungs·kurs *der* exchange rate

um|reißen[1] *unr. tr. V.* pull ⟨*mast, tree*⟩ down; knock ⟨*person*⟩ down; ⟨*wind*⟩ tear ⟨*tent etc.*⟩ down

um-reißen[2] *unr. tr. V.* outline; summarize ⟨*subject, problem, situation*⟩

um|rennen *unr. tr. V.* [run into and] knock down

um-ringen *tr. V.* surround

Um·riss, *Um·riß *der* (auch fig.) outline

um|rühren *tr.* (*auch itr.*) *V.* stir

um|rüsten *tr. V.* (Technik) convert (**auf** + *Akk.* to, **zu** into)

ums /ʊms/ *Präp. + Art.* (a) = **um das**; (b) ~ **Leben kommen** lose one's life

um|satteln *itr. V.* (ugs.) change jobs; ⟨*student*⟩ change courses

Um·satz *der* turnover; (Verkauf) sales *pl.* (**an** + *Dat.* of); ~ **machen** (ugs.) make money

um|säumen *tr. V.* hem

um|schalten [1] *tr. V.* (auch fig.) switch [over] (**auf** + *Akk.* to); move ⟨*lever*⟩
[2] *itr. V.* switch or change over (**auf** + *Akk.* to)

Um·schlag *der* (a) cover
(b) (Briefumschlag) envelope
(c) (Schutzumschlag) jacket; (einer Broschüre, eines Heftes) cover
(d) (Med.: Wickel) compress; (warm) poultice

um|schlagen [1] *unr. tr. V.* (a) turn up ⟨*sleeve, collar, trousers*⟩; turn over ⟨*page*⟩
(b) (umladen, verladen) turn round, trans-ship ⟨*goods*⟩
[2] *unr. itr. V.; mit sein* change (**in** + *Akk.* into); ⟨*wind*⟩ veer [round]

um|schreiben[1] *unr. tr. V.* rewrite

um-schreiben[2] *unr. tr. V.* (a) (in Worte fassen) describe; (definieren) define ⟨*meaning, sb.'s task, etc.*⟩; (paraphrasieren) paraphrase ⟨*word, expression*⟩
(b) (Sprachw.) construct (**mit** with)

Um·schreibung *die* description; (Definition) definition; (Verhüllung) circumlocution (*Gen.* for)

Um·schrift *die* (Sprachw.) transcription

um|schulen [1] *tr. V.* (beruflich) retrain
[2] *itr. V.* retrain (**auf** + *Akk.* as)

Um·schulung *die;* ~: retraining (**auf** + *Akk.* as)

um|schütten *tr. V.* (a) pour [into another container]; decant ⟨*liquid*⟩
(b) (verschütten) spill

Um·schweif *der* circumlocution; **ohne** ~**e** without beating about the bush

Um·schwung *der* complete change; (in der Politik usw.) U-turn

um|sehen *unr. refl. V.* (a) look; **sich im Zimmer** ~: look [a]round the room
(b) (zurücksehen) look round or back

umseitig *Adj., adv.* overleaf

um|setzen *tr. V.* (a) move; (auf anderen Posten usw.) move, transfer (**in** + *Akk.* to); (umpflanzen) transplant; (in anderen Topf) repot
(b) (verwirklichen) implement ⟨*plan*⟩; translate ⟨*plan, intention, etc.*⟩ into action or reality; realize ⟨*ideas*⟩
(c) (Wirtsch.) turn over, have a turnover of ⟨*x euros etc.*⟩; sell ⟨*shares, goods*⟩

Um·sicht *die* circumspection

um·sichtig [1] *Adj.* circumspect
[2] *adv.* circumspectly

um|siedeln [1] *tr. V.* resettle
[2] *itr. V.; mit sein* move (**in** + *Akk., nach* to)

um-so *Konj.* **je ...** ~: the ..., the; ~ **besser/ schlimmer!** all the better/worse!

um-sonst *Adv.* (a) (unentgeltlich) free; for nothing
(b) (vergebens) in vain

Um·stand *der* (a) (Gegebenheit) circumstance; (Tatsache) fact; **unter Umständen** possibly
(b) (Aufwand) business; **macht keine [großen] Umstände** please don't go to any bother

umstände·halber *Adv.* owing to circumstances; „~ **zu verkaufen**" 'forced to sell'

umständlich [1] *Adj.* involved, elaborate ⟨*procedure, method, description, explanation, etc.*⟩; elaborate, laborious ⟨*preparation, check, etc.*⟩; awkward, difficult ⟨*journey, job*⟩; (weitschweifig) long-winded; (Umstände machend) awkward ⟨*person*⟩
[2] *adv.* in an involved or roundabout way; (weitschweifig) at great length

Umstands·kleid *das* maternity dress

umstehend *Adj.* standing round *postpos.*

um|steigen *unr. itr. V.* change (**in** + *Akk.* [on] to)

um|stellen[1] [1] *tr. V.* (a) rearrange, change round ⟨*furniture, books, etc.*⟩; reorder ⟨*words etc.*⟩; transpose ⟨*two words*⟩
(b) (anders einstellen) reset ⟨*lever, switch, points, clock*⟩
(c) (ändern) change or switch over (**auf** + *Akk.* to)
[2] *refl. V.* adjust (**auf** + *Akk.* to)

um-stellen[2] *tr. V.* surround

um|stimmen *tr. V.* win ⟨*person*⟩ round

um|stoßen *unr. tr. V.* (a) knock over
(b) (rückgängig machen) change ⟨*plan, decision*⟩; (zunichte machen) upset, wreck ⟨*plan, theory*⟩

umstritten *Adj.* disputed; controversial ⟨*book, author, policy, etc.*⟩

Um·sturz *der* coup

um|stürzen [1] *tr. V.* overturn; (fig.) topple, overthrow ⟨*political system, government*⟩
[2] *itr. V.* overturn; ⟨*wall, building, chimney*⟩ fall down

umstürzlerisch *Adj.* subversive

Ụmsturz·versuch der attempted coup

Ụm·tausch der exchange

ụm|tauschen tr. V. exchange ⟨goods, article⟩ (**gegen** for); change ⟨dollars, pounds, etc.⟩ (**in** + Akk. into)

ụm|topfen tr. V. repot ⟨plant⟩

Ụm·trunk der communal drink

ụm|tun unr. refl. V. (ugs.) look [a]round; **sich nach etw. ~:** be on the lookout for sth.

Ụmwälzung die; ~, ~en (fig.) revolution

ụm|wandeln tr. V. convert ⟨substance, building, etc.⟩ (**in** + Akk. into); (ändern) change; alter

Ụm·weg der detour

Ụm·welt die (a) environment (b) (Menschen) people pl. around sb.

ụmwelt-, Ụmwelt-: ~**bedingt** Adj. caused by the or one's environment postpos.; ~**belastung** die environmental pollution no indef. art.; ~**bewusst,** *~**bewußt** Adj. environmentally conscious or aware; ~**feindlich** 1 Adj. inimical to the environment postpos.; ecologically undesirable; 2 adv. in an ecologically undesirable way; ⟨drive, behave⟩ without regard for the environment; ~**freundlich** 1 Adj. environmentally friendly; 2 adv. in an environmentally friendly way; ~**katastrophe** die environmental disaster; ~**schädlich** 1 Adj. harmful to the environment postpos.; ecologically harmful; 2 adv. in an ecologically harmful way; ~**schutz** der environmental protection no art.; ~**schützer** der; ~~s, ~~, ~**schützerin** die; ~~, ~, ~**nen** environmentalist; conservationist; ~**verschmutzung** die pollution [of the environment]

ụm|wenden regelm. (auch unr.) tr. V. (a) turn over ⟨page, joint, etc.⟩ (b) turn round ⟨vehicle, horse⟩

um·wẹrben unr. tr. V. court; woo; **viel umworben** much-courted

ụm|werfen unr. tr. V. (a) knock over; knock ⟨person⟩ down or over; (fig. ugs.: aus der Fassung bringen) bowl ⟨person⟩ over; stun ⟨person⟩ (b) (fig. ugs.: umstoßen) knock ⟨plan⟩ on the head (coll.)

ụmwerfend (ugs.) 1 Adj. fantastic (coll.); stunning (coll.) 2 adv. fantastically [well] (coll.); brilliantly

um·wịckeln tr. V. wrap; bind; (mit einem Verband) bandage

Umzäunung die; ~, ~en fence, fencing (Gen. round)

ụm|ziehen 1 unr. itr. V.; mit sein move (**an** + Akk., **in** + Akk., **nach** to) 2 unr. tr. V. jmdn. ~: change sb. or get sb. changed; **sich** ~: change or get changed

um·zịngeln tr. V. surround; encircle

Umzịngelung die; ~: encirclement

Ụm·zug der (a) move; (von Möbeln) removal (b) (Festzug) procession

UN Pl. UN sing.

unabänderlich 1 Adj. unalterable; irrevocable ⟨decision⟩ 2 adv. irrevocably

unabhängig 1 Adj. independent (**von** of); (unbeeinflusst) unaffected (**von** by) 2 adv. independently (**von** of); ~ **davon, ob** .../**was** .../**wo** ... usw. irrespective or regardless of whether .../what .../where ... etc

Ụnabhängigkeit die; ~: independence

unabkǫmmlich Adj. indispensable; **sie ist im Moment** ~: she is otherwise engaged

unablässig 1 Adj. incessant 2 adv. incessantly

unabsichtlich 1 Adj. unintentional 2 adv. unintentionally

unabwẹndbar Adj. inevitable

unachtsam 1 Adj. (a) inattentive (b) (nicht sorgfältig) careless 2 adv. (ohne Sorgfalt) carelessly

Ụnachtsamkeit die; ~ (a) inattentiveness (b) (mangelnde Sorgfalt) carelessness

unangebracht Adj. inappropriate

unangefochten Adj. unchallenged; (Rechtsw.) uncontested ⟨verdict, will, etc.⟩

unangenehm 1 Adj. unpleasant (Dat. for); (peinlich) embarrassing ⟨question, situation⟩ 2 adv. unpleasantly

unannẹhmbar Adj. unacceptable

Ụnannehmlichkeit die; ~, ~en trouble

unansehnlich Adj. unprepossessing; plain ⟨girl⟩

unanstạ̈ndig 1 Adj. improper; (anstößig) indecent; dirty ⟨joke⟩; rude ⟨word, song⟩ 2 adv. improperly

Ụnanständigkeit die; ~, ~en impropriety; indecency; (Obszönität) obscenity

unappetitlich 1 Adj. unappetizing; (fig.) unsavoury ⟨joke⟩; disgusting ⟨washbasin, nails, etc.⟩ 2 adv. unappetizingly

Ụnart die; ~, ~en bad habit

unartig Adj. naughty

unästhetisch Adj. unpleasant ⟨sight etc.⟩; ugly ⟨building etc.⟩

unauffällig 1 Adj. inconspicuous; unobtrusive ⟨scar, defect, skill, behaviour, surveillance, etc.⟩; discreet ⟨signal, elegance⟩ 2 adv. inconspicuously; unobtrusively

unauffịndbar Adj. untraceable; ~ **sein** od. **bleiben** be nowhere to be found

unaufgefordert Adv. without being asked

unaufhạltsam 1 Adj. inexorable 2 adv. inexorably

unaufmerksam Adj. inattentive (gegenüber to); careless ⟨driver⟩

unaufrichtig Adj. insincere

u

Unaufrichtigkeit die; ~, ~en insincerity
unausbleiblich Adj. inevitable
unausgegoren Adj. (abwertend) immature
unausstehlich Adj. unbearable ⟨person, noise, smell, etc.⟩; insufferable ⟨person⟩; intolerable ⟨noise, smell⟩
unausweichlich Adj. unavoidable; inevitable
unbändig ①Adj. (a) boisterous
  (b) (überaus groß/stark) unbridled
  ②adv. (a) wildly
  (b) (sehr, äußerst) unrestrainedly; tremendously (coll.)
unbarmherzig Adj. merciless
unbeabsichtigt ①Adj. unintentional
  ②adv. unintentionally
unbeachtet Adj. unnoticed
unbedacht ①Adj. rash; thoughtless
  ②adv. rashly; thoughtlessly
unbedenklich adv. without second thoughts
unbedeutend ①Adj. insignificant; minor ⟨artist, poet⟩; slight, minor ⟨improvement, change, error⟩
  ②adv. slightly
unbedingt ①Adj. absolute
  ②adv. absolutely
  ③Adv. (auf jeden Fall) whatever happens
unbefangen Adj. (a) (ungehemmt) uninhibited
  (b) (unvoreingenommen) impartial
Unbefangenheit die; ▶ UNBEFANGEN A, B: uninhibitedness; impartiality
unbefriedigend Adj. unsatisfactory
unbefristet ①Adj. for an indefinite period postpos.; indefinite ⟨strike⟩; unlimited ⟨visa⟩
  ②adv. for an indefinite period
unbefugt ①Adj. unauthorized
  ②adv. without authorization
unbegreiflich Adj. incomprehensible (Dat., für to); incredible ⟨love, goodness, stupidity, carelessness, etc.⟩
unbegrenzt ①Adj. unlimited
  ②adv. ⟨stay, keep, etc.⟩ indefinitely
Unbehagen das; ~s uneasiness, disquiet; (Sorge) concern (an + Dat. about)
unbehaglich ①Adj. uneasy ⟨feeling, atmosphere⟩; uncomfortable ⟨thought, room⟩
  ②adv. uneasily
unbeherrscht Adj. uncontrolled; er ist ~: he has no self-control
Unbeherrschtheit die; ~: lack of self-control
unbeholfen ①Adj. clumsy
  ②adv. clumsily
unbekannt Adj. (a) unknown; (nicht vertraut) unfamiliar; unidentified ⟨caller, donor⟩; „Empfänger ~" 'not known at this address'

*alte Schreibung - vgl. Hinweis auf S. xiv

(b) (nicht vielen bekannt) little known; obscure ⟨poet, painter, etc.⟩
Unbekannte¹ der/die; adj. Dekl. unknown or unidentified man/woman; (Fremde[r]) stranger
Unbekannte² die; adj. Dekl. (Math.; auch fig.) unknown
unbekleidet Adj. without any clothes on postpos.; bare ⟨torso etc.⟩; naked ⟨corpse⟩
unbekümmert ①Adj. carefree; (ohne Bedenken, lässig) casual
  ②adv. (a) in a carefree way
  (b) (ohne Bedenken) without caring or worrying
unbeleuchtet Adj. unlit ⟨street, corridor, etc.⟩; ⟨vehicle⟩ without [any] lights
unbeliebt Adj. unpopular (bei with)
unbemannt Adj. unmanned
unbemerkt Adj., adv. unnoticed
unbenutzt Adj. unused
unbequem ①Adj. (a) uncomfortable
  (b) (lästig) awkward, embarrassing ⟨question, opinion⟩; troublesome ⟨politician etc.⟩; unpleasant ⟨criticism, truth, etc.⟩
  ②adv. uncomfortably
unberechenbar ①Adj. unpredictable
  ②adv. unpredictably
unberechtigt Adj. (a) (ungerechtfertigt) unjustified
  (b) (unbefugt) unauthorized
unberührt Adj. untouched; sie ist noch ~: she is still a virgin
unbescheiden Adj. presumptuous
unbeschrankt Adj. ⟨crossing⟩ without gates, with no gates
unbeschreiblich ①Adj. indescribable; unimaginable ⟨fear, beauty⟩; ⟨fear, beauty⟩ beyond description
  ②adv. indescribably ⟨beautiful⟩; unbelievably ⟨busy⟩
unbesorgt Adj. unconcerned; seien Sie ~: don't [you] worry
unbeständig Adj. changeable ⟨weather⟩; fickle ⟨lover etc.⟩
unbestimmt ①Adj. (a) indefinite; indeterminate ⟨age, number⟩; (ungewiss) uncertain
  (b) (ungenau) vague
  (c) (Sprachw.) indefinite ⟨article, pronoun⟩
  ②adv. (ungenau) vaguely
unbestreitbar Adj. indisputable; unquestionable
unbestritten ①Adj. undisputed; ~ ist, dass ... it is undisputed that ...; there is no disputing that ...
  ②adv. indisputably
unbewacht Adj. unsupervised; unattended ⟨car park⟩
unbewaffnet Adj. unarmed
unbeweglich Adj. motionless; still ⟨air, water⟩; fixed ⟨gaze, expression⟩

unbewegt *Adj.* motionless; fixed ⟨*expression*⟩

unbewohnbar *Adj.* uninhabitable

unbewohnt *Adj.* uninhabited ⟨*area*⟩; unoccupied ⟨*house, flat*⟩

unbewusst, *unbewußt *Adj.* unconscious

unbrauchbar *Adj.* unusable; (untauglich) useless ⟨*method, person*⟩

und *Konj.* and; (folglich) [and] so; **ich ~ tanzen?** what, me dance?; **sei so gut ~ mach das Fenster zu** be so good as to shut the window

Undank *der;* ~[e]s: ingratitude

undankbar *Adj.* ungrateful ⟨*person, behaviour*⟩

undenkbar *Adj.* unthinkable; inconceivable

undeutlich ⟨1⟩ *Adj.* unclear; indistinct; (ungenau) vague ⟨*idea, memory, etc.*⟩ ⟨2⟩ *adv.* indistinctly; (ungenau) vaguely

undicht *Adj.* leaky; leaking; ~e **Fenster** windows which do not fit tightly

Unding *das* **ein ~ sein** be preposterous *or* ridiculous

undurchführbar *Adj.* impracticable

undurchlässig *Adj.* impermeable; (wasserdicht) watertight; waterproof; (luftdicht) airtight

uneben *Adj.* uneven

Unebenheit *die;* ~, ~en (a) unevenness (b) (unebene Stelle) lumpy *or* uneven patch

unehelich *Adj.* illegitimate ⟨*child*⟩; unmarried ⟨*mother*⟩

unehrlich ⟨1⟩ *Adj.* dishonest ⟨2⟩ *adv.* dishonestly; by dishonest means

uneigennützig *Adj.* unselfish

Uneigennützigkeit *die;* ~: unselfishness

uneinig *Adj.* ⟨*party*⟩ divided by disagreement; [**sich** (*Dat.*)] ~ **sein** disagree

Uneinigkeit *die;* ~: disagreement (**in** + *Dat.* on)

uneins *Adj.* ~ **sein** be divided (**in** + *Dat.* on); ⟨*persons*⟩ be at variance *or* at cross purposes (**in** + *Dat.* over)

unempfindlich *Adj.* (a) insensitive (**gegen** to) (b) (immun) immune (**gegen** to, against) (c) (strapazierfähig) hard-wearing

unendlich ⟨1⟩ *Adj.* infinite; boundless; (zeitlich) endless; (Math.) infinite ⟨2⟩ *adv.* infinitely ⟨*lovable, sad*⟩; immeasurably ⟨*happy*⟩; ⟨*happy*⟩ beyond measure

unentbehrlich *Adj.* indispensable (*Dat.,* **für** to)

unentgeltlich */od.* '----/ ⟨1⟩ *Adj.* free ⟨2⟩ *adv.* free of charge; ⟨*work*⟩ for nothing

unentschieden ⟨1⟩ *Adj.* unsettled; undecided ⟨*question*⟩; (Sport, Schach) drawn ⟨2⟩ *adv.* ~ **spielen** draw

Unentschieden *das;* ~s, ~ (Sport, Schach) draw

unentwegt */od.* --'-/ ⟨1⟩ *Adj.* (a) (beharrlich) persistent ⟨*fighter, champion, efforts*⟩ (b) (unaufhörlich) constant; incessant ⟨2⟩ *adv.* (a) (beharrlich) persistently (b) (unaufhörlich) constantly; incessantly

unerbittlich ⟨1⟩ *Adj.* (auch fig.) inexorable; unsparing ⟨*critic*⟩; relentless ⟨*battle, struggle*⟩; implacable ⟨*hate, enemy*⟩ ⟨2⟩ *adv.* (auch fig.) inexorably

unerfahren *Adj.* inexperienced

unerfreulich ⟨1⟩ *Adj.* unpleasant; bad ⟨*news*⟩ ⟨2⟩ *adv.* unpleasantly

unerheblich *Adj.* insignificant

unerhört ⟨1⟩ *Adj.* (empörend) outrageous ⟨2⟩ *adv.* outrageously

unerlaubt ⟨1⟩ *Adj.* unauthorized ⟨2⟩ *adv.* without authorization

unerledigt *Adj.* not dealt with *postpos.*

unermüdlich ⟨1⟩ *Adj.* tireless, untiring (**bei, in** + *Dat.* in) ⟨2⟩ *adv.* tirelessly

unerreichbar *Adj.* inaccessible; (fig.) unattainable

unerreicht *Adj.* unequalled

unersättlich *Adj.* insatiable

unerschöpflich *Adj.* inexhaustible

unersetzlich *Adj.* irreplaceable

unerträglich */od.* '----/ *Adj.* unbearable; intolerable ⟨*situation, conditions, etc.*⟩

unerwartet ⟨1⟩ *Adj.* unexpected; **es kam für alle ~:** it came as a surprise to everybody ⟨2⟩ *adv.* unexpectedly

unerwünscht *Adj.* unwanted; unwelcome ⟨*interruption, visit, visitor*⟩; undesirable ⟨*side effects*⟩

unethisch ⟨1⟩ *Adj.* unethical ⟨2⟩ *adv.* unethically

unfähig *Adj.* (a) ~ **sein, etw. zu tun** (ständig) be incapable of doing sth.; (momentan) be unable to do sth. (b) (inkompetent) incompetent

Unfähigkeit *die* (a) inability (b) (Inkompetenz) incompetence

unfair ⟨1⟩ *Adj.* unfair (**gegen** to) ⟨2⟩ *adv.* unfairly

Un·fall: *der;* ~[e]s, **Unfälle** accident

Unfall-: ~**arzt** *der,* ~**ärztin** *die* casualty doctor; ~**flucht** *die* (Rechtsspr.) ~**flucht begehen** fail to stop after [being involved in] an accident; ~**opfer** *das* accident victim; ~**stelle** *die* scene of an/the accident; ~**versicherung** *die* accident insurance

unfehlbar *Adj.* infallible

Unfehlbarkeit *die;* ~: infallibility

unförmig *Adj.* shapeless; huge ⟨*legs, hands, body*⟩; bulky, ungainly ⟨*shape, shoes*⟩

unfrei *Adj.* not free *pred.*; subject, dependent ⟨*people*⟩; ⟨*life*⟩ of bondage

u

unfreiwillig ① *Adj.* involuntary;
(erzwungen) enforced ⟨*stay*⟩; (nicht beabsichtigt)
unintended ⟨*publicity, joke, humour*⟩
② *adv.* involuntarily; without wanting to;
(unbeabsichtigt) unintentionally

unfreundlich ① *Adj.* unfriendly (**zu,
gegen** to); unkind ⟨*words, remark*⟩
② *adv.* in an unfriendly way

Unfreundlichkeit *die;* ∼: unfriendliness

unfrisiert *Adj.* ungroomed ⟨*hair*⟩

unfruchtbar *Adj.* infertile; (fig.)
unproductive

Unfruchtbarkeit *die;* ∼: infertility; (fig.)
unproductiveness

Unfug *der;* ∼[e]s **(a)** [piece of] mischief;
grober ∼: public nuisance
(b) (Unsinn) nonsense

Ungar *der;* ∼n, ∼n, **Ungarin** *die;* ∼,
∼nen Hungarian

ungarisch *Adj.* Hungarian

Ungarn (*das*) ∼s Hungary

ungeachtet *Präp. mit Gen.* (geh.)
notwithstanding; despite

ungebildet *Adj.* uneducated

ungeboren *Adj.* unborn

ungebräuchlich *Adj.* uncommon; rare;
rarely used ⟨*method, process*⟩

ungebrochen *Adj.* (fig.) unbroken ⟨*will,
person*⟩; undiminished ⟨*strength, courage*⟩

ungedeckt *Adj.* uncovered ⟨*cheque*⟩

Ungeduld *die;* ∼: impatience

ungeduldig ① *Adj.* impatient
② *adv.* impatiently

ungeeignet *Adj.* unsuitable; (für eine
Aufgabe) unsuited (**für, zu** to, for)

ungefähr ① *Adj.* approximate; rough
⟨*idea, outline*⟩
② *adv.* approximately; roughly

ungefährlich *Adj.* safe; harmless ⟨*animal,
person, illness, etc.*⟩

ungeheizt *Adj.* unheated

ungeheuer ① *Adj.* enormous; tremendous
⟨*strength, energy, effort, enthusiasm, fear,
success, pressure, etc.*⟩; vast, immense
⟨*fortune, knowledge*⟩; (schrecklich) terrible
(coll.), terrific (coll.) ⟨*pain, rage*⟩
② *adv.* tremendously; terribly (coll.)
⟨*difficult, clever*⟩

Ungeheuer *das;* ∼s, ∼ (auch fig.) monster

ungeheuerlich *Adj.* monstrous;
outrageous

Ungeheuerlichkeit *die;* ∼, ∼en **(a)**
monstrous nature; outrageousness
(b) (Vorgang) monstrous or outrageous thing

ungehindert *Adj.* unimpeded

ungehörig ① *Adj.* improper; (frech)
impertinent
② *adv.* improperly; (frech) impertinently

ungehorsam *Adj.* disobedient (**gegenüber**
to)

Ungehorsam *der;* ∼s disobedience
(**gegenüber** to)

ungekürzt *Adj.* unabridged ⟨*edition, book*⟩;
uncut ⟨*film, speech*⟩

ungelegen ① *Adj.* das kommt mir sehr ∼/
nicht ∼: that is very inconvenient or
awkward/quite convenient for me
② *adv.* inconveniently

ungelernt *Adj.* unskilled

ungemütlich ① *Adj.* uninviting, cheerless
⟨*room, flat*⟩; uncomfortable, unfriendly
⟨*atmosphere*⟩
② *adv.* uncomfortably ⟨*furnished*⟩

ungenau ① *Adj.* inaccurate; imprecise,
inexact ⟨*definition, formulation, etc.*⟩;
(undeutlich) vague ⟨*memory, idea, impression*⟩
② *adv.* inaccurately; ⟨*define*⟩ imprecisely,
inexactly; ⟨*remember*⟩ vaguely

ungeniert /ˈʊnʒeniːɐ̯t/ ① *Adj.* free and
easy; uninhibited
② *adv.* openly; ⟨*yawn*⟩ unconcernedly;
⟨*undress etc.*⟩ without any embarrassment

ungenießbar *Adj.* (nicht essbar) inedible;
(nicht trinkbar) undrinkable; (fig. ugs.)
unbearable

ungenügend ① *Adj.* inadequate; die Note
„∼"/ein Ungenügend (Schulw.) the/an
'unsatisfactory' [mark]
② *adv.* inadequately

ungepflegt *Adj.* neglected ⟨*garden, park,
car, etc.*⟩; unkempt ⟨*person, appearance,
hair*⟩; uncared-for ⟨*hands*⟩

ungerade *Adj.* odd ⟨*number*⟩

ungerecht ① *Adj.* unjust, unfair (**gegen,
zu, gegenüber** to)
② *adv.* unjustly; unfairly

Ungerechtigkeit *die;* ∼, ∼en injustice

ungern *Adv.* reluctantly; etw. ∼ tun not like
or dislike doing sth.

ungerührt *Adj.* unmoved

ungeschält *Adj.* unpeeled ⟨*fruit*⟩

ungeschehen *Adj.* etw. ∼ machen undo
sth.

Ungeschicklichkeit *die;* ∼, ∼en
(a) clumsiness
(b) (etwas Ungeschicktes) piece of clumsiness

ungeschickt ① *Adj.* clumsy; awkward
② *adv.* clumsily; awkwardly

ungesetzlich ① *Adj.* unlawful; illegal
② *adv.* unlawfully; illegally

ungestempelt *Adj.* uncancelled ⟨*stamp*⟩

ungestört *Adj.* undisturbed; uninterrupted
⟨*development*⟩

ungesund *Adj.* (auch fig.) unhealthy

Ungetüm *das;* ∼s, ∼e monster

ungewiss, *ungewiß *Adj.* uncertain;
über etw. (*Akk.*) im Ungewissen sein be
uncertain or unsure about sth.

Ungewissheit, *Ungewißheit *die;* ∼,
∼en uncertainty

ungewöhnlich ① *Adj.* **(a)** unusual

(b) (sehr groß) exceptional ⟨*strength, beauty, ability, etc.*⟩; outstanding ⟨*achievement, success*⟩
2 *adv.* **(a)** ⟨*behave*⟩ abnormally, strangely **(b)** (enorm) exceptionally

ungewohnt 1 *Adj.* unaccustomed; (nicht vertraut) unfamiliar ⟨*method, work, surroundings, etc.*⟩
2 *adv.* unusually

ungewollt 1 *Adj.* unwanted; (unbeabsichtigt) unintentional; inadvertent
2 *adv.* unintenionally; inadvertently

Ungeziefer *das;* ~s vermin *pl.*

ungezogen 1 *Adj.* naughty; badly behaved; bad ⟨*behaviour*⟩; (frech) cheeky
2 *adv.* naughtily; ⟨*behave*⟩ badly

ungezwungen *Adj.* natural, unaffected ⟨*person, behaviour, cheerfulness*⟩; (nicht förmlich) informal, free and easy ⟨*tone, conversation, etc.*⟩

ungläubig 1 *Adj.* **(a)** disbelieving **(b)** (Rel.) unbelieving
2 *adv.* in disbelief

unglaublich 1 *Adj.* incredible
2 *adv.* (ugs.: äußerst) incredibly (coll.)

unglaubwürdig *Adj.* implausible; untrustworthy, unreliable ⟨*witness etc.*⟩

ungleich 1 *Adj.* unequal; odd, unmatching ⟨*socks, gloves, etc.*⟩; (unähnlich) dissimilar
2 *adv.* **(a)** unequally **(b)** (ungleichmäßig) unevenly

ungleichmäßig 1 *Adj.* uneven
2 *adv.* unevenly

Unglück *das;* ~[e]s, ~e **(a)** (Unfall) accident; (Flugzeugunglück, Zugunglück) crash; accident **(b)** (Not) misfortune; (Leid) suffering **(c)** (Pech) bad luck; ~ haben be unlucky; das bringt ~: that's unlucky **(d)** (Schicksalsschlag) misfortune

unglücklich 1 *Adj.* **(a)** unhappy **(b)** (nicht vom Glück begünstigt) unfortunate ⟨*person*⟩; (bedauernswert, arm) hapless ⟨*person, animal*⟩ **(c)** (ungünstig, ungeschickt) unfortunate ⟨*moment, combination, meeting, etc.*⟩; unhappy ⟨*end, choice, solution*⟩
2 *adv.* **(a)** unhappily **(b)** (ungünstig) unfortunately; (ungeschickt) unhappily, clumsily ⟨*translated, expressed*⟩

unglücklicher·weise *Adv.* unfortunately

Unglücks·fall *der* accident

Ungnade *die* [bei jmdm.] in ~ (*Akk.*) fallen/in ~ (*Dat.*) sein fall/be out of favour [with sb.]

ungnädig *Adj.* bad-tempered; grumpy

ungültig *Adj.* invalid; void (esp. Law); spoilt ⟨*vote, ballot paper*⟩; disallowed ⟨*goal*⟩

Ungunst *die* zu jmds. ~en to sb.'s disadvantage

ungünstig 1 *Adj.* **(a)** unfavourable; unfortunate, bad ⟨*shape, layout*⟩ **(b)** (unpassend) inconvenient ⟨*time*⟩; (ungeeignet) inappropriate, inconvenient ⟨*time, place*⟩
2 *adv.* **(a)** unfavourably; badly ⟨*designed, laid out*⟩ **(b)** (unpassend) inconveniently

ungut *Adj.* nichts für ~! no offence [meant]! (coll.)

unhandlich *Adj.* unwieldy

Unheil *das;* ~s disaster

unheilbar 1 *Adj.* incurable
2 *adv.* incurably

unheil·voll *Adj.* disastrous; (verhängnisvoll) fateful

unheimlich 1 *Adj.* **(a)** eerie **(b)** (ugs.) (schrecklich) terrible (coll.) ⟨*hunger, headache, etc.*⟩ terrific (coll.) ⟨*fun etc.*⟩
2 *adv.* **(a)** eerily **(b)** (ugs.: äußerst) terribly (coll.); incredibly (coll.) ⟨*quick, long*⟩

unhöflich 1 *Adj.* impolite
2 *adv.* impolitely

Unhöflichkeit *die;* ~, ~en impoliteness

unhygienisch 1 *Adj.* unhygienic
2 *adv.* unhygienically

Uni *die;* ~, ~s (ugs.) university

Uniform *die;* ~, ~en uniform

uninteressant *Adj.* uninteresting; (nicht von Belang) of no interest *postpos.;* unimportant

Union *die;* ~, ~en union

Universität *die;* ~, ~en university

Universum *das;* ~s universe

unkenntlich *Adj.* unrecognizable ⟨*person, face*⟩; indecipherable ⟨*writing, stamp*⟩

Unkenntnis *die;* ~: ignorance

unklar *Adj.* unclear; sich (*Dat.*) über etw. (*Akk.*) im Unklaren sein be unclear *or* unsure about sth.

unkonventionell 1 *Adj.* unconventional
2 *adv.* unconventionally

Unkosten *Pl.* **(a)** [extra] expense *sing.;* expenses **(b)** (ugs.: Ausgaben) costs; expenditure *sing.*

Unkosten·beitrag *der* contribution towards expenses

Unkraut *das;* ~[e]s, Unkräuter weeds *pl.*

unkultiviert *Adj.* uncultivated

unlauter *Adj.* (geh.) dishonest; ~er Wettbewerb (Rechtsspr.) unfair competition

unleserlich 1 *Adj.* illegible
2 *adv.* illegibly

unmäßig 1 *Adj.* immoderate; excessive
2 *adv.* excessively; ⟨*eat, drink*⟩ to excess

Unmenge *die* mass; enormous number/ amount

Unmensch *der;* ~en, ~en brute

unmenschlich 1 *Adj.* **(a)** inhuman; brutal; appalling ⟨*conditions*⟩ **(b)** (entsetzlich) appalling ····❖

② *adv.* **(a)** in an inhuman way
(b) (entsetzlich) appallingly (coll.)

unmissverständlich,
*unmißverständlich ① *Adj.* **(a)**
(eindeutig) unambiguous
(b) (offen, direkt) blunt ⟨*answer, refusal*⟩;
unequivocal ⟨*language*⟩
② *adv.* **(a)** (eindeutig) unambiguously
(b) (offen, direkt) bluntly; unequivocally

unmittelbar ① *Adj.* immediate; direct
⟨*contact, connection, influence, etc.*⟩
② *adv.* immediately; directly

unmöbliert *Adj.* unfurnished

unmodern ① *Adj.* old-fashioned; (nicht
modisch) unfashionable
② *adv.* in an old-fashioned way; (nicht
modisch) unfashionably

unmöglich ① *Adj.* impossible; (ugs.:
seltsam) incredible
② *adv.* (ugs.) ⟨*behave*⟩ impossibly; ⟨*dress*⟩
ridiculously
③ *Adv.* (ugs.) **ich/es** *usw.* **kann ∼ …:** I/it *etc.*
can't possibly …

unmoralisch ① *Adj.* immoral
② *adv.* immorally

unmündig *Adj.* under-age

Unmut *der;* ∼[e]s (geh.) displeasure;
annoyance

unnachsichtig ① *Adj.* merciless;
unmerciful
② *adv.* mercilessly; ⟨*punish*⟩ unmercifully

unnahbar *Adj.* unapproachable

unnatürlich ① *Adj.* unnatural; forced
⟨*laugh*⟩
② *adv.* unnaturally; ⟨*laugh*⟩ in a forced way;
⟨*speak*⟩ affectedly

unnötig ① *Adj.* unnecessary
② *adv.* unnecessarily

unnütz *Adj.* useless

UNO *die;* ∼: UN

unordentlich ① *Adj.* **(a)** untidy
(b) (ungeregelt) disorderly ⟨*life*⟩
② *adv.* untidily; ⟨*tie, treat, etc.*⟩ carelessly

Unordnung *die;* ∼: disorder; mess

unparteiisch ① *Adj.* impartial
② *adv.* impartially

unpassend ① *Adj.* inappropriate;
unsuitable ⟨*dress etc.*⟩
② *adv.* inappropriately; unsuitably ⟨*dressed
etc.*⟩

unpersönlich ① *Adj.* impersonal; distant,
aloof ⟨*person*⟩
② *adv.* impersonally; ⟨*answer, write*⟩ in
impersonal terms

unpraktisch ① *Adj.* unpractical
② *adv.* in an unpractical way

unproblematisch *Adj.* unproblematic

unproduktiv *Adj.* unproductive

unpünktlich ① *Adj.* unpunctual ⟨*person*⟩;
late, unpunctual ⟨*payment*⟩
② *adv.* late

Unpünktlichkeit *die;* ∼: lack of
punctuality

Unrecht *das;* ∼[e]s wrong; **zu** ∼: wrongly;
∼ **haben** be wrong; **jmdm.** ∼ **tun** do sb. an
injustice

unrechtmäßig ① *Adj.* unlawful
② *adv.* unlawfully

unredlich (geh.) ① *Adj.* dishonest
② *adv.* dishonestly

Unredlichkeit *die;* ∼, ∼en **(a)** dishonesty
(b) (Handlung) dishonest act

unregelmäßig ① *Adj.* irregular
② *adv.* irregularly

Unregelmäßigkeit *die;* ∼, ∼en
irregularity

unreif *Adj.* **(a)** unripe
(b) (nicht erwachsen) immature

unrentabel *Adj.* unprofitable

Unruhe *die;* ∼, ∼n (auch fig.) unrest; (Lärm)
noise; (Unrast) restlessness; (Besorgnis) anxiety

unruhig ① *Adj.* **(a)** restless; (besorgt)
anxious; unsettled, troubled ⟨*time*⟩
(b) (laut) noisy
(c) (ungleichmäßig) uneven ⟨*breathing, pulse,
etc.*⟩; fitful ⟨*sleep*⟩; disturbed ⟨*night*⟩
② *adv.* **(a)** restlessly; (besorgt) anxiously
(b) (ungleichmäßig) unevenly; ⟨*sleep*⟩ fitfully

uns ① **(a)** *Akk. von* WIR us
(b) *Dat. von* WIR; **gib es** ∼: give it to us; **bei**
∼: at our home *or* (coll.) place
② *Reflexivpron. der 1. Pers. Pl.* **(a)** *refl.*
ourselves
(b) *reziprok* one another

unsachlich ① *Adj.* unobjective
② *adv.* without objectivity

unsauber ① *Adj.* **(a)** dirty
(b) (nachlässig) untidy; sloppy
② *adv.* (nachlässig) untidily

unschädlich *Adj.* harmless

unscharf *Adj.* blurred ⟨*photo, picture*⟩

unscheinbar *Adj.* inconspicuous

unschlagbar *Adj.* unbeatable

Unschuld *die;* ∼: innocence; (Jungfräulichkeit)
virginity

unschuldig ① *Adj.* innocent
② *adv.* innocently

unselbständig, unselbstständig
Adj. dependent [on other people]

unser[1] *Possessivpron. der 1. Pers. Pl.* our;
das ist ∼**s** that is ours

unser[2] *Gen. von* WIR (geh.) of us; **in** ∼ **aller/
beider Interesse** in the interest of all/both of
us

unser·einer, unsereins *Indefinitpron.*
(ugs.) the likes of us *pl.*; our sort (coll.)

unserer·seits *Adv.* for our part; (von uns)
on our part

unser[e]s**·gleichen** *indekl. Indefinitpron.*
people *pl.* like us

unsert·wegen *Adv.:* ▶ MEINETWEGEN:
because of us; for our sake; about us; as far
as we are concerned

---

u

unsicher ☐1 *Adj.* uncertain; (nicht
selbstsicher) insecure
  ☐2 *adv.* ⟨*walk, stand, etc.*⟩ unsteadily; (nicht
selbstsicher) ⟨*smile, look*⟩ diffidently

Unsicherheit *die;* ~: uncertainty;
(fehlende Selbstsicherheit) insecurity

unsichtbar *Adj.* invisible (**für** to)

Unsinn *der;* ~[e]s nonsense; ~ **machen**
mess *or* fool about

unsinnig *Adj.* nonsensical ⟨*statement, talk,
etc.*⟩; absurd, ridiculous ⟨*demand etc.*⟩

Unsitte *die;* ~, ~n bad habit

unsittlich ☐1 *Adj.* indecent
  ☐2 *adv.* indecently

unsr... ▶ UNSER[1]

unsterblich *Adj.* immortal

Unsterblichkeit *die;* ~: immortality

unstreitig ☐1 *Adj.* indisputable
  ☐2 *adv.* indisputably

unsympathisch *Adj.* uncongenial,
disagreeable ⟨*person*⟩; unpleasant
⟨*characteristic, nature, voice*⟩

Untat *die;* ~, ~en misdeed; evil deed

untätig *Adj.* idle; ~ **herumsitzen/zusehen**
sit around doing nothing/stand idly by

untauglich *Adj.* unsuitable; (für Militärdienst)
unfit [for service] *postpos.*

unten *Adv.* (a) down; **hier/da** ~: down
here/there; **von** ~: from below
  (b) (in Gebäuden) downstairs; **nach** ~:
downstairs
  (c) (am unteren Ende, zum unteren Ende hin) at
the bottom; ~ **[links] auf der Seite/im
Schrank** at the bottom [left] of the page/
cupboard
  (d) (an der Unterseite) underneath
  (e) (im Text) below; ~ **genannt**
undermentioned (Brit.); mentioned below
postpos.

*unten·genannt ▶ UNTEN E

unter ☐1 *Präp. mit Dat.* (Lage, Standort)
under; (zwischen) among[st]; ~ **100
Stück** quantities of less than 100; ~ **Angst/
Tränen** in *or* out of fear/in tears
  ☐2 *Präp. mit Akk.* under; (zwischen)
among[st]; ~ **Null sinken** drop below zero
  ☐3 *Adv.* less than; ~ **30 [Jahre alt] sein** be
under 30 [years of age]

unter... *Adj.* lower; bottom; (ganz unten)
bottom; (in der Rangfolge o. Ä.) lower

Unter·arm *der* forearm

unterbelichten *tr. V.;* **ich unterbelichte,
unterbelichtet, unterzubelichten** (Fot.)
underexpose

**Unter·bewusstsein,
*Unter·bewußtsein** *das* subconscious

unter·bleiben *unr. itr. V.; mit sein* **etw.
unterbleibt** sth. does not occur *or* happen

unter·brechen *unr. tr. V.* interrupt;
break ⟨*journey, silence*⟩

Unter·brechung *die* ▶ UNTERBRECHEN:
interruption; break (*Gen.* in)

unter|bringen *unr. tr. V.* (a) put
  (b) (beherbergen) put up

Unterbringung *die;* ~, ~en
accommodation *no indef. art.*

unter|buttern *tr. V.* (ugs.) push aside (fig.)

*unter·der·hand ▶ HAND

unter·dessen ▶ INZWISCHEN

unter·drücken *tr. V.* suppress; hold back
⟨*comment, question, answer, criticism, etc.*⟩;
oppress ⟨*minority etc.*⟩

Unterdrückung *die;* ~, ~en (a) (das
Unterdrücken) suppression
  (b) (das Unterdrücktwerden, -sein) oppression

unter·einander *Adv.* (a) (räumlich) one
below the other
  (b) (miteinander) among[st] ourselves/
themselves *etc.*

unter·ernährt *Adj.* undernourished

Unter·ernährung *die* malnutrition

Unter·führung *die* underpass; (für
Fußgänger) subway (Brit.); [pedestrian]
underpass (Amer.)

unter-, Unter-: ~**gang** *der* (a)
(Sonnenuntergang, Monduntergang usw.) setting;
  (b) (von Schiffen) sinking; (c) (das
Zugrundegehen) decline; ~|**gehen** *unr. itr.
V.; mit sein* (a) ⟨*sun, star, etc.*⟩ set; ⟨*ship*⟩
sink, go down; ⟨*person*⟩ drown, go under; (b)
(zugrunde gehen) come to an end;
  ~**geordnet** *Adj.* secondary ⟨*role,
importance, etc.*⟩; subordinate ⟨*position, post,
etc.*⟩; ~**geschoss, *~geschoß** *das*
basement; ~**gewicht** *das* underweight;
~**grund** *der* (bes. Politik) underground;
~**grund·bahn** *die* underground [railway]
(Brit.); subway (Amer.); ~|**haken** *tr. V.* (ugs.)
jmdn. ~**haken** take sb.'s arm; ~**halb**
☐1 *Adv.* below; ~**halb von** below; ☐2 *Präp.
mit Gen.* below; ~**halt** *der* (a) living; (b)
(Zahlung) maintenance; (c)
(Instandhaltung[skosten]) upkeep

unter-, Unter-: ~**halten** ☐1 *unr. tr. V.*
(a) support; (b) (instand halten) maintain
⟨*building*⟩; (c) (betreiben) run, keep ⟨*car,
hotel*⟩; (d) (pflegen) maintain, keep up
⟨*contact, correspondence*⟩; (e) entertain
⟨*guest, audience*⟩; ☐2 *unr. refl. V.* (a) talk;
converse; (b) (sich vergnügen) enjoy oneself;
~**haltsam** *Adj.* entertaining; ~**haltung**
die (a) (Versorgung) support; (b) (Instandhaltung)
maintenance; (c) (Gespräch) conversation; (d)
(Zeitvertreib) entertainment

unter-, Unter-: ~**händler** *der,*
~**händlerin** *die* (bes. Politik) negotiator;
~**hemd** *das* vest (Brit.); undershirt (Amer.);
~**holz** *das* underwood; undergrowth;
~**hose** *die* (für Männer) briefs *pl.;*
[under]pants *pl.;* (für Frauen) panties *pl.;*
knickers *pl.* (Brit.); ~**irdisch** ☐1 *Adj.*
underground; ☐2 *adv.* underground;
~|**jubeln** *tr. V.* (ugs.) **jmdm. etw.** ~**jubeln**
palm sth. off on sb.; ~**kiefer** *der* lower   ⸱⸱⸱⸺

jaw; ~|**kommen** *unr. itr. V.; mit sein* find accommodation; ~**kühlt** *Adj.* ~kühlt sein be suffering from hypothermia *or* exposure

Unterkunft *die;* ~, Unterkünfte accommodation *no indef. art.;* lodging *no indef. art.;* ~ und Frühstück bed and breakfast; ~ und Verpflegung board and lodging

Unter·lage *die* (a) (Schreibunterlage) pad; (für eine Schreibmaschine usw.) mat (b) *Pl.* documents; papers

unter-, Unter-: ~**lassen** *unr. tr. V.* refrain from [doing]; ~**lassung** *die;* ~~, ~~en omission; failure;

~**lassungs·sünde** *die* (ugs.) sin of omission; ~**laufen** *unr. itr. V.; mit sein* occur; jmdm. ist ein Fehler/Irrtum ~laufen sb. made a mistake; ~**legen** *Adj.* inferior; jmdm. ~legen sein be inferior to sb. (an + *Dat.* in); ~**leib** *der* lower abdomen

unter·liegen *unr. itr. V.* (a) *mit sein* (besiegt werden) lose; be beaten *or* defeated (b) (unterworfen sein) be subject to

Unter·lippe *die* lower lip

unterm *Präp. + Art.* = unter dem

unter·malen *tr. V.* accompany

Unter·malung *die;* ~, ~en accompaniment (*Gen.* to)

unter·mauern *tr. V.* (mit Argumenten, Fakten absichern) back up

Unter-: ~**miete** *die* subtenancy; sublease; ~**mieter** *der,* ~**mieterin** *die* subtenant; lodger

untern (ugs.) *Präp. + Art.* = unter den

unter-, Unter-: ~**nehmen** *unr. tr. V.* (a) (durchführen) undertake; make; take ⟨steps⟩; (b) etwas ~nehmen do something; ~**nehmen** *das;* ~~s, ~~ (a) (Vorhaben) enterprise; (b) (Firma) concern; ~**nehmer** *der;* ~~s, ~~, ~**nehmerin** *die;* ~~, ~~nen employer

unternehmerisch **1** *Adj.* entrepreneurial **2** *adv.* ⟨think⟩ in an entrepreneurial *or* businesslike way

unter·nehmungs·lustig *Adj.* active; sie ist sehr ~ she is always out doing things

Unter·offizier *der* (a) non-commissioned officer (b) (Dienstgrad) corporal

unter·ordnen **1** *tr. V.* subordinate **2** *refl. V.* accept a subordinate role

Unter·redung *die;* ~, ~en discussion

Unter·richt *der;* ~[e]s, ~e instruction; (Schulunterricht) teaching; (Schulstunden) classes *pl.*

unter·richten **1** *tr. V.* (a) teach (b) (informieren) inform (**über** + *Akk.* of, about) **2** *itr. V.* (Unterricht geben) teach **3** *refl. V.* (sich informieren) inform oneself (**über** + *Akk.* about)

Unterrichts·stunde *die* lesson; period

Unter·rock *der* [half] slip

unter|rühren *tr. V.* stir in

unters *Präp. + Art.* = **unter das**

unter·sagen *tr. V.* forbid; prohibit

Unter·satz *der* ▶ UNTERSETZER

unter-, Unter-: ~**schätzen** *tr. V.* underestimate ⟨amount, effect, etc.⟩; underrate ⟨talent, ability, etc.⟩; ~**scheiden** **1** *unr. tr. V.* distinguish; **2** *unr. refl. V.* differ (**durch** in, **von** from); ~**scheidung** *die* (Vorgang) differentiation; (Resultat) distinction

Unter-: ~**schenkel** *der* shank; lower leg; ~**schicht** *die* (Soziol.) lower class

Unter·schied *der;* ~[e]s, ~e difference

unterschiedlich **1** *Adj.* different; (uneinheitlich) variable; varying **2** *adv.* [sehr/ganz] ~: in [very/quite] different ways

unterschieds·los **1** *Adj.* uniform; equal ⟨treatment⟩ **2** *adv.* ⟨treat⟩ equally; (ohne Benachteiligung) without discrimination

unter·schlagen *unr. tr. V.* embezzle ⟨money, funds, etc.⟩; (unterdrücken) intercept ⟨letter⟩; withhold ⟨fact, news, information, etc.⟩

Unter·schlupf *der;* ~[e]s, ~e shelter; (Versteck) hiding place; hideout

unter|schlüpfen *itr. V.; mit sein* (ugs.) hide out

unter·schreiben *unr. itr., tr. V.* sign

Unter-: ~**schrift** *die* signature; (Bild~) caption; ~**see·boot** *das* submarine; ~**setzer** *der* mat; (für Gläser) coaster

untersetzt *Adj.* stocky

Unter·stand *der* (Schutzbunker) dugout; (Unterschlupf) shelter

unter|stehen **1** *unr. itr. V.* jmdm. ~: be subordinate *or* answerable to sb. **2** *unr. refl. V.* dare

unter|stellen[1] **1** *tr. V.* (zur Aufbewahrung) keep; store ⟨furniture⟩ **2** *refl. V.* take shelter

unter·stellen[2] *tr. V.* (a) jmdm. eine Abteilung ~: put sb. in charge of a department; die Behörde ist dem Ministerium unterstellt the office is under the ministry (b) (unterschieben) jmdm. böse Absichten *usw.* ~: insinuate that sb.'s intentions *etc.* are bad

Unter·stellung *die* (falsche Behauptung) insinuation

unter·streichen *unr. tr. V.* (a) underline (b) (hervorheben) emphasize

Unter·streichung *die;* ~, ~en (a) underlining (b) (das Betonen) emphasizing

unter·stützen *tr. V.* support

Unter·stützung *die;* ~, ~en (a) support (b) (finanzielle Hilfe) allowance; (für Arbeitslose) [unemployment] benefit *no art.*

unter·suchen *tr. V.* examine; (überprüfen)

test (**auf** + *Akk.* for); (aufzuklären suchen) investigate; (durchsuchen) search (**auf** + *Akk.*, **nach** for)

Untersuchung *die;* ∼, ∼en (a)
▶ UNTERSUCHEN: examination; test; investigation; search
(b) (wissenschaftliche Arbeit) study

Untersuchungs·haft *die* imprisonment *or* detention while awaiting trial

Unter·tasse *die* saucer

unter|tauchen 1 *itr. V.; mit sein* (a) (im Wasser) dive [under]
(b) (verschwinden) disappear
2 *tr. V.* duck

Unter·teil *das od. der* bottom part

unter·teilen *tr. V.* divide; (gliedern) subdivide

Unter·titel *der* subtitle

unter·treiben *unr. itr. V.* play things down

Untertreibung *die;* ∼, ∼en understatement

unter·vermieten *tr., itr. V.* sublet

unter·wandern *tr. V.* infiltrate

Unter·wanderung *die* infiltration *no indef. art.*

Unter·wäsche *die* underwear

unterwegs *Adv.* on the way; (nicht zu Hause) out [and about]

unter·weisen *unr. tr. V.* (geh.) instruct

Unter·welt *die;* ∼: underworld

unter·werfen 1 *unr. tr. V.* (a) subjugate ⟨*people, country*⟩
(b) (unterziehen) subject (*Dat.* to)
2 *unr. refl. V.* **sich** [jmdm./einer Sache] ∼: submit [to sb./sth.]

Unterwerfung *die;* ∼, ∼en (a) (das Unterwerfen) subjugation (**unter** + *Akk.* to)
(b) (das Sichunterwerfen) submission (**unter** + *Akk.* to)

unterwürfig 1 *Adj.* obsequious
2 *adv.* obsequiously

unter·zeichnen *tr. V.* sign

unter·ziehen 1 *unr. tr. V.* etw. einer Untersuchung/Überprüfung (*Dat.*) ∼: examine/check sth.
2 *unr. refl. V.* **sich einer Operation** (*Dat.*) ∼: undergo *or* have an operation

untragbar *Adj.* unbearable

untreu *Adj.* disloyal; (in der Ehe, Liebe) unfaithful

Untreue *die;* ∼: disloyalty; (in der Ehe, Liebe) unfaithfulness

untröstlich *Adj.* inconsolable

Untugend *die;* ∼, ∼en bad habit

unüberlegt 1 *Adj.* rash
2 *adv.* rashly

unübersehbar 1 *Adj.* (a) (offenkundig) conspicuous
(b) (sehr groß) enormous
2 *adv.* (sehr) extremely

unübersichtlich 1 *Adj.* unclear; confusing ⟨*arrangement*⟩; blind ⟨*bend*⟩; broken ⟨*country etc.*⟩
2 *adv.* unclearly; confusingly ⟨*arranged*⟩

unübertrefflich 1 *Adj.* superb
2 *adv.* superbly

unübertroffen *Adj.* unsurpassed

unumgänglich *Adj.* [absolutely] necessary

Unumgänglichkeit *die;* ∼: absolute necessity

unumwunden 1 *Adj.* frank
2 *adv.* frankly; openly

ununterbrochen 1 *Adj.* incessant
2 *adv.* incessantly

unveränderlich *Adj.* unchangeable

unverantwortlich 1 *Adj.* irresponsible
2 *adv.* irresponsibly

unverbesserlich *Adj.* incorrigible

unverbindlich 1 *Adj.* (a) not binding *pred.;* without obligation *postpos;*
(b) (reserviert) non-committal ⟨*answer, words*⟩; impersonal ⟨*attitude*⟩
2 *adv.* ⟨*send, reserve*⟩ without obligation

unverbleit *Adj.* unleaded

unverblümt 1 *Adj.* blunt
2 *adv.* bluntly

unverbraucht *Adj.* untouched; unspent ⟨*energy*⟩; fresh ⟨*air*⟩

unverdaut *Adj.* undigested

unverdorben *Adj.* unspoilt

unverdrossen *Adj.* undeterred; (unverzagt) undaunted

unvereinbar *Adj.* incompatible (**mit** with)

Unvereinbarkeit *die;* ∼: incompatibility (**mit** with)

unverfänglich *Adj.* harmless

unverfroren *Adj.* insolent; impudent

unvergänglich *Adj.* immortal ⟨*fame*⟩; unchanging ⟨*beauty*⟩; abiding ⟨*recollection*⟩

unvergesslich, *unvergeßlich *Adj.* unforgettable

unvergleichlich 1 *Adj.* incomparable
2 *adv.* incomparably

unverheiratet *Adj.* unmarried

unverhofft 1 *Adj.* unexpected
2 *adv.* unexpectedly

unverhohlen 1 *Adj.* unconcealed
2 *adv.* openly

unverkäuflich *Adj.* **diese Vase ist** ∼: this vase is not for sale/(nicht absetzbar) unsaleable

unvermeidlich *Adj.* unavoidable; (sich als Folge ergebend) inevitable

Unvermögen *das;* ∼s lack of ability

unvermutet 1 *Adj.* unexpected
2 *adv.* unexpectedly

unvernünftig *Adj.* stupid; foolish

unverrichtet *Adj.* ∼**er Dinge** without having achieved anything

u

unverschämt ① *Adj.* (a) impertinent
⟨*person, manner, words, etc.*⟩; barefaced ⟨*lie*⟩
(b) (ugs.: sehr groß) outrageous ⟨*price, luck,
etc.*⟩
② *adv.* impertinently; ⟨*lie*⟩ barefacedly;
blatantly

Unverschämtheit *die;* ~, ~en
impertinence

unversehens *Adv.* suddenly

unversehrt *Adj.* unscathed; (unbeschädigt)
undamaged

unverständlich *Adj.* incomprehensible

Unverständnis *das;* ~ses lack of
understanding

unverträglich *Adj.* (a) quarrelsome
(b) incompatible ⟨*blood groups, medicines,
transplant tissue*⟩

unverwechselbar *Adj.* unmistakable;
distinctive

unverwüstlich *Adj.* indestructible

unverzeihlich *Adj.* unforgivable

unverzüglich ① *Adj.* prompt
② *adv.* promptly

unvollkommen ① *Adj.* (a) imperfect
(b) (unvollständig) incomplete
② *adv.* (a) imperfectly
(b) (unvollständig) incompletely

Unvollkommenheit *die;* ~: (a)
imperfectness
(b) (Unvollständigkeit) incompleteness

unvollständig *Adj.* incomplete

Unvollständigkeit *die;* ~:
incompleteness

unvorhergesehen *Adj.* unforeseen;
unexpected ⟨*visit*⟩

unvorhersehbar *Adj.* unforeseeable

unvorsichtig ① *Adj.* careless; (unüberlegt)
rash
② *adv.* carelessly; (unüberlegt) rashly

Unvorsichtigkeit *die;* ~ ▶ UNVORSICHTIG
1: carelessness; rashness

unvorstellbar ① *Adj.* inconceivable
② *adv.* unimaginably

unvorteilhaft *Adj.* (a) unattractive
⟨*figure, appearance*⟩
(b) (ohne Vorteil) unfavourable, poor
⟨*purchase, exchange*⟩; unprofitable ⟨*business*⟩

unwahr *Adj.* untrue

Unwahrheit *die;* ~, ~en (a)
untruthfulness
(b) (Äußerung) untruth

unwahrscheinlich ① *Adj.* (a)
improbable; unlikely
(b) (ugs.: sehr viel) incredible (coll.)
② *adv.* (ugs.: sehr) incredibly (coll.)

Unwahrscheinlichkeit *die;* ~:
improbability

unwegsam *Adj.* [almost] impassable

unweiblich *Adj.* unfeminine

unweigerlich ① *Adj.* inevitable

② *adv.* inevitably

Unwesen *das:* **sein** ~ **treiben** (abwertend) be
up to one's mischief *or* one's tricks

Unwetter *das;* ~s, ~: [thunder]storm

unwichtig *Adj.* unimportant

Unwichtigkeit *die;* ~, ~en (a)
unimportance
(b) (etw. Unwichtiges) unimportant thing

unwiderruflich ① *Adj.* irrevocable
② *adv.* irrevocably

unwiderstehlich *Adj.* irresistible

unwiederbringlich (geh.) ① *Adj.*
irretrievable
② *adv.* irretrievably

Unwille[n] *der;* Unwillens displeasure

unwillig ① *Adj.* indignant; (widerwillig)
unwilling
② *adv.* indignantly; (widerwillig) unwillingly

unwillkürlich ① *Adj.* (a) spontaneous
⟨*cry, sigh*⟩; instinctive ⟨*reaction, movement,
etc.*⟩
(b) (Physiol.) involuntary ⟨*movement etc.*⟩
② *adv.* (a) ⟨*shout etc.*⟩ spontaneously; ⟨*react,
move, etc.*⟩ instinctively
(b) (Physiol.) ⟨*move etc.*⟩ involuntarily

unwirklich (geh.) *Adj.* unreal

Unwirklichkeit *die;* ~, ~en unreality

unwirksam *Adj.* ineffective

Unwirksamkeit *die;* ~: ineffectiveness

unwirsch ① *Adj.* surly; ill-natured
② *adv.* ill-naturedly

unwirtschaftlich ① *Adj.* uneconomic
⟨*procedure etc.*⟩; (nicht sparsam) uneconomical
⟨*driving etc.*⟩
② *adv.* ⟨*work, drive, etc.*⟩ uneconomically

Unwissenheit *die;* ~: ignorance

unwissentlich ① *Adj.* unconscious
② *adv.* unknowingly; unwittingly

unwohl *Adv.* unwell; **mir ist** ~: I don't feel
well

Unwohlsein *das;* ~s indisposition

unwürdig *Adj.* (a) undignified ⟨*person,
behaviour*⟩; degrading ⟨*treatment*⟩
(b) (unangemessen) unworthy

unzählig *Adj.* innumerable; countless

Unze *die;* ~, ~n ounce

unzeitgemäß *Adj.* anachronistic

unzerbrechlich *Adj.* unbreakable

unzertrennlich *Adj.* inseparable

Unzucht *die:* ~ **treiben** fornicate;
gewerbsmäßige ~: prostitution

unzüchtig ① *Adj.* obscene ⟨*letter, gesture*⟩
② *adv.* ⟨*touch, approach, etc.*⟩ indecently;
⟨*speak*⟩ obscenely

unzufrieden *Adj.* dissatisfied; (stärker)
unhappy

Unzufriedenheit *die;* ~: dissatisfaction;
(stärker) unhappiness

unzugänglich *Adj.* inaccessible ⟨*area,
building, etc.*⟩; unapproachable ⟨*character,
person, etc.*⟩

---

*alte Schreibung - vgl. Hinweis auf S. xiv

unzulänglich (geh.) ①*Adj.* insufficient
②*adv.* insufficiently

unzumutbar *Adj.* unreasonable

unzurechnungsfähig *Adj.* not
responsible for one's actions *pred.;*
(geistesgestört) of unsound mind *postpos.*

unzustellbar *Adj.* (Postw.) „~": 'not
known [at this address]'

unzutreffend *Adj.* inappropriate; (falsch)
incorrect

unzuverlässig *Adj.* unreliable

Unzuverlässigkeit *die;* ~: unreliability

unzweckmäßig ①*Adj.* unsuitable;
(unpraktisch) impractical
②*adv.* unsuitably; (unpraktisch) impractically

Update /'apdeit/ *das;* ~s, ~s (DV) update

üppig ①*Adj.* lush ⟨*vegetation*⟩; thick ⟨*hair,
beard*⟩; full ⟨*bosom, lips*⟩; voluptuous ⟨*figure,
woman*⟩; (fig.) sumptuous, opulent ⟨*meal*⟩
②*adv.* luxuriantly; (fig.) sumptuously

Ur·abstimmung *die* [esp. strike] ballot

Ural *der;* ~[s] Urals *pl.;* Ural Mountains *pl.*

ur·alt *Adj.* very old; ancient

Uran *das;* ~s uranium

Ur·aufführung *die* première; first night *or*
performance; (eines Films) première; first
showing

urbar *Adj.* ein Stück Land ~ machen
cultivate a piece of land

Ur·einwohner *der,* **Ur·einwohnerin**
die native inhabitant

Ur·enkel *der* great-grandson

Urgroß-: ~**eltern** *Pl.* great-grandparents;
~**mutter** *die; Pl.* ~mütter great-
grandmother; ~**vater** *der* great-
grandfather

Ur·heber *der;* ~s, ~: originator; initiator;
(bes. Rechtsspr.: Verfasser, Autor) author

Urheber·recht *das* copyright

urig *Adj.* natural ⟨*person*⟩; real ⟨*beer*⟩; cosy
⟨*pub*⟩

Urin *der;* ~s, ~e (Med.) urine

urinieren *itr. V.* urinate

Ur·knall *der* big bang

Ur·kunde *die;* ~, ~n document;
(Bescheinigung, Siegerurkunde, Diplom usw.)
certificate

Urlaub *der;* ~[e]s, ~e holiday[s] (Brit.);
vacation (esp. Amer.); (bes. Milit.) leave

urlaubs-, Urlaubs-: ~**geld** *das* holiday
pay *or* money; (gespartes Geld) holiday
money; ~**ort** *der* holiday resort; ~**reif**
Adj. ~reif sein (ugs.) be ready for a holiday;
~**reise** *die* holiday [trip]; ~**zeit** *die*
holiday period *or* season

Urne *die;* ~, ~n urn; (Wahlurne) [ballot] box

Ur·oma *die* (fam.) great-granny (coll./child
lang.)

Ur·opa *der* (fam.) great-grandpa (coll./child
lang.)

Ur·sache *die* cause

Ur·sprung *der* origin

ur·sprünglich ①*Adj.* (a) original ⟨*plan,
price, form, material, etc.*⟩
(b) (natürlich) natural
②*adv.* (a) originally
(b) (natürlich) naturally

Urteil *das;* ~s, ~e judgement; (Strafe)
sentence; (Gerichtsurteil) verdict

urteilen *itr. V.* form an opinion; judge;
über etw./jmdn. ~: judge sth./sb.

urteils-, Urteils-: ~**fähig** *Adj.*
competent *or* able to judge *postpos.;*
~**fähigkeit** *die* competence *or* ability to
judge; ~**vermögen** *das* competence to
judge

Ur·wald *der* primeval forest; (tropisch)
jungle

ur·wüchsig *Adj.* natural ⟨*landscape,
power*⟩; earthy ⟨*language, humour*⟩

Urwüchsigkeit *die;* ~ ▶ URWÜCHSIG:
naturalness; earthiness

USA *Pl.* USA

User /'ju:ze/ *der;* ~s, ~, **Userin** *die;* ~,
~nen (bes. DV, Drogenjargon) user

usw. *Abk.* = **und so weiter** etc.

Utensil *das;* ~s, ~ien /...jən/ piece of
equipment; ~ien equipment *sing.*

Utopie *die;* ~, ~n utopian dream

utopisch *Adj.* utopian

UV *Abk.* = **Ultraviolett** UV

Vv

v, V /vau:/ *das;* ∼, ∼: v/V
v. *Abk.* = **von**
vage /'va:ga/ ① *Adj.* vague
　② *adv.* vaguely
Vagina /va'gi:na/ *die;* ∼, **Vaginen** (Anat.)
　vagina
vaginal *Adj.* (Anat.) vaginal
vakant /va'kant/ *Adj.* vacant
Vakuum *das;* ∼s, **Vakuen** vacuum
vakuum·verpackt *Adj.* vacuum-packed
Valentins·tag /'va:lɛntǐ:ns-/ *der* [St]
　Valentine's Day
Van /væn/ *der;* ∼s, ∼s (Kfz.-W.) multi-
　purpose vehicle; MPV
Vandale /van'da:la/ *usw.* ▶ WANDALE
Vanille /va'nɪlja/ *die;* ∼: vanilla
Vanille-: ∼**eis** *das* vanilla ice cream;
　∼**pudding** *der* vanilla pudding; ∼**zucker**
　der vanilla sugar
variabel /va'rǐa:bl̩/ ① *Adj.* variable
　② *adv.* variably
Variante /va'rǐanta/ *die;* ∼, ∼n (geh.)
　variant; variation
variieren *tr., itr. V.* vary
Vase /'va:za/ *die;* ∼, ∼n vase
Vaseline /vaze'li:na/ *die;* ∼: Vaseline ®
Vater *der;* ∼s, **Väter** father; **Gott** ∼: God the
　Father
Vater·land *das* fatherland
väterlich ① *Adj.* (a) paternal ⟨*line, love,
　instincts, etc.*⟩
　(b) (fürsorglich) fatherly
　② *adv.* in a fatherly way
väterlicherseits *Adv.* on the/his/her *etc.*
　father's side
Vaterschaft *die;* ∼, ∼en fatherhood
Vater-: ∼**tag** *der* Father's Day *no def. art.;*
　∼**unser** *das;* ∼s, ∼s: Lord's Prayer
Vati *der;* ∼s, ∼s (fam.) dad[dy] (coll.)
Vatikan /vati'ka:n/ *der;* ∼s Vatican
v. Chr. *Abk.* = **vor Christus** BC
Vegetarier /vege'ta:rǐɐ/ *der;* ∼s, ∼,
　Vegetarierin *die;* ∼, ∼nen vegetarian
vegetarisch ① *Adj.* vegetarian
　② *adv.* **er isst** *od.* **lebt** ∼: he is a vegetarian
Vegetation *die;* ∼, ∼en vegetation *no
　indef. art.*
vegetieren *itr. V.* vegetate
Veilchen *das;* ∼s, ∼: violet
Vene /'ve:na/ *die;* ∼, ∼n vein
Venedig /ve'ne:dɪç/ (*das*); ∼s Venice

Venezolaner /venets:o'la:nɐ/ *der;* ∼s, ∼,
　Venezolanerin *die;* ∼, ∼nen Venezuelan
venezolanisch *Adj.* Venezuelan
Venezuela (*das*) ∼s Venezuela
Ventil /vɛn'ti:l/ *das;* ∼s, ∼e valve
Ventilator /vɛnti'la:tɔr/ *der;* ∼s, ∼en
　ventilator
Venus /'ve:nʊs/ *die;* ∼: Venus *no def. art.*
verabreden ① *tr. V.* arrange
　② *refl. V.* **sich im Park/zum Tennis/für den
　folgenden Abend** ∼: arrange to meet in the
　park/for tennis/next evening
Verabredung *die;* ∼, ∼en (a)
　arrangement
　(b) (verabredete Zusammenkunft) appointment;
　eine ∼ **absagen** call off a meeting
verabscheuen *tr. V.* detest; loathe
verabschieden ① *tr. V.* (a) say goodbye
　to
　(b) (aus dem Dienst) retire ⟨*general, civil
　servant, etc.*⟩
　② *refl. V.* **sich [von jmdm.]** ∼: say goodbye
　[to sb.]
Verabschiedung *die;* ∼, ∼en (a) leave-
　taking
　(b) (aus dem Dienst) retirement
verachten *tr. V.* despise
verächtlich ① *Adj.* (a) contemptuous
　(b) (verachtenswürdig) contemptible
　② *adv.* contemptuously
Verächtlichkeit *die;* ∼: contempt;
　contemptuousness
Verachtung *die;* ∼: contempt
verallgemeinern *tr., itr. V.* generalize
Verallgemeinerung *die;* ∼, ∼en
　generalization
veralten *itr. V.; mit sein* become obsolete
Veranda /ve'randa/ *die;* ∼, **Veranden**
　veranda; porch
veränderlich *Adj.* changeable
verändern *tr., refl. V.* change
Veränderung *die;* ∼, ∼en change (*Gen.*
　in)
verängstigen *tr. V.* frighten; scare
verankern *tr. V.* fix ⟨*tent, mast, pole, etc.*⟩;
　(mit einem Anker) anchor
veranlagen *tr. V.* (Steuerw.) assess (**mit** at)
veranlagt *Adj.* **künstlerisch/praktisch** ∼
　sein have an artistic bent/be practically
　minded
Veranlagung *die;* ∼, ∼en [pre]disposition
veranlassen *tr. V.* cause; induce; ∼, **dass**
　... see to it that ...

*old spelling - see note on page xiv

Veranlassung *die;* ~, ~en reason
veranschaulichen *tr. V.* illustrate
veranschlagen *tr. V.* estimate (**mit** at)
veranstalten *tr. V.* organize; hold, give
⟨party⟩; hold ⟨auction⟩; do ⟨survey⟩
Veranstalter *der;* ~s, ~,
Veranstalterin *die;* ~, ~nen organizer
Veranstaltung *die;* ~, ~en (a) (das
Veranstalten) organizing; organization
(b) (etw., was veranstaltet wird) event
verantworten ⓵ *tr. V.* **etw.** ~: take
responsibility for sth.
⓶ *refl. V.* **sich für etw.** ~: answer for sth.;
sich vor jmdm. ~: answer to sb
verantwortlich *Adj.* responsible
Verantwortung *die;* ~, ~en
responsibility (**für** for)
verantwortungs-: ~**bewusst,**
*~**bewußt** *Adj.* responsible; ~**los** *Adj.*
irresponsible; ~**voll** *Adj.* responsible
verarbeiten *tr. V.* use; **etw. zu etw.** ~:
make sth. into sth.; (geistig bewältigen)
assimilate ⟨film, experience, impressions⟩
Verarbeitung *die;* ~, ~en (a) (das
Verarbeiten) use
(b) (Art der Fertigung) finish; **Schuhe in
erstklassiger** ~: shoes with a first-class
finish
verärgern *tr. V.* annoy
verarzten *tr. V.* (ugs.) patch up (coll.)
⟨person⟩; fix (coll.) ⟨wound etc.⟩
verausgaben *refl. V.* wear oneself out; **sie
hat sich total verausgabt** (finanziell) she has
completely spent out
veräußern *tr. V.* dispose of ⟨property⟩
Verb /vɛrp/ *das;* ~s, ~en verb
verbal /vɛr'baːl/ *Adj.* ⓵ (auch Sprachw.)
verbal
⓶ *adv.* verbally
Verband *der* (a) (Binde) bandage; dressing
(b) (Vereinigung) association
verbandeln *tr. V.* link closely
Verband[s]-: ~**kasten** *der* first-aid box;
~**material** *das* dressing materials *pl.*
Verband-zeug *das* first-aid things *pl.*
Verbannung *die;* ~, ~en banishment
verbeamten *tr. V.* make ⟨person⟩ a civil
servant
verbergen *unr. tr. V.* hide; conceal
verbessern ⓵ *tr. V.* (a) improve
(b) (korrigieren) correct
⓶ *refl. V.* (a) improve
(b) ([beruflich] aufsteigen) better oneself
Verbesserung *die* (a) improvement
(b) (Korrektur) correction
Verbesserungs-vorschlag *der*
suggestion for improvement
verbeugen *refl. V.* bow (**vor** + *Dat.* to)
Verbeugung *die;* ~, ~en bow
verbeulen *tr. V.* dent
verbieten *unr. tr. V.* (a) forbid; **jmdm. etw.**

~: forbid sb. sth.; „**Betreten des Rasens/
Rauchen verboten**" 'keep off the grass'/'no
smoking'
(b) (für unzulässig erklären) ban
verbinden ⓵ *unr. tr. V.* (a) (bandagieren)
bandage; dress
(b) (zubinden) bind; **jmdm. die Augen** ~:
blindfold sb.
(c) (zusammenfügen) join
(d) (in Beziehung bringen) connect (**durch** by);
link ⟨towns, lakes, etc.⟩ (**durch** by)
(e) (verknüpfen) combine ⟨abilities, qualities,
etc.⟩
(f) *auch itr.* (telefonisch) **jmdn.** [**mit jmdm.**] ~:
put sb. through [to sb.]
⓶ *unr. refl. V.* (a) (auch Chemie) combine (**mit**
with)
(b) (sich zusammentun) join [together]; join
forces
verbindlich ⓵ *Adj.* (a) friendly
(b) (bindend) obligatory; compulsory; binding
⟨agreement, decision, etc.⟩
⓶ *adv.* (a) (freundlich) in a friendly manner
(b) ~ **zusagen** definitely agree; **jmdm. etw.**
~ **zusagen** make sb. a firm offer of sth
Verbindung *die;* ~, ~en (a) (das
Verknüpfen) linking
(b) (Zusammenhalt) join; connection
(c) (verknüpfende Strecke) link
(d) (durch Telefon, Funk, Verkehrsmittel)
connection (**nach** to)
(e) (Kombination) combination; **in** ~ **mit etw.**
in conjunction with sth.
(f) (Kontakt) contact; **sich mit jmdm. in** ~
setzen get in touch *or* contact with sb.
(g) (Zusammenhang) connection
verbissen ⓵ *Adj.* dogged; doggedly
determined
⓶ *adv.* doggedly
verbitten *unr. refl. V.* **sich** (*Dat.*) **etw.** ~:
refuse to tolerate sth.
verbittern *tr. V.* embitter
Verbitterung *die;* ~, ~en bitterness;
embitterment
verblassen *itr. V.; mit sein* (auch fig. geh.)
fade
Verbleib *der;* ~[e]s (geh.) whereabouts *pl.*
verbleiben *unr. itr. V.; mit sein* remain;
wie seid ihr verblieben? what did you
arrange?
verbleien *tr. V.* (Technik) lead ⟨petrol⟩
Verblendung *die;* ~, ~en blindness
verblüffen *tr.* (auch itr.) *V.* amaze
verblüffend ⓵ *Adj.* amazing
⓶ *adv.* amazingly
Verblüffung *die;* ~, ~en amazement
verblühen *itr. V.; mit sein* (auch fig.) fade
verbluten *itr.* (auch refl.) *V.; mit sein* bleed
to death
verbohrt *Adj.* pigheaded
verborgen *Adj.* (abgelegen) secluded; (nicht
sichtbar) hidden
Verbot *das;* ~[e]s, ~e ban (*Gen.,* **von** on)

Verbots·schild *das; Pl.* ~er sign (prohibiting sth.); (Verkehrsw.) prohibitive sign

Verbrauch *der;* ~[e]s consumption (**von**, **an** + *Dat.* of)

verbrauchen *tr. V.* use; consume *⟨food, drink⟩*; use up *⟨provisions⟩*; spend *⟨money⟩*; consume, use *⟨fuel⟩*; (fig.) use up *⟨strength, energy⟩*

Verbraucher *der;* ~s, ~,
Verbraucherin *die;* ~, ~nen consumer

Verbraucher·schutz *der* consumer protection

Verbrechen *das;* ~s, ~: crime (**an** + *Dat.*, **gegen** against)

Verbrechens-: ~**rate** *die* crime rate; ~**verhütung** *die* crime prevention

Verbrecher *der;* ~s, ~, **Verbrecherin** *die;* ~, ~nen criminal

verbrecherisch *Adj.* criminal

verbreiten ⒈ *tr. V.* spread; radiate *⟨optimism, calm, etc.⟩* ⒉ *refl. V.* spread

Verbreitung *die;* ~, ~en (a) ▶ VERBREITEN 1: spreading; radiation (b) (Ausbreitung) spread

verbrennen ⒈ *unr. itr. V.; mit sein* burn ⒉ *tr. V.* burn; cremate *⟨dead person⟩*; **sich** (*Dat.*) **den Mund** ~ (fig.) say too much

Verbrennung *die;* ~, ~en (a) ▶ VERBRENNEN 2: burning; cremation (b) (Wunde) burn

Verbrennungs·anlage *die* incineration plant; incinerator

verbringen *unr. tr. V.* spend

verbummeln *tr. V.* (ugs.) (a) waste *⟨time⟩* (b) (vergessen) forget [all] about; clean forget; (verlieren) lose

verbünden *refl. V.* form an alliance

Verbündete *der/die; adj. Dekl.* ally

verbüßen *tr. V.* serve *⟨sentence⟩*

Verdacht *der;* ~[e]s, ~e *od.* **Verdächte** suspicion; **wen hast du in** ~? who do you suspect?

verdächtig ⒈ *Adj.* suspicious ⒉ *adv.* suspiciously

Verdächtige *der/die; adj. Dekl.* suspect

verdächtigen *tr. V.* suspect

Verdächtigung *die;* ~, ~en suspicion

verdammen *tr. V.* condemn; (Rel.) damn

verdampfen ⒈ *itr. V.; mit sein* evaporate ⒉ *tr. V.* evaporate

verdanken *tr. V.* **jmdm./einer Sache etw.** ~: owe sth. to sb./sth.

verdarb *1. u. 3. Pers. Sg. Prät. v.* VERDERBEN

verdattert (ugs.) *Adj.* flabbergasted; (verwirrt) dazed; stunned

verdauen ⒈ *tr. V.* (auch fig.) digest ⒉ *itr. V.* digest [one's food]

verdaulich *Adj.* digestible

Verdauung *die;* ~: digestion

Verdeck *das;* ~[e]s, ~e top; hood (Brit.); (bei Kinderwagen) hood

verdecken *tr. V.* hide; cover

verderben ⒈ *unr. itr. V.; mit sein* go bad or off; spoil ⒉ *unr. tr. V.* spoil; (stärker) ruin; spoil *⟨appetite, enjoyment, fun, etc.⟩* ⒊ *unr. refl. V.* **sich** (*Dat.*) **den Magen/die Augen** ~: give oneself an upset stomach/ ruin one's eyesight

Verderben *das;* ~s ruin

verderblich *Adj.* perishable *⟨food⟩*; pernicious *⟨influence, effect, etc.⟩*

verdeutlichen *tr. V.* **etw.** ~: make sth. clear; (erklären) explain sth.

verdichten *refl. V.* *⟨fog, smoke⟩* thicken, become thicker; (fig.) *⟨suspicion, rumour⟩* grow; *⟨feeling⟩* intensify

verdienen ⒈ *tr. V.* (a) earn (b) (wert sein) deserve ⒉ *itr. V.* **beide Eheleute** ~: husband and wife are both earning

Verdiener *der;* ~s, ~, **Verdienerin** *die;* ~, ~nen wage earner

Verdienst[1] *der;* ~[e]s, ~e income

Verdienst[2] *das;* ~[e]s, ~e merit

verdienst·voll ⒈ *Adj.* commendable; *⟨person⟩* of outstanding merit ⒉ *adv.* commendably

verdient ⒈ *Adj.* (a) *⟨person⟩* of outstanding merit; **sich um etw.** ~ **machen** render outstanding services to sth. (b) (gerecht, zustehend) well-deserved ⒉ *adv.* deservedly

verdientermaßen *Adv.* deservedly

verdoppeln ⒈ *tr. V.* double; (fig.) double, redouble *⟨efforts etc.⟩* ⒉ *refl. V.* double

verdorben *2. Part. v.* VERDERBEN

verdorren *itr. V.; mit sein* wither [and die]; *⟨meadow⟩* scorch

verdrängen *tr. V.* (a) drive out *⟨inhabitants⟩*; (fig.: ersetzen) displace (b) (Psych.) repress; (bewusst) suppress

verdrehen *tr. V.* (a) twist *⟨joint⟩*; roll *⟨eyes⟩* (b) (ugs. abwertend: entstellen) twist *⟨words, facts, etc.⟩*

verdrießen *unr. tr. V.* (geh.) irritate; annoy

verdrießlich ⒈ *Adj.* morose ⒉ *adv.* morosely

verdross, *verdroß *1. u. 3. Pers. Sg. Prät. v.* VERDRIESSEN

verdrossen ⒈ *Adj.* (missmutig) morose; (missmutig und lustlos) sullen ⒉ *adv.* (missmutig) morosely; (missmutig und lustlos) sullenly

Verdruss, *Verdruß *der;* Verdrusses, Verdrusse annoyance

verdunkeln *tr. V.* darken; (vollständig) black out *⟨room, house, etc.⟩*

Verdunk[e]lung die; ∼, ∼en darkening; (vollständig) blackout

verdünnen tr. V. dilute

verdunsten itr. V.; mit sein evaporate

verdünnen tr. V. dilute

verdunsten itr. V.; mit sein evaporate

Verdunstung die; ∼: evaporation

verdursten itr. V.; mit sein die of thirst

verdutzt Adj. taken aback pred.; nonplussed; (verwirrt) baffled

Verdutztheit die; ∼: bafflement

verehren tr. V. (a) venerate
(b) (geh.: bewundern) admire; (ehrerbietig lieben) worship

Verehrer der; ∼s, ∼, **Verehrerin** die; ∼, ∼en admirer

Verehrung die; ∼ (a) veneration
(b) (Bewunderung) admiration

vereidigen tr. V. swear in

Vereidigung die; ∼, ∼en swearing in

Verein der; ∼s, ∼e organization; (der Kunstfreunde usw.) association; society; (Sportverein) club

vereinbar Adj. compatible

vereinbaren tr. V. agree; arrange ⟨meeting etc.⟩

Vereinbarung die; ∼, ∼en (a) agreeing; (eines Termins usw.) arranging
(b) (Abmachung) agreement

vereinfachen tr. V. simplify

Vereinfachung die; ∼, ∼en simplification

vereinheitlichen tr. V. standardize

Vereinheitlichung die; ∼, ∼en standardization

vereinigen tr., refl. V. unite; (in der Wirtschaft) merge

vereinigt Adj. united

Vereinigung die; ∼, ∼en (a) organization
(b) (das Vereinigen) uniting; (von Unternehmen) merging

vereinsamen itr. V.; mit sein become [increasingly] lonely or isolated

Vereinsamung die; ∼: loneliness; isolation

vereinzelt [1] Adj. occasional
[2] adv. (zeitlich) occasionally; (örtlich) here and there

Vereinzelung die; ∼, ∼en isolation

vereisen itr. V.; mit sein freeze or ice over; ⟨wing⟩ ice up; ⟨lock⟩ freeze up

vereiteln tr. V. thwart

Vereitelung die; ∼: thwarting

vereitern itr. V.; mit sein go septic

verenden itr. V.; mit sein perish; die

verengen refl. V. narrow; ⟨pupils⟩ contract

vererben tr. V. leave, bequeath ⟨property⟩ (Dat., an + Akk. to)

Vererbung die; ∼, ∼en heredity no art.

verewigen [1] tr. V. immortalize

⌐2⌐ refl. V. (ugs.: Spuren hinterlassen) leave one's mark

verfahren [1] unr. refl. V. lose one's way
[2] unr. itr. V.; mit sein proceed

Verfahren das; ∼s, ∼ (a) procedure; (Technik) process; (Methode) method
(b) (Rechtsw.) proceedings pl.

Verfall der; ∼[e]s (a) decay; (fig.: der Preise, einer Währung) collapse
(b) (Auflösung) decline

verfallen unr. itr. V.; mit sein (a) (baufällig werden) fall into disrepair
(b) (körperlich) ⟨strength⟩ decline
(c) (untergehen) ⟨empire⟩ decline; ⟨morals, morale⟩ deteriorate
(d) (ungültig werden) expire

Verfalls·datum das use-by date; (ugs.: Mindesthaltbarkeitsdatum) best-before date

verfälschen tr. V. distort, misrepresent ⟨statement, message⟩; falsify, misrepresent ⟨facts, history, truth⟩; falsify ⟨painting, banknote⟩; adulterate ⟨wine, milk, etc.⟩

Verfälschung die ▸ VERFÄLSCHEN: distortion; misrepresentation; falsification; adulteration

verfassen tr. V. write; draw up ⟨resolution⟩

Verfasser der; ∼s, ∼, **Verfasserin** die; ∼, ∼nen writer; (eines Buchs, Artikels usw.) author; writer

Verfassung die; ∼, ∼en (a) (Politik) constitution
(b) (Zustand) state [of health/mind]; in guter/ schlechter ∼ sein be in good/poor shape

verfassungs·gemäß [1] Adj. constitutional; in accordance with the constitution postpos.;
[2] adv. constitutionally; in accordance with the constitution

verfaulen itr. V.; mit sein rot

verfehlen tr. V. miss

Verfehlung die; ∼, ∼en misdemeanour; (Rel.: Sünde) transgression

verfeinden refl. V. sich ∼ mit make an enemy of

verfeinern tr. V. improve; refine ⟨method, procedure⟩

Verfeinerung die; ∼, ∼en ▸ VERFEINERN: improvement; refinement

verfertigen tr. V. produce

verfilmen tr. V. film; make a film of

Verfilmung die; ∼, ∼en (a) (das Verfilmen) filming
(b) (Film) film [version]

verfinstern [1] tr. V. obscure ⟨sun etc.⟩
[2] refl. V. (auch fig.) darken

Verfinsterung die; ∼, ∼en darkening

verflixt (ugs.) [1] Adj. (a) (ärgerlich) awkward, unpleasant ⟨situation, business, etc.⟩
(b) (verdammt) blasted (Brit.); blessed; confounded; ∼ [noch mal]! [damn and] blast! (Brit. coll.) ⋯⋯▸

(c) (sehr groß) **er hat ~es Glück gehabt** he was damned lucky (coll.)
2 *adv.* (sehr) damned (coll.)
verflossen *Adj.* (ugs.) former
verfluchen *tr. V.* curse
verflucht 1 *Adj.* (salopp) damned (coll.); bloody (Brit. sl.); **~ [noch mal]!** damn [it]! (coll.)
2 *adv.* (sehr) damned (coll.)
verfolgen *tr. V.* pursue; hunt, track ⟨animal⟩; **etw. [strafrechtlich] ~:** prosecute sth.
Verfolgte *der/die; adj. Dekl.* victim of persecution
Verfolgung *die; ~, ~en* **(a)** pursuit; (eines Ziels, Plans usw.) pursuance
(b) [strafrechtliche] **~:** prosecution
Verfolgungs-: ~jagd *die* pursuit; chase; **~wahn** *der* (Psych.) persecution mania
verfressen *Adj.* (salopp) greedy
verfügen 1 *tr. V.* (anordnen) order; (dekretieren) decree
2 *itr. V.* **über etw.** (Akk.) **[frei] ~ können** be free to do what to do with sth.; **über etw.** (Akk.) **~** (etw. haben) have sth. at one's disposal
Verfügung *die; ~, ~en* **(a)** (Anordnung) order; (Dekret) decree
(b) (Disposition) **etw. zur ~ haben** have sth. at one's disposal; **jmdm. etw. zur ~ stellen** put sth. at sb.'s disposal
verführen *tr. V.* **(a)** (verleiten) tempt
(b) (sexuell) seduce
Verführer *der; ~s, ~:* seducer
Verführerin *der; ~, ~nen* seductress
verführerisch 1 *Adj.* **(a)** (verlockend) tempting
(b) (aufreizend) seductive
2 *adv.* **(a)** (verlockend) temptingly
(b) (aufreizend) seductively
Verführung *die; ~, ~en* **(a)** temptation
(b) (sexuell) seduction
vergangen *Adj.* **(a)** (vorüber, vorbei) bygone, former ⟨times, years, etc.⟩
(b) (letzt...) last ⟨year, week, etc.⟩
Vergangenheit *die; ~* **(a)** past
(b) (Grammatik: Präteritum) past tense
vergänglich *Adj.* transient; transitory; ephemeral
Vergänglichkeit *die; ~:* transience
Vergaser *der; ~s, ~:* carburettor
vergaß 1. u. 3. Pers. Sg. Prät. v. VERGESSEN
Vergasung *die; ~, ~en* **(a)** (von Kohle) gasification
(b) (Tötung) gassing
(c) bis zur ~ (ugs.) ad nauseam
vergeben *unr. tr. V.* **(a)** auch itr. (geh.: verzeihen) forgive; **jmdm. etw. ~:** forgive sb. [for] sth.
(b) throw away ⟨chance, goal, etc.⟩

(c) (geben) place ⟨order⟩ (an + Akk. with); award ⟨grant, prize⟩ (an + Akk. to)
vergebens 1 *Adv.* in vain; vainly
2 *adj.* **es war ~:** it was of or to no avail
vergeblich 1 *Adj.* futile; vain, futile ⟨attempt, efforts⟩
2 *adv.* in vain
Vergebung *die; ~:* (geh.) forgiveness
vergegenwärtigen /od. ---'---/ *refl. V.* **sich** (Dat.) **etw. ~:** imagine sth.; (erinnern) recall sth.
vergehen *unr. itr. V.; mit sein* ⟨time⟩ pass [by], go by; ⟨pain⟩ wear off, pass; ⟨pleasure⟩ fade
Vergehen *das; ~s, ~:* crime; (Rechtsspr.) offence
vergeigen *tr. V.* (ugs.) botch up ⟨test, performance, etc.⟩; lose ⟨game, match⟩
vergelten *unr. tr. V.* repay
vergessen *unr. tr.* (auch itr.) *V.* forget
Vergessenheit *die; ~:* oblivion
vergesslich, *vergeßlich *Adj.* forgetful
vergeuden *tr. V.* waste
Vergeudung *die; ~, ~en* waste
vergewaltigen *tr. V.* rape
Vergewaltigung *die; ~, ~en* rape
vergewissern *refl. V.* make sure (Gen. of)
vergießen *unr. tr. V.* spill; **Tränen ~:** shed tears
vergiften *tr. V.* (auch fig.) poison
Vergiftung *die; ~, ~en* poisoning
vergiss, *vergiß *Imper. Sg. v.* VERGESSEN
Vergiss·mein·nicht, *Vergiß·mein·nicht *das; ~[e]s, ~[e]* forget-me-not
vergisst, *vergißt 2. u. 3. Pers. Sg. Präs. v. VERGESSEN
Vergleich *der; ~[e]s, ~e* **(a)** comparison; **im ~ zu** od. **mit etw.** in comparison with sth.; compared with or to sth.
(b) (Rechtsw.) settlement
vergleichbar *Adj.* comparable
vergleichen *unr. tr. V.* compare
Vergleichs·form *die* (Sprachw.) comparative/superlative form
verglühen *itr. V.; mit sein* ⟨log, wick, fire, etc.⟩ smoulder and go out; ⟨satellite, rocket, wire, etc.⟩ burn out
vergnügen *refl. V.* enjoy oneself; have a good time
Vergnügen *das; ~s, ~:* pleasure; (Spaß) fun; **viel ~!** (auch iron.) have fun!
vergnüglich *Adj.* amusing; entertaining
vergnügt 1 *Adj.* cheerful
2 *adv.* cheerfully
Vergnügungs·viertel *das* pleasure district
vergolden *tr. V.* gold-plate ⟨jewellery etc.⟩; (mit Blattgold) gild
vergraben *unr. tr. V.* bury
vergrämt *Adj.* careworn

---
*old spelling - see note on page xiv

vergraulen tr. V. (ugs.) put off
vergreifen unr. refl. V. **sich an jmdm. ~:** assault sb.
vergriffen Adj. out of print pred.
vergrößern ① tr. V. (a) (erweitern) extend ⟨room, area, building, etc.⟩
(b) (vermehren) increase
(c) (größer reproduzieren) enlarge ⟨photograph etc.⟩
② refl. V. (a) (größer werden) ⟨firm, business, etc.⟩ expand
(b) (zunehmen) increase
③ itr. V. ⟨lens etc.⟩ magnify
Vergrößerung die; ~, ~en (a)
▶ VERGRÖSSERN 1, 2: extension; increase; enlargement; expansion
(b) (Foto) enlargement
Vergrößerungs·glas das magnifying glass
Vergünstigung die; ~, ~en privilege
vergüten tr. V. (a) (erstatten) **jmdm. etw. ~:** reimburse sb. for sth.
(b) (bes. Papierdt.: bezahlen) remunerate, pay for ⟨work, services⟩
Vergütung die; ~, ~en (a) (Rückerstattung) reimbursement
(b) (Geldsumme) remuneration
verhaften tr. V. arrest; **Sie sind verhaftet** you are under arrest
Verhaftung die; ~, ~en arrest
verhalten unr. refl. V. (a) behave; (reagieren) react
(b) (beschaffen sein) be
Verhalten das; ~s behaviour
Verhaltens·weise die behaviour
Verhältnis das; ~ses, ~se ~se ein ~ von drei zu eins a ratio of three to one
(b) (persönliche Beziehung) relationship (**zu** with); **mit jmdm. ein ~ haben** (ugs.) have an affair with sb.
(c) Pl. (Umstände) conditions
verhältnis·mäßig Adv. relatively; comparatively
Verhältnis·wort das; Pl. ~wörter (Sprachw.) preposition
verhandeln ① itr. V. (a) negotiate (**über** + Akk. about)
(b) (strafrechtlich) try a case; (zivilrechtlich) hear a case
② tr. V. (a) **etw. ~:** negotiate over sth.
(b) (strafrechtlich) try ⟨case⟩; (zivilrechtlich) hear ⟨case⟩
Verhandlung die; ~, ~en (a) ~en negotiations
(b) (strafrechtlich) trial; (zivilrechtlich) hearing; **die ~ gegen X** the trial of X
verhängen tr. V. impose ⟨fine, punishment⟩ (**über** + Akk. on); declare ⟨state of emergency, state of siege⟩; (Sport) award, give ⟨penalty etc.⟩
Verhängnis das; ~ses, ~se undoing
verhängnis·voll Adj. disastrous
verharmlosen tr. V. play down

Verharmlosung die; ~, ~en playing down
verhärmt Adj. careworn
verharren itr. V. (geh.) remain
verhärten ① tr. V. harden; make ⟨person⟩ hard
② refl. V. ⟨tissue⟩ become hardened
verhasst, *verhaßt Adj. hated; detested
verhätscheln tr. V. (ugs.) pamper
verhauen (ugs.) unr. tr. V. beat up; (als Strafe) beat
verheben unr. refl. V. do oneself an injury [while lifting sth.]
verheeren tr. V. devastate; lay waste [to]
verheerend Adj. (a) devastating
(b) (ugs.: scheußlich) ghastly (coll.)
verhehlen tr. V. (geh.) conceal (Dat. from)
verheilen itr. V.; mit sein ⟨wound⟩ heal [up]
verheimlichen tr. V. [jmdm.] etw. ~: keep sth. secret [from sb.]
Verheimlichung die; ~, ~en concealment
verheiraten refl. V. get married; **sich mit jmdm. ~:** marry sb.; get married to sb.
Verheiratete der/die; adj. Dekl. married person; married man/woman
Verheiratung die; ~, ~en marriage
verheizen tr. V. (a) burn; use as fuel
(b) (abwertend: rücksichtslos einsetzen) burn out ⟨athlete, skier, etc.⟩; use ⟨troops⟩ as cannon fodder
verhelfen unr. itr. V. jmdm./einer Sache zu etw. ~: help sb./sth. to get/achieve sth.
verherrlichen tr. V. glorify
Verherrlichung die; ~, ~en glorification
verheult Adj. (ugs.) ⟨eyes⟩ red from crying; ⟨face⟩ puffy or swollen from crying
verhexen tr. V. (auch fig.) bewitch
verhindern tr. V. prevent
Verhinderung die; ~, ~en prevention
verhöhnen tr. V. mock
Verhöhnung die; ~, ~en mockery
Verhör das; ~[e]s, ~e interrogation; questioning; (bei Gericht) examination
verhören ① tr. V. interrogate; question; (bei Gericht) examine
② refl. V. mishear
verhüllen tr. V. cover; (fig.) disguise
verhüllend Adj. (Literaturw.) euphemistic
Verhüllung die; ~, ~en covering; (fig.) disguising
verhungern itr. V.; mit sein die of starvation; starve [to death]
verhunzen tr. V. (ugs. abwertend) ruin; mess up; ruin ⟨landscape, townscape, etc.⟩
verhüten tr. V. prevent
Verhütung die; ~, ~en prevention; (Empfängnisverhütung) contraception
Verhütungs·mittel das contraceptive

verirren *refl. V.* (a) get lost; lose one's way; ⟨*animal*⟩ stray
(b) (irgendwohin gelangen) stray (**in, an** + *Akk.*
into)

verjagen *tr. V.* chase away

verjüngen ☐ *tr. V.* rejuvenate
☐ *refl. V.* (schmaler werden) taper; become
narrower; narrow

verkalken *itr. V.; mit sein* (a) ⟨*tissue*⟩
calcify; ⟨*arteries*⟩ become hardened
(b) (ugs.: senil werden) become senile

Verkauf *der;* ∼[e]s, Verkäufe sale

verkaufen *tr. V.* (auch fig.) sell ⟨*Dat.,* an +
Akk. to); „**zu** ∼" 'for sale'

Verkäufer *der;* ∼s, ∼ **Verkäuferin** *die;*
∼, ∼nen (a) seller; vendor (formal)
(b) (Berufsbez.) sales *or* shop assistant; (im
Außendienst) salesman/saleswoman

verkäuflich *Adj.* (zum Verkauf geeignet)
saleable; (zum Verkauf bestimmt) for sale
postpos.

verkaufs·offen *Adj.* der ∼e Samstag
Saturday on which the shops are open all
day

Verkaufs·preis *der* retail price

Verkehr *der;* ∼s (a) traffic
(b) (Kontakt) contact; communication
(c) (Geschlechtsverkehr) intercourse

verkehren *itr. V.* (a) *auch mit sein* (fahren)
run; ⟨*aircraft*⟩ fly
(b) (in Kontakt stehen) **mit jmdm.** ∼: associate
with sb.
(c) (zu Gast sein) **bei jmdm.** ∼: visit sb.
regularly

verkehrs-, Verkehrs-: ∼**ampel** *die*
traffic lights *pl.;* ∼**amt** *das* tourist
information office; ∼**aufkommen** *das*
volume of traffic; ∼**hindernis** *das*
obstruction to traffic; ∼**knotenpunkt** *der*
[traffic] junction; ∼**kontrolle** *die* traffic
check; ∼**meldung** *die* traffic
announcement *or* flash; ∼**mittel** *das*
means of transport; **die öffentlichen** ∼**mittel**
public transport *sing.;* ∼**polizist** *der* traffic
policeman; ∼**polizistin** *die* traffic
policewoman; ∼**schild** *das; Pl.* ∼∼**er**
traffic sign; road sign; ∼**sicher** *Adj.*
roadworthy; ∼**teilnehmer** *der,*
∼**teilnehmerin** *die* road user; ∼**unfall**
der road accident; ∼**weg** *der* traffic route;
∼**zeichen** *das* traffic sign; road sign

verkehrt ☐ *Adj.* wrong
☐ *adv.* wrongly; **alles** ∼ **machen** do
everything wrong

verkennen *unr. tr. V.* fail to recognize;
misjudge ⟨*situation*⟩

verklagen *tr. V.* sue; take to court; **eine
Firma auf Schadenersatz** ∼: sue a company
for damages

verkleben ☐ *itr. V.; mit sein* stick together
☐ *tr. V.* (zukleben) seal up ⟨*hole*⟩; (festkleben)
stick [down] ⟨*floor covering etc.*⟩

*alte Schreibung - vgl. Hinweis auf S. xiv

verkleiden *tr. V.* disguise; (kostümieren)
dress up; **sich** ∼: disguise oneself/dress
[oneself] up

Verkleidung *die;* ∼, ∼en (a) disguising;
(das Kostümieren) dressing up
(b) (Kleidung) disguise; (bei einer Party) fancy
dress

verkleinern ☐ *tr. V.* (a) make smaller
(b) (verringern) reduce ⟨*size, number, etc.*⟩
(c) (kleiner reproduzieren) reduce ⟨*photograph
etc.*⟩
☐ *refl. V.* become smaller; ⟨*number*⟩
decrease

Verkleinerungs·form *die* (Sprachw.)
diminutive form

verknallen *refl. V.* (ugs.: sich verlieben) fall
head over heels in love (**in** + *Akk.* with); **in
jmdn. verknallt sein** be crazy about sb. (coll.)

verknittern *tr. V.* crumple

verknoten *tr. V.* tie; knot

verknüpfen *tr. V.* (a) (knoten) tie; knot
(b) (in Beziehung setzen) link

verkochen *itr. V.; mit sein* (a) boil away
(b) (breiig werden, zerfallen) boil down to a pulp

verkohlen *itr. V.* char

verkommen[1] *unr. itr. V.; mit sein* go to
the dogs; (moralisch, sittlich) go to the bad

verkommen[2] *Adj.* depraved

verköstigen *tr. V.* feed; provide with
meals

verkraften *tr. V.* cope with

verkrampfen *refl. V.* ⟨*muscle*⟩ become
cramped; ⟨*person*⟩ tense up

Verkrampfung *die;* ∼, ∼en tenseness;
tension

verkriechen *unr. refl. V.* ⟨*animal*⟩ creep
[away]; ⟨*person*⟩ hide [oneself away]

verkrümeln *refl. V.* (ugs.: sich entfernen) slip
off *or* away

verkrümmt *Adj.* bent ⟨*person*⟩; crooked
⟨*finger*⟩; curved ⟨*spine*⟩

Verkrümmung *die;* ∼, ∼en crookedness

verkrüppeln *tr. V.* cripple

verkümmern *itr. V.; mit sein* ⟨*person,
animal*⟩ go into a decline; ⟨*plant etc.*⟩ become
stunted; ⟨*talent, emotional life, etc.*⟩ wither
away

verkünden *tr. V.* announce; pronounce
⟨*judgement*⟩; promulgate ⟨*law, decree*⟩

verkündigen *tr. V.* (geh.) announce;
proclaim

Verkündigung *die;* ∼, ∼en
announcement; proclamation

Verkündung *die;* ∼, ∼en announcement;
(von Urteilen) pronouncement; (von Gesetzen,
Verordnungen) promulgation

verkürzen *tr. V.* (a) (verringern) reduce;
(abkürzen) shorten
(b) (abbrechen) cut short ⟨*stay, life*⟩; put an
end to, end ⟨*suffering*⟩

verladen *unr. tr. V.* load

Verlag ⋯⋗ verloren ⋯⋅

Verlag *der;* ~[e]s, ~e publishing house *or* firm; publisher's

verlagern *tr. V.* shift; (an einen anderen Ort) move; (fig.) transfer; shift ⟨emphasis⟩

Verlagerung *die* moving; **eine** ~ **des Schwergewichts** (fig.) a shift in emphasis

verlanden *itr. V.; mit sein* silt up

Verlandung *die;* ~, ~en silting up

verlangen *tr. V.* demand; (nötig haben) ⟨task etc.⟩ require, call for ⟨patience, knowledge, experience, skill, etc.⟩; (berechnen) charge; (sehen/sprechen wollen) ask for; **du wirst am Telefon verlangt** you're wanted on the phone (coll.)

Verlangen *das;* ~s, ~ (a) desire (**nach** for)
(b) **auf** ~: on request

verlängern *tr. V.* extend; lengthen, make longer ⟨skirt, sleeve, etc.⟩; renew ⟨passport, driving licence, etc.⟩

Verlängerung *die;* ~, ~en
▶ VERLÄNGERN: extension; lengthening; renewal

Verlängerungs-schnur *die* extension lead *or* (Amer.) cord

verlangsamen *tr. V.* **das Tempo/seine Schritte** ~: reduce speed/slacken one's pace; slow down

verlassen[1] [1] *unr. refl. V.* rely, depend (**auf** + *Akk.* on)
[2] *unr. tr. V.* (a) leave
(b) (sich trennen von) desert; abandon; forsake; leave, desert ⟨wife, family, etc.⟩

verlassen[2] *Adj.* deserted ⟨street etc.⟩; empty ⟨house⟩; (öd) desolate ⟨region etc.⟩

verlässlich, *verläßlich [1] *Adj.* reliable
[2] *adv.* reliably

Verlauf *der;* ~[e]s, Verläufe course

verlaufen [1] *unr. itr. V.; mit sein* (a) (sich erstrecken) run
(b) (ablaufen) ⟨test, rehearsal, etc.⟩ go; ⟨party etc.⟩ go off
[2] *unr. refl. V.* get lost; lose one's way

Verlaufs-form *die* (Sprachw.) progressive *or* continuous form

verlautbaren *tr. V.* announce [officially]

Verlautbarung *die;* ~, ~en announcement

verlauten *itr. V.; mit sein* be reported; **wie verlautet** according to reports

verleben *tr. V.* spend

verlebt *Adj.* dissipated

verlegen[1] *tr. V.* (a) mislay
(b) (verschieben) postpone (**auf** + *Akk.* until); (vor~) bring forward (**auf** + *Akk.* to); **einen Termin** ~: alter an appointment
(c) (verlagern) move; transfer ⟨patient⟩
(d) (legen) lay ⟨cable, pipe, carpet, etc.⟩

verlegen[2] [1] *Adj.* embarrassed
[2] *adv.* in embarrassment

Verlegenheit *die;* ~, ~en (a) (Befangenheit) embarrassment; **jmdn. in** ~ **bringen** embarrass sb.
(b) (Unannehmlichkeit) embarrassing situation

Verleger *der;* ~s, ~, **Verlegerin** *die;* ~, ~nen publisher

Verleih *der;* ~[e]s, ~e (a) hiring out; (von Autos) renting *or* hiring out
(b) (Unternehmen) hire firm; (Filmverleih) distribution company; (Videoverleih) video library; (Autoverleih) rental *or* hire firm

verleihen *unr. tr. V.* (a) hire out; rent *or* hire out ⟨car⟩; (umsonst) lend [out]
(b) (überreichen) award; confer ⟨award, honour⟩

Verleihung *die;* ~, ~en (a) ▶ VERLEIHEN A: hiring out; renting out; lending [out]
(b) ▶ VERLEIHEN B: awarding; conferring; (Zeremonie) award; conferment

verleiten *tr. V.* **jmdn. dazu** ~, **etw. zu tun** lead *or* induce sb. to do sth.

verlernen *tr. V.* forget

verlesen [1] *unr. tr. V.* read out
[2] *unr. refl. V.* (falsch lesen) make a mistake/ mistakes in reading

verletzen *tr. V.* (a) injure; (durch Schuss, Stich) wound
(b) (kränken) hurt ⟨person, feelings⟩
(c) (verstoßen gegen) violate; infringe ⟨regulation⟩; break ⟨agreement, law⟩

verletzlich *Adj.* vulnerable

Verletzlichkeit *die;* ~: vulnerability

Verletzte *der/die; adj. Dekl.* casualty; (durch Schuss, Stich) wounded person

Verletzung *die;* ~, ~en (a) (Wunde) injury
(b) (Kränkung) hurting
(c) ▶ VERLETZEN C: violation; infringement; breaking

verleugnen *tr. V.* deny; disown ⟨friend, relation⟩

Verleugnung *die;* ~, ~en denial; (eines Freundes, Verwandten) disownment

verleumden *tr. V.* slander; (schriftlich) libel

verleumderisch *Adj.* slanderous; (in Schriftform) libellous

Verleumdung *die;* ~, ~en slander; (in Schriftform) libel

verlieben *refl. V.* fall in love (**in** + *Akk.* with)

Verliebte *der/die; adj. Dekl.* lover

verlieren *unr. tr., itr. V.* lose

Verlierer *der;* ~s, ~, **Verliererin** *die;* ~, ~nen loser

verloben *refl. V.* get engaged; **verlobt sein** be engaged

Verlobte *der/die; adj. Dekl.* fiancé/fiancée

verlockend *Adj.* tempting

Verlockung *die;* ~, ~en temptation

verlogen *Adj.* lying, mendacious ⟨person⟩; false ⟨morality etc.⟩

verlor *1. u. 3. Pers. Sg. Prät. v.* VERLIEREN

verloren [1] *2. Part. v.* VERLIEREN ⋯⋗

[2] *Adj.* lost; wasted ⟨*effort*⟩; ~ **gehen** get lost
*verloren|gehen ▸ VERLOREN 2
verlosen *tr. V.* raffle
Verlosung *die;* ~, ~**en** raffle; draw
verlottern *itr. V.; mit sein* ⟨*person*⟩ go to
seed
Verlust *der;* ~[e]s, ~e loss (**an** + *Dat.* of)
vermachen *tr. V.* jmdm. etw. ~: leave *or*
bequeath sth. to sb.; (fig.: schenken, überlassen)
give sth. to sb.
vermählen *refl. V.* (geh.) **sich** [jmdm. *od.*
mit jmdm.] ~: marry *or* wed [sb.]
Vermählung *die;* ~, ~**en** (geh.) **(a)**
marriage
(b) (Fest) wedding ceremony
vermarkten *tr. V.* market ⟨*goods etc.*⟩
Vermarktung *die;* ~, ~**en** marketing
vermehren [1] *tr. V.* increase (**um** by)
[2] *refl. V.* **(a)** increase
(b) (sich fortpflanzen) reproduce
Vermehrung *die;* ~, ~**en** **(a)** increase
(*Gen.* in)
(b) (Fortpflanzung) reproduction
vermeiden *unr. tr. V.* avoid
Vermeidung *die;* ~, ~**en** avoidance
vermeintlich *Adj.* supposed
vermengen *tr. V.* mix (**miteinander**
together)
Vermerk *der;* ~[e]s, ~e note; (amtlich)
remark
vermerken *tr. V.* make a note of; note
[down]; (in Akten, Wachbuch usw.) record
vermessen¹ *unr. tr. V.* measure; survey
⟨*land, site*⟩
vermessen² *Adj.* (geh.) presumptuous
vermieten *tr.* (*auch itr.*) *V.* rent [out], let
[out] (**an** + *Akk.* to); hire [out] ⟨*boat, car,
etc.*⟩; „**Zimmer zu** ~" 'room to let'
Vermieter *der;* ~s, ~: landlord
Vermieterin *die;* ~, ~**nen** landlady
Vermietung *die;* ~, ~**en** ▸ VERMIETEN:
renting [out]; letting [out]; hiring [out]
vermindern [1] *tr. V.* reduce; decrease;
reduce, lessen ⟨*danger, stress*⟩; lower
⟨*resistance*⟩; reduce ⟨*debt*⟩
[2] *refl. V.* decrease; ⟨*resistance*⟩ diminish
Verminderung *die* ▸ VERMINDERN 1:
reduction; decreasing; lessening; lowering;
eine ~ **der Einnahmen** a decrease in
revenues
verminen *tr. V.* mine
vermischen [1] *tr. V.* mix (**miteinander**
together); blend ⟨*teas, tobaccos, etc.*⟩
[2] *refl. V.* mix; (fig.) mingle; ⟨*races, animals*⟩
interbreed
Vermischung *die;* ~ ▸ VERMISCHEN:
mixing; blending; (fig.) mingling
vermissen *tr. V.* **(a)** miss
(b) (nicht haben) **ich vermisse meinen Ausweis**
my identity card is missing

Vermisste, *Vermißte *der/die; adj.
Dekl.* missing person
vermitteln [1] *itr. V.* mediate, act as [a]
mediator (**in** + *Dat.* in)
[2] *tr. V.* **(a)** (herbeiführen) arrange; negotiate
⟨*transaction, ceasefire, compromise*⟩
(b) (besorgen) **jmdm. eine Stelle** ~: find sb. a
job
(c) (weitergeben) impart ⟨*knowledge, insight,
values, etc.*⟩; communicate ⟨*message,
information, etc.*⟩; convey ⟨*feeling*⟩; pass on
⟨*experience*⟩
Vermittler *der;* ~s, ~, **Vermittlerin**
die; ~, ~**nen** **(a)** (Mittler) mediator
(b) ▸ VERMITTELN 2c: imparter;
communicator; conveyer
(c) (von Berufs wegen) agent
Vermittlung *die;* ~, ~**en** **(a)** (Schlichtung)
mediation
(b) ▸ VERMITTELN 2A: arrangement;
negotiation
(c) ▸ VERMITTELN 2c: imparting;
communicating; conveying
(d) (Telefonzentrale) exchange; (in einer Firma)
switchboard
vermöbeln *tr. V.* (ugs.) beat up; (als Strafe)
thrash
vermögen (geh.) *unr. tr. V.* **etw. zu tun** ~:
be able to do sth.; be capable of doing sth.
Vermögen *das;* ~s, ~ **(a)** (geh.: Fähigkeit)
ability
(b) (Besitz) fortune; **er hat** ~: he has money
vermögend *Adj.* wealthy; well-off
Vermögen[s]-steuer *die* wealth tax
vermummen *tr. V.* wrap up [warmly];
(verbergen) disguise
vermurksen *tr. V.* (ugs.) mess up; muck up
(Brit. sl.)
vermuten *tr. V.* suspect; **das ist zu** ~: that
is what one would suppose *or* expect; we
may assume that;
vermutlich [1] *Adj.* probable
[2] *Adv.* presumably; (wahrscheinlich) probably
Vermutung *die;* ~, ~**en** supposition
vernachlässigen *tr. V.* neglect;
(unberücksichtigt lassen) ignore; disregard
Vernachlässigung *die;* ~, ~**en** neglect
vernarben *itr. V.; mit sein* [form a] scar;
heal (lit. or fig.)
vernehmbar *Adj.* (geh.) audible
vernehmen *unr. tr. V.* **(a)** (geh.: hören,
erfahren) hear
(b) (verhören) question
vernehmlich [1] *Adj.* [clearly] audible
[2] *adv.* audibly
Vernehmung *die;* ~, ~**en** questioning
verneigen *refl. V.* (geh.) bow (**vor** + *Dat.* to,
(literary) before)
verneinen *tr.* (*auch itr.*) *V.* **(a)** say 'no' to
⟨*question*⟩; answer ⟨*question*⟩ in the negative
(b) (Sprachw.) negate
Verneinung *die;* ~, ~**en** (Sprachw.)
negation

---

vernetzen *tr. V.* (Chemie, Technik) interlink

vernichten *tr. V.* destroy; exterminate ⟨*pests, vermin*⟩

vernichtend ⟦1⟧ *Adj.* crushing ⟨*defeat*⟩; shattering ⟨*blow*⟩; (fig.) devastating ⟨*criticism*⟩; devastating, withering ⟨*glance*⟩ ⟦2⟧ *adv.* **den Feind ∼ schlagen** inflict a crushing defeat on the enemy

Vernichtung *die; ∼, ∼en* destruction; (von Schädlingen) extermination

Vernichtungs-: **∼lager** *das* extermination camp; **∼waffe** *die* weapon of annihilation

Vernunft *die; ∼:* reason

vernünftig ⟦1⟧ *Adj.* (a) sensible (b) (ugs.: ordentlich, richtig) decent ⟦2⟧ *adv.* (a) sensibly (b) (ugs.: ordentlich, richtig) ⟨*talk, eat*⟩ properly; ⟨*dress*⟩ sensibly

veröffentlichen *tr. V.* publish

Veröffentlichung *die; ∼, ∼en* publication

verordnen *tr. V.* [jmdm. etw.] **∼:** prescribe [sth. for sb.]

Verordnung *die; ∼, ∼en* prescribing

verpachten *tr. V.* lease

verpacken *tr. V.* pack; wrap up ⟨*present, parcel*⟩

Verpackung *die* (a) packing (b) (Umhüllung) packaging *no pl.;* wrapping

verpassen *tr. V.* miss

verpennen (salopp) ⟦1⟧ *itr. V.* oversleep ⟦2⟧ *tr. V.* (a) (vergessen) forget (b) (verschlafen) sleep through ⟨*morning etc.*⟩

verpesten *tr. V.* (abwertend) pollute

Verpestung (abwertend) *die; ∼, ∼en* pollution

verpflanzen *tr. V.* (auch Med.) transplant; graft ⟨*skin*⟩

Verpflanzung *die; ∼, ∼en* (Med.) transplant[ing]; (von Haut) graft

verpflegen *tr. V.* cater for; feed

Verpflegung *die; ∼, ∼en* (a) catering *no indef. art.* (Gen. for) (b) (Nahrung) food; **Unterkunft und ∼:** board and lodging

verpflichten ⟦1⟧ *tr. V.* (a) oblige; commit; (festlegen, binden) bind (b) (einstellen, engagieren) engage ⟨*manager, actor, etc.*⟩ ⟦2⟧ *refl. V.* undertake; promise; **sich vertraglich ∼:** sign a contract

Verpflichtung *die; ∼, ∼en* (a) obligation; commitment (b) (Engagement) engaging; engagement

verpfuschen *tr. V.* (ugs.) make a mess of; muck up (Brit. sl.)

verpissen *refl. V.* (salopp) piss off (Brit. sl.); beat it (coll.)

verpönt *Adj.* scorned; (tabu) taboo

verprügeln *tr. V.* beat up; (zur Strafe) thrash

Verputz *der; ∼es* plaster; (auf Außenwänden) rendering

verputzen *tr. V.* plaster; render ⟨*outside wall*⟩

verquer *Adj.* (absonderlich) weird, outlandish ⟨*idea*⟩

verquirlen *tr. V.* mix [with a whisk]; whisk

verquollen *Adj.* swollen

verrammeln *tr. V.* barricade

Verrat *der; ∼[e]s* betrayal (**an** + *Dat.* of)

verraten *unr. tr. V.* (a) betray (**an** + *Akk.* to) (b) (ugs.: mitteilen) **jmdm. den Grund** *usw.* **∼:** tell sb. the reason *etc.;* (c) (erkennen lassen) show, betray ⟨*feelings, surprise, fear, etc.*⟩; show ⟨*influence, talent*⟩

Verräter *der; ∼s, ∼:* traitor

Verräterin *die; ∼, ∼nen* traitress

verräterisch *Adj.* treacherous ⟨*plan, purpose, act, etc.*⟩

verraucht *Adj.* smoke-filled; smoky

verrechnen ⟦1⟧ *tr. V.* include ⟨*amount etc.*⟩; (gutschreiben) credit ⟨*cheque etc.*⟩ to another account ⟦2⟧ *refl. V.* miscalculate

Verrechnungs·scheck *der* crossed cheque

verregnen *itr. V.; mit sein* be spoilt *or* ruined by rain

verreiben *unr. tr. V.* rub in

verreisen *itr. V.; mit sein* go away

verrenken *tr. V.* dislocate

Verrenkung *die; ∼, ∼en* dislocation

verrichten *tr. V.* perform

verriegeln *tr. V.* bolt

verringern ⟦1⟧ *tr. V.* reduce ⟦2⟧ *refl. V.* decrease

Verringerung *die; ∼:* reduction; decrease (Gen., **von** in)

Verriss, *Verriß *der* (ugs.) damning review *or* criticism (**über** + *Akk.* of)

verrosten *itr. V.; mit sein* rust; **verrostet** rusty

verrückt (ugs.) ⟦1⟧ *Adj.* (a) mad *or* insane **∼ werden** go mad *or* insane (b) (überspannt, ausgefallen) crazy ⟨*idea, fashion, prank, day, etc.*⟩ ⟦2⟧ *adv.* crazily; ⟨*behave*⟩ crazily *or* like a madman; ⟨*dress etc.*⟩ in a mad *or* crazy way

Verrückte *der/die; adj. Dekl.* (ugs.) madman/madwoman; lunatic

verrufen *Adj.* disreputable

verrühren *tr. V.* stir together; mix

verrutschen *itr. V.* slip

Vers *der; ∼es, ∼e* verse

versagen *itr. V.* fail; ⟨*machine, engine*⟩ stop [working]; **menschliches Versagen** human error

Versager *der; ∼s, ∼,* **Versagerin** *die; ∼, ∼nen* failure

V

versalzen *unr. tr. V.* put too much salt in/ on; (fig. ugs.) spoil

versammeln *tr., refl. V.* assemble

Versammlung *die;* ~, ~en **(a)** meeting **(b)** (Gremium) assembly

Versand *der;* ~[e]s **(a)** dispatch **(b)** (ugs.: Versandhaus) mail order firm

Versand-: ~**handel** *der* mail order business; ~**haus** *das* mail order firm

versauen *tr. V.* (salopp) **(a)** (verschmutzen) mess up; make mucky (coll.) **(b)** (verderben) foul up (coll.)

versäumen *tr. V.* **(a)** (verpassen) miss; lose ⟨time, sleep⟩ **(b)** (vernachlässigen, unterlassen) neglect ⟨duty, task⟩

verschaffen *tr. V.* jmdm. etw. ~: provide sb. with sth.; get sb. sth.; **sich** (*Dat.*) **etw.** ~: get hold of sth.; obtain sth.

verschämt [1] *Adj.* bashful [2] *adv.* bashfully

verschandeln *tr. V.* (ugs.) spoil; ruin

verschenken *tr. V.* give away

verscheuchen *tr. V.* chase away

verscheuern *tr. V.* (ugs.) flog (Brit. sl.) (*Dat.,* **an** + *Akk.* to)

verschicken *tr. V.* ▶ VERSENDEN

verschieben [1] *unr. tr. V.* **(a)** shift; move **(b)** (aufschieben) put off, postpone (**auf** + *Akk.* till) [2] *unr. refl. V.* be postponed (**um** for); ⟨start⟩ be put back *or* delayed (**um** by)

Verschiebung *die;* ~, ~en postponement

verschieden [1] *Adj.* **(a)** different (**von** from) **(b)** (vielfältig) various; **die** ~**sten** ...: all sorts of ...; **die** ~**en** ...: the various ... **(c) Verschiedenes** various things *pl.;* [2] *adv.* differently

verschieden·artig [1] *Adj.* different in kind *pred.;* (mehr als zwei) diverse [2] *adv.* diversely

Verschiedenheit *die;* ~, ~en difference; (unter mehreren) diversity

verschiedentlich *Adv.* on various occasions

verschimmeln *itr. V.; mit sein* go mouldy; **verschimmelt** mouldy

verschlafen¹ [1] *unr. itr. (auch refl.) V.* oversleep [2] *unr. tr. V.* **(a)** (schlafend verbringen) sleep through ⟨morning, journey, etc.⟩ **(b)** (versäumen) not wake up in time for ⟨appointment⟩; not wake up in time to catch ⟨train, bus⟩ **(c)** (ugs.: vergessen) forget about ⟨appointment etc.⟩

verschlafen² *Adj.* half asleep; (fig.) sleepy ⟨town⟩

Verschlag *der;* ~[e]s, **Verschläge** shed

verschlagen¹ *unr. tr. V.* **die Seite** ~: lose one's place *or* page; **jmdm. die Sprache** ~: leave sb. speechless

verschlagen² [1] *Adj.* sly; shifty [2] *adv.* slyly; shiftily

verschlechtern [1] *tr. V.* make worse [2] *refl. V.* get worse; deteriorate

Verschlechterung *die;* ~, ~en worsening, deterioration (Gen. in)

Verschleiß *der;* ~es, ~e **(a)** wear *no indef. art.;* **(b)** (Verbrauch) consumption (**an** + *Dat.* of)

verschleißen [1] *unr. itr. V.; mit sein* wear out [2] *unr. tr. V.* wear out; (fig.) run down, ruin ⟨one's nerves, one's health⟩; use up ⟨energy, ability, etc.⟩

verschleppen *tr. V.* **(a)** carry off; take away ⟨person⟩ **(b)** (weiterverbreiten) carry, spread ⟨disease, bacteria, mud, etc.⟩ **(c)** (verzögern) delay; (in die Länge ziehen) draw out; let ⟨illness⟩ drag on [and get worse]

verschleudern *tr. V.* **(a)** sell dirt cheap (coll.); (mit Verlust) sell at a loss **(b)** (verschwenden) squander

verschließbar *Adj.* closable; lockable ⟨suitcase, drawer, etc.⟩; [luftdicht] ~: sealable ⟨container etc.⟩

verschließen *unr. tr. V.* **(a)** close; stop, (mit einem Korken) cork ⟨bottle⟩ **(b)** (abschließen) lock; lock up ⟨house etc.⟩ **(c)** (wegschließen) lock away (**in** + *Dat. od. Akk.* in)

verschlimmern [1] *tr. V.* make worse [2] *refl. V.* get worse; ⟨position, conditions⟩ deteriorate, worsen

Verschlimmerung *die;* ~, ~en worsening

verschlingen *unr. tr. V.* **(a)** [inter]twine ⟨threads etc.⟩ (**zu** into) **(b)** (essen, fressen) devour ⟨food⟩; (fig.) devour ⟨novel, money, etc.⟩

verschlissen *2. Part. v.* VERSCHLEISSEN 2

verschlossen *Adj.* (wortkarg) taciturn; (zurückhaltend) reserved

Verschlossenheit *die;* ~: taciturnity; (Zurückhaltung) reserve

verschlucken [1] *tr. V.* swallow [2] *refl. V.* choke

Verschluss, *Verschluß *der* (am BH, an Schmuck usw.) fastener; fastening; (an Taschen, Schmuck) clasp; (an Schuhen, Gürteln) buckle; (am Schrank, Fenster, Koffer usw.) catch; (an Flaschen) top; (Stöpsel) stopper

verschmähen *tr. V.* (geh.) spurn

verschmerzen *tr. V.* get over

verschmieren *tr. V.* smear ⟨window etc.⟩; (beim Schreiben) mess up ⟨paper⟩; scrawl all over ⟨page⟩; smudge ⟨ink⟩

verschmitzt [1] *Adj.* mischievous [2] *adv.* mischievously

verschmutzen ① *itr. V.; mit sein* get dirty; ⟨*river etc.*⟩ become polluted

② *tr. V.* dirty; soil; pollute ⟨*air, water, etc.*⟩

Verschmutzung *die; ~, ~en* (der Umwelt) pollution; (von Stoffen, Teppichen usw.) soiling

verschnaufen *itr. V.* (*auch refl.*) V. have *or* take a breather

verschneit *Adj.* snow-covered *attrib.;* covered with snow *postpos.*

verschnörkelt *Adj.* ornate

verschnüren *tr. V.* tie up

verschollen *Adj.* missing

verschonen *tr. V.* spare; jmdn. mit etw. ~: spare sb. sth.

verschönern *tr. V.* brighten up

verschränken *tr. V.* fold ⟨*arms*⟩; cross ⟨*legs*⟩; clasp ⟨*hands*⟩

verschrecken *tr. V.* frighten *or* scare [off *or* away]

verschreiben ① *unr. tr. V.* (Med.: verordnen) prescribe

② *unr. refl. V.* (a) make a slip of the pen (b) sich einer Sache (*Dat.*) ~: devote oneself to sth.

verschreibungs·pflichtig *Adj.* available only on prescription *postpos.*

verschrie[e]n *Adj.* notorious (**wegen** for)

verschroben *Adj.* eccentric, cranky ⟨*person*⟩; cranky, weird ⟨*ideas*⟩

verschrotten *tr. V.* scrap

Verschrottung *die; ~, ~en* scrapping

verschulden ① *tr. V.* be to blame for ⟨*accident, death, etc.*⟩

② *refl. V.* get into debt

Verschulden *das; ~s* guilt; durch eigenes ~: through one's own fault

verschuldet *Adj.* in debt *postpos.* (**bei** to); hoch ~: deeply in debt

verschütt: ~ gehen (ugs.) do a vanishing trick *or* disappearing act (coll.)

verschütten *tr. V.* (a) spill (b) (begraben) bury ⟨*person*⟩ [alive]

**verschütt|gehen ▶ VERSCHÜTT

verschwägert *Adj.* related by marriage *postpos.*

verschweigen *unr. tr. V.* conceal (*Dat.* from)

verschwenden *tr. V.* waste (**an** + *Akk.* on)

Verschwender *der; ~s, ~,* **Verschwenderin** *die; ~, ~nen* (von Geld) spendthrift; (von Dingen) wasteful person

verschwenderisch ① *Adj.* wasteful ⟨*person*⟩; ⟨*life*⟩ of extravagance

② *adv.* wastefully

Verschwendung *die; ~, ~en* wastefulness; extravagance

verschwiegen *Adj.* discreet; (still, einsam) secluded

Verschwiegenheit *die; ~:* secrecy; (Diskretion) discretion

verschwimmen *unr. itr. V.; mit sein* blur

verschwinden *unr. itr. V.; mit sein* disappear; vanish; **verschwinde [hier]!** off with you!; go away!; hop it! (coll.); **ich muss mal ~** (ugs. verhüll.) I have to pay a visit (coll.) *or* (Brit. coll.) spend a penny

verschwindend ① *Adj.* tiny

② *adv.* ~ klein tiny; minute; ~ wenig a tiny amount

verschwommen ① *Adj.* blurred ⟨*photograph, vision*⟩; blurred, hazy ⟨*outline*⟩; vague, woolly ⟨*idea, concept, formulation, etc.*⟩

② *adv.* vaguely; ⟨*remember*⟩ hazily

versehen ① *unr. tr. V.* (a) (ausstatten) provide; equip ⟨*car, factory, machine, etc.*⟩ (b) (ausüben, besorgen) perform ⟨*duty etc.*⟩

② *unr. refl. V.* make a slip; slip up

Versehen *das; ~s, ~:* oversight; slip; **aus ~:** by mistake; inadvertently

versehentlich ① *Adv.* by mistake; inadvertently

② *adj.* inadvertent

Versehrte *der/die; adj. Dekl.* disabled person; **die ~n** the disabled

versenden *unr.* (*auch regelm.*) *tr. V.* send ⟨*letter, parcel*⟩; send out ⟨*invitations*⟩; dispatch ⟨*goods*⟩

versetzen ① *tr. V.* (a) move; transfer, move ⟨*employee*⟩; (in die nächsthöhere Klasse) move ⟨*pupil*⟩ up, (Amer.) promote ⟨*pupil*⟩ (in + *Akk.* to); (umpflanzen) transplant, move ⟨*plant*⟩; (fig.) transport (**in** + *Akk.* to) (b) (nicht geradlinig anordnen) stagger (c) (verpfänden) pawn (d) (verkaufen) sell (e) (ugs.: vergeblich warten lassen) stand ⟨*person*⟩ up (coll.) (f) (vermischen) mix (g) (erwidern) retort (h) etw. in Bewegung/Tätigkeit ~: set sth. in motion/operation; jmdn. in die Lage ~, etw. zu tun put sb. in a position to do sth.; jmdm. einen Stoß/Fußtritt/Schlag usw. ~: give sb. a push/kick/deal sb. a blow *etc.;*

② *refl. V.* sich in jmds. Lage (*Akk.*) ~: put oneself in sb.'s position *or* place

Versetzung *die; ~, ~en* (eines Schülers) moving up, (Amer.) promotion (**in** + *Akk.* to); (eines Angestellten) transfer

verseuchen *tr. V.* (auch fig.) contaminate; **radioaktiv ~:** contaminate with radioactivity

Verseuchung (auch fig.) *die; ~, ~en* contamination

Versicherer *der; ~s, ~,* **Versicherin** *die; ~, ~nen* insurer

versichern *tr. V.* (a) assert ⟨*sth.*⟩ (b) (vertraglich schützen) insure (**bei** with)

Versicherte *der/die; adj. Dekl.* insured [person]

Versicherung *die* (a) (Beteuerung) assurance (b) (Schutz durch Vertrag) insurance; (Vertrag) insurance [policy] (**über** + *Akk.* for); (Gesellschaft) insurance [company]

Versicherungs-: ~**beitrag** der insurance premium; ~**betrug** der insurance fraud; ~**gesellschaft** die insurance company; ~**nehmer** der; ~~**s**; ~~, ~**nehmerin** die; ~~, ~~**nen** policy holder; ~**police** die insurance policy

versickern itr. V.; mit sein ⟨river etc.⟩ drain or seep away

versiegeln tr. V. seal

versiegen itr. V.; mit sein (geh.) dry up; run dry

versinken unr. itr. V.; mit sein sink; im Schlamm ~: sink into the mud

verslumen /...'slamən/ itr. V.; mit sein turn into a slum; ein verslumter Stadtteil a slum district

versoffen Adj. (salopp abwertend) boozy (coll.)

versöhnen [1] refl. V. sich [miteinander] ~: become reconciled; sich mit jmdm. ~: make it up with sb. [2] tr. V. reconcile

Versöhnung die; ~, ~en reconciliation

versonnen [1] Adj. dreamy [2] adv. dreamily

versorgen tr. V. **(a)** supply **(b)** (unterhalten, ernähren) provide for ⟨children, family⟩ **(c)** (sorgen für) look after; jmdn. ärztlich ~: give sb. medical care; (kurzzeitig) give sb. medical attention

Versorger der; ~s, ~, **Versorgerin** die; ~, ~nen breadwinner

Versorgung die; ~, ~en **(a)** supply[ing] **(b)** (Unterhaltung, Ernährung) support[ing] **(c)** (Bedienung, Pflege) care; ärztliche ~: medical care or treatment; (kurzzeitig) medical attention

Verspannung die (Med.: der Muskulatur) tension

verspäten refl. V. be late

verspätet Adj. late ⟨arrival etc.⟩; belated ⟨greetings, thanks⟩; ~ eintreffen arrive late

Verspätung die; ~, ~en lateness; (verspätetes Eintreffen) late arrival; [fünf Minuten] ~ haben be [five minutes] late

versperren tr. V. block; obstruct ⟨view⟩

verspielen tr. V. gamble away; (fig.) squander, throw away ⟨opportunity, chance⟩; forfeit ⟨right, credibility, etc⟩

verspielt [1] Adj. (auch fig.) playful; fanciful, fantastic ⟨form, design, etc.⟩ [2] adv. playfully (lit. or fig.); ⟨dress, designed⟩ fancifully, fantastically

verspotten tr. V. mock; ridicule

Verspottung die; ~, ~en mocking; ridiculing

versprechen [1] unr. tr. V. promise; sich (Dat.) etw. von etw./jmdm. ~: hope for sth. or to get sth. from sth./sb. [2] unr. refl. V. make a slip/slips of the tongue

Versprechen das; ~s, ~, **Versprechung** die; ~, ~en promise

versprühen tr. V. spray

verspüren tr. V. feel

verstaatlichen tr. V. nationalize

Verstaatlichung die; ~, ~en nationalization

Verstand der; ~[e]s (Fähigkeit zu denken) reason no art.; (Fähigkeit, Begriffe zu bilden) mind; (Vernunft) [common] sense no art.; hast du denn den ~ verloren? (ugs.) have you taken leave of your senses?

verständig [1] Adj. sensible [2] adv. sensibly

verständigen [1] tr. V. notify, inform (von, über + Akk. of) [2] refl. V. **(a)** make oneself understood; sich mit jmdm. ~: communicate with sb. **(b)** (sich einigen) sich [mit jmdm.] über/auf etw. (Akk.) ~: come to an understanding [with sb.] about or on sth.

Verständigkeit die; ~: understanding; intelligence

Verständigung die; ~, ~en **(a)** notification **(b)** (das Sichverständlichmachen) communication no art.; **(c)** (Einigung) understanding

Verständigungs·schwierigkeit die difficulty of communication

verständlich [1] Adj. **(a)** comprehensible; (deutlich) clear ⟨pronunciation, presentation, etc.⟩; sich ~ machen make oneself understood; jmdm. etw. ~ machen make sth. clear to sb. **(b)** (begreiflich, verzeihlich) understandable [2] adv. comprehensibly; (deutlich) ⟨speak, express oneself, present⟩ clearly

verständlicher·weise Adv. understandably

Verständlichkeit die; ~: comprehensibility; clarity

Verständnis das; ~ses, ~se understanding; ich habe volles ~ dafür, dass ...: I fully understand that ...; für die Unannehmlichkeiten bitten wir um [Ihr] ~: we apologize for the inconvenience caused

verständnis-: ~**los** [1] Adj. uncomprehending; [2] adv. uncomprehendingly; ~**voll** [1] Adj. understanding; [2] adv. understandingly

verstärken [1] tr. V. **(a)** strengthen **(b)** (zahlenmäßig) reinforce ⟨troops etc.⟩ (um by); enlarge ⟨orchestra, choir⟩ (um by) **(c)** (intensiver machen) intensify, increase ⟨effort, contrast⟩; strengthen, increase ⟨impression, suspicion⟩; (größer machen) increase ⟨pressure, voltage, effect, etc.⟩; (lauter machen) amplify ⟨signal, sound, guitar, etc.⟩ [2] refl. V. increase

Verstärker der; ~s, ~: amplifier

Verstärkung die; ~, ~en **(a)** strengthening

(b) (zahlenmäßig) reinforcement (esp. Mil.)
(c) (Zunahme) increase (*Gen.* in); (der Lautstärke) amplification
(d) (zusätzliche Person[en]) reinforcements *pl.*
verstauben *itr. V.; mit sein* get dusty; gather dust (lit. or fig.)
verstaubt *Adj.* (fig. abwertend) old-fashioned; outmoded
verstauchen *tr. V.* sprain; **sich** (*Dat.*) **den Fuß/die Hand ~:** sprain one's ankle/wrist
Verstauchung *die; ~, ~en* sprain
verstauen *tr. V.* pack (**in** + *Dat. od. Akk.* in[to]); (bes. im Boot/Auto) stow (**in** + *Dat. od. Akk.* in)
Versteck *das; ~[e]s, ~e* hiding place: **~ spielen** play hide-and-seek
verstecken ① *tr. V.* hide (**vor** + *Dat.* from)
  ② *refl. V.* **sich** [**vor jmdm./etw.**] **~:** hide [from sb./sth.]
versteckt *Adj.* hidden; (heimlich) secret ⟨*malice, activity, etc.*⟩; disguised ⟨*foul*⟩
verstehen ① *unr. tr. V.* understand; **wie soll ich das ~?** how am I to interpret that?; **jmdn./etw. falsch ~:** misunderstand sb./sth.
  ② *unr. refl. V.* **sich mit jmdm. ~:** get on with sb.; **das versteht sich [von selbst]** that goes without saying
versteigern *tr. V.* auction; **etw. ~ lassen** put sth. up for auction
Versteigerung *die; ~, ~en* auction
versteinern *itr. V.; mit sein* ⟨*plant, animal*⟩ fossilize, become fossilized; ⟨*wood etc.*⟩ petrify, become petrified
Versteinerung *die; ~, ~en* **(a)** (das Versteinern) fossilization; (von Holz) petrification
  (b) (Fossil) fossil
verstellbar *Adj.* adjustable
verstellen ① *tr. V.* **(a)** (falsch platzieren) misplace
  (b) (anders einstellen) adjust ⟨*seat etc.*⟩; alter [the adjustment of] ⟨*mirror etc.*⟩; reset ⟨*alarm clock, points, etc.*⟩
  (c) (versperren) block, obstruct
  (d) (zur Täuschung verändern) disguise ⟨*voice, handwriting*⟩
  ② *refl. V.* pretend
Verstellung *die; ~, ~en* pretence; (der Stimme, Schrift) disguising
versteuern *tr. V.* pay tax on
verstimmen *tr. V.* put ⟨*person*⟩ in a bad mood; (verärgern) annoy
verstimmt *Adj.* **(a)** (Musik) out of tune *pred.;*
  (b) (verärgert) put out, peeved, disgruntled (**über** + *Akk.* by, about); **ein ~er Magen** an upset stomach
Verstimmung *die; ~, ~en* bad mood
verstockt *Adj.* obdurate; stubborn
Verstocktheit *die; ~:* obduracy; stubbornness
verstohlen ① *Adj.* furtive

  ② *adv.* furtively
verstopfen ① *tr. V.* block; **verstopft sein** ⟨*pipe, drain, jet, nose, etc.*⟩ be blocked [up] (**durch, von** with)
  ② *itr. V.; mit sein* become blocked
Verstopfung *die; ~, ~en* (Med.) constipation
verstorben *Adj.* late (*deceased*)
Verstorbene *der/die; adj. Dekl.* (geh.) deceased
verstören *tr. V.* distress
verstört *Adj.* distraught
Verstoß *der; ~es, Verstöße* violation (**gegen** of)
verstoßen ① *unr. tr. V.* disown
  ② *unr. itr. V.* **gegen etw. ~:** infringe sth
verstreichen ① *unr. tr. V.* apply, put on ⟨*paint*⟩; spread ⟨*butter etc.*⟩
  ② *unr. itr. V.; mit sein* (geh.) ⟨*time*⟩ pass [by]
verstreuen *tr. V.* scatter; put down ⟨*bird food, salt*⟩; (versehentlich) spill
verstricken ① *tr. V.* **jmdn. in etw.** (*Akk.*) **~:** involve sb. in sth.; draw sb. into sth.
  ② *refl. V.* **sich in etw.** (*Akk.*) **~:** become entangled *or* caught up in sth
verstümmeln *tr. V.* mutilate; (fig.) garble ⟨*report*⟩; chop, mutilate ⟨*text*⟩
verstummen *itr. V.; mit sein* (geh.) fall silent; ⟨*music, noise, conversation*⟩ cease
Versuch *der; ~[e]s, ~e* attempt; (Experiment) experiment (**an** + *Dat.* on); (Probe) test
versuchen *tr. V.* **(a)** try; attempt
  (b) (probieren) try ⟨*cake etc.*⟩
versündigen *refl. V.* **sich an jmdm./etw. ~:** sin against sb./sth.
versüßen *tr. V.* **jmdm./sich etw. ~** (fig.) make sth. more pleasant for sb./oneself
vertauschen *tr. V.* exchange; switch; reverse ⟨*roles, poles*⟩; **etw. mit od. gegen etw. ~:** exchange sth. for sth.
verteidigen *tr. V.* defend
Verteidiger *der; ~s, ~,* **Verteidigerin** *die; ~, ~nen* (auch Sport) defender; (Rechtsw.) defence counsel
Verteidigung *die; ~, ~en* defence
Verteidigungs-minister *der,* **Verteidigungs-ministerin** *die* minister of defence
verteilen *tr. V.* distribute, hand out ⟨*leaflets, prizes, etc.*⟩ (**an** + *Akk.* to, **unter** + *Akk.* among); share [out], distribute ⟨*money, food*⟩ (**an** + *Akk.* to, **unter** + *Akk.* among); allocate ⟨*work*⟩; distribute ⟨*weight etc.*⟩ (**auf** + *Akk.* over); spread ⟨*cost*⟩ (**auf** + *Akk.* among); distribute, spread ⟨*butter, seed, dirt, etc.*⟩
Verteilung *die; ~, ~en* distribution; (der Rollen, der Arbeit) allocation
verteuern ① *tr. V.* make ⟨*goods*⟩ more expensive
  ② *refl. V.* become more expensive

verteufeln *tr. V.* condemn; denigrate

Verteufelung *die;* ∼, ∼en condemnation; denigration

vertiefen [1] *tr. V.* (auch fig.) deepen (**um** by) [2] *refl. V.* **sich** ∼ **in** (+ *Akk.*) bury oneself in ⟨*book, work, etc.*⟩; **in etw.** (*Akk.*) **vertieft sein** be engrossed in sth

Vertiefung *die;* ∼, ∼en (Mulde) depression; hollow

vertikal [1] *Adj.* vertical [2] *adv.* vertically

Vertikale *die;* ∼, ∼n ▶ SENKRECHTE

vertilgen *tr. V.* (a) (vernichten) exterminate ⟨*vermin*⟩; kill off ⟨*weeds*⟩ (b) (ugs.: verzehren) devour, (joc.) demolish ⟨*food*⟩

vertonen *tr. V.* set ⟨*text, poem*⟩ to music

Vertonung *die;* ∼, ∼en setting

Vertrag *der;* ∼[e]s, Verträge contract; (zwischen Staaten) treaty

vertragen [1] *unr. tr. V.* endure; tolerate (esp. Med.); (aushalten, leiden können) stand; bear; **ich vertrage keinen Kaffee** coffee disagrees with me [2] *unr. refl. V.* **sich mit jmdm.** ∼: get on *or* along with sb.; (passen) **sich mit etw.** ∼: go with sth

vertraglich [1] *Adj.* contractual [2] *adv.* contractually; by contract

verträglich *Adj.* (a) digestible ⟨*food*⟩ (b) (umgänglich) goodnatured; easy to get on with *pred.*

vertrauen *itr. V.* **jmdm./einer Sache** ∼: trust sb./sth.; **auf etw.** (*Akk.*) ∼: [put one's] trust in sth.

Vertrauen *das;* ∼s trust; confidence; **jmdn. ins** ∼ **ziehen** take sb. into one's confidence

vertrauen-erweckend *Adj.* inspiring

vertrauens-, Vertrauens-: ∼**bruch** *der* breach of trust; ∼**lehrer** *der,* ∼**lehrerin** *die* (Schulw.) liaison teacher (liaising between staff and pupils); ∼**person** *die* person in a position of trust; ∼**sache** *die* matter *or* question of trust; ∼**selig** *Adj.* all too trusting; ∼**voll** [1] *Adj.* trusting ⟨*relationship*⟩; ⟨*collaboration, cooperation*⟩ based on trust; (zuversichtlich) confident; [2] *adv.* trustingly; (zuversichtlich) confidently; ∼**würdig** *Adj.* trustworthy

vertraulich [1] *Adj.* (a) confidential (b) (freundschaftlich, intim) familiar ⟨*manner, tone, etc.*⟩; intimate ⟨*conversation*⟩ [2] *adv.* (a) confidentially (b) (freundschaftlich, intim) in a familiar way

Vertraulichkeit *die;* ∼, ∼en (a) confidentiality (b) (vertrauliche Information) confidence (c) (distanzloses Verhalten) familiarity; (Intimität) intimacy

vertraut *Adj.* (a) close ⟨*friend etc.*⟩; intimate ⟨*circle, conversation, etc.*⟩

(b) (bekannt) familiar; **jmdn./sich mit etw.** ∼ **machen** familiarize sb./oneself with sth.

Vertraute *der/die; adj. Dekl.* close friend

vertreiben *unr. tr. V.* (a) drive out ⟨**aus** of⟩; drive away ⟨*animal, smoke, clouds*⟩ ⟨**aus** from⟩; fight off ⟨*tiredness, troubles*⟩ (b) (verkaufen) sell

vertreten [1] *unr. tr. V.* (a) stand in *or* deputize for ⟨*colleague etc.*⟩; ⟨*teacher*⟩ cover for ⟨*colleague*⟩ (b) (eintreten für, repräsentieren) represent ⟨*person, firm, interests, constituency, country, etc.*⟩; (Rechtsw.) act for ⟨*person, prosecution, etc.*⟩; ∼ **sein** be represented (c) (einstehen für, verfechten) support ⟨*point of view, principle*⟩; hold ⟨*opinion*⟩; advocate ⟨*thesis etc.*⟩ [2] *unr. refl. V.* **sich** (*Dat.*) **die Füße** *od.* **Beine** ∼ (ugs.) stretch one's legs

Vertreter *der;* ∼s, ∼, **Vertreterin** *die;* ∼, ∼nen (a) (Stellvertreter[in]) deputy; stand-in (b) (Repräsentant[in]) representative; (Handelsvertreter[in]) sales representative; commercial traveller (c) (Verfechter[in], Anhänger[in]) supporter; advocate

Vertretung *die;* ∼, ∼en deputy; (Delegierte[r]) representative; (Delegation) delegation (Handelsvertretung) [sales] agency; **eine diplomatische** ∼: a diplomatic mission

Vertriebene *der/die; adj. Dekl.* expellee [from his/her homeland]

vertrocknen *itr. V.; mit sein* dry up

vertrödeln *tr. V.* (ugs. abwertend) dawdle away, waste ⟨*time*⟩

vertrösten *tr. V.* put ⟨*person*⟩ off (**auf** + *Akk.* until)

vertun [1] *unr. tr. V.* waste [2] *unr. refl. V.* (ugs.) make a slip

vertuschen *tr. V.* hush up ⟨*scandal etc.*⟩; keep ⟨*truth etc.*⟩ secret

Vertuschung *die;* ∼, ∼en hushing up; **eine** ∼: a hush-up *or* cover-up

verübeln *tr. V.* **jmdm. eine Äußerung** *usw.* ∼: take sb.'s remark *etc.* amiss

verüben *tr. V.* commit ⟨*crime etc.*⟩

verunglücken *itr. V.; mit sein* have an accident; ⟨*car etc.*⟩ be involved in an accident; **mit dem Auto/Flugzeug** ∼: be in a car/an air accident *or* crash

Verunglückte *der/die; adj. Dekl.* accident victim; casualty

verunreinigen *tr. V.* pollute; contaminate ⟨*water, milk, flour, oil*⟩

verunsichern *tr. V.* **jmdn.** ∼: make sb. feel unsure *or* uncertain

verunstalten *tr. V.* disfigure

Verunstaltung *die;* ∼, ∼en disfigurement

veruntreuen *tr. V.* embezzle

Veruntreuung *die;* ∼, ∼en embezzlement

verunzieren *tr. V.* spoil the look of

verursachen *tr. V.* cause

---

*alte Schreibung - vgl. Hinweis auf S. xiv

verurteilen *tr. V.* pass sentence on; sentence; (fig.) condemn ⟨*behaviour, action*⟩; **jmdn. zum Tode** ~: sentence *or* condemn sb. to death

Verurteilte *der/die; adj. Dekl.* convicted man/woman

Verurteilung *die;* ~, ~en sentencing; (fig.) condemnation

vervollkommnen *tr. V.* perfect

vervollständigen *tr. V.* complete

verwachsen *Adj.* deformed

verwählen *refl. V.* misdial

verwahren ① *tr. V.* keep [safe]
② *refl. V.* protest

verwahrlosen *itr. V.; mit sein* get in a bad state; ⟨*house, building*⟩ fall into disrepair; ⟨*garden, hedge*⟩ become overgrown; ⟨*person*⟩ let oneself go; **verwahrlost** neglected; overgrown ⟨*hedge, garden*⟩; dilapidated ⟨*house, building*⟩; unkempt ⟨*person, appearance, etc.*⟩; (in der Kleidung) ragged ⟨*person*⟩

Verwahrlosung *die;* ~: (eines Gebäudes) dilapidation; (einer Person) advancing decrepitude

verwaisen *itr. V.* be orphaned

verwalten *tr. V.* (a) administer ⟨*estate, property*⟩; run ⟨*house*⟩; hold ⟨*money*⟩ in trust (b) (leiten) run, manage ⟨*hostel, kindergarten, etc.*⟩; (regieren) administer ⟨*area, colony, etc.*⟩; govern ⟨*country*⟩

Verwalter *der;* ~s, ~, **Verwalterin** *die;* ~, ~nen administrator; (eines Amts usw.) manager; (eines Nachlasses) trustee

Verwaltung *die;* ~, ~en (a) administration; (eines Landes) government; (eines Amtes) tenure; (einer Aufgabe) performance (b) (Organ) administration

verwandeln ① *tr. V.* convert (in + *Akk.*, **zu** into); (völlig verändern) transform (in + *Akk.*, **zu** into)
② *refl. V.* **sich in etw.** (*Akk.*) *od.* **zu etw.** ~: turn *or* change into sth.; (bei chemischen Vorgängen usw.) be converted into sth

Verwandlung *die;* ~, ~en conversion (in + *Akk.*, **zu** into); (völlige Veränderung, das Sichverwandeln) transformation (in + *Akk.*, **zu** into)

verwandt¹ 2. *Part. v.* VERWENDEN

verwandt² *Adj.* related (**mit** to); (fig.) similar ⟨*views, ideas, forms*⟩

Verwandte *der/die; adj. Dekl.* relative; relation

Verwandtschaft *die;* ~, ~en (a) relationship (**mit** to); (fig.) affinity (b) (Verwandte) relatives *pl.;* relations *pl.;* **die ganze** ~: all one's relatives

verwandtschaftlich *Adj.* family ⟨*ties, relationships, etc.*⟩

verwarnen *tr. V.* warn, caution (**wegen** for)

Verwarnung *die;* ~, ~en warning; caution

verwechseln *tr. V.* (a) [miteinander] ~: confuse ⟨*two things/people*⟩; **etw. mit etw./jmdn. mit jmdm.** ~: mistake sth. for sth./sb. for sb.; confuse sth. with sth./sb. with sb. (b) (vertauschen) mix up

Verwechslung *die;* ~, ~en (a) [case of] confusion (b) (Vertauschung) mixing up; **eine** ~: a mix-up

verwegen ① *Adj.* daring; (auch fig.) audacious
② *adv.* (auch fig.) audaciously

Verwegenheit *die;* ~: daring; (auch fig.) audacity

verwehren *tr. V.* **jmdm. etw.** ~: refuse *or* deny sb. sth.

Verwehung *die;* ~, ~en [snow]drift

verweigern *tr. V.* refuse

Verweigerung *die;* ~, ~en refusal

Verweis *der;* ~es, ~e (a) reference (**auf** + *Akk.* to); (Querverweis) cross reference (b) (Tadel) reprimand

verweisen *unr. tr. V.* (a) **jmdn./einen Fall** *usw.* **an jmdn./etw.** ~ (auch Rechtsspr.) refer sb./a case *etc.* to sb./sth. (b) (wegschicken) **jmdn. von der Schule/aus dem Saal** ~: expel sb. from the school/send sb. out of the room; **einen Spieler vom Platz** ~: send a player off [the field] (c) *auch itr.* (hinweisen) **[jmdn.] auf etw.** (*Akk.*) ~: refer [sb.] to sth.

verwelken *itr. V.; mit sein* wilt

verwendbar *Adj.* usable

Verwendbarkeit *die;* ~: usability

verwenden *unr. od. regelm. tr. V.* (a) use (**zu, für** for) (b) (aufwenden) spend ⟨*time*⟩ (**auf** + *Akk.* on)

Verwendung *die;* ~, ~en use

verwerfen *unr. tr. V.* reject; dismiss ⟨*thought*⟩

verwerflich (geh.) ① *Adj.* reprehensible
② *adv.* reprehensibly

verwertbar *Adj.* utilizable; usable

verwerten *tr. V.* utilize, use (**zu** for); make use of ⟨*suggestion, experience, knowledge, etc.*⟩

verwesen *itr. V.; mit sein* decompose

Verwesung *die;* ~: decomposition

verwickeln ① *refl. V.* get tangled up *or* entangled; **sich in etw.** (*Akk. od. Dat.*) ~: get caught [up] in sth.
② *tr. V.* involve

Verwicklung *die;* ~, ~en complication

verwildern *itr. V.* ⟨*garden*⟩ become overgrown; ⟨*domestic animal*⟩ return to the wild

verwirklichen ① *tr. V.* realize ⟨*dream*⟩; realize, put into practice ⟨*plan, proposal, idea, etc.*⟩; carry out ⟨*project, intention*⟩
② (a) *refl. V.* ⟨*hope, dream*⟩ be realized

····⫶

V

(b) (sich voll entfalten) **sich [selbst]** ∼: realize one's [full] potential; fulfil oneself

Verwirklichung *die;* ∼, ∼**en** realization; (eines Wunsches, einer Hoffnung) fulfilment

verwirren *tr. (auch itr.) V.* confuse; **verwirrt** confused; ∼**d** bewildering

Verwirrung *die;* ∼, ∼**en** confusion

verwischen *tr. V.* smudge ⟨*signature, writing, etc.*⟩; smear ⟨*paint*⟩; (fig.) cover up ⟨*tracks*⟩

verwittern *itr. V.; mit sein* weather

Verwitterung *die;* ∼, ∼**en** weathering

verwitwet *Adj.* widowed

verwöhnen *tr. V.* spoil

verwöhnt *Adj.* spoilt; (anspruchsvoll) discriminating; ⟨*taste, palate*⟩ of a gourmet

verworren *Adj.* confused, muddled ⟨*ideas, situation, etc.*⟩

verwunden *tr. V.* wound; injure

Verwundete *der/die; adj. Dekl.* casualty; **die** ∼**n** the wounded

Verwundung *die;* ∼, ∼**en** wound

verwünschen *tr. V.* curse

verwüsten *tr. V.* devastate

Verwüstung *die;* ∼, ∼**en** devastation

verzagen *itr. V.; mit sein od. haben* despair; lose heart; **verzagt sein** be despondent

Verzagtheit *die;* ∼: despondency; despair

verzählen *refl. V.* miscount

verzanken *refl. V.* (ugs.) **sich [mit jmdm. wegen etw.]** ∼: fall out [with sb. over sth.]

verzaubern *tr. V.* cast a spell on; bewitch; (fig.) enchant; **jmdn. in etw.** *(Akk.)* ∼: transform sb. into sth.

Verzehr *der;* ∼**[e]s** consumption

verzehren *tr. V.* consume

Verzeichnis *das;* ∼**ses**, ∼**se** list; (Register) index

verzeihen *unr. tr., itr. V.* forgive; (entschuldigen) excuse ⟨*behaviour, remark, etc.*⟩; ∼ **Sie [bitte], können Sie mir sagen …?** excuse me, could you tell me …?

Verzeihung *die;* ∼: forgiveness; ∼**!** sorry!; **jmdn. um** ∼ **bitten** apologize to sb.

verzerren *tr. V.* **(a)** contort ⟨*face etc.*⟩ (**zu** into)

(b) (akustisch, optisch) distort ⟨*sound, image*⟩; **etw. verzerrt darstellen** (fig.) present a distorted account *or* picture of sth.

Verzicht *der;* ∼**[e]s**, ∼**e (a)** renunciation (**auf** + *Akk.* of)

(b) (auf Reichtum, ein Amt usw.) relinquishment (**auf** + *Akk.* of)

verzichten *itr. V.* do without; ∼ **auf** (+ *Akk.*) do without; (sich enthalten) refrain from; (aufgeben) give up ⟨*share, smoking, job, etc.*⟩; renounce ⟨*inheritance*⟩; relinquish ⟨*right, privilege*⟩; (opfern) sacrifice ⟨*holiday, salary*⟩

verziehen¹ *2. Part. v.* VERZEIHEN

---

verziehen² ⎡1⎤ *unr. tr. V.* **(a)** screw up ⟨*face, mouth, etc.*⟩

(b) (schlecht erziehen) spoil

⎡2⎤ *unr. refl. V.* **(a)** (aus der Form geraten) go out of shape; ⟨*wood*⟩ warp

(b) (wegziehen) ⟨*clouds, storm*⟩ move away, pass over; ⟨*fog, mist*⟩ disperse

(c) (ugs.: weggehen) take oneself off

⎡3⎤ *unr. itr. V.; mit sein* move [away]; „**Empfänger [unbekannt] verzogen**" 'no longer at this address'

verzieren *tr. V.* decorate

Verzierung *die;* ∼, ∼**en** decoration

verzögern ⎡1⎤ *tr. V.* **(a)** delay (**um** by)

(b) (verlangsamen) slow down

⎡2⎤ *refl. V.* be delayed (**um** by)

Verzögerung *die;* ∼, ∼**en** delay (*Gen.* in); (Verlangsamung) slowing down

verzollen *tr. V.* pay duty on

Verzug *der;* ∼**[e]s** delay; **im** ∼ **sein/in** ∼ **kommen** be/fall behind

verzweifeln *itr. V.; mit sein* despair; **über etw./jmdn.** ∼: despair at sth./of sb.

verzweifelt ⎡1⎤ *Adj.* despairing ⟨*person*⟩; desperate ⟨*situation, attempt, effort, struggle, etc*⟩; ∼ **sein** be in despair

⎡2⎤ *adv.* desperately

Verzweiflung *die;* ∼: despair

verzweigen *refl. V.* branch [out]

Veteran /vete'raːn/ *der;* ∼**en**, ∼**en**, **Veteranin** *die;* ∼, ∼**nen** (auch fig.) veteran

Vetter *der;* ∼**s**, ∼**n** cousin

vgl. *Abk.* = **vergleiche** cf.

v. H. *Abk.* = **vom Hundert** per cent

via /'viːa/ *Präp.* via

Viadukt /via'dʊkt/ *das od. der;* ∼**[e]s**, ∼**e** viaduct

Viagra Ⓦ/'viagra/ *das;* ∼**s** Viagra ®

vibrieren /vi'briːrən/ *itr. V.* vibrate

Video *das;* ∼**s**, ∼**s** (ugs.) video

video-, Video- /'viːdeo-/: video

Video-: ∼**clip** *der;* ∼**s**, ∼**s** video; ∼**gerät** *das* video machine; ∼**kassette** *die* video cassette; ∼**recorder**, ∼**rekorder** *der* video recorder; ∼**text** *der* videotex[t]

Videothek *die;* ∼, ∼**en** video library

Vieh *das;* ∼**[e]s (a)** (Nutztiere) livestock *sing. or pl.;*

(b) (Rinder) cattle *pl.*

Vieh·zucht *die* [live]stock/cattle breeding *no art.*

viel ⎡1⎤ *Indefinitpron. u. unbest. Zahlw.* **(a)** *Sg.* a great deal of; a lot of (coll.); **wie/nicht/zu** ∼: how/not/too much; ∼**[es]** (vielerlei) much; **der** ∼**e Regen** all the rain; **um** ∼**es jünger** a great deal younger

(b) *Pl.* many; **gleich** ∼**[e]** the same number of; **die** ∼**en Menschen** all the people

⎡2⎤ *Adv.* **(a)** (oft, lange) much; a great deal (coll.)

(b) (wesentlich) much; a great deal; a lot (coll.); ∼ **zu klein** much too small

vielerlei *indekl. Adj.* (a) *attr.* many different; all kinds *or* sorts of (b) *allein stehend* all kinds of things

viel-, Viel-: ~**fach** ⓵ *Adj.* (a) multiple; **die** ~**fache Menge** many times the amount; (b) (vielfältig) many kinds of; ⓶ *adv.* many times; ~**falt** *die;* ~~: diversity; ~**fältig** ⓵ *Adj.* many and diverse; ⓶ *adv.* in many different ways

vielleicht *Adv.* perhaps; maybe

viel-: ~**mals** *Adv.* ich bitte ~mals um Entschuldigung I'm very sorry; **danke** ~**mals** thank you very much; ~**mehr** */od. ·ʼ-/ Konj. u. Adv.* rather; ~**sagend** ⓵ *Adj.* meaningful; ⓶ *adv.* meaningfully; ~**seitig** *Adj.* versatile ⟨*person*⟩; ~**versprechend** ⓵ *Adj.* [very] promising; ⓶ *adv.* [very] promisingly

vier *Kardinalz.* four

Vier *die;* ~, ~**en** four; **eine** ~ **schreiben/ bekommen** (Schulw.) ≈ get a D

vier-, Vier-: (*s. auch* ACHT-, ACHT-); ~**beiner** *der;* ~~s, ~~ (ugs.) four-legged friend; ~**beinig** *Adj.* four-legged; ~**eck** *das* quadrilateral; (Rechteck) rectangle; (Quadrat) square; ~**eckig** *Adj.* quadrilateral; (rechteckig) rectangular; ~**fach** *Vervielfältigungsz.* fourfold; quadruple; ~**fache** *das; adj. Dekl.* **um das** ~**fache:** fourfold; by four times the amount; ~**hundert** *Kardinalz.* four hundred

Vierling *der;* ~~s, ~e quadruplet

vier-, Vier-: ~**mal** *Adv.* four times; ~**spurig** *Adj.* four-lane ⟨*road, motorway*⟩; ~**spurig sein** have four lanes; ~**stellig** *Adj.* four-figure *attrib.;* ~**sterne·hotel** */·ʼ----/ das* four-star hotel

viert... *Ordinalz.* fourth

vier·tausend *Kardinalz.* four thousand;

viertel /ʼfɪrtl̩ / *Bruchz.* quarter; **ein** ~ **Pfund** a quarter of a pound; **drei** ~ **Liter** three quarters of a litre

Viertel /ʼfɪrtl̩ / *das* (schweiz. meist *der*); ~~s, ~ **(a)** quarter; ~ **vor/nach eins** [a] quarter to/past one; **drei** ~: three-quarters **(b)** (Stadtteil) quarter; district

viertel-, Viertel-: ~**finale** *das* (Sport) quarter-final; ~**jahr** *das* three months *pl.;* ~**jährlich** ⓵ *Adj.* quarterly; ⓶ *adv.* quarterly; ~**liter** *der* quarter of a litre; ~**note** *die* (Musik) crotchet (Brit.); quarter note (Amer.); ~**pfund** *das* quarter [of a] pound; ~**stunde** *die* quarter of an hour; ~**stündig** *Adj.* quarter-of-an-hour; ~**stündlich** *Adj., adv* every quarter of an hour

viertens *Adv.* fourthly

viertürig *Adj.* four-door *attrib.;* ~ **sein** have four doors

Vierwaldstätter See, (schweiz.:) **Vierwaldstättersee** *der* Lake Lucerne

vier- /ʼfɪr-:/ ~**zehn** *Kardinalz.* fourteen; **für vierzehn Tage** for a fortnight;

~**zehn·tägig** *Adj.* two-week; ~**zehn·täglich** ⓵ *Adj.* fortnightly; ⓶ *adv.* fortnightly

vierzig /ʼfɪrtsɪç/ *Kardinalz.* forty; *s. auch* ACHTZIG

vierzigst... *Ordinalz.* fortieth; *s. auch* ACHT...

Vikar /vɪˈkaːɐ̯/ *der;* ~s, ~e, **Vikarin** *die;* ~, ~nen (a) (kath. Kirche) locum tenens (b) (ev. Kirche) ≈ [trainee] curate

Villa /ʼvɪla/ *die;* ~, **Villen** villa

Villen·viertel *das* exclusive residential district

violett /vi̯oˈlɛt/ purple; violet

Violett *das;* ~s, ~e *od. ugs.* ~s purple; violet; (im Spektrum) violet

Violine /vi̯oˈliːnə/ *die;* ~, ~n (Musik) violin

Viper /ʼviːpɐ/ *die;* ~, ~n viper; adder

Viren ▶ VIRUS

Viren·schutz *der* (DV, Med.) virus protection

virtuell /vɪrˈtu̯ɛl/ ⓵ *Adj.* (a) potential (b) (DV, Optik) virtual ⟨*memory, image;*⟩ ~**e Wirklichkeit** virtual reality ⓶ *adv.* virtually

virtuos /vɪrˈtu̯oːs/ ⓵ *Adj.* virtuoso ⟨*performance etc.*⟩ ⓶ *adv.* in a virtuoso manner

Virtuose *der;* ~n, ~n, **Virtuosin** *die;* ~, ~nen virtuoso

Virtuosität *die;* ~: virtuosity

Virus /ʼviːrʊs/ *das;* ~, **Viren** virus

Visa ▶ VISUM

Visage /viˈzaːʒə/ *die;* ~, ~n (salopp abwertend) mug (coll.); (Miene) expression

Visen ▶ VISUM

Visier /viˈziːɐ̯/ *das;* ~s, ~e (am Helm) visor; (an der Waffe) backsight

Vision /viˈzi̯oːn/ *die;* ~, ~en vision

Visite /viˈziːtə/ *die;* ~, ~n round; ~ **machen** do one's round

Visiten·karte *die* visiting card

Visum /ʼviːzʊm/ *das;* ~s, **Visa** *od.* **Visen** visa

vital *Adj.* vital

Vitalität *die;* ~: vitality

Vitamin /vita̯ˈmiːn/ *das;* ~s, ~e vitamin

vitamin-, Vitamin-: ~**arm** *Adj.* low in vitamins *postpos.;* ~**mangel** *der* vitamin deficiency; ~**reich** *Adj.* rich in vitamins *postpos.*

Vitrine /viˈtriːnə/ *die;* ~, ~n display case; (Möbel) display cabinet

Vize- vice-

Vogel *der;* ~s, **Vögel** bird; **einen** ~ **haben** (salopp) be off one's rocker (coll.)

Vogel-: ~**grippe** *die* bird flu; ~**käfig** *der* birdcage; ~**nest** *das* bird's nest; ~**perspektive** *die* bird's-eye view; ~**scheuche** *die;* ~~, ~~n scarecrow

Vokabel /voˈkaːbl̩ / *die;* ~, ~n word; ~n vocabulary *sing.*

V

Vokal /vo'ka:l/ *der;* ∼s, ∼e (Sprachw.) vowel

Volk *das;* ∼[e]s, Völker people

volks-, Volks-: ∼**abstimmung** *die* plebiscite; ∼**eigen** *Adj.* (DDR) publicly *or* nationally owned; ∼**entscheid** *der* (Politik) referendum; ∼**fest** *das* public festival; (Jahrmarkt) fair; ∼**hochschule** *die* adult education centre; ∼**kammer** *die* (DDR) Volkskammer; People's Chamber; ∼**kunde** *die* folklore; ∼**lied** *das* folk song; ∼**musik** *die* folk music; ∼**polizei** *die* (DDR) People's Police; ∼**republik** *die* People's Republic; ∼**stamm** *der* tribe; ∼**tanz** *der* folk dance; ∼**tracht** *die* traditional costume; (eines Landes) national costume; ∼**trauer·tag** *der* (Bundesrepublik Deutschland) national remembrance day

volkstümlich ① *Adj.* popular ② *adv.* ∼ schreiben write in terms readily comprehensible to the layman

volks-, Volks-: ∼**verhetzung** *die;* ∼∼: incitement of the people; ∼**vertreter** *der,* ∼**vertreterin** *die* representative of the people; ∼**wirt** *der,* ∼**wirtin** *die* economist; ∼**wirtschaft** *die* national economy; (Fach) economics *sing., no art.;* ∼**wirtschaftlich** ① *Adj.* economic; ② *adv.* economically; ∼**zählung** *die* [national] census; ∼**zorn** *der* public anger

voll ① *Adj.* full; ample ⟨bosom⟩; (salopp: betrunken) plastered (sl.); ∼ von *od.* mit etw. sein be full of sth.; ∼ laufen fill up; etw. ∼ laufen lassen fill sth. [up]; etw. ∼ füllen fill sth. up; etw. ∼ gießen fill sth. [up]; etw. ∼ tanken fill sth. up; bitte ∼ tanken fill it up, please; etw. ∼ machen fill sth. up; [sich] (*Dat.*)] die Hosen/Windeln ∼ machen (ugs.) mess one's pants/nappy; jmdn. nicht für ∼ nehmen not take sb. seriously ② *adv.* fully; ∼ und ganz completely

*∼**vollabern▶** VOLLLABERN

voll·auf /*od.* '--/ *Adv.* completely

*∼**vollaufen ▶** VOLL 1

voll-, Voll-: ∼**automatisch** ① *Adj.* fully automatic; ② *adv.* fully automatically; ∼**bad** *das* bath; ∼**bart** *der* full beard; ∼**bringen** /-'--/ *unr. tr. V.* (geh.) accomplish

Völle-gefühl *das* feeling of fullness

voll·enden *tr. V.* complete

vollendet ① *Adj.* accomplished ⟨performance⟩; perfect ⟨gentleman, host, manners, reproduction⟩ ② *adv.* ⟨play⟩ in an accomplished manner

vollends *Adv.* completely

Voll·endung *die* completion

voller *indekl. Adj.* full of; ∼ Flecken covered with stains

Volley·ball /'vɔlibal/ *der* volleyball

voll-, Voll-: ∼**führen** /-'--/ *tr. V.* perform;

*alte Schreibung - vgl. Hinweis auf S. xiv

*∼|**füllen ▶** VOLL 1; ∼**gas** *das* ∼gas geben put one's foot down; mit ∼**gas** at full throttle; *∼|**gießen ▶** VOLL 1

völlig ① *Adj.* complete; total ② *adv.* completely; totally; du hast ∼ Recht you are absolutely right

voll-, Voll-: ∼**jährig** *Adj.* of age *pred.;* ∼jährig werden come of age; ∼**jährigkeit** *die;* ∼: majority *no art.;* ∼**kasko·versicherung** *die* fully comprehensive insurance

voll·kommen ① *Adj.* (a) /-'-- *od.* '---/ (vollendet) perfect (b) /'---/ (vollständig) complete; total ② /'---/ *adv.* completely; totally

voll-, Voll-: ∼**korn·brot** *das* wholemeal (Brit.) *or* (Amer.) wholewheat bread; ∼|**labern** *tr. V.* (ugs.) jmdn. ∼labern rabbit on at sb. (coll.); *∼|**laufen ▶** VOLL 1; *∼|**machen ▶** VOLL 1; ∼**macht** *die;* ∼∼, ∼∼en (a) authority; (b) (Urkunde) power of attorney; ∼**milch** *die* full-cream milk; ∼**milch·schokolade** *die* full-cream milk chocolate; ∼**mond** *der* full moon; ∼**pension** *die* full board *no art.;* ∼**ständig** ① *Adj.* complete; full ⟨text, address, etc.⟩; ② *adv.* completely; ⟨list⟩ in full; ∼**ständigkeit** *die;* ∼: completeness; ∼**strecken** /-'--/ *tr. V.* enforce ⟨penalty, fine, law⟩; carry out ⟨sentence⟩ (an + *Dat.* on); *∼|**tanken ▶** VOLL 1; ∼**treffer** *der* direct hit; ein ∼treffer sein (fig.) hit the bull's eye; ∼**versammlung** *die* general meeting; (der UNO) General Assembly; ∼**zählig** *Adj.* complete; ∼**zeit·beschäftigt** *Adj.* emloyed full-time *postpos.;* ∼**zeit·beschäftigte** *der/die* full-time employee

voll·ziehen *unr. tr. V.* carry out (an + *Dat.* on); execute, carry out ⟨order⟩; perform ⟨sacrifice, ceremony, sexual intercourse⟩

Voll·zug *der:* ▶ VOLLZIEHEN: carrying out; execution; performance

Volt /vɔlt/ *das;* ∼ *od.* ∼[e]s, ∼: (Physik, Elektrot.) volt

Volumen /vo'lu:mən/ *das;* ∼s, ∼: volume

vom *Präp.* + *Art.* (a) = von dem; (b) (räumlich) from the; links/rechts ∼ Eingang to the left/right of the entrance; ∼ Stuhl aufspringen jump up out of one's chair (c) (zeitlich) ∼ Morgen bis zum Abend from morning till night; ∼ ersten Januar an [as] from the first of January (d) (zur Angabe der Ursache) das kommt ∼ Rauchen/Alkohol that comes from smoking/drinking alcohol; jmdn. ∼ Sehen kennen know sb. by sight

von *Präp. mit Dat.* (a) (räumlich) from; nördlich/südlich ∼ Mannheim to the north/ south of Mannheim; rechts/links ∼ mir on my right/left; ∼ hier an *od.* (ugs.) ab from here on[ward]; ∼ Mannheim aus from Mannheim (b) (zeitlich) from; ∼ jetzt an *od.* (ugs.) ab from now on; ∼ heute/morgen an [as] from today/ tomorrow; starting today/tomorrow; in der

Nacht ~ Freitag auf *od.* zu Samstag during Friday night; **das Brot ist ~ gestern** it's yesterday's bread
(c) (anstelle eines Genitivs) of; **acht ~ hundert/ zehn** eight out of a hundred/ten
(d) (zur Angabe des Urhebers, der Ursache, beim Passiv) by; **der Roman ist ~ Fontane** the novel is by Fontane; **müde ~ der Arbeit sein** be tired from work[ing]; **sie hat ein Kind ~ ihm** she has a child by him
(e) (zur Angabe von Eigenschaften) of; **eine Fahrt ~ drei Stunden** a three-hour drive

von·ein·ạnder *Adv.* from each other *or* one another

vonstạtten *Adv.* ~ **gehen** proceed

vor ⓵ *Präp. mit Dat.* **(a)** (räumlich) in front of; (weiter vorn) ahead of; in front of; (nicht ganz so weit wie) before; (außerhalb) outside; **kurz ~ der Abzweigung** just before the turn-off; **~ der Stadt** outside the town; **etw. ~ sich haben** (fig.) have sth. before one; **das liegt noch ~ mir** (fig.) I still have that to come *or* have that ahead of me
(b) (zeitlich) before; **es ist fünf [Minuten] ~ sieben** it is five [minutes] to seven
(c) (bei Reihenfolge, Rangordnung) before; **knapp ~ jmdm. siegen** win just ahead *or* in front of sb.
(d) (aufgrund von) with; **~ Freude strahlen** beam with joy; **~ Hunger/Durst umkommen** (ugs.) die of hunger/thirst
(e) ~ fünf Minuten/10 Jahren/Wochen *usw.* five minutes/ten years/weeks ago; **heute ~ einer Woche** a week ago today
⓶ *Präp. mit Akk.* in front of; **~ sich hin** to oneself

Vor·abend *der* evening before; (fig.) eve

Vor·ahnung *die* premonition; presentiment; **dunkle/schlimme ~en** dark forebodings

vor·ạn *Adv.* forward[s] ahead; first

vorạn-: ~|**gehen** *unr. itr. V.; mit sein* **(a)** go first; **(b)** (Fortschritte machen) make progress; ~|**kommen** *unr. itr. V.; mit sein* **(a)** make headway; **(b)** (Fortschritte machen) make progress; ~|**treiben** *unr. tr. V.* push ahead

Vor·arbeiter *der* foreman

Vor·arbeiterin *die* forewoman

vor·aus ⓵ /⋅'⋅/ *Präp. mit Dat., nachgestellt* in front; **jmdm./seiner Zeit ~ sein** (fig.) be ahead of sb./one's time
⓶ *Adv.* **im Voraus** /'⋅⋅/ in advance

vorạus-, Vorạus-: ~|**gehen** *unr. itr. V.; mit sein* **(a)** go [on] ahead; **(b)** (zeitlich) **einem Ereignis ~gehen** precede an event; ~**sage** *die* ▶ VORHERSAGE; ~|**sagen** *tr. V.* predict; ~|**sehen** *unr. tr. V.* foresee; ~|**setzen** *tr. V.* **(a)** (als gegeben ansehen) assume; ~**gesetzt, [dass] ...:** provided [that] ...; **(b)** (erfordern) require ⟨skill, experience, etc.⟩; presuppose ⟨good organization, planning, etc.⟩; ~**setzung** *die;* ~~, ~~**en (a)** (Annahme) assumption; (Prämisse) premiss;

(b) (Vorbedingung) prerequisite; **unter der ~setzung, dass ...:** on condition *or* on the precondition that ...; ~**sichtlich** ⓵ *Adj.* anticipated; ⓶ *adv.* probably

Vor·bau *der; Pl.* ~**ten** porch

Vorbehalt *der;* ~[e]s, ~e reservation; **unter dem ~, dass ...:** with the reservation that ...

vor|behalten *unr. tr. V.* **sich** (*Dat.*) **etw. ~:** reserve oneself sth.; „**Änderungen ~**" 'subject to alterations'

vorbehalt·los ⓵ *Adj.* unreserved; unconditional
⓶ *adv.* unreservedly; without reservation[s]

vor·bei *Adv.* **(a)** (räumlich) past; by; **an etw.** (*Dat.*) **~:** past sth.
(b) (zeitlich) past; over; (beendet) finished; over; **es ist acht Uhr ~** (ugs.) it is past *or* gone eight o'clock

vorbei-: ~|**fahren** *unr. itr. V.; mit sein* **(a)** drive/ride past; pass; **an jmdm. ~fahren** drive/ride past *or* pass sb.; **(b)** (ugs.: einen kurzen Besuch machen) [bei jmdm./der Post] ~**fahren** drop in (coll.) [at sb.'s/at the post office]; ~|**gehen** *unr. itr. V.; mit sein* **(a)** pass; go past; **an jmdm./etw. ~gehen** pass *or* go past sb./sth.; **der Schuss ist ~gegangen** the shot missed; **(b)** (ugs.: einen kurzen Besuch machen) [bei jmdm./der Post] ~**gehen** drop in (coll.) [at sb.'s/at the post office]; **(c)** (vergehen) pass; ~|**kommen** *unr. itr. V.; mit sein* pass; **an etw.** (*Dat.*) **~kommen** pass sth.; ~|**reden** *itr. V.* **an etw.** (*Dat.*) **~reden** talk round sth. without getting to the point; **aneinander ~reden** talk at cross purposes; ~|**schießen** *unr. itr. V.* miss

vor·belastet *Adj.* handicapped (durch by); **erblich ~ sein** have an inherited defect

vor|bereiten *tr. V.* prepare; **jmdn./sich auf** *od.* **für etw. ~:** prepare sb./oneself for sth.

Vor·bereitung *die;* ~, ~**en** preparation; ~**en** [für etw.] **treffen** make preparations for sth.

vor|bestellen *tr. V.* order in advance

Vor·bestellung *die* advance order

vor·bestraft *Adj.* with a previous conviction/previous convictions *postpos., not pred.*

vor|beugen ⓵ *tr. V.* bend ⟨head, upper body⟩ forward; **sich ~:** lean forward
⓶ *itr. V.* **einer Sache** (*Dat.*) *od.* **gegen etw. ~:** prevent sth.

Vor·beugung *die* prevention (gegen of); **zur ~:** as a preventive

Vor·bild *das* model; **jmdm. ein gutes ~ sein** be a good example to sb.

vor·bildlich ⓵ *Adj.* exemplary
⓶ *adv.* in an exemplary way

vor|bringen *unr. tr. V.* say; **eine Forderung/ein Anliegen ~:** make a demand/ express a desire; **Argumente ~:** present arguments

vor·christlich *Adj.* pre-Christian

vor|datieren *tr. V.* postdate

vorder... *Adj.* front; **der Vordere Orient** the Middle East

Vorder-: ~grund *der* foreground; **im ~grund stehen** (fig.) be prominent *or* to the fore; **~mann** *der; Pl.* **~männer** person in front; **jmdn. auf ~mann bringen** (ugs.) lick sb. into shape

vor|drängen *refl. V.* push [one's way] forward *or* to the front; (fig.) push oneself forward

vor|dringen *unr. itr. V.; mit sein* push forward; advance

vor·dringlich [1] *Adj.* (a) priority *attrib.* ⟨treatment⟩ (b) (dringlich) urgent [2] *adv.* (a) as a matter of priority (b) (dringlich) as a matter of urgency

Vor·druck *der; Pl.* **~e** form

vor·eilig [1] *Adj.* rash [2] *adv.* rashly

vor·einander *Adv.* (a) one in front of the other (b) (einer dem anderen gegenüber) opposite each other; face to face (c) **Angst ~ haben** be afraid of each other

vor·eingenommen *Adj.* prejudiced; biased; **für/gegen jmdn. ~ sein** be prejudiced in sb.'s favour/against sb.

Vor·eingenommenheit *die; ~, ~en* prejudice; bias

vor|enthalten *unr. tr. V.; ich enthalte vor* (*od. seltener:* vorenthalte), vorenthalten, vorzuenthalten: **jmdm. etw. ~:** withhold sth. from sb.

vor·erst /*od.* -'-/ *Adv.* for the present

Vor·fahr *der; ~en, ~en* forefather

vor|fahren *unr. itr. V.; mit sein* (a) (ankommen) drive/ride up (b) (weiter nach vorn fahren) ⟨person⟩ drive *or* move forward; ⟨car⟩ move forward (c) (vorausfahren) drive *or* go on ahead

Vor·fahrt *die* right of way; „**~ beachten/gewähren**" 'give way'

Vorfahrt[s]-: ~schild *das; Pl.* **~~er** right-of-way sign; **~straße** *die* main road

Vor·fall *der* incident; occurrence

vor|fallen *unr. itr. V.; mit sein* (a) (sich ereignen) happen; occur (b) (nach vorn fallen) fall forward

Vor·film *der* supporting film

vor|finden *unr. tr. V.* find

Vor·freude *die* anticipation

vor|führen *tr. V.* show ⟨film, slides, etc.⟩; present ⟨circus act, programme⟩; perform ⟨play, trick, routine⟩; (demonstrieren) demonstrate; **jmdn. dem Richter ~:** bring sb. before the judge

Vor·führung *die* show; (eines Theaterstücks) performance

---

*old spelling - see note on page xiv

Vor·gang *der* occurrence; (Amtsspr.) file

Vorgänger *der; ~s, ~,* **Vorgängerin** *die; ~, ~nen* predecessor

Vor·garten *der* front garden

vor|geben *unr. tr. V.* pretend

Vor·gebirge *das* promontory

vor·gefasst, *vor·gefaßt *Adj.* preconceived

vor|gehen *unr. itr. V.; mit sein* (a) (ugs.: nach vorn gehen) go forward (b) (vorausgehen) go on ahead; **jmdn. ~ lassen** let sb. go first (c) ⟨clock⟩ be fast (d) (einschreiten) **gegen jmdn./etw. ~:** take action against sb./sth. (e) (verfahren) proceed (f) (sich abspielen) happen; go on (g) (Vorrang haben) have priority; come first

Vor·geschmack *der* foretaste

Vor·gesetzte *der/die; adj. Dekl.* superior

vor·gestern *Adv.* the day before yesterday

vor|greifen *unr. itr. V.* **jmdn. ~:** anticipate sb.; jump in ahead of sb.

vor|haben *unr. tr. V.* intend; (geplant haben) plan

Vor·haben *das; ~s, ~:* plan; (Projekt) project

Vor·halle *die* entrance hall; (eines Theaters, Hotels) foyer

vor|halten *unr. tr. V.* (a) hold up; **mit vorgehaltener Schusswaffe** at gunpoint (b) (zum Vorwurf machen) **jmdm. etw. ~:** reproach sb. for sth.

Vor·haltungen *Pl.* **jmdm. [wegen etw.] ~ machen** reproach sb. [for sth.]

vorhanden *Adj.* existing; (verfügbar) available; **~ sein** exist *or* be in existence/be available

Vor·hang *der* (auch Theater) curtain

Vorhänge·schloss, *Vorhänge·schloß *das* padlock

Vor·haut *die* foreskin

vor·her /*od.* -'-/ beforehand; (davor) before

vorher|gehen *unr. itr. V.; mit sein* **in den ~den Wochen** in the preceding weeks

Vor·herrschaft *die* supremacy

vor|herrschen *itr. V.* predominate

vorher-, Vorher-: ~sage *die* prediction; (des Wetters) forecast; **~|sagen** *tr. V.* predict; forecast ⟨weather⟩; **~|sehen** *unr. tr. V.* ▶ VORAUSSEHEN

vor·hin /*od.* -'-/ *Adv.* a short time *or* while ago

vorig... *Adj.* last

Vor·jahr *das* previous year

vor·jährig *Adj.* of the previous year

Vor·kämpfer *der,* **Vor·kämpferin** *die* pioneer

Vorkehrungen *Pl.* precautions

Vor·kenntnis *die* background knowledge

vor|kommen *unr. itr. V.; mit sein* **(a)** (sich ereignen) happen
(b) (vorhanden sein) occur
(c) (erscheinen) seem; **das Lied kommt mir bekannt vor** I seem to know the song
Vorkommnis *das;* ~**ses,** ~**se** incident; occurrence
vor|laden *unr. tr. V.* summon
Vor·ladung *die* summons
Vor·lage *die* **(a)** ▸ VORLEGEN: presentation; showing; production; submission; tabling
(b) (Entwurf) draft
(c) (Muster) pattern; (Modell) model
Vor·lauf *der* (eines Bandgeräts) fast forward
Vor·läufer *der*, **Vor·läuferin** *die* precursor; forerunner
vor·läufig ① *Adj.* temporary; provisional; interim ⟨order, agreement⟩
② *adv.* for the time being
vor·laut ① *Adj.* forward
② *adv.* forwardly
vor|legen *tr. V.* present; show, produce ⟨certificate, identity card, etc.⟩; show ⟨sample⟩; submit ⟨evidence⟩; table ⟨parliamentary bill⟩
vor|lesen *unr. tr., itr. V.* read aloud *or* out; read ⟨story, poem, etc.⟩ aloud; **jmdm. [etw.]** ~: read [sth.] to sb.
Vor·lesung *die* lecture; (Vorlesungsreihe) series *or* course of lectures
vor·letzt... *Adj.* last but one; penultimate ⟨page, episode, etc.⟩
vorlieb: **mit jmdm./etw.** ~ **nehmen** put up with sb./sth.; (sich begnügen) make do with sb./sth.
Vor·liebe *die* preference
*****vorlieb|nehmen** ▸ VORLIEB
vor|liegen *unr. itr. V.* **jmdm.** ~: be with sb.; **die Ergebnisse liegen uns noch nicht vor** we do not have the results yet; **im** ~**den Fall** in the present case
vor|lügen *unr. tr. V.* (ugs.) **jmdm. etwas** ~: lie to sb.
vorm *Präp. + Art.* **(a)** = vor dem;
(b) (räumlich) in front of the
(c) (zeitlich, bei Reihenfolge) before the
vor|machen *tr. V.* (ugs.) **jmdm. etw.** ~: show sb. sth.; (vortäuschen) kid (coll.) *or* fool sb.
vormalig *Adj.* former
vormals *Adv.* formerly
Vor·marsch *der* (auch fig.) advance
vor|merken *tr. V.* make a note of; **ich habe Sie für den Kurs vorgemerkt** I've put you down for the course
*****vor·mittag** ▸ VORMITTAG
Vor·mittag *der* morning; **heute/morgen/gestern** ~: this/tomorrow/yesterday morning
vor·mittags *Adv.* in the morning
Vor·mund *der; Pl.* ~**e** *od.* **Vormünder** guardian

Vor·name *der* first *or* Christian name
vorn[e] *Adv.* at the front; **nach** ~: to the front; **von** ~: from the front; **noch einmal von** ~ **anfangen** start afresh; **von** ~ **bis hinten** (ugs.) from beginning to end
vornehm ① *Adj.* (nobel; adelig) noble; (kultiviert) distinguished; (elegant) exclusive ⟨district, hotel, restaurant, resort⟩; elegant ⟨villa, clothes⟩
② *adv.* nobly; (elegant) elegantly
vor|nehmen *unr. refl. V.* **sich** (*Dat.*) **etw.** ~: plan sth.; **sich** (*Dat.*) ~, **mit dem Rauchen aufzuhören** resolve to give up smoking
vorn-: ~**herein: von** ~**herein** from the outset; ~**über** *Adv.* forwards
Vor·ort *der* suburb
vor|programmieren *tr. V.* (auch fig.) pre-programme
Vor·rang *der* **(a)** priority (**vor** + *Dat.* over)
(b) (bes. österr.: Vorfahrt) right of way
Vor·rat *der* supply, stock (**an** + *Dat.* of)
vorrätig *Adj.* in stock *postpos.*
Vor·raum *der* anteroom
vor|rechnen *tr. V.* **jmdm. etw.** ~: work sth. out *or* calculate sth. for sb.; **jmdm. seine Fehler** ~ (fig.) enumerate sb.'s mistakes
Vor·recht *das* privilege
Vor·redner *der*, **Vor·rednerin** *die* previous speaker; **mein Vorredner:** the previous speaker
Vor·richtung *die* device
vor|rücken ① *tr. V.* move forward; advance ⟨chess piece⟩
② *itr. V.; mit sein* move forward; **auf den 5. Platz** ~: move up to fifth place
Vor·ruhestand *der* early retirement
vors *Präp. + Art.* = vor das
vor|sagen *tr. V.* **(a)** *auch itr.* **jmdm. [die Antwort]** ~: tell sb. the answer; (flüsternd) whisper the answer to sb.
(b) (aufsagen) recite
Vor·saison *die* start of the season; early [part of the] season
Vor·satz *der* intention
vorsätzlich ① *Adj.* intentional; wilful ⟨murder, arson, etc.⟩
② *adv.* intentionally
Vor·schau *die* preview
Vor·schein *der:* **zum** ~ **kommen** appear; (entdeckt werden) come to light
vor|schieben *unr. tr. V.* **(a)** push ⟨bolt⟩ across
(b) (nach vorn schieben) push forward
vor|schießen *unr. tr. V.* **jmdm. Geld** ~: advance sb. money
Vorschlag *der* suggestion; proposal
vor|schlagen *unr. tr. V.* **[jmdm.] etw.** ~: suggest *or* propose sth. [to sb.]
vor|schreiben *unr. tr. V.* stipulate, set ⟨conditions⟩; lay down ⟨rules⟩; prescribe ⟨dose⟩

Vor·schrift *die* instruction; order; (gesetzliche od. amtliche Bestimmung) regulation

vorschrifts·mäßig ① *Adj.* correct; proper
② *adv.* correctly; properly

Vor·schub *der* jmdm./einer Sache ∼ leisten encourage sb./encourage *or* promote *or* foster sth.

Vorschul·alter *das* preschool age

Vor·schuss, *Vor·schuß *der* advance

vor|schwärmen *itr. V.* jmdm. von jmdm./ etw. ∼: rave about sb./sth. to sb. (coll.)

vor|schweben *itr. V.* jmdm. schwebt etw. vor sb. has sth. in mind

vor|sehen ① *unr. tr. V.* (a) plan; etw. für/ als etw. ∼: intend sth. for/as sth.
(b) ⟨law, plan, contract, etc.⟩ provide for
② *unr. refl. V.* sich [vor jmdm./etw.] ∼: be careful [of sb./sth.]

vor|setzen *tr. V.* jmdm. etw. ∼: serve sb. sth.; (fig.) serve *or* dish sb. up sth.

Vor·sicht *die* care; (bei Risiko, Gefahr) caution; care; **zur** ∼: as a precaution; ∼! be careful!; „∼, Stufe!" 'mind the step!'

vorsichtig ① *Adj.* careful; (bei Risiko, Gefahr) cautious; **sei** ∼! be careful!; take care!
② *adv.* carefully; with care

vorsichts·halber *Adv.* as a precaution; to be on the safe side

Vorsichts·maßnahme *die* precautionary measure; precaution

Vor·silbe *die* [monosyllabic] prefix

vor|singen *unr. tr. V.* [jmdm.] etw. ∼: sing sth. [to sb.]

Vor·sitz *der* chairmanship

Vorsitzende *der/die; adj. Dekl.* chair[person]; (bes. Mann) chairman; (Frau auch) chairwoman

Vor·sorge *die* precautions *pl.;* (für den Todesfall, Krankheit, Alter) provisions *pl.*

vor|sorgen *itr. V.* für etw. ∼: make provisions for sth.; provide for sth.

Vorsorge·untersuchung *die* (Med.) medical check-up

vorsorglich *adv.* as a precaution

Vor·spann *der* (Film, Ferns.) opening credits *pl.*

Vor·speise *die* starter; hors d'œuvre

Vor·spiel *das* (Theater) prologue; (Musik) prelude

vor|spielen *tr. V.* (a) play ⟨piece of music⟩ (Dat. to, for); act out, perform ⟨scene⟩ (Dat. for, in front of)
(b) (vorspiegeln) jmdm. etw. ∼: feign sth. to sb.

vor|sprechen ① *unr. tr. V.* (a) (zum Nachsprechen) jmdm. etw. ∼: pronounce *or* say sth. first for sb.
(b) (zur Prüfung) recite
② *unr. itr. V.* audition

Vor·sprung *der* lead (**vor** + *Dat.* over)

---

*alte Schreibung - vgl. Hinweis auf S. xiv

Vor·stadt *die* suburb

Vor·stand *der* (einer Firma) board [of directors]; (eines Vereins, einer Gesellschaft) executive committee; (einer Partei) executive

vor|stehen *unr. itr. V.* (a) project; jut out; ⟨teeth, chin⟩ stick out; ∼**de Zähne** buck teeth; projecting teeth
(b) (geh.: leiten) einer Institution ∼: be the head of an institution

vorstell·bar *Adj.* conceivable; imaginable; es ist durchaus/[nur] schwer ∼, dass ...: it is quite/scarcely conceivable that ...

vor|stellen ① *tr. V.* jmdn./sich jmdm. ∼: introduce sb./oneself to sb.; (bei Bewerbung) sich ∼: come/go for [an] interview; die Uhr [um eine Stunde] ∼: put the clock forward [one hour]
② *refl. V.* sich (Dat.) etw. ∼: imagine sth.

Vor·stellung *die* (a) (Begriff) idea
(b) (Fantasie) imagination
(c) (Aufführung) performance; (im Kino) showing

Vorstellungs·gespräch *das* interview

Vor·stoß *der* advance

vor|stoßen *unr. itr. V.; mit sein* advance; push forward

Vor·strafe *die* previous conviction

vor|strecken *tr. V.* stretch ⟨arm, hand⟩ out; advance ⟨money, sum⟩

Vor·tag *der* day before

vor|täuschen *tr. V.* feign; simulate ⟨reality etc.⟩; fake ⟨crime⟩

Vor·teil */od.* 'fortail/ *der* advantage

vorteilhaft ① *Adj.* advantageous
② *adv.* advantageously

Vortrag *der;* ∼[e]s, Vorträge talk; (wissenschaftlich) lecture; einen ∼ halten give a talk/lecture

vor|tragen *unr. tr. V.* (a) sing ⟨song⟩, perform, play ⟨piece of music⟩; recite ⟨poem⟩
(b) (darlegen) present ⟨case, matter, request, demands⟩; lodge, make ⟨complaint⟩; express ⟨wish, desire⟩

vor·trefflich ① *Adj.* excellent
② *adv.* excellently

Vor·trefflichkeit *die;* ∼: excellence

vorüber *Adv.* over; (räumlich) past

vorüber|gehen *unr. itr. V.; mit sein* (a) pass *or* walk past; pass by; an jmdm./etw. ∼: go past sb./sth.; pass sb./sth.; (achtlos) pass sb./ sth. by
(b) (vergehen) pass; ⟨pain⟩ go

vorübergehend ① *Adj.* temporary; passing ⟨interest, infatuation⟩; brief ⟨illness, stay⟩
② *adv.* temporarily; (für kurze Zeit) for a short time; briefly

Vor·urteil *das* bias; (voreilige Schlussfolgerung) prejudice

Vor·vergangenheit *die* (Sprachw.) pluperfect

Vor·verkauf *der* advance sale of tickets

vor|verlegen *tr. V.* (zeitlich) bring forward (auf + *Akk.* to; um by)

Vor·wahl *die,* **Vorwähl·nummer** *die* (Fernspr.) dialling code

Vorwand *der;* ~[e]s, V<u>o</u>rwände pretext; (Ausrede) excuse

vor|warnen *tr. V.* jmdn. ~: give sb. advance warning; warn sb. [in advance]; **vorgewarnt sein** be forewarned

Vor·warnung *die* [advance] warning

vor·wärts *Adv.* forwards; (weiter) onwards; ~ kommen make progress; (im Beruf, Leben) get on; get ahead

*****vorwärts|kommen** ▶ VORWÄRTS

vor·weg *Adv.* beforehand

vorweg|nehmen *unr. tr. V.* anticipate

vor|weisen *unr. tr. V.* produce

vor|werfen *unr. tr. V.* jmdm. etw. ~: reproach sb. with sth.; (beschuldigen) accuse sb. of sth.

vor·wiegend *Adv.* mainly

vor·witzig *Adj.* bumptious; pert ‹*child*›

Vor·wort *das; Pl.* ~e foreword

Vor·wurf *der* reproach; (Beschuldigung) accusation

vorwurfs·voll ①*Adj.* reproachful
②*adv.* reproachfully

Vor·zeichen *das* (a) (Omen) omen
(b) (Math.) [algebraic] sign

vor|zeigen *tr. V.* produce; show

Vor·zeit *die* prehistory

vorzeitig ①*Adj.* premature; early ‹*retirement*›
②*adv.* prematurely

vor|ziehen *unr. tr. V.* prefer

Vor·zimmer *das* outer office

Vor·zug *der* (a) preference (gegenüber over)
(b) (gute Eigenschaft) good quality; merit

vorzüglich ①*Adj.* excellent; first-rate
②*adv.* excellently

vulgär /vʊlˈgɛːɐ̯/ ①*Adj.* vulgar
②*adv.* in a vulgar way

Vulgarität /vʊlɡariˈtɛːt/ *die;* ~, ~en vulgarity

Vulkan /vʊlˈkaːn/ *der;* ~s, ~e volcano

vulkanisch *Adj.* volcanic

vulkanisieren *tr. V.* vulcanize

v. u. Z. *Abk.* = **vor unserer Zeit[rechnung]** BC

· ·

Ww

· ·

w, W /veː/ *das;* ~s, ~: w/W

W *Abk.* (a) = **West, Westen** W.
(b) = **Watt** W.

Waage *die;* ~, ~n (a) [pair *sing.* of] scales *pl.*
(b) (Astrol.) [die] ~: Libra; **er ist [eine]** ~: he is a Libra *or* Libran

waage·recht ①*Adj.* horizontal
②*adv.* horizontally

Waage·rechte *die;* ~, ~n; *also adj. Dekl.* horizontal

Waag·schale *die* scale pan

Wabe *die;* ~, ~n honeycomb

wach ①*Adj.* awake
②*adv.* alertly; attentively

Wache *die;* ~, ~n (a) (Milit.) guard *or* sentry duty; (Seew.) watch [duty]
(b) (Wächter, Milit.) guard; (Seew.) watch
(c) (Polizei~) police station

wachen *itr. V.* (geh.) be awake; **bei jmdm.** ~: stay up at sb.'s bedside; sit up with sb.

Wachheit *die;* ~: alertness

Wach·hund *der* guard dog

Wacholder *der;* ~s, ~: juniper

Wach·posten *der* (Milit.) guard

Wachs *das;* ~es, ~e wax

wachsam *Adj.* watchful; vigilant

Wachsamkeit *die;* ~: vigilance

wachsen[1] *unr. itr. V.; mit sein* grow

wachsen[2] *tr. V.* wax

Wachs-: ~**figur** *die* waxwork; ~**figuren·kabinett** *das* waxworks *sing. or pl.;* waxworks museum

wächst 2. u. 3. Pers. Sg. Präsens v. WACHSEN

Wachs·tuch *das Pl.* W<u>a</u>chstücher (Tischtuch) oilcloth tablecloth

Wachstum *das;* ~s growth

Wachtel *die;* ~, ~n quail

Wächter *der;* ~s, ~: guard; (Nacht-, Turmwächter) watchman; (Parkwächter) [park-]keeper

Wächterin *die;* ~, ~nen ▶ WÄCHTER

Wach[t]·turm *der* watchtower

wackelig *Adj.* (a) wobbly ‹*chair, table, etc.*›; loose ‹*tooth*›
(b) (ugs.: kraftlos, schwach) frail

Wackel·kontakt *der* (Elektrot.) loose connection

wackeln *itr. V.* wobble; ‹*tooth etc.*› be loose; ‹*house, window, etc.*› shake; **mit dem Kopf/den Ohren** ~: waggle one's head/ears

wacker (veralt.) ①*Adj.* upright ·····⁝

W

[2] *adv.* valiantly; **sich ~ halten** put up a good show

Wade *die; ~, ~n* (Anat.) calf

Waden·krampf *der* cramp in one's calf

Waffe *die; ~, ~n* weapon

Waffel *die; ~, ~n* waffle; (dünne Waffel, Eiswaffel) wafer; (Eistüte) cone

Waffen-: **~gewalt** *die* **mit ~gewalt** by force of arms; **~handel** *der* arms trade; **~händler** *der*, **~händlerin** *die* arms dealer; **~schein** *der* firearms licence; **~stillstand** *der* armistice

Wage·mut *der* daring

wage·mutig *Adj.* daring

wagen [1] *tr. V.* risk; **[es] ~, etw. zu tun** dare to do sth.
[2] *refl. V.* **sich irgendwohin/nicht irgendwohin ~:** venture somewhere/not dare to go somewhere

Wagen *der; ~s, ~:* (PKW) car; (Pferdewagen) cart; (Eisenb.: Personenwagen) coach; (Eisenb.: Güterwagen) truck; (Straßenbahnwagen) car; (Kinder-, Puppenwagen) pram (Brit.); baby carriage (Amer.); (Sportwagen) pushchair (Brit.); stroller (Amer.)

Wagen·heber *der* jack

Waggon /va'gɔŋ, *südd., österr.:* va'goːn/ *der; ~s, ~s, südd., österr.: ~s, ~e* wagon; truck (Brit.); car (Amer.)

waghalsig [1] *Adj.* daring; (leichtsinnig) reckless
[2] *adv.* daringly; ⟨*speculate*⟩ riskily; (leichtsinnig) recklessly

Wagnis *das; ~ses, ~se* daring exploit *or* feat; (Risiko) risk

Wahl *die; ~, ~en* (a) choice; **eine/seine ~ treffen** make a/one's choice
(b) (in ein Gremium, Amt usw.) election; **geheime ~:** secret ballot

wahl·berechtigt *Adj.* eligible *or* entitled to vote *postpos.*

Wahl·beteiligung *die* turn-out

wählen [1] *tr. V.* (a) choose; (aus~) select
(b) (Fernspr.) dial ⟨*number*⟩
(c) (durch Stimmabgabe) elect
(d) (stimmen für) vote for ⟨*party, candidate*⟩
[2] *itr. V.* (a) choose
(b) (Fernspr.) dial
(c) (stimmen) vote

Wähler *der; ~s, ~:* voter

Wahl·ergebnis *das* election result

Wählerin *die; ~, ~nen* voter

wählerisch *Adj.* choosy; particular (**in +** *Dat.* about)

Wählerschaft *die; ~, ~en* electorate; **die ~ der SPD** the SPD's voters *pl.;* those who vote for the SPD

wahl-, Wahl-: **~fach** *das* (Schulw.) optional subject; **~gang** *der* ballot; **~geheimnis** *das* secrecy of the ballot; **~geschenk** *das* pre-election bonus;

~kabine *die* polling booth; **~kampf** *der* election campaign; **~kreis** *der* constituency; **~lokal** *das* polling station; **~los** [1] *Adj.* indiscriminate; [2] *adv.* indiscriminately; **~niederlage** *die* election defeat; **~recht** *das* right to vote

Wähl·scheibe *die* (Fernspr.) dial

Wahl-: **~sieg** *der* election victory; **~spruch** *der* motto; **~system** *das* electoral system; **~urne** *die* ballot box

Wahn *der; ~[e]s* mania; delusion

Wahn·sinn *der* (a) insanity; madness
(b) (ugs.: Unvernunft) madness; lunacy

wahnsinnig [1] *Adj.* (a) (geistesgestört) insane; mad
(b) (ugs.: ganz unvernünftig) mad; crazy
(c) (ugs.: groß, heftig, intensiv) terrific (coll.) ⟨*effort, speed, etc.*⟩; terrible (coll.) ⟨*fright, job, pain*⟩
[2] *adv.* (ugs.) incredibly (coll.); terribly (coll.)

wahr *Adj.* (a) true; **nicht ~?** *translation depends on preceding verb form:* **du hast Hunger, nicht ~?** you're hungry, aren't you?; **nicht ~, er weiß es doch?** he does know, doesn't he?
(b) (wirklich) real ⟨*reason, motive, feelings, joy, etc.*⟩; actual ⟨*culprit*⟩; (echt) true, real ⟨*friend, friendship, love, art*⟩

wahren *tr. V.* (geh.) preserve ⟨*balance, equality, neutrality, etc.*⟩; maintain ⟨*authority, right*⟩; (verteidigen) defend

währen *itr. V.* (geh.) last

während [1] *Konj.* (a) (zeitlich) while
(b) (adversativ) whereas
[2] *Präp. mit Gen.* during; (über einen Zeitraum von) for

wahr|haben *unr. tr. V.* **etw. nicht ~ wollen** not want to admit sth.

wahrhaft (geh.) [1] *Adj.* true
[2] *adv.* truly

wahrhaftig [1] *Adj.* (geh.) truthful ⟨*person*⟩
[2] *adv.* really; genuinely

Wahrheit *die; ~, ~en* truth

wahrheits·getreu [1] *Adj.* truthful; faithful ⟨*account*⟩
[2] *adv.* truthfully; ⟨*portray*⟩ faithfully

wahr|nehmen *unr. tr. V.* (a) (mit den Sinnen erfassen) perceive; (spüren) feel; detect ⟨*sound, smell*⟩; (bemerken) notice; (erkennen, ausmachen) make out
(b) (nutzen) take advantage of ⟨*opportunity*⟩; exploit ⟨*advantage*⟩; exercise ⟨*right*⟩
(c) (vertreten) look after ⟨*sb.'s interests, affairs*⟩
(d) (erfüllen, ausführen) carry out, perform ⟨*function, task, duty*⟩; fulfil ⟨*responsibility*⟩

Wahrnehmung *die; ~, ~en* (a) perception; (eines Sachverhalts) awareness; (eines Geruchs, eines Tons) detection
(b) (Nutzung) (eines Rechts) exercise; (einer Gelegenheit, eines Vorteils) exploitation
(c) (Vertretung) representation
(d) (einer Funktion, Aufgabe, Pflicht) performance; execution; (einer Verantwortung) fulfilment

---

*old spelling - see note on page xiv

wahr·sagen *2. Part.* gewahrsagt ⓵ *itr. V.* tell fortunes

⓶ *tr. V.* predict, foretell ⟨*future*⟩

Wahrsager *der;* ∼s, ∼, **Wahrsagerin** *die;* ∼, ∼nen fortune-teller

wahrscheinlich ⓵ *Adj.* probable; likely

⓶ *adv.* probably

Wahrscheinlichkeit *die;* ∼, ∼en probability; likelihood

Währung *die;* ∼, ∼en currency

Währungs-: ∼**reform** *die* currency reform; ∼**union** *die* currency union; ∼-, Wirtschafts- und Sozialunion social, economic, and currency union

Wahr·zeichen *das* symbol; (einer Stadt, einer Landschaft) [most famous] landmark

Waise *die;* ∼, ∼n orphan

Waisen·haus *das* orphanage

Wal *der;* ∼[e]s, ∼e whale

Wald *der;* ∼[e]s, Wälder wood; (größer) forest

Wald·brand *der* forest fire

Wäldchen *das;* ∼s, ∼: copse

Wald-: ∼**meister** *der* (Bot.) woodruff; ∼**sterben** *das;* ∼∼s death of the forest [as a result of pollution]

Wal·fang *der* whaling *no def. art.;* **auf** ∼ gehen/sein go/be whaling

Waliser *der;* ∼s, ∼: Welshman

Waliserin *die;* ∼, ∼nen Welshwoman

walisisch *Adj.* Welsh

Walkman ⓦ /'wɔkmən/ *der;* ∼s, Walkmen /'wɔkmən/ Walkman ®; personal stereo

Wall *der;* ∼[e]s, Wälle earthwork; embankment; rampart (esp. Mil.)

Wall-: ∼**fahrer** *der* pilgrim; ∼**fahrt** *die* pilgrimage; ∼**fahrts·ort** *der* place of pilgrimage

Wal·nuss, *Wal·nuß *die* walnut

Wal·ross, *Wal·roß *das; Pl.* -rosse walrus

walten *itr. V.* (geh.) ⟨*good sense, good spirit*⟩ prevail; ⟨*peace, silence, harmony, etc.*⟩ reign

Walze *die;* ∼, ∼n roller; (Straßen∼) [road] roller; (Schreib∼) platen

walzen *tr. V.* roll ⟨*field, road, steel, etc.*⟩

wälzen ⓵ *tr. V.* roll; heave ⟨*heavy object*⟩; (fig.) shove ⟨*blame, responsibility*⟩ (auf + Akk. on); **etw. in Mehl** *usw.* ∼ (Kochk.) toss sth. in flour *etc.;* **Probleme** ∼ (fig. ugs.) mull over problems

⓶ *refl. V.* roll; (auf der Stelle) roll about *or* around; (im Krampf, vor Schmerzen) writhe around

Walzer *der;* ∼s, ∼: waltz

wand *1. u. 3. Pers. Sg. Prät. v.* WINDEN

Wand *die;* ∼, Wände wall; (Trennwand) partition; (bewegliche Trennwand) screen; (eines Behälters, Schiffs) side

Wandale *der;* ∼n, ∼n, **Wandalin** *die;* ∼, ∼nen vandal

Wandalismus *der;* ∼: vandalism

Wandel *der;* ∼s change

wandeln *refl., tr. V.* change (in + Akk. into)

Wanderer *der;* ∼s, ∼, **Wanderin** *die;* ∼, ∼nen rambler; hiker

Wander·karte *die* rambler's [path] map

wandern *itr. V.; mit sein* (a) hike; ramble

(b) (ugs.: gehen; fig.) wander (lit. or fig.)

(c) (ziehen, reisen) travel; (ziellos) roam; ⟨*exhibition, circus, theatre*⟩ tour, travel; ⟨*animal, people, tribe*⟩ migrate

Wander·tag *der* day's hike (*for a class or school*)

Wanderung *die;* ∼, ∼en (a) hike; walking tour; **eine** ∼ **machen** go on a hike *or* a walking tour

(b) (Zool., Soziol.) migration

Wander-: ∼**urlaub** *der* walking holiday; ∼**weg** *der* footpath (*constructed for ramblers*)

Wand-: ∼**gemälde** *das* mural; ∼**lampe** *die* wall light

Wandlung *die;* ∼, ∼en change; (grundlegend) transformation

Wand-: ∼**malerei** *die* (Bild) mural; ∼**schrank** *der* wall cupboard *or* (Amer.) closet

wandte *1. u. 3. Pers. Prät. v.* WENDEN

Wange *die;* ∼, ∼n (geh.) cheek

Wankelmut *der* (geh.) vacillation

wankel·mütig *Adj.* (geh.) vacillating

wanken *itr. V.* (a) sway; ⟨*person*⟩ totter; (unter einer Last) stagger

(b) *mit sein* (unsicher gehen) stagger; totter

wann *Adv.* when; **seit** ∼ **wohnst du dort?** how long have you been living there?

Wanne *die;* ∼, ∼n bath[tub]

Wanze *die;* ∼, ∼n bug (coll.)

Wappen *das;* ∼s, ∼: coat of arms

wappnen *refl. V.* (geh.) forearm oneself

war *1. u. 3. Pers. Sg. Prät. v.* SEIN

warb *1. u. 3. Pers. Sg. Prät. v.* WERBEN

ward (geh.) *1. u. 3. Pers. Sg. Prät. v.* WERDEN

Ware *die;* ∼, ∼n (a) ∼[n] goods *pl.;*

(b) (Artikel) article; commodity (Econ., fig.); (Erzeugnis) product

Waren-: ∼**angebot** *das* supply [of goods]; (Sortiment) range of goods; ∼**haus** *das* department store; ∼**korb** *der* (Statistik) basket of goods; ∼**lager** *das* (einer Fabrik o. Ä.) stores *pl.;* (eines Geschäftes) stockroom; (größer) warehouse; ∼**muster** *das,* ∼**probe** *die* sample; ∼**zeichen** *das* trade mark

warf *1. u. 3. Pers. Sg. Prät. v.* WERFEN

warm; wärmer, wärmst ... ⓵ *Adj.* (auch fig.) warm; hot ⟨*meal, food, bath, spring*⟩; keen, lively ⟨*interest*⟩ **das Essen** ∼ **machen** heat up the food; „∼" (auf Wasserhahn) 'hot'

⓶ *adv.* warmly; ∼ **essen/duschen** have a hot meal/shower

Wärme *die;* ∼: warmth; (Hitze; auch Physik) heat

W

wärmen ① *tr. V.* warm; (aufwärmen) warm up ⟨*food, drink*⟩
② *itr. V.* be warm; (warm halten) keep one warm

Wärme·pumpe *die* (Technik) heat pump

Warm·front *die* (Met.) warm front

warm|halten *unr. tr. V.* (ugs.) **sich** (*Dat.*) **jmdn.** ∼: keep on the right side of sb.

Warm·wasser-: ∼**bereiter** *der;* ∼**s,** ∼: water heater; ∼**heizung** *die* hot-water heating

Warn-: ∼**blinkanlage** *die* (Kfz-W.) hazard warning lights *pl.;* ∼**dreieck** *das* (Kfz-W.) hazard warning triangle

warnen *tr.* (*auch itr.*) *V.* warn (**vor** + *Dat.* of, about); **jmdn.** [**davor**] ∼, **etw. zu tun** warn sb. against doing sth.

Warn-: ∼**schild** *das; Pl.* ∼∼**er** warning sign; ∼**schuss,** ***∼**schuß** *der* warning shot; ∼**signal** *das* warning signal; ∼**streik** *der* token strike

Warnung *die;* ∼, ∼**en** warning (**vor** + *Dat.* of, about)

Warschau (*das*); ∼**s** Warsaw

Warte-: ∼**halle** *die* waiting room; (Flugw.) departure lounge; ∼**liste** *die* waiting list

warten ① *itr. V.* wait (**auf** + *Akk.* for)
② *tr. V.* service ⟨*car etc.*⟩

Wärter *der;* ∼**s,** ∼, **Wärterin** *die;* ∼, ∼**nen** attendant; (Tier-, Zoo-, Leuchtturmwärter[in]) keeper; (Krankenwärter[in]) orderly; (Gefängniswärter[in]) warder

Warte-: ∼**saal** *der* waiting room; ∼**zimmer** *das* waiting room

Wartung *die;* ∼, ∼**en** service; (das Warten) servicing; (Instandhaltung) maintenance

warum *Adv.* why

Warze *die;* ∼, ∼**n** wart; (Brust∼) nipple

was ① *Interrogativpron. Nom. u. Akk. u.* (*nach Präp.*) *Dat. Neutr.;* ∼ **kostet das?** what *or* how much does that cost?; **ach** ∼! (ugs.) oh, come on!; ∼ **für ein …/**∼ **für …:** what sort *or* kind of …
② *Relativpron. Nom. u. Akk. u.* (*nach Präp.*) *Dat. Neutr.;* [**das,**] ∼: what; **alles,** ∼ …: everything *or* all that …; **vieles/nichts/etwas,** ∼ …: much/nothing/something that …; ∼ **mich betrifft,** [**so**] …: as far as I'm concerned, …
③ *Indefinitpron. Nom. u. Akk. u.* (*nach Präp.*) *Dat. Neutr.* (ugs.) ▶ ETWAS;
④ *Adv.* (ugs.) (warum, wozu) why; what … for

Wasch-: ∼**anlage** *die* car wash; ∼**automat** *der* washing machine; ∼**becken** *das* washbasin

Wäsche *die;* ∼, ∼**n** (a) (zu waschende Textilien) washing; (für die Wäscherei) laundry
(b) (Unterwäsche) underwear
(c) (das Waschen) washing *no pl.;* (einmalig) wash; **in der** ∼ **sein** be in the wash

wasch·echt *Adj.* (a) colour-fast ⟨*textile, clothes*⟩; fast ⟨*colour*⟩
(b) (fig.) genuine

Wäsche-: ∼**klammer** *die* clothes peg (Brit.); clothespin (Amer.); ∼**korb** *der* laundry basket; ∼**leine** *die* clothes line

waschen ① *unr. tr. V.* wash; **sich** ∼: wash [oneself]; have a wash; **Wäsche** ∼: do the/ some washing
② *unr. itr. V.* do the washing

Wäscherei *die;* ∼, ∼**en** laundry

Wäsche-: ∼**schleuder** *die* spin drier; ∼**trockner** *der* (a) (Maschine) tumble drier; (b) (Gestell) clothes airer

wasch-, Wasch-: ∼**gelegenheit** *die* washing facilities *pl.;* ∼**küche** *die* laundry room; ∼**lappen** *der* [face] flannel; washcloth (Amer.); ∼**maschine** *die* washing machine; ∼**maschinen·fest** *Adj.* machine washable; ∼**mittel** *das* detergent; ∼**pulver** *das* washing powder; ∼**raum** *der* washing room; ∼**schüssel** *die* washing bowl; ∼**straße** *die* [automatic] car wash

wäscht *3. Pers. Sg. Präsens v.* WASCHEN

Wasch·wasser *das* washing water

Wasser *das;* ∼**s,** ∼/**Wässer** (a) water
(b) *Pl.* **Wässer** (Mineral-, Tafelwasser) mineral water; (Heilwasser) water
(c) (Gewässer) **ein fließendes/stehendes** ∼: a moving/stagnant stretch of water
(d) ∼ **lassen** pass water

wasser-, Wasser-: ∼**bad** *das* (Kochk.) bain-marie; ∼**ball** *der* (a) beachball; (b) (Spiel) water polo; ∼**dampf** *der* steam; ∼**dicht** *Adj.* waterproof ⟨*clothing, watch, etc.*⟩; watertight ⟨*container, seal, etc.*⟩; ∼**fall** *der* waterfall; ∼**farbe** *die* watercolour; ∼**hahn** *der* water tap; faucet (Amer.)

wässerig ▶ WÄSSRIG

Wasser-: ∼**kessel** *der* kettle; ∼**leitung** *die* water pipe; (Hauptleitung) water main; ∼**mann** *der* (Astrol.) [der] ∼**mann** Aquarius; **er/sie ist** [**ein**] ∼∼: he/she is an Aquarian

wässern *itr. V.; mit sein* land [on the water]

wässern *tr. V.* soak; (Fot.) wash ⟨*negative, print*⟩

wasser-, Wasser-: ∼**pflanze** *die* aquatic plant; ∼**qualität** *die* water quality; ∼**rohr** *das* water pipe; ∼**scheu** *Adj.* scared of water; ∼**schlauch** *der* [water] hose; ∼**schutz·polizei** *die* river/lake police; ∼**ski**[1] *der* waterski; ∼**ski fahren** waterski; ∼**ski** *das;* ∼∼**s** waterskiing *no art.;* ∼**spiegel** *der* (a) (Oberfläche) surface [of the water]; (b) (Niveau) water level; ∼**sport** *der* water sport *no art.;* ∼**spülung** *die* flush

Wasser·stoff *der* hydrogen

Wasser·stoff-: ∼**bombe** *die* hydrogen

bomb; ∼**per·oxid,** ∼**per·oxyd,**
∼**super·oxid,** ∼**super·oxyd** *das*
(Chemie) hydrogen peroxide

Wasser-: ∼**strahl** *der* jet of water;
∼**straße** *die* waterway; ∼**temperatur**
die water temperature; ∼**tiefe** *die* depth of
the water; ∼**tropfen** *der* drop of water;
∼**turm** *der* water tower; ∼**werfer** *der*
water cannon; ∼**werk** *das* waterworks
sing.; ∼**zeichen** *das* watermark

wässrig, *wäßrig *Adj.* watery

waten *itr. V.; mit sein* wade

Waterloo *das;* ∼**s,** ∼**s** Waterloo *no art.;*
sein ∼ erleben meet one's Waterloo

watscheln *itr. V.; mit sein* waddle

Watt¹ *das;* ∼**[e]s,** ∼**en** mudflats *pl.*

Watt² *das;* ∼**s,** ∼ (Technik, Physik) watt

Watte *die;* ∼, ∼**n** cotton wool

Watte·bausch *der* wad of cotton wool

Watten·meer *das* tidal shallows *pl.*

wattiert *Adj.* quilted; padded ‹*shoulder
etc., envelope*›

WC *das;* ∼**[s],** ∼**[s]** toilet; WC

weben *tr., itr. V.* weave

Weber *der;* ∼**s,** ∼, **Weberin** *die;* ∼, ∼**nen**
weaver

Website /web'saɪt/ *die;* ∼, ∼**s** (DV) Web
site

Web·stuhl *der* loom

Wechsel *der;* ∼**s,** ∼ (a) (das Auswechseln)
change; (Geldwechsel) exchange
(b) (Aufeinanderfolge) alternation; im ∼:
alternately; (bei mehr als zwei) in rotation
(c) (das Überwechseln) move; (Sport) transfer
(d) (Bankw.) bill of exchange (über + *Akk.*
for)

wechsel-, Wechsel-: ∼**geld** *das*
change; ∼**haft** *Adj.* changeable; ∼**jahre**
Pl. change of life *sing.;* menopause *sing.;*
∼**kurs** *der* exchange rate

wechseln ① *tr. V.* (a) change; das Hemd
∼: change one's shirt; die Wohnung ∼:
move home
(b) ([aus]tauschen) exchange ‹*letters, glances,
etc.*›
(c) (umwechseln) change ‹*money, note, etc.*› (in
+ *Akk.* into)
② *itr. V.* change

wechsel-, Wechsel-: ∼**seitig** ① *Adj.*
mutual; ② *adv.* mutually; ∼**strom** *der*
(Elektrot.) alternating current; ∼**stube** *die*
bureau de change; ∼**wähler** *der,*
∼**wählerin** *die* (Politik) floating voter;
∼**wirkung** *die* interaction

wecken *tr. V.* jmdn. [aus dem Schlaf] ∼:
wake sb. [up]; (fig.: hervorrufen) arouse
‹*interest, curiosity, anger*›

Wecker *der;* ∼**s,** ∼ alarm clock

wedeln *itr. V.* ‹*tail*› wag; [mit dem
Schwanz] ∼ ‹*dog*› wag its tail

weder *Konj.* ∼ **A** noch **B** neither A nor B

weg *Adv.* away; (verschwunden, weggegangen)
gone; **er ist schon seit einer Stunde** ∼: he
left an hour ago; **weit** ∼: far away; a long
way away

Weg *der;* ∼**[e]s,** ∼**e** (a) (Fußweg) path;
(Feldweg) track
(b) (Zugang) way; (Passage, Durchgang) passage;
sich (*Dat.*) **einen** ∼ **durch etw. bahnen** clear
a path *or* way through sth.
(c) (Route, Verbindung) way; route
(d) (Strecke, Entfernung) distance; (Gang) walk;
(Reise) journey; **auf dem kürzesten** ∼: by the
shortest route; **auf halbem** ∼**[e]** (auch fig.)
half-way; **sich auf den** ∼ **machen** set off;
etw. in die ∼**e leiten** get sth. under way
(e) (ugs.: Besorgung) errand
(f) (Methode) way; (Mittel) means

weg-: ∼**|bleiben** *unr. itr. V.; mit sein*
(nicht kommen) stay away; (nicht nach Hause
kommen) stay out; ∼**|bringen** *unr. tr. V.*
take away; (zur Reparatur, Wartung usw.) take in

Wegelagerei *die;* ∼: highway robbery

Wegelagerer *der;* ∼**s,** ∼: highwayman

Wegelagerin *die;* ∼, ∼**nen**
highwaywoman

wegen *Präp. mit Gen.* (a) because of; ∼
Umbau[s] geschlossen closed for alterations
(b) (um ... willen) for the sake of; ∼ **der
Kinder/**(ugs.) **dir** for the children's/your sake
(c) (bezüglich) about; regarding

weg-: ∼**|fahren** ① *unr. itr. V.; mit sein*
(a) leave; (im Auto) drive off; (losfahren) set off;
(b) (irgendwohin fahren) go away; ② *unr. tr. V.*
drive away; (mit dem Handwagen usw.) take
away; ∼**|fallen** *unr. itr. V.; mit sein* be
discontinued; (nicht mehr zutreffen) no longer
apply; ∼**|fliegen** *unr. itr. V.; mit sein* fly
away; (weggeblasen werden) fly off; ∼**|gehen**
unr. itr. V. (a) leave; (ugs.: ausgehen) go out;
(ugs.: wegziehen) move away; (b) (verschwinden)
‹*spot, fog, etc.*› go away; (c) (sich entfernen
lassen) ‹*stain*› come out; ∼**|jagen** *tr. V.*
chase away; ∼**|kommen** *unr. itr. V.; mit
sein* (a) get away; (b) (abhanden kommen) go
missing; (c) **gut/schlecht** *usw.* [bei etw.]
∼**kommen** (ugs.) come off well/badly *etc.* [in
sth.]; ∼**|kriegen** *tr. V.* get rid of ‹*cold,
pain, etc.*›; get out, get rid of ‹*stain*›;
∼**|lassen** *unr. tr. V.* (a) jmdn. ∼**lassen** let
sb. go; (ausgehen lassen) let sb. go out; (b)
(auslassen) leave out; omit; ∼**|laufen** *unr.
itr. V.; mit sein* run away (**von, vor** + *Dat.*
from); ∼**|legen** *tr. V.* put aside; (an seinen
Platz legen) put away; ∼**|nehmen** *unr. tr. V.*
(a) take away; move ‹*head, arm*›; (b) jmdm.
etw. ∼**nehmen** take sth. away from sb.;
∼**|schicken** *tr. V.* (a) send off ‹*letter,
parcel*›; (b) send ‹*person*› away;
∼**|schmeißen** *unr. tr. V.* (ugs.) chuck
away (coll.); ∼**|schnappen** *tr. V.* (ugs.)
jmdm. etw. ∼**schnappen/vor der Nase**
∼**schnappen** snatch sth. away from sb./from
under sb.'s nose; ∼**|schütten** *tr. V.* pour
away; ∼**|sehen** *unr. itr. V.* look away;
∼**|stellen** *tr. V.* put away; (beiseite stellen) ···⁝

w

put aside; ~|**stoßen** *unr. tr. V.* push *or* shove away; ~|**tragen** *unr. tr. V.* carry away

Weg·weiser *der;* ~s, ~: signpost

weg-: ~|**werfen** *unr. tr. V.* (auch fig.) throw away; ~**werfend** *Adj.* dismissive ⟨*gesture, remark*⟩; ~|**wischen** *tr. V.* wipe away; ~**zappen** (ugs.) ① *tr. V.* etw. ~**zappen** switch sth. off [by changing channels]; ② *itr. V.* switch to another channel; ~**ziehen** ① *unr. tr. V.* pull away; draw back curtain; pull off blanket; ② *unr. itr. V.; mit sein* (a) (umziehen) move away; (b) (wandern) ⟨*animals, nomads, etc.*⟩ leave [on their migration]

weh (ugs.) *Adj.* sore; *s. auch* WEHTUN

Wehe *die;* ~, ~n: ~n haben have contractions; **in den** ~n **liegen** be in labour

wehen *itr. V.* (a) (blasen) blow (b) (flattern) flutter

weh-, Weh-: ~**leidig** (abwertend) ① *Adj.* (überempfindlich) soft; (weinerlich) whining *attrib.;* ② *adv.* self-pityingly; (weinerlich) whiningly; ~**mut** *die;* ~ (geh.) wistful nostalgia; ~**mütig** *Adj.* wistfully nostalgic

Wehr¹ *die;* ~, ~en: **sich [gegen jmdn./etw.] zur** ~ **setzen** make a stand [against sb./sth.]; resist [sb./sth.]

Wehr² *das;* ~[e]s, ~e weir

Wehrdienst *der* military service *no art.;* **seinen** ~ **ableisten** do one's military service

Wehr·dienst-: ~**verweigerer** *der;* ~s, ~: conscientious objector; ~**verweigerung** *die* conscientious objection

wehren *refl. V.* defend oneself

wehr-, Wehr-: ~**los** *Adj.* defenceless; ~**losigkeit** *die;* ~~: defencelessness; ~**pflicht** *die* military service; **die allgemeine** ~**pflicht** compulsory military service; ~**pflichtig** *Adj.* liable for military service *postpos.;* ~**sold** *der* military pay; ~**übung** *die* reserve duty [re]training exercise

weh|tun *unr. itr. V.* (ugs.) hurt; **mir tut der Magen/Kopf/Rücken weh** my stomach/head/back is aching *or* hurts; **jmdm./sich** ~: hurt sb./oneself

Weib *das;* ~[e]s, ~er (veralt., ugs.) woman; female (derog.)

Weibchen *das;* ~s, ~: female

Weiber·held *der* (ugs.) ladykiller

weiblich ① *Adj.* (a) female (b) (für die Frau typisch; Sprachw.) feminine ② *adv.* femininely

Weiblichkeit *die;* ~: femininity

Weibs·bild *das* (a) (ugs.) woman (b) (salopp abwertend) female

weich ① *Adj.* (auch fig.) soft; **ein** ~**es** *od.* ~ **gekochtes Ei** a soft-boiled egg ② *adv.* softly

Weiche¹ *die;* ~, ~n (Flanke) flank

Weiche² *die;* ~, ~n points *pl.* (Brit.); switch (Amer.)

weichen *unr. itr. V.; mit sein* move; **vor jmdm./einer Sache** ~: give way to sb./sth.

*weich·gekocht ▶ WEICH 1

weichlich ① *Adj.* soft; (ohne innere Festigkeit) weak ② *adv.* softly

Weich·macher *der* (Chemie, Technik) plasticizer

Weide¹ *die;* ~, ~n willow

Weide² *die;* ~, ~n pasture

weiden *itr., tr. V.* graze

Weiden·kätzchen *das* willow catkin

weigern *refl. V.* refuse

Weigerung *die;* ~, ~en refusal

Weih·bischof *der* (kath. Kirche) suffragan bishop

Weihe *die;* ~, ~n (Rel.) consecration; (kath. Kirche: Priester-, Bischofsweihe) ordination

weihen *tr. V.* (a) (Rel.) consecrate; (zueignen) dedicate (*Dat.* to) (b) (kath. Kirche: ordinieren) ordain

Weiher *der;* ~s, ~: [small] pond

Weihnachten *das;* ~, ~: Christmas; **frohe** *od.* **fröhliche** *od.* **gesegnete** ~! Merry *or* Happy Christmas!

weihnachtlich *Adj.* Christmassy

Weihnachts-: ~**baum** *der* Christmas tree; ~**feiertag** *der:* **der erste/zweite** ~**feiertag** Christmas Day/Boxing Day; ~**fest** *das* Christmas; ~**geld** *das* Christmas bonus; ~**geschenk** *das* Christmas present *or* gift; ~**lied** *das* Christmas carol; ~**mann** *der; Pl.* ~**männer** Father Christmas; Santa Claus; ~**markt** *der* Christmas fair; ~**tag** *der:* ▶ ~FEIERTAG; ~**zeit** *die* Christmas time

Weih-: ~**rauch** *der* incense; ~**wasser** *das* (kath. Kirche) holy water

weil *Konj.* because

Weile *die;* ~: while

weilen *itr. V.* (geh.) stay; (sein) be

Wein *der;* ~[e]s, ~e wine

Wein-: ~**berg** *der* vineyard; ~**berg·schnecke** *die* [edible] snail; ~**brand** *der* brandy

weinen *itr. V.* cry (**über** + *Akk.* over, about); (aus Trauer, Kummer) cry, weep (**um** for)

weinerlich ① *Adj.* tearful; weepy ② *adv.* tearfully

wein-, Wein-: ~**essig** *der* wine vinegar; ~**flasche** *die* wine bottle; ~**glas** *das* wineglass; ~**handlung** *die* wine merchant's; ~**karte** *die* wine list; ~**krampf** *der* crying fit; fit of crying; ~**lokal** *das* wine bar; ~**probe** *die* wine-tasting [session]; ~**rebe** *die* grapevine; ~**rot** *Adj.* wine-red; ~**schaum·creme**

---

die (Kochk.) zabaglione; ~**stock** *der; Pl.*
~stöcke [grape]vine; ~**stube** *die* wine
bar; ~**traube** *die* grape
weise ①*Adj.* wise
②*adv.* wisely
Weise *die;* ~, ~n (a) (Art, Verfahren) way
(b) (Melodie) tune; melody
weisen ①*unr. tr. V.* (geh.: zeigen) show;
jmdn. aus dem Zimmer ~: send sb. out of
the room
②*unr. itr. V.* (irgendwohin zeigen) point
Weisheit *die;* ~, ~en (a) wisdom
(b) (Erkenntnis) wise insight; (Spruch) wise
saying
Weisheits·zahn *der* wisdom tooth
weis|machen *tr. V.* (ugs.) das kannst du
mir nicht ~! you can't expect me to swallow
that!
weiß[1] *1. u. 3. Pers. Sg. Präsens v.* WISSEN
weiß[2] *Adj.* white
Weiß *das;* ~[e]s, ~: white
weis·sagen *tr. V.* prophesy
Weissagung *die;* ~, ~en prophecy
Weiß-: ~**bier** *das* wheat beer; white beer;
~**brot** *das* white bread; ~**dorn** *der;* ~~s,
~~e hawthorn
Weiße *der/die; adj. Dekl.* white; white man/
woman
weißen *tr. V.* paint white; (tünchen)
whitewash
weiß-, Weiß-: ~**gold** *das* white gold;
~**haarig** *Adj.* white-haired; ~haarig sein
have white hair; ~**herbst** *der* ≈ rosé
wine; ~**kohl** *der,* (bes. südd., österr.)
~**kraut** *das* white cabbage
weißlich *Adj.* whitish
Weiß·macher *der* whitener
weißt *2. Pers. Sg. Präsens v.* WISSEN
Weiß-: ~**wein** *der* white wine; ~**wurst**
die veal sausage
Weisung *die;* ~, ~en (geh., sonst Amtsspr.)
instruction; (Direktive) directive
Weisungs·befugnis *die* authority to
issue instructions/directives
weit [1]*Adj.* wide; long ⟨*way*⟩; jmdm. zu ~
sein ⟨*clothes*⟩ be too loose on sb.
②*adv.* (a) (räumlich ausgedehnt) ~ geöffnet
wide open; ~ und breit war niemand zu
sehen there was no one to be seen
anywhere; ~ verbreitet widespread;
common; common ⟨*plant, animal*⟩; ~ gereist
widely travelled
(b) (lang) far; ~er further; farther; am
~esten [the] furthest *or* farthest; ~ [entfernt
od. weg] wohnen live a long way away *or*
off; live far away; ~ reichend long-range;
(fig.) far-reaching ⟨*importance, consequences*⟩;
sweeping ⟨*changes, powers*⟩; extensive
⟨*relations, influence*⟩; von ~em from a
distance; das geht zu ~ (fig.) that is going
too far
(c) (zeitlich entfernt) ~ nach Mitternacht well
past midnight

(d) (in der Entwicklung) far
Weit·blick *der* far-sightedness
Weite *die;* ~, ~n (a) (räumliche Ausdehnung)
expanse
(b) (bes. Sport: Entfernung) distance
(c) (eines Kleidungsstückes) width
weiten ①*tr. V.* widen
②*refl. V.* widen; ⟨*pupil*⟩ dilate
weiter *Adv.* (a) ▶ WEIT 2;
(b) und so ~: and so on
(c) (weithin, anschließend) then
(d) (außerdem, sonst) ~ nichts nothing more
or else
weiter... *Adj.* further; bis auf ~es for the
time being; *s. auch* OHNE
weiter-, Weiter-: ~|**bilden** *tr. V.:*
▶ FORTBILDEN; ~**bildung** *die:*
▶ FORTBILDUNG; ~|**bringen** *unr. tr. V.* die
Diskussion brachte uns nicht ~: the
discussion did not get us any further
[forward]; ~|**erzählen** *tr. V.* (a) continue
telling; *itr.* erzähl weiter! do carry *or* go on;
(b) (~sagen) pass on; ~|**fahren** *unr. itr. V.;*
mit sein continue [on one's way]; (weiterreisen)
travel on; ~|**führen** *tr. V.* continue;
~|**geben** *unr. tr. V.* pass on; ~|**gehen**
unr. itr. V.; mit sein go on; bitte ~gehen!
please move along *or* keep moving!; ~**hin**
Adv. (a) (immer noch) still; (b) (künftig) in
future; (c) (außerdem) in addition;
~|**kommen** *unr. itr. V.; mit sein* (a) get
further; (b) (Fortschritte machen) make
progress; im Beruf ~kommen get on in one's
career; ~|**machen** (ugs.) *itr. V.* carry on;
go on; ~|**reichen** *tr. V.* pass on;
~|**sagen** *tr. V.* pass on; ~|**sehen** *unr.*
itr. V. see
Weiterungen *Pl.* complications;
difficulties
weiter-, Weiter-:
~**verarbeiten** *tr. V.* process;
~**verarbeitung** *die* processing
weit-, Weit-: ~**gehend** ①*Adj.*
extensive, wide, sweeping ⟨*powers*⟩; far-
reaching ⟨*support, concessions, etc.*⟩; wide
⟨*support, agreement, etc.*⟩; general
⟨*renunciation*⟩; ②*adv.* to a large *or* great
extent; *~**gereist** ▶ WEIT 2A; ~**hin** *Adv.*
for miles around; ~**läufig** ①*Adj.* (a)
(ausgedehnt) extensive; (geräumig) spacious; (b)
(entfernt) distant; ②*adv.* (a) (ausgedehnt)
spaciously; (b) (entfernt) distantly;
~**räumig** ①*Adj.* spacious ⟨*room, area,*
etc.⟩; wide ⟨*gap, space*⟩; ②*adv.* spaciously;
*~**reichend** ▶ WEIT 2B; ~**sichtig** *Adj.*
long-sighted; ~**sichtigkeit** *die;* ~~: long-
sightedness; ~**sprung** *der* (Sport) long
jump (Brit.); broad jump (Amer.);
*~**verbreitet** ▶ WEIT 2A;
~**winkel·objektiv** *das* wide-angle lens
Weizen *der;* ~s wheat
Weizen·bier *das:* ▶ WEISSBIER
welch [1]*Interrogativpron.* (bei Wahl aus einer ···⊹

unbegrenzten Menge) what; (bei Wahl aus einer begrenzten Menge) (*adj.*) which; (*subst.*) which one

[2] *Relativpron.* (bei Menschen) who; (bei Sachen) which

[3] *Indefinitpron.* some; (in Fragen) any

welk *Adj.* withered ‹*skin, hands, etc.*›; wilted ‹*leaves, flower*›; limp ‹*lettuce*›

welken *itr. V.; mit sein* ‹*plant, flower*› wilt

Well·blech *das* corrugated iron

Welle *die;* ∼, ∼**n (a)** (auch fig.) wave; (Rundf.: Wellenlänge) wavelength **(b)** (Technik) shaft

wellen-, Wellen-: ∼**bad** *das* artificial wave pool; ∼**bereich** *der* (Rundf.) waveband; ∼**brecher** *der* breakwater; ∼**gang** *der* swell; **bei starkem** ∼**gang** in heavy seas; ∼**länge** *die* wavelength; ∼**sittich** *der* budgerigar

Well·fleisch *das* boiled belly pork

wellig *Adj.* wavy ‹*hair*›; undulating ‹*scenery, hills, etc.*›; uneven ‹*surface, track, etc.*›

Well·pappe *die* corrugated cardboard

Wels *der;* ∼**es,** ∼**e** catfish

Welt *die;* ∼, ∼**en (a)** world; **auf der** ∼: in the world; **die Alte/Neue** ∼: the Old/New World; **die Dritte/Vierte** ∼ the Third/Fourth World; **auf die** *od.* **zur** ∼ **kommen** be born; **alle** ∼ (fig. ugs.) the whole world; everybody **(b)** (Weltall) universe

welt-, Welt-: ∼**all** *das* universe; ∼**anschauung** *die* world view; ∼**ausstellung** *die* world fair; ∼**berühmt** *Adj.* world-famous; ∼**bevölkerung** *die* world population; population of the world

Welten·bummler *der;* ∼**s,** ∼, **Welten·bummlerin** *die;* ∼, ∼**nen** globetrotter

welt-, Welt-: ∼**erfolg** *der* worldwide success; ∼**fremd** [1] *Adj.* unworldly; [2] *adv.* unrealistically; ∼**frieden** *der* world peace; ∼**karte** *die* map of the world; ∼**klima** *das* world climate; ∼**krieg** *der* world war; **der Erste/Zweite** ∼**krieg** the First/Second World War

weltlich *Adj.* **(a)** worldly **(b)** (nicht geistlich) secular

welt-, Welt-: ∼**literatur** *die* world literature *no art.;* ∼**macht** *die* world power; ∼**markt** *der* (Wirtsch.) world market; ∼**meister** *der,* ∼**meisterin** *die* world champion; ∼**meisterschaft** *die* world championship; ∼**politik** *die* world politics *pl.;* ∼**rangliste** *die* world ranking list; world rankings *pl.;* ∼**raum** *der* space *no art.;* ∼**reise** *die* world tour; ∼**rekord** *der* world record; ∼**religion** *die* world religion; ∼**sicherheits·rat** *der* (Pol.) [United Nations] Security Council; ∼**sprache** *die* world language; ∼**stadt**

die cosmopolitan city; ∼**weit** [1] *Adj.* worldwide; [2] *adv.* throughout the world; ∼**wirtschaft** *die* world economy; ∼**wunder** *das:* **die sieben** ∼**wunder** the Seven Wonders of the World

wem *Dat. von* WER [1] *Interrogativpron.* to whom; who ... to; **mit/von/zu** ∼: with/from/ to whom; who ... with/from/to [2] *Relativpron.* the person to whom ...; the person who ... to [3] *Indefinitpron.* (ugs.: jemandem) to somebody *or* someone; (fragend *od.* verneint) to anybody *or* anyone

wen *Akk. von* WER [1] *Interrogativpron.* whom; who (coll.); **an/für** ∼: to/for whom ...; who ... to/for [2] *Relativpron.* the person whom [3] *Indefinitpron.* (ugs.: jemanden) somebody; someone; (fragend *od.* verneint) anybody; anyone

Wende *die;* ∼, ∼**n** change (**zu** for)

Wende·kreis *der* **(a)** (Geogr.) tropic **(b)** (Kfz-W.) turning circle

Wendel·treppe *die* spiral staircase

wenden[1] [1] *tr. u. itr. V.* (auf die andere Seite) turn [over]; (in die entgegengesetzte Richtung) turn [round]; **bitte** ∼! please turn over [2] *itr. V.* turn [round] [3] *refl. V.* **sich zum Besseren/Schlechteren** ∼: take a turn for the better/worse

wenden[2] [1] *unr. (auch regelm.) tr. V.* turn [2] *unr. (auch regelm.) refl. V.* **(a)** ‹*person*› turn **(b)** (sich richten) **sich an jmdn. [um Rat]** ∼: turn to sb. [for advice]

Wende-: ∼**platz** *der* turning area; ∼**punkt** *der* turning point

wendig [1] *Adj.* **(a)** agile; manœuvrable ‹*vehicle, boat, etc.*› **(b)** (gewandt) astute [2] *adv.* **(a)** (beweglich) agilely **(b)** (gewandt) astutely

Wendigkeit *die;* ∼ **(a)** agility; (eines Flugzeugs) manœuvrability **(b)** (Gewandtheit) astuteness

Wendung *die;* ∼, ∼**en (a)** (Änderung der Richtung) turn **(b)** (Veränderung) change

wenig [1] *Indefinitpron. u. unbest. Zahlw.* **(a)** *Sing.* little; **das ist** ∼: that isn't much; **zu** ∼ **Zeit/Geld haben** not have enough time/ money; **ein Exemplar/50 Euro zu** ∼: one copy too few/50 euros too little **(b)** *Pl.* a few; **mit** ∼**en Worten** in a few words [2] *Adv.* little; ∼ **mehr** not much more

weniger [1] *Komp. von* WENIG; *Indefinitpron. u. unbest. Zahlw.* (+ *Sg.*) less; (+ *Pl.*) fewer; **immer** ∼: less and less [2] *Komp. von* WENIG; *Adv.* less; **das ist** ∼ **angenehm/erfreulich/schön** that is not very pleasant/pleasing/nice; *s. auch* MEHR 1; [3] *Konj.* less; **fünf** ∼ **drei** five, take away three

w<u>e</u>nigst... [1] *Sup. von* WENIG 1; least; **am ~en** least
[2] *Sup. von* WENIG 2: **am ~en** the least

w<u>e</u>nigstens *Adv.* at least

wenn *Konj.* (a) (konditional) if; **außer ~:** unless; **~ es nicht anders geht** if there's no other way
(b) (temporal) when; **jedes Mal** *od.* **immer, ~:** whenever
(c) (konzessiv) **wenn ... auch** even though
(d) (in Wunschsätzen) if only

wenn-gl<u>ei</u>ch *Konj.* (geh.) even though; although

wer *Nom. Mask. u. Fem.; s. auch* (*Gen.*) WESSEN; (*Dat.*) WEM; (*Akk.*) WEN
[1] *Interrogativpron.* who; **~ von ...:** which of ...
[2] *Relativpron.* the person who; (jeder, der) anyone *or* anybody who
[3] *Indefinitpron.* (ugs.: jemand) someone; (in Fragen, Konditionalsätzen) anyone; anybody

W<u>e</u>rbe-: ~abteilung *die* advertising *or* publicity department; **~agentur** *die* advertising agency; **~aktion** *die* advertising campaign; **~block** *der; pl.* **~blöcke** commercial break; **~fernsehen** *das* television commercials *pl.;* **~funk** *der* radio commercials *pl.;* **~geschenk** *das* [promotional] free gift

w<u>e</u>rben [1] *unr. itr. V.* advertise; **für etw. ~:** advertise sth.
[2] *unr. tr. V.* attract ⟨*readers, customers, etc.*⟩; recruit ⟨*soldiers, members, etc.*⟩

W<u>e</u>rbe-: ~pause *die* commercial break; **~spot** *der* commercial; advertisement; ad (coll.); **~spruch** *der* advertising slogan

W<u>e</u>rbung *die; ~:* advertising; **für etw. ~ machen** advertise sth.

W<u>e</u>rde-gang *der* career

w<u>e</u>rden [1] *unr. itr. V.; mit sein* become; get; **älter ~:** get *or* grow old[er]; **wahnsinnig** *od.* **verrückt ~:** go mad; **das muss anders ~:** things have to change; **wach ~:** wake up; **rot ~:** go *or* turn red; **Arzt/Professor ~:** become a doctor/professor; **zu etw. ~:** become sth.; **es wird [höchste] Zeit** it is [high] time; **es wird 10 Uhr** it is nearly 10 o'clock; **es wird Herbst** autumn is coming; **sind die Fotos [etwas] geworden?** (ugs.) have the photos turned out [well]?
[2] *Hilfsverb; 2. Part.* **worden** (a) (zur Bildung des Futurs) **wir ~ uns um ihn kümmern** we will take care of him; **es wird gleich regnen** it is going to rain any minute; **es wird um die 80 Euro kosten** (ich vermute, es kostet um die 80 Euro) it will cost around 80 euros
(b) (zur Bildung des Passivs) **du wirst gerufen** you are being called; **er wurde gebeten** he was asked

w<u>e</u>rfen [1] *unr. tr. V.* throw; drop ⟨*bombs*⟩
[2] *unr. itr. V.* (a) throw; **mit etw. ~:** throw sth.
(b) (Junge kriegen) give birth; ⟨*dog, cat*⟩ litter

[3] *unr. refl. V.* throw oneself; **sich vor einen Zug ~:** throw oneself under a train

W<u>e</u>rft *die; ~, ~en* shipyard

Werk *das; ~[e]s, ~e* (a) work
(b) (Betrieb, Fabrik) factory; works *sing. or pl.;* **ab ~:** ex works

W<u>e</u>rk·bank *die; Pl.* **W<u>e</u>rkbänke** workbench

w<u>e</u>rken *itr. V.* work

W<u>e</u>rken *das; ~s* (Schulw.) handicraft

W<u>e</u>rk[s]-: ~angehörige *der/die* factory *or* works employee; **~arzt** *der,* **~ärztin** *die* factory *or* works doctor

werk-, Werk-: ~statt *die; ~statt,* **~stätten** workshop; (Kfz-W.) garage; **~stoff** *der* material; **~tag** *der* working day; workday; **~tags** *Adv.* on weekdays; **~tätig** *Adj.* working; **~tätige** *der/die; adj. Dekl.* worker; **~zeug** *das* (auch fig.) tool; (Gesamtheit von Werkzeugen) tools *pl.*

Werkzeug-: ~kasten *der* toolbox; **~macher** *der,* **~macherin** *die* tool maker

W<u>e</u>rmut *der; ~[e]s, ~s* (a) (Pflanze) wormwood
(b) (Wein) vermouth

wert *Adj.* (geh.) esteemed; (als Anrede) my dear ...; **etw./nichts ~ sein** be worth sth./be worthless

Wert *der; ~[e]s, ~e* value; **im ~[e] von ...:** worth ...; **~ auf etw.** (*Akk.*) **legen** set great store by *or* on sth.

wert·beständig *Adj.* of lasting value *postpos.*

w<u>e</u>rten *tr., itr. V.* judge; assess

wert-, Wert-: ~gegenstand *der* valuable object; **~gegenstände** valuables; **~los** *Adj.* worthless; valueless; **~papier** *das* (Wirtsch.) security; **~sache** *die* valuable item; **~sachen** valuables; **~sendung** *die* (Postw.) registered item; **~stoff** *der* recyclable material

W<u>e</u>rtung *die; ~, ~en* judgement

Wert·urteil *das* value judgement

wert·voll *Adj.* valuable; (moralisch) estimable

W<u>e</u>sen *das; ~s* nature

w<u>e</u>sentlich [1] *Adj.* fundamental (**für** to); **im W~en** essentially
[2] *adv.* (erheblich) considerably; much

wes·h<u>a</u>lb *Adv.* ▶ WARUM

W<u>e</u>spe *die; ~, ~n* wasp

W<u>e</u>spen·nest *das* wasp's nest; **in ein ~stechen** (fig. ugs.) stir up a hornets' nest

w<u>e</u>ssen *Interrogativpron.* (a) *Gen. von* WER whose
(b) *Gen. von* WAS: **~ wird er beschuldigt?** what is he accused of?

W<u>e</u>ssi *der; ~s, ~s* (salopp) West German

West (bes. Seemannsspr., Met.) ▶ WESTEN

west·d<u>eu</u>tsch *Adj.* Western German; (hist.: auf die alte BRD bezogen) West German

W

West·deutschland (das) Western Germany; (hist.: alte BRD) West Germany

Weste die; ~, ~n waistcoat (Brit.); vest (Amer.)

Westen der; ~s west; der ~: the West

Western der; ~[s], ~: western

West·europa (das) Western Europe

Westfalen (das); ~s Westphalia

westfälisch Adj. Westphalian

West·indien (das) the West Indies pl.

westlich ①Adj. (a) western (b) (nach Westen) westerly (c) (aus dem Westen) Western ②adv. westwards ③Präp. mit Gen. [to the] west of

west·wärts Adv. [to the] west

West·wind der west[erly] wind

wes·wegen Adv. ▶ WARUM

Wett·bewerb der; ~[e]s, ~e (a) competition (b) (Wirtsch.) competition no indef. art.

Wette die; ~, ~n bet; eine ~ [mit jmdm.] abschließen make a bet [with sb.]; mit jmdm. um die ~ laufen race sb.

wett·eifern itr. V.; 2. Part. gewetteifert: mit jmdm. [um etw.] ~: compete with sb. [for sth.]

wetten itr. V. bet; mit jmdm. ~: have a bet with sb.; mit jmdm. um etw. ~: bet sb. sth.

Wetter das; ~s weather

wetter-, Wetter-: ~aussichten Pl. weather outlook sing.; ~bedingungen Pl. weather conditions; ~bericht der weather report; (Vorhersage) weather forecast; ~dienst der weather or meteorological service; ~fühlig Adj. sensitive to [changes in] the weather postpos.; ~fühligkeit die; ~~: sensitivity to [changes in] the weather; ~karte die weather chart; weather map; ~lage die weather situation; ~satellit der weather satellite; ~vorhersage die weather forecast; ~warte die weather station

wett-, Wett-: ~kampf der competition; ~lauf der race; ~|machen tr. V. make up for (durch with); ~rennen das race; ~rüsten das; ~~s arms race; ~streit der contest

wetzen tr. V. sharpen; whet

WEZ Abk. = **Westeuropäische Zeit** GMT

Whirlpool /'wə:lpu:l/ der; ~s, ~s whirlpool [bath]

Whiskey /'vɪskɪ/ der; ~s ~s whiskey

Whisky /'vɪskɪ/ der; ~s, ~s whisky

wich 1. u. 3. Pers. Sg. Prät. v. WEICHEN

wichtig Adj. important

Wichtigkeit die; ~: importance

Wicke die; ~, ~n vetch; (im Garten) sweet pea

Wickel der; ~s, ~: compress

wickeln tr. V. wind; (einwickeln) wrap (in + Akk. in); (auswickeln) unwrap (aus + Dat. from); (abwickeln) unwind (von from); ein Kind ~: change a baby's nappy

Widder der; ~s, ~: (a) ram (b) (Astrol.) Aries

wider Präp. mit Akk. (geh.) against

wider-: ~fahren unr. itr. V.; mit sein (geh.) etw. ~fährt jmdm. sth. happens to sb.; ~legen tr. V. etw. ~legen refute sth.; jmdn. ~legen prove sb. wrong

widerlich ①Adj. revolting; repulsive ⟨person, behaviour, etc.⟩; awful ⟨headache⟩ ②adv. revoltingly; ⟨behave⟩ in a repugnant or repulsive manner; awfully ⟨cold, sweet, etc.⟩

Widerlichkeit die; ~, ~en (abwertend) (a) repulsiveness (b) (Äußerung/Handlung) revolting remark/action

wider-, Wider-: ~rede die: keine ~rede! don't argue!; ~ruf der retraction; [bis] auf ~ruf until revoked; ~rufen /-'--/ unr. tr., auch itr. V. retract ⟨statement, claim, confession, etc.⟩; ~setzen /-'--/ refl. V. sich jmdm./einer Sache ~setzen oppose sb./sth.; ~spenstig ①Adj. unruly; stubborn ⟨horse, mule, etc.⟩; ②adv. wilfully; ~|spiegeln, ~spiegeln /-'--/ ①tr. V. mirror; (fig.) reflect; ②refl. V. be mirrored; (fig.) be reflected; ~sprechen /-'--/ unr. itr. V. contradict; ~spruch der (a) (Widerrede, Protest) opposition; protest; (b) (etw. Unvereinbares) contradiction; in ~spruch zu od. mit etw. stehen contradict sth.; be contradictory to sth.; ~sprüchlich Adj. contradictory ⟨news, statements, etc.⟩; inconsistent ⟨behaviour, attitude, etc.⟩

Wider·stand der (a) resistance (gegen to) (b) (Hindernis) opposition

widerstands-, Widerstands-: ~fähig Adj. robust; resistant ⟨material etc.⟩; hardy ⟨animal, plant⟩; ~fähigkeit die robustness; (von Material usw.) resistance; (von Tier, Pflanze) hardiness; ~los Adj., adv. without resistance postpos.

wider-, Wider-: ~stehen /-'--/ unr. itr. V. (a) (nicht nachgeben) [jmdm./einer Sache] ~stehen resist [sb./sth.]; (b) (standhalten) jmdm./einer Sache ~stehen withstand sb./sth.; ~streben /-'--/ itr. V. etw. ~strebt jmdm. sb. dislikes or detests sth.; ~wärtig ①Adj. revolting, repugnant ⟨smell, taste, etc.⟩; offensive ⟨person, behaviour, etc.⟩; ②adv. ⟨behave etc.⟩ in an offensive manner; ~wille der aversion (gegen to); ~willig ①Adj. reluctant; unwilling; ②adv. reluctantly; unwillingly

widmen ①tr. V. (a) dedicate (b) (verwenden für/auf) devote ②refl. V. sich jmdm./einer Sache ~: attend to sb./sth.; (ausschließlich) devote oneself to sb./sth.

W

Widmung *die;* ~, ~en dedication (an + *Akk.* to)

widrig *Adj.* unfavourable; adverse

Widrigkeit *die;* ~, ~en adversity

wie ① *Interrogativadv.* how; ~ viel/viele how much/many; ~ [bitte]? I beg your] pardon?; ~ spät ist es? what time is it? ② *Relativadv.* ~ er es tut the way *or* manner in which he does it ③ *Konj.* (a) *Vergleichspartikel* as; [so] … ~ …: as … as …; ich fühlte mich ~ …: I felt as if I were …; „N" ~ „Nordpol" N for November (b) (zum Beispiel) like; such as (c) (und, sowie) as well as; both

wieder *Adv.* again; alles ist ~ beim Alten everything is back as it was before; ich bin gleich ~ da I'll be right back (coll.); etw. ~ finden find sth. again; etw. ~ gutmachen make sth. good; put sth. right; den Schaden ~ gutmachen pay for the damage; jmdn. ~ wählen re-elect sb.; jmdn. ~ beleben revive *or* resuscitate sb.; jmdn./etw. ~ erkennen recognize sb./sth.

wieder-, Wieder-: ~aufbau /-'--/ *der* reconstruction; rebuilding; der wirtschaftliche ~aufbau economic recovery; ~|bekommen *unr. tr. V.* get back; **~|beleben ▶* WIEDER; ~belebungs·versuch *der* attempt at resuscitation; ~eingliederung *die* reintegration (in + *Akk.* in); **~|erkennen ▶* WIEDER; **~|finden ▶* WIEDER; **~|gabe die* (Bericht) report; (Übersetzung) rendering; (Reproduktion) reproduction; ~|geben *unr. tr. V.* (a) (zurückgeben) give back; (b) (berichten) report; (wiederholen) repeat; ~geburt *die* (christl. Rel., fig. geh.) rebirth

*wieder·gut|machen ▶ WIEDER

wieder|haben *unr. tr. V.* (auch fig.) have back

wieder-: ~her|stellen *tr. V.* (a) re-establish ⟨contact, peace⟩; (b) (reparieren) restore ⟨building⟩; ~holen ① *tr. V.* repeat; (repetieren) revise ⟨lesson, vocabulary, etc.⟩; ② *refl. V.* (a) (wieder dasselbe sagen) repeat oneself; (b) (erneut geschehen) happen again; (c) (wiederkehren) be repeated; recur

wieder|holen *tr. V.* fetch *or* get back

wiederholt ① *Adj.* repeated ② *adv.* repeatedly

Wiederholung *die;* ~, ~en repetition; (eines Fußballspiels usw.) replay; (einer Sendung) repeat; (einer Aufführung) repeat performance; (von Lernstoff) revision

Wiederholungs·täter *der,* **Wiederholungs·täterin** *die* habitual offender

Wieder·hören *das:* [auf *od.* Auf] ~! goodbye! (*at end of telephone call*)

wieder-, Wieder-: ~kehr *die;* ~~ (geh.) return; ~|kehren *itr. V.;* mit sein (geh.) return; ~|kommen *unr. itr. V.;* mit sein (a) (zurückkommen) return; come back; (b)

(noch einmal kommen) come back *or* again; (c) (sich noch einmal ereignen) ⟨opportunity, past⟩ come again; ~|kriegen *tr. V.* (ugs.) get back; ~schauen *das:* [auf] ~schauen! (südd., österr.) goodbye!; ~|sehen *unr. tr. V.* see again; ~sehen *das;* ~s, ~: reunion; [auf] ~sehen! goodbye!; ~um *Adv.* (a) (erneut) again; (b) (andererseits) on the other hand; ~verwendung *die* reuse; ~verwertung *die* recycling; ~wahl *die* re-election; **~|wählen tr. V.* WIEDER

Wiege *die;* ~, ~n (auch fig.) cradle

wiegen¹ *unr. itr., tr. V.* weigh

wiegen² *tr. V.* rock; shake ⟨head⟩

Wiegen·lied *das* lullaby; cradle song

wiehern *itr. V.* whinny; (lauter) neigh

Wien (*das*) ~s Vienna

Wiener¹ *der;* ~s, ~: Viennese

Wiener² *Adj.* Viennese; *s. auch* WÜRSTCHEN

Wienerin *die;* ~, ~nen Viennese

wienerisch *Adj.* Viennese

wies *1. u. 3. Pers. Sg. Prät. v.* WEISEN

Wiese *die;* ~, ~n meadow; (Rasen) lawn

wie·so *Interrogativadv.* why

*wie·viel /od. '--/ ▶ VIEL, WIE, UHR B

wie·viel·mal /od. -'--/ *Interrogativadv.* how many times

wievielt… /od. '-:-/ *Interrogativadj.* der ~e Band? which number volume?; der Wievielte ist heute? what is the date today?

wie·weit *Interrogativadv.* to what extent; how far

wild ① *Adj.* (auch fig.) wild; (wütend) furious ⟨cursing, shouting, etc.⟩; ~es Parken illegal parking; ~er Streik wildcat strike; ~ auf etw./jmdn. sein (ugs.) be mad *or* crazy about sth./sb. (coll.); ~ werden get furious; jmdn. ~ machen infuriate sb. ② *adv.* (a) wildly; wie ~ (ugs.) like mad (coll.) (b) (ordnungswidrig) illegally

Wild *das;* ~[e]s (a) (Tiere, Fleisch) game (b) (einzelnes Tier) [wild] animal

Wild·bret /-brɛt/ *das;* ~s (geh.) game

Wilde *der/die; adj. Dekl.* savage

Wilderei *die;* ~, ~en poaching *no pl., no art.*

Wilderer *der;* ~s, ~, **Wilderin** *die;* ~, ~nen poacher

wild·fremd *Adj.* completely strange

Wild·gans *die* wild goose

Wildheit *die;* ~: wildness

Wild-: ~katze *die* wild cat; ~leder *das* suede

Wildnis *die;* ~, ~se wilderness

Wild-: ~pferd *das* wild horse; ~schwein *das* wild boar; ~wasser *das Pl.* ~~: mountain torrent; ~wechsel *der* game crossing; ~west·film *der* western

will *1. u. 3. Pers. Sg. Präsens v.* WOLLEN

Wille *der;* ~ns will; (Wunsch) wish

willen *Präp. mit Gen.* um jmds./einer Sache ∼: for sb.'s/sth.'s sake

Willen *der;* ∼s ▶ WILLE

willen·los ⓵ *Adj.* will-less
⓶ *adv.* will-lessly

willens *Adj.* ∼ sein, etw. zu tun (geh.) be willing to do sth.

willens-, Willens-: ∼**schwach** *Adj.* weak-willed; ∼**schwäche** *die* weakness of will; ∼**stark** *Adj.* strong-willed; ∼**stärke** *die* strength of will

willentlich ⓵ *Adj.* deliberate
⓶ *adv.* deliberately; on purpose

willig ⓵ *Adj.* willing
⓶ *adv.* willingly

will·kommen *Adj.* welcome; jmdn. ∼ heißen welcome sb.

Will·kür *die;* ∼: arbitrary use of power; (Handlung o. Ä.) arbitrariness

willkürlich ⓵ *Adj.* arbitrary; (vom Willen gesteuert) voluntary ⟨*muscle, movement, etc.*⟩
⓶ *adv.* arbitrarily; (vom Willen gesteuert) voluntarily

wimmeln *itr. V.* von Fischen/Fehlern ∼: be teeming with fish/mistakes

wimmern *itr. V.* whimper

Wimpel *der;* ∼s, ∼: pennant

Wimper *die;* ∼, ∼n [eye]lash

Wimpern·tusche *die* mascara

Wind *der;* ∼[e]s, ∼e wind

Wind·beutel *der* cream puff

Winde *die;* ∼, ∼n winch

Windel *die;* ∼, ∼n nappy (Brit.); diaper (Amer.)

Windel·höschen *das* nappy pants pl.

winden ⓵ *unr. tr. V.* (geh.) make ⟨*wreath, garland*⟩; etw. um etw. ∼: wind sth. around sth.
⓶ *unr. refl. V.* ⟨*plant, tendrils*⟩ wind (um around); ⟨*snake*⟩ coil [itself], wind itself (um around); sich vor Schmerzen ∼: writhe in pain

Windes·eile *die:* in ∼: in next to no time

Wind-: ∼**hose** *die* (Met.) whirlwind; ∼**hund** *der* greyhound

windig *Adj.* windy

Wind-: ∼**kanal** *der* (Technik) wind tunnel; ∼**mühle** *die* windmill; ∼**pocken** *Pl.* chickenpox *sing.*; ∼**schatten** *der* lee; ∼**schutz·scheibe** *die* windscreen (Brit.); windshield (Amer.); ∼**stärke** *die;* ∼stärke 7/9 *usw.* wind force 7/9 *etc.*; ∼**still** *Adj.* windless; still; ∼**stoß** *der* gust of wind; ∼**surfer** *der*, ∼**surferin** *die* windsurfer; ∼**surfing** *das;* ∼∼s windsurfing *no art.*

Windung *die;* ∼, ∼en (a) bend
(b) (spiralförmiger Verlauf) spiral; (einer Spule usw.) winding

Wink *der;* ∼[e]s, ∼e sign; (Hinweis) hint; (Ratschlag) tip; hint

Winkel *der;* ∼s, ∼ (a) (Math.) angle; toter ∼: blind spot
(b) (Ecke; auch fig.) corner

winkelig *Adj.* twisty ⟨*streets*⟩

winken ⓵ *itr. V.* (a) wave; mit etw. ∼: wave sth.
(b) (auffordern heranzukommen) jmdn. ∼: beckon sb. over; einem Taxi ∼: hail a taxi
⓶ *tr. V.* beckon; jmdn. zu sich ∼: beckon sb. over [to one]

winklig *Adj.* ▶ WINKELIG

winseln *itr. V.* ⟨*dog*⟩ whimper

Winter *der;* ∼s, ∼: winter

Winter-: ∼**anfang** *der* beginning of winter; ∼**garten** *der* conservatory

winterlich ⓵ *Adj.* wintry; winter attrib. ⟨*clothing, break*⟩
⓶ *adv.* ∼ kalt cold and wintry

Winter-: ∼**reifen** *der* winter tyre; ∼**schlussverkauf,** *∼**schlußverkauf** *der* winter sale[s *pl.*]; ∼**sport** *der* winter sports *pl.*; ∼**urlaub** *der* winter holiday; ∼**zeit** *die* wintertime

Winzer *der;* ∼s, ∼, **Winzerin** *die;* ∼, ∼nen winegrower

winzig ⓵ *Adj.* tiny
⓶ *adv.* ∼ klein tiny; minute

Winzigkeit *die;* ∼, ∼en (a) tininess; minuteness
(b) (Kleinigkeit) tiny thing; triviality

Wipfel *der;* ∼s, ∼: treetop

Wippe *die;* ∼, ∼n see-saw

wippen *itr. V.* bob up and down; (hin und her) bob about; (auf einer Wippe) see-saw

wir *Personalpron.;* 1. Pers. Pl. Nom. we; s. auch (Gen.) UNSER; (Dat.) UNS; (Akk.) UNS

wirb *Imperativ Sg. v.* WERBEN

Wirbel *der;* ∼s, ∼ (a) (kreisende Bewegung) (im Wasser) whirlpool; (in der Luft) whirlwind; (kleiner) eddy; (von Rauch, beim Tanz) whirl
(b) (Trubel) hurly-burly
(c) (Aufsehen) fuss
(d) (Anat.) vertebra

wirbeln ⓵ *itr. V.* mit sein whirl; ⟨*water, snowflakes*⟩ swirl
⓶ *tr. V.* swirl ⟨*leaves, dust*⟩; whirl ⟨*dancer*⟩

Wirbel-: ∼**säule** *die* spinal column; ∼**sturm** *der* cyclone

wirbt 3. Pers. Sg. Präsens v. WERBEN

wird 3. Pers. Sg. Präsens v. WERDEN

wirf *Imperativ Sg. v.* WERFEN

wirft 3. Pers. Sg. Präsens v. WERFEN

wirken *itr. V.* (a) (eine Wirkung haben) have an effect; gegen etw. ∼: be effective against sth.
(b) (erscheinen) seem; appear

wirklich ⓵ *Adj.* real
⓶ *Adv.* really

Wirklichkeit *die;* ∼, ∼en reality; in ∼: in reality

wirksam ⓵ *Adj.* effective
⓶ *adv.* effectively

Wirksamkeit *die;* ∼: effectiveness

Wirk·stoff *der* active agent

Wirkung *die;* ~, ~en effect (auf + *Akk.* on); mit ~ vom 1. Juli (Amtsspr.) with effect from 1 July

wirkungs-, Wirkungs-: ~**grad** *der* (Technik) efficiency; ~**los** [1] *Adj.* ineffective; [2] *adv.* ineffectively; ~**losigkeit** *die;* ~~: ineffectiveness; ~**voll** [1] *Adj.* effective; [2] *adv.* effectively

wirr *Adj.* (unordentlich) tousled ⟨*hair, beard*⟩; tangled ⟨*ropes, roots*⟩; (unklar, verwirrt) confused

Wirren *Pl.* turmoil *sing.*

Wirrwarr *der;* ~s chaos; (von Stimmen) clamour

Wirsing *der;* ~s, **Wirsing·kohl** *der* savoy [cabbage]

Wirt *der;* ~[e]s, ~e landlord

Wirtin *die;* ~, ~nen landlady

Wirtschaft *die;* ~, ~en (a) economy; (Geschäftsleben) commerce and industry (b) (Gaststätte) public house; pub (Brit. coll.); bar (Amer.) (c) (Haushalt) household (d) (ugs. abwertend: Unordnung) mess; shambles *sing.*

wirtschaften *itr. V.* mit dem Geld gut ~: manage one's money well; mit Verlust/ Gewinn ~: run at a loss/profit

wirtschaftlich [1] *Adj.* (a) economic (b) (finanziell) financial (c) (sparsam, rentabel) economical [2] *adv.; s. Adj.:* economically; financially

Wirtschaftlichkeit *die;* ~: economic viability

Wirtschafts-: ~**hilfe** *die* economic aid *no indef. art.;* ~**krieg** *der* economic war; (Kriegsführung) economic warfare; ~**kriminalität** *die* economic crime *no art.;* ~**krise** *die* economic crisis; ~**lehre** *die* economics *sing.;* ~**minister** *der,* ~**ministerin** *die* minister for economic affairs; ~**politik** *die* economic policy; ~**union** *die* economic union; *s. auch* WÄHRUNGSUNION; ~**wunder** *das* (ugs.) economic miracle

Wirts-: ~**haus** *das* pub (Brit. coll.); ~**leute** *Pl.* landlord and landlady

Wisch *der;* ~[e]s, ~e (salopp) piece *or* bit of paper

wischen *itr., tr. V.* wipe; Staub ~: do the dusting; dust

wispern *itr., tr. V.* whisper

wiss-, *wiß-, Wiss, *Wiß-: ~**begier,** ~**begierde** *die* thirst for knowledge; ~**begierig** *Adj.* eager for knowledge; ⟨*child*⟩ eager to learn

wissen [1] *unr. tr. V.* know; von jmdm./etw. nichts [mehr] ~ wollen want to have nothing [more] to do with sb./sth. [2] *unr. itr. V.* von etw./um etw. ~: know about sth.

Wissen *das;* ~s knowledge; meines/ unseres ~s to my/our knowledge

Wissenschaft *die;* ~, ~en science

Wissenschaftler *der;* ~s ~, **Wissenschaftlerin** *die;* ~, ~nen academic; (Naturwissenschaft) scientist

wissenschaftlich [1] *Adj.* scholarly; (naturwissenschaftlich) scientific [2] *adv.* in a scholarly manner; (naturwissenschaftlich) scientifically

wissens·wert *Adj.* ~ sein be worth knowing

wissentlich [1] *Adj.* deliberate [2] *adv.* knowingly; deliberately

wittern [1] *itr. V.* sniff the air [2] *tr. V.* get wind of; (fig.: ahnen) sense

Witterung *die;* ~, ~en (a) (Wetter) weather *no indef. art;* (b) (Jägerspr.) (Geruchssinn) sense of smell; (Geruch) scent

Witwe *die;* ~, ~n widow; ~ werden be widowed

Witwen·rente *die* widow's pension

Witwer *der;* ~s, ~: widower; ~ werden be widowed

Witz *der;* ~es, ~e joke

Witz-: ~**blatt** *das* humorous magazine; ~**bold** *der;* ~~es, ~~e joker

Witzelei *die;* ~, ~en (a) teasing (b) (witzelnde Bemerkung) joke

witzeln *itr. V.* joke (über + *Akk.* about)

Witz·figur *die* (a) (in Witzen) joke character (b) (ugs. abwertend) figure of fun

witzig [1] *Adj.* funny [2] *adv.* amusingly

witz·los *Adj.* (a) dull (b) (ugs.: sinnlos) pointless

wo [1] *Adv.* where [2] *Konj.* (a) (da, weil) seeing that (b) (obwohl) although; when

wo·anders *Adv.* somewhere else

wo·bei *Adv.* (a) (interrogativ) ~ hast du sie ertappt? what did you catch her doing? (b) (relativisch) er gab sechs Schüsse ab, ~ einer der Täter getötet wurde he fired six shots – one of the criminals was killed

Woche *die;* ~, ~n week; in dieser/der nächsten/der letzten ~: this/next/last week; heute in/vor einer ~: a week today/a week ago today

wochen-, Wochen-: ~**bett** *das:* im ~bett liegen be lying in; ~**ende** *das* weekend; ~**lang** [1] *Adj.* lasting weeks *postpos;* [2] *adv.* for weeks [on end]; ~**stunde** *die* (Schulw.) period per week; ~**tag** *der* weekday *(including Saturday)*; ~**tags** *Adv.* on weekdays [and Saturdays]

wöchentlich *Adj., adv.* weekly

Wochen·zeitung *die* weekly newspaper

-wöchig (a) (... Wochen alt) ... -week-old (b) (... Wochen dauernd) ... week's/weeks'; ...-week

Wöchnerin *die;* ~, ~nen woman who has just given birth

Wodka *der;* ~s, ~s vodka

wo·durch *Adv.* **(a)** (interrogativ) how **(b)** (relativisch) as a result of which

wo·für *Adv.* **(a)** (interrogativ) for what **(b)** (relativisch) for which

wog *1. u. 3. Pers. Sg. Prät. v.* WIEGEN

Woge *die;* ~, ~n wave

wo·gegen [1] *Adv.* **(a)** (interrogativ) against what; what ... against **(b)** (relativisch) against which; which ... against [2] *Konj.* whereas

wogen *itr. V.* (geh.) ⟨*sea*⟩ surge; (fig.) ⟨*corn*⟩ wave

wo·her *Adv.* **(a)** (interrogativ) where ... from; ~ weißt du das? how do you know that? **(b)** (relativisch) where ... from

wo·hin *Adv.* **(a)** (interrogativ) where [... to] **(b)** (relativisch) where

wo·hingegen *Konj.* whereas

wohl [1] *Adv.* **(a)** well; jmdm. ist nicht ~, jmd. fühlt sich nicht ~: sb. does not feel well **(b)** (behaglich) at ease; happy; leb ~!/leben Sie ~! farewell! **(c)** (durchaus) well **(d)** (ungefähr) about **(e)** etw. tut jmdm. ~: sth. does sb. good [2] *Partikel* probably; ~ kaum hardly

Wohl *das;* ~[e]s welfare; auf jmds. ~ trinken drink sb.'s health; zum ~! cheers!

wohl-, Wohl-: ~**auf** /-'-/ *Adj.* (geh.) ~auf sein be well; ~**befinden** *das* well-being; ~**behagen** *das* sense of well-being; ~**behalten** *Adj.* safe and well ⟨*person*⟩; undamaged ⟨*thing*⟩; ~**fahrts·staat** *der* welfare state; ~**gefallen** *das;* ~~s pleasure; ~**gemerkt** *Adv.* please note; ~**habend** *Adj.* prosperous; ~**habenheit** *die;* ~~: prosperity

wohlig [1] *Adj.* pleasant; agreeable [2] *adv.* ⟨*sigh, purr, etc.*⟩ with pleasure

wohl-, Wohl-: ~**klang** *der* (geh.) melodious sound; ~**schmeckend** *Adj.* (geh.) delicious; ~**stand** *der* prosperity; ~**stands·gesellschaft** *die* affluent society; ~**tat** *die* **(a)** (gute Tat) good deed; (Gefallen) favour; **(b)** (*Genuss*) blissful relief; ~**tätig** *Adj.* charitable; ~**tuend** *Adj.* agreeable; ***~|**tun** ▶ WOHL 1 E; ~**verdient** *Adj.* well-earned; ~**weislich** *Adv.* deliberately; ~**wollen** *das;* ~~s goodwill; ~**wollend** [1] *Adj.* benevolent; favourable ⟨*judgement, opinion*⟩; [2] *adv.* benevolently; ⟨*judge, consider*⟩ favourably

Wohn-: ~**anhänger** *der* caravan; trailer (Amer.); ~**block** *der; Pl.* ~~s, *od.* ~blöcke residential block

wohnen *itr. V.* live; (kurzfristig) stay

wohn-, Wohn-: ~**gemeinschaft** *die* group sharing a flat (Brit.) *or* (Amer.) apartment/house; ~**haft** *Adj.* resident (in + *Dat.* in); ~**heim** *das* (für Alte, Behinderte) home; (für Obdachlose, Lehrlinge) hostel; (für Studenten) hall of residence

wohnlich *Adj.* homely

Wohn-: ~**mobil** *das;* ~~s, ~~e motor home; ~**ort** *der* place of residence; ~**siedlung** *die* residential estate; (mit gleichartigen Häusern) housing estate; ~**sitz** *der* place of residence; ohne festen ~sitz of no fixed abode

Wohnung *die;* ~, ~en **(a)** flat (Brit.); apartment (Amer.) **(b)** (Unterkunft) lodging

Wohnungs-: ~**not** *die* housing crisis; serious housing shortage; ~**schlüssel** *der* key to the flat (Brit.) *or* (Amer.) apartment; ~**suche** *die* search for a flat (Brit.) *or* (Amer.) apartment; auf ~suche sein be flat-hunting; ~**tür** *die* door of the flat (Brit.) *or* (Amer.) apartment; ~**verlust** *der* loss of one's home

Wohn-: ~**verhältnisse** *Pl.* living conditions; ~**wagen** *der* caravan; trailer (Amer.); ~**zimmer** *das* living room

wölben [1] *tr. V.* curve; vault, arch ⟨*roof, ceiling*⟩ [2] *refl. V.* curve; ⟨*bridge, ceiling*⟩ arch

Wölbung *die;* ~, ~en curve; (einer Decke) arch; vault

Wolf *der;* ~[e]s, **Wölfe** wolf

Wolke *die;* ~, ~n cloud

wolken-, Wolken-: ~**bruch** *der* cloudburst; ~**bruch-artig** *Adj.* torrential; ~**decke** *die* [unbroken] cloud *no indef. art.;* die ~decke riss auf the clouds broke; ~**kratzer** *der* skyscraper; ~**los** *Adj.* cloudless

wolkig *Adj.* cloudy

Wolle *die;* ~, ~n wool

wollen¹ *Adj.* woollen

wollen² [1] *unr. Modalverb; 2. Part.* wollen: etw. tun ~ (den Wunsch haben, etw. zu tun) want to do sth.; (die Absicht haben, etw. zu tun) be going to do sth.; die Wunde will nicht heilen the wound [just] won't heal [2] *unr. itr. V.* du musst nur ~, dann ... you only have to want to enough, then ... ganz wie du willst just as you like; ich will nach Hause (ugs.) I want to go home; zu wem ~ Sie? whom do you want to see? [3] *unr. tr. V.* want; das habe ich nicht gewollt I never meant that to happen

wo·mit *Adv.* **(a)** (interrogativ) ~ schreibst du? what do you write with? **(b)** (relativisch) ~ du schreibst which *or* that you write with; (more formal) with which you write

wo·möglich *Adv.* possibly

wo·nach *Adv.* **(a)** (interrogativ) after what; what ... after; ~ suchst du? what are you looking for?

W

(b) (relativisch) after which; which ... after

Wọnne *die;* ∼, ∼**n** (geh.) bliss *no pl.;* ecstasy; (etw., was Freude macht) joy

wọnnig *Adj.* sweet

worạn *Adv.* **(a)** (interrogativ) ∼ **denkst du?** what are you thinking of? **(b)** (relativisch) **nichts,** ∼ **man sich anlehnen könnte** nothing one could lean against

worạuf (a) (interrogativ) ∼ **wartest du?** what are you waiting for? **(b)** (relativisch) **etwas,** ∼ **man sich verlassen kann** something one can rely on **(c)** (relativisch: woraufhin) whereupon

worạus *Adv.* **(a)** (interrogativ) ∼ **schließt du das?** what do you infer that from? **(b)** (relativisch) **es gab nichts,** ∼ **wir den Wein hätten trinken können** there was nothing for us to drink the wine out of

wọrden 2. *Part. v.* WERDEN 2

worịn *Adv.* **(a)** (interrogativ) in what; what ... in **(b)** (relativisch) in which; which ... in

Workaholic /wə:kə'hɔlɪk/ *der;* ∼**s,** ∼**s:** workaholic

Wọrt *das;* ∼[e]s, Wörter/∼e **(a)** *Pl.* Wörter, (auch:) ∼e word; ∼ **für** ∼: word for word; **1 000** € (in ∼**en: tausend)** 1,000 € (in words: one thousand) **(b)** *Pl.* ∼e (Äußerung) word; **mir fehlen die** ∼e I'm lost for words; **Dr. Meyer hat das** ∼: it's Dr Meyer's turn to speak **(c)** *Pl.* ∼e (Spruch) saying; (Zitat) quotation **(d)** *Pl.* ∼e (geh.: Text) words *pl.;* **in** ∼ **und Bild** in words and pictures **(e)** *Pl.* ∼e (Versprechen) word; [**sein**] ∼ **halten** keep one's word

Wọrt·bruch *der* breaking one's word *no art.*

wọrt·brüchig *Adj.* ∼ **werden** break one's word

Wörter·buch *das* dictionary

wọrt-, Wọrt-: ∼**getreu** *Adj.* word-for-word; ∼**karg** ① *Adj.* taciturn ⟨person⟩; ② *adv.* taciturnly; ∼**kargheit** *die* taciturnity; ∼**laut** *der* wording; **im [vollen]** ∼**laut** verbatim

wörtlich ① *Adj.* **(a)** word-for-word **(b)** (der eigentlichen Bedeutung entsprechend) literal ② *adv.: s. Adj.:* word for word; literally

wọrt-, Wọrt-: ∼**los** ① *Adj.* silent; wordless; ② *adv.* without saying a word; ∼**meldung** *die:* **gibt es noch** ∼**meldungen?** does anyone else wish to speak?; ∼**spiel** *das* play on words; pun; ∼**wechsel** *der* exchange of words; ∼**wörtlich** *Adj.* word-for-word

worüber *Adv.* **(a)** (interrogativ) over what ...; what ... over **(b)** (relativisch) over which; which ... over

worụm *Adv.* **(a)** (interrogativ) around what; what ... around

(b) (relativisch) around which; which ... around

worụnter *Adv.* **(a)** (interrogativ) under what; what ... under **(b)** (relativisch) under which; which ... under

wo·vọn *Adv.* **(a)** (interrogativ) from where; where ... from **(b)** (relativisch) from which; which ... from

wo·vọr *Adv.* **(a)** (interrogativ) in front of what; what ... in front of **(b)** (relativisch) in front of which; which ... in front of

wo·zụ *Adv.* **(a)** (interrogativ) to what; what ... to; (wofür) what ... for **(b)** (relativisch) ∼ **du dich auch entschließt** whatever you decide on

Wrạck *das;* ∼[e]s, ∼s *od.* ∼e wreck

wrạng 1. *und* 3. *Pers. Sg. Prät. v.* WRINGEN

wrịngen *unr. tr. V.* (bes. nordd.) wring

Wụcher *der;* ∼s profiteering; (beim Verleihen von Geld) usury

wụchern *itr. V.* **(a)** auch mit sein ⟨plants, weeds, etc.⟩ proliferate, run wild **(b)** (Wucher treiben) [mit etw.] ∼: profiteer [on sth.]; (beim Verleihen von Geld) lend [sth.] at extortionate interest rates

Wụcherung *die;* ∼, ∼**en** growth

wụchs 1. *u.* 3. *Pers. Sg. Prät. v.* WACHSEN

Wụchs *der;* ∼es (Gestalt) stature

Wụcht *die;* ∼: force; (von Schlägen) power; weight

wụchtig ① *Adj.* **(a)** (voller Wucht) powerful; mighty **(b)** (schwer, massig) massive ② *adv.* powerfully

wühlen ① *itr. V.* **(a)** dig; (mit der Schnauze, dem Schnabel) root (nach for); ⟨mole⟩ tunnel, burrow **(b)** (ugs.: suchen) rummage [around] (nach for) ② *tr. V.* burrow; tunnel out ⟨burrow⟩

wụlstig *Adj.* bulging

wụnd *Adj.* sore; **sich** ∼ **liegen** get bed sores

Wụnde *die;* ∼, ∼**n** wound

wụnder, Wụnder¹ (ugs.): **er denkt, er sei** ∼ **wer** he thinks he's really something; **sie bildet sich** ∼ **was darauf ein** she's terribly pleased with herself about it (coll.)

Wụnder² *das;* ∼**s,** ∼ **(a)** miracle; ∼ **wirken** (fig. ugs.) work wonders; **ein/kein** ∼ **sein** (ugs.) be a/no wonder **(b)** (etw. Erstaunliches) wonder

wụnderbar ① *Adj.* **(a)** miraculous **(b)** (sehr schön, herrlich) wonderful; marvellous ② *adv.* **(a)** (sehr schön, herrlich) wonderfully; marvellously **(b)** (ugs.: sehr) wonderfully

Wụnder-: ∼**kerze** *die* sparkler; ∼**kind** *das* child prodigy

wụnderlich ① *Adj.* strange; odd ② *adv.* strangely; oddly

w

wundern [1] *tr. V.* surprise; **mich wundert** *od.* **es wundert mich, dass …**: I'm surprised that … [2] *refl. V.* **sich über jmdn./etw. ~**: be surprised at sb./sth

wunder-: ~schön [1] *Adj.* simply beautiful; (herrlich) simply wonderful; [2] *adv.* quite beautifully; **~voll** [1] *Adj.* wonderful; [2] *adv.* wonderfully

*wund|liegen ▸ WUND

Wund·starr·krampf *der* (Med.) tetanus

Wunsch *der;* **~[e]s, Wünsche** wish (**nach** to have); (Sehnen) desire (**nach** for); **haben Sie [sonst] noch einen ~?** will there be anything else?; **auf jmds. ~**: at sb.'s wish; **mit den besten/herzlichsten Wünschen** with best/warmest wishes

wünschbar *Adj.* (bes. schweiz.) desirable

Wünschel-: ~rute *die* divining rod; **~ruten·gänger** *der;* **~~s, ~~, ~ruten·gängerin** *die;* **~~, ~~nen** diviner

wünschen *tr. V.* (a) **sich** (*Dat.*) **etw. ~**: want sth.; (im Stillen) wish for sth. (b) (in formelhaften Wünschen) wish; **jmdm. alles Gute/frohe Ostern ~**: wish sb. all the best/a happy Easter (c) *auch itr. V.* (begehren) want; **was ~ Sie?, Sie ~?** (im Lokal) what would you like?; (in einem Geschäft) can I help you?

Wunsch-: ~kind *das* wanted child; **~konzert** *das* request concert; (im Rundfunk) request programme; **~zettel** *der* (zum Geburtstag *usw.*) list of presents one would like

wurde *1. u. 3. Pers. Sg. Prät. v.* WERDEN

würde *1. u. 3. Pers. Sg. Konjunktiv II v.* WERDEN

Würde *die;* **~**: dignity

würde·los [1] *Adj.* undignified; (schimpflich) disgraceful [2] *adv.* in an undignified way; (schimpflich) disgracefully

Würdelosigkeit *die;* **~** ▸ WÜRDELOS: lack of dignity; disgracefulness

Würden·träger *der,* **Würden·trägerin** *die* dignitary

würde·voll [1] *Adj.* dignified [2] *adv.* with dignity

würdig [1] *Adj.* (a) dignified (b) (wert) worthy [2] *adv.* (a) with dignity (b) (angemessen) worthily

würdigen *tr. V.* (a) (anerkennen, beachten) recognize; (schätzen) appreciate; (lobend hervorheben) acknowledge (b) (für wert halten) **jmdn. keines Blickes/keiner Antwort ~**: not deign to look at/answer sb.

Wurf *der;* **~[e]s, Würfe (a)** throw; (beim Kegeln) bowl

(b) *o. Pl.* (das Werfen) throwing/pitching/bowling **(c)** (Zool.) litter

Würfel *der;* **~s, ~**: cube; (Spielwürfel) dice; die (formal)

Würfel·becher *der* dice cup

würfeln [1] *itr. V.* throw the dice; **um etw. ~**: play dice for sth. [2] *tr. V.* (a) throw (b) (in Würfel schneiden) dice

Würfel-: ~spiel *das* dice; (Brettspiel) dice game; **~zucker** *der* cube sugar

Wurf·geschoss, *Wurf·geschoß *das* missile

würgen [1] *tr. V.* strangle; throttle [2] *itr. V.* (Brechreiz haben) retch

Wurm *der;* **~[e]s, Würmer** worm; (Made) maggot

wurmig *Adj.,* **wurm·stichig** *Adj.* worm-eaten; (madig) maggoty

Wurst *die;* **~, Würste** sausage; **es geht um die ~** (fig. ugs.) the crunch has come; **jmdm. ist jmd./etw. ~** (ugs.) sb. doesn't care about sb./sth.

Wurst·bude *die* ▸ WÜRSTCHENBUDE

Würstchen *das;* **~s, ~ (a)** [small] sausage; **Frankfurter/Wiener ~**: frankfurter/wienerwurst **(b)** (fig. ugs.) nobody; (hilfloser Mensch) poor soul

Würstchen·bude *die* sausage stand

Wurstelei *die;* **~, ~en** (ugs. abwertend) pottering about *no pl.*

wursteln *itr. V.* (ugs.) potter

Wurst·salat *der:* piquant salad with pieces of sausage, onion rings, boiled eggs and/or cheese

Würze *die;* **~, ~n** spice; seasoning

Wurzel *die;* **~, ~n** (auch fig.) root

wurzeln *itr. V.* take root

würzen *tr. V.* season

würzig *Adj.* tasty; full-flavoured ‹beer, wine›; aromatic ‹fragrance›; tangy ‹air›

Würzigkeit *die;* **~** ▸ WÜRZIG 1: tastiness; full flavour; aromatic fragrance; tanginess

wusch *1. u. 3. Pers. Sg. Prät. v.* WASCHEN

wusste, *wußte *1. und 3. Pers. Sg. Prät. v.* WISSEN

wüsste, *wüßte *1. und 3. Pers. Sg. Konjunktiv II v.* WISSEN

wüst [1] *Adj.* (a) (öde) desolate **(b)** (unordentlich) chaotic **(c)** (ungezügelt) wild; (unanständig) rude [2] *adv.* (a) (unordentlich) chaotically **(b)** (ungezügelt) wildly

Wust *der;* **~[e]s** (abwertend) jumble; (fig.) welter; **ein ~ von Daten/Vorschriften** a mass of data/regulations

Wüste *die;* **~, ~n** desert

Wut *die;* **~**: rage; fury

*alte Schreibung - vgl. Hinweis auf S. xiv

wüten *itr. V.* (auch fig.) rage; (zerstören) wreak havoc

wütend ① *Adj.* furious; angry ⟨*voice, mob*⟩ ② *adv.* furiously; in a fury

x¹, X /ɪks/ *das;* ~, ~: x/X
x² *unbest. Zahlwort* (ugs.) umpteen (coll.)
x-Achse *die* (Math.) x-axis
X-Beine *Pl.* knock knees
x-beinig *Adj.* knock-kneed
x-beliebig *Adj.* (ugs.) [irgend]ein ~er/ [irgend]eine ~e/[irgend]ein ~es any old (coll. attrib.); jeder ~e Ort any old place (coll.)

X-Chromosom *das* (Biol.) X-chromosome
x-fach ① *Vervielfältigungsz.* die ~e Menge (Math.) x times the amount; (ugs.) umpteen times the amount (coll.)
② *adv.* (ugs.) ~ erprobt sein ⟨*tested etc.*⟩ umpteen times (coll.)
x-mal *Adv.* (ugs.) umpteen times (coll.)
x-t... *Ordinalz.* (ugs.) umpteenth (coll.)
Xylophon *das;* ~s, ~e xylophone

y, Y /ˈʏpsilɔn/ *das;* ~, ~: y/Y
y-Achse *die* (Math.) y-axis
Yacht ▶ JACHT
Y-Chromosom *das* (Biol.) Y-chromosome

Yoga ▶ JOGA
Ypsilon *das;* ~[s], ~s y, Y; (im griechischen Alphabet) upsilon

z, Z /tsɛt/ *das;* ~, ~: z/Z
Zack: auf ~ sein (ugs.: tüchtig sein) be on the ball (coll.) *or* one's toes; jmdn. auf ~ bringen (ugs.) knock sb. into shape (coll.)
Zacke *die;* ~, ~n point; peak; (einer Säge, eines Kamms) tooth; (einer Gabel, Harke) prong
Zacken *der;* ~s: ▶ ZACKE
zackig ① *Adj.* (a) (gezackt) jagged; (mit kleinen, regelmäßigen Zacken) serrated
(b) (schneidig) dashing; smart; rousing ⟨*music*⟩; brisk ⟨*orders, tempo*⟩; lively ⟨*organization*⟩
② *adv.* (a) (gezackt) jaggedly
(b) (schneidig) smartly; ⟨*play music*⟩ rousingly
zaghaft ① *Adj.* timid; (zögernd) hesitant
② *adv.* timidly; (zögernd) hesitantly
Zaghaftigkeit *die;* ~: timidity; (Zögern) hesitancy
zäh ① *Adj.* (a) tough; heavy ⟨*dough, soil*⟩; (dickflüssig) glutinous; viscous ⟨*oil*⟩

(b) (widerstandsfähig) tough ⟨*person*⟩
(c) (beharrlich) tenacious; tough ⟨*negotiations*⟩; dogged ⟨*resistance*⟩
② *adv.* (beharrlich) tenaciously; ⟨*resist*⟩ doggedly

Zähheit *die;* ~: (a) (Festigkeit) toughness; (des Teigs, Bodens) heaviness; (Dickflüssigkeit) glutinousness; (von Öl) viscosity
(b) (Widerstandsfähigkeit) toughness
(c) (Beharrlichkeit) tenacity; (des Widerstands) doggedness
Zähigkeit *die;* ~ (a) (Widerstandsfähigkeit) toughness
(b) (Beharrlichkeit) tenacity; mit ~: tenaciously
Zahl *die;* ~, ~en number; (Ziffer) numeral; (Zahlenangabe, Geldmenge) figure; in den roten/ schwarzen ~en in the red/black
zahlbar *Adj.* (Kaufmannsspr.) payable
zahlen ① *tr. V.* pay ⟨an + *Akk.* to⟩ ···✦

2 *itr. V.* pay; [ich möchte] bitte ~ (im Lokal) [can I have] the bill, please!

zählen 1 *itr. V.* (a) count; **zu einer Gruppe** *usw.* ~: be one of *or* belong to a group *etc.*; (b) **auf jmdn./etw.** ~: count on sb./sth

2 *tr. V.* count; **jmdn. zu seinen Freunden** ~: count sb. among one's friends

zahl-, Zahl-: ~**karte** *die* (Postw.) paying-in slip; ~**los** *Adj.* countless; ~**reich** *Adj.* numerous

Zahlung *die;* ~, ~**en** payment

Zählung *die;* ~, ~**en** counting; **eine** ~: a count

zahlungs-, Zahlungs-: ~**bilanz** *die* (Wirtsch.) balance of payments; ~**fähig** *Adj.* solvent; ~**fähigkeit** *die* solvency; ~**mittel** *das* means of payment; ~**unfähig** *Adj.* insolvent; ~**unfähigkeit** *die* insolvency

Zahl·wort *das; Pl.* Z**ahl·wörter** (Sprachw.) numeral

zahm 1 *Adj.* tame
2 *adv.* tamely

zähmen *tr. V.* (auch fig.) tame

Zahn *der;* ~[e]s, Zähne tooth; (Reißzahn) fang; (an einer Briefmarke usw.) serration

Zahn-: ~**arzt** *der,* ~**ärztin** *die* dentist; (mit chirurgischer Ausbildung) dental surgeon; ~**bürste** *die* toothbrush

zahnen *itr. V.* ⟨*baby*⟩ be teething

zahn-, Zahn-: ~**ersatz** *der* denture; ~**fleisch** *das* gum; (als Ganzes) gums *pl.;* ~**fleisch·bluten** *das;* ~~s bleeding gums *pl.;* ~**los** *Adj.* toothless; ~**lücke** *die* gap in one's teeth; ~**pasta** *die;* ~~, ~**pasten** toothpaste; ~**pflege** *die* dental care; ~**prothese** *die* dentures *pl.;* [set *sing.* of] false teeth *pl.;* ~**rad** *das* gearwheel; (für Ketten) sprocket; ~**schmerzen** *Pl.* toothache *sing.;* ~**seide** *die* dental floss; ~**spange** *die* [tooth] brace; ~**stein** *der* tartar; ~**stocher** *der;* ~~s, ~~: toothpick; ~**weh** *das* (ugs.) toothache

Zange *die;* ~, ~**n** (a) (Werkzeug) pliers *pl.;* (Eiswürfel-, Zuckerzange) tongs *pl.;* (Geburtszange) forceps *pl.;* (Kneifzange) pincers *pl.;* **eine** ~: a pair of pliers/tongs/forceps/pincers (b) (bei Tieren) pincer

Zank *der;* ~[e]s squabble; row

zanken *refl.* (*auch itr.*) *V.* squabble, bicker (um *od.* über + *Akk.* over)

zänkisch *Adj.* quarrelsome

Zäpfchen *das;* ~s, ~: suppository

zapfen *tr. V.* tap, draw ⟨*beer, wine*⟩

Zapfen *der;* ~s, ~ (a) (Bot.) cone (b) (Stöpsel) bung

Zapf·säule *die* petrol pump (Brit.); gasoline pump (Amer.)

zappeln *itr. V.* wriggle; ⟨*child*⟩ fidget

zappen /'zɛpn̩/ *itr. V.* (ugs.) zap (coll.)

Zar *der;* ~en, ~en (hist.) Tsar

Zarin *die;* ~, ~**nen** (hist.) Tsarina

zart 1 *Adj.* (auch fig.) delicate; soft ⟨*skin*⟩; tender ⟨*bud, shoot; meat, vegetables*⟩; fine ⟨*biscuits*⟩; gentle ⟨*kiss, touch*⟩; soft ⟨*pastel colours*⟩
2 *adv.* (empfindlich) delicately; ⟨*kiss, touch*⟩ gently

Zartheit *die;* ~: delicacy; (der Haut) softness; (von Fleisch, Gemüse) tenderness; (eines Kusses, einer Berührung) gentleness

zärtlich 1 *Adj.* tender
2 *adv.* tenderly

Zärtlichkeit *die;* ~, ~**en** (a) (Zuneigung) tenderness; affection (b) (Liebkosung) caress

Zauber *der;* ~s, ~ (a) (auch fig.) magic; (Bann) [magic] spell (b) (ugs. abwertend: Aufheben) fuss

Zauberei *die;* ~, ~**en** (a) (das Zaubern) magic (b) (Zaubertrick) magic trick

Zauberer *der;* ~s, ~: magician

zauber·haft 1 *Adj.* enchanting
2 *adv.* enchantingly

Zauberin *die;* ~, ~**nen** (a) sorceress (b) (Zauberkünstlerin) conjurer

Zauber·künstler *der,* **Zauberkünstlerin** *die* conjurer; magician

zaubern 1 *itr. V.* (a) do magic (b) (Zaubertricks ausführen) do conjuring tricks
2 *tr. V.* (auch fig.) conjure

zaudern *itr. V.* (geh.) delay

Zaum *der;* ~[e]s, Zäume bridle

zäumen *tr. V.* bridle

Zaum·zeug *das* bridle

Zaun *der;* ~[e]s, Zäune fence

Zaun·könig *der* wren

z. B. *Abk.* = **zum Beispiel** e.g.

ZDF *das;* ~: *Abk.* = **Zweites Deutsches Fernsehen** Second German Television Channel

Zebra *das;* ~s, ~s zebra

Zebra·streifen *der* zebra crossing (Brit.); pedestrian crossing

Zeche *die;* ~, ~**n** (a) (Rechnung) bill (Brit.); check (Amer.) (b) (Bergwerk) pit; mine

zechen *itr. V.* (veralt., scherzh.) tipple

Zecke *die;* ~, ~**n** (Zool.) tick

Zeder *die;* ~, ~**n** cedar

Zedern·holz *das* cedarwood

Zeh *der;* ~s, ~en, **Zehe** *die;* ~, ~**n** (a) toe (b) (Knoblauchzehe) clove

Zehen·spitze *die:* auf ~**n** on tiptoe

zehn *Kardinalz.* ten

Zehn *die;* ~, ~**en** ten

Zehner *der;* ~s, ~ (a) (ugs.: Geldschein, Münze) ten (b) (ugs.: Autobus) number ten (c) (Math.) ten

---

zehn·fach *Vervielfältigungsz.* tenfold
Zehnfache *das; adj. Dekl.* **das ∼:** ten times as much
zehn-, Zehn-: ∼**kampf** *der* (Sport) decathlon; ∼**mal** *Adv.* ten times; ∼**mark·schein** *der* ten-mark note; ∼**pfennig·[brief]marke** *die* ten-pfennig stamp; ∼**pfennig·stück** *das* ten-pfennig piece
zehnt... *Ordinalz.* tenth;
zehn·tausend *Kardinalz.* ten thousand
zehntel *Bruchz.* tenth
Zehntel *das* (schweiz. meist *der*); ∼**s, ∼:** tenth
zehntens *Adv.* tenthly
zehren *itr. V.* **von etw. ∼:** live on *or* off sth.
Zeichen *das; ∼s, ∼:* sign; (Markierung) mark; (Chemie, Math., auf Landkarten usw.) symbol; (Schrift∼) character; **jmdm. ein ∼ geben** signal to sb.
Zeichen-: ∼**setzung** *die;* ∼∼: punctuation; ∼**sprache** *die* sign language
zeichnen [1] *tr. V.* draw; (fig.) portray ⟨*character*⟩
  [2] *itr. V.* draw
Zeichner *der; ∼s, ∼,* **Zeichnerin** *die; ∼, ∼nen* graphic artist; (Technik) draughtsman/-woman
Zeichnung *die; ∼, ∼en* drawing
zeichnungs·berechtigt *Adj.* with signatory powers *postpos.;* ∼ **sein** have signatory powers
Zeige·finger *der* index finger; forefinger
zeigen [1] *itr. V.* point
  [2] *tr. V.* show
  [3] *refl. V.* (a) (sich sehen lassen) appear
  (b) (sich erweisen) prove to be; **es wird sich ∼, ...:** time will tell ...
Zeiger *der; ∼s, ∼:* pointer; (Uhrzeiger) hand
Zeile *die; ∼, ∼n* line; (Reihe) row
zeit *Präp. mit Gen.* ∼ **meines** *usw.*/**unseres** *usw.* **Lebens** all my *etc.* life/our *etc.* lives
Zeit *die; ∼, ∼en* (a) time *no art.;* **mit der ∼:** with *or* in time; (allmählich) gradually; **eine ∼ lang** for a while
  (b) (Zeitpunkt) time; **alles zu seiner ∼:** all in good time; *****zur ∼:** at the moment
  (c) (Zeit-, Lebensabschnitt) time; period; (Geschichtsabschnitt) age; period
  (d) (Sprachw.) tense
zeit-, Zeit-: ∼**alter** *das* age; era; ∼**arbeit** *die* (Wirtsch.) temporary work; work as a temp (coll.); ∼**druck** *der* pressure of time; **unter ∼druck** under pressure; **unter ∼druck stehen** be pressed for time; ∼**geist** *der* spirit of the age; ∼**gemäß** *Adj.* (modern) up-to-date; (aktuell) topical ⟨*theme*⟩; contemporary ⟨*views*⟩; ∼**genosse** *der,* ∼**genossin** *die* contemporary; ∼**genössisch** *Adj.* contemporary; ∼**geschehen** *das:* **das** [**aktuelle**] ∼**geschehen** current events *pl.;* ∼**geschichte** *die* contemporary history

zeitig *Adj., adv.* early
zeit-, Zeit-: ∼**karte** *die* (Verkehrsw.) season ticket; *****∼lang** ▶ ZEIT A; ∼**lebens** *Adv.* all my/his/her *etc.* life
zeitlich [1] *Adj.* ⟨*length, interval*⟩ in time; chronological ⟨*order, sequence*⟩
  [2] *adv.* with regard to time
zeit-, Zeit-: ∼**los** [1] *Adj.* timeless; classic ⟨*fashion, shape*⟩; [2] *adv.* timelessly; ∼**lupe** *die* slow motion; ∼**mangel** *der* lack of time; ∼**punkt** *der* moment; ∼**raubend** *Adj.* time-consuming; ∼**raum** *der* period; ∼**schrift** *die* magazine; (bes. wissenschaftlich) journal; periodical; ∼**spanne** *die* period
Zeitung *die; ∼, ∼en* [news]paper
Zeitungs-: ∼**ausschnitt** *der* newspaper cutting; ∼**bericht** *der* newspaper report; ∼**notiz** *die* newspaper item
zeit-, Zeit-: ∼**unterschied** *der* time difference; ∼**verschwendung** *die* waste of time; ∼**vertreib** *der;* ∼∼[e]s, ∼∼e pastime; **zum ∼vertreib** to pass the time; ∼**weilig** [1] *Adj.* temporary; [2] *adv.* temporarily; ∼**weise** *Adv.* (gelegentlich) occasionally; (von Zeit zu Zeit) from time to time; ∼**wort** *das; Pl.* ∼wörter (Sprachw.) verb; ∼**zünder** *der* time fuse
Zelle *die; ∼, ∼n* cell
Zelluloid /tsɛlu'lɔy:t/ *das;* ∼[e]s celluloid
Zelt *das;* ∼[e]s, ∼e tent; (Festzelt) marquee; (Zirkuszelt) big top
zelten *itr. V.* camp
Zelt-: ∼**lager** *das* camp; ∼**plane** *die* tarpaulin
Zement *der;* ∼[e]s, ∼e cement
Zensur *die; ∼, ∼en* (a) (Schulw.: Note) mark; grade (Amer.)
  (b) (Kontrolle) censorship
  (c) (Behörde) censors *pl.*
Zenti-: ∼**meter** *der, auch: das* centimetre; ∼**meter·maß** *das* [centimetre] measuring tape
Zentner *der; ∼s, ∼* (a) metric hundredweight
  (b) (österr., schweiz.) ▶ DOPPELZENTNER
zentral [1] *Adj.* central
  [2] *adv.* centrally
Zentral·bank *die; Pl.* ∼en (Finanzw.) central bank
Zentrale *die; ∼, ∼n* (a) (zentrale Stelle) head *or* central office; (der Polizei, einer Partei) headquarters *sing. or pl.;* (Funkzentrale) control centre
  (b) (Telefonzentrale) [telephone] exchange; (eines Hotels, einer Firma o. Ä.) switchboard
Zentral-: ∼**figur** *die* central figure; ∼**heizung** *die* central heating; ∼**speicher** *der* (DV) main memory
Zentren ▶ ZENTRUM
Zentrifugal·kraft *die* (Physik) centrifugal force

Z

Zentrifuge die; ~, ~n centrifuge

Zentrum das; ~s, Zentren centre; im ~: at the centre; (im Stadtzentrum) in the town/city centre

Zeppelin der; ~s, ~e Zeppelin

Zepter das, auch: der; ~s, ~: sceptre

zerbeißen unr. tr. V. bite in two

zerbersten unr. itr. V.; mit sein burst apart

zerbrechen ① unr. itr. V.; mit sein break [into pieces]; smash [to pieces]; ⟨glass⟩ shatter; (fig.) ⟨marriage, relationship⟩ break up

② unr. tr. V. break; smash, shatter ⟨dishes, glass⟩

zerbrechlich Adj. fragile; (fig.) frail

Zerbrechlichkeit die; ~: fragility; (fig.) frailty

zerbröckeln ① itr. V.; mit sein crumble away

② tr. V. break into small pieces

zerdrücken tr. V. mash

Zeremonie die; ~, ~n ceremony; (fig.) ritual

Zeremoniell das; ~s, ~e ceremonial

zerfallen unr. itr. V.; mit sein (auch fig.) disintegrate (in + Akk., zu into); ⟨building⟩ fall into ruin, decay; ⟨corpse⟩ decompose, decay

zerfetzen tr. V. rip or tear to pieces; (fig.) tear apart ⟨body, limb⟩

zerfleischen tr. V. tear ⟨person, animal⟩ limb from limb

zerfressen unr. tr. V. (a) eat away; ⟨moth etc.⟩ eat holes in

(b) (zersetzen) corrode ⟨metal⟩; eat away ⟨bone⟩

zergehen unr. itr. V.; mit sein melt; (in Wasser, im Mund) ⟨tablet etc.⟩ dissolve

zerhacken tr. V. chop up (zu into)

zerhauen unr. tr. V. chop up

zerkleinern tr. V. chop up; (zermahlen) crush ⟨rock etc.⟩

zerknautschen tr. V. (ugs.) crumple

zerknirscht ① Adj. remorseful

② adv. remorsefully

zerknittern tr. V. crease; crumple

zerknüllen tr. V. crumple up [into a ball]

zerkratzen tr. V. scratch

zerkrümeln tr. V. crumble up

zerlegen tr. V. (a) dismantle; take to pieces

(b) (zerschneiden) cut up ⟨animal, meat⟩; carve ⟨joint⟩

zerlumpt Adj. ragged ⟨clothes, person⟩

zerplatzen itr. V.; mit sein burst

Zerr·bild das distorted image

zerreiben unr. tr. V. crush

zerreißen ① unr. tr. V. (a) tear up; (in kleine Stücke) tear to pieces; break ⟨thread⟩

(b) (beschädigen) tear ⟨stocking, trousers, etc.⟩ (an + Dat. on)

② unr. itr. V.; mit sein ⟨thread, string, rope⟩ break; ⟨paper, cloth, etc.⟩ tear

Zerreiß·probe die acid test

zerren ① tr. V. (a) drag

(b) sich (Dat.) einen Muskel/eine Sehne ~: pull a muscle/tendon

② itr. V. an etw. (Dat.) ~: tug or pull at sth

Zerrung die; ~, ~en pulled muscle/tendon

zerrütten tr. V. ruin; shatter ⟨nerves⟩

zerschellen itr. V.; mit sein be dashed or smashed to pieces

zerschlagen ① unr. tr. V. smash ⟨plate, windscreen, etc.⟩; smash up ⟨furniture⟩; (fig.) smash ⟨spy ring etc.⟩

② unr. refl. V. ⟨plan, deal⟩ fall through

zerschmettern tr. V. smash; shatter ⟨glass, leg, bone⟩

zerschneiden unr. tr. V. cut; (in Stücke) cut up; (in zwei Teile) cut in two

zersetzen tr. V. corrode ⟨metal⟩; decompose ⟨organism⟩

zersplittern itr. V.; mit sein ⟨wood, bone⟩ splinter; ⟨glass⟩ shatter

zerspringen unr. itr. V.; mit sein shatter; (Sprünge bekommen) crack

zerstäuben tr. V. spray

zerstören tr. V. destroy; ⟨hooligan⟩ smash up, vandalize; (fig.) ruin ⟨health, life⟩

Zerstörung die; ~, ~en ▶ ZERSTÖREN: destruction; smashing up; vandalization; (fig.) ruin[ation]

Zerstörungs·wut die destructive frenzy

zerstreuen ① tr. V. scatter; disperse ⟨crowd⟩; jmdn./sich ~ (ablenken) take sb.'s/ one's mind off things

② refl. V. disperse; (schneller) scatter

zerstreut ① Adj. distracted; (vergesslich) absent-minded

② adv. absentmindedly

Zerstreuung die; ~, ~en (Ablenkung) diversion

zerstückeln tr. V. break ⟨sth.⟩ up into small pieces; (zerschneiden) cut or chop ⟨sth.⟩ up into small pieces; dismember ⟨corpse⟩

zerteilen tr. V. divide into pieces; (zerschneiden) cut into pieces; cut up

Zertifikat das; ~[e]s, ~e certificate

zertrampeln tr. V. trample all over ⟨flower bed etc.⟩; trample ⟨child etc.⟩ underfoot

zertreten unr. tr. V. stamp on; stamp out ⟨cigarette, match⟩

zertrümmern tr. V. smash; smash, shatter ⟨glass⟩; smash up ⟨furniture⟩; wreck ⟨car, boat⟩; reduce ⟨building⟩ to ruins

Zerwürfnis das; ~ses, ~se (geh.) quarrel; dispute; (Bruch) rift

zerzausen tr. V. ruffle; zerzaust aussehen look dishevelled

zetern itr. V. scold [shrilly]; (sich beklagen) moan (über + Akk. about)

Zẹttel *der;* ~s, ~: slip *or* piece of paper; (mit einigen Zeilen) note; (Bekanntmachung) notice; (Formular) form; (Kassenzettel) receipt; (Handzettel) leaflet

Zeug *das;* ~[e]s, ~e (a) (ugs.) stuff; **dummes** ~: nonsense; rubbish **(b)** (Kleidung) things *pl.*

Zeuge *der;* ~n, ~n witness

zeugen *tr. V.* procreate; ⟨man⟩ father ⟨child⟩

Zeugen·aussage *die* testimony

Zeugin *die;* ~, ~nen witness

Zeugnis *das;* ~ses, ~se (a) (Schulw.) report **(b)** (Arbeitszeugnis) reference; testimonial **(c)** (Gutachten) certificate

Zeugung *die;* ~, ~en procreation; (eines Kindes) fathering

zeugungs·fähig *Adj.* fertile

z. Hd. *Abk.* = **zu Händen** attn.

Zicke *die;* ~, ~n (a) ▶ ZIEGE; **(b)** *Pl.* (ugs.: Dummheiten) stupid tricks; monkey business *sing.* (coll.); ~n **machen** mess about; (Schwierigkeiten machen) make trouble

Zickzack *der;* ~[e]s, ~e zigzag

Ziege *die;* ~, ~n goat; (Schimpfwort: Frau) cow (sl. derog.)

Ziegel *der;* ~s, ~ brick; (Dachziegel) tile

Ziegelei *die;* ~, ~en brickworks *sing.*

Ziegel·stein *der* brick

Ziegen-: ~**bock** *der* he- *or* billy goat; ~**käse** *der* goat's cheese

ziehen ⟨1⟩ *unr. tr. V.* **(a)** pull; (sanfter) draw; (zerren) tug; (schleppen) drag; **etw. nach sich** ~ (fig.) result in sth.; entail sth. **(b)** (herausziehen) extract ⟨tooth⟩; take out, remove ⟨stitches⟩; draw ⟨cord, sword, pistol⟩; **den Hut** ~: raise one's hat; **die [Quadrat]wurzel** ~ (Math.) extract the square root **(c)** (dehnen) stretch ⟨elastic etc.⟩; stretch out ⟨sheets etc.⟩ **(d)** (Gesichtspartien bewegen) make ⟨face, grimace⟩ **(e)** (bei Brettspielen) move ⟨chessman etc.⟩ **(f)** (zeichnen) draw ⟨line etc.⟩ **(g)** (anlegen) dig ⟨trench⟩; build ⟨wall⟩; erect ⟨fence⟩; put up ⟨washing line⟩; run, lay ⟨cable, wires⟩; draw ⟨frontier⟩ **(h)** (aufziehen) grow ⟨plants, flowers⟩; breed ⟨animals⟩ ⟨2⟩ *unr. itr. V.* **(a)** (reißen) pull; **an etw.** (Dat.) ~: pull on sth. **(b)** (funktionieren) ⟨stove, pipe, chimney⟩ draw **(c)** *mit sein* (umziehen) move (**nach, in** + *Akk.* to) **(d)** *mit sein* (gehen) go; (marschieren) march; (umherstreifen) roam; (weggehen) go away; leave; ⟨fog, clouds⟩ drift **(e)** (saugen) draw; **an einer Zigarette/Pfeife** ~: draw on a cigarette/pipe **(f)** ⟨tea, coffee⟩ draw **(g)** (Kochk.) simmer **(h)** *unpers.* **es zieht** there's a draught

⟨3⟩ *unr. refl. V.* ⟨road⟩ run, stretch; ⟨frontier⟩ run

Zieh·harmonika *die* piano accordion

Ziehung *die;* ~, ~en draw

Ziel *das;* ~[e]s, ~e **(a)** destination **(b)** (Sport) finish; (Ziellinie) finishing line; (Pferderennen) finishing post **(c)** (Zielscheibe; auch Milit.) target **(d)** (Zweck) aim; goal; **sein** ~ **erreichen** achieve one's objective *or* aim

ziel·bewusst, *ziel·bewußt ⟨1⟩ *Adj.* determined ⟨2⟩ *adv.* determinedly

zielen *itr. V.* aim (**auf** + *Akk.*, at); (fig.) **auf jmdn./etw.** ~ ⟨reproach, efforts, etc.⟩ be aimed at sb./sth.

ziel-, Ziel-: ~**gruppe** *die* target group; ~**los** ⟨1⟩ *Adj.* aimless; ⟨2⟩ *adv.* aimlessly; ~**losigkeit** *die;* ~~: aimlessness; ~**scheibe** *die* (auch fig.) target (*Gen.* for); ~**strebig** ⟨1⟩ *Adj.* **(a)** purposeful; **(b)** (energisch) single-minded ⟨person⟩; ⟨2⟩ *adv.* **(a)** purposefully; **(b)** (energisch) single-mindedly; ~**strebigkeit** *die;* ~~ ▶ ~STREBIG: **(a)** purposefulness; **(b)** single-mindedness; ~**wahl** *die* (Fernspr.) one-touch dialling

ziemlich ⟨1⟩ *Adj.* (ugs.) fair, sizeable ⟨quantity, number⟩ ⟨2⟩ *adv.* **(a)** quite; fairly **(b)** (ugs.: fast) pretty well

Zierde *die;* ~, ~n (auch fig.) ornament

zieren *refl. V.* be coy

zierlich ⟨1⟩ *Adj.* dainty; petite, dainty ⟨woman, figure⟩ ⟨2⟩ *adv.* daintily

Zierlichkeit *die;* ~: daintiness; (einer Frau, Gestalt) petiteness; daintiness

Zier·pflanze *die* ornamental plant

Ziffer *die;* ~, ~n numeral; (in einer mehrstelligen Zahl) digit; figure

Ziffer·blatt *das* dial; face

zig *unbest. Zahlwort* (ugs.) umpteen (coll.)

Zigarẹtte *die;* ~, ~n cigarette

Zigarẹtten·werbung *die* cigarette advertising

Zigarịllo *der od. das;* ~s, ~s cigarillo; small cigar

Zigạrre *die;* ~, ~n cigar

Zigeuner *der;* ~s, ~, **Zigeunerin** *die;* ~, ~nen gypsy

zig·mal *Adv.* (ugs.) umpteen times (coll.)

zig·tausend *unbest. Zahlwort* (ugs.) umpteen thousand (coll.)

Zimmer *das;* ~s, ~: room

Zimmer·mädchen *das* chambermaid

zimmern *tr. V.* make ⟨shelves etc.⟩

Zimmer-: ~**suche** *die* room-hunt; ~**vermittlung** *die* accommodation office

zimperlich ⟨1⟩ *Adj.* timid; (leicht angeekelt) squeamish; (prüde) prissy ⟨2⟩ *adv.: s. Adj.:* timidly; squeamishly; prissily

Z

Zimperlichkeit *die;* ~, ~en (abwertend) timidity; (Neigung zum Ekel) squeamishness; (Prüderie) prissiness

Zimt *der;* ~[e]s, ~e cinnamon

Zink *das;* ~[e]s zinc

Zinke *die;* ~, ~n prong; (eines Kamms) tooth

Zinn *das;* ~[e]s tin; (Gegenstände) pewter[ware]

Zins *der;* ~es, ~en interest

Zinses·zins *der* compound interest

zins·los 1 *Adj.* interest-free
2 *adv.* free of interest

Zins·satz *der* interest rate

Zipfel *der;* ~s, ~ (einer Decke, eines Tisch-, Handtuchs usw.) corner; (Wurstzipfel, eines Halstuchs) [tail] end

Zipfel·mütze *die* [long-]pointed cap

zirka *Adv.* about; approximately

Zirkulation *die,* ~, ~en circulation

zirkulieren *itr. V.; auch mit sein* circulate

Zirkus *der;* ~, ~se (a) circus (b) (ugs.) (Trubel) hustle and bustle; (Krach) to-do

zirpen *itr. V.* chirp

zischeln *tr. V.* whisper angrily

zischen *itr. V.* (a) hiss; ⟨*hot fat*⟩ sizzle (b) *mit sein* hiss

Zitat *das;* ~[e]s, ~e quotation (aus from)

zitieren *tr., itr. V.* (a) quote; (Rechtsspr.) cite (b) (rufen) summon

Zitronat *das;* ~[e]s candied lemon peel

Zitrone *die;* ~, ~n lemon

Zitronen-: ~**limonade** *die* lemonade; ~**presse** *die* lemon squeezer; ~**saft** *der* lemon juice

Zitrus·frucht *die* citrus fruit

zittern *itr. V.* tremble (vor + *Dat.* with); (vor Kälte) shiver; (beben) ⟨*walls, windows*⟩ shake; vor jmdm./etw. ~: be terrified of sb./sth.

Zitter·partie *die* nail-biting affair

zittrig *Adj.* shaky; doddery ⟨*old man*⟩

Zitze *die;* ~, ~n teat

zivil 1 *Adj.* (a) civilian; non-military ⟨*purposes*⟩; civil ⟨*aviation, marriage, law, defence*⟩ (b) (annehmbar) decent
2 *adv.* (annehmbar) decently

Zivil *das;* ~s civilian clothes *pl.*

Zivil·bevölkerung *die* civilian population

Zivilisation /tsːːivilizaʹtsːioːn/ *die;* ~, ~en civilization

zivilisieren *tr. V.* civilize

zivilisiert 1 *Adj.* civilized
2 *adv.* in a civilized way

Zivilist *der;* ~en, ~en, **Zivilistin** *die;* ~, ~nen civilian

Zivil·kleidung *die* civilian clothes *pl.*

Zofe *die;* ~, ~n (hist.) lady's maid

zoffen *refl. V.* (ugs.) quarrel (mit with)

zog *1. u. 3. Pers. Sg. Prät. v.* ZIEHEN

zögerlich 1 *Adj.* hesitant; tentative
2 *adv.* hesitantly; tentatively

zögern *itr. V.* hesitate; **ohne zu** ~: without hesitation

Zoll *der;* ~[e]s, **Zölle** (a) [customs] duty (b) (Behörde) customs *pl.*

zoll-, Zoll-: ~**amt** *das* customs house *or* office; ~**beamte** *der,* ~**beamtin** *die* customs officer; ~**erklärung** *die* customs declaration; ~**frei** 1 *Adj.* duty-free; free of duty *pred.;* 2 *adv.* free of duty; ~**kontrolle** *die* customs examination *or* check; ~**stock** *der* folding rule

Zone *die;* ~, ~n zone

Zoo *der;* ~s, ~s zoo

Zoologe *der;* ~n, ~n zoologist

Zoologie *die;* ~: zoology *no art.*

Zoologin *die;* ~, ~nen zoologist

zoologisch *Adj.* zoological; ~**er Garten** zoological gardens *pl.*

Zoom *das;* ~s, ~s (Film, Fot.) zoom

Zoom-objektiv *das* (Film, Fot.) zoom lens

Zopf *der;* ~[e]s, **Zöpfe** plait; (am Hinterkopf) pigtail

Zorn *der;* ~[e]s anger; (stärker) wrath; fury

zornig 1 *Adj.* furious
2 *adv.* furiously

Zote *die;* ~, ~n dirty joke

zotig 1 *Adj.* smutty; dirty ⟨*joke*⟩
2 *adv.* smuttily

zottig *Adj.* shaggy

zu 1 *Präp. mit Dat.* (a) (Richtung) to; **zu ... hin** towards ... (b) (zusammen mit) with; **zu dem Käse gab es Wein** there was wine with the cheese (c) (Lage) at; **zu beiden Seiten** on both sides (d) (zeitlich) at; **zu Weihnachten** at Christmas (e) (Art u. Weise) **zu meiner Zufriedenheit/Überraschung** to my satisfaction/surprise; (bei Mengenangaben) **zu Dutzenden/zweien** by the dozen/in twos (f) (ein Zahlenverhältnis ausdrückend) **ein Verhältnis von 3 zu 1** a ratio of 3 to 1 (g) (einen Preis zuordnend) at; for (h) (Zweck) for (i) (Ziel, Ergebnis) into; **zu etw. werden** turn into sth. (j) (über) about; on; **sich zu etw. äußern** comment on sth. (k) (gegenüber) **freundlich/hässlich zu jmdm. sein** be friendly/nasty to sb.; *s. auch* ZUM; ZUR; 2 *Adv.* (a) (allzu) too; **zu sehr/viel** too much; **zu wenig** too little (b) *nachgestellt* (Richtung) towards 3 *Konj.* (a) *mit Infinitiv* to; **was gibts da zu lachen?** what is there to laugh about? (b) *mit 1. Part.* **die zu erledigende Post** the letters *pl.* to be dealt with

Zubehör *das;* ~[e]s, ~e *od. schweiz.* ~den accessories *pl.;* (eines Staubsaugers, Mixers usw.) attachments *pl.;* (Ausstattung) equipment

---

*old spelling - see note on page xiv

zu|bereiten *tr. V.* prepare ‹*meal etc.*›; make up ‹*medicine, ointment*›; (kochen) cook ‹*fish, meat, etc.*›

zu|billigen *tr. V.* jmdm. etw. ∼: grant *or* allow sb. sth.

zu|binden *unr. tr. V.* tie [up]

zu|blinzeln *itr. V.* jmdm. ∼: wink at sb.

zu|bringen *unr. tr. V.* spend

Zu-bringer *der;* ∼s, ∼ **(a)** (Straße) access road

(b) (Verkehrsmittel) shuttle

Zucht *die;* ∼, ∼en **(a)** breeding; (von Pflanzen) cultivation; **ein Pferd aus deutscher** ∼: a German-bred horse

(b) (geh.: Disziplin) discipline

züchten *tr. V.* (auch fig.) breed; cultivate ‹*plants*›; culture ‹*bacteria, pearls*›

Züchter *der;* ∼s, ∼, **Züchterin** *die;* ∼, ∼nen breeder; (von Pflanzen) grower [of new varieties]

züchtigen *tr. V.* (geh.) beat; thrash; (fig.: bestrafen) castigate

Züchtigung *die;* ∼, ∼en (geh.) beating; thrashing; (fig.: Bestrafung) castigation

Züchtung *die;* ∼, ∼en **(a)** breeding; (von Pflanzen) cultivation

(b) (Zuchtergebnis) strain

zucken *itr. V.; mit Richtungsangabe mit sein* twitch; ‹*body, arm, leg, etc.*› jerk; (vor Schreck) start; ‹*flames*› flicker; **mit den Achseln/Schultern** ∼: shrug one's shoulders

zücken *tr. V.* draw ‹*sword, dagger, knife*›

Zucker *der;* ∼s, ∼ **(a)** sugar

(b) (ugs.: Diabetes) diabetes; ∼ **haben** be a diabetic

zucker-, Zucker-: ∼**dose** *die* sugar bowl; ∼**hut** *der* sugar loaf; ∼**krank** *Adj.* diabetic

zuckern *tr. V.* sugar

Zucker·wasser *das* sugar water

Zuckung *die;* ∼, ∼en twitch

zu|decken *tr. V.* cover up; cover [over] ‹*well, ditch*›; jmdn./sich ∼: tuck sb./oneself up

zu|drehen *tr. V.* **(a)** (abdrehen) turn off

(b) (zuwenden) jmdm. den Rücken ∼: turn one's back on sb.

zu-dringlich ⓵ *Adj.* pushy (coll.), pushing ‹*person, manner*›; (sexuell) importunate ‹*person, manner*›; prying ‹*glance*›

⓶ *adv.* importunately

Zu-dringlichkeit *die;* ∼, ∼en **(a)** pushiness (coll.); (in sexueller Hinsicht) importunate manner

(b) (Handlung) ∼en insistent advances *or* attentions

zu|drücken *tr. V.* press shut; push ‹*door*› shut; jmdm. die Kehle ∼: choke *or* throttle sb.

zu-einander *Adv.* to one another

zu-erst *Adv.* **(a)** first

(b) (anfangs) at first; to start with

(c) (erstmals) first

Zu-fahrt *die* **(a)** access [for vehicles]

(b) (Straße, Weg) access road; (zum Haus) driveway

Zufahrts·straße *die* access road

Zu-fall *der* chance; (zufälliges Zusammentreffen von Ereignissen) coincidence; **durch** ∼: by chance

zu|fallen *unr. itr. V.; mit sein* **(a)** ‹*door etc.*› slam shut; ‹*eyes*› close

(b) (zukommen) jmdm. ∼ ‹*task*› fall to sb.; ‹*prize, inheritance*› go to sb.

zu-fällig ⓵ *Adj.* accidental; chance *attrib.* ‹*meeting, acquaintance*›; random ‹*selection*›

⓶ *adv.* by chance; **wissen Sie** ∼, **wie spät es ist?** (ugs.) do you by any chance know the time?

Zufalls·treffer *der* fluke

zu|fassen *itr. V.* make a snatch *or* grab

zu|faxen *tr.V.* jmdm. etw. ∼: fax sth. to sb.; fax sb. sth.

zu|fliegen *unr. itr. V.; mit sein* (ugs.) ‹*door, window, etc.*› slam shut

Zu-flucht *die* refuge (vor + *Dat.* from); (vor Unwetter o. Ä.) shelter (vor + *Dat.* from)

Zufluchts·ort *der* place of refuge; sanctuary

Zu-fluss, *Zu-fluß *der* **(a)** (das Zufließen) inflow; supply; (fig.) influx

(b) (Gewässer) feeder stream/river

zu|flüstern *tr. V.* jmdm. etw. ∼: whisper sth. to sb.

zu-folge *Präp. mit Dat.; nachgestellt* according to

zu-frieden ⓵ *Adj.* contented; (befriedigt) satisfied; **mit etw.** ∼ **sein** be satisfied with sth.; **sich** ∼ **geben** be satisfied; **jmdn.** ∼ **stellen** satisfy sb.

⓶ *adv.* contentedly

***zufrieden|geben** ▸ ZUFRIEDEN 1

Zufriedenheit *die;* ∼: contentment; (Befriedigung) satisfaction

***zufrieden|stellen** ▸ ZUFRIEDEN 1

zufriedenstellend ⓵ *Adj.* satisfactory

⓶ *adv.* satisfactorily

zu|frieren *unr. itr. V.; mit sein* freeze over

zu|fügen *tr. V.* jmdm. etw. ∼: inflict sth. on sb.; jmdm. Schaden/[ein] Unrecht ∼: do sb. harm/an injustice

Zufuhr *die;* ∼: supply; (Material) supplies *pl.*

zu|führen ⓵ *itr. V.* auf etw. (*Akk.*) ∼: lead towards sth.

⓶ *tr. V.* **(a)** (zuleiten) einer Sache (*Dat.*) etw. ∼: supply sth. to sth.

(b) (bringen) einer Partei Mitglieder ∼: bring new members to a party

Zug *der;* ∼[e]s, Züge **(a)** (Bahn) train

(b) (Kolonne) column; (Umzug) procession; (Demonstrationszug) march

(c) (das Ziehen) pull; traction (Phys.)

(d) (Vorrichtung) pull

(e) (Wanderung) migration

(f) (beim Brettspiel) move

∲

Z

(g) (Schluck) swig (coll.); mouthful; (großer Schluck) gulp; **das Glas auf einen** *od.* **in einem** ~ **leeren** empty the glass at one go
(h) (beim Rauchen) pull; drag (coll.)
(i) (Atemzug) breath
(j) (Zugluft; beim Ofen) draught
(k) (Gesichtszug) feature; (Wesenszug) characteristic; trait

Zu·gabe *die* **(a)** (Geschenk) [free] gift
(b) (im Konzert, Theater) encore

Zu·gang *der* **(a)** (Weg, auch fig.) access; (Eingang) entrance
(b) (das Hinzukommen) (von Personen) intake; (von Patienten) admission
(c) (Zuwachs) increase (**von** in)

zu·gange: ~ **sein** (ugs.) be busy *or* occupied

zugänglich *Adj.* **(a)** accessible; (geöffnet) open
(b) (zur Verfügung stehend) available (*Dat.,* **für** to); (verständlich) accessible (*Dat.,* **für** to)
(c) (aufgeschlossen) approachable ⟨*person*⟩

zu|geben *unr. tr. V.* admit; admit to ⟨*deed, crime*⟩

zu·gegen *Adj.* ~ **sein** be present

zu|gehen *unr. itr. V.; mit sein* **(a) auf** jmdn./etw. ~: approach sb./sth.
(b) jmdm. ~ (zugeschickt werden) be sent to sb.
(c) (ugs.: sich schließen) close; shut; **die Tür geht nicht zu** the door will not shut

zu·gehörig *Adj.* belonging to it/them *postpos., not pred.*

Zugehörigkeit *die;* ~: belonging (**zu** to)

Zügel *der;* ~**s,** ~: rein

zügel·los (fig.) ①*Adj.* unrestrained; unbridled ⟨*rage, passion*⟩
②*adv.* without restraint

Zügellosigkeit *die;* ~, ~**en** lack of restraint; (Unzüchtigkeit) licentiousness

zügeln *tr. V.* rein [in] ⟨*horse*⟩; (fig.) curb, restrain ⟨*desire etc.*⟩

zu|gesellen *refl. V.* **sich** jmdm./einer Sache ~: join sb./sth.

Zu·geständnis *das* concession

zu|gestehen *unr. tr. V.* admit; concede

zu·getan *Adj.* jmdm. [herzlich] ~ **sein** (geh.) be [very] attached to sb.

zugig *Adj.* draughty, (im Freien) windy

zügig ①*Adj.* speedy; rapid
②*adv.* speedily; rapidly

Zügigkeit *die;* ~: speediness; rapidity

zu·gleich *Adv.* at the same time

Zug-: ~**luft** *die* draught; ~**maschine** *die* tractor; (von Sattelzug) tractor [unit]

zu|greifen *unr. itr. V.* **(a)** take hold
(b) (sich bedienen) help oneself
(c) (fleißig arbeiten) [**hart** *od.* **kräftig**] ~: [really] knuckle down to it

Zu·griff *der* (Zugang) access (**auf** + *Akk.* to)

zu·grunde *Adv.* **(a)** ~ **gehen** (sterben) die

(an + *Dat.* of); (zerstört werden) be destroyed **(an** + *Dat.* by); ~ **richten** destroy; (finanziell) ruin ⟨*company, person*⟩
(b) etw. einer Sache (*Dat.*) ~ **legen** base sth. on sth.; **etw. liegt einer Sache** ~: sth. is based on sth.

zu|gucken *itr. V.* (ugs.) ▶ ZUSEHEN

zu·gunsten ①*Präp. mit Gen.* in favour of
②*Adv.* ~ **von** in favour of

zu·gute *Adv.* jmdm. **seine Unerfahrenheit** *usw.* ~ **halten** (geh.) make allowances for sb.'s inexperience *etc.;* **sich** (*Dat.*) **etwas/viel auf etw.** (*Akk.*) ~ **tun** *od.* **halten** (geh.) be proud/very proud of sth.; jmdm./einer Sache ~ **kommen** stand sb./sth. in good stead

zu|haben *unr. itr. V.* (ugs.) ⟨*shop, office*⟩ be shut *or* closed

zu|halten *unr. tr. V.* hold closed; (nicht öffnen) keep closed

zu|hängen *tr. V.* cover ⟨*window, cage*⟩

zu|hauen (ugs.) ①*unr. itr. V.* bang *or* slam ⟨*door, window*⟩ shut
②*unr. itr. V.* hit *or* strike out

Zu·hause *das;* ~**s** home

Zuhilfenahme *die;* ~: utilization; **ohne/ unter** ~ **einer Sache** (*Gen.*)/**von etw.** without/ with the aid of sth.

zu|hören *itr. V.* jmdm./einer Sache ~: listen to sb./sth.

Zu·hörer *der,* **Zu·hörerin** *die* listener

zu|kleben *tr. V.* seal ⟨*letter, envelope*⟩

zu|knallen (ugs.) ①*tr. V.* slam
②*itr. V.; mit sein* slam

zu|knöpfen *tr. V.* button up

zu|kommen *itr. V.; mit sein* **auf** jmdn. ~: approach sb.

Zukunft *die;* ~: future

Zukunfts·technologie *die* technology of the future

Zu·lage *die* extra pay *no indef. art.;* additional allowance *no indef. art.*

zu|lassen *unr. tr. V.* **(a)** allow; permit
(b) (teilnehmen lassen) admit
(c) (mit einer Lizenz usw. versehen) **jmdn. als Arzt** ~: register sb. as a doctor
(d) (Kfz-W.) register ⟨*vehicle*⟩
(e) (geschlossen lassen) leave closed *or* shut

zu·lässig *Adj.* permissible; admissible ⟨*appeal*⟩

Zulassung *die;* ~, ~**en** registration

Zu·lauf *der* [viel] ~ **haben** ⟨*shop, restaurant, etc.*⟩ enjoy a large clientele; ⟨*doctor, lawyer*⟩ have a large practice

zu|laufen *unr. itr. V.; mit sein* **(a) auf** jmdn./etw. ~ (auch fig.) run towards sb./sth.
(b) jmdm. ~ ⟨*cat, dog, etc.*⟩ adopt sb. as a new owner

zu|legen *refl. V.* **sich** (*Dat.*) **etw.** ~: get oneself sth.

zu·letzt *Adv.* **(a)** last [of all]
(b) (als Letzter/Letzte/Letztes) last
(c) (fig.: am wenigsten) least of all
(d) (schließlich, am Ende) in the end; **bis** ~: [right up] to *or* until the end

---

Z

zu·liebe *Adv.* jmdm./einer Sache ~: for sb.'s sake/for the sake of sth.

Zulieferer *der;* ~s, ~, **Zulieferin** *die;* ~, ~nen supplier

zum *Präp.* + *Art.* **(a)** = zu dem; **(b)** (räumlich: Richtung) to the **(c)** (räumlich: Lage) etw. ~ **Fenster hinauswerfen** throw sth. out of the window **(d)** (Hinzufügung) **Milch** ~ **Tee nehmen** take milk with [one's] tea **(e)** (zeitlich) at the; **spätestens** ~ **15. April** by 15 April at the latest **(f)** (Zweck) ~ **Spaß/Vergnügen** for fun/pleasure **(g)** (Folge) ~ **Ärger seines Vaters** to the annoyance of his father

zu|machen *tr. V.* close; fasten, do up ⟨*dress*⟩; seal ⟨*envelope, letter*⟩; turn off ⟨*tap*⟩; put the top on ⟨*bottle*⟩; (stilllegen) close *or* shut down ⟨*factory, mine, etc.*⟩

zu·mal **1** *Adv.* especially; particularly **2** *Konj.* especially *or* particularly since

zumindest *Adv.* at least

zu|müllen *tr. V.* (ugs.) etw. ~: bury sth. under rubbish; **mit etw. zugemüllt werden** be buried under sth.; **von etw. zugemüllt werden** (fig.) be buried under sth.

zu·mute *Adj.* jmdm. ist unbehaglich *usw.* ~: sb. feels uncomfortable *etc.;* **mir war nicht danach** ~: I didn't feel like it

zu|muten *tr. V.* jmdm. etw. ~ (abverlangen) expect *or* ask sth. of sb.; (antun) expect sb. to put up with sth.

Zumutung *die;* ~, ~en unreasonable demand; **eine** ~ **sein** be unreasonable

zu·nächst *Adv.* **(a)** (als erstes) first; (anfangs) at first **(b)** (im Moment, vorläufig) for the moment

Zunahme *die;* ~, ~n increase (*Gen.*, an + *Dat.* in)

Zu·name *der* surname; last name

zünden **1** *tr. V.* ignite ⟨*gas, fuel, etc.*⟩; detonate ⟨*bomb, explosive device, etc.*⟩; let off ⟨*fireworks*⟩; fire ⟨*rocket*⟩ **2** *itr. V.* ⟨*rocket, engine*⟩ fire; ⟨*lighter, match*⟩ light; ⟨*gas, fuel, explosive*⟩ ignite

Zünd-: ~**holz** *das* (bes. südd., österr.) match; ~**schlüssel** *der* (Kfz-W.) ignition key

Zündung *die;* ~, ~en (a) ▶ ZÜNDEN 1: ignition; detonation; letting off; firing **(b)** (Kfz-W.: Anlage) ignition

zu|nehmen *unr. itr. V.* **(a)** increase (an + *Dat.* in); ⟨*moon*⟩ wax **(b)** (schwerer werden) put on *or* gain weight

Zu·neigung *die* affection

Zunge *die;* ~, ~n tongue; **[jmdm.] die** ~ **herausstrecken** put one's tongue out [at sb.]

zu·nichte *Adj.* etw. ~ **machen** ruin sth.

zu·oberst *Adv.* [right] on [the] top

zu·pass, *zu·paß: jmdm. ~ **kommen** come [to sb.] at just the right moment

zupfen **1** *itr. V.* an etw. (*Dat.*) ~: pluck *or* pull at sth.

2 *tr. V.* **(a)** etw. aus/von *usw.* etw. ~: pull sth. out of/from *etc.* sth. **(b)** (auszupfen) pull out; pluck ⟨*eyebrows*⟩ **(c)** pluck ⟨*string, guitar, tune*⟩ **(d)** jmdn. am Ärmel ~: pull *or* tug [at] sb.'s sleeve

zur *Präp.* + *Art.* **(a)** = zu der; **(b)** (räumlich, fig.: Richtung) to the; ~ **Schule/Arbeit gehen** go to school/work **(c)** (räumlich: Lage) ~ **Tür hereinkommen** come [in] through the door **(d)** (Zusammengehörigkeit, Hinzufügung) with the **(e)** (zeitlich) at the; ~ **Stunde** at the moment; at present ~ **Zeit** ▶ ZURZEIT **(f)** (Zweck) ~ **Entschuldigung** by way of [an] excuse **(g)** (Folge) ~ **vollen Zufriedenheit ihres Chefs** to the complete satisfaction of her boss

zurechnungs·fähig *Adj.* sound of mind *pred.*

zurecht-: ~**finden** *unr. refl. V.* find one's way [around]; ~**kommen** *unr. itr. V.;* mit sein get on (mit with); ~**legen** *tr. V.* lay out [ready]; jmdm. etw. ~legen lay sth. out ready for sb.; ~**machen** *tr. V.* (ugs.) **(a)** (vorbereiten) get ready; **(b)** (herrichten) do up; **(c)** jmdn./sich ~machen get sb. ready/get [oneself] ready; (schminken) make sb. up/put on one's make-up; ~**weisen** *unr. tr. V.* rebuke; reprimand ⟨*pupil, subordinate, etc.*⟩

zu|reden *itr. V.* jmdm. ~: persuade sb.; (ermutigen) encourage sb.

Zürich *(das);* ~s Zurich

zu·rück *Adv.* back; (weiter hinten) behind; **einen Schritt** ~: a step backwards; ~**!** get *or* go back!

zurück-, Zurück-: ~**behalten** *unr. tr. V.* **(a)** keep [back]; retain; **(b)** be left with ⟨*scar, heart defect, etc.*⟩; ~**bekommen** *unr. tr. V.* get back; **Sie bekommen 10 Euro** ~: you get 10 euros change; ~**bleiben** *unr. itr. V.; mit sein* **(a)** remain; **(b)** (nicht mithalten) lag behind; (fig.) fall behind; **(c)** (bleiben) remain; ~**blicken** *itr. V.* look back; ~**erstatten** *tr. V.* refund; jmdm. etw. ~erstatten refund sth. to sb.; ~**fahren** *unr. itr. V.; mit sein* **(a)** go back; return; **(b)** (nach hinten fahren) go back[wards]; ~**fallen** *unr. itr. V.; mit sein* **(a)** (in Rückstand geraten) fall behind; **(b)** (auf einen niedrigeren Rang) drop (auf + *Akk.* to); **(c)** an jmdn. ~fallen ⟨*property*⟩ revert to sb.; **(d)** auf jmdn. ~fallen ⟨*actions, behaviour*⟩ reflect [up]on sb.; ~**fliegen** *unr. itr. V.; mit sein* fly back; ~**führen** *tr. V.* etw. auf etw. (*Akk.*) ~führen attribute sth. to sth.; ~**geben** *unr. tr. V.* give back; return; take back ⟨*defective goods*⟩; ~**gehen** *unr. itr. V.; mit sein* **(a)** go back; return; **(b)** (nach hinten) go back; **(c)** (verschwinden) disappear; ⟨*swelling, inflammation*⟩ go down; ⟨*pain*⟩ subside; **(d)** (sich verringern) decrease; ⟨*fever*⟩ abate; ⟨*flood*⟩ subside; ⟨*business*⟩ fall off; **(e)** (zurückgeschickt werden) be returned *or* sent back; ~**greifen** *unr. itr. V.* auf jmdn./etw. ···⟶

Z

~**zurückgreifen** fall back on sb./sth.;
~|**halten** ① *unr. tr. V.* (a) jmdn. ~halten
hold sb. back; (von etw. abhalten) stop sb.; (b)
(am Vordringen hindern) keep back ⟨*crowd, mob,
etc.*⟩; (c) (behalten) withhold ⟨*news, letter, etc.*⟩;
(d) (nicht austreten lassen) hold back ⟨*tears etc.*⟩;
② *unr. refl. V.* restrain *or* control oneself;
sich in einer Diskussion ~halten keep in the
background in a discussion; ~**haltend**
① *Adj.* (a) reserved; (b) (kühl, reserviert) cool,
restrained ⟨*reception, response*⟩; (c) (Wirtsch.:
schwach) slack ⟨*demand*⟩; ② *adv.* ⟨*behave*⟩
with reserve *or* restraint; (kühl, reserviert)
coolly; ~**haltung** *die* reserve; (Kühle,
Reserviertheit) coolness; (Wirtsch.) caution;
~|**kehren** *itr. V.; mit sein* return; come
back; ~|**kommen** *unr. itr. V.; mit sein*
come back; return; (zurückgelangen) get back;
~**kommen auf** (+ *Akk.*) come back to
⟨*subject, question, point, etc.*⟩; ~|**kriegen**
tr. V. (ugs.) ▶ ~BEKOMMEN; ~|**lassen** *unr.
tr. V.* leave; ~|**legen** *tr. V.* (a) put back; (b)
(reservieren) put aside, keep (*Dat.*, **für** for); (c)
(sparen) put away; (d) (hinter sich bringen) cover
⟨*distance*⟩; ~|**lehnen** *refl. V.* lean back;
~|**nehmen** *unr. tr. V.* (auch fig. widerrufen)
take back; ~|**rufen** *unr. tr. V.* (a) call back;
recall ⟨*ambassador*⟩; (b) *auch itr.* (telefonisch)
call *or* (Brit.) ring back; ~|**schauen** *itr. V.*
(bes. südd., österr., schweiz.) ▶ ~BLICKEN;
~|**schicken** *tr. V.* send back;
~|**schlagen** ① *unr. tr. V.* (a) (nach hinten
schlagen) fold back ⟨*cover, hood, etc.*⟩; turn
down ⟨*collar*⟩; (b) (durch einen Schlag
zurückbefördern) hit back; (mit dem Fuß) kick
back; (c) (zum Rückzug zwingen, abwehren) beat
off, repulse ⟨*enemy, attack*⟩; ② *unr. itr. V.* (a)
hit back; ⟨*enemy*⟩ strike back, retaliate; (b)
mit sein ⟨*pendulum*⟩ swing back;
~|**schrecken** *regelm.*, (veralt.) *unr., itr. V.,
mit sein* **vor etw.** (*Dat.*) ~**schrecken** (fig.)
shrink from sth.; **er schreckt vor nichts ~:**
he will stop at nothing; ~|**senden** *unr. od.
regelm. tr. V.* (geh.) ▶ ~SCHICKEN; ~|**treten**
unr. itr. V.; mit sein step back; (von einem Amt)
resign; step down; ⟨*government*⟩ resign; (von
einem Vertrag usw.) withdraw (**von** from); back
out (**von** of); (fig.: in den Hintergrund treten)
become less important; ~|**weisen** *unr.
tr. V.* reject ⟨*proposal, question, demand,
application, etc.*⟩; turn down, refuse ⟨*offer,
request, help, etc.*⟩; turn away ⟨*petitioner,
unwelcome guest*⟩; repudiate ⟨*accusation,
claim, etc.*⟩; ~|**werfen** *unr. tr. V.* throw
back; reflect ⟨*light, sound*⟩; repulse ⟨*enemy*⟩;
(fig.: in einer Entwicklung) set back; ~|**zahlen**
tr. V. pay back; ~|**ziehen** ① *unr. tr. V.* (a)
pull back; draw back ⟨*bolt, curtains, one's
hand, etc.*⟩; (b) (abziehen, zurückbeordern)
withdraw ⟨*troops*⟩; recall ⟨*ambassador*⟩; (c)
(rückgängig machen) withdraw; cancel ⟨*order,
instruction*⟩; ② *unr. refl. V.* withdraw
Zu·ruf *der* shout

zu|**rufen** *unr. tr. V.* jmdm. etw. ~: shout sth.
to sb.
zur·zeit *Adv.* at the moment
Zu·sage *die* (a) (auf eine Einladung hin)
acceptance; (auf eine Stellenbewerbung hin) offer
(b) (Versprechen) promise; undertaking
zu|**sagen** ① *itr. V.* (a) accept
(b) jmdm. ~ (gefallen) appeal to sb.
② *tr. V.* promise
zusammen *Adv.* together; ~ **sein**
(zusammenleben) be *or* live together
zusammen-, Zusammen-: ~**arbeit**
die cooperation *no indef. art.;* ~|**arbeiten**
itr. V. cooperate; ~|**binden** *unr. tr. V.* tie
together; ~|**brechen** *unr. itr. V.; mit sein*
collapse; (fig.) ⟨*order, communications, system,
telephone network*⟩ break down; ⟨*traffic*⟩
come to a standstill; ~**bruch** *der* collapse;
(fig., auch psychisch, nervlich) breakdown;
~|**drücken** *tr. V.* press together;
~|**fahren** *unr. itr. V.; mit sein*
(zusammenzucken) start; jump; ~|**fallen** *unr.
itr. V.; mit sein* (a) collapse; (b) [zeitlich]
~**fallen** coincide; ~|**fassen** *tr. V.*
summarize; ~**fassung** *die* summary;
~|**fegen** *tr. V.* (bes. nordd.) sweep together;
~|**fließen** *unr. itr. V.; mit sein* ⟨*rivers,
streams*⟩ flow into each other; ~**fluss,**
*****~**fluß** *der* confluence; ~|**fügen** *tr. V.* fit
together; ~|**führen** *tr. V.* bring together;
~|**gehören** *itr. V.* belong together;
~**gehörig** *Adj.* [closely] related *or*
connected ⟨*subjects, problems, etc.*⟩; matching
attrib. ⟨*pieces of tea service, cutlery, etc.*⟩;
~**gehörigkeit** *die;* ~~~: **ein starkes
Gefühl der ~gehörigkeit** a strong sense of
belonging together;
~**gehörigkeits·gefühl** *das* sense *or*
feeling of belonging together; ~**hang** *der*
connection; (einer Geschichte, Rede) coherence;
(Kontext) context; ~|**hängen** *unr. itr. V.* (a)
be joined [together]; (b) **mit etw. ~hängen**
(fig.) be related to sth.; (durch etw. [mit]
verursacht sein) be the result of sth.;
~|**kehren** *tr. V.* (bes. südd.) sweep together;
~**klappbar** *Adj.* folding; ~|**klappen** *tr.
V.* fold up; ~|**kommen** *unr. itr. V.; mit sein*
(a) meet; **mit jmdm. ~kommen** meet sb.; (b)
(zueinanderkommen; auch fig.) get together;
(gleichzeitig auftreten) occur *or* happen together;
~**kunft** *die;* ~~, ~**künfte** meeting;
~|**laufen** *unr. itr. V.; mit sein* (a) ⟨*people,
crowd*⟩ gather, congregate; (b) ⟨*rivers,
streams*⟩ flow into each other, join up;
~|**leben** *itr. V.* live together; ~**leben** *das*
living together *no art.;* ~|**legen** ① *tr. V.*
(a) put *or* gather together; (b) (zusammenfalten)
fold [up]; (c) (miteinander verbinden)
amalgamate, merge ⟨*classes, departments,
etc.*⟩; combine ⟨*events*⟩; (d) put ⟨*patients,
guests, etc.*⟩ together [in the same room];
② *itr. V.* club together; ~|**nehmen** ① *unr.
tr. V.* summon up ⟨*courage, strength,
understanding*⟩; ② *unr. refl. V.* get *or* take a
grip on oneself; **nimm dich ~!** pull yourself

---

*old spelling - see note on page xiv

z

together!; ~|**passen** *itr. V.* go together; ⟨*persons*⟩ be suited to each other; ~**prall** *der;* ~~[e]s, ~~e collision; ~|**prallen** *itr. V.; mit sein* collide (mit with); ~|**schlagen** *unr. tr. V.* (verprügeln) beat up; **~*|**sein**
▶ ZUSAMMEN; ~|**setzen** ⟨1⟩ *tr. V.* put together; ⟨2⟩ *refl. V.* (a) sich aus etw. ~**setzen** be made up *or* composed of sth.; (b) (sich zueinander setzen) sit together; (zu einem Gespräch) get together; ~**setzung** *die;* ~~, ~~en (a) putting together; (b) (Aufbau) composition; „~**setzung**: ..." (als Aufschrift auf Medikamentenpackung) 'ingredients: ...'; (c) (Sprachw.) compound; ~**spiel** *das* (a) (von Musikern) ensemble playing; (von Darstellern) ensemble acting; (einer Mannschaft) teamwork; (b) (fig.) interplay; ~|**stehen** *unr. itr. V.* stand together; ~|**stellen** *tr. V.* put together; draw up ⟨*list*⟩; ~**stoß** *der* collision; (fig.) clash (mit with); ~|**stoßen** *unr. itr. V.; mit sein* collide (mit with); ~|**treffen** *unr. itr. V.; mit sein* (a) meet; mit jmdm. ~**treffen** meet sb.; (b) (zeitlich) coincide; ~|**wachsen** *unr. itr. V.; mit sein* grow together; join [up]; ⟨*bones*⟩ knit together; (fig.) ⟨*towns*⟩ merge into one; ~|**zählen** *tr. V.* add up; ~|**ziehen** *unr. itr. V.; mit sein* move in together; mit jmdm. ~**ziehen** move in with sb.; ~|**zucken** *itr. V.; mit sein* start; jump

Zu·satz *der* addition; (Zugesetztes, Additiv) additive

zusätzlich ⟨1⟩ *Adj.* additional ⟨2⟩ *adv.* in addition

zu|**schauen** *itr. V.* (südd., österr., schweiz.)
▶ ZUSEHEN

Zu·schauer *der,* **Zu·schauerin** *die;* ~, ~nen spectator; (im Theater, Kino) member of the audience; (an einer Unfallstelle) onlooker; (Fernsehzuschauer) viewer; **die Zuschauer** (im Theater, Kino) the audience *sing.*

Zuschauer·zahl *die* (bes. Ferns.) audience [numbers]; (Sport) attendance

zu|**schicken** *tr. V.* send; jmdm. etw. ~: send sth. to sb.

zu|**schieben** *unr. V.* (a) push ⟨*drawer, door*⟩ shut
(b) (fig.) jmdm. die Schuld ~: lay the blame on sb.

Zu·schlag *der* (a) additional *or* extra charge; (für Nacht-, Feiertagsarbeit usw.) additional *or* extra payment
(b) (Eisenb.) supplement

zu|**schlagen** ⟨1⟩ *unr. tr. V.* bang *or* slam ⟨*door, window, etc.*⟩ shut; close ⟨*book*⟩; (heftig) slam ⟨*book*⟩ shut
⟨2⟩ *unr. itr. V.* (a) *mit sein* ⟨*door, trap*⟩ slam *or* bang shut
(b) (einen Schlag/Schläge führen) throw a blow/ blows; (losschlagen) hit *or* strike out; (fig.) ⟨*army, police, murderer*⟩ strike

zu|**schließen** ⟨1⟩ *unr. tr. V.* lock ⟨2⟩ *unr. itr. V.* lock up

zu|**schnüren** *tr. V.* tie up

zu|**schrauben** *tr. V.* screw the lid *or* top on ⟨*jar, flask*⟩; screw ⟨*lid, top*⟩ on

Zu·schrift *die* letter; (auf eine Anzeige) reply

Zu·schuss, *****Zu·schuß** *der* contribution (zu towards)

zu|**sehen** *unr. itr. V.* (a) watch; jmdm. [beim Arbeiten *usw.*] ~: watch sb. [working *etc.*]
(b) (dafür sorgen) make sure; see to it

zu|**senden** *unr. od. regelm. tr. V.*
▶ ZUSCHICKEN

Zu·sendung *die* sending

zu|**spitzen** *refl. V.* become aggravated

zu|**sprechen** ⟨1⟩ *unr. tr. V.* (a) er sprach ihr Trost/Mut zu his words gave her comfort/ courage
(b) jmdm. ein Erbe *usw.* ~: award sb. an inheritance *etc.;*
⟨2⟩ *unr. itr. V.* jmdm. ermutigend/tröstend ~: speak encouragingly/comfortingly to sb.

Zu·stand *der* (a) condition; (bes. abwertend) state
(b) (Stand der Dinge) state of affairs

zu·stande *Adv.* etw. ~ bringen [manage to] bring about sth.; ~ kommen come into being; (geschehen) take place

zu·ständig *Adj.* appropriate relevant ⟨*authority, office, etc.*⟩; [für etw.] ~ sein (verantwortlich) be responsible [for sth.]

Zuständigkeit *die;* ~, ~en (Verantwortlichkeit) responsibility; (Kompetenz) competence

zu|**stehen** *unr. itr. V.* etw. steht jmdm. zu sb. is entitled to sth.

zu|**steigen** *unr. itr. V.; mit sein* get on; ist noch jemand zugestiegen? (im Bus) ≈ any more fares, please?; (im Zug) ≈ tickets, please!

zu|**stellen** *tr. V.* deliver ⟨*letter, parcel, etc.*⟩

zu|**stimmen** *itr. V.* agree; jmdm. [in einem Punkt] ~: agree with sb. [on a point]; einer Sache (*Dat.*) ~: agree to sth.

Zu·stimmung *die* (Billigung) approval (zu of); (Einverständnis) agreement (zu to, with)

zu|**stoßen** *unr. itr. V.; mit sein* jmdm. ~: happen to sb.

Zu·tat *die* ingredient

zu·teil *Adv.* jmdm./einer Sache ~ werden (geh.) be granted to sb./sth.

zu|**teilen** *tr. V.* jmdm. jmdn./etw. ~: allot *or* assign sb./sth. to sb.; jmdm. seine Portion ~: mete out his/her share to sb.

zu|**tragen** *unr. refl. V.* (geh.) occur

zuträglich *Adj.* healthy ⟨*climate*⟩; jmdm./ einer Sache ~ sein be good for sb./sth.; be beneficial to sb./sth.

zu|**trauen** *tr. V.* jmdm. etw. ~: believe sb. [is] capable of [doing] sth.; sich (*Dat.*) etw. ~: think one can do sth.

Zutrauen *das;* ~s confidence, trust (zu in)

zutraulich ⟨1⟩ *Adj.* trusting ⟨2⟩ *adv.* trustingly

Z

Zutraulichkeit *die;* ∼: trust[fulness]
zu|treffen *unr. itr. V.* **(a)** be correct
(b) auf *od.* für jmdn./etw. ∼: apply to sb./sth.
zutreffend 1 *Adj.* **(a)** correct; (treffend) accurate
(b) (geltend) applicable; relevant
2 *adv.* correctly
zu|trinken *unr. itr. V.* jmdm. ∼: raise one's glass and drink to sb.
Zu·tritt *der* entry; admittance; „kein ∼", „∼ verboten" 'no entry'; 'no admittance'; ∼ [zu etw.] haben have access [to sth.]
Zu·tun *das;* ∼s: ohne jmds. ∼: without sb.'s being involved
zu·unterst *Adv.* right at the bottom
zuverlässig 1 *Adj.* reliable; (verlässlich) dependable ⟨person⟩
2 *adv.* reliably
Zuverlässigkeit *die;* ∼: reliability; (Verlässlichkeit) dependability
Zuversicht *die;* ∼: confidence
zuversichtlich 1 *Adj.* confident
2 *adv.* confidently
***zuviel** ▶ ZU 2A
zu·vor *Adv.* before
zuvor|kommen *unr. itr. V.; mit sein* **(a)** jmdm. ∼: beat sb. to it
(b) einer Sache (*Dat.*) ∼: anticipate sth.
zuvorkommend 1 *Adj.* obliging; (höflich) courteous
2 *adv.* obligingly; (höflich) courteously
Zuvorkommenheit *die;* ∼: courteousness; courtesy
Zuwachs *der;* ∼es, Zuwächse increase (*Gen.,* an + *Dat.* in)
Zuwachs·rate *die* (bes. Wirtsch.) growth rate
Zu·wanderer *der,* **Zu·wanderin** *die* immigrant
Zu·wanderung *die* immigration
zu·weilen *Adv.* (geh.) now and again
zu|weisen *unr. tr. V.* jmdm. etw. ∼: allocate *or* allot sb. sth.
zu|wenden *unr. od. regelm. refl. V.* sich jmdm./einer Sache ∼ (auch fig.) turn to sb./sth.
***zu·wenig** ▶ ZU 2A
zuwider *Adj.* jmdm. ∼ sein be repugnant to sb.
zu|winken *itr. V.* jmdm./einander ∼: wave to sb./one another
zu|zahlen *tr. V.* pay ⟨five euros etc.⟩ extra
zu|ziehen 1 *unr. tr. V.* pull ⟨door⟩ shut; draw ⟨curtain⟩; do up ⟨zip⟩
2 *unr. refl. V.* sich (*Dat.*) eine Krankheit ∼: catch an illness
3 *unr. itr. V.; mit sein* move into the area
Zu·zug *der* influx
zuzüglich *Präp. mit Gen.* plus
zwang *1. u. 3. Pers. Sg. Prät. v.* ZWINGEN

---

*alte Schreibung - vgl. Hinweis auf S. xiv

Zwang *der;* ∼[e]s, Zwänge **(a)** compulsion
(b) (unwiderstehlicher Drang) irresistible urge
zwängen 1 *tr. V.* squeeze
2 *refl. V.* squeeze [oneself]
zwanghaft *Adj.* obsessive
zwanglos 1 *Adj.* **(a)** informal; casual ⟨behaviour⟩
(b) (unregelmäßig) haphazard ⟨arrangement⟩
2 *adv.* **(a)** informally
(b) (unregelmäßig) haphazardly ⟨arranged⟩
Zwanglosigkeit *die;* ∼: **(a)** informality
(b) (Unregelmäßigkeit) haphazard *or* casual manner
Zwangs·lage *die* predicament
zwangs·läufig 1 *Adj.* inevitable
2 *adv.* inevitably
zwanzig *Kardinalz.* twenty; *s. auch* ACHTZIG
zwanziger *indekl. Adj.* die ∼ Jahre the twenties
Zwanzig·mark·schein *der* twenty-mark note
zwanzigst... *Ordinalz.* twentieth
zwar *Adv.* **(a)** admittedly
(b) und ∼: to be precise
Zweck *der;* ∼[e]s, ∼e purpose; (Sinn) point; es hat keinen ∼: it's pointless; es hat keinen ∼, das zu tun there is no point in doing that
zweck-, Zweck-: ∼**entfremden** *tr. V.* use for another purpose; ∼**los** *Adj.* pointless; ∼**losigkeit** *die;* ∼∼: pointlessness; ∼**mäßig** 1 *Adj.* appropriate; expedient ⟨behaviour, action⟩; functional ⟨building, fittings, furniture⟩;
2 *adv.* appropriately ⟨arranged, clothed⟩; ⟨act⟩ expediently; ⟨equip, furnish⟩ functionally; ∼**mäßigkeit** *die* appropriateness; (einer Handlung) expediency; (eines Gebäudes) functionalism
zwecks *Präp. mit Gen.* (Papierdt.) for the purpose of
zwei *Kardinalz.* two; *s. auch* ACHT[1]
Zwei *die;* ∼, ∼en **(a)** (Zahl) two
(b) (Schulnote) B
zwei-, Zwei-: ∼**bettzimmer** *das* twin-bedded room; ∼**deutig** 1 *Adj.* ambiguous; (fig.: schlüpfrig) suggestive ⟨remark, joke⟩;
2 *adv.* ambiguously; (fig.) suggestively; ∼**deutigkeit** *die;* ∼∼, ∼∼en ambiguity; (fig.) suggestiveness; ∼**dimensional** 1 *Adj.* two-dimensional; 2 *adv.* two-dimensionally; ∼**ein·halb** *Bruchz.* two and a half
zweierlei *indekl. Adj.* **(a)** *attr.* two sorts *or* kinds of; two different ⟨sizes, kinds, etc.⟩; odd ⟨socks, gloves⟩
(b) *allein stehend* two [different] things
zwei·fach *Vervielfältigungsz.* double; (zweimal) twice
Zwei·fache *das; adj. Dekl.* das ∼: twice as much
Zweifel *der;* ∼s, ∼: doubt (an + *Dat.* about); etw. in ∼ ziehen question sth.
zweifelhaft *Adj.* **(a)** doubtful

(b) (fragwürdig) dubious; (suspekt) suspicious
zweifel·los *Adv.* undoubtedly
zweifeln *itr. V.* doubt; **an jmdm./etw.** ∼: doubt sb./sth.; have doubts about sb./sth.
zweifels-, Zweifels-: ∼**fall** *der* case of doubt; doubtful *or* problematic case; **im** ∼**fall[e]** in case of doubt; if in doubt; ∼**ohne** *Adv.* undoubtedly; without doubt
Zweig *der;* ∼**[e]s,** ∼**e** [small] branch; (meist ohne Blätter) twig
zwei-, Zwei-: ∼**hundert** *Kardinalz.* two hundred; ∼**mal** *Adv.* twice; ∼**mark·stück** *das* two-mark piece; ∼**pfennig·stück** *das* two-pfennig piece; ∼**reiher** *der* double-breasted suit/coat/jacket; ∼**schneidig** *Adj.* double-edged; ∼**sprachig** ① *Adj.* bilingual; ⟨sign⟩ in two languages; ② *adv.* bilingually; ⟨written⟩ in two languages; ⟨published⟩ in a bilingual edition; ∼**spurig** *Adj.* **(a)** two-lane ⟨road⟩; **(b)** two-track ⟨vehicle⟩; **(c)** two- *or* twin-track ⟨recording⟩; ∼**stellig** *Adj.* two-figure *attrib.* ⟨number, sum⟩; ∼**stöckig** *Adj.* two-storey *attrib.;* ∼**stöckig sein** have two storeys
zweit… *Ordinalz.* second; **jeder Zweite** every other one; *s. auch* ERST…
zwei·tägig *Adj.* (2 Tage alt) two-day-old *attrib.;* (2 Tage dauernd) two-day *attrib.*
zweit·ältest… *Adj.* second oldest
zwei·tausend *Kardinalz.* two thousand
zweit·best… *Adj.* second best
*****zweite·mal** ▶ MAL¹
*****zweiten·mal** ▶ MAL¹
zweitens *Adv.* secondly; in the second place
Zweite[r]-Klasse-Abteil *das* second-class compartment
zweit·rangig *Adj.* of secondary importance *postpos.;* (zweitklassig) second-rate
Zweit·stimme *die* second vote
zwei·türig *Adj.* two-door ⟨car⟩
Zweit-: ∼**wagen** *der* second car; ∼**wohnung** *die* second home
Zwei-zimmer·wohnung *die* two-room flat (Brit.) *or* (Amer.) apartment
Zwerch·fell *das* (Anat.) diaphragm
Zwerg *der;* ∼**[e]s,** ∼**e** dwarf; (Gartenzwerg) gnome
Zwetsche *die;* ∼, ∼**n** damson plum
Zwieback *der;* ∼**[e]s,** ∼**e** *od.* **Zwiebäcke** rusk; (unzählbar) rusks *pl.*
Zwiebel *die;* ∼, ∼**n** onion; (Blumenzwiebel) bulb
zwie-, Zwie-: ∼**gespräch** *das* (geh.) dialogue; ∼**spalt** *der;* ∼∼**[e]s,** ∼∼**e** *od.* ∼**spälte** [inner] conflict; ∼**spältig** *Adj.* conflicting ⟨mood, feelings⟩; discordant ⟨impression⟩; (widersprüchlich) contradictory ⟨nature, attitude, person, etc.⟩
Zwilling *der;* ∼**s,** ∼**e** **(a)** twin **(b)** *Pl.* (Astrol.) Gemini; the Twins; **er/sie ist [ein]** ∼: he/she is a Gemini

Zwillings-: ∼**bruder** *der* twin brother; ∼**paar** *das* pair of twins; ∼**schwester** *die* twin sister
zwingen *unr. tr. V.* force; **jmdn. [dazu]** ∼, **etw. zu tun** force *or* compel sb. to do sth.
zwingend *Adj.* compelling ⟨reason, logic⟩; conclusive ⟨proof, argument⟩; imperative ⟨necessity⟩
zwinkern *itr. V.* **[mit den Augen]** ∼: blink; (als Zeichen) wink
Zwirn *der;* ∼**[e]s,** ∼**e** [strong] thread *or* yarn
zwischen *Präp. mit Dat./Akk.* between; (mitten unter) among[st]
zwischen-, Zwischen-: ∼**durch** /-'-/ *Adv.* (zeitlich) between times; (zwischen zwei Zeitpunkten) in between; (von Zeit zu Zeit) from time to time; ∼**fall** *der* incident; ∼**landen** *itr. V.; mit sein* **in X** ∼**landen** land in X on the way; ∼**mahlzeit** *die* snack [between meals]; ∼**menschlich** ① *Adj.* interpersonal ⟨relations⟩; ⟨contacts⟩ between people; ② *adv.* on a personal level; ∼**raum** *der* space; gap; (Lücke) gap; ∼**ruf** *der* interruption; **viele** ∼**rufe** a great deal of heckling *sing.;* ∼**wand** *die* dividing wall; partition; ∼**zeit** *die* interim
Zwist *der;* ∼**[e]s,** ∼**e** (geh.) strife *no indef. art.;* (Fehde) feud; dispute
Zwistigkeit *die;* ∼, ∼**en** (geh.) dispute
zwitschern *itr. V.* (auch tr.) V. chirp
Zwitter *der;* ∼**s,** ∼ (Biol.) hermaphrodite
zwo *Kardinalz.* (ugs.; bes. zur Verdeutlichung) two
zwölf *Kardinalz.* twelve; ∼ **Uhr mittags/nachts** [twelve o'clock] midday/midnight; *s. auch* ACHT¹
zwölft… *Ordinalz.* twelfth; *s. auch* ACHT…
zwölftel *Bruchz.* twelfth; *s. auch* ACHTEL
Zwölftel *das* (schweiz. meist *der*); ∼**s,** ∼: twelfth
zwot… *Ordinalz.* (ugs.; bes. zur Verdeutlichung) second
zwotens *Adv.* (ugs.; bes. zur Verdeutlichung) secondly
Zylinder /tsi'lɪndɐ/ *der;* ∼**s,** ∼ **(a)** cylinder; **(b)** (Hut) top hat
zylindrisch ① *Adj.* cylindrical ② *adv.* cylindrically
Zyniker *der;* ∼**s,** ∼, **Zynikerin** *die;* ∼, ∼**nen** cynic
zynisch ① *Adj.* cynical ② *adv.* cynically
Zynismus *der;* ∼: cynicism
Zypern (*das*) ∼**s** Cyprus
Zyprer *der;* ∼**s,** ∼, **Zyprerin** *die;* ∼, ∼**nen** Cypriot
Zypresse *die;* ∼, ∼**n** cypress
Zypriot *der;* ∼**en,** ∼**en,** **Zypriotin** *die;* ∼, ∼**nen** Cypriot
zypriotisch, zyprisch *Adj.* Cypriot
Zyste *die;* ∼, ∼**n** (Med.) cyst

Z

. . . .

Contents

. . . .

Calendar
Culture
Letters

Traditions, festivals, and holidays in German-speaking countries

1 January Neujahr (New Year's Day) is always a public holiday and tends to be a quiet day when people are recovering from the Silvester celebrations.

6 January Heilige Drei Könige Epiphany or Twelfth Night is a public holiday in Austria and some parts of southern Germany. In some areas, children dress up as the Three Kings and go from house to house to bless homes for the coming year and collect money for charity.

2 February Mariä Lichtmess Candlemas is celebrated in the Catholic Church but is not a public holiday.

1 April Erster April April Fool's Day is the time to make an April fool of your family and friends (*jdn. in den April schicken*) or to play an April fool trick (*Aprilscherz*).

1 May Erster Mai May Day is a public holiday in Germany, Austria, and Switzerland. It is celebrated by trade unions as Labour Day, often with rallies and demonstrations. Many people go on a family outing; in rural areas maypoles are put up in the villages.

3 October Tag der deutschen Einheit Germany's national holiday, the Day of German Unity, commemorates German reunification on 3 October 1990.

26 October Nationalfeiertag Austria's national holiday.

31 October Reformationstag Reformation Day is a public holiday in some mainly Protestant parts of Germany and commemorates the Reformation.

1 November Allerheiligen All Saints' Day is a public holiday in Catholic parts of Germany and Austria.

2 November Allerseelen All Souls' Day is the day when Catholics remember their dead by visiting the cemeteries to pray and place wreaths, flowers, and candles on the graves. This is often done on 1 November as Allerseelen is not a public holiday.

11 November Martinstag (St Martin's Day) is not a public holiday, but in Catholic areas the charitable saint is commemorated with processions where children carry lanterns and sing songs. Traditional food includes the *Martinsgans* (roast goose) and *Martinsbrezel* (a soft pretzel).

6 December Nikolaustag On the eve of St Nicholas' Day, children put out their boots in the hope of finding presents and fruit, nuts, and sweets in the morning. St Nicholas is always depicted as looking much like Santa Claus or Father Christmas.

25 December Weihnachten (Christmas) is a family event in Germany, and preparations begin with the *Adventskranz*, an Advent wreath with four candles. On each Sunday of Advent one more candle is lit. Christmas decorations are generally very traditional, with fir branches, candles and wooden Christmas figurines, which can be bought at the *Weihnachtsmarkt* (Christmas market). Typical Christmas baking includes *Stollen* or *Christstollen* (a rich fruit bread), *Lebkuchen* (spicy honey biscuits), and lots of biscuits in the shape of stars, bells, etc. The decorated Christmas tree should only be seen by the children on Heiligabend (Christmas Eve), when presents are given out. The erster Weihnachtstag (Christmas Day) is a public holiday in Germany, Austria, and Switzerland. It tends to be a quiet day for family gatherings, often with a traditional lunch of goose or carp.

The zweiter Weihnachtstag (Boxing Day) is also a public holiday; in Austria and Switzerland it is called Stephanstag (St Stephen's Day).

31 December Silvester New Year's Eve is not a bank holiday, but firms and shops tend to close early. Many people celebrate with a party, or a meal with friends, toasting in the new year at midnight with Sekt (German sparkling wine), and watching fireworks.

Movable feasts

Rosenmontag The day before Shrove Tuesday is not an official holiday but many people, especially in the Rhineland, get the day off to take part in the *Karneval* celebrations, including masked balls, fancy-dress parties, and parades. Almost every town has its own carnival prince and princess. The street parades in Düsseldorf, Cologne, Mainz, and other cities are attended by thousands of revellers wearing fancy dress and shown live on television.

Faschingsdienstag Shrove Tuesday is the final day of *Fasching* (Carnival) in southern Germany, with processions and fancy-dress parties similar to Rosenmontag in the northwest. In the far south, ancient customs to drive out the winter with bells and drums survive.

Aschermittwoch Ash Wednesday marks the end of the carnival season and the beginning of Lent. It is celebrated in the Catholic Church but it is not a pubic holiday.

Karfreitag Good Friday is a public holiday and generally quiet. Catholics traditionally eat fish on this day.

Ostern Easter traditions include hiding Easter eggs (often dyed hardboiled eggs, or the chocolate variety) in the garden for the children, supposedly left by the *Osterhase* (Easter bunny). Ostermontag (Easter Monday) is also a public holiday.

Weißer Sonntag (Sunday after Easter) In the Catholic Church, first communion is traditionally taken on this Sunday.

Muttertag (second Sunday in May). On Mother's Day, children of all ages give their mothers small gifts, cards, or flowers.

Christi Himmelfahrt (40 days after Easter). Ascension Day is a public holiday in Germany, Austria, and Switzerland. This is also Father's Day, when fathers traditionally go out on day trips or pub crawls.

Pfingsten (Whitsun – seventh Sunday after Easter). As Pfingstmontag (Whit Monday) is a public holiday in Germany, Austria, and Switzerland, Whitsun is a popular time to have a long weekend away.

Fronleichnam (second Thursday after Whitsun). Corpus Christi is a public holiday in Austria and in parts of Germany and Switzerland. In Catholic areas, processions and open-air masses are held.

Erntedankfest Harvest festival is not a legal holiday in Germany, but is celebrated with church services on the first Sunday in October in many rural areas. In Switzerland there is a harvest thanksgiving holiday in mid-September.

Buß- und Bettag (third Wednesday in November). This day of 'repentance and prayer' is a public holiday only in some parts of Germany.

Volkstrauertag (second Sunday before the beginning of Advent). In Germany, this is a national day of mourning to commemorate the dead of both world wars, and the victims of the Nazis.

Totensonntag (last Sunday before the beginning of Advent). Protestants remember their dead on this day.

Advent The four weeks leading up to Christmas, beginning with the 1. Adventssonntag (first Sunday in Advent), still have a special significance in Germany, even for people who are not religious.

Calendar

A–Z of life and culture in German-speaking countries

Abendbrot, Abendessen For most Germans, MITTAGESSEN is still the main meal of the day. *Abendbrot* or *Abendessen* normally consists of bread, cheese, meats, perhaps a salad, and a hot drink. It is eaten by the whole family at about 6 or 7 p.m. *Abendessen* can also refer to a cooked meal, especially for people who are out at work all day.

Abitur The *Abitur*, or *Matura* in Austria, is the final exam taken by pupils at a GYMNASIUM, usually when they are aged about 19. The result is based on continuous assessment during the last two years before the *Abitur*, plus examinations in four subjects. On passing the *Abitur*, a *Zeugnis der allgemeinen Hochschulreife* is issued. This certificate is the obligatory qualification for university entrance.

Adventskranz A garland made of fir springs, traditionally decorated with ribbons and four candles. The wreath is either suspended from the ceiling or put on a table. One candle is lit on the first Sunday in Advent, two on the next, and so on until the fourth Sunday.

Allerheiligen ▶ TRADITIONS, FESTIVALS, AND HOLIDAYS

Allerseelen ▶ TRADITIONS, FESTIVALS, AND HOLIDAYS

Amerikahaus In Germany and Austria, Amerikahäuser are US information centres. They have reference libraries and offer language courses and lectures.

Ampelkoalition A term describing any coalition between the SPD (the party colour is red), the FDP (yellow), and the Green Party (*see* BÜNDNIS 90). This type of coalition has become increasingly common in local government over the last ten years, with some LÄNDER ruled in this way.

Amtsgericht *Amtsgerichte* (local or district courts) are the lowest level of ordinary courts in Germany. They work in a two-tier system with the *Landgerichte* (regional courts) and deal with minor cases. There are four levels of ordinary courts hearing both civil and criminal cases: beside the *Amtsgericht* and *Landgericht* there are the *Oberlandesgericht* (higher regional court) and the *Bundesgerichtshof* (federal supreme court). Most legal proceedings at the local court are handled by magistrates. The regional courts handle more serious cases and deal with local court appeals; a panel of lay judges sits with a professional judge in a regional court.

Arbeitsagentur The local employment office to be found in every German town (formerly called *Arbeitsamt*). It provides career guidance, helps the unemployed find new jobs, and processes all claims for ARBEITSLOSENGELD I and related benefits. Unemployed people have to report to the *Arbeitsagentur* once every three months to prove that they are still looking for work.

Arbeitsgericht Industrial tribunals are held at administrative courts (local, higher, and federal), which handle all proceedings under administrative law. They deal with disputes between employers and employees, between employers and trade unions, and matters connected with the *Betriebsverfassungsgesetz* (industrial relations law).

Arbeitslosengeld I, or earnings-related unemployment benefit, is paid to all unemployed people who are looking for a new job and have already made a minimum contribution to the ARBEITSLOSENVERSICHERUNG. The benefit is a proportion of the person's previous pay, and is higher for people supporting children. It is generally paid for up to one year. People unemployed for longer than twelve months, or those who are not entitled to *Arbeitslosengeld I*, can apply for the so-called *Arbeitslosengeld II* (unemployment benefit II), which has replaced *Arbeitslosenhilfe* and is a reduced-rate benefit.

Arbeitsamt ▶ ARBEITSAGENTUR

Arbeitslosenversicherung This is the compulsory state-run insurance against unemployment. All employees have to pay into this scheme, and in return are entitled to ARBEITSLOSENGELD I and related benefits. Employees and employers each pay half of the contributions. This area has been subject to wide-ranging reforms in recent years.

Archiv der Jugendkulturen Since 1998 the Archive of Youth Culture in Berlin has been collecting and cataloguing books, magazines, CDs, and other materials of special interest to young people. The Archive is open to the public and publishes a magazine called *Journal der Jugendkulturen* (Journal of Youth Culture).

ARD – Arbeitsgemeinschaft der öffentlich-rechtlichen Rundfunkanstalten der Bundesrepublik Deutschland An umbrella organization for the regional broadcasting stations of the various German LÄNDER, financed by licence fees plus a certain amount of advertising. The ARD broadcasts das ERSTE.

Aschermittwoch ▶ TRADITIONS, FESTIVALS, AND HOLIDAYS

AStA — Allgemeiner Studentenausschuss A students' union which consists of twelve student boards elected by a student parliament that is voted in annually. AStA deals with all student issues, including financial, cultural, and social concerns, offering advice and support.

Ausbildungsplatz Over 500,000 firms in all branches of the economy, including the independent professions and the public sector, provide trainee posts for AZUBIS. Young people can only apply for these in state-recognized occupations for which vocational training is required. Large firms have their own training workshops, but smaller firms train their apprentices on the job.

Autobahn Germany's motorway network is very extensive and not subject to a general speed limit, other than a recommended limit of about 80 mph (130 km/h). But increasingly speed limits are in force on long stretches of the *Autobahn*. Many motorways have only two lanes. To ease congestion, lorries are not allowed to use the *Autobahn* on Sundays. German motorways are free for passenger traffic. Lorries over twelve tonnes pay a toll known as *Autobahngebühren*. On Austrian and Swiss motorways, all vehicles must display a VIGNETTE.

Azubi Trainees and apprentices are known as *Azubis* or *Auszubildende*. They are trained within the German dual system (*das duale Ausbildungssystem*), which combines practical on-the-job training in recognized occupations with theoretical instruction at a BERUFSSCHULE. During the training period, *Azubis* receive a small wage from their employer. In order to gain professional qualifications, *Azubis* take an examination at the end of their two- or three-year apprenticeship; this is conducted by a board of examiners such as the chamber of industry and commerce, the chamber of crafts, or representatives of employers and vocational schoolteachers.

Bachfest This ten-day music festival is held annually in honour of the great German composer Johann Sebastian Bach (1685–1750), and takes place in Leipzig, where Bach spent many years of his life. The Bachfest is one of more than a hundred important music festivals in Germany.

BAföG – Bundesausbildungsförderungsgesetz Federal education and training assistance, which about a quarter of German students receive from the state. Whether they are entitled to a *BAföG* grant or loan, and how much they get, depends on the students' and their parents' financial circumstances. Half of this assistance is awarded in the form of a grant, and the rest as an interest-free loan which usually has to be repaid within five years of the end of the maximum entitlement period. The payments are made by the STUDENTENWERKE (student welfare services).

BahnCard A rail pass for frequent rail travellers within Germany. *Bahncard 25/Bahncard 50/Bahncard 100* entitle the holder to 25 per cent, 50 per cent, or 100 per cent discount respectively. There are a number of other passes and saver tickets offering reductions throughout Germany, Austria, Switzerland, and neighbouring countries.

Bauhaus   A school of architecture and the applied arts founded in 1919 in Weimar and later housed at Dessau. Under the leadership of Walter Gropius (1883–1969) and Ludwig Mies van der Rohe (1886–1969), it became the centre of modern design in the 1920s and played a key role in establishing a relationship between architecture, technology, and functionality. The Bauhaus was closed down by the Nazis in 1933.

Bausparen   German building societies expect people to have saved up a sizeable sum towards the purchase of a house before they will give them a mortgage. For this reason, many Germans have a *Bausparvertrag* (a tax-efficient savings contract for an agreed sum) with a building society, even if they are not planning to buy their EIGENHEIM for some time.

Bayern   Bayern, or Bavaria, the largest and most southerly of Germany's LÄNDER, is known for its beautiful scenery (the Alps and their foothills, as well as forests, rivers, and lakes, picturesque towns and villages), its excellent BIER (beer) and food, and its lively cosmopolitan capital, München (Munich). The Bavarians are said to be warm and hospitable, but also fiercely independent and very conservative.

Bayreuth   The Franconian city of Bayreuth in Bavaria is a magnet for opera fans. The German composer Richard Wagner (1813–83) lived there from 1872. Since 1876 the Richard Wagner Festival has been staged annually in the Festspielhaus, the festival theatre built between 1872 and 1876 with funding by the Bavarian King Ludwig II, one of Wagner's greatest admirers.

Beamte   This term, meaning 'official', covers civil servants and other local government officers, but also teachers and lecturers. *Beamte* are legally obliged to support the democratic system in Germany and are not allowed to go on strike. In return, they enjoy many privileges, such as total job security, private health insurance, and exemption from social security contributions.

Berlin   After WIEDERVEREINIGUNG, Berlin took over from Bonn as the capital of Germany, though the German government did not start moving there until 1998. This vibrant city lies on the River Spree. It has about 3.5 million inhabitants and is a major cultural and commercial centre.

Berlinale   This is the short name for the Internationale Filmfestspiele Berlin, an annual film festival that was first held in 1951. A *Goldener Bär* (Golden Bear) statuette is awarded for the best film, and a *Gläserner Bär* (Glass Bear) for the best children's film. The bear is Berlin's symbol.

Berliner Theatertreffen   Founded in 1964, the Berlin Theatre Encounter presents the best German-language plays. Some dramatic productions are broadcast on 3SAT, which also presents one of the Theatertreffen prizes, awarded for innovative drama.

Berufsfachschule A full-time vocational college that offers preparation courses for a period of one to three years. Only pupils with a *Haupt-* or *Realschulabschluss* (school-leaving certificates) can attend a *Berufsfachschule*. The courses count as part of an apprenticeship, or can even replace it. *See also* SCHULE.

Berufsschule A college for young people who are doing a LEHRE. They attend *Berufsschule* one or two days a week (or sometimes in blocks of several weeks) to continue their general education and receive formal training in their chosen type of job.

Besenwirtschaft An inn set up temporarily by a local winegrower for a few weeks after the new wine has been made. A blown-up pig's bladder hung outside the door indicates that the new vintage may be sampled here. This is mainly found in southern Germany and is similar to the Austrian HEURIGE. *See also* STRAUSSWIRTSCHAFT.

Culture

Betriebsrat The staff in any German company with at least five employees are entitled to have a *Betriebsrat*. This is a committee elected by the workers to represent their interests, as opposed to those of management. It allows workers to participate in decisions on pay and other benefits, redundancies, and even some business matters.

Bier Germany and Austria rank among the world's top beer producers and consumers, with a vast range of beer varieties (Bock, Alt, Dunkel, Export, Hell, Kölsch, Lager, Malzbier, Pils, Märzen, Weizenbier or Weißbier, and Berliner Weiße) to choose from. Germans brew more than 5,000 varieties, and each beer tastes different depending on the ratio of ingredients, brewing temperature and technique, alcoholic content, ageing time, and colour. Although there are now some big brewing conglomerates, the local brews from small independent breweries (there are about 1,300 in Germany) are still the best and most popular. German beer is brewed according to the *Reinheitsgebot* (beer purity regulation) of 1516, which stipulates that no ingredients other than hops, malted barley, yeast, and water can be used. Dortmund and Munich are among the top beer-producing cities in the world. Drinking beer is a vital part of everyday life for many people; they regularly meet up at their STAMMTISCH in a *Kneipe* (pub) or BIERGARTEN.

Biergarten A rustic open-air pub, or beer garden, which is traditional in Bavaria and Austria but can now also be found throughout Germany. It is usually set up for the summer in the yard of a pub or restaurant and serves beer and simple meals. In Munich beer gardens, the drink comes in a litre-sized glass, called a *Maß*. The standard everyday pale beer most people order is a *Helles*, a dark beer is a *Dunkles*, and a wheat beer is a *Weißbier*.

Bild Zeitung Germany's largest-selling daily newspaper, *Bild* is a typical tabloid with huge headlines, lots of photos, scandal stories, gossip, and nude models. It is known for its right-wing views. *Bild* sells about 4.5 million copies every day, almost eight times more than any other newspaper in Germany. Its Sunday edition is called *Bild am Sonntag*.

Bioladen A health-food shop which sells only organically grown products.

Biotonne ▶ RECYCLING

BKJ ▶ DBJR

Blauer Brief A letter sent by a school to inform parents that their son or daughter is in danger of having to repeat the year, a concept colloquially known as SITZEN BLEIBEN.

Blauer Engel The Blue Angel label on goods for sale shows consumers that the product is environmentally friendly.

Bodensee This is the German name for Lake Constance, Germany's biggest lake, bordered by Germany, Switzerland, and Austria. The River Rhine flows through it. This popular recreation area enjoys a particularly mild climate, especially on the three islands, Lindau, Mainau, and Reichenau.

Bonn Bonn was the capital of the Federal Republic of Germany (*see* BUNDESREPUBLIK DEUTSCHLAND) from 1949 until Berlin was made the capital of reunified Germany in 1991. It is still home to a number of government institutions. This relatively small city of about 300,000 inhabitants enjoys a picturesque location on the River Rhine.

Brandenburger Tor Once a symbol of divided Berlin, the Brandenburg Gate triumphal arch has become a symbol of reunited Germany. It was designed in the neoclassical style by Karl Gotthard Langhans (1732–1808) and opened in 1791 as an entrance to the boulevard Unter den Linden. Topped by the goddess of peace, the monument was part of the closed border between East and West Berlin from 1961 to 1989.

Brothers Grimm ▶ KINDER- UND HAUSMÄRCHEN

Bund This term refers to the federal state as the top level of government, as opposed to the individual LÄNDER which make up the BUNDESREPUBLIK. *Bund* and *Länder* have different responsibilities, with the *Bund* in charge of foreign policy, defence, transport, health, employment, etc.

Bundesbank Properly called the Deutsche Bundesbank, Germany's central bank is an autonomous non-governmental institution located in Frankfurt am Main. With the introduction of the EURO in 1999, some of the bank's functions passed to the European Central Bank (also in Frankfurt).

Bundesheer The Bundesheer is the Austrian federal army, which ensures the country's neutrality. All 18-year-old Austrian males must serve for a compulsory six months, plus two further months reserve duty at later dates. Conscientious objectors do public service. No foreign military bases are allowed on Austrian territory. *See also* WEHRDIENST, ZIVILDIENST.

Bundeskanzler The chancellor is the head of government in Germany and Austria. The German chancellor is normally elected for four years by the ministers in the BUNDESTAG after being proposed by the BUNDESPRÄSIDENT. The *Bundeskanzler* chooses the ministers and decides on government policies.

Bundesländer ▶ LÄNDER

Bundesliga The German national soccer league is split into two divisions of eighteen teams: *Bundesliga* and *2nd Bundesliga*. League games attract hundreds of thousands of spectators every week during the regular season.

Bundesminister The Federal Government consists of the BUNDESKANZLER and the *Bundesministerin* (federal ministers). The chancellor appoints ministers and determines their number and responsibilities in the Cabinet. Ministers run their ministries independently but within the framework of the guidelines of the chancellor's policy.

Bundespräsident The president is the head of state in Germany and Austria. The German president is elected for five years by the members of the BUNDESTAG and delegates from the LÄNDER. The *Bundespräsident* acts mainly as a figurehead, representing Germany abroad, and does not get involved in party politics, although he often takes a moral lead in major issues and can exercise personal authority through his neutral mediating function. The *Bundespräsident* can only be re-elected once.

Bundesrat This is the upper house of the German parliamentary system. The Bundesrat members are appointed by the LÄNDER governments and represent them. The Bundesrat has to approve laws affecting the *Länder*, and also any changes to the GRUNDGESETZ. The opposition parties can sometimes hold a majority in the Bundesrat, which allows them to influence German legislation.

Bundesrepublik Deutschland, or Bundesrepublik for short, is the official name of the German state (the Federal Republic of Germany, or FRG). Before reunification, the shortened form was used to distinguish the West German state from the East German (*see* GDR), but it is now commonly used to refer to the reunified state. Established on 23 May 1949, the republic became fully independent from British, French, and US control in May 1955. In October 1990 the Federal Republic merged with the GDR to form a single, unified Germany. *See also* WIEDERVEREINIGUNG.

Bundestag The lower house of the German parliament, which is elected every four years by the German people. The Bundestag is responsible for federal legislation, the federal budget, and electing the BUNDESKANZLER. Half of the ministers are elected directly and half by proportional representation, in a system in which each voter has two votes. *See also* NATIONALRAT.

Bundesverfassungsgericht As the supreme court in Germany, the federal constitutional court in Karlsruhe is the guardian of the GRUNDGESETZ and the final arbiter in any German legal appeal. It passes judgement on constitutional complaints and has the power to order a party's dissolution if it is unconstitutional and may pose a threat to democracy. The Federal Government has to accept the judges' ruling, however controversial the case may be. The Bundesverfassungsgericht consists of two panels, each with eight judges, who are elected for a single twelve-year term. Half of the panel is elected by the BUNDESTAG and half by the BUNDESRAT.

Bundeswappen The federal coat of arms is the eagle. This heraldic bird – emblem of the Roman emperors – was adopted by Charlemagne and became the coat of arms of the German Empire when it was founded in 1871. The Weimar Republic adopted it in its present form in 1919, and since 1950 it has been used by the BUNDESREPUBLIK DEUTSCHLAND.

Bundeswehr This is the name for the Federal Armed Forces, which come under the control of the defence minister. The Bundeswehr consists of professional soldiers and conscripts serving their WEHRDIENST. Until 1994, the GRUNDGESETZ did not allow German forces to be deployed abroad, but they now take part in certain operations, notably UN peacekeeping missions.

Bündnis 90/Die Grünen This party came into being in 1993 as a result of the merger of the West German Green party and civil-rights movements of the former East Germany (GDR). It is an important force in the German parliament, committed to environmental and social issues.

Burschenschaft A students' duelling society, like a fraternity, which was founded in Jena in 1815 to strengthen patriotic feeling. The tradition was abolished in 1935, but a decade later male students formed a new fraternity, the Deutsche Burschenschaft. Most of these generally right-wing social organizations for students are now called studentische Verbindungen (*Verbindung* means 'link' or 'connection'). There are now also Verbindungen for women.

CDU – Christlich-Demokratische Union One of the main German political parties, it was founded in 1945 and is committed to Christian and conservative values. Led by Angela Merkel, the CDU and its sister party, the CSU, were well ahead in opinion polls at the start of the 2005 election

Culture

campaign. However, results announced after the 18 September ballot
showed the CDU/CSU had gained only four more seats than its rivals, the
SPD, headed by former chancellor Gerhard Schröder. Extended negotiations
between the SPD and CDU/CSU resulted in an agreement to form a Grand
Coalition between the parties, with Merkel as BUNDESKANZLER.

Christkind Traditionally, it is *das* Christkind (the Christ child) who
brings Christmas presents to children on Christmas Eve. The concept of
der Weihnachtsmann (Father Christmas or Santa Claus) is relatively new
in Germany.

Christopher Street Day Gay Pride festivals and parades in Germany
and Switzerland are called Christopher Street Days (or CSDs), after the
New York street in which the gay protests known as the Stonewall
Rebellion took place in 1969. Pride parades are held in most German cities,
and the most famous are in Berlin and Cologne. In Austria, the parade is
called the Regenbogenparade (Rainbow Parade).

CSU – Christlich-Soziale Union The Bavarian sister party
of the CDU was founded in 1946 and has enjoyed an absolute
majority in Bavaria for over 30 years. It now forms part of the
governing Grand Coalition in Germany.

DAAD – Deutscher Akademischer Austauschdienst
The German Academic Exchange Service is a joint
organization of universities and other institutions of higher
education for the promotion of academic exchange. The
DAAD is the central source of information on study and
research opportunities in Germany and abroad. It awards
scholarships to students and academics and acts as a national
agency for grants from the European Union.

DBJR – Deutscher Bundesjugendring The German Federal Youth
Association, based in Berlin, is made up of twenty-four national youth
organizations and sixteen regional youth councils. The Bundesjugendring
aims to represent young people in their everyday lives. The
Bundesvereinigung Kulturelle Jugendbildung (BKJ), a separate Federation
of Youth Cultural Associations based in Remscheid, specializes in cultural
activities that are followed by more than 12 million young people.

Deutsche Bibliothek The German Library in Frankfurt am Main is the
central archive of all German-language writing, and the national
bibliographical information centre of the BUNDESREPUBLIK. The first
national library bringing together all German-language literature under
one roof was set up in Leipzig in 1912. The division of Germany after the
Second World War resulted in a new national library, established in 1947 in
Frankfurt. After reunification in 1990, the German library in Leipzig was
merged with the Frankfurt library.

(sidebar) Culture

Deutsche Post The previously state-run German postal system has undergone wide-ranging reforms in recent years, which will effectively remove the Deutsche Post monopoly by 2007. The number of post offices has been reduced, but small post-office agencies can now be found in shops, newsagents, and petrol stations. German letter boxes are yellow. Postal charges are relatively high, but the service is very reliable.

Deutsche Telekom The previously state-run German telecommunications service has undergone extensive reforms and gradual privatization and is now a public limited company. Since 1998, when the market was opened up to competition, Deutsche Telekom has ceased to have a monopoly.

Deutsche Welle Aimed at listeners abroad, this radio station is financed and controlled by the German government and broadcasts programmes on German politics, business, arts, and culture.

Deutscher Kulturrat The German Arts Council was founded in 1982 as a non-governmental commission representing cultural associations and institutions. The Arts Council comprises eight independent organizations, among them the Sociocultural Council (SOZIOKULTUR). The function of the Kulturrat is to coordinate, advise, and inform on matters concerning cultural affairs, make recommendations on cultural policy, and further international cultural relations.

Deutscher Sportbund – DSB Around 27 million people are members of a sports club in Germany, while another 12 million take part in sport. The German Sports Federation (DSB) has 16 regional sports federations and many individual sports associations. There are more than 2.5 million volunteer coaches and officials working for the Sports Federation. The DSB also promotes programmes such as *Trimm dich* (Get fit), a programme aimed at physical fitness, and *Sport für alle* (Sport for all), a programme encouraging people to run, swim, cycle, ski, and hike. About 750,000 people a year pass DSB tests and qualify for a gold, silver, or bronze sports medal.

Deutschlandlied This has been the German national anthem since 1922, when it was chosen by the first president of the Weimar Republic. The song entitled *Lied der Deutschen* (Song of the Germans) was written by Hoffmann von Fallersleben in 1841 and set to a melody composed by Joseph Haydn (1732–1809). Only the third stanza of the song is now used as the national anthem.

Diplomprüfung Final (degree) examination at a university or equivalent higher education institution in a technical or scientific subject, especially in engineering, business administration, design, agriculture, and social work. On passing the exam, a degree or diploma is awarded.

Duales System This waste-disposal and recycling system was
introduced in Germany in 1993 and is operated by the private company
DSD. All packaging materials marked with the GRÜNER PUNKT symbol are
collected separately, and sorted into plastics, glass, paper, and metal for
recycling. All other waste is still collected by the local refuse collection
service. *See also* RECYCLING.

Eigenheim Germany and Switzerland have the lowest levels of home
ownership in Europe, while Austria has among the highest. In Germany,
many people happily live in rented flats or houses, but most dream of
buying or building their *Eigenheim* (own home) one day, and save up
towards it through the system of BAUSPAREN. First-time buyers are usually
middle-aged and expect to stay in their home for the rest of their lives.

Einwohnermeldeamt (residents' registration office) Anybody who
moves to Germany or relocates within Germany is legally obliged to
register their address with the *Einwohnermeldeamt* within a
week.

Eisschießen, Eisstockschießen Ice-stick shooting or
Bavarian curling is a popular sport in Bavaria and Austria.
There are two kinds of *Eisschießen*: in one, the aim is to slide
the ice stick, a heavy metal plate with a handle, as far as
possible across the ice; in the other, players slide a metal-
plated wooden ice stick as close as possible to the *Daube*, a
wooden tee.

Elternzeit A German mother or father who looks after a
child at home is entitled to up to three years' extended
maternity or paternity leave. At the end of this *Elternzeit* –
formerly called *Erziehungsurlaub* (parental leave) – they are entitled to
return to their old job. Around 95 per cent of German mothers take time
out of work for at least one year after the birth.

Entwerter In many German cities, *Entwerter* (ticket-cancelling
machines) are located on U-Bahn and S-Bahn platforms, or on trains,
trams, or buses. When travelling on public transport in Germany, it is
important to remember to cancel (*entwerten*) the ticket in one of the
machines. Even if just bought from the driver, your ticket is not valid
without this stamp.

Erntedankfest ▶ TRADITIONS, FESTIVALS, AND HOLIDAYS

Erste, Das Also called Erstes Programm, this is the first German public
TV channel, broadcast by ARD. Programming includes news, information,
films, and entertainment. There is a limited amount of advertising, which
is concentrated in blocks at certain times of day and not after 8 p.m.

Erziehungsgeld A state benefit paid for up to two years to any mother or
father who stays at home after the birth of a child to look after it. In 98 per

cent of cases, it is still the mother who claims *Erziehungsgeld*. In addition to this, parents receive *Kindergeld* (child benefit) for each child.

Erziehungsurlaub ▶ ELTERNZEIT

Euro The *Euro* was introduced as a *gemeinsame Währung* (common currency) in twelve states of the European Union in 2002. It replaced the *Mark* in Germany and the *Schilling* in Austria. Switzerland is not a member of the EU and retained the *Franken*.

Eurocheque The *Eurocheque* is the standard cheque issued by banks in Germany. It is backed up by the *Eurochequekarte*, which can also be used at cash machines and for payments in shops. Although plastic cards have become more popular in Germany, many people (and shops and restaurants) still prefer cash.

Fachhochschule This type of college provides shorter, more vocational and practical courses than those available at a HOCHSCHULE. A third of new students now enrol at a *Fachhochschule* to take the DIPLOMPRÜFUNG.

Fachhochschulreife ▶ FACHOBERSCHULE

Fachoberschule This vocationally orientated college takes students with an intermediate school certificate and leads to the *Fachhochschulreife*, a certificate qualifying students for the FACHHOCHSCHULE. Courses last for two to three years and cover theoretical instruction as well as on-the-job training.

Fasching, Fastnachtszeit This is the carnival season, which begins in November and ends on Aschermittwoch for Lent. Depending on the region it is called *Karneval*, *Fastnacht*, *Fasnet*, or *Fasching*, and is celebrated in Germany, Austria, and Switzerland. Every town and village has its own carnival customs. Whether it is the Kölner Karneval or the Münchner Fasching, celebrations reach a climax in the last week, especially on Rosenmontag and Faschingsdienstag. On Ash Wednesday everything returns to normal. *See also* ASCHERMITTWOCH, FASCHINGSDIENSTAG, ROSENMONTAG in TRADITIONS, FESTIVALS, AND HOLIDAYS.

Faschingsdienstag ▶ TRADITIONS, FESTIVALS, AND HOLIDAYS

FDP – Freie Demokratische Partei The German Liberal party, founded in 1948. This relatively small party has held the balance of power in coalitions in the past, even though it tends to gain only 5 to 10 per cent of the vote at general elections (9.9 per cent in 2005). It supports a free-market economy and the freedom of the individual.

Flohmarkt There is a *Flohmarkt* (flea market) on Sundays in most big cities. Stalls are set up along a main street, in a park or central square, to sell knick-knacks, second-hand clothes, furniture, and other bargains.

Focus A relatively new weekly news and current affairs magazine published in Munich. It was set up in 1993 and is aimed at a centre-right, professional readership. *Focus* has become a serious competitor of DER SPIEGEL, with shorter, easier-to-read articles, and a more modern presentation.

Formel 1 Formula 1 motor racing enjoys a large following in Germany, particularly since local hero Michael Schumacher has won the drivers' world championship seven times between 1994 and 2004. The German Grand Prix, which has been won three times by Michael and once by his brother Ralf, takes place each year at Hockenheim near Mannheim. The European Grand Prix has been held at the Nürburgring in Rheinland-Pfalz since 1999.

FPÖ – Freiheitliche Partei Österreichs The Austrian Freedom Party, also known as Die Freiheitlichen, was founded in 1955. It is right wing and is the third largest party. It advocates a minimum monthly wage and stricter asylum policies.

Frankfurter Allgemeine Zeitung (FAZ) One of Germany's most serious and widely respected daily newspapers. It tends to have a centre-left to liberal outlook.

Frankfurter Buchmesse The annual Book Fair was first held in Frankfurt in 1964. Since then it has become the most important publishing trade fair in the world. Held every October, it includes the award of the Friedenspreis des deutschen Buchhandels (Peace Prize of the German Book Trade). Leipzig also stages an important annual book fair.

Die Freiheitlichen ▶ FPÖ

FRG – Federal Republic of Germany ▶ BUNDESREPUBLIK DEUTSCHLAND

Frühstück Breakfast in Germany typically consists of strong coffee, slices of bread or fresh rolls with butter, jam, honey, sliced cheese and meat, and maybe a boiled egg. For working people and schoolchildren, who have little time for breakfast first thing in the morning, a *zweites Frühstück* is common at around 10 a.m.

Fünfprozentklausel The 5 per cent clause, introduced in 1953, stipulates that only parties gaining at least 5 per cent of the valid second votes, or at least three constituency seats, can be represented in parliament.

Fußballweltmeisterschaft The Football World Cup takes place in Germany in 2006, with matches spread across twelve cities, including the opening match in Munich and the final in Berlin. The German team won the *Weltmeisterschaft* (World Cup) in 1954, 1974, and 1990, and has been runner-up four times. Women's football is also strong in Germany; the German team won the Women's World Cup in 2003.

Gastarbeiter The term used for workers from foreign countries, mainly Turkey, former Yugoslavia, and Italy, many of whom came to Germany in the 1960s and 1970s. Despite the time that they have lived in Germany, and the fact that their children have grown up there, the issue of integration is still widely discussed.

GDR – German Democratic Republic The communist state, established in the Soviet-occupied zone of Germany after the Second World War. Also known as East Germany, or the Deutsche Demokratische Republik (DDR), it lasted from 1949 to 1990. *See also* BUNDESREPUBLIK DEUTSCHLAND, MAUER, WIEDERVEREINIGUNG.

Gemeinde The lowest level of local government, run by a local council chaired by the *Bürgermeister* (mayor). *Gemeinden* have their own budget, with income from local taxes. They pass local legislation and administer local affairs.

Gesamthochschule A type of university established in some LÄNDER following reforms in the 1960s and combining HOCHSCHULE and FACHHOCHSCHULE under one roof, thereby offering greater flexibility and a wider choice of subjects to the student.

Gesamtschule A comprehensive secondary school introduced in the 1970s and designed to replace the traditional division into GYMNASIUM, REALSCHULE, and HAUPTSCHULE. Pupils are taught different subjects at their own level and may take any of the school-leaving exams, including the ABITUR.

Glascontainer ▶ RECYCLING

Goethe-Institut An organization promoting German language and culture abroad. It is based in Munich and runs about 140 institutes in over seventy countries, offering German language classes, cultural events such as exhibitions, films, and seminars, and a library, which is open to the public, of German books and magazines and other documentation.

Goldener Bär ▶ BERLINALE

Grundgesetz The written German constitution which came into force in May 1949. It lays down the basic rights of German citizens, the relationship between BUND and LÄNDER, and the legal framework of the German state.

Grundschule The primary school which all German children attend for four years from the age of six (some children do not start until they are seven). Lessons are intense but pupils only attend school for about four hours a day. At the end of the *Grundschule*, teachers and parents decide together which type of secondary school – HAUPTSCHULE, REALSCHULE, GESAMTSCHULE, or GYMNASIUM – the child should attend.

Grünen, Die ▶ BÜNDNIS 90

Grüner Punkt A symbol used to mark packaging materials that can be recycled. Any packaging carrying this logo is collected separately under the DUALES SYSTEM recycling scheme. Manufacturers have to buy a licence from the recycling company DSD (Duales System Deutschland) to entitle them to use this symbol.

Gruppe 47 This German literary group was founded (in 1947, hence its name) by the writer Hans Werner Richter (1908–93), who organized regular meetings to encourage young German-language authors in the postwar era. The group's two most famous representatives both won Nobel Prizes in Literature: Heinrich Böll in 1972, for his 'renewal of German literature', and Günter Grass, in 1999, for portraying 'the forgotten face of history'.

Gymnasium The secondary school which prepares pupils for the ABITUR. The GYMNASIUM is attended after the GRUNDSCHULE by the most

academically inclined pupils. They spend nine years at this school, and during the last three years they have some choice as to which subjects they study. *See also* SCHULE.

Hansestadt Hansestädte (Hanseatic cities), such as Bremen and Hamburg, were once part of an association of trading cities along the North Sea and Baltic coasts. The Hanse (Hanseatic League or Hansa) was formed in the 13th century to protect the economic interests of its members. Meetings were held at Lübeck, where members developed a system of commercial laws. The Hanse remained a powerful force until the late sixteenth century, after which it declined.

Hauptschule The secondary school which prepares pupils for the *Hauptschulabschluss* (school-leaving certificate). The *Hauptschule* aims to give less academically inclined pupils a sound educational grounding. Pupils stay at the *Hauptschule* for five or six years after the GRUNDSCHULE. *See also* LEHRE, SCHULE.

Hausordnung These 'house rules' are what a tenant has to adhere to in order to maintain a harmonious relationship with neighbours. They might cover the maintenance of common areas and the appearance of the house or apartment block; for example, forbidding a tenant from hanging washing from a front window. But usually the *Hausordnung*, whether written or unwritten, refer to restrictions on noise, possibly even including running a late-night bath. *See also* RUHEZEIT.

Heiligabend ▶ TRADITIONS, FESTIVALS, AND HOLIDAYS

Heilige Drei Könige ▶ TRADITIONS, FESTIVALS, AND HOLIDAYS

Heurige This is an Austrian term for both a new wine and an inn with new wine on tap, especially an inn with its own vineyard in the environs of

Vienna. On warm, late summer evenings Viennese wine devotees sit on wooden benches and sample the new wine of the year. A garland of pine twigs outside the gates of the *Heurige* shows that the barrel has been breached. *See also* BESENWIRTSCHAFT and STRAUßWIRTSCHAFT.

Hochdeutsch There are many regional variations and dialects in Germany, Austria, and Switzerland (64 per cent of Swiss people speak Schwyzerdütsch). Hochdeutsch is the standard German that can be understood by all German speakers. It is probably the only way for a Bavarian, Austrian, or Swiss to communicate with a North German. Newspapers and other publications are generally printed in Hochdeutsch, which is regarded as 'proper' German.

Hochschule German *Hochschulen* (universities and colleges) have up to now generally not charged fees, but at least some LÄNDER will in the near future introduce them. Anybody who has passed the ABITUR is entitled to go to university (except for some subjects which have a restriction on numbers, or NUMERUS CLAUSUS). They tend to be very large and impersonal institutions. Students may receive a BAFÖG grant and often take more than the minimum eight semesters (four years) to complete their course.

Hochzeit Church weddings are not legally recognized in Germany, Austria, or Switzerland, and all couples must be married in a civil ceremony. The civil ceremony is held in a *Standesamt* (registry office, called a *Zivilstandsamt* in Switzerland). The civil marriage tends to be a private family affair; if the couple also has a church ceremony afterwards, that is usually a more public event. Various traditions are associated with weddings: often a car procession takes place (where the wedding party and guests drive around honking their horns, and well-wishers honk back), or children strew flowers in front of the couple for good luck. The bachelor party or stag night is known as *Junggesellenabschied*, and there is often also an informal party held before the wedding known as POLTERABEND. Since 2001, same-sex couples have been able to register a civil union called a *Lebenspartnerschaft*.

ICE – Intercityexpresszug This high-speed train runs at one- or two-hour intervals on a number of main routes in Germany, offering shorter journey times and better facilities than ordinary trains.

IM – inoffizieller Mitarbeiter This term refers to 'unofficial collaborators' of the STASI. These informers were often ordinary people in the former GDR who had been recruited or pressurized by the Stasi to spy on neighbours, family, and friends. However, some were prominent figures in the West.

Jüdisches Museum The new Jewish Museum in Berlin opened in 1999, a

stunning, angular silver building designed by the American architect
Daniel Libeskind. It stands in dramatic contrast to its Baroque neighbour,
a former appeal court built in 1734–35. The collection covers two millennia
of German Jewish history, and includes a Holocaust Tower memorial.

Kaffee This refers not only to coffee as a drink but also to the small meal
taken at about four in the afternoon, consisting of coffee and cakes or
biscuits. It is often a social occasion, as it is common to invite family or
friends for *Kaffee und Kuchen* (rather than for tea or dinner), especially on
birthdays and other family occasions.

Kanton The name for the individual autonomous states that make up
Switzerland. There are 26 *Kantone*, each with its own government and
constitution.

Karneval ▶ FASCHING, FASTNACHTSZEIT

Kfz-Kennzeichen This is the number plate on German motor vehicles,
which have to be licensed by the *Zulassungsstelle* (vehicle
registration office) for the owner's registered place of
residence. The first letter, or first two or three letters, on the
Kfz-Kennzeichen indicate where the car comes from.

Kl.KA – Kinderkanal This publicly funded children's TV
channel was set up in 1997 by ARD and ZDF. Based in Erfurt,
the channel broadcasts German children's favourites, as well
as classic programmes from around the world.

Kindergarten Every German pre-school child has the right
to attend *Kindergarten* (nursery or play school) between the
ages of three and six. *Kindergarten* concentrates on play,
crafts, singing, etc., and aims to foster the child's social and emotional
development. There is no formal teaching at all, this being reserved for the
GRUNDSCHULE.

Kindertagesstätte Often called *Kita* for short, these day nurseries are
intended for the children of working parents and usually cater for babies to
6-year-olds, though some *Kitas* also offer after-school care for older children.

Kinder- und Hausmärchen Jakob Grimm (1785–1863) and his brother
Wilhelm (1786–1859) collected fairy tales for their book of *Kinder- und
Hausmärchen* (Household and Nursery Tales). In 1852 they started
compiling a comprehensive German dictionary, but the work was so vast
that it was only completed in 1961, a century after their deaths.

Kirchensteuer Any taxpayer who is a member of one of the established
churches in Germany (mainly Catholic and Protestant) has to pay
Kirchensteuer (church tax). It is calculated as a proportion of income tax
and is collected at source by the tax office, which then passes on the money
to the relevant church.

Kita ▶ KINDERTAGESSTÄTTE

Knecht Ruprecht ▶ KRAMPUS

Krampus – Knecht Ruprecht The legendary figure known as Krampus in Austria and Bavaria, and Knecht Ruprecht in other regions, is St Nicholas's helper. While St Nicholas carries presents, Krampus is a scary – sometimes horned – figure, who carries a sack in which he is supposed to place disobedient children. Other traditions have him carrying a birch and a sack full of coal for the naughty ones. He visits on St Nicholas' Day (6 December). He is also believed to help the CHRISTKIND carry Christmas presents. *See also* TRADITIONS, FESTIVALS, AND HOLIDAYS.

Krankenkasse There are many different health insurance organizations in Germany. Contributions are high, due to the high standard (and cost) of health care in Germany. Members of the *Krankenkassen* are given plastic cards entitling them to treatment by the doctor of their choice.

Kriminalpolizei – Kripo The criminal investigation department deals with serious offences, including murder, terrorism, and organized crime.

Kulturstadt Weimar This thousand-year-old city has played an important role in Germany's cultural history. The composer Johann Sebastian Bach (1685–1750) and the artist Lucas Cranach (1472–1553) lived and worked here. Other important writers and poets such as Johann Wolfgang von Goethe (1749–1832), Johann Gottfried von Herder (1744–1803) and Christoph Martin Wieland (1733–1813) – who translated Shakespeare's plays – made the city their home. Friedrich von Schiller (1759–1805) wrote many of his plays in Weimar, while the composer Franz Liszt (1811–86) composed and gave concerts here. In 1919 the Bauhaus was founded in Weimar; in the same year, the constitution of the first German republic – the Weimar Republic – was drafted in the city.

Kur A health cure in a spa town lasting about three to six weeks and usually involving a special diet, exercise programmes, physiotherapy, massage, etc. These are intended for people with minor complaints or recovering from illness. *Kuren* are paid for by the KRANKENKASSEN, with the patient making a contribution. The *Kur* is not taken as frequently as it once was.

Kuratorium Junger Deutscher Film Young creative directors are given financial support by the LÄNDER. The Young German Film Board awards prizes for first films (sometimes also second films) of artistic value. The Filmförderungsanstalt – FFA (German Film Board) – provides financial assistance for film productions and cinemas.

Ladenschlusszeit Strict regulations governing *Ladenschlusszeit* (shop closing times) in Germany were relaxed in 1996. Shops are allowed to stay open until 8 p.m. on weekdays and 4 p.m. on Saturdays, and bakeries may open for three hours on Sundays. However, actual opening times vary, depending on the location and size of the shop.

Länder Germany is a federal republic consisting of sixteen member states called *Länder* or *Bundesländer*. Five so-called *neue Bundesländer* were added after reunification in 1990. Each *Land* has a degree of autonomy and is responsible for educational and cultural affairs, the police, the environment, and local government. Austria is a federal state consisting of nine *Länder*. The Swiss equivalent of a German or Austrian *Land* is a KANTON.

Landtag The parliament of a *Land*. It is elected every four to five years using a similar mixed system of voting as for the BUNDESTAG elections.

Lebenspartnerschaft ▶ HOCHZEIT

Lehre This type of apprenticeship is still the normal way to learn a trade or train for a practical career in Germany. A *Hauptschulabschluss* is the minimum requirement, although many young people with a *Realschulabschluss* or ABITUR opt to train in this way. A *Lehre* takes about two to three years and involves practical training by a MEISTER(IN) backed up by lessons at a BERUFSSCHULE, with an exam at the end.

Linkspartei, Die (Left Party) Formerly known as the PDS, this ultra left-wing party formed in 1990 from the old East German SED, the Communist party which ruled in the former GDR. In the 2005 federal elections, the Left Party joined forces with the newly formed Arbeit & soziale Gerechtigkeit – Die Wahlalternative, or WASG (the Labour and Social Justice Party) and won an 8.7 per cent share of the vote.

Loveparade A techno music and dance festival which takes place in Berlin every summer, with hundreds of thousands of mainly young people attending. Originally a celebration of youth culture, it has become a major tourist attraction.

Markt Weekly markets are still held in most German cities and towns, usually laid out very attractively in the picturesque market squares. Fresh fruit and vegetables, flowers, eggs, cheese and other dairy products, bread, meat, and fish are available directly from the producer. Many Germans still buy most of their provisions '*auf dem Markt*'.

Matura ▶ ABITUR

Mauer *Die Mauer*, or the Berlin Wall, a 42-km (26-mile) structure of concrete blocks, was put up almost overnight in 1961. It was designed to halt the exodus of inhabitants from the Communist-controlled East of the city to the West. Over the following twenty-eight years, numerous people were killed trying to escape East Berlin. On 9 November 1989, an announcement by the East German Government that border checkpoints in the city had been abandoned resulted in a flood of people crossing to the West, the gradual dismantling of the wall, and eventually the WIEDERVEREINIGUNG. Parts of the Berlin Wall were sold to museums and private collectors. A few small sections remain as a memorial and tourist attraction.

Meister(in) A master craftsman or craftswoman who has completed rigorous training in his/her trade or vocation and has passed a final exam after several years' experience in a job. A *Meister(in)* is allowed to set up in business and train young people who are doing their LEHRE.

Meldepflicht An 'obligation to register' that applies to all German residents, regardless of nationality. Residents must inform the EINWOHNERMELDEAMT every time they change their address. The applicant is issued with an *Abmeldebestätigung* (notification of intention to leave) and must then register the new address. The system means that every resident can quickly be traced.

Mitfahrzentrale An agency that puts drivers and passengers in contact with each other (including via the Internet) to save petrol costs and reduce pollution. The Mitfahrzentrale charges a small fee, complies with particular requests (non-smoking, female drivers, etc.), and is popular throughout Germany for long-distance travel.

Mittagessen This is a cooked meal eaten in the middle of the day and is the main meal of the day for most Germans. Schoolchildren come home from school in time for *Mittagessen*, and most large companies have canteens where hot meals are served at lunchtime. On a Sunday, *Mittagessen* might consist of a starter such as clear broth, followed by a roast with gravy, boiled potatoes and vegetables, and a dessert.

Museumsinsel The Museum Island on the River Spree in Berlin is home to the renowned Pergamon Museum of Antiquities, attracting more than 850,000 visitors a year, as well as to the Altes Museum and Neues Museum. The island was designated a World Heritage Site by UNESCO in 1999.

Namenstag This day is celebrated by many Germans, especially Catholics, in the same way as a birthday. It is the day dedicated to the saint whose name the person carries, so someone called Martin, for example, would celebrate their *Namenstag* on Martinstag (11 November). *See also* TRADITIONS, FESTIVALS, AND HOLIDAYS.

Nationalrat In Austria the Nationalrat is the Federal Assembly's lower house, whose 183 members are elected for four years under a system of proportional representation. The BUNDESKANZLER commands the majority in the Nationalrat. The BUNDESRAT, the 64-member upper house, is elected by provincial assemblies. In Switzerland, the National Council is made up of 200 representatives, and together with the STÄNDERAT forms the Federal Assembly.

Neue Kronen Zeitung An Austrian tabloid that is published in Vienna and is read by around half the population. It is regarded as right wing, as is the *Kurier*, Austria's other tabloid.

Neue Zürcher Zeitung A Swiss quality daily which is held in high esteem at home and abroad.

Numerus clausus The *Numerus clausus* system is used to limit the number of students studying certain oversubscribed subjects such as medicine at German universities. It means that only those students who have achieved a minimum average mark in their ABITUR are admitted.

Oktoberfest Germany's most famous beer festival (the Munich October Festival) actually starts each year in September. Over 5 million litres of beer

are drunk over a period of sixteen days. The Oktoberfest goes back to the year 1810, when the Bavarian crown prince (later King Ludwig I) married Therese of Saxony-Hildburghausen. A horse race was organized in honour of the couple on the Theresienwiese (Therese's Meadow, named after the bride), and almost the entire population of Munich joined in the celebrations. The party was such a success that it became an annual event. Today the *Wies'n* (meadow), as the locals call the Oktoberfest, looks more like a giant fairground, with huge marquees in which the big breweries set up beer halls for visitors to drink many a *Maß* (a litre of beer), eat *Weißwurst* (veal sausage), *Schweinshaxe* (pork knuckles) and giant *Brezen* (pretzels) while listening and singing along to Bavarian music.

Orientierungsstufe A two-year orientation stage following GRUNDSCHULE, during which pupils can find out if they are more suited to a HAUPTSCHULE, GESAMTSCHULE, GYMNASIUM, or REALSCHULE. Students can transfer to a different school during this phase.

Ossi A colloquial and sometimes derogatory term for someone from the former East Germany (GDR), as opposed to a WESSI (someone from the former West Germany).

Ostern ▸ TRADITIONS, FESTIVALS, AND HOLIDAYS

ÖVP – Österreichische Volkspartei The conservative People's Party is Austria's centrist party. It was founded in 1945 and is the second largest party.

Papiertonne ▸ RECYCLING

Parkscheibe In Germany, some areas only allow limited parking time; here you have to display a *Parkscheibe* (parking disc) on your windscreen, with the hands of its clock set to your arrival time. These blue cardboard or plastic discs are available at newsagents and department stores.

Passionsspiel The famous Passion Play is held every ten years in the small Bavarian mountain village of Oberammergau. It has its origin in a vow sworn by the villagers in 1633 that they would perform the passion of Jesus if God delivered them from the plague.

PDS – Partei des Demokratischen Sozialismus ▶ LINKSPARTIE

Personalausweis The standard German identity card, with the holder's photograph and particulars, should in theory be carried at all times. If you are stopped by the police without any ID, you might be taken to a police station and kept there for up to six hours. The *Personalausweis* acts as a passport for Germans and Austrians travelling within the EU.

Pflegeversicherung Compulsory nursing-care insurance which all employees have to pay into as part of their SOZIALABGABEN. It was introduced in Germany in 1995 and pays for the long-term nursing care of the elderly and the severely disabled. Employers and employees make equal contributions to the scheme.

Pinakothek der Moderne This gallery of modern art, design, graphics, and architecture opened in Munich in 2002. Its collections concentrate on 20th- and 21st-century art, complementing the nearby Neue Pinakothek (exhibiting 19th-century art) and Alte Pinakothek (14th–18th century art).

Polterabend In Germany the *Polterabend* usually takes place a few days before the wedding and takes the form of a large party for the family and friends of both bride and groom. Traditionally, the guests smash some crockery, as this is supposed to bring good luck to the couple. *See also* HOCHZEIT.

Popmusik At the beginning of the 1980s, the *Neue Deutsche Welle* (New German Wave) of popular music brought German pop groups to the fore. Today all the different pop genres are represented by German groups, and in 2005 the German hip-hop band *Die Fantastischen Vier* won an ECHO music award. Some chart-topping German pop groups such as No Angels and Bro'Sis were discovered via the Popstars REALITY-TV show.

Post ▶ DEUTSCHE POST

Prater Vienna's largest and most popular amusement park. In 1766 Joseph II, the son of Empress Maria Theresa, decreed that Der Prater should be open to everyone. Earlier it had been forbidden to enter forests and meadows reserved for imperial hunts. The Prater has old-fashioned swings, skittle alleys, and merry-go-rounds, including the oldest carousel in Europe. A *Riesenrad* (big wheel) with a diameter of 67 m (200 ft) was put up for the World Exhibition of 1897 and is a famous Viennese landmark.

Premiere Germany's main pay-TV channel, introduced in 1991, can be received via satellite or cable. Premiere subscribers can watch feature films, sports events, documentaries, and so on, uninterrupted by advertising.

Pro 7 Germany's third largest private television channel, Pro 7 is financed entirely by advertising. It offers documentaries, films, and news programmes.

profil An Austrian news and current affairs magazine, with a circulation of over 100,000. It has a reputation for hard-hitting journalism.

Reality-TV *Reality-Shows* are as popular in the German-speaking world as elsewhere. They include *Big Brother* (shown on RTL II in Germany and TV3 in Switzerland) and a mobile version called *Taxi Orange*, shown on ORF, the public broadcaster in Austria, in which contestants have to run a taxi company in Vienna and live off the profits. So-called *Casting-Shows* such as Popstars have produced chart-topping pop groups. *See also* POPMUSIK.

Realschule The secondary school that prepares pupils for the *Realschulabschluss* (school-leaving certificate). It is in between HAUPTSCHULE and GYMNASIUM, catering for less academic students who will probably train for a practical career. Pupils stay at the *Realschule* for six years after the GRUNDSCHULE. *See also* LEHRE, SCHULE.

Rechtschreibreform After much controversy, a reform aiming to simplify the rules governing German spelling was implemented in 1998. The old spellings were officially acceptable for a transitional period until 2005, and further modifications to the reform were agreed during that period. The new spellings are still controversial and are only binding for schools and public authorities. Some newspapers have retained or returned to the old spellings, so it remains to be seen whether the changes will gain general acceptance.

Recycling All *Hausmüll* (domestic waste) in Germany is collected in at least three bins, and waste materials are recycled and reused. The *Biotonne* is for biodegradable kitchen waste (vegetable and fruit peel, meat, cheese, nutshells, tea leaves, and coffee filters, etc.). The *Wertstofftonne* can be used for plastic containers, metal objects, cans, aluminium, textiles, etc., and anything with a GRÜNER PUNKT. A separate *Papiertonne* is used for paper and cardboard, although most wrapping is discarded at source or reused – German supermarkets don't hand out a free supply of plastic bags. The *Restmüll* is for sweepings and general household rubbish. Bottles and glass are taken to the *Glascontainer* (bottle bank). A deposit on drinks bottles encourages returning empties to the shop. There are also collection points for fridges, freezers, and bulky items. *See also* DUALES SYSTEM.

Regenbogenparade ▶ CHRISTOPHER STREET DAY

Reichstag This historic building in the centre of Berlin became the seat of the BUNDESTAG in 1999. The refurbishment of the REICHSTAG included the addition of a glass cupola, with a walkway open to visitors, which provides a spectacular viewing platform and further enhances the Berlin skyline.

Religion In Germany, the Christian community is divided almost equally between Roman Catholics (26.6 million people) and Protestants (mostly Lutheran, 26.3 million). In April 2005, a German, Cardinal Joseph Ratzinger, was appointed head of the Roman Catholic Church as Papst Benedikt XVI (Pope Benedict XVI). There are also more than 3 million Muslims, mostly from Turkey and former Yugoslavia, living in Germany. Eighty-eight per cent of Austrians are Catholic, while in Switzerland there are slightly more Catholics than Protestants, with Muslims – again mainly from Turkey and former Yugoslavia – making up just over 4 per cent of the population. *See also* KIRCHENSTEUER.

Culture

Rentenversicherung This is the compulsory state pension insurance in Germany. All employees have to pay into it as part of their SOZIALABGABEN, with employers and the state also making a contribution. The amount of the German state pension depends on the contributions made by the individual, with allowances for years spent as a student or carer.

Restmüll ▶ RECYCLING

Rosenmontag ▶ TRADITIONS, FESTIVALS, AND HOLIDAYS

RTL – Radio Télévision Luxembourg Germany's largest privately owned television channel is the market leader in commercial television. It broadcasts films, sport, news, and entertainment, and regularly achieves top viewing figures.

Ruhezeit This is the accepted 'quiet time', usually between one and three o'clock in the afternoon, late evening, and on Sundays. *Ruhezeit* prohibits loud music and any noisy work, including drilling and vacuuming. But many young Germans no longer adhere to the letter of the *Ruhezeit*. *See also* HAUSORDNUNG.

Salzburger Festspiele Since 1920, this annual festival has been held in Salzburg, the home of Wolfgang Amadeus Mozart (1756–91), as a tribute to the great composer.

SAT 1 Germany's second largest privately owned television channel broadcasts films, news, sport, and entertainment. It was the first commercial channel in the country.

3SAT This satellite TV channel is run jointly by ARD, ZDF, and Swiss and

Austrian TV. It offers programmes that are not broadcast by other TV stations, and almost half of 3SAT's output is devoted to cultural reports.

S-Bahn ▶ U-BAHN

Schnellimbiss Usually a *Schnellimbiss* is just a stand, selling different kinds of *Würstchen* (sausages), rissoles, *Döner* (doner kebab) or *Leberkäse* (meat loaf), depending on which region you are in. You can eat there or take the snack away. *Currywurst* – sausages served with ketchup (or a tomato-based sauce) mixed with curry powder – is a *Schnellimbiss* favourite.

Schrebergarten A *Schrebergarten* is an enclosed mini-garden in a large common garden, usually just outside an urban area. As most German city-dwellers live in blocks of flats, many rent a *Schrebergarten* to provide them with a place where they can grow fruit and flowers and relax. The gardens are named after the Leipzig physician D. G. M. Schreber (1808–61), who had the idea of creating playgrounds for children and small gardens for adults,

set within a common plot. By law, the size of each mini-garden is limited to no more than 400 sq. m (4,306 sq. ft). Most *Schrebergärten* have a shed or summer house at one end that often looks like a fairy-tale cottage, and tidy flower beds. The gardeners are members of an association (*Schrebergartenverein*) which represents their interests.

Schule German children have to attend school from the ages of 6 to 18. Full-time schooling is compulsory for nine or ten years, until pupils are at least 15. All children go to a GRUNDSCHULE for four years (six in Berlin) and move on to a HAUPTSCHULE, REALSCHULE, GYMNASIUM, or GESAMTSCHULE, depending on their ability. From the age of 15, some pupils attend a BERUFSSCHULE, a part-time vocational school. Some students stay at school until they are over 20, due to the system of SITZEN BLEIBEN.

Schultüte The first day at school (*der 1. Schultag*) is a big event for a German child, involving a ceremony at school and sometimes at church. The child is given a *Schultüte*, a large cardboard cone containing pens, small gifts, and sweets, to mark this special occasion.

Schützenfest An annual festival celebrated in most towns, involving a shooting competition, parade, and fair. The winners of the shooting competition are crowned *Schützenkönig* and *Schützenkönigin* (shooting king and queen) for the year.

Schutzpolizei (Schupo) Colloquially referred to as the Schupo, the Schutzpolizei is the general police force dealing with public security, order, and traffic offences. Most people know the Schupo only as traffic police.

Schwarzwald The Black Forest, a mountainous area in Baden-Württemberg in southwestern Germany, is a popular holiday destination for Germans and foreign tourists alike. The name refers to the large coniferous forests in the region. *See also* WALDSTERBEN.

Schweizerische Eidgenossenschaft The Swiss Confederation is the official name for Switzerland. The confederation was established in 1291 when farmers from the mountain cantons of Uri, Schwyz, and Unterwalden swore that they would jointly defend their traditional rights against the House of Habsburg. The unified federal state as it is today, with twenty-six self-governing cantons, was formed in 1848. *See also* KANTON.

Seniorenbüro There are 170 *Seniorenbüros* (senior citizens' offices) spread throughout Germany. They were set up in the early 1990s to organize events, publicize sources of help and advice, and help older people take part in volunteer work. They are government funded.

siezen/duzen German has two forms for 'you', the formal *Sie* and the familiar *du*. *Du* is used when speaking to a friend, a child, or a family member. Young people always address each other as *du*. If someone says, *wir duzen uns* (we call each other *du*), it means that they are friends. When speaking to a person you do not know very well, the polite form *Sie* is used. Even though there has been a tendency for less formality in recent years, it is still best to say *Sie*, especially in work situations and when you would normally address someone in English as Mrs or Mr.

sitzen bleiben If German pupils fail more than one subject in their end-of-year school report, they have to repeat the year. This is colloquially referred to as *sitzen bleiben*. Some students might even have to repeat two years, not sitting their ABITUR until they are 20.

Skat A popular card game for three players playing with thirty-two German cards. Keen players even join a *Skat* club.

Solidaritätszuschlag A tax surcharge introduced to help pay for the cost of German reunification and rebuilding the economy in former East Germany (GDR). It is payable by every German taxpayer and firm.

Sozialabgaben This term refers to the contributions every German taxpayer has to make towards the four main state insurance schemes: pension, health, nursing care, and unemployment. This amounts to over 40 per cent of gross income, with employee and employer paying half each.

Soziokultur The sociocultural movement has its origins in the alternative cultural scene which developed in the 1970s in Germany. Groups of artists and performers developed new, independent centres such as theatres, art schools, and women's cultural groups.

SPD — Sozialdemokratische Partei Deutschlands One of the main German political parties. Reformed after the war in 1945, it is a workers'

Culture

party supporting social-democratic values. In the 2005 federal elections, the SPD gained only 1 per cent fewer votes than the CDU/CSU; after protracted negotiations, the three parties agreed to form a Grand Coalition, headed by the CDU leader, Angela Merkel.

Der Spiegel One of Germany's best-selling weekly news and current affairs magazines, *Der Spiegel* was founded in 1947 and is published in Hamburg. It has a liberal outlook and has become synonymous with investigative journalism in Germany, as it has brought to light a number of major scandals in German business and politics over the years.

SPÖ — Sozialistische Partei Österreichs The Austrian Social-Democratic Party was founded in 1888 as the Sozialdemokratische Arbeiterpartei Österreichs (Social Democratic Workers' Party of Austria). It was reformed in 1945 and is the largest political party in Austria.

Stadtumbau Ost This government programme was set up to regenerate inner-city housing and improve the urban environment between the years 2002 and 2009 in the eastern part of Germany (the former GDR).

Stammtisch A large table reserved for regulars in most German pubs. The word is also used to refer to the group of people who meet around the table for a drink and lively discussion.

Der Standard An Austrian daily printed on pink paper and considered to be liberal in its views.

Ständerat The Ständerat (Council of States) is the upper chamber in Switzerland. It is composed of forty-six representatives from the various cantons. *See also* KANTON.

Stasi, Staatssicherheitsdienst *Stasi* is the shortened nickname of the State Security Service, the much-despised secret police and their agents in the former GDR. With the help of an extensive network of informers, the *Stasi* built up personal files on a third of the East German population. It was disbanded a year before the WIEDERVEREINIGUNG. Since then there have been many charges relating to political crimes committed by *Stasi* agents, as well as enquiries into the number of former GDR citizens who cooperated with the *Stasi*. *See also* IM.

Straußwirtschaft An inn set up temporarily by a local winegrower for a few weeks after the new wine has been made. A bunch of flowers and vine leaves above the door shows that the new vintage is ready for tasting. *See also* BESENWIRTSCHAFT and HEURIGE.

Studentenwerke The *Studentenwerke* (student welfare services) are responsible for the economic, social, cultural, and health care of students at higher educational institutions.

Culture

Süddeutsche Zeitung This respected daily national newspaper was founded in 1945 and is published in Munich. It has a liberal outlook and is read mainly in southern Germany.

Tempolimit Speed limits are either compulsory – 50 km/h (30 mph) in towns, 100 km/h (60 mph) on other roads – or recommended when driving in bad weather conditions, on dangerous stretches, and in urban areas. On the *Autobahn* the *Richtgeschwindigkeit* (recommended maximum speed) is 130 km/h (80 mph). In residential areas the limit can be as low as 30 km/h (20 mph); the 30-Zone was introduced to protect children and pedestrians.

Trabant A make of car produced in the former GDR. A Trabant, or Trabi, with its two-stroke engine and plastic body, was a prized possession, and people had to wait for years to get one. After reunification, the Trabant came to symbolize the GDR era and has achieved cult status in Germany.

U-Bahn Most large cities have a *U-Bahn* (*Untergrundbahn*) (underground railway network) that connects with an *S-Bahn* (*Schnellbahn* or *Stadtbahn*) (city and suburban railway). The same ticket can normally be used for both services.

Umweltschutz (Environmental protection) Most Germans feel a strong sense of responsibility for the environment, especially after seeing so many forests dying (WALDSTERBEN). The *Bundesumweltministerium* is the government ministry responsible for all environmental matters. Its policy is based on the 'polluter must pay' principle, by which manufacturers are obliged to collect, sort, and recycle their waste; on the cooperation principle, by which every individual is responsible for the environment; and on the prevention principle, which encourages manufacturers to develop environmentally friendly products. Other focal points are a more efficient use of energy, a clean air and water programme, less road traffic, and cleaner fuels, nature conservation, and soil protection. *See also* DUALES SYSTEM, GRÜNER PUNKT, RECYCLING.

Verein There are over 300,000 officially registered *Vereine* (clubs or associations) with their own constitution and by-laws. Millions of Germans belong to a club; nearly one in four is a member of a sports club, and there are around 15 million hiking-club members. Stamp collectors, marksmen, dog breeders, music fans – in fact those who follow any kind of activity or hobby – are soon organized into a *Verein*. Membership fees are usually low, and everybody is encouraged to socialize at club level.

Vignette In order to be able to use Austrian and Swiss motorways, all vehicles must display a sticker on the windscreen called a *Vignette*. These stickers are usually valid for one year, but foreign tourists in Austria can buy stickers for a period of ten days or two months. The sticker can be bought at all Austrian border crossings and petrol stations.

Culture

Volkshochschule (VHS) A local adult education centre that can be found in every German town. The *VHS* offers low-cost day and evening classes in a wide range of subjects, including crafts, languages, music, and exercise.

Waldsterben *Waldsterben* (the death of forests) is due mainly to pollution from factories and cars. By 1996 over half of Germany's trees were damaged. The threat to forests has strengthened support for Germany's ecological political movement, BÜNDNIS 90/DIE GRÜNEN.

WASG ▶ LINKSPARTEI

Wehrdienst Compulsory military service for young men in Germany (nine months), Switzerland (three months), and Austria (six months). Young Germans are generally called up when they are 18 or 19, although there are certain exemptions. Conscientious objectors may apply to do ZIVILDIENST instead.

Weihnachten ▶ TRADITIONS, FESTIVALS, AND HOLIDAYS

Weihnachtsmarkt During the weeks of Advent, Christmas markets take place in most German towns, selling Christmas decorations, handmade toys and crib figures, traditional Christmas biscuits, and mulled wine to sustain the shoppers.

Wein Germany, Switzerland, and Austria are wine-producing countries, best known for their white wines. Germany's main wine regions are Franconia, the Rhineland-Palatinate, the Moselle area, and Baden-Württemberg. Rhine wine (or hock) is sold in tall brown bottles and wine from the Moselle in green bottles; Franconian Bocksbeutel comes in wide, bulbous bottles. There are two categories of German wine, the cheap *Tafelwein* (table wine) and the superior *Qualitätswein* (quality wine). The best wines are designated *Qualitätswein mit Prädikat*. Sekt is a champagne-like sparkling wine. In August and September there are festivals in German wine towns and villages. Austria grows red and white wines, mainly in the Burgenland, in Styria, and around the Neusiedler See where the HEURIGE is celebrated. More than a third of the total area of grape cultivation in Austria is devoted to Grüner Veltliner, a full-bodied, fruity white wine. Wines from Switzerland are mostly drunk locally and are produced in the Thurgau region. The Swiss reputation rests with their spirits, such as Kirsch, Pflümli, Mirabelle, and Enzian. *See also* BESENWIRTSCHAFT and STRAUßWIRTSCHAFT.

Weinstube A cosy wine bar which offers a wide choice of wines and usually also serves a few dishes that are considered to go well with wine. A *Weinstube* can be more upmarket than an ordinary pub, or else fairly rustic, especially in wine-growing areas.

Culture

Die Welt A national daily newspaper published in Hamburg. It has a large business section and is considered right-wing in its views.

Wende This word can refer to any major political or social change or turning point, but it is used especially to refer to the collapse of Communism in 1989, symbolized by the fall of die MAUER (the Berlin Wall), which eventually led to the WIEDERVEREINIGUNG in 1990.

Wertstofftonne ▶ RECYCLING

Wessi A colloquial and sometimes derogatory term for someone from West Germany, as opposed to an OSSI. The expression *Besserwessi*, a pun on *Besserwisser* (know-all), is sometimes used to describe overly confident West Germans.

Westdeutsche Allgemeine Zeitung (WAZ) Germany's highest-circulation serious national paper. It is published in Essen, and caters mainly for the densely populated Ruhr area.

Wiedervereinigung The German word for the reunification of Germany, which officially took place on 3 October 1990, when the former GDR was incorporated into the BUNDESREPUBLIK. The huge financial and social costs of reunification are still being felt throughout Germany. *See also* SOLIDARITÄTSZUSCHLAG.

Wirtschaftswunder, or German economic miracle, which resulted from the country's rapid reconstruction after the Second World War. The economy boomed in the decades after 1950.

Die Woche A relatively new weekly newspaper, which was founded in 1993 and is published in Hamburg. It is less comprehensive and easier to read than DIE ZEIT, but is also an important opinion leader with a liberal outlook offering background information, analyses, and reports.

ZDF – Zweites Deutsches Fernsehen The second German public TV channel, founded in 1961. It broadcasts the Zweites Programm with entertainment, news, information, and a limited amount of advertising.

Die Zeit Germany's 'heaviest' weekly newspaper, published in Hamburg, is considered essential reading for academics and intellectuals. Former BUNDESKANZLER Helmut Schmidt is a joint editor. The paper offers in-depth analysis of current issues in politics, society, culture, and the arts.

Zeugnis der allgemeinen Hochschulreife ▶ ABITUR

Zivildienst Community service, which recognized conscientious objectors in Germany, Austria, and Switzerland can choose to carry out instead of WEHRDIENST. It lasts longer than WEHRDIENST and usually involves caring for children, the elderly, the disabled, or the sick.

Letter-writing / Briefeschreiben

Holiday postcard

- *Beginnings (informal):* 'Lieber' here because it's a man; if it's a woman, use e.g. Liebe Elke.

  To two people, repeat 'Liebe(r)': Lieber Hans, liebe Elke.

  To a family: Liebe Schmidts, Liebe Familie Schmidt, *or just* Liebe Leute.

- *Address: Note that the title (Herrn, Frau, Fräulein) stands on the line above the name. Herr always has an n on the end in addresses.*

  The house number comes after the street name.

  The postcode comes before the place, and if you're writing from outside the country put a D- for Germany, A- for Austria or CH- for Switzerland in front of it.

Letters

Heidelberg, den 6.8. 2000

Lieber Hans!

Einen schönen Gruß aus Alt-Heidelberg! Wir sind erst zwei Tage hier, aber schon sehr angetan von der Stadt und Umgebung, trotz der vielen Touristen. Allerdings ist es ziemlich schwül. Wir waren gestern abend in einem Konzert im Schlosshof, eine wunderbare Stimmung! Und dann die herrliche Aussicht auf Altstadt und Neckar von der Terrasse. Morgen machen wir eine Bootsfahrt, dann geht's am Donnerstag wieder nach Hause. Hoffentlich ist deine Mutter inzwischen wieder gesund.

Bis bald

Max und Sophie

Herrn

Hans Matthäus

Brucknerstr. 26

91052 Erlangen

- *Endings (informal):* Herzlich *or* Herzlichst, Herzliche Grüße; *more affectionately:* Alles Liebe; Bis bald = *See you soon .*

Postkarte aus dem Urlaub

- *Anrede: sehr einfach auf Postkarten, immer 'Dear' und der Vorname, der im englischen Sprachraum viel häufiger verwendet wird. Die Anrede kann auch entfallen.*

- *Meist keine Ortsangabe, wenn der Ort aus dem Inhalt oder dem Bild auf der Postkarte klar hervorgeht.*
  Datum – in den USA verwendet man die Reihenfolge Monat, Tag, Jahr, wenn ein Datum mit Ziffern angegeben ist – 8.6.2000

- *Adresse: Der Titel (Mr, Mrs, Miss, Ms) steht direkt vor dem Namen auf der gleichen Zeile.*

  Das Haus hat oft einen Namen anstelle einer (oder zusätzlich zur) Hausnummer, die übrigens vor dem Straßennamen steht.

  Es folgen (in GB) Ortschaft, meist auch Grafschaft, dann Postleitzahl (postcode), alles jeweils auf einer eigenen Zeile; in den USA Ortschaft und Postleitzahl (zipcode), mit dem auf zwei Buchstaben abgekürzten Namen des Staates davor:

  John Splaine Jr.
  1067 Blackwall Avenue
  Studio City
  CA 91604
  USA

6.8.2000

Dear John,

Greetings from old Heidelberg! Got here ① a couple of days ago, but already in love with the place (in spite of all the tourists). It's pretty sultry though. Last night we went to a concert in the castle courtyard, very atmospheric. And a terrific view of the river and the old town from the terrace. Tomorrow we're taking a boat trip, and then on Thursday we head for home. Hope ① your mother's fully recovered by now.

Mr J. Roberts
The Willows
49 North Terrace
Kings Barton
Nottinghamshire
NG8 4LQ
England

See you soon,

Mark and Juliet

- *Schlussformel:*
  All the best, Best wishes, oder einfach Yours; auch Love (from), wenn man den Addressaten näher steht.

- *① Telegrammstil: die Angabe der Person entfällt auf Postkarten oft.*

Letters

. . . .

Christmas and New Year wishes

On a card:

Frohe Weihnachten und viel Glück im neuen Jahr

A bit more formal: Ein gesegnetes Weihnachtsfest und die besten Wünsche zum neuen Jahr

A bit less formal: Fröhliche Weihnachten und einen guten Rutsch ins neue Jahr

In a letter:

- *On most personal letters German speakers don't put their address at the top, but just the name of the place and the date*

Würzburg, den 20.12.2000

Liebe Karin, lieber Ferdinand,

euch und euren Kindern wünschen wir von Herzen frohe Weihnachten und ein glückliches neues Jahr. Wir hoffen, es geht euch allen gut, und dass wir uns bald mal wieder sehen werden. Es kommt uns so vor, als hätten wir uns eine Ewigkeit nicht gesehen.

Das vergangene Jahr war für uns sehr ereignisreich. Thomas hatte im Sommer einen Unfall mit dem Fahrrad, und brach sich den Arm und das Schlüsselbein. Sabine hat das Abitur gerade noch bestanden und ist jetzt an der Uni in Erlangen, studiert Sport. Der arme Michael ist im Oktober arbeitslos geworden und sucht immer noch nach einer Stelle.

Ihr müsst unbedingt vorbeikommen, wenn ihr das nächste Mal in der Gegend seid. Ruft doch einfach ein paar Tage vorher an, damit wir etwas ausmachen können.

Mit herzlichen Grüßen

Eure Gabi und Michael

Letters

● ●

Weihnachts- und Neujahrsgrüße

Auf einer Karte:

> *[Best wishes for a] Happy* ① *Christmas and a Prosperous New Year*
>
> *All best wishes for Christmas and the New Year*
>
> *Wishing you every happiness this Christmas[tide] and in the New Year*

① *Oder etwas altmodisch:* Merry

In einem Brief:

> *44 Louis Gardens*
> *London NW6 4GM*
>
> *December 20th 2000*
>
> *Dear Peter and Claire,*
>
> *First of all, a very happy Christmas and all the best for the New Year to you and the children.*① *We hope you're all well*② *and that we'll see you again soon. It seems ages since we last met up.*
>
> *We've had a very eventful year. Last summer Gavin came off his bike and broke his arm and collarbone. Kathy scraped through her A levels and is now at Sussex doing European Studies. Poor Tony was made redundant in October and is still looking for a job.*
>
> *Do come and see us next time you are over this way. Just give us a ring a couple of days before so we can fix something.*
>
> *All best wishes*
>
> *Tony and Ann*

Letters

① *Oder (vor allem, wenn die Kinder älter sind):* to you and the family.
② *Informeller:* flourishing.

. . . .

Invitation (informal)

> *Hamm, den 22.4.2000*
>
> *Liebe Jennie,*
>
> *wäre es möglich, dass du ① in den Sommerferien zu uns kommst? Katrin und Gottfried würden sich riesig freuen (ich und mein Mann natürlich auch). Wir planen eine Reise zum Bodensee Ende Juli/Anfang August, du ① könntest gerne mitfahren. Es ist wirklich sehr schön dort unten. Wir werden wahrscheinlich zelten – hoffentlich hast du ① nichts dagegen!*
>
> *Schreib bald, ob das für dich ① in Frage kommt.*
>
> *Herzliche Grüße*
>
> *Monika Pfortner*

- *Beginning: if you put a comma after the name on the first line (which is usual), the letter proper should start with a small letter.*

① *du, dich, dein etc.: although many people still write these with a capital in letters, this is not necessary. But the formal Sie, Ihnen, Ihr must always have a capital.*

Invitation (formal)

Invitations to parties are usually by word of mouth, while for weddings, announcements rather than invitations are usually sent out:

> *Irene Brinkmann*   *Stefan Hopf*
>
> Wir heiraten am Samstag, den 20. April 2000, um 14 Uhr in der Pfarrkirche Landsberg.
>
> Goethestraße 12   Ulrichsweg 4
>
> Landsberg   Altötting

Letters

Einladung (informell)

- *Die Absenderadresse befindet sich oben auf dem Brief selbst, entweder rechts oder in der Mitte, darunter das Datum.*

- *Das Datum im Englischen hat viele Formen:* May 10, 10 May, May 10th, 10th May *sind alle möglich und gleichermaßen richtig. In den USA verwendet man die Reihenfolge Monat, Tag, Jahr, wenn das Datum in Ziffern angegeben wird:* 05/10/2000

35 Winchester Drive
Stoke Gifford
Bristol
BS34 8PD

April 22nd 2000

Dear Klaus,

Is there any chance of your coming to stay with us in the summer holidays? Roy and Debbie would be delighted if you could (as well as David and me, of course). We hope to go to North Wales at the end of July/beginning of August, and you'd be very welcome to come too. It's really beautiful up there. We'll probably take tents — I hope that's OK by you.

Let me know as soon as possible if you can manage it.

All best wishes

Rachel Hemmings

Letters

Einladung (förmlich)

Zu einer Hochzeit mit anschließendem Empfang

Mr and Mrs Peter Thompson

request the pleasure of your company
at the marriage of their daughter

Hannah Louise
to
Steven David Warner

at St. Mary's Church, Little Bourton
on Saturday 25th July 2000 at 2 p.m.
and afterwards at the
Golden Cross Hotel, Billing

R.S.V.P.   23 Santers Lane
Little Bourton
Northampton
NN6 1AZ

Accepting an invitation

Edinburgh, den 2.5.2000

Liebe Frau Pfortner,

recht herzlichen Dank für Ihre liebe Einladung. Da ich noch keine festen Pläne für die Sommerferien habe, möchte ich sie sehr gerne annehmen. Allerdings darf ich nicht mehr als vier bis fünf Tage weg sein, da es meiner Mutter nicht sehr gut geht. Sie ① müssen mir sagen, was ich mitbringen soll (außer Edinburgh Rock!). Ist es sehr warm am Bodensee? Kann man im See schwimmen?

Natürlich habe ich nichts gegen Zelten. Auch hier in Schottland bei Wind und Regen macht es mir Spaß!

Ich freue mich auf ein baldiges Wiedersehen.

Herzliche Grüße

Jennie Stewart

① Since this is a letter from a younger person writing to the mother of a friend, she uses the formal *Sie* form and possessive Ihr *(always with capitals), and writes to her as* "Frau Pfortner". *On the other hand it was quite natural for* Frau Pfortner *to use the du form to her.*

Antwort auf eine Einladung (informell)

> Mozartstraße 5
> 32756 Detmold
> Germany
>
> 2 May 2000

Dear Mrs Hemmings,

Many thanks for your letter and kind invitation. Since I don't have anything fixed yet for the summer holidays, I'd be delighted to come. However I mustn't be away for more than four or five days since my mother hasn't been very well.

You must let me know what I should bring. How warm is it in North Wales? Can one swim in the sea? Camping is fine as far as I'm concerned, we take our tent everywhere.

Looking forward to seeing you again soon,

Yours

Klaus

Letters

Antwort auf eine Einladung (förmlich)

> Greenacres
> Westway
> Balsall Common
> West Midlands
> CV7 8RR

- Man wiederholt die Details von der Einladung, etwas vereinfacht.

Annahme:
Richard Willis has great pleasure in accepting Mr and Mrs Peter Thompson's kind invitation to the marriage of their daughter Hannah Louise to Steven Warner at St. Mary's Church, Little Bourton, on Saturday 25th July.

- Im Falle einer Absage ist es oft höflicher, einen Brief zu schreiben, vor allem wenn man die Brauteltern gut kennt.

Absage:
Richard Willis regrets that he is unable to accept Mr and Mrs Peter Thompson's kind invitation ... , due to a prior engagement.

Replying to a job advertisement

David Baker
67 Whiteley Avenue
St George
Bristol
BS5 6TW

Softwarehaus WSO GmbH
Personalabteilung
Kanalstr. 75
D-75757 Pforzheim   Bristol, den 26.2.2000

Ihre Stellenanzeige im Tagblatt vom 23.2.2000

Sehr geehrte Damen und Herren, ①

ich interessiere mich für die von Ihnen im Tagblatt vom 23. September
ausgeschriebene Stelle eines Computergrafikers und würde mich freuen, wenn
Sie mir nähere Informationen zuschicken könnten. ②

Derzeit bin ich bei der Firma Wondersoft Ltd in Bristol tätig, aber mein Vertrag
läuft schon Ende des Monats aus, ③ und ich möchte gerne in Deutschland
arbeiten. Wie Sie meinem Lebenslauf entnehmen können, verfüge ich über
ausgezeichnete Sprachkenntnisse sowie die geforderten Qualifikationen und
einschlägige Berufserfahrung.

Zu einem Vorstellungsgespräch stehe ich jederzeit ab dem 6. Oktober zur
Verfügung. Sie können mich ab diesem Datum unter der folgenden Adresse in
Deutschland erreichen:

bei Gerber
Rudolfstr. 22
81925 München
Tel. (089) 460 99 507

Ich freue mich darauf, von Ihnen zu hören. ④

Mit freundlichen Grüßen

David Baker

Anlage: Lebenslauf

① Correct if the letter is addressed to the personnel department, but if it is addressed to the personnel manager (An den Personalleiter, …) the letter begins: Sehr geehrter Herr XY or Sehr geehrte Frau XY.
② Or if you have enough details and want to apply for the job right away: und möchte mich um diese Stellung bewerben.
③ Or if you are unemployed: Derzeit bin ich arbeitslos, …
④ Or: Ihre Antwort erwarte ich mit Interesse.

Letters

• •

Bewerbung auf eine Stellenanzeige hin

Humboldtweg 16
60247 Frankfurt a. M.
Germany
Tel. (069) 724 689

13th February 2000

The Personnel Manager ①
Patterson Software plc
Milton Estate
Bath BA6 8YZ

Dear Sir or Madam, ②

I am interested in the post of programmer advertised in the Guardian of 12th
February and would be grateful if you could send me further particulars. ③

I am currently working for the Sempo Corporation in Frankfurt, but my contract
finishes at the end of the month, and I would like ④ to come and work in the
UK. As you can see from my CV (enclosed), I have an excellent command of
English and also the required qualifications and experience.

I will be available for interview any time after 6th October, from which date I
can be contacted at the following address in the UK:

c/o Lewis
51 Dexter Road
London N7 6BW
Tel. 0207 607 5512

I look forward to hearing from you. ⑤

Yours sincerely

Rita Steinmüller

Encl.

Letters

① *Den Brief so addressieren, wenn in der Anzeige kein Name vorkommt; aber wenn es z.B. heißt*
"Reply to Angela Summers", *dann* "Ms Angela Summers, ..."
② *Wenn der Name bekannt ist, dann* "Dear Ms Summers", "Dear Mr Wright" *etc.*
③ *Oder falls Sie schon genügend Informationen haben und sich bewerben wollen:* "and would like
to apply for this position".
④ *Oder falls Sie arbeitslos sind:* "I am currently unemployed and would like ..."
⑤ *Oder:* "Thanking you in anticipation".

Letter-writing / Briefeschreiben

Curriculum Vitae (CV) or (*Amer.*) Résumé

Lebenslauf

David Baker
67 Whiteley Avenue
St George
Bristol
BS5 6TW
Großbritannien

Tel. +43 (0)117 945 3421

geboren am 30.06.1970 in London, ledig①

Ausbildung

1986 O Levels in 7 Fächern (ungefähr = mittlere Reife), John Radcliffe School, Croydon

1988 A Levels in Mathematik, Höherer Mathematik, Informatik, Deutsch (ungefähr = Abitur), Croydon Sixth Form College

1989 Teilzeitarbeit in München, Abendkurse an der VHS

1990-94 University of Aston, Birmingham, B.Sc in Informatik

Berufstätigkeit

08/94 - 08/97 Traineeausbildung, anschließend Sotwareentwickler bei IBM

seit 09/97 Programmierer bei Wondersoft plc, Bristol

Entwicklung von Programmen für die Industrie; Schwerpunkt: Grafiksoftware

Besondere Kenntnisse

Fremdsprachen: Deutsch (fließend), Französisch (gut)

① *Or:* Verheiratet (mit einem Kind/zwei Kindern etc.); Geschieden (mit einem Kind/zwei Kindern etc.)

Lebenslauf

CURRICULUM VITAE ①

Name:	Rita Steinmüller
Address:	Humboldtweg 16 60247 Frankfurt a. M. Germany
Telephone:	+44 (0)69 724 689
Nationality:	German
Date of Birth:	11/3/1973
Marital status:	Single ②

Education:

1991-1995	Degree Course in Information Technology at Stuttgart University
1984-1991	Theodor-Heuss-Gymnasium, Eichborn Abitur examination (approx. A Level) in Mathematics, Physics, Economics and English

Employment:

1996-present	Program development engineer with Sempo-Informatik, Frankfurt, specializing in computer graphics
1995-1996	Trainee programmer with Oregon Germany, Rüsselsheim

Further skills:

Languages:	German (mother tongue), English (fluent spoken and written), French (good)
Interests:	Travel (many trips to the UK), chess, tennis

Letters

① *Oder (Amer.):* RÉSUMÉ
② *Oder:* Married (with one/two/three etc. children), Divorced (with one/two/three etc. children)

Letter-writing / Briefeschreiben

• •

Booking a hotel room

Hotel Goldener Pflug   Tobias Schwarz
Ortsstraße 7   Gartenstr. 19
69235 Steinbach   76530 Baden-Baden

16. Juli 2000

Sehr geehrte Damen und Herren,

Ich wurde durch die Broschüre "Hotels und Pensionen im Naturpark Odenwald (Ausgabe 2000)" auf ihr Hotel aufmerksam.

Ich möchte für mich und meine Frau für die Zeit vom 2. bis 11. August (neun Nächte) ein ruhiges Doppelzimmer mit Dusche reservieren, sowie ein Einzelzimmer für unseren Sohn.

Falls Sie für diese Zeit etwas Passendes haben, informieren Sie mich doch bitte über den Preis und darüber, ob Sie eine Anzahlung wünschen.

Mit freundlichen Grüßen

Tobias Schwarz

Letters

Booking a campsite

Camilla Stumpf
Saalgasse 10
60311 Frankfurt

Camping am See
Frau Bettina Sattler   ■ For a business letter to a particular person, use "Sehr geehrte(r)"
Auweg 6-10   and the name. (If this letter were to a man, it would start "Sehr geehrter
87654 Waldenkirchen   Herr Sattler").

                                      Frankfurt, den 16.04.2000

Sehr geehrte Frau Sattler,

Ihr Campingplatz wurde mir von Herrn Stephan Seidel empfohlen, der schon mehrmals bei Ihnen war. ① Ich würde nun gerne vom 18. bis 25. Juli mit zwei Freunden eine Woche bei Ihnen verbringen. Könnten Sie uns bitte einen Zeltplatz ② möglichst in unmittelbarer Nähe des Sees ③ reservieren?

Würden Sie mir freundlicherweise mitteilen, ob Sie meine Reservierung annehemen können und ob Sie eine Anzahlung wünschen?

Außerdem wäre ich Ihnen dankbar für eine kurze Wegbeschreibung von der Autobahn.

Mit vielem Dank im Voraus und freundlichen Grüßen

Camilla Stumpf

① Or if you have found the campsite in a guide, say e.g.: "Ich habe Ihre Anschrift dem ACDA-Campingführer 2000 entnommen".
② Or if you have a caravan: "einen Stellplatz für einen Wohnwagen".
③ Alternatives: "in schattiger/geschützter Lage".

Hotelzimmerreservierung

The Manager	35 Prince Edward Road
Torbay Hotel	Oxford OX7 3AA
Dawlish	
Devon	Tel. 01865 322435
EX37 2LR	23rd April 2000

Dear Sir or Madam,

I saw your hotel listed in the Inns of Devon guide for last year, and wish to reserve a double (or twin-bedded) room with shower ① in a quiet position from August 2nd - 11th (nine nights), also a single room for our son.

If you have anything suitable for this period please let me know the price and whether you require a deposit.

Yours sincerely

Charles Fairhurst

① *Alternativen:* "with bath", "with ensuite".

Campingplatzreservierung

22 Daniel Avenue
Caldwood
Leeds LS8 7RR
Tel. 01132 998767

25th April 2000

Mr Joseph Vale
Lakeside Park
Rydal
Cumbria
LA22 9RZ

Dear Mr Vale

Your campsite was recommended to me by James Dallas, who knows it from several visits. ① I and two friends would like to come for a week from July 18th to 25th Could you please reserve us a site for one tent. ② preferably close to the shore. ③

Please confirm the booking and let me know if you require a deposit. Would you also be good enough to send me instructions on how to reach you from the motorway.

Yours sincerely

Frances Good

① *Oder falls Sie den Campingplatz einem Führer entnommen haben, etwa:* "I found your site in the Tourist Board's list/ the Good Camper's Guide" *etc.*

② *Oder falls Sie einen Wohnwagen haben:* "a caravan site".

③ *Andere Möglichkeiten:* "in a shady/sheltered spot".

Cancelling a reservation

Herrn
Hans Knauer
Gasthaus Sonnenblick
Hauptstr. 6
D-94066 Bad Füssing
Germany   Aberdeen, den 2.6.2000

Sehr geehrter Herr Knauer,

leider muss ich meine/unsere Reservierung für die Woche vom 7. bis 13. August
① rückgängig machen. Wegen unvorhergesehener Umstände ② muss
ich/müssen wir auf meinen/unseren Urlaub verzichten.

Es tut mir aufrichtig Leid, dass ich so spät abbestellen muss, und hoffe, dass Sie
deswegen keine Unannehmlichkeiten haben.

Mit freundlichen Grüßen

Robert McDonald

① Or: "für die Zeit vom 7. bis 20. August" etc.
② Or more precisely: "Durch den überraschenden Tod meines Vaters/die Krankheit meines
Mannes" etc.

Stornierung einer Reservierung

Mrs J. Warrington   Wernerstr. 17
Downlands   49835 Wietmarschen
Steyning   Germany
West Sussex
BN44 6LZ

                                  July 20th 2000

Dear Mrs Warrington,

Unfortunately I have to cancel my/our reservation for the week
of August 7th. ① Due to unforeseen circumstances ② I/we have
had to abandon my/our holiday plans.

I very much regret having to cancel [at such a late stage] and
hope it does not cause you undue inconvenience.

Yours sincerely

Elke Nordrup

① Oder: "for the period from August 7th to 14th".
② Oder genauer: "Owing to my father's sudden death/my husband's illness" etc

Letters / Briefe

. . . .

Sending an e-mail

The illustration shows a typical interface for sending e-mail.

Das Verschicken von E-Mails

Die Abbildung zeigt eine typische Oberfläche zum Verschicken von E-Mails.

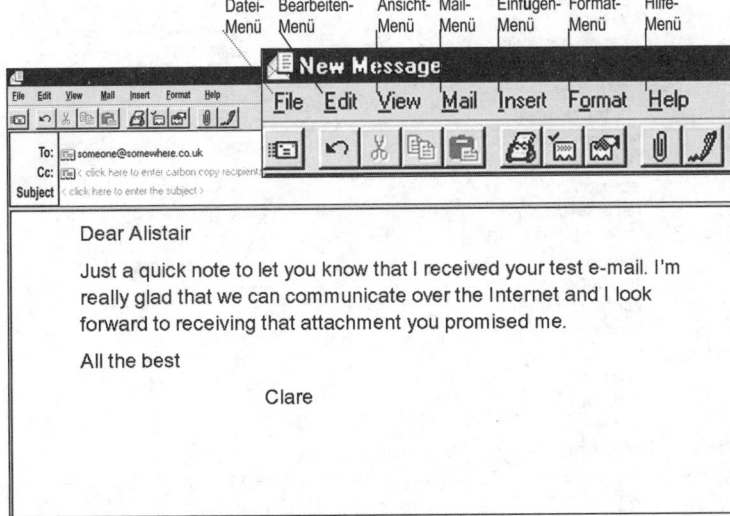

SMS (electronic text-messaging)

The basic principles governing German SMS abbreviations are similar to those governing English SMS. Certain words or syllables are represented by letters or numbers that sound the same. Most punctuation is usually omitted, umlauts are rarely used, and there are no strict rules about upper and lower case. For example 'viele Grüße' can be 'vlg'. Sentences are shortened by leaving out certain letters – 'bist du noch wach?' might read 'bidunowa'. Often just the initial letter of a word is used, as in 'ff' for 'Fortsetzung folgt'. Many English abbreviations have made it into German text messages. For example '4u' (for you) is often used for 'für dich'.

Glossary of German SMS abbreviations

Abbreviation	Meaning
8ung	Achtung
ads	alles deine Schuld
akla?	alles klar?
aws	auf Wiedersehen
bb	bis bald
bda	bis dann
bidunowa?	bist du noch wach?
braduhi?	brauchst du Hilfe?
bs	bis später
dad	denke an dich
d	der
div	danke im Voraus
dubido	du bist doof
ff	Fortsetzung folgt
g	grinsen
g&k	Gruß und Kuss
gn8	gute Nacht
gngn	geht nicht, gibts nicht
hahu	habe Hunger
hdl	habe dich lieb
hdos	halt die Ohren steif
hegl	herzlichen Glückwunsch
ild	ich liebe dich
jon	jetzt oder nie
katze?	kannst du tanzen?
ko5mispä	komme 5 Minuten später
l8er	later = später
lg	liebe Grüße
lidumino	liebst du mich noch?
mamima	mail mir mal
mumidire	muss mit dir reden
n8	Nacht
nfd	nur für dich
pg	Pech gehabt
rumian	ruf mich an
sfh	Schluss für heute
siw	soweit ich weiß

Abbreviation	Meaning
sms	schreib mir schnell
sz	schreib zurück
tabu	tausend Bussis
vegimini	vergiss mich nicht
vlg	viele Grüße
vv	viel Vergnügen
wamaduheu?	was machst du heute?
waudi	warte auf dich
we	Wochenende
zdom?	zu dir oder zu mir?

Emoticons

:-)	lächeln, glücklich
:-))	sehr glücklich
:-|	Stirnrunzeln
:-e	enttäuscht
:-(	unglücklich, traurig
:-((	sehr unglücklich
:->	sarkastisch
%-)	verwirrt
:~-(or :'-(	weinen
;-)	zwinkern
|-o	müde
:-\	skeptisch
:-D	lachen
:-<>	erstaunt
:-p	rausgestreckte Zunge
:-O	schreien
O:-)	Engel
:-* or :-x	Kuss
:-o	Schock
@}-,-'–	Rose

SMS (elektronische Textmitteilungen über das Handy)

SMS ist die englische Abkürzung für "Short Message Service", was sich als "Kurznachrichtendienst" übersetzen lässt. Im Englischen gibt es zahllose Abkürzungen, die es erlauben, viele Informationen mit wenigen Zeichen und Zahlen zu übermitteln. Zum Beispiel: 2L8 = 'too late'. Für die meisten Nachrichten tippt man nur die Anfangsbuchstaben jedes Wortes ein, zum Beispiel: ttyl = 'talk to you later' oder fyi = 'for your information'.

Verzeichnis von englischen SMS-Abkürzungen

Abkürzung	Bedeutung
adn	any day now
afaik	as far as I know
atb	all the best
b	be
b4	before
b4n	bye for now
bbl	be back late(r)
bcnu	be seeing you
bfn	bye for now
brb	be right back
btw	by the way
bwd	backward
c	see
cu	see you
cul8r	see you later
f2f	face to face
f2t	free to talk
fwd	forward
fwiw	for what it's worth
fyi	for your information
gal	get a life
gr8	great
h8	hate
hand	have a nice day
hak	hugs and kisses
hth	hope this helps
ic	I see
iluvu	I love you
imho	in my humble opinion
imo	in my opinion
iow	in other words
jic	just in case
jk	just kidding
kit	keep in touch
kwim	know what I mean?
l8	late
l8r	later

Abkürzung	Bedeutung
lol	lots of luck/ laughing out loud
mob	mobile
msg	message
myob	mind your own business
ne	any
ne1	anyone
no1	no one
oic	oh, I see
otoh	on the other hand
pcm	please call me
pls	please
ppl	people
r	are
rofl	rolling on the floor, laughing
ru	are you
ruok	are you OK?
sit	stay in touch
som1	someone
spk	speak
thkq	thank you
ttyl	talk to you later
tx	thanks
u	you
ur	you are
w/	with
wan2	want to
wan2 tlk	want to talk?
werv u bin	where have you been?
wknd	weekend
wot	what
wu	what's up?
x	kiss
xlnt	excellent
xoxoxo	hugs and kisses

Abkürzung	Bedeutung
yr	your
2	to, too
2day	today
2l8	too late
2moro	tomorrow
2nite	tonight
3sum	threesome
4	for

Emoticons

:-)	smiling, happy face
:-))	very happy face
:-|	frowning
:-e	disappointed
:-(	unhappy, sad face
:-((	very unhappy face
:->	sarcastic
%-)	confused
:~(or :'-(	crying
;-)	winking happy face
|-o	tired, asleep
:-\	sceptical
:-D	big smile, laughing face
:-<>	amazed
X=	fingers crossed
:-p	tongue sticking out
:-O	shouting
O:-)	angel
:-* or :-x	big kiss!
:-o	shocked face
@}-,-'—	a rose

SMS

A, a¹ /eɪ/ *n.* A, a, *das;* **A road** Straße 1.
Ordnung; ≈ Bundesstraße, *die*

a² /ə, *stressed* eɪ/ *indef. art.* ein/eine/ein; **he
is a gardener/a Frenchman** er ist Gärtner/
Franzose; **she did not say a word** sie sagte
kein Wort

AA *abbr.* (Brit.) = **Automobile
Association** *britischer Automobilklub*

aback /ə'bæk/ *adv.* **be taken ~:** erstaunt
sein

abacus /'æbəkəs/ *n., pl.* **~es** *or* **abaci**
/'æbəsaɪ/ Abakus, *der*

abandon /ə'bændən/ *v.t.* verlassen ⟨*Ort,
Person*⟩; aufgeben ⟨*Prinzip*⟩; **~ed** verlassen,
ausgesetzt ⟨*Kind, Tier*⟩

abase /ə'beɪs/ *v.t.* erniedrigen

abashed /ə'bæʃt/ *adj.* beschämt

abate /ə'beɪt/ *v.i.* nachlassen

abattoir /'æbətwɑː(r)/ *n.* Schlachthof, *der*

abbey /'æbɪ/ *n.* Abtei, *die*

abbot /'æbət/ *n.* Abt, *der*

abbreviate /ə'briːvɪeɪt/ *v.t.* abkürzen

ab'breviated dialling *n.* (Teleph.)
Kurzwahl, *die*

abbreviation /əbriːvɪ'eɪʃn/ *n.* Abkürzung,
die

abdicate /'æbdɪkeɪt/ *v.t.* abdanken

abdication /æbdɪ'keɪʃn/ *n.* Abdankung,
die

abdomen /'æbdəmən/ *n.* Bauch, *der*

abdominal /æb'dɒmɪnl/ *adj.* Bauch-

abduct /əb'dʌkt/ *v.t.* entführen

abduction /əb'dʌkʃn/ *n.* Entführung, *die*

aberration /æbə'reɪʃn/ *n.* Abweichung,
die

abet /ə'bet/ *v.t.,* **-tt-** helfen (+ *Dat.*); **aid and
~:** Beihilfe leisten (+ *Dat.*)

abhor /əb'hɔː(r)/ *v.t.,* **-rr-** verabscheuen

abhorrent /əb'hɒrənt/ *adj.* abscheulich

abide /ə'baɪd/ ①*v.i.* **~ by** befolgen ⟨*Gesetz,
Vorschrift*⟩; [ein]halten ⟨*Versprechen*⟩
②*v.t.* ertragen; **I can't ~ dogs** ich kann
Hunde nicht ausstehen

ability /ə'bɪlɪtɪ/ *n.* **(a)** (capacity) Fähigkeit,
die; **have the ~ to do sth.** etw. können
(b) (cleverness) Intelligenz, *die*
(c) (talent) Begabung, *die*

abject /'æbdʒekt/ *adj.* elend; bitter
⟨*Armut*⟩; demütig ⟨*Entschuldigung*⟩

ablaze /ə'bleɪz/ *adj.* **be ~:** in Flammen
stehen

able /'eɪbl/ *adj.* **(a) be ~ to do sth.** etw. tun
können
(b) (competent) fähig

able-bodied /'eɪblbɒdɪd/ *adj.* kräftig;
tauglich ⟨*Soldat, Matrose*⟩

ably /'eɪblɪ/ *adv.* geschickt; gekonnt

abnormal /æb'nɔːml/ *adj.* abnorm;
a[b]normal ⟨*Interesse, Verhalten*⟩

abnormality /æbnɔː'mælɪtɪ/ *n.*
Abnormität, *die*

aboard /ə'bɔːd/ ① *adv.* an Bord
② *prep.* an Bord (+ *Gen.*); **~ the bus** imC
~ ship an Bord

abode /ə'bəʊd/ *n.* **of no fixed ~:** ohne
festen Wohnsitz

abolish /ə'bɒlɪʃ/ *v.t.* abschaffen

abolition /æbə'lɪʃn/ *n.* Abschaffung, *die*

abominable /ə'bɒmɪnəbl/ *adj.*
abscheulich; scheußlich

aborigine /æbə'rɪdʒɪnɪ/ *n.* Ureinwohner,
der

abort /ə'bɔːt/ *v.t.* abtreiben ⟨*Baby*⟩

abortion /ə'bɔːʃn/ *n.* Abtreibung, *die;*
1776991/ann>**back-street ~:** illegale
Abtreibung (durch Engelmacherin)

a'bortion pill *n.* Abtreibungspille, *die*

abortive /ə'bɔːtɪv/ *adj.* misslungen ⟨*Plan*⟩;
fehlgeschlagen ⟨*Versuch*⟩

abound /ə'baʊnd/ *v.i.* **~ in sth.** an etw.
(*Dat.*) reich sein

about /ə'baʊt/ ① *adv.* **(a)** (all around)
rings[her]um; (here and there) überall; **all ~:**
ringsumher
(b) (near) **be ~:** da sein; hier sein
(c) be ~ to do sth. gerade etw. tun wollen
(d) be out and ~: aktiv sein
(e) (approximately) ungefähr
② *prep.* **(a)** (all round) um [… herum]
(b) (concerning) über (+ *Akk.*); **know ~ sth.**
von etw. wissen; **a question ~ sth.** eine
Frage zu etw.; **what was it ~?** worum ging
es?

above /ə'bʌv/ ① *adv.* **(a)** (position) oben;
(higher up) darüber
(b) (direction) nach oben
② *prep.* (position) über (+ *Dat.*); (direction, more
than) über (+ *Akk.*); **~ all** vor allem

above 'board *pred. adj.* einwandfrei;
korrekt

a'bove-mentioned *adj.* oben erwähnt
od. genannt

abrasion /ə'breɪʒn/ *n.* (graze)
Hautabschürfung, *die*

abrasive /ə'breɪsɪv/ ① *adj.* **(a)** scheuernd;
Scheuer-
(b) (fig.: harsh) aggressiv
② *n.* Scheuermittel, *das*

abreast /ə'brest/ *adv.* **(a)** nebeneinander ⋯⋗

(b) (fig.) keep ∼ of sth. sich über etw. (*Akk.*) auf dem Laufenden halten

abroad /ə'brɔːd/ *adv.* im Ausland; (direction) ins Ausland

abrupt /ə'brʌpt/ *adj.*, **a'bruptly** *adv.* **(a)** (sudden[ly]) abrupt; plötzlich
(b) (brusque[ly]) schroff

ABS *abbr.* = **anti-lock brake** *or* **braking system** ABS

abscess /'æbsɪs/ *n.* Abszess, *der*

abscond /əb'skɒnd/ *v.t.* sich entfernen

absence /'æbsəns/ *n.* Abwesenheit, *die;* the ∼ of sth. der Mangel an etw. (*Dat.*)

absent /'æbsənt/ *adj.* abwesend; be ∼ from school/work in der Schule/am Arbeitsplatz fehlen

absentee /æbsən'tiː/ *n.* Fehlende, *der/die;* Abwesende, *der/die;* ∼ballot (Amer.) Briefwahl, *die;* ∼ landlord nicht auf seinem Gut lebender Gutsherr

absenteeism /æbsən'tiːɪzm/ *n.* [häufiges] Fernbleiben; (without good reason) Krankfeiern, *das* (ugs.)

absent-minded /æbsənt'maɪndɪd/ *adj.* geistesabwesend; (habitually) zerstreut

absolute /'æbsəluːt/ *adj.* absolut; ausgemacht ⟨Lüge, Skandal⟩; ∼ majority absolute Mehrheit

abso'lutely *adv.* absolut; völlig ⟨verrückt⟩; you're ∼ right! du hast völlig Recht; ∼ not! auf keinen Fall!

absolve /əb'zɒlv/ *v.t.* ∼ from entbinden von ⟨Pflichten⟩; lossprechen von ⟨Schuld⟩

absorb /əb'sɔːb/ *v.t.* **(a)** aufsaugen ⟨Flüssigkeit⟩
(b) abfangen ⟨Schlag, Stoß⟩

absorbency /əb'sɔːbənsɪ/ *n.* Saugfähigkeit, *die*

absorbent /əb'sɔːbənt/ *adj.* saugfähig

ab'sorbing *adj.* faszinierend

abstain /əb'steɪn/ *v.i.* ∼ from sth. sich einer Sache (*Gen.*) enthalten; ∼ [from voting] sich der Stimme enthalten

abstemious /əb'stiːmɪəs/ *adj.* enthaltsam

abstention /əb'stenʃn/ *n.* (from voting) Stimmenthaltung, *die*

abstinence /'æbstɪnəns/ *n.* Abstinenz, *die*

abstinent /'æbstɪnənt/ *adj.* abstinent

abstract /'æbstrækt/ ① *adj.* abstrakt ② *n.* Zusammenfassung, *die*

absurd /əb'sɜːd/ *adj.* absurd; (ridiculous) lächerlich

absurdity /əb'sɜːdɪtɪ/ *n.* Absurdität, *die*

ab'surdly *adv.* lächerlich

abundance /ə'bʌndəns/ *n.* [an] ∼ of sth. eine Fülle von etw.

abundant /ə'bʌndənt/ *adj.* reich (in an + *Dat.*)

abuse ① /ə'bjuːz/ *v.t.* beschimpfen ② /ə'bjuːs/ *n.* Beschimpfungen *Pl.*

abusive /ə'bjuːsɪv/ *adj.* beleidigend; become ∼: ausfallend werden

abysmal /ə'bɪzml/ *adj.* (coll.: bad) katastrophal (ugs.)

abyss /ə'bɪs/ *n.* Abgrund, *der*

AC *abbr.* = **alternating current** Ws

academic /ækə'demɪk/ *adj.* akademisch

academy /ə'kædəmɪ/ *n.* Akademie, *die*

accede /æk'siːd/ *v.i.* **(a)** zustimmen (to *Dat.*)
(b) ∼ [to the throne] den Thron besteigen

accelerate /ək'seləreɪt/ ① *v.t.* beschleunigen
② *v.i.* sich beschleunigen; ⟨Auto, Fahrer:⟩ beschleunigen

acceleration /əkselə'reɪʃn/ *n.* Beschleunigung, *die*

accelerator /ək'seləreɪtə(r)/ *n.* ∼ [pedal] Gas[pedal], *das*

accent /'æksənt/ *n.* Akzent, *der*

accentuate /ək'sentjʊeɪt/ *v.t.* betonen

accept /ək'sept/ *v.t.* **(a)** annehmen; entgegennehmen ⟨Dank, Spende⟩; übernehmen ⟨Verantwortung⟩
(b) (acknowledge) akzeptieren

acceptable /ək'septəbl/ *adj.* akzeptabel; annehmbar ⟨Preis, Gehalt⟩

acceptance /ək'septəns/ *n.* **(a)** Annahme, *die*
(b) (acknowledgement) Anerkennung, *die*

access /'ækses/ *n.* **(a)** (admission) gain ∼: Einlass finden
(b) (opportunity to use or approach) Zugang, *der* (to zu)

accessible /ək'sesɪbl/ *adj.* **(a)** (reachable) erreichbar
(b) (available, understandable) zugänglich (to für)

accession /ək'seʃn/ *n.* Amtsantritt, *der;* ∼ [to the throne] Thronbesteigung, *die*

accessory /ək'sesərɪ/ *n.* **(a)** accessories *pl.* Zubehör, *das*
(b) (dress article) Accessoire, *das*

'access road *n.* Zufahrtsstraße, *die*

accident /'æksɪdənt/ *n.* **(a)** Unfall, *der*
(b) (chance) Zufall, *der;* by ∼: zufällig
(c) (mistake) Versehen, *das;* by ∼: versehentlich

accidental /æksɪ'dentl/ *adj.* (chance) zufällig; (unintended) unbeabsichtigt

acci'dentally *adv.* (by chance) zufällig; (by mistake) versehentlich

'accident-prone *adj.* ∼ person Unfäller, *der* (Psych.); he's such an ∼ boy mit dem Jungen ist aber auch immer irgendwas (ugs.)

acclaim /ə'kleɪm/ *v.t.* feiern

acclimatisation, acclimatise
▶ ACCLIMATIZ-

acclimatization /əklaɪmətaɪ'zeɪʃn/ *n.* (lit. or fig.) Akklimatisation, *die*

acclimatize /ə'klaɪmətaɪz/ *v.t.* get *or* become ∼d sich akklimatisieren

accolade /'ækəleɪd/ *n.* ∼[s] (praise) Lob, *das*

accommodate /əˈkɒmədeɪt/ *v.t.* (a) unterbringen; (hold) Platz bieten (+ *Dat.*) (b) (oblige) gefällig sein (+ *Dat.*)

accommodating /əˈkɒmədeɪtɪŋ/ *adj.* zuvorkommend

accommodation /əkɒməˈdeɪʃn/ *n.* Unterkunft, *die*

accommo'dation address *n.* Gefälligkeitsadresse, *die*

accompaniment /əˈkʌmpənɪmənt/ *n.* Begleitung, *die*

accompanist /əˈkʌmpənɪst/ *n.* Begleiter, *der*/Begleiterin, *die*

accompany /əˈkʌmpənɪ/ *v.t.* begleiten

accomplice /əˈkʌmplɪs/ *n.* Komplize, *der*/ Komplizin, *die*

accomplish /əˈkʌmplɪʃ/ *v.t.* vollbringen ⟨*Tat*⟩; erfüllen ⟨*Aufgabe*⟩

accomplished /əˈkʌmplɪʃt/ *adj.* fähig; **he is an ∼ speaker/dancer** er ist ein erfahrener Redner/vollendeter Tänzer

ac'complishment *n.* (a) (completion) Vollendung, *die* (b) (achievement) Leistung, *die;* (skill) Fähigkeit, *die*

accord /əˈkɔːd/ [1] *n.* Übereinstimmung, *die;* **of one's own ∼:** aus eigenem Antrieb; **with one ∼:** geschlossen [2] *v.t.* **∼ sb. sth.** jmdm. etw. gewähren

accordance /əˈkɔːdəns/ *n.* **in ∼ with** in Übereinstimmung mit

ac'cording *adv.* **∼ to** nach; **∼ to him** nach seiner Aussage

ac'cordingly *adv.* (as appropriate) entsprechend; (therefore) folglich

accordion /əˈkɔːdɪən/ *n.* Akkordeon, *das*

accost /əˈkɒst/ *v.t.* ansprechen

account /əˈkaʊnt/ *n.* (a) (Finance) Rechnung, *die;* (at bank, shop) Konto, *das* (b) (consideration) **take ∼ of sth., take sth. into ∼:** etw. berücksichtigen; **take no ∼ of sth./ sb.** etw./jmdn. unberücksichtigt lassen; **don't change your plans on my ∼:** ändert nicht meinetwegen eure Pläne; **on ∼ of** wegen; **on no ∼:** auf [gar] keinen Fall (c) (report) Bericht, *der* (d) **call sb. to ∼:** jmdn. zur Rechenschaft ziehen

▪ **ac'count for** *v.t.* Rechenschaft ablegen über; (explain) erklären

accountable /əˈkaʊntəbl/ *adj.* verantwortlich

accountancy /əˈkaʊntənsɪ/ *n.* Buchhaltung, *die*

accountant /əˈkaʊntənt/ *n.* [Bilanz]buchhalter, *der*/-halterin, *die*

account: ∼ holder *n.* Kontoinhaber, *der*/-inhaberin, *die;* **∼ number** *n.* Kontonummer, *die*

accredited /əˈkredɪtɪd/ *adj.* anerkannt ⟨*Schule, Anstalt, Buch, Regierung*⟩; akkreditiert ⟨*Botschafter, Diplomat*⟩; zugelassen ⟨*Journalist*⟩

accrue /əˈkruː/ *v.i.* ⟨*Zinsen:*⟩ auflaufen; **∼ to sb.** ⟨*Reichtümer, Einnahmen:*⟩ jmdm. zufließen

accumulate /əˈkjuːmjʊleɪt/ [1] *v.t.* sammeln [2] *v.i.* ⟨*Menge, Staub:*⟩ sich ansammeln; ⟨*Geld:*⟩ sich anhäufen

accumulation /əkjuːmjʊˈleɪʃn/ *n.* [An]sammeln, *das;* (being accumulated) Anhäufung, *die*

accuracy /ˈækjʊrəsɪ/ *n.* Genauigkeit, *die*

accurate /ˈækjʊrət/ *adj.*, **'accurately** *adv.* genau; (correct[ly]) richtig

accusation /ækjuːˈzeɪʃn/ *n.* Anschuldigung, *die;* (Law) Anklage, *die*

accusative /əˈkjuːzətɪv/ *adj. & n.* **∼ [case]** Akkusativ, *der*

accuse /əˈkjuːz/ *v.t.* beschuldigen; (Law) anklagen (**of** wegen + *Gen.*)

accustom /əˈkʌstəm/ *v.t.* gewöhnen (**to** an + *Akk.*); **grow/be ∼ed to sth.** sich an etw. (*Akk.*) gewöhnen/an etw. (*Akk.*) gewöhnt sein

accustomed /əˈkʌstəmd/ *attrib. adj.* gewohnt; üblich

ace /eɪs/ [1] *n.* As, *das* [2] *adj.* (coll.) klasse (ugs.); spitze (ugs.)

ache /eɪk/ [1] *v.i.* schmerzen; wehtun [2] *n.* Schmerz, *der*

achieve /əˈtʃiːv/ *v.t.* zustande bringen; erreichen ⟨*Ziel, Standard*⟩

a'chievement *n.* (a) ▸ ACHIEVE: Zustandebringen, *das;* Erreichen, *das* (b) (thing accomplished) Leistung, *die*

acid /ˈæsɪd/ [1] *adj.* sauer [2] *n.* Säure, *die*

'acid house *n.* Acidhouse, *das;* **∼ music/ party** Acidhousemusik, *die*/Acidhouseparty, *die*

'acid: ∼'rain *n.* saurer Regen; **∼ test** *n.* (fig.) Feuerprobe, *die*

acidic /əˈsɪdɪk/ *adj.* säuerlich

acidity /əˈsɪdɪtɪ/ *n.* Säure, *die*

acknowledge /əkˈnɒlɪdʒ/ *v.t.* (a) zugeben ⟨*Tatsache, Fehler, Schuld*⟩ (b) sich erkenntlich zeigen für ⟨*Dienste, Bemühungen*⟩; erwidern ⟨*Gruß*⟩ (c) bestätigen ⟨*Empfang, Bewerbung*⟩; **∼ a letter** den Empfang eines Briefes bestätigen

acknowledg[e]ment /əkˈnɒlɪdʒmənt/ *n.* (a) (admission) Eingeständnis, *das* (b) (thanks) Dank, *der* (**of** für) (c) (of letter) Bestätigung [des Empfangs]

acne /ˈæknɪ/ *n.* Akne, *die*

acorn /ˈeɪkɔːn/ *n.* Eichel, *die*

acoustic /əˈkuːstɪk/ *adj.* akustisch

a'coustics *n. pl.* Akustik, *die*

acquaint /əˈkweɪnt/ *v.t.* **be ∼ed with sb.** mit jmdm. bekannt sein

acquaintance /əˈkweɪntəns/ *n.* (a) **∼ with sb.** Bekanntschaft mit jmdm.; **make sb.'s ∼:** jmds. Bekanntschaft machen ⸱⸱⸽

(b) (person) Bekannte, *der/die*

acquiesce /ækwɪ'es/ *v.i.* einwilligen (**in** in + *Akk.*)

acquire /ə'kwaɪə(r)/ *v.t.* sich (*Dat.*) anschaffen ‹*Gegenstände*›; erwerben ‹*Besitz, Kenntnisse*›

acquisition /ækwɪ'zɪʃn/ *n.* Erwerb, *der;* (thing) Anschaffung, *die*

acquisitive /ə'kwɪzɪtɪv/ *adj.* raffsüchtig

acquit /ə'kwɪt/ *v.t.,* **-tt-** freisprechen

acquittal /ə'kwɪtl/ *n.* Freispruch, *der*

acre /'eɪkə(r)/ *n.* Acre, *der*

acrid /'ækrɪd/ *adj.* beißend ‹*Geruch, Rauch*›; bitter ‹*Geschmack*›

acrimonious /ækrɪ'məʊnɪəs/ *adj.* bitter; erbittert ‹*Streit*›

acrobat /'ækrəbæt/ *n.* Akrobat, *der/* Akrobatin, *die*

acrobatic /ækrə'bætɪk/ *adj.* akrobatisch

acrobatics /ækrə'bætɪks/ *n.* Akrobatik, *die*

acronym /'ækrənɪm/ *n.* Akronym, *das*

across /ə'krɒs/ ⊡ *adv.* (from one side to the other) darüber; (from here to there) hinüber; **be 9 miles ~:** 9 Meilen breit sein
⊡ *prep.* über (+ *Akk.*); (on the other side of) auf der anderen Seite (+ *Gen.*)

a'cross-the-board *adj.* pauschal; **an ~ pay rise** eine pauschale *od.* generelle Lohnerhöhung

acrylic /ə'krɪlɪk/ ⊡ *adj.* aus Acryl *nachgestellt;* Acryl-; **~ paint/fibre** Acrylfarbe, *die*/-faser, *die*
⊡ *n.* Acryl, *das*

act /ækt/ ⊡ *n.* **(a)** (deed) Tat, *die*
(b) (Theatre) Akt, *der*
(c) (pretence) Theater, *das;* **put on an ~:** Theater spielen
(d) (Law) Gesetz, *das*
⊡ *v.t.* spielen ‹*Stück*›
⊡ *v.i.* **(a)** (perform actions) handeln
(b) (behave) sich verhalten; **~ as** fungieren als
(c) (perform play) spielen
(d) (have effect) **~ on sth.** auf etw. (*Akk.*) wirken

action: **~ committee, ~ group** *ns.* [Eltern-/Bürger- *usw.*]initiative, *die;*
~-packed *adj.* spannend ‹*Buch, Roman*›; **an ~-packed film** ein Film mit viel Action;
~'replay *n.* Wiederholung (in Zeitlupe)

activate /'æktɪveɪt/ *v.t.* **(a)** in Gang setzen
(b) (Chem., Phys.) aktivieren

'acting ⊡ *n.* (Theatre etc.) die Schauspielerei
⊡ *adj.* (temporary) stellvertretend

action /'ækʃn/ *n.* **(a)** (doing sth.) Handeln, *das;* **take ~:** Schritte *od.* etwas unternehmen; **put a plan into ~:** einen Plan in die Tat umsetzen; **put sth. out of ~:** etw. außer Betrieb setzen
(b) (act) Tat, *die*
(c) (legal process) [Gerichts]verfahren, *das*
(d) **die in ~:** im Kampf fallen

active /'æktɪv/ *adj.,* **'actively** *adv.* aktiv

activist /'æktɪvɪst/ *n.* Aktivist, *der/* Aktivistin, *die*

activity /æk'tɪvɪtɪ/ *n.* Aktivität, *die;* **outdoor activities** Betätigung an der frischen Luft; **~ holiday** Aktivurlaub, *der*

actor /'æktə(r)/ *n.* Schauspieler, *der*

actress /'æktrɪs/ *n.* Schauspielerin, *die*

actual /'æktʃʊəl/ *adj.* eigentlich; wirklich ‹*Name*›

'actually *adv.* (in fact) eigentlich; (by the way) übrigens; (believe it or not) sogar

acumen /'ækjʊmen/ Scharfsinn, *der;* **business ~:** Geschäftssinn, *der*

acupressure /'ækjuːpreʃə(r)/ *n.* (Med.) Akupressur, *die*

acupuncture /'ækjʊpʌnktʃə(r)/ *n.* Akupunktur, *die*

acute /ə'kjuːt/ *adj.* **(a)** spitz ‹*Winkel*›
(b) (critical; Med.) akut

ad /æd/ *n.* (coll.) Annonce, *die*

AD *abbr.* = **Anno Domini** n.Chr.

adamant /'ædəmənt/ *adj.* unnachgiebig; **be ~ that ...:** darauf bestehen, dass ...

adapt /ə'dæpt/ *v.t.* **(a)** anpassen (**to** *Dat.*); **~ oneself to sth.** sich an etw. (*Akk.*) gewöhnen
(b) bearbeiten ‹*Text, Theaterstück*›

adaptable /ə'dæptəbl/ *adj.* anpassungsfähig

adaptation /ædəp'teɪʃn/ *n.* **(a)** Anpassung, *die*
(b) (version) Adap[ta]tion, *die;* (of story, text) Bearbeitung, *die*

adapter, adaptor /ə'dæptə(r)/ *n.* Adapter, *der*

add /æd/ ⊡ *v.t.* hinzufügen (**to** *Dat.*); **~ two and two** zwei und zwei zusammenzählen
⊡ *v.i.* **~ to** vergrößern ‹*Schwierigkeiten, Einkommen*›
■ **add 'up** ⊡ *v.i.* **~ up to sth.** (fig.) auf etw. (*Akk.*) hinauslaufen
⊡ *v.t.* zusammenzählen

adder /'ædə(r)/ *n.* Viper, *die*

addict ⊡ /ə'dɪkt/ *v.t.* **be ~ed** süchtig sein (**to** nach); **be ~ed to alcohol/smoking/drugs** alkohol-/nikotin-/drogensüchtig sein
⊡ /'ædɪkt/ *n.* Süchtige, *der/die*

addiction /ə'dɪkʃn/ *n.* Sucht, *die* (**to** nach)

addictive /ə'dɪktɪv/ *adj.* **be ~:** süchtig machen

addition /ə'dɪʃn/ *n.* **(a)** Hinzufügen, *das;* (adding up) Addieren, *das;* (process) Addition, *die;* **in ~:** außerdem; **in ~ to** zusätzlich zu
(b) (thing added) Ergänzung, *die* (**to** zu)

additional /ə'dɪʃənl/ *adj.* zusätzlich

additionally /ə'dɪʃənəlɪ/ *adv.* außerdem

additive /'ædɪtɪv/ *n.* Zusatz, *der*

'add-on ⊡ *n.* (accessory) Zubehörteil, *das;* (for electrical appliance) Zusatzgerät, *das;* (addition) Zusatz, *der*

2 *adj.* ~ **accessory** Zubehörteil, *das*; (for electrical appliance) Zusatzgerät, *das*

address /ə'dres/ **1** *v.t.* (a) (mark with ~) adressieren (**to** an + *Akk.*)
(b) (speak to) anreden; sprechen zu ⟨*Zuhörern*⟩
2 *n.* (a) (on letter) Adresse, *die*
(b) (speech) Ansprache, *die*

ad'dress book *n.* Adressenbüchlein, *das*

addressee /ædre'si:/ *n.* Adressat, *der*/ Adressatin, *die*

ad'dress label *n.* Adressenaufkleber, *der*

adept /'ædept, ə'dept/ *adj.* geschickt (**in, at** in + *Dat.*)

adequate /'ædɪkwət/ *adj.* (a) angemessen (**to** *Dat.*); (suitable) passend
(b) (sufficient) ausreichend

'adequately *adv.* (a) (sufficiently) ausreichend
(b) (suitably) angemessen ⟨*gekleidet, qualifiziert usw.*⟩

adhere /əd'hɪə(r)/ *v.i.* haften, (by glue) kleben (**to** an + *Dat.*)

adhesion /əd'hi:ʒn/ *n.* Haften, *das*

adhesive /əd'hi:sɪv/ **1** *adj.* gummiert ⟨*Briefmarke*⟩; Klebe⟨*band*⟩; ~ **plaster** Heftpflaster, *das*
2 *n.* Klebstoff, *der*

adjacent /ə'dʒeɪsənt/ *adj.* angrenzend; ~ **to** neben (*position:* + *Dat.; direction:* + *Akk.*)

adjective /'ædʒɪktɪv/ *n.* Adjektiv, *das*

adjoin /ə'dʒɔɪn/ *v.t.* grenzen an (+ *Akk.*)

adjourn /ə'dʒɜːn/ **1** *v.t.* (break off) unterbrechen; (put off) aufschieben
2 *v.i.* sich vertagen; ~ **for lunch/half an hour** eine Mittagspause/halbstündige Pause einlegen

a'djournment *n.* (of court) Vertagung, *die;* (of meeting) Unterbrechung, *die*

adjudicate /ə'dʒuːdɪkeɪt/ *v.i.* (in court, tribunal) das Urteil fällen; (in contest) entscheiden

adjust /ə'dʒʌst/ **1** *v.t.* einstellen; ~ **sth.** [**to sth.**] etw. [an etw. (*Akk.*)] anpassen
2 *v.i.* ⟨*Person:*⟩ sich anpassen (**to** an + *Akk.*)

adjustable /ə'dʒʌstəbl/ *adj.* einstellbar; verstellbar ⟨*Gerät*⟩

a'djustment *n.* Einstellung, *die;* (to situation etc.) Anpassung, *die*

ad-lib /æd'lɪb/ **1** *adj.* improvisiert
2 *v.i., -bb-* improvisieren

admin /'ædmɪn/ *n.* (coll.) Verwaltung, *die;* **an** ~ **problem** ein Verwaltungsproblem

administer /æd'mɪnɪstə(r)/ (a) (manage) verwalten
(b) leisten ⟨*Hilfe*⟩; verabreichen ⟨*Medikamente*⟩

administration /ədmɪnɪ'streɪʃn/ *n.* Verwaltung, *die*

administrative /əd'mɪnɪstrətɪv/ *adj.* Verwaltungs-; **an** ~ **job** ein Verwaltungsposten

administrator /əd'mɪnɪstreɪtə(r)/ *n.* Administrator, *der;* Verwalter, *der*

admirable /'ædmərəbl/ *adj.* bewundernswert

admiral /'ædmərəl/ *n.* Admiral, *der*

admiration /ædmə'reɪʃn/ *n.* Bewunderung, *die* (**of, for** für)

admire /əd'maɪə(r)/ *v.t.* bewundern

admirer /əd'maɪərə(r)/ *n.* Bewunderer, *der*/ Bewunderin, *die*

admiring /əd'maɪərɪŋ/ *adj.* bewundernd

admission /əd'mɪʃn/ *n.* (a) (entry) Zutritt, *der*
(b) (charge) Eintritt, *der*
(c) (confession) Eingeständnis, *das*

admission: ~ **charge,** ~ **fee** *ns.* Eintrittspreis, *der;* ~ **money** *n.* Eintrittsgeld, *das;* ~**price** *n.* Eintrittspreis, *der;* ~ **ticket** *n.* Eintrittskarte, *die*

admit /əd'mɪt/ *v.t., -tt-:* (a) (let in) hinein-/ hereinlassen
(b) (acknowledge) zugeben

admittance /əd'mɪtəns/ *n.* Zutritt, *der*

admittedly /əd'mɪtɪdlɪ/ *adv.* zugegeben[ermaßen]

admonish /əd'mɒnɪʃ/ *v.t.* ermahnen

ado /ə'duː/ *n.* **without more** ~: ohne weiteres Aufheben

adolescence /ædə'lesns/ *n.* die Zeit des Erwachsenwerdens

adolescent /ædə'lesnt/ **1** *n.* Heranwachsende, *der*/*die*
2 *adj.* heranwachsend

adopt /ə'dɒpt/ *v.t.* (a) adoptieren
(b) (take over) annehmen ⟨*Glaube, Kultur*⟩
(c) (take up) übernehmen ⟨*Methode*⟩; einnehmen ⟨*Standpunkt, Haltung*⟩

adoption /ə'dɒpʃn/ *n.* (a) Adoption, *die*
(b) (taking over) Annahme, *die*
(c) (taking up) Übernahme, *die;* (of point of view) Einnahme, *die*

adorable /ə'dɔːrəbl/ *adj.* bezaubernd

adoration /ædə'reɪʃn/ *n.* Verehrung, *die*

adore /ə'dɔː(r)/ *v.t.* verehren

adorn /ə'dɔːn/ *v.t.* schmücken

a'dornment *n.* Verzierung, *die;* ~**s** Schmuck, *der*

adrenalin /ə'drenəlɪn/ *n.* Adrenalin, *das*

Adriatic /eɪdrɪ'ætɪk/ *pr. n.* ~ [**Sea**] Adriatisches Meer

adrift /ə'drɪft/ *adj.* **be** ~: treiben

adroit /ə'drɔɪt/ *adj.* geschickt

ADSL *abbr.* (Teleph.) = **asymmetric digital subscriber line** ADSL

adulation /ædjʊ'leɪʃn/ *n.* Vergötterung, *die*

adult /'ædʌlt, ə'dʌlt/ **1** *adj.* erwachsen; ein ~ **film/book** *etc.* ein Film/Buch *usw.* [nur] für Erwachsene
2 *n.* Erwachsene, *der*/*die;* ~ **education** Erwachsenenbildung, *die*

adulterate /ə'dʌltəreɪt/ *v.t.* verunreinigen

adultery /ə'dʌltərɪ/ *n.* Ehebruch, *der*

advance /əd'vɑːns/ 1 *v.t.* **(a)** (also Mil.) vorrücken lassen
(b) (put forward) vorbringen ⟨*Plan, Meinung*⟩
(c) (further) fördern
(d) (pay before due date) vorschießen; ⟨*Bank:*⟩ leihen
2 *v.i.* **(a)** (also Mil.) vorrücken; ⟨*Prozession:*⟩ sich vorwärts bewegen
(b) (fig.: make progress) vorankommen
3 *n.* **(a)** Vorrücken, *das;* (fig.: progress) Fortschritt, *der*
(b) *usu. in pl.* (personal approach) Annäherungsversuch, *der*
(c) (on salary) Vorschuss, *der*
(d) in ~: im Voraus

ad'vance booking *n.* (for a film, play) [vorherige] Kartenreservierung; (of a table in a restaurant) [vorherige] Tischreservierung

advanced /əd'vɑːnst/ *adj.* fortgeschritten

advance: ~ 'notice *n.* **a week's ~ notice** Benachrichtigung eine Woche [im] Voraus; **give sb. ~ notice of sth.** jmdn. im Voraus von etw. in Kenntnis setzen; **~ 'payment** *n.* Vorauszahlung, *die*

advantage /əd'vɑːntɪdʒ/ *n.* Vorteil, *der;* **take ~ of sb.** jmdn. ausnutzen; **be to one's ~:** für jmdn. von Vorteil sein; **turn sth. to [one's] ~:** etw. ausnutzen

advantageous /ædvən'teɪdʒəs/ *adj.* vorteilhaft

advent /'ædvent/ *n.* Beginn, *der;* **A~:** Advent, *der*

adventure /əd'ventʃə(r)/ *n.* Abenteuer, *das*

adventure: ~ holiday *n* Abenteuerurlaub, *der;* **~ playground** *n.* (Brit.) Abenteuerspielplatz, *der*

adventurous /əd'ventʃərəs/ *adj.* abenteuerlustig

adverb /'ædvɜːb/ *n.* Adverb, *das*

adversary /'ædvəsərɪ/ *n.* (enemy) Widersacher, *der*/Widersacherin, *die;* (opponent) Kontrahent, *der*/Kontrahentin, *die*

adverse /'ædvɜːs/ *adj.* **(a)** (unfavourable) ungünstig
(b) (contrary) widrig ⟨*Wind, Umstände*⟩

adversity /əd'vɜːsɪtɪ/ *n.* **(a)** *no pl.* Not, *die*
(b) *usu. in pl.* Widrigkeit, *die*

advert /'ædvɜːt/ *n.* (Brit. coll.) ▸ ADVERTISEMENT

advertise /'ædvətaɪz/ 1 *v.t.* werben für; (by small ad) inserieren; ausschreiben ⟨*Stelle*⟩
2 *v.i.* werben; (in newspaper) inserieren; annoncieren

advertisement /əd'vɜːtɪsmənt/ *n.* Anzeige, *die;* **TV ~:** Fernsehspot, *der;* **classified ~:** Kleinanzeige, *die*

advertiser /'ædvətaɪzə(r)/ *n.* (in newspaper) Inserent, *der*/Inserentin, *die;* (on radio, TV) Auftraggeber/Auftraggeberin [der Werbesendung]

advertising /'ædvətaɪzɪŋ/ *n.* Werbung, *die;*

attrib. Werbe-; **~ agency/campaign/industry** Werbeagentur, *die*/-kampagne, *die*/-branche, *die*

advice /əd'vaɪs/ *n.* Rat, *der;* **take sb.'s ~:** jmds. Rat (*Dat.*) folgen

advisable /əd'vaɪzəbl/ *adj.* ratsam

advise /əd'vaɪz/ *v.t.* beraten; **~ sth.** zu etw. raten; (inform) unterrichten (**of** über + *Akk.*); **~ sb. to do sth.** jmdm. raten, etw. zu tun

adviser, advisor /əd'vaɪzə(r)/ *n.* Berater, *der*/Beraterin, *die*

advisory /əd'vaɪzərɪ/ *adj.* beratend

advocate 1 /'ædvəkət/ *n.* (of a cause) Befürworter, *der*/Befürworterin, *die;* (Law) [Rechts]anwalt, *der*/-anwältin, *die*
2 /'ædvəkeɪt/ *v.t.* befürworten

advt. *abbr.* = **advertisement**

aerial /'eərɪəl/ 1 *adj.* Luft-;
~ bombardment Bombardierung [aus der Luft]; **~ photograph/photography** Luftaufnahme, *die*/Luftaufnahmen Pl.
2 *n.* Antenne, *die*

aero- /eərəʊ/ *in comb.* Aero-

aerobic /eə'rəʊbɪk/ *adj.* (Biol.) aerob

ae'robics *n.* Aerobic, *das*

aerody'namic *adj.* aerodynamisch

aeronautics /eərə'nɔːtɪks/ *n.* Aeronautik, *die*

aeroplane /'eərəpleɪn/ *n.* (Brit.) Flugzeug, *das*

aerosol /'eərəsɒl/ *n.* (spray) Spray, *der od. das;* (container) **~ [spray]** Spraydose, *die*

'aerospace *n., no art.* Erdatmosphäre und Weltraum; (technology) Luft- und Raumfahrt, *die*

aesthetic /iːs'θetɪk/ *adj.* ästhetisch

afar /ə'fɑː/ *adv.* **from ~:** aus der Ferne

affable /'æfəbl/ *adj.* freundlich

affair /ə'feə/ *n.* **(a)** (concern) Angelegenheit, *die*
(b) *in pl.* (business) Geschäfte Pl.
(c) (love) ~ Affäre, *die;* **have an ~ with sb.** eine Affäre *od.* ein Verhältnis mit jmdm. haben

affect /ə'fekt/ *v.t.* **(a)** sich auswirken auf (+ *Akk.*)
(b) (emotionally) betroffen machen

affectation /æfek'teɪʃn/ *n.* (studied display) Verstellung, *die;* (artificiality) Affektiertheit, *die*

affected /ə'fektɪd/ *adj.* affektiert; gekünstelt ⟨*Sprache, Stil*⟩

affection /ə'fekʃn/ *n.* Zuneigung, *die*

affectionate /ə'fekʃənət/ *adj.* anhänglich; liebevoll ⟨*Umarmung*⟩

af'fectionately *adv.* liebevoll

affiliate /ə'fɪlɪeɪt/ *v.t.* **be ~d to sth.** an etw. (*Akk.*) angegliedert sein

affinity /ə'fɪnɪtɪ/ *n.* **(a)** (relationship) Verwandtschaft, *die* (**to** mit)
(b) (liking) Neigung, *die* (**for** zu); **feel an ~ to** *or* **for sb./sth.** sich zu jmdm./etw. hingezogen fühlen

affirm /ə'fɜːm/ v.t. (assert) bekräftigen ‹Absicht›; beteuern ‹Unschuld›; (state as a fact) bestätigen

affirmation /æfə'meɪʃn/ n. (of intention) Bekräftigung, die; (of fact) Bestätigung, die

affirmative /ə'fɜːmətɪv/ ⬚1 adj. affirmativ; bejahend ‹Antwort›
⬚2 n. answer in the ~: bejahend antworten

affirmative 'action n. (Amer.) positive Diskriminierung (fachspr.); Bevorzugung, die

afflict /ə'flɪkt/ v.t. (physically) plagen; (mentally) quälen; peinigen; **be ~ed with sth.** von etw. befallen sein

affliction /ə'flɪkʃn/ n. Leiden, das

affluence /'æflʊəns/ n. Reichtum, der

affluent /'æflʊənt/ adj. reich; **the ~ society** die Überflussgesellschaft

afford /ə'fɔːd/ v.t. (a) sich (Dat.) leisten
(b) (provide) bieten; gewähren ‹Schutz›

affordable /ə'fɔːdəbl/ adj. erschwinglich

affray /ə'freɪ/ n. Schlägerei, die

affront /ə'frʌnt/ ⬚1 v.t. beleidigen
⬚2 n. Beleidigung, die

afield /ə'fiːld/ adv. **far ~** (direction) weit hinaus; (place) weit draußen

afloat /ə'fləʊt/ pred. adj. (a) (floating) über Wasser; flott ‹Schiff›
(b) (at sea) auf See; **be ~:** auf dem Meer treiben

afoot /ə'fʊt/ pred. adj. im Gange

aforementioned /ə'fɔːmenʃnd/,
aforesaid /ə'fɔːsed/ adjs. oben erwähnt od. genannt

afraid /ə'freɪd/ adj. **be ~ [of sb./sth.]** [vor jmdm./etw.] Angst haben; **be ~ to do sth.** Angst davor haben, etw. zu tun; **I'm ~ so/ not** ich fürchte ja/nein

afresh /ə'freʃ/ adv. von neuem

Africa /'æfrɪkə/ pr. n. Afrika (das)

African /'æfrɪkən/ ⬚1 adj. afrikanisch; **sb. is ~:** jmd. ist Afrikaner/Afrikanerin
⬚2 n. Afrikaner, der/Afrikanerin, die

Afro-Carib'bean ⬚1 adj. afrokaribisch
⬚2 n. Mensch afrokaribischer Herkunft od. Abstammung

after /'ɑːftə(r)/ ⬚1 adv. (a) (later) danach
(b) (behind) hinterher
⬚2 prep. (a) (in time) nach; **two days ~:** zwei Tage danach
(b) (behind) hinter (+ Dat.)
(c) **ask ~ sb./sth.** nach jmdm./etw. fragen
(d) **~ all** schließlich
⬚3 conj. nachdem

after: ~care n. (Med.) Nachbehandlung, die **~-effect** n. Nachwirkung, die

aftermath /'ɑːftəmæθ, 'ɑːftəmɑːθ/ n. Nachwirkungen Pl.

after: ~'noon n. Nachmittag, der; **this/ tomorrow ~noon** heute/morgen Nachmittag; **in the ~noon** am Nachmittag; (regularly) nachmittags; **~-sales service** n.

Kundendienst, der; **~shave** n. Aftershave, das; **~taste** n. Nachgeschmack, der; **~thought** n. nachträglicher Einfall

afterwards /'ɑːftəwədz/ adv. danach

again /ə'gen, ə'geɪn/ adv. wieder; (one more time) noch einmal; **~ and ~, time and [time] ~:** immer wieder; **back ~:** wieder zurück

against /ə'genst, ə'geɪnst/ prep. gegen

age /eɪdʒ/ ⬚1 n. (a) Alter, das; **what ~ are you?** wie alt bist du?; **at the ~ of** im Alter von; **come of ~:** volljährig werden; **be under ~:** zu jung sein
(b) (great period) Zeitalter, das; **~s** (coll.: a long time) eine Ewigkeit
⬚2 v.t. altern lassen
⬚3 v.i. altern

'age bracket n. Altersstufe, die

aged adj. (a) /eɪdʒd/ **be ~ five** fünf Jahre alt sein; **a boy ~ five** ein fünfjähriger Junge
(b) /'eɪdʒɪd/ (elderly) bejahrt

'age group n. Altersgruppe, die

ageism /'eɪdʒɪzm/ n. Diskriminierung aufgrund des Alters

ageist /'eɪdʒɪst/ adj. das Alter diskriminierend

ageless /'eɪdʒlɪs/ adj. nicht alternd ‹Person›; (eternal) zeitlos

'age limit n. Altersgrenze, die

agency /'eɪdʒənsɪ/ n. (business establishment) Geschäftsstelle, die; (news/advertising ~) Agentur, die

agenda /ə'dʒendə/ n. Tagesordnung, die

agent /'eɪdʒənt/ n. Vertreter, der/ Vertreterin, die; (spy) Agent, der/Agentin, die

age: ~old adj. uralt; **~ range** n. Altersstufe, die

aggravate /'ægrəveɪt/ v.t. (a) (make worse) verschlimmern
(b) (annoy) aufregen; ärgern

aggravating /'ægrəveɪtɪŋ/ adj. ärgerlich

aggravation /ægrə'veɪʃn/ n. (a) Verschlimmerung, die
(b) (annoyance) Ärger, der

aggregate /'ægrɪgət/ ⬚1 n. Gesamtmenge, die
⬚2 adj. gesamt

aggression /ə'greʃn/ n. Aggression, die

aggressive /ə'gresɪv/ adj.,
ag'gressively adv. aggressiv

ag'gressiveness n. Aggressivität, die

aggressor /ə'gresə(r)/ n. Aggressor, der

aggrieved /ə'griːvd/ v.t. (resentful) verärgert; (offended) gekränkt

aggro /'ægrəʊ/ n. (Brit. sl.) Zoff, der (ugs.); Krawall, der; **they are looking for ~:** sie suchen Streit

aghast /ə'gɑːst/ pred. adj. bestürzt (über + Akk.)

agile /'ædʒaɪl/ adj. beweglich; flink ‹Bewegung›

agility /ə'dʒɪlɪtɪ/ n. Beweglichkeit, die; (of movement) Flinkheit, die

a

agitate /ˈædʒɪteɪt/ 1 *v.t.* (a) (shake) schütteln

(b) (disturb) erregen

2 *v.i.* agitieren

agitation /ædʒɪˈteɪʃn/ *n.* (a) (shaking) Schütteln, *das*

(b) (emotional) Erregung, *die*

agitator /ˈædʒɪteɪtə(r)/ *n.* Agitator, *der*

AGM *abbr.* = **Annual General Meeting** JHV

agnostic /ægˈnɒstɪk/ *n.* Agnostiker, *der*/ Agnostikerin, *die*

ago /əˈgəʊ/ *adv.* ten years ∼: vor zehn Jahren; [not] long ∼: vor [nicht] langer Zeit

agog /əˈgɒg/ *pred. adj.* gespannt

agonize /ˈægənaɪz/ *v.i.* ∼ over sth. sich (*Dat.*) den Kopf über etw. (*Akk.*) zermartern

agony /ˈægənɪ/ *n.* Todesqualen *Pl.*

'agony aunt *n.* (coll.) Briefkastentante, *die* (ugs. scherzh.)

agoraphobia /ægərəˈfəʊbɪə/ *n.* (Psych.) Agoraphobie, *die;* Platzangst, *die*

agoraphobic /ægərəˈfəʊbɪk/ *adj.* (Psych.) an Agoraphobie *od.* Platzangst leidend; be ∼: an Agoraphobie *od.* Platzangst leiden

agree /əˈgriː/ 1 *v.i.* (a) (consent) einverstanden sein (to, with mit)

(b) (hold similar opinion) einer Meinung sein; they ∼d [with me] sie waren derselben Meinung [wie ich]

(c) (reach similar opinion) ∼ on sth. sich über etw. (*Akk.*) einigen

(d) (harmonize) übereinstimmen

(e) ∼ with sb. (suit) jmdm. bekommen

2 *v.t.* vereinbaren

agreeable /əˈgriːəbl/ *adj.* (a) (pleasing) angenehm

(b) be ∼ [to sth.] [mit etw.] einverstanden sein

agreeably /əˈgriːəblɪ/ *adv.* angenehm

agreed /əˈgriːd/ *adj.* einig; vereinbart ⟨Summe, Zeit⟩

a'greement *n.* Übereinstimmung, *die;* be in ∼ [about sth.] sich (*Dat.*) [über etw. (*Akk.*)] einig sein

agricultural /ægrɪˈkʌltʃərl/ *adj.* landwirtschaftlich

agriculture /ˈægrɪkʌltʃə(r)/ *n.* Landwirtschaft, *die*

aground /əˈgraʊnd/ *adj.* go *or* run ∼: auf Grund laufen

aha /ɑːˈhɑː/ *int.* aha

ahead /əˈhed/ *adv.* voraus; ∼ of vor (+ *Dat.*); be ∼ of the others (fig.) den anderen voraus sein

AI *abbr.* = **artificial intelligence** KI

aid /eɪd/ 1 *v.t.* (a) ∼ sb. [to do sth.] jmdm. helfen[, etw. zu tun]; ∼ed by unterstützt von

(b) (promote) fördern

2 *n.* (a) (help) Hilfe, *die;* with the ∼ of sth./ sb. mit Hilfe einer Sache (*Gen.*)/mit jmds. Hilfe; in ∼ of sb./sth. zugunsten von jmdm./ etw.

(b) (source of help) Hilfsmittel, *das* (to für)

'aid agency *n.* Hilfsorganisation, *die;* Hilfswerk, *das*

aide /eɪd/ *n.* Berater, *der*/Beraterin, *die*

Aids /eɪdz/ *n.* Aids (*das*); ∼ test Aidstest, *der*

'Aids-related *adj.* ∼ disease/illness durch Aids hervorgerufene Krankheit

'aid worker *n.* Helfer, *der*/Helferin, *die;* ∼s Hilfskräfte *Pl.*; Hilfspersonal, *das*

ailment /ˈeɪlmənt/ *n.* Gebrechen, *das*

aim /eɪm/ 1 *v.t.* ausrichten ⟨Schusswaffe, Rakete⟩; ∼ sth. at sb./sth. etw. auf jmdn./etw. richten

2 *v.i.* (a) zielen (at auf + *Akk.*)

(b) ∼ to do sth. beabsichtigen, etw. zu tun; ∼ at *or* for sth. (fig.) etwas anstreben

3 *n.* Ziel, *das;* take ∼ [at sth./sb.] [auf etw./ jmdn.] zielen

'aimless *adj.,* **'aimlessly** *adv.* ziellos

air /eə(r)/ 1 *n.* (a) (source of help) Luft, *die;* be/go on the ∼: senden; ⟨Programm:⟩ gesendet werden; by ∼: mit dem Flugzeug; (by ∼ mail) mit Luftpost

(b) (facial expression) Miene, *die*

(c) put on ∼s sich aufspielen

2 *v.t.* (ventilate) lüften; (make public) [öffentlich] darlegen

air: ∼ **bag** *n.* (Motor Veh.) Airbag *der;* side ∼ bag Seitenairbag, *der;* ∼**base** *n.* Luftwaffenstützpunkt, *der;* ∼**bed** *n.* Luftmatratze, *die;* ∼**borne** *adj.* be ∼borne sich in der Luft befinden; ∼ **brake** *n.* Druckluftbremse, *die;* (flap) Luftbremse, *die;* ∼**brush** *n.* Spritzpistole, *die;* ∼ **bubble** *n.* Luftblase, *die;* ∼ **bus** *n.* Airbus, *der;* ∼**-conditioned** *adj.* klimatisiert; ∼ **conditioner** *n.* Klimaanlage, *die;* ∼ **conditioning** *n.* Klimaanlage, *die;* ∼**-cooled** *adj.* luftgekühlt; ∼**craft** *n., pl. same* Flugzeug, *das;* ∼**craft carrier** *n.* Flugzeugträger, *der;* ∼ **crew** *n.* Besatzung, *die;* Flugpersonal, *das;* ∼ **cushion** *n.* Luftkissen, *das;* ∼ **fare** *n.* Flugpreis, *der;* ∼**field** *n.* Flugplatz, *der;* ∼ **force** *n.* Luftwaffe, *die;* ∼ **freshener** *n.* Lufterfrischer, *der;* Luftverbesserer, *der;* ∼**gun** *n.* Luftgewehr, *das;* ∼ **hostess** *n.* Stewardess, *die*

airing /ˈeərɪŋ/ *n.* Auslüften, *das;* these clothes need a good ∼: diese Kleider müssen gründlich gelüftet werden

airless /ˈeəlɪs/ *adj.* stickig ⟨Zimmer, Büro⟩; windstill ⟨Nacht⟩

air: ∼ **letter** *n.* Aerogramm, *das;* ∼**lift** *n.* Luftbrücke, *die* (of für); ∼**line** *n.* Fluggesellschaft, *die;* Fluglinie, *die;* ∼**line pilot** [für eine Fluggesellschaft fliegender] Pilot; ∼ **liner** *n.* Verkehrsflugzeug, *das;* ∼ **mail** *n.* Luftpost, *die;* by ∼ mail mit Luftpost; ∼**man** /ˈeəmən/ *n., pl.* ∼**men** / -mən/ Flieger, *der;* ∼ **mile** *n.* Flugmeile, *die;* ∼**plane** *n.* (Amer.) Flugzeug, *das;* ∼ **play** *n.* (Radio) *das Spielen einer Platte im Radio;*

the record receives *or* gets no/a great deal of
~play die Platte wird [überhaupt] nicht/
wird sehr häufig im Radio gespielt;
~ **pocket** *n.* (Aeronaut.) Luftloch, *das;*
~ **pollution** *n.* Luftverschmutzung, *die;*
~port *n.* Flughafen, *der;* ~port tax
Flughafengebühr, *die;* ~ **pressure** *n.*
Luftdruck, *der;* ~ **raid** *n.* Luftangriff, *der;*
~-**raid shelter** *n.* Luftschutzraum, *der;*
~ **rifle** *n.* Luftgewehr, *das;* ~-**sea**
'**rescue** *n.* Seenotrettungseinsatz aus der
Luft; ~**ship** *n.* Luftschiff, *das;* ~ **show** *n.*
Flugschau, *die;* ~**sick** *adj.* luftkrank;
~**stream** *n.* (Meteorol.) Luftströmung, *die;*
~**strike** *n.* Luftanschlag, *der;*
~ **terminal** *n.* (Air-)Terminal, *der od. das;*
~**tight** *adj.* luftdicht; ~**time** *n.* Sendezeit,
die; ~ **traffic** *n.* Flugverkehr, *der;*
~-**traffic control** *n.* Flugsicherung, *die;*
~-**traffic controller** *n.* Fluglotse, *der;*
~ **travel** *n.* Fliegen, *das;* ~**waves** *n. pl.*
Äther, *der*
'**airy** *adj.* luftig ‹Büro, Zimmer›
aisle /aɪl/ *n.* Gang, *der;* (of church)
Seitenschiff, *das*
ajar /əˈdʒɑː(r)/ *adj.* be ~: einen Spaltbreit
offen stehen
a.k.a. *abbr.* = **also known as** al.
akin /əˈkɪn/ *adj.* be ~ to sth. einer Sache
(*Dat.*) ähnlich sein
alarm /əˈlɑːm/ ①*n.* (a) Alarm, *der;* give *or*
raise the ~: Alarm schlagen
(b) (fear) Angst, *die*
② *v.t.* aufschrecken
alarm: ~ **call** *n.* Weck[an]ruf, *der;*
~ '**clock** *n.* Wecker, *der*
alas /əˈlæs/ *int.* ach
Albania /ælˈbeɪnɪə/ *pr. n.* Albanien (*das*)
Albanian /ælˈbeɪnɪən/ ①*adj.* albanisch;
sb. is ~: jmd. ist Albaner/Albanerin
② *n.* (a) (person) Albaner, *der*/Albanerin, *die*
(b) (language) Albanisch, *das; see also*
ENGLISH 2 A
albatross /ˈælbətrɒs/ *n.* Albatros, *der*
album /ˈælbəm/ *n.* Album, *das*
alcohol /ˈælkəhɒl/ *n.* Alkohol, *der*
'**alcohol-free** *adj.* alkoholfrei
alcoholic /ælkəˈhɒlɪk/ ①*adj.* alkoholisch
② *n.* Alkoholiker, *der*/Alkoholikerin, *die*
Alcoholics A'nonymous *n.* die
Anonymen Alkoholiker
alcoholism /ˈælkəhɒlɪzm/ *n.*
Alkoholismus, *der*
alcopop /ˈælkəʊpɒp/ *n.* Alcopop, *der od.
das*
alcove /ˈælkəʊv/ *n.* Alkoven, *der*
ale /eɪl/ *n.* Ale, *das*
alert /əˈlɜːt/ ①*adj.* wachsam
② *n.* Alarmbereitschaft, *die;* on the ~: auf
der Hut
③ *v.t.* alarmieren; ~ sb. [to sth.] jmdn. [vor
etw. (*Dat.*)] warnen
'**A level** *n.* (Brit. Sch.) ≈ Abitur, *das*

algebra /ˈældʒɪbrə/ *n.* Algebra, *die*
Algeria /ælˈdʒɪərɪə/ *pr. n.* Algerien (*das*)
Algerian /ælˈdʒɪərɪən/ ①*adj.* algerisch;
sb. is ~: jmd. ist Algerier/Algerierin
② *n.* Algerier, *der*/Algerierin, *die*
alias /ˈeɪlɪəs/ ①*adv.* alias
② *n.* (a) angenommener Name;
(b) (Comp.) Alias, *das*
alibi /ˈælɪbaɪ/ *n.* Alibi, *das*
alien /ˈeɪlɪən/ ①*adj.* (a) (strange) fremd
(b) (foreign) ausländisch
② *n.* (a) (from another world) Außerirdische,
der/die
(b) (Admin.: foreigner) Ausländer, *der*/
Ausländerin, *die*
alienate /ˈeɪlɪəneɪt/ *v.t.* befremden
alienation /eɪlɪəˈneɪʃn/ *n.* Entfremdung,
die
alight¹ /əˈlaɪt/ *v.i.* (a) aussteigen (**from** aus)
(b) ‹Vogel:› sich niedersetzen
alight² *adj.* be/catch ~: brennen; set sth.
~: etw. in Brand setzen
align /əˈlaɪn/ *v.t.* (a) (place in a line)
ausrichten
(b) (bring into line) in eine Linie bringen
a'lignment *n.* Ausrichtung, *die;* out of ~:
nicht richtig ausgerichtet
alike /əˈlaɪk/ *pred. adj.* ähnlich;
(indistinguishable) gleich
alimony /ˈælɪmənɪ/ *n.* Unterhaltszahlung,
die
alive /əˈlaɪv/ *pred. adj.* (a) lebendig
(b) (aware) be ~ to sth. sich (*Dat.*) einer
Sache (*Gen.*) bewusst sein
(c) (swarming) be ~ with wimmeln von
alkali /ˈælkəlaɪ/ *n., pl.* ~s *or* ~es Alkali,
das
alkaline /ˈælkəlaɪn/ *adj.* alkalisch
all /ɔːl/ ①*attrib. adj.* (a) (entire extent or
quantity of) ganz; ~ **day** den ganzen Tag;
~ **my money** mein ganzes Geld
(b) (entire number of) alle; ~ **the books** alle
Bücher; ~ **my books** all[e] meine Bücher;
~ **the others** alle anderen
(c) (any whatever) jeglicher/jegliche/jegliches
(d) (greatest possible) in ~ **innocence** in aller
Unschuld
② *n.* (a) (~ persons) alle; ~ **of us** wir alle;
the happiest of ~: der/die Glücklichste
unter *od.* von allen
(b) (every bit) ~ **of it** alles; ~ **of the money**
das ganze Geld
(c) ~ **of** (coll.: as much as) be ~ **of seven feet
tall** gut sieben Fuß groß sein
(d) (~ things) alles; ~ **I need is the money**
ich brauche nur das Geld; **that is** ~: das ist
alles; **the most beautiful of** ~: der/die/das
Schönste von allen; **most of** ~: am meisten;
it was ~ **but impossible** es war fast
unmöglich; **it's** ~ **the same to me** es ist mir
ganz egal; **can I help you at** ~? kann ich
Ihnen irgendwie behilflich sein?; **she has no
talent at** ~: sie hat überhaupt kein Talent; ⋯❖

nothing at ~: gar nichts; not at ~ happy/well überhaupt nicht glücklich/gesund; not at ~! überhaupt nicht!; (acknowledging thanks) gern geschehen!; if at ~: wenn überhaupt; in ~: insgesamt; ~ in ~: alles in allem
(e) (Sport) two [goals] ~: zwei zu zwei; (Tennis) thirty ~: dreißig beide
3 *adv.* ganz; ~ but fast; ~ the better/worse [for that] um so besser/schlimmer; ~ at once (suddenly) plötzlich; be ~ 'in (exhausted) total erledigt sein (ugs.); sth. is ~ right etw. ist in Ordnung; (tolerable) etw. ist ganz gut; I'm ~ right mir geht es ganz gut; yes, ~ right ja, gut; it's ~ right by me das ist mir recht

allay /ə'leɪ/ *v.t.* zerstreuen ⟨Besorgnis, Befürchtungen⟩

all: ~-'clear *n.* Entwarnung, *die;* ~-day *adj.* ganztägig ⟨Ausflug, Versammlung⟩

allegation /ælɪ'geɪʃn/ *n.* Behauptung, *die;* make ~s against sb. Beschuldigungen gegen jmdn. erheben

allege /ə'ledʒ/ *v.t.* behaupten

alleged /ə'ledʒd/ *adj.*, **allegedly** /ə'ledʒɪdlɪ/ *adv.* angeblich

allegiance /ə'li:dʒəns/ *n.* Loyalität, *die* (to gegenüber)

allegorical /ælɪ'gɒrɪkl/ *adj.* allegorisch

allegory /'ælɪgərɪ/ *n.* Allegorie, *die*

allergic /ə'lɜ:dʒɪk/ *adj.* allergisch (to gegen)

allergy /'ælədʒɪ/ *n.* Allergie, *die*

alleviate /ə'li:vɪeɪt/ *v.t.* abschwächen

alley /'ælɪ/ *n.* [schmale] Gasse

alliance /ə'laɪəns/ *n.* Bündnis, *das;* (league) Allianz, *die*

allied /'ælaɪd/ *adj.* be ~ to *or* with sb./sth. mit jmdm./etw. verbündet sein

alligator /'ælɪgeɪtə(r)/ *n.* Alligator, *der*

all: ~-in *adj.* Pauschal-; ~-night *adj.* die ganze Nacht dauernd ⟨Sitzung⟩; nachts durchgehend geöffnet ⟨Gaststätte⟩

allocate /'æləkeɪt/ *v.t.* zuweisen, zuteilen (to *Dat.*)

allocation /ælə'keɪʃn/ *n.* Zuweisung, *die;* (ration) Zuteilung, *die*

allot /ə'lɒt/ *v.t.*, **-tt-:** ~ sth. to sb. jmdm. etw. zuteilen

al'lotment *n.* (Brit.: plot of land) ≈ Schrebergarten, *der*

all: ~-out *attrib. adj.* mit allen [verfügbaren] Mitteln *nachgestellt;* ~-over *attrib. adj.* ~-over tan nahtlose Bräune

allow /ə'laʊ/ **1** *v.t.* erlauben; zulassen; ~ sb. to do sth. jmdm. erlauben, etw. zu tun; be ~ed to do sth. etw. tun dürfen
2 *v.i.* ~ for sth. etw. berücksichtigen

allowance /ə'laʊəns/ *n.* (a) Zuteilung, *die;* (for special expenses) Zuschuss, *der.* (b) make ~s for sth./sb. etw./jmdn. berücksichtigen

alloy /'ælɔɪ/ *n.* Legierung, *die*

all: ~-purpose *adj.* Universal-; Allzweck-; ~-risks *attrib. adj.* an ~-risks insurance

eine alle gängigen Risiken abdeckende Versicherung; ~-round *adj.* Allround-; ~-'rounder *n.* Allroundtalent, *das;* ~-seater *adj.* voll bestuhlt ⟨Stadion⟩; ~-time *adj.* ~-time record absoluter Rekord

allude /ə'lu:d/ *v.i.* ~ to sich beziehen auf (+ *Akk.*); (indirectly) anspielen auf (+ *Akk.*)

allusion /ə'lu:ʒn/ *n.* Hinweis, *der;* (indirect) Anspielung, *die*

ally /'ælaɪ/ *n.* Verbündete, *der/die;* the Allies die Alliierten

almighty /ɔ:l'maɪtɪ/ *adj.* allmächtig; the A~: der Allmächtige

almond /'ɑ:mənd/ *n.* Mandel, *die*

almost /'ɔ:lməʊst/ *adv.* fast; beinahe

alms /ɑ:mz/ *n.* Almosen, *das*

alone /ə'ləʊn/ **1** *pred. adj.* allein; alleine (ugs.)
2 *adv.* allein

along /ə'lɒŋ/ **1** *prep.* entlang ⟨position: + *Dat.*; direction: + *Akk.*⟩
2 *adv.* weiter; I'll be ~ shortly ich komme gleich; all ~: die ganze Zeit [über]

along'side **1** *adv.* daneben
2 *prep.* neben ⟨position: + *Dat.*; direction: + *Akk.*⟩

aloof /ə'lu:f/ **1** *adv.* abseits; hold ~ from sb. sich von jmdm. fern halten
2 *adj.* distanziert

aloud /ə'laʊd/ *adv.* laut; read [sth.] ~: [etw.] vorlesen

alphabet /'ælfəbet/ *n.* Alphabet, *das*

alphabetical /ælfə'betɪkl/ *adj.*, **alpha'betically** *adv.* alphabetisch

alpine /'ælpaɪn/ *adj.* alpin

Alps /ælps/ *pr. n. pl.* the ~: die Alpen

already /ɔ:l'redɪ/ *adv.* schon

Alsation /æl'seɪʃn/ *n.* [deutscher] Schäferhund

also /'ɔ:lsəʊ/ *adv.* auch; (moreover) außerdem

altar /'ɔ:ltə(r), 'ɒltə(r)/ *n.* Altar, *der*

alter /'ɔ:ltə(r), 'ɒltə(r)/ **1** *v.t.* ändern
2 *v.i.* sich verändern

alteration /ɔ:ltə'reɪʃn, ɒltə'reɪʃn/ *n.* Änderung, *die*

alternate **1** /ɔ:l'tɜ:nət/ *adj.* sich abwechselnd
2 /'ɔ:ltənət/ *v.t.* abwechseln lassen
3 /'ɔ:ltənət/ *v.i.* sich abwechseln

al'ternately *adv.* abwechselnd

'alternating current *n.* (Electr.) Wechselstrom, *der*

alternative /ɔ:l'tɜ:nətɪv/ **1** *adj.* alternativ; Alternativ-; ~ energy alternative Energie; ~ fuel Alternativkraftstoff, *der* (*für Verbrennungsmotoren*); ~ medicine Alternativmedizin, *die*
2 *n.* (a) (choice) Alternative, *die*
(b) (possibility) Möglichkeit, *die*

al'ternatively *adv.* oder aber; or ~: oder aber auch

although /ɔːˈðəʊ/ *conj.* obwohl

altimeter /ˈæltɪmiːtə(r)/ *n.* Höhenmesser, *der*

altitude /ˈæltɪtjuːd/ *n.* Höhe, *die*

altogether /ɔːltəˈgeðə(r)/ *adv.* völlig; (on the whole) im Großen und Ganzen; (in total) insgesamt; **not** ~ **[true/convincing]** nicht ganz [wahr/überzeugend]

altruist /ˈæltrʊɪst/ *n.* Altruist, *der*/ Altruistin, *die* (geh.)

altruistic /æltrʊˈɪstɪk/ *adj.* altruistisch

aluminium /æljʊˈmɪniəm/ (Brit.), **aluminum** /əˈluːmɪnəm/ (Amer.) *ns.* Aluminium, *das*

always /ˈɔːlweɪz/ *adv.* immer; (repeatedly) ständig

Alzheimer's disease /ˈæltshaɪmez dɪziːz/ *n.* Alzheimerkrankheit, *die*

am ▶ BE

AM *abbr.* = **amplitude modulation** AM

a.m. /eɪˈem/ *adv.* vormittags; [at] one/four ~: [um] ein/vier Uhr früh

amalgamate /əˈmælgəmeɪt/ ① *v.t.* vereinigen
② *v.i.* sich vereinigen; ⟨*Firmen:*⟩ fusionieren

amalgamation /əmælgəˈmeɪʃn/ *n.* Vereinigung, *die;* (of firms) Fusion, *die*

amass /əˈmæs/ *v.t.* anhäufen

amateur /ˈæmətə(r)/ *n.* Amateur, *der; attrib.* Amateur-; Laien-

'amateurish *adj.* laienhaft; amateurhaft

amaze /əˈmeɪz/ *v.t.* verblüffen; verwundern

a'mazement *n.* Verblüffung, *die;* Verwunderung, *die*

amazing /əˈmeɪzɪŋ/ *adj.* (remarkable) erstaunlich; (astonishing) verblüffend

Amazon /ˈæməzən/ *pr. n.* the ~: der Amazonas

ambassador /æmˈbæsədə(r)/ *n.* Botschafter, *der*/Botschafterin, *die*

amber /ˈæmbə(r)/ ① *n.* (a) Bernstein, *der* (b) (traffic light) Gelb, *das*
② *adj.* Bernstein-; (colour) bernsteinfarben; gelb ⟨*Verkehrslicht*⟩

ambiguity /æmbɪˈgjuːɪtɪ/ *n.* Zweideutigkeit, *die*

ambiguous /æmˈbɪgjʊəs/ *adj.* zweideutig

ambition /æmˈbɪʃn/ *n.* Ehrgeiz, *der;* (aspiration) Ambition, *die*

ambitious /æmˈbɪʃəs/ *adj.* ehrgeizig

ambivalent /æmˈbɪvələnt/ *adj.* ambivalent

amble /ˈæmbl/ *v.i.* schlendern

ambulance /ˈæmbjʊləns/ *n.* Krankenwagen, *der;* Ambulanz, *die*

ambulance: ~ **chaser** *n.* (Amer.) *Anwalt oder sein Agent, der Unfallopfer dazu überredet, auf Schadenersatz zu klagen;*

~ **driver** *n.* Fahrer/Fahrerin eines/des Krankenwagens; ~ **man** *n.* Sanitäter, *der;* ~ **service** *n.* Rettungsdienst, *der*

ambush /ˈæmbʊʃ/ ① *n.* Hinterhalt, *der;* **lie in** ~: im Hinterhalt liegen
② *v.t.* [aus dem Hinterhalt] überfallen

amen /ɑːˈmen, eɪˈmen/ ① *int.* amen
② *n.* Amen, *das*

amenable /əˈmiːnəbl/ *adj.* zugänglich, aufgeschlossen (**to** *Dat.*)

amend /əˈmend/ *v.t.* berichtigen; abändern ⟨*Gesetzentwurf, Antrag*⟩

a'mendment *n.* (to motion) Abänderungsantrag, *der;* (to bill) Änderungsantrag, *der*

amends /əˈmendz/ *n. pl.* **make** ~ **[to sb.]** es [bei jmdm.] wieder gutmachen; **make** ~ **for sth.** etw. wieder gutmachen

amenity /əˈmiːnɪtɪ/ *n., usu. in pl.* **amenities** (of town) kulturelle und Freizeiteinrichtungen

America /əˈmerɪkə/ *pr. n.* Amerika (*das*)

American /əˈmerɪkən/ ① *adj.* amerikanisch; **sb. is** ~: jmd. ist Amerikaner/Amerikanerin; ~ **English** amerikanisches Englisch
② *n.* (person) Amerikaner, *der*/ Amerikanerin, *die*

American: ~ **'football** *n.* Football, *der;* ~ **'Indian** *n.* Indianer, *der*/Indianerin, *die*

Americanism /əˈmerɪkənɪzm/ *n.* (Ling.) Amerikanismus, *der*

Americanization /əmerɪkənaɪˈzeɪʃn/ *n.* Amerikanisierung, *die*

Americanize /əˈmerɪkənaɪz/ *v.t.* amerikanisieren

amiable /ˈeɪmɪəbl/ *adj.* umgänglich

amicable /ˈæmɪkəbl/ *adj.* freundschaftlich; gütlich ⟨*Einigung*⟩

amicably /ˈæmɪkəblɪ/ *adv.* in [aller] Freundschaft

amid[st] /əˈmɪd(st)/ *prep.* inmitten; (fig.: during) bei

amiss /əˈmɪs/ ① *pred. adj.* verkehrt; **is anything** ~? stimmt irgendetwas nicht?
② *adv.* **take sth.** ~: etw. übel nehmen

ammonia /əˈməʊnɪə/ *n.* Ammoniak, *das*

ammunition /æmjʊˈnɪʃn/ *n.* Munition, *die*

amnesia /æmˈniːzɪə/ *n.* Amnesie, *die*

amnesty /ˈæmnɪstɪ/ *n.* Amnestie, *die*

amniocentesis /æmnɪəʊsenˈtiːsɪs/ *n.* (Med.) Fruchtwasserentnahme, *die*

amok /əˈmɒk/ *adv.* **run** ~: Amok laufen

among[st] /əˈmʌŋ(st)/ *prep.* unter (+ *Dat.*); ~ **other things** unter anderem; **they often quarrel** ~ **themselves** sie streiten oft miteinander

amoral /eɪˈmɒrl/ *adj.* amoralisch

amorous /ˈæmərəs/ *adj.* verliebt; amourös ⟨*Abenteuer, Beziehung*⟩

amorphous /əˈmɔːfəs/ *adj.* formlos; amorph ⟨*Masse*⟩

amount /əˈmaʊnt/ ① *v.i.* ~ **to sth.** sich auf etw. (*Akk.*) belaufen; (fig.) etw. bedeuten ② *n.* (a) (total) Betrag, *der;* Summe, *die* (b) (quantity) Menge, *die*

amp /æmp/ *n.* Ampere, *das*

amphetamine /æmˈfetəmɪn/ *n.* (Med.) Amphetamin, *das*

amphibian /æmˈfɪbɪən/ ① *adj.* amphibisch ② *n.* Amphibie, *die*

amphibious /æmˈfɪbɪəs/ *adj.* amphibisch

amphitheatre /ˈæmfɪθɪətə(r)/ *n.* Amphitheater, *das*

ample /ˈæmpl/ *adj.* (a) (spacious) weitläufig ‹*Garten, Räume*›; reichhaltig ‹*Mahl*› (b) (enough) ~ **room/food** reichlich Platz/zu essen

amplifier /ˈæmplɪfaɪə(r)/ *n.* Verstärker, *der*

amplify /ˈæmplɪfaɪ/ *v.t.* verstärken; (enlarge on) weiter ausführen

amputate /ˈæmpjʊteɪt/ *v.t.* amputieren

amputation /æmpjʊˈteɪʃn/ *n.* Amputation, *die*

amuse /əˈmjuːz/ *v.t.* (a) (interest) unterhalten; ~ **oneself by doing sth.** sich (*Dat.*) die Zeit damit vertreiben, etw. zu tun (b) (make laugh or smile) amüsieren

a'musement *n.* Belustigung, *die;* ~ **arcade** Spielhalle, *die*

amusing /əˈmjuːzɪŋ/ *adj.* amüsant

an /ən, *stressed* æn/ *indef. art. see also* A²: ein/eine/ein

anaemia /əˈniːmɪə/ *n.* Blutarmut, *die;* Anämie, *die*

anaemic /əˈniːmɪk/ *adj.* blutarm; anämisch

anaesthetic /ænɪsˈθetɪk/ *n.* Anästhetikum, *das;* **general** ~: Narkosemittel, *das;* **local** ~: Lokalanästhetikum, *das*

anaesthetist /əˈniːsθətɪst/ *n.* Anästhesist, *der*/Anästhesistin, *die;* Narkose[fach]arzt, *der*/-ärztin, *die*

anagram /ˈænəgræm/ *n.* Anagramm, *das*

analgesia /ænælˈdʒiːzɪə/ *n.* (Med.) Analgesie, *die*

analgesic /ænælˈdʒiːsɪk/ (Med.) ① *adj.* analgetisch ② *n.* Analgetikum, *das*

analog (Amer.) ▶ ANALOGUE

analogue /ˈænəlɒg/ *n.* Entsprechung, *die;* Analogon, *das* (geh.); ~ **computer** Analogrechner, *der;* ~ **watch** Analoguhr, *die*

analogy /əˈnælədʒɪ/ *n.* Analogie, *die*

analyse /ˈænəlaɪz/ *v.t.* analysieren

analysis /əˈnælɪsɪs/ *n., pl.* **analyses** /əˈnælɪsiːz/ Analyse, *die*

analyst /ˈænəlɪst/ *n.* (a) (Psych.) Analytiker, *der*/Analytikerin, *die* (b) (Econ., Polit., etc.) Experte, *der*/Expertin, *die*

analytic /ænəˈlɪtɪk/, **analytical** /ænəˈlɪtɪkl/ *adj.* analytisch

analyze (Amer.) ▶ ANALYSE

anarchic /əˈnɑːkɪk/, **anarchical** /əˈnɑːkɪkl/ *adj.* anarchisch; (anarchistic) anarchistisch

anarchist /ˈænəkɪst/ *n.* Anarchist, *der*/Anarchistin, *die*

anarchy /ˈænəkɪ/ *n.* Anarchie, *die*

anatomical /ænəˈtɒmɪkl/ *adj.* anatomisch

anatomy /əˈnætəmɪ/ *n.* Anatomie, *die*

ANC *abbr.* = **African National Congress** ANK

ancestor /ˈænsestə(r)/ *n.* Vorfahr, *der*

ancestry /ˈænsestrɪ/ *n.* Abstammung, *die*

anchor /ˈæŋkə(r)/ ① *n.* Anker, *der* ② *v.t.* verankern ③ *v.i.* ankern

anchorage /ˈæŋkərɪdʒ/ *n.* Ankerplatz, *der*

anchorman /ˈæŋkəmæn/ *n.* (Telev., Radio) Moderator, *der*

anchovy /ˈæntʃəvɪ/ *n.* Sardelle, *die*

ancient /ˈeɪnʃənt/ *adj.* alt; historisch ‹*Gebäude usw.*›; (of antiquity) antik

and /ənd, *stressed* ænd/ *conj.* und; **for weeks** ~ **weeks** wochenlang; **better** ~ **better** immer besser

androgynous /ænˈdrɒdʒɪnəs/ *adj.* (Biol.) zwittrig

anecdote /ˈænɪkdəʊt/ *n.* Anekdote, *die*

anemia, anemic (Amer.) ▶ ANAEM-

anesthetic *etc.* (Amer.) ▶ ANAESTHETIC *etc.*

angel /ˈeɪndʒl/ *n.* Engel, *der*

angelic /ænˈdʒelɪk/ *adj.* engelhaft

anger /ˈæŋgə(r)/ ① *n.* Zorn, *der* (at über + Akk.); (fury) Wut, *die* (at über + Akk.) ② *v.t.* verärgern; (infuriate) wütend machen

angina [pectoris] /ænˈdʒaɪnə (ˈpektərɪs)/ *n.* (Med.) Angina pectoris, *die*

angle¹ /ˈæŋgl/ *n.* (a) (Geom.) Winkel, *der;* **at an** ~ **of 60°** im Winkel von 60°; **at an** ~: schief (b) (fig.) Gesichtspunkt, *der*

angle² *v.i.* angeln; (fig.) ~ **for sth.** sich um etw. bemühen

angle: ~ **brackets** *n. pl.* spitze Klammern; ~ **grinder** *n.* Winkelschleifer, *der;* (with cutting disc) Flex, *die;* ~**-parking** *n.* Schrägparken, *das*

angler /ˈæŋglə(r)/ *n.* Angler, *der*/Anglerin, *die*

Anglican /ˈæŋglɪkən/ ① *adj.* anglikanisch ② *n.* Anglikaner, *der*/Anglikanerin, *die*

Anglo- /æŋgləʊ/ *in comb.* anglo-/Anglo-

Anglo-Saxon /-ˈsæksn/ ① *n.* Angelsachse, *der*/Angelsächsin, *die;* (language) Angelsächsisch, *das* ② *adj.* angelsächsisch

angora [wool] /æŋˈgɔːrə/ *n.* Angorawolle, *die;* Mohair, *der*

angrily /ˈæŋgrɪlɪ/ *adv.* verärgert; (stronger) zornig

angry /ˈæŋgrɪ/ *adj.* böse; verärgert ‹*Person, Stimme, Geste*›; (stronger) zornig; wütend; **be**

~ **at** *or* **about sth.** wegen etw. böse sein; **be** ~ **with** *or* **at sb.** mit jmdm. *od.* auf jmdn. böse sein; **get** ~: böse werden

anguish /'æŋgwɪʃ/ *n.* Qualen *Pl.*

angular /'æŋgjʊlə(r)/ *adj.* eckig ⟨*Gebäude, Struktur*⟩; kantig ⟨*Gesicht*⟩

animal /'ænɪməl/ ① *n.* Tier, *das* ② *adj.* tierisch

animal: A~ Libe'ration Front *n.* Tierbefreiungsfront, *die;* ~ **lover** *n.* Tierfreund, *der*/-freundin, *die;* ~ **pro'tectionist** *n.* Tierschützer, *der*/ -schützerin, *die;* ~ **'rights** *n. pl.* Tierrechte *Pl.;* ~ **rights supporter** Tierrechtler, *der*/ Tierrechtlerin, *die*

animate ① /'ænɪmeɪt/ *v.t.* beleben ② /'ænɪmət/ *adj.* beseelt ⟨*Leben, Körper*⟩; belebt ⟨*Objekt, Welt*⟩

animated /'ænɪmeɪtɪd/ *adj.* lebhaft ⟨*Diskussion, Gebärde*⟩; ~ **cartoon** Zeichentrickfilm, *der*

animation /ænɪ'meɪʃn/ *n.* **(a)** Lebhaftigkeit, *die* **(b)** (Cinemat.) Animation, *die*

animosity /ænɪ'mɒsɪtɪ/ *n.* Feindseligkeit, *die*

aniseed /'ænɪsiːd/ *n.* Anis[samen], *der*

ankle /'æŋkl/ *n.* Fußgelenk, *das*

ankle: ~**-deep** *adj.* knöcheltief; ~ **sock** *n.* Socke, *die;* (esp. for children) Söckchen, *das*

annex ① /ə'neks/ *v.t.* annektieren ⟨*Land, Territorium*⟩ ② /'æneks/ *n.* Anbau, *der*

annexation /ænɪk'seɪʃn/ *n.* Annexion, *die;* Annektierung, *die*

annexe ▶ ANNEX 2

annihilate /ə'naɪɪleɪt/ *v.t.* vernichten

annihilation /ənaɪ'leɪʃn/ *n.* Vernichtung, *die*

anniversary /ænɪ'vɜːsərɪ/ *n.* Jahrestag, *der;* wedding ~: Hochzeitstag, *der*

annotate /'ænəteɪt/ *v.t.* kommentieren

announce /ə'naʊns/ *v.t.* bekannt geben; ansagen ⟨*Programm*⟩; (over Tannoy etc.) durchsagen; (in newspaper) anzeigen ⟨*Heirat usw.*⟩

an'nouncement *n.* Bekanntgabe, *die;* (over Tannoy etc.) Durchsage, *die;* (in newspaper) Anzeige, *die*

an'nouncer *n.* Ansager, *der*/Ansagerin, *die*

annoy /ə'nɔɪ/ *v.t.* **(a)** ärgern **(b)** (harass) schikanieren

annoyance /ə'nɔɪəns/ *n.* Verärgerung, *die;* (nuisance) Plage, *die*

annoyed /ə'nɔɪd/ *adj.* **be** ~ [at *or* with sb./ sth.] ärgerlich [auf *od.* über jmdn./über etw.] sein; **he got very** ~: er hat sich darüber sehr geärgert

an'noying *adj.* ärgerlich; lästig ⟨*Gewohnheit, Person*⟩

annual /'ænjʊəl/ ① *adj.* **(a)** (reckoned by the year) Jahres-; ~ **income/subscription/rent/ turnover/production/leave/salary** Jahreseinkommen, *das*/-abonnement, *das*/ -miete, *die*/-umsatz, *der*/-produktion, *die*/ -urlaub, *der*/-gehalt, *das;* ~ **rainfall** jährliche Regenmenge **(b)** (recurring yearly) [all]jährlich ⟨*Ereignis, Feier*⟩; Jahres⟨*bericht, -hauptversammlung*⟩ ② *n.* **(a)** Jahrbuch, *das;* (of comic etc.) Jahresalbum, *das* **(b)** (plant) einjährige Pflanze

'annually *adv.* jährlich

annul /ə'nʌl/ *v.t.,* **-ll-** annullieren; auflösen ⟨*Vertrag*⟩

anodyne /'ænədaɪn/ *adj.* (fig.) wohltuend; (soothing) einlullend

anon. /ə'nɒn/ *abbr.* = **anonymous [author]** anon.

anonymity /ænə'nɪmɪtɪ/ *n.* Anonymität, *die*

anonymous /ə'nɒnɪməs/ *adj.* anonym

anorak /'ænəræk/ *n.* Anorak, *der*

anorexia /ænə'reksɪə/ *n.* Anorexie, *die* (Med.); Magersucht, *die*

anorexic /ænə'reksɪk/ *adj.* anorektisch (fachspr.); magersüchtig; **be** ~: an Anorexie (Med.) *od.* Magersucht leiden

another /ə'nʌðə(r)/ ① *pron.* **(a)** (an additional one) noch einer/eine/eins; ein weiterer/eine weitere/ein weiteres **(b)** (counterpart) wieder einer/eine/eins **(c)** (a different one) ein anderer/eine andere/ ein anderes ② *adj.* **(a)** (additional) noch ein/eine; ein weiterer/eine weitere/ein weiteres; **after** ~ **six weeks** nach weiteren sechs Wochen **(b)** (different) ein anderer/eine andere/ein anderes

answer /'ɑːnsə(r)/ ① *n.* **(a)** (reply) Antwort, *die* (to auf + *Akk.*) **(b)** (to problem) Lösung, *die* (to *Gen.*); (to calculation) Ergebnis, *das* ② *v.t.* **(a)** beantworten ⟨*Brief, Frage*⟩; antworten auf (+ *Akk.*) ⟨*Frage, Hilferuf, Einladung, Inserat*⟩; eingehen auf (+ *Akk.*) ⟨*Angebot, Vorschlag*⟩; sich stellen zu ⟨*Beschuldigung*⟩; erhören ⟨*Gebet*⟩; erfüllen ⟨*Bitte, Wunsch*⟩; ~ **sb.** jmdm. antworten **(b)** ~ **the door/bell** an die Tür gehen ③ *v.i.* **(a)** (reply) antworten; ~ **to sth.** sich zu etw. äußern **(b)** (be responsible) ~ **for sth.** für etw. die Verantwortung übernehmen **(c)** ~ **to a description** einer Beschreibung (*Dat.*) entsprechen

answerable /'ɑːnsərəbl/ *adj.* verantwortlich (for für; to *Dat.*)

answering: ~**machine** *n.* Anrufbeantworter, *der;* ~ **service** *n.* Fernsprechauftragsdienst, *der*

'answerphone (Brit.) ▶ ANSWERING MACHINE

ant /ænt/ *n.* Ameise, *die*

a

antagonism /æn'tægənɪzm/ n. Feindseligkeit, die (**towards, against** gegenüber)

antagonist /æn'tægənɪst/ n. Gegner, der/ Gegnerin, die

antagonistic /æntægə'nɪstɪk/ adj. feindlich

antagonize /æn'tægənaɪz/ v.t. ~ **sb.** sich (Dat.) jmdn. zum Feind machen

antarctic /ænt'ɑːktɪk/ [1] adj. antarktisch [2] n. **the A~:** die Antarktis

antelope /'æntɪləʊp/ n. Antilope, die

antenatal /æntɪ'neɪtl/ adj. (concerning pregnancy) Schwangerschafts-; Schwangeren-; ~ **care** Schwangerenfürsorge, die; ~ **clinic** Klinik für werdende Mütter

antenna /æn'tenə/ n. (a) pl. ~e /æn'teniː/ (Zool.) Fühler, der
(b) pl. ~s (tech., Amer.: aerial) Antenne, die

anthem /'ænθəm/ n. Chorgesang, der

anthology /æn'θɒlədʒɪ/ n. Anthologie, die

anthropologist /ænθrə'pɒlədʒɪst/ n. Anthropologe, der/Anthropologin, die

anthropology /ænθrə'pɒlədʒɪ/ n. Anthropologie, die

anti /'æntɪ/ [1] prep. gegen [2] adj. ablehnend

anti- /æntɪ/ pref. anti-/Anti-

anti: ~**a'bortion** attrib. adj. ~**-abortion protester** Abtreibungsgegner, der/-gegnerin, die; ~**-abortion protest/law** Protest/Gesetz gegen Abtreibung; ~**-abortion demonstration/movement** Antiabtreibungsdemonstration, die/ -bewegung, die; ~**-abortionist** /æntɪə'bɔːʃənɪst/ n. Abtreibungsgegner, der/ -gegnerin, die; ~**-'aircraft** adj. (Mil.) Flugabwehr-; ~**-aircraft gun** Flak, die

antibiotic /æntɪbaɪ'ɒtɪk/ n. Antibiotikum, das

'antibody n. Antikörper, der

antic /'æntɪk/ n. (trick) Mätzchen, das (ugs.); (of clown) Possen, der

anticipate /æn'tɪsɪpeɪt/ v.t. (a) (expect) erwarten; (foresee) voraussehen; ~ **trouble** mit Ärger rechnen
(b) (consider before due time) vorwegnehmen

anticipation /æntɪsɪ'peɪʃn/ n. Erwartung, die

anti'climax n. Abstieg, der

anti'clockwise adv., adj. gegen den Uhrzeigersinn

anti'cyclone n. Hochdruckgebiet, das

antidepressant /æntɪdɪ'presənt/ n. Antidepressivum, das

antidote /'æntɪdəʊt/ n. Gegenmittel, das (**for, against, to** gegen)

'antifreeze n. Frostschutzmittel, das

antiglobalization /æntɪɡləʊbəlaɪ'zeɪʃn/ n. Antiglobalisierung, die

'anti-hero n. Antiheld, der

antihistamine /æntɪ'hɪstəmɪn/ n. (Med.) Antihistamin[ikum], das

'anti-lock adj. Antiblockier-; ~ **brake** or **braking system** Antiblockiersystem, das

anti'nuclear adj. Anti-Atom[kraft]-

antipathy /æn'tɪpəθɪ/ n. Antipathie, die; Abneigung, die

anti-person'nel adj. gegen Menschen gerichtet; ~ **mine** Schützenmine, die

antiperspirant /æntɪ'pɜːspɪrənt/ [1] adj. schweißhemmend; ~ **spray** Deodorantspray, der od. das [2] n. Antitranspirant, das

antiquated /'æntɪkweɪtɪd/ adj. antiquiert; veraltet

antique /æn'tiːk/ [1] adj. antik [2] n. Antiquität, die; ~ **shop** Antiquitätenladen, der

antiquity /æn'tɪkwɪtɪ/ n. Altertum, das; Antike, die

anti-Semitic /æntɪsɪ'mɪtɪk/ adj. antisemitisch; judenfeindlich

anti-Semitism /æntɪ'semɪtɪzm/ n. Antisemitismus, der; Judenhass, der

anti'septic [1] adj. antiseptisch [2] n. Antiseptikum, das

anti'social adj. asozial

anti-'theft attrib. adj. Antidiebstahl-

antithesis /æn'tɪθəsɪs/ n., pl. **antitheses** /æn'tɪθəsiːz/ Gegenstück, das (**of, to** zu)

anti: ~**'toxin** n. (Med.) Antitoxin, das; ~**'virus** attrib. adj. (Comp.) Antivirus-; ~**virus software** Antivirensoftware, die

antivivisectionist /æntɪvɪvɪ'sekʃənɪst/ n. Vivisektionsgegner, der/-gegnerin, die

antler /'æntlə(r)/ n. Geweihsprosse, die; [pair of] ~**s** Geweih, das

anvil /'ænvɪl/ n. Amboss, der

anxiety /æŋ'zaɪətɪ/ n. Angst, die; (concern about future) Sorge, die (**about** wegen)

anxious /'æŋkʃəs/ adj. (a) (troubled) besorgt (**about** um)
(b) (eager) sehnlich; **be** ~ **for sth.** sich nach etw. sehnen

'anxiously adv. (a) besorgt
(b) (eagerly) sehnsüchtig

any /'enɪ/ [1] adj. (a) (some) [irgend]ein/ [irgend]eine; **not** ~: kein/keine; **have you** ~ **wool/wine?** haben Sie Wolle/Wein?
(b) (one) ein/eine
(c) (all, every) jeder/jede/jedes; [at] ~ **time** jederzeit
(d) (whichever) jeder/jede/jedes [beliebige]; **choose** ~ [one] **book/**~ **books you like** suchen Sie sich (Dat.) irgenden Buch/ irgendwelche Bücher aus
[2] pron. (a) (some) in condit., interrog., or neg. sentence (replacing sing. n.) einer/eine/ ein[e]s; (replacing collect. n.) welcher/welche/ welches; (replacing pl. n.) welche; **not** ~: keiner/keine/kein[e]s/Pl. keine
(b) (no matter which) irgendeiner/irgendeine/ irgenden[e]s/irgendwelche Pl.

3 *adv.* **do you feel ~ better today?** fühlen Sie sich heute [etwas] besser?; **if it gets ~ colder** wenn es noch kälter wird; **I can't wait ~ longer** ich kann nicht [mehr] länger warten

'anybody *n. & pron.* **(a)** (whoever) jeder **(b)** (somebody) [irgend]jemand; *after neg.* niemand

'anyhow *adv.* **(a)** ▶ ANYWAY **(b)** (haphazardly) irgendwie

'anyone ▶ ANYBODY

'anything **1** *n. & pron.* **(a)** (whatever thing) was [immer]; alles, was **(b)** (something) irgendetwas; *after neg.* nichts **(c)** (a thing of any kind) alles **2** *adv.* **not ~ like as ... as** keineswegs so ... wie

'anyway *adv.* **(a)** (in any case, besides) sowieso **(b)** (at any rate) jedenfalls

'anywhere *adv.* **(a)** (in any place) (wherever) überall, wo; wo [immer]; (somewhere) irgendwo; **not ~ near as ... as** (coll.) nicht annähernd so ... wie **(b)** (to any place) (wherever) wohin [auch immer]; (somewhere) irgendwohin

aorta /eɪˈɔːtə/ *n.* (Anat.) Aorta, *die*

apart /əˈpɑːt/ *adv.* **(a)** (separately) getrennt; **~ from ...:** außer ... **(b)** (into pieces) auseinander

apartheid /əˈpɑːteɪt/ *n.* Apartheid, *die*

apartment /əˈpɑːtmənt/ *n.* **(a)** (room) Apartment, *das* **(b)** (Amer.: flat) Wohnung, *die*

apathetic /æpəˈθetɪk/ *adj.* apathisch **(about** gegenüber**)**

apathy /ˈæpəθɪ/ *n.* Apathie, *die* **(about** gegenüber**)**

ape /eɪp/ **1** *n.* [Menschen]affe, *der* **2** *v.t.* nachahmen

aperitif /əperrˈtiːf/ *n.* Aperitif, *der*

aperture /ˈæpətʃə(r)/ *n.* Öffnung, *die*

apex /ˈeɪpeks/ *n.* Spitze, *die*

aphid /ˈeɪfɪd/ *n.* Blattlaus, *die*

aphrodisiac /æfrəˈdɪziæk/ *n.* Aphrodisiakum, *das*

apiece /əˈpiːs/ *adv.* je; **they cost a penny ~:** sie kosten einen Penny das Stück

apolitical /eɪpəˈlɪtɪkl/ *adj.* apolitisch; unpolitisch

apologetic /əpɒləˈdʒetɪk/ *adj.* entschuldigend; **be ~:** sich entschuldigen

apologize /əˈpɒlədʒaɪz/ *v.i.* sich entschuldigen (**to** bei)

apology /əˈpɒlədʒɪ/ *n.* Entschuldigung, *die;* **make an ~:** sich entschuldigen (**to** bei)

apoplectic /æpəˈplektɪk/ *adj.* apoplektisch; **~ fit** Schlaganfall, *der*

apoplexy /ˈæpəpleksɪ/ *n.* Apoplexie, *die* (fachspr.); Schlaganfall, *der*

apostle /əˈpɒsl/ *n.* Apostel, *der*

apostrophe /əˈpɒstrəfɪ/ *n.* Apostroph, *der;* Auslassungszeichen, *das*

appal (*Amer.:* **appall**) /əˈpɔːl/ *v.t.,* **-ll-** entsetzen

apˈpalling *adj.* entsetzlich

apparatus /æpəˈreɪtəs/ *n.* (equipment) Gerät, *das;* (gymnastic ~) Geräte *Pl.;* (machinery, lit. or fig.) Apparat, *der;* **a piece of ~:** ein Gerät

apparel /əˈpærəl/ *n.* Kleidung, *die;* Gewänder *Pl.* (geh.)

apparent /əˈpærənt/ *adj.* **(a)** (clear) offensichtlich; offenbar ⟨Bedeutung, Wahrheit⟩ **(b)** (seeming) scheinbar

apˈparently *adv.* **(a)** (clearly) offensichtlich **(b)** (seemingly) scheinbar

apparition /æpəˈrɪʃn/ *n.* [Geister]erscheinung, *die*

appeal /əˈpiːl/ **1** *v.i.* **(a)** (Law etc.) Einspruch einlegen **(b)** (make earnest request) **~ to sb. for sth./to do sth.** jmdn. um etw. ersuchen/jmdn. ersuchen, etw. zu tun **(c)** (address oneself) **~ to sb./sth.** an jmdn./ etw. appellieren **(d)** (be attractive) **~ to sb.** jmdm. zusagen **2** *n.* **(a)** (Law etc.) Einspruch, *der* (**to** bei); (to higher court) Berufung, *die* (**to** bei) **(b)** (request) Appell, *der;* **an ~ to sb. for sth.** eine Bitte an jmdn. um etw. **(c)** (attraction) Reiz, *der*

apˈpealing *adj.* **(a)** (imploring) flehend **(b)** (attractive) ansprechend; verlockend ⟨Idee⟩

appear /əˈpɪə(r)/ *v.i.* **(a)** (become visible, arrive) erscheinen; ⟨Licht, Mond:⟩ auftauchen; (present oneself) auftreten **(b)** (occur) vorkommen **(c)** (seem) **~ [to be] ...:** scheinen ... [zu sein]

appearance /əˈpɪərəns/ *n.* **(a)** (becoming visible) Auftauchen, *das;* (arrival) Erscheinen, *das;* (of performer etc.) Auftritt, *der* **(b)** (look) Äußere, *das;* **to all ~s** allem Anschein nach **(c)** (semblance) Anschein, *der* **(d)** (occurrence) Vorkommen, *das*

appease /əˈpiːz/ *v.t.* besänftigen; (Polit.) beschwichtigen

append /əˈpend/ *v.t.* anhängen (**to** an + *Akk.*); (add) anfügen (+ *Dat.*)

appendage /əˈpendɪdʒ/ *n.* Anhängsel, *das;* (addition) Anhang, *der*

appendicitis /əpendɪˈsaɪtɪs/ *n.* Blinddarmentzündung, *die*

appendix /əˈpendɪks/ *n., pl.* **appendices** /əˈpendɪsiːz/ *or* **~es** **(a)** (Anhang, *der* (**to** zu) **(b)** (Anat.) Blinddarm, *der*

appetite /ˈæpɪtaɪt/ *n.* **(a)** Appetit, *der* (**for** auf + *Akk.*) **(b)** (fig.) Verlangen, *das* (**for** nach)

appetizer /ˈæpɪtaɪzə(r)/ *n.* Appetitanreger, *der*

appetizing /ˈæpɪtaɪzɪŋ/ *adj.* appetitlich

applaud /əˈplɔːd/ **1** *v.i.* applaudieren; [Beifall] klatschen
2 *v.t.* applaudieren (+ *Dat.*)
applause /əˈplɔːz/ *n.* Beifall, *der;* Applaus, *der*
apple /ˈæpl/ *n.* Apfel, *der*
apple: ~ **'pie** gedeckte Apfeltorte; ~ **'sauce** *n.* Apfelmus, *das*
applet /ˈæplɪt/ *n.* (Comp.) Applet, *das*
'apple tree *n.* Apfelbaum, *der*
appliance /əˈplaɪəns/ *n.* Gerät, *das*
applicable /əˈplɪkəbl/ *adj.* **(a)** anwendbar (**to** auf + *Akk.*)
(b) (appropriate) geeignet; zutreffend ⟨*Fragebogenteil*⟩
applicant /ˈæplɪkənt/ *n.* Bewerber, *der/* Bewerberin, *die* (**for** um); (claimant) Antragsteller, *der/*-stellerin, *die*
application /æplɪˈkeɪʃn/ *n.* **(a)** (request) Bewerbung, *die* (**for** um); (for passport, licence, etc.) Antrag, *der* (**for** auf + *Akk.*); ~ **form** Antragsformular, *das*
(b) (putting) Auftragen, *das* (**to** auf + *Akk.*)
(c) (use) Anwendung, *die*
(d) (Comp.) Applikation, *die*
applicator /ˈæplɪkeɪtə(r)/ *n.* Applikator, *der*
apply /əˈplaɪ/ **1** *v.t.* **(a)** auftragen ⟨*Creme, Farbe*⟩ (**to** auf + *Akk.*)
(b) (make use of) anwenden
2 *v.i.* **(a)** (have relevance) zutreffen (**to** auf + *Akk.*)
(b) ~ [**to sb.**] **for sth.** [jmdn.] um etw. bitten; (for passport etc.) [bei jmdm.] etw. beantragen; (for job) sich [bei jmdm.] um etw. bewerben
appoint /əˈpɔɪnt/ *v.t.* **(a)** (fix) bestimmen; festlegen ⟨*Zeitpunkt, Ort*⟩
(b) (to job) einstellen; (to office) ernennen
appointee /əpɔɪnˈtiː/ *n.* Ernannte, *der/die;* Berufene, *der/die*
ap'pointment *n.* **(a)** (to job) Einstellung, *die;* (to office) Ernennung, *die* (**as** zum/zur)
(b) (job) Stelle, *die*
(c) (arrangement) Termin, *der;* **make an** ~ **with sb.** sich (*Dat.*) von jmdm. einen Termin geben lassen; **by** ~: nach Anmeldung
appraisal /əˈpreɪzl/ *n.* (evaluation) Bewertung, *die*
appraise /əˈpreɪz/ *v.t.* (evaluate) bewerten
appreciable /əˈpriːʃəbl/ *adj.* **(a)** (perceptible) nennenswert ⟨*Unterschied, Einfluss*⟩; spürbar ⟨*Veränderung, Wirkung*⟩; merklich ⟨*Verringerung, Anstieg*⟩
(b) (considerable) beträchtlich
appreciably /əˈpriːʃəblɪ/ *adv.* **(a)** (perceptibly) spürbar ⟨*verändern*⟩; merklich ⟨*sich unterscheiden*⟩
(b) (considerably) beträchtlich
appreciate /əˈpriːʃɪeɪt/ **1** *v.t.* **(a)** ([correctly] estimate) [richtig] einschätzen; (understand) verstehen; (be aware of) sich (*Dat.*) bewusst sein (+ *Gen.*)
(b) (be grateful for) schätzen; (enjoy) genießen

2 *v.i.* im Wert steigen
appreciation /əpriːʃɪˈeɪʃn/ *n.* **(a)** ([correct] estimation) [richtige] Einschätzung; (understanding) Verständnis, *das* (**of** für); (awareness) Bewusstsein, *das*
(b) (gratefulness) Dankbarkeit, *die;* (enjoyment) Gefallen, *das* (**of** an + *Dat.*)
appreciative /əˈpriːʃətɪv/ *adj.* (grateful) dankbar (**of** für); (approving) anerkennend
apprehend /æprɪˈhend/ *v.t.* **(a)** (arrest) festnehmen
(b) (understand) erfassen
apprehension /æprɪˈhenʃn/ *n.* Besorgnis, *die*
apprehensive /æprɪˈhensɪv/ *adj.* besorgt
apprentice /əˈprentɪs/ *n.* Lehrling, *der* (**to** bei)
ap'prenticeship *n.* (training) Lehre, *die;* (learning period) Lehrzeit, *die*
approach /əˈprəʊtʃ/ **1** *v.i.* sich nähern; (in time) nahen
2 *v.t.* **(a)** (come near to) sich nähern (+ *Dat.*)
(b) (approximate to) nahe kommen (+ *Dat.*)
(c) (appeal to) sich wenden an (+ *Akk.*)
3 *n.* **(a)** [Heran]nahen, *das*
(b) (approximation) Annäherung, *die* (**to** an + *Akk.*)
(c) (appeal) Herantreten, *das* (**to** an + *Akk.*)
(d) (access) Zugang, *der;* (road) Zufahrtsstraße, *die*
approachable /əˈprəʊtʃəbl/ *adj.* **(a)** (friendly) umgänglich
(b) (accessible) zugänglich
ap'proach road *n.* Zufahrtsstraße, *die*
appropriate **1** /əˈprəʊprɪət/ *adj.* geeignet (**to, for** für)
2 /əˈprəʊprɪeɪt/ *v.t.* sich (*Dat.*) aneignen
appropriately /əˈprəʊprɪətlɪ/ *adv.* gebührend; passend ⟨*gekleidet, genannt*⟩
approval /əˈpruːvl/ *n.* **(a)** (sanctioning) Genehmigung, *die;* (of proposal) Billigung, *die;* (agreement) Zustimmung, *die*
(b) on ~ (Commerc.) zur Probe
approve /əˈpruːv/ **1** *v.t.* **(a)** (sanction) genehmigen ⟨*Plan, Projekt*⟩; billigen ⟨*Vorschlag*⟩
(b) (find good) gutheißen
2 *v.i.* ~ **of** billigen; zustimmen (+ *Dat.*) ⟨*Plan*⟩
approving /əˈpruːvɪŋ/ *adj.* zustimmend ⟨*Worte*⟩; anerkennend ⟨*Blicke*⟩
approx. /əˈprɒks/ *abbr.* = **approximately** ca.
approximate /əˈprɒksɪmət/ *adj.* ungefähr *attr.*
ap'proximately *adv.* ungefähr
approximation /əprɒksɪˈmeɪʃn/ *n.* **(a)** Annäherung, *die* (**to** an + *Dat.*)
(b) (estimate) Annäherungswert, *der*
APR *abbr.* = **annualized percentage rate** Jahreszinssatz, *der*
Apr. *abbr.* = **April** Apr.

après-ski /æpreɪˈski:/ *n.* Après-Ski, *der;* *attrib.* Après-Ski-

apricot /ˈeɪprɪkɒt/ *n.* Aprikose, *die*

April /ˈeɪprəl/ *n.* April, *der;* ~ **fool** April[s]narr, *der; see also* AUGUST

apron /ˈeɪprən/ *n.* Schürze, *die*

apt /æpt/ *adj.* **(a)** (suitable) passend; treffend ⟨*Bemerkung*⟩ **(b)** be ~ **to do** sth. dazu neigen, etw. zu tun

aptitude /ˈæptɪtjuːd/ *n.* Begabung, *die*

'aptly *adv.* passend

'aqualung /ˈækwəlʌŋ/ *n.* Tauchgerät, *das*

aquaplane /ˈækwəpleɪn/ *v.i.* ⟨*Reifen:*⟩ aufschwimmen; ⟨*Fahrzeug:*⟩ [durch Aquaplaning] ins Rutschen geraten

aquarium /əˈkweərɪəm/ *n., pl.* ~s *or* aquaria /əˈkweərɪə/ Aquarium, *das*

Aquarius /əˈkweərɪəs/ *n.* (Astrol., Astron.) der Wassermann

aquatic /əˈkwætɪk/ *adj.* aquatisch; Wasser-; ~ **plant** Wasserpflanze, *die*

aqueduct /ˈækwɪdʌkt/ *n.* Aquädukt, *der od. das*

aqueous /ˈeɪkwɪəs, ˈækwɪəs/ *adj.* wässerig; wässrig

Arab /ˈærəb/ ①*adj.* arabisch ②*n.* Araber, *der*/Araberin, *die*

Arabian /əˈreɪbɪən/ ①*adj.* arabisch ②*n.* Araber, *der*/Araberin, *die*

Arabic /ˈærəbɪk/ ①*adj.* arabisch ②*n.* Arabisch, *das; see also* ENGLISH 2A

arable /ˈærəbl/ *adj.* bebaubar, landwirtschaftlich nutzbar ⟨*Land*⟩; ~ **land** (cultivated) Ackerland, *das*

arbitrary /ˈɑːbɪtrərɪ/ *adj.* willkürlich

arbitrate /ˈɑːbɪtreɪt/ ①*v.t.* schlichten ⟨*Streit*⟩ ②*v.i.* ~ **[upon** sth.] [in einer Sache] vermitteln

arbitration /ɑːbɪˈtreɪʃn/ *n.* Vermittlung, *die;* (in industry) Schlichtung, *die*

arbitrator /ˈɑːbɪtreɪtə(r)/ *n.* Vermittler, *der;* (in industry) Schlichter, *der*

arboretum /ɑːbəˈriːtəm/ *n., pl.* arboreta /ɑːbəˈriːtə/ *or* (Amer.) ~s Arboretum, *das;* Baumgarten, *der*

arbour /ˈɑːbə(r)/ *n.* (Brit.) Laube, *die*

arc /ɑːk/ *n.* [Kreis]bogen, *der;* ~ **lamp,** ~ **light** Lichtbogenlampe, *die;* ~ **welding** Lichtbogen-, Elektroschweißung, *die*

arcade /ɑːˈkeɪd/ *n.* Arkade, *die*

arch /ɑːtʃ/ ①*n.* Bogen, *der;* (of foot) Wölbung, *die* ②*v.t.* beugen ⟨*Rücken*⟩; ~ **its back** ⟨*Katze:*⟩ einen Buckel machen

arch- *pref.* Erz-

archaeological /ɑːkɪəˈlɒdʒɪkl/ *adj.* archäologisch

archaeologist /ɑːkɪˈɒlədʒɪst/ *n.* Archäologe, *der*/Archäologin, *die*

archaeology /ɑːkɪˈɒlədʒɪ/ *n.* Archäologie, *die*

archaic /ɑːˈkeɪɪk/ *adj.* veraltet

arch'bishop *n.* Erzbischof, *der*

arch-'enemy *n.* Erzfeind, *der*/Erzfeindin, *die*

archeology *etc.* (Amer.) ▶ ARCHAEOLOGY *etc.*

archer /ˈɑːtʃə(r)/ *n.* Bogenschütze, *der*

archery /ˈɑːtʃərɪ/ *n.* Bogenschießen, *das*

archetype /ˈɑːkɪtaɪp/ *n.* (original) Urfassung, *die;* (typical specimen) Prototyp, *der*

architect /ˈɑːkɪtekt/ *n.* Architekt, *der*/Architektin, *die*

architectural /ɑːkɪˈtektʃərl/ *adj.* architektonisch

architecture /ˈɑːkɪtektʃə(r)/ *n.* Architektur, *die*

archive /ˈɑːkaɪv/ ①*n.* Archiv, *das;* ~s Archiv, *das* ②*v.t.* archivieren

arctic /ˈɑːktɪk/ ①*adj.* arktisch; A~ **Circle** nördlicher Polarkreis; A~ **Ocean** Nordpolarmeer, *das* ②*n.* the A~: die Arktis

ardent /ˈɑːdənt/ *adj.* leidenschaftlich; brennend ⟨*Wunsch*⟩; (eager) begeistert

ardor (Amer.), **ardour** (Brit.) /ˈɑːdə(r)/ *n.* Leidenschaft, *die*

arduous /ˈɑːdjʊəs/ *adj.* anstrengend

are ▶ BE

area /ˈeərɪə/ *n.* **(a)** (surface measure) Fläche, *die;* Flächeninhalt, *der* **(b)** (region) Gelände, *das;* (of wood, marsh, desert) Gebiet, *das;* (of city, country) Gegend, *die;* **parking/picnic** ~: Park-/Picknickplatz, *der* **(c)** (subject field) Gebiet, *das*

'area code *n.* (Amer. Teleph.) Gebietsvorwahl[nummer], *die*

arena /əˈriːnə/ *n.* Arena, *die;* **the political** ~: die politische Arena

aren't /ɑːnt/ (coll.) = are not; ▶ BE

Argentina /ɑːdʒənˈtiːnə/ *pr. n.* Argentinien (*das*)

Argentinian /ɑːdʒənˈtɪnɪən/ ①*adj.* argentinisch; **sb. is** ~: jmd. ist Argentinier/Argentinierin ②*n.* Argentinier, *der*/Argentinierin, *die*

arguable /ˈɑːgjʊəbl/ *adj.* (questionable) fragwürdig

arguably /ˈɑːgjʊəblɪ/ *adv.* möglicherweise

argue /ˈɑːgjuː/ ①*v.t.* **(a)** (maintain) ~ **that** ...: die Ansicht vertreten, dass ... **(b)** (with reasoning) darlegen ⟨*Grund, Standpunkt*⟩ ②*v.i.* ~ **with** sb. sich mit jmdm. streiten; ~ **for/against** sth. für/gegen etw. eintreten; ~ **about** sth. sich über/um etw. (*Akk.*) streiten

argument /ˈɑːgjʊmənt/ *n.* **(a)** (reason) Begründung, *die;* ~s **for/against** sth. Argumente für/gegen etw. **(b)** (reasoning process) Argumentieren, *das* ⋯❖

(c) (disagreement, quarrel) Auseinandersetzung, *die*

argumentative /ɑːgjʊ'mentətɪv/ *adj.* widerspruchsfreudig

arid /'ærɪd/ *adj.* trocken

Aries /'eəriːz/ *n.* (Astrol; Astron.) der Widder

arise /ə'raɪz/ *v.i.,* **arose** /ə'rəʊz/, **arisen** /ə'rɪzn/ (a) (originate) entstehen
(b) (present itself) auftreten; ‹*Gelegenheit:*› sich bieten
(c) (result) ~ **from** *or* **out of sth.** von etw. herrühren

aristocracy /ærɪ'stɒkrəsɪ/ *n.* Aristokratie, *die*

aristocrat /'ærɪstəkræt/ *n.* Aristokrat, *der/* Aristokratin, *die*

aristocratic /ærɪstə'krætɪk/ *adj.* aristokratisch

arithmetic /ə'rɪθmətɪk/ *n.* Arithmetik, *die*

arm¹ /ɑːm/ *n.* Arm, *der*

arm² ① *n.* (a) *usu. in pl.* (weapon) Waffe, *die;* **up in** ~s (fig.) in Harnisch (**about** wegen)
(b) *in pl.* (heraldic device) Wappen, *das*
② *v.t.* bewaffnen

armada /ɑː'mɑːdə/ *n.* Armada, *die*

arm: ~**band** *n.* Armbinde, *die;* ~**chair** *n.* Sessel, *der;* ~**chair politician/strategist** politischer Amateur/Amateurstratege, *der;* ~**chair critic** Hobby- *od.* Amateurkritiker, *der;* ~**chair travel** Reisen *Pl.* in der Fantasie

armed /ɑːmd/ *adj.* bewaffnet; ~ **forces** Streitkräfte *Pl.*

armistice /'ɑːmɪstɪs/ *n.* Waffenstillstand, *der*

armor (Amer.), **armour** (Brit.) /'ɑːmə(r)/ *n.* (a) (Hist.) Rüstung, *die*
(b) (steel plates) Panzerung, *die*

arm: ~**pit** *n.* Achselhöhle, *die;* ~**rest** *n.* Armlehne, *die*

arms: ~ **control** *n.* Rüstungskontrolle, *die; attrib.* Rüstungskontroll-; ~ **race** *n.* Rüstungswettlauf, *der;* ~ **trade** *n.* Waffenhandel, *der*

army /'ɑːmɪ/ *n.* Heer, *das;* **join the** ~: zum Militär gehen

aroma /ə'rəʊmə/ *n.* Duft, *der*

aromatherapy /ərəʊmə'θerəpɪ/ *n.* Aromatherapie, *die*

aromatic /ærə'mætɪk/ *adj.* aromatisch

arose ▶ ARISE

around /ə'raʊnd/ ① *adv.* (a) (on every side) [all] ~: überall
(b) (round) herum
(c) (in various places) **ask/look** ~: herumfragen/sich umsehen
② *prep.* (a) um [... herum]
(b) (approximately) ~ **3 o'clock** gegen 3 Uhr; **sth. [costing]** ~ **£2** etw. für ungefähr 2 Pfund

arouse /ə'raʊz/ *v.t.* (a) (awake) [auf]wecken
(b) (excite) erregen; erwecken ‹*Interesse, Begeisterung*›; ~ **suspicion** Verdacht erregen

arrange /ə'reɪndʒ/ ① *v.t.* (a) (order) anordnen
(b) (settle, agree) ausmachen, vereinbaren ‹*Termin*›; planen ‹*Urlaub*›; **they** ~**d to meet the following day** sie verabredeten sich für den nächsten Tag
② *v.i.* (plan) sorgen (**for** für)

ar'rangement *n.* (a) (ordering, order) Anordnung, *die*
(b) (settling, agreement) Vereinbarung, *die*
(c) *in pl.* (plans) Vorkehrungen *Pl.;* **make** ~s Vorkehrungen treffen

arrears /ə'rɪəz/ *n. pl.* Schulden *Pl.;* **be in** ~ **with sth.** mit etw. im Rückstand sein; **be paid in** ~: rückwirkend bezahlt werden

arrest /ə'rest/ ① *v.t.* (a) verhaften, (temporarily) festnehmen ‹*Person*›
(b) (stop) aufhalten
② *n.* Verhaftung, *die;* **under** ~: festgenommen

arrival /ə'raɪvl/ *n.* Ankunft, *die;* **new** ~s Neuankömmlinge

arrive /ə'raɪv/ *v.i.* (a) ankommen; ~ **at a conclusion/an agreement** zu einem Schluss/ einer Einigung kommen
(b) ‹*Stunde, Tag, Augenblick:*› kommen

arrogance /'ærəgəns/ *n.* Arroganz, *die*

arrogant /'ærəgənt/ *adj.* arrogant

arrow /'ærəʊ/ *n.* Pfeil, *der*

arse /ɑːs/ *n.* (coarse) Arsch, *der* (derb)
■ **arse a'bout, arse a'round** *v. i.* (Brit. coarse) herumalbern (ugs.); herumblödeln (ugs.)

'arsehole *n.* (coarse) Arschloch, *das* (derb)

arsenal /'ɑːsənl/ *n.* Waffenlager, *das*

arsenic /'ɑːsənɪk/ *n.* (a) Arsenik, *das*
(b) (element) Arsen, *das*

arson /'ɑːsn/ *n.* Brandstiftung, *die;* ~ **attack** Brandanschlag, *der*

arsonist /'ɑːsənɪst/ *n.* Brandstifter, *der/* Brandstifterin, *die*

art /ɑːt/ *n.* (a) Kunst, *die;* **works of** ~: Kunstwerke *Pl.;* ~ **college** *or* **school** Kunsthochschule, *die;* ~s **and crafts** Kunsthandwerk, *das*
(b) *in pl.* (branch of study) Geisteswissenschaften *Pl.*

artery /'ɑːtərɪ/ *n.* (Anat.) Schlagader, *die;* Arterie, *die* (bes. fachspr.)

artful /'ɑːtfl/ *adj.* schlau

'art gallery *n.* Kunstgalerie, *die*

arthritic /ɑː'θrɪtɪk/ *adj.* arthritisch

arthritis /ɑː'θraɪtɪs/ *n.* Arthritis, *die* (fachspr.); Gelenkentzündung, *die*

artichoke /'ɑːtɪtʃəʊk/ *n.* [**globe**] ~: Artischocke, *die*

article /'ɑːtɪkl/ *n.* (a) (in magazine, newspaper; Ling.) Artikel, *der*
(b) **an** ~ **of furniture/clothing** ein Möbel-/ Kleidungsstück; **an** ~ **of value** ein Wertgegenstand

articulate ⋯⋗ ass ⋯⋯

articulate /ɑːˈtɪkjʊlət/ *adj.* redegewandt; **be ~/not very ~**: sich gut/nicht sehr gut ausdrücken [können]

articulated /ɑːˈtɪkjʊleɪtɪd/ *adj.* **~ 'lorry** Sattelzug, *der*

artificial /ɑːtɪˈfɪʃl/ *adj.* **(a)** künstlich; Kunst-; (not real) unecht; **~ limb** Prothese, *die* **(b)** (affected) gekünstelt

artificial: ~ insemi'nation *n.* künstliche Befruchtung; (of animal) künstliche Besamung; **~ in'telligence** *n.* künstliche Intelligenz; **~ 'language** *n.* Kunstsprache, *die;* **~ respi'ration** *n.* künstliche Beatmung

artillery /ɑːˈtɪləri/ *n.* Artillerie, *die*

artisan /ˈɑːtɪzn, ɑːtɪˈzæn/ *n.* [Kunst]handwerker, *der*

artist /ˈɑːtɪst/ *n.* Künstler, *der*/Künstlerin, *die*

artiste /ɑːˈtiːst/ *n.* Artist, *der*/Artistin, *die*

artistic /ɑːˈtɪstɪk/ *adj.* **(a)** (of art) Kunst-; künstlerisch **(b)** (naturally skilled in art) künstlerisch veranlagt

'artless *adj.* arglos

art nouveau /ɑː nuːˈvəʊ/ *n.* Jugendstil, *der*

'art room *n.* Zeichensaal, *der*

'arts centre *n.* Kunstzentrum, *das*

'art work *n.* Bildmaterial, *das*

as /əz, stressed æz/ ① *adv., conj.* **(a)** he is as tall as I am er ist so groß wie ich; **as quickly as you can/as possible** so schnell du kannst/wie möglich **(b)** (though) small as he was obwohl er klein war **(c)** (however much) try as he might/would, he could not concentrate sosehr er sich auch bemühte, er konnte sich nicht konzentrieren **(d)** *expr. manner* wie; **as you may already have heard, ...**: wie Sie vielleicht schon gehört haben, ...; **as it were** sozusagen **(e)** *expr. time* als; während; **as we climbed the stairs** als wir die Treppe hinaufgingen; **as we were talking** während wir uns unterhielten **(f)** *expr. reason* da ② *prep.* **(a)** (in the function of) als; **as an artist** als Künstler; **speaking as a mother ...**: als Mutter ... **(b)** (like) wie **(c)** **the same as ...**: der-/die-/dasselbe wie ...; **such as** wie zum Beispiel ③ **as for ...**: was ... angeht *od.* betrifft; **as [it] is** wie die Dinge liegen; **the place is untidy enough as it is** es ist hier [so] schon unordentlich genug; **as of ...** (Amer.) von ... an; **as to** hinsichtlich (+ *Gen.*); **as yet** bis jetzt; noch

a.s.a.p. *abbr.* = **as soon as possible**

asbestos /æzˈbestɒs/ *n.* Asbest, *der*

asbestosis /æzbesˈtəʊsɪs/ *n.* (Med.) Asbestose, *die*

ASBO /ˈæzbəʊ/ *abbr.* (Brit.) = **antisocial behaviour order** Verfügung gegen antisoziales Verhalten

ascend /əˈsend/ ① *v.i.* **(a)** (go up) hinaufsteigen; (climb up) hinaufklettern; (by vehicle) hinauffahren **(b)** (rise) aufsteigen; ⟨*Hubschrauber:*⟩ höhersteigen **(c)** (slope upwards) ⟨*Hügel, Straße:*⟩ ansteigen ② *v.t.* **(a)** (go up) hinaufsteigen ⟨*Treppe, Leiter, Berg*⟩ **(b)** **~ the throne** den Thron besteigen

Ascension Day /əˈsenʃn/ *n.* Himmelfahrtstag, *der*

ascent /əˈsent/ *n.* Aufstieg, *der*

ascertain /æsəˈteɪn/ *v.t.* feststellen; ermitteln ⟨*Fakten, Daten*⟩

ascribe /əˈskraɪb/ *v.t.* zuschreiben (**to** *Dat.*)

ash¹ /æʃ/ *n.* (tree) Esche, *die*

ash² *n.* (from fire etc.) Asche, *die*

ashamed /əˈʃeɪmd/ *adj.* beschämt; **be ~**: sich schämen (**of** wegen)

ash: ~ bin *n.* Mülleimer, *der;* **~ blonde** ① *adj.* aschblond; ② *n.* Aschblonde, *der*/*die;* **~can** (Amer.) ▶ **~ BIN**

ashen /ˈæʃn/ *adj.* aschfahl ⟨*Gesicht*⟩

ashore /əˈʃɔː(r)/ *adv.* an Land

'ashtray *n.* Aschenbecher, *der*

Ash 'Wednesday *n.* Aschermittwoch, *der*

Asia /ˈeɪʃə/ *pr. n.* Asien (*das*)

Asian /ˈeɪʃən/ ① *adj.* asiatisch ② *n.* Asiat, *der*/Asiatin, *die*

aside /əˈsaɪd/ *adv.* beiseite; zur Seite

ask /ɑːsk/ ① *v.t.* **(a)** fragen; **~ sb. [sth.]** jmdn. [nach etw.] fragen **(b)** (seek to obtain) **~ sth.** um etw. bitten; **how much are you ~ing for that car?** wie viel verlangen Sie für das Auto?; **~ sb. to do sth.** jmdn. [darum] bitten, etw. zu tun **(c)** (invite) einladen ② *v.i.* **~ after sb./sth.** nach jmdm./etw. fragen; **~ for sth./sb.** etw./jmdn. verlangen

askance /əˈskæns, əˈskɑːns/ *adv.* **look ~ at sb.** jmdn. befremdet ansehen

askew /əˈskjuː/ *adv., pred. adj.* schief

asleep /əˈsliːp/ *pred. adj.* schlafend; **be/lie ~**: schlafen; **fall ~**: einschlafen

asparagus /əˈspærəgəs/ *n.* Spargel, *der*

aspect /ˈæspekt/ *n.* Aspekt, *der*

aspersion /əˈspɜːʃn/ *n.* **cast ~s on sb./sth.** jmdn./etw in den Schmutz ziehen

asphalt /ˈæsfælt/ *n.* Asphalt, *der*

asphyxiate /æsˈfɪksɪeɪt/ *v.t. & i.* ersticken

aspiration /æspəˈreɪʃn/ *n.* Streben, *das*

aspire /əˈspaɪə(r)/ *v.i.* **~ to** or **after sth.** nach etw. streben

aspirin /ˈæspərɪn/ *n.* Aspirin ⓦ, *das;* Kopfschmerztablette, *die*

ass¹ /æs/ *n.* Esel, *der*

ass² (Amer.) ▶ ARSE

a

assailant /əˈseɪlənt/ *n.* Angreifer, *der*/Angreiferin, *die*
assassin /əˈsæsɪn/ *n.* Mörder, *der*/Mörderin, *die*
assassinate /əˈsæsɪneɪt/ *v.t.* ermorden; **be ~d** einem Attentat zum Opfer fallen
assassination /əsæsɪˈneɪʃn/ *n.* Mord, *der* (**of** an + *Dat.*); **~ attempt** Attentat, *das* (**on** auf + *Akk.*)
assault /əˈsɔːlt/ **1** *n.* Angriff, *der;* (fig.) Anschlag, *der*
2 *v.t.* angreifen
assemble /əˈsembl/ **1** *v.t.* **(a)** zusammentragen; zusammenrufen ‹*Menschen*›
(b) (fit together) zusammenbauen
2 *v.i.* sich versammeln
assembly /əˈsemblɪ/ *n.* **(a)** (meeting) Versammlung, *die;* (in school) Morgenandacht, *die*
(b) (fitting together) Zusammenbau, *der*
asˈsembly line *n.* Fließband, *das*
assent /əˈsent/ **1** *v.i.* zustimmen (**to** *Dat.*)
2 *n.* Zustimmung, *die*
assert /əˈsɜːt/ *v.t.* **(a)** geltend machen; **~ oneself** sich durchsetzen
(b) (declare) behaupten; beteuern ‹*Unschuld*›
assertion /əˈsɜːʃn/ *n.* **(a)** Geltendmachen, *das*
(b) (declaration) Behauptung, *die*
assertive /əˈsɜːtɪv/ *adj.* energisch ‹*Person*›; bestimmt ‹*Ton, Verhalten*›
assertiveness /əˈsɜːtɪvnɪs/ *n.* Bestimmtheit, *die*
assess /əˈses/ *v.t.* einschätzen; festsetzen ‹*Steuer*› (**at** auf + *Akk.*)
asˈsessment *n.* **(a)** Einschätzung, *die*
(b) (tax to be paid) Steuerbescheid, *der*
asset /ˈæset/ *n.* **(a)** Vermögenswert, *der*
(b) (useful quality) Vorzug, *der* (**to** für); (person) Stütze, *die;* (thing) Hilfe, *die*
ˈasset-stripping *n.: Ankauf unrentabler Unternehmen, von denen einzelne Teile Gewinn bringend weiterverkauft werden*
assiduous /əˈsɪdjʊəs/ *adj.* **(a)** (diligent) eifrig
(b) (conscientious) gewissenhaft
assign /əˈsaɪn/ *v.t.* **(a)** (allot) zuweisen (**to** *Dat.*)
(b) (appoint) zuteilen; **~ sb. to do sth.** jmdn. damit betrauen, etw. zu tun
asˈsignment *n.* **(a)** (allotment) Zuweisung, *die;* (appointment) Zuteilung, *die*
(b) (task) Aufgabe, *die*
assimilate /əˈsɪmɪleɪt/ *v.t.* angleichen (**to, with** an + *Akk.*)
assimilation /əsɪmɪˈleɪʃn/ *n.* Angleichung, *die* (**to, with** an + *Akk.*)
assist /əˈsɪst/ **1** *v.t.* helfen (+ *Dat.*)
2 *v.i.* helfen; **~ with sth./in doing sth.** bei etw. helfen/helfen, etw. zu tun
assistance /əˈsɪstəns/ *n.* Hilfe, *die*
assistant /əˈsɪstənt/ *n.* (helper) Helfer, *der*/Helferin, *die;* (subordinate) Mitarbeiter, *der*/Mitarbeiterin, *die;* (of professor, artist) Assistent, *der*/Assistentin, *die;* (in shop) Verkäufer, *der*/Verkäuferin, *die;* **~ manager** stellvertretender Geschäftsführer
associate **1** /əˈsəʊʃɪət, əˈsəʊsɪət/ *n.* (partner) Partner, *der*/Partnerin, *die;* (colleague) Kollege, *der*/Kollegin, *die*
2 /əˈsəʊʃɪeɪt, əˈsəʊsɪeɪt/ *v.t.* in Verbindung bringen; **be ~d** in Verbindung stehen
3 /əˈsəʊʃɪeɪt, əˈsəʊsɪeɪt/ *v.i.* **~ with sb.** mit jmdm. Umgang haben
association /əsəʊsɪˈeɪʃn/ *n.* **(a)** (organization) Vereinigung, *die*
(b) (mental connection) Assoziation, *die*
(c) (connection) Verbindung, *die*
assorted /əˈsɔːtɪd/ *adj.* gemischt
assortment /əˈsɔːtmənt/ *n.* Sortiment, *das;* **a good ~ of hats [to choose from]** eine gute Auswahl an Hüten
Asst. *abbr.* = **Assistant** Ass.
assume /əˈsjuːm/ *v.t.* **(a)** voraussetzen; **assuming that ...:** vorausgesetzt, dass ...
(b) (undertake) übernehmen ‹*Amt, Pflichten*›
(c) (take on) annehmen ‹*Namen, Rolle*›
assumption /əˈsʌmpʃn/ *n.* Annahme, *die;* **going on the ~ that ...:** vorausgesetzt, dass ...; **the A~** (Relig.) Mariä Himmelfahrt
assurance /əˈʃʊərəns/ *n.* **(a)** Zusicherung, *die*
(b) (self-confidence) Selbstsicherheit, *die*
assure /əˈʃʊə(r)/ *v.t.* **(a)** versichern (+ *Dat.*)
(b) (convince) **~ sb./oneself** jmdn./sich überzeugen
(c) (make certain or safe) gewährleisten
assured /əˈʃʊəd/ *adj.* gewährleistet ‹*Erfolg*›; **be ~ of sth.** sich (*Dat.*) einer Sache (*Gen.*) sicher sein
asterisk /ˈæstərɪsk/ *n.* Sternchen, *das*
astern /əˈstɜːn/ *adv.* (Naut., Aeronaut.) achtern; (towards the rear) achteraus
asteroid /ˈæstərɔɪd/ *n.* Asteroid, *der*
asthma /ˈæsmə/ *n.* Asthma, *das*
asthmatic /æsˈmætɪk/ **1** *adj.* asthmatisch
2 *n.* Asthmatiker, *der*/Asthmatikerin, *die*
astonish /əˈstɒnɪʃ/ *v.t.* erstaunen
aˈstonishing *adj.* erstaunlich
aˈstonishment *n.* Erstaunen, *das*
astound /əˈstaʊnd/ *v.t.* verblüffen
aˈstounding *adj.* erstaunlich
astray /əˈstreɪ/ *adv.* **sth. goes ~** (is mislaid) etw. wird verlegt; (is lost) etw. geht verloren; **go/lead ~** (fig.) in die Irre gehen/führen
astride /əˈstraɪd/ **1** *adv.* rittlings ‹*sitzen*›
2 *prep.* rittlings auf (+ *Dat.*)
astringent /əˈstrɪndʒənt/ **1** *adj.* scharf
2 *n.* Adstringens, *das*
astrologer /əˈstrɒlədʒə(r)/ *n.* Astrologe, *der*/Astrologin, *die*
astrological /æstrəˈlɒdʒɪkl/ *adj.* astrologisch
astrology /əˈstrɒlədʒɪ/ *n.* Astrologie, *die*

astronaut /'æstrənɔːt/ n. Astronaut, der/ Astronautin, die

astronautics /æstrəˈnɔːtɪks/ n. Astronautik, die; Raumfahrt, die

astronomer /əˈstrɒnəmə(r)/ n. Astronom, der/Astronomin, die

astronomical /æstrəˈnɒmɪkl/ adj. astronomisch

astronomy /əˈstrɒnəmɪ/ n. Astronomie, die

astrophysics /æstrəʊˈfɪzɪks/ n. Astrophysik, die

astute /əˈstjuːt/ adj. scharfsinnig

asylee /æsaɪˈliː/ n. Asylant, der/Asylantin, die

asylum /əˈsaɪləm/ n. (a) (Polit.) Asyl, das; grant sb. ~: jmdm. Asyl gewähren; ~ seeker Asylsuchende, der/die
(b) ▶ LUNATIC ASYLUM

asymmetric /æsɪˈmetrɪk, eɪsɪˈmetrɪk/ adj. asymmetrisch; unsymmetrisch

at /ət, stressed æt/ prep. (a) expr. place an (+ Dat.); at the station am Bahnhof; at the baker's/butcher's/grocer's beim Bäcker/ Fleischer/Kaufmann; at the chemist's in der Apotheke/Drogerie; at the supermarket im Supermarkt; at the party auf der Party; at the office/hotel im Büro/Hotel; at Dover in Dover
(b) expr. time at Christmas [zu od. an] Weihnachten; at six o'clock um sechs Uhr; at midnight um Mitternacht; at midday am Mittag; at [the age of] 40 mit 40; im Alter von 40; at this/the moment in diesem/im Augenblick od. Moment
(c) expr. price at £2.50 [each] zu od. für [je] 2,50 Pfund
(d) expr. speed at 30 m.p.h. etc. mit dreißig Meilen pro Stunde usw.
(e) at that (at that point) dabei; (at that provocation) daraufhin; (moreover) noch dazu

ate ▶ EAT

atheism /'eɪθɪɪzm/ n. Atheismus, der

atheist /'eɪθɪɪst/ n. Atheist, der/Atheistin, die

Athens /'æθɪnz/ pr. n. Athen (das)

athlete /'æθliːt/ n. Athlet, der/Athletin, die; (runner, jumper) Leichtathlet, der/-athletin, die

athletic /æθ'letɪk/ adj. sportlich

ath'letics n. Leichtathletik, die

Atlantic /ət'læntɪk/ 1 adj. atlantisch; ~ Ocean Atlantischer Ozean
2 pr. n. Atlantik, der

atlas /'ætləs/ n. Atlas, der

ATM abbr. = **automated teller machine**

atmosphere /'ætməsfɪə(r)/ n. Atmosphäre, die

atmospheric /ætməsˈferɪk/ adj. (a) atmosphärisch
(b) (fig.: evocative) stimmungsvoll

atom /'ætəm/ n. Atom, das

'**atom bomb** n. Atombombe, die

atomic /əˈtɒmɪk/ adj. Atom-

atomizer /'ætəmaɪzə(r)/ n. Zerstäuber, der

atone /əˈtəʊn/ v.i. es wieder gutmachen; ~ for sth. etw. wieder gutmachen

a'tonement n. Buße, die

atrocious /əˈtrəʊʃəs/ adj. grauenhaft; scheußlich ⟨Wetter, Benehmen⟩

atrocity /əˈtrɒsɪtɪ/ n. (a) (wickedness) Grauenhaftigkeit, die
(b) (deed) Gräueltat, die

'**at sign** n. At-Zeichen, das; Klammeraffe, der (ugs.)

attach /əˈtætʃ/ v.t. (a) (fasten) befestigen (to an + Dat.); please find ~ed a copy of the letter beigeheftet ist eine Kopie des Briefes
(b) (fig.) ~ importance to sth. einer Sache (Dat.) Gewicht beimessen

attaché /əˈtæʃeɪ/ n. Attaché, der

at'taché case n. Diplomatenkoffer, der

attached /əˈtætʃt/ adj. (emotionally) be ~ to sb./sth. an jmdm./etw. hängen

at'tachment n. (a) (act or means of fastening) Befestigung, die
(b) (affection) Anhänglichkeit, die (to an + Akk.)
(c) (accessory) Zusatzgerät, das
(d) (Comp.) Attachment, das; Anlage, die

attack /əˈtæk/ 1 v.t. (a) angreifen; (ambush, raid) überfallen; (fig.: criticize) attackieren
(b) (affect) ⟨Krankheit:⟩ befallen
2 v.i. angreifen
3 n. Angriff, der; (ambush) Überfall, der; (fig.: criticism) Attacke, die; (of illness) Anfall, der

at'tacker n. Angreifer, der/Angreiferin, die

attacking /əˈtækɪŋ/ adj. offensiv ⟨Spielweise, Spieler⟩; angreifend ⟨Truppen⟩

attain /əˈteɪn/ v.t. erreichen

attainable /əˈteɪnəbl/ adj. erreichbar ⟨Ziel⟩; realisierbar ⟨Hoffnung, Ziel⟩

at'tainment n. Verwirklichung, die

attempt /əˈtempt/ 1 v.t. versuchen
2 n. Versuch, der

attend /əˈtend/ 1 v.i. (a) (give care and thought) aufpassen; (apply oneself) ~ to sth. (deal with sth.) sich um etw. kümmern
(b) (be present) anwesend sein (at bei)
2 v.t. (be present at) teilnehmen an (+ Dat.); (go regularly to) besuchen

attendance /əˈtendəns/ n. Anwesenheit, die; (number of people) Teilnehmerzahl, die

attendant /əˈtendənt/ n. (a) [lavatory] ~: Toilettenmann, der/-frau, die; [cloakroom] ~: Garderobenmann, der/-frau, die; museum ~: Museumswärter, der/-wärterin, die
(b) (member of entourage) Begleiter, der/ Begleiterin, die

attention /əˈtenʃn/ 1 n. (a) Aufmerksamkeit, die; attract [sb.'s] ~: [jmdn.] auf sich (Akk.) aufmerksam machen; pay ~ to sb./sth. jmdn./etw. beachten; pay ⋯⋮

~! gib Acht!; pass auf!; **hold sb.'s** ~: jmds.
Interesse wach halten; ~ **Miss Jones** (on
letter) zu Händen [von] Miss Jones
(b) (Mil.) **stand to** ~: stillstehen
 2 *int.* (a) Achtung
(b) (Mil.) stillgestanden
attentive /ə'tentɪv/ *adj.* aufmerksam
attic /'ætɪk/ *n.* (room) Dachboden, *der;*
(habitable) Dachkammer, *die*
attire /ə'taɪə(r)/ *n.* Kleidung, *die*
attitude /'ætɪtjuːd/ *n.* (a) Haltung, *die*
(b) (mental ~) Einstellung, *die*
attn. *abbr.* = **for the attention of**
z. H[d].
attorney /ə'tɜːnɪ/ *n.* (a) Bevollmächtigte,
der/die; **power of** ~: Vollmacht, *die*
(b) (Amer.: lawyer) [Rechts]anwalt, *der/*
-anwältin, *die*
attract /ə'trækt/ *v.t.* (a) (draw) anziehen; auf
sich (*Akk.*) ziehen ⟨*Interesse, Blick, Kritik*⟩
(b) (arouse pleasure in) anziehend wirken auf
(+ *Akk.*)
(c) (arouse interest in) reizen (**about** an + *Dat.*)
attraction /ə'trækʃn/ *n.* (a) Anziehung,
die; (force, lit. or fig.) Anziehung[skraft], *die*
(b) (fig.: thing that attracts) Attraktion, *die;*
(charm) Verlockung, *die;* Reiz, *der*
attractive /ə'træktɪv/ *adj.* (a) anziehend
(b) (fig.) attraktiv; reizvoll ⟨*Vorschlag,
Möglichkeit, Idee*⟩
attribute 1 /'ætrɪbjuːt/ *n.* Eigenschaft, *die*
 2 /ə'trɪbjuːt/ *v.t.* zuschreiben (**to** *Dat.*)
attributive /ə'trɪbjʊtɪv/ *adj.* (Ling.)
attributiv
atypical /eɪ'tɪpɪkl/ *adj.* atypisch; untypisch
aubergine /'əʊbəʒiːn/ *n.* Aubergine, *die*
auburn /'ɔːbən/ *adj.* rötlich braun
auction /'ɔːkʃn/ 1 *n.* Versteigerung, *die*
 2 *v.t.* versteigern
auctioneer /ɔːkʃə'nɪə(r)/ *n.* Auktionator,
der/Auktionatorin, *die*
audacious /ɔː'deɪʃəs/ *adj.* (a) (daring) kühn;
verwegen
(b) (impudent) dreist
audacity /ɔː'dæsɪtɪ/ *n.* (a) (daringness)
Kühnheit, *die;* Verwegenheit, *die*
(b) (impudence) Dreistigkeit, *die*
audible /'ɔːdɪbl/ *adj.* hörbar
audience /'ɔːdɪəns/ *n.* (a) Publikum, *das*
(b) (formal interview) Audienz, *die* (**with** bei)
audio /'ɔːdɪəʊ/ *adj.* Ton-; ~ **frequency**
Tonfrequenz, *die;* ~ **equipment** Audioanlage,
die
audio: ~**book** *n.* Hörbuch, *das;*
~ **cassette,** *n.* Audiokassette, *die;*
Tonkassette, *die;* ~ **typist** *n.* Phonotypist,
der/-typistin, *die;* ~**visual** *adj.* audiovisuell
audit /'ɔːdɪt/ 1 *n.* ~ **[of the accounts]**
Rechnungsprüfung, *die*
 2 *v.t.* prüfen
audition /ɔː'dɪʃn/ 1 *n.* (singing) Vorsingen,
das; (dancing) Vortanzen, *das;* (acting)
Vorsprechen, *das*

 2 *v.i.* (sing) vorsingen; (dance) vortanzen;
(act) vorsprechen
 3 *v.t.* vorsingen/vortanzen/vorsprechen
lassen
auditor /'ɔːdɪtə(r)/ *n.* Buchprüfer, *der/*
-prüferin, *die*
auditorium /ɔːdɪ'tɔːrɪəm/ *n.*
Zuschauerraum, *der*
Aug. *abbr.* = **August** Aug.
augment /ɔːg'ment/ *v.t.* verbessern
⟨*Einkommen*⟩; aufstocken ⟨*Fonds*⟩
augur /'ɔːgə(r)/ 1 *v.t.* bedeuten;
versprechen ⟨*Erfolg*⟩
 2 *v.i.* ~ **well/ill for sth./sb.** ein gutes/
schlechtes Zeichen für etw./jmdn. sein
August /'ɔːgəst/ *n.* August, *der;* **in** ~: im
August; **last/next** ~: letzten/nächsten
August; **the first of/on the first of** ~: der
erste/am ersten August
aunt /ɑːnt/ *n.* Tante, *die*
auntie, aunty /'ɑːntɪ/ *n.* (coll.) Täntchen,
das; (with name) Tante, *die*
au pair /əʊ 'peə(r)/ *n.* Aupairmädchen, *das*
aura /'ɔːrə/ *n.* Aura, *die*
auspices /'ɔːspɪsɪs/ *n. pl.* **under the** ~ **of**
sb./sth. unter jmds./einer Sache
Schirmherrschaft
auspicious /ɔː'spɪʃəs/ *adj.* günstig;
viel versprechend ⟨*Anfang*⟩
Aussie /'ɒzɪ/ (coll.) 1 *adj.* australisch
 2 *n.* Australier, *der*/Australierin, *die*
austere /ɒ'stɪə(r)/ *adj.* (a) (strict, stern)
streng
(b) (severely simple) karg
austerity /ɒ'sterɪtɪ/ *n.* (a) (strictness)
Strenge, *die*
(b) (severe simplicity) Kargheit, *die*
(c) (lack of luxuries) wirtschaftliche
Einschränkung
Australia /ɒ'streɪlɪə/ *pr. n.* Australien (*das*)
Australian /ɒ'streɪlɪən/ 1 *adj.* australisch;
sb. is ~: jmd. ist Australier/Australierin
 2 *n.* Australier, *der*/Australierin, *die*
Austria /'ɒstrɪə/ *pr. n.* Österreich (*das*)
Austrian /'ɒstrɪən/ 1 *adj.* österreichisch;
sb. is ~: jmd. ist Österreicher/Österreicherin
 2 *n.* Österreicher, *der*/Österreicherin, *die*
authentic /ɔː'θentɪk/ *adj.* authentisch
authenticate /ɔː'θentɪkeɪt/ *v.t.*
authentifizieren; ~ **sth.** die Echtheit einer
Sache (*Gen.*) bestätigen
authentication /ɔːθentɪ'keɪʃn/ *n.*
Bestätigung der Echtheit; (of information, report)
Bestätigung, *die*
authenticity /ɔːθen'tɪsɪtɪ/ *n.* Authentizität,
die
author /'ɔːθə(r)/ *n.* Autor, *der*/Autorin, *die;*
(profession) Schriftsteller, *der*/Schriftstellerin,
die
authoritarian /ɔːθɒrɪ'teərɪən/ 1 *adj.*
autoritär
 2 *n.* autoritäre Person

authoritative /ɔːˈθɒrɪtətɪv/ adj. maßgebend; zuverlässig ⟨Bericht, Information⟩

authority /ɔːˈθɒrɪtɪ/ n. (a) Autorität, die; in ~: verantwortlich

(b) the authorities die Behörde[n]

authorization /ɔːθəraɪˈzeɪʃn/ n. Genehmigung, die

authorize /ˈɔːθəraɪz/ v.t. (a) ermächtigen; bevollmächtigen

(b) (sanction) genehmigen

auto /ˈɔːtəʊ/ n., pl. ~s (Amer. coll.) Auto, das

auto- /ˈɔːtəʊ/ in comb. auto-/Auto-

autobio'graphical adj. autobiographisch

autobi'ography n. Autobiographie, die

autocrat /ˈɔːtəkræt/ n. Autokrat, der/ Autokratin, die

autocratic /ɔːtəˈkrætɪk/ adj. autokratisch

'autocross n. Autocross, das

Autocue ® /ˈɔːtəʊkjuː/ n. Teleprompter (Wz), der

'autofocus n. (Photog.) Autofokus, der

autograph /ˈɔːtəgrɑːf/ ① n. Autogramm, das

② v.t. signieren

auto-im'mune adj. (Med.) autoimmun; ~ response Autoimmunantwort, die

automat /ˈɔːtəmæt/ n. (Amer.) (a) (slot machine) [Münz]automat, der

(b) (cafeteria) Automatenrestaurant, das

automate /ˈɔːtəmeɪt/ v.t. automatisieren

automated 'teller machine n. Geldautomat, der

automatic /ɔːtəˈmætɪk/ ① adj. automatisch; ~ gear system, ~ transmission Automatikgetriebe, das

② n. (weapon) automatische Waffe; (vehicle) Fahrzeug mit Automatikgetriebe

automatically /ɔːtəˈmætɪkəlɪ/ adv. automatisch

automation /ɔːtəˈmeɪʃn/ n. Automation, die

automaton /ɔːˈtɒmətən/ n., pl. ~s or automata /ɔːˈtɒmətə/ Automat, der

automobile /ˈɔːtəməbiːl/ n. (Amer.) Auto, das

autonomous /ɔːˈtɒnəməs/ adj. autonom

autonomy /ɔːˈtɒnəmɪ/ n. Autonomie, die

'autopilot n. Autopilot, der; [fly] on ~: mit Autopilot [fliegen]

autopsy /ˈɔːtɒpsɪ/ n. Autopsie, die

auto: ~save (Comp.) ① n. automatisches Speichern; ② v.t. automatisch speichern; ~-suggestion n. Autosuggestion, die; ~timer n. [automatische] Schaltuhr

autumn /ˈɔːtəm/ n. Herbst, der; in [the] ~: im Herbst

autumnal /ɔːˈtʌmnl/ adj. herbstlich

auxiliary /ɔːgˈzɪljərɪ/ ① adj. Hilfs-

② n. (a) Hilfskraft, die

(b) (Ling.) Hilfsverb, das

avail /əˈveɪl/ ① n. be of no ~: nichts nützen; to no ~: vergebens

② v. refl. ~ oneself of sth. von etw. Gebrauch machen

available /əˈveɪləbl/ adj. (a) (at one's disposal) verfügbar

(b) (obtainable) erhältlich; lieferbar ⟨Waren⟩

avalanche /ˈævəlɑːnʃ/ n. Lawine, die

avarice /ˈævərɪs/ n. Geldgier, die; Habsucht, die

avaricious /ævəˈrɪʃəs/ adj. geldgierig; habsüchtig

avenge /əˈvendʒ/ v.t. rächen

avenue /ˈævənjuː/ n. Allee, die; (fig.) Weg, der (to zu)

average /ˈævərɪdʒ/ ① n. Durchschnitt, der; on ~: im Durchschnitt; durchschnittlich

② adj. durchschnittlich

③ v.t. (a) (find the ~ of) den Durchschnitt ermitteln von

(b) (amount on ~ to) durchschnittlich betragen

④ v.i. ~ out at im Durchschnitt betragen

averse /əˈvɜːs/ adj. be ~ to sth. einer Sache ⟨Dat.⟩ abgeneigt sein

aversion /əˈvɜːʃn/ n. Abneigung, die (to gegen)

avert /əˈvɜːt/ v.t. abwenden; verhüten ⟨Unfall⟩

aviary /ˈeɪvɪərɪ/ n. Vogelhaus, das

aviation /eɪvɪˈeɪʃn/ n. Luftfahrt, die

avid /ˈævɪd/ adj. (enthusiastic) begeistert; be ~ for sth. (eager, greedy) begierig auf etw. ⟨Akk.⟩ sein

avocado /ævəˈkɑːdəʊ/ n., pl. ~s: ~ [pear] Avocado[birne], die

avoid /əˈvɔɪd/ v.t. (a) meiden ⟨Ort⟩; ~ a cyclist einem Radfahrer ausweichen; ~ the boss when he's in a temper geh dem Chef aus dem Weg, wenn er schlechte Laune hat

(b) (refrain from, escape) vermeiden

avoidable /əˈvɔɪdəbl/ adj. vermeidbar

avoidance /əˈvɔɪdəns/ n. Vermeidung, die

await /əˈweɪt/ v.t. erwarten

awake /əˈweɪk/ ① v.i., awoke /əˈwəʊk/, awoken /əˈwəʊkn/ erwachen

② v.t., awoke, awoken wecken

③ pred. adj. wach; wide ~: hellwach

awaken /əˈweɪkn/ v.t. & i. (esp. fig.)
▶ AWAKE 1, 2

award /əˈwɔːd/ ① v.t. verleihen ⟨Preis, Auszeichnung⟩; zusprechen ⟨Sorgerecht, Entschädigung⟩; gewähren ⟨Zahlung, Gehaltserhöhung⟩

② n. (prize) Auszeichnung, die

a'ward-winning adj. preisgekrönt

aware /əˈweə(r)/ adj. be ~ of sth. sich ⟨Dat.⟩ einer Sache ⟨Gen.⟩ bewusst sein; be ~ that …: sich ⟨Dat.⟩ [dessen] bewusst sein, dass …

a'wareness n. Bewusstsein, das

awash /əˈwɒʃ/ *adj.* be ~ (flooded) unter Wasser stehen

away /əˈweɪ/ ① *adv.* (a) (at a distance) entfernt; **play** ~ (Sport) auswärts spielen (b) (to a distance) weg; fort (c) (absent) nicht da ② *adj.* (Sport) auswärts *präd.*; Auswärts-; ~ **match** Auswärtsspiel, *das;* ~ **team** Gastmannschaft, *die*

awe /ɔː/ *n.* Ehrfurcht, *die* (of vor + *Dat.*)

'awe-inspiring *adj.* Ehrfurcht gebietend; beeindruckend

awesome /ˈɔːsəm/ *adj.* überwältigend; eindrucksvoll ⟨*Schweigen*⟩; übergroß ⟨*Verantwortung*⟩

awe: ~**stricken,** ~**struck** *adj.* [von Ehrfurcht] ergriffen; ehrfurchtsvoll ⟨*Ausdruck, Staunen*⟩

awful /ˈɔːfl/ *adj.*, **'awfully** *adv.* furchtbar

awkward /ˈɔːkwəd/ *adj.* (a) (difficult to use) ungünstig; be ~ **to use** unhandlich sein (b) (clumsy) unbeholfen (c) (embarrassing) peinlich (d) (difficult) schwierig; ungünstig ⟨*Zeitpunkt*⟩

awning /ˈɔːnɪŋ/ *n.* (on house) Markise, *die;* (of tent) Vordach, *das*

awoke, awoken ▶ AWAKE

awry /əˈraɪ/ *adv.* schief; **go** ~ (fig.) schief gehen (ugs.); ⟨*Plan:*⟩ fehlschlagen

axe (*Amer.:* **ax**) /æks/ *n.* Axt, *die;* Beil, *das*

axis /ˈæksɪs/ *n., pl.* **axes** /ˈæksiːz/ Achse, *die*

axle /ˈæksl/ *n.* Achse, *die*

Bb

B, b /biː/ *n.* B, b, *das;* **B road** Straße 2. Ordnung; ≈ Landstraße, *die*

BA *abbr.* = **Bachelor of Arts**

babble /ˈbæbl/ *v.i.* (a) (talk incoherently) stammeln (b) (talk foolishly) [dumm] schwatzen (c) ⟨*Bach:*⟩ plätschern

baboon /bəˈbuːn/ *n.* Pavian, *der*

baby /ˈbeɪbɪ/ *n.* (a) Baby, *das;* **have a** ~/**be going to have a** ~: ein Kind bekommen; **throw out** *or* **away the** ~ **with the bathwater** (fig.) das Kind mit dem Bade ausschütten (b) (childish person) **be a** ~: sich wie ein kleines Kind benehmen

baby: ~ **boom** *n.* Babyboom, *der;* ~**-bouncer** *n.:* federnd aufgehängter Sitz *für Kleinkinder, in dem sie durch Wippen ihre Beine kräftigen sollen;* ~ **buggy,** ~ **carriage** *ns.* (Amer.) Kinderwagen, *der;* ~ **clothes** *n. pl.* Babykleidung, *die;* ~ **food** *n.* Babynahrung, *die*

'babyish *adj.* kindlich ⟨*Aussehen*⟩; kindisch ⟨*Benehmen, Person*⟩

baby: ~**-minder** *n.* Tagesmutter, *die;* ~**sit** *v.i., forms as* SIT 1: babysitten (ugs.); auf das Kind/die Kinder aufpassen; ~**sitter** *n.* Babysitter, *der*/Babysitterin, *die;* ~**sitting** *n.* Babysitting, *das;* ~**-snatcher** *n.* Kindesentführer, *der* /-entführerin, *die;* ~**-talk** *n.* Babysprache, *die;* ~ **walker** *n.* Laufstuhl, *der;* ~ **wipe** *n.* feuchtes Baby[pflege]tuch

bachelor /ˈbætʃələ(r)/ *n.* (a) Junggeselle, *der*

(b) (Univ.) **B**~ **of Arts/Science** Bakkalaureus der philosophischen Fakultät/der Naturwissenschaften

back /bæk/ ① *n.* (a) (of person, animal) Rücken, *der;* (of house, cheque) Rückseite, *die;* (of vehicle) Heck, *das;* (inside car) Rücksitz, *der;* **stand** ~ **to** ~: Rücken an Rücken stehen; ~ **to front** verkehrt rum; **turn one's** ~ **on sb.** jmdm. den Rücken zuwenden; (fig.) jmdn. im Stich lassen; **turn one's** ~ **on sth.** (fig.) sich um etw. nicht kümmern; **get** *or* **put sb.'s** ~ **up** (fig.) jmdn. wütend machen; **be glad to see the** ~ **of sb./sth.** (fig.) froh sein, jmdn./ etw. nicht mehr sehen zu müssen; **have one's** ~ **to the wall** (fig.) mit dem Rücken zur Wand stehen; **put one's** ~ **into sth.** (fig.) für etw. mit allen Kräften einsetzen; **with the** ~ **of one's hand** mit dem Handrücken; **at the** ~ **[of the book]** hinten [im Buch] (b) (Sport: player) Verteidiger, *der* ② *adj.* hinter... ③ *adv.* zurück; **two miles** ~: vor zwei Meilen; ~ **and forth** hin und her; **there and** ~: hin und zurück; **a week/month** ~: vor einer Woche/vor einem Monat ④ *v.t.* (a) (assist) unterstützen (b) (bet on) wetten *od.* setzen auf (+ *Akk.*) (c) zurücksetzen [mit] ⟨*Fahrzeug*⟩ ⑤ *v.i.* zurücksetzen; ~ **into/out of sth.** rückwärts in etw. (*Akk.*)/aus etw. fahren; ~ **on to sth.** hinten an etw. (*Akk.*) grenzen

■ **back 'down** *v.i.* nachgeben

■ **back 'out** *v.i.* rückwärts herausfahren; ~ **out of sth.** (fig.) von etw. zurücktreten

■ **back 'up** *v.t.* (a) unterstützen; untermauern ⟨*Anspruch, These*⟩

(b) (Comp.) sichern ‹*Daten, Dokumente*›; ∼ **up a file on to a floppy disk** von einer Datei eine Sicherungskopie auf Diskette machen

back: ∼**ache** n. Rückenschmerzen *Pl.;* ∼**-bencher** /bæk'bentʃə(r)/ n. (Brit. Parl.) [einfacher] Abgeordneter/[einfache] Abgeordnete; ∼**bone** n. Rückgrat, *das;* ∼**chat** n. (coll.) [freche] Widerrede; ∼**date** *v.t.* zurückdatieren (**to** auf + *Akk.*); ∼ **'door** n. Hintertür, *die*

'backer n. Geldgeber, *der*

back: ∼**'fire** *v.i.* knallen; (fig.) fehlschlagen; **it** ∼**fired on me/him** *etc.* der Schuss ging nach hinten los (ugs.); ∼**gammon** /'bækgæmən/ n. (game) Backgammon, *das;* ≈ Tricktrack, *das;* ≈ Puff, *das;* ∼**ground** n. Hintergrund, *der;* (social status) Herkunft, *die;* ∼**hand** (Tennis etc.) 1 *adj.* Rückhand-; 2 n. Rückhand, *die;* ∼**'handed** *adj.* **(a)** (Tennis etc.) Rückhand-; **(b)** (fig.) indirekt; zweifelhaft ‹*Kompliment*›; ∼**'hander** n. (coll.: bribe) Schmiergeld, *das*

'backing n. (support) Unterstützung, *die*

back: ∼ **issue** ▶≈ NUMBER; ∼**lash** n. (fig.) Gegenreaktion, *die;* ∼**log** n. Rückstand, *der;* ∼ **number** n. (of periodical, magazine) alte Nummer; ∼**pack** 1 n. Rucksack, *der;* 2 *v.i.* mit dem Rucksack [ver]reisen; ∼**packer** n. Rucksackreisende, *der/die;* Rucksacktourist, *der/*-touristin, *die;* (hiker) Wanderer, *der/* Wanderin, *die* mit Rucksack; ∼**packing** n. das [Ver]reisen mit dem Rucksack; (hiking) das Wandern mit dem Rucksack; *attrib.* ‹*Reise usw.*› mit dem Rucksack; ∼ **pay** n. ausstehender Lohn/ausstehendes Gehalt; **he was reinstated with** ∼ **pay** er wurde wieder eingestellt und erhielt eine Lohn-/ Gehaltsnachzahlung; **she was awarded £7,850 in** ∼ **pay** sie erhielt eine Nachzahlung von 7 850 Pfund; ∼**'pedal** *v.i.* **(a)** die Pedale rückwärts treten; **(b)** (fig.) einen Rückzieher machen (ugs.); ∼**scratching** n. (fig. coll.) [mutual] ∼**scratching** Klüngelei, *die* (abwertend); ∼ **'seat** n. Rücksitz, *der;* ∼**side** n. Hinterteil, *das* (ugs.); ∼**'space** *v.i.* die Rücktaste betätigen; ∼**'stage** *adv.* **go** ∼**stage** hinter die Bühne gehen; ∼ **street** n. kleine Seitenstraße; ∼**stroke** n. Rückenschwimmen, *das;* ∼**track** *v.i.* wieder zurückgehen; (fig.) eine Kehrtwendung machen; ∼**-up** n. (support) Unterstützung, *die;* ∼**-up** [copy] (Comp.) Sicherungskopie, *die*

backward /'bækwəd/ 1 *adj.* **(a)** rückwärts gerichtet; Rückwärts-; **(b)** (reluctant, shy) zurückhaltend; **(c)** (underdeveloped) rückständig ‹*Land, Region*› 2 *adv.* ▶ BACKWARDS

backwards /'bækwədz/ *adv.* **(a)** nach hinten; **the child fell [over]** ∼ **into the water**

das Kind fiel rückwärts ins Wasser; **bend** *or* **lean over** ∼ **to do sth.** (fig. coll.) sich zerreißen, um etw. zu tun (ugs.) **(b)** (oppositely to normal direction) rückwärts; ∼ **and forwards** hin und her

back: ∼**water** n. (fig.) Kaff, *das* (ugs.); ∼ **'yard** n. Hinterhof, *der*

bacon /'beɪkn/ n. [Frühstücks]speck, *der*

bacterial /bæk'tɪərɪəl/ *adj.* bakteriell

bacterium /bæk'tɪərɪəm/ n., *pl.* **bacteria** /bæk'tɪərɪə/ Bakterie, *die*

bad /bæd/ *adj.,* **worse** /wɜːs/, **worst** /wɜːst/ **(a)** schlecht; (rotten) schlecht, verdorben ‹*Fleisch, Fisch, Essen*›; faul ‹*Ei, Apfel*›; **not** ∼ (coll.) nicht schlecht; nicht übel **(b)** (naughty) ungezogen, böse ‹*Kind, Hund*› **(c)** (offensive) [use] ∼ **language** Kraftausdrücke [benutzen] **(d)** (regretful) **feel** ∼ **about sth.** etw. bedauern; **I feel** ∼ **about him** ich habe seinetwegen ein schlechtes Gewissen **(e)** (serious) schlimm ‹*Sturz, Krise*›; schwer ‹*Fehler, Krankheit, Unfall*› **(f)** (Commerc.) **a** ∼ **debt** eine uneinbringliche Schuld

bade ▶ BID 1B

badge /bædʒ/ n. Abzeichen, *das*

badger /'bædʒə(r)/ n. Dachs, *der*

'badly *adv.,* **worse** /wɜːs/, **worst** /wɜːst/ **(a)** schlecht **(b)** schwer ‹*verletzt, beschädigt*› **(c)** (urgently) dringend

bad-mannered /bæd'mænəd/ *adj.* **be** ∼: schlechte Manieren haben

badminton /'bædmɪntən/ n. Federball, *der;* (als Sport) Badminton, *das*

bad-tempered /bæd'tempəd/ *adj.* griesgrämig

baffle /'bæfl/ *v.t.* ∼ **sb.** jmdm. unverständlich sein

baffling /'bæflɪŋ/ *adj.* rätselhaft

bag /bæg/ 1 n. Tasche, *die;* (sack) Sack, *der;* (hand∼) Handtasche, *die;* (plastic ∼) Beutel, *der;* (small paper ∼) Tüte, *die;* ∼**s of** (coll.: large amount) jede Menge 2 *v.t.,* **-gg-:** **(a)** in Säcke/Beutel/Tüten füllen **(b)** (claim possession of) sich (*Dat.*) schnappen (ugs.)

baggage /'bægɪdʒ/ n. Gepäck, *das*

baggage: ∼ **allowance** n. Freigepäck, *das;* **be over/within one's** ∼ **allowance** Übergepäck/kein Übergepäck haben; ∼ **handler** n. Gepäckverlader, *der/* -verladerin, *die;* ∼ **handling** n. Gepäckverladung, *die;* ∼ **reclaim** n. Gepäckausgabe, *die*

baggy /'bægɪ/ *adj.* weit [geschnitten] ‹*Kleid, Hose*›; (through long use) ausgebeult ‹*Hose*›

'bagpipe[s] n. [*pl.*] Dudelsack, *der*

baguette /bæ'get/ n. Baguette, *die;* [französisches] Stangenweißbrot

Bahamas /bəˈhɑːməz/ *pr. n. pl.* the ~: die Bahamas *Pl.*

bail[1] /beɪl/ **1** *n.* Kaution, *die;* **be [out] on ~:** gegen Kaution auf freiem Fuß sein
2 *v.t.* ~ **sb. out** jmdn. gegen Kaution freibekommen; *(fig.)* jmdm. aus der Klemme helfen (ugs.)

bail[2] *v.t.* (scoop) ~ **[out]** ausschöpfen
■ ˈ**bail out** *v.i.* ⟨*Pilot:*⟩ abspringen

bailiff /ˈbeɪlɪf/ *n.* ≈ Gerichtsvollzieher, *der*

bait /beɪt/ **1** *v.t.* mit einem Köder versehen
2 *n.* Köder, *der*

bake /beɪk/ *v.t. & i.* backen; **~d beans** gebackene Bohnen [in Tomatensoße]; **~d potato** [in der Schale] gebackene Kartoffel

ˈ**baker** *n.* Bäcker, *der*

bakery /ˈbeɪkərɪ/ *n.* Bäckerei, *die*

baking: ~ **powder** *n.* Backpulver, *das;* ~ **sheet** *n.* Backblech, *das;* ~ **soda** *n.* Natron, *das;* ~ **tin** *n.* Backform, *die;* ~ **tray** *n.* Kuchenblech, *das*

balance /ˈbæləns/ **1** *n.* **(a)** (instrument) Waage, *die*
(b) *(fig.)* be *or* hang in the ~: in der Schwebe sein
(c) (steady position) Gleichgewicht, *das;* **keep/lose one's ~:** das Gleichgewicht halten/verlieren; *(fig.)* sein Gleichgewicht bewahren/verlieren; **strike a ~ between** *(fig.)* den Mittelweg finden zwischen (+ *Dat.*)
(d) (Bookk.: difference) Bilanz, *die;* (state of bank account) Kontostand, *der;* **on ~** *(fig.)* alles in allem; ~ **sheet** Bilanz, *die*
(e) (Econ.) ~ **of payments** Zahlungsbilanz, *die;* ~ **of trade** Handelsbilanz, *die*
(f) (remainder) Rest, *der*
2 *v.t.* **(a)** (weigh up) abwägen
(b) (bring into or keep in ~) balancieren; auswuchten ⟨*Rad*⟩
(c) (equal, neutralize) ausgleichen; ~ **each other, be ~d** sich (*Dat.*) die Waage halten

ˈ**balanced** *adj.* ausgewogen; ausgeglichen ⟨*Person, Team, Gemüt*⟩

balcony /ˈbælkənɪ/ *n.* Balkon, *der*

bald /bɔːld/ *adj.* kahl ⟨*Kopf*⟩; kahlköpfig, glatzköpfig ⟨*Person*⟩; **be/go ~:** eine Glatze haben/bekommen

bald: ~**head** *n.* kahlköpfiger *od.* glatzköpfiger Mensch; Kahlkopf, *der* (ugs.); Glatzkopf, *der* (ugs.); ~-ˈ**headed** *adj.* glatzköpfig; kahlköpfig

ˈ**balding** *adj.* mit beginnender Glatze *nachgestellt;* **be ~:** kahl werden

ˈ**baldness** *n.* Kahlheit, *die*

bale /beɪl/ *n.* Ballen, *der*

balk /bɔːlk/ **1** *v.t.* they were ~ed in their plan ihr Plan wurde blockiert
2 *v.i.* sich sträuben (**at** gegen)

Balkan /ˈbɔːlkn/ **1** *adj.* Balkan-
2 *n. pl.* the ~s der Balkan

ball[1] /bɔːl/ *n.* **(a)** Ball, *der;* (Billiards etc., Croquet) Kugel, *die;* **be on the ~** (coll.: be alert) auf Zack sein (ugs.)

(b) (of wool, string, fluff, etc.) Knäuel, *das*

ball[2] *n.* (dance) Ball, *der*

ballad /ˈbæləd/ *n.* Ballade, *die*

ballast /ˈbæləst/ *n.* Ballast, *der*

ball: ~ ˈ**bearing** *n.* Kugellager, *das;* ~**boy** *n.* Balljunge, *der;* ~**cock** *n.* Schwimmer[regel]ventil, *das*

ballerina /bæləˈriːnə/ *n.* Ballerina, *die*

ballet /ˈbæleɪ/ *n.* Ballett, *das;* ~ **dancer** Balletttänzer, *der*/-tänzerin, *die*

ˈ**ball game** *n.* **(a)** Ballspiel, *das*
(b) (Amer.) Baseballspiel, *das;* **a whole new ~** *(fig. coll.)* eine ganz neue Geschichte (ugs.); **a different ~** *(fig. coll.)* eine andere Sache

ballistic /bəˈlɪstɪk/ *adj.* ballistisch; **go ~** *(fig. coll.)* ausrasten (salopp)

balloon /bəˈluːn/ *n.* **(a)** Ballon, *der;* **hot-air ~:** Heißluftballon, *der*
(b) (toy) Luftballon, *der*

ballot /ˈbælət/ *n.* Abstimmung, *die;* [secret] ~: geheime Wahl

ballot: ~ **box** *n.* Wahlurne, *die;* ~ **paper** *n.* Stimmzettel, *der*

ball: ~**park** *n.* (Amer.) Baseballfeld, *das;* **your estimate is not in the right ~park** *(fig.)* mit deiner Schätzung liegst du völlig falsch (ugs.); ~ **pen,** ~**point** ˈ**pen** *ns.* Kugelschreiber, *der;* ~**room** *n.* Tanzsaal, *der*

balls-up /ˈbɔːlzʌp/ *n.* (coarse) Scheiß, *der* (salopp abwertend); **make a ~ of sth.** bei etw. Scheiße bauen (derb)

balm /bɑːm/ *n.* Balsam, *der*

balmy /ˈbɑːmɪ/ *adj.* (mild) mild

balsa /ˈbɔːlsə, ˈbɒlsə/ *n.* ~ [**wood**] Balsaholz, *das*

Baltic /ˈbɔːltɪk/ **1** *pr. n.* Ostsee, *die*
2 *adj.* ~ **Sea** Ostsee, *die*

balustrade /bæləˈstreɪd/ *n.* Balustrade, *die*

bamboo /bæmˈbuː/ *n.* Bambus, *der*

ban /bæn/ **1** *v.t.*, **-nn-** verbieten; ~ **sb. from doing sth.** jmdm. verbieten, etw. zu tun
2 *n.* Verbot, *das*

banal /bəˈnɑːl/ *adj.* banal

banality /bəˈnælɪtɪ/ *n.* Banalität, *die*

banana /bəˈnɑːnə/ *n.* Banane, *die*

baˈnana skin *n.* Bananenschale, *die*

band /bænd/ **1** *n.* **(a)** Band, *das;* **a ~ of light/colour** ein Streifen Licht/Farbe
(b) (range of values) Bandbreite, *die*
(c) (organized group) Gruppe, *die;* (of robbers, outlaws, etc.) Bande, *die*
(d) (Mus.) [Musik]kapelle, *die;* (pop group, jazz ~) Band, *die*
2 *v.i.* ~ **together [with sb.]** sich [mit jmdm.] zusammenschließen

bandage /ˈbændɪdʒ/ **1** *n.* Verband, *der;* (as support) Bandage, *die*
2 *v.t.* verbinden; bandagieren ⟨*verstauchtes] Gelenk usw.*⟩

b. & b. /biː ən ˈbiː/ *abbr.* = **bed & breakfast**

b

bandit /'bændɪt/ *n.* Bandit, *der*

band: ∼**stand** *n.* Musiktribüne, *die;* ∼**wagon** *n.* climb *or* jump on [to] the ∼**wagon** (fig.) auf den fahrenden Zug aufspringen (fig.)

bandy[1] /'bændɪ/ *v.t.* they were ∼ing words/ insults sie stritten sich/beschimpften sich gegenseitig

bandy[2] *adj.* krumm; he is ∼-legged er hat O-Beine (ugs.)

bang /bæŋ/ [1] *v.t.* knallen (ugs.); schlagen; zuknallen (ugs.) ⟨Tür, Fenster, Deckel⟩; ∼ one's head on sth. mit dem Kopf an etw. (*Akk.*) knallen (ugs.)
[2] *v.i.* (strike) ∼ [against sth.] [gegen etw.] knallen (ugs.); ∼ shut ⟨Tür:⟩ zuknallen (ugs.)
[3] *n.* (a) (blow) Schlag, *der*
(b) (noise) Knall, *der*
[4] *adv.* go ∼ ⟨Gewehr, Feuerwerkskörper:⟩ krachen

'banger *n.* (coll.) (a) (sausage) Würstchen, *das*
(b) (firework) Kracher, *der* (ugs.)
(c) (car) Klapperkiste, *die* (ugs.)

bangle /'bæŋgl/ *n.* Armreif, *der*

banish /'bænɪʃ/ *v.t.* verbannen (from aus)

banister /'bænɪstə(r)/ *n.* [Treppen]geländer, *das*

banjo /'bændʒəʊ/ *n., pl.* ∼s *or* ∼es Banjo, *das*

bank[1] /bæŋk/ *n.* (a) (slope) Böschung, *die*
(b) (of river) Ufer, *das*

bank[2] [1] *n.* (Finance) Bank, *die*
[2] *v.i.* ∼ at/with …: ein Konto haben bei …; ∼ on sth. (fig.) auf etw. (*Akk.*) zählen
[3] *v.t.* zur Bank bringen

bank: ∼˙ **account** *n.* Bankkonto, *das;* ∼ **balance** *n.* Kontostand, *der;* ∼ **book** *n.* Sparbuch, *das;* ∼ **card** *n.* Scheckkarte, *die;* ∼ **charges** *n. pl.* Kontoführungskosten *Pl.;* ∼ **clerk** *n.* Bankangestellte, *der/die;* ∼ **draft** *n.* Bankakzept, *das*

'banker *n.* Bankier, *der*

banker's: ∼ **card** ▶ BANK CARD; ∼ **draft** ▶ BANK DRAFT; ∼ **'order** *n.* Bankanweisung, *die*

bank 'holiday *n.* (Brit.) Feiertag, *der*

'banking *n.* Bankwesen, *das*

bank: ∼ **loan** *n.* Bankdarlehen, *das;* take out a ∼ loan bei einer Bank einen Kredit *od.* ein Darlehen aufnehmen; ∼ **manager** *n.* Zweigstellenleiter/-leiterin [einer/der Bank]; ∼**note** *n.* Banknote, *die*

bankrupt /'bæŋkrʌpt/ [1] *n.* Bankrotteur, *der*
[2] *adj.* go ∼: Bankrott machen
[3] *v.t.* Bankrott machen

bankruptcy /'bæŋkrʌptsɪ/ *n.* Konkurs, *der;* Bankrott, *der*

'bank statement *n.* Kontoauszug, *der*

banner /'bænə(r)/ *n.* Banner, *das;* (on two poles) Spruchband, *das*

banns /bænz/ *n. pl.* Aufgebot, *das*

banquet /'bæŋkwɪt/ *n.* Bankett, *das*

bap /bæp/ *n.* ≈ Brötchen, *das*

baptism /'bæptɪzm/ *n.* Taufe, *die*

Baptist /'bæptɪst/ *n.* Baptist, *der*/Baptistin, *die*

baptize /bæp'taɪz/ *v.t.* taufen

bar /bɑː(r)/ [1] *n.* (a) Stange, *die;* (shorter, thinner also) Stab, *der;* (of cage, prison) Gitterstab, *der;* a ∼ of soap ein Stück Seife; a ∼ of chocolate eine Tafel Schokolade
(b) (for refreshment) Bar, *die;* (counter) Theke, *die*
[2] *v.t.*, -rr-: (a) (fasten) verriegeln
(b) ∼ sb.'s way jmdm. den Weg versperren
(c) (prohibit, hinder) verbieten; ∼ sb. from doing sth. jmdn. daran hindern, etw. zu tun
[3] *prep.* abgesehen von; ∼ none ohne Einschränkung

barb /bɑːb/ *n.* Widerhaken, *der*

barbarian /bɑː'beərɪən/ *n.* Barbar, *der*

barbaric /bɑː'bærɪk/ *adj.* barbarisch

barbarity /bɑː'bærɪtɪ/ *n.* Grausamkeit, *die*

barbecue /'bɑːbɪkjuː/ [1] *n.* (a) (party) Grillparty, *die*
(b) (food) Grillgericht, *das;* ∼ sauce Grillsoße, *die;* Barbecuesoße, *die*
[2] *v.t.* grillen

barbed wire /bɑːbd 'waɪə(r)/ *n.* Stacheldraht, *der*

barber /'bɑːbə(r)/ *n.* [Herren]friseur, *der;* ∼'s shop (Brit.) Friseursalon, *der*

barbiturate /bɑː'bɪtjʊrət/ *n.* (Chem.) Barbiturat, *das*

bar: ∼ **chart** *n.* Stabdiagramm, *das;* ∼ **code** *n.* Strichcode, *der*

bare /beə(r)/ [1] *adj.* nackt; (leafless, unfurnished) kahl; (empty) leer; äußerst ⟨Notwendige⟩; do sth. with one's ∼ hands etw. mit den bloßen Händen tun
[2] *v.t.* entblößen ⟨Kopf, Arm, Bein⟩; blecken ⟨Zähne⟩

bare: ∼**faced** /'beəfeɪst/ *adj.* (fig.) unverhüllt; ∼**foot** [1] *adj.* barfüßig; [2] *adv.* barfuß

barely /'beəlɪ/ *adv.* kaum; knapp ⟨vermeiden, entkommen⟩

bargain /'bɑːgɪn/ [1] *n.* (a) (agreement) Abmachung, *die;* into the ∼: darüber hinaus
(b) (thing offered cheap) günstiges Angebot; (thing acquired cheaply) guter Kauf
[2] *v.i.* (a) (discuss) handeln
(b) ∼ for *or* on sth. (expect sth.) mit etw. rechnen

bargain: ∼ **'basement** *n.* Untergeschoss mit Sonderangeboten; ∼ **hunter** *n.* Schnäppchenjäger, *der/*-jägerin, *die;* ∼ **price** *n.* Sonderpreis, *der*

barge /bɑːdʒ/ [1] *n.* Kahn, *der*
[2] *v.i.* ∼ into sb. jmdn. anrempeln; ∼ in (intrude) hineinplatzen/hereinplatzen (ugs.)

baritone /'bærɪtəʊn/ [1] *n.* Bariton, *der*
[2] *adj.* Bariton-

bark¹ /bɑːk/ n. (of tree) Rinde, die

bark² 1 n. (of dog) Bellen, das 2 v.i. bellen; be ~ing up the wrong tree auf dem Holzweg sein

barley /'bɑːlɪ/ n. Gerste, die

bar: ~maid n. (Brit.) Bardame, die; ~**man** /'bɑːmən/ n., pl. ~**men** /'bɑːmən/ Barmann, der

barmy /'bɑːmɪ/ adj. (coll.: crazy) bescheuert (salopp)

barn /bɑːn/ n. (Brit.: for grain etc.) Scheune, die; (Amer.: for animals) Stall, der

barnacle /'bɑːnəkl/ n. Rankenfüßer, der

barn: ~ **dance** n. ≈ Schottische, der; ~**storming** /'bɑːnstɔːmɪŋ/ adj. mitreißend

barometer /bə'rɒmɪtə(r)/ n. Barometer, das

baron /'bærn/ n. Baron, der; Freiherr, der

baroness /'bærənɪs/ n. Baronin, die; Freifrau, die

baroque /bə'rɒk/ 1 n. Barock, das 2 adj. barock

barracks /'bærəks/ n. pl. Kaserne, die

barrage /'bærɑːʒ/ n. (Mil.) Sperrfeuer, das; a ~ of questions ein Bombardement von Fragen

barrel /'bærl/ n. (a) Fass, das (b) (of gun) Lauf, der

barren /'bærn/ adj. unfruchtbar

barricade /bærɪ'keɪd/ 1 n. Barrikade, die 2 v.t. verbarrikadieren

barrier /'bærɪə(r)/ n. Barriere, die; (at level crossing etc.) Schranke, die

barring /'bɑːrɪŋ/ prep. außer im Falle (+ Gen.)

barrister /'bærɪstə(r)/ n. (Brit.) ~[-at-law] Barrister, der; ≈ [Rechts]anwalt/-anwältin vor höheren Gerichten

barrow /'bærəʊ/ n. (a) Karre, die; Karren, der (b) ▸ WHEELBARROW

barter /'bɑːtə(r)/ 1 v.t. [ein]tauschen; ~ sth. for sth. [else] etw. für od. gegen etw. [anderes] [ein]tauschen 2 v.i. Tauschhandel treiben 3 n. Tauschhandel, der

base /beɪs/ 1 n. (a) (of lamp, mountain) Fuß, der; (of cupboard, statue) Sockel, der; (fig.: support) Basis, die (b) (Mil.) Basis, die; Stützpunkt, der 2 v.t. (a) be ~d on sth. sich auf etw. (Akk.) gründen; ~ sth. on sth. etw. auf etw. (Dat.) aufbauen (b) in pass. be ~d in Paris (permanently) in Paris sitzen; (temporarily) in Paris sein

base: ~**ball** n. Baseball, der; ~**line** n. Grundlinie, die

basement /'beɪsmənt/ n. Untergeschoss, das; a ~ flat eine Kellerwohnung

'base rate n. (Finance) Eckzins, der

bash /bæʃ/ v.t. [heftig] schlagen

bashful /'bæʃfl/ adj. schüchtern

basic /'beɪsɪk/ adj. grundlegend; Grund⟨prinzip, -bestandteil, -lohn, -gehalt usw.⟩; Haupt⟨problem, -grund, -sache⟩; ~ to sth. wesentlich für etw. sein

basically /'beɪsɪkəlɪ/ adv. im Grunde; grundsätzlich ⟨übereinstimmen⟩; (mainly) hauptsächlich

basil /'bæzɪl/ n. Basilikum, das

basin /'beɪsn/ n. (a) Becken, das; (wash~) Waschbecken, das; (bowl) Schüssel, die (b) (of river) Becken, das

basis /'beɪsɪs/ n., pl. bases /'beɪsiːz/ Basis, die; Grundlage, die

bask /bɑːsk/ v.i. sich [wohlig] wärmen

basket /'bɑːskɪt/ n. Korb, der

'basketball n. Basketball, der

Basle /bɑːl/ pr. n. Basel (das)

bass /beɪs/ 1 n. (a) Bass, der (b) (coll.) (double ~) [Kontra]bass, der; (~ guitar) Bass, der 2 adj. Bass-

bass gui'tar n. Bassgitarre, die

bassoon /bə'suːn/ n. Fagott, das

'bass player n. Bassist, der/Bassistin, die

bastard /'bɑːstəd/ 1 adj. unehelich 2 n. (a) uneheliches Kind (b) (sl.: disliked person) Schweinehund, der (derb)

baste /beɪst/ v.t. [mit Fett] begießen

bastion /'bæstɪən/ n. Bastei, die

bat¹ /bæt/ n. (Zool.) Fledermaus, die

bat² 1 n. (Sport) Schlagholz, das; (for table tennis) Schläger, der; do sth. off one's own ~ (fig.) etw. auf eigene Faust tun 2 v.t., -tt- schlagen

bat³ v.t. not ~ an eyelid nicht mit der Wimper zucken

batch /bætʃ/ n. (a) (of loaves) Schub, der (b) (of people) Gruppe, die; (of books, papers) Stapel, der

batch: ~ **file** n. (Comp.) Stapeldatei, die; ~ '**processing** n. (Comp.) Schub-, Stapelverarbeitung, die

bated /'beɪtɪd/ v.t. with ~ breath mit angehaltenem Atem

bath /bɑːθ/ 1 n., pl. ~s /bɑːðz/ (a) Bad, das; have od. take a ~: ein Bad nehmen (b) (tub) Badewanne, die; room with ~: Zimmer mit Bad (c) usu. in pl. (building) Bad, das 2 v.t. & i. baden

'bath cubes n. pl. Badesalz, das

bathe /beɪð/ v.t. & i. baden

bather /'beɪðə(r)/ n. Badende, der/die

bathing /'beɪðɪŋ/ n. Baden, das

bathing: ~ **beach** n. Badestrand, der; ~ **costume,** ~ **suit** ns. Badeanzug, der; ~ **trunks** n. pl. Badehose, die

bath: ~ **mat** n. Bademattе, die; ~**robe** n. Bademantel, der; ~**room** n. Badezimmer,

das; ~ **salts** *n. pl.* Badesalz, *das;*
~ **towel** *n.* Badetuch, *das;* ~**tub** ▶ BATH
1B; ~**water** *n.* Badewasser, *das*

baton /'bætn/ *n.* **(a)** (truncheon) Schlagstock,
der
(b) (Mus.) Taktstock, *der*

batsman /'bætsmən/ *n., pl.* **batsmen**
/'bætsmən/ Schlagmann, *der*

battalion /bə'tæljən/ *n.* Bataillon, *das*

batter¹ /'bætə(r)/ *v.t.* (strike) einschlagen
auf (+ *Akk.*)

batter² *n.* (Cookery) [Back]teig, *der*

battery /'bætərɪ/ *n.* Batterie, *die*

battery: ~ **charger** *n.* Batterieladegerät,
das; ~ '**chicken** *n.* Batteriehuhn, *das;*
~ '**farming** *n.* Batteriehaltung, *die;*
~ '**hen** *n.* Batteriehuhn, *das;*
~**-operated** *adj.* batteriebetrieben

battle /'bætl/ ① *n.* Schlacht, *die;* (fig.)
Kampf, *der*
② *v.i.* kämpfen

battle: ~**axe** *n.* (coll.: woman)
Schreckschraube, *die* (ugs.); ~**field,**
~**ground** *ns.* Schlachtfeld, *das*

battlements /'bætlmənts/ *n. pl.* Zinnen
Pl.

'**battleship** *n.* Schlachtschiff, *das*

batty /'bætɪ/ *adj.* (coll.) bekloppt (salopp)

bauble /'bɔːbl/ *n.* Flitter, *der*

baulk ▶ BALK

Bavaria /bə'veərɪə/ *pr. n.* Bayern *(das)*

Bavarian /bə'veərɪən/ ① *adj.* bay[e]risch;
sb. is ~: jmd. ist Bayer/Bayerin
② *n.* Bayer, *der*/Bayerin, *die*

bawdy /'bɔːdɪ/ *adj.* zweideutig; (stronger)
obszön

bay¹ /beɪ/ *n.* (of sea) Bucht, *die*

bay² *n.* **(a)** (space in room) Erker, *der*
(b) [parking] ~: Stellplatz, *der*

bay³ *n.* **hold** *or* **keep sb./sth. at** ~: sich
(Dat.) jmdn./etw. vom Leib halten

'**bayleaf** *n.* Lorbeerblatt, *das*

bayonet /'beɪənɪt/ *n.* Bajonett, *das*

bayonet: ~ **fitting** *n.* Bajonettfassung,
die; ~ **plug** *n.* Stecker mit
Bajonettverschluss *od.* -fassung; ~ **socket**
n. Steckdose mit Bajonettfassung

bay 'window *n.* Erkerfenster, *das*

bazaar /bə'zɑː(r)/ *n.* Basar, *der*

BBC *abbr.* = **British Broadcasting
Corporation** BBC, *die*

BC *abbr.* = **before Christ** v.Chr.

be /biː/ *v., pres. t.* **I am** /əm, *stressed* æm/, **he
is** /ɪz/, **we are** /ə(r), *stressed* ɑː(r)/; *p.t.* **I was**
/wəz, *stressed* wɒz/, **we were** /wə(r), *stressed*
wɜː(r)/; *pres.p.* **being** /'biːɪŋ/; *p.p.* **been** /bɪn,
stressed biːn/ ① **copula (a)** sein; **she is a
mother/an Italian/a teacher** sie ist Mutter/
Italienerin/Lehrerin; **be sensible!** sei
vernünftig!; **be ill/unwell** krank sein/sich
nicht wohl fühlen; **I am well** es geht mir gut;
I am hot mir ist heiß; **I am freezing** mich

friert es; **how are you/is she?** wie gehts
(ugs.)/geht es ihr?; **it is the 5th today** heute
haben wir den Fünften; **who's that?** wer ist
das?; **if I were you** an deiner Stelle; **it's hers**
es ist ihrs
(b) (cost) kosten; **how much are the eggs?**
was kosten die Eier?; **two times three is six,
two threes are six** zweimal drei ist *od.* sind
sechs
(c) (constitute) bilden
② *v.i.* **(a)** (exist) [vorhanden] sein; **there is/
are ...:** es gibt ...; **for the time being**
vorläufig; **be that as it may** wie dem auch
sei
(b) (remain) bleiben; **I shan't be a moment** ich
komme sofort; **let it be** lass es sein; **let him/
her be** lass ihn/sie in Ruhe
(c) (happen) stattfinden; sein
(d) (go, come) **be off with you!** geh/geht!; **I'm
off home** ich gehe jetzt nach Hause; **she's
from Australia** sie stammt *od.* ist aus
Australien
(e) (go or come on visit) sein; **have you [ever]
been to London?** bist du schon einmal in
London gewesen?; **has anyone been?** ist
jemand da gewesen?
③ *v. aux.* **(a)** *forming passive* werden; **the
child was found** das Kind wurde gefunden;
German is spoken here hier wird Deutsch
gesprochen
(b) *forming continuous tenses, active* **he is
reading** er liest [gerade]; **I am leaving
tomorrow** ich reise morgen [ab]; **the train
was departing when I got there** der Zug fuhr
gerade ab, als ich ankam
(c) *forming continuous tenses, passive* **the
house is/was being built** das Haus wird/
wurde [gerade] gebaut
(d) *expr. arrangement, obligation* **be to**
sollen; **I am to go/to inform you** ich soll
gehen/Sie unterrichten
(e) *expr. destiny* **they were never to meet
again** sie sollten sich nie wieder treffen
(f) *expr. condition* **if I were to tell you that
...:** wenn ich dir sagen würde, dass ...
④ **bride-/husband-to-be** zukünftige Braut/
zukünftiger Ehemann

beach /biːtʃ/ *n.* Strand, *der;* **on the** ~: am
Strand; ~ **hat/holiday/shoe** Strandhut/
-urlaub/-schuh, *der*

beach: ~**ball** *n.* Wasserball, *der;* ~**wear**
n. Strandkleidung, *die*

beacon /'biːkn/ *n.* Leuchtfeuer, *das;* (Naut.)
Leuchtbake, *die*

bead /biːd/ *n.* Perle, *die;* ~**s** Perlen *Pl.;*
Perlenkette, *die;* ~**s of dew/sweat** Tau-/
Schweißtropfen

beady /'biːdɪ/ *adj.* ~ **eyes** Knopfaugen *Pl.*

beak /biːk/ *n.* Schnabel, *der*

beaker /'biːkə(r)/ *n.* Becher, *der*

beam /biːm/ ① *n.* **(a)** (timber etc.) Balken,
der
(b) (ray etc.) [Licht]strahl, *der*
② *v.i.* **(a)** (shine) strahlen; glänzen ⋯⋗

(b) (smile) strahlen; ~ **at sb.** jmdn. anstrahlen

bean /biːn/ *n.* Bohne, *die;* **full of** ~**s** (fig. coll.) putzmunter (ugs.)

bean: ~**bag** *n.* (a) *mit Bohnen gefülltes Säckchen zum Spielen;* (b) (cushion) Knautschsessel, *der;* ~ **curd** *n.* Soja[bohnen]quark, *der;* ~**pole** *n.* (lit. or fig.) Bohnenstange, *die;* ~**sprout** *n.* Sojabohnenkeim, *der*

bear[1] /beə(r)/ *n.* Bär, *der*

bear[2] 1 *v.t.,* bore /bɔː(r)/, borne /bɔːn/ (a) tragen; aufweisen ⟨*Spuren, Ähnlichkeit*⟩; tragen, führen ⟨*Namen, Titel*⟩; ~ **some/little relation to sth.** einen gewissen/wenig Bezug zu etw. haben
(b) (endure, tolerate) ertragen ⟨*Schmerz, Kummer*⟩; *with neg.* ertragen, aushalten ⟨*Schmerz*⟩; ausstehen ⟨*Geruch, Lärm*⟩
(c) (be fit for) vertragen; **it will not** ~ **scrutiny** es hält einer Überprüfung nicht stand; **it does not** ~ **thinking about** daran darf man gar nicht denken
(d) (give birth to) gebären ⟨*Kind, Junges*⟩
2 *v.i.,* bore, borne: ~ **left** ⟨*Person:*⟩ sich links halten; **the path** ~**s to the left** der Weg führt nach links
■ **bear 'out** *v.t.* (fig.) bestätigen ⟨*Bericht, Erklärung*⟩; ~ **sb. out** jmdm. Recht geben
■ **bear 'with** *v.t.* Nachsicht haben mit

bearable /'beərəbl/ *adj.* erträglich

beard /bɪəd/ *n.* Bart, *der*

bearded *adj.* bärtig. **be** ~: einen Bart haben

bearer *n.* (carrier) Träger, *der*/Trägerin, *die;* (of message, cheque) Überbringer, *der*/Überbringerin, *die*

bear hug *n.* kräftige Umarmung

bearing *n.* (a) (behaviour) Verhalten, *das*
(b) (relation) Bezug, *der;* **have some/no** ~ **on sth.** relevant/irrelevant für etw. sein
(c) (Mech. Engin.) Lager, *das*
(d) (compass ~) Position, *die;* **take a compass** ~: den Kompasskurs feststellen; **get one's** ~**s** sich orientieren; (fig.) sich zurechtfinden

beast /biːst/ *n.* Tier, *das;* (fig.: brutal person) Bestie, *die*

beastly *adj., adv.* (coll.) scheußlich

beat /biːt/ 1 *v.t.,* **beat, beaten** /'biːtn/ schlagen; klopfen ⟨*Teppich*⟩; (surpass) brechen ⟨*Rekord*⟩; **hard to** ~: schwer zu schlagen; **it** ~**s me how/why ...:** es ist mir ein Rätsel wie/warum ...; ~ **time** den Takt schlagen; ~ **it!** (coll.) hau ab! (ugs.); *see also* BEATEN 2
2 *v.i.,* **beat, beaten** schlagen (**on** auf + *Akk.*); ⟨*Regen, Hagel:*⟩ prasseln (**against** gegen)
3 *n.* (a) (stroke, throbbing) Schlagen, *das;* (*Mus.*) (rhythm) Takt, *der;* (single ~) Schlag, *der*
(b) (of policeman) Runde, *die*
■ **beat 'off** *v.t.* abwehren ⟨*Angriff*⟩
■ **beat 'up** *v.t.* zusammenschlagen ⟨*Person*⟩

beaten /'biːtn/ 1 ▶ BEAT 1, 2
2 *adj.* (a) **off the** ~ **track** weit abgelegen

(b) gehämmert ⟨*Silber, Gold*⟩

beating *n.* (a) (punishment) **a** ~: Schläge *Pl.;* Prügel *Pl.*
(b) (defeat) Niederlage, *die*
(c) **take some/a lot of** ~: nicht leicht zu übertreffen sein

beat-up *adj.* (coll.) ramponiert (ugs.)

beautician /bjuːˈtɪʃn/ *n.* Kosmetiker, *der*/Kosmetikerin, *die*

beautiful /'bjuːtɪfl/ *adj.* schön; wunderschön ⟨*Augen, Aussicht, Morgen*⟩

beautify /'bjuːtɪfaɪ/ *v.t.* verschönern

beauty /'bjuːtɪ/ *n.* Schönheit, *die;* (beautiful feature) Schöne, *das;* **the** ~ **of it** das Schöne daran

beauty: ~ **competition,** ~ **contest** *ns.* Schönheitswettbewerb, *der;* ~ **parlour** ▶ ~ SALON; ~ **queen** *n.* Schönheitskönigin, *die;* ~ **salon** *n.* Kosmetiksalon, *der;* ~ **spot** *n.* Schönheitsfleck, *der;* (place) schönes Fleckchen [Erde]; ~ **treatment** *n.* Schönheitsbehandlung, *die*

beaver /'biːvə(r)/ *n.* Biber, *der*

became ▶ BECOME

because /bɪˈkɒz/ 1 *conj.* weil
2 *adv.* ~ **of** wegen (+ *Gen.*)

beckon /'bekn/ *v.t. & i.* winken (**to sb.** jmdm.); (fig.) locken

become /bɪˈkʌm/ 1 *copula,* **became** /bɪˈkeɪm/, **become** werden; ~ **a politician** Politiker werden; ~ **a nuisance/rule** zu einer Plage/zur Regel werden
2 *v.i.,* **became, become** werden; **what has** ~ **of him?** was ist aus ihm geworden?
3 *v.t.,* **became, become** (suit) ~ **sb.** jmdm. stehen

becoming /bɪˈkʌmɪŋ/ *adj.* (a) (fitting) schicklich (geh.)
(b) (flattering) vorteilhaft ⟨*Hut, Kleid, Frisur*⟩

bed /bed/ *n.* (a) Bett, *das;* (without bedstead) Lager, *das;* **in** ~: im Bett; ~ **and breakfast** Zimmer mit Frühstück; **get out of/into** ~: aufstehen/ins Bett gehen; **go to** ~: ins Bett gehen; **put sb. to** ~: jmdn. ins Bett bringen; **make the** ~: das Bett machen
(b) (flat base) Unterlage, *die;* (of machine) Bett, *das*
(c) (in garden) Beet, *das*
(d) (of sea, lake) Grund, *der;* (of river) Bett, *das*

bedclothes *n. pl.* Bettzeug, *das*

bedding /'bedɪŋ/ *n.* Matratze und Bettzeug

bedding plant *n.* Freilandpflanze, *die*

bedlam /'bedləm/ *n., no indef. art.* Tumult, *der*

bed: ~**linen** *n.* Bettwäsche, *die;* ~**pan** *n.* Bettpfanne, *die*

bedraggled /bɪˈdrægld/ *adj.* (soaked) durchnässt; (with mud) verdreckt

bed: ~**ridden** *adj.* bettlägerig; ~**room** *n.* Schlafzimmer, *das;* ~ **set'tee** *n.* Bettcouch, *die;* ~**side** *n.* Seite des Bettes, *die;* ~**side table/lamp** Nachttisch, *der*/Nachttischlampe, *die;* ~**sit,** ~**sitter** *ns.* (coll.)

Wohnschlafzimmer, *das;* ~**spread** *n.*
Tagesdecke, *die;* ~**stead** *n.* Bettgestell,
das; ~**time** *n.* Schlafenszeit, *die;* **at** ~**time**
vor dem Zubettgehen; **a** ~**time story** eine
Gutenachtgeschichte; ~**-wetting** *n.*
Bettnässen, *das*

bee /biː/ *n.* Biene, *die*

beech /biːtʃ/ *n.* Buche, *die*

beef /biːf/ **1** *n.* **(a)** Rindfleisch, *das*
(b) (coll.: muscles) Muskeln *Pl.*
2 *v.t.* ~ **up** stärken

beef: ~**burger** *n.* Beefburger, *der;*
~**cake** *n.* (Amer. coll.) Muskeln *Pl.;* Bizeps,
der (ugs.)

bee: ~**hive** *n.* Bienenstock, *der;*
~**-keeper** *n.* Imker, *der*/Imkerin, *die;*
~**-keeping** *n.* Imkerei, *die;* ~**line** *n.*
make a ~**line for sth./sb.** schnurstracks auf
etw./jmdn. zustürzen

been ▶ BE

beep /biːp/ **1** *n.* Piepton, *der;* (of car horn)
Tuten, *das*
2 *v.i.* piepen; ⟨Signalhorn:⟩ hupen
3 *v.t.* (esp. Amer.) ▶ BLEEP 3

beeper /ˈbiːpə(r)/ *n.* Piepser, *der*

beer /bɪə(r)/ *n.* Bier, *das*

beer: ~ **barrel** *n.* Bierfass, *das;* ~ **belly**
n. (coll.) Bierbauch, *der* (ugs.); ~ **bottle** *n.*
Bierflasche, *die;* ~ **can** *n.* Bierdose, *die;*
~ **cellar** *n.* Bierkeller, *der;* ~ **drinker** *n.*
Biertrinker, *der;* ~ **garden** *n.* Biergarten,
der; ~ **glass** *n.* Bierglas, *das;* ~ **mat** *n.*
Bierdeckel, *der;* Bieruntersetzer, *der;*
~ **mug** *n.* Bierkrug, *der*

beet /biːt/ *n.* Rübe, *die*

beetle /ˈbiːtl/ *n.* Käfer, *der*

'**beetroot** *n.* rote Beete *od.* Rübe

before /bɪˈfɔː(r)/ **1** *adv.* **(a)** (of time) vorher;
(already) schon; **the day** ~: am Tag zuvor;
never ~: noch nie
(b) (ahead in position) vor[aus]
2 *prep.* (of time; position) vor (+ *Dat.*);
(direction) vor (+ *Akk.*); **the day** ~ **yesterday**
vorgestern; ~ **now/then** früher/vorher;
~ **Christ** vor Christus; ~ **leaving, he phoned**
bevor er wegging, rief er an
3 *conj.* bevor

be'forehand *adv.* vorher; (in anticipation) im
Voraus

befriend /bɪˈfrend/ *v.t.* **(a)** (act as a friend to)
sich anfreunden mit
(b) (help) sich annehmen (+ *Gen.*)

beg /beg/ **1** *v.t.,* **-gg-:** **(a)** betteln um
(b) (ask earnestly for) ~ **sth.** um etw. bitten
2 *v.i.,* **-gg-** betteln (**for** um)

began ▶ BEGIN

beggar /ˈbegə(r)/ *n.* **(a)** Bettler, *der*/
Bettlerin, *die*
(b) (coll.) **poor** ~: armer Teufel

begin /bɪˈgɪn/ **1** *v.t.,* **-nn-,** **began** /bɪˈgæn/,
begun /bɪˈgʌn/ ~ **sth.** [mit] etw. beginnen;
~ **doing** *or* **to do sth.** anfangen *od.*
beginnen, etw. zu tun

2 *v.i.,* **-nn-,** **began, begun** anfangen;
~ **[up]on sth.** etw. anfangen

be'ginner *n.* Anfänger, *der*/Anfängerin, *die*

be'ginning *n.* Anfang, *der;* **at** *or* **in the** ~:
am Anfang; **at the** ~ **of February/the month**
Anfang Februar/des Monats; **from the** ~:
von Anfang an

begrudge /bɪˈgrʌdʒ/ *v.t.* ~ **sb. sth.** jmdm.
etw. missgönnen; ~ **doing sth.** etw. ungern
tun

begun ▶ BEGIN

behalf /bɪˈhɑːf/ *n.* **on** *or* (Amer.) **in** ~ **of sb./
sth.** für jmdn./etw.; (more formally) im Namen
von jmdm./etw.

behave /bɪˈheɪv/ *v.i.* sich verhalten;
sich benehmen; **well-/ill-** *or* **badly** ~**d** brav/
ungezogen
2 *v. refl.* ~ **oneself** sich benehmen

behaviour /bɪˈheɪvjə(r)/ *n.* Verhalten, *das*

behead /bɪˈhed/ *v.t.* enthaupten

behind /bɪˈhaɪnd/ **1** *adv.* hinten; (further
back) **be miles** ~: kilometerweit
zurückliegen; **stay** ~: dableiben; **leave sb./
sth.** ~: jmdn./etw. zurücklassen; **fall** ~:
zurückbleiben; (fig.) in Rückstand geraten;
be/get ~ **with one's payments/rent** mit
seinen Zahlungen/der Miete im Rückstand
sein/in Rückstand geraten
2 *prep.* **(a)** hinter (+ *Dat.*); **one** ~ **the other**
hintereinander
(b) (towards rear of) hinter (+ *Akk.*)

beige /beɪʒ/ **1** *n.* Beige, *das*
2 *adj.* beige

being /ˈbiːɪŋ/ *n.* **(a)** (existence) Dasein, *das;*
in ~: bestehend; **come into** ~: entstehen
(b) (person etc.) Wesen, *das*

belated /bɪˈleɪtɪd/ *adj.,* **be'latedly** *adv.*
verspätet

belch /beltʃ/ **1** *v.i.* heftig aufstoßen;
rülpsen (ugs.)
2 *n.* Rülpser, *der* (ugs.)

beleaguer /bɪˈliːgə(r)/ *v.t.* (lit. or fig.)
belagern

belfry /ˈbelfrɪ/ *n.* Glockenturm, *der*

Belgian /ˈbeldʒən/ **1** *adj.* belgisch; **sb. is**
~: jmd. ist Belgier/Belgierin
2 *n.* Belgier, *der*/Belgierin, *die*

Belgium /ˈbeldʒəm/ *pr. n.* Belgien (*das*)

belie /bɪˈlaɪ/ *v.t.,* **belying** /bɪˈlaɪɪŋ/
hinwegtäuschen über ⟨Tatsachen, wahren
Zustand⟩; nicht erfüllen ⟨Versprechen⟩; nicht
entsprechen ⟨Vorstellung (Dat.)⟩

belief /bɪˈliːf/ *n.* **(a)** Glaube, *der* (in an
+ *Akk.*); **in the** ~ **that ...:** in der
Überzeugung, dass ...
(b) (Relig.) Glaube[n], *der*

believable /bɪˈliːvəbl/ *adj.* glaubhaft

believe /bɪˈliːv/ **1** *v.i.* glauben (**in an**
+ *Dat.*); (have faith) glauben (**in an** + *Akk.*)
⟨Gott, Himmel usw.⟩; **I** ~ **so/not** ich glaube
schon/nicht

2 *v.t.* glauben; ~ sb. jmdm. glauben; **I don't ~ you** das glaube ich dir nicht; **make ~ that ...:** so tun, als ob ...

believer /brˈliːvə(r)/ *n.* (a) Gläubige, *der/die* (b) **be a great** *or* **firm ~ in sth.** viel von etw. halten

Belisha beacon /bəliˌʃə ˈbiːkn/ *n.* (Brit.) *gelbes Blinklicht an Zebrastreifen*

belittle /brˈlɪtl/ *v.t.* herabsetzen

bell /bel/ *n.* Glocke, *die;* (door~) Klingel, *die*

belligerent /brˈlɪdʒərənt/ *adj.* Krieg führend ⟨Nation⟩; streitlustig ⟨Person⟩

bellow /ˈbeləʊ/ 1 *v.i.* brüllen
2 *v.t.* ~ [out] brüllen ⟨Befehl⟩

bellows /ˈbeləʊz/ *n. pl.* Blasebalg, *der*

bell: ~-ringer *n.* Glöckner, *der;* **~-ringing** *n.* Glockenläuten, *das*

belly /ˈbelɪ/ *n.* Bauch, *der*

belly: ~ache *n.* Bauchschmerzen *Pl.;* **~ button** *n.* (coll.) Bauchnabel, *der;* **~ dance** *n.* Bauchtanz, *der*

belong /brˈlɒŋ/ *v.i.* ~ **to sb./sth.** jmdm./zu etw. gehören; ~ **to a club** einem Verein angehören; **where does this ~?** wo gehört das hin?

be'longings *n. pl.* Habe, *die;* Sachen *Pl.;* **personal ~:** persönlicher Besitz; persönliches Eigentum

beloved /brˈlʌvɪd/ 1 *adj.* geliebt
2 *n.* Geliebte, *der/die*

below /brˈləʊ/ 1 *adv.* (a) (position) unten; (lower down) darunter; **from ~:** von unten [herauf]
(b) (direction) nach unten; hinunter
2 *prep.* unter (*position: + Dat.; direction: + Akk.*)

belt /belt/ *n.* Gürtel, *der;* (for tools, weapons, ammunition) Gurt, *der;* (of trees) Streifen, *der*
■ **belt along** *v.i.* (coll.) rasen (ugs.)
■ **belt 'up** *v.i.* (Brit. coll.) die Klappe halten (salopp)

bemused /brˈmjuːzd/ *adj.* verwirrt

bench /bentʃ/ *n.* Bank, *die;* (work table) Werkbank, *die*

bench: ~mark *n.* Höhenmarke, *die;* (fig.) Maßstab, *der;* Fixpunkt, *der;* **~marking** *n.* Benchmarking, *das* (fachspr.); Leistungsvergleich, *der;*

bend /bend/ 1 *n.* Beuge, *die;* (in road) Kurve, *die*
2 *v.t.,* bent /bent/ biegen; beugen ⟨Arm, Knie⟩; anwinkeln ⟨Bein⟩
3 *v.i.,* bent sich biegen; (bow) sich bücken
■ **bend 'down** *v.i.* sich bücken
■ **bend 'over** *v.i.* sich nach vorn beugen

beneath /brˈniːθ/ *prep.* (a) (unworthy of) ~ **sb.,** ~ **sb.'s dignity** unter jmds. Würde (*Dat.*)
(b) (arch./literary: under) unter (+ *Dat.*)

benefactor /ˈbenɪfæktə(r)/ *n.* Wohltäter, *der;* (patron) Gönner, *der*

beneficial /benɪˈfɪʃl/ *adj.* nützlich; vorteilhaft ⟨Einfluss⟩

benefit /ˈbenɪfɪt/ 1 *n.* (a) Vorteil, *der;* **be of ~ to sb./sth.** jmdm./einer Sache von Nutzen sein; **have the ~ of** den Vorteil (+ *Gen.*) haben; **with the ~ of** mit Hilfe (+ *Gen.*); **for sb.'s ~:** in jmds. Interesse (*Dat.*)
(b) (allowance) Beihilfe, *die;* **unemployment ~:** Arbeitslosenunterstützung, *die*
2 *v.t.* nützen (+ *Dat.*)
3 *v.i.* ~ **by/from sth.** von etw. profitieren

benevolent /brˈnevələnt/ *adj.* (a) gütig (b) wohltätig ⟨Institution, Verein⟩

benign /brˈnaɪn/ *adj.* gütig; (Med.) gutartig

bent /bent/ 1 ▶ BEND 2, 3
2 *n.* (liking) Neigung, *die* (**for** zu)
3 (a) *adj.* krumm
(b) (Brit. sl.: corrupt) link (salopp)

bequeath /brˈkwiːð/ *v.t.* ~ **sth. to sb.** jmdm. etw. hinterlassen

bequest /brˈkwest/ *n.* Legat, *das* (**to** an + *Akk.*)

bereaved /brˈriːvd/ *n.* **the ~:** der/die Hinterbliebene/die Hinterbliebenen

bereavement /brˈriːvmənt/ *n.* Trauerfall, *der*

beret /ˈbereɪ/ *n.* Baskenmütze, *die*

Berlin /bɜːˈlɪn/ *pr. n.* Berlin (*das*)

Berne /bɜːn/ *pr. n.* Bern (*das*)

berry /ˈberɪ/ *n.* Beere, *die*

berserk /bəˈsɜːk/ *adj.* rasend; **go ~:** durchdrehen (ugs.)

berth /bɜːθ/ *n.* (for ship) Liegeplatz, *der;* (sleeping place) (in ship) Koje, *die;* (in train) Schlafwagenbett, *das*

beside /brˈsaɪd/ *prep.* (a) neben (+ *Dat.*); ~ **the sea/lake** am Meer/See
(b) **be ~ the point** nichts damit zu tun haben
(c) ~ **oneself** außer sich

besides /brˈsaɪdz/ 1 *adv.* außerdem
2 *prep.* außer

besiege /brˈsiːdʒ/ *v.t.* belagern

besotted /brˈsɒtɪd/ *adj.* **be ~ by** *or* **with sb.** in jmdn. vernarrt sein

bespectacled /brˈspektəkld/ *adj.* bebrillt

best /best/ 1 *adj.* best...; **the ~ part of an hour** fast eine ganze Stunde
2 *adv.* am besten
3 *n.* **the ~:** der/die/das Beste; **do one's ~:** sein Bestes tun; **make the ~ of it** das Beste daraus machen; **at ~:** bestenfalls

best: ~-before date *n.* Mindesthaltbarkeitsdatum, *das;* ~ **'friend** *n.* bester Freund/beste Freundin; **be ~ friends with sb.** sehr gut mit jmdm. befreundet sein; ~ **'man** *n.* Trauzeuge, *der* (des Bräutigams); ~ **'seller** *n.* Bestseller, *der;* (author) Bestsellerautor, *der;* **~-selling** *attrib. adj.* meistverkauft ⟨Schallplatte⟩; **~-selling book/novel** Bestseller, *der;* **a ~-selling author/novelist** ein Bestsellerautor

bet /bet/ 1 *v.t. & i.,* -tt-, ~ *or* ~ted wetten; **I ~ him £10** ich habe mit ihm um 10 Pfund gewettet; ~ **on sth.** auf etw. (*Akk.*) setzen

2 *n.* Wette, *die;* (fig. coll.) Tipp, *der*
beta-blocker /'biːtəblɒkə(r)/ *n.* (Med.)
Beta[rezeptoren]blocker, *der*
betray /bɪ'treɪ/ *v.t.* verraten (**to** an + *Akk.*)
betrayal /bɪ'treɪəl/ *n.* Verrat, *der*
better /'betə(r)/ 1 *adj.* besser; ~ **and** ~:
immer besser; **be much** ~ (recovered) sich
viel besser fühlen; **get** ~ (recover) besser
werden; **the** ~ **part of sth.** der größte Teil
einer Sache (*Gen.*)
2 *adv.* besser; ~ **'off** (financially) [finanziell]
besser gestellt; **be** ~ **off than sb.** besser als
jmd. dran sein (ugs.); **be** ~ **off without sb./
sth.** ohne jmdn./etw. besser dran sein; **I'd**
~ **be off now** ich gehe jetzt besser
3 *n.* **get the** ~ **of sb./sth.** jmdn./etw.
unterkriegen (ugs.); **a change for the** ~: eine
vorteilhafte Veränderung
4 *v.t.* übertreffen
better-'quality *attrib. adj.* qualitativ
besser
'betting shop *n.* Wettbüro, *das*
between /bɪ'twiːn/ 1 *prep.* (a) [in] ~:
zwischen (*position:* + *Dat.; direction:* + *Akk.*)
(b) (amongst) unter (+ *Dat.*); ~ **ourselves,**
~ **you and me** unter uns (*Dat.*) gesagt
(c) ~ **them/us** (by joint action of) gemeinsam;
~ **us we had 40p** wir hatten zusammen 40
Pence
2 *adv.* [in] ~: dazwischen; (in time)
zwischendurch
beverage /'bevərɪdʒ/ *n.* Getränk, *das*
beware /bɪ'weə(r)/ *v.t. & i.; only in imper.
and inf.* ~ **[of]** sb./sth. sich vor jmdm./etw.
in Acht nehmen; ~ **of doing sth.** sich davor
hüten, etw. zu tun; '~ **of the dog'** „Vorsicht,
bissiger Hund!"
bewilder /bɪ'wɪldə(r)/ *v.t.* verwirren
be'wildering *adj.* verwirrend
be'wilderment *n.* Verwirrung, *die*
bewitch /bɪ'wɪtʃ/ *v.t.* verzaubern; (fig.)
bezaubern
beyond /bɪ'jɒnd/ 1 *adv.* (a) (in space)
jenseits; (on other side of wall, mountain range,
etc.) dahinter
(b) (in time) darüber hinaus
(c) (in addition) außerdem
2 *prep.* (a) (at far side of) jenseits (+ *Gen.*)
(b) (later than) nach
(c) (out of reach or comprehension or range) über
... (+ *Akk.*) hinaus
bias /'baɪəs/ 1 *n.* Voreingenommenheit, *die*
2 *v.t.*, **-s-** *or* **-ss-** beeinflussen; **be** ~**ed in
favour of/against sth./sb.** für etw./jmdn.
eingestellt sein/gegen etw./jmdn.
voreingenommen sein
bib /bɪb/ *n.* Lätzchen, *das*
Bible /'baɪbl/ *n.* Bibel, *die*
biblical /'bɪblɪkl/ *adj.* biblisch
bibliography /bɪblɪ'ɒɡrəfɪ/ *n.*
Bibliographie, *die*
biceps /'baɪseps/ *n.* Bizeps, *der*
bicker /'bɪkə(r)/ *v.i.* sich zanken

bicycle /'baɪsɪkl/ 1 *n.* Fahrrad, *das;*
attrib. Fahrrad-
2 *v.i.* Rad fahren
bicycle: ~ **clip** *n.* Hosenklammer, *die;*
~ **courier** *n.* Fahrradkurier, *der/*
-kurierin, *die;* ~ **lane** *n.* (reserved for cyclists)
Radfahrstreifen, *der;* (with priority for cyclists)
Schutzstreifen, *der* [für Radfahrer]; ~ **path**
n. [Fahr]radweg, *der*
bid /bɪd/ 1 *v.t.* (a) **-dd-, bid** (at auction)
bieten
(b) **-dd-, bade** /bæd, beɪd/ *or* **bid, bidden**
/'bɪdn/ *or* **bid:** ~ **sb. welcome/goodbye**
jmdn. willkommen heißen/sich von jmdm.
verabschieden
2 *v.i.,* **-dd-, bid** (a) werben (**for** um)
(b) (at auction) bieten
3 *n.* (a) (at auction) Gebot, *das*
(b) (attempt) Versuch, *der*
bidden ▶ BID 1B
'bidder *n.* Bieter, *der*/Bieterin, *die*
bide /'baɪd/ *v.t.* ~ **one's time** den richtigen
Augenblick abwarten
biennial /baɪ'enɪəl/ *n.* (Bot.) zweijährige
Pflanze; Bienne, *die* (fachspr.)
bifocal /baɪ'fəʊkl/ 1 *adj.* Bifokal-
2 *n.* in *pl.* Bifokalgläser *Pl.*
big /bɪɡ/ *adj.* groß
bigamist /'bɪɡəmɪst/ *n.* Bigamist, *der/*
Bigamistin, *die*
bigamy /'bɪɡəmɪ/ *n.* Bigamie, *die*
big: ~**head** *n.* (coll.) Fatzke, *der* (ugs.
abwertend); ~-**'headed** *adj.* (coll.)
eingebildet
bigot /'bɪɡət/ *n.* bornierter Mensch; (Relig.)
bigotter Mensch
bigoted /'bɪɡətɪd/ *adj.* borniert
big: ~ **'toe** *n.* große Zehe; ~ **'top** *n.*
Zirkuszelt, *das;* ~ **'wheel** *n.* (at fair)
Riesenrad, *das*
bike /baɪk/ (coll.) 1 *n.* (bicycle) Rad, *das;*
(motor cycle) Maschine, *die*
2 *v.i.* Rad fahren/[mit dem] Motorrad
fahren
bike: ~ **courier,** ~ **messenger** *ns.* (on
motorbike) Motorradkurier, *der/*-kurierin, *die;*
(on bicycle) Fahrradkurier, *der/*-kurierin, *die;*
~ **path** (esp. Amer.) ▶ BICYCLE PATH
bikini /bɪ'kiːnɪ/ *n.* Bikini, *der*
bilingual /baɪ'lɪŋɡwəl/ *adj.* zweisprachig
bilious /'bɪljəs/ *adj.* (Med.) Gallen-; ~ **attack**
Gallenanfall, *der*
bill[1] /bɪl/ *n.* (of bird) Schnabel, *der*
bill[2] *n.* (a) (Parl.) Gesetzentwurf, *der*
(b) (note of charges) Rechnung, *die;* **could we
have the** ~ **please?** wir möchten zahlen
(c) (poster) **'stick no** ~**s'** „[Plakate]
ankleben verboten"
'billboard *n.* Reklametafel, *die*
billet /'bɪlɪt/ 1 *n.* Quartier, *das*
2 *v.t.* einquartieren (**with, on** bei)
'billfold *n.* (Amer.) Brieftasche, *die*

'billiard ball n. Billardkugel, *die*

billiards /'bɪljədz/ n. Billard[spiel], *das*

billion /'bɪljən/ n. (thousand million) Milliarde, *die*

billionaire /bɪljə'neə(r)/ n. Milliardär, *der*

bimbo /'bɪmbəʊ/ n. (coll. derog.) Puppe, *die* (salopp)

bin /bɪn/ n. Behälter, *der;* (for bread) Brotkasten, *der;* (for rubbish) Mülleimer, *der*

binary /'baɪnərɪ/ adj. binär

'bin bag n. Müllbeutel, *der*

bind /baɪnd/ v.t., **bound** /baʊnd/ **(a)** fesseln ⟨*Person, Tier*⟩; (bandage) wickeln ⟨*Glied, Baum*⟩; verbinden ⟨*Wunde*⟩ (with mit)
(b) binden ⟨*Buch*⟩
(c) be bound up with sth. (fig.) eng mit etw. verbunden sein
(d) be bound to do sth. (required) verpflichtet sein, etw. zu tun; (certain) etw. ganz bestimmt tun; **it is bound to rain** es wird bestimmt regnen

'binder n. (for papers) Hefter, *der;* (for magazines) Mappe, *die*

'binding ☐1 adj. bindend ⟨*Vertrag, Abkommen*⟩ (on für)
☐2 n. (of book) Einband, *der*

bingo /'bɪŋgəʊ/ n. Bingo, *das*

'bin liner n. Müllbeutel, *der*

binoculars /bɪ'nɒkjʊləz/ n. pl. [pair of] ~: Fernglas, *das*

bio'chemistry n. Biochemie, *die*

biodegradable /baɪəʊdɪ'greɪdəbl/ adj. biologisch abbaubar

biode'grade v.i. sich biologisch abbauen

brodi'versity n. biologische Vielfalt

biographer /baɪ'ɒgrəfə(r)/ n. Biograph, *der*/Biographin, *die*

biographical /baɪə'græfɪkl/ adj. biographisch

biography /baɪ'ɒgrəfɪ/ n. Biographie, *die*

'biohazard n. Biogefahr, *die*

biological /baɪə'lɒdʒɪkl/ adj. biologisch

biological: ~ **'clock** n. biologische Uhr; ~ **'warfare** n. biologische Kriegführung; Bakterienkrieg, *der;* ~ **'waste** n. Bio-Abfall, *der;* Biomüll, *der*

biologist /baɪ'ɒlədʒɪst/ n. Biologe, *der*/Biologin, *die*

biology /baɪ'ɒlədʒɪ/ n. Biologie, *die*

biopsy /'baɪɒpsɪ/ n. Biopsie, *die*

'biorhythm n. Biorhythmus, *der*

'biosphere n. Biosphäre, *die*

biotech'nology n. Biotechnologie, *die*

bio'terrorism n. Bioterrorismus, *der*

birch /bɜːtʃ/ n. Birke, *die*

bird /bɜːd/ n. Vogel, *der*

bird: ~ **bath** n. Vogelbad, *das;* ~ **cage** n. Vogelkäfig, *der;* ~ **flu** n. Vogelgrippe, *die;* ~**'s-eye 'view** n. Vogelperspektive, *die;*

~**'s nest** n. Vogelnest, *das;* ~ **table** n. Futterstelle für Vögel; ~**watcher** n. Vogelbeobachter, *der*/-beobachterin, *die;* ~**-watching** n. das Beobachten von Vögeln

Biro ® /'baɪrəʊ/ n., pl. ~s Kugelschreiber, *der;* Kuli, *der* (ugs.)

birth /bɜːθ/ n. **(a)** Geburt, *die;* **give** ~ ⟨*Frau:*⟩ entbinden; ⟨*Tier:*⟩ jungen; werfen; **give** ~ **to a child** ein Kind zur Welt bringen
(b) (of movement, fashion, etc.) Aufkommen, *das*

birth: ~ **certificate** n. Geburtsurkunde, *die;* ~ **control** n. Geburtenkontrolle, *die;* ~**day** n. Geburtstag, *der;* attrib. Geburtstags; ~**mark** n. Muttermal, *das;* ~**place** n. Geburtsort, *der;* ~ **rate** n. Geburtenrate, *die*

biscuit /'bɪskɪt/ n. (Brit.) Keks, *der*

bisect /baɪ'sekt/ v.t. halbieren

bisexual /baɪ'seksjʊəl/ ☐1 adj. bisexuell
☐2 n. Bisexuelle, *der*/*die*

bishop /'bɪʃəp/ n. **(a)** (Eccl.) Bischof, *der*
(b) (Chess) Läufer, *der*

bit¹ /bɪt/ n. **(a)** (for horse) Gebiss, *das*
(b) (of drill) [Bohr]einsatz, *der*

bit² n. (piece) Stück, *das;* **not a** or **one** ~ (not at all) überhaupt nicht; **a** ~ **tired/too early** ein bisschen müde/zu früh; **be a** ~ **of a coward/ bully** ein ziemlicher Feigling sein/den starken Mann markieren (ugs.)

bit³ n. (Comp.) Bit, *das*

bit⁴ ▸ BITE 1, 2

bitch /bɪtʃ/ n. **(a)** (dog) Hündin, *die*
(b) (sl. derog.: woman) Miststück, *das* (derb)

bitchy /'bɪtʃɪ/ adj. (coll.) gemein; gehässig

bite /baɪt/ ☐1 v.t., **bit** /bɪt/, **bitten** /'bɪtn/ beißen; ⟨*Moskito usw.:*⟩ stechen
☐2 v.i., **bit, bitten** beißen/stechen; (take bait) anbeißen
☐3 n. Biss, *der;* (piece) Bissen, *der;* (wound) Bisswunde, *die;* (by mosquito etc.) Stich, *der*
■ **bite 'off** v.t. abbeißen

'bite-size adj. mundgerecht

biting /'baɪtɪŋ/ adj. beißend

bitten ▸ BITE 1, 2

bitter /'bɪtə(r)/ adj. bitter

'bitterly adv. bitterlich ⟨*weinen, sich beschweren*⟩; ~ **cold** bitterkalt

'bitterness n. Bitterkeit, *die*

bizarre /bɪ'zɑː(r)/ adj. bizarr

black /blæk/ ☐1 adj. **(a)** schwarz; ~ **and blue** (fig.) grün und blau; **in** ~ **and white** (fig.) schwarz auf weiß; ~ **and white film** Schwarzweißfilm, *der;* **in the** ~ (in credit) in den schwarzen Zahlen
(b) B~ (dark-skinned) schwarz
☐2 n. **(a)** Schwarz, *das*
(b) B~ (person) Schwarze, *der*/*die*
☐3 v.t. bestreiken ⟨*Betrieb*⟩; boykottieren ⟨*Arbeit*⟩
■ **black 'out** ☐1 v.t. verdunkeln
☐2 v.i. das Bewusstsein verlieren

black: ~**berry** /'blækbərɪ/ n. Brombeere, die; ~**bird** n. Amsel, die; ~**board** n. [Wand]tafel, die; ~ **'box** n. (flight recorder) Flugschreiber, der; ~**'currant** n. schwarze Johannisbeere

blacken /'blækn/ v.t. schwärzen; verfinstern ⟨Himmel⟩

black: ~ **'eye** n. blaues Auge; **B**~ **'Forest** pr. n. Schwarzwald, der; ~ **'hole** n. (Astron.) schwarzes Loch; ~ **'ice** n. Glatteis, das; ~**leg** n. (Brit.) Streikbrecher, der/-brecherin, die; ~ **list** n. schwarze Liste; ~**list** v.t. auf die schwarze Liste setzen; ~**mail** [1] v.t. erpressen; [2] n. Erpressung, die; ~ **market** n. schwarzer Markt

'blackness n. Schwärze, die; (darkness) Finsternis, die

black: ~**out** n. (a) Verdunkelung, die; (Theatre, Radio) Blackout, der; (b) (Med.) **have a** ~**out** das Bewusstsein verlieren; ~ **'pudding** n. Blutwurst, die; **B**~ **'Sea** pr. n. Schwarze Meer, das; ~**smith** n. Schmied, der; ~ **spot** n. Gefahrenstelle, die

bladder /'blædə(r)/ n. Blase, die

blade /bleɪd/ n. (a) (of sword, knife, razor, etc.) Klinge, die; (of saw, oar, propeller) Blatt, das (b) (of grass) Spreite, die

Blairite /'bleəraɪt/ [1] adj. blairsch; Blairsch [2] n. Blair-Anhänger, der/-Anhängerin, die

blame /bleɪm/ [1] v.t. ~ **sb. [for sth.]** jmdm. die Schuld [an etw. (Dat.)] geben; **be to** ~ **[for sth.]** an etw. (Dat.) schuld sein; ~ **sth. [for sth.]** etw. [für etw.] verantwortlich machen [2] n. Schuld, die

'blameless adj. untadelig

blancmange /blə'mɒnʒ/ n. Flammeri, der

bland /blænd/ adj. mild; (suave) verbindlich

blank /blæŋk/ [1] adj. (a) leer; kahl ⟨Wand, Fläche⟩ (b) (empty) frei [2] n. (a) (space) Lücke, die (b) (cartridge) Platzpatrone, die (c) **draw a** ~: kein Glück haben

blank 'cheque n. Blankoscheck, der; (fig.) Blankovollmacht, die

blanket /'blæŋkɪt/ n. Decke, die; **wet '**~ (fig.) Trauerkloß, der (ugs.)

blare /'bleə(r)/ [1] v.i. ⟨Lautsprecher:⟩ plärren; ⟨Trompete:⟩ schmettern [2] v.t. ~ **[out]** [hinaus]plärren ⟨Worte⟩; [hinaus]schmettern ⟨Melodie⟩

blasé /'blɑːzeɪ/ adj. blasiert

blasphemous /'blæsfəməs/ adj. lästerlich

blasphemy /'blæsfəmɪ/ n. Blasphemie, die

blast /blɑːst/ [1] n. (a) **a** ~ **[of wind]** ein Windstoß (b) (of horn) Tuten, das [2] v.t. (blow up) sprengen [3] int. verdammt
■ **blast 'off** v.i. abheben

blasted /'blɑːstɪd/ adj. (damned) verdammt (salopp)

'blast-off n. Abheben, das

blatant /'bleɪtənt/ adj. (a) (flagrant) eklatant (b) (unashamed) unverhohlen; unverfroren ⟨Lüge⟩

'blatantly adv. ▶ BLATANT: eklatant; unverhohlen

blaze /bleɪz/ [1] n. Feuer, das [2] v.i. brennen; lodern (geh.)

blazer /'bleɪzə(r)/ n. Blazer, der

bleach /bliːtʃ/ [1] v.t. bleichen [2] n. Bleichmittel, das

bleak /'bliːk/ adj. (a) öde ⟨Landschaft usw.⟩ (b) (unpromising) düster

bleat /bliːt/ v.i. ⟨Schaf:⟩ blöken; ⟨Ziege:⟩ meckern

bled ▶ BLEED

bleed /bliːd/ v.i., bled /bled/ bluten

bleep /bliːp/ [1] n. Piepen, das [2] v.i. ⟨Geigerzähler, Funksignal:⟩ piepen [3] v.t. ~ **sb.** jmdn. über seinen Kleinempfänger od. (ugs.) Piepser rufen

'bleeper /'bliːpə(r)/ n. Kleinempfänger, der; Piepser, der (ugs.)

blemish /'blemɪʃ/ n. Fleck, der

blend /blend/ [1] v.t. mischen [2] v.i. sich mischen lassen [3] n. Mischung, die

'blender n. Mixer, der

bless /bles/ v.t. segnen; ~ **you!** (after sb. sneezes) Gesundheit!

blessed /'blesɪd/ adj. (a) (revered) heilig (b) (cursed) verdammt (salopp)

'blessing n. Segen, der

blew ▶ BLOW[1]

blight /blaɪt/ n. (fig.) Fluch, der

blind /blaɪnd/ [1] adj. blind; ~ **in one eye** auf einem Auge blind [2] adv. blindlings [3] n. (a) Jalousie, die; (made of cloth) Rouleau, das; (of shop) Markise, die (b) pl. **the** n~: die Blinden Pl. [4] v.t. blenden

blind: ~ **'alley** n. (lit. or fig.) Sackgasse, die; ~ **'corner** n. unübersichtliche Ecke; ~ **'date** n. Verabredung mit einem/einer Unbekannten; ~**fold** [1] v.t. die Augen verbinden (+ Dat.); [2] adj. mit verbundenen Augen nachgestellt

'blinding adj. blendend; **a** ~ **headache** rasende Kopfschmerzen Pl.

'blindly adv. [wie] blind; (fig.) blindlings

'blindness n. Blindheit, die

'blind spot n. (Motor Veh.) toter Winkel; (fig.: weak spot) schwacher Punkt;

blink /blɪŋk/ v.i. (a) blinzeln (b) (shine intermittently) blinken

'blinkers n. pl. Scheuklappen Pl.

bliss /blɪs/ n. [Glück]seligkeit, die

blissful /'blɪsfl/ adj. [glück]selig

blister /'blɪstə(r)/ [1] n. Blase, die ┈╳

2 *v.i.* ⟨*Haut:*⟩ Blasen bekommen; ⟨*Anstrich:*⟩ Blasen werfen

'blister pack *n.* Klarsichtpackung, *die*

blizzard /'blɪzəd/ *n.* Schneesturm, *der*

bloated /'bləʊtɪd/ *adj.* (having overeaten) aufgedunsen; **I feel** ~: ich bin voll (ugs.)

blob /blɒb/ *n.* (drop) Tropfen, *der;* (small mass) Klacks, *der* (ugs.)

block /blɒk/ 1 *n.* (a) Klotz, *der;* (for chopping on) Hackklotz, *der;* (of concrete or stone, building stone) Block, *der*
(b) (building) [Häuser]block, *der;* ~ **of flats**/ **offices** Wohnblock, *der*/Bürohaus, *das*
2 *v.t.* versperren ⟨*Tür, Straße, Durchgang, Sicht*⟩; verstopfen ⟨*Pfeife, Abfluss*⟩; verhindern ⟨*Fortschritt*⟩

■ **block 'out** *v.t.* ausschließen ⟨*Licht, Lärm*⟩

■ **block 'up** *v.t.* verstopfen; versperren ⟨*Eingang*⟩

blockade /blɒ'keɪd/ 1 *n.* Blockade, *die*
2 *v.t.* blockieren

blockage /'blɒkɪdʒ/ *n.* Block, *der;* (of pipe, gutter) Verstopfung, *die*

block: ~ **'booking** *n.* Gruppenbuchung, *die;* ~**buster** *n.* (a) (bomb) [große] Fliegerbombe; (b) (fig.) Knüller, *der* (ugs.); ~ **'capital** *n.* Blockbuchstabe, *der;* ~**head** *n.* Dummkopf, *der;* ~ **'letters** *n. pl.* Blockschrift, *die*

blog /blɒg/ (Comp.) 1 *n.* Blog, *das* (Jargon)
2 *v.i.* ein Weblog unterhalten

blogger /'blɒgə(r)/ *n.* (author of a weblog) Weblogautor, *der*/-autorin, *die*

bloke /bləʊk/ *n.* (Brit. coll.) Typ, *der* (ugs.)

blonde /blɒnd/ 1 *adj.* blond
2 *n.* Blondine, *die*

blood /blʌd/ *n.* Blut, *das*

blood: ~ **bank** *n.* Blutbank, *die;* ~**bath** *n.* Blutbad, *das;* ~ **cell** *n.* Blutkörperchen, *das;* ~ **clot** *n.* Blutgerinnsel, *das;* ~ **donor** *n.* Blutspender, *der*/-spenderin, *die;* ~ **group** *n.* Blutgruppe, *die;* ~**hound** *n.* Bluthund, *der;* ~ **plasma** *n.* Blutplasma, *das;* ~ **poisoning** *n.* Blutvergiftung, *die;* ~ **pressure** *n.* Blutdruck, *der;* ~ **sample** *n.* Blutprobe, *die;* ~**shed** *n.* Blutvergießen, *das;* ~**shot** *adj.* blutunterlaufen; ~ **sports** *n. pl.* Hetzjagd, *die;* ~**stain** *n.* Blutfleck, *der;* ~**stained** *adj.* blutbefleckt; ~**stream** *n.* Blutstrom, *der;* ~ **sugar** *n.* Blutzucker, *der;* ~ **test** *n.* Blutprobe, *die;* ~**thirsty** *adj.* blutrünstig; ~ **transfusion** *n.* Bluttransfusion, *die;* ~ **vessel** *n.* Blutgefäß, *das*

'bloody 1 *adj.* (a) blutig; (running with blood) blutend
(b) (sl.: damned) verdammt (salopp)
2 *adv.* (sl.: damned) verdammt (salopp)

bloom /bluːm/ 1 *n.* Blüte, *die;* **be in** ~: in Blüte stehen
2 *v.i.* blühen

blossom /'blɒsəm/ 1 *n.* (flower) Blüte, *die;* (mass) Blütenmeer, *das* (geh.)
2 *v.i.* blühen; ⟨*Mensch:*⟩ aufblühen

blot /blɒt/ 1 *n.* (of ink) Tintenklecks, *der;* (stain) Fleck, *der*
2 *v.t.,* **-tt-** ablöschen ⟨*Tinte, Papier*⟩

■ **blot 'out** *v.t.* (fig.) auslöschen

'blotting paper *n.* Löschpapier, *das*

blouse /blaʊz/ *n.* Bluse, *die*

blow[1] /bləʊ/ 1 *v.i.,* **blew** /bluː/, **blown** /bləʊn/ ⟨*Wind:*⟩ wehen; ⟨*Sturm:*⟩ blasen
2 *v.t.,* **blew, blown:** (a) blasen; ⟨*Wind:*⟩ wehen; machen ⟨*Seifenblase*⟩; ~ **sb. a kiss** jmdm. eine Kusshand zuwerfen
(b) ~ **one's nose** sich ⟨*Dat.*⟩ die Nase putzen
(c) ~ **sth. to pieces** etw. in die Luft sprengen

■ **blow 'out** 1 *v.t.* ausblasen
2 *v.i.* ausgeblasen werden

■ **blow 'over** 1 *v.i.* umgeblasen werden; ⟨*Streit, Sturm:*⟩ sich legen
2 *v.t.* umblasen

■ **blow 'up** 1 *v.t.* (a) (shatter) [in die Luft] sprengen
(b) aufblasen ⟨*Ballon*⟩; aufpumpen ⟨*Reifen*⟩
(c) (coll.: exaggerate) hochspielen
2 *v.i.* (explode) explodieren

blow[2] *n.* (a) Schlag, *der;* (with axe) Hieb, *der;* **come to ~s** handgreiflich werden
(b) (disaster) [schwerer] Schlag

blow: ~**dry** *v.t.* fönen; ~**lamp,** ~**torch** *n.* Lötlampe, *die*

blown ▶ BLOW[1]

blubber /'blʌbə(r)/ *n.* Walspeck, *der*

blue /bluː/ 1 *adj.* blau
2 *n.* (a) Blau, *das*
(b) **have the ~s** deprimiert sein
(c) (Mus.) **the ~s** der Blues
(d) **out of the ~:** aus heiterem Himmel

blue: ~**bell** *n.* Glockenblume, *die;* ~**bottle** *n.* Schmeißfliege, *die;* ~ **'cheese** *n.* Blauschimmelkäse, *der;* Edelpilzkäse, *der;* ~**collar** *adj.* ~**collar worker** Arbeiter, *der*/Arbeiterin, *die;* ~**eyed** *adj.* blauäugig; **be ~eyed** blaue Augen haben; ~ **'moon** *n.* **once in a ~ moon** alle Jubeljahre (ugs.); ~**print** *n.* (fig.) Entwurf, *der;* ~ **tit** *n.* (Ornith.) Blaumeise, *die;* ~ **'whale** *n.* Blauwal, *der*

bluff /blʌf/ 1 *n.* Bluff, *der* (ugs.); **call sb.'s ~:** es darauf ankommen lassen (ugs.)
2 *v.i. & t.* bluffen (ugs.)

blunder /'blʌndə(r)/ 1 *n.* [schwerer] Fehler
2 *v.i.* (a) (make mistake) einen [schweren] Fehler machen
(b) (move blindly) tappen

blunt /blʌnt/ 1 *adj.* (a) stumpf
(b) (outspoken) direkt; glatt (ugs.) ⟨*Ablehnung*⟩
2 *v.t.* ~ **[the edge of]** stumpf machen

'bluntly *adv.* direkt; glatt ⟨*ablehnen*⟩

blur /blɜː(r)/ *v.t.,* **-rr-:** verwischen; **his vision was ~red** er sah alles verschwommen

blurt /blɜːt/ v.t. ~ **out** herausplatzen mit (ugs.)

blush /blʌʃ/ 1 v.i. rot werden
2 n. Rotwerden, das

bluster /ˈblʌstə(r)/ v.i. sich aufplustern (ugs.)

blustery /ˈblʌstərɪ/ adj. stürmisch

BO abbr. (coll.) = **body odour** Körpergeruch, der

boar /bɔː(r)/ n. [wild] ~: Keiler, der

board /bɔːd/ 1 n. (a) Brett, das; (black~) Tafel, die; (notice~) schwarzes Brett; above ~ (fig.) einwandfrei; korrekt
(b) (Commerc.) ~ [of directors] Vorstand, der; (supervisory ~) Aufsichtsrat, der
(c) (Naut., Aeronaut.) on ~: an Bord
(d) ~ and lodging Unterkunft und Verpflegung; full ~: Vollpension, die
2 v.t. ~ the ship/plane an Bord des Schiffes/Flugzeuges gehen; ~ the train/bus in den Zug/Bus einsteigen
■ **board 'up** v.t. mit Brettern vernageln

'boarder n. (Sch.) Internatsschüler, der/ -schülerin, die

'board game n. Brettspiel, das

boarding: ~ **house** n. Pension, die; ~ **pass** n. Bordkarte, die; ~ **school** n. Internat, das

board: ~ **meeting** n. Vorstandssitzung, die; ~**room** n. Sitzungssaal, der

boast /bəʊst/ v.i. prahlen

boastful /ˈbəʊstfl/ adj. prahlerisch

boat /bəʊt/ n. Boot, das

boat: ~**house** n. Bootshaus, das; ~ **trip** n. Bootsfahrt, die

bob¹ /bɒb/ v.i., -bb-: ~ [up and down] sich auf und nieder bewegen

bob² n. (~sled) Bob, der

bob: ~**sled,** ~**sleigh** ns. Bobschlitten, der

bodice /ˈbɒdɪs/ n. Mieder, das; (part of dress) Oberteil, das

bodily /ˈbɒdɪlɪ/ adj. körperlich; ~ needs leibliche Bedürfnisse

body /ˈbɒdɪ/ n. (a) Körper, der
(b) (corpse) Leiche, die
(c) (group) Gruppe, die; (with particular function) Organ, das

body: ~ **bag** n. Leichensack, der; ~**building** 1 n. Bodybuilding, das; 2 adj. ~building food Aufbaukost, die; ~ **clock** ▶ BIOLOGICAL CLOCK; ~**guard** n. (single) Leibwächter, der; (group) Leibwache, die; ~ **language** n. Körpersprache, die; ~ **odour** n. Körpergeruch, der; ~ **part** n. Körperteil, der; ~ **piercing** n. Piercing, das; ~ **weight** n. Körpergewicht, das; ~**work** n. Karosserie, die

bog /bɒg/ 1 n. Moor, das; (marsh, swamp) Sumpf, der
2 v.t., -gg-: be/get ~ged down (fig.) sich verzettelt haben/sich verzetteln

boggle /ˈbɒgl/ v.i. (coll.) the mind ~s da kann man nur [noch] staunen

bogus /ˈbəʊgəs/ adj. falsch

boil¹ /bɔɪl/ 1 v.i. & t. kochen
2 n. come to/go off the ~: zu kochen anfangen/aufhören; bring to the ~: zum Kochen bringen
■ **boil 'down** v.i. ~ down to sth. (fig.) auf etw. hinauslaufen
■ **boil 'over** v.i. überkochen

boil² n. (Med.) Furunkel, der

'boiler n. Kessel, der

boiler: ~**room** n. Kesselraum, der; ~ **suit** n. Overall, der

'boiling point n. Siedepunkt, der

boisterous /ˈbɔɪstərəs/ adj. ausgelassen

bold /bəʊld/ adj. (a) (courageous) mutig; (daring) kühn
(b) auffallend ⟨Farbe, Muster⟩

'boldly adv. (courageously) mutig; (daringly) kühn

Bolivia /bəˈlɪvɪə/ pr. n. Bolivien (das)

bollard /ˈbɒlɑːd/ n. (Brit.) Poller, der

bollocks /ˈbɒləks/ (coarse) 1 n. pl. Eier (derb)
2 int. Scheiße

bolster /ˈbəʊlstə(r)/ 1 n. (pillow) Nackenrolle, die
2 v.t. (fig.) stärken

bolt /bəʊlt/ 1 n. (a) (on door or window) Riegel, der; (on gun) Kammerverschluss, der
(b) (metal pin) Schraube, die; (without thread) Bolzen, der
2 v.i. davonlaufen; ⟨Pferd:⟩ durchgehen; ⟨Fuchs, Kaninchen:⟩ flüchten
3 v.t. (a) verriegeln ⟨Tür, Fenster⟩
(b) (fasten with ~s) verschrauben/mit Bolzen verbinden
(c) ~ [down] hinunterschlingen ⟨Essen⟩
4 adv. ~ upright kerzengerade

bomb /bɒm/ 1 n. Bombe, die; ~ attack Bombenanschlag, der
2 v.t. bombardieren

bombard /bɒmˈbɑːd/ v.t. beschießen

bom'bardment n. Beschuss, der

bombastic /bɒmˈbæstɪk/ adj. bombastisch

bomb: ~ **blast** n. (blast wave) Druckwelle, die; (explosion) Bombenexplosion, die; ~ **disposal** n. Räumung von Bomben; ~ **disposal squad** Bombenräumkommando, das

bomber /ˈbɒmə(r)/ n. (Air Force) Bomber, der (ugs.)

bombing /ˈbɒmɪŋ/ n. Bombardierung, die

bomb: ~ **scare** n. Bombendrohung, die; ~**shell** n. Bombe, die; (fig.) Sensation, die

bond /bɒnd/ n. (a) Band, das; in pl. (shackles) Fesseln Pl.
(b) (adhesion) Verbindung, die
(c) (Commerc.) Anleihe, die

bone /bəʊn/ 1 n. Knochen, der; (of fish) Gräte, die   ⋯⟶

② *v.t.* den/die Knochen herauslösen aus; entgräten ⟨*Fisch*⟩

bone: ~ **'china** *n.* Knochenporzellan, *das;* ~ **'dry** *adj.* knochentrocken (ugs.); ~ **'idle** *adj.* stinkfaul (salopp); ~ **marrow** *n.* (Anat.) Knochenmark, *das;* ~**meal** *n.* Knochenmehl, *das*

bonfire /'bɒnfaɪə(r)/ *n.* Freudenfeuer, *das;* (for rubbish) Feuer, *das;* B~ **Night** (Brit.) [Abend des] Guy Fawkes Day (*mit Feuerwerk*)

bonnet /'bɒnɪt/ *n.* (a) (woman's) Haube, *die;* (child's) Häubchen, *das*
(b) (Brit. Motor Veh.) Motorhaube, *die*

bonus /'bəʊnəs/ *n.* zusätzliche Leistung; (to shareholders) Bonus, *der;* **Christmas** ~: Weihnachtsgratifikation, *die*

bony /'bəʊnɪ/ *adj.* (a) Knochen-; (like bone) knochenartig
(b) (skinny) knochendürr (ugs.); spindeldürr

boo /buː/ ① *int.* (to surprise sb.) huh; (expr. disapproval, contempt) buh
② *n.* Buh, *das* (ugs.)
③ *v.t.* ausbuhen (ugs.)
④ *v.i.* buhen (ugs.)

boob /buːb/ (Brit. coll.) *n.* (a) (mistake) Fehler, *der;* Schnitzer, *der* (ugs.)
(b) (breast) Titte, *die* (derb)

booby /'buːbɪ/ *n.* Trottel, *der* (ugs.)

booby: ~ **prize** *n.*: Preis für den schlechtesten Teilnehmer an einem Wettbewerb; ~ **trap** *n.* (a) Falle, mit der man jmdm. einen Streich spielen will; **(b)** (Mil.) versteckte Sprengladung

book /bʊk/ ① *n.* Buch, *das;* (for accounts) Rechnungsbuch, *das;* (for exercises) [Schreib]heft, *das*
② *v.t.* buchen ⟨*Reise, Flug, Platz [im Flugzeug]*⟩; [vor]bestellen ⟨*Eintrittskarte, Tisch, Zimmer, Platz [im Theater]*⟩
③ *v.i.* buchen
▪ **book 'in** ① *v.i.* sich eintragen
② *v.t.* eintragen
▪ **book 'up** *v.i. & t.* buchen; be ~ed up ⟨*Hotel usw.:*⟩ ausgebucht sein

book: ~**case** *n.* Bücherschrank, *der;* ~ **club** *n.* Buchklub, *der;* Buchgemeinschaft, *die;* ~**ends** *n. pl.* Buchstützen *Pl.*

bookie /'bʊkɪ/ *n.* (coll.) Buchmacher, *der*

'booking office *n.* [Fahrkarten]schalter, *der*

book: ~**keeper** *n.* Buchhalter, *der/* -halterin, *die;* ~**keeping** *n.* Buchführung, *die;* Buchhaltung, *die*

booklet /'bʊklɪt/ *n.* Broschüre, *die*

book: ~**maker** *n.* (in betting) Buchmacher, *der;* ~**mark** *n.* ① (also Comp.) Lesezeichen, *das;* ② *v.t.* (Comp.) mit einem Lesezeichen versehen; ~**seller** *n.* Buchhändler, *der/* -händlerin, *die;* ~**shelf** *n.* Bücherbord, *das;* ~**shop** *n.* Buchhandlung, *die;* ~**stall** *n.* Bücherstand, *der;* ~**store** *n.* (Amer.)

Buchhandlung, *die;* ~ **token** *n.* Büchergutschein, *der;* ~**worm** *n.* Bücherwurm, *der*

boom¹ /buːm/ *n.* (a) (for camera or microphone) Ausleger, *der*
(b) (Naut.) Baum, *der*

boom² ① *v.i.* (a) dröhnen
(b) ⟨*Geschäft, Verkauf, Gebiet:*⟩ sich sprunghaft entwickeln
② *n.* (a) Dröhnen, *das*
(b) (in business or economy) Boom, *der*

boomerang /'buːməræŋ/ *n.* Bumerang, *der*

boon /buːn/ *n.* Segen, *der* (**to** für)

boor /bʊər/ *n.* Rüpel, *der*

boorish /'bʊərɪʃ/ *adj.* rüpelhaft

boost /buːst/ ① *v.t.* ankurbeln ⟨*Wirtschaft*⟩; in die Höhe treiben ⟨*Preis, Wert*⟩; stärken ⟨*Selbstvertrauen, Moral*⟩
② *n.* Auftrieb, *der*

boot /buːt/ ① *n.* (a) Stiefel, *der;* **give sb. the** ~ (fig. coll.) jmdn. rausschmeißen (ugs.)
(b) (Brit.: of car) Kofferraum, *der*
② *v.t.* (a) (coll.: kick) kicken (ugs.)
(b) (Comp.) ~ [**up**] booten

bootable /'buːtəbl/ *adj.* (Comp.) bootbar ⟨*System*⟩; ~ **disk** Bootdiskette, *die*

'boot disk *n.* (Comp.) Bootdiskette, *die*

booth /buːð/ *n.* (a) Bude, *die*
(b) (telephone ~) Zelle, *die*

'bootleg *adj.* (illegally sold/distilled) schwarz verkauft/gebrannt

booze /buːz/ (coll.) ① *v.i.* saufen (derb)
② *n.* Alkohol, *der*

'booze-up *n.* (coll.) Besäufnis, *das* (salopp); **have a** ~: saufen gehen (salopp) (ugs.)

border /'bɔːdə(r)/ ① *n.* (a) Rand, *der;* (of tablecloth, handkerchief) Bordüre, *die*
(b) (of country) Grenze, *die*
(c) (flower bed) Rabatte, *die*
② *attrib. adj.* Grenz⟨*stadt, -streit*⟩
③ *v.t.* (a) (adjoin) [an]grenzen an (+ Akk.)
(b) (put a ~ to, act as ~ to) umranden; einfassen
④ *v.i.* ~ **on** (a) ▶ 3A
(b) (resemble) grenzen an (+ Akk.)

border: ~ **crossing** *n.* Grenzübergang, *der;* ~**line** ① *n.* Grenzlinie, *die;* ② *adj.* be ~line auf der Grenze liegen; **a** ~line case/candidate ein Grenzfall

bore¹ /bɔː(r)/ ① *v.t.* bohren
② *n.* (of firearm) Kaliber, *das*

bore² ① *n.* (a) it's a real ~: es ist wirklich ärgerlich; **what a** ~! wie ärgerlich!
(b) (person) Langweiler, *der* (ugs.)
② *v.t.* langweilen; be ~d sich langweilen

bore³ ▶ BEAR²

boredom /'bɔːdəm/ *n.* Langeweile, *die*

'borehole *n.* Bohrloch, *das*

boring /'bɔːrɪŋ/ *adj.* langweilig

born /bɔːn/ ① be ~: geboren werden
② *adj.* geboren; be a ~ orator der geborene Redner sein

borne ▶ BEAR²

borough /'bʌrə/ n. (town) Stadt, die; (village) Gemeinde, die

borrow /'bɒrəʊ/ v.t. leihen (from von, bei); (from library) entleihen

'borrower n. (from bank) Kreditnehmer, der; (from library) Entleiher, der

Bosnia /'bɒznɪə/ n. Bosnien (das)

Bosnian /'bɒznɪən/ **1** adj. bosnisch; sb. is ∼: jmd. ist Bosnier/Bosnierin **2** n. Bosnier, der/Bosnierin, die

bosom /'bʊzəm/ n. Brust, die

boss /bɒs/ (coll.) **1** n. Boss, der (ugs.); Chef, der **2** v.t. ∼ [about or around] herumkommandieren (ugs.)

'bossy adj. (coll.) herrisch

botanical /bə'tænɪkl/ adj. botanisch

botanist /'bɒtənɪst/ n. Botaniker, der/ Botanikerin, die

botany /'bɒtənɪ/ n. Botanik, die

botch /bɒtʃ/ **1** v.t. pfuschen bei (ugs.) **2** v.i. pfuschen (ugs.)

■ **botch 'up** v.t. (bungle) verpfuschen (ugs.)

both /bəʊθ/ **1** adj. beide; ∼ [the] brothers beide Brüder **2** pron. beide; ∼ [of them] are dead beide sind tot; ∼ of you/them are ...: ihr seid/sie sind beide ... **3** adv. ∼ A and B sowohl A als [auch] B; he and I were ∼ there er und ich waren beide da

bother /'bɒðə(r)/ **1** v.t. (a) I can't be ∼ed ich habe keine Lust (b) (annoy) lästig sein (+ Dat.); ⟨Lärm, Licht:⟩ stören; ⟨Schmerz, Zahn:⟩ zu schaffen machen (+ Dat.); I'm sorry to ∼ you, but ...: es tut mir Leid, wenn ich Sie störe, aber ... (c) (worry) Sorgen machen (+ Dat.); ⟨Problem, Frage:⟩ beschäftigen **2** v.i. don't ∼ to do it Sie brauchen es nicht zu tun; you needn't/shouldn't have ∼ed das wäre nicht nötig gewesen; don't ∼! nicht nötig! **3** n. (a) (trouble) Ärger, der (b) (effort) Mühe, die **4** int. (coll.) wie ärgerlich!

bottle /'bɒtl/ **1** n. Flasche, die; a ∼ of beer eine Flasche Bier **2** v.t. (a) (put into ∼s) in Flaschen [ab]füllen (b) ∼d beer Flaschenbier, das (c) (preserve in jars) einmachen

■ **bottle 'up** v.t. (a) (conceal) in sich (Dat.) aufstauen (b) (trap) einschließen

bottle: ∼ **bank** n. Altglasbehälter, der; ∼**neck** n. Flaschenhals, der (ugs.); ∼**-opener** n. Flaschenöffner, der; ∼ **top** n. Flaschenverschluss, der

bottom /'bɒtəm/ **1** n. (a) unteres Ende; (of cup, glass, box) Boden, der; (of valley, well, shaft) Sohle, die; (of hill, cliff, stairs) Fuß, der (b) (buttocks) Hinterteil, das (ugs.) (c) (of sea, lake) Grund, der (e) (farthest point) at the ∼ of the garden/street hinten im Garten/am Ende der Straße (e) (underside) Unterseite, die (f) (fig.) start at the ∼: ganz unten anfangen; be ∼ of the class der/die Letzte in der Klasse sein **2** adj. (a) (lowest) unterst...; (lower) unter... (b) (fig.: last) letzt...

'bottomless adj. bodenlos; unendlich tief ⟨Meer, Ozean⟩

'botulism /'bɒtjuːlɪzm/ n. (Med.) Botulismus, der

bough /baʊ/ n. Ast, der

bought ▶ BUY 1

boulder /'bəʊldə(r)/ n. Felsbrocken, der

boulevard /'buːləvɑːd/ n. Boulevard, der

bounce /baʊns/ **1** v.i. (a) springen (b) (coll.) ⟨Scheck:⟩ platzen (ugs.) **2** v.t. aufspringen lassen ⟨Ball⟩ **3** n. Aufprall, der

'bouncer n. (coll.) Rausschmeißer, der (ugs.)

bouncing /'baʊnsɪŋ/ adj. stramm ⟨Baby⟩

bouncy /'baʊnsɪ/ adj. gut springend ⟨Ball⟩; (fig.: lively) munter

bound¹ /baʊnd/ **1** n., usu. in pl. (limit) Grenze, die; within the ∼s of possibility im Bereich des Möglichen; sth. is out of ∼s [to sb.] der Zutritt zu etw. ist [für jmdn.] verboten **2** v.t. be ∼ed by sth. durch etw. begrenzt werden

bound² **1** v.i. hüpfen **2** n. Satz, der

bound³ pred. adj. be ∼ for home/Frankfurt auf dem Heimweg/nach Frankfurt unterwegs sein; homeward ∼: auf dem Weg nach Hause

bound⁴ ▶ BIND

boundary /'baʊndərɪ/ n. Grenze, die

'boundless adj. grenzenlos

bounty /'baʊntɪ/ n. Kopfgeld, das

bouquet /bʊ'keɪ/ n. [Blumen]strauß, der

bourgeois /'bʊəʒwɑː/ **1** n., pl. same Bürger, der/Bürgerin, die **2** adj. bürgerlich

bout /baʊt/ n. (a) (contest) Wettkampf, der (b) (fit) Anfall, der

boutique /buː'tiːk/ n. Boutique, die

bow¹ /bəʊ/ n. (a) (curve, weapon, Mus.) Bogen, der (b) (knot, ribbon) Schleife, die

bow² /baʊ/ **1** v.i. (a) ∼ [to sb.] sich [vor jmdm.] verbeugen (b) (submit) sich beugen (to Dat.) **2** n. Verbeugung, die

bow³ /baʊ/ n. (Naut.) Bug, der

bowel /'baʊəl/ n. (Anat.) ∼s pl., (Med.) ∼: Darm, der

bowl¹ /bəʊl/ n. (basin) Schüssel, die; (shallower) Schale, die; (of spoon) Schöpfteil, der; (of pipe) Kopf, der

bowl² **1** n. (a) (ball) Kugel, die   ····❖

(b) *in pl.* (game) Bowls, *das*
2 *v.i.* (a) (play ~s) Bowls spielen
(b) (Cricket) werfen
bow-legged /'bəʊlegɪd/ o-beinig (ugs.)
bowler¹ /'bəʊlə(r)/ *n.* (Cricket) Werfer, *der*
bowler² *n.* ~ [hat] Bowler, *der*
'**bowling** *n.* [tenpin] ~: Bowling, *das;* go ~: bowlen gehen
bowling: ~ **alley** *n.* Bowlingbahn, *die;* ~ **green** *n.: Rasenfläche für Bowls*
bow /bəʊ/: ~**string** *n.* Bogensehne, *die;* ~ '**tie** *n.* Fliege, *die;* ~ **window** *n.* Erkerfenster, *das*
box¹ /bɒks/ *n.* (a) Kasten, *der;* (bigger) Kiste, *die;* (of cardboard) Schachtel, *die*
(b) the ~ (coll.: television) der Kasten (ugs. abwertend); die Flimmerkiste (scherzh.)
box² 1 *n.* he gave him a ~ on the ear[s] er gab ihm eine Ohrfeige
2 *v.t.* (a) he ~ed his ears *or* ~ed him round the ears er ohrfeigte ihn
(b) (Sport) ~ sb. gegen jmdn. boxen
3 *v.i.* (Sport) boxen
■ **box 'in** *v.t.* (enclose tightly) einklemmen
'**boxer** *n.* Boxer, *der*
'**boxer shorts** *n. pl.* Boxershorts *Pl.*
'**boxing** *n.* Boxen, *das*
boxing: B~ Day *n.* zweiter Weihnachtsfeiertag; ~ **glove** *n.* Boxhandschuh, *der;* ~ **match** *n.* Boxkampf, *der;* ~ **ring** *n.* Boxring, *der*
box: ~ **junction** *n.* (Brit.) *gelb markierter Kreuzungsbereich, in den man bei Stau nicht einfahren darf;* ~ **number** *n.* (at newspaper office) Chiffre, *die;* (at post office) Postfach, *das;* ~ **office** *n.* Kasse, *die;* be a ~ office success ein Kassenerfolg sein; ~**room** *n.* (Brit.) Abstellraum, *der*
boy /bɔɪ/ *n.* Junge, *der*
'**boy band** *n.* Boyband, *die*
boycott /'bɔɪkɒt/ 1 *v.t.* boykottieren
2 *n.* Boykott, *der*
'**boyfriend** *n.* Freund, *der*
'**boyish** *adj.* jungenhaft
boy 'scout ▸ SCOUT 1A
bra /brɑː/ *n.* BH, *der* (ugs.)
brace /breɪs/ 1 *n.* (a) (connecting piece) Klammer, *die;* (strut) Strebe, *die;* (Dent.) [Zahn]spange, *die*
(b) *in pl.* (trouser straps) Hosenträger *Pl.*
2 *v. refl.* ~ oneself for sth. sich auf etw. (*Akk.*) vorbereiten
bracelet /'breɪslɪt/ *n.* Armband, *das*
bracing /'breɪsɪŋ/ *adj.* belebend
bracken /'brækn/ *n.* [Adler]farn, *der*
bracket /'brækɪt/ 1 *n.* (a) (support) Konsole, *die*
(b) (mark) Klammer, *die*
2 *v.t.* einklammern
brag /bræg/ *v.i. & t.,* -gg- prahlen (about mit)

braid /breɪd/ 1 *n.* (a) (plait) Flechte, *die* (geh.); Zopf, *der*
(b) (woven band) Borte, *die;* (on uniform) Litze, *die*
2 *v.t.* flechten
Braille /breɪl/ *n.* Blindenschrift, *die*
brain /breɪn/ *n.* Gehirn, *das*
brain: ~**child** *n.* (coll.) Geistesprodukt, *das;* ~-**dead** *adj.* (a) (Med.) hirntot; (b) (coll. derog.) hirnlos ⟨*Person*⟩; ~**less** *adj.* hirnlos; ~**storm** *n.* (a) Anfall geistiger Umnachtung; (b) (Amer. coll.) ▸ ~WAVE; ~**storming** *n.* Brainstorming, *das;* ~ **tumour** *n.* Gehirntumor, *der;* ~**wash** *v.t.* einer Gehirnwäsche unterziehen; ~**wave** *n.* (coll.: inspiration) genialer Einfall
'**brainy** *adj.* intelligent
brake /breɪk/ 1 *n.* Bremse, *die*
2 *v.t. & i.* bremsen
brake: ~ **block** *n.* Bremsklotz, *der;* ~ **cable** *n.* Bremszug, *der;* Bremsseil, *das;* ~ **fluid** *n.* Bremsflüssigkeit, *die;* ~ **light** *n.* Bremslicht, *das;* ~ **pad** *n.* Bremsbelag, *der;* ~ **shoe** *n.* Bremsbacke, *die*
'**braking distance** *n.* Bremsweg, *der*
bramble /'bræmbl/ *n.* Dornenstrauch, *der*
bran /bræn/ *n.* Kleie, *die*
branch /brɑːntʃ/ 1 *n.* (a) (bough) Ast, *der;* (twig) Zweig, *der*
(b) (of artery, antlers) Ast, *der*
(c) (office) Zweigstelle, *die;* (shop) Filiale, *die*
2 *v.i.* sich verzweigen
■ **branch 'off** *v.i.* abzweigen
■ **branch 'out** *v.i.* (fig.) ~ out into sth. sich auch mit etw. befassen
branch: ~ **line** *n.* (Railw.) Nebenstrecke, *die;* ~ **manager** *n.* Filialleiter, *der/* -leiterin, *die;* ~ **office** *n.* Zweigstelle, *die*
brand /brænd/ *n.* (a) (trade mark) Markenzeichen, *das;* (goods of particular make) Marke, *die*
(b) (mark) Brandmal, *das*
'**brand image** *n.* Markenimage, *das*
brandish /'brændɪʃ/ *v.t.* schwenken; schwingen ⟨*Waffe*⟩
brand: ~ **leader** *n.* (product) marktführendes Produkt; (brand) führende Marke; ~ **name** *n.* Markenname, *der;* ~-'**new** *adj.* nagelneu (ugs.)
brandy /'brændɪ/ *n.* Weinbrand, *der;* Kognak, *der*
brash /bræʃ/ *adj.* dreist
brass /brɑːs/ *n.* Messing, *das; attrib.* Messing-; the ~ (Mus.) das Blech; ~ **player** (Mus.) Blechbläser, *der;* get down to ~ tacks zur Sache kommen
brass 'band *n.* Blaskapelle, *die*
brassière /'bræzjə(r)/ *n.* Büstenhalter, *der*
brat /bræt/ *n.* Balg, *das od. der* (ugs.)
bravado /brə'vɑːdəʊ/ *n.* do sth. out of ~: so waghalsig sein, etw. zu tun
brave /breɪv/ 1 *adj.* tapfer
2 *n.* [indianischer] Krieger

3 *v.t.* trotzen (+ *Dat.*)

'bravely *adv.* tapfer

bravery /'breɪvərɪ/ *n.* Tapferkeit, *die*

bravo /brɑː'vəʊ/ *int.* bravo

brawl /brɔːl/ **1** *v.i.* sich schlagen
2 *n.* Schlägerei, *die*

brawny /'brɔːnɪ/ *adj.* muskulös

bray /breɪ/ **1** *n.* Iah, *das*
2 *v.i.* ⟨*Esel:*⟩ iahen

brazen /'breɪzn/ **1** *adj.* dreist; (shameless) schamlos
2 *v.t.* ∼ **[out]** trotzen (+ *Dat.*); ∼ **it out** (deny guilt) es abstreiten; (not admit guilt) es nicht zugeben

brazier /'breɪzɪə(r)/ *n.* Kohlenbecken, *das*

Brazil /brə'zɪl/ *pr. n.* Brasilien (*das*)

Bra'zil nut *n.* Paranuss, *die*

breach /briːtʃ/ **1** *n.* (a) (violation) Verstoß, *der* (of gegen); ∼ **of faith/duty** Vertrauensbruch, *der*/Pflichtverletzung, *die*
(b) (of relations) Bruch, *der*
(c) (gap) Bresche, *die;* (fig.) Riss, *der*
2 *v.t.* durchbrechen

bread /bred/ *n.* Brot, *das;* **a piece of** ∼ **and butter** ein Butterbrot

bread: ∼ **bin** *n.* Brotkasten, *der;* ∼**board** *n.* [Brot]brett, *das;* ∼**crumb** *n.* Brotkrume, *die;* ∼**crumbs** (coating) Paniermehl, *das;* ∼ **knife** *n.* Brotmesser, *das;* ∼**line** *n.* be *or* live on/below the ∼**line** gerade noch/nicht einmal mehr das Notwendigste zum Leben haben; ∼ **'roll** *n.* Brötchen, *das*

breadth /bredθ/ *n.* Breite, *die*

'breadwinner *n.* Ernährer, *der*/ Ernährerin, *die*

break /breɪk/ **1** *v.t.,* broke /brəʊk/, broken /'brəʊkn/ **(a)** brechen; (so as to damage) zerbrechen; kaputtmachen (ugs.); zerreißen ⟨*Seil*⟩; (fig.: interrupt) unterbrechen; brechen ⟨*Bann, Zauber, Schweigen*⟩; **the TV/my watch is broken** der Fernseher/meine Uhr ist kaputt (ugs.); ∼ **the habit** es sich (*Dat.*) abgewöhnen
(b) (fracture) sich (*Dat.*) brechen ⟨*Arm, Bein usw.*⟩
(c) brechen ⟨*Vertrag, Versprechen*⟩; verstoßen gegen ⟨*Regel, Gesetz*⟩
(d) (surpass) brechen ⟨*Rekord*⟩
(e) (cushion) auffangen ⟨*Schlag, jmds. Fall*⟩
2 *v.i.,* broke, broken **(a)** kaputtgehen (ugs.); ⟨*Faden, Seil:*⟩ [zer]reißen; ⟨*Glas, Tasse, Teller:*⟩ zerbrechen; ⟨*Eis:*⟩ brechen; ∼ **in two/ in pieces** durchbrechen/zerbrechen
(b) ∼ **into** einbrechen in (+ *Akk.*) ⟨*Haus*⟩; aufbrechen ⟨*Auto, Safe*⟩; ∼ **into laughter/ tears** in Gelächter/Tränen ausbrechen; ∼ **into a trot/run** zu traben/laufen anfangen
(c) (escape) ∼ **out of prison** aus dem Gefängnis ausbrechen; ∼ **free** *or* **loose** sich losreißen
(d) ⟨*Welle:*⟩ sich brechen (**on/against** an + *Dat.*)
(e) ⟨*Tag:*⟩ anbrechen; ⟨*Sturm:*⟩ losbrechen

(f) sb's voice is ∼ing jmd. kommt in den Stimmbruch
3 *n.* **(a)** Bruch, *der;* (of rope) Reißen, *das;* **a** ∼ **with sb./sth.** ein Bruch mit jmdm./etw.
(b) (gap) Lücke, *die;* (broken place) Sprung, *der*
(c) (dash) **they made a sudden** ∼: sie stürmten plötzlich davon
(d) (interruption) Unterbrechung, *die;* (pause, holiday) Pause, *die;* **take** *or* **have a** ∼: Pause machen
(e) (coll.: chance) Chance, *die*
▪ **break 'down** **1** *v.i.* zusammenbrechen; ⟨*Verhandlungen:*⟩ scheitern; ⟨*Auto:*⟩ eine Panne haben
2 *v.t.* **(a)** aufbrechen ⟨*Tür*⟩; brechen ⟨*Widerstand*⟩; niederreißen ⟨*Barriere, Schranke*⟩
(b) (analyse) aufgliedern
▪ **break 'in** **1** *v.i.* (into building etc.) einbrechen
2 *v.t.* **(a)** zureiten ⟨*Pferd*⟩
(b) einlaufen ⟨*Schuhe*⟩
(c) ∼ **the door** in die Tür aufbrechen
▪ **'break into** ▶ ∼ 2B
▪ **break 'off** **1** *v.t.* abbrechen; abreißen ⟨*Faden*⟩; auflösen ⟨*Verlobung*⟩
2 *v.i.* **(a)** abbrechen
(b) (cease) aufhören
▪ **break 'out** *v.i.* ausbrechen; ∼ **out in spots/a rash** Pickel/einen Ausschlag bekommen
▪ **break 'up** **1** *v.t.* **(a)** (∼ into pieces) zerkleinern; ausschlachten ⟨*Auto*⟩; aufbrechen ⟨*Erde*⟩
(b) (disband) auflösen
2 *v.i.* **(a)** (∼ into pieces, lit. or fig.) zerbrechen
(b) (disband) sich auflösen; ⟨*Schule:*⟩ schließen; ⟨*Schüler, Lehrer:*⟩ in die Ferien gehen
(c) ∼ **up [with sb.]** sich [von jmdm.] trennen

breakable /'breɪkəbl/ **1** *adj.* zerbrechlich
2 *n.* ∼s zerbrechliche Dinge

breakage /'breɪkɪdʒ/ *n.* Zerbrechen, *das;* ∼s must be paid for zerbrochene Ware muss bezahlt werden

'breakdown *n.* **(a)** (of vehicle) Panne, *die;* (in machine) Störung, *die;* ∼ **truck/van** Abschleppwagen, *der*
(b) (Med.) Zusammenbruch, *der*
(c) (analysis) Aufschlüsselung, *die*

'breaker *n.* **(a)** (wave) Brecher, *der*
(b) ∼'s [yard] Autoverwertung, *die*

breakfast /'brekfəst/ **1** *n.* Frühstück, *das;* for ∼: zum Frühstück
2 *v.i.* frühstücken

breakfast: ∼ **cereal** *n.* ≈ Frühstücksflocken *Pl.;* ∼ **'television** *n.* Frühstücksfernsehen, *das*

'break-in *n.* Einbruch, *der*

'breaking *n.* ∼ **and entering** (Law) Einbruch, *der;* **be at** ∼ **point** (mentally) die Grenze der Belastbarkeit erreicht haben

break: ∼**neck** *adj.* halsbrecherisch;   ···⟩

~**through** n. Durchbruch, der; ~**up** n. Auflösung, die; (of relationship) Bruch, der; ~**water** n. Wellenbrecher, der

breast /brest/ n. Brust, die

breast: ~**bone** n. Brustbein, das; ~ **cancer** n. Brustkrebs, der; ~**feed** v.t. & i. stillen; ~**stroke** n. Brustschwimmen, das

breath /breθ/ n. (a) Atem, der; get one's ~ back wieder zu Atem kommen; hold one's ~: den Atem anhalten; be out of ~: außer Atem sein; say sth. under one's ~: etw. vor sich (Akk.) hin murmeln (b) (one respiration) Atemzug, der

Breathalyser (Brit.), **Breathalyzer** ® /'breθəlaɪzə(r)/ n. Alcotest-Röhrchen ⓌⓏ, das; ~ test Alcotest ⓌⓏ, der

breathe /briːð/ ① v.i. atmen; ~ in einatmen; ~ out ausatmen ② v.t. (a) ~ [in/out] ein-/ausatmen (b) (utter) hauchen

'**breather** /'briːðə(r)/ n. Verschnaufpause, die

'**breathing space** n. Zeit zum Luftholen; (fig.) Atempause, die

'**breathless** adj. atemlos (with vor + Dat.)

breath: ~**taking** adj. atemberaubend; ~ **test** n. Alcotest ⓌⓏ, der

bred ▶ BREED 1, 2

breeches /'brɪtʃɪz/ n. pl. [pair of] ~: [Knie]bundhose, die; [riding]~: Reithose, die

breed /briːd/ ① v.t., bred /bred/ (a) (cause) erzeugen (b) züchten 〈Tiere, Pflanzen〉 ② v.i., bred sich vermehren ③ n. (of animals) Rasse, die

'**breeding** n. [good] ~: gute Erziehung

'**breeding ground** n. (lit. or fig.) Brutstätte, die

breeze /briːz/ n. Brise, die

'**breeze block** n. (Building) ≈ Leichtstein, der

breezy /'briːzɪ/ adj. windig

brevity /'brevɪtɪ/ n. Kürze, die

brew /bruː/ ① v.t. brauen 〈Bier〉; ~ [up] kochen 〈Kaffee, Tee usw.〉 ② v.i. (a) 〈Bier:〉 gären; 〈Kaffee, Tee:〉 ziehen (b) 〈Unwetter:〉 sich zusammenbrauen ③ n. (brewed beer/tea) Bier, das/Tee, der

'**brewer** n. Brauer, der; (firm) Brauerei, die

brewery /'bruːərɪ/ n. Brauerei, die

bribe /braɪb/ ① n. Bestechung, die ② v.t. bestechen; ~ sb. to do/into doing sth. jmdn. bestechen, damit er etw. tut

bribery /'braɪbərɪ/ n. Bestechung, die

brick /brɪk/ ① n. Ziegelstein, der; (toy) Bauklötzchen, das ② adj. Ziegelstein-

brick: ~**layer** n. Maurer, der; ~**laying** n. Mauern, das; ~ '**wall** n. Backsteinmauer, die; bang one's head against a ~ wall (fig.) mit dem Kopf gegen die Wand rennen (fig.)

bridal /'braɪdl/ adj. Braut-

bride /braɪd/ n. Braut, die

'**bridegroom** n. Bräutigam, der

bridesmaid /'braɪdzmeɪd/ n. Brautjungfer, die

bridge¹ /brɪdʒ/ ① n. (a) Brücke, die (b) (Naut.) [Kommando]brücke, die (c) (of nose) Nasenbein, das (d) (of spectacles) Steg, der ② v.t. eine Brücke bauen über (+ Akk.)

bridge² n. (Cards) Bridge, das

'**bridging loan** n. (Commerc.) Überbrückungskredit, der

bridle /'braɪdl/ n. Zaum, der

'**bridle path** n. Reitweg, der

brief¹ /briːf/ adj. (a) kurz; gering 〈Verspätung〉 (b) (concise) knapp; in ~, to be ~: kurz gesagt

brief² ① n. (instructions) Instruktionen Pl.; (Law: case) Mandat, das ② v.t. Instruktionen geben (+ Dat.); (inform) unterrichten

'**briefcase** n. Aktentasche, die

'**briefing** n. Briefing, das; (of reporters) Unterrichtung, die

'**briefly** adv. (a) kurz (b) (concisely) knapp; kurz

briefs /briːfs/ n. pl. [pair of] ~: Slip, der

brigade /brɪ'geɪd/ n. (Mil.) Brigade, die

brigadier /brɪgə'dɪə(r)/ n. Brigadegeneral, der

bright /braɪt/ adj. (a) hell; grell 〈Scheinwerfer[licht], Sonnenlicht〉; strahlend 〈Sonnenschein, Augen, Tag〉; leuchtend 〈Farbe, Blume〉; ~ intervals/periods Aufheiterungen Pl. (b) (cheerful) fröhlich (c) (clever) intelligent

brighten /'braɪtn/ ① v.t. ~ [up] aufhellen ② v.i. the weather or it is ~ing [up] es klärt sich auf

'**brightly** adv. (a) hell (b) (cheerfully) fröhlich

'**brightness** n. ▶ BRIGHT: (a) Helligkeit, die; Grelle, die; Strahlen, das; Leuchtkraft, die (b) Fröhlichkeit, die (c) Intelligenz, die

brilliance /'brɪlɪəns/ n. ▶ BRILLIANT: (a) Helligkeit, die; Leuchten, das (b) Genialität, die; Glanz, der

brilliant /'brɪljənt/ adj. (a) hell 〈Licht〉; leuchtend 〈Farbe〉 (b) genial 〈Mensch, Gedanke, Leistung〉; glänzend 〈Verstand, Aufführung, Idee〉

brim /brɪm/ ① n. Rand, der; (of hat) [Hut]krempe, die ② v.i., -mm-: be ~ming with sth. randvoll mit etw. sein

brim-'full pred. adj. randvoll (with mit)

brine /braɪn/ n. Salzwasser, das

bring /brɪŋ/ *v.t.*, **brought** /brɔːt/ (a) bringen; (as a present or favour) mitbringen; ∼ sth. with one etw. mitbringen
(b) ∼ **sb. to do sth.** jmdn. dazu bringen, etw. zu tun; **I could not** ∼ **myself to do it** ich konnte es nicht über mich bringen, es zu tun
■ **bring a'bout** *v.t.* verursachen
■ **bring 'back** *v.t.* (a) (return) zurückbringen; (from a journey) mitbringen
(b) (recall) in Erinnerung bringen
(c) (restore, reintroduce) wieder einführen
■ **bring 'down** *v.t.* (a) herunterbringen
(b) (kill, wound) zur Strecke bringen
(c) senken ⟨Preise, Inflationsrate, Fieber⟩
■ **bring 'forward** *v.t.* (a) nach vorne bringen
(b) vorverlegen ⟨Termin⟩ (**to** auf + *Akk.*)
■ **bring 'in** *v.t.* hereinbringen; einbringen ⟨Gesetzesvorlage, Verdienst, Summe⟩
■ **bring 'off** *v.t.* (conduct successfully) zustande bringen
■ **bring 'on** *v.t.* (a) (cause) verursachen
(b) (Sport) einsetzen
■ **bring 'out** *v.t.* (a) herausbringen
(b) hervorheben ⟨Unterschied⟩
(c) einführen ⟨Produkt⟩; herausbringen ⟨Buch, Zeitschrift⟩
■ **bring 'up** *v.t.* (a) heraufbringen
(b) (educate) erziehen; (rear) aufziehen
(c) zur Sprache bringen ⟨Angelegenheit, Thema, Problem⟩

brink /brɪŋk/ *n.* Rand, *der;* **be on the** ∼ **of doing sth.** nahe daran sein, etw. zu tun

brisk /brɪsk/ *adj.* flott ⟨Gang⟩; forsch ⟨Person, Art⟩; frisch ⟨Wind⟩; (fig.) rege ⟨Handel, Nachfrage⟩; lebhaft ⟨Geschäft⟩

'briskly *adv.* flott

bristle /'brɪsl/ [1] *n.* Borste, *die*
[2] *v.i.* (a) ∼ [up] ⟨Haare:⟩ sich sträuben
(b) ∼ **with** (fig.) starren vor (+ *Dat.*)

bristly /'brɪslɪ/ *adj.* borstig

Brit /brɪt/ *n.* (coll.) Brite, *der*/Britin, *die;* Engländer, *der*/Engländerin, *die* (ugs.)

Britain /'brɪtn/ *pr. n.* Großbritannien (*das*)

British /'brɪtɪʃ/ [1] *adj.* britisch; **he/she is** ∼: er ist Brite/sie ist Britin
[2] *n. pl.* **the** ∼: die Briten

British 'Isles *pr. n. pl.* Britische Inseln

Briton /'brɪtn/ *n.* Brite, *der*/Britin, *die*

Brittany /'brɪtənɪ/ *pr. n.* Bretagne, *die*

brittle /'brɪtl/ *adj.* spröde ⟨Material⟩

broach /brəʊtʃ/ *v.t.* anschneiden ⟨Thema⟩

broad /brɔːd/ *adj.* (a) breit; (extensive) weit ⟨Ebene, Land⟩
(b) (explicit) klar ⟨Hinweis⟩; breit ⟨Lächeln⟩
(c) (main) grob; (generalized) allgemein
(d) stark ⟨Akzent⟩

'broadband *n.* (Comp.) Breitband, *das; attrib.* Breitband-

broad 'bean *n.* Saubohne, *die*

broadcast /'brɔːdkɑːst/ [1] *n.* Sendung, *die;* (live) Übertragung, *die*

[2] *v.t.*, **broadcast** senden; übertragen ⟨Livesendung⟩
[3] *v.i.*, **broadcast** senden

'broadcaster *n.* (Radio, Telev.) jmd., *der* durch häufige Auftritte im Rundfunk und Fernsehen, besonders als Interviewpartner, Diskussionsteilnehmer od. Kommentator, bekannt ist

'broadcasting *n.* Senden, *das;* (live) Übertragen, *das;* **work in** ∼: beim Funk arbeiten

broaden /'brɔːdn/ [1] *v.t.* (a) verbreitern
(b) ausweiten ⟨Diskussion⟩
[2] *v.i.* sich verbreitern; (fig.) sich erweitern

'broadly *adv.* (a) deutlich ⟨hinweisen⟩; breit ⟨grinsen, lächeln⟩
(b) (in general) allgemein ⟨beschreiben⟩; ∼ **speaking** allgemein gesagt

broad: ∼**'minded** *adj.* tolerant;
∼**sheet** *n.* (a) (Printing) Einblattdruck, *der;*
(b) (pamphlet) Flugblatt, *das;*
∼**'shouldered** *adj.* breitschultrig;
∼**side** *n.* Breitseite, *die*

brocade /brə'keɪd/ *n.* Brokat, *der*

broccoli /'brɒkəlɪ/ *n.* Brokkoli, *der*

brochure /'brəʊʃə(r)/ *n.* Broschüre, *die;* Prospekt, *der*

broil /'brɔɪl/ *v.t.* (esp. Amer.) grillen

broke /brəʊk/ [1] ▸ BREAK 1, 2
[2] *pred. adj.* (coll.) pleite (ugs.)

broken /'brəʊkn/ [1] ▸ BREAK 1, 2
[2] *adj.* (a) zerbrochen; gebrochen ⟨Bein, Hals⟩; verletzt ⟨Haut⟩; abgebrochen ⟨Zahn⟩; gerissen ⟨Seil⟩; kaputt (ugs.) ⟨Uhr, Fernsehen, Fenster⟩; ∼ **glass** Glasscherben *Pl.*
(b) (imperfect) gebrochen; **in** ∼ **English** in gebrochenem Englisch
(c) (fig.) ruiniert ⟨Ehe⟩; gebrochen ⟨Mensch, Herz⟩

broken: ∼**-down** *adj.* baufällig ⟨Gebäude⟩; kaputt (ugs.) ⟨Wagen⟩;
∼**'hearted** *adj.* untröstlich

broker /'brəʊkə(r)/ *n.* Makler, *der*

brolly /'brɒlɪ/ *n.* (Brit. coll.) [Regen]schirm, *der*

bronchitis /brɒŋ'kaɪtɪs/ *n.* Bronchitis, *die*

bronze /brɒnz/ [1] *n.* Bronze, *die*
[2] *attrib. adj.* Bronze-; (coloured like ∼) bronzefarben

brooch /brəʊtʃ/ *n.* Brosche, *die*

brood /bruːd/ [1] *n.* Brut, *die*
[2] *v.i.* [vor sich (*Akk.*) hin] brüten

brook /brʊk/ *n.* Bach, *der*

broom /bruːm/ *n.* (a) Besen, *der*
(b) (Bot.) Ginster, *der*

broom: ∼ **cupboard** *n.* Besenschrank, *der;* ∼**stick** *n.* Besenstiel, *der*

broth /brɒθ/ *n.* Brühe, *die*

brothel /'brɒθl/ *n.* Bordell, *das*

brother /'brʌðə(r)/ *n.* Bruder, *der;* **my** ∼**s and sisters** meine Geschwister

'brotherhood *n.* (organization) Bruderschaft, *die*

'brother-in-law *n., pl.* **brothers-in-law** Schwager, *der*

brought ▶ BRING

brow /braʊ/ *n.* (a) (eye~) Braue, *die* (b) (forehead) Stirn, *die* (c) (of hill) Kuppe, *die*

'browbeat *v.t., forms as* BEAT 1 einschüchtern

brown /braʊn/ [1] *adj.* braun [2] *n.* Braun, *das*

brown: ~ **'bread** *n.* ≈ Mischbrot, *das;* ~**-eyed** *adj.* braunäugig; **be** ~**-eyed** braune Augen haben

Brownie /'braʊnɪ/ *n.* Wichtel, *die*

brown: ~ **'paper** *n.* Packpapier, *das;* ~ **'rice** *n.* Naturreis, *der*

browse /braʊz/ *v.i.* [1] (a) weiden (b) (in shop) sich umsehen; (read) blättern (**through** in + *Dat.*) (c) (Comp.) suchen; ~ **through** sth. etw. durchsuchen [2] (a) abgrasen ⟨*Weide*⟩; abfressen ⟨*Blätter*⟩ (b) (Comp.) ~ **sth** in etw. (*Dat.*) suchen

browser /'braʊzə(r)/ *n.* (Comp.) Browser, *der*

bruise /bruːz/ [1] *n.* (a) (Med.) blauer Fleck (b) (on fruit) Druckstelle, *die* [2] *v.t.* quetschen ⟨*Obst, Pflanzen*⟩; ~ **oneself/one's leg** sich stoßen/sich am Bein stoßen

brunch /brʌntʃ/ *n.* (coll.) Brunch, *der;* ausgedehntes, spätes Frühstück

brunette /bruː'net/ [1] *n.* Brünette, *die* [2] *adj.* brünett

brunt /brʌnt/ *n.* **bear the** ~ **of the attack/ financial cuts** von dem Angriff/von den Einsparungen am meisten betroffen sein

brush /brʌʃ/ [1] *n.* (a) Bürste, *die;* (for sweeping) Besen, *der;* (with short handle) Handfeger, *der;* (for painting or writing) Pinsel, *der* (b) (skirmish) Zusammenstoß, *der* (c) (light touch) flüchtige Berührung [2] *v.t.* (a) kehren; fegen; abbürsten ⟨*Kleidung*⟩; ~ **one's teeth/hair** sich (*Dat.*) die Zähne putzen/die Haare bürsten (b) (touch in passing) streifen [3] *v.i.* ~ **past sb./sth.** jmdn./etw. streifen ■ **brush 'up** *v.t. & i.* ~ **up [on]** auffrischen ⟨*Kenntnisse usw.*⟩

brusque /brʌsk/ *adj.,* **'brusquely** *adv.* schroff

Brussels /'brʌslz/ *pr. n.* Brüssel (*das*)

Brussels 'sprouts *n. pl.* Rosenkohl, *der*

brutal /'bruːtl/ *adj.* brutal

brutality /bruː'tælɪtɪ/ *n.* Brutalität, *die*

brutally /'bruːtəlɪ/ *adv.* brutal

brute /bruːt/ [1] *n.* (a) (animal) Bestie, *die* (b) (person) Rohling, *der* [2] *attrib. adj.* **by** ~ **force** mit roher Gewalt

B.Sc. *abbr.* = **Bachelor of Science**

BSE *abbr.* = **bovine spongiform encephalopathy** BSE

BST *abbr.* = **British Summer Time** Britische Sommerzeit

bubble /'bʌbl/ [1] *n.* Blase, *die;* (small) Perle, *die* [2] *v.i.* ⟨*Wasser, Schlamm, Lava:*⟩ Blasen bilden

bubble: ~ **bath** *n.* Schaumbad, *das;* ~ **pack** *n.* Klarsichtpackung, *die;* ~**-wrapped** *adj.* in Luftpolsterfolie verpackt

buck[1] /bʌk/ *n.* (deer, chamois) Bock, *der;* (rabbit, hare) Rammler, *der*

buck[2] *n.* **pass the** ~ **to sb.** jmdm. die Verantwortung aufhalsen

buck[3] (coll.) [1] *v.i.* ~ **'up (a)** (make haste) sich ranhalten (ugs.) (b) (cheer up) ~ **up!** Kopf hoch! [2] *v.t.* ~ **one's ideas up** (coll.) sich zusammenreißen

buck[4] *n.* (Amer. coll.) Dollar, *der*

bucket /'bʌkɪt/ *n.* Eimer, *der*

bucketful /'bʌkɪtfʊl/ *n.* Eimer [voll]

bucket: ~ **seat** *n.* Schalensitz, *der;* ~ **shop** *n.* [nicht ganz seriöses] Maklerbüro; (for air tickets) Reisebüro (*das vor allem Billigflüge vermittelt*)

buckle /'bʌkl/ [1] *n.* Schnalle, *die* [2] *v.t.* (a) zuschnallen; ~ **sth. on/up** etw. anschnallen/festschnallen (b) verbiegen ⟨*Stoßstange, Rad*⟩ [3] *v.i.* ⟨*Rad, Metallplatte:*⟩ [sich] verbiegen

bud /bʌd/ [1] *n.* Knospe, *die;* **come into** ~**/be in** ~: Knospen treiben [2] *v.i.,* **-dd-** Knospen treiben

Buddha /'bʊdə/ *n.* Buddha, *der*

Buddhism /'bʊdɪzm/ *n.* Buddhismus, *der*

Buddhist /'bʊdɪst/ [1] *n.* Buddhist, *der/* Buddhistin, *die* [2] *adj.* buddhistisch

budge /bʌdʒ/ [1] *v.i.* sich rühren; ⟨*Gegenstand:*⟩ sich bewegen [2] *v.t.* bewegen

budgerigar /'bʌdʒərɪgɑː(r)/ *n.* Wellensittich, *der*

budget /'bʌdʒɪt/ [1] *n.* Etat, *der;* Haushalt[splan], *der* [2] *v.i.* ~ **for sth.** etw. [im Etat] einplanen

'budget account *n.* Konto für laufende Zahlungen

budgie /'bʌdʒɪ/ *n.* (coll.) Wellensittich, *der*

buff /bʌf/ [1] *adj.* gelbbraun [2] *n.* (coll.: enthusiast) Fan, *der* (ugs.)

buffalo /'bʌfələʊ/ *n., pl.* ~**es or same** Büffel, *der*

buffer /'bʌfə(r)/ *n.* Prellbock, *der;* (on vehicle; also fig.) Puffer, *der*

buffet /'bʊfeɪ/ *n.* Büfett, *das*

'buffet car *n.* Büfettwagen, *der*

bug /bʌg/ *n.* (also coll.: microphone) Wanze, *die*

bugger /'bʌgə(r)/ (coarse) ⊡ *n.* (as insult) Scheißkerl, *der* (derb)

⊡ *v.t.* (damn) ~ you/him du kannst/der kann mich mal (derb); ~ it! ach du Scheiße! (derb)

■ ~ **'off** *v.i.* abhauen (ugs.)

buggy /'bʌgɪ/ *n.* (pushchair) Sportwagen, *der*

bugle /'bjuːgl/ *n.* Bügelhorn, *das*

build /bɪld/ ⊡ *v.t.*, *built* /bɪlt/ bauen; (fig.) aufbauen ⟨System, Gesellschaft, Zukunft⟩

⊡ *v.i.*, *built* bauen

⊡ *n.* Körperbau, *der*

■ **build 'in** *v.t.* einbauen

■ **build 'on** *v.t.* aufbauen auf (+ *Dat.*); bebauen ⟨Gebiet⟩

■ **build 'up** ⊡ *v.t.* aufhäufen ⟨Reserven, Mittel⟩; kräftigen ⟨Personen, Körper⟩; steigern ⟨Produktion, Kapazität⟩; stärken ⟨[Selbst]vertrauen⟩; aufbauen ⟨Firma, Geschäft⟩

⊡ *v.i.* ⟨Spannung, Druck:⟩ zunehmen; ⟨Schlange, Rückstau:⟩ sich bilden; ⟨Verkehr:⟩ sich verdichten

'builder *n.* Bauunternehmer, *der*

'building *n.* (a) Bau, *der*

(b) (structure) Gebäude, *das*

building: ~ **site** *n.* Baustelle, *die;* ~ **society** *n.* (Brit.) Bausparkasse, *die*

built ▶ BUILD 1, 2

built: ~**-in** *adj.* (a) eingebaut; Einbau⟨schrank, küche usw.⟩; (b) (fig.: instinctive) angeboren; ~**-up** *adj.* bebaut; ~**-up area** Wohngebiet, *das;* (Motor Veh.) geschlossene Ortschaft

bulb /bʌlb/ *n.* (a) (Bot., Hort.) Zwiebel, *die* (b) (of lamp) [Glüh]birne, *die*

Bulgaria /bʌl'geərɪə/ *pr. n.* Bulgarien (*das*)

Bulgarian /bʌl'geərɪən/ ⊡ *adj.* bulgarisch; **sb. is** ~: jmd. ist Bulgare/Bulgarin

⊡ *n.* (a) (person) Bulgare, *der*/Bulgarin, *die* (b) (language) Bulgarisch, *das; see also* ENGLISH 2A

bulge /bʌldʒ/ ⊡ *n.* Ausbeulung, *die;* ausgebeulte Stelle

⊡ *v.i.* sich wölben

bulimia (nervosa) /bʊ'liːmɪə (nɜː'vəʊsə)/ *n.* Bulimie, *die;* Bulimia nervosa, *die* (fachspr.)

bulimic /bʊ'lɪmɪk/ ⊡ *n.* Bulimiker, *der*/ Bulimikerin, *die*

⊡ *adj.* bulimisch

bulk /bʌlk/ *n.* (a) (large quantity) **in** ~: in großen Mengen

(b) (large shape) massige Gestalt

(c) (size) Größe, *die*

(d) (greater part) der größte Teil; (of population, votes) Mehrheit, *die*

bulk 'buying *n.* Großeinkauf, *der*

'bulky *adj.* sperrig ⟨Gegenstand⟩; massig ⟨Gestalt, Körper⟩

bull /bʊl/ *n.* Bulle, *der;* (esp. for bullfight) Stier, *der*

bull: ~ **bar** *n.* Rammschutz, *der;* Rammbügel, *der;* ~**dog** *n.* Bulldogge, *die*

bulldozer /'bʊldəʊzə(r)/ *n.* Planierraupe, *die*

bullet /'bʊlɪt/ *n.* Kugel, *die*

'bullet hole *n.* Einschuss, *der;* Einschussloch, *das*

bulletin /'bʊlɪtɪn/ *n.* Bulletin, *das*

'bulletin board *n.* (Comp.) schwarzes Brett

'bulletproof *adj.* kugelsicher

bull: ~**fight** *n.* Stierkampf, *der;* ~**fighter** *n.* Stierkämpfer, *der;* ~**fighting** *n.* Stierkämpfe *Pl.*

bullion /'bʊljən/ *n.* **gold** ~: Goldbarren *Pl.*

'bull neck *n.* Stiernacken, *der*

bullock /'bʊlək/ *n.* Ochse, *der*

bull: ~**ring** *n.* Stierkampfarena, *die;* ~**seye** *n.* (of target) Schwarze, *das;* ~**shit** (coarse) *n.* Scheiße, *der* (salopp abwertend)

bully /'bʊlɪ/ ⊡ *n.* (schoolboy etc.) ≈ Rabauke, *der;* (boss) Tyrann, *der*

⊡ *v.t.* schikanieren; (frighten) einschüchtern

bullying /'bʊlɪɪŋ/ *n.* Schikanieren, *das*

bum¹ /bʌm/ *n.* (Brit. coll.) Hintern, *der* (ugs.)

bum² *n.* (Amer. coll.: tramp) Penner, *der* (salopp)

bumble-bee /'bʌmblbiː/ *n.* Hummel, *die*

bumf /bʌmf/ *n.* (Brit. coll. derog.: papers) Papierkram, *der* (ugs.)

bump /bʌmp/ ⊡ *n.* (a) (sound) Bums, *der;* (impact) Stoß, *der*

(b) (swelling) Beule, *die*

(c) (hump) Buckel, *der* (ugs.)

⊡ *adv.* bums

⊡ *v.t.* anstoßen

■ **'bump into** *v.t.* (a) stoßen an (+ *Akk.*)

(b) (meet by chance) zufällig [wieder]treffen

'bumper ⊡ *n.* Stoßstange, *die;* ~**-to-**~ Stoßstange an Stoßstange

⊡ *attrib. adj.* Rekord⟨ernte, -jahr⟩

'bumpy *adj.* holp[e]rig ⟨Straße, Fahrt, Fahrzeug⟩; uneben ⟨Fläche⟩; unruhig ⟨Flug⟩

bun /bʌn/ *n.* süßes Brötchen; (currant ~) Korinthenbrötchen, *das*

bunch /bʌntʃ/ *n.* (a) (of flowers) Strauß, *der;* (of grapes, bananas) Traube, *die;* (of parsley, radishes) Bund, *das;* ~ **of flowers/grapes** Blumenstrauß, *der*/Traube, *die;* **a** ~ **of keys** ein Schlüsselbund

(b) (lot) Anzahl, *die;* **the best** *or* **pick of the** ~: der/die/das Beste [von allen]

(c) (of people) Haufen, *der* (ugs.)

bundle /'bʌndl/ *n.* Bündel, *das;* (of papers) Packen, *der*

bung /bʌŋ/ ⊡ *n.* Spund, *der*

⊡ *v.t.* (coll.) schmeißen (ugs.)

■ **bung 'up** *v.i.* be/get ~ed up verstopft sein/verstopfen

bungalow /'bʌŋgələʊ/ *n.* Bungalow, *der*

'bungee jumping /'bʌndʒɪ/ *n.* Bungeespringen, *das*

bungle /'bʌŋgl/ *v.t.* stümpern bei

bunk /bʌŋk/ *n.* (in ship, lorry) Koje, *die;* (in sleeping car) Bett, *das;* (~ bed) Etagenbett, *das*

bunker /'bʌŋkə(r)/ n. Bunker, der

bunny /'bʌnɪ/ n. Häschen, das

buoy /bɔɪ/ n. Boje, die

buoyancy /'bɔɪənsɪ/ n. Auftrieb, der

buoyant /'bɔɪənt/ adj. (a) schwimmend; be ∼: schwimmen
(b) (fig.) rege, lebhaft ⟨Markt⟩; heiter, munter ⟨Person⟩; in ∼ spirits in Hochstimmung

burden /'bɜːdn/ ① n. Last, die; become a ∼ (fig.) zur Last werden
② v.t. belasten (with mit)

bureau /'bjʊərəʊ, bjʊəˈrəʊ/ n. (a) (Brit.: writing desk) Sekretär, der
(b) (office) Büro, das

bureaucracy /bjʊəˈrɒkrəsɪ/ n. Bürokratie, die

bureaucrat /'bjʊərəkræt/ n. Bürokrat, der/Bürokratin, die

bureaucratic /bjʊərəˈkrætɪk/ adj. bürokratisch

burger /'bɜːgə(r)/ n. (coll.) Hamburger, der

'burger bar n. (coll.) Hamburgerlokal, das

burglar /'bɜːglə(r)/ n. Einbrecher, der

burglar: ∼ **alarm** n. Alarmanlage, die; ∼**-proof** adj. einbruch[s]sicher

burglary /'bɜːglərɪ/ n. Einbruch, der

burgle /'bɜːgl/ v.t. einbrechen in (+ Akk.); the shop/he was ∼d in dem Laden/bei ihm wurde eingebrochen

burial /'berɪəl/ n. Begräbnis, das

burly /'bɜːlɪ/ adj. stämmig

Burma /'bɜːmə/ pr. n. Birma (das)

Burmese /bɜːˈmiːz/ ① adj. birmanisch; sb. is ∼: jmd. ist Birmane/Birmanin
② n., pl. same (a) (person) Birmane, der/Birmanin, die
(b) (language) Birmanisch, das; see also ENGLISH 2A

burn /bɜːn/ ① n. (on the skin) Verbrennung, die; (on material) Brandfleck, der
② v.t., ∼t /bɜːnt/ or ∼ed (a) verbrennen; ∼ oneself/one's hand sich verbrennen/sich (Dat.) die Hand verbrennen; ∼ a hole in sth. ein Loch in etw. (Akk.) brennen
(b) als Brennstoff verwenden ⟨Gas, Öl usw.⟩; heizen mit ⟨Kohle, Holz, Torf⟩
(c) (spoil) anbrennen lassen ⟨Fleisch, Kuchen⟩; be ∼t angebrannt sein
(d) (Comp.) brennen ⟨CD, CD-ROM⟩
③ v.i., ∼t or ∼ed brennen; ∼ to death verbrennen; she ∼s easily sie bekommt leicht einen Sonnenbrand
■ **burn 'down** v.t. & i. niederbrennen

'burned-out adj. (lit. or fig.) ausgebrannt

'burner n. Brenner, der

'burning adj. glühend ⟨Leidenschaft, Hass, Wunsch⟩; brennend ⟨Wunsch, Frage⟩

'burn-out n. Burn-out, das (Med.); totale Erschöpfung od. Entkräftung; risk ∼: Gefahr laufen, sich zu übernehmen

burnt ▶ BURN 2, 3

'burnt-out ▶ BURNED-OUT

burp /bɜːp/ (coll.) ① n. Rülpser, der (ugs.)
② v.i. rülpsen (ugs.)

burrow /'bʌrəʊ/ ① n. Bau, der
② v.i. [sich (Dat.)] einen Gang graben

burst /bɜːst/ ① n. (a) (split) Bruch, der
(b) (of firing) Salve, die
(c) (fig.) a ∼ of applause/cheering ein Beifallsausbruch/Beifallsrufe Pl.
② v.t., burst zum Platzen bringen; platzen lassen ⟨Luftballon⟩; ∼ pipe Rohrbruch, der
③ v.i., burst (a) platzen; ⟨Bombe:⟩ explodieren; ⟨Damm:⟩ brechen; ⟨Flussufer:⟩ überschwemmt werden; ⟨Furunkel, Geschwür:⟩ aufgehen
(b) be ∼ing with sth. zum Bersten voll sein mit etw.; be ∼ing with pride/impatience/excitement vor Stolz/Ungeduld platzen/vor Aufregung außer sich sein
■ **'burst into** v.t. (a) eindringen in
(b) ∼ into tears/laughter in Tränen/Gelächter ausbrechen; ∼ into flames in Brand geraten
■ **burst 'out** v.i. (a) herausstürzen
(b) (exclaim) losplatzen
(c) ∼ out laughing/crying in Lachen/Tränen ausbrechen

bury /'berɪ/ v.t. (a) begraben
(b) (hide) vergraben; ∼ one's face in one's hands das Gesicht in den Händen vergraben
(c) ∼ one's teeth in sth. seine Zähne in etw. (Akk.) graben

bus /bʌs/ n. Bus, der

bus: ∼ **company** n. ≈ Verkehrsbetrieb, der; ∼ **conductor** n. Busschaffner, der/-schaffnerin, die; ∼ **depot** ▶ ∼ GARAGE; ∼ **driver** n. Busfahrer, der/-fahrerin, die; ∼ **fare** n. [Bus]fahrpreis, der; ∼ **garage** n. Busdepot, das

bush /bʊʃ/ n. (a) Busch, der
(b) (shrubs) Gebüsch, das

'bushy adj. buschig

busily /'bɪzɪlɪ/ adj. eifrig

business /'bɪznɪs/ n. (a) (trading operation) Geschäft, das; (company, firm) Betrieb, der; (large) Unternehmen, das; how's ∼ with you? (lit. or fig.) was machen die Geschäfte [bei Ihnen]?; ∼ is ∼ (fig.) Geschäft ist Geschäft; go out of ∼: Pleite gehen (ugs.); go into ∼: Geschäftsmann/-frau werden
(b) (buying and selling) Geschäfte Pl.
(c) (task, province) Aufgabe, die; mind your own ∼! kümmere dich um deine [eigenen] Angelegenheiten!
(d) (difficult matter) Problem, das

business: ∼ **address** n. Geschäftsadresse, die; ∼ **card** n. Geschäftskarte, die; ∼ **class** ① n., no pl. Businessklasse-; attrib. ② adv. fly/travel ∼ class in der Businessklasse fliegen/reisen; ∼ **correspondence** n. Geschäftskorrespondenz, die; ∼ **hours** n. pl. Geschäftszeit, die; (in office) Dienstzeit, die; ∼ **letter** n. Geschäftsbrief, der; ∼**-like**

adj. geschäftsmäßig ⟨Art⟩; geschäftstüchtig ⟨Person⟩; ~ **lunch** n. Arbeitsessen, das; ~**man** n. Geschäftsmann, der; ~ **park** n. Gewerbepark, der; ~ **plan** n. Geschäftsplan, der; ~ **premises** n. pl. Geschäftsräume Pl.; ~ **school** n. kaufmännische Fachschule; ~ **studies** n. pl. Wirtschaftslehre, die; ~ **trip** n. Geschäftsreise, die; on a ~ trip auf Geschäftsreise; ~**woman** n. Geschäftsfrau, die

busker /'bʌskə(r)/ n. Straßenmusikant, der

bus: ~ **lane** n. (Brit.) Busspur, die; ~ **ride** n. Busfahrt, die; B. is only an hour's ~ ride away B. ist nur eine Busstunde entfernt; ~ **route** n. Buslinie, die; ~ **service** n. Omnibusverkehr, der; (specific service) Busverbindung, die; ~ **shelter** n. Wartehäuschen, das; ~ **station** n. Omnibusbahnhof, der; ~ **stop** n. Bushaltestelle, die

bust¹ /bʌst/ n. (a) (sculpture) Büste, die (b) ~ [measurement] Oberweite, die

bust² (coll.) [1] adj. kaputt (ugs.) [2] v.t., ~ed or bust (break) kaputtmachen (ugs.); ~ sth. open etw. aufbrechen [3] v.i., ~ed or bust kaputtgehen (ugs.)

bus: ~ **terminal** n. Busbahnhof, der; ~ **ticket** n. Busfahrkarte, die; Busfahrschein, der

bustle /'bʌsl/ [1] v.i. ~ about geschäftig hin und her eilen [2] n. Betrieb, der

bustling /'bʌslɪŋ/ adj. belebt ⟨Straße, Stadt, Markt usw.⟩; rege ⟨Tätigkeit⟩

busy /'bɪzɪ/ [1] adj. (a) beschäftigt (at, with mit); arbeitsreich ⟨Leben⟩; ziemlich hektisch ⟨Zeit⟩; I'm ~ now ich habe jetzt zu tun; he was ~ packing er war mit Packen beschäftigt (b) (Amer. Teleph.) besetzt [2] v. refl. ~ oneself sich beschäftigen (with mit)

'**busybody** n. G[e]schaftlhuber, der

but [1] /bət, stressed bʌt/ conj. aber; correcting after a negative sondern; **not that book** ~ **this one** nicht das Buch, sondern dieses [2] /bət/ prep. außer (+ Dat.); **the next/last** ~ **one** der/die/das übernächste/vorletzte

butcher /'bʊtʃə(r)/ [1] n. Fleischer, der/ Fleischerin, die [2] v.t. (murder) niedermetzeln

butler /'bʌtlə(r)/ n. Butler, der

butt¹ /bʌt/ n. (a) (of rifle) Kolben, der (b) (of cigarette, cigar) Stummel, der

butt² n. (object of teasing or ridicule) Zielscheibe, die

butt³ [1] n. (push) (by person) [Kopf]stoß, der; (by animal) Stoß [mit den Hörnern] [2] v.t. & i. mit dem Kopf/den Hörnern stoßen

■ **butt 'in** v.i. dazwischenreden

butter /'bʌtə(r)/ [1] n. Butter, die

[2] v.t. buttern

butter: ~ **bean** n. Mondbohne, die; ~**cup** n. Butterblume, die; ~ **dish** n. Butterdose, die; ~**fingers** n. sing. Tollpatsch, der (beim Fangen usw.); ~**fly** n. (a) Schmetterling, der; (b) ~fly [stroke] Delphinstil, der; ~ **mountain** n. Butterberg, der

buttock /'bʌtək/ n. Hinterbacke, die; Gesäßhälfte, die; ~s Gesäß, das

button /'bʌtn/ [1] n. Knopf, der [2] v.t. ~ [up] zuknöpfen

'**buttonhole** [1] n. (a) Knopfloch, das (b) (flower) Knopflochblume, die [2] v.t. zu fassen kriegen (ugs.)

buttress /'bʌtrɪs/ n. (Archit.) Mauerstütze, die

buxom /'bʌksəm/ adj. drall

buy /baɪ/ [1] v.t., bought /bɔːt/ kaufen; ~ sb./oneself sth. jmdm./sich etw. kaufen [2] n. [Ein]kauf, der; be a good ~: preiswert sein

■ **buy 'up** v.t. aufkaufen

'**buyer** n. (a) Käufer, der/Käuferin, die (b) (Commerc.) Einkäufer, der/Einkäuferin, die

'**buying power** /'baɪɪŋ/ n. Kaufkraft, die

'**buyout** n. Aufkauf, der; Management-Buy-Out, das (Wirtsch.)

buzz /bʌz/ [1] n. Summen, das [2] v.i. summen

■ **buzz 'off** v.i. (coll.) abhauen (salopp)

'**buzzer** n. Summer, der

by /baɪ/ [1] prep. (a) (near, beside) an (+ Dat.); bei; (next to) neben; ~ **the window/river** am Fenster/Fluss (b) (to position beside) zu (c) (about, in the possession of) bei (d) [all] by herself/himself etc. [ganz] allein[e] (e) (along) entlang; (via) über (+ Akk.) (f) (passing) vorbei an (+ Dat.) (g) (during) bei; **by day/night** bei Tag/Nacht (h) (through the agency of) von; **written by ...**: geschrieben von ... (i) (through the means of) durch; **by bus/ship** etc. mit dem Bus/Schiff usw.; **by air/sea** mit dem Flugzeug/Schiff (j) (not later than) bis; **by now/this time** inzwischen (k) (indicating unit) pro; **by the minute/hour** pro Minute/Stunde; **day by day/month by month** Tag für Tag/Monat für Monat; **10 ft. by 20 ft.** 10 [Fuß] mal 20 Fuß (l) (indicating amount) **one by one** einzeln; **two by two/three by three** zu zweit/dritt (m) (indicating factor) durch; **8 divided by 2 is 4** 8 geteilt durch 2 ist 4 (n) (indicating extent) um; **wider by a foot** um einen Fuß breiter (o) (according to) nach [2] adv. (a) (past) vorbei (b) (near) **close/near by** in der Nähe (c) **by and large** im Großen und Ganzen

bye[-bye] /'baɪ(baɪ)/ *int.* (coll.) tschüs (ugs.)

bye-law ▸ BY-LAW

'by-election *n.* Nachwahl, *die*

bygone /'baɪɡɒn/ *adj.* vergangen

'by-law *n.* (esp. Brit.) Verordnung, *die*

'bypass ① *n.* **(a)** Umgehungsstraße, *die*
(b) (Med.) Bypass, *der;* ~ **surgery** (Med.) eine
Bypassoperation/Bypassoperationen *Pl.*
② *v.t.* **(a) the road** ~**es the town** die Straße
führt um die Stadt herum

(b) (fig.) übergehen

'by-product *n.* Nebenprodukt, *das*

'byroad *n.* Nebenstraße, *die*

bystander /'baɪstændə(r)/ *n.* Zuschauer,
*der/*Zuschauerin, *die*

byte /'baɪt/ *n.* (Comp.) Byte, *das*

'byway *n.* Seitenweg, *der*

'byword *n.* Inbegriff, *der* (**for** *Gen.*)

Cc

C, c /siː/ *n.* C, c, *das*

C. *abbr.* **(a)** = **Celsius** C
(b) = **Centigrade** C

cab /kæb/ *n.* **(a)** (taxi) Taxi, *das*
(b) (of lorry, truck) Fahrerhaus, *das;* (of train)
Führerstand, *der*

cabaret /'kæbəreɪ/ *n.* Varietee, *das;*
(satirical) Kabarett, *das*

cabbage /'kæbɪdʒ/ *n.* Kohl, *der;* **red/white**
~: Rot-/Weißkohl, *der*

'cab driver *n.* Taxifahrer, *der/*-fahrerin, *die*

cabin /'kæbɪn/ *n.* (in ship) (for passengers)
Kabine, *die;* (for crew) Kajüte, *die;* (in aircraft)
Kabine, *die*

cabinet /'kæbɪnɪt/ *n.* **(a)** Schrank, *der;* (in
bathroom, for medicines) Schränkchen, *das;*
[**display**] ~: Vitrine, *die*
(b) the C~ (Polit.) das Kabinett; **C**~ **Minister**
Minister, *der*

cable /'keɪbl/ ① *n.* **(a)** (rope) Kabel, *das;* (of
~ car etc.) Seil, *das*
(b) (Electr., Teleph.) Kabel, *das*
(c) (message) Kabel, *das*
② *v.t.* kabeln ⟨*Mitteilung, Nachricht*⟩

cable: ~ **car** *n.* Drahtseilbahn, *die;*
~ **'television,** ~ **T'V** *ns.* Kabelfernsehen,
das

'cab rank *n.* (Brit.) Taxistand, *der;*
Droschken[halte]platz, *der* (Amtsspr.)

cache /kæʃ/ *n.* geheimes [Waffen-/Proviant-]
lager

cackle /'kækl/ ① *n.* **(a)** (of hen) Gackern,
das
(b) (laughter) [meckerndes] Gelächter
② *v.i.* **(a)** ⟨*Henne:*⟩ gackern
(b) (laugh) meckernd lachen

cactus /'kæktəs/ *n., pl.* **cacti** /'kæktaɪ/ *or*
~**es** Kaktus, *der*

CAD *abbr.* = **computer-aided design**
CAD

caddie /'kædɪ/ *n.* (Golf) Caddie, *der*

caddy /'kædɪ/ *n.* Dose, *die*

cadet /kə'det/ *n.* Offiziersschüler, *der;*
naval/police ~: Marinekadett/Anwärter für
den Polizeidienst

cadge /kædʒ/ *v.t.* [sich (*Dat.*)] erbetteln

café, cafe /'kæfeɪ/ *n.* Lokal, *das;* (tea room)
Café, *das*

cafeteria /kæfɪ'tɪərɪə/ *n.* Cafeteria, *die*

cafetière /kæfə'tjeə/ *n.* Kaffeebereiter, *der*

caffeinated /'kæfɪneɪtɪd/ *adj.* koffeinhaltig

caffeine /'kæfiːn/ *n.* Koffein, *das*

cage /keɪdʒ/ ① *n.* **(a)** Käfig, *der*
(b) (of lift) Fahrkabine, *die*
② *v.t.* einsperren

cagey /'keɪdʒɪ/ *adj.* (coll.) zugeknöpft (ugs.);
be ~ **about sth.** mit etw. hinterm Berg
halten (ugs.)

Cairo /'kaɪərəʊ/ *pr. n.* Kairo (*das*)

cajole /kə'dʒəʊl/ *v.t.* ~ **sb. into sth./doing
sth.** jmdm. etw. einreden/jmdm. einreden,
etw. zu tun

cake /keɪk/ ① *n.* **(a)** Kuchen, *der;* **a** ~ **of soap**
ein Riegel *od.* Stück Seife
② *v.t.* verkrusten; ~**d with dirt/blood**
schmutz-/blutverkrustet

cal. *abbr.* = **calorie[s]** cal.

calamity /kə'læmɪtɪ/ *n.* Unheil, *das*

calcium /'kælsɪəm/ *n.* Kalzium, *das*

calculate /'kælkjʊleɪt/ ① *v.t.* **(a)**
berechnen; (by estimating) ausrechnen
(b) be ~**d to do sth.** darauf abzielen, etw. zu
tun
② *v.i.* ~ **on doing sth.** damit rechnen, etw.
zu tun

'calculated *adj.* kalkuliert ⟨*Risiko*⟩;
vorsätzlich ⟨*Handlung*⟩

calculation /kælkjʊ'leɪʃn/ *n.* **(a)** (result)
Rechnung, *die;* **he is out in his** ~**s** er hat
sich verrechnet
(b) (calculating) Berechnung, *die*

calculator /'kælkjʊleɪtə(r)/ *n.* Rechner, *der*

calculus /ˈkælkjuːləs/ *n.* differential/ integral ∼: Differenzial-/Integralrechnung, *die*

calendar /ˈkælɪndə(r)/ *n.* Kalender, *der; attrib.* Kalender-

calf¹ /kɑːf/ *n., pl.* **calves** Kalb, *das*

calf² *n., pl.* **calves** (Anat.) Wade, *die*

calibre (*Brit.; Amer.:* **caliber**) /ˈkælɪbə(r)/ *n.* Kaliber, *das*

calico /ˈkælɪkəʊ/ *n.* Kattun, *der*

California /kælɪˈfɔːnɪə/ *pr. n.* Kalifornien (*das*)

caliper ▶ CALLIPER

call /kɔːl/ ① *v.i.* (a) rufen; ∼ **to sb.** jmdm. etwas zurufen; ∼ **[out] for help** um Hilfe rufen
(b) (*pay brief visit*) [kurz] besuchen (**at** *Akk.*); ∼ **on sb.** jmdn. besuchen; ∼ **round** vorbeikommen (ugs.); ∼ **at a port/station** einen Hafen anlaufen/an einem Bahnhof halten
(c) (Teleph.) **who is** ∼**ing, please?** wer spricht da, bitte?; **thank you for** ∼**ing** vielen Dank für Ihren Anruf!
② *v.t.* (a) rufen; aufrufen ⟨*Namen, Nummer*⟩
(b) (*cry to, summon*) rufen; (*to a duty, to do sth.*) aufrufen
(c) (*by radio/telephone*) rufen/anrufen; (*initially*) Kontakt aufnehmen mit
(d) (*rouse*) wecken
(e) einberufen ⟨*Konferenz*⟩; ausrufen ⟨*Streik*⟩
(f) (*name*) nennen; **he is** ∼**ed Bob** er heißt Bob; **what is it** ∼**ed in English?** wie heißt das auf Englisch?
③ *n.* (a) Ruf, *der;* **a** ∼ **for help** ein Hilferuf; **be on** ∼: Bereitschaftsdienst haben
(b) (*visit*) Besuch, *der;* **make** *or* **pay a** ∼ **on sb., make** *or* **pay sb. a** ∼: jmdn. besuchen
(c) (*telephone* ∼) Anruf, *der;* **give sb. a** ∼: jmdn. anrufen; **make a** ∼: telefonieren
(d) (*invitation, summons*) Aufruf, *der*
(e) (*need, occasion*) Anlass, *der*

▪ **call ˈback** ① *v.t.* zurückrufen
② *v.i.* zurückrufen; (*come back*) zurückkommen

▪ **ˈcall for** *v.t.* (a) (*send for, order*) bestellen
(b) (*collect*) abholen
(c) (*require, demand*) erfordern; **this** ∼**s for a celebration** das muss gefeiert werden

▪ **call ˈin** ① *v.i.* vorbeikommen (ugs.) (**on** bei)
② *v.t.* zu Rate ziehen ⟨*Fachmann usw.*⟩

▪ **call ˈoff** *v.t.* absagen ⟨*Treffen, Verabredung*⟩; rückgängig machen ⟨*Geschäft*⟩; lösen ⟨*Verlobung*⟩; (*end*) abbrechen ⟨*Streik*⟩

▪ **ˈcall on** *v.t.* (a) ▶ ∼ 1B
(b) ▶ ∼ [UP]ON

▪ **call ˈout** ① *v.t.* alarmieren ⟨*Truppen*⟩; zum Streik aufrufen ⟨*Arbeitnehmer*⟩
② *v.i.* ▶ ∼ 1A

▪ **call ˈup** *v.t.* (a) (*by telephone*) anrufen
(b) (Mil.) einberufen

▪ **ˈcall [up]on** *v.t.* ∼ **upon sb.'s generosity**

an jmds. Großzügigkeit (*Akk.*) appellieren; ∼ **[up]on sb. to do sth.** jmdn. auffordern, etw. zu tun

ˈcall box *n.* Telefonzelle, *die*

ˈcaller *n.* (*visitor*) Besucher, *der*/Besucherin, *die;* (*on telephone*) Anrufer, *der*/Anruferin, *die*

ˈcall girl *n.* Callgirl, *das*

ˈcalling *n.* Beruf, *der*

calliper /ˈkælɪpə(r)/ *n.* (a) [**a pair of**] ∼**s** Tasterzirkel, *der*
(b) (Med.) Beinschiene, *die*

callous /ˈkæləs/ *adj.* gefühllos; herzlos ⟨*Handlung, Verhalten*⟩

ˈcall-up *n.* (Mil.) Einberufung, *die*

calm /kɑːm/ ① *n.* (*stillness*) Stille, *die;* (*serenity*) Ruhe, *die*
② *adj.* ruhig
③ *v.t.* ∼ **sb.** [**down**] jmdn. beruhigen
④ *v.i.* ∼ [**down**] sich beruhigen

ˈcalmly *adv.* ruhig; gelassen

ˈcalmness *n.* Ruhe, *die;* (*of water*) Stille, *die*

Calor gas ® /ˈkælə gæs/ *n.* Butangas, *das*

calorie /ˈkælərɪ/ *n.* Kalorie, *die*

calorific /kæləˈrɪfɪk/ *adj.* ∼ **value** Heizwert, *der*

calves *pl. of* CALF¹, ²

CAM *abbr.* = **computer-aided manufacturing** CAM

camber /ˈkæmbə(r)/ *n.* Wölbung, *die*

camcorder /ˈkæmkɔːdə(r)/ *n.* Camcorder, *der;* Kamerarecorder, *der*

came ▶ COME

camel /ˈkæml/ *n.* Kamel, *das*

camera /ˈkæmərə/ *n.* Kamera, *die*

camera: ∼ **case** *n.* Kameratasche, *die;* ∼ **crew** *n.* Kamerateam, *das;* ∼**man** *n.* Kameramann, *der;* ∼**work** *n., no indef. art.* Kameraführung, *die*

camomile /ˈkæməmaɪl/ *n.* Kamille, *die;* ∼ **tea** Kamillentee, *der*

camouflage /ˈkæməflɑːʒ/ ① *n.* Tarnung, *die*
② *v.t.* tarnen

camp /kæmp/ ① *n.* Lager, *das*
② *v.i.* ∼ [**out**] campen; (*in tent*) zelten; **go** ∼**ing** Campen/Zelten fahren/gehen

campaign /kæmˈpeɪn/ ① *n.* (a) (Mil.) Feldzug, *der*
(b) (*organized action*) Kampagne, *die;* **publicity** ∼: Werbekampagne, *die*
② *v.i.* ∼ **for/against sth.** sich für etw. einsetzen/gegen etw. etwas unternehmen; **be** ∼**ing** ⟨*Politiker:*⟩ im Wahlkampf stehen

ˈcamp bed *n.* Campingliege, *die*

ˈcamper *n.* (*person*) Camper, *der*/Camperin, *die*

ˈcampfire *n.* Lagerfeuer, *das*

ˈcamping *n.* Camping, *das;* (*in tent*) Zelten, *das*

camping: ∼ **ground** ▶ ∼ SITE;

~ **holiday** *n.* Campingurlaub, *der;* ~ **site** *n.* Campingplatz, *der;* ~ **stove** *n.* Campingkocher, *der*

'**campsite** *n.* Campingplatz, *der*

campus /'kæmpəs/ *n.* Campus, *der*

can¹ /kæn/ 1 *n.* (a) (milk ~, watering ~) Kanne, *die;* (for oil, petrol) Kanister, *der;* (Amer.: for refuse) Eimer, *der*
(b) (for preserving) [Konserven]dose, *die;* a ~ of tomatoes/beer eine Dose Tomaten/Bier
2 *v.t.,* -**nn**- konservieren

can² /kən, *stressed* kæn/ *v. aux., only in pres.* **can,** *neg.* **cannot** /'kænət/, (coll.) **can't** /kɑːnt/, *past* **could** /kʊd/, *neg.* (coll.) **couldn't** /'kʊdnt/ können; (have right, be permitted) dürfen; können; **I can't do that** das kann ich nicht; (it would be wrong) das kann ich nicht tun; **you can't smoke here** hier dürfen Sie nicht rauchen; **could you ring me tomorrow?** könnten Sie mich morgen anrufen?; **I could have killed him** ich hätte ihn umbringen können; **[that] could be [so]** das könnte *od.* kann sein

Canada /'kænədə/ *pr. n.* Kanada (*das*)

Canadian /kə'neɪdɪən/ 1 *adj.* kanadisch; **sb. is** ~; jmd. ist Kanadier/Kanadierin
2 *n.* Kanadier, *der*/Kanadierin, *die*

canal /kə'næl/ *n.* Kanal, *der*

canary /kə'neərɪ/ *n.* Kanarienvogel, *der*

Ca'nary Islands *pr. n. pl.* Kanarische Inseln *Pl.*

cancel /'kænsl/ 1 *v.t.,* (Brit.) -**ll**- (a) absagen ⟨Besuch, Urlaub, Reise, Sportveranstaltung⟩; ausfallen lassen ⟨Veranstaltung, Vorlesung, Zug, Bus⟩; fallen lassen ⟨Pläne⟩; rückgängig machen ⟨Einladung, Vertrag⟩; zurücknehmen ⟨Befehl⟩; stornieren ⟨Bestellung, Auftrag⟩; kündigen ⟨Abonnement⟩; abbestellen ⟨Zeitung⟩
(b) (Comp.) abbrechen
2 *v.i.,* (Brit.) -**ll**-: (a) ~ [out] sich [gegenseitig] aufheben
(b) (Comp.) abbrechen

cancellation /kænsə'leɪʃn/ *n.* ▶ CANCEL 1A: Absage, *die;* Ausfall, *der;* Fallenlassen, *das;* Rückgängigmachen, *das;* Zurücknahme, *die;* Stornierung, *die;* Kündigung, *die;* Abbestellung, *die*

cancer /'kænsə(r)/ *n.* (a) (Med.) Krebs, *der;* ~ **of the liver** Leberkrebs, *der*
(b) C~ (Astrol., Astron.) der Krebs

candelabra /kændɪ'lɑːbrə/ *n.* Leuchter, *der*

candid /'kændɪd/ *adj.* offen; ehrlich ⟨Ansicht, Bericht⟩

candidate /'kændɪdət, 'kændɪdeɪt/ *n.* Kandidat, *der*/Kandidatin, *die*

candle /'kændl/ *n.* Kerze, *die*

candle: ~**light** *n.* Kerzenlicht, *das;* ~**stick** *n.* Kerzenhalter, *der;* (elaborate) Leuchter, *der;* ~**wick** *n.* (material) Frottierplüsch, *der*

candour (*Brit., Amer.:* **candor**) /'kændə(r)/ *n.* ▶ CANDID: Offenheit, *die;* Ehrlichkeit, *die*

candy /'kændɪ/ *n.* (Amer.) (sweets) Süßigkeiten *Pl.;* (sweet) Bonbon, *das od. der*

'**candyfloss** /'kændɪflɒs/ *n.* Zuckerwatte, *die*

cane /keɪn/ 1 *n.* (a) (stem) Rohr, *das;* (of raspberry, blackberry) Spross, *der*
(b) (material) Rohr, *das*
(c) (stick) [Rohr]stock, *der*
2 *v.t.* [mit dem Stock] schlagen

'**cane sugar** *n.* Rohrzucker, *der*

canine /'keɪnaɪn/ *adj.* (a) (of dog[s]) Hunde-
(b) ~ **tooth** Eckzahn, *der*

canister /'kænɪstə(r)/ *n.* Büchse, *die;* (for petrol, oil, etc.) Kanister, *der*

cannabis /'kænəbɪs/ *n.* (hashish) Haschisch, *das;* (marijuana) Marihuana, *das*

canned /kænd/ *adj.* Dosen-; in Dosen *nachgestellt;* ~ **meat/fruit** Fleisch-/ Obstkonserven *Pl.;* ~ **beer** Dosenbier; ~ **food** [Lebensmittel]konserven *Pl.;* ~ **music** Musikkonserve, *die*

cannibal /'kænɪbl/ *n.* Kannibale, *der*/ Kannibalin, *die*

cannibalism /'kænɪbəlɪzm/ *n.* Kannibalismus, *der*

cannon /'kænən/ 1 *n.* Kanone, *die*
2 *v.i.* (Brit.) ~ **into sb./sth.** mit etw./jmdm. zusammenprallen

'**cannon ball** *n.* Kanonenkugel, *die*

cannot ▶ CAN²

canny /'kænɪ/ *adj.* (shrewd) schlau

canoe /kə'nuː/ *n.* Paddelboot, *das;* (Indian ~, Sport) Kanu, *das*

canoeing /kə'nuːɪŋ/ *n.* Paddeln, *das;* (Sport) Kanufahren, *das;* Kanusport, *der*

canoeist /kə'nuːɪst/ *n.* Paddelbootfahrer, *der*/-fahrerin, *die*

canon /'kænən/ *n.* (a) (general law, criterion) Grundregel, *die*
(b) (Eccl.: person) Kanoniker, *der*

canonize /'kænənaɪz/ *v.t.* kanonisieren ⟨Heiligen⟩; heilig sprechen ⟨Märtyrer⟩

'**can-opener** *n.* Dosenöffner, *der*

canopy /'kænəpɪ/ *n.* Baldachin, *der;* (over entrance) Vordach, *das*

can't /kɑːnt/ (coll.) = CANNOT; ▶ CAN²

cantankerous /kæn'tæŋkərəs/ *adj.* streitsüchtig

canteen /kæn'tiːn/ *n.* Kantine, *die*

canter /'kæntə(r)/ 1 *n.* Handgalopp, *der*
2 *v.i.* leicht galoppieren

canvas /'kænvəs/ *n.* Leinwand, *die*

canvass /'kænvəs/ 1 *v.t.* Wahlwerbung treiben in ⟨einem Wahlkreis, Gebiet⟩; Wahlwerbung treiben bei ⟨Wählern, Bürgern⟩
2 *v.i.* werben (**on behalf of** für); ~ **for votes** um Stimmen werben

'**canvasser** *n.* (for votes) Wahlhelfer, *der*/

-helferin, *die*

canyon /'kænjən/ *n.* Cañon, *der*

cap /kæp/ ① *n.* (a) Mütze, *die;* (nurse's, servant's) Haube, *die;* (with peak) Schirmmütze, *die;* (skull∼) Kappe, *die*
(b) (of bottle, jar) [Verschluss]kappe, *die;* (petrol ∼, radiator ∼) Deckel, *der*
② *v.t.,* -pp-: (a) verschließen ⟨*Flasche*⟩; zudecken ⟨*Bohrloch*⟩; mit einer Schutzkappe versehen ⟨*Zahn*⟩
(b) (fig.) überbieten; **to ∼ it all** obendrein

CAP *abbr.* = **Common Agricultural Policy** gemeinsame Agrarpolitik

capability /keɪpə'bɪlɪtɪ/ *n.* Fähigkeit, *die*

capable /'keɪpəbl/ *adj.* (a) **be ∼ of sth.** ⟨*Person:*⟩ zu etw. imstande sein
(b) (gifted, able) fähig

capacity /kə'pæsɪtɪ/ *n.* (a) Fassungsvermögen, *das;* **the machine is working to ∼:** die Maschine ist voll ausgelastet; **a seating ∼ of 300** 300 Sitzplätze
(b) (measure) Rauminhalt, *der;* Volumen, *das;* **measure of ∼:** Hohlmaß, *das*
(c) (position) Eigenschaft, *die;* **in his ∼ as ...:** in seiner Eigenschaft als ...

cape¹ /keɪp/ *n.* (garment) Umhang, *der;* Cape, *das*

cape² *n.* (Geog.) Kap, *das;* **the C∼** [of Good Hope] das Kap der Guten Hoffnung; **C∼ Town** Kapstadt (*das*)

caper /'keɪpə(r)/ *v.i.* ∼ [about] [herum]tollen

capful /'kæpfʊl/ *n.* **one ∼:** der Inhalt einer Verschlusskappe

capillary /kə'pɪlərɪ/ *n.* Kapillare, *die* (fachspr.)

capital /'kæpɪtl/ ① *attrib. adj.* (a) Todes⟨*strafe, -urteil*⟩; Kapital⟨*verbrechen*⟩
(b) groß, Groß⟨*buchstabe*⟩
(c) (principal) Haupt⟨*stadt*⟩
② *n.* (a) (letter) Großbuchstabe, *der*
(b) (city, town) Hauptstadt, *die*
(c) (stock, wealth) Kapital, *das*

capitalism /'kæpɪtəlɪzm/ *n.* Kapitalismus, *der*

capitalist /'kæpɪtəlɪst/ ① *n.* Kapitalist, *der*/Kapitalistin, *die*
② *adj.* kapitalistisch

capitalize /'kæpɪtəlaɪz/ ① *v.t.* großschreiben ⟨*Buchstabe, Wort*⟩
② *v.i.* ∼ **on sth.** aus etw. Kapital schlagen (ugs.)

capital 'punishment *n.* Todesstrafe, *die*

capitulate /kə'pɪtjʊleɪt/ *v.i.* kapitulieren
capitulation /kəpɪtjʊ'leɪʃn/ *n.* Kapitulation, *die*

cappuccino /kɑːpʊ'tʃiːnəʊ/ *n., pl.* ∼s Cappuccino, *der*

capricious /kə'prɪʃəs/ *adj.* launisch

Capricorn /'kæprɪkɔːn/ *n.* (Astrol., Astron.) der Steinbock

capsize /kæp'saɪz/ ① *v.t.* zum Kentern bringen

② *v.i.* kentern

capsule /'kæpsjuːl/ *n.* Kapsel, *die*

Capt. *abbr.* = **Captain** Kapt.; Hptm.

captain /'kæptɪn/ ① *n.* Kapitän, *der;* (Army) Hauptmann, *der*
② *v.t.* ∼ **a team** Kapitän einer Mannschaft sein

caption /'kæpʃn/ *n.* (heading) Überschrift, *die;* (under photograph, drawing) Bildunterschrift, *die;* (Cinemat., Telev.) Untertitel, *der*

captivate /'kæptɪveɪt/ *v.t.* fesseln

captivating /'kæptɪveɪtɪŋ/ *adj.* bezaubernd; einnehmend ⟨*Lächeln*⟩

captive /'kæptɪv/ ① *adj.* gefangen; **be taken ∼:** gefangen genommen werden; **∼ audience** unfreiwilliges Publikum
② *n.* Gefangener, *der*/Gefangene, *die*

captivity /kæp'tɪvɪtɪ/ *n.* Gefangenschaft, *die;* **be held in ∼:** gefangen gehalten werden

captor /'kæptə(r)/ *n.* **his ∼:** der, der/die, die ihn gefangen nahm

capture /'kæptʃə(r)/ ① *n.* (a) (of thief etc.) Festnahme, *die;* (of town) Einnahme, *die*
(b) (thing, person) Fang, *der*
② *v.t.* festnehmen ⟨*Person*⟩; [ein]fangen ⟨*Tier*⟩; einnehmen ⟨*Stadt*⟩; gefangen nehmen ⟨*Fantasie*⟩

car /kɑː(r)/ *n.* Auto, *das;* Wagen, *der;* **by ∼:** mit dem Auto

carafe /kə'ræf/ *n.* Karaffe, *die*

caramel /'kærəmel/ *n.* Karamell, *der;* (toffee) Karamellbonbon, *das*

carat /'kærət/ *n.* Karat, *das;* **a 22-∼ gold ring** ein 22-karätiger Goldring

caravan /'kærəvæn/ *n.* (Brit.) Wohnwagen, *der*

'caravan site *n.* Campingplatz für Wohnwagen

carbohydrate /kɑːbəʊ'haɪdreɪt/ *n.* Kohlenhydrat, *das*

'car bomb *n.* Autobombe, *die*

carbon /'kɑːbən/ *n.* Kohlenstoff, *der*

carbon: ∼ **'copy** *n.* Durchschlag, *der;* ∼ **dioxide** /- daɪ'ɒksaɪd/ *n.* Kohlendyoxid, *das;* ∼ **mo'noxide** /-mə'nɒksaɪd/ *n.* (Chem.) Kohlenmonoxyd, *das;* ∼ **paper** *n.* Kohlepapier, *das*

car 'boot sale *n.:* Trödelmarkt, bei dem die Händler ihre Waren aus dem Kofferraum ihrer Autos heraus verkaufen

carburettor (*Amer.:* **carburetor**) /kɑːbə'retə(r)/ *n.* Vergaser, *der*

carcass (*Brit. also:* **carcase**) /'kɑːkəs/ *n.* Kadaver, *der*

'car crash *n.* Autounfall, *der*

card /kɑːd/ *n.* Karte, *die;* **play ∼s** Karten spielen

card: ∼**board** *n.* Pappe, *die;* ∼**board 'box** *n.* [Papp]karton, *der;* (smaller) [Papp]schachtel, *die;* ∼ **game** *n.* Kartenspiel, *das;* ∼**holder** *n.* Karteninhaber, *der*/-inhaberin, *die*

cardiac /ˈkɑːdɪæk/ adj. (of heart) Herz-
cardiac ar'rest n. Herzstillstand, der
cardigan /ˈkɑːdɪgən/ n. Strickjacke, die
cardinal /ˈkɑːdɪnl/ 1 adj. grundlegend
⟨Frage, Doktrin, Pflicht⟩; Kardinal⟨fehler,
-problem⟩; Haupt⟨punkt, -merkmal⟩
2 n. (Eccl.) Kardinal, der
cardinal: ~ 'number n. Kardinalzahl,
die; ~ 'sin n. Todsünde, die
'**cardphone** n. Kartentelefon, das
care /keə(r)/ 1 n. (a) (anxiety) Sorge, die
(b) (pains) Sorgfalt, die
(c) (caution) Vorsicht, die; take ~: aufpassen
(d) medical ~: ärztliche Betreuung
(e) (charge) Obhut, die (geh.); put sb. in ~/
take sb. into ~: jmdn. in Pflege geben/
nehmen; ~ of (on letter) bei; take ~ of sb./sth.
(ensure safety of) auf jmdn./etw. aufpassen;
(attend to) sich um jmdn./etw. kümmern
2 v.i. ~ for sb./sth. (look after) sich um
jmdn./etw. kümmern; (like) jmdn./etw. mögen;
~ to do sth. etw. tun mögen; I don't
~ [whether/how/what etc.] es ist mir
gleich[, ob/wie/was usw.]
career /kəˈrɪə(r)/ 1 n. Beruf, der
2 v.i. rasen; ⟨Pferd, Reiter:⟩ galoppieren
career: ~ **break** n. Karriereknick, der;
~s **adviser** n. Berufsberater, der/
-beraterin, die; ~s [**advisory**] **service**
n. Berufsberatung, die; ~ **woman** n.
Karrierefrau, die
'**carefree** adj. sorgenfrei
careful /ˈkeəfl/ adj. (thorough) sorgfältig;
(cautious) vorsichtig; [be] ~! Vorsicht!; be
~ of sb./sth. (be cautious of) sich vor jmdm./
etw. in Acht nehmen; be ~ with sb./sth.
vorsichtig mit jmdn./etw. umgehen
'**carefully** adv. (thoroughly) sorgfältig;
(attentively) aufmerksam; (cautiously) vorsichtig
careless /ˈkeəlɪs/ adj. (a) (inattentive)
unaufmerksam; (thoughtless) gedankenlos;
leichtsinnig ⟨Fahrer⟩; nachlässig ⟨Arbeiter,
Arbeit⟩; gedankenlos ⟨Bemerkung,
Handlung⟩; unachtsam ⟨Fahren⟩
(b) (nonchalant) ungezwungen
'**carelessly** adv. (without care) nachlässig;
(thoughtlessly) gedankenlos
'**carelessness** n. (lack of care)
Nachlässigkeit, die; (thoughtlessness)
Gedankenlosigkeit, die
carer /ˈkeərə(r)/ n. (for sick person) Pfleger,
der/Pflegerin, die
caress /kəˈres/ 1 n. Liebkosung, die
2 v.t. liebkosen
'**caretaker** n. Hausmeister, der/-meisterin,
die
'**car ferry** n. Autofähre, die
cargo /ˈkɑːgəʊ/ n. Fracht, die
'**cargo boat**, '**cargo ship** ns. Frachter,
der
'**car hire** n. Autovermietung, die
Caribbean /kærɪˈbiːən/ 1 n. the ~: die
Karibik

2 adj. karibisch
caricature /ˈkærɪkətjʊə(r)/ 1 n.
Karikatur, die
2 v.t. karikieren
caring /ˈkeərɪŋ/ adj. sozial ⟨Gesellschaft⟩;
fürsorglich ⟨Person⟩
carnage /ˈkɑːnɪdʒ/ n. Gemetzel, das
carnal /ˈkɑːnl/ adj. sinnlich
carnation /kɑːˈneɪʃn/ n. [Garten]nelke, die
carnet /ˈkɑːneɪ/ n. (of motorist) Triptyk, das;
[camping] ~: Ausweis für Camper
carnival /ˈkɑːnɪvl/ n. Volksfest, das
carnivorous /kɑːˈnɪvərəs/ adj. Fleisch
fressend
carol /ˈkærl/ n. [Christmas] ~:
Weihnachtslied, das
'**car owner** n. Autobesitzer, der/-besitzerin,
die
carp /kɑːp/ n., pl. same Karpfen, der
car: ~ **park** n. Parkplatz, der; (building)
Parkhaus, das; ~ **parking** n. Parken, das;
~ **parking facilities are available** Parkplätze
[sind] vorhanden
carpenter /ˈkɑːpɪntə(r)/ n. Zimmermann,
der; (for furniture) Tischler, der/Tischlerin, die
carpentry /ˈkɑːpɪntrɪ/ n.
Zimmerhandwerk, das; (in furniture)
Tischlerhandwerk, das
carpet /ˈkɑːpɪt/ n. Teppich, der
carpet: ~ **slipper** n. Hausschuh, der;
~ **sweeper** n. Teppichkehrer, der
car: ~ **phone** n. Autotelefon, das; ~**port**
n. Einstellplatz, der; ~ **radio** n. Autoradio,
das; ~ **rental** ▶ CAR HIRE
carriage /ˈkærɪdʒ/ n. (a) (horse-drawn)
Kutsche, die
(b) (Railw.) Wagen, der
'**carriageway** n. Fahrbahn, die
'**car ride** n. Autofahrt, die
carrier /ˈkærɪə(r)/ n. (a) (bearer) Träger, der
(b) (firm) Transportunternehmen, das
carrier: ~ **bag** n. Tragetasche, die;
~ **pigeon** n. Brieftaube, die
carrot /ˈkærət/ n. Möhre, die
carry /ˈkærɪ/ v.t. (a) tragen; (emphasizing
destination) bringen
(b) (possess) besitzen ⟨Autorität, Gewicht⟩
■ **carry a'way** v.t. forttragen; be or get
carried away sich hinreißen lassen
■ **carry 'on** 1 v.t. fortführen; ~ on [doing
sth.] weiterhin etw. tun
2 v.i. weitermachen
■ **carry 'out** v.t. durchführen; ausführen
⟨Anweisung, Auftrag⟩; vornehmen
⟨Verbesserungen⟩
carry: ~**cot** n. Babytragetasche, die;
~-**out** n. ~-out [meal] Essen od. Mahlzeit
zum Mitnehmen; **get a** ~-**out** sich (Dat.) in
einem Restaurant was zu essen holen
'**carsick** adj. children are often ~: Kindern
wird beim Autofahren oft schlecht
cart /kɑːt/ 1 n. Wagen, der

2 *v.t.* (coll.) schleppen
'**car thief** *n.* Autodieb, *der*/-diebin, *die*
cartilage /'kɑːtɪlɪdʒ/ *n.* Knorpel, *der*
carton /'kɑːtn/ *n.* [Papp]karton, *der;* (of drink) Tüte, *die;* (of cream, yoghurt) Becher, *der*
cartoon /kɑː'tuːn/ *n.* humoristische Zeichnung; (satirical) Karikatur, *die;* (film) Zeichentrickfilm, *der*
cartridge /'kɑːtrɪdʒ/ *n.* (a) (for gun) Patrone, *die*
(b) (of film; cassette) Kassette, *die*
'**cartwheel** *n.* (Gymnastics) Rad, *das;* **turn** or **do ~s** Rad schlagen
carve /kɑːv/ 1 *v.t.* (a) tranchieren ⟨*Fleisch, Braten, Hähnchen*⟩
(b) (from wood) schnitzen; (from stone) meißeln
2 *v.i.* **~ in wood/stone** in Holz schnitzen/in Stein meißeln
carving /'kɑːvɪŋ/ *n.* (in or from wood) Schnitzerei, *die;* (in or from stone) Skulptur, *die*
'**carving knife** *n.* Tranchiermesser, *das*
'**car wash** *n.* Waschanlage, *die*
cascade /kæs'keɪd/ *n.* Kaskade, *die*
case¹ /keɪs/ *n.* (a) (instance, matter, set of arguments) Fall, *der;* **it is [not] the ~ that …:** es trifft [nicht] zu, dass …; **in ~ …:** falls …; **[just] in ~:** für alle Fälle; **in ~ of emergency** im Notfall; **in any ~:** jedenfalls; **in that ~:** in diesem Fall; **in any ~** (regardless of anything else) jedenfalls; **I don't need it in any ~:** ich brauche es sowieso nicht
(b) (Med., Police, Soc. Serv., etc.) Fall, *der*
(c) (Law) Fall, *der;* (action) Verfahren, *das*
(d) (Ling.) Fall, *der;* Kasus, *der* (fachspr.)
case² *n.* (a) Koffer, *der;* (brief~) [Akten]tasche, *die*
(b) (for spectacles, cigarettes) Etui, *das*
(c) (crate) Kiste, *die*
(d) [display] ~: Schaukasten, *der*
cash /kæʃ/ 1 *n.* Bargeld, *das;* **pay [in] ~, pay ~ down** bar zahlen
2 *v.t.* einlösen ⟨*Scheck*⟩
cash: ~ account *n.* Kassekonto, *das;* **~ and 'carry** *n.* cash and carry; (store) Cash-and-carry-Laden, *der;* **~back** *n., no art.:* Barauszahlung eines Differenzbetrages bei Kauf mit Geldkarte; **~card** *n.* Geldautomatenkarte, *die;* **~ desk** *n.* (Brit.) Kasse, *die;* **~ discount** *n.* Skonto, *der od. das;* Barzahlungsrabatt, *der;* **~ dispenser** *n.* Geldautomat, *der*
cashew nut /'kæʃuː/ *n.* Cashewnuss, *die*
'**cash flow** *n.* Cashflow, *der*
cashier /kæ'ʃɪə(r)/ *n.* Kassierer, *der*/ Kassiererin, *die*
'**cashless** *adj.* bargeldlos; **the ~ society** die bargeldlose Gesellschaft
cashmere /'kæʃmɪə(r)/ *n.* Kaschmir, *der;* **~ wool/sweater** Kaschmirwolle, *die*/ Kaschmirpullover, *der*
cash: ~ payment *n.* Barzahlung, *die;*

make ~ payment bar bezahlen; **~point** *n.* Geldautomat, *der;* **~ register** *n.* [Registrier]kasse, *die*
casino /kə'siːnəʊ/ *n.* Kasino, *das*
cask /kɑːsk/ *n.* Fass, *das*
casket /'kɑːskɪt/ *n.* (a) Kästchen, *das*
(b) (Amer.: coffin) Sarg, *der*
casserole /'kæsərəʊl/ *n.* Schmortopf, *der*
cassette /kə'set, kæ'set/ *n.* Kassette, *die*
cassette: ~ deck *n.* Kassettendeck, *das;* **~ player** *n.* Kassettengerät, *das;* **~ recorder** *n.* Kassettenrekorder, *der*
cast /kɑːst/ 1 *v.t.,* **cast (a)** werfen
(b) (shape, form) gießen
(c) abgeben ⟨*Stimme*⟩
2 *n.* (a) (Med.) Gipsverband, *der*
(b) (actors) Besetzung, *die*
■ **cast a'side** *v.t.* beiseite schieben ⟨*Vorschlag*⟩; vergessen ⟨*Sorgen*⟩; fallen lassen ⟨*Hemmungen*⟩
■ **cast 'off** *v.i. & t.* (Naut.) losmachen
castanets /kæstə'nets/ *n. pl.* Kastagnetten *Pl.*
'**castaway** *n.* Schiffbrüchige, *der*/*die*
caste /kɑːst/ *n.* Kaste, *die*
cast 'iron *n.* Gusseisen, *das*
castle /'kɑːsl/ *n.* Burg, *die;* (mansion) Schloss, *das*
'**cast-offs** *n. pl.* abgelegte Sachen *Pl.*
castor /'kɑːstə(r)/ *n.* (wheel) Rolle, *die*
castor: ~ 'oil *n.* Rizinusöl, *das;* **~ sugar** *n.* Raffinade, *die*
castrate /kæ'streɪt/ *v.t.* kastrieren
castration /kæ'streɪʃn/ *n.* Kastration, *die*
casual /'kæʒjʊəl/ *adj.* ungezwungen; leger ⟨*Kleidung*⟩; beiläufig ⟨*Bemerkung*⟩; flüchtig ⟨*Bekannter, Bekanntschaft, Blick*⟩; unbekümmert ⟨*Haltung, Einstellung*⟩
casual 'labour *n.* Gelegenheitsarbeit, *die*
'**casually** *adv.* ungezwungen; beiläufig ⟨*bemerken*⟩; flüchtig ⟨*anschauen*⟩; leger ⟨*sich kleiden*⟩
casualty /'kæʒjʊəltɪ/ *n.* (a) (injured person) Verletzte, *der*/*die;* (battle) Verwundete, *der*/ *die;* (dead person) Tote, *der*/*die*
(b) (hospital department) Unfallstation, *die*
'**casualty ward** *n.* Unfallstation, *die*
cat /kæt/ *n.* Katze, *die*
catalogue (*Amer.:* **catalog**) /'kætəlɒg/ 1 *n.* Katalog, *der*
2 *v.t.* katalogisieren
catalyst /'kætəlɪst/ *n.* Katalysator, *der*
catalytic /kætə'lɪtɪk/ *adj.* **~ converter** Katalysator, *der*
catamaran /kætəmə'ræn/ *n.* Katamaran, *der*
catapult /'kætəpʌlt/ 1 *n.* Katapult, *das*
2 *v.t.* katapultieren
cataract /'kætərækt/ *n.* (a) Katarakt, *der*
(b) (Med.) grauer Star
catarrh /kə'tɑː(r)/ *n.* Katarrh, *der*

catastrophe /kə'tæstrəfi/ n. Katastrophe, *die*

catastrophic /kætə'strɒfɪk/ *adj.* katastrophal

catch /kætʃ/ [1] *v.t.*, **caught** /kɔːt/ (a) fangen; ~ **hold of sb./sth.** jmdn./etw. festhalten; (to stop oneself falling) sich an jmdm./etw. festhalten; **get sth. caught** *or* ~ **sth. on/in sth.** mit etw. an/in etw. (*Dat.*) hängen bleiben; ~ **one's finger in the door** sich (*Dat.*) den Finger in der Tür einklemmen
(b) (travel by) nehmen; (be in time for) [noch] erreichen
(c) (surprise) ~ **sb. doing sth.** jmdn. [dabei] erwischen, wie er etw. tut (ugs.)
(d) (become infected with) sich (*Dat.*) zuziehen; ~ **sth. from sb.** sich bei jmdm. mit etw. anstecken; ~ **a cold** sich erkälten; ~ **it** (fig. coll.) etwas kriegen (ugs.)
(e) ~ **sb.'s attention/interest** jmds. Aufmerksamkeit erregen/jmds. Interesse wecken.
[2] *v.i.*, **caught (a)** (begin to burn) [anfangen zu] brennen
(b) (become hooked up) hängenbleiben; ⟨*Haar, Faden:*⟩ sich verfangen
[3] *n.* (a) (of ball) **make a** ~: fangen
(b) (amount caught, lit. or fig.) Fang, *der*
(c) (difficulty) Haken, *der* (in an + *Dat.*)
(d) (of door) Schnapper, *der*
■ **catch 'on** *v.i.* (coll.) (a) (become popular) [gut] ankommen (ugs.)
(b) (understand) kapieren (ugs.)
■ **catch 'up** [1] *v.t.* ~ **sb. up,** ~ **up with sb.** jmdn. einholen
[2] *v.i.* ~ **up** gleichziehen; ~ **up on sth.** etw. nachholen

'catching *adj.* ansteckend

'catchphrase *n.* Slogan, *der*

'catchy *adj.* eingängig

'cat door *n.* Katzentür, *die*

categorical /kætɪ'gɒrɪkl/ *adj.* kategorisch

categorize (categorise) /'kætɪgəraɪz/ *v.t.* kategorisieren

category /'kætɪgərɪ/ *n.* Kategorie, *die*

cater /'keɪtə(r)/ *v.i.* ~ **for sb./sth.** für jmdn./ etw. [die] Speisen und Getränke liefern; (fig.) auf jmdn./etw. eingestellt sein

'caterer *n.* Lieferant von Speisen und Getränken

'catering *n.* (a) (trade) Gastronomie, *die*
(b) (service) Lieferung von Speisen und Getränken

caterpillar /'kætəpɪlə(r)/ *n.* Raupe, *die*

'cat flap ▶ CAT DOOR

cathedral /kə'θiːdrl/ *n.* Dom, *der*

Catherine wheel /'kæθrɪn wiːl/ *n.* Feuerrad, *das*

Catholic /'kæθəlɪk/ [1] *adj.* katholisch
[2] *n.* Katholik, *der*/Katholikin, *die*

Catholicism /kə'θɒlɪsɪzm/ *n.* Katholizismus, *der*

catkin /'kætkɪn/ *n.* (Bot.) Kätzchen, *das*

'Cat's-eye ® *n.* (Brit.: on road) Bodenrückstrahler, *der*

cattle /'kætl/ *n. pl.* Rinder *Pl.*

'cattle market *n.* Viehmarkt, *der;* (fig.) Fleischbeschau, *die* (ugs. scherzh.)

'catwalk *n.* Laufsteg, *der*

caught ▶ CATCH 1, 2

cauldron /'kɔːldrən/ *n.* Kessel, *der*

cauliflower /'kɒlɪflaʊə(r)/ *n.* Blumenkohl, *der*

cause /kɔːz/ [1] *n.* (a) Ursache, *die* (of für od. Gen.); (person) Verursacher, *der*/ Verursacherin, *die;* **be the** ~ **of sth.** etw. verursachen
(b) (reason) Grund, *der;* ~ **for sth.** Grund zu etw.
(c) (object of support) Sache, *die;* [in] **a good** ~: [für] eine gute Sache
[2] *v.t.* verursachen; erregen ⟨*Aufsehen, Ärgernis*⟩; hervorrufen ⟨*Unruhe, Verwirrung*⟩; ~ **sb. worry/pain** jmdm. Sorge/ Schmerzen bereiten; ~ **sb. to do sth.** jmdn. veranlassen, etw. zu tun

causeway /'kɔːzweɪ/ *n.* Damm, *der*

caustic /'kɔːstɪk/ *adj.* ätzend; (fig.) bissig; beißend ⟨*Spott*⟩

caution /'kɔːʃn/ [1] *n.* (a) Vorsicht, *die*
(b) (warning) Warnung, *die*
[2] *v.t.* (warn) warnen; (warn and reprove) verwarnen (for wegen)

cautious /'kɔːʃəs/ *adj.,* **'cautiously** *adv.* vorsichtig

cavalry /'kævəlrɪ/ *n.* Kavallerie, *die*

cave /keɪv/ *n.* Höhle, *die*
■ **cave 'in** *v.i.* einbrechen

'caveman *n.* Höhlenbewohner, *der*

cavern /'kævən/ *n.* Höhle, *die*

cavernous /'kævənəs/ *adj.* höhlenartig

caviar[e] /'kævɪɑː(r)/ *n.* Kaviar, *der*

cavity /'kævɪtɪ/ *n.* Hohlraum, *der;* (in tooth) Loch, *das*

'cavity wall *n.* Hohlmauer, *die*

cc /siː'siː/ *abbr.* = **cubic centimetre(s)** cm^3

CCTV *abbr.* = **closed-circuit television** CCTV

CD *abbr.* = **compact disc** CD, *die;* **CD burner, CD writer** CD-Brenner; **CD player** CD-Spieler, *der*

CD-ROM /siːdiː'rɒm/ *n.* CD-ROM, *die;* ~ **drive** CD-ROM-Laufwerk, *das*

cease /siːs/ [1] *v.i.* aufhören
[2] *v.t.* (a) (stop) aufhören
(b) (end) aufhören mit; einstellen ⟨*Bemühungen*⟩

'ceasefire *n.* Waffenruhe, *die*

cedar /'siːdə(r)/ *n.* Zeder, *die*

Ceefax ® /'siːfæks/ *n.* (Brit.) Bildschirmtextdienst der BBC

ceiling /'siːlɪŋ/ *n.* (a) Decke, *die*
(b) (upper limit) Maximum, *das*

celebrate /'selɪbreɪt/ v.t. & i. feiern

'celebrated adj. berühmt

celebration /selɪ'breɪʃn/ n. Feier, die

celebrity /sɪ'lebrɪtɪ/ n. Berühmtheit, die

celery /'selərɪ/ n. Sellerie, der od. die

celibate /'selɪbət/ adj. zölibatär (Rel.);
ehelos

cell /sel/ n. Zelle, die

cellar /'selə(r)/ n. Keller, der

cellist /'tʃelɪst/ n. Cellist, der/Cellistin, die

cello /'tʃeləʊ/ n., pl. ~s Cello, das

Cellophane ® /'seləfeɪn/ n. Cellophan
Ⓦ, das

'cellphone, cellular 'phone
/'seljʊlə(r)/ ns. Mobiltelefon, das

cellulite /'seljʊlaɪt/ n., no indef. art.:
überschüssige Fettdepots an Oberschenkeln
und Hüften

Celsius /'selsɪəs/ adj. Celsius

cement /sɪ'ment/ ①n. Zement, der
②v.t. zementieren; (stick together)
zusammenkleben

ce'ment mixer n. Betonmischmaschine,
die

cemetery /'semɪtərɪ/ n. Friedhof, der

censor /'sensə(r)/ ①n. Zensor, der
②v.t. zensieren

'censorship n. Zensur, die

censure /'senʃə(r)/ v.t. tadeln

census /'sensəs/ n. Volkszählung, die

cent /sent/ n. Cent, der

centenary /sen'tiːnərɪ/ adj. & n.
~ [celebrations] Hundertjahrfeier, die

center (Amer.) ▶ CENTRE

centigrade /'sentɪɡreɪd/ ▶ CELSIUS

centimetre (Brit.; Amer.: **centimeter**)
/'sentɪmiːtə(r)/ n. Zentimeter, der

centipede /'sentɪpiːd/ n. Tausendfüßler,
der

central /'sentrl/ adj. zentral

Central: ~ A'merica pr. n.
Mittelamerika (das); ~ **'Europe** pr. n.
Mitteleuropa (das); ~ **Euro'pean** adj.
mitteleuropäisch; **c~ 'heating** n.
Zentralheizung, die

centralize /'sentrəlaɪz/ v.t. zentralisieren

central: ~ 'locking n. (Motor Veh.)
Zentralverriegelung, die; ~ **'nervous
system** n. Zentralnervensystem, das;
~ **'processing unit** n. (Comp.)
Zentraleinheit, die; ~ **reservation** n.
(Brit.) Mittelstreifen, der

centre /'sentə(r)/ (Brit.) ①n. (a) Mitte, die;
(of circle) Mittelpunkt, der
(b) (of area, city) Zentrum, das
②adj. mittler...
③v.i. ~ **on sth.** sich auf etw. (Akk.)
konzentrieren; ~ **[a]round sth.** sich um etw.
drehen
④v.t. **(a)** in der Mitte anbringen

(b) (concentrate) **be** ~d **[a]round sth.** etw. zum
Mittelpunkt haben; ~ **sth. on sth.** etw. auf
etw. (Akk.) konzentrieren

centre 'forward n. Mittelstürmer, der

centrifugal /sentrɪ'fjuːɡl/ adj. ~ **force**
Zentrifugalkraft, die; Fliehkraft, die

century /'sentʃərɪ/ n. (hundred-year period from
a year ..00) Jahrhundert, das; (hundred years)
hundert Jahre

ceramic /sɪ'ræmɪk/ adj. keramisch

cereal /'sɪərɪəl/ n. Getreide, das; (breakfast
dish) Getreideflocken Pl.

cerebral /'serɪbrl/ adj. (intellectual)
intellektuell

ceremonial /serɪ'məʊnɪəl/ ① adj.
feierlich; (prescribed for ceremony) zeremoniell
② n. Zeremoniell, das

ceremony /'serɪmənɪ/ n. Feier, die; (formal
act) Zeremonie, die

certain /'sɜːtn, 'sɜːtɪn/ adj. (a) (settled,
definite) bestimmt
(b) be ~ **to do sth.** etw. bestimmt tun
(c) (confident, sure to happen) sicher
(d) (indisputable) unbestreitbar
(e) a ~ **Mr Smith** ein gewisser Herr Smith;
to a ~ **extent** in gewisser Weise

'certainly adv. (a) (admittedly) sicher[lich];
(definitely) bestimmt
(b) (in answer) [aber] sicher; [most] ~ **'not!**
auf [gar] keinen Fall!

certainty /'sɜːtntɪ, 'sɜːtɪntɪ/ n. (a) **be a** ~:
sicher sein
(b) (absolute conviction) Gewissheit, die

certificate /sə'tɪfɪkət/ n. Urkunde, die; (of
action performed) Schein, der

certify /'sɜːtɪfaɪ/ v.t. bescheinigen;
bestätigen; **this is to** ~ **that ...:** hiermit wird
bescheinigt od. bestätigt, dass ...

cf. abbr. = **compare** vgl.

CFC abbr. = **chlorofluorocarbon**
FCKW, das; ~**free** FCKW-frei

chafe /tʃeɪf/ v.t. wund scheuern

chaff /tʃɑːf/ n. Spreu, die

chaffinch /'tʃæfɪntʃ/ n. Buchfink, der

chagrin /'ʃæɡrɪn/ n. Kummer, der

chain /tʃeɪn/ ①n. Kette, die; ~ **of shops/
hotels** Laden-/Hotelkette, die
②v.t. [an]ketten (**to** an + Akk.)

chain: ~ **re'action** n. Kettenreaktion,
die; ~**saw** n. Kettensäge, die; ~**smoke**
v.t. & i. Kette rauchen (ugs.); ~**smoker** n.
Kettenraucher, der/-raucherin, die;
~ **store** n. Kettenladen, der

chair /tʃeə(r)/ ①n. (a) Stuhl, der; (arm~,
easy ~) Sessel, der
(b) (professorship) Lehrstuhl, der
(c) (at meeting) Vorsitz, der; (~person)
Vorsitzende, der/die
②v.t. den Vorsitz haben bei

chair: ~ **back** n. Rückenlehne, die; ~**lift**
n. Sessellift, der; ~**man** /'tʃeəmən/ n., pl. ····⊹

∼**men** /'tʃeəmən/ Vorsitzende, *der/die;*
∼**person** n. Vorsitzende, *der/die;*
∼**woman** n. Vorsitzende, *die*

chalet /'ʃæleɪ/ n. Chalet, *das*

chalk /tʃɔːk/ ⊡ n. Kreide, *die*
⊡ v.t. mit Kreide schreiben/malen *usw*

challenge /'tʃælɪndʒ/ ⊡ n.
Herausforderung, *die*
⊡ v.t. (a) (to contest etc.) herausfordern
(b) (fig.) auffordern; (question) infrage stellen

challenged /'tʃælɪndʒd/ adj. (euphem. or
joc.) behindert; **mentally** ∼: geistig behindert

'**challenger** n. Herausforderer, *der/*
Herausforderin, *die*

challenging /'tʃælɪndʒɪŋ/ adj.
herausfordernd; fesselnd ⟨*Problem*⟩;
anspruchsvoll ⟨*Arbeit*⟩

chamber /'tʃeɪmbə(r)/ n. Kammer, *die*

chamber: ∼**maid** n. Zimmermädchen,
das; ∼ **music** n. Kammermusik, *die;*
C∼ **of** '**Commerce** n. Industrie- und
Handelskammer, *die;* ∼ **pot** n. Nachttopf,
der

chameleon /kə'miːljən/ n. Chamäleon, *das*

chamois /'ʃæmwɑː/ n. (a) Gämse, *die*
(b) /'ʃæmɪ/ ∼ [leather] Chamois[leder], *das*

champagne /ʃæm'peɪn/ n. Sekt, *der;* (from
Champagne) Champagner, *der*

cham'pagne glass n. Sektglas, *das*

champion /'tʃæmpɪən/ ⊡ n. (a) (defender)
Verfechter, *der/*Verfechterin, *die*
(b) (Sport) Meister, *der/*Meisterin, *die*
⊡ v.t. verfechten ⟨*Sache*⟩; sich einsetzen für
⟨*Person*⟩

'**championship** n. Meisterschaft, *die*

chance /tʃɑːns/ ⊡ n. (a) (fortune, trick of fate)
Zufall, *der;* attrib. zufällig; ∼ **encounter**
Zufallsbegegnung, *die;* **game of** ∼:
Glücksspiel, *das;* **by** ∼: zufällig; **take a** ∼: es
riskieren; **the** ∼**s are that** ...: es ist
wahrscheinlich, dass ...; **by [any]** ∼, **by some**
∼ **or other** zufällig
(b) (opportunity, possibility) Chance, *die;* **get a/the**
∼ **to do sth.** eine/die Gelegenheit haben,
etw. zu tun
⊡ v.t. riskieren

chancellor /'tʃɑːnsələ(r)/ n. Kanzler, *der;*
C∼ **of the Exchequer** (Brit.) Schatzkanzler, *der*

chandelier /ʃændə'lɪə(r)/ n. Kronleuchter,
der

change /tʃeɪndʒ/ ⊡ n. (a) Veränderung,
die; Änderung, *die;* (of job, surroundings,
government, etc.) Wechsel, *der*
(b) (for the sake of variety) Abwechslung, *die;*
for a ∼: zur Abwechslung
(c) (money) Wechselgeld, *das;* [loose *or* small]
∼: Kleingeld, *das;* [here is] £5 ∼:
5 Pfund zurück; **keep the** ∼: [es] stimmt so
⊡ v.t. (a) (switch) wechseln; auswechseln
⟨*Glühbirne, Batterie*⟩; ∼ **one's clothes** sich
umziehen; ∼ **one's address/name** seine
Anschrift/seinen Namen ändern; ∼ **trains/**
buses umsteigen

(b) (transform) verwandeln (**into** in + *Akk.*);
(alter) ändern
(c) (exchange) eintauschen (**for** für); wechseln
⟨*Geld*⟩
⊡ v.i. (a) (alter) sich ändern; ⟨*Person, Land:*⟩
sich verändern
(b) (into something else) sich verwandeln
(c) (put on other clothes) sich umziehen
(d) (∼trains, buses, etc.) umsteigen
■ **change 'over** v.i. ∼ **over from sth. to**
sth. von etw. zu etw. übergehen

changeable /'tʃeɪndʒəbl/ adj.
veränderlich

'**change[-giving] machine** n.
Geldwechsler, *der*

'**changeover** n.Wechsel, *der;* ∼ **from sth.**
to sth. Umstellung von etw. auf etw. (*Akk.*)

'**changing room** n. (Brit.) Umkleideraum,
der

channel /'tʃænl/ ⊡ n. (also Telev., Radio)
Kanal, *der;* **the C**∼ (Brit.) der [Ärmel]kanal
⊡ v.t. (fig.) lenken

Channel: c∼**hop** v.i. (coll.) (a) (Telev.)
zappen (ugs.); (b) (cross the English Channel)
kurz mal über den Kanal fahren;
∼ **Islands** pr. n. pl. Kanalinseln *Pl.;*
∼ '**Tunnel** n. [Ärmel]kanaltunnel, *der*

chant /tʃɑːnt/ ⊡ v.t. skandieren; (Eccl.)
singen
⊡ v.i. Sprechchöre anstimmen; (Eccl.) singen
⊡ n. Sprechchor, *der;* (Eccl.) Gesang, *der*

chaos /'keɪɒs/ n. Chaos, *das*

chaotic /keɪ'ɒtɪk/ adj. chaotisch

chap[1] /tʃæp/ n. (Brit. coll.) Bursche, *der;* Kerl,
der

chap[2] v.t., -pp- aufplatzen lassen

chapel /'tʃæpl/ n. Kapelle, *die*

chaperon /'ʃæpərəʊn/ ⊡ n.
Anstandsdame, *die*
⊡ v.t. beaufsichtigen

chaplain /'tʃæplɪn/ n. Kaplan, *der*

chapter /'tʃæptə(r)/ n. Kapitel, *das*

char /tʃɑː(r)/ v.t. & i., -rr- verkohlen

character /'kærɪktə(r)/ n. (a) Charakter,
der
(b) (in novel etc.) Figur, *die*
(c) (coll.: extraordinary person) Original, *das*
(d) (symbol) Zeichen, *das*

characteristic /kærɪktə'rɪstɪk/ ⊡ adj.
charakteristisch (**of** für)
⊡ n. charakteristisches Merkmal

characterize /'kærɪktəraɪz/ v.t.
charakterisieren

'**characterless** adj. nichts sagend

charade /ʃə'rɑːd/ n. Scharade, *die;* (fig.)
Farce, *die*

charcoal /'tʃɑːkəʊl/ n. Holzkohle, *die*

charge /tʃɑːdʒ/ ⊡ n. (a) (price) Preis, *der;*
(for services) Gebühr, *die*
(b) **be in** ∼ **of sth.** für etw. die
Verantwortung haben; **take** ∼: die
Verantwortung übernehmen
(c) (Law: accusation) Anklage, *die*

543

charge account ⋯▷ cheer ⋯⋯

(d) (attack) Angriff, *der*
(e) (of explosives, electricity) Ladung, *die*
② *v.t.* (a) ~ **sb. sth.,** ~ **sth. to sb.** jmdm.
etw. berechnen
(b) (Law: accuse) anklagen (**with** wegen)
(c) (Electr.) [auf]laden ⟨*Batterie*⟩
(d) (rush at) angreifen
③ *v.i.* (a) (attack) angreifen
(b) (coll.: hurry) sausen
charge: ~ **account** *n.* (Amer.)
Kreditkonto, *das;* ~ **card** *n.* Kreditkarte,
die
charisma /kə'rızmə/ *n.* Charisma, *das*
charitable /'tʃærıtəbl/ *adj.* (a) wohltätig
(b) (lenient) großzügig
charity /'tʃærıtı/ *n.* (a) Wohltätigkeit, *die*
(b) (organization) wohltätige Organisation
charity: ~ **concert** *n.* Benefizkonzert,
das; ~ **match** *n.* Benefizspiel, *das;*
~ **performance** *n.* Benefizvorstellung,
die; Wohltätigkeitsvorstellung, *die;* ~ **shop**
*n.: Secondhandladen, dessen Erlöse einem
wohltätigen Zweck dienen*
charlady /'tʃɑːleıdı/ *n.* (Brit.) Putzfrau, *die*
charlatan /'ʃɑːlətən/ *n.* Scharlatan, *der*
charm /tʃɑːm/ ① *n.* (a) (act) Zauber, *der*
(b) (talisman) Talisman, *der*
(c) (attractiveness) Reiz, *der;* (of person)
Charme, *der*
② *v.t.* bezaubern
'**charming** *adj.* bezaubernd
chart /tʃɑːt/ ① *n.* (a) (map) Karte, *die*
(b) (graph etc.) Schaubild, *das*
(c) the ~s die Hitliste
② *v.t.* (fig.: describe) schildern
charter /'tʃɑːtə(r)/ ① *n.* (a) Charta, *die*
(b) on ~ gechartert
② *v.t.* chartern ⟨*Schiff, Flugzeug*⟩
chartered: ~ **ac'countant** *n.* (Brit.)
Wirtschaftsprüfer, *der*/-prüferin, *die;*
~ '**aircraft** *n.* Charterflugzeug, *das;*
Chartermaschine, *die*
charter: ~ **flight** *n.* Charterflug, *der;*
~ **plane** ▶ CHARTERED AIRCRAFT
charwoman /'tʃɑːwʊmən/ *n.* Putzfrau, *die*
chase /tʃeıs/ ① *n.* Verfolgungsjagd, *die*
② *v.t.* (pursue) jagen; ~ **sth.** (fig.) einer Sache
(*Dat.*) nachjagen
③ *v.i.* ~ **after sb./sth.** hinter jmdm./etw.
herjagen
■ **chase 'up** *v.t.* (coll.) ausfindig machen
chasm /'kæzm/ *n.* Kluft, *die*
chassis /'ʃæsı/ *n., pl. same* /'ʃæsız/
Chassis, *das;* Fahrgestell, *das*
chaste /tʃeıst/ *adj.* keusch
chastening /'tʃeısənıŋ/ *adj.* ernüchternd
chastise /tʃæ'staız/ *v.t.* züchtigen
chastity /'tʃæstıtı/ *n.* Keuschheit, *die*
chat /tʃæt/ ① *n.* Schwätzchen, *das*
② *v.i.,* **-tt-:** (a) plaudern; ~ **with** *or* **to sb.**
about sth. mit jmdm. von etw. plaudern
(b) (Comp.) chatten
■ **chat 'up** *v.t.* (Brit. coll.) anmachen (ugs.)

chat: ~ **line** *n.* Chatline, *die;* ~ **room** *n.*
(Comp.) Chat-Room, *der;* ~ **show** *n.*
Talkshow, *die*
chattels /'tʃætlz/ *n. pl.* bewegliche Habe
(geh.)
chatter /'tʃætə(r)/ ① *v.i.* (a) schwatzen
(b) ⟨*Zähne:*⟩ klappern
② *n.* Schwatzen, *das*
'**chatterbox** *n.* Quasselstrippe, *die* (ugs.)
chatty /'tʃætı/ *adj.* gesprächig
chauffeur /'ʃəʊfə(r)/ ① *n.* Fahrer, *der;*
Chauffeur, *der*
② *v.t.* fahren
chauvinist /'ʃəʊvɪnɪst/ *n.* Chauvinist, *der*/
Chauvinistin, *die*
chauvinistic /ʃəʊvɪ'nɪstɪk/ *adj.*
chauvinistisch
cheap /tʃiːp/ *adj., adv.* billig
cheapen /'tʃiːpn/ *v.t.* (fig.) herabsetzen
'**cheaply** *adv.* billig
cheat /tʃiːt/ ① *n.* Schwindler, *der*/
Schwindlerin, *die*
② *v.t. & i.* betrügen
check¹ /tʃek/ ① *n.* (a) Kontrolle, *die;*
make/keep a ~ on kontrollieren
(b) (Amer.: bill) Rechnung, *die*
② *v.t.* (a) (restrain) unter Kontrolle halten
(b) (examine) nachprüfen; kontrollieren
⟨*Fahrkarte*⟩
(c) (stop) aufhalten
③ *v.i.* ~ **on sth.** etw. überprüfen; ~ **with sb.**
bei jmdm. nachfragen
■ **check 'in** *v.t. & i.* (at airport) einchecken
■ **check 'out** ① *v.t.* überprüfen
② *v.i.* abreisen
■ **check 'up** *v.i.* ~ **up [on]** überprüfen
check² *n.* (pattern) Karo, *das*
checkers /'tʃekəz/ (Amer.) ▶ DRAUGHTS
check: ~**-in** *n.* Abfertigung, *die;* ~**list** *n.*
Checkliste, *die;* ~**mate** ① *n.* [Schach]matt,
das; ② *int.* [schach]matt; ~**out [desk]** *n.*
Kasse, *die;* ~**point** *n.* Kontrollpunkt, *der;*
~**-up** *n.* (Med.) Untersuchung, *die*
cheek /tʃiːk/ *n.* (a) Backe, *die;* Wange, *die*
(geh.)
(b) (impertinence) Frechheit, *die*
'**cheekbone** *n.* Backenknochen, *der*
'**cheekily** *adv.,* '**cheeky** *adj.* frech
cheep /tʃiːp/ ① *v.i.* piep[s]en
② *n.* Piep[s]en, *das*
cheer /tʃıə(r)/ ① *n.* (a) (applause)
Beifallsruf, *der*
(b) *in pl.* (Brit. coll.: as a toast) prost!
(c) (Brit. coll.: thank you) danke
② *v.t.* (a) (applaud) ~ **sth./sb.** etw. bejubeln/
jmdm. zujubeln
(b) (gladden) aufmuntern
③ *v.i.* jubeln
■ **cheer 'on** *v.t.* anfeuern ⟨*Sportler*⟩
■ **cheer 'up** ① *v.t.* aufheitern
② *v.i.* bessere Laune bekommen; ~ **up!**
Kopf hoch!

cheerful /'tʃɪəfl/ *adj.* (in good spirits) fröhlich; (bright, pleasant) heiter

'cheerfully *adv.* vergnügt

'cheering ① *adj.* fröhlich stimmend ② *n.* Jubeln, *das*

cheerio /tʃɪərɪ'əʊ/ *int.* (Brit. coll.) tschüs (ugs.)

'cheery *adj.* fröhlich

cheese /tʃiːz/ *n.* Käse, *der*

cheese: ∼board *n.* Käseplatte, *die;* ∼**cake** *n.* Käsetorte, *die*

cheetah /'tʃiːtə/ *n.* Gepard, *der*

chef /ʃef/ *n.* Küchenchef, *der;* (as profession) Koch, *der*

chemical /'kemɪkl/ ① *adj.* chemisch ② *n.* Chemikalie, *die*

chemical 'warfare *n.* chemische Krieg[s]führung

chemist /'kemɪst/ *n.* (a) (scientist) Chemiker, *der*/Chemikerin, *die* (b) (Brit.: pharmacist) Drogist, *der*/Drogistin, *die;* ∼**'s [shop]** Drogerie, *die*

chemistry /'kemɪstrɪ/ *n.* Chemie, *die*

chemotherapy /kiːmə'θerəpɪ/ *n.* Chemotherapie, *die*

cheque /tʃek/ *n.* Scheck, *der;* **pay by ∼:** mit [einem] Scheck bezahlen

cheque: ∼book *n.* Scheckbuch, *das;* ∼**book 'journalism** *n.* Scheckbuchjournalismus, *der;* ∼ **card** *n.* Scheckkarte, *die*

cherish /'tʃerɪʃ/ *v.t.* hegen ⟨*Hoffnung, Gefühl*⟩; in Ehren halten ⟨*[Erinnerungs]gegenstand*⟩

cherry /'tʃerɪ/ *n.* Kirsche, *die*

chess /tʃes/ *n., no art.* das Schach[spiel]

chess: ∼board *n.* Schachbrett, *das;* ∼**man** *n.* Schachfigur, *die;* ∼ **player** *n.* Schachspieler, *der*/-spielerin, *die*

chest /tʃest/ *n.* (a) Kiste, *die* (b) (Anat.) Brust, *die;* **get sth. off one's ∼** (fig. coll.) sich (*Dat.*) etw. von der Seele reden (c) ∼ **[measurement]** Brustumfang, *der*

chestnut /'tʃesnʌt/ ① *n.* (a) Kastanie, *die* (b) (colour) Kastanienbraun, *das* ② *adj.* (colour) ∼**[-brown]** kastanienbraun

'chestnut tree *n.* Kastanie, *die*

chest of 'drawers *n.* Kommode, *die*

chew /tʃuː/ *v.t. & i.* kauen

'chewing gum *n.* Kaugummi, *der od. das*

chic /ʃiːk/ *adj.* schick; elegant

chick /tʃɪk/ *n.* (a) Küken, *das* (b) (sl.: young woman) Biene, *die* (ugs.)

chicken /'tʃɪkɪn/ ① *n.* (a) Huhn, *das;* (grilled, roasted) Hähnchen, *das* (b) (coll.: coward) Angsthase, *der* ② *adj.* (coll.) feig[e] ③ *v.i.* ∼ **out** (coll.) kneifen

chicken: ∼pox /-pɒks/ *n.* Windpocken *Pl.;* ∼ **'soup** *n.* Hühnersuppe, *die;* ∼ **wire** *n.* Maschendraht, *der*

'chickpea *n.* Kichererbse, *die*

chicory /'tʃɪkərɪ/ *n.* (plant) Chicorée, *der od. die;* (for coffee) Zichorie, *die*

chief /tʃiːf/ ① *n.* (a) Oberhaupt, *das;* (of tribe) Häuptling, *der* (b) (of department) Leiter, *der;* ∼ **of police** Polizeipräsident, *der* ② *adj., usu. attrib.* (a) Haupt- (b) (leading) führend

'chiefly *adv.* hauptsächlich

chieftain /'tʃiːftən/ *n.* Stammesführer, *der*

chilblain /'tʃɪlbleɪn/ *n.* Frostbeule, *die*

child /tʃaɪld/ *n., pl.* ∼**ren** /'tʃɪldrən/ Kind, *das*

child: ∼ abuse *n.* Kindesmisshandlung, *die;* ∼**bearing** ① *n.* Schwangerschaften *Pl.;* ② *adj.* ∼**bearing age** Gebäralter, *das;* **of** ∼**bearing age** im gebärfähigen Alter; ∼**birth** *n.* Geburt, *die;* ∼**care** *n.* Kinderbetreuung *die*

'childhood *n.* Kindheit, *die*

childish /'tʃaɪldɪʃ/ *adj.,* **'childishly** *adv.* kindisch

'childishness *n.* (behaviour) kindisches Benehmen

child: ∼less *adj.* kinderlos; ∼**like** *adj.* kindlich; ∼**minder** /-maɪndə(r)/ *n.* (Brit.) Tagesmutter, *die;* ∼**proof** *adj.* kindersicher; ∼**proof door lock** (in car) Kindersicherung, *die*

children *pl. of* CHILD

'child's play *n.* (fig.) ein Kinderspiel

Chile /'tʃɪlɪ/ *pr. n.* Chile (*das*)

chill /tʃɪl/ ① *n.* Kühle, *die;* (illness) Erkältung, *die* ② *v.t.* kühlen ▪ **chill out** *v.i.* (coll.) (relax) sich entspannen; (calm down) sich abregen (ugs.)

chilli /'tʃɪlɪ/ *n., pl.* ∼**es** Chili, *der*

chilling /'tʃɪlɪŋ/ *adj.* (fig.) ernüchternd

'chilly *adj.* kühl; **I am rather ∼:** mir ist ziemlich kühl

chime /tʃaɪm/ ① *n.* Geläute, *das* ② *v.i.* läuten; ⟨*Turmuhr:*⟩ schlagen

chimney /'tʃɪmnɪ/ *n.* Schornstein, *der*

chimney: ∼ breast *n.* Kaminmantel, *der;* ∼ **pot** *n.* ≈ Schornsteinkopf, *der;* ∼ **sweep** *n.* Schornsteinfeger, *der*

chimpanzee /tʃɪmpən'ziː/ *n.* Schimpanse, *der*

chin /tʃɪn/ *n.* Kinn, *das*

china *n.* Porzellan, *das;* (crockery) Geschirr, *das*

China /'tʃaɪnə/ *pr. n.* China (*das*)

Chinese /tʃaɪ'niːz/ ① *adj.* chinesisch; **sb. is ∼:** jmd. ist Chinese/Chinesin ② *n.* (a) *pl. same* (person) Chinese, *der*/Chinesin, *die* (b) (language) Chinesisch, *das; see also* ENGLISH 2A

chink *n.* (gap) Spalt, *der*

chip /tʃɪp/ ① *n.* (a) Splitter, *der* (b) *in pl.* (Brit.: potato ∼s) Pommes frites *Pl.*

(c) (Gambling, Comp.) Chip, *der*
②*v.t.,* **-pp-** anschlagen
■ **chip 'in** (coll.) ①*v.i.* **(a)** (interrupt) sich einmischen
(b) (contribute money) etwas beisteuern
②*v.t.* (contribute) beisteuern
'**chipboard** *n.* Spanplatte, *die*
chipmunk /'tʃɪpmʌŋk/ *n.* Chipmunk, *das*
chippy /'tʃɪpɪ/ *n.* (Brit. coll.) Pommes-frites-Bude, *die;* Frittenbude, *die* (ugs.)
'**chip shop** (Brit.) ▶ CHIPPY
chiropodist /kɪ'rɒpədɪst/ *n.* Fußpfleger, *der*/-pflegerin, *die*
chiropody /kɪ'rɒpədɪ/ *n.* Fußpflege, *die*
chirp /tʃɜːp/ ①*v.i.* zwitschern; ⟨Grille:⟩ zirpen
②*n.* Zwitschern, *das;* Zirpen, *das*
chisel /'tʃɪzl/ ①*n.* Meißel, *der;* (for wood) Stemmeisen, *das*
②*v.t.,* (Brit.) **-ll-** meißeln; (in wood) hauen
chit /tʃɪt/ *n.* Notiz, *die*
chit-chat /'tʃɪttʃæt/ *n.* Plauderei, *die*
chivalrous /'ʃɪvlrəs/ *adj.* ritterlich
chivalry /'ʃɪvlrɪ/ *n.* Ritterlichkeit, *die*
chives /tʃaɪvz/ *n.* Schnittlauch, *der*
chloride /'klɔːraɪd/ *n.* Chlorid, *das*
chlorine /'klɔːriːn/ *n.* Chlor, *das*
chlorofluorocarbon /klɔːrəʊflʊərəʊ'kɑːbən/ *n.* Chlorfluorkohlenstoff, *der*
chock /tʃɒk/ *n.* Bremsklotz, *der*
'**chock-a-block** *pred adj.* voll gepfropft
chocolate /'tʃɒklət/ *n.* Schokolade, *die*
chocolate 'biscuit *n.* Schokoladenkeks, *der*
choice /tʃɔɪs/ ①*n.* **(a)** Wahl, *die;* **from** ∼: freiwillig
(b) (variety) Auswahl, *die*
②*adj.* ausgewählt
choir /kwaɪə(r)/ *n.* Chor, *der*
'**choirboy** *n.* Chorknabe, *der*
choke /tʃəʊk/ ①*v.t.* **(a)** ersticken
(b) (block up) verstopfen
②*v.i.* (temporarily) keine Luft [mehr] bekommen; (permanently) ersticken (**on** an + *Dat.*)
③*n.* (Motor Veh.) Choke, *der*
cholera /'kɒlərə/ *n.* Cholera, *die*
cholesterol /kə'lestərɒl/ *n.* Cholesterin, *das*
choose /tʃuːz/ ①*v.t.,* **chose** /tʃəʊz/, **chosen** /'tʃəʊzn/ **(a)** wählen
(b) (decide) ∼/∼ **not to do sth.** sich dafür/dagegen entscheiden, etw. zu tun
②*v.i.,* **chose, chosen** wählen (**between** zwischen); ∼ **from sth.** aus etw./(from several) unter etw. (*Dat.*) [aus]wählen
choos[e]y /'tʃuːzɪ/ *adj.* wählerisch
chop /tʃɒp/ ①*n.* **(a)** Hieb, *der*
(b) (of meat) Kotelett, *das*
(c) get the ∼ (coll.: be dismissed) rausgeworfen werden (ugs.)

②*v.t.,* **-pp-** hacken ⟨Holz⟩; klein schneiden ⟨Fleisch, Gemüse⟩
'**chopper** *n.* (axe) Beil, *das;* (cleaver) Hackbeil, *das*
'**chopping board** *n.* Hackbrett, *das*
'**choppy** *adj.* bewegt
'**chopstick** *n.* [Ess]stäbchen, *das*
choral /'kɔːrl/ *adj.* Chor-
chord /kɔːd/ *n.* (Mus.) Akkord, *der*
chore /tʃɔː(r)/ *n.* [lästige] Routinearbeit
choreographer /kɒrɪ'ɒɡrəfə(r)/ *n.* Choreograph, *der*/Choreographin, *die*
choreography /kɒrɪ'ɒɡrəfɪ/ *n.* Choreographie, *die*
chortle /'tʃɔːtl/ ①*v.i.* vor Lachen glucksen
②*n.* Glucksen, *das*
chorus /'kɔːrəs/ *n.* **(a)** Chor, *der*
(b) (of song) Refrain, *der;* (in jazz) Chorus, *der*
chose, chosen ▶ CHOOSE
chow /tʃaʊ/ *n.* (Amer. sl.: food) Futter, *das* (salopp)
Christ /kraɪst/ *n.* Christus (*der*)
christen /'krɪsn/ *v.t.* taufen
'**christening** *n.* Taufe, *die*
Christian /'krɪstjən/ ①*adj.* christlich
②*n.* Christ, *der*/Christin, *die*
Christianity /krɪstɪ'ænɪtɪ/ *n.* das Christentum
'**Christian name** *n.* Vorname, *der*
Christmas /'krɪsməs/ *n.* Weihnachten, *das od. Pl.;* **merry** *or* **happy** ∼: frohe *od.* fröhliche Weihnachten; **at** ∼: [zu] Weihnachten
Christmas: ∼ **cake** *n.* Weihnachtskuchen, *der;* ∼ **card** *n.* Weihnachtskarte, *die;* ∼ '**carol** *n.* Weihnachtslied, *das;* ∼ '**Day** *n.* erster Weihnachtsfeiertag; ∼ '**Eve** *n.* Heiligabend, *der;* ∼ **present** *n.* Weihnachtsgeschenk, *das;* ∼ **tree** *n.* Weihnachtsbaum, *der*
chrome /krəʊm/**, chromium** /'krəʊmɪəm/ *ns.* Chrom, *das*
'**chromium-plated** *adj.* verchromt
chromosome /'krəʊməsəʊm/ *n.* Chromosom, *das*
chronic /'krɒnɪk/ *adj.* chronisch; ∼ **fatigue syndrome** chronisches Müdigkeitssyndrom
chronically /'krɒnɪkəlɪ/ *adv.* chronisch
chronicle /'krɒnɪkl/ *n.* Chronik, *die*
chronological /krɒnə'lɒdʒɪkl/ *adj.* chronologisch
chrysalis /'krɪsəlɪs/ *n., pl.* ∼**es** Puppe, *die*
chrysanthemum /krɪ'sænθɪməm/ *n.* Chrysantheme, *die*
chubby /'tʃʌbɪ/ *adj.* pummelig
chuck /tʃʌk/ *v.t.* (coll.) schmeißen (ugs.)
■ **chuck 'away, chuck 'out** *v.t.* (coll.) wegschmeißen (ugs.)
chuckle /'tʃʌkl/ ①*v.i.* leise [vor sich hin] lachen (**at** über + *Akk.*)
②*n.* leises, glucksendes Lachen

chug /tʃʌg/ *v.i.*, **-gg-** tuckern

chum /tʃʌm/ *n.* (coll.) Kumpel, *der* (salopp)

chunk /tʃʌŋk/ *n.* dickes Stück

'**chunky** *adj.* (a) (small and sturdy) stämmig
(b) dick ‹*Pullover*›

Chunnel /'tʃʌnl/ *n.* (Brit. coll.)
[Ärmel]kanaltunnel, *der*

church /tʃɜ:tʃ/ *n.* Kirche, *die;* **go to ~:** in
die Kirche gehen; **the C~ of England** die
Kirche von England

'**churchyard** *n.* Friedhof, *der* (*bei einer
Kirche*); Kirchhof, *der* (veralt.)

churlish /'tʃɜ:lɪʃ/ *adj.* (ill-bred) ungehobelt;
(surly) griesgrämig

churn /tʃɜ:n/ *n.* (Brit.) Butterfass, *das*

churn 'out *v.t.* massenweise produzieren
(ugs.)

chute /ʃu:t/ *n.* Schütte, *die;* (for persons)
Rutsche, *die*

chutney /'tʃʌtnɪ/ *n.* Chutney, *das*

CIA *abbr.* (Amer.) = **Central
Intelligence Agency** CIA, *der od. die*

cicada /sɪ'kɑ:də/ *n.* Zikade, *die*

CID *abbr.* (Brit.) = **Criminal
Investigation Department** C.I.D.; **the
~:** die Kripo

cider /'saɪdə(r)/ *n.* ≈ Apfelwein, *der*

cigar /sɪ'gɑ:(r)/ *n.* Zigarre, *die*

cigarette /sɪgə'ret/ *n.* Zigarette, *die*

cigarette: ~ end *n.* Zigarettenstummel,
der; **~ lighter** *n.* Feuerzeug, *das;*
~ packet *n.* Zigarettenschachtel, *die;*
~ paper *n.* Zigarettenpapier, *das*

cinders /'sɪndəz/ *n. pl.* Asche, *die*

cine /'sɪnɪ/: **~ camera** *n.* Filmkamera,
die; **~ film** *n.* Schmalfilm, *der*

cinema /'sɪnɪmə/ *n.* Kino, *das;* **go to the ~:**
ins Kino gehen

cinema: ~ complex *n.* Kinocenter, *das;*
~-goer *n.* (Brit.) Kinogänger, *der*/-gängerin,
die

cinematography /sɪnɪmə'tɒgrəfɪ/ *n.*
Kinematographie, *die*

cinnamon /'sɪnəmən/ *n.* Zimt, *der*

cipher /'saɪfə(r)/ *n.* Geheimschrift, *die;* **in
~:** chiffriert

circle /'sɜ:kl/ ① *n.* Kreis, *der*
② *v.i.* kreisen
③ *v.t.* umkreisen

circuit /'sɜ:kɪt/ *n.* (a) (Electr.) Schaltung, *die*
(b) (Motor racing) Rundkurs, *der*

circular /'sɜ:kjʊlə(r)/ ① *adj.* (round)
kreisförmig
② *n.* (letter, notice) Rundbrief, *der;*
Rundschreiben, *das;* (advertisement)
Werbeprospekt, *der*

circular: ~ 'letter ▶ CIRCULAR 2; **~ 'saw**
n. Kreissäge, *die*

circulate /'sɜ:kjʊleɪt/ ① *v.i.* zirkulieren
‹*Personen, Wein usw.*›: herumgehen (ugs.)
② *v.t.* in Umlauf setzen; herumgehen lassen
‹*Buch, Bericht*› (around in + *Dat.*)

circulation /sɜ:kjʊ'leɪʃn/ *n.* (a) (Physiol.)
Kreislauf, *der;* **poor ~:** Kreislaufstörungen
Pl.
(b) (copies sold) verkaufte Auflage

circulatory /sɜ:kjʊ'leɪtərɪ, 'sɜ:kjʊleɪtərɪ/
adj. (Physiol., Bot.) Kreislauf-; **~ system**
Kreislauf, *der*

circumcise /'sɜ:kəmsaɪz/ *v.t.* beschneiden

circumcision /sɜ:kəm'sɪʒn/ *n.*
Beschneidung, *die*

circumference /sə'kʌmfərəns/ *n.*
Umfang, *der*

circumstances /'sɜ:kəmstənsɪz/ *n. pl.*
Umstände *Pl.;* **in** *or* **under the ~:** unter
diesen Umständen; **under no ~:** unter
keinen Umständen

circus /'sɜ:kəs/ *n.* Zirkus, *der*

CIS *abbr.* = **Commonwealth of
Independent States** GUS

cissy /'sɪsɪ/ *n.* ▶ SISSY

cistern /'sɪstən/ *n.* Wasserkasten, *der;* (in
roof) Wasserbehälter, *der*

citation /saɪ'teɪʃn/ *n.* Zitat, *das*

cite /saɪt/ *v.t.* (quote) zitieren; anführen
‹*Beispiel*›

citizen /'sɪtɪzən/ *n.* (a) (of town, city) Bürger,
der/Bürgerin, *die*
(b) (of state) [Staats]bürger, *der*/-bürgerin, *die*

'**citizenship** *n.* Staatsbürgerschaft, *die*

citrus /'sɪtrəs/ *n.* ~ [fruit] Zitrusfrucht, *die*

city /'sɪtɪ/ *n.* [Groß]stadt, *die*

city 'centre *n.* Stadtzentrum, *das*

civic /'sɪvɪk/ *adj.* [staats]bürgerlich;
~ centre Verwaltungszentrum der Stadt

civil /'sɪvl/ *adj.* (a) (not military) zivil
(b) (polite, obliging) höflich
(c) (Law) Zivil-

civil: ~ engi'neer *n.* Bauingenieur, *der*/
-ingenieurin, *die;* **~ engi'neering** *n.*
Hoch- und Tiefbau, *der*

civilian /sɪ'vɪljən/ ① *n.* Zivilist, *der*
② *adj.* Zivil-

civility /sɪ'vɪlɪtɪ/ *n.* Höflichkeit, *die*

civilization /sɪvɪlaɪ'zeɪʃn/ *n.* Zivilisation,
die

civilized /'sɪvɪlaɪzd/ *adj.* zivilisiert

civil: ~ 'law *n.* Zivilrecht, *das;* **~ 'rights**
n. pl. Bürgerrechte *Pl.;* **~ 'servant** *n.* ≈
Staatsbeamte, *der*/-beamtin, *die;*
C~ 'Service *n.* öffentlicher Dienst;
~ 'war *n.* Bürgerkrieg, *der*

CJD *abbr.* = **Creutzfeldt-Jakob
disease**

clad /klæd/ *adj.* (arch./literary) gekleidet (**in** in
+ *Akk.*)

claim /kleɪm/ ① *v.t.* (a) beanspruchen
‹*Thron, Gebiete*›; fordern ‹*Lohnerhöhung,
Schadensersatz*›; beantragen ‹*Sozialhilfe
usw.*›
(b) (assert) behaupten
② *v.i.* (Insurance) Ansprüche geltend machen

3 *n.* Anspruch, *der* (**to** auf + *Akk.*); **lay ~ to** sth. auf etw. (*Akk.*) Anspruch erheben

claimant /'kleɪmənt/ *n.* Antragsteller, *der*/ -stellerin, *die*

'claim form *n.* (a) (Insurance) Antragsformular, *das*
(b) (for expenses) Spesenabrechnungsformular, *das*

clairvoyant /kleə'vɔɪənt/ **1** *n.* Hellseher, *der*/Hellseherin, *die*
2 *adj.* hellseherisch

clam /klæm/ **1** *n.* Klaffmuschel, *die*
2 *v.i.*, **-mm-:** **~ up** (coll.) den Mund nicht [mehr] aufmachen

clamber /'klæmbə(r)/ *v.i.* klettern

clammy /'klæmɪ/ *adj.* feucht; kalt und schweißig ⟨*Haut*⟩; klamm ⟨*Kleidung*⟩

clamour (*Brit.; Amer.:* **clamor**) /'klæmə(r)/ **1** *n.* (noise, shouting) Lärm, *der;* lautes Geschrei
2 *v.i.* **~ for sth.** nach etw. schreien

clamp /klæmp/ **1** *n.* Klammer, *die;* (for holding) Schraubzwinge, *die*
2 *v.t.* klemmen; einspannen ⟨*Werkstück*⟩
3 *v.i.* (fig.) **~ down on sb./sth.** gegen jmdn./ etw. rigoros vorgehen

clan /klæn/ *n.* Sippe, *die;* (of Scottish Highlanders) Clan, *der*

clandestine /klæn'destɪn/ *adj.* heimlich

clang /klæŋ/ **1** *n.* (of bell) Läuten, *das;* (of hammer) Klingen, *das*
2 *v.i.* ⟨*Glocke:*⟩ läuten; ⟨*Hammer:*⟩ klingen

clap /klæp/ **1** *n.* (a) Klatschen, *das*
(b) **~ of thunder** Donnerschlag, *der*
2 *v.i.*, **-pp-** klatschen
3 *v.t.*, **-pp-:** **~ one's hands** in die Hände klatschen; **~ sth.** etw. beklatschen; **~ sb.** jmdm. Beifall klatschen

'clapping *n.* Applaus, *der*

claret /'klærət/ **1** *n.* roter Bordeauxwein
2 *adj.* weinrot

clarification /klærɪfɪ'keɪʃn/ *n.* Klarstellung, *die*

clarify /'klærɪfaɪ/ *v.t.* klären ⟨*Situation usw.*⟩; (by explanation) klarstellen; erläutern ⟨*Bedeutung, Aussage*⟩

clarinet /klærɪ'net/ *n.* Klarinette, *die*

clarity /'klærɪtɪ/ *n.* Klarheit, *die*

clash /klæʃ/ **1** *v.i.* (a) scheppern (ugs.)
(b) (meet in conflict) zusammenstoßen
(c) (disagree) sich streiten
(d) ⟨*Interesse, Ereignis:*⟩ kollidieren; ⟨*Farbe:*⟩ sich beißen (ugs.) (**with** mit)
2 *v.t.* gegeneinander schlagen
3 *n.* (a) (of cymbals) Dröhnen, *das*
(b) (meeting in conflict) Zusammenstoß, *der*
(c) (disagreement) Auseinandersetzung, *die*
(d) (of personalities, colours) Unverträglichkeit, *die;* (of events) Überschneiden, *das*

clasp /klɑ:sp/ **1** *n.* Verschluss, *der*
2 *v.t.* umklammern

class /klɑ:s/ **1** *n.* Klasse, *die;* (in society) Gesellschaftsschicht, *die;* (Sch.: lesson) Stunde, *die*
2 *v.t.* einstufen (**as** als)

'class-conscious *adj.* klassenbewusst

classic /'klæsɪk/ **1** *adj.* klassisch
2 *n.* Klassiker, *der;* **~s** Altphilologie, *die*

classical /'klæsɪkl/ *adj.* klassisch

classifiable /'klæsɪfaɪəbl/ *adj.* klassifizierbar

classification /klæsɪfɪ'keɪʃn/ *n.* Klassifikation, *die*

classified /'klæsɪfaɪd/ *adj.* (a) (secret) geheim
(b) **~ advertisement** Kleinanzeige, *die*

classify /'klæsɪfaɪ/ *v.t.* klassifizieren

'classless *adj.* klassenlos ⟨*Gesellschaft*⟩

class: **~mate** *n.* Klassenkamerad, *der*/ -kameradin, *die;* **~room** *n.* Klassenzimmer, *das;* **~room assistant** Unterrichtsassistent, *der*/-assistentin, *die;* **~ trip** *n.* Klassenfahrt, *die;* Klassenausflug, *der*

'classy *adj.* (coll.) klasse

clatter /'klætə(r)/ **1** *n.* Klappern, *das*
2 *v.i.* (a) klappern
(b) (move or fall with a **~**) poltern

clause /klɔ:z/ *n.* (a) Klausel, *die*
(b) (Ling.) Teilsatz, *der;* [**subordinate**] **~:** Nebensatz, *der*

claustrophobia /klɒstrə'fəʊbɪə/ *n.* Klaustrophobie, *die*

claustrophobic /klɒstrə'fəʊbɪk/ *adj.* beengend ⟨*Ort*⟩

claw /klɔ:/ **1** *n.* Kralle, *die;* (of crab etc.) Schere, *die*
2 *v.t.* kratzen

clay /kleɪ/ *n.* Lehm, *der;* (for pottery) Ton, *der*

clean /kli:n/ **1** *adj.* sauber; frisch ⟨*Wäsche, Hemd*⟩
2 *adv.* glatt
3 *v.t.* sauber machen; putzen ⟨*Zimmer, Schuh*⟩; reinigen ⟨*Teppich, Kleidung, Wunde*⟩; **~ one's teeth** sich (*Dat.*) die Zähne putzen
4 *n.* **give sth. a ~:** etw. putzen
■ **clean 'out** *v.t.* (a) sauber machen
(b) (coll.) **~ sb. out** (take all sb.'s money) jmdn. [total] schröpfen (ugs.)
■ **clean 'up** **1** *v.t.* (a) aufräumen
(b) (fig.) säubern
2 *v.i.* aufräumen

'clean-cut *adj.* klar [umrissen]; **his ~ features** seine klar geschnittenen Gesichtszüge

'cleaner *n.* (a) Raumpfleger, *der*/-pflegerin, *die;* (woman also) Putzfrau, *die*
(b) *usu. in pl.* (dry-**~**) Reinigung, *die;* **take sth. to the ~'s** etw. in die Reinigung bringen

cleanliness /'klenlɪnɪs/ *n.* Reinlichkeit, *die*

'clean-living *adj.* von untadeligem Lebenswandel *nachgestellt*

cleanse /klenz/ v.t. [gründlich] reinigen

'**cleanser** n. Reinigungsmittel, das

'**clean-shaven** adj. glatt rasiert

'**cleansing cream** n. Reinigungscreme, die

clear /klɪə(r)/ ① adj. (a) klar; scharf ⟨Bild⟩; make oneself ~: sich deutlich [genug] ausdrücken; make it ~ [to sb.] that ...: [jmdm.] klar und deutlich sagen, dass ...
(b) (complete) three ~ days volle drei Tage
(c) (unobstructed) frei; keep sth. ~ (not block) etw. freihalten
② adv. keep ~ of sth./sb. etw./jmdn. meiden; please stand or keep ~ of the door bitte von der Tür zurücktreten
③ v.t. (a) räumen ⟨Straße⟩; abräumen ⟨Schreibtisch⟩; freimachen ⟨Abfluss, Kanal⟩; ~ a space for sb./sth. für jmdn./etw. Platz machen
(b) (empty) räumen; leeren ⟨Briefkasten⟩
(c) (remove) wegräumen; beheben ⟨Verstopfung⟩
(d) (show to be innocent) freisprechen
(e) (get permission for) ~ sth. with sb. etw. von jmdm. genehmigen lassen
④ v.i. (a) ⟨Wetter, Himmel:⟩ sich aufheitern
(b) (disperse) sich verziehen
⑤ n. we're in the ~ (free of suspicion) auf uns fällt kein Verdacht; (free of trouble) wir haben es geschafft
∎ **clear 'off** v.i. abhauen (salopp)
∎ **clear 'out** ① v.t. ausräumen
② v.i. (coll.) verschwinden
∎ **clear 'up** ① v.t. (a) wegräumen ⟨Abfall⟩; aufräumen ⟨Platz, Sachen⟩
(b) (explain) klären
② v.i. (a) aufräumen
(b) ⟨Wetter:⟩ sich aufhellen

clearance /'klɪərəns/ n. (a) (of obstruction) Beseitigung, die
(b) (clear space) Spielraum, der

'**clearance sale** n. Räumungsverkauf, der

'**clear cut** adj. klar umrissen; klar ⟨Abgrenzung, Ergebnis⟩

'**clearing** n. Lichtung, die

'**clearing bank** n. Clearingbank, die

'**clearly** adv. (a) (distinctly) klar; deutlich ⟨sprechen⟩
(b) (manifestly, unambiguously) eindeutig; klar ⟨denken⟩

'**clearway** n. (Brit.) Straße mit Halteverbot

cleavage /'kliːvɪdʒ/ n. (between breasts) Dekolleté, das

cleaver /'kliːvə(r)/ n. Hackbeil, das

clef /klef/ n. Notenschlüssel, der

cleft /kleft/ n. Spalte, die

clematis /'klemətɪs, klə'meɪtɪs/ n. Klematis, die

clementine /'klementiːn, 'klementaɪn/ n. Klementine, die

clench /klentʃ/ v.t. zusammenpressen; ~ one's fist or fingers die Faust ballen; ~ one's teeth die Zähne zusammenbeißen

clergy /'klɜːdʒɪ/ n. pl. Geistlichkeit, die; Klerus, der

clergyman /'klɜːdʒɪmən/ n., pl. ~men /'klɜːdʒɪmən/ Geistliche, der

clerical /'klerɪkl/ adj. Büro⟨arbeit, -personal⟩; ~ error Schreibfehler, der

clerk /klɑːk/ n. (in bank) Bankangestellte, der/die; (in office) Büroangestellte, der/die

clever /'klevə(r)/ adj. (a) klug
(b) (skilful) geschickt
(c) (ingenious) geistreich ⟨Idee, Argument⟩
(d) (smart, cunning) clever

'**cleverly** adv. (a) klug
(b) (skilfully) geschickt

cliché /'kliːʃeɪ/ n. Klischee, das

click /klɪk/ ① n. Klicken, das
② v.i. klicken
③ v.t. (Comp.) drücken ⟨Maustaste⟩
∎ **click on** v.t. (Comp.) anklicken

client /'klaɪənt/ n. (a) Klient, der/Klientin, die
(b) (customer) Kunde, der/Kundin, die

clientele /kliːɒn'tel/ n. (of shop) Kundschaft, die

cliff /klɪf/ n. Kliff, das

'**cliffhanger** n. Thriller, der

climate /'klaɪmət/ n. Klima, das

'**climate change** n. Klimawandel, der

climatic /klaɪ'mætɪk/ adj. klimatisch

climax /'klaɪmæks/ n. Höhepunkt, der

climb /klaɪm/ ① v.t. hinaufsteigen; klettern auf ⟨Baum⟩; hinaufkommen ⟨Hügel⟩
② v.i. (a) klettern (up auf + Akk.)
(b) ⟨Flugzeug, Sonne:⟩ aufsteigen
③ n. Aufstieg, der
∎ **climb 'down** v.i. (a) hinunterklettern
(b) (fig.) nachgeben

'**climbdown** n. Rückzieher, der (ugs.)

climber /'klaɪmə(r)/ n. Bergsteiger, der

'**climbing frame** n. Klettergerüst, das

clinch /klɪntʃ/ ① v.t. zum Abschluss bringen; perfekt machen (ugs.) ⟨Geschäft⟩
② n. (Boxing) Clinch, der

cling /klɪŋ/ v.i., clung /klʌŋ/ sich klammern (to an + Akk.)

'**cling film** n. Klarsichtfolie, die

clinic /'klɪnɪk/ n. Klinik, die

clinical /'klɪnɪkl/ adj. (a) (Med.) klinisch
(b) (dispassionate) nüchtern

clink /klɪŋk/ ① n. (of glasses) Klirren, das; (of coins) Klimpern, das
② v.i. ⟨Flaschen:⟩ klirren; ⟨Münzen:⟩ klimpern
③ v.t. klirren mit ⟨Glas⟩

clip¹ /klɪp/ ① n. Klammer, die; (for paper) Büroklammer, die
② v.t., -pp- klammern ([on] to an + Akk.)

clip² v.t., -pp- schneiden ⟨Fingernägel, Haar, Hecke⟩; stutzen ⟨Flügel⟩

clip: ~**board** n. (a) Klemmbrett, das; (b) (Comp.) Zwischenablage, die; ~ **frame** n. [rahmenloser] Bilderhalter

clipping /'klɪpɪŋ/ n. (a) (piece clipped off) Schnipsel, der od. das (b) (newspaper cutting) Ausschnitt, der

clique /kliːk/ n. Clique, die

clitoris /'klɪtərɪs/ n. Kitzler, der; Klitoris, die (fachspr.)

cloak /kləʊk/ 1 n. Umhang, der 2 v.t. [ein]hüllen

'cloakroom n. Garderobe, die; (Brit. euphem.: lavatory) Toilette, die

clock /klɒk/ 1 n. (a) Uhr, die; [work] against the ~: gegen die Zeit [arbeiten]; round the ~: rund um die Uhr (b) (coll.) (speedometer) Tacho, der (ugs.); (milometer) ≈ Kilometerzähler, der 2 v.t. ~ [up] zu verzeichnen haben ‹Erfolg›; erreichen ‹Geschwindigkeit›

■ **clock 'in, clock 'on** v.i. [bei Arbeitsantritt] stechen

■ **clock 'off, clock 'out** v.i. [bei Arbeitsschluss] stechen

clock 'radio n. Radiowecker, das

'clockwise adv., adj. im Uhrzeigersinn

'clockwork n. Uhrwerk, das; a ~ car ein Aufziehauto; as regular as ~ (fig.) absolut regelmäßig

clod /klɒd/ n. (of earth) Scholle, die

clog /klɒg/ 1 n. Clog, der; (traditional) Holzschuh, der 2 v.t., -gg-: ~ [up] verstopfen

cloister /'klɔɪstə(r)/ n. Kreuzgang, der

clone /kləʊn/ 1 n. Klon, der 2 v.t. klonen

close 1 /kləʊs/ adj. (a) (in space) dicht; nahe; be ~ to sth. nahe bei od. an etw. (Dat.) sein; at ~ quarters aus der Nähe betrachtet (b) (in time) nahe (to an + Dat.) (c) eng ‹Freund, Zusammenarbeit›; nahe ‹Verwandte, Bekanntschaft› (d) eingehend ‹Untersuchung, Prüfung usw.› (e) hart ‹Wett[kampf], Spiel›; knapp ‹Ergebnis›; that was a ~ call or shave! (coll.) das war knapp! 2 /kləʊs/ adv. nah[e]; ~ by in der Nähe; ~ to sb./sth. nahe bei jmdm./etw. 3 /kləʊz/ v.t. (a) (shut) schließen; zuziehen ‹Vorhang›; schließen ‹Laden, Fabrik›; sperren ‹Straße› (b) (conclude) schließen ‹Diskussion, Versammlung› 4 /kləʊz/ v.i. (a) (shut) sich schließen (b) ‹Laden, Fabrik:› schließen, (ugs.) zumachen 5 /kləʊz/ n. Ende, das; Schluss, der; come or draw to a ~: zu Ende gehen; bring or draw sth. to a ~: etw. zu Ende bringen

■ **close 'down** /kləʊz/ 1 v.t. schließen; stilllegen ‹Werk› 2 v.i. geschlossen werden; ‹Werk:› stillgelegt werden

■ **close 'in** v.i. ‹Nacht, Dunkelheit:› hereinbrechen; ‹Tage:› kürzer werden; ~ in on umzingeln

■ **close 'off** v.t. [ab]sperren

close-cropped /'kləʊskrɒpt/ adj. kurz geschoren

closed /kləʊzd/ adj. geschlossen; we're ~: wir haben geschlossen

'closed-circuit adj. ~ television interne Fernsehanlage; (for supervision) Videoüberwachungsanlage, die

close-down /'kləʊzdaʊn/ n. (Radio, Telev.) Sendeschluss, der

closed 'shop n. Closed Shop, der

'close-knit /kləʊs'nɪt/ adj. fest zusammengewachsen

closely /'kləʊslɪ/ adv. (a) dicht (b) (intimately) eng (c) genau ‹befragen, prüfen›; streng ‹bewachen›

'close-range /'kləʊsreɪndʒ/ adj. ‹Sicht, Betrachtung› aus nächster Nähe

closet /'klɒzɪt/ n. (Amer.: cupboard) Schrank, der

close-up /'kləʊsʌp/ n. ~ [picture/shot] Nahaufnahme, die

closing /'kləʊzɪŋ/: ~ **date** n. (for competition) Einsendeschluss, der; (to take part) Meldefrist, die; ~ **time** n. (of pub) Polizeistunde, die

closure /'kləʊʒə(r)/ n. Schließung, die; (of road) Sperrung, die

clot /klɒt/ 1 n. (a) (blood) Gerinnsel, das (b) (Brit. coll.: stupid person) Trottel, der 2 v.i., -tt- ‹Blut:› gerinnen

cloth /klɒθ/ n., pl. ~s /klɒθs/ (a) Stoff, der; Tuch, das (b) (dish~) Spültuch, das; (table~) [Tisch]decke, die

clothe /kləʊð/ v.t. kleiden

clothes /kləʊðz/ n. pl. Kleider Pl.; put one's ~ on sich anziehen; take one's ~ off sich ausziehen

clothes: ~ **brush** n. Kleiderbürste, die; ~ **hanger** n. Kleiderbügel, der; ~ **horse** n. Wäscheständer, der; ~ **line** n. Wäscheleine, die; ~ **peg** (Brit.), ~**pin** (Amer.) ns. Wäscheklammer, die

clothing /'kləʊðɪŋ/ n. Kleidung, die

clotted cream /klɒtɪd 'kriːm/ n. sehr fetter Rahm

cloud /klaʊd/ n. (a) Wolke, die; every ~ has a silver lining (prov.) es hat alles sein Gutes (b) ~ of dust/smoke Staub-/Rauchwolke, die

■ **cloud 'over** v.i. sich bewölken

'cloudburst n. Wolkenbruch, der

'cloudless adj. wolkenlos

'cloudy adj. bewölkt ‹Himmel›; trübe ‹Wetter, Flüssigkeit, Glas›

clout /klaʊt/ (coll.) 1 n. Schlag, der 2 v.t. hauen (ugs.)

clove¹ /kləʊv/ n. ~ [of garlic] [Knoblauch]zehe, die

clove² n. (spice) [Gewürz]nelke, die

clover /'kləʊvə(r)/ n. Klee, der

'cloverleaf *n.* Kleeblatt, *das*
clown /klaʊn/ ① *n.* Clown, *der*
② *v.i.* ~ **[about** *or* **around]** den Clown
spielen
cloying /'klɔɪɪŋ/ *adj.* süßlich
club /klʌb/ ① *n.* **(a)** (weapon) Keule, *die;* (golf
~) Schläger, *der*
(b) (association) Klub, *der;* Verein, *der*
(c) (Cards) Kreuz, *das;* ~s are trumps Kreuz
ist Trumpf; **the ace/seven of** ~s das
Kreuzas/die Kreuzsieben
② *v.t.*, **-bb-** (beat) prügeln; (with ~) knüppeln
③ *v.i.*, **-bb-:** ~ **together** (to buy something)
zusammenlegen
club 'sandwich *n.* (Amer.) Club-Sandwich,
das; Doppeldecker, *der* (ugs.)
cluck /klʌk/ ① *n.* Gackern, *das*
② *v.i.* gackern
clue /kluː/ *n.* Anhaltspunkt, *der;* (in criminal
investigation) Spur, *die;* **not have a** ~: keine
Ahnung haben
'clueless *adj.* (coll.) unbedarft (ugs.)
clump /klʌmp/ *n.* Gruppe, *die;* (of grass)
Büschel, *das*
clumsily /'klʌmzɪlɪ/ *adv.* ▶ CLUMSY:
schwerfällig; unbeholfen; plump
clumsiness /'klʌmzɪnɪs/ *n.* ▶ CLUMSY:
Schwerfälligkeit, *die;* Plumpheit, *die*
clumsy /'klʌmzɪ/ *adj.* schwerfällig,
unbeholfen ⟨Person, Bewegung⟩; plump
⟨Form, Figur, Nachahmung⟩
clung ▶ CLING
cluster /'klʌstə(r)/ ① *n.* (of grapes, berries)
Traube, *die;* (of fruit, flowers) Büschel, *das;* (of
stars, huts) Haufen, *der*
② *v.i.* ~ **[a]round sb./sth.** sich um jmdn./
etw. scharen *od.* drängen
clutch /klʌtʃ/ ① *v.t.* umklammern
② *v.i.* ~ **at sth.** nach etw. greifen; (fig.) sich
an etw. (Akk.) klammern
③ *n.* **(a)** in pl. (fig.: control) Klauen *Pl.*
(b) (Motor Veh.) Kupplung, *die*
clutter /'klʌtə(r)/ ① *n.* Durcheinander, *das*
② *v.t.* ~ **[up] the table/room** überall auf dem
Tisch/im Zimmer herumliegen
cm. *abbr.* = **centimetre[s]** cm
c/o *abbr.* = **care of** bei; c/o
Co. *abbr.* **(a)** = **company** Co.
(b) = **county**
coach /kəʊtʃ/ ① *n.* **(a)** (horse-drawn)
Kutsche, *die*
(b) (Railw.) Wagen, *der*
(c) (bus) [Reise]bus, *der;* **by** ~: mit dem Bus
(d) (Sport) Trainer, *der*/Trainerin, *die*
② *v.t.* trainieren
coaching /'kəʊtʃɪŋ/ *n.* **(a)** (teaching)
Privatunterricht, *der*
(b) (Sport) Training, *das*
coach: ~ **party** *n.* Reisegesellschaft, *die;*
~ **station** *n.* Busbahnhof, *der;* ~ **tour** *n.*
Rundreise [im Omnibus]
coagulate /kəʊ'ægjʊleɪt/ ① *v.t.* gerinnen
lassen

② *v.i.* gerinnen
coal /kəʊl/ *n.* Kohle, *die*
coal: ~**field** *n.* Kohlenrevier, *das;*
~ **fire** *n.* Kohlenfeuer, *das;* ~**fired** *adj.* mit
Kohle beheizt; kohlebeheizt
coalition /kəʊə'lɪʃn/ *n.* (Polit.) Koalition, *die*
coal: ~ **mine** *n.* [Kohlen]bergwerk, *das;*
~ **miner** *n.* [im Kohlenbergbau tätiger]
Grubenarbeiter; ~ **mining** *n.*
Kohlenbergbau, *der*
coarse /kɔːs/ *adj.* **(a)** (in texture) grob
(b) (unrefined, obscene) derb
coast /kəʊst/ ① *n.* Küste, *die*
② *v.i.* im Freilauf fahren
coastal /'kəʊstl/ *adj.* Küsten-
'coaster *n.* **(a)** (mat) Untersetzer, *der*
(b) (ship) Küstenmotorschiff, *das*
coast: ~**guard** *n.* Küstenwache, -wacht,
die; ~**line** *n.* Küste, *die*
coat /kəʊt/ ① *n.* **(a)** Mantel, *der*
(b) (layer) Schicht, *die;* (of paint) Anstrich, *der*
(c) (animal's hair, fur, etc.) Fell, *das*
② *v.t.* überziehen; (with paint) streichen
'coat hanger *n.* Kleiderbügel, *der*
'coating *n.* Schicht, *die*
coat of 'arms *n.* Wappen, *das*
coax /kəʊks/ *v.t.* überreden
cobble /'kɒbl/ *n.* Kopfstein, *der*
cobbler /'kɒblə(r)/ *n.* Schuster, *der*
'cobblestone ▶ COBBLE
cobra /'kɒbrə/ *n.* Kobra, *die*
cobweb /'kɒbweb/ *n.* Spinnengewebe, *das;*
Spinnennetz, *das*
cocaine /kə'keɪn/ *n.* Kokain, *das*
cock /kɒk/ ① *n.* Hahn, *der*
② *v.t.* spitzen ⟨Ohren⟩; ~ **a/the gun** den
Hahn spannen
cock-a-hoop /kɒkə'huːp/ *adj.*
überschwänglich
cockatoo /kɒkə'tuː/ *n.* Kakadu, *der*
'cockcrow *n.* **at** ~: beim ersten
Hahnenschrei
cockerel /'kɒkərəl/ *n.* junger Hahn
cock-eyed /'kɒkaɪd/ *adj.* **(a)** (crooked)
schief
(b) (absurd) verrückt
cockle /'kɒkl/ *n.* Herzmuschel, *die*
cockney /'kɒknɪ/ ① *adj.* Cockney-
② *n.* Cockney, *der*
'cockpit *n.* Cockpit, *das*
cockroach /'kɒkrəʊtʃ/ *n.* [Küchen-, Haus-]
schabe, *die*
cocktail /'kɒkteɪl/ *n.* Cocktail, *der*
cocktail: ~ **cabinet** *n.* Hausbar, *die;*
~ **party** *n.* Cocktailparty, *die*
cocoa /'kəʊkəʊ/ *n.* Kakao, *der*
coconut /'kəʊkənʌt/ *n.* Kokosnuss, *die*
cocoon /kə'kuːn/ *n.* (Zool.) Kokon, *der*
cod /kɒd/ *n., pl. same* Kabeljau, *der*
COD *abbr.* = **cash on delivery,** (Amer.)
= **collect on delivery** p. Nachn.

code /kəʊd/ ① *n.* **(a)** (statutes etc.)
Gesetzbuch, *das;* ~s of behaviour
Verhaltensnormen
(b) (system of signals) Code, *der;* be in ~:
verschlüsselt sein
② *v.t.* chiffrieren; verschlüsseln
code: ~ **name** *n.* Deckname, *der;*
~ **word** *n.* Kennwort, *das*
cod-liver 'oil *n.* Lebertran, *der*
co-driver /'kəʊdraɪvə(r)/ *n.* Beifahrer, *der/*
-fahrerin, *die*
coed /'kəʊed/ (esp. Amer. coll.) ① *n.*
Studentin, *die*
② *adj.* ~ **school** gemischte Schule
coeducational /kəʊedjʊ'keɪʃənl/ *adj.*
koedukativ; Koedukations-
coerce /kəʊ'ɜːs/ *v.t.* zwingen; ~ sb. into
sth. jmdn. zu etw. zwingen
coercion /kəʊ'ɜːʃn/ *n.* Zwang, *der*
coexist /kəʊɪg'zɪst/ *v.i.* koexistieren
coexistence /kəʊɪg'zɪstəns/ *n.*
Koexistenz, *die*
C. of E. /siːəv'iː/ *abbr.* = **Church of
England**
coffee /'kɒfɪ/ *n.* Kaffee, *der;* three black/
white ~s drei [Tassen] Kaffee ohne/mit
Milch
coffee: ~ **bar** *n.* Café, *das;* ~ **bean** *n.*
Kaffeebohne, *die;* ~ **break** *n.* Kaffeepause,
die; ~ **cup** *n.* Kaffeetasse, *die;*
~ **machine,** ~ **maker** *ns.*
Kaffeeautomat, *der;* ~ **pot** *n.* Kaffeekanne,
die; ~ **shop** *n.* Kaffeestube, *die;* ~ **table**
n. Couchtisch, *der*
coffin /'kɒfɪn/ *n.* Sarg, *der*
cog /kɒg/ *n.* (Mech.) Zahn, *der*
cogent /'kəʊdʒənt/ *adj.* überzeugend
⟨*Argument*⟩; zwingend ⟨*Grund*⟩
cognac /'kɒnjæk/ *n.* Cognac, *der* Ⓦ
cog: ~ **railway** *n.* Zahnradbahn, *die;*
~**wheel** *n.* Zahnrad, *das*
cohabit /kəʊ'hæbɪt/ *v.i.* zusammenleben;
in eheähnlicher Gemeinschaft leben
(Rechtsspr.)
cohere /kəʊ'hɪə(r)/ *v.i.* zusammenhalten
coherent /kəʊ'hɪərənt/ *adj.*
zusammenhängend
coherently /kəʊ'hɪərəntlɪ/ *adv.*
zusammenhängend; im Zusammenhang
coil /kɔɪl/ ① *v.t.* aufwickeln; (twist)
aufdrehen
② *v.i.* ~ round sth. etw. umschlingen
③ *n.* **(a)** ~s of rope/wire aufgerollte Seile
*Pl./*aufgerollter Draht
(b) (single turn) Windung, *die*
(c) (Electr.) Spule, *die*
'coil spring *n.* Spiralfeder, *die*
coin /kɔɪn/ ① *n.* Münze, *die*
② *v.t.* prägen ⟨*Wort, Redewendung*⟩
coincide /kəʊɪn'saɪd/ *v.i.* **(a)** (in time)
zusammenfallen
(b) (agree) übereinstimmen (with mit)

coincidence /kəʊ'ɪnsɪdəns/ *n.* Zufall, *der*
coincidental /kəʊɪnsɪ'dentl/ *adj.* zufällig
coincidentally /kəʊɪnsɪ'dentəlɪ/ *adv.*
gleichzeitig; (by coincidence) zufälligerweise
'coin-operated *adj.* Münz-
coke /kəʊk/ *n.* Koks, *der*
Col. *abbr.* = **Colonel** Obst.
colander /'kʌləndə(r)/ *n.* Sieb, *das*
cold /kəʊld/ ① *adj.* **(a)** kalt; I am/feel ~:
mir ist kalt
(b) (fig.) [betont] kühl ⟨*Person, Aufnahme,
Begrüßung*⟩
② *adv.* kalt
③ *n.* **(a)** Kälte, *die*
(b) (illness) Erkältung, *die;* ~ [in the head]
Schnupfen, *der;* have a ~: eine Erkältung/
[einen] Schnupfen haben
cold-blooded /'kəʊldblʌdɪd/ *adj.* **(a)**
wechselwarm ⟨*Tier*⟩
(b) kaltblütig ⟨*Person, Mord*⟩
'coldly *adv.* [betont] kühl
cold: ~'**shoulder** *v.t.* schneiden (fig.);
~ '**storage** *n.* Kühllagerung, *die;* ~ '**war**
n. kalter Krieg
coleslaw /'kəʊlslɔː/ *n.* Krautsalat, *der*
collaborate /kə'læbəreɪt/ *v.i.* **(a)**
zusammenarbeiten; ~ [with sb.] on sth.
zusammen [mit jmdm.] an etw. (*Dat.*)
arbeiten
(b) (with enemy) kollaborieren
collaboration /kəlæbə'reɪʃn/ *n.*
Zusammenarbeit, *die;* (with enemy)
Kollaboration, *die*
collaborator /kə'læbəreɪtə(r)/ *n.*
Mitarbeiter, *der/*-arbeiterin, *die;* (with enemy)
Kollaborateur, *der/*Kollaborateurin, *die*
collage /'kɒlɑːʒ/ *n.* Collage, *die*
collapse /kə'læps/ ① *n.* **(a)** (of person)
Zusammenbruch, *der*
(b) (of structure) Einsturz, *der*
(c) (of negotiations) Scheitern, *das;* (of company)
Zusammenbruch, *der*
② *v.i.* **(a)** ⟨*Person:*⟩ zusammenbrechen
(b) ⟨*Stuhl:*⟩ zusammenbrechen; ⟨*Gebäude:*⟩
einstürzen
(c) ⟨*Verhandlungen:*⟩ scheitern;
⟨*Unternehmen:*⟩ zusammenbrechen
(d) (fold down) ⟨*Regenschirm, Fahrrad, Tisch:*⟩
sich zusammenklappen lassen
collapsible /kə'læpsɪbl/ *adj.* Klapp⟨*stuhl,
-tisch, -fahrrad*⟩
collar /'kɒlə(r)/ ① *n.* **(a)** Kragen, *der*
(b) (for dog) [Hunde]halsband, *das*
② *v.t.* schnappen (ugs.)
'collarbone *n.* Schlüsselbein, *das*
colleague /'kɒliːg/ *n.* Kollege, *der/*
Kollegin, *die*
collect /kə'lekt/ ① *v.i.* sich versammeln;
⟨*Staub, Müll usw.:*⟩ sich ansammeln
② *v.t.* sammeln; aufsammeln ⟨*Müll, leere
Flaschen usw.*⟩; (fetch) abholen ⟨*Menschen,
Dinge*⟩; ~ one's wits/thoughts seine
Gedanken sammeln

col'lected adj. (a) (gathered) gesammelt
(b) (calm) gesammelt; gelassen

collection /kə'lekʃn/ n. (a) (collecting)
Sammeln, das; (of goods, persons) Abholen, das
(b) (amount of money collected) Sammlung, die;
(in church) Kollekte, die
(c) (from postbox) Leerung, die
(d) (of stamps etc.) Sammlung, die

collective /kə'lektɪv/ adj. kollektiv nicht
präd

collective 'bargaining n.
Tarifverhandlungen Pl.

collector /kə'lektə(r)/ n. (a) (of stamps etc.)
Sammler, der/Sammlerin, die
(b) (of taxes) Einnehmer, der/Einnehmerin,
die

col'lector's item, col'lector's piece
ns. Sammlerstück, das

college /'kɒlɪdʒ/ n. (a) (esp. Brit. Univ.)
College, das
(b) (place of further education) Fach[hoch]schule,
die; go to ~ (esp. Amer.) studieren

collide /kə'laɪd/ v.i. zusammenstoßen (with
mit)

collie /'kɒlɪ/ n. Collie, der

colliery /'kɒljərɪ/ n. Kohlengrube, die

collision /kə'lɪʒn/ n. Zusammenstoß, der;
on a ~ course (lit. or fig.) auf Kollisionskurs

colloquial /kə'ləʊkwɪəl/ adj.
umgangssprachlich

collusion /kə'luːʒn/ n. geheime Absprache

cologne ▶ EAU-DE-COLOGNE

Cologne /kə'ləʊn/ [1] pr. n. Köln (das)
[2] attrib. adj. Kölner

Colombia /kə'lɒmbɪə/ pr. n. Kolumbien
(das)

colon[1] /'kəʊlən/ n. Doppelpunkt, der

colon[2] /'kəʊlən, 'kəʊlɒn/ n. (Anat.)
Grimmdarm, der

colonel /kɜːnl/ n. Oberst, der

colonial /kə'ləʊnɪəl/ adj. Kolonial-; kolonial

colonize /'kɒlənaɪz/ v.t. kolonisieren

colony /'kɒlənɪ/ n. Kolonie, die

color etc. (Amer.) ▶ COLOUR etc.

colossal /kə'lɒsl/ adj. ungeheuer; gewaltig
⟨Bauwerk⟩

colour /'kʌlə(r)/ (Brit.) [1] n. Farbe, die; what
~ is it? welche Farbe hat es?; change ~: die
Farbe ändern; he is off ~: ihm ist nicht gut
[2] v.t. (a) (give ~ to) Farbe geben (+ Dat.)
(b) (paint) malen
(c) (stain, dye) färben
[3] v.i. ~ [up] erröten

'colour-blind adj. farbenblind

coloured /'kʌləd/ (Brit.) [1] adj. (a) farbig
(b) (of non-white descent) farbig; ~ people
Farbige Pl.
[2] n. Farbige, der/die

colour: ~-fast adj. farbecht; ~ **film** n.
Farbfilm, der

colourful /'kʌləfl/ adj. (Brit.) bunt;
anschaulich ⟨Sprache, Stil, Bericht⟩

'colouring n. (Brit.) (a) (colours) Farben Pl.
(b) ~ [matter] (in food etc.) Farbstoff, der

'colourless adj. (Brit.) farblos

colour: ~ photograph n.
Farbaufnahme, die; ~ **printer** n.
Farbdrucker, der; ~ **scheme** n.
Farb[en]zusammenstellung, die;
~ **supplement** n. Farbbeilage, die;
~ **television** n. Farbfernsehen, das; (set)
Farbfernsehgerät, das; ~ **transparency**
n. Farbdia, das

colt /kəʊlt/ n. [Hengst]fohlen, das

column /'kɒləm/ n. (a) Säule, die
(b) (of page) Spalte, die; sports ~: Sportteil,
der

columnist /'kɒləmɪst/ n. Kolumnist, der/
Kolumnistin, die

coma /'kəʊmə/ n. Koma, das; in a ~: im
Koma

comb /kəʊm/ [1] n. Kamm, der
[2] v.t. (a) kämmen; ~ sb.'s/one's hair
jmdm./sich die Haare kämmen
(b) (search) durchkämmen

combat /'kɒmbæt/ [1] n. Kampf, der
[2] v.t. bekämpfen

combatant /'kɒmbətənt/ n. Kombattant,
der

combination /kɒmbɪ'neɪʃn/ n.
Kombination, die; in ~: zusammen

combi'nation lock n.
Kombinationsschloss, das

combine [1] /kəm'baɪn/ v.t.
zusammenfügen (into zu); verbinden
⟨Substanzen⟩
[2] v.i. (join together) ⟨Stoffe:⟩ sich verbinden
[3] /'kɒmbaɪn/ n. ~ [harvester] Mähdrescher,
der

combustible /kəm'bʌstɪbl/ adj. brennbar

combustion /kəm'bʌstʃn/ n.
Verbrennung, die

come /kʌm/ v.i., came /keɪm/, come /kʌm/
kommen; ~ here! komm [mal] her!; [I'm]
coming! [ich] komme schon!; the train came
into the station der Zug fuhr in den Bahnhof
ein; Christmas is coming bald ist
Weihnachten; the handle has ~ loose der
Griff ist lose; nothing came of it es ist nichts
daraus geworden
■ **come a'bout** v.i. passieren
■ **come across** [1] /--'-/ v.i. (be understood)
verstanden werden
[2] /'---/ v.t. begegnen (+ Dat.)
■ **come a'long** v.i. (coll.) (a) (hurry up)
~ along! komm/kommt!
(b) (make progress) ~ along nicely gute
Fortschritte machen
(c) (to place) mitkommen (with mit)
■ **come 'back** v.i. zurückkommen
■ **come by** [1] /-'-/ v.t. (obtain) bekommen
[2] /'-'-/ v.i. vorbeikommen
■ **come 'down** v.i. (a) (fall) ⟨Schnee, Regen,
Preis:⟩ fallen
(b) (~ lower) herunterkommen
(c) (land) [not]landen; (crash) abstürzen

■ **come 'in** *v.i.* (enter) hereinkommen; ~ **in!**
herein!

■ **'come into** *v.t.* (a) (enter) hereinkommen
in (+ *Akk.*)
(b) (inherit) erben

■ **come off** [1] /-'-/ *v.i.* (a) ⟨*Griff, Knopf:*⟩
abgehen; (be removable) sich abnehmen lassen
(b) (succeed) ⟨*Pläne, Versuche:*⟩ Erfolg haben
(c) (take place) stattfinden
[2] /'--/ *v.t.* ~ **off a horse/bike** vom Pferd/
Fahrrad fallen; ~ **'off it!** (coll.) nun mach mal
halblang! (ugs.)

■ **come on** [1] /-'-/ *v.i.* (a) (continue coming,
follow) kommen; ~ **on!** komm, komm/kommt,
kommt!; (encouraging) na, komm!
(b) (make progress) ~ **on very well** gute
Fortschritte machen
[2] /'--/ *v.t.* ▶ ~ UPON

■ **come 'out** *v.i.* (a) (continue coming) herauskommen
(b) (fig.) ⟨*Sonne, Wahrheit, Buch:*⟩
herauskommen
(c) ~ **out with** herausrücken mit (ugs.)

■ **come 'over** [1] *v.i.* herüberkommen
[2] *v.t.* kommen über (+ *Akk.*)

■ **come 'round** *v.i.* (a) (visit)
vorbeischauen
(b) (recover) wieder zu sich kommen

■ **come 'through** [1] *v.i.* durchkommen
[2] *v.t.* (survive) überleben

■ **come to** [1] /'--/ *v.t.* (amount to) ⟨*Rechnung,
Kosten:*⟩ sich belaufen auf (+ *Akk.*), machen
[2] /-'-/ *v.i.* wieder zu sich kommen

■ **'come under** *v.t.* (a) (be classed as or
among) kommen unter (+ *Akk.*)
(b) (be subject to) kommen unter (+ *Akk.*)

■ **come 'up** *v.i.* (a) (~ higher) hochkommen
(b) ~ **up to sb.** (approach for talk) auf jmdn.
zukommen
(c) (present itself) sich ergeben
(d) ~ **up to** (reach) reichen bis an (+ *Akk.*);
entsprechen (+ *Dat.*) ⟨*Erwartungen*⟩
(e) ~ **up against sth.** (fig.) auf etw. (*Akk.*)
stoßen
(f) ~ **up with** vorbringen ⟨*Vorschlag*⟩;
wissen ⟨*Lösung, Antwort*⟩

■ **'come upon** *v.t.* (meet by chance)
begegnen (+ *Dat.*)

'comeback *n.* (to profession etc.) Come-back,
das

comedian /kə'miːdɪən/ *n.* Komiker, *der*

comedienne /kəmi:dr'en/ *n.* Komikerin,
die

'comedown *n.* Abstieg, *der*

comedy /'kɒmɪdɪ/ (a) *n.* Lustspiel, *das;*
Komödie, *die*
(b) (humour) Witz; Witzigkeit, *die*

comer /'kʌmə(r)/ *n.* **the competition is
open to all** ~s an dem Wettbewerb kann
sich jeder beteiligen; **the first** ~: derjenige,
der zuerst kommt

comet /'kɒmɪt/ *n.* Komet, *der*

comeuppance /kʌm'ʌpəns/ *n.* **get one's**
~: die Quittung kriegen (fig.)

comfort /'kʌmfət/ [1] *n.* (a) (consolation)
Trost, *der*

(b) (physical well-being) Behaglichkeit, *die*
(c) *in pl.* Komfort, *der*
[2] *v.t.* trösten

comfortable /'kʌmfətəbl/ *adj.* (a) bequem
⟨*Bett, Schuhe*⟩; komfortabel ⟨*Haus, Zimmer*⟩;
a ~ **victory** ein leichter Sieg
(b) (at ease) **be/feel** ~: sich wohl fühlen

comfortably /'kʌmfətəblɪ/ *adv.* bequem;
leicht ⟨*gewinnen*⟩

comforting /'kʌmfətɪŋ/ *adj.* beruhigend
⟨*Gedanke*⟩; tröstend ⟨*Worte*⟩; wohlig ⟨*Wärme*⟩

'comfort station *n.* (Amer.) öffentliche
Toilette

comfy /'kʌmfɪ/ *adj.* (coll.) bequem;
gemütlich ⟨*Haus, Zimmer*⟩

comic /'kɒmɪk/ [1] *adj.* komisch
[2] *n.* (a) (comedian) Komiker, *der*/Komikerin,
die
(b) (periodical) Comicheft, *das*

comical /'kɒmɪkl/ *adj.* komisch

coming /'kʌmɪŋ/ [1] *adj.* **in the** ~ **week**
kommende Woche
[2] *n.* ~**s and goings** das Kommen und
Gehen

comma /'kɒmə/ *n.* Komma, *das*

command /kə'mɑːnd/ [1] *v.t.* (a) (order)
befehlen (**sb.** jmdm.)
(b) (be in ~ of) befehligen ⟨*Schiff, Armee*⟩
(c) verfügen über (+ *Akk.*) ⟨*Gelder,
Wortschatz*⟩
[2] *n.* (a) Kommando, *das;* (in writing) Befehl,
der; **have/take** ~ **of** das Kommando über
(+ *Akk.*) ... haben/übernehmen
(b) (mastery, possession) Beherrschung, *die*

commandeer /kɒmən'dɪə(r)/ *v.t.*
requirieren

com'mander *n.* Führer, *der*

com'manding *adj.* (a) gebieterisch
⟨*Erscheinung, Stimme*⟩; imposant ⟨*Gestalt*⟩
(b) beherrschend ⟨*Ausblick, Lage*⟩

commanding 'officer *n.* Befehlshaber,
der/Befehlshaberin, *die*

com'mandment *n.* Gebot, *das*

commemorate /kə'meməreɪt/ *v.t.*
gedenken (+ *Gen.*)

commemoration /kəmemə'reɪʃn/ *n.*
Gedenken, *das;* **in** ~ **of** zum Gedenken an
(+ *Akk.*)

commemorative /kə'memərətɪv/ *adj.*
Gedenk-; ~ **of** zum Gedenken an (+ *Akk.*)

commence /kə'mens/ *v.t.* & *i.* beginnen

com'mencement *n.* Beginn, *der*

commend /kə'mend/ *v.t.* (praise) loben

commendable /kə'mendəbl/ *adj.*
lobenswert; löblich

commendation /kɒmen'deɪʃn/ *n.* (praise)
Lob, *das;* (official) Belobigung, *die;* (award)
Auszeichnung, *die*

comment /'kɒment/ [1] *n.* Bemerkung, *die*
(**on** über + *Akk.*); (note) Anmerkung, *die* (**on**
über + *Akk.*); **no** ~! (coll.) kein Kommentar! ···⫶

2 *v.i.* ~ **on sth.** über etw. (*Akk.*)
Bemerkungen machen; **he** ~**ed that** ...: er
bemerkte, dass ...

commentary /'kɒməntərɪ/ *n.* (a)
Kommentar, *der* (**on** zu)
(b) (Radio, Telev.) [**live** *or* **running**] ~:
Livereportage, *die*

commentate /'kɒmənteɪt/ *v.i.* ~ **on sth.**
etw. kommentieren

commentator /'kɒmənteɪtə(r)/ *n.*
Kommentator, *der*/Kommentatorin, *die;*
(Sport) Reporter, *der*/Reporterin, *die*

commerce /'kɒmɜːs/ *n.* Handel, *der*

commercial /kə'mɜːʃl/ 1 *adj.* Handels-;
kaufmännisch ⟨*Ausbildung*⟩
2 *n.* Werbespot, *der*

commercial: ~ **'bank** *n.* private
Geschäftsbank; ~ **'break** *n.* Werbepause,
die

commercialism /kə'mɜːʃəlɪzm/ *n.*
Kommerzialismus, *der*

commercialize /kə'mɜːʃəlaɪz/ *v.t.*
kommerzialisieren

commercial: ~ **'radio** *n.* Werbefunk,
der; ~ **'television** *n.* Werbefernsehen,
das; ~ **'traveller** *n.* Handelsvertreter, *der*/
-vertreterin, *die;* ~ **'vehicle** *n.*
Nutzfahrzeug, *das*

commiserate /kə'mɪzəreɪt/ *v.i.* ~ **with sb.**
jmdm. sein Mitgefühl aussprechen (**on** zu)

commission /kə'mɪʃn/ 1 *n.* (a) (official
body) Kommission, *die*
(b) (instruction, piece of work) Auftrag, *der*
(c) (Mil.) Ernennungsurkunde, *die*
(d) (pay of agent) Provision, *die*
(e) **in/out of** ~ ⟨*Auto, Maschine*⟩ in/außer
Betrieb
2 *v.t.* beauftragen ⟨*Künstler*⟩; in Auftrag
geben ⟨*Gemälde usw.*⟩

commissionaire /kəmɪʃə'neə(r)/ *n.* (esp.
Brit.) Portier, *der*

commissioner /kə'mɪʃənə(r)/ *n.* (of police)
Präsident, *der*

commit /kə'mɪt/ *v.t.,* -tt-: (a) begehen
⟨*Verbrechen, Fehler, Ehebruch*⟩
(b) (pledge, bind) ~ **oneself/sb. to doing sth.**
sich/jmdn. verpflichten, etw. zu tun
(c) (entrust) anvertrauen (**to** *Dat.*)
(d) ~ **sb. for trial** jmdm. dem Gericht
überstellen

com'mitment *n.* Verpflichtung (**to**
gegenüber)

com'mitted *adj.* engagiert

committee /kə'mɪtɪ/ *n.* Ausschuss, *der*

commodity /kə'mɒdɪtɪ/ *n.* (a) **household**
~: Haushaltsartikel, *der*
(b) (St. Exch.) [vertretbare] Ware; (raw material)
Rohstoff, *der*

common /'kɒmən/ 1 *adj.* (a) (belonging to
all) gemeinsam
(b) (public) öffentlich
(c) (usual) gewöhnlich; (frequent) häufig;
allgemein verbreitet ⟨*Sitte, Redensart*⟩

(d) (vulgar) ordinär
2 *n.* (a) (land) Gemeindeland, *das*
(b) **have sth./nothing/a lot in** ~ [**with sb.**]
etw./nichts/viel [mit jmdm.] gemein[sam]
haben

common 'cold *n.* Erkältung, *die*

'commoner *n.* Bürgerliche *der/die*

common: ~ **'ground** *n.* gemeinsame
Basis; ~ **'knowledge** *n.* **it's [a matter of]**
~ **knowledge that** ... es ist allgemein
bekannt, dass ...; ~**-law** *adj.* **she's his**
~**-law wife** sie lebt mit ihm in eheähnlicher
Gemeinschaft

'commonly *adv.* im Allgemeinen

common: **C**~ **'Market** *n.* gemeinsamer
Markt; ~**place** 1 *n.* Gemeinplatz, *der;*
2 *adj.* alltäglich; ~ **room** *n.* (Brit.)
Gemeinschaftsraum, *der;* (for lecturers)
Dozentenzimmer, *das*

Commons /'kɒmənz/ *n. pl.* **the [House of]**
~: das Unterhaus

common: ~ **'sense** *n.* gesunder
Menschenverstand; ~**-sense** *adj.*
vernünftig; gesund ⟨*Ansicht, Standpunkt*⟩;
~**wealth** *n.* **the [British] C**~**wealth** das
Commonwealth

commotion /kə'məʊʃn/ *n.* Tumult, *der*

communal /'kɒmjʊnl/ *adj.* (a) (of or for the
community) gemeindlich
(b) (for common use) gemeinsam

commune /'kɒmjuːn/ *n.* Kommune, *die*

communicate /kə'mjuːnɪkeɪt/ 1 *v.t.*
übertragen ⟨*Krankheit*⟩; übermitteln
⟨*Informationen*⟩; vermitteln ⟨*Gefühle, Ideen*⟩
2 *v.i.* ~ **with sb.** mit jmdm. kommunizieren

communication /kəmjuːnɪ'keɪʃn/ *n.* (a)
(of information) Übermittlung, *die*
(b) (message) Mitteilung, *die* (**to** an + *Akk.*)

communication: ~ **cord** *n.* Notbremse,
die; ~**s satellite** *n.* Nachrichtensatellit,
der

communicative /kə'mjuːnɪkətɪv/ *adj.*
gesprächig

Communion /kə'mjuːnɪən/ *n.* **[Holy]** ~
(Protestant Ch.) das [heilige] Abendmahl; (RC
Ch.) die [heilige] Kommunion

communiqué /kə'mjuːnɪkeɪ/ *n.*
Kommuniqué, *das*

communism /'kɒmjʊnɪzm/ *n.*
Kommunismus, *der;* C~: der Kommunismus

Communist, communist /'kɒmjʊnɪst/
1 *n.* Kommunist, *der*/Kommunistin, *die*
2 *adj.* kommunistisch

community /kə'mjuːnɪtɪ/ *n.* (a) (organized
body) Gemeinwesen, *das;* **the Jewish** ~: die
jüdische Gemeinde
(b) *no pl.* (public) Öffentlichkeit, *die*

community: ~ **'care** *n.* ≈ ambulante
Betreuung; ~ **centre** *n.*
Gemeindezentrum, *das;* ~ **'charge** *n.* (Brit.)
Gemeindesteuer, *die;* ~ **'service** *n.:*

[*freiwilliger od. als Strafe auferlegter*]
sozialer Dienst; ~ **spirit** *n.*
Gemeinschaftsgeist, *der*

commute /kə'mju:t/ [1] *v.t.* umwandeln
⟨*Strafe*⟩ (**to** in + *Akk.*)
[2] *v.i.* pendeln

commuter /kə'mju:tə(r)/ *n.* Pendler, *der*/
Pendlerin, *die*

com'muter: ~ **belt** *n.* großstädtischer
Einzugsbereich; ~ **train** *n.* Pendlerzug, *der*

compact¹ /kəm'pækt/ *adj.* kompakt

compact² /'kɒmpækt/ *n.* Puderdose [mit
Puder(stein)]

compact 'disc *n.* Compactdisc, *die;*
~ **player** CD-Spieler, *der*

companion /kəm'pænjən/ *n.* Begleiter,
der/Begleiterin, *die*

com'panionship *n.* Gesellschaft, *die*

company /'kʌmpəni/ *n.* **(a)** (persons
assembled, companionship) Gesellschaft, *die;*
expect ~: Besuch *od.* Gäste erwarten; **keep
sb.** ~: jmdm. Gesellschaft leisten
(b) (firm) Gesellschaft, *die;* ~ **car**
Firmenwagen, *der;* ~ **policy**
Unternehmenspolitik, *die;* Firmenpolitik, *die*
(c) (of actors) Truppe, *die;* Ensemble, *das*
(d) (Mil.) Kompanie, *die*

comparable /'kɒmpərəbl/ *adj.*
vergleichbar (**to, with** mit)

comparably /'kɒmpərəblɪ/ *adv.* in
vergleichbarer Weise; vergleichbar

comparative /kəm'pærətɪv/ [1] *adj.* **(a)**
(relative) relativ; **in** ~ **comfort** relativ
komfortabel
(b) (Ling.) komparativ (fachspr.); **a**
~ **adjective/adverb** ein Adjektiv/Adverb im
Komparativ
[2] *n.* (Ling.) Komparativ, *der*

com'paratively *adv.* verhältnismäßig

compare /kəm'peə(r)/ [1] *v.t.* vergleichen
(**to, with** mit) or/; ~**d with** or **to sb./sth.**
verglichen mit *od.* im Vergleich zu jmdm./
etw.
[2] *v.i.* sich vergleichen lassen

comparison /kəm'pærɪsn/ *n.* Vergleich,
der; **in** or **by** ~ [**with sb./sth.**] im Vergleich
[zu jmdm./etw.]

compartment /kəm'pɑ:tmənt/ *n.* (in
drawer, desk, etc.) Fach, *das;* (of railway carriage)
Abteil, *das*

compass /'kʌmpəs/ *n.* **(a)** *in pl.* [**a pair of**]
~**es** ein Zirkel
(b) (for navigating) Kompass, *der*

compassion /kəm'pæʃn/ *n.* Mitgefühl,
das (**for** mit)

compassionate /kəm'pæʃənət/ *adj.*
mitfühlend; **on** ~ **grounds** aus persönlichen
Gründen; (for family reasons) aus familiären
Gründen

compatibility /kəmpætɪ'bɪlɪtɪ/ *n.*
Vereinbarkeit, *die;* (of people)
Zueinanderpassen, *das;* (Comp.)
Kompatibilität, *die*

compatible /kəm'pætɪbl/ *adj.* vereinbar;
zueinander passend ⟨*Personen*⟩; (Comp.)
kompatibel

compel /kəm'pel/ *v.t.,* **-ll-** zwingen

compelling /kəm'pelɪŋ/ *adj.* bezwingend

compendium /kəm'pendɪəm/ *n.*
Kompendium, *das*

compensate /'kɒmpenseɪt/ [1] *v.i.* ~ **for**
sth. etw. ersetzen
[2] *v.t.* ~ **sb. for sth.** jmdn. für etw.
entschädigen

compensation /kɒmpen'seɪʃn/ *n.* Ersatz,
der; (for damages, injuries, etc.)
Schaden[s]ersatz, *der*

compère /'kɒmpeə(r)/ *n.* (Brit.)
Conférencier, *der*

compete /kəm'pi:t/ *v.i.* konkurrieren (**for**
um); (Sport) kämpfen

competence /'kɒmpɪtəns/ *n.* Fähigkeiten
Pl.

competent /'kɒmpɪtənt/ *adj.* fähig; **not**
~ **to do sth.** nicht kompetent, etw. zu tun

'competently *adv.* kompetent

competition /kɒmpɪ'tɪʃn/ *n.* **(a)** (contest)
Wettbewerb, *der;* (in magazine etc.)
Preisausschreiben, *das*
(b) (those competing) Konkurrenz, *die*

competitive /kəm'petɪtɪv/ *adj.*
wettbewerbsfähig ⟨*Preis, Unternehmen*⟩;
~ **sports** Leistungssport, *der*

competitor /kəm'petɪtə(r)/ *n.* Konkurrent,
der/Konkurrentin, *die;* (in contest, race)
Teilnehmer, *der*/-nehmerin, *die*

compile /kəm'paɪl/ *v.t.* zusammenstellen

complacency /kəm'pleɪsənsɪ/ *n.*
Selbstzufriedenheit, *die*

complacent /kəm'pleɪsənt/ *adj.*
selbstzufrieden

complain /kəm'pleɪn/ *v.i.* sich beklagen
(**about, at** über + *Akk.;* **to** bei); ~ **of sth.**
über etw. (*Akk.*) klagen

complaint /kəm'pleɪnt/ *n.* **(a)** Beschwerde,
die
(b) (ailment) Leiden, *das*

complement [1] /'kɒmplɪmənt/ *n.* **(a)**
(what completes) Vervollständigung, *die*
(b) (full number) **a** [**full**] ~: die volle Zahl; (of
people) die volle Stärke
[2] /'kɒmplɪment/ *v.t.* ergänzen

complementary /kɒmplɪ'mentərɪ/ *adj.*
(a) (completing) ergänzend
(b) (completing each other) einander ergänzend

complementary 'medicine *n.*
Komplementärmedizin, *die*

complete /kəm'pli:t/ [1] *adj.* **(a)**
vollständig; (in number) vollzählig
(b) (finished) fertig
(c) (absolute) völlig ⟨*Idiot*⟩; absolut
⟨*Katastrophe*⟩; total, (ugs.) blutig ⟨*Anfänger*⟩
[2] *v.t.* **(a)** (finish) beenden; fertig stellen
⟨*Gebäude, Arbeit*⟩
(b) ausfüllen ⟨*Formular*⟩

C

com'pletely *adv.* völlig; absolut ⟨*erfolgreich*⟩

completion /kəm'pliːʃn/ *n.* Beendigung, *die;* (of building, work) Fertigstellung, *die*

complex /'kɒmpleks/ **1** *adj.* kompliziert **2** *n.* Komplex, *der*

complexion /kəm'plekʃn/ *n.* Gesichtsfarbe, *die;* (fig.) Gesicht, *das*

-complexioned /kəm'plekʃnd/ *adj.* in *comb.* sallow-/fair-~: mit gelblichem Teint/ mit hellem Teint

complexity /kəm'pleksɪtɪ/ *n.* Kompliziertheit, *die*

complicate /'kɒmplɪkeɪt/ *v.t.* komplizieren.

'complicated *adj.* kompliziert

complication /kɒmplɪ'keɪʃn/ *n.* Komplikation, *die*

complicity /kəm'plɪsɪtɪ/ *n.* Mittäterschaft, *die* (**in** bei)

compliment **1** /'kɒmplɪmənt/ *n.* Kompliment, *das; in pl.* (formal greetings) Grüße *Pl.;* **pay sb. a ~:** jmdn. ein Kompliment machen **2** /'kɒmplɪment/ *v.t.* ~ **sb. on sth.** jmdm. Komplimente wegen etw. machen

complimentary /kɒmplɪ'mentərɪ/ *adj.* **(a)** schmeichelhaft **(b)** (free) Frei-

comply /kəm'plaɪ/ *v.i.* ~ **with sth.** sich nach etw. richten; **he refused to ~:** er wollte sich nicht danach richten

component /kəm'pəʊnənt/ **1** *n.* Bestandteil, *der* **2** *adj.* a ~ part ein Bestandteil

compose /kəm'pəʊz/ *v.t.* **(a)** bilden; **be ~d of** sich zusammensetzen aus **(b)** verfassen ⟨*Rede, Gedicht*⟩; abfassen ⟨*Brief*⟩ **(c)** (Mus.) komponieren

com'posed *adj.* (calm) gefasst

com'poser *n.* Komponist, *der/* Komponistin, *die*

composition /kɒmpə'zɪʃn/ *n.* **(a)** (constitution) (of soil etc.) Zusammensetzung, *die;* (of picture) Aufbau, *der* **(b)** (essay) Aufsatz, *der;* (Mus.) Komposition, *die*

compost /'kɒmpɒst/ *n.* Kompost, *der*

compostable /'kɒmpʊstəbl/ *adj.* kompostierbar

'compost heap *n.* Komposthaufen, *der*

composure /kəm'pəʊʒə(r)/ *n.* Gleichmut, *der*

compound¹ **1** /'kɒmpaʊnd/ *adj.* **(a)** zusammengesetzt **(b)** (Med.) ~ **fracture** komplizierter Bruch **2** /'kɒmpaʊnd/ *n.* **(a)** (mixture) Mischung, *die* **(b)** (Ling.) Kompositum, *das* **(c)** (Chem.) Verbindung, *die* **3** /'kəm'paʊnd/ *v.t.* verschlimmern ⟨*Schwierigkeiten, Verletzung usw.*⟩

compound² /'kɒmpaʊnd/ *n.* umzäuntes Gelände

compound 'interest *n.* Zinseszinsen *Pl.*

comprehend /kɒmprɪ'hend/ *v.t.* verstehen

comprehensible /kɒmprɪ'hensɪbl/ *adj.* verständlich

comprehension /kɒmprɪ'henʃn/ *n.* Verständnis, *das*

comprehensive /kɒmprɪ'hensɪv/ **1** *adj.* **(a)** umfassend **(b)** ~ **school** Gesamtschule, *die* **(c)** (insurance) Vollkasko- **2** *n.* Gesamtschule, *die*

compress **1** /kəm'pres/ *v.t.* **(a)** (squeeze) zusammenpressen (**into** zu) **(b)** komprimieren ⟨*Luft, Gas, Bericht*⟩ **(c)** (Comp.) komprimieren **2** /'kɒmpres/ *n.* Kompresse, *die*

compression /kəm'preʃn/ *n.* Kompression, *die*

compressor /kəm'presə(r)/ *n.* Kompressor, *der*

comprise /kəm'praɪz/ *v.t.* (include) umfassen; (consist of) bestehen aus

compromise /'kɒmprəmaɪz/ **1** *n.* Kompromiss, *der* **2** *v.i.* Kompromisse/einen Kompromiss schließen **3** *v.t.* kompromittieren

compromising /'kɒmprəmaɪzɪŋ/ *adj.* kompromittierend

compulsion /kəm'pʌlʃn/ *n.* Zwang, *der;* **be under no ~ to do sth.** keineswegs etw. tun müssen

compulsive /kəm'pʌlsɪv/ *adj.* **(a)** zwanghaft; **he is a ~ gambler** er ist dem Spiel verfallen **(b)** **this book is ~ reading** von diesem Buch kann man sich nicht losreißen

compulsory /kəm'pʌlsərɪ/ *adj.* obligatorisch

compunction /kəm'pʌŋkʃn/ *n.* Schuldgefühle

computer /kəm'pjuːtə(r)/ *n.* Computer, *der*

computer: ~-aided *adj.* computergestützt; ~ **ani'mation** *n.* Computeranimation, *die;* **~-assisted** *adj.* computergestützt; ~ **'dating** *n.* Partnervermittlung per Computer; ~ **dating agency/service** Computer-Partnervermittlung[sagentur], *die;* ~ **game** *n.* Computerspiel, *das;* ~ **'graphics** *n. pl.* Computergraphik, *die*

computerisation, computerise ▶ COMPUTERIZ-

computerization /kəmpjuːtəraɪ'zeɪʃn/ *n.* Computerisierung, *die*

computerize /kəm'pjuːtəraɪz/ *v.t.* computerisieren

computer: ~-'literate *adj.* mit Computern vertraut; **~-'operated** *adj.* computergesteuert; rechnergesteuert; ~ **program** *n.* Programm, *das;*

~ **programmer** *n.* Programmierer, *der*/ Programmiererin, *die*; ~ **programming** *n.* Programmieren, *das*; ~ **room** *n.* Computerraum, *der*; ~ '**science** *n.* Computerwissenschaft, *die*; ~ **terminal** *n.* Terminal, *das*; ~ '**typesetting** *n.* Computersatz, *der*; ~ **virus** *n.* [Computer]virus, *das od. der*

computing /kəmˈpjuːtɪŋ/ *n.* EDV, *die*; elektronische Datenverarbeitung; ~ **skills** Computerkenntnisse *Pl.*

comrade /ˈkɒmreɪd, ˈkɒmrɪd/ *n.* Kamerad, *der*/Kameradin, *die*

'**comradeship** *n.* Kameradschaft, *die*

con /kɒn/ (coll.) ⟦1⟧ *n.* Schwindel, *der* ⟦2⟧ *v.t.*, **-nn-** reinlegen (ugs.); ~ **sb. into sth.** jmdm. etw. aufschwatzen (ugs.)

concave /ˈkɒnkeɪv/ *adj.* konkav

conceal /kənˈsiːl/ *v.t.* verbergen (**from** vor + *Dat.*)

con'cealment *n.* Verbergen, *das*

concede /kənˈsiːd/ *v.t.* zugeben

conceit /kənˈsiːt/ *n.* Einbildung, *die*

con'ceited *adj.* eingebildet

conceivable /kənˈsiːvəbl/ *adj.* vorstellbar; **it is scarcely ~ that …**: man kann sich (*Dat.*) kaum vorstellen, dass …

conceivably /kənˈsiːvəblɪ/ *adj.* möglicherweise; **he cannot ~ have done it** er kann es unmöglich getan haben

conceive /kənˈsiːv/ ⟦1⟧ *v.t.* (a) empfangen ⟨*Kind*⟩ (b) (form in mind) sich (*Dat.*) vorstellen; haben ⟨*Idee, Plan*⟩ ⟦2⟧ *v.i.* (a) (become pregnant) empfangen (b) ~ **of sth.** sich (*Dat.*) etw. vorstellen

concentrate /ˈkɒnsəntreɪt/ ⟦1⟧ *v.t.* konzentrieren ⟦2⟧ *v.i.* sich konzentrieren (**on** auf + *Akk.*)

'**concentrated** *adj.* konzentriert

concentration /kɒnsənˈtreɪʃn/ *n.* Konzentration, *die*

concen'tration camp *n.* Konzentrationslager, *das*; KZ, *das*

concentric /kənˈsentrɪk/ *adj.* konzentrisch

concept /ˈkɒnsept/ *n.* Begriff, *der*; (idea) Vorstellung, *die*

conception /kənˈsepʃn/ (a) Vorstellung, *die* (**of** von) (b) (of child) Empfängnis, *die*

conceptual /kənˈseptjʊəl/ *adj.* begrifflich

conceptualize /kənˈseptjʊəlaɪz/ *v.t.* begrifflich fassen

concern /kənˈsɜːn/ ⟦1⟧ *v.t.* (a) (affect) betreffen; **so far as … is ~ed** was … betrifft; '**to whom it may ~**' ≈ „Bestätigung"; (on certificate, testimonial) ≈ „Zeugnis" (b) (interest) ~ **oneself with** *or* **about sth.** sich mit etw. befassen (c) (trouble) beunruhigen ⟦2⟧ *n.* (a) (anxiety) Besorgnis, *die*; (interest) Interesse, *das*

(b) (matter) Angelegenheit, *die* (c) (firm) Unternehmen, *das*

con'cerned /kənˈsɜːnd/ *adj.* (a) (involved) betroffen; (interested) interessiert; **as** *or* **so far as I'm ~**: was mich betrifft (b) (troubled) besorgt

con'cerning *prep.* bezüglich

concert /ˈkɒnsət/ *n.* Konzert, *das*

concerted /kənˈsɜːtɪd/ *adj.* vereint

concert: ~**goer** *n.* Konzertbesucher, *der*/-besucherin, *die*; ~ **hall** *n.* Konzertsaal, *der*

concertina /kɒnsəˈtiːnə/ *n.* Konzertina, *die*

concerto /kənˈtʃeətəʊ/ *n.* Konzert, *das*

concession /kənˈseʃn/ *n.* Konzession, *die*

concessionary /kənˈseʃənərɪ/ *adj.* Konzessions-; ~ **rate/fare** ermäßigter Tarif

conciliatory /kənˈsɪljətərɪ/ *adj.* versöhnlich

concise /kənˈsaɪs/ *adj.* kurz und prägnant; knapp, konzis ⟨*Stil*⟩

conclude /kənˈkluːd/ ⟦1⟧ *v.t.* (a) (end) beschließen (b) (infer) schließen (**from** aus) (c) (reach decision) beschließen ⟦2⟧ *v.i.* (end) schließen

concluding /kənˈkluːdɪŋ/ *adj.* abschließend

conclusion /kənˈkluːʒn/ *n.* (a) (end) Abschluss, *der*; **in ~**: zum Abschluss (b) (result) Ausgang, *der* (c) (inference) Schluss, *der*; **draw** *or* **reach a ~**: zu einem Schluss kommen

conclusive /kənˈkluːsɪv/ *adj.*, **con'clusively** *adv.* schlüssig

concoct /kənˈkɒkt/ *v.t.* zubereiten; zusammenbrauen ⟨*Trank*⟩

concoction /kənˈkɒkʃn/ *n.* Gebräu, *das*

concourse /ˈkɒnkɔːs/ *n.* Halle, *die*; **station ~**: Bahnhofshalle, *die*

concrete /ˈkɒnkriːt/ ⟦1⟧ *adj.* konkret ⟦2⟧ *n.* Beton, *der*; *attrib.* Beton-; **aus Beton** *präd*

concrete/ˈkɒnkriːt/**:** ~ **mixer** *n.* Betonmischer, *der*; Betonmischmaschine, *die*; ~ '**poetry** *n.* konkrete Poesie

concur /kənˈkɜː(r)/ *v.i.*, **-rr-**: ~ [**with sb.**] [**in sth.**] [jmdm.] [in etw. (*Dat.*)] zustimmen

concurrent /kənˈkʌrənt/ *adj.*, **con'currently** *adv.* gleichzeitig

concussion /kənˈkʌʃn/ *n.* Gehirnerschütterung, *die*

condemn /kənˈdem/ *v.t.* (a) (censure) verdammen (b) (Law: sentence) verurteilen (**to** zu) (c) für unbewohnbar erklären ⟨*Gebäude*⟩

condemnation /kɒndemˈneɪʃn/ *n.* Verdammung, *die*

condensation /kɒndenˈseɪʃn/ *n.* (a) (condensing) Kondensation, *die* (b) (water) Kondenswasser, *das*

condense /kən'dens/ ① *v.t.* (a)
komprimieren; ∼d milk Kondensmilch, *die*
(b) (Phys., Chem.) kondensieren
② *v.i.* kondensieren

condescend /kɒndɪ'send/ *v.i.* ∼ to do sth.
sich dazu herablassen, etw. zu tun

conde'scending *adj.* herablassend

condescension /kɒndɪ'senʃn/ *n.* (derog.:
patronizing manner) Herablassung, *die*

condiment /'kɒndɪmənt/ *n.* Gewürz, *das*

condition /kən'dɪʃn/ *n.* (a) (stipulation)
[Vor]bedingung, *die;* on [the] ∼ that ...: unter
der Voraussetzung, dass ...
(b) *in pl.* (circumstances) Umstände *Pl.;*
weather/living ∼s Witterungs-/
Wohnverhältnisse; working ∼s
Arbeitsbedingungen
(c) (of athlete etc.) Form, *die;* (of thing) Zustand,
der; (of patient) Verfassung, *die*
(d) (Med.) Leiden, *das*

conditional /kən'dɪʃənl/ *adj.* (a) bedingt;
be ∼ [up]on sth. von etw. abhängen
(b) (Ling.) Konditional-

con'ditioner *n.* Frisiermittel, *das*

condolence /kən'dəʊləns/ *n.*
Anteilnahme, die; letter of ∼: Beileidsbrief,
der

condom /'kɒndɒm/ *n.* Kondom, *das od. der*

condominium /'kɒndə'mɪnɪəm/ *n.* (Amer.)
Appartementhaus [mit
Eigentumswohnungen]

condone /kən'dəʊn/ *v.t.* hinwegsehen über
(+ *Akk.*); (approve) billigen

conducive /kən'dju:sɪv/ *adj.* be ∼ to sth.
einer Sache (*Dat.*) förderlich sein

conduct ① /'kɒndʌkt/ *n.* (a) (behaviour)
Verhalten, *das*
(b) (way of ∼ing) Führung, *die*
② /kən'dʌkt/ *v.t.* (a) führen
(b) (Mus.) dirigieren
(c) (Phys.) leiten
(d) ∼ed tour Führung, *die*

conduction /kən'dʌkʃn/ *n.* (Phys.) Leitung,
die

conductor /kən'dʌktə(r)/ *n.* (a) (Mus.)
Dirigent, *der*/Dirigentin, *die*
(b) (of bus, tram) Schaffner, *der*

conductress /kən'dʌktrɪs/ *n.* Schaffnerin,
die

conduit /'kɒndjʊɪt/ *n.* (a) Leitung, *die;*
Kanal, *der* (auch fig.)
(b) (Electr.) Isolierrohr, *das*

cone /kəʊn/ *n.* (a) Kegel, *der;* (traffic ∼)
Leitkegel, *der*
(b) (Bot.) Zapfen, *der*
(c) ice-cream ∼: Eistüte, *die*

confectioner /kən'fekʃənə(r)/ *n.* ∼'s
[shop] Süßwarengeschäft, *das*

con'fectionery *n.* Süßwaren *Pl.*

confederate /kən'fedərət/ *adj.* verbündet

confederation /kən'fedə'reɪʃn/ *n.*
[Staaten]bund, *der*

confer /kən'fɜ:(r)/ ① *v.t.,* -rr-: ∼ sth. [up]on
sb. jmdm. etw. verleihen
② *v.i.,* -rr-: ∼ with sb. sich mit jmdm.
beraten

conference /'kɒnfərəns/ *n.* (a) Konferenz,
die
(b) be in ∼: in einer Besprechung sein

conference: ∼ room *n.* Konferenzraum,
der; ∼ table *n.* Konferenztisch, *der*

confess /kən'fes/ ① *v.t.* (a) gestehen
(b) (Eccl.) beichten
② *v.i.* (a) ∼ to sth. etw. gestehen
(b) (Eccl.) beichten (to sb. jmdm.)

confession /kən'feʃn/ *n.* (a) Geständnis,
das
(b) (Eccl.: of sins etc.) Beichte, *die*

confetti /kən'fetɪ/ *n.* Konfetti, *das*

confidant /'kɒnfɪdænt, kɒnfɪ'dænt/ *n.*
Vertraute, *der*

confidante /'kɒnfɪdænt, kɒnfɪ'dænt/ *n.*
Vertraute, *die*

confide /kən'faɪd/ ① *v.i.* ∼ in sb. sich
jmdm. anvertrauen
② *v.t.* ∼ sth. to sb. jmdm. etw. anvertrauen

confidence /'kɒnfɪdəns/ *n.* (a) (firm trust)
Vertrauen, *das;* have ∼ in sb./sth. Vertrauen
zu jmdm./etw. haben; have [absolute] ∼ that
...: [absolut] sicher sein, dass ...
(b) (assured expectation) Gewissheit, *die*
(c) (self-reliance) Selbstvertrauen, *das*
(d) in ∼: im Vertrauen; this is in [strict] ∼:
das ist [streng] vertraulich

'confidence trick *n.* (Brit.) Trickbetrug,
der

confident /'kɒnfɪdənt/ *adj.* zuversichtlich
(about in Bezug auf + *Akk.*)

confidential /kɒnfɪ'denʃl/ *adj.* vertraulich

confidentiality /kɒnfɪdenʃɪ'ælɪtɪ/ *n.*
Vertraulichkeit, *die*

confi'dentially *adv.* vertraulich

'confidently *adv.* zuversichtlich

configure /kən'fɪgə(r)/ *v.t.* (esp. Comp.)
konfigurieren

confine /kən'faɪn/ *v.t.* (a) einsperren; be
∼d to bed/the house ans Bett/Haus gefesselt
sein
(b) (fig.) ∼ oneself to doing sth. sich darauf
beschränken, etw. zu tun

con'fined *adj.* begrenzt

con'finement *n.* (imprisonment)
Einsperrung, *die*

confines /'kɒnfaɪnz/ *n. pl.* Grenzen

confirm /kən'fɜ:m/ *v.t.* bestätigen

confirmation /kɒnfə'meɪʃn/ *n.* (a)
Bestätigung, *die*
(b) (Protestant Ch.) Konfirmation, *die;* (RC Ch.)
Firmung, *die*

con'firmed *adj.* eingefleischt ‹*Junggeselle*›;
überzeugt ‹Vegetarier›

confiscate /'kɒnfɪskeɪt/ *v.t.*
beschlagnahmen

confiscation /kɒnfɪsˈkeɪʃn/ *n.*
Beschlagnahme, *die*

conflict ⓵ /ˈkɒnflɪkt/ *n.* **(a)** (fight) Kampf, *der*
(b) (clashing) Konflikt, *der*
⓶ /kənˈflɪkt/ *v.i.* (be incompatible) sich (*Dat.*) widersprechen; ∼ **with sth.** einer Sache (*Dat.*) widersprechen

conˈflicting *adj.* widersprüchlich

conform /kənˈfɔːm/ *v.i.* **(a)** entsprechen (**to** *Dat.*)
(b) (comply) sich einfügen; ∼ **to** *or* **with sth./ with sb.** sich nach etw./jmdm. richten

conformist /kənˈfɔːmɪst/ *n.* Konformist, *der*/Konformistin, *die*

conformity /kənˈfɔːmɪtɪ/ *n.*
Übereinstimmung, *die* (**with, to** mit)

confound /kənˈfaʊnd/ *v.t.* **(a)** (defeat) vereiteln
(b) (confuse) verwirren

conˈfounded *adj.* (coll. derog.) verdammt

confront /kənˈfrʌnt/ *v.t.* **(a)** gegenüberstellen; ∼ **sb. with sth./sb.** jmdn. mit etw./[mit] jmdm. konfrontieren
(b) (stand facing) gegenüberstehen (+ *Dat.*)

confrontation /kɒnfrənˈteɪʃn/ *n.*
Konfrontation, *die*

confuse /kənˈfjuːz/ *v.t.* **(a)** (disorder) durcheinander bringen
(b) (mix up mentally) verwechseln
(c) (perplex) verwirren

conˈfused *adj.* konfus; wirr ‹*Gedanken, Gerüchte*›; verworren ‹*Lage, Situation*›

confusing /kənˈfjuːzɪŋ/ *adj.* verwirrend

confusion /kənˈfjuːʒn/ *n.* **(a)** Verwirrung, *die;* (mixing up) Verwechslung, *die*
(b) (embarrassment) Verlegenheit, *die*

congeal /kənˈdʒiːl/ *v.i.* gerinnen

congenial /kənˈdʒiːnɪəl/ *adj.* (agreeable) angenehm

congenital /kənˈdʒenɪtl/ *adj.* angeboren; kongenital (fachspr.)

conger /ˈkɒŋɡə(r)/ *n.* ∼ [**eel**] Seeaal, *der*

congested /kənˈdʒestɪd/ *adj.* verstopft ‹*Straße, Nase*›

congestion /kənˈdʒestʃn/ *n.* (of traffic) Stauung, *die;* **nasal** ∼: verstopfte Nase

conglomerate /kənˈɡlɒmərət/ *n.* (Commerc.) Großkonzern, *der*

conglomeration /kənɡlɒməˈreɪʃn/ *n.*
Anhäufung, *die*

congratulate /kənˈɡrætjʊleɪt/ *v.t.* gratulieren (+ *Dat.*); ∼ **sb./oneself on sth.** jmdm./sich zu etw. gratulieren

congratulations /kənɡrætjʊˈleɪʃnz/
⓵ *int.* ∼! herzlichen Glückwunsch! (**on** zu); (on passing exam etc.) ich gratuliere!
⓶ *n. pl.* Glückwünsche *Pl.*

congregate /ˈkɒŋɡrɪɡeɪt/ *v.i.* sich versammeln

congregation /kɒŋɡrɪˈɡeɪʃn/ *n.* (Eccl.) Gemeinde, *die*

congress /ˈkɒŋɡres/ *n.* Kongress, *der;* C∼ (Amer.) der Kongress

congressional /kənˈɡreʃənl/ *adj.*
Kongress-

conical /ˈkɒnɪkl/ *adj.* kegelförmig

conifer /ˈkɒnɪfə(r)/ *n.* Nadelbaum, *der*

coniferous /kəˈnɪfərəs/ *adj.* Nadel-; ∼ **tree** Nadelbaum, *der;* Konifere, *die*

conjecture /kənˈdʒektʃə(r)/ ⓵ *n.*
Vermutung, *die*
⓶ *v.t.* vermuten
⓷ *v.i.* Vermutungen anstellen

conjugate /ˈkɒndʒʊɡeɪt/ *v.t.* (Ling.) konjugieren

conjugation /kɒndʒʊˈɡeɪʃn/ *n.* (Ling.) Konjugation, *die*

conjunction /kənˈdʒʌŋkʃn/ *n.* **(a)**
Verbindung, *die;* **in** ∼ **with** in Verbindung mit
(b) (Ling.) Konjunktion, *die*

conjure /ˈkʌndʒə(r)/ *v.i.* zaubern; **conjuring trick** Zaubertrick, *der*
■ **conjure ˈup** *v.t.* heraufbeschwören

conjurer, conjuror /ˈkʌndʒərə(r)/ *n.*
Zauberkünstler, *der*/-künstlerin, *die*

connect /kəˈnekt/ ⓵ *v.t.* verbinden (**to, with** mit)
⓶ *v.i.* ∼ **with sth.** mit etw. zusammenhängen

conˈnected *adj.* zusammenhängend

connection, (Brit. also) **connexion** /kəˈnekʃn/ *n.* **(a)** (act, state) Verbindung, *die*
(b) (fig.: of ideas) Zusammenhang, *der;* **in** ∼ **with** im Zusammenhang mit
(c) (train, bus, etc.) Anschluss, *der*

connoisseur /kɒnəˈsɜː(r)/ *n.* Kenner, *der*

connotation /kɒnəˈteɪʃn/ *n.* Assoziation, *die*

conquer /ˈkɒŋkə(r)/ *v.t.* besiegen; erobern ‹*Land*›

conqueror /ˈkɒŋkərə(r)/ *n.* (of a country) Eroberer, *der*

conquest /ˈkɒŋkwest/ *n.* Eroberung, *die*

conscience /ˈkɒnʃəns/ *n.* Gewissen, *das;* **have a clear/guilty** ∼: ein gutes/schlechtes Gewissen haben

ˈconscience-stricken, ˈconscience-struck *adjs.*
schuldbewusst

conscientious /kɒnʃɪˈenʃəs/ *adj.*
pflichtbewusst; (meticulous) gewissenhaft; ∼ **objector** Wehrdienstverweigerer [aus Gewissensgründen]

consciˈentiously *adv.* pflichtbewusst; (meticulously) gewissenhaft

conscious /ˈkɒnʃəs/ *adj.* **(a) he is not** ∼ **of it** es ist ihm nicht bewusst
(b) *pred.* (awake) bei Bewusstsein *präd.*
(c) (realized by doer) bewusst ‹*Versuch, Bemühung*›

ˈconsciously *adv.* bewusst

ˈconsciousness *n.* Bewusstsein, *das*

conscript ① /kənˈskrɪpt/ v.t. einberufen ② /ˈkɒnskrɪpt/ n. Einberufene, der/die

conscription /kənˈskrɪpʃn/ n. Wehrpflicht, die

consecrate /ˈkɒnsɪkreɪt/ v.t. weihen

consecutive /kənˈsekjʊtɪv/ adj. aufeinander folgend ⟨Monate, Jahre⟩; fortlaufend ⟨Zahlen⟩

con'secutively adv. hintereinander

consensus /kənˈsensəs/ n. Einigkeit, die

consent /kənˈsent/ ① v.i. zustimmen ② n. (agreement) Zustimmung, die (to zu); by common or general ~: nach allgemeiner Auffassung; age of ~: Ehemündigkeitsalter, das

consequence /ˈkɒnsɪkwəns/ n. (a) (result) Folge, die; in ~: folglich; as a ~: infolgedessen (b) (importance) Bedeutung, die

consequent /ˈkɒnsɪkwənt/ adj. daraus folgend

'consequently adv. infolgedessen

conservation /kɒnsəˈveɪʃn/ n. Erhaltung, die; wildlife ~: Schutz wild lebender Tierarten

conser'vation area n. (Brit.) (rural) Landschaftsschutzgebiet, das; (urban) unter Denkmalschutz stehendes Gebiet

conservationist /kɒnsəˈveɪʃənɪst/ n. Naturschützer, der/-schützerin, die

conservative /kənˈsɜːvətɪv/ ① adj. (a) konservativ (b) vorsichtig ⟨Schätzung⟩ (c) C~ (Brit. Polit.) konservativ; the C~ Party die Konservative Partei ② n. C~ (Brit. Polit.) Konservative, der/die

con'servatively adv. vorsichtig ⟨geschätzt⟩

conservatory /kənˈsɜːvətəri/ n. Wintergarten, der

conserve /kənˈsɜːv/ v.t. erhalten; schonen ⟨Kräfte⟩

consider /kənˈsɪdə(r)/ v.t. (a) (think about) ~ sth. an etw. (Akk.) denken; he's ~ing emigrating er denkt daran, auszuwandern (b) (reflect on) sich (Dat.) überlegen (c) (regard as) halten für; all things ~ed alles in allem

considerable /kənˈsɪdərəbl/ adj., **con'siderably** adv. erheblich

considerate /kənˈsɪdərət/ adj. rücksichtsvoll; (thoughtfully kind) entgegenkommend

considerately /kənˈsɪdərətli/ adv. rücksichtsvoll; (obligingly) entgegenkommend

consideration /kənsɪdəˈreɪʃn/ n. (a) Überlegung, die; take sth. into ~: etw. berücksichtigen; the matter is under ~: die Angelegenheit wird geprüft (b) (thoughtfulness) Rücksichtnahme, die

considered /kənˈsɪdəd/ adj. (a) ~ opinion feste od. ernsthafte Überzeugung

(b) be highly ~ [by others] [bei anderen] in hohem Ansehen stehen

con'sidering prep. ~ sth. wenn man etw. bedenkt; ~ [that] ...: wenn man bedenkt, dass ...

consign /kənˈsaɪn/ v.t. anvertrauen (to Dat.)

con'signment n. (Commerc.) Sendung, die; (large) Ladung, die

consist /kənˈsɪst/ v.i. ~ of bestehen aus

consistency /kənˈsɪstənsi/ n. (a) (density) Konsistenz, die (b) (being consistent) Konsequenz, die

consistent /kənˈsɪstənt/ adj. (a) (compatible) [miteinander] vereinbar (b) (uniform) gleich bleibend ⟨Qualität⟩ (c) (unchanging) konsequent

consolation /kɒnsəˈleɪʃn/ n. Trost, der

conso'lation prize n. Trostpreis, der

console /kənˈsəʊl/ v.t. trösten

consolidate /kənˈsɒlɪdeɪt/ v.t. festigen

consolidation /kənsɒlɪˈdeɪʃn/ n. Festigung, die

consoling /kənˈsəʊlɪŋ/ adj. tröstlich

consonant /ˈkɒnsənənt/ n. Konsonant, der

consort /kənˈsɔːt/ v.i. verkehren (with mit)

consortium /kənˈsɔːtɪəm/ n., pl. consortia /kənˈsɔːtɪə/ Konsortium, das

conspicuous /kənˈspɪkjʊəs/ adj. (a) (visible) unübersehbar (b) (obvious) auffallend

con'spicuously adv. (a) (visibly) unübersehbar (b) (obviously) auffallend

conspiracy /kənˈspɪrəsi/ n. (conspiring) Verschwörung, die; (plot) Komplott, das

conspire /kənˈspaɪə(r)/ v.i. sich verschwören

constable /ˈkʌnstəbl, ˈkɒnstəbl/ n. (Brit.) Polizist, der/Polizistin, die

constabulary /kənˈstæbjʊləri/ n. Polizei, die

constant /ˈkɒnstənt/ adj. (a) (unceasing) ständig (b) (unchanging) gleich bleibend

'constantly adv. (a) (unceasingly) ständig (b) (unchangingly) konstant

constellation /kɒnstəˈleɪʃn/ n. Sternbild, das

consternation /kɒnstəˈneɪʃn/ n. Bestürzung, die

constipated /ˈkɒnstɪpeɪtɪd/ adj. be ~: an Verstopfung leiden

constipation /kɒnstɪˈpeɪʃn/ n. Verstopfung, die

constituency /kənˈstɪtjʊənsi/ n. Wahlkreis, der

constituent /kənˈstɪtjʊənt/ n. (a) (part) Bestandteil, der (b) (Polit.) Wähler, der/Wählerin, die

constitute /ˈkɒnstɪtjuːt/ v.t. (a) (form, be) sein; ~ a threat to eine Gefahr sein für

(b) (make up) bilden

constitution /kɒnstɪˈtjuːʃn/ *n.* **(a)** (of person) Konstitution, *die*
(b) (of state) Verfassung, *die*

constitutional /kɒnstɪˈtjuːʃənl/ *adj.* (of constitution) der Verfassung *nachgestellt;* (in harmony with constitution) verfassungsmäßig

constrain /kənˈstreɪn/ *v.t.* zwingen

constraint /kənˈstreɪnt/ *n.* (limitation) Einschränkung, *die*

constrict /kənˈstrɪkt/ *v.t.* verengen

constriction /kənˈstrɪkʃn/ *n.* Verengung, *die*

construct /kənˈstrʌkt/ *v.t.* bauen; (fig.) erstellen ‹Plan›

construction /kənˈstrʌkʃn/ *n.* **(a)** (constructing) Bau, *der;* **be under** ∼: im Bau sein
(b) (thing constructed) Bauwerk, *das*

constructive /kənˈstrʌktɪv/ *adj.* konstruktiv

consul /ˈkɒnsl/ *n.* Konsul, *der*

consulate /ˈkɒnsjʊlət/ *n.* Konsulat, *das*

consult /kənˈsʌlt/ *v.t.* konsultieren ‹Arzt, Fachmann›; ∼ **a book** in einem Buch nachsehen

consultant /kənˈsʌltənt/ *n.* Berater, *der/* Beraterin, *die;* (Med.) Chefarzt, *der/*-ärztin, *die*

consultation /kɒnsəlˈteɪʃn/ *n.* Beratung, *die*

conˈsulting room *n.* Sprechzimmer, *das*

consume /kənˈsjuːm/ *v.t.* verbrauchen; (eat, drink) konsumieren

conˈsumer *n.* Verbraucher, *der/* Verbraucherin, *die*

conˈsumer goods *n. pl.* Konsumgüter *Pl.*

consumerism /kənˈsjuːmərɪzm/ *n., no art.* Konsumerismus, *der*

consumer: ∼ **proˈtection** *n.* Verbraucherschutz, *der;* ∼ **research** *n.* Verbrauchsforschung, *die;* Konsumforschung, *die*

consumption /kənˈsʌmpʃn/ *n.* Verbrauch, *der* (of an + *Dat.*); (eating or drinking) Verzehr, *der* (of von)

cont. *abbr.* = **continued** Forts.

contact ☐1 /ˈkɒntækt/ *n.* Berührung, *die;* (fig.) Kontakt, *der;* **be in** ∼ **with sth.** etw. berühren; **be in** ∼ **with sb.** (fig.) mit jmdm. Kontakt haben
☐2 /ˈkɒntækt, kənˈtækt/ *v.t.* sich in Verbindung setzen mit

ˈcontact lens *n.* Kontaktlinse, *die*

contagious /kənˈteɪdʒəs/ *adj.* ansteckend

contain /kənˈteɪn/ *v.t.* **(a)** (hold, include) enthalten
(b) (prevent from spreading) aufhalten

conˈtainer *n.* Behälter, *der;* (cargo ∼) Container, *der;* **cardboard/wooden** ∼: Pappkarton, *der/*Holzkiste, *die*

contaminate /kənˈtæmɪneɪt/ *v.t.* verunreinigen; (with radioactivity) verseuchen

contamination /kəntæmɪˈneɪʃn/ *n.* Verunreinigung, *die;* (with radioactivity) Verseuchung, *die*

contemplate /ˈkɒntəmpleɪt/ *v.t.* **(a)** betrachten; (mentally) nachdenken über (+ *Akk.*)
(b) (expect) rechnen mit; (consider) ∼ **sth./ doing sth.** an etw. (*Akk.*) denken/daran denken, etw. zu tun

contemplation /kɒntəmˈpleɪʃn/ *n.* Betrachtung, *die;* (mental) Nachdenken, *das* (of über + *Akk.*)

contemporary /kənˈtempərərɪ/ ☐1 *adj.* zeitgenössisch
☐2 *n.* Zeitgenosse, *der/*-genossin, *die*

contempt /kənˈtempt/ *n.* Verachtung, *die* (of, for für)

contemptible /kənˈtemptɪbl/ *adj.* verachtenswert

contemptuous /kənˈtemptjʊəs/ *adj.* verächtlich

contend /kənˈtend/ *v.i.* **be able/have to** ∼ **with** fertig werden können/müssen mit

conˈtender *n.* Bewerber, *der/*Bewerberin, *die*

content[1] /ˈkɒntent/ *n.* **(a)** *in pl.* Inhalt, *der;* [table of] ∼**s** Inhaltsverzeichnis, *das*
(b) (amount contained) Gehalt, *der* (of an + *Dat.*)

content[2] /kənˈtent/ ☐1 *pred. adj.* zufrieden
☐2 *v.t.* zufrieden stellen; ∼ **oneself with sth./ sb.** sich mit etw./jmdm. zufrieden geben

conˈtented *adj.,* **conˈtentedly** *adv.* zufrieden

contention /kənˈtenʃn/ *n.* **(a)** Streit, *der*
(b) (point asserted) Behauptung, *die*

contentious /kənˈtenʃəs/ *adj.* strittig ‹Punkt, Thema›

conˈtentment *n.* Zufriedenheit, *die*

contest ☐1 /ˈkɒntest/ *n.* Wettbewerb, *der*
☐2 /kənˈtest/ *v.t.* **(a)** bestreiten; infrage stellen ‹Behauptung›
(b) (Brit.: compete for) kandidieren für

contestant /kənˈtestənt/ *n.* (competitor) Teilnehmer, *der/*Teilnehmerin, *die*

context /ˈkɒntekst/ *n.* Kontext, *der;* **in/out of** ∼: im/ohne Kontext; **in this** ∼: in diesem Zusammenhang

contextual /kənˈtekstjʊəl/ *adj.* kontextuell

contextualize /kənˈtekstjʊəlaɪz/ *v.t.* (place in context) in einen Kontext einordnen

continent /ˈkɒntɪnənt/ *n.* Kontinent, *der;* **the C**∼: das europäische Festland

continental /kɒntɪˈnentl/ *adj.* **(a)** kontinental
(b) **C**∼ (mainland European) kontinental[europäisch]

continental: ∼ **ˈbreakfast** *n.* kontinentales Frühstück; ∼ **ˈquilt** *n.* (Brit.) [Stepp]federbett, *das*

con'tingency plan /kən'tɪndʒənsɪ/ n.
Alternativplan, der

contingent /kən'tɪndʒənt/ n. Kontingent,
das

continual /kən'tɪnjʊəl/ adj.,
con'tinually adv. (frequent[ly]) ständig;
(without stopping) unaufhörlich

continuation /kəntɪnjʊ'eɪʃn/ n.
Fortsetzung, die

continue /kən'tɪnju:/ ① v.t. fortsetzen; '~d
on page 2' „Fortsetzung auf Seite 2";
~ doing or to do sth. etw. weiter tun; it ~d
to rain es regnete weiter
② v.i. (persist) ⟨Wetter, Zustand, Krise usw.:⟩
andauern; (persist in doing sth.) nicht aufhören;
~ with sth. mit etw. fortfahren

continuity /kɒntɪ'nju:ɪtɪ/ n. Kontinuität,
die

continuous /kən'tɪnjʊəs/ adj. (a)
ununterbrochen; anhaltend ⟨Regen,
Sonnenschein⟩; ständig ⟨Kritik, Streit⟩;
durchgezogen ⟨Linie⟩
(b) (Ling.) ~ [form] Verlaufsform, die

con'tinuously adv. ununterbrochen;
ständig ⟨sich ändern⟩

contort /kən'tɔ:t/ v.t. verdrehen

contortion /kən'tɔ:ʃn/ n. Verdrehung, die

contour /'kɒntʊə(r)/ n. Kontur, die; ~ map
Höhenlinienkarte, die

contraband /'kɒntrəbænd/ n.
Schmuggelware, die

contraception /kɒntrə'sepʃn/ n.
Empfängnisverhütung, die

contraceptive /kɒntrə'septɪv/ ① adj.
empfängnisverhütend
② n. Verhütungsmittel, das

contract ① /'kɒntrækt/ n. Vertrag, der;
~ of employment Arbeitsvertrag, der; be
under ~ to do sth. vertraglich verpflichtet
sein, etw. zu tun
② /kən'trækt/ v.t. (Med.) sich ⟨Dat.⟩ zuziehen
③ /kən'trækt/ v.i. (a) ~ to do sth. sich
vertraglich verpflichten, etw. zu tun
(b) (become smaller, be drawn together) sich
zusammenziehen

contraction /kən'trækʃn/ n. Kontraktion,
die

'**contract killer** n. Auftragskiller, der/
-killerin, die

contractor /kən'træktə(r)/ n.
Auftragnehmer, der/-nehmerin, die

contradict /kɒntrə'dɪkt/ v.t.
widersprechen (+ Dat.)

contradiction /kɒntrə'dɪkʃn/ n.
Widerspruch, der; in ~ to sb./sth. im
Widerspruch zu jmdm./etw.

contradictory /kɒntrə'dɪktərɪ/ adj.
widersprüchlich

contraflow /'kɒntrəfləʊ/ n. ~ system
Gegenverkehr auf einem Fahrstreifen

contralto /kən'træltəʊ/ n., pl. ~s Alt, der

contraption /kən'træpʃn/ n. (coll.)
[komisches] Gerät

contrary /'kɒntrərɪ/ ① adj. (a)
entgegengesetzt; be ~ to sth. im Gegensatz
zu etw. stehen
(b) /kən'treərɪ/ (perverse) widerspenstig
② n. the ~: das Gegenteil; on the ~: im
Gegenteil
③ adv. ~ to sth. entgegen einer Sache

contrast ① /kɒn'trɑ:st/ v.t.
gegenüberstellen
② /'kɒntrɑ:st/ n. Kontrast, der (with zu); in
~, ...: im Gegensatz dazu, ...; [be] in ~ with
sth. im Gegensatz zu etw. [stehen]

con'trasting adj. gegensätzlich

contravene /kɒntrə'vi:n/ v.t. verstoßen
gegen

contravention /kɒntrə'venʃn/ n. Verstoß,
der (of gegen)

contribute /kən'trɪbju:t/ ① v.t. ~ sth. [to
or towards sth.] etw. [zu etw.] beitragen
② v.i. ~ to charity für karitative Zwecke
spenden; ~ to the success of sth. zum Erfolg
einer Sache (Gen.) beitragen

contribution /kɒntrɪ'bju:ʃn/ n. Beitrag,
der; (for charity) Spende, die (to für); make a
~: einen Beitrag leisten; (to charity) etwas
spenden

contributor /kən'trɪbjʊtə(r)/ n. (to
encyclopaedia etc.) Mitarbeiter, der/
Mitarbeiterin, die

'**con trick** (Brit. coll.) ▶ CONFIDENCE TRICK

contrite /'kɒntraɪt/ adj. zerknirscht

contrive /kən'traɪv/ v.t. ~ to do sth. es
fertig bringen, etw. zu tun

contrived /kən'traɪvd/ adj. künstlich

control /kən'trəʊl/ ① n. (a) Kontrolle, die
(of über + Akk.); keep ~ of sth. etw. unter
Kontrolle halten; be in ~ [of sth.] die
Kontrolle [über etw. (Akk.)] haben; [go or
get] out of ~: außer Kontrolle [geraten]; [get
sth.] under ~: [etw.] unter Kontrolle
[bringen]
(b) (device) Regler, der; ~s Schalttafel, die
② v.t., -ll- kontrollieren; lenken ⟨Auto⟩;
zügeln ⟨Zorn⟩; regeln ⟨Verkehr⟩

control: ~ centre n. Kontrollzentrum,
das; ~ **con'trol desk** n. Schaltpult, das

con'troller n. (director) Leiter, der/Leiterin,
die

control: ~ panel n. Schalttafel, die;
~ **room** n. Kontrollraum, der; ~ **tower**
n. Kontrollturm, der

controversial /kɒntrə'vɜ:ʃl/ adj.
umstritten

controversy /'kɒntrəvɜ:sɪ, kən'trɒvəsɪ/ n.
Auseinandersetzung, die

conurbation /kɒnɜ:'beɪʃn/ n. Konurbation,
die (Soziol.); ≈ Stadtregion, die

convalesce /kɒnvə'les/ v.i. genesen

convalescence /kɒnvə'lesəns/ n.
Genesung, die

convection /kən'vekʃn/ n. (Phys., Meteorol.)
Konvektion, die

convector /kən'vektə(r)/ n. Konvektor, der

convene /kən'viːn/ [1] v.t. einberufen
[2] v.i. zusammenkommen

convenience /kən'viːnɪəns/ n. (a) for
sb.'s ~ zu jmds. Bequemlichkeit; at your ~:
wann es Ihnen passt
(b) (toilet) [public] ~: [öffentliche] Toilette

con'venience food n. Fertignahrung,
die

convenient /kən'viːnɪənt/ adj. günstig;
(useful) praktisch; would it be ~ to or for
you? würde es Ihnen passen?

con'veniently adv. (a) günstig ⟨gelegen,
angebracht⟩
(b) (opportunely) angenehmerweise

convent /'kɒnvənt/ n. Kloster, das

convention /kən'venʃn/ n. (a) Brauch,
der
(b) (assembly) Konferenz, die
(c) (agreement) Konvention, die

conventional /kən'venʃənl/ adj.
konventionell

converge /kən'vɜːdʒ/ v.i. ~ [on each
other] aufeinander zulaufen

conversant /kən'vɜːsənt/ pred. adj.
vertraut (with mit)

conversation /kɒnvə'seɪʃn/ n.
Unterhaltung, die; have a ~: ein Gespräch
führen

conversational /kɒnvə'seɪʃənl/ adj.
~ English gesprochenes Englisch

converse[1] /kən'vɜːs/ v.i. (formal) ~ [with
sb.] [about or on sth.] sich [mit jmdm.]
[über etw. (Akk.)] unterhalten

converse[2] /'kɒnvɜːs/ [1] adj.
entgegengesetzt; umgekehrt ⟨Fall, Situation⟩
[2] n. Gegenteil, das

conversely /kən'vɜːslɪ/ adv. umgekehrt

conversion /kən'vɜːʃn/ n. (a)
Umwandlung, die (into in + Akk.)
(b) (adaptation) Umbau, der
(c) (of person) Bekehrung, die (to zu)

con'version table n.
Umrechnungstabelle, die

convert [1] /kən'vɜːt/ v.t. umwandeln (into
in + Akk.); (Comp.) konvertieren ⟨Daten⟩;
~ sb. [to sth.] jmdn. [zu etw.] bekehren
[2] /kən'vɜːt/ v.i. ~ into sth. sich in etw.
(Akk.) umwandeln lassen
[3] /'kɒnvɜːt/ n. Konvertit, der/Konvertitin,
die

convertible /kən'vɜːtɪbl/ [1] adj. be ~ into
sth. sich in etw. (Akk.) umwandeln lassen
[2] n. Kabrio[lett], das

convex /'kɒnveks/ adj. konvex

convey /kən'veɪ/ v.t. (a) befördern
(b) (impart) vermitteln

conveyance /kən'veɪəns/ n. (a)
(transportation) Beförderung, die
(b) (formal: vehicle) Beförderungsmittel, das

con'veyancing n. (Law) ~ [of property]
[Eigentums]übertragung, die

conveyor /kən'veɪə(r)/ n. ~ [belt]
Förderband, das

convict [1] /'kɒnvɪkt/ n. Strafgefangene,
der/die
[2] /kən'vɪkt/ v.t. verurteilen

conviction /kən'vɪkʃn/ n. (a) (Law)
Verurteilung, die (for wegen)
(b) (belief) Überzeugung, die

convince /kən'vɪns/ v.t. überzeugen; ~ sb.
that …: jmdn. davon überzeugen, dass …; be
~d that …: davon überzeugt sein, dass …

convincing /kən'vɪnsɪŋ/ adj.,
con'vincingly adv. überzeugend

convivial /kən'vɪvɪəl/ adj. fröhlich

convoluted /'kɒnvəluːtɪd/ adj. (complex)
kompliziert

convoy /'kɒnvɔɪ/ n. Konvoi, der; in ~: im
Konvoi

convulse /kən'vʌls/ v.t. be ~d with sich
krümmen vor (+ Dat.)

convulsions /kən'vʌlʃnz/ n. pl. Krämpfe
Pl.

convulsive /kən'vʌlsɪv/ adj.,
con'vulsively adv. konvulsivisch

coo /kuː/ v.i. gurren

cook /kʊk/ [1] n. Koch, der/Köchin, die
[2] v.t. kochen ⟨Mahlzeit⟩; (fry, roast) braten;
(boil) kochen
[3] v.i. kochen
■ **cook 'up** v.t. erfinden ⟨Geschichte⟩

'cookbook n. (Amer.) Kochbuch, das

'cooker n. (Brit.) Herd, der

cookery /'kʊkərɪ/ n. Kochen, das

'cookery book n. (Brit.) Kochbuch, das

cookie /'kʊkɪ/ n. (a) (Amer.) Keks, der
(b) (Comp.) Cookie, der

'cooking n. Kochen, das

cooking: ~ **apple** n. Kochapfel, der;
~ **utensil** n. Küchengerät, das

cool /kuːl/ [1] adj. (a) kühl; store in a
~ place kühl aufbewahren
(b) (unemotional, unfriendly) kühl; (calm) ruhig
[2] n. Kühle, die
[3] v.i. abkühlen
[4] v.t. kühlen; (from high temperature) abkühlen
■ **cool 'down, cool 'off** v.i. & t.
abkühlen

cool: ~ **box** n. Kühlbox, die; ~**-headed**
adj. kühl; nüchtern

coolly /'kuːllɪ/ adv. (calmly) ruhig;
(unemotionally) kühl

coop /kuːp/ [1] n. (for poultry) Hühnerstall,
der
[2] v.t. ~ up einpferchen

cooperate /kəʊ'ɒpəreɪt/ v.i. mitarbeiten
(in bei); (with each other) zusammenarbeiten
(in bei)

cooperation /kəʊɒpə'reɪʃn/ n.
Zusammenarbeit, die

cooperative /kəʊ'ɒpərətɪv/ [1] adj.
kooperativ; (helpful) hilfsbereit
[2] n. Genossenschaft, die

coordinate /kəʊ'ɔːdmeɪt/ v.t. koordinieren

coordination /kəʊɔːdɪ'neɪʃn/ n. Koordination, die

co-owner /kəʊ'əʊnə(r)/ n. Miteigentümer, der/-eigentümerin, die; (of business) Mitinhaber, der/-inhaberin, die

cop /kɒp/ n. (coll.: police officer) Bulle, der (salopp)

cope /kəʊp/ v.i. ~ **with sb./sth.** mit jmdm./ etw. fertig werden

Copenhagen /kəʊpn'heɪgn/ pr. n. Kopenhagen (das)

copier /'kɒpɪə(r)/ n. (machine) Kopiergerät, das

co-pilot /'kəʊpaɪlət/ n. Kopilot, der/ Kopilotin, die

copious /'kəʊpɪəs/ adj. reichhaltig

'**cop-out** n. (coll.) Drückebergerei, die (ugs. abwertend); **that's a ~:** das ist Drückebergerei (ugs. abwertend)

copper[1] /'kɒpə(r)/ n. Kupfer, das

copper[2] (Brit. coll.) ▶ COP

coppice /'kɒpɪs/, **copse** /kɒps/ ns. Wäldchen, das

'**cop shop** n. (Brit. coll.) Wache, die; Revier, das

copula /'kɒpjʊlə/ n. (Ling.) Kopula, die

copulate /'kɒpjʊleɪt/ v.i. kopulieren

copy /'kɒpɪ/ 1 n. (a) (reproduction) Kopie, die (b) (specimen) Exemplar, das
2 v.t. & i. kopieren; (transcribe) abschreiben

copy: ~**cat** n. (coll.) **you're such a ~cat!** du musst immer alles nachmachen!; ~ **editor** n. Redakteur, der/Redakteurin, die (der/die nur nach schriftlichen Vorlagen arbeitet);
~ **protection** n. (Comp.) Kopierschutz, der; ~**right** n. Urheberrecht, das ~**writer** n. [Werbe]texter, der/-texterin, die

coral /'kɒrl/ n. Koralle, die

cord /kɔːd/ n. (a) (thin) Kordel, die; (strong string) Schnur, die
(b) (cloth) Cord, der
(c) in pl. (trousers) [pair of] ~s Cordhose, die

cordial /'kɔːdɪəl/ 1 adj. herzlich
2 n. (drink) Sirup, der

cordiality /kɔːdɪ'ælɪtɪ/ n. Herzlichkeit, die

'**cordially** adv. herzlich

'**cordless phone** /'kɔːdlɪs/ n. Schnurlostelefon, das

cordon /'kɔːdn/ 1 n. Kordon, der
2 v.t. ~ [**off**] absperren

corduroy /'kɔːdərɔɪ, 'kɔːdjʊrɔɪ/ n. Cordsamt, der

core /kɔː(r)/ 1 n. (of fruit) Kerngehäuse, das
2 v.t. entkernen

co-respondent /kəʊrɪ'spɒndənt/ n. Mitbeklagte, der/die (im Scheidungsprozess)

cork /kɔːk/ 1 n. (a) (bark) Kork, der
(b) (bottle stopper) Korken, der
2 v.t. zukorken

cork: ~**screw** n. Korkenzieher, der; ~ '**tile** n. Korkplatte, die

cormorant /'kɔːmərənt/ n. Kormoran, der

corn[1] /kɔːn/ n. Getreide, das

corn[2] n. (on foot) Hühnerauge, das

cornea /'kɔːnɪə/ n. (Anat.) Hornhaut, die; Cornea, die (fachspr.)

corned beef /kɔːnd 'biːf/ n. Cornedbeef, das

corner /'kɔːnə(r)/ 1 n. (a) Ecke, die; (curve) Kurve, die; **on the ~:** an der Ecke/in der Kurve
(b) (of mouth, eye) Winkel, der
2 v.t. (fig.) in die Enge treiben
3 v.i. die Kurve nehmen

corner: ~ **kick** n. (Footb.) Eckball, der; ~ **shop** n. Tante-Emma-Laden, der (ugs.); ~**stone** n. (fig.) Eckpfeiler, der

cornet /'kɔːnɪt/ n. (a) (Brit.: for ice cream) [Eis]tüte, die
(b) (Mus.) Kornett, das

corn: ~**flakes** n. pl. Cornflakes Pl.; ~**flour** (Brit.) n. Maismehl, das; ~**flower** n. Kornblume, die; ~ **starch** (Amer.) n. Maismehl, das

'**corny** adj. (coll.: trite) abgedroschen

coronary /'kɒrənərɪ/ 1 adj. (Anat.) koronar
2 n. (Med.) ▶ CORONARY THROMBOSIS

coronary: ~ '**artery** n. Herzkranzarterie, die; Koronararterie, die (fachspr.); ~ **throm'bosis** n. Koronarthrombose, die

coronation /kɒrə'neɪʃn/ n. Krönung, die

coroner /'kɒrənə(r)/ n. Coroner, der; Beamter, der gewaltsame od. unnatürliche Todesfälle untersucht

coronet /'kɒrənet/ n. Krone, die

corporal[1] /'kɔːpərl/ adj. körperlich

corporal[2] n. ≈ Hauptgefreite, der

corporate /'kɔːpərət/ adj. körperschaftlich

corporation /kɔːpə'reɪʃn/ n. Stadtverwaltung, die

corpo'ration tax n. Körperschaftsteuer, die

corps /kɔː(r)/ n., pl. same /kɔːz/ Korps, das

corpse /kɔːps/ n. Leiche, die

corpulent /'kɔːpjʊlənt/ adj. korpulent

Corpus Christi /kɔːpəs 'krɪstɪ/ n. (Eccl.) Fronleichnam (der)

corpuscle /'kɔːpəsl/ n. [blood] ~ Blutkörperchen, das

corral /kə'rɑːl/ (Amer.) 1 n. Pferch, der
2 v.t., -ll- einpferchen

correct /kə'rekt/ 1 v.t. korrigieren
2 adj. korrekt; **that is ~:** das stimmt

correction /kə'rekʃn/ n. Korrektur, die

cor'rectly adv. korrekt

correspond /kɒrɪ'spɒnd/ v.i. (a) ~ [to each other] einander entsprechen; ~ **to sth.** einer Sache (Dat.) entsprechen
(b) (communicate) ~ **with sb.** mit jmdm. korrespondieren

correspondence /kɒrɪ'spɒndəns/ n. (a) Übereinstimmung, die (with, to mit)
(b) (communication) Briefwechsel, der

corre'spondence course *n.* Fernkurs, *der*

correspondent /kɒrɪ'spɒndənt/ *n.* (reporter) Korrespondent, *der*/ Korrespondentin, *die*

corre'sponding *adj.* entsprechend (**to** *Dat.*)

corre'spondingly *adv.* entsprechend

corridor /'kɒrɪdɔ:(r)/ *n.* (a) Flur, *der* (b) (Railw.) [Seiten]gang, *der*

corroborate /kə'rɒbəreɪt/ *v.t.* bestätigen

corroboration /kərɒbə'reɪʃn/ *n.* Bestätigung, *die*

corrode /kə'rəʊd/ [1] *v.t.* zerfressen [2] *v.i.* zerfressen werden

corrosion /kə'rəʊʒn/ *n.* Korrosion, *die*

corrugated /'kɒrəgeɪtɪd/ *adj.* ~ **cardboard** Wellpappe, *die;* ~ **iron** Wellblech, *das*

corrupt /kə'rʌpt/ [1] *adj.* (depraved) verdorben (geh.); (influenced by bribery) korrupt [2] *v.t.* (deprave) korrumpieren; (bribe) bestechen

corruption /kə'rʌpʃn/ *n.* (moral deterioration) Verdorbenheit, *die* (geh.); (corrupt practices) Korruption, *die*

corset /'kɔ:sɪt/ *n.* Korsett, *das*

Corsica /'kɔ:sɪkə/ *pr. n.* Korsika (*das*)

cortège /kɔ:'teɪʒ/ *n.* Trauerzug, *der*

cortisone /'kɔ:tɪzəʊn/ *n.* Kortison, *das;* Cortison, *das* (fachspr.)

cosh /kɒʃ/ (Brit. coll.) [1] *n.* Totschläger, *der* [2] *v.t.* niederknüppeln

cosmetic /kɒz'metɪk/ [1] *adj.* kosmetisch [2] *n.* Kosmetikum, *das*

cosmic /'kɒzmɪk/ *adj.* kosmisch

cosmonaut /'kɒzmənɔ:t/ *n.* Kosmonaut, *der*/Kosmonautin, *die*

cosmopolitan /kɒzmə'pɒlɪtən/ *adj.* kosmopolitisch

cosmos /'kɒzmɒs/ *n.* Kosmos, *der*

cosset /'kɒsɪt/ *v.t.* [ver]hätscheln

cost /kɒst/ [1] *n.* (a) Kosten *Pl.* (b) (fig.) Preis, *der;* **at all ~s, at any ~:** um jeden Preis
[2] *v.t.* (a) *p.t., p.p.* **cost** (lit. or fig.) kosten; **how much does it ~?** was kostet es? (b) *p.t., p.p.* **costed** (Commerc.: fix price of) ~ **sth.** den Preis für etw. kalkulieren

co-star /'kəʊstɑ:(r)/ (Cinemat., Theatre) [1] *n.* **be a/the ~:** eine der Hauptrollen/die zweite Hauptrolle spielen
[2] *v.i.,* **-rr-** eine der Hauptrollen spielen
[3] *v.t.,* **-rr-:** **the film ~red Robert Redford** der Film zeigte Robert Redford in einer der Hauptrollen

cost: ~ **cutting** *n.* Kostensenkung, *die;* ~-**cutting** *adj.* Spar-; ~-**effective** *adj.* rentabel

'costly *adj.* teuer

cost: ~ **of 'living** *n.*

Lebenshaltungskosten *Pl.;* ~-**of-living index** Lebenshaltungsindex, *der;* ~ **price** *n.* Selbstkostenpreis, *der*

costume /'kɒstjuːm/ *n.* Kleidermode, *die;* (theatrical ~) Kostüm, *das*

costume 'jewellery *n.* Modeschmuck, *der*

cosy /'kəʊzɪ/ *adj.* gemütlich

cot /kɒt/ *n.* Kinderbett, *das*

'cot death *n.* (Brit.) plötzlicher Kindstod; Cot-death, *der* (Med.)

cottage /'kɒtɪdʒ/ *n.* Cottage, *das*

cottage: ~ **'cheese** *n.* Hüttenkäse, *der;* ~ **'hospital** *n.:* kleines [Land]krankenhaus ohne ständige ärztliche Betreuung; ~ **industry** *n.* Heimarbeit, *die;* ~ **'pie** *n.:* mit Kartoffelbrei überbackenes Hackfleisch

cotton /'kɒtən/ [1] *n.* Baumwolle, *die;* (thread) Baumwollgarn, *das* [2] *attrib. adj.* Baumwoll- [3] *v.i.* ~ **'on** (coll.) kapieren (ugs.)

cotton: ~ **reel** *n.* [Näh]garnrolle, *die;* ~ **'wool** *n.* Watte, *die*

couch /kaʊtʃ/ *n.* Couch, *die*

couchette /ku:'ʃet/ *n.* (Railw.) Liegewagenplatz, *der*

couch po'tato *n.* (coll.) Couchpotato[e], *der*

cough /kɒf/ [1] *n.* Husten, *der* [2] *v.i.* husten

cough: ~ **medicine** *n.* Hustenmittel, *das;* ~ **mixture** *n.* Hustensaft, *der*

could ▶ CAN²

couldn't /'kʊdnt/ (coll.) = could not; ▶ CAN²

council /'kaʊnsl/ *n.* Rat, *der;* local ~: Gemeinderat, *der;* **city/town** ~: Stadtrat, *der;* **C~ of Ministers** Ministerrat, *der*

council: ~ **estate** *n.* Wohnviertel mit Sozialwohnungen; ~ **flat** *n.* Sozialwohnung, *die;* ~ **house** *n.* Haus des sozialen Wohnungsbaus; ~ **housing** *n.* sozialer Wohnungsbau

councillor /'kaʊnsələ(r)/ *n.* Ratsmitglied, *das*

'council tax *n.* (Brit.) Gemeindesteuer, *die*

counsel /'kaʊnsl/ [1] *n.* (a) Rat[schlag], *der* (b) *pl. same* (Law) Rechtsanwalt, *der*/ -anwältin, *die* [2] *v.t.,* (Brit.) **-ll-** beraten

counselling (*Amer.:* **counseling**) /'kaʊnsəlɪŋ/ *n.* Beratung, *die;* **marriage** ~: Eheberatung, *die*

counsellor, (*Amer.* **counselor**) /'kaʊnsələ(r)/ *n.* Berater, *der*/Beraterin, *die*

count¹ /kaʊnt/ [1] *n.* Zählen, *das;* **keep** ~ **[of sth.]** [etw.] zählen; **lose** ~: sich verzählen
[2] *v.t.* (a) zählen (b) (include) mitzählen; **not ~ing** abgesehen von (c) (consider) halten für; ~ **oneself lucky** sich glücklich schätzen können ⋯⟩

3 *v.i.* (a) zählen; ~ [up] to ten bis zehn zählen

(b) (be included) zählen

■ **'count on** *v.t.* ~ on sb./sth. sich auf jmdn./etw. verlassen

■ **count 'up** *v.t.* zusammenzählen

count² *n.* (nobleman) Graf, *der*

'countdown *n.* Count-down, *der od. das*

countenance /'kaʊntɪnəns/ 1 *n.* (literary: face) Antlitz, *das*

2 *v.t.* (formal: approve) gutheißen

counter¹ /'kaʊntə(r)/ *n.* (a) (in shop) Ladentisch, *der;* (in cafeteria) Büfett, *das;* (in bank) Schalter, *der*

(b) (for games) Spielmarke, *die*

counter² 1 *adj.* Gegen-

2 *v.t.* (a) (oppose) begegnen (+ *Dat.*)

(b) (act against) kontern

3 *adv.* go ~ to zuwiderlaufen (+ *Dat.*)

counter: ~'**act** *v.t.* entgegenwirken (+ *Dat.*); ~-**attack** *n.* Gegenangriff, *der;* ~**balance** *v.t.* (fig.) ausgleichen; ~-'**espionage** *n.* Spionageabwehr, *die*

counterfeit /'kaʊntəfɪt/ 1 *adj.* gefälscht; ~ money Falschgeld, *das*

2 *v.t.* fälschen

'counterfeiter *n.* Fälscher, *der*/Fälscherin, *die*

counterfoil /'kaʊntəfɔɪl/ *n.* Kontrollabschnitt, *der*

counter: ~**part** *n.* Gegenstück, *das* (of zu); ~**pro'ductive** *adj.* sth. is ~productive etw. bewirkt das Gegenteil des Gewünschten; ~**sign** *v.t.* gegenzeichnen; ~**weight** *n.* Gegengewicht, *das*

countess /'kaʊntɪs/ *n.* Gräfin, *die*

'countless *adj.* zahllos

countrified /'kʌntrɪfaɪd/ *adj.* ländlich

country /'kʌntrɪ/ *n.* (a) Land, *das;* sb's [home] ~: jmds. Heimat

(b) (~side) Landschaft, *die;* in the ~: auf dem Land; ~ road/air Landstraße, *die*/Landluft, *die*

country 'dancing *n.* Kontertanz, *der*

countryfied ▶ COUNTRIFIED

country: ~**man** /'kʌntrɪmən/, *n. pl.* ~**men** /'kʌntrɪmən/ Landsmann, *der;* ~**side** *n.* (a) (rural areas) Land, *das;* (b) (rural scenery) Landschaft, *die*

county /'kaʊntɪ/ *n.* (Brit.) Grafschaft, *die*

coup /ku:/ *n.* (a) Coup, *der*

(b) ▶ COUP D'ÉTAT

coup d'état /ku: deɪ'ta:/ *n.* Staatsstreich, *der*

coupé /'ku:peɪ/ *n.* Coupé, *das*

couple /kʌpl/ 1 *n.* (a) (pair) Paar, *das;* (married) [Ehe]paar, *das*

(b) a ~ [of] (a few) ein paar; (two) zwei

2 *v.t.* koppeln

coupon /'ku:pɒn/ *n.* (a) (for rations) Marke, *die*

(b) (in advertisement) Coupon, *der*

courage /'kʌrɪdʒ/ *n.* Mut, *der*

courageous /kə'reɪdʒəs/ *adj.,* **cou'rageously** *adv.* mutig

courgette /kʊə'ʒet/ *n.* (Brit.) Zucchino, *der*

courier /'kʊrɪə(r)/ *n.* (a) (Tourism) Reiseleiter, *der*/-leiterin, *die*

(b) (messenger) Kurier, *der*

'courier company *n.* Kurierdienst, *der*

course /kɔ:s/ *n.* (a) (of ship, plane) Kurs, *der;* ~ [of action] Vorgehensweise, *die*

(b) of ~: natürlich

(c) in due ~: zu gegebener Zeit; in the ~ of the day/his life im Lauf[e] des Tages/seines Lebens

(d) (of meal) Gang, *der*

(e) (Sport) Kurs, *der;* [golf]~: [Golf]platz, *der*

(f) (Educ.) Kurs[us], *der;* go to or attend/do a ~ in sth. einen Kurs in etw. (*Dat.*) besuchen/machen

(g) (Med.) a ~ of treatment eine Kur

court /kɔ:t/ 1 *n.* (a) Hof, *der*

(b) (Tennis, Squash) Platz, *der*

(c) (Law) Gericht, *das*

2 *v.t.* ~ sb. jmdn. umwerben

courteous /'kɜːtɪəs/ *adj.* höflich

courtesy /'kɜːtəsɪ/ *n.* Höflichkeit, *die*

'courtesy light *n.* (Motor Veh.) Innenbeleuchtung, *die*

court: ~ **house** *n.* (Law) Gerichtsgebäude, *das;* ~ '**martial** *n., pl.* ~s martial (Mil.) Kriegsgericht, *das;* ~**room** *n.* (Law) Gerichtssaal, *der*

courtship /'kɔ:tʃɪp/ *n.* Werben, *das*

court: ~ **shoe** *n.* Pumps, *der;* ~**yard** *n.* Hof, *der*

cousin /'kʌzn/ *n.* [first] ~: Cousin, *der*/Cousine, *die*

couturier /ku:'tjʊərɪeɪ/ *n.* Couturier, *der;* Modeschöpfer, *der*

cove /kəʊv/ *n.* (Geog.) [kleine] Bucht

covenant /'kʌvənənt/ *n.* formelle Übereinkunft

cover /'kʌvə(r)/ 1 *n.* (a) (piece of cloth) Decke, *die;* (of cushion, bed) Bezug, *der;* (lid) Deckel, *der;* (of hole, engine, typewriter, etc.) Abdeckung, *die*

(b) (of book) Einband, *der;* (of magazine) Umschlag, *der*

(c) [send sth.] under separate ~: [etw.] mit getrennter Post [schicken]

(d) take ~ [from sth.] Schutz [vor etw. (*Dat.*)] suchen; under ~ (from rain) überdacht

2 *v.t.* (a) bedecken; beziehen ‹Sessel, Kissen›; zudecken ‹Pfanne›; the roses are ~ed with greenfly die Rosen sind voller Blattläuse

(b) (include) abdecken

(c) (Journ.) berichten über (+ *Akk.*)

(d) decken ‹Kosten›

■ **cover 'up** 1 *v.t.* zudecken; (fig.) vertuschen

2 *v.i.* ~ up for sb. jmdn. decken

coverage /'kʌvərɪdʒ/ *n.* (Journ.) Berichterstattung, *die*

'cover charge n. [Preis für das] Gedeck

'covering n. Decke, die; (of chair, bed) Bezug, der

'covering letter n. Begleitbrief, der

'cover story n. (Journ.) Titelgeschichte, die

covert /'kʌvət/ adj. versteckt

cover: ∼-**up** n. Verschleierung, die; ∼ **version** n. Coverversion, die

covet /'kʌvɪt/ v.t. begehren (geh.)

covetous /'kʌvɪtəs/ adj. begehrlich (geh.)

cow /kaʊ/ n. Kuh, die

coward /'kaʊəd/ n. Feigling, der

cowardice /'kaʊədɪs/ n. Feigheit, die

'cowardly adj. feig[e]

'cowboy n. Cowboy, der

cower /'kaʊə(r)/ v.i. sich ducken

cowherd n. Kuhhirte, der

'co-worker n. Kollege, der/Kollegin, die

cow: ∼ **parsley** n. (Bot.) Wiesenkerbel, der; ∼**pat** n. Kuhfladen, der; ∼**shed** n. Kuhstall, der; ∼**slip** n. Schlüsselblume, die

coy /kɔɪ/ adj. gespielt schüchtern

cozy (Amer.) ▶ cosy

CPU abbr. (Comp.) = **central processing unit** ZE

crab /kræb/ n. Krabbe, die

'crab apple n. Holzapfel, der

crack /kræk/ ⓵ n. (a) (noise) Krachen, das (b) (in china etc.) Sprung, der; (in rock) Spalte, die; (chink) Spalt, der (c) (coll.: try) have a ∼ at sth./doing sth. versuchen, etw. zu tun (d) (sl.: drug) ∼ [**cocaine**] Crack, das ⓶ attrib. adj. (coll.) erstklassig ⓷ v.t. (a) knacken ⟨Nuss, Problem, Kode⟩ (b) (make a ∼ in) anschlagen ⟨Porzellan usw.⟩ (c) ∼ a joke einen Witz machen (d) ∼ a whip mit einer Peitsche knallen ⓸ v.i. ⟨Porzellan usw.:⟩ einen Sprung/ Sprünge bekommen ■ **crack 'down** v.i. (coll.) ∼ **down** [**on sb.**/ **sth.**] [gegen jmdn./etw.] [hart] vorgehen ■ **crack 'up** v.i. (coll.) ⟨Person:⟩ zusammenbrechen

'crack-down n. (coll.) there will be a ∼: man wird hart durchgreifen; have/order a ∼ on sb./sth. drastische Maßnahmen gegen jmdn./etw. ergreifen/anordnen

cracked /krækt/ adj. gesprungen ⟨Porzellan usw.⟩; rissig ⟨Verputz⟩

cracker /'krækə(r)/ n. (a) [Christmas] ∼ ≈ Knallbonbon, der od. das (b) (biscuit) Cracker, der

'crackers pred. adj. (Brit. coll.) übergeschnappt (ugs.)

crackle /'krækl/ ⓵ v.i. knistern; ⟨Feuer:⟩ prasseln ⓶ n. Knistern, das

cradle /'kreɪdl/ ⓵ n. Wiege, die ⓶ v.t. wiegen

cradle: ∼ -**snatch** v.i. (coll.) Your boyfriend/girlfriend is much younger than

you. You're ∼-snatching Dein Freund/deine Freundin ist viel jünger als du. Du vergreifst dich ja an kleinen Kindern (ugs. scherzh.); ∼ -**snatcher** n. (fig. coll.) jmd., der mit einer sehr viel jüngeren Person eine Liebesbeziehung eingeht

craft /krɑːft/ n. (a) (trade) Handwerk, das; (art) Kunsthandwerk, das (b) pl. same (boat) Boot, das

craftily /'krɑːftɪlɪ/ adv. listig

craftsman /'krɑːftsmən/ n., pl. **craftsmen** /'krɑːftsmən/ Handwerker, der

craftsmanship /'krɑːftsmənʃɪp/ n. (skilled workmanship) handwerkliches Können

crafty /'krɑːftɪ/ adj. listig

crag /kræg/ n. Felsspitze, die

'craggy adj. (a) felsig (b) zerfurcht ⟨Gesicht⟩

cram /kræm/ ⓵ v.t., -mm- (overfill) voll stopfen (ugs.); (force) stopfen ⓶ v.i., -mm- (for exam) büffeln (ugs.)

cramp /kræmp/ ⓵ n. (Med.) Krampf, der ⓶ v.t. einengen

cramped /kræmpt/ adj. eng ⟨Raum⟩; gedrängt ⟨Handschrift⟩

cranberry /'krænbərɪ/ n. Preiselbeere, die

crane /kreɪn/ ⓵ n. Kran, der ⓶ v.t. ∼ one's neck den Hals recken

crane: ∼ **driver** n. Kranführer, der/ -führerin, die; ∼ **fly** n. Schnake, die

crank[1] /kræŋk/ n. (Mech. Engin.) [Hand]kurbel, die

crank[2] n. Irre, der/die (salopp)

crank: ∼ **arm** n. (of bicycle) Tretkurbel, die; ∼**shaft** n. (Mech. Engin.) Kurbelwelle, die

'cranky adj. (eccentric) schrullig

cranny /'krænɪ/ n. Ritze, die

crap /kræp/ n. (coarse) (a) (faeces) Scheiße, die (derb); have a ∼: scheißen (derb) (b) (nonsense) Scheiß, der (salopp)

crash /kræʃ/ ⓵ n. (a) (noise) Krachen, das (b) (collision) Zusammenstoß, der; have a ∼: einen Unfall haben ⓶ v.i. (a) (make a noise, go noisily) krachen (b) (have a collision) einen Unfall haben; ⟨Flugzeug, Flieger:⟩ abstürzen; ∼ into sth. gegen etw. krachen (c) (Finance etc., Computing) zusammenbrechen ⓷ v.t. (a) (smash) schmettern (b) (cause to have collision) einen Unfall haben mit

crash: ∼ **barrier** n. Leitplanke, die; ∼ **course** n. Intensivkurs, der; ∼ **diet** n. radikale Diät; ≈ Nulldiät, die; ∼ **helmet** n. Sturzhelm, der; ∼-**land** ⓵ v.t. ∼-land a plane mit einem Flugzeug bruchlanden; ⓶ v.i. bruchlanden; ∼-**landing** n. Bruchlandung, die

crass /kræs/ adj. haarsträubend ⟨Dummheit, Unwissenheit⟩; (grossly stupid) strohdumm

crate /kreɪt/ n. Kiste, die

crater /'kreɪtə(r)/ n. Krater, der

cravat /krə'væt/ *n.* Krawatte, *die*

crave /kreɪv/ *v.t.* **(a)** (beg) erbitten **(b)** (long for) sich sehnen nach

'craving *n.* Verlangen, *das* (for nach)

crawl /krɔːl/ 1 *v.i.* **(a)** kriechen; ⟨*Baby, Insekt:*⟩ krabbeln **(b)** (coll.) ~ to sb. vor jmdm. kriechen 2 *n.* **(a)** go at a ~: im Schneckentempo fahren **(b)** (swimming stroke) Kraulen, *das*

'crawler lane *n.* Kriechspur, *die*

crayfish /'kreɪfɪʃ/ *n., pl.* same Flusskrebs, *der*

crayon /'kreɪən/ *n.* [coloured] ~: Buntstift, *der;* (wax) Wachsmalstift, *der*

craze /kreɪz/ *n.* Begeisterung, *die*

crazy /'kreɪzɪ/ *adj.* verrückt; be ~ about sb./sth. (coll.) nach jmdm./etw. verrückt sein (ugs.)

creak /kriːk/ 1 *n.* Knarren, *das* 2 *v.i.* knarren

cream /kriːm/ 1 *n.* **(a)** Sahne, *die* **(b)** (dessert, cosmetic) Creme, *die* 2 *adj.* ~[-coloured] creme[farben]

cream: ~ **cake** *n.* Cremetorte, *die;* (small) Cremetörtchen, *das;* (with whipped ~) Sahnetorte, *die*/Sahnetörtchen, *das;* ~ **'cheese** *n.* ≈ Frischkäse, *der;* ~ **'cracker** *n.* ≈ Cracker, *der;* ~ **'tea** *n.* Tee mit Marmeladetörtchen und Sahne

'creamy *adj.* (with cream) sahnig; (like cream) cremig

crease /kriːs/ 1 *n.* (pressed) Bügelfalte, *die;* (accidental) Falte, *die* 2 *v.t.* (press) eine Falte bügeln in (+ *Akk.*); (accidentally) zerknittern 3 *v.i.* Falten bekommen; knittern

'crease-resistant *adj.* knitterfrei

create /kriː'eɪt/ *v.t.* schaffen; verursachen ⟨*Verwirrung*⟩; machen ⟨*Eindruck*⟩

creation /kriː'eɪʃn/ *n.* Schaffung, *die;* (of the world) Schöpfung, *die* (geh.)

creative /kriː'eɪtɪv/ *adj.* kreativ

creator /kriː'eɪtə(r)/ *n.* Schöpfer, *der*/ Schöpferin, *die*

creature /'kriːtʃə(r)/ *n.* Geschöpf, *das*

crèche /kreʃ/ *n.* [Kinder]krippe, *die*

credentials /krɪ'denʃlz/ *n. pl.* Zeugnis, *das*

credibility /kredɪ'bɪlɪtɪ/ *n.* Glaubwürdigkeit, *die*

credible /'kredɪbl/ *adj.* glaubwürdig

credit /'kredɪt/ 1 *n.* **(a)** (honour) Ehre, *die;* take the ~ for sth. die Anerkennung für etw. einstecken **(b)** (Commerc.) Kredit, *der* **(c)** ~s, ~ titles (at beginning of film) Vorspann, *der;* (at end) Nachspann, *der* 2 *v.t.* **(a)** glauben **(b)** (Finance) gutschreiben

creditable /'kredɪtəbl/ *adj.* anerkennenswert

creditably /'kredɪtəblɪ/ *adv.* achtbar

credit: ~ **account** *n.* Kreditkonto, *das;* ~ **card** *n.* Kreditkarte, *die;* ~ **facilities** *n. pl.* [Kredit]fazilität, *die* (fachspr.); ~ **limit** *n.* Kreditlinie, *die*

creditor /'kredɪtə(r)/ *n.* Gläubiger, *der*/ Gläubigerin, *die*

credit: ~ **rating** *n.* [Einschätzung der] Kreditwürdigkeit; have a good/bad ~ rating als kreditwürdig/kreditunwürdig eingeschätzt werden; ~**worthy** *adj.* kreditwürdig

creed /kriːd/ *n.* Glaubensbekenntnis, *das*

creek /kriːk/ *n.* **(a)** (Brit.: of coast) [kleine] Bucht **(b)** (of river) [kurzer] Flussarm

creep /kriːp/ 1 *v.i.*, crept [krept] kriechen; (move timidly, slowly, stealthily) schleichen 2 *n.* **(a)** (coll.: person) Fiesling, *der* (salopp) **(b)** (coll.) give sb. the ~s jmdn. nicht [ganz] geheuer sein

'creeper *n.* Kletterpflanze, *die*

'creepy *adj.* unheimlich

cremate /krɪ'meɪt/ *v.t.* einäschern

cremation /krɪ'meɪʃn/ *n.* Einäscherung, *die*

crematorium /kremə'tɔːrɪəm/ *n.* Krematorium, *das*

creosote /'kriːəsəʊt/ *n.* Kreosot, *das*

crept ▸ CREEP 1

crescendo /krɪ'ʃendəʊ/ *n., pl.* ~s (Mus.) Crescendo, *das;* (fig.) Zunahme, *die*

crescent /'kresənt/ *n.* Mondsichel, *die*

cress /kres/ *n.* Kresse, *die*

crest /krest/ *n.* Kamm, *der*

'crestfallen *adj.* niedergeschlagen

Crete /kriːt/ *pr. n.* Kreta (*das*)

cretin /'kretɪn/ *n.* (coll.) Trottel, *der*

Creutzfeldt-Jakob disease /'krɔɪtsfelt'jækɒb/ *n.* Creutzfeldt-Jakob-Krankheit, *die*

crevasse /krɪ'væs/ *n.* Gletscherspalte, *die*

crevice /'krevɪs/ *n.* Spalt, *der*

crew /kruː/ *n.* Besatzung, *die*

crew: ~**cut** *n.* Bürstenschnitt, *der;* ~ **neck** *n.* enger, runder Halsausschnitt; a ~-neck pullover ein Pullover mit engem, rundem Halsausschnitt

crib /krɪb/ 1 *n.* Krippe, *die* 2 *v.t.*, -bb- (coll.) abkupfern (salopp)

crick /krɪk/ *n.* a ~ [in one's neck/back] ein steifer Hals/Rücken

cricket[1] /'krɪkɪt/ *n.* Kricket, *das*

cricket[2] *n.* (Zool.) Grille, *die*

cricket: ~ **ball** *n.* Kricketball, *der;* ~ **bat** *n.* Schlagholz, *das*

'cricketer *n.* Kricketspieler, *der*/-spielerin, *die*

'cricket match *n.* Kricketspiel, *das*

cried ▸ CRY

crime /kraɪm/ *n.* **(a)** Verbrechen, *das*

(b) *collect.* **a wave of** ∼: eine Welle von Straftaten; ∼ **doesn't pay** Verbrechen lohnen sich nicht

crime: ∼ **prevention** *n.* Verbrechensverhütung, *die;* C∼ **Prevention Officer** *Polizeibeamter, dessen/-beamtin, deren Aufgabe aktive, vorbeugende Verbrechensbekämpfung ist;* ∼ **rate** *n.* Kriminalitätsrate, *die;* ∼ **wave** *n.* Welle von Straftaten; ∼ **writer** *n.* Kriminalschriftsteller, *der/*-schriftstellerin, *die*

criminal /'krɪmɪnl/ **1** *adj.* kriminell; strafbar; ∼ **act** *or* **deed/offence** Straftat, *die* **2** *n.* Kriminelle, *der/die*

criminal: ∼ **charge** *n.* Anklage, *die;* **face** ∼ **charges [for sth.]** sich [wegen etw.] vor Gericht zu verantworten haben; **there are** ∼ **charges against him** er steht unter Anklage; ∼ **'court** *n.* Strafgericht, *das;* ∼ **'law** *n.* Strafrecht, *das;* ∼ **'lawyer** *n.* Anwalt/Anwältin für Strafsachen; ∼ **'record** *n.* Strafregister, *das;* **have a** ∼ **record** vorbestraft sein

crimson /'krɪmzn/ **1** *adj.* purpurrot **2** *n.* Purpurrot, *das*

cringe /krɪndʒ/ *v.i.* zusammenzucken

crinkle /'krɪŋkl/ **1** *n.* Knitterfalte, *die* **2** *v.t.* zerknittern **3** *v.i.* knittern

cripple /'krɪpl/ **1** *n.* Krüppel, *der* **2** *v.t.* zum Krüppel machen; (fig.) lähmen

crippled /'krɪpld/ *adj.* verkrüppelt

crippling /'krɪplɪŋ/ *adj.* zur Verkrüppelung führend ⟨*Krankheit, Verletzung*⟩; (fig.) erdrückend ⟨*Preise, Inflationsrate, Steuern, Mieten*⟩; lähmend ⟨*Streik, Schmerzen*⟩

crisis /'kraɪsɪs/ *n., pl.* **crises** /'kraɪsiːz/ Krise, *die*

crisis: ∼ **area** *n.* Krisengebiet, *das;* ∼ **'management** *n.* Krisenmanagement, *das*

crisp /krɪsp/ **1** *adj.* knusprig **2** *n.* **(a)** *usu. in pl.* (Brit.: potato ∼) [Kartoffel]chip, *der* **(b) be burned to a** ∼: verbrannt sein

'crispbread *n.* Knäckebrot, *das*

'crispy *adj.* knusprig

criss-cross /'krɪskrɒs/ **1** *adj.* ∼ **pattern** Muster aus gekreuzten Linien **2** *adv.* kreuz und quer **3** *v.t.* wiederholt schneiden

criterion /kraɪ'tɪərɪən/ *n., pl.* **criteria** /kraɪ'tɪərɪə/ Kriterium, *das*

critic /'krɪtɪk/ *n.* Kritiker, *der/*Kritikerin, *die*

critical /'krɪtɪkl/ *adj.* kritisch; **be** ∼ **of sb./sth.** jmdn./etw. kritisieren

critically /'krɪtɪkəlɪ/ *adv.* kritisch; ∼ **ill** ernstlich krank

critical 'mass *n.* (Phys.) kritische Masse

criticism /'krɪtɪsɪzm/ *n.* Kritik, *die* (**of an** + *Dat.*)

criticize /'krɪtɪsaɪz/ *v.t.* kritisieren (**for** wegen)

critique /krɪ'tiːk/ *n.* Kritik, *die*

croak /krəʊk/ **1** *n.* (of frog) Quaken, *das;* (of person) Krächzen, *das* **2** *v.i.* ⟨*Frosch:*⟩ quaken; ⟨*Person:*⟩ krächzen **3** *v.t.* krächzen

Croat /'krəʊæt/ *n.* **(a)** (person) Kroate, *der/* Kroatin, *die* **(b)** (language) Kroatisch, *das*

Croatia /krəʊ'eɪʃə/ *pr. n.* Kroatien (*das*)

Croatian /krəʊ'eɪʃən/ **1** *adj.* kroatisch; **sb. is** ∼: jmd. ist Kroate/Kroatin **2** *n.* ▶ CROAT

crochet /'krəʊʃeɪ/ **1** *n.* Häkelarbeit, *die;* ∼ **hook** Häkelhaken, *der* **2** *v.t.* häkeln

crock /krɒk/ *n.* (coll.) **[old]** ∼ (person) altes Wrack, *das* (fig.); (vehicle) [alte] Klapperkiste (ugs.)

crockery /'krɒkərɪ/ *n.* Geschirr, *das*

crocodile /'krɒkədaɪl/ *n.* Krokodil, *das*

crocus /'krəʊkəs/ *n.* Krokus, *der*

croft /krɒft/ *n.* **(a)** [kleines] Stück Acker-/ Weideland **(b)** (smallholding) [kleines] Pachtgut

'crofter *n.* (Brit.) Pächter, *der/*Pächterin, *die*

croissant /'krwɑːsã/ *n.* Hörnchen, *das*

crony /'krəʊnɪ/ *n.* Kumpel, *der* (ugs.)

crook /krʊk/ *n.* **(a)** (coll.: rogue) Gauner, *der* **(b)** (shepherd's) Hirtenstab, *der*

crooked /'krʊkɪd/ *adj.* krumm; (fig.: dishonest) betrügerisch

crop /krɒp/ **1** *n.* [Feld]frucht, *die;* (season's yield) Ernte, *die* **2** *v.t.* stutzen ⟨*Haare usw.*⟩ ■ **crop 'up** *v.i.* auftauchen

'crop dusting *n.* Schädlingsbekämpfung aus der Luft

'cropper *n.* (coll.) **come a** ∼: einen Sturz bauen (ugs.)

crop: ∼**-spraying** *n.* Schädlingsbekämpfung (*mit Sprühmitteln*); ∼ **top** *n.* bauch- od. nabelfreies Top

croquet /'krəʊkeɪ/ *n.* Krocket[spiel], *das*

croquette /krə'ket/ *n.* Krokette, *die*

cross /krɒs/ **1** *n.* **(a)** Kreuz, *das* **(b)** (mixture) Mischung, *die* (**between** aus) **2** *v.t.* **(a)** [über]kreuzen; ∼ **one's arms/legs** die Arme verschränken/die Beine übereinander schlagen; **keep one's fingers** ∼**ed [for sb.]** (fig.) [jmdm.] die *od.* den Daumen drücken **(b)** (go across) kreuzen; überqueren ⟨*Straße, Gebirge*⟩; durchqueren ⟨*Land, Zimmer*⟩; ∼ **sb.'s mind** (fig.) jmdm. einfallen; '∼ **now**' „Gehen" **(c)** (Brit.) **a** ∼**ed cheque** ein Verrechnungsscheck **(d)** ∼ **oneself** sich bekreuzigen **3** *v.i.* aneinander vorbeigehen; ∼ **[in the post]** ⟨*Briefe:*⟩ sich kreuzen ⋯⟩

4 *adj.* verärgert; *sb.* will be ∼: jmd. wird ärgerlich *od.* böse werden; be ∼ with *sb.* böse auf jmdn. sein

■ **cross 'out** *v.t.* ausstreichen

■ **cross 'over** *v.t.* überqueren; *abs.* hinüberberehen

cross: ∼**bar** *n.* (a) [Fahrrad]stange, *die;* (b) (Sport) Querlatte, *die;* ∼**bones** *n. pl.* gekreuzte Knochen *Pl. (unter Totenkopf);* ∼**bow** /ˈkrɒsbəʊ/ *n.* Armbrust, *die;* ∼**breed** **1** *n.* Hybride, *die;* (animal) Bastard, *der;* **2** *v.t.* kreuzen; ∼-**Channel** *adj.* ∼-Channel traffic/ferry Verkehr/Fähre über den Kanal; ∼-**check** **1** *n.* Gegenprobe, *die;* **2** *v.t.* [nochmals] nachprüfen; kreuzkontrollieren; ∼-**country** **1** *adj.* Querfeldein-; **2** *adv.* querfeldein; ∼-**cultural** *adj.* interkulturell; ∼-**dressing** *n.* Crossdressing, *das;* ∼-**examination** *n.* Kreuzverhör, *das;* ∼-**examine** *v.t.* ins Kreuzverhör nehmen; ∼-**eyed** /ˈkrɒsaɪd/ *adj.* [nach innen] schielend; be ∼-eyed schielen; ∼-ˈ**fertilize** *v.t.* fremdbestäuben; kreuzbefruchten; (fig.) sich gegenseitig befruchten; ∼**fire** *n.* Kreuzfeuer, *das;* get caught in the ∼fire (fig.) ins Kreuzfeuer geraten

ˈ**crossing** *n.* (a) (act) Überquerung, *die* (b) (pedestrian ∼) Überweg, *der*

cross-legged /ˈkrɒslegd/ *adv.* mit gekreuzten Beinen; (with feet across thighs) im Schneidersitz

ˈ**crossly** *adv.* verärgert

cross: ∼ ˈ**purposes** *n. pl.* talk at ∼ purposes aneinander vorbeireden; ∼-ˈ**question** *v.t.* ins Kreuzverhör nehmen; ∼-**refer** *v.i.* einen Querverweis machen (to auf + *Akk.*); ∼ **reference** *n.* Querverweis, *der;* ∼**roads** *n. sing.* Kreuzung, *die;* (fig.) Wendepunkt, *der;* ∼ **section** *n.* Querschnitt, *der;* ∼**word** *n.* ∼word [puzzle] Kreuzworträtsel, *das*

crotch /krɒtʃ/ *n.* (of trousers, body) Schritt, *der*

crotchet /ˈkrɒtʃɪt/ *n.* (Brit. Mus.) Viertelnote, *die*

crouch /krautʃ/ *v.i.* [sich zusammen]kauern

croupier /ˈkruːpɪə(r), ˈkruːpɪeɪ/ *n.* Croupier, *der*

crow /krəʊ/ *n.* Krähe, *die;* as the ∼ flies Luftlinie

ˈ**crowbar** *n.* Brechstange, *die*

crowd /kraʊd/ **1** *n.* [Menschen]menge, *die* **2** *v.t.* füllen **3** *v.i.* sich sammeln

ˈ**crowded** *adj.* überfüllt

ˈ**crowd-puller** *n.* (coll.) Publikumsmagnet, *der*

crown /kraʊn/ **1** *n.* Krone, *die* **2** *v.t.* (a) krönen (b) überkronen ⟨*Zahn*⟩

crown 'jewels *n. pl.* Kronjuwelen *Pl.*

ˈ**crow's-foot** *n., usu. in pl.* Krähenfuß, *der*

crucial /ˈkruːʃl/ *adj.* entscheidend (to für)

crucially /ˈkruːʃəlɪ/ *adv.* entscheidend; be ∼ important von entscheidender Wichtigkeit sein

crucifix /ˈkruːsɪfɪks/ *n.* Kruzifix, *das*

crucifixion /kruːsɪˈfɪkʃn/ *n.* Kreuzigung, *die*

crucify /ˈkruːsɪfaɪ/ *v.t.* kreuzigen

crude /kruːd/ *adj.* (a) roh; ∼ oil Rohöl, *das* (b) (fig.) grob ⟨*Entwurf, Worte*⟩

cruel /ˈkruːəl/ *adj.* grausam

cruelty /ˈkruːəltɪ/ *n.* Grausamkeit, *die*

cruet /ˈkruːɪt/ *n.* (a) Essig-/Ölfläschchen, *das* (b) ▸ CRUET STAND

ˈ**cruet stand** *n.* Menage, *die*

cruise /kruːz/ **1** *v.i.* (at random) ⟨*Fahrzeug, Fahrer:*⟩ herumfahren **2** *n.* Kreuzfahrt, *die*

ˈ**cruise missile** *n.* Marschflugkörper, *der*

ˈ**cruiser** *n.* Kreuzer, *der*

crumb /krʌm/ *n.* Krümel, *der*

crumble /ˈkrʌmbl/ **1** *v.t.* zerkrümeln ⟨*Keks, Kuchen*⟩ **2** *v.i.* ⟨*Mauer:*⟩ zusammenfallen

crumbly /ˈkrʌmblɪ/ *adj.* krümelig ⟨*Keks, Kuchen*⟩; bröckelig ⟨*Gestein*⟩

crumpet /ˈkrʌmpɪt/ *n.* weiches Hefeküchlein zum Toasten

crumple /ˈkrʌmpl/ **1** *v.t.* (a) (crush) zerdrücken (b) (wrinkle) zerknittern **2** *v.i.* knittern

ˈ**crumple zone** *n.* (Motor Veh.) Knautschzone, *die*

crunch /krʌntʃ/ **1** *v.t.* [geräuschvoll] knabbern ⟨*Keks*⟩ **2** *v.i.* ⟨*Schnee, Kies:*⟩ knirschen **3** *n.* Knirschen, *das;* when it comes to the ∼: wenn es hart auf hart geht

ˈ**crunchy** *adj.* knusprig

crusade /kruːˈseɪd/ **1** *n.* (Hist.; also fig.) Kreuzzug, *der* **2** *v.i.* (fig.) zu Felde gehen

cru'sader *n.* (Hist.) Kreuzfahrer, *der*

crush /krʌʃ/ **1** *v.t.* (a) quetschen (b) (powder) zerstampfen (c) (fig.) niederschlagen **2** *n.* (a) (crowd) Gedränge, *das* (b) (coll.) have/get a ∼ on *sb.* in jmdn. verknallt sein/sich in jmdn. verknallen (ugs.)

crush: ∼ **bar** *n.* Bar, *die (im Foyer eines Theaters);* ∼-**barrier** *n.* Absperrgitter, *das*

crushing /ˈkrʌʃɪŋ/ *adj.* niederschmetternd ⟨*Antwort*⟩; vernichtend ⟨*Niederlage, Schlag*⟩

crust /krʌst/ *n.* Kruste, *die*

ˈ**crusty** *adj.* knusprig

crutch /krʌtʃ/ *n.* Krücke, *die;* go about on ∼es an Krücken gehen

crux /krʌks/ *n.* the ∼ of the matter der springende Punkt bei der Sache

cry /kraɪ/ ① *n.* (of grief) Schrei, *der;* (of words) Schreien, *das;* **a far ~ from ...** (fig.) etwas ganz anderes als ...

② *v.i.* **(a)** rufen; (loudly) schreien **(b)** (weep) weinen (**over** wegen)

■ **cry 'off** *v.i.* absagen

■ **cry 'out** *v.i.* aufschreien

'crying *adj.* **it's a ~ shame** es ist eine wahre Schande

crypt /krɪpt/ *n.* Krypta, *die*

cryptic /'krɪptɪk/ *adj.* geheimnisvoll

crystal /'krɪstl/ ① *n.* **(a)** Kristall, *der* **(b)** (glass) Bleikristall, *das* ② *adj.* (made of ~ glass) kristallen; Kristalle⟨schale, -vase⟩

crystal: **~ clear** *adj.* kristallklar; ; (fig.) glasklar; **~ 'glass** *n.* Bleikristall, *das;* Kristallglas, *das*

crystallize /'krɪstəlaɪz/ *v.i.* kristallisieren; (fig.) feste Form annehmen

cub /kʌb/ *n.* **(a)** Junge, *das;* (of wolf, fox, dog) Welpe, *der* **(b)** Cub ▶ CUB SCOUT

Cuba /'kju:bə/ *pr. n.* Kuba (*das*)

cubby[hole] /'kʌbɪ(həʊl)/ *n.* Kämmerchen, *das*

cube /kju:b/ *n.* Würfel, *der*

'cube sugar *n.* Würfelzucker, *der*

cubic /'kju:bɪk/ *adj.* **(a)** würfelförmig **(b)** Kubik⟨meter usw.⟩

cubicle /'kju:bɪkl/ *n.* Kabine, *die*

cubism /'kju:bɪzm/ *n.* (Art) Kubismus, *der*

cubist /'kju:bɪst/ *n.* (Art) Kubist, *der*/ Kubistin, *die*

'Cub Scout *n.* Wölfling, *der*

cuckoo /'kʊku:/ *n.* Kuckuck, *der*

'cuckoo clock *n.* Kuckucksuhr, *die*

cucumber /'kju:kʌmbə(r)/ *n.* [Salat]gurke, *die*

cuddle /'kʌdl/ ① *n.* enge Umarmung ② *v.t.* schmusen mit; hätscheln ⟨kleines Kind⟩ ③ *v.i.* schmusen

cuddly /'kʌdlɪ/ *adj.* zum Schmusen *nachgestellt*

cuddly 'toy *n.* Plüschtier, *das*

cudgel /'kʌdʒl/ *n.* Knüppel, *der*

cue[1] /kju:/ *n.* (Billiards etc.) Queue, *das*

cue[2] *n.* (Theatre) Stichwort, *das*

cuff[1] /kʌf/ *n.* **(a)** Manschette, *die;* **off the ~** (fig.) aus dem Stegreif **(b)** (Amer.: trouser turn-up) [Hosen]aufschlag, *der*

cuff[2] ① *v.t.* **~ sb.** jmdm. einen Klaps geben ② *n.* Klaps, *der*

'cuff link *n.* Manschettenknopf, *der*

cuisine /kwɪ'zi:n/ *n.* Küche, *die*

cul-de-sac /'kʌldəsæk/ *n.* Sackgasse, *die*

culinary /'kʌlɪnərɪ/ *adj.* kulinarisch

culminate /'kʌlmɪneɪt/ *v.i.* gipfeln; **~ in** sth. in etw. (*Dat.*) seinen Höchststand erreichen

culmination /kʌlmɪ'neɪʃn/ *n.* Höhepunkt, *der*

culottes /kju:'lɒts/ *n. pl.* Hosenrock, *der*

culpable /'kʌlpəbl/ *adj.* schuldig ⟨Person⟩; strafbar ⟨Handlung⟩

culprit /'kʌlprɪt/ *n.* Täter, *der*/Täterin, *die*

cult /kʌlt/ *n.* Kult, *der*

cultivate /'kʌltɪveɪt/ *v.t.* kultivieren (auch fig.); bestellen ⟨Acker, Land⟩; anbauen ⟨Pflanzen⟩

cultivated /'kʌltɪveɪtɪd/ *adj.* kultiviert ⟨Manieren, Sprache, Geschmack⟩; kultiviert, gebildet ⟨Person⟩

cultivation /kʌltɪ'veɪʃn/ *n.* ▶ CULTIVATE: Kultivierung, *die;* Bestellen *das;* Anbau, *der*

culture /'kʌltʃə(r)/ *n.* Kultur, *die*

'cultured *adj.* kultiviert

'culture shock *n.* Kulturschock, *der*

cumbersome /'kʌmbəsəm/ *adj.* hinderlich ⟨Kleider⟩; sperrig ⟨Pakete⟩; schwerfällig ⟨Arbeitsweise⟩

cunning /'kʌnɪŋ/ ① *n.* Schläue, *die* ② *adj.* schlau

cup /kʌp/ *n.* **(a)** Tasse, *die* **(b)** (prize, competition) Pokal, *der* **(c)** (~ful) Tasse, *die;* **a ~ of coffee/tea** eine Tasse Kaffee/Tee

cupboard /'kʌbəd/ *n.* Schrank, *der*

'Cup Final *n.* Pokalendspiel, *das*

cupful /'kʌpfl/ *n.* Tasse, *die;* **a ~ of water** eine Tasse Wasser

'cup tie *n.* Pokalspiel, *das*

curable /'kjʊərəbl/ *adj.* heilbar

curate /'kjʊərət/ *n.* Kurat, *der*

curator /kjʊə'reɪtə(r)/ *n.* (of museum) Direktor, *der*/Direktorin, *die*

curb /kɜ:b/ *v.t.* zügeln

'curd cheese *n.* ≈ Quark, *der*

curdle /'kɜ:dl/ *v.i.* gerinnen

cure /kjʊə(r)/ ① *n.* [Heil]mittel, *das* (**for** gegen); (fig.) Mittel, *das* ② *v.t.* **(a)** heilen **(b)** [ein]pökeln ⟨Fleisch⟩

'cure-all *n.* Allheilmittel, *das*

curfew /'kɜ:fju:/ *n.* Ausgangssperre, *die*

curiosity /kjʊərɪ'ɒsɪtɪ/ *n.* **(a)** Neugier[de], *die* **(b)** (object) Wunderding, *das*

curious /'kjʊərɪəs/ *adj.* **(a)** (inquisitive) neugierig **(b)** (strange, odd) seltsam

curl /kɜ:l/ ① *n.* Locke, *die* ② *v.t.* locken ③ *v.i.* **(a)** sich locken **(b)** ⟨Straße, Fluss:⟩ sich winden

'curler *n.* Lockenwickler, *der*

'curly *adj.* lockig

'curly-haired *adj.* lockenköpfig; mit lockigem Haar

currant /'kʌrənt/ *n.* Korinthe, *die*

currency /'kʌrənsı/ *n.* (money) Währung, *die;* foreign currencies Devisen *Pl.*

current /'kʌrənt/ **1** *adj.* (a) verbreitet ⟨*Meinung*⟩; gebräuchlich ⟨*Wort*⟩ (b) laufend ⟨*Jahr, Monat*⟩ (c) (the present) aktuell ⟨*Ereignis, Mode*⟩; Tages⟨*politik, -preis*⟩; ∼ affairs Tagespolitik, *die* **2** *n.* (a) (of water, air) Strömung, *die* (b) (Electr.) Strom, *der*

'current account *n.* Girokonto, *das*

'currently *adv.* zur Zeit

curriculum /kə'rıkjʊləm/ *n.* Lehrplan, *der*

curriculum vitae /- 'vi:taı/ *n.* Lebenslauf, *der*

curry[1] /'kʌrı/ *n.* Curry[gericht], *das*

curry[2] *v.t.* ∼ favour [with sb.] sich [bei jmdm.] einschmeicheln

curse /kɜ:s/ **1** *n.* Fluch, *der* **2** *v.t.* verfluchen **3** *v.i.* fluchen

cursor /'kɜ:sə(r)/ *n.* Läufer, *der;* (on screen) Cursor, *der;* Schreibmarke, *die*

cursory /'kɜ:sərı/ *adj.* flüchtig

curt /kɜ:t/ *adj.* kurz angebunden; kurz und schroff ⟨*Brief*⟩

curtail /kɜ:'teıl/ *v.t.* kürzen; abkürzen ⟨*Urlaub*⟩; beschneiden ⟨*Macht*⟩

curtain /'kɜ:tən/ *n.* Vorhang, *der;* **draw** or **pull the** ∼s (open) die Vorhänge aufziehen; (close) die Vorhänge zuziehen

curtain: ∼ **call** *n.* Vorhang, *der;* ∼ **hook** *n.* Gardinenhaken, *der;* ∼ **rod** *n.* Gardinenstange, *die*

curtsy /'kɜ:tsı/ **1** *n.* Knicks, *der* **2** *v.i.* einen Knicks machen (**to** vor + *Dat.*)

curvaceous /kɜ:'veıʃəs/ *adj.* kurvenreich (ugs.); **a** ∼ **figure** eine üppige Figur

curve /kɜ:v/ **1** *v.t.* krümmen **2** *v.i.* ⟨*Straße, Fluss:*⟩ eine Biegung machen **3** *n.* Kurve, *die*

cushion /'kʊʃn/ **1** *n.* Kissen, *das* **2** *v.t.* dämpfen ⟨*Aufprall, Stoß*⟩

cushy /'kʊʃı/ *adj.* (coll.) bequem

custard /'kʌstəd/ *n.* ≈ Vanillesoße, *die*

'custard powder *n.* Vanillesoßenpulver, *das*

custodian /kʌs'təʊdıən/ *n.* (of museum) Wächter, *der*/Wächterin, *die;* (of valuables) Hüter, *der*/Hüterin, *die*

custody /'kʌstədı/ *n.* (a) (care) Obhut, *die* (b) (imprisonment) [be] **in** ∼: in Haft [sein]; **take sb. into** ∼: jmdn. verhaften *od.* festnehmen

custom /'kʌstəm/ *n.* (a) Brauch, *der* (b) in *pl.* (duty on imports) Zoll, *der*

customary /'kʌstəmərı/ *adj.* üblich

'custom-built *adj.* spezial[an]gefertigt

customer /'kʌstəmə(r)/ *n.* Kunde, *der*/ Kundin, *die*

customize (**customise**) /'kʌstəmaız/ *v.t.* speziell anfertigen; (alter) umbauen

'custom-made *adj.* spezial[an]gefertigt; maßgeschneidert ⟨*Kleidung*⟩

customs: ∼ **duty** *n.* Zoll, *der;* ∼ **inspection** *n.* Zollkontrolle, *die;* ∼ **officer** *n.* Zollbeamter, *der*/-beamtin, *die*

cut /kʌt/ **1** *v.t.*, **-tt-**, **cut** (a) schneiden; durchschneiden ⟨*Seil*⟩; ∼ **one's leg** sich (*Dat. od. Akk.*) ins Bein schneiden (b) abschneiden ⟨*Scheibe*⟩; schneiden ⟨*Hecke*⟩; mähen ⟨*Getreide, Gras*⟩; ∼ **one's nails** sich (*Dat.*) die Nägel schneiden (c) (reduce) senken ⟨*Preise*⟩; kürzen ⟨*Lohn*⟩; abbauen ⟨*Arbeitsplätze*⟩ (d) ∼ **sth. short** (interrupt) etw. abbrechen (e) (Comp.) ∼ **and paste** ausschneiden und einfügen **2** *v.i.*, **-tt-**, **cut** (a) ⟨*Messer:*⟩ schneiden (b) ∼ **through** or **across the field/park** [quer] über das Feld/durch den Park gehen **3** *n.* (a) (act of cutting) Schnitt, *der* (b) (stroke, blow) (with knife) Schnitt, *der;* (with sword, whip) Hieb, *der* (c) (reduction) Kürzung, *die;* (in prices) Senkung, *die;* (in services) Verringerung, *die* (d) (of meat) Stück, *das* ■ **cut a'way** *v.t.* abschneiden ■ **cut 'back** *v.t.* (a) (reduce) einschränken (b) (prune) stutzen ■ **cut 'down** **1** *v.t.* (a) fällen ⟨*Baum*⟩ (b) (reduce) einschränken **2** *v.i.* ∼ **down on sth.** etw. einschränken ■ **cut 'off** *v.t.* abschneiden; unterbrechen ⟨*Telefongespräch, Sprecher*⟩ ■ **cut 'out** **1** *v.t.* (a) ausschneiden (of aus) (b) be ∼ out for geeignet sein zu **2** *v.i.* ⟨*Motor:*⟩ aussetzen ■ **cut 'up** *v.t.* zerschneiden

cut: ∼**back** *n.* (reduction) Kürzung, *die;* ∼ **'glass** *n.* Kristall[glas], *das;* ∼**-glass** *adj.* Kristall-

cutlery /'kʌtlərı/ *n.* Besteck, *das*

cutlet /'kʌtlıt/ *n.* Kotelett, *das*

cut: ∼**-off** *n.* ∼**-off point** Trennungslinie, *die;* ∼**-out** *n.* (figure) Ausschneidefigur, *die;* ∼**-price** *adj.* herabgesetzt; ∼**-price offer** Billigangebot, *das*

'cutting **1** *adj.* beißend ⟨*Bemerkung, Antwort*⟩ **2** *n.* (from newspaper) Ausschnitt, *der*

'cutting edge *n.* be at the ∼ of technology auf dem Gebiet der Technologie führend sein; die Speerspitze der Technologie sein; be at the ∼ of fashion auf dem Gebiet der Mode führend sein

c. v. *abbr.* = **curriculum vitae**

cyber: ∼**cafe** /'saıbəkæfeı/ *n.* Internet-Café *das;* ∼**sex** /'saıbəseks/ *n.*, no art. Cybersex, *der;* ∼**space** /'saıbəspeıs/ *n.*, no art. Cyberspace, *der*

cycle /'saɪkl/ ⓵ n. (a) (recurrent period) Zyklus, *der* (b) (bicycle) Rad, *das* ⓶ v.i. Rad fahren

cycle: ~ **lane** n. Fahrradspur, *die;* ~ **race** n. Radrennen, *das;* ~ **track** n. Rad[fahr]weg, *der;* (for racing) Radrennbahn, *die*

cycling /'saɪklɪŋ/ n. (activity) Radfahren, *das;* (sport) Radsport, *der;* ~ **shorts** Radlerhose, *die*

cyclist /'saɪklɪst/ n. Radfahrer, *der*/-fahrerin, *die*

cyclone /'saɪkləʊn/ n. (violent hurricane) Zyklon, *der*

cylinder /'sɪlɪndə(r)/ n. Zylinder, *der*

cylindrical /sɪ'lɪndrɪkl/ adj. zylindrisch

cymbal /'sɪmbl/ n. Beckenteller, *der;* ~s Becken *Pl.*

cynic /'sɪnɪk/ n. Zyniker, *der*

cynical /'sɪnɪkl/ adj. zynisch; bissig ⟨*Bemerkung, Worte*⟩

cynicism /'sɪnɪsɪzm/ n. Zynismus, *der*

Cyprus /'saɪprəs/ pr. n. Zypern (*das*)

czar ▶ TSAR

Czech /tʃek/ ⓵ adj. tschechisch; *sb. is* ~: jmd. ist Tscheche/Tschechin ⓶ n. (a) (language) Tschechisch, *das* (b) (person) Tscheche, *der*/Tschechin, *die*

Czechoslovakia /tʃekəʊslə'vækɪə/ pr. n. (Hist.) die Tschechoslowakei

Czechoslovakian /tʃekəʊslə'vækɪən/ (Hist.) ⓵ adj. tschechoslowakisch ⓶ n. Tschechoslowake, *der*/Tschechoslowakin, *die*

Czech Re'public pr. n. Tschechische Republik; Tschechien (*das*)

d

Dd

D, d /di:/ n. D, d, *das*

dab /dæb/ ⓵ n. Tupfer, *der* ⓶ v.t., **-bb-** abtupfen; ~ **sth. on** *or* **against sth.** etw. auf etw. (*Akk.*) tupfen

dabble /'dæbl/ v.i. ~ **in sth.** sich in etw. (*Dat.*) versuchen

dachshund /'dækshʊnd/ n. Dackel, *der*

dad /dæd/ n. (coll.) Vater, *der*

daddy /'dædɪ/ n. (coll.) Vati, *der* (fam.)

daddy-'long-legs n. Schnake, *die*

daffodil /'dæfədɪl/ n. Osterglocke, *die*

daft /dɑ:ft/ adj. doof (ugs.)

dagger /'dægə(r)/ n. Dolch, *der*

daily /'deɪlɪ/ ⓵ adj. täglich; ~ **[news]paper** Tageszeitung, *die* ⓶ adv. täglich ⓷ n. Tageszeitung, *die*

dainty /'deɪntɪ/ adj. zierlich; anmutig ⟨*Bewegung, Person*⟩; zart ⟨*Gesichtszüge*⟩

dairy /'deərɪ/ n. (a) Molkerei, *die* (b) (shop) Milchladen, *der*

dairy: ~ **cattle** n. Milchvieh, *das;* ~ **farm** n. Milchbetrieb, *der;* ~ **farmer** n. Milchbauer, *der;* ~ **produce** n., ~ **products** n. pl. Molkereiprodukte

dais /'deɪɪs/ n. Podium, *das*

daisy /'deɪzɪ/ n. Gänseblümchen, *das*

'daisy chain n. Kranz aus Gänseblümchen

dam /dæm/ ⓵ n. [Stau]damm, *der* ⓶ v.t., **-mm-:** (a) ~ **[up] sth.** etw. abblocken (b) aufstauen ⟨*Fluss*⟩

damage /'dæmɪdʒ/ ⓵ n. Schaden, *der*

⓶ v.t. beschädigen

damaging /'dæmɪdʒɪŋ/ adj. schädlich (**to** für)

damn /dæm/ ⓵ v.t. verdammen ⓶ adj., adv., int. (coll.) verdammt (ugs.) ⓷ n. **he doesn't give** *or* **care a** ~: ihm ist es völlig wurscht (ugs.)

damp /dæmp/ ⓵ adj. feucht ⓶ v.t. ▶ DAMPEN ⓷ n. Feuchtigkeit, *die*

dampen /'dæmpn/ v.t. befeuchten; (fig.) dämpfen ⟨*Begeisterung, Eifer*⟩

'dampness n. Feuchtigkeit, *die*

'damp-proof adj. feuchtigkeitsbeständig; ~ **course** Sperrschicht, *die* (*gegen aufsteigende Bodenfeuchtigkeit*)

dance /dɑ:ns/ ⓵ v.i. & t. tanzen ⓶ n. (a) Tanz, *der* (b) (party) Tanzveranstaltung, *die;* (private) Tanzparty, *die*

dance: ~ **floor** n. Tanzfläche, *die;* ~ **hall** n. Tanzsaal, *der*

'dancer n. Tänzer, *der*/Tänzerin, *die*

'dance step n. Tanzschritt, *der*

dandelion /'dændɪlaɪən/ n. Löwenzahn, *der*

dandruff /'dændrʌf/ n. [Kopf]schuppen *Pl.*

Dane /deɪn/ n. Däne, *der*/Dänin, *die*

danger /'deɪndʒə(r)/ n. Gefahr, *die;* **in/out of** ~: in/außer Gefahr; **be in** ~ **of doing sth.** ⟨*Person:*⟩ Gefahr laufen, etw. zu tun

danger: ~ **area** n. Gefahrenzone, die; ~ **list** n. be on/off the ~ list in/außer Lebensgefahr sein
dangerous /'deɪndʒərəs/ adj., **'dangerously** adv. gefährlich
danger: ~ **signal** n. Warnzeichen, das; ~ **zone** n. Gefahrenzone, die
dangle /'dæŋgl/ [1] v.i. baumeln (**from** an + Dat.)
[2] v.t. baumeln lassen
Danish /'deɪnɪʃ/ [1] adj. dänisch; **sb. is** ~: jmd. ist Däne/Dänin
[2] n. Dänisch, das; see also ENGLISH 2A
dank /dæŋk/ adj. feucht
Danube /'dænjuːb/ pr. n. Donau, die
dare /deə(r)/ [1] v.t. (a) [es] wagen; ~ **to do sth.** [es] wagen, etw. zu tun
(b) (challenge) ~ **sb. to do sth.** jmdn. aufstacheln, etw. zu tun; **I** ~ **you!** trau dich!
[2] n. Mutprobe, die
daring /'deərɪŋ/ adj. (bold) kühn; waghalsig ⟨Kunststück, Tat⟩; (fearless) wagemutig
dark /dɑːk/ [1] adj. dunkel; (dark-haired) dunkelhaarig; ~-**blue**/-**brown** dunkelblau/ -braun; ~ **glasses** dunkle Brille
[2] n. (a) Dunkel, das; **in the** ~: im Dunkeln; **keep sb. in the** ~ (fig.) jmdn. im Dunkeln lassen
(b) no art. (nightfall) Einbruch der Dunkelheit
darken /'dɑːkn/ v.t. verdunkeln
dark: ~-**haired** adj. dunkelhaarig; ~ **'horse** n. be a ~ horse ein stilles Wasser sein
'darkness n. Dunkelheit, die
'darkroom n. Dunkelkammer, die
darling /'dɑːlɪŋ/ n. Liebling, der
darn /dɑːn/ v.t. stopfen
dart /dɑːt/ [1] n. (a) (missile) Pfeil, der
(b) (Sport) Wurfpfeil, der; ~**s** sing. (game) Darts, das
[2] v.i. sausen
'dartboard n. Dartsscheibe, die
dash /dæʃ/ [1] v.i. sausen
[2] v.t. (fling) schleudern
[3] n. (a) **make a** ~: rasen (ugs.) (**for** zu)
(b) (horizontal stroke) Gedankenstrich, der
(c) (small amount) Schuss, der
'dashboard n. Armaturenbrett, das
data /'deɪtə, 'dɑːtə/ n. Daten Pl.
data: ~**base** n. Datenbank, die; ~ **capture** n. (Comp.) Datenerfassung, die; ~ **file** n. (Comp.) Datei, die; ~ **highway** n. (Comp.) Datenautobahn, die; ~ **pro'tection** n. (Comp.) Datenschutz, der; ~ **retrieval** n. (Comp.) Retrieval, das; Datenabruf, der; ~ **security** n. (Comp.) Datensicherung, die; ~ **storage** n. (Comp.) Datenspeicherung, die; (capacity) Speicherkapazität, die
date[1] /deɪt/ n. (Bot.) Dattel, die
date[2] [1] n. (a) Datum, das; (on coin etc.) Jahreszahl, die; ~ **of birth** Geburtsdatum, das; **be out of** ~: altmodisch sein; **to** ~: bis heute

(b) (coll.: appointment) Verabredung, die; **have**/ **make a** ~ **with sb.** mit jmdm. verabredet sein/sich mit jmdm. verabreden
[2] v.t. (a) datieren
(b) (coll.: make seem old) alt machen
[3] v.i. ~ **back to**/~ **from** stammen aus
dated /'deɪtɪd/ adj. altmodisch
date: ~ **line** n. Datumsgrenze, die; ~ **rape** n.: Vergewaltigung der eigenen Freundin oder Vergewaltigung einer Frau während einer Verabredung mit ihr; ~ **stamp** n. Datumsstempel, der; ~-**stamp** v.t. abstempeln; mit einem Datumsstempel versehen
'dating agency /'deɪtɪŋ/ n. Partnervermittlung, die
dative /'deɪtɪv/ adj. & n. ~ [**case**] Dativ, der
daub /dɔːb/ v.t. (smear) beschmieren; (put crudely) schmieren
daughter /'dɔːtə(r)/ n. Tochter, die
'daughter-in-law n., pl. **daughters-in-law** Schwiegertochter, die
daunt /dɔːnt/ v.t. entmutigen
dawdle /'dɔːdl/ v.i. bummeln (ugs.)
dawn /dɔːn/ [1] v.i. dämmern; **sth.** ~**s** [**up**]**on sb.** etw. dämmert jmdm
[2] n. [Morgen]dämmerung, die; **at** ~: im Morgengrauen
dawn 'chorus n. morgendlicher Gesang der Vögel
day /deɪ/ n. Tag, der; **all** ~ [**long**] den ganzen Tag [lang]; **for two** ~**s** zwei Tage [lang]; **the** ~ **before yesterday**/**after tomorrow** vorgestern/übermorgen; ~ **after** ~: Tag für Tag; ~ **in** ~ **out** tagaus, tagein; **in the** ~**s when** ...: zu der Zeit, als ...; **these** ~**s** heutzutage; **in those** ~**s** damals
day: ~**bed** n. Liegesofa, das; ~**break** n. Tagesanbruch, der; ~ **care** n. Ganztagsbetreuung, die; ~**dream** [1] n. Tagtraum, der; [2] v.i. träumen; ~**dreamer** n. Tagträumer, der/-träumerin, die; ~**light** n. Tageslicht, das; **in broad** ~**light** am helllichten Tag[e]; ~ **release** n. (Brit.) [tageweise] Freistellung zur Fortbildung; ~ **re'turn** n. Tagesrückfahrkarte, die; ~**time** n. Tag, der; ~-**to**-~ adj. [tag]täglich; ~ **trip** n. Tagesausflug, der; ~ **tripper** n. Tagesausflügler, der/ -ausflüglerin, die
daze /deɪz/ v.t. benommen machen
dazed /deɪzd/ adj. benommen
dazzle /'dæzl/ v.t. blenden
DC abbr. = **direct current** GS
dead /ded/ [1] adj. (a) tot
(b) plötzlich ⟨Halt⟩; genau ⟨Mitte⟩
(c) (numb) taub
[2] adv. völlig; ~ **straight** schnurgerade; ~ **easy**/**slow** kinderleicht/ganz langsam; ~ **on time** auf die Minute; ~ **tired** todmüde
[3] n. pl. **the** ~: die Toten Pl.
deaden /'dedn/ v.t. dämpfen; betäuben ⟨Schmerz⟩

dead: ～ **'end** *n.* Sackgasse, *die;* ～ **'heat** *n.* totes Rennen; ～**line** *n.* [letzter] Termin; ～**lock** *n.* völliger Stillstand; ～ **'loss** *n.* (coll.) (worthless thing) totaler Reinfall (ugs.); (person) hoffnungsloser Fall (ugs.)

deadly /'dedlɪ/ *adj.* tödlich; (fig. coll.: boring) todlangweilig

dead: ～**pan** *adj.* unbewegt; **he looked** ～**pan** *or* **had a** ～**pan expression** er verzog keine Miene; **D**～ **'Sea** *pr. n.* Totes Meer; ～ **'wood** *n.* (fig.) **be just** ～ **wood** völlig überflüssig sein

deaf /def/ *adj.* 1 taub; ～ **and dumb** taubstumm
2 *n. pl.* **the** ～: die Gehörlosen *Pl.*

'deaf aid *n.* Hörgerät, *das*

deafen /'defn/ *v.t.* ～ **sb.** bei jmdm. zur Taubheit führen; **I was** ～**ed by the noise** (fig.) ich war von dem Lärm wie betäubt

'deafening *adj.* ohrenbetäubend

'deafness *n.* Taubheit, *die*

deal¹ /diːl/ 1 *v.t.,* dealt /delt/ **(a)** (Cards) austeilen
(b) ～ **sb. a blow** jmdm. einen Schlag versetzen
2 *v.i.,* dealt **(a)** (do business) ～ **in sth.** mit etw. handeln
(b) ～ **with sth.** (occupy oneself) sich mit etw. befassen; (manage) mit etw. fertig werden; (be about) von etw. handeln; ～ **with sb.** mit jmdm. fertig werden
3 *n.* (coll.: arrangement) Geschäft, *das;* **it's a** ～**!** abgemacht!; **big** ～**!** (iron.) na, und?
■ **deal 'out** *v.t.* verteilen

deal² *n.* **a great** *or* **good** ～: viel; (often) ziemlich viel; **a great** *or* **good** ～ **of** viel

'dealer *n.* **(a)** Händler, *der*
(b) (Cards) Geber, *der;* **he's the** ～: er gibt

'dealings *n. pl.* **have** ～ **with sb.** mit jmdm. zu tun haben

dealt ▶ DEAL¹ 1, 2

dean /diːn/ *n.* (Eccl.) Dechant, *der*

dear /dɪə(r)/ 1 *adj.* **(a)** lieb; **sb./sth. is** ～ **to sb.['s heart]** jmd. liebt jmdn./etw.; (beginning letter) **D**～ **Sir/Madam** Sehr geehrter Herr/Sehr geehrte Dame; **D**～ **Mr Jones/Mrs Jones** Sehr geehrter Herr Jones/Sehr geehrte Frau Jones; **D**～ **Malcolm/Emily** Lieber Malcolm/Liebe Emily
(b) (expensive) teuer
2 *int.* ～, ～**!,** ～ **me!, oh** ～**!** [ach] du liebe *od.* meine Güte!

'dearly *adv.* **(a)** von ganzem Herzen
(b) (at high price) teuer

dearth /dɜːθ/ *n.* Mangel, *der* (**of** an + *Dat.*)

death /deθ/ *n.* **(a)** Tod, *der;* ... **to** ～: zu Tode ...; **bleed to** ～: verbluten
(b) (instance) Todesfall, *der*

death: ～**bed** *n.* Totenbett, *das;* **on one's** ～**bed** auf dem Sterbebett; ～ **certificate** *n.* (from doctor) Totenschein, *der*

deathly /'deθlɪ/ 1 *adj.* tödlich
2 *adv.* tödlich; ～ **still/quiet** totenstill

death: ～ **penalty** *n.* Todesstrafe, *die;* ～ **sentence** *n.* Todesurteil, *das;* ～ **trap** *n.* lebensgefährliche Sache; ～ **threat** *n.* Morddrohung, *die*

debatable /dɪ'beɪtəbl/ *adj.* (questionable) fraglich

debate /dɪ'beɪt/ *n.* Debatte, *die*

debilitating /dɪ'bɪlɪteɪtɪŋ/ *adj.* anstrengend ⟨*Klima*⟩; schwächend ⟨*Krankheit*⟩

debit /'debɪt/ 1 *n.* Soll, *das*
2 *v.t.* belasten ⟨*Konto*⟩

debris /'debriː/ *n.* Trümmer *Pl.*

debt /det/ *n.* Schuld, *die;* **be in** ～: Schulden haben; **get into** ～: in Schulden geraten

debtor /'detə(r)/ *n.* Schuldner, *der*/Schuldnerin, *die*

debug /diː'bʌg/ *v.t.,* -gg- (coll.: remove defects from) von Fehlern befreien

début (*Amer.:* **debut**) /'deɪbuː, 'deɪbjuː/ *n.* Debüt, *das*

Dec. *abbr.* = **December** Dez.

decade /'dekeɪd/ *n.* Jahrzehnt, *das*

decadent /'dekədənt/ *adj.* dekadent

decaf, decaff /'diːkæf/ *n.* (coll.) *or* ® koffeinfreier Kaffee

decaffeinated /diː'kæfɪneɪtɪd/ *adj.* entkoffeiniert

decanter /dɪ'kæntə(r)/ *n.* Karaffe, *die*

decay /dɪ'keɪ/ 1 *v.i.* verrotten; ⟨*Gebäude:*⟩ zerfallen; ⟨*Zahn:*⟩ faul werden
2 *n.* Verrotten, *das;* (of building) Zerfall, *der;* (of tooth) Fäule, *die*

deceased /dɪ'siːst/ 1 *adj.* verstorben
2 *n.* Verstorbene, *der/die*

deceit /dɪ'siːt/ *n.* Täuschung, *die*

deceitful /dɪ'siːtfl/ *adj.* falsch ⟨*Person, Art*⟩; hinterlistig ⟨*Trick*⟩

deceive /dɪ'siːv/ *v.t.* täuschen; (be unfaithful to) betrügen

December /dɪ'sembə(r)/ *n.* Dezember, *der; see also* AUGUST

decency /'diːsənsɪ/ *n.* Anstand, *der*

decent /'diːsənt/ *adj.* anständig

decentralization /diːsentrəlaɪ'zeɪʃn/ *n.* Dezentralisierung, *die*

decentralize /diː'sentrəlaɪz/ *v.t.* dezentralisieren

deception /dɪ'sepʃn/ *n.* Betrug, *der;* (being deceived) Täuschung, *die*

deceptive /dɪ'septɪv/ *adj.* trügerisch

decibel /'desɪbel/ *n.* Dezibel, *das*

decide /dɪ'saɪd/ 1 *v.t.* **(a)** (settle, judge) entscheiden über (+ *Akk.*)
(b) (resolve) ～ **that** ...: beschließen, dass ...; ～ **to do sth.** sich entschließen, etw. zu tun
2 *v.i.* sich entscheiden (**in favour of** zugunsten von, **against** gegen)

de'cided *adj.,* **de'cidedly** *adv.* entschieden

deciduous /dɪ'sɪdjʊəs/ *adj.* ～ **tree** ≈ Laubbaum, *der*

decimal /'desɪml/ ☐1 *n.* Dezimalbruch, *der*
☐2 *adj.* Dezimal-

decimal: ∼ **'currency** *n.*
Dezimalwährung, *die;* ∼ **'fraction** *n.*
Dezimalbruch, *der;* ∼ **'point** *n.* Komma,
das

decimate /'desɪmeɪt/ *v.t.* dezimieren

decipher /dɪ'saɪfə(r)/ *v.t.* entziffern

decision /dɪ'sɪʒn/ *n.* Entscheidung, *die*

decisive /dɪ'saɪsɪv/ *adj.* entscheidend

deck /dek/ *n.* (a) Deck, *das;* on ∼: an Deck;
below ∼[s] unter Deck
(b) (Amer.: pack) a ∼ of cards ein Spiel
Karten

'deckchair *n.* Liegestuhl, *der*

declaration /deklə'reɪʃn/ *n.* Erklärung,
die

declare /dɪ'kleə(r)/ *v.t.* erklären; kundtun
(geh.) ⟨*Wunsch, Absicht*⟩; ∼ **sth./sb. [to be]**
sth. etw./jmdn. für etw. erklären

declension /dɪ'klenʃn/ *n.* Deklination, *die*

decline /dɪ'klaɪn/ ☐1 *v.i.* nachlassen;
⟨*Anzahl:*⟩ sinken
☐2 *v.t.* (a) ablehnen
(b) (Ling.) deklinieren
☐3 *n.* ▸1: Nachlassen, *das*/Sinken, *das* (in
Gen.); be on the ∼: nachlassen/sinken

decode /diː'kəʊd/ *v.t.* entziffern

decommission /diːkə'mɪʃən/ *v.t.*
stilllegen; außer Dienst stellen ⟨*Schiff*⟩

decompose /diːkəm'pəʊz/ *v.i.* sich
zersetzen

décor /'deɪkɔː(r)/ *n.* Ausstattung, *die*

decorate /'dekəreɪt/ *v.t.* (a) schmücken
⟨*Raum, Straße, Baum*⟩; verzieren ⟨*Kuchen,
Kleid*⟩; (paint) streichen; (wallpaper) tapezieren
(b) (award medal etc. to) auszeichnen

decoration /dekə'reɪʃn/ *n.* (a) Schmücken,
das; (with paint) Streichen, *das;* (with wallpaper)
Tapezieren, *das;* (of cake, dress) Verzieren, *das*
(b) (adornment) Schmuck, *der*
(c) (medal etc.) Auszeichnung, *die*

decorative /'dekərətɪv/ *adj.* dekorativ

decorator /'dekəreɪtə(r)/ *n.* Maler, *der;*
(paperhanger) Tapezierer, *der*

decorous /'dekərəs/ *adj.,* **'decorously**
adv. schicklich (geh.)

decorum /dɪ'kɔːrəm/ *n.* Schicklichkeit, *die*
(geh.)

decoy /'diːkɔɪ/ *n.* Lockvogel, *der*

decrease ☐1 /dɪ'kriːs/ *v.i.* abnehmen;
⟨*Stärke:*⟩ nachlassen
☐2 /dɪ'kriːs/ *v.t.* [ver]mindern ⟨*Wert, Lärm*⟩;
schmälern ⟨*Popularität, Macht*⟩
☐3 /'diːkriːs/ *n.* Rückgang, *der;* (in weight)
Abnahme, *die;* (in strength) Nachlassen, *das;* (in
value, noise) Minderung, *die*

decree /dɪ'kriː/ ☐1 *n.* Dekret, *das;* Erlass,
der
☐2 *v.t.* verfügen

decrepit /dɪ'krepɪt/ *adj.* altersschwach;
(dilapidated) heruntergekommen

decriminalize /diː'krɪmɪnəlaɪz/ *v.t.*
entkriminalisieren

dedicate /'dedɪkeɪt/ *v.t.* ∼ sth. to sb.
jmdm. etw. widmen

'dedicated *adj.* (a) (devoted) be ∼ to sth./
sb. nur für etw./jmdn. leben
(b) (to vocation) hingebungsvoll; a ∼ teacher
ein Lehrer mit Leib und Seele

dedication /dedɪ'keɪʃn/ *n.* (a) Widmung,
die (to *Dat.*)
(b) (devotion) Hingabe, *die*

deduce /dɪ'djuːs/ *v.t.* ∼ sth. [from sth.] etw.
[aus etw.] schließen

deduct /dɪ'dʌkt/ *v.t.* ∼ sth. [from sth.] etw.
[von etw.] abziehen

deduction /dɪ'dʌkʃn/ *n.* (a) (deducting)
Abzug, *der*
(b) (deducing, thing deduced) Ableitung, *die*
(c) (amount) Abzüge *Pl.*

deed /diːd/ *n.* (a) Tat, *die*
(b) (Law) Urkunde, *die*

deejay /diː'dʒeɪ/ *n.* (coll.) Diskjockey, *der*

deem /diːm/ *v.t.* erachten für

deep /diːp/ ☐1 *adj.* (lit. or fig.) tief; tiefgründig
⟨*Bemerkung*⟩; water ten feet ∼: drei Meter
tiefes Wasser; take a ∼ breath tief Atem
holen; be ∼ in thought in Gedanken
versunken sein
☐2 *adv.* tief

'deepen ☐1 *v.t.* vertiefen
☐2 *v.i.* sich vertiefen

deep: ∼-**'freeze** *v.t.* tiefgefrieren;
∼-**fried** *adj.* frittiert

'deeply *adv.* (lit. or fig.) tief; äußerst
⟨*interessiert, dankbar*⟩

deep-'rooted *adj.* tief ⟨*Abneigung*⟩; tief
verwurzelt ⟨*Tradition*⟩

deer /dɪə(r)/ *n., pl. same* Hirsch, *der;* (roe ∼)
Reh, *das*

de-escalate /diː'eskəleɪt/ *v.t.* deeskalieren

deface /dɪ'feɪs/ *v.t.* verunstalten

defamation /defə'meɪʃn/ *n.* Diffamierung,
die

defamatory /dɪ'fæmətərɪ/ *adj.*
diffamierend

default /dɪ'fɔːlt, dɪ'fɒlt/ ☐1 *n.* (a) lose/go by
∼: durch Abwesenheit verlieren/nicht zur
Geltung kommen; win by ∼: durch
Nichterscheinen des Gegners gewinnen
(b) (Comp.) Voreinstellung, *die*
☐2 *v.i.* ∼ on one's payments/debts seinen
Zahlungsverpflichtungen nicht nachkommen

defeat /dɪ'fiːt/ ☐1 *v.t.* besiegen
☐2 *n.* (being ∼ed) Niederlage, *die;* (∼ing) Sieg,
der (of über + *Akk.*)

de'featist *adj.* defätistisch

defect ☐1 /'diːfekt/ *n.* (a) (lack) Mangel, *der*
(b) (shortcoming) Fehler, *der*
☐2 /dɪ'fekt/ *v.i.* überlaufen (to zu)

defection /dɪ'fekʃn/ *n.* Flucht, *die*

defective /dɪˈfektɪv/ adj. defekt ⟨Maschine⟩; fehlerhaft ⟨Material, Arbeiten, Methode⟩

defector /dɪˈfektə(r)/ n. Überläufer, der/ -läuferin, die

defence /dɪˈfens/ n. (Brit.) Verteidigung, die; (means of ~) Schutz, der

de'fenceless adj. wehrlos

de'fence mechanism n. (Physiol., Psych.) Abwehrmechanismus, der

defend /dɪˈfend/ v.t. verteidigen

defendant /dɪˈfendənt/ n. (Law) (accused) Angeklagte, der/die; (sued) Beklagte, der/die

de'fender n. Verteidiger, der

defense etc. (Amer.) ▶ DEFENCE etc.

defensive /dɪˈfensɪv/ ① adj. defensiv ② n. be on the ~: in der Defensive sein

defer¹ /dɪˈfɜː(r)/ v.t., -rr- aufschieben

defer² v.i., -rr-: ~ [to sb.] sich [jmdm.] beugen

deference /ˈdefərəns/ n. Respekt, der; in ~ to sb./sth. aus Achtung vor jmdm./etw.

deferential /defəˈrenʃl/ adj. respektvoll

defiance /dɪˈfaɪəns/ n. Trotz, der; in ~ of sb./sth. jmdm./einer Sache zum Trotz

defiant /dɪˈfaɪənt/ adj., **de'fiantly** adv. trotzig

deficiency /dɪˈfɪʃənsɪ/ n. Mangel, der

deficient /dɪˈfɪʃənt/ adj. unzulänglich; sb./ sth. is ~ in sth. jmdm./einer Sache mangelt es an etw. (Dat.)

deficit /ˈdefɪsɪt/ n. Defizit, das (of an + Dat.)

defile /dɪˈfaɪl/ v.t. verpesten ⟨Luft⟩; beflecken ⟨Reinheit, Unschuld⟩

define /dɪˈfaɪn/ v.t. definieren

definite /ˈdefɪnɪt/ adj. bestimmt; eindeutig ⟨Antwort, Entscheidung, Beschluss, Verbesserung⟩; klar umrissen ⟨Ziel, Plan⟩; klar ⟨Vorstellung⟩; genau ⟨Zeitpunkt⟩

'definitely ① adv. bestimmt; eindeutig ⟨festlegen, größer sein, verbessert⟩; endgültig ⟨entscheiden⟩
② int. (coll.) na, klar (ugs.)

definition /defɪˈnɪʃn/ n. Definition, die; (Telev., Phot.) Schärfe, die

definitive /dɪˈfɪnɪtɪv/ adj. endgültig ⟨Beschluss, Antwort, Urteil⟩; (authoritative) maßgeblich

deflate /dɪˈfleɪt/ v.t. die Luft ablassen aus; (fig.) ernüchtern

deflation /dɪˈfleɪʃn/ n. (Econ.) Deflation, die

deflect /dɪˈflekt/ v.t. brechen ⟨Licht⟩; ~ sb./sth. [from sb./sth.] jmdn./etw. [von jmdm./einer Sache] ablenken

deforestation /diːforɪˈsteɪʃn/ n. Entwaldung, die; Abholzung, die

deform /dɪˈfɔːm/ v.t. deformieren

deformed /dɪˈfɔːmd/ adj. entstellt ⟨Gesicht⟩; verunstaltet ⟨Person, Körperteil⟩

deformity /dɪˈfɔːmɪtɪ/ n. (malformation) Verunstaltung, die

defraud /dɪˈfrɔːd/ v.t. ~ sb. [of sth.] jmdn. [um etw.] betrügen

defray /dɪˈfreɪ/ v.t. bestreiten

defrost /diːˈfrɒst/ v.t. auftauen ⟨Speisen⟩; abtauen ⟨Kühlschrank⟩

deft /deft/ adj., **'deftly** adv. sicher und geschickt

defunct /dɪˈfʌŋkt/ adj. defekt ⟨Maschine⟩; veraltet ⟨Gesetz⟩

defuse /diːˈfjuːz/ v.t. entschärfen

defy /dɪˈfaɪ/ v.t. (a) (resist openly) ~ sb. jmdm. trotzen
(b) (refuse to obey) ~ sb./sth. sich jmdm./ einer Sache widersetzen

degenerate /dɪˈdʒenəreɪt/ v.i. ~ [into sth.] [zu etw.] verkommen

degradation /degrəˈdeɪʃn/ n. Erniedrigung, die

degrade /dɪˈgreɪd/ v.t. erniedrigen

degrading /dɪˈgreɪdɪŋ/ adj. entwürdigend; erniedrigend

degree /dɪˈɡriː/ n. (a) Grad, der; 20 ~s 20 Grad
(b) (academic rank) [akademischer] Grad

de'gree course n. Studium, das

dehydrate /diːˈhaɪdreɪt/ v.t. austrocknen ⟨Körper⟩; ~d dehydratisiert (fachspr.)

dehydration /diːhaɪˈdreɪʃn/ n. Dehydration, die (fachspr.); Austrocknung, die

de-ice /diːˈaɪs/ v.t. enteisen

deign /deɪn/ v.t. ~ to do sth. sich [dazu] herablassen, etw. zu tun

deity /ˈdiːɪtɪ/ n. Gottheit, die

dejected /dɪˈdʒektɪd/ adj. niedergeschlagen

dejection /dɪˈdʒekʃn/ n. Niedergeschlagenheit, die

delay /dɪˈleɪ/ ① v.t. (make late) aufhalten; verzögern ⟨Ankunft, Abfahrt⟩; the train has been ~ed der Zug hat Verspätung
② v.i. warten
③ n. (a) Verzögerung, die (to bei)
(b) (Transport) Verspätung, die

delectable /dɪˈlektəbl/ adj. köstlich

delegate ① /ˈdelɪgət/ n. Delegierte, der/ die
② /ˈdelɪgeɪt/ v.t. delegieren (to an + Akk.)

delegation /delɪˈgeɪʃn/ n. Delegation, die

delete /dɪˈliːt/ v.t. streichen (from in + Dat.); (Comp.) löschen

de'lete key n. (Comp.) Löschtaste, die

deletion /dɪˈliːʃn/ n. Streichung, die; (Comp.) Löschung, die

deli /ˈdelɪ/ (coll.) ▶ DELICATESSEN

deliberate /dɪˈlɪbərət/ adj. (a) (intentional) absichtlich; bewusst ⟨Lüge, Irreführung⟩
(b) (fully considered) wohl überlegt

de'liberately adv. absichtlich

deliberation /dɪlɪbəˈreɪʃn/ n. Überlegung, die; (discussion) Beratung, die

delicacy /ˈdelɪkəsɪ/ n. (a) (tactfulness and care) Feingefühl, das ⋯⊳

(b) (food) Delikatesse, *die*

delicate /'delɪkət/ *adj.* zart; (requiring careful handling) empfindlich; delikat ‹*Frage, Angelegenheit*›

delicatessen /delɪkə'tesən/ *n.* Feinkostgeschäft, *das*

delicious /dɪ'lɪʃəs/ *adj.* köstlich

delight /dɪ'laɪt/ ① *v.t.* erfreuen
② *v.i.* sb. ⁓s in doing sth. es macht jmdm. Freude, etw. zu tun
③ *n.* Freude, *die* (at über + *Akk.;* in an + *Dat.*)

de'lighted *adj.* be ⁓ ‹*Person:*› hocherfreut sein; be ⁓ by or with sth. sich über etw. (*Akk.*) freuen

delightful /dɪ'laɪtfl/ *adj.* wunderbar; köstlich ‹*Geschmack*›; reizend ‹*Person, Landschaft*›

de'lightfully *adv.* wunderbar

delinquent /dɪ'lɪŋkwənt/ ① *n.* Randalierer, *der*
② *adj.* kriminell

delirious /dɪ'lɪrɪəs/ *adj.* be ⁓: im Delirium sein; be ⁓ [with sth.] (fig.) außer sich [vor etw. (*Dat.*)] sein

delirium /dɪ'lɪrɪəm/ *n.* Delirium, *das*

deliver /dɪ'lɪvə(r)/ *v.t.* (a) bringen; liefern ‹*Ware*›; zustellen ‹*Post, Telegramm*›; überbringen ‹*Botschaft*›
(b) halten ‹*Rede*›

delivery /dɪ'lɪvərɪ/ *n.* Lieferung, *die;* (of letters, parcels) Zustellung, *die*

delivery: ⁓ **date** *n.* Liefertermin, *der;* ⁓ **note** *n.* Lieferschein, *der;* ⁓ **service** *n.* Zustelldienst, *der;* ⁓ **van** *n.* Lieferwagen, *der*

delta /'deltə/ *n.* Delta, *das*

delude /dɪ'lju:d/ *v.t.* täuschen

deluge /'delju:dʒ/ ① *n.* sintflutartiger Regen
② *v.t.* überschwemmen

delusion /dɪ'lju:ʒn/ *n.* Illusion, *die*

de luxe /də'lʌks/ *adj.* Luxus-

demand /dɪ'mɑ:nd/ ① *n.* Forderung, *die* (for nach); (for commodity) Nachfrage, *die;* sth./ sb. is in ⁓: etw. ist gefragt/jmd. ist begehrt
② *v.t.* verlangen (of, from von); fordern ‹*Recht*›

de'manding *adj.* anspruchsvoll

demean /dɪ'mi:n/ *v. refl.* (lower one's dignity) ⁓ oneself [to do sth.] sich [dazu] erniedrigen[, etw. zu tun]; ⁓ oneself by sth./ doing sth. sich durch etw. erniedrigen/sich dadurch erniedrigen, dass man etw. tut

demeaning /dɪ'mi:nɪŋ/ *adj.* erniedrigend

demeanour (*Brit.; Amer.:* **demeanor**) /dɪ'mi:nə(r)/ *n.* Benehmen, *das*

demented /dɪ'mentɪd/ *adj.* wahnsinnig

dementia /dɪ'menʃə/ *n.* (Med.) Demenz, *die*

demerara /demə'reərə/ *n.* ⁓ [sugar] brauner Zucker; Farin, *der*

demise /dɪ'maɪz/ *n.* (death) Ableben, *das* (geh.); (of firm, party, etc.) Untergang, *der*

demo /'deməʊ/ *n., pl.* ⁓s (coll.) Demo, *die* (ugs.)

de'mobilize *v.t.* demobilisieren ‹*Armee*›; aus dem Kriegsdienst entlassen ‹*Soldat*›

democracy /dɪ'mɒkrəsɪ/ *n.* Demokratie, *die*

Democrat /'deməkræt/ *n.* (Amer. Polit.) Demokrat, *der*/Demokratin, *die*

democratic /demə'krætɪk/ *adj.,* **democratically** /demə'krætɪkəlɪ/ *adv.* demokratisch

demolish /dɪ'mɒlɪʃ/ *v.t.* abreißen

demolition /demə'lɪʃn/ *n.* Abriss, *der;* ⁓ work Abbrucharbeit, *die*

demon /'di:mən/ *n.* Dämon, *der*

demonstrably /'demənstrəblɪ, dɪ'mɒnstrəblɪ/ *adv.* nachweislich

demonstrate /'demənstreɪt/ ① *v.t.* zeigen; (be proof of) zeigen; beweisen
② *v.i.* demonstrieren

demonstration /demən'streɪʃn/ *n.* (also Pol. etc.) Demonstration, *die;* (proof) Beweis, *der*

demonstrative /də'mɒnstrətɪv/ *adj.* (a) offen ‹*Person*›
(b) (Ling.) Demonstrativ-

demonstrator /'demənstreɪtə(r)/ *n.* (Pol. etc.) Demonstrant, *der*/Demonstrantin, *die*

demoralize /dɪ'mɒrəlaɪz/ *v.t.* demoralisieren

demote /di:'məʊt/ *v.t.* degradieren (to zu)

demotion /di:'məʊʃn/ *n.* Degradierung, *die* (to zu)

demur /dɪ'mɜ:(r)/ *v.i.,* -rr- Einwände erheben

demure /dɪ'mjʊə(r)/ *adj.* betont zurückhaltend

den /den/ *n.* Höhle, *die*

denial /dɪ'naɪəl/ *n.* (refusal) Verweigerung, *die;* (of request) Ablehnung, *die;* be in ⁓: die Augen vor der Wahrheit schließen

denier /'denjə(r)/ *n.* Denier, *das;* 20 ⁓ stockings 20-den-Strümpfe

denim /'denɪm/ *n.* Denim Ⓦ, *der;* Jeansstoff, *der;* ⁓ jacket Jeansjacke, *die;* ⁓s Bluejeans *Pl.*

Denmark /'denmɑ:k/ *pr. n.* Dänemark (*das*)

denomination /dɪnɒmɪ'neɪʃn/ *n.* (Relig.) Konfession, *die*

denote /dɪ'nəʊt/ *v.t.* bezeichnen

dénouement, denouement /deɪ'nu:mɑ̃/ *n.* Ausgang, *der*

denounce /dɪ'naʊns/ *v.t.* denunzieren; (accuse publicly) beschuldigen

dense /dens/ *adj.* (a) dicht; massiv ‹*Körper*›
(b) (stupid) dumm

'densely *adv.* dicht; ⁓ packed dicht gedrängt

density /'densɪtɪ/ *n.* Dichte, *die*

dent /dent/ ① *n.* Beule, *die*

2 *v.t.* einbeulen

dental /'dentl/ *adj.* Zahn-; ~ **care** Zahnpflege, *die;* ~ **treatment** zahnärztliche Behandlung

dental: ~ **floss** /'dentl flɒs/ *n.* Zahnseide, *die;* ~ **practitioner,** ~ **surgeon** *ns.* Zahnarzt, *der*/-ärztin, *die*

dentist /'dentɪst/ *n.* Zahnarzt, *der*/-ärztin, *die*

dentistry /'dentɪstrɪ/ *n.* Zahnheilkunde, *die*

denture /'dentʃə(r)/ *n.* ~[s] Zahnprothese, *die*

denunciation /dɪnʌnsɪ'eɪʃn/ *n.* Denunziation, *die;* (public accusation) Beschuldigung, *die*

deny /dɪ'naɪ/ *v.t.* (declare untrue) bestreiten; (refuse) ~ **sb. sth.** jmdm. etw. verweigern; ~ **sb.'s request** jmdm. seine Bitte abschlagen

deodorant /diː'əʊdərənt/ **1** *adj.* deodorierend
2 *n.* Deodorant, *das*

depart /dɪ'pɑːt/ *v.i.* (a) (go away) weggehen
(b) (set out, leave) abfahren; (on one's journey) abreisen
(c) (fig.: deviate) abweichen (**from** von)

department /dɪ'pɑːtmənt/ *n.* Abteilung, *die;* (government ~) Ministerium, *das;* (of university) Seminar, *das*

de'partment store *n.* Kaufhaus, *das*

departure /dɪ'pɑːtʃə(r)/ *n.* (a) Abreise, *die;* (of train, bus, ship) Abfahrt, *die;* (of aircraft) Abflug, *der*
(b) (deviation) ~ **from sth.** Abweichen von etw.

departure: ~ **gate** *n.* Flugsteig, *der;* ~ **lounge** *n.* Abflughalle, *die;* ~ **time** *n.* (of train, bus) Abfahrtzeit, *die;* (of aircraft) Abflugzeit, *die*

depend /dɪ'pend/ *v.i.* (a) ~ [up]on abhängen von; **it/that** ~**s** es kommt drauf an
(b) (rely, trust) ~ [up]on sich verlassen auf (+ *Akk.*); (have to rely on) angewiesen sein auf (+ *Akk.*)

dependable /dɪ'pendəbl/ *adj.* zuverlässig

dependant /dɪ'pendənt/ *n.* Abhängige, *der*/*die*

dependence /dɪ'pendəns/ *n.* Abhängigkeit, *die*

dependent /dɪ'pendənt/ **1** *n.*
▶ DEPENDANT
2 *adj.* abhängig

depict /dɪ'pɪkt/ *v.t.* darstellen

deplete /dɪ'pliːt/ *v.t.* erheblich verringern

deplorable /dɪ'plɔːrəbl/ *adj.* beklagenswert

deplore /dɪ'plɔː(r)/ *v.t.* (a) (disapprove of) verurteilen
(b) (regret) beklagen

deploy /dɪ'plɔɪ/ *v.t.* einsetzen

deport /dɪ'pɔːt/ *v.t.* ausweisen

deportation /diːpɔː'teɪʃn/ *n.* Ausweisung, *die*

depose /dɪ'pəʊz/ *v.t.* absetzen

deposit /dɪ'pɒzɪt/ **1** *n.* (a) (in bank) Depot, *das;* (credit) Guthaben, *das;* (Brit.: at interest) Sparguthaben, *das*
(b) (first instalment) Anzahlung, *die;* **put down a** ~ **on sth.** eine Anzahlung für etw. leisten
(c) (on bottle) Pfand, *das*
2 *v.t.* (a) (lay down) ablegen; abstellen ‹*etw. Senkrechtes*›
(b) (in bank) deponieren

de'posit account *n.* (Brit.) Sparkonto, *das*

depot /'depəʊ/ *n.* Depot, *das*

depraved /dɪ'preɪvd/ *adj.* verdorben

depravity /dɪ'prævɪtɪ/ *n.* Verdorbenheit, *die*

depreciate /dɪ'priːʃɪeɪt/ *v.i.* an Wert verlieren

depreciation /dɪpriːʃɪ'eɪʃn/ *n.* Wertverlust, *der*

depress /dɪ'pres/ *v.t.* (a) (deject) deprimieren
(b) (push down) herunterdrücken

depressed /dɪ'prest/ *adj.* deprimiert

de'pressing *adj.,* **de'pressingly** *adv.* deprimierend

depression /dɪ'preʃn/ *n.* (a) Depression, *die*
(b) (sunk place) Vertiefung, *die*
(c) (Meteorol.) Tief[druckgebiet], *das*
(d) (Econ.) Wirtschaftskrise, *die*

deprivation /deprɪ'veɪʃn/ *n.* Entbehrung, *die*

deprive /dɪ'praɪv/ *v.t.* ~ **sb. of sth.** jmdm. etw. nehmen; (prevent from having) jmdm. etw. vorenthalten

deprived /dɪ'praɪvd/ *adj.* benachteiligt ‹*Kind, Familie usw.*›

depth /depθ/ *n.* Tiefe, *die;* **in** ~: gründlich; **in the** ~**s of winter** im tiefsten Winter

'depth charge *n.* Wasserbombe, *die*

deputation /depjʊ'teɪʃn/ *n.* Abordnung, *die*

deputize /'depjʊtaɪz/ *v.i.* ~ **for sb.** jmdn. vertreten

deputy /'depjʊtɪ/ *n.* [Stell]vertreter, *der*/-vertreterin, *die; attrib.* stellvertretend

derail /dɪ'reɪl/ *v.t.* **be** ~**ed** entgleisen

de'railment *n.* Entgleisung, *die*

deranged /dɪ'reɪndʒd/ *adj.* [mentally] ~: geistesgestört

deregulate /diː'regjʊleɪt/ *v.t.* deregulieren (fachspr.); dem freien Wettbewerb überlassen

deregulation /diːregjʊ'leɪʃn/ *n.* Deregulation, *die* (fachspr.); Deregulierung, *die* (fachspr.)

derelict /'derɪlɪkt/ **1** *adj.* verlassen und verfallen
2 *n.* Ausgestoßene, *der*/*die*

deride /dɪˈraɪd/ v.t. sich lustig machen über (+ Akk.)

derision /dɪˈrɪʒn/ n. Spott, der

derisive /dɪˈraɪsɪv/ adj. (ironical) spöttisch; (scoffing) verächtlich

derisory /dɪˈraɪzərɪ/ adj. (ridiculously inadequate) lächerlich

derivation /derɪˈveɪʃn/ n. Ableitung, die

derivative /dɪˈrɪvətɪv/ [1] adj. abgeleitet; (lacking originality) nachahmend
[2] n. Ableitung, die

derive /dɪˈraɪv/ [1] v.t. ~ sth. from sth. etw. aus etw. gewinnen; ~ **pleasure from sth.** Freude an etw. (Dat.) haben
[2] v.i. ~ **from** beruhen auf (+ Dat.)

derogatory /dɪˈrɒgətərɪ/ adj. abfällig

derrick /ˈderɪk/ n. [Derrick]kran, der

derv /dɜːv/ n. Diesel[kraftstoff], der

descale /diːˈskeɪl/ v.t. entkalken

descend /dɪˈsend/ [1] v.i. (a) (go down) hinuntergehen/-steigen/-klettern/-fahren; (come down) herunterkommen; ⟨Fallschirm, Flugzeug:⟩ niedergehen
(b) (slope downwards) abfallen
(c) ~ **on sb.** jmdn. überfallen
[2] v.t. (go/come down) hinunter-/heruntergehen/-steigen/-klettern/-fahren

descendant /dɪˈsendənt/ n. Nachkomme, der

de'scended adj. be ~ **from sb.** von jmdm. abstammen

descent /dɪˈsent/ n. (a) Abstieg, der; (of parachute, plane) Niedergehen, das
(b) (lineage) Herkunft, die; **be of Russian** ~: russischer Abstammung sein

describe /dɪˈskraɪb/ v.t. beschreiben

description /dɪˈskrɪpʃn/ n. (a) Beschreibung, die
(b) (sort, class) Art, die

descriptive /dɪˈskrɪptɪv/ adj. beschreibend; (vivid) anschaulich; **a purely** ~ **report** ein reiner Tatsachenbericht

desecrate /ˈdesɪkreɪt/ v.t. entweihen

desert¹ /ˈdezət/ n. Wüste, die

desert² /dɪˈzɜːt/ [1] v.t. verlassen
[2] v.i. ⟨Soldat:⟩ desertieren

de'serted adj. verlassen

de'serter n. Deserteur, der

desertion /dɪˈzɜːʃn/ n. Desertion, die

desert 'island /dezət ˈaɪlənd/ n. einsame Insel

deserts /dɪˈzɜːts/ n. pl. **get one's [just]** ~: das bekommen, was man verdient hat

deserve /dɪˈzɜːv/ v.t. verdienen

deserving /dɪˈzɜːvɪŋ/ adj. verdienstvoll; **a** ~ **cause** ein guter Zweck

design /dɪˈzaɪn/ [1] n. Entwurf, der; (pattern) Muster, das; (established form of machine, engine, etc.) Bauweise, die; (general idea, construction) Konstruktion, die
[2] v.t. entwerfen; **be** ~**ed to do sth.** etw. tun sollen

designate /ˈdezɪgneɪt/ v.t. (a) bezeichnen
(b) (appoint) designieren (geh.)

designation /dezɪgˈneɪʃn/ n. Bezeichnung, die

'**designer** n. Designer, der/Designerin, die; (of machines) Konstrukteur, der/Konstrukteurin, die; attrib. Modell‹-kleidung, -jeans›

desirability /dɪzaɪərəˈbɪlɪtɪ/ n. Wunschbarkeit, die

desirable /dɪˈzaɪərəbl/ adj. wünschenswert

desire /dɪˈzaɪə(r)/ [1] n. Wunsch, der (for nach); (longing) Sehnsucht, die (for nach)
[2] v.t. sich (Dat.) wünschen; (long for) sich sehnen nach

desist /dɪˈzɪst/ v.i. (literary) einhalten (geh.); ~ **from sth.** von etw. ablassen (geh.)

desk /desk/ n. (a) Schreibtisch, der; (in school) Tisch, der
(b) (cash ~) Kasse, die; (reception ~) Rezeption, die

desk: **~-bound** adj. an den Schreibtisch gefesselt (fig.); ~ **calendar,** ~ **diary** ns. Tischkalender, der; ~ **editor** n. Manuskriptbearbeiter, der/-bearbeiterin, die; Lektor, der/Lektorin, die; ~ **lamp** n. Schreibtischlampe, die; ~**top** adj. ~**top publishing** Desktoppublishing, das; ~**top computer** Tischcomputer, der

desolate /ˈdesələt/ adj. trostlos

desolation /desəˈleɪʃn/ n. Trostlosigkeit, die

despair /dɪˈspeə(r)/ [1] n. Verzweiflung, die; **be the** ~ **of sb.** jmdn. zur Verzweiflung bringen
[2] v.i. verzweifeln

desperate /ˈdespərət/ adj. verzweifelt; extrem ⟨Maßnahmen⟩; **be** ~ **for sth.** etw. dringend brauchen

desperation /despəˈreɪʃn/ n. Verzweiflung, die

despicable /dɪˈspɪkəbl/ adj. verabscheuungswürdig

despise /dɪˈspaɪz/ v.t. verachten

despite /dɪˈspaɪt/ prep. trotz

despondent /dɪˈspɒndənt/ adj. bedrückt

despot /ˈdespɒt/ n. Despot, der

dessert /dɪˈzɜːt/ n. Nachtisch, der

dessert: **~spoon** n. Esslöffel, der; ~**spoonful** n. Esslöffel, der; ~ **wine** n. Dessertwein, der

destabilize /diːˈsteɪbɪlaɪz/ v.t. (Polit.) destabilisieren

destination /destɪˈneɪʃn/ n. Reiseziel, das; (of goods) Bestimmungsort, der; (of train, bus) Zielort, der

destine /ˈdestɪn/ v.t. bestimmen; **be** ~**d to do sth.** dazu bestimmt sein, etw. zu tun

destiny /ˈdestɪnɪ/ n. Schicksal, das

destitute /ˈdestɪtjuːt/ adj. mittellos

destroy /dɪˈstrɔɪ/ v.t. zerstören

de'stroyer n. (also Naut.) Zerstörer, der

destruction /dɪ'strʌkʃn/ *n.* Zerstörung, *die*

destructive /dɪ'strʌktɪv/ *adj.* zerstörerisch; verheerend ⟨*Sturm, Feuer*⟩

desultory /'desəltərɪ/ *adj.* sprunghaft; zwanglos, ungezwungen ⟨*Gespräch*⟩

detach /dɪ'tætʃ/ *v.t.* entfernen; abnehmen ⟨*wieder zu Befestigendes*⟩; herausnehmen ⟨*innen Befindliches*⟩

detachable /dɪ'tætʃəbl/ *adj.* abnehmbar

detached /dɪ'tætʃt/ *adj.* **(a)** (impartial) unvoreingenommen; (unemotional) unbeteiligt **(b)** a ~ house ein Einzelhaus

de'tachment *n.* **(a)** ▶ DETACH: Entfernen, *das;* Abnehmen, *das;* Herausnehmen, *das* **(b)** (Mil.) Abteilung, *die*

detail /'diːteɪl/ ① *n.* Einzelheit, *die;* Detail, *das;* in ~: Punkt für Punkt; **go into** ~[s] ins Detail gehen
② *v.t.* **(a)** einzeln ausführen **(b)** (Mil.) abkommandieren

detailed /'diːteɪld/ *adj.* detailliert; eingehend ⟨*Studie*⟩

detain /dɪ'teɪn/ *v.t.* **(a)** festhalten; (take into confinement) verhaften **(b)** (delay) aufhalten

detainee /diːteɪ'niː/ *n.* Verhaftete, *der/die*

detect /dɪ'tekt/ *v.t.* entdecken; wahrnehmen ⟨*Bewegung*⟩; aufdecken ⟨*Irrtum, Verbrechen*⟩

detection /dɪ'tekʃn/ *n.* Entdeckung, *die;* (of error, crime) Aufdeckung, *die*

detective /dɪ'tektɪv/ *n.* Detektiv, *der;* **private** ~: Privatdetektiv, *der;* ~ **work** Ermittlungsarbeit, *die;* ~ **story** Detektivgeschichte, *die*

detector /dɪ'tektə(r)/ *n.* Detektor, *der*

detention /dɪ'tenʃn/ *n.* **(a)** Festnahme, *die;* (confinement) Haft, *die* **(b)** (Sch.) Nachsitzen, *das*

de'tention centre *n.* (Brit.) Jugendstrafanstalt, *die*

deter /dɪ'tɜː(r)/ *v.t.,* **-rr-** abschrecken

detergent /dɪ'tɜːdʒənt/ *n.* Waschmittel, *das*

deteriorate /dɪ'tɪərɪəreɪt/ *v.i.* sich verschlechtern; ⟨*Haus:*⟩ verfallen

deterioration /dɪtɪərɪə'reɪʃn/ *n.* ▶ DETERIORATE: Verschlechterung, *die;* Verfall, *der*

determination /dɪtɜːmɪ'neɪʃn/ *n.* Entschlossenheit, *die*

determine /dɪ'tɜːmɪn/ *v.t.* **(a)** (decide) beschließen **(b)** (be a decisive factor for) bestimmen **(c)** (ascertain) feststellen

determined /dɪ'tɜːmɪnd/ *adj.* **(a)** be ~ **to do sth.** etw. unbedingt tun wollen **(b)** (resolute) entschlossen

deterrent /dɪ'terənt/ *n.* Abschreckungsmittel, *das* **(to** für)

detest /dɪ'test/ *v.t.* verabscheuen

detestable /dɪ'testəbl/ *adj.* verabscheuenswert

detonate /'detəneɪt/ ① *v.t.* zünden ② *v.i.* detonieren

detonation /detə'neɪʃn/ *n.* Detonation, *die*

detonator /'detəneɪtə(r)/ *n.* Sprengkapsel, *die*

detour /'diːtʊə(r)/ *n.* Umweg, *der;* (diversion) Umleitung, *die*

detoxify /diː'tɒksɪfaɪ/ *v.t.* entgiften; unschädlich machen ⟨*Gift usw.*⟩

detract /dɪ'trækt/ *v.i.* ~ **from sth.** etw. beeinträchtigen

detriment /'detrɪmənt/ *n.* **to the** ~ **of sth.** zum Nachteil einer Sache (Gen.)

detrimental /detrɪ'mentl/ *adj.* schädlich; **be** ~ **to sth.** einer Sache (Dat.) schaden

deuce /djuːs/ *n.* (Tennis) Einstand, *der*

devaluation /diːvæljuː'eɪʃn/ *n.* Abwertung, *die*

devalue /diː'væljuː/ *v.t.* abwerten

devastate /'devəsteɪt/ *v.t.* verwüsten; (fig.) niederschmettern

devastating /'devəsteɪtɪŋ/ *adj.* verheerend; (fig.) niederschmetternd

devastation /devə'steɪʃn/ *n.* Verwüstung, *die*

develop /dɪ'veləp/ ① *v.t.* entwickeln; erschließen ⟨*natürliche Ressourcen*⟩; bekommen ⟨*Krankheit, Fieber, Lust*⟩; ~ **a taste for sth.** Geschmack an etw. (Akk.) finden
② *v.i.* sich entwickeln (**from** aus; **into** zu)

de'veloper *n.* **(a)** (Photog.) Entwickler, *der* **(b)** (of land) Bauunternehmer, *der*

developing: ~ **country** *n.* Entwicklungsland, *das;* ~ **world** *n.* Entwicklungsländer *Pl.*

de'velopment *n.* Entwicklung, *die* (**from** aus; **into** zu); (of natural resources etc.) Erschließung, *die*

de'velopment area *n.* (Brit.) Entwicklungsgebiet, *das*

deviant /'diːvɪənt/ *adj.* abweichend

deviate /'diːvɪeɪt/ *v.i.* abweichen

deviation /diːvɪ'eɪʃn/ *n.* Abweichung, *die*

device /dɪ'vaɪs/ *n.* Gerät, *das;* (as part of sth.) Vorrichtung, *die;* **leave sb. to his own** ~s jmdn. sich (Dat.) selbst überlassen

devil /'devl/ *n.* Teufel, *der;* **the D**~: der Teufel

'devilish *adj.* teuflisch

devious /'diːvɪəs/ *adj.* **(a)** (winding) verschlungen; ~ **route** Umweg, *der* **(b)** (unscrupulous, insincere) hinterhältig

devise /dɪ'vaɪz/ *v.t.* entwerfen; schmieden ⟨*Pläne*⟩

devoid /dɪ'vɔɪd/ *adj.* ~ **of sth.** (lacking) ohne etw.; (free from) frei von etw.

devolution /diːvə'luːʃn/ *n.* (Polit.) Dezentralisierung, *die*

devote /dɪ'vəʊt/ *v.t.* widmen (**to** Dat.)

de'voted adj. treu; aufrichtig ⟨Freundschaft, Liebe, Verehrung⟩; be ∼ to sb. jmdn. innig lieben

devotion /dɪ'vəʊʃn/ n. ∼ to sb./sth. Hingabe an jmdn./etw.

devour /dɪ'vaʊə(r)/ v.t. verschlingen

devout /dɪ'vaʊt/ adj. fromm

dew /dju:/ n. Tau, der

'dewdrop n. Tautropfen, der

dexterity /dek'sterɪtɪ/ n. Geschicklichkeit, die

dextrous /'dekstrəs/ adj. geschickt

diabetes /daɪə'bi:ti:z/ n. Zuckerkrankheit, die

diabetic /daɪə'betɪk/ 1 adj. zuckerkrank ⟨Person⟩
2 n. Diabetiker, der/Diabetikerin, die

diabolical /daɪə'bɒlɪkl/ adj. teuflisch

diagnose /daɪəg'nəʊz/ v.t. diagnostizieren; feststellen ⟨Fehler⟩

diagnosis /daɪəg'nəʊsɪs/ n., pl. **diagnoses** /daɪəg'nəʊsi:z/ Diagnose, die; make a ∼: eine Diagnose stellen

diagonal /daɪ'ægənl/ 1 adj. diagonal
2 n. Diagonale, die

di'agonally adv. diagonal

diagram /'daɪəgræm/ n. Diagramm, das

dial /'daɪəl/ 1 n. (of clock or watch) Zifferblatt, das; (of gauge, meter, etc.) Skala, die; (Teleph.) Wählscheibe, die
2 v.t. & i., (Brit.) -ll- (Teleph.) wählen; ∼ direct selbst wählen; (dial extension) durchwählen

dialect /'daɪəlekt/ n. Dialekt, der

dialling, (Amer.) **dialing:** ∼ **code** n. Vorwahl, die; ∼ **tone** Wählton, der

dialogue /'daɪəlɒg/ n. Dialog, der

'dialogue box n. (Comp.) Dialogbox, die; Dialogfenster, das

'dial tone n. (Amer.) Wählton, der

dialysis /daɪ'ælɪsɪs/ n. [Hämo]dialyse, die (fachspr.); Blutwäsche, die; ∼ **machine** Dialyseapparat, der

diameter /daɪ'æmɪtə(r)/ n. Durchmesser, der

diametrical /daɪə'metrɪkl/ adj., **dia'metrically** adv. diametral

diamond /'daɪəmənd/ n. (a) Diamant, der
(b) (figure) Raute, die
(c) (Cards) Karo, das; see also CLUB 1c

diaper /'daɪəpə(r)/ n. (Amer.) Windel, die

diaphragm /'daɪəfræm/ n. Diaphragma, das (Fachspr.); ⟨Anat. also⟩ Zwerchfell, das; ⟨Photog. also⟩ Blende, die

diarrhoea ⟨Amer.: **diarrhea**⟩ /daɪə'ri:ə/ n. Durchfall, der

diary /'daɪərɪ/ n. (a) Tagebuch, das
(b) (for appointments) Terminkalender, der

dice /daɪs/ 1 n. Würfel, der
2 v.t. (Cooking) würfeln

dicey /'daɪsɪ/ adj. (coll.) riskant

Dictaphone ® /'dɪktəfəʊn/ n. Diktaphon, das (fachspr.); Diktiergerät, das

dictate /dɪk'teɪt/ v.t. & i. diktieren; (prescribe) vorschreiben; ∼ to Vorschriften machen (+ Dat.)

dic'tating machine n. Diktiergerät, das

dictation /dɪk'teɪʃn/ n. Diktat, das

dictator /dɪk'teɪtə(r)/ n. Diktator, der

dictatorial /dɪktə'tɔ:rɪəl/ adj. diktatorisch

dic'tatorship n. Diktatur, die

dictionary /'dɪkʃənərɪ/ n. Wörterbuch, das

did ▶ DO

diddle /'dɪdl/ v.t. (coll.) übers Ohr hauen (ugs.)

didn't /'dɪdnt/ (coll.) = did not; ▶ DO

die /daɪ/ v.i., **dying** /'daɪɪŋ/ sterben (of, from an + Dat.); ⟨Tier, Pflanze:⟩ eingehen; be dying to do sth. darauf brennen, etw. zu tun; be dying for sth. etw. unbedingt brauchen
■ **die 'down** v.i. ⟨Sturm, Wind, Protest:⟩ sich legen; ⟨Flammen:⟩ kleiner werden; ⟨Feuer:⟩ herunterbrennen; ⟨Lärm:⟩ leiser werden
■ **die 'out** v.i. aussterben

'diehard n. Ewiggestrige, der/die

diesel /'di:zl/ n. ∼ **[engine]** Diesel[motor], der; ∼ **[fuel]** Diesel[kraftstoff], der

diet /'daɪət/ 1 n. Diät, die; be/go on a ∼: eine Schlankheitskur machen
2 v.i. eine Schlankheitskur machen

'diet sheet n. Diätplan, der

differ /'dɪfə(r)/ v.i. (be different) sich unterscheiden

difference /'dɪfərəns/ n. (a) Unterschied, der; make no ∼ [to sb.] [jmdm.] nichts ausmachen; it makes a ∼: es ist ein od. (ugs.) macht einen Unterschied
(b) (disagreement) Meinungsverschiedenheit, die

different /'dɪfərənt/ adj. verschieden; ⟨pred. also⟩ anders; ⟨attrib. also⟩ ander...; be ∼ from or (esp. Brit.) to or (Amer.) than ...: anders sein als ...

differentiate /dɪfə'renʃɪeɪt/ v.t. & i. unterscheiden (between zwischen + Dat.)

'differently adv. anders (from, esp. Brit. to als)

difficult /'dɪfɪkəlt/ adj. schwierig

'difficulty n. Schwierigkeit, die; with [great] ∼: [sehr] mühsam; get into difficulties in Schwierigkeiten kommen

diffident /'dɪfɪdənt/ adj. zaghaft; (modest) zurückhaltend

diffuse 1 /dɪ'fju:z/ v.t. verbreiten
2 v.i. sich ausbreiten (through in + Dat.)
3 /dɪ'fju:s/ adj. diffus

dig /dɪg/ 1 v.i., **-gg-**, dug /dʌg/ graben (for nach)
2 v.t., **-gg-**, dug graben; umgraben ⟨Erde, Garten⟩
■ **dig 'out** v.t. ausgraben

■ **dig 'up** v.t. ausgraben; umgraben ⟨*Garten*⟩; aufreißen ⟨*Straße*⟩

digest /dɪ'dʒest, daɪ'dʒest/ v.t. verdauen

digestion /dɪ'dʒestʃn, daɪ'dʒestʃn/ n. Verdauung, *die*

'digger n. Bagger, *der*

digit /'dɪdʒɪt/ n. Ziffer, *die*

digital /'dɪdʒɪtl/ adj. Digital-; ∼ **audio tape** Digitaltonband, *das;* ∼ **camera** Digitalkamera, *die;* ∼ **television** Digitalfernsehen, *das;* ∼ **video disc** DVD, *die;* Digital Video Disc, *die*

dignified /'dɪgnɪfaɪd/ adj. würdig; (stately) würdevoll

dignify /'dɪgnɪfaɪ/ v.t. Würde verleihen (+ *Dat.*)

dignitary /'dɪgnɪtərɪ/ n. Würdenträger, *der;* dignitaries (prominent people) Honoratioren *Pl.*

dignity /'dɪgnɪtɪ/ n. Würde, *die*

digress /daɪ'gres/ v.i. abschweifen

digression /daɪ'greʃn/ n. Abschweifung, *die*

dike /daɪk/ n. Deich, *der*

dilapidated /dɪ'læpɪdeɪtɪd/ adj. verfallen ⟨*Gebäude*⟩; verwahrlost ⟨*Erscheinung*⟩

dilate /daɪ'leɪt/ [1] v.i. sich weiten [2] v.t. ausdehnen

dilemma /dɪ'lemə, daɪ'lemə/ n. Dilemma, *das*

diligence /'dɪlɪdʒəns/ n. Fleiß, *der*

diligent /'dɪlɪdʒənt/ adj., **'diligently** adv. fleißig

dilute [1] /daɪ'lju:t, 'daɪlju:t/ adj. verdünnt [2] /daɪ'lju:t/ v.t. verdünnen

dim /dɪm/ [1] adj. (a) schwach ⟨*Licht, Flackern*⟩; dunkel ⟨*Zimmer*⟩; verschwommen ⟨*Gestalt*⟩ (b) (vague) verschwommen (c) (coll.: stupid) beschränkt [2] v.i. schwächer werden

dime /daɪm/ n. (Amer. coll.) Zehncentstück, *das*

dimension /dɪ'menʃn, daɪ'menʃn/ n. Dimension, *die;* ∼s (measurements) Abmessungen; Maße

diminish /dɪ'mɪnɪʃ/ [1] v.i. nachlassen; ⟨*Vorräte, Einfluss:*⟩ abnehmen; ⟨*Wert, Ansehen:*⟩ geringer werden [2] v.t. verringern; schmälern ⟨*Ansehen, Ruf*⟩

dimple /'dɪmpl/ n. Grübchen, *das*

dim: ∼**wit** n. (coll.) Dummkopf, *der* (ugs.); ∼**-witted** /'dɪmwɪtɪd/ adj. (coll.) dusselig (salopp)

din /dɪn/ n. Lärm, *der*

dine /daɪn/ v.i. [zu Mittag/zu Abend] essen

'diner n. Gast, *der*

dinghy /'dɪŋgɪ, 'dɪŋɪ/ n. Ding[h]i, *das;* (inflatable) Schlauchboot, *das*

dingy /'dɪndʒɪ/ adj. schmuddelig

dining /'daɪnɪŋ/**:** ∼ **area** n. ≈ Essecke,

die; ∼ **car** n. Speisewagen, *der;* ∼ **room** n. Esszimmer, *das;* (in hotel etc.) Speisesaal, *der;* ∼ **table** n. Esstisch, *der*

dinner /'dɪnə(r)/ n. (at midday) Mittagessen, *das;* (in the evening) Abendessen, *das;* (formal) Diner, *das*

dinner: ∼ **jacket** n. (Brit.) Dinnerjacket, *das;* ∼ **party** n. Abendeinladung, *das* (*mit Essen*); (more formal) Abendgesellschaft, *die;* ∼ **plate** n. flacher Teller; Essteller, *der;* ∼ **table** n. Esstisch, *der;* ∼ **time** n. Essenszeit, *die;* at ∼ time zur Essenszeit; (12-2 p.m.) mittags

dinosaur /'daɪnəsɔ:(r)/ n. Dinosaurier, *der*

dint /dɪnt/ n. by ∼ of durch; by ∼ of doing sth. indem jmd. etw. tut

dip /dɪp/ [1] v.t., -pp-: (a) [ein]tauchen (in in + *Akk.*) (b) ∼ one's headlights abblenden [2] v.i. sinken; (incline) abfallen [3] n. (a) (in road) Senke, *die* (b) (bathe) [kurzes] Bad

diphtheria /dɪf'θɪərɪə/ n. Diphtherie, *die*

diphthong /'dɪfθɒŋ/ n. Diphthong, *der*

diploma /dɪ'pləʊmə/ n. Diplom, *das*

diplomacy /dɪ'pləʊməsɪ/ n. Diplomatie, *die*

diplomat /'dɪpləmæt/ n. Diplomat, *der/* Diplomatin, *die*

diplomatic /dɪplə'mætɪk/ adj., **diplo'matically** adv. diplomatisch

diplo'matic service n. diplomatischer Dienst

'dipstick n. (Öl-/Benzin]messstab, *der*

dire /'daɪə(r)/ adj. furchtbar

direct /dɪ'rekt, daɪ'rekt/ [1] v.t. (a) (turn) richten (to[wards] auf + *Akk.*); ∼ sb. to a place jmdn. den Weg zu einem Ort weisen (b) (control) leiten; regeln ⟨*Verkehr*⟩ (c) (order) anweisen (d) (Theatre, Cinemat., etc.) Regie führen bei [2] adj. direkt; durchgehend ⟨*Zug*⟩; unmittelbar ⟨*Ursache, Auswirkung, Erfahrung, Verantwortung*⟩; genau ⟨*Gegenteil*⟩; direkt ⟨*Widerspruch*⟩; diametral ⟨*Gegensatz*⟩; ∼ speech direkte Rede [3] adv. direkt

direct: ∼ **'current** n. (Electr.) Gleichstrom, *der;* ∼ **'debit** n. (Brit.) Lastschriftverfahren, *das;* ∼ **'dialling** n. Durchwahl, *die;* we will soon have ∼ dialling wir werden bald ein Durchwahlsystem haben; ∼ **'flight** n. Direktflug, *der;* ∼ **'hit** n. Volltreffer, *der*

direction /dɪ'rekʃn, daɪ'rekʃn/ n. (a) Richtung, *die;* in the ∼ of London in Richtung London (b) (guidance) Führung, *die;* (Theatre, Cinemat., etc.) Regie, *die;* Spielleitung, *die* (c) usu. in pl. (order) Anordnung, *die;* ∼s [for use] Gebrauchsanweisung, *die*

di'rectly adv. (a) direkt; unmittelbar ⟨*folgen, verantwortlich sein*⟩ ⋯▸

(b) (exactly) genau
(c) (at once) umgehend
(d) (shortly) gleich
di'rect object *n.* direktes Objekt
director /daɪ'rektə(r), dɪ'rektə(r)/ *n.* **(a)**
(Commerc.) Direktor, *der*/Direktorin, *die;*
board of ∼s Aufsichtsrat, *der*
(b) (Theatre, Cinemat., etc.) Regisseur, *der*/
Regisseurin, *die*
directory /daɪ'rektərɪ, dɪ'rektərɪ/ *n.*
(telephone ∼) Telefonbuch, *das;* (of tradesmen
etc.) Branchenverzeichnis, *das;* (Comp.)
Verzeichnis, *das;* ∼ **enquiries** (Brit.),
∼ **information** (Amer.) [Fernsprech]auskunft,
die
dirt /dɜːt/ *n.* Schmutz, *der;* ∼ **cheap** (coll.)
spottbillig
'dirty ①︎ *adj.* schmutzig; **get sth.** ∼: etw.
schmutzig machen
②︎ *v.t.* schmutzig machen
disa'bility *n.* Behinderung, *die*
disa'bility allowance *n.*
Erwerbsunfähigkeitsentschädigung, *die*
disabled /dɪs'eɪbld/ *adj.* behindert
disad'vantage *n.* Nachteil, *der;* **at a** ∼: im
Nachteil
disad'vantaged *adj.* benachteiligt
disa'gree *v.i.* anderer Meinung sein;
∼ **with sb.**/**sth.** mit jmdm./etw. nicht
übereinstimmen; ∼ [**with sb.**] **about** *or* **over**
sth. sich [mit jmdm.] über etw. (*Akk.*) nicht
einig sein
disa'greeable *adj.* unangenehm
disa'greement *n.* **(a)** (difference of opinion)
Uneinigkeit, *die;* **be in** ∼ **with sb.**/**sth.** mit
jmdm./etw. nicht übereinstimmen
(b) (quarrel) Meinungsverschiedenheit, *die*
(c) (discrepancy) Diskrepanz, *die*
disal'low *v.t.* verbieten; (Sport) nicht geben
⟨Tor⟩
disap'pear *v.i.* verschwinden; ⟨Brauch,
Tierart:⟩ aussterben
disap'pearance *n.* Verschwinden, *das*
disap'point *v.t.* enttäuschen
disap'pointed *adj.* enttäuscht
disap'pointing *adj.* enttäuschend
disap'pointment *n.* Enttäuschung, *die*
disap'proval *n.* Missbilligung, *die*
disap'prove *v.i.* dagegen sein; ∼ **of sb.**/
sth. jmdn. ablehnen/etw. missbilligen
dis'arm *v.t.* entwaffnen
disarmament /dɪs'ɑːməmənt/ *n.*
Abrüstung, *die*
disarray /dɪsə'reɪ/ *n.* Unordnung, *die;* **in** ∼:
in Unordnung
disaster /dɪ'zɑːstə(r)/ *n.* Katastrophe, *die;*
∼ **area** Katastrophengebiet, *das;* ∼ **fund**
Nothilfefonds, *der*
disastrous /dɪ'zɑːstrəs/ *adj.* katastrophal;
verhängnisvoll ⟨Irrtum, Entscheidung,
Politik⟩
dis'band ①︎ *v.t.* auflösen

②︎ *v.i.* sich auflösen
disbe'lief *n.* Unglaube, *der;* **in** ∼: ungläubig
disbe'lieve *v.t.* ∼ **sb.**/**sth.** jmdm./etw. nicht
glauben
disc /dɪsk/ *n.* **(a)** Scheibe, *die;* (record) Platte,
die
(b) (Comp.) ▶ DISK A
discard /dɪs'kɑːd/ *v.t.* wegwerfen;
fallenlassen ⟨Vorschlag, Idee⟩
'disc brake *n.* Scheibenbremse, *die*
discern /dɪ'sɜːn/ *v.t.* wahrnehmen
discernible /dɪ'sɜːnɪbl/ *adj.* erkennbar
di'scerning *adj.* kritisch
discharge ①︎ /dɪs'tʃɑːdʒ/ *v.t.* **(a)** entlassen
(from aus); freisprechen ⟨Angeklagte⟩
(b) ablassen ⟨Flüssigkeit, Gas⟩
②︎ /'dɪstʃɑːdʒ/ *n.* **(a)** Entlassung, *die* (from
aus); (of defendant) Freispruch, *der*
(b) (emission) Ausfluss, *der*
disciple /dɪ'saɪpl/ *n.* **(a)** (Relig.) Jünger, *der*
(b) (follower) Anhänger, *der*/Anhängerin, *die*
disciplinary /dɪsɪ'plɪnərɪ/ *adj.*
disziplinarisch; ∼ **action**
Disziplinarmaßnahmen *Pl.*
discipline /'dɪsɪplɪn/ ①︎ *n.* Disziplin, *die*
②︎ *v.t.* disziplinieren; (punish) bestrafen
disciplined /'dɪsɪplɪnd/ *adj.* diszipliniert
'disc jockey *n.* Diskjockey, *der*
dis'claim *v.t.* abstreiten
dis'claimer *n.* Gegenerklärung, *die;* (Law)
Verzichterklärung, *die*
disclose /dɪs'kləʊz/ *v.t.* enthüllen; bekannt
geben ⟨Information, Nachricht⟩
dis'closure *n.* Enthüllung, *die;* (of
information, news) Bekanntgabe, *die*
disco /'dɪskəʊ/ *n., pl.* ∼**s** (coll.) Disko, *die*
'disco dancing *n.* Diskotanz, *der*
dis'colour (Brit.; Amer.: **discolor**) *v.t.*
verfärben
dis'comfort *n.* **(a)** *no pl.* (slight pain)
Beschwerden *Pl.*
(b) (hardship) Unannehmlichkeit, *die*
'disco music *n.* Diskomusik, *die*
disconcert /dɪskən'sɜːt/ *v.t.* irritieren
discon'nect *v.t.* abtrennen; abstellen
⟨Telefon⟩
disconsolate /dɪs'kɒnsələt/ *adj.* **(a)**
(unhappy) unglücklich
(b) (inconsolable) untröstlich
discon'tent *n.* Unzufriedenheit, *die*
discon'tented *adj.* unzufrieden
discon'tinue *v.t.* einstellen
discord /'dɪskɔːd/ *n.* **(a)** Zwietracht, *die*
(b) (Mus.) Dissonanz, *die*
discordant /dɪs'kɔːdənt/ *adj.* **(a)** (conflicting)
gegensätzlich
(b) a ∼ **note** ein Misston
discothèque /'dɪskətek/ *n.* Diskothek, *die*
discount ①︎ /'dɪskaʊnt/ *n.* (Commerc.)
Rabatt, *der* (on auf + *Akk.*)

2 /dɪ'skaʊnt/ *v.t.* (disbelieve)
unberücksichtigt lassen

discourage /dɪ'skʌrɪdʒ/ *v.t.* **(a)**
entmutigen
(b) (advise against) abraten

di'scouragement *n.* **(a)** Entmutigung,
die
(b) (depression) Mutlosigkeit, *die*

discouraging /dɪ'skʌrɪdʒɪŋ/ *adj.*
entmutigend

dis'courteous *adj.* unhöflich

dis'courtesy *n.* Unhöflichkeit, *die*

discover /dɪ'skʌvə(r)/ *v.t.* entdecken; (by
search) herausfinden

di'scovery *n.* Entdeckung, *die*

dis'credit **1** *n.* Misskredit, *der;* **bring
~ on sb./sth., bring sb./sth. into ~:** jmdn./
etw. in Misskredit bringen
2 *v.t.* in Misskredit bringen

discreet /dɪ'skri:t/ *adj.*, **di'screetly** *adv.*
diskret

discrepancy /dɪ'skrepənsɪ/ *n.*
Diskrepanz, *die*

discrepant /dɪ'skrepənt/ *adj.*
[voneinander] abweichend

discretion /dɪ'skreʃn/ *n.* (prudence)
Umsicht, *die*

discriminate /dɪ'skrɪmɪneɪt/ *v.i.* **(a)**
unterscheiden
(b) ~ against/in favour of sb. jmdn.
diskriminieren/bevorzugen

discrimination /dɪskrɪmɪ'neɪʃn/ *n.* **(a)**
Unterscheidung, *die* **(against** *Gen.*); **~ in
favour of** Bevorzugung (+ *Gen.*)

discus /'dɪskəs/ *n.* Diskus, *der*

discuss /dɪ'skʌs/ *v.t.* besprechen; (debate)
diskutieren über (+ *Akk.*)

discussion /dɪ'skʌʃn/ *n.* Gespräch, *das;*
(debate) Diskussion, *die*

disdain /dɪs'deɪn/ **1** *n.* Verachtung, *die*
2 *v.t.* verachten; **~ to do sth.** zu stolz sein,
etw. zu tun

disdainful /dɪs'deɪnfl/ *adj.* verächtlich

disease /dɪ'zi:z/ *n.* Krankheit, *die*

diseased /dɪ'zi:zd/ *adj.* krank

disem'bark *v.i.* von Bord gehen

disen'chant *v.t.* ernüchtern; **he became
~ed with her/it** sie/es hat ihn desillusioniert

disen'gage *v.t.* lösen (from aus, von);
~ the clutch auskuppeln

disen'tangle *v.t.* entwirren; (extricate)
befreien (from aus)

dis'figure *v.t.* entstellen

disgrace /dɪs'greɪs/ **1** *n.* Schande, *die* (to
für)
2 *v.t.* Schande machen (+ *Dat.*); **~ oneself**
sich blamieren

dis'graceful /dɪs'greɪsfl/ *adj.* skandalös;
it's ~: es ist ein Skandal

disgruntled /dɪs'grʌntld/ *adj.* verstimmt

disguise /dɪs'gaɪz/ **1** *v.t.* verkleiden
⟨*Person*⟩; verstellen ⟨*Stimme*⟩; tarnen
⟨*Gegenstand*⟩
2 *n.* Verkleidung, *die*

disgust /dɪs'gʌst/ **1** *n.* (nausea) Ekel, *der*
(at vor + *Dat.*); (revulsion) Abscheu, *der* (at
vor + *Dat.*); (indignation) Empörung, *die* (at
über + *Akk.*)
2 *v.t.* anwidern; (fill with nausea) ekeln; (fill
with indignation) empören

dis'gusted *adj.* angewidert; (nauseated)
angeekelt; (indignant) empört

dis'gusting *adj.* widerlich

dish /dɪʃ/ *n.* **(a)** Schale, *die;* (deeper)
Schüssel, *die;* ~**es** (crockery) Geschirr, *das;*
wash *or* (coll.) **do the** ~**es** Geschirr spülen
(b) (type of food) Gericht, *das*
■ **dish 'out** *v.t.* **(a)** austeilen ⟨*Essen*⟩
(b) (coll.: distribute) verteilen
■ **dish 'up** *v.t.* auftragen

'dishcloth *n.* Spültuch, *das*

dis'hearten *v.t.* entmutigen

dishevelled (*Amer.:* **disheveled**)
/dɪ'ʃevld/ *adj.* zerzaust ⟨*Haar*⟩; ungepflegt
⟨*Erscheinung*⟩

dis'honest *adj.*, **dis'honestly** *adv.*
unehrlich

dis'honesty *n.* Unehrlichkeit, *die*

dis'honour **1** *n.* Unehre, *die*
2 *v.t.* beleidigen

dishonourable /dɪs'ɒnərəbl/ *adj.*
unehrenhaft

dish: ~ rack *n.* Abtropfgestell, *das;* (in
dishwasher) Geschirrwagen, *der;* ~**washer**
n. Geschirrspülmaschine, *die*

disil'lusion **1** *v.t.* ernüchtern
2 *n.* Desillusion, *die* (with über + *Akk.*)

disil'lusionment *n.* Desillusionierung,
die

disincentive /dɪsɪn'sentɪv/ *n.* Hemmnis,
das; **act as** *or* **be a ~ to sb. to do sth.** jmdn.
davon abhalten, etw. zu tun

disin'fect *v.t.* desinfizieren

disinfectant /dɪsɪn'fektənt/ **1** *adj.*
desinfizierend
2 *n.* Desinfektionsmittel, *das*

disinformation /dɪsɪnfə'meɪʃn/ *n.*
Desinformation, *die*

disingenuous /dɪsɪn'dʒenjʊəs/ *adj.*
unaufrichtig

dis'integrate *v.i.* zerfallen

disinte'gration *n.* Zerfall, *der*

dis'interested *adj.* **(a)** (impartial)
unvoreingenommen
(b) (coll.: uninterested) desinteressiert

disjointed /dɪs'dʒɔɪntɪd/ *adj.*
unzusammenhängend

disk *n.* **(a)** (Comp.) **[floppy]** ~**:** Floppydisk,
die; Diskette, *die;* **[hard]** ~ (exchangeable)
[harte] Magnetplatte; (fixed) Festplatte, *die*
(b) ▶ DISC A

'disk drive n. (Comp.) Diskettenlaufwerk, *das*

diskette /dɪ'skɛt/ n. Diskette, *die*

dis'like ⟦1⟧ v.t. nicht mögen; ∼ **doing sth.** etw. ungern tun
⟦2⟧ n. Abneigung, *die* (**of, for** gegen); **take a** ∼ **to sb./sth.** eine Abneigung gegen jmdn./ etw. empfinden

dislocate /'dɪsləkeɪt/ v.t. ausrenken; auskugeln ⟨*Schulter, Hüfte*⟩

dis'lodge v.t. entfernen (**from** aus)

dis'loyal adj. illoyal (**to** gegenüber)

dis'loyalty n. Illoyalität, *die* (**to** gegenüber)

dismal /'dɪzməl/ adj. trist

dismantle /dɪs'mæntl/ v.t. demontieren; abbauen ⟨*Schuppen, Gerüst*⟩

dismay /dɪs'meɪ/ ⟦1⟧ v.t. bestürzen
⟦2⟧ n. Bestürzung, *die* (**at** über + *Akk.*)

dismiss /dɪs'mɪs/ v.t. entlassen; (reject) ablehnen

dismissal /dɪs'mɪsl/ n. Entlassung, *die*

dismissive /dɪs'mɪsɪv/ adj. abweisend; (disdainful) abschätzig

dis'mount v.i. absteigen

diso'bedience n. Ungehorsam, *der*

diso'bedient adj. ungehorsam

diso'bey v.t. nicht gehorchen (+ *Dat.*); nicht befolgen ⟨*Befehl*⟩

dis'order n. (a) Durcheinander, *das* (b) (Med.) Störung, *die*

dis'orderly adj. (untidy) unordentlich; ∼ **conduct** ungebührliches Benehmen

dis'organized adj. chaotisch

dis'orientated, dis'oriented adjs. desorientiert

dis'own v.t. verleugnen

disparage /dɪ'spærɪdʒ/ v.t. herabsetzen

disparaging /dɪ'spærɪdʒɪŋ/ adj. abschätzig

disparity /dɪ'spærɪtɪ/ n. Ungleichheit, *die*

dispatch /dɪ'spætʃ/ ⟦1⟧ v.t. (a) schicken (b) (kill) töten
⟦2⟧ n. Bericht, *der*

di'spatch note n. Versandanzeige, *die*

dispel /dɪ'spɛl/ v.t., -II- vertreiben; zerstreuen ⟨*Besorgnis, Befürchtung*⟩

dispensable /dɪ'spɛnsəbl/ adj. entbehrlich

dispensary /dɪ'spɛnsərɪ/ n. Apotheke, *die*

dispense /dɪ'spɛns/ v.i. ∼ **with** verzichten auf (+ *Akk.*)

dispensing 'chemist n. Apotheker, *der*/ Apothekerin, *die*

dispersal /dɪ'spɜːsl/ n. Zerstreuung, *die*

disperse /dɪ'spɜːs/ ⟦1⟧ v.t. zerstreuen
⟦2⟧ v.i. sich zerstreuen

dispirited /dɪ'spɪrɪtɪd/ adj. entmutigt

dis'place v.t. verschieben; (supplant) ersetzen

displaced 'person n. Vertriebene, *der*/ *die*

display /dɪ'spleɪ/ ⟦1⟧ v.t. (a) zeigen; ausstellen ⟨*Waren*⟩

(b) (Comp.) anzeigen
⟦2⟧ n. (a) Ausstellung, *die;* (of goods) Auslage, *die;* (ostentatious show) Zurschaustellung, *die* (b) (Comp. etc.) Display, *das;* Anzeige, *die*

dis'please v.t. ∼ **sb.** jmds. Missfallen erregen

dis'pleasure n. Missfallen, *das*

disposable /dɪ'spəʊzəbl/ adj. Wegwerf-

disposal /dɪ'spəʊzl/ n. Beseitigung, *die;* **have sth./sb. at one's** ∼: etw./jmdn. zur Verfügung haben; **be at sb.'s** ∼: jmdm. zur Verfügung stehen

dispose /dɪ'spəʊz/ v.t. ∼ **sb. to sth.** jmdn. zu etw. veranlassen; ∼ **sb. to do sth.** jmdn. dazu veranlassen, etw. zu tun
■ **di'spose of** v.t. beseitigen; (settle) erledigen

disposed /dɪ'spəʊzd/ adj. **be** ∼ **to do sth.** dazu neigen, etw. zu tun; **be well** ∼ **towards sb./sth.** jmdm. wohl gesinnt sein/einer Sache (*Dat.*) positiv gegenüberstehen

disposition /dɪspə'zɪʃn/ n. Veranlagung, *die;* (nature) Art, *die*

dis'prove v.t. widerlegen

disputable /dɪ'spjuːtəbl, 'dɪspjʊtəbl/ adj. strittig

dispute /dɪ'spjuːt/ ⟦1⟧ n. Streit, *der* (**over** um)
⟦2⟧ v.t. (a) (discuss) sich streiten über (+ *Akk.*) (b) (oppose) bestreiten

disqualifi'cation n. Ausschluss, *der;* (Sport) Disqualifikation, *die*

dis'qualify v.t. ausschließen (**from** von); (Sport) disqualifizieren

disre'gard ⟦1⟧ v.t. ignorieren
⟦2⟧ n. Missachtung, *die* (**of, for** *Gen.*); (of wishes, feelings) Gleichgültigkeit, *die* (**for, of** gegenüber)

dis'reputable adj. verrufen

disre'pute /dɪsrɪ'pjuːt/ n. Verruf, *der;* **bring sb./sth. into** ∼: jmdn./etw. in Verruf bringen

disre'spect n. Missachtung, *die;* **show** ∼ **for sb./sth.** keine Achtung vor jmdm./etw. haben

disre'spectful adj. respektlos

disrupt /dɪs'rʌpt/ v.t. stören

disruption /dɪs'rʌpʃn/ n. Störung, *die*

disruptive /dɪs'rʌptɪv/ adj. störend

dissatis'faction n. Unzufriedenheit, *die*

dis'satisfied adj. unzufrieden

dissect /dɪ'sɛkt/ v.t. sezieren

disseminate /dɪ'sɛmɪneɪt/ v.t. verbreiten

dissent /dɪ'sɛnt/ ⟦1⟧ v.i. (a) (refuse to assent) nicht zustimmen; ∼ **from sth.** mit etw. nicht übereinstimmen (b) (disagree) ∼ **from sth.** von etw. abweichen
⟦2⟧ n. Ablehnung, *die;* (from majority) Abweichung, *die*

dissertation /dɪsə'teɪʃn/ n. Dissertation, *die*

dis'service n. **do sb. a** ∼: jmdm. einen schlechten Dienst erweisen

dissident /'dɪsɪdənt/ n. Dissident, der/ Dissidentin, die

dis'similar adj. unähnlich (to Dat.)

dissociate /dɪ'səʊʃɪeɪt/ v.t. trennen; ∼ **oneself** sich distanzieren (from von)

dissolve /dɪ'zɒlv/ **1** v.t. auflösen
2 v.i. sich auflösen

dissuade /dɪ'sweɪd/ v.t. abbringen (from von)

distance /'dɪstəns/ n. (a) Entfernung, die (from zu)
(b) (way to cover) Strecke, die; from a ∼: von weitem; in/into the ∼: in der/die Ferne

'distance learning n. Fernstudium, das

distant /'dɪstənt/ adj. (a) fern; entfernt ⟨Ähnlichkeit, Verwandtschaft, Verwandte⟩
(b) (reserved) distanziert

dis'taste n. Abneigung, die (for gegen)

dis'tasteful adj. unangenehm

distend /dɪ'stend/ v.t. erweitern

distil, (Amer.) **distill** /dɪ'stɪl/ v.t. destillieren; brennen ⟨Branntwein⟩

distillation /dɪstɪ'leɪʃn/ n. Destillation, die

distillery /dɪ'stɪlərɪ/ n. Brennerei, die

distinct /dɪ'stɪŋkt/ adj. deutlich; (different) verschieden

distinction /dɪ'stɪŋkʃn/ n. Unterschied, der

distinctive /dɪ'stɪŋktɪv/ adj. unverwechselbar

dis'tinctly adv. deutlich

distinguish /dɪ'stɪŋgwɪʃ/ **1** v.t. (a) (make out) erkennen
(b) (differentiate) unterscheiden
(c) (characterize) kennzeichnen
(d) ∼ **oneself [by sth.]** sich [durch etw.] hervortun
2 v.i. unterscheiden; ∼ **between** auseinander halten

distinguished /dɪ'stɪŋgwɪʃt/ adj. angesehen; glänzend ⟨Laufbahn⟩; vornehm ⟨Aussehen⟩

distort /dɪ'stɔːt/ v.t. verzerren; (fig.) verdrehen

distortion /dɪ'stɔːʃn/ n. Verzerrung, die; (fig.) Verdrehung, die

distract /dɪ'strækt/ v.t. ablenken; ∼ **sb.['s attention from sth.]** jmdn. [von etw.] ablenken

di'stracted adj. von Sinnen nachgestellt; (mentally far away) abwesend

distraction /dɪ'strækʃn/ n. (a) (diversion) Ablenkung, die; (interruption) Störung, die
(b) **drive sb. to** ∼: jmdn. zum Wahnsinn treiben

distraught /dɪ'strɔːt/ adj. aufgelöst (with vor + Dat.); verstört ⟨Blick⟩

distress /dɪ'stres/ **1** n. (a) Kummer, der (at über + Akk.)
(b) (pain) Qualen Pl.
(c) an aircraft/ship in ∼: ein Flugzeug in Not/ein Schiff in Seenot

2 v.t. nahe gehen (+ Dat.)

di'stressing adj. erschütternd

di'stress signal n. Notsignal, das

distribute /dɪ'strɪbjuːt/ v.t. verteilen (to an + Akk.; among unter + Akk.); (Commerc.) vertreiben

distribution /dɪstrɪ'bjuːʃn/ n. Verteilung, die; (Commerc.) Vertrieb, der

distributor /dɪ'strɪbjʊtə(r)/ n. Verteiler, der/Verteilerin, die; (Commerc.) Vertreiber, der

district /'dɪstrɪkt/ n. Gegend, die; (Admin.) Bezirk, der

district: ∼ **at'torney** n. (Amer. Law) [Bezirks]staatsanwalt, der/-anwältin, die; ∼ **'nurse** n. (Brit.) Gemeindeschwester, die

dis'trust /dɪs'trʌst/ **1** n. Misstrauen, das (of gegen)
2 v.t. misstrauen (+ Dat.)

dis'trustful adj. misstrauisch

disturb /dɪ'stɜːb/ v.t. (a) stören; **'do not** ∼**!'** „bitte nicht stören!"
(b) (worry) beunruhigen

disturbance /dɪ'stɜːbəns/ n. Störung, die; **political** ∼**s** politische Unruhen

disturbed /dɪ'stɜːbd/ adj. besorgt; **[mentally]** ∼: geistig gestört

disturbing /dɪs'tɜːbɪŋ/ adj. bestürzend

disuse /dɪs'juːs/ n. **fall into** ∼: außer Gebrauch kommen

disused /dɪs'juːzd/ adj. stillgelegt; leer stehend ⟨Gebäude⟩

ditch /dɪtʃ/ **1** n. Graben, der
2 v.t. (coll.) sausen lassen ⟨Plan⟩; sitzen lassen ⟨Familie, Freund⟩

dither /'dɪðə(r)/ v.i. schwanken

ditto /'dɪtəʊ/ n., pl. ∼**s** ebenso; ditto; ∼ **marks** Unterführungszeichen, das

divan /dɪ'væn/ n. [Polster]liege, die

dive /daɪv/ **1** v.i., dived or (Amer.) dove /dəʊv/ **(a)** einen Kopfsprung machen; (when already in water) tauchen
(b) ⟨Vogel, Flugzeug usw.:⟩ einen Sturzflug machen
2 n. (a) Kopfsprung, der; (of bird, aircraft, etc.) Sturzflug, der
(b) (coll.: place) Spelunke, die

'diver n. (a) (Sport) Kunstspringer, der/-springerin, die
(b) (as profession) Taucher, der/Taucherin, die

diverge /daɪ'vɜːdʒ/ v.i. auseinander gehen

divergent /daɪ'vɜːdʒənt/ adj. auseinander gehend

diverse /daɪ'vɜːs/ adj. verschieden

diversify /daɪ'vɜːsɪfaɪ, dɪ'vɜːsɪfaɪ/ v.i. ⟨Firma:⟩ sich auf neue Produktions-/ Produktbereiche umstellen

diversion /daɪ'vɜːʃn/ n. (a) Ablenkung, die; **create a** ∼: ein Ablenkungsmanöver durchführen
(b) (Brit.: alternative route) Umleitung, die

diversity /daɪ'vɜːsɪtɪ/ n. Vielfalt, die

divert /daɪ'vɜːt/ v.t. umleiten ‹Verkehr, Fluss›; ablenken ‹Aufmerksamkeit›

divide /dɪ'vaɪd/ 🔲 v.t. (a) teilen; ~ sth. in two etw. [in zwei Teile] zerteilen

(b) (distribute) aufteilen (among/between unter + Akk. od. Dat.)

(c) (Math.) dividieren (fachspr.), teilen (by durch)

🔲 v.i. sich teilen; ~ [from sth.] von etw. abzweigen

■ **divide 'out** v.t. aufteilen (among/between unter + Akk. od. Dat.); (distribute) verteilen an (+ Akk.)

■ **divide 'up** v.t. aufteilen

dividend /'dɪvɪdend/ n. Dividende, die

dividers /dɪ'vaɪdəz/ n. pl. Stechzirkel, der

divine /dɪ'vaɪn/ adj. göttlich

diving /'daɪvɪŋ/ n. Kunstspringen, das

diving: ~ **board** n. Sprungbrett, das; ~ **suit** n. Taucheranzug, der

divinity /dɪ'vɪnɪtɪ/ n. (a) Göttlichkeit, die (b) (god) Gottheit, die

divisible /dɪ'vɪzɪbl/ adj. teilbar (by durch)

division /dɪ'vɪʒn/ n. (a) Teilung, die

(b) (Math.) Dividieren, das; do ~: dividieren; long ~: ausführliche Division (mit Aufschreiben der Zwischenprodukte); short ~: verkürzte Division (ohne Aufschreiben der Zwischenprodukte)

(c) (section, part) Abteilung, die

(d) (group) Gruppe, die

(e) (Mil. etc.) Division, die

(f) (Footb. etc.) Liga, die; Spielklasse, die; (in British football) Division, die

divorce /dɪ'vɔːs/ 🔲 n. [Ehe]scheidung, die 🔲 v.t. ~ one's husband/wife sich von seinem Mann/seiner Frau scheiden lassen

divorcee /dɪvɔː'siː/ n. Geschiedene, der/die; be a ~: geschieden sein

divorced /dɪ'vɔːst/ adj. geschieden; get ~: sich scheiden lassen

divulge /daɪ'vʌldʒ/ v.t. preisgeben

DIY abbr. = **do-it-yourself**

dizzy /'dɪzɪ/ adj. schwind[e]lig; I feel ~: mir ist schwindlig

DJ /diː'dʒeɪ/ abbr. = **disc jockey** Diskjockey, der

DNA abbr. = **deoxyribonucleic acid** DNS

do /də, stressed duː/ 🔲 v.t., neg. (coll.) **don't** /dəʊnt/, pres.t. **he does** /dʌz/, neg. (coll.) **doesn't** /'dʌznt/, p.t. **did** /dɪd/, neg. (coll.) **didn't** /'dɪdnt/, pres.p. **doing** /'duːɪŋ/, p.p. **done** /dʌn/ (a) machen ‹Hausaufgaben, Hausarbeit, Examen, Übersetzung, Kopie, Bett, Handstand›; erfüllen ‹Pflicht›; verrichten ‹Arbeit›; vorführen ‹Trick, Nummer, Tanz›; durchführen ‹Test›; schaffen ‹Pensum›; (clean) putzen; (arrange) [zurecht]machen ‹Haare›; schminken ‹Lippen, Augen, Gesicht›; machen (ugs.) ‹Nägel›; (cut) schneiden ‹Nägel›; (paint) machen (ugs.) ‹Zimmer›; streichen ‹Haus,

Möbel›; (repair) in Ordnung bringen; **do the shopping/washing-up/cleaning** einkaufen [gehen]/abwaschen/sauber machen; **what can I do for you?** (in shop) was darfs sein?; **do sth. about sth./sb.** etw. gegen etw./jmdn. unternehmen

(b) (cook) braten; **well done** durch[gebraten]

(c) (solve) lösen ‹Problem, Rätsel›; machen ‹Puzzle, Kreuzworträtsel›

(d) (coll.: swindle) reinlegen (ugs.); **do sb. out of sth.** jmdn. um etw. bringen

(e) (satisfy) zusagen (+ Dat.)

🔲 v.i., forms as 1: (a) (act) tun; **do as they do** mach es wie sie

(b) (fare) **how are you doing?** wie gehts dir?

(c) (get on) vorankommen; (in exams) abschneiden; **do well/badly at school** gut/ schlecht in der Schule sein

(d) **how do you do?** (formal) guten Tag/ Morgen/Abend!

(e) (serve purpose) es tun; (suffice) [aus]reichen; (be suitable) gehen; **that won't do** das geht nicht; **that will do!** jetzt aber genug!

🔲 v. substitute, forms as 1: **you mustn't act as he does** du darfst nicht so wie er handeln; **You went to Paris, didn't you? – Yes, I did** Du warst doch in Paris, nicht wahr? – Ja[, stimmt]; **come in, do!** komm doch herein!

🔲 v. aux. forms as 1: **I do love Greece** Griechenland gefällt mir wirklich gut; **little did he know that …:** er hatte keine Ahnung, dass …; **do you know him?** kennst du ihn?; **what does he want?** was will er?; **I don't** or **do not wish to take part** ich möchte nicht teilnehmen; **don't be so noisy!** seid [doch] nicht so laut!

🔲 n. /duː/, pl. **do's** or **dos** /duːz/ (Brit. coll.) Feier, die; Fete, die (ugs.)

■ **do a'way with** v.t. abschaffen

■ **'do for** v.t. (coll.) **do for sb.** jmdn. fertig machen (ugs.); **be done for** erledigt sein

■ **do 'in** v.t. (sl.) kaltmachen (salopp)

■ **do 'up** v.t. (a) (fasten) zumachen; binden ‹Schnürsenkel, Fliege›

(b) (wrap) einpacken

■ **'do with** v.t. **I could do with …:** ich brauche …

■ **'do without** v.t. **do without sth.** auf etw. (Akk.) verzichten

docile /'dəʊsaɪl/ adj. sanft; (submissive) unterwürfig

dock¹ /dɒk/ 🔲 n. (a) Dock, das

(b) usu. in pl. (area) Hafen, der

🔲 v.t. [ein]docken

🔲 v.i. anlegen

dock² n. (in lawcourt) Anklagebank, die; **stand/be in the ~:** ≈ auf der Anklagebank sitzen

'docker n. Hafenarbeiter, der

dock: ~**land** n. das Hafenviertel; ~**yard** n. Schiffswerft, die

doctor /'dɒktə(r)/ 🔲 n. (a) Arzt, der/Ärztin, die; **as address** Herr/Frau Doktor

(b) (holder of degree) Doktor, der

② *v.t.* (coll.) verfälschen

doctorate /'dɒktərət/ *n.* Doktorwürde, *die*

doctrine /'dɒktrɪn/ *n.* Lehre, *die*

document /'dɒkjʊmənt/ *n.* **(a)** Dokument, *das;* Urkunde, *die*
(b) (Comp.) Dokument, *das*

documentary /dɒkjʊ'mentərɪ/ ① *adj.* dokumentarisch
② *n.* (film) Dokumentarfilm, *der*

documentation /dɒkjʊmen'teɪʃn/ *n.* (material) beweiskräftige Dokumente *Pl.*

dodge /dɒdʒ/ ① *v.i.* ausweichen
② *v.t.* ausweichen (+ *Dat.*) ‹Schlag, Hindernis usw.›; entkommen (+ *Dat.*) ‹Polizei, Verfolger›
③ *n.* (trick) Trick, *der*

dodgems /'dɒdʒəmz/ *n. pl.* [Auto]skooterbahn, *die;* **have a ride/go on the ~:** Autoskooter fahren

dodgy /'dɒdʒɪ/ *adj.* (Brit. coll.) (unreliable) unsicher; (risky) gewagt

doe /dəʊ/ *n.* (deer) Damtier, *das;* (rabbit) [Kaninchen]weibchen, *das*

does /dʌz/ ▶ DO

doesn't /'dʌznt/ (coll.) = does not; ▶ DO

dog /dɒg/ ① *n.* Hund, *der*
② *v.t.,* **-gg-** verfolgen; (fig.) heimsuchen

dog: ~ **biscuit** *n.* Hundekuchen, *der;* ~ **collar** *n.* [Hunde]halsband, *das;* (joc.: clerical collar) Kollar, *das;* ~-**eared** *adj.* a ~-**eared book** ein Buch mit Eselsohren; ~-**end** *n.* (coll.) Kippe, *die* (ugs.)

dogged /'dɒgɪd/ *adj.* hartnäckig ‹Weigerung, Verurteilung›; zäh ‹Durchhaltevermögen, Ausdauer›

'dog licence *n.* Hundesteuerbescheinigung, *die*

dogma /'dɒgmə/ *n.* Dogma, *das*

dogmatic /dɒg'mætɪk/ *adj.* dogmatisch

do-gooder /du:'gʊdə(r)/ *n.* Wohltäter, *der* (iron.)

dog: ~**sbody** *n.* (Brit. coll.) Mädchen für alles; ~**'s life** *n.* a ~'s life ein Hundeleben; **give** *or* **lead sb. a** ~'s **life** jmdn. schäbig behandeln; ~'**tired** *adj.* hundemüde

doing /'du:ɪŋ/ *n.* Tun, *das*

do-it-yourself /du:ɪtjə'self/ ① *adj.* Do-it-yourself-
② *n.* Heimwerken, *das*

doldrums /'dɒldrəmz/ *n. pl.* **in the** ~ (in low spirits) niedergeschlagen; (Econ.) in einer Flaute

dole /dəʊl/ ① *n.* (coll.) **the** ~: Stempelgeld, *das* (ugs.); **be/go on the** ~: stempeln gehen (ugs.)
② *v.t.* ~ **out** [in kleinen Mengen] verteilen

doll /dɒl/ *n.* Puppe, *die*

dollar /'dɒlə(r)/ *n.* Dollar, *der*

dollar: ~ '**bill** *n.* Dollarnote, *die;* Dollarschein, *der;* ~ **sign** *n.* Dollarzeichen, *das*

dollop /'dɒləp/ *n.* (coll.) Klacks, *der* (ugs.)

'doll's house *n.* Puppenhaus, *das*

dolphin /'dɒlfɪn/ *n.* Delphin, *der*

domain /də'meɪn/ *n.* **(a)** Gebiet, *das*
(b) (Comp.) Domäne, *die;* Domain, *die;* ~ **name** Domänenname, *der*

dome /dəʊm/ *n.* Kuppel, *die*

domestic /də'mestɪk/ *adj.* **(a)** (household) häuslich; (family) familiär ‹Angelegenheit, Reibereien›
(b) (Econ.) inländisch; Binnen-
(c) ~ **animal/cat** Haustier, *das*/-katze, *die*

domesticated /də'mestɪkeɪtɪd/ *adj.* gezähmt ‹Tier›; (fig.) häuslich

domesticity /dəʊmes'tɪsɪtɪ, dɒmes'tɪsɪtɪ/ *n.* (being domestic) Häuslichkeit, *die*

domestic 'science *n.* Hauswirtschaftslehre, *die*

dominant /'dɒmɪnənt/ *adj.* vorherrschend

dominate /'dɒmɪneɪt/ *v.t.* beherrschen

domination /dɒmɪ'neɪʃn/ *n.* [Vor]herrschaft, *die* (over über + *Akk.*)

domineering /dɒmɪ'nɪərɪŋ/ *adj.* herrisch

domino /'dɒmɪnəʊ/ *n.* Domino[stein], *der;* ~**es** *sing.* (game) Domino[spiel], *das;* **play** ~**es** Domino spielen

'domino effect *n.* Dominoeffekt, *der*

don¹ /dɒn/ *v.t.* (Liter.) anlegen (geh.)

don² *n.* (Univ.) Dozent, *der*

donate /də'neɪt/ *v.t.* spenden; (on large scale) stiften

donation /də'neɪʃn/ *n.* Spende, *die* (to für); (large-scale) Stiftung, *die*

done /dʌn/ ▶ DO

donkey /'dɒŋkɪ/ *n.* Esel, *der*

donor /'dəʊnə(r)/ *n.* Spender, *der*/ Spenderin, *die*

don't /dəʊnt/ (coll.) = do not; ▶ DO

doodle /'du:dl/ *v.i.* [herum]kritzeln

doom /du:m/ ① *n.* Verhängnis, *das*
② *v.t.* verurteilen; **be** ~**ed** verloren sein; **be** ~**ed to fail** *or* **failure** zum Scheitern verurteilt sein

door /dɔ:(r)/ *n.* Tür, *die;* (of castle, barn) Tor, *das;* **out of** ~**s** im Freien; **go out of** ~**s** nach draußen gehen

door: ~**bell** *n.* Türklingel, *die;* ~**frame** *n.* Türrahmen, *der;* ~ **handle** *n.* Türklinke, *die;* ~**keeper** *n.* Pförtner, *der;* Portier, *der;* ~**knob** *n.* Türknopf, -knauf, *der;* ~**man** *n.* Portier, *der;* ~**mat** *n.* Fußmatte, *die;* ~**step** *n.* Türstufe, *die;* **on one's/the** ~**step** (fig.) vor jmds. Tür; ~**way** *n.* Eingang, *der*

dope /dəʊp/ ① *n.* **(a)** (sl.: narcotic) Stoff, *der* (salopp)
(b) (coll.: fool) Dussel, *der*
② *v.t.* dopen ‹Pferd, Athleten›

dormant /'dɔ:mənt/ *adj.* ruhend ‹Tier, Pflanze›; untätig ‹Vulkan›

dormitory /'dɔ:mɪtərɪ/ *n.* Schlafsaal, *der*

dormouse /'dɔ:maʊs/ *n., pl.* **dormice** /'dɔ:maɪs/ Haselmaus, *die*

DOS /dɒs/ abbr. (Comp.) = **disk operating system** DOS

dosage /'dəʊsɪdʒ/ n. (size of dose) Dosis, die

dose /dəʊs/ ⓵ n. Dosis, die
⓶ v.t. ~ sb. with sth. jmdm. etw. geben

dot /dɒt/ n. Punkt, der; on the ~: auf den Punkt genau

dot.com /'dɒtkɒm/ ⓵ adj. Dot-com-
⓶ n. Dot-com-Firma, die

dote /dəʊt/ v.i. ~ on sb./sth. jmdn./etw. abgöttisch lieben

'**dot matrix** n. (Comp.) Punktmatrix, die; ~ **printer** Nadeldrucker, der

dotted /'dɒtɪd/ adj. gepunktet

dotty /'dɒtɪ/ adj. (coll.) (silly) dümmlich; (feeble-minded) vertrottelt (ugs.); (absurd) blödsinnig (ugs.)

double /'dʌbl/ ⓵ adj. doppelt; ~ **bed/room** Doppelbett, das/-zimmer, das; be ~ the **height/width/length** doppelt so hoch/breit/lang sein
⓶ adv. doppelt
⓷ n. (a) Doppelte, das
(b) (twice as much) doppelt so viel; (twice as many) doppelt so viele
(c) (person) Doppelgänger, der/-gängerin, die
(d) in pl. (Tennis etc.) Doppel, das
(e) at the ~ (Mil.) im Laufschritt; (fig.) ganz schnell
⓸ v.t. verdoppeln
⓹ v.i. sich verdoppeln
■ **double 'back** v.i. kehrtmachen (ugs.).
■ **double 'up** v.i. sich krümmen (**with** vor + Dat.)

double: ~ 'agent n. Doppelagent, der/-agentin, die; **~-barrelled** (Amer.: **~-barreled**) /'dʌblbærəld/ adj. doppelläufig; **~-barrelled surname** (Brit.) Doppelname, der; ~ **'bass** n. Kontrabass, der; ~ **'bill** n. Doppelprogramm, das; **~-breasted** /dʌbl'brestɪd/ adj. zwei- od. doppelreihig; **~-breasted jacket** Zweireiher, der; **~-'check** v.t. (verify twice) zweimal kontrollieren; (verify in two ways) zweifach überprüfen; ~ **'chin** n. Doppelkinn, das; **~-click** (Comp.) ⓵ v.i. doppelklicken; ⓶ v.t. **~click sth.** auf etw. (Dat.) doppelklicken; ~ **'cream** n. Sahne mit hohem Fettgehalt; **~-'cross** v.t. ein Doppelspiel treiben mit; **~-decker** /dʌbl'dekə(r)/ n. Doppeldeckerbus, der

double entendre /du:bl ã'tãdr/ n. Zweideutigkeit, die

double: ~-'glazed adj. Doppel⟨fenster⟩; ~ **'glazing** n. Doppelverglasung, die; **~-'jointed** adj. sehr gelenkig; ~ **lesson** n. Doppelstunde, die; **~-'lock** v.t. zweimal abschließen; ~ **'meaning** ▶ DOUBLE ENTENDRE; **~-page 'spread** n. the advertisement was a **~-page spread** die Anzeige war doppelseitig; **~-'parking** n. Parken in der zweiten Reihe; ~ **'room** n. Doppelzimmer, das; ~ **'standard** n. (rule) Doppelmoral, die; **apply** or **operate a**

~ **standard** or ~ **standards** mit zweierlei Maß messen; ~ **'vision** n. Doppeltsehen, das; ~ **yellow 'lines** n. pl.: am Fahrbahnrand verlaufende gelbe Doppellinie, die ein Halteverbot signalisiert

doubly /'dʌblɪ/ adv. doppelt

doubt /daʊt/ ⓵ n. Zweifel, der (**about, as to, of** an + Dat.); **~[s]** (**about** or **as to sth./as to whether** ...] (as to future) Ungewissheit, (as to fact) Unsicherheit [über etw. (Akk.)/darüber, ob ...]; there's no ~ **that** ...: es besteht kein Zweifel daran, dass ...; **~[s]** (hesitations) Bedenken Pl. (**about** gegen); no ~ (certainly) gewiss; (probably) sicherlich
⓶ v.i. zweifeln
⓷ v.t. zweifeln an (+ Dat.); I don't ~ **that** or it ich bezweifle das nicht; I ~ **whether** or if or **that** ...: ich bezweifle, dass ...

doubtful /'daʊtfl/ adj. skeptisch ⟨Wesen⟩; ungläubig ⟨Blick⟩

doubtless /'daʊtlɪs/ adv. (a) (certainly) gewiss
(b) (probably) sicherlich

dough /dəʊ/ n. (a) Teig, der
(b) (coll.: money) Knete, die (salopp)

'**doughnut** n. [Berliner] Pfannkuchen, der

douse /daʊs/ v.t. übergießen; (extinguish) ausmachen

dove[1] /dʌv/ n. Taube, die

dove[2] /dəʊv/ ▶ DIVE 1

dovecot, dovecote /'dʌvkɒt/ n. Taubenschlag, der; **flutter the ~cots** (fig.) für einige Aufregung sorgen

dowdy /'daʊdɪ/ adj. unansehnlich; (shabby) schäbig

down[1] /daʊn/ n. (feathers) Daunen Pl.

down[2] /daʊn/ ⓵ adv. (a) (to lower place) herunter/hinunter; (in lift) abwärts
(b) (in lower place, downstairs) unten; ~ **there/here** da/hier unten; **the next floor ~:** ein Stockwerk tiefer; **be ~ with an illness** eine Krankheit haben; **be three points/games ~:** mit drei Punkten/Spielen zurückliegen
⓶ prep. herunter/hinunter; **lower ~ the river** weiter unten am Fluss; **walk ~ the hill/road** den Berg/die Straße heruntergehen; **fall ~ the stairs/steps** die Treppe/Stufen herunterstürzen; **fall ~ a hole/ditch** in ein Loch/ einen Graben fallen; **go ~ the pub** in die Kneipe gehen; **live just ~ the road** ein Stück weiter unten in der Straße wohnen; **be ~ the pub/town** in der Kneipe/Stadt sein; **I've got coffee [all] ~ my skirt** mein ganzer Rock ist voll Kaffee
⓷ v.t. (coll.) schlucken (ugs.) ⟨Getränk⟩; ~ **tools** die Arbeit niederlegen

down: ~-and-'out n. Stadtstreicher, der/-streicherin, die; **~cast** adj. niedergeschlagen; **~fall** n. Untergang, der; **~-hearted** adj. niedergeschlagen; **~hill** adv. bergab; **~load** v.t. (Comp.) herunterladen; **~market** adj. weniger anspruchsvoll; ~ **payment** n. Anzahlung, die; **~pour** n. Regenguss, der; **~right** adj.

ausgemacht; glatt ⟨*Lüge*⟩; ∼**size** 1 *v.t.* verschlanken; 2 *v.i.* abspecken; ∼**stairs** 1 /-'-/ *adv.* die Treppe hinunter⟨*gehen, -fallen, -kommen*⟩; unten ⟨*wohnen, sein*⟩; 2 /'--/ *adj.* im Erdgeschoss *nachgestellt;* ∼'**stream** *adv.* flussabwärts; ∼**to-** '**earth** *adj.* sachlich; ∼**town** *adv.* im/ (direction) ins Stadtzentrum; ∼**trodden** *adj.* unterdrückt; ∼**turn** *n.* (Econ., Commerc.) Abschwung, *der;* ∼ '**under** *adv.* (coll.) in/ (to) nach Australien/Neuseeland

downward /'daʊnwəd/ 1 *adj.* nach unten gerichtet
   2 *adv.* abwärts ⟨*sich bewegen*⟩; nach unten ⟨*sehen, gehen*⟩

downwards /'daʊnwədz/ ▶ DOWNWARD 2

dowry /'daʊrɪ/ *n.* Aussteuer, *die*

doz. *abbr.* = **dozen** Dtzd.

doze /dəʊz/ 1 *v.i.* dösen (ugs.)
   2 *n.* Nickerchen, *das* (ugs.)
■ **doze 'off** *v.i.* eindösen (ugs.)

dozen /'dʌzn/ *n.* (a) Dutzend, *das;* half a ∼: sechs
   (b) *in pl.* (coll.: many) Dutzende *Pl.*

Dr *abbr.* = **doctor** Dr.

drab /dræb/ *adj.* langweilig; trostlos ⟨*Landschaft*⟩; eintönig ⟨*Leben*⟩

draft /drɑːft/ 1 *n.* (a) (of speech) Konzept, *das;* (of treaty, bill) Entwurf, *der*
   (b) (Amer.) ▶ DRAUGHT
   2 *v.t.* entwerfen

drafty (Amer.) ▶ DRAUGHTY

drag /dræg/ 1 *v.t.,* -**gg-** schleppen; (Comp.) ziehen; ∼ **and drop** ziehen und ablegen
   2 *v.i.,* -**gg-** schleifen; (fig.: pass slowly) sich [hin]schleppen
   3 *n.* (a) (coll.) **in** ∼: in Frauenkleidung
   (b) (coll.: at cigarette) Zug, *der*
■ **drag 'down** *v.t.* nach unten ziehen; ∼ **sb. down to one's own level** (fig.) jmdn. auf sein Niveau herabziehen
■ **drag 'on** *v.i.* sich [da]hinschleppen

dragon /'drægn/ *n.* Drache, *der*

'**dragonfly** *n.* Libelle, *die*

drain /dreɪn/ 1 *n.* Abflussrohr, *das;* (underground) Kanalisationsrohr, *das;* (grating at roadside) Gully, *der;* **go down the** ∼ (fig. coll.) für die Katz sein (ugs.)
   2 *v.t.* (a) trockenlegen ⟨*Teich*⟩; entwässern ⟨*Land*⟩; ableiten ⟨*Wasser*⟩
   (b) (Cookery) abgießen ⟨*Wasser, Gemüse*⟩
   (c) austrinken ⟨*Glas*⟩
   3 *v.i.* ⟨*Flüssigkeit:*⟩ ablaufen; ⟨*Geschirr, Gemüse:*⟩ abtropfen

drainage /'dreɪnɪdʒ/ *n.* Kanalisation, *die*

'**draining board** (*Brit.;* Amer.: '**drainboard**) *n.* Abtropfbrett, *das*

'**drainpipe** *n.* Regen[abfall]rohr, *das*

drake /dreɪk/ *n.* Enterich, *der*

drama /'drɑːmə/ *n.* Drama, *das*

dramatic /drə'mætɪk/ *adj.* dramatisch

dramatist /'dræmətɪst/ *n.* Dramatiker, *der*/Dramatikerin, *die*

dramatize /'dræmətaɪz/ *v.t.* dramatisieren

drank ▶ DRINK 2

drape /dreɪp/ 1 *v.t.* drapieren
   2 *n.* (Amer.: curtain) Vorhang, *der*

'**draper** *n.* (Brit.) Textilkaufmann, *der;* ∼'s [shop] Textilgeschäft, *das*

drastic /'dræstɪk/ *adj.* drastisch

draught /drɑːft/ *n.* [Luft]zug, *der;* **there's a** ∼: es zieht

draught: ∼ '**beer** *n.* Fassbier, *das;* ∼ **board** *n.* (Brit.) Damebrett, *das;* ∼ **excluder** *n.* Abdichtvorrichtung, *die;* Zugluft-Verhinderer, *der;* ∼**proof** *adj.* winddicht

draughts /drɑːfts/ *n.* (Brit.) Damespiel, *das*

'**draughtsman** /-mən/ *n., pl.* **draughtsmen** /-mən/ Zeichner, *der*/Zeichnerin, *die*

'**draughty** *adj.* zugig

draw /drɔː/ 1 *v.t.,* drew /druː/, drawn /drɔːn/ (a) (pull) ziehen; ∼ **the curtains**/ **blinds** (close) die Vorhänge zuziehen/die Jalousien herunterlassen; ∼ **sth. towards one** etw. zu sich heranziehen
   (b) (attract) anlocken; **be** ∼**n to sb.** von jmdm. angezogen werden
   (c) (take out) herausziehen; schöpfen ⟨*Wasser*⟩; ∼ **money from the bank** Geld bei der Bank holen/abheben
   (d) beziehen ⟨*Gehalt, Rente, Arbeitslosenunterstützung*⟩
   (e) ziehen ⟨*Strich*⟩; zeichnen ⟨*geometrische Figur, Bild*⟩
   (f) ziehen ⟨*Parallele, Vergleich*⟩; herausstellen ⟨*Unterschied*⟩
   2 *v.i.* (a) drew, drawn: ∼ **to an end** zu Ende gehen
   (b) (Sport) **they drew [three-all]** sie spielten [3 : 3] unentschieden
   3 *n.* (a) (raffle) Tombola, *die*
   (b) (of lottery) Ziehung, *die*
   (c) ([result of] game) Unentschieden, *das;* **end in a** ∼: mit einem Unentschieden enden
■ **draw 'back** 1 *v.t.* zurückziehen
   2 *v.i.* zurückweichen
■ **draw 'in** *v.i.* einfahren; ⟨*Tage:*⟩ kürzer werden
■ **draw 'out** *v.i.* abfahren; ⟨*Tage:*⟩ länger werden
■ **draw 'up** 1 *v.t.* (a) aufsetzen ⟨*Vertrag*⟩; aufstellen ⟨*Liste*⟩
   (b) (pull closer) heranziehen
   2 *v.i.* [an]halten

draw: ∼**back** *n.* Nachteil, *der;* ∼**bridge** *n.* Zugbrücke, *die*

drawer /drɔː(r), 'drɔːə(r)/ *n.* Schublade, *die*

'**drawing** *n.* (sketch) Zeichnung, *die*

drawing: ∼ **board** *n.* Zeichenbrett, *das;* ∼ **pin** *n.* (Brit.) Reißzwecke, *die;* ∼ **room** *n.* Salon, *der*

drawl /drɔːl/ 1 *v.i.* gedehnt sprechen
   2 *n.* gedehntes Sprechen

drawn ▶ DRAW 1, 2

dread /dred/ [1] v.t. sich sehr fürchten vor (+ Dat.); **the ~ed day/moment** der gefürchtete Tag/Augenblick
[2] n. Angst, die

dreadful /'dredfl/ adj. schrecklich; (coll.: very bad) fürchterlich; **I feel ~** (unwell) ich fühle mich scheußlich (ugs.)

dreadfully adv. schrecklich; (coll.: very badly) fürchterlich

'**dream** /driːm/ [1] n. Traum, der; attrib. traumhaft; Traum⟨haus, -auto, -urlaub⟩; **have a ~ about sb./sth.** von jmdm./etw. träumen
[2] v.i. & t. dreamt /dremt/ or dreamed träumen

'**dreamer** n. (in sleep) Träumende, der/die; (day~) Träumer, der/Träumerin, die

dreary /'drɪərɪ/ adj. trostlos

dredge /dredʒ/ v.t. ausbaggern

'**dredger** n. Bagger, der

dregs /dregz/ n. pl. [Boden]satz, der

drench /drentʃ/ v.t. durchnässen

dress /dres/ [1] n. Kleid, das; (clothing) Kleidung, die
[2] v.t. (a) anziehen; **be well ~ed** gut gekleidet sein; **get ~ed** sich anziehen
(b) verbinden ⟨Wunde⟩
[3] v.i. sich anziehen
■ **dress 'up** v.i. sich fein machen

dress: ~ circle n. (Theatre) erster Rang; **~ designer** n. Modeschöpfer, der/-schöpferin, die

'**dresser** n. (a) Anrichte, die
(b) (Amer.) ▶ DRESSING TABLE

'**dressing** n. (a) no pl. Anziehen, das
(b) (Cookery) Dressing, das
(c) (Med.) Verband, der

dressing: ~ gown n. Bademantel, der; **~ room** n. (Sport) Umkleideraum, der; (for actor) Garderobe, die; **~ table** n. Frisierkommode, die

dress: ~maker n. Damenschneider, der/-schneiderin, die; **~making** n. Damenschneiderei, die; **~ rehearsal** n. Generalprobe, die

drew ▶ DRAW 1, 2

dribble /'drɪbl/ v.i. (a) (slobber) sabbern
(b) (Sport) dribbeln

dried /draɪd/ adj. getrocknet; **~ fruit[s]** Dörrobst, das; **~ milk** Trockenmilch, die

drier /'draɪə(r)/ n. (for hair) Trockenhaube, die; (hand-held) Föhn, der; (for laundry) [Wäsche]trockner, der

drift /drɪft/ [1] n. (a) (of snow or sand) Verwehung, die
(b) (gist) **get** or **catch the ~ of sth.** etw im Wesentlichen verstehen
[2] v.i. (a) treiben; ⟨Wolke:⟩ ziehen
(b) ⟨Sand, Schnee:⟩ zusammengeweht werden

'**driftwood** n. Treibholz, das

drill /drɪl/ [1] n. (a) (tool) Bohrer, der
(b) (Mil.: training) Drill, der
[2] v.t. & i. bohren (**for** nach)

'**drill bit** n. Bohrer, der

drink /drɪŋk/ [1] n. Getränk, das; (alcoholic) Glas, das; (not with food) Drink, der; **have a ~:** [etwas] trinken; (alcoholic) ein Glas trinken
[2] v.t. & i. **drank** /dræŋk/, **drunk** /drʌŋk/ trinken

drinkable /'drɪŋkəbl/ adj. trinkbar

'**drink-driving** n. Fahren unter Alkoholeinfluss; Alkohol am Steuer; **~ offence** Alkoholdelikt, das

drinker /'drɪŋkə(r)/ n. Trinker, der/Trinkerin, die

drinking /'drɪŋkɪŋ/: **~ fountain** n. Trinkbrunnen, der; **~ water** n. Trinkwasser, das

drip /drɪp/ [1] n. (a) Tropfen, das
(b) (coll.: feeble person) Schlappschwanz, der (salopp)
[2] v.i., -pp- tropfen; **be ~ping with water/moisture** triefend nass sein

'**drip-dry** adj. bügelfrei

'**dripping** n. (Cookery) Schmalz, das

drive /draɪv/ [1] n. (a) Fahrt, die
(b) (private road) Zufahrt, die; (entrance) (to small building) Einfahrt, die; (to large building) Auffahrt, die
(c) (energy) Tatkraft, die
(d) (Psych.) Trieb, der
(e) (Motor Veh.) **left-hand/right-hand ~:** Links-/Rechtssteuerung, die
[2] v.t., **drove** /drəʊv/, **driven** /'drɪvn/ (a) fahren
(b) treiben ⟨Tier⟩
(c) (compel to move) vertreiben (**out of, from** aus)
(d) (fig.) **~ sb. to sth.** jmdn. zu etw. treiben; **~ sb. to do sth.** or **into doing sth.** jmdn. dazu treiben, etw. zu tun
(e) (power) antreiben
[3] v.i., **drove, driven** (a) fahren; **can you ~?** kannst du Auto fahren?
(b) (go by car) mit dem [eigenen] Auto fahren
■ '**drive at** v.t. (fig.) hinauswollen auf (+ Akk.); **what are you driving at?** worauf wollen Sie hinaus?
■ **drive a'way** [1] v.i. wegfahren
[2] v.t. (a) wegfahren
(b) (chase away) vertreiben
■ **drive 'off** ▶ DRIVE AWAY
■ **drive 'on** v.i. weiterfahren
■ **drive 'up** v.i. vorfahren (**to** vor + Dat.)

'**drive-in** adj. Drive-in-; **~ cinema** or (Amer.) movie [theater] Autokino, das

drivel /'drɪvl/ n. Gefasel, das (ugs.); **talk ~:** faseln (ugs.)

driven ▶ DRIVE 2, 3

driver /'draɪvə(r)/ n. (a) Fahrer, der/Fahrerin, die; (of locomotive) Führer, der/Führerin, die; **~'s license** (Amer.) Führerschein, der
(b) (Comp.) Treiber, der

driving /'draɪvɪŋ/ [1] n. Fahren, das
[2] adj. peitschend ⟨Regen⟩

driving: ~ force n. treibende Kraft;

Triebfeder, *die; the* ∼ **force behind sth.** die treibende Kraft hinter etw.; ∼ **gloves** *n. pl.* Autohandschuhe *Pl.;* ∼ **instructor** *n.* Fahrlehrer, *der/-*lehrerin, *die;* ∼ **lesson** *n.* Fahrstunde, *die;* ∼ **licence** *n.* Führerschein, *der;* ∼ **mirror** *n.* Rückspiegel, *der;* ∼ **school** *n.* Fahrschule, *die;* ∼ **test** *n.* Fahrprüfung, *die*

drizzle /'drɪzl/ ① *n.* Nieseln, *das* ② *v.i.* **it's drizzling** es nieselt

drone /drəʊn/ ① *v.i.* (a) ⟨*Biene:*⟩ summen; ⟨*Maschine:*⟩ brummen (b) ⟨*Rezitator:*⟩ leiern ② *n.* ▶ 1: Summen, *das;* Brummen, *das;* Geleier, *das*

drool /druːl/ *v.i.* ∼ **over** eine kindische Freude haben an (+ *Dat.*)

droop /druːp/ *v.i.* herunterhängen; ⟨*Blume:*⟩ den Kopf hängen lassen

drop /drɒp/ ① *n.* (a) Tropfen, *der;* **in** ∼**s** tropfenweise (b) (decrease) Rückgang, *der* ② *v.i.,* **-pp-:** (a) (fall) (accidentally) [herunter]fallen; (deliberately) sich [hinunter]fallen lassen (b) (in amount etc.) sinken; ⟨*Preis, Wert:*⟩ sinken, fallen; ⟨*Wind:*⟩ sich legen; ⟨*Stimme:*⟩ sich senken ③ *v.t.,* **-pp-:** (a) fallen lassen; abwerfen ⟨*Bomben, Nachschub*⟩ (b) (discontinue, abandon) fallen lassen; ∼ **out of university/the course** das Studium abbrechen *od.* aufgeben (c) (omit) auslassen

■ **drop 'by, drop 'in** *v.i.* vorbeikommen
■ **drop 'off** ① *v.i.* (a) (fall off) abfallen (b) (fall asleep) einnicken ② *v.t.* absetzen ⟨*Fahrgast*⟩
■ **drop 'out** *v.i.* (a) herausfallen (of aus) (b) (withdraw) aussteigen (ugs.) (of aus); (beforehand) seine Teilnahme absagen

drop: ∼**-down menu** *n.* (Comp.) Dropdownmenü, *das;* ∼ **handlebars** *n. pl.* Rennlenker, *der;* ∼ **kick** *n.* (Football) Dropkick, *der*

droplet /'drɒplɪt/ *n.* Tröpfchen, *das*

dropout /'drɒpaʊt/ *n.* Aussteiger, *der/* Aussteigerin, *die*

dropper /'drɒpə(r)/ *n.* (esp. Med.) Tropfer, *der*

drop shot *n.* (Tennis etc.) Stoppball, *der*

drought /draʊt/ *n.* Dürre, *die*

drove ▶ DRIVE 2, 3

drown /draʊn/ ① *v.i.* ertrinken ② *v.t.* ertränken; **be** ∼**ed** ertrinken

drowse /draʊz/ *v.i.* [vor sich hin]dösen

drowsy /'draʊzɪ/ *adj.* schläfrig; (on just waking) verschlafen

drudgery /'drʌdʒərɪ/ *n.* Schufterei, *die*

drug /drʌɡ/ ① *n.* (a) (Med.) [Arznei]mittel, *das* (b) (narcotic) Droge, *die;* **be on** ∼**s** Rauschgift nehmen

② *v.t.,* **-gg-** betäuben ⟨*Person*⟩; ∼ **sb.'s food/ drink** jmds. Essen/Getränk (*Dat.*) ein Betäubungsmittel beimischen

drug: ∼ **abuse** *n.* Drogenmissbrauch, *der;* ∼ **abuser** *n.* Drogenmissbrauch Treibender/Treibende; ∼ **addict** *n.* Drogensüchtige, *der/die;* ∼ **addiction** *n.* Drogensucht, *die;* ∼ **dealer** *n.* Drogenhändler, *der/-*händlerin, *die;* Dealer, *der/*Dealerin, *die* (Drogenjargon); ∼ **peddler** ▶ DRUG DEALER; ∼**-related** *adj.* Drogen⟨*-tote, -kriminalität, -delikt, -probleme*⟩; ∼ **scene** *n.* Drogenszene, *die;* ∼**store** *n.* (Amer.) Drugstore, *der;* ∼**-taking** *n.* Drogeneinnahme, *die;* ∼ **trafficking** *n.* Drogenhandel, *der;* ∼ **test** *n.* Dopingkontrolle, *die;* Dopingtest, *der;* ∼**user** *n.* Drogenkonsument, *der/* -konsumentin, *die*

drum /drʌm/ ① *n.* (a) Trommel, *die* (b) *in pl.* (in jazz or pop) Schlagzeug, *das* (c) (container) Fass, *das* ② *v.i.* trommeln
■ **drum 'up** *v.i.* auftreiben

'drum beat *n.* Trommelschlag, *der*

'drummer *n.* Schlagzeuger, *der*

'drumstick *n.* (a) Trommelschlägel, *der* (b) (Cookery) Keule, *die*

drunk /drʌŋk/ ① *adj.* **be** ∼: betrunken sein; **get** ∼: betrunken werden (**on** von); (intentionally) sich betrinken (**on** mit) ② *n.* Betrunkene, *der/die*

drunkard /'drʌŋkəd/ *n.* Trinker, *der/* Trinkerin, *die*

drunken /'drʌŋkn/ *attrib. adj.* betrunken; (habitually) ständig betrunken; ∼ **driving** Trunkenheit am Steuer

'drunkenness *n.* Betrunkenheit, *die;* (habitual) Trunksucht, *die*

dry /draɪ/ ① *adj.* trocken; trocken, (very ∼) herb ⟨*Wein*⟩; ausgetrocknet ⟨*Flussbett*⟩; **get** *or* **become** ∼: trocknen ② *v.t.* (a) trocknen ⟨*Haare, Wäsche*⟩; abtrocknen ⟨*Geschirr, Baby*⟩; ∼ **oneself** sich abtrocknen; ∼ **one's eyes** *or* **tears/hands** sich (*Dat.*) die Tränen abwischen/die Hände abtrocknen (b) (preserve) trocknen; dörren ⟨*Obst, Fleisch*⟩ ③ *v.i.* trocknen
■ **dry 'out** *v.t. & i.* trocknen
■ **dry 'up** ① *v.t.* abtrocknen ② *v.i.* (a) (∼ the dishes) abtrocknen (b) ⟨*Brunnen, Quelle:*⟩ versiegen; ⟨*Fluss, Teich:*⟩ austrocknen

dry: ∼**-'clean** *v.t.* chemisch reinigen; ∼**-'cleaner's** *n.* chemische Reinigung; ∼**-'cleaning** *n.* chemische Reinigung **'dryer** ▶ DRIER

dry: ∼**-eyed** *adj.* ohne Rührung; ∼ **'ice** *n.* Trockeneis, *das*

drying-'up *n.* Abtrocknen, *das;* **do the** ∼ abtrocknen; *attrib.* ∼ **cloth** Geschirrtuch, *das*

'dryness n. Trockenheit, die

dry 'rot n. Trockenfäule, die

dual /'dju:əl/ adj. doppelt

dual: ~ **'carriageway** n. (Brit.) Straße mit Mittelstreifen; ~ **con'trol** n. (Aeronaut.) Doppelsteuerung, die; (Motor Veh.) doppelte Bedienungselemente Pl.; ~**'purpose** adj. zweifach verwendbar

dub /dʌb/ v.t., **-bb-** (Cinemat.) synchronisieren

dubious /'dju:bɪəs/ adj. (doubting) unschlüssig; (suspicious) zweifelhaft

duchess /'dʌtʃɪs/ n. Herzogin, die

duck /dʌk/ [1] n. Ente, die
[2] v.i. sich [schnell] ducken
[3] v.t. ~ one's head den Kopf einziehen

duckling /'dʌklɪŋ/ n. Entenküken, das

'duck pond n. Ententeich, der

duct /dʌkt/ n. Rohr, das; (for air) Ventil, das

dud /dʌd/ [1] n. (useless thing) Niete, die (ugs.); (counterfeit) Fälschung, die
[2] adj. mies (ugs.); schlecht; (fake) gefälscht; geplatzt ⟨Scheck⟩

dude /dju:d, du:d/ n. (esp. Amer. coll.) Typ, der (ugs.)

due /dju:/ [1] adj. (a) (owed) geschuldet; zustehend ⟨Eigentum, Recht usw.⟩; **there's sth. ~ to me, I've got sth. ~:** mir steht etw. zu
(b) (immediately payable) fällig
(c) (that it is proper to give or use) gebührend; angemessen ⟨Belohnung⟩; **be ~ to sb.** jmdm. gebühren; **with all ~ respect** bei allem gebotenen Respekt
(d) (attributable) **the mistake was ~ to negligence** der Fehler war durch Nachlässigkeit verursacht; **it's ~ to her that we missed the train** ihretwegen verpassten wir den Zug
(e) (scheduled, expected); **be ~ to do sth.** etw. tun sollen; **be ~ [to arrive]** ankommen sollen
(f) (likely to get, deserving) **be ~ for sth.** etw. verdienen
[2] adv. (a) ~ **north** genau nach Norden
(b) ~ **to** aufgrund (+ Gen.); auf Grund (+ Gen.)
[3] n. (a) **give sb. his ~:** jmdm. Gerechtigkeit widerfahren lassen
(b) ~**s** (fees) Gebühren Pl.

duel /'dju:əl/ n. Duell, das

duet /dju:'et/ n. (for voices) Duett, das; (instrumental) Duo, das

duffle /'dʌfl/**:** ~ **bag** n. Matchbeutel, der; ~ **coat** n. Dufflecoat, der

dug /dʌɡ/ ▶ DIG

duke /dju:k/ n. Herzog, der

dull /dʌl/ [1] adj. (a) (stupid) beschränkt; (slow to understand) begriffsstutzig
(b) (boring) langweilig
(c) (gloomy) trübe ⟨Wetter, Tag⟩
[2] v.t. abstumpfen ⟨Geist, Sinne, Verstand⟩

duly /'dju:lɪ/ adv. ordnungsgemäß

dumb /dʌm/ adj. (a) stumm
(b) (coll.: stupid) doof (ugs.)

■ **dumb down** v.t. & i. (coll.) verflachen

dumbfounded /dʌm'faʊndɪd/ adj. sprachlos

dummy /'dʌmɪ/ n. (a) (of tailor) Schneiderpuppe, die; (in shop) Schaufensterpuppe, die; (of ventriloquist) Puppe, die; (stupid person) Dummkopf, der (ugs.); **like a stuffed ~** wie ein Ölgötze (ugs.)
(b) (imitation) Attrappe, die
(c) (esp. Brit.: for baby) Schnuller, der

dump /dʌmp/ [1] n. (a) (place) Müllkippe, die; (heap) Müllhaufen, der; (permanent) Müllhalde, die
(b) (Mil.) Depot, das
(c) (coll.: town) Kaff, das (ugs.)
[2] v.t. (dispose of) werfen; (deposit) abladen ⟨Sand, Müll usw.⟩; (leave) lassen; (place) abstellen

'dumping ground n. Müllkippe, die; (fig.) Abstellplatz, der

dumpling /'dʌmplɪŋ/ n. Kloß, der

dumps /dʌmps/ n. pl. **be** or **feel down in the ~:** ganz down sein (ugs.)

'dump truck n. Kipper, der

dunce /dʌns/ n. Null, die (ugs.)

dune /dju:n/ n. Düne, die

dung /dʌŋ/ n. Dung, der

dungarees /dʌŋɡə'ri:z/ n. pl. Latzhose, die

dungeon /'dʌndʒən/ n. Kerker, der

dunk /dʌŋk/ v.t. tunken

dupe /dju:p/ [1] v.t. übertölpeln
[2] n. Dumme, der/die

duplex /'dju:pleks/ adj. (esp. Amer.) (two-storey) zweistöckig ⟨Wohnung⟩; (two-family) Zweifamilien⟨haus⟩

duplicate [1] /'dju:plɪkət/ adj. (a) (identical) Zweit-
(b) (twofold) doppelt
[2] n. Kopie, die; (second copy of letter/document/ key) Duplikat, das; **in ~:** in doppelter Ausfertigung
[3] /'dju:plɪkeɪt/ v.t. (a) (make a copy of, make in ~) ~ **sth.** eine zweite Anfertigung von etw. machen
(b) (on machine) vervielfältigen
(c) (do twice) noch einmal tun

duplicity /dju:'plɪsɪtɪ/ n. Falschheit, die

durability /djʊərə'bɪlɪtɪ/ n. (of friendship, peace, etc.) Dauerhaftigkeit, die; (of garment, material) Haltbarkeit, die

durable /'djʊərəbl/ adj. haltbar; dauerhaft ⟨Friede, Freundschaft usw.⟩

duration /djʊə'reɪʃn/ n. Dauer, die

duress /djʊə'res/ n. Zwang, der

during /'djʊərɪŋ/ prep. während; (at a point in) in (+ Dat.)

dusk /dʌsk/ n. Einbruch der Dunkelheit

dust /dʌst/ [1] n. Staub, der
[2] v.t. abstauben ⟨Möbel⟩; ~ **a room/ house** in einem Zimmer/Haus Staub wischen
[3] v.i. Staub wischen

dustbin ⋯▸ earplug ⋯

dust: ∼bin *n.* (Brit.) Mülltonne, *die;* **∼cart** *n.* (Brit.) Müllwagen, *der;* **∼ cloth** *n.* Schonbezug, *der;* (duster) Staubtuch, *das*

'duster *n.* Staubtuch, *das*

dust: ∼ jacket *n.* Schutzumschlag, *der;* **∼man** /-mən/ *n., pl.* **∼men** /-mən/ (Brit.) Müllmann, *der;* **∼pan** *n.* Kehrschaufel, *die*

'dusty *adj.* staubig; verstaubt ⟨Bücher, Möbel⟩

Dutch /dʌtʃ/ ⓵ *adj.* holländisch; **sb. is ∼:** jmd. ist Holländer/Holländerin
⓶ *n.* **(a)** (language) Holländisch, *das; see also* ENGLISH 2A
(b) the **∼** *pl.* die Holländer *Pl.*

Dutch: ∼ 'courage *n.* angetrunkener Mut; **∼ 'elm disease** *n.* Ulmensterben, *das;* **∼man** /-mən/ *n., pl.* **∼men** /-mən/ Holländer, *der;* **∼woman** *n.* Holländerin, *die*

dutiful /'djuːtɪfl/ *adj.,* **'dutifully** *adv.* pflichtbewusst

duty /'djuːtɪ/ *n.* **(a)** Pflicht, *die;* (task) Aufgabe, *die;* **be on ∼:** Dienst haben; **off ∼:** nicht im Dienst; **be off ∼:** keinen Dienst haben; ⟨ab … Uhr⟩ dienstfrei sein
(b) (tax) Zoll, *der;* **pay ∼ on sth.** Zoll für etw. bezahlen

'duty-free *adj., adv.* zollfrei

duvet /'duːveɪ/ *n.* Federbett, *das;* **∼ cover** Bettbezug, *der*

DVD *abbr.* = **digital video disc** DVD

dwarf /dwɔːf/ *n., pl.* **∼s** *or* dwarves /'dwɔːvz/ Zwerg, *der*/Zwergin, *die*

dwell /dwel/ *v.i.,* dwelt /dwelt/ (literary) wohnen
■ **'dwell [up]on** *v.t.* (in discussion) sich ausführlich befassen mit; (in thought) in Gedanken verweilen bei

'dwelling *n.* Wohnung, *die*

dwelt ▸ DWELL

dwindle /'dwɪndl/ *v.i.* **∼ [away]** abnehmen; ⟨Unterstützung, Interesse:⟩ nachlassen; ⟨Vorräte:⟩ schrumpfen

dye /daɪ/ ⓵ *n.* Färbemittel, *das*
⓶ *v.t.,* **∼ing** /'daɪŋ/ färben

dying /'daɪŋ/ *adj.* sterbend; absterbend ⟨Baum⟩

dyke ▸ DIKE

dynamic /daɪ'næmɪk/ *adj.* dynamisch

dynamism /'daɪnəmɪzm/ *n.* Dynamik, *die*

dynamite /'daɪnəmaɪt/ *n.* Dynamit, *das*

dynamo /'daɪnəməʊ/ *n.* Dynamo, *der;* (in car) Lichtmaschine, *die*

dynasty /'dɪnəstɪ/ *n.* Dynastie, *die*

dysentry /'dɪsəntrɪ/ *n.* Ruhr, *die*

Ee

E, e /iː/ *n.* E, e, *das*

E. *abbr.* **(a)** = **east** O
(b) = **eastern** ö

each /iːtʃ/ ⓵ *adj.* jeder/jede/jedes; **they cost** *or* **are a pound ∼:** sie kosten ein Pfund pro Stück
⓶ *pron.* **(a)** jeder/jede/jedes
(b) **∼ other** sich

eager /'iːgə(r)/ *adj.* eifrig; **be ∼ to do sth.** etw. unbedingt tun wollen

'eagerly *adv.* eifrig; gespannt ⟨warten⟩

eagle /'iːgl/ *n.* Adler, *der*

eagle-'eyed *adj.* adleräugig

ear¹ /ɪə(r)/ *n.* Ohr, *das;* **up to one's ∼s in work/debt** bis zum Hals in Arbeit/Schulden; **be[come] all ∼s** [plötzlich] ganz Ohr sein; **play by ∼** (Mus.) nach dem Gehör spielen

ear² *n.* (Bot.) Ähre, *die*

ear: ∼ache *n.* Ohrenschmerzen *Pl.;* **∼ clip** *n.* Ohr[en]klipp, *der;* **∼ drops** *n. pl.* **(a)** (Med.) Ohrentropfen *Pl.;* **(b)** (earrings) Ohrgehänge, *das;* **∼drum** *n.* Trommelfell, *das*

earl /ɜːl/ *n.* Graf, *der*

'ear lobe *n.* Ohrläppchen, *das*

early /'ɜːlɪ/ ⓵ *adj.* früh
⓶ *adv.* früh; **I am a bit ∼:** ich bin etwas zu früh gekommen; **∼ next week** Anfang der nächsten Woche; **∼ in June** Anfang Juni; **from ∼ in the morning till late at night** von früh [morgens] bis spät [nachts]; **∼ on** schon früh

early: ∼ 'closing *n.* **it is ∼ closing** die Geschäfte haben nachmittags geschlossen; **∼-'closing day** *n.: Tag, an dem die Geschäfte nachmittags geschlossen haben*

ear: ∼mark *v.t.* vorsehen; **∼muffs** *n. pl.* Ohrenschützer *Pl.*

earn /ɜːn/ *v.t.* verdienen; (bring in as income or interest) einbringen

earnest /'ɜːnɪst/ ⓵ *adj.* ernsthaft
⓶ *n.* **in ∼:** mit vollem Ernst

earnings /'ɜːnɪŋz/ *n. pl.* Verdienst, *der;* (of business etc.) Ertrag, *der*

ear: ∼phones *n. pl.* Kopfhörer, *der;* **∼piece** *n.* Hörmuschel, *die;* **∼piercing** ⓵ *adj.* durch Mark und Bein gehend ⟨Lärm⟩; ⓶ *n.* Durchstechen der Ohrläppchen; **∼plug** *n.* Ohropax, *das* Ⓦ;

~ring *n.* Ohrring, *der;* **~shot** *n.* out of/ within ~shot außer/in Hörweite; **~-splitting** *adj.* ohrenbetäubend

earth /ɜ:θ/ ☐ *n.* (also Brit. Electr.) Erde, *die;* how/what *etc.* on ~ ...? wie/was *usw.* in aller Welt ...? ☐ *v.t.* (Brit. Electr.) erden

earthenware /'ɜ:θnweə(r)/ ☐ *n.* Tonwaren *Pl.* ☐ *adj.* irden

earthly /'ɜ:θlı/ *adj.* irdisch; **no** ~ **use** *etc.* (coll.) nicht der geringste Nutzen *usw.*

earth: **~quake** *n.* Erdbeben, *das;* ~ **sciences** *n. pl.* Geowissenschaften *Pl.;* **~worm** *n.* Regenwurm, *der*

'earthy *adj.* (a) erdig (b) (coarse) derb

'earwax *n.* Ohrenschmalz, *das*

earwig /'ɪəwıg/ *n.* Ohrwurm, *der*

ease /i:z/ ☐ *n.* (a) set sb. at ~: jmdn. beruhigen; **at [one's]** ~: entspannt; **be** *or* **feel at [one's]** ~: sich wohl fühlen; **[stand] at** ~! (Mil.) rührt euch! (b) **with** ~ (without difficulty) mit Leichtigkeit ☐ *v.t.* lindern ⟨Schmerz, Kummer⟩; entspannen ⟨Lage⟩; verringern ⟨Belastung, Druck, Spannung⟩ ☐ *v.i.* nachlassen

easel /'i:zl/ *n.* Staffelei, *die*

easily /'i:zılı/ *adv.* leicht

east /i:st/ ☐ *n.* (a) Osten, *der;* **in/to[wards]/ from the** ~: im/nach/von Osten; **to the** ~ **of** östlich von (b) *usu.* E~ (Geog., Polit.) Osten, *der* ☐ *adj.* östlich; Ost⟨küste, -wind, -grenze⟩ ☐ *adv.* nach Osten; ~ **of** östlich von

'East Ber'lin *pr. n.* (Hist.) Ostberlin, *das*

'eastbound *adj.* ⟨Zug, Verkehr *usw.*⟩ in Richtung Osten

Easter /'i:stə(r)/ *n.* Ostern, *das od. Pl.*

'Easter egg *n.* Osterei, *das*

easterly /'i:stəlı/ *adj.* östlich; ⟨Wind⟩ aus östlichen Richtungen

Easter 'Monday *n.* Ostermontag, *der*

eastern /'i:stən/ *adj.* östlich; Ost⟨grenze, -hälfte, -seite⟩; ~ **Germany** Ostdeutschland (*das*)

Eastern: ~ **'Europe** *pr. n.* Osteuropa, (*das*); ~ **Euro'pean** ☐ *adj.* osteuropäisch; ☐ *n.* Osteuropäer, *der*/ Osteuropäerin, *die*

Easter 'Sunday *n.* Ostersonntag, *der*

East: ~ **'German** (Hist.) ☐ *adj.* ostdeutsch; **he/she is** ~ **German** er ist Ostdeutscher/sie ist Ostdeutsche; ☐ *n.* Ostdeutsche, *der/die;* ~ **'Germany** *pr. n.* (Hist.) Ostdeutschland (*das*); ~ **'Timor** /'ti:mɔ:(r)/ *pr. n.* Osttimor (*das*)

eastward(s) /'i:stwəd(z)/ *adv.* ostwärts

easy /'i:zı/ ☐ *adj.* (a) leicht; **on** ~ **terms** auf Raten ⟨kaufen⟩ (b) sorglos ⟨Leben, Zeit⟩

☐ *adv.* leicht; **easier said than done** leichter gesagt als getan; **take it** ~! (calm down!) beruhige dich!

easy: **~-care** *attrib. adj.* pflegeleicht; ~ **chair** *n.* Sessel, *der;* **~-'going** *adj.* gelassen; (lax) nachlässig; ~ **'money** *n.* leicht verdientes Geld

eat /i:t/ *v.t. & i.,* **ate** /et, eıt/, **eaten** /'i:tn/ essen; ⟨Tier:⟩ fressen
∎ **eat a'way** *v.t.* ⟨Rost, Säure:⟩ zerfressen
∎ **eat 'out** *v.i.* essen gehen
∎ **eat 'up** *v.t.* aufessen; ⟨Tier:⟩ auffressen

'eat-by date *n.* Verfallsdatum, *das*

eaten ▶ EAT

eating: ~ **apple** *n.* Essapfel, *der;* ~ **disorder** *n.* Essstörung, *die* (*meist Pl.*); ~ **place** *n.* Essgelegenheit, *die*

eau-de-Cologne /əʊdəkə'ləʊn/ *n.* Kölnischwasser, *das*

eaves /i:vz/ *n. pl.* Dachgesims, *das*

'eavesdrop *v.i.* lauschen; ~ **on** belauschen

'eavesdropper *n.* Lauscher, *der*/ Lauscherin, *die*

'e-banking *n.* E-Banking, *das*

ebb /eb/ ☐ *n.* Ebbe, *die;* **be at a low** ~ (fig.) ⟨Person, Stimmung, Moral:⟩ auf dem Nullpunkt sein ☐ *v.i.* zurückgehen; ~ **away** (fig.) dahinschwinden

'ebb tide *n.* Ebbe, *die*

ebony /'ebənı/ *n.* Ebenholz, *das*

EC *abbr.* = **European Community** EG

eccentric /ık'sentrık/ ☐ *adj.* exzentrisch ☐ *n.* Exzentriker, *der*/Exzentrikerin, *die*

eccentricity /eksen'trısıtı/ *n.* Exzentrizität, *die*

ecclesiastical /ıklı:zı'æstıkl/ *adj.* kirchlich; geistlich ⟨Musik⟩

ECG *abbr.* = **electrocardiogram** EKG

echo /'ekəʊ/ ☐ *n.* Echo, *das* ☐ *v.t.* zurückwerfen; (fig.: repeat) wiederholen

éclair /eı'kleə(r)/ *n.* Eclair, *das*

eclipse /ı'klıps/ *n.* (Astron.) Finsternis, *die;* ~ **of the sun** Sonnenfinsternis, *die*

'eco-friendly *adj.* umweltfreundlich

ecological /i:kə'lɒdʒıkl/ *adj.* ökologisch

eco'logically *adv.* ökologisch; ~ **aware/ sound/harmful** umweltbewusst/-gerecht/ -schädlich

ecologist /i:'kɒlədʒıst/ *n.* Ökologe, *der*/ Ökologin, *die*

ecology /i:'kɒlədʒı/ *n.* Ökologie, *die*

e-commerce /i:'kɒmɜ:s/ *n.* (Comp.) elektronischer Handel; E-Commerce, *der*

economic /i:kə'nɒmık/ *adj.* (a) Wirtschafts⟨politik, -abkommen, -system, -krise, -wunder⟩; wirtschaftlich ⟨Entwicklung, Zusammenbruch⟩; ~ **refugee** Wirtschaftsflüchtling, *der* (b) (giving adequate return) wirtschaftlich

economical /i:kə'nɒmıkl/ *adj.* wirtschaftlich; sparsam ⟨Person⟩; **be** ~ **with** **sth.** mit etw. haushalten

eco'nomically *adv.* wirtschaftlich; (not wastefully) sparsam

economics /iːkə'nɒmɪks/ *n.* Wirtschaftswissenschaft, *die (meist Pl.)*

economist /ɪ'kɒnəmɪst/ *n.* Wirtschaftswissenschaftler, *der/* -wissenschaftlerin, *die*

economize /ɪ'kɒnəmaɪz/ *v.i.* sparen; **~ on sth.** etw. sparen

economy /ɪ'kɒnəmɪ/ *n.* (a) (frugality) Sparsamkeit, *die* (b) (instance) Einsparung, *die;* **make economies** zu Sparmaßnahmen greifen (c) (of country etc.) Wirtschaft, *die*

economy: ~ class *n.* Touristenklasse, *die;* Economyklasse, *die;* **~-class syndrome** Economyclasssyndrom, *das;* **~ size** *n.* Haushaltspackung, *die*

'ecosystem *n.* Ökosystem, *das*

ecstasy /'ekstəsɪ/ *n.* (a) Ekstase, *die* (b) E~ (drug) Ecstasy, *das*

ecstatic /ɪk'stætɪk/ *adj.* ekstatisch

eddy /'edɪ/ *n.* Strudel, *der*

edge /edʒ/ ☐ *n.* (a) (of knife, razor, weapon) Schneide, *die;* **on ~** (fig.) nervös *od.* gereizt (**about** wegen) (b) (of solid, bed, table) Kante, *die;* (of sheet of paper, road, forest, cliff) Rand, *der* ☐ *v.i.* sich schieben

edgy /'edʒɪ/ *adj.* nervös

edible /'edɪbl/ *adj.* essbar

edict /'iːdɪkt/ *n.* Erlass, *der*

edit /'edɪt/ *v.t.* herausgeben ⟨*Zeitung*⟩; redigieren ⟨*Buch, Artikel, Manuskript*⟩

edition /ɪ'dɪʃn/ *n.* Ausgabe, *die*

editor /'edɪtə(r)/ *n.* Redakteur, *der/* Redakteurin, *die;* (of particular work) Bearbeiter, *der/*Bearbeiterin, *die;* (of newspaper) Herausgeber, *der/*Herausgeberin, *die*

editorial /edɪ'tɔːrɪəl/ ☐ *n.* Leitartikel, *der* ☐ *adj.* redaktionell

EDP *abbr.* = **electronic data processing** EDV

educate /'edjʊkeɪt/ *v.t.* (a) (bring up) erziehen; (train mind and character of) bilden (b) (provide schooling for) **he was ~d at ...:** er hat seine Ausbildung in ... erhalten

educated /'edjʊkeɪtɪd/ *adj.* gebildet

education /edjʊ'keɪʃn/ *n.* Erziehung, *die;* (system) Bildungswesen, *das*

educational /edjʊ'keɪʃənl/ *adj.* pädagogisch; Lehr⟨*film, -spiele, -anstalt*⟩; Erziehungs⟨*methoden, -arbeit*⟩

edu'cation system *n.* Bildungssystem, *das*

EEC *abbr.* = **European Economic Community** EWG

eel /iːl/ *n.* Aal, *der*

eerie /'ɪːrɪ/ *adj.* unheimlich

eff /ef/ *v.i.* (sl.) **~ and blind** fluchen

effect /ɪ'fekt/ *n.* (a) Wirkung, *die* (**on** auf + *Akk.*); **the ~s of sth. on sth.** die Auswirkungen einer Sache (*Gen.*) auf etw. (*Akk.*); **take ~:** die erwünschte Wirkung erzielen; **in ~:** in Wirklichkeit (b) **come into ~:** gültig werden; ⟨*Gesetz:*⟩ in Kraft treten; **put into ~:** in Kraft setzen ⟨*Gesetz*⟩; verwirklichen ⟨*Plan*⟩; **with ~ from 2 November/Monday** mit Wirkung vom 2. November/von Montag (c) **personal ~s** persönliches Eigentum; Privateigentum, *das;* **household ~s** Hausrat, *der*

effective /ɪ'fektɪv/ *adj.* (a) wirksam ⟨*Mittel, Maßnahmen*⟩; **be ~** ⟨*Arzneimittel:*⟩ wirken (b) (in operation) gültig; **~ from/as of** mit Wirkung vom

ef'fectively *adv.* (in fact) effektiv; (with effect) wirkungsvoll

effectual /ɪ'fektjʊəl/ *adj.* wirksam

effeminate /ɪ'femɪnət/ *adj.* unmännlich

effervescent /efə'vesənt/ *adj.* sprudelnd; (fig.) übersprudelnd

effete /e'fiːt/ *adj.* verweichlicht

efficiency /ɪ'fɪʃənsɪ/ *n.* (of person) Fähigkeit, *die;* Tüchtigkeit, *die;* (of machine, factory, engine) Leistungsfähigkeit, *die;* (of organization, method) gutes Funktionieren

efficient /ɪ'fɪʃənt/ *adj.* fähig ⟨*Person*⟩; tüchtig ⟨*Arbeiter, Sekretärin*⟩; leistungsfähig ⟨*Maschine, Motor, Fabrik*⟩; gut funktionierend ⟨*Methode, Organisation*⟩

ef'ficiently *adj.* gut

effigy /'efɪdʒɪ/ *n.* Bildnis, *das*

effing /'efɪŋ/ *adj.* (sl.) Scheiß- (salopp)

effluent /'eflʊənt/ Abwässer *Pl.*

effort /'efət/ *n.* (a) Anstrengung, *die;* Mühe, *die;* **make an/every ~** (physically) sich anstrengen; (mentally) sich bemühen (b) (attempt) Versuch, *der*

'effortless *adj.* mühelos

effrontery /ɪ'frʌntərɪ/ *n.* Dreistigkeit, *die;* **have the ~ to do sth.** die Stirn besitzen, etw. zu tun

effusive /ɪ'fjuːsɪv/ *adj.* überschwänglich; exaltiert (geh.) ⟨*Person*⟩

EFL *abbr.* = **English as a foreign language**

e.g. /iː'dʒiː/ *abbr.* = **for example** z.B.

egg /eg/ *n.* Ei, *das*

■ **egg 'on** *v.t.* anstacheln

egg: ~cup *n.* Eierbecher, *der;* **~plant** *n.* Aubergine, *die;* (fruit also) Eierfrucht, *die;* (plant also) Eierpflanze, *die;* **~shell** *n.* Eierschale, *die;* **~ timer** *n.* Eieruhr, *die;* **~ white** *n.* Eiweiß, *das;* **~ yolk** *n.* Eigelb, *das*

ego /'egəʊ, 'iːgəʊ/ *n., pl.* **~s** (a) (Psych.) Ego, *das* (b) (self-esteem) Selbstbewusstsein, *das*

egotism /'egətɪzm/ *n.* (a) Egotismus, *der* (fachspr.); Ichbezogenheit, *die* ⸱⸱⸱⸽

(b) (self-conceit) Egotismus, *der;* Selbstgefälligkeit, *die*

egotist /'egətɪst/ *n.* Egotist, *der*/Egotistin, *die* (fachspr.); (self-centred person) Egozentriker, *der*/Egozentrikerin, *die*

egotistic /egə'tɪstɪk/, **egotistical** /egə'tɪstɪkl/ *adj.* **(a)** ichbezogen ⟨Rede, Gespräch⟩

(b) selbstsüchtig, selbstgefällig ⟨Person⟩

Egypt /'iːdʒɪpt/ *pr. n.* Ägypten (*das*)

Egyptian /ɪ'dʒɪpʃn/ **1** *adj.* ägyptisch; **sb. is ∼:** jmd. ist Ägypter/Ägypterin

2 *n.* (person) Ägypter, *der*/Ägypterin, *die*

eiderdown /'aɪdədaʊn/ *n.* Federbett, *das*

eight /eɪt/ **1** *adj.* acht; **at ∼:** um acht; **half past ∼:** halb neun; **∼ thirty** acht Uhr dreißig; **∼ ten/fifty** zehn nach acht/vor neun; (esp. in timetable) acht Uhr zehn/fünfzig; **∼-year-old boy** achtjähriger Junge; **an ∼-year-old** ein Achtjähriger/eine Achtjährige; **at [the age of] ∼, aged ∼:** mit acht Jahren; **∼ times** achtmal

2 *n.* Acht, *die;* **the first/last ∼:** die ersten/letzten acht; **there were ∼ of us present** wir waren [zu] acht

eighteen /eɪ'tiːn/ **1** *adj.* achtzehn

2 *n.* Achtzehn, *die. See also* EIGHT

eighteenth /eɪ'tiːnθ/ **1** *adj.* achtzehnt...

2 *n.* (fraction) Achtzehntel, *das. See also* EIGHTH

eighth /eɪtθ/ **1** *adj.* acht...; **be/come ∼:** Achter sein/als Achter ankommen; **∼largest** achtgrößt...

2 *n.* (in sequence, rank) Achte, *der/die/das;* (fraction) Achtel, *das;* **the ∼ of May** der achte Mai

eightieth /'eɪtɪɪθ/ *adj.* achtzigst...

eighty /'eɪtɪ/ **1** *adj.* achtzig

2 *n.* Achtzig, *die;* **the eighties** (years) die Achtzigerjahre; **be in one's eighties** in den Achtzigern sein. *See also* EIGHT

Eire /'eərə/ *pr. n.* Irland, *das;* Eire, *das*

either /'aɪðə(r), 'iːðə(r)/ **1** *adj.* **(a)** (each) **at ∼ end of the table** an beiden Enden des Tisches

(b) (one or other) [irgend]ein ... [von beiden]; **take ∼ one** nimm einen/eine/eins von [den] beiden

2 *pron.* **(a)** (each) beide *Pl.;* **I can't cope with ∼:** ich kann mit keinem von beiden fertig werden

(b) (one or other) einer/eine/ein[e]s [von beiden]

3 *adv.* auch [nicht]; **'I don't like that ∼:** ich mag es auch nicht

4 *conj.* **∼ ... or ...:** entweder ... oder ...; (after negation) weder ... noch ...

ejaculate /ɪ'dʒækjʊleɪt/**1** *v.t.* (utter suddenly) ausstoßen

2 *v.i.* (eject semen) ejakulieren

eject /'ɪdʒekt/ **1** *v.t.* **(a)** (from hall, meeting) hinauswerfen **(from** aus)

(b) ⟨Gerät:⟩ auswerfen, ⟨Person:⟩ herausholen ⟨Kassette⟩

2 *v.i.* sich hinauskatapultieren

ejector seat /ɪ'dʒektə siːt/ *n.* Schleudersitz, *der*

eke out /iːk 'aʊt/ *v.t.* strecken; **∼ out a living** sich (*Dat.*) seinen Lebensunterhalt notdürftig verdienen

elaborate **1** /ɪ'læbərət/ *adj.* kompliziert; kunstvoll [gearbeitet] ⟨Arrangement, Verzierung⟩

2 /ɪ'læbəreɪt/ *v.i.* mehr ins Detail gehen; **∼ on** näher ausführen

elapse /ɪ'læps/ *v.i.* ⟨Zeit:⟩ vergehen

elastic /ɪ'læstɪk/ **1** *adj.* elastisch

2 *n.* (∼ band) Gummiband, *das*

elastic 'band *n.* Gummiband, *das*

elated /ɪ'leɪtɪd/ *adj.* freudig erregt; **be** *or* **feel ∼:** in Hochstimmung sein

elation /ɪ'leɪʃn/ *n.* freudige Erregung

elbow /'elbəʊ/ **1** *n.* Ell[en]bogen, *der*

2 *v.t.* **∼ sb. aside** jmdn. mit dem Ellenbogen zur Seite stoßen

elbow: ∼ grease *n.* (joc.) Muskelkraft, *die;* **∼ room** *n.* Ell[en]bogenfreiheit, *die*

elder¹ /'eldə(r)/ **1** *attrib. adj.* älter...

2 *n.* **(a)** (senior) Ältere, *der/die*

(b) (village ∼, church ∼) Älteste, *der/die*

elder² *n.* (Bot.) Holunder, *der*

'elderberry *n.* Holunderbeere, *die*

elderly /'eldəlɪ/ **1** *adj.* älter

2 *n. pl.* **the ∼:** ältere Menschen

eldest /'eldɪst/ *adj.* ältest...

elect /ɪ'lekt/ **1** *adj. postpos.* gewählt; **the President ∼:** der designierte Präsident

2 *v.t.* wählen; **∼ sb. chairman** jmdn. zum Vorsitzenden wählen

election /ɪ'lekʃn/ *n.* Wahl, *die;* **general ∼:** allgemeine Wahlen *Pl.;* **∼ results** Wahlergebnisse *Pl.*

e'lection campaign *n.* Wahlkampagne, *die*

electioneer /ɪlekʃə'nɪə(r)/ *v.i.* **be/go ∼ing** Wahlkampf machen

elector /ɪ'lektə(r)/ *n.* Wähler, *der*/Wählerin, *die*

electoral /ɪ'lektərl/ *adj.* Wahl-

electoral 'college *n.* Wahlmännergremium, *das;* Wahlausschuss, *der*

electorate /ɪ'lektərət/ *n.* Wähler *Pl.*

electric /ɪ'lektrɪk/ *adj.* elektrisch; Elektro⟨kabel, -motor, -herd, -kessel⟩; Strom⟨versorgung⟩; (fig.) spannungsgeladen ⟨Atmosphäre⟩

electrical /ɪ'lektrɪkl/ *adj.* elektrisch; Elektro⟨abteilung, -handel, -geräte⟩

electric: ∼ 'blanket *n.* Heizdecke, *die;* **∼ 'chair** *n.* elektrischer Stuhl; **∼ cooker** *n.* Elektroherd, *der;* **∼ 'fire** *n.* [elektrischer] Heizofen; **∼ gui'tar** *n.* elektrische Gitarre; E-Gitarre, *die*

electrician /ɪlek'trɪʃn/ *n.* Elektriker, *der*/Elektrikerin, *die*

electricity /ɪlek'trɪsɪtɪ/ n. Elektrizität, *die*
electricity: ~ **bill** n. Stromrechnung, *die;*
~ **man** n. (fitter) Elektroinstallateur, *der;*
(meter reader, collector) Stromableser, *der;*
~ **meter** n. Stromzähler, *der*

electric 'shock n. Stromschlag, *der*

electrify /ɪ'lektrɪfaɪ/ v.t. elektrifizieren;
(fig.) elektrisieren

electro'cardiogram n.
Elektrokardiogramm, *das*

electrocute /ɪ'lektrəkjuːt/ v.t. durch
Stromschlag töten

electrode /ɪ'lektrəʊd/ n. Elektrode, *die*

electro'magnet n. Elektromagnet, *der*

electromag'netic adj.
elektromagnetisch

electron /ɪ'lektrɒn/ n. Elektron, *das*

electronic /ɪlek'trɒnɪk/ adj. elektronisch

electronic: ~ **'cash** n. elektronisches
Geld; ~ **'mail** n. elektronische Post;
~ **'publishing** n. elektronisches
Publizieren

electronics /ɪlek'trɒnɪks/ n. Elektronik,
die

electronic: ~ **'shopping basket** n.
elektronischer Warenkorb; ~**'storefront**
n. elektronisches Schaufenster

electron 'microscope n.
Elektronenmikroskop, *das*

elegance /'elɪgəns/ n. Eleganz, *die*

elegant /'elɪgənt/ adj. elegant

elegy /'elɪdʒɪ/ n. Elegie, *die*

element /'elɪmənt/ n. (a) Element, *das*
(b) (Electr.) Heizelement, *das*
(c) ~s (rudiments) Grundlagen *Pl.*

elementary /elɪ'mentərɪ/ adj. elementar;
grundlegend ⟨Fakten, Wissen⟩;
Grundschul⟨bildung⟩; Grund⟨kurs,
-ausbildung, -kenntnisse⟩

elementary: ~ **'particle** n. (Phys.)
Elementarteilchen, *das;* ~ **school** n.
Grundschule, *die*

elephant /'elɪfənt/ n. Elefant, *der;* white ~
(fig.) nutzloser Besitz; (Gebäude,
⟨Gebäude, Einkaufszentrum usw.:⟩ reine
Geldverschwendung sein

elevate /'elɪveɪt/ v.t. [empor]heben

elevation /elɪ'veɪʃn/ n. (a) (height) Höhe, *die*
(b) (Archit.) Aufriss, *der*

elevator /'elɪveɪtə(r)/ n. (Amer.) Aufzug,
der; Fahrstuhl, *der*

eleven /ɪ'levn/ [1] adj. elf
[2] n. (also Sport) Elf, *die. See also* EIGHT

elevenses /ɪ'levnzɪz/ n. sing. or pl. (Brit.
coll.) ≈ zweites Frühstück [gegen elf Uhr]

eleventh /ɪ'levnθ/ [1] adj. elft...; at the
~ hour in letzter Minute
[2] n. (fraction) Elftel, *das. See also* EIGHTH

elf /elf/ n., pl. **elves** /elvz/ Elf, *der;* Elfe, *die*

elicit /ɪ'lɪsɪt/ v.t. entlocken (from *Dat.*);
gewinnen ⟨Unterstützung⟩

eligible /'elɪdʒɪbl/ adj. be ~ for sth. (fit) für
etw. geeignet sein; (entitled) zu etw. berechtigt
sein

eliminate /ɪ'lɪmɪneɪt/ v.t. (a) (remove)
beseitigen; ausschließen ⟨Möglichkeit⟩
(b) (exclude) ausschließen; be ~d (Sport)
ausscheiden

elimination /ɪlɪmɪ'neɪʃn/ n. (a) (removal)
Beseitigung, *die;* process of ~:
Ausleseverfahren, *das*
(b) (exclusion) Ausschluss, *der;* (Sport)
Ausscheiden, *das*

élite /eɪ'liːt/ n. Elite, *die*

élitist /eɪ'liːtɪst/ adj. elitär; Elite⟨denken⟩

elk /elk/ n., pl. ~s or same (a) (deer) Elch,
der
(b) (moose) Riesenelch, *der*

ellipse /ɪ'lɪps/ n. Ellipse, *die*

elliptical /ɪ'lɪptɪkl/ adj. elliptisch

elm /elm/ n. Ulme, *die*

elongated /'iːlɒŋgeɪtɪd/ adj. lang gestreckt

elope /ɪ'ləʊp/ v.i. durchbrennen (ugs.)

eloquence /'eləkwəns/ n. Beredtheit, *die*

eloquent /'eləkwənt/ adj. beredt ⟨Person⟩;
gewandt ⟨Stil, Redner⟩

else /els/ adv. (a) (besides) sonst [noch];
somebody/something ~: [noch] jemand
anders/noch etwas; everybody/everything ~:
alle anderen/alles andere; who/what/when/
how ~? wer/was/wann/wie sonst noch?;
why ~? warum sonst?
(b) (instead) ander...; sb. ~'s hat der Hut von
jmd. anders; anybody/anything ~?
[irgend]jemand anders/[irgend]etwas
anderes?; somebody/something ~: jemand
anders/etwas anderes; everybody/everything
~: alle anderen/alles andere
(c) (otherwise) sonst; or ~: oder aber; do it or
~ ...! tun Sie es, sonst ...!

'elsewhere adv. woanders

elude /ɪ'ljuːd/ v.t. (avoid) ausweichen
(+ *Dat.*); (escape from) entkommen (+ *Dat.*)

elusive /ɪ'ljuːsɪv/ adj. schwer zu erreichen
⟨Person⟩; schwer zu fassen ⟨Straftäter⟩;
schwer definierbar ⟨Begriff, Sinn⟩

elves pl. of ELF

emaciated /ɪ'meɪsɪeɪtɪd/ adj. abgezehrt

e-mail /'iːmeɪl/ [1] n. E-Mail, *die;* ~ address
E-Mail-Adresse, *die;* ~ message E-Mail, *die*
[2] v.t. per E-Mail übermitteln ⟨Ergebnisse,
Datei usw.⟩; ~ sb. jmdm. eine E-Mail
schicken

emancipated /ɪ'mænsɪpeɪtɪd/ adj.
emanzipiert: become ~: sich emanzipieren

emancipation /ɪmænsɪ'peɪʃn/ n.
Emanzipation, *die*

embalm /ɪm'baːm/ v.t. einbalsamieren

embankment /ɪm'bæŋkmənt/ n. Damm,
der

embargo /em'baːgəʊ/ n., pl. ~es Embargo,
das; put or lay an ~ on sth. etw. mit einem
Embargo belegen

embark /ɪmˈbɑːk/ v.i. (a) sich einschiffen (for nach)
(b) ~ [up]on sth. etw. in Angriff nehmen

embarkation /embɑːˈkeɪʃn/ n. Einschiffung, die

embarrass /ɪmˈbærəs/ v.t. in Verlegenheit bringen

embarrassed /ɪmˈbærəst/ adj. verlegen; feel ~: verlegen sein

em'barrassing adj. peinlich

em'barrassment n. Verlegenheit, die

embassy /ˈembəsɪ/ n. Botschaft, die

embed /ɪmˈbed/ v.t., -dd-: (a) (fix) einlassen; ~ sth. in cement/concrete etw. einzementieren/einbetonieren; ~ded in the mud im Schlamm versunken; ~ded journalist eingebetteter Journalist; ~ded sentence (Ling.) eingeschobener Satz

embellish /emˈbelɪʃ/ v.t. beschönigen ⟨Wahrheit⟩; ausschmücken ⟨Geschichte, Bericht⟩

embers /ˈembəz/ n. pl. Glut, die

embezzle /ɪmˈbezl/ v.t. unterschlagen

embitter /ɪmˈbɪtə(r)/ v.t. verbittern

emblem /ˈembləm/ n. Emblem, das

embody /ɪmˈbɒdɪ/ v.t. verkörpern

embrace /ɪmˈbreɪs/ ① v.t. umarmen; (fig.: accept, adopt) annehmen
② v.i. sich umarmen
③ n. Umarmung, die

embroider /ɪmˈbrɔɪdə(r)/ v.t. sticken ⟨Muster⟩; besticken ⟨Tuch, Kleid⟩; (fig.) ausschmücken

embroidery /ɪmˈbrɔɪdərɪ/ n. Stickerei, die

embroil /ɪmˈbrɔɪl/ v.t. become/be ~ed in sth. in etw. (Akk.) verwickelt werden/sein

embryo /ˈembrɪəʊ/ n. Embryo, der; ~ research Embryonenforschung, die

embryonic /embrɪˈɒnɪk/ adj. (Biol., fig.) Embryonal⟨entwicklung, -struktur, -zustand, -stadium⟩; unausgereift ⟨Vorstellung⟩

emerald /ˈemərəld/ ① n. Smaragd, der
② adj. smaragdgrün; the E~ Isle die Grüne Insel

emerald 'green n. Smaragdgrün, das

emerge /ɪˈmɜːdʒ/ v.i. auftauchen (from aus, from behind hinter + Dat.); ⟨Wahrheit:⟩ an den Tag kommen; it ~s that ...: es stellt sich heraus, dass ...

emergency /ɪˈmɜːdʒənsɪ/ ① n. Notfall, der; in an or in case of ~: im Notfall; declare a state of ~: den Ausnahmezustand ausrufen
② adj. Not-

emergency: ~ exit n. Notausgang, der; **~ services** n. pl. Hilfsdienste Pl.

'emery paper n. Schmirgelpapier, das

emigrant /ˈemɪɡrənt/ n. Auswanderer, der/ Auswanderin, die

emigrate /ˈemɪɡreɪt/ v.i. auswandern (to nach, from aus)

emigration /emɪˈɡreɪʃn/ n. Auswanderung, die (to nach, from aus)

eminence /ˈemɪnəns/ n. hohes Ansehen

eminent /ˈemɪnənt/ adj. bedeutend; herausragend

emission /ɪˈmɪʃn/ n. Emission, die (fachspr.); (process also) Abgabe, die

emit /ɪˈmɪt/ v.t., -tt- abgeben, emittieren (fachspr.) ⟨Wärme, Strahlung usw.⟩; ausstoßen ⟨Rauch⟩

emoticon /ɪˈmɒtɪkɒn/ n. (Comp.) Emoticon, das

emotion /ɪˈməʊʃn/ n. Gefühl, das

emotional /ɪˈməʊʃənl/ adj. emotional; Gemüts⟨zustand, -störung⟩; gefühlvoll ⟨Stimme⟩

e'motionally adv. emotional; gefühlvoll ⟨sprechen⟩; ~ disturbed seelisch gestört

emotive /ɪˈməʊtɪv/ adj. emotional

empathize /ˈempəθaɪz/ v.i. ~ with sb. sich in jmdn. hineinversetzen; ~ with sth. etw. nachempfinden

empathy /ˈempəθɪ/ n. Empathie, die (Psych.); Einfühlung, die

emperor /ˈempərə(r)/ n. Kaiser, der

emphasis /ˈemfəsɪs/ n., pl. **emphases** /ˈemfəsiːz/ Betonung, die; lay or place or put ~ on sth. etw. betonen

emphasize /ˈemfəsaɪz/ v.t. betonen

emphatic /ɪmˈfætɪk/ adj. nachdrücklich; demonstrativ ⟨Ablehnung⟩; be ~ that ...: darauf bestehen, dass ...

em'phatically adv. nachdrücklich

empire /ˈempaɪə(r)/ n. Reich, das

empirical /ɪmˈpɪrɪkl/ adj. empirisch

employ /ɪmˈplɔɪ/ v.t. (a) (take on) einstellen; (have working for one) beschäftigen; be ~ed by a company bei einer Firma arbeiten
(b) (use) einsetzen (for, in, on für); anwenden ⟨Methode, List⟩ (for, in, on bei)

employee (Amer.: **employe**) /emplɔɪˈiː, emˈplɔɪiː/ n. Angestellte, der/die

employer /ɪmˈplɔɪə(r)/ n. Arbeitgeber, der/ -geberin, die

employment /ɪmˈplɔɪmənt/ n. (a) (work) Arbeit, die
(b) (regular trade or profession) Beschäftigung, die

employment: ~ agency n. Stellenvermittlung, die; **~ office** n. (Brit.) Arbeitsamt, das

empower /ɪmˈpaʊə(r)/ v.t. (authorize) ermächtigen; (enable) befähigen

empress /ˈemprɪs/ n. Kaiserin, die

emptiness /ˈemptɪnɪs/ n. Leere, die

empty /ˈemptɪ/ ① adj. leer; frei ⟨Sitz, Parkplatz⟩
② v.t. leeren; (pour) schütten (over über + Akk.)
③ v.i. sich leeren

'empty-handed adj. mit leeren Händen

EMS *abbr.* = **European Monetary System** EWS

emu /'i:mju:/ *n.* (Ornith.) Emu, *der*

EMU *abbr.* = **Economic and Monetary Union** WWU

emulate /'emjʊleɪt/ *v.t.* nacheifern (+ *Dat.*)

emulsion /ɪ'mʌlʃn/ *n.* (a) Emulsion, *die*
(b) ▶ EMULSION PAINT

e'mulsion paint *n.* Dispersionsfarbe, *die*

enable /ɪ'neɪbl/ *v.t.* ~ sb. to do sth. es jmdm. ermöglichen, etw. zu tun

enamel /ɪ'næml/ ⃞1 *n.* Email, *das*
⃞2 *v.t.*, (Brit.) -ll- emaillieren

enchant /ɪn'tʃɑ:nt/ *v.t.* verzaubern; (delight) entzücken

en'chanted *adj.* verzaubert

en'chanting *adj.* entzückend

en'chantment *n.* Verzauberung, *die;* (fig.) Zauber, *der*

encircle /ɪn'sɜ:kl/ *v.t.* umgeben

encl. *abbr.* = **enclosed, enclosure[s]** Anl.

enclave /'enkleɪv/ *n.* Enklave, *die*

enclose /ɪn'kləʊz/ *v.t.* (a) (surround) umgeben; (shut up or in) einschließen
(b) (with letter) beilegen (**with, in** *Dat.*); **please find ~d** anbei erhalten Sie

enclosure /ɪn'kləʊʒə(r)/ *n.* (a) (in zoo) Gehege, *das*
(b) (with letter) Anlage, *die*

encode /ɪn'kəʊd/ *v.t.* verschlüsseln; chiffrieren

encore /'ɒŋkɔ:(r)/ ⃞1 *int.* Zugabe!
⃞2 *n.* Zugabe, *die*

encounter /ɪn'kaʊntə(r)/ ⃞1 *v.t.* (as adversary) treffen auf (+ *Akk.*); (by chance) begegnen (+ *Dat.*); stoßen auf (+ *Akk.*) ⟨*Problem, Widerstand usw.*⟩
⃞2 *n.* (chance meeting) Begegnung, *die*

encourage /ɪn'kʌrɪdʒ/ *v.t.* ermutigen; (promote) fördern

encouragement *n.* Ermutigung, *die* (**from** durch)

encroach /ɪn'krəʊtʃ/ *v.i.* ~ **on** eindringen in (+ *Akk.*); in Anspruch nehmen ⟨*Zeit*⟩

encrypt /en'krɪpt/ *v.t.* (Comp.) verschlüsseln ⟨*Daten etc.*⟩

encumber /ɪn'kʌmbə(r)/ *v.t.* belasten

encumbrance /ɪn'kʌmbrəns/ *n.* Belastung, *die*

encyclopaedia /ɪnsaɪklə'pi:dɪə/ *n.* Lexikon, *das;* Enzyklopädie, *die*

encyclopaedic /ɪnsaɪklə'pi:dɪk/ *adj.* enzyklopädisch

end /end/ ⃞1 *n.* (a) Ende, *das;* (of nose, hair, finger) Spitze, *die;* **from ~ to ~:** von einem Ende zum anderen; **at the ~ of 1987/March** Ende 1987/März; **in the ~:** schließlich; **come to an ~:** ein Ende nehmen; **be at an ~:** zu Ende sein
(b) (of box, packet, etc.) Schmalseite, *die;* (top/ bottom surface) Ober-/Unterseite, *die;* **on ~:**

hochkant; **make ~s meet** (fig.) zurechtkommen; **no ~ of** (coll.) unendlich viel/viele
(c) (remnant) Rest, *der;* (of cigarette) Stummel, *der*
(d) (purpose, object) Ziel, *das;* ~ **in itself** Selbstzweck, *der*
⃞2 *v.t.* beenden
⃞3 *v.i.* enden

■ **end 'up** *v.i.* enden; ~ **up in** (coll.) landen in (+ *Dat.*); ~ **up [as] a teacher** (coll.) schließlich Lehrer werden

endanger /ɪn'deɪndʒə(r)/ *v.t.* gefährden

endear /ɪn'dɪə(r)/ *v.t.* ~ **sb./sth./oneself to sb.** jmdn./etw./sich bei jmdm. beliebt machen

en'dearing *adj.* reizend; gewinnend ⟨*Lächeln, Art*⟩

endeavour (*Brit.; Amer.:* **endeavor**) /ɪn'devə(r)/ ⃞1 *v.i.* ~ **to do sth.** sich bemühen, etw. zu tun
⃞2 *n.* Bemühung, *die;* (attempt) Versuch, *der*

'ending *n.* Schluss, *der;* (of word) Endung, *die*

endive /'endaɪv/ *n.* Endivie, *die*

'endless *adj.* endlos

'endlessly *adv.* unaufhörlich ⟨*streiten, schwatzen*⟩

endorse /ɪn'dɔ:s/ *v.t.* (a) indossieren ⟨*Scheck*⟩
(b) beipflichten (+ *Dat.*) ⟨*Meinung*⟩; billigen ⟨*Entscheidung, Handlung*⟩; unterstützen ⟨*Vorschlag*⟩
(c) (Brit. Law) einen Strafvermerk machen auf (+ *Akk. od. Dat.*)

en'dorsement *n.* (a) (of cheque) Indossament, *das*
(b) (support) Billigung, *die;* (of proposal) Unterstützung, *die*
(c) (Brit. Law) Strafvermerk, *der*

endow /ɪn'daʊ/ *v.t.* [über Stiftungen/ eine Stiftung] finanzieren; stiften ⟨*Preis, Lehrstuhl*⟩; **be ~ed with charm/a talent for music** Charme/musikalisches Talent besitzen

en'dowment mortgage *n.* ≈ Tilgungslebensversicherung, *die;*

end: ~ **'product** *n.* Endprodukt, *das;* ~ **re'sult** *n.* Ergebnis, *das;* (consequence) Folge, *die*

endurable /ɪn'djʊərəbl/ *adj.* erträglich

endurance /ɪn'djʊərəns/ *n.* Ausdauer, *die*

en'durance test *n.* Belastungsprobe, *die*

endure /ɪn'djʊə(r)/ *v.t.* ertragen

enema /'enəmə/ *n.* Einlauf, *der*

enemy /'enəmɪ/ ⃞1 *n.* Feind, *der* (**of, to** *Gen.*)
⃞2 *adj.* feindlich

energetic /enə'dʒetɪk/ *adj.* energiegeladen; (active) tatkräftig

energy /'enədʒɪ/ *n.* Energie, *die*

energy: ~ **consumption** *n.* Energieverbrauch, *der;* ~ **crisis** *n.* ⋯⁞

Energiekrise, *die;* ~ **resources** *n. pl.*
Energieressourcen *Pl.;* ~**saving** *adj.*
Energie sparend; ~**saving lamp**
Energiesparlampe, *die*

enforce /ɪnˈfɔːs/ *v.t.* durchsetzen; sorgen
für ‹*Disziplin*›; ~**d** erzwungen ‹*Schweigen*›;
unfreiwillig ‹*Untätigkeit*›

ENG *abbr.* = **electronic news-**
gathering elektronische
Berichterstattung; EB

engage /ɪnˈɡeɪdʒ/ **1** *v.t.* (a) (hire) einstellen
‹*Arbeiter*›; engagieren ‹*Sänger*›
(b) wecken ‹*Interesse*›; auf sich (*Akk.*) ziehen
‹*Aufmerksamkeit*›
(c) ~ **the clutch/first gear** einkuppeln/den
ersten Gang einlegen
2 *v.i.* ~ **in sth.** sich an etw. (*Dat.*)
beteiligen; ~ **in politics** sich politisch
engagieren

engaged /ɪnˈɡeɪdʒd/ *adj.* (a) **be** ~ [**to be**
married] [**to sb.**] [**mit jmdm.**] verlobt sein; **get**
~ [**to be married**] [**to sb.**] sich [mit jmdm.]
verloben
(b) **be** ~ **in sth./in doing sth.** mit etw.
beschäftigt sein/damit beschäftigt sein, etw.
zu tun; **be otherwise** ~: etwas anderes
vorhaben
(c) besetzt ‹*Toilette,* [*Telefon*]*anschluss,*
Nummer›; ~ **signal** *or* **tone** (Brit.)
Besetztzeichen, *das*

en'gagement *n.* (a) (to be married)
Verlobung, *die* (to mit)
(b) (appointment) Verabredung, *die*

en'gagement ring *n.* Verlobungsring,
der

engaging /ɪnˈɡeɪdʒɪŋ/ *adj.* bezaubernd;
einnehmend ‹*Persönlichkeit, Art*›

engine /ˈendʒɪn/ *n.* (a) Motor, *der;* (rocket/jet
~) Triebwerk, *das*
(b) (locomotive) Lok[omotive], *die*

'engine driver *n.* Lok[omotiv]führer, *der*

engineer /endʒɪˈnɪə(r)/ **1** *n.* (a) Ingenieur,
der/Ingenieurin, *die;* (service ~, installation ~)
Techniker, *der*/Technikerin, *die*
(b) (Amer.: engine driver) Lok[omotiv]führer,
der
2 *v.t.* arrangieren

engi'neering *n.* Technik, *die*

England /ˈɪŋɡlənd/ *pr. n.* England (*das*)

English /ˈɪŋɡlɪʃ/ **1** *adj.* englisch; **he/she is**
~: er ist Engländer/sie ist Engländerin
2 *n.* (a) Englisch, *das;* **say sth. in** ~: etw.
auf Englisch sagen; **I cannot** *or* **do not speak**
~: ich spreche kein Englisch; **translate into/**
from [**the**] ~: ins Englische/aus dem
Englischen übersetzen
(b) *pl.* **the** ~: die Engländer *Pl.*

English: ~ **'breakfast** *n.* englisches
Frühstück; ~ **'Channel** *pr. n.* **the**
~ **Channel** der [Ärmel]kanal; ~**man** /-mən/
n., pl. ~**men** /-mən/ Engländer, *der;*
~**woman** *n.* Engländerin, *die*

engrave /ɪnˈɡreɪv/ *v.t.* gravieren;
eingravieren ‹*Namen, Figur usw.*›

engraving /ɪnˈɡreɪvɪŋ/ *n.* Stich, *der;* (from
wood) Holzschnitt, *der*

engross /ɪnˈɡrəʊs/ *v.t.* fesseln; **be** ~**ed in**
sth. in etw. (*Akk.*) vertieft sein; **become** *or*
get ~**ed in sth.** sich in etw. (*Akk.*) vertiefen

engrossing /ɪnˈɡrəʊsɪŋ/ *adj.* fesselnd

engulf /ɪnˈɡʌlf/ *v.t.* verschlingen

enhance /ɪnˈhɑːns/ *v.t.* erhöhen ‹*Wert,*
Aussichten, Schönheit›; verstärken
‹*Wirkung*›; heben ‹*Aussehen*›

enigma /ɪˈnɪɡmə/ *n.* Rätsel, *das*

enigmatic /enɪɡˈmætɪk/ *adj.* rätselhaft

enjoy /ɪnˈdʒɔɪ/ **1** *v.t.* (a) **I** ~**ed the book/**
work das Buch/die Arbeit hat mir gefallen;
he ~**s reading/travelling** er liest/reist gern
(b) genießen ‹*Rechte, Privilegien, Vorteile*›
2 *v. refl.* sich amüsieren

enjoyable /ɪnˈdʒɔɪəbl/ *adj.* schön;
angenehm ‹*Empfindung, Arbeit*›;
unterhaltsam ‹*Buch, Film, Stück*›

en'joyment *n.* Vergnügen, *das* (**of** an
+ *Dat.*)

enlarge /ɪnˈlɑːdʒ/ **1** *v.t.* vergrößern;
verbreitern ‹*Straße, Durchgang*›
2 *v.i.* ~ [**up**]**on sth.** etw. weiter ausführen

en'largement *n.* Vergrößerung, *die;*
(making wider) Verbreiterung, *die*

enlighten /ɪnˈlaɪtn/ *v.t.* aufklären (**on, as to**
über + *Akk.*).

en'lightenment *n.* Aufklärung, *die*

enlist /ɪnˈlɪst/ **1** *v.t.* (obtain) gewinnen
2 *v.i.* ~ [**for the army/navy**] in die Armee/
Marine eintreten; ~ [**as a soldier**] Soldat
werden

enliven /ɪnˈlaɪvn/ *v.t.* beleben

enmity /ˈenmɪtɪ/ *n.* Feindschaft, *die*

enormous /ɪˈnɔːməs/ *adj.* enorm; riesig,
gewaltig ‹*Figur, Tier, Menge*›

e'normously *adv.* enorm

enough /ɪˈnʌf/ **1** *adj.* genug; **there's**
~ **room** es ist Platz genug
2 *n.* genug; **be** ~ **to do sth.** genügen, etw.
zu tun; **have had** ~ [**of sb./sth.**] genug [von
jmdm./etw.] haben; **I've had** ~**!** jetzt reicht's
mir aber!
3 *adv.* genug; **oddly/funnily** ~:
merkwürdigerweise/(ugs.) komischerweise

enquire /ɪnˈkwaɪə(r)/ **1** *v.i.* sich
erkundigen (**about, after** nach, **of** bei); ~ **into**
untersuchen
2 *v.t.* sich erkundigen nach ‹*Weg, Namen*›

enquiring /ɪnˈkwaɪərɪŋ/ *adj.* fragend;
forschend ‹*Geist*›

enquiry /ɪnˈkwaɪərɪ/ *n.* (a) (question)
Erkundigung, *die* (**into** über + *Akk.*); **make**
enquiries Erkundigungen einziehen; ~ **desk,**
~ **office** Auskunft, *die*
(b) (investigation) Untersuchung, *die*

enrage /ɪnˈreɪdʒ/ *v.t.* wütend machen; **be**
~**d by sth.** über etw. (*Akk.*) wütend werden

enrich /ɪnˈrɪtʃ/ *v.t.* reich machen; (fig.)
bereichern

enrol (*Amer.*: **enroll**) /ɪn'rəʊl/ 1 *v.i.*, -ll-
sich einschreiben; ~ **for a course** sich zu
einem Kurs anmelden
2 *v.t.* einschreiben

en'rolment (*Amer.*: **en'rollment**) *n.*
Einschreibung, *die*

en route /ɑ̃ 'ruːt/ *adv.* unterwegs; ~ **to
Scotland/for Edinburgh** auf dem Weg nach
Schottland/Edinburgh

ensign /'ensaɪn, 'ensn/ *n.* Hoheitszeichen,
das

enslave /ɪn'sleɪv/ *v.t.* versklaven

ensue /ɪn'sjuː/ *v.i.* folgen (**from** aus); **the
discussion which** ~**d** die anschließende
Diskussion

ensure /ɪn'ʃʊə(r)/ *v.t.* ~ **that ...** (see to it
that) gewährleisten, dass ...; ~ **sth.** etw.
gewährleisten

entail /ɪn'teɪl/ *v.t.* mit sich bringen; **sth.** ~**s
doing sth.** etw. bedeutet, dass man etw. tun
muss

entangle /ɪn'tæŋgl/ *v.t.* sich verfangen
lassen; **get** *or* **become** ~**d in** *or* **with sth.**
sich in etw. (*Dat.*) verfangen

enter /'entə(r)/ 1 *v.i.* **(a)** hineingehen;
⟨*Fahrzeug:*⟩ hineinfahren; (come in)
hereinkommen; (into room) eintreten
(b) (register as competitor) sich zur Teilnahme
anmelden (**for** an + *Dat.*)
2 *v.t.* **(a)** [hinein]gehen in (+ *Akk.*);
⟨*Fahrzeug:*⟩ [hinein]fahren in (+ *Akk.*);
betreten ⟨*Gebäude, Zimmer*⟩; einlaufen in
(+ *Akk.*) ⟨*Hafen*⟩; einreisen in (+ *Akk.*)
⟨*Land*⟩; (come into) [herein]kommen in
(+ *Akk.*)
(b) teilnehmen an (+ *Dat.*) ⟨*Rennen,
Wettbewerb*⟩
(c) (in book etc.) eintragen (**in** in + *Akk.*)
(d) (Comp.) eingeben ⟨*Daten usw.*⟩; **press** ~:
'Enter' drücken

■ **'enter in** *v.t.* aufnehmen
⟨*Verhandlungen*⟩; eingehen ⟨*Verpflichtung*⟩;
schließen ⟨*Vertrag*⟩

■ **'enter [up]on** *v.t.* beginnen

'enter key *n.* (Comp.) Entertaste, *die;*
Eingabetaste, *die*

enterprise /'entəpraɪz/ *n.* **(a)** (undertaking)
Unternehmen, *das;* **free/private** ~: freies/
privates Unternehmertum
(b) (enterprising spirit) Unternehmungsgeist,
der

enterprising /'entəpraɪzɪŋ/ *adj.*
unternehmungslustig

entertain /entə'teɪn/ *v.t.* **(a)** (amuse)
unterhalten
(b) (receive as guest) bewirten
(c) haben ⟨*Vorstellung*⟩; hegen (geh.) ⟨*Gefühl,
Verdacht, Zweifel*⟩; (consider) in Erwägung
ziehen

enter'tainer *n.* Unterhalter, *der/*
Unterhalterin, *die*

enter'taining *adj.* unterhaltsam

enter'tainment *n.* **(a)** (amusement)
Unterhaltung, *die*

(b) (performance, show) Veranstaltung, *die*

enthral (*Amer.*: **enthrall**) /ɪn'θrɔːl/ *v.t.*,
-ll- gefangen nehmen (fig.)

enthuse /ɪn'θjuːz/ 1 *v.i.* in Begeisterung
ausbrechen (**about** über + *Akk.*)
2 *v.t.* begeistern

enthusiasm /ɪn'θjuːzɪæzm/ *n.*
Begeisterung, *die*

enthusiast /ɪn'θjuːzɪæst/ *n.* Enthusiast,
der; (for sports) Fan, *der;* **a great DIY** ~: ein
begeisterter Heimwerker

enthusiastic /ɪnθjuːzɪ'æstɪk/ *adj.*
begeistert; **not be very** ~ **about doing sth.**
keine große Lust haben, etw. zu tun

entice /ɪn'taɪs/ *v.t.* locken (**into** in + *Akk.*);
~ **sb. into doing** *or* **to do sth.** jmdn. dazu
verleiten, etw. zu tun

entire /ɪn'taɪə(r)/ *adj.* **(a)** (whole) ganz
(b) (intact) vollständig

en'tirely *adv.* **(a)** (wholly) völlig
(b) (solely) ganz ⟨*für sich behalten*⟩; voll
⟨*verantwortlich sein*⟩; **it's up to you** ~: es
liegt ganz bei dir

entirety /ɪn'taɪərətɪ/ *n.* **in its** ~: in seiner/
ihrer Gesamtheit

entitle /ɪn'taɪtl/ *v.t.* berechtigen (**to** zu);
~ **sb. to do sth.** jmdm. das Recht geben, etw.
zu tun; **be** ~**d to [claim] sth.** Anspruch auf
etw. (*Akk.*) haben; **be** ~**d to do sth.** das
Recht haben, etw. zu tun

entomologist /entə'mɒlədʒɪst/ *n.*
Entomologe, *der/*Entomologin, *die*

entomology /entə'mɒlədʒɪ/ *n.*
Entomologie, *die;* Insektenkunde, *die*

entourage /ɒntʊ'rɑːʒ/ *n.* Gefolge, *das*

entrails /'entreɪlz/ *n. pl.* Eingeweide *Pl.*

entrance¹ /ɪn'trɑːns/ *v.t.* hinreißen

entrance² /'entrəns/ *n.* (way in) Eingang,
der (**to** *Gen. od.* zu); (for vehicles) Einfahrt, *die*

entrance /'entrəns/**: ~ examination**
n. Aufnahmeprüfung, *die;* ~ **fee** *n.*
Eintrittsgeld, *das;* ~ **hall** *n.* Eingangshalle,
die; ~ **ticket** *n.* Eintrittskarte, *die*

entrant /'entrənt/ *n.* (for competition, race, etc.)
Teilnehmer, *der/*Teilnehmerin, *die* (**for** *Gen.,*
an + *Dat.*)

entreat /ɪn'triːt/ *v.t.* anflehen

en'treaty *n.* flehentliche Bitte

entrepreneur /ɒntrəprə'nɜː(r)/ *n.*
Unternehmer, *der/*Unternehmerin, *die*

entrepreneurial /ɒntrəprə'nɜːrɪəl/ *adj.*
unternehmerisch

entrust /ɪn'trʌst/ *v.t.* ~ **sb. with sth.** jmdm.
etw. anvertrauen; ~ **sb./sth. to sb./sth.**
jmdn./etw. jmdm./einer Sache anvertrauen;
~ **a task to sb.** jmdn. mit einer Aufgabe
betrauen

entry /'entrɪ/ *n.* **(a)** Eintritt, *der* (**into** in
+ *Akk.*); (into country) Einreise, *die;* **'no** ~**'** (for
people) „Zutritt verboten"; (for vehicles)
„Einfahrt verboten"
(b) (way in) Eingang, *der;* (for vehicle) Einfahrt,
die   ⸱⸱⸱❖

(c) (registration, item) Eintragung, *die* (in, into in + *Akk. od. Dat.*); (in dictionary, encyclopaedia) Eintrag, *der*

entry: ~ **fee** *n.* Eintrittsgeld, *das;* ~ **form** *n.* Anmeldeformular, *das;* ~ **visa** *n.* Einreisevisum, *das*

envelop /ɪnˈveləp/ *v.t.* [ein]hüllen (in in + *Akk.*); be ~**ed in flames** ganz von Flammen umgeben sein

envelope /ˈenvələʊp, ˈɒnvələʊp/ *n.* [Brief]umschlag, *der*

enviable /ˈenvɪəbl/ *adj.* beneidenswert

envious /ˈenvɪəs/ *adj.* neidisch (of auf + *Akk.*)

environment /ɪnˈvaɪərənmənt/ *n.* Umwelt, *die;* (surrounding objects, region) Umgebung, *die*

environmental /ɪnvaɪərənˈmentl/ *adj.* Umwelt⟨verschmutzung, -schutz, -katastrophe⟩; for ~ **reasons** aus Gründen des Umweltschutzes; ~ **group** Umweltschutzorganisation, *die;* ~ **protection** Umweltschutz, *der*

environmental 'health *n.* Umwelthygiene, *die;* ~ **health officer** Umwelthygienebeauftragte, *der/die;* ~ **health department** Umwelthygieneamt, *das*

environ'mentalist *n.* Umweltschützer, *der/*-schützerin, *die*

environ'mentally *adv.* ~ **friendly** umweltfreundlich; ~ **sensitive** ökologisch sensibel; ~ **sound** umweltverträglich; umweltgerecht

envisage /ɪnˈvɪzɪdʒ/, **envision** /ɪnˈvɪʒn/ *v.t.* sich (*Dat.*) vorstellen

envoy /ˈenvɔɪ/ *n.* Gesandte, *der/*Gesandtin, *die*

envy /ˈenvɪ/ ① *n.* Neid, *der;* **you'll be the** ~ **of all your friends** alle deine Freunde werden dich beneiden

② *v.t.* beneiden; ~ **sb. sth.** jmdn. um etw. beneiden

enzyme /ˈenzaɪm/ *n.* Enzym, *das*

ephemeral /ɪˈfemərl/ *adj.* kurzlebig

epic /ˈepɪk/ ① *adj.* episch

② *n.* Epos, *das*

epidemic /epɪˈdemɪk/ ① *adj.* epidemisch

② *n.* Epidemie, *die*

epilepsy /ˈepɪlepsɪ/ *n.* Epilepsie, *die*

epileptic /epɪˈleptɪk/ ① *adj.* epileptisch; ~ **fit** epileptischer Anfall

② *n.* Epileptiker, *der/*Epileptikerin, *die*

Epiphany /ɪˈpɪfənɪ/ *n.* [Feast of the] ~: Epiphanias, *das;* Dreikönigsfest, *das;* at ~: am Dreikönigstag

episode /ˈepɪsəʊd/ *n.* **(a)** Episode, *die*

(b) (of serial) Folge, *die*

epistle /ɪˈpɪsl/ *n.* Epistel, *die*

epitaph /ˈepɪtɑːf/ *n.* Grab[in]schrift, *die*

epithet /ˈepɪθet/ *n.* Beiname, *der;* (as term of abuse) Schimpfname, *der*

epitome /ɪˈpɪtəmɪ/ *n.* Inbegriff, *der*

epitomize /ɪˈpɪtəmaɪz/ *v.t.* ~ **sth.** der Inbegriff einer Sache (*Gen.*) sein

epoch /ˈiːpɒk/ *n.* Epoche, *die*

'epoch-making *adj.* Epoche machend

equal /ˈiːkwl/ ① *adj.* **(a)** gleich; ~ **in** *or* **of** ~ **height/size/importance** etc. gleich hoch/ groß/wichtig *usw.*

(b) be ~ **to sth./sb.** (strong, clever, etc. enough) einer Sache/jmdm. gewachsen sein

② *n.* Gleichgestellte, *der/die;* **have no** ~: nicht seines-/ihresgleichen haben

③ *v.t.,* (Brit.) -**ll**-: ~ **sb.** es jmdm. gleichtun; **three times four** ~**s twelve** drei mal vier ist [gleich] zwölf

equality /ɪˈkwɒlɪtɪ/ *n.* Gleichheit, *die;* (equal rights) Gleichberechtigung, *die;* ~ **between the sexes** Gleichheit von Mann und Frau

equalize /ˈiːkwəlaɪz/ *v.i.* (Sport) den Ausgleich[streffer] erzielen

'equalizer *n.* (Sport) Ausgleich[streffer], *der*

'equally *adv.* gleich; (just as) ebenso; in gleiche Teile ⟨aufteilen⟩; gleichmäßig ⟨verteilen⟩

Equal Oppor'tunities Commission *n.* (Brit.) *Ausschuss für Chancengleichheit;* ≈ Gleichstellungsausschuss, *der*

equal oppor'tunity *n.* Chancengleichheit, *die*

'equals sign *n.* (Math.) Gleichheitszeichen, *das*

equanimity /ekwəˈnɪmɪtɪ/ *n.* Gelassenheit, *die*

equate /ɪˈkweɪt/ *v.t.* gleichsetzen (with mit)

equation /ɪˈkweɪʒn/ *n.* (Math.) Gleichung, *die*

equator /ɪˈkweɪtə(r)/ *n.* Äquator, *der*

equilibrium /iːkwɪˈlɪbrɪəm/ *n., pl.* **equilibria** /iːkwɪˈlɪbrɪə/ *or* ~**s** Gleichgewicht, *das*

equinox /ˈekwɪnɒks/ *n.* Tagundnachtgleiche, *die*

equip /ɪˈkwɪp/ *v.t.,* -**pp**- ausrüsten ⟨Fahrzeug, Armee⟩; ausstatten ⟨Küche⟩; fully ~**ped** komplett ausgerüstet/ausgestattet; ~ **sb./oneself** [with sth.] jmdn./sich [mit etw.] ausrüsten

e'quipment *n.* Ausrüstung, *die;* (of kitchen, laboratory) Ausstattung, *die;* (needed for activity) Geräte *Pl.*

equity /ˈekwɪtɪ/ *n.***(a)** (fairness) Gerechtigkeit, *die;* with ~: gerecht

(b) in *pl.* (stocks and shares without fixed interest) [Stamm]aktien *Pl.*

(c) (value of shares) Eigenkapital, *das*

(d) (net value of mortgaged property) *Wert eines Besitzes nach Abzug der Belastungen*

'equity market *n.* (Commerc.) Aktienmarkt, *der*

equivalent /ɪˈkwɪvələnt/ ① *adj.* gleichwertig; be ~ **to sth.** einer Sache (*Dat.*) entsprechen

② *n.* **(a)** (thing, person) Pendant, *das;* Gegenstück, *das* (of zu)

(b) be the ~ of sth. (have same result) einer Sache (*Dat.*) entsprechen

equivocal /ɪ'kwɪvəkl/ *adj.* zweideutig

er /ɜ:(r)/ *int.* äh

era /'ɪərə/ *n.* Ära, *die*

eradicate /ɪ'rædɪkeɪt/ *v.t.* ausrotten

erase /ɪ'reɪz/ *v.t.* auslöschen; (with rubber, knife) ausradieren; (from tape, also Comp.) löschen

e'raser *n.* [pencil] ~: Radiergummi, *der*

erect /ɪ'rekt/ **1** *adj.* aufrecht

2 *v.t.* errichten; aufstellen ⟨*Standbild, Mast, Verkehrsschild, Gerüst, Zelt*⟩

erection /ɪ'rekʃn/ *n.* **(a)** ▶ ERECT 2: Errichtung, *die;* Aufstellen, *das*

(b) (Physiol.) Erektion, *die*

ergonomic /ɜ:gə'nɒmɪk/ *adj.*, **ergo'nomically** *adv.* ergonomisch

ermine /'ɜ:mɪn/ *n.* Hermelin, *der*

erode /ɪ'rəʊd/ *v.t.* **(a)** ⟨*Säure, Rost:*⟩ angreifen; ⟨*Wasser:*⟩ auswaschen; ⟨*Wind:*⟩ verwittern lassen

(b) (fig.) unterminieren

erosion /ɪ'rəʊʒn/ *n.* **(a)** ▶ ERODE A: Angreifen, *das;* Auswaschung, *die;* Verwitterung, *die*

(b) (fig.) Unterminierung, *die*

erotic /ɪ'rɒtɪk/ *adj.* erotisch

err /ɜ:(r)/ *v.i.* sich irren

errand /'erənd/ *n.* Botengang, *der;* (shopping) Besorgung, *die;* **go an** *or* **run an ~:** einen Botengang/eine Besorgung machen

'errand boy *n.* Laufbursche, *der*

erratic /ɪ'rætɪk/ *adj.* unregelmäßig; sprunghaft ⟨*Wesen, Person, Art*⟩; launenhaft ⟨*Verhalten*⟩

erroneous /ɪ'rəʊnɪəs/ *adj.* falsch; irrig ⟨*Schlussfolgerung, Annahme*⟩

error /'erə(r)/ *n.* (mistake) Fehler, *der;* (wrong opinion) Irrtum, *der;* **in ~:** irrtümlich[erweise]

'error message *n.* (Comp.) Fehlermeldung, *die*

erudite /'eru:daɪt/ *adj.* gelehrt

erupt /ɪ'rʌpt/ *v.i.* ausbrechen

eruption /ɪ'rʌpʃn/ *n.* Ausbruch, *der*

escalate /'eskəleɪt/ *v.i.* **1** sich ausweiten (into zu); ⟨*Preise, Kosten:*⟩ [ständig] steigen

2 *v.t.* ausweiten (into zu)

escalator /'eskəleɪtə(r)/ *n.* Rolltreppe, *die*

escapade /eskə'peɪd/ *n.* Eskapade, *die* (geh.)

escape /ɪ'skeɪp/ **1** *n.* Flucht, *die* (from aus); **have a narrow ~:** gerade noch einmal davonkommen

2 *v.i.* **(a)** fliehen (from aus); (successfully) entkommen (from *Dat.*)

(b) ⟨*Gas:*⟩ ausströmen; ⟨*Flüssigkeit:*⟩ auslaufen

3 *v.t.* **(a)** entkommen (+ *Dat.*) ⟨*Verfolger,*

Feind⟩; entgehen (+ *Dat.*) ⟨*Bestrafung, Gefangennahme, Tod*⟩; verschont bleiben von ⟨*Zerstörung, Auswirkungen*⟩

(b) (not be remembered by) entfallen sein (+ *Dat.*)

escape: ~ artist ▶ ESCAPOLOGIST;

~ attempt, ~ bid *ns.* Fluchtversuch, *der;* (from prison) Ausbruchsversuch, *der;* **~ hatch** *n.* Notausstieg, *der;* (fig.) Rettungsanker, *der;* **~ key** *n.* (Comp.) Escapetaste, *die;* **~ road** *n.* Auslaufstrecke, *die;* **~ route** *n.* Fluchtweg, *der*

escapism /ɪ'skeɪpɪzm/ *n.* Realitätsflucht, *die*

escapologist /eskə'pɒlədʒɪst/ *n.* (Brit.) Entfesselungskünstler, *der*/-künstlerin, *die*

escarpment /ɪ'skɑ:pmənt/ *n.* (Geog.) Steilhang, *der*

escort **1** /'eskɔ:t/ *n.* **(a)** Begleitung, *die;* (Mil.) Eskorte, *die*

(b) (hired companion) Begleiter, *der*/ Begleiterin, *die*

2 /ɪ'skɔ:t/ *v.t.* begleiten; (lead) führen; (Mil.) eskortieren

Eskimo /'eskɪməʊ/ **1** *adj.* Eskimo-

2 *n., pl.* **~s** or same Eskimo, *der*/ Eskimofrau, *die;* **the ~[s]** die Eskimos

esoteric /esəʊ'terɪk/ *adj.* esoterisch

especial /ɪ'speʃl/ *attrib. adj.* [ganz] besonder...

especially /ɪ'speʃəlɪ/ *adv.* besonders

espionage /'espɪənɑ:ʒ/ *n.* Spionage, *die*

esplanade /esplə'neɪd, esplə'nɑ:d/ *n.* Esplanade, *die* (geh.)

espouse /ɪ'spaʊz/ *v.t.* eintreten für

espresso /e'spresəʊ/ *n., pl.* **~s** (coffee) Espresso, *der*

e'spresso bar *n.* Espressobar, *die*

Esq. /ɪ'skwaɪə(r)/ *abbr.* = **Esquire** ≈ Hr.; (on letter) ≈ Hrn.; **Jim Smith, ~:** Hr./Hrn. Jim Smith

essay /'eseɪ/ *n.* Essay, *der;* Aufsatz, *der* (bes. Schulw.)

essence /'esəns/ *n.* **(a)** Wesen, *das;* (gist) Wesentliche, *das;* **in ~:** im Wesentlichen

(b) (Cookery) Essenz, *die*

essential /ɪ'senʃl/ **1** *adj.* **(a)** (fundamental) wesentlich

(b) (indispensable) unentbehrlich; lebensnotwendig ⟨*Versorgungseinrichtungen, Güter*⟩; unabdingbar ⟨*Qualifikation, Voraussetzung*⟩; **it is ~ that ...:** es ist unbedingt notwendig, dass ...

2 *n. pl.* **the ~s** (fundamentals) das Wesentliche; (items) das Notwendigste

es'sentially *adv.* im Grunde

establish /ɪ'stæblɪʃ/ *v.t.* **(a)** schaffen ⟨*Einrichtung, Präzedenzfall*⟩; gründen ⟨*Organisation, Institut*⟩; errichten ⟨*Geschäft, System*⟩

(b) (secure acceptance for) etablieren; **become ~ed** sich einbürgern

(c) (prove) beweisen

···⟶

(d) (discover) feststellen

established /ɪˈstæblɪʃt/ *adj.* bestehend ⟨*Ordnung*⟩; etabliert ⟨*Schriftsteller*⟩; (accepted) üblich; fest ⟨*Brauch*⟩; feststehend ⟨*Tatsache*⟩; become ∼: sich durchsetzen

e'stablishment *n.* **(a)** (setting up, foundation) Gründung, *die* **(b)** [business] ∼: Unternehmen, *das*

estate /ɪˈsteɪt/ *n.* **(a)** (landed property) Gut, *das* **(b)** (Brit.: housing ∼) [Wohn]siedlung, *die* **(c)** (of deceased person) Erbmasse, *die*

estate: ∼ **agent** *n.* (Brit.) Grundstücksmakler, *der*/-maklerin, *die;* ∼ **car** *n.* (Brit.) Kombiwagen, *der;* ∼ **duty** (Brit.), **e'state tax** (Amer.) *ns.* Erbschaftssteuer, *die*

esteem /ɪˈstiːm/ ① *n.* Wertschätzung, *die* (geh.) (for *Gen.,* für) ② *v.t.* schätzen; **highly** ∼**ed** hoch geschätzt

estimate ① /ˈestɪmət/ *n.* **(a)** Schätzung, *die;* **at a rough** ∼: grob geschätzt **(b)** (Commerc.) Kostenvoranschlag, *der* ② /ˈestɪmeɪt/ *v.t.* schätzen (at auf + *Akk.*)

estimation /estɪˈmeɪʃn/ *n.* Schätzung, *die;* **in sb.'s** ∼: nach jmds. Schätzung

Estonia /eˈstəʊnɪə/ *pr. n.* Estland (*das*)

Estonian /eˈstəʊnɪən/ ① *adj.* estländisch; estnisch; **sb. is** ∼: jmd. ist Este/Estin ② *n.* **(a)** (language) Estnisch, *das;* Estländisch, *das; see also* ENGLISH 2A **(b)** (person) Este, *der*/Estin, *die;* Estländer, *der*/Estländerin, *die*

estuary /ˈestjʊərɪ/ *n.* [Trichter]mündung, *die*

ETA *abbr.* = **estimated time of arrival** voraussichtliche Ankunftszeit

etc. *abbr.* = **et cetera** usw.

etch /etʃ/ *v.t.* ätzen (on auf + *Akk.*); (on metal also) ⟨*bes. Künstler:*⟩ radieren; (fig.) einprägen (in, on *Dat.*)

'etching *n.* (Art) Radierung, *die*

eternal /ɪˈtɜːnl/ *adj.,* **e'ternally** *adv.* ewig

eternity /ɪˈtɜːnɪtɪ/ *n.* Ewigkeit, *die*

ether /ˈiːθə(r)/ *n.* Äther, *der*

ethereal /ɪˈθɪərɪəl/ *adj.* ätherisch

ethical /ˈeθɪkl/ *adj.* ethisch

ethics /ˈeθɪks/ *n.* **(a)** Moral, *die;* (moral philosophy) Ethik, *die* **(b)** *usu. constr. as pl.* (moral code) Ethik, *die* (geh.)

Ethiopia /iːθɪˈəʊpɪə/ *pr. n.* Äthiopien (*das*)

Ethiopian /iːθɪˈəʊpɪən/ ① *adj.* äthiopisch; **sb. is** ∼: jmd. ist Äthiopier/Äthiopierin ② *n.* Äthiopier, *der*/Äthiopierin, *die*

ethnic /ˈeθnɪk/ *adj.* ethnisch; ∼ **minority** ethnische Minderheit

ethnic 'cleansing *n.* ethnische Säuberung

ethnology /eθˈnɒlədʒɪ/ *n.* Ethnologie, *die*

ethos /ˈiːθɒs/ *n.* (guiding beliefs) Gesinnung, *die;* (fundamental values) Ethos, *das* (geh.)

etiquette /ˈetɪket/ *n.* Etikette, *die*

etymology /etɪˈmɒlədʒɪ/ *n.* Etymologie, *die*

EU *abbr.* = **European Union** EU

eulogy /ˈjuːlədʒɪ/ *n.* Lobrede, *die*

euphemism /ˈjuːfəmɪzm/ *n.* Euphemismus, *der*

euphemistic /juːfəˈmɪstɪk/ *adj.* verhüllend

euphoria /juːˈfɔːrɪə/ *n.* Euphorie, *die* (geh.)

euro /ˈjʊərəʊ/ *n.* Euro, *der*

Euro-: ∼**cheque** *n.* Euroscheck, *der;* ∼**land** *n.* Euroland, *das;* ∼**-MP** *n.* Europaabgeordnete, *der*/*die*

Europe /ˈjʊərəp/ *pr. n.* Europa (*das*)

European /jʊərəˈpiːən/ ① *adj.* europäisch; **sb. is** ∼: jmd. ist Europäer/Europäerin; ∼ **[Economic] Community** Europäische [Wirtschafts]gemeinschaft ② *n.* Europäer, *der*/Europäerin, *die*

European: ∼ **Central 'Bank** *n.* Europäische Zentralbank; ∼ **Com'mission** *n.* Europäische Kommission; ∼ **'Council** *n.* Europäischer Rat; ∼ **Court of 'Justice** *n.* Europäischer Gerichtshof; ∼ **'Cup** *n.* (Footb.) Europacup, *der;* Europapokal, *der;* ∼ **'currency unit** *n.* Europäische Währungseinheit; ∼ **'Monetary System** *n.* Europäisches Währungssystem; ∼ **Monetary 'Union** *n.* Europäische Währungsunion; ∼ **'Parliament** *n.* Europäisches Parlament; ∼ **'Union** *n.* Europäische Union

Euro-: ∼**-rebel** *n.* (esp. Brit.) [innerparteilicher] Europagegner/ [innerparteiliche] Europagegnerin; ∼**sceptic** *n.* Euroskeptiker, *der*/ -skeptikerin, *die;* ∼**star** ® *n.* Eurostar, *der;* **go by** ∼**star** mit dem Eurostar fahren; ∼**zone** *n.* Eurozone, *die*

euthanasia /juːθəˈneɪzɪə/ *n.* Euthanasie, *die*

evacuate /ɪˈvækjʊeɪt/ *v.t.* evakuieren (from aus)

evacuation /ɪvækjʊˈeɪʃn/ *n.* Evakuierung, *die* (from aus)

evade /ɪˈveɪd/ *v.t.* ausweichen (+ *Dat.*) ⟨*Angriff, Angreifer, Schlag, Problem, Frage*⟩; sich entziehen (+ *Dat.*) ⟨*Verhaftung, Verantwortung*⟩; entkommen (+ *Dat.*) ⟨*Verfolger, Verfolgung*⟩; hinterziehen ⟨*Steuern*⟩; ∼ **doing sth.** vermeiden, etw. zu tun

evaluate /ɪˈvæljʊeɪt/ *v.t.* einschätzen; bewerten ⟨*Daten*⟩

evangelical /iːvænˈdʒelɪkl/ *adj.* missionarisch (fig.); (Protestant) evangelikal

evangelist /ɪˈvændʒəlɪst/ *n.* Evangelist, *der*

evaporate /ɪˈvæpəreɪt/ ① *v.i.* verdunsten ② *v.t.* verdunsten lassen

evaporated 'milk *n.* Kondensmilch, *die*

evaporation /ɪvæpə'reɪʃn/ n. Verdunstung, die

evasion /ɪ'veɪʒn/ n. Umgehung, die; (of responsibility, question) Ausweichen, das (of vor + Dat.); **tax** ~: Steuerhinterziehung, die

evasive /ɪ'veɪsɪv/ adj. (a) be/become ~: ausweichen
(b) ausweichend ⟨Antwort⟩

eve /iːv/ n. Vorabend, der (of Gen.); (day) Vortag, der (of Gen.)

even /'iːvn/ ① adj. (a) eben ⟨Boden, Fläche⟩; gleich hoch ⟨Stapel, Stuhl-, Tischbein⟩; **be of ~ height/length** gleich hoch/lang sein
(b) gerade ⟨Zahl, Seite, Hausnummer⟩
(c) **be** or **get ~ with sb.** (quits) es jmdm. heimzahlen; **break ~:** die Kosten decken
② adv. sogar; selbst; sogar noch ⟨weniger, schlimmer usw.⟩; ~ **if** selbst wenn; ~ **so** [aber] trotzdem; **not** or **never ~ ...:** [noch] nicht einmal ...

■ **even 'up** v.t. ausgleichen

evening /'iːvnɪŋ/ n. Abend, der; **this/ tomorrow ~:** heute/morgen Abend; **in the ~:** am Abend; (regularly) abends

evening: ~ **class** n. Abendkurs, der; ~ **dress** n. Abendkleidung, die; ~ '**meal** n. Abendessen, das; ~ '**paper** n. Abendzeitung, die

'**evenly** adv. gleichmäßig

'**even-numbered** adj. gerade

event /ɪ'vent/ n. (a) **in the ~ of his dying** or **death** im Falle seines Todes; **in the ~:** letzten Endes; **in the ~ of rain** bei Regenwetter
(b) (occurrence) Ereignis, das
(c) (planned public or social occasion) Veranstaltung, die

e'ventful adj. ereignisreich

eventual /ɪ'ventjʊəl/ adj. **predict sb.'s ~ downfall** vorhersagen, dass jmd. schließlich zu Fall kommen wird; **the career of Napoleon and his ~ defeat** der Aufstieg Napoleons und schließlich seine Niederlage

eventuality /ɪventjʊ'ælɪtɪ/ n. Eventualität, die

e'ventually adv. schließlich

ever /'evə(r)/ adv. (a) (always) immer; **for ~:** für immer; ewig ⟨lieben, da sein, leben⟩; ~ **since** [then] seit [dieser Zeit]
(b) (at any time) je[mals]; **hardly ~:** so gut wie nie; **as ~:** wie gewöhnlich
(c) in comb. with compar. adj. or adv. noch; ~-**increasing** ständig zunehmend
(d) **what ~ does he want?** was will er nur?; **why ~ not?** warum denn nicht?

'**ever:** ~**green** ① adj. immergrün;
② n. immergrüne Pflanze; ~**lasting** adj. (a) (eternal) immer während; ewig ⟨Leben⟩; unvergänglich ⟨Ruhm, Ehre⟩; (b) (incessant) endlos

every /'evrɪ/ adj. (a) jeder/jede/jedes; ~ **one** jeder/jede/jedes [einzelne]; **your ~ wish** all[e] deine Wünsche; **she comes ~ day** sie kommt jeden Tag; ~ **three/few days** alle drei/paar Tage; ~ **other** (~ second, almost ~) jeder/jede/jedes zweite
(b) (the greatest possible) all ⟨Respekt, Aussicht⟩

every: ~**body** n. & pron. jeder; ~**body else** alle anderen; ~**day** attrib. adj. alltäglich; Alltags⟨kleidung, -sprache⟩; **in ~day life** im Alltag; ~**one** ▶ ~BODY; ~**place** (Amer.) ▶ ~WHERE; ~**thing** n. & pron. alles; ~**where** adv. überall; ~**where you go/look** wohin man auch geht/sieht

evict /ɪ'vɪkt/ v.t. ~ **sb.** [from his home] jmdn. zur Räumung [seiner Wohnung] zwingen

eviction /ɪ'vɪkʃn/ n. Zwangsräumung, die; **the ~ of the tenant** die zwangsweise Vertreibung des Mieters

evidence /'evɪdəns/ n. (a) Beweis, der; (indication) Anzeichen, das; **be ~ of sth.** etw. beweisen
(b) (Law) Beweismaterial, das; **give ~:** aussagen

evident /'evɪdənt/ adj. offensichtlich; **be ~ to sb.** jmdm. klar sein; **it soon became ~ that ...:** es stellte sich bald heraus, dass ...

'**evidently** adv. offensichtlich

evil /'iːvl, 'iːvɪl/ ① adj. böse; schlecht ⟨Charakter, Einfluss, System⟩
② n. (a) Böse, das
(b) (bad thing) Übel, das

evocative /ɪ'vɒkətɪv/ adj. **be ~ of sth.** etw. heraufbeschwören

evoke /ɪ'vəʊk/ v.t. heraufbeschwören; hervorrufen ⟨Bewunderung, Überraschung⟩; erregen ⟨Interesse⟩

evolution /iːvə'luːʃn/ n. Entwicklung, die; (Biol.) Evolution, die

evolve /ɪ'vɒlv/ ① v.i. sich entwickeln (**from** aus, **into** zu)
② v.t. entwickeln

ewe /juː/ n. Mutterschaf, das

ex¹ /eks/ n. (coll.) Verflossene, der/die (ugs.)

ex² prep. (Commerc.) **ex works/store** ⟨Güter⟩ ab Werk/Lager

ex- pref. Ex-⟨Freundin, Präsident, Champion⟩; Alt-⟨[bundes]kanzler⟩

exacerbate /ek'sæsəbeɪt/ v.t. verschärfen ⟨Lage⟩; verschlechtern ⟨Zustand⟩

exact /ɪg'zækt/ ① adj. genau
② v.t. fordern; erheben ⟨Gebühr⟩

exacting /ɪg'zæktɪŋ/ n. anspruchsvoll; hoch ⟨Anforderung⟩

exactitude /ɪg'zæktɪtjuːd/ Genauigkeit, die

exactly /ɪg'zæktlɪ/ adv. genau; **not ~** (coll. iron.) nicht gerade

exactness /ɪg'zæktnɪs/ n. Genauigkeit, die

exaggerate /ɪg'zædʒəreɪt/ v.t. übertreiben

exaggeration /ɪgzædʒə'reɪʃn/ n. Übertreibung, die

exam /ɪg'zæm/ (coll.) ▶ EXAMINATION B

examination /ɪgzæmɪ'neɪʃn/ *n.* **(a)** (inspection; Med.) Untersuchung, *die* **(b)** (Sch. etc.) Prüfung, *die;* (final ~ at university) Examen, *das*

exami'nation paper *n.* **(a)** ~[s] schriftliche Prüfungsaufgaben *Pl.* **(b)** (with candidate's answers) ≈ Klausurarbeit, *die*

examine /ɪg'zæmɪn/ *v.t.* **(a)** (inspect; Med.) untersuchen (for auf + *Akk.*); prüfen ⟨Dokument, Gewissen⟩; kontrollieren ⟨Ausweis, Gepäck⟩ **(b)** (Sch. etc.) prüfen (in in + *Dat.*) **(c)** (Law) verhören

examiner /ɪg'zæmɪnə(r)/ *n.* Prüfer, *der*/ Prüferin, *die*

example /ɪg'zɑːmpl/ *n.* Beispiel, *das;* for ~: zum Beispiel; **make an** ~ **of sb.** ein Exempel an jmdm. statuieren

exasperate /ɪg'zæspəreɪt/ *v.t.* (irritate) verärgern; (infuriate) zur Verzweiflung bringen

exasperation /ɪg'zæspəreɪʃn/ *n.* ▶ EXASPERATE: Ärger, *der*/Verzweiflung, *die* (with über + *Akk.*); in ~: verärgert/ verzweifelt

excavate /'ekskəveɪt/ *v.t.* **(a)** ausschachten; (with machine) ausbaggern **(b)** (Archaeol.) ausgraben

excavation /ekskə'veɪʃn/ *n.* **(a)** Ausschachtung, *die;* (with machine) Ausbaggerung, *die* **(b)** (Archaeol.) Ausgrabung, *die*

excavator /'ekskəveɪtə(r)/ *n.* Bagger, *der*

exceed /ɪk'siːd/ *v.t.* **(a)** (be greater than) übertreffen (in an + *Dat.*); ⟨Kosten, Summe, Anzahl:⟩ übersteigen (by um) **(b)** (go beyond) überschreiten; hinausgehen über (+ *Akk.*) ⟨Auftrag, Befehl⟩

ex'ceedingly *adv.* äußerst; ausgesprochen ⟨hässlich, dumm⟩

excel /ɪk'sel/ **1** *v.t.,* **-ll-** übertreffen; ~ **oneself** (lit. or iron.) sich selbst übertreffen **2** *v.i.,* **-ll-** sich hervortun (at, in in + *Dat.*)

excellence /'eksələns/ *n.* hervorragende Qualität

excellent /'eksələnt/ *adj.* hervorragend

except /ɪk'sept/ **1** *prep.* ~ [for] außer (+ *Dat.*); ~ **for** (in all respects other than) abgesehen von **2** *v.t.* ausnehmen (from bei); ~ed ausgenommen

ex'cepting *prep.* außer (+ *Dat.*)

exception /ɪk'sepʃn/ *n.* Ausnahme, *die;* **take** ~ **to** Anstoß nehmen an (+ *Dat.*)

exceptional /ɪk'sepʃənl/ *adj.* außergewöhnlich

ex'ceptionally *adv.* **(a)** (as an exception) ausnahmsweise **(b)** (remarkably) ungewöhnlich

excerpt /'eksɜːpt/ *n.* Auszug, *der* (from aus)

excess /ɪk'ses/ *n.* **(a)** Übermaß, *das* (of an + *Dat.*); **eat/drink to** ~: übermäßig essen/ trinken

(b) *esp. in pl.* (over-indulgence) Exzess, *der* **(c)** be in ~ of sth. etw. übersteigen **(d)** (surplus) Überschuss, *der*

excess /'ekses/: ~ **'baggage** *n.* Mehrgepäck, *das;* ~ **'fare** *n.* Mehrpreis, *der;* **pay the** ~ fare nachlösen

excessive /ɪk'sesɪv/ *adj.* übermäßig; übertrieben ⟨Forderung, Lob, Ansprüche⟩; unmäßig ⟨Esser, Trinker⟩

ex'cessively *adv.* übertrieben; unmäßig ⟨essen, trinken⟩

excess: ~ **'luggage** ▶ ~ BAGGAGE; ~ **'postage** *n.* Nachgebühr, *die*

exchange /ɪks'tʃeɪndʒ/ **1** *v.t.* **(a)** tauschen ⟨Plätze, Ringe, Küsse⟩; umtauschen ⟨Geld⟩; wechseln ⟨Blicke, Worte⟩; ~ **insults** sich beleidigen **(b)** (give in place of another) eintauschen (for für, gegen); umtauschen ⟨[gekaufte] Ware⟩ (for gegen) **2** *n.* **(a)** Tausch, *der;* in ~: dafür; in ~ for sth. für etw. **(b)** (Educ.) Austausch, *der;* **an** ~ **student** ein Austauschstudent/eine Austauschstudentin **(c)** (of money) Umtausch, *der;* ~ **rate, rate of** ~: Wechselkurs, *der* **(d)** (Teleph.) Fernmeldeamt, *das*

exchequer /ɪks'tʃekə(r)/ *n.* (Brit.) Schatzamt, *das*

excise /'eksaɪz/ *n.* Verbrauchsteuer, *die;* **Customs and E**~ (Brit.) *Amt für Zölle und Verbrauchsteuer*

excitable /ek'saɪtəbl/ *adj.* leicht erregbar

excite /ɪk'saɪt/ *v.t.* **(a)** (thrill) begeistern **(b)** (agitate) aufregen

ex'cited *adj.* aufgeregt (at über + *Akk.*); **get** ~: sich aufregen

ex'citement *n.* Aufregung, *die;* (enthusiasm) Begeisterung, *die*

exciting /ɪk'saɪtɪŋ/ *adj.* aufregend; (full of suspense) spannend

exclaim /ɪk'skleɪm/ **1** *v.t.* ausrufen **2** *v.i.* aufschreien

exclamation /eksklə'meɪʃn/ *n.* Ausruf, *der*

excla'mation mark, (Amer.) **excla'mation point** *ns.* Ausrufezeichen, *das*

exclude /ɪk'skluːd/ *v.t.* ausschließen

excluding /ɪk'skluːdɪŋ/ *prep.* ~ **drinks/VAT** Getränke ausgenommen/ohne Mehrwertsteuer

exclusion /ɪk'skluːʒn/ *n.* Ausschluss, *der*

exclusive /ɪk'skluːsɪv/ *adj.* **(a)** alleinig ⟨Besitzer, Kontrolle⟩; Allein⟨eigentum⟩; (Journ.) Exklusiv⟨bericht, -interview⟩ **(b)** (select) exklusiv **(c)** ~ **of** ohne

ex'clusively *adv.* ausschließlich

excommunicate /ekskə'mjuːnɪkeɪt/ *v.t.* exkommunizieren

excrement /'ekskrɪmənt/ *n.* Kot, *der* (geh.)

excrete /ɪk'skriːt/ *v.t.* ausscheiden

excruciating /ɪkˈskruːˈʃɪeɪtɪŋ/ *adj.* unerträglich

excursion /ɪkˈskɜːʃn/ *n.* Ausflug, *der*

excusable /ɪkˈskjuːzəbl/ *adj.* entschuldbar; verzeihlich

excuse ① /ɪkˈskjuːz/ *v.t.* (a) entschuldigen; ~ oneself sich entschuldigen; ~ me Entschuldigung (b) (release, exempt) befreien (**from** von) ② /ɪkˈskjuːs/ *n.* Entschuldigung, *die*

ex-diʹrectory *adj.* (Brit. Teleph.) Geheim⟨*nummer, -anschluss*⟩; be ~: nicht im Telefonbuch stehen

execute /ˈeksɪkjuːt/ *v.t.* (a) hinrichten (b) ⟨put into effect⟩ ausführen

execution /eksɪˈkjuːʃn/ *n.* (a) Hinrichtung, *die* (b) ⟨putting into effect⟩ Ausführung, *die*

exeʹcutioner *n.* Scharfrichter, *der*

executive /ɪɡˈzekjʊtɪv/ ① *n.* leitender Angestellter/leitende Angestellte ② *adj.* leitend ⟨*Stellung, Funktion*⟩

executive: ~ ʹstress *n.* Managerstress, *der;* ~ ʹtoy *n.* Managerspielzeug, *das*

executor /ɪɡˈzekjʊtə(r)/ *n.* (Law) Testamentsvollstrecker, *der*

exemplary /ɪɡˈzemplərɪ/ *adj.* (a) ⟨model⟩ vorbildlich (b) ⟨deterrent⟩ exemplarisch

exemplify /ɪɡˈzemplɪfaɪ/ *v.t.* veranschaulichen

exempt /ɪɡˈzempt/ ① *adj.* [be] ~ [**from** sth.] [von etw.] befreit [sein] ② *v.t.* befreien

exemption /ɪɡˈzempʃn/ *n.* Befreiung, *die*

exercise /ˈeksəsaɪz/ ① *n.* (a) Übung, *die* (b) *no pl.* (physical exertion) Bewegung, *die;* take ~: sich (*Dat.*) Bewegung schaffen ② *v.t.* ausüben ⟨*Recht, Macht, Einfluss*⟩; walten lassen ⟨*Vorsicht*⟩ ③ *v.i.* sich (*Dat.*) Bewegung schaffen

exercise: ~ **bicycle,** (coll.) ~ **bike** *ns.* Heimtrainer, *der;* ~ **book** *n.* [Schul]heft, *das*

exert /ɪɡˈzɜːt/ ① *v.t.* aufbieten ⟨*Kraft*⟩; ausüben ⟨*Einfluss, Druck*⟩ ② *v. refl.* sich anstrengen

exertion /ɪɡˈzɜːʃn/ *n.* (a) (of strength, force) Aufwendung, *die;* (of influence, pressure) Ausübung, *die* (b) (effort) Anstrengung, *die*

exhale /eksˈheɪl/ *v.t. & i.* ausatmen

exhaust /ɪɡˈzɔːst/ ① *v.t.* erschöpfen; erschöpfend behandeln ⟨*Thema*⟩ ② *n.* (Motor Veh.) Auspuff, *der;* (gases) Auspuffgase *Pl.;* ~ **emissions** Auspuffabgase *Pl.;* ~ **emissions test** Abgasuntersuchung, *die*

exʹhausted *adj.* erschöpft

exʹhausting *adj.* anstrengend

exhaustion /ɪɡˈzɔːstʃn/ *n.* Erschöpfung, *die*

exhaustive /ɪɡˈzɔːstɪv/ *adj.* umfassend

exʹhaust pipe *n.* Auspuffrohr, *das*

exhibit /ɪɡˈzɪbɪt/ ① *v.t.* ausstellen; zeigen ⟨*Mut, Symptome, Angst usw.*⟩ ② *n.* Ausstellungsstück, *das*

exhibition /eksɪˈbɪʃn/ *n.* Ausstellung, *die;* make an ~ of oneself sich unmöglich aufführen

exhibitionism /eksɪˈbɪʃənɪzm/ *n.* Exhibitionismus, *der*

exhibitionist /eksɪˈbɪʃənɪst/ *n.* Exhibitionist, *der*/Exhibitionistin, *die*

exhibitor /ɪɡˈzɪbɪtə(r)/ *n.* Aussteller, *der*/Ausstellerin, *die*

exhilarated /ɪɡˈzɪləreɪtɪd/ *adj.* belebt

exhilarating /ɪɡˈzɪləreɪtɪŋ/ *adj.* belebend

exhilaration /ɪɡzɪləˈreɪʃn/ *n.* [feeling of] ~: Hochgefühl, *das*

exhort /ɪɡˈzɔːt/ *v.t.* ermahnen

exile /ˈeksaɪl/ ① *n.* (a) Exil, *das;* in/into ~: im/ins Exil (b) ⟨person⟩ Verbannte, *der*/die ② *v.t.* verbannen

exist /ɪɡˈzɪst/ *v.i.* existieren; ⟨*Zweifel, Gefahr, Problem, Einrichtung:*⟩ bestehen; ~ on sth. von etw. leben

existence /ɪɡˈzɪstəns/ *n.* Existenz, *die;* (mode of living) Dasein, *das;* be in/come into ~: existieren/entstehen

exit /ˈeksɪt/ *n.* (way out) Ausgang, *der* (**from** aus); (for vehicle) Ausfahrt, *die*

exit: ~ **permit** *n.* Ausreiseerlaubnis, *die;* ~ **poll** *n.:* Befragung der ein Wahllokal verlassenden Wähler; ~ **visa** *n.* Ausreisevisum, *das*

exonerate /ɪɡˈzɒnəreɪt/ *v.t.* entlasten

exorbitant /ɪɡˈzɔːbɪtənt/ *adj.* [maßlos] überhöht

exorcize /ˈeksɔːsaɪz/ *v.t.* austreiben

exotic /ɪɡˈzɒtɪk/ *adj.* exotisch

expand /ɪkˈspænd/ ① *v.i.* (a) sich ausdehnen; (Commerc.) expandieren (b) ~ on weiter ausführen ② *v.t.* ausdehnen; (Commerc.) erweitern

expanse /ɪkˈspæns/ *n.* [weite] Fläche

expansion /ɪkˈspænʃn/ *n.* Ausdehnung, *die;* (Commerc.) Expansion, *die*

expect /ɪkˈspekt/ *v.t.* (a) erwarten; ~ to do sth. damit rechnen, etw. zu tun; ~ sb. to do sth. damit rechnen, dass jmd. etw. tut; (require) von jmdm. erwarten, dass er etw. tut (b) (coll.: think, suppose) glauben; I ~ so ich glaube schon

expectancy /ɪkˈspektənsɪ/ *n.* Erwartung, *die*

expectant /ɪkˈspektənt/ *adj.* erwartungsvoll; ~ mother werdende Mutter

exʹpectantly *adv.* erwartungsvoll; gespannt ⟨*warten*⟩

expectation /ekspekˈteɪʃn/ *n.* Erwartung, *die*

expedient /ɪkˈspiːdɪənt/ ① *adj.* angebracht

2 *n.* Mittel, *das*

expedition /eksprˈdɪʃn/ *n.* Expedition, *die*

expel /ɪkˈspel/ *v.t.,* **-ll-** ausweisen (**from** aus); ∼ **sb. from school** jmdn. von der Schule verweisen

expend /ɪkˈspend/ *v.t.* (a) aufwenden ([up]on für) (b) (use up) aufbrauchen ([up]on für)

expendable /ɪkˈspendəbl/ *adj.* entbehrlich; **be** ∼: geopfert werden können

expenditure /ɪkˈspendɪtʃə(r)/ *n.* (a) (amount spent) Ausgaben *Pl.* (**on** für) (b) (spending) Ausgabe, *die*

expense /ɪkˈspens/ *n.* (a) Kosten *Pl.;* **at sb.'s** ∼: auf jmds. Kosten (*Akk.*); **at one's own** ∼: auf eigene Kosten (b) *usu. in pl.* (Commerc. etc.: amount spent [and repaid]) Spesen *Pl.* (c) (fig.) [**be**] **at the** ∼ **of sth.** auf Kosten von etw. [gehen]

ex'pense account *n.* Spesenabrechnung, *die;* **put sth. on one's** ∼: etw. als Spesen abrechnen

expensive /ɪkˈspensɪv/ *adj.,* **ex'pensively** *adv.* teuer

experience /ɪkˈspɪərɪəns/ **1** *n.* Erfahrung, *die;* (incident) Erlebnis, *das* **2** *v.t.* erleben; haben ⟨*Schwierigkeiten*⟩; verspüren ⟨*Kälte, Schmerz, Gefühl*⟩

ex'perienced *adj.* erfahren

experiment **1** /ɪkˈsperɪmənt/ *n.* (a) Experiment, *das,* Versuch, *der* (**on** an + *Dat.*) (b) (fig.) Experiment, *das* **2** /ɪkˈsperɪment/ *v.i.* Versuche anstellen (**on** an + *Dat.*)

experimental /ɪksperɪˈmentl/ *adj.* experimentell; Experimentier⟨*theater, -kino*⟩

expert /ˈeksp3:t/ **1** *adj.* ausgezeichnet; **be** ∼ **in** *or* **at sth.** Fachmann *od.* Experte für etw. sein; **be** ∼ **in** *or* **at doing sth.** etw. ausgezeichnet können **2** *n.* Fachmann, *der;* Experte, *der/*Expertin, *die;* **be an** ∼ **in** *or* **at/on sth.** Fachmann *od.* Experte in etw. (*Dat.*)/für etw. sein

expertise /eksp3:ˈti:z/ *n.* Fachkenntnisse *Pl.;* (skill) Können, *das*

expert: ∼ **system** *n.* (Comp.) Expertensystem, *das;* ∼ **'witness** *n.* sachverständiger Zeuge

expire /ɪkˈspaɪə(r)/ *v.i.* ablaufen

expiry /ɪkˈspaɪərɪ/ *n.* Ablauf, *der*

explain /ɪkˈsplein/ **1** *v.t., also abs.* erklären **2** *v. refl., often abs.* **please** ∼ [**yourself**] bitte erklären Sie mir das ■ **explain a'way** *v.t.* eine [plausible] Erklärung finden für

explanation /ekspləˈneɪʃn/ *n.* Erklärung, *die;* **need** ∼: einer Erklärung bedürfen

explanatory /ɪkˈsplænətərɪ/ *adj.* erklärend; erläuternd ⟨*Bemerkung*⟩

explicable /ɪkˈsplɪkəbl/ *adj.* erklärbar

explicit /ɪkˈsplɪsɪt/ *adj.* klar; ausdrücklich ⟨*Zustimmung, Erwähnung*⟩

ex'plicitly *adv.* ausdrücklich; deutlich ⟨*beschreiben, ausdrücken*⟩

explode /ɪkˈspləʊd/ **1** *v.i.* explodieren **2** *v.t.* zur Explosion bringen

exploit **1** /ˈeksplɔɪt/ *n.* Heldentat, *die* **2** /ɪkˈsplɔɪt/ *v.t.* ausbeuten ⟨*Arbeiter usw.*⟩; ausnutzen ⟨*Gutmütigkeit, Freund, Unwissenheit*⟩

exploitation /eksplɔɪˈteɪʃn/ *n.* ▶ EXPLOIT 2: Ausbeutung, *die;* Ausnutzung, *die*

exploration /ekspləˈreɪʃn/ *n.* Erforschung, *die;* (fig.) Untersuchung, *die*

exploratory /ɪkˈsplɒrətərɪ/ *adj.* Forschungs-

explore /ɪkˈsplɔː(r)/ *v.t.* erforschen; (fig.) untersuchen

ex'plorer *n.* Entdeckungsreisende, *der/die*

explosion /ɪkˈspləʊʒn/ *n.* Explosion, *die*

explosive /ɪkˈspləʊzɪv/ **1** *adj.* explosiv **2** *n.* Sprengstoff, *der*

export **1** /ɪkˈspɔːt, ˈekspɔːt/ *v.t.* exportieren; ausführen **2** /ˈekspɔːt/ *n.* Export, *der*

export /ˈekspɔːt/: ∼ **drive** *n.* Exportkampagne, *die;* ∼ **duty** *n.* Exportzoll, *der*

ex'porter *n.* Exporteur, *der*

export /ˈekspɔːt/: ∼ **licence** *n.* Ausfuhrlizenz, *die;* ∼ **market** *n.* Exportmarkt, *der;* ∼ **permit** *n.* Exporterlaubnis, *die;* Ausfuhrerlaubnis, *die*

expose /ɪkˈspəʊz/ *v.t.* (a) (uncover) freilegen; entblößen ⟨*Haut, Körper*⟩ (b) offenbaren ⟨*Schwäche*⟩; aufdecken ⟨*Missstände, Verbrechen*⟩; entlarven ⟨*Täter, Spion*⟩ (c) (subject) ∼ **to sth.** einer Sache (*Dat.*) aussetzen (d) (Photog.) belichten

exposed /ɪkˈspəʊzd/ *adj.* (unprotected) ungeschützt; ∼ **position** exponierte Stellung

exposure /ɪkˈspəʊʒə(r)/ *n.* (a) (to cold etc.) **die of/suffer from** ∼: an Unterkühlung (*Dat.*) sterben/leiden (b) (Photog.) (exposing time) Belichtung, *die;* (picture) Aufnahme, *die*

ex'posure meter *n.* Belichtungsmesser, *der*

expound /ɪkˈspaʊnd/ *v.t.* darlegen

express /ɪkˈspres/ **1** *v.t.* ausdrücken; äußern ⟨*Meinung, Wunsch, Dank, Bedauern*⟩; ∼ **oneself** sich ausdrücken **2** *attrib. adj.* (a) Eil⟨*brief, -bote usw.*⟩; Schnell⟨*paket, -sendung*⟩ (b) ausdrücklich ⟨*Wunsch, Absicht*⟩ **3** *adv.* als Eilsache ⟨*senden*⟩ **4** *n.* (train) Schnellzug, *der*

express de'livery *n.* Eilzustellung, *die*

expression /ɪkˈspreʃn/ *n.* Ausdruck, *der*

expressive /ɪkˈspresɪv/ *adj.* ausdrucksvoll

express: ~ **'letter** n. Eilbrief, der;
~ **'lift** n. Schnellaufzug, der

ex'pressly adv. ausdrücklich

express: ~ **'train** n. D-Zug, der; ~**way**
n. (Amer.) Schnellstraße, die

expulsion /ɪk'spʌlʃn/ n. Ausweisung, die
(from aus); (from school) Verweisung, die
(from von)

exquisite /'ekskwɪzɪt, ɪk'skwɪzɪt/ adj.
erlesen

ex'quisitely adv. vorzüglich; kunstvoll
⟨verziert, geschnitzt⟩

extend /ɪk'stend/ **1** v.t. verlängern;
ausstrecken ⟨Arm, Bein, Hand⟩; ausziehen
⟨Leiter, Teleskop⟩; verlängern lassen
⟨Leihbuch, Visum⟩; ausdehnen ⟨Einfluss,
Macht⟩; vergrößern ⟨Haus, Geschäft,
Fabrik⟩; gewähren ⟨[Gast]freundschaft, Hilfe,
Kredit⟩ (to Dat.); ~ **the time limit** den
Termin hinausschieben
2 v.i. sich erstrecken; **the season** ~**s from
November to March** die Saison geht von
November bis März

extended 'family n. Großfamilie, die

extension /ɪk'stenʃn/ n. (a) Verlängerung,
die
(b) (part of house) Anbau, der
(c) (telephone) Nebenanschluss, der; (number)
Apparat, der

extension: ~ **cord** (Amer.) ▶ ~ LEAD;
~ **ladder** n. Ausziehleiter, die; ~ **lead** n.
(Brit.) Verlängerungsschnur, die

extensive /ɪk'stensɪv/ adj. ausgedehnt;
umfangreich ⟨Reparatur, Wissen,
Nachforschungen⟩; beträchtlich ⟨Schäden⟩;
weit reichend ⟨Änderungen⟩

ex'tensively adv. beträchtlich ⟨ändern,
beschädigen⟩; ausführlich ⟨berichten,
schreiben⟩

extent /ɪk'stent/ n. Ausdehnung, die;
(scope) Umfang, der; (of damage) Ausmaß, das;
to what ~? inwieweit?

exterior /ɪk'stɪərɪə(r)/ **1** adj. äußer...;
Außen⟨fläche, -wand⟩
2 n. Äußere, das; (of house) Außenwände Pl.

exterminate /ɪk'stɜːmɪneɪt/ v.t. ausrotten
⟨Nation, Volk⟩; vertilgen ⟨Ungeziefer⟩;
liquidieren ⟨Person⟩

extermination /ɪkstɜːmɪ'neɪʃn/ n.
Ausrottung, die; (of pests) Vertilgung, die

extermi'nation camp n.
Vernichtungslager, das

external /ɪk'stɜːnl/ adj. äußer...;
Außen⟨fläche, -abmessungen⟩; **purely** ~: rein
äußerlich; **for** ~ **use only** nur äußerlich
anzuwenden

extinct /ɪk'stɪŋkt/ adj. erloschen ⟨Vulkan⟩;
ausgestorben ⟨Art, Rasse, Gattung⟩

extinction /ɪk'stɪŋkʃn/ n. Aussterben, das

extinguish /ɪk'stɪŋgwɪʃ/ v.t. löschen

ex'tinguisher n. Feuerlöscher, der

extol /ɪk'stɒl/ v.t., **-ll-** rühmen; preisen

extort /ɪk'stɔːt/ v.t. erpressen (out of von)

extortion /ɪk'stɔːʃn/ n. Erpressung, die

extortionate /ɪk'stɔːʃənət/ adj.
Wucher⟨preis, -zinsen usw.⟩; maßlos
überzogen ⟨Forderung⟩

extra /'ekstrə/ **1** adj. zusätzlich;
Mehr⟨arbeit, -kosten, -ausgaben⟩;
Sonder⟨bus, -zug⟩
2 adv. (a) (more than usually) besonders; extra
⟨lang, stark, fein⟩
(b) (additionally) extra; **packing and postage**
~: zuzüglich Verpackung und Porto
3 n. (a) (added to services, salary, etc.)
zusätzliche Leistung; (on car etc.) Extra, das
(b) (in play, film, etc.) Statist, der/Statistin, die

extract **1** /'ekstrækt/ n. (a) Extrakt, der
(fachspr. auch: das)
(b) (from book, music, etc.) Auszug, der
2 /ɪk'strækt/ v.t. ziehen ⟨Zahn⟩;
herausziehen ⟨Dorn, Splitter usw.⟩

extraction /ɪk'strækʃn/ n. (of tooth)
Extraktion, die; (of thorn, splinter, etc.)
Herausziehen, das

ex'tractor fan n. Entlüfter, der

extra-curricular /ekstrəkə'rɪkjʊlə(r)/
adj. extracurricular (fachspr.); ⟨Aktivität⟩
außerhalb des Lehrplans

extradite /'ekstrədaɪt/ v.t. ausliefern

extradition /ekstrə'dɪʃn/ n. Auslieferung,
die

extra'marital adj. außerehelich

extraordinary /ɪk'strɔːdɪnərɪ/ adj.
außergewöhnlich; merkwürdig ⟨Benehmen⟩;
how ~! wie seltsam!

extravagance /ɪk'strævəgəns/ n. (a)
Extravaganz, die
(b) (extravagant thing) Luxus, der

extravagant /ɪk'strævəgənt/ adj.
verschwenderisch; aufwendig ⟨Lebensstil⟩

extreme /ɪk'striːm/ **1** adj. (a) äußerst...
⟨Spitze, Rand, Ende⟩; extrem ⟨Gegensätze,
Hitze, Kälte⟩; höchst... ⟨Gefahr⟩; äußerst...
⟨Notfall, Höflichkeit, Bescheidenheit⟩;
stärkst... ⟨Schmerzen⟩; größt... ⟨Wichtigkeit⟩;
at the ~ **edge/left** ganz am Rand/ganz links
(b) (not moderate) extrem; drastisch
⟨Maßnahme⟩
2 n. Extrem, das; **go to** ~**s** vor nichts
zurückschrecken; **go from one** ~ **to the
other** von einem Extrem ins andere fallen

ex'tremely adv. äußerst

extreme 'sport n. Extremsportart, die

extremist /ɪk'striːmɪst/ n. Extremist, der/
Extremistin, die; attrib. extremistisch

extremity /ɪk'stremɪtɪ/ n. äußerstes Ende

extricate /'ekstrɪkeɪt/ v.t. ~ **sth. from sth.**
etw. aus etw. herausziehen; ~ **oneself/sb.
from sth.** sich/jmdn. aus etw. befreien

extrovert /'ekstrəvɜːt/ **1** n.
extravertierter Mensch; **be an** ~:
extravertiert sein
2 adj. extravertiert

exuberant /ɪg'zjuːbərənt/ adj. **be** ~: sich
überschwänglich freuen

exude /ɪgˈzjuːd/ v.t. absondern; (fig.) ausstrahlen

exult /ɪgˈzʌlt/ v.i. jubeln (**in, at, over** über + *Akk.*)

eye /aɪ/ ① n. (a) Auge, *das;* **keep an ~ on** sb./sth. auf jmdn./etw. aufpassen; **see ~ to ~:** einer Meinung sein; **with one's ~s shut** (fig.) blind; (easily) im Schlaf; **be up to one's ~s in** work/debt bis über beide Ohren in Arbeit/Schulden stecken (ugs.) (b) (of needle) Öhr, *das;* (metal loop) Öse, *die* ② v.t., beäugen; **~ sb. up and down** jmdn. von oben bis unten mustern

eye: ~ball n. Augapfel, *der;* **~brow** n. Augenbraue, *die;* **~catching** adj. ins Auge springend *od.* fallend ⟨*Inserat, Plakat,* *Buchhülle usw.*⟩; **be** [very] **~catching** ein [wirkungsvoller] Blickfang sein; **~ drops** n. pl. (Med.) Augentropfen Pl.; **~ hospital** n. Augenklinik, *die;* **~lash** n. Augenwimper, *die;* **~ level** n. Augenhöhe, *die;* **~-level** attrib. in Augenhöhe nachgestellt; **at ~ level** in Augenhöhe; **~lid** n. Augenlid, *das;* **~ make-up** n. Augen-Make-up, *das;* **~shadow** n. Lidschatten, *der;* **~sight** n. Sehkraft, *die;* **have good ~sight** gute Augen haben; **his ~sight is poor** er hat schlechte Augen; **~sore** n. Schandfleck, *der;* **~wash** n. (a) (Med.: lotion) Augenwasser, *das;* (b) (coll.) (nonsense) Gewäsch, *das* (ugs.); (concealment) Augen[aus]wischerei, *die* (ugs.); **~witness** n. Augenzeuge, *der*/-zeugin, *die*

Ff

F, f /ef/ n. F, f, *das*

fable /ˈfeɪbl/ n. Fabel, *die;* (myth, lie) Märchen, *das*

fabric /ˈfæbrɪk/ n. Gewebe, *das*

fabricate /ˈfæbrɪkeɪt/ v.t. (invent) erfinden

fabrication /fæbrɪˈkeɪʃn/ n. Erfindung, *die*

'fabric softener /ˈsʊfənə(r)/ n. Weichspülmittel, *das;* Weichspüler, *der*

fabulous /ˈfæbjʊləs/ adj. (a) sagenhaft (b) (coll.: marvellous) fabelhaft (ugs.)

façade /fəˈsɑːd/ n. (lit. or fig.) Fassade, *die;* **that's just a ~** (fig.) das ist alles nur Fassade

face /feɪs/ ① n. (a) Gesicht, *das;* **lie ~ down[ward]** ⟨*Person/Buch:*⟩ auf dem Bauch/Gesicht liegen; **make** or **pull a ~**/~s Grimassen schneiden; **on the ~ of it** dem Anschein nach; **in the ~ of sth.** trotz etw. (Gen.) (b) (of mountain, cliff) Wand, *die;* (of clock, watch) Zifferblatt, *das;* (of dice) Seite, *die;* (of coin, playing card) Vorderseite, *die* ② v.t. (a) sich wenden zu; [stand] **facing one another** sich ⟨*Dat.*⟩ gegenüber[stehen] (b) (fig.) ins Auge sehen (+ *Dat.*) ⟨*Tod,* *Vorstellung:*⟩; stehen vor (+ *Dat.*) ⟨*Ruin,* *Entscheidung:*⟩; **~ the facts** den Tatsachen ins Gesicht sehen; **be ~d with sth.** sich einer Sache (*Dat.*) gegenübersehen (c) (coll.: bear) verkraften ③ v.i. (in train etc.) **~ backwards/forwards** ⟨*Person:*⟩ entgegen der/in Fahrtrichtung sitzen

■ **face 'up to** v.t. ins Auge sehen (+ *Dat.*); sich abfinden mit ⟨*Möglichkeit*⟩

face: ~ cream n. Gesichtscreme, *die;* **~ flannel** n. (Brit.) Waschlappen, *der;* **~less** /ˈfeɪslɪs/ adj. (anonymous) anonym (fig.); **~lift** n. (a) Facelifting, *das;* **have** or **get a ~lift** sich liften lassen; (b) (fig.) Verschönerung, *die;* **~ pack** n. [Gesichts]maske, *die;* **~-saving** adj. zur Wahrung des Gesichts nachgestellt

facet /ˈfæsɪt/ n. Facette, *die;* (fig.) Aspekt, *der*

facetious /fəˈsiːʃəs/ adj. [gewollt] witzig

face: ~-to-~ adj. persönlich ⟨*Gespräch,* *Treffen*⟩; **~ value** n. Nennwert, *der;* **accept sth. at** [its] **~ value** (fig.) etw. für bare Münze nehmen

facial /ˈfeɪʃl/ adj. Gesichts-

facile /ˈfæsaɪl/ adj. nichts sagend

facilities /fəˈsɪlɪtɪz/ n. pl. Einrichtungen Pl.; **cooking/washing ~:** Koch-/ Waschgelegenheit, *die;* **sports ~:** Sportanlagen Pl.; **shopping ~:** Einkaufsmöglichkeiten Pl.

facsimile /fækˈsɪmɪlɪ/ n. (a) Faksimile, *das* (b) ▶ FAX 1

fact /fækt/ n. Tatsache, *die;* **~s and figures** Fakten und Zahlen; **the ~ remains that ...:** Tatsache bleibt: ...; **the true ~s of the case** or **matter** der wahre Sachverhalt; **know for a ~ that ...:** genau wissen, dass ...; **in ~:** tatsächlich

faction /ˈfækʃn/ n. Splittergruppe, *die*

factor /ˈfæktə(r)/ n. Faktor, *der*

factory /ˈfæktərɪ/ n. Fabrik, *die*

factory: ~ 'farm n. [voll]automatisierter landwirtschaftlicher Betrieb; **~ 'farming** n. [fabrikmäßige] Massentierhaltung; **the ~ farming of salmon** die massenweise Lachsproduktion; **~ worker** n. Fabrikarbeiter, *der*/-arbeiterin, *die*

'fact sheet n. Infoblatt, *das*

factual /ˈfæktjʊəl/ adj. sachlich

faculty /'fækəltɪ/ n. (a) Fähigkeit, die; mental ∼: geistige Kraft
(b) (Univ.) Fakultät, die

fad /fæd/ n. Marotte, die

fade /feɪd/ v.i. (a) ⟨Blätter, Blumen:⟩ [ver]welken
(b) ∼ [in colour] [ver]bleichen; the light ∼d es dunkelte
(c) ⟨Laut:⟩ verklingen
(d) (fig.) verblassen; ⟨Schönheit:⟩ verblühen; ⟨Hoffnung:⟩ schwinden
(e) (blend) übergehen (into in + Akk.).
■ **fade a'way** v.i. schwinden; ⟨Laut:⟩ verklingen (into in + Dat.)

faded /'feɪdɪd/ adj. welk ⟨Blume, Blatt, Laub⟩; verblichen ⟨Stoff, Farbe⟩

faeces /'fi:si:z/ n. pl. Fäkalien Pl.

fag /fæg/ n. (a) (Brit. coll.) Schinderei, die (ugs.)
(b) (coll.: cigarette) Stäbchen, das (ugs.)

fail /feɪl/ ①v.i. (a) scheitern; (in examination) nicht bestehen, (ugs.) durchfallen (in in + Dat.)
(b) (become weaker) ⟨Augenlicht, Gehör, Stärke:⟩ nachlassen
(c) (break down, stop) ⟨Versorgung:⟩ zusammenbrechen; ⟨Motor:⟩ aussetzen; ⟨Batterie, Pumpe:⟩ ausfallen; ⟨Bremse:⟩ versagen
② v.t. (a) ∼ to do sth. (not succeed in doing) etw. nicht tun [können]; ∼ to achieve one's purpose/aim seine Absicht/sein Ziel verfehlen
(b) (be unsuccessful in) nicht bestehen, (ugs.) durchfallen in (+ Dat.) ⟨Prüfung⟩
(c) (reject) durchfallen lassen (ugs.) ⟨Prüfling⟩
(d) ∼ to do sth. (not do) etw. nicht tun; (neglect to do) [es] versäumen, etw. zu tun; not ∼ to do sth. etw. tun
(e) words ∼ me mir fehlen die Worte; his courage ∼ed him ihn verließ der Mut
③ n. without ∼: auf jeden Fall

'failing ① n. Schwäche, die
② prep. ∼ that andernfalls

failure /'feɪljə(r)/ n. (a) (omission, neglect) Versäumnis, das
(b) (lack of success) Scheitern, das; end in ∼: scheitern
(c) (person or thing) Versager, der; our plan/attempt was a ∼: unser Plan/Versuch war fehlgeschlagen

faint /feɪnt/ ① adj. (a) matt ⟨Licht, Farbe, Stimme, Lächeln⟩; schwach ⟨Geruch, Duft⟩; leise ⟨Flüstern, Geräusch, Stimme⟩; entfernt ⟨Ähnlichkeit⟩; undeutlich ⟨Umriss, Linie, Spur, Fotokopie⟩
(b) (giddy, weak) matt; she felt ∼: ihr war schwindelig
② v.i. ohnmächtig werden (from vor + Dat.)
③ n. Ohnmacht, die

faint-'hearted adj. hasenherzig; zaghaft ⟨Versuch⟩

'faintly adv. schwach; entfernt ⟨sich ähneln⟩

fair¹ /feə(r)/ n. (fun∼) Jahrmarkt, der; (exhibition) Messe, die; book/trade ∼: Buch-/Handelsmesse, die

fair² adj. (a) (just) gerecht; begründet ⟨Beschwerde, Annahme⟩; fair ⟨Spiel, Kampf, Prozess, Preis, Beurteilung, Handel⟩; ∼ play Fairness, die
(b) (not bad, pretty good) ganz gut ⟨Bilanz, Anzahl, Chance⟩; ziemlich ⟨Maß, Geschwindigkeit⟩
(c) (blond) blond ⟨Haar, Person⟩; (light) hell ⟨Haut⟩; (∼-skinned) hellhäutig ⟨Person⟩
(d) schön ⟨Wetter, Tag⟩

fair: ∼ground n. Festplatz, der; **∼-haired** adj. blond; **∼-haired boy** (Amer. fig.) Liebling, der; Favorit, der

'fairly adv. (a) fair ⟨kämpfen, spielen⟩; gerecht ⟨bestrafen, beurteilen, behandeln⟩
(b) (rather) ziemlich

'fair-minded adj. unvoreingenommen

'fairness n. Gerechtigkeit, die; in all ∼ [to sb.] um fair [gegen jmdn.] zu sein

fairy /'feərɪ/ n. Fee, die

fairy: ∼ 'godmother n. gute Fee; **∼ story**, **∼ tale** ns. Märchen, das

faith /feɪθ/ n. (a) (reliance, trust) Vertrauen, das (in in zu); have ∼ in oneself Selbstvertrauen haben; in good ∼: in gutem Glauben
(b) (religious belief) Glaube, der

faithful /'feɪθfl/ adj. (a) treu (to Dat.)
(b) (conscientious) pflichtbewusst; [ge]treu ⟨Diener⟩
(c) (accurate) [wahrheits]getreu; originalgetreu ⟨Wiedergabe, Kopie⟩

'faithfully adv. (a) treu ⟨dienen⟩; pflichtbewusst ⟨überbringen, zustellen⟩; hoch und heilig ⟨versprechen⟩
(b) (accurately) wahrheitsgetreu ⟨erzählen⟩; originalgetreu ⟨wiedergeben⟩; genau ⟨befolgen⟩
(c) yours ∼: hochachtungsvoll

faith: ∼ healer n. Gesundbeter, der/ -beterin, die; **∼ healing** n. Gesundbeten, das

fake /feɪk/ ① adj. unecht; gefälscht ⟨Dokument, Banknote, Münze⟩
② n. (a) Imitation, die; (painting) Fälschung, die
(b) (person) Schwindler, der/Schwindlerin, die
③ v.t. fälschen ⟨Unterschrift⟩; vortäuschen ⟨Krankheit, Unfall⟩

falcon /'fɔːlkn/ n. Falke, der

fall /fɔːl/ ① n. (a) Fallen, das; (of person) Sturz, der; ∼ of snow/rain Schnee-/Regenfall, der; have a ∼: stürzen
(b) (collapse, defeat) Fall, der; (of dynasty, empire) Untergang, der
(c) (decrease) Rückgang, der
(d) (Amer.: autumn) Herbst, der
② v.i., fell /fel/, fallen /'fɔːln/ (a) fallen; ⟨Baum:⟩ umstürzen; ⟨Pferd:⟩ stürzen; ∼ off sth., ∼ down from sth. von etw. ···⫶

f

[herunter]fallen; ∼ **down** [into] sth. in etw. (Akk.) [hinein]fallen; ∼ **to the ground** auf den Boden fallen; ∼ **down the stairs** or **downstairs** die Treppe herunter-/ hinunterfallen

(b) ⟨Nacht, Dunkelheit:⟩ hereinbrechen; ⟨Abend:⟩ anbrechen

(c) ⟨Blätter:⟩ [ab]fallen

(d) (sink) sinken; ⟨Barometer:⟩ fallen; ⟨Absatz, Verkauf:⟩ zurückgehen; ∼ **by 10 per cent/ from 10[°C] to 0[°C]** um 10%/von 10[°C] auf 0[°C] sinken

(e) (be killed) ⟨Soldat:⟩ fallen

(f) (collapse) einstürzen; ∼ **to pieces**, ∼ **apart** auseinander fallen

(g) (occur) fallen (on auf + Akk.)

■ **fall 'back** v.i. zurückweichen

■ **fall 'back on** v.t. zurückgreifen auf (+ Akk.)

■ **fall 'down** v.i. (a) ▶ FALL 2A
(b) ⟨Brücke, Gebäude:⟩ einstürzen

■ **fall for** v.t. (coll.) ∼ **for sb.** sich in jmdn. verknallen (ugs.); ∼ **for sth.** auf etw. (Akk.) hereinfallen (ugs.)

■ **fall 'in** v.i. (a) hineinfallen
(b) (Mil.) antreten; ∼ **in!** angetreten!
(c) ⟨Gebäude, Wand usw.:⟩ einstürzen

■ **fall 'off** v.i. (a) herunterfallen
(b) (diminish) nachlassen

■ **fall 'out** v.i. (a) herausfallen; ⟨Haare, Federn⟩ ausfallen
(b) (quarrel) ∼ **out** [**with sb.**] sich [mit jmdm.] streiten

■ **fall 'over** v.i. umfallen; ⟨Person:⟩ [hin]fallen

■ **fall 'through** v.i. (fig.) ins Wasser fallen (ugs.)

fallacy /'fæləsɪ/ n. Irrtum, der

fallen ▶ FALL 2

fallible /'fælɪbl/ adj. nicht unfehlbar; fehlbar ⟨Person⟩

'fallout n. radioaktiver Niederschlag

fallow /'fæləʊ/ adj. brachliegend; ∼ **ground/ land** Brache, die/Brachland, das; **lie** ∼: brachliegen

false /fɔːls, fɒls/ adj. falsch; gefälscht ⟨Urkunde, Dokument⟩; künstlich ⟨Wimpern⟩; **under a** ∼ **name** unter falschem Namen

false 'alarm n. blinder Alarm

'falsely adv. falsch; fälschlich[erweise] ⟨annehmen, glauben, behaupten, beschuldigen⟩

false: ∼ **'move** ▶ FALSE STEP; ∼ **pre'tences** n. pl. Vorspiegelung falscher Tatsachen; ∼ **'start** n. Fehlstart, der; ∼ **'step** n. (lit. or fig.) falscher Schritt; **make a** ∼ **step** einen falschen Schritt tun; ∼ **'teeth** n. pl. [künstliches] Gebiss

falsify /'fɔːlsɪfaɪ/ v.t. (alter) fälschen; (misrepresent) verfälschen ⟨Tatsachen, Wahrheit⟩

falter /'fɔːltə(r)/ v.i. stocken

fame /feɪm/ n. Ruhm, der

familiar /fə'mɪljə(r)/ adj. (a) vertraut; bekannt ⟨Gesicht, Name, Lied⟩; **he looks** ∼: er kommt mir bekannt vor
(b) (informal) ungezwungen ⟨Sprache, Art⟩

familiarity /fəmɪlɪ'ærɪtɪ/ n. Vertrautheit, die

familiarize /fə'mɪljəraɪz/ v.t. vertraut machen (**with** mit)

family /'fæməlɪ/ n. Familie, die

family: ∼ **'doctor** n. Hausarzt, der; ∼ **name** n. Familienname, der; ∼ **'planning** n. Familienplanung, die; ∼ **'tree** n. Stammbaum, der

famine /'fæmɪn/ n. Hungersnot, die

famished /'fæmɪʃt/ adj. ausgehungert; **I'm absolutely** ∼ (coll.) ich sterbe vor Hunger (ugs.)

famous /'feɪməs/ adj. berühmt

fan[1] /fæn/ ① n. Fächer, der; (apparatus) Ventilator, der
② v.t., -nn- fächeln ⟨Gesicht⟩; anfachen ⟨Feuer⟩; ∼ **oneself/sb.** sich/jmdm. Luft zufächeln

■ **fan 'out** v.i. fächern; ⟨Soldaten:⟩ ausfächern

fan[2] n. (devotee) Fan, der

fanatic /fə'nætɪk/ n. Fanatiker, der/ Fanatikerin, die

fanatical /fə'nætɪkl/ adj. fanatisch

fanaticism /fə'nætɪsɪzm/ n. Fanatismus, der

'fan belt n. Keilriemen, der

fanciful /'fænsɪfl/ adj. überspannt ⟨Vorstellung, Gedanke⟩; fantastisch ⟨Gemälde, Design⟩

'fan club n. Fanklub, der

fancy /'fænsɪ/ ① n. (a) (taste, inclination) **he has taken a** ∼ **to a new car/her** ein neues Auto/sie hat es ihm angetan; **take** or **catch sb.'s** ∼: jmdm. gefallen
(b) (whim) Laune, die; **tickle sb.'s** ∼: jmdn. reizen
② attrib. adj. kunstvoll ⟨Arbeit, Muster⟩; fein[st...] ⟨Kuchen, Spitzen⟩
③ v.t. (a) (imagine) sich ⟨Dat.⟩ einbilden; ∼ **that!** (coll.) sieh mal einer an!
(b) (suppose) glauben
(c) (wish to have) mögen; **what do you** ∼ **for dinner?** was hättest du gern zum Abendessen?; **do you think she fancies him?** glaubst du, sie mag ihn?

fancy 'dress n. [Masken]kostüm, das; **in** ∼: kostümiert; **fancy-dress party** Kostümfest, das; **fancy-dress ball** Maskenball, der

fanfare /'fænfeə(r)/ n. Fanfare, die

fang /fæŋ/ n. Reißzahn, der; (of snake) Giftzahn, der

fan: ∼ **heater** n. Heizlüfter, der; ∼**light** n. Oberlicht, das; ∼ **mail** n. Fanpost, die; ∼ **oven** n. Heißluftofen, der

fantastic /fæn'tæstɪk/ adj. (a) (grotesque, quaint) bizarr
(b) (coll.: excellent) fantastisch (ugs.)

fantasy /ˈfæntəzɪ/ n. Fantasie, die; (mental image) Fantasiegebilde, das

FAQ /fæk/ abbr. (Comp.) FAQ

far /fɑː(r)/ ① adv. weit; ~ **above/below** hoch über/tief unter (+ Dat.); hoch oben/tief unten; **as ~ as Munich/the church** bis [nach] München/bis zur Kirche; ~ **and wide** weit und breit; **from ~ and wide** von fern und nah; ~ **too** viel zu; ~ **longer/better** weit[aus] länger/besser; **as ~ as I remember/know** soweit ich mich erinnere/weiß; **go so ~ as to do sth.** so weit gehen und etw. tun; **so ~** (until now) bisher; **so ~ so good** so weit, so gut; **by ~:** bei weitem; ~ **from easy/good** alles andere als leicht/gut
② adj. **(a)** (remote) weit entfernt; (in time) fern; **in the ~ distance** in weiter Ferne **(b)** (more remote) weiter entfernt; **the ~ bank of the river/side of the road** das andere Flussufer/die andere Straßenseite; **the ~ door/wall** etc. die hintere Tür/Wand usw.

farce /fɑːs/ n. Farce, die

farcical /ˈfɑːsɪkl/ adj. (absurd) farcenhaft

fare /feə(r)/ n. **(a)** (price) Fahrpreis, der; (money) Fahrgeld, das; **what** or **how much is the ~?** was kostet die Fahrt? **(b)** (food) Kost, die

Far: ~ 'East n. **the ~ East** der Ferne Osten; ~ **'Eastern** adj. fernöstlich; des Fernen Ostens nachgestellt

farewell /feəˈwel/ ① int. leb[e] wohl (veralt.)
② n. attrib. ~ **speech/gift** Abschiedsrede, die/-geschenk, das

far-'fetched adj. weit hergeholt

farm /fɑːm/ ① n. [Bauern]hof, der; (larger) Gut, das; ~ **animals** Nutzvieh, das
② v.t. bebauen ⟨Land⟩
③ v.i. Landwirtschaft treiben

'farmer n. Landwirt, der/-wirtin, die

farm: ~hand n. Landarbeiter, der/-arbeiterin, die; **~house** n. Bauernhaus, das; (larger) Gutshaus, das

'farming n. Landwirtschaft, die

farm: ~land n. Acker- und Weideland, das; **~worker** n. Landarbeiter, der/-arbeiterin, die; **~yard** n. Hof, der

far: ~-'reaching adj. weit reichend; **~sighted** adj. **(a)** (fig.) weit blickend; **(b)** (Amer.: long-sighted) weitsichtig

fart /fɑːt/ (coarse) ① v.i. furzen (derb)
② n. Furz, der (derb)

farther /ˈfɑːðə(r)/ ▶ FURTHER 1A, 2

farthest /ˈfɑːðɪst/ ▶ FURTHEST

fascinate /ˈfæsɪneɪt/ v.t. fesseln; bezaubern

fascinated /ˈfæsɪneɪtɪd/ adj. fasziniert

fascinating /ˈfæsɪneɪtɪŋ/ adj. faszinierend (geh.); bezaubernd; hochinteressant ⟨Thema, Faktum, Meinung⟩; spannend, fesselnd ⟨Buch⟩

fascination /fæsɪˈneɪʃn/ n. Zauber, der; **have a ~ for sb.** einen besonderen Reiz auf jmdn. ausüben

fascism /ˈfæʃɪzm/ n. Faschismus, der

fascist /ˈfæʃɪst/ ① n. Faschist, der/ Faschistin, die
② adj. faschistisch

fashion /ˈfæʃn/ ① n. **(a)** Mode, die **(b)** (manner) Art [und Weise]; **talk/behave in a peculiar ~:** merkwürdig sprechen/sich merkwürdig verhalten
② v.t. formen **(out of, from** aus; **[in]to** zu)

fashionable /ˈfæʃənəbl/ adj. modisch; vornehm ⟨Hotel, Restaurant⟩; Mode⟨farbe, -autor⟩

fashionably /ˈfæʃənəblɪ/ adv. modisch

fashion: ~-conscious adj. modebewusst; ~ **designer** n. Modeschöpfer, der/-schöpferin, die; ~ **parade,** ~ **show** ns. Mode[n]schau, die

fast¹ /fɑːst/ ① v.i. fasten
② n. Fasten, das

fast² ① adj. **(a)** (fixed, attached) fest; **make [the boat] ~:** das Boot festmachen; **hard and ~:** fest; bindend ⟨Regel⟩; klar ⟨Entscheidung⟩ **(b)** (rapid) schnell; ~ **train** Schnellzug, der; D-Zug, der **(c) be [ten minutes] ~** ⟨Uhr:⟩ [zehn Minuten] vorgehen
② adv. **(a) be ~ asleep** fest schlafen; (when one should be awake) fest eingeschlafen sein **(b)** (quickly) schnell

'fastback n. (back of car) Fließheck, das; Fastback, das; (car) Wagen mit Fließheck; Fastback, das

fasten /ˈfɑːsn/ v.t. befestigen **(on, to** an + Dat.); zumachen ⟨Kleid, Spange, Jacke⟩; [ab]schließen ⟨Tür⟩; anstecken ⟨Brosche⟩ **(to** an + Akk.); ~ **one's seat belt** sich anschnallen

'fastener, 'fastening ns. Verschluss, der

fast: ~ 'food n.: im Schnellrestaurant angebotenes Essen; Fastfood, das; attrib. **~-food restaurant** Schnellrestaurant, das; ~ **'forward** n. schneller Vorlauf; ⟨playback⟩ Zeitrafferwiedergabe, die; ⟨video⟩ **~-forward** ① attrib. adj. Vorspul⟨taste, -funktion⟩; ② v.t. & i. vorspulen

fastidious /fæˈstɪdɪəs/ adj. wählerisch; (hard to please) heikel

fast: ~ lane n. Überholspur, die; **life in the ~ lane** (fig.) Leben auf Touren (ugs.); ~ **track** n. Überholspur, die; **a career on the ~ track** eine Blitzkarriere; **be on the ~ track** eine Blitzkarriere machen; **~-track** ① v.t. beschleunigen ⟨Projekt⟩; ② attrib. adj. Schnell-

fat /fæt/ ① adj. dick; rund ⟨Wangen, Gesicht⟩
② n. Fett, das; **animal/vegetable ~:** tierisches/pflanzliches Fett

fatal /'feɪtl/ *adj.* (a) (disastrous) verheerend (to für); **it would be ~**: das wäre das Ende (b) (deadly) tödlich ⟨*Unfall, Verletzung*⟩

fatality /fə'tælɪtɪ/ *n.* Todesopfer, *das*

'fatally *adv.* tödlich; **be ~ ill** todkrank sein

fate /feɪt/ *n.* Schicksal, *das*

fat-free *adj.* fettfrei

'fathead *n.* Dummkopf, *der* (ugs.)

father /'fɑːðə(r)/ *n.* Vater, *der*

father: F~ 'Christmas *n.* der Weihnachtsmann; **~ figure** *n.* Vaterfigur, *die*

fatherhood /'fɑːðəhʊd/ *n.* Vaterschaft, *die*

'father-in-law *n., pl.* **~s-in-law** Schwiegervater, *der*

'fatherly *adj.* väterlich

'Father's Day *n.* Vatertag, *der*

fathom /'fæðəm/ ① *n.* (Naut.) Faden, *der* ② *v.t.* (comprehend) verstehen; **~ sb./sth. out** jmdn./etw. ergründen

fatigue /fə'tiːg/ ① *n.* Ermüdung, *die* ② *v.t.* ermüden

'fatness *n.* Dicke, *die*

fatten /'fætn/ *v.t.* herausfüttern ⟨*Person*⟩; mästen ⟨*Tier*⟩

'fattening *adj.* **be ~**: dick machen

fatty /'fætɪ/ *adj.* fett ⟨*Fleisch, Soße*⟩; fetthaltig ⟨*Speise, Nahrungsmittel*⟩

faucet /'fɔːsɪt/ *n.* (Amer.) Wasserhahn, *der*

fault /fɔːlt, fɒlt/ *n.* (a) Fehler, *der* (b) (responsibility) Schuld, *die*; **it's your ~**: du bist schuld; **it isn't my ~**: ich habe keine Schuld; **be at ~**: im Unrecht sein (c) (in machinery; also Electr.) Defekt, *der*

'faultless *adj.* einwandfrei

'faulty *adj.* fehlerhaft; defekt ⟨*Gerät, usw.*⟩

fauna /'fɔːnə/ *n., pl.* **~e** /'fɔːniː/ *or* **~s** Fauna, *die*

favor etc. (Amer.) ▶ FAVOUR etc.

favour /'feɪvə(r)/ ① *n.* (a) Gunst, *die* (b) (kindness) Gefallen, *der*; **ask sb. a ~, ask a ~ of sb.** jmdn. um einen Gefallen bitten; **do sb. a ~, do a ~ for sb.** jmdm. einen Gefallen tun; **as a ~**: aus Gefälligkeit (c) **be in ~ of sth.** für etw. sein ② *v.t.* bevorzugen

favourable /'feɪvərəbl/ *adj.* (Brit.) (a) günstig ⟨*Eindruck, Licht*⟩; gewogen ⟨*Haltung, Einstellung*⟩; freundlich ⟨*Erwähnung*⟩; positiv ⟨*Bericht[erstattung], Bemerkung*⟩ (b) (helpful) günstig (**to** für) ⟨*Wetter, Wind, Umstand*⟩

favourably /'feɪvərəblɪ/ *adv.* (Brit.) wohlwollend; **be ~ disposed towards sb./sth.** jmdn./einer Sache positiv gegenüberstehen

favourite /'feɪvərɪt/ (Brit.) ① *adj.* Lieblings- ② *n.* (a) Liebling, *der*; ⟨food/country etc.⟩ Lieblingsessen, *das*/-land, *das usw.*; **this/he is my ~**: das/ihn mag ich am liebsten (b) (Sport) Favorit, *der*/Favoritin, *die*

favouritism /'feɪvərɪtɪzm/ *n.* (Brit.) Begünstigung, *die*; (when selecting sb. for a post etc.) Günstlingswirtschaft, *die*

fawn /fɔːn/ ① *n.* (a) (colour) Rehbraun, *das* (b) (young deer) [Dam]kitz, *das* ② *adj.* rehfarben

fax /fæks/ ① *n.* [Tele]fax, *das* ② *v.t.* faxen

fax: ~ machine *n.* Faxgerät, *das*; **~ modem** *n.* (Comp.) Faxmodem, *das*; **~ number** *n.* Faxnummer, *die*

FBI *abbr.* (Amer.) = **Federal Bureau of Investigation** FBI, *das*

fear /fɪə(r)/ ① *n.* Angst, *die* (**of** vor + *Dat.*); (instance) Befürchtung, *die*; **~ of death** *or* **dying/heights** Todes-/Höhenangst, *die*; **~ of doing sth.** Angst davor, etw. zu tun; **in ~**: angstvoll; **no ~!** (coll.) keine Bange! (ugs.) ② *v.t.* (a) **~ sb./sth.** vor jmdm./etw. Angst haben; **~ to do** *or* **doing sth.** Angst haben, etw. zu tun (b) (be worried about) befürchten; **~ [that ...]** fürchten[, dass ...]

fearful /'fɪəfl/ *adj.* (a) (terrible) furchtbar (b) (frightened) ängstlich; **be ~ of sth./sb.** vor etw./jmdm. Angst haben

'fearless *adj.*, **'fearlessly** *adv.* furchtlos

feasibility /fiːzɪ'bɪlɪtɪ/ *n.* Durchführbarkeit, *die*

feasible /'fiːzɪbl/ *adj.* durchführbar

feast /fiːst/ ① *n.* (a) (Relig.) Fest, *das* (b) (banquet) Festessen, *das* ② *v.i.* schlemmen; **~ on sth.** sich an etw. (*Dat.*) gütlich tun

feat /fiːt/ *n.* Meisterleistung, *die*

feather /'feðə(r)/ *n.* Feder, *die*

feather: ~ 'bed *n.* mit Federn gefüllte Matratze; **~ 'duster** *n.* Flederwisch, *der*; **~weight** *n.* (Boxing) Federgewicht, *das*

feature /'fiːtʃə(r)/ ① *n.* (a) *usu. in pl.* (of face) Gesichtszug, *der* (b) (characteristic) [charakteristisches] Merkmal; **be a ~ of sth.** charakteristisch für etw. sein (c) (Journ.) Feature, *das* (d) (Cinemat.) **~ [film]** Hauptfilm, *der* ② *v.t.* vorrangig vorstellen; (in film) in der Hauptrolle zeigen ③ *v.i.* vorkommen; **~ in** (be important) eine bedeutende Rolle haben bei

Feb. *abbr.* = **February** Febr.

February /'februərɪ/ *n.* Februar, *der*

feces (Amer.) ▶ FAECES

fed /fed/ ① ▶ FEED 1, 2 ② *pred. adj.* (coll.) **be/get ~ up with sb./sth.** jmdn./etw. satt haben/kriegen (ugs.); **I'm ~ up** ich hab die Nase voll (ugs.)

federal /'fedərl/ *adj.* Bundes-; föderativ ⟨*System*⟩

federation /fedə'reɪʃn/ *n.* Föderation, *die*

fee /fiː/ *n.* Gebühr, *die*; (of doctor, lawyer, etc.) Honorar, *das*

feeble /'fiːbl/ adj. schwach; wenig überzeugend ⟨Entschuldigung⟩; zaghaft ⟨Versuch⟩; lahm (ugs.) ⟨Witz⟩

feed /fiːd/ 1 v.t., fed /fed/ (a) füttern; ~ sb./an animal with sth. jmdm. etw. zu essen/einem Tier [etw.] zu fressen geben (b) (provide food for) ernähren (on, with mit) 2 v.i., fed ⟨Tier:⟩ fressen (from aus); ⟨Person:⟩ essen (off von); ~ on sth. ⟨Tier:⟩ etw. fressen 3 n. (a) (for baby) Mahlzeit, die (b) (fodder) Futter, das

'feedback n. Reaktion, die

feel /fiːl/ 1 v.t., felt /felt/ (a) (explore by touch) befühlen (b) (perceive by touch) fühlen; (become aware of) bemerken; (have sensation of) spüren (c) (experience) empfinden; verspüren ⟨Drang⟩; ~ the cold/heat unter der Kälte/ Hitze leiden; ~ [that] …: das Gefühl haben, dass …; (think) glauben, dass … 2 v.i., felt: (a) ~ [about] in sth. [for sth.] in etw. (Dat.) [nach etw.] [herum]suchen (b) (be conscious that one is) sich … fühlen; ~ angry/sure/disappointed böse/sicher/ enttäuscht sein; ~ like sth./doing sth. auf etw. (Akk.) Lust haben/Lust haben, etw. zu tun (c) (be consciously perceived as) sich … anfühlen
▪ **'feel for** v.t. ~ for sb. mit jmdm. Mitleid haben

'feeler n. Fühler, der

'feeling n. (a) Gefühl, das; (sense of touch) [sense of] ~: Tastsinn, der; hurt sb.'s ~s jmdn. verletzen (b) (opinion) Ansicht, die

feet pl. of FOOT

feign /feɪn/ v.t. vortäuschen; ~ to do sth. vorgeben, etw. zu tun

feline /'fiːlaɪn/ adj. (of cat[s]) Katzen-; (catlike) katzenartig; katzenhaft

fell¹ ▶ FALL 2

fell² /fel/ v.t. fällen ⟨Baum⟩

fell³ adj. in one ~ swoop auf einen Schlag

fellow /'feləʊ/ 1 n. (a) (comrade) Kamerad, der (b) (Brit. Univ.) Fellow, der (c) (of academy or society) Mitglied, das (d) (coll.: man, boy) Kerl, der (ugs.) 2 attrib. adj. Mit-; ~ man or human being Mitmensch, der

fellowship /'feləʊʃɪp/ n. (companionship) Gesellschaft, die

felt¹ /felt/ n. Filz, der

felt² ▶ FEEL

felt[-tipped] 'pen n. Filzstift, der

female /'fiːmeɪl/ 1 adj. weiblich; Frauen⟨stimme, -chor, -verein⟩ 2 n. Frau, die; (foetus, child) Mädchen, das; (animal) Weibchen, das

feminine /'femɪnɪn/ adj. weiblich; Frauen⟨angelegenheit, -leiden⟩; (womanly) feminin

femininity /femɪ'nɪnɪtɪ/ n. Weiblichkeit, die

feminism /'femɪnɪzm/ n. Feminismus, der

feminist /'femɪnɪst/ 1 adj. feministisch; Feministen⟨bewegung, -gruppe⟩ 2 n. Feministin, die/Feminist, der

fence /fens/ 1 n. Zaun, der 2 v.i. (Sport) fechten 3 v.t. ~ [in] einzäunen

'fencer n. Fechter, der/Fechterin, die

fencing /'fensɪŋ/ n. (Sport) Fechten, das

fend /fend/ v.i. ~ for oneself für sich selbst sorgen; (in hostile surroundings) sich allein durchschlagen
▪ **fend 'off** v.t. abwehren

fender /'fendə(r)/ n. (a) (for fire) Kaminschutz, der (b) (Amer.) (car bumper) Stoßstange, die; (car mudguard) Kotflügel, der

ferment /fə'ment/ 1 v.i. gären 2 v.t. zur Gärung bringen

fermentation /fɜːmen'teɪʃn/ n. Gärung, die

fern /fɜːn/ n. Farnkraut, das

ferocious /fə'rəʊʃəs/ adj. wild

ferocity /fə'rɒsɪtɪ/ n. Wildheit, die

ferret /'ferɪt/ n. Frettchen, das

ferrous /'ferəs/ adj. (containing iron) eisenhaltig; Eisen-

ferry /'ferɪ/ 1 n. Fähre, die; (service) Fährverbindung, die 2 v.t. (in boat) ~ [across or over] übersetzen

'ferry service n. (a) Fährverbindung, die (b) (business) Fährbetrieb, der

fertile /'fɜːtaɪl/ adj. (fruitful) fruchtbar; (capable of developing) befruchtet

fertility /fɜː'tɪlɪtɪ/ n. Fruchtbarkeit, die

fer'tility drug n. Hormonpräparat, das (zur Steigerung der Fruchtbarkeit)

fertilization /fɜːtɪlaɪ'zeɪʃn/ n. (a) (Biol.) Befruchtung, die (b) (Agric.) Düngung, die

fertilize /'fɜːtɪlaɪz/ v.t. befruchten

'fertilizer n. Dünger, der

fervent /'fɜːvənt/ adj. leidenschaftlich; inbrünstig ⟨Gebet, Wunsch, Hoffnung⟩

fervour (Brit.; Amer.: fervor) /'fɜːvə(r)/ n. Leidenschaftlichkeit, die

fester /'festə(r)/ v.i. eitern

festival /'festɪvl/ n. (a) (feast day) Fest, das (b) (of music etc.) Festival, das

festive /'festɪv/ adj. festlich; fröhlich; the ~ season die Weihnachtszeit

festivity /fe'stɪvɪtɪ/ n. (a) (gaiety) Feststimmung, die (b) (celebration) Feier, die; festivities Feierlichkeiten Pl.

festoon /fe'stuːn/ 1 n. Girlande, die 2 v.t. schmücken (with mit)

fetch /fetʃ/ *v.t.* **(a)** holen; (collect) abholen (from von); ∼ *sb.* *sth.*, ∼ *sth.* for *sb.* jmdm. etw. holen
(b) (be sold for) erzielen ⟨*Preis*⟩
'fetching *adj.* einnehmend
fête /feɪt/ *n.* [Wohltätigkeits]basar, *der*
fetish /'fetɪʃ/ *n.* Fetisch, *der*
fetishism /'fetɪʃɪzm/ *n.* Fetischismus, *der*
fetishist /'fetɪʃɪst/ *n.* Fetischist, *der*/ Fetischistin, *die*
fetter /'fetə(r)/ *v.t.* fesseln
fetus (Amer.) ▶ FOETUS
feud /fjuːd/ *n.* Fehde, *die*
feudal /'fjuːdl/ *adj.* Feudal-; feudalistisch; ∼ **system** Feudalsystem, *das*
fever /'fiːvə(r)/ *n.* **(a)** (high temperature) Fieber, *das;* **have a [high]** ∼: [hohes] Fieber haben
(b) (disease) Fieberkrankheit, *die*
'feverish *adj.* **(a)** (Med.) fiebrig; **be** ∼: Fieber haben
(b) (excited) fiebrig
'fever pitch *n.* Siedepunkt, *der* (fig.); **reach** ∼: auf dem Siedepunkt angelangt sein; **at** ∼: auf dem Siedepunkt
few /fjuː/ ⓵ *adj.* **(a)** (not many) wenige; *abs.* nur wenige; **with very** ∼ **exceptions** mit ganz wenigen Ausnahmen; **his** ∼ **belongings** seine paar Habseligkeiten; **a** ∼ ...: wenige ...
(b) (some) wenige; **a** ∼ ...: ein paar ...; **a** ∼ **more** ...: noch ein paar ...
⓶ *n.* **(a)** (not many) wenige; **a** ∼: wenige; **just a** ∼ **of you/her friends** nur ein paar von euch/ihrer Freunde
(b) (some) **with a** ∼ **of our friends** mit einigen unserer Freunde; **quite a** ∼: ziemlich viele
fiancé /fɪ'ɑ̃seɪ/ *n.* Verlobte, *der*
fiancée /fɪ'ɑ̃seɪ/ *n.* Verlobte, *die*
fiasco /fɪ'æskəʊ/ *n., pl.* ∼**s** Fiasko, *das*
fib /fɪb/ ⓵ *n.* Flunkerei, *die* (ugs.); **tell** ∼**s** flunkern (ugs.)
⓶ *v.i.,* **-bb-** flunkern (ugs.)
fibre (Brit.; Amer.: **fiber**) /'faɪbə(r)/ *n.* **(a)** Faser, *die*
(b) (material) [Faser]gewebe, *das*
fibre: ∼**glass** *n.* (plastic) glasfaserverstärkter Kunststoff; ∼ **optic 'cable** *n.* Glasfaserkabel, *das;* ∼ **'optics** *n.* Faseroptik, *die*
fibrous /'faɪbrəs/ *adj.* faserig ⟨*Aufbau, Beschaffenheit, Eigenschaft*⟩; Faser⟨*gewebe, -holz, -stoff*⟩
fiche /fiːʃ/ *n., pl. same or* ∼**s** Mikrofiche, *das od. der*
fickle /'fɪkl/ *adj.* unberechenbar
fiction /'fɪkʃn/ *n.* erzählende Literatur; **a** ∼/ ∼**s** eine Erfindung
fictional /'fɪkʃənl/ *adj.* erfunden ⟨*Geschichte*⟩; fiktiv ⟨*Figur*⟩
'fiction writer *n.* Belletrist, *der*/ Belletristin, *die*
fictitious /fɪk'tɪʃəs/ *adj.* fingiert; falsch ⟨*Name, Identität*⟩

fiddle /'fɪdl/ ⓵ *n.* **(a)** (Mus.) (coll./derog.) Fiedel, *die;* (violin for traditional music) Geige, *die;* [**as**] **fit as a** ∼: kerngesund
(b) (coll.: swindle) Gaunerei, *die*
⓶ *v.t.* (coll.) frisieren (ugs.) ⟨*Bücher, Rechnungen*⟩
⓷ *v.i.* herumspielen (with mit)
fiddler /'fɪdlə(r)/ *n.* Geiger, *der*/Geigerin, *die*
fiddly /'fɪdlɪ/ *adj.* (coll.) knifflig
fidelity /fɪ'delɪtɪ/ *n.* Treue, *die* (to zu)
fidget /'fɪdʒɪt/ ⓵ *v.i.* ∼ [**about**] herumrutschen
⓶ *n.* (person) Zappelphilipp, *der* (ugs.)
'fidgety *adj.* unruhig; zappelig ⟨*Kind*⟩
field /fiːld/ *n.* **(a)** Feld, *das*
(b) (for game) Platz, *der;* [Spiel]feld, *das*
(c) (subject area) [Fach]gebiet, *das;* **in the** ∼ **of medicine** auf dem Gebiet der Medizin; **that is outside my** ∼: das fällt nicht in mein Fach
field: ∼ **day** *n.* **have a** ∼ **day** seinen großen Tag haben; ∼ **events** *n. pl.* technische Disziplinen *Pl.* ∼ **glasses** *n. pl.* Feldstecher, *der;* **F∼ 'Marshal** *n.* (Brit. Mil.) Feldmarschall, *der;* ∼ **mouse** *n.* Brandmaus, *die;* ∼ **trip** *n.* Exkursion, *die*
fiend /fiːnd/ *n.* **(a)** (wicked person) Scheusal, *das*
(b) (evil spirit) böser Geist
'fiendish *adj.* **(a)** teuflisch
(b) (very awkward) höllisch
fierce /fɪəs/ *adj.* wild; erbittert ⟨*Widerstand, Kampf*⟩; scharf ⟨*Kritik*⟩
'fiercely *adv.* heftig ⟨*angreifen, Widerstand leisten*⟩; wütend ⟨*brüllen*⟩; aufs heftigste ⟨*kritisieren, bekämpfen*⟩
fiery /'faɪərɪ/ *adj.* glühend; (looking like fire) feurig; (blazing red) feuerrot
fifteen /fɪf'tiːn/ ⓵ *adj.* fünfzehn
⓶ *n.* Fünfzehn, *die.* See also EIGHT
fifteenth /fɪf'tiːnθ/ ⓵ *adj.* fünfzehnt...
⓶ *n.* (fraction) Fünfzehntel, *das.* See also EIGHTH
fifth /fɪfθ/ ⓵ *adj.* fünft...
⓶ *n.* (in sequence, rank) Fünfte, *der/die/das;* (fraction) Fünftel, *das.* See also EIGHTH
fiftieth /'fɪftɪɪθ/ *adj.* fünfzigst...
fifty /'fɪftɪ/ ⓵ *adj.* fünfzig
⓶ *n.* Fünfzig, *die.* See also EIGHT; EIGHTY 2
fig /fɪg/ *n.* Feige, *die*
fig. *abbr.* = **figure** Abb.
fight /faɪt/ ⓵ *v.i.,* **fought** /fɔːt/ **(a)** kämpfen; (with fists) sich schlagen
(b) (squabble) [sich] streiten (about wegen)
⓶ *v.t.,* **fought: (a)** ∼ *sb.*/*sth.* gegen jmdn./ etw. kämpfen; (using fists) ∼ *sb.* sich mit jmdm. schlagen
(b) (seek to overcome) bekämpfen; (resist) ∼ *sb.*/*sth.* gegen jmdn./etw. ankämpfen
(c) ∼ **a battle** einen Kampf austragen
(d) kandidieren bei ⟨*Wahl*⟩
⓷ *n.* Kampf, *der* (for um)
■ **'fight against** *v.t.* kämpfen gegen; ankämpfen gegen ⟨*Wellen, Wind*⟩

■ **fight 'back** ① *v.i.* zurückschlagen
② *v.t.* (suppress) zurückhalten
■ **fight 'off** *v.t.* abwehren
■ **'fight with** *v.t.* **(a)** kämpfen mit
(b) (squabble with) [sich] streiten mit
'fighter *n.* Kämpfer, *der/*Kämpferin, *die;*
(aircraft) Kampfflugzeug, *das*
'fighting *n.* Kämpfe *Pl.*
fighting 'chance *n.* have a ∼ of
succeeding/of doing sth. Aussicht auf Erfolg
haben/gute Chancen haben, etw. zu tun
'fig leaf *n.* (lit. or fig.) Feigenblatt, *das*
figment /'fɪgmənt/ *n.* a ∼ of one's *or* the
imagination pure Einbildung
'fig tree *n.* Feigenbaum, *der*
figurative /'fɪgərətɪv/ *adj.* übertragen
figure /'fɪgə(r)/ ① *n.* **(a)** (shape) Form, *die*
(b) (carving, sculpture, one's bodily shape) Figur,
die
(c) (illustration) Abbildung, *die*
(d) (person as seen) Gestalt, *die;* (literary ∼)
Figur, *die*
(e) (numerical symbol) Ziffer, *die;* (number) Zahl,
die; (amount of money) Betrag, *der*
(f) ∼ of speech Redewendung, *die*
② *v.i.* **(a)** vorkommen
(b) that ∼s (coll.) das kann gut sein
■ **figure 'out** *v.t.* **(a)** (by arithmetic)
ausrechnen
(b) (understand) verstehen
figure: ∼**head** *n.* (lit. or fig.) Galionsfigur,
die; ∼ **skating** *n.* Eiskunstlauf, *der*
filament /'fɪləmənt/ *n.* **(a)** Faden, *der*
(b) (Electr.) Glühfaden, *der*
filch /'fɪltʃ/ *v.t.* stibitzen (ugs.)
file¹ /faɪl/ ① *n.* Feile, *die*
② *v.t.* feilen ⟨*Fingernägel*⟩; mit der Feile
bearbeiten ⟨*Holz, Eisen*⟩
file² ① *n.* **(a)** (holder) Ordner, *der;* (box)
Kassette, *die*
(b) (papers) Ablage, *die;* (cards) Kartei, *die*
② *v.t.* **(a)** [in die Kartei] einordnen/[in die
Akten] aufnehmen
(b) einreichen ⟨*Antrag*⟩
file³ ① *n.* (Mil. etc.) Reihe, *die;* [in] single *or*
Indian ∼: [im] Gänsemarsch
② *v.i.* ∼ [in/out] in einer Reihe [hinein-/
hinaus]gehen
file: ∼ **copy** *n.* Belegexemplar, *das;* (of
letter) Kopie für die Akten; ∼ **extension**
n. (Comp.) Dateierweiterung, *die;* ∼ **name**
n. (Comp.) Dateiname, *der*
filigree /'fɪlɪgriː/ *n.* Filigran, *das*
'filing cabinet *n.* Aktenschrank, *der*
filings /'faɪlɪŋz/ *n. pl.* Späne *Pl.*
fill /fɪl/ ① *v.t.* **(a)** füllen; besetzen
⟨*Sitzplätze*⟩; (fig.) ausfüllen ⟨*Gedanken, Zeit*⟩;
(pervade) erfüllen; ∼ed with voller ⟨*Reue,
Bewunderung, Neid usw.*⟩
(b) (appoint sb. to) besetzen ⟨*Posten*⟩
② *v.i.* ∼ [with sth.] sich [mit etw.] füllen
③ *n.* eat/drink one's ∼: sich satt essen/
trinken

■ **fill 'in** ① *v.t.* **(a)** füllen; zuschütten
⟨*Erdloch*⟩
(b) (complete) ausfüllen
(c) ∼ sb. in [on sth.] (coll.) jmdn. [über etw.
(*Akk.*)] ins Bild setzen
② *v.i.* ∼ in for sb. für jmdn. einspringen
■ **fill 'out** *v.t.* ausfüllen
■ **fill 'up** *v.t.* **(a)** füllen (with mit)
(b) (put petrol into) ∼ up the tank tanken; ∼
her up! (coll.) voll [tanken]!
fillet /'fɪlɪt/ ① *n.* Filet, *das*
② *v.t.* entgräten ⟨*Fisch*⟩
'filling *n.* **(a)** (for teeth) Füllung, *die*
(b) (for pancakes etc.) Füllung, *die;* (for
sandwiches etc.) Belag, *der;* (for spreading)
Aufstrich, *der*
'filling station *n.* Tankstelle, *die*
filly /'fɪlɪ/ *n.* junge Stute
film /fɪlm/ ① *n.* **(a)** Film, *der*
(b) (thin layer) Schicht, *die*
② *v.t.* filmen; drehen ⟨*Kinofilm, Szene*⟩
film: ∼ **crew** *n.* Kamerateam, *das;*
∼ **director** *n.* Filmregisseur, *der/*
-regisseurin, *die;* ∼ **industry** *n.*
Filmindustrie, *die;* ∼ **music** *n.*
Filmmusik, *die;* ∼ **poster** *n.* Filmplakat,
das; ∼ **projector** *n.* Projektor, *der;*
∼ **script** *n.* Drehbuch, *das;* ∼ **set** *n.*
Dekoration, *die;* ∼ **star** *n.* Filmstar, *der;*
∼**strip** *n.* Filmstreifen, *der;* ∼ **studio** *n.*
Filmstudio, *die*
filter /'fɪltə(r)/ ① *n.* Filter, *der*
② *v.t.* filtern
■ **filter 'through** *v.t.* durchsickern
filter: ∼ **ciga'rette** *n.* Filterzigarette, *die;*
∼ **coffee** *n.* Filterkaffee, *der;* ∼ **lane** *n.*
Abbiegespur, *die;* ∼**-tip** *n.* **(a)** Filter, *der;*
(b) ∼-tip [cigarette] Filterzigarette, *die*
filth /fɪlθ/ *n.* Dreck, *der*
'filthy *adj.* dreckig (ugs.); schmutzig
fin /fɪn/ *n.* Flosse, *die*
final /'faɪnl/ ① *adj.* letzt...; End⟨*spiel,
-stadium, -stufe, -ergebnis*⟩; endgültig
⟨*Entscheidung*⟩
② *n.* **(a)** (Sport etc.) Finale, *das*
(b) ∼s *pl.* (university examination) Examen, *das*
finale /fɪ'nɑːlɪ/ *n.* Finale, *das*
finalist /'faɪnəlɪst/ *n.* Teilnehmer/
Teilnehmerin in der Endausscheidung;
(Sport) Finalist, *der/*Finalistin, *die*
finality /faɪ'nælɪtɪ/ *n.* Endgültigkeit, *die;* (of
tone of voice) Entschiedenheit, *die*
finalize /'faɪnəlaɪz/ *v.t.* [endgültig]
beschließen; (complete) zum Abschluss
bringen
finally /'faɪnəlɪ/ *adv.* **(a)** (in the end)
schließlich; (expressing impatience etc.) endlich
(b) (in conclusion) abschließend
(c) (conclusively) entschieden ⟨*sagen*⟩
finance /faɪ'næns, 'faɪnæns/ ① *n.* **(a)** *in pl.*
(resources) Finanzen *Pl.*
(b) (management of money) Geldwesen, *das*
(c) (support) Geldmittel *Pl.*

2 *v.t.* finanzieren

'**finance company** *n.*
Finanzierungsgesellschaft, *die*

financial /faɪˈnænʃl/ *adj.* finanziell;
Finanz⟨mittel, -experte, -lage⟩; ~ **year**
Geschäftsjahr, *das*

fi'nancially *adv.* finanziell

financier /faɪˈnænsɪə(r)/ *n.* Finanzexperte,
der/-expertin, *die*

finch /fɪntʃ/ *n.* Fink[envogel], *der*

find /faɪnd/ 1 *v.t.*, **found** /faʊnd/ finden;
(come across unexpectedly) entdecken;
auftreiben ⟨Geld, Gegenstand⟩; aufbringen
⟨Kraft, Energie⟩; **want to** ~: suchen; ~ **that**
…: herausfinden, dass …; ~ **sth. necessary**
etw. für nötig erachten; ~ **sth./sb. to be** …:
herausfinden, dass etw./jmd. … ist/war; **you**
will ~ **[that]** …: Sie werden sehen, dass …
2 *n.* Fund, *der*
■ **find 'out** *v.t.* herausfinden

'**finder** *n.* Finder, *der*/Finderin, *die*

'**findings** *n. pl.* Ergebnisse *Pl.*

fine¹ /faɪn/ 1 *n.* Geldstrafe, *die*
2 *v.t.* mit einer Geldstrafe belegen

fine² *adj.* (a) hochwertig ⟨Qualität,
Lebensmittel⟩; fein ⟨Gewebe, Spitze⟩; edel
⟨Holz, Wein⟩
(b) (delicate) fein; zart ⟨Porzellan⟩; (thin)
hauchdünn; **cut** *or* **run it** ~: knapp
kalkulieren
(c) (in small particles) [hauch]fein ⟨Sand,
Staub⟩; ~ **rain** Nieselregen, *der*
(d) (sharp) scharf ⟨Spitze, Klinge⟩; spitz
⟨Nadel, Schreibfeder⟩
(e) (excellent) ausgezeichnet ⟨Sänger,
Schauspieler⟩
(f) (satisfactory) schön; **that's** ~ **by** *or* **with me**
ja, ist mir recht
(g) (in good health or state) gut; **feel** ~: sich
wohl fühlen
(h) schön ⟨Wetter⟩

fine 'arts *n. pl.* schöne Künste *Pl.*

finery /ˈfaɪnərɪ/ *n.* Pracht, *die;* (garments etc.)
Staat, *der*

finger /ˈfɪŋɡə(r)/ 1 *n.* Finger, *der*
2 *v.t.* berühren; (meddle with) befingern

finger: ~**mark** *n.* Fingerabdruck, *der;*
~**nail** *n.* Fingernagel, *der;* ~**print** *n.*
Fingerabdruck, *der;* ~**tip** *n.* Fingerspitze,
die; **have sth. at one's** ~**tips** (fig.) etw. im
kleinen Finger haben (ugs.)

finish /ˈfɪnɪʃ/ 1 *v.t.* (a) beenden
⟨Unterhaltung⟩; erledigen ⟨Arbeit⟩;
abschließen ⟨Kurs, Ausbildung⟩; **have** ~**ed**
sth. etw. fertig haben; ~ **writing/reading sth.**
etw. zu Ende schreiben/lesen
(b) aufessen ⟨Mahlzeit⟩; auslesen ⟨Buch,
Zeitung⟩; austrinken ⟨Flasche, Glas⟩
2 *v.i.* (a) aufhören; **have you** ~**ed?** sind Sie
fertig?; **when does the concert** ~? wann ist
das Konzert aus?; **have you** ~**ed with the**
sugar? brauchen Sie den Zucher noch?; ~
with one's boyfriend/girlfriend mit seinem
Freund/seiner Freundin Schluss machen

(b) (in race) das Ziel erreichen
3 *n.* (a) Ende, *das*
(b) (~ing line) Ziel, *das*
■ **finish 'off** *v.t.* abschließen

finishing: ~ **post** *n.* Zielpfosten, *der;*
~ '**touch** *n.* **as a** ~ **touch to sth.** zur
Vollendung *od.* Vervollkommnung einer
Sache; **put the** ~ **touches to sth.** einer Sache
(*Dat.*) den letzten Schliff geben

finite /ˈfaɪnaɪt/ *adj.* begrenzt

Finland /ˈfɪnlənd/ *pr. n.* Finnland (*das*)

Finn /fɪn/ *n.* Finne, *der*/Finnin, *die*

Finnish /ˈfɪnɪʃ/ 1 *adj.* finnisch; **sb. is** ~:
jmd. ist Finne/Finnin
2 *n.* Finnisch, *das; see also* ENGLISH 2A

fiord /fɪˈɔːd/ *n.* Fjord, *der*

fir /fɜː(r)/ *n.* Tanne, *die*

fire /ˈfaɪə(r)/ 1 *n.* (a) Feuer, *das;* **be on** ~:
brennen; **catch** ~: Feuer fangen; ⟨Wald,
Gebäude:⟩ in Brand geraten; **set** ~ **to sth.**
etw. anzünden
(b) (in grate) [offenes] Feuer; (electric or gas ~)
Heizofen, *der;* **light the** ~: den Ofen
anstecken; (in grate) das [Kamin]feuer
anmachen
(c) (destructive burning) Brand, *der*
(d) (of guns) **come/be under** ~: unter
Beschuss geraten/beschossen werden
2 *v.t.* (a) abschießen ⟨Gewehr⟩; abfeuern
⟨Kanone⟩; abgeben ⟨Schuss⟩; ~ **one's gun/**
pistol/rifle at sb. auf jmdn. schießen; **two**
shots were ~**d** es fielen zwei Schüsse;
~ **questions at sb.** jmdn. mit Fragen
bombardieren
(b) (coll.: dismiss) feuern (ugs.)
3 *v.i.* feuern; ~ **at/on** schießen auf (+ *Akk.*);
~! Feuer!

fire: ~ **alarm** *n.* Feuermelder, *der;* ~**arm**
n. Schusswaffe, *die;* ~**bomb** *n.* Brandsatz,
der; (aerial bomb) Brandbombe, *die;*
~ **brigade** (Brit.)**,** ~ **department** (Amer.)
ns. Feuerwehr, *die;* ~ **drill** *n.*
Probe[feuer]alarm, *der;* ~ **engine** *n.*
Löschfahrzeug, *das;* ~ **escape** *n.* (staircase)
Feuertreppe, *die;* ~ **exit** *n.* Notausgang,
der; ~ **extinguisher** *n.* Feuerlöscher, *der;*
~**fighter** *n.* Feuerwehrmann, *der*/-frau, *die;*
~**fighting** *n.* Feuerbekämpfung, *die;*
Brandbekämpfung, *die;* ~ **hazard** *n.*
Brandrisiko, *das;* ~**lighter** *n.* (Brit.)
Feueranzünder, *der;* ~**man** /ˈfaɪəmən/ *n.*,
pl. ~**men** /-mən/ Feuerwehrmann, *der;*
~**place** *n.* Kamin, *der;* ~ **precautions**
n. pl. Feuerschutz, *der;* ~**proof** 1 *adj.*
feuerfest; 2 *v.t.* feuerfest machen;
~**-resistant** *adj.* feuerbeständig; ~ **risk**
▶ ~ HAZARD; ~**side** *n.* **at** *or* **by the** ~**side**
am Kamin; ~ **station** *n.* Feuerwache, *die;*
~ **tongs** *n. pl.* Feuerzange, *die;* **a pair of**
~ **tongs** eine Feuerzange; ~**wood** *n.*
Brennholz, *das;* ~**work** *n.*
Feuerwerkskörper, *der;* ~**works** (display)
Feuerwerk, *das*

firm¹ /fɜːm/ *n.* Firma, *die*

firm² *adj.* (a) fest; stabil ⟨Konstruktion, Stuhl⟩
(b) (resolute, strict) bestimmt

'firmly *adv.* (a) fest
(b) (resolutely, strictly) bestimmt

first /fɜ:st/ ①*adj.* erst...; **he was ∼ to arrive** er kam als Erster an
②*adv.* (a) (before anyone else) zuerst; als Erster/Erste ⟨sprechen, ankommen⟩; (before anything else) an erster Stelle ⟨stehen, kommen⟩; **∼ come ∼ served** wer zuerst kommt, mahlt zuerst (Spr.)
(b) (beforehand) vorher
(c) (for the ∼ time) zum ersten Mal
(d) **∼ of all** zuerst; (in importance) vor allem
③*n.* (a) **the ∼** (in sequence, rank) der/die/das Erste; *pl.* die Ersten
(b) **at ∼:** zuerst; **from the ∼:** von Anfang an

first: ∼ 'aid *n.* erste Hilfe; **∼-aid box/kit** Verbandkasten, *der*/Erste-Hilfe-Ausrüstung, *die;* **∼-class** ①/'--/ *adj.* (a) erster Klasse *nachgestellt;* Erste[r]-Klasse-⟨Fahrkarte, Abteil, Post, Brief usw.⟩; (b) (excellent) erstklassig; ②/-'-/ *adv.* erster Klasse ⟨reisen⟩

'firstly *adv.* zunächst [einmal]; (followed by 'secondly') erstens

first: ∼ name *n.* Vorname, *der;* **∼ 'night** *n.* (Theatre) Premiere, *die;* **∼ offender** *n.* Ersttäter, *der*/-täterin, *die;* **∼-rate** *adj.* erstklassig; **∼ school** *n.* (Brit.) ≈ Grundschule, *die*

'fir tree *n.* Tanne, *die*

fish /fɪʃ/ ①*n.* Fisch, *der*
②*v.i.* fischen; (with rod) angeln; **go ∼ing** fischen/angeln gehen
▪ **fish 'out** *v.t.* (coll.) herausfischen (ugs.)

fish: ∼ bone *n.* [Fisch]gräte, *die;* **∼ cake** *n.* Fischfrikadelle, *die*

fisherman /'fɪʃəmən/ *n., pl.* **fishermen** /'fɪʃəmən/ Fischer, *der;* (angler) Angler, *der*

fish: ∼eye lens *n.* Fischaugenobjektiv, *das;* **∼ farm** *n.* Fischzucht[anlage], *die;* **∼ farming** *n.* Fischzucht, *die;* **∼ 'finger** *n.* Fischstäbchen, *das;* **∼ hook** *n.* Angelhaken, *der*

'fishing *n.* Fischen, *das;* (with rod) Angeln, *das*

fishing: ∼ boat *n.* Fischerboot, *das;* **∼ industry** *n.* Fischerei[industrie], *die;* **∼ net** *n.* Fischernetz, *das;* **∼ rod** *n.* Angelrute, *die;* **∼ tackle** *n.* Angelgeräte *Pl.;* **∼ vessel** *n.* Fischereifahrzeug, *das;* **∼ village** *n.* Fischerdorf, *das*

fish: ∼ kettle *n.* Fischkessel, *der;* **∼monger** /'fɪʃmʌŋɡə(r)/ *n.* (Brit.) Fischhändler, *der*/-händlerin, *die;* **∼ pond** *n.* Fischteich, *der;* **∼ shop** *n.* Fischgeschäft, *das;* **∼ slice** *n.* Wender, *der;* **∼ tank** *n.* Fischkasten, *der;* Fischbehälter, *der*

'fishy *adj.* (a) fischartig; Fisch⟨geschmack, -geruch⟩
(b) (coll.: suspicious) verdächtig

fist /fɪst/ *n.* Faust, *die*

fit¹ /fɪt/ *n.* Anfall, *der;* (fig.) [plötzliche] Anwandlung; **be in ∼s of laughter** sich vor Lachen biegen; **in a ∼ of ...:** in einem Anfall von ...

fit² ①*adj.* (a) (suitable) geeignet; **∼ to eat** essbar
(b) (worthy) würdig; wert
(c) (proper) richtig; **see** *or* **think ∼ [to do sth.]** es für richtig halten[, etw. zu tun]
(d) (healthy) fit (ugs.); **keep ∼:** sich fit halten
②*n.* Passform, *die;* **it is a good/bad ∼:** es sitzt *od.* passt gut/nicht gut
③*v.t.,* **-tt-:** (a) ⟨Kleider:⟩ passen (+ Dat.); ⟨Deckel, Bezug:⟩ passen auf (+ Akk.)
(b) (put into place) ⟨anbringen (**to** an + Dat. *od.* Akk.); ⟨einbauen ⟨Motor, Ersatzteil⟩
④*v.i.,* **-tt-** passen
▪ **fit 'in** ①*v.t.* unterbringen
②*v.i.* (a) ⟨Person:⟩ sich anpassen (**with** an + Akk.)
(b) (be in accordance with) **∼ in with sth.** mit etw. übereinstimmen

fitful /'fɪtfl/ *adj.* unbeständig; unruhig ⟨Schlaf⟩; launisch ⟨Brise⟩

'fitment *n.* Einrichtung, *die*

'fitness *n.* (a) (physical) Fitness, *die*
(b) (suitability) Eignung, *die*

'fitness studio *n.* Fitnessstudio, *das*

'fitted *adj.* (a) (suited) geeignet (**for** für, zu)
(b) (shaped) tailliert ⟨Kleider⟩; Einbau⟨küche, schrank⟩; **∼ carpet** Teppichboden, *der*

'fitter *n.* Monteur, *der;* (of pipes) Installateur, *der;* (of machines) Maschinenschlosser, *der*

'fitting ①*adj.* (a) (appropriate) passend; (becoming) schicklich (geh.) ⟨Benehmen⟩
②*n.* (a) *usu. in pl.* (fixture) Anschluss, *der;* **∼s** (furniture) Ausstattung, *die*
(b) (Brit.: size) Größe, *die*

'fitting-room *n.* Anprobe, *die*

five /faɪv/ ①*adj.* fünf
②*n.* Fünf, *die. See also* EIGHT

fiver /'faɪvə(r)/ *n.* (Brit. coll.) Fünfpfundschein, *der*

five: ∼-star *adj.* Fünf-Sterne-⟨Hotel, General⟩; (fig.) ausgezeichnet; **∼-'year plan** *n.* Fünfjahresplan, *der*

fix /fɪks/ ①*v.t.* (a) befestigen
(b) festsetzen ⟨Termin, Preis, Grenze⟩; (agree on) ausmachen
(c) (repair) reparieren
(d) (arrange) arrangieren
②*n.* (coll.: predicament) Klemme, *die* (ugs.); **be in a ∼:** in der Klemme sitzen
▪ **fix 'up** *v.t.* (a) (arrange) arrangieren; festsetzen ⟨Termin, Treffpunkt⟩
(b) (provide) versorgen; **∼ sb. up with sth.** jmdm. etw. verschaffen

fixed: ∼ price Festpreis, *der;* **∼-rate** *attrib. adj.* Festzins-; mit festem Zins *nachgestellt*

fixture /'fɪkstʃə(r)/ *n.* (a) (furnishing) eingebautes Teil
(b) (Sport) Veranstaltung, *die*

fizz /fɪz/ v.i. [zischend] sprudeln

fizzle /'fɪzl/ v.i. zischen

■ **fizzle 'out** v.i. ⟨Kampagne:⟩ im Sande verlaufen

fizzy /'fɪzɪ/ adj. sprudelnd; ∼ **lemonade** Brause[limonade], die

flabbergast /'flæbəgɑːst/ v.t. umhauen (ugs.)

flabby /'flæbɪ/ adj. schlaff

flag[1] /flæg/ n. Fahne, die; (national ∼, on ship) Flagge, die

flag[2] v.i., **-gg-** ⟨Person:⟩ abbauen; ⟨Kraft, Begeisterung usw.:⟩ nachlassen

flagon /'flægn/ n. Kanne, die

'**flagpole** n. Flaggenmast, der

flagrant /'fleɪgrənt/ adj. eklatant; flagrant ⟨Verstoß⟩

'**flagstone** n. Steinplatte, die

flair /fleə(r)/ n. Gespür, das; (special ability) Talent, das

flak /flæk/ n. Flakfeuer, das (Milit.); (gun) Flak, die (Milit.); **get a lot of ∼ for sth.** (fig.) wegen etw. [schwer] unter Beschuss geraten

flake /fleɪk/ ① n. Flocke, die; (of dry skin) Schuppe, die
② v.i. abblättern

'**flak jacket** n. kugelsichere Weste

flaky /'fleɪkɪ/ adj. blättrig ⟨Kruste⟩; ∼ **pastry** Blätterteig, der

flamboyant /flæm'bɔɪənt/ adj. extravagant

flame /fleɪm/ n. Flamme, die; **be in ∼s** in Flammen stehen

'**flameproof** nicht entflammbar; flammfest

flan /flæn/ n. [fruit] ∼: [Obst]torte, die

flank /flæŋk/ n. Seite, die; (of animal; also Mil.) Flanke, die

flannel /'flænl/ n. (a) (fabric) Flanell, der
(b) (Brit.: for washing) Waschlappen, der

flap /flæp/ ① v.t., **-pp-:** ∼ **its wings** mit den Flügeln schlagen
② v.i., **-pp-** ⟨Flügel:⟩ schlagen; ⟨Segel, Fahne, Vorhang:⟩ flattern
③ n. (a) Klappe, die; (envelope seal, of shoe) Lasche, die
(b) (fig. coll.) **in a ∼:** furchtbar aufgeregt

flare /fleə(r)/ ① v.i. flackern; (fig.) ausbrechen; **tempers ∼d** die Gemüter erhitzten sich
② n. Leuchtsignal, das

■ **flare 'up** v.i. (a) aufflackern
(b) (break out) [wieder] ausbrechen

flash /flæʃ/ ① n. Aufleuchten, das; (as signal) Lichtsignal, das; ∼ **of lightning** Blitz, der; **in a ∼:** (quickly) im Nu
② v.t. (a) aufleuchten lassen; ∼ **one's headlights** die Lichthupe betätigen; ∼ **sb. a smile/glance** jmdm. ein Lächeln/einen Blick zuwerfen
(b) (display briefly) kurz zeigen
③ v.i. aufleuchten; ∼ **by** or **past** ⟨Zeit, Ferien:⟩ wie im Fluge vergehen

flash: ∼**back** n. Rückblende, die (**to** auf + Akk.); ∼ **bulb** n. Blitzbirnchen, das; ∼ **cube** n. Blitzwürfel, der; ∼ **flood** n. Überschwemmung, die (durch heftige Regenfälle); ∼**gun** n. Blitzgerät, das; ∼**light** n. (a) (for signals) Blinklicht, das; (b) (Amer.: torch) Taschenlampe, die; ∼**point** n. Flammpunkt, der; (fig.) Siedepunkt, der

'**flashy** adj. auffällig

flask /flɑːsk/ n. (a) ▶ THERMOS
(b) (for wine, oil) [bauchige] Flasche
(c) (Chem.) Kolben, der

flat[1] /flæt/ n. (Brit.) Wohnung, die

flat[2] ① adj. (a) flach; eben ⟨Fläche⟩; platt ⟨Nase, Reifen⟩
(b) (downright) glatt (ugs.) ⟨Absage, Weigerung, Widerspruch⟩
(c) (Mus.) [um einen Halbton] erniedrigt ⟨Note⟩
(d) schal, abgestanden ⟨Bier, Sekt⟩
(e) leer ⟨Batterie⟩
② adv. (Mus.) zu tief

flat: ∼**-chested** /flæt'tʃestɪd/ adj. flachbrüstig; flachbusig; ∼ '**feet** n. pl. Plattfüße Pl.; ∼'**fish** n. Plattfisch, der; ∼'**footed** adj. plattfüßig; ∼**-heeled** adj. ⟨Schuh⟩ mit flachem Absatz; flach ⟨Schuh⟩

'**flatly** adv. rundweg

flat: ∼ **mate** n. (Brit.) Mitbewohner, der/ Mitbewohnerin, die; **they were ∼ mates** sie haben zusammen gewohnt; ∼ '**out** adv. (at top speed) **he ran/worked ∼ out** er rannte/ arbeitete, so schnell er konnte; ∼**-pack** adj. ⟨Möbel⟩ zum Selbstbauen; ∼ **rate** n. Einheitstarif, der; ∼ **screen** n. (Comp.) Flachbildschirm, der; ∼ '**spin** n. (Aeronaut.) Flachtrudeln, das; **go into a ∼ spin** (fig. coll.) durchdrehen (ugs.)

flatten /'flætn/ ① v.t. flach drücken ⟨Schachtel⟩; dem Erdboden gleichmachen ⟨Stadt, Gebäude⟩
② v. refl. ∼ **oneself against sth.** sich flach gegen etw. drücken

flatter /'flætə(r)/ v.t. schmeicheln (+ Dat.)

'**flattering** adj. schmeichelhaft

'**flattery** n. Schmeichelei, die

flat 'tyre n. Reifenpanne, die

flatulence /'flætjʊləns/ n. Blähungen Pl.; Flatulenz, die (Med.)

flaunt /flɔːnt/ v.t. zur Schau stellen

flavor etc. (Amer.) ▶ FLAVOUR etc.

flavour /'fleɪvə(r)/ (Brit.) ① n. (a) Geschmack, der
(b) (fig.) Anflug, der
② v.t. abschmecken

'**flavouring** n. (Brit.) Aroma, das

'**flavourless** adj. (Brit.) fade

flavoursome /'fleɪvəsəm/ adj. (Brit.) schmackhaft

flaw /flɔː/ n. Fehler, der; (imperfection) Makel, der; (in workmanship or goods) Mangel, der

flax /flæks/ n. Flachs, der

flea /fliː/ n. Floh, der

flea: ∼ **bite** n. Flohbiss, der; ∼ **market** n. (coll.) Flohmarkt, der

fled ▶ FLEE

flee /fliː/ ① v.i., fled /fled/ fliehen; ∼ from sth./sb. aus etw./vor jmdm. flüchten ② v.t., fled fliehen aus

fleece /fliːs/ ① n. [Schaf]fell, das ② v.t. (fig.) ausplündern

fleecy /'fliːsɪ/ adj. flauschig

fleet /fliːt/ n. Flotte, die

fleeting /'fliːtɪŋ/ adj. flüchtig

flesh /fleʃ/ n. Fleisch, das; (of fruit, plant) [Frucht]fleisch, das

flesh: ∼-**coloured** adj. fleischfarben; ∼ **wound** n. Fleischwunde, die

'fleshy adj. fett; fleischig ⟨Hände⟩

flew ▶ FLY² 1, 2

flex¹ /fleks/ n. (Brit. Electr.) Kabel, das

flex² v.t. beugen ⟨Arm, Knie⟩; ∼ one's muscles seine Muskeln spielen lassen

flexible /'fleksɪbl/ adj. (a) biegsam; elastisch
(b) (fig.) flexibel; ∼ working hours or time gleitende Arbeitszeit

flexitime /'fleksɪtaɪm/ (Brit.)**, flextime** /'flekstaɪm/ (Amer.) ns. Gleitzeit, die; be on or work ∼: gleitende Arbeitszeit haben

flick /flɪk/ v.t. schnippen; anknipsen ⟨Schalter⟩; verspritzen ⟨Tinte⟩
■ **'flick through** v.t. durchblättern

flicker /'flɪkə(r)/ ① v.i. flackern; ⟨Fernsehapparat:⟩ flimmern ② n. Flackern, das; (of TV) Flimmern, das

'flick knife n. (Brit.) Schnappmesser, das

flight¹ /flaɪt/ n. (a) Flug, der
(b) ∼ [of stairs or steps] Treppe, die

flight² n. (fleeing) Flucht, die; take ∼: die Flucht ergreifen; put to ∼: in die Flucht schlagen

flight: ∼ **attendant** n. Flugbegleiter, der/-begleiterin, die; ∼ **control** n. ≈ Flugsicherung, die; ∼ **controller** n. (Aeronaut.) Fluglotse, der; ∼ **deck** n. (a) (of aircraft carrier) Flugdeck, das; (b) (of aircraft) Cockpit, das; ∼ **number** n. Flugnummer, die; ∼ **path** n. (Aeronaut.) Flugweg, der; (Astronaut.) Flugbahn, die; ∼ **recorder** n. Flugschreiber, der

flimsy /'flɪmzɪ/ adj. (a) dünn; nicht sehr haltbar ⟨Verpackung⟩
(b) (fig.) fadenscheinig ⟨Entschuldigung, Argument⟩

flinch /flɪntʃ/ v.i. zurückschrecken (from vor + Dat.); (wince) zusammenzucken

fling /flɪŋ/ ① n. have a or one's ∼: sich ausleben ② v.t., flung /flʌŋ/ werfen; ∼ oneself into sth. (fig.) sich in etw. (Akk.) stürzen

flint /flɪnt/ n. Feuerstein, der

flip /flɪp/ v.t., -pp- schnippsen; ∼ [over] (turn over) umdrehen
■ **'flip through** v.t. durchblättern

flippant /'flɪpənt/ adj. leichtfertig

flipper /'flɪpə(r)/ n. Flosse, die

'flip side n. B-Seite, die

flirt /flɜːt/ v.i. flirten

flirtation /flɜː'teɪʃn/ n. Flirt, der

flirtatious /flɜː'teɪʃəs/ adj. kokett ⟨Blick, Art⟩

flit /flɪt/ v.i. huschen

float /fləʊt/ ① v.i. treiben; (in air) schweben ② n. (for carnival) Festwagen, der ③ v.t. (set afloat) flottmachen; (fig.) lancieren ⟨Plan, Idee⟩

floating: ∼ **'dock** n. Schwimmdock, das; ∼ **'voter** n. Wechselwähler, der/-wählerin, die

flock /flɒk/ ① n. (a) Herde, die; (of birds) Schwarm, der
(b) (of people) Schar, die ② v.i. strömen; ∼ round sb. sich um jmdn. scharen

flog /flɒg/ v.t., -gg-: (a) auspeitschen
(b) (Brit. coll.: sell) verscheuern (salopp)

flood /flʌd/ ① n. Überschwemmung, die; the F∼ (Bibl.) die Sintflut ② v.i. ⟨Fluss:⟩ über die Ufer treten; (fig.) strömen ③ v.t. überschwemmen

flood: ∼ **damage** n. Hochwasserschaden, der; the area suffered extensive ∼ damage in dem Gebiet gab es beträchtliche Hochwasserschäden; ∼**gate** n. (Hydraulic Engin.) Schütze, die; open the ∼gates to sth. (fig.) einer Sache (Dat.) Tür und Tor öffnen; ∼**light** ① n. Scheinwerfer, der. ② v.t., floodlit /'flʌdlɪt/ anstrahlen; ∼ **tide** n. Flut, die; ∼ **warning** n. Hochwasserwarnung, die; ∼ **water** n. Hochwasser, das

floor /flɔː(r)/ ① n. (a) Boden, der
(b) (storey) Stockwerk, das; first ∼ (Amer.) Erdgeschoss, das; first ∼ (Brit.), second ∼ (Amer.) erster Stock; ground ∼: Erdgeschoss, das; Parterre, das ② v.t. (a) (confound) überfordern
(b) (knock down) zu Boden schlagen

floor: ∼**board** n. Dielenbrett, das; ∼**cloth** n. (Brit.) Scheuertuch, das; ∼ **polish** n. Bohnerwachs, das; ∼ **show** n. ≈ Unterhaltungsprogramm, das

flop /flɒp/ ① v.i., -pp-: (a) plumpsen
(b) (coll.: fail) fehlschlagen; ⟨Theaterstück, Show:⟩ durchfallen ② n. (coll.: failure) Reinfall, der (ugs.)

floppy /'flɒpɪ/ adj. weich und biegsam

floppy disk n. (Comp.) Floppy Disk, die; Diskette, die

flora /'flɔːrə/ n. Flora, die

floral /'flɔːrl, 'flɒrl/ adj. geblümt ⟨Kleid, Stoff⟩; Blumen⟨muster⟩

Florence /'flɒrəns/ pr. n. Florenz (das)

florid /'flɒrɪd/ adj. blumig ⟨Stil, Redeweise⟩; gerötet ⟨Teint⟩

florist /'flɒrɪst/ n. Florist, der/Floristin, die

flotsam /'flɒtsəm/ n. ~ [and jetsam] Treibgut, *das*

flounder /'flaʊndə(r)/ v.i. taumeln

flour /'flaʊə(r)/ n. Mehl, *das*

flourish /'flʌrɪʃ/ ① v.i. gedeihen; ⟨Geschäft:⟩ florieren, gut gehen
② v.t. schwingen
③ n. do sth. with a ~: etw. schwungvoll tun

flout /flaʊt/ v.t. missachten

flow /fləʊ/ ① v.i. fließen; ⟨Körner, Sand:⟩ rinnen, rieseln; ⟨Gas:⟩ strömen
② n. (a) Fließen, *das;* ~ of water/people Wasser-/Menschenstrom, *der;* ~ of information Informationsfluss, *der*
(b) (of tide, river) Flut, *die*

'flow chart n. Flussdiagramm, *das*

flower /'flaʊə(r)/ ① n. (blossom) Blüte, *die;* (plant) Blume, *die;* come into ~: zu blühen beginnen
② v.i. blühen

'flower bed n. Blumenbeet, *das*

flowering /'flaʊərɪŋ/ adj. ~ cherry/shrub Zierkirsche, *die*/Blütenstrauch, *der*

'flowerpot n. Blumentopf, *der*

'flowery adj. geblümt ⟨Stoff, Muster⟩; (fig.) blumig ⟨Sprache⟩

'flowing adj. fließend; wallend ⟨Haar⟩

flown ▸ FLY² 1, 2

flu /fluː/ n. (coll.) Grippe, *die*

fluctuate /'flʌktjʊeɪt/ v.i. schwanken

fluctuation /flʌktjʊ'eɪʃn/ n. Schwankung, *die*

fluency /'fluːənsɪ/ n. Gewandtheit, *die;* (spoken) Redegewandtheit, *die*

fluent /'fluːənt/ adj. gewandt ⟨Stil, Redeweise, Redner, Schreiber⟩; be ~ in Russian, speak ~ Russian fließend Russisch sprechen

fluff /flʌf/ n. Flusen *Pl.;* Fusseln *Pl.*

fluffy /'flʌfɪ/ adj. [flaum]weich ⟨Kissen, Küken⟩; flauschig ⟨Spielzeug, Decke⟩

fluid /'fluːɪd/ ① n. Flüssigkeit, *die*
② adj. flüssig

fluke /fluːk/ n. (piece of luck) Glücksfall, *der*

flung ▸ FLING 2

fluorescent /flʊə'resənt/ adj. fluoreszierend

fluorescent 'light n. Leuchtstofflampe, *die*

fluoride /'flʊəraɪd/ n. Fluorid, *das;* ~ toothpaste fluorhaltige Zahnpasta

flurry /'flʌrɪ/ n. (a) Aufregung, *die* (b) (of rain/snow) [Regen-/Schnee]schauer, *der*

flush¹ /flʌʃ/ ① v.i. rot werden
② v.t. ausspülen ⟨Becken⟩; ~ the toilet or lavatory spülen
③ n. Rotwerden, *das*

flush² adj. (level) bündig; be ~ with sth. mit etw. bündig abschließen

flush 'toilet n. Toilette mit Wasserspülung

fluster /'flʌstə(r)/ v.t. aus der Fassung bringen

flustered /'flʌstəd/ adj. nervös

flute /fluːt/ n. Flöte, *die*

flutter /'flʌtə(r)/ ① v.i. flattern
② v.t. flattern mit ⟨Flügel⟩

flux /flʌks/ n. in a state of ~: im Fluss

fly¹ /flaɪ/ n. Fliege, *die*

fly² ① v.i., flew /fluː/, flown /fləʊn/ (a) fliegen; ~ away or off wegfliegen
(b) (fig.) ~ [by or past] wie im Fluge vergehen
(c) ⟨Fahne:⟩ gehisst sein
② v.t., flew, flown fliegen ⟨Flugzeug, Fracht, Einsatz usw.⟩; fliegen über (+ Akk.) ⟨Strecke⟩
③ n. in sing. or pl. (on trousers) Hosenschlitz, *der*

■ **fly 'in** v.i. [mit dem Flugzeug] eintreffen (from aus)

■ **fly 'out** v.i. abfliegen (of von)

'fly-fishing n. Fliegenfischerei, *die*

flying /'flaɪɪŋ/: ~ 'doctor n.: Arzt, der seine Krankenbesuche mit dem Flugzeug macht; ~ 'saucer n. fliegende Untertasse; ~ 'start n. (Sport) fliegender Start; ~ 'visit n. Stippvisite, *die* (ugs.)

fly: ~leaf n. Vorsatzblatt, *das;* ~over n. (Brit.) [Straßen]überführung, *die;* ~ spray n. Insektenspray, *der od. das;* ~ swatter n. Fliegenklappe, *die;* Fliegenklatsche, *die*

foal /fəʊl/ n. Fohlen, *das*

foam /fəʊm/ ① n. Schaum, *der*
② v.i. schäumen

foam: ~-backed adj. schaumstoffverstärkt; ~ 'mattress n. Schaumgummimatratze, *die;* ~ 'rubber n. Schaumgummi, *der*

fob /fɒb/ v.t., -bb-: ~ sb. off with sth. jmdn. mit etw. abspeisen (ugs.)

'focal point n. Brennpunkt, *der* (auch fig.)

focus /'fəʊkəs/ ① n., pl. ~es or foci /'fəʊsaɪ/ Brennpunkt, *der;* out of/in ~: unscharf/scharf eingestellt; unscharf/scharf ⟨Foto, Film usw.⟩; (fig.) be the ~ of attention im Brennpunkt des Interesses stehen
② v.t., -s- or -ss- einstellen (on auf + Akk.); bündeln ⟨Licht, Strahlen⟩
③ v.i., -s- or -ss- (fig.) sich konzentrieren (on auf + Akk.)

'focus group n. Fokusgruppe, *die*

fodder /'fɒdə(r)/ n. [Vieh]futter, *das*

foe /fəʊ/ n. (poet./rhet.) Feind, *der*

foetus /'fiːtəs/ n. Fötus, *der*

fog /fɒg/ n. Nebel, *der*

'foglight n. Nebelscheinwerfer, *der*

foggy /'fɒgɪ/ adj. neblig

fogy /'fəʊgɪ/ n. [old] ~: [alter] Opa (salopp)/ [alte] Oma (salopp)

foible /'fɔɪbl/ n. Eigenheit, *die*

foil¹ /fɔɪl/ n. Folie, *die*

foil² v.t. vereiteln

foist /fɔɪst/ v.t. ~ [off] on to sb. jmdm. andrehen (ugs.); auf jmdn. abwälzen ⟨Probleme, Verantwortung⟩

fold /fəʊld/ ⊡ *v.t.* [zusammen]falten;
∼ **one's arms** die Arme verschränken
⊡ *v.i.* **(a)** (become ∼ed) sich zusammenfalten
(b) (be able to be ∼ed) sich falten lassen
(c) (go bankrupt) Konkurs machen
⊡ *n.* Falte, *die;* (line made by ∼ing) Kniff, *der*
■ **fold 'up** *v.t.* zusammenfalten ⟨*Laken*⟩;
zusammenklappen ⟨*Stuhl*⟩

'folder *n.* **(a)** Mappe, *die*
(b) (Comp.) Ordner, *der*

foliage /'fəʊlɪɪdʒ/ *n.* Blätter *Pl.;* (of tree also)
Laub, *das*

folk /fəʊk/ *n.* **(a)** Volk, *das*
(b) *in pl.* ∼[s] (people) Leute *Pl.*

folk: ∼ **dance** *n.* Volkstanz, *der;* ∼ **hero**
n. Volksheld, *der;* ∼**lore** /-lɔ:(r)/ *n.*
Folklore, *die;* ∼ **music** *n.* Volksmusik, *die;*
∼ **singer** *n.* Sänger/Sängerin von
Volksliedern; (modern) Folksänger, *der/*
-sängerin, *die;* ∼ **song** Volkslied, *das;*
(modern) Folksong, *der*

follow /'fɒləʊ/ ⊡ *v.t.* **(a)** folgen (+ *Dat.*)
(b) entlanggehen/-fahren ⟨*Straße usw.*⟩
(c) (come after) folgen auf (+ *Akk.*)
(d) (result from) die Folge sein von
(e) (treat or take as guide) sich orientieren an
(+ *Dat.*)
(f) folgen (+ *Dat.*) ⟨*Prinzip, Instinkt, Trend*⟩;
verfolgen ⟨*Politik*⟩; befolgen ⟨*Regel,
Vorschrift, Warnung*⟩; sich halten an
(+ *Akk.*) ⟨*Konventionen, Diät*⟩
(g) (grasp meaning of) folgen (+ *Dat.*); **do you
∼ me?** verstehst du, was ich meine?
⊡ *v.i.* **(a)** (go, come) ∼ **after sb./sth.** jmdm./
einer Sache folgen
(b) (come next in order or time) folgen; **as ∼s**
wie folgt
(c) ∼ **from sth.** (result) die Folge von etw.
sein; (be deducible) aus etw. folgen
■ **follow 'on** *v.i.* (continue) ∼ **on from sth.**
die Fortsetzung von etw. sein
■ **follow 'up** *v.t.* **(a)** ausbauen ⟨*Erfolg,
Sieg*⟩
(b) nachgehen (+ *Dat.*) ⟨*Hinweis*⟩

'follower *n.* Anhänger, *der/*Anhängerin,
die

'following ⊡ *adj.* folgend; **the ∼:**
Folgendes
⊡ *prep.* nach
⊡ *n.* Anhängerschaft, *die*

folly /'fɒlɪ/ *n.* Torheit, *die* (geh.)

fond /fɒnd/ *adj.* liebevoll; lieb ⟨*Erinnerung*⟩;
be ∼ of sb. jmdn. mögen; **be ∼ of doing sth.**
etw. gern tun

fondle /'fɒndl/ *v.t.* streicheln

'fondness *n.* Liebe, *die;* ∼ **for sth.** Vorliebe
für etw.

font[1] /fɒnt/ *n.* Taufstein, *der*

font[2] *n.* (Comp., Printing) Schrift, *die;* Font, *die*
(fachspr.); ∼ **size** Schriftgröße, *die;* Fontgröße,
die

food /fu:d/ *n.* **(a)** Nahrung, *die;* (for animals)
Futter, *das*
(b) (as commodity) Lebensmittel *Pl.*
(c) (in solid form) Essen, *das*
(d) (particular kind) Nahrungsmittel, *das;* Kost,
die

food: ∼ **chain** *n.* Nahrungskette, *die;*
∼ **poisoning** *n.* Lebensmittelvergiftung,
die; ∼ **processor** *n.* Küchenmaschine,
die; ∼ **shop,** ∼ **store** *ns.*
Lebensmittelgeschäft, *das;* ∼**stuff** *n.*
Nahrungsmittel, *das;* perishable ∼stuffs
leicht verderbliche Lebensmittel

fool /fu:l/ ⊡ *n.* Dummkopf, *der* (ugs.)
⊡ *v.t.* ∼ **sb. into doing sth.** jmdn. [durch
Tricks] dazu bringen, etw. zu tun
■ **fool a'bout, fool a'round** *v.i.* Unsinn
machen

foolhardy /'fu:lhɑ:dɪ/ *adj.* tollkühn

'foolish *adj.* töricht; verrückt (ugs.) ⟨*Idee,
Vorschlag*⟩

'foolproof *adj.* (infallible) absolut sicher

foot /fʊt/ ⊡ *n.*, *pl.* **feet** /fi:t/ **(a)** Fuß, *der;* **on
∼:** zu Fuß; **put one's ∼ in it** (fig. coll.) ins
Fettnäpfchen treten (ugs.)
(b) (far end) unteres Ende; (of bed) Fußende,
das
(c) (measure) Fuß, *der* (30,48 cm)
⊡ *v.t.* ∼ **the bill** die Rechnung bezahlen

football /'fʊtbɔ:l/ *n.* (game, ball) Fußball, *der*

'football boot *n.* Fußballschuh, *der*

'footballer *n.* Fußballspieler, *der/*
-spielerin, *die*

football: ∼ **pitch** *n.* Fußballplatz, *der;*
∼ **pools** *n. pl.* **the ∼ pools** das Fußballtoto

foot: ∼ **brake** *n.* Fußbremse, *die;*
∼ **bridge** *n.* Fußgängerbrücke, *die;*
∼**hold** *n.* Halt, *der*

'footing *n.* **(a)** (fig.) **be on an equal ∼ [with
sb.]** [jmdm.] gleichgestellt sein
(b) (foothold) Halt, *der*

foot: ∼**note** *n.* Fußnote, *die;*
∼ **passenger** *n.* Fußpassagier, *der;*
∼**path** *n.* Fußweg, *der;* ∼**print** *n.*
Fußabdruck, *der;* ∼**rest** *n.* Fußstütze, *die;*
(on bicycle or motorcycle) Fußraste, *die;* ∼**step**
n. Schritt, *der;* **follow in sb.'s ∼steps** (fig.) in
jmds. Fußstapfen (*Akk.*) treten; ∼**stool** *n.*
Fußbank, *die;* Fußschemel, *der;* ∼**wear** *n.*
Schuhe *Pl.;* ∼**work** *n.* (Sport, Dancing)
Beinarbeit, *die*

for /fə(r), stressed fɔ:(r)/ ⊡ *prep.* **(a)** für;
what is it ∼? wofür ist das?; **reason ∼ living**
Grund zu leben; **a request ∼ help** eine Bitte
um Hilfe; **study ∼ a university degree** auf
einen Hochschulabschluss hin studieren;
take sb. ∼ a walk mit jmdm. einen
Spaziergang machen; **be '∼ doing sth.** (in
favour) dafür sein, etw. zu tun; **cheque/bill
∼ £5** Scheck/Rechnung über 5 Pfund; **what
have you got ∼ a cold?** was haben Sie
gegen Erkältungen da?
(b) (on account of, as penalty of) wegen; **were it
not ∼ you/ your help** ohne dich/deine Hilfe;
∼ **fear of** aus Angst vor (+ *Dat.*)
(c) (in spite of) ∼ **all …:** trotz …; ∼ **all that,
…:** trotzdem … ⋯⊹

(d) ~ all I know/care ...: möglicherweise/was mich betrifft, ...; ~ one thing, ...: zunächst einmal ...

(e) (during) stay ~ a week eine Woche bleiben; we've/we haven't been here ~ three years wir sind seit drei Jahren hier/nicht mehr hier gewesen

(f) walk ~ 20 miles 20 Meilen gehen

2 *conj.* denn

forage /ˈfɒrɪdʒ/ 1 *n.* Futter, *das*

2 *v.i.* ~ for sth. auf der Suche nach etw. sein

forbad, forbade ▶ FORBID

forbid /fəˈbɪd/ *v.t.,* **-dd-, forbad** /fəˈbæd/ *or* **forbade** /fəˈbæd, fəˈbeɪd/, **forbidden** /fəˈbɪdn/ ~ sb. to do sth. jmdm. verbieten, etw. zu tun; ~ [sb.] sth. [jmdm.] etw. verbieten; it is ~den [to do sth.] es ist verboten[, etw. zu tun]

forbidden ▶ FORBID

for'bidding *adj.* Furcht einflößend

force /fɔːs/ 1 *n.* **(a)** (strength, power) Stärke, *die;* (of explosion, storm) Wucht, *die;* (Phys.; physical strength) Kraft, *die;* in ~: mit einem großen Aufgebot

(b) (validity) Kraft, *die;* in ~: in Kraft; come into ~ ⟨Gesetz usw.⟩ in Kraft treten

(c) (violence) Gewalt, *die;* by ~: gewaltsam

(d) (group) (of workers) Kolonne, *die;* Trupp, *der;* (Mil.) Armee, *die;* the ~ (Police) die Polizei; the ~s die Armee; be in the ~s beim Militär sein

2 *v.t.* **(a)** zwingen; ~ sth. [up]on sb. jmdm. etw. aufzwingen

(b) ~ [open] aufbrechen; ~ one's way in sich ⟨Dat.⟩ mit Gewalt Zutritt verschaffen

forced /fɔːst/ *adj.* **(a)** (contrived, unnatural) gezwungen

(b) (compelled by force) erzwungen; Zwangs⟨arbeit⟩

forced 'landing *n.* Notlandung, *die*

'force-feed *v.t.* zwangsernähren

forceful /ˈfɔːsfl/ *adj.* stark ⟨Persönlichkeit, Charakter⟩; energisch ⟨Person, Art⟩; eindrucksvoll ⟨Sprache⟩

forceps /ˈfɔːseps/ *n., pl. same* [pair of] ~: Zange, *die*

forcible /ˈfɔːsɪbl/ *adj.,* **forcibly** /ˈfɔːsɪblɪ/ *adv.* gewaltsam

ford /fɔːd/ 1 *n.* Furt, *die*

2 *v.t.* durchqueren; (wade through) durchwaten

fore /fɔː(r)/ 1 *adj., esp. in comb.* vorder...; Vorder⟨teil, -front usw.⟩

2 *n.* to the ~: im Vordergrund

'forearm *n.* Unterarm, *der*

foreboding /fɔːˈbəʊdɪŋ/ *n.* Vorahnung, *die*

'forecast 1 *v.t.,* **forecast** *or* **forecasted** vorhersagen

2 *n.* Voraussage, *die*

'forecaster *n.* Meteorologe, *der*/ Meteorologin, *die*

'forecourt *n.* Vorhof, *der*

'forefather *n., usu. in pl.* Vorfahr, *der*

'forefinger *n.* Zeigefinger, *der*

'forefront *n.* [be] in the ~ of in vorderster Linie (+ Gen.) [stehen]

'foregone *adj.* be a ~ conclusion von vornherein feststehen; (be certain) so gut wie sicher sein

'foreground *n.* Vordergrund, *der*

forehead /ˈfɒrɪd, ˈfɔːhed/ *n.* Stirn, *die*

foreign /ˈfɒrɪn/ *adj.* **(a)** (from abroad) ausländisch; Fremd⟨kapital, -sprache⟩; he is ~: er ist Ausländer

(b) (abroad) fremd; Außen⟨politik, -handel⟩; from a ~ country aus einem anderen Land; aus dem Ausland; ~ countries Ausland, *das*

(c) (from outside) fremd; ~ body/substance Fremdkörper, *der*

foreign corre'spondent *n.* (Journ.) Auslandskorrespondent, *der*/ -korrespondentin, *die*

'foreigner *n.* Ausländer, *der*/Ausländerin, *die*

foreign: ~ ex'change *n.* Devisen *Pl.;* ~ 'language *n.* Fremdsprache, *die;* ~-language assistant Fremdsprachenassistent, *der*/-assistentin, *die;* ~-language newspaper/broadcast fremdsprachige Zeitung/Rundfunksendung; ~-language teaching Fremdsprachenunterricht, *der;* F~ 'Minister *n.* Außenminister, *der*/ -ministerin, *die;* F~ 'Ministry *n.* Außenministerium, *das;* F~ Office *n.* (Brit. Hist./coll.) Außenministerium, *das;* ~ policy *n.* Außenpolitik, *die;* F~ 'Secretary *n.* (Brit.) Außenminister, *der*/-ministerin, *die;* ~ trade *n.* Außenhandel, *der*

foreman /ˈfɔːmən/ *n., pl.* **foremen** /ˈfɔːmən/ Vorarbeiter, *der*

foremost /ˈfɔːməʊst, ˈfɔːməst/ 1 *adj.* **(a)** vorderst...

(b) (fig.) führend

2 *adv.* first and ~: zunächst einmal

'forename *n.* Vorname, *der*

forensic /fəˈrensɪk/ *adj.* ~ medicine Gerichtsmedizin, *die;* ~ science Kriminaltechnik, *die*

'foreplay *n.* Vorspiel, *das*

'forerunner *n.* Vorläufer, *der*/Vorläuferin, *die*

foresaw ▶ FORESEE

foresee /fɔːˈsiː/ *v.t., forms as* SEE voraussehen

foreseeable /fɔːˈsiːəbl/ *adj.* vorhersehbar; in the ~ future in nächster Zukunft

foreseen ▶ FORESEE

'foresight *n.* Weitblick, *der*

foreskin *n.* (Anat.) Vorhaut, *die*

forest /ˈfɒrɪst/ *n.* Wald, *der;* (commercially exploited) Forst, *der*

fore'stall *v.t.* zuvorkommen (+ Dat.)

forested /ˈfɒrɪstɪd/ *adj.* bewaldet

forestry /'fɒrɪstrɪ/ n. Forstwirtschaft, die

'foretaste n. Vorgeschmack, der

fore'tell v.t., **fore'told** voraussagen

'forethought n. (prior deliberation) [vorherige] Überlegung; (care for the future) Vorausdenken, das

forever /fə'revə(r)/ adv. (constantly) ständig

fore'warn v.t. vorwarnen

fore'warning n. Vorwarnung, die

'foreword n. Vorwort, das

forfeit /'fɔːfɪt/ [1] v.t. verlieren; verwirken (geh.) ⟨Recht, jmds. Gunst⟩
[2] n. Strafe, die; (games) Pfand, das

forgave ▶ FORGIVE

forge¹ /fɔːdʒ/ [1] n. (a) (workshop) Schmiede, die
(b) (blacksmith's hearth) Esse, die
[2] v.t. (a) schmieden (into zu)
(b) (fig.) schmieden ⟨Plan⟩; schließen ⟨Vereinbarung, Freundschaft⟩
(c) (counterfeit) fälschen

forge² v.i. ~ **ahead** [das Tempo] beschleunigen; (fig.) Fortschritte machen

'forger n. Fälscher, der/Fälscherin, die

forgery /'fɔːdʒərɪ/ n. Fälschung, die

forget /fə'get/ [1] v.t., **-tt-**, **forgot** /fə'gɒt/, **forgotten** /fə'gɒtn/ vergessen; (~ learned ability) verlernen
[2] v.i., **-tt-**, **forgot**, **forgotten** es vergessen; ~ **about sth.** etw. vergessen; ~ **about it!** (coll.) schon gut!

forgettable /fə'getəbl/ adj. **easily** ~: leicht zu vergessen

forgetful /fə'getfl/ adj. vergesslich

for'getfulness n. Vergesslichkeit, die

for'get-me-not n. (Bot.) Vergissmeinnicht, das

forgive /fə'gɪv/ v.t., **forgave** /fə'geɪv/, **forgiven** /fə'gɪvn/ verzeihen; vergeben ⟨Sünden⟩; ~ **sb.** [**sth.** or for **sth.**] jmdm. [etw.] verzeihen

for'giveness n. Verzeihung, die; (of sins) Vergebung, die

for'giving /fə'gɪvɪŋ/ adj. versöhnlich

forgo /fɔː'gəʊ/ v.t., forms as GO: verzichten auf (+ Akk.)

forgone ▶ FORGO

forgot, forgotten ▶ FORGET

fork /fɔːk/ [1] n. (a) Gabel, die; **knives and** ~**s** Besteck, das
(b) (in road) Gabelung, die; (one branch) Abzweigung, die
[2] v.i. (divide) sich gabeln; (turn) abbiegen; ~ **left** links abbiegen
■ **fork 'out** v.i. (coll.) blechen (ugs.)

forked 'lightning n., no indef. art. Linienblitz, der

'forklift truck n. Gabelstapler, der

forlorn /fə'lɔːn/ adj. (a) (desperate) verzweifelt
(b) (forsaken) verlassen

form /fɔːm/ [1] n. (a) (shape, type, style) Form, die; **take** ~: Gestalt annehmen
(b) (printed sheet) Formular, das
(c) (Brit. Sch.) Klasse, die
(d) (bench) Bank, die
(e) (Sport: physical condition) Form, die; (fig.) **true to** ~: wie üblich
[2] v.t. (a) bilden
(b) (shape) formen, gestalten (**into** zu)
(c) sich (Dat.) bilden ⟨Meinung, Urteil⟩; gewinnen ⟨Eindruck⟩; fassen ⟨Plan⟩; entwickeln ⟨Vorliebe, Gewohnheit⟩; schließen ⟨Freundschaft⟩
(d) (set up) bilden ⟨Regierung⟩; gründen ⟨Bund, Firma, Partei⟩
[3] v.i. sich bilden; ⟨Idee:⟩ Gestalt annehmen

formal /'fɔːml/ adj. formell; förmlich ⟨Person, Art, Einladung, Begrüßung⟩; (official) offiziell; **a** ~ **'yes'/'no'** eine bindende Zusage/endgültige Absage

formality /fɔː'mælɪtɪ/ n. (a) (requirement) Formalität, die
(b) (being formal) Förmlichkeit, die

formalize /'fɔːməlaɪz/ v.t. (a) (specify and systematize) formalisieren
(b) (make official) formell bekräftigen

format /'fɔːmæt/ n. [1] (also Comp.) Format, das
[2] v.t., **-tt-** (Comp.) formatieren

formation /fɔː'meɪʃn/ n. (a) ▶ FORM 2A, D: Bildung, die; Gründung, die
(b) (Mil., Aeronaut.) Formation, die

formative /'fɔːmətɪv/ adj. formend, prägend ⟨Einfluss⟩; **the** ~ **years of life** die entscheidenden Lebensjahre

former /'fɔːmə(r)/ attrib. adj. ehemalig; **in** ~ **times** früher; **the** ~: der/die/das Erstere; pl. die Ersteren

'formerly adv. früher

formidable /'fɔːmɪdəbl/ adj. gewaltig; gefährlich ⟨Herausforderung, Gegner⟩

formula /'fɔːmjʊlə/ n. Formel, die

formulate /'fɔːmjʊleɪt/ v.t. formulieren; (devise) entwickeln

formulation /fɔːmjʊ'leɪʃn/ n. Formulierung, die

forsake /fə'seɪk/ v.t., **forsook** /fə'sʊk/, ~**n** /fə'seɪkn/ (a) (give up) verzichten auf (+ Akk.)
(b) (desert) verlassen

for'saken adj. verlassen

forsook ▶ FORSAKE

fort /fɔːt/ n. (Mil.) Fort, das

forte /'fɔːteɪ/ n. Stärke, die

forth /fɔːθ/ adv. ~ **and so** ~: und so weiter; see also BACK 3

forthcoming /'---, -'-/ adj. (a) (approaching) bevorstehend; in Kürze erscheinend ⟨Buch usw.⟩
(b) pred. **be** ~ ⟨Geld, Antwort:⟩ kommen; ⟨Hilfe:⟩ geleistet werden; **not be** ~: ausbleiben
(c) (responsive) mitteilsam ⟨Person⟩

'forthright adj. direkt

forth'with adv. unverzüglich

fortieth /'fɔːtɪɪθ/ adj. vierzigst...

fortify /'fɔːtɪfaɪ/ v.t. **(a)** (Mil.) befestigen
(b) (strengthen) stärken

fortitude /'fɔːtɪtjuːd/ n. innere Stärke

fortnight /'fɔːtnaɪt/ n. vierzehn Tage Pl.

fortnightly /'fɔːtnaɪtlɪ/ ⏞**1** adj.
vierzehntäglich; zweiwöchentlich
⏞**2** adv. alle vierzehn Tage; alle zwei Wochen

fortress /'fɔːtrɪs/ n. Festung, die

fortuitous /fɔːˈtjuːɪtəs/ adj.,
for'tuitously adv. zufällig

fortunate /'fɔːtʃənət/ adj. glücklich

'fortunately adv. glücklicherweise

fortune /'fɔːtʃən, ˈfɔːtʃuːn/ n. **(a)** (wealth)
Vermögen, das
(b) (luck) Schicksal, das; **bad/good** ∼: Pech/
Glück, das

'fortune teller n. Wahrsager, der/
Wahrsagerin, die

forty /'fɔːtɪ/ ⏞**1** adj. vierzig; **have** ∼ 'winks
ein Nickerchen machen (ugs.)
⏞**2** n. Vierzig, die. See also EIGHT; EIGHTY 2

forum /'fɔːrəm/ n. Forum, das

forward /'fɔːwəd/ ⏞**1** adv. **(a)** (in direction
faced) vorwärts
(b) (to the front) nach vorn; vor⟨laufen,
-rücken, -schieben⟩
(c) (closer) heran; **he came** ∼ **to greet me** er
kam auf mich zu, um mich zu begrüßen
(d) come ∼ ⟨Zeuge, Helfer:⟩ sich melden
⏞**2** adj. **(a)** (directed ahead) vorwärts gerichtet
(b) (at or to the front) Vorder-; vorder...
⏞**3** n. (Sport) Stürmer, der/Stürmerin, die
⏞**4** v.t. (send on) nachschicken ⟨Post⟩ **(to an**
+ Akk.)

forwarding ad'dress /'fɔːwədɪŋ/ n.
Nachsendeanschrift, die

forward: ∼**-looking** adj.
vorausschauend; ∼ **'planning** n.
Vorausplanung, die

forwards /'fɔːwədz/ ▶ FORWARD 1A, B

forwent ▶ FORGO

fossil /'fɒsɪl/ n. Fossil, das; ∼ **fuel** fossiler
Brennstoff

foster /'fɒstə(r)/ ⏞**1** v.t. **(a)** fördern; pflegen
⟨Freundschaft⟩
(b) in Pflege haben ⟨Kind⟩
⏞**2** adj. ∼-: Pflege⟨kind, -eltern, -sohn usw.⟩

fought ▶ FIGHT 1, 2

foul /faʊl/ ⏞**1** adj. **(a)** abscheulich ⟨Geruch,
Geschmack⟩
(b) (polluted) verschmutzt ⟨Wasser, Luft⟩;
(putrid) faulig ⟨Wasser⟩; stickig ⟨Luft⟩
(c) (coll.: awful) scheußlich (ugs.); anstößig
⟨Sprache⟩
⏞**2** n. (Sport) Foul, das
⏞**3** v.t. **(a)** beschmutzen; verpesten ⟨Luft⟩
(b) (Sport) foulen

foul: ∼**-mouthed** /'faʊlmaʊðd/ adj.
unanständig; unflätig; ∼**-smelling** adj.
übel riechend

found¹ /faʊnd/ v.t. **(a)** (establish) gründen;
stiften ⟨Krankenhaus, Kloster⟩; begründen
⟨Wissenschaft, Religion⟩
(b) (fig.: base) begründen; **be** ∼**ed [up]on sth.**
[sich] auf etw. (Akk.) gründen

found² ▶ FIND 1

foundation /faʊnˈdeɪʃn/ n. **(a)** Gründung,
die; (of hospital, monastery) Stiftung, die
(b) usu. in pl. ∼**[s]** (lit. or fig.) Fundament,
das; **be without** ∼ (fig.) unbegründet sein

foundation: ∼ **course** n. (Univ. etc.)
Grundkurs, der; ∼ **cream** n.
Grundierungscreme, die; ∼ **stone** n. (lit. or
fig.) Grundstein, der

'founder¹ n. Gründer, der/Gründerin, die;
(of hospital) Stifter, der/Stifterin, die

founder² v.i. **(a)** ⟨Schiff:⟩ sinken
(b) (fig.: fail) sich zerschlagen

foundry /'faʊndrɪ/ n. Gießerei, die

fountain /'faʊntɪn/ n. Fontäne, die; (structure)
Springbrunnen, der; (fig.) Quelle, die

'fountain pen n. Füllfederhalter, der

four /fɔː(r)/ ⏞**1** adj. vier
⏞**2** n. Vier, die; **on all** ∼**s** auf allen vieren
(ugs.). See also EIGHT

four: ∼**-by-**∼ ⏞**1** adj. Allrad-; ⏞**2** n.
Allradler, der/Allradfahrzeug, das; ∼**-door**
attrib. adj. viertürig ⟨Auto⟩; ∼**fold**
/'fɔːfəʊld/ adj., adv. vierfach; **a** ∼**fold**
increase ein Anstieg auf das Vierfache;
∼**-legged** /'fɔːleɡɪd, ˈfɔːleɡd/ adj.
vierbeinig; ∼**-letter 'word** n. vulgärer
Ausdruck; (expressing anger) ≈ Kraftausdruck,
der; ∼**-poster** n. Himmelbett, das;
∼**some** /'fɔːsəm/ n. Quartett, das; **go in** or
as a ∼**some** zu viert gehen; ∼**-star** n.
∼**-star [petrol]** Super[benzin], das

fourteen /fɔːˈtiːn/ ⏞**1** adj. vierzehn
⏞**2** n. Vierzehn, die. See also EIGHT

fourteenth /fɔːˈtiːnθ/ ⏞**1** adj. vierzehnt...
⏞**2** n. (fraction) Vierzehntel, das. See also
EIGHTH

fourth /fɔːθ/ ⏞**1** adj. viert...
⏞**2** n. (in sequence, rank) Vierte, der/die/das;
(fraction) Viertel, das. See also EIGHTH

'fourthly adv. viertens

four-wheel 'drive n. (Motor Veh.) Vier- od.
Allradantrieb, der

fowl /faʊl/ n. Haushuhn, das; (collectively)
Geflügel, das

fox /fɒks/ ⏞**1** n. Fuchs, der
⏞**2** v.t. verwirren

'fox-hunting n. Fuchsjagd, die

foyer /'fɔɪeɪ/ n. Foyer, das

fraction /'frækʃn/ n. **(a)** (Math.) Bruch, der
(b) (small part) Bruchteil, der

fracture /'fræktʃə(r)/ ⏞**1** n. Bruch, der
⏞**2** v.t. brechen

fragile /'frædʒaɪl/ adj. zerbrechlich

fragility /frəˈdʒɪlɪtɪ/ n. Zerbrechlichkeit, die

fragment /'fræɡmənt/ n. Bruchstück, das

fragmentary ⋯⋙ freezer · · · ·

fragmentary /'frægməntərɪ/ *adj.* bruchstückhaft

fragrance /'freɪgrəns/ *n.* Duft, *der*

fragrant /'freɪgrənt/ *adj.* duftend

frail /freɪl/ *adj.* zerbrechlich; gebrechlich ⟨Greis, Greisin⟩

frame /freɪm/ ① *n.* (a) (of vehicle) Rahmen, *der;* (of bed) Gestell, *das* (b) (border) Rahmen, *der;* [spectacle] ∼s [Brillen]gestell, *das* ② *v.t.* (a) rahmen (b) formulieren ⟨Frage, Antwort⟩ (c) (coll.: incriminate) ∼ sb. jmdm. etwas anhängen (ugs.)

frame: ∼**up** *n.* (coll.) abgekartetes Spiel (ugs.); ∼**work** *n.* Gerüst, *das*

franc /fræŋk/ *n.* Franc, *der;* (Swiss) Franken, *der*

France /frɑːns/ *pr. n.* Frankreich (*das*)

franchise /'frænt∫aɪz/ *n.* (a) Stimmrecht, *das* (b) (Commerc.) Lizenz, *die*

frank¹ *adj.* offen; freimütig ⟨Geständnis, Äußerung⟩; be ∼ with sb. zu jmdm. offen sein

frank² *v.t.* (Post) frankieren

frankfurter /'fræŋkfɜːtə(r)/ (*Amer.:* **frankfurt** /'fræŋkfɜːt/) *n.* Frankfurter [Würstchen]

frankly *adv.* offen; (honestly) offen gesagt

frantic /'fræntɪk/ *adj.* (a) verzweifelt ⟨Hilferufe, Gestikulieren⟩; be ∼ with fear/ rage *etc.* außer sich (*Dat.*) sein vor Angst/ Wut *usw.* (b) hektisch ⟨Aktivität, Suche⟩

frantically /'fræntɪkəlɪ/, **franticly** *adv.* verzweifelt

fraternal /frə'tɜːnl/ *adj.* brüderlich

fraternize /'frætənaɪz/ *v.i.* ∼ [with sb.] sich verbrüdern [mit jmdm.]

fraud /frɔːd/ *n.* (a) *no pl.* Betrug, *der* (b) (trick) Schwindel, *der* (c) (person) Betrüger, *der*/Betrügerin, *die*

fraudulent /'frɔːdjʊlənt/ *adj.* betrügerisch

fraught /frɔːt/ *adj.* be ∼ with danger voller Gefahren sein

fray¹ /freɪ/ *n.* [Kampf]getümmel, *das;* enter *or* join the ∼: sich in den Kampf stürzen

fray² *v.i.* [sich] durchscheuern; ⟨Hosenbein, Teppich, Seilende:⟩ ausfransen; our nerves/ tempers began to ∼ (fig.) wir verloren langsam die Nerven/unsere Gemüter erhitzten sich

freak /friːk/ *n.* (a) Missgeburt, *die; attrib.* ungewöhnlich ⟨Wetter, Ereignis⟩ (b) (coll.: fanatic) Freak, *der*

freakish /'friːkɪ∫/ *adj.* (capricious) launisch; verrückt (ugs.); (abnormal) absonderlich

freaky /'friːkɪ/ *adj.*(a) ▶ FREAKISH (b) (coll.: bizarre) irre (salopp); verrückt (ugs.)

freckle /'frekl/ *n.* Sommersprosse, *die*

freckled *adj.* sommersprossig

free /friː/ ① *adj.,* freer /'friːə(r)/, freest /'friːɪst/ (a) frei; get ∼: freikommen; set ∼: freilassen; ∼ of charge/cost gebührenfrei/ kostenlos; sb. is ∼ to do sth. es steht jmdm. frei, etw. zu tun; ∼ time Freizeit, *die;* he's ∼ in the mornings er hat morgens Zeit (b) (without payment) kostenlos; frei ⟨Unterkunft, Verpflegung⟩; Frei⟨karte, -exemplar⟩; Gratis⟨probe⟩; 'admission ∼' „Eintritt frei"; for ∼ (coll.) umsonst ② *adv.* gratis; umsonst ③ *v.t.* (set at liberty) freilassen; (disentangle) befreien (of, from von); ∼ sb./oneself from jmdn./sich befreien aus ⟨Gefängnis, Sklaverei⟩

free 'agent *n.* be a ∼: sein eigener Herr sein

freedom /'friːdəm/ *n.* Freiheit, *die;* ∼ of the press Pressefreiheit, *die;* ∼ of action/ speech/movement Handlungs-/Rede-/ Bewegungsfreiheit, *die;* ∼ of information Auskunftsrecht, *das*

'freedom fighter *n.* Freiheitskämpfer, *der*/-kämpferin, *die*

free: ∼ 'enterprise *n.* freies Unternehmertum; ∼ 'fall *n.* freier Fall; ∼-fall parachuting Fallschirmspringen mit freiem Fall; F∼fone ® /'friːfəʊn/ *n.* ≈ Service 130; phone us on F∼fone 0800 343 027 rufen Sie uns unter 0800 343 027 zum Nulltarif an; ∼ 'gift *n.* Gratisgabe, *die;* ∼hold ① *n.* Besitzrecht, *das;* ② *adj.* Eigentums-; ∼holder *n.* Grundeigentümer, *der;* ∼ house *n.* (Brit.) brauereiunabhängiges Wirtshaus; ∼ 'kick *n.* (Footb.) Freistoß, *der;* ∼lance ① *n.* freier Mitarbeiter/freie Mitarbeiterin; ② *adj.* freiberuflich; ∼lancer /'friːlɑːnsə(r)/ ▶ ∼LANCE 1

freely *adv.* (willingly) großzügig; freimütig ⟨eingestehen⟩; (without restriction) frei; (frankly) offen

free: ∼ 'market *n.* (Econ.) freier Markt; F∼mason *n.* Freimaurer, *der;* F∼phone ▶ FREEFONE; ∼-'range *adj.* frei laufend ⟨Huhn⟩; ∼-range eggs Eier von frei laufenden Hühnern; ∼ speech *n.* Redefreiheit; ∼-standing *adj.* frei stehend; ∼ware /'friːweə(r)/ *n., no indef. art.* (Comp.) Freeware, *die;* kostenlose Software; ∼way *n.* (Amer.) Autobahn, *die;* ∼-wheel *v.i.* im Freilauf fahren; ∼ 'world *n.* freie Welt

freeze /friːz/ ① *v.i.,* froze /frəʊz/, frozen /'frəʊzn/ (a) frieren; (become covered with ice) zufrieren; ⟨Straße:⟩ vereisen; ⟨Flüssigkeit:⟩ gefrieren; ⟨Rohr, Schloss:⟩ einfrieren (b) (become rigid) steif frieren ② *v.t.,* froze, frozen (a) (preserve) tiefkühlen (b) einfrieren ⟨Kredit, Löhne, Preise usw.⟩

'freeze-dry *v.t.* gefriertrocknen

'freezer *n.* Tiefkühltruhe, *die;* [upright] ∼: Tiefkühlschrank, *der;* ∼ compartment Tiefkühlfach, *das*

freezing /ˈfriːzɪŋ/ ⟦1⟧ *adj.* (lit. or fig.) frostig; it's ∼: es ist eiskalt
⟦2⟧ *n.* above/below ∼: über/unter dem/den Gefrierpunkt

freezing: ∼ **'fog** *n.* gefrierender Nebel; ∼ **point** *n.* Gefrierpunkt, *der*

freight /freɪt/ *n.* Fracht, *die*

'freighter *n.* Frachter, *der*

'freight train *n.* Güterzug, *der*

French /frentʃ/ ⟦1⟧ *adj.* französisch; he/she is ∼: er ist Franzose/sie ist Französin
⟦2⟧ *n.* **(a)** (language) Französisch, *das; see also* ENGLISH 2A
(b) the ∼ *pl.* die Franzosen *Pl.*

French: ∼ **'bean** *n.* (Brit.) Gartenbohne, *die;* ∼ **'bread** *n.* französisches [Stangen]weißbrot; ∼ **'dressing** *n.* Vinaigrette, *die;* ∼ **'fries** *n. pl.* Pommes frites *Pl.;* ∼ **'kiss** *n.* französischer Kuss (ugs.); Zungenkuss, *der;* ∼**man** /ˈfrentʃmən/ *n., pl.* ∼**men** /ˈfrentʃmən/ Franzose, *der;* ∼ **'polish** *n.* Schellackpolitur, *die;* ∼ **'window** *n.* französisches Fenster; ∼**woman** *n.* Französin, *die*

frenzied /ˈfrenzɪd/ *adj.* rasend

frenzy /ˈfrenzɪ/ *n.* Wahnsinn, *der;* (fury) Raserei, *die*

frequency /ˈfriːkwənsɪ/ *n.* **(a)** Häufigkeit, *die*
(b) (Phys.) Frequenz, *die*

frequent ⟦1⟧ /ˈfriːkwənt/ *adj.* **(a)** häufig; become less ∼: seltener werden
(b) (habitual) eifrig
⟦2⟧ /friˈkwent/ *v.t.* häufig besuchen ⟨Café, Klub, usw.⟩

frequently /ˈfriːkwəntlɪ/ *adv.* häufig

fresco /ˈfreskəʊ/ *n. pl.* ∼es *or* ∼s Fresko, *das*

fresh /freʃ/ *adj.* frisch; neu ⟨Beweise, Anstrich, Mut, Energie⟩; ∼ **supplies** Nachschub, *der* (of an + *Dat.*); **make a** ∼ **start** noch einmal von vorne anfangen; (fig.) neu beginnen

freshen /ˈfreʃn/ *v.i.* auffrischen

■ **freshen 'up** *v.i.* sich auffrischen

'freshly *adv.* frisch

'freshness *n.* Frische, *die*

fresh 'water *n.* Süßwasser, *das*

fret /fret/ *v.i.,* **-tt-** sich (*Dat.*) Sorgen machen

fretful /ˈfretfl/ *adj.* verdrießlich; quengelig (ugs.)

'fretsaw *n.* Laubsäge, *die*

Fri. *abbr.* = **Friday** Fr.

friar /ˈfraɪə(r)/ *n.* Ordensbruder, *der*

friction /ˈfrɪkʃn/ *n.* Reibung, *die*

Friday /ˈfraɪdeɪ, ˈfraɪdɪ/ *n.* Freitag, *der;* on ∼: [am] Freitag; on a ∼, on ∼s freitags; ∼ **13 August** Freitag, der 13. August; (at top of letter etc.) Freitag, den 13. August; next/last ∼: [am] nächsten/letzten Freitag; Good ∼: Karfreitag, *der*

fridge /frɪdʒ/ *n.* (Brit. coll.) Kühlschrank, *der*

fried ▶ FRY[1]

friend /frend/ *n.* Freund, *der*/Freundin, *die;* be ∼s with sb. mit jmdm. befreundet sein; make ∼s [with sb.] [mit jmdm.] Freundschaft schließen

friendliness /ˈfrendlɪnɪs/ *n.* Freundlichkeit, *die*

'friendly ⟦1⟧ *adj.* freundlich (to zu); freundschaftlich ⟨Rat, Beziehungen, Wettkampf⟩
⟦2⟧ *n.* (Sport) Freundschaftsspiel, *das*

'friendship *n.* Freundschaft, *die*

fries /fraɪz/ *n. pl.* (Amer.) Pommes frites *Pl.*

frigate /ˈfrɪɡət/ *n.* (Naut.) Fregatte, *die*

fright /fraɪt/ *n.* Schreck, *der;* take ∼: erschrecken

frighten /ˈfraɪtn/ *v.t.* ⟨Explosion, Schuss:⟩ erschrecken; ⟨Gedanke, Drohung:⟩ Angst machen (+ *Dat.*); be ∼ed at *or* by sth. vor etw. (*Dat.*) erschrecken

'frightful *adj.,* **'frightfully** *adv.* furchtbar

frigid /ˈfrɪdʒɪd/ *adj.* frostig; (sexually) frigid[e]

frill /frɪl/ *n.* **(a)** Rüsche, *die*
(b) in *pl.* (embellishments) Beiwerk, *das*

'frilly *adj.* mit Rüschen besetzt; Rüschen⟨kleid, -bluse⟩

fringe /frɪndʒ/ *n.* **(a)** Fransenkante, *die* (on an + *Dat.*)
(b) (hair) [Pony]fransen *Pl.* (ugs.)
(c) (edge) Rand, *der*

frisk /frɪsk/ ⟦1⟧ *v.i.* ∼ [about] [herum]springen
⟦2⟧ *v.t.* (coll.) filzen (ugs.)

'frisky *adj.* munter

fritter¹ /ˈfrɪtə(r)/ *n.* apple *etc.* ∼s Apfelstücke *usw.* in Pfannkuchenteig

fritter² *v.t.* ∼ **away** vergeuden

frivolity /frɪˈvɒlɪtɪ/ *n.* Oberflächlichkeit, *die*

frivolous /ˈfrɪvələs/ *adj.* **(a)** frivol
(b) (trifling) belanglos

frizzy /ˈfrɪzɪ/ *adj.* kraus

fro /frəʊ/ *adv.* ▶ TO 2

frock /frɒk/ *n.* Kleid, *das*

frog /frɒɡ/ *n.* Frosch, *der*

frog: ∼**man** /ˈfrɒɡmən/ *n., pl.* ∼**men** /ˈfrɒɡmən/ Froschmann, *der;* ∼**spawn** *n.* Froschlaich, *der*

frolic /ˈfrɒlɪk/ *v.i.,* **-ck-:** ∼ [about *or* around] [herum]springen

from /frəm, *stressed* frɒm/ *prep.* von; (∼ within; expr. origin) aus; ∼ **Paris** aus Paris; ∼ **Paris to Munich** von Paris nach München; **be a mile** ∼ **sth.** eine Meile von etw. entfernt sein; **where do you come** ∼?, **where are you** ∼?** woher kommen Sie?; **painted** ∼ **life** nach dem Leben gemalt; **weak** ∼ **hunger** schwach vor Hunger; ∼ **the year 1972** seit 1972; ∼ **[the age of] 18** ab 18 Jahre; ∼ **4 to 6 eggs** 4 bis 6 Eier

front /frʌnt/ ⟦1⟧ *n.* **(a)** Vorderseite, *die;* (of house) Vorderfront, *die;* in *or* at the ∼ [of

sth.] vorn [in etw. *position: Dat., movement: Akk.*]; **to the ~:** nach vorn; **in ~:** vorn[e]; **be in ~ of sth./sb.** vor etw./jmdm. sein
(b) (Mil.) Front, *die*
(c) (at seaside) Strandpromenade, *die*
(d) (Metereol.) Front, *die*
(e) (bluff) Fassade, *die*
2 *adj.* vorder...; Vorder⟨*rad, -zimmer, -zahn*⟩; **~ garden** Vorgarten, *der;* **~ row** erste Reihe
frontal /'frʌntl/ *adj.* Frontal-
front 'door *n.* (of flat) Wohnungstür, *die;* (of house) Haustür, *die*
frontier /'frʌntɪə(r)/ *n.* Grenze, *die*
front: ~ 'page *n.* Titelseite, *die;* **~-wheel drive** 1 *n.* Vorderradantrieb, *der;* Frontantrieb, *der;* 2 *adj.* **a ~-wheel drive vehicle** ein Fahrzeug mit Vorderrad- od. Frontantrieb
frost /frɒst/ 1 *n.* Frost, *der;* **ten degrees of ~** (Brit.) zehn Grad minus
2 *v.t.* **~ed glass** Mattglas, *das*
'**frostbite** *n.* Erfrierung, *die*
'**frosting** *n.* (esp. Amer.) Glasur, *die*
'**frosty** *adj.* frostig
froth /frɒθ/ 1 *n.* Schaum, *der*
2 *v.i.* schäumen
'**frothy** *adj.* schaumig
frown /fraʊn/ 1 *v.i.* die Stirn runzeln ([up]on über + *Akk.*)
2 *n.* Stirnrunzeln, *das*
froze ▸ FREEZE
frozen /'frəʊzn/ 1 ▸ FREEZE
2 *adj.* **(a)** zugefroren ⟨*Fluss, See*⟩; eingefroren ⟨*Wasserleitung*⟩; **I'm ~** (fig.) mir ist eiskalt
(b) (to preserve) tiefgekühlt; **~ food** Tiefkühlkost, *die*
frugal /'fru:gl/ *adj.* genügsam ⟨*Lebensweise, Mensch*⟩; frugal ⟨*Mahl*⟩
fruit /fru:t/ *n.* Frucht, *die; collect.* Obst, *das*
'**fruit cake** *n.* englischer Teekuchen
fruitful /'fru:tfl/ *adj.* fruchtbar
'**fruit juice** *n.* Obstsaft, *der*
'**fruitless** *adj.* nutzlos ⟨*Versuch, Gespräch*⟩; fruchtlos ⟨*Verhandlung, Suche*⟩
fruit: ~ machine *n.* (Brit.) Spielautomat, *der;* **~ 'salad** *n.* Obstsalat, *der*
'**fruity** *adj.* fruchtig ⟨*Geschmack, Wein*⟩
frustrate /frʌ'streɪt/ *v.t.* vereiteln ⟨*Plan, Versuch*⟩; zunichte machen ⟨*Hoffnung, Bemühungen*⟩
'**frustrated** *adj.* frustriert
frustration /frʌ'streɪʃn/ *n.* Frustration, *die*
fry¹ /fraɪ/ *v.t. & i.,* fried /fraɪd/ braten; **fried egg** Spiegelei, *das*
fry² *n.* (fishes) Brut, *die;* **small ~** (fig.) unbedeutende Leute
'**frying pan** *n.* Bratpfanne, *die*
ft. *abbr.* = **feet, foot** ft.
fuchsia /'fju:ʃə/ *n.* (Bot.) Fuchsie, *die*

fuck /fʌk/ (coarse) 1 *v.t. & i.* ficken (vulg.); [oh,] **~!,** [oh,] **~ it!** [au,] Scheiße! (derb.)
2 *n.* Fick, *der* (vulg.)
fuddy-duddy /'fʌdɪdʌdɪ/ (coll.) 1 *adj.* verkalkt (ugs.)
2 *n.* Fossil, *das* (fig.)
fudge /fʌdʒ/ *n.* Karamellbonbon, *der od. das*
fuel /'fju:əl/ *n.* Brennstoff, *der;* (for vehicle) Kraftstoff, *der;* (for ship, aircraft) Treibstoff, *der*
fuel: ~ consumption *n.* (of vehicle) Kraftstoffverbrauch, *der;* **~ gauge** *n.* Kraftstoffanzeiger *der;* **~ injection** *n.* Benzineinspritzung, *die*
fugitive /'fju:dʒɪtɪv/ *n.* Flüchtige, *der/die*
fugue /fju:g/ *n.* (Mus.) Fuge, *die*
fulfil (*Amer.:* **fulfill**) /fʊl'fɪl/ *v.t.,* -ll- erfüllen; halten ⟨*Versprechen;*⟩ **~ oneself** sich selbst verwirklichen
ful'filment (*Amer.:* **ful'fillment**) *n.* Erfüllung, *die*
full /fʊl/ 1 *adj.* **(a)** voll; satt ⟨*Person*⟩; **~ of** voller; **be ~ up** voll [besetzt] sein; ⟨*Behälter:*⟩ randvoll sein; ⟨*Flug:*⟩ völlig ausgebucht sein; **I'm ~ [up]** (coll.) ich bin voll [bis obenhin] (ugs.); **be ~ of oneself** sehr von sich eingenommen sein
(b) ausführlich ⟨*Bericht, Beschreibung*⟩; erfüllt ⟨*Leben*⟩; ganz ⟨*Stunde, Jahr, Monat, Seite*⟩; voll ⟨*Name, Bezahlung, Verständnis*⟩; **~ details** alle Einzelheiten; **at ~ speed** mit Höchstgeschwindigkeit
(c) voll ⟨*Gesicht*⟩; füllig ⟨*Figur*⟩; weit ⟨*Rock*⟩
2 *n.* **in ~:** vollständig
3 *adv.* (exactly) genau
full: ~-blown *adj.* ausgewachsen ⟨*Skandal*⟩; ausgereift ⟨*Theorie, Plan, Gedanke*⟩; **~-blown AIDS** Vollbild-Aids, *das;* **~-bodied** *adj.* vollmundig, (fachspr.) körperreich ⟨*Wein*⟩; **~-cream** *adj.* **~-cream milk/cheese** Vollmilch, *die/* Vollfettkäse, *der;* **~ -length** *adj.* lang ⟨*Kleid*⟩; **~ 'moon** *n.* Vollmond, *der;* **~-scale** *adj.* **(a)** in Originalgröße; **(b)** groß angelegt ⟨*Untersuchung, Suchaktion*⟩; **~ 'stop** *n.* Punkt, *der;* **~-time** *adj.* ganztägig; Ganztags⟨*arbeit*⟩; **~-'timer** *n.* Ganztagsbeschäftigte, *der/die*
fully /'fʊlɪ/ *adv.* voll [und ganz]; reich ⟨*belohnt*⟩; ausführlich ⟨*erklären*⟩
fulsome /'fʊlsəm/ *adj.* übertrieben
fumble /'fʌmbl/ *v.i.* **~ at** *or* **with** [herum]fingern an (+ *Dat.*); **~ in one's pockets for sth.** in seinen Taschen nach etw. kramen (ugs.)
fume /fju:m/ 1 *n.* in *pl.* **~s** Dämpfe *Pl.;* (from car exhaust) Abgase *Pl.*
2 *v.i.* vor Wut schäumen
fumigate /'fju:mɪgeɪt/ *v.t.* ausräuchern
fun /fʌn/ *n.* Spaß, *der;* **have ~!** viel Spaß!; **make ~ of sb.** sich über jmdn. lustig machen; **for ~, for the ~ of it** zum Spaß

function /ˈfʌŋkʃn/ **1** n. Aufgabe, die; Funktion, die; (formal event) Veranstaltung, die **2** v.i. ⟨Maschine, System:⟩ funktionieren; ~ **as** fungieren als; (serve as) dienen als

functional /ˈfʌŋkʃənl/ adj. (a) (useful) funktionell
(b) (working) funktionsfähig

'function key n. (Comp.) Funktionstaste, die

fund /fʌnd/ **1** n. (a) (money) Fonds, der
(b) (fig.: stock) Fundus, der ⟨of von, an + Dat.⟩ **2** v.t. finanzieren

fundamental /fʌndəˈmentl/ adj. grundlegend (**to** für); elementar ⟨Bedürfnisse⟩

fundamentalism /fʌndəˈmentəlɪzm/ n. Fundamentalismus, der

fundamentalist /fʌndəˈmentəlɪst/ n. Fundamentalist, der/Fundamentalistin, die

funda'mentally adv. grundlegend; von Grund auf ⟨verschieden, ehrlich⟩

fund: ~-raiser /ˈfʌndreɪzə(r)/ n. (a) (person) Geldbeschaffer, der/-beschafferin, die; (b) (event) Benefizveranstaltung, die; **~-raising** /ˈfʌndreɪzɪŋ/ n. Geldbeschaffung, die; attrib. zur Geldbeschaffung nachgestellt

funeral /ˈfjuːnərl/ n. Beerdigung, die. ~ **director** Bestattungsunternehmer, der; ~ **service** Trauerfeier, die

'funfair n. (Brit.) Jahrmarkt, der

fungus /ˈfʌŋgəs/ n., pl. fungi /ˈfʌŋgaɪ, ˈfʌndʒaɪ/ or ~es Pilz, der

funicular /fjuːˈnɪkjʊlə(r)/ adj. & n. ~ [railway] [Stand]seilbahn, die

'fun-loving adj. lebenslustig

funnel /ˈfʌnl/ n. Trichter, der; (of ship etc.) Schornstein, der

funnily /ˈfʌnɪlɪ/ adv. komisch; ~ **enough** komischerweise

funny /ˈfʌnɪ/ adj. (a) komisch; lustig; witzig ⟨Mensch, Einfall⟩
(b) (strange) komisch

'funny bone n. Musikantenknochen, der

fur /fɜː(r)/ n. (a) Fell, das; (garment) Pelz, der; ~ **coat** Pelzmantel, der
(b) (in kettle) Kesselstein, der

furious /ˈfjʊərɪəs/ adj. wütend; heftig ⟨Streit⟩; wild ⟨Tanz, Tempo, Kampf⟩; **be** ~ **with sb.** wütend auf jmdn. sein

'furiously adv. wütend; wild ⟨kämpfen⟩: wie wild (ugs.) ⟨arbeiten⟩

furl /fɜːl/ v.t. einrollen ⟨Segel, Flagge⟩

furnace /ˈfɜːnɪs/ n. Ofen, der

furnish /ˈfɜːnɪʃ/ v.t. (a) möblieren
(b) (supply) liefern; ~ **sb. with sth.** jmdm. etw. liefern

'furnishings n. pl. Einrichtungsgegenstände Pl.

furniture /ˈfɜːnɪtʃə(r)/ n. Möbel Pl.; **piece of** ~: Möbel[stück], das

furniture: ~ polish n. Möbelpolitur, die; ~ **van** n. Möbelwagen, der

furrow /ˈfʌrəʊ/ n. Furche, die

furry /ˈfɜːrɪ/ adj. haarig; ~ **animal** (toy) Plüschtier, das

further /ˈfɜːðə(r)/ **1** adj. (a) (in space) weiter entfernt
(b) (additional) weiter...
2 adv. weiter
3 v.t. fördern

further edu'cation n. Weiterbildung, die; (for adults also) Erwachsenenbildung, die

further'more adv. außerdem

'furthermost adj. äußerst...

furthest /ˈfɜːðɪst/ **1** adj. am weitesten entfernt
2 adv. am weitesten ⟨springen, laufen⟩; am weitesten entfernt ⟨sein, wohnen⟩

furtive /ˈfɜːtɪv/ adj., **furtively** adv. verstohlen

fury /ˈfjʊərɪ/ n. Wut, die; (of sea, battle) Wüten, das

fuse¹ /fjuːz/ **1** v.t. (blend) verschmelzen (into zu)
2 v.i. ~ **together** miteinander verschmelzen

fuse² n. [time] ~: [Zeit]zünder, der; (cord) Zündschnur, die

fuse³ (Electr.) **1** n. Sicherung, die
2 v.i. **the lights have ~d** die Sicherung ist durchgebrannt

'fuse box n. Sicherungskasten, der

fuselage /ˈfjuːzəlɑːʒ/ n. [Flugzeug]rumpf, der

fusion /ˈfjuːʒn/ n. (a) Verschmelzung, die
(b) (Phys.) Fusion, die

fuss /fʌs/ **1** n. Theater, das (ugs.); **make a** ~ [about sth.] einen Wirbel [um etw.] machen
2 v.i. Wirbel machen; (get agitated) sich [unnötig] aufregen

'fussy adj. (fastidious) eigen; penibel; **I'm not** ~ (I don't mind) ich bin nicht wählerisch

futile /ˈfjuːtaɪl/ adj. vergeblich ⟨Versuch, Bemühung⟩; zum Scheitern verurteilt ⟨Plan⟩

futility /fjuːˈtɪlɪtɪ/ n. (of attempt, effort) Vergeblichkeit, die; (of plan) Zwecklosigkeit, die

futon /ˈfuːtɒn/ n. Futon, der

future /ˈfjuːtʃə(r)/ **1** adj. [zu]künftig; **at some ~ date** zu einem späteren Zeitpunkt
2 n. (a) Zukunft, die; **in** ~: in Zukunft; künftig
(b) (Ling.) Futur, das; Zukunft, die
(c) in pl. (Commerc.) Terminware, die; (contracts) Lieferungsverträge Pl.

futuristic /fjuːtʃəˈrɪstɪk/ adj. futuristisch

fuze /fjuːz/ ▶ FUSE²

fuzzy /ˈfʌzɪ/ adj. (a) (frizzy) kraus
(b) (blurred) verschwommen

Gg

G, g /dʒiː/ *n.* G, g, *das*

gab /gæb/ *n.* (coll.) **have the gift of the ~:** reden können

gabble /'gæbl/ *v.i.* brabbeln (ugs.)

gable /'geɪbl/ *n.* Giebel, *der*

gad /gæd/ *v.i.,* -dd- (coll.) **~ about** herumziehen (ugs.)

gadget /'gædʒɪt/ *n.* Gerät, *das*

gadgetry /'gædʒɪtrɪ/ *n.* [hoch technisierte] Ausstattung

Gaelic /'geɪlɪk, 'gælɪk/ 1 *adj.* gälisch 2 *n.* Gälisch, *das*

gaffe /gæf/ *n.* Fauxpas, *der*

gag /gæg/ 1 *n.* (a) Knebel, *der* (b) (joke) Gag, *der* 2 *v.t.,* -gg- knebeln

gaiety /'geɪətɪ/ *n.* Fröhlichkeit, *die*

gaily /'geɪlɪ/ *adv.* fröhlich; in leuchtenden Farben ‹bemalt, geschmückt›

gain /geɪn/ 1 *n.* (a) Gewinn, *der* (b) (increase) Zunahme, *die* (in an + *Dat.*) 2 *v.t.* (a) gewinnen; finden ‹Zugang, Zutritt›; erwerben ‹Wissen, Ruf›; erlangen ‹Freiheit›; erzielen ‹Vorteil, Punkte›; verdienen ‹Lebensunterhalt, Geldsumme›; **~ weight/five pounds [in weight]** zunehmen/fünf Pfund zunehmen; **~ speed** schneller werden (b) ‹Uhr:› vorgehen um 3 *v.i.* (a) **~ by sth.** von etw. profitieren (b) ‹Uhr:› vorgehen

gainful /'geɪnfl/ *adj.* **~ employment** Erwerbstätigkeit, *die*

gainfully /'geɪnfəlɪ/ *adv.* **~ employed** erwerbstätig

gait /geɪt/ *n.* Gang, *der*

gala /'gɑːlə, 'geɪlə/ *n.* Festveranstaltung, *die; attrib.* Gala‹abend, -vorstellung›; **swimming ~:** Schwimmfest, *das*

galaxy /'gæləksɪ/ *n.* Galaxie, *die*

gale /geɪl/ *n.* Sturm, *der*

gall /gɔːl/ *n.* Unverschämtheit, *die*

gallant /'gælənt/ *adj.* (brave) tapfer; (chivalrous) ritterlich

gallantry /'gæləntrɪ/ *n.* (bravery) Tapferkeit, *die*

'gall bladder *n.* Gallenblase, *die*

gallery /'gælərɪ/ *n.* (a) Galerie, *die* (b) (Theatre) dritter Rang

galley /'gælɪ/ *n.* (a) (ship's kitchen) Kombüse, *die* (b) (Hist.) Galeere, *die*

gallivant /'gælɪvænt/ *v.i.* (coll.) herumziehen (ugs.)

gallon /'gælən/ *n.* Gallone, *die*

gallop /'gæləp/ 1 *n.* Galopp, *der* 2 *v.i.* ‹Pferd, Reiter:› galoppieren

gallows /'gæləʊz/ *n. sing.* Galgen, *der*

Gallup poll ® /'gæləp pəʊl/ *n.* Meinungsumfrage, *die*

galore /gə'lɔː(r)/ *adv.* im Überfluss; in Hülle und Fülle

galvanize /'gælvənaɪz/ *v.t.* wachrütteln; **~ sb. into action** jmdn. veranlassen, sofort aktiv zu werden

gambit /'gæmbɪt/ *n.* Gambit, *das*

gamble /'gæmbl/ *v.i.* (a) [um Geld] spielen; **~ at cards/on horses** um Geld Karten spielen/auf Pferde wetten (b) (fig.) spekulieren; **~ on sth.** sich auf etw. (*Akk.*) verlassen

gambler /'gæmblə(r)/ *n.* Glücksspieler, *der*

gambling /'gæmblɪŋ/ *n.* Spiel[en], *das;* Glücksspiel, *das;* (on horses, dogs) Wetten, *das*

game¹ /geɪm/ *n.* (a) Spiel, *das;* (of [table] tennis, chess, cards, cricket) Partie, *die* (b) (fig.: scheme) Vorhaben, *das* (c) *in pl.* (athletic contests) Spiele *Pl.;* (in school) (sports) Sport, *der;* (athletics) Leichtathletik, *die* (d) (Hunting, Cookery) Wild, *das*

game² *adj.* mutig; **be ~ to do sth.** bereit sein, etw. zu tun

'gamekeeper *n.* Wildheger, *der*

gamma rays /'gæmə/ *n. pl.* (Phys.) Gammastrahlen *Pl.*

gammon /'gæmən/ *n.* Räucherschinken, *der*

gamut /'gæmət/ *n.* Skala, *die*

gander /'gændə(r)/ *n.* Gänserich, *der*

gang /gæŋ/ 1 *n.* Bande, *die;* (of workmen, prisoners) Trupp, *der* 2 *v.i.* **~ up against** *or* **on** (coll.) sich verbünden gegen

gangling /'gæŋglɪŋ/ schlaksig (ugs.)

gangster /'gæŋstə(r)/ *n.* Gangster, *der*

'gang warfare *n.* Bandenkrieg, *der*

'gangway *n.* Gangway, *die;* (Brit.: between seats) Gang, *der*

gaol /dʒeɪl/ ▶ JAIL

gap /gæp/ *n.* (a) Lücke, *die* (b) (in time) Pause, *die* (c) (divergence) Kluft, *die*

gape /geɪp/ *v.i.* (a) den Mund aufsperren; ‹Loch, Abgrund, Wunde:› klaffen (b) (stare) Mund und Nase aufsperren (ugs.); **~ at sb./sth.** jmdn./etw. mit offenem Mund anstarren

garage /'gærɪdʒ/ n. Garage, die; (selling petrol) Tankstelle, die; (for repairing cars) [Kfz-]Werkstatt, die

garb /gɑːb/ n. Tracht, die

garbage /'gɑːbɪdʒ/ n. **(a)** Abfall, der; Müll, der **(b)** (coll.: nonsense) Quatsch, der (salopp)

garbage: ~ **can** n. (Amer.) Mülltonne, die; ~ **dis'posal unit,** ~ **disposer** ns. Abfallvernichter, der; Müllwolf, der

garble /'gɑːbl/ v.t. verstümmeln

garden /'gɑːdn/ n. Garten, der

garden: ~ **centre** n. Gartencenter, das; ~ **'city** n. Gartenstadt, die

gardener /'gɑːdnə(r)/ n. Gärtner, der/ Gärtnerin, die

gardening /'gɑːdnɪŋ/ n. Gartenarbeit, die

garden: ~ **'shed** n. Geräteschuppen, der ~ **'waste** n. Gartenabfälle Pl.; Gartenabfall, der

gargle /'gɑːgl/ v.i. gurgeln

gargoyle /'gɑːgɔɪl/ n. (Archit.) Wasserspeier, der

garish /'geərɪʃ/ adj. grell ‹Farbe, Licht›; knallbunt ‹Kleidung›

garland /'gɑːlənd/ n. Girlande, die

garlic /'gɑːlɪk/ n. Knoblauch, der

garment /'gɑːmənt/ n. Kleidungsstück, das; ~s pl. (clothes) Kleidung, die; Kleider Pl.

garnish /'gɑːnɪʃ/ 1 v.t. garnieren 2 n. Garnierung, die

garret /'gærət/ n. Dachkammer, die

garrison /'gærɪsn/ n. Garnison, die

garter /'gɑːtə(r)/ n. Strumpfband, das

gas /gæs/ 1 n. **(a)** pl. ~es /'gæsɪz/ Gas, das **(b)** (Amer. coll.: petrol) Benzin, das 2 v.t., -ss- mit Gas vergiften

gas: ~ **chamber** n. Gaskammer, die; ~ **'cooker** n. (Brit.) Gasherd, der; ~ **cylinder** n. Gasflasche, die; ~ **'fire** n. Gasofen, der

gash /gæʃ/ 1 n. Schnittwunde, die 2 v.t. aufritzen ‹Haut›; ~ one's finger sich (Dat. od. Akk.) in den Finger schneiden

gas: ~ **heater** n. Gasofen, der; ~ **mask** n. Gasmaske, die; ~ **meter** n. Gaszähler, der

gasoline (**gasolene**) /'gæsəliːn/ n. (Amer.) Benzin, das

gasometer /gæ'sɒmɪtə(r)/ n. Gasometer, der

gasp /gɑːsp/ 1 v.i. nach Luft schnappen (with vor); he was ~ing for air er rang nach Luft 2 v.t. ~ out hervorstoßen 3 n. Keuchen, das

'gas station n. (Amer.) Tankstelle, die

gastric: ~ **'flu** (coll.), ~ **influ'enza** ns. Darmgrippe, die; ~ **'ulcer** n. Magengeschwür, das

gastro-enteritis /gæstrəʊentə'raɪtɪs/ n. Gastroenteritis, die (fachspr.); Magen-Darm-Katarrh, der

gastronomy /gæ'strɒnəmɪ/ n. Gastronomie, die

'gasworks n. sing. Gaswerk, das

gate /geɪt/ n. Tor, das; (barrier) Sperre, die; (to field etc.) Gatter, das; (of level crossing) [Bahn]schranke, die; (in airport) Flugsteig, der

gateau /'gætəʊ/ n., pl. ~s or ~x /'gætəʊz/ Torte, die

gate: ~**crasher** /'geɪtkræʃə(r)/ n. ungeladener Gast; ~**way** n. Tor, das

gather /'gæðə(r)/ 1 v.t. **(a)** sammeln; zusammentragen ‹Informationen›; pflücken ‹Obst, Blumen› **(b)** (infer, deduce) schließen (from aus) **(c)** ~ speed/force schneller/stärker werden 2 v.i. sich versammeln; ‹Wolken:› sich zusammenziehen

'gathering n. Versammlung, die

GATT /gæt/ abbr. = **General Agreement on Tariffs and Trade** GATT, das

gauche /gəʊʃ/ adj. linkisch

gaudy /'gɔːdɪ/ adj. protzig; grell ‹Farben›

gauge /geɪdʒ/ n. 1 **(a)** (measure) Maß, das **(b)** (instrument) Messgerät, das 2 v.t. messen; (fig.) beurteilen

gaunt /gɔːnt/ adj. hager

gauntlet /'gɔːntlɪt/ n. Stulpenhandschuh, der

gauze /gɔːz/ n. Gaze, die

gave ▸ GIVE 1, 2

gay /geɪ/ 1 adj. **(a)** fröhlich; (brightly coloured) farbenfroh **(b)** (coll.: homosexual) schwul (ugs.); Schwulen‹lokal› 2 n. (coll.) Schwule, der (ugs.)

gay 'rights n. pl. Schwulenrechte Pl.

gaze /geɪz/ v.i. blicken; (fixedly) starren; ~ at sb./sth. jmdn./etw. anstarren

GB abbr. = **Great Britain** GB

GCSE abbr. (Brit.) = **General Certificate of Secondary Education**

gear /gɪə(r)/ 1 n. **(a)** (Motor Veh.) Gang, der; top/bottom ~ (Brit.) der höchste/erste Gang; change or shift ~: schalten; put the car into ~: einen Gang einlegen; out of ~: im Leerlauf **(b)** (coll.: clothes) Aufmachung, die **(c)** (equipment) Gerät, das; Ausrüstung, die 2 v.t. ausrichten (to auf + Akk.)

gear: ~**box** n. Getriebekasten, der; ~ **lever,** (Amer.) ~ **shift** ns. Schalthebel, der

geese pl. of GOOSE

geezer /'giːzə(r)/ n. (coll.: old man) Opa, der (ugs.)

gel /dʒel/ n. Gel, das

gelatin ⋯▷ **germinate** ⋯⋯

gelatin /'dʒelətɪn/, (Brit.) **gelatine** /'dʒeləti:n/ n. Gelatine, *die*

gelignite /'dʒelɪgnaɪt/ n. Gelatinedynamit, *das*

gem /dʒem/ n. Edelstein, *der*

Gemini /'dʒemɪnaɪ, 'dʒemɪnɪ/ n. (Astrol., Astron.) Zwillinge *Pl.*

'gemstone n. Edelstein, *der*

gender /'dʒendə(r)/ n. (Ling.) [grammatisches] Geschlecht

gene /dʒi:n/ n. (Biol.) Gen, *das*

general /'dʒenrl/ [1] adj. allgemein; weit verbreitet ⟨*Ansicht*⟩; (true of [nearly] all cases) allgemein gültig; ungefähr ⟨*Vorstellung, Beschreibung usw.*⟩; **the ~ public** weite Kreise der Bevölkerung; **in ~ use** allgemein verbreitet; **as a ~ rule, in ~:** im Allgemeinen

[2] n. (Mil.) General, *der*

general: ~ e'lection ▶ ELECTION; **~ 'hospital** n. Allgemeinkrankenhaus, *das*

generalization /dʒenrəlaɪ'zeɪʃn/ n. Verallgemeinerung, *die*

generalize /'dʒenrəlaɪz/ [1] v.t. verallgemeinern

[2] v.i. **~ about sth.** etw. verallgemeinern

general 'knowledge n. Allgemeinwissen, *das*

generally /'dʒenrəlɪ/ adv. (a) allgemein; **~ available** überall erhältlich; **~ speaking** im Allgemeinen

(b) (usually) im Allgemeinen

general: ~ 'manager n. [leitender] Direktor/[leitende] Direktorin; **~ 'meeting** n. Generalversammlung, *die;* Hauptversammlung, *die;* **~ National Vo'cational Qualification** n. (Brit.) staatliches Berufsausbildungsprogramm; **~ prac'titioner** n. (Med.) Arzt/Ärztin für Allgemeinmedizin

generate /'dʒenəreɪt/ v.t. erzeugen (**from** aus); (result in) führen zu

generation /dʒenə'reɪʃn/ n. **(a)** Generation, *die*

(b) (production) Erzeugung, *die*

generator /'dʒenəreɪtə(r)/ n. Generator, *der*

generosity /dʒenə'rɒsɪtɪ/ n. Großzügigkeit, *die*

generous /'dʒenərəs/ adj. großzügig; reichlich ⟨*Vorrat, Portion*⟩

'generously adv. großzügig

genetic /dʒɪ'netɪk/ adj. genetisch

genetically /dʒɪ'netɪkəlɪ/ adv. genetisch; **~ modified** gentechnisch verändert; **~ engineered** gentechnisch verändert ⟨*Organismen, Pflanzen, Tiere, Nahrungsmittel*⟩; genetisch hergestellt ⟨*Medikament, Enzym*⟩

genetic engi'neering n. Gentechnologie, *die*

genetics /dʒɪ'netɪks/ n. Genetik, *die*

Geneva /dʒɪ'ni:və/ [1] pr. n. Genf (*das*)

[2] attrib. adj. Genfer

genial /'dʒi:nɪəl/ adj. freundlich

genitals /'dʒenɪtlz/ n. pl. Geschlechtsorgane *Pl.*

genitive /'dʒenɪtɪv/ adj. & n. **~ [case]** Genitiv, *der*

genius /'dʒi:nɪəs/ n. **(a)** (person) Genie, *das* **(b)** (ability) Talent, *das*

genome /'dʒi:nəʊm/ n. (Biol.) Genom, *das*

genre /'ʒɑ̃rə/ n. Genre, *das*

gent /dʒent/ n. **(a)** (coll./joc.) Gent, *der* (iron.) **(b) the G~s** (Brit. coll.) die Herrentoilette

genteel /dʒen'ti:l/ adj. vornehm

gentle /'dʒentl/ adj., **~r** /'dʒentlə(r)/, **~st** /'dʒentlɪst/ sanft; liebenswürdig ⟨*Person, Verhalten*⟩; leicht, schwach ⟨*Brise*⟩; leise ⟨*Geräusch*⟩; gemächlich ⟨*Spaziergang, Tempo*⟩; mäßig ⟨*Hitze*⟩

gentleman /'dʒentlmən/ n., pl. **gentlemen** /'dʒentlmən/ Herr, *der;* (well-mannered) Gentleman, *der;* **Ladies and Gentlemen!** meine Damen und Herren!; **'Gentlemen'** (sign) „Herren"

'gentleness n. Sanftheit, *die;* (of nature) Sanftmütigkeit, *die*

gently /'dʒentlɪ/ adv. (tenderly) zart; zärtlich; (mildly) sanft; (carefully) behutsam; (quietly, softly) leise

genuine /'dʒenjʊɪn/ adj. **(a)** (real) echt **(b)** (true) aufrichtig; wahr ⟨*Grund, Not*⟩

'genuinely adv. wirklich

genus /'dʒi:nəs, 'dʒenəs/ n., pl. **genera** /'dʒenərə/ (Biol.) Gattung, *die*

geographical /dʒi:ə'græfɪkl/ adj. geographisch

geography /dʒɪ'ɒgrəfɪ/ n. Geographie, *die;* Erdkunde, *die* (Schulw.)

geological /dʒi:ə'lɒdʒɪkl/ adj. geologisch

geologist /dʒɪ'ɒlədʒɪst/ n. Geologe, *der/* Geologin, *die*

geology /dʒɪ'ɒlədʒɪ/ n. Geologie, *die*

geometric /dʒi:ə'metrɪk/, **geometrical** /dʒi:ə'metrɪkl/ adj. geometrisch

geometry /dʒɪ'ɒmɪtrɪ/ n. Geometrie, *die*

geranium /dʒə'reɪnɪəm/ n. Geranie, *die;* Pelargonie, *die*

geriatric /dʒerɪ'ætrɪk/ adj. geriatrisch

germ /dʒɜ:m/ n. Keim, *der*

German /'dʒɜ:mən/ [1] adj. deutsch; **he/she is ~:** er ist Deutscher/sie ist Deutsche [2] n. **(a)** (person) Deutsche, *der/die* **(b)** (language) Deutsch, *das; see also* ENGLISH 2A

German Democratic Re'public pr. n. (Hist.) Deutsche Demokratische Republik

Germanic /dʒɜ:'mænɪk/ adj. germanisch

German 'measles n. Röteln *Pl.*

Germany /'dʒɜ:mənɪ/ pr. n. Deutschland (*das*); **Federal Republic of ~:** Bundesrepublik Deutschland, *die*

germinate /'dʒɜ:mɪneɪt/ v.i. keimen

germ 'warfare n. Bakterienkrieg, *der*

gesticulate /dʒe'stɪkjʊleɪt/ *v.i.* gestikulieren

gesticulation /dʒestɪkjʊ'leɪʃn/ n. Gesten *Pl.*

gesture /'dʒestʃə(r)/ n. Geste, *die*

get /get/ ① *v.t.*, **-tt-**, got /gɒt/, got *or* (Amer.) gotten /'gɒtn/ **(a)** (obtain, receive) bekommen; kriegen (ugs.); sich ⟨*Dat.*⟩ besorgen ⟨*Visum, Genehmigung*⟩; sich ⟨*Dat.*⟩ beschaffen ⟨*Geld*⟩; (find) finden ⟨*Zeit*⟩; (fetch) holen; (buy) kaufen; **where did you ~ that?** wo hast du das her?; **~ sb. a job/taxi, ~ a job/taxi for sb.** jmdn. einen Job verschaffen/ein Taxi besorgen; **~ oneself sth.** sich ⟨*Dat.*⟩ etw. zulegen **(b) ~ the bus** *etc.* (be in time for, catch) den Bus *usw.* erreichen *od.* (ugs.) kriegen; (travel by) den Bus *usw.* nehmen **(c)** (prepare) machen (ugs.), zubereiten ⟨*Essen*⟩ **(d)** (win) bekommen; finden ⟨*Anerkennung*⟩; erzielen ⟨*Tor, Punkt, Treffer*⟩; gewinnen ⟨*Spiel, Preis, Belohnung*⟩; **~ permission** die Erlaubnis erhalten **(e)** finden ⟨*Schlaf, Ruhe*⟩; bekommen ⟨*Einfall, Vorstellung, Gefühl, Kopfschmerzen, Grippe*⟩; gewinnen ⟨*Eindruck*⟩ **(f) have got** (coll.: have) haben; **have got a cold** eine Erkältung haben; **have got to do sth.** etw. tun müssen **(g)** (succeed in placing, bringing, etc.) bringen; kriegen (ugs.); **~ a message to sb.** jmdm. eine Nachricht zukommen lassen; **~ things going** *or* **started** die Dinge in Gang bringen **(h) ~ everything packed/prepared** alles [ein]packen/vorbereiten; **~ sth. ready/done** etw. fertig machen; **~ one's feet wet** nasse Füße kriegen; **~ one's hands dirty** sich ⟨*Dat.*⟩ die Hände schmutzig machen; **~ one's hair cut** sich (Dat.) die Haare schneiden lassen; **~ sb. to do sth.** (induce) jmdn. dazu bringen, etw. zu tun **(i) ~ sb. [on the telephone]** jmdn. [telefonisch] erreichen **(j)** (coll.) (understand) kapieren (ugs.); (hear) mitkriegen (ugs.) ② *v.i.*, **-tt-**, got, got *or* (Amer.) gotten **(a)** (succeed in coming or going) kommen; **~ to London before dark** London vor Einbruch der Dunkelheit erreichen **(b)** (come to be) **~ working** sich an die Arbeit machen; **~ going** *or* **started** (leave) losgehen; (become lively or operative) in Schwung kommen; **~ going on** *or* **with sth.** mit etw. anfangen **(c) ~ to know sb.** jmdn. kennen lernen **(d)** (become) werden; **~ ready/washed** sich fertig machen/waschen; **~ frightened/hungry** Angst/Hunger kriegen

▪ **get a'bout** *v.i.* **(a)** (travel) herumkommen **(b)** ⟨*Gerücht:*⟩ sich verbreiten

▪ **'get at** *v.t.* **(a)** herankommen an (+ *Akk.*) **(b)** (find out) [he]rausfinden ⟨*Wahrheit usw.*⟩; **what are you ~ting at?** worauf wollen Sie hinaus? **(c)** (coll.: attack, taunt) anmachen (salopp)

▪ **get a'way** *v.i.* **(a)** (leave) wegkommen **(b)** (escape) entkommen

▪ **get 'back** ① *v.i.* zurückkommen; **~ back home** nach Hause kommen ② *v.t.* (recover) zurückbekommen; **~ one's own back** (coll.) sich rächen

▪ **get 'by** *v.i.* **(a)** vorbeikommen **(b)** (coll.: manage) über die Runden kommen (ugs.)

▪ **get 'down** ① *v.i.* hinunter-/heruntersteigen; **~ down to sth.** (start) sich an etw. ⟨*Akk.*⟩ machen ② *v.t.* **(a) ~ sb./sth. down** jmdn./etw. hinunter-/herunterbringen **(b)** (coll.: depress) fertig machen (ugs.)

▪ **get 'in** ① *v.i.* (into bus etc.) einsteigen; (arrive) ankommen ② *v.t.* (fetch) reinholen

▪ **get 'off** ① *v.i.* **(a)** (alight) aussteigen; (dismount) absteigen **(b)** (leave) [weg]gehen **(c)** (escape punishment) davonkommen ② *v.t.* **(a)** (remove) ausziehen ⟨*Kleidung usw.*⟩; entfernen ⟨*Fleck usw.*⟩; abbekommen ⟨*Deckel usw.*⟩ **(b)** (alight from) aussteigen aus; absteigen von ⟨*Fahrrad*⟩ **(c) ~ off the subject** vom Thema abkommen

▪ **get 'on** *v.i.* **(a)** (mount) aufsteigen; (enter vehicle) einsteigen **(b)** (make progress) vorankommen; **he's ~ting on well** es geht ihm gut **(c)** (manage) zurechtkommen

▪ **get 'on with** *v.t.* **(a)** weitermachen mit **(b) ~ on [well] with sb.** mit jmdm. [gut] auskommen

▪ **get 'out** ① *v.i.* **(a)** rausgehen/rausfahren (of aus) **(b)** (alight) aussteigen **(c)** (escape) ausbrechen (of aus); (fig.) herauskommen; **~ out of** (avoid) herumkommen um (ugs.) ② *v.t.* **(a)** (cause to leave) rausbringen **(b)** (withdraw) abheben ⟨*Geld*⟩ (of von)

▪ **get 'over** *v.t.* **(a)** (cross) gehen über (+ *Akk.*); (climb) klettern über (+ *Akk.*) **(b)** (recover from) überwinden; hinwegkommen über (+ *Akk.*)

▪ **get 'round** *v.i.* **~ round to doing sth.** dazu kommen, etw. zu tun

▪ **get 'through** *v.i.* durchkommen

▪ **get 'up** *v.i.* aufstehen

▪ **get 'up to** *v.t.* **~ up to mischief** etwas anstellen

get: ~away n. Flucht, *die; attrib.* Flucht⟨*plan, -wagen*⟩; **make one's ~away** entkommen; **~-together** n. (coll.) gemütliches Beisammensein; **~-up** n. (coll.) Aufmachung, *die*

geyser /'giːzə(r)/ n. **(a)** (spring) Geysir, *der* **(b)** (Brit.) Durchlauferhitzer, *der*

ghastly /'ɡɑːstlɪ/ *adj.* grauenvoll; entsetzlich ⟨*Verletzungen*⟩; schrecklich ⟨*Fehler*⟩

gherkin /'ɡɜːkɪn/ n. Essiggurke, *die*

ghetto /'getəʊ/ n., pl. ~s Getto, das
ghetto blaster /'getəʊblɑːstə(r)/ n. (coll.) [großer, tragbarer] Radiorekorder
ghost /gəʊst/ n. Geist, der; Gespenst, das
'ghostly adj. gespenstisch
ghost: ~ story n. Gespenstergeschichte, die; **~ writer** n. Ghostwriter, der
giant /'dʒaɪənt/ ① n. Riese, der ② attrib. adj. riesig
gibberish /'dʒɪbərɪʃ/ n. Kauderwelsch, das
gibe /dʒaɪb/ n. Stichelei, die
giblets /'dʒɪblɪts/ n. pl. [Geflügel]klein, das
giddiness /'gɪdɪnɪs/ n. Schwindel, der
giddy /'gɪdɪ/ adj. schwind[e]lig
gift /gɪft/ n. (a) Geschenk, das; **make sb. a ~ of sth., make a ~ of sth. to sb.** jmdm. etw. schenken; **a ~ box/pack** eine Geschenkpackung
(b) (talent) Begabung, die; **have a ~ for languages/ mathematics** sprachbegabt/ mathematisch begabt sein
'gifted adj. begabt (**in, at** für)
gift: ~ shop n. Geschenkboutique, die; Geschenkladen, der; **~ token, ~ voucher** ns. Geschenkgutschein, der; **~-wrap** v.t. als Geschenk einpacken; in Geschenkpapier einpacken
gigantic /dʒaɪ'gæntɪk/ adj. gigantisch; riesig; enorm ⟨Verbesserung, Appetit⟩
giggle /'gɪgl/ ① n. Kichern, das ② v.i. kichern
gild /gɪld/ v.t. vergolden
gill /gɪl/ n. Kieme, die
gilt /gɪlt/ ① n. Goldauflage, die; (paint) Goldfarbe, die ② adj. vergoldet
gimmick /'gɪmɪk/ n. (coll.) Gag, der
gin /dʒɪn/ n. Gin, der
ginger /'dʒɪndʒə(r)/ n. (a) Ingwer, der (b) (colour) Rötlichgelb, das
ginger: ~ 'beer n. Ingwerbier, das; **~bread** n. Pfefferkuchen, der
gingerly /'dʒɪndʒəlɪ/ adv. vorsichtig
gipsy ▶ GYPSY
giraffe /dʒɪ'rɑːf/ n. Giraffe, die
girder /'gɜːdə(r)/ n. Träger, der
girl /gɜːl/ n. Mädchen, das; (teenager) junges Mädchen
girl: ~ band n. Girlgroup, die; **~friend** n. Freundin, die
'girlish adj. mädchenhaft
'girl power n. (coll.) Girlpower, die
giro /'dʒaɪərəʊ/ n. (a) Giro, das; attrib. Giro-; **bank ~:** Giroverkehr, der (b) (cheque) Scheck, der
girth /gɜːθ/ n. (a) Umfang, der (b) (for horse) Bauchgurt, der
gismo /'gɪzməʊ/ n. (coll.) Ding, das (ugs.)
gist /dʒɪst/ n. Wesentliche, das; (of tale, question, etc.) Kern, der

give /gɪv/ ① v.t., gave /geɪv/, given /'gɪvn/ (a) geben (**to** Dat.)
(b) (as gift) schenken; **~ sb. sth., ~ sth. to sb.** jmdm. etw. schenken; **~ and take** (fig.) Kompromisse eingehen
(c) (assign) aufgeben ⟨Hausaufgaben usw.⟩; (grant, award, offer, allow to have) geben; verleihen ⟨Preis, Titel usw.⟩; lassen ⟨Wahl, Zeit⟩; verleihen ⟨Gewicht, Nachdruck⟩; bereiten, machen ⟨Freude, Mühe, Kummer⟩; bieten ⟨Schutz⟩; leisten ⟨Hilfe⟩; gewähren ⟨Unterstützung⟩; **be ~n sth.** etw. bekommen; **~n that** (because) da; (if) wenn; **~ sb. hope** jmdm. Hoffnung machen
(d) (tell) angeben ⟨Namen, Anschrift, Alter, Grund⟩; nennen ⟨Einzelheiten⟩; geben ⟨Rat, Befehl, Anweisung, Antwort⟩; fällen ⟨Urteil, Entscheidung⟩; sagen ⟨Meinung⟩; bekannt geben ⟨Nachricht⟩; **~ him my best wishes** richte ihm meine besten Wünsche aus
(e) ⟨perform, sing, etc.⟩ geben ⟨Vorstellung, Konzert⟩; halten ⟨Vortrag, Seminar⟩
(f) ⟨produce⟩ geben ⟨Licht, Milch⟩; ergeben ⟨Zahlen, Resultat⟩
(g) (make, show) geben ⟨Zeichen, Stoß, Tritt⟩; machen ⟨Satz, Ruck⟩; ausstoßen ⟨Schrei, Seufzer, Pfiff⟩; **~ sb. a [friendly] look** jmdm. einen [freundlichen] Blick zuwerfen
(h) (inflict) versetzen ⟨Schlag, Stoß⟩; **sth. ~s me a headache** von etw. bekomme ich Kopfschmerzen
(i) geben ⟨Party, Essen usw.⟩
② v.i., gave, given (yield) nachgeben; ⟨Knie:⟩ weich werden; ⟨Bett:⟩ federn
③ n. Nachgiebigkeit, die; (elasticity) Elastizität, die
■ **give a'way** v.t. (a) verschenken
(b) (in marriage) dem Bräutigam zuführen
(c) (betray) verraten
■ **give 'back** v.t. zurückgeben
■ **give in** ① /'--/ v.t. abgeben ② /-'-/ v.i. nachgeben (**to** Dat.)
■ **give 'off** v.t. ausströmen ⟨Geruch⟩; aussenden ⟨Strahlen⟩
■ **give 'up** ① v.i. aufgeben ② v.t. aufgeben; widmen ⟨Zeit⟩; **~ sth. up** (abandon habit) sich (Dat.) etw. abgewöhnen; **~ oneself up** sich stellen
■ **give 'way** v.i. (a) (yield) nachgeben
(b) (in traffic) **~ way [to traffic from the right]** [dem Rechtsverkehr] die Vorfahrt lassen; **'G~ Way'** „Vorfahrt beachten"
(c) (collapse) einstürzen

given ▶ GIVE 1, 2
'given name n. (Amer.) Vorname, der
give-'way sign n. (Brit.) Vorfahrtsschild, das
gizmo ▶ GISMO
glacier /'glæsɪə(r)/ n. Gletscher, der
glad /glæd/ adj. froh; **be ~ of sth.** über etw. (Akk.) froh sein; für etw. dankbar sein
gladden /'glædn/ v.t. erfreuen
glade /gleɪd/ n. Lichtung, die
'gladly adv. gern

glamor (Amer.) ▶ GLAMOUR

glamorous /'glæmərəs/ *adj.* glanzvoll; glamourös ⟨*Filmstar*⟩

glamour /'glæmə(r)/ *n.* Glanz, *der;* (of person) Ausstrahlung, *die*

glance /glɑ:ns/ ① *n.* Blick, *der*
② *v.i.* blicken; ~ **at sb./sth.** jmdn./etw. anblicken; ~ **at one's watch** auf seine Uhr blicken; ~ **at the newspaper** *etc.* einen Blick in die Zeitung *usw.* werfen; ~ **round [the room]** sich [im Zimmer] umsehen

gland /glænd/ *n.* Drüse, *die*

glandular /'glændjʊlə(r)/ *adj.* Drüsen-

glare /gleə(r)/ ① *n.* **(a)** grelles Licht
(b) (hostile look) feindseliger Blick; **with a** ~: feindselig
② *v.i.* (glower) [finster] starren; ~ **at sb./sth.** jmdn./etw. anstarren

glaring /'gleərɪŋ/ *adj.* grell; (fig.: conspicuous) schreiend; grob ⟨*Fehler*⟩; krass ⟨*Gegensatz*⟩

glass /glɑ:s/ *n.* **(a)** (substance) Glas, *das;* pieces of/broken ~: Glasscherben *Pl.;* (smaller) Glassplitter *Pl.*
(b) (drinking ~) Glas, *das;* **a** ~ **of milk** ein Glas Milch
(c) (pane) [Glas]scheibe, *die*
(d) *in pl.* (spectacles) [a pair of] ~es eine Brille

glass 'ceiling *n.* (fig.) unsichtbare Barriere

'glassy *adj.* gläsern

glaze /gleɪz/ ① *n.* Glasur, *die*
② *v.t.* **(a)** glasieren
(b) (fit with glass) verglasen

glazed /gleɪzd/ *adj.* glasig ⟨*Blick*⟩

glazier /'gleɪzɪə(r)/ *n.* Glaser, *der*

gleam /gli:m/ ① *n.* Schein, *der;* (fainter) Schimmer, *der;* ~ **of hope** Hoffnungsschimmer, *der*
② *v.i.* ⟨*Licht:*⟩ scheinen; ⟨*Fußboden, Stiefel:*⟩ glänzen; ⟨*Zähne:*⟩ blitzen; ⟨*Augen:*⟩ leuchten

'gleaming *adj.* glänzend

glean /gli:n/ *v.t.* zusammentragen ⟨*Informationen usw.*⟩; ~ **sth. from sth.** einer Sache (*Dat.*) etw. entnehmen

glee /gli:/ *n.* Freude, *die;* (gloating joy) Schadenfreude, *die*

gleeful /'gli:fl/ *adj.* freudig; (gloating) schadenfroh

glen /glen/ *n.* [schmales] Tal

glib /glɪb/ *adj.* aalglatt ⟨*Person*⟩; leicht dahingesagt ⟨*Antwort*⟩

glide /glaɪd/ *v.i.* gleiten; (through the air) schweben

'glider *n.* Segelflugzeug, *das*

glimmer /'glɪmə(r)/ ① *n.* Schimmer, *der* (**of** von); (of fire) Glimmen, *das*
② *v.i.* glimmen

glimpse /glɪmps/ ① *n.* [kurzer] Blick; **catch** *or* **have** *or* **get a** ~ **of sb./sth.** jmdn./ etw. [kurz] zu sehen bekommen
② *v.t.* flüchtig sehen

glint /glɪnt/ ① *n.* Schimmer, *der*
② *v.i.* blinken; glitzern

glisten /'glɪsn/ *v.i.* glitzern

glitter /'glɪtə(r)/ ① *v.i.* glitzern; ⟨*Juwelen, Sterne:*⟩ funkeln
② *n.* Glitzern, *das;* (of diamonds) Funkeln, *das*

glitz /glɪts/ *n.* Glanz, *der*

glitzy /'glɪtsɪ/ *adj.* glanzvoll

gloat /gləʊt/ *v.i.* ~ **over sth.** sich hämisch über etw. (*Akk.*) freuen

global /'gləʊbl/ *adj.* weltweit;
G~ Positioning System GPS[-Navigationssystem] *das;* ~ **warming** globaler Temperaturanstieg; **the** ~ **village** das Weltdorf

globalization /gləʊbəlaɪ'zeɪʃn/ *n.* Globalisierung, *die*

globalize /'gləʊbəlaɪz/ *v.t.* globalisieren

globe /gləʊb/ *n.* **(a)** (*sphere*) Kugel, *die*
(b) (with map) Globus, *der*
(c) (world) **the** ~: der Globus; der Erdball

'globetrotter *n.* Globetrotter, *der;* Weltenbummler, *der*

gloom /glu:m/ *n.* **(a)** (darkness) Dunkel, *das* (geh.)
(b) (despondency) düstere Stimmung

'gloomy *adj.* **(a)** (*dark*) düster; finster
(b) (depressing) düster; (depressed) trübsinnig

glorify /'glɔ:rɪfaɪ/ *v.t.* verherrlichen; **a glorified messenger boy** ein besserer Botenjunge

glorious /'glɔ:rɪəs/ *adj.* **(a)** (illustrious) ruhmreich ⟨*Held, Sieg*⟩
(b) (delightful) wunderschön; herrlich

glory /'glɔ:rɪ/ ① *n.* **(a)** (splendour) Schönheit, *die;* (majesty) Herrlichkeit, *die*
(b) (fame) Ruhm, *der*
② *v.i.* ~ **in sth.** (be proud of) sich einer Sache (*Gen.*) rühmen

gloss /glɒs/ *n.* Glanz, *der;* ~ **paint** Lackfarbe, *die*

■ **'gloss over** *v.t.* bemänteln; beschönigen ⟨*Fehler*⟩

glossary /'glɒsərɪ/ *n.* Glossar, *das*

'glossy ① *adj.* glänzend; (fig.) glanzvoll
② *n.* (coll.) (magazine) auf [Hoch]glanzpapier gedruckte Zeitschrift

glove /glʌv/ *n.* Handschuh, *der*

glove: ~ **box** *n.* **(a)** ▶ ~ COMPARTMENT; **(b)** (for toxic material etc.) Handschuhkasten, *der;* ~ **compartment** *n.* Handschuhfach, *das;* ~ **puppet** *n.* Handpuppe, *die*

glow /gləʊ/ *v.i.* **(a)** glühen; ⟨*Lampe, Leuchtfarbe:*⟩ schimmern, leuchten
(b) (fig.) (with warmth or pride) ⟨*Gesicht, Wangen:*⟩ glühen (**with** vor + *Dat.*); (with health or vigour) strotzen (**with** vor + *Dat.*)

glower /'glaʊə(r)/ *v.i.* finster dreinblicken; ~ **at sb.** jmdn. finster anstarren

'glowing *adj.* glühend; begeistert ⟨*Bericht*⟩

'glow-worm *n.* Glühwürmchen, *das*

glucose /'glu:kəʊz/ *n.* Glucose, *die*

glue /glu:/ ① *n.* Klebstoff, *der*

2 *v.t.* kleben; ~ **sth. to sth.** etw. an etw. (*Dat.*) an- *od.* festkleben

'**glue-sniffing** *n.* Schnüffeln, *das* (ugs.); Sniefen, *das* (ugs.)

glum /glʌm/ *adj.* verdrießlich

glut /glʌt/ *n.* Überangebot, *das* (**of** an, von + *Dat.*)

glutton /'glʌtən/ *n.* Vielfraß, *der* (ugs.); **a ~ for punishment** (iron.) ein Masochist (fig.)

gluttony /'glʌtənɪ/ *n.* Gefräßigkeit, *die*

glycerine /'glɪsəriːn/ (*Amer.*: **glycerin** /'glɪsərɪn/) *n.* Glyzerin, *das*

GM *abbr.* = **genetically modified**; GM **crops/food** gentechnisch veränderte Feldfrüchte *Pl.*/Nahrungsmittel *Pl.*

gm. *abbr.* = **gram[s]** g

GMO *abbr.* = **genetically modified organism** GVO

GMT *abbr.* = **Greenwich Mean Time** GMT; WEZ

gnarled /nɑːld/ *adj.* knorrig; knotig ⟨*Hand*⟩

gnash /næʃ/ *v.t.* ~ **one's teeth** mit den Zähnen knirschen

gnat /næt/ *n.* [Stech]mücke, *die*

gnaw /nɔː/ 1 *v.i.* ~ **[away] at sth.** an etw. (*Dat.*) nagen
2 *v.t.* nagen an (+ *Dat.*); abnagen ⟨*Knochen*⟩

gnome /nəʊm/ *n.* Gnom, *der*

GNVQ *abbr.* = **General National Vocational Qualification**

go /gəʊ/ 1 *v.i., pres.* he goes /gəʊz/, *p.t.* went /went/, *pres. p.* going /'gəʊɪŋ/, *p.p.* gone /gɒn/ (a) gehen; ⟨*Fahrzeug:*⟩ fahren; ⟨*Flugzeug:*⟩ fliegen; ⟨*Vierfüßer:*⟩ laufen; (on horseback etc.) reiten; (in lift) fahren; (on outward journey) weg-, abfahren; (travel regularly) ⟨*Verkehrsmittel:*⟩ verkehren (**from ... to** zwischen + *Dat.* ... und); **go by bicycle/car/ bus/train** *or* **rail/boat** *or* **sea** *or* **ship** mit dem [Fahr]rad/Auto/Bus/Zug/Schiff fahren; **go by plane** *or* **air** fliegen; **go on foot** zu Fuß gehen; laufen (ugs.); **go on a journey** verreisen; **have far to go** es weit haben; **go to the toilet/cinema/a museum** auf die Toilette/ins Kino/ins Museum gehen; **go to the doctor['s]** *etc.* zum Arzt *usw.* gehen; **go bathing** baden gehen; **go cycling** Rad fahren; **go to see sb.** jmdn. aufsuchen; **go and see whether ...**: nachsehen [gehen], ob ...; **I'll go!** ich geh schon!; (answer phone) ich geh ran *od.* nehme ab; (answer door) ich mache auf
(b) (start) losgehen; (in vehicle) losfahren
(c) (pass, circulate) gehen; **a shiver went up** *or* **down my spine** ein Schauer lief mir über den Rücken; **go to** (be given to) ⟨*Preis, Gelder, Job:*⟩ gehen an (+ *Akk.*); ⟨*Titel, Besitz:*⟩ übergehen auf (+ *Akk.*); **go towards** (be of benefit to) zugute kommen (+ *Dat.*)
(d) (act, function effectively) gehen; ⟨*Mechanismus, Maschine:*⟩ laufen; **keep going** (in movement) weitergehen/-fahren; (in activity) weitermachen; (not fail) sich aufrecht

halten; **keep sth. going** etw. in Gang halten; **make sth. go, get/set sth. going** etw. in Gang bringen
(e) **go to work** zur Arbeit gehen; **go to school** in die Schule gehen; **go to a comprehensive school** auf eine Gesamtschule gehen
(f) (depart) gehen; ⟨*Bus, Zug:*⟩ [ab]fahren; ⟨*Post:*⟩ rausgehen (ugs.)
(g) (cease to function) kaputtgehen; ⟨*Sicherung:*⟩ durchbrennen; (break) brechen; ⟨*Seil usw.:*⟩ reißen
(h) (disappear) weggehen; ⟨*Mantel, Hut, Fleck:*⟩ verschwinden; ⟨*Geruch, Rauch:*⟩ sich verziehen; ⟨*Geld, Zeit:*⟩ draufgehen (ugs.) (**in**, on für)
(i) **to go** (still remaining) have sth. [still] **to go** [noch] etw. übrig haben; **one week** *etc.* **to go to ...:** noch eine Woche *usw.* bis ...; **there's hours to go** es dauert noch Stunden
(j) (be sold) weggehen; verkauft werden; **going! going! gone!** zum Ersten! zum Zweiten! zum Dritten!; **go to sb.** an jmdn. gehen
(k) (run) ⟨*Grenze, Straße usw.:*⟩ verlaufen, gehen; (lead) gehen; führen; (extend) reichen; **as** *or* **so far as he/it goes** so weit
(l) (turn out, progress) ⟨*Projekt, Interview, Abend:*⟩ verlaufen; **how did your holiday go?** wie war Ihr Urlaub?; **things have been going well/badly** in der letzten Zeit läuft alles gut/schief
(m) (be, have form or nature) sein; ⟨*Sprichwort, Gedicht, Titel:*⟩ lauten; **that's the way it goes** so ist es nun mal; **go hungry** hungern; **go without food/water** es ohne Essen/Wasser aushalten
(n) (become) werden; **the tyre has gone flat** der Reifen ist platt
(o) (have usual place) kommen; (belong) gehören; **where does the box go?** wo kommt *od.* gehört die Kiste hin?
(p) (fit) passen; **go in[to] sth.** in etw. (*Akk.*) gehen *od.* [hinein]passen; **go through sth.** durch etw. [hindurch]gehen
(q) (match) passen (**with** zu)
(r) ⟨*Turmuhr, Gong:*⟩ schlagen; ⟨*Glocke:*⟩ läuten
(s) (coll.: be acceptable or permitted) erlaubt sein; **it/that goes without saying** es/das ist doch selbstverständlich. See also GOING 2
2 *n., pl.* **goes** /gəʊz/ (coll.) (a) (attempt, try) Versuch, *der;* (chance) Gelegenheit, *die;* **have a go** es versuchen; **let me have a go/can I have a go?** lass mich [auch ein]mal/kann ich [auch ein]mal? (ugs.); **it's 'my go** ich bin an der Reihe *od.* dran; **at one go** auf einmal; **at the first go** auf Anhieb
(b) (vigorous activity) **it's all go** es ist alles eine einzige Hetzerei (ugs.); **be on the go** auf Trab sein (ugs.)
(c) (success) **make a go of sth.** mit etw. Erfolg haben

■ **go a'head** *v.i.* (a) (in advance) vorausgehen (**of** *Dat.*)

(b) (proceed) weitermachen; (make progress) ⟨*Arbeit:*⟩ fortschreiten, vorangehen
■ **go a'long with** *v.t.* **go along with sth.** (agree to) sich einer Sache (*Dat.*) anschließen
■ **go a'way** *v.i.* weggehen; (on holiday or business) verreisen
■ **go 'back** *v.i.* zurückgehen/-fahren; (restart) ⟨*Schule, Fabrik:*⟩ wieder anfangen; (fig.) zurückgehen; **go back to the beginning** noch mal von vorne anfangen
■ **go by** ⟨1⟩ /'--/ *v.t.* **go by sth.** sich nach etw. richten; (adhere to) sich an etw. (*Akk.*) halten ⟨2⟩ /-'-/ *v.i.* ⟨*Zeit:*⟩ vergehen
■ **go 'down** *v.i.* hinuntergehen/-fahren; ⟨*Sonne:*⟩ untergehen; ⟨*Schiff:*⟩ untergehen; (fall to ground) ⟨*Flugzeug usw.:*⟩ abstürzen
■ **'go for** *v.t.* **go for sb./sth.** (go to fetch) jmdn./etw. holen; (apply to) für jmdn./etw. gelten; (like) jmdn./etw. gut finden
■ **go 'in** *v.i.* hineingehen; reingehen (ugs.)
■ **go 'off** ⟨1⟩ *v.i.* (a) **go off with sb./sth.** sich mit jmdm./etw. auf- und davonmachen (ugs.) (b) ⟨*Alarm, Schusswaffe:*⟩ losgehen; ⟨*Wecker:*⟩ klingeln; ⟨*Bombe:*⟩ hochgehen (c) (turn bad) schlecht werden (d) ⟨*Strom:*⟩ ausfallen ⟨2⟩ *v.t.* (begin to dislike) **go off sth.** von etw. abkommen
■ **go 'on** *v.i.* (a) weitergehen/-fahren (b) (continue) weitermachen (c) (happen) passieren
■ **go 'out** *v.i.* ausgehen; **go out to work/for a meal** arbeiten/essen gehen; **go out with sb.** (date sb.) mit jmdm. gehen (ugs.)
■ **go over** ⟨1⟩ /-'-/ *v.i.* hinübergehen ⟨2⟩ /'---, -'-/ *v.t.* (re-examine) durchgehen
■ **go 'round** *v.i.* (a) (call) **go round and** *or* **to see sb.** bei jmdm. vorbeigehen (ugs.) (b) (look round) sich umschauen (c) (suffice) reichen; langen (ugs.) (d) (spin) sich drehen
■ **go through** ⟨1⟩ /-'-/ *v.i.* ⟨*Ernennung:*⟩ durchkommen; ⟨*Antrag:*⟩ durchgehen ⟨2⟩ /'--/ (a) (rehearse) durchgehen (b) (examine) durchsehen (c) (endure) durchmachen
■ **go 'through with** *v.t.* zu Ende führen
■ **go 'under** *v.i.* untergehen; (fig.: fail) eingehen
■ **go 'up** *v.i.* (a) hinaufgehen/-fahren; ⟨*Ballon:*⟩ aufsteigen; (Theatre) ⟨*Vorhang:*⟩ aufgehen; ⟨*Lichter:*⟩ angehen (b) (increase) ⟨*Zahl:*⟩ wachsen; ⟨*Preis, Wert, Niveau:*⟩ steigen; (in price) ⟨*Ware:*⟩ teurer werden
■ **go without** ⟨1⟩ /'---/ *v.t.* verzichten auf (+ *Akk.*) ⟨2⟩ /-'-/ *v.i.* verzichten

goad /gəʊd/ *v.t.* ~ **sb. into sth./doing sth.** jmdn. zu etw. anstacheln/dazu anstacheln, etw. zu tun

'go-ahead ⟨1⟩ *adj.* unternehmungslustig; (progressive) fortschrittlich ⟨2⟩ *n.* **give sb./sth. the** ~: jmdm./einer Sache grünes Licht geben

goal /gəʊl/ *n.* (a) (aim) Ziel, *das* (b) (Footb., Hockey) Tor, *das;* **score/kick a** ~: einen Treffer erzielen

goalie /'gəʊlɪ/ *n.* (coll.) Tormann, *der*

goal: ~**keeper** *n.* Torwart, *der;* ~**post** *n.* Torpfosten, *der;* **move the** ~**posts** (fig. coll.) sich nicht an die Spielregeln halten

goat /gəʊt/ *n.* Ziege, *die*

gobble /'gɒbl/ ⟨1⟩ *v.t.* ~ [**down** *or* **up**] hinunterschlingen ⟨2⟩ *v.i.* schlingen

'go-between *n.* Vermittler, *der*/ Vermittlerin, *die*

goblet /'gɒblɪt/ *n.* Kelchglas, *das*

goblin /'gɒblɪn/ *n.* Kobold, *der*

god /gɒd/ *n.* (a) Gott, *der* (b) **God** (Theol.) Gott

god: ~**child** *n.* Patenkind, *das;* ~**daughter** *n.* Patentochter, *die*

goddess /'gɒdɪs/ *n.* Göttin, *die*

god: ~**father** *n.* Pate, *der;* **G**~**-forsaken** *adj.* gottverlassen; ~**mother** *n.* Patentante, *die;* ~**send** *n.* Gottesgabe, *die;* **be a** ~**send to sb.** für jmdn. ein Geschenk des Himmels sein; ~**son** *n.* Patensohn, *der*

'go-getter *n.* Draufgänger, *der*

'goggle-box *n.* (Brit. coll.) Glotze, *die* (salopp); Glotzkiste, *die* (salopp)

goggles /'gɒglz/ *n. pl.* Schutzbrille, *die*

going /'gəʊɪŋ/ ⟨1⟩ *n.* (progress) Vorankommen, *das;* **while the** ~ **is good** solange es noch geht ⟨2⟩ *adj.* (a) (available) erhältlich; **there is sth.** ~: es gibt etw. (b) **be** ~ **to do sth.** etw. tun [werden/wollen]; **I was** ~ **to say** ich wollte sagen; **it's** ~ **to snow** es wird schneien; **a** ~ **concern** eine gesunde Firma (c) (current) [derzeit/damals/dann] geltend; **the** ~ **rate of exchange** der augenblickliche Wechselkurs (d) **a** ~ **concern** eine gesunde Firma

goings-'on *n. pl.* Ereignisse *Pl.*

gold /gəʊld/ ⟨1⟩ *n.* Gold, *das* ⟨2⟩ *attrib. adj.* golden; Gold⟨münze, -kette *usw.*⟩

'gold-digger *n.* Goldgräber, *der;* **she's a** ~**-digger** (fig. coll.) sie ist nur auf das Geld der Männer aus

golden /'gəʊldn/ *adj.* golden

golden 'wedding *n.* goldene Hochzeit

gold: ~**fish** *n.* Goldfisch, *der;* ~**fish bowl** *n.* Goldfischglas, *das;* **like being in a** ~**fish bowl** (fig.) wie auf dem Präsentierteller; ~ **'medal** *n.* Goldmedaille, *die;* ~ **'medallist** *n.* Goldmedaillengewinner, *der*/-gewinnerin, *die;* ~ **mine** *n.* Goldmine, *die;* (fig.) Goldgrube, *die;* ~**-plated** *adj.* vergoldet; ~**smith** *n.* Goldschmied, *der*/-schmiedin, *die*

golf /gɒlf/ *n.* Golf, *das*

golf ball ⋯

golf: ~ **ball** n. Golfball, der; ~ **club** n. (a) (implement) Golfschläger, der; (b) (association) Golfklub, der; ~**course** n. Golfplatz, der

'golfer n. Golfer, der/Golferin, die

golf links n. Golfplatz, der

gondola /'gɒndələ/ n. Gondel, die

gondolier /gɒndə'lɪə(r)/ n. Gondoliere, der

gone /gɒn/ ① ▶ GO 1
② pred. adj. (a) (away) weg; it's time you were ~: es ist od. wird Zeit, dass du gehst (b) (of time: after) nach; it's ~ ten o'clock es ist zehn Uhr vorbei

gong /gɒŋ/ n. Gong, der

good /gʊd/ ① adj., better /'betə(r)/, best /best/ (a) gut; günstig ⟨Gelegenheit, Angebot⟩; ausreichend ⟨Vorrat⟩; ausgiebig ⟨Mahl⟩; as ~ as so gut wie; his ~ eye/leg sein gesundes Auge/Bein; in ~ time frühzeitig; all in ~ time alles zu seiner Zeit; be ~ at sth. in etw. (Dat.) gut sein; too ~ to be true zu schön, um wahr zu sein; apples are ~ for you Äpfel sind gesund; be too much of a ~ thing zu viel des Guten sein; ~ times eine schöne Zeit; feel ~: sich wohl fühlen; take a ~ look round sich gründlich umsehen; give sb. a ~ beating/scolding jmdn. tüchtig verprügeln/ausschimpfen; ~ afternoon/day guten Tag!; ~ evening/ morning guten Abend/Morgen!; ~ night gute Nacht!
(b) (enjoyable) schön ⟨Leben, Urlaub, Wochenende⟩; the ~ life das angenehme[, sorglose] Leben; have a ~ time! viel Spaß!; have a ~ journey! gute Reise!
(c) (well-behaved) gut; brav; be ~!, be a ~ girl/boy! sei brav od. lieb!; [as] ~ as gold ganz artig od. brav
(d) (virtuous) rechtschaffen; (kind) nett; gut ⟨Absicht, Wünsche, Benehmen, Tat⟩; be ~ to sb. gut zu jmdm. sein; would you be so ~ as to or ~ enough to do that? wären Sie so freundlich od. nett, das zu tun?; that/it is ~ of you das/es ist nett od. lieb von dir
(e) (commendable) gut; ~ for 'you etc. (coll.) bravo!
(f) (attractive) schön; gut ⟨Figur⟩; look ~: gut aussehen
(g) (considerable) [recht] ansehnlich ⟨Menschenmenge⟩; ganz schön, ziemlich (ugs.) ⟨Entfernung, Strecke⟩; gut ⟨Preis, Erlös⟩
(h) make ~ (succeed) erfolgreich sein; (compensate for) wieder gutmachen; (indemnify) ersetzen
② n. (a) (use) Nutzen, der; be some ~ to sb./sth. jmdm./einer Sache nützen; be no ~ to sb./sth. für jmdn./etw. nicht zu gebrauchen sein; it is no/not much ~ doing sth. es hat keinen/kaum einen Sinn, etw. zu tun; what's the ~ of ...?, what ~ is ...? was nützt ...?
(b) (benefit) for your/his etc. own ~: zu deinem/seinem usw. Besten; do no/little ~: nichts/wenig helfen od. nützen; do sb./sth.

~: jmdm./einer Sache nütz[...] Erholung:⟩ jmdm./einer Sa[...] ⟨Arznei:⟩ jmdm./einer Sac[...]
(c) (goodness) Gute, das; b[...] nichts Gutes im Sinn hab[...]
(d) for ~ (finally) ein für a[...] (permanently) für immer
(e) in pl. (wares etc.) Waren Pl.; (belongings) Habe, die; (Brit. Railw.) Fracht, die; attrib. Güter⟨wagen, -zug⟩

good: ~'bye (Amer.: ~'by) int. auf Wiedersehen!; (on telephone) auf Wiederhören!; ~-for-nothing ① adj. nichtsnutzig; ② n. Taugenichts, der; ~-'looking adj. gut aussehend

'goodness ① n. Güte, die
② int. [my] ~! meine Güte! (ugs.)

good: ~s train n. (Brit.) Güterzug, der; ~-'tempered adj. ausgeglichen; verträglich ⟨Person⟩; ~'will n. guter Wille; attrib. Goodwill⟨botschaft, -reise usw.⟩

'goody n. (coll.: hero) Gute, der/die

gooey /'guːɪ/ adj., gooier /'guːɪə(r)/, gooiest /'guːɪɪst/ (coll.) klebrig

goose /guːs/ n., pl. geese /giːs/ Gans, die

gooseberry /'gʊzbərɪ/ n. Stachelbeere, die

goose bumps (Amer.), **goose pimples** ns. pl. have ~: eine Gänsehaut haben

gore[1] /gɔː(r)/ v.t. [mit den Hörnern] aufspießen od. durchbohren

gore[2] n. Blut, das

gorge /gɔːdʒ/ ① n. Schlucht, die
② v.i. & refl. ~ [oneself] sich voll stopfen (ugs.) (on mit)

gorgeous /'gɔːdʒəs/ adj. prächtig; hinreißend ⟨Frau, Mann, Lächeln⟩

gorilla /gə'rɪlə/ n. Gorilla, der

gormless /'gɔːmlɪs/ adj. (Brit. coll.) dämlich (ugs.)

gorse /gɔːs/ n. Stechginster, der

gory /'gɔːrɪ/ adj. (fig.) blutrünstig

gosh /gɒʃ/ int. (coll.) Gott!

'go-slow n. (Brit.) Bummelstreik, der

gospel /'gɒspl/ n. Evangelium, das

'gospel singer n. Gospelsänger, der/ -sängerin, die

gossamer /'gɒsəmə(r)/ n. Altweibersommer, der; attrib. hauchdünn

gossip /'gɒsɪp/ ① n. (a) (talk) Klatsch, der (ugs.)
(b) (person) Klatschbase, die (ugs.)
② v.i. klatschen (ugs.)

gossip: ~ column n. Klatschspalte, die (ugs.); ~ columnist n. Klatschspaltenkolumnist, der/-kolumnistin, die

got ▶ GET

Gothic /'gɒθɪk/ adj. gotisch

gotten ▶ GET

gouge /gaʊdʒ/ v.t. aushöhlen

goulash /'guːlæʃ/ n. Gulasch, das od. der

gourmet /'guəmeɪ/ n. Gourmet, der

govern /'gʌvn/ ① v.t. (a) regieren ⟨Land, Volk⟩; verwalten ⟨Provinz⟩
(b) (dictate) bestimmen
② v.i. regieren

governess /'gʌvənɪs/ n. Gouvernante, die (veraltet); Hauslehrerin, die

government /'gʌvnmənt/ n. Regierung, die; attrib. Regierungs-

government: ~ **department** n. Regierungsstelle, die; ~**-funded** adj. staatlich finanziert; ~ **official** n. Regierungsbeamte, der/-beamtin, die

governor /'gʌvənə(r)/ n. (a) (of province etc.) Gouverneur, der
(b) (of institution) Direktor, der/Direktorin, die; [board of] ~s Vorstand, der
(c) (coll.: employer) Boss, der (ugs.)

gown /gaʊn/ n. (a) [elegantes] Kleid
(b) (official or uniform robe) Talar, der

GP abbr. = **general practitioner**

GPS abbr. = **Global Positioning System**

grab /græb/ ① v.t., -bb- greifen nach; (seize) packen; ~ the chance die Gelegenheit ergreifen; ~ hold of sb./sth. sich ⟨Dat.⟩ jmdn./etw. schnappen (ugs.)
② v.i., -bb-: ~ at sth. nach etw. greifen
③ n. make a ~ at or for sb./sth. nach jmdn./etw. greifen

grace /greɪs/ n. (a) (charm) Anmut, die (geh.)
(b) (decency) have the ~ to do sth. so anständig sein und etw. tun
(c) (delay) Frist, die; give sb. a day's ~: jmdm. einen Tag Aufschub gewähren
(d) (prayers) say ~: das Tischgebet sprechen

graceful /'greɪsfl/ adj. elegant; graziös ⟨Bewegung, Eleganz⟩

gracious /'greɪʃəs/ ① adj. (a) liebenswürdig
(b) (merciful) gnädig
② int. good ~! [ach] du meine Güte!

grade /greɪd/ ① n. (a) Rang, der; (Mil.) Dienstgrad, der
(b) (position) Stufe, die
(c) (Amer. Sch.: class) Klasse, die
(d) (Sch., Univ.: mark) Note, die; Zensur, die
② v.t. (a) einstufen ⟨Schüler⟩; [nach Größe/ Qualität] sortieren ⟨Eier, Kartoffeln⟩
(b) (mark) benoten

gradient /'greɪdɪənt/ n. (ascent) Steigung, die; (descent) Gefälle, das

gradual /'grædʊəl/ adj., **'gradually** adv. allmählich

graduate ① /'grædʒʊət/ n. Graduierte, der/die; (who has left university) Akademiker, der/Akademikerin, die; university ~: Hochschulabsolvent, der/-absolventin, die
② /'grædʒʊeɪt/ v.i. einen akademischen Grad/Titel erwerben; (Amer. Sch.) die [Schul]abschlussprüfung bestehen (from an + Dat.)

graduation /grædʒʊ'eɪʃn/ n. (a) (Univ.) Graduierung, die

(b) (Amer. Sch.) Entlassung, die

graffiti /grə'fiːtiː/ n. sing. or pl. Graffiti Pl.; ~ artist Graffitikünstler, der/-künstlerin, die

graft /grɑːft/ ① n. (a) (Bot.) Edelreis, das
(b) (Med.) (operation) Transplantation, die; (thing ~ed) Transplantat, das
(c) (Brit. coll.: work) Plackerei, die (ugs.)
② v.t. (a) (Bot.) pfropfen
(b) (Med.) transplantieren
③ v.i. (Brit. coll.) schuften (ugs.)

grain /greɪn/ n. (a) Korn, das; collect. Getreide, das
(b) (particle) Korn, das
(c) (in wood) Maserung, die; (in paper) Faser, die; (in leather) Narbung, die; go against the ~ [for sb.] (fig.) jmdm. gegen den Strich gehen (ugs.)

'grainy adj. körnig; gemasert ⟨Holz⟩; genarbt ⟨Leder⟩

gram /græm/ n. Gramm, das

grammar /'græmə(r)/ n. Grammatik, die

grammar: ~ **book** n. Grammatik, die; ~ **school** n. (Brit.) ≈ Gymnasium, das

grammatical /grə'mætɪkl/ adj. (a) grammat[ikal]isch richtig od. korrekt
(b) (of grammar) grammatisch

grammatically /grə'mætɪkəlɪ/ adv. grammati[kal]isch ⟨richtig, falsch⟩

gramme ▸ GRAM

gramophone /'græməfəʊn/ n. (dated) Plattenspieler, der

gran /græn/ n. (coll./child lang.) Oma, die (Kinderspr./ugs.)

granary /'grænərɪ/ n. Getreidesilo, der od. das; Kornspeicher, der

'granary bread n. Ganzkornbrot, das

grand /grænd/ adj. (a) (most or very important) groß; ~ finale großes Finale
(b) (splendid) grandios
(c) (coll.: excellent) großartig

grandad /'grændæd/ n. (coll./child lang.); Opa, der (Kinderspr./ugs.)

grand: ~**child** n. Enkel, der/Enkelin, die; Enkelkind, das; ~**dad[dy]** /'grændæd(i)/ ▸ GRANDAD; ~**daughter** n. Enkelin, die

grandeur /'grændʒə(r), 'grændjə(r)/ n. Erhabenheit, die

'grandfather n. Großvater, der; ~ **clock** Standuhr, die

grandiose /'grændɪəʊs/ adj. grandios; (pompous) bombastisch

grand: ~**ma** n. (coll./child lang.) Oma, die (Kinderspr./ugs.); ~**mother** n. Großmutter, die; ~**pa** n. (coll./child lang.) Opa, der (Kinderspr./ugs.); ~**parent** n. (male) Großvater, der; (female) Großmutter, die; ~**parents** Großeltern Pl.; ~ **pi'ano** n. [Konzert]flügel, der; ~**son** n. Enkel, der; ~**stand** n. [Haupt]tribüne, die

granite /'grænɪt/ n. Granit, der

granny /'grænɪ/ n. (coll./child lang.) Oma, die (Kinderspr./ugs.)

'granny flat n. Einliegerwohnung, die

grant /grɑːnt/ ① *v.t.* **(a)** erfüllen ‹*Wunsch*›; stattgeben (+ *Dat.*) ‹*Gesuch*› **(b)** (concede, give) gewähren; geben ‹*Zeit*›; bewilligen ‹*Geldmittel*›; zugestehen ‹*Recht*›; erteilen ‹*Erlaubnis*› **(c)** (in argument) zugeben; **take sb./sth. for** ∼**ed** sich (*Dat.*) jmds. sicher sein/etw. für selbstverständlich halten ② *n.* Zuschuss, *der;* (financial aid [to student]) [Studien]beihilfe, *die;* (scholarship) Stipendium, *das*

granulated sugar /ˈɡrænjʊleɪtɪd ˈʃʊɡə(r)/ *n.* Kristallzucker, *der*

granule /ˈɡrænjuːl/ *n.* Körnchen, *das*

grape /ɡreɪp/ *n.* Weintraube, *die;* **a bunch of** ∼**s** eine Traube

grape: ∼**fruit** *n.*, *pl. same* Grapefruit, *die;* ∼ **juice** *n.* Traubensaft, *der;* ∼**vine** *n.* (fig.) **the** ∼**vine** die Flüsterpropaganda; **I heard on the** ∼**vine that …**: es wird geflüstert, dass …

graph /ɡrɑːf/ *n.* grafische Darstellung; ∼ **paper** Diagrammpapier, *das*

graphic /ˈɡræfɪk/ *adj.* **(a)** grafisch **(b)** (vivid) plastisch; anschaulich

graphically /ˈɡræfɪkəlɪ/ *adv.* **(a)** (vividly) plastisch **(b)** (using graphics) grafisch

graphic 'arts *n. pl.* Grafik, *die*

graphics /ˈɡræfɪks/ *n.* (use of diagrams) grafische Darstellung; **computer** ∼: Computergraphik, *die*

grapple /ˈɡræpl/ *v.i.* handgemein werden; ∼ **with** (fig.) sich auseinander setzen mit

grasp /ɡrɑːsp/ ① *v.i.* ∼ **at** ergreifen; sich stürzen auf (+ *Akk.*) ‹*Angebot*› ② *v.t.* **(a)** (seize) ergreifen **(b)** (hold firmly) festhalten **(c)** (understand) verstehen; erfassen ‹*Bedeutung*› ③ *n.* **(a)** (firm hold) Griff, *der* **(b)** (mental ∼) **have a good** ∼ **of sth.** etw. gut beherrschen

grasping *adj.* habgierig

grass /ɡrɑːs/ *n.* **(a)** Gras, *das* **(b)** (lawn) Rasen, *der* **(c)** (Brit. sl.: police informer) Spitzel, *der*

grass: ∼**hopper** *n.* Grashüpfer, *der;* ∼**root[s]** *attrib. adj.* (Polit.) Basis-; ∼ **seed** *n.* Grassamen, *der;* (collect.) Grassamen *Pl.*

grassy /ˈɡrɑːsɪ/ *adj.* mit Gras bewachsen

grate¹ /ɡreɪt/ *n.* Rost, *der;* (recess) Kamin, *der*

grate² *v.t.* **(a)** reiben; (less finely) raspeln **(b)** (grind) ∼ **one's teeth** mit den Zähnen knirschen

grateful /ˈɡreɪtfl/ *adj.* dankbar (**to** *Dat.*)

gratefully *adv.* dankbar

grater *n.* Reibe, *die;* Raspel, *die*

gratify /ˈɡrætɪfaɪ/ *v.t.* freuen; **be gratified by** *or* **with** *or* **at sth.** über etw. (*Akk.*) erfreut sein

gratifying *adj.* erfreulich

grating /ˈɡreɪtɪŋ/ *n.* Gitter, *das*

gratitude /ˈɡrætɪtjuːd/ *n.* Dankbarkeit, *die* (**to** gegenüber)

gratuitous /ɡrəˈtjuːɪtəs/ *adj.* (motiveless) grundlos

gratuity /ɡrəˈtjuːɪtɪ/ *n.* Trinkgeld, *das*

grave¹ /ɡreɪv/ *n.* Grab, *das*

grave² *adj.* **(a)** (important, solemn) ernst **(b)** (serious) schwer ‹*Fehler, Irrtum*›; ernst ‹*Situation, Lage*›; groß ‹*Gefahr*›; schlimm ‹*Nachricht*›

gravedigger *n.* Totengräber, *der*

gravel /ˈɡrævl/ *n.* Kies, *der*

grave: ∼**stone** *n.* Grabstein, *der;* ∼**yard** *n.* Friedhof, *der*

gravity /ˈɡrævɪtɪ/ *n.* **(a)** (of mistake, offence) Schwere, *die;* (of situation) Ernst, *der* **(b)** (Phys., Astron.) Gravitation, *die;* Schwerkraft, *die*

gravy /ˈɡreɪvɪ/ *n.* **(a)** (juices) Bratensaft, *der* **(b)** (dressing) [Braten]soße, *die*

gravy: ∼ **boat** *n.* Sauciere, *die;* Soßenschüssel, *die;* ∼ **train** *n.* **ride/board the** ∼ **train** (coll.) leichtes Geld machen (ugs.)

gray etc. (*Amer.*) ▶ GREY etc.

graze¹ /ɡreɪz/ *v.i.* grasen; weiden

graze² ① *n.* Schürfwunde, *die* ② *v.t.* **(a)** (touch lightly) streifen **(b)** (scrape) abschürfen ‹*Haut*›; zerkratzen ‹*Oberfläche*›

grease /ɡriːs/ ① *n.* Fett, *das;* (lubricant) Schmierfett, *das* ② *v.t.* einfetten; (lubricate) schmieren

greaseproof *adj.* fettdicht; ∼ **paper** Pergament- *od.* Butterbrotpapier, *das*

greasy /ˈɡriːsɪ/ *adj.* fettig; fett ‹*Essen*›; (lubricated) geschmiert; (dirty with lubricant) schmierig

great /ɡreɪt/ *adj.* **(a)** groß; **a** ∼ **many** sehr viele; sehr gut ‹*Freund*›; (impressive; coll.: splendid) großartig; **be a** ∼ **one for sth.** etw. sehr gern tun **(b)** Groß‹*onkel, -tante, -neffe, -nichte*›; Ur‹*großmutter, -großvater, -enkel, -enkelin*›

great: G∼ **'Bear** *n.* (Astron.) Großer Bär; **G**∼ **'Britain** *pr. n.* Großbritannien (*das*)

greatly *adv.* sehr; höchst ‹*verärgert*›; stark ‹*beeinflusst*›; bedeutend ‹*verbessert*›

greatness *n.* Größe, *die*

Great 'War *n.* Erster Weltkrieg

Greece /ɡriːs/ *pr. n.* Griechenland (*das*)

greed /ɡriːd/ *n.* Gier, *die* (**for** nach); (gluttony) Gefräßigkeit, *die*

greedy *adj.* gierig; (gluttonous) gefräßig

Greek /ɡriːk/ ① *adj.* griechisch; **sb. is** ∼: jmd. ist Grieche/Griechin ② *n.* **(a)** (person) Grieche, *der*/Griechin, *die* **(b)** (language) Griechisch, *das; see also* ENGLISH 2A

green /ɡriːn/ ① *adj.* **(a)** grün **(b)** (environmentally safe) ökologisch ⋯⋯

(c) (gullible) naiv; (inexperienced) grün
(d) (Polit.) G∼: grün; **the G∼s** die Grünen
2 *n.* **(a)** (colour) Grün, *das*
(b) (piece of land) Grünfläche, *die;* **village** ∼:
Dorfanger, *der*
(c) *in pl.* (∼ vegetables) Grüngemüse, *das*

green: ∼ **belt** *n.* Grüngürtel, *der;*
∼ **'card** *n.* (Motor Veh.) grüne Karte

greenery /'gri:nərı/ *n.* Grün, *das*

green: ∼**fly** *n.* (Brit.) grüne Blattlaus;
∼**gage** /'gri:ngeɪdʒ/ *n.* Reineclaude, *die;*
∼**grocer** *n.* (Brit.) Obst- und
Gemüsehändler, *der/*-händlerin, *die*

'greenhouse *n.* Gewächshaus, *das*

greenhouse: ∼ **effect** *n.*
Treibhauseffekt, *der;* ∼ **gas** *n.*
Treibhausgas, *das*

green: ∼ **light** *n.* **(a)** grünes Licht; (as
signal) Grün, *das;* **(b)** (fig.) **give sb./get the** ∼:
jmdm. grünes Licht geben/grünes Licht
erhalten; **G**∼ **Party** *n.* (Polit.) die Grünen
Pl.

greet /gri:t/ *v.t.* begrüßen; (in passing)
grüßen; (receive) empfangen

'greeting *n.* Begrüßung, *die;* (in passing)
Gruß, *der;* (words) Grußformel, *die*

'greetings card *n.* Grußkarte, *die;* (for
birthday) Glückwunschkarte, *die*

gregarious /grɪ'geərɪəs/ *adj.* gesellig

grenade /grɪ'neɪd/ *n.* Granate, *die*

grew ▸ GROW

grey /greɪ/ **1** *adj.* grau
2 *n.* Grau, *das*

grey: ∼**haired** *adj.* grauhaarig;
∼**hound** *n.* Windhund, *der;* ∼**hound**
racing *n.* Windhundrennen, *das*

greyish /'greɪʃ/ *adj.* gräulich

grid /grɪd/ *n.* **(a)** (grating) Rost, *der*
(b) (of lines) Gitter[netz], *das*
(c) (for supply) Versorgungsnetz, *das*

grid: ∼**lock** *n.* Verkehrsinfarkt, *der;* (fig.)
völliger Stillstand; ∼**locked** /'grɪdlɒkt/
adj. total verstopft ⟨Straße, Stadt⟩; (fig.)
festgefahren

grief /gri:f/ *n.* Kummer, *der* (**over, at** über
+ *Akk.,* um); (at loss of sb.) Trauer, *die* (**for**
um); **come to** ∼ (fail) scheitern

'grief-stricken *adj.* untröstlich (**at** über
+ *Akk.*)

grievance /'gri:vəns/ *n.* (complaint)
Beschwerde, *die;* (grudge) Groll, *der*

grieve /gri:v/ **1** *v.t.* betrüben; bekümmern
2 *v.i.* trauern (**for** um)

grievous /'gri:vəs/ *adj.* schwer
⟨Verwundung, Krankheit;⟩ ∼ **bodily harm**
(Law) schwere Körperverletzung

grill¹ /grɪl/ **1** *v.t.* (cook) grillen; (fig.: question)
in die Mangel nehmen (ugs.)
2 *n.* **(a) mixed** ∼: gemischte Grillplatte
(b) (on cooker) Grill, *der*

grille (grill²) *n.* **(a)** Gitter, *das*
(b) (Motor Veh.) [Kühler]grill, *der*

grim /grɪm/ *adj.* (stern) streng; grimmig
⟨Lächeln, Schweigen⟩; (unrelenting) erbittert
⟨Widerstand, Kampf⟩; (ghastly) grauenvoll
⟨Aufgabe, Nachricht⟩; trostlos ⟨Aussichten⟩

grimace /grɪ'meɪs/ **1** *n.* Grimasse, *die*
2 *v.i.* Grimassen schneiden; ∼ **with pain** vor
Schmerz das Gesicht verziehen

grime /graɪm/ *n.* Schmutz, *der*

grimy /'graɪmɪ/ *adj.* schmutzig

grin /grɪn/ **1** *n.* Grinsen, *das*
2 *v.i.,* **-nn-** grinsen; ∼ **at sb.** jmdn.
angrinsen

grind /graɪnd/ **1** *v.t.,* **ground** /graʊnd/ **(a)**
∼ [up] zermahlen; mahlen ⟨Kaffee, Pfeffer,
Getreide⟩
(b) (sharpen) schleifen ⟨Schere, Messer⟩;
schärfen ⟨Klinge⟩
(c) (rub harshly) zerquetschen; ∼ **one's teeth**
mit den Zähnen knirschen
2 *v.i.,* **ground:** ∼ **to a halt** ⟨Fahrzeug:⟩
quietschend zum Stehen kommen; (fig.)
⟨Verkehr:⟩ zum Erliegen kommen
3 *n.* (coll.) Plackerei, *die* (ugs.)

'grinder *n.* Schleifmaschine, *die;* (coffee
∼ etc.) Mühle, *die*

'grindstone *n.* Schleifstein, *der*

grip /grɪp/ **1** *n.* **(a)** (firm hold) Halt, *der;* (fig.:
power) Umklammerung, *die;* **have a** ∼ **on sth.**
etw. festhalten; (fig.) etwas im Griff haben;
loosen one's ∼: loslassen; **lose one's** ∼ (fig.)
nachlassen
(b) (strength or way of ∼ping) Griff, *der*
2 *v.t.,* **-pp-** [fest] halten; ⟨Reifen:⟩ greifen;
(fig.) fesseln ⟨Publikum, Aufmerksamkeit⟩
3 *v.i.,* **-pp-** ⟨Räder, Bremsen usw.:⟩ greifen

gripe /graɪp/ *v.i.* (coll.) meckern (ugs.) (**about**
über + *Akk.*)

gripping /'grɪpɪŋ/ *adj.* (fig.) packend

grisly /'grɪzlɪ/ *adj.* grausig

gristle /'grɪsl/ *n.* Knorpel, *der*

grit /grɪt/ **1** *n.* **(a)** Sand, *der*
(b) (coll.: courage) Schneid, *der* (ugs.)
2 *v.t.,* **-tt-:** **(a)** streuen ⟨Straßen⟩
(b) ∼ **one's teeth** die Zähne
zusammenbeißen (ugs.)

grizzly /'grɪzlɪ/ *n.* ∼ [**bear**] Grislybär, *der*

groan /grəʊn/ **1** *n.* Stöhnen, *das;* (of thing)
Ächzen, *das*
2 *v.i.* [auf]stöhnen (**at** bei); ⟨Tisch, Planken:⟩
ächzen
3 *v.t.* stöhnen

grocer /'grəʊsə(r)/ *n.* Lebensmittelhändler,
der/-händlerin, *die*

grocery /'grəʊsərɪ/ *n.* **(a)** *in pl.* (goods)
Lebensmittel *Pl.*
(b) ∼ [**store**] Lebensmittelgeschäft, *das*

groggy /'grɒgɪ/ *adj.* groggy *präd.* (ugs.)

groin /grɔɪn/ *n.* Leistengegend, *die*

groom /gru:m, grʊm/ **1** *n.* **(a)** (stable boy)
Stallbursche, *der*
(b) (bride∼) Bräutigam, *der*
2 *v.t.* striegeln ⟨Pferd⟩; (fig.) vorbereiten (**for**
auf + *Akk.*)

groove /gruːv/ n. Rille, *die*

grope /grəʊp/ v.i. tasten (**for** nach)

gross[1] /grəʊs/ adj. **(a)** (flagrant) grob 〈*Fahrlässigkeit, Fehler*〉
(b) (obese) fett
(c) (total) Brutto-

gross[2] n., pl. same Gros, *das*

'grossly adj. (flagrantly) äußerst; grob 〈*übertreiben*〉

grotesque /grəʊˈtesk/ adj. grotesk

grotto /ˈgrɒtəʊ/ n., pl. ~es or ~s Grotte, *die*

grotty /ˈgrɒtɪ/ adj. (Brit. coll.) mies (ugs.)

ground[1] /graʊnd/ ⟦1⟧ n. **(a)** Boden, *der;* **get off the ~** (coll.) konkrete Gestalt annehmen
(b) [sports] ~: Sportplatz, *der*
(c) in pl. (attached to house) Anlage, *die*
(d) (reason) Grund, *der;* **on the ~[s] of** auf Grund (+ *Gen.*); **on the ~[s] that …:** unter Berufung auf die Tatsache, dass …
(e) in pl. (sediment) Satz, *der*
⟦2⟧ v.t. (Aeronaut.) am Boden festhalten

ground[2] ⟦1⟧ ▶ GRIND 1, 2
⟦2⟧ adj. gemahlen 〈*Kaffee, Getreide*〉

ground: ~ control n. (Aeronaut.: personnel, equipment, etc.;) Flugsicherungskontrolldienst, *der;* **~ 'floor** ▶ FLOOR 1B; **~ forces** n. pl. Bodentruppen *Pl.;* **~ frost** n. Bodenfrost, *der*

'grounding n. Grundkenntnisse *Pl.*

'groundless adj. unbegründet

ground: ~sheet n. Bodenplane, *die;*
~sman /ˈgraʊndzmən/ n., pl. -smen /ˈgraʊndzmən/ (Sport) Platzwart, *der;*
~work n. Vorarbeiten *Pl.;* **~ 'zero** n. [Boden]nullpunkt, *der*

group /gruːp/ ⟦1⟧ n. Gruppe, *die*
⟦2⟧ v.t. gruppieren

group: ~ practice n. Gemeinschaftspraxis, *die;* **~ therapy** n. Gruppentherapie, *die*

grouse[1] /graʊs/ n., pl. same Raufußhuhn, *das;* [red] ~ (Brit.) Schottisches Moorschneehuhn

grouse[2] v.i. (coll.) meckern (ugs.)

grove /grəʊv/ n. Wäldchen, *das*

grovel /ˈgrɒvl/ v.i., (Brit.) -ll- (fig.) katzbuckeln

grow /grəʊ/ ⟦1⟧ v.i., grew /gruː/, grown /grəʊn/ **(a)** wachsen; **~ out of** or **from sth.** sich aus etw. entwickeln; (from sth. abstract) von etw. herrühren; **~ in** gewinnen an (+ *Dat.*) 〈*Größe, Bedeutung*〉
(b) (become) werden; **~ apart** (fig.) sich auseinander leben; **~ to love/hate sb./sth.** jmdn./etw. lieben lernen/hassen lernen; **~ to like sb./sth.** nach und nach Gefallen an jmdm./etw. finden
⟦2⟧ v.t., grew, grown (on a large scale) anpflanzen; züchten 〈*Blumen*〉

■ **grow 'up** v.i. **(a)** aufwachsen; (become adult) erwachsen werden
(b) 〈*Legende:*〉 entstehen

growl /graʊl/ ⟦1⟧ n. Knurren, *das;* (of bear) Brummen, *das*
⟦2⟧ v.i. knurren; 〈*Bär:*〉 [böse] brummen

grown /grəʊn/ ⟦1⟧ ▶ GROW
⟦2⟧ adj. erwachsen

'grown-up ⟦1⟧ n. Erwachsene, *der/die*
⟦2⟧ adj. erwachsen

growth /grəʊθ/ n. **(a)** Wachstum, *das* (of, in *Gen.*); (increase) Zunahme, *die* (of, in *Gen.*)
(b) (Med.) Gewächs, *das*

growth: ~ area n. Wachstumsbereich, *der;* **~ industry** n. Wachstumsindustrie, *die;* **~ rate** n. Wachstumsrate, *die*

grub /grʌb/ n. **(a)** Larve, *die;* (maggot) Made, *die*
(b) (coll.: food) Fressen, *das* (salopp)

grubby /ˈgrʌbɪ/ adj. schmudd[e]lig (ugs.)

grudge /grʌdʒ/ ⟦1⟧ v.t. ~ sb. sth. jmdm. etw. missgönnen; ~ doing sth. etw. ungern tun
⟦2⟧ n. Groll, *der;* **bear sb. a ~** or **a ~ against sb.** jmdm. gegenüber nachtragend sein

grudging /ˈgrʌdʒɪŋ/ adj. widerwillig; widerwillig gewährt 〈*Zuschuss*〉

'grudgingly adv. widerwillig

gruelling (Amer.: **grueling**) /ˈgruːəlɪŋ/ adj. aufreibend; strapaziös 〈*Reise*〉

gruesome /ˈgruːsəm/ adj. grausig

gruff /grʌf/ adj. barsch; rau 〈*Stimme*〉

grumble /ˈgrʌmbl/ v.i. murren; ~ about or over sth. sich über etw. (*Akk.*) beklagen

grumpily /ˈgrʌmpɪlɪ/ adv. unleidlich

grumpy /ˈgrʌmpɪ/ adj. unleidlich

grunge /grʌndʒ/ n. Grunge, *der*

grunt /grʌnt/ ⟦1⟧ n. Grunzen, *das*
⟦2⟧ v.i. grunzen

guarantee /gærənˈtiː/ ⟦1⟧ v.t. **(a)** garantieren für; [eine] Garantie geben auf (+ *Akk.*); **the clock is ~d for a year** die Uhr hat ein Jahr Garantie
(b) (promise) garantieren (ugs.); (ensure) bürgen für 〈*Qualität*〉
⟦2⟧ n. **(a)** (Commerc. etc.) Garantie, *die;* (document) Garantieschein, *der*
(b) (promise) Garantie, *die* (ugs.); **give sb. a ~ that …:** jmdm. garantieren, dass …

guarantor /ˈgærəntə(r), gærənˈtɔː(r)/ n. Bürge, *der*/Bürgin, *die*

guaranty /ˈgærəntɪ/ n. (basis of security) Garantie, *die;* Gewähr, *die*

guard /gɑːd/ ⟦1⟧ n. **(a)** (guardsman) Wachtposten, *der;* (group of soldiers) Wache, *die;* **be on ~:** Wache haben; **be on [one's] ~** (lit. or fig.) sich hüten
(b) (Brit. Railw.) [Zug]schaffner, *der*/-schaffnerin, *die*
(c) (Amer.: prison warder) [Gefängnis]wärter, *der*/-wärterin, *die*
⟦2⟧ v.t. bewachen; hüten 〈*Geheimnis*〉; schützen 〈*Leben*〉; beschützen 〈*Prominenten*〉 ⋯⟡

■ **'guard against** *v.t.* sich hüten vor (+ *Dat.*); vorbeugen (+ *Dat.*) ⟨*Krankheit, Irrtum*⟩

guard: ~ **dog** *n.* Wachhund, *der;* ~ **duty** *n.* Wachdienst, *der*

'guarded *adj.* zurückhaltend

guardian /'gɑːdɪən/ *n.* (a) Hüter, *der;* Wächter, *der*
(b) (Law) Vormund, *der*

guardian 'angel *n.* Schutzengel, *der*

guerrilla /gəˈrɪlə/ *n.* Guerillakämpfer, *der/* -kämpferin, *die; attrib.* Guerilla-

guess /ges/ ⟨1⟩ *v.t.* (a) (estimate) schätzen; (surmise) raten; (surmise correctly) erraten; raten ⟨*Rätsel*⟩; ~ **what!** (coll.) stell dir vor!
(b) (esp. Amer.: suppose) I ~: ich glaube ⟨2⟩ *v.i.* (estimate) schätzen; (make assumption) vermuten; (surmise correctly) es erraten; ~ **at** **sth.** etw. schätzen; **keep sb.** ~**ing** (coll.) jmdn. im Unklaren lassen
⟨3⟩ *n.* Schätzung, *die;* **make** *or* **have a** ~: schätzen

'guesswork *n.* be ~: eine Vermutung sein

guesstimate /'gestɪmət/ *n.* (coll.) grobe Schätzung

guest /gest/ *n.* Gast, *der*

guest: ~ **house** *n.* Pension, *die;* ~ **list** *n.* Gästeliste, *die;* ~ **room** *n.* Gästezimmer, *das;* ~ **worker** *n.* Gastarbeiter, *der/* -arbeiterin, *die*

guffaw /gʌˈfɔː/ ⟨1⟩ *n.* brüllendes Gelächter ⟨2⟩ *v.i.* brüllend lachen

guidance /'gaɪdəns/ *n.* (a) (leadership) Führung, *die;* (by teacher etc.) [An]leitung, *die*
(b) (advice) Rat, *der*

guide /gaɪd/ ⟨1⟩ *n.* (a) Führer, *der/*Führerin, *die;* (Tourism) [Fremden]führer, *der/*-führerin, *die*
(b) (indicator) be a [good] ~ to sth. ein [guter] Anhaltspunkt für etw. sein; be no ~ to sth. keine Rückschlüsse auf etw. (*Akk.*) zulassen
(c) (Brit.) [Girl] G~: Pfadfinderin, *die*
(d) (handbook) Handbuch, *das*
(e) (for tourists) [Reise]führer, *der*
⟨2⟩ *v.t.* führen; (fig.) bestimmen ⟨*Handeln, Urteil*⟩; **be** ~**d by sth./sb.** sich von etw./ jmdm. leiten lassen

'guidebook *n.* [Reise]führer, *der*

guided 'missile *n.* Lenkflugkörper, *der*

'guide dog *n.* Blinden[führ]hund, *der*

guided 'tour *n.* Führung, *die* (of durch)

'guideline *n.* Richtlinie, *die*

guild /gɪld/ *n.* (a) Verein, *der*
(b) (Hist.) Gilde, *die;* Zunft, *die*

guile /gaɪl/ *n.* Hinterlist, *die*

guillotine /'gɪlətiːn/ *n.* Guillotine, *die*

guilt /gɪlt/ *n.* (a) Schuld, *die* (of, for an + *Dat.*)
(b) (guilty feeling) Schuldgefühle *Pl.*

'guiltless *adj.* unschuldig (of an + *Dat.*)

'guilty *adj.* (a) schuldig; **be** ~ **of murder** des Mordes schuldig sein; **find sb.** ~/**not** ~ [of

sth.] jmdn. [an etw. (*Dat.*)] schuldig sprechen/[von etw.] freisprechen; **feel** ~ ein schlechtes Gewissen haben
(b) schuldbewusst ⟨*Miene, Blick, Verhalten*⟩; schlecht ⟨*Gewissen*⟩

guinea: ~**fowl**, ~ **hen** *ns.* Perlhuhn, *das;* ~ **pig** *n.* (a) (animal) Meerschweinchen, *das;*
(b) (fig.: subject of experiment) (person) Versuchsperson, *die;* Versuchskaninchen, *das* (ugs. abwertend); (thing) Versuchsobjekt, *das;* **act as** ~ **pig** Versuchskaninchen spielen

guise /gaɪz/ *n.* Gestalt, *die;* **in the** ~ **of** in Gestalt (+ *Gen.*)

guitar /gɪˈtɑː(r)/ *n.* Gitarre, *die*

guitarist /gɪˈtɑːrɪst/ *n.* Gitarrist, *der/* Gitarristin, *die*

gulf /gʌlf/ *n.* (a) (Geog.) Golf, *der*
(b) (wide gap) Kluft, *die*

gull /gʌl/ *n.* Möwe, *die*

gullet /'gʌlɪt/ *n.* (a) Speiseröhre, *die*
(b) (throat) Kehle, *die*

gullible /'gʌlɪbl/ *adj.* leichtgläubig

gully /'gʌlɪ/ *n.* (artificial channel) Abzugsrinne, *die;* (drain) Gully, *der*

gulp /gʌlp/ ⟨1⟩ *v.t.* hinunterschlingen; hinuntergießen ⟨*Getränk*⟩
⟨2⟩ *n.* (a) Schlucken, *das*
(b) (large mouthful of drink) kräftiger Schluck

■ **gulp 'down** *v.t.* hinunterschlingen; hinuntergießen ⟨*Getränk*⟩

gum¹ /gʌm/ *n.* (Anat.) ~[s] Zahnfleisch, *das*

gum² ⟨1⟩ *n.* (a) Gummi, *das;* (glue) Klebstoff, *der*
(b) (Amer.) ▶ CHEWING GUM
⟨2⟩ *v.t.,* -mm-: (a) (smear with ~) mit Klebstoff bestreichen; gummieren ⟨*Briefmarken, Etiketten usw.*⟩
(b) (fasten with ~) kleben

'gumboot *n.* Gummistiefel, *der*

gumption /'gʌmpʃn/ *n.* (coll.) Grips, *der*

gun /gʌn/ *n.* Schusswaffe, *die;* (rifle) Gewehr, *das;* (pistol) Pistole, *die;* (revolver) Revolver, *der*

■ **gun 'down** *v.t.* niederschießen

gun: ~**fight** *n.* (Amer. coll.) Schießerei, *die;* ~**fire** *n.* Geschützfeuer, *das;* ~ **laws** *pl.* Waffengesetze *Pl.;* ~**man** /'gʌnmən/ *n., pl.* ~**men** /'gʌnmən/ bewaffneter Mann; ~**powder** *n.* Schießpulver, *das;* ~**shot** *n.* Schuss, *der;* ~**shot wound** Schusswunde, *die;* ~**smith** *n.* Büchsenmacher, *der*

gurgle /'gɜːgl/ ⟨1⟩ *n.* Gluckern, *das;* (of brook) Plätschern, *das*
⟨2⟩ *v.i.* gluckern; ⟨*Bach:*⟩ plätschern; ⟨*Baby:*⟩ lallen; (with delight) glucksen

guru /'gʊruː/ *n.* Guru, *der*

gush /gʌʃ/ ⟨1⟩ *n.* Schwall, *der*
⟨2⟩ *v.i.* (a) strömen; ~ **out** herausströmen
(b) (fig.: enthuse) schwärmen

'gushing *adj.* (a) reißend ⟨*Strom*⟩
(b) (effusive) exaltiert

gust /gʌst/ *n.* ~ [of wind] Bö[e], *die*

gusto /'gʌstəʊ/ *n.* Genuss, *der;* (vitality) Schwung, *der*

'gusty adj. böig

gut /gʌt/ ① n. (a) (material) Darm, der
(b) in pl. (bowels) Eingeweide Pl.; Gedärme Pl.
(c) in pl. (coll.: courage) Schneid, der (ugs.)
② v.t., -tt-: (a) (remove ~s of) ausnehmen
(b) (remove fittings from) ausräumen; **the house was ~ted [by fire]** das Haus brannte aus
③ attrib. adj. ~ **feeling** instinktives Gefühl; **have a ~ feeling that ...** es im Gefühl od. (salopp) Urin haben, dass ...

gutter /'gʌtə(r)/ n. (below edge of roof) Dachrinne, die; (at side of street) Rinnstein, der; Gosse, die

'guttering n. (on roof) Dachrinnen Pl.

gutter 'press n. Sensationspresse, die

guttural /'gʌtərl/ adj. guttural; kehlig

guy /gaɪ/ n. (a) (coll.: man) Typ, der (ugs.)
(b) in pl. (Amer.: everyone) [listen,] you ~s! [hört mal,] Kinder! (ugs.)

'guy rope n. Zelt[spann]leine, die

guzzle /'gʌzl/ ① v.t. (eat) hinunterschlingen; (drink) hinuntergießen

② v.i. schlingen

gym /dʒɪm/ n. (coll.) (a) (gymnasium) Turnhalle, die
(b) (gymnastics) Turnen, das

gymnasium n. /dʒɪm'neɪzɪəm/ n., pl. ~s or **gymnasia** /dʒɪm'neɪzɪə/ Turnhalle, die

gymnast /'dʒɪmnæst/ n. Turner, der/ Turnerin, die

gymnastic /dʒɪm'næstɪk/ adj. turnerisch ⟨Können⟩; ~ **equipment** Turngeräte Pl.

gymnastics /dʒɪm'næstɪks/ n. Gymnastik, die; (esp. with apparatus) Turnen, das

'gymslip n. Trägerrock, der

gynaecologist /gaɪnɪ'kɒlədʒɪst/ n. Frauenarzt, der/-ärztin, die

gynaecology /gaɪnɪ'kɒlədʒɪ/ n. Gynäkologie, die

gypsy, Gypsy /'dʒɪpsɪ/ n. Zigeuner, der/ Zigeunerin, die

gyrate /dʒaɪə'reɪt/ v.i. sich drehen

H h

H¹, h /eɪtʃ/ n. H, h, das

haberdashery /'hæbədæʃərɪ/ n. (goods) Kurzwaren Pl.; (Amer.: menswear) Herrenmoden Pl.

habit /'hæbɪt/ n. (a) Gewohnheit, die; **good/ bad ~:** gute/schlechte [An]gewohnheit; **get or fall into a or the ~ of doing sth.** [es] sich (Dat.) angewöhnen, etw. zu tun
(b) (coll.: addiction) Süchtigkeit, die

habitable /'hæbɪtəbl/ adj. bewohnbar

habitat /'hæbɪtæt/ n. Habitat, das

habitation /hæbɪ'teɪʃn/ n. **fit/unfit for human ~:** bewohnbar/unbewohnbar

habitual /hə'bɪtjʊəl/ adj. (a) gewohnt
(b) (given to habit) gewohnheitsmäßig; Gewohnheits⟨trinker⟩

ha'bitually adv. (regularly) regelmäßig

hack¹ /hæk/ v.t. (a) hacken ⟨Holz⟩; ~ sth. **to bits** or **pieces** etw. in Stücke hacken
(b) (Comp.) eindringen in (+ Akk.) ⟨Computersystem⟩; ~ **into sth.** in etw. (Akk.) eindringen
■ **hack 'off** v.t. abhacken
■ **hack 'out** v.t. heraushauen (**from** aus)

hack² n. (derog.: writer) Schreiberling, der

hacker /'hækə(r)/ n. (Comp.) Hacker, der

hackneyed /'hæknɪd/ adj. abgegriffen; abgedroschen (ugs.)

'hacksaw n. [Metall]bügelsäge, die

had ▶ HAVE

haddock /'hædək/ n., pl. same Schellfisch, der

hadn't /'hædnt/ (coll.) = **had not;** ▶ HAVE

haemoglobin /hiːmə'gləʊbɪn/ n. Hämoglobin, das

haemophilia /hiːmə'fɪlɪə/ n. Hämophilie, die (fachspr.); Bluterkrankheit, die

haemophiliac /hiːmə'fɪlɪæk/ n. Bluter, der/Bluterin, die

haemorrhage /'hemərɪdʒ/ n. Blutung, die

haemorrhoid /'hemərɔɪd/ n. Hämorrhoide, die

hag /hæg/ n. [alte] Hexe

haggard /'hægəd/ adj. ausgezehrt; (with worry) abgehärmt

haggle /'hægl/ v.i. sich zanken (**over, about** wegen); (over price) feilschen (**over, about** um)

Hague /heɪg/ pr. n. **The ~:** Den Haag (das)

hail¹ /heɪl/ ① n. Hagel, der
② v.i. **it ~s** or **is ~ing** es hagelt; ~ **down** (fig.) niederprasseln (**on** auf + Akk.)

hail² v.t. (a) (call out to) anrufen; (signal to) anhalten ⟨Taxi⟩
(b) (acclaim) zujubeln (+ Dat.); bejubeln (**as** als)

'hailstone n. Hagelkorn, das

hair /heə(r)/ n. (a) (one strand) Haar, das ···:

(b) *collect.* Haar, *das;* Haare *Pl.; attrib.* Haar-; **have** *or* **get one's** ∼ **done** sich (*Dat.*) das Haar *od.* die Haare machen lassen (ugs.)

hair: ∼**brush** n. Haarbürste, *die;* ∼ **conditioner** n. Pflegespülung, *die;* ∼ **cream** n. Haarcreme, *die;* Pomade, *die;* ∼ **curler** n. Lockenwickler, *der;* ∼**cut** n. (a) (act) Haareschneiden, *das;* **go for/need a** ∼**cut** zum Friseur gehen/müssen; **get/have a** ∼**cut** sich (*Dat.*) die Haare schneiden lassen; (b) (style) Haarschnitt, *der;* ∼**do** n. (style) Frisur, *die;* ∼**dresser** n. Friseur, *der/* Friseurin, *die;* **go to the** ∼**dresser's** zum Friseur gehen; ∼ **dye** n. Haarfärbemittel, *das;* ∼**grip** n. (Brit.) Haarklammer, *die;* ∼**line** n. (a) (edge of hair) Haaransatz, *der;* **his** ∼**line is receding, he has a receding** ∼**line** er bekommt eine Stirnglatze; (b) (crack) Haarriss; ∼**line fracture** (Med.) Fissur, *die;* ∼**pin** n. Haarnadel, *die;* ∼**pin 'bend** n. Haarnadelkurve, *die;* ∼**-raising** /'heəreɪzɪŋ/ *adj.* haarsträubend; ∼**spray** n. Haarspray, *das;* ∼**style** n. Frisur, *die*

'**hairy** *adj.* (a) behaart; flauschig ⟨*Pullover, Teppich*⟩

(b) (coll.: difficult) haarig

hale /heɪl/ *adj.* ∼ **and hearty** gesund und munter

half /hɑːf/ ⟨**1**⟩ n., *pl.* **halves** /hɑːvz/ (a) Hälfte, *die;* ∼ [**of sth.**] die Hälfte [von etw.]; ∼ **of Europe** halb Europa; **one and a** ∼ **hours, one hour and a** ∼: anderthalb *od.* eineinhalb Stunden; **divide sth. in** ∼ *or* **into halves** etw. halbieren; **she is three and a** ∼: sie ist dreieinhalb

(b) (Footb. etc.: period) Halbzeit, *die*

⟨**2**⟩ *adj.* halb; ∼ **the house/books/time** die Hälfte des Hauses/der Bücher/der Zeit; ∼ **an hour** eine halbe Stunde

⟨**3**⟩ *adv.* (a) zur Hälfte; halb ⟨*schließen, aufessen, fertig, voll, geöffnet*⟩; (almost) fast ⟨*ersticken, tot sein*⟩; ∼ **as much/many** halb so viel/viele; **only** ∼ **hear what ...:** nur zum Teil hören, was ...

(b) ∼ **past** *or* (coll.) ∼ **one/two/three** *etc.* halb zwei/drei/vier *usw.;* ∼ **past twelve** halb eins

half: ∼**-'board** n. Halbpension, *die;* ∼**caste** n. Mischling, *der;* ∼**-'hearted** *adj.* halbherzig; ∼**-'hour** n. halbe Stunde; ∼ '**mast** n. **be [flown] at** ∼ **mast** auf Halbmast stehen; ∼ '**moon** n. Halbmond, *der;* ∼ **note** n. (Amer. Mus.) halbe Note; ∼**-'price** ⟨**1**⟩ n. halber Preis; ⟨**2**⟩ *adj.* zum halben Preis *nachgestellt;* ⟨**3**⟩ *adv.* zum halben Preis; ∼**-'term** n. (Brit.) (holiday) ∼**-term** [**holiday/break**] Ferien in der Mitte des Trimesters; ∼**-'time** n. (Sport) Halbzeit, *die;* ∼'**way** ⟨**1**⟩ *adj.* ∼**way point** Mitte, *die;* ⟨**2**⟩ *adv.* die Hälfte des Weges ⟨*begleiten, fahren*⟩; ∼**wit** n. Schwachkopf, *der;* (scatterbrain) Schussel, *der*

halibut /'hælɪbət/ n., *pl.* same Heilbutt, *der*

hall /hɔːl/ n. (a) Saal, *der;* (building) Halle, *die;* **school/church** ∼: Aula, *die/*Gemeindehaus, *das*

(b) (entrance ∼) Flur, *der*

(c) (Univ.) ∼ [**of residence**] Studentenwohnheim, *das*

'**hallmark** n. [Feingehalts]stempel, *der;* (fig.) Kennzeichen, *das*

hallo /hə'ləʊ/ *int.* (a) (to call attention) hallo (b) (Brit.) ▶ HELLO

Hallowe'en /hæləʊ'iːn/ n. Halloween, *das;* Abend vor Allerheiligen

hallucination /həluːsɪ'neɪʃn/ n. Halluzination, *die*

hallucinogen /hə'luːsɪnədʒen/ n. (Med.) Halluzinogen, *das*

hallucinogenic /həluːsɪnə'dʒenɪk/ *adj.* (Med.) halluzinogen

'**hallway** n. Flur, *der*

halo /'heɪləʊ/ n., *pl.* ∼**es** Heiligenschein, *der*

halt /hɒlt, hɔːlt/ ⟨**1**⟩ n. (a) Pause, *die;* (interruption) Unterbrechung, *die;* **call a** ∼ **to sth.** mit etw. Schluss machen

(b) (Brit. Railw.) Haltepunkt, *der*

⟨**2**⟩ *v.i.* (a) stehen bleiben; ⟨*Fahrer:*⟩ anhalten; (for a rest) eine Pause machen; (esp. Mil.) Halt machen; ∼, **who goes there?** (Mil.) halt, wer da?

(b) (end) eingestellt werden

⟨**3**⟩ *v.t.* anhalten; einstellen ⟨*Projekt*⟩

'**halting** *adj.* schleppend; zögernd ⟨*Antwort*⟩

halve /hɑːv/ *v.t.* halbieren

halves *pl. of* HALF

ham /hæm/ n. Schinken, *der*

hamburger /'hæmbɜːgə(r)/ n. Hacksteak, *das;* (in roll) Hamburger, *der*

hamlet /'hæmlɪt/ n. Weiler, *der*

hammer /'hæmə(r)/ ⟨**1**⟩ n. Hammer, *der* ⟨**2**⟩ *v.t.* hämmern

⟨**3**⟩ *v.i.* hämmern (**at** an + *Dat.*)

■ **hammer 'out** *v.t.* ausklopfen ⟨*Delle, Beule*⟩; (fig.: devise) ausarbeiten

hammock /'hæmək/ n. Hängematte, *die*

hamper¹ /'hæmpə(r)/ n. [Deckel]korb, *der*

hamper² *v.t.* behindern

hamster /'hæmstə(r)/ n. Hamster, *der*

'**hamstring** ⟨**1**⟩ n. (Anat.) Kniesehne, *die* ⟨**2**⟩ *vt.* (fig.) lähmen

hand /hænd/ ⟨**1**⟩ n. (a) Hand, *die;* **by** ∼ (manually) mit der *od.* von Hand; **give** *or* **lend** [**sb.**] **a** ∼ [**with** *or* **in sth.**] [jmdm.] [bei etw.] helfen

(b) (share) **have a** ∼ **in sth.** bei etw. seine Hände im Spiel haben

(c) (worker) Arbeiter, *der;* (Naut.: seaman) Matrose, *der*

(d) (of clock or watch) Zeiger, *der*

(e) **at** ∼: in der Nähe; **on the one** ∼ **..., [but] on the other** [∼] **...:** einerseits ..., andererseits ...

(f) (Cards) Karte, *die*

⟨**2**⟩ *v.t.* geben; ⟨*Überbringer:*⟩ übergeben ⟨*Sendung, Lieferung*⟩

■ **hand 'in** *v.t.* abgeben (**to, at** bei); einreichen ⟨*Petition*⟩

■ **hand 'out** *v.t.* austeilen

■ **hand 'over** *v.t.* übergeben (**to** *Dat.*)
hand: ∼**bag** *n.* Handtasche, *die;*
∼ **baggage** *n.* Handgepäck, *das;* ∼**book**
n. Handbuch, *das;* ∼**brake** *n.* Handbremse,
die; ∼**cuff** ⓵ *n., usu. in pl.* Handschelle,
die; ⓶ *v.t.* ∼**cuff sb.** jmdm. Handschellen
anlegen
handful /'hændful/ *n.* Handvoll, *die;* **be a** ∼:
(fig. coll.) einen ständig auf Trab halten (ugs.)
hand: ∼ **grenade** *n.* Handgranate, *die;*
∼**gun** *n.* Faustfeuerwaffe, *die;* ∼**-held** *adj.*
∼**-held camera** Handkamera, *die*
handicap /'hændıkæp/ ⓵ *n.* (a) (Sport, also
fig.) Handikap, *das*
(b) (physical) Behinderung, *die*
⓶ *v.t.,* **-pp-** benachteiligen
handicapped /'hændıkæpt/ *adj.*
[mentally/physically] ∼: [geistig/körperlich]
behindert
handicraft /'hændıkrɑːft/ *n.*
[Kunst]handwerk, *das;* (needlework, knitting,
etc.) Handarbeit, *die*
handiwork /'hændıwɜːk/ *n.*
handwerkliche Arbeit; **it's all his own** ∼:
das hat er selbst gemacht
handkerchief /'hæŋkətʃɪf/ *n., pl.* ∼**s** or
handkerchieves /'hæŋkətʃiːvz/ Taschentuch,
das
handle /'hændl/ ⓵ *n.* Griff, *der;* (of door)
Klinke, *die;* (of axe, brush, comb, broom,
saucepan) Stiel, *der;* (of cup, jug) Henkel, *der*
⓶ *v.t.* (a) (touch, feel) anfassen
(b) (control) handhaben ⟨*Fahrzeug, Flugzeug*⟩
(c) (deal/cope with) umgehen/fertig werden mit
'handlebars *n. pl.* Lenkstange, *die*
'handling charge /'hændlıŋ/ *n.*
(Commerc.) Bearbeitungsgebühr, *die*
hand: ∼ **lotion** *n.* Handlotion, *die;*
∼ **luggage** *n.* Handgepäck, *das;* ∼**made**
adj. handgearbeitet; ∼**over** *n.* Übergabe,
die; ∼**-painted** *adj.* handbemalt;
∼**picked** *adj.* sorgfältig ausgewählt; ∼**s-**
free *adj.* Freisprech⟨einrichtung, -betrieb⟩;
∼**s-free kit** Freisprechanlage, *die;*
Freisprecheinrichtung, *die;* ∼**shake** *n.*
Händedruck, *der*
handsome /'hænsəm/ *adj.* gut aussehend
hand: ∼**s-'on** *adj.* praktisch; ∼**stand** *n.*
Handstand, *der;* ∼ **towel** *n.*
[Hände]handtuch, *das;* ∼**writing** *n.*
[Hand]schrift, *die;* ∼**written** *adj.*
handgeschrieben; handschriftlich
handy /'hændı/ *adj.* greifbar; **keep/have**
sth. ∼: etw. greifbar haben
'handyman *n.* Handwerker, *der;* [home]
∼: Heimwerker, *der*
hang /hæŋ/ ⓵ *v.t.* (a) *p.t., p.p.* **hung** /hʌŋ/
hängen; aufhängen ⟨*Bild, Gardinen*⟩;
ankleben ⟨*Tapete*⟩
(b) *p.t., p.p.* **hanged** (execute) hängen (**for**
wegen); ∼ **oneself** sich erhängen
⓶ *v.i.,* **hung** (a) hängen; ⟨*Kleid usw.:*⟩ fallen
(b) (be executed) hängen

⓷ *n.* **get the** ∼ **of** sth. (coll.) mit etw.
klarkommen (ugs.)
■ **hang a'bout, hang a'round** *v.i.* (a)
(loiter) herumlungern (salopp)
(b) (coll.: wait) warten
■ **hang 'on** *v.i.* (a) sich festhalten (**to an**
+ *Dat.*)
(b) (coll.: wait) warten
(c) ∼ **on to** (coll.: keep) behalten
■ **hang 'out** ⓵ *v.t.* aufhängen ⟨*Wäsche*⟩
⓶ *v.i.* (a) heraushängen
(b) (coll.) (live) wohnen; (be often present) sich
herumtreiben (ugs.)
■ **hang 'up** *v.t.* ⓵ aufhängen
⓶ *v.i.* (Teleph.) auflegen
hangar /'hæŋə(r)/ *n.* Hangar, *der*
'hanger *n.* Bügel, *der*
hang: ∼**-glider** *n.* Hängegleiter, *der;*
Drachen, *der;* ∼**-glider pilot** Drachenflieger,
der/-fliegerin, *die;* ∼**-gliding** *n.*
Drachenfliegen, *das*
'hanging ⓵ *n.* (execution) Hinrichtung, *die*
[durch den Strang]
⓶ *adj.* ∼ **basket** Hängekorb, *der*
hang: ∼**man** /hæŋmən/ *n., pl.* ∼**men**
/hæŋmən/ Henker, *der;* ∼**over** *n.* Kater,
der (ugs.); ∼**-up** *n.* (coll.) Macke, *die* (ugs.)
hanker /'hæŋkə(r)/ *v.i.* ∼ **after** ein heftiges
Verlangen haben nach
hanky /'hæŋkı/ *n.* (coll.) Taschentuch, *das*
haphazard /hæp'hæzəd/ *adj.,*
hap'hazardly *adv.* willkürlich
happen /'hæpn/ *v.i.* geschehen;
⟨*Vorhergesagtes:*⟩ eintreffen; ∼ **to sb.** jmdm.
passieren; ∼ **to do sth./be sb.** zufällig etw.
tun/jmd. sein; **as it** ∼**s** or **it so** ∼**s I have** ...:
zufällig habe ich ...
'happening *n.* Ereignis, *das*
happily /'hæpılı/ *adv.* (a) glücklich
⟨*lächeln*⟩; vergnügt ⟨*spielen, lachen*⟩
(b) (gladly) mit Vergnügen
happiness /'hæpınıs/ *n.* ▶ HAPPY A: Glück,
das; Heiterkeit, *die;* Zufriedenheit, *die*
happy /'hæpı/ *adj.* (a) (joyful) glücklich;
heiter ⟨*Bild, Veranlagung*⟩; erfreulich
⟨*Erinnerung, Szene*⟩; froh ⟨*Ereignis*⟩;
(contented) zufrieden
(b) **be** ∼ **to do sth.** (glad) etw. gern tun
happy: ∼ **'ending** *n.* Happyend, *das;*
∼**-go-'lucky** *adj.* sorglos
harass /'hærəs/ *v.t.* schikanieren
harassed /'hærəst/ *adj.* geplagt (**with** von);
gequält ⟨*Blick, Ausdruck*⟩
'harassment *n.* Schikanierung, *die;*
sexual ∼: [sexuelle] Belästigung
harbour (*Brit.; Amer.:* **harbor**) /'hɑːbə(r)/
⓵ *n.* Hafen, *der;* **in** ∼: im Hafen
⓶ *v.t.* Unterschlupf gewähren (+ *Dat.*)
⟨*Verbrecher, Flüchtling*⟩; hegen (geh.) ⟨*Groll,
Verdacht*⟩
hard /hɑːd/ ⓵ *adj.* (a) hart; fest ⟨*Gelee*⟩;
stark ⟨*Regen*⟩; streng ⟨*Frost, Winter*⟩;
gesichert ⟨*Beweis, Daten*⟩ ····:·

(b) (difficult) schwer; **this is ~ to believe** das ist kaum zu glauben; **do sth. the ~ way** es sich (*Dat.*) bei etw. unnötig schwer machen
(c) (strenuous) hart
(d) (vigorous) kräftig ⟨*Schlag, Stoß, Tritt*⟩
(e) (harsh) hart
2 *adv.* (a) (strenuously) hart ⟨*arbeiten, trainieren*⟩; fleißig ⟨*studieren, üben*⟩; genau ⟨*überlegen*⟩; gut ⟨*aufpassen, zuhören*⟩; **try ~:** sich sehr bemühen
(b) (vigorously) heftig; fest ⟨*schlagen, drücken, klopfen*⟩
(c) (severely) hart; **be ~ up** knapp bei Kasse sein (ugs.); **feel ~ done by** sich schlecht behandelt fühlen

hard: ~back *n.* gebundene Ausgabe; **~board** *n.* Hartfaserplatte, *die;* **~-boiled** *adj.* (a) hart gekocht ⟨*Ei*⟩; (b) (tough) hartgesotten; **~ 'cash** *n.* in **~ cash** in bar ⟨*bezahlen*⟩; **~ copy** *n.* (Comp.) Hardcopy, *die;* **~-core** *attrib. adj.* hart ⟨*Pornographie*⟩; **~ court** *n.* (Tennis) Hartplatz, *der;* **~ 'currency** *n.* harte Währung; **~ 'disk** ▶ DISK A; **~ drug** *n.* harte Droge; **~-earned** *adj.* schwer verdient

harden /ˈhɑːdn/ **1** *v.t.* härten; (fig.) abhärten (**to** gegen)
2 *v.i.* hart werden; (become confirmed) sich verhärten

hardened /ˈhɑːdnd/ *adj.* abgehärtet (**to** gegen); hartgesotten ⟨*Verbrecher*⟩

hard: ~ 'hat *n.* Schutzhelm, *der;* **~-headed** *adj.* nüchtern; **~-hearted** *adj.* hartherzig (**towards** gegenüber); **~-'hitting** *adj.* (fig.) aggressiv ⟨*Rede, Politik, Kritik*⟩; **~ 'labour** *n.* Zwangsarbeit, *die*

hardly /ˈhɑːdlɪ/ *adv.* kaum; **~ anyone** *or* anybody/anything fast niemand/nichts; **~ ever** so gut wie nie; **~ at all** fast überhaupt nicht

'hardness *n.* Härte, *die*

hard: ~ porn (coll.)**, ~ pornography** *ns.* harte Pornographie; harte Pornos *Pl.* (ugs.); **~ 'pressed** *adj.* hart bedrängt; **be ~ pressed** große Schwierigkeiten haben; **~ sell** *n.* aggressive Verkaufsmethoden *Pl.*

'hardship *n.* (a) Not, *die;* Elend, *das*
(b) (instance) Notlage, *die*

hard: ~ 'shoulder *n.* (Brit.) Standspur, *die;* **~ware** *n.* (a) (goods) Eisenwaren *Pl.;* attrib. Eisenwaren⟨*geschäft*⟩; (b) (Comp.) Hardware, *die;* **~-wearing** *adj.* strapazierfähig; **~-working** *adj.* fleißig; **~wood** *n.* Hartholz, *das*

hardy /ˈhɑːdɪ/ *adj.* abgehärtet; zäh ⟨*Rasse*⟩; winterhart ⟨*Pflanze*⟩

hare /heə(r)/ *n.* Hase, *der*

harem /ˈhɑːriːm, hɑːˈriːm/ *n.* Harem, *der*

hark /hɑːk/ *v.i.* [just] **~ at him** hör ihn dir/ hört ihn euch nur an!; **~ back to** zurückkommen auf (+ *Akk.*)

harm /hɑːm/ **1** *n.* Schaden, *der;* **do sb. ~, do ~ to sb.** jmdm. schaden
2 *v.t.* etwas [zuleide] tun (+ *Dat.*); schaden (+ *Dat.*) ⟨*Beziehungen, Land, Ruf*⟩

harmful /ˈhɑːmfl/ *adj.* schädlich (**to** für)

'harmless *adj.* harmlos

harmonica /hɑːˈmɒnɪkə/ *n.* Mundharmonika, *die*

harmonious /hɑːˈməʊnɪəs/ *adj.* harmonisch

harmonize /ˈhɑːmənaɪz/ **1** *v.t.* aufeinander abstimmen
2 *v.i.* harmonieren (**with** mit)

harmony /ˈhɑːmənɪ/ *n.* Harmonie, *die;* **be in ~:** harmonieren

harness /ˈhɑːnɪs/ **1** *n.* Geschirr, *das*
2 *v.t.* anschirren; (fig.) nutzen

harp /hɑːp/ **1** *n.* Harfe, *die*
2 *v.i.* **~ on [about]** sth. immer wieder von etw. reden; (critically) auf etw. (*Dat.*) herumreiten (salopp)

harpoon /hɑːˈpuːn/ *n.* Harpune, *die*

harpsichord /ˈhɑːpsɪkɔːd/ *n.* Cembalo, *das*

harrowing /ˈhærəʊɪŋ/ *adj.* entsetzlich; grauenhaft ⟨*Anblick, Geschichte*⟩

harsh /hɑːʃ/ *adj.* (a) rau ⟨*Gewebe, Klima*⟩; schrill ⟨*Ton, Stimme*⟩; grell ⟨*Licht*⟩; hart ⟨*Bedingungen, Leben*⟩
(b) (excessively severe) [sehr] hart; [äußerst] streng ⟨*Disziplin*⟩; rücksichtslos ⟨*Tyrann, Herrscher, Politik*⟩

'harshly *adv.* [sehr] hart

harvest /ˈhɑːvɪst/ **1** *n.* Ernte, *die*
2 *v.t.* ernten

harvest 'festival *n.* Erntedankfest, *das*

has ▶ HAVE

has-been /ˈhæzbiːn/ *n.* (coll.) **be a ~:** seine besten Jahre hinter sich haben

hash /hæʃ/ *n.* (a) (Cookery) Haschee, *das*
(b) **make a ~ of sth.** (coll.) etw. verpfuschen (ugs.)

'hash browns *n. pl.:* Bratkartoffeln mit Zwiebeln; ≈ Rösti mit Zwiebeln

hashish /ˈhæʃɪʃ/ *n.* Haschisch, *das*

hasn't /ˈhæznt/ = **has not;** ▶ HAVE

hassle /ˈhæsl/ **1** *n.* Ärger, *der*
2 *v.t.* schikanieren

haste /heɪst/ *n.* Eile, *die;* (rush) Hast, *die;* **make ~:** sich beeilen

hasten /ˈheɪsn/ **1** *v.t.* beschleunigen
2 *v.i.* eilen

hastily /ˈheɪstɪlɪ/ *adv.* (hurriedly) eilig; (rashly) übereilt

hasty /ˈheɪstɪ/ *adj.* eilig; flüchtig ⟨*Skizze, Blick*⟩; (rash) übereilt

hat /hæt/ *n.* Hut, *der*

hatch¹ /hætʃ/ *n.* Luke, *die;* (serving ~) Durchreiche, *die*

hatch² **1** *v.t.* ausbrüten
2 *v.i.* [aus]schlüpfen

■ **hatch 'out** **1** *v.i.* ausschlüpfen
2 *v.t.* ausbrüten

'hatchback *n.* (car) Schräghecklimousine, *die*

hatchet /'hætʃɪt/ *n.* Beil, *das;* **bury the ~** (fig.) das Kriegsbeil begraben

hate /heɪt/ ⟨1⟩ *n.* Hass, *der*
⟨2⟩ *v.t.* hassen; **I ~ to say this** (coll.) ich sage das nicht gern

hateful /'heɪtfl/ *adj.* abscheulich

'hate mail *n.* hasserfüllte Briefe *Pl.*

'hatpin *n.* Hutnadel, *die*

hatred /'heɪtrɪd/ *n.* Hass, *der*

hat: ~stand *n.* Hutständer, *der;* **~ trick** *n.* Hattrick, *der*

haughty /'hɔːtɪ/ *adj.* hochmütig

haul /hɔːl/ ⟨1⟩ *v.i. & t.* ziehen
⟨2⟩ *n.* (a) Ziehen, *das*
(b) (catch) Fang, *der;* (fig.) Beute, *die*

haulage /'hɔːlɪdʒ/ *n.* Transport, *der*

haunch /hɔːntʃ/ *n.* **sit on one's/its ~es** auf seinem Hinterteil sitzen

haunt /hɔːnt/ *v.t.* **~ a house/castle** in einem Haus/Schloss spuken; **a ~ed house** ein Haus, in dem es spukt

'haunting *adj.* sehnsüchtig

have ⟨1⟩ /hæv/ *v.t., pres.* **he has** /hæz/, *p.t. & p.p.* **had** /hæd/ haben; (obtain) bekommen; (take) nehmen; bekommen ⟨Kind⟩; **~ breakfast/dinner/lunch** frühstücken/zu Abend/zu Mittag essen; **~ a cup of tea** eine Tasse Tee trinken; **~ sb. to stay** jmdn. zu Besuch haben; **you've had it now** (coll.) jetzt ist es aus (ugs.); **~ a game of football** Fußball spielen
⟨2⟩ /həv, əv, *stressed* hæv/ *v. aux.,* **he has** /həz, əz, *stressed* hæz/, **had** /həd, əd, *stressed* hæd/ **I ~/I had read** ich habe/hatte gelesen; **I ~/I had gone** ich bin/war gegangen; **if I had known ...:** wenn ich gewusst hätte ...; **~ sth. made** etw. machen lassen; **~ to** müssen
▪ **have 'on** *v.t.* (a) (wear) tragen
(b) (Brit. coll.: deceive) **~ sb. on** jmdn. auf den Arm nehmen (ugs.)
▪ **have 'out** *v.t.* (a) **~ a tooth/one's tonsils out** sich (*Dat.*) einen Zahn ziehen lassen/sich (*Dat.*) die Mandeln herausnehmen lassen
(b) **~ it out with sb.** mit jmdm. offen sprechen

haven /'heɪvn/ *n.* geschützte Anlegestelle, *die;* (fig.) Zufluchtsort, *der*

haven't /'hævnt/ = **have not;** ▶ HAVE

haversack /'hævəsæk/ *n.* Brotbeutel, *der*

havoc /'hævək/ *n.* (a) (devastation) Verwüstungen *Pl.;* **cause** *or* **wreak ~:** Verwüstungen anrichten
(b) (confusion) Chaos; **play ~ with sth.** etw. völlig durcheinander bringen

hawk[1] /hɔːk/ *n.* Falke, *der*

hawk[2] *v.t.* hausieren mit

'hawker *n.* Hausierer, *der*/Hausiererin, *die*

hawthorn /'hɔːθɔːn/ *n.* (Bot.) (white) Weißdorn, *der;* (red) Rotdorn, *der*

hay /heɪ/ *n.* Heu, *das*

hay: ~ fever *n.* Heuschnupfen, *der;* **~making** *n.* Heuernte, *die;* **~stack** *n.* Heuschober, *der* (südd.); Heudieme, *die* (nordd.); **~wire** *adj.* (coll.) **go ~wire** ⟨Instrument:⟩ verrückt spielen (ugs.)

hazard /'hæzəd/ ⟨1⟩ *n.* Gefahr, *die*
⟨2⟩ *v.t.* **~ a guess** es mit Raten probieren

'hazard lights *n. pl.* Warnblinkanlage, *die*

hazardous /'hæzədəs/ *adj.* gefährlich; **~ waste** Sondermüll, *der*

hazard 'warning lights ▶ HAZARD LIGHTS

haze /heɪz/ *n.* Dunst[schleier], *der*

hazel /'heɪzl/ *adj.* haselnussbraun

hazelnut /'heɪzlnʌt/ *n.* Haselnuss, *die*

hazy /'heɪzɪ/ *adj.* dunstig; (fig.) vage

HDTV *abbr.* = **high-definition television** HDTV

he /hi, *stressed* hiː/ *pron.* er

head /hed/ ⟨1⟩ *n.* (a) Kopf, *der;* **~ first** mit dem Kopf voran; **~ over heels** kopfüber; **keep/lose one's ~:** einen klaren Kopf behalten/den Kopf verlieren; **in one's ~:** im Kopf; **enter sb.'s ~:** jmdm. in den Sinn kommen; **use your ~:** gebrauch deinen Verstand; **a** *or* **per ~:** pro Kopf
(b) *in pl.* (on coin) **~s** Kopf; **~s or tails?** Kopf oder Zahl?
(c) (leader) Leiter, *der*/Leiterin, *die*
(d) (on beer) Blume, *die*
⟨2⟩ *attrib. adj.* **~ waiter** Oberkellner, *der;* **~ office** Hauptverwaltung, *die;* **~ boy/girl** ≈ Schulsprecher, *der*/-sprecherin, *die* (*vom Lehrkörper eingesetzt*)
⟨3⟩ *v.t.* (a) (stand at top of) anführen ⟨Liste⟩; (lead) leiten; führen ⟨Bewegung⟩
(b) (Football) köpfen
⟨4⟩ *v.i.* steuern; **~ for London** ⟨Flugzeug, Schiff:⟩ Kurs auf London nehmen; ⟨Auto:⟩ in Richtung London fahren; **you're ~ing for trouble** du wirst Ärger bekommen

head: ~ache *n.* Kopfschmerzen *Pl.;* **~band** *n.* Stirnband, *das;* **~board** *n.* Kopfende, *das;* **~ count** *n.* Kopfzahl, *die*

'header *n.* (Footb.) Kopfball, *der*

'headgear *n.* Kopfbedeckung, *die*

'heading *n.* Überschrift, *die*

head: ~lamp *n.* Scheinwerfer, *der;* **~land** *n.* Landspitze, *die;* **~light** *n.* Scheinwerfer, *der;* **~line** *n.* Schlagzeile, *die;* **be ~line news, make [the] ~lines, hit the ~lines** Schlagzeilen machen; **~long** *adv.* kopfüber; **~'master** *n.* Schulleiter, *der;* **~'mistress** *n.* Schulleiterin, *die;* **~ 'office** *n.* Hauptsitz, *der;* **~-on** ⟨1⟩ /'·-/ *adj.* frontal; Frontal⟨zusammenstoß⟩; ⟨2⟩ /'·-'/ *adv.* frontal; **~phones** *n. pl.* Kopfhörer, *der;* **~'quarters** *n. sing. or pl.* Hauptquartier, *das;* **~rest** *n.* Kopfstütze, *die;* **~room** *n.* [lichte] Höhe, *die;* **~scarf** *n.* Kopftuch, *das;* **~set** *n.* Kopfhörer, *der;* **~stone** *n.* (a) (gravestone) Grabstein, *der;* (b) (of building) Grundstein, *der;* (fig.) Grundpfeiler, *der;* **~strong** *adj.* ⋯⟩

eigensinnig; ~ **'teacher ▶** ~MASTER;
~MISTRESS; ~**way** n. make ~way
Fortschritte machen; ~ **wind** n.
Gegenwind, der

heady /'hedɪ/ adj. berauschend

heal /hiːl/ ① v.t. heilen
② v.i. ~ [up] [ver]heilen

healer /'hiːlə(r)/ n. (person) Heilkundige,
der/die

health /helθ/ n. Gesundheit, die; in good/
very good ~: bei guter/bester Gesundheit;
good or your ~! auf deine Gesundheit!

health: ~ **care** n. Gesundheitsfürsorge,
die; ~ care worker im Gesundheitswesen
Beschäftigte, der/die; inadequate ~ care
unzureichende medizinische Versorgung;
~ **centre** n. Poliklinik, die;
~ **certificate** n. Gesundheitszeugnis, das;
~ **check** n. Gesundheitsuntersuchung, die;
~ **farm** n. Gesundheitsfarm, die (ugs.);
~ **food** n. Reformhauskost, die; ~ food
shop Reformhaus, das; ~ **hazard** n.
Gesundheitsrisiko, das

healthily /'helθɪlɪ/ adv. gesund

health: ~ **insurance** n.
Krankenversicherung, die; ~ **resort** n.
Kurort, der; ~ **service** n.
Gesundheitsdienst, der; ~ **visitor** n.
Krankenschwester/-pfleger im Sozialdienst;
~ **warning** n. Warnhinweis, der; Hinweis
auf die Gesundheitsgefährdung

healthy /'helθɪ/ adj. gesund

heap /hiːp/ ① n. Haufen, der; ~s of (coll.)
jede Menge (ugs.)
② v.t. aufhäufen

hear /hɪə(r)/ ① v.t., **heard** /hɜːd/ (a) hören
(b) (understand) verstehen
② v.i., **heard:** ~ **about** sb./sth. von jmdm./
etw. [etwas] hören; he wouldn't ~ of it er
wollte nichts davon hören
③ int. H~! H~! bravo!; richtig!
■ **hear 'out** v.t. ausreden lassen

heard ▶ HEAR 1, 2

'hearing n. Gehör, das; be hard of ~:
schwerhörig sein

'hearing aid n. Hörgerät, das

hearsay /'hɪəseɪ/ n. Gerücht, das; it's only
~: es ist nur ein Gerücht

hearse /hɜːs/ n. Leichenwagen, der

heart /hɑːt/ n. (also Cards) Herz, das; by ~:
auswendig; at ~: im Grunde seines/ihres
Herzens; take/lose ~: Mut schöpfen/
verlieren; my ~ sank mein Mut sank; the
~ of the matter der wahre Kern der Sache;
see also CLUB 1C

heart: ~**ache** n. [seelische] Qual;
~ **attack** n. Herzanfall, der; (fatal)
Herzschlag, der; ~**beat** n. Herzschlag, der;
~**breaking** adj. herzzerreißend;
~**broken** adj. she was ~broken ihr Herz
war gebrochen; ~**burn** n. Sodbrennen, das;
~ **disease** n. Herzkrankheiten Pl.

hearten /'hɑːtn/ v.t. ermutigen

'heartening adj. ermutigend

heart: ~ **failure** n. Herzversagen, das;
~**felt** adj. tief empfunden ⟨Beileid⟩;
aufrichtig ⟨Dankbarkeit⟩

hearth /hɑːθ/ n.: Platz vor dem Kamin

'hearthrug n. Kaminvorleger, der

heartily /'hɑːtɪlɪ/ adv. von Herzen; eat ~:
tüchtig essen

'heartless adj. herzlos

heart: ~ **rate** n. Herzfrequenz, die;
~**-shaped** adj. herzförmig; ~**-throb** n.
Idol, das; ~ **transplant** n.
Herztransplantation, die (fachspr.);
~**-warming** adj. herzerfreuend

hearty /'hɑːtɪ/ adj. herzlich; ungeteilt
⟨Zustimmung⟩; herzhaft ⟨Mahlzeit⟩

heat /hiːt/ ① n. (a) (hotness) Hitze, die
(b) (Phys.) Wärme, die
(c) (Sport) Vorlauf, der
② v.t. heizen
■ **heat 'up** v.t. heiß machen

'heated adj. (angry) hitzig

'heater n. Ofen, der; (for water) Boiler, der

heath /hiːθ/ n. Heide, die

heathen /'hiːðn/ ① adj. heidnisch
② n. Heide, der/Heidin, die

heather /'heðə(r)/ n. Heidekraut, das

'heating n. Heizung, die

heat: ~**proof** adj. feuerfest; ~ **rash** n.
Hitzebläschen Pl.; ~**-resistant** adj.
hitzebeständig; ~**stroke** n. Hitzschlag, der;
~ **treatment** n. (Med.) Wärmebehandlung,
die; ~**wave** n. Hitzewelle, die

heave /hiːv/ ① v.t. (a) heben
(b) (coll.: throw) schmeißen (ugs.)
(c) ~ a sigh aufseufzen
② v.i. (pull) ziehen
③ n. Zug, der

heaven /'hevn/ n. Himmel, der; in ~: im
Himmel; for H~'s sake! um Gottes willen!

'heavenly adj. himmlisch

heavily /'hevɪlɪ/ adj. schwer; (to a great
extent) stark; schwer ⟨bewaffnet⟩; tief
⟨schlafen⟩; dicht ⟨bevölkert⟩; smoke/drink ~:
ein starker Raucher/Trinker sein; it rained/
snowed ~: es regnete/schneite stark

heavy /'hevɪ/ adj. schwer; unmäßig
⟨Trinken, Rauchen⟩; a ~ smoker/drinker ein
starker Raucher/Trinker; be a ~ sleeper
sehr fest schlafen

heavy: ~**-duty** adj. strapazierfähig
⟨Kleidung, Material⟩; schwer ⟨Werkzeug,
Maschine⟩; ~ **'goods vehicle** n. (Brit.)
Schwerlastwagen, der; ~**-'handed** adj.
(clumsy) ungeschickt ⟨Person⟩; ~ **'industry**
n. Schwerindustrie, die; ~ **'metal** n. (a)
Schwermetall, das; (b) (Mus.) Heavy metal,
das; ~**weight** n. Schwergewicht, das

Hebrew /'hiːbruː/ ① adj. hebräisch
② n. (language) Hebräisch, das

heckle /'hekl/ v.t. durch Zwischenrufe
unterbrechen

heckler /ˈheklə(r)/ *n.* Zwischenrufer, *der*/ Zwischenruferin, *die*

hectic /ˈhektɪk/ *adj.* hektisch

he'd /hɪd, *stressed* hi:d/ (a) = he had; (b) = he would

hedge /hedʒ/ 1 *n.* Hecke, *die*
2 *v.t.* ~ one's bets (fig.) nicht alles auf eine Karte setzen
3 *v.i.* sich nicht festlegen

'hedge clippers *n. pl.* Heckenschere, *die*

hedgehog /ˈhedʒhɒg/ *n.* Igel, *der*

'hedgerow *n.* Hecke, *die* [als Feldbegrenzung]

hedonism /ˈhi:dənɪzm/ *n.* Hedonismus, *der*

hedonist /ˈhi:dənɪst/ *n.* Hedonist, *der*/ Hedonistin, *die*

heed /hi:d/ 1 *v.t.* beachten; beherzigen ⟨Rat, Lektion⟩; ~ the danger/risk sich (*Dat.*) der Gefahr/des Risikos bewusst sein
2 *n.* give *or* pay ~ to, take ~ of Beachtung schenken (+ *Dat.*)

'heedless *adj.* unachtsam; be ~ of sth. auf etw. (*Akk.*) nicht achten

heel /hi:l/ *n.* Ferse, *die;* (of shoe) Absatz, *der; * Achilles' ~ (fig.) Achillesferse, *die;* down at ~ (fig.) heruntergekommen; take to one's ~s Fersengeld geben (ugs.)

hefty /ˈheftɪ/ *adj.* kräftig; (heavy) schwer

height /haɪt/ *n.* (a) Höhe, *die;* (of person, animal, building) Größe, *die* (b) (fig.: highest point) Höhepunkt, *der*

heighten /ˈhaɪtn/ *v.t.* aufstocken; (fig.) verstärken

heir /eə(r)/ *n.* Erbe, *der*/Erbin, *die*

heiress /ˈeərɪs/ *n.* Erbin, *die*

heirloom /ˈeəlu:m/ *n.* Erbstück, *das*

held ▶ HOLD² 1, 2

helicopter /ˈhelɪkɒptə(r)/ *n.* Hubschrauber, *der*

heliport /ˈhelɪpɔ:t/ *n.* Heliport, *der*

helium /ˈhi:lɪəm/ *n.* Helium, *das*

hell /hel/ *n.* (a) Hölle, *die* (b) (coll.) [oh] ~! verdammter Mist! (ugs.); what the ~! ach, zum Teufel! (ugs.); run like ~: wie der Teufel rennen (ugs.)

he'll /hɪl, *stressed* hi:l/ = he will

hello /həˈləʊ, heˈləʊ/ *int.* (greeting) hallo; (surprise) holla

hell's 'angel *n.* Rocker, *der*

helm /helm/ *n.* (Naut.) Ruder, *das*

helmet /ˈhelmɪt/ *n.* Helm, *der*

help /help/ 1 *v.t.* (a) ~ sb. [to do sth.] jmdm. helfen[, etw. zu tun]; can I ~ you? (in shop) was möchten Sie bitte? (b) (serve) ~ oneself sich bedienen; ~ oneself to sth. sich (*Dat.*) etw. nehmen; (coll.: steal) etw. mitgehen lassen (ugs.) (c) (avoid) if I/you can ~ it wenn es irgend zu vermeiden ist; (remedy) I can't ~ it ich kann nichts dafür (ugs.); it can't be ~ed es lässt sich nicht ändern (d) (refrain from) I can't ~ thinking *or* can't

~ but think that …: ich kann mir nicht helfen, ich glaube, …; I can't ~ laughing ich muss einfach lachen
2 *n.* Hilfe, *die;* with the ~ of …: mit Hilfe … (+ *Gen.*); be of [some]/no/much ~ to sb. jmdm. eine gewisse/keine/eine große Hilfe sein

■ **help 'out** 1 *v.i.* aushelfen
2 *v.t.* ~ sb. out jmdm. helfen

'help desk *n.* Help Desk, *das* (fachspr.); *Auskunftsstelle für Computerbenutzer*

'helper *n.* Helfer, *der*/Helferin, *die*

helpful /ˈhelpfl/ *adj.* (willing) hilfsbereit; (useful) hilfreich; nützlich

'helping 1 *adj.* lend [sb.] a ~ hand [with sth.] (fig.) [jmdm.] [bei etw.] helfen
2 *n.* Portion, *die*

'helpless *adj.*, **'helplessly** *adv.* hilflos

'helpline *n.* Hotline, *die*

helter-skelter /heltəˈskeltə(r)/ *n.* [spiralförmige] Rutschbahn

hem /hem/ 1 *n.* Saum, *der*
2 *v.t.,* -mm- säumen

■ **hem 'in** *v.t.* einschließen; feel ~med in sich eingeengt fühlen

hemisphere /ˈhemɪsfɪə(r)/ *n.* Halbkugel, *die*

'hemline *n.* Saum, *der*

hemo- (*Amer.*) ▶ HAEMO-

hemp /hemp/ *n.* Hanf, *der*

hen /hen/ *n.* Huhn, *das;* Henne, *die*

hence /hens/ *adv.* (therefore) daher

hence'forth *adv.* von nun an

henchman /ˈhentʃmən/ *n., pl.* henchmen /ˈhentʃmən/ Handlanger, *der*

hen: ~ party *n.* (coll.) [Damen]kränzchen, *das;* ~pecked /ˈhenpekt/ *adj.* a ~ husband ein Pantoffelheld, *der* (ugs.)

hepatitis /hepəˈtaɪtɪs/ *n.* (Med.) Leberentzündung, *die*

her¹ /hə(r), *stressed* hɜ:(r)/ *pron.* sie; *as indirect object* ihr; it was ~: sie wars

her² *poss. pron. attr.* ihr

herald /ˈherəld/ 1 *n.* Herold, *der*
2 *v.t.* ankündigen

heraldic /heˈrældɪk/ *adj.* heraldisch

heraldry /ˈherəldrɪ/ *n.* Heraldik, *die*

herb /hɜ:b/ *n.* Kraut, *das*

herbaceous /hɜ:ˈbeɪʃəs/ *adj.* krautartig; ~ border Staudenrabatte, *die*

herbal /ˈhɜ:bl/ *attrib. adj.* Kräuter-

herbivore /ˈhɜ:bɪvɔ:(r)/ *n.* Pflanzenfresser, *der*

'herb tea *n.* Kräuteraufguss, *der*

herd /hɜ:d/ 1 *n.* Herde, *die;* (of wild animals) Rudel, *das*
2 *v.t.* (a) treiben; ~ people together Menschen zusammenpferchen (b) (tend) hüten

here /hɪə(r)/ 1 *adv.* (a) (in or at this place) hier; down/in/up ~: hier unten/drin/oben; ~ you are (coll.: giving sth.) hier ⋯⟩

(b) (to this place) hierher; **in[to]** ~: hierherein; **come/bring** ~: hierher kommen/bringen
2 *int.* (attracting attention) he

here'by *adv.* (formal) hiermit

hereditary /hɪˈredɪtərɪ/ *adj.* **(a)** erblich ⟨*Titel, Amt*⟩
(b) (Biol.) angeboren

heresy /ˈherɪsɪ/ *n.* Ketzerei, *die*

heretic /ˈherɪtɪk/ *n.* Ketzer, *der*/Ketzerin, *die*

heretical /hɪˈretɪkl/ *adj.* ketzerisch

here'with *adv.* in der Anlage

heritage /ˈherɪtɪdʒ/ *n.* Erbe, *das*

hermetic /hɜːˈmetɪk/ *adj.* luftdicht

hermetically /hɜːˈmetɪkəlɪ/ *adv.* hermetisch

hermit /ˈhɜːmɪt/ *n.* Einsiedler, *der*/ Einsiedlerin, *die*

hernia /ˈhɜːnɪə/ *n.* Bruch, *der*

hero /ˈhɪərəʊ/ *n.*, *pl.* ~es Held, *der*

heroic /hɪˈrəʊɪk/ *adj.* heldenhaft

heroin /ˈherəʊɪn/ *n.* Heroin, *das*

heroine /ˈherəʊɪn/ *n.* Heldin, *die*

heroism /ˈherəʊɪzm/ *n.* Heldentum, *das*

heron /ˈhern/ *n.* Reiher, *der*

herpes /ˈhɜːpiːz/ *n.* (Med.) Herpes, *der*

herring /ˈherɪŋ/ *n.* Hering, *der*

hers /hɜːz/ *poss. pron. pred.* ihrer/ihre/ihres; **the book is** ~: das Buch gehört ihr

her'self *pron.* **(a)** *emphat.* selbst; **[all] by** ~: [ganz] allein[e]
(b) *refl.* sich; allein[e] ⟨*tun, wählen*⟩; **younger than/as heavy as** ~: jünger als/so schwer wie sie selbst

he's /hɪz, *stressed* hiːz/ **(a)** = he is; **(b)** = he has

hesitant /ˈhezɪtənt/ *adj.* zögernd ⟨*Reaktion*⟩; stockend ⟨*Rede*⟩

hesitate /ˈhezɪteɪt/ *v.i.* zögern; (falter) ins Stocken geraten; ~ **to do sth.** Bedenken haben, etw. zu tun

hesitation /hezɪˈteɪʃn/ *n.* **(a)** (indecision) Unentschlossenheit, *die;* **without** ~: ohne zu zögern
(b) (instance of faltering) Unsicherheit, *die*
(c) (reluctance) Bedenken *Pl.*

hetero /ˈhetərəʊ/ *n.* (coll.) **1** Hetero *der*/*die*

heterosexual /hetərəʊˈseksjʊəl/ **1** *adj.* heterosexuell
2 *n.* Heterosexuelle, *der*/*die*

het up /het ˈʌp/ *adj.* aufgeregt

hew /hjuː/ *v.t., p.p.* **hewn** /hjuːn/ *or* **hewed** /hjuːd/ hacken ⟨*Holz*⟩; losschlagen ⟨*Kohle, Gestein*⟩

hewn ▶ HEW

hexagon /ˈheksəgən/ *n.* Sechseck, *das*

hey /heɪ/ *int.* he; ~ **presto!** simsalabim!

heyday /ˈheɪdeɪ/ *n.* Blütezeit, *die*

HGV *abbr.* (Brit.) = **heavy goods vehicle**

hi /haɪ/ *int.* hallo (ugs.)

---

hiatus /haɪˈeɪtəs/ *n.* Unterbrechung, *die*

hibernate /ˈhaɪbəneɪt/ *v.i.* Winterschlaf halten

hibernation /haɪbəˈneɪʃn/ *n.* Winterschlaf, *der*

hiccup /ˈhɪkʌp/ **1** *n.* **(a)** Schluckauf, *der;* **have/get [the]** ~**s** den Schluckauf haben/ bekommen
(b) (fig.: stoppage) Störung, *die*
2 *v.i.* schlucksen (ugs.)

hid ▶ HIDE[1]

hidden ▶ HIDE[1]

hide[1] /haɪd/ **1** *v.t.,* **hid** /hɪd/, **hidden** /ˈhɪdn/ **(a)** verstecken ⟨*Gegenstand, Person usw.*⟩ (**from** vor + *Dat.*); verbergen ⟨*Gefühle, Sinn usw.*⟩ (**from** vor + *Dat.*); verheimlichen ⟨*Tatsache, Absicht usw.*⟩ (**from** *Dat.*)
(b) (obscure) verdecken
2 *v.i.,* **hid, hidden** sich verstecken (**from** vor + *Dat.*)

hide[2] *n.* Haut, *die;* (of furry animal) Fell, *das;* (dressed) Leder, *das*

hide-and-'seek *n.* Versteckspiel, *das;* **play** ~: Verstecken spielen

hideous /ˈhɪdɪəs/ *adj.* scheußlich

'hideout *n.* Versteck, *das*

hiding[1] /ˈhaɪdɪŋ/ *n.* **go into** ~: sich verstecken; (to avoid police, public attention) untertauchen; **be in** ~: sich versteckt halten; (to avoid police, public attention) untergetaucht sein

hiding[2] *n.* (coll.: beating) Tracht Prügel; **give sb. a [good]** ~: jmdm. eine [ordentliche] Tracht Prügel verpassen (ugs.)

'hiding place *n.* Versteck, *das*

hierarchic /haɪəˈrɑːkɪk/, **hierarchical** /haɪəˈrɑːkɪkl/ *adj.* hierarchisch

hierarchy /ˈhaɪərɑːkɪ/ *n.* Hierarchie, *die*

hi-fi /ˈhaɪfaɪ/ (coll.) **1** *adj.* Hi-Fi-
2 *n.* Hi-Fi-Anlage, *die*

high /haɪ/ **1** *adj.* **(a)** hoch; groß ⟨*Höhe*⟩; stark ⟨*Wind*⟩
(b) (coll.: on a drug) high (ugs.)
(c) it's ~ **time you left** es ist höchste Zeit, dass du gehst
2 *adv.* hoch; **search** *or* **look** ~ **and low** überall suchen
3 *n.* **(a)** (~est level/figure) Höchststand, *der*
(b) (Meteorol.) Hoch, *das*
(c) (coll.: drug-induced euphoria) Rausch[zustand], *der;* **give sb. a** ~ ⟨*Droge:*⟩ jmdn. high machen (ugs.)

high: ~**brow** **1** *n.* Intellektuelle, *der*/*die;*
2 *adj.* intellektuell ⟨*Person, Gerede usw.*⟩; hochgestochen (abwertend) ⟨*Person, Musik, Literatur usw.*⟩; ~ **chair** *n.* Hochstuhl, *der;*
~**-definition 'television** *n.* hoch auflösendes Fernsehen

higher edu'cation *n.* Hochschulbildung, *die*

high: ~ **fi'nance** *n.* Hochfinanz, *die;*
~**-'flier,** ~**-'flyer** *n.* (successful person) Senkrechtstarter, *der;* (person with great

high frequency ⋯⋗ hit ⋯⋅

potential) Hochbegabte, *der/die;*
~ **'frequency** *n.* Hochfrequenz, *die;*
~**-'handed** *adj.* selbstherrlich;
~**-heeled** /haɪ'hiːld/ *adj.* ⟨*Schuhe*⟩ mit
hohen Absätzen; ~**-income** *adj.*
einkommensstark; ~ **jump** *n.* Hochsprung,
der; ~**land** /'haɪlənd/ *n.* Hochland, *das;*
~**light** ⟨1⟩ *n.* (a) Höhepunkt, *der;* (b) (bright
area) Licht, *das;* ⟨2⟩ *v.t.,* ~**lighted** ein
Schlaglicht werfen auf (+ *Akk.*) ⟨*Probleme
usw.*⟩

'highly *adv.* sehr; hoch ⟨*angesehen, bezahlt*⟩;
hoch⟨*interessant, -gebildet*⟩; leicht
⟨*entzündlich*⟩; stark ⟨*gewürzt*⟩; **think** ~ **of
sb./sth.** eine hohe Meinung von jmdm./etw.
haben; **speak** ~ **of sb./sth.** jmdn./etw. sehr
loben

highly-strung /'haɪlɪstrʌŋ/ *adj.*
übererregbar

Highness /'haɪnɪs/ *n.* **His/her** *etc.* ~:
Seine/Ihre *usw.* Hoheit

high: ~**-pitched** /'haɪpɪtʃt/ *adj.* hoch
⟨*Ton, Stimme*⟩; ~**-powered** /'haɪpaʊəd/
adj. (forceful) dynamisch ⟨*Geschäftsmann*⟩;
~ **'pressure** *n.* (a) (Meteorol.) Hochdruck,
der; (b) (Mech. Engin.) Überdruck, *der;*
~**-rise** *adj.* ~**-rise building** Hochhaus, *das;*
~**-rise block of flats/office block** Wohn-/
Bürohochhaus, *das;* ~**-risk** *attrib. adj.*
risikoreich; Risiko⟨*gruppe, -sportart*⟩; **a**
~**-risk investment** eine Geldanlage mit
hohem Risiko; ~ **school** *n.* ≈ Oberschule,
die; ~ **'seas** *n. pl.* **the** ~ **seas** die hohe
See; ~ **season** *n.* Hochsaison, *die;*
~**-speed** *adj.* ~**-speed train**
Hochgeschwindigkeitszug, *der;* ~ **street**
n. Hauptstraße, *die;* ~ **'tech** (coll.)
▶ ~ TECHNOLOGY; ~**-tech** *adj.* (coll.)
Hightech-; ~ **tech'nology** *n.*
Spitzentechnologie, *die;* Hochtechnologie,
die; ~**-'voltage** *adj.* Hochspannungs-;
~**way** *n.* öffentliche Straße

hijack /'haɪdʒæk/ *v.t.* entführen

'hijacker *n.* Entführer, *der;* (of aircraft)
Hijacker, *der*

hike /haɪk/ *n.* Wanderung, *die*

'hiker *n.* Wanderer, *der/*Wanderin, *die*

hilarious /hɪ'leərɪəs/ *adj.* urkomisch

hill /hɪl/ *n.* Hügel, *der;* (higher) Berg, *der;*
(slope) Hang, *der*

hill: ~**billy** /'hɪlbɪlɪ/ *n.* (Amer.)
Hinterwäldler, *der/*Hinterwäldlerin, *die;*
~**side** *n.* Hang, *der;* ~**top** *n.* [Berg]gipfel,
der

'hilly *adj.* hüg[e]lig

hilt /hɪlt/ *n.* Griff, *der;* [up] **to the** ~ (fig.)
voll und ganz

him /ɪm, *stressed* hɪm/ *pron.* ihn; *as indirect
object* ihm; **it was** ~: er war's

Himalayas /hɪmə'leɪəz/ *pr. n. pl.*
Himalaya, *der*

him'self *pron.* (a) *emphat.* selbst
(b) *refl.* sich. *See also* HERSELF

hind /haɪnd/ *adj.* hinter...; ~ **legs**
Hinterbeine *Pl.*

hinder /'hɪndə(r)/ *v.t.* (impede) behindern;
(delay) verzögern ⟨*Vollendung einer Arbeit,
Vorgang*⟩; aufhalten ⟨*Person*⟩; ~ **sb. from
doing sth.** jmdn. daran hindern, etw. zu tun

'hindquarters *n. pl.* Hinterteil, *das*

hindrance /'hɪndrəns/ *n.* Hindernis, *das*
(to für)

'hindsight *n.* **with** [**the benefit of**] ~: im
Nachhinein

Hindu /'hɪnduː, hɪn'duː/ ⟨1⟩ *n.* Hindu, *der*
⟨2⟩ *adj.* hinduistisch; Hindu⟨*gott, -tempel*⟩

Hinduism /'hɪnduːɪzm/ *n.* Hinduismus, *der*

hinge /hɪndʒ/ ⟨1⟩ *n.* Scharnier, *das*
⟨2⟩ *v.t.* mit Scharnieren versehen
⟨3⟩ *v.i.* (depend) abhängen ([up]on von)

hint /hɪnt/ ⟨1⟩ *n.* (a) (suggestion) Wink, *der*
(b) (slight trace) Spur, *die* (of von); **the** ~/**no**
~ **of a smile** der Anflug/nicht die Spur eines
Lächelns
(c) (information) Tipp, *der* (on für)
⟨2⟩ *v.i.* ~ **at** andeuten

hip /hɪp/ *n.* Hüfte, *die*

hip: ~ **bone** *n.* Hüftbein, *das;* ~ **flask** *n.*
Taschenflasche, *die;* ~ **joint** *n.* Hüftgelenk,
das

hippie /'hɪpɪ/ *n.* (coll.) Hippie, *der*

hippopotamus /hɪpə'pɒtəməs/ *n.*
Nilpferd, *das*

hippy ▶ HIPPIE

hire /haɪə(r)/ ⟨1⟩ *n.* Mieten, *das;* **be on** ~ [**to
sb.**] [an jmdn.] vermietet sein; **for** ~: zu
vermieten
⟨2⟩ *v.t.* (a) (employ) anwerben; engagieren
⟨*Anwalt, Berater usw.*⟩
(b) (obtain use of) mieten; ~ **sth. from sb.**
etw. bei jmdm. mieten
(c) (grant use of) ~ [**out**] vermieten; ~ **sth.**
[**out**] **to sb.** etw. jmdm. *od.* an jmdn.
vermieten

hire: ~ **car** *n.* Mietwagen, *der;* ~
'purchase *n.* (Brit.) Ratenkauf, *der; attrib.*
Raten-; **pay for/buy sth. on** ~ **purchase** etw.
in Raten bezahlen/auf Raten kaufen

his /ɪz, *stressed* hɪz/ *poss. pron.* (a) *attrib.*
sein
(b) *pred.* seiner/seine/sein[e]s; *see also* HERS

hiss /hɪs/ ⟨1⟩ *n.* Zischen, *das*
⟨2⟩ *v.i.* zischen

historian /hɪ'stɔːrɪən/ *n.* Historiker, *der/*
Historikerin, *die*

historic /hɪ'stɒrɪk/ *adj.* historisch

historical /hɪ'stɒrɪkl/ *adj.* historisch;
geschichtlich ⟨*Belege, Hintergrund*⟩

history /'hɪstərɪ/ *n.* Geschichte, *die*

hit /hɪt/ ⟨1⟩ *v.t.,* **-tt-,** hit schlagen; (with missile)
treffen; ⟨*Geschoss, Ball usw.*⟩ treffen;
⟨*Fahrzeug:*⟩ prallen gegen; ⟨*Schiff:*⟩ laufen
gegen; ~ **one's head on sth.** mit dem Kopf
gegen etw. stoßen; ~ **it off with sb.** gut mit
jmdm. auskommen
⟨2⟩ *v.i.,* **-tt-,** hit schlagen ⋯⋗

3 *n.* **(a)** (blow) Schlag, *der;* (shot or bomb striking target) Treffer, *der*
(b) (success) Erfolg, *der;* (in entertainment) Schlager, *der;* Hit, *der* (ugs.)
■ **hit 'back** *v.t. & i.* zurückschlagen
■ **'hit [up]on** *v.t.* kommen auf (+ *Akk.*) ⟨*Idee*⟩; finden ⟨*richtige Antwort, Methode*⟩
hit-and-'run *adj.* unfallflüchtig ⟨*Fahrer*⟩; ~ **accident** Unfall mit Fahrerflucht

hitch /hɪtʃ/ **1** *v.t.* **(a)** binden ⟨*Seil*⟩ (round um + *Akk.*); [an]koppeln ⟨*Anhänger usw.*⟩ (to an + *Akk.*); spannen ⟨*Zugtier usw.*⟩ (to vor + *Akk.*).
(b) ~ **a lift** *or* **ride** (coll.) per Anhalter fahren
2 *n.* (problem) Problem, *das*
■ **hitch 'up** *v.t.* hochheben ⟨*Rock*⟩
'hitch-hike *v.i.* per Anhalter fahren
'hitch-hiker *n.* Anhalter, *der*/Anhalterin, *die*

hit: ~ **man** *n.* (Amer.) Killer, *der* (salopp); ~**-or-'miss** *adj.* (coll.: random) unsicher, unzuverlässig ⟨*Methode*⟩; ~ **parade** *n.* Hitparade, *die;* ~ **'record** *n.* Hit, *der* (ugs.)

HIV *abbr.* = **human immunodeficiency virus** HIV; ~**-positive/-negative** HIV-positiv/-negativ

hive /haɪv/ *n.* [Bienen]stock, *der*

HMS *abbr.* (Brit.) = **Her/His Majesty's Ship** H.M.S.

hoard /hɔːd/ **1** *n.* Vorrat, *der*
2 *v.t.* ~ **[up]** horten; hamstern ⟨*Lebensmittel*⟩

hoarding /'hɔːdɪŋ/ *n.* (fence) Bauzaun, *der;* (Brit.: for advertisements) Reklamewand, *die*

hoar frost /'hɔːfrɒst/ *n.* [Rau]reif, *der*

hoarse /hɔːs/ *adj.* heiser

hoax /həʊks/ **1** *v.t.* anführen (ugs.); foppen
2 *n.* (deception) Schwindel, *der;* (practical joke) Streich, *der;* (false alarm) blinder Alarm

hob /hɒb/ *n.* [Koch]platte, *die*

hobble /'hɒbl/ *v.i.* ~ **[about]** [herum]humpeln

hobby /'hɒbɪ/ *n.* Hobby, *das*

'hobby horse *n.* Steckenpferd, *das*

hobnailed /'hɒbneɪld/ *adj.* Nagel⟨*schuh, -stiefel*⟩

hobo /'həʊbəʊ/ *n., pl.* **-es** (Amer.) Landstreicher, *der*/-streicherin, *die*

hockey /'hɒkɪ/ *n.* Hockey, *das*

'hockey stick *n.* Hockeyschläger, *der*

hoe /həʊ/ **1** *n.* Hacke, *die*
2 *v.t. & i.* hacken

hog /hɒg/ **1** *n.* [Mast]schwein
2 *v.t.,* **-gg-** (coll.) mit Beschlag belegen

hoist /hɔɪst/ **1** *v.t.* hochziehen, hissen ⟨*Flagge usw.*⟩; hieven ⟨*Last*⟩; setzen ⟨*Segel*⟩
2 *n.* [Lasten]aufzug, *der*

hold[1] /həʊld/ *n.* (of ship) Laderaum, *der;* (of aircraft) Frachtraum, *der*

hold[2] **1** *v.t.,* held /held/ **(a)** halten; (carry)

tragen; (keep fast) festhalten; ~ **the door open for sb.** jmdm. die Tür aufhalten; ~ **sth. in place** etw. halten
(b) (contain) enthalten; (be able to contain) fassen ⟨*Liter, Personen usw.*⟩
(c) (possess) besitzen; haben
(d) (keep possession of) halten ⟨*Stützpunkt, Stadt, Stellung*⟩; ~ **the line** (Teleph.) am Apparat bleiben; ~ **one's own** sich behaupten
(e) (cause to take place) stattfinden lassen; abhalten ⟨*Veranstaltung, Konferenz, Gottesdienst, Sitzung*⟩; veranstalten ⟨*Festival, Auktion*⟩; austragen ⟨*Meisterschaften*⟩; führen ⟨*Unterhaltung, Gespräch*⟩; durchführen ⟨*Untersuchung*⟩; halten ⟨*Vortrag, Rede*⟩
(f) (think, believe) ~ **a view** *or* **an opinion** eine Ansicht haben (on über + *Akk.*); ~ **that ...:** der Ansicht sein, dass ...; ~ **oneself responsible for sth.** sich für etw. verantwortlich fühlen; ~ **sth. against sb.** jmdm. etw. vorwerfen
2 *v.i.,* held halten; ⟨*Wetter:*⟩ sich halten
3 *n.* **(a)** (grasp) Griff, *der;* **grab** *or* **seize** ~ **of sth.** etw. ergreifen; **get** *or* **lay** *or* **take** ~ **of sth.** etw. fassen *od.* packen; **keep** ~ **of sth.** etw. festhalten; **get** ~ **of sth.** (fig.) etw. auftreiben; **get** ~ **of sb.** (fig.) jmdn. erreichen
(b) (influence) Einfluss, *der* (on, over auf + *Akk.*)
(c) (Sport) Griff, *der*
■ **hold 'back** **1** *v.t.* zurückhalten
2 *v.i.* zögern
■ **hold 'on** **1** *v.t.* [fest]halten
2 *v.i.* **(a)** sich festhalten; ~ **on to** sich festhalten an (+ *Dat.*); (keep) behalten
(b) (coll.: wait) warten
■ **hold 'out** **1** *v.t.* ausstrecken ⟨*Hand, Arm usw.*⟩; hinhalten ⟨*Tasse, Teller*⟩
2 *v.i.* (resist) sich halten
■ **hold 'up** *v.t.* **(a)** (raise) hochhalten; heben ⟨*Hand, Kopf*⟩
(b) (delay) aufhalten
(c) (rob) überfallen
■ **'hold with** *v.t.* **not** ~ **with sth.** etw. ablehnen

'holdall *n.* Reisetasche, *die*

'holder *n.* **(a)** (of post, title) Inhaber, *der*/Inhaberin, *die*
(b) ⟨*Zigaretten*⟩spitze, *die;* ⟨*Papier-, Zahnputzglas*⟩halter, *der*

'hold-up *n.* **(a)** (robbery) [Raub]überfall, *der*
(b) (delay) Verzögerung, *die*

hole /həʊl/ *n.* Loch, *das;* (of fox, badger, rabbit) Bau, *der;* **pick** ~**s in** (fig.) zerpflücken (ugs.)

holiday /'hɒlɪdeɪ/ *n.* **(a)** [arbeits]freier Tag; (public ~) Feiertag, *der*
(b) *in sing. or pl.* (Brit.: vacation) Urlaub, *der;* (Sch.) [Schul]ferien *Pl.*

holiday: ~ **home** *n.* Feriendomizil, *das;* ~ **job** *n.* Ferienjob, *der;* ~**maker** *n.* Urlauber, *der*/Urlauberin, *die;* ~ **resort** *n.* Ferienort, *der;* ~ **season** *n.* Urlaubszeit, *die*

Holland /'hɒlənd/ *pr. n.* Holland (*das*)

hollow /ˈhɒləʊ/ [1] *adj.* hohl; eingefallen ‹*Wangen, Schläfen*›; (fig.) leer ‹*Versprechen*›
[2] *n.* [Boden]senke, *die*
[3] *v.t.* ~ **out** aushöhlen

holly /ˈhɒlɪ/ *n.* Stechpalme, *die*

holocaust /ˈhɒləkɔːst/ *n.* (destruction) Massenvernichtung, *die;* **the H~**: der Holocaust

hologram /ˈhɒləɡræm/ *n.* Hologramm, *der*

holster /ˈhəʊlstə(r)/ *n.* [Pistolen]halfter, *die od. das*

holy /ˈhəʊlɪ/ *adj.* heilig

Holy: H~ ˈ**Bible** *n.* Heilige Schrift; ~ ˈ**Ghost** ▶ ~ SPIRIT; ~ **Land** *n.* the ~ **Land** das Heilige Land; ~ ˈ**Spirit** *n.* Heiliger Geist

homage /ˈhɒmɪdʒ/ *n.* Huldigung, *die* (**to** an + *Akk.*); **pay** *or* **do** ~ **to sb./sth.** jmdm./einer Sache huldigen

home /həʊm/ [1] *n.* (a) Heim, *das;* (flat) Wohnung, *die;* (house) Haus, *das;* (household) [Eltern]haus, *das;* (native country) Heimat, *die;* **at** ~: zu Hause; **be/feel at** ~: (fig.) sich wohl fühlen; **make yourself at** ~: fühl dich wie zu Hause
(b) (institution) Heim, *das*
[2] *adj.* (a) Haus-
(b) (Sport) Heim-; ~ **match** Heimspiel, *das*
[3] *adv.* nach Hause

home: ~ ˈ**address** *n.* Privatanschrift, *die;* ~ ˈ**banking** *n.* Homebanking, *das;* ~**-based** /ˈhəʊmbeɪst/ *adj.* zu Hause arbeitend; **be** ~**-based** zu Hause arbeiten; seinen Arbeitsplatz zu Hause haben; ~**coming** *n.* Heimkehr, *die;* ~ **com'puter** *n.* Heimcomputer, *der;* ~ ˈ**ground** *n.* **on** ~ **ground** auf heimischem Boden; (fig.) zu Hause (ugs.); ~**-grown** *adj.* selbst gezogen; ~**land** *n.* Heimat, *die;* ~**land security** (esp. Amer.) Heimatschutz, *der*

ˈ**homeless** [1] *adj.* obdachlos
[2] *n. pl.* **the** ~: die Obdachlosen *Pl.*

ˈ**homelessness** *n.* Obdachlosigkeit, *die*

homely /ˈhəʊmlɪ/ *adj.* wohnlich ‹*Zimmer usw.*›; behaglich ‹*Atmosphäre*›

home: ~**-made** *adj.* selbst gemacht; selbst gebacken ‹*Brot*›; hausgemacht ‹*Lebensmittel*›; **H~ Office** *n.* (Brit.) Innenministerium, *das*

homeopathic *etc.* (Amer.) ▶ HOMOEO-

home: ~**owner** *n.* Eigenheimbesitzer, *der/*-besitzerin, *die;* ~ **page** *n.* (Comp.) Homepage, *die;* **H~** ˈ**Secretary** *n.* (Brit.) Innenminister, *der;* ~ ˈ**shopping** *n.* Teleshopping, *das;* ~**sick** *adj.* heimwehkrank; **become/be** ~**sick** Heimweh bekommen/haben; ~**sickness** *n.* Heimweh, *das;* ~ ˈ**town** *n.* Heimatstadt, *die;* ~**work** *n.* Hausaufgaben *Pl.;* **piece of** ~**work** Hausaufgabe, *die*

homicide /ˈhɒmɪsaɪd/ *n.* Tötung, *die;* (manslaughter) Totschlag, *der*

homoeopathic /həʊmɪəˈpæθɪk, hɒmɪəˈpæθɪk/ *adj.* homöopathisch

homoeopathy /həʊmɪˈɒpəθɪ, hɒmɪˈɒpəθɪ/ *n.* Homöopathie, *die*

homosexual /həʊməʊˈseksjʊəl/ [1] *adj.* homosexuell
[2] *n.* Homosexuelle, *der/die*

homosexu'ality *n.* Homosexualität, *die*

hone /həʊn/ *v.t.* wetzen

honest /ˈɒnɪst/ *adj.* ehrlich

ˈ**honestly** *adv.* ehrlich; redlich ‹*handeln*›; ~! ehrlich!; (annoyed) also wirklich!

honesty /ˈɒnɪstɪ/ *n.* Ehrlichkeit, *die*

honey /ˈhʌnɪ/ *n.* Honig, *der*

honey: ~ **bee** *n.* Honigbiene, *die;* ~**comb** *n.* Honigwabe, *die;* ~**moon** *n.* Flitterwochen *Pl.;* (journey) Hochzeitsreise, *die;* ~**suckle** *n.* Geißblatt, *das*

honk /hɒŋk/ [1] *v.i.* ‹*Fahrzeug, Fahrer:*› hupen
[2] *n.* Hupen, *das*

honor, honorable (Amer.) ▶ HONOUR, HONOURABLE

honorary /ˈɒnərərɪ/ *adj.* Ehren‹*mitglied, -präsident, -doktor, -bürger*›

honour /ˈɒnə(r)/ (Brit.) [1] *n.* (a) Ehre, *die*
(b) (distinction) Auszeichnung, *die*
[2] *v.t.* ehren; (Commerc.) honorieren

honourable /ˈɒnərəbl/ *adj.* (Brit.) ehrenwert (geh.)

ˈ**honours degree** *n.* Examen mit Auszeichnung

hood /hʊd/ *n.* (a) Kapuze, *die*
(b) (Amer. Motor Veh.) Motorhaube, *die*
(c) (of pram) Verdeck, *das*

hoodlum /ˈhuːdləm/ *n.* Rowdy, *der*

hoodwink /ˈhʊdwɪŋk/ *v.t.* hinters Licht führen

hoof /huːf/ *n., pl.* ~**s** *or* **hooves** /huːvz/ Huf, *der*

hook /hʊk/ [1] *n.* Haken, *der;* **by** ~ **or by crook** mit allen Mitteln
[2] *v.t.* (a) (grasp) mit Haken/mit einem Haken greifen
(b) (fasten) mit Haken/mit einem Haken befestigen (**to** an + *Dat.*)
(c) **be** ~**ed [on sth.]** (addicted) [von etw.] abhängig sein; (harmlessly) auf etw. (*Akk.*) stehen (ugs.)

■ **hook 'up** *v.t.* festhaken (**to** an + *Akk.*)

hooligan /ˈhuːlɪɡən/ *n.* Rowdy, *der*

hooliganism /ˈhuːlɪɡənɪzm/ *n.* Rowdytum, *das*

hoop /huːp/ *n.* Reifen, *der*

hooray /hʊˈreɪ/ *int.* hurra

hoot /huːt/ [1] *v.i.* (a) (call out) johlen
(b) ‹*Eule:*› schreien
(c) ‹*Fahrzeug, Fahrer:*› hupen
[2] *n.* (a) (shout) ~**s of derision** verächtliches Gejohle
(b) (of owl) Schrei, *der*   ⋯⟡

'hooter n. (Brit.: siren) Sirene, die
hoover /'hu:və(r)/ (Brit.) **1** n. (a) H~ ®
[Hoover]staubsauger, der
(b) (made by any company) Staubsauger, der
2 v.t. staubsaugen
hooves pl. of HOOF
hop¹ /hɒp/ n. (a) (plant) Hopfen, der
(b) in pl. (Brewing) Hopfen, der
hop² **1** v.i., -pp-: (a) hüpfen; ⟨Hase:⟩
hoppeln
(b) (fig. coll.) ~ out of bed aus dem Bett
springen; ~ into the car/on [to] the bus/train
sich ins Auto/in den Bus/Zug schwingen
(ugs.)
2 v.t., -pp- (Brit. coll.) ~ it sich verziehen
(ugs.)
3 n. (a) Hüpfer, der
(b) (Brit. coll.) catch sb. on the ~: jmdn.
überraschen
hope /həʊp/ **1** n. Hoffnung, die; sb.'s ~[s]
of sth. jmds. Hoffnung auf etw. (Akk.); raise
sb.'s ~s jmdm. Hoffnung machen
2 v.i. & t. hoffen (for auf + Akk.); I ~ so/not
hoffentlich/hoffentlich nicht; ~ for the best
das Beste hoffen
hopeful /'həʊpfl/ adj. (a) zuversichtlich; be
~ of sth./of doing sth. auf etw. (Akk.) hoffen/
voller Hoffnung sein, etw. zu tun
(b) (promising) viel versprechend
'hopefully adv. (a) (expectantly) voller
Hoffnung
(b) (coll.: it is hoped that) hoffentlich
'hopeless adj., **'hopelessly** adv. (a)
hoffnungslos
(b) (inadequate) miserabel
'hopelessness n. Hoffnungslosigkeit, die
hopscotch /'hɒpskɒtʃ/ n. Himmel-und-
Hölle-Spiel, das
horde /hɔ:d/ n. Horde, die
horizon /hə'raɪzn/ n. Horizont, der; on the
~: am Horizont; (fig.) broaden one's/sb.'s ~s
seinen/jmds. Horizont erweitern
horizontal /hɒrɪ'zɒntl/ adj. horizontal;
waagerecht
hori'zontally adv. horizontal; (flat)
waagerecht
hormone /'hɔ:məʊn/ n. Hormon, das
hormone re'placement therapy n.
Hormonsubstitutionstherapie, die
horn /hɔ:n/ n. Horn, das; (of vehicle) Hupe, die
hornet /'hɔ:nɪt/ n. Hornisse, die
'horny adj. (hard) hornig
horoscope /'hɒrəskəʊp/ n. Horoskop, das
horrendous /hə'rendəs/ adj. (coll.)
schrecklich (ugs.)
horrible /'hɒrɪbl/ adj. grauenhaft; grausig
⟨Monster⟩; grauenvoll ⟨Verbrechen,
Albtraum⟩
horrid /'hɒrɪd/ adj. scheußlich
horrific /hə'rɪfɪk/ adj. schrecklich
horrify /'hɒrɪfaɪ/ v.t. mit Schrecken
erfüllen; be horrified (shocked, scandalized)
entsetzt sein (at, by über + Akk.)

'horrifying adj. grauenhaft
horror /'hɒrə(r)/ **1** n. Entsetzen, das (at
über + Akk.); (repugnance) Grausen, das;
(horrifying thing) Gräuel, der
2 attrib. adj. Horror-; ~ film/story
Horrorfilm, der/-geschichte, die
'horror-stricken, 'horror-struck adjs.
von Entsetzen gepackt
hors d'œuvre /ɔ:'dɜ:vr/ n. Horsd'œuvre,
das; ≈ Vorspeise, die
horse /hɔ:s/ n. Pferd, das
horse: ~**back** n. on ~back zu Pferd;
~ '**chestnut** n. Rosskastanie, die; ~**fly** n.
Pferdebremse, die; ~**man** /'hɔ:smən/ n., pl.
~**men** /'hɔ:smən/ ([skilled] rider) [guter] Reiter;
~**play** n. Balgerei, die; ~**power** n., pl.
same (Mech.) Pferdestärke, die; ~**racing** n.
Pferderennsport, der; ~**radish** n.
Meerrettich, der; ~**shoe** n. Hufeisen, das
horticulture /'hɔ:tɪkʌltʃə(r)/ n. Gartenbau,
der
hose /həʊz/, **'hosepipe** ns. Schlauch, der
hospice /'hɒspɪs/ n. (Brit.: for the terminally ill)
Sterbehospiz, das
hospitable /hɒ'spɪtəbl/ adj. gastfreundlich
⟨Person, Wesensart⟩; be ~ to sb. jmdn.
gastfreundlich aufnehmen
hospital /'hɒspɪtl/ n. Krankenhaus, das; in
~ (Brit.), in the ~ (Amer.) im Krankenhaus
'hospital bed n. Krankenhausbett, das
hospitality /hɒspɪ'tælɪtɪ/ n.
Gastfreundschaft, die
'hospital nurse n. ≈ Krankenschwester,
die
host¹ /həʊst/ n. (large number) Menge, die; a
~ of people/children eine Menge Leute/eine
Schar von Kindern
host² n. Gastgeber, der/-geberin, die
hostage /'hɒstɪdʒ/ n. Geisel, die
'host country n. Gastland, das
hostel /'hɒstl/ n. (Brit.) Wohnheim, das
hostess /'həʊstɪs/ n. Gastgeberin, die; (in
nightclub) Animierdame, die
hostile /'hɒstaɪl/ adj. (a) feindlich
(b) (unfriendly) feindselig (to[wards]
gegenüber); be ~ to sth. etw. ablehnen
hostility /hɒ'stɪlɪtɪ/ n. Feindseligkeit, die
hot /hɒt/ adj. (a) heiß; warm ⟨Mahlzeit,
Essen⟩; I am/feel ~: mir ist heiß
(b) (pungent) scharf ⟨Gewürz, Senf usw.⟩;
scharf gewürzt ⟨Essen⟩
(c) (recent) noch warm ⟨Nachrichten⟩
(d) (coll.: illegally obtained) heiß ⟨Ware, Geld⟩
hot: ~ '**air** n. (coll.) leeres Gerede (ugs.);
~**bed** n. (Hort.) Mistbeet, das; (fig.: of vice,
corruption) Brutstätte, die (of für)
hotchpotch /'hɒtʃpɒtʃ/ n. Mischmasch,
der (ugs.) (of aus)
hot: ~-**desking** n.: Mehrfachnutzung von
Arbeitsplätzen; ~ **dog** n. (coll.) Hotdog, der
od. das
hotel /həʊ'tel/ n. Hotel, das

hotelier /hə'telɪə(r)/ n. Hotelier, *der*

ho'tel room n. Hotelzimmer, *das*

hot: ~**head** n. Hitzkopf, *der;* ~**house** n. Treibhaus, *das;* ~ **line** n. Hotline, *die;* (Polit.) heißer Draht

'**hotly** *adv.* heftig

hot: ~**plate** n. Kochplatte, *die;* (to keep food ~) Warmhalteplatte, *die;* ~ **seat** n. (coll.) be in the ~ seat den Kopf hinhalten müssen (ugs.); ~**-tempered** *adj.* heißblütig; ~**-'water bottle** n. Wärmflasche, *die*

hound /haʊnd/ ⃞1 n. Jagdhund, *der* ⃞2 *v.t.* verfolgen

hour /'aʊə(r)/ n. (a) Stunde, *die;* half an ~: eine halbe Stunde; an ~ and a half anderthalb Stunden; **be paid by the** ~: stundenweise bezahlt werden; **the 24-**~ **clock** die Vierundzwanzigstundenuhr **(b)** (time o'clock) Zeit, *die;* **the small** ~**s** [of the morning] die frühen Morgenstunden; **0100/ 0200/1700/1800** ~**s** (on 24-~ clock) 1.00/2.00/ 17.00/18.00 Uhr

'**hourly** *adj., adv.* stündlich; **be paid** ~: stundenweise bezahlt werden

house ⃞1 /haʊs/ *n., pl.* ~**s** /'haʊzɪz/ Haus, *das;* **to/at my** ~: zu mir [nach Hause]/bei mir [zu Hause] ⃞2 /haʊz/ *v.t.* **(a)** ein Heim geben (+ *Dat.*) **(b)** (keep, store) unterbringen

house/haʊs/**:** ~ **arrest** n. Hausarrest, *der;* ~**-boat** n. Hausboot, *das;* ~**-bound** *adj.* ans Haus gefesselt

household /'haʊshəʊld/ n. Haushalt, *der; attrib.* Haushalts-

'**householder** n. Wohnungsinhaber, *der/* -inhaberin, *die*

household 'name n. geläufiger Name; **be a** ~: ein Begriff sein

house /haʊs/**:** ~ **husband** n. Hausmann, *der;* ~**keeper** n. Haushälterin, *die;* ~**keeping** n. Hauswirtschaft, *die;* ~ **plant** n. Zimmerpflanze, *die;* ~**-proud** *adj.* he/she is ~-proud Ordnung und Sauberkeit [im Haushalt] gehen ihm/ihr über alles; ~**-sit** *v.i.* das Haus hüten; ~**-sitter** n. Housesitter, *der* (ugs.); *Person, die für jemanden das Haus hütet;* ~**-trained** *adj.* (Brit.) stubenrein ‹Hund, Katze›; ~**-warming** n. ~**-warming [party]** Einzugsfeier, *die;* ~**wife** n. Hausfrau, *die;* ~**work** n. Hausarbeit, *die*

housing /'haʊzɪŋ/ n. (dwellings) Wohnungen Pl.; (provision of dwellings) Wohnungsbeschaffung, *die*

housing: ~ **association** n. (Brit.) Gesellschaft für sozialen Wohnungsbau; ~ **benefit** n. (Brit.) Wohngeld, *das;* ~ **estate** n. (Brit.) Wohnsiedlung, *die;* ~ **shortage** n. Wohnraummangel, *der*

hovel /'hɒvl/ n. [armselige] Hütte

hover /'hɒvə(r)/ *v.i.* **(a)** schweben **(b)** (linger) sich herumdrücken (ugs.)

'**hovercraft** n., *pl. same* Hovercraft, *das;* Luftkissenfahrzeug, *das*

'**hover mower** n. Luftkissenmäher, *der*

how /haʊ/ *adv.* wie; **learn** ~ **to ride a bike/ swim** Rad fahren/schwimmen lernen; ~ '**are you?** wie geht es dir?; (greeting) guten Morgen/Tag/Abend!; ~ **do you 'do?** (formal) guten Morgen/Tag/Abend!; ~ **much?** wieviel?; ~ **many?** wie viel?; wie viele?

however /haʊ'evə(r)/ *adv.* **(a)** wie … auch **(b)** (nevertheless) jedoch; aber

howl /haʊl/ ⃞1 n. (of animal) Heulen, *das;* (of distress) Schrei, *der;* ~s **of laughter** brüllendes Gelächter ⃞2 *v.i.* ‹Tier, Wind:› heulen; (with distress) schreien ⃞3 *v.t.* [hinaus]schreien

howler /'haʊlə(r)/ n. (coll.: blunder) Schnitzer, *der* (ugs.)

HP *abbr.* (Brit.) = **hire purchase**

HQ *abbr.* = **headquarters** HQ

HTML *abbr.* (Comp.) = **hypertext markup language** HTML

hub /hʌb/ n. [Rad]nabe, *die;* (fig.) Mittelpunkt, *der*

hubbub /'hʌbʌb/ n. Lärm, *der;* a ~ **of voices** ein Stimmengewirr

hub: ~**cap** n. Radkappe, *die;* ~ **dynamo** n. Nabendynamo, *der;* ~ **gear** n. Nabenschaltung, *die*

huddle /'hʌdl/ *v.i.* sich drängen; ~ **together** sich zusammendrängen
▪ **huddle 'up** *v.i.* (nestle up) sich zusammenkauern; (crowd together) sich [zusammen]drängen

hue¹ /hju:/ n. Farbton, *der*

hue² n. ~ **and cry** lautes Geschrei; (protest) Gezeter, *das*

huff /hʌf/ ⃞1 *v.i.* ~ **and puff** schnaufen und keuchen ⃞2 n. **in a** ~: beleidigt

hug /hʌg/ ⃞1 n. Umarmung, *die;* **give sb. a** ~: jmdn. umarmen ⃞2 *v.t.,* **-gg-** umarmen

huge /hju:dʒ/ *adj.* riesig; gewaltig ‹Unterschied, Verbesserung, Interesse›

hulking /'hʌlkɪŋ/ *adj.* (coll.) ~ **great** klobig

hull /hʌl/ n. (Naut.) Schiffskörper, *der*

hum /hʌm/ ⃞1 *v.i.,* **-mm-:** **(a)** summen; ‹Maschine:› brummen **(b)** ~ **and haw** (coll.) herumdrucksen (ugs.) ⃞2 *v.t.,* **-mm-** summen ⃞3 n. **(a)** Summen, *das;* (of machinery) Brummen, *das* **(b)** (of voices, conversation) Gemurmel, *das;* (of traffic) Brausen, *das*

human /'hju:mən/ ⃞1 *adj.* menschlich; **the** ~ **race** die menschliche Rasse ⃞2 n. Mensch, *der*

human 'being n. Mensch, *der*

humane /hju:'meɪn/ *adj.* human

humanitarian /hju:mænɪ'teərɪən/ *adj.* humanitär

humanity /hju:ˈmænɪtɪ/ n. **(a)** (mankind) Menschheit, die; (people collectively) Menschen Pl.
(b) (being humane) Humanität, die
human 'rights n. pl. Menschenrechte Pl.; ∼ **activist** Menschenrechtsaktivist, der/-aktivistin, die; ∼ **group** Menschenrechtsorganisation, die
humble /ˈhʌmbl/ **1** adj. **(a)** demütig
(b) (modest) bescheiden
(c) (low-ranking) einfach; niedrig ⟨Status, Rang⟩
2 v.t. **(a)** demütigen; ∼ **oneself** sich demütigen od. erniedrigen
(b) (defeat decisively) [vernichtend] schlagen
humbly /ˈhʌmblɪ/ adv. demütig
humdrum /ˈhʌmdrʌm/ adj. alltäglich; eintönig ⟨Leben⟩
humid /ˈhju:mɪd/ adj. feucht
humidifier /hju:ˈmɪdɪfaɪə(r)/ n. Luftbefeuchter, der
humidify /hju:ˈmɪdɪfaɪ/ v.t. befeuchten
humidity /hju:ˈmɪdɪtɪ/ n. Feuchtigkeit, die
humiliate /hju:ˈmɪlɪeɪt/ v.t. demütigen
humiliation /hju:mɪlɪˈeɪʃn/ n. Demütigung, die
humility /hju:ˈmɪlɪtɪ/ n. Demut, die
humor (Amer.) ▶ HUMOUR
humorous /ˈhju:mərəs/ adj. lustig, komisch ⟨Geschichte, Name, Situation⟩; witzig ⟨Bemerkung⟩
humour /ˈhju:mə(r)/ (Brit.) **1** n. **(a)** Humor, der; **sense of** ∼: Sinn für Humor; **have no sense of** ∼: keinen Humor haben
(b) (mood) Laune, die
2 v.t. ∼ **sb.** jmdm. seinen Willen lassen
hump /hʌmp/ **1** n. **(a)** (of person) Buckel, der; (of animal) Höcker, der
(b) (mound) Hügel, der
2 v.t. (Brit. coll.: carry) schleppen
humpback 'bridge n. gewölbte Brücke
hunch¹ /hʌntʃ/ v.t. ∼ **[up]** hochziehen
hunch² n. (feeling) Gefühl, das
'hunchback n. (back) Buckel, der; (person) Bucklige, der/die; **be a** ∼: einen Buckel haben
hundred /ˈhʌndrəd/ **1** adj. hundert; **a** or **one** ∼: [ein]hundert; **two/several** ∼: zweihundert/mehrere hundert; **a** or **one** ∼ **and one** [ein]hundert[und]eins
2 n. **(a)** (number) hundert; **a** or **one/two** ∼: [ein]hundert/zweihundert
(b) (written figure; group) Hundert, das
(c) (indefinite amount) ∼s Hunderte. See also EIGHT
hundredth /ˈhʌndrədθ/ **1** adj. hundertst...; **a** ∼ **part** ein Hundertstel
2 n. (fraction) Hundertstel, das; (in sequence, rank) Hundertste, der/die/das
'hundredweight n., pl. same (Brit.) 50,8 kg; ≈ Zentner, der
hung ▶ HANG 1, 2
Hungarian /hʌŋˈgeərɪən/ **1** adj. ungarisch; **sb. is** ∼: jmd. ist Ungar/Ungarin
2 n. **(a)** (person) Ungar, der/Ungarin, die

(b) (language) Ungarisch, das; see also ENGLISH 2A
Hungary /ˈhʌŋgərɪ/ pr. n. Ungarn (das)
hunger /ˈhʌŋgə(r)/ **1** n. Hunger, der
2 v.i. ∼ **after** or **for sb./sth.** [heftiges] Verlangen nach jmdm./etw. haben
'hunger strike n. Hungerstreik, der; **go on** ∼: in den Hungerstreik treten
hung 'over adj. (coll.) verkatert (ugs.)
hungry /ˈhʌŋgrɪ/ adj. hungrig; **be** ∼: Hunger haben; **go** ∼: hungern
hunk /hʌŋk/ n. [großes] Stück
hunt /hʌnt/ **1** n. Jagd, die; (search) Suche, die
2 v.t. jagen; (search for) Jagd machen auf (+ Akk.) ⟨Mörder usw.⟩
3 v.i. jagen; **go** ∼**ing** auf die Jagd gehen; ∼ **after** or **for** Jagd machen auf (+ Akk.); (seek) suchen
'hunter n. Jäger, der
'hunting n. die Jagd (**of** auf + Akk.); (searching) Suche, die (**for** nach)
hurdle /ˈhɜ:dl/ n. Hürde, die
hurl /hɜ:l/ v.t. werfen; (violently) schleudern; ∼ **insults at sb.** jmdm. Beleidigungen ins Gesicht schleudern
hurly-burly /ˈhɜ:lɪbɜ:lɪ/ n. Tumult, der; **the** ∼ **of city life** der Großstadttrummel (ugs.)
hurrah /hʊˈrɑː/, **hurray** /hʊˈreɪ/ int. hurra
hurricane /ˈhʌrɪkən/ n. (tropical cyclone) Hurrikan, der; (storm, lit. or fig.) Orkan, der
hurried /ˈhʌrɪd/ adj. eilig; überstürzt ⟨Abreise⟩; in Eile ausgeführt ⟨Arbeit⟩
hurry /ˈhʌrɪ/ **1** n. Eile, die; **in a** ∼: eilig; **be in a** ∼: es eilig haben; **there's no** ∼: es eilt nicht
2 v.t. antreiben ⟨Person⟩; hinunterschlingen ⟨Essen⟩; ∼ **one's work** seine Arbeit in zu großer Eile erledigen
3 v.i. sich beeilen; (to or from place) eilen
■ **hurry 'up** **1** v.i. sich beeilen
2 v.t. antreiben
hurt /hɜ:t/ **1** v.t., hurt **(a)** wehtun (+ Dat.); (injure) verletzen; ∼ **oneself** sich (Dat.) weh tun; (injure oneself) sich verletzen; ∼ **one's arm/back** sich (Dat.) am Arm/Rücken wehtun; (injure) sich (Dat.) den Arm/am Rücken verletzen
(b) (damage, be detrimental to) schaden (+ Dat.)
(c) (upset) verletzen ⟨Person, Stolz⟩
2 v.i., hurt **(a)** wehtun
(b) (cause damage, be detrimental) schaden
3 adj. gekränkt ⟨Tonfall, Miene⟩
4 n. (emotional pain) Schmerz, der
hurtful /ˈhɜ:tfl/ adj. verletzend
hurtle /ˈhɜ:tl/ v.i. rasen (ugs.)
husband /ˈhʌzbənd/ n. Ehemann, der; **my/your/her** ∼: mein/dein/ihr Mann; ∼ **and wife** Mann und Frau
hush /hʌʃ/ **1** n. (silence) Schweigen, das; (stillness) Stille, die
2 v.t. (silence) zum Schweigen bringen; (still) beruhigen
3 v.i. still sein; ∼! still!

■ **hush 'up** *v.t.* vertuschen

husk /hʌsk/ *n.* Spelze, *die*

husky¹ /'hʌskɪ/ *adj.* heiser

husky² *n.* Eskimohund, *der*

hustle /'hʌsl/ ⟦1⟧ *v.t.* drängen (**into** zu) ⟦2⟧ *n.* ∼ **and bustle** geschäftiges Treiben

hut /hʌt/ *n.* Hütte, *die*

hutch /hʌtʃ/ *n.* Stall, *der*

hyacinth /'haɪəsɪnθ/ *n.* Hyazinthe, *die*

hybrid /'haɪbrɪd/ ⟦1⟧ *n.* Hybride, *die od. der* (**between** aus); (fig.: mixture) Mischung, *die* ⟦2⟧ *adj.* hybrid ⟨*Züchtung*⟩

'hybrid bike *n.* Crossrad, *das*

hydrangea /haɪ'dreɪndʒə/ *n.* Hortensie, *die*

hydrant /'haɪdrənt/ *n.* Hydrant, *der*

hydraulic /haɪ'drɔːlɪk/ *adj.* hydraulisch

hydrochloric acid /haɪdrəklɔːrɪk 'æsɪd/ *n.* Salzsäure, *die*

hydroelectric /haɪdrəʊɪ'lektrɪk/ *adj.* hydroelektrisch; ∼ **power station** Wasserkraftwerk, *das*

hydrofoil /'haɪdrəfɔɪl/ *n.* Tragflächenboot, *das*

hydrogen /'haɪdrədʒən/ *n.* Wasserstoff, *der;* ∼ **bomb** Wasserstoffbombe, *die*

hyena /haɪ'iːnə/ *n.* Hyäne, *die*

hygiene /'haɪdʒiːn/ *n.* Hygiene, *die*

hygienic /haɪ'dʒiːnɪk/ *adj.* hygienisch

hymn /hɪm/ *n.* Hymne, *die;* (sung in service) Kirchenlied, *das*

'hymn book *n.* Gesangbuch, *das*

hyper /'haɪpə(r)/ *adj.* (coll.) aufgedreht (ugs.)

hyperactive /haɪpə'ræktɪv/ *adj.* überaktiv

hyperbole /haɪ'pɜːbəlɪ/ *n.* Hyperbel, *die*

hyper: ∼**link** *n.* (Comp.) Hyperlink, *der;* ∼**market** *n.* (Brit.) Verbrauchermarkt, *der;* ∼**text** *n.* (Comp.) Hypertext, *der;* ∼**'ventilate** *v.i.* hyperventilieren

hyphen /'haɪfn/ ⟦1⟧ *n.* Bindestrich, *der* ⟦2⟧ *v.t.* mit Bindestrich schreiben

hyphenate /'haɪfəneɪt/ ▶ HYPHEN 2

hyphenation /haɪfə'neɪʃn/ *n.* Kopplung, *die*

hypnosis /hɪp'nəʊsɪs/ *n., pl.* **hypnoses** /hɪp'nəʊsiːz/ Hypnose, *die;* (act, process) Hypnotisierung, *die;* **under** ∼: in Hypnose (*Dat.*)

hypnotic /hɪp'nɒtɪk/ *adj.* hypnotisch

hypnotism /'hɪpnətɪzm/ *n.* Hypnotik, *die;* (act) Hypnotisieren, *das*

hypnotist /'hɪpnətɪst/ *n.* Hypnotiseur, *der/* Hypnotiseurin, *die*

hypnotize /'hɪpnətaɪz/ *v.t.* hypnotisieren

hypochondria /haɪpə'kɒndrɪə/ *n.* Hypochondrie, *die*

hypochondriac /haɪpə'kɒndrɪæk/ *n.* Hypochonder, *der*

hypocrisy /hɪ'pɒkrɪsɪ/ *n.* Heuchelei, *die*

hypocrite /'hɪpəkrɪt/ *n.* Heuchler, *der/* Heuchlerin, *die*

hypocritical /hɪpə'krɪtɪkl/ *adj.* heuchlerisch

hypodermic /haɪpə'dɜːmɪk/ *adj. & n.* ∼ [**syringe**] Injektionsspritze, *die*

hypotenuse /haɪ'pɒtənjuːz/ *n.* Hypotenuse, *die*

hypothermia /haɪpə'θɜːmɪə/ *n.* (Med.) Hypothermie, *die* (fachspr.); Unterkühlung, *die*

hypothesis /haɪ'pɒθɪsɪs/ *n., pl.* **hypotheses** /haɪ'pɒθɪsiːz/ Hypothese, *die*

hypothetical /haɪpə'θetɪkl/ *adj.* hypothetisch

hysterectomy /hɪstə'rektəmɪ/ *n.* (Med.) Hysterektomie, *die* (fachspr.)

hysteria /hɪ'stɪərɪə/ *n.* Hysterie, *die*

hysterical /hɪ'sterɪkl/ *adj.* hysterisch

hysterics /hɪ'sterɪks/ *n. pl.* (laughter) hysterischer Lachanfall; (crying) hysterischer Weinkrampf; **have** ∼: hysterisch lachen/ weinen

• •

I i

• •

I¹, i /aɪ/ *n.* I, i, *das*

I² *pron.* ich

ice /aɪs/ ⟦1⟧ *n.* (a) Eis, *das;* **feel/be like** ∼ (be very cold) eiskalt sein (b) (∼ cream) [Speise]eis, *das;* **an** ∼/**two** ∼**s** ein/zwei Eis ⟦2⟧ *v.t.* glasieren ⟨*Kuchen*⟩

■ **ice 'over, ice 'up** *v.i.* ⟨*Gewässer:*⟩ zufrieren

'ice age *n.* Eiszeit, *die*

iceberg /'aɪsbɜːg/ *n.* Eisberg, *der*

ice: ∼**box** *n.* (Amer.) Kühlschrank, *der;* ∼ **bucket** *n.* Eisbehälter, *der;* ∼**cold** *adj.* eiskalt; ∼ **'cream** *n.* Eis, *das;* Eiscreme, *die;* **one** ∼ **cream/two/too many** ∼ **creams** ein/zwei/zu viel Eis; ∼ **'cream parlour** *n.* Eisdiele, *die;* ∼ **cube** *n.* Eiswürfel, *die;* ∼ **hockey** *n.* Eishockey, *das*

Iceland /'aɪslənd/ *pr. n.* Island (*das*)

Icelandic /aɪsˈlændɪk/ ① *adj.* isländisch
② *n.* Isländisch, *das; see also* ENGLISH 2A

ice: ~ **'lolly** *n.* Eis am Stiel; ~ **rink** *n.*
Eisbahn, *die;* ~ **skate** *n.* Schlittschuh, *der;*
~**skate** *v.i.* Schlittschuh laufen;
~ **skating** *n.* Schlittschuhlaufen, *das*

icicle /'aɪsɪkl/ *n.* Eiszapfen, *der*

icing /'aɪsɪŋ/ *n.* Zuckerguss, *der*

'icing sugar *n.* (Brit.) Puderzucker, *der*

icon /'aɪkɒn/ *n.* (a) Ikone, *die*
(b) (Comp.) Icon, *das*

icy /'aɪsɪ/ *adj.* (a) vereist ⟨Berge, Landschaft,
Straße⟩; eisreich ⟨Region, Land⟩; in
~ **conditions** bei Eis
(b) (very cold) eiskalt; eisig; (fig.) frostig

I'd /aɪd/ (a) = I had;
(b) = I would

idea /aɪˈdɪə/ *n.* Idee, *die;* Gedanke, *der;*
(mental picture) Vorstellung, *die;* (vague notion)
Ahnung, *die;* **have you any** ~ [of] **how ...?**
weißt du ungefähr, wie ...?; **have no** ~ [of]
where ...: keine Ahnung haben, wo ...; **not
have the slightest** *or* **faintest** ~: nicht die
leiseste Ahnung haben

ideal /aɪˈdɪəl/ ① *adj.* ideal; vollendet
⟨Ehemann, Gastgeber⟩; vollkommen ⟨Welt⟩
② *n.* Ideal, *das*

idealism /aɪˈdɪəlɪzm/ *n.* Idealismus, *der*

idealist /aɪˈdɪəlɪst/ *n.* Idealist, *der/*
Idealistin, *die*

idealistic /aɪdɪəˈlɪstɪk/ *adj.* idealistisch

idealize /aɪˈdɪəlaɪz/ *v.t.* idealisieren

ideally /aɪˈdɪəlɪ/ *adv.* ideal; ~, ...:
idealerweise *od.* im Idealfall ...

identical /aɪˈdentɪkl/ *adj.* identisch; **be** ~:
sich (*Dat.*) völlig gleichen; ~ **twins** eineiige
Zwillinge

identification /aɪdentɪfɪˈkeɪʃn/ *n.*
Identifizierung, *die;* (of plants, animals)
Bestimmung, *die*

identifi'cation parade *n.* (Brit.)
Gegenüberstellung [zur Identifizierung], *die*

identify /aɪˈdentɪfaɪ/ ① *v.t.* identifizieren;
bestimmen ⟨Pflanze, Tier⟩
② *v.i.* ~ **with sb.** sich mit jmdm.
identifizieren

Identikit ® /aɪˈdentɪkɪt/ *n.* Phantombild,
das

identity /aɪˈdentɪtɪ/ *n.* Identität, *die;* **proof
of** ~: Identitätsnachweis, *der;* [**case of**]
mistaken ~: [Personen]verwechslung, *die*

identity: ~ **card** *n.* [Personal]ausweis,
der; ~ **crisis** *n.* Identitätskrise, *die;*
~ **parade** ▶ IDENTIFICATION PARADE;
~ **theft** *n.* Identitätsdiebstahl, *der*

ideological /aɪdɪəˈlɒdʒɪkl/ *adj.* ideologisch

ideology /aɪdɪˈɒlədʒɪ/ *n.* Ideologie, *die*

idiocy /'ɪdɪəsɪ/ *n.* Idiotie, *die*

idiom /'ɪdɪəm/ *n.* [Rede]wendung, *die*

idiomatic /ɪdɪəˈmætɪk/ *adj.* idiomatisch

idiosyncrasy /ɪdɪəˈsɪŋkrəsɪ/ *n.*
Eigentümlichkeit, *die*

idiosyncratic /ɪdɪəsɪŋˈkrætɪk/ *adj.*
eigenwillig

idiot /'ɪdɪət/ *n.* Idiot, *der* (ugs.)

idiotic /ɪdɪˈɒtɪk/ *adj.* idiotisch (ugs.)

idle /'aɪdl/ ① *adj.* (a) (lazy) faul
(b) (not in use) außer Betrieb *nachgestellt;* **be**
~ ⟨Maschinen, Fabrik:⟩ stillstehen
(c) bloß ⟨Neugier, Spekulation⟩; leer
⟨Geschwätz⟩
② *v.i.* ⟨Motor:⟩ leer laufen

▪ **idle a'way** *v.t.* vertun

'idleness *n.* Faulheit, *die*

idol /'aɪdl/ *n.* Idol, *das*

idolize /'aɪdəlaɪz/ *v.t.* vergöttern

idyllic /ɪˈdɪlɪk/ *adj.* idyllisch

i.e. /aɪˈiː/ *abbr.* = **that is** d.h.; i.e.

if /ɪf/ *conj.* (a) wenn; **if anyone should ask ...:**
falls jemand fragt, ...; **if I knew what to do ...:**
wenn ich wüsste, was ich tun soll ...; **if I
were you** an deiner Stelle; **if so/not** wenn ja/
nein *od.* nicht; **if then/that/at all** wenn
überhaupt; **if** als ob; **if I only knew, if only
I knew!** wenn ich das nur wüsste!; **if it isn't
Ronnie!** das ist doch Ronnie!
(b) (whenever) [immer] wenn
(c) (whether) ob
(d) (though) auch *od.* selbst wenn
(e) (despite being) wenn auch

iffy /'ɪfɪ/ *adj.* (coll.) ungewiss; zweifelhaft

igloo /'ɪɡluː/ *n.* Iglu, *der od. das*

ignite /ɪɡˈnaɪt/ ① *v.t.* anzünden
② *v.i.* sich entzünden

ignition /ɪɡˈnɪʃn/ *n.* (a) (igniting) Zünden, *das*
(b) (Motor Veh.) Zündung, *die;* ~ **key**
Zündschlüssel, *der*

ignorance /'ɪɡnərəns/ *n.* Unwissenheit,
die; **keep sb. in** ~ **of sth.** jmdn. in
Unkenntnis über etw. (*Akk.*) lassen

ignorant /'ɪɡnərənt/ *adj.* unwissend; **be**
~ **of sth.** (uninformed) über etw. (*Akk.*) nicht
informiert sein

ignore /ɪɡˈnɔː(r)/ *v.t.* ignorieren; nicht
befolgen ⟨Befehl, Rat⟩; übergehen ⟨Frage,
Bemerkung⟩

ill /ɪl/ ① *adj.,* **worse** /wɜːs/, **worst** /wɜːst/
krank; **fall** ~: krank werden
② *adv.* **be** ~ **at ease** sich nicht wohl fühlen
③ *n.* Übel, *das*

I'll /aɪl/ (a) = I shall
(b) = I will

'ill-advised *adj.* unklug

illegal /ɪˈliːɡl/ *adj.,* **il'legally** *adv.* illegal

il'legal immigrant *n.* illegaler
Einwanderer/illegale Einwanderin

illegality /ɪlɪˈɡælɪtɪ/ *n.* Ungesetzlichkeit, *die*

illegible /ɪˈledʒɪbl/ *adj.* unleserlich

illegitimate /ɪlɪˈdʒɪtɪmət/ *adj.* unehelich
⟨Kind⟩

ill 'health n. schwache Gesundheit

illicit /ɪˈlɪsɪt/ adj. unerlaubt ⟨Beziehung, [Geschlechts]verkehr⟩; Schwarz⟨handel, -verkauf, -arbeit⟩

'ill-informed adj. schlecht informiert

illiteracy /ɪˈlɪtərəsɪ/ n. Analphabetentum, das

illiterate /ɪˈlɪtərət/ adj. des Lesens und Schreibens unkundig; analphabetisch ⟨Bevölkerung⟩

illness /ˈɪlnɪs/ n. Krankheit, die

illogical /ɪˈlɒdʒɪkl/ adj. unlogisch

ill-'treat v.t. misshandeln

ill-'treatment n. Misshandlung, die

illuminate /ɪˈluːmɪneɪt/ v.t. beleuchten

illuminating /ɪˈluːmɪneɪtɪŋ/ adj. aufschlussreich

illumination /ɪluːmɪˈneɪʃn/ n. Beleuchtung, die

illusion /ɪˈluːʒn/ n. Illusion, die; **be under the** ∼ **that** ...: sich (Dat.) einbilden, dass ...

illusory /ɪˈluːsərɪ/ adj. illusorisch

illustrate /ˈɪləstreɪt/ v.t. (a) (serve as example of) veranschaulichen
(b) illustrieren ⟨Buch, Erklärung⟩

illustration /ɪləˈstreɪʃn/ n. (a) (example) Beispiel, das (of für)
(b) (picture) Abbildung, die

illustrious /ɪˈlʌstrɪəs/ adj. berühmt ⟨Person⟩

ill 'will n. Böswilligkeit, die

I'm /aɪm/ = I am

image /ˈɪmɪdʒ/ n. (a) Bildnis, das (geh.)
(b) (Optics) Bild, das
(c) [public] ∼: Image, das

'image-conscious adj. imagebewusst

imaginable /ɪˈmædʒɪnəbl/ adj. **the best solution** ∼: die denkbar beste Lösung

imaginary /ɪˈmædʒɪnərɪ/ adj. imaginär (geh.); eingebildet ⟨Krankheit⟩

imagination /ɪmædʒɪˈneɪʃn/ n. (a) Fantasie, die
(b) (fancy) Einbildung, die

imaginative /ɪˈmædʒɪnətɪv/ adj. fantasievoll; (showing imagination) einfallsreich

imagine /ɪˈmædʒɪn/ v.t. (a) sich (Dat.) vorstellen
(b) (suppose) glauben
(c) (get the impression) ∼ **that** ...: sich (Dat.) einbilden[, dass ...]

imbalance /ɪmˈbæləns/ n. Unausgeglichenheit, die

imbecile /ˈɪmbɪsiːl/ n. Idiot, der (ugs.)

IMF abbr. = **International Monetary Fund** IWF, der

imitate /ˈɪmɪteɪt/ v.t. nachahmen

imitation /ɪmɪˈteɪʃn/ n. (a) Nachahmung, die
(b) (counterfeit) Imitation, die

immaculate /ɪˈmækjʊlət/ adj. (spotless) makellos; (faultless) tadellos

immaterial /ɪməˈtɪərɪəl/ adj. unerheblich

immature /ɪməˈtjʊə(r)/ adj. unreif; noch nicht voll entwickelt ⟨Lebewesen⟩

immaturity /ɪməˈtjʊərɪtɪ/ n. Unreife, die

immediate /ɪˈmiːdjət/ adj. (a) unmittelbar; (nearest) nächst... ⟨Nachbar[schaft], Umgebung, Zukunft⟩; engst... ⟨Familie⟩
(b) (occurring at once) prompt; unverzüglich ⟨Handeln, Maßnahmen⟩; umgehend ⟨Antwort⟩

im'mediately ① adv. (a) unmittelbar
(b) (without delay) sofort
② conj. sobald

immemorial /ɪmɪˈmɔːrɪəl/ adj. **from time** ∼: seit undenklichen Zeiten

immense /ɪˈmens/ adj. (a) ungeheuer
(b) (coll.: great) enorm

im'mensely adv. (a) ungeheuer
(b) (coll.: very much) unheimlich (ugs.)

immerse /ɪˈmɜːs/ v.t. [ein]tauchen; **be** ∼**d in thought/one's work** in Gedanken versunken/in seine Arbeit vertieft sein

immersion /ɪˈmɜːʃn/ n. Eintauchen, das

im'mersion heater n. Heißwasserbereiter, der

immigrant /ˈɪmɪɡrənt/ ① n. Einwanderer, der/Einwanderin, die
② adj. Einwanderer-; ∼ **workers** ausländische Arbeitnehmer Pl.

immigration /ɪmɪˈɡreɪʃn/ n. Einwanderung die (into nach, from aus); attrib. Einwanderungs⟨kontrolle, -gesetz⟩; ∼ **officer** Beamter/Beamtin der Einwanderungsbehörde; ∼ **authorities** Einwanderungsbehörden Pl.; **go through** ∼: durch die Passkontrolle gehen

imminent /ˈɪmɪnənt/ adj. unmittelbar bevorstehend; drohend ⟨Gefahr⟩; **be** ∼: unmittelbar bevorstehen/drohen

immobile /ɪˈməʊbaɪl/ adj. (immovable) unbeweglich

immobilize /ɪˈməʊbɪlaɪz/ v.t. verankern; (fig.) lähmen

immobilizer /ɪˈməʊbɪlaɪzə(r)/ n. (Motor Veh.) Wegfahrsperre, die

immodest /ɪˈmɒdɪst/ adj. unbescheiden; (improper) unanständig

immoral /ɪˈmɒrəl/ adj. unmoralisch; (in sexual matters) sittenlos

immorality /ɪməˈrælɪtɪ/ n. Unmoral, die; (in sexual matters) Sittenlosigkeit, die

immortal /ɪˈmɔːtl/ adj. unsterblich

immortality /ɪmɔːˈtælɪtɪ/ n. Unsterblichkeit, die

immortalize /ɪˈmɔːtəlaɪz/ v.t. unsterblich machen

immovable /ɪˈmuːvəbl/ adj. unbeweglich; **be** ∼: sich nicht bewegen lassen

immune /ɪˈmjuːn/ adj. (a) (exempt) sicher (from vor + Dat.)
(b) (not susceptible) unempfindlich (to gegen) ···❖

(c) (Med.) immun (**to** gegen); ~ **system** Immunsystem, *das;* ~ **therapy** *n.* Immuntherapie, *die*

immunity /ı'mju:nıtı/ *n.* (a) diplomatic ~: diplomatische Immunität (b) (Med.) Immunität, *die*

immunization /ımjʊnaɪ'zeɪʃn/ *n.* Immunisierung, *die*

immunize /'ımjʊnaɪz/ *v.t.* immunisieren

immunodeficiency /ı'mju:nəʊdɪfıʃənsı/ *n.* Immunschwäche, *die*

immunology /ımjʊ'nɒlədʒı/ *n.* Immunologie, *die*

immunotherapy /ımju:nəʊ'θerəpı/ *n.* Immuntherapie, *die*

immutable /ı'mju:təbl/ *adj.* unveränderlich

imp /ımp/ *n.* (a) Kobold, *der* (b) (fig.: child) Racker, *der* (fam.)

impact /'ımpækt/ *n.* (a) Aufprall, *der* (**on, against** auf + *Akk.*); (collision) Zusammenprall, *der* (b) (fig.) Wirkung, *die*

impair /ım'peə(r)/ *v.t.* beeinträchtigen; schaden (+ *Dat.*) ⟨Gesundheit⟩

impale /ım'peıl/ *v.t.* aufspießen

impart /ım'pɑ:t/ *v.t.* (a) (give) [ab]geben (**to** an + *Akk.*) (b) (communicate) kundtun (geh.) (**to** *Dat.*); vermitteln ⟨Kenntnisse⟩ (**to** *Dat.*)

impartial /ım'pɑ:ʃl/ *adj.* unparteiisch; gerecht ⟨Entscheidung, Urteil⟩

impassable /ım'pɑ:səbl/ *adj.* unpassierbar (**to** für); (to vehicles) unbefahrbar (**to** für)

impasse /'æmpɑ:s/ *n.* Sackgasse, *die*

impassive /ım'pæsıv/ *adj.* ausdruckslos

impatience /ım'peıʃəns/ *n.* Ungeduld, *die* (**at** über + *Akk.*)

impatient /ım'peıʃənt/ *adj.* ungeduldig; ~ **at sth./with sb.** ungeduldig über etw. (*Akk.*)/mit jmdm.

im'patiently *adv.* ungeduldig

impeccable /ım'pekəbl/ *adj.* makellos; tadellos ⟨Manieren⟩

impeccably /ım'pekəblı/ *adv.* tadellos; makellos ⟨rein⟩

impede /ım'pi:d/ *v.t.* behindern

impediment /ım'pedımənt/ *n.* (a) Hindernis, *das* (**to** für) (b) (speech defect) Sprachfehler, *der*

impel /ım'pel/ *v.t.,* **-ll-** treiben; **feel** ~**led to do sth.** sich genötigt *od.* gezwungen fühlen, etw. zu tun

impending /ım'pendıŋ/ *adj.* bevorstehend

impenetrable /ım'penıtrəbl/ *adj.* undurchdringlich (**by, to** für)

imperative /ım'perətıv/ 1 *adj.* dringend erforderlich
2 *n.* (Ling.) Imperativ, *der*

imperceptible /ımpə'septıbl/ *adj.* nicht wahrnehmbar; (very slight or gradual) unmerklich

imperfect /ım'pɜ:fıkt/ 1 *adj.* (a) (incomplete) unvollständig (b) (faulty) mangelhaft
2 *n.* (Ling.) Imperfekt, *das*

imperfection /ımpə'fekʃn/ *n.* (a) (incompleteness) Unvollständigkeit, *die* (b) (fault) Mangel, *der*

im'perfectly *adv.* (a) (incompletely) unvollständig (b) (faultily) fehlerhaft

imperial /ım'pıərıəl/ *adj.* kaiserlich

imperialism /ım'pıərıəlızm/ *n.* Imperialismus, *der*

imperious /ım'pıərıəs/ *adj.* herrisch

impermeable /ım'pɜ:mıəbl/ *adj.* undurchlässig

impersonal /ım'pɜ:sənl/ *adj.* unpersönlich

impersonate /ım'pɜ:səneıt/ *v.t.* sich ausgeben als; (to entertain) imitieren; nachahmen

impertinence /ım'pɜ:tınəns/ *n.* Unverschämtheit, *die*

impertinent /ım'pɜ:tınənt/ *adj.* unverschämt

imperturbable /ımpə'tɜ:bəbl/ *adj.* gelassen; **be completely** ~: durch nichts zu erschüttern sein

impervious /ım'pɜ:vıəs/ *adj.* undurchlässig; **be** ~ **to sth.** (fig.) unempfänglich für etw. sein

impetuous /ım'petjʊəs/ *adj.* unüberlegt; impulsiv ⟨Person⟩

impetus /'ımpıtəs/ *n.* (a) Kraft, *die* (b) (fig.) Motivation, *die*

impinge /ım'pındʒ/ *v.i.* ~ **on sth.** auf etw. (*Akk.*) Einfluss nehmen

'impish *adj.* lausbübisch

implacable /ım'plækəbl/ *adj.* unversöhnlich; erbittert ⟨Gegner⟩

implausible /ım'plɔ:zıbl/ *adj.* unglaubwürdig

implement 1 /'ımplımənt/ *n.* Gerät, *das*
2 /'ımplıment/ *v.t.* [in die Tat] umsetzen ⟨Politik, Plan usw.⟩

implicate /'ımplıkeıt/ *v.t.* belasten; **be** ~**d in a scandal** in einen Skandal verwickelt sein

implication /ımplı'keıʃn/ *n.* Implikation, *die;* **by** ~: implizit

implicit /ım'plısıt/ *adj.* (a) (implied) implizit (geh.); unausgesprochen ⟨Drohung, Zweifel⟩ (b) (resting on authority) unbedingt; blind ⟨Vertrauen⟩

implicitly /ım'plısıtlı/ *adv.* (a) (by implication) implizit (geh.) (b) (unquestioningly) blind ⟨vertrauen, gehorchen usw.⟩

implode /ım'pləʊd/*v.i.* implodieren

implore /ım'plɔ:(r)/ *v.t.* anflehen (**for** um)

imply /ım'plaı/ *v.t.* (a) implizieren (geh.); (say indirectly) hindeuten auf (+ *Akk.*) (b) (insinuate) unterstellen

impolite /ˌɪmpəˈlaɪt/ adj. unhöflich

import ① /ɪmˈpɔːt/ v.t. importieren, einführen ⟨Waren⟩ (from aus, into nach) ② /ˈɪmpɔːt/ n. (a) (process) Import, der (b) (article) Importgut, das

importance /ɪmˈpɔːtəns/ n. Wichtigkeit, die (to für); (significance) Bedeutung, die; be of ∼: wichtig sein; full of one's own ∼: von seiner eigenen Wichtigkeit überzeugt

important /ɪmˈpɔːtənt/ adj. wichtig (to für); (significant) bedeutend

'import duty n. Einfuhrzoll, der

im'porter n. Importeur, der

impose /ɪmˈpəʊz/ v.t. auferlegen (geh.) ⟨Bürde, Verpflichtung⟩ ([up]on Dat.); erheben ⟨Steuer⟩ (on auf + Akk.); verhängen ⟨Kriegsrecht⟩; anordnen ⟨Rationierung⟩ ▪ **im'pose on** v.t. ausnutzen ⟨Gutmütigkeit, Toleranz usw.⟩; ∼ on sb. sich jmdm. aufdrängen

imposing /ɪmˈpəʊzɪŋ/ adj. imposant

imposition /ˌɪmpəˈzɪʃn/ n. (a) Auferlegung, die; (of tax) Erhebung, die (b) (unreasonable demand) Zumutung, die

impossibility /ɪmˌpɒsɪˈbɪlɪtɪ/ n. Unmöglichkeit, die

impossible /ɪmˈpɒsɪbl/ adj., **impossibly** /ɪmˈpɒsɪblɪ/ adv. unmöglich

impostor /ɪmˈpɒstə(r)/ n. Hochstapler, der/-staplerin, die; (swindler) Betrüger, der/ Betrügerin, die

impotence /ˈɪmpətəns/ n. (a) (powerlessness) Machtlosigkeit, die (b) (lack of sexual power) Impotenz, die

impotent /ˈɪmpətənt/ adj. (a) (powerless) machtlos (b) (lacking in sexual power; in popular use: sterile) impotent

impound /ɪmˈpaʊnd/ v.t. beschlagnahmen

impoverished /ɪmˈpɒvərɪʃt/ adj. be/ become ∼: verarmt sein/verarmen

impracticable /ɪmˈpræktɪkəbl/ adj. undurchführbar

impractical /ɪmˈpræktɪkl/ adj. (a) (unpractical) unpraktisch (b) ▶ IMPRACTICABLE

imprecise /ˌɪmprɪˈsaɪs/ adj. ungenau

impregnable /ɪmˈpregnəbl/ adj. uneinnehmbar ⟨Festung, Bollwerk⟩; (fig.) unanfechtbar ⟨Ruf, Stellung⟩

impregnate /ˈɪmpregneɪt/ v.t. imprägnieren

impress /ɪmˈpres/ v.t. beeindrucken; abs. Eindruck machen; be ∼ed by or with sth. von etw. beeindruckt sein ▪ **im'press [up]on** v.t. einschärfen (+ Dat.); ∼ sth. [up]on sb.'s memory jmdm. etw. einschärfen

impression /ɪmˈpreʃn/ n. (a) Eindruck, der; form an ∼ of sb. sich (Dat.) ein Bild von jmdm. machen (b) (impersonation) do an ∼ of sb. jmdn. imitieren; do ∼s andere Leute imitieren

impressionable adj. beeinflussbar

impressionist /ɪmˈpreʃənɪst/ n. Impressionist, der/Impressionistin, die

impressive /ɪmˈpresɪv/ adj. beeindruckend; imponierend

imprint ① /ˈɪmprɪnt/ n. Abdruck, der; (fig.) Stempel, der ② /ɪmˈprɪnt/ v.t. aufdrucken; (fig.) einprägen (on Dat.)

imprison /ɪmˈprɪzn/ v.t. in Haft nehmen; be ∼ed sich in Haft befinden

im'prisonment n. Haft, die; a long term of ∼: eine lange Haftstrafe

improbable /ɪmˈprɒbəbl/ adj. unwahrscheinlich

impromptu /ɪmˈprɒmptjuː/ ① adj. improvisiert; an ∼ speech eine Stegreifrede ② adv. aus dem Stegreif

improper /ɪmˈprɒpə(r)/ adj. (a) (wrong) unrichtig (b) (unseemly) unpassend; (indecent) unanständig

im'properly adv. ▶ IMPROPER: unrichtig; unpassend; unanständig

improvable /ɪmˈpruːvəbl/ adj. verbesserungsfähig

improve /ɪmˈpruːv/ ① v.i. besser werden; ⟨Person, Wetter:⟩ sich bessern ② v.t. verbessern ③ v. refl. ∼ oneself sich weiterbilden ▪ **im'prove [up]on** v.t. überbieten ⟨Rekord, Angebot⟩; verbessern ⟨Leistung⟩

improvement /ɪmˈpruːvmənt/ n. Verbesserung, die (on, over gegenüber); make ∼s to sth. Verbesserungen an etw. (Dat.) vornehmen

improvisation /ˌɪmprəvaɪˈzeɪʃn/ n. Improvisieren, das

improvise /ˈɪmprəvaɪz/ v.t. improvisieren

imprudent /ɪmˈpruːdənt/ adj. unklug; (showing rashness) unbesonnen

impudence /ˈɪmpjʊdəns/ n. Unverschämtheit, die; (brazenness) Dreistigkeit, die

impudent /ˈɪmpjʊdənt/ adj., **'impudently** adv. unverschämt; (brazen[ly]) dreist

impulse /ˈɪmpʌls/ n. Impuls, der; on [an] ∼: impulsiv

'impulse buying n. Spontankäufe Pl.

impulsive /ɪmˈpʌlsɪv/ adj. impulsiv

impunity /ɪmˈpjuːnɪtɪ/ v.t. with ∼: ungestraft

impure /ɪmˈpjʊə(r)/ adj. unrein

impurity /ɪmˈpjʊərɪtɪ/ n. Unreinheit, die; (foreign body) Fremdstoff, der

impute /ɪmˈpjuːt/ v.t. zuschreiben (to Dat.)

in /ɪn/ ① prep. (position; also fig.) in (+ Dat.); (into) in (+ Akk.); in this heat bei dieser Hitze; two feet in diameter mit einem Durchmesser von zwei Fuß; there are three feet in a yard ein Yard hat drei Fuß; draw in ⋯⋯▷

crayon/ink mit Kreide/Tinte zeichnen; **pay in pounds/dollars** in Pfund/Dollars bezahlen; **in fog/rain** *etc.* bei Nebel/Regen *usw.;* **in the 20th century** im 20. Jahrhundert; **4 o'clock in the morning/afternoon** 4 Uhr morgens/abends; **in 1990** [im Jahre] 1990; **in three minutes/years** in drei Minuten/Jahren; **in doing this, he ...:** indem er das tut/tat, ... er ...; **in that ...:** insofern als...
2 *adv.* **(a)** (inside) hinein⟨*gehen usw.*⟩; herein⟨*kommen usw.*⟩
(b) (at home, work, etc.) **be in** da sein
(c) have it in for sb. es auf jmdn. abgesehen haben (ugs.); **sb. is in for sth.** (about to undergo) jmdm. steht etw. bevor
3 *adj.* (coll.: in fashion) in (ugs.)
4 *n.* **know the ins and outs of sth.** sich in einer Sache genau auskennen

in. *abbr.* = **inch[es]**
ina'bility *n.* Unfähigkeit, *die*
inaccessible /ɪnək'sesɪbl/ *adj.* unzugänglich
in'accuracy *n.* **(a)** (incorrectness) Unrichtigkeit, *die*
(b) (imprecision) Ungenauigkeit, *die*
in'accurate *adj.* **(a)** (incorrect) unrichtig
(b) (imprecise) ungenau
in'active *adj.* untätig
inac'tivity *n.* Untätigkeit, *die*
inadequacy /ɪn'ædɪkwəsɪ/ *n.* **(a)** Unzulänglichkeit, *die*
(b) (incompetence) mangelnde Eignung
in'adequate *adj.* unzulänglich; (incompetent) ungeeignet; **feel** ∼: sich überfordert fühlen
inadvertent /ɪnəd'vɜːtənt/ *adj.,* **inad'vertently** *adv.* versehentlich
inad'visable *adj.* nicht ratsam
inane /ɪn'eɪn/ *adj.* dümmlich
in'animate *adj.* unbelebt
inap'plicable *adj.* nicht zutreffend
inap'propriate *adj.* unpassend
in'apt *adj.* unpassend
inar'ticulate *adj.* **(a) she's rather/very** ∼: sie kann sich ziemlich schlecht/sehr schlecht ausdrücken
(b) (indistinct) unverständlich
inat'tentive *adj.* unaufmerksam (**to** gegenüber)
in'audible *adj.* unhörbar
inau'spicious *adj.* (ominous) unheilvoll; (unlucky) unglücklich
'inborn *adj.* angeboren (**in** *Dat.*)
'in-box *n.* (Comp.) Inbox, *die;* Posteingang, *der*
in'bred *adj.* **they are/have become** ∼: bei ihnen herrscht Inzucht
in'breeding *n.* Inzucht, *die*
'inbuilt *adj.* jmdm./einer Sache eigen
Inc. *abbr.* (Amer.) = **Incorporated** e. G.
incalculable /ɪn'kælkjʊləbl/ *adj.* (very great) unermesslich

in'capable *adj.* **(a) be** ∼ **of doing sth.** außerstande sein, etw. zu tun; **be** ∼ **of sth.** zu etw. unfähig sein
(b) be ∼ **of** nicht zulassen ⟨*Beweis, Messung usw.*⟩
incapacitate /ɪnkə'pæsɪteɪt/ *v.t.* unfähig machen
incarcerate /ɪn'kɑːsəreɪt/ *v.t.* einkerkern (geh.)
incarceration /ɪnkɑːsə'reɪʃn/ *n.* Einkerkerung, *die* (geh.)
incendiary /ɪn'sendɪərɪ/ *adj. & n.* ∼ **device** Brandsatz, *der;* ∼ **[bomb]** Brandbombe, *die*
incense¹ /'ɪnsens/ *n.* Weihrauch, *der*
incense² /ɪn'sens/ *v.t.* erzürnen
incentive /ɪn'sentɪv/ *n.* Anreiz, *der*
incessant /ɪn'sesənt/ *adj.,* **in'cessantly** *adv.* unablässig
incest /'ɪnsest/ *n.* Inzest, *der*
incestuous /ɪn'sestjʊəs/ *adj.* inzestuös
inch /ɪntʃ/ **1** *n.* Inch, *der;* Zoll, *der* (veralt.)
2 *v.t. & i.* ∼ **[one's way] forward** sich Zoll für Zoll vorwärts bewegen
incident /'ɪnsɪdənt/ *n.* **(a)** (notable event) Vorfall, *der*
(b) (clash) Zwischenfall, *der*
incidental /ɪnsɪ'dentl/ *adj.* beiläufig ⟨*Bemerkung*⟩; Neben⟨*ausgaben, -einnahmen*⟩
incidentally /ɪnsɪ'dentəlɪ/ *adv.* nebenbei [bemerkt]
inci'dental music *n.* Begleitmusik, *die*
incinerate /ɪn'sɪnəreɪt/ *v.t.* verbrennen
incinerator /ɪn'sɪnəreɪtə(r)/ *n.* Verbrennungsofen, *der*
incision /ɪn'sɪʒn/ *n.* Einschnitt, *der*
incisive /ɪn'saɪsɪv/ *adj.* schneidend ⟨*Ton*⟩; scharf ⟨*Verstand*⟩; scharfsinnig ⟨*Kritik, Frage, Bemerkung, Argument*⟩
incite /ɪn'saɪt/ *v.t.* anstiften; aufstacheln ⟨*Massen, Volk*⟩
in'citement *n.* Anstiftung, *die/* Aufstachelung, *die*
incl. *abbr.* = **including** inkl.
inclination /ɪnklɪ'neɪʃn/ *n.* Neigung, *die*
incline **1** /ɪn'klaɪn/ *v.t.* **(a)** (bend) neigen
(b) (dispose) veranlassen
2 *v.i.* (be disposed) neigen (**to[wards]** zu)
3 /'ɪnklaɪn/ *n.* Steigung, *die*
inclined /ɪn'klaɪnd/ *adj.* geneigt; **they are** ∼ **to be slow** sie neigen zur Langsamkeit; **if you feel [so]** ∼: wenn Sie Lust [dazu] haben
include /ɪn'kluːd/ *v.t.* einschließen; (contain) enthalten; ∼**d in the price** im Preis inbegriffen
including /ɪn'kluːdɪŋ/ *prep.* einschließlich (+ *Gen.*); ∼ **VAT** inklusive Mehrwertsteuer
inclusion /ɪn'kluːʒn/ *n.* Aufnahme, *die*
inclusive /ɪn'kluːsɪv/ *adj.* einschließlich; **be** ∼ **of sth.** etw. einschließen; **from 2 to 6 January** ∼: vom 2. bis einschließlich 6. Januar; **cost £50** ∼: 50 Pfund kosten, alles inbegriffen

incognito /ɪnkɒgˈniːtəʊ/ adj., adv.
inkognito

inco'herent adj. zusammenhanglos

income /ˈɪnkəm/ n. Einkommen, das

income: ~ bracket, ~ group ns.
Einkommensklasse, die; **~ sup'port** n.
(Brit.) zusätzliche Hilfe zum Lebensunterhalt;
~ tax n. Einkommensteuer, die; (on wages,
salary) Lohnsteuer, die

'incoming adj. ankommend; landend
⟨Flugzeug⟩; einfahrend ⟨Zug⟩; eingehend
⟨Telefongespräch, Auftrag⟩

incomings /ˈɪnkʌmɪŋz/ n. pl. (revenue,
income) Einnahmen Pl.

in'comparable adj. unvergleichlich

incom'patible adj. unvereinbar; be ~
⟨Menschen:⟩ nicht zueinander passen

in'competence /ɪnˈkɒmpɪtəns/ n.
Unfähigkeit, die; Unvermögen, das

in'competent adj. unfähig

incom'plete adj. unvollständig

incompre'hensible adj. unbegreiflich;
unverständlich ⟨Rede, Argument⟩

incon'ceivable adj. unvorstellbar

incon'clusive adj. ergebnislos; nicht
schlüssig ⟨Beweis, Argument⟩

incongruous /ɪnˈkɒŋgrʊəs/ adj.
unpassend

inconsequential /ɪnkɒnsɪˈkwenʃl/ adj.
belanglos

incon'siderate adj. rücksichtslos

incon'sistency n. ▶ INCONSISTENT:
Widersprüchlichkeit, die; Inkonsequenz, die;
Unbeständigkeit, die

incon'sistent adj. widersprüchlich;
(illogical) inkonsequent; (irregular) unbeständig

inconsolable /ɪnkənˈsəʊləbl/ adj.
untröstlich

incon'spicuous adj. unauffällig

incontinence /ɪnˈkɒntɪnəns/ n. (Med.)
Inkontinenz, die

incontinent /ɪnˈkɒntɪnənt/ adj. (Med.)
inkontinent; be ~: an Inkontinenz leiden

incontrovertible /ɪnkɒntrəˈvɜːtəbl/ adj.
unbestreitbar; unwiderlegbar ⟨Beweis⟩

incon'venience 1 n.
Unannehmlichkeiten Pl. (to für); **put sb. to a
lot of ~:** jmdm. große Unannehmlichkeiten
bereiten
2 v.t. Unannehmlichkeiten bereiten
(+ Dat.); (disturb) stören

incon'venient adj. unbequem; ungünstig
⟨Lage, Standort⟩; **come at an ~ time** zu
ungelegener Zeit kommen; **be ~ for sb.**
jmdm. nicht passen

incorporate /ɪnˈkɔːpəreɪt/ v.t. aufnehmen
(in[to], with in + Akk.)

incorporated /ɪnˈkɔːpəreɪtɪd/ adj.
eingetragen ⟨[Handels]gesellschaft⟩

incor'rect adj. (a) unrichtig; **be ~:** nicht
stimmen; **it is ~ to say that ...:** es stimmt
nicht, dass ...

(b) (improper) inkorrekt

incor'rectly adv. (a) unrichtigerweise;
falsch ⟨beantworten, aussprechen⟩
(b) (improperly) inkorrekt

incorrigible /ɪnˈkɒrɪdʒɪbl/ adj.
unverbesserlich

increase 1 /ɪnˈkriːs/ v.i. zunehmen;
⟨Lärm:⟩ größer werden; ⟨Preise, Nachfrage:⟩
steigen; **~ in weight/size/price** schwerer/
größer/teurer werden
2 v.t. (a) (make greater) erhöhen
(b) (intensify) verstärken
3 /ˈɪnkriːs/ n. Zunahme, die (in Gen.); **be on
the ~:** ständig zunehmen

increasing /ɪnˈkriːsɪŋ/ adj. steigend; **an
~ number of people** mehr und mehr
Menschen

in'creasingly adv. in zunehmendem
Maße; **become ~ apparent** immer deutlicher
werden

in'credible adj. (also coll.: remarkable)
unglaublich

in'credibly adv. (also coll.: remarkably)
unglaublich

incredulity /ɪnkrɪˈdjuːlɪtɪ/ n.
Ungläubigkeit, die

incredulous /ɪnˈkredjʊləs/ adj. ungläubig

increment 1 /ˈɪnkrɪmənt/ n. Erhöhung, die;
(amount of growth) Zuwachs, die

incriminate /ɪnˈkrɪmɪneɪt/ v.t. belasten

incubate /ˈɪŋkjʊbeɪt/ v.t. bebrüten; (to
hatching) ausbrüten

incubation /ɪŋkjʊˈbeɪʃn/ n. Bebrütung, die

incubator /ɪŋkjʊˈbeɪtə(r)/ n. Inkubator,
der; (for babies also) Brutkasten, der

incur /ɪnˈkɜː(r)/ v.t., **-rr-** sich (Dat.) zuziehen
⟨Unwillen, Ärger⟩; **~ debts/expenses/risks**
Schulden machen/Ausgaben haben/Risiken
eingehen

in'curable adj. unheilbar

incurably /ɪnˈkjʊərəblɪ/ adv. unheilbar
⟨krank⟩

incursion /ɪnˈkɜːʃn/ n. Eindringen, das; (by
sudden attack) Einfall, der

indebted /ɪnˈdetɪd/ pred. adj. **be [much]
~ to sb. for sth.** jmdm. für etw. [sehr] zu
Dank verpflichtet sein

in'decency n. Unanständigkeit, die

in'decent adj., **in'decently** adv.
unanständig

indecipherable /ɪndɪˈsaɪfərəbl/ adj.
unentzifferbar

inde'cision n. Unentschlossenheit, die

inde'cisive adj. (a) ergebnislos ⟨Streit,
Diskussion⟩; nichtssagend ⟨Ergebnis⟩
(b) (hesitating) unentschlossen

indeed /ɪnˈdiːd/ adv. (a) in der Tat; **thank
you very much ~:** haben Sie vielen
herzlichen Dank; **~ it is** in der Tat
(b) (in fact) ja sogar; **~, he can ...:** ja, er
kann sogar ...
(c) (admittedly) zugegebenermaßen

indefatigable /ɪndɪˈfætɪgəbl/ adj.
unermüdlich

indefensible /ɪndɪˈfensɪbl/ adj. (intolerable)
unverzeihlich

in'definite adj. (a) (vague) unbestimmt
(b) (unlimited) unbegrenzt

in'definitely adv. (a) (vaguely) unbestimmt
(b) (unlimitedly) unbegrenzt; auf unbestimmte
Zeit ‹verschieben›

indelible /ɪnˈdelɪbl/ adj. unauslöschlich;
~ ink Wäschetinte, die

indelibly /ɪnˈdelɪblɪ/ adv. unauslöschlich

indemnify /ɪnˈdemnɪfaɪ/ v.t. absichern
(against gegen); (compensate) entschädigen

indemnity /ɪnˈdemnɪtɪ/ n. Absicherung,
die; (compensation) Entschädigung, die

indentation /ɪndenˈteɪʃn/ n. (a) (indenting,
notch) Einkerbung, die
(b) (recess) Einschnitt, der

inde'pendence n. Unabhängigkeit, die

inde'pendent adj., **inde'pendently**
adv. unabhängig (of von)

indescribable /ɪndɪˈskraɪbəbl/ adj.
unbeschreiblich

indestructible /ɪndɪˈstrʌktɪbl/ adj.
unzerstörbar

indeterminable /ɪndɪˈtɜːmɪnəbl/ adj.
unbestimmbar

indeterminate /ɪndɪˈtɜːmɪnət/ adj.
unbestimmt; unklar ‹Konzept›

index /ˈɪndeks/ [1] n. Register, das
[2] v.t. mit einem Register versehen

index: ~**card** n. Karteikarte, die;
~ **finger** n. Zeigefinger, der; ~ **gears** pl.
Indexschaltung, die; ~**linked** adj. (Econ.)
indexiert; dynamisch ‹Rente›; ~ **number**
n. Indexzahl, die

India /ˈɪndɪə/ n. Indien (das)

Indian /ˈɪndɪən/ [1] adj. (a) indisch; sb. is
~: jmd. ist Inder/Inderin
(b) [American] ~: indianisch
[2] n. (a) Inder, der/Inderin, die
(b) [American] ~: Indianer, der/Indianerin,
die

Indian: ~ **'Ocean** pr. n. Indischer Ozean;
~ **'summer** n. Altweibersommer, der

indicate /ˈɪndɪkeɪt/ [1] v.t. (a) (be a sign of)
erkennen lassen
(b) (state briefly) andeuten
(c) (mark, point out) anzeigen
(d) (suggest, make evident) zum Ausdruck
bringen (to gegenüber)
[2] v.i. (Motor Veh.) blinken

indication /ɪndɪˈkeɪʃn/ n. [An]zeichen, das
(of Gen., für)

indicative /ɪnˈdɪkətɪv/ [1] adj. (a) be ~ of
sth. auf etw. (Akk.) schließen lassen
(b) (Ling.) indikativisch
[2] n. (Ling.) Indikativ, der

indicator /ˈɪndɪkeɪtə(r)/ n. (on vehicle)
Blinker, der

indict /ɪnˈdaɪt/ v.t. anklagen (for, on a
charge of Gen.)

indie /ˈɪndɪ/ (coll.) [1] adj. Indie-‹Gruppe,
Szene, Charts etc.›
[2] n. (record company) Indie-Label, das; (band)
Indie-Band, die

in'difference n. Gleichgültigkeit, die
(to[wards] gegenüber)

in'different adj. (a) gleichgültig
(b) (not good) mittelmäßig

indigenous /ɪnˈdɪdʒɪnəs/ adj. einheimisch;
eingeboren ‹Bevölkerung›

indigestible /ɪndɪˈdʒestɪbl/ adj. (lit. or fig.)
unverdaulich

indi'gestion n. Magenverstimmung, die;
(chronic) Verdauungsstörungen Pl.

indignant /ɪnˈdɪgnənt/ adj. entrüstet (at,
over, about über + Akk.); indigniert ‹Blick,
Geste›

in'dignantly adv. entrüstet; indigniert

indignation /ɪndɪgˈneɪʃn/ n. Entrüstung,
die (about, at, against, over über + Akk.)

in'dignity n. Demütigung, die

indigo /ˈɪndɪgəʊ/ [1] adj. ~ [blue] indigoblau
[2] n. ~ [blue] Indigoblau, das

indi'rect adj. indirekt; ~ **speech** indirekte
Rede

indi'rectly adv. indirekt

indirect 'object n. indirektes Objekt; (in
German) Dativobjekt, das

indiscipline /ɪnˈdɪsɪplɪn/ n., no indef. art.
Disziplinlosigkeit, die

indi'screet adj. indiskret

indi'scretion n. Indiskretion, die

indiscriminate /ɪndɪˈskrɪmɪnət/ adj.
(lacking judgement) unkritisch; (random,
unrestrained) wahllos

indi'spensable adj. unentbehrlich (to
für); unabdingbar ‹Voraussetzung›

indisposed /ɪndɪˈspəʊzd/ adj. (unwell)
unpässlich; indisponiert ‹Sänger,
Schauspieler›

indisputable /ɪndɪˈspjuːtəbl/ adj.,
indisputably /ɪndɪˈspjuːtəblɪ/ adv.
unbestreitbar

indi'stinct adj., **indi'stinctly** adv.
undeutlich

indi'stinguishable adj. nicht
unterscheidbar

individual /ɪndɪˈvɪdjʊəl/ [1] adj. (a) einzeln
(b) (distinctive, characteristic) individuell
[2] n. Einzelne, der/die

individualist /ɪndɪˈvɪdjʊəlɪst/ n.
Individualist, der/Individualistin, die

individualistic /ɪndɪvɪdjʊəˈlɪstɪk/ adj.
individualistisch

individuality /ɪndɪvɪdjʊˈælɪtɪ/ n. (character)
eigene Persönlichkeit

indi'vidually adv. einzeln

indi'visible adj. unteilbar

indoctrinate /ɪnˈdɒktrɪneɪt/ v.t.
indoktrinieren

indoctrination /ɪndɒktrɪˈneɪʃn/ n.
Indoktrination, die

indolence /'ɪndələns/ n. Trägheit, die
indolent /'ɪndələnt/ adj. träge
indomitable /ɪn'dɒmɪtəbl/ adj.
unbeugsam
Indonesia /ɪndə'niːzɪə/ pr. n. Indonesien
(das)
'indoor adj. ~ swimming pool/sports
Hallenbad, das/-sport, der; ~ plants
Zimmerpflanzen; ~ games Spiele im Haus;
(Sport) Hallenspiele
indoors /ɪn'dɔːz/ adv. drinnen; im Haus;
go/come ~: nach drinnen gehen/kommen
indubitable /ɪn'djuːbɪtəbl/ adj.
unzweifelhaft
indubitably /ɪn'djuːbɪtəblɪ/ adv.
zweifellos; zweifelsohne
induce /ɪn'djuːs/ v.t. ~ sb. to do sth. jmdn.
dazu bringen, etw. zu tun
in'ducement n. (incentive) Anreiz, der
induction /ɪn'dʌkʃn/ n. Amtseinführung,
die; ~ course Einführungskurs[us], der
indulge /ɪn'dʌldʒ/ 1 v.t. (a) nachgeben
(+ Dat.) ⟨Wunsch, Verlangen, Verlockung⟩;
frönen (geh.) (+ Dat.) ⟨Leidenschaft⟩
(b) (please) verwöhnen
2 v.i. ~ in frönen (geh.) (+ Dat.)
⟨Leidenschaft⟩
indulgence /ɪn'dʌldʒəns/ n. (a)
Nachsicht, die; (humouring) Nachgiebigkeit,
die (with gegenüber)
(b) (thing indulged in) Luxus, der
indulgent /ɪn'dʌldʒənt/ adj. nachsichtig
(with, to[wards] gegenüber)
industrial /ɪn'dʌstrɪəl/ adj. industriell;
Arbeits⟨unfall, -medizin, -psychologie⟩
industrial: ~ 'action n.
Arbeitskampfmaßnahmen Pl.; take ~ action
in den Ausstand treten; ~ area n.
Industriegebiet, das; ~ di'sease n.
Berufskrankheit, die; ~ dispute n.
Arbeitskonflikt, der; ~ 'espionage n.
Industriespionage, die; ~ estate n.
Industriegebiet, das ~ 'injury n.
Arbeitsverletzung, die
industrialist /ɪn'dʌstrɪəlɪst/ n.
Industrielle, der/die
industrialization /ɪndʌstrɪəlar'zeɪʃn/ n.
Industrialisierung, die
industrialize /ɪn'dʌstrɪəlaɪz/ v.t.
industrialisieren
industrial: ~ park n. Industriegebiet,
das; ~ plant n. Industrieanlage, die;
~ re'lations n. pl. Industrialrelations Pl.;
~ town n. Industriestadt, die;
~ tribunal n. Arbeitsgericht, das;
~ 'waste n. Industriemüll, der
industrious /ɪn'dʌstrɪəs/ adj. fleißig;
(busy) emsig
industry /'ɪndəstrɪ/ n. (a) Industrie, die
(b) ▶ INDUSTRIOUS: Fleiß, der; Emsigkeit, die
inebriated /ɪ'niːbrɪeɪtɪd/ adj. betrunken
inebriation /iniːbrɪ'eɪʃn/ n.
Betrunkenheit, die; betrunkener Zustand

in'edible adj. ungenießbar
ineffective adj. unwirksam; fruchtlos
⟨Anstrengung, Versuch⟩
ineffectual /ɪnɪ'fektjʊəl/ adj. unwirksam;
fruchtlos ⟨Versuch, Bemühung⟩; ineffizient
⟨Methode, Person⟩
inefficiency n. Leistungsschwäche, die;
(of organization, method) schlechtes
Funktionieren
inefficient adj. leistungsschwach;
schlecht funktionierend ⟨Organisation,
Methode⟩
in'elegant adj. unelegant
in'eligible adj. ungeeignet; be ~ for nicht
infrage kommen für ⟨Beförderung, Position⟩;
nicht berechtigt sein zu ⟨Leistungen des
Staats usw.⟩
inept /ɪ'nept/ adj. unbeholfen
ineptitude /ɪ'neptɪtjuːd/ n.
Unbeholfenheit, die
ine'quality n. Ungleichheit, die
inert /ɪ'nɜːt/ adj. (a) reglos; (sluggish) träge
(b) (Chem.) inert; ~ gas Edelgas, das
inertia /ɪ'nɜːʃə/ n. Trägheit, die
inertia reel 'seat belt n.
Automatikgurt, der
inescapable /ɪnɪ'skeɪpəbl/ adj.
unausweichlich
ines'sential adj. unwesentlich;
(dispensable) entbehrlich
inestimable /ɪn'estɪməbl/ adj.
unschätzbar
inevitable /ɪn'evɪtəbl/ adj. unvermeidlich;
unabwendbar ⟨Ereignis, Krieg, Schicksal⟩;
zwangsläufig ⟨Ergebnis, Folge⟩
inevitably /ɪn'evɪtəblɪ/ adv. zwangsläufig
ine'xact adj. ungenau
inex'cusable adj. unverzeihlich
inexhaustible /ɪnɪg'zɔːstɪbl/ adj.
unerschöpflich; unverwüstlich ⟨Person⟩
inexorable /ɪn'eksərəbl/ adj. unerbittlich
inex'pensive adj. preisgünstig
inex'perience n. Unerfahrenheit, die
inex'perienced adj. unerfahren; ~ in
sth. wenig vertraut mit etw.
inexpert /ɪn'ekspɜːt/ adj. unerfahren
inex'plicable adj. unerklärlich
inexpressive /ɪnɪk'spresɪv/ adj.
ausdruckslos ⟨Gesicht, Augen⟩; trocken
⟨Ausdrucksweise, Sprache⟩
inextricably /ɪn'ekstrɪkəblɪ/ adv. become
~ entangled sich vollkommen verheddern
(ugs.); [be] ~ linked untrennbar verbunden
[sein]
infallibility /ɪnfælr'bɪlɪtɪ/ n. Unfehlbarkeit,
die
in'fallible adj. unfehlbar
infamous /'ɪnfəməs/ adj. berüchtigt
infancy /'ɪnfənsɪ/ n. frühe Kindheit; be in
its ~ (fig.) noch in den Anfängen stecken
infant /'ɪnfənt/ n. kleines Kind

infantile /'ɪnfəntaɪl/ *adj.* kindlich; (childish) kindisch

infant mor'tality *n.* Säuglingssterblichkeit, *die*

infantry /'ɪnfəntrɪ/ *n.* Infanterie, *die*

'infant school *n.* (Brit.) ≈ Vorschule, *die*

infatuated /ɪn'fætjʊeɪtɪd/ *adj.* be ∼ with sb. in jmdn. vernarrt sein

infect /ɪn'fekt/ *v.t.* anstecken; infizieren; **the wound became** ∼ed die Wunde entzündete sich

infection /ɪn'fekʃn/ *n.* Infektion, *die;* **throat/ear/eye** ∼: Hals-/Ohren-/ Augenentzündung, *die*

infectious /ɪn'fekʃəs/ *adj.* ansteckend; **be** ∼ ⟨*Person:*⟩ eine ansteckende Krankheit haben

infer /ɪn'fɜ:(r)/ *v.t.*, **-rr-** schließen (**from** aus); ziehen ⟨*Schlussfolgerung*⟩

inference /'ɪnfərəns/ *n.* [Schluss]folgerung, *die*

inferior /ɪn'fɪərɪə(r)/ **1** *adj.* (of lower quality) minderwertig ⟨*Ware*⟩; minder... ⟨*Qualität*⟩; unterlegen ⟨*Gegner*⟩; ∼ **to sth.** schlechter als etw.; **feel** ∼: Minderwertigkeitsgefühle haben **2** *n.* Untergebene, *der/die*

inferiority /ɪnfɪərɪ'ɒrɪtɪ/ *n.* Minderwertigkeit, *die;* (of opponent) Unterlegenheit, *die*

inferi'ority complex *n.* Minderwertigkeitskomplex, *der*

infernal /ɪn'fɜ:nl/ *adj.* (a) (of hell) höllisch (b) (coll.) verdammt (salopp)

inferno /ɪn'fɜ:nəʊ/ *n.* Inferno, *das*

in'fertile *adj.* unfruchtbar

infer'tility *n.* Unfruchtbarkeit, *die*

infest /ɪn'fest/ *v.t.* ⟨*Ungeziefer:*⟩ befallen; ⟨*Unkraut:*⟩ überwuchern; ∼ed with befallen/ überwuchert von

infestation /ɪnfes'teɪʃn/ *n.* ∼ **of rats/ insects** Ratten-/Insektenplage, *die*

infidelity /ɪnfɪ'delɪtɪ/ *n.* Untreue, *die* (**to** gegenüber)

'infighting *n.* (in organization) interne Machtkämpfe *Pl.*

infiltrate /'ɪnfɪltreɪt/ *v.t.* (a) infiltrieren; unterwandern ⟨*Partei, Organisation*⟩ (b) einschleusen ⟨*Agenten*⟩

infinite /'ɪnfɪnɪt/ *adj.* (a) (endless) unendlich (b) (very great) ungeheuer

infinitesimal /ɪnfɪnɪ'tesɪml/ *adj.* (a) (Math.) infinitesimal (b) (very small) äußerst gering; winzig ⟨*Menge*⟩

infinitive /ɪn'fɪnɪtɪv/ *n.* Infinitiv, *der*

infinity /ɪn'fɪnɪtɪ/ *n.* Unendlichkeit, *die*

infirm /ɪn'fɜ:m/ *adj.* gebrechlich

infirmary /ɪn'fɜ:mərɪ/ *n.* (hospital) Krankenhaus, *das*

infirmity /ɪn'fɜ:mɪtɪ/ *n.* Gebrechlichkeit, *die;* (malady) Gebrechen, *das*

inflamed /ɪn'fleɪmd/ *adj.* (Med.) be/become ∼: entzündet sein/sich entzünden

inflammable /ɪn'flæməbl/ *adj.* feuergefährlich

inflammation /ɪnflə'meɪʃn/ *n.* (Med.) Entzündung, *die*

inflammatory /ɪn'flæmətərɪ/ *adj.* aufrührerisch; **an** ∼ **speech** eine Hetzrede

inflatable /ɪn'fleɪtəbl/ *adj.* aufblasbar; ∼ **dinghy** Schlauchboot, *das*

inflate /ɪn'fleɪt/ *v.t.* aufblasen; (with pump) aufpumpen

inflated /ɪn'fleɪtɪd/ *adj.* (lit or fig.) aufgeblasen

inflation /ɪn'fleɪʃn/ *n.* (Econ.) Inflation, *die*

in'flexible *adj.* (a) (stiff) unbiegsam (b) (obstinate) [geistig] unbeweglich

inflict /ɪn'flɪkt/ *v.t.* zufügen ⟨*Leid, Schmerzen*⟩, beibringen ⟨*Wunde*⟩, versetzen ⟨*Schlag*⟩ (on Dat.)

infliction /ɪn'flɪkʃn/ *n.* ▶ INFLICT: Zufügen, *das;* Beibringen, *das;* Versetzen, *das*

'in-flight *adj.* Bord⟨*verpflegung, -programm*⟩

influence /'ɪnfluəns/ **1** *n.* Einfluss, *der;* **be a good/bad** ∼ [**on sb.**] einen guten/ schlechten Einfluss [auf jmdn.] ausüben **2** *v.t.* beeinflussen

influential /ɪnflʊ'enʃl/ *adj.* einflussreich

influenza /ɪnflʊ'enzə/ *n.* Grippe, *die*

influx /'ɪnflʌks/ *n.* Zustrom, *der*

info /'ɪnfəʊ/ *n.* (coll.) Infos *Pl.* (ugs.)

inform /ɪn'fɔ:m/ **1** *n.* informieren (**of, about** über + *Akk.*); **keep sb.** ∼ed jmdn. auf dem Laufenden halten **2** *v.i.* ∼ **against** *or* **on sb.** jmdn. denunzieren (**to** bei)

in'formal *adj.* (a) zwanglos (b) (unofficial) informell

infor'mality *n.* Zwanglosigkeit, *die*

informant /ɪn'fɔ:mənt/ *n.* Informant, *der/* Informantin, *die*

information /ɪnfə'meɪʃn/ *n.* Informationen *Pl.;* **give** ∼ **on sth.** Auskunft über etw. (*Akk.*) erteilen; **piece** *or* **bit of** ∼: Information, *die*

information: ∼ **bureau,** ∼ **centre** *ns.* Auskunftsbüro, *das;* ∼ **desk** *n.* Informationsschalter, *der;* ∼ **explosion** *n.* Informationsflut, *die;* ∼ **highway** *n.* (Comp.) Datenautobahn, *die;* ∼ **office** ▶ ∼ BUREAU; ∼ **pack** *n.* Informationspaket, *das;* (folder etc.) Informationsmappe, *die;* ∼ **retrieval** *n.* (Comp.) Retrieval, *das;* ∼ **science** *n.* Informatik, *die;* ∼ **superhighway** *n.* (Comp.) Datenautobahn, *die;* Datensuperhighway, *der;* ∼ **system** *n.* Informationssystem, *das;* ∼ **technology** *n.* Informationstechnologie, *die*

informative /ɪn'fɔ:mətɪv/ *adj.* informativ; **not very** ∼: nicht sehr aufschlussreich ⟨*Dokument, Schriftstück*⟩

informed /ɪn'fɔ:md/ *adj.* informiert

in'former *n.* Denunziant, *der/* Denunziantin, *die*

infra-red /ˌɪnfrəˈred/ *adj.* infrarot

infrastructure /ˈɪnfrəstrʌktʃə(r)/ *n.* Infrastruktur, *die*

infrequency /ɪnˈfriːkwənsɪ/ *n.* Seltenheit, *die*

in'frequent *adj.*, **in'frequently** *adv.* selten

infringe /ɪnˈfrɪndʒ/ *v.t. & i.* ~ [on] verstoßen gegen

in'fringement *n.* Verstoß, *der* (of gegen)

infuriate /ɪnˈfjʊərɪeɪt/ *v.t.* wütend machen; **be** ~**d** wütend sein (**by** über + *Akk.*)

infuriating /ɪnˈfjʊərɪeɪtɪŋ/ *adj.* ärgerlich

ingenious /ɪnˈdʒiːnɪəs/ *adj.* einfallsreich; genial ⟨*Methode, Idee*⟩; raffiniert ⟨*Spielzeug, Maschine*⟩

ingenuity /ˌɪndʒɪˈnjuːɪtɪ/ *n.* Genialität, *die*

ingot /ˈɪŋgət/ *n.* Ingot, *der*

ingratiate /ɪnˈgreɪʃɪeɪt/ *v. refl.* ~ **oneself with sb.** sich bei jmdm. einschmeicheln

in'gratitude *n.* Undankbarkeit, *die* (to[wards] gegenüber)

ingredient /ɪnˈgriːdɪənt/ *n.* Zutat, *die*

ingrowing /ˈɪngrəʊɪŋ/ *adj.* eingewachsen ⟨*Zehennagel usw.*⟩

inhabit /ɪnˈhæbɪt/ *v.t.* bewohnen

inhabitable /ɪnˈhæbɪtəbl/ *adj.* bewohnbar

inhabitant /ɪnˈhæbɪtənt/ *n.* Bewohner, *der/*Bewohnerin, *die*

inhale /ɪnˈheɪl/ *v.t. & i.* einatmen; inhalieren (ugs.) ⟨*Zigarettenrauch usw.*⟩

inherent /ɪnˈhɪərənt, ɪnˈherənt/ *adj. adj.* (belonging by nature) innewohnend (geh.); natürlich ⟨*Anmut, Eleganz*⟩

inherit /ɪnˈherɪt/ *v.t.* erben

inheritance /ɪnˈherɪtəns/ *n.* Erbe, *das;* (inheriting) Erbschaft, *die*

in'heritance tax *n.* Erbschaftssteuer, *die*

inhibit /ɪnˈhɪbɪt/ *v.t.* hemmen

in'hibited *adj.* gehemmt

inhibition /ˌɪnhɪˈbɪʃn/ *n.* Hemmung, *die*

inho'spitable *adj.* ungastlich ⟨*Person, Verhalten*⟩; unwirtlich ⟨*Gegend, Klima*⟩

'in-house *adj.* hausintern

in'human *adj.* unmenschlich

inhumane /ˌɪnhjuːˈmeɪn/ *adj.* unmenschlich

initial /ɪˈnɪʃl/ ① *adj.* anfänglich; Anfangs⟨*stadium, -schwierigkeiten*⟩ ② *n. esp. in pl.* Initiale, *die* ③ *v.t.,* (Brit.) abzeichnen ⟨*Scheck, Quittung*⟩; paraphieren ⟨*Vertrag, Abkommen usw.*⟩

initial 'letter *n.* Anfangsbuchstabe, *der*

i'nitially *adv.* anfangs; am Anfang

initiate /ɪˈnɪʃɪeɪt/ *v.t.* (a) (introduce) einführen (**into** in + *Akk.*); (into knowledge, mystery) einweihen (**into** in + *Akk.*) (b) (begin) einleiten

initiation /ɪˌnɪʃɪˈeɪʃn/ *n.* (a) (introduction) Einführung, *die* (b) (into knowledge, mystery) Einweihung, *die*

initiative /ɪˈnɪʃətɪv/ *n.* Initiative, *die;* **lack** ~: keine Initiative haben

inject /ɪnˈdʒekt/ *v.t.* [ein]spritzen; injizieren (Med.)

injection /ɪnˈdʒekʃn/ *n.* Spritze, *die;* Injektion, *die*

injure /ˈɪndʒə(r)/ *v.t.* (a) verletzen; **his leg was** ~**d** er wurde/(state) war am Bein verletzt (b) (impair) schaden (+ *Dat.*)

injured /ˈɪndʒəd/ *adj.* verletzt; verwundet ⟨*Soldat*⟩

injury /ˈɪndʒərɪ/ *n.* Verletzung, *die* (**to** *Gen.*)

'injury time *n.* (Brit. Footb.) Nachspielzeit, *die;* **be into/play** ~: nachspielen

in'justice *n.* Ungerechtigkeit, *die*

ink /ɪŋk/ *n.* Tinte, *die*

'ink-jet printer *n.* Tintenstrahldrucker, *der*

inkling /ˈɪŋklɪŋ/ *n.* Ahnung, *die;* **have an** ~ **of sth.** etw. ahnen

'ink pad *n.* Stempelkissen, *das*

inland /ˈɪnlənd, ˈɪnlænd/ *adj.* Binnen-; binnenländisch

Inland 'Revenue *n.* (Brit.) ≈ Finanzamt, *das*

'in-laws *n. pl.* (coll.) Schwiegereltern *Pl.*

inlet /ˈɪnlət/ *n.* [schmale] Bucht

'inmate *n.* Insasse, *der/*Insassin, *die*

inn /ɪn/ *n.* (hotel) Gasthof, *der;* (pub) Wirtshaus, *das*

innate /ɪˈneɪt/ *adj.* angeboren

inner /ˈɪnə(r)/ *adj.* inner...; Innen⟨*hof, -tür, -fläche, -seite usw.*⟩; ~ **tube** Schlauch, *der*

inner 'city *n.* Innenstadt, *die;* ~ **areas** Innenbezirke

innermost /ˈɪnəməʊst/ *adj.* innerst...

'innkeeper *n.* [Gast]wirt, *der/*-wirtin, *die*

innocence /ˈɪnəsəns/ *n.* (a) Unschuld, *die* (b) (naïvity) Naivität, *die*

innocent /ˈɪnəsənt/ *adj.* (a) unschuldig (**of** an + *Dat.*) (b) (naïve) naiv

innocuous /ɪˈnɒkjʊəs/ *adj.* harmlos

innovation /ˌɪnəˈveɪʃn/ *n.* Innovation, *die;* (thing, change) Neuerung, *die*

innovative /ˈɪnəvətɪv/ *adj.* innovativ

innuendo /ˌɪnjuːˈendəʊ/ *n., pl.* ~**es** *or* ~**s** versteckte Andeutung

innumerable /ɪˈnjuːmərəbl/ *adj.* unzählig

innumeracy /ɪˈnjuːmərəsɪ/ *n.* Nicht-Rechnen-Können, *das*

innumerate /ɪˈnjuːmərət/ *adj.* **be** ~: nicht rechnen können

inoculate /ɪˈnɒkjʊleɪt/ *v.t.* impfen

inoculation /ɪˌnɒkjʊˈleɪʃn/ *n.* Impfung, *die*

inof'fensive *adj.* harmlos

inoperable /ɪnˈɒpərəbl/ *adj.* (Surg.)
inoperabel (fachspr.)

inoperative /ɪnˈɒpərətɪv/ *adj.* ungültig

in'opportune *adj.* unpassend;
unangebracht ‹*Bemerkung*›

inordinate /ɪˈnɔːdɪnət/ *adj.* unmäßig;
ungeheuer ‹*Menge*›

inor'ganic *adj.* anorganisch

'inpatient *n.* stationär behandelter Patient/
behandelte Patientin

'input *n.* Input, der od. das

inquest /ˈɪŋkwest/ *n.* gerichtliche
Untersuchung der Todesursache

inquire, inquiry ▶ ENQUIR-

inquisitive /ɪnˈkwɪzɪtɪv/ *adj.* neugierig

'inroad *n.* Eingriff, der (on, into in + *Akk.*);
make ~s into sb.'s savings jmds.
Ersparnisse angreifen

in'sane *adj.* geisteskrank

in'sanitary *adj.* unhygienisch

in'sanity *n.* Geisteskrankheit, die

insatiable /ɪnˈseɪʃəbl/ *adj.* unersättlich;
unstillbar ‹*Verlangen*›

inscribe /ɪnˈskraɪb/ *v.t.* schreiben; (on stone,
rock) einmeißeln; mit einer Inschrift
versehen ‹*Denkmal, Grabstein*›

inscription /ɪnˈskrɪpʃn/ *n.* Inschrift, die;
(on coin) Aufschrift, die

inscrutable /ɪnˈskruːtəbl/ *adj.*
unergründlich; undurchdringlich ‹*Miene*›

insect /ˈɪnsekt/ *n.* Insekt, das

insect: ~ bite *n.* Insektenstich, der;
~-borne *adj.* durch Insekten übertragen
‹*Krankheit*›

insecticide /ɪnˈsektɪsaɪd/ *n.* Insektizid,
das

'insect repellent *n.*
Insektenschutzmittel, das

inse'cure *adj.* unsicher

inse'curity *n.* Unsicherheit, die

insemination /ɪnsemɪˈneɪʃn/ *n.* (of woman)
Befruchtung, die (of animal) Besamung, die

in'sensitive *adj.* (a) gefühllos ‹*Person,
Art*›; (unappreciative) unempfänglich (to für)
(b) (physically) unempfindlich (to gegen)

in'separable *adj.* untrennbar; (fig.)
unzertrennlich

insert /ɪnˈsɜːt/ *v.t.* (a) einlegen ‹*Film*›;
einwerfen ‹*Münze*›; hineinstecken
‹*Schlüssel*›; einstechen ‹*Nadel*›
(b) (Comp.) einfügen; **~ key** Einfügetaste, die

insertion /ɪnˈsɜːʃn/ *n.* ▶ INSERT: Einlegen,
das; Einwerfen, das; Hineinstecken, das;
Einstechen, das; Einfügen, das

'inset *n.* (small map) Nebenkarte, die; (small
photograph, diagram) Nebenbild, das

inside ⟨1⟩ /-ˈ-, ˈ--/ *n.* (a) (internal side)
Innenseite, die; **on the ~:** innen; **to/from the
~:** nach/von innen
(b) (inner part) Innere, das
⟨2⟩ /ˈ--/ *adj.* inner...; Innen⟨*wand,
-einrichtung, -ansicht*⟩; (fig.) intern

⟨3⟩ /-ˈ-/ *adv.* (on or in the **~**) innen; (to the **~**)
nach innen hinein/herein; (indoors) drinnen;
come ~: hereinkommen; **take a look ~:**
hineinsehen; **go ~:** [ins Haus] hineingehen;
turn a jacket ~ out eine Jacke nach links
wenden; **know sth. ~ out** etw. in- und
auswendig kennen
⟨4⟩ /-ˈ-/ *prep.* (position) in (+ *Dat.*); (direction) in
(+ *Akk.*) hinein

inside-'leg *adj.* **~ measurement**
Schrittlänge, die

insidious /ɪnˈsɪdɪəs/ *adj.* heimtückisch

'insight *n.* (discernment) Verständnis, das;
gain an ~ into sth. Einblick in etw. (*Akk.*)
gewinnen

insig'nificant *adj.* unbedeutend;
geringfügig ‹*Summe*›

insin'cere *adj.* unaufrichtig

insin'cerity *n.* Unaufrichtigkeit, die

insinuate /ɪnˈsɪnjʊeɪt/ *v.t.* andeuten (**to sb.**
jmdm. gegenüber)

insinuation /ɪnsɪnjʊˈeɪʃn/ *n.* Anspielung,
die (**about** auf + *Akk.*)

insipid /ɪnˈsɪpɪd/ *adj.* fade

insist /ɪnˈsɪst/ *v.i.* bestehen ([up]on auf
+ *Dat.*); **~ on doing sth./on sb.'s doing sth.**
darauf bestehen, etw. zu tun/dass jmd. etw.
tut; **if you ~:** wenn du darauf bestehst

insistence /ɪnˈsɪstəns/ *n.* Bestehen, das
(**on** auf + *Dat.*)

insistent /ɪnˈsɪstənt/ *adj.* **be ~ that ...:**
darauf bestehen, dass ...

insolence /ˈɪnsələns/ *n.* Unverschämtheit,
die; Frechheit, die

insolent /ˈɪnsələnt/ *adj.,* **'insolently** *adv.*
unverschämt; frech

in'soluble *adj.* (a) (esp. Chem.) unlöslich
(b) (not solvable) unlösbar

insolvency /ɪnˈsɒlvənsɪ/ *n.*
Zahlungsunfähigkeit, die

in'solvent *adj.* zahlungsunfähig

insomnia /ɪnˈsɒmnɪə/ *n.* Schlaflosigkeit, die

insomniac /ɪnˈsɒmnɪæk/ *n.* **be an ~:** an
Schlaflosigkeit leiden

inspect /ɪnˈspekt/ *v.t.* prüfend betrachten;
(examine officially) überprüfen; kontrollieren
‹*Räumlichkeiten*›

inspection /ɪnˈspekʃn/ *n.* Überprüfung,
die; (of premises) Kontrolle, die; Inspektion,
die; **on [closer] ~:** bei näherer Betrachtung

inspector /ɪnˈspektə(r)/ *n.* (a) (on bus, train,
etc.) Kontrolleur, der/Kontrolleurin, die
(b) (Brit.) ≈ Polizeiinspektor, der

inspiration /ɪnspəˈreɪʃn/ *n.* Inspiration, die
(geh.)

inspire /ɪnˈspaɪə(r)/ *v.t.* (a) inspirieren
(geh.) ‹*Person*›
(b) (instil) einflößen (**in** *Dat.*)

inspiring /ɪnˈspaɪərɪŋ/ *adj.* inspirierend
(geh.)

insta'bility *n.* Instabilität, die; (of person)
Labilität, die

install /ɪn'stɔːl/ v.t. installieren; einbauen ⟨Badezimmer⟩; anschließen ⟨Telefon, Herd⟩; ∼ oneself sich installieren

installation /ɪnstə'leɪʃn/ n. (a) Installation, die; (of bathroom) Einbau, der; (of telephone, cooker) Anschluss, der (b) (apparatus etc. installed) Anlage, die

instalment (Amer.: **installment**) /ɪn'stɔːlmənt/ n. (a) (part payment) Rate, die; pay by or in ∼s in Raten zahlen (b) (of serial, novel) Fortsetzung, die; (Radio, Telev.) Folge, die

instance /'ɪnstəns/ n. (example) Beispiel, das (of für); for ∼: zum Beispiel; in many ∼s (cases) in vielen Fällen; in the first ∼: zunächst einmal

instant /'ɪnstənt/ 1 adj. unmittelbar; sofortig ⟨Wirkung, Linderung, Ergebnis⟩; ∼ coffee/tea Pulverkaffee/Instanttee, der; ∼ potatoes fertiger Kartoffelbrei
2 n. Augenblick, der; at that very ∼: genau in dem Augenblick; come here this ∼: komm sofort her; in an ∼: augenblicklich

instantaneous /ɪnstən'teɪnɪəs/ adj. unmittelbar; his reaction was ∼: er reagierte sofort

'instantly adv. sofort

instead /ɪn'sted/ adv. stattdessen; ∼ of doing sth. [an]statt etw. zu tun; ∼ of sth. anstelle einer Sache (Gen.); I will go ∼ of you ich gehe an deiner Stelle

'instep n. (of foot) Spann, der; Fußrücken, der; (of shoe) Blatt, das

instigate /'ɪnstɪgeɪt/ v.t. anstiften (to zu); initiieren (geh.) ⟨Reformen, Projekt usw.⟩

instigation /ɪnstɪ'geɪʃn/ n. Anstiftung, die; (of reforms, project, etc.) Initiierung, die; at sb.'s ∼: auf jmds. Betreiben (Akk.)

instil (Amer.: **instill**) /ɪn'stɪl/ v.t., -ll- einflößen (in Dat.); beibringen ⟨gutes Benehmen, Wissen⟩ (in Dat.)

instinct /'ɪnstɪŋkt/ n. Instinkt, der

instinctive /ɪn'stɪŋktɪv/ adj., **in'stinctively** adv. instinktiv

institute /'ɪnstɪtjuːt/ 1 n. Institut, das
2 v.t. einführen; einleiten ⟨Suche, Verfahren⟩; anstrengen ⟨Prozess⟩

institution /ɪnstɪ'tjuːʃn/ n. Institution, die; (home) Heim, das; Anstalt, die

instruct /ɪn'strʌkt/ v.t. (a) (teach) unterrichten ⟨Klasse, Fach⟩ (b) (direct, command) anweisen

instruction /ɪn'strʌkʃn/ n. (a) (teaching) Unterricht, der (b) esp. in pl. (direction, order) Anweisung, die; ∼ manual/∼s for use Gebrauchsanleitung, die

instructive /ɪn'strʌktɪv/ adj. aufschlussreich; lehrreich ⟨Erfahrung, Buch⟩

instructor /ɪn'strʌktə(r)/ n. Lehrer, der/ Lehrerin, die; (Mil.) Ausbilder, der

instrument /'ɪnstrʊmənt/ n. Instrument, das

instrumental /ɪnstrə'mentl/ adj. (a) (Mus.) Instrumental- (b) (helpful) dienlich (to Dat.); he was ∼ in finding me a job er hat mir zu einer Stelle verholfen

instrumentalist /ɪnstrʊ'mentəlɪst/ n. Instrumentalist, der/Instrumentalistin, die

insubordinate /ɪnsə'bɔːdɪnət/ adj. aufsässig

insubordination /ɪnsəbɔːdɪ'neɪʃn/ n. Aufsässigkeit, die

insubstantial /ɪnsəb'stænʃl/ adj. wenig substanziell (geh.)

insufferable /ɪn'sʌfərəbl/ adj. (unbearably arrogant) unausstehlich

insuf'ficient adj. nicht genügend; unzulänglich ⟨Beweise⟩; unzureichend ⟨Versorgung, Beleuchtung⟩

insuf'ficiently adv. ungenügend

insular /'ɪnsjʊlə(r)/ adj. (a) Insel-; insular (fachspr.) (b) (fig.: narrow-minded) provinziell (abwertend)

insulate /'ɪnsjʊleɪt/ v.t. isolieren (against, from gegen); insulating tape Isolierband, das

insulation /ɪnsjʊ'leɪʃn/ n. Isolierung, die

insulin /'ɪnsjʊlɪn/ n. Insulin, das

insult 1 /'ɪnsʌlt/ n. Beleidigung, die (to Gen.)
2 /ɪn'sʌlt/ v.t. beleidigen

insulting /ɪn'sʌltɪŋ/ adj. beleidigend

insuperable /ɪn'suːpərəbl/ adj. unüberwindlich

insupportable /ɪnsə'pɔːtəbl/ adj. (undurable) unerträglich

insurance /ɪn'ʃʊərəns/ n. Versicherung, die; (fig.) Sicherheit, die; take out ∼ against/ on sth. eine Versicherung gegen etw. abschließen/etw. versichern lassen; travel ∼: Reisegepäck- und -unfallversicherung, die

insurance: ∼ **agent** n. Versicherungsvertreter, der/-vertreterin, die; ∼ **broker** n. Versicherungsmakler, der/ -maklerin, die; ∼ **claim** n. Versicherungsanspruch, der; ∼ **company** n. Versicherungsgesellschaft, die; ∼ **stamp** n. (Brit.) Versicherungsmarke, die

insure /ɪn'ʃʊə(r)/ v.t. versichern ⟨Person⟩; versichern lassen ⟨Gepäck, Gemälde usw.⟩; ∼ [oneself] against sth. [sich] gegen etw. versichern

insurer /ɪn'ʃʊərə(r)/ n. Versicherer, der

insurmountable /ɪnsə'maʊntəbl/ adj. unüberwindlich

intact /ɪn'tækt/ adj. (a) (entire) unbeschädigt; intakt ⟨Uhr, Maschine usw.⟩ (b) (unimpaired) unversehrt

'intake n. (a) (action) Aufnahme, die (b) (persons, things) Neuzugänge Pl.; (amount) aufgenommene Menge

in'tangible *adj.* nicht greifbar; (mentally) unbestimmbar

integral /'ɪntɪgrl/ *adj.* **(a)** wesentlich ⟨*Bestandteil*⟩ **(b)** (whole) vollständig

integrate /'ɪntɪgreɪt/ *v.t.* integrieren (into in + *Akk.*)

integration /ɪntɪ'greɪʃn/ *n.* Integration, *die* (into in + *Akk.*)

integrity /ɪn'tegrɪti/ *n.* Redlichkeit, *die*

intellect /'ɪntəlekt/ *n.* Verstand, *der;* Intellekt, *der*

intellectual /ɪntə'lektjʊəl/ ① *adj.* intellektuell; geistig anspruchsvoll ⟨*Person, Publikum*⟩ ② *n.* Intellektuelle, *der/die*

intelligence /ɪn'telɪdʒəns/ *n.* **(a)** Intelligenz, *die* **(b)** (information) Informationen *Pl.* **(c)** military ~ (organization) militärischer Geheimdienst

intelligence: ~ **quotient** *n.* Intelligenzquotient, *der;* ~ **test** *n.* Intelligenztest, *der*

intelligent /ɪn'telɪdʒənt/ *adj.* intelligent

intelligible /ɪn'telɪdʒɪbl/ *adj.* verständlich (to für)

intend /ɪn'tend/ *v.t.* beabsichtigen; it was ~ed as a joke das sollte ein Witz sein

in'tended *adj.* beabsichtigt ⟨*Wirkung*⟩; be ~ for sb./sth. für jmdn./etw. gedacht sein

intense /ɪn'tens/ *adj.* **(a)** intensiv; groß ⟨*Hitze, Belastung, Interesse*⟩; stark ⟨*Schmerzen*⟩ **(b)** (earnest) ernst

in'tensely *adv.* äußerst; intensiv ⟨*studieren, fühlen*⟩

intensify /ɪn'tensɪfaɪ/ ① *v.t.* intensivieren ② *v.i.* zunehmen

intensity /ɪn'tensɪti/ *n.* ▶ INTENSE A: Intensität, *die;* Größe, *die;* Stärke, *die*

intensive /ɪn'tensɪv/ *adj.* intensiv; Intensiv⟨*kurs*⟩; be in ~ care auf der Intensivstation sein

in'tensively *adv.* intensiv

intent /ɪn'tent/ ① *n.* Absicht, *die;* to all ~s and purposes im Grunde ② *adj.* be ~ on achieving sth. etw. unbedingt erreichen wollen

intention /ɪn'tenʃn/ *n.* Absicht, *die*

intentional /ɪn'tenʃənl/ *adj.,* **in'tentionally** *adv.* absichtlich

in'tently *adv.* aufmerksam

interact /ɪntər'ækt/ *v.i.* interagieren

interaction /ɪntər'ækʃn/ *n.* Interaktion, *die*

interactive /ɪntər'æktɪv/ *adj.* (Sociol., Psych., Comp.) interaktiv; ~ television interaktives Fernsehen

intercede /ɪntə'siːd/ *v.i.* sich einsetzen (with bei; for, on behalf of für)

intercept /ɪntə'sept/ *v.t.* abfangen

interchange ① /'ɪntətʃeɪndʒ/ *n.* **(a)** Austausch, *der* **(b)** (road junction) [Autobahn]kreuz, *das* ② /ɪntə'tʃeɪndʒ/ *v.t.* austauschen

interchangeable /ɪntə'tʃeɪndʒəbl/ *adj.* austauschbar

inter-city /ɪntə'sɪti/ *adj.* Intercity-; ~ train Intercity[-Zug], *der*

intercom /'ɪntəkɒm/ *n.* (coll.) Gegensprechanlage, *die*

interconnect /ɪntəkə'nekt/ ① *v.t.* miteinander verbinden ② *v.i.* miteinander in Zusammenhang stehen

intercontinental /ɪntəkɒntɪ'nentl/ *adj.* interkontinental

intercourse /'ɪntəkɔːs/ *n.* (sexual) [Geschlechts]verkehr, *der*

interest /'ɪntrəst/ ① *n.* **(a)** Interesse, *das;* take *or* have an ~ in sb./sth. sich für jmdn./etw. interessieren; [just] for *or* out of ~: [nur] interessehalber; with ~: interessiert; act in one's own/sb.'s ~[s] im eigenen/in jmds. Interesse handeln; be of ~: interessant sein (to für) **(b)** (Finance) Zinsen *Pl.* ② *v.t.* interessieren; be ~ed sich interessieren (in für)

interest-'free *adj., adv.* unverzinslich ⟨*Schuldverschreibung*⟩; zinsfrei ⟨*Darlehen*⟩

'interesting *adj.* interessant

'interest rate *n.* Zinssatz, *der;* Zinsfuß, *der*

interface /'ɪntəfeɪs/ *n.* (Comp.) Schnittstelle, *die*

interfere /ɪntə'fɪə(r)/ *v.i.* sich einmischen (in in + *Akk.*); ~ with sth. sich (*Dat.*) an etw. (*Dat.*) zu schaffen machen

interference /ɪntə'fɪərəns/ *n.* **(a)** (interfering) Einmischung, *die* **(b)** (Radio, Telev.) Störung, *die*

interim /'ɪntərɪm/ ① *n.* in the ~: in der Zwischenzeit ② *adj.* vorläufig

interior /ɪn'tɪərɪə(r)/ ① *adj.* inner...; Innen⟨*fläche, -wand*⟩ ② *n.* Innere, *das*

interior: ~ **deco'ration** *n.* Raumgestaltung, *die;* ~ **'decorator** *n.* Raumgestalter, *der*/-gestalterin, *die;* ~ **de'sign** *n.* Innenarchitektur, *die;* ~ **de'signer** *n.* Innenarchitekt, *der*/-architektin, *die*

interject /ɪntə'dʒekt/ *v.t.* einwerfen

interjection /ɪntə'dʒekʃn/ *n.* Ausruf, *der*

interloper /'ɪntələʊpə(r)/ *n.* Eindringling, *der*

interlude /'ɪntəluːd/ *n.* Pause, *die;* (music) Zwischenspiel, *das*

intermediary /ɪntə'miːdɪərɪ/ *n.* Vermittler, *der*/Vermittlerin, *die*

intermediate /ɪntə'miːdjət/ *adj.* Zwischen-

interminable /ɪn'tɜːmɪnəbl/ *adj.* endlos

intermingle /ɪntə'mɪŋgl/ v.i. sich
vermischen
intermission /ɪntə'mɪʃn/ n. Pause, die
intermittent /ɪntə'mɪtənt/ adj. in
Abständen auftretend
inter'mittently adv. in Abständen
intern /ɪn'tɜ:n/ v.t. gefangen halten
internal /ɪn'tɜ:nl/ adj. inner...;
Innen⟨fläche, -abmessungen⟩
internally /ɪn'tɜ:nəlɪ/ adv. innerlich
international /ɪntə'næʃənl/ [1] adj.
international
[2] n. (a) (Sport) (contest) Länderspiel, das
(b) (participant) Nationalspieler, der/
-spielerin, die
international: ∼ **call** n.
Auslandsgespräch, das; ∼ **'law** n.
Völkerrecht, das
inter'nationally adv. international
International 'Monetary Fund n.
Internationaler Währungsfonds
internee /ɪntɜ:'ni:/ n. Internierte, der/die
Internet /'ɪntənet/ n. the ∼ das Internet;
on the ∼: im Internet
Internet: ∼ **access** n. Internetzugang,
der; ∼ **cafe** n. Internetcafé, das;
∼ **'Service Provider** n.
Internetprovider, der; ∼ **site** n.
Internetseite, die
in'ternment n. Internierung, die
interplay /'ɪntəpleɪ/ n. Zusammenspiel,
das
interpret /ɪn'tɜ:prɪt/ [1] v.t. (a)
interpretieren; deuten ⟨Traum, Zeichen⟩
(b) (between languages) dolmetschen
[2] v.i. dolmetschen
interpretation /ɪntɜ:prɪ'teɪʃn/ n.
Interpretation, die; (of dream, symptoms)
Deutung, die
in'terpreter n. Dolmetscher, der/
Dolmetscherin, die
interrogate /ɪn'terəgeɪt/ v.t. verhören;
ausfragen ⟨Freund, Kind usw.⟩
interrogation /ɪnterə'geɪʃn/ n. Verhör,
das
interrogative /ɪntə'rɒgətɪv/ adj. (Ling.)
Interrogativ-
interrogator /ɪn'terəgeɪtə(r)/ n.
Vernehmer, der
interrupt /ɪntə'rʌpt/ [1] v.t. unterbrechen;
don't ∼ me when I'm busy stör mich nicht,
wenn ich zu tun habe
[2] v.i. unterbrechen; stören
interruption /ɪntə'rʌpʃn/ n.
Unterbrechung, die; Störung, die
intersect /ɪntə'sekt/ v.i. (a) ⟨Straßen:⟩ sich
kreuzen
(b) (Geom.) sich schneiden
intersection /ɪntə'sekʃn/ n. (a) (road
junction) Kreuzung, die
(b) (Geom.) Schnittpunkt, der
intersperse /ɪntə'spɜ:s/ v.t. be ∼d with
durchsetzt sein mit

interval /'ɪntəvl/ n. (a) [Zeit]abstand, der;
at ∼s in Abständen
(b) (break; also Brit. Theatre etc.) Pause, die;
sunny ∼s Aufheiterungen Pl.
intervene /ɪntə'vi:n/ v.i. (a) [vermittelnd]
eingreifen (in in + Akk.)
(b) the intervening years die
dazwischenliegenden Jahre
intervention /ɪntə'venʃn/ n. Eingreifen,
das; Intervention, die (bes. Politik)
interview /'ɪntəvju:/ [1] n. (a) (for job)
Vorstellungsgespräch, das
(b) (Journ., Radio, Telev.) Interview, das
[2] v.t. ein Vorstellungsgespräch führen mit;
interviewen ⟨Politiker, Filmstar usw.⟩
'interviewer n. Interviewer, der/
Interviewerin, die
intestine /ɪn'testɪn/ n. Darm, der
intimacy /'ɪntɪməsɪ/ n. (a) Vertrautheit,
die
(b) (sexual) Intimität, die
intimate [1] /'ɪntɪmət/ adj. (a) eng
⟨Freund, Verhältnis⟩; genau, (geh.) intim
⟨Kenntnis⟩
(b) (sexually) intim
[2] /'ɪntɪmeɪt/ v.t. (imply) andeuten
intimately /'ɪntɪmətlɪ/ adv. genau[estens]
⟨kennen⟩; eng ⟨verbinden⟩
intimidate /ɪn'tɪmɪdeɪt/ v.t. einschüchtern
intimidation /ɪntɪmɪ'deɪʃn/ n.
Einschüchterung, die
into /before vowel 'ɪntʊ, before consonant
'ɪntə/ prep. in (+ Akk.); (against) gegen; I went
out ∼ the street ich ging auf die Straße
hinaus; translate sth. ∼ English etw. ins
Englische übersetzen
in'tolerable adj. unerträglich
in'tolerance n. Intoleranz, die
in'tolerant adj. intolerant (of gegenüber)
intonation /ɪntə'neɪʃn/ n. Intonation, die
intoxicant /ɪn'tɒksɪkənt/ n. Rauschmittel,
das
intoxicate /ɪn'tɒksɪkeɪt/ v.t. betrunken
machen
intoxication /ɪntɒksɪ'keɪʃn/ n. Rausch,
der
intractable /ɪn'træktəbl/ adj. hartnäckig
⟨Problem⟩
intransigent /ɪn'trænsɪdʒənt/ adj.
unnachgiebig
in'transitive adj. (Ling.) intransitiv
intra-uterine /ɪntrə'ju:təraɪn/ adj. (Med.)
intrauterin; ∼ [contraceptive] device
Intrauterinpessar, das
intravenous /ɪntrə'vi:nəs/ adj. (Med.)
intravenös
'in-tray n. Eingangskorb, der
intrepid /ɪn'trepɪd/ adj. unerschrocken
intricacy /'ɪntrɪkəsɪ/ n. Kompliziertheit,
die
intricate /'ɪntrɪkət/ adj. kompliziert
intrigue /ɪn'tri:g/ v.t. faszinieren

intriguing /ɪnˈtriːɡɪŋ/ adj. faszinierend
intrinsic /ɪnˈtrɪnsɪk/ adj. innewohnend; inner...; ~ **value** innerer Wert
intrinsically /ɪnˈtrɪnsɪkəlɪ/ adv. im Wesentlichen
intro /ˈɪntrəʊ/ n., pl. ~**s** (coll.) (presentation) Vorstellung, die; (Mus.) Einleitung, die
introduce /ɪntrəˈdjuːs/ v.t. einführen; ~ **oneself/sb.** [**to sb.**] sich/jmdn. [jmdm.] vorstellen
introduction /ɪntrəˈdʌkʃn/ n. Einführen, das; Einführung, die; (to person) Vorstellung, die; (to book) Einleitung, die
intro'duction agency n. Partnervermittlung[sagentur], die
introductory /ɪntrəˈdʌktərɪ/ adj. einleitend; Einführungs⟨kurs, -vortrag⟩
introspective /ɪntrəˈspektɪv/ adj. in sich (Akk.) gerichtet
introvert /ˈɪntrəvɜːt/ [1] n. Introvertierte, der/die; **be an** ~: introvertiert sein [2] adj. introvertiert
introverted /ˈɪntrəvɜːtɪd/ adj. introvertiert
intrude /ɪnˈtruːd/ v.i. stören
in'truder n. Eindringling, der
in'truder alarm n. Einbruchmeldeanlage, die
intrusion /ɪnˈtruːʒn/ n. Störung, die
intrusive /ɪnˈtruːsɪv/ adj. aufdringlich
intuition /ɪntjuːˈɪʃn/ n. Intuition, die
intuitive /ɪnˈtjuːɪtɪv/ adj., **in'tuitively** adv. intuitiv
inundate /ˈɪnəndeɪt/ v.t. überschwemmen
inure /ɪˈnjʊə(r)/ v.t. gewöhnen (**to** an + Akk.)
invade /ɪnˈveɪd/ v.t. einfallen in (+ Akk.)
in'vader n. Angreifer, der
invalid[1] /ˈɪnvəlɪd/ (Brit.) [1] n. Kranke, der/die; (disabled) Körperbehinderte, der/die [2] adj. körperbehindert
invalid[2] /ɪnˈvælɪd/ adj. nicht schlüssig ⟨Argument, Theorie⟩; ungültig ⟨Fahrkarte, Garantie, Vertrag⟩
invalidate /ɪnˈvælɪdeɪt/ v.t. aufheben; widerlegen ⟨Theorie, These⟩
in'valuable adj. unersetzlich ⟨Person⟩; unschätzbar ⟨Dienst, Hilfe⟩; außerordentlich wichtig ⟨Rolle⟩
in'variable adj. unveränderlich
invariably /ɪnˈveərɪəblɪ/ adv. immer; ausnahmslos ⟨falsch, richtig⟩
invasion /ɪnˈveɪʒn/ n. Invasion, die
invective /ɪnˈvektɪv/ n. Beschimpfungen Pl.
invent /ɪnˈvent/ v.t. erfinden
invention /ɪnˈvenʃn/ n. Erfindung, die
inventive /ɪnˈventɪv/ adj. (a) schöpferisch ⟨Person, Begabung⟩ (b) (original) originell
inventor /ɪnˈventə(r)/ n. Erfinder, der/ Erfinderin, die

inventory /ˈɪnvəntərɪ/ n. Bestandsliste, die; **make** or **take an** ~ **of sth.** von etw. ein Inventar aufstellen
inverse /ˈɪnvɜːs/ adj. umgekehrt
invert /ɪnˈvɜːt/ v.t. umstülpen
in'vertebrate n. wirbelloses Tier
inverted 'commas n. pl. (Brit.) Anführungszeichen Pl.
invest /ɪnˈvest/ v.t. (a) (Finance) anlegen (**in** in + Dat.); investieren (**in** in + Dat. od. Akk.) (b) (fig.) investieren; ~ **sb. with sth.** jmdm. etw. übertragen; ~ **sth. with sth.** einer Sache (Dat.) etw. verleihen
investigate /ɪnˈvestɪɡeɪt/ v.t. untersuchen
investigation /ɪnvestɪˈɡeɪʃn/ n. Untersuchung, die
investigative /ɪnˈvestɪɡətɪv/ adj. detektivisch; ~ **journalism** Enthüllungsjournalismus, der
investigator /ɪnˈvestɪɡeɪtə(r)/ n. [**private**] ~: [Privat]detektiv, der/-detektivin, die
in'vestment n. Investition, die; (money invested) angelegtes Geld; **be a good** ~ (fig.) sich bezahlt machen
investor /ɪnˈvestə(r)/ n. [Kapital]anleger, der/-anlegerin, die
inveterate /ɪnˈvetərət/ adj. eingefleischt ⟨Trinker, Raucher⟩; unverbesserlich ⟨Lügner⟩
invigilate /ɪnˈvɪdʒɪleɪt/ v.i. (Brit.: in examination) Aufsicht führen
invigilator /ɪnˈvɪdʒɪleɪtə(r)/ n. (Brit.) Aufsichtsperson, die
invigorate /ɪnˈvɪɡəreɪt/ v.t. stärken; (physically) kräftigen
invigorating /ɪnˈvɪɡəreɪtɪŋ/ adj. kräftigend ⟨Getränk, Klima⟩
invincible /ɪnˈvɪnsɪbl/ adj. unbesiegbar
in'visible adj. unsichtbar
invitation /ɪnvɪˈteɪʃn/ n. Einladung, die; **at sb.'s** ~: auf jmds. Einladung (Akk.)
invite /ɪnˈvaɪt/ v.t. (a) (request to come) einladen (b) (request to do sth.) auffordern (c) (bring on) herausfordern ⟨Kritik, Verhängnis⟩
inviting /ɪnˈvaɪtɪŋ/ adj. einladend; verlockend ⟨Gedanke, Vorstellung⟩
in-vitro fertili'zation /ɪnˈviːtrəʊ fɜːtɪlaɪˈzeɪʃn/ n. künstliche Befruchtung [im Reagenzglas]; In-vitro-Fertilisation, die (fachspr.)
invoice /ˈɪnvɔɪs/ [1] n. (bill) Rechnung, die [2] v.t. ~ **sb.** jmdm. eine Rechnung schicken; ~ **sb. for sth.** jmdm. etw. in Rechnung stellen
invoke /ɪnˈvəʊk/ v.t. anrufen
in'voluntarily adv., **in'voluntary** adj. unwillkürlich
involve /ɪnˈvɒlv/ v.t. (a) (implicate) verwickeln

(b) become *or* get ~d in a fight in eine Schlägerei verwickelt werden; get ~d with sb. sich mit jmdm. einlassen
(c) (entail) mit sich bringen
involved /ɪnˈvɒlvd/ *adj.* verwickelt; (complicated) kompliziert
invulnerable /ɪnˈvʌlnərəbl/ *adj.* unverwundbar; (fig.) unantastbar
inward /ˈɪnwəd/ ⊡ *adj.* inner...
⊡ *adv.* einwärts ⟨*gerichtet, gebogen*⟩; open ~: nach innen öffnen
'inwardly *adv.* im Inneren; innerlich
inwards /ˈɪnwədz/ ▶ INWARD 2
iodine /ˈaɪədiːn/ *n.* Jod, *das*
ion /ˈaɪən/ *n.* Ion, *das*
iota /aɪˈəʊtə/ *n.* not one *or* an ~: nicht ein Jota (geh.)
IOU /aɪəʊˈjuː/ *n.* Schuldschein, *der*
IQ *abbr.* = **intelligence quotient** IQ, *der;* IQ-Test IQ-Test, *der*
IRA *abbr.* = **Irish Republican Army** IRA, *die*
Iran /ɪˈrɑːn/ *pr. n.* Iran, *der od.* (*das*)
Iraq /ɪˈrɑːk/ *pr. n.* Irak, *der od.* (*das*)
Iraq 'War *n.* Irakkrieg, *der*
irate /aɪˈreɪt/ *adj.* wütend
Ireland /ˈaɪələnd/ *pr. n.* Irland (*das*)
iris /ˈaɪərɪs/ *n.* (Bot., Anat.) Iris, *die*
Irish /ˈaɪərɪʃ/ ⊡ *adj.* irisch; sb. is ~: jmd. ist Ire/Irin
⊡ *n.* **(a)** (language) Irisch, *das; see also* ENGLISH 2A
(b) *constr. as pl.* the ~: die Iren *Pl.*
Irish: ~man /ˈaɪərɪʃmən/ *n., pl.* ~men /ˈaɪərɪʃmən/ Ire, *der;* ~ **Re'public** *pr. n.* Irische Republik; ~ **'Sea** *pr. n.* Irische See; ~**woman** *n.* Irin, *die*
irk /ɜːk/ *v.t.* ärgern
irksome /ˈɜːksəm/ *adj.* lästig
iron /ˈaɪən/ ⊡ *n.* **(a)** (metal) Eisen, *das*
(b) (for smoothing) Bügeleisen, *das*
⊡ *attrib. adj.* eisern; Eisen⟨*platte usw.*⟩
⊡ *v.t. & i.* bügeln
■ **iron 'out** *v.t.* herausbügeln; (fig.) aus dem Weg räumen
Iron 'Curtain *n.* (Hist.) Eiserner Vorhang
ironic /aɪˈrɒnɪk/, **ironical** /aɪˈrɒnɪkl/ *adj.* ironisch
ironing /ˈaɪənɪŋ/ *n.* Bügeln, *das;* (items) Bügelwäsche, *die;* do the ~: bügeln
'ironing board *n.* Bügelbrett, *das*
ironmonger /ˈaɪənmʌŋɡə(r)/ *n.* (Brit.) Eisenwarenhändler, *der*/-händlerin, *die*
irony /ˈaɪrənɪ/ *n.* Ironie, *die;* the ~ was that ...: die Ironie lag darin, dass ...
irradiate /ɪˈreɪdɪeɪt/ *v.t.* bestrahlen
irrational /ɪˈræʃənl/ *adj.* irrational
irreconcilable /ɪˈrekənsaɪləbl/ *adj.* (incompatible) unvereinbar
irrefutable /ɪrɪˈfjuːtəbl/ *adj.* unwiderlegbar

irregular /ɪˈreɡjʊlə(r)/ *adj.* unregelmäßig; unkorrekt ⟨*Verhalten, Handlung usw.*⟩
irregularity /ɪreɡjʊˈlærɪtɪ/ *n.* ▶ IRREGULAR: Unregelmäßigkeit, *die;* Unkorrektheit, *die*
irrelevance /ɪˈrelɪvəns/, **irrelevancy** /ɪˈrelɪvənsɪ/ *ns.* Belanglosigkeit, *die;* Irrelevanz, *die* (geh.)
irrelevant /ɪˈrelɪvənt/ *adj.* belanglos; irrelevant (geh.)
irreparable /ɪˈrepərəbl/ *adj.* nicht wieder gutzumachend *nicht präd.;* irreparabel (geh., Med.)
irreplaceable /ɪrɪˈpleɪsəbl/ *adj.* unersetzlich
irrepressible /ɪrɪˈpresɪbl/ *adj.* nicht zu unterdrücken *nicht präd.;* she is ~: sie ist nicht unterzukriegen (ugs.)
irresistible /ɪrɪˈzɪstɪbl/ *adj.* unwiderstehlich; bestechend ⟨*Argument*⟩
irresolute /ɪˈrezəluːt/ *adj.* unentschlossen
irrespective /ɪrɪˈspektɪv/ *adj.* ~ of ungeachtet (+ *Gen.*)
irresponsible /ɪrɪˈspɒnsɪbl/ *adj.* verantwortungslos ⟨*Person*⟩; unverantwortlich ⟨*Benehmen*⟩
irretrievable /ɪrɪˈtriːvəbl/ *adj.* nicht mehr wiederzubekommen *nicht attr.*
irreverence /ɪˈrevərəns/ *n.* Respektlosigkeit, *die*
irreverent /ɪˈrevərənt/ *adj.* respektlos
irreversible /ɪrɪˈvɜːsɪbl/, **irrevocable** /ɪˈrevəkəbl/ *adjs.* unwiderruflich
irrigate /ˈɪrɪɡeɪt/ *v.t.* bewässern
irrigation /ɪrɪˈɡeɪʃn/ *n.* Bewässerung, *die*
irritable /ˈɪrɪtəbl/ *adj.* (quick to anger) reizbar; (temporarily) gereizt
irritant /ˈɪrɪtənt/ *n.* Reizstoff, *der*
irritate /ˈɪrɪteɪt/ *v.t.* **(a)** ärgern; get ~d ärgerlich werden; be ~d by sth. sich über etw. (*Akk.*) ärgern
(b) (Med.) reizen
irritating /ˈɪrɪteɪtɪŋ/ *adj.* lästig
irritation /ɪrɪˈteɪʃn/ *n.* **(a)** Ärger, *der;*
(b) (Med.) Reizung, *die*
is ▶ BE
Islam /ˈɪzlɑːm/ *n.* Islam, *der*
Islamist /ˈɪzlæmɪst/ ⊡ *n.* Islamist, *der*/ Islamistin *die*
⊡ *adj.* islamistisch
island /ˈaɪlənd/ *n.* Insel, *die*
'islander *n.* Inselbewohner, *der*/ -bewohnerin, *die*
island: ~hop *v.i.* go ~-hopping eine Inselhoppingtour machen; ~**-hopping** *n.* Inselhopping, *das*
isle /aɪl/ *n.* Insel, *die*
isn't /ˈɪznt/ (coll.) = is not; ▶ BE
isolate /ˈaɪsəleɪt/ *v.t.* isolieren
isolated /ˈaɪsəleɪtɪd/ *adj.* **(a)** (single) einzeln; ~ cases/instances Einzelfälle
(b) (remote) abgelegen

isolation /aɪsə'leɪʃn/ *n.* (a) (act) Isolierung, *die*
(b) (state) Isolation, *die*

ISP *abbr.* = **Internet service provider** ISP

Israel /'ɪzreɪl/ *pr. n.* Israel (*das*)

Israeli /ɪz'reɪlɪ/ **1** *adj.* israelisch; **sb. is ~:** jmd. ist Israeli
2 *n.* Israeli, *der*/*die*

issue /'ɪʃuː, 'ɪsjuː/ **1** *n.* (a) (point in question) Frage, *die;* **make an ~ of sth.** etw. aufbauschen; **evade** *or* **dodge the ~:** ausweichen
(b) (of magazine etc.) Ausgabe, *die*
(c) (result, outcome) Ergebnis, *das*
2 *v.t.* (a) (give out) ausgeben; ausstellen ⟨*Pass*⟩; erteilen ⟨*Lizenz, Befehl*⟩; **~ sb. with sth.** etw. an jmdn. austeilen
(b) (publish) herausgeben ⟨*Publikation*⟩

it /ɪt/ *pron.* (a) es; **I can't cope with it any more** ich halte das nicht mehr länger aus; **what is it?** was ist los?
(b) (the thing, animal, young child previously mentioned) er/sie/es; *as direct obj.* ihn/sie/es; *as indirect obj.* ihm/ihr/ihm
(c) (the person in question) **who is it?** wer ist da?; **it was the children** es waren die Kinder; **is it you, Dad?** bist du es, Vater?

IT *abbr.* = **information technology** IT

Italian /ɪ'tæljən/ **1** *adj.* italienisch; **sb. is ~:** jmd. ist Italiener/Italienerin
2 *n.* (a) (person) Italiener, *der*/Italienerin, *die*
(b) (language) Italienisch, *das; see also* ENGLISH 2A

italic /ɪ'tælɪk/ **1** *adj.* kursiv
2 *n. in pl.* Kursivschrift, *die;* **in ~s** kursiv

Italy /'ɪtəlɪ/ *pr. n.* Italien (*das*)

itch /ɪtʃ/ **1** *n.* Juckreiz, *der;* **I have an ~:** es juckt mich
2 *v.i.* (a) einen Juckreiz haben; **it ~es** es juckt
(b) **~** *or* **be ~ing to do sth.** darauf brennen, etw. zu tun

'itchy *adj.* kratzig; **be ~** ⟨*Körperteil:*⟩ jucken

it'd /'ɪtəd/ (coll.) (a) = **it had**
(b) = **it would**

item /'aɪtəm/ *n.* (a) Ding, *das;* Sache, *die;* (in shop, catalogue) Artikel, *der;* (on radio, TV) Nummer, *die;* **~ of clothing** Kleidungsstück, *das*
(b) **~** [of news] Nachricht, *die*

itemize /'aɪtəmaɪz/ *v.t.* einzeln aufführen

itinerary /aɪ'tɪnərərɪ/ *n.* Reiseroute, *die*

it'll /ɪtl/ (coll.) = **it will**

its /ɪts/ *poss. pron. attrib.* sein/ihr/sein

it's /ɪts/ (a) = **it is**
(b) = **it has**

itself /ɪt'self/ *pron.* (a) *emphat.* selbst
(b) *refl.* sich

IUD *abbr.* = **intrauterine device** IUP

I've /aɪv/ = **I have**

IVF *abbr.* = **in-vitro fertilization** IVF

ivory /'aɪvərɪ/ *n.* Elfenbein, *das; attrib.* elfenbeinern; Elfenbein-

ivy /'aɪvɪ/ *n.* Efeu, *der*

J j

J, j /dʒeɪ/ *n.* J, j, *das*

jab /dʒæb/ **1** *v.t.*, **-bb-** stoßen
2 *n.* (a) Stoß, *der;* (with needle) Stich, *der*
(b) (Brit. coll.: injection) Spritze, *die*

jabber /'dʒæbə(r)/ *v.i.* plappern (ugs.)

jack /dʒæk/ *n.* (a) (for car) Wagenheber, *der*
(b) (Cards) Bube, *der*

jackal /'dʒækl/ *n.* Schakal, *der*

jackdaw /'dʒækdɔː/ *n.* Dohle, *die*

jacket /'dʒækɪt/ *n.* (a) Jacke, *die;* (of suit) Jackett, *das;* **sports ~:** Sakko, *der*
(b) (of book) Schutzumschlag, *der*
(c) **~ potatoes** in der Schale gebackene Kartoffeln

jack: ~-knife *v.i.* **the lorry ~-knifed** der Anhänger des Lastwagens stellte sich quer; **~pot** *n.* Jackpot, *der;* **hit the ~pot** (fig.) das große Los ziehen

jacuzzi (Amer.: ®) /dʒə'kuːzɪ/ *n.* ≈ Whirlpool, *der*

jaded /'dʒeɪdɪd/ *adj.* abgespannt

jagged /'dʒægɪd/ *adj.* gezackt

jaguar /'dʒægjʊə(r)/ *n.* Jaguar, *der*

jail /dʒeɪl/ **1** *n.* Gefängnis, *das*
2 *v.t.* ins Gefängnis bringen

jail: ~bird Knastbruder, *der* (ugs.); **~break** *n.* Gefängnisausbruch, *der*

jailer, jailor /'dʒeɪlə(r)/ *n.* Gefängniswärter, *der*/-wärterin, *die*

jam¹ /dʒæm/ **1** *v.t.*, **-mm-:** (a) (between two surfaces) einklemmen
(b) (make immovable) blockieren; (fig.) lähmen
2 *v.i.*, **-mm-:** (a) (become wedged) sich verklemmen
(b) ⟨*Maschine:*⟩ klemmen
3 *n.* (a) (crush, stoppage) Blockierung, *die*

(b) (coll.: dilemma) **be in a** ∼: in der Klemme stecken (ugs.)

■ **jam 'on** v.t. ∼ **the brakes** [full] **on** [voll] auf die Bremse steigen (ugs.)

jam² n. Marmelade, die

Jamaica /dʒə'meɪkə/ pr. n. Jamaika (das)

jamb /dʒæm/ n. (of doorway, window) Pfosten, der

'**jam-packed** adj. (coll.) knallvoll (ugs.), proppenvoll (ugs.) **(with** von)

Jan. abbr. = **January** Jan.

jangle /'dʒæŋgl/ [1] v.i. klimpern; ⟨Klingel:⟩ bimmeln

  [2] v.t. rasseln mit

janitor /'dʒænɪtə(r)/ n. Hausmeister, der

January /'dʒænjʊərɪ/ n. Januar, der; see also AUGUST

Japan /dʒə'pæn/ n. Japan (das)

Japanese /dʒæpə'niːz/ [1] adj. japanisch; **sb. is** ∼ jmd. ist Japaner/Japanerin

  [2] n., pl. same **(a)** (person) Japaner, der/ Japanerin, die

  (b) (language) Japanisch, das; see also ENGLISH 2A

jar¹ /dʒɑː(r)/ [1] v.i., -rr- quietschen; (fig.) ∼ **on sb./sb.'s nerves** jmdm. auf die Nerven gehen

  [2] v.t., -rr- erschüttern

jar² n. Topf, der; (glass ∼) Glas, das

jargon /'dʒɑːgən/ n. Jargon, der

jasmin[e] /'dʒæsmɪn/ n. Jasmin, der

jaundice /'dʒɔːndɪs/ n. (Med.) Gelbsucht, die

jaundiced /'dʒɔːndɪst/ adj. (fig.) verbittert

jaunt /dʒɔːnt/ n. Ausflug, der

jaunty /'dʒɔːntɪ/ adj. unbeschwert; keck ⟨Hut⟩; **he wore his hat at a** ∼ **angle** er hatte sich (Dat.) den Hut keck aufs Ohr gesetzt

javelin /'dʒævlɪn/ n. **(a)** Speer, der

  (b) (Sport: event) Speerwerfen, das

jaw /dʒɔː/ n. Kiefer, der

'**jawbone** n. Kieferknochen, der

jay /dʒeɪ/ n. Eichelhäher, der

'**jay-walk** v.i. als Fußgänger im Straßenverkehr unachtsam sein

jazz /dʒæz/ [1] n. Jazz, der; attrib. Jazz-

  [2] v.t. ∼ **up** aufpeppen (ugs.)

jazz: ∼ **band** n. Jazzband, die; ∼ **dance** n. Jazztanz, der; ∼ '**rock** n. Jazzrock, der

jazzy /'dʒæzɪ/ adj. poppig; **a** ∼ **sports car** ein aufgemotzter Sportwagen (ugs.)

jealous /'dʒeləs/ adj. eifersüchtig **(of** auf + Akk.)

'**jealousy** n. Eifersucht, die

jeans /dʒiːnz/ n. pl. Jeans Pl.

Jeep ® /dʒiːp/ n. Jeep Ⓦ, der

jeer /dʒɪə(r)/ v.i. höhnen (geh.); ∼ **at sb.** jmdn. verhöhnen

jelly /'dʒelɪ/ n. Gelee, das; (dessert) Götterspeise, die

'**jellyfish** n. Qualle, die

jeopardize /'dʒepədaɪz/ v.t. gefährden

jeopardy /'dʒepədɪ/ n. **in** ∼: in Gefahr; gefährdet

jerk /dʒɜːk/ [1] n. Ruck, der

  [2] v.t. reißen an (+ Dat.)

  [3] v.i. zucken

jersey /'dʒɜːzɪ/ n. Pullover, der; (Sport) Trikot, das

jest /dʒest/ [1] n. Scherz, der; **in** ∼: im Scherz

  [2] v.i. scherzen

Jesus /'dʒiːzəs/ pr. n. Jesus (der)

jet /dʒet/ n. **(a)** (stream) Strahl, der

  (b) (nozzle) Düse, die

  (c) (aircraft) Düsenflugzeug, das; Jet, der

jet: ∼**-black** adj. pechschwarz; ∼ **engine** n. Düsentriebwerk, das; ∼**foil** n. [Jetfoil-]Tragflügelboot, das; ∼ **lag** n. Jetlag, der; ∼**-lagged** adj. **sb. is** ∼**-lagged** jmdm. macht der Jetlag zu schaffen; ∼ **plane** n. Düsenflugzeug, das; ∼**-propelled** adj. düsengetrieben; ∼ **pro'pulsion** n. Düsen- od. Strahlantrieb, der

jetsam /'dʒetsəm/ n. ▶ FLOTSAM

jet: ∼ **set** n. Jet-set, der; ∼ **ski** n. Jetski, der

jettison /'dʒetɪsən/ v.t. über Bord werfen; (discard) wegwerfen

jetty /'dʒetɪ/ n. Landungsbrücke, die

Jew /dʒuː/ n. Jude, der/Jüdin, die

jewel /'dʒuːəl/ n. Juwel, das od. der

'**jewel box,** '**jewel case** ns. Schmuckkasten, der

jeweller (Amer.: **jeweler**) /'dʒuːələ(r)/ n. Juwelier, der

jewellery (Brit.), **jewelry** /'dʒuːəlrɪ/ n. Schmuck, der

Jewish /'dʒuːɪʃ/ adj. jüdisch; **he/she is** ∼: er ist Jude/sie ist Jüdin

jib /dʒɪb/ v.i., -bb- sich sträuben **(at** gegen)

jibe ▶ GIBE

jiffy /'dʒɪfɪ/ n. (coll.) **in a** ∼: sofort

'**Jiffy bag** ® n. gefütterte Versandtasche

jig /dʒɪg/ n. Jig, die

'**jigsaw** n. **(a)** Dekupiersäge, die; (electric) Stichsäge, die

  (b) ∼ [**puzzle**] Puzzle, das

jilt /dʒɪlt/ v.t. sitzenlassen (ugs.)

jingle /'dʒɪŋgl/ [1] n. (Commerc.) Werbespruch, der; Jingle, der (Werbespr.)

  [2] v.i. klimpern; ⟨Glöckchen:⟩ bimmeln

  [3] v.t. klimpern mit ⟨Münzen, Schlüsseln⟩

jinx /dʒɪŋks/ (coll.) [1] n. Fluch, der

  [2] v.t. verhexen

jitters /'dʒɪtəz/ n. pl. (coll.) großes Zittern

jittery /'dʒɪtərɪ/ adj. (coll.) (nervous) nervös; (frightened) verängstigt

job /dʒɒb/ n. **(a)** (piece of work) Arbeit, die; **I have a** ∼ **for you** ich habe eine Aufgabe für dich

  (b) (employment) Stelle, die; Job, der (ugs.)

job: ∼ **advert** n. Stellenanzeige, die; ∼**centre** n. (Brit.) Arbeitsvermittlungsstelle, die; ∼ **creation scheme** n. Beschäftigungsprogramm, das; Arbeitsbeschaffungsprogramm, das; ∼ **description** n. Arbeitsplatzbeschreibung, die; ∼ **evaluation** n. Arbeitsbewertung, die; ∼**-hunt** v.i. go/be ∼-hunting auf Arbeitsod. Stellensuche gehen/sein; ∼**-hunter** n. Stellen- od. Arbeitssuchende, der/die; ∼**-hunting** n. Arbeitssuche, die; Stellensuche, die

'jobless adj. arbeitslos

job: ∼ **market** n. Arbeitsmarkt, der; Stellenmarkt, der; ∼ **offer** n. Stellenangebot, das; ∼ **satisfaction** n. Arbeitszufriedenheit, die; ∼ **security** n. Arbeitsplatzsicherheit, die; ∼**-share** 1 n. geteilter Arbeitsplatz; 2 v.i. sich (Dat.) einen Arbeitsplatz teilen (with mit); ∼**-sharing** n. Jobsharing, das

jockey /'dʒɒkɪ/ n. Jockei, der

jockey shorts n. pl. (Amer.) Unterhose, die; Unterhosen Pl.

jocular /'dʒɒkjʊlə(r)/ adj. lustig

jodhpurs /'dʒɒdpəz/ n. pl. Reithose, die

jog /dʒɒg/ 1 v.t., -gg-: (a) (shake) rütteln (b) (nudge) [an]stoßen (c) ∼ sb.'s memory jmds. Gedächtnis (Dat.) auf die Sprünge helfen 2 v.i., -gg-: (a) (up and down) auf und ab hüpfen (b) (trot) ⟨Pferd:⟩ [dahin]trotten (c) (Sport) joggen 3 n. go for a ∼: joggen gehen

jogger /'dʒɒgə(r)/ n. Jogger, der/Joggerin, die

'jogging n. Jogging, das

'jogtrot n. (lit. or fig.) Trott, der

john /dʒɒn/ n. (Amer. sl.: lavatory) Lokus, der (salopp)

join /dʒɔɪn/ 1 v.t. (a) (connect) verbinden (to mit) (b) (come into company of) sich gesellen zu (c) (eintreten in (+ Akk.) ⟨Armee, Firma, Verein, Partei⟩ 2 v.i. ⟨Straßen:⟩ zusammenlaufen ■ **join in** 1 /-'-/ v.i. mitmachen (with bei) 2 /'--/ v.t. mitmachen bei ■ **join 'up** 1 v.i. (Mil.) einrücken 2 v.t. miteinander verbinden

'joiner n. Tischler, der/Tischlerin, die

joinery /'dʒɔɪnərɪ/ n., no art. (craft) Tischlerei, die; Tischlerhandwerk, das

joint /dʒɔɪnt/ 1 n. (a) (Building) Fuge, die (b) (Anat.) Gelenk, das (c) a ∼ [of meat] ein Stück Fleisch; (for roasting) ein Braten (d) (coll.: place) Laden, der (e) (sl.: marijuana cigarette) Joint, der 2 adj. (a) (of two or more) gemeinsam (b) Mit⟨autor, -erbe, -besitzer⟩

'jointly adv. gemeinsam

joint 'venture n. (Commerc.) Jointventure, das

joist /dʒɔɪst/ n. (Building) Deckenbalken, der; (steel) [Decken]träger, der

joke /dʒəʊk/ 1 n. Witz, der; Scherz, der 2 v.i. scherzen, Witze machen (about über + Akk.); joking apart Scherz beiseite!

'joker n. (a) Spaßvogel, der (b) (Cards) Joker, der

jollity /'dʒɒlɪtɪ/ n. Fröhlichkeit, die; (merrymaking) Festlichkeit, die

jolly /'dʒɒlɪ/ 1 adj. fröhlich 2 adv. (Brit. coll.) ganz schön (ugs.); ∼ **good!** ausgezeichnet!

jolt /dʒəʊlt/ 1 v.t. ⟨Fahrzeug:⟩ durchrütteln 2 v.i. ⟨Fahrzeug:⟩ holpern 3 n. (a) (jerk) Stoß, der; Ruck, der (b) (fig.: shock) Schock, der

Jordan /'dʒɔːdn/ pr. n. Jordanien (das)

jostle /'dʒɒsl/ 1 v.i. ∼ [against each other] aneinander stoßen 2 v.t. stoßen

jot /dʒɒt/ n. [not] a ∼: [k]ein bisschen ■ **jot 'down** v.t. [rasch] aufschreiben

jotter /'dʒɒtə(r)/ n. Notizblock, der

journal /'dʒɜːnl/ n. Zeitschrift, die

journalism /'dʒɜːnəlɪzm/ n. Journalismus, der

journalist /'dʒɜːnəlɪst/ n. Journalist, der/Journalistin, die

journey /'dʒɜːnɪ/ n. (a) Reise, die (b) (of vehicle) Fahrt, die

jovial /'dʒəʊvɪəl/ adj. herzlich ⟨Gruß⟩; fröhlich ⟨Person⟩

jowl /dʒaʊl/ n. (jaw) Unterkiefer, der; (lower part of face) Kinnbacken Pl.; (double chin) Doppelkinn, das

joy /dʒɔɪ/ n. Freude, die

joyful /'dʒɔɪfl/ adj. froh [gestimmt] ⟨Person⟩; freudig ⟨Blick, Ereignis, Gesang⟩

joy: ∼**ride** n. (coll.) Spritztour, die [im gestohlenen Auto]; ∼**stick** n. (a) (Aeronaut.) Knüppel, der; (b) (on computer etc.) Hebel, der; Joystick, der

JP abbr. = **Justice of the Peace**

jubilant /'dʒuːbɪlənt/ adj. jubelnd; be ∼ ⟨Person⟩ frohlocken

jubilation /dʒuːbɪ'leɪʃn/ n. Jubel, der

jubilee /'dʒuːbɪliː/ n. Jubiläum, das

Judaism /'dʒuːdeɪɪzm/ n., no art. Judentum, das; Judaismus, der

judge /dʒʌdʒ/ 1 n. (a) Richter, der/Richterin, die (b) (in contest) Preisrichter, der/-richterin, die (c) (fig.: critic) Kenner, der/Kennerin, die 2 v.t. (a) (sentence) richten (geh.) (b) (form opinion about) [be]urteilen

'judg[e]ment n. (a) Urteil, das (b) (critical faculty) Urteilsvermögen, das

judicial /dʒuː'dɪʃl/ adj. gerichtlich

judiciary /dʒuː'dɪʃərɪ/ n. Richterschaft, die

judicious /dʒuː'dɪʃəs/ adj. klar blickend

judo /'dʒuːdəʊ/ n. Judo, das

jug /dʒʌg/ n. Krug, der; (with lid, water ∼) Kanne, die

juggernaut /'dʒʌgənɔːt/ n. (Brit.: lorry) schwerer Brummer (ugs.)

juggle /'dʒʌgl/ v.i. jonglieren

juggler /'dʒʌglə(r)/ n. Jongleur, der/ Jongleurin, die

juice /dʒuːs/ n. Saft, der

juicy /'dʒuːsɪ/ adj. saftig

jukebox /'dʒuːkbɒks/ n. Jukebox, die; Musikbox, die

Jul. abbr. = **July** Jul.

July /dʒʊ'laɪ/ n. Juli, der; see also AUGUST

jumble /'dʒʌmbl/ 1 v.t. ∼ up durcheinander bringen
2 n. Durcheinander, das

'jumble sale n. (Brit.) Trödelmarkt, der

jumbo jet /dʒʌmbəʊ 'dʒet/ n. Jumbojet, der

jump /dʒʌmp/ 1 n. (a) Sprung, der
(b) (in prices) sprunghafter Anstieg
2 v.i. (a) springen; ∼ for joy einen Freudensprung machen
(b) ∼ to conclusions voreilige Schlüsse ziehen
3 v.t. (a) überspringen
(b) ∼ the queue (Brit.) sich vordrängeln
▪ **jump a'bout, jump a'round** v.i. herumspringen (ugs.)
▪ **'jump at** v.t. (fig.) sofort zugreifen bei ⟨Angebot, Gelegenheit⟩

jumped-up /'dʒʌmptʌp/ adj. (coll.) emporgekommen

'jumper n. Pullover, der

jump: ∼ **jet** n. Senkrechtstarter, der; ∼ **leads** n. pl. (Brit. Motor Veh.) Starthilfekabel Pl. ; ∼**start** 1 v.t. Starthilfe geben (+ Dat.) ⟨Auto⟩; (fig.) [wieder] in Gang bringen; [wieder] ankurbeln ⟨Wirtschaft, Industrie⟩; 2 n. Start durch Starthilfe; (fig.) neuer Impuls od. Auftrieb; ∼**suit** n. Overall, der

jumpy /'dʒʌmpɪ/ adj. nervös

Jun. abbr. = **June** Jun.

junction /'dʒʌŋkʃn/ n. (a) (of railway lines, roads) ≈ Einmündung, die
(b) (crossroads) Kreuzung, die

'junction box n. (Electr.) Verteilerkasten, der

juncture /'dʒʌŋktʃə(r)/ n. at this ∼: zu diesem Zeitpunkt

June /dʒuːn/ n. Juni, der; see also AUGUST

jungle /'dʒʌŋgl/ n. Dschungel, der

junior /'dʒuːnɪə(r)/ adj. (a) (in age) jünger; ∼ **team** (Sport) Juniorenmannschaft, die
(b) (in rank) rangniedriger ⟨Person⟩; niedriger ⟨Rang⟩

junior: ∼ **'partner** n. Juniorpartner, der/ -partnerin, die; ∼ **school** n. (Brit.) Grundschule, die

junk /dʒʌŋk/ n. Trödel, der (ugs.); (trash) Ramsch, der (ugs.)

junk 'e-mail n. Junkmail, die

'junk food n. minderwertige Kost

junkie /'dʒʌŋkɪ/ n. (sl.) Junkie, der (Drogenjargon)

junk: ∼ **mail** n. Postwurfsendungen Pl.; Reklame, die; (e-mail) Junkmail, die; ∼ **shop** n. Trödelladen, der (ugs.)

Jupiter /'dʒuːpɪtə(r)/ pr. n. (Astron.) Jupiter, der

jurisdiction /dʒʊərɪs'dɪkʃn/ n. Gerichtsbarkeit, die

juror /'dʒʊərə(r)/ n. Geschworene, der/die

jury /'dʒʊərɪ/ n. (a) (in court) the ∼: die Geschworenen Pl.
(b) (in competition) Jury, die

just /dʒʌst/ 1 adj. (morally right) gerecht
2 adv. (a) (exactly) genau; ∼ **then/enough** gerade da/genug; ∼ **as** (exactly as) genauso wie; (when) gerade, als; ∼ **as you like** or **please** ganz wie Sie wünschen/du magst; ∼ **as good** etc. genauso gut usw.
(b) (barely) gerade [eben]; (with little time to spare) gerade noch; (no more than) nur; ∼ **under £10** nicht ganz zehn Pfund
(c) (at this moment) gerade; **not** ∼ **now** im Moment nicht
(d) (coll.) (simply) einfach; (only) nur; esp. with imper. mal [eben]; ∼ **look at that!** guck dir das mal an!; ∼ **a moment** einen Moment mal; ∼ **in case** für alle Fälle

justice /'dʒʌstɪs/ n. (a) Gerechtigkeit, die
(b) (magistrate) Schiedsrichter, der/-richterin, die; J∼ **of the Peace** Friedensrichter, der/ -richterin, die

justifiable /dʒʌstɪ'faɪəbl/ adj. berechtigt

justifiably /dʒʌstɪ'faɪəblɪ/ adv. zu Recht

justification /dʒʌstɪfɪ'keɪʃn/ n. Rechtfertigung, die

justify /'dʒʌstɪfaɪ/ v.t. rechtfertigen; **be justified in doing sth.** etw. zu Recht tun

jut /dʒʌt/ v.i., -tt-: ∼ [out] [her]vorragen; herausragen

juvenile /'dʒuːvənaɪl/ 1 adj. (a) jugendlich
(b) (immature) kindisch
2 n. Jugendliche, der/die

juvenile delinquency /dɪ'lɪŋkwənsɪ/ n. Jugendkriminalität, die

juvenile delinquent /dɪ'lɪŋkwənt/ n. jugendlicher Straftäter/jugendliche Straftäterin

juxtapose /dʒʌkstə'pəʊz/ v.t. nebeneinander stellen (with, to und)

juxtaposition /dʒʌkstəpə'zɪʃn/ n. Nebeneinanderstellung, die

Kk

K, k /keɪ/ *n.* K, k, *das*

kale /keɪl/ *n.* Grünkohl, *der;* Krauskohl, *der*

kaleidoscope /kə'laɪdəskəʊp/ *n.* Kaleidoskop, *das*

kangaroo /kæŋgə'ruː/ *n.* Känguru, *das*

karaoke /kærɪ'əʊkɪ/ *n., no indef. art.* Karaoke, *das; attrib.* Karaoke-

karate /kə'rɑːtɪ/ *n.* Karate, *das*

kebab /kɪ'bæb/ *n.* Kebab, *der*

keel /kiːl/ *n.* ① (Naut.) Kiel, *der*
② *v.i.* ~ **over** umstürzen; ⟨*Schiff:*⟩ kentern; ⟨*Person:*⟩ umkippen

keen /kiːn/ *adj.* **(a)** (sharp) scharf
(b) (cold) schneidend ⟨*Wind, Kälte*⟩
(c) (eager) begeistert ⟨*Fußballfan, Sportler*⟩; lebhaft ⟨*Interesse*⟩; **be ~ to do sth.** darauf erpicht sein, etw. zu tun; **be ~ on doing sth.** etw. gern[e] tun
(d) (sensitive) scharf ⟨*Augen*⟩; fein ⟨*Sinne*⟩

'keenly *adv.* **(a)** (sharply) scharf
(b) (eagerly) eifrig; brennend ⟨*interessiert sein*⟩
(c) (acutely) **be ~ aware of sth.** sich ⟨*Dat.*⟩ einer Sache ⟨*Gen.*⟩ voll bewusst sein

keep /kiːp/ ① *v.t.,* **kept** /kept/ **(a)** halten ⟨*Versprechen, Schwur, Sabbat, Fasten*⟩; einhalten ⟨*Verabredung, Vereinbarung*⟩; begehen, feiern ⟨*Fest*⟩
(b) (have charge of) aufbewahren
(c) (retain) behalten; (not lose or destroy) aufheben ⟨*Quittung, Rechnung*⟩
(d) halten ⟨*Bienen, Hund usw*⟩
(e) führen ⟨*Tagebuch, Geschäft, Ware*⟩
(f) (support) versorgen ⟨*Familie*⟩
(g) (detain) festhalten; ~ **sb. waiting** jmdn. warten lassen; **what kept you?** wo bleibst du denn?
(h) (reserve) aufheben
② *v.i.,* **kept (a)** (remain) bleiben; **are you ~ing well?** gehts dir gut?
(b) ~ **[to the] left/right** sich links/rechts halten; ~ **doing sth.** (repeatedly) etw. immer wieder tun; ~ **talking/working** *etc.* **until** ...: weiterreden/-arbeiten usw., bis ...
(c) (remain good) ⟨*Lebensmittel:*⟩ sich halten
③ *n.* **(a)** (maintenance) Unterhalt, *der*
(b) for ~s (coll.) auf Dauer
(c) (Hist.: tower) Bergfried, *der*

▪ **keep 'back** ① *v.i.* zurückbleiben
② *v.t.* **(a)** (restrain) zurückhalten ⟨*Menschenmenge, Tränen*⟩
(b) (withhold) verschweigen ⟨*Informationen, Tatsachen*⟩ (from *Dat.*)

▪ **keep 'down** ① *v.i.* unten bleiben
② *v.t.* **(a)** niedrig halten ⟨*Steuern, Preise usw.*⟩; ~ **one's weight down** nicht zunehmen
(b) keep your voice down! rede nicht so laut!

▪ **keep 'off** ① *v.i.* ⟨*Person:*⟩ wegbleiben
② *v.t.* fern halten; '~ **off the grass'** „Betreten des Rasens verboten"

▪ **keep 'on** *v.i.* weitermachen (**with** Akk.); ~ **on doing sth.** etw. [immer] weiter tun; (repeatedly) etw. immer wieder tun

▪ **keep 'out** ① *v.i.* '~**out** „Zutritt verboten"
② *v.t.* nicht hereinlassen

▪ **keep 'up** ① *v.i.* ~ **up with sb./sth.** mit jmdm./etw. Schritt halten
② *v.t.* aufrechterhalten ⟨*Freundschaft, jmds. Moral:*⟩; ~ **one's strength up** sich bei Kräften halten; ~ **it up!** weiter so!

keep-'fit *n.* Fitnesstraining, *das*

keep-'fit class *n.* Fitnessgruppe, *die;* **go to ~es** zu Fitnessübungen gehen

'keeping *n.* **be in ~ with sth.** einer Sache ⟨*Dat.*⟩ entsprechen

'keepsake *n.* Andenken, *das*

keg /keg/ *n.* [kleines] Fass

kelp /kelp/ *n.* [See]tang, *der*

kennel /'kenl/ *n.* Hundehütte, *die*

Kenya /'kenjə/ *pr. n.* Kenia (*das*)

kept ▸ KEEP 1, 2

kerb /kɜːb/ *n.* (Brit.) Bordstein, *der*

kerb: ~-crawling *n.* (Brit.) (*langsames*) *Fahren auf dem Autostrich zur Kontaktaufnahme mit einer Prostituierten;* **~stone** *n.* (Brit.) Bordstein, *der*

kernel /'kɜːnl/ *n.* Kern, *der*

kerosene, kerosine /'kerəsiːn/ *n.* (Amer., Austral., NZ/as tech. term) Paraffin[öl], *das;* (for jet engines) Kerosin, *das*

kestrel /'kestrəl/ *n.* Turmfalke, *der*

ketchup /'ketʃʌp/ *n.* Ketschup, *der od. das*

kettle /'ketl/ *n.* [Wasser]kessel, *der*

key /kiː/ ① *n.* **(a)** Schlüssel, *der*
(b) (on piano, typewriter, computer, etc.) Taste, *die*
(c) (Mus.) Tonart, *die*
② *v.t.* (Comp.) eintasten

key: ~board *n.* (of piano etc.) Klaviatur, *die;* (of typewriter, computer, etc.) Tastatur, *die;* **~board operator** Taster, *der*/Tasterin, *die;* **~boarder** *n.* Taster, *der*/Tasterin, *die;* **~boarding** *n.* Tasten, *das;* **~boarding error** Tastfehler, *der;* ~ **card** *n.* Schlüsselkarte, *die;* **~hole** *n.* Schlüsselloch, *das;* **~hole surgery** *n.* Schlüssellochchirurgie, *die;* Knopflochchirurgie, *die*

'keying ▸ KEYBOARDING

key: ~ring *n.* Schlüsselring, *der;* **~stone** *n.* (Archit.) Schlussstein, *der;* (fig.) Grundpfeiler, *der;* **~stroke** *n.* Anschlag, *der*

683

kg. *abbr.* = **kilogram[s]** kg

khaki /'kɑːkɪ/ ① *adj.* khakifarben
② *n.* (cloth) Khaki, *der*

kick /kɪk/ ① *n.* **(a)** [Fuß]tritt, *der;* (Footb.)
Schuss, *der;* **give sb. a ∼:** jmdm. einen Tritt
geben
(b) (coll.: thrill) **do sth. for ∼s** etw. zum Spaß
tun; **he gets a ∼ out of it** er hat Spaß daran
② *v.i.* treten; ⟨Pferd:⟩ ausschlagen
③ *v.t.* einen Tritt geben (+ *Dat.*) ⟨Person,
Hund⟩; treten gegen ⟨Gegenstand⟩; kicken
(ugs.), schießen ⟨Ball⟩
■ **kick a'bout, kick a'round** *v.t.* [in der
Gegend] herumkicken (ugs.)
■ **kick 'off** *v.i.* (Footb.) anstoßen
■ **kick 'up** *v.t.* (coll.) **∼ up a fuss/row** Krach
schlagen/anfangen (ugs.)
kick: **∼-off** *n.* (Footb.) Anstoß, *der;*
∼-start ① *n.* **(a)** Kickstarter, *der;* **(b)** (fig.)
[neuer] Auftrieb; ② *v.t.* **(a)** [mit dem
Kickstarter] starten; **(b)** (fig.) ankurbeln
⟨Industrie, Wirtschaft⟩; vorantreiben,
forcieren ⟨Friedensprozess, Entwicklung⟩
kid /kɪd/ ① *n.* **(a)** (young goat) Kitz, *das*
(b) (coll.: child) Kind, *das*
② *v.t.,* **-dd-** (coll.) auf den Arm nehmen (ugs.);
∼ oneself sich (*Dat.*) was vormachen
kiddie /'kɪdɪ/ *n.* (coll.) Kindchen, *das*
kid-'glove *adj.* sanft
kidnap /'kɪdnæp/ *v.t.,* (Brit.) **-pp-** entführen
'kidnapper *n.* Entführer, *der*/Entführerin,
die
kidney /'kɪdnɪ/ *n.* Niere, *die*
kidney: **∼ bean** *n.* Gartenbohne, *die;*
(scarlet runner bean) Feuerbohne, *die;* **red
∼ bean** Kidneybohne, *die;* **∼ machine** *n.*
künstliche Niere; **∼-shaped** *adj.*
nierenförmig
kill /kɪl/ *v.t.* **(a)** töten; (deliberately)
umbringen; **be ∼ed in action** im Kampf
fallen; **be ∼ed in a car crash** bei einem
Autounfall ums Leben kommen
(b) **∼ time** die Zeit totschlagen
'killer *n.* Mörder, *der*/Mörderin, *die*
'killer whale *n.* Mörderwal, *der*
'killing *n.* **(a)** Töten, *das*
(b) **make a ∼** (coll.: great profit) einen
[Mords]reibach machen (ugs.)
'killjoy *n.* Spielverderber, *der*/-verderberin,
die
kiln /kɪln/ *n.* Brennofen, *der*
kilo /'kiːləʊ/ *n., pl.* **∼s** Kilo, *das*
kilogram, kilogramme /'kɪləɡræm/ *n.*
Kilogramm, *das*
kilometre (Brit.; Amer.: **kilometer**)
/'kɪləmiːtə(r) (Brit.), kɪ'lɒmɪtə(r)/ *n.*
Kilometer, *der*
kilowatt *n.* /'kɪləwɒt/ Kilowatt, *das*
kilt /kɪlt/ *n.* Kilt, *der*
kimono /kɪ'məʊnəʊ/ *n., pl.* **∼s** Kimono, *der*
kin /kɪn/ *n.* (relatives) Verwandte *Pl.;* (relative)
Verwandte, *der*/*die*
kind¹ /kaɪnd/ *n.* **(a)** (class, sort) Art, *die;*

several **∼s of apples** mehrere Sorten Äpfel;
all ∼s of things/excuses alles Mögliche/alle
möglichen Ausreden; **no ... of any ∼:**
keinerlei ...; **what ∼ is it?** was für einer/
eine/eins ist es?; **what ∼ of [a] tree is this?**
was für ein Baum ist das?
(b) (implying vagueness) **a ∼ of ...:** [so] eine
Art ...; **∼ of cute** (coll.) irgendwie niedlich
(ugs.)
kind² *adj.* liebenswürdig; (showing friendliness)
freundlich; **be ∼ to animals** gut zu Tieren
sein; **how ∼!** wie nett [von ihm/Ihnen *usw.*]!
kindergarten /'kɪndəɡɑːtn/ *n.*
Kindergarten, *der*
kind-hearted /kaɪnd'hɑːtɪd/ *adj.*
gutherzig
kindle /'kɪndl/ (fig.) wecken
kindly /'kaɪndlɪ/ ① *adv.* **(a)** freundlich;
nett
(b) *in polite request etc.* freundlicherweise;
thank you ∼: herzlichen Dank
② *adj.* freundlich; nett; (kind-hearted) gütig
'kindness *n.* **(a)** *no pl.* (kind nature)
Freundlichkeit, *die*
(b) **do sb. a ∼** (kind act) jmdm. eine
Gefälligkeit erweisen
kindred /'kɪndrɪd/ *adj.* verwandt; **∼ 'spirit**
Gleichgesinnte, *der*/*die*
king /kɪŋ/ *n.* König, *der*
kingdom /'kɪŋdəm/ *n.* Königreich, *das*
'kingfisher *n.* Eisvogel, *der*
'king-size[d] *adj.* extragroß; King-size-
⟨Zigaretten⟩
kink /kɪŋk/ *n.* (in pipe, wire, etc.) Knick, *der;*
(in hair, wool) Welle, *die*
'kinky *adj.* (coll.) spleenig; (sexually) abartig
kinsman /'kɪnzmən/ *n., pl.* **kinsmen**
/'kɪnzmən/ Verwandte, *der*
kinswoman /'kɪnzwʊmn/ *n.* Verwandte,
die
kiosk /'kiːɒsk/ *n.* **(a)** Kiosk, *der*
(b) (telephone booth) [Telefon]zelle, *die*
kip /kɪp/ *n.* (Brit. coll.: sleep) **have a/get some
∼:** eine Runde pennen (salopp)
kipper /'kɪpə(r)/ *n.* Kipper, *der*
kiss /kɪs/ ① *n.* Kuss, *der*
② *v.t.* küssen; **∼ sb. good night/goodbye**
jmdm. einen Gutenacht-/Abschiedskuss
geben
③ *v.i.* **they ∼ed** sie küssten sich
kit /kɪt/ *n.* **(a)** (Brit.: set of items) Set, *das*
(b) (Brit.: clothing etc.) **sports ∼:** Sportzeug,
das; **riding/skiing ∼:** Reit-/Skiausrüstung,
die
'kitbag *n.* Tornister, *der*
kitchen /'kɪtʃɪn/ *n.* Küche, *die; attrib.*
Küchen-
kitchen: **∼ paper** *n.* Küchenkrepp, *der;*
∼ roll *n.* Küchenrolle, *die;* (kitchen paper)
Küchenkrepp, *der;* **∼ 'sink** *n.*
[Küchen]ausguss, *der;* **∼ unit** *n.*   ⋯⃗

Küchenelement, *das;* ~ units Küchenmöbel *Pl.;* ~ **utensil** *n.* Küchengerät, *das;* ~**ware** *n.* Küchengeräte *Pl.*

kite /kaɪt/ *n.* Drachen, *der*

kith /kɪθ/ *n.* ~ **and kin** Freunde und Verwandte

kitten /ˈkɪtn/ *n.* Kätzchen, *das*

kitty /ˈkɪtɪ/ *n.* (money) Kasse, *die*

kleptomania /kleptəˈmeɪnɪə/ *n.* Kleptomanie, *die*

kleptomaniac /kleptəˈmeɪnɪæk/ *n.* Kleptomane, *der*/Kleptomanin, *die*

km. *abbr.* = **kilometre[s]** km

knack /næk/ *n.* Talent, *das;* **get the ~ [of doing sth.]** den Bogen rauskriegen [, wie man etw. macht] (ugs.); **have lost the ~:** es nicht mehr zustande bringen

knapsack /ˈnæpsæk/ *n.* Rucksack, *der;* (Mil.) Tornister, *der*

knead /niːd/ *v.t.* kneten

knee /niː/ *n.* Knie, *das*

knee: ~**cap** *n.* Kniescheibe, *die;* ~**-deep** *adj.* knietief; ~**-high** *adj.* kniehoch; ~**-jerk reaction** *n.* (fig.) automatische Reaktion; ~ **joint** *n.* Kniegelenk, *das*

kneel /niːl/ *v.i.,* knelt /nelt/ *or* (esp. Amer.) kneeled knien; ~ **down** niederknien

'knee-length *adj.* knielang

knelt ▶ KNEEL

knew ▶ KNOW

knickers /ˈnɪkəz/ *n. pl.* (Brit.) [Damen]schlüpfer, *der*

knife /naɪf/ ⒈ *n., pl.* **knives** /naɪvz/ Messer, *das* ⒉ *v.t.* (stab) einstechen auf (+ *Akk.*); (kill) erstechen

'knife-edge *n.* Schneide, *die;* **be [balanced] on a ~** (fig.) auf des Messers Schneide stehen

knight /naɪt/ *n.* (a) (Hist.) Ritter, *der* (b) (Chess) Springer, *der*

'knighthood *n.* Ritterwürde, *die*

knit /nɪt/ *v.t.,* -tt- stricken; ~ **one's brow** die Stirn runzeln

'knitting *n.* Stricken, *das;* (work being knitted) Strickarbeit, *die*

'knitting needle *n.* Stricknadel, *die*

'knitwear *n.* Strickwaren *Pl.*

knives *pl. of* KNIFE 1

knob /nɒb/ *n.* (a) (on door, walking stick, etc.) Knauf, *der* (b) (control on radio etc.) Knopf, *der* (c) (of butter) Klümpchen, *das*

knock /nɒk/ ⒈ *v.t.* (a) (strike) (lightly) klopfen an (+ *Akk.*); (forcefully) schlagen gegen *od.* an (+ *Akk.*); ~ **a hole in sth.** ein Loch in etw. (*Akk.*) schlagen (b) (coll.: criticize) herziehen über (+ *Akk.*) (ugs.) ⒉ *v.i.* klopfen (**at** an + *Akk.*) ⒊ *n.* Klopfen, *das*

■ **knock 'down** *v.t.* (a) (in car) umfahren (b) (demolish) abreißen

■ **knock 'off** ⒈ *v.t.* (a) ~ off work (coll.: leave) Feierabend machen (b) (deduct) ~ **five pounds off the price** es fünf Pfund billiger machen (c) (coll.: do quickly) aus dem Ärmel schütteln (ugs.) (d) (coll.: steal) klauen (salopp) ⒉ *v.i.* (coll.) Feierabend machen

■ **knock 'out** *v.t.* (a) (make unconscious) bewusstlos umfallen lassen (b) (Boxing) k.o. schlagen (c) (coll.: exhaust) kaputtmachen (ugs.)

■ **knock 'over** *v.t.* umstoßen; ⟨Fahrer, Fahrzeug:⟩ umfahren ⟨Person⟩

'knock-down *adj.* ~ **prices** Schleuderpreise

'knocker *n.* [Tür]klopfer, *der*

knock: ~**-kneed** /ˈnɒkniːd/ *adj.* x-beinig ⟨Person⟩; ~**out** *n.* (Boxing) K.-o.-Schlag, *der*

knot /nɒt/ ⒈ *n.* Knoten, *der* ⒉ *v.t.,* -tt- knoten ⟨Seil, Faden usw.⟩

'knotty *adj.* (fig.: puzzling) verwickelt

know /nəʊ/ *v.t.,* knew /njuː/, known /nəʊn/ (a) (recognize) erkennen (**by** an + *Dat.,* **for** als + *Akk.*) (b) (be able to distinguish) ~ **sth. from sth.** etw. von etw. unterscheiden können (c) (be aware of) wissen (d) (have understanding of) können ⟨ABC, Einmaleins, Deutsch usw.⟩; ~ **how to mend fuses** wissen, wie man Sicherungen repariert; ~ **how to drive a car** Auto fahren können (e) kennen ⟨Person⟩

'know-all *n.* Neunmalkluge, *der/die*

'know-how *n.* praktisches Wissen; (technical expertise) Know-how, *das*

'knowing *adj.* (a) wissend ⟨Blick, Lächeln⟩ (b) (cunning) verschlagen

'knowingly *adv.* (a) (intentionally) wissentlich (b) viel sagend ⟨lächeln, anblicken⟩

knowledge /ˈnɒlɪdʒ/ *n.* (a) (familiarity) Kenntnisse *Pl.* (**of** in + *Dat.*) (b) (awareness) Wissen, *das;* **have no ~ of sth.** nichts von etw. wissen; keine Kenntnis von etw. haben (geh.) (c) [a] ~ **of languages/French** Sprach-/Französischkenntnisse *Pl.*

knowledgeable /ˈnɒlɪdʒəbl/ *adj.* **be ~ about** *or* **on sth.** viel über etw. (*Akk.*) wissen

known /nəʊn/ ⒈ ▶ KNOW ⒉ *adj.* bekannt

knuckle /ˈnʌkl/ *n.* [Finger]knöchel, *der*

Koran /kɔːˈrɑːn, kəˈrɑːn/ *n.* Koran, *der*

Korea /kəˈrɪə/ *pr. n.* Korea (*das*)

Korean /kəˈriːən/ ⒈ *adj.* koreanisch; **sb. is ~:** jmd. ist Koreaner/Koreanerin ⒉ *n.* (a) (person) Koreaner, *der*/Koreanerin, *die* (b) (language) Koreanisch, *das; see also* ENGLISH 2A

kosher /ˈkəʊʃə(r)/ *adj.* koscher

Kosovan /'kɒsəvən/ [1] *adj.* ~ **town**/ **immigrant** Stadt im Kosovo/Einwanderer aus dem Kosovo; ~ **Albanian** Kosovoalbaner, *der*/-albanerin, *die*; **he/she is** ~: er ist Kosovarer/sie ist Kosovarin
[2] *n.* (person) Kosovare, *der*/Kosovarin, *die*

Kosovo /'kɒsəvə/ *pr. n.* Kosovo, *der od. das od. (das)*

kudos /'kjuːdɒs/ *n.* Prestige, *das*

Kurd /kɜːd/ *n.* Kurde, *der*/Kurdin, *die*

Kurdish /'kɜːdɪʃ/ [1] *adj.* kurdisch; **sb. is** ~: jmd. ist Kurde/Kurdin
[2] *n.* (language) Kurdisch, *das*

Kurdistan /kɜːdɪ'stɑːn/ *pr. n.* Kurdistan *(das)*

Kuwait /kʊ'weɪt/ *pr. n.* Kuwait *(das)*

Kuwaiti /kʊ'weɪtɪ/ [1] *adj.* kuwaitisch; **sb. is** ~: jmd. ist Kuwaiti
[2] *n.* Kuwaiti, *der*/die

kW *abbr.* = **kilowatt[s]** kW

Ll

L, l /el/ *n.* L, l, *das*

l. *abbr.* = **litre[s]** l

£ *abbr.* = **pound[s]** £; **cost £5** 5 £ *od.* Pfund kosten

lab /læb/ *n.* (coll.) Labor, *das*

label /'leɪbl/ [1] *n.* Schildchen, *das*; (on bottles, in clothes) Etikett, *das*; (tied/stuck to an object) Anhänger/Aufkleber, *der*
[2] *v.t.*, (Brit.) **-ll-:** (a) etikettieren; auszeichnen ⟨Waren⟩; (write on) beschriften (b) (fig.) ~ **sb.**/**sth. [as] sth.** jmdn./etw. als etw. etikettieren

labor (Amer.) ▶ LABOUR

laboratory /lə'bɒrətərɪ/ *n.* Labor[atorium], *das*

labored, laborer (Amer.) ▶ LABOUR-

laborious /lə'bɔːrɪəs/ *adj.* mühsam

la'boriously *adv.* mühevoll

labour /'leɪbə(r)/ (Brit.) [1] *n.* (a) Arbeit, *die* (b) (workers) Arbeiterschaft, *die*; **immigrant** ~: ausländische Arbeitskräfte *Pl.* (c) **L**~, **the L**~ **Party** (Polit.) die Labour Party (d) (childbirth) Wehen *Pl.*; **be in** ~: in den Wehen liegen
[2] *v.i.* hart arbeiten (**at, on an** + *Dat.*)
[3] *v.t.* ~ **the point** sich lange darüber verbreiten

laboured /'leɪbəd/ *adj.* (Brit.) mühsam; schwerfällig ⟨Stil⟩; **his breathing was** ~: er atmete schwer

'labourer *n.* (Brit.) Arbeiter, *der*/Arbeiterin, *die*

labour: ~ **pains** *n. pl.* Wehenschmerzen *Pl.*; ~**-saving** *adj.* arbeit[s]sparend

laburnum /lə'bɜːnəm/ *n.* (Bot.) Goldregen, *der*

labyrinth /'læbərɪnθ/ *n.* Labyrinth, *das*

lace /leɪs/ [1] *n.* (a) (for shoe) Schnürsenkel, *der* (b) (fabric) Spitze, *die*; *attrib.* Spitzen-
[2] *v.t.* ~ [**up**] [zu]schnüren

lacerate /'læsəreɪt/ *v.t.* aufreißen

'lace-up [1] *attrib. adj.* Schnür-
[2] *n.* Schnürschuh/-stiefel, *der*

lack /læk/ [1] *n.* Mangel, *der* (**of an** + *Dat.*)
[2] *v.t.* **sb.**/**sth.** ~**s sth.** jmdm./einer Sache fehlt es an etw. (*Dat.*)

lackey /'lækɪ/ *n.* Lakai, *der*

'lacking *adj.* **be** ~: fehlen

laconic /lə'kɒnɪk/ *adj.* lakonisch

lacquer /'lækə(r)/ *n.* Lack, *der*

lacrosse /lə'krɒs/ *n.* Lacrosse, *das*

lacy /'leɪsɪ/ *adj.* Spitzen-

lad /læd/ *n.* Junge, *der*

ladder /'lædə(r)/ [1] *n.* (a) Leiter, *die* (b) (Brit.: in tights etc.) Laufmasche, *die*
[2] *v.i.* (Brit.) Laufmaschen/eine Laufmasche bekommen
[3] *v.t.* (Brit.) Laufmaschen/eine Laufmasche machen in (+ *Akk.*)

laden /'leɪdn/ *adj.* beladen (**with** mit)

ladle /'leɪdl/ *n.* Schöpfkelle, *die*

lady /'leɪdɪ/ *n.* (a) Dame, *die*; ~**-in-waiting** (Brit.) Hofdame, *die* (b) '**Ladies**' (WC) „Damen" (c) (as form of address) **Ladies** meine Damen (d) (Brit.) (as title) **L**~: Lady

lady: ~**bird,** (Amer.) ~**bug** *ns.* Marienkäfer, *der*; ~**like** *adj.* damenhaft

lag¹ /læg/ *v.i.,* **-gg-:** ~ [**behind**] zurückbleiben; (fig.) im Rückstand sein

lag² *v.t.,* **-gg-** (insulate) isolieren

lager /'lɑːgə(r)/ *n.* Lagerbier, *das*

'lager lout *n.* Bier trinkender Rüpel

'lagging *n.* Isolierung, *die*

lagoon /lə'guːn/ *n.* Lagune, *die*

laid ▶ LAY²

'laid-back *adj.* (coll.) gelassen

lain ▶ LIE²

lair /leər/ *n.* (of wild animal) Unterschlupf, *der*; (of pirates, bandits) Schlupfwinkel, *der*

lake /leɪk/ *n.* See, *der*

Lake Constance /leɪk 'kɒnstəns/ *pr. n.* der Bodensee

lama /'lɑːmə/ n. Lama, der
lamb /læm/ n. (a) Lamm, das
(b) (meat) Lamm[fleisch], das
lamb 'chop n. Lammkotelett, das
lambswool /'læmzwʊl/ n. Lambswool, die
lame /leɪm/ adj., **'lamely** adv. lahm
lament /lə'ment/ 1 n. Klage, die (for um)
2 v.t. ~ that ...: beklagen, dass ...
3 v.i. klagen (geh.); ~ over sth. etw.
beklagen (geh.)
lamentable /'læməntəbl/ adj.
beklagenswert
laminated /'læmɪneɪtɪd/ adj. lamelliert;
~ **glass** Verbundglas, das
lamp /læmp/ n. Lampe, die; (in street)
[Straßen]laterne, die
lamp: ~ **post** n. Laternenpfahl, der;
~**shade** n. Lampenschirm, der
lance /lɑːns/ 1 n. Lanze, die
2 v.t. (Med.) mit der Lanzette öffnen
lance 'corporal n. Obergefreite, der
land /lænd/ 1 n. Land, das; **have** or **own** ~:
Grundbesitz haben
2 v.t. (a) (set ashore) [an]landen
(b) (Aeronaut.) landen
(c) ~ **oneself in trouble** sich in
Schwierigkeiten bringen; ~ **sb. with sth.**,
~ **sth. on sb.** jmdm. etw. aufhalsen (ugs.)
3 v.i. (a) ⟨Boot usw.:⟩ anlegen, landen;
⟨Passagier:⟩ aussteigen (**from** aus); **we** ~**ed at**
Dieppe wir gingen in Dieppe an Land
(b) (Aeronaut.) landen
(c) ~ **on one's feet** (fig.) [wieder] auf die
Füße fallen
'landed adj. ~ **gentry/aristrocracy** Landadel,
der
'landing n. (a) (of ship, aircraft) Landung, die
(b) (on stairs) Treppenabsatz, der; (passage)
Treppenflur, der
landing: ~ **card** n. Landekarte, die;
~ **stage** n. Landesteg, der
land: ~**lady** n. (a) (of rented property)
Vermieterin, die; (b) (of public house)
[Gast]wirtin, die; ~**locked** adj. vom Land
eingeschlossen ⟨Bucht, Hafen⟩; ⟨Staat⟩ ohne
Zugang zum Meer; ~**lord** n. (a) (of rented
property) Vermieter, der; (b) (of public house)
[Gast]wirt, der; ~**mark** n. (a)
Orientierungspunkt, der; (b) (fig.) Markstein,
der; ~ **mass** n. Landmasse, die; ~**mine** n.
Landmine, die; ~**owner** n. Grundbesitzer,
der/-besitzerin, die; ~**scape** /'lændskeɪp/
n. Landschaft, die; ~**scape architect** n.
Landschaftsarchitekt, der/-architektin, die;
~**scape gardener** n.
Landschaftsgärtner, der/-gärtnerin, die;
~**scape gardening** n.
Landschaftsgärtnerei, die; ~**slide** n.
Erdrutsch, der; **a** ~**slide [victory]** (Polit.) ein
Erdrutsch[wahl]sieg
lane /leɪn/ n. (a) (in the country)
Landsträßchen, das; Weg, der
(b) (in town) Gasse, die

(c) (part of road) [Fahr]spur, die; **'get in** ~'
„bitte einordnen"
(d) (Sport) Bahn, die
language /'læŋgwɪdʒ/ n. Sprache, die;
(style) Ausdrucksweise, die
language: ~ **course** n. Sprachkurs[us],
der; ~ **school** n. Sprachenschule; die;
~ **teacher** n. Sprachlehrer, der/-lehrerin,
die
languid /'læŋgwɪd/ adj. träge
languish /'læŋgwɪʃ/ v.i. (a) (lose vitality)
ermatten (geh.)
(b) ~ **under sth.** unter etw. (Dat.)
schmachten (geh.)
lank /læŋk/ adj. (a) hager
(b) glatt herabhängend ⟨Haar⟩
lanky /'læŋkɪ/ adj. schlaksig (ugs.)
lantern /'læntən/ n. Laterne, die
lap¹ /læp/ n. (part of body) Schoß, der
lap² n. (Sport) Runde, die
lap³ 1 v.i., -pp- schlecken
2 v.t., -pp-: ~ [**up**] [auf]schlecken
■ **lap 'up** v.t. (fig.) schlucken
'lap belt n. Beckengurt, der
lapel /lə'pel/ n. Revers, das
Lapland /'læplænd/ pr. n. Lappland (das)
lapse /læps/ 1 n. (a) (interval) **a/the** ~ **of** ...:
eine/die Zeitspanne von ...
(b) (mistake) Fehler, der; ~ **of memory**
Gedächtnislücke, die
2 v.i. (a) ⟨Vertrag, usw.:⟩ ungültig werden
(b) ~ **into** verfallen in (+ Akk.)
'laptop 1 adj. tragbar, Laptop⟨gerät, -PC⟩
2 n. Laptop, der; tragbarer PC
larceny /'lɑːsənɪ/ n. Diebstahl, der
lard /lɑːd/ n. Schweineschmalz, das
larder /'lɑːdə(r)/ n. Speisekammer, die
large /lɑːdʒ/ 1 adj. groß
2 n. **at** ~ (not in prison etc.) auf freiem Fuß
3 adv. ▶ BY 2D
'largely adv. weitgehend
larger-than-'life attrib. adj.
überlebensgroß
large: ~**-scale** attrib. adj. groß angelegt;
groß ⟨Erfolg, Misserfolg⟩; ⟨Katastrophe⟩
großen Ausmaßes; ⟨Modell⟩ in großem
Maßstab; ~**-scale manufacture**
Massenproduktion, die; ~**-size[d]** adj. groß
lark¹ /lɑːk/ n. (Ornith.) Lerche, die
lark² (coll.) 1 n. Jux, der (ugs.)
2 v.i. ~ [**about** or **around**] herumalbern
(ugs.)
larva /'lɑːvə/ n., pl. ~**e** /'lɑːvɪː/ Larve, die
laryngitis /lærɪn'dʒaɪtɪs/ n.
Kehlkopfentzündung, die
larynx /'lærɪŋks/ n. Kehlkopf, der
lascivious /lə'sɪvɪəs/ adj. lüstern (geh.)
laser /'leɪzə(r)/ n. Laser, der
laser: ~ **beam** n. Laserstrahl, der;
~**disc** n. Laserplatte, die; ~ **printer** n.
Laserdrucker, der

lash /læʃ/ ⒈ *n.* (a) (stroke) [Peitschen]hieb,
der
(b) (on eyelid) Wimper, *die*
⒉ *v.i.* ‹Welle, Regen:› peitschen (**against**
gegen, **on** auf + *Akk.*)
⒊ *v.t.* (a) (fasten) festbinden (**to** an + *Dat.*)
(b) (as punishment) auspeitschen
■ **lash 'down** ⒈ *v.t.* festbinden
⒉ *v.i.* ‹Regen:› niederprasseln
■ **lash 'out** *v.i.* (a) (hit out) um sich
schlagen; ~ **out at sb.** nach jmdm. schlagen
(b) ~ **out on sth.** (coll.: spend freely) sich (*Dat.*)
etw. leisten
lashings /'læʃɪŋz/ *n. pl.* ~ **of sth.**
Unmengen von etw.
lass /læs/ *n.* Mädchen, *das*
lasso /lə'suː/ Lasso, *das*
last¹ /lɑːst/ ⒈ *adj.* letzt...; **be** ~ **to arrive**
als Letzter/Letzte ankommen; ~ **night**
gestern Nacht/Abend
⒉ *adv.* (a) [ganz] zuletzt; als Letzter/Letzte
‹sprechen, ankommen›
(b) (on ~ previous occasion) das letzte Mal;
zuletzt
⒊ *n.* (a) (person or thing) **the** ~: der/die/das
Letztere; *pl.* die Letzteren
(b) **at** [**long**] ~: endlich
last² *v.i.* (a) (continue) dauern; ‹Wetter,
Ärger:› anhalten
(b) (suffice) reichen
'last-ditch *adj.* ~ **attempt** letzter
verzweifelter Versuch
'lasting *adj.* bleibend; dauerhaft
‹Beziehung›; nachhaltig ‹Eindruck,
Wirkung›
'lastly *adv.* schließlich
last: ~**-minute** *attrib. adj.* in letzter
Minute vorgebracht ‹Plan, Aufruf,
Ergänzung, Gesuch, Bewerbung›; ~ **name**
n. Zuname, *der;* Nachname, *der*
latch /lætʃ/ *n.* Riegel, *der;* **on the** ~: nur
eingeklinkt
■ **latch 'on to** *v.t.* (coll.:) kapieren (ugs.)
late /leɪt/ ⒈ *adj.* (a) spät; **am I** ~? komme
ich zu spät?; **be** ~ **for the train** den Zug
verpassen; **the train is** [**an hour**] ~: der Zug
hat [eine Stunde] Verspätung; ~ **shift**
Spätschicht, *die;* ~ **summer** Spätsommer,
der
(b) (dead) verstorben
(c) (former) ehemalig. *See also* LATER 1;
LATEST
⒉ *adv.* (a) (after proper time) verspätet
(b) (at/till a ~ hour) spät; **be up** ~: bis spät in
die Nacht aufbleiben; **work** ~ **at the office**
[abends] lange im Büro arbeiten; [**a bit**] ~ **in
the day** (fig. coll.) reichlich spät
⒊ *n.* **of** ~: in letzter Zeit
latecomer /'leɪtkʌmə(r)/ *n.*
Zuspätkommende, *der/die*
'lately *adv.* in letzter Zeit
'lateness *n.* (a) (delay) Verspätung, *die*
(b) **the** ~ **of the performance** der späte
Beginn der Vorstellung

'late-night *attrib. adj.* Spät‹programm,
-vorstellung›
latent /'leɪtənt/ *adj.* latent
later /'leɪtə(r)/ ⒈ *adv.* ~ [**on**] später
⒉ *adj.* später; (more recent) neuer
lateral /'lætərl/ *adj.* seitlich (**to** von);
~ **thinking** Querdenken, *das*
latest /'leɪtɪst/ *adj.* (a) (modern) neu[e]st...
(b) (most recent) letzt...
(c) **at** [**the**] ~/**the very** ~: spätestens/
allerspätestens
lathe /leɪð/ *n.* Drehbank, *die*
lather /'lɑːðə(r)/ ⒈ *n.* [Seifen]schaum, *der*
⒉ *v.t.* einschäumen
Latin /'lætɪn/ ⒈ *adj.* lateinisch
⒉ *n.* Latein, *das; see also* ENGLISH 2A
Latin A'merica *pr. n.* Lateinamerika
(*das*)
Latin-A'merican *adj.* lateinamerikanisch
latitude /'lætɪtjuːd/ *n.* (a) (freedom)
Freiheit, *die*
(b) (Geog.) Breite, *die*
latrine /lə'triːn/ *n.* Latrine, *die*
latter /'lætə(r)/ *attrib. adj.* letzter...; **the** ~:
der/die/das Letztere; *pl.* die Letzteren
'latterly *adv.* in letzter Zeit
lattice /'lætɪs/ *n.* Gitter, *das*
laudable /'lɔːdəbl/ *adj.* lobenswert
laugh /lɑːf/ ⒈ *n.* Lachen, *das;* (continuous)
Gelächter, *das*
⒉ *v.i.* lachen; ~ **out loud** laut auflachen;
~ **at sb./sth.** über jmdn./etw. lachen; (jeer)
jmdn. auslachen/etw. verlachen
■ **laugh 'off** *v.t.* mit einem Lachen abtun
laughable /'lɑːfəbl/ *adj.* lachhaft;
lächerlich
'laughing *n.* **be no** ~ **matter** nicht zum
Lachen sein
laughing: ~ **gas** *n.* Lachgas, *das;*
~ **stock** *n.* **make sb. a** ~ **stock, make a**
~ **stock of sb.** jmdn. zum Gespött machen
laughter /'lɑːftə(r)/ *n.* Lachen, *das;*
(continuous) Gelächter, *das*
'laughter lines *n. pl.* Lachfältchen *Pl.*
launch /lɔːntʃ/ *v.t.* (a) zu Wasser lassen
‹Boot›; vom Stapel lassen ‹neues Schiff›;
abschießen ‹Harpune, Torpedo›; schleudern
‹Speer›
(b) (fig.) auf den Markt bringen ‹Produkt›;
vorstellen ‹Buch, Schallplatte, Sänger›; ~ **an
attack** einen Angriff durchführen
■ **launch 'out** *v.i.* (fig.) ~ **out into films/a
new career/on one's own** sich beim Film
versuchen/beruflich etwas ganz Neues
anfangen/sich selbstständig machen
'launching pad, launch pad *ns.*
[Raketen]abschussrampe, *die*
launder /'lɔːndə(r)/ *v.t.* waschen und
bügeln
launderette /lɔːndə'ret/**, laundrette**
/lɔːn'dret/, (Amer.) **laundromat**
/'lɔːndrəmæt/ *ns.* Waschsalon, *der*

laundry /'lɔːndrɪ/ n. (a) (place) Wäscherei, *die*
(b) (clothes etc.) Wäsche, *die*

'laundry basket n. Wäschekorb, *der*

lava /'lɑːvə/ n. Lava, *die*

lavatory /'lævətərɪ/ n. Toilette, *die*

lavender /'lævɪndə(r)/ n. Lavendel, *der*

lavish /'lævɪʃ/ 1 adj. großzügig
2 v.t. ~ sth. on sb. jmdn. mit etw. überhäufen

law /lɔː/ n. (a) Gesetz, *das;* break the ~: gegen das Gesetz verstoßen; take the ~ into one's own hands sich (Dat.) selbst Recht verschaffen; ~ and order Ruhe und Ordnung
(b) (of game) Regel, *die*
(c) (as subject) Jura o. Art.

law: ~-abiding /'lɔːəbaɪdɪŋ/ adj. gesetzestreu; **~court** n. Gerichtsgebäude, *das;* (room) Gerichtssaal, *der;* ~ **firm** n. (Amer.) Anwaltskanzlei, *die*

lawful /'lɔːfl/ adj. rechtmäßig ‹Besitzer, Erbe›; legal, gesetzmäßig ‹Vorgehen, Maßnahme›

'lawless adj. gesetzlos

lawn /lɔːn/ n. Rasen, *der*

lawn: ~mower n. Rasenmäher, *der;* ~ **sprinkler** n. Rasensprenger, *der;* ~ **tennis** n. Rasentennis, *das*

'law suit n. Prozess, *der*

lawyer /'lɔːjə(r)/ n. Rechtsanwalt, *der/* Rechtsanwältin, *die*

lax /læks/ adj. lax; be ~ about hygiene/ paying the rent etc. es mit der Hygiene/der Zahlung der Miete usw. nicht so genau nehmen

laxative /'læksətɪv/ n. Abführmittel, *das*

laxity /'læksɪtɪ/, **'laxness** ns. Laxheit, *die*

lay¹ /leɪ/ adj. Laien-

lay² v.t., laid /leɪd/ (a) legen ‹Teppichboden, Rohr, Kabel›
(b) (impose) auferlegen ‹Verantwortung, Verpflichtung› (on Dat.); verhängen ‹Strafe› (on über + Akk.)
(c) ~ the table den Tisch decken
(d) (Biol.) legen ‹Ei›
■ **lay a'side** v.t. beiseite legen
■ **lay 'by** v.t. beiseite legen
■ **lay 'down** v.t. (a) hinlegen
(b) festlegen ‹Regeln, Bedingungen›
■ **lay 'off** 1 v.t. (from work) vorübergehend entlassen
2 v.i. (coll.: stop) aufhören
■ **lay 'out** v.t. (a) (spread out) ausbreiten
(b) anlegen ‹Garten›
■ **lay 'up** v.t. (a) (store) lagern
(b) I was laid up in bed for a week ich musste eine Woche das Bett hüten

lay³ ▶ LIE²

lay: ~about n. (Brit.) Gammler, *der* (ugs.); **~-by** n., pl. **~-bys** (Brit.) Parkbucht, *die;* Haltebucht, *die*

layer /'leɪə(r)/ n. Schicht, *die*

layette /leɪ'et/ n. [baby's] ~: Babyausstattung, *die*

lay: ~man /'leɪmən/ n., pl. **~men** /'leɪmən/ Laie, *der;* **~out** n. (of garden, park) Anlage, *die;* (of book, advertisement, etc.) Layout, *das*

laze /leɪz/ v.i. faulenzen; ~ around or about herumfaulenzen (ugs.)

lazily /'leɪzɪlɪ/ adv. faul

laziness /'leɪzɪnɪs/ n. Faulheit, *die*

lazy /'leɪzɪ/ adj. faul

'lazybones n. sing. Faulpelz, *der*

lb. abbr. = **pound[s]** ≈ Pfd.

LCD abbr. = **liquid crystal display** LCD

lead¹ /led/ 1 n. (a) (metal) Blei, *das*
(b) (in pencil) [Bleistift]mine, *die*
2 attrib. adj. Blei-
3 v.t. (a) in Blei fassen ‹Fenster›; ~ed bleigefasst
(b) ~ed petrol bleihaltiges Benzin

lead² /liːd/ 1 v.t., led /led/ (a) führen; ~ sb. to do sth. (fig.) jmdn. dazu bringen, etw. zu tun
(b) (fig.: influence) ~ sb. to do sth. jmdn. veranlassen, etw. zu tun; be easily led sich leicht beeinflussen lassen; he led me to believe that ...: er machte mich glauben, dass ...
(c) (be first in) anführen
(d) (direct) anführen ‹Bewegung, Abordnung›; leiten ‹Diskussion, Orchester›
2 v.i., led (a) ‹Straße usw., Tür:› führen
(b) (be first) führen; (go in front) vorangehen
3 n. (a) (precedent) Beispiel, *das;* (clue) Anhaltspunkt, *der;* follow sb.'s ~: jmds. Beispiel (Dat.) folgen
(b) (first place) Führung, *die;* be in the ~: in Führung liegen
(c) (distance ahead) Vorsprung, *der*
(d) (leash) Leine, *die;* on a ~: an der Leine
(e) (Electr.) Kabel, *das*
(f) (Theatre) Hauptrolle, *die*
■ **lead a'way** v.t. abführen ‹Gefangenen, Verbrecher›
■ **lead 'off** 1 v.t. abführen
2 v.i. beginnen
■ **lead 'on** 1 v.t. ~ sb. on (entice) jmdn. reizen; (deceive) jmdn. auf den Leim führen
2 v.i. ~ on to the next topic etc. zum nächsten Thema usw. führen
■ **lead 'up to** v.t. schließlich führen zu

'leader n. (a) Führer, *der/*Führerin, *die;* (of political party) Vorsitzende, *der/die;* (of expedition) Leiter, *der/*Leiterin, *die*
(b) (Brit. Journ.) Leitartikel, *der*

'leadership n. Führung, *die*

'leader writer n. Leitartikelschreiber, *der/*-schreiberin, *die;* Leitartikler, *der/* -artiklerin, *die* (Pressejargon)

lead-free /'ledfriː/ adj. bleifrei

leading /'liːdɪŋ/ adj. führend

leading: ~ 'lady n. Hauptdarstellerin, *die;* ~ **'man** n. Hauptdarsteller, *der;*

~ **'question** n. Suggestivfrage, die; ~ **role** n. Hauptrolle, die; (fig.) führende Rolle

lead: ~ **'pencil** /led 'pensl/ n. Bleistift, der; ~ **poisoning** /'led pɔɪzənɪŋ/ n. Bleivergiftung, die; ~ **singer** /liːd 'sɪŋə(r)/ n. Leadsänger der/-sängerin, die; ~ **story** /'liːd stɔːrɪ/ n. (Journ.) Titelgeschichte, die; ~ **time** /'liːd taɪm/ n. (Econ.) Entwicklungszeit, die

leaf /liːf/ n., pl. **leaves** /liːvz/ Blatt, das; (of table) Platte die
■ **leaf 'through** v.t. durchblättern

leaflet /'liːflɪt/ n. [Hand]zettel, der; (advertising) Reklamezettel, der; (political) Flugblatt, das

'leafy adj. belaubt

league /liːg/ n. (a) (agreement) Bündnis, das; be in ~ **with sb.** mit jmdm. im Bunde sein (b) (Sport) Liga, die

league: ~ **'football** n. Ligafußball, der; ~ **match** n. Ligaspiel, das; ~ **table** n. Tabelle, die (Sport); **be at the top/bottom of the** ~ **table** an der Tabellenspitze/am Tabellenende sein (fig.); an der Spitze rangieren/das Schlusslicht bilden (ugs.) (of unter + Dat.)

leak /liːk/ [1] n. (a) (hole) Leck, das; (in roof, tent; also fig.) undichte Stelle
(b) (escaping gas) durch ein Leck austretendes Gas
[2] v.i. (a) (escape) austreten (from aus)
(b) ⟨Fass, Tank, Schiff:⟩ lecken; ⟨Rohr, Leitung, Dach:⟩ undicht sein; ⟨Gefäß, Füller:⟩ auslaufen
(c) (fig.) ~ [out] durchsickern
[3] v.t. ~ **sth. to sb.** jmdm. etw. zuspielen

leakage /'liːkɪdʒ/ n. Auslaufen, das; (of fluid, gas) Ausströmen, das

'leaky adj. undicht; leck ⟨Boot⟩

lean¹ /liːn/ [1] adj. mager
[2] n. (meat) Magere, das

lean² [1] v.i., **leaned** /liːnd, lent/ or (Brit.) **leant** /lent/ (a) sich beugen; ~ **against the door** sich gegen die Tür lehnen; ~ **down/ forward** sich herab-/vorbeugen; ~ **back** sich zurücklehnen
(b) (support oneself) ~ **against/on sth.** sich gegen/an etw (Akk.) lehnen
(c) (be supported) lehnen (**against** an + Dat.)
(d) (fig.) ~ [up]on sb. (rely) auf jmdn. bauen; ~ **to[wards]** sth. (tend) zu etw. neigen
[2] v.t., **leaned** or (Brit.) **leant** lehnen (**against** gegen od. an + Akk.)
■ **lean 'over** v.i. sich hinüberbeugen

'leaning n. Neigung, die

leant ▶ LEAN²

leap /liːp/ [1] v.i., **leaped** /liːpt, lept/ or **leapt** /lept/ (a) springen; ⟨Herz:⟩ hüpfen
(b) (fig.) ~ **at the chance** die Gelegenheit beim Schopf packen
[2] v.t., **leaped** or **leapt** überspringen

[3] n. Sprung, der; **with** or **in one** ~: mit einem Satz; **by** ~**s and bounds** (fig.) mit Riesenschritten

'leapfrog [1] n. Bockspringen, das
[2] v.i., **-gg-** Bockspringen machen
[3] v.t. (a) ~**frog sb.** einen Bocksprung über jmdn. machen
(b) (fig.) übertreffen ⟨Konkurrenz, Kollegen usw.⟩

leapt ▶ LEAP 1, 2

'leap year n. Schaltjahr, das

learn /lɜːn/ [1] v.t., **learned** /lɜːnd, lɜːnt/ or **learnt** /lɜːnt/ (a) lernen; ~ **to swim** schwimmen lernen
(b) (find out) erfahren
[2] v.i., **learned** or **learnt** (a) lernen; ~ **about** sth. etwas über etw. (Akk.) lernen
(b) (get to know) erfahren (**of** von)

learned /'lɜːnɪd/ adj. gelehrt

'learner n. (beginner) Anfänger, der/ Anfängerin, die; ~ [**driver**] Fahrschüler, der/-schülerin, die

'learning n. (of person) Gelehrsamkeit, die

learning: ~ **curve** n. Lernkurve, die; ~ **difficulties** n. pl. Lernschwierigkeiten Pl.; ~ **disability** n. Lernbehinderung, die

learnt ▶ LEARN

lease /liːs/ [1] n. (of land, business premises) Pachtvertrag, der; (of house, flat, office) Mietvertrag, der
[2] v.t. (a) (grant ~ on) verpachten ⟨Grundstück, Geschäft, Rechte⟩; vermieten ⟨Haus, Wohnung, Büro⟩
(b) (take ~ on) pachten ⟨Grundstück, Geschäft⟩; mieten ⟨Haus, Wohnung, Büro⟩

'leasehold n. ▶ LEASE 2: **have the** ~ **of** or **on sth.** etw. gepachtet/gemietet haben

leash /liːʃ/ n. Leine, die

least /liːst/ [1] adj. (smallest) kleinst…; (in quantity) wenigst…; (in status) geringst…
[2] n. Geringste, das; **the** ~ **I can do** das Mindeste, was ich tun kann; **at** ~: mindestens; (anyway) wenigstens; **at the** [**very**] ~: [aller]mindestens; **not** [**in**] **the** ~: nicht im Geringsten
[3] adv. am wenigsten

leather /'leðə(r)/ [1] n. Leder, das
[2] adj. ledern; Leder⟨jacke, -mantel⟩

'leather goods n. pl. Lederwaren Pl.

'leathery adj. ledern

leave¹ /liːv/ n. (a) (permission) Erlaubnis, die
(b) (from duty or work) Urlaub, der; ~ [**of absence**] Urlaub, der
(c) **take one's** ~ sich verabschieden

leave² v.t., **left** /left/ (a) (make or let remain) hinterlassen; (leave to do, etw. zu tun); (in will) ~ **sb. sth.,** ~ **sth. to sb.** jmdm. etw. hinterlassen
(b) (refrain from doing, using, etc.) stehen lassen ⟨Abwasch, Essen⟩ ⋯⋮

(c) (in given state) lassen; ~ **sb. alone** (allow to be alone) jmdn. allein lassen; (stop bothering) jmdn. in Ruhe lassen
(d) (refer, entrust) ~ **sth. to sb.**/**sth.** etw. jmdm./einer Sache überlassen
(e) (go away from, quit, desert) verlassen; ~ **home at 6 a.m.** um 6 Uhr früh von zu Hause weggehen/-fahren; ~ **Bonn at 6 p.m.** (by car, in train) um 18 Uhr von Bonn abfahren; (by plane) um 18 Uhr in Bonn abfliegen; *abs.* **the train** ~**s at 8.30 a.m.** der Zug fährt *od.* geht um 8.30 Uhr; ~ **on the 8 a.m. train/flight** mit dem Achtuhrzug fahren/der Achtuhrmaschine fliegen
■ **leave a'side** *v.t.* beiseite lassen
■ **leave be'hind** *v.t.* zurücklassen; (by mistake) vergessen; liegen lassen
■ **leave 'off** *v.t.* (stop) aufhören mit; *abs.* aufhören
■ **leave 'out** *v.t.* auslassen
■ **leave 'over** *v.t.* **be left over** übrig [geblieben] sein

leaves *pl. of* LEAF

Lebanon /'lebənən/ *pr. n.* [the] ~: [der] Libanon

lecherous /'letʃərəs/ *adj.* lüstern (geh.)

lecture /'lektʃə(r)/ ① **(a)** *n.* Vortrag, *der;* (Univ.) Vorlesung, *die*
(b) (reprimand) Strafpredigt, *die* (ugs.)
② *v.i.* ~ **[to sb.]** **[on sth.]** [vor jmdm.] einen Vortrag/(Univ.) eine Vorlesung [über etw. (*Akk.*)] halten
③ *v.t.* (scold) ~ **sb.** jmdm. eine Strafpredigt halten

'lecture hall *n.* Hörsaal, *der*

'lecturer *n.* Vortragende, *der/die;* **senior** ~: Dozent, *der*/Dozentin, *die*

'lecture room *n.* Vortragsraum, *der;* (Univ.) Vorlesungsraum, *der*

lectureship /'lektʃəʃɪp/ *n.* Dozentur, *die*

lecture: ~ **theatre** *n.* Hörsaal, *der;* ~ **tour** *n.* Vortragsreise, *die*

led ► LEAD² 1, 2

LED *abbr.* = **light-emitting diode** LED

ledge /ledʒ/ *n.* Sims, *der od. das;* (of rock) Vorsprung, *der*

ledger /'ledʒə(r)/ *n.* Hauptbuch, *das*

lee /liː/ *n.* **(a)** (shelter) Schutz, *der*
(b) ~ **[side]** (Naut.) Leeseite, *die*

leech /liːtʃ/ *n.* [Blut]egel, *der*

leek /liːk/ *n.* Stange Porree *od.* Lauch; ~**s** Porree, *der;* Lauch, *der*

leek 'soup *n.* Lauch[creme]suppe, *die*

leer /lɪə(r)/ ① *n.* anzüglicher Blick
② *v.i.* ~ **at sb.** jmdm. einen anzüglichen/ spöttischen [Seiten]blick zuwerfen

leeward /'liːwəd/ ① *adj.* **to/on the** ~ **side of the ship** nach/in Lee
② *n.* Leeseite, *die;* **to** ~: leewärts

'leeway *n.* **(a)** (Naut.) Leeweg, *der;* Abdrift, *die*
(b) (fig.) Spielraum, *der*

left¹ ► LEAVE²

left² /left/ ① *adj.* **(a)** link...; **on the** ~ **side** auf der linken Seite; links
(b) **L**~ (Polit.) link...
② *adv.* nach links
③ *n.* **(a)** (~-hand side) linke Seite; **on** *or* **to the** ~ [of sb.'s.] links [von jmdm./etw.]
(b) (Polit.) **the L**~: die Linke

left: ~**-hand** *adj.* link...; ~**-'handed** ① *adj.* linkshändig; ⟨Werkzeug⟩ für Linkshänder; **be** ~**-handed** Linkshänder/ Linkshänderin sein; ② *adv.* linkshändig; ~ **'luggage [office]** *n.* (Brit. Railw.) Gepäckaufbewahrung, *die;* ~**overs** *n. pl.* Reste *Pl.* ~ **'wing** *n.* linker Flügel; ~**-wing** *adj.* (Polit.) linksgerichtet; Links⟨extremist, -intellektueller⟩; ~**-'winger** *n.* **(a)** (Sport) Linksaußen, *der;* **(b)** (Polit.) Angehöriger/Angehörige des linken Flügels

leg /leg/ *n.* **(a)** Bein, *das;* **pull sb.'s** ~ (fig.) jmdn. auf den Arm nehmen (ugs.); **stretch one's** ~**s** sich (*Dat.*) die Beine vertreten
(b) ~ **of lamb** Lammkeule, *die*
(c) (of journey) Etappe, *die*

legacy /'legəsɪ/ *n.* Vermächtnis, *das* (Rechtsspr.); Erbschaft, *die*

legal /'liːgl/ *adj.* **(a)** (concerning the law) juristisch; Rechts⟨beratung, -streit, -experte, -schutz⟩; gesetzlich ⟨Vertreter⟩; rechtlich ⟨Gründe, Stellung⟩; Gerichts⟨kosten⟩
(b) (required by law) gesetzlich ⟨Verpflichtung⟩; gesetzlich verankert ⟨Recht⟩
(c) (lawful) legal; rechtsgültig ⟨Vertrag, Testament⟩

legal: ~ **'action** *n.* Gerichtsverfahren, *das;* Prozess, *der;* **take** ~ **action against sb.** gerichtlich gegen jmdn. vorgehen; ~ **'aid** *n.* ≈ Prozesskostenhilfe, *die*

legality /lɪ'gælɪtɪ/ *n.* Legalität, *die*

legalization /liːgəlar'zeɪʃn/ *n.* Legalisierung, *die*

legalize /'liːgəlaɪz/ *v.t.* legalisieren

legend /'ledʒənd/ *n.* Sage, *die;* (unfounded belief) Legende, *die*

legendary /'ledʒəndərɪ/ *adj.* legendär

leggings /'legɪnz/ *n. pl.* Ledergamaschen *Pl.* (veralt.); (of baby) Strampelhose, *die*

legibility /ledʒɪ'bɪlɪtɪ/ *n.* Leserlichkeit, *die*

legible /'ledʒɪbl/ *adj.* leserlich; **easily/ scarcely** ~: leicht/kaum lesbar

legion /'liːdʒn/ *n.* Legion, *die*

legion'naires' disease *n.* (Med.) Legionärskrankheit, *die*

legislate /'ledʒɪsleɪt/ *v.i.* Gesetze verabschieden

legislation /ledʒɪs'leɪʃn/ *n.* **(a)** (laws) Gesetze *Pl.*
(b) (legislating) Gesetzgebung, *die*

legislative /'ledʒɪslətɪv/ *adj.* gesetzgebend

legislator /'ledʒɪsleɪtə(r)/ *n.* Gesetzgeber, *der*

legislature /'ledʒɪsleɪtʃə(r)/ *n.* Legislative, *die*

legitimacy /lɪ'dʒɪtɪməsɪ/ *n.* **(a)**
Rechtmäßigkeit, *die;* Legitimität, *die*
(b) (of child) Ehelichkeit, *die*
legitimate /lɪ'dʒɪtɪmət/ *adj.* **(a)** (lawful)
legitim; rechtmäßig ‹*Besitzer, Regierung*›
(b) (valid) berechtigt
(c) ehelich ‹*Kind*›
legitimatize (legitimatise)
/lɪ'dʒɪtɪmətaɪz/, **legitimize (legitimise)**
/lɪ'dʒɪtɪmaɪz/ *v.t.* legitimieren
leisure /'leʒə(r)/ *n.* Freizeit, *die; attrib.*
Freizeit-
'leisurely *adj.* gemächlich
'leisurewear *n., no indef. art.*
Freizeitkleidung, *die*
lemon /'lemən/ *n.* Zitrone, *die*
lemonade /lemə'neɪd/ *n.*
[Zitronen]limonade, *die*
lend /lend/ *v.t.,* **lent** /lent/ leihen; ∼ sth. to
sb. jmdm. etw. leihen
'lender *n.* Verleiher, *der*/Verleiherin, *die*
length /leŋθ, leŋkθ/ *n.* **(a)** (also of time)
Länge, *die;* be six feet in ∼: sechs Fuß lang
sein; a short ∼ of time kurze Zeit
(b) at ∼ (for a long time) lange; (eventually)
schließlich; at [great] ∼ (in great detail) lang
und breit; at some ∼: ziemlich ausführlich
(c) go to any/great ∼s alles nur/alles
Erdenkliche tun
(d) (piece of material) Länge, *die;* Stück, *das*
lengthen /'leŋθən/ **1** *v.i.* länger werden
2 *v.t.* verlängern; länger machen ‹*Kleid*›
lengthways /'leŋθweɪz/ *adv.* der Länge
nach; längs
'lengthy *adj.* überlang
lenient /'liːnɪənt/ *adj.* nachsichtig
lens /lenz/ *n.* Linse, *die;* (of spectacles) Glas,
das
lens cap *n.* Objektivdeckel, *der*
lent ▶ LEND
Lent /lent/ *n.* Fastenzeit, *die*
lentil /'lentl/ *n.* Linse, *die*
Leo /'liːəʊ/ *n., pl.* ∼s (Astrol., Astron.) der
Löwe
leopard /'lepəd/ *n.* Leopard, *der*
leotard /'liːətɑːd/ *n.* Turnanzug, *der*
leper /'lepə(r)/ *n.* Leprakranke, *der*/*die*
leprosy /'leprəsɪ/ *n.* Lepra, *die*
lesbian /'lezbɪən/ **1** *n.* Lesbierin, *die*
2 *adj.* lesbisch
less /les/ **1** *adj.* weniger; of ∼ value/
importance weniger wertvoll/wichtig
2 *adv.* weniger; ∼ and ∼: immer weniger;
∼ and ∼ [often] immer seltener
3 *n.* weniger
4 *prep.* (deducting) ten ∼ three zehn weniger
drei
lessen /'lesn/ **1** *v.t.* verringern
2 *v.i.* sich verringern
lesser /'lesə(r)/ *attrib. adj.* geringer...
lessee /le'siː/ *n.* Pächter, *der*/Pächterin,
die; Mieter, *der*/Mieterin, *die*

lesson /'lesn/ *n.* **(a)** (class)
[Unterrichts]stunde, *die*
(b) (example, warning) Lehre, *die*
(c) (Eccl.) Lesung, *die*
let /let/ **1** *v.t.,* -tt-, **let (a)** (allow to) lassen;
∼ sb. do sth. jmdn. etw. tun lassen; ∼ alone
(far less) geschweige denn
(b) (cause to) ∼ sb. know jmdn. wissen
lassen
(c) (Brit.: rent out) vermieten
2 *v. aux.,* -tt-, **let** lassen; **Let's go to the
cinema.** – **Yes,** ∼'s/**No,** ∼'s not Komm/
Kommt, wir gehen ins Kino. – Ja, gut/Nein,
lieber nicht; ∼ them come in sie sollen
hereinkommen
■ **let 'down** *v.t.* **(a)** (lower) herunter-/
hinunterlassen
(b) (Dressm.) auslassen
(c) (disappoint, fail) im Stich lassen
■ **let 'in** *v.t.* **(a)** (admit) herein-/hineinlassen
(b) ∼ oneself in for sth. sich auf etw. (*Akk.*)
einlassen
(c) ∼ sb. in on a secret/plan *etc.* jmdn. in
ein Geheimnis/einen Plan *usw.* einweihen
■ **'let into** *v.t.* **(a)** (admit into) lassen in
(+ *Akk.*)
(b) (fig.: acquaint with) ∼ sb. into a secret
jmdn. in ein Geheimnis einweihen
■ **let 'off** *v.t.* **(a)** (excuse) laufen lassen (ugs.);
∼ sb. off sth. jmdm. etw. erlassen
(b) (allow to alight) aussteigen lassen
(c) abbrennen ‹*Feuerwerk*›
■ **let 'on** (coll.) **1** *v.i.* don't ∼ on! nichts
verraten!
2 *v.t.* sb. ∼ on to me that ...: man hat mir
gesteckt, dass ... (ugs.)
■ **let 'out** *v.t.* **(a)** ∼ sb./an animal out
jmdn./ein Tier heraus-/hinaus lassen
(b) ausstoßen ‹*Schrei*›; ∼ out a groan
aufstöhnen
(c) verraten ‹*Geheimnis*›
(d) (Dressm.) auslassen
(e) (Brit.: rent out) vermieten
■ **let 'through** *v.t.* durchlassen
■ **let 'up** *v.i.* (coll.) nachlassen
'let-down *n.* Enttäuschung, *die*
lethal /'liːθl/ *adj.* tödlich
lethargic /lɪ'θɑːdʒɪk/ *adj.* träge; (apathetic)
lethargisch
lethargy /'leθədʒɪ/ *n.* Trägheit, *die;* (apathy)
Lethargie, *die*
letter /'letə(r)/ *n.* **(a)** Brief, *der* (to an
+ *Akk.*)
(b) (of alphabet) Buchstabe, *der*
letter: ∼ **bomb** *n.* Briefbombe, *die;*
∼ **box** *n.* Briefkasten, *der;* ∼**head,**
∼**-heading** *ns.* Briefkopf, *der*
'lettering *n.* Typographie, *die*
letter: ∼ **pad** *n.* Briefblock, *der;* ∼**s
page** *n.* Leserbriefseite, *die*
lettuce /'letɪs/ *n.* [Kopf]salat, *der*
leukaemia, (Amer.) **leukemia**
/luː'kiːmɪə/ *n.* Leukämie, *die*

level /'levl/ **1** *n.* (a) Höhe, *die;* (storey) Etage, *die*
(b) (fig.: steady state) Niveau, *das;* **be on a ~ [with sb./sth.]** auf dem gleichen Niveau sein [wie jmd./etw.]
(c) (of computer game) Level, *der*
2 *adj.* (a) waagerecht; eben ⟨*Boden, Land*⟩
(b) (on a ~) **be ~ [with sth./sb.]** auf gleicher Höhe [mit etw./jmdm.] sein
(c) (fig.) **keep a ~ head** einen kühlen Kopf bewahren; **do one's ~ best** (coll.) sein Möglichstes tun
3 *v.t.,* (Brit.) **-ll-:** (a) (make ~) ebnen
(b) (aim) richten ⟨*Blick, Gewehr*⟩ (at auf + *Akk.*); (fig.) richten ⟨*Kritik usw.*⟩ (at gegen)

level: ~ **'crossing** *n.* (Brit. Railw.) [schienengleicher] Bahnübergang;
~-'headed *adj.* besonnen

lever /'liːvə(r)/ **1** *n.* Hebel, *der*
2 *v.t.* ~ **sth. open** etw. aufhebeln

leverage /'liːvərɪdʒ/ *n.* Hebelwirkung, *die*

levity /'levɪtɪ/ *n.* (frivolity) Unernst, *der*

levy /'levɪ/ **1** *n.* (tax) Steuer, *die*
2 *v.t.* erheben

lewd /ljuːd/ *adj.* geil; anzüglich ⟨*Geste*⟩; schlüpfrig ⟨*Witz*⟩

lexicon /'leksɪkən/ *n.* (a) (dictionary) Wörterbuch, *das;* Lexikon, *das* (veralt.)
(b) (vocabulary) Wortschatz, *der*

liability /laɪə'bɪlɪtɪ/ *n.* (a) Haftung, *die*
(b) (handicap) Belastung, *die* (to für)

liable /'laɪəbl/ *pred. adj.* (a) (legally bound) **be ~ for sth.** für etw. haftbar sein *od.* haften
(b) (prone) **be ~ to sth.** ⟨*Person:*⟩ zu etw. neigen; **be ~ to do sth.** ⟨*Sache:*⟩ leicht etw. tun; ⟨*Person:*⟩ dazu neigen, etw. zu tun

liaise /lɪ'eɪz/ *v.i.* eine Verbindung herstellen; ~ **on a project** bei einem Projekt zusammenarbeiten

liaison /lɪ'eɪzɒn/ *n.* (cooperation) Zusammenarbeit, *die*

liar /'laɪə(r)/ *n.* Lügner, *der*/Lügnerin, *die*

libel /'laɪbl/ **1** *n.* Verleumdung, *die*
2 *v.t.,* (Brit.) **-ll-** verleumden

libellous (*Amer.:* **libelous**) /'laɪbələs/ *adj.* verleumderisch

liberal /'lɪbərl/ **1** *adj.* (a) großzügig
(b) (Polit.) liberal; **the L~ Democrats** (Brit.) die Liberaldemokraten
2 *n.* **L~** (Polit.) Liberale, *der/die*

liberate /'lɪbəreɪt/ *v.t.* befreien (**from** aus); **a ~d woman** eine emanzipierte Frau

liberation /lɪbə'reɪʃn/ *n.* Befreiung, *die; see also* WOMEN'S LIBERATION

liberator /'lɪbəreɪtə(r)/ *n.* Befreier, *der/* Befreierin, *die*

liberty /'lɪbətɪ/ *n.* Freiheit, *die;* **take the ~ of doing sth.** sich (*Dat.*) die Freiheit nehmen, etw. zu tun; **take liberties with sb.** sich (*Dat.*) Freiheiten gegen jmdn. herausnehmen (ugs.)

Libra /'liːbrə/ *n.* (Astrol., Astron.) die Waage

librarian /laɪ'breərɪən/ *n.* Bibliothekar, *der/* Bibliothekarin, *die*

library /'laɪbrərɪ/ *n.* Bibliothek, *die;* **public ~:** öffentliche Bücherei

library: ~ **book** *n.* Buch aus der Bibliothek; ~ **ticket** *n.* Lesekarte, *die*

Libya /'lɪbɪə/ *pr. n.* Libyen (*das*)

lice *pl. of* LOUSE

licence /'laɪsəns/ **1** *n.* [behördliche] Genehmigung; Lizenz, *die;* [**driving**] ~: Führerschein, *der*
2 *v.t.* ▶ LICENSE 1

'licence fee *n.* Lizenzgebühr, *die*

license /'laɪsəns/ **1** *v.t.* ermächtigen; **the restaurant is ~d to sell drinks** das Restaurant hat eine Schankerlaubnis *od.* -konzession; ~**d** ⟨*Händler, Makler, Buchmacher*⟩ mit [einer] Lizenz; **licensing laws** Schankgesetze; ~**d premises** Gaststätte mit Schankerlaubnis; **get a car ~d** ≈ die Kfz-Steuer für ein Auto bezahlen
2 *n.* (Amer.) ▶ LICENCE 1

'license plate *n.* (Amer.) Nummernschild, *das*

licentious /laɪ'senʃəs/ *adj.* zügellos ⟨*Person*⟩; unzüchtig ⟨*Benehmen*⟩

lichen /'laɪkn, 'lɪtʃn/ *n.* Flechte, *die*

lick /lɪk/ **1** *v.t.* (a) lecken
(b) (coll.: beat) verdreschen (ugs.)
2 *n.* Lecken, *das*
■ **lick 'off** *v.t.* ablecken

lid /lɪd/ *n.* (a) Deckel, *der*
(b) (eyelid) Lid, *das*

lido /'liːdəʊ/ *n., pl.* ~**s** Freibad, *das*

lie¹ /laɪ/ **1** *n.* Lüge, *die;* **tell ~s/a ~:** lügen
2 *v.i., lying* /'laɪɪŋ/ lügen; ~ **to sb.** jmdn. be- *od.* anlügen

lie² *v.i., lying* /'laɪɪŋ/, **lay** /leɪ/, **lain** /leɪn/ (a) liegen; (assume horizontal position) sich legen
(b) ~ **idle** ⟨*Maschine, Fabrik:*⟩ stillstehen
■ **lie a'bout, lie a'round** *v.i.* herumliegen (ugs.).
■ **lie 'back** *v.i.* sich zurücklegen; (sitting) sich zurücklehnen
■ **lie 'down** *v.i.* sich hinlegen

lie detector /'laɪdɪtektə(r)/ *n.* Lügendetektor, *der*

'lie-in *n.* (coll.) **have a ~:** [sich] ausschlafen

lieu /ljuː/ *n.* **in ~ of sth.** anstelle einer Sache (*Gen.*); **get holiday in ~:** stattdessen Urlaub bekommen

lieutenant /lef'tenənt/ *n.* (Army) Oberleutnant, *der*

life /laɪf/ *n., pl.* **lives** /laɪvz/ Leben, *das;* **for ~:** lebenslänglich ⟨*inhaftiert*⟩; **true to ~:** wahrheitsgetreu; **get a ~:** (coll.) was aus seinem Leben machen

life: ~**-and-death** *adj.* ⟨*Kampf*⟩ auf Leben und Tod; (fig.) überaus wichtig ⟨*Frage, Brief*⟩; ~ **assurance** *n.* (Brit.) Lebensversicherung, *die;* ~**belt** *n.* Rettungsring, *der;* ~**boat** *n.* Rettungsboot, *das;* ~**buoy** *n.* Rettungsring, *der;* ~ **cycle**

n. Lebenszyklus, *der;* ~ **expectancy** *n.* Lebenserwartung, *die;* ~**guard** *n.* Rettungsschwimmer, *der/*-schwimmerin, *die;* ~ **insurance** *n.* Lebensversicherung, *die;* ~ **jacket** *n.* Schwimmweste, *die;* ~**less** *adj.* leblos; (fig.) farblos; ~**line** *n.* Rettungsleine, *die;* (fig.) Rettungsanker, *der;* ~**long** *adj.* lebenslang

lifer /ˈlaɪfə(r)/ *n.* (coll.) Lebenslängliche, *der/ die* (ugs.)

life: ~**-saving** *n.* Rettungsschwimmen, *das; attrib.* Rettungs-; ~ **sciences** *n. pl.* Biowissenschaften *Pl.;* ~ **sentence** *n.* lebenslängliche Freiheitsstrafe; ~**sized** *adj.* lebensgroß; in Lebensgröße *nachgestellt;* ~**span** *n.* Lebenserwartung, *die;* (Biol.) Lebensdauer, *die;* ~**style** *n.* Lebensstil, *der;* ~**time** *n.* Lebenszeit, *die;* **during my** ~**time** während meines Lebens; **once in a** ~**time** einmal im Leben; ~ **vest** *n.* Schwimmweste, *die*

lift /lɪft/ 1 *v.t.* heben; (fig.) erheben ⟨Gemüt, Geist⟩

2 *n.* **(a)** (in vehicle) **get a** ~: mitgenommen werden; **give sb. a** ~: jmdn. mitnehmen **(b)** (Brit.: elevator) Aufzug, *der* 3 *v.i.* ⟨Nebel:⟩ sich auflösen

■ **'lift off** *v.t. & i.* abheben

■ **lift 'up** *v.t.* hochheben; heben ⟨Kopf⟩

'lift-off *n.* Abheben, *das*

ligament /ˈlɪɡəmənt/ *n.* Band, *das*

light¹ /laɪt/ 1 *n.* **(a)** Licht, *das;* ~ **of day** Tageslicht, *das* **(b)** (lamp) Licht, *das;* (fitting) Lampe, *die* **(c)** (signal to traffic) Ampel, *die;* **as far as the** ~**s** bis zur Ampel **(d)** (to ignite) **have you got a** ~? haben Sie Feuer? **set** ~ **to sth.** etw. anzünden **(e) bring sth. to** ~: etw. ans [Tages]licht bringen; **throw** *or* **shed** ~ **[up]on sth.** Licht in etw. (Akk.) bringen **(f)** (aspect) **in that** ~: aus dieser Sicht; **seen in this** ~: so gesehen; **in the** ~ **of** angesichts (+ Gen.); **show sb. in a bad** ~: ein schlechtes Licht auf jmdn. werfen 2 *adj.* hell; ~**-blue/-brown** etc. hellblau/ -braun usw. 3 *v.t.,* **lit** /lɪt/ *or* **lighted (a)** (ignite) anzünden **(b)** (illuminate) erhellen

■ **light 'up** 1 *v.i.* **(a)** (become lit) erleuchtet werden **(b)** (become bright) aufleuchten **(with** vor) 2 *v.t.* **(a)** (illuminate) erleuchten **(b)** anzünden ⟨Zigarette⟩

light² 1 *adj.* leicht; (mild) mild ⟨Strafe⟩ 2 *adv.* **travel** ~: mit wenig *od.* leichtem Gepäck reisen

light: ~ **'aircraft** *n.* Leichtflugzeug, *das;* ~**bulb** *n.* Glühbirne, *die*

'lighted *adj.* brennend ⟨Kerze, Zigarette⟩; angezündet ⟨Streichholz⟩

light-emitting 'diode /ˈdaɪəʊd/ *n.* Leuchtdiode, *die*

lighten¹ /ˈlaɪtn/ *v.t.* (make less heavy, difficult) leichter machen

lighten² 1 *v.t.* (make brighter) aufhellen; heller machen ⟨Raum⟩ 2 *v.i.* sich aufhellen

'lighter *n.* Feuerzeug, *das*

light: ~**'headed** *adj.* leicht benommen; ~**-'hearted** *adj.* **(a)** (humorous) unbeschwert; **(b)** (optimistic) unbekümmert; ~**house** *n.* Leuchtturm, *der;* ~ **'industry** *n.* Leichtindustrie, *die*

'lighting *n.* Beleuchtung, *die*

'lightly *adv.* **(a)** leicht **(b)** (without serious consideration) leichtfertig **(c)** (cheerfully) leichthin; **not treat sth.** ~: etw. nicht auf die leichte Schulter nehmen **(d) get off** ~: glimpflich davonkommen

'light meter *n.* Lichtmesser, *der;* (exposure meter) Belichtungsmesser, *der*

'lightness¹ *n.* (of weight; also fig.) Leichtigkeit, *die*

lightness² *n.* (of colour) Helligkeit, *die*

lightning /ˈlaɪtnɪŋ/ *n.* Blitz, *der;* **flash of** ~: Blitz, *der*

lightning: ~ **conductor** *n.* Blitzableiter, *der;* ~ **strike** *n.* Blitzschlag, *der*

light: ~**weight** 1 *adj.* leicht. 2 *n.* Leichtgewicht, *das;* ~ **year** *n.* Lichtjahr, *das*

like¹ /laɪk/ 1 *adj.* **(a)** (resembling) wie; **your dress is** ~ **mine** dein Kleid ist so ähnlich wie meins; **in a case** ~ **that** in so einem Fall; **what is sb./sth.** ~? wie ist jmd./etw.? **(b)** (characteristic of) typisch für ⟨dich, ihn usw.⟩ **(c)** (similar) ähnlich 2 *prep.* (in the manner of) wie; **[just]** ~ **that** [einfach] so 3 *n.* **(a)** (equal) **his/her** ~: seines-/ ihresgleichen **(b)** (similar things) **the** ~: so etwas; **and the** ~: und dergleichen

like² 1 *v.t.* (be fond of, wish for) mögen; ~ **vegetables** Gemüse mögen; gern Gemüse essen; ~ **doing sth.** etw. gern tun; **would you** ~ **a drink?** möchtest du etwas trinken?; **would you** ~ **me to do it?** möchtest du, dass ich es tue?; **how do you** ~ **it?** wie gefällt es dir?; **if you** ~ *expr. assent* wenn du willst 2 *n., in pl.* ~**s and dislikes** Vorlieben und Abneigungen

likeable /ˈlaɪkəbl/ *adj.* nett; sympathisch

likelihood /ˈlaɪklɪhʊd/ *n.* Wahrscheinlichkeit, *die*

likely /ˈlaɪklɪ/ 1 *adj.* wahrscheinlich; **there are** ~ **to be [traffic] hold-ups** man muss mit [Verkehrs]staus rechnen; **they are [not]** ~ **to come** sie werden wahrscheinlich [nicht] kommen; **is it** ~ **to rain tomorrow?** wird es morgen wohl regnen?; **this is not** ~ **to happen** es ist unwahrscheinlich, dass das geschieht ⋯⟶

2 *adv.* wahrscheinlich; **as** ∼ **as not** höchstwahrscheinlich; **not** ∼! (coll.) auf keinen Fall!

'like-minded *adj.* gleich gesinnt

liken /'laɪkn/ *v.t.* ∼ **sth./sb. to sth./sb.** etw./ jmdn. mit etw./jmdm. vergleichen

'likeness *n.* Ähnlichkeit, *die* **(to** mit)

likewise /'laɪkwaɪz/ *adv.* ebenso

liking /'laɪkɪŋ/ *n.* Vorliebe, *die;* **take a** ∼ **to sb./sth.** an jmdm./etw. Gefallen finden; **sth. is [not] to sb.'s** ∼: etw. ist [nicht] nach jmds. Geschmack

lilac /'laɪlək/ 1 *n.* (a) (Bot.) Flieder, *der* (b) (colour) Zartlila, *das* 2 *adj.* zartlila; fliederfarben

Lilo ® /'laɪləʊ/ *n.* Luftmatratze, *die*

lily /'lɪlɪ/ *n.* Lilie, *die*

limb /lɪm/ *n.* (a) (Anat.) Glied, *das* (b) **be out on a** ∼ (fig.) exponiert sein

limber up /lɪmbər 'ʌp/ *v.i.* (loosen up) die Muskeln lockern

lime¹ /laɪm/ *n.* [quick]∼: [ungelöschter] Kalk

lime² *n.* (fruit) Limone, *die*

lime³ ▶ LIME TREE

'limelight *n.* **be in the** ∼: im Rampenlicht [der Öffentlichkeit] stehen

limerick /'lɪmərɪk/ *n.* Limerick, *der*

lime: ∼**stone** *n.* Kalkstein, *der;* ∼ **tree** *n.* Linde, *die*

limit /'lɪmɪt/ 1 *n.* (a) Grenze, *die;* **set** *or* **put a** ∼ **on sth.** etw. begrenzen; **be over the** ∼ ⟨*Autofahrer:*⟩ zu viele Promille haben; **lower/ upper** ∼: Untergrenze/Höchstgrenze, *die;* **without** ∼: unbegrenzt; **within** ∼**s** innerhalb gewisser Grenzen (b) (coll.) **this is the** ∼! das ist [doch] die Höhe!; **he/she is the [very]** ∼: er/sie ist [einfach] unmöglich 2 *v.t.* begrenzen (**to** auf + *Akk.*); einschränken ⟨*Freiheit*⟩

limitation /lɪmɪ'teɪʃn/ *n.* Beschränkung, *die*

'limited *adj.* (a) (restricted) begrenzt (b) (intellectually narrow) beschränkt

'limitless *adj.* grenzenlos

limousine /'lɪməʊziːn/ *n.* Limousine, *die*

limp¹ /lɪmp/ 1 *v.i.* hinken 2 *n.* Hinken, *das*

limp² *adj.* schlaff

'limply *adv.* schlaff; (weakly) schwach

limpet /'lɪmpɪt/ *n.* (Zool.) Napfschnecke, *die*

limpid /'lɪmpɪd/ *adj.* klar

linctus /'lɪŋktəs/ *n.* Hustensaft, *der*

line¹ /laɪn/ 1 *n.* (a) (string, cord, rope, etc.) Leine, *die* (b) (telephone cable) Leitung, *die* (c) (long mark; also Math., Phys.) Linie, *die* (d) (row, series) Reihe, *die;* (Amer.: queue) Schlange, *die;* **bring sb. into** ∼: dafür sorgen, dass jmd. nicht aus der Reihe tanzt (ugs.) (e) (row of words on a page) Zeile, *die*

(f) (wrinkle) Falte, *die* (g) (direction, course) Richtung, *die;* **on the** ∼**s of** nach Art (+ *Gen.*); **be on the right/wrong** ∼**s** in die richtige/falsche Richtung gehen; **along** *or* **on the same** ∼**s** in der gleichen Richtung (h) (Railw.) Bahnlinie, *die;* (track) Gleis, *das* (i) (field of activity) Branche, *die* (j) (Commerc.: product) Artikel, *der;* Linie, *die* (fachspr.) 2 *v.t.* (a) linieren ⟨*Papier*⟩; **a** ∼**d face** ein faltiges Gesicht (b) säumen (geh.) ⟨*Straße, Strecke*⟩

■ **line 'up** 1 *v.t.* antreten lassen ⟨*Gefangene, Soldaten usw.*⟩; [in einer Reihe] aufstellen ⟨*Gegenstände*⟩ 2 *v.i.* ⟨*Gefangene, Soldaten:*⟩ antreten; (queue up) sich anstellen

line² *v.t.* füttern ⟨*Kleidungsstück*⟩; ausschlagen ⟨*Schublade usw.*⟩

lineage /'lɪnɪɪdʒ/ *n.* Abstammung, *die*

linear /'lɪnɪə(r)/ *adj.* linear

line: ∼ **dance** 1 *n.* Linedance, *der;* 2 *v.i.* Linedance tanzen; ∼ **dancing** *n.* Linedance-Tanzen, *das;* ∼ **manager** *n.* [unmittelbarer] Vorgesetzter; Linienmanager, *der*

linen /'lɪnɪn/ 1 *n.* (a) Leinen, *das* (b) (shirts, sheets, etc.) Wäsche, *die* 2 *adj.* Leinen⟨faden, -bluse⟩; Lein⟨tuch⟩

linen: ∼ **basket** *n.* (Brit.) Wäschekorb, *der;* ∼ **cupboard** *n.* Wäscheschrank, *der*

'line printer *n.* (Comp.) Zeilendrucker, *der*

liner /'laɪnə(r)/ Linienschiff, *das*

'line-up *n.* Aufstellung, *die*

linger /'lɪŋɡə(r)/ *v.i.* verweilen (geh.); bleiben

lingerie /'læʒərɪ/ *n.* **[women's]** ∼: Damenunterwäsche, *die*

lingo /'lɪŋɡəʊ/ *n.* (coll.) Sprache, *die*

linguist /'lɪŋɡwɪst/ *n.* Sprachkundige, *der/ die*

linguistic /lɪŋ'ɡwɪstɪk/ *adj.* (of ∼s) linguistisch; (of language) sprachlich

linguistics /lɪŋ'ɡwɪstɪks/ *n.* Linguistik, *die*

lining /'laɪnɪŋ/ *n.* (of clothes) Futter, *das;* (of objects, machines, etc.) Auskleidung, *die*

'lining paper *n.* Schrankpapier, *das*

link /lɪŋk/ 1 *n.* (a) (of chain) Glied, *das* (b) (connection) Verbindung, *die* 2 *v.t.* verbinden; ∼ **arms** sich unterhaken

■ **link 'up** *v.t.* miteinander verbinden

links /lɪŋks/ *n.* **[golf]** ∼: Golfplatz, *der*

lino /'laɪnəʊ/ *n., pl.* ∼**s** Linoleum, *das*

linoleum /lɪ'nəʊlɪəm/ *n.* Linoleum, *das*

linseed /'lɪnsiːd/ *n.* Leinsamen, *der*

linseed 'oil *n.* Leinöl, *das*

lint /lɪnt/ *n.* Mull, *der*

lintel /'lɪntl/ *n.* (Archit.) Sturz, *der*

lion /'laɪən/ *n.* Löwe, *der*

lioness /'laɪənɪs/ *n.* Löwin, *die*

lip /lɪp/ *n.* (a) Lippe, *die;* **lower/upper** ∼: Unter-/Oberlippe, *die*

(b) (of cup) [Gieß]rand, *der;* (of jug) Schnabel, *der*

liposuction /'laɪpəʊsʌkʃn, 'lɪpəʊsʌkʃn/ *n.* Fettabsaugung, *die;* Liposuktion, *die*

lip: ~-**read** *v.i.* von den Lippen lesen; ~-**reading** *n.* Lippenlesen, *das;* ~ **service** *n.* pay ~ service to sth. ein Lippenbekenntnis zu etw. ablegen; ~**stick** *n.* Lippenstift, *der*

liquefy /'lɪkwɪfaɪ/ ① *v.t.* verflüssigen ② *v.i.* sich verflüssigen

liqueur /lɪ'kjʊə(r)/ *n.* Likör, *der*

liquid /'lɪkwɪd/ ① *adj.* flüssig ② *n.* Flüssigkeit, *die*

liquidate /'lɪkwɪdeɪt/ *v.t.* (Commerc.) liquidieren

liquidation /lɪkwɪ'deɪʃn/ *n.* (Commerc.) Liquidation, *die*

liquid crystal dis'play *n.* Flüssigkristallanzeige, *die*

liquidize /'lɪkwɪdaɪz/ *v.t.* auflösen; (Cookery) [im Mixer] pürieren

'liquidizer *n.* Mixer, *der*

liquid 'measure *n.* Flüssigkeitsmaß, *das*

liquor /'lɪkə(r)/ *n.* (drink) Alkohol, *der*

liquorice /'lɪkərɪs/ *n.* Lakritze, *die*

Lisbon /'lɪzbən/ *pr. n.* Lissabon (*das*)

lisp /lɪsp/ ① *v.i. & t.* lispeln ② *n.* Lispeln, *das*

list¹ /lɪst/ ① *n.* Liste, *die* ② *v.t.* aufführen; auflisten; (verbally) aufzählen

list² *v.i.* (Naut.) Schlagseite haben

listed 'building *n.* (Brit.) Gebäude unter Denkmalsschutz

listen /'lɪsn/ *v.i.* zuhören; ~ to music/the radio Musik/Radio hören; they ~ed to his words sie hörten ihm zu

listener /'lɪsnə(r)/ *n.* Zuhörer, *der/* Zuhörerin, *die;* (to radio) Hörer, *der/*Hörerin, *die*

listless /'lɪstlɪs/ *adj.* lustlos

'list price *n.* Katalogpreis, *der*

lit ▶ LIGHT¹ 3

litany /'lɪtənɪ/ *n.* Litanei, *die*

lite, Lite ® /laɪt/ ① *adj.* kalorienreduziert ⟨Bier, Käse etc.⟩ ② *n.* Leichtbier, *das*

liter (Amer.) ▶ LITRE

literacy /'lɪtərəsɪ/ *n.* Lese- und Schreibfertigkeit, *die*

literal /'lɪtərl/ *adj.* **(a)** wörtlich **(b)** (not exaggerated) buchstäblich

literally /'lɪtərəlɪ/ *adv.* **(a)** wörtlich **(b)** (actually) buchstäblich **(c)** (coll.: with some exaggeration) geradezu

literary /'lɪtərərɪ/ *adj.* literarisch

literary 'agent *n.* Literaturagent, *der/* -agentin, *die*

literate /'lɪtərət/ *adj.* des Lesens und Schreibens kundig; (educated) gebildet

literature /'lɪtrətʃə(r)/ *n.* Literatur, *die*

lithe /laɪð/ *adj.* geschmeidig

litigation /lɪtɪ'geɪʃn/ *n.* Rechtsstreit, *der*

litre /'liːtə(r)/ *n.* (Brit.) Liter, *der od. das*

litter /'lɪtə(r)/ ① *n.* **(a)** (rubbish) Abfall, *der* **(b)** (of animals) Wurf, *der* ② *v.t.* verstreuen

litter: ~ **basket** *n.* Abfallkorb, *der;* ~ **bin** *n.* Abfalleimer, *der;* ~**bug**, ~ **lout** *ns.* Schmutzfink, *der* (ugs.)

little /'lɪtl/ ① *adj.,* ~*r* /'lɪtlə(r)/, ~**st** /'lɪtlɪst/ (*Note: it is more common to use the compar. and superl. forms* **smaller, smallest**) **(a)** klein; a ~ **way** ein kurzes Stück; after a ~ **while** nach kurzer Zeit **(b)** (not much) wenig; there is very ~ **tea** left es ist kaum noch Tee da; a ~ ... (a small quantity of) etwas ...; ein bisschen ... ② *n.* wenig; a ~ (a small quantity) etwas; (somewhat) ein wenig; ~ **by** ~: nach und nach

little: ~ '**finger** *n.* kleiner Finger; ~-**known** *adj.* wenig bekannt

liturgy /'lɪtədʒɪ/ *n.* Liturgie, *die*

live¹ /laɪv/ ① *adj. attrib.* (alive) lebend **(b)** (Radio, Telev.) ~ **performance** Liveaufführung, *die;* ~ **broadcast** Livesendung, *die* **(c)** (Electr.) Strom führend ② *adv.* (Radio, Telev.) live ⟨übertragen usw.⟩

live² /lɪv/ ① *v.i.* **(a)** leben **(b)** (make permanent home) wohnen; leben ② *v.t.* leben

■ **live 'down** *v.t.* Gras wachsen lassen über (+ *Akk.*); he will never be able to ~ it down das wird ihm ewig anhängen

■ **live on** ① /'--/ *v.t.* leben von ② /-'-/ *v.i.* weiterleben

■ **live 'up to** *v.t.* gerecht werden (+ *Dat.*)

live-in /'lɪvɪn/ *attrib. adj.* im Haus wohnend ⟨*Personal*⟩

livelihood /'laɪvlɪhʊd/ *n.* Lebensunterhalt, *der*

liveliness /'laɪvlɪnɪs/ *n.* Lebhaftigkeit, *die*

lively /'laɪvlɪ/ *adj.* lebhaft; lebendig ⟨*Schilderung*⟩; rege ⟨*Handel*⟩

liven up /laɪvn 'ʌp/ ① *v.t.* Leben bringen in (+ *Akk.*) ② *v.i.* ⟨*Person:*⟩ aufleben

liver /'lɪvə(r)/ *n.* Leber, *die*

livery /'lɪvərɪ/ *n.* Livree, *die*

lives *pl. of* LIFE

live /laɪv/**:** ~**stock** *n. pl.* Vieh, *das;* ~ '**wire** *n.* (fig.) Energiebündel, *das* (ugs.)

livid /'lɪvɪd/ *adj.* (Brit. coll.) fuchtig (ugs.)

living /'lɪvɪŋ/ ① *n.* **(a)** Leben, *das* **(b)** make a ~: seinen Lebensunterhalt verdienen **(c)** *pl.* the ~: die Lebenden *Pl.* ② *adj.* lebend; within ~ **memory** seit Menschengedenken

living: ~ **room** *n.* Wohnzimmer, *das;* ~ '**will** *n.* Patientenverfügung, *die*

lizard /'lɪzəd/ n. Eidechse, die

llama /'lɑːmə/ n. Lama, das

load /ləʊd/ **1** n. (burden, weight; also fig.) Last, die; (amount carried) Ladung, die

2 v.t. (a) (put ~ on) beladen; (put as load) ~ sb. with work (fig.) jmdm. Arbeit auftragen

(b) (load a camera) ⟨Gewehr⟩; ~ a camera einen Film [in einen Fotoapparat] einlegen

■ **load 'up** v.i. laden (with Akk.)

'loaded adj. a ~ question eine suggestive Frage; be ~ (coll.: rich) [schwer] Kohle haben (salopp)

'loading bay n. Ladeplatz, der

loaf¹ /ləʊf/ n., pl. **loaves** /ləʊvz/ Brot, das; [Brot]laib, der; a ~ of bread ein Laib Brot

loaf² v.i. ~ round town/the house in der Stadt/zu Hause herumlungern (ugs.)

loan /ləʊn/ **1** n. (a) (thing lent) Leihgabe, die; be out on ~: ausgeliehen sein; have sth. on ~ [from sb.] etw. [von jmdm.] geliehen haben

(b) (money lent) Darlehen, das

2 v.t. ~ sth. to sb. jmdm. etw. leihen

loan shark n. (coll.) Kredithai, der (ugs.)

loath /ləʊθ/ pred. adj. be ~ to do sth. etw. ungern tun

loathe /ləʊð/ v.t. verabscheuen

loathing /'ləʊðɪŋ/ n. Abscheu, der (of, for vor + Dat.)

loathsome /'ləʊðsəm/ adj. abscheulich; widerlich

loaves pl. of LOAF¹

lobby /'lɒbɪ/ n. (a) (pressure group) Lobby, die

(b) (of hotel) Eingangshalle, die; (of theatre) Foyer, das

lobe /ləʊb/ n. (ear~) Ohrläppchen, das

lobster /'lɒbstə(r)/ n. Hummer, der

'lobster pot n. Hummerkorb, der

local /'ləʊkl/ **1** adj. lokal (bes. Zeitungsw.); Kommunal⟨wahl, -abgaben⟩; (of this area) hiesig; (of that area) dortig; ortsansässig ⟨Firma, Familie⟩; ⟨Wein, Produkt, Spezialität⟩ [aus] der Gegend; she's a ~ girl sie ist von hier/dort

2 n. (a) (person) Einheimische, der/die

(b) (Brit. coll.: pub) [Stamm]kneipe, die

local: ~ **anaes'thetic** n. Lokalanästhetikum, das; ~ **au'thority** n. (Brit.) Kommunalverwaltung, die; ~ **call** n. (Teleph.) Ortsgespräch, das; ~ **'government** n. Kommunalverwaltung, die

locality /ləʊ'kælɪtɪ/ n. Ort, der

localization /ləʊkəlaɪ'zeɪʃn/ n. (Comp.) Lokalisierung, die

'locally adv. im/am Ort

locate /ləʊ'keɪt/ v.t. (a) be ~d liegen

(b) (determine position of) ausfindig machen

location /ləʊ'keɪʃn/ n. (a) Lage, die

(b) (Cinemat.) Drehort, der; be on ~: bei Außenaufnahmen sein

loch /lɒx, lɒk/ n. (Scot.) See, der

lock¹ /lɒk/ n. (of hair) [Haar]strähne, die

lock² **1** n. (a) (of door etc.) Schloss, das

(b) (on canal etc.) Schleuse, die

2 v.t. zuschließen

■ **lock a'way** v.t. einschließen; einsperren ⟨Person⟩

■ **lock 'in** v.t. einschließen; (deliberately) einsperren

■ **lock 'out** v.t. aussperren (of aus); ~ oneself out sich aussperren

■ **lock 'up** **1** v.i. abschließen

2 v.t. (a) abschließen ⟨Haus, Tür⟩

(b) (imprison) einsperren

locker /'lɒkə(r)/ n. Schließfach, das

locket /'lɒkɪt/ n. Medaillon, das

lock: ~**jaw** n. (Med.) Kieferklemme, die; ~**out** n. Aussperrung, die; ~**smith** n. Schlosser, der

locomotive /ləʊkə'məʊtɪv/ n. Lokomotive, die

locust /'ləʊkəst/ n. Heuschrecke, die

lodge /lɒdʒ/ **1** n. (a) (cottage) Pförtner-/ Gärtnerhaus, das

(b) (porter's room) [Pförtner]loge, die

2 v.t. (a) einlegen ⟨Beschwerde, Protest usw.⟩

(b) einreichen ⟨Klage⟩

3 v.i. [zur Miete] wohnen

'lodger n. Untermieter, der/Untermieterin, die

lodging /'lɒdʒɪŋ/ n. [möbliertes] Zimmer

loft /lɒft/ n. (attic) [Dach]boden, der

lofty /'lɒftɪ/ adj. (a) (exalted) hoch

(b) (haughty) hochmütig

log /lɒg/ n. (a) (timber) [geschlagener] Baumstamm; (as firewood) [Holz]scheit, das

(b) ~[book] (Naut.) Logbuch, das

■ **log 'in** ▶ LOG ON

■ **log 'off** v.i. (Comp.) sich abmelden

■ **log 'on** v.i. (Comp.) sich anmelden

■ **log 'out** ▶ LOG OFF

log: ~ **'cabin** n. Blockhütte, die; ~ **'fire** n. Holzfeuer, das

loggerheads /'lɒgəhedz/ n. pl. be at ~ with sb. mit jmdm. im Clinch liegen

logic /'lɒdʒɪk/ n. Logik, die

logical /'lɒdʒɪkl/ adj. logisch; she has a ~ mind sie denkt logisch

logically /'lɒdʒɪkəlɪ/ adv. logisch

logistics /lə'dʒɪstɪks/ n. pl. Logistik, die

logo /'ləʊgəʊ/ n., pl. ~s Signet, das

loin /lɔɪn/ n. Lende, die

'loincloth n. Lendenschurz, der

loiter /'lɔɪtə(r)/ v.i. trödeln; (linger suspiciously) herumlungern

loll /lɒl/ v.i. sich lümmeln (ugs.)

lollipop /'lɒlɪpɒp/ n. Lutscher, der

London /'lʌndən/ **1** pr. n. London (das)

2 attrib. adj. Londoner

'Londoner n. Londoner, der/Londonerin, die

lone /ləʊn/ attrib. adj. einsam

loneliness /ˈləʊnlɪnɪs/ *n.* Einsamkeit, *die*

lonely /ˈləʊnlɪ/ *adj.* einsam

lone 'parent *n.* allein erziehender Elternteil; **she/he is a ~:** sie/er ist allein erziehend

loner /ˈləʊnə(r)/ *n.* Einzelgänger, *der*/ -gängerin, *die*

lonesome /ˈləʊnsəm/ *adj.* einsam

long¹ /lɒŋ/ ① *adj.,* ~er /ˈlɒŋgə(r)/, ~est /ˈlɒŋgɪst/ **(a)** lang; weit ⟨*Reise, Weg*⟩ **(b)** (elongated) länglich; schmal **(c)** in the '~ **run** auf die Dauer
② *n.* (~ interval) **take ~:** lange dauern; **for ~:** lange; (since ~ ago) seit langem; **before ~:** bald
③ *adv.,* ~er, ~est **(a)** lang[e]; **as** *or* **so ~ as** solange; **you should have finished ~ before now** du hättest schon längst fertig sein sollen; **much ~er** viel länger **(b)** as *or* so ~ as (provided that) solange; wenn

long² *v.i.* ~ **for sb./sth.** sich nach jmdm./ etw. sehnen; ~ **to do sth.** sich danach sehnen, etw. zu tun

long-distance ① /'---/ *adj.* Fern⟨*gespräch, -verkehr usw.*⟩; Langstrecken⟨*läufer, -flug usw.*⟩ ② /'-'--/ *adv.* **phone ~:** ein Ferngespräch führen

longevity /lɒn'dʒevɪtɪ/ *n.* Langlebigkeit, *die*

long: ~-haired *adj.* langhaarig; Langhaar⟨*dackel, -katze*⟩; ~**hand** *n.* Langschrift, *die;* ~**haul** *adj.* Fern⟨*verkehr, -lastwagen*⟩; Langstrecken⟨*[flug]verkehr*⟩

'longing ① *n.* Sehnsucht, *die* ② *adj.* sehnsüchtig

'longingly *adv.* sehnsüchtig

longitude /ˈlɒŋgɪtjuːd/ *n.* (Geog.) Länge, *die*

long: ~ jump *n.* (Brit. Sport) Weitsprung, *der;* ~**lasting** *adj.* langandauernd; dauerhaft ⟨*Beziehung, Freundschaft*⟩; ~**legged** *adj.* langbeinig; ~ **'lens** *n.* Fernobjektiv, *das;* ~**life** *adj.* haltbar [gemacht]; ~**life battery** Batterie mit langer Lebensdauer; ~**life milk** H-Milch, *die;* ~**lived** /ˈlɒŋlɪvd/ *adj.* langlebig; ~**playing 'record** *n.* Langspielplatte, *die;* ~**range** *adj.* **(a)** Langstrecken⟨*flugzeug, -rakete usw.*⟩; **(b)** (relating to time) langfristig; ~**sighted** /lɒŋ'saɪtɪd/ *adj.* weitsichtig; (fig.) weitblickend; ~**sleeved** /ˈlɒŋsliːvd/ *adj.* langärmelig; ~**standing** *attrib. adj.* seit langem bestehend; alt ⟨*Schulden, Streit*⟩; ~**suffering** *adj.* schwer geprüft; ~**term** *adj.* langfristig; ~ **wave** *n.* (Radio) Langwelle, *die;* ~**winded** /lɒŋ'wɪndɪd/ *adj.* langatmig

loo /luː/ *n.* (Brit. coll.) Klo, *das* (ugs.)

look /lʊk/ ① *v.i.* **(a)** sehen; gucken (ugs.) **(b)** (search) nachsehen **(c)** (face) zugewandt sein (**to[wards]** *Dat.*)

(d) (appear) aussehen; ~ **well/ill** gut/schlecht aussehen
② *n.* **(a)** Blick, *der;* **have** *or* **take a ~ at sb./ sth.** sich (*Dat.*) jmdn./etw. ansehen **(b)** (appearance) Aussehen, *das;* **good ~s** gutes Aussehen
▪ **look 'after** *v.t.* (care for) sorgen für
▪ **look a'head** *v.i.* (fig.) an die Zukunft denken
▪ **'look at** *v.t.* **(a)** (regard) ansehen **(b)** (consider) betrachten
▪ **look 'back** *v.i.* **(a)** sich umsehen **(b)** ~ **back on** *or* **to sth.** an etw. (*Akk.*) zurückdenken
▪ **look 'down [up]on** *v.t.* **(a)** herunter-/ hinuntersehen auf (+ *Akk.*) **(b)** (fig.: despise) herabsehen auf (+ *Akk.*)
▪ **'look for** *v.t.* **(a)** (seek) suchen nach **(b)** (expect) erwarten
▪ **look 'out** *v.i.* **(a)** hinaus-/herausehen (**of** aus) **(b)** (take care) aufpassen **(c)** ~ **out on sth.** ⟨*Zimmer, Wohnung usw.:*⟩ zu etw. hin liegen
▪ **look 'out for** *v.t.* (be prepared for) achten auf (+ *Akk.*); (keep watching for) Ausschau halten nach ⟨*Arbeit, Gelegenheit, Sammelobjekt usw.*⟩
▪ **look 'over** *v.t.* **(a)** sehen über (+ *Akk.*) **(b)** (survey) sich (*Dat.*) ansehen ⟨*Haus*⟩
▪ **look 'round** *v.i.* sich umsehen
▪ **'look through** *v.t.* **(a)** ~ **through sth.** durch etw. [hindurch] sehen **(b)** (inspect) durchsehen ⟨*Papiere*⟩
▪ **'look to** *v.t.* (rely on) ~ **to sb./sth. for sth.** etw. von jmdm./etw. erwarten
▪ **look 'up** ① *v.i.* **(a)** aufblicken **(b)** (improve) besser werden ② *v.t.* nachschlagen ⟨*Wort*⟩; heraussuchen ⟨*Telefonnummer, Zugverbindung usw.*⟩
▪ **look 'up to** *v.t.* ~ **up to sb.** zu jmdm. aufsehen

'look-alike *n.* Doppelgänger, *der*/-gängerin, *die*

looker-'on *n.* Zuschauer, *der*/Zuschauerin, *die*

'looking glass *n.* Spiegel, *der*

'lookout *n.,* *pl.* ~**s (a)** (observation post) Ausguck, *der* **(b)** (person) Wache, *die* **(c)** (Brit. fig.) **that's a bad ~:** das sind schlechte Aussichten; **that's his ~:** das ist sein Problem **(d)** **keep a ~ [for sb./sth.]** [nach jmdm./etw] Ausschau halten

loom¹ /luːm/ *n.* (Weaving) Webstuhl, *der*

loom² *v.i.* auftauchen

loop /luːp/ ① *n.* **(a)** Schleife, *die* **(b)** (cord) Schlaufe, *die* ② *v.t.* zu einer Schlaufe formen

'loophole *n.* (fig.) Lücke, *die*

loopy /ˈluːpɪ/ *adj.* (coll.) verrückt (ugs.)

loose /luːs/ *adj.* **(a)** (not firm) locker ⟨*Zahn, Schraube, Knopf*⟩ ┄┅▶

(b) (not fixed) lose ⟨*Knopf, Buchseite, Brett, Stein*⟩; offen ⟨*Haar*⟩

(c) be at a ∼ end (fig.) nichts zu tun haben

(d) (inexact) ungenau

loose: ∼**-fitting** *adj.* bequem geschnitten; ∼**-leaf** *adj.* Loseblatt-; ∼**-leaf file** Ringbuch, *das;* ∼**-limbed** *adj.* gelenkig

'**loosely** *adv.* locker; lose ⟨*zusammenhängen*⟩; frei ⟨*übersetzen*⟩

loosen /'luːsn/ *v.t.* lockern
■ **loosen 'up** *v.i.* sich auflockern; (relax) auftauen

'**looseness** *n.* Lockerheit, *die*

loot /luːt/ ① *v.t.* plündern
② *n.* Beute, *die*

'**looter** *n.* Plünderer, *der*

lop /lɒp/ *v.t.* ∼ sth. [off *or* away] etw. abbauen *od.* abhacken

lopsided /lɒp'saɪdɪd/ *adj.* schief

loquacious /lə'kweɪʃəs/ *adj.* redselig

lord /lɔːd/ ① *n.* **(a)** (master) Herr, *der*
(b) L∼ (Relig.) Herr, *der*
(c) (Brit.: as title) Lord, *der;* **the House of L**∼**s** (Brit.) das Oberhaus
② *int.* (coll.) Gott; **oh/good L**∼! du lieber Himmel!

'**lordship** *n.* Lordschaft, *die*

lore /lɔː(r)/ *n.* Überlieferung, *die*

lorry /'lɒrɪ/ *n.* (Brit.) Lastwagen, *der;* Lkw, *der*

'**lorry driver** *n.* (Brit.) Lastwagenfahrer, *der;* Lkw-Fahrer, *der*

lose /luːz/ ① *v.t.,* lost /lɒst/ **(a)** verlieren; ∼ **one's way** sich verlaufen/verfahren
(b) ⟨*Uhr:*⟩ nachgehen
(c) (waste) vertun ⟨*Zeit*⟩; (miss) versäumen ⟨*Gelegenheit*⟩
(d) ∼ **weight** abnehmen
② *v.i.,* lost **(a)** (in match, contest) verlieren
(b) ⟨*Uhr:*⟩ nachgehen

'**loser** *n.* Verlierer, *der*/Verliererin, *die*

loss /lɒs/ *n.* **(a)** Verlust, *der* (of *Gen.*); **sell at a** ∼: mit Verlust verkaufen
(b) be at a ∼: nicht [mehr] weiterwissen; **be at a** ∼ **for words** um Worte verlegen sein; **be at a** ∼ **what to do** nicht wissen, was zu tun ist

loss: ∼ **adjuster** *n.* (Finance) Schaden[s]regulierer, *der*/-reguliererin, *die;* ∼**-making** *adj.* mit Verlust arbeitend

lost /lɒst/ ① ▸ LOSE
② *adj.* **(a)** verloren; **get** ∼ ⟨*Person:*⟩ sich verlaufen/verfahren; **get** ∼! (coll.) verdufte! (salopp); ∼ **cause** aussichtslose Sache
(b) (wasted) vertan ⟨*Zeit*⟩; (missed) versäumt ⟨*Gelegenheit*⟩

lot /lɒt/ *n.* **(a)** (destiny) Los, *das*
(b) (set of persons) Haufen, *der;* **the** ∼: [sie] alle
(c) (set of things) Menge, *die;* **the** ∼: alle/alles
(d) (coll.: large quantity) ∼**s** *or* **a** ∼ **of money** *etc.* viel *od.* eine Menge Geld *usw.;* **sing** *etc.* **a** ∼: viel singen *usw.;* **like sth. a** ∼: etw. sehr mögen; **have** ∼**s to do** viel zu tun haben

(e) (for choosing) Los, *das;* **draw/cast/throw** ∼**s** [for sth.] um etw. losen

lotion /'ləʊʃn/ *n.* Lotion, *die*

lottery /'lɒtərɪ/ *n.* Lotterie, *die*

'**lottery number** *n.* Lottozahl, *die*

loud /laʊd/ ① *adj.* **(a)** laut; lautstark ⟨*Protest, Kritik*⟩
(b) (flashy, conspicuous) aufdringlich; grell ⟨*Farbe*⟩
② *adv.* laut; **laugh out** ∼: laut auflachen; **say sth. out** ∼: etw. aussprechen

loud'hailer *n.* Megaphon, *das*

'**loudly** *adv.* laut

loud: ∼**mouth** *n.* Großmaul, *das;* ∼**-mouthed** /'laʊdmaʊðd/ *adj.* großmäulig (ugs.)

'**loudness** *n.* Lautstärke, *die*

loud'speaker *n.* Lautsprecher, *der*

lounge /laʊndʒ/ ① *v.i.* ∼ [about *or* around] [faul] herumliegen/-sitzen/-stehen
② *n.* **(a)** (in hotel) [Hotel]halle, *die;* (at airport) Wartehalle, *die*
(b) (sitting room) Wohnzimmer, *das*

lounger /'laʊndʒə(r)/ *n.* (sunbed) Liege, *die*

'**lounge suit** *n.* (Brit.) Straßenanzug, *der*

louse /laʊs/ *n., pl.* lice /laɪs/ Laus, *die*

lousy /'laʊzɪ/ *adj.* (coll.) **(a)** (disgusting) ekelhaft
(b) (very poor) lausig (ugs.); **feel** ∼: sich mies (ugs.) fühlen

lout /laʊt/ *n.* Rüpel, *der;* Flegel, *der*

loutish /'laʊtɪʃ/ *adj.* rüpelhaft; flegelhaft

louver, louvre /'luːvə(r)/ *n.* ∼ **window** Jalousiefenster, *das;* ∼ **door** Jalousietür, *die*

lovable /'lʌvəbl/ *adj.* liebenswert

love /lʌv/ ① *n.* **(a)** Liebe, *die* (of, for zu); **in** ∼ [with] verliebt [in (+ *Akk.*)]; **fall in** ∼ [with] sich verlieben [in (+ *Akk.*)]; **for** ∼: aus Liebe; ∼ **from Beth** (in letter) herzliche Grüße von Beth; **send one's** ∼ **to sb.** jmdn. grüßen lassen
(b) (sweetheart) Geliebte, *der/die;* [my] ∼ (coll.: form of address) [mein] Liebling *od.* Schatz
(c) (Tennis) **fifteen/thirty** ∼: fünfzehn/dreißig null
② *v.t.* **(a)** lieben; **our/their** ∼**d ones** unsere/ihre Lieben
(b) (like) **I'd** ∼ **a cigarette** ich hätte sehr gerne eine Zigarette; ∼ **to do** *or* ∼ **doing sth.** etw. gern tun

love: ∼ **affair** *n.* Liebesverhältnis, *das;* ∼ **letter** *n.* Liebesbrief, *der;* ∼ **life** *n.* Liebesleben, *das*

loveliness /'lʌvlɪnɪs/ *n.* Schönheit, *die*

lovely /'lʌvlɪ/ *adj.* [wunder]schön; herrlich ⟨*Tag, Essen*⟩

lover /'lʌvə(r)/ *n.* **(a)** Liebhaber, *der;* Geliebte, *der;* (woman) Geliebte, *die;* **be** ∼**s** ein Liebespaar sein
(b) (person who likes sth.) Freund, *der*/Freundin, *die*

love: ∼**sick** *adj.* an Liebeskummer

leidend; liebeskrank (geh.); ～ **song** n.
Liebeslied, das; ～ **story** n.
Liebesgeschichte, die
loving /'lʌvɪŋ/ adj. (a) (affectionate) liebend
(b) (expressing love) liebevoll
'**lovingly** adv. liebevoll
low /ləʊ/ ① adj. (a) niedrig; tief
ausgeschnitten ⟨Kleid⟩; tief ⟨Ausschnitt⟩; tief
liegend ⟨Grund⟩
(b) (of humble rank) nieder...; niedrig
(c) (inferior) niedrig; gering ⟨Intelligenz,
Bildung⟩
(d) (in pitch) tief; (in loudness) leise
② adv. (a) (to a ～ position) tief
(b) (not loudly) leise
(c) lie ～ (hide) untertauchen
low: ～-**alcohol** adj. alkoholarm
⟨Getränk⟩; ～**brow** adj. schlicht ⟨Person⟩;
[geistig] anspruchslos ⟨Buch, Programm⟩;
～-**budget** adj. Lowbudget-, Billig⟨film,
-produktion usw.⟩; ～-**calorie** adj.
kalorienarm ⟨Kost, Getränk⟩; ～-**cost** adj.
preiswert; ～-**cut** adj. [tief] ausgeschnitten
⟨Kleid⟩; ～-**cut neck** tiefer Ausschnitt; ～-**cut
shoes** Halbschuhe
lower[1] /'ləʊə(r)/ v.t. (a) herab-/hinablassen
(b) senken ⟨Blick⟩; auslassen ⟨Saum⟩;
senken ⟨Preis, Miete, Zins usw.⟩; ～ one's
voice leiser sprechen
lower[2] ① compar. adj. unter...;
Unter⟨grenze, -arm, -lippe usw.⟩
② compar. adv. tiefer
lower 'case ① n. Kleinbuchstaben Pl.;
② adj. klein ⟨Buchstabe⟩
low: ～-**fat** adj. fettarm; ～-**flying** adj. tief
fliegend; ～-**flying aircraft** Tiefflieger, der;
～ '**frequency** n. Niederfrequenz, die;
～-**grade** adj. minderwertig; ～-**income**
adj. einkommensschwach; ～-**income families**
Familien mit niedrigem Einkommen;
～-**key** adj. zurückhaltend; unaufdringlich
⟨Beleuchtung, Unterhaltung⟩; unauffällig
⟨Einsatz⟩; ～-**land** /'ləʊlənd/ n. Tiefland, das
lowly /'ləʊli/ adj. (modest) bescheiden
low: ～-**lying** adj. tief liegend;
～-**nicotine** adj. nikotinarm; ～-**paid** adj.
niedrig bezahlt; ～-**paid families** Familien
mit geringem Einkommen; ～ **point** n.
Tiefpunkt, der; ～ **pressure** n. (Meteorol.)
Tiefdruck, der; ～-**priced** adj. preisgünstig;
～ **season** n. Nebensaison, die; ～-**tech**
adj. Lowtech⟨-system, -ausrüstung etc.⟩;
～-**voltage** Niederspannungs-;
～-**wage** attrib. adj. schlecht bezahlt;
Niedriglohn⟨land⟩
loyal /'lɔɪəl/ adj. treu
loyalty /'lɔɪəlti/ n. Treue, die
'**loyalty card** n. Treuekarte, die ⟨für
Kunden⟩
lozenge /'lɒzɪndʒ/ n. Pastille, die
LP abbr. = **long-playing record** LP, die
'**L-plate** n. (Brit.) 'L'-Schild, das; ≈
„Fahrschule"-Schild, das

Ltd. abbr. = **Limited** GmbH
lubricant /'lu:brɪkənt/ n. Schmiermittel,
das
lubricate /'lu:brɪkeɪt/ v.t. schmieren
lubrication /lu:brɪ'keɪʃn/ n. Schmierung,
die; attrib. Schmier⟨system, -vorrichtung⟩
lucid /'lu:sɪd/ adj. klar
lucidity /lu:'sɪdɪtɪ/ n. Klarheit, die
luck /lʌk/ n. Glück, das; good ～: Glück,
das; bad or hard ～: Pech, das; good ～! viel
Glück!; be in/out of ～: Glück/kein Glück
haben; no such ～: schön wärs
luckily /'lʌkɪlɪ/ adv. glücklicherweise
lucky /'lʌkɪ/ adj. (a) glücklich; be ～: Glück
haben
(b) (bringing good luck) Glücks⟨zahl, -tag usw.⟩;
～ **charm** Glücksbringer, der
lucrative /'lu:krətɪv/ adj. einträglich;
lukrativ
ludicrous /'lu:dɪkrəs/ adj. lächerlich;
lachhaft ⟨Angebot, Ausrede⟩
lug /lʌg/ v.t. -gg- (drag) schleppen
luggage /'lʌgɪdʒ/ n. Gepäck, das
luggage: ～ **locker** n.
[Gepäck]schließfach, das; ～ **rack** n.
Gepäckablage, die
lugubrious /lu:'gu:brɪəs/ adj. (mournful)
kummervoll; (dismal) düster
lukewarm /'lu:kwɔ:m/ adj. lauwarm
lull /lʌl/ ① v.t. (a) (soothe) lullen
(b) (fig.) einlullen; ～ **sb. into a false sense of
security** jmdn. in einer trügerischen
Sicherheit wiegen
② n. Pause, die
lullaby /'lʌləbaɪ/ n. Schlaflied, das
lumbago /lʌm'beɪgəʊ/ n., pl. ～s (Med.)
Hexenschuss, der
lumber /'lʌmbə(r)/ ① n. (a) (furniture)
Gerümpel, das
(b) (useless material) Kram, der (ugs.)
(c) (Amer.: timber) [Bau]holz, das
② v.t. ～ **sb. with sth./sb.** jmdm. etw./jmdn.
aufhalsen (ugs.)
'**lumbering** adj. schwerfällig
lumberjack /'lʌmbədʒæk/ n. (Amer.)
Holzfäller, der
luminous /'lu:mɪnəs/ adj. [hell] leuchtend;
Leucht⟨anzeige, -zeiger usw.⟩
lump /lʌmp/ ① n. (a) Klumpen, der; (of
sugar, butter, etc.) Stück, das; (of wood) Klotz,
der; (of dough) Kloß, der; (of bread) Brocken,
der
(b) (swelling) Beule, die
② v.t. ～ **sth. with sth.** etw. und etw.
zusammentun
lump: ～ '**payment** n. einmalige Zahlung
[einer größeren Summe]; ～ '**sum** n.
Pauschalsumme, die
'**lumpy** adj. klumpig ⟨Brei⟩; ⟨Kissen,
Matratze⟩ mit klumpiger Füllung
lunacy /'lu:nəsɪ/ n. Wahnsinn, der
lunar /'lu:nə(r)/ adj. Mond-

lunatic /'luːnətɪk/ [1] *adj.* wahnsinnig
[2] *n.* Wahnsinnige, *der/die*; Irre, *der/die*
lunch /lʌntʃ/ [1] *n.* Mittagessen, *das;* have *or* eat [one's] ~: zu Mittag essen
[2] *v.i.* zu Mittag essen
lunch: ~ **box** *n.* Lunchbox, *die;* ~ **break**
▸ ~ HOUR
luncheon: ~ **meat** *n.* Frühstücksfleisch, *das;* ~ **voucher** *n.* (Brit.) Essenmarke, *die*
lunch: ~ **hour** *n.* Mittagspause, *die;*
~**time** *n.* Mittagszeit, *die;* at ~**time** mittags
lung /lʌŋ/ *n.* (right or left) Lungenflügel, *der;*
~s Lunge, *die*
'lung cancer *n.* Lungenkrebs, *der*
lunge /lʌndʒ/ [1] *n.* Sprung nach vorn
[2] *v.i.* ~ at sb. with a knife jmdn. mit einem Messer angreifen
lurch¹ /lɜːtʃ/ *n.* leave sb. in the ~: jmdn. im Stich lassen
lurch² [1] *n.* Rucken, *das*
[2] *v.i.* rucken; ⟨Betrunkener:⟩ torkeln
lure /ljʊə(r), lʊə(r)/ [1] *v.t.* locken
[2] *n.* Lockmittel, *das*
lurid /'ljʊərɪd, 'lʊərɪd/ *adj.* (a) (in colour) grell
(b) (sensational) reißerisch
lurk /lɜːk/ *v.i.* lauern
lurker /'lɜːkə(r)/ *n.* (Comp. sl.) Lurker, *der/*Lurkerin, *die*
luscious /'lʌʃəs/ *adj.* köstlich [süß]; saftig [süß] ⟨Obst⟩
lush /lʌʃ/ *adj.* saftig ⟨Wiese⟩; grün ⟨Tal⟩; üppig ⟨Vegetation⟩

lust /lʌst/ [1] *n.* (a) (sexual) Sinnenlust, *die*
(b) (strong desire) Gier, *die* (for nach)
[2] *v.i.* ~ after [lustvoll] begehren (geh.)
lustful /'lʌstfl/ *adj.* lüstern (geh.)
lustily /'lʌstɪlɪ/ *adv.* kräftig; aus voller Kehle ⟨rufen, singen⟩
lustre /'lʌstə(r)/ *n.* (Brit.) (a) Schimmer, *der*
(b) (fig.: splendour) Glanz, *der*
lusty /'lʌstɪ/ *adj.* kräftig
Luxembourg, Luxemburg
/'lʌksəmbɜːg/ *pr. n.* Luxemburg (*das*)
luxuriant /lʌg'zjʊərɪənt/ *adj.* üppig
luxuriate /lʌg'zjʊərɪeɪt/ *v.i.* ~ in sich aalen in (+ *Dat.*)
luxurious /lʌg'zjʊərɪəs/ *adj.* luxuriös
luxury /'lʌkʃərɪ/ *n.* (a) Luxus, *der; attrib.* Luxus-
(b) (article) Luxusgegenstand, *der;* luxuries Luxus, *der*
LW *abbr.* (Radio) = **long wave** LW
lying /'laɪŋ/ *adj.* verlogen ⟨Person⟩. See also LIE¹ 2
lymph gland *n.* Lymphknoten, *der*
lynch /lɪntʃ/ *v.t.* lynchen
lynx /lɪŋks/ *n.* Luchs, *der*
lyre /'laɪə(r)/ *n.* Lyra, *die*
lyric /'lɪrɪk/ [1] *adj.* lyrisch; ~ poetry Lyrik, *die*
[2] *n.* in pl. (of song) Text, *der*
lyrical /'lɪrɪkl/ *adj.* (a) lyrisch
(b) (coll.: enthusiastic) gefühlvoll

Mm

M, m /em/ *n.* M, m, *das*
m. *abbr.* (a) = **masculine** m.
(b) = **metre[s]** m
(c) = **million[s]** Mill.
(d) = **minute[s]** Min.
MA *abbr.* = **Master of Arts** M.A.
mac /mæk/ *n.* (Brit. coll.) Regenmantel, *der*
macaroni /mækə'rəʊnɪ/ *n.* Makkaroni *Pl.*
Macedonia /mæsɪ'dəʊnɪə/ *pr. n.* Makedonien (*das*)
machine /mə'ʃiːn/ *n.* Maschine, *die*
machine: ~ **gun** *n.* Maschinengewehr, *das;* ~**-made** *adj.* maschinell hergestellt; ~ **operator** *n.* [Maschinen]bediener, *der/*-bedienerin, *die;* ~**-readable** *adj.* (Comp.) maschinenlesbar
machinery /mə'ʃiːnərɪ/ *n.* (a) (machines) Maschinen *Pl.*
(b) (mechanism) Mechanismus, *der*
machine: ~ **tool** *n.* Werkzeugmaschine,

die; ~**-wash** *v.t.* in der Waschmaschine waschen; ~**-washable** *adj.* waschmaschinenfest
machinist /mə'ʃiːnɪst/ *n.* Maschinist, *der/*Maschinistin, *die;* [sewing] ~: [Maschinen]näherin, *die/*-näher, *der*
machismo /mə'tʃɪzməʊ, mə'kɪzməʊ/ *n.* Machismo, *der;* Männlichkeitswahn, *der*
macho /'mætʃəʊ/ *adj.* Macho-; he is ~: er ist ein Macho
mackerel /'mækərl/ *n., pl. same or* ~s Makrele, *die*
mackintosh /'mækɪntɒʃ/ *n.* Regenmantel, *der*
macro /'mækrəʊ/ *n.* (Comp.) Makro, *das*
macrobiotic /mækrəʊbaɪ'ɒtɪk/ *adj.* makrobiotisch
mad /mæd/ *adj.* (a) (insane) geisteskrank
(b) (frenzied) wahnsinnig; drive sb. mad jmdn. um den Verstand bringen

(c) (foolish) verrückt (ugs.)
(d) (very enthusiastic) be ~ about or on sb./
sth. auf jmdn./etw. wild sein (ugs.)
(e) (coll.: annoyed) ~ [with or at sb.] sauer
[auf jmdn.] (ugs.)
(f) (with rabies) toll[wütig]; [run etc.] like ~
(coll.) wie wild [laufen usw.]
madam /'mædəm/ n. gnädige Frau; **Dear
M~** (in letter) Sehr geehrte Dame
mad 'cow disease n. (coll.)
Rinderwahnsinn, der
madden /'mædn/ v.t. (irritate) [ver]ärgern
maddening /'mædənɪŋ/ adj. (irritating)
[äußerst] ärgerlich
made ▶ MAKE 1
made-to-'measure attrib. adj. Maß-
'madly adv. (coll.) wahnsinnig (ugs.)
madman /'mædmən/ n., pl. **madmen**
/'mædmən/ n. Wahnsinnige, der
'madness n. Wahnsinn, der
magazine /mægə'ziːn/ n. **(a)** Zeitschrift,
die
(b) (of firearm) Magazin, das
maggot /'mægət/ n. Made, die
magic /'mædʒɪk/ ☐1 n. **(a)** Magie, die; **work
like ~:** wie ein Wunder wirken
(b) (conjuring) Zauberei, die
☐2 adj. **(a)** magisch; Zauber⟨trank, -baum⟩
(b) (fig.) wunderbar
magical /'mædʒɪkl/ adj. zauberhaft
magician /mə'dʒɪʃn/ n. Magier, der/
Magierin, die; (conjurer) Zauberer, der/
Zauberin, die
magic 'wand n. Zauberstab, der
magistrate /'mædʒɪstreɪt/ n.
Friedensrichter, der/-richterin, die
magnanimity /mægnə'nɪmɪtɪ/ n.
Großmut, die
magnanimous /mæg'nænɪməs/ adj.
großmütig (**towards** gegen)
magnate /'mægneɪt/ n. Magnat, der/
Magnatin, die
magnesium /mæg'niːzɪəm/ n.
Magnesium, das
magnet /'mægnɪt/ n. Magnet, der
magnetic /mæg'netɪk/ adj. magnetisch
magnetic: ~ 'north magnetisch Nord,
das; ~ 'tape n. Magnetband, das
magnetism /'mægnɪtɪzm/ n. **(a)** (force, lit.
or fig.) Magnetismus, der
(b) (fig.: charm) Anziehungskraft, die
magnetize /'mægnɪtaɪz/ v.t.
magnetisieren
magnification /mægnɪfɪ'keɪʃn/ n.
Vergrößerung, die
magnificence /mæg'nɪfɪsəns/ n. Pracht,
die; (beauty) Herrlichkeit, die; (lavishness)
Üppigkeit, die
magnificent /mæg'nɪfɪsənt/ adj. **(a)**
prächtig; herrlich ⟨Garten, Kunstwerk,
Wetter⟩; (lavish) üppig ⟨Mahl⟩
(b) (coll.: excellent) fabelhaft (ugs.)

magnifier /'mægnɪfaɪə(r)/ n. (Optics) Lupe,
die
magnify /'mægnɪfaɪ/ v.t. **(a)** vergrößern
(b) (exaggerate) aufbauschen
'magnifying glass n. Lupe, die
magnitude /'mægnɪtjuːd/ n. **(a)** (size)
Größe, die
(b) (importance) Wichtigkeit, die
magnolia /mæg'nəʊlɪə/ n. Magnolie, die
magnum /'mægnəm/ n. (bottle) Magnum,
die
magpie /'mægpaɪ/ n. Elster, die
mahogany /mə'hɒgənɪ/ n. Mahagoni[holz],
das; attrib. Mahagoni-
maid /meɪd/ n. Dienstmädchen, das
maiden /'meɪdn/ ☐1 n. Jungfrau, die
☐2 adj. **(a)** (unmarried) unverheiratet
(b) (first) ~ **voyage/speech** Jungfernfahrt/
-rede, die
'maiden name n. Mädchenname, der
mail /meɪl/ ☐1 n. ▶ POST² 1
☐2 v.t. abschicken
mail: ~**bag** n. Postsack, der; ~**box** n.
(Amer.) Briefkasten, der; ~**ing address** n.
Postanschrift, die; ~**ing list** n.
Adressenliste, die; ~**man** n. (Amer.)
Briefträger, der; ~ **order** n. Bestellung per
Post; ~ **order catalogue** n.
Versandhauskatalog, der; ~ **order firm** n.
Versandhaus, das; ~ **room** n. Poststelle,
die
maim /meɪm/ v.t. verstümmeln
main /meɪn/ ☐1 n. **(a)** (channel, pipe)
Hauptleitung, die; ~s (Electr.) Stromnetz, das
(b) in the ~: im Großen und Ganzen
☐2 attrib. adj. Haupt-; **the ~ thing is that …:**
die Hauptsache ist, dass …
main: ~ **beam** n. (Motor Veh.) **on ~ beam**
aufgeblendet; ~ **course** n. Hauptgang,
der; Hauptgericht, das; ~**frame** n. (Comp.)
Großrechner, der; ~**land** /'meɪnlənd/ n.
Festland, das; ~ **'line** n. (Railw.)
Hauptstrecke, die; ~**-line station/train**
Fernbahnhof/-zug, der
'mainly adv. hauptsächlich
main: ~ **'road** n. Hauptstraße, die;
~**stay** n. [wichtigste] Stütze; ~ **street**
/Brit. -'-, Amer. '--/ n. Hauptstraße, die
maintain /meɪn'teɪn/ v.t. **(a)** (keep up)
aufrechterhalten
(b) (provide for) ~ **sb.** für jmds. Unterhalt
aufkommen
(c) (preserve) instand halten; warten
⟨Maschine⟩
(d) ~ **that …:** behaupten, dass …
maintenance /'meɪntənəns/ n. **(a)** (keeping
up) Aufrechterhaltung, die
(b) (preservation) Instandhaltung, die; (of
machinery) Wartung, die
(c) (Law: money paid to support sb.) Unterhalt,
der
maintenance-'free adj. wartungsfrei

maison[n]ette /meɪzə'net/ n. [zweistöckige] Wohnung

maize /meɪz/ n. Mais, der

majestic /mə'dʒestɪk/ adj., **majestically** /mə'dʒestɪkəlɪ/ adv. majestätisch

majesty /'mædʒɪstɪ/ n. Majestät, die (geh.); Your/Her etc. M~: Eure/Seine usw. Majestät

major /'meɪdʒə(r)/ 1 adj. (a) attrib. (greater) größer... (b) attrib. (important) bedeutend...; (serious) schwer; ~ road Hauptverkehrsstraße, die (c) (Mus.) Dur-; C ~: C-Dur 2 n. (Mil.) Major, der 3 v.i. (Amer. Univ.) ~ in sth. etw. als Hauptfach haben

Majorca /mə'jɔːkə/ pr. n. Mallorca (das)

majority /mə'dʒɒrɪtɪ/ n. Mehrheit, die; be in the ~: in der Mehrzahl sein

majority 'rule n. Mehrheitsregierung, die

make /meɪk/ 1 v.t., made /meɪd/ (a) machen (of aus); bauen ⟨Straße, Flugzeug⟩; anlegen ⟨Teich, Weg usw.⟩; zimmern ⟨Tisch, Regal⟩; basteln ⟨Spielzeug, Vogelhäuschen usw.⟩; nähen ⟨Kleider⟩; (manufacture) herstellen; (prepare) zubereiten ⟨Mahlzeit⟩; machen, kochen ⟨Kaffee, Tee⟩; backen ⟨Brot, Kuchen⟩ (b) (establish, enact) treffen ⟨Unterscheidung, Übereinkommen⟩; ziehen ⟨Vergleich⟩; erlassen ⟨Gesetz⟩; aufstellen ⟨Regeln, Behauptung⟩; stellen ⟨Forderung⟩; geben ⟨Bericht⟩; vornehmen ⟨Zahlung⟩; erheben ⟨Protest, Beschwerde⟩ (c) (cause to be or become) ~ happy/known etc. glücklich/bekannt usw. machen; ~ sb. captain jmdn. zum Kapitän machen (d) ~ sb. do sth. (cause) jmdn. dazu bringen, etw. zu tun; (compel) jmdn. zwingen, etw. zu tun; be made to do sth. etw. tun müssen (e) (earn) machen ⟨Profit, Verlust⟩; verdienen ⟨Lebensunterhalt⟩ (f) what do you ~ of him? was hältst du von ihm? (g) (arrive at) erreichen; make it (succeed in arriving) es schaffen (h) ~ 'do vorlieb nehmen; ~ 'do with/ without sth. mit/ohne etw. auskommen 2 n. (brand) Marke, die

■ **'make for** v.t. zusteuern auf (+ Akk.)

■ **make 'off** v.i. sich davonmachen

■ **make 'off with** v.t. ~ off with sb./sth. sich mit jmdm./etw. auf und davon machen

■ **make 'out** 1 v.t. (a) (write) ausstellen; ~ out a cheque to sb. einen Scheck auf jmdn. ausstellen (b) (claim) behaupten (c) (manage to see or hear) ausmachen; (manage to read) entziffern (d) (pretend) vorgeben 2 v.i. (coll.) zurechtkommen (at bei)

■ **make 'over** v.t. überschreiben (to auf + Akk.)

■ **make 'up** 1 v.t. (a) (assemble) zusammenstellen

(b) (invent) erfinden (c) (constitute) bilden; be made up of ...: bestehen aus ... (d) (apply cosmetics to) schminken; ~ up one's face sich schminken 2 v.i. (be reconciled) sich wieder vertragen

■ **make 'up for** v.t. wieder gutmachen; ~ up for lost time Versäumtes nachholen

make: ~**believe** 1 n. it's only ~-believe das ist bloß Fantasie; 2 adj. nicht echt; ~**-or-'break** attrib. adj. alles entscheidend; ~**over** n. (of a person's appearance) [grundlegende] Verwandlung; (of a building) Umbau, der

'maker n. (manufacturer) Hersteller, der

make: ~**shift** adj. behelfsmäßig; ~**-up** n. Make-up, das; ~**-up bag** Kosmetiktasche, die

making /'meɪkɪŋ/ n. in the ~: im Entstehen; have the ~s of a leader das Zeug zum Führer haben (ugs.)

maladjusted /mælə'dʒʌstɪd/ adj. verhaltensgestört

malady /'mælədɪ/ n. Leiden, das

malaise /mæ'leɪz/ n. Unbehagen, das

malaria /mə'leərɪə/ n. Malaria, die

Malaysia /mə'leɪzɪə/ pr. n. Malaysia (das)

male /meɪl/ 1 adj. männlich; Männer⟨stimme, -chor, -verein⟩; ~ doctor/ nurse Arzt, der/Krankenpfleger, der 2 n. (person) Mann, der; (animal) Männchen, das

'male-dominated adj. von Männern dominiert

malevolence /mə'levələns/ n. Boshaftigkeit, die

malevolent /mə'levələnt/ adj. boshaft

malfunction /mæl'fʌŋkʃn/ 1 n. Störung, die; (Med.) Funktionsstörung, die 2 v.i. nicht richtig funktionieren

malice /'mælɪs/ n. Bosheit, die

malicious /mə'lɪʃəs/ adj. böse

malign /mə'laɪn/ v.t. verleumden

malignant /mə'lɪgnənt/ adj. bösartig

malinger /mə'lɪŋgə(r)/ v.i. simulieren

ma'lingerer n. Simulant, der/Simulantin, die

malleable /'mælɪəbl/ adj. formbar

mallet /'mælɪt/ n. Holzhammer, der

malnourished /mæl'nʌrɪʃt/ adj. unterernährt

malnutrition /mælnjuː'trɪʃn/ n. Unterernährung, die

malpractice /mæl'præktɪs/ n. (Law, Med.) Kunstfehler, der

malt /mɔːlt/ n. Malz, das

Malta /'mɔːltə/ pr. n. Malta (das)

maltreat /mæl'triːt/ v.t. misshandeln

mal'treatment n. Misshandlung, die

malt 'whisky n. Malzwhisky, der

mammal /'mæml/ n. Säugetier, das

mammoth /'mæməθ/ 1 n. Mammut, das

2 *adj.* Mammut-; gigantisch ‹*Vorhaben*›

man /mæn/ **1** *n.* **(a)** *pl.* **men** [men] Mann, *der*
(b) (human race) der Mensch
2 *v.t.*, **-nn-** bemannen ‹*Schiff*›; besetzen ‹*Büro, Stelle usw.*›; bedienen ‹*Telefon, Geschütz*›

manacle /'mænəkl/ **1** *n.*, *usu. in pl.* [Hand]fessel, *die*
2 *v.t.* Handfesseln anlegen (+ *Dat.*)

manage /'mænɪdʒ/ **1** *v.t.* **(a)** leiten ‹*Geschäft*›
(b) (Sport) betreuen ‹*Mannschaft*›
(c) (cope with) schaffen
(d) ~ to do sth. es fertig bringen, etw. zu tun; he ~d to do it es gelang ihm, es zu tun
2 *v.i.* zurechtkommen; ~ without sth. ohne etw. auskommen; I can ~: es geht

manageable /'mænɪdʒəbl/ *adj.* leicht frisierbar ‹*Haar*›; fügsam ‹*Person, Tier*›; überschaubar ‹*Größe, Menge*›

'management *n.* **(a)** (of a business) Leitung, *die*
(b) (managers) **the** ~: die Geschäftsleitung

management: ~ **consultancy** *n.* Unternehmensberatung, *die;*
~ **consultant** *n.* Unternehmensberater, *der/*-beraterin, *die*

'manager *n.* (of shop or bank) Filialleiter, *der/*-leiterin, *die;* (of football team) [Chef]trainer, *der/*-trainerin, *die;* (of restaurant, shop, hotel) Geschäftsführer, *der/*-führerin, *die*

manageress /mænɪdʒə'res/ *n.* Geschäftsführerin, *die*

managerial /mænə'dʒɪərɪəl/ *adj.* führend, leitend ‹*Stellung*›; ~ **skills** Führungsqualitäten

managing /'mænɪdʒɪŋ/ *adj.* ~ **director** Geschäftsführer, *der/*-führerin, *die*

mandarin[1] /'mændərɪn/ *n.* ~ **[orange]** Mandarine, *die*

mandarin[2] *n.* (bureaucrat) Bürokrat, *der/* Bürokratin, *die*

mandarine /'mændəri:n/ *n.* ► MANDARIN[1]

mandate /'mændeɪt/ *n.* Mandat, *das*

mandatory /'mændətərɪ/ *adj.* obligatorisch

mandolin[e] /mændə'lɪn/ *n.* Mandoline, *die*

mane /meɪn/ *n.* Mähne, *die*

maneuver[able] (Amer.) ► MANŒUVR-

manful /'mænfl/ *adj.*, **manfully** /'mænfəlɪ/ *adv.* mannhaft

manger /'meɪndʒə(r)/ *n.* Krippe, *die*

mangetout /mɑ̃ʒ'tu:/ *n.* Zuckererbse, *die*

mangle /'mæŋgl/ *v.t.* verstümmeln ‹*Person*›; demolieren ‹*Sache*›

mango /'mæŋgəʊ/ *n.*, *pl.* ~**es** *or* ~**s** (fruit) Mango[frucht], *die*

mangy /'meɪndʒɪ/ *adj.* **(a)** (Vet. Med.) räudig
(b) (shabby) schäbig

man ⋯⟶ manual ⋯⋯

man: ~**handle** *v.t.* **(a)** von Hand bewegen ‹*Gegenstand*›; **(b)** grob behandeln ‹*Person*›;
~**hole** *n.* Mannloch, *das*

'manhood *n.* Mannesalter, *das*

man: ~**-hour** *n.* Arbeitsstunde, *die;*
~**hunt** *n.* Verbrecherjagd, *die*

mania /'meɪnɪə/ *n.* Manie, *die*

maniacal /mə'naɪəkl/ *adj.* wahnsinnig

manicure /'mænɪkjʊə(r)/ **1** *n.* Maniküre, *die*
2 *v.t.* maniküren

manifest /'mænɪfest/ **1** *adj.* offenkundig
2 *v.t.* (reveal) offenbaren

'manifestly *adv.* offenkundig

manifesto /mænɪ'festəʊ/ *n.*, *pl.* ~**s** Manifest, *das*

manifold /'mænɪfəʊld/ *adj.* (literary) mannigfaltig (geh.)

manipulate /mə'nɪpjʊleɪt/ *v.t.* **(a)** manipulieren
(b) (handle) handhaben

manipulation /mənɪpjʊ'leɪʃn/ *n.* **(a)** Manipulation, *die*
(b) (handling) Handhabung, *die*

manipulative /mə'nɪpjʊlətɪv/ *adj.* manipulativ

mankind /mæn'kaɪnd/ *n.* Menschheit, *die*

manly /'mænlɪ/ *adj.* männlich

'man-made *adj.* künstlich; (synthetic) Kunst‹*faser, -stoff*›

manned /mænd/ *adj.* bemannt

manner /'mænə(r)/ *n.* **(a)** Art, *die;* Weise, *die;* in this ~: auf diese Art und Weise
(b) (general behaviour) Art, *die*
(c) *in pl.* Manieren *Pl.*

mannerism /'mænərɪzm/ *n.* Eigenart, *die*

manœuvrable /mə'nu:vrəbl/ *adj.* (Brit.) manövrierfähig

manœuvre /mə'nu:və(r)/ (Brit.) **1** *n.* Manöver, *das*
2 *v.t. & i.* manövrieren

manor /'mænə(r)/ *n.* **(a)** (land) [Land]gut, *das*
(b) ► MANOR HOUSE

'manor house *n.* Herrenhaus, *das*

'manpower *n.* Arbeitskräfte *Pl.*

mansion /'mænʃn/ *n.* Herrenhaus, *das*

manslaughter /'mænslɔ:tə(r)/ *n.* Totschlag, *der*

mantel: ~**piece** /'mæntlpi:s/ *n.* **(a)** (above fireplace) Kaminsims, *der od. das; (b)** (around fireplace) Kamineinfassung, *die;* ~**shelf** ► ~PIECE A

mantle /'mæntl/ *n.* Umhang, *der*

manual /'mænjʊəl/ **1** *adj.* **(a)** manuell; ~ **work** Handarbeit; ~ **worker** Handarbeiter, *der/*-arbeiterin, *die*
(b) (not automatic) handbetrieben; ‹*Bedienung, Schaltung*› von Hand
2 *n.* Handbuch, *das*

manually /'mænjʊəlɪ/ adv. manuell; a ~ **operated machine** eine handbetriebene Maschine

manufacture /mænjʊ'fæktʃə(r)/ **1** n. Herstellung, die
2 v.t. herstellen

manu'facturer n. Hersteller, der

manure /mə'njʊə(r)/ **1** n. Dung, der
2 v.t. düngen

manuscript /'mænjʊskrɪpt/ n. Manuskript, das

many /'menɪ/ **1** adj. viele; **how ~ people/ books?** wie viele od. wie viel Leute/Bücher?
2 n. viele [Leute]; **~ of us** viele von uns; **a good/great ~:** eine Menge

map /mæp/ **1** n. [Land]karte, die; (street plan) Stadtplan, der
2 v.t., **-pp-** kartographieren
■ **map 'out** v.t. im Einzelnen festlegen

maple /'meɪpl/ n. Ahorn, der

'map-reading n. Kartenlesen, das

mar /mɑː(r)/ v.t. verderben

marathon /'mærəθən/ n. (a) Marathon[lauf], der
(b) (fig.) Marathon, das

marauder /mə'rɔːdə(r)/ n. Plünderer, der

marble /'mɑːbl/ n. (a) (stone) Marmor, der
(b) (toy) Murmel, die; [game of] ~s Murmelspiel, das

march **1** n. Marsch, der; [protest] ~: Protestmarsch, der
2 v.i. marschieren
■ **march 'off** **1** v.i. losmarschieren
2 v.t. abführen
■ **march 'past** v.i. vorbeimarschieren

March /mɑːtʃ/ n. März, der; see also AUGUST

'marcher n. [protest] ~: Demonstrant, der/ Demonstrantin, die

mare /meə(r)/ n. Stute, die

margarine /mɑːdʒə'riːn/, (coll.) **marge** /mɑːdʒ/ ns. Margarine, die

margin /'mɑːdʒɪn/ n. (a) (of page) Rand, der
(b) (extra amount) Spielraum, der; [profit] ~: [Gewinn]spanne, die; **by a narrow ~:** knapp

marginal /'mɑːdʒɪnl/ adj., **'marginally** adv. unwesentlich

marigold /'mærɪɡəʊld/ n. Ringelblume, die

marijuana /mærɪjʊ'ɑːnə/ n. Marihuana, das

marina /mə'riːnə/ n. Jachthafen, der

marinade /mærɪ'neɪd/ **1** n. Marinade, die
2 ▶ MARINATE

marinate /'mærɪneɪt/ v.t. marinieren

marine /mə'riːn/ **1** adj. Meeres-; See⟨versicherung, -recht usw.⟩; Schiffs⟨ausrüstung, -turbine usw.⟩
2 n. (person) Marineinfanterist, der

mariner /'mærɪnə(r)/ n. Seemann, der

marionette /mærɪə'net/ n. Marionette, die

marital /'mærɪtl/ adj. ehelich; **~ status** Familienstand, der

maritime /'mærɪtaɪm/ adj. See-

mark¹ /mɑːk/ **1** n. (a) (trace) Spur, die; (stain etc.) Fleck, der; (scratch) Kratzer, der
(b) (sign) Zeichen, das
(c) (Sch.) Note, die
(d) (target) Ziel, das
2 v.t. (a) (dirty) schmutzig machen; (scratch) zerkratzen
(b) (put distinguishing ~ on) kennzeichnen, markieren (with mit)
(c) (Sch.) (correct) korrigieren; (grade) benoten
(d) **~ time** auf der Stelle treten
■ **mark 'off** v.t. abgrenzen (from von, gegen)
■ **mark 'out** v.t. markieren

mark² n. (monetary unit) Mark, die

marked /mɑːkt/ adj., **markedly** /'mɑːkɪdlɪ/ adv. deutlich

'marker n. Markierung, die

'marker pen n. Markierstift, der

market /'mɑːkɪt/ **1** n. Markt, der
2 v.t. vermarkten

market: ~ day n. Markttag, der;
~ e'conomy n. Marktwirtschaft, die;
~ 'forces n. pl. Kräfte des freien Marktes;
~ 'gardening n. (Brit.) Gemüseanbau, der

'marketing n. Marketing, das

market: ~ 'leader n. (company, brand) Marktführer, der; (product) meistverkauftes Produkt; **the company is the ~ leader in its field** die Firma ist marktführend auf ihrem Gebiet; **~ place** n. Marktplatz, der; (fig.) Markt, der; **~ 'price** n. Marktpreis, der;
~ 'research n. Marktforschung, die;
~ share n. Marktanteil, der; **~ town** n. Marktort, der; **~ 'value** n. Marktwert, der

'marking n. (a) Markierung, die
(b) (on animal) Zeichnung, die

marksman /'mɑːksmən/ n., pl. **marksmen** /'mɑːksmən/ Scharfschütze, der

marmalade /'mɑːməleɪd/ n. [orange] ~: Orangenmarmelade, die

maroon¹ /mə'ruːn/ **1** adj. kastanienbraun
2 n. Kastanienbraun, das

maroon² v.t. (a) (Naut.: put ashore) aussetzen
(b) ⟨Flut, Hochwasser:⟩ von der Außenwelt abschneiden

marquee /mɑː'kiː/ n. Festzelt, das

marquess, marquis /'mɑːkwɪs/ n. Marquis, der

marquetry /'mɑːkɪtrɪ/ n. Marketerie, die

marriage /'mærɪdʒ/ n. (a) Ehe, die (to mit)
(b) (wedding) Hochzeit, die

marriage: ~ broker n. Heiratsvermittler, der/-vermittlerin, die;
~ bureau n. Eheanbahnungs- od. Ehevermittlungsinstitut, das;
~ certificate n. Trauschein, der; (record of civil marriage also) Heiratsurkunde, die;
~ 'guidance n. Eheberatung, die;
~ licence n. Heirats- od. Eheerlaubnis, die

married /'mærɪd/ adj. (a) verheiratet;
~ couple Ehepaar, das
(b) (marital) Ehe⟨leben, -name⟩

marrow /'mærəʊ/ n. (a) [vegetable] ~: Speisekürbis, der
(b) (Anat.) [Knochen]mark, das

marry /'mærɪ/ ① v.t. (a) heiraten
(b) (join) trauen; **they were** or **got/have got married** sie haben geheiratet
② v.i. heiraten

Mars /mɑːz/ pr. n. (Astron.) Mars, der

marsh /mɑːʃ/ n. Sumpf, der

marshal /'mɑːʃl/ ① n. (a) (officer in army) Marschall, der
(b) (Sport) Ordner, der
② v.t., (Brit.) -ll- aufstellen ⟨Truppen⟩; ordnen ⟨Fakten⟩

'marshalling yard n. Rangierbahnhof, der

marshmallow /mɑːʃ'mæləʊ/ n. (sweet) ≈ Mohrenkopf, der

'marshy adj. sumpfig

marsupial /mɑː'sjuːpɪəl/ n. Beuteltier, das

martial /'mɑːʃl/ adj. kriegerisch

martial 'law n. Kriegsrecht, das

martyr /'mɑːtə(r)/ ① n. Märtyrer, der/ Märtyrerin, die
② v.t. **be** ~**ed** den Märtyrertod sterben

marvel /'mɑːvl/ ① n. Wunder, das
② v.i., (Brit.) -ll- (literary) ~ **at sth.** über etw (Akk.) staunen

marvellous /'mɑːvələs/ adj.,
'marvellously adv. wunderbar
marvelous[ly] (Amer.) ▶ MARVELLOUS[LY]

Marxism /'mɑːksɪzm/ n. Marxismus, der

Marxist /'mɑːksɪst/ ① n. Marxist, der/ Marxistin, die
② adj. marxistisch

marzipan /'mɑːzɪpæn/ n. Marzipan, das

mascara /mæ'skɑːrə/ n. Mascara, das

mascot /'mæskɒt/ n. Maskottchen, das

masculine /'mæskjʊlɪn/ adj. männlich

masculinity /mæskju'lɪnɪtɪ/ n. Männlichkeit, die

mash /mæʃ/ ① n. (a) Brei, der
(b) (Brit. coll.: ~ed potatoes) Kartoffelbrei, der
② v.t. zerdrücken; ~**ed potatoes** Kartoffelbrei, der

mask /mɑːsk/ ① n. Maske, die
② v.t. maskieren

'masking tape n. Abklebeband, das

masochism /'mæsəkɪzm/ n. Masochismus, der

masochist /'mæsəkɪst/ n. Masochist, der/ Masochistin, die

masochistic /mæsə'kɪstɪk/ adj. masochistisch

mason /'meɪsn/ n. (a) Steinmetz, der
(b) M~ (Free~) [Frei]maurer, der

Masonic /mə'sɒnɪk/ adj. [frei]maurerisch; ~ **lodge** [Frei]maurerloge, die

masonry /'meɪsnrɪ/ n. Mauerwerk, das

masquerade /mæskə'reɪd, mɑːskə'reɪd/ ① n. Maskerade, die

② v.i. ~ **as sb./sth.** sich als jmd./etw. ausgeben

mass¹ /mæs/ n. (Eccl.) Messe, die

mass² ① n. (a) Masse, die
(b) **a** ~ **of** ...: eine Unmenge von ...
(c) attrib. (for many people) Massen-
② v.t. anhäufen
③ v.i. sich ansammeln; ⟨Truppen:⟩ sich massieren

massacre /'mæsəkə(r)/ ① n. Massaker, das
② v.t. massakrieren

massage /'mæsɑːʒ/ ① n. Massage, die
② v.t. massieren

mass communi'cations n. pl. Massenkommunikation, die

masseur /mæ'sɜː(r)/ n. Masseur, der

masseuse /mæ'sɜːz/ n. fem. Masseurin, die

mass hy'steria n. Massenhysterie, die

massive /'mæsɪv/ adj. massiv; gewaltig ⟨Aufgabe⟩; enorm ⟨Schulden⟩

mass: ~ **market** attrib. adj. für den Massenmarkt nachgestellt; ~ **'media** n. pl. Massenmedien Pl.; ~ **'murderer** n. Massenmörder, der/-mörderin, die; ~**-pro'duced** adj. serienmäßig produziert; ~ **pro'duction** n. Massenproduktion, die

mast /mɑːst/ n. Mast, der

mastectomy /mæ'stektəmɪ/ n. (Med.) Mastektomie, die

master /'mɑːstə(r)/ ① n. (a) Herr, der
(b) (of dog) Herrchen, das; (of ship) Kapitän, der
(c) (Sch.: teacher) Lehrer, der
(d) (expert, great artist) Meister, der (at in + Dat.)
(e) M~ **of Arts/Science** Magister Artium/ rerum naturalium
② adj. Haupt-
③ v.t. (learn) erlernen; **have** ~**ed a language** eine Sprache beherrschen

masterful /'mɑːstəfl/ adj. (masterly) meisterhaft

'master key n. Hauptschlüssel, der

masterly /'mɑːstəlɪ/ adj. meisterhaft

master: ~**mind** ① n. führender Kopf;
② v.t. ~**mind the plot** der Kopf des Komplotts sein; ~**piece** n. (work of art) Meisterwerk, das; ~ **stroke** n. Geniestreich, der; **be a** ~ **stroke** genial sein; ~ **switch** n. Hauptschalter, der

mastery /'mɑːstərɪ/ n. (a) (skill) Meisterschaft, die
(b) (knowledge) Beherrschung, die (of Gen.)

masturbate /'mæstəbeɪt/ v.i. & t. masturbieren

masturbation /mæstə'beɪʃn/ n. Masturbation, die

mat /mæt/ n. (a) Matte, die
(b) (to protect table etc.) Untersetzer, der

matador /'mætədɔː(r)/ n. Matador, der

m

match¹ /mætʃ/ ☐ *n.* **(a)** be no ~ for sb. sich mit jmdm. nicht messen können; **meet one's** ~: seinen Meister finden **(b)** be a [good *etc.*] ~ for sth. [gut *usw.*] zu etw. passen **(c)** (Sport) Spiel, *das;* (Boxing) Kampf, *der* ☐ *v.t.* **(a)** (equal) ~ sb. at chess es mit jmdm. im Schach aufnehmen [können] **(b)** (harmonize with) passen zu; **a handbag and** ~ing shoes eine Handtasche und [dazu] passende Schuhe; ~ **each other** zueinander passen ☐ *v.i.* zusammenpassen

match² *n.* (~stick) Streichholz, *das*

'**matchbox** *n.* Streichholzschachtel, *die*

'**matchless** *adj.* unvergleichlich

match: ~**maker** *n.* Ehestifter, *der*/ Ehestifterin, *die;* ~**stick** *n.* Streichholz, *das*

mate¹ /meɪt/ ☐ *n.* **(a)** Kumpel, *der* (ugs.); **look** *or* **listen,** ~, ...: jetzt hör [mir] mal gut zu, Freundchen, ... **(b)** (Naut.) ≈ Kapitänleutnant, *der* **(c)** (workman's assistant) Gehilfe, *der* **(d)** (Zool.) (male) Männchen, *das;* (female) Weibchen, *das* ☐ *v.i.* sich paaren ☐ *v.t.* paaren ‹*Tiere*›

mate² (Chess) ▶ CHECKMATE

material /mə'tɪərɪəl/ ☐ *adj.* **(a)** materiell **(b)** (relevant) wesentlich ☐ *n.* **(a)** ~[s] Material, *das;* **building/writing** ~s Bau-/Schreibmaterial, *das* **(b)** (cloth) Stoff, *der*

materialism /mə'tɪərɪəlɪzm/ *n.* Materialismus, *der*

materialistic /mətɪərɪə'lɪstɪk/ *adj.* materialistisch

materialize /mə'tɪərɪəlaɪz/ *v.i.* ‹*Plan, Idee:*› sich verwirklichen; ‹*Treffen:*› zustande kommen

maternal /mə'tɜ:nl/ *adj.* mütterlich; Mutter‹*instinkt*›

maternity /mə'tɜ:nɪtɪ/ *n.* Mutterschaft, *die*

maternity: ~ **benefit** *n.* Mutterschaftsgeld, *das;* ~ **dress** *n.* Umstandskleid, *das;* ~ **hospital** *n.* Entbindungsheim, *das;* ~ **leave** *n.* Mutterschaftsurlaub, *der;* ~ **nurse** *n.* Hebamme, *die;* ~ **pay** *n.* Mutterschaftsgeld, *das;* ~ **unit,** ~ **ward** *ns.* Entbindungsstation, *die;* ~ **wear** *n.* Umstandskleidung, *die*

matey /'meɪtɪ/ *adj.,* **matier** /'meɪtɪə(r)/, **matiest** /'meɪtɪɪst/ (Brit. coll.) kameradschaftlich

math /mæθ/ (Amer. coll.) ▶ MATHS

mathematical /mæθɪ'mætɪkl/ *adj.,* **mathematically** /mæθɪ'mætɪkəlɪ/ *adv.* mathematisch

mathematician /mæθɪmə'tɪʃn/ *n.* Mathematiker, *der*/Mathematikerin, *die*

mathematics /mæθɪ'mætɪks/ *n.* Mathematik, *die*

maths /mæθs/ *n.* (Brit. coll.) Mathe, *die* (Schülerspr.)

matinée /'mætɪneɪ/ *n.* Nachmittagsvorstellung, *die*

matriarchal /meɪtrɪ'ɑ:kl/ *adj.* matriarchalisch

matriarchy /'meɪtrɪɑ:kɪ/ *n.* Matriarchat, *das*

matrices *pl. of* MATRIX

matriculate /mə'trɪkjʊleɪt/ ☐ *v.t.* immatrikulieren (**in** an + *Dat.*) ☐ *v.i.* sich immatrikulieren

matriculation /mətrɪkjʊ'leɪʃn/ *n.* Immatrikulation, *die*

matrimonial /mætrɪ'məʊnɪəl/ *adj.* Ehe-

matrimony /'mætrɪmənɪ/ *n.* Ehestand, *der*

matrix /'meɪtrɪks/ *n., pl.* **matrices** /'meɪtrɪsi:z/ *or* ~**es** Matrix, *die*

matron /'meɪtrən/ *n.* (in school) ≈ Hausmutter, *die;* (in hospital) Oberschwester, *die*

matt /mæt/ *adj.* matt

'**matted** *adj.* verfilzt

'**matter** /'mætə(r)/ ☐ *n.* **(a)** (affair) Angelegenheit, *die;* ~s die Dinge; **money** ~s Geldangelegenheiten **(b)** it's a ~ **of taste** das ist Geschmackssache; **[only] a** ~ **of time** [nur noch] eine Frage der Zeit **(c)** what's the ~? was ist [los]? **(d)** (physical material) Materie, *die* ☐ *v.i.* etwas ausmachen; **what does it** ~? was macht das schon?; **[it] doesn't** ~: [das] macht nichts (ugs.)

'**matter-of-fact** *adj.* sachlich

mattress /'mætrɪs/ *n.* Matratze, *die*

mature /mə'tjʊə(r)/ ☐ *adj.* reif; ausgereift ‹*Stil, Käse, Portwein, Sherry*› ☐ *v.t.* reifen lassen ☐ *v.i.* reifen

maturity /mə'tjʊərɪtɪ/ *n.* Reife, *die*

Maundy Thursday /mɔ:ndɪ 'θɜ:zdɪ/ *n.* Gründonnerstag, *der*

mausoleum /mɔ:sə'li:əm/ *n.* Mausoleum, *das*

mauve /məʊv/ *adj.* mauve

mawkish /'mɔ:kɪʃ/ *adj.* rührselig

max. *abbr.* = **maximum** (*adj.*) max., (*n.*) Max.

maxim /'mæksɪm/ *n.* Maxime, *die*

maximum /'mæksɪməm/ ☐ *n., pl.* **maxima** /'mæksɪmə/ Maximum, *das* ☐ *adj.* maximal; Maximal-; ~ **speed**/ **temperature** Höchstgeschwindigkeit, *die*/ -temperatur, *die*

'**maximum-security** *attrib. adj.* Hochsicherheits‹*gefängnis*›*trakt*›

may *v. aux., only in pres.* **may,** *neg.* (coll.) **mayn't** /meɪnt/, *past* **might** /maɪt/, *neg.* (coll.) **mightn't** /'maɪtnt/ **(a)** (expr. possibility) können; **it** ~ **be true** das kann stimmen; **I** ~ **be wrong** vielleicht irre ich mich; **it** ~ **not be possible**

das wird vielleicht nicht möglich sein; he ~ have missed his train vielleicht hat er seinen Zug verpasst; it ~ or might rain es könnte regnen; we ~ or might as well go wir könnten eigentlich ebenso gut [auch] gehen **(b)** (expr. permission) dürfen **(c)** (expr. wish) mögen; ~ the best man win! auf dass der Beste gewinnt!

May /meɪ/ n. Mai, der; see also AUGUST

maybe /ˈmeɪbiː, ˈmeɪbɪ/ adv. vielleicht

'May Day n. der Erste Mai; the ~ holiday der Maifeiertag

'mayfly n. Eintagsfliege, die

mayhem /ˈmeɪhem/ n. Chaos, das

mayn't /meɪnt/ (coll.) = may not; ▶ MAY

mayonnaise /meɪəˈneɪz/ n. Mayonnaise, die

mayor /meə(r)/ n. Bürgermeister, der

mayoress /ˈmeərɪs/ n. (woman mayor) Bürgermeisterin, die; (mayor's wife) [Ehe]frau des Bürgermeisters

maze /meɪz/ n. Labyrinth, das

MBA abbr. = **Master of Business Administration** Diplom in Betriebswirtschaft

me /mɪ, stressed miː/ pron. mich; as indirect object mir; who, me? wer, ich?; not me ich nicht; it's me ich bins

ME abbr. (Med.) = **myalgic encephalomyelitis**

meadow /ˈmedəʊ/ n. Wiese, die

meagre /ˈmiːgə(r)/ adj. dürftig

meal /miːl/ n. Mahlzeit, die; go out for a ~: essen gehen; enjoy your ~: guten Appetit!; ~s on wheels (Brit.) Essen auf Rädern

meal: ~ **ticket** n. Essensmarke, die; (fig. coll.) melkende Kuh (ugs.); ~**time** n. Essenszeit, die; ~ **voucher** n. Essensmarke, die

mean¹ /miːn/ n. **(a)** Mittelweg, der **(b)** (Math.) Mittelwert, der

mean² adj. **(a)** (miserly) geizig **(b)** (unkind) gemein **(c)** (shabby) schäbig

mean³ v.t., meant /ment/ **(a)** (intend) beabsichtigen; ~ to do sth. etw. tun wollen **(b)** (design, destine) be ~t to do sth. etw. tun sollen **(c)** (intend to convey) meinen; I [really] ~ it ich meine das ernst; what do you ~ by that? was hast du damit gemeint? **(d)** (signify) bedeuten

meander /mɪˈændə(r)/ v.i. **(a)** ⟨Fluss:⟩ sich winden **(b)** ⟨Person:⟩ schlendern

'meaning n. Bedeutung, die; (of text etc., life) Sinn, der

meaningful /ˈmiːnɪŋfl/ adj. bedeutungsvoll ⟨Blick, Ergebnis⟩; sinnvoll ⟨Aufgabe, Gespräch⟩

'meaningless adj. ⟨Wort, Gespräch:⟩ ohne Sinn; sinnlos ⟨Aktivität⟩

means /miːnz/ n. **(a)** Möglichkeit, die; [Art und] Weise; by this ~: hierdurch; ~ of transport Transportmittel, das **(b)** pl. (resources) Mittel Pl.; live within/ beyond one's ~: seinen Verhältnissen entsprechend/über seine Verhältnisse leben **(c)** by all ~! selbstverständlich!; by no [manner of] ~: ganz und gar nicht; by ~ of durch; mit [Hilfe von]

'means test n. Überprüfung der Bedürftigkeit

meant ▶ MEAN³

mean: ~**time** 1 n. in the ~time inzwischen; 2 adv inzwischen; ~**while** adv. inzwischen

measles /ˈmiːzlz/ n. Masern Pl.

measly /ˈmiːzlɪ/ adj. (coll.) pop[e]lig (ugs.)

measurable /ˈmeʒərəbl/ adj. messbar

measure /ˈmeʒə(r)/ 1 n. **(a)** Maß, das; for good ~: sicherheitshalber; (as an extra) zusätzlich; made to ~: maßgeschneidert **(b)** (degree) in some/large ~: in gewisser Hinsicht/ in hohem Maße **(c)** (for measuring) Maß, das **(d)** (step) Maßnahme, die; take ~s Maßnahmen treffen 2 v.t. messen ⟨Größe, Menge usw.⟩; ausmessen ⟨Raum⟩ 3 v.i. messen ▪ **measure 'up to** v.t. entsprechen (+ Dat.)

'measured /ˈmeʒəd/ adj. gemessen ⟨Schritt, Worte⟩

'measurement n. **(a)** Messung, die **(b)** (dimension) Maß, das

'measuring tape n. Bandmaß, das

meat /miːt/ n. Fleisch, das

'meaty adj. **(a)** fleischig **(b)** (fig.) gehaltvoll

mechanic /mɪˈkænɪk/ n. Mechaniker, der/ Mechanikerin, die

mechanical /mɪˈkænɪkl/ adj. mechanisch

mechanical engi'neering n. Maschinenbau, der

me'chanically adv. mechanisch

mechanical 'pencil n. (Amer.) Drehbleistift, der

me'chanics n. **(a)** Mechanik, die **(b)** pl. (mechanism) Mechanismus, der

mechanism /ˈmekənɪzm/ n. Mechanismus, der

mechanize /ˈmekənaɪz/ v.t. mechanisieren

medal /ˈmedl/ n. Medaille, die; (decoration) Orden, der

medallion /mɪˈdæljən/ n. [große] Medaille

medallist /ˈmedəlɪst/ n. Medaillengewinner, der/-gewinnerin, die

meddle /ˈmedl/ v.i. ~ with sth. sich (Dat.) an etw. (Dat.) zu schaffen machen; ~ in sth. sich in etw. (Akk.) einmischen

media /ˈmiːdɪə/ ▶ MASS MEDIA; MEDIUM 1

mediaeval ▶ MEDIEVAL

'media studies *n. sing.*
Medienwissenschaft, *die;* (school subject)
Medienkunde, *die*

mediate /'mi:dɪeɪt/ *v.i.* vermitteln

mediator /'mi:dɪeɪtə(r)/ *n.* Vermittler, *der*/
Vermittlerin, *die*

medical /'medɪkl/ *adj.* medizinisch;
ärztlich ⟨*Behandlung, Untersuchung*⟩

medical: ∼ **certificate** *n.* Attest, *das;*
∼ **exami'nation** *n.* ärztliche
Untersuchung; ∼ **'history** *n.* (of person)
Krankengeschichte, *die;* ∼ **insurance** *n.*
Krankenversicherung, *die;* **have** ∼ **insurance**
krankenversichert sein; ∼ **prac'titioner**
n. praktischer Arzt/praktische Ärztin;
∼ **report** *n.* medizinisches Gutachten;
∼ **school** *n.* medizinische Hochschule;
∼ **student** *n.* Medizinstudent, *der*/
-studentin *die*

medicament /mɪ'dɪkəmənt, 'medɪkəmənt/
n. Medikament, *das*

Medicare /'medɪkeə(r)/ *n.* (Amer.)
[*bundes*]staatliches
*Krankenversicherungssystem für Personen
über 65 Jahre*

medicated /'medɪkeɪtɪd/ *adj.* medizinisch

medication /medɪ'keɪʃn/ *n.* (medicine)
Medikament, *das*

medicinal /mɪ'dɪsɪnl/ *adj.* medizinisch

medicine /'medsən, 'medɪsɪn/ *n.* (a)
(science) Medizin, *die*
(b) (preparation) Medikament, *das*

'medicine chest *n.*
Medikamentenschränkchen, *das;* (in home)
Hausapotheke, *die*

medieval /medɪ'i:vl/ *adj.* mittelalterlich

mediocre /mi:dɪ'əʊkə(r)/ *adj.* mittelmäßig

mediocrity /mi:dɪ'ɒkrɪtɪ/ *n.*
Mittelmäßigkeit, *die*

meditate /'medɪteɪt/ *v.i.* nachdenken, (esp.
Relig.) meditieren ([up]on über + *Akk.*)

meditation /medɪ'teɪʃn/ *n.* (a) (act)
Nachdenken, *das*
(b) (Relig.) Meditation, *die*

Mediterranean /medɪtə'reɪnɪən/ *pr. n.* the
∼: das Mittelmeer

medium /'mi:dɪəm/ ① *n., pl.* **media**
/'mi:dɪə/ *or* ∼**s** (a) (substance) Medium, *das*
(b) (means) Mittel, *das;* **by** *or* **through the**
∼ **of** durch
(c) *pl.* ∼**s** (Spiritualism) Medium, *das*
(d) *in pl.* **media** (mass media) Medien *Pl.*
② *adj.* mittler ...; medium *nur präd.* ⟨*Steak*⟩

medium: ∼-**range** *adj.*
Mittelstrecken⟨*flugzeug, -rakete*⟩; ∼-**size[d]**
adj. mittelgroß

medley /'medlɪ/ *n.* (a) buntes Gemisch
(b) (Mus.) Potpourri, *das*

meek /mi:k/ *adj.* (a) (humble) sanftmütig
(b) (submissive) zu nachgiebig

meet /mi:t/ ① *v.t.,* met /met/ (a) treffen;
(collect) abholen

(b) (make the acquaintance of) kennen lernen;
pleased to ∼ **you** [sehr] angenehm
(c) (experience) stoßen auf (+ *Akk.*)
⟨*Widerstand, Problem*⟩
(d) (satisfy) entsprechen (+ *Dat.*) ⟨*Wunsch,
Bedürfnis, Kritik*⟩; einhalten ⟨*Termin,
Zeitplan*⟩
(e) (pay) decken ⟨*Kosten*⟩; bezahlen
⟨*Rechnung*⟩
② *v.i.,* **met (a)** (by chance) sich ⟨*Dat.*⟩
begegnen; (by arrangement) sich treffen; **we've
met before** wir kennen uns bereits
(b) ⟨*Komitee, Ausschuss usw.*⟩ tagen
■ **meet 'up** *v.i.* sich treffen; ∼ **up with sb.**
(coll.) sich treffen
■ **'meet with** *v.t.* (a) begegnen (+ *Dat.*)
(b) (experience) haben ⟨*Erfolg, Unfall*⟩; stoßen
auf (+ *Akk.*) ⟨*Widerstand*⟩

'meeting *n.* (a) Begegnung, *die;* (by
arrangement) Treffen, *das*
(b) (assembly) Versammlung, *die;* (of committee
etc.) Sitzung, *die*

'meeting place *n.* Treffpunkt, *der*

mega /'megə/ (coll.) ① *adj.* (a) (enormous)
Mega- (Jugendspr.)
(b) (excellent) geil (Jugendspr.)
② *adv.* äußerst; **be** ∼ **rich** super- *od.*
(Jugendspr.) megareich sein

'megabyte *n.* (Comp.) Megabyte, *das*

megalomania /megələ'meɪnɪə/ *n.*
Größenwahn, *der*

megaphone /'megəfəʊn/ *n.* Megaphon, *das*

melancholic /melən'kɒlɪk/ *adj.*
melancholisch

melancholy /'melənkəlɪ/ ① *n.*
Melancholie, *die*
② *adj.* melancholisch

mellow /'meləʊ/ ① *adj.* (a) (softened by age
or experience) abgeklärt
(b) (ripe, well-matured) reif
② *v.i.* reifen

melodic /mɪ'lɒdɪk/**, melodious**
/mɪ'ləʊdɪəs/ *adjs.,* **me'lodiously** *adv.*
melodisch

melodrama /'melədrɑ:mə/ *n.* Melodrama,
das

melodramatic /melədrə'mætɪk/ *adj.*
melodramatisch

melody /'melədɪ/ *n.* Melodie, *die*

melon /'melən/ *n.* Melone, *die*

melt /melt/ ① *v.i.* schmelzen
② *v.t.* schmelzen; zerlassen ⟨*Butter*⟩
■ **melt a'way** *v.i.* [weg]schmelzen
■ **melt 'down** ① *v.i.* schmelzen
② *v.t.* einschmelzen

melting: ∼ **point** *n.* Schmelzpunkt, *der;*
∼ **pot** *n.* (fig.) Schmelztiegel, *der*

member /'membə(r)/ *n.* (a) Mitglied, *das;*
be a ∼: Mitglied sein; ∼ **of a/the family**
Familienangehörige, *der*/*die*
(b) M∼ **[of Parliament]** (Brit.) Abgeordnete
[des Unterhauses], *der*/*die*

'membership n. (a) Mitgliedschaft, die (of in + Dat.)
(b) (number of members) Mitgliederzahl, die
(c) (members) Mitglieder Pl.

'member state n. Mitglied[s]staat, der

membrane /'membreɪn/ n. (Biol.) Membran, die

memento /mɪ'mentəʊ/ n., pl. ~es or ~s Andenken, das (of an + Akk.)

memo /'meməʊ/ n., pl. ~s (coll.)
▶ MEMORANDUM

memoirs /'memwɑːz/ n. pl. Memoiren Pl.

memorable /'memərəbl/ adj. denkwürdig ⟨Ereignis, Tag⟩; unvergesslich ⟨Film, Buch, Aufführung⟩

memorandum /memə'rændəm/ n., pl. memoranda /memə'rændə/ or ~s Mitteilung, die

memorial /mɪ'mɔːrɪəl/ 1 adj. Gedenk-
2 n. Denkmal, das (to für)

memorize /'meməraɪz/ v.t. sich (Dat.) merken od. einprägen; (learn by heart) auswendig lernen

memory /'memərɪ/ n. (a) Gedächtnis, das
(b) (thing remembered, act of remembering) Erinnerung, die (of an + Akk.); from ~: aus dem Gedächtnis; in ~ of zur Erinnerung an (+ Akk.)
(c) (Comp.) Speicher, der

memory: ~ **bank** n. Speicherbank, die; ~ **stick** n. (Comp.) Memorystick, der; Speicherstab, der

men pl. of MAN

menace /'menəs/ 1 v.t. bedrohen
2 n. Plage, die

menacing /'menəsɪŋ/ adj. drohend

mend /mend/ 1 v.t. reparieren; ausbessern ⟨Kleidung⟩; kleben ⟨Glas, Porzellan⟩
2 v.i. ⟨Knochen, Bein usw.⟩ heilen
3 n. be on the ~: auf dem Wege der Besserung sein

'menfolk n. pl. Männer Pl.

menial /'miːnɪəl/ adj. niedrig; untergeordnet ⟨Aufgabe⟩

meningitis /menɪn'dʒaɪtɪs/ n. Hirnhautentzündung, die

menopause /'menəpɔːz/ n. Wechseljahre Pl.

menstruate /'menstrʊeɪt/ v.i. menstruieren

menstruation /menstrʊ'eɪʃn/ n. Menstruation, die

menswear /'menzweə(r)/ n. Herrenbekleidung, die

mental /'mentl/ adj. (a) (of the mind) geistig; Geistes⟨zustand, -störung⟩
(b) (Brit. coll.: mad) verrückt (salopp)

mental: ~ **a'rithmetic** n. Kopfrechnen, das; ~ **'health** n. seelische Gesundheit; ~ **hospital** n. Nervenklinik, die (ugs.); ~ **'illness** n. Geisteskrankheit, die

mentality /men'tælɪtɪ/ n. Mentalität, die

'mentally adv. geistig

mention /'menʃn/ 1 n. Erwähnung, die
2 v.t. erwähnen (to gegenüber); don't ~ it keine Ursache

menu /'menjuː/ n. (a) [Speise]karte, die
(b) (Comp., Telev.) Menü, das

'menu bar n. (Comp.) Menüleiste, die

mercenary /'mɜːsɪnərɪ/ 1 adj. gewinnsüchtig
2 n. Söldner, der

merchandise /'mɜːtʃəndaɪz/ n. [Handels]ware, die

merchant /'mɜːtʃənt/ n. Kaufmann, der

merchant: ~ **'bank** n. Handelsbank, die; ~ **'navy** n. (Brit.) Handelsmarine, die

merciful /'mɜːsɪfl/ adj. gnädig

mercifully /'mɜːsɪfəlɪ/ adv. (fortunately) glücklicherweise

merciless /'mɜːsɪlɪs/ adj., **'mercilessly** adv. gnadenlos

mercury /'mɜːkjʊrɪ/ 1 n. Quecksilber, das
2 pr. n. M~ (Astron.) Merkur, der

mercy /'mɜːsɪ/ n. Erbarmen, das (on mit); show ~: [no] ~: mit jmdm. [kein] Erbarmen haben; be at the ~ of sb./sth. jmdm./einer Sache [auf Gedeih und Verderb] ausgeliefert sein

mere /mɪə(r)/ adj., **'merely** adv. bloß

merge /mɜːdʒ/ 1 v.t. (a) (combine) zusammenschließen
(b) (blend gradually) verschmelzen (with mit)
2 v.i. (a) (combine) fusionieren (with mit)
(b) ⟨Straße:⟩ zusammenlaufen (with mit)

merger /'mɜːdʒə(r)/ n. Fusion, die

meringue /mə'ræŋ/ n. Meringe, die; Baiser, das

merit /'merɪt/ 1 n. (a) (worth) Verdienst, das
(b) (good feature) Vorzug, der
2 v.t. verdienen

mermaid /'mɜːmeɪd/ n. Nixe, die

merrily /'merɪlɪ/ adv. munter

merriment /'merɪmənt/ n. Fröhlichkeit, die

merry /'merɪ/ adj. fröhlich; ~ Christmas! frohe od. fröhliche Weihnachten!

'merry-go-round n. Karussell, das

'merrymaking n. Feiern, das

mesh /meʃ/ n. (a) Masche, die
(b) (netting; also fig.: network) Geflecht, das; wire ~: Maschendraht, der

mesmerize /'mezməraɪz/ v.t. faszinieren

mess /mes/ n. (a) (dirty/untidy state) [be] a ~ or in a ~: schmutzig/unaufgeräumt [sein]; what a ~! was für ein Dreck (ugs.)/ Durcheinander!
(b) (bad state) be [in] a ~: sich in einem schlimmen Zustand befinden; ⟨Person:⟩ schlimm dran sein; get into a ~: in Schwierigkeiten geraten; make a ~ of verpfuschen (ugs.) ⟨Arbeit, Leben⟩
(c) (Mil.) Kasino, das ⋯⟶

■ **mess a'bout, mess a'round** ⓵ *v.i.*
(potter) herumwerken; (fool about)
herumalbern
⓶ *v.t.* ~ **sb. about** *or* **around** mit jmdm.
nach Belieben umspringen
■ **mess 'up** *v.t.* **(a)** (make dirty) schmutzig
machen; (make untidy) in Unordnung bringen
(b) (bungle) ~ **it/things up** Mist bauen (ugs.)
message /'mesɪdʒ/ *n.* Nachricht, *die;* **give**
sb. a ~: jmdm. etwas ausrichten
messenger /'mesɪndʒə(r)/ *n.* Bote, *der/*
Botin, *die*
Messiah /mɪˈsaɪə/ *n.* Messias, *der*
Messrs /'mesəz/ *n. pl.* **(a)** (in name of firm) ≈
Fa.
(b) *pl. of* Mʀ; (in list of names) ~ **A and B** die
Herren A und B
'**messy** *adj.* (dirty) schmutzig; (untidy)
unordentlich
met ▶ MEET
metabolism /mɪˈtæbəlɪzm/ *n.*
Stoffwechsel, *der*
metal /'metl/ ⓵ *n.* Metall, *das*
⓶ *adj.* Metall-
'**metal detector** *n.* Metallsuchgerät, *das*
metallic /mɪˈtælɪk/ *adj.* metallisch; **have a**
~ **taste** nach Metall schmecken
metallurgy /mɪˈtælədʒɪ/ *n.* Metallurgie, *die*
'**metalwork** *n.* (products) Metallarbeiten *Pl.*
metamorphosis /metəˈmɔːfəsɪs/ *n., pl.*
metamorphoses /metəˈmɔːfəsiːz/
Metamorphose, *die*
metaphor /'metəfə(r)/ *n.* Metapher, *die*
metaphorical /metəˈfɒrɪkl/ *adj.,*
metaphorically /metəˈfɒrɪkəlɪ/ *adv.*
metaphorisch
meteor /'miːtɪə(r)/ *n.* Meteor, *der*
meteoric /miːtɪˈɒrɪk/ *adj.* (fig.) kometenhaft
meteorological /miːtɪərəˈlɒdʒɪkl/ *adj.*
meteorologisch ⟨*Instrument*⟩; Wetter⟨*ballon,*
-bericht⟩
meteorologist /miːtɪəˈrɒlədʒɪst/ *n.*
Meteorologe, *der/*Meteorologin, *die*
meteorology /miːtɪəˈrɒlədʒɪ/ *n.*
Meteorologie, *die*
meter¹ /'miːtə(r)/ *n.* **(a)** Zähler, *der;* (for
coins) Münzzähler, *der*
(b) (parking ~) Parkuhr, *die*
meter² (Amer.) ▶ METRE¹⸴ ²
methane /'miːθeɪn/ *n.* Methan, *das*
method /'meθəd/ *n.* Methode, *die*
methodical /mɪˈθɒdɪkl/ *adj.,*
me'thodically *adv.* systematisch
Methodist /'meθədɪst/ *n.* Methodist, *der/*
Methodistin, *die*
meths /meθs/ *n.* (Brit. coll.) [Brenn]spiritus,
der
methylated spirit[s] /meθɪleɪtɪd
'spɪrɪt(s)/ *n.* [*pl.*] Brennspiritus, *der*
meticulous /mɪˈtɪkjʊləs/ *adj.,*
me'ticulously *adv.* (scrupulous[ly])
sorgfältig; (overscrupulous[ly]) übergenau

metre¹ /'miːtə/ *n.* (Brit.: poetic rhythm)
Metrum, *das*
metre² *n.* (Brit.: unit) Meter, *der od. das*
metric /'metrɪk/ *adj.* metrisch; ~ **system**
metrisches System
metrication /metrɪˈkeɪʃn/ *n.* Umstellung
auf das metrische System
metro /'metrəʊ/ *n., pl.* ~**s** U-Bahn, *die;* **the**
Paris M~ die [Pariser] Metro
metronome /'metrənəʊm/ *n.* Metronom,
das
metropolis /mɪˈtrɒpəlɪs/ *n.* Metropole, *die*
metropolitan /metrəˈpɒlɪtən/ *adj.* ~ **New**
York der Großraum New York; ~ **London**
Großlondon (*das*)
Mexican /'meksɪkən/ ⓵ *adj.* mexikanisch;
sb. is ~: jmd. ist Mexikaner/Mexikanerin
⓶ *n.* Mexikaner, *der/*Mexikanerin, *die*
Mexico /'meksɪkəʊ/ *pr. n.* Mexiko (*das*)
miaow /mɪˈaʊ/ ⓵ *v.i.* miauen
⓶ *n.* Miauen, *das*
mice *pl. of* MOUSE
microbe /'maɪkrəʊb/ *n.* Mikrobe, *die*
micro /'maɪkrəʊ/: ~**chip** *n.* Mikrochip,
der; ~**computer** *n.* Mikrocomputer, *der;*
~**dot** *n.* Mikrat, *das;* ~**fibre** *n.*
Mikrofaser, *die;* ~**fiche** *n.* Mikrofiche, *das*
od. der; ~**film** ⓵ *n.* Mikrofilm, *der;* ⓶ *v.t.*
auf Mikrofilm aufnehmen; ~**light**
['aircraft] *n.* Ultraleichtflugzeug, *das*
microphone /'maɪkrəfəʊn/ *n.* Mikrofon,
das
microprocessor /maɪkrəʊˈprəʊsesə(r)/ *n.*
Mikroprozessor, *der*
microscope /'maɪkrəskəʊp/ *n.* Mikroskop,
das
microscopic /maɪkrəˈskɒpɪk/ *adj.*
mikroskopisch; (fig.: very small) winzig
'**microwave** *n.* Mikrowelle, *die;* ~ [**oven**]
Mikrowellenherd, *der*
mid- /mɪd/ *in comb.* **in ~-air** in der Luft; **in**
~-sentence mitten im Satz; **~-July** Mitte
Juli; **the ~-60s** die Mitte der Sechzigerjahre;
a man in his ~-fifties ein Mittfünfziger; **be in**
one's ~-thirties Mitte dreißig sein
midday /'mɪddeɪ, mɪdˈdeɪ/ *n.* **(a)** (noon) zwölf
Uhr
(b) (middle of day) Mittag, *der; attrib.* Mittags-
middle /'mɪdl/ ⓵ *attrib. adj.* mittler...
⓶ *n.* **(a)** Mitte, *die;* **in the ~ of the forest/**
night mitten im Wald/in der Nacht
(b) (waist) Taille, *die*
middle: ~ '**age** *n.* mittleres [Lebens]alter;
~**-aged** /'mɪdleɪdʒd/ *adj.* mittleren Alters
nachgestellt; **M~** '**Ages** *n. pl.* **the M~ Ages**
das Mittelalter; ~ '**class** *n.* Mittelstand,
der; ~**-class** *adj.* bürgerlich; **M~** '**East**
pr. n. **the M~ East** der Nahe [und Mittlere]
Osten; **M~** '**Eastern** *adj.* nahöstlich;
~**man** *n.* (Commerc.) Zwischenhändler, *der/*
-händlerin, *die;* (fig.) Vermittler, *der/*

Vermittlerin, *die;* ～ **'management** *n.*
mittleres Management; ～ **name** *n.* zweiter
Vorname
middling /'mɪdlɪŋ/ *adj.* mittelmäßig
'midfield *n.* (Footb.) Mittelfeld, *das*
midge /mɪdʒ/ *n.* Stechmücke, *die*
midget /'mɪdʒɪt/ ☐1 *n.* Liliputaner, *der/*
Liliputanerin, *die*
☐2 *adj.* winzig
Midlands /'mɪdləndz/ *n. pl.* the ～ (Brit.)
Mittelengland (*das*)
midlife crisis /mɪdlaɪf 'kraɪsɪs/ *n.*
Midlifecrisis, *die*
'midnight *n.* Mitternacht, *die*
'midpoint *n.* Mitte, *die*
midriff /'mɪdrɪf/ *n.* Bauch, *der*
midst /mɪdst/ *n.* in the ～ of sth. mitten in
einer Sache; in our/their/your ～: in unserer/
ihrer/eurer Mitte
midsummer /'---, -'--/ *n.* die [Zeit der]
Sommersonnenwende
midway /'--, -'-/ *adv.* auf halbem Weg[e]
⟨*sich treffen, sich befinden*⟩
midweek /'mɪdwiːk, mɪd'wiːk/ *n.* in ～: in
der Wochenmitte
'midwife *n., pl.* **'midwives** Hebamme, *die*
midwifery /'mɪdwɪfrɪ, mɪd'wɪfərɪ/ *n., no
art.* Geburtshilfe, *die*
mid'winter *n.* die [Zeit der]
Wintersonnenwende
might¹ ▶ MAY
might² /maɪt/ *n.* (a) (force) Gewalt, *die*
(b) (power) Macht, *die*
mightn't /'maɪtnt/ (coll.) = might not; ▶ MAY
mighty /'maɪtɪ/ ☐1 *adj.* mächtig
☐2 *adv.* (coll.) verdammt (ugs.)
migraine /'miːgreɪn/ *n.* Migräne, *die*
migrant /'maɪgrənt/ *n.* (a) Auswanderer,
*der/*Auswanderin, *die*
(b) (bird) Zugvogel, *der*
migrate /maɪ'greɪt/ *v.i.* (a) (to a town)
abwandern; (to another country) auswandern
(b) ⟨*Vogel:*⟩ fortziehen
migration /maɪ'greɪʃn/ *n.* (a) (to a town)
Abwandern, *das;* (to another country)
Auswandern, *das*
(b) (of birds) Zug, *der*
migratory /maɪ'greɪtərɪ/ *adj.* ～ **bird/fish**
Zugvogel, *der/*Wanderfisch, *der*
mike /maɪk/ *n.* (coll.) Mikro, *das*
Milan /mɪ'læn/ *pr. n.* Mailand (*das*)
mild /maɪld/ *adj.* mild; sanft ⟨*Person*⟩
mildew /'mɪldjuː/ *n.* (a) Schimmel, *der*
(b) (on plant) Mehltau, *der*
'mildly *adv.* (a) (gently) mild[e]
(b) (slightly) ein bisschen
(c) to put it ～: gelinde gesagt
mile /maɪl/ *n.* (a) Meile, *die*
(b) (fig. coll.) ～s **better/too big** tausendmal
besser/viel zu groß; **be** ～**s ahead of sb.**
jmdm. weit voraus sein

mileage /'maɪlɪdʒ/ *n.* [Anzahl der] Meilen
Pl.; a low ～: ein niedriger Meilenstand
'milestone *n.* Meilenstein, *der*
militant /'mɪlɪtənt/ ☐1 *adj.* militant
☐2 *n.* Militante, *der/die*
military /'mɪlɪtərɪ/ ☐1 *adj.* militärisch;
Militär⟨*regierung, -akademie, -uniform,
-parade*⟩; ～ **service** Militärdienst, *der*
☐2 *n.* the ～: das Militär
militate /'mɪlɪteɪt/ *v.i.* ～ **against/in favour
of** sth. [deutlich] gegen/für etw. sprechen
militia /mɪ'lɪʃə/ *n.* Miliz, *die*
milk /mɪlk/ ☐1 *n.* Milch, *die*
☐2 *v.t.* melken
milk: ～ **bottle** *n.* Milchflasche, *die;*
～ **'chocolate** *n.* Milchschokolade, *die;*
～ **float** *n.* (Brit.) Milchwagen, *der*
milking /'mɪlkɪŋ/ *n.* Melken, *das*
milk: ～ **jug** *n.* Milchkännchen, *das;*
～**man** /'mɪlkmən/ *n., pl.* ～**men** /'mɪlkmən/
Milchmann, *der;* ～ **shake** *n.* Milchshake,
der; ～ **tooth** *n.* Milchzahn, der
'milky *adj.* milchig
Milky 'Way *n.* Milchstraße, *die*
mill /mɪl/ ☐1 *n.* (a) Mühle, *die*
(b) (factory) Fabrik, *die*
☐2 *v.t.* (a) mahlen ⟨*Getreide*⟩
(b) fräsen ⟨*Metallgegenstand*⟩
mill a'bout (Brit.), **mill a'round** *v.i.*
durcheinander laufen
millennium /mɪ'lenɪəm/ *n., pl.* ～**s** *or*
millennia /mɪ'lenɪə/ Jahrtausend, *das;*
Millennium, *das*
mil'lennium bug *n.* (Comp.)
Jahrtausendvirus, *der od. das*
'miller *n.* Müller, *der*
millet /'mɪlɪt/ *n.* Hirse, *die*
milligram /'mɪlɪgræm/ *n.* Milligramm, *das*
millilitre (*Brit.; Amer.:* **milliliter**)
/'mɪlɪliːtə(r)/ *n.* Milliliter, *der od. das*
millimetre (*Brit.; Amer.:* **millimeter**)
/'mɪlɪmiːtə(r)/ *n.* Millimeter, *der*
milliner /'mɪlɪnə(r)/ *n.* Modist, *der/*
Modistin, *die*
'millinery *n.* Hutmacherei, *die*
million /'mɪljən/ ☐1 *adj.* a *or* one/two ～:
eine Million/zwei Millionen; **half a** ～: eine
halbe Million
☐2 *n.* (a) Million, *die*
(b) (indefinite amount) ～**s of people** eine
Unmenge Leute
millionaire /mɪljə'neə(r)/ *n.* Millionär,
*der/*Millionärin, *die*
millionth /'mɪljənθ/ ☐1 *adj.* millionst...
☐2 *n.* (fraction) Millionstel, *das*
'millstone *n.* Mühlstein, *der*
mime /maɪm/ ☐1 *n.* (a) (performance)
Pantomime, *die*
(b) (art) Pantomimik, *die*
☐2 *v.i.* pantomimisch agieren
☐3 *v.t.* pantomimisch darstellen
mimic /'mɪmɪk/ ☐1 *n.* Imitator, *der*   ⋯⊱

2 *v.t.*, **-ck-** nachahmen

min. *abbr.* (a) = **minute[s]** Min.
(b) = **minimum** (*adj.*) mind., (*n.*) Min.

mince /mɪns/ 1 *n.* Hackfleisch, *das*
2 *v.t.* durch den [Fleisch]wolf drehen
⟨*Fleisch*⟩

'**mincemeat** *n.* (a) Hackfleisch, *das*
(b) (sweet) *süße Pastetenfüllung aus Obst,
Rosinen, Gewürzen, Nierenfett usw.*

mince 'pie *n.* mit „mincemeat" B gefüllte
Pastete

'**mincer** *n.* Fleischwolf, *der*

mind /maɪnd/ 1 *n.* (a) Geist, *der*
(b) (remembrance) bear *or* keep sth. in ∼: an
etw. (*Akk.*) denken; **have [got] sb./sth. in** ∼:
an jmdn./etw. denken
(c) (opinion) **give sb. a piece of one's** ∼:
jmdm. gründlich die Meinung sagen; **to my**
∼: meiner Meinung *od.* Ansicht nach;
change one's ∼: seine Meinung ändern; **I
have a good** ∼ **to do that** ich hätte große
Lust, das zu tun; **make up one's** ∼, **make
one's** ∼ **up** sich entscheiden
(d) ([normal] mental powers) Verstand, *der*; **be
out of one's** ∼: den Verstand verloren haben
(e) (frame of ∼) [seelische] Verfassung
2 *v.t.* (a) **I can't afford a bicycle, never** ∼ **a
car** ich kann mir kein Fahrrad leisten,
geschweige denn ein Auto; **we've got some
decorations up, - not many,** ∼ wir haben
etwas dekoriert, allerdings nicht viel
(b) *usu. neg. or interrog.* (object to) **would you**
∼ **opening the door?** würdest du bitte die
Tür öffnen?; **I wouldn't** ∼ **a walk** ich hätte
nichts gegen einen Spaziergang
(c) (take care) ∼ **you don't go too near the
cliff edge!** pass auf, dass du nicht zu nah an
den Felsenrand gehst!; ∼ **how you go!** pass
auf!
(d) (have charge of) aufpassen auf (+ *Akk.*)
3 *v.i.* (a) ∼! Vorsicht!; Achtung!
(b) (care, object) **do you** ∼ **if I smoke?** stört es
Sie, wenn ich rauche?
(c) **never** ∼ (it's not important) macht nichts
■ **mind 'out** *v.i.* aufpassen (**for** auf + *Akk.*);
∼ **out!** Vorsicht!

mind: ∼**-bending**, (coll.) ∼**-blowing**
adjs. bewusstseinsverändernd;
∼**-boggling** /'maɪndbɒglɪŋ/ *adj.* (coll.)
wahnsinnig (ugs.)

'**minded** *adj.* **mechanically** ∼: technisch
veranlagt; **not politically** ∼: unpolitisch

minder /'maɪndə(r)/ *n.* (a) (for child) **we need
a** ∼ **for the child** wir brauchen jemanden,
der auf das Kind aufpasst *od.* das Kind
betreut
(b) (sl.: protector of criminal) Gorilla, *der* (salopp)

mindful /'maɪndfl/ *adj.* **be** ∼ **of sth.** etw.
berücksichtigen

'**mindless** *adj.* geistlos ⟨*Person*⟩; sinnlos
⟨*Gewalt*⟩

mine¹ /maɪn/ *n.* (a) Bergwerk, *das*
(b) (explosive) Mine, *die*

mine² *poss. pron. pred.* meiner/meine/
mein[e]s; *see also* HERS

mine: ∼**-detector** *n.* Minensuchgerät,
das; ∼**field** *n.* Minenfeld, *das*

'**miner** *n.* Bergmann, *der*

mineral /'mɪnərl/ 1 *adj.* mineralisch;
Mineral⟨*salz, -quelle*⟩
2 *n.* (a) Mineral, *das*
(b) (Brit.: soft drink) Erfrischungsgetränk, *das*

'**mineral water** *n.* Mineralwasser, *das*

minesweeper /'maɪnswiːpə(r)/ *n.*
Minensuchboot, *das*

mingle /'mɪŋgl/ 1 *v.t.* [ver]mischen
2 *v.i.* sich [ver]mischen (**with** mit)

mini /'mɪnɪ/ *n.* (coll.) (a) (car) **M**∼ ® Mini, *der*
(b) (skirt) Mini, *der* (ugs.)

mini- /'mɪnɪ/ *in comb.* Mini-; Klein⟨*bus,
-wagen, -taxi*⟩

miniature /'mɪnɪtʃə(r)/ 1 *n.* (picture)
Miniatur, *die*
2 *adj.* Miniatur-

mini: ∼**bus** *n.* Kleinbus, *der;* ∼**cab** *n.*
Minicar, *das*

minim /'mɪnɪm/ *n.* (Brit. Mus.) halbe Note

minimal /'mɪnɪml/ *adj.* minimal

minimize /'mɪnɪmaɪz/ *v.t.* (a) (reduce) auf
ein Mindestmaß reduzieren
(b) (understate) bagatellisieren

minimum /'mɪnɪməm/ 1 *n., pl.* minima
/'mɪnɪmə/ Minimum, *das* (**of** an + *Dat.*)
2 *attrib. adj.* Mindest-

minimum: ∼ '**lending rate** *n.*
Mindestausleihsatz [*der Bank von England*];
≈ Mindestdiskontsatz, *der;* ∼ '**wage** *n.*
Mindestlohn, *der*

mining /'maɪnɪŋ/ *n.* Bergbau, *der; attrib.*
Bergbau-

mining: ∼ **industry** *n.* Bergbau, *der;*
∼ **town** *n.* Bergbaustadt, *die*

minion /'mɪnjən/ *n.* Lakai, *der*

mini: ∼ **roundabout** *n.* (Brit.) *sehr kleiner,
oft nur aufs Pflaster aufgezeichneter
Kreisverkehr;* ∼**skirt** *n.* Minirock, *der*

minister /'mɪnɪstə(r)/ 1 *n.* (a) (Polit.)
Minister, *der*/Ministerin, *die*
(b) (Eccl.) Geistliche, *der/die;* Pfarrer, *der/*
Pfarrerin, *die*
2 *v.i.* ∼ **to sb.** sich um jmdn. kümmern

ministerial /mɪnɪ'stɪərɪəl/ *adj.* (Polit.)
Minister-; ministeriell

ministry /'mɪnɪstrɪ/ *n.* (a) (Polit.)
Ministerium, *das*
(b) (Eccl.) geistliches Amt

mink /mɪŋk/ *n.* Nerz, *der*

minnow /'mɪnəʊ/ *n.* Elritze, *die*

minor /'maɪnə(r)/ 1 *adj.* (a) (lesser)
kleiner...
(b) (unimportant) weniger bedeutend; (not
serious) leicht; ∼ **road** kleine Straße
(c) (Mus.) Moll-; **A** ∼: a-Moll
2 *n.* Minderjährige, *der/die*

minority /maɪˈnɒrɪtɪ, mɪˈnɒrɪtɪ/ *n.*
Minderheit, *die;* **in the ∼:** in der Minderheit

minstrel /ˈmɪnstrl/ *n.* fahrender Sänger

mint¹ /mɪnt/ ① *n.* (place) Münzanstalt, *die* ② *adj.* funkelnagelneu (ugs.); **in ∼ condition** in tadellosem Zustand ③ *v.t.* prägen

mint² *n.* (a) (plant) Minze, *die* (b) (peppermint) Pfefferminz, *das; attrib.* Pfefferminz-

mint ʼsauce *n.* Minzsoße, *die*

minuet /mɪnjʊˈet/ *n.* Menuett, *das*

minus /ˈmaɪnəs/ *prep.* minus; weniger; (without) abzüglich (+ *Gen.*)

minuscule /ˈmɪnəskjuːl/ *adj.* winzig

minute¹ /ˈmɪnɪt/ *n.* (a) Minute, *die;* (moment) Moment, *der* (b) ∼s (of meeting) Protokoll, *das;* **take the ∼s of a meeting** bei einer Sitzung [das] Protokoll führen

minute² /maɪˈnjuːt/ *adj.* (tiny) winzig

minute hand /ˈmɪnɪthænd/ *n.* Minutenzeiger, *der;* großer Zeiger

minutiae /maɪˈnjuːʃiː, mɪˈnjuːʃiː/ *n. pl.* Details *Pl.*

miracle /ˈmɪrəkl/ *n.* Wunder, *das*

miraculous /mɪˈrækjʊləs/ *adj.* wunderbar

mirage /ˈmɪrɑːʒ/ *n.* Fata Morgana, *die*

mire /maɪə(r)/ *n.* Morast, *der*

mirror /ˈmɪrə(r)/ ① *n.* Spiegel, *der* ② *v.t.* [wider]spiegeln

mirror ʼimage *n.* Spiegelbild, *das*

misadventure /mɪsədˈventʃə(r)/ *n.* Missgeschick, *das*

misanthropist /mɪˈzænθrəpɪst/ *ns.* Misanthrop, *der* (geh.); Menschenfeind, *der*

misanthropy /mɪˈzænθrəpɪ/ *n.* Menschenfeindlichkeit, *die*

misapprehension /mɪsæprɪˈhenʃn/ *n.* Missverständnis, *das;* **be under a ∼:** einem Irrtum unterliegen

misbehave /mɪsbɪˈheɪv/ *v.i. & refl.* sich schlecht benehmen

misbehaviour (*Amer.:* **misbehavior**) /mɪsbɪˈheɪvjə(r)/ *n.* schlechtes Benehmen

miscalculate /mɪsˈkælkjʊleɪt/ ① *v.t.* falsch berechnen; (misjudge) falsch einschätzen ② *v.i.* sich verrechnen

miscalculation /mɪskælkjʊˈleɪʃn/ *n.* Rechenfehler, *der;* (misjudgement) Fehleinschätzung, *die*

miscarriage /mɪsˈkærɪdʒ/ *n.* (a) Fehlgeburt, *die* (b) ∼ of justice Justizirrtum, *der*

miscarry /mɪsˈkærɪ/ *v.i.* (a) (Med.) eine Fehlgeburt haben (b) ⟨Plan, Vorhaben usw.:⟩ fehlschlagen

miscellaneous /mɪsəˈleɪnɪəs/ *adj.* (a) [kunter]bunt (b) *with pl. n.* verschieden

miscellany /mɪˈselənɪ/ *n.* [bunte] Sammlung; [buntes] Gemisch

mischief /ˈmɪstʃɪf/ *n.* (a) Unfug, *der;* **get up to ∼:** etwas anstellen (b) (harm) Schaden, *der*

mischievous /ˈmɪstʃɪvəs/ *adj.* spitzbübisch; schelmisch

misconception /mɪskənˈsepʃn/ *n.* falsche Vorstellung (**about** von); **be [labouring] under a ∼ about sth.** sich (*Dat.*) eine falsche Vorstellung von etw. machen

misconduct /mɪsˈkɒndʌkt/ *n.* unkorrektes Verhalten

misconstrue /mɪskənˈstruː/ *v.t.* missverstehen

miscount /mɪsˈkaʊnt/ ① *v.i.* sich verzählen ② *v.t.* falsch zählen

misdeed /mɪsˈdiːd/ *n.* Missetat, *die* (veralt., scherzh.)

misdemeanour (*Amer.:* **misdemeanor**) /mɪsdɪˈmiːne(r)/ *n.* Missetat, *die* (veralt., scherzh.)

misdirect /mɪsdɪˈrekt, mɪsdaɪˈrekt/ *v.t.* falsch adressieren ⟨*Brief*⟩; in die falsche Richtung schicken ⟨*Person*⟩

miser /ˈmaɪzə(r)/ *n.* Geizhals, *der*

miserable /ˈmɪzərəbl/ *adj.* (a) unglücklich; **feel ∼:** sich elend fühlen (b) trist ⟨*Wetter, Urlaub*⟩

miserably /ˈmɪzərəblɪ/ *adv.* unglücklich; jämmerlich ⟨*versagen*⟩; **∼ poor** bettelarm

miserly /ˈmaɪzəlɪ/ *adj.* geizig

misery /ˈmɪzərɪ/ *n.* (a) Elend, *das* (b) (coll.: discontented person) **∼ [guts]** Miesepeter, *der* (ugs.)

misfire /mɪsˈfaɪə(r)/ *v.i.* (a) ⟨*Motor:*⟩ Fehlzündungen haben (b) ⟨*Plan, Versuch:*⟩ fehlschlagen; ⟨*Streich, Witz:*⟩ danebengehen

misfit /ˈmɪsfɪt/ *n.* Außenseiter, *der/* Außenseiterin, *die*

misfortune /mɪsˈfɔːtʃuːn/ *n.* Missgeschick, *das*

misgiving /mɪsˈɡɪvɪŋ/ *n.* **∼[s]** Bedenken *Pl.*

misguided /mɪsˈɡaɪdɪd/ *adj.* töricht

mishandle /mɪsˈhændl/ *v.t.* falsch behandeln

mishap /ˈmɪshæp/ *n.* Missgeschick, *das*

mishear /mɪsˈhɪə(r)/ ① *v.i.,* misheard /mɪsˈhɜːd/ sich verhören ② *v.t.,* misheard falsch verstehen

mishit ① /ˈmɪshɪt/ *n.* Fehlschlag, *der* ② /mɪsˈhɪt/ *v.t.,* -tt-, mishit verschlagen

mishmash /ˈmɪʃmæʃ/ *n.* Mischmasch, *der* (ugs.) (**of** aus)

misinform /mɪsɪnˈfɔːm/ *v.t.* falsch informieren

misinterpret /mɪsɪnˈtɜːprɪt/ *v.t.* (make wrong inference from) falsch deuten; missdeuten ···⟩

misinterpretation /mɪsɪntɜːprɪˈteɪʃn/ *n.*
be open to ∼: leicht missdeutet werden
können

misjudge /mɪsˈdʒʌdʒ/ *v.t.* falsch
einschätzen; falsch beurteilen ⟨*Person*⟩

misjudgement, misjudgment
/mɪsˈdʒʌdʒmənt/ *n.* Fehleinschätzung, *die;* (of
person) falsche Beurteilung

mislay /mɪsˈleɪ/ *v.t.,* **mislaid** /mɪsˈleɪd/
verlegen

mislead /mɪsˈliːd/ *v.t.,* **misled** /mɪsˈled/
irreführen

misˈleading *adj.* irreführend

mismanage /mɪsˈmænɪdʒ/ *v.t.* schlecht
abwickeln ⟨*Geschäft, Projekt*⟩

mismanagement /mɪsˈmænɪdʒmənt/ *n.*
schlechte Abwicklung

misnomer /mɪsˈnəʊmə(r)/ *n.* unzutreffende
Bezeichnung

misogynist /mɪˈsɒdʒɪnɪst/ *n.*
Frauenhasser, *der*

misplace /mɪsˈpleɪs/ *v.t.* an den falschen
Platz stellen/legen/setzen *usw.*

misprint 1 /ˈmɪsprɪnt/ *n.* Druckfehler, *der*
2 /mɪsˈprɪnt/ *v.t.* verdrucken

mispronounce /mɪsprəˈnaʊns/ *v.t.* falsch
aussprechen

misquote /mɪsˈkwəʊt/ *v.t.* falsch zitieren;
he was ∼d as saying that …: man
unterstellte ihm, gesagt zu haben, dass …

misread /mɪsˈriːd/ *v.t.,* **misread** /mɪsˈred/
falsch lesen

misrepresent /mɪsreprɪˈzent/ *v.t.* falsch
darstellen

misrepresentation /mɪsreprɪzenˈteɪʃn/
n. falsche Darstellung

miss 1 *n.* Fehlschlag, *der;* (shot) Fehlschuss,
der; (throw) Fehlwurf, *der*
2 *v.t.* **(a)** (fail to hit) verfehlen
(b) (let slip) verpassen; **∼ an opportunity** sich
(*Dat.*) eine Gelegenheit entgehen lassen
(c) (fail to catch) verpassen ⟨*Zug*⟩
(d) (fail to take part in) versäumen; **∼ school** in
der Schule fehlen
(e) (fail to see) übersehen; (fail to hear) nicht
mitbekommen
(f) (feel the absence of) vermissen; **she ∼es
him** er fehlt ihr
3 *v.i.* (not hit sth.) danebentreffen
■ **miss ˈout** 1 *v.t.* weglassen
2 *v.i.* **∼ out on sth.** (coll.) sich (*Dat.*) etw.
entgehen lassen

Miss /mɪs/ *n.* **∼ Brown** (unmarried woman)
Frau Brown; Fräulein Brown (veralt.); (girl)
Fräulein Brown

misshapen /mɪsˈʃeɪpn/ *adj.* missgebildet

missile /ˈmɪsaɪl/ *n.* **(a)** (thrown)
[Wurf]geschoss, *das*
(b) (Mil.) Rakete, *die*

ˈmissile base, ˈmissile site *ns.*
Raketenbasis, *die*

ˈmissing *adj.* fehlend; **be ∼:** fehlen;
⟨*Person:*⟩ (Mil. etc.) vermisst werden; (not
present) fehlen; **∼ person** Vermisste, *der/die*

mission /ˈmɪʃn/ *n.* **(a)** Mission, *die*
(b) (planned operation) Einsatz, *der*

missionary /ˈmɪʃənərɪ/ *n.* Missionar, *der/*
Missionarin, *die*

ˈmission statement *n.*
Unternehmensleitbild, *das*

misspell /mɪsˈspel/ *v.t.,* forms as SPELL[1]
falsch schreiben

mist /mɪst/ *n.* (fog) Nebel, *der;* (haze) Dunst,
der; (on windscreen etc.) Beschlag, *der*
■ **mist ˈup** *v.i.* [sich] beschlagen

mistake /mɪˈsteɪk/ 1 *n.* Fehler, *der;* **by ∼:**
versehentlich
2 *v.t.,* forms as TAKE 1: **(a)** falsch verstehen
(b) **∼ x for y** x mit y verwechseln

mistaken /mɪˈsteɪkn/ *adj.* **be ∼:** sich
täuschen; **a case of ∼ identity** eine
Verwechslung

miˈstakenly *adv.* irrtümlicherweise

mistletoe /ˈmɪsltəʊ/ *n.* Mistel, *die*

mistook ▶ MISTAKE 2

mistranslate /mɪstrænsˈleɪt/ *v.t.* falsch
übersetzen

mistreat /mɪsˈtriːt/ *v.t.* schlecht behandeln;
(violently) misshandeln

mistreatment /mɪsˈtriːtmənt/ *n.* schlechte
Behandlung; (violent) Misshandlung, *die*

mistress /ˈmɪstrɪs/ *n.* **(a)** (Brit. Sch.: teacher)
Lehrerin, *die*
(b) (lover) Geliebte, *die*

mistrust /mɪsˈtrʌst/ 1 *v.t.* misstrauen
(+ *Dat.*)
2 *n.* Misstrauen, *das* (of gegenüber + *Dat.*)

mistrustful /mɪsˈtrʌstfl/ *adj.* misstrauisch
(of gegenüber)

ˈmisty *adj.* dunstig

misunderstand /mɪsʌndəˈstænd/ *v.t.,*
forms as UNDERSTAND: missverstehen

misunderˈstanding *n.* Missverständnis,
das

misuse 1 /mɪsˈjuːz/ *v.t.* missbrauchen
2 /mɪsˈjuːs/ *n.* Missbrauch, *der*

mite /maɪt/ *n.* **(a)** (Zool.) Milbe, *die*
(b) (small child) Würmchen, *das* (fam.); **poor
little ∼:** armes Kleines

miter (Amer.) ▶ MITRE

mitigate /ˈmɪtɪgeɪt/ *v.t.* **(a)** (reduce) lindern
(b) (make less severe) mildern; **mitigating
circumstances** mildernde Umstände

mitre /ˈmaɪtə(r)/ *n.* (Brit. Eccl.) Mitra, *die*

mitten /ˈmɪtn/ *n.* Fausthandschuh, *der*

mix /mɪks/ 1 *v.t.* [ver]mischen; verrühren
⟨*Zutaten*⟩
2 *v.i.* **(a)** (become ∼ed) sich vermischen
(b) (be sociable, participate) Umgang mit
anderen [Menschen] haben; **∼ with** Umgang
haben mit; **∼ well** kontaktfreudig sein
3 *n.* (coll.) Mischung, *die;* [cake] **∼:**
Backmischung, *die*

■ **mix 'up** *v.t.* (a) vermischen
(b) (muddle) durcheinander bringen; (confuse)
verwechseln
(c) be/get ~ed up in sth. in etw. (*Akk.*)
verwickelt sein/werden

mixed /mɪkst/ *adj.* (a) gemischt
(b) (diverse) unterschiedlich

mixed: ~ **'bag** *n.* bunte Mischung;
~ **'blessing** *n.* be a ~ blessing nicht nur
Vorteile haben; ~ **'grill** *n.* Mixedgrill, *der*
(Gastr.); gemischte Grillplatte;
~ **'marriage** *n.* Mischehe, *die;* ~ **'up** *adj.*
(fig. coll.) verwirrt, konfus ⟨*Person*⟩; be/feel
very ~ up völlig durcheinander sein

'mixer *n.* (for food) Küchenmaschine, *die;*
hand ~: Handrührgerät, *das*

mixture /'mɪkstʃə(r)/ *n.* (a) Mischung, *die*
(of aus)
(b) (Med.) Mixtur, *die*

'mix-up *n.* Durcheinander, *das;*
(misunderstanding) Missverständnis, *das*

mm. *abbr.* = **millimetre[s]** mm

moan /məʊn/ ①*n.* (a) Stöhnen, *das*
(b) have a ~ (complain) jammern
②*v.i.* (a) stöhnen (with vor + *Dat.*)
(b) (complain) jammern (about über + *Akk.*)
③*v.t.* stöhnen

moat /məʊt/ *n.* [castle] ~: Burggraben, *der*

mob /mɒb/ ①*n.* (a) (rabble) Mob, *der*
(b) (coll.: group) Peter and his ~: Peter und
seine ganze Blase (salopp)
②*v.t.,* **-bb-** belagern (ugs.) ⟨*Star*⟩

mobile /'məʊbaɪl/ ①*adj.* beweglich; (on
wheels) fahrbar; upwardly ~: sozial
aufsteigend
②*n.* Mobile, *das;* (~ phone) Handy, *das*

mobile: ~ **'home** *n.* transportable
Wohneinheit; ~ **'phone** *n.* Mobiltelefon,
das

mobility /mə'bɪlɪtɪ/ *n.* Beweglichkeit, *die*

mobilization /məʊbɪlaɪ'zeɪʃn/ *n.*
Mobilisierung, *die*

mobilize /'məʊbɪlaɪz/ *v.t.* mobilisieren

moccasin /'mɒkəsɪn/ *n.* Mokassin, *der*

mocha /'mɒkə/ *n.* Mokka, *der*

mock /mɒk/ ①*v.t.* sich lustig machen über
(+ *Akk.*)
②*v.i.* sich lustig machen (at über + *Akk.*)
③*adj.* Schein⟨*kampf, -angriff, -ehe*⟩

mockery /'mɒkərɪ/ *n.* Spott, *der;* make a
~ of sth. etw. zur Farce machen

'mock-up *n.* Modell [in Originalgröße]

mode /məʊd/ *n.* (a) Art [und Weise], *die*
(b) (fashion) Mode, *die*

model /'mɒdl/ ①*n.* (a) Modell, *das*
(b) (example to be imitated) Vorbild, *das*
(c) (Art) Modell, *das;* (Fashion) Mannequin,
das; (male) Dressman, *der*
②*adj.* (a) (exemplary) Muster-
(b) (miniature) Modell-
③*v.t.,* (Brit.) **-ll-:** (a) modellieren; ~ sth. after
or [up]on sth. etw. einer Sache (*Dat.*)
nachbilden

(b) (Fashion) vorführen
④*v.i.* (Fashion) als Mannequin/Dressman
arbeiten; (Art) Modell stehen/sitzen

modem /'məʊdem/ *n.* Modem, *der*

moderate ① /'mɒdərət/ *adj.* (a) gemäßigt
⟨*Ansichten*⟩; maßvoll ⟨*Trinker, Forderungen*⟩
(b) mittler... ⟨*Größe, Menge, Wert*⟩;
(reasonable) angemessen ⟨*Preis, Summe*⟩
② /'mɒdərət/ *n.* Gemäßigte, *der/die*
③ /'mɒdəreɪt/ *v.t.* mäßigen
④*v.i.* nachlassen

moderately /'mɒdərətlɪ/ *adv.*
einigermaßen; mäßig ⟨*begeistert, groß,
begabt*⟩

moderation /mɒdə'reɪʃn/ *n.* Mäßigkeit,
die; in ~: mit Maßen

modern /'mɒdn/ *adj.* modern; heutig
⟨*Zeit[alter], Welt, Mensch*⟩; ~ art/music
moderne Kunst/Musik; ~ history neuere
Geschichte; ~ languages neuere Sprachen

modernize /'mɒdənaɪz/ *v.t.* modernisieren

modest /'mɒdɪst/ *adj.* bescheiden; einfach
⟨*Haus, Kleidung*⟩

'modestly *adv.* bescheiden

'modesty *n.* Bescheidenheit, *die*

modification /mɒdɪfɪ'keɪʃn/ *n.*
[Ab]änderung, *die*

modify /'mɒdɪfaɪ/ *v.t.* [ab]ändern

modulate /'mɒdjʊleɪt/ *v.t. & i.* modulieren

modulation /mɒdjʊ'leɪʃn/ *n.* Modulation,
die

module /'mɒdjuːl/ *n.* (a) Bauelement, *das*
(b) (Astronaut.) command ~:
Kommandoeinheit, *die*
(c) (Educ.) Unterrichtseinheit, *die*

mohair /'məʊheə(r)/ *n.* Mohair, *der*

moist /mɔɪst/ *adj.* feucht (with von)

moisten /'mɔɪsn/ *v.t.* anfeuchten

moisture /'mɔɪstʃə(r)/ *n.* Feuchtigkeit, *die*

moisturize /'mɔɪstjʊraɪz, 'mɔɪstʃəraɪz/ *v.t.*
befeuchten; ~ the skin der Haut (*Dat.*)
Feuchtigkeit zuführen; ⟨*Creme:*⟩ der Haut
(*Dat.*) Feuchtigkeit verleihen

moisturizer /'mɔɪstʃəraɪzə(r)/,
moisturizing cream /'mɔɪstʃəraɪzɪŋ
kriːm/ *ns.* Feuchtigkeitscreme, *die*

molar /'məʊlə(r)/ *n.* Backenzahn, *der*

molasses /mə'læsɪz/ *n.* Melasse, *die*

mold (Amer.) ▶ MOULD¹, ²

molder, molding, moldy (Amer.)
▶ MOULD-

mole¹ /məʊl/ *n.* (on skin) Leberfleck, *der*

mole² *n.* (animal) Maulwurf, *der*

molecular /mə'lekjʊlə(r)/ *adj.* molekular

molecule /'mɒlɪkjuːl/ *n.* Molekül, *das*

'molehill *n.* Maulwurfshügel, *der*

molest /mə'lest/ *v.t.* belästigen

mollify /'mɒlɪfaɪ/ *v.t.* besänftigen

mollusc, (Amer.) **mollusk** /'mɒləsk/ *n.*
Weichtier, *das*

mollycoddle /ˈmɒlɪkɒdl/ v.t. [ver]hätscheln

molt (Amer.) ▶ MOULT

molten /ˈməʊltn/ adj. geschmolzen

mom /mɒm/ (Amer. coll.) ▶ MUM²

moment /ˈməʊmənt/ n. Augenblick, der; at any ~, (coll.) any ~: jeden Augenblick; one or just a or wait a ~! einen Augenblick!; in a ~ (very soon) sofort; at the ~: im Augenblick; the ~ of truth die Stunde der Wahrheit

momentarily /ˈməʊməntərɪlɪ/ adv. einen Augenblick lang

momentary /ˈməʊməntərɪ/ adj. kurz

momentous /məˈmentəs/ adj. (important) bedeutsam; (of consequence) folgenschwer

momentum /məˈmentəm/ n. Schwung, der

Mon. abbr. = **Monday** Mo.

monarch /ˈmɒnək/ n. Monarch, der/ Monarchin, die

'monarchy n. Monarchie, die

monastery /ˈmɒnəstrɪ/ n. Kloster, das

monastic /məˈnæstɪk/ adj. mönchisch

Monday /ˈmʌndeɪ, ˈmʌndɪ/ n. Montag, der; see also FRIDAY

monetary /ˈmʌnɪtərɪ/ adj. (a) (of currency) monetär; Währungs‹politik, -system›; ~ union Währungsunion, die (b) (of money) finanziell

money /ˈmʌnɪ/ n. Geld, das; make ~ ‹Person:› [viel] Geld verdienen; ‹Geschäft:› etwas einbringen; for 'my ~: wenn man mich fragt

money: ~ **bag** n. Geldsack, der; ~ **belt** n. Geldgürtel, der; ~ **box** n. Sparbüchse, die; ~**making** adj. Gewinn bringend; ~ **order** n. Postanweisung, die

Mongolia /mɒŋˈɡəʊlɪə/ pr. n. Mongolei, die

Mongolian /mɒŋˈɡəʊlɪən/ 1 adj. mongolisch; **sb. is** ~: jmd. ist Mongole/ Mongolin 2 n. (person) Mongole, der/Mongolin, die

mongrel /ˈmʌŋɡrəl/ n. ~ [dog] Promenadenmischung, die

monitor /ˈmɒnɪtə(r)/ 1 n. (a) (Sch.) Aufsichtsschüler, der/-schülerin, die (b) (Med., Telev., Comp.) Monitor, der 2 v.t. beobachten ‹Wetter, Flugzeug›; abhören ‹Sendung, Telefongespräch›

monk /mʌŋk/ n. Mönch, der

monkey /ˈmʌŋkɪ/ n. Affe, der

monkey: ~ **business** n. (coll.: mischief) Schabernack, der; ~ **nut** n. Erdnuss, die; ~ **wrench** n. Universalschraubenschlüssel, der

mono /ˈmɒnəʊ/ adj. Mono‹platte[nspieler], -wiedergabe›

monochrome /ˈmɒnəkrəʊm/ adj. monochrom (fachspr.); einfarbig; Schwarzweiß- (Ferns.)

monocle /ˈmɒnəkl/ n. Monokel, das

monogamous /məˈnɒɡəməs/ adj. monogam

monogamy /məˈnɒɡəmɪ/ n. Monogamie, die; Einehe, die

monogram /ˈmɒnəɡræm/ n. Monogramm, das

monogrammed /ˈmɒnəɡræmd/ adj. monogrammiert; ‹Taschentuch usw.:› mit Monogramm

monologue (Amer.: **monolog**) /ˈmɒnəlɒɡ/ n. Monolog, der

monopolize /məˈnɒpəlaɪz/ v.t. (Econ.) monopolisieren; (fig.) mit Beschlag belegen; ~ **the conversation** den/die anderen nicht zu Wort kommen lassen

monopoly /məˈnɒpəlɪ/ n. (a) (Econ.) Monopol, das (of auf + Akk.) (b) (exclusive possession) alleiniger Besitz

monotone /ˈmɒnətəʊn/ n. gleich bleibender Ton

monotonous /məˈnɒtənəs/ adj., **mo'notonously** adv. eintönig

monotony /məˈnɒtənɪ/ n. Eintönigkeit, die

monsoon /mɒnˈsuːn/ n. Monsun, der

monster /ˈmɒnstə(r)/ n. (a) (creature) Ungeheuer, das; (huge thing) Ungetüm, das (b) (inhuman person) Unmensch, der

monstrosity /mɒnˈstrɒsɪtɪ/ n. (a) (outrageous thing) Ungeheuerlichkeit, die (b) (hideous building etc.) Ungetüm, das

monstrous /ˈmɒnstrəs/ adj. (a) (huge) riesig (b) (outrageous) ungeheuerlich (c) (atrocious) scheußlich

month /mʌnθ/ n. Monat, der; **for a** ~/~s einen Monat [lang]/monatelang

'monthly 1 adj. monatlich; Monats‹einkommen, -gehalt› 2 adv. einmal im Monat 3 n. Monatsschrift, die

monument /ˈmɒnjʊmənt/ n. Denkmal, das

monumental /mɒnjʊˈmentl/ adj. (a) (massive) monumental (b) gewaltig ‹Misserfolg, Irrtum›

moo /muː/ 1 n. Muhen, das 2 v.i. muhen

mooch /muːtʃ/ v.i. (coll.) ~ **about** or **around**/ **along** herumschleichen (ugs.)/zockeln (ugs.)

mood /muːd/ n. (a) Stimmung, die; **be in a good/bad** ~: [bei] guter/schlechter Laune sein; **I'm not in the** ~: ich hab keine Lust dazu (b) (bad ~) Verstimmung, die

'moody adj. (a) (sullen) missmutig (b) (subject to moods) launenhaft

moon /muːn/ n. Mond, der

moon: ~**beam** n. Mondstrahl, der; ~**light** 1 n. Mondlicht, das; Mondschein, der; 2 v.i. (coll.) nebenberuflich abends arbeiten; ~**lit** adj. mondbeschienen (geh.)

moor¹ /mʊə(r), mɔː(r)/ n. (Geog.) [Hoch]moor, das

moor² v.t. & i. festmachen; vertäuen

'moorhen n. [Grünfüßiges] Teichhuhn

'**mooring** n. ~[s] Anlegestelle, *die*

'**mooring post** n. Pfahl, *der;*
≈ Duckdalben, *der*

moorland /'mʊələnd, 'mɔːlənd/ n.
Moorland, *das*

moose /muːs/ n., pl. *same* Amerikanischer
Elch

moot /muːt/ ①adj. umstritten; offen
⟨*Frage*⟩; strittig ⟨*Punkt*⟩
②v.t. erörtern ⟨*Frage, Punkt*⟩

mop /mɒp/ ①n. (a) Mopp, *der*
(b) ~ [of hair] Wuschelkopf, *der*
②v.t., -pp- moppen ⟨*Fußboden*⟩; (wipe)
abwischen ⟨*Träne, Schweiß, Stirn*⟩
∎ **mop 'up** v.t. aufwischen

mope /məʊp/ v.i. Trübsal blasen

moped /'məʊped/ n. Moped, *das*

moral /'mɒrl/ ①adj. (a) moralisch; sittlich
⟨*Wert*⟩; Moral⟨*begriff, -prinzip*⟩
(b) (virtuous) moralisch ⟨*Leben, Person*⟩
②n. (a) Moral, *die*
(b) in pl. (habits) Moral, *die*

morale /məˈrɑːl/ Moral, *die;* low/high ~:
schlechte/gute Moral

mo'rale-booster n. be a or act as a ~ for
sb. jds. Moral heben od. stärken

morality /məˈrælɪtɪ/ n. Moral, *die*

moral sup'port n. moralische
Unterstützung

morbid /'mɔːbɪd/ adj. krankhaft; morbid
(geh.) ⟨*Faszination, Neigung*⟩

more /mɔː(r)/ ①adj. mehr; any or some ~
(apples, books, etc.) noch welche; any or some
~ (tea, paper, etc.) noch etwas; any or some
~ **apples/tea** noch Äpfel/Tee; I haven't any
~ [apples/tea] ich habe keine [Äpfel]/keinen
[Tee] mehr; ~ **and** ~: immer mehr
②n. mehr; ~ **and** ~: immer mehr; **six or**
~: mindestens sechs
③adv. (a) mehr; ~ **interesting**
interessanter
(b) (nearer, rather) eher
(c) (again) wieder; **no** ~, **not any** ~: nicht
mehr; **once** ~: noch einmal
(d) ~ **and** ~: immer mehr; ~ **and** ~ **absurd**
immer absurder
(e) ~ **or less** (fairly) mehr oder weniger;
(approximately) annähernd

moreish /'mɔːrɪʃ/ adj. (coll.) lecker

more'over adv. und außerdem

morgue /mɔːg/ ▶ MORTUARY

morning /'mɔːnɪŋ/ n. Morgen, *der;* (not
afternoon) Vormittag, *der; attrib.* morgendlich;
Morgen-; **this** ~: heute Morgen; **tomorrow**
~, (coll.) **in the** ~: morgen früh; [early] **in the**
~: am [frühen] Morgen; (regularly)
[früh]morgens

morning: ~ '**after** n. ~-'**after** [feeling]
(coll.: hangover) Katzenjammer, *der;* ~-'**after**
pill n. Pille [für den Morgen] danach;
~ '**star** n. Morgenstern, *der*

Moroccan /məˈrɒkən/ ①adj.
marokkanisch; **sb. is** ~: jmd. ist
Marokkaner/Marokkanerin
②n. Marokkaner, *der*/Marokkanerin, *die*

Morocco /məˈrɒkəʊ/ pr. n. Marokko (*das*)

moron /'mɔːrɒn/ n. (coll.) Schwachkopf, *der*
(ugs.)

morose /məˈrəʊs/ adj. verdrießlich

morphine /'mɔːfiːn/ n. Morphin, *das*

Morse [code] /mɔːs ('kəʊd)/ n.
Morsealphabet, *das*

morsel /'mɔːsl/ n. (of food) Bissen, *der*

mortal /'mɔːtl/ ①adj. (a) sterblich
(b) (fatal) tödlich (**to** für)
②n. Sterbliche, *der*/*die*

mortality /mɔːˈtælɪtɪ/ n. (a) Sterblichkeit,
die
(b) ~ [rate] Sterblichkeitsrate, *die*

'**mortally** adv. tödlich

mortar /'mɔːtə(r)/ n. (a) Mörtel, *der*
(b) (vessel) Mörser, *der*
(c) (weapon) Minenwerfer, *der;* Mörser, *der*

mortgage /'mɔːgɪdʒ/ ①n. Hypothek, *die*
②v.t. mit einer Hypothek belasten

mortuary /'mɔːtjʊərɪ/ n. (building)
Leichenschauhaus, *das;* (room)
Leichenkammer, *die*

mosaic /məʊˈzeɪɪk/ n. Mosaik, *das*

Moscow /'mɒskəʊ/ pr. n. Moskau (*das*)

Moselle /məʊˈzel/ pr. n. Mosel, *die*

Moslem /'mɒzləm/ n. ▶ MUSLIM

mosque /mɒsk/ n. Moschee, *die*

mosquito /mɒsˈkiːtəʊ/ n., pl. ~es
Stechmücke, *die;* (in tropics) Moskito, *der*

mos'quito net n. Moskitonetz, *das*

moss /mɒs/ n. Moos, *das*

'**mossy** adj. moosig

most /məʊst/ ①adj. (in number, majority of)
die meisten; (in amount) meist…; **make the**
~ **mistakes/the** ~ **noise** die meisten Fehler/
den größten Lärm machen; **for the** ~ **part**
größtenteils
②n. (a) (greatest amount) **the** ~ **it will cost is**
£10 es wird höchstens zehn Pfund kosten;
pay the ~: am meisten bezahlen
(b) (greater part) ~ **of the girls** die meisten
Mädchen; ~ **of his friends** die meisten
seiner Freunde; ~ **of the poem** der größte
Teil des Gedichts; ~ **of the time** die meiste
Zeit
(c) (on ~ occasions) meistens
③adv. (a) am meisten; **the** ~ **interesting**
book das interessanteste Buch; ~ **often** am
häufigsten
(b) (exceedingly) äußerst

'**mostly** adv. (most of the time) meistens;
(mainly) größtenteils

MOT ▶ MOT TEST

motel /məʊˈtel/ n. Motel, *das*

moth /mɒθ/ n. Nachtfalter, *der;* (in clothes)
Motte, *die*

moth: ∼**ball** n. Mottenkugel, *die;*
∼**-eaten** adj. von Motten zerfressen

mother /'mʌðə(r)/ [1] n. Mutter, *die*
[2] v.t. (over-protect) bemuttern

'**motherboard** n. (Comp.) Mutterplatine, *die*

'**motherhood** n. Mutterschaft, *die*

Mothering Sunday /'mʌðərɪŋ sʌndɪ/
(Brit. Eccl.) ▶ MOTHER'S DAY

mother: ∼**-in-law** n., pl. ∼**s-in-law**
Schwiegermutter, *die;* ∼**land** n. Vaterland,
das

motherly /'mʌðəlɪ/ adj. mütterlich; ∼ **love**
Mutterliebe, *die*

mother: ∼**-of-'pearl** n. Perlmutt, *das;*
M∼'s Day n. Muttertag, *der;* ∼ '**tongue**
n. Muttersprache, *die*

moth: ∼ **hole** n. Mottenloch, *das;* ∼**proof**
adj. mottenfest

motif /məʊ'tiːf/ n. Motiv, *das*

motion /'məʊʃn/ [1] n. (a) Bewegung, *die*
(b) (proposal) Antrag, *der*
[2] v.t. & i. ∼ [to] sb. to do sth. jmdm.
bedeuten (geh.), etw. zu tun

'**motionless** adj. bewegungslos

motivate /'məʊtɪveɪt/ v.t. motivieren

motivation /məʊtɪ'veɪʃn/ n. Motivation,
die

motive /'məʊtɪv/ n. Beweggrund, *der;* **the**
∼ **for the crime** das Tatmotiv

motley /'mɒtlɪ/ adj. bunt gemischt

motor /'məʊtə(r)/ [1] n. (a) Motor, *der*
(b) (Brit.: car) Auto, *das*
[2] adj. Motor⟨mäher, -jacht usw.⟩
[3] v.i. (Brit.) [mit dem Auto] fahren

motor: ∼**bike** n. (coll.) Motorrad, *das;*
∼ **boat** n. Motorboot, *das*

motorcade /'məʊtəkeɪd/ n. Fahrzeug- od.
Wagenkolonne, *die*

motor: ∼ **car** n. (Brit.) Kraftfahrzeug, *das;*
∼ **cycle** n. Motorrad, *das;* ∼**cyclist** n.
Motorradfahrer, *der/*-fahrerin, *die*

'**motoring** n. (Brit.) Autofahren, *das*

'**motorist** n. Autofahrer, *der/*-fahrerin, *die*

motorize /'məʊtəraɪz/ v.t. motorisieren

motor: ∼ **racing** n. Autorennsport, *der;*
∼ **show** n. Auto[mobil]ausstellung, *die;*
∼ **vehicle** n. Kraftfahrzeug, *das;* ∼**way**
n. (Brit.) Autobahn, *die*

MOT test n. (Brit.) ≈ TÜV, *der*

mottled /'mɒtld/ adj. gesprenkelt

motto /'mɒtəʊ/ n., pl. ∼**es** Motto, *das*

mould¹ /məʊld/ [1] n. (hollow container) Form,
die
[2] v.t. formen (**out of, from** aus)·

mould² n. (Bot.) Schimmel, *der*

moulder /'məʊldə(r)/ v.i. ∼ [**away**]
[ver]modern

'**moulding** n. (a) Formteil, *das* (**of, in** aus);
(Archit.) Zierleiste, *die*
(b) (wooden) Leiste, *die*

'**mouldy** adj. schimmlig; **go** ∼: schimmeln

moult /məʊlt/ v.i. ⟨Vogel:⟩ sich mausern;
⟨Hund, Katze:⟩ sich haaren

mound /maʊnd/ n. (a) (of earth) Hügel, *der*
(b) (heap) Haufen, *der*

mount /maʊnt/ [1] n. (a) M∼ **Vesuvius/**
Everest der Vesuv/der Mount Everest
(b) (animal) Reittier, *das;* (horse) Pferd, *das*
(c) (of picture, photograph) Passepartout, *das*
(d) (for gem) Fassung, *die*
[2] v.t. (a) hinaufsteigen ⟨Treppe⟩; steigen auf
(+ Akk.) ⟨Plattform, Reittier, Fahrzeug⟩
(b) aufziehen ⟨Bild⟩; einfassen ⟨Edelstein
usw.⟩
(c) inszenieren ⟨Stück, Oper⟩; organisieren
⟨Ausstellung⟩; durchführen ⟨Angriff,
Operation⟩
[3] v.i. ∼ [**up**] (increase) steigen (**to** auf + Akk.)

mountain /'maʊntɪn/ n. Berg, *der;* **in the**
∼**s** im Gebirge

mountain: ∼ **bike** n. Mountainbike, *das;*
∼ **chain** n. Gebirgszug, *der*

mountaineer /maʊntɪ'nɪə(r)/ n.
Bergsteiger, *der/*Bergsteigerin, *die*

mountai'neering n. Bergsteigen, *das*

mountainous /'maʊntɪnəs/ adj. (a)
gebirgig
(b) (huge) riesig

mountain: ∼ '**range** n. Gebirgszug, *der;*
∼**side** n. [Berg][ab]hang, *der;* ∼ **top** n.
Berggipfel, *der*

mourn /mɔːn/ [1] v.i. trauern; ∼ **for** or **over**
trauern um ⟨Toten⟩
[2] v.t. betrauern

'**mourner** n. Trauernde, *der/die*

mournful /'mɔːnfl/ adj. klagend ⟨Stimme,
Ton, Schrei⟩; trauervoll (geh.) ⟨Person⟩

'**mourning** n. Trauer, *die;* **be in/go into** ∼:
Trauer tragen/anlegen

mouse /maʊs/ n., pl. **mice** /maɪs/ Maus, *die*

mouse: ∼ **button** n. (Comp.) Maustaste,
die; ∼ **click** n. (Comp.) Mausklick, *der;*
∼ **mat** n. (Comp.) Mauspad, *das;*
∼ **pointer** n. (Comp.) Mauszeiger, *der;*
∼**trap** n. Mausefalle, *die*

mousse /muːs/ n. Mousse, *die*

moustache /mə'stɑːʃ/ n. Schnurrbart, *der*

mousy /'maʊsɪ/ adj. (a) mattbraun ⟨Haar⟩
(b) (timid) scheu

mouth [1] /maʊθ/ n. (a) (of person) Mund,
der; (of animal) Maul, *das;* **with one's** ∼ **open/**
full mit offenem/vollem Mund
(b) (harbour entrance) [Hafen]einfahrt, *die;* (of
tunnel, cave) Eingang, *der;* (of river) Mündung,
die
[2] /maʊð/ v.t. mit Lippenbewegungen sagen

mouthful /'maʊθfʊl/ n. Mundvoll, *der*

mouth: ∼ **organ** n. Mundharmonika, *die;*
∼**piece** n. (a) Mundstück, *das;* (b) (fig.)
Sprachrohr, *das*

movable /'muːvəbl/ adj. beweglich

move /muːv/ [1] n. (a) (change of home)
Umzug, *der*

(b) (action taken) Schritt, *der;* (Footb. etc.) Spielzug, *der*

(c) (turn in game) Zug, *der;* **make a ~**: ziehen; **it's your ~**: du bist am Zug

(d) be on the **~** ⟨*Person:*⟩ unterwegs sein

(e) **make a ~** ⟨do sth.⟩ etwas tun; (coll.: leave) losziehen (ugs.)

(f) **get a ~ on** (coll.) einen Zahn zulegen (ugs.); **get a ~ on!** (coll.) [mach] Tempo! (ugs.)

2 *v.t.* **(a)** (change position of) bewegen; wegräumen ⟨*Hindernis, Schutt*⟩; (transport) befördern; **~ sth. to a new position** etw. an einen neuen Platz bringen; **~ house** umziehen

(b) (in game) ziehen

(c) (affect) bewegen; **~ sb. to tears** jmdn. zu Tränen rühren; **be ~d by sth.** über etw. (*Akk.*) gerührt sein

(d) (prompt) **~ sb. to do sth.** jmdn. dazu bewegen, etw. zu tun

(e) (propose) beantragen

3 *v.i.* **(a)** sich bewegen; (in vehicle) fahren

(b) (in games) ziehen

(c) (do sth.) handeln

(d) (change home) umziehen (**to** nach); **~ into a flat** in eine Wohnung einziehen; **~ out of a flat** aus einer Wohnung ausziehen; **~ to London** nach London ziehen

(e) (change posture or state) sich bewegen; **don't ~!** keine Bewegung!

■ **move a'bout** **1** *v.i.* zugange sein; (travel) unterwegs sein

2 *v.t.* herumräumen

■ **move a'long** **1** *v.i.* **(a)** gehen/fahren

(b) **~ along, please!** gehen/fahren Sie bitte weiter!

2 *v.t.* zum Weitergehen/-fahren auffordern

■ **move 'in** **1** *v.i.* **(a)** (to home etc.) einziehen

(b) **~ in on** ⟨*Truppen, Polizeikräfte:*⟩ vorrücken gegen

2 *v.t.* hineinbringen

■ **move 'off** *v.i.* sich in Bewegung setzen

■ **move 'on** **1** *v.i.* weitergehen/-fahren; **~ on to another question** (fig.) zu einer anderen Frage übergehen

2 *v.t.* zum Weitergehen/-fahren auffordern

■ **move 'out** *v.t.* ausziehen (of aus)

■ **move 'over** *v.i.* rücken

■ **move 'up** *v.i.* **(a)** rücken

(b) (in queue, hierarchy) aufrücken

'**movement** *n.* **(a)** Bewegung, *die;* (trend, tendency) Tendenz, *die* (**towards** zu)

(b) *in pl.* Aktivitäten *Pl.*

(c) (Mus.) Satz, *der*

movie /'muːvɪ/ *n.* (Amer. coll.) Film, *der;* the **~s** der Film; **go to the ~s** ins Kino gehen

moving /'muːvɪŋ/ *adj.* **(a)** beweglich

(b) (affecting) ergreifend

mow /məʊ/ *v.t., p.p.* **mown** /məʊn/ *or* **mowed** /məʊd/ mähen

■ **mow 'down** *v.t.* (shoot) niedermähen ⟨*Menschen*⟩

'**mower** *n.* Rasenmäher, *der*

mown ▶ MOW

MP *abbr.* = **Member of Parliament**

m.p.g. *abbr.* = **miles per gallon**

m.p.h. *abbr.* = **miles per hour**

MPV *abbr.* = **multi-purpose vehicle**

Mr /'mɪstə(r)/ *n.* Herr; (in an address) Herrn

Mrs /'mɪsɪz/ *n.* Frau

Ms /mɪz/ *n.* Frau

MS *abbr.* (Med.) = **multiple sclerosis** MS

Mt. *abbr.* = **Mount**

much /mʌtʃ/ **1** *adj.,* more /mɔː(r)/, most /məʊst/ viel; **too ~**: zu viel *indekl*

2 *n.* vieles; **~ of the day** der Großteil des Tages; **not be ~ to look at** nicht sehr ansehnlich sein

3 *adv.,* more, most **(a)** viel ⟨*besser, schöner usw.*⟩; **~ more lively/attractive** viel lebhafter/attraktiver

(b) mit Abstand ⟨*der/die/das Beste, Klügste usw.*⟩

(c) (greatly) sehr ⟨*lieben, genießen usw.*⟩; (for **~** of the time) viel ⟨*lesen, spielen usw.*⟩; (often) oft ⟨*sehen, besuchen usw.*⟩

(d) [pretty *or* very] **~ the same** fast [genau] der-/die-/dasselbe

muck /mʌk/ *n.* **(a)** (coll.: something disgusting) Dreck, *der* (ugs.)

(b) (coll.: nonsense) Mist, *der* (ugs.)

■ **muck a'bout, muck a'round** (Brit. coll.) *v.i.* **(a)** herumalbern (ugs.)

(b) (tinker) herumfummeln (**with** an + *Dat.*)

■ **muck 'in** *v.i.* (coll.) mit anpacken (**with** bei)

■ **muck 'up** *v.t.* **(a)** (Brit. coll.: bungle) vermurksen (ugs.)

(b) (make dirty) dreckig machen (ugs.)

(c) (coll.: spoil) vermasseln (salopp)

'**mucky** *adj.* dreckig (ugs.)

mucus /'mjuːkəs/ *n.* Schleim, *der*

mud /mʌd/ *n.* Schlamm, *der*

muddle /'mʌdl/ **1** *n.* Durcheinander, *das*

2 *v.t.* **~ [up]** durcheinander bringen; **~ up** (mix up) verwechseln (**with** mit)

■ **muddle a'long, muddle 'on** *v.i.* vor sich (*Akk.*) hin wursteln (ugs.)

■ **muddle 'through** *v.i.* sich durchwursteln (ugs.)

muddy /'mʌdɪ/ *adj.* schlammig; **get** *or* **become ~**: verschlammen

'**mudguard** *n.* Schutzblech, *das;* (of car) Kotflügel, *der*

muesli /'mjuːzlɪ/ *n.* Müsli, *das*

muff¹ /mʌf/ *n.* Muff, *der*

muff² *v.t.* verpatzen (ugs.)

muffin /'mʌfɪn/ *n.* Muffin, *der*

muffle /'mʌfl/ *v.t.* **(a)** (envelop) **~ [up]** einhüllen

(b) dämpfen ⟨*Geräusch*⟩

'**muffler** *n.* **(a)** (wrap, scarf) Schal, *der*

(b) (Amer. Motor Veh.) Schalldämpfer, *der*

mug /mʌg/ **1** *n.* **(a)** Becher, *der* (meist mit Henkel); (for beer etc.) Krug, *der*

(b) (coll.: face, mouth) Visage, *die* (salopp)   ⋯⋗

(c) (Brit. coll.: gullible person) Trottel, *der* (ugs.)
② *v.t.*, **-gg-** (rob) überfallen und berauben

'mugger *n.* Straßenräuber, *der*/-räuberin, *die*

'mugging *n.* Straßenraub, *der*

muggy /'mʌgɪ/ *adj.* schwül

mule /mjuːl/ *n.* Maultier, *das*

multi: ~**coloured** (Brit.; Amer.: ~**colored**) *adj.* mehrfarbig; bunt ⟨*Stoff, Kleid*⟩; ~**'cultural** *adj.* multikulturell; ~**function button** *n.* Multifunktionstaste, *die;* ~**media** *n. sing.* Multimedia, *das;* ~**millio'naire** *n.* Multimillionär, *der*/-millionärin, *die;* ~**national** /mʌltɪ'næʃənl/ ① *adj.* multinational; ② *n.* multinationaler Konzern, *der;* Multi, *der* (ugs.)

multiple /'mʌltɪpl/ *adj.* mehrfach

multiple: ~**'choice** *adj.* Multiplechoice⟨*test, -frage*⟩; ~ **'store** *n.* (Brit.) Kettenladen, *der*

multiplication /mʌltɪplɪ'keɪʃn/ *n.* Multiplikation, *die*

multiply /'mʌltɪplaɪ/ ① *v.t.* multiplizieren, malnehmen **(by** mit) ② *v.i.* sich vermehren

multi: ~**-purpose** *adj.* Mehrzweck-; ~**-purpose 'vehicle** *n.* Großraumlimousine, *die;* '~**-storey** *adj.* mehrstöckig; mehrgeschossig; ~**-storey car park/block of flats** Parkhaus/Wohnhochhaus, *das;* ~**track** *adj.* mehrspurig; Mehrspur⟨*aufnahme, -ton, -tonbandgerät*⟩

multitude /'mʌltɪtjuːd/ *n.* (crowd) Menge, *die;* (great number) Vielzahl, *die*

mum¹ /mʌm/ (coll.) ① *int.* ~'**s the word** nicht weitersagen! ② *adj.* **keep** ~: den Mund halten (ugs.)

mum² *n.* (Brit. coll.: mother) Mama, *die* (fam.)

mumble /'mʌmbl/ *v.i. & t.* nuscheln (ugs.)

mummy¹ *n.* (Brit. coll.: mother) Mutti, *die* (fam.)

mummy² /'mʌmɪ/ *n.* Mumie, *die*

mumps /mʌmps/ *n.* Mumps, *der*

munch /mʌntʃ/ *v.t. & i.* ~ **[one's food]** mampfen (salopp)

mundane /mʌn'deɪn/ *adj.* (a) (dull) banal (b) (worldly) weltlich

Munich /'mjuːnɪk/ *pr. n.* München (*das*)

municipal /mjʊ'nɪsɪpl/ *adj.* kommunal; Kommunal⟨*politik, -verwaltung*⟩

munition /mjuː'nɪʃn/ *n., usu. in pl.* Kriegsmaterial, *das;* ~**[s] factory** Rüstungsbetrieb, *der*

mural /'mjʊərl/ *n.* Wandbild, *das*

murder /'mɜːdə(r)/ ① *n.* Mord, *der* **(of** an + *Dat.*) ② *v.t.* ermorden

'murderer *n.* Mörder, *der*/Mörderin, *die*

murderess /'mɜːdərɪs/ *n.* Mörderin, *die*

murderous /'mɜːdərəs/ *adj.* tödlich; Mord⟨*absicht, -drohung*⟩; mörderisch (ugs.) ⟨*Kampf*⟩

murk /mɜːk/ *n.* Dunkelheit, *die*

'murky *adj.* (a) (dark) düster (b) (dirty) schmutzig-trüb ⟨*Wasser*⟩

murmur /'mɜːmə(r)/ ① *n.* (a) (subdued sound) Rauschen, *das* (b) (expression of discontent) Murren, *das* (c) (soft speech) Murmeln, *das* ② *v.t.* murmeln ③ *v.i.* ⟨*Person:*⟩ murmeln; (complain) murren

muscle /'mʌsl/ *n.* Muskel, *der*

muscular /'mʌskjʊlə(r)/ *adj.* (a) (Anat.) Muskel- (b) (strong) muskulös

muse /mjuːz/ (literary) *v.i.* [nach]sinnen (geh.) **(on,** over über + *Akk.*)

museum /mjuː'ziːəm/ *n.* Museum, *das*

mush /mʌʃ/ *n.* Brei, *der*

mushroom /'mʌʃrʊm, 'mʌʃruːm/ ① *n.* Pilz, *der;* (cultivated) Champignon, *der* ② *v.i.* wie Pilze aus dem Boden schießen

'mushroom cloud *n.* Rauchpilz, *der;* (after nuclear explosion) Atompilz, *der*

'mushy *adj.* breiig

music /'mjuːzɪk/ *n.* (a) Musik, *die;* **piece of** ~: Musikstück, *das;* **set sth. to** ~: etw. vertonen (b) (score) Noten *Pl.*

musical /'mjuːzɪkl/ ① *adj.* musikalisch; Musik⟨*instrument, -verständnis, -notation, -abend*⟩ ② *n.* Musical, *das*

'musical box *n.* (Brit.) Spieldose, *die*

musician /mjuː'zɪʃn/ *n.* Musiker, *der*/Musikerin, *die*

music: ~ **lesson** *n.* Musikstunde, *die;* ~ **room** *n.* Musiksaal, *der;* ~ **stand** *n.* Notenständer, *der;* ~ **teacher** *n.* Musiklehrer, *der*/-lehrerin, *die;* ~ **video** *n.* Musikvideo, *das*

Muslim /'mʊslɪm, 'mʌzlɪm/ ① *adj.* moslemisch ② *n.* Moslem, *der*/Moslime, *die*

muslin /'mʌzlɪn/ *n.* Musselin, *der*

mussel /'mʌsl/ *n.* Muschel, *die*

must /məst, stressed mʌst/ ① *v. aux., only in pres., neg.* (coll.) **mustn't** /'mʌsnt/ müssen; *with neg.* dürfen ② *n.* (coll.) Muss, *das*

mustache ▶ MOUSTACHE

mustard /'mʌstəd/ *n.* Senf, *der*

muster /'mʌstə(r)/ ① *n.* **pass** ~: akzeptabel sein ② *v.t.* versammeln; (Mil., Naut.) [zum Appell] antreten lassen; (fig.) zusammennehmen ⟨*Kraft, Mut, Verstand*⟩ ③ *v.i.* sich [ver]sammeln

■ **muster 'up** *v.t.* aufbringen

mustn't /'mʌsnt/ (coll.) = **must not;** ▶ MUST 1

musty /'mʌstɪ/ *adj.* muffig

mutant /'mjuːtənt/ ① *adj.* mutiert
② *n.* Mutante, *die*
mutation /mjuːˈteɪʃn/ *n.* Mutation, *die*
mute /mjuːt/ ① *adj.* stumm
② *n.* Stumme, *der/die*
'muted *adj.* gedämpft
mutilate /'mjuːtɪleɪt/ *v.t.* verstümmeln
mutilation /mjuːtɪˈleɪʃn/ *n.*
Verstümmelung, *die*
mutinous /'mjuːtɪnəs/ *adj.* meuternd
mutiny /'mjuːtɪnɪ/ ① *n.* Meuterei, *die*
② *v.i.* meutern
mutter /'mʌtə(r)/ *v.i. & t.* murmeln
'muttering *n.* Gemurmel, *das*
mutton /'mʌtn/ *n.* Hammelfleisch, *das*
mutual /'mjuːtjʊəl/ *adj.* **(a)** gegenseitig
(b) (coll.: shared) gemeinsam
'mutually *adv.* **(a)** gegenseitig; **be
~ exclusive** sich [gegenseitig] ausschließen
(b) (in common) gemeinsam
muzak /'mjuːzæk/ *n.* (often derog.)
Hintergrundmusik, *die*
muzzle /'mʌzl/ ① *n.* **(a)** (of dog) Schnauze,
die; (of horse, cattle) Maul, *das*
(b) (of gun) Mündung, *die*
(c) (put over animal's mouth) Maulkorb, *der*
② *v.t.* **(a)** einen Maulkorb anlegen (+ *Dat.*)
⟨*Hund*⟩
(b) (fig.) mundtot machen (ugs.) (+ *Dat.*)
muzzy /'mʌzɪ/ *adj.* verschwommen; **feel ~:**
ein dumpfes Gefühl haben
MW *abbr.* (Radio) = **medium wave** MW

my /maɪ/ *poss. pron. attrib.* mein; **my[, my]!,
[my] oh my!** [ach du] meine Güte! (ugs.)
myalgic encephalomyelitis
/maɪældʒɪk ensefələʊmaɪəˈlaɪtɪs/ *n.* (Med.)
myalgische Enzephalomyelitis
myopia /maɪˈɒpɪə/ *n.* Kurzsichtigkeit, *die*
(auch fig.)
myopic /maɪˈɒpɪk/ *adj.* kurzsichtig (auch
fig.)
myself /maɪˈself/ *pron.* **(a)** *emphat.* selbst; **I
thought so ~:** das habe ich auch gedacht
(b) *refl.* mich/mir. See also HERSELF
mysterious /mɪˈstɪərɪəs/ *adj.* rätselhaft;
geheimnisvoll ⟨*Fremder, Orient*⟩
my'steriously *adv.* auf rätselhafte Weise;
geheimnisvoll ⟨*lächeln usw.*⟩
mystery /'mɪstərɪ/ *n.* **(a)** Rätsel, *das*
(b) (secrecy) Geheimnis, *das*
mystery: ~ tour *n.* Fahrt ins Blaue (ugs.);
~ writer Kriminalschriftsteller, *der/*
-schriftstellerin, *die*
mystic /'mɪstɪk/ ① *adj.* mystisch
② *n.* Mystiker, *der/*Mystikerin, *die*
mystical /'mɪstɪkl/ *adj.* mystisch
mysticism /'mɪstɪsɪzm/ *n.* Mystik, *die*
mystify /'mɪstɪfaɪ/ *v.t.* verwirren
myth /mɪθ/ *n.* Mythos, *der*
mythical /'mɪθɪkl/ *adj.* **(a)** (based on myth)
mythisch
(b) (invented) fiktiv
mythological /mɪθəˈlɒdʒɪkl/ *adj.*
mythologisch
mythology /mɪˈθɒlədʒɪ/ *n.* Mythologie, *die*

Nn

N, n /en/ *n.* N, n, *das*
N. *abbr.* **(a)** = **north** N
(b) = **northern** n.
NAAFI /'næfɪ/ *abbr.* (Brit.) **Navy, Army and
Air Force Institutes** *Kaufhaus für Angehörige
der britischen Truppen*
nab /næb/ *v.t.,* **-bb-** (coll.) **(a)** (arrest)
schnappen (ugs.)
(b) (seize) sich (*Dat.*) schnappen
nag /næg/ *v.i. & t.* **-gg-:** **~ [at]** sb. an jmdm.
herumnörgeln; **~ [at]** sb. **to do** sth. jmdm.
zusetzen (ugs.), dass er etw. tut
'nagging ① *adj.* (persistent) quälend;
bohrend ⟨*Schmerz*⟩
② *n.* Genörgel, *das*
nail /neɪl/ ① *n.* Nagel, *der;* **hit the ~ on the
head** (fig.) den Nagel auf den Kopf treffen
(ugs.)
② *v.t.* nageln (**to** an + *Akk.*)

■ **nail 'down** *v.t.* festnageln; zunageln
⟨*Kiste*⟩

nail: ~ brush *n.* Nagelbürste, *die;*
~ clippers *n. pl.* [pair of] **~ clippers**
Nagelknipser, *der;* **~ file** *n.* Nagelfeile, *die;*
~ polish *n.* Nagellack, *der;* **~ polish
remover** Nagellackentferner, *der;*
~ scissors *n. pl.* [pair of] **~ scissors**
Nagelschere, *die;* **~ varnish** (Brit.)
▶ ~ POLISH

naive, naïve /naɪˈiːv/ *adj.,* **na'ively,
na'ïvely** *adv.* naiv
naked /'neɪkɪd/ *adj.* nackt; **visible to** *or*
with the ~ eye mit bloßem Auge zu
erkennen
'nakedness *n.* Nacktheit, *die*
name /neɪm/ ① *n.* **(a)** Name, *der;* **what's
your ~/the ~ of this place?** wie heißt du/
dieser Ort?; **my ~ is Jack** ich heiße Jack; ····✦

last ~: Nachname, *der;* **by ~**: namentlich
⟨*erwähnen, aufrufen usw.*⟩; **know sb. by ~**:
jmdn. mit Namen kennen
(b) (reputation) Ruf, *der;* **make a ~ for oneself**
sich (*Dat.*) einen Namen machen
(c) call sb. ~s jmdn. beschimpfen
② *v.t.* **(a)** (give ~ to) einen Namen geben
(+ *Dat.*); **~ sb.** John jmdn. John nennen;
~ sb./sth. after *or* (Amer.) **for sb.** jmdn./etw.
nach jmdm. benennen; **be ~d John** John
heißen; **a man ~d Smith** ein Mann namens
Smith
(b) (call by right ~) benennen
(c) (nominate) **~ sb. [as] sth.** jmdn. zu etw.
ernennen
'name-drop *v.i.* [scheinbar beiläufig]
bekannte Namen fallen lassen
'nameless *adj.* namenlos
'namely *adv.* nämlich
'namesake *n.* Namensvetter, *der*/
-schwester, *die*
nanny /'nænɪ/ *n.* (Brit.) Kindermädchen, *das*
nanny: ~ goat *n.* Ziege, *die;* **~ 'state** *n.*
(derog.) Versorgungsstaat, *der*
nap /næp/ **①** *n.* Nickerchen, *das* (fam.); **have
a ~**: ein Nickerchen halten
② *v.i.,* **-pp-** dösen (ugs.); **catch sb. ~ping** (fig.)
jmdn. überrumpeln
nape /neɪp/ *n.* **~ [of the neck]** Nacken, *der;*
Genick, *das*
napkin /'næpkɪn/ *n.* Serviette, *die*
Naples /'neɪplz/ *pr. n.* Neapel (*das*)
nappy /'næpɪ/ *n.* (Brit.) Windel, *die*
narcissistic /nɑːsɪ'sɪstɪk/ *adj.* narzisstisch
narcissus /nɑː'sɪsəs/ *n., pl.* **narcissi**
/nɑː'sɪsaɪ/ *or* **~es** Narzisse, *die*
narcotic /nɑː'kɒtɪk/ **①** *n.* **(a)** (drug)
Rauschgift, *das*
(b) (active ingredient) Betäubungsmittel, *das*
② *adj.* **(a)** narkotisch; **~ drug** Rauschgift,
das
(b) (causing drowsiness) einschläfernd
narrate /nə'reɪt/ *v.t.* erzählen;
kommentieren ⟨*Film*⟩
narration /nə'reɪʃn/ *n.* Erzählung, *die*
narrative /'nærətɪv/ **①** *n.* Erzählung, *die*
② *adj.* erzählend
narrator /nə'reɪtə(r)/ *n.* Erzähler, *der*/
Erzählerin, *die*
narrow /'nærəʊ/ **①** *adj.* **(a)** schmal; schmal
geschnitten ⟨*Rock, Hose, Ärmel usw.*⟩; eng
⟨*Tal, Gasse*⟩
(b) (limited) eng; begrenzt ⟨*Auswahl*⟩
(c) knapp ⟨*Sieg, Mehrheit*⟩; **have a ~ escape**
mit knapper Not entkommen (**from** *Dat.*)
(d) (not tolerant) engstirnig
② *v.i.* sich verschmälern; ⟨*Tal:*⟩ sich
verengen
③ *v.t.* verschmälern; (fig.) einengen
■ **narrow 'down** *v.t.* einengen (**to** auf
+ *Akk.*)
narrow-'minded *adj.* engstirnig
nasal /'neɪzl/ *adj.* **(a)** (Anat.) Nasen-

(b) näselnd; **speak in a ~ voice** näseln
nastily /'nɑːstɪlɪ/ *adv.* **(a)** (unpleasantly)
scheußlich
(b) (ill-naturedly) gemein; **behave ~**: hässlich
sein
nasty /'nɑːstɪ/ *adj.* **(a)** (unpleasant) scheußlich
⟨*Geruch, Geschmack*⟩; gemein ⟨*Trick,
Person*⟩; hässlich ⟨*Angewohnheit*⟩; **that was a
~ thing to say/do** das war gemein
(b) (ill-natured) böse; **be ~ to sb.** hässlich zu
jmdm. sein
(c) (serious) übel; schlimm ⟨*Krankheit,
Husten, Verletzung*⟩; **she had a ~ fall** sie ist
übel gefallen
nation /'neɪʃn/ *n.* Nation, *die;* (people) Volk,
das
national /'næʃənl/ **①** *adj.* national;
National⟨*flagge, -held, -theater, -gericht,
-charakter*⟩; Staats⟨*sicherheit, -religion*⟩;
überregional ⟨*Rundfunkstation, Zeitung*⟩;
landesweit ⟨*Streik*⟩
② *n.* (citizen) Staatsbürger, *der*/-bürgerin, *die;*
foreign ~: Ausländer, *der*/Ausländerin, *die*
national: ~ 'anthem *n.* Nationalhymne,
die; **~ call** *n.* (Brit. Teleph.) Inlandsgespräch,
das; **~ 'costume** *n.* Nationaltracht, *die;*
N~ 'Health [Service] *n.* (Brit.)
staatlicher Gesundheitsdienst; **N~ Health
doctor/patient/spectacles** ≈ Kassenarzt, *der*/
-patient, *der*/-brille, *die;* **N~ In'surance**
n. (Brit.) Sozialversicherung, *die*
nationalism /'næʃənəlɪzm/ *n.*
Nationalismus, *der*
nationalist /'næʃənəlɪst/ **①** *n.* Nationalist,
der/Nationalistin, *die*
② *adj.* nationalistisch
nationality /næʃə'nælɪtɪ/ *n.*
Staatsangehörigkeit, *die;* **what's his ~?**
welche Staatsangehörigkeit hat er?
nationalization /næʃənəlaɪ'zeɪʃn/ *n.*
Verstaatlichung, *die*
nationalize /'næʃənəlaɪz/ *v.t.*
verstaatlichen
'nationally *adv.* landesweit
National: n~ 'park *n.* Nationalpark, *der;*
~ 'Savings *n. pl.* (Brit.)
Staatsschuldverschreibungen *Pl.;* **~ Savings
certificate** Sparkassengutschein, *der;*
öffentlicher Sparbrief; **N~ 'service** *n.*
(Brit.) Wehrdienst, *der;* **do n~ service** seinen
Wehrdienst ableisten; **~ 'Socialist** *n.*
Nationalsozialist, *der*/-sozialistin, *die; attrib.*
nationalsozialistisch; **~ Vo'cational
Qualification** *n.* (Brit.) *staatliches
Berufsausbildungsprogramm*
native /'neɪtɪv/ **①** *n.* **(a)** (of specified place) **a
~ of Britain** ein gebürtiger Brite/eine
gebürtige Britin
(b) (person born in a place) Eingeborene, *der*/
die
(c) (local inhabitant) Einheimische, *der*/*die*
② *adj.* eingeboren; einheimisch ⟨*Pflanze,
Tier*⟩; **~ inhabitant** Eingeborene/

Einheimische, *der/die;* ∼ **land** Geburts- *od.* Heimatland, *das;* ∼ **language** Muttersprache, *die*

nativity /nə'tɪvɪtɪ/ *n.* **the N**∼ **[of Christ]** die Geburt Christi

na'tivity play *n.* Krippenspiel, *das*

NATO, Nato /'neɪtəʊ/ *abbr.* = **North Atlantic Treaty Organization** NATO, *die*

natter /'nætə(r)/ (Brit. coll.) **1** *v.i.* quatschen (ugs.)
2 *n.* **have a** ∼: quatschen (ugs.)

natural /'nætʃrəl/ *adj.* natürlich; Natur⟨*zustand, -seide, -gewalt*⟩

natural: ∼ **'childbirth** *n.* natürliche Geburt; ∼ **'gas** *n.* Erdgas, *das;* ∼ **'history** *n.* Naturkunde, *die*

naturalism /'nætʃrəlɪzm/ *n.* Naturalismus, *der*

naturalist /'nætʃrəlɪst/ *n.* Naturforscher, *der/*-forscherin, *die*

naturalization /nætʃrəlaɪ'zeɪʃn/ *n.* Einbürgerung, *die*

naturalize /'nætʃrəlaɪz/ *v.t.* einbürgern

'naturally *adv.* **(a)** (by nature) von Natur aus ⟨*blass, fleißig usw.*⟩; (in a true-to-life way) naturgetreu
(b) (of course) natürlich

'naturalness Natürlichkeit, *die*

nature /'neɪtʃə(r)/ *n.* **(a)** Natur, *die*
(b) (essential qualities) Beschaffenheit, *die;* **in the** ∼ **of things** naturgemäß
(c) (kind) Art, *die;* **things of this** ∼: derartiges
(d) (character) Wesen, *das;* **be proud/friendly** *etc.* **by** ∼: ein stolzes/freundliches *usw.* Wesen haben

nature: ∼ **conservation** *n.* Naturschutz, *der;* ∼ **lover** *n.* Naturfreund, *der/*-freundin, *die;* ∼ **reserve** *n.* Naturschutzgebiet, *das;* ∼ **study** *n.* Naturkunde, *die;* ∼ **trail** *n.* Naturlehrpfad, *der*

naturist /'neɪtʃərɪst/ *n.* (nudist) Naturist, *der/*Naturistin, *die;* FKK-Anhänger, *der/* FKK-Anhängerin, *die*

naught /nɔːt/ *n.* (arch./dial.) **come to** ∼: zunichte werden

naughtily /'nɔːtɪlɪ/ *adv.* ungezogen

naughtiness /'nɔːtɪnɪs/ *n.* Ungezogenheit, *die*

naughty /'nɔːtɪ/ *adj.* ungezogen; **you** ∼ **boy/dog** du böser Junge/Hund

nausea /'nɔːzɪə/ *n.* Übelkeit, *die*

nauseate /'nɔːzɪeɪt/ *v.t.* (disgust) anwidern

'nauseating *adj.* (disgusting) widerlich

nauseous /'nɔːzɪəs/ *adj.* **sb. is** *or* **feels** ∼: jmdm. ist übel

nautical /'nɔːtɪkl/ *adj.* nautisch

nautical 'mile *n.* Seemeile, *die*

naval /'neɪvl/ *adj.* Marine-; See⟨*schlacht, -macht, -streitkräfte*⟩; ∼ **ship** Kriegsschiff, *das*

naval: ∼ **base** *n.* Flottenstützpunkt, *der;* ∼ **officer** *n.* Marineoffizier, *der*

nave /neɪv/ *n.* [Mittel]schiff, *das*

navel /'neɪvl/ *n.* Nabel, *der*

navigate /'nævɪgeɪt/ *v.t.* **(a)** navigieren ⟨*Schiff, Flugzeug*⟩
(b) befahren ⟨*Fluss usw.*⟩

navigation /nævɪ'geɪʃn/ *n.* Navigation, *die*

navigator /'nævɪgeɪtə(r)/ *n.* Navigator, *der/*Navigatorin, *die*

navy /'neɪvɪ/ **1** *n.* **(a)** [Kriegs]marine, *die*
(b) ▶ NAVY BLUE
2 *adj* ▶ NAVY-BLUE

navy: ∼ **'blue** *n.* Marineblau, *das;* ∼**-blue** *adj.* marineblau

Nazi /'nɑːtsɪ/ **1** *n.* Nazi, *der*
2 *adj.* nazistisch; Nazi-

NB *abbr.* = **nota bene** NB

NCO *abbr.* = **non-commissioned officer** Uffz.

NE *abbr.* = **north-east** NO

near /nɪə(r)/ **1** *adv.* nah[e]; **stand/live [quite]** ∼: [ganz] in der Nähe stehen/wohnen; **come** *or* **draw** ∼/∼**er** ⟨*Tag, Zeitpunkt:*⟩ nahen/näher rücken; **get** ∼**er together** näher zusammenrücken; ∼ **at hand** in Reichweite (*Dat.*); ⟨*Ort*⟩ ganz in der Nähe; ∼ **to** = 2
2 *prep.* **(a)** (position) nahe an/bei (+ *Dat.*); (fig.) in der Nähe (+ *Gen.*); **keep** ∼ **me** halte dich in meiner Nähe; **it's** ∼ **here** es ist hier in der Nähe
(b) (motion) nahe an (+ *Akk.*); (fig.) in der Nähe (+ *Gen.*); **don't come** ∼ **me** komm mir nicht zu nahe
3 *adj.* **(a)** (in space or time) nahe; **in the** ∼ **future** in nächster Zukunft; **the** ∼**est man** der am nächsten stehende Mann
(b) (in nature) **£30 or** ∼/∼**est offer** 30 Pfund oder nächstbestes Angebot; ∼ **escape** Entkommen mit knapper Not; **that was a** ∼ **miss/thing!** das war knapp!
4 *v.t.* sich nähern (+ *Dat.*); **the building is** ∼**ing completion** das Gebäude steht kurz vor seiner Vollendung
5 *v.i.* ⟨*Zeitpunkt:*⟩ näher rücken

'nearby *adj.* nahe gelegen

'nearly *adv.* fast; **be** ∼ **in tears** den Tränen nahe sein; **it is** ∼ **six o'clock** es ist kurz vor sechs Uhr; **are you** ∼ **ready?** bist du bald fertig?

'nearness *n.* Nähe, *die*

'near-sighted *adj.* (Amer.) kurzsichtig

neat /niːt/ *adj.* **(a)** (tidy) ordentlich
(b) (undiluted) pur
(c) (smart) gepflegt ⟨*Erscheinung, Kleidung*⟩
(d) (deft) geschickt

'neatly *adv.* ▶ NEAT A, C, D: ordentlich; gepflegt; geschickt

'neatness n. ▶ NEAT A, C, D: Ordentlichkeit, *die;* Gepflegtheit, *die;* Geschicktheit, *die*

necessarily /nesɪˈserɪlɪ/ adv. zwangsläufig; **it is not ~ true** es muss nicht [unbedingt] stimmen

necessary /ˈnesɪsərɪ/ ① adj. nötig; notwendig; **do everything ~:** das Nötige od. Notwendige tun

② n. **the necessaries of life** das Lebensnotwendige

necessitate /nɪˈsesɪteɪt/ v.t. erforderlich machen

necessity /nɪˈsesɪtɪ/ n. Notwendigkeit, *die;* **do sth. out of or from ~:** etw. notgedrungen tun; **of ~:** notwendigerweise

neck /nek/ n. **(a)** Hals, *der;* **be a pain in the ~** (coll.) jmdm. auf die Nerven gehen (ugs.); **break one's ~** (fig. coll.) sich den Hals brechen; **~ and ~:** Kopf an Kopf **(b)** (of garment) Kragen, *der*

neck: ~lace /ˈneklɪs/ n. [Hals]kette, *die;* (with jewels) Kollier, *das;* **~line** n. [Hals]ausschnitt, *der;* **~tie** n. Krawatte, *die*

nectar /ˈnektə(r)/ n. Nektar, *der*

née (*Amer.:* **nee**) /neɪ/ adj. geborene

need /niːd/ ① n. **(a)** Notwendigkeit, *die* (**for,** **of** *Gen.*); (demand) Bedarf, *der* (**for, of** an + *Dat.*); **as the ~ arises** nach Bedarf; **if ~ be** nötigenfalls; **there's no ~ for that** [das ist] nicht nötig; **there's no ~ to do sth.** es ist nicht nötig, etw. zu tun; **be in ~ of sth.** etw. brauchen; **there's no ~ for you to come** du brauchst nicht zu kommen **(b)** *no pl.* (emergency) Not, *die;* **in case of ~:** im Notfall **(c)** (thing) Bedürfnis, *das* ② v.t. **(a)** (require) brauchen; **sth. that urgently ~s doing** etw., was dringend gemacht werden muss; **it ~s a coat of paint** es muss gestrichen werden **(b)** (expr. necessity) müssen; **I ~ to do it** ich muss es tun; **it ~s/doesn't ~ to be done** es muss getan werden/es braucht nicht getan zu werden **(c)** *pres.* **he ~,** *neg.* **~ not** *or* (coll.) **~n't** /ˈniːdnt/ (expr. desirability) müssen; *with neg.* brauchen zu

needle /ˈniːdl/ ① n. Nadel, *die* ② v.t. (coll.) nerven (ugs.)

needless /ˈniːdlɪs/ adj. unnötig; **~ to add** *or* **say, ...:** überflüssig zu sagen, dass ...

'needlessly adv. unnötig

'needlework n. Handarbeit, *die;* **do ~:** handarbeiten

needn't /ˈniːdnt/ (coll.) = **need not;** ▶ NEED 2C

'needy adj. notleidend; bedürftig

negation /nɪˈgeɪʃn/ n. Verneinung, *die*

negative /ˈnegətɪv/ ① adj. negativ ② n. **(a)** (Photog.) Negativ, *das* **(b)** (~ statement) negative Aussage; (answer) Nein, *das*

negative 'equity n. Negativwert, *der*

'negatively adv. negativ

neglect /nɪˈglekt/ ① v.t. vernachlässigen; **she ~ed to write** sie hat es versäumt zu schreiben ② n. Vernachlässigung, *die;* **be in a state of ~** ⟨*Gebäude:*⟩ verwahrlost sein

neglectful /nɪˈglektfl/ adj. gleichgültig (**of** gegenüber); **be ~ of** sich nicht kümmern um

negligence /ˈneglɪdʒəns/ n. Nachlässigkeit, *die;* (Law, Insurance, etc.) Fahrlässigkeit, *die*

negligent /ˈneglɪdʒənt/ adj. nachlässig; **be ~ about sth.** sich um etw. nicht kümmern

negligible /ˈneglɪdʒɪbl/ adj. unerheblich

negotiable /nɪˈgəʊʃəbl/ adj. **(a)** verhandlungsfähig ⟨*Forderung,* *Bedingungen*⟩ **(b)** passierbar ⟨*Straße, Fluss*⟩

negotiate /nɪˈgəʊʃɪeɪt/ ① v.i. verhandeln (**for, on, about** über + *Akk.*) ② v.t. **(a)** (arrange) aushandeln **(b)** überwinden ⟨*Hindernis*⟩; passieren ⟨*Straße, Fluss*⟩; nehmen ⟨*Kurve*⟩

negotiation /nɪgəʊʃɪˈeɪʃn/ n. Verhandlung, *die*

negotiator /nɪˈgəʊʃɪeɪtə(r)/ n. Unterhändler, *der*/-händlerin, *die*

Negress /ˈniːgrɪs/ n. (dated/offensive) Negerin, *die*

Negro /ˈniːgrəʊ/ ① n., *pl.* **~es** (dated/offensive) Neger, *der* ② adj. Neger-

neigh /neɪ/ ① v.i. wiehern ② n. Wiehern, *das*

neighbor etc. (*Amer.*) ▶ NEIGHBOUR etc.

neighbour /ˈneɪbə(r)/ ① n. Nachbar, *der*/ Nachbarin, *die;* **my next-door ~s** meine Nachbarn von nebenan ② v.t. & i. **~ [upon]** grenzen an (+ *Akk.*)

'neighbourhood n. (district) Gegend, *die;* (neighbours) Nachbarschaft, *die;* **[somewhere] in the ~ of £100** [so] um [die] 100 Pfund

'neighbourhood watch n.: Programm fur Verhütung von Straftaten, bes. von Wohnungseinbrüchen, durch erhöhte Wachsamkeit aller in einem Wohngebiet lebenden Menschen

'neighbouring adj. Nachbar-; angrenzend ⟨*Felder*⟩

neighbourly /ˈneɪbəlɪ/ adj. [gut]nachbarlich

neither /ˈnaɪðə(r), niːˈðə(r)/ ① adj. keiner/ keine/keins der beiden ② pron. keiner/keine/keins von od. der beiden ③ adv. (also not) auch nicht; **~ am I,** (coll.) **me ~:** ich auch nicht ④ conj. (not either) weder; **~ ... nor ...:** weder ... noch ...

neo'classical adj. klassizistisch

neo'conservative ① adj. neokonservativ ② n. Neokonservative, *der/die*

neo'fascist *adj.* neofaszistisch

neon /'niːɒn/ *n.* Neon, *das*

neo-'nazi 1 *n.* Neonazi, *der*
2 *adj.* neonazistisch; **a** ~ **group** eine Neonazigruppe

neon: ~ **'lamp,** ~ **'light** *ns.* Neonlampe, *die;* ~ **'sign** *n.* Neonreklame, *die*

nephew /'nevjuː, 'nefjuː/ *n.* Neffe, *der*

nepotism /'nepətɪzm/ *n.* Vetternwirtschaft, *die*

Neptune /'neptjuːn/ *pr. n.* (Astron.) Neptun, *der*

nerve /nɜːv/ *n.* Nerv, *der;* **get on sb.'s** ~**s** jmdm. auf die Nerven gehen (ugs.); **lose one's** ~: die Nerven verlieren; **what** [a] ~! [so eine] Frechheit!

nerve: ~ **cell** *n.* Nervenzelle, *die;* ~ **centre** *n.* (fig.) Schaltzentrale, *die;* ~ **gas** *n.* Nervengas, *das;* ~**-racking** *adj.* nervenaufreibend

nervous /'nɜːvəs/ *adj.* **(a)** (Anat., Med.) Nerven-; ~ **breakdown** Nervenzusammenbruch, *der*
(b) (having delicate nerves) nervös; **be a** ~ **wreck** mit den Nerven völlig am Ende sein
(c) (Brit.: timid) **be** ~ **of** *or* **about** Angst haben vor (+ *Dat.*); **be a** ~ **person** ängstlich sein

'nervously *adv.* nervös

'nervousness *n.* Ängstlichkeit, *die*

nervy /'nɜːvɪ/ *adj.* **(a)** nervös
(b) (Amer. coll.: impudent) unverschämt

nest 1 *n.* Nest, *das*
2 *v.i.* nisten

'nest egg *n.* (fig.) Notgroschen, *der*

nestle /'nesl/ *v.i.* **(a)** sich schmiegen (**to, up against** an + *Akk.*)
(b) (lie half hidden) eingebettet sein

net¹ /net/ 1 *n.* **(a)** Netz, *das*
(b) the Net (Comp.) das Netz
2 *v.t.,* **-tt-** [mit einem Netz] fangen

net² *adj.* **(a)** netto; Netto‹*einkommen, -[verkaufs]preis usw.*›; ~ **weight** Nettogewicht, *das*
(b) (ultimate) End‹*ergebnis, -effekt*›

net: ~**ball** *n.* Netzball, *der;* ~ **'curtain** *n.* Store, *der*

Netherlands /'neðələndz/ *pr. n. sing. or pl.* Niederlande *Pl.*

net 'profit *n.* Reingewinn, *der*

'netspeak *n.* Internetjargon, *der*

nett ▶ NET² A

'netting *n.* ([piece of] net) Netz, *das;* **wire** ~: Maschendraht, *der*

nettle /'netl/ *n.* Nessel, *die*

'network *n.* Netz, *das;* (Comp.) Netzwerk, *das*

'network provider *n.* (Comp) Netzanbieter, *der*

neuralgia /njʊə'rældʒə/ *n.* Neuralgie, *die*

neurological /njʊərə'lɒdʒɪkl/ *adj.* neurologisch

neurologist /njʊə'rɒlədʒɪst/ *n.* Neurologe, *der*/Neurologin, *die*

neurology /njʊə'rɒlədʒɪ/ *n.* Neurologie, *die*

neurosis /njʊə'rəʊsɪs/ *n., pl.* **neuroses** /njʊə'rəʊsiːz/ Neurose, *die*

neurotic /njʊə'rɒtɪk/ *adj.* **(a)** nervenkrank
(b) (coll.) neurotisch

neuter /'njuːtə(r)/ *adj.* sächlich

neutral /'njuːtrl/ 1 *adj.* neutral
2 *n.* (~ gear) Leerlauf, *der*

neutrality /njuː'trælɪtɪ/ *n.* Neutralität, *die*

neutralize /'njuːtrəlaɪz/ *v.t.* neutralisieren

neutron /'njuːtrɒn/ *n.* Neutron, *das*

never /'nevə(r)/ *adv.* **(a)** nie; ~**-ending** endlos
(b) (coll.) **you** ~ **believed that, did you?** du hast das doch wohl nicht geglaubt?; **well, I** ~ [**did**]! [na] so was!

neverthe'less *adv.* trotzdem

new /njuː/ *adj.* neu

new: New Age *n.* Newage, *das; attrib.* Newage-; ~**-born** *adj.* neugeboren; ~**comer** /'njuːkʌmə(r)/ *n.* Neuankömmling, *der;* ~**fangled** /'njuːfæŋgld/ *adj.* neumodisch; ~**found** *adj.* neu; ~**-laid** *adj.* frisch [gelegt]; **New 'Left** *n.* neue Linke; ~ **'look** *n.* (coll.) neuer Stil

'newly *adv.* (recently) neu; ~ **married** seit kurzem verheiratet

'newly-wed *n.* Jungverheiratete, *der*/*die*

new: New 'Man *n.* der neue Mann; ~ **'moon** *n.* Neumond, *der*

'newness *n.* Neuheit, *die*

news /njuːz/ *n.* **(a)** Nachricht, *die;* **be in the** ~: Schlagzeilen machen; **good/bad** ~: schlechte/gute Nachrichten *Pl.*
(b) (Radio, Telev.) Nachrichten *Pl.*

news: ~ **agency** *n.* Nachrichtenagentur, *die;* ~**agent** *n.* Zeitungshändler, *der*/-händlerin, *die;* ~ **bulletin** *n.* Nachrichten *Pl.;* ~**cast** *n.* Nachrichtensendung, *die;* ~**caster** *n.* Nachrichtensprecher, *der*/-sprecherin, *die;* ~ **desk** *n.* Nachrichtenredaktion, *die;* **this is Joe Smith at the** ~ **desk** (Radio) hier ist Joe Smith mit den Nachrichten; ~**flash** *n.* Kurzmeldung, *die;* ~**group** *n.* (Comp.) Newsgroup, *die;* ~ **'headline** *n.* Schlagzeile, *die;* ~**letter** *n.* Rundschreiben, *das;* ~**paper** *n.* **(a)** Zeitung, *die;* ~**paper boy/girl** Zeitungsausträger, *der*/-austrägerin, *die;* **(b)** (material) Zeitungspapier, *das;* ~**reader** *n.* Nachrichtensprecher, *der*/-sprecherin, *die;* ~**reel** *n.* Wochenschau, *die;* ~**room** *n.* Nachrichtenredaktion, *die;* ~**sheet** *n.* Informationsblatt, *das;* ~**stand** *n.* Zeitungskiosk, *der;* Zeitungsstand, *der;* ~ **summary** *n.* Kurznachrichten *Pl.;* ~ **vendor** *n.* Zeitungsverkäufer, *der*/-verkäuferin, *die;* ~**worthy** *adj.* [für die Medien] interessant

newt /njuːt/ *n.* [Wasser]molch, *der*

n

New: new town *n.*: mit Unterstützung der Regierung völlig neu entstandene Ansiedlung; **new 'year** *n.* Neujahr, *das;* over the new year über Neujahr; a Happy New Year ein glückliches *od.* gutes neues Jahr; ~ **'Year's** (Amer.), ~ **Year's 'Day** *ns.* Neujahrstag, *der;* ~ **Year's 'Eve** *n.* Silvester, *der od. das;* ~ **Zealand** /-'ziːlənd/ *pr. n.* Neuseeland *(das);* ~ **'Zealander** *n.* Neuseeländer, *der* /-länderin, *die*

next /nekst/ **1** *adj.* nächst...; the ~ but one der/die/das Übernächste; ~ to (fig.: almost) fast; nahezu; [the] ~ time das nächste Mal; the ~ best der/die/das Nächstbeste; am I ~? komme ich jetzt dran?
2 *adv.* (in the ~ place) als Nächstes; (on the ~ occasion) das nächste Mal; it's my turn ~: ich komme als Nächster dran; sit/stand ~ to **sb.** neben jmdm. stehen/sitzen; **place sth.** ~ **to sb./sth.** etw. neben jmdn./etw. stellen
3 *n.* (a) the week after ~: [die] übernächste Woche
(b) (person) ~ of kin nächster/nächste Angehörige; ~, please! der Nächste, bitte!

'next-door *adj.* gleich nebenan *nachgestellt*

NHS *abbr.* (Brit.) = **National Health Service**

nib /nɪb/ *n.* Feder, *die*

nibble /'nɪbl/ *v.t. & i.* knabbern (at, on an + *Dat.*)

nice /naɪs/ *adj.* nett; angenehm ⟨Stimme⟩; schön ⟨Wetter⟩; (iron.: disgraceful, difficult) schön; ~ [and] warm/fast schön warm/schnell; ~-looking gut aussehen

'nicely *adv.* (coll.) (a) (well) nett; gut ⟨arbeiten, sich benehmen, platziert sein⟩
(b) (all right) gut; that will do ~: das reicht völlig

niceties /'naɪsɪtɪz/ *n. pl.* Feinheiten *Pl.*

niche /nɪtʃ, niːʃ/ *n.* (a) (in wall) Nische, *die*
(b) (fig.: suitable place) Platz, *der*

nick **1** *n.* (a) (notch) Kerbe, *die*
(b) (sl. prison) Knast, *der* (salopp)
(c) (Brit.: police station) Wache, *die*
(d) in good/poor ~ (coll.) gut/nicht gut im Schuss (ugs.)
2 *v.t.* (a) einkerben
(b) (Brit. coll.: arrest) einlochen (salopp)
(c) (Brit. coll.: steal) klauen (salopp)

nickel /'nɪkl/ *n.* (a) Nickel, *das*
(b) (Amer. coll.: coin) Fünfcentstück, *das*

nickname /'nɪkneɪm/ *n.* Spitzname, *der;* (affectionate) Koseform, *die*

nicotine /'nɪkətiːn/ *n.* Nikotin, *das*

'nicotine patch *n.* Nikotinpflaster, *das*

niece /niːs/ *n.* Nichte, *die*

Nigeria /naɪ'dʒɪərɪə/ *pr. n.* Nigeria *(das)*

niggardly /'nɪgədlɪ/ *adj.* knaus[e]rig (ugs.)

niggling /'nɪglɪŋ/ *adj.* (a) (petty) belanglos
(b) (trivial) nichts sagend
(c) (nagging) nagend

night /naɪt/ *n.* Nacht, *die;* (evening) Abend, *der;* the following ~: die Nacht/der Abend darauf; the previous ~: die vorausgegangene Nacht/der vorausgegangene Abend; on Sunday ~: Sonntagnacht/[am] Sonntagabend; for the ~: über Nacht; at ~: nachts/abends; late at ~: spätabends

night: ~**bird** *n.* (person) Nachteule, *die* (ugs. scherzh.); ~ **blindness** *n.* Nachtblindheit, *die;* ~**cap** *n.* (drink) Schlaftrunk, *der;* ~**clothes** *n. pl.* Nachtwäsche, *die;* ~**club** *n.* Nachtklub, *der;* ~**dress** *n.* Nachthemd, *das;* ~ **duty** *n.* Nachtdienst, *der;* be on ~ duty Nachtdienst haben; ~**fall** *n.* Einbruch der Dunkelheit

nightie /'naɪtɪ/ *n.* (coll.) Nachthemd, *das*

nightingale /'naɪtɪŋgeɪl/ *n.* Nachtigall, *die*

'nightlife *n.* Nachtleben, *das*

nightly /'naɪtlɪ/ **1** *adj.* (happening every night/ evening) allnächtlich/allabendlich
2 *adv.* (every night) jede Nacht; (every evening) jeden Abend

night: ~**mare** *n.* Albtraum, *der;* ~**marish** /'naɪtmeərɪʃ/ *adj.* albtraumhaft; ~ **owl** *n.* (a) (Ornith.) Eule, *die;* (b) (coll.: person) Nachteule, *die* (ugs. scherzh.); ~ **porter** *n.* Nachtportier, *der;* ~ **safe** *n.* Nachttresor, *der;* ~ **school** *n.* Abendschule, *die;* ~ **shelter** *n.* Nachtasyl, *das;* ~ **shift** *n.* Nachtschicht, *die;* ~ **'sky** *n.* Nachthimmel, *der;* ~ **'storage heater** *n.* Nachtspeicherofen, *der;* ~**-time** *n.* Nacht, *die;* in the *or* at ~-time nachts; ~**'watchman** *n.* Nachtwächter, *der;* ~**wear** *n. sing.* ▶ NIGHTCLOTHES

nihilistic /naɪɪ'lɪstɪk, nɪhɪ'lɪstɪk/ *adj.* nihilistisch

nil /nɪl/ *n.* null

Nile /naɪl/ *pr. n.* Nil, *der*

nimble /'nɪmbl/ *adj.,* **nimbly** /'nɪmblɪ/ *adv.* flink

nine /naɪn/ **1** *adj.* neun
2 *n.* Neun, *die. See also* EIGHT

nineteen /naɪn'tiːn/ **1** *adj.* neunzehn
2 *n.* Neunzehn, *die. See also* EIGHT

nineteenth /naɪn'tiːnθ/ **1** *adj.* neunzehnt...
2 *n.* (fraction) Neunzehntel, *das. See also* EIGHTH

ninetieth /'naɪntɪɪθ/ *adj.* neunzigst...

ninety /'naɪntɪ/ **1** *adj.* neunzig
2 *n.* Neunzig, *die. See also* EIGHT; EIGHTY 2

ninth /naɪnθ/ **1** *adj.* neunt...
2 *n.* (in sequence, rank) Neunte, *der/die/das;* (fraction) Neuntel, *das. See also* EIGHTH

nip **1** *v.t.,* -pp- zwicken
2 *v.i.,* -pp- (Brit. coll.) ~ in hinein-/ hereinflitzen (ugs.); ~ out hinaus-/ herausflitzen (ugs.)
3 *n.* (pinch, squeeze) Kniff, *der;* (bite) Biss, *der*

'nipper *n.* (Brit. coll.: child) Balg, *das* (ugs.)

nipple /'nɪpl/ *n.* (a) Brustwarze, *die*
(b) (of feeding bottle) Sauger, *der*

nitrate /'naɪtreɪt/ *n.* (a) (salt) Nitrat, *das* (b) (fertilizer) Nitratdünger, *der*

nitric acid /'naɪtrɪk æsɪd/ *n.* Salpetersäure, *die*

nitrogen /'naɪtrədʒən/ *n.* Stickstoff, *der*

'**nitrogen cycle** *n.* Stickstoffkreislauf, *der*

nitwit /'nɪtwɪt/ *n.* (coll.) Trottel, *der* (ugs.)

no /nəʊ/ [1] *adj.* kein
[2] *adv.* (a) (by no amount) nicht; **no less [than]** nicht weniger [als]; **no more wine?** keinen Wein mehr?
(b) (as answer) nein
[3] *n., pl.* **noes** /nəʊz/ Nein, *das*

No. *abbr.* = **number** Nr.

Noah's ark /nəʊəz 'ɑːk/ *n.* die Arche Noah

Nobel prize /nəʊbel 'praɪz/ *n.* Nobelpreis, *der*

nobility /nə'bɪlɪtɪ/ *n.* Adel, *der;* **many of the ~:** viele Adlige

noble /'nəʊbl/ [1] *adj.* ad[e]lig; edel ⟨*Gedanken, Gefühle*⟩
[2] *n.* Adlige, *der/die*

nobleman /'nəʊblmən/ *n., pl.* **noblemen** /'nəʊblmən/ Adlige, *der*

nobly /'nəʊblɪ/ *adv.* (a) edel [gesinnt]
(b) (generously) edelmütig (geh.)

nobody /'nəʊbədɪ/ *n. & pron.* niemand; keiner; (person of no importance) Niemand, *der*

no-'claim[s] bonus *n.* (Insurance) Schadenfreiheitsrabatt, *der*

nocturnal /nɒk'tɜːnl/ *adj.* nächtlich; **~ animal/bird** Nachttier, *das*/-vogel, *der*

nod /nɒd/ [1] *v.i.,* **-dd-** nicken
[2] *v.t.,* **-dd-: ~ one's head [in greeting]** [zum Gruß] mit dem Kopf nicken
[3] *n.* [Kopf]nicken, *das*
■ **nod 'off** *v.i.* einnicken (ugs.)

nodule /'nɒdjuːl/ *n.* (a) Klümpchen, *das*
(b) (Bot.) Knötchen, *das*

no-'fly zone *n.* Flugverbotszone, *die*

no-'go *adj.* Sperr⟨*gebiet, -zone*⟩

'**no-good** *adj.* (coll.) nichtsnutzig (abwertend)

no-hoper /nəʊ'həʊpə(r)/ *n.* absoluter Außenseiter; **be a ~:** keine Chance haben

nohow /'nəʊhaʊ/ *adv.* (Amer. coll.) in keiner Weise

noise /nɔɪz/ *n.* Geräusch, *das;* (loud, harsh, unwanted) Lärm, *der*

'**noise abatement** *n.* Lärmbekämpfung, *die*

'**noiseless** *adj.,* '**noiselessly** *adv.* lautlos

noise: ~ level *n.* Geräuschpegel, *der;* (of unpleasant noise) Lärmpegel, *der;*
~ pollution *n.* Lärmbelästigung, *die*

noisily /'nɔɪzɪlɪ/ *adv.,* **noisy** /'nɔɪzɪ/ *adj.* laut

nomad /'nəʊmæd/ *n.* Nomade, *der*

nomadic /nəʊ'mædɪk/ *adj.* nomadisch; **~ tribe** Nomadenstamm, *der*

'**no man's land** *n.* Niemandsland, *das*

nominal /'nɒmɪnl/ *adj.* (a) (in name only) nominell
(b) (virtually nothing) äußerst gering

nominally /'nɒmɪnəlɪ/ *adv.* namentlich

nominate /'nɒmɪneɪt/ *v.t.* (a) (propose) nominieren
(b) (appoint) ernennen

nomination /nɒmɪ'neɪʃn/ *n.* ▶ NOMINATE: Nominierung, *die;* Ernennung, *die*

nominative /'nɒmɪnətɪv/ *adj. & n.* **~ [case]** Nominativ, *der*

nominee /nɒmɪ'niː/ *n.* (candidate) Kandidat, *der*/Kandidatin, *die*

non- /nɒn/ *pref.* nicht-

non-alco'holic *adj.* alkoholfrei

nonchalant /'nɒnʃələnt/ *adj.* unbekümmert

non-commissioned 'officer *n.* Unteroffizier, *der*

non-committal /nɒnkə'mɪtl/ *adj.* unverbindlich; **he was ~:** er hat sich nicht klar geäußert

noncon'formist *n.* Nonkonformist, *der/* Nonkonformistin, *die*

non-con'tributory *adj.* beitragsfrei

nondescript /'nɒndɪskrɪpt/ *adj.* unscheinbar; undefinierbar ⟨*Farbe*⟩

'**non-drip** *adj.* nicht tropfend ⟨*Farbe*⟩

non-'driver *n.* Nicht[auto]fahrer, *der*

none /nʌn/ [1] *pron.* kein...; **~ of them** keiner/keine/keines von ihnen; **~ of this** nichts davon
[2] *adv.* keineswegs; **I'm ~ the wiser now** jetzt bin ich um nichts klüger; **~ the less** nichtsdestoweniger

nonentity /nɒ'nentɪtɪ/ *n.* Nichts, *das*

non-existent /nɒnɪg'zɪstənt/ *adj.* nicht vorhanden

non-'fiction *n.* Sachliteratur, *die*

non-'iron *adj.* bügelfrei

non-'member *n.* Nichtmitglied, *das*

'**no-no** *n., pl.* **~es** (coll.) **be a ~:** nicht infrage kommen (ugs.)

non-'payment *n.* Nichtzahlung, *die*

nonplus /nɒn'plʌs/ *v.t.,* **-ss-** verblüffen

non-'profit[-making] *adj.* nicht auf Gewinn ausgerichtet

non-prolife'ration *n.* Nichtverbreitung von Atomwaffen; **~ treaty** Atom[waffen]sperrvertrag, *der*

non-re'cyclable *adj.* nicht recyclebar

non-'resident *n.* (outside a country) Nichtansässige, *der/die;* **the bar is open to ~s** die Bar ist auch für Gäste geöffnet, die nicht im Hotel wohnen

nonsense /'nɒnsəns/ [1] *n.* Unsinn, *der*
[2] *int.* Unsinn

nonsensical /nɒn'sensɪkl/ *adj.* unsinnig

non sequitur /nɒn 'sekwɪtə(r)/ *n.* unlogische Folgerung

n

non-'smoker n. (a) (person) Nichtraucher, der/-raucherin, die
(b) (train compartment) Nichtraucherabteil, das
non-'starter n. (fig. coll.) Reinfall, der (ugs.)
non-'stick adj. ~ frying pan etc.
Bratpfanne usw. mit Antihaftbeschichtung
non-stop ⏜1⏜ /'-·/ adj. durchgehend ‹Zug, Busverbindung›; Nonstop‹flug, -revue›
⏜2⏜ /-'-/ adv. ohne Unterbrechung ‹tanzen, reden, reisen, senden›; nonstop ‹fliegen, tanzen, fahren›
'non-toxic adj. ungiftig
noodle /'nuːdl/ n., usu. pl. Nudel, die
nook /nʊk/ n. Winkel, der; Ecke, die
noon /nuːn/ n. Mittag, der; zwölf Uhr [mittags]; **at/before** ~: um/vor zwölf [Uhr mittags]
'no one pron. ▶ NOBODY
noose /nuːs/ n. Schlinge, die
nor /nə(r), stressed nɔː(r)/ conj. noch; **neither/ not ... ~ ...**: weder ... noch ...
norm /nɔːm/ n. Norm, die
normal /'nɔːml/ ⏜1⏜ adj. normal
⏜2⏜ n. (a) (~ value) Normalwert, der
(b) (usual state) normaler Stand; **everything is back to** or **has returned to** ~: es hat sich wieder alles normalisiert
normality /nɔː'mælɪtɪ/ Normalität, die
'normally adv. (a) (in normal way) normal
(b) (ordinarily) normalerweise
north /nɔːθ/ ⏜1⏜ n. (a) Norden, der; **in/ to[wards]/from the** ~: im/nach/von Norden; **to the** ~ **of** nördlich von
(b) usu. N~ (Geog., Polit.) Norden, der
⏜2⏜ adj. nördlich; Nord‹wind, -küste, -grenze›
⏜3⏜ adv. nach Norden; ~ **of** nördlich von
north: N~ 'Africa pr. n. Nordafrika (das);
N~ A'merica pr. n. Nordamerika (das);
N~ A'merican ⏜1⏜ adj. nordamerikanisch;
⏜2⏜ n. Nordamerikaner, der/-amerikanerin, die; **~bound** adj. ‹Zug, Verkehr usw.› in Richtung Norden; **~-'east** ⏜1⏜ n. Nordosten, der; ⏜2⏜ adj. nordöstlich; Nordost‹wind, -küste›; ⏜3⏜ adv. nordostwärts; nach Nordosten; **~-'eastern** adj. nordöstlich
northerly /'nɔːðəlɪ/ adj. nördlich; ‹Wind› aus nördlichen Richtungen
northern /'nɔːðən/ adj. nördlich; Nord‹grenze, -hälfte, -seite›
northern: N~ 'Ireland pr. n. Nordirland (das); ~ **'lights** n. pl. Nordlicht, das
North: ~ 'Germany pr. n. Norddeutschland (das); ~ **'Pole** pr. n. Nordpol, der; ~ **'Sea** pr. n. Nordsee, die
northward[s] /'nɔːθwəd(z)/ adv. nordwärts
north: ~-'west ⏜1⏜ n. Nordwesten, der; ⏜2⏜ adj. nordwestlich; Nordwest‹wind, -küste›; ⏜3⏜ adv. nordwestwärts; nach Nordwesten; **~-'western** adj. nordwestlich
Norway /'nɔːweɪ/ pr. n. Norwegen (das)
Norwegian /nɔː'wiːdʒn/ ⏜1⏜ adj. norwegisch; **sb. is** ~: jmd. ist Norweger/ Norwegerin

⏜2⏜ n. (a) (person) Norweger, der/Norwegerin, die
(b) (language) Norwegisch, das; see also ENGLISH 2A
Nos. abbr. = **numbers** Nrn.
nose /nəʊz/ ⏜1⏜ n. Nase, die
⏜2⏜ v.t. ~ **one's way** sich (Dat.) vorsichtig seinen Weg bahnen
⏜3⏜ v.i. sich vorsichtig bewegen
■ **nose a'bout, nose a'round** v.i. (coll.) herumschnüffeln (ugs.)
nose: ~bleed n. Nasenbluten, das; ~**dive** ⏜1⏜ n. Sturzflug, der; ⏜2⏜ v.i. im Sturzflug hinuntergehen
nosey ▶ NOSY
nostalgia /nɒ'stældʒə/ n. Nostalgie, die; ~ **for sth.** Sehnsucht nach etw.
nostalgic /nɒ'stældʒɪk/ adj. nostalgisch
nostril /'nɒstrɪl/ n. Nasenloch, das; (of horse) Nüster, die
nosy /'nəʊzɪ/ adj. (coll.) neugierig
not /nɒt/ adv. nicht; **he is** ~ **a doctor** er ist kein Arzt; ~ **at all** überhaupt nicht; ~ **... but** ...: nicht ..., sondern ...; ~ **a thing** gar nichts
notable /'nəʊtəbl/ adj. bemerkenswert; **be** ~ **for sth.** für etw. bekannt sein
notably /'nəʊtəblɪ/ adv. besonders
notation /nəʊ'teɪʃn/ n. Notierung, die
notch /nɒtʃ/ ⏜1⏜ n. Kerbe, die
⏜2⏜ v.t. kerben
■ **notch 'up** v.t. erreichen
note /nəʊt/ ⏜1⏜ n. (a) (Mus.) (sign) Note, die; (key of piano) Taste, die; (sound) Ton, der
(b) (jotting) Notiz, die; **take** or **make** ~**s** sich (Dat.) Notizen machen; **take** or **make a** ~ **of sth.** sich (Dat.) etw. notieren
(c) (comment, footnote) Anmerkung, die
(d) (short letter) [kurzer] Brief
(e) (importance) **a person/something of** ~: eine bedeutende Persönlichkeit/etwas Bedeutendes; **be of** ~: bedeutend sein
⏜2⏜ v.t. (a) (pay attention to) beachten
(b) (notice) bemerken
(c) (write) ~ **[down]** [sich (Dat.)] notieren
'notebook n. (a) Notizbuch, das; (for lecture notes) Kollegheft, das
(b) ~**book [computer]** Notebook, das
'noted adj. bekannt (**for** für, wegen)
note: ~pad n. Notizblock, der; ~**paper** n. Briefpapier, das; ~**worthy** adj. bemerkenswert
nothing /'nʌθɪŋ/ n. nichts; ~ **interesting** nichts Interessantes; ~ **much** nichts Besonderes; ~ **more than** nur; ~ **more,** ~ **less** nicht mehr, nicht weniger; **next to** ~: so gut wie nichts; **have [got]** or **be** ~ **to do with sb./sth.** (not concern) nichts zu tun haben mit jmdm./etw.; **have** ~ **to do with sb.** (avoid) jmdm. aus dem Weg gehen
notice /'nəʊtɪs/ ⏜1⏜ n. (a) Anschlag, der; (in newspaper) Anzeige, die

(b) (warning) **at short/a moment's** ~:
kurzfristig/von einem Augenblick zum
andern
(c) (formal notification) Ankündigung, *die; until
further* ~: bis auf weiteres
(d) (ending an agreement) Kündigung, *die;* **give
sb. a month's** ~: jmdm. mit einer Frist von
einem Monat kündigen; **hand in one's** ~,
give ~ (Brit.), **give one's** ~ (Amer.) kündigen
(e) (attention) **bring sb./sth. to sb.'s** ~: jmdn.
auf jmdn./etw. aufmerksam machen; **take no**
~ **of sb./sth.** (disregard) keine Notiz von
jmdm./etw. nehmen; **take no** ~: sich nicht
darum kümmern
  2 *v.t.* bemerken
noticeable /'nəʊtɪsəbl/ *adj.* wahrnehmbar
⟨*Fleck, Schaden, Geruch*⟩; merklich
⟨*Verbesserung*⟩; spürbar ⟨*Mangel*⟩
noticeably /'nəʊtɪsəblɪ/ *adv.* sichtlich
⟨*größer, kleiner*⟩; merklich ⟨*verändern*⟩;
spürbar ⟨*kälter*⟩
'noticeboard *n.* (Brit.) Anschlagbrett, *das;*
schwarzes Brett
notifiable /'nəʊtɪfaɪəbl/ *adj.* meldepflichtig
⟨*Krankheit*⟩
notification /nəʊtɪfɪ'keɪʃn/ *n.* Mitteilung,
die (of sth. über etw. [*Akk.*])
notify /'nəʊtɪfaɪ/ *v.t.* **(a)** (make known)
ankündigen
(b) (inform) benachrichtigen (of über + *Akk.*)
notion /'nəʊʃn/ *n.* Vorstellung, *die;* **not
have the faintest/least** ~ **of how/what** *etc.*
nicht die blasseste/geringste Ahnung haben,
wie/was *usw.*
notoriety /nəʊtə'raɪətɪ/ *n.* traurige
Berühmtheit
notorious /nə'tɔːrɪəs/ *adj.* berüchtigt (**for**
wegen); notorisch ⟨*Lügner*⟩
nougat /'nuːgɑː/ *n.* Nougat, *das od. der*
nought /nɔːt/ *n.* Null, *die*
noun /naʊn/ *n.* (Ling.) Substantiv, *das*
nourish /'nʌrɪʃ/ *v.t.* ernähren (**on** mit)
'nourishing *adj.* nahrhaft
'nourishment *n.* Nahrung, *die*
Nov. *abbr.* = **November** Nov.
novel /'nɒvl/ **1** *n.* Roman, *der*
  2 *adj.* neuartig
novelist /'nɒvəlɪst/ *n.* Romanautor, *der/*
-autorin, *die*
novella /nə'velə/ *n.* Novelle, *die*
novelty /'nɒvltɪ/ *n.* **(a) be a/no** ~: etwas/
nichts Neues sein
(b) (newness) Neuheit, *die*
(c) (gadget) Überraschung, *die*
November /nə'vembə(r)/ *n.* November,
der; see also AUGUST
novice /'nɒvɪs/ *n.* Anfänger, *der/*
Anfängerin, *die*
now /naʊ/ **1** *adv.* jetzt; (nowadays)
heutzutage; (immediately) [jetzt] sofort; **just** ~
(very recently) gerade eben; **[every]** ~ **and then**
or **again** hin und wieder; **well** ~: also; ~, ~:
na, na; ~ **then** na (ugs.)

  2 *conj.* ~ **[that]** …: jetzt, wo …
  3 *n.* **before** ~: früher; **by** ~: inzwischen; **a
week from** ~: [heute] in einer Woche
nowadays /'naʊədeɪz/ *adv.* heutzutage
nowhere /'nəʊweə(r)/ *adv.* nirgends;
nirgendwo; (to no place) nirgendwohin
no-'win *attrib. adj.* Verlierer-
noxious /'nɒkʃəs/ *adj.* giftig
nozzle /'nɒzl/ *n.* Düse, *die*
nuance /'njuːɑːs/ *n.* Nuance, *die*
nuclear /'njuːklɪə(r)/ *adj.* Atom-;
Kern⟨*explosion*⟩; atomar ⟨*Antrieb,
Gefechtskopf, Wettrüsten, Abrüstung*⟩;
nuklear ⟨*Sprengkörper*⟩; atomgetrieben
⟨*Unterseeboot*⟩
nuclear: ~ **'bomb** *n.* Atombombe, *die;*
~ **capa'bility** *n.* nukleares Potenzial; **a
missile with** ~ **capability** eine nuklearfähige
Rakete; **have** ~ **capability** nuklearfähig sein;
~ **de'terrent** *n.* atomare *od.* nukleare
Abschreckung; ~ **'energy** *n.* Atom- *od.*
Kernenergie, *die;* ~ **'family** *n.*
Kernfamilie, *die;* ~**-free** *adj.*
atomwaffenfrei ⟨*Zone*⟩; ~ **'fuel** *n.*
Kernbrennstoff, *der;* ~ **'physics** *n.*
Kernphysik, *die;* ~ **'power** *n.* **(a)** Atom-
od. Kernkraft, *die;* **(b)** (country) Atom- *od.*
Nuklearmacht, *die;* ~**-'powered** *adj.*
atomgetrieben; ~ **'power station** *n.*
Atom- *od.* Kernkraftwerk, *das;* ~ **'test** *n.*
Atom[waffen]test, *der;* ~ **'testing** *n.*
Atomversuche *Pl.;* ~ **'warfare** *n.*
Atomkrieg, *der;* ~ **'waste** *n.* Atommüll,
der
nucleus /'njuːklɪəs/ *n., pl.* **nuclei**
/'njuːklɪaɪ/ Kern, *der*
nude /njuːd/ **1** *adj.* nackt
  2 *n.* **(a)** (figure) Akt, *der*
(b) in the ~: nackt
nudge /nʌdʒ/ **1** *v.t.* anstoßen
  2 *n.* Stoß, *der*
nudism /'njuːdɪzm/ *n.* Nudismus, *der;*
Freikörperkultur, *die*
nudist /'njuːdɪst/ *n.* Nudist, *der/*Nudistin,
die; attrib. Nudisten-
nudity /'njuːdɪtɪ/ *n.* Nacktheit, *die*
nugget /'nʌgɪt/ *n.* Klumpen, *der;* (of gold)
Goldklumpen, *der;* (fig.) ~**s of wisdom**
goldene Weisheiten
nuisance /'njuːsəns/ *n.* Ärgernis, *das;*
what a ~**!** so etwas Dummes!
null /nʌl/ *adj.* ~ **and void** null und nichtig
numb /nʌm/ **1** *adj.* gefühllos, taub (**with**
vor + *Dat.*); (without emotion) benommen
  2 *v.t.* betäuben
number /'nʌmbə(r)/ **1** *n.* **(a)** (in series)
Nummer, *die;* **you've got the wrong** ~
(Teleph.) Sie sind falsch verbunden; **dial a
wrong** ~: sich verwählen (ugs.)
(b) (esp. Math.: numeral) Zahl, *die*
(c) (sum, total, quantity) [An]zahl, *die;* **a** ~ **of
people/things** einige Leute/Dinge; **a** ~ **of
times** mehrmals   **·⃗**

2 *v.t.* **(a)** (assign ∼ to) nummerieren
(b) (amount to, comprise) zählen
(c) (include) zählen (**among, with** zu)
(d) sb.'s days are ∼ed jmds. Tage sind gezählt
'numbering *n.* Nummerierung, *die*
'numberless *adj.* unzählig; zahllos
'number plate *n.* Nummernschild, *das*
numeracy /'nju:mərəsı/ *n.* rechnerische Fähigkeiten *Pl.*
numeral /'nju:mərl/ *n.* Ziffer, *die*
numerate /'nju:mərət/ *adj.* be ∼: rechnen können
numerical /nju:'merıkl/ *adj.* numerisch; Zahlen⟨wert, -folge⟩; zahlenmäßig ⟨Stärke, Überlegenheit⟩
numerically /nju:'merıkəlı/ *adv.* numerisch
numerous /'nju:mərəs/ *adj.* zahlreich
nun /nʌn/ *n.* Nonne, *die*
nurse /nɜ:s/ **1** *n.* Krankenschwester, *die;* [male] ∼: Krankenpfleger, *der*
2 *v.t.* **(a)** pflegen ⟨Kranke⟩
(b) (fig.) hegen (geh.) ⟨Gefühl, Groll⟩
'nursemaid *n.* (lit. or fig.) Kindermädchen, *das*
nursery /'nɜ:sərı/ *n.* **(a)** (room) Kinderzimmer, *das*
(b) (crèche) Kindertagesstätte, *die*
(c) ▶ NURSERY SCHOOL
(d) (for plants) Gärtnerei, *die*
nursery: ∼ **rhyme** *n.* Kinderreim, *der;* ∼ **school** *n.* Kindergarten, *der;* ∼**-school teacher** *n.* (female) Kindergärtnerin, *die;* Erzieherin, *die;* (male) Erzieher, *der;* ∼ **slopes** *n. pl.* (Skiing) Idiotenhügel, *der* (ugs. scherzh.)

nursing /'nɜ:sıŋ/ *n.* Krankenpflege, *die; attrib.* Pflege⟨personal, -beruf⟩
'nursing home *n.* Pflegeheim, *das*
nurture /'nɜ:tʃə(r)/ *v.t.* (rear) aufziehen; (fig.) nähren
nut /nʌt/ *n.* **(a)** Nuss, *die*
(b) (Mech. Engin.) [Schrauben]mutter, *die*
(c) (crazy person) Verrückte, *der/die* (ugs.)
nut: ∼ **case** *n.* (coll.) Verrückte, *der/die* (ugs.); ∼ **crackers** *n. pl.* Nussknacker, *der*
nutmeg /'nʌtmeg/ *n.* Muskat, *der*
nutrient /'nju:trıənt/ *n.* Nährstoff, *der*
nutrition /nju:'trıʃn/ *n.* Ernährung, *die;* (food) Nahrung, *die*
nutritional /nju:'trıʃənl/ *adj.* nahrhaft; ∼ **value** Nährwert, *der*
nutritionist /nju:'trıʃənıst/ *n.* Ernährungswissenschaftler, *der/* -wissenschaftlerin, *die*
nutritious /nju:'trıʃəs/ *adj.* nahrhaft
'nutshell *n.* Nussschale, *die;* in a ∼ (fig.) hurz [gesagt]
nutty /'nʌtı/ *adj.* **(a)** (in taste) nussig
(b) (coll.: crazy) verrückt (ugs.)
nuzzle /'nʌzl/ *v.i.* sich kuscheln (**up to, against** an + *Akk.*)
NVQ *abbr.* (Brit.) = **National Vocational Qualification**
NW *abbr.* = **north-west** NW
nylon /'naılɒn/ *n.* **(a)** Nylon, *das; attrib.* Nylon-
(b) *in pl.* (stockings) Nylonstrümpfe *Pl.*
nymph /nımf/ *n.* Nymphe, *die*
nymphomaniac /nımfə'meınıæk/ *n.* Nymphomanin, *die*
NZ *abbr.* = **New Zealand**

Oo

O, o /əʊ/ *n.* O, o, *das*
oaf /əʊf/ *n.* Stoffel, *der* (ugs.)
oak /əʊk/ *n.* Eiche, *die*
'oak tree *n.* Eiche, *die*
OAP *abbr.* (Brit.) = **old-age pensioner** Rentner, *der/*Rentnerin, *die*
oar /ɔ:(r)/ *n.* Ruder, *das*
oarsman /'ɔ:zmən/ *n., pl.* **oarsmen** /'ɔ:zmən/ Ruderer, *der*
oasis /əʊ'eısıs/ *n., pl.* **oases** /əʊ'eısi:z/ Oase, *die*
oat /əʊt/ *n.* ∼s Hafer, *der*
'oatcake *n.* [flacher] Haferkuchen
oath /əʊθ/ *n.* **(a)** Eid, *der;* Schwur, *der;* take *or* swear an ∼: einen Eid schwören

(b) (swear word) Fluch, *der*
'oatmeal *n.* Hafermehl, *das*
obedience /ə'bi:dıəns/ *n.* Gehorsam, *der*
obedient /ə'bi:dıənt/ *adj.* gehorsam; be ∼ to sb./sth. jmdm./einer Sache gehorchen
o'bediently *adv.* gehorsam
obelisk /'ɒbəlısk/ *n.* Obelisk, *der*
obese /əʊ'bi:s/ *adj.* fettleibig
obesity /əʊ'bi:sıtı/ *n.* Fettleibigkeit, *die*
obey /əʊ'beı/ **1** *v.t.* gehorchen (+ *Dat.*); sich halten an (+ *Akk.*) ⟨Vorschrift, Regel⟩; befolgen ⟨Befehl⟩
2 *v.i.* gehorchen
obituary /ə'bıtjʊərı/ *n.* Nachruf, *der* (**to, of** auf + *Akk.*)

object ⟦1⟧ /'ɒbdʒɪkt/ n. (a) (thing)
Gegenstand, der
(b) (purpose) Ziel, das
(c) (obstacle) **money/time** etc. **is no ~:** Geld/
Zeit usw. spielt keine Rolle
(d) (Ling.) Objekt, das
⟦2⟧ /əb'dʒekt/ v.i. (a) Einwände/einen
Einwand erheben (**to** gegen)
(b) (have objection or dislike) etwas dagegen
haben; **~ to sb./sth.** etwas gegen jmdn./etw.
haben
⟦3⟧ /əb'dʒekt/ v.t. einwenden

objection /əb'dʒekʃn/ n. (a) Einwand, der;
raise or **make an ~** [**to sth.**] einen Einwand
[gegen etw.] erheben
(b) (dislike) Abneigung, die; **have an/no ~ to**
sb./sth. etw./nichts gegen jmdn./etw. haben;
have no ~s nichts dagegen haben

objectionable /əb'dʒekʃənəbl/ adj.
unangenehm ⟨Anblick, Geruch⟩; anstößig
⟨Bemerkung, Wort, Benehmen⟩

objective /əb'dʒektɪv/ ⟦1⟧ adj. objektiv
⟦2⟧ n. (goal) Ziel, das

ob'jectively adv. objektiv

objectivity /ɒbdʒek'tɪvɪtɪ/ n. Objektivität,
die

obligation /ɒblɪ'geɪʃn/ n. Verpflichtung,
die; **be under an ~ to sb.** jmdm. verpflichtet
sein; **without ~:** unverbindlich

obligatory /ə'blɪɡətərɪ/ adj. obligatorisch;
it has become ~ to ...: es ist jetzt Pflicht,
zu ...

oblige /ə'blaɪdʒ/ v.t. (a) (be binding on) **~ sb.**
to do sth. jmdm. vorschreiben, etw. zu tun
(b) (compel) zwingen; **be ~d to do sth.**
gezwungen sein, etw. zu tun; **feel ~d to do**
sth. sich verpflichtet fühlen, etw. zu tun
(c) (be kind to) **~ sb. by doing sth.** jmdm. den
Gefallen tun und etw. tun
(d) (grateful) **be much/greatly ~d to sb.** [**for**
sth.] jmdm. [für etw.] sehr verbunden sein;
much ~d! besten Dank!

obliging /ə'blaɪdʒɪŋ/ adj.
entgegenkommend

oblique /ə'bliːk/ adj. schief ⟨Gerade,
Winkel⟩; (fig.) indirekt

obliterate /ə'blɪtəreɪt/ v.t. auslöschen

oblivion /ə'blɪvɪən/ n. Vergessenheit, die;
sink or **fall into ~:** in Vergessenheit geraten

oblivious /ə'blɪvɪəs/ adj. **be ~ to** or **of sth.**
sich (Dat.) einer Sache (Gen.) nicht bewusst
sein

oblong /'ɒblɒŋ/ ⟦1⟧ adj. rechteckig
⟦2⟧ n. Rechteck, das

obnoxious /əb'nɒkʃəs/ adj. widerlich

oboe /'əʊbəʊ/ n. Oboe, die

obscene /əb'siːn/ adj. obszön

obscenity /əb'senɪtɪ/ n. Obszönität, die

obscure /əb'skjʊə(r)/ ⟦1⟧ adj. (a)
(unexplained) dunkel
(b) (hard to understand) schwer verständlich
⟨Argument, Dichtung, Autor, Stil⟩
(c) (unknown) unbekannt

object ⟦2⟧ v.t. (a) (make indistinct) verdunkeln;
versperren ⟨Aussicht⟩
(b) (make unintelligible) unverständlich machen

obsequious /əb'siːkwɪəs/ adj. unterwürfig

observance /əb'zɜːvəns/ n. Einhaltung,
die

observant /əb'zɜːvənt/ adj. aufmerksam

observation /ɒbzə'veɪʃn/ n. (a)
Beobachtung, die; **be [kept] under ~:**
beobachtet werden; (by police) überwacht
werden
(b) (remark) Bemerkung, die (**on** über + Akk.)

obser'vation post n.
Beobachtungsposten, der

observatory /əb'zɜːvətərɪ/ n. (Astron.)
Sternwarte, die

observe /əb'zɜːv/ v.t. (a) (watch)
beobachten; (perceive) bemerken
(b) (abide by, keep) einhalten
(c) (say) bemerken

ob'server n. Beobachter, der/Beobachterin,
die

obsess /əb'ses/ v.t. **~ sb.** von jmdm. Besitz
ergreifen (fig.); **be/become ~ed with** or **by**
sb./sth. von jmdm./etw. besessen sein/
werden

obsession /əb'seʃn/ n. Zwangsvorstellung,
die

obsessive /əb'sesɪv/ adj. zwanghaft; **be**
~ about sth. von etw. besessen sein

obsolescent /ɒbsə'lesənt/ adj. veraltend

obsolete /'ɒbsəliːt/ adj. veraltet

obstacle /'ɒbstəkl/ n. Hindernis, das (**to**
für)

obstacle: ~ course n.
Hindernisparcours, der; **~ race** n.
Hindernisrennen, das

obstetrics /ɒb'stetrɪks/ n. (Med.)
Obstetrik, die (fachspr.)

obstinacy /'ɒbstɪnəsɪ/ n. ▶ OBSTINATE:
Starrsinn, der; Hartnäckigkeit, die

obstinate /'ɒbstɪnət/ adj. starrsinnig;
(adhering to particular course of action) hartnäckig

obstruct /əb'strʌkt/ v.t. (a) (block)
blockieren; behindern ⟨Verkehr⟩; **~ sb.'s**
view jmdm. die Sicht versperren
(b) (fig.: impede; also Sport) behindern

obstruction /əb'strʌkʃn/ n. Blockierung,
die; (of progress; also Sport) Behinderung, die

obstructive /əb'strʌktɪv/ adj. hinderlich;
obstruktiv ⟨Politik, Taktik⟩; **be ~** ⟨Person:⟩
sich quer legen (ugs.)

obtain /əb'teɪn/ v.t. bekommen; erzielen
⟨Resultat, Wirkung⟩

obtainable /əb'teɪnəbl/ adj. erhältlich

obtrusive /əb'truːsɪv/ adj. aufdringlich;
(conspicuous) auffällig

obtuse /əb'tjuːs/ adj. (a) stumpf ⟨Winkel⟩
(b) (stupid) begriffsstutzig

obvious /'ɒbvɪəs/ adj. offenkundig; (easily
seen) augenfällig; **be ~ [to sb.] that ...:**
[jmdm.] klar sein, dass ...

o

'obviously *adv.* offenkundig; sichtlich ⟨*enttäuschen, überraschen usw.*⟩

occasion /əˈkeɪʒn/ **1** *n.* **(a)** Gelegenheit, *die;* **rise to the** ∼: sich der Situation gewachsen zeigen; **on several** ∼**s** bei mehreren Gelegenheiten; **on** ∼**[s]** gelegentlich
(b) (special occurrence) Anlass, *der;* **it was quite an** ∼: es war ein Ereignis
(c) (reason) Grund, *der* **(for** zu)
2 *v.t.* verursachen

occasional /əˈkeɪʒənl/ *adj.* gelegentlich; vereinzelt ⟨*Regenschauer*⟩

oc'casionally *adv.* gelegentlich; [only] **very** ∼: gelegentlich einmal

occult /ɒˈkʌlt, ˈɒkʌlt/ *adj.* okkult; **the** ∼: das Okkulte

occupant /ˈɒkjʊpənt/ *n.* Bewohner, *der*/ Bewohnerin, *die;* (of car, bus, etc.) Insasse, *der*/ Insassin, *die*

occupation /ɒkjʊˈpeɪʃn/ *n.* **(a)** (Mil.) Besetzung, *die;* (period) Besatzungszeit, *die*
(b) (activity) Beschäftigung, *die*
(c) (profession) Beruf, *der*

occupational /ɒkjʊˈpeɪʃənl/ *adj.* Berufs⟨*beratung, -risiko*⟩; ∼ **therapy** Beschäftigungstherapie, *die;* ∼ **therapist** Beschäftigungstherapeut, *der*/-therapeutin, *die*

occupier /ˈɒkjʊpaɪə(r)/ *n.* (Brit.) Besitzer, *der*/Besitzerin, *die;* (tenant) Bewohner, *der*/ Bewohnerin, *die*

occupy /ˈɒkjʊpaɪ/ *v.t.* **(a)** (Mil.; as demonstration) besetzen
(b) (live in) bewohnen
(c) (take up, fill) einnehmen; belegen ⟨*Zimmer*⟩; in Anspruch nehmen ⟨*Zeit, Aufmerksamkeit*⟩
(d) (busy, employ) beschäftigen

occur /əˈkɜː(r)/ *v.i.,* **-rr-:** **(a)** (be met with) vorkommen; ⟨*Gelegenheit:*⟩ sich bieten; ⟨*Problem:*⟩ auftreten
(b) (happen) ⟨*Veränderung:*⟩ eintreten; ⟨*Unfall, Vorfall:*⟩ sich ereignen
(c) ∼ **to sb.** (be thought of) jmdm. in den Sinn kommen; ⟨*Idee:*⟩ jmdm. kommen

occurrence /əˈkʌrəns/ *n.* **(a)** (incident) Ereignis, *das;* Begebenheit, *die*
(b) (occurring) Vorkommen, *das*

ocean /ˈəʊʃn/ *n.* Ozean, *der;* Meer, *das*

o'clock /əˈklɒk/ *adv.* **it is two/six** ∼: es ist zwei/sechs Uhr; **at two/six** ∼: um zwei/sechs Uhr; **six** ∼ *attrib.* Sechsuhr⟨*zug, -maschine, -nachrichten*⟩

Oct. *abbr.* = **October** Okt.

octagon /ˈɒktəgən/ *n.* Achteck, *das*

octane /ˈɒkteɪn/ *n.* Oktan, *das*

octave /ˈɒktɪv/ *n.* Oktave, *die*

October /ɒkˈtəʊbə(r)/ *n.* Oktober, *der; see also* AUGUST

octopus /ˈɒktəpəs/ *n.* Tintenfisch, *der*

odd /ɒd/ *adj.* **(a)** (surplus, spare) übrig ⟨*Stück, Silbergeld*⟩; **£25 and a few** ∼ **pence** 25 Pfund und ein paar Pence
(b) (occasional) gelegentlich; ∼ **job**/∼**-job man** Gelegenheitsarbeit, *die*/-arbeiter, *der*
(c) (one of pair or group) einzeln; ∼ **socks** nicht zusammengehörende Socken; **be the** ∼ **man out** ⟨*Gegenstand:*⟩ nicht dazu passen
(d) (uneven) ungerade ⟨*Zahl, Seite, Hausnummer*⟩
(e) (plus something) **forty** ∼: über vierzig; **twelve pounds** ∼: etwas mehr als zwölf Pfund
(f) (strange, eccentric) seltsam

oddity /ˈɒdɪtɪ/ *n.* (object, event) Kuriosität, *die*

'oddly *adv.* seltsam; ∼ **enough** seltsamerweise

odd 'man *n.* ∼ **out** Außenseiter, *der*/ Außenseiterin, *die;* **be the** ∼ **out** (extra person) überzählig sein

'odd-numbered *adj.* ungerade

odds /ɒdz/ *n. pl.* **(a)** (Betting) Odds *Pl.*
(b) [the] ∼ **are that she did it** wahrscheinlich hat sie es getan; **the** ∼ **are against/in favour of sb./sth.** jmds. Aussichten/die Aussichten für etw. sind gering/gut
(c) ∼ **and ends** Kleinigkeiten; (of food) Reste
(d) **be at** ∼ **with sb. over sth.** mit jmdm. in etw. (*Dat.*) uneinig sein
(e) **it makes no/little** ∼ [whether ...] es ist völlig/ziemlich gleichgültig[, ob ...]

'odds-on **1** *adj.* gut ⟨*Chance, Aussicht*⟩; hoch, klar ⟨*Favorit*⟩
2 *adv.* wahrscheinlich

odious /ˈəʊdɪəs/ *adj.* widerwärtig

odor etc. (*Amer.*) ▶ ODOUR etc.

odour /ˈəʊdə(r)/ *n.* Geruch, *der*

'odourless *adj.* geruchlos

oedema /ɪˈdiːmə/ *n.* Ödem, *das*

oestrogen /ˈiːstrədʒən/ *n.* Östrogen, *das*

œuvre /ˈɜːvr/ *n.* Œuvre, *das* (geh.); Werk, *das*

of /əv, *stressed* ɒv/ *prep.* von; (indicating material, substance) aus; **articles of clothing** Kleidungsstücke; **a friend of mine** ein Freund von mir; **where's that pencil of mine?** wo ist mein Bleistift?; **it was clever of you to do that** es war klug von dir, das zu tun; **the approval of sb.** jmds. Zustimmung; **the works of Shakespeare** Shakespeares Werke; **be made of ...:** aus ... [hergestellt] sein; **the fifth of January** der fünfte Januar; **his love of his father** seine Liebe zu seinem Vater; **person of extreme views** jemand mit extremen Ansichten; **a boy of 14 years** ein vierzehnjähriger Junge; **the five of us** wir fünf

off /ɒf/ **1** *adv.* **(a)** (away) **be a few miles** ∼: wenige Meilen entfernt sein; **the lake is not far** ∼: der See ist nicht weit [weg]; **I'm** ∼ **now** ich gehe jetzt; ∼ **we go!** los gehts! **(b)** (not on or attached or supported) ab; **get the lid** ∼: den Deckel abbekommen

(c) be ~ (switched or turned ~) ⟨*Wasser, Gas, Strom:*⟩ abgestellt sein; **the light/radio** etc. **is ~:** das Licht/Radio usw. ist aus
(d) the meat etc. **is ~:** das Fleisch usw. ist schlecht [geworden]
(e) be ~ (cancelled) abgesagt sein; ⟨*Verlobung:*⟩ [auf]gelöst sein; **~ and on** immer mal wieder (ugs.)
(f) (not at work) frei; **on my day ~:** an meinem freien Tag; **have a week ~:** eine Woche Urlaub bekommen
(g) (no longer available) **[the] soup** etc. **is ~:** es gibt keine Suppe usw. mehr
(h) (situated as regards money etc.) **he is badly** etc. **~:** er ist schlecht usw. gestellt
2 *prep.* von; **be ~ school/work** in der Schule/am Arbeitsplatz fehlen; **be ~ one's food** keinen Appetit haben; **just ~ the square** ganz in der Nähe des Platzes

offal /'ɒfl/ *n.* Innereien *Pl.*

off: ~beat *adj.* (fig.: eccentric) unkonventionell; **~-'centre** *adv.* nicht [genau] in der Mitte; **~ 'colour** *adj.* unwohl; **~cut** *n.* Rest, *der;* **~-'duty** *attrib. adj.* Freizeit-; ⟨*Polizist usw.*⟩, der dienstfrei hat

offence /ə'fens/ *n.* (Brit.) **(a)** (hurting of sb.'s feelings) Kränkung, *die;* **I meant no ~:** ich wollte Sie/ihn usw. nicht kränken
(b) (annoyance) **give ~:** Missfallen erregen; **take ~:** verärgert sein
(c) (crime) Straftat, *die;* **criminal ~:** strafbare Handlung

offend /ə'fend/ **1** *v.i.* verstoßen **(against** gegen)
2 *v.t.* **~ sb.** bei jmdm. Anstoß erregen; (hurt feelings of) jmdn. kränken

of'fender *n.* Straffällige, *der/die*

offense (Amer.) ▶ OFFENCE

offensive /ə'fensɪv/ **1** *adj.* **(a)** (aggressive) offensiv; Angriffs⟨*waffe*⟩
(b) (giving offence) ungehörig; (indecent) anstößig
2 *n.* Offensive, *die;* **take the** *or* **go on the ~:** in die *od.* zur Offensive übergehen

offer /'ɒfə(r)/ **1** *v.t.* anbieten; vorbringen ⟨*Entschuldigung*⟩; bieten ⟨*Chance*⟩; aussprechen ⟨*Beileid*⟩; **~ to help** seine Hilfe anbieten; **~ resistance** Widerstand leisten
2 *n.* Angebot, *das;* **[have/be] on ~:** im Angebot [haben/sein]

'offering *n.* (thing) Angebot, *das;* (to a deity) Opfer, *das*

off'hand **1** *adv.* **(a)** (without preparation) auf Anhieb ⟨*sagen, wissen*⟩; spontan ⟨*beschließen, entscheiden*⟩
(b) (casually) leichthin
2 *adj.* **(a)** (without preparation) spontan
(b) (casual) beiläufig; **be ~ with sb.** zu jmdm. kurz angebunden sein

office /'ɒfɪs/ *n.* **(a)** Büro, *das*
(b) (branch) Zweigstelle, *die*
(c) (position) Amt, *das;* **hold ~:** amtieren

office: ~ block *n.* Bürogebäude, *das;* **~ hours** *n. pl.* Dienststunden *Pl.;* **~ job** *n.* Bürotätigkeit, *die*

officer /'ɒfɪsə(r)/ *n.* **(a)** (Army etc.) Offizier, *der*
(b) (official) Beamte, *der*/Beamtin, *die*
(c) (constable) Polizeibeamte, *der*/-beamtin, *die*

office: ~ technology *n.* Bürotechnik, *die;* **~ worker** *n.* Büroangestellte, *der/die*

official /ə'fɪʃl/ **1** *adj.* offiziell; amtlich ⟨*Verlautbarung*⟩; regulär ⟨*Streik*⟩
2 *n.* Beamte, *der*/Beamtin, *die;* (party, union, or sports ~) Funktionär, *der*/Funktionärin, *die*

officialdom /ə'fɪʃldəm/ *n., no art.* Beamtentum, *das;* Bürokratie, *die*

officially *adv.* offiziell

officious /ə'fɪʃəs/ *adj.* übereifrig

offing /'ɒfɪŋ/ *n.* **be in the ~:** bevorstehen; ⟨*Gewitter:*⟩ aufziehen

off: ~licence *n.* (Brit.) ≈ Wein- und Spirituosenladen, *der;* **~line** (Comp.) **1** /'--/ *adj.* Offline-; **2** /-'-/ *adv.* offline; **~load** *v.t.* abladen; **~peak** *attrib. adj.* during **~peak hours** außerhalb der Spitzenlastzeiten; **~peak power** *or* **electricity** Nachtstrom, *der;* **~putting** /'ɒfpʊtɪŋ/ *adj.* (Brit.) abstoßend; **~print** *n.* Sonderdruck, *der;* **~road** *attrib. adj.* Gelände-, Offroad⟨*fahrzeug, -fahrrad, -wagen, -fahrt, -einsatz*⟩; **~road driving** Fahren im Gelände; **~set** /'--, -'-/ *v.t., forms as* SET: ausgleichen; **~ season** *n.* Nebensaison, *die;* **~shore** *adj.* küstennah; **~'side** *adj.* Abseits-; **be ~side** abseits sein; **~spring** *n., pl. same* Nachkommenschaft, *die;* (of animal) Junge *Pl.;* **~-the-peg** *attrib. adj.* Konfektions-; **~-the-shoulder** *attrib. adj.* schulterfrei ⟨*Kleid*⟩; **~-the-wall** *attrib. adj.* (esp. Amer. coll.) ausgeflippt (ugs.); **~'white** *adj.* gebrochen weiß

Oftel /'ɒftel/ *abbr.* (Brit.) = **Office of Telecommunications** *Regulierungsbehörde für Telekommunikation*

often /'ɒfn, 'ɒftn/ *adv.* oft; **every so ~:** gelegentlich

Ofwat /'ɒfwɒt/ *abbr.* (Brit.) = **Office of Water Services** *Regulierungsbehörde für Wasserwirtschaft*

oh /əʊ/ *int.* oh; *expr. pain* au

OHP *abbr.* (Brit.) = **overhead projector** OHP

oil /ɔɪl/ **1** *n.* Öl, *das*
2 *v.t.* ölen

oil: ~burner *n.* Ölbrenner, *der;* **~can** *n.* Ölkanne, *die;* **~ change** *n.* (Motor Veh.) Ölwechsel, *der;* **~ drum** *n.* Ölfass, *das;* **~field** *n.* Ölfeld, *das;* **~ lamp** *n.* Öllampe, *die;* **~ painting** *n.* Ölgemälde, *das;* **~producing** *adj.* [Erd]öl fördernd ⟨*Land*⟩; **~ refinery** *n.* [Erd]ölraffinerie, ⋯⧁

O

die; ∼ **rig** ▶ RIG[1] 1; ∼**skins** *n. pl.* Ölzeug, *das;* ∼ **slick** *n.* Ölteppich, *der;* ∼ **tanker** *n.* Öltanker, *der;* ∼ **well** *n.* Ölquelle, *die*

oily /'ɔɪlɪ/ *adj.* ölig; ölverschmiert ⟨*Gesicht, Hände*⟩

ointment /'ɔɪntmənt/ *n.* Salbe, *die*

OK /əʊ'keɪ/ (coll.) [1] *adj.* in Ordnung; okay (ugs.)
[2] *adv.* gut
[3] *int.* okay (ugs.)
[4] *v.t.* (approve) zustimmen (+ *Dat.*); **be OK'd by sb.** von jmdm. das Okay bekommen (ugs.)

okay /əʊ'keɪ/ ▶ OK

old /əʊld/ *adj.* alt; **be [more than] 30 years** ∼: [über] 30 Jahre alt sein

old: ∼ **'age** *n.* [fortgeschrittenes] Alter; ∼**-age** *attrib. adj.* Alters⟨rente, -ruhegeld⟩; ∼**-age pensioner** Rentner, *der*/Rentnerin, *die;* ∼**-fashioned** /əʊld'fæʃnd/ *adj.* altmodisch; ∼ **'people's home** *n.* Altenheim, *das;* Altersheim, *das;* ∼ **'wives' tale** *n.* Ammenmärchen, *das*

olive /'ɒlɪv/ *n.* Olive, *die*

olive 'oil *n.* Olivenöl, *das*

Olympic /ə'lɪmpɪk/ *adj.* olympisch; ∼ **Games** Olympische Spiele

Olympics /ə'lɪmpɪks/ *n. pl.* Olympiade, *die;* **Winter** ∼: Winterolympiade, *die*

omelette (**omelet**) /'ɒmlɪt/ *n.* Omelett, *das*

omen /'əʊmən/ *n.* Vorzeichen, *das*

ominous /'ɒmɪnəs/ *adj.* (of evil omen) ominös; (worrying) beunruhigend

omission /ə'mɪʃn/ *n.* Auslassung, *die;* (failure to act) Unterlassung, *die*

omit /ə'mɪt/ *v.t.* **-tt-** weglassen; ∼ **to do sth.** es versäumen, etw. zu tun

omnipotence /ɒm'nɪpətəns/ *n.* Allmacht, *die* (geh.)

omnipotent /ɒm'nɪpətənt/ *adj.* allmächtig

on /ɒn/ [1] *prep.* auf (*position: + Dat.; direction: + Akk.*); (attached to sth.) an (+ *Dat.*/ *Akk.*); (concerning, about) über (+ *Akk.*); (in expressions of time) an ⟨*einem Abend, Tag usw.*⟩; **write sth. on the wall** etw. an die Wand schreiben; **be hanging on the wall** an der Wand hängen; **have sth. on one** etw. bei sich haben; **on the bus/train** im Bus/Zug; (by bus/ train) mit dem Bus/Zug; **on Oxford 556767** unter der Nummer Oxford 556767; **on Sundays** sonntags; **on [his] arrival** bei seiner Ankunft; **on entering the room ...:** beim Betreten des Zimmers ...; **it's just on 9** es ist fast 9 Uhr; **the drinks are on me** (coll.) die Getränke gehen auf mich
[2] *adv.* **with/without a hat/coat on** mit/ohne Hut/Mantel; **have a hat on** einen Hut aufhaben; **on and on** immer weiter; **speak/ wait/work** *etc.* **on** weiterreden/-warten/ -arbeiten *usw.;* **from now on** von jetzt an; **the light/radio** *etc.* **is on** das Licht/Radio *usw.* ist an; **is Sunday's picnic on?** findet das Picknick am Sonntag statt?; **what's on at the**

cinema? was läuft im Kino?; **on and off** immer mal wieder (ugs.); **on to, onto** auf (+ *Akk.*)

once /wʌns/ [1] *adv.* **(a)** einmal; ∼ **a week/ month/year** einmal die Woche/im Monat/im Jahr; ∼ **again** *or* **more** noch einmal; ∼ **[and] for all** ein für alle Mal; **never/not** ∼: nicht ein einziges Mal
(b) (multiplied by one) ein mal
(c) (formerly) früher einmal; ∼ **upon a time there lived a king** es war einmal ein König
(d) at ∼ (immediately) sofort; (at the same time) gleichzeitig; **all at** ∼ (suddenly) plötzlich; (simultaneously) alle[s] zugleich
[2] *conj.* wenn; (with past tense) als
[3] *n.* [just *or* only] **this** ∼: [nur] dieses eine Mal

'oncoming *adj.* entgegenkommend ⟨*Fahrzeug, Verkehr*⟩

one /wʌn/ [1] *adj.* ein; *see also* EIGHT 1; (single, only) einzig; **no/not** ∼: kein; **the** ∼ **thing** das Einzige; **at** ∼ **time** einmal; ∼ **morning/night** eines Morgens/Nachts
[2] *n.* **(a)** eins
(b) (number, symbol) Eins, *die*
(c) (unit) **in** ∼**s** einzeln
[3] *pron.* **(a)** ein... (of + *Gen.*); **big** ∼**s and little** ∼**s** Große und Kleine; **the older/younger** ∼: der/die/das Ältere/Jüngere; **this** ∼: dieser/diese/dieses [da]; **that** ∼: der/die/das [da]; **which** ∼? welcher/welche/welches?; **which** ∼**s?** welche?; ∼ **by** ∼: einzeln; **love/ hate** ∼ **another** sich lieben/hassen; **be kind to** ∼ **another** nett zueinander sein
(b) (people in general; coll.: I, we) man; *as indirect object* einem; *as direct object* einen; ∼**'s** sein

one: ∼**-night 'stand** *n.* (coll.) [sexuelles] Abenteuer für eine Nacht; ∼**-off** (Brit.) [1] *n.* (article) Einzelstück, *das;* [2] *adj.* einmalig; ∼**-parent family** *n.* Einelternfamilie, *die*

onerous /'əʊnərəs/ *adj.* schwer

one: ∼**'self** *pron.* **(a)** *emphat.* selbst; **be** ∼**self** man selbst sein; **(b)** *refl.* sich; *see also* HERSELF; ∼**-sided** *adj.* einseitig; ∼**-stop shopping** *n.* Einkaufen in einem Einkaufszentrum [mit Komplettangebot]; ∼**-storey** *adj.* eingeschossig; ∼**-touch** *adj.* ∼**-touch dialling** Zielwahl, *die;* ∼**-track** *adj.* eingleisig; **have a** ∼**-track mind** (be obsessed) nur eins im Kopf haben; ∼**-upmanship** /wʌn'ʌpmənʃɪp/ *n., no indef. art.* die Kunst, den anderen immer um eine Nasenlänge voraus zu sein; ∼**-way** *adj.* **(a)** in einer Richtung *nachgestellt;* Einbahn⟨straße, -verkehr⟩; **(b)** einfach ⟨*Fahrpreis, Flug*⟩

'ongoing *adj.* aktuell ⟨*Problem, Debatte*⟩; andauernd ⟨*Situation*⟩

onion /'ʌnjən/ *n.* Zwiebel, *die*

onion: ∼ **skin** *n.* Zwiebelschale, *die;* ∼ **'soup** *n.* Zwiebelsuppe, *die*

online (Comp.) [1] /'--/ *adj.* Online-
[2] /'-'-/ *adv.* online

onlooker ⋯⋮ opinion ⋯ ⋯

'**onlooker** *n.* Zuschauer, *der*/Zuschauerin, *die*

only /'əʊnlɪ/ ⓵ *attrib. adj.* einzig...; **the ~ person** der/die Einzige; **an ~ child** ein Einzelkind

⓶ *adv.* nur; **we had been waiting ~ 5 minutes when ...**: wir hatten erst 5 Minuten gewartet, als ...; **it's ~/~ just 6 o'clock** es ist erst 6 Uhr/gerade erst 6 Uhr vorbei; **he ~ just made it** er hat es gerade noch geschafft; **~ if** nur [dann] ..., wenn; **~ the other day/week** erst neulich

on-screen *adj.* (Comp., TV) Bildschirm-

'**onset** *n.* (of winter) Einbruch, *der;* (of disease) Ausbruch, *der*

onslaught /'ɒnslɔːt/ *n.* [heftige] Attacke (fig.)

'**on-target** *attrib. adj.* **~ earnings £50,000** Verdienst bei erfolgreicher Tätigkeit 50 000 Pfund

onto ▶ ON 2

onus /'əʊnəs/ *n.* **the ~ is on him to do it** es ist seine Sache, es zu tun

onward[s] /'ɒnwədz/ *adv.* (in space) vorwärts; **from X ~**: von X an; **from that day ~**: von diesem Tag an

onyx /'ɒnɪks/ *n.* Onyx, *der*

ooze /uːz/ ⓵ *v.i.* sickern (**from** aus) ⓶ *v.t.* triefen von *od.* vor (+ *Dat.*); (fig.) ausstrahlen

op /ɒp/ *n.* (coll.) Operation, *die*

opaque /əʊ'peɪk/ *adj.* lichtundurchlässig; opak (fachspr.)

open /'əʊpn/ ⓵ *adj.* (a) offen; (not blocked or obstructed) frei; (available) frei ⟨*Stelle*⟩; **in the ~ air** im Freien; **be ~** ⟨*Laden, Museum, Bank usw.*⟩ geöffnet sein; **have an ~ mind about** *or* **on sth.** einer Sache gegenüber aufgeschlossen sein

(b) unverhohlen ⟨*Bewunderung, Hass, Verachtung*⟩

(c) (frank, communicative) offen ⟨*Wesen, Streit, Abstimmung, Regierungsstil*⟩; (not secret) öffentlich ⟨*Wahl*⟩

(d) geöffnet ⟨*Regenschirm*⟩; aufgeblüht ⟨*Blume, Knospe*⟩; aufgeschlagen ⟨*Zeitung, Landkarte*⟩

⓶ *n.* **in the ~** (outdoors) unter freiem Himmel; **[out] in the ~** (fig.) öffentlich bekannt

⓷ *v.t.* (a) öffnen

(b) eröffnen ⟨*Konferenz, Diskussion, Laden*⟩; beginnen ⟨*Verhandlungen, Spiel*⟩

(c) (unfold, spread out) aufschlagen ⟨*Zeitung, Buch, Landkarte*⟩; öffnen ⟨*Schirm*⟩

⓸ *v.i.* (a) sich öffnen; **~ into/on to sth.** zu etw. führen

(b) (become ~ to customers) öffnen; (start trading etc.) eröffnet werden

(c) (start) beginnen ⟨*Ausstellung.*⟩ eröffnet werden; ⟨*Theaterstück.*⟩ Premiere haben

■ **open 'up** ⓵ *v.t.* öffnen; (establish) eröffnen ⓶ *v.i.* sich öffnen; ⟨*Filiale*⟩ eröffnet werden; ⟨*Firma*⟩ sich niederlassen

open: ~-air *attrib. adj.* Openair⟨*konzert*⟩; **~-air [swimming] pool** Freibad, *das;* **~-and-'shut case** *n.* (coll.) klarer Fall; **~ day** *n.* Tag der offenen Tür

'**opener** *n.* Öffner, *der*

'**opening** ⓵ *n.* (a) Öffnen, *das;* (becoming open) Sichöffnen, *das;* (of exhibition, new centre) Eröffnen, *das*

(b) (establishment, ceremony) Eröffnung, *die*

(c) (initial part) Anfang, *der*

(d) (gap, aperture) Öffnung, *die*

(e) (opportunity) Möglichkeit, *die;* (vacancy) freie Stelle

⓶ *adj.* einleitend

opening: ~ hours *n. pl.* Öffnungszeiten *Pl.;* **~ time** *n.* Öffnungszeit, *die*

'**openly** *adv.* (a) (publicly) in der Öffentlichkeit; öffentlich ⟨*zugeben, verurteilen*⟩

(b) (frankly) offen

open: ~ 'market *n.* offener *od.* freier Markt; **~-'minded** *adj.* aufgeschlossen

openness /'əʊpnnɪs/ *n.* (frankness) Offenheit, *die*

open: ~-'plan *adj.* **~-plan office** Großraumbüro, *das;* **~ 'prison** *n.* offene Anstalt; **~ 'sandwich** *n.* belegtes Brot

opera /'ɒpərə/ *n.* Oper, *die*

opera: ~ glasses *n. pl.* Opernglas, *das;* **~ house** *n.* Opernhaus, *das;* **~ singer** *n.* Opernsänger, *der*/-sängerin, *die*

operate /'ɒpəreɪt/ ⓵ *v.i.* (a) (be in action) in Betrieb sein; ⟨*Bus, Zug usw.*⟩ verkehren

(b) (function) arbeiten; **the torch ~s on batteries** die Taschenlampe arbeitet mit Batterien

(c) **~ [on sb.]** (Med.) [jmdn.] operieren

⓶ *v.t.* bedienen ⟨*Maschine*⟩; unterhalten ⟨*Busverbindung, Telefondienst*⟩; betätigen ⟨*Hebel, Bremse*⟩

operating: ~ system *n.* (Comp.) Betriebssystem, *das;* **~ theatre** *n.* (Brit. Med.) Operationssaal, *der*

operation /ɒpə'reɪʃn/ *n.* (a) (causing to work) (of machine) Bedienung, *die;* (of bus service, telephone service, etc.) Unterhaltung, *die;* (of lever, brake) Betätigung, *die*

(b) **come into ~** ⟨*Gesetz, Gebühr usw.*⟩ in Kraft treten; **be in/out of ~** ⟨*Maschine, Gerät usw.*⟩ in/außer Betrieb sein

(c) (Med.) Operation, *die;* **have an ~**: operiert werden

operational /ɒpə'reɪʃənl/ *adj.* (esp. Mil.: ready to function) einsatzbereit

operative /'ɒpərətɪv/ *adj.* **become ~** ⟨*Gesetz.*⟩ in Kraft treten; **the scheme is ~**: das Programm läuft

operator /'ɒpəreɪtə(r)/ *n.* [Maschinen]bediener, *der*/-bedienerin, *die;* (Teleph.) (at exchange) Vermittlung, *die;* (at switchboard) Telefonist, *der*/Telefonistin, *die*

ophthalmic op'tician *n.* (Brit.) Augenoptiker, *der*/-optikerin, *die*

opinion /ə'pɪnjən/ *n.* Meinung, *die* (**on** über ⋯⋮

+ *Akk.,* zu); **have a high/low** ∼ **of sb.** eine/
keine hohe Meinung von jmdm. haben; **in
my** ∼: meiner Meinung nach
opinionated /ə'pɪnjəneɪtɪd/ *adj.*
rechthaberisch
o'pinion poll *n.* Meinungsumfrage, *die*
opium /'əʊpɪəm/ *n.* Opium, *das*
opponent /ə'pəʊnənt/ *n.* Gegner, *der/*
Gegnerin, *die*
opportune /'ɒpətjuːn/ *adj.* **(a)** (favourable)
günstig
(b) (well-timed) zur rechten Zeit *nachgestellt*
opportunism /ɒpə'tjuːnɪzm/ *n.*
Opportunismus, *der*
opportunist /ɒpə'tjuːnɪst/ *n.* Opportunist,
*der/*Opportunistin, *die*
opportunity /ɒpə'tjuːnɪti/ *n.* Gelegenheit,
die
oppose /ə'pəʊz/ **1** *v.t.* sich wenden gegen
2 *v.i.* **the opposing team** die gegnerische
Mannschaft
opposed /ə'pəʊzd/ *adj.* **as** ∼ **to** im
Gegensatz zu; **be** ∼ **to sth.** ⟨*Person.*⟩ gegen
etw. sein
opposite /'ɒpəzɪt/ **1** *adj.* gegenüberliegend
⟨*Straßenseite, Ufer*⟩; entgegengesetzt ⟨*Ende,
Weg, Richtung*⟩; **the** ∼ **sex** das andere
Geschlecht
2 *n.* Gegenteil, *das* **(of** von)
3 *adv.* gegenüber
4 *prep.* gegenüber
opposite 'number *n.* (fig.) Pendant, *das*
opposition /ɒpə'zɪʃn/ *n.* **(a)** Opposition,
die; (resistance) Widerstand, *der* **(to** gegen); **in**
∼ **to** entgegen
(b) (Brit. Polit.) **the O**∼: die Opposition
oppress /ə'pres/ *v.t.* unterdrücken; (fig.)
⟨*Gefühl:*⟩ bedrücken
oppression /ə'preʃn/ *n.* Unterdrückung,
die
oppressive /ə'presɪv/ *adj.* repressiv; (fig.)
bedrückend ⟨*Ängste, Atmosphäre*⟩; (hot and
close) drückend ⟨*Wetter, Klima, Tag*⟩
opt /ɒpt/ *v.i.* sich entscheiden (**for** für); ∼ **to
do sth.** sich dafür entscheiden, etw. zu tun;
∼ **out** nicht mitmachen/(stop taking part) nicht
länger mitmachen (**of** bei)
optic /'ɒptɪk/ **1** *adj.* (Anat.) Seh⟨*nerv, -bahn*⟩
2 *n. or* **O**∼ ® (Brit.: for spirits) Portionierer,
der
optical /'ɒptɪkl/ *adj.* optisch
optical 'character reader *n.* (Comp.)
Klarschriftleser, *der*
optician /ɒp'tɪʃn/ *n.* Optiker, *der/*
Optikerin, *die*
optics /'ɒptɪks/ *n.* Optik, *die*
optima *pl. of* OPTIMUM
optimise ▶ OPTIMIZE
optimism /'ɒptɪmɪzm/ *n.* Optimismus, *der*
optimist /'ɒptɪmɪst/ *n.* Optimist, *der/*
Optimistin, *die*
optimistic /ɒptɪ'mɪstɪk/ *adj.* optimistisch

optimize /'ɒptɪmaɪz/ *v.t.* (make the most of)
das Beste machen aus
optimum /'ɒptɪməm/ **1** *n., pl.* optima
/'ɒptɪmə/ Optimum, *das*
2 *adj.* optimal
option /'ɒpʃn/ *n.* (choice) Wahl, *die;* (thing)
Wahlmöglichkeit, *die*
optional /'ɒpʃənl/ *adj.* nicht zwingend;
∼ **subject** Wahlfach, *das*
opulence /'ɒpjʊləns/ *n.* Wohlstand, *der*
opulent /'ɒpjʊlənt/ *adj.* wohlhabend; feudal
⟨*Auto, Haus usw.*⟩
or /ə(r), *stressed* ɔː(r)/ *conj.* **(a)** oder; **he
cannot read or write** er kann weder lesen
noch schreiben; **without food or water** ohne
Essen und Wasser; **15 or 20 minutes** 15 bis 20
Minuten; **in a day or two** in ein, zwei Tagen
(b) (introducing explanation) das heißt; **or rather**
beziehungsweise
oracle /'ɒrəkl/ *n.* Orakel, *das*
oral /'ɔːrəl/ *adj.* mündlich; (Med.) oral
orally /'ɔːrəli/ *adv.* **take** ∼: einnehmen
orange /'ɒrɪndʒ/ **1** *n.* **(a)** (fruit) Orange, *die;*
Apfelsine, *die*
(b) (colour) Orange, *das*
2 *adj.* orange[farben]
orange: ∼ **juice** *n.* Orangensaft, *der;*
∼ **peel** *n.* Orangenschale, *die;* ∼ **'squash**
n. Orangensaftgetränk, *das*
orator /'ɒrətə(r)/ *n.* Redner, *der/*Rednerin,
die
oratory /'ɒrətəri/ *n.* Redekunst, *die*
orb /ɔːb/ *n.* Kugel, *die*
orbit /'ɔːbɪt/ **1** *n.* (Astron.) [Umlauf]bahn, *die*
2 *v.i.* kreisen
3 *v.t.* umkreisen
orbital /'ɔːbɪtl/ *adj.* ∼ **road** Ringstraße, *die*
orchard /'ɔːtʃəd/ *n.* Obstgarten, *der;*
(commercial) Obstplantage, *die*
orchestra /'ɔːkɪstrə/ *n.* Orchester, *das*
orchestral /ɔː'kestrl/ *adj.* Orchester-
orchestrate /'ɔːkɪstreɪt/ *v.t.* orchestrieren
orchid /'ɔːkɪd/ *n.* Orchidee, *die*
ordain /ɔː'deɪn/ *v.t.* **(a)** (Eccl.) ordinieren
(b) (decree) verfügen
ordeal /ɔː'diːl/ *n.* Qual, *die*
order /'ɔːdə(r)/ **1** *n.* **(a)** (sequence)
Reihenfolge, *die;* **out of** ∼: durcheinander
(b) (regular arrangement, normal state) Ordnung,
die; **be/not be in** ∼: in Ordnung/nicht in
Ordnung sein (ugs.); **be out of/in** ∼ (not in/in
working condition) nicht funktionieren/
funktionieren; **'out of** ∼' „außer Betrieb"; **in
good/bad** ∼: in gutem/schlechtem Zustand
(c) (command) Anweisung, *die;* (Mil.) Befehl,
der
(d) in ∼ **to do sth.** um etw. zu tun
(e) (Commerc.) Auftrag, *der* (**for** über + *Akk.*);
(to waiter, ∼ed goods) Bestellung, *die*
(f) keep ∼: Ordnung [be]wahren; *see also*
LAW B
(g) (religious ∼) Orden, *der*

2 *v.t.* (a) (command) befehlen; ⟨*Richter:*⟩ verfügen; ~ **sb. to do sth.** jmdn. anweisen/ (Milit.) jmdm. befehlen, etw. zu tun
(b) (Commerc.) bestellen (**from** bei)
(c) (arrange) ordnen
■ **order a'bout, order a'round** *v.t.* herumkommandieren

'**order form** *n.* Bestellformular, *das*

orderly /'ɔːdəlɪ/ 1 *adj.* friedlich; diszipliniert ⟨*Menge*⟩; (methodical) methodisch; (tidy) ordentlich
2 *n.* (a) (Mil.) [Offiziers]bursche, *der*
(b) medical ~: ≈ Krankenpflegehelfer, *der*

ordinal /'ɔːdɪml/ *adj. & n.* ~ [**number**] Ordinalzahl, *die*

ordinarily /'ɔːdɪnərɪlɪ/ *adv.* normalerweise; gewöhnlich

ordinary /'ɔːdɪnərɪ/ *adj.* (normal) normal ⟨*Gebrauch*⟩; üblich ⟨*Verfahren*⟩; (not exceptional) gewöhnlich

ordination /ɔːdɪ'neɪʃn/ *n.* (Eccl.) Ordination, *die;* Ordinierung, *die*

ordnance 'survey /'ɔːdnəns/ *n.* (Brit.) amtliche Landesvermessung; ~ **survey map** amtliche topographische Karte

ore /ɔː(r)/ *n.* Erz, *das*

organ /'ɔːgən/ *n.* (a) (Mus.) Orgel, *die*
(b) (Biol.) Organ, *das*

'**organ donor** *n.* Organspender, *der*/ -spenderin, *die;* ~ **card** Organspende[r]ausweis, *der*

organic /ɔː'gænɪk/ *adj.* organisch; biologisch-dynamisch ⟨*Ackerbau*⟩; biodynamisch ⟨*Nahrungsmittel*⟩

organically /ɔː'gænɪkəlɪ/ *adv.* (a) (also Med.) organisch
(b) (without chemicals) biologisch

organism /'ɔːgənɪzm/ *n.* Organismus, *der*

organist /'ɔːgənɪst/ *n.* Organist, *der*/ Organistin, *die*

organization /ɔːgənaɪ'zeɪʃn/ *n.* Organisation, *die;* ~ **of time/work** Zeit-/ Arbeitseinteilung, *die*

organize /'ɔːgənaɪz/ *v.t.* organisieren; einteilen ⟨*Arbeit, Zeit*⟩; veranstalten ⟨*Konferenz, Festival*⟩; ~ **into groups** in Gruppen einteilen

organized /'ɔːgənaɪzd/ *adj.* organisiert

'**organizer** *n.* Organisator, *der*/ Organisatorin, *die;* (of event, festival) Veranstalter, *der*/Veranstalterin, *die*

'**organ transplant** *n.* Organverpflanzung, *die*

orgasm /'ɔːgæzm/ *n.* Orgasmus, *der*

orgy /'ɔːdʒɪ/ *n.* Orgie, *die*

orient 1 /'ɔːrɪənt/ *n.* **the O~:** der Orient
2 /'ɒrɪent/ *v.t.* ausrichten (**towards** nach); ~ **oneself** sich orientieren

oriental /ɒrɪ'entl/ 1 *adj.* orientalisch
2 *n.* Asiat, *der*/Asiatin, *die*

orientate /'ɒrɪənteɪt/ ▸ ORIENT 2

orientation /ɒrɪən'teɪʃn/ *n.* Orientierung, *die*

orienteering /ɒrɪən'tɪərɪŋ/ *n.* (Brit.) Orientierungslauf, *der*

orifice /'ɒrɪfɪs/ *n.* Öffnung, *die*

origin /'ɒrɪdʒɪn/ *n.* (derivation) Herkunft, *die;* (beginnings) Anfänge *Pl.;* (source) Ursprung, *der;* **country of** ~: Herkunftsland, *das;* **have its** ~ **in sth.** seinen Ursprung in etw. (*Dat.*) haben

original /ə'rɪdʒɪml/ 1 *adj.* ursprünglich; Ur⟨*text, -fassung*⟩; eigenständig ⟨*Forschung*⟩; (inventive) originell; **an** ~ **painting** ein Original
2 *n.* Original, *das*

original 'gravity *n.* Stammwürze, *die*

originality /ərɪdʒɪ'nælɪtɪ/ *n.* Originalität, *die*

originally /ə'rɪdʒɪnəlɪ/ *adv.* (a) ursprünglich
(b) originell ⟨*schreiben usw.*⟩

originate /ə'rɪdʒɪneɪt/ *v.i.* ~ **from** entstehen aus; ~ **in** seinen Ursprung haben in (+ *Dat.*)

ornament /'ɔːnəmənt/ *n.* Ziergegenstand, *der*

ornamental /ɔːnə'mentl/ *adj.* dekorativ; Zier⟨*pflanze, -naht usw.*⟩

ornate /ɔː'neɪt/ *adj.* reich verziert; prunkvoll ⟨*Dekoration*⟩

ornithologist /ɔːnɪ'θɒlədʒɪst/ *n.*. Ornithologe, *der*/Ornithologin, *die*

ornithology /ɔːnɪ'θɒlədʒɪ/ *n.* Ornithologie, *die*

orphan /'ɔːfn/ 1 *n.* Waise, *die*
2 *v.t.* **be** ~**ed** [zur] Waise werden

orphanage /'ɔːfənɪdʒ/ *n.* Waisenhaus, *das*

orthodox /'ɔːθədɒks/ *adj.* orthodox

orthopaedic /ɔːθə'piːdɪk/ *adj.* orthopädisch

orthopaedics /ɔːθə'piːdɪks/ *n.* Orthopädie, *die*

oscillate /'ɒsɪleɪt/ *v.i.* schwingen

oscillation /ɒsɪ'leɪʃn/ *n.* Schwingen, *das;* (single ~) Schwingung, *die*

osmosis /ɒz'məʊsɪs/ *n.*, *pl.* **osmoses** /ɒz'məʊsiːz/ Osmose, *die*

ostensible /ɒ'stensɪbl/ *adj.* vorgeschoben

ostensibly /ɒ'stensɪblɪ/ *adv.* vorgeblich

ostentatious /ɒsten'teɪʃəs/ *adj.* prunkhaft ⟨*Kleidung, Schmuck*⟩; prahlerisch ⟨*Art*⟩

osteopath /'ɒstɪəpæθ/ *n.* Osteopath, *der*/ Osteopathin, *die*

osteoporosis /ɒstɪəʊpə'rəʊsɪs/ *n.* Osteoporose, *die*

ostrich /'ɒstrɪtʃ/ *n.* Strauß, *der*

other /'ʌðə(r)/ 1 *adj.* (a) (not the same) ander...; **the** ~ **two/three** *etc.* (the remaining) die beiden/drei *usw.* anderen; **the** ~ **one** der/die/das andere; **some** ~ **time** ein andermal   ···⟩

O

(b) (further) one ∼ thing noch eins; **some/six ∼ people** noch ein paar/noch sechs [andere *od.* weitere] Leute; **no ∼ questions** keine weiteren Fragen

(c) ∼ **than** (different from) anders als; (except) außer

(d) the ∼ day/evening neulich/neulich abends

2 *n.* anderer/andere/anderes; **there are six ∼s** es sind noch sechs andere da; **any ∼:** irgendein anderer/-eine andere/-ein anderes; **not any ∼:** kein anderer/keine andere/kein anderes; **one after the ∼:** einer/eine/eins nach dem/der/dem anderen

3 *adv.* anders; ∼ **than that, ...:** abgesehen davon, ...

otherwise /'ʌðəwaɪz/ **1** *adv.* **(a)** (in a different way) anders

(b) (or else) anderenfalls

(c) (in other respects) im Übrigen

2 *pred. adj.* anders

otter /'ɒtə(r)/ *n.* [Fisch]otter, *der*

ouch /aʊtʃ/ *int.* autsch

ought /ɔːt/ *v. aux. only in pres. and past* ought, neg. (coll.) **oughtn't** /'ɔːtnt/ **I ∼ to do/ have done it** (expr. moral duty) ich müsste es tun/hätte es tun müssen; (expr. desirability) ich sollte es tun/hätte es tun sollen; ∼ **not** *or* ∼**n't you to have left by now?** müsstest du nicht schon weg sein?; **one ∼ not to do it** man sollte es nicht tun; **he ∼ to be hanged/ in hospital** er gehört an den Galgen/ins Krankenhaus; **that ∼ to be enough** das dürfte reichen; **he ∼ to win** er müsste [eigentlich] gewinnen

oughtn't /'ɔːtnt/ (coll.) = ought not

ounce /aʊns/ *n.* (measure) Unze, *die*

our /'aʊə(r)/ *poss. pron. attrib.* unser

ours /'aʊəz/ *poss. pron. pred.* unserer/ unsere/unseres; *see also* HERS

ourselves /aʊə'selvz/ *pron.* **(a)** *emphat.* selbst

(b) *refl.* uns. See also HERSELF

oust /aʊst/ *v.t.* verdrängen; ∼ **sb. from his job/from power** jmdn. von seinem Arbeitsplatz vertreiben/jmdn. entmachten

out /aʊt/ *adv.* **(a)** (away from place) ∼ **here/ there** hier/da draußen; **be ∼ in the garden** draußen im Garten sein; **what's it like ∼?** wie ist es draußen?; **go ∼ shopping** *etc.* einkaufen *usw.* gehen; **be ∼** (not at home, not in one's office, etc.) nicht da sein; **she was ∼ all night** sie war eine/die ganze Nacht weg; **have a day ∼ in London** einen Tag in London verbringen; **row ∼ to ...:** hinaus-/ herausrudern zu ...; **be ∼ at sea** auf See sein **(b)** (Sport, Games) **be ∼** ⟨*Ball:*⟩ aus *od.* im Aus sein; ⟨*Mitspieler:*⟩ ausscheiden; ⟨*Schlagmann:*⟩ aus[geschlagen] sein; **not ∼:** nicht aus

(c) be ∼ (asleep) weg sein (ugs.); (unconscious) bewusstlos sein

(d) (no longer burning) aus[gegangen]

(e) (in error) **be 3% ∼ in one's calculations** sich um 3% verrechnet haben; **this is £5 ∼:** das stimmt um 5 Pfund nicht

(f) (not in fashion) passee (ugs.); out (ugs.)

(g) say it ∼ loud es laut sagen; ∼ **with it!** heraus mit der Sprache; **their secret is ∼:** ihr Geheimnis ist bekannt geworden; [the] **truth will ∼:** die Wahrheit wird an den Tag kommen; **the sun/moon is ∼:** die Sonne/der Mond scheint; **the third volume is just ∼:** der dritte Band ist soeben erschienen; **the roses are ∼:** die Rosen blühen

(h) be ∼ for sth./to do sth. auf etw. (*Akk.*) aus sein/darauf aus sein, etw. zu tun; **be ∼ for trouble** Streit suchen

(i) (to or at an end) **before the day/month was ∼:** am selben Tag/vor Ende des Monats. *See also* OUT OF

out: ∼back *n.* (esp. Austral.) Hinterland, *das;* ∼'**bid** *v.t.,* ∼**bid** überbieten; ∼**board** *adj.* ∼**board motor** Außenbordmotor, *der;* ∼**break** *n.* Ausbruch, *der;* **at the ∼break of war** bei Kriegsausbruch; **an ∼break of flu** eine Grippeepidemie; ∼**building** *n.* Nebengebäude, *das;* ∼**burst** *n.* Ausbruch, *der;* **an ∼burst of weeping/laughter** ein Weinkrampf/Lachanfall; **an ∼burst of temper** ein Wutanfall; ∼**cast** *n.* Ausgestoßene, *der/ die;* **a social ∼cast** ein Geächteter/eine Geächtete; ∼**come** *n.* Ergebnis, *das;* Resultat, *das;* ∼**cry** *n.* [Aufschrei der] Empörung; ∼'**dated** *adj.* überholt; ∼'**do** *v.t., forms as* DO: überbieten (in an + *Dat.*); ∼**door** *adj.* ∼**door shoes/things** Straßenschuhe/-kleidung, *die;* ∼**door games/ pursuits** Spiele/Beschäftigungen im Freien; ∼**door swimming pool** Freibad, *das;* ∼'**doors** **1** *adv.* draußen; **go ∼doors** nach draußen gehen; **2** *n.* **the [great] ∼doors** die freie Natur

outer /'aʊtə(r)/ *adj.* äußer...; Außen⟨*fläche, -seite, -wand, -tür*⟩

outer 'space *n.* Weltraum, *der*

out: ∼fit *n.* **(a)** (clothes) Kleider *Pl.;* **(b)** (equipment) Ausrüstung, *die;* **(c)** (coll.: organization) Laden, *der* (ugs.); ∼**going** **1** *adj.* **(a)** [aus dem Amt] scheidend ⟨*Regierung, Präsident*⟩; **(b)** (friendly) kontaktfreudig ⟨*Person*⟩; **2** *n., in pl.* ∼**s** (expenditure) Ausgaben *Pl.;* ∼'**grow** *v.t., forms as* GROW: herauswachsen aus ⟨*Kleider*⟩; (leave behind) entwachsen (+ *Dat.*); ∼**growth** *n.* Auswuchs, *der;* ∼**house** *n.* Nebengebäude, *das*

'**outing** *n.* Ausflug, *der*

out: ∼landish /aʊt'lændɪʃ/ *adj.* ausgefallen; ∼'**last** *v.t.* überdauern; überleben ⟨*Person, Jahrhundert*⟩; ∼**law** **1** *n.* Bandit, *der*/Banditin, *die;* **2** *v.t.* verbieten; ∼**lay** *n.* Ausgaben *Pl.* (on für); ∼**let** /'aʊtlet, 'aʊtlɪt/ *n.* **(a)** Ablauf, Abfluss, *der;* Auslauf, Auslass, *der;* **(b)** (fig.) Ventil, *das;* **(c)** (market) Absatzmarkt, *der;* (shop) Verkaufsstelle, *die;* ∼**line** **1** *n.* **(a)** in sing. or pl. Umriss, *der;* **(b)** (short account)

Grundriss, *der;* (of topic) Übersicht, die **(of
über + *Akk.*); [2]** *v.t.* (describe) umreißen;
∼live /aʊtˈlɪv/ *v.t.* überleben; **∼look** *n.* **(a)**
(view) Aussicht, die **(over** über + *Akk.,* **on** to
auf + *Akk.*); (fig.; Meteorol.) Aussichten *Pl.;* **(b)**
(mental attitude) Einstellung, die **(on** zu);
∼lying *adj.* entlegen; **∼maˈnœuvre** *v.t.*
überlisten ‹*Truppen*›; **∼moded**
/aʊtˈməʊdɪd/ *adj.* antiquiert; **∼ˈnumber**
v.t. zahlenmäßig überlegen sein (+ *Dat.*)

ˈ**out of** *prep.* **(a)** (from within) aus; **go ∼ the
door** zur Tür hinausgehen
(b) (not within) **be ∼ the country** im Ausland
sein; **be ∼ town/the room** nicht in der Stadt/
im Zimmer sein; **feel ∼ it** *or* **things** sich
ausgeschlossen fühlen
(c) (from among) **one ∼ every three smokers**
jeder dritte Raucher; **58 ∼ every 100** 58 von
hundert
(d) (beyond range of) außer ‹*Reich-/Hörweite,
Sicht, Kontrolle*›
(e) (from) aus; **get money ∼ sb.** Geld aus
jmdm. herausholen; **do well ∼ sb./sth.** von
jmdm./etw. profitieren
(f) aus ‹*Mitleid, Furcht, Neugier usw.*›
(g) (without) **∼ money** ohne Geld; **we're ∼ tea**
wir haben keinen Tee mehr
(h) (away from) von … entfernt; **ten miles
∼ London** 10 Meilen außerhalb von London

out: ∼-of-court settlement *n.* (Law)
(agreement) außergerichtlicher Vergleich;
(payment) Vergleichssumme, die; **∼-ofˈdate**
attrib. adj. veraltet; (expired) ungültig ‹*Karte*›;
∼-ofˈpocket *attrib. adj.* Bar‹*auslagen*›;
∼-of-print *attrib. adj.* vergriffen; **∼-of-
work** *attrib. adj.* arbeitslos; **∼patient** *n.*
ambulanter Patient/ambulante Patientin;
∼patients[' department] Poliklinik, *die;*
∼ˈplay *v.t.* (Sport) besser spielen als;
∼post *n.* Außenposten, *der;* (of civilization etc.;
also Mil.) Vorposten, *der;* **∼put** *n.* **(a)**
Produktion, *die;* (of liquid, electricity, etc.)
Leistung, *die;* **(b)** (Comp.) Ausgabe, *die*

outrage [1] /ˈaʊtreɪdʒ/ *n.* **(a)** (deed)
Verbrechen, *das;* (during war) Gräueltat, *die;*
(against decency) grober Verstoß
(b) (strong resentment) Empörung, die **(at**
gegen)
[2] /aʊˈtreɪdʒ/ *v.t.* empören

outrageous /aʊtˈreɪdʒəs/ *adj.*
unverschämt; unverschämt hoch ‹*Preis*›;
unerhört ‹*Frechheit, Skandal*›

out: ∼right [1] /-'-'-/ *adv.* **(a)** (wholly)
‹*kaufen, verkaufen*›; **(b)** (openly) freiheraus
‹*erzählen, sagen, lachen*›; [2] /'--/ *adj.*
ausgemacht ‹*Unehrlichkeit*›; glatt (ugs.)
‹*Ablehnung, Absage, Lüge*›; klar ‹*Sieg,
Niederlage, Sieger*›; **∼set** *n.* Anfang, *der;* **at
the ∼set** zu Anfang; **from the ∼set** von
Anfang an; **∼ˈshine** *v.t.,* **∼shone** /aʊtˈʃɒn/
(fig.) in den Schatten stellen

outside [1] /-'-', '--'/ *n.* **(a)** Außenseite, *die;*
on the ∼: außen; **to/from the ∼:** nach/von
außen; **∼ lane** Überholspur, *die*
(b) (external appearance) Äußere, *das*

(c) at the [very] ∼ äußerstenfalls; höchstens
[2] /'--/ *adj.* **(a)** äußer…; Außen‹*wand,
-antenne, -kajüte, -toilette, -durchmesser*›;
∼ lane Überholspur, *die*
(b) have only an **∼ chance** nur eine sehr
geringe Chance haben
[3] /-'-/ *adv.* (on the **∼**) draußen; (to the **∼**)
nach draußen
[4] /-'-/ *prep.* **(a)** (position) außerhalb (+ *Gen.*);
∼ the door vor der Tür
(b) (to the **∼** of) aus … hinaus; **go ∼ the
house** nach draußen gehen

outˈsider *n.* (Sport; also fig.) Außenseiter, *der*

out: ∼size *adj.* überdimensional; **∼size
clothes** Kleidung in Übergröße; **∼skirts**
n. pl. Stadtrand, *der;* **the ∼skirts of the town**
die Außenbezirke der Stadt; **∼ˈsmart** *v.t.*
(coll.) ausschmieren (ugs.); **∼source** *v.t.*
extern vergeben ‹*Arbeit, Aufträge*›;
∼ sourcing /ˈautsɔːsɪŋ/ *n.* Outsourcing,
das (fachspr.); Fremdbezug, *der* (fachspr.);
∼ˈspoken *adj.* freimütig; **be ∼spoken
about sth.** sich freimütig über etw. äußern;
∼ˈstanding *adj.* **(a)** (exceptional)
hervorragend; überragend ‹*Bedeutung*›;
außergewöhnlich ‹*Person, Mut, Fähigkeit*›;
(b) (not yet settled) ausstehend ‹*Schuld,
Geldsumme*›; unbezahlt ‹*Rechnung*›;
ungelöst ‹*Problem*›; **∼ˈstretched** *adj.*
ausgestreckt; (spread out) ausgebreitet;
∼ˈstrip *v.t.* (in competition) überflügeln;
∼tray *n.* Ablage für Ausgänge; **∼ˈvote**
v.t. überstimmen

outward /ˈautwəd/ [1] *adj.* **(a)** (external,
apparent) [rein] äußerlich; äußer…
‹*Erscheinung, Bedingung*›
(b) Hin‹*reise, -fracht*›
[2] *adv.* nach außen ‹*aufgehen, richten*›

ˈ**outwardly** *adv.* nach außen hin ‹*Gefühle
zeigen*›; öffentlich ‹*Loyalität erklären*›

ˈ**outwards ▸** OUTWARD 2

out: ∼ˈweigh *v.t.* schwerer wiegen als;
überwiegen ‹*Nachteile*›; **∼ˈwit** *v.t.,* **-tt-**
überlisten; **∼ˈworn** *adj.* veraltet

oval /ˈəʊvl/ [1] *adj.* oval
[2] *n.* Oval, *das*

ovary /ˈəʊvəri/ *n.* (Anat.) Eierstock, *der*

ovation /əˈveɪʃn/ *n.* Ovation, *die;* **a
standing ∼:** stehende Ovationen *Pl.*

oven /ˈʌvn/ *n.* [Back]ofen, *der*

oven: ∼ cloth *n.* Topflappen, *der;*
∼ glove *n.* Topfhandschuh, *der;* **∼proof**
adj. feuerfest; **∼-ready** *adj.* backfertig
‹*Pommes frites, Pastete*›; bratfertig
‹*Geflügel*›; **∼ware** *n.* feuerfestes Geschirr

over /ˈəʊvə(r)/ [1] *adv.* **(a)** (outward and
downward) hinüber; **climb/look/jump ∼:**
hinüber- *od.* (ugs.) rüberklettern/-sehen/
-springen
(b) (so as to cover surface) **board/cover ∼:**
zunageln/-decken
(c) (across a space) hinüber; (towards speaker)
herüber; **he swam ∼ to us/the other side** er
schwamm zu uns herüber/hinüber zur ····⟫

anderen Seite; ∼ **here/there** (direction) hier
herüber/dort hinüber; (location) hier/dort;
[**come in, please,**] ∼ (Radio) übernehmen Sie
bitte; ∼ **and out** (Radio) Ende
(d) (in excess etc.) **children of 12 and** ∼:
Kinder im Alter von zwölf Jahren und
darüber; **be** [**left**] ∼: übrig [geblieben] sein
(e) (from beginning to end) von Anfang bis
Ende; **say sth. twice** ∼: etw. zweimal sagen;
[**all**] ∼ **again,** (Amer.) ∼: noch einmal [ganz
von vorn]; ∼ **and** ∼ [**again**] immer wieder
(f) (at an end) vorbei; vorüber; **be** ∼: vorbei
sein; ⟨*Aufführung:*⟩ zu Ende sein; **get sth.**
∼ **with** etw. hinter sich ⟨*Akk.*⟩ bringen; **be**
∼ **and done with** erledigt sein
(g) all ∼ (completely finished) aus [und vorbei]; **I
ache all** ∼: mir tut alles weh; **be shaking all**
∼: am ganzen Körper zittern
[2] *prep.* **(a)** (above, on, round about) über
(*position:* + *Dat.; direction:* + *Akk.*); (across)
über (+ *Akk.*); **look** ∼ **a wall** über eine Mauer
sehen; **fall** ∼ **a cliff** von einem Felsen stürzen;
the pub ∼ **the road** die Wirtschaft gegenüber;
hit sb. ∼ **the head** jmdm. auf den Kopf
schlagen; ∼ **the page** auf der nächsten Seite
(b) (in or across every part of) [überall] in
(+ *Dat.*); (to and fro upon) über (+ *Akk.*); (all
through) durch; **all** ∼ (in or on all parts of)
überall in (+ *Dat.*); **travel all** ∼ **the country**
das ganze Land bereisen; **all** ∼ **Spain** in ganz
Spanien; **all** ∼ **the world** in der ganzen Welt
(c) (on account of) wegen
(d) (engaged with) bei; **take trouble** ∼ **sth.** sich
(*Dat.*) mit etw. Mühe geben; **be a long time**
∼ **sth.** lange für etw. brauchen; ∼ **work/
dinner** bei der Arbeit/beim Essen
(e) (superior to, in charge of) über (+ *Akk.*); **have
command/authority** ∼ **sb.** Befehlsgewalt über
jmdn./Weisungsbefugnis gegenüber jmdm.
haben; **be** ∼ **sb.** (in rank) über jmdm. stehen
(f) (beyond, more than) über (+ *Akk.*); ∼ **and
above** zusätzlich zu
(g) (throughout, during) über (+ *Akk.*); ∼ **the
weekend/summer** übers Wochenende/den
Sommer über; ∼ **the past years** in den
letzten Jahren

over: ∼**'active** *adj.* hyperaktiv; ∼**all**
[1] *n.* (Brit.: garment) Arbeitskittel, *der;* [2] *adj.*
(a) Gesamt⟨*breite, -einsparung, -abmessung*⟩;
have an ∼**all majority** die absolute Mehrheit
haben; **(b)** (general) allgemein; [3] /'-'-, --'-/
adv. **(a)** (in all parts) insgesamt; **(b)** (taken as a
whole) im Großen und Ganzen; ∼**'awe** *v.t.*
Ehrfurcht einflößen (+ *Dat.*); ∼**'balance**
v.i. das Gleichgewicht verlieren;
∼**'bearing** *adj.* herrisch; ∼**'blown** *adj.*
(past its prime, lit. or fig.) verblühend; ∼**board**
adv. über Bord; **fall** ∼**board** über Bord
gehen; ∼**'cast** *adj.* trübe; bewölkt ⟨*Himmel*⟩;
∼**'charge** *v.t.* **(a)** (beyond reasonable price) zu
viel abverlangen (+ *Dat.*); **(b)** (beyond right
price) zu viel berechnen (+ *Dat.*); ∼**'coat** *n.*
Mantel, *der;* ∼**'come** *v.t., forms as* COME:
(a) überwinden; bezwingen ⟨*Feind*⟩;
⟨*Dämpfe:*⟩ betäuben; **(b) he was** ∼**come by
grief/with emotion** Kummer/Rührung

überwältigte ihn; ∼**'confidence** *n.*
übersteigertes Selbstvertrauen;
∼**'confident** *adj.* übertrieben
zuversichtlich; ∼**'cooked** *adj.* verkocht;
∼**'critical** *adj.* zu kritisch; ∼**'crowded**
adj. überfüllt; ∼**'crowding** *n.* (of room, bus,
train) Überfüllung, *die;* (of city) Übervölkerung,
die; ∼**'do** *v.t., forms as* DO: (carry to excess)
übertreiben; ∼**do it** *or* **things** (work too hard)
sich übernehmen; ∼**'done** *adj.*
(a) (exaggerated) übertrieben; **(b)** (∼cooked)
verkocht; verbraten ⟨*Fleisch*⟩; ∼**dose** [1] *n.*
Überdosis, *die;* [2] *v.i.* ∼**dose on heroin** eine
Überdosis Heroin nehmen; ∼**draft** *n.*
Kontoüberziehung, *die;* **have an** ∼**draft of £50**
sein Konto um 50 Pfund überzogen haben;
∼**'draw** *v.t., forms as* DRAW 1: überziehen
⟨*Konto*⟩; ∼**'drawn** *adj.* überzogen ⟨*Konto*⟩;
I am ∼**drawn** [**at the bank**] mein Konto ist
überzogen; ∼**drive** *n.* Schongang, *der;*
∼**'due** *adj.* überfällig; **the train is 15 minutes**
∼**due** der Zug hat schon 15 Minuten
Verspätung; ∼**'eager** *adj.* übereifrig;
∼**'eat** *v.i., forms as* EAT: zu viel essen;
∼**estimate** [1] /-'estɪmeɪt/ *v.t.*
überschätzen; [2] /-'estɪmət/ *n.* zu hohe
Schätzung; ∼**ex'ert** *v. refl.* sich
überanstrengen; ∼**ex'pose** *v.t.* (Photog.)
überbelichten; ∼**'fill** *v.t.* zu voll machen;
∼**'fish** *v.t.* überfischen; ∼**flow** [1] /--'-/ *v.t.*
laufen über (+ *Akk.*) ⟨*Rand*⟩; (flow over brim of)
überlaufen aus; ∼**flow its banks** ⟨*Fluss:*⟩ über
die Ufer treten; [2] /--'-/ *v.i.* überlaufen;
[3] /'---/ *n.* ∼**flow** [**pipe**] Überlauf, *der;* ∼**flow
car park** Ausweichparkplatz, *der;* ∼**'full** *adj.*
zu voll; übervoll; ∼**grown** *adj.*
überwachsen (with von); ∼**hang** [1] /--'-/ *v.t.,*
∼**hung** /əʊvə'hʌŋ/ ⟨*Felsen, Stockwerk:*⟩
hinausragen über (+ *Akk.*); [2] /'---/ *n.*
Überhang, *der;* ∼**'hanging** *adj.*
überhängend; ∼**haul** [1] /--'-/ *v.t.* überholen;
überprüfen ⟨*System*⟩; [2] /'---/ *n.* Überholung,
die; ∼**head** [1] /--'-/ *adv.* über mir/ihm/uns
usw.; [2] /'---/ *adj.* ∼**head wires** Oberleitung,
die; ∼**head lighting** Deckenbeleuchtung, *die;*
[3] /'---/ *n.* ∼**heads,** (Amer.) ∼**head** (Commerc.)
Gemeinkosten *Pl.;* ∼**'hear** *v.t., forms as*
HEAR 1 (accidentally) zufällig [mit]hören;
(intentionally) belauschen; ∼**'heat** *v.i.* zu heiß
werden; ⟨*Maschine, Lager:*⟩ heißlaufen;
∼**in'dulge** *v.i.* es übertreiben; ∼**indulge
in food and drink** sich am Essen und Trinken
mehr als gütlich tun; ∼**in'dulgence** *n.*
übermäßiger Genuss (**in** von); (towards a
person) zu große Nachgiebigkeit;
∼**in'dulgent** *adj.* unmäßig; (towards a
person) zu nachgiebig

overjoyed /əʊvə'dʒɔɪd/ *adj.* überglücklich
(**at** über + *Akk.*)

over: ∼**land** /--'-/ *adv.* auf dem Landweg;
∼**lap** [1] /--'-/ *v.t.* überlappen; [2] /--'-/ *v.i.*
⟨*Flächen, Dachziegel:*⟩ sich überlappen;
⟨*Aufgaben:*⟩ sich überschneiden; [3] *n.*
Überlappung, *die;* ∼**'leaf** *adv.* auf der
Rückseite; ∼**load** *v.t.* überladen; ∼**'look**
v.t. **(a)** ⟨*Hotel, Zimmer, Haus:*⟩ Aussicht

bieten auf (+ *Akk.*); **(b)** (ignore, not see)
übersehen; (allow to go unpunished)
hinwegsehen über (+ *Akk.*)

'**overly** *adv.* allzu

over: ~'**man** *v.t.* überbesetzen;
~**manning** *n.* [personelle] Überbesetzung;
~'**modest** *adj.* zu bescheiden; ~'**much**
[1] *adj.* allzu viel; [2] *adv.* allzu sehr;
~**night** [1] /--'-/ *adv.* (also fig.: suddenly) über
Nacht; **stay** ~ **night** übernachten; [2] /'---/
adj. ~**night stay** Übernachtung, *die;* **be an**
~**night success** (fig.) über Nacht Erfolg
haben; ~'**pay** *v.t., forms as* PAY 2:
überbezahlen; ~'**populated** *adj.*
überbevölkert; ~**popu'lation** *n.*
Übervölkerung, *die;* ~'**power** *v.t.*
überwältigen; ~'**powering** *adj.*
überwältigend; durchdringend ⟨*Geruch*⟩;
~'**priced** *adj.* zu teuer; ~'**qualified** *adj.*
überqualifiziert; ~'**rate** *v.t.* überschätzen;
~**re'act** *v.i.* unangemessen heftig
reagieren (**to** auf + *Akk.*); ~**re'action** *n.*
Überreaktion, *die* (**to** auf + *Akk.*); ~'**ride**
v.t. forms as RIDE 3: sich hinwegsetzen über
(+ *Akk.*); ~'**riding** *adj.* vorrangig; **be of**
~**riding importance** wichtiger als alles
andere sein; ~'**ripe** *adj.* überreif; ~'**rule**
v.t. aufheben ⟨*Entscheidung*⟩; zurückweisen
⟨*Einwand, Argument*⟩; ~**rule sb.** jmds.
Vorschlag ablehnen; ~'**run** *v.t., forms as*
RUN 3: **be** ~**run with** überlaufen sein von
⟨*Touristen*⟩; überwuchert sein von
⟨*Unkraut*⟩; ~**seas** [1] /--'-/ *adv.* in Übersee
⟨*leben, sein*⟩; nach Übersee ⟨*gehen*⟩; [2] /'---/
adj. Übersee-; ~'**see** *v.t., forms as* SEE 1:
überwachen; (manage) leiten ⟨*Abteilung*⟩;
~'**sensitive** *adj.* überempfindlich;
~-**sexed** /əʊvə'sekst/ *adj.* sexbesessen;
~'**shadow** *v.t.* überschatten; ~'**shoot**
v.t., forms as SHOOT 2: hinausschießen über
(+ *Akk.*); ~**shoot [the runway]** ⟨*Pilot,*
Flugzeug:⟩ zu weit kommen; ~**sight** *n.*
Versehen, *das;* ~**simplifi'cation** *n.* zu
starke Vereinfachung; ~'**simplify** *v.t.* zu
stark vereinfachen; ~'**sleep** *v.i., forms as*
SLEEP 2: verschlafen; ~'**spend** *v.i., forms*
as SPEND: zu viel [Geld] ausgeben;
~**statement** *n.* Übertreibung, *die;*
~'**stay** *v.t.* überziehen ⟨*Urlaub*⟩; ~'**step**
v.t. überschreiten; ~'**stretch** *v.t.*
überdehnen; (fig.) überfordern

'**overt** /əʊ'vɜːt/ *adj.* unverhohlen

over: ~'**take** *v.t., forms as* TAKE:
überholen; '**no** ~**taking**' (Brit.) „Überholen
verboten"; ~-**the-top** *adj.* übergroßen;
~'**throw** [1] /--'-/ *v.t., forms as* THROW 1:
stürzen; [2] /'---/ *n.* Sturz, *der;* ~'**time** [1] *n.*
Überstunden *Pl.;* [2] *adv.* **work** ~**time**
Überstunden machen; ~'**tire** *v.t.*
übermüden; ~**tire oneself** sich übernehmen
od. überanstrengen

overtly /'əʊvətlɪ, əʊ'vɜːtlɪ/ *adv.*
unverhohlen

'**overtone** *n.* (fig.) Unterton, *der*

overture /'əʊvətjʊə(r)/ *n.* (Mus.) Ouvertüre,
die

over: ~'**turn** [1] *v.t.* umstoßen; [2] *v.i.*
⟨*Auto, Boot:*⟩ umkippen; ⟨*Boot:*⟩ kentern;
~**use** /əʊvə'juːz/ *v.t.* zu oft verwenden

overweening /əʊvə'wiːnɪŋ/ *adj.* maßlos
⟨*Ehrgeiz, Gier, Stolz*⟩

'**overweight** *adj.* übergewichtig ⟨*Person*⟩;
be ~**weight** Übergewicht haben

overwhelm /əʊvə'welm/ *v.t.* überwältigen

over'whelming *adj.* überwältigend

over: ~'**work** [1] *v.t.* mit Arbeit
überlasten; [2] *v.i.* sich überarbeiten;
~'**wrought** *adj.* überreizt

ovulate /'ɒvjʊleɪt/ *v.i.* (Physiol.) ovulieren

ovulation /ɒvjʊ'leɪʃn/ *n.* Ovulation, *die*

owe /əʊ/ *v.t.,* owing /'əʊɪŋ/ schulden; ~ **sb.**
sth., ~ **sth. to sb.** jmdm. etw. schulden; (fig.)
jmdm. etw. verdanken

owing /'əʊɪŋ/ *pred. adj.* ausstehend; **be** ~:
ausstehen

'**owing to** *prep.* wegen

owl /aʊl/ *n.* Eule, *die*

own /əʊn/ [1] *adj.* eigen; **be sb.'s**
~ [property] jmdm. selbst gehören; **a house/**
ideas of one's ~: ein eigenes Haus/eigene
Ideen; **on one's/its** ~: allein
[2] *v.t.* besitzen; **be** ~**ed by sb.** jmdm.
gehören

■ **own 'up** *v.i.* gestehen; ~ **up to sth.** etw.
zugeben

'**own-brand,** '**own-label** [1] *attrib. adjs.*
Eigenmarken-
[2] *n.* Hausmarke, *die*

'**owner** *n.* Besitzer, *der*/Besitzerin, *die;* (of
shop, hotel, firm, etc.) Inhaber, *der*/Inhaberin,
die

owner-'occupier *n.* (Brit.)
Eigenheimbesitzer, *der*/-besitzerin, *die*

'**ownership** *n.* Besitz, *der*

own 'goal *n.* (lit. or fig.) Eigentor, *das*

ox /ɒks/ *n., pl.* **oxen** /'ɒksn/ Ochse, *der*

oxidize (**oxidise**) /'ɒksɪdaɪz/ *v.t.* & *i.*
(Chem.) oxidieren; oxydieren (fachspr.)

oxtail 'soup *n.* Ochsenschwanzsuppe, *die*

oxygen /'ɒksɪdʒən/ *n.* Sauerstoff, *der*

'**oxygen mask** *n.* Sauerstoffmaske, *die*

oyster /'ɔɪstə(r)/ *n.* Auster, *die*

oz. *abbr.* = **ounce[s]**

ozone /'əʊzəʊn/ *n.* Ozon, *das*

ozone: ~ **depletion** *n.* Ozonabbau, *der;*
~-**friendly** *adj.* ozonsicher; (not using CFCs)
FCKW-frei; ~ **hole** *n.* Ozonloch, *das* (ugs.);
~ **layer** *n.* Ozonschicht, *die*

Pp

P, p /piː/ n. P, p, *das*

p. *abbr.* (a) = **page** S.
(b) (Brit.) = **penny/pence** p

pace /peɪs/ ① n. (a) (step) Schritt, *der*
(b) (speed) Tempo, *das;* **keep** ~ **with** Schritt
halten mit
② v.i. ~ **up and down** auf und ab gehen
③ v.t. ~ auf und ab gehen in (+ *Dat.*)

'pacemaker n. (Sport, Med.) Schrittmacher,
der

Pacific /pəˈsɪfɪk/ ① adj. (Geog.) ~ **Ocean**
Pazifischer od. Stiller Ozean
② n. the ~: der Pazifik

pacifier /ˈpæsɪfaɪə(r)/ n. (Amer.: dummy)
Schnuller, *der*

pacifism /ˈpæsɪfɪzm/ n. Pazifismus, *der*

pacifist /ˈpæsɪfɪst/ ① n. Pazifist, *der/*
Pazifistin, *die*
② adj. pazifistisch

pacify /ˈpæsɪfaɪ/ v.t. besänftigen

pack /pæk/ ① n. (a) (bundle) Bündel, *das;*
(Mil.) Tornister, *der;* (rucksack) Rucksack, *der*
(b) (derog.: lot) (people) Bande, *die;* **a** ~ **of lies/**
nonsense ein Sack voll Lügen/eine Menge
Unsinn
(c) (Brit.) ~ **[of cards]** [Karten]spiel, *das*
(d) (of wolves, wild dogs) Rudel, *das;* (of hounds)
Meute, *die*
(e) (packet) Packung, *die*
② v.t. (a) einpacken; (fill) packen; ~ **one's**
bags seine Koffer packen
(b) (cram) voll stopfen (ugs.)
(c) (wrap) verpacken (**in** in + *Dat. od. Akk.*)
③ v.i. packen; **send sb.** ~**ing** (fig.) jmdn.
rausschmeißen (ugs.)
∎ **pack 'up** ① v.t. zusammenpacken
⟨*Sachen, Werkzeug*⟩; packen ⟨*Paket*⟩
② v.i. (coll.: stop) aufhören

package /ˈpækɪdʒ/ ① n. Paket, *das*
② v.t. verpacken

package: ~ **deal** n. Paket, *das;*
~ **holiday,** ~ **tour** ns. Pauschalreise, *die*

packaging /ˈpækɪdʒɪŋ/ n. (material)
Verpackung, *die*

packed /pækt/ adj. (a) gepackt; ~ **lunch**
Lunchpaket, *das*
(b) (crowded) [über]voll; ~ **out** gerammelt voll
(ugs.)

packet /ˈpækɪt/ n. Päckchen, *das;* (box)
Schachtel, *die;* **a** ~ **of cigarettes** ein
Päckchen/eine Schachtel Zigaretten; **cost/**
earn a ~: ein Heidengeld kosten (ugs.)/ein
Schweinegeld verdienen (ugs.)

packet 'soup n. Instantsuppe, *die*

'packing n. (material) Verpackungsmaterial,
das; **postage and** ~: Porto und Verpackung

'packing case n. [Pack]kiste, *die*

pact /pækt/ n. Pakt, *der*

pad¹ /pæd/ ① n. Polster, *das;* (block of paper)
Block, *der*
② v.t., **-dd-** polstern ⟨*Jacke, Schulter*⟩
∎ **pad 'out** v.t. (fig.) auswalzen

pad² v.i., **-dd-** tappen

padded /ˈpædɪd/ adj. gepolstert

padded 'envelope n. wattierter
Umschlag

padding /ˈpædɪŋ/ n., no indef. art.
Polsterung, *die;* (fig.) Füllsel, *das*

paddle¹ /ˈpædl/ ① n. [Stech]paddel, *das*
② v.t. & i. paddeln

paddle² ① v.i. (with feet) planschen
② n. **have a/go for a** ~: ein bisschen
planschen/planschen gehen

paddling pool /ˈpædlɪŋpuːl/ n.
Planschbecken, *das*

paddock /ˈpædək/ n. Koppel, *die*

'padlock ① n. Vorhängeschloss, *das*
② v.t. [mit einem Vorhängeschloss]
verschließen

paediatrician /piːdɪəˈtrɪʃn/ n. Kinderarzt,
der/-ärztin, *die*

paediatrics /piːdɪˈætrɪks/ n. Pädiatrie, *die*
(fachspr.); Kinderheilkunde, *die*

paedophile /ˈpiːdəfaɪl/ ① n. Pädophile,
der
② adj. pädophil

pagan /ˈpeɪgən/ ① n. Heide, *der/*Heidin, *die*
② adj. heidnisch

page¹ /peɪdʒ/ n. (boy) Page, *der*

page² n. (of book etc.) Seite, *die*

pageant /ˈpædʒənt/ n. (spectacle)
Schauspiel, *das*

pageantry /ˈpædʒəntrɪ/ n. Prunk, *der*

page: ~ **break** n. (Comp.) Seitenbruch, *der;*
~ **number** n. Seitenzahl, *die*

pager /ˈpeɪdʒə(r)/ n. Piepser, *der* (ugs.)

paginate /ˈpædʒɪneɪt/ v.t. paginieren

pagination /pædʒɪˈneɪʃn/ n. Paginierung,
die

'paging device ▶ PAGER

paid /peɪd/ ① ▶ PAY 2, 3
② adj. (a) bezahlt ⟨*Urlaub, Arbeit*⟩
(b) **put** ~ **to** (Brit. coll.) zunichte machen;
kurzen Prozess machen mit (ugs.) ⟨*Person*⟩

pail /peɪl/ n. Eimer, *der*

pain /peɪn/ n. (a) (suffering) Schmerzen *Pl.;*
(mental ~) Qualen *Pl.;* **be in** ~: Schmerzen
haben
(b) (instance) Schmerz, *der;* **I have a** ~ **in my**
knee/stomach mein Knie/Magen tut weh

(c) *in pl.* (trouble taken) Mühe, *die;* **take** ∼**s** sich (*Dat.*) Mühe geben (**over** mit, bei)
painful /'peɪnfl/ *adj.* **(a)** schmerzhaft; **be** ∼ ⟨*Körperteil:*⟩ wehtun
(b) (distressing) schmerzlich ⟨*Gedanke, Erinnerung*⟩; traurig ⟨*Pflicht*⟩
'**painkiller** *n.* schmerzstillendes Mittel
'**painless** *adj.* schmerzlos; (fig.) unproblematisch
painstaking /'peɪnzteɪkɪŋ/ *adj.* gewissenhaft
paint /peɪnt/ 1 *n.* Farbe, *die;* (on car) Lack, *der*
2 *v.t.* (cover, colour) [an]streichen; (make picture of, make by ∼ing) malen; bemalen ⟨*Wand, Vase, Decke*⟩
paint: ∼**box** *n.* Malkasten, *der;* ∼**brush** *n.* Pinsel, *der*
'**painter** *n.* Maler, *der*/Malerin, *die*
'**painting** *n.* (art) Malerei, *die;* (picture) Gemälde, *das;* Bild, *das*
'**painting book** *n.* Malbuch, *das*
paint: ∼ **stripper** *n.* Abbeizer, *der;* ∼**work** *n.* (on walls etc.) Anstrich, *der;* (of car) Lack, *der*
pair /peə(r)/ 1 *n.* Paar, *das;* **a** ∼ **of** gloves/ socks/shoes *etc.* ein Paar Handschuhe/ Socken/Schuhe *usw.;* **in** ∼**s** paarweise; **a** ∼ **of trousers/jeans** eine Hose/Jeans
2 *v.t.* paaren
▪ **pair 'off** *v.i.* Zweiergruppen bilden
pajamas /pə'dʒɑːməz/ (Amer.) ▶ PYJAMAS
Pakistan /pɑːkɪ'stɑːn/ *pr. n.* Pakistan (*das*)
Pakistani /pɑːkɪ'stɑːnɪ/ 1 *adj.* pakistanisch; **sb. is** ∼: jmd. ist Pakistani
2 *n.* Pakistani, *der/die*
pal /pæl/ *n.* (coll.) Kumpel, *der* (ugs.)
palace /'pælɪs/ *n.* Palast, *der*
palate /'pælət/ *n.* Gaumen, *der*
palatial /pə'leɪʃl/ *adj.* palastartig
pale[1] /peɪl/ *adj.* blass, (nearly white) bleich ⟨*Gesichtsfarbe, Haut, Gesicht*⟩; blass ⟨*Farbe*⟩; fahl ⟨*Licht*⟩; **go** ∼: blass/bleich werden; (fig.) ∼ **imitation** schlechte Nachahmung
pale[2] *n.* **beyond the** ∼: unmöglich
Palestine /'pælɪstaɪn/ *pr. n.* Palästina (*das*)
Palestinian /pælɪ'stɪnɪən/ 1 *adj.* palästinensisch; **sb. is** ∼ jmd. ist Palästinenser/Palästinenserin
2 *n.* Palästinenser, *der*/Palästinenserin, *die*
palette /'pælɪt/ *n.* Palette, *die*
pall[1] /pɔːl/ *n.* **(a)** (over coffin) Sargtuch, *das* **(b)** (fig.) Schleier, *der*
pall[2] *v.i.* ∼ **[on sb.]** [jmdm.] langweilig werden
pallor /'pælə(r)/ *n.* Blässe, *die*
palm[1] /pɑːm/ *n.* (tree) Palme, *die*
palm[2] *n.* Handteller, *der*
▪ **palm 'off** *v.t.* ∼ sth. off on sb., ∼ sb. off with sth. jmdm. etw. andrehen (ugs.)

palmistry /'pɑːmɪstrɪ/ *n.* Handlesekunst, *die*
palm: P∼ '**Sunday** *n.* Palmsonntag, *der;* ∼**top** *n.* ∼top [computer] Palmtop, *der;* ∼ **tree** *n.* Palme, *die*
palpitation /pælpɪ'teɪʃn/ *n. in pl.* (Med.: of heart) Palpitation, *die* (fachspr.); **suffer from** ∼**s** Herzklopfen haben
paltry /'pɔːltrɪ, 'pɒltrɪ/ *adj.* schäbig
pamper /'pæmpə(r)/ *v.t.* verhätscheln; ∼ **oneself** sich verwöhnen
pamphlet /'pæmflɪt/ *n.* (leaflet) Prospekt, *der;* (booklet) Broschüre, *die*
pan /pæn/ *n.* [Koch]topf, *der;* (for frying) Pfanne, *die*
panacea /pænə'sɪə/ *n.* Allheilmittel, *das*
Panama /pænə'mɑː/ *pr. n.* Panama (*das*); ∼ **Ca'nal** Panamakanal, *der*
'**pancake** *n.* Pfannkuchen, *der*
pancreas /'pæŋkrɪəs/ *n.* Bauchspeicheldrüse, *die*
panda /'pændə/ *n.* Panda, *der*
pandemonium /pændɪ'məʊnɪəm/ *n.* Chaos, *das;* (uproar) Tumult, *der*
pander /'pændə(r)/ *v.i.* ∼ **to** allzu sehr entgegenkommen (+ *Dat.*)
pane /peɪn/ *n.* Scheibe, *die*
panel /'pænl/ *n.* **(a)** Paneel, *das* **(b)** (esp. Telev., Radio, etc.) (quiz team) Rateteam, *das;* (in public discussion) Podium, *das*
panelling /'pænəlɪŋ/ *n.* Täfelung, *die*
panellist /'pænəlɪst/ *n.* (Telev., Radio) (on quiz programme) Mitglied des Rateteams; (on discussion panel) Diskussionsteilnehmer, *der*/ -teilnehmerin, *die*
'**pan-fry** *v.t.* [in der Pfanne] braten
pang /pæŋ/ *n.* (of pain) Stich, *der;* **feel** ∼**s of** conscience/guilt Gewissensbisse haben; ∼**[s] of hunger** quälender Hunger
panic /'pænɪk/ 1 *n.* Panik, *die;* **hit the** ∼ **button** (fig. coll.) Alarm schlagen; (∼) durchdrehen (ugs.)
2 *v.i.,* -ck- in Panik (*Akk.*) geraten; **don't** ∼! nur keine Panik!
panic: ∼ **attack** *n.* Angstanfall, *der;* ∼-**stricken,** ∼-**struck** *adjs.* von Panik erfasst
panorama /pænə'rɑːmə/ *n.* Panorama, *das*
pansy /'pænzɪ/ *n.* Stiefmütterchen, *das*
pant /pænt/ *v.i.* keuchen; ⟨*Hund:*⟩ hecheln
panther /'pænθə(r)/ *n.* Panther, *der*
panties /'pæntɪz/ *n. pl.* (coll.) [pair of] ∼: Schlüpfer, *der*
pantomime /'pæntəmaɪm/ *n.* (Brit.) *Märchenspiel im Varieteestil, das um Weihnachten aufgeführt wird*
pantry /'pæntrɪ/ *n.* Speisekammer, *die*
pants /pænts/ *n. pl.* **(a)** (esp. Amer. coll.: trousers) [pair of] ∼: Hose, *die* **(b)** (Brit. coll.: underpants) Unterhose, *die*

paparazzo /pæpæ'rɑːtsəʊ/ *n.*, *pl.* **paparazzi**
/pæpæ'rɑːtsi:/ Paparazzo, *der*
paper /'peɪpə(r)/ **1** *n.* **(a)** (material) Papier,
das
(b) *in pl.* (documents) Unterlagen *Pl.;* (to prove
identity etc.) Papiere *Pl.*
(c) (in examination) (Univ.) Klausur, *die;* (Sch.)
Arbeit, *die*
(d) (newspaper) Zeitung, *die*
(e) (learned article) Referat, *das*
2 *adj.* aus Papier *nachgestellt;* Papier‹*mütze,
-taschentuch*›
3 *v.t.* tapezieren
paper: ~**back** **1** *n.* Paperback, *das;*
2 *adj.* ~**back book** Paperback, *das;* ~ **'bag**
n. Papiertüte, *die;* ~ **'boy** *n.* Zeitungsjunge,
der; ~ **clip** *n.* Büroklammer, *die;* (larger)
Aktenklammer, *die;* ~ **'handkerchief** *n.*
Papiertaschentuch, *das;* ~ **mill** *n.*
Papierfabrik *od.* -mühle, *die;* ~ **money** *n.*
Papiergeld, *das;* ~ **'napkin** *n.*
Papierserviette, *die;* ~ **round** *n.*
Zeitungenaustragen, *das;* ~ **servi'ette**
▶ ~ NAPKIN; ~ **'towel** *n.* Papierhandtuch,
das; ~**weight** *n.* Briefbeschwerer, *der;*
~**work** *n.* Schreibarbeit, *die*
par /pɑː(r)/ *n.* **feel below** ~: nicht ganz auf
dem Posten sein (ugs.); **be on a** ~ **with sb./
sth.** jmdm./einer Sache gleichkommen
parable /'pærəbl/ *n.* Gleichnis, *das*
parachute /'pærəʃuːt/ **1** *n.* Fallschirm,
der
2 *v.i.* ‹*Truppen:*› abspringen (**into** über
+ *Dat.*)
parade /pə'reɪd/ **1** *n.* **(a)** (display)
Zurschaustellung, *die*
(b) (Mil.) Appell, *der*
(c) (procession) Umzug, *der;* (of troops) Parade,
die
2 *v.t.* zur Schau stellen
3 *v.i.* paradieren
pa'rade ground *n.* Exerzierplatz, *der*
paradise /'pærədaɪs/ *n.* Paradies, *das*
paradox /'pærədɒks/ *n.* Paradox[on], *das*
paradoxical /pærə'dɒksɪkl/ *adj.* paradox
paraffin /'pærəfɪn/ *n.* Paraffin, *das;* (Brit.:
fuel) Petroleum, *das*
paragliding /'pærəglaɪdɪŋ/ *n.* Paragliding,
das
paragon /'pærəgən/ Muster, *das* (**of an**
+ *Dat.*); ~ **of virtue** Tugendheld, *der*/-heldin,
die
paragraph /'pærəgrɑːf/ *n.* Absatz, *der*
parallel /'pærəlel/ **1** *adj.* parallel; (fig.:
similar) vergleichbar; ~ **bars** Barren, *der*
2 *n.* Parallele, *die;* ~ **[of latitude]**
Breitenkreis, *der*
Paralympics /pærə'lɪmpɪks/ *n. pl.*
Paralympics *Pl.*
paralyse /'pærəlaɪz/ *v.t.* lähmen; (fig.) lahm
legen ‹*Verkehr, Industrie*›
paralysis /pə'rælɪsɪs/ *n.* Lähmung, *die*
paralyze (Amer.) ▶ PARALYSE

paramedic /pærə'medɪk/ *n.* medizinische
Hilfskraft; (ambulance worker) Sanitäter, *der*/
Sanitäterin, *die*
parameter /pə'ræmɪtə(r)/ *n.* Faktor, *der*
paramilitary /pærə'mɪlɪtərɪ/ *adj.*
paramilitärisch
paramount /'pærəmaʊnt/ *adj.* größt...
‹*Wichtigkeit*›; Haupt‹*überlegung*›; **be** ~:
Vorrang haben
paranoia /pærə'nɔɪə/ *n.* Paranoia, *die*
(Med.); (tendency) Verfolgungswahn, *der*
paranoid /'pærənɔɪd/ *adj.* **be** ~ ‹*Person:*›
an Verfolgungswahn leiden
parapet /'pærəpɪt/ *n.* Brüstung, *die*
paraphernalia /pærəfə'neɪlɪə/ *n. sing.*
Apparat, *der*
paraphrase /'pærəfreɪz/ **1** *n.*
Umschreibung, *die*
2 *v.t.* umschreiben
paraplegic /pærə'pliːdʒɪk/ **1** *adj.*
doppelseitig gelähmt
2 *n.* doppelseitig Gelähmter/Gelähmte
parasite /'pærəsaɪt/ *n.* Schmarotzer, *der*
parasitic /pærə'sɪtɪk/ *adj.* **(a)** (Biol.)
parasitisch
(b) (fig.) schmarotzerhaft
parasol /'pærəsɒl/ *n.* Sonnenschirm, *der*
paratroops /'pærətruːps/ *n. pl.*
Fallschirmjäger *Pl.*
parcel /'pɑːsl/ *n.* Paket, *das*
parched /pɑːtʃt/ *adj.* ausgedörrt; trocken
‹*Lippen*›
parchment /'pɑːtʃmənt/ *n.* Pergament, *das*
pardon /'pɑːdn/ **1** *n.* Verzeihung, *die;* **beg
sb.'s** ~: jmdn. um Entschuldigung bitten; **I
beg your** ~: entschuldigen Sie bitte
2 *v.t.* **(a)** ~ **sb.** [**for**] **sth.** jmdm. etw.
verzeihen
(b) (excuse) entschuldigen
pardonable /'pɑːdənəbl/ *adj.* verzeihlich
pare /peə(r)/ *v.t.* (trim) schneiden; (peel)
schälen
parent /'peərənt/ *n.* Elternteil, *der;* ~**s**
Eltern *Pl.*
parental /pə'rentl/ *adj.* Eltern‹*pflicht,
-haus, -liebe*›
parenthesis /pə'renθɪsɪs/ *n.*, *pl.*
parentheses /pə'renθɪsiːz/ (bracket) runde
Klammer
'parents' evening *n.* Elternabend, *der*
'parents-in-law *pl.* Schwiegeeltern *Pl.*
Paris /'pærɪs/ *pr. n.* Paris (*das*)
parish /'pærɪʃ/ *n.* Gemeinde, *die*
parish: ~ **'church** *n.* Pfarrkirche, *die;*
~ **'council** *n.* (Brit.) Gemeinderat, *der*
parishioner /pə'rɪʃənə(r)/ *n.*
Gemeinde[mit]glied, *das*
parish 'priest *n.* Gemeindepfarrer, *der*
park /pɑːk/ **1** *n.* Park, *der*
2 *v.i.* parken
3 *v.t.* abstellen; parken ‹*Kfz*›; **a** ~**ed car** ein
parkendes Auto

park-and-'ride *n.* Park-and-ride-System, *das;* (place) Park-and-ride-Parkplatz, *der*

'parking *n.* Parken, *das;* 'no ∼' „Parken verboten"

parking: ∼ **fine** *n.* Geldbuße für falsches Parken; ∼ **light** *n.* Parkleuchte, *die;* ∼ **lot** *n.* (Amer.) Parkplatz, *der;* ∼ **meter** *n.* Parkuhr, *die;* ∼ **offence** *n.* Verstoß gegen das Parkverbot; ∼ **space** *n.* (a) *no pl.* Parkraum, *der;* (b) (single space) Parkplatz, *der;* ∼ **ticket** *n.* Strafzettel [für falsches Parken]

'park-keeper *n.* Parkwächter, *der/* -wächterin, *die*

parliament /'pɑːləmənt/ *n.* Parlament, *das;* [Houses of] P∼ (Brit.) Parlament, *das*

parliamentary /pɑːlə'mentərɪ/ *adj.* parlamentarisch; Parlaments⟨*geschäfte, -wahlen, -reform*⟩

parlour (*Brit.; Amer.:* **parlor**) /'pɑːlə(r)/ *n.* (dated) Wohnzimmer, *das*

parochial /pə'rəʊkɪəl/ *adj.* krähwinklig

parody /'pærədɪ/ ①*n.* Parodie, *die* (of auf + *Akk.*)
② *v.t.* parodieren

parole /pə'rəʊl/ *n.* bedingter Straferlass (Rechtsw.); **on** ∼: auf Bewährung

paroxysm /'pærəksɪzm/ *n.* Krampf, *der;* (fit, convulsion) Anfall, *der* (of von)

parquet /'pɑːkɪ, 'pɑːkeɪ/ *n.* ∼ [floor/ flooring] Parkett, *das*

parrot /'pærət/ *n.* Papagei, *der*

parry /'pærɪ/ *v.t.* abwehren ⟨*Faustschlag*⟩; (Fencing; also fig.) parieren

parsley /'pɑːslɪ/ *n.* Petersilie, *die*

parsnip /'pɑːsnɪp/ *n.* Gemeiner Pastinak, *der*

parson /'pɑːsn/ *n.* Pfarrer, *der*

part /pɑːt/ ①*n.* (a) Teil, *der;* **the greater** ∼: der größte Teil; der Großteil; **for the most** ∼: größtenteils; **in** ∼: teilweise; **in large** ∼: groß[en]teils; **in** ∼s zum Teil
(b) (of machine) [Einzel]teil, *das*
(c) (share) Anteil, *der*
(d) (Theatre) Rolle, *die*
(e) (Mus.) Part, *der;* Stimme, *die*
(f) *usu. in pl.* (region) Gegend, *die;* (of continent, world) Teil, *der*
(g) (side) Partei, *die;* **take sb.'s** ∼: jmds. od. für jmdn. Partei ergreifen
(h) **take [no]** ∼ [in sth.] sich [an etw. (*Dat.*)] [nicht] beteiligen
(i) **take sth. in good** ∼: etw. nicht übel nehmen
② *adv.* teils
③ *v.t.* (a) (divide into ∼s) teilen; scheiteln ⟨*Haar*⟩
(b) (separate) trennen
④ *v.i.* ⟨*Seil, Tau, Kette:*⟩ reißen; ⟨*Wege, Personen:*⟩ sich trennen; ∼ **with** sich trennen von ⟨*Besitz, Geld*⟩

part ex'change *n.* **accept sth. in** ∼ **for sth.** etw. für etw. in Zahlung nehmen; **sell sth. in** ∼: etw. in Zahlung geben

partial /'pɑːʃl/ *adj.* (a) (biased) voreingenommen
(b) **be/not be** ∼ **to sth.** eine Schwäche/keine besondere Vorliebe für etw. haben
(c) partiell ⟨*Lähmung, Sonnenfinsternis*⟩; **a** ∼ **success** ein Teilerfolg

'partially *adv.* teilweise

participant /pɑː'tɪsɪpənt/ *n.* Beteiligte, *der/die* (in an + *Dat.*)

participate /pɑː'tɪsɪpeɪt/ *v.i.* sich beteiligen (in an + *Dat.*); (in arranged event) teilnehmen (in an + *Dat.*)

participation /pɑːtɪsɪ'peɪʃn/ *n.* Beteiligung, *die* (in an + *Dat.*); (in arranged event) Teilnahme, *die* (in bei, an + *Dat.*)

participle /'pɑːtɪsɪpl/ *n.* Partizip, *das*

particle /'pɑːtɪkl/ *n.* Teilchen, *das*

particular /pə'tɪkjʊlə(r)/ ①*adj.* (a) besonder...; **here in** ∼: besonders hier; **nothing/anything [in]** ∼: nichts/irgendetwas Besonderes
(b) (fastidious) genau; **I am not** ∼: es ist mir gleich; **be** ∼ **about sth.** es mit etw. genau nehmen
② *n., in pl.* Einzelheiten *Pl.*; Details *Pl.*; (of person) Personalien *Pl.*

par'ticularly *adv.* besonders

'parting ①*n.* (a) [final] ∼: Abschied, *der*
(b) (Brit.: in hair) Scheitel, *der*
② *attrib. adj.* Abschieds-

partisan /'pɑːtɪzæn/ *n.* Partisan, *der/* Partisanin, *die*

partition /pɑː'tɪʃn/ ①*n.* (a) (Polit.) Teilung, *die*
(b) (room divider) Trennwand, *die*
② *v.t.* (a) (divide) aufteilen ⟨*Land, Zimmer*⟩
(b) (Polit.) teilen ⟨*Land*⟩
■ **partition 'off** *v.t.* abteilen

'partly *adv.* zum Teil; teilweise

partner /'pɑːtnə(r)/ *n.* Partner, *der/* Partnerin, *die*

'partnership *n.* Partnerschaft, *die;* **business** ∼: [Personen]gesellschaft, *die*

'part-owner *n.* Mitbesitzer, *der/* -besitzerin, *die*

partridge /'pɑːtrɪdʒ/ *n., pl. same or* ∼s Rebhuhn, *das*

part: ∼-**time** ①/'--/ *adj.* Teilzeit⟨*arbeit, -arbeiter*⟩; ② /-'-/ *adv.* stundenweise, halbtags ⟨*arbeiten, studieren*⟩; ∼-**'timer** *n.* Teilzeitkraft, *die;* **study as a** ∼-**timer** halbtags *od.* stundenweise studieren

party /'pɑːtɪ/ *n.* (a) (Polit., Law) Partei, *die; attrib.* Partei-
(b) (group) Gruppe, *die*
(c) (social gathering) Party, *die*

party: ∼ **po'litical** *adj.* parteipolitisch; ∼ '**politics** *n.* Parteipolitik, *die;* ∼ **wall** *n.* Mauer zum Nachbargrundstück/-gebäude

pass /pɑːs/ ①*n.* (a) (passing of an ⋯⟶

examination) bestandene Prüfung; '∼' (mark)
Ausreichend, *das;* **get a ∼ in maths** die
Mathematikprüfung bestehen
(b) (written permission) Ausweis, *der*
(c) (Footb.) Pass, *der* (fachspr.); Ballabgabe, *die*
(d) (in mountains) Pass, *der*
[2] *v.i.* **(a)** (go by) ⟨Fußgänger:⟩ vorbeigehen;
⟨Fahrer, Fahrzeug:⟩ vorbeifahren; ⟨Zeit,
Sekunde:⟩ vergehen; (by chance) ⟨Person,
Fahrzeug:⟩ vorbeikommen
(b) (come to an end) vorbeigehen; ⟨Gewitter,
Unwetter:⟩ vorüberziehen
(c) (be accepted) durchgehen (**as** als, **for** für)
(d) (in exam) bestehen
[3] *v.t.* **(a)** ⟨Fußgänger:⟩ vorbeigehen an
(+ *Dat.*); ⟨Fahrer, Fahrzeug:⟩ vorbeifahren an
(+ *Dat.*); (by chance) ⟨Person, Fahrzeug:⟩
vorbeikommen an (+ *Dat.*)
(b) (overtake) vorbeifahren an (+ *Dat.*)
(c) bestehen ⟨Prüfung⟩
(d) (approve) verabschieden ⟨Gesetzentwurf⟩;
annehmen ⟨Vorschlag⟩; bestehen lassen
⟨Prüfungskandidaten⟩
(e) (Footb. etc.) abgeben (**to** an + *Akk.*)
(f) (spend) verbringen ⟨Leben, Zeit, Tag⟩
(g) (hand) ∼ **sb. sth.** jmdm. etw. reichen
(h) fällen ⟨Urteil⟩; machen ⟨Bemerkung⟩
(i) ∼ **water** Wasser lassen
■ **pass a'way** *v.i.* (euphem.) verscheiden
(geh.)
■ **pass 'off** *v.t.* ∼ **sth. off as sth.** etw. als
etw. ausgeben
■ **pass 'on** *v.t.* weitergeben (**to** an + *Akk.*)
■ **pass 'out** *v.i.* ohnmächtig werden
■ **pass 'up** *v.t.* entgehen lassen
⟨Gelegenheit⟩; ablehnen ⟨Angebot⟩
passable /'pɑːsəbl/ *adj.* **(a)** (acceptable)
passabel
(b) befahrbar ⟨Straße⟩
passage /'pæsɪdʒ/ *n.* **(a)** (voyage) Überfahrt,
die
(b) (way) Durchgang, *der;* (corridor) Korridor,
der
(c) (part of book etc.) Textstelle, *die*
'**passageway** *n.* Gang, *der;* (between houses)
Durchgang, *der*
passenger /'pæsɪndʒə(r)/ *n.* Passagier, *der;*
(on train) Reisende, *der/die;* (on bus, in taxi)
Fahrgast, *der;* (in car, on motor cycle) Mitfahrer,
*der/*Mitfahrerin, *die;* (in front seat of car)
Beifahrer, *der/*Beifahrerin, *die*
passenger: ∼ **aircraft** *n.*
Passagierflugzeug, *das;* ∼ **door** *n.*
Beifahrertür, *die;* ∼ **lounge** *n.* Warteraum,
der; ∼ **plane** *n.* Passagierflugzeug, *das;*
∼ **seat** *n.* Beifahrersitz, *der;* ∼ **service**
n. (train) Personenzugverbindung, *die;* (ferry)
Personenfährverbindung, *die*
passer-by /pɑːsə'baɪ/ *n.* Passant, *der/*
Passantin, *die*
'**passing** [1] *n.* (of time, years) Lauf, *der;* **in** ∼:
beiläufig ⟨bemerken usw.⟩
[2] *adj.* **(a)** vorbeifahrend ⟨Zug, Auto⟩;
vorbeikommend ⟨Person⟩
(b) flüchtig ⟨Blick⟩; vorübergehend ⟨Mode,
Interesse⟩; flüchtig ⟨Bekanntschaft⟩

'**passing place** *n.* Ausweichstelle, *die*
passion /'pæʃn/ *n.* Leidenschaft, *die;*
(enthusiasm) leidenschaftliche Begeisterung;
he has a ∼ for steam engines Dampfloks
sind seine Leidenschaft
passionate /'pæʃənət/ *adj.*
leidenschaftlich; heftig ⟨Verlangen⟩
passive /'pæsɪv/ [1] *adj.* passiv;
∼ **smoker** Passivraucher, *der/*-raucherin,
die; ∼ **smoking** passives Rauchen
(b) (Ling.) Passiv-
[2] *n.* (Ling.) Passiv, *das*
pass: ∼ **key** *n.* (master key) Hauptschlüssel,
der; ∼ **mark** *n.* Mindestpunktzahl, *die;*
∼**port** *n.* **(a)** [Reise]pass, *der; attrib.* Pass-;
∼**port control** Passkontrolle, *die;* **(b)** (fig.)
Schlüssel, *der* (**to** zu); ∼**word** *n.* **(a)** Parole,
die; Losung, *die;* **(b)** (Comp.) Passwort, *das*
∼**word-protected** passwortegeschützt
past /pɑːst/ [1] *adj.* **(a)** *pred.* (over) vorbei
(b) *attrib.* (previous) früher; vergangen;
ehemalig ⟨Präsident, Vorsitzende usw.⟩
(c) *attrib.* (just gone by) letzt...; vergangen; **in
the ∼ few days** während der letzten Tage
(d) (Ling.) ∼ **tense** Vergangenheit, *die*
[2] *n.* Vergangenheit, *die;* **in the ∼:** früher; **in
der Vergangenheit** ⟨leben⟩; **be a thing of the
∼:** der Vergangenheit angehören
[3] *prep.* (in time) nach; (in place) hinter
(+ *Dat.*); **half ∼ three** halb vier; **five [minutes]
∼ two** fünf [Minuten] nach zwei; **gaze/walk
∼ sb./sth.** an jmdm./etw. vorbeiblicken/
vorbeigehen; ∼ **repair** nicht mehr zu
reparieren
[4] *adv.* vorbei; **hurry ∼:** vorübereilen
pasta /'pæstə/ *n.* Teigwaren *Pl.*
paste /peɪst/ [1] *n.* **(a)** Brei, *der*
(b) (glue) Kleister, *der*
(c) (of meat, fish, etc.) Paste, *die*
[2] *v.t.* **(a)** kleben; ∼ **sth. into sth.** etw. in
etw. (*Akk.*) einkleben
(b) (Comp.) einfügen (**into** in + *Akk.*); *see also*
CUT 1E
pastel /'pæstl/ [1] *n.* (crayon) Pastellstift, *der*
[2] *adj.* pastellfarben; Pastell⟨farben, -töne,
-zeichnung⟩
pasteurize /'pɑːstʃəraɪz/ *v.t.*
pasteurisieren
pastille /'pæstɪl/ *n.* Pastille, *die*
pastime /'pɑːstaɪm/ *n.* Zeitvertreib, *der;*
(person's specific ∼) Hobby, *das*
past 'master *n.* (fig.) Meister, *der*
pastor /'pɑːstə(r)/ *n.* Pfarrer, *der/*Pfarrerin,
die; Pastor, *der/*Pastorin, *die*
pastoral /'pɑːstərl/ *adj.* Weide-; ländlich
⟨Reiz, Idylle, Umgebung⟩
pastry /'peɪstrɪ/ *n.* Teig, *der;* (article of food)
Gebäckstück, *das;* **pastries** *collect.*
[Fein]gebäck, *das*
pasture /'pɑːstʃə(r)/ *n.* Weide, *die*
'**pastureland** *n.* Weideland, *das*
pasty /'pæstɪ/ *n.* Pastete, *die*

pat¹ /pæt/ [1] n. (a) (tap) Klaps, der
(b) (of butter) Stückchen, das
[2] v.t., -tt- leicht klopfen auf (+ Akk.);
tätscheln, (once) einen Klaps geben (+ Dat.)
⟨Person, Hund, Pferd⟩; ~ sb. on the arm/
head jmdm. den Arm/Kopf tätscheln

pat² adv. have sth. off ~: etw. parat haben

patch /pætʃ/ [1] n. (a) Stelle, die; fog ~es
Nebelfelder
(b) (on worn garment) Flicken, der; be not a
~ on sth. (fig. coll.) nichts gegen etw. sein
[2] v.t. flicken
■ **patch 'up** v.t. reparieren; (fig.) beilegen
⟨Streit⟩

patchwork n. Patchwork, das

patchy /'pætʃɪ/ adj. uneinheitlich
⟨Qualität⟩; ungleichmäßig ⟨Arbeit⟩; sehr
lückenhaft ⟨Wissen⟩

pâté /'pæteɪ/ n. Pastete, die

patent /'peɪtənt, 'pætənt/ [1] adj. (obvious)
offenkundig
[2] n. Patent, das
[3] v.t. patentieren lassen

patent 'leather n. Lackleder, das;
~ shoes Lackschuhe Pl.

'patently adv. offenkundig; ~ obvious
ganz offenkundig

paternal /pə'tɜːnl/ adj. väterlich

paternity /pə'tɜːnɪtɪ/ n. (fatherhood)
Vaterschaft, die

pa'ternity leave n. Vaterschaftsurlaub,
der

path /pɑːθ/ n. Weg, der; (line of motion) Bahn,
die

pathetic /pə'θetɪk/ adj. (a) (pitiful) Mitleid
erregend
(b) (contemptible) armselig ⟨Entschuldigung⟩;
erbärmlich ⟨Person, Leistung⟩

pathogen /'pæθədʒən/ n.
[Krankheits]erreger, der

pathological /pæθə'lɒdʒɪkl/ adj. (a)
pathologisch
(b) (fig.: obsessive) krankhaft

pathologist /pə'θɒlədʒɪst/ n. Pathologe,
der/Pathologin, die

pathology /pə'θɒlədʒɪ/ n. Pathologie, die;
the ~ of a disease das Krankheitsbild

'pathway n. Weg, der

patience /'peɪʃəns/ n. Geduld, die

patient /'peɪʃənt/ [1] adj. geduldig
[2] n. Patient, der/Patientin, die

'patiently adv. geduldig

patio /'pætɪəʊ/ n., pl. ~s Veranda, die;
Terrasse, die

patio 'door n. große Glasschiebetür (zum
Garten)

patriarch /'peɪtrɪɑːk/ n. (of family)
Familienoberhaupt, das

patriarchal /peɪtrɪ'ɑːkl/ adj.
patriarchalisch

patriot /'peɪtrɪət/ n. Patriot, der/Patriotin,
die

patriotic /peɪtrɪ'ɒtɪk/ adj. patriotisch

patriotism /'peɪtrɪətɪzm/ n. Patriotismus,
der

patrol /pə'trəʊl/ [1] n. (Police) Streife, die;
(Mil.) Patrouille, die; be on ~: patrouillieren
[2] v.i., -ll- patrouillieren; ⟨Polizei:⟩ Streife
laufen/fahren
[3] v.t., -ll- patrouillieren durch (+ Akk.);
abpatrouillieren ⟨Straßen, Gegend, Lager⟩;
patrouillieren vor (+ Dat.) ⟨Küste, Grenze⟩;
⟨Polizei:⟩ Streife laufen/fahren in (+ Dat.)
⟨Straßen, Stadtteil⟩

patrol: ~ **boat** n. Patrouillenboot, das;
~ **car** n. Streifenwagen, der

patron /'peɪtrən/ n. (a) Gönner, der/
Gönnerin, die; (of institution, campaign)
Schirmherr, der/Schirmherrin, die
(b) (customer) (of shop) Kunde, der/Kundin,
die; (of restaurant, hotel) Gast, der; (of theatre,
cinema) Besucher, der/Besucherin, die
(c) ~ [saint] Schutzheilige, der/die

patronage /'pætrənɪdʒ/ n. Gönnerschaft,
die; (for campaign, institution) Schirmherrschaft,
die

patronize /'pætrənaɪz/ v.t. (a) (frequent)
besuchen
(b) (condescend to) ~ sb. jmdn. herablassend
behandeln

patronizing /'pætrənaɪzɪŋ/ adj.
gönnerhaft; herablassend

patter /'pætə(r)/ [1] n. (of rain) Prasseln, das;
(of feet) Trappeln, das
[2] v.i. ⟨Regen:⟩ prasseln

pattern /'pætən/ n. Muster, das; (model)
Vorlage, die; (for sewing) Schnittmuster, das;
(for knitting) Strickmuster, das

paunch /pɔːntʃ/ n. Bauch, der

pauper /'pɔːpə(r)/ n. Arme, der/die

pause /pɔːz/ [1] n. Pause, die
[2] v.i. eine Pause machen; ⟨Redner:⟩
innehalten; (hesitate) zögern

pave /peɪv/ v.t. befestigen; (with stones)
pflastern; ~ the way for sth. (fig.) einer
Sache (Dat.) den Weg ebnen

'pavement n. (a) (Brit.: footway) Bürgersteig,
der
(b) (Amer.: roadway) Fahrbahn, die

'pavement café n. Straßencafé, das

pavilion /pə'vɪljən/ n. Pavillon, der; (Brit.
Sport) Klubhaus, das

'paving stone n. Platte, die; Pflasterstein,
der

paw /pɔː/ n. Pfote, die; (of bear, lion, tiger)
Pranke, die

pawn¹ /pɔːn/ n. (Chess) Bauer, der; (fig.)
Schachfigur, die

pawn² [1] n. Pfand, das; in ~: verpfändet
[2] v.t. verpfänden

pawn: ~**broker** n. Pfandleiher, der/
-leiherin, die; ~**shop** n. Leihhaus, das

pay /peɪ/ [1] n. (wages) Lohn, der; (salary)
Gehalt, das; be in the ~ of sb./sth. für
jmdn./etw. arbeiten ···⋗

2 *v.t.*, paid /peɪd/ bezahlen; zahlen ‹Geld›; ~ sb. to do sth. jmdn. dafür bezahlen, dass er etw. tut; ~ sb. £10 jmdm. 10 Pfund zahlen 3 *v.i.*, paid (a) zahlen; ~ for sth./sb. etw./ für jmdn. bezahlen; sth. ~s for itself etw. macht sich bezahlt

(b) (be profitable) sich lohnen; ‹Geschäft:› rentabel sein; it ~s to be careful es lohnt sich, vorsichtig zu sein. See also PAID

■ **pay 'back** *v.t.* zurückzahlen; I'll ~ you back later ich gebe dir das Geld später zurück

■ **pay 'in** *v.t.* einzahlen

■ **pay 'off** *v.t.* auszahlen ‹Arbeiter›; abbezahlen ‹Schulden›; ablösen ‹Hypothek›; befriedigen ‹Gläubiger›

■ **pay 'out** *v.t.* auszahlen; (spend) ausgeben

■ **pay 'up** *v.i.* zahlen

payable /ˈpeɪəbl/ *adj.* zahlbar; be ~ to sb. an jmdn. zu zahlen sein; make a cheque ~ to the Post Office/to sb. einen Scheck auf die Post/auf jmds. Namen ausstellen

pay: ~ and display 1 *n.* Parken mit Parkschein; *attrib.* Parkschein-; 2 *n.* ~ and display car park Parkplatz mit Parkscheinautomat; ~ cheque *n.* Lohn-/ Gehaltsscheck, *der;* ~ claim *n.* Lohn-/ Gehaltsforderung, *die;* ~ day *n.* Zahltag, *der;* ~ increase ▶ PAY RISE

payee /peɪˈiː/ *n.* Zahlungsempfänger, *der/* -empfängerin, *die*

paying /ˈpeɪɪŋ/**:** ~ 'guest *n.* zahlender Gast; ~'in slip *n.* (Brit. Banking) Einzahlungsschein, *der*

'**payment** *n.* (a) (of sum, bill, debt, fine) Bezahlung, *die;* (of interest, instalment, tax, fee) Zahlung, *die;* in ~ [for sth.] als Bezahlung [für etw.]

(b) (amount) Zahlung, *die*

pay: ~ packet *n.* (Brit.) Lohntüte, *die;* ~phone *n.* Münzfernsprecher, *der;* ~ rise *n.* Lohn-/Gehaltserhöhung, *die;* ~roll *n.* Lohnliste, *die;* be on sb.'s ~roll für jmdn. arbeiten; ~slip *n.* Lohnstreifen, *der/* Gehaltszettel, *der;* ~ station *n.* (Amer.) ▶ ~PHONE

p.c. *abbr.* = **per cent** v. H.

PC *abbr.* (a) (Brit.) = **police constable** Wachtm.

(b) = **personal computer** PC

(c) = **politically correct** politisch korrekt

PE *abbr.* = **physical education**

pea /piː/ *n.* Erbse, *die*

peace /piːs/ *n.* Frieden, *der;* (tranquillity) Ruhe, *die;* ~ of mind Seelenfrieden, *der*

peaceable /ˈpiːsəbl/ *adj.* friedfertig; (calm) friedlich

peaceful /ˈpiːsfl/ *adj.* friedlich; friedfertig ‹Person, Volk›

'**peacefully** *adv.* friedlich; die ~: sanft entschlafen

peace: ~keeper *n.* Friedenswächter, *der;* ~keeping force Friedenstruppe, *die;*

~maker *n.* Friedensstifter, *der/*-stifterin, *die;* ~ movement *n.* Friedensbewegung, *die;* ~ process *n.* Friedensprozess, *der* ~ treaty *n.* Friedensvertrag, *der*

peach /piːtʃ/ *n.* Pfirsich, *der*

'**peacock** *n.* Pfau, *der*

'**pea-green** *adj.* erbsengrün; maigrün

peak /piːk/ 1 *n.* (a) (of cap) Schirm, *der* (b) (of mountain) Gipfel, *der;* (fig.) Höhepunkt, *der*

2 *attrib. adj.* Höchst-, Spitzen‹preise, -werte›; ~-hour traffic Stoßverkehr, *der*

peaked /piːkt/ *adj.* ~ cap Schirmmütze, *die*

'**peak season** *n.* Hochsaison, *die*

peal /piːl/ *n.* Läuten, *das;* ~ of bells Glockenläuten, *das;* a ~/~s of laughter schallendes Gelächter

peanut /ˈpiːnʌt/ *n.* Erdnuss, *die;* ~ butter Erdnussbutter, *die;* ~s (coll.: little money) ein paar Kröten (salopp)

pear /peə(r)/ *n.* Birne, *die*

pearl /pɜːl/ *n.* Perle, *die*

pear: ~-shaped *adj.* birnenförmig: ~tree *n.* Birnbaum, *der*

peasant /ˈpezənt/ *n.* [armer] Bauer, *der;* Landarbeiter, *der*

pea 'soup Erbsensuppe, *die*

peat /piːt/ *n.* Torf, *der*

pebble /ˈpebl/ *n.* Kiesel[stein], *der*

peck /pek/ 1 *v.t.* hacken; picken ‹Körner› 2 *v.i.* picken (at nach); ~ at one's food im Essen herumstochern

3 *n.* (kiss) flüchtiger Kuss

'**pecking order** *n.* Hackordnung, *die*

peckish /ˈpekɪʃ/ *adj.* (coll.) feel/get ~: Hunger haben/bekommen

peculiar /pɪˈkjuːlɪə(r)/ *adj.* (a) (strange) seltsam; I feel [slightly] ~: mir ist [etwas] komisch

(b) (especial) besonder…

(c) (belonging exclusively) eigentümlich (to *Dat.*)

peculiarity /pɪkjuːlɪˈærɪtɪ/ *n.* (a) (odd trait) Eigentümlichkeit, *die*

(b) (distinguishing characteristic) [charakteristisches] Merkmal

pe'culiarly *adv.* (a) (strangely) seltsam

(b) (especially) besonders

pedal /ˈpedl/ 1 *n.* Pedal, *das* 2 *v.i.*, (Brit.) -ll- in die Pedale treten

'**pedal bin** *n.* Treteimer, *der*

pedalo /ˈpedələʊ/ *n., pl.* ~s Tretboot, *das*

pedant /ˈpedənt/ *n.* Pedant, *der/*Pedantin, *die*

pedantic /pɪˈdæntɪk/ *adj.* pedantisch

peddle /ˈpedl/ *v.t.* auf der Straße verkaufen; (door to door) hausieren mit

pedestal /ˈpedɪstl/ *n.* Sockel, *der*

pedestrian /pɪˈdestrɪən/ 1 *adj.* (uninspired) trocken; langweilig

2 *n.* Fußgänger, *der/*-gängerin, *die*

pedestrian 'crossing *n.* Fußgängerüberweg, *der*

pedestrianize (**pedestrianise**) /pɪˈdestrɪənaɪz/ *v.t.* zur Fußgängerzone machen; ∼**d zone** Fußgängerzone, *die*

pedestrian ˈprecinct ▶ PRECINCT A

pediatrician *etc.* ▶ PAEDIATRICIAN *etc.*

pedicure /ˈpedɪkjʊə(r)/ *n.*, *no art.* Pediküre, *die*

pedigree /ˈpedɪɡriː/ **1** *n.* Stammbaum, *der* **2** *adj.* mit Stammbaum *nachgestellt*

pedlar /ˈpedlə(r)/ *n.* Straßenhändler, *der*/ -händlerin, *die*; (door to door) Hausierer, *der*/ Hausiererin, *die*

pee /piː/ (coll.) **1** *v.i.* pinkeln (salopp); Pipi machen (Kinderspr.) **2** *n.* (a) have a ∼: pinkeln (salopp) (b) (urine) Pipi, *das* (Kinderspr.)

peek /piːk/ ▶ PEEP²

peel /piːl/ **1** *v.t.* schälen **2** *v.i.* ⟨Person, Haut:⟩ sich schälen; ⟨Farbe:⟩ abblättern **3** *n.* Schale, *die*

ˈpeelings *n. pl.* Schalen *Pl.*

peep¹ /piːp/ **1** *v.i.* ⟨Maus, Vogel:⟩ piep[s]en **2** *n.* Piepsen, *das*; (coll.: remark etc.) Piep[s], *der*

peep² **1** *v.i.* gucken (ugs.); (furtively) verstohlen gucken (ugs.) **2** *n.* kurzer/verstohlener Blick

peep: ∼**hole** *n.* Guckloch, *das*; ∼**ing ˈTom** *n.* Spanner, *der* (ugs.)

peer¹ /pɪə(r)/ *n.* Peer, *der*; (equal) Gleichgestellte, *der/die*

peer² *v.i.* forschend schauen; (with difficulty) angestrengt schauen; ∼ **at sth./sb.** [sich (*Dat.*)] etw. genau ansehen/jmdn. forschend ansehen; (with difficulty) [sich (*Dat.*)] etw./ jmdn. angestrengt ansehen

peerage /ˈpɪərɪdʒ/ *n.* Peerswürde, *die*

ˈpeer pressure *n.* Gruppenzwang, *der*

peevish /ˈpiːvɪʃ/ *adj.* nörgelig

peg /peɡ/ *n.* (for holding together) Stift, *der*; (for tying things to) Pflock, *der*; (for hanging things on) Haken, *der*; (clothes ∼) Wäscheklammer, *die*; (tent ∼) Hering, *der*; **off the** ∼ (Brit.: ready-made) von der Stange (ugs.)

pejorative /pɪˈdʒɒrətɪv/ *adj.*, **peˈjoratively** *adv.* abwertend

pelican /ˈpelɪkən/ *n.* Pelikan, *der*

ˈpelican crossing *n.* (Brit.) Ampelübergang, *der*

pellet /ˈpelɪt/ *n.* Kügelchen, *das*

pelmet /ˈpelmɪt/ *n.* Blende, *die*

pelt¹ /pelt/ *n.* Fell, *das*

pelt² **1** *v.t.* ∼ **sb. with sth.** jmdn. mit etw. bewerfen **2** *v.i.* (a) **it was** ∼**ing down** [**with rain**] es goss wie aus Kübeln (ugs.) (b) (run fast) rasen (ugs.)

pelvic /ˈpelvɪk/ *adj.* Becken-

pelvis /ˈpelvɪs/ *n.*, *pl.* **pelves** /ˈpelviːz/ *or* ∼**es** (Anat.) Becken, *das*

pen¹ /pen/ **1** *n.* (enclosure) Pferch, *der* **2** *v.t.*, **-nn-:** ∼ **sb. in a corner** jmdn. in eine Ecke drängen ∎ **pen ˈin** *v.t.* einpferchen

pen² **1** *n.* Federhalter, *der*; (fountain ∼) Füller, *der*; (ball ∼) Kugelschreiber, *der*; (felt-tip ∼) Filzstift, *der* **2** *v.t.*, **-nn-** schreiben

penal /ˈpiːnl/ *adj.* Straf-

penalize /ˈpiːnəlaɪz/ *v.t.* bestrafen; (Sport) eine Strafe verhängen gegen

penalty /ˈpenltɪ/ *n.* (a) Strafe, *die*; **pay the** ∼/**the** ∼ **for** *or* **of sth.** dafür/für etw. büßen [müssen] (b) (Footb.) Elfmeter, *der*

penalty: ∼ **box** *n.* (Footb.) Strafraum, *der*; (Ice Hockey) Strafbank, *die*; ∼ **kick** *n.* (Footb.) Strafstoß, *der*

penance /ˈpenəns/ *n.* Buße, *die*; **act of** ∼: Bußwerk, *das*; **do** ∼: Buße tun

pence ▶ PENNY

pencil /ˈpensɪl/ **1** *n.* Bleistift, *der*; **red/coloured** ∼: Rot-/Buntstift, *der* **2** *v.t.*, (Brit.) **-ll-** mit einem Bleistift/Farbstift schreiben

pencil: ∼ **case** *n.* Griffelkasten, *der*; (of soft material) Federmäppchen, *das*; ∼ **sharpener** *n.* Bleistiftspitzer, *der*

pendant /ˈpendənt/ *n.* Anhänger, *der*

pending /ˈpendɪŋ/ **1** *adj.* unentschieden ⟨Angelegenheit, Sache⟩; schwebend ⟨Verfahren⟩ **2** *prep.* ∼ **his return** bis zu seiner Rückkehr

pendulum /ˈpendjʊləm/ *n.* Pendel, *das*

penetrate /ˈpenɪtreɪt/ *v.t.* eindringen in (+ *Akk.*); (pass through) durchdringen

penetrating /ˈpenɪtreɪtɪŋ/ *adj.* durchdringend

penetration /penɪˈtreɪʃn/ *n.* Eindringen, *das* (of in + *Akk.*); (passing through) Durchdringen, *das*

ˈpenfriend *n.* Brieffreund, *der*/-freundin, *die*

penguin /ˈpeŋɡwɪn/ *n.* Pinguin, *der*

penicillin /penɪˈsɪlɪn/ *n.* Penizillin, *das*

peninsula /pɪˈnɪnsjʊlə/ *n.* Halbinsel, *die*

penis /ˈpiːnɪs/ *n.* Penis, *der*

penitence /ˈpenɪtəns/ *n.* Reue, *die*

penitent /ˈpenɪtənt/ *adj.* reuevoll (geh.); reuig (geh.) ⟨Sünder⟩

penitentiary /penɪˈtenʃərɪ/ *n.* (Amer.) Straf[vollzugs]anstalt, *die*

pen: ∼**knife** *n.* Taschenmesser, *das*; ∼ **light** *n.* [Mini]stablampe, *die*

pennant /ˈpenənt/ *n.* Wimpel, *der*; (on official car etc.) Stander, *der*

penniless /ˈpenɪlɪs/ *adj.* mittellos

penny /ˈpenɪ/ *n.*, *pl. usu.* **pennies** /ˈpenɪz/ (for separate coins), **pence** /pens/ (for sum of money) Penny, *der*; **fifty pence** fünfzig Pence; **two/fifty pence [piece]** Zwei-/Fünfzigpencestück, *das*

p

pension /'penʃn/ n. Rente, die; (payment to retired civil servant) Pension, die; **widow's ~**: Witwenrente, die /-pension, die; **be on a ~**: eine Rente beziehen

■ **pension 'off** v.t. berenten (Amtsspr.); auf Rente setzen (ugs.); pensionieren ⟨Lehrer, Beamten⟩

'**pensioner** n. Rentner, der/Rentnerin, die; (retired civil servant) Pensionär, der/Pensionärin, die

pensive /'pensɪv/ adj. nachdenklich

pentagon /'pentəgən/ n. Fünfeck, das; **the P~** (Amer. Polit.) das Pentagon

Pentecost /'pentɪkɒst/ n. Pfingsten, das

pent: ~house n. Penthaus, das; **~-up** adj. angestaut ⟨Ärger, Wut⟩; unterdrückt ⟨Sehnsucht, Gefühle⟩

penultimate /pe'nʌltɪmət/ adj. vorletzt...

people /'piːpl/ n. (a) constr. as pl. Leute Pl.; Menschen Pl.; (as opposed to animals) Menschen Pl.; **city/country ~** (inhabitants) Stadt-/Landbewohner Pl.; **local ~**: Einheimische Pl.; **working ~**: arbeitende Menschen; **coloured/white ~**: Farbige/Weiße Pl.; **~ say ...**: man sagt ...; **a crowd of ~**: eine Menschenmenge
(b) (nation) Volk, das

pepper /'pepə(r)/ 1 n. (a) Pfeffer, der
(b) (vegetable) Paprikaschote, die; **red/green ~**: roter/grüner Paprika
2 v.t. (a) pfeffern
(b) (pelt) bombardieren (ugs.)

pepper: ~corn n. Pfefferkorn, das; **~ mill** n. Pfeffermühle, die; **~mint** n. (sweet) Pfefferminz, das; **~ pot** n. Pfefferstreuer, der

peppery /'pepərɪ/ adj. pfeff[e]rig; (spicy) scharf

per /pə(r), stressed pɜː(r)/ prep. pro

perceive /pə'siːv/ v.t. wahrnehmen; (with the mind) spüren; **~d** vermeintlich ⟨Bedrohung, Gefahr, Wert⟩

per cent (Brit.; Amer.: **percent**) /pə'sent/ 1 adv. **ninety ~ effective** zu 90 Prozent wirksam
2 adj. **a 5 ~ increase** ein Zuwachs von 5 Prozent
3 n. (a) Prozent, das
(b) ▶ PERCENTAGE

percentage /pə'sentɪdʒ/ n. Prozentsatz, der

per'centage sign n. Prozentzeichen, das

perceptible /pə'septɪbl/ adj. wahrnehmbar

perception /pə'sepʃn/ n. (act) Wahrnehmung, die; (result) Erkenntnis, die; (faculty) Wahrnehmungsvermögen, das

perceptive /pə'septɪv/ adj. einfühlsam ⟨Person, Bemerkung⟩

perch /pɜːtʃ/ 1 n. Sitzstange, die
2 v.i. (a) sich niederlassen
(b) (be supported) sitzen
3 v.t. setzen/stellen/legen

percolate /'pɜːkəleɪt/ v.i. [durch]sickern

percolator /'pɜːkəleɪtə(r)/ n. Kaffeemaschine, die

percussion /pə'kʌʃn/ n. (Mus.) Schlagzeug, das; **~ instrument** Schlaginstrument, das

perennial /pə'renjəl/ 1 adj. (a) (Bot.) ausdauernd
(b) immer wieder auftretend ⟨Problem⟩
2 n. (Bot.) ausdauernde Pflanze

perfect 1 /'pɜːfɪkt/ adj. vollkommen; perfekt ⟨Englisch, Timing⟩; tadellos ⟨Zustand⟩; (coll.: unmitigated) absolut; **a ~ stranger** ein völlig Fremder
2 /pə'fekt/ v.t. vervollkommnen

perfection /pə'fekʃn/ n. Perfektion, die; **to ~**: perfekt

perfectionism /pə'fekʃənɪzm/ n. Perfektionismus, der

perfectionist /pə'fekʃənɪst/ n. Perfektionist, der/Perfektionistin, die

'**perfectly** adv. (a) (completely) vollkommen; **be ~ entitled to do sth.** durchaus berechtigt sein, etw. zu tun
(b) (faultlessly) perfekt; tadellos ⟨sich verhalten⟩

perfect 'pitch n. (Mus.) absolutes Gehör

perforate /'pɜːfəreɪt/ v.t. perforieren; (make opening into) durchlöchern

perforation /pɜːfə'reɪʃn/ n. (a) (hole) Loch, das
(b) in pl. **~s** Perforation, die; (in sheets of stamps) Zähnung, die

perform /pə'fɔːm/ 1 v.t. ausführen ⟨Arbeit, Operation⟩; erfüllen ⟨Pflicht, Aufgabe⟩; vollbringen ⟨[Helden]tat, Leistung⟩; ausfüllen ⟨Funktion⟩; vollbringen ⟨Wunder⟩; anstellen ⟨Berechnungen⟩; durchführen ⟨Experiment, Sektion⟩; vorführen ⟨Trick⟩; aufführen ⟨Theaterstück, Scharade⟩; vortragen ⟨Lied, Sonate usw.⟩
2 v.i. eine Vorführung geben; (sing) singen; (play) spielen

performance /pə'fɔːməns/ n. (a) (of duty, task) Erfüllung, die
(b) ([notable] achievement; Motor Veh.) Leistung, die
(c) (at theatre, cinema, etc.) Vorstellung, die; **her ~ as Desdemona** ihre Darstellung der Desdemona; **the ~ of a play/opera** die Aufführung eines Theaterstücks/einer Oper

performance: ~ art n. Performance-Art, die; **~ artist** n. Performancekünstler, der/ -künstlerin, die **~-enhancing** adj. **~-enhancing drug/substance** leistungsfördernde od. -steigernde Droge/ Substanz

per'former n. Künstler, der/Künstlerin, die

per'forming attrib. adj. dressiert ⟨Tier⟩

performing 'arts n. pl. darstellende Künste

perfume /'pɜːfjuːm/ n. Duft, der; (fluid) Parfüm, das

perfunctory /pə'fʌŋktərɪ/ *adj.*
oberflächlich ⟨*Arbeit, Überprüfung*⟩; flüchtig
⟨*Erkundigung, Bemerkung*⟩

perhaps /pə'hæps/ *adv.* vielleicht

peril /'perl/ *n.* Gefahr, *die*

perilous /'perələs/ *adj.* gefahrvoll; **be ~:**
gefährlich sein

perimeter /pə'rɪmɪtə(r)/ *n.* [äußere]
Begrenzung; Grenze, *die*

period /'pɪərɪəd/ **1** *n.* **(a)** (of history or life)
Periode, *die;* Zeit, *die;* (any portion of time)
Zeitraum, *der;* **the Classical/Romantic ~:** die
Klassik/Romantik
(b) (Sch.) Stunde, *die;* **chemistry/English ~:**
Chemie-/Englischstunde, *die*
(c) (menstruation) Periode, *die*
(d) (punctuation mark) Punkt, *der*
2 *adj.* zeitgenössisch ⟨*Tracht, Kostüm*⟩;
antik ⟨*Möbel*⟩

periodic /pɪərɪ'ɒdɪk/ *adj.* regelmäßig;
(intermittent) gelegentlich

periodical /pɪərɪ'ɒdɪkl/ **1** *adj.* ▶ PERIODIC
2 *n.* Zeitschrift, *die;* **weekly/monthly ~:**
Wochenzeitschrift/Monatsschrift, *die*

peri'odically *adv.* regelmäßig; (intermittently)
gelegentlich

peripheral /pə'rɪfərl/ **1** *adj.* peripher
(geh.); Rand⟨*problem, -erscheinung*⟩
2 *n.* (Comp.) Peripheriegerät, *das*

periphery /pə'rɪfərɪ/ *n.* Peripherie, *die*

periscope /'perɪskəʊp/ *n.* Periskop, *das*

perish /'perɪʃ/ *v.i.* **(a)** (die) umkommen
(b) (rot) verderben; ⟨*Gummi:*⟩ altern

perishable /'perɪʃəbl/ *adj.* [leicht]
verderblich

'perishing (coll.) **1** *adj.* mörderisch
⟨*Kälte*⟩; **it's/I'm ~:** es ist bitterkalt/ich
komme um vor Kälte (ugs.)
2 *adv.* mörderisch ⟨*kalt*⟩

perjury /'pɜːdʒərɪ/ *n.* Meineid, *der;* **commit
~:** einen Meineid leisten

perk¹ /pɜːk/ (coll.) **1** *v.i.* **~ up** munter
werden
2 *v.t.* **~ up** aufmuntern

perk² *n.* (Brit. coll.) [Sonder]vergünstigung,
die

perky /'pɜːkɪ/ *adj.* lebhaft; munter

perm /pɜːm/ **1** *n.* Dauerwelle, *die*
2 *v.t.* **have one's hair ~ed** sich (*Dat.*) eine
Dauerwelle machen lassen

permanence /'pɜːmənəns/ *n.*
Dauerhaftigkeit, *die*

permanent /'pɜːmənənt/ *adj.* fest ⟨*Sitz,
Bestandteil, Mitglied*⟩; ständig ⟨*Wohnsitz,
Adresse, Kampf*⟩; Dauer⟨*stellung, -visum*⟩;
bleibend ⟨*Schaden*⟩

'permanently *adv.* dauernd; auf Dauer
⟨*verhindern, bleiben*⟩

permanent 'wave *n.* Dauerwelle, *die*

permeable /'pɜːmɪəbl/ *adj.* durchlässig; **be
~ to sth.** etw. durchlassen

permeate /'pɜːmɪeɪt/ **1** *v.t.* dringen
durch; **be ~d with** *or* **by sth.** (fig.) von etw.
durchdrungen sein
2 *v.i.* **~ through sth.** etw. durchdringen

permissible /pə'mɪsɪbl/ *adj.* zulässig; **be
~ to** *or* **for sb.** jmdm. erlaubt sein

permission /pə'mɪʃn/ *n.* Erlaubnis, *die;*
(given by official body) Genehmigung, *die;* **give
sb. ~ to do sth.** jmdm. erlauben, etw. zu tun

permissive /pə'mɪsɪv/ *adj.* **the ~ society**
die permissive Gesellschaft

permit **1** /pə'mɪt/ *v.t.,* **-tt-** zulassen
⟨*Berufung, Einspruch usw.*⟩; **~ sb. sth.**
jmdm. etw. erlauben; **sb. is ~ted to do sth.**
es ist jmdm. erlaubt, etw. zu tun
2 *v.i.,* **-tt-** es zulassen
3 /'pɜːmɪt/ *n.* Genehmigung, *die*

pernicious /pə'nɪʃəs/ *adj.* verderblich;
bösartig ⟨*Krankheit*⟩

peroxide /pə'rɒksaɪd/ *n.* Peroxid, *das;*
~ blonde Wasserstoffblondine, *die*

perpendicular /pɜːpən'dɪkjʊlə(r)/ *adj.*
senkrecht

perpetrate /'pɜːpɪtreɪt/ *v.t.* begehen;
verüben ⟨*Gräuel*⟩

perpetual /pə'petjʊəl/ *adj.* **(a)** (eternal) ewig
(b) (continuous; coll.: repeated) ständig

per'petually *adv.* **(a)** (eternally) ewig
(b) (continuously; coll.: repeatedly) ständig

perpetuate /pə'petjʊeɪt/ *v.t.*
aufrechterhalten

perplex /pə'pleks/ *v.t.* verwirren

perplexed /pə'plekst/ *adj.* verwirrt;
(puzzled) ratlos

perplexity /pə'pleksɪtɪ/ *n.* Verwirrung,
die; (puzzlement) Ratlosigkeit, *die*

persecute /'pɜːsɪkjuːt/ *v.t.* verfolgen

persecution /pɜːsɪ'kjuːʃn/ *n.* Verfolgung,
die

persecutor /'pɜːsɪkjuːtə(r)/ *n.* Verfolger,
der/Verfolgerin, *die*

perseverance /pɜːsɪ'vɪərəns/ *n.*
Beharrlichkeit, *die;* Ausdauer, *die*

persevere /pɜːsɪ'vɪə(r)/ *v.i.* ausharren;
~ with *or* **at** *or* **in sth.** bei etw. dabeibleiben

Persian /'pɜːʃn/ *adj.* persisch; Perser⟨*katze,
-teppich*⟩

persist /pə'sɪst/ *v.i.* **(a)** nicht nachgeben;
~ in doing sth. etw. weiterhin [beharrlich]
tun
(b) (continue to exist) anhalten

persistence /pə'sɪstəns/ Hartnäckigkeit,
die

persistent /pə'sɪstənt/ *adj.* **(a)** hartnäckig
(b) (constantly repeated) dauernd; hartnäckig
⟨*Gerüchte*⟩

per'sistently *adv.* hartnäckig

person /'pɜːsn/ *n.* Mensch, *der;* **in ~:**
persönlich; selbst

personal /'pɜːsənl/ *adj.* persönlich; ⋯⋗

p

Privat⟨*angelegenheit, -leben*⟩; ∼ **computer** Personalcomputer, *der;* ∼ **stereo** Walkman, *der;* ∼ **hygiene** Körperpflege, *die*

personal: ∼ **ad** *n.* Privatanzeige, *die;* (seeking friendship, romance) Kontaktanzeige, *die;* ∼ **as'sistant** *n.* persönlicher Referent/ persönliche Referentin; ∼ **'best** *n.* (Sport) persönliche Bestleistung; ∼ **call** *n.* (Brit. Teleph.) Anruf mit Voranmeldung; ∼ **column** *n.* Rubrik für private [Klein]anzeigen; ∼ **identifi'cation number** *n.* persönliche Identifikationsnummer; Geheimnummer, *die*

personality /pɜːsə'nælɪtɪ/ *n.* Persönlichkeit, *die*

'personal loan *n.* Personal- *od.* Privatdarlehen, *das;* Personal- *od.* Privatkredit, *der*

'personally *adv.* persönlich

personal: ∼ **'organizer** *n.* Terminplaner, *der;* ∼ **'pension plan** *n.* persönlicher Renten[vorsorge]plan; ∼ **'property** *n.* persönliches Eigentum

personification /pəsɒnɪfɪ'keɪʃn/ *n.* Verkörperung, *die*

personify /pə'sɒnɪfaɪ/ *v.t.* verkörpern; **be kindness personified** die Freundlichkeit in Person sein

personnel /pɜːsə'nel/ *n.* Belegschaft, *die;* (of shop, restaurant, etc.) Personal, *das; attrib.* Personal-; ∼ **department** Personalabteilung, *die*

person-to-'person *adj.* (Amer. Teleph.) ∼ **call** Anruf mit Voranmeldung

perspective /pə'spektɪv/ *n.* Perspektive, *die;* (fig.) Blickwinkel, *der*

perspiration /pɜːspɪ'reɪʃn/ *n.* Schweiß, *der*

perspire /pə'spaɪə(r)/ *v.i.* schwitzen

persuade /pə'sweɪd/ *v.t.* (a) (convince) überzeugen (**of** von); ∼ **oneself [that]** ...: sich (*Dat.*) einreden, dass ... (b) (induce) überreden

persuasion /pə'sweɪʒn/ *n.* Überzeugung, *die;* **it didn't take much** ∼: es brauchte nicht viel Überredungskunst

persuasive /pə'sweɪsɪv/ *adj.,* **per'suasively** *adv.* überzeugend

pert /pɜːt/ *adj.* keck

pertinent /'pɜːtɪnənt/ *adj.* relevant (**to** für)

perturb /pə'tɜːb/ *v.t.* beunruhigen

Peru /pə'ruː/ *pr. n.* Peru (*das*)

Peruvian /pə'ruːvɪən/ ① *adj.* peruanisch; **sb. is** ∼: jmd. ist Peruaner/Peruanerin ② *n.* Peruaner, *der*/Peruanerin, *die*

peruse /pə'ruːz/ *v.t.* genau durchlesen; (fig.: examine) untersuchen

pervade /pə'veɪd/ *v.t.* durchdringen

pervasive /pə'veɪsɪv/ *adj.* durchdringend ⟨*Geruch, Kälte*⟩; weit verbreitet ⟨*Ansicht*⟩; sich ausbreitend ⟨*Gefühl*⟩

perverse /pə'vɜːs/ *adj.* starrköpfig

perversion /pə'vɜːʃn/ *n.* (a) (sexual) Perversion, *die* (b) ∼ **of justice** Rechtsbeugung, *die*

pervert ① /pə'vɜːt/ *v.t.* (morally) verderben ② /'pɜːvɜːt/ *n.* perverser Mensch

perverted /pə'vɜːtɪd/ *adj.* (sexually) pervers

pessimism /'pesɪmɪzm/ *n.* Pessimismus, *der*

pessimist /'pesɪmɪst/ *n.* Pessimist, *der*/ Pessimistin, *die*

pessimistic /pesɪ'mɪstɪk/ *adj.* pessimistisch

pest /pest/ *n.* (thing) Ärgernis, *das;* (person) Nervensäge, *die* (ugs.); (animal) Schädling, *der*

pester /'pestə(r)/ *v.t.* belästigen; nerven (ugs.); ∼ **sb. for sth.** jmdm. wegen etw. in den Ohren liegen

pesticide /'pestɪsaɪd/ *n.* Pestizid, *das*

pestle /'pesl/ *n.* Stößel, *der*

pet /pet/ ① *n.* (a) (animal) Haustier, *das* (b) (as term of endearment) Schatz, *der* ② *adj.* (favourite) Lieblings- ③ *v.i., -tt-* knutschen (ugs.)

petal /'petl/ *n.* Blütenblatt, *das*

peter /'piːtə(r)/ *v.i.* ∼ **out** [allmählich] zu Ende gehen; ⟨*Weg:*⟩ sich verlieren

'pet food *n.* Tierfutter, *das*

petite /pə'tiːt/ *adj.* zierlich

petition /pə'tɪʃn/ ① *n.* Petition, *die;* Eingabe, *die* ② *v.t.* eine Eingabe richten an (+ *Akk.*)

petitioner /pə'tɪʃənə(r)/ *n.* Antragsteller, *der*/Antragstellerin, *die*

petrify /'petrɪfaɪ/ *v.t.* **be petrified with fear/ shock** starr vor Angst/Schrecken sein

petrol /'petrl/ *n.* (Brit.) Benzin, *das*

petrol: ∼ **bomb** *n.* Benzinbombe, *die;* ∼ **can** *n.* (Brit.) Benzinkanister, *der;* ∼ **cap** *n.* (Brit.) Tankverschluss, *der*

petroleum /pɪ'trəʊlɪəm/ *n.* Erdöl, *das*

petroleum 'jelly *n.* Vaseline, *die*

petrol: ∼ **pump** *n.* (Brit.) Zapfsäule, *die;* ∼ **station** *n.* (Brit.) Tankstelle, *die;* ∼ **tank** *n.* (Brit.) Benzintank, *der;* ∼ **tanker** *n.* (Brit.) Benzintankwagen, *der*

'pet shop *n.* Tierhandlung, *die*

petticoat /'petɪkəʊt/ *n.* Unterrock, *der*

petty /'petɪ/ *adj.* kleinlich ⟨*Vorschrift, Einwand*⟩; belanglos ⟨*Detail, Sorgen*⟩; ∼ **criminal** Kleinkriminelle, *der*/*die;* ∼ **theft** Bagatelldiebstahl, *der;* ∼ **thief** kleiner Dieb/ kleine Diebin

petty 'cash *n.* kleine Kasse; Portokasse, *die*

petulance /'petjʊləns/ *n.* Bockigkeit, *die*

petulant /'petjʊlənt/ *adj.* bockig

pew /pjuː/ *n.* Kirchenbank, *die*

pewter /'pjuːtə(r)/ *n.* Zinn, *das*

phallic /'fælɪk/ *adj.* phallisch; ∼ **symbol** Phallussymbol, *das*

phantom /'fæntəm/ *n.* Phantom, *das*

pharmacist ···⳾ pick ····

pharmacist /ˈfɑːməsɪst/ n. Apotheker, der/Apothekerin, die

pharmacy /ˈfɑːməsɪ/ n. (dispensary) Apotheke, die

phase /feɪz/ n. Phase, die
■ **phase 'in** v.t. stufenweise einführen
■ **phase 'out** v.t. allmählich abschaffen ⟨Verfahrensweise, Methode⟩; (stop producing) [langsam] auslaufen lassen

Ph.D. /piːeɪtʃˈdiː/ abbr. = **Doctor of Philosophy** Dr. phil.

pheasant /ˈfezənt/ n. Fasan, der

phenomenal /fɪˈnɒmɪnl/ adj., **phenomenally** /fɪˈnɒmɪnəlɪ/ adv. phänomenal

phenomenon /fɪˈnɒmɪnən/ n., pl. **phenomena** /fɪˈnɒmɪnə/ Phänomen, das

phew /fjuː/ int. puh

philanderer /fɪˈlændərə(r)/ n. Schürzenjäger, der (spött.)

philanthropist /fɪˈlænθrəpɪst/ n. Philanthrop, der/Philanthropin, die (geh.)

philanthropy /fɪˈlænθrəpɪ/ n. Philanthropie, die (geh.)

Philippines /ˈfɪlɪpiːnz/ pr. n. pl. Philippinen Pl.

philistine /ˈfɪlɪstaɪn/ n. Banause, der/ Banausin, die

Phillips /ˈfɪlɪps/ n. ~ **screw** ® Kreuz[schlitz]schraube, die; ~ **screwdriver** ® Kreuz[schlitz]schraubenzieher, der

philosopher /fɪˈlɒsəfə(r)/ n. Philosoph, der/Philosophin, die

philosophical /fɪləˈsɒfɪkl/ adj. (a) philosophisch
(b) (resigned) abgeklärt

philosophize (philosophise) /fɪˈlɒsəfaɪz/ v.i. philosophieren (about, on über + Akk.)

philosophy /fɪˈlɒsəfɪ/ n. Philosophie, die

phlegm /flem/ n. Schleim, der

phobia /ˈfəʊbɪə/ n. Phobie, die

phobic /ˈfəʊbik/ adj. phobisch

phone /fəʊn/ n. (coll.) [1] n. Telefon, das; by ~: telefonisch; be on the ~: Telefon haben; (be phoning) telefonieren
[2] v.t. & i. anrufen
■ **phone 'back** v.t. & i. zurückrufen; (make further call) wieder anrufen
■ **phone 'up** v.t. & i. anrufen

phone: ~ **book** n. Telefonbuch, das; ~ **booth,** ~ **box** ns. Telefonzelle, die; ~ **call** n. Anruf, der; ~ **card** n. Telefonkarte, die; ~**in** n. ~**in [programme]** (Radio) Hörersendung, die; (Telev.) Phone-in-Sendung, die (Jargon); ~ **number** n. Telefonnummer, die

phonetic /fəˈnetɪk/ adj. phonetisch

phonetics /fəˈnetɪks/ n. Phonetik, die

phoney /ˈfəʊnɪ/ adj. (coll.) (sham) falsch; gefälscht ⟨Brief, Dokument⟩

phonograph /ˈfəʊnəɡrɑːf/ n. (Amer.) Plattenspieler, der

phony ▶ PHONEY

phosphate /ˈfɒsfeɪt/ n. Phosphat, das

phosphorus /ˈfɒsfərəs/ n. Phosphor, der

photo /ˈfəʊtəʊ/ n., pl. ~s Foto, das

photo: ~ **album** n. Fotoalbum, das; ~**call** n. Fototermin, der; ~**copier** n. Fotokopiergerät, das; ~**copy** [1] n. Fotokopie, die; [2] v.t. fotokopieren

photogenic /fəʊtəˈdʒiːnɪk/ adj. fotogen

photograph /ˈfəʊtəɡrɑːf/ [1] n. Fotografie, die; Foto, das; take a ~ [of sb./sth.] [jmdn./etw.] fotografieren
[2] v.t. & i. fotografieren

'photograph album n. Fotoalbum, das

photographer /fəˈtɒɡrəfə(r)/ n. Fotograf, der/Fotografin, die

photographic /fəʊtəˈɡræfɪk/ adj. fotografisch; Foto⟨ausrüstung, -apparat, -ausstellung⟩

photography /fəˈtɒɡrəfɪ/ n. Fotografie, die

photo: ~ **session,** ~ **shoot** ns. Shooting, das; ~'**synthesis** n. Photosynthese, die

phrase /freɪz/ [1] n. [Rede]wendung, die [2] v.t. formulieren

'phrase book n. Sprachführer, der

physical /ˈfɪzɪkl/ adj. (a) physisch ⟨Gewalt⟩; dinglich ⟨Welt, Universum⟩
(b) (of physics) physikalisch
(c) (bodily) körperlich

physical edu'cation n. (Sch.) Sport, der

'physically adv. (relating to the body) körperlich

physical 'training n. Sport, der; (Sch.) Sport[unterricht], der

physician /fɪˈzɪʃn/ n. Arzt, der/Ärztin, die

physicist /ˈfɪzɪsɪst/ n. Physiker, der/ Physikerin, die

physics /ˈfɪzɪks/ n. Physik, die

physiology /fɪzɪˈɒlədʒɪ/ n. Physiologie, die

physiotherapist /fɪzɪəʊˈθerəpɪst/ n. Physiotherapeut, der/-therapeutin, die

physiotherapy /fɪzɪəʊˈθerəpɪ/ n. Physiotherapie, die

physique /fɪˈziːk/ n. Körperbau, der

pianist /ˈpiːənɪst/ n. Pianist, der/Pianistin, die

piano /pɪˈænəʊ/ n., pl. ~s (upright) Klavier, das; (grand) Flügel, der

piano: ~ **ac'cordion** n. Akkordeon, das; ~ **music** n. Klaviermusik, die; ~ **player** n. Klavierspieler, der/-spielerin, die; ~ **stool** n. Klavierschemel, der; ~ **tuner** n. Klavierstimmer, der/-stimmerin, die

pick¹ /pɪk/ n. (tool) Spitzhacke, die

pick² [1] n. (a) (choice) Wahl, die; take your ~: du hast die Wahl
(b) (best part) Elite, die; the ~ of the fruit die besten Früchte ···⳾

2 *v.t.* (a) pflücken ⟨*Blumen, Äpfel usw.*⟩; lesen ⟨*Trauben*⟩
(b) (select) auswählen; ~ one's way sich (*Dat.*) vorsichtig [s]einen Weg suchen
(c) ~ one's nose in der Nase bohren
(d) ~ sb.'s pocket jmdn. bestehlen; he had his pocket ~ed er wurde von einem Taschendieb bestohlen
(e) ~ a lock ein Schloss knacken (salopp)
3 *v.i.* ~ and choose wählerisch sein
■ **'pick at** *v.t.* herumstochern in (+ *Dat.*) ⟨*Essen*⟩
■ **'pick on** *v.t.* (victimize) es abgesehen haben auf (+ *Akk.*)
■ **pick 'out** *v.t.* (a) (choose) auswählen; (for oneself) sich (*Dat.*) aussuchen
(b) (distinguish) entdecken ⟨*Detail, jmds. Gesicht in der Menge*⟩
■ **pick up** **1** /'--/ *v.t.* (a) [in die Hand] nehmen; hochnehmen ⟨*Baby*⟩; (after dropping) aufheben; aufnehmen ⟨*Masche*⟩; ~ up the telephone den [Telefon]hörer abnehmen
(b) (collect) mitnehmen; (by arrangement) abholen (at, from von); (obtain) holen
(c) (become infected by) sich (*Dat.*) holen (ugs.) ⟨*Virus, Grippe*⟩
(d) ⟨*Bus, Autofahrer:*⟩ mitnehmen
(e) (rescue from the sea) [aus Seenot] bergen
(f) empfangen ⟨*Signal, Funkspruch usw.*⟩
(g) (coll.: make acquaintance of) aufreißen (ugs.)
2 /'-'-/ *v.i.* (a) sich bessern
(b) ⟨*Wind:*⟩ auffrischen
'pickaxe (*Amer.*: **'pickax**) ▶ PICK¹
picket /'pɪkɪt/ **1** *n.* Streikposten, *der*
2 *v.i.* Streikposten stehen
3 *v.t.* Streikposten stellen vor (+ *Dat.*)
'picket fence *n.* Palisadenzaun, *der*
'picketing /'pɪkɪtɪŋ/ *n.* Aufstellen von Streikposten
'picket line *n.* Streikpostenkette, *die*
pickle /'pɪkl/ **1** *n., usu. in pl.* (food) Mixedpickles *Pl.*
2 *v.t.* einlegen ⟨*Gurken, Zwiebeln, Eier*⟩; marinieren ⟨*Hering*⟩
pick: ~-me-up *n.* Stärkungsmittel, *das;*
~pocket *n.* Taschendieb, *der/-diebin, die;*
~up. (a) ~up [truck] Kleinlastwagen, *der;*
(b) (of record player, guitar) Tonabnehmer, *der*
picnic /'pɪknɪk/ **1** *n.* Picknick, *das;* go for *or* on/have a ~: ein Picknick machen
2 *v.i.,* -ck- picknicken; Picknick machen
picnic: ~ basket *n.* Picknickkorb, *der;*
~ site *n.* Picknickplatz, *der*
pictorial /pɪk'tɔːrɪəl/ *adj.* illustriert ⟨*Bericht, Zeitschrift*⟩; bildlich ⟨*Darstellung*⟩
picture /'pɪktʃə(r)/ **1** *n.* (a) Bild, *das;* get the ~ (coll.) verstehen[, worum es geht]; put sb. in the ~: jmdn. ins Bild setzen
(b) (film) Film, *der*
(c) *in pl.* (Brit.: cinema) Kino, *das;* go to the ~s ins Kino gehen; what's on at the ~s? was läuft im Kino?
2 *v.t.* ~ [to oneself] sich (*Dat.*) vorstellen

picture: ~ book *n.* Bilderbuch, *das;*
~ frame *n.* Bilderrahmen, *der;*
~ 'postcard *n.* Ansichtskarte, *die*
picturesque /pɪktʃə'resk/ *adj.* malerisch
pidgin /'pɪdʒɪn/ *n.* Pidgin, *das*
pidgin 'English *n.* Pidginenglisch, *das*
pie /paɪ/ *n.* (of meat, fish, etc.) Pastete, *die;* (of fruit etc.) ≈ Obstkuchen, *der*
piece /piːs/ **1** *n.* (a) Stück, *das;* (of broken glass or pottery) Scherbe, *die;* (of jigsaw puzzle, crashed aircraft, etc.) Teil, *der;* (Amer.: distance) [kleines] Stück; a ~ of meat/cake ein Stück Fleisch/Kuchen; ~ of furniture/luggage Möbel-/Gepäckstück, *das;* a three-~ suite eine dreiteilige Sitzgarnitur; ~ of luck Glücksfall, *der;* ~ of news/gossip/ information Nachricht, *die*/Klatsch, *der*/ Information, *die*
(b) (Chess) Figur, *die*
(c) (coin) gold ~: Goldstück, *das;* a 10p ~: ein 10-Pence-Stück
(d) (literary or musical composition) Stück, *das;* ~ of music Musikstück, *das*
2 *v.t.* ~ to'gether zusammenfügen (**from** aus)
piece: ~meal *adv., adj.* stückweise;
~work *n.* Akkordarbeit, *die*
pie: ~ chart *n.* Kreisdiagramm, *das;*
~crust *n.* Teigmantel, *der*
pier /pɪə(r)/ *n.* (at seaside) Pier, *der*
pierce /pɪəs/ *v.t.* (prick) durchstechen; (penetrate) [ein]dringen in (+ *Akk.*) ⟨*Körper, Fleisch, Herz*⟩; ~ a hole in sth. ein Loch in etw. (*Akk.*) stechen
piercing /'pɪəsɪŋ/ *adj.* durchdringend ⟨*Stimme, Schrei, Blick*⟩
piety /'paɪətɪ/ *n.* Frömmigkeit, *die*
pig /pɪg/ *n.* (a) Schwein, *das;* ~s might fly (iron.) da müsste schon ein Wunder geschehen
(b) (coll.: greedy person) Vielfraß, *der* (ugs.)
pigeon /'pɪdʒɪn/ *n.* Taube, *die*
'pigeonhole *n.* [Ablage]fach, *das;* (for letters) Postfach, *das*
piggy /'pɪgɪ/**: ~back** *n.* give sb. a ~back jmdn. huckepack nehmen; ~ bank *n.* Sparschwein[chen], *das*
pig'headed *adj.* dickschädelig (ugs.)
piglet /'pɪglɪt/ *n.* Ferkel, *das*
pigment /'pɪgmənt/ *n.* Pigment, *das*
pigmentation /pɪgmən'teɪʃn/ *n.* Pigmentierung, *die*
pig's 'ear *n.* (Brit. coll.) make a ~'s ear of sth. etw. verpfuschen od. (ugs.) vermurksen
pig: ~sty *n.* (lit. or fig.) Schweinestall, *der;*
~tail *n.* (plaited) Zopf, *der;* ~tails (at either side of head) Rattenschwänzchen *Pl.* (ugs.)
pike /paɪk/ *n., pl. same* Hecht, *der*
pilchard /'pɪltʃəd/ *n.* Sardine, *die*
pile¹ /paɪl/ **1** *n.* (a) (of dishes, plates) Stapel, *der;* (of paper, books, letters) Stoß, *der;* (of clothes) Haufen, *der*
(b) (coll.: large quantity) Haufen, *der* (ugs.)

2̲ *v.t.* **(a)** (load) [voll] beladen
(b) (heap up) aufstapeln ⟨*Holz, Steine*⟩; aufhäufen ⟨*Abfall, Schnee*⟩
■ **pile 'in** *v.i.* (seen from outside) hineindrängen; (seen from inside) hereindrängen
■ **'pile into** *v.t.* sich zwängen in (+ *Akk.*) ⟨*Auto, Zimmer, Zugabteil*⟩
■ **pile 'on** 1̲ ▶ PILE IN
2̲ *v.t.* (fig.) ~ **on the pressure** Druck machen
■ **'pile on to** *v.t.* drängen in (+ *Akk.*) ⟨*Bus usw.*⟩
■ **pile 'out** *v.i.* nach draußen drängen
■ **pile 'up** 1̲ *v.i.* **(a)** ⟨*Waren, Post, Arbeit, Schnee:*⟩ sich auftürmen; ⟨*Verkehr:*⟩ sich stauen
(b) (crash) aufeinander auffahren
2̲ *v.t.* aufstapeln ⟨*Steine, Bücher usw.*⟩; aufhäufen ⟨*Abfall, Schnee*⟩
pile² *n.* (of fabric etc.) Flor, *der*
pile³ *n.* (stake) Pfahl, *der*
'piledriver *n.* [Pfahl]ramme, *die*
piles /paɪlz/ *n. pl.* (Med.) Hämorrhoiden *Pl.*
'pile-up *n.* Massenkarambolage, *die*
pilfer /'pɪlfə(r)/ *v.t.* stehlen
pilgrim /'pɪlgrɪm/ *n.* Pilger, *der*/Pilgerin, *die*
pilgrimage /'pɪlgrɪmɪdʒ/ *n.* Pilgerfahrt, *die*
pill /pɪl/ *n.* **(a)** Tablette, *die;* Pille, *die* (ugs.)
(b) (coll.: contraceptive) **the** ~ **or P**~: die Pille (ugs.); **be on the** ~: die Pille nehmen (ugs.)
pillage /'pɪlɪdʒ/ *v.t.* [aus]plündern
pillar /'pɪlə(r)/ *n.* Säule, *die*
'pillar box *n.* (Brit.) Briefkasten, *der*
'pillbox *n.* Pillenschachtel, *die*
pillion /'pɪljən/ *n.* Beifahrersitz, *der;* **ride** ~: als Beifahrer/Beifahrerin mitfahren
pillow /'pɪləʊ/ *n.* [Kopf]kissen, *das*
'pillowcase, 'pillowslip *ns.* [Kopf]kissenbezug, *der*
'pill-popping *n.* (coll.) Pillenschluckerei, *die* (ugs.)
pilot /'paɪlət/ 1̲ *n.* **(a)** (Aeronaut.) Pilot, *der*/Pilotin, *die*
(b) (Naut.) Lotse, *der*
2̲ *adj.* Pilot⟨*programm, -studie, -projekt usw.*⟩
3̲ *v.t.* **(a)** (Aeronaut.) fliegen
(b) (Naut.; fig.) lotsen
'pilot light *n.* Zündflamme, *die*
pimp /pɪmp/ *n.* Zuhälter, *der*
pimple /'pɪmpl/ *n.* Pickel, *der*
pimply /'pɪmplɪ/ *adj.* pick[e]lig
pin 1̲ *n.* **(a)** Stecknadel, *die;* ~**s and needles** (fig.) Kribbeln, *das*
(b) (peg) Stift, *der*
(c) (Electr.) **a two-/three-**~ **plug** ein zwei-/dreipoliger Stecker
2̲ *v.t., -nn-:* **(a)** nageln ⟨*Knochen, Bein*⟩; ~ **a badge to one's lapel** sich (*Dat.*) ein Abzeichen ans Revers stecken
(b) (fig.) ~ **one's hopes on sb./sth.** seine

[ganze] Hoffnung auf jmdn./etw. setzen; ~ **the blame for sth. on sb.** jmdm. die Schuld an etw. (*Dat.*) zuschieben
(c) ~ **sb. against the wall** jmdn. an die Wand drängen
■ **pin 'down** *v.t.* **(a)** (fig.) festnageln (**to** or **on** auf + *Akk.*)
(b) (trap) festhalten
■ **pin 'up** *v.t.* aufhängen ⟨*Bild, Foto*⟩; anschlagen ⟨*Bekanntmachung, Liste*⟩; aufstecken ⟨*Haar*⟩; abstecken ⟨*Saum*⟩
PIN /pɪn/ *abbr.* = **PIN [number]**
▶ PERSONAL IDENTIFICATION NUMBER
pinafore /'pɪnəfɔ:(r)/ *n.* Schürze, *die* (mit Oberteil)
pincers /'pɪnsəz/ *n. pl.* **(a)** [pair of] ~: Beißzange, *die*
(b) (of crab etc.) Schere, *die*
pinch /pɪntʃ/ 1̲ *n.* **(a)** (squeezing) Kniff, *der;* **give sb. a** ~ **on the arm/cheek** jmdn. od. jmdm. in den Arm/die Backe kneifen
(b) (fig.) **feel the** ~: knapp bei Kasse sein (ugs.); **at a** ~: zur Not
(c) (small amount) Prise, *die*
2̲ *v.t.* **(a)** kneifen; ~ **sb.'s cheek/bottom** jmdn. in die Wange/den Hintern (ugs.) kneifen
(b) (coll.: steal) klauen (salopp)
'pincushion *n.* Nadelkissen, *das*
pine¹ /paɪn/ *n.* (tree) Kiefer, *die*
pine² *v.i.* sich [vor Kummer] verzehren (geh.)
■ **pine a'way** *v.i.* dahinkümmern
pineapple /'paɪnæpl/ *n.* Ananas, *die*
'pine tree *n.* Kiefer, *die*
ping-pong (Amer.: **Ping-Pong**®) /'pɪŋpɒŋ/ *n.* Tischtennis, *das*
pinhole 'camera *n.* Lochkamera, *die;* Camera obscura, *die*
pink /pɪŋk/ 1̲ *n.* Rosa, *das*
2̲ *adj.* rosa
pinkie /'pɪŋkɪ/ *n.* (Amer., Scot.) kleiner Finger
'pin money *n.* Taschengeld, *das*
pinnacle /'pɪnəkl/ *n.* Gipfel, *der;* (fig.) Höhepunkt, *der*
pin: ~**point** *v.t.* genau festlegen; ~**prick** *n.* Nadelstich, *der;* ~**stripe** *n.* Nadelstreifen, *der;* ~**stripe suit** Nadelstreifenanzug, *der*
pint /paɪnt/ *n.* Pint, *das;* ≈ halber Liter
pint 'mug *n.* ≈ Halbliterglas, *das od.* -humpen, *der*
'pin-up (coll.) *n.* Pin-up-Girl, *das;* (picture) (of beautiful girl) Pin-up[-Foto], *das;* (of sports, film or pop star) Starfoto, *das*
pioneer /paɪə'nɪə(r)/ 1̲ *n.* Pionier, *der*
2̲ *v.t.* Pionierarbeit leisten für
pious /'paɪəs/ *adj.* fromm
pip /pɪp/ *n.* (seed) Kern, *der*
pipe /paɪp/ 1̲ *n.* **(a)** (tube) Rohr, *das*
(b) (Mus.) Pfeife, *die*
(c) [tobacco] ~: [Tabaks]pfeife, *die* ⋯⊹

2 *v.t.* [durch ein Rohr/durch Rohre] leiten
■ **pipe 'down** *v.i.* (coll.) ruhig sein
■ **pipe 'up** *v.i.* (coll.) etwas sagen
pipe: ∼ **dream** *n.* Wunschtraum, *der;* Hirngespinst, *das* (abwertend); ∼**line** *n.* Pipeline, *die;* **in the** ∼**line** (fig.) in Vorbereitung

piper /'paɪpə(r)/ *n.* Pfeifer, *der*/Pfeiferin, *die;* (bagpiper) Dudelsackspieler, *der*/-spielerin, *die*

piping hot /'paɪpɪŋ hɒt/ *adj.* kochend heiß

piquant /'piːkənt/ *adj.* pikant

pique /piːk/ *n.* **in a [fit of]** ∼: verstimmt

piracy /'paɪrəsɪ/ *n.* Seeräuberei, *die*

piranha /pɪˈrɑːnə, pɪˈrɑːnjə/ *n.* Piranha, *der*

pirate /'paɪrət/ *n.* (a) Pirat, *der;* Seeräuber, *der*
(b) (Radio) ∼ **radio station** Piratensender, *der*

Pisces /'paɪsiːz/ *n.* (Astrol, Astron.) Fische *Pl.*

piss /pɪs/ (coarse) 1 *n.* (a) (urine) Pisse, *die* (derb)
(b) **have a/go for a** ∼: pissen/pissen gehen (derb)
2 *v.i.* pissen (derb)
■ **'piss down** *v.i.* (sl.) ∼ **down** [with rain] schiffen (salopp)
■ **piss 'off** (Brit. sl.) 1 *v.i.* sich verpissen (salopp)
2 *v.t.* ankotzen (derb)

pissed /pɪst/ *adj.* (sl.) (a) (drunk) voll (salopp)
(b) (Amer.: angry) [stock]sauer (**with** auf + *Akk.*) (salopp)

pissed 'off *adj.* (sl.) stocksauer (**with** auf + *Akk.*) (salopp)

'piss-up *n.* (sl.) Sauferei, *die* (salopp)

pistol /'pɪstl/ *n.* Pistole, *die*

piston /'pɪstən/ *n.* Kolben, *der*

pit /pɪt/ 1 *n.* (hole, mine) Grube, *die;* (natural) Vertiefung, *die*
2 *v.t.,* -tt-: ∼ **one's wits/skill** *etc.* **against sth.** seinen Verstand/sein Können *usw.* an etw. (*Dat.*) messen

'pit bull terrier *n.* Pitbullterrier, *der*

pitch[1] /pɪtʃ/ 1 *n.* (a) (Brit.: usual place) [Stand]platz, *der;* (Sport: playing area) Feld, *das;* Platz, *der*
(b) (Mus.) Tonhöhe, *die*
(c) (slope) Neigung, *die*
2 *v.t.* (a) (erect) aufschlagen; ∼ **camp** ein/ das Lager aufschlagen
(b) (throw) werfen
3 *v.i.* stürzen; ⟨Schiff:⟩ stampfen; ∼ **forward** vornüberstürzen

pitch[2] *n.* (substance) Pech, *das*

pitch: ∼-**'black** *adj.* pechschwarz; stockdunkel (ugs.) ⟨*Nacht*⟩; ∼-**'dark** *adj.* stockdunkel (ugs.)

pitcher /'pɪtʃə(r)/ *n.* [Henkel]krug, *der*

'pitchfork *n.* Heugabel, *die*

'pitfall *n.* Fallstrick, *der*

pith /pɪθ/ *n.* (a) (of orange etc.) weiße Haut
(b) (fig.) Kern, *der*

'pith helmet *n.* Tropenhelm, *der*

'pithy *adj.* (fig.) prägnant

pitiable /'pɪtɪəbl/, **pitiful** /'pɪtɪfl/ *adjs.* (a) Mitleid erregend
(b) (contemptible) jämmerlich

pitifully /'pɪtɪfəlɪ/ *adv.* erbärmlich; jämmerlich

'pitiless *adj.* unbarmherzig

'pit stop *n.* (Motor racing) Boxenstopp, *der*

pittance /'pɪtəns/ *n.* Hungerlohn, *der*

pity /'pɪtɪ/ 1 *n.* Mitleid, *das;* **feel** ∼ **for sb.** Mitgefühl für jmdn. empfinden; **have/take** ∼ **on sb.** Erbarmen mit jmdm. haben; **[what a]** ∼! [wie] schade!
2 *v.t.* bemitleiden; **I** ∼ **you** du tust mir leid

pivot /'pɪvət/ 1 *n.* [Dreh]zapfen, *der*
2 *v.i.* sich drehen

pivotal /'pɪvətl/ *adj.* (fig.: crucial) zentral

pixel /'pɪksel/ *n.* (Comp. etc.) Bildpunkt, *der;* Pixel, *das*

pixie /'pɪksɪ/ *n.* Kobold, *der*

pizza /'piːtsə/ *n.* Pizza, *die*

pizzeria /piːtsəˈriːə/ *n.* Pizzeria, *die*

placard /'plækɑːd/ *n.* Plakat, *das*

placate /pləˈkeɪt/ *v.t.* beschwichtigen

place /pleɪs/ 1 *n.* (a) Ort, *der;* (spot) Stelle, *die;* **a [good]** ∼ **to park/to stop** ein [guter] Platz zum Parken/eine [gute] Stelle zum Halten; **do you know a good/cheap** ∼ **to eat?** weißt du, wo man gut/billig essen kann?; ∼ **of worship** Andachtsort, *der;* **all over the** ∼: überall; (coll.: in a mess) ganz durcheinander (ugs.)
(b) (rank, position) Stellung, *die;* **put sb. in his** ∼: jmdn. in seine Schranken weisen
(c) (country, town) Ort, *der;* ∼ **of birth** Geburtsort, *der;* ∼ **of residence** Wohnort, *der;* **'go** ∼**s** (coll.: fig.) es [im Leben] zu was bringen (ugs.)
(d) (coll.: premises) Bude, *die* (ugs.); **she is at his** ∼: sie ist bei ihm
(e) (seat etc.) [Sitz]platz, *der;* **change** ∼**s [with sb.]** [mit jmdm.] die Plätze tauschen; (fig.) [mit jmdm.] tauschen
(f) (step, stage) **in the first** ∼: zuerst; **why didn't you say so in the first** ∼? warum hast du das nicht gleich gesagt?
(g) (proper ∼) Platz, *der;* **everything fell into** ∼ (fig.) alles wurde klar; **out of** ∼: nicht am richtigen Platz; (several things) in Unordnung
(h) (position in competition) Platz, *der*
2 *v.t.* (a) (vertically) stellen; (horizontally) legen
(b) **in** *p.p.* (situated) gelegen
(c) (find situation or home for) unterbringen (**with** bei)
(d) (class) einordnen; einstufen; **be** ∼**d second in the race** im Rennen den zweiten Platz belegen

placebo /pləˈsiːbəʊ/ *n.,* *pl.* ∼**s** Placebo, *das*

'place mat *n.* Set, *der* od. *das*

placement /'pleɪsmənt/ *n.* Platzierung, *die*

'place name *n.* Ortsname, *der*

placenta /pləˈsentə/ *n.,* *pl.* ∼**e** /pləˈsentiː/ or ∼**s** Plazenta, *die*

'place setting n. Gedeck, das
placid /'plæsɪd/ adj. ruhig
plagiarism /'pleɪdʒərɪzm/ n. Plagiat, das
plagiarize /'pleɪdʒəraɪz/ v.t. plagiieren
plague /pleɪg/ ⓵ n. (a) (esp. Hist.: epidemic) Seuche, die; **the** ∼ (bubonic) die Pest
(b) (infestation) ∼ **of rats** Rattenplage, die
⓶ v.t. plagen; ∼**d with** or **by sth.** von etw. geplagt
plaice /pleɪs/ n., pl. same Scholle, die
plain /pleɪn/ ⓵ adj. (a) (clear) klar; (obvious) offensichtlich
(b) (frank) offen; schlicht ‹Wahrheit›; **be** ∼ **sailing** (fig.) [ganz] einfach sein
(c) (unsophisticated) einfach; schlicht ‹Kleidung›; unliniert ‹Papier›; ‹Stoff› ohne Muster
(d) wenig attraktiv ‹Mädchen›
⓶ adv. (a) (clearly) deutlich
(b) (simply) einfach
⓷ n. Ebene, die
plain: ∼ **'chocolate** n. halbbittere Schokolade; ∼ **'clothes** n. pl. **in** ∼ **clothes** in Zivil
'plainly adv. (a) (clearly) deutlich
(b) (obviously) offensichtlich; (undoubtedly) eindeutig
(c) (frankly) offen
(d) (simply) schlicht
plaintiff /'pleɪntɪf/ n. Kläger, der/Klägerin, die
plaintive /'pleɪntɪv/ adj. klagend
plait /plæt/ ⓵ n. Zopf, der
⓶ v.t. flechten
plan /plæn/ ⓵ n. Plan, der; **[go] according to** ∼: nach Plan [gehen]; planmäßig [verlaufen]
⓶ v.t., -nn- planen; (design) entwerfen
⓷ v.i., -nn- planen
plane¹ /pleɪn/ n. ∼ **[tree]** Platane, die
plane² ⓵ n. (tool) Hobel, der
⓶ v.t. hobeln
plane³ n. (a) (Geom.: fig.) Ebene, die
(b) (aircraft) Flugzeug, das; Maschine, die (ugs.)
'planeload n. Flugzeugladung, die
planet /'plænɪt/ n. Planet, der
planetarium /plænɪ'teərɪəm/ n., pl. ∼**s** or **planetaria** /plænɪ'teərɪə/ Planetarium, das
planetary /'plænɪtərɪ/ adj. planetarisch
plank /plæŋk/ n. Brett, das; (thicker) Bohle, die; (on ship) Planke, die
plankton /'plæŋktən/ n. Plankton, das
planned e'conomy n. Planwirtschaft, die
'planner n. Planer, der/Planerin, die
'planning n. Planen, das; Planung, die
plant /plɑːnt/ ⓵ n. (a) (Bot.) Pflanze, die
(b) no indef. art. (machinery) Maschinen Pl.
(c) (factory) Fabrik, die; Werk, das
⓶ v.t. (a) pflanzen

(b) (coll.: conceal) anbringen ‹Wanze›; legen ‹Bombe›; ∼ **sth. on sb.** jmdm. etw. unterschieben
plantation /plɑːn'teɪʃn/ n. Plantage, die
planter /'plɑːntə(r)/ n. (container) Pflanzgefäß, das
'plant food n. Pflanzennahrung, die
plaque /plɑːk, plæk/ n. (a) Platte, die; (commemorating sb.) [Gedenk]tafel, die
(b) (Dent.) Zahnbelag, der
plasma /'plæzmə/ n. Plasma, das
plaster /'plɑːstə(r)/ ⓵ n. (a) (for walls etc.) [Ver]putz, der
(b) ∼ **[of Paris]** Gips, der; **have one's leg in** ∼: ein Gipsbein haben
(c) ▶ STICKING PLASTER
⓶ v.t. (a) verputzen ‹Wand›
(b) (daub) ∼ **sth. on sth.** etw. dick auf etw. (Akk.) auftragen
plaster: ∼**board** n. Gipsplatte, die; ∼ **cast** n. (Med.) Gipsverband, der
plastered /'plɑːstəd/ adj. (sl.: drunk) voll (salopp); **get** ∼: sich voll laufen lassen (salopp)
'plasterer n. Gipser, der
plastic /'plæstɪk/ ⓵ n. (a) Plastik, das; Kunststoff, der
(b) (coll.: credit cards etc.) Plastikgeld, das
⓶ adj. aus Plastik od. Kunststoff nachgestellt; ∼ **bag** Plastiktüte, die; ∼ **money** (joc.) Kreditkarten Pl.
plastic 'bullet n. Plastikgeschoss, das
Plasticine ® /'plæstɪsiːn/ n. Plastilin, das
plastic: ∼ **'surgeon** n. Facharzt für plastische Chirurgie; ∼ **'surgery** n. plastische Chirurgie
plate /pleɪt/ ⓵ n. (a) Teller, der; (serving ∼) Platte, die
(b) (metal ∼ with name etc.) Schild, das
(c) (for printing) Platte, die; (illustration) [Bild]tafel, die
⓶ v.t. ∼ **sth. [with gold/silver]** etw. vergolden/versilbern
plateau /'plætəʊ/ n., pl. ∼**x** /'plætəʊz/ or ∼**s** Hochebene, die; Plateau, das
plate: ∼ **'glass** n. Flachglas, das; ∼ **rack** n. (Brit.) Abtropfständer, der; Geschirrablage, die
platform /'plætfɔːm/ n. (a) (Brit. Railw.) Bahnsteig, der; ∼ **4** Gleis 4
(b) (stage) Podium, das
platinum /'plætɪnəm/ n. Platin, das
platitude /'plætɪtjuːd/ n. Plattitüde, die (geh.); Gemeinplatz, der
platonic /plə'tɒnɪk/ adj. platonisch ‹Liebe, Freundschaft›
platoon /plə'tuːn/ n. (Mil.) Zug, der
plausible /'plɔːzɪbl/ adj. plausibel; einleuchtend
play /pleɪ/ ⓵ n. (a) (Theatre) [Theater]stück, das; **television** ∼: Fernsehspiel, das
(b) (recreation) Spielen, das; Spiel, das; ∼ **on words** Wortspiel, das
(c) (Sport) Spiel, das   ···⟩

(d) come into ∼, **be brought** or **called into**
∼: ins Spiel kommen
[2] *v.i.* (a) spielen; ∼ **safe** sichergehen; ∼ **for**
time Zeit gewinnen wollen
(b) (Mus.) spielen (**on** auf + *Dat.*)
[3] *v.t.* (also Sport, Theatre, Cards, Mus.) spielen;
abspielen ⟨*Schallplatte, Tonband*⟩; schlagen
⟨*Ball*⟩; spielen gegen ⟨*Mannschaft, Gegner*⟩;
∼ **the violin** etc. Geige *usw.* spielen; ∼ **a**
trick/joke on sb. jmdn. hereinlegen (ugs.)/
jmdm. einen Streich spielen; ∼ **one's cards**
right (fig.) es richtig anfassen (fig.)
▪ **play a'bout, play a'round** *v.i.*
spielen; **stop** ∼**ing about** or **around** hör doch
auf mit dem Unsinn!
▪ **play a'long** *v.i.* mitspielen
▪ **play 'back** *v.t.* abspielen ⟨*Tonband*⟩
▪ **play 'down** *v.t.* herunterspielen
▪ **play 'up** [1] *v.i.* (coll.) ⟨*Kinder:*⟩ nichts als
Ärger machen
[2] *v.t.* (coll.: annoy) ärgern

play: ∼**-acting** *n.* Theater, *das* (ugs.);
∼ **area** *n.* Spielplatz, *der;* ∼**back** *n.*
Wiedergabe, *die;* **listen to the** ∼**back** die
Aufnahme anhören; ∼**boy** *n.* Playboy, *der*

'**player** *n.* Spieler, *der*/Spielerin, *die*

playful /'pleɪfl/ *adj.* spielerisch; (frolicsome)
verspielt

play: ∼**ground** *n.* Spielplatz, *der;* (Sch.)
Schulhof, *der;* ∼ **group** *n.* Spielgruppe, *die*

playing: ∼ **area** *n.* (Sport) Spielfeld, *das;*
∼ **card** *n.* Spielkarte, *die;* ∼ **field** *n.*
Sportplatz, *der*

play: ∼**mate** *n.* Spielkamerad, *der/*
-kameradin, *die;* ∼**off** *n.*
Entscheidungsspiel, *das;* ∼**pen** Laufgitter,
das; ∼ **school** *n.* Kindergarten, *der;*
∼**thing** *n.* Spielzeug, *das;* ∼**wright**
/'pleɪraɪt/ *n.* Dramatiker, *der*/Dramatikerin,
die

PLC, plc *abbr.* (Brit.) = **public limited**
company ≈ GmbH

plea /pliː/ *n.* Bitte, *die;* (public appeal) Appell,
der (**for** zu)

plead /pliːd/ [1] *v.i.* (a) inständig bitten (**for**
um); (imploringly) flehen (**for** um); ∼ **with sb.**
for sth. jmdn. inständig um etw. bitten
(b) (Law; also fig.) plädieren
[2] *v.t.* (a) inständig bitten; (imploringly) flehen
(b) (Law) ∼ **guilty/not guilty** sich schuldig/
nicht schuldig bekennen

'**pleading** *adj.* flehend

pleasant /'plezənt/ *adj.* angenehm

pleasantry /'plezəntrɪ/ *n.* Nettigkeit, *die*

please /pliːz/ [1] *v.t.* gefallen (+ *Dat.*);
∼ **oneself** tun, was man will; ∼ **yourself**
ganz wie du willst
[2] *v.i.* **I come and go as I** ∼: ich komme und
gehe, wie es mir gefällt; **if you** ∼: bitte schön
[3] *int.* bitte; ∼ **do!** aber bitte od. gern!

pleased /pliːzd/ *adj.* (satisfied) zufrieden (**by**
mit); (happy) erfreut (**by** über + *Akk.*); **be** ∼ **at**
or **about sth.** sich über etw. (*Akk.*) freuen

pleasing /'pliːzɪŋ/ *adj.* gefällig

pleasure /'pleʒə(r)/ *n.* (joy) Freude, *die;*
(enjoyment) Vergnügen, *das;* **have the** ∼ **of**
doing sth. das Vergnügen haben, etw. zu tun;
with ∼: mit Vergnügen

'**pleasure cruise** *n.* Vergnügungsfahrt,
die

pleat /pliːt/ *n.* Falte, *die*

'**pleated** *adj.* gefältelt; Falten⟨*rock*⟩

plebiscite /'plebɪsɪt, 'plebɪsaɪt/ *n.* Plebiszit,
das

pledge /pledʒ/ [1] *n.* Versprechen, *das*
[2] *v.t.* versprechen; geloben ⟨*Treue*⟩

plentiful /'plentɪfl/ *adj.* reichlich; **be** ∼:
reichlich vorhanden sein

plenty /'plentɪ/ *n.* ∼ **of** viel; eine Menge;
(coll.: enough) genug

pleurisy /'plʊərɪsɪ/ *n.* Pleuritis, *die;*
Brustfellentzündung, *die*

pliable /'plaɪəbl/ *adj.* biegsam

plied ▸ PLY

pliers /'plaɪəz/ *n. pl.* [**pair of**] ∼: Zange, *die*

plight /plaɪt/ *n.* Notlage, *die*

plimsoll /'plɪmsl/ *n.* (Brit.) Turnschuh, *der*

plinth /plɪnθ/ *n.* Sockel, *der*

plod /plɒd/ *v.i.*, **-dd-** trotten
▪ **plod 'on** *v.i.* (fig.) sich weiterkämpfen

plonk /plɒŋk/ *n.* (coll.) [billiger] Wein

plot /plɒt/ [1] *n.* (a) (conspiracy)
Verschwörung, *die*
(b) (of play, novel) Handlung, *die*
(c) (of ground) Stück Land
[2] *v.t.*, **-tt-:** (a) [heimlich] planen
(b) (mark on map) einzeichnen
[3] *v.i.*, **-tt-:** ∼ **against sb.** sich gegen jmdn.
verschwören

'**plotter** *n.* Verschwörer, *der*/Verschwörerin,
die

plough /plaʊ/ [1] *n.* Pflug, *der*
[2] *v.t.* pflügen
▪ **plough 'back** *v.t.* (Finance) reinvestieren

plow (Amer./arch.) ▸ PLOUGH

ploy /plɔɪ/ *n.* Trick, *der*

pluck /plʌk/ [1] *v.t.* (a) pflücken ⟨*Obst*⟩;
∼ [**out**] auszupfen ⟨*Federn, Haare*⟩
(b) (pull at) zupfen an (+ *Dat.*)
(c) (strip of feathers) rupfen
[2] *v.i.* ∼ **at sth.** an etw. (*Dat.*) zupfen
[3] *n.* Mut, *der*
▪ **pluck 'up** *v.t.* ∼ **up** [**one's**] **courage** all
seinen Mut zusammennehmen

pluckily /'plʌkɪlɪ/ *adv.,* '**plucky** *adj.*
tapfer

plug /plʌg/ [1] *n.* (a) (filling hole) Pfropfen, *der;*
(in cask) Spund, *der;* (for basin etc.) Stöpsel, *der*
(b) (Electr.) Stecker, *der*
[2] *v.t.*, **-gg-:** (a) ∼ [**up**] zustopfen ⟨*Loch usw.*⟩
(b) (coll.: advertise) Schleichwerbung machen
für
▪ **plug 'in** *v.t.* anschließen

'**plughole** *n.* Abfluss, *der*

plum /plʌm/ *n.* (a) Pflaume, *die*

(b) (fig.) Leckerbissen, *der;* **a ~ job** ein Traumjob (ugs.)

plumage /ˈpluːmɪdʒ/ *n.* Gefieder, *das*

plumb¹ /plʌm/ ① *v.t.* [aus]loten ② *adv.* (a) lotrecht (b) (fig.) genau

plumb² *v.t.* **~ in** fest anschließen

plumber /ˈplʌmə(r)/ *n.* Klempner, *der*

plumbing /ˈplʌmɪŋ/ *n.* (a) Klempnerarbeiten *Pl.* (b) (waterpipes) Wasserleitungen *Pl.*

'plumb line *n.* Lot, *das*

plume /pluːm/ *n.* Feder, *die;* (ornamental bunch) Federbusch, *der*

plummet /ˈplʌmɪt/ *v.i.* stürzen

plump /plʌmp/ *adj.* mollig; rundlich

■ **'plump for** *v.t.* sich entscheiden für

plunder /ˈplʌndə(r)/ ① *v.t.* [aus]plündern ⟨*Gebäude, Gebiet*⟩ ② *n.* Plünderung, *die;* (booty) Beute, *die*

plunge /plʌndʒ/ ① *v.t.* stecken; (into liquid) tauchen ② *v.i.* (a) **~ into sth.** in etw. (*Akk.*) stürzen (b) ⟨*Straße usw.:*⟩ steil abfallen ③ *n.* Sprung, *der;* **take the ~** (fig. coll.) den Sprung wagen

plunger /ˈplʌndʒə(r)/ *n.* (suction cup) Stampfer, *der*

plural /ˈplʊərl/ ① *adj.* pluralisch; Plural-; **~ noun** Substantiv im Plural ② *n.* Mehrzahl, *die;* Plural, *der*

pluralism /ˈplʊərəlɪzm/ *n.* Pluralismus, *der*

plus /plʌs/ ① *prep.* plus (+ *Dat.*) ② *n.* (advantage) Pluspunkt, *der*

plush /plʌʃ/ ① *n.* Plüsch, *der* ② *adj.* (coll.) feudal (ugs.)

Pluto /ˈpluːtəʊ/ *pr. n.* (Astron.) Pluto, *der*

plutonium /pluːˈtəʊnɪəm/ *n.* Plutonium, *das*

ply /plaɪ/ ① *v.t.* (a) (use) gebrauchen (b) nachgehen (+ *Dat.*) ⟨*Handwerk, Arbeit*⟩ (c) (supply) **~ sb. with sth.** jmdn. mit etw. versorgen (d) (assail) überhäufen ② *v.i.* **~ between** zwischen ⟨*Orten*⟩ [hin- und her]pendeln

'plywood *n.* Sperrholz, *das*

PM *abbr.* = **Prime Minister**

p.m. /piːˈem/ *adv.* nachmittags; **one ~:** ein Uhr mittags

PMT *abbr.* = **premenstrual tension** PMS

pneumatic /njuːˈmætɪk/ *adj.* pneumatisch

pneumatic 'drill *n.* Pressluftbohrer, *der*

pneumonia /njuːˈməʊnɪə/ *n.* Lungenentzündung, *die*

PO *abbr.* (a) = **postal order** PA (b) = **Post Office** PA

poach¹ /pəʊtʃ/ *v.t.* (a) (catch illegally) wildern; illegal fangen ⟨*Fische*⟩ (b) stehlen, (ugs.) klauen ⟨*Idee*⟩

poach² *v.t.* (Cookery) pochieren ⟨*Ei*⟩; dünsten ⟨*Fisch, Fleisch, Gemüse*⟩; **~ed eggs** verlorene Eier

'poacher *n.* Wilderer, *der*

PO box ▶ POST OFFICE BOX

pocket /ˈpɒkɪt/ ① *n.* (a) Tasche, *die* (b) (fig.) **be in ~:** Geld verdient haben; **be out of ~:** draufgelegt haben ② *adj.* Taschen⟨rechner, -uhr, -ausgabe⟩ ③ *v.t.* (a) einstecken (b) (steal) in die eigene Tasche stecken (ugs.)

pocket: ~book *n.* (wallet) Brieftasche, *die;* (notebook) Notizbuch, *das;* **~ 'handkerchief** *n.*Taschentuch, *das;* **~ knife** *n.* Taschenmesser, *das;* **~ money** *n.* Taschengeld, *das;* **~-size[d]** *adj.* im Taschenformat *nachgestellt*

'pockmarked *adj.* (a) pockennarbig ⟨*Gesicht, Haut*⟩ (b) **a wall ~ with bullets** eine mit Einschüssen übersäte Wand

pod /pɒd/ *n.* Hülse, *die;* (of pea) Schote, *die*

podgy /ˈpɒdʒɪ/ *adj.* dicklich

poem /ˈpəʊɪm/ *n.* Gedicht, *das*

poet /ˈpəʊɪt/ *n.* Dichter, *der/*Dichterin, *die*

poetic /pəʊˈetɪk/ *adj.* dichterisch

poetry /ˈpəʊɪtrɪ/ *n.* [Vers]dichtung, *die;* Lyrik, *die*

pogrom /ˈpɒgrəm/ *n.* Pogrom, *das od. der*

poignant /ˈpɔɪnjənt/ *adj.* tief ⟨*Bedauern, Trauer*⟩; ergreifend ⟨*Anblick*⟩

point /pɔɪnt/ ① *n.* (a) (tiny mark, dot) Punkt, *der* (b) (of tool, pencil, etc.) Spitze, *die* (c) (single item; unit of scoring) Punkt, *der* (d) (stage, degree) **up to a ~:** bis zu einem gewissen Grad; **he gave up at this ~:** an diesem Punkt gab er auf (e) (moment) Zeitpunkt, *der;* **be on the ~ of doing sth.** etw. gerade tun wollen (f) (distinctive trait) Seite, *die;* **best/strong ~:** starke Seite; Stärke, *die* (g) (thing to be discussed) **come to or get to the ~:** zum Thema kommen; **be beside the ~:** keine Rolle spielen; **make a ~ of doing sth.** [großen] Wert darauf legen, etw. zu tun (h) (of story, joke, remark) Pointe, *die* (i) (purpose) Zweck, *der;* Sinn, *der;* **there's no ~ in protesting** es hat keinen Sinn *od.* Zweck zu protestieren (j) (precise place, spot) Punkt, *der;* Stelle, *die;* **~ of view** (fig.) Standpunkt, *der* (k) (Brit.) [power *or* electric] **~:** Steckdose, *die* (l) *usu in pl.* (Brit. Railw.) Weiche, *die* ② *v.t.* (a) zeigen, weisen (**to,** **at** auf + *Akk.*) (b) **~ towards** *or* **to** (fig.) [hin]deuten auf (+ *Akk.*) ③ *v.t.* richten ⟨*Waffe, Kamera*⟩ (**at** auf + *Akk.*); **~ one's finger at sth./sb.** mit dem Finger auf etw./jmdn. zeigen

■ **point 'out** *v.t.* hinweisen auf (+ *Akk.*); **~ sth./sb. out to sb.** jmdn. auf etw./jmdn. hinweisen

point-'blank ① *adj.* (lit. or fig.) direkt; glatt ⟨*Weigerung*⟩; ∼ **range** kürzeste Entfernung ② *adv.* (at very close range) aus kürzester Entfernung

'pointed *adj.* (a) spitz
(b) (fig.) unmissverständlich

'pointer *n.* (a) Zeiger, *der;* (rod) Zeigestock, *der*
(b) (coll.: indication) Hinweis, *der* (**to** auf + *Akk.*)

'pointless *adj.* sinnlos; belanglos ⟨*Bemerkung, Geschichte*⟩

poise /pɔɪz/ *n.* (composure) Haltung, *die;* (self-confidence) Selbstvertrauen, *das*

poised /pɔɪzd/ *adj.* selbstsicher

poison /'pɔɪzn/ ① *n.* Gift, *das*
② *v.t.* vergiften

'poisoning *n.* Vergiftung, *die*

poisonous /'pɔɪzənəs/ *adj.* giftig

poke ① *v.t.* (a) ∼ sth. [with sth.] [mit etw.] gegen etw. stoßen; ∼ sth. into sth. etw. in etw. (*Akk.*) stoßen; ∼ **the fire** das Feuer schüren
(b) stecken ⟨*Kopf*⟩
② *v.i.* (a) [herum]stochern (**at, in, among** in + *Dat.*)
(b) (pry) schnüffeln (ugs.)
③ *n.* (thrust) Stoß, *der;* **give sb. a** ∼ [**in the ribs**] jmdm. einen [Rippen]stoß versetzen; **give the fire a** ∼: das Feuer [an]schüren
∎ **poke a'bout, poke a'round** *v.i.* herumschnüffeln (ugs.)

'poker¹ *n.* Schüreisen, *das*

'poker² *n.* (Cards) Poker, *das od. der*

'poker-faced *adj.* mit unbewegter Miene *nachgestellt*

poky /'pəʊkɪ/ *adj.* winzig

Poland /'pəʊlənd/ *pr. n.* Polen (*das*)

polar /'pəʊlə(r)/ *adj.* polar ⟨*Kaltluft, Gewässer*⟩; Polar⟨*eis, -gebiet, -fuchs*⟩

polar: ∼ **'bear** *n.* Eisbär, *der;* ∼ **'cap** *n.* Polkappe, *die*

pole¹ *n.* (support) Stange, *die;* **drive sb. up the** ∼ (Brit. coll.) jmdn. zum Wahnsinn treiben (ugs.)

pole² *n.* (Astron., Geog., Magn., Electr., fig.) Pol, *der*

Pole /pəʊl/ *n.* Pole, *der*/Polin, *die*

pole: ∼ **star** *n.* Polarstern, *der;* ∼**-vault** *n.* Stabhochsprung, *der;* ∼ **vaulter** *n.* Stabhochspringer, *der*/-springerin, *die*

police /pə'liːs/ ① *n. pl.* Polizei, *die;* (members) Polizisten *Pl.; attrib.* Polizei- ② *v.t.* [polizeilich] überwachen ⟨*Fußballspiel*⟩; kontrollieren ⟨*Gebiet*⟩

police: ∼ **force** *n.* **the** ∼ **force** die Polizei; ∼**man** /pə'liːsmən/ *n., pl.* **-men** /pə'liːsmən/ Polizist, *der;* ∼ **officer** *n.* Polizeibeamte, *der*/-beamtin, *die;* ∼ **state** *n.* Polizeistaat, *der;* ∼ **station** *n.* Polizeirevier, *das;* ∼**woman** *n.* Polizistin, *die*

policy¹ /'pɒlɪsɪ/ *n.* Politik, *die*

policy² *n.* (Insurance) Police, *die*

'policy holder *n.* Versicherte, *der/die*

polio /'pəʊlɪəʊ/ *n., no art.* Polio, *die;* [spinale] Kinderlähmung

polish /'pɒlɪʃ/ ① *v.t.* (a) polieren; bohnern ⟨*Fußboden*⟩; putzen ⟨*Schuhe*⟩
(b) (fig.) ausfeilen ⟨*Text, Theorie, Stil*⟩
② *n.* (a) (smoothness) Glanz, *der*
(b) (substance) Politur, *die*
(c) (fig.) Schliff, *der*
∎ **polish 'off** *v.t.* (coll.) (a) (consume) verdrücken (ugs.)
(b) (complete quickly) durchziehen (ugs.)
∎ **polish 'up** *v.t.* (a) polieren
(b) ausfeilen ⟨*Stil*⟩; aufpolieren ⟨*Kenntnisse*⟩

Polish /'pəʊlɪʃ/ ① *adj.* polnisch; **sb. is** ∼: jmd. ist Pole/Polin
② *n.* Polnisch, *das; see also* ENGLISH 2A

polite /pə'laɪt/ *adj.,* ∼**r** /pə'laɪtə(r)/, ∼**st** /pə'laɪtɪst/ höflich

po'liteness *n.* Höflichkeit, *die*

political /pə'lɪtɪkl/ *adj.* politisch

politically /pə'lɪtɪkəlɪ/ *adv.* politisch; ∼ **correct** politisch korrekt

political 'prisoner *n.* politischer Gefangener/politische Gefangene

politician /pɒlɪ'tɪʃn/ *n.* Politiker, *der*/Politikerin, *die*

politicize (**politicise**) /pə'lɪtɪsaɪz/ *v.t.* politisieren

politics /'pɒlɪtɪks/ *n.* Politik, *die;* (of individual) politische Einstellung

polka /'pɒlkə, 'pəʊlkə/ *n.* Polka, *die*

'polka dot *n.* [großer] Tupfen

poll /pəʊl/ ① *n.* (a) (voting) Abstimmung, *die;* (to elect sb.) Wahl, *die;* **go to the** ∼**s** zur Wahl gehen
(b) (opinion ∼) Umfrage, *die*
② *v.t.* (a) (take vote[s] of) abstimmen/wählen lassen
(b) (take opinion of) befragen

pollen /'pɒlən/ *n.* Pollen, *der;* Blütenstaub, *der*

'pollen count *n.* Pollenmenge, *die*

pollinate /'pɒlɪneɪt/ *v.t.* bestäuben

pollination /pɒlɪ'neɪʃn/ *n.* Bestäubung, *die*

polling /'pəʊlɪŋ/**:** ∼ **booth** *n.* Wahlkabine, *die;* ∼ **station** *n.* (Brit.) Wahllokal, *das*

'poll tax *n.* Kopfsteuer, *die*

pollutant /pə'luːtənt/ *n.* [Umwelt]schadstoff, *der*

pollute /pə'luːt/ *v.t.* verschmutzen ⟨*Luft, Boden, Wasser*⟩

pollution /pə'luːʃn/ *n.* [**environmental**] ∼: [Umwelt]verschmutzung, *die;* **noise** ∼: Lärmbelästigung, *die*

polo /'pəʊləʊ/ *n.* Polo, *das*

polo: ∼ **neck** *n.* Rollkragen, *der;* ∼ **shirt** *n.* Polohemd, *das*

poly /'pɒlɪ/ *n., pl.* ∼**s** (coll.) Polytechnikum, *das;* ≈ TH, *die*

polyester /pɒlɪ'estə(r)/ *n.* Polyester, *der*

polygamy /pə'lɪgəmɪ/ *n.* Polygamie, *die*

polystyrene /pɒlɪ'staɪriːn/ *n.* Polystyrol,
das; ～ **foam** Styropor Ⓦ, *das*

polytechnic /pɒlɪ'teknɪk/ *n.* (Brit.) ≈
technische Hochschule

polythene /'pɒlɪθiːn/ *n.* Polyäthylen, *das;*
～ **bag** Plastikbeutel, *der*

polyunsaturated /pɒlɪʌn'sætʃəreɪtɪd/
adj. mehrfach ungesättigt

polyunsaturates /pɒlɪʌn'sætʃʊrəts/ *n.*
pl. mehrfach ungestättigte Fettsäuren *Pl.*

pomegranate /'pɒmɪgrænɪt/ *n.*
Granatapfel, *der*

'pommel horse *n.* Seitpferd, *das*

pomp /pɒmp/ *n.* Pomp, *der*

pompom /'pɒmpɒm/ *n.* Pompon, *der;* ～ **hat**
Pudelmütze, *die*

pompous /'pɒmpəs/ *adj.* großspurig;
gespreizt ⟨*Sprache*⟩

pond /pɒnd/ *n.* Teich, *der*

ponder /'pɒndə(r)/ ① *v.t.* nachdenken über
(+ *Akk.*) ⟨*Frage, Ereignis*⟩; abwägen
⟨*Vorteile, Worte*⟩
② *v.i.* nachdenken (**over, on** über + *Akk.*)

ponderous /'pɒndərəs/ *adj.* schwer

pong /pɒŋ/ (Brit. coll.) ① *n.* Mief, *der* (ugs.)
② *v.i.* miefen (ugs.)

pony /'pəʊnɪ/ *n.* Pony, *das*

pony: ～**tail** *n.* Pferdeschwanz, *der;*
～**-trekking** /'pəʊnɪtrekɪŋ/ *n.* (Brit.)
Ponyreiten, *das*

poodle /'puːdl/ *n.* Pudel, *der*

pool¹ /puːl/ *n.* **(a)** Tümpel, *der*
(b) (temporary) Lache, *die;* ～ **of blood**
Blutlache, *die*
(c) (swimming ～) Schwimmbecken, *das;*
(public) Schwimmbad, *das;* (in house or garden)
Pool, *der*

pool² ① *n.* **(a)** (Gambling) [gemeinsame
Spiel]kasse; **the** ～**s** (Brit.) das Toto
(b) (common supply) Topf, *der;* **a** ～ **of**
experience ein Erfahrungsschatz
(c) (game) Pool[billard], *das*
② *v.t.* zusammenlegen ⟨*Geld, Ersparnisse*⟩;
bündeln ⟨*Anstrengungen*⟩

'pool table *n.* Pool[billard]tisch, *der*

poor /pʊə(r)/ ① *adj.* **(a)** arm
(b) (inadequate) schlecht; schwach ⟨*Spiel,
Gesundheit, Leistung, Rede*⟩; dürftig
⟨*Kleidung, Essen, Unterkunft*⟩; **of** ～ **quality**
minderer Qualität
(c) (paltry) schwach ⟨*Trost*⟩; schlecht
⟨*Aussichten*⟩
(d) (unfortunate) arm (auch iron.)
(e) karg ⟨*Boden*⟩
(f) (deficient) arm (**in** an + *Dat.*); ～ **in**
vitamins vitaminarm
② *n. pl.* **the** ～: die Armen *Pl.*

poorly /'pʊəlɪ/ *adv., pred. adj.* schlecht

pop¹ /pɒp/ ① *v.i.,* **-pp-: (a)** (make sound)
knallen
(b) (coll.: go quickly) **let's** ～ **round to Fred's**
komm, wir gehen kurz bei Fred vorbei (ugs.)

② *v.t.,* **-pp-: (a)** (coll.: put) ～ **the meat in the**
fridge das Fleisch in den Kühlschrank tun
(b) platzen ⟨*Luftballon*⟩
③ *n.* **(a)** Knall, *der;* Knallen, *das*
(b) (coll.: drink) Brause, *die* (ugs.)
④ *adv.* **go** ～: knallen

■ **pop 'out** *v.i.* hervorschießen; ～ **out to the**
shops schnell einkaufen gehen

pop² (coll.) ① *n.* Popmusik, *die;* Pop, *der*
② *adj.* Pop⟨*star, -musik usw.*⟩

'popcorn *n.* Popcorn, *das*

pope /pəʊp/ *n.* Papst, *der/*Päpstin, *die*

poplar /'pɒplə(r)/ *n.* Pappel, *die*

'pop music *n.* Popmusik, *die*

popper /'pɒpə(r)/ *n.* (Brit. coll.) Druckknopf,
der

poppy /'pɒpɪ/ *n.* Mohn, *der*

popular /'pɒpjʊlə(r)/ *adj.* **(a)** (well liked)
beliebt; populär ⟨*Entscheidung, Maßnahme*⟩;
～ **music** Unterhaltungsmusik, *die*
(b) verbreitet ⟨*Aberglaube, Irrtum,
Meinung*⟩; allgemein ⟨*Wahl, Unterstützung*⟩

popularity /pɒpjʊ'lærɪtɪ/ *n.* Beliebtheit,
die; (of decision, measure) Popularität, *die*

popularize /'pɒpjʊləraɪz/ *v.t.* **(a)** (make
popular) populär machen
(b) (make understandable) breiteren Kreisen
zugänglich machen

'popularly *adv.* allgemein

populate /'pɒpjʊleɪt/ *v.t.* bevölkern;
bewohnen ⟨*Insel*⟩

population /pɒpjʊ'leɪʃn/ *n.* Bevölkerung,
die; Britain has a ～ of 56 million
Großbritannien hat 56 Millionen
Einwohner; ～ **density** Bevölkerungsdichte,
die

popu'lation explosion *n.*
Bevölkerungsexplosion, *die*

'pop-up *adj.* Stehauf⟨*buch, -illustration*⟩;
～ **toaster** Toaster mit
Auswerfmechanismus; ～ **menu** (Comp.)
Pop-up-Menü, *das;* ～ **window** (Comp.)
Pop-up-Fenster, *das*

porcelain /'pɔːslɪn/ *n.* Porzellan, *das*

porch /pɔːtʃ/ *n.* Vordach, *das;* (with side walls)
Vorbau, *der;* (enclosed) Windfang, *der*

porcupine /'pɔːkjʊpaɪn/ *n.*
Stachelschwein, *das*

pore¹ /pɔː(r)/ *n.* Pore, *die*

pore² *v.i.* ～ **over sth.** etw. [genau] studieren

pork /pɔːk/ *n.* Schweinefleisch, *das; attrib.*
Schweine-

pork: ～ **'chop** *n.* Schweinekotelett, *das;*
～ **'pie** *n.* Schweinepastete, *die*

porn /pɔːn/ *n.* (coll.) Pornographie, *die;*
Pornos *Pl.* (ugs.)

pornographic /pɔːnə'græfɪk/ *adj.*
pornographisch; Porno- (ugs.)

pornography /pɔː'nɒgrəfɪ/ *n.*
Pornographie, *die*

porous /'pɔːrəs/ *adj.* porös

porridge /'pɒrɪdʒ/ *n.* [Hafer]brei, *der*

port¹ /pɔːt/ **1** *n.* (a) Hafen, *der*
(b) (Naut., Aeronaut.: left side) Backbord, *das*
2 *adj.* (Naut., Aeronaut.: left) Backbord-;
backbordseitig

port² *n.* (wine) Portwein, *der*

portable /'pɔːtəbl/ *adj.* tragbar

port au'thority *n.* Hafenbehörde, *die*

porter¹ /'pɔːtə(r)/ *n.* (Brit.: doorman) Pförtner,
der; (of hotel) Portier, *der*

porter² *n.* [Gepäck]träger, *der/*-trägerin, *die;*
(in hotel) Hausdiener, *der*

portfolio /pɔːt'fəʊlɪəʊ/ *n. pl.* ~s (a) (Polit.)
Geschäftsbereich, *der*
(b) (case, contents) Mappe, *die*

porthole /'pɔːthəʊl/ *n.* (Naut.) Seitenfenster,
das; (round) Bullauge, *das*

portion /'pɔːʃn/ *n.* (a) (part) Teil, *der;* (of
ticket) Abschnitt, *der*
(b) (of food) Portion, *die*

portly /'pɔːtlɪ/ *adj.* beleibt

portrait /'pɔːtrɪt/ *n.* Porträt, *das*

portray /pɔː'treɪ/ *v.t.* darstellen; (make
likeness of) porträtieren

Portugal /'pɔːtjʊgl/ *pr. n.* Portugal (*das*)

Portuguese /pɔːtjʊ'giːz/ **1** *adj.*
portugiesisch; *sb.* is ~: jmd. ist Portugiese/
Portugiesin
2 *n., pl. same* (a) (person) Portugiese, *der/*
Portugiesin, *die*
(b) (language) Portugiesisch, *das; see also*
ENGLISH 2A

pose /pəʊz/ **1** *v.t.* aufwerfen ⟨Frage,
Problem⟩; darstellen ⟨Bedrohung⟩; mit sich
bringen ⟨Schwierigkeiten⟩
2 *v.i.* (a) (assume attitude) posieren; (fig.) sich
geziert benehmen
(b) ~ as sich geben als
3 *n.* Pose, *die;* strike a ~: eine Pose
einnehmen

poser /'pəʊzə(r)/ *n.* (question) knifflige Frage

posh /pɒʃ/ *adj.* (coll.) vornehm; nobel (spött.);
stinkvornehm (salopp)

position /pə'zɪʃn/ **1** *n.* (a) (place occupied)
Platz, *der;* (of player in team, of plane, ship, etc.)
Position, *die;* (of hands of clock, words, stars)
Stellung, *die;* (of building) Lage, *die;* be in/out
of ~: an seinem Platz/nicht an seinem Platz
sein
(b) (Mil.) Stellung, *die*
(c) (fig.: mental attitude) Standpunkt, *der*
(d) (fig.: situation) be in a good ~ [financially]
[finanziell] gut gestellt sein; be in a ~ of
strength eine starke Position haben
(e) (rank) Stellung, *die*
(f) (job) Stelle, *die*
(g) (posture) Haltung, *die*
2 *v.t.* platzieren; postieren ⟨Polizisten,
Wachen⟩; ~ oneself sich stellen/(sit) setzen

positive /'pɒzɪtɪv/ *adj.* (a) (also Math.)
positiv; konstruktiv ⟨Vorschlag⟩; (definite)
eindeutig; (convinced) sicher; I'm ~ of it ich
bin [mir] [dessen] ganz sicher

(b) (Electr.) positiv ⟨Elektrode, Ladung⟩;
Plus⟨platte, -leiter⟩
(c) *as intensifier* (coll.) echt

positive: ~ discrimi'nation *n.* positive
Diskriminierung; ~ vetting *n., no indef.
art.* (Brit.) Sicherheitsüberprüfung, *die*

possess /pə'zes/ *v.t.* besitzen; (as faculty or
quality) haben; ⟨Furcht usw.:⟩ ergreifen; what
~ed you? was ist in dich gefahren?

possessed /pə'zest/ *adj.* besessen

possession /pə'zeʃn/ *n.* (a) (thing possessed)
Besitz, *der;* some of my ~s einige meiner
Sachen
(b) *in pl.* (property) Besitz, *der*
(c) (possessing) Besitz, *der;* be in ~ of sth. im
Besitz einer Sache (Gen.) sein; take ~ of in
Besitz nehmen; beziehen ⟨Haus, Wohnung⟩

possessive /pə'zesɪv/ *adj.* (a) be ~ about
sth./sb. etw. eifersüchtig hüten/an jmdn.
Besitzansprüche stellen
(b) (Ling.) possessiv; Possessiv⟨pronomen⟩

possessor /pə'zesə(r)/ *n.* Besitzer, *der/*
Besitzerin, *die*

possibility /pɒsɪ'bɪlɪtɪ/ *n.* Möglichkeit, *die*

possible /'pɒsɪbl/ *adj.* möglich; (likely) [gut]
möglich; if ~: wenn möglich; as ... as ~: so
... wie möglich; möglichst ...

possibly /'pɒsɪblɪ/ *adv.* (a) as often as I
~ can sooft ich irgend kann; I cannot
~ commit myself ich kann mich unmöglich
festlegen
(b) (perhaps) möglicherweise

post¹ /pəʊst/ *n.* (a) (as support) Pfosten, *der*
(b) (stake) Pfahl, *der*
(c) (starting/finishing ~) Start-/Zielpfosten, *der*

post² **1** *n.* (a) (Brit.: one dispatch/delivery of
letters) Postausgang, *der/*Post[zustellung], *die;*
by return of ~: postwendend
(b) *no indef. art.* (Brit.: official conveying) Post,
die; by ~: mit der Post; per Post
(c) (~ office) Post, *die*
2 *v.t.* (a) abschicken
(b) (fig. coll.) keep sb. ~ed jmdn. auf dem
Laufenden halten

post³ **1** *n.* (a) (job) Stelle, *die;* Posten, *der*
(b) (Mil.; also fig.) Posten, *der*
2 *v.t.* postieren; aufstellen

postage /'pəʊstɪdʒ/ *n.* Porto, *das;* ~ paid
freigemacht; frankiert; Frei⟨umschlag⟩

'postage stamp *n.* Briefmarke, *die*

postal /'pəʊstl/ *adj.* Post-; postalisch
⟨Aufgabe, Einrichtung⟩; (by post) per Post
nachgestellt

'postal order *n.* ≈ Postanweisung, *die*

post: ~box *n.* (Brit.) Briefkasten, *der;*
~card *n.* Postkarte, *die;* ~code *n.* (Brit.)
Postleitzahl, *die;* ~'date *v.t.* (give later date to)
vordatieren

poster /'pəʊstə(r)/ *n.* Plakat, *das*

poste restante /pəʊst re'stãt/ *n.*
Abteilung/Schalter für postlagernde
Sendungen; write to sb. [at the] ~ in Rome
jmdm. postlagernd nach Rom schreiben

posterior /pɒˈstɪərɪə(r)/ *n.* (joc.) Hinterteil, *das* (ugs.)

posterity /pɒˈsterɪtɪ/ *n., no art.* Nachwelt, *die*

postgrad /pəʊstˈgræd/ (coll.)**,**
postˈgraduate ① *adj.* Graduierten-
② *n.* Graduierte, *der/die*

posthumous /ˈpɒstjʊməs/ *adj.* postum

post: ~**man** /ˈpəʊstmən/, *pl.* ~**men**
/ˈpəʊstmən/ *n.* Briefträger, *der;* ~**mark**
① *n.* Poststempel, *der;* ② *v.t.* abstempeln;
~**modern** ▶ ~MODERNIST 1;
~**modernist** ① *adj.* postmodernistisch;
② *n.* Postmodernist, *der*/Postmodernistin,
die

postmortem /pəʊstˈmɔːtəm/ *n.*
Obduktion, *die*

post: ~ **office** *n.* (a) (organization) the
P~ Office die Post; (b) (place) Postamt, *das;*
Post, *die;* ~ **office box** *n.* Postfach, *das*

postpone /pəˈspəʊn/ *v.t.* verschieben; (for
an indefinite period) aufschieben

postˈponement *n.* Verschiebung, *die*/
Aufschub, *der*

ˈpost room *n.* Poststelle, *die*

postscript /ˈpəʊskrɪpt/ *n.* Nachschrift, *die;*
(fig.) Nachtrag, *der*

posture /ˈpɒstʃə(r)/ *n.* [Körper]haltung, *die*

ˈpost-war *adj.* Nachkriegs-; der
Nachkriegszeit *nachgestellt*

posy /ˈpəʊzɪ/ *n.* Sträußchen, *das*

pot¹ /pɒt/ ① *n.* (a) (Koch]topf, *der;* go to ~
(coll.) den Bach runtergehen (ugs.).
(b) (container, contents) Topf, *der;* (teapot, coffee
pot) Kanne, *die*
(c) (coll.: large sum) **a** ~ **of**/~**s of**
massenweise
② *v.t.* ~ **[up]** eintopfen ‹*Pflanze*›

pot² *n.* (sl.: marijuana) Pot, *das* (Jargon)

potassium /pəˈtæsɪəm/ *n.* Kalium, *das*

potato /pəˈteɪtəʊ/ *n., pl.* ~**es** Kartoffel, *die*

potato ˈsalad *n.* Kartoffelsalat, *der*

pot: ~**belly** *n.* Schmerbauch, *der* (ugs.);
~**boiler** *n.* (derog.) Fließbandprodukt, *das*

potent /ˈpəʊtənt/ *adj.* [hoch]wirksam
‹*Droge*›; stark ‹*Schnaps usw.*›; schlagkräftig
‹*Waffe*›

potential /pəˈtenʃl/ ① *adj.* potenziell
(geh.); möglich
② *n.* Potenzial, *das* (geh.); Möglichkeiten *Pl.*

potentially /pəˈtenʃəlɪ/ *adv.* potenziell
(geh.); **he's** ~ **dangerous** er kann gefährlich
werden; **a** ~ **rich country** ein Land, das
reich sein könnte

pot: ~**hole** *n.* (a) Schlagloch, *das;* (b)
(cave) [tiefe] Höhle; ~**holer** *n.*
Höhlenforscher, *der*/-forscherin, *die;*
~ **plant** *n.* Topfpflanze, *die*

potpourri /pəʊpʊəˈriː/ *n.* Duftmischung,
die

pot: ~ **roast** *n.* Schmorbraten, *der;*
~**shot** *n.* take a ~shot [at sb./sth.] aufs
Geratewohl [auf jmdn./etw.] schießen

ˈpotted *adj.* (a) (planted) Topf-
(b) (abridged) kurz [gefasst]

ˈpotter¹ *n.* Töpfer, *der*/Töpferin, *die*

ˈpotter² *v.i.* ~ **[about]** [he]rumwerkeln
(ugs.)

pottery /ˈpɒtərɪ/ *n.* (a) Töpferware, *die*
(b) (workshop, craft) Töpferei, *die*

potty¹ /ˈpɒtɪ/ *adj.* (Brit. coll.) verrückt (ugs.)
(about, on nach)

potty² *n.* (Brit. coll.) Töpfchen, *das*

pouch /paʊtʃ/ *n.* Beutel, *der*

pouffe /puːf/ *n.* Sitzpolster, *das*

poultry /ˈpəʊltrɪ/ *n.* Geflügel, *das*

pounce /paʊns/ *v.i.* (a) sich auf sein Opfer
stürzen; ‹*Raubvogel:*› herabstoßen auf
(+ *Akk.*)
(b) (fig.) ~ **[up]on/at** sich stürzen auf
(+ *Akk.*)

pound¹ /paʊnd/ *n.* (a) (unit of weight)
[britisches] Pfund (*453,6 Gramm*); **two** ~**[s]**
of apples 2 Pfund Äpfel
(b) (unit of currency) Pfund, *das*

pound² *n.* (enclosure) Pferch, *der;* (for stray
dogs) Zwinger, *der;* (for cars) Abstellplatz, *der*

pound³ ① *v.t.* (crush) zerstoßen
② *v.i.* (a) (make one's way heavily) stampfen
(b) ‹*Herz:*› heftig schlagen

ˈpound[s] sign *n.* Pfundzeichen, *das*

pour /pɔː(r)/ ① *v.t.* gießen; (into cup, glass)
einschenken
② *v.i.* (a) (flow) strömen; ‹*Rauch:*›
hervorquellen (**from** aus); ~ **[with rain]** in
Strömen regnen
(b) (fig.) strömen; ~ **in** herein-/
hineinströmen; ~ **out** heraus-/
hinausströmen
■ **pour ˈdown** *v.i.* it's ~ing down es gießt
[in Strömen] (ugs.)

pout /paʊt/ ① *v.i.* einen Schmollmund
machen
② *v.t.* aufwerfen ‹*Lippen*›

poverty /ˈpɒvətɪ/ *n.* Armut, *die*

poverty: ~ **line** *n.* Armutsgrenze, *die;* **be**
on the ~ **line** an der Armutsgrenze liegen;
live below the ~ **line** unterhalb der
Armutsgrenze leben; ~**-stricken** *adj.* Not
leidend

powder /ˈpaʊdə(r)/ ① *n.* (a) Pulver, *das*
(b) (cosmetic) Puder, *der*
② *v.t.* (a) pudern
(b) (reduce to ~) pulverisieren; ~**ed milk**
Milchpulver, *das*

ˈpowdery *adj.* pulv[e]rig

power /ˈpaʊə(r)/ ① *n.* (a) (ability) Kraft, *die;*
do all in one's ~ **to help sb.** alles in seiner
Macht Stehende tun, um jmdm. zu helfen
(b) (faculty) Fähigkeit, *die*
(c) (strength, intensity) Kraft, *die;* (of blow)
Wucht, *die*

P

(d) (authority, political ∿) Macht, *die* (over über + *Akk.*); come into ∿: an die Macht kommen
(e) (authorization) Vollmacht, *die*
(f) (State) Macht, *die*
(g) (Math.) Potenz, *die*
(h) (Mech., Electr.) Kraft, *die;* (electric current) Strom, *der*
2 *v.t.* ⟨*Treibstoff, Strom:*⟩ antreiben; ⟨*Batterie:*⟩ mit Energie versorgen

power: ∿**-assisted** *adj.* ∿**-assisted steering/brakes** Servolenkung, *die*/-bremsen *Pl.;* ∿ **brakes** *n. pl.* Servobremsen *Pl.;* ∿ **cable** *n.* Hochspannungsleitung, *die;* ∿ **cut** *n.* Stromsperre, *die;* ∿ **dressing** *n.: das Tragen betont streng wirkender Kleidung;* ∿ **failure** *n.* Stromausfall, *der*

powerful /ˈpaʊəfl/ *adj.* (a) (strong) stark; kräftig ⟨*Tritt, Schlag, Tier*⟩; heftig ⟨*Gefühl, Empfindung*⟩; hell, strahlend ⟨*Licht*⟩
(b) mächtig ⟨*Clique, Person, Herrscher*⟩

powerless *adj.* machtlos

power: ∿ **plant** ▶ ∿ STATION; ∿ **point** *n.* (Brit.) Steckdose, *die;* ∿ **station** *n.* Kraftwerk, *das;* ∿ **steering** *n.* Servolenkung, *die;* ∿ **supply** *n.* Energieversorgung, *die* (to *Gen.*)

pp. *abbr.* = **pages**

p.p. /ˈpiːˈpiː/ *abbr.* = **by proxy** pp[a].

practicable /ˈpræktɪkəbl/ *adj.* durchführbar ⟨*Projekt, Plan*⟩

practical /ˈpræktɪkl/ *adj.* (a) praktisch; praktisch veranlagt ⟨*Person*⟩
(b) (virtual) tatsächlich
(c) (feasible) möglich

practical ʹjoke *n.* Streich, *der*

ʹpractically *adv.* praktisch; (almost) so gut wie; praktisch (ugs.)

practice¹ /ˈpræktɪs/ *n.* (a) (repeated exercise) Übung, *die;* be out of ∿: außer Übung sein
(b) (session) Übungen *Pl.;* piano ∿: Klavierüben, *das*
(c) (of doctor, lawyer, etc.) Praxis, *die*
(d) (action) put sth. into ∿: etw. in die Praxis umsetzen
(e) (custom) Gewohnheit, *die;* regular ∿: Brauch, *der*

practice², practiced, practicing (Amer.) ▶ PRACTIS-

practise /ˈpræktɪs/ 1 *v.t.* (a) (apply) anwenden; praktizieren
(b) ausüben ⟨*Beruf, Religion*⟩
(c) trainieren in (+ *Dat.*) ⟨*Sportart*⟩; ∿ the piano/flute Klavier/Flöte üben
2 *v.i.* üben

practised /ˈpræktɪst/ *adj.* geübt

practising /ˈpræktɪsɪŋ/ *adj.* praktizierend ⟨*Arzt, Katholik usw.*⟩

practitioner /prækˈtɪʃənə(r)/ *n.* Fachmann, *der; see also* GENERAL PRACTITIONER

pragmatic /prægˈmætɪk/ *adj.* pragmatisch

Prague /prɑːg/ *pr. n.* Prag ⟨*das*⟩

prairie /ˈpreərɪ/ *n.* Grassteppe, *die;* (in North America) Prärie, *die*

praise /preɪz/ 1 *v.t.* loben; (more strongly) rühmen
2 *n.* Lob, *das*

ʹpraiseworthy *adj.* lobenswert

pram /præm/ *n.* (Brit.) Kinderwagen, *der*

prance /prɑːns/ *v.i.* (a) ⟨*Pferd:*⟩ tänzeln
(b) (fig.) stolzieren; ∿ about *or* around herumhüpfen

prank /præŋk/ *n.* Streich, *der*

prattle /ˈprætl/ 1 *v.i.* plappern (ugs.)
2 *n.* Geplapper, *das* (ugs.)

prawn /prɔːn/ *n.* Garnele, *die*

prawn ʹcocktail *n.* Krabbencocktail, *der*

pray /preɪ/ *v.i.* beten (for um)

prayer /preə(r)/ *n.* (a) Gebet, *das*
(b) *no art.* (praying) Beten, *das*

ʹprayer book *n.* Gebetbuch, *das*

preach /priːtʃ/ 1 *v.i.* predigen (to zu, vor + *Dat.;* on über + *Akk.*)
2 *v.t.* halten ⟨*Predigt*⟩; predigen ⟨*Evangelium, Botschaft*⟩

ʹpreacher *n.* Prediger, *der*/Predigerin, *die*

pre-arrange /priːəˈreɪndʒ/ *v.t.* vorher absprechen; vorher ausmachen ⟨*Treffpunkt, Zeichen*⟩

precarious /prɪˈkeərɪəs/ *adj.* (a) (uncertain) labil; prekär; make a ∿ living eine unsichere Existenz haben
(b) (insecure, dangerous) gefährlich

precaution /prɪˈkɔːʃn/ *n.* Vorsichts-, Schutzmaßnahme, *die;* as a ∿: vorsichtshalber

precede /prɪˈsiːd/ *v.t.* (in order or time) vorangehen (+ *Dat.*)

precedence /ˈpresɪdəns/ *n.* Priorität, *die* (geh.), Vorrang, *der* (over vor + *Dat.*)

precedent /ˈpresɪdənt/ *n.* Präzedenzfall, *der*

precinct /ˈpriːsɪŋkt/ *n.* (a) [pedestrian] ∿: Fußgängerzone, *die*
(b) (Amer.: district) Bezirk, *der*

precious /ˈpreʃəs/ 1 *adj.* (a) kostbar ⟨*Schmuckstück, Zeit*⟩; Edel⟨*metall, -stein*⟩
(b) (beloved) lieb
(c) (affected) affektiert
2 *adv.* (coll.) herzlich ⟨*wenig, wenige*⟩

precipice /ˈpresɪpɪs/ *n.* Abgrund, *der*

precipitate 1 /prɪˈsɪpɪtət/ *adj.* eilig ⟨*Flucht*⟩; übereilt ⟨*Entschluss*⟩
2 /prɪˈsɪpɪteɪt/ *v.t.* (hasten) beschleunigen; (trigger) auslösen

precipitation /prɪsɪpɪˈteɪʃn/ *n.* (Meteorol.) Niederschlag, *der*

precipitous /prɪˈsɪpɪtəs/ *adj.* (a) (steep) sehr steil
(b) ▶ PRECIPITATE 1

précis /ˈpreɪsiː/ *n., pl. same* /ˈpreɪsiːz/ Zusammenfassung, *die*

precise /prɪ'saɪs/ *adj.* genau; präzise; fein ⟨*Instrument*⟩; förmlich ⟨*Art*⟩; **be [more]** ~: sich präzise[r] ausdrücken

pre'cisely *adv.* genau

precision /prɪ'sɪʒn/ *n.* Genauigkeit, *die*

precision 'instrument *n.* Präzisions[mess]gerät, *das*

preclude /prɪ'kluːd/ *v.t.* ausschließen

precocious /prɪ'kəʊʃəs/ *adj.* frühreif ⟨*Kind*⟩; altklug ⟨*Äußerung*⟩

preconceived /priːkən'siːvd/ *adj.* vorgefasst ⟨*Ansicht, Vorstellung*⟩

preconception /priːkən'sepʃn/ *n.* vorgefasste Meinung (**of** über + *Akk.*)

precondition /priːkən'dɪʃn/ *n.* Vorbedingung, *die* (**of für**)

pre-cooked /priː'kʊkt/ *adj.* vorgekocht

precursor /priː'kɜːsə(r)/ *n.* Wegbereiter, *der*/-bereiterin, *die*

predator /'predətə(r)/ *n.* Raubtier, *das;* (fish) Raubfisch, *der*

'predatory *adj.* räuberisch; ~ **animal** Raubtier, *das*

predecessor /'priːdɪsesə(r)/ *n.* Vorgänger, *der*/-gängerin, *die*

predestine /priː'destɪn/ *v.t.* von vornherein bestimmen (**to** zu)

predicament /prɪ'dɪkəmənt/ *n.* Dilemma, *das*

predicate /'predɪkət/ *n.* (Ling.) Prädikat, *das*

predicative /prɪ'dɪkətɪv/ *adj.* (Ling.) prädikativ

predict /prɪ'dɪkt/ *v.t.* voraus-, vorhersagen; vorhersehen ⟨*Folgen*⟩

predictable /prɪ'dɪktəbl/ *adj.* voraussagbar; vorhersehbar ⟨*Ereignis, Reaktion*⟩; berechenbar ⟨*Person*⟩

prediction /prɪ'dɪkʃn/ *n.* Vorhersage, *die*

predominance /prɪ'dɒmɪnəns/ *n.* **(a)** (control) Vorherrschaft, *die* (**over** über + *Akk.*) **(b)** (majority) Überzahl, *die* (**of** von)

predominant /prɪ'dɒmɪnənt/ *adj.* (having more power) dominierend; (prevailing) vorherrschend

pre'dominantly *adv.* überwiegend

predominate /prɪ'dɒmɪneɪt/ *v.i.* (be more powerful) dominierend sein; (be more important) vorherrschen

pre-eminent /priː'emɪnənt/ *adj.* herausragend

pre-empt /priː'empt/ *v.t.* zuvorkommen (+ *Dat.*)

preen /priːn/ *v.t.* putzen ⟨*Federn*⟩

prefab /'priːfæb/ *n.* (coll.) Fertighaus, *das*

prefabricated /priː'fæbrɪkeɪtɪd/ *adj.* vorgefertigt

preface /'prefəs/ ① *n.* Vorwort, *das* (**to** *Gen.*)
② *v.t.* (introduce) einleiten

prefect /'priːfekt/ *n.* (Sch.) die Aufsicht führender älterer Schüler/führende ältere Schülerin

prefer /prɪ'fɜː(r)/ *v.t.,* **-rr-** vorziehen; ~ **to do sth.** etw. lieber tun; ~ **sth. to sth.** etw. einer Sache (*Dat.*) vorziehen

preferable /'prefərəbl/ *adj.* vorzuziehen *präd.;* vorzuziehend *attr.;* besser (**to** als)

preferably /'prefərəblɪ/ *adv.* am besten; (as best liked) am liebsten; **Wine or beer?** – **Wine,** ~! Wein oder Bier? – Lieber Wein!

preference /'prefərəns/ *n.* **(a)** (greater liking) Vorliebe, *die;* **for** ~ ▶ PREFERABLY; **have a** ~ **for sth.** [**over** etc.] etw. [einer Sache (*Dat.*)] vorziehen; **do sth. in** ~ **to sth. else** etw. lieber als etw. anderes tun **(b)** (thing preferred) **what are your** ~**s?** was wäre dir am liebsten? **(c)** **give** ~ **to sb.** jmdn. bevorzugen

preferential /prefə'renʃl/ *adj.* bevorzugt ⟨*Behandlung*⟩

preferred /prɪ'fɜːd/ *adj.* bevorzugt; **my** ~ **solution** *etc.* die Lösung *usw.*, der ich den Vorzug gebe

prefix /'priːfɪks/ *n.* Präfix, *das*

pregnancy /'pregnənsɪ/ *n.* (of woman) Schwangerschaft, *die;* (of animal) Trächtigkeit, *die*

'pregnancy test *n.* Schwangerschaftstest, *der*

pregnant /'pregnənt/ *adj.* schwanger ⟨*Frau*⟩; trächtig ⟨*Tier*⟩

preheat /priː'hiːt/ *v.t.* vorheizen ⟨*Backofen*⟩; vorwärmen ⟨*Geschirr, Essen*⟩

prehistoric /priːhɪ'stɒrɪk/ *adj.* prähistorisch

prehistory /priː'hɪstərɪ/ Vorgeschichte, *die*

prejudge /priː'dʒʌdʒ/ *v.t.* vorschnell urteilen über (+ *Akk.*)

prejudice /'predʒʊdɪs/ ① *n.* Vorurteil, *das* ② *v.t.* beeinflussen

prejudiced /'predʒʊdɪst/ *adj.* voreingenommen (**about** gegenüber, **against** gegen)

preliminary /prɪ'lɪmɪnərɪ/ ① *adj.* Vor-; vorbereitend ⟨*Forschung, Maßnahme*⟩ ② *n., usu. in pl.* **preliminaries** Präliminarien *Pl.;* **as a** ~ **to sth.** als Vorbereitung auf etw. (*Akk.*)

prelude /'preljuːd/ *n.* **(a)** (introduction) Anfang, *der* (**to** *Gen.*) **(b)** (Theatre, Mus.) Vorspiel, *das*

premature /'premətjʊə(r)/ *adj.* **(a)** (hasty) übereilt **(b)** (early) vorzeitig ⟨*Altern, Ankunft*⟩; verfrüht ⟨*Bericht, Eile*⟩; ~ **baby** Frühgeburt, *die*

prema'turely *adv.* (early) vorzeitig; zu früh ⟨*geboren werden*⟩; (hastily) übereilt

premeditated /priː'medɪteɪtɪd/ *adj.* vorsätzlich

premeditation /priːmedɪ'teɪʃn/ *n.* Vorsatz, *der*

p

premenstrual /priː'menstrʊəl/ *adj.*
prämenstruell; ~ **tension** prämenstruelles
Syndrom

premier /'premɪə(r)/ *n.* Premier[minister],
der/Premierministerin, *die*

première /'premjeə(r)/ *n.* Premiere, *die;*
Erstaufführung, *die*

premise /'premɪs/ *n.* **(a)** ~s *pl.* (building)
Gebäude, *das;* (buildings and land) Gelände, *das;*
(rooms) Räumlichkeiten *Pl.*
(b) ▶ PREMISS

premiss /'premɪs/ *n.* Prämisse, *die*

premium /'priːmɪəm/ *n.* Prämie, *die;* **be at
a** ~ (fig.) sehr gefragt sein

'**Premium Bond** *n.* (Brit.) Prämienanleihe,
die; Losanleihe, *die*

premonition /premə'nɪʃn/ *n.* Vorahnung,
die

pre-natal /priː'neɪtl/ *adj.* pränatal (fachspr.);
~ **care** Schwangerschaftsfürsorge, *die*

preoccupation /prɪɒkjʊ'peɪʃn/ *n.* Sorge,
die (with um)

preoccupied /prɪ'ɒkjʊpaɪd/ *adj.* (lost in
thought) gedankenverloren; (concerned) besorgt
(with um)

pre-'packed *adj.* abgepackt

prepaid /priː'peɪd/ *adj.* ~ **envelope**
frankierter Umschlag

preparation /prepə'reɪʃn/ *n.* Vorbereitung,
die; ~s *pl.* Vorbereitungen *Pl.* (for für)

preparatory /prɪ'pærətərɪ/ ① *adj.*
vorbereitend ⟨Maßnahme, Schritt⟩; ~ **work**
Vorarbeiten *Pl.*
② *adv.* ~ **to sth.** vor etw. (*Dat.*)

prepare /prɪ'peə(r)/ ① *v.t.* **(a)** vorbereiten;
ausarbeiten ⟨Plan, Rede⟩; vorbereiten
⟨Person⟩ (for auf + *Akk.*); **be** ~**d to do sth.**
(be willing) bereit sein, etw. zu tun
(b) herstellen ⟨Chemikalie usw.⟩; zubereiten
⟨Essen⟩
② *v.i.* sich vorbereiten (for auf + *Akk.*)

preponderance /prɪ'pɒndərəns/ *n.*
Überlegenheit, *die* (over über + *Akk.*)

preposition /prepə'zɪʃn/ *n.* (Ling.)
Präposition, *die*

prepossessing /priːpə'zesɪŋ/ *adj.*
einnehmend

preposterous /prɪ'pɒstərəs/ *adj.* absurd;
grotesk ⟨Äußeres, Kleidung⟩

'**pre-program** *v.t.*, **-mm-**
[vor]programmieren

prerequisite /priː'rekwɪzɪt/ ① *n.*
[Grund]voraussetzung, *die*
② *adj.* unbedingt erforderlich

prerogative /prɪ'rɒgətɪv/ *n.* Privileg, *das;*
Vorrecht, *das*

Presbyterian /prezbɪ'tɪərɪən/ ① *adj.*
presbyterianisch
② *n.* Presbyterianer, *der*/Presbyterianerin,
die

prescribe /prɪ'skraɪb/ *v.t.* **(a)** (impose)
vorschreiben
(b) (Med.; also fig.) verschreiben

prescription /prɪ'skrɪpʃn/ *n.* **(a)**
Vorschreiben, *das*
(b) (Med.) Rezept, *das*

pre'scription charge *n.* Rezeptgebühr,
die

presence /'prezəns/ *n.* **(a)** (of person)
Anwesenheit, *die;* (of things) Vorhandensein,
das; **in the** ~ **of** in Anwesenheit (+ *Gen.*)
(b) ~ **of mind** Geistesgegenwart, *die*

present¹ /'prezənt/ ① *adj.* **(a)** anwesend
(at bei); **all those** ~: alle Anwesenden
(b) (existing now) gegenwärtig; jetzig ⟨Bischof,
Chef usw.⟩
(c) (Ling.) ~ **tense** Präsens, *das;* Gegenwart,
die
② *n.* **(a) the** ~: die Gegenwart; **at** ~:
zurzeit; **for the** ~: vorläufig
(b) (Ling.) Präsens, *das;* Gegenwart, *die*

present² ① /'prezənt/ *n.* (gift) Geschenk,
das
② /prɪ'zent/ *v.t.* **(a)** schenken; überreichen
⟨Preis, Medaille, Geschenk⟩; ~ **sth. to sb.** *or*
sb. with sth. jmdm. etw. schenken/
überreichen; ~ **sb. with difficulties/a
problem** jmdn. vor Schwierigkeiten/ein
Problem stellen
(b) überreichen ⟨Gesuch⟩ (to bei); vorlegen
⟨Scheck, Bericht, Rechnung⟩ (to *Dat.*);
~ **one's case** seinen Fall darlegen
(c) (exhibit) zeigen; bereiten ⟨Schwierigkeit⟩
(d) (introduce) vorstellen (to *Dat.*); vorlegen
⟨Abhandlung⟩; moderieren ⟨Sendung⟩
③ *v. refl.* ⟨Problem:⟩ auftreten; ⟨Möglichkeit:⟩
sich ergeben; ~ **oneself for an interview** zu
einem Gespräch erscheinen

presentable /prɪ'zentəbl/ *adj.* ansehnlich;
I'm not ~: ich kann mich nicht so zeigen

presentation /prezən'teɪʃn/ *n.* **(a)** (giving)
Schenkung, *die;* (of prize, medal) Überreichung,
die
(b) (ceremony) Verleihung, *die*
(c) (of petition) Überreichung, *die;* (of cheque,
report, account) Vorlage, *die;* (of case)
Darlegung, *die*

present-day /prezənt'deɪ/ *adj.* heutig

presenter /prɪ'zentə(r)/ *n.* (Radio, Telev.)
Moderator, *der*/Moderatorin, *die*

presentiment /prɪ'zentɪmənt/ *n.*
Vorahnung, *die*

presently /'prezəntlɪ/ *adv.* bald; (Amer.,
Scot.: now) zurzeit

preservation /prezə'veɪʃn/ *n.* Erhaltung,
die; (of leather, wood, etc.) Konservierung, *die*

preservative /prɪ'zɜːvətɪv/ *n.*
Konservierungsmittel, *das*

preserve /prɪ'zɜːv/ ① *n.* **(a)** *in sing. or pl.*
(fruit) Eingemachte, *das*
(b) (fig.: special sphere) Domäne, *die* (geh.)
(c) wildlife/game ~: Tierschutzgebiet, *das*/
Wildpark, *der*
② *v.t.* **(a)** (keep safe) schützen (from vor
+ *Dat.*)
(b) bewahren ⟨Brauch⟩; wahren ⟨Anschein,
Reputation⟩

preside /prɪ'zaɪd/ v.i. präsidieren, vorsitzen (**over** Dat.); (at meeting etc.) den Vorsitz haben (**at** bei)

presidency /'prezɪdənsɪ/ n. (a) Präsidentschaft, die (b) (of society) Vorsitz, der

president /'prezɪdənt/ n. (a) Präsident, der/Präsidentin, die (b) (of society) Vorsitzende, der/die

presidential /prezɪ'denʃl/ adj. Präsidenten-

press¹ /pres/ ① n. (a) (newspapers etc.) Presse, die; attrib. Presse-
(b) ▶ PRINTING PRESS
(c) (for flattening, compressing, etc.) Presse, die ② v.t. (a) drücken; drücken auf (+ Akk.) ⟨Klingel, Knopf⟩; treten auf (+ Akk.) ⟨Gas-, Brems-, Kupplungspedal usw.⟩
(b) (urge) drängen ⟨Person⟩; (force) aufdrängen ([up]on Dat.); nachdrücklich vorbringen ⟨Forderung, Argument⟩; **he did not ~ the point** er ließ die Sache auf sich beruhen
(c) (compress) pressen; auspressen ⟨Orangen, Saft⟩; keltern ⟨Trauben, Äpfel⟩
(d) (iron) bügeln
(e) **be ~ed for time/money** zu wenig Zeit/ Geld haben ③ v.i. (a) (exert pressure) drücken
(b) (be urgent) drängen
(c) (make demand) **~ for sth.** auf etw. (Akk.) drängen
■ **press a'head, press 'on** v.i. (continue) [zügig] weitermachen; (continue travelling) [zügig] weitergehen/-fahren; **~ on with one's work** sich mit der Arbeit ranhalten (ugs.)

press² v.t. **~ into service/use** in Dienst nehmen; einsetzen

press: ~ agent n. Presseagent, der/ -agentin, die; **~ conference** n. Pressekonferenz, die; **~ coverage** n. Berichterstattung in der Presse; **~ cutting** n. (Brit.) Zeitungsausschnitt, der

'pressing adj. (urgent) dringend

press: ~man n. (Brit.: journalist) Journalist, der; **~ release** n. Presseinformation, die; **~ stud** n. (Brit.) Druckknopf, der; **~-up** n. Liegestütz, der

pressure /'preʃə(r)/ ① n. Druck, der; **put ~ on sb.** jmdn. unter Druck setzen; **atmospheric ~:** Luftdruck, der ② v.t. unter Druck setzen ⟨Person⟩; **~ sb. into doing sth.** jmdn. [dazu] drängen, etw. zu tun

pressure: ~ cooker n. Schnellkochtopf, der; **~ group** n. Pressuregroup, die

pressurize /'preʃəraɪz/ v.t. (a) ▶ PRESSURE 2
(b) **~d cabin** Druckkabine, die

prestige /pre'stiːʒ/ n. Prestige, das

prestigious /pre'stɪdʒəs/ adj. angesehen

presumably /prɪ'zjuːməblɪ/ adv. vermutlich

presume /prɪ'zjuːm/ ① v.t. (a) **~ to do sth.** sich (Dat.) anmaßen, etw. zu tun; (take the liberty) sich (Dat.) erlauben, etw. zu tun
(b) (suppose) annehmen ② v.i. **[up]on sth.** etw. ausnützen

presumption /prɪ'zʌmpʃn/ n. (a) (arrogance) Anmaßung, die
(b) (assumption) Annahme, die

presumptuous /prɪ'zʌmptjʊəs/ adj. anmaßend

presuppose /priːsə'pəʊz/ v.t. voraussetzen

pre-teen /'priːtiːn/ adj. ≈ zehn- bis zwölfjährig

pretence /prɪ'tens/ n. (Brit.) (a) (pretext) Vorwand, der
(b) no art. (make-believe, insincere behaviour) Verstellung, die; **it is all** or **just a ~:** das ist alles nicht echt

pretend /prɪ'tend/ ① v.t. (a) vorgeben; **she ~ed to be asleep** sie tat, als ob sie schlief[e]
(b) (imagine in play) **~ to be sth.** so tun, als ob man etw. sei ② v.i. sich verstellen; **she's only ~ing** sie tut nur so

pretense (Amer.) ▶ PRETENCE

pretension /prɪ'tenʃn/ n. (a) Anspruch, der (**to** auf + Akk.)
(b) (pretentiousness) Überheblichkeit, die

pretentious /prɪ'tenʃəs/ adj. hochgestochen; wichtigtuerisch ⟨Person⟩; (ostentatious) großspurig

pretext /'priːtekst/ n. Vorwand, der; **[up]on** or **under the ~ of doing sth.** unter dem Vorwand, etw. tun zu wollen

prettily /'prɪtɪlɪ/ adv. hübsch; sehr schön ⟨singen, tanzen⟩

pretty /'prɪtɪ/ ① adj. (also iron.) hübsch ② adv. ziemlich; **I am ~ well** es geht mir ganz gut

prevail /prɪ'veɪl/ v.i. (a) die Oberhand gewinnen (**against, over** über + Akk.); **~ [up]on sb. to do sth.** jmdn. dazu bewegen, etw. zu tun
(b) (predominate) ⟨Zustand, Bedingung:⟩ vorherrschen
(c) (be current) herrschen

prevalence /'prevələns/ n. Vorherrschen, das

prevalent /'prevələnt/ adj. (a) (existing) herrschend; weit verbreitet ⟨Krankheit⟩
(b) (predominant) vorherrschend

prevent /prɪ'vent/ v.t. (hinder) verhindern; (forestall) vorbeugen; **~ sb. from doing sth., ~ sb.'s doing sth.,** (coll.) **~ sb. doing sth.** jmdn. daran hindern, etw. zu tun

preventable /prɪ'ventəbl/ adj. vermeidbar

prevention /prɪ'venʃn/ n. Verhinderung, die; (forestalling) Vorbeugung, die

p

preventive /prɪˈventɪv/ adj. vorbeugend; Präventiv‹maßnahme›

preventive ˈmedicine n. Präventivmedizin, die

preview /ˈpriːvjuː/ n. (of film, play) Voraufführung, die; (of exhibition) Vernissage, die (geh.)

previous /ˈpriːvɪəs/ ① adj. (a) früher ‹Anstellung, Gelegenheit›; vorherig ‹Abend›; vorig ‹Besitzer, Wohnsitz›; **the ~ page** die Seite davor
(b) (prior) **~ to** vor (+ Dat.)
② adv. **~ to** vor (+ Dat.)

ˈpreviously adv. vorher

pre-war /ˈpriːwɔː(r)/ adj. Vorkriegs-

prey /preɪ/ ① n., pl. same (a) (animal[s]) Beute, die; **beast/bird of ~:** Raubtier, das/ -vogel, der
(b) (victim) Opfer, das
② v.i. **~ [up]on** ‹Raubtier, Raubvogel:› schlagen; (plunder) ausplündern ‹Person›; Jagd machen auf (+ Akk.); **~ [up]on sb.'s mind** jmdm. keine Ruhe lassen

price /praɪs/ n. (lit. or fig.) Preis, der; **at a ~ of** zum Preis von; **what is the ~ of this?** was kostet das?; **at/not at any ~:** um jeden/ keinen Preis

price: ~ bracket ▶ ~ RANGE; **~ cut** n. Preissenkung, die; **~-cutting** n. Preisschleuderei, die; **~ increase** n. Preiserhöhung, die

ˈpriceless adj. (a) (invaluable) unbezahlbar; (b) (coll.: amusing) köstlich

price: ~ list n. Preisliste, die; **~ range** n. Preisspanne, die; **~ rise** n. Preisanstieg, der; **~ tag** n. Preisschild, das; **~ war** n. Preiskrieg, der

pricey /ˈpraɪsɪ/ adj. (Brit. coll.) teuer

prick /prɪk/ ① v.t. stechen; stechen in ‹Ballon›; aufstechen ‹Blase›
② v.i. stechen
③ n. Stich, der
■ **ˈprick up** v.t. aufrichten ‹Ohren›; **~ up one's/its ears** die Ohren spitzen

prickle /ˈprɪkl/ ① n. (a) Dorn, der
(b) (Zool., Bot.) Stachel, der
② v.i. kratzen

prickly /ˈprɪklɪ/ adj. dornig; stachelig; (fig.) empfindlich

pride /praɪd/ ① n. (a) Stolz, der; (arrogance) Hochmut, der; **take [a] ~ in sb./sth.** auf jmdn./etw. stolz sein; **sb's ~ and joy** jmds. ganzer Stolz
(b) (of lions) Rudel, das
② v. refl. **~ oneself [up]on sth.** auf etw. (Akk.) stolz sein

pried ▶ PRY

priest /priːst/ n. Priester, der

ˈpriesthood n. geistliches Amt

prig /prɪg/ n. Tugendbold, der (ugs., iron.)

priggish /ˈprɪgɪʃ/ adj. übertrieben tugendhaft

prim /prɪm/ adj. spröde; (prudish) zimperlich

primarily /ˈpraɪmərɪlɪ/ adv. in erster Linie

primary /ˈpraɪmərɪ/ ① adj. (a) (first) primär (geh.); grundlegend
(b) (chief) Haupt‹rolle, -ziel, -zweck›
② n. (Amer.: election) Vorwahl, die

ˈprimary school n. Grundschule, die

primate /ˈpraɪmeɪt/ n. (a) (Eccl.) Primas, der
(b) (Zool.) Primat, der

prime¹ /praɪm/ ① n. Höhepunkt, der; **be in one's ~:** in den besten Jahren sein
② adj. (a) Haupt-; hauptsächlich
(b) (excellent) erstklassig; vortrefflich ‹Beispiel›

prime² v.t. (a) (equip) vorbereiten; **~ sb. with information/advice** jmdn. instruieren/ jmdm. Ratschläge erteilen
(b) grundieren ‹Wand, Decke›
(c) schärfen ‹Sprengkörper›

prime: ~ ˈminister n. Premierminister, der/-ministerin, die; **~ ˈnumber** n. (Math.) Primzahl, die

ˈprimer n. (a) (explosive) Zündvorrichtung, die
(b) (paint) Grundierlack, der

ˈprime time n. Hauptsendezeit, die; **~-time** TV Hauptsendezeit im Fernsehen

primeval /praɪˈmiːvl/ adj. urzeitlich; Ur‹zeiten, -wälder›

primitive /ˈprɪmɪtɪv/ adj. primitiv; (prehistoric) urzeitlich ‹Mensch›

primrose /ˈprɪmrəʊz/ n. gelbe Schlüsselblume

Primus ® /ˈpraɪməs/ n. **~ [stove]** Primuskocher, der

prince /prɪns/ n. Prinz, der

ˈprincely adj. fürstlich

princess /prɪnˈses/ n. Prinzessin, die

principal /ˈprɪnsɪpl/ ① adj. Haupt-; (most important) wichtigst...
② n. (of college) Rektor, der/Rektorin, die

principality /prɪnsɪˈpælɪtɪ/ n. Fürstentum, das

ˈprincipally adv. in erster Linie

principle /ˈprɪnsɪpl/ n. Prinzip, das; **on the ~ that ...:** nach dem Grundsatz, dass ...; **in ~:** im Prinzip; **do sth. on ~ or as a matter of ~:** etw. prinzipiell od. aus Prinzip tun

print /prɪnt/ ① n. (a) (impression) Abdruck, der; (finger~) Fingerabdruck, der
(b) (~ed lettering) Gedruckte, das; (typeface) Druck, der
(c) **be in/out of ~** ‹Buch:› erhältlich/ vergriffen sein
(d) (~ed picture or design) Druck, der
(e) (Photog.) Abzug, der
② v.t. (a) drucken ‹Buch, Zeitschrift usw.›
(b) (write) in Druckschrift schreiben
■ **ˈprint ˈout** v.t. (Comp.) ausdrucken

ˈprinted adj. (a) gedruckt
(b) (published) veröffentlicht

ˈprinted matter n. (Post) Drucksachen Pl.

ˈprinter n. (a) (worker) Drucker, der/ Druckerin, die; (firm) Druckerei, die

(b) (Comp.) Drucker, *der*

'printing *n.* **(a)** Drucken, *das*
(b) (writing like print) Druckschrift, *die*
(c) (edition) Auflage, *die*

'printing press *n.* Druckerpresse, *die*

print: ~**out** *n.* (Comp.) Ausdruck, *der;*
~ **run** *n.* (Publishing) Auflage, die; **what is
the ~ run?** wie hoch ist die Auflage?

prion /'pri:ɒn/ *n.* (Biol.) Prion, *das*

prior /'praɪə(r)/ ☐ *adj.* vorherig ⟨Warnung,
Zustimmung usw.⟩; früher ⟨Verabredung⟩;
Vor⟨geschichte, -kenntnis⟩
☐ *adv.* ~ **to** vor (+ *Dat.*); ~ **to doing sth.**
bevor man etw. tut/tat; ~ **to that** vorher

priority /praɪ'ɒrɪtɪ/ *n.* **(a)** (precedence)
Vorrang, *der; attrib.* vorrangig; **have** *or* **take**
~: Vorrang haben (**over** vor + *Dat.*); **have** ~
(on road) Vorfahrt haben; **give** ~ **to sb./sth.**
jmdm./einer Sache den Vorrang geben; **give
top** ~ **to sth.** einer Sache (*Dat.*) höchste
Priorität einräumen
(b) (matter) vordringliche Angelegenheit

prioritize (**prioritise**) /praɪ'ɒrɪtaɪz/ *v.t.*
nach Vordringlichkeit ordnen

prism /'prɪzm/ *n.* Prisma, *das*

prison /'prɪzn/ *n.* **(a)** Gefängnis, *das; attrib.*
Gefängnis-
(b) (custody) Haft, die; **in** ~: im Gefängnis; **go
to** ~: ins Gefängnis gehen

'prison camp *n.* Gefangenenlager, *das*

'prisoner *n.* Gefangene, *der/die;* **take sb.** ~:
jmdn. gefangen nehmen

prisoner of 'war *n.* Kriegsgefangene,
der/die

prison: ~ **sentence** *n.* Gefängnisstrafe,
die; ~ **service** *n.* Strafvollzugsbehörde,
die

pristine /'prɪstiːn/ *adj.* unberührt; **in**
~ **condition** in tadellosem Zustand

privacy /'prɪvəsɪ/ *n.* Privatsphäre, *die;*
(being undisturbed) Ungestörtheit, *die;* **invasion
of** ~: Eindringen in die Privatsphäre; **in the
strictest** ~: unter strengster Geheimhaltung

private /'praɪvət/ ☐ *adj.* **(a)** (outside State
system) privat; Privat⟨schule, -industrie,
-klinik usw.⟩
(b) persönlich ⟨Dinge, Meinung, Interesse⟩;
nichtöffentlich ⟨Versammlung, Sitzung⟩;
privat ⟨Telefongespräch, Vereinbarung⟩;
Privat⟨strand, -parkplatz, -leben⟩; geheim
⟨Verhandlung, Geschäft⟩; persönlich
⟨Gründe⟩; (confidential) vertraulich
☐ *n.* **(a)** (Brit. Mil.) einfacher Soldat
(b) **in** ~: privat; in kleinem Kreis ⟨feiern⟩;
(confidentially) ganz im Vertrauen

private: ~ **de'tective** *n.*
[Privat]detektiv, *der/*-detektivin, *die;*
~ '**enterprise** *n.* das freie
Unternehmertum; [spirit of] ~ **enterprise**
(fig.) Unternehmungsgeist, *der;* ~ '**income**
n. private Einkünfte *Pl.;* ~ **investigator**
n. Privatdetektiv, *der/*-detektivin, *die*

'privately *adv.* privat ⟨erziehen, zugeben⟩;
vertraulich ⟨jmdn. sprechen⟩; insgeheim
⟨denken, glauben⟩; ~ **owned** in Privatbesitz

private: ~ '**parts** *n. pl.* Geschlechtsteile
Pl.; ~ '**practice** *n.* (Med.) Privatpraxis,
die; ~ '**property** *n.* Privateigentum, *das;*
~ '**view[ing]** *n.* (Art) Vernissage, *die*

privation /praɪ'veɪʃn/ *n.* Not, *die;* **suffer
many** ~**s** viele Entbehrungen erleiden

privatize /'praɪvətaɪz/ *v.t.* privatisieren

privet /'prɪvɪt/ *n.* Liguster, *der*

privilege /'prɪvɪlɪdʒ/ *n.* (right, immunity)
Privileg, *das;* (special benefit) Sonderrecht,
das; (honour) Ehre, *die*

'privileged *adj.* privilegiert

privy /'prɪvɪ/ *adj.* **be** ~ **to sth.** in etw. (*Akk.*)
eingeweiht sein

prize¹ /praɪz/ ☐ *n.* **(a)** (reward, money) Preis,
der; **win** *or* **take first** ~: den ersten Preis
gewinnen
(b) (in lottery) Gewinn, *der*
☐ *v.t.* ~ **sth.** [highly] etw. hoch schätzen

prize² *v.t.* ~ [**open**] aufstemmen

prize: ~**giving** *n.* Preisverleihung, *die;*
~ **money** *n.* Geldpreis, *der;* (Sport)
Preisgeld, *das;* ~**winner** *n.* Preisträger,
der/-trägerin, *die;* (in lottery) Gewinner, *der/*
Gewinnerin, *die*

pro /prəʊ/ *n. in pl.* **the** ~**s and cons** das Pro
und Kontra

proactive /prəʊ'æktɪv/ *adj.* aktiv
⟨Haltung, Rolle⟩; **be** ~ ⟨Person:⟩ [selbst] die
Initiative ergreifen

probability /prɒbə'bɪlɪtɪ/ *n.*
Wahrscheinlichkeit, *die;* **in all** ~: aller
Wahrscheinlichkeit nach

probable /'prɒbəbl/ *adj.* wahrscheinlich;
highly ~: höchstwahrscheinlich

probably /'prɒbəblɪ/ *adv.* wahrscheinlich

probation /prə'beɪʃn/ *n.* **(a)** Probezeit, *die*
(b) (Law) Bewährung, *die;* **on** ~: auf
Bewährung

probationary /prə'beɪʃənərɪ/ *adj.* Probe-;
~ **period** Probezeit, *die*

pro'bation officer *n.* Bewährungshelfer,
der/-helferin, *die*

probe /prəʊb/ ☐ *n.* **(a)** Untersuchung, *die*
(**into** Gen.)
(b) (Med., Astron.) Sonde, *die*
☐ *v.t.* untersuchen

problem /'prɒbləm/ *n.* Problem, *das;*
(puzzle) Rätsel, *das;* **what's the** ~? (coll.) wo
fehlts denn?; **the** ~ **about** *or* **with sb./sth.**
das Problem mit jmdm./bei etw.

problematic /prɒblə'mætɪk/,
problematical /prɒblə'mætɪkl/ *adj.*
problematisch

procedure /prə'siːdjə(r)/ *n.* Verfahren, *das*

proceed /prə'siːd/ *v.i.* (formal) **(a)** (on foot)
gehen; (as or by vehicle) fahren; (after
interruption) weitergehen/-fahren ⋯⟡

(b) (begin and carry on) beginnen; (after interruption) fortfahren; ∼ **in** or **with sth.** (begin) [mit] etw. beginnen; (continue) etw. fortsetzen **(c)** (be under way) ⟨*Verfahren:*⟩ laufen; (be continued after interruption) fortgesetzt werden

pro'ceedings *n. pl.* **(a)** (events) Vorgänge *Pl.*
(b) (Law) Verfahren, *das;* **legal** ∼: Gerichtsverfahren, *das;* **start/take [legal]** ∼: gerichtlich vorgehen **(against** gegen)

proceeds /'prəʊsiːdz/ *n. pl.* Erlös, *der* **(from** aus)

process¹ /'prəʊses/ ⟦1⟧ *n.* **(a)** (of time or history) Lauf, *der;* **he learnt a lot in the** ∼: er lernte eine Menge dabei; **be in the** ∼ **of doing sth.** gerade etw. tun
(b) (proceeding, natural operation) Vorgang, *der*
(c) (method) Verfahren, *das*
⟦2⟧ *v.t.* verarbeiten ⟨*Rohstoff, Signal, Daten*⟩; bearbeiten ⟨*Antrag, Akte*⟩; (Photog.) entwickeln ⟨*Film*⟩

process² /prəʊ'ses/ *v.i.* ziehen

'process cheese (Amer.)**, 'processed cheese** *ns.* Schmelzkäse, *der*

procession /prə'seʃn/ *n.* Zug, *der;* (religious) Prozession, *die;* (festive) Umzug, *der;* **go/march in** ∼: ziehen

proclaim /prə'kleɪm/ *v.t.* erklären ⟨*Absicht*⟩; geltend machen ⟨*Recht, Anspruch*⟩; verkünden ⟨*Amnestie*⟩; ausrufen ⟨*Republik*⟩

proclamation /prɒklə'meɪʃn/ *n.* **(a)** (proclaiming) Verkündung, *die*
(b) (notice) Bekanntmachung, *die;* (decree) Erlass, *der*

procreation /prəʊkrɪ'eɪʃn/ *n.* Fortpflanzung, *die*

procure /prə'kjʊə(r)/ *v.t.* beschaffen

prod /prɒd/ ⟦1⟧ *v.t.,* **-dd-** (poke) stupsen (ugs.); stoßen mit ⟨*Stock, Finger usw.*⟩; ∼ **sb. gently** jmdn. anstupsen
⟦2⟧ *n.* Stupser, *der;* **give sb. a** ∼: jmdm. einen Stupser geben

prodigal /'prɒdɪgl/ *adj.* verschwenderisch; ∼ **son** verlorener Sohn

prodigious /prə'dɪdʒəs/ *adj.* ungeheuer

prodigy /'prɒdɪdʒɪ/ *n.* [außergewöhnliches] Talent; **child** ∼: Wunderkind, *das*

produce ⟦1⟧ /'prɒdjuːs/ *n.* Produkte *Pl.;* Erzeugnisse *Pl.*
⟦2⟧ /prə'djuːs/ *v.t.* **(a)** vorzeigen ⟨*Pass, Fahrkarte*⟩
(b) produzieren ⟨*Show, Film*⟩; inszenieren ⟨*Theaterstück, Hörspiel*⟩; herausgeben ⟨*Schallplatte, Buch*⟩
(c) (manufacture) herstellen; (in nature; Agric.) produzieren
(d) (cause) hervorrufen; bewirken ⟨*Änderung*⟩
(e) (bring into being) erzeugen; führen zu ⟨*Situation*⟩
(f) (yield) geben ⟨*Milch*⟩; legen ⟨*Eier*⟩
(g) ⟨*Baum, Blume:*⟩ tragen ⟨*Früchte, Blüten*⟩; entwickeln ⟨*Triebe*⟩; bilden ⟨*Keime*⟩

producer /prə'djuːsə(r)/ *n.* **(a)** (Cinemat., Theatre, Radio, Telev.) Produzent, *der/* Produzentin, *die*
(b) (Brit. Theatre/Radio/Telev.) Regisseur, *der/* Regisseurin, *die*

product /'prɒdʌkt/ *n.* **(a)** Produkt, *das;* (of industrial process) Erzeugnis, *das;* (of art or intellect) Werk, *das*
(b) (result) Folge, *die*
(c) (Math.) Produkt, *das* **(of** aus)

production /prə'dʌkʃn/ *n.* **(a)** (Cinemat.) Produktion, *die;* (Theatre) Inszenierung, *die;* (of record, book) Herausgabe, *die*
(b) (making) Produktion, *die;* (manufacturing) Herstellung, *die;* (thing produced) Produkt, *das;* (thing created) Werk, *das*
(c) (yielding) Produktion, *die;* (yield) Ertrag, *der*

production: ∼ **line** *n.* Fertigungsstraße, *die;* ∼ **manager** *n.* Produktionsleiter, *der/*-leiterin, *die*

productive /prə'dʌktɪv/ *adj.* leistungsfähig ⟨*Betrieb, Bauernhof*⟩; fruchtbar ⟨*Gespräch, Verhandlungen*⟩

productivity /prɒdʌk'tɪvɪtɪ/ *n.* Produktivität, *die*

'product range *n.* Produktpalette, *die*

Prof. /prɒf/ *abbr.* = **Professor** Prof.

profane /prə'feɪn/ *adj.* **(a)** (irreligious) gotteslästerlich
(b) (secular) weltlich
(c) (irreverent) respektlos ⟨*Bemerkung*⟩; profan ⟨*Sprache*⟩

profess /prə'fes/ *v.t.* **(a)** (declare openly) bekunden ⟨*Vorliebe, Abneigung*⟩; ∼ **to be/do sth.** erklären, etw. zu sein/tun
(b) (claim) vorgeben; ∼ **to be/do sth.** behaupten, etw. zu sein/tun

profession /prə'feʃn/ *n.* **(a)** Beruf, *der;* **be a pilot by** ∼: von Beruf Pilot sein
(b) (body of people) Berufsstand, *der*

professional /prə'feʃənl/ ⟦1⟧ *adj.* **(a)** Berufs⟨*ausbildung, -leben*⟩; beruflich ⟨*Qualifikation*⟩
(b) (worthy of profession) (in technical expertise) fachmännisch; (in attitude) professionell; (in experience) routiniert
(c) ∼ **people** Angehörige *Pl.* hoch qualifizierter Berufe
(d) (by profession) gelernt; (not amateur) Berufs⟨*musiker, -sportler*⟩; Profi⟨*sportler*⟩
(e) (paid) Profi⟨*sport, -boxen*⟩
⟦2⟧ *n.* (trained person) Fachmann, *der/*Fachfrau, *die;* (non-amateur; also Sport) Profi, *der*

professor /prə'fesə(r)/ *n.* **(a)** (Univ.) Professor, *der/*Professorin, *die* **(of** für)
(b) (Amer.: teacher at university) Dozent, *der/* Dozentin, *die*

proficiency /prə'fɪʃənsɪ/ *n.* Können, *das*

proficient /prə'fɪʃənt/ *adj.* fähig; gut ⟨*Pianist, Reiter usw.*⟩; geschickt ⟨*Radfahrer, Handwerker*⟩; **be** ∼ **at** or **in maths** viel von Mathematik verstehen

profile /'prəʊfaɪl/ *n.* **(a)** (side aspect) Profil, *das*

(b) (biographical sketch) Porträt, *das*
(c) (fig.) **keep a low** ~: sich zurückhalten
profit /'prɒfɪt/ *n.* Gewinn, *der;* Profit, *der;*
make a ~ from *or* out of sth. mit etw. Geld
verdienen; **make [a few pence]** ~ **on sth.**
[ein paar Pfennige] an etw. (*Dat.*) verdienen;
~ **and loss** Gewinn und Verlust; ~**-and-loss**
account Gewinn-und-Verlust-Rechnung, *die*
■ '**profit by** *v.t.* profitieren von; Nutzen
ziehen aus 〈*Fehler, Erfahrung*〉
■ '**profit from** *v.t.* profitieren von
profitable /'prɒfɪtəbl/ *adj.* rentabel;
einträglich; (fruitful) nützlich
profiteer /prɒfɪ'tɪə(r)/ [1] *n.* Profitmacher,
der/-macherin, *die*
[2] *v.i.* sich bereichern
profi'teering *n.* Wucher, *der*
profit: ~ **margin** *n.* Gewinnspanne, *die;*
~**-sharing** *n.* Gewinnbeteiligung, *die*
profligate /'prɒflɪgət/ *adj.*
verschwenderisch; **be** ~ **of** *or* **with sth.**
verschwenderisch umgehen mit etw.
profound /prə'faʊnd/ *adj.* tief; nachhaltig
〈*Wirkung, Einfluss*〉; tief greifend 〈*Wandel,*
Veränderung〉; tief empfunden 〈*Beileid,*
Mitgefühl〉; tief sitzend 〈*Misstrauen*〉
prognosis /prɒg'nəʊsɪs/ *n., pl.* prognoses
/prɒg'nəʊsiːz/ Prognose, *die*
program /'prəʊgræm/ [1] *n.* **(a)** (Amer.)
▶ PROGRAMME 1
(b) (Comp.) Programm, *das;* ~ **file**
Programmdata, *die*
[2] *v.t.,* **-mm-** (Comp.) programmieren
programme /'prəʊgræm/ *n.* **(a)** ([notice of]
events) Programm, *das*
(b) (Radio, Telev.) Sendung, *die*
(c) (plan, instructions for machine) Programm,
das
programmer /'prəʊgræmə(r)/ *n.* (Comp.)
Programmierer, *der*/Programmiererin, *die*
progress [1] /'prəʊgres/ *n.* **(a)** no pl., no
indef. art. (onward movement)
[Vorwärts]bewegung, *die*
(b) (advance) Fortschritt, *der;* **make** ~:
vorankommen; 〈*Student, Patient:*〉
Fortschritte machen; **in** ~: im Gange
[2] /prə'gres/ *v.i.* **(a)** (move forward)
vorankommen
(b) (be carried on, develop) Fortschritte machen
progression /prə'greʃn/ *n.* **(a)**
(development) Fortschritt, *der*
(b) (succession) Folge, *die*
progressive /prə'gresɪv/ *adj.* **(a)**
fortschreitend 〈*Verbesserung,*
Verschlechterung〉; schrittweise 〈*Reform*〉;
allmählich 〈*Veränderung*〉
(b) (favouring reform; in culture) fortschrittlich;
progressiv
pro'gressively *adv.* immer 〈*schlechter,*
weiter〉
prohibit /prə'hɪbɪt/ *v.t.* (forbid) verbieten;
~ **sb.'s doing sth.,** ~ **sb. from doing sth.**
jmdm. verbieten, etw. zu tun

prohibition /prəʊhɪ'bɪʃn, prəʊɪ'bɪʃn/ *n.*
Verbot, *das*
prohibitive /prə'hɪbɪtɪv/ *adj.*
unerschwinglich 〈*Preis, Miete*〉; untragbar
〈*Kosten*〉
project [1] /prə'dʒekt/ *v.t.* werfen 〈*Schein*〉;
senden 〈*Strahl*〉; (Cinemat.) projizieren
[2] /prə'dʒekt/ *v.i.* (jut out) 〈*Felsen:*〉
vorspringen; 〈*Zähne, Brauen:*〉 vorstehen
[3] /'prɒdʒekt/ *n.* Projekt, *das*
projectile /prə'dʒektaɪl/ *n.* Geschoss, *das*
projection /prə'dʒekʃn/ *n.* **(a)** (protruding
thing) Vorsprung, *der*
(b) (estimate) Hochrechnung, *die;* (forecast)
Voraussage, *die*
projectionist /prə'dʒekʃənɪst/ *n.* (Cinemat.)
Filmvorführer, *der*/-vorführerin, *die*
pro'jection room *n.* (Cinemat.)
Vorführraum, *der*
projector /prə'dʒektə(r)/ *n.* Projektor, *der*
proletarian /prəʊlɪ'teərɪən/ [1] *adj.*
proletarisch
[2] *n.* Proletarier, *der*/Proletarierin, *die*
'**pro-life** *adj.* Lebensschutz-
'**pro-lifer** *n.* Verfechter, *der*/Verfechterin,
die des Rechts auf Leben
proliferate /prə'lɪfəreɪt/ *v.i.* (increase) sich
ausbreiten
proliferation /prəlɪfə'reɪʃn/ *n.* starke
Zunahme
prolific /prə'lɪfɪk/ *adj.* **(a)** (fertile) fruchtbar
(b) (productive) produktiv
prologue (*Amer.:* **prolog**) /'prəʊlɒg/ *n.*
Prolog, *der* (**to** zu)
prolong /prə'lɒŋ/ *v.t.* verlängern
prolonged /prə'lɒŋd/ *adj.* lang; lang
anhaltend 〈*Beifall*〉
promenade /prɒmə'nɑːd/ *n.* Promenade,
die
prominence /'prɒmɪnəns/ *n.* **(a)**
(conspicuousness) Auffälligkeit, *die*
(b) (distinction) Bekanntheit, *die*
prominent /'prɒmɪnənt/ *adj.* **(a)**
(conspicuous) auffallend
(b) (foremost) herausragend; **he was** ~ **in**
politics er war ein prominenter Politiker
(c) (projecting) vorspringend; vorstehend
〈*Backenknochen, Brauen*〉
promiscuity /prɒmɪ'skjuːɪtɪ/ *n.*
Promiskuität, *die* (geh.)
promiscuous /prə'mɪskjʊəs/ *adj.*
promiskuitiv (geh.); **a** ~ **man** ein Mann, der
häufig die Partnerin wechselt
promise /'prɒmɪs/ [1] *n.* **(a)** Versprechen,
das; **sb.'s** ~**s** jmds. Versprechungen; **give** *or*
make a ~ **[to sb.]** [jmdm.] ein Versprechen
geben; **give** *or* **make a** ~ **[to sb.] to do sth.**
[jmdm.] versprechen, etw. zu tun
(b) (fig.: reason for expectation) Hoffnung, *die;* **a**
painter of *or* **with** ~: ein viel versprechender
Maler
[2] *v.t.* **(a)** versprechen; ~ **sth. to sb.,** ~ **sb.**
sth. jmdm. etw. versprechen ···⊹

(b) (fig.: give reason for expectation of) verheißen (geh.); ~ **sb. sth.** jmdm. etw. in Aussicht stellen
3 v.i. ~ **well** or **favourably** viel versprechend sein; **I can't** ~: ich kann es nicht versprechen

promising /'prɒmɪsɪŋ/ adj. viel versprechend

promote /prə'məʊt/ v.t. **(a)** (to more senior job) befördern
(b) (encourage) fördern
(c) (publicize) Werbung machen für
(d) (Footb.) **be** ~**d** aufsteigen

pro'moter n. Veranstalter, der/ Veranstalterin, die

promotion /prə'məʊʃn/ n. **(a)** Beförderung, die; **win** or **gain** ~: befördert werden
(b) (furtherance) Förderung, die
(c) (publicization) Werbung, die; (instance) Werbekampagne, die
(d) (Footb.) Aufstieg, der

promotional /prə'məʊʃənl/ adj. Werbe⟨kampagne, -broschüre usw.⟩

prompt /prɒmpt/ 1 adj. **(a)** (ready to act) bereitwillig; **be** ~ **in doing sth.** or **to do sth.** etw. unverzüglich tun
(b) (done readily) sofortig; **her** ~ **answer** ihre prompte Antwort; **take** ~ **action** sofort handeln
(c) (punctual) pünktlich
2 adv. pünktlich; **at 6 o'clock** ~: Punkt 6 Uhr
3 v.t. **(a)** (incite) veranlassen
(b) (supply with words) soufflieren (+ Dat.); (give suggestion to) weiterhelfen (+ Dat.)
(c) hervorrufen ⟨Kritik⟩; provozieren ⟨Antwort⟩

'**promptly** adv. **(a)** (quickly) prompt
(b) (punctually) pünktlich

prone /prəʊn/ adj. (liable) **be** ~ **to** anfällig sein für ⟨Krankheiten⟩; **be** ~ **to do sth.** dazu neigen, etw. zu tun

prong /prɒŋ/ n. (of fork) Zinke, die

pronoun /'prəʊnaʊn/ n. (Ling.) Pronomen, das; Fürwort, das

pronounce /prə'naʊns/ 1 v.t. **(a)** (declare) verkünden; ~ **sb./sth. [to be] sth.** jmdn./etw. für etw. erklären; ~ **sb. fit for work** jmdn. für arbeitsfähig erklären
(b) aussprechen ⟨Wort, Buchstaben usw.⟩
2 v.i. ~ **on sth.** zu etw. Stellung nehmen; ~ **for** or **in favour of/against sth.** sich für/ gegen etw. aussprechen

pronounced /prə'naʊnst/ adj. (marked) ausgeprägt

pro'nouncement n. Erklärung, die; **make a** ~ **[about sth.]** eine Erklärung [zu etw.] abgeben

pronunciation /prənʌnsɪ'eɪʃn/ n. Aussprache, die; **what is the** ~ **of this word?** wie wird dieses Wort ausgesprochen?

proof /pruːf/ 1 n. **(a)** (fact, evidence) Beweis, der
(b) no indef. art. (Law) Beweismaterial, das

(c) (proving) **in** ~ **of** zum Beweis (+ Gen.)
(d) no art. (standard of strength) Proof o. Art.; **100°** ~ **(Brit.), 128°** ~ **(Amer.)** 64 Vol.-% Alkohol
(e) (Printing) [Korrektur]abzug, der
2 adj. **(a) be** ~ **against sth.** unempfindlich gegen etw. sein; (fig.) gegen etw. immun sein
(b) in comb. ⟨kugel-, einbruch-, idioten⟩sicher; ⟨schall-, wasser⟩dicht; **flame-** ~: nicht brennbar

proof ~**-read** v.t. Korrektur lesen; ~**-reader** n. Korrektor, der/Korrektorin, die

prop¹ /prɒp/ 1 n. Stütze, die; (Mining) Strebe, die
2 v.t., **-pp-** stützen; **the ladder was** ~**ped against the house** die Leiter war gegen das Haus gelehnt
■ **prop 'up** v.t. stützen; (fig.) vor dem Konkurs bewahren ⟨Firma⟩; stützen ⟨Regierung⟩

prop² n. (Theatre, Cinemat.: also fig.) Requisit, das

propaganda /prɒpə'gændə/ n. Propaganda, die

propagate /'prɒpəgeɪt/ 1 v.t. **(a)** (Hort., Agric.) vermehren (**from, by** durch)
(b) (spread) verbreiten
2 v.i. **(a)** (Bot.) sich vermehren
(b) (spread) sich ausbreiten

propagation /prɒpə'geɪʃn/ n. **(a)** (Hort., Agric.) Züchtung, die
(b) (Bot.) Vermehrung, die
(c) (spreading) Verbreitung, die

propel /prə'pel/ v.t., **-ll-** antreiben

propellant /prə'pelənt/ n. **(a)** Treibstoff, der
(b) (of aerosol spray) Treibgas, das

pro'peller n. Propeller, der

propelling 'pencil n. (Brit.) Drehbleistift, der

propensity /prə'pensɪtɪ/ n. **have a** ~ **to do sth.** or **for doing sth.** dazu neigen, etw. zu tun

proper /'prɒpə(r)/ adj. **(a)** (accurate) richtig; zutreffend ⟨Beschreibung⟩; eigentlich ⟨Wortbedeutung⟩
(b) postpos. (strictly so called) im engeren Sinn nachgestellt; **in London** ~: in London selbst
(c) (genuine) echt; richtig ⟨Wirbelsturm, Schauspieler⟩
(d) (satisfactory) richtig; zufrieden stellend ⟨Antwort⟩
(e) (suitable) angemessen; (morally fitting) gebührend; **do sth. the** ~ **way** etw. richtig machen
(f) attrib. (coll.: thorough) richtig

'**properly** adv. richtig; (rightly) zu Recht; ~ **speaking** genau genommen

proper 'name, proper 'noun ns. (Ling.) Eigenname, der

property /'prɒpətɪ/ n. **(a)** (possession[s]) Eigentum, das; **lost** ~ **[department** or **office]** Fundbüro, das

(b) (estate) Besitz, *der;* Immobilie, *die* (fachspr.)
(c) (attribute) Eigenschaft, *die;* (effect, special power) Wirkung, *die*

'**property developer** *n.* ≈ Bauunternehmer, *der*/-unternehmerin, *die*

prophecy /'prɒfɪsɪ/ *n.* (prediction) Vorhersage, *die;* (prophetic utterance) Prophezeiung, *die*

prophesy /'prɒfɪsaɪ/ *v.t.* (predict) vorhersagen; (fig.) prophezeien ⟨*Unglück*⟩; (as fortune teller) weissagen

prophet /'prɒfɪt/ *n.* Prophet, *der*

prophetic /prə'fetɪk/ *adj.* prophetisch

proportion /prə'pɔːʃn/ ① *n.* **(a)** (portion) Teil, *der*
(b) (ratio) Verhältnis, *das;* the ∼ of sth. to sth. das Verhältnis von etw. zu etw.
(c) (correct relation; Math.) Proportion, *die;* be in ∼ [to *or* with sth.] im richtigen Verhältnis [zu *od.* mit etw.] stehen; **keep things in** ∼ (fig.) die Dinge im richtigen Licht sehen; **be out of** ∼/**all** *or* **any** ∼ [to *or* with sth.] in keinem/keinerlei Verhältnis zu etw. stehen
(d) *in pl.* (size) Dimensionen *Pl.*
② *v.t.* proportionieren

proportional /prə'pɔːʃənl/ *adj.* **(a)** (in proportion) entsprechend; **be** ∼ **to sth.** einer Sache (*Dat.*) entsprechen
(b) (Math.) **be directly/indirectly** ∼ **to sth.** einer Sache (*Dat.*) direkt/umgekehrt proportional sein

proportionate /prə'pɔːʃənət/
▶ PROPORTIONAL A

proposal /prə'pəʊzl/ *n.* Vorschlag, *der;* (offer) Angebot, *das;* ∼ **[of marriage]** [Heirats]antrag, *der*

propose /prə'pəʊz/ ① *v.t.* **(a)** vorschlagen; ∼ **sth. to sb.** jmdm. etw. vorschlagen; ∼ **marriage [to sb.]** [jmdm.] einen Heiratsantrag machen
(b) (nominate) ∼ **sb. as/for sth.** jmdn. als/für etw. vorschlagen
(c) (intend) ∼ **doing** *or* **to do sth.** beabsichtigen, etw. zu tun
② *v.i.* (offer marriage) ∼ **[to sb.]** jmdm. einen Heiratsantrag machen

proposition /prɒpə'zɪʃn/ *n.* **(a)** (proposal) Vorschlag, *der;* **make** *or* **put a** ∼ **to sb.** jmdm. einen Vorschlag machen
(b) (statement; Logic) Aussage, *die*

propound /prə'paʊnd/ *v.t.* darlegen

proprietary /prə'praɪətərɪ/ *adj.* ∼ **name** *or* **term** Markenname, *der*

proprietor /prə'praɪətə(r)/ *n.* Inhaber, *der*/ Inhaberin, *die*

propriety /prə'praɪətɪ/ *n.* Anstand, *der;* **breach of** ∼: Verstoß gegen die guten Sitten

propulsion /prə'pʌlʃn/ *n.* Antrieb, *der*

prosaic /prə'zeɪɪk/ *adj.* prosaisch (geh.); nüchtern

proscribe /prə'skraɪb/ *v.t.* verbieten

prose /prəʊz/ *n.* Prosa, *die; attrib.* Prosa⟨*werk, -stil*⟩

prosecute /'prɒsɪkjuːt/ ① *v.t.* strafrechtlich verfolgen; ∼ **sb. for sth.**/**doing sth.** jmdn. wegen etw. strafrechtlich verfolgen/jmdn. strafrechtlich verfolgen, weil er etw. tut/getan hat
② *v.i.* Anzeige erstatten

prosecution /prɒsɪ'kjuːʃn/ *n.* (bringing to trial) [strafrechtliche] Verfolgung; (court procedure) Anklage, *die;* (prosecuting party) Anklage[vertretung], *die;* **the** ∼: die Anklage

prosecutor /'prɒsɪkjuːtə(r)/ *n.* Ankläger, *der*/Anklägerin, *die;* **public** ∼ ≈ Generalstaatsanwalt, *der*/-anwältin, *die*

prospect ① /'prɒspekt/ *n.* **(a)** (expectation) Erwartung, *die* (of hinsichtlich); **[at the]** ∼ **of sth.**/**doing sth.** [bei der] Aussicht auf etw. (*Akk.*)/[darauf], etw. zu tun
(b) *in pl.* (hope of success) Zukunftsaussichten *Pl.;* **a man with [good]** ∼**s** ein Mann mit Zukunft; **sb.'s** ∼**s of sth.**/**doing sth.** jmds. Chancen auf etw. (*Akk.*)/darauf, etw. zu tun; **the** ∼**s for sb.**/**sth.** die Aussichten für jmdn./ etw.
② /prə'spekt/ *v.i.* nach Bodenschätzen suchen

prospective /prə'spektɪv/ *adj.* voraussichtlich; zukünftig ⟨*Erbe, Braut*⟩; potenziell ⟨*Käufer, Kandidat*⟩

prospector /prə'spektə(r)/ *n.* Prospektor, *der;* (for gold) Goldsucher, *der*

prospectus /prə'spektəs/ *n.* Prospekt, *der;* (Brit. Univ.) Studienführer, *der*

prosper /'prɒspə(r)/ *v.i.* gedeihen; ⟨*Geschäft:*⟩ florieren; ⟨*Berufstätiger:*⟩ Erfolg haben

prosperity /prɒ'sperɪtɪ/ *n.* Wohlstand, *der*

prosperous /'prɒspərəs/ *adj.* wohlhabend; florierend ⟨*Unternehmen*⟩

prostitute /'prɒstɪtjuːt/ *n.* Prostituierte, *die*

prostitution /prɒstɪ'tjuːʃn/ *n.* Prostitution, *die*

prostrate ① /'prɒstreɪt/ *adj.* [auf dem Bauch] ausgestreckt
② /prə'streɪt/ *v. refl.* ∼ **oneself [at sth.**/ **before sb.]** sich [vor etw./jmdm.] niederwerfen

protagonist /prəʊ'tægənɪst/ *n.* (Lit.) Protagonist, *der*/Protagonistin, *die*

protect /prə'tekt/ *v.t.* **(a)** schützen (from vor + *Dat.,* against gegen)
(b) (preserve) unter [Natur]schutz stellen ⟨*Pflanze, Tier*⟩

protection /prə'tekʃn/ *n.* Schutz, *der* (from vor + *Dat.,* against gegen)

protective /prə'tektɪv/ *adj.* schützend; Schutz⟨*hülle, -anstrich, -vorrichtung, -maske*⟩; **be** ∼ **towards sb.** fürsorglich gegenüber jmdm. sein

protein /'prəʊtiːn/ *n.* Protein, *das* (fachspr.); Eiweiß, *das*

protest ⒈ /'prəʊtest/ *n.* **(a)** Beschwerde, *die;* **make** *or* **lodge a** ∼ **[against sb./sth.]** eine Beschwerde [gegen jmdn./etw.] einreichen **(b)** (gesture of disapproval) ∼**[s]** Protest, *der;* **under** ∼: unter Protest; **in** ∼ **[against sth.]** aus Protest [gegen etw.]
(c) *no art.* (dissent) Protest, *der*
⒉ /prə'test/ *v.t.* (affirm) beteuern
⒊ /prə'test/ *v.i.* protestieren **(about** gegen); (make written or formal ∼) Protest einlegen **(to** bei)

Protestant /'prɒtɪstənt/ ⒈ *n.* Protestant, *der*/Protestantin, *die*
⒉ *adj.* protestantisch; evangelisch

Protestantism /'prɒtɪstəntɪzm/ *n., no art.* Protestantismus, *der*

pro'tester *n.* Protestierende, *der/die;* (at demonstration) Demonstrant, *der*/Demonstrantin, *die*

protocol /'prəʊtəkɒl/ *n.* Protokoll, *das*

proton /'prəʊtɒn/ *n.* Proton, *das*

prototype /'prəʊtətaɪp/ *n.* Prototyp, *der*

protract /prə'trækt/ *v.t.* verlängern

protractor /prə'træktə(r)/ *n.* (Geom.) Winkelmesser, *der*

protrude /prə'truːd/ *v.i.* herausragen **(from** aus); ⟨*Zähne*⟩ vorstehen

protuberance /prə'tjuːbərəns/ *n.* Auswuchs, *der*

proud /praʊd/ ⒈ *adj.* **(a)** stolz; ∼ **to do sth.** *or* **to be doing sth.** stolz darauf, etw. zu tun; ∼ **of sb./sth./doing sth.** stolz auf jmdn./etw./darauf, etw. zu tun
(b) (arrogant) hochmütig
⒉ *adv.* (Brit. coll.) **do sb.** ∼: jmdn. verwöhnen

'proudly *adv.* **(a)** stolz
(b) (arrogantly) hochmütig

provable /'pruːvəbl/ *adj.* beweisbar

prove /pruːv/ ⒈ *v.t., p.p.* ∼**d** *or* **proven** /'pruːvn/ beweisen; nachweisen ⟨*Identität*⟩; ∼ **one's ability** sein Können unter Beweis stellen; ∼ **sb. right/wrong** ⟨*Ereignis:*⟩ jmdm. recht/unrecht geben; **be** ∼**d wrong** *or* **to be false** ⟨*Theorie:*⟩ widerlegt werden; ∼ **one's/ sb.'s case** *or* **point** beweisen, dass man recht hat/jmdm. recht geben
⒉ *v. refl., p. p.* **proved** *or* **proven:** ∼ **oneself** sich bewähren
⒊ *v.i., p. p.* **proved** *or* **proven:** ∼ **[to be]** sich erweisen als

proven ▶ PROVE

proverb /'prɒvɜːb/ *n.* Sprichwort, *das*

proverbial /prə'vɜːbɪəl/ *adj.* sprichwörtlich

provide /prə'vaɪd/ *v.t.* **(a)** (supply) liefern ⟨*Beweis*⟩; bereitstellen ⟨*Dienst, Geld*⟩; ∼ **a home/a car for sb.** jmdm. Unterkunft/ein Auto [zur Verfügung] stellen
(b) ⟨*Vertrag, Gesetz:*⟩ vorsehen

■ **pro'vide for** *v.t.* **(a)** (make provision for) vorsorgen für; ⟨*Plan, Gesetz:*⟩ vorsehen
(b) (maintain) sorgen für, versorgen ⟨*Familie, Kind*⟩

pro'vided *conj.* ∼ **[that]** ...: vorausgesetzt, [dass] ...

providence /'prɒvɪdəns/ *n.* **(a)** [divine] ∼: die [göttliche] Vorsehung
(b) P∼ (God) der Himmel

province /'prɒvɪns/ *n.* **(a)** Provinz, *die*
(b) the ∼**s** (regions outside capital) die Provinz
(c) (sphere of action) [Tätigkeits]bereich, *der;* (area of responsibility) Zuständigkeitsbereich, *der*

provincial /prə'vɪnʃl/ *adj.* Provinz-

provision /prə'vɪʒn/ *n.* **(a)** (providing) Bereitstellung, *die;* **make** ∼ **for** vorsorgen *od.* Vorsorge treffen für ⟨*Notfall*⟩
(b) ∼**s** *pl.* (food) Lebensmittel *Pl.*

provisional /prə'vɪʒənl/ *adj.,*
provisionally /prə'vɪʒənəlɪ/ *adv.* vorläufig; provisorisch

proviso /prə'vaɪzəʊ/ *n., pl.* ∼**s** Vorbehalt, *der*

provocation /prɒvə'keɪʃn/ *n.* Provokation, *die*

provocative /prə'vɒkətɪv/ *adj.* provozierend; (sexually) aufreizend

provoke /prə'vəʊk/ *v.t.* **(a)** provozieren ⟨*Person*⟩; reizen ⟨*Person, Tier*⟩; ∼ **sb. into doing sth.** jmdn. so sehr provozieren, dass er etw. tut
(b) (give rise to) hervorrufen; erregen

prow /praʊ/ *n.* (Naut.) Bug, *der*

prowl /praʊl/ ⒈ *v.i.* streifen
⒉ *v.t.* durchstreifen
⒊ *n.* **be on the** ∼: auf einem Streifzug sein

proximity /prɒk'sɪmɪtɪ/ *n.* Nähe, *die*

proxy /'prɒksɪ/ *n.* **by** ∼: durch einen Bevollmächtigten/eine Bevollmächtigte

prude /pruːd/ *n.* prüder Mensch

prudence /'pruːdəns/ *n.* Besonnenheit, *die*

prudent /'pruːdənt/ *adj.* **(a)** (careful) besonnen
(b) (circumspect) vorsichtig

prudish /'pruːdɪʃ/ *adj.* prüde

prune[1] /pruːn/ *n.* Backpflaume, *die*

prune[2] *v.t.* **(a)** (trim) [be]schneiden
(b) (fig.) reduzieren

pry /praɪ/ *v.i.* neugierig sein
■ **'pry into** *v.t.* seine Nase stecken in (+ *Akk.*) (ugs.) ⟨*Angelegenheit*⟩

PS *abbr.* = **postscript** PS

psalm /sɑːm/ *n.* Psalm, *der*

pseudo /'sjuːdəʊ/ ⒈ *adj.* **(a)** (sham) unecht
(b) (insincere) verlogen
⒉ *n., pl.* ∼**s** (pretentious person) Möchtegern, *der* (ugs. spött.)

pseudonym /'sjuːdənɪm/ *n.* Pseudonym, *das*

psychiatric /saɪkɪ'ætrɪk/ *adj.* psychiatrisch

psychiatrist /saɪ'kaɪətrɪst/ *n.* Psychiater, *der*/Psychiaterin, *die*

psychiatry /saɪ'kaɪətrɪ/ *n.* Psychiatrie, *die*

psychic /'saɪkɪk/ *adj.* be ~:
übernatürliche Fähigkeiten haben

psychoanalyse /saɪkəʊˈænəlaɪz/ *v.t.*
psychoanalysieren

psychoa'nalysis *n.* Psychoanalyse, *die*

psycho'analyst *n.* Psychoanalytiker,
der/-analytikerin, *die*

psychological /saɪkəˈlɒdʒɪkl/ *adj.*
psychologisch; psychisch ⟨*Problem*⟩

psychologist /saɪˈkɒlədʒɪst/ *n.*
Psychologe, *der*/Psychologin, *die*

psychology /saɪˈkɒlədʒɪ/ *n.* Psychologie,
die

psychopath /'saɪkəpæθ/ *n.* Psychopath,
der/Psychopathin, *die*

psychopathic /saɪkəˈpæθɪk/ *adj.*
psychopathisch

psychosis /saɪˈkəʊsɪs/ *n.*, *pl.* **psychoses**
/saɪˈkəʊsiːz/ Psychose, *die*

psychotherapist /saɪkəʊˈθerəpɪst/ *n.*
Psychotherapeut, *der*/-therapeutin, *die*

psycho'therapy *n.* Psychotherapie, *die*

psychotic /saɪˈkɒtɪk/ *adj.* psychotisch

PTO *abbr.* = **please turn over** b.w.

pub /ʌb/ *n.* (Brit. coll.) Kneipe, *die* (ugs.)

'pub crawl *n.* (Brit. coll.) Zechtour, *die* (ugs.)

puberty /'pjuːbətɪ/ *n.*, *no art.* Pubertät, *die*

'pub grub *n.* (Brit. coll.) Kneipenessen, *das*
(ugs.)

pubic /'pjuːbɪk/ *adj.* Scham-

public /'pʌblɪk/ [1] *adj.* öffentlich; **make
sth. ~**: etw. bekannt machen
[2] *n.*, *sing. or pl.* (a) (the people)
Öffentlichkeit, *die*
(b) (section of community) Publikum, *das*
(c) **in ~**: öffentlich

publican /'pʌblɪkən/ *n.* (Brit.) [Gast]wirt,
der/-wirtin, *die*

publication /pʌblɪˈkeɪʃn/ *n.*
Veröffentlichung, *die*

public: ~ **'building** *n.* öffentliches
Gebäude; ~ **con'venience** *n.* öffentliche
Toilette; ~ **'figure** *n.* Persönlichkeit des
öffentlichen Lebens; ~ **'footpath** *n.*
öffentlicher Fußweg; ~ **'holiday** *n.*
gesetzlicher Feiertag; ~ **'house** *n.* (Brit.)
Gastwirtschaft, *die;* Gaststätte, *die*

publicity /pʌbˈlɪsɪtɪ/ *n.* Publicity, *die;*
(advertising) Werbung, *die;* ~ **campaign**
Werbekampagne, *die*

pub'licity agent *n.* Publicitymanager,
der/-managerin, *die*

publicize /'pʌblɪsaɪz/ *v.t.* publik machen
⟨*Ungerechtigkeit*⟩; werben für, Reklame
machen für ⟨*Produkt*⟩

public: ~ **'library** *n.* öffentliche Bücherei;
~ **limited company** *n.* (Brit.) ≈
Aktiengesellschaft, *die*

'publicly *adv.* öffentlich; ~ **owned**
staatseigen

public: ~ **property** *n.* Staatsbesitz, *der;*
~ **re'lations** *n.*, *sing. or pl.*

Publicrelations *Pl.;* ~ **school** *n.* (a) (Brit.)
Privatschule, *die;* (b) (Scot., Amer.) staatliche
od. öffentliche Schule; ~ **'servant** *n.*
Inhaber/Inhaberin eines öffentlichen Amtes;
~ **'transport** *n.* öffentlicher
Personenverkehr

publish /'pʌblɪʃ/ *v.t.* ⟨*Verlag:*⟩ verlegen
⟨*Buch, Zeitschrift, Musik usw.*⟩; ⟨*Autor:*⟩
veröffentlichen ⟨*Text*⟩

'publisher *n.* Verleger, *der*/Verlegerin, *die;*
~[s] (company) Verlag, *der*

'publishing *n.*, *no art.* Verlagswesen, *das*

puck /pʌk/ *n.* (Ice Hockey) Puck, *der*

pucker /'pʌkə(r)/ [1] *v.t.* ~ [up] runzeln
⟨*Brauen, Stirn*⟩; kräuseln ⟨*Lippen*⟩
[2] *v.i.* ~ [up] ⟨*Stoff:*⟩ sich kräuseln

pudding /'pʊdɪŋ/ *n.* (a) Pudding, *der*
(b) (dessert) süße Nachspeise

puddle /'pʌdl/ *n.* Pfütze, *die*

puerile /'pjʊəraɪl/ *adj.* kindisch

puff /pʌf/ [1] *n.* (a) Stoß, *der;* ~ **of breath/
wind** Atem-/Windstoß, *der*
(b) ~ **of smoke** Rauchstoß, *der*
(c) (pastry) Blätterteigteilchen, *das*
[2] *v.i.* (a) ~ **[and blow]** schnaufen [und
keuchen]
(b) (~ cigarette smoke etc.) paffen (ugs.) (**at** an
+ *Dat.*)
(c) ⟨*Person:*⟩ keuchen; ⟨*Zug, Lokomotive*⟩
schnaufend fahren
[3] *v.t.* blasen ⟨*Rauch*⟩; stäuben ⟨*Puder*⟩
■ **puff 'out** *v.t.* (a) bauschen ⟨*Segel*⟩
(b) (put out of breath) außer Atem bringen
⟨*Person*⟩; be ~ed [out] außer Atem sein

puff 'pastry *n.* Blätterteig, *der*

puffy /'pʌfɪ/ *adj.* verschwollen

pugnacious /pʌɡˈneɪʃəs/ *adj.* kampflustig

puke /pjuːk/ (coarse) [1] *v.i.* kotzen (salopp)
[2] *n.* Kotze, *die* (salopp)

pull /pʊl/ [1] *v.t.* (a) (draw, tug) ziehen an
(+ *Dat.*); ziehen ⟨*Hebel*⟩; ~ **sb.'s** *or* **sb. by
the hair/ears/sleeve** jmdn. an den Haaren/
Ohren/am Ärmel ziehen; ~ **sth. over one's
ears/head** sich (*Dat.*) etw. über die Ohren/
den Kopf ziehen; ~ **to pieces** in Stücke
reißen; (fig.) zerpflücken ⟨*Argument usw.*⟩
(b) (extract) [her]ausziehen; [heraus]ziehen
⟨*Zahn*⟩
(c) (strain) sich (*Dat.*) zerren ⟨*Muskel*⟩
[2] *v.i.* (a) ziehen; **'P~'** „Ziehen“
(b) ~ **[to the left/right]** ⟨*Auto, Boot:*⟩ [nach
links/rechts] ziehen
(c) (pluck) ~ **at** ziehen an (+ *Dat.*); ~ **at sb.'s
sleeve** jmdn. am Ärmel ziehen
[3] *n.* (a) Zug, *der*
(b) (influence) Einfluss, *der* (with auf + *Akk.*,
bei)
■ **pull a'part** *v.t.* (a) (take to pieces)
auseinander nehmen
(b) (fig.: criticize) zerpflücken; verreißen
⟨*Buch, [literarisches] Werk*⟩
■ **pull 'down** *v.t.* (a) herunterziehen
(b) (demolish) abreißen
■ **pull 'in** [1] *v.t.* hereinziehen   ⋯⟿

p

② *v.i.* **(a)** ⟨*Zug:*⟩ einfahren
(b) (move to side of road) an die Seite fahren; (stop) anhalten
■ **pull 'off** *v.t.* **(a)** (remove) abziehen; (violently) abreißen
(b) (accomplish) an Land ziehen (ugs.)
■ **pull 'out** ① *v.t.* herausziehen
② *v.i.* **(a)** (depart) abfahren
(b) (away from roadside) ausscheren
■ **pull 'through** *v.i.* ⟨*Patient:*⟩ durchkommen
■ **pull to'gether** *v. refl.* sich zusammennehmen
■ **pull 'up** ① *v.t.* **(a)** hochziehen
(b) [he]rausziehen ⟨*Unkraut, Pflanze*⟩
(c) (reprimand) zurechtweisen
② *v.i.* (stop) anhalten
'pull-down menu *n.* (Comp.) Pull-down-Menü, *das*
pulley /ˈpʊlɪ/ *n.* Rolle, *die*
pullover /ˈpʊləʊvə(r)/ *n.* Pullover, *der*
pulp /pʌlp/ ① *n.* Brei, *der*
② *v.t.* zerdrücken ⟨*Rübe*⟩; einstampfen ⟨*Druckerzeugnis*⟩
pulpit /ˈpʊlpɪt/ *n.* Kanzel, *die*
pulsate /pʌlˈseɪt/ *v.i.* pulsieren
pulse¹ /pʌls/ *n.* Puls, *der;* (single beat) Pulsschlag, *der*
pulse² *n.* (Cookery) Hülsenfrucht, *die*
'pulse rate *n.* Pulsfrequenz, *die*
pulverize /ˈpʌlvəraɪz/ *v.t.* pulverisieren
puma /ˈpjuːmə/ *n.* Puma, *der*
pumice /ˈpʌmɪs/ *n.* ~ **[stone]** Bimsstein, *der*
pummel /ˈpʌml/ *v.t.,* (Brit) **-ll-** einschlagen auf (+ *Akk.*)
pump /pʌmp/ ① *n.* Pumpe, *die*
② *v.i.* pumpen
③ *v.t.* pumpen; ~ **sth. dry** etw. leer pumpen; ~ **sb. for information** Auskünfte aus jmdm. herausholen; ~ **up** aufpumpen
'pump-action *adj.* ~ **spray** Pumpspray, *das od. der*
pumpkin /ˈpʌmpkɪn/ *n.* Kürbis, *der*
pun /pʌn/ *n.* Wortspiel, *das*
punch¹ ① *v.t.* **(a)** (with fist) boxen
(b) (pierce) lochen; ~ **a hole** ein Loch stanzen; ~ **a hole/holes in sth.** etw. lochen
② *n.* **(a)** (blow) Faustschlag, *der*
(b) (for making holes) (in leather, tickets) Lochzange, *die;* (in paper) Locher, *der*
punch² *n.* (drink) Punsch, *der*
punch: ~ **line** *n.* Pointe, *die;* ~**-up** *n.* (Brit. coll.) Prügelei, *die*
punctual /ˈpʌŋktjʊəl/ *adj.* pünktlich
punctuality /pʌŋktjʊˈælɪtɪ/ *n.* Pünktlichkeit, *die*
'punctually *adv.* pünktlich
punctuate /ˈpʌŋktjʊeɪt/ *v.t.* mit Satzzeichen versehen
punctuation /pʌŋktjʊˈeɪʃn/ *n.* Zeichensetzung, *die*

punctu'ation mark *n.* Satzzeichen, *das*
puncture /ˈpʌŋktʃə(r)/ ① *n.* **(a)** (flat tyre) Reifenpanne, *die*
(b) (hole) Loch, *das*
② *v.t.* durchstechen; **be** ~**d** ⟨*Reifen:*⟩ platt sein
pundit /ˈpʌndɪt/ *n.* Experte, *der/*Expertin, *die*
pungent /ˈpʌndʒənt/ *adj.* beißend, ätzend ⟨*Rauch*⟩; scharf ⟨*Soße*⟩; stechend riechend ⟨*Gas*⟩
punish /ˈpʌnɪʃ/ *v.t.* bestrafen
punishable /ˈpʌnɪʃəbl/ *adj.* strafbar
'punishment *n.* **(a)** (punishing) Bestrafung, *die*
(b) (penalty) Strafe, *die*
punitive /ˈpjuːnɪtɪv/ *adj.* **(a)** (penal) Straf-
(b) (severe) [allzu] rigoros
punk /pʌŋk/ *n.* **(a)** (Amer. sl.: worthless person) Dreckskerl, *der* (salopp)
(b) (admirer of ~ rock) Punk, *der;* (performer) Punk[rock]er, *der/*-[rock]erin, *die*
(c) (music) Punkrock, *der*
punnet /ˈpʌnɪt/ *n.* (Brit.) Körbchen, *das*
punt /pʌnt/ *n.* Stechkahn, *der*
punter *n.* (coll.) **the** ~**s** (customers) die Leutchen (ugs.)
puny /ˈpjuːnɪ/ *adj.* **(a)** (undersized) zu klein ⟨*Baby, Junge*⟩
(b) (feeble) gering ⟨*Kraft*⟩; schwach ⟨*Waffe, Person*⟩
pup /pʌp/ *n.* Welpe, *der*
pupa /ˈpjuːpə/ *n., pl.* ~**e** /ˈpjuːpiː/ Puppe, *die*
pupate /pjuːˈpeɪt/ *v.i.* sich verpuppen
pupil /ˈpjuːpɪl/ *n.* **(a)** Schüler, *der/*Schülerin, *die*
(b) (Anat.) Pupille, *die*
puppet /ˈpʌpɪt/ *n.* Puppe, *die;* (marionette; also fig.) Marionette, *die*
puppy /ˈpʌpɪ/ *n.* Hundejunge, *das;* Welpe, *der*
puppy: ~ **fat** *n.* (Brit.) Babyspeck, *der;* ~ **love** *n.* Jugendschwärmerei, *die*
purchase /ˈpɜːtʃəs/ ① *n.* **(a)** Kauf, *der;* **make a** ~: etwas kaufen
(b) (hold) Halt, *der;* (leverage) Hebelwirkung, *die*
② *v.t.* kaufen
'purchase price *n.* Kaufpreis, *der*
'purchaser *n.* Käufer, *der/*Käuferin, *die*
'purchasing power *n.* Kaufkraft, *die*
pure /pjʊə(r)/ *adj.* rein
purée /ˈpjʊəreɪ/ *n.* Püree, *das*
'purely *adv.* **(a)** (solely) rein
(b) (merely) lediglich
purgatory /ˈpɜːgətərɪ/ *n.* **it was** ~ (fig.) es war eine Strafe
purge /pɜːdʒ/ ① *v.t.* **(a)** (cleanse) reinigen (**of** von)
(b) (remove) entfernen
(c) (rid) säubern ⟨*Partei*⟩ (**of** von)
② *n.* Säuberung[saktion], *die*

purification /pjʊərɪfɪˈkeɪʃn/ *n*. Reinigung, *die*

purify /ˈpjʊərɪfaɪ/ *v.t*. reinigen

purist /ˈpjʊərɪst/ *n*. Purist, *der*/Puristin, *die*

puritan, (Hist.) **Puritan** /ˈpjʊərɪtn/ *n*. Puritaner, *der*/Puritanerin, *die*

puritanical /pjʊərɪˈtænɪkl/ *adj*. puritanisch

purity /ˈpjʊərɪtɪ/ *n*. Reinheit, *die*

purl /pɜːl/ 1 *n*. linke Masche
2 *v.t*. links stricken; ~ **three** [**stitches**] drei linke Maschen stricken

purple /ˈpɜːpl/ 1 *adj*. lila; violett
2 *n*. Lila, *das;* Violett, *das*

purport /pəˈpɔːt/ *v.t*. ~ **to do sth.** (profess) [von sich] behaupten, etw. zu tun; (be intended to seem) den Anschein erwecken sollen, etw. zu tun

purpose /ˈpɜːpəs/ *n*. (a) (object) Zweck, *der;* (intention) Absicht, *die;* **what is the ~ of doing that?** was hat es für einen Zweck, das zu tun?; **on ~:** mit Absicht; absichtlich
(b) (effect) **to no ~:** ohne Erfolg; **to some/good ~:** mit einigem/gutem Erfolg
(c) (determination) Entschlossenheit, *die*

ˈpurpose-built *adj*. [eigens] zu diesem Zweck errichtet ⟨Gebäude⟩

purposeful /ˈpɜːpəsfl/ *adj*. zielstrebig; (with specific aim) entschlossen

ˈpurposely *adv*. absichtlich

ˈpurpose-made *adj*. spezialgefertigt

purr /pɜː(r)/ 1 *v.i*. schnurren
2 *n*. Schnurren, *das*

purse /pɜːs/ 1 *n*. Portemonnaie, *das*
2 *v.t*. kräuseln ⟨Lippen⟩

purser /ˈpɜːsə(r)/ *n*. Zahlmeister, *der*/-meisterin, *die*

pursue /pəˈsjuː/ *v.t*. (a) (chase) verfolgen
(b) (look into) nachgehen (+ *Dat.*)
(c) (engage in) betreiben

pursuer /pəˈsjuːə(r)/ *n*. Verfolger, *der*/Verfolgerin, *die*

pursuit /pəˈsjuːt/ *n*. (a) Verfolgung, *die;* (of knowledge, truth, etc.) Streben, *das* (of nach); **in ~ of** auf der Jagd nach ⟨Wild, Dieb usw.⟩; in Ausführung (+ *Gen.*) ⟨Beschäftigung⟩; **with the police in [full] ~:** mit der Polizei [dicht] auf den Fersen
(b) (pastime) Beschäftigung, *die*

pus /pʌs/ *n*. Eiter, *der*

push /pʊʃ/ 1 *v.t*. (a) schieben; (make fall) stoßen; drücken gegen ⟨Tür⟩; ~ **one's way through/into/on to** etc. sich (*Dat.*) einen Weg durch/in/auf usw. etw. (*Akk.*) bahnen
(b) (fig.: impel) drängen
(c) (tax) ~ **sb.** [**hard**] jmdn. [stark] fordern; **be ~ed for sth.** (coll.: find it difficult to provide sth.) mit etw. knapp sein; **be ~ed for money** *or* **cash** knapp bei Kasse sein (ugs.)
(d) (sell illegally, esp. drugs) pushen (Drogenjargon)

2 *v.i*. (a) schieben; (in queue) drängeln; (at door) drücken; ~ **and shove** schubsen und drängeln
(b) (make demands) ~ **for sth.** etw. fordern
(c) (make one's way) **he ~ed between us** er drängte sich zwischen uns; ~ **through the crowd** sich durch die Menge drängeln
3 *n*. (a) Stoß, *der;* **give sth. a ~:** etw. schieben
(b) (effort) Anstrengungen *Pl.;* (Mil.: attack) Vorstoß, *der*
(c) (crisis) **when it comes to the ~,** (Amer. coll.) **when ~ comes to shove** wenn es ernst wird
(d) (Brit. coll.: dismissal) **get the ~:** rausfliegen (ugs.)

■ **push aˈhead** *v.i*. ~ **ahead with sth.** etw. vorantreiben

■ **push ˈin** *v.i*. sich hineindrängen

■ **push ˈoff** *v.i*. (a) (Boating) abstoßen
(b) (coll.: leave) abhauen (salopp)

■ **push ˈon** 1 *v.i*. (with plans etc.) weitermachen
2 *v.t*. draufdrücken ⟨Deckel usw.⟩

■ **push ˈup** *v.t*. hochschieben; (fig.) hochtreiben

push: ~bike *n*. (Brit. coll.) Fahrrad, *das;* **~-button** *n*. [Druck]knopf, *der;* Drucktaste, *die;* **~chair** *n*. (Brit.) Sportwagen, *der*

pusher /ˈpʊʃə(r)/ *n*. (seller of drugs) Dealer, *der*/Dealerin, *die*

ˈpushover *n*. (coll.) Kinderspiel, *das*

pushy /ˈpʊʃɪ/ *adj*. (coll.) [übermäßig] ehrgeizig ⟨Person⟩

pussy /ˈpʊsɪ/ *n*. (child lang.: cat) Miezekatze, *die* (fam.)

p

put /pʊt/ 1 *v.t.*, **-tt-**, **put** (a) (place) tun; (vertically) stellen; (horizontally) legen; ~ **plates on the table** Teller auf den Tisch stellen; ~ **a stamp on the letter** eine Briefmarke auf den Brief kleben; ~ **the letter in an envelope/the letter box** den Brief in einen Umschlag/in den Briefkasten stecken; ~ **sth. in one's pocket** etw. in die Tasche stecken; ~ **petrol in the tank** Benzin in den Tank füllen; ~ **the car in[to] the garage** das Auto in die Garage stellen; ~ **the plug in the socket** den Stecker in die Steckdose stecken; ~ **one's hands over one's eyes** sich (*Dat.*) die Hände auf die Augen legen; **where shall I ~ it?** wo soll ich es hintun (ugs.)/-stellen/-legen usw.?; (fig.) **be ~ in a difficult position** in eine schwierige Lage geraten; ~ **sb. on to sth.** jmdn. auf etw. (*Akk.*) hinweisen; ~ **sb. to work** jmdn. arbeiten lassen; ~ **sb. on antibiotics** jmdn. auf Antibiotika setzen; ~ **oneself in sb.'s place** *or* **situation** sich in jmds. Lage (*Akk.*) versetzen
(b) (submit) unterbreiten ⟨Vorschlag, Plan⟩ (to *Dat.*)
(c) (express) ausdrücken; **let's ~ it like this: ...:** sagen wir so: ...; ~ **sth. into English** etc. etw. ins Englische usw. übertragen; ~ **sth. into words** etw. in Worte fassen
(d) (write) schreiben; ~ **one's name on the** ⋯✢

list seinen Namen auf die Liste setzen;
~ **sth. on the bill** etw. auf die Rechnung
setzen
(e) (stake) setzen (**on** auf + *Akk.*)
(f) (estimate) ~ **sb./sth. at** jmdn./etw.
schätzen auf (+ *Akk.*)
② *v.i.* **-tt-, put** (Naut.) ~ [out] **to sea** in See
stechen
■ **put a'cross** *v.t.* **(a)** (communicate)
vermitteln (**to** *Dat.*)
(b) (make acceptable) ankommen mit
■ **put a'way** *v.t.* **(a)** wegräumen; reinstellen
‹*Auto*›; (in file) abheften
(b) (save) beiseite legen
(c) (coll.) (eat) verdrücken (ugs.); (drink)
runterkippen (ugs.)
(d) (coll.: confine) einsperren (ugs.)
■ **put 'back** *v.t.* **(a)** ~ **the book back** das
Buch zurücktun
(b) ~ **the clock back** die Uhr zurückstellen
(c) (postpone) verschieben
■ **put 'down** *v.t.* **(a)** (set down) (vertically)
hinstellen; (horizontally) hinlegen; auflegen
‹*Hörer*›
(b) (suppress) niederwerfen
(c) (humiliate) herabsetzen
(d) (kill) töten
(e) (write) notieren
(f) (attribute) ~ **sth. down to sth.** etw. auf etw.
(*Akk.*) zurückführen
■ **put 'forward** *v.t.* **(a)** (propose) aufwarten
mit
(b) (nominate) vorschlagen
(c) ~ **the clock forward** die Uhr vorstellen
■ **put 'in** ① *v.t.* **(a)** (install) einbauen
(b) (submit) stellen ‹*Forderung*›; einreichen
‹*Bewerbung*›
(c) (devote) aufwenden ‹*Mühe*›; (perform)
einlegen ‹*Sonderschicht, Überstunden*›
② *v.i.* ~ **in for** sich bewerben um ‹*Stellung*›;
beantragen ‹*Urlaub*›
■ **put 'off** *v.t.* **(a)** (postpone) verschieben
(**until** auf + *Akk.*); (postpone engagement with)
vertrösten (**until** auf + *Akk.*)
(b) (switch off) ausmachen
(c) (repel) abstoßen; ~ **sb. off sth.** jmdm. etw.
verleiden
(d) (distract) stören
(e) (dissuade) ~ **sb. off doing sth.** jmdn.
davon abbringen, etw. zu tun
■ **put 'on** *v.t.* **(a)** (wear) anziehen ‹*Kleidung, Hose
usw.*›; aufsetzen ‹*Hut, Brille*›; draufsetzen
‹*Deckel*›; ~ **it on** (coll.) [nur] Schau machen
(ugs.)
(b) anmachen ‹*Radio, Licht*›; aufsetzen
‹*Wasser, Kessel*›

(c) (gain) ~ **on weight** zunehmen
(d) (stage) spielen ‹*Stück*›; zeigen ‹*Film*›
■ **put 'out** *v.t.* **(a)** rausbringen
(b) ausmachen ‹*Licht*›; löschen ‹*Feuer*›
(c) (inconvenience) in Verlegenheit bringen
■ **put 'through** *v.t.* **(a)** (carry out)
durchführen ‹*Plan, Programm*›
(b) (Teleph.) verbinden (**to** mit)
■ **put 'up** ① *v.t.* **(a)** heben ‹*Hand*›; errichten
‹*Gebäude, Denkmal*›; aufstellen ‹*Gerüst*›
(b) (display) aushängen
(c) hochnehmen ‹*Fäuste*›; leisten
‹*Widerstand, Gegenwehr*›
(d) (propose) vorschlagen; (nominate) aufstellen
(e) (incite) ~ **sb. up to sth.** jmdn. zu etw.
anstiften
(f) (accommodate) unterbringen
(g) (increase) [he]raufsetzen ‹*Preis, Miete*›
② *v.i.* (lodge) übernachten
■ **put 'up with** *v.t.* sich (*Dat.*) bieten lassen
‹*Beleidigung, Benehmen*›; sich abfinden mit
‹*Lärm, Elend*›; sich abgeben mit ‹*Person*›
'put-down *n.* Herabsetzung, *die;* (snub)
Abfuhr, *die*
putrefaction /pjuːtrɪˈfækʃn/ *n., no indef.
art.* Zersetzung, *die*
putrefy /ˈpjuːtrɪfaɪ/ *v.i.* sich zersetzen
putrid /ˈpjuːtrɪd/ *adj.* (rotten) faul; ~ **smell**
Fäulnisgeruch, *der*
putt /pʌt/ (Golf) ① *v.i. & t.* putten
② *n.* Putt, *der*
'putter *n.* Putter, *der*
putty /ˈpʌtɪ/ *n.* Kitt, *der*
'put-up *adj.* **a** ~ **job** ein abgekartetes Spiel
(ugs.)
puzzle /ˈpʌzl/ ① *n.* (problem, enigma) Rätsel,
das; (toy) Geduldsspiel, *das*
② *v.t.* rätselhaft *od.* ein Rätsel sein (+ *Dat.*)
③ *v.i.* ~ **over** *or* **about sth.** sich (*Dat.*) über
etw. den Kopf zerbrechen
puzzled /ˈpʌzld/ *adj.* ratlos
puzzling /ˈpʌzlɪŋ/ *adj.* rätselhaft
PVC *abbr.* = **polyvinyl chloride** PVC,
das
pygmy /ˈpɪɡmɪ/ *n.* Pygmäe, *der*
pyjamas /prˈdʒɑːməz/ *n. pl.* [**pair of**] ~:
Schlafanzug, *der*
pylon /ˈpaɪlən/ *n.* Mast, *der*
pyramid /ˈpɪrəmɪd/ *n.* Pyramide, *die*
Pyrenees /pɪrəˈniːz/ *pr. n. pl.* **the** ~: die
Pyrenäen
python /ˈpaɪθən/ *n.* Python, *der*

Qq

Q, q /kjuː/ *n.* Q, q, *das*

quack /kwæk/ **1** *v.i.* ⟨Ente:⟩ quaken
2 *n.* Quaken, *das*

quadrangle /'kwɒdræŋgl/ *n.* [viereckiger] Innenhof

quadruped /'kwɒdrʊped/ *n.* Vierfüßler, *der*

quadruple /'kwɒdrʊpl/ **1** *adj.* vierfach
2 *v.t.* vervierfachen
3 *v.i.* sich vervierfachen

quagmire /'kwægmaɪə(r)/ *n.* Sumpf, *der;* Morast, *der*

quail¹ /kweɪl/ *n.* (Ornith.) Wachtel, *die*

quail² *v.i.* ⟨Person:⟩ [ver]zagen

quaint /kweɪnt/ *adj.* drollig ⟨Häuschen, Einrichtung⟩; malerisch ⟨Ort⟩; (odd) kurios ⟨Bräuche, Anblick⟩

quake /kweɪk/ **1** *n.* (coll.) [Erd]beben, *das*
2 *v.i.* beben; ~ **with fear** vor Angst zittern

Quaker /'kweɪkə(r)/ *n.* Quäker, *der*/ Quäkerin, *die*

qualification /kwɒlɪfɪ'keɪʃn/ *n.* **(a)** Qualifikation, *die;* (condition) Voraussetzung, *die*
(b) (limitation) Vorbehalt, *der;* **without ~**: vorbehaltlos

qualified /'kwɒlɪfaɪd/ *adj.* **(a)** qualifiziert; (by training) ausgebildet
(b) (restricted) nicht uneingeschränkt; **a ~ success** kein voller Erfolg; **~ acceptance** bedingte Annahme

qualify /'kwɒlɪfaɪ/ **1** *v.t.* **(a)** (make competent) berechtigen **(for** zu)
(b) (modify) einschränken
2 *v.i.* **(a)** ~ **in law/medicine** seinen [Studien]abschluss in Jura/Medizin machen; **~ as a doctor/lawyer** sein Examen als Arzt/ Anwalt machen
(b) (fulfil a condition) in Frage kommen **(for** für)
(c) (Sport) sich qualifizieren

qualifying /'kwɒlɪfaɪɪŋ/ *adj.* (Sport) **~ match** Qualifikationsspiel, *das*

quality /'kwɒlɪtɪ/ **1** *n.* **(a)** Qualität, *die*
(b) (characteristic) Eigenschaft, *die*
2 *adj.* Qualitäts-

quality: ~ control *n.* Qualitätskontrolle, *die;* **~ time** *n.:* ganz dem Miteinander gewidmete Zeit

qualm /kwɑːm/ *n.* Bedenken, *das* **(over, about** gegen)

quandary /'kwɒndərɪ/ *n.* Dilemma, *das*

quantify /'kwɒntɪfaɪ/ *v.t.* quantifizieren

quantity /'kwɒntɪtɪ/ *n.* **(a)** Quantität, *die*
(b) (amount, sum) Menge, *die*

'quantity surveyor *n.* Baukostenkalkulator, *der*/-kalkulatorin, *die*

quantum: ~ jump, ~ leap *ns.* (Phys.; also fig.) Quantensprung, *der;*
~ me'chanics *n.* Quantenmechanik, *die*

quarantine /'kwɒrəntiːn/ *n.* Quarantäne, *die;* **be in ~**: unter Quarantäne stehen

quarrel /'kwɒrl/ **1** *n.* **(a)** Streit, *der;* **have/ pick a ~ with sb.** [about/over sth.] sich mit jmdm. [über etw. (*Akk.*)] streiten/mit jmdm. [wegen etw.] Streit anfangen
(b) (cause of complaint) Einwand, *der* **(with** gegen)
2 *v.i.,* (Brit.) **-ll-** [sich] streiten **(over** um, **about** über + *Akk.*); **~ with each other** [sich] [miteinander] streiten; (fall out) sich [zer]streiten **(over** um, **about** über + *Akk.*)

quarrelsome /'kwɒrlsəm/ *adj.* streitsüchtig

quarry¹ /'kwɒrɪ/ *n.* Steinbruch, *der*

quarry² *n.* (prey) Beute, *die*

quart /kwɔːt/ *n.* Quart, *das*

quarter /'kwɔːtə(r)/ **1** *n.* **(a)** Viertel, *das;* **a** *or* **one ~ of** ein Viertel (+ *Gen.*); **a ~ of a mile/an hour** eine Viertelmeile/-stunde
(b) (of year) Quartal, *das;* Vierteljahr, *das*
(c) **[a] ~ to/past six** Viertel vor/nach sechs
(d) (direction) Richtung, *die*
(e) (area of town) [Stadt]viertel, *das*
(f) **~s** *pl.* (lodgings) Quartier, *das* (bes. Milit.); Unterkunft, *die*
(g) (Amer. coin) Vierteldollar, *der*
2 *v.t.* **(a)** (divide) vierteln
(b) (lodge) einquartieren ⟨Soldaten⟩

quarter-'final *n.* Viertelfinale, *das*

'quarterly **1** *adj.* vierteljährlich
2 *n.* Vierteljahr[e]sschrift, *die*

quarter-'pounder *n.* Viertelpfünder, *der*

quartet /kwɔː'tet/ *n.* Quartett, *das*

quartz /kwɔːts/ *n.* Quarz, *der*

quash /kwɒʃ/ *v.t.* **(a)** (annul) aufheben
(b) (suppress) niederschlagen

quaver /'kweɪvə(r)/ **1** *n.* (Brit. Mus.) Achtelnote, *die*
2 *v.i.* (vibrate) zittern

quay /kiː/, **'quayside** *ns.* Kai, *der*

queasy /'kwiːzɪ/ *adj.* unwohl

queen /kwiːn/ *n.* **(a)** Königin, *die*
(b) (Chess, Cards) Dame, *die*

queen: ~ 'bee *n.* Bienenkönigin, *die;*
~ 'mother *n.* Königinmutter, *die*

queer /kwɪə(r)/ **1** *adj.* **(a)** (strange) sonderbar; (eccentric) verschroben
(b) (shady) merkwürdig
(c) (Brit. coll. dated: out of sorts) unwohl ⋯⟶

(d) (sl. derog.: homosexual) schwul (ugs.)
2 *n.* (sl. derog.: homosexual) Schwule, *der* (ugs.)

quell /kwel/ *v.t.* (literary) niederschlagen
⟨*Aufstand*⟩; zügeln ⟨*Furcht*⟩

quench /kwentʃ/ *v.t.* löschen

query /'kwɪərɪ/ 1 *n.* Frage, *die*
2 *v.t.* in Frage stellen ⟨*Anweisung,
Glaubwürdigkeit*⟩; beanstanden ⟨*Rechnung*⟩

quest /kwest/ *n.* Suche, *die* (**for** nach)

question /'kwestʃn/ 1 *n.* **(a)** Frage, *die;*
ask sb. a ∼: jmdm. eine Frage stellen
(b) (doubt, objection) Zweifel, *der* (**about** an
+ *Dat.*); **there is no ∼ about sth.** es besteht
kein Zweifel an etw. (*Dat.*); **beyond all** *or*
without ∼: ohne Frage
(c) (problem, concern) Frage, *die;* **sth./it is only
a ∼ of time** etw./es ist [nur] eine Frage der
Zeit; **it is [only] a ∼ of doing sth.** es geht
[nur] darum, etw. zu tun; **the person/thing in
∼:** die fragliche Person/Sache; **sth./it is out
of the ∼:** etw./es ist ausgeschlossen
2 *v.t.* **(a)** befragen; ⟨*Polizei, Gericht usw.:*⟩
vernehmen
(b) (throw doubt upon, raise objections to)
bezweifeln

questionable /'kwestʃənəbl/ *adj.*
fragwürdig

'question mark *n.* Fragezeichen, *das*

questionnaire /kwestʃə'neə(r)/ *n.*
Fragebogen, *der*

queue /kju:/ 1 *n.* Schlange, *die;* **join the ∼:**
sich anstellen
2 *v.i.* ∼ [up] Schlange stehen

'queue-jumping *n.* (Brit.) Vordrängen, *das*

quibble /'kwɪbl/ 1 *n.* Spitzfindigkeit, *die*
2 *v.i.* streiten

quibbling /'kwɪblɪŋ/ *adj.* spitzfindig

quiche /ki:ʃ/ *n.* Quiche, *die*

quick /kwɪk/ 1 *adj.* schnell; kurz ⟨*Rede,
Pause*⟩; flüchtig ⟨*Kuss, Blick*⟩; **be ∼!** mach
schnell! (ugs.); **be ∼ to do sth.** etw. schnell
tun; **a ∼ temper** ein aufbrausendes Wesen
2 *adv.* schnell
3 *n.* empfindliches Fleisch; **be cut to the ∼**
(fig.) tief getroffen sein

quicken /'kwɪkn/ 1 *v.t.* beschleunigen
2 *v.i.* sich beschleunigen

'quickly *adv.* schnell

'quickness *n.* **(a)** (speed) Schnelligkeit, *die*
(b) (∼ of perception) Schärfe, *die*

quick: ∼**sand** *n.* Treibsand, *der;*
∼**-tempered** /-'tempəd/ *adj.* hitzig; **be
∼-tempered** leicht aufbrausen; ∼**-witted**
adj. geistesgegenwärtig

quid /kwɪd/ *n., pl. same* (Brit. coll.) Pfund, *das*

quiet /'kwaɪət/ 1 *adj.,* ∼**er** /'kwaɪətə(r)/,
∼**est** /'kwaɪətɪst/ **(a)** (silent) still; (not loud)
leise; **keep ∼ about sth.** (fig.) etw. geheim
halten
(b) (peaceful, not busy) ruhig
(c) (not overt) versteckt; **on the ∼:** still und
heimlich
2 *n.* Ruhe, *die;* (silence, stillness) Stille, *die*

quieten /'kwaɪətn/ *v.t.* beruhigen
■ **quieten 'down** *v.i.* sich beruhigen

'quietly *adv.* **(a)** (silently) still; (not loudly) leise
(b) (peacefully) ruhig

'quietness *n.* (absence of noise) Stille, *die;*
(peacefulness) Ruhe, *die*

quill /kwɪl/ *n.* (feather) Kielfeder, *die;* (of
porcupine) Stachel, *der*

quilt /kwɪlt/ 1 *n.* Schlafdecke, *die*
2 *v.t.* wattieren

quince /kwɪns/ *n.* Quitte, *die*

quintessential /kwɪntɪ'senʃl/ *adj.*
typisch; wesentlich

quintet /kwɪn'tet/ *n.* Quintett, *das*

quip /kwɪp/ 1 *n.* Witzelei, *die*
2 *v.i.,* -pp- witzeln (**at** über + *Akk.*)

quirk /kwɜ:k/ *n.* Marotte, *die;* **a ∼ of fate**
eine Laune des Schicksals

quirky /'kwɜ:kɪ/ *adj.* schrullig (ugs.)

quit /kwɪt/ *v.t.,* -tt-, (Amer.) **quit (a)** (give up)
aufgeben; (stop) aufhören mit; **∼ doing sth.**
aufhören, etw. zu tun; **they were given notice
to ∼ [the flat]** ihnen wurde [die Wohnung]
gekündigt
(b) (Comp.) beenden

quite /kwaɪt/ *adv.* **(a)** (entirely) ganz; völlig;
fest ⟨*entschlossen*⟩; ∼ [so]! [ja,] genau!
(b) (to some extent) ziemlich; ganz ⟨*gern*⟩; ∼ **a
few** ziemlich viele

quits /kwɪts/ *pred. adj.* **be ∼ [with sb.]** [mit
jmdm.] quitt sein (ugs.)

quiver¹ /'kwɪvə(r)/ *v.i.* zittern (**with** vor
+ *Dat.*); ⟨*Stimme, Lippen:*⟩ beben (geh.); ⟨*Lid:*⟩
zucken

quiver² *n.* (for arrows) Köcher, *der*

quiz /kwɪz/ 1 *n., pl.* ∼**zes** Quiz, *das*
2 *v.t.,* -zz- ausfragen (**about sth.** nach etw.,
about sb. über jmdn.)

quizzical /'kwɪzɪkl/ *adj.* fragend

'quiz programme, 'quiz show *ns.*
(Radio, Telev.) Quizsendung, *die*

quoit /kɔɪt/ *n.* [Gummi]ring, *der*

quorum /'kwɔ:rəm/ *n.* Quorum, *das*

quota /'kwəʊtə/ *n.* **(a)** (share) Anteil, *der*
(b) (goods to be produced)
Produktionsmindestquote, *die*
(c) (maximum number) Höchstquote, *die*

quotation /kwəʊ'teɪʃn/ *n.* **(a)** (Zitieren, *das;*
(passage) Zitat, *das*
(b) (estimate) Kosten[vor]anschlag, *der*

quo'tation marks *n. pl.*
Anführungszeichen *Pl.*

quote /kwəʊt/ 1 *v.t. also abs.* zitieren
(**from** aus); zitieren aus ⟨*Buch, Text*⟩; (mention)
anführen; nennen ⟨*Preis*⟩
2 *n.* (coll.) **(a)** (passage) Zitat, *das*
(b) (estimate) Kosten[vor]anschlag, *der*
(c) *usu. in pl.* (quotation mark)
Anführungszeichen, *das*

quotient /'kwəʊʃnt/ *n.* (Math.) Quotient, *der;*
see also INTELLIGENCE QUOTIENT

Rr

R, r /ɑː(r)/ *n.* R, r, *das*

R. *abbr.* = **River** Fl.

rabbi /'ræbaɪ/ *n.* Rabbi[ner], *der;* (as title) Rabbi, *der*

rabbit /'ræbɪt/ *n.* Kaninchen, *das*

rabbit: ~ burrow *n.* Kaninchenbau, *der;* **~ hutch** *n.* (also fig.) Kaninchenstall, *der;* **~ warren** *n.* Kaninchengehege, *das;* (fig.) Labyrinth, *das*

rabble /'ræbl/ *n.* Mob, *der*

rabid /'ræbɪd/ *adj.* (a) tollwütig **(b)** (extreme) fanatisch

rabies /'reɪbiːz/ *n.* Tollwut, *die*

race¹ /reɪs/ ① *n.* Rennen, *das;* (fig.) **a ~ against time** ein Wettlauf mit der Zeit ② *v.i.* (a) (in swimming, running, etc.) um die Wette schwimmen/laufen *usw.* (with, against mit) **(b)** ⟨*Motor:*⟩ durchdrehen; ⟨*Puls:*⟩ jagen **(c)** (rush) sich sehr beeilen; **~ after sb.** jmdn. hinterherhetzen ③ *v.t.* um die Wette schwimmen/laufen *usw.* mit

race² *n.* (Anthrop., Biol.) Rasse, *die;* **the human ~:** die Menschheit

race: ~course *n.* Rennbahn, *die;* **~ hatred** *n.* Rassenhass, *der;* **~horse** *n.* Rennpferd, *das;* **~ meeting** *n.* Renntag, *der;* (on successive days) Renntage *Pl.* **~ relations** *n. pl.* Beziehung zwischen den Rassen; **~ riot** *n.* Rassenkrawall, *der;* **~track** *n.* Rennbahn, *die*

racial /'reɪʃl/ *adj.* Rassen⟨diskriminierung, -konflikt, -gleichheit, -spannung, -vorurteil⟩; rassisch ⟨Gruppe, Minderheit⟩

racialism /'reɪʃəlɪzm/ *n.* Rassismus, *der*

racialist /'reɪʃəlɪst/ ① *n.* Rassist, *der/* Rassistin, *die* ② *adj.* rassistisch

racially /'reɪʃəlɪ/ *adv.* rassisch; **be ~ prejudiced** Rassenvorurteile haben

racing /'reɪsɪŋ/ *n.* Rennsport, *der;* (with horses) Pferdesport, *der*

racing: ~ bicycle *n.* Rennrad, *das;* Rennmaschine, *die;* **~ car** *n.* Rennwagen, *der;* **~ driver** *n.* Rennfahrer, *der/*-fahrerin, *die*

racism /'reɪsɪzm/ *n.* Rassismus, *der*

racist /'reɪsɪst/ ① *n.* Rassist, *der/*Rassistin, *die* ② *adj.* rassistisch

rack /ræk/ ① *n.* (for luggage) Ablage, *die;* (for toast, plates) Ständer, *der;* (on bicycle, motor cycle) Gepäckträger, *der*

② *v.t.* **~ one's brain[s]** (fig.) sich (*Dat.*) den Kopf zerbrechen (ugs.)

racket¹ /'rækɪt/ *n.* Schläger, *der*

racket² *n.* **(a)** (disturbance) Lärm, *der;* Krach, *der* **(b)** (scheme) Schwindelgeschäft, *das* (ugs.)

racketeer /rækɪ'tɪə(r)/ *n.* Ganove, *der;* (profiteer) Wucherer, *der*

racketeering /rækɪ'tɪərɪŋ/ *n.* kriminelle Geschäfte *Pl.*

racoon /rə'kuːn/ *n.* Waschbär, *der*

racy /'reɪsɪ/ *adj.* flott (ugs.) ⟨Stil⟩

radar /'reɪdɑː(r)/ *n.* Radar, *das od. der*

'radar screen *n.* Radarschirm, *der*

radiant /'reɪdɪənt/ *adj.* strahlend; fröhlich ⟨Stimmung⟩; **be ~:** strahlen (**with** vor + *Dat.*)

radiate /'reɪdɪeɪt/ ① *v.i.* (a) ⟨Hitze, Wärme:⟩ ausstrahlen; ⟨Schein, Wellen:⟩ ausgehen (**from** von) **(b)** (from central point) strahlenförmig ausgehen (**from** von) ② *v.t.* ausstrahlen ⟨Licht, Wärme; Glück, Liebe⟩; aussenden ⟨Strahlen, Wellen⟩

radiation /reɪdɪ'eɪʃn/ *n.* (of energy) Emission, *die;* (of signals) Ausstrahlung, *die;* (energy transmitted) Strahlung, *die*

radiator /'reɪdɪeɪtə(r)/ *n.* **(a)** (for heating) Heizkörper, *der* **(b)** (Motor Veh.) Kühler, *der*

'radiator cap *n.* Kühlverschraubung, *die*

radical /'rædɪkl/ *adj.* ① **(a)** (thorough; also Polit.) radikal; drastisch ⟨Maßnahme⟩ **(b)** (progressive) radikal **(c)** (fundamental) grundlegend ② *n.* (Polit.) Radikale, *der/die*

radio /'reɪdɪəʊ/ ① *n., pl.* **~s (a)** no indef. art. Funk, *der;* (for private communication) Sprechfunk, *der* **(b)** no indef. art. (Broadcasting) Rundfunk, *der;* **on the ~:** im Radio **(c)** (apparatus) Radio, *das* ② *attrib. adj.* (Broadcasting) Rundfunk-; Radio⟨welle, -teleskop⟩; Funk⟨mast, -turm, -taxi⟩ ③ *v.t.* funken

radio: ~'active *adj.* radioaktiv; **~ac'tivity** *n.* Radioaktivität, *die;* **~ cas'sette player** *n.* Kassettenradio, *das;* Radio mit Kassettenteil; **~con'trolled** *adj.* funkgesteuert; **~ frequency** *n.* Hochfrequenz, *die; attrib.* **~-frequency** Hochfrequenz-; **~ play** *n.* Hörspiel, *das;* **~ station** *n.* Rundfunkstation, *die;* Rundfunk- *od.* ⋯❖

Radiosender, *der;* ∼ **'telescope** *n.*
Radioteleskop, *das;* ∼**'therapy** *n.*
Strahlentherapie, *die*

radish /'rædɪʃ/ *n.* Rettich, *der;* (small, red)
Radieschen, *das*

radius /'reɪdɪəs/ *n., pl.* **radii** /'reɪdɪaɪ/ *or*
∼**es** (Math.) Radius, *der;* (fig.) Umkreis, *der*

RAF /ɑːreɪ'ef, (coll.) ræf/ *abbr.* = **Royal Air
Force**

raffle /'ræfl/ 1 *n.* Tombola, *die;* ∼ **ticket**
Los, *das*
2 *v.t.* ∼ [off] verlosen

raft /rɑːft/ *n.* Floß, *das*

rafter /'rɑːftə(r)/ *n.* Sparren, *der*

rag¹ /ræg/ *n.* **(a)** [Stoff]fetzen, *der*
(b) *in pl.* (old and torn clothes) Lumpen *Pl.*
(c) (derog.: newspaper) Käseblatt, *das* (salopp)

rag² *v.t.,* **-gg-** (tease) aufziehen

rag: ∼**bag** *n.* (fig.) Sammelsurium, *das;*
∼ **doll** *n.* Stoffpuppe, *die*

rage /reɪdʒ/ 1 *n.* **(a)** (violent anger) Wut, *die;*
(fit of anger) Wutausbruch, *der*
(b) sth. is [all] the ∼: etw. ist [ganz] groß in
Mode
2 *v.i.* **(a)** (rave) toben; ∼ **at** *or* **against sth./
sb.** gegen etw./jmdn. wüten
(b) (be violent, unchecked) toben; ⟨*Krankheit:*⟩
wüten

ragged /'rægɪd/ *adj.* zerrissen

⊸rag trade *n.* (coll.) Modebranche, *die* (ugs.)

raid /reɪd/ 1 *n.* Einfall, *der;* Überfall, *der;*
(Mil.) Überraschungsangriff, *der;* (by police)
Razzia, *die* (on in + *Dat.*)
2 *v.t.* ⟨*Polizei:*⟩ eine Razzia machen auf
(+ *Akk.*); ⟨*Räuber, Soldaten:*⟩ überfallen

'raider *n.* Räuber, *der/*Räuberin, *die*

rail /reɪl/ *n.* **(a)** Stange, *die;* (on ship) Reling,
die; (as protection against contact) Barriere, *die*
(b) (Railw.: of track) Schiene, *die*
(c) (∼way) [Eisen]bahn, *die; attrib.* Bahn-; **by**
∼: mit der Bahn

'rail card *n.* Bahnkarte, *die*

railing /'reɪlɪŋ/ *n.* (round park) Zaun, *der;* (on
staircase) Geländer, *das*

rail: ∼**road** (Amer.) ▶ ∼WAY; **R**∼**track** *n.,*
no art. (Brit.) *Betreibergesellschaft des
britischen Schienennetzes;* ∼**way** *n.* **(a)**
(track) Bahnlinie, *die;* Bahnstrecke, *die;* **(b)**
(system) [Eisen]bahn, *die*

railway: ∼ **carriage** *n.* Eisenbahnwagen,
der; ∼ **crossing** *n.* Bahnübergang, *der;*
∼ **engine** *n.* Lokomotive, *die;* ∼ **line** *n.*
[Eisen]bahnlinie, *die;* ∼ **station** *n.*
Bahnhof, *der;* ∼ **worker** *n.* Bahnarbeiter,
der/-arbeiterin, *die*

rain /reɪn/ 1 *n.* **(a)** Regen, *der*
(b) (fig.: of arrows, blows, etc.) Hagel, *der*
2 *v.i. impers.* **it is** ∼**ing** es regnet
3 *v.t.* hageln lassen ⟨*Schläge, Hiebe*⟩

rain: ∼**bow** /'reɪnbəʊ/ *n.* Regenbogen, *der;*
∼ **check** *n.* (Amer. fig.) **take a** ∼ **check on**
sth. auf etw. (*Akk.*) später wieder
zurückkommen; ∼ **cloud** *n.* Regenwolke,

die; ∼**coat** *n.* Regenmantel, *der;* ∼**fall** *n.*
Niederschlag, *der;* ∼**forest** *n.* Regenwald,
der; ∼**proof** *adj.* regendicht; ∼**water** *n.*
Regenwasser, *das;* ∼**wear** *n.*
Regenkleidung, *die*

'rainy *adj.* regnerisch ⟨*Tag, Wetter*⟩;
regenreich ⟨*Gebiet, Sommer*⟩; ∼ **season**
Regenzeit, *die;* **keep sth. for a** ∼ **day** (fig.) sich
(*Dat.*) etw. für schlechte Zeiten aufheben

raise /reɪz/ *v.t.* **(a)** (lift up) heben; erhöhen
⟨*Temperatur, Miete, Gehalt*⟩; hochziehen
⟨*Fahne*⟩; aufziehen ⟨*Vorhang*⟩; hochheben
⟨*Arm*⟩; ∼ **one's glass to sb.** das Glas auf
jmdn. erheben
(b) (set upright) aufrichten; erheben ⟨*Banner*⟩;
∼ **sb.'s spirits** jmds. Stimmung heben
(c) erheben ⟨*Forderungen, Einwände*⟩;
aufwerfen ⟨*Frage*⟩; zur Sprache bringen
⟨*Thema, Problem*⟩
(d) aufziehen ⟨*Vieh, [Haus]tiere*⟩; großziehen
⟨*Familie, Kinder*⟩
(e) aufbringen ⟨*Geld, Betrag*⟩
(f) aufheben ⟨*Belagerung, Blockade,
Embargo, Verbot*⟩

raisin /'reɪzn/ *n.* Rosine, *die*

rake /reɪk/ 1 *n.* Rechen, *der;* Harke, *die*
2 *v.t.* **(a)** harken
(b) ∼ **the fire** die Asche entfernen
(c) (with eyes, shots) bestreichen
∎ **rake 'in** *v.t.* (coll.) scheffeln (ugs.).
∎ **rake 'up** *v.t.* zusammenharken; (fig.)
wieder ausgraben

'rake-off *n.* (coll.) [Gewinn]anteil, *der*

rakish /'reɪkɪʃ/ *adj.* flott; kess

rally /'rælɪ/ 1 *v.i.* (regain health) sich wieder
[ein wenig] erholen
2 *v.t.* **(a)** (reassemble) wieder zusammenrufen
(b) einigen ⟨*Partei, Kräfte*⟩; sammeln
⟨*Anhänger*⟩
3 *n.* **(a)** (mass meeting) Versammlung, *die*
(b) [motor] ∼: Rallye, *die*
(c) (Tennis) Ballwechsel, *der*

ram /ræm/ 1 *n.* (Zool.) Schafbock, *der;*
Widder, *der*
2 *v.t.,* **-mm-**: **(a)** (force) stopfen; ∼ **a post into
the ground** einen Pfosten in die Erde
rammen; ∼ **sth. home to sb.** jmdm. etw.
deutlich vor Augen führen
(b) (collide with) rammen

RAM /ræm/ *abbr.* (Comp.) = **random
access memory** RAM

ramble /'ræmbl/ 1 *n.* [nature] ∼:
Wanderung, *die*
2 *v.i.* **(a)** (walk) umherstreifen (**through, in** in
+ *Dat.*)
(b) (in talk) zusammenhangloses Zeug reden;
keep rambling on about sth. sich endlos über
etw. (*Akk.*) auslassen

rambler /'ræmblə(r)/ *n.* Wanderer, *der/*
Wanderin, *die*

rambling /'ræmblɪŋ/ 1 *n.* Wandern, *das*
2 *adj.* **(a)** (irregularly arranged) verschachtelt;
verwinkelt ⟨*Straßen*⟩

(b) (incoherent) unzusammenhängend ⟨*Erklärung*⟩
(c) ∼ **rose** Kletterrose, *die*
ramp /ræmp/ *n.* Rampe, *die*
rampage ① /'ræmpeɪdʒ/ *n.* Randale, *die* (ugs.); **be/go on the** ∼ (coll.) randalieren ② /ræm'peɪdʒ/ *v.i.* randalieren
rampant /'ræmpənt/ *adj.* zügellos ⟨*Gewalt, Rassismus*⟩; steil ansteigend ⟨*Inflation*⟩; üppig ⟨*Wachstum*⟩
rampart /'ræmpɑːt/ *n.* Wehrgang, *der*
ram: ∼ **raid** ① *v.t.* [durch Rammen mit einem Fahrzeug] einbrechen in (+ *Akk.*); ② *n.* [durch Rammen eines Gebäudes verübter] Einbruch; ∼**-raider** *n.:* Einbrecher, der sich durch Einrammen bes. eines Schaufensters mit einem Fahrzeug Zutritt verschafft
'ramshackle *adj.* klapprig ⟨*Auto*⟩; verkommen ⟨*Gebäude*⟩
ran ▶ RUN 2, 3
ranch /rɑːntʃ/ *n.* Ranch, *die*
'ranch hand *n.* Farmarbeiter, *der*/-arbeiterin, *die*
rancid /'rænsɪd/ *adj.* ranzig
rancour (Brit.; Amer.: **rancor**) /'ræŋkə(r)/ *n.* [tiefe] Verbitterung
R&B *abbr.* = **rhythm and blues** R&B
R&D *abbr.* = **research and development** F&E
random /'rændəm/ ① *n.* **at** ∼: wahllos; willkürlich; (aimlessly) ziellos; **choose at** ∼: aufs Geratewohl wählen ② *adj.* willkürlich
random 'access memory *n.* (Comp.) Schreib-Lese-Speicher, *der*
randy /'rændɪ/ *adj.* geil; scharf (ugs.)
rang ▶ RING² 2, 3
range /reɪndʒ/ ① *n.* **(a)** ∼ **of mountains** Bergkette, *die* **(b)** (of subjects) Palette, *die;* (of knowledge, voice) Umfang, *der* **(c)** (of missile etc.) Reichweite, *die;* **at a** ∼ **of 200 metres** auf eine Entfernung von 200 Metern **(d)** (series, selection) Kollektion, *die* **(e)** (stove) Herd, *der* ② *v.i.* ⟨*Preise, Temperaturen:*⟩ schwanken, sich bewegen (**from ... to** zwischen [+ *Dat.*] ... und)
'ranger *n.* Förster, *der*/Försterin, *die*
rank¹ /ræŋk/ ① *n.* **(a)** (position in hierarchy) Rang, *der;* (Mil. also) Dienstgrad, *der* **(b)** (social position) [soziale] Stellung **(c)** (row) Reihe, *die;* **the** ∼ **and file** (fig.) die breite Masse; **the** ∼**s** (enlisted men) die Mannschaften und Unteroffiziere ② *v.t.* ∼ **among** zählen zu ③ *v.i.* ∼ **among** zählen zu
rank² *adj.* **(a)** krass ⟨*Außenseiter*⟩ **(b)** ∼ **weeds** [wild]wucherndes Unkraut
rankings /'ræŋkɪŋz/ *n. pl.* (Sport) Rangliste,

die; **the team has fallen in the** ∼: die Mannschaft ist in der Tabelle nach unten gerutscht
ransack /'rænsæk/ *v.t.* **(a)** (search) durchsuchen (**for** nach) **(b)** (pillage) plündern
ransom /'rænsəm/ *n.* ∼ **[money]** Lösegeld, *das;* **hold to** ∼: als Geisel festhalten
rant /rænt/ *v.i.* ∼ **[and rave]** wettern (ugs.) (**about** über + *Akk.*)
rap /ræp/ ① *n.* [energisches] Klopfen ② *v.t.,* **-pp-** klopfen ③ *v.i.,* **-pp-** klopfen (**on** an + *Akk.*)
rape¹ /reɪp/ ① *n.* Vergewaltigung, *die* ② *v.t.* vergewaltigen
rape² *n.* (Bot., Agric.) Raps, *der*
rape: ∼**seed** *n.* Rapssamen, *der;* ∼**seed oil** *n.* Rapsöl, *das*
rapid /'ræpɪd/ ① *adj.* schnell ⟨*Bewegung, Wachstum, Puls*⟩; rasch ⟨*Fortschritt, Ausbreitung*⟩ ② *n. in pl.* Stromschnellen *Pl.*
rapid-'fire *adj.* Schnellfeuer⟨*waffe, -schießen*⟩; (fig.) schnell aufeinander folgend ⟨*Wiederholung*⟩; Schnellfeuer⟨*witze, -fragen*⟩
rapidity /rə'pɪdɪtɪ/ *n.* Schnelligkeit, *die*
'rapidly *adv.* schnell
rapist /'reɪpɪst/ *n.* Vergewaltiger, *der*
rapport /ræ'pɔː(r)/ *n.* [harmonisches] Verhältnis
rapt /ræpt/ *adj.* gespannt ⟨*Miene*⟩
rapture /'ræptʃə(r)/ *n.* **[state of]** ∼: Verzückung, *die*
rapturous /'ræptʃərəs/ *adj.* begeistert
rare¹ /reə(r)/ *adj.,* **'rarely** *adv.* selten
rare² *adj.* (Cookery) englisch gebraten
rarefied /'reərɪfaɪd/ *adj.* dünn ⟨*Luft*⟩; (fig.) exklusiv
rarity /'reərɪtɪ/ *n.* Seltenheit, *die*
rash¹ /ræʃ/ *n.* [Haut]ausschlag, *der*
rash² *adj.* voreilig ⟨*Urteil, Entscheidung*⟩; überstürzt ⟨*Versprechung*⟩
rasher /'ræʃə(r)/ *n.* Speckscheibe, *die*
'rashly *adv.* voreilig
rasp /rɑːsp/ ① *n.* (tool) Raspel, *die* ② *v.t.* (say gratingly) schnarren
raspberry /'rɑːzbərɪ/ *n.* Himbeere, *die*
rat /ræt/ *n.* **(a)** Ratte, *die;* **smell a** ∼ (fig.) Lunte riechen (ugs.) **(b)** (coll. derog.: person) Ratte, *die* (derb)
ratchet /'rætʃɪt/ *n.* **(a)** (Mech. Engin.) (set of teeth) Zahnkranz, *der* **(b)** ∼ **[wheel]** Klinkenrad, *das*
'ratchet screwdriver *n.* Drillschraubenzieher, *der*
rate /reɪt/ ① *n.* **(a)** (proportion) Rate, *die;* ∼ **of inflation** Inflationsrate, *die* **(b)** (tariff) Satz, *der;* ∼ **[of pay]** Lohnsatz, *der* **(c)** (speed) Geschwindigkeit, *die;* Tempo, *das* **(d)** (Brit.: levy) **[local or council]** ∼**s** Gemeindeabgaben *Pl.* **(e)** (coll.) **at any** ∼ (at least) zumindest; ⋯❖

wenigstens; (whatever happens) auf jeden Fall;
at this ∼ we won't get any work done so
kriegen wir gar nichts fertig (ugs.)
2 v.t. (a) einschätzen ⟨Intelligenz, Leistung⟩
(b) (consider) betrachten; rechnen (among zu)
3 v.i. ∼ as gelten als

'ratepayer n. (Brit.) Realsteuerpflichtige,
der/die

rather /'rɑːðə(r)/ adv. (a) (by preference)
lieber
(b) (somewhat) ziemlich; I ∼ think that ...: ich
bin ziemlich sicher, dass ...
(c) (more truly) vielmehr; or ∼:
beziehungsweise

ratification /rætɪfɪ'keɪʃn/ n. Ratifizierung,
die

ratify /'rætɪfaɪ/ v.t. ratifizieren

rating /'reɪtɪŋ/ n. (a) (estimated standing)
Einschätzung, die
(b) (Radio, Telev.) [popularity] ∼:
Einschaltquote, die
(c) (Brit. Navy) Matrose, der

ratio /'reɪʃɪəʊ/ n., pl. ∼s Verhältnis, das

ration /'ræʃn/ 1 n. ∼[s] Ration, die (of an
+ Dat.)
2 v.t. rationieren ⟨Benzin, Zucker usw.⟩

rational /'ræʃənl/ adj. (having reason)
rational ⟨Wesen⟩; (sensible) vernünftig ⟨Person,
Art usw.⟩

rationalist /'ræʃənəlɪst/ n. Rationalist,
der/Rationalistin, die

rationalize /'ræʃənəlaɪz/ v.t.
rationalisieren

rationing /'ræʃənɪŋ/ n. Rationierung, die

rat: ∼ **poison** n. Rattengift, das; ∼ **race**
n. erbarmungsloser Konkurrenzkampf;
∼ **run** n. (Brit. coll.) Schleichweg, der

rattle /'rætl/ 1 v.i. (a) ⟨Fenster:⟩ klappern;
⟨Flaschen:⟩ klirren; ⟨Kette:⟩ rasseln
(b) ⟨Zug, Bus:⟩ rattern
2 v.t. (a) klappern mit ⟨Würfel, Geschirr⟩;
klirren lassen ⟨Fenster[scheiben]⟩; rasseln
mit ⟨Kette⟩
(b) (coll.: disconcert) ∼ sb., get sb. ∼d jmdn.
durcheinander bringen
3 n. (a) (of baby) Rassel, die
(b) (sound) Klappern, das
■ **rattle 'off** v.t. (coll.) herunterrasseln (ugs.)

'rattlesnake n. Klapperschlange, die

raucous /'rɔːkəs/ adj. rau

raunchy /'rɔːntʃɪ/ adj. (lewd) vulgär;
(suggestive) scharf (salopp)

ravage /'rævɪdʒ/ 1 v.t. heimsuchen
⟨Gebiet, Stadt⟩
2 n. in pl. verheerende Wirkung

rave /reɪv/ 1 v.i. (a) (talk wildly) irrereden
(b) (speak admiringly) schwärmen (about von)
2 attrib. adj. (coll.) begeistert ⟨Kritik⟩
3 n. (coll.: dancing party) Rave, der od. das

raven /'reɪvn/ n. Rabe, der

ravenous /'rævənəs/ adj. I'm ∼: ich habe
einen Bärenhunger (ugs.)

'rave-up n. (Brit. coll.) [wilde] Fete (ugs.)

ravine /rə'viːn/ n. Schlucht, die

raving /'reɪvɪŋ/ 1 adj. irreredend ⟨Idiot⟩
2 adv. be ∼ mad völlig verrückt sein (ugs.)

ravish /'rævɪʃ/ v.t. (charm) entzücken

'ravishing adj. bildschön ⟨Anblick, Person⟩;
hinreißend ⟨Schönheit⟩

raw /rɔː/ adj. (a) (uncooked) roh
(b) (inexperienced) unerfahren
(c) (stripped of skin) blutig ⟨Fleisch⟩; offen
⟨Wunde⟩
(d) (chilly) nasskalt

raw ma'terial n. Rohstoff, der

Rawlplug ® /'rɔːlplʌg/ n. Dübel, der

ray /reɪ/ n. Strahl, der; ∼ of sunshine/light
Sonnen-/Lichtstrahl, der

raze /reɪz/ v.t. ∼ to the ground dem
Erdboden gleichmachen

razor /'reɪzə(r)/ n. Rasiermesser, das;
[electric] ∼: [elektrischer] Rasierapparat

razor: ∼ **blade** n. Rasierklinge, die;
∼**-sharp** adj. sehr scharf ⟨Messer⟩; (fig.)
messerscharf ⟨Verstand, Intellekt⟩;
scharfsinnig ⟨Person⟩

RC abbr. = **Roman Catholic** r.-k.;
röm.-kath.

Rd. abbr. = **Road** Str.

re /riː/ prep. (Commerc.) betreffs

RE abbr. (Brit.) = **Religious Education**
Religionslehre, die

reach /riːtʃ/ 1 v.t. (a) (arrive at) erreichen;
ankommen in (+ Dat.) ⟨Stadt, Land⟩;
erzielen ⟨Übereinstimmung⟩; kommen zu
⟨Entscheidung; Ausgang, Eingang⟩; you can
∼ her at this number du kannst sie unter
dieser Nummer erreichen
(b) (extend to) ⟨Straße:⟩ führen bis zu; ⟨Leiter,
Haar:⟩ reichen bis zu
2 v.i. (a) (stretch out hand) ∼ for sth. nach
etw. greifen; ∼ across the table über den
Tisch langen
(b) (be long/tall enough) sth. will/won't ∼: etw.
ist/ist nicht lang genug; I can't ∼: ich
komme nicht daran
(c) (go as far as) ⟨Wasser, Gebäude, Besitz:⟩
reichen ([up] to bis [hinauf] zu)
3 n. Reichweite, die; be within easy ∼ ⟨Ort:⟩
leicht erreichbar sein; be out of ∼ ⟨Ort:⟩
nicht erreichbar sein; ⟨Gegenstand:⟩ außer
Reichweite sein
■ **reach 'out** v.i. die Hand ausstrecken (for
nach)

react /rɪ'ækt/ v.i. reagieren (to auf + Akk.)

reaction /rɪ'ækʃn/ n. Reaktion, die (to auf
+ Akk.)

reactionary /rɪ'ækʃənərɪ/ (Polit.) 1 adj.
reaktionär
2 n. Reaktionär, der/Reaktionärin, die

reactor /rɪ'æktə(r)/ n. [nuclear] ∼:
Kernreaktor, der

read /riːd/ 1 v.t., read /red/ (a) lesen; ∼ sb.
sth., ∼ sth. to sb. jmdm. etwas vorlesen;
∼ the gas meter das Gas ablesen

(b) (interpret) deuten; ~ **between the lines** zwischen den Zeilen lesen **(c)** (study) studieren ②*v.i.*, read **(a)** lesen; ~ **to sb.** jmdm. vorlesen **(b)** (convey meaning) lauten; **the contract** ~**s as follows** der Vertrag hat folgenden Wortlaut ∎ **read 'out** *v.t.* laut vorlesen ∎ **read 'over, read 'through** *v.t.* durchlesen ∎ **read 'up** *v.t.* sich informieren (**on** über + *Akk.*)

readable /'riːdəbl/ *adj.* **(a)** (pleasant to read) lesenswert **(b)** (legible) leserlich

'**reader** *n.* **(a)** Leser, *der*/Leserin, *die* **(b)** (book) Lesebuch, *das*

'**readership** *n.* Leserschaft, *die*

readily /'redɪlɪ/ *adv.* **(a)** (willingly) bereitwillig **(b)** (easily) ohne weiteres

readiness /'redɪnɪs/ *n.* Bereitschaft, *die;* **be in** ~: bereit sein (**for** für)

'**reading** *n.* **(a)** Lesen, *das* **(b)** (figure shown) Anzeige, *die* **(c)** (recital) Lesung, *die* (**from** aus) **(d)** (Parl.) Lesung, *die*

reading: ~ **glasses** *n. pl.* Lesebrille, *die;* ~ **lamp,** ~ **light** *ns.* Leselampe, *die;* ~ **matter** *n.* Lesestoff, *der;* Lektüre, *die*

readjust /riːə'dʒʌst/① *v.t.* neu einstellen; neu anpassen ⟨*Gehalt, Zinssatz*⟩ ② *v. refl. & i.* ~ [oneself] **to** sich wieder gewöhnen an (+ *Akk.*)

read /riːd/: ~'**only memory** *n.* (Comp.) Fest[wert]speicher, *der;* ~**out** *n.* (Comp.) Ausgabe, *die;* ~**write** *n. attrib.* (Comp.) Schreib-Lese-; ~**write head** Schreib-Lese-Kopf, *der*

ready /'redɪ/ ① *adj.* **(a)** (prepared) fertig; **be** ~ **to do sth.** bereit sein, etw. zu tun; **get** ~: sich fertig machen **(b)** (willing) bereit **(c)** (within reach) griffbereit ② *adv.* fertig ③ *n.* **at the** ~ ⟨*Schusswaffe*⟩ im Anschlag

ready: ~ '**cash** ▶ ~ MONEY; ~**cooked** *adj.* vorgekocht; ~**cooked meal** Fertiggericht, *das;* Fertigmahlzeit, *die;* ~'**made** *adj.* **(a)** Konfektions⟨*anzug, -kleidung*⟩; **(b)** (fig.) vorgefertigt; ~ '**money** *n.* Bargeld, *das;* ~**to-eat** *adj.* Fertig⟨*mahlzeit, -dessert*⟩; ~**to-serve** *adj.* tischfertig; ~**to-wear** *adj.* Konfektions⟨*anzug, -kleidung*⟩

real /rɪəl/ *adj.* **(a)** (actually existing) real ⟨*Ereignis, Lebewesen*⟩; wirklich ⟨*Macht*⟩ **(b)** (genuine) echt ⟨*Interesse, Gold, Seide*⟩ **(c)** (complete) total (ugs.) ⟨*Desaster, Enttäuschung*⟩ **(d)** (true) wahr ⟨*Grund, Name, Glück*⟩; echt ⟨*Mitleid, Sieg*⟩; **the** ~ **thing** der/die/das Echte

(e) be for ~ (coll.) echt sein

'**real estate** *n.* (Amer.) Immobilien *Pl.*

realism /'rɪəlɪzm/ *n.* Realismus, *der*

'**realist** *n.* Realist, *der*/Realistin, *die*

realistic /rɪə'lɪstɪk/ *adj.* realistisch

reality /rɪ'ælɪtɪ/ *n.* Realität, *die;* **in** ~: in Wirklichkeit

reality TV *n.* Reality-TV, *das*

realization /rɪəlaɪ'zeɪʃn/ *n.* Erkenntnis, *die*

realize /'rɪəlaɪz/ *v.t.* **(a)** (be aware of) bemerken; erkennen ⟨*Fehler*⟩; **I didn't** ~ *abs.* ich habe es nicht gewusst; ~ [that] ...: merken, dass ... **(b)** (make happen) verwirklichen **(c)** erbringen ⟨*Summe, Preis*⟩

real-life *attrib. adj.* real

really /'rɪəlɪ/ *adv.* wirklich; **not** ~: eigentlich nicht; [**well,**] ~! [also] so was!

realm /relm/ *n.* Reich, *das*

realtor /'riːəltə(r)/ (Amer.) Grundstücksmakler, *der*

reap /riːp/ *v.t.* (cut) schneiden ⟨*Getreide*⟩; (gather in) einfahren ⟨*Getreide, Ernte*⟩

reappear /riːə'pɪə(r)/ *v.i.* wieder auftauchen; (come back) [wieder] zurückkommen

rear¹ /rɪə(r)/ ① *n.* **(a)** (back part) hinterer Teil **(b)** (back) Rückseite, *die* **(c)** (Mil.) Rücken, *der* ② *adj.* hinter...; ~ **axle** Hinterachse, *die*

rear² ① *v.t.* großziehen ⟨*Kind, Familie*⟩; halten ⟨*Vieh*⟩ ② *v.i.* ⟨*Pferd:*⟩ sich aufbäumen

rear: ~**guard** *n.* (Mil.) Nachhut, *die;* ~ **light** *n.* Rücklicht, *das;* ~**wheel drive** ① *n.* Hinterradantrieb, *der;* ② *adj.* a ~**wheel drive vehicle** ein Fahrzeug mit Hinterradantrieb

rearm /riː'ɑːm/ *v.i. & t.* wieder aufrüsten

rearrange /riːə'reɪndʒ/ *v.t.* umräumen ⟨*Möbel*⟩; verlegen ⟨*Spiel*⟩ (**for** auf + *Akk.*); ändern ⟨*Programm*⟩

rear-view 'mirror *n.* Rückspiegel, *der*

reason /'riːzn/ ① *n.* **(a)** (cause) Grund, *der;* **have no** ~ **to complain** sich nicht beklagen können; **for that** [**very**] ~: aus [eben] diesem Grund **(b)** (power to understand; sense) Vernunft, *die;* (power to think) Verstand, *der;* **in** *or* **within** ~: innerhalb eines vernünftigen Rahmens; **it stands to** ~ **that** ...: es ist unzweifelhaft, dass ... ② *v.i.* **(a)** schlussfolgern (**from** aus) **(b)** ~ **with sb.** diskutieren mit (**about, on** über + *Akk.*); **you can't** ~ **with her** mit ihr kann man nicht vernünftig reden ③ *v.t.* schlussfolgern

reasonable /'riːzənəbl/ *adj.* **(a)** vernünftig **(b)** (inexpensive) günstig ····>

reasonably /'riːzənəblɪ/ adv. (a) (within reason) vernünftig
(b) (fairly) ganz ‹gut›; ziemlich ‹gesund›

reasoned /'riːznd/ adj. durchdacht

reasoning /'riːzənɪŋ/ n. logisches Denken

reassurance /riːə'ʃʊərəns/ n. (a) (calming) give sb. ~: jmdn. beruhigen
(b) (confirmation) Bestätigung, die

reassure /riːə'ʃʊə(r)/ v.t. beruhigen; ~ sb. about his health. jmdm. versichern, dass er gesund ist

reassuring /riːə'ʃʊərɪŋ/ adj. beruhigend

rebate /'riːbeɪt/ n. (a) (refund) Rückzahlung, die
(b) (discount) Preisnachlass, der (on auf + Akk.)

rebel ① /'rebl/ n. Rebell, der/Rebellin, die
② attrib. adj. Rebellen-
③ /rɪ'bel/ v.i., -ll- rebellieren

rebellion /rɪ'beljən/ n. Rebellion, die

rebellious /rɪ'beljəs/ adj. rebellisch

rebirth /riː'bɜːθ/ n. (revival) Wiederaufleben, das

reboot /riː'buːt/ (Comp.) v.t. & i. neu booten

rebound ① /rɪ'baʊnd/ v.i. (a) (spring back) abprallen (from von)
(b) (fig.) zurückfallen (upon auf + Akk.)
② /'riːbaʊnd/ n. Abprall, der

rebuff /rɪ'bʌf/ ① n. [schroffe] Abweisung
② v.t. [schroff] zurückweisen

rebuild /riː'bɪld/ v.t., rebuilt /riː'bɪlt/ wieder aufbauen

rebuke /rɪ'bjuːk/ ① v.t. tadeln, rügen (for wegen)
② n. Rüge, die

recall ① /rɪ'kɔːl/ v.t. (a) (remember) sich erinnern an (+ Akk.)
(b) (serve as reminder of) erinnern an (+ Akk.)
(c) abberufen ‹Botschafter›
② /rɪ'kɔːl, 'riːkɔːl/ n. (a) [powers of] ~: Gedächtnis, das
(b) beyond ~: unwiderruflich

recant /rɪ'kænt/ v.i. [öffentlich] widerrufen

recap /'riːkæp/ v.t. & i., -pp- (coll.) rekapitulieren

recapitulate /riːkə'pɪtjʊleɪt/ v.t. & i. rekapitulieren

recapture /riː'kæptʃə(r)/ v.t. wieder ergreifen ‹Gefangenen›; wieder einfangen ‹Tier›

recede /rɪ'siːd/ v.i. ‹Hochwasser, Flut:› zurückgehen; ~ [into the distance] in der Ferne verschwinden

receding /rɪ'siːdɪŋ/ adj. fliehend ‹Kinn, Stirn›

receipt /rɪ'siːt/ n. (a) (receiving) Empfang, der
(b) (written acknowledgement) Quittung, die
(c) in pl. (amount received) Einnahmen Pl. (from aus)

receive /rɪ'siːv/ v.t. (a) (get) erhalten; beziehen ‹Gehalt, Rente›

(b) (accept) entgegennehmen ‹Strauß, Lieferung›
(c) (entertain) empfangen ‹Gast›

re'ceiver n. (a) Empfänger, der/ Empfängerin, die
(b) (Teleph.) [Telefon]hörer, der
(c) (of stolen goods) Hehler, der/Hehlerin, die

recent /'riːsənt/ adj. jüngst… ‹Ereignisse, Vergangenheit usw.›; the ~ closure of the factory die kürzlich erfolgte Schließung der Fabrik

'recently adv. (a short time ago) vor kurzem; (in the recent past) in der letzten Zeit

receptacle /rɪ'septəkl/ n. Behälter, der; Gefäß, das

reception /rɪ'sepʃn/ n. (a) (welcome) Aufnahme, die
(b) (party) Empfang, der
(c) (Brit.: foyer) die Rezeption

reception: ~ com'mittee n. Empfangskomitee, das; ~ desk n. Rezeption, die

re'ceptionist n. (in hotel) Empfangschef, der/-dame, die; (at doctor's) Sprechstundenhilfe, die

receptive /rɪ'septɪv/ adj. aufgeschlossen, empfänglich (to für)

recess /rɪ'ses, 'riːses/ n. (a) (alcove) Nische, die
(b) (Brit. Parl.; Amer.: short vacation) Ferien Pl.; (Amer. Sch.; between classes) Pause, die

recession /rɪ'seʃn/ n. (Econ.) Rezession, die (fachspr.); Konjunkturrückgang, der

recharge /riː'tʃɑːdʒ/ v.t. aufladen ‹Batterie›

rechargeable /riː'tʃɑːdʒəbl/ adj. wieder aufladbar

recipe /'resɪpɪ/ n. Rezept, das

recipient /rɪ'sɪpɪənt/ n. Empfänger, der/ Empfängerin, die

reciprocal /rɪ'sɪprəkl/ adj. gegenseitig ‹Abkommen, Zuneigung›

reciprocate /rɪ'sɪprəkeɪt/ v.t. erwidern

recital /rɪ'saɪtl/ n. (performance) [Solisten]konzert, das; (of literature also) Rezitation, die

recitation /resɪ'teɪʃn/ n. Rezitation, die

recite /rɪ'saɪt/ v.t. (a) rezitieren ‹Gedicht›
(b) (list) aufzählen

reckless /'reklɪs/ adj. unbesonnen; rücksichtslos ‹Fahrweise›; ~ of the dangers/ consequences ungeachtet der Gefahren/ Folgen

reckon /'rekn/ v.t. (a) (work out) ausrechnen ‹Kosten›; bestimmen ‹Position›
(b) (consider) halten (as für)
(c) (estimate) schätzen

■ **'reckon on** v.t. (a) (rely on) zählen auf (+ Akk.)
(b) (expect) rechnen mit

■ **'reckon with** v.i. rechnen mit

'reckoning n. Berechnung, die; by my ~: nach meiner Rechnung

reclaim /rɪˈkleɪm/ v.t. (a) zurückbekommen ⟨Steuern⟩ (b) urbar machen ⟨Land⟩

recline /rɪˈklaɪn/ v.i. liegen; **reclining seat** Liegesitz, der

recluse /rɪˈkluːs/ n. Einsiedler, der/ Einsiedlerin, die

recognition /rekəgˈnɪʃn/ n. (a) Wiedererkennen, das; **be beyond all ~:** nicht wieder zu erkennen sein (b) (acknowledgement) Anerkennung, die; **in ~ of** als Anerkennung für

recognize /ˈrekəgnaɪz/ v.t. (a) (know again) wieder erkennen (**by** an + Dat., **from** durch) (b) (acknowledge) erkennen; anerkennen ⟨Gültigkeit, Land⟩; **be ~d as** gelten als

recoil ① /rɪˈkɔɪl/ v.i. zurückfahren ② /ˈriːkɔɪl, rɪˈkɔɪl/ n. Rückstoß, der

recollect /rekəˈlekt/ ① v.t. sich erinnern an (+ Akk.) ② v.i. sich erinnern

recollection /rekəˈlekʃn/ n. Erinnerung, die

recommend /rekəˈmend/ v.t. empfehlen

recommendation /rekəmenˈdeɪʃn/ n. Empfehlung, die; **on sb.'s ~:** auf jmds. Empfehlung (Akk.)

recompense /ˈrekəmpens/ ① v.t. entschädigen ② n. Entschädigung, die

reconcile /ˈrekənsaɪl/ v.t. (a) (restore to friendship) versöhnen (b) **~ oneself to sth.** sich mit etw. versöhnen

reconciliation /rekənsɪlɪˈeɪʃn/ n. Versöhnung, die

recondition /riːkənˈdɪʃn/ v.t. [general]überholen; **~ed engine** Austauschmotor, der

reconnaissance /rɪˈkɒnɪsəns/ n. (Mil.) Aufklärung, die

reconnoitre (Brit.; Amer.: **reconnoiter**) /rekəˈnɔɪtə(r)/ v.i. auf Erkundung [aus]gehen

reconsider /riːkənˈsɪdə(r)/ v.t. [noch einmal] überdenken

reconstruct /riːkənˈstrʌkt/ v.t. wieder aufbauen; (fig.) rekonstruieren

reconstruction /riːkənˈstrʌkʃn/ n. Wiederaufbau, der; (thing reconstructed) Rekonstruktion, die

record ① /rɪˈkɔːd/ v.t. (a) aufzeichnen; **~ a new CD** eine neue CD aufnehmen (b) (register officially) dokumentieren; protokollieren ⟨Verhandlung⟩ ② /ˈrekɔːd/ n. (a) **be on ~** ⟨Prozess, Verhandlung, Besprechung:⟩ protokolliert sein; **have sth. on ~:** etw. dokumentiert haben (b) (report) Protokoll, das (c) (document) Dokument, das; [strictly] **off the ~:** [ganz] inoffiziell (d) (for ~ player) [Schall]platte, die

(e) **have a [criminal/police] ~:** vorbestraft sein (f) (Sport) Rekord, der

record /ˈrekɔːd/: **~-breaking** adj. Rekord-; **~ deck** n. Plattenspieler, der

recorded /rɪˈkɔːdɪd/ adj. aufgezeichnet ⟨Konzert, Rede⟩; **~ music** Musikaufnahmen Pl.

recorded deˈlivery n. (Brit. Post.) eingeschriebene Sendung (ohne Versicherung)

recorder /rɪˈkɔːdə(r)/ n. (Mus.) Blockflöte, die

ˈrecord holder n. (Sport) Rekordhalter, der/-halterin, die

recording /rɪˈkɔːdɪŋ/ n. (a) (process) Aufzeichnung, die (b) (what is recorded) Aufnahme, die

recording: **~ head** n. Aufnahmekopf, der; **~ studio** n. Tonstudio, das

record /ˈrekɔːd/: **~ player** n. Plattenspieler, der; **~ sleeve** n. Plattenhülle, die; **~ token** n. [Schall]plattengutschein, der

re-count ① /riːˈkaʊnt/ v.t. [noch einmal] nachzählen ② /ˈriːkaʊnt/ n. Nachzählung, die

recoup /rɪˈkuːp/ v.t. [wieder] hereinbekommen ⟨[Geld]einsatz⟩

recourse /rɪˈkɔːs/ n. **have ~ to sb./sth.** bei jmdm./zu etw. Zuflucht nehmen

recover /rɪˈkʌvə(r)/ ① v.t. zurückbekommen ② v.i. **~ from sth.** sich von etw. [wieder] erholen; **be [fully] ~ed** [völlig] wiederhergestellt sein

recovery /rɪˈkʌvərɪ/ n. Erholung, die; **make a quick/good ~:** sich schnell/gut erholen

recovery: **~ position** n. (Med.) stabile Seitenlage; **~ vehicle** n. Bergungsfahrzeug, das

recreation /rekrɪˈeɪʃn/ n. Freizeitbeschäftigung, die; Hobby, das

recreational /rekrɪˈeɪʃənl/ adj. Freizeit-

recreational: **~ ˈdrug** n. Freizeitdroge, die; **~ ˈvehicle** n. (Amer.) Wohnmobil, das

recreˈation centre n. Freizeitzentrum, das

recrimination /rɪkrɪmɪˈneɪʃn/ n. Gegenbeschuldigung, die

recruit /rɪˈkruːt/ ① n. (a) (Mil.) Rekrut, der (b) (new member) neues Mitglied ② v.t. (Mil.: enlist) anwerben; (into party etc.) werben ⟨Mitglied⟩; einstellen ⟨neuen Mitarbeiter⟩

reˈcruitment n. (Mil.) Anwerbung, die; (of new staff) Neueinstellung, die; **~ of members** Mitgliederwerbung, die

rectangle /ˈrektæŋgl/ n. Rechteck, das

rectangular /rekˈtæŋgjʊlə(r)/ adj. rechteckig

rector /ˈrektə(r)/ n. (a) Pfarrer, der (b) (Univ.) Rektor, der/Rektorin, die   ····﹢

rectory /'rektərɪ/ n. Pfarrhaus, das

recuperate /rɪ'kjuːpəreɪt/ v.i. sich erholen

recuperation /rɪkjuːpə'reɪʃn/ n. Erholung, die

recur /rɪ'kəː(r)/ v.i., -rr- sich wiederholen; ‹Krankheit:› wiederkehren; ‹Symptom:› wieder auftreten

recurrence /rɪ'kʌrəns/ n. Wiederholung, die; (of illness, thought, feeling) Wiederkehr, die; (of symptom) Wiederauftreten, das

recurrent /rɪ'kʌrənt/ adj. immer wiederkehrend

recycle /riː'saɪkl/ v.t. wieder verwerten; ∼d paper Recyclingpapier, das

recyclable /riː'saɪkləbl/ adj. recycelbar

recycling /riː'saɪklɪŋ/ n. Recycling, das

red /red/ 1 adj. rot
2 n. (a) Rot, das
(b) (debt) [be] in the ∼: in den roten Zahlen [sein]

red: ∼ 'card n. (Footb.) rote Karte, die; **Red 'Crescent** n. Roter Halbmond; **Red 'Cross** n. Rotes Kreuz; ∼'currant n. [rote] Johannisbeere

redden /'redn/ v.i. ‹Gesicht, Himmel:› sich röten; ‹Person:› rot werden

reddish /'redɪʃ/ adj. rötlich

redecorate /riː'dekəreɪt/ v.t. renovieren; (with wallpaper) neu tapezieren; (with paint) neu streichen

redeem /rɪ'diːm/ v.t. (a) [wieder] einlösen ‹Pfand›; einlösen ‹Gutschein, Coupon›
(b) (save) retten

redemption /rɪ'dempʃn/ n. (from sin) Erlösung, die

redeploy /riːdɪ'plɔɪ/ v.t. woanders einsetzen ‹Arbeitskräfte›

red: ∼'handed adj. catch sb. ∼-handed jmdn. auf frischer Tat ertappen; ∼ 'herring n. (fig.) Ablenkungsmanöver, das; ∼-hot adj. [rot] glühend

redial 1 /riː'daɪəl/ v.t. noch einmal wählen ‹Telefonnummer›
2 /'riːdaɪəl/ n. Wahlwiederholung, die; ∼ button Wahlwiederholungstaste, die

Red 'Indian (Brit. dated) 1 n. Indianer, der/ Indianerin, die
2 adj. Indianer-

redirect /riːdaɪ'rekt/ v.t. nachsenden ‹Post, Brief usw.›; umleiten ‹Verkehr›

rediscover /riːdɪ'skʌvə(r)/ v.t. wieder entdecken

redistribute /riːdɪ'strɪbjuːt/ v.t. umverteilen ‹Besitz, Einkommen›

redistribution /riːdɪstrɪ'bjuːʃn/ n. (of land, wealth) Umverteilung, die

red: ∼-'letter day n. großer Tag; ∼ 'light n. rotes Warnlicht; (traffic light) rote Ampel; **drive through a** ∼ **light** bei Rot über

die Ampel fahren; ∼-'light district n. Strich, der (salopp); ∼ **meat** n. dunkles Fleisch ‹z.B. vom Rind›

redo /riː'duː/ v.t. forms as DO: noch einmal machen ‹Bett, Hausaufgabe›; neu frisieren ‹Haare›

redouble /riː'dʌbl/ v.t. verdoppeln

red 'pepper n. rote Paprika[schote]

redress /rɪ'dres/ 1 n. Entschädigung, die
2 v.t. wieder gutmachen; ∼ **the balance** das Gleichgewicht wiederherstellen

red 'tape n. (fig.) [unnötige] Bürokratie

reduce /rɪ'djuːs/ v.t. (a) senken ‹Preis, Gebühr, Fieber, Aufwendungen, Blutdruck usw.›; reduzieren ‹Geschwindigkeit, Gewicht›; **at** ∼d **prices** zu herabgesetzten Preisen
(b) ∼ **to silence/tears** verstummen lassen/ zum Weinen bringen

reduction /rɪ'dʌkʃn/ n. (in price, costs, speed, etc.) Senkung, die (in Gen.); ∼ **in wages/ weight** Lohnsenkung, die/Gewichtsabnahme, die

redundancy /rɪ'dʌndənsɪ/ n. (Brit.) Arbeitslosigkeit, die; redundancies Pl.; Entlassungen Pl.; **take** or **accept voluntary** ∼: seiner betriebsbedingten Kündigung zustimmen; ∼ **payment** Abfindung, die

redundant /rɪ'dʌndənt/ adj. (Brit.) arbeitslos; **be made** ∼: den Arbeitsplatz verlieren; **make** ∼: entlassen

red 'wine n. Rotwein, der

reed /riːd/ n. Schilf[rohr], das

re-educate /riː'edjʊkeɪt/ v.t. umerziehen

reef /riːf/ n. Riff, das

'reef knot n. Kreuzknoten, der

reek /riːk/ v.i. stinken (of nach)

reel /riːl/ 1 n. ‹Garn-, Angel›rolle, die; ‹Film-, Tonband›spule, die
2 v.i. (a) (be in a whirl) sich drehen
(b) (sway) torkeln

re-establish /riːɪ'stæblɪʃ/ v.t. wiederherstellen

re-examine /riːɪg'zæmɪn/ v.t. (scrutinize) erneut überprüfen

ref /ref/ n. (Sport coll.) Schiri, der (Sportjargon)

ref. abbr. = **reference** Verw.; **your/our ref.** Ihr/unser Zeichen

refashion /riː'fæʃn/ v.t. umgestalten

refectory /rɪ'fektərɪ/ n. Mensa, die

refer /rɪ'fɜː(r)/ 1 v.i., -rr-: (a) ∼ **to** (allude to) sich beziehen auf (+ Akk.) ‹Buch, Person usw.›; (speak of) sprechen von ‹Person, Problem usw.›
(b) ∼ **to** (apply to, relate to) betreffen
(c) ∼ **to** (consult, cite as proof) nachsehen in (+ Dat.)
2 v.t., -rr-: ∼ sb./sth. to sb./sth. jmdn./etw. an jmdn./auf etw. (Akk.) verweisen

referee /refə'riː/ (Sport) 1 n. (umpire) Schiedsrichter, der/-richterin, die; (Boxing) Ringrichter, der
2 v.t. als Schiedsrichter/-richterin leiten

reference /'refrəns/ *n.* (a) (allusion) Hinweis, *der* (to auf + *Akk.*); **make no ~ to sth.** etw. nicht ansprechen
(b) (testimonial) Zeugnis, *das*
reference: ~ book *n.* Nachschlagewerk, *das;* **~ number** *n.* [Kenn]nummer, *die;* **~ point** *n.* Bezugspunkt, *der*
referendum /refə'rendəm/ *n.* Volksentscheid, *der*
refill ① /ri:'fɪl/ *v.t.* nachfüllen; **~ the glasses** nachschenken
② /'ri:fɪl/ *n.* (for ball pen) Ersatzmine, *die*
refine /rɪ'faɪn/ *v.t.* (a) (purify) raffinieren
(b) (make cultured) kultivieren
(c) (improve) verbessern; verfeinern ‹*Stil, Technik*›
refined /rɪ'faɪnd/ *adj.* kultiviert
re'finement *n.* Kultiviertheit, *die;* (improvement) Verbesserung, *die*
refinery /rɪ'faɪnərɪ/ *n.* Raffinerie, *die*
reflate /ri:'fleɪt/ *v.t.* (Econ.) ankurbeln
reflation /ri:'fleɪʃn/ *n.* (Econ.) Reflation, *die*
reflect /rɪ'flekt/ *v.t.* (a) reflektieren
(b) (fig.) widerspiegeln ‹*Ansichten*›
(c) (contemplate) nachdenken über (+ *Akk.*); **~ what/how …:** überlegen, was/wie …
■ **re'flect [up]on** *v.t.* (a) (consider) nachdenken über (+ *Akk.*)
(b) **~ badly [up]on sb./sth.** auf jmdn./etw. ein schlechtes Licht werfen
reflection /rɪ'flekʃn/ *n.* (a) Reflexion, *die;* (by surface of water) Spiegelung, *die*
(b) (image) Spiegelbild, *das*
(c) (consideration) Nachdenken, *das* (**upon** über + *Akk.*); **on ~:** bei weiterem Nachdenken
reflective /rɪ'flektɪv/ *adj.* (a) reflektierend
(b) (thoughtful) nachdenklich
reflector /rɪ'flektə(r)/ *n.* Rückstrahler, *der*
reflex /'ri:fleks/ ① *n.* Reflex, *der*
② *adj.* **~ action** Reflexhandlung, *die*
reflexive /rɪ'fleksɪv/ *adj.* (Ling.) reflexiv
reforestation /ri:fɒrɪ'steɪʃn/ *n.* Wiederaufforstung, *die*
reform /rɪ'fɔ:m/ ① *v.t.* (make better) bessern ‹*Person*›; reformieren ‹*Institution*›
② *n.* Reform, *die* (**in** *Gen.*)
reformation /refə'meɪʃn/ *n.* (of character) Wandlung, *die;* **the R~** (Hist.) die Reformation
re'former *n.* [political] ~: Reformpolitiker, *der/*-politikerin, *die*
refract /rɪ'frækt/ *v.t.* (Phys.) brechen
refrain¹ /rɪ'freɪn/ *n.* Refrain, *der*
refrain² *v.i.* **~ from doing sth.** es unterlassen, etw. zu tun
refresh /rɪ'freʃ/ *v.t.* erfrischen
re'fresher course *n.* Auffrischungskurs, *der*
re'freshing *adj.* erfrischend; wohltuend ‹*Abwechslung*›
re'freshment *n.* Erfrischung, *die*

refrigerate /rɪ'frɪdʒəreɪt/ *v.t.* (a) kühl lagern ‹*Lebensmittel*›
(b) (chill) kühlen; (freeze) einfrieren
refrigeration /rɪfrɪdʒə'reɪʃn/ *n.* kühle Lagerung; (chilling) Kühlung, *die;* (freezing) Einfrieren, *das*
refrigerator /rɪ'frɪdʒəreɪtə(r)/ *n.* Kühlschrank, *der*
refuel /ri:'fju:əl/, (Brit.) -ll- ① *v.t.* auftanken
② *v.i.* [auf]tanken
refuge /'refju:dʒ/ *n.* Zuflucht, *die;* **take ~ in** Schutz *od.* Zuflucht suchen in (+ *Dat.*) (**from** vor + *Dat.*); **women's ~:** Frauenhaus, *das*
refugee /refjʊ'dʒi:/ *n.* Flüchtling, *der*
refu'gee camp *n.* Flüchtlingslager, *das*
refund ① /ri:'fʌnd/ *v.t.* (pay back) zurückzahlen ‹*Geld*›; erstatten ‹*Kosten*›
② /'ri:fʌnd/ *n.* Rückzahlung, *die;* (of expenses) [Rück]erstattung, *die*
refundable /ri:'fʌndəbl/ *adj.* **be ~:** zurückerstattet werden
refurbish /ri:'fɜ:bɪʃ/ *v.t.* renovieren ‹*Haus*›
refurnish /ri:'fɜ:nɪʃ/ *v.t.* neu einrichten
refusal /rɪ'fju:zl/ *n.* Ablehnung, *die;* (after a period of time) Absage, *die;* **~ to do sth.** Weigerung, etw. zu tun
refuse¹ /rɪ'fju:z/ ① *v.t.* ablehnen; verweigern ‹*Zutritt, Einreise, Erlaubnis*›; **~ sb. admittance/entry/permission** jmdm. den Zutritt/die Einreise/die Erlaubnis verweigern; **~ to do sth.** sich weigern, etw. zu tun
② *v.i.* ablehnen; (after request) sich weigern
refuse² /'refju:s/ *n.* Abfall, *der*
refuse /'refju:s/**: ~ collection** *n.* Müllabfuhr, *die;* **~ collector** *n.* Müllwerker, *der;* **~ disposal** *n.* Abfallbeseitigung, *die*
refute /rɪ'fju:t/ *v.t.* widerlegen
regain /rɪ'geɪn/ *v.t.* zurückgewinnen ‹*Zuversicht, Vertrauen, Augenlicht*›; **~ one's strength** wieder zu Kräften kommen
regal /'ri:gl/ *adj.* majestätisch
regalia /rɪ'geɪlɪə/ *n. pl.* (of royalty) Krönungsinsignien *Pl.*
regard /rɪ'gɑ:d/ ① *v.t.* (a) (look at) betrachten
(b) (give heed to) beachten
(c) (fig.: look upon, contemplate) betrachten; **~ sb. as a friend/fool/genius** jmdn. als Freund betrachten/für einen Dummkopf/ein Genie halten; **be ~ed as** gelten als
(d) (concern, have relation to) betreffen; **as ~s sb./sth., ~ing sb./sth.** was jmdn./etw. angeht *od.* betrifft
② *n.* (a) (attention) **pay** *or* **have ~ to sb./sth.** jmdm./etw. Beachtung schenken; **without ~ to** ohne Rücksicht auf (+ *Akk.*)
(b) (esteem) Achtung, *die;* **hold sb./sth. in high ~:** jmdn./etw. sehr schätzen
(c) in *pl.* Grüße *Pl.;* **give her my ~s** grüße sie von mir; **with kind[est] ~s** mit herzlich[st]en Grüßen

r

re'gardless *adj.* ohne Rücksicht (**of** auf + *Akk.*)

regatta /rɪ'gætə/ *n.* Regatta, *die*

regenerate /rɪ'dʒenəreɪt/ *v.t.* erneuern

reggae /'regeɪ/ *n.* Reggae, *der*

regime, régime /reɪ'ʒiːm/ *n.* [Regierungs]system, *das*

regiment /'redʒɪmənt/ *n.* Regiment, *das*

regimental /redʒɪ'mentl/ *adj.* Regiments-

region /'riːdʒn/ *n.* (a) (area) Gebiet, *das* (b) (administrative division) Bezirk, *der;* **in the ~ of** (fig.) ungefähr

regional /'riːdʒənl/ *adj.* regional

regionalism /'riːdʒənəlɪzm/ *n.* (Polit., Ling.) Regionalismus, *der*

regionalize /'riːdʒənəlaɪz/ *v.t.* regionalisieren

register /'redʒɪstə(r)/ ☐ *n.* Register, *das;* (at school) Klassenbuch, *das* ② *v.t.* (a) (enter) registrieren; (cause to be entered) registrieren lassen; anmelden ⟨*Auto, Patent*⟩; (at airport) einchecken ⟨*Gepäck*⟩; *abs.* (at hotel) sich ins Fremdenbuch eintragen; **~ with the police** sich polizeilich anmelden (b) (enrol) anmelden; (Univ.) sich einschreiben (c) zum Ausdruck bringen ⟨*Überraschung*⟩; **~ a protest** Protest anmelden

registered /'redʒɪstəd/ *adj.* eingetragen ⟨*Firma*⟩; eingeschrieben ⟨*Student, Brief*⟩; **~ trade mark** eingetragenes Warenzeichen; **by ~ post** per Einschreiben

registrar /'redʒɪstrɑː(r)/ *n.* Standesbeamte, *der*/-beamtin, *die*

registration /redʒɪ'streɪʃn/ *n.* Registrierung, *die;* (enrolment) Anmeldung, *die;* (of students) Einschreibung, *die*

registration: ~ document *n.* (Brit.) Kraftfahrzeugbrief, *der;* **~ form** *n.* Anmeldeformular, *das;* **~ number** *n.* amtliches Kennzeichen; **~ plate** *n.* (Motor Veh.) Nummernschild, *das*

registry /'redʒɪstrɪ/ *n.* **~ [office]** Standesamt, *das*

regret /rɪ'gret/ ☐ *v.t.,* -tt- bedauern; **I ~ to say that ...:** ich muss leider sagen, dass ... ② *n.* Bedauern, *das;* **have no ~s** nichts bereuen

regretfully /rɪ'gretfəlɪ/ *adv.* mit Bedauern

regrettable /rɪ'gretəbl/ *adj.* bedauerlich

regrettably /rɪ'gretəblɪ/ *adv.* bedauerlicherweise

regroup /riː'gruːp/ ☐ *v.t.* umgruppieren ② *v.i.* (a) (form new group) sich neu gruppieren (b) (Mil.) sich neu formieren

regular /'regjʊlə(r)/ ☐ *adj.* regelmäßig; geregelt ⟨*Arbeit*⟩; fest ⟨*Anstellung*⟩; **~ customer** Stammkunde, *der*/-kundin, *die;* **~ army** reguläre Armee ② *n.* (coll.: ~ customer) Stammkunde, *der*/-kundin, *die;* (in pub) Stammgast, *der*

regularity /regjʊ'lærɪtɪ/ *n.* Regelmäßigkeit, *die*

'regularly *adv.* regelmäßig

regulate /'regjʊleɪt/ *v.t.* (control) regeln; (restrict) begrenzen; (adjust) regulieren

regulation /regjʊ'leɪʃn/ *n.* (a) ▶ REGULATE: Regelung, *die;* Begrenzung, *die;* Regulierung, *die* (b) (rule) Vorschrift, *die*

rehabilitate /riːhə'bɪlɪteɪt/ *v.t.* rehabilitieren; **~ [back into society]** wieder [in die Gesellschaft] eingliedern

rehabilitation /riːhəbɪlɪ'teɪʃn/ *n.* **~ [in society]** Wiedereingliederung, *die* [in die Gesellschaft]

rehash ☐ /riː'hæʃ/ *v.t.* aufwärmen ② /'riːhæʃ/ *n.* Aufguss, *der*

rehearsal /rɪ'hɜːsl/ *n.* Probe, *die*

rehearse /rɪ'hɜːs/ *v.t.* proben

reheat /riː'hiːt/ *v.t.* wieder erwärmen; aufwärmen ⟨*Essen*⟩

rehouse /riː'haʊz/ *v.t.* umquartieren

reign /reɪn/ ☐ *n.* Herrschaft, *die* ② *v.i.* herrschen (**over** über + *Akk.*)

reimburse /riːɪm'bɜːs/ *v.t.* [zurück]erstatten ⟨[*Un*]*kosten, Spesen*⟩; entschädigen ⟨*Person*⟩

rein /reɪn/ *n.* Zügel, *der*

reincarnation /riːɪnkɑː'neɪʃn/ *n.* (Relig.) Reinkarnation, *die*

reindeer /'reɪndɪə(r)/ *n., pl. same* Ren[tier], *das*

reinforce /riːɪn'fɔːs/ *v.t.* verstärken; **~d concrete** Stahlbeton, *der*

rein'forcement *n.* Verstärkung, *die;* **~[s]** (additional men etc.) Verstärkung, *die*

reinstate /riːɪn'steɪt/ *v.t.* (in job) wieder einstellen

reintegrate /riː'ɪntɪgreɪt/ ☐ *v.t.* wieder eingliedern (**into** in + *Akk.*) ② *v. refl.* sich wieder eingliedern (**into** in + *Akk.*)

reintegration /riːɪntɪ'greɪʃn/ *n.* Wiedereingliederung, *die* (**into** in + *Akk.*)

reinvigorate /riːɪn'vɪgəreɪt/ *v.t.* neu beleben; **feel ~d** sich gestärkt fühlen

reissue /riː'ɪʃuː/ *v.t.* neu herausbringen

reiterate /riː'ɪtəreɪt/ *v.t.* wiederholen

reject ☐ /rɪ'dʒekt/ *v.t.* ablehnen; zurückweisen ⟨*Bitte, Annäherungsversuch*⟩ ② /'riːdʒekt/ (thing) Ausschuss, *der*

rejection /rɪ'dʒekʃn/ *n.* Ablehnung, *die*/ Zurückweisung, *die*

re'jection slip *n.* Absage, *die*

rejoice /rɪ'dʒɔɪs/ *v.i.* sich freuen (**over, at** über + *Akk.*)

rejoin¹ /rɪ'dʒɔɪn/ *v.t.* (reply) erwidern (**to** auf + *Akk.*)

rejoin² /riː'dʒɔɪn/ *v.t.* wieder eintreten in (+ *Akk.*) ⟨*Partei, Verein*⟩

rejoinder /rɪ'dʒɔɪndə(r)/ *n.* Erwiderung, *die* (**to** auf + *Akk.*)

rejuvenate /rɪ'dʒuːvəneɪt/ *v.t.* verjüngen

rekindle /riːˈkɪndl/ *v.t.* wieder anfachen; wieder aufleben lassen ‹*Verlangen, Hoffnungen*›

relapse /rɪˈlæps/ ☐1 *v.i.* ‹*Kranker:*› einen Rückfall bekommen
☐2 *n.* Rückfall, *der*

relate /rɪˈleɪt/ ☐1 *v.t.* (a) erzählen ‹*Geschichte*›; erzählen von ‹*Abenteuer*›
(b) (bring into relation) in Zusammenhang bringen (**to, with** mit)
☐2 *v.i.* (a) ~ **to** (have reference to) in Zusammenhang stehen mit; betreffen ‹*Person*›
(b) ~ **to** (feel involved with) eine Beziehung haben zu

reˈlated *adj.* verwandt (**to** mit)

relation /rɪˈleɪʃn/ *n.* (a) (connection) Beziehung, *die*, Zusammenhang, *der* (**of ... and** zwischen ... und); **in** *or* **with** ~ **to** in Bezug auf (+ *Akk.*)
(b) *in pl.* (dealings) Verhältnis, *das* (**with** zu)
(c) (relative) Verwandte, *der/die*

reˈlationship *n.* (a) (mutual tie) Beziehung, *die* (**with** zu)
(b) (kinship) Verwandtschaftsverhältnis, *das*
(c) (connection) Beziehung, *die;* (between cause and effect) Zusammenhang, *der*
(d) (sexual) Verhältnis, *das*

relative /ˈrelətɪv/ ☐1 *n.* Verwandte, *der/die*
☐2 *adj.* relativ; Relativ‹*satz, -pronomen*›

ˈrelatively *adv.* relativ; verhältnismäßig

relative ˈpronoun *n.* (Ling.) Relativpronomen, *das*

relax /rɪˈlæks/ ☐1 *v.t.* (a) entspannen ‹*Muskel, Körper[teil]*›; lockern ‹*Griff*›
(b) (make less strict) lockern ‹*Gesetz, Disziplin*›
☐2 *v.i.* sich entspannen

relaxation /riːlækˈseɪʃn/ *n.* Entspannung, *die;* **for** ~: zur Entspannung

relaxed /rɪˈlækst/ *adj.* entspannt, gelöst ‹*Atmosphäre, Person*›

reˈlaxing *adj.* entspannend

relay ☐1 /ˈriːleɪ/ *n.* (a) (race) Staffel, *die*
(b) (gang) Schicht, *die;* **work in** ~**s** schichtweise arbeiten
(c) (Electr.) Relais, *das*
☐2 /riːˈleɪ/ *v.t.* (a) weiterleiten
(b) (Radio, Telev.) übertragen

ˈrelay race *n.* Staffellauf, *der;* (Swimming) Staffelschwimmen, *das*

release /rɪˈliːs/ ☐1 *v.t.* (a) (free) freilassen ‹*Tier, Häftling, Sklaven*›; (from jail) entlassen (**from** aus)
(b) (let go) loslassen; lösen ‹*Handbremse*›
(c) (make known) veröffentlichen ‹*Erklärung, Nachricht*›; (issue) herausbringen ‹*Film, Schallplatte*›
☐2 *n.* (a) ▶ 1A: Freilassung, *die;* Entlassung, *die*
(b) (of published item) Veröffentlichung, *die*
(c) (handle, lever, button) Auslöser, *der*

relegate /ˈrelɪgeɪt/ *v.t.* (a) ~ **sb. to the position of ...:** jmdn. zu ... degradieren

(b) (Sport) absteigen lassen; **be** ~**d** absteigen (**to** in + *Akk.*)

relegation /relɪˈgeɪʃn/ *n.* (Sport) Abstieg, *der*

relent /rɪˈlent/ *v.i.* nachgeben

reˈlentless *adj.*, **reˈlentlessly** *adv.* unerbittlich

relevance /ˈrelɪvəns/ *n.* Relevanz, *die* (**to** für)

relevant /ˈrelɪvənt/ *adj.* relevant (**to** für); wichtig ‹*Information*›

reliability /rɪlaɪəˈbɪlɪtɪ/ *n.* Zuverlässigkeit, *die*

reliable /rɪˈlaɪəbl/ *adj.*, **reliably** /rɪˈlaɪəblɪ/ *adv.* zuverlässig

reliance /rɪˈlaɪəns/ *n.* Abhängigkeit, *die* (**on** von)

reliant /rɪˈlaɪənt/ *adj.* **be** ~ **on sb./sth.** auf jmdn./etw. angewiesen sein

relief¹ /rɪˈliːf/ *n.* (a) Erleichterung, *die;* **give** [**sb.**] ~ [**from pain**] [jmdm.] [Schmerz]linderung verschaffen; **what a** ~**!, that's a** ~**!** da bin ich aber erleichtert!
(b) (assistance) Hilfe, *die*

relief² *n.* (Art) Relief, *das*

relief: ~ **bus** *n.* Entlastungsbus, *der;* (as replacement) Ersatzbus, *der;* ~ **map** *n.* Reliefkarte, *die;* ~ **road** *n.* Entlastungsstraße, *die;* ~ **worker** *n.* Helfer, *der*

relieve /rɪˈliːv/ *v.t.* (a) erleichtern; unterbrechen ‹*Eintönigkeit*›; abbauen ‹*Anspannung*›; stillen ‹*Schmerzen*›; **I am** *or* **feel** ~**d to hear that ...:** es erleichtert mich zu hören, dass ...
(b) ablösen ‹*Wache, Truppen*›

religion /rɪˈlɪdʒn/ *n.* Religion, *die*

religious /rɪˈlɪdʒəs/ *adj.* religiös; Religions‹*freiheit, -unterricht*›

reˈligiously *adv.* (conscientiously) gewissenhaft

relinquish /rɪˈlɪŋkwɪʃ/ *v.t.* (a) (give up) aufgeben
(b) ~ **one's hold** *or* **grip on sb./sth.** jmdn./ etw. loslassen

relish /ˈrelɪʃ/ ☐1 *n.* (a) (liking) Vorliebe, *die;* **do sth. with** [**great**] ~: etw. mit [großem] Genuss tun
(b) (condiment) Relish, *das*
☐2 *v.t.* genießen

relive /riːˈlɪv/ *v.t.* noch einmal durchleben

reload /riːˈləʊd/ *v.t.* nachladen ‹*Schusswaffe*›

relocate /riːləˈkeɪt/ ☐1 *v.t.* verlegen ‹*Fabrik, Büro*›; versetzen ‹*Angestellten*›
☐2 *v.i.* (settle) sich niederlassen

relocation /riːləˈkeɪʃn/ *n.* (of factory, office) Verlegung, *die;* (of employee) Versetzung, *die;* ~ **expenses** Umzugskosten *Pl.*

reluctance /rɪˈlʌktəns/ *n.* Widerwille, *der;* **have a** [**great**] ~ **to do sth.** etw. nur mit Widerwillen tun

r

reluctant /rɪˈlʌktənt/ adj. unwillig; **be ~ to do sth.** etw. nur ungern tun

re'luctantly adv. nur ungern

rely /rɪˈlaɪ/ v.i. (have trust) sich verlassen/(be dependent) angewiesen sein ([up]on auf + Akk.)

remain /rɪˈmeɪn/ v.i. (a) (be left over) übrigbleiben

(b) (stay) bleiben; **~ behind** noch dableiben

(c) (continue to be) bleiben; **it ~s to be seen** es wird sich zeigen

remainder /rɪˈmeɪndə(r)/ n. Rest, der

re'maining adj. restlich

re'mains n. pl. (a) Reste Pl.

(b) (human) sterbliche [Über]reste Pl. (verhüll.)

remand /rɪˈmɑːnd/ **1** v.t. **~ sb. [in custody]** jmdn. in Untersuchungshaft behalten

2 n. **on ~:** in Untersuchungshaft

remark /rɪˈmɑːk/ **1** v.t. bemerken (to gegenüber)

2 v.i. eine Bemerkung machen ([up]on zu, über + Akk.)

3 n. Bemerkung, die (on über + Akk.)

remarkable /rɪˈmɑːkəbl/ adj. (a) (notable) bemerkenswert

(b) (extraordinary) außergewöhnlich

remarkably /rɪˈmɑːkəblɪ/ adv. (a) (notably) bemerkenswert

(b) (exceptionally) außergewöhnlich

remarry /riːˈmærɪ/ v.i. & t. wieder heiraten

remedy /ˈremɪdɪ/ **1** n. [Heil]mittel, das (for gegen)

2 v.t. beheben ⟨Problem⟩; retten ⟨Situation⟩

remember /rɪˈmembə(r)/ v.t. (a) sich erinnern an (+ Akk.); **I ~ed to bring the book** ich habe daran gedacht, das Buch mitzubringen; **an evening to ~:** ein unvergesslicher Abend

(b) (convey greetings) **~ me to them** grüße sie von mir

remembrance /rɪˈmembrəns/ n. Gedenken, das; **in ~ of sb.** zu jmds. Gedächtnis

Remembrance Day, Remembrance Sunday ns. (Brit.) ≈ Volkstrauertag, der

remind /rɪˈmaɪnd/ v.t. erinnern (of an + Akk.); **~ sb. to do sth.** jmdn. daran erinnern, etw. zu tun; **that ~s me, ...:** dabei fällt mir ein, ...

re'minder n. Erinnerung, die (of an + Akk.); (letter) Mahnung, die; Mahnbrief, der

reminisce /remɪˈnɪs/ v.i. sich in Erinnerungen (Dat.) ergehen (about an + Akk.)

reminiscences /remɪˈnɪsənsɪz/ n. pl. Erinnerungen Pl.; (memoirs) [Lebens]erinnerungen Pl.

reminiscent /remɪˈnɪsənt/ adj. **be ~ of sth.** an etw. (Akk.) erinnern

remiss /rɪˈmɪs/ adj. nachlässig (of von)

remission /rɪˈmɪʃn/ n. (a) (of debt, punishment) Erlass, der

(b) (of prison sentence) Straferlass, der

remit /rɪˈmɪt/ v.t., **-tt-** (send) überweisen ⟨Geld⟩

remittance /rɪˈmɪtəns/ n. Überweisung, die

remnant /ˈremnənt/ n. Rest, der

remonstrate /ˈremənstreɪt/ v.i. protestieren (against gegen); **~ with sb.** jmdm. Vorhaltungen machen (about, on wegen)

remorse /rɪˈmɔːs/ n. Reue, die (for, about über + Akk.)

re'morseful /rɪˈmɔːsfl/ adj. reumütig

re'morseless adj. unerbittlich

remote /rɪˈməʊt/ adj., **~r** /rɪˈməʊtə(r)/, **~st** /rɪˈməʊtɪst/ (a) fern ⟨Vergangenheit, Zukunft, Zeit⟩; abgelegen ⟨Ort, Gebiet⟩; **~ from** weit entfernt von

(b) (slight) gering ⟨Chance⟩

remote: ~ con'trol n. (of vehicle) Fernlenkung, die; (for TV set) Fernbedienung, die; **~-con'trol[led]** adj. ferngelenkt; fernbedient ⟨Anlage⟩

re'motely adv. entfernt ⟨verwandt⟩; **they are not ~ alike** sie haben nicht die entfernteste Ähnlichkeit miteinander

removable /rɪˈmuːvəbl/ adj. abnehmbar; entfernbar ⟨Trennwand⟩; herausnehmbar ⟨Futter⟩

removal /rɪˈmuːvl/ n. (a) Entfernung, die; (of obstacle, problem) Beseitigung, die

(b) (transfer of furniture) Umzug, der

removal: ~ expenses n. pl. Umzugskosten Pl.; **~ firm** n. Spedition, die; **~ man** n. Möbelpacker, der; **~ van** n. Möbelwagen, der

remove /rɪˈmuːv/ v.t. entfernen; beseitigen ⟨Spur, Hindernis⟩; (take off) abnehmen; ausziehen ⟨Kleidungsstück⟩; **~ a book from the shelf** ein Buch vom Regal nehmen

re'mover n. (a) (of paint/varnish/hair/rust) Farb-/Lack-/Haar-/Rostentferner, der

(b) (man) Möbelpacker, der; [firm of] **~s** Spedition[sfirma], die

remunerate /rɪˈmjuːnəreɪt/ v.t. bezahlen

remuneration /rɪmjuːnəˈreɪʃn/ n. Bezahlung, die

Renaissance /rəˈneɪsəns, rɪˈneɪsəns/ n. (Hist.) Renaissance, die

rename /riːˈneɪm/ v.t. umbenennen

render /ˈrendə(r)/ v.t. (a) (make) machen

(b) erweisen ⟨Dienst⟩

(c) (translate) übersetzen (by mit)

'rendering n. (translation) Übersetzung, die

rendezvous /ˈrɒndeɪvuː/ n., pl. same /ˈrɒndeɪvuːz/ (a) (meeting place) Treffpunkt, der

(b) (meeting) Verabredung, die

renegade /ˈrenɪgeɪd/ **1** n. Abtrünnige, der/die

2 adj. abtrünnig

renegotiate /riːnɪˈgəʊʃɪeɪt/ v.t. neu aushandeln

renew /rɪ'nju:/ *v.t.* erneuern; fortsetzen ⟨*Angriff, Bemühungen*⟩; (extend) erneuern ⟨*Vertrag, Ausweis usw.*⟩; **~ a library book** ⟨*Bibliothekar/Benutzer:*⟩ ein Buch [aus der Bücherei] verlängern/verlängern lassen

re'newable /rɪ'nju:əbl/ *adj.* regenerationsfähig ⟨*Energiequelle*⟩; verlängerbar ⟨*Vertrag, Genehmigung, Ausweis*⟩

renewal /rɪ'nju:əl/ *n.* Erneuerung, *die*

renounce /rɪ'naʊns/ *v.t.* verzichten auf (+ *Akk.*); verstoßen ⟨*Person*⟩; **~ the devil/ one's faith** dem Teufel/seinem Glauben abschwören

renovate /'renəveɪt/ *v.t.* renovieren ⟨*Gebäude*⟩; restaurieren ⟨*Möbel usw.*⟩

renovation /renə'veɪʃn/ *n.* ▶ RENOVATE: Renovierung, *die;* Restaurierung, *die*

renown /rɪ'naʊn/ *n.* Renommee, *das*

renowned /rɪ'naʊnd/ *adj.* berühmt (**for** wegen, für)

rent /rent/ ①*n.* (for house etc.) Miete, *die;* (for land) Pacht, *die*
② *v.t.* **(a)** (use) mieten ⟨*Haus, Wohnung usw.*⟩; pachten ⟨*Land*⟩; mieten ⟨*Auto*⟩
(b) (let) vermieten ⟨*Haus, Auto usw.*⟩ (**to** *Dat.*, an + *Akk.*); verpachten ⟨*Land*⟩ (**to** *Dat.*, an + *Akk.*)

▪ **rent 'out** *v.t.* ▶ RENT 2B

rental /'rentl/ *n.* Miete, *die*

rent-: ~ boy *n.* (coll.) Strichjunge, *der* (salopp); **~ rebate** *n.* Mietermäßigung, *die;* **~ tribunal** *n.* Mietgericht, *das*

renunciation /rɪnʌnsɪ'eɪʃn/ *n.*
▶ RENOUNCE: Verzicht, *der;* Verstoßung, *die*

reopen /ri:'əʊpn/ ①*v.t.* wieder öffnen; wieder aufmachen; wieder eröffnen ⟨*Geschäft, Lokal usw.*⟩; wieder aufnehmen ⟨*Diskussion, Verhandlung*⟩
② *v.i.* ⟨*Geschäft, Lokal usw.:*⟩ wieder öffnen

reorder /ri:'ɔ:də(r)/ *v.t.* **(a)** (Commerc.) nachbestellen ⟨*Ware*⟩
(b) (rearrange) umordnen

reorganization /ri:ɔ:gənaɪ'zeɪʃn/ *n.* Umorganisation, *die;* (of time, work) Neueinteilung, *die*

reorganize /ri:'ɔ:gənaɪz/ *v.t.* umorganisieren; neu einteilen ⟨*Zeit, Arbeit*⟩

rep /rep/ *n.* (coll.: representative) Vertreter, *der/* Vertreterin, *die*

repaid ▶ REPAY

repair /rɪ'peə(r)/ ①*v.t.* (mend) reparieren; ausbessern ⟨*Kleidung, Straße*⟩
② *n.* Reparatur, *die;* **be in good/bad ~:** in gutem/schlechtem Zustand sein

repair: ~ man *n.* Mechaniker, *der;* (in house) Handwerker, *der;* **~ shop** *n.* Reparaturwerkstatt, *die*

repaper /ri:'peɪpə(r)/ *v.t.* neu tapezieren

repatriate /ri:'pætrɪeɪt/ *v.t.* repatriieren

repatriation /ri:pætrɪ'eɪʃn/ *n.* Repatriierung, *die*

repay /ri:'peɪ/ *v.t.*, **repaid** /ri:'peɪd/

zurückzahlen ⟨*Schulden usw.*⟩; erwidern ⟨*Besuch, Gruß, Freundlichkeit*⟩; **~ sb. for** sth. jmdm. etw. vergelten

re'payment *n.* Rückzahlung, *die*

re'payment mortgage *n.* Tilgungshypothek, *die*

repeal /rɪ'pi:l/ ①*v.t.* aufheben ⟨*Gesetz, Erlass usw.*⟩
② *n.* Aufhebung, *die*

repeat /rɪ'pi:t/ ①*n.* Wiederholung, *die*
② *v.t.* wiederholen; **please ~ after me:** ...: sprich/sprecht/sprechen Sie mir bitte nach: ...

re'peated *adj.* wiederholt; (several) mehrere; **make ~ efforts to** ...: wiederholt *od.* mehrfach versuchen, ...zu...

re'peatedly *adv.* mehrmals

repel /rɪ'pel/ *v.t.*, **-ll-:** **(a)** (drive back) abwehren
(b) (be repulsive to) abstoßen

repellent /rɪ'pelənt/ ①*adj.* abstoßend
② *n.* [insect] **~:** Insektenschutzmittel, *das*

repent /rɪ'pent/ *v.i.* bereuen (**of** *Akk.*)

repentance /rɪ'pentəns/ *n.* Reue, *die*

repentant /rɪ'pentənt/ *adj.* reuig

repercussion /ri:pə'kʌʃn/ *n., usu. in pl.* Auswirkung, *die* ([up]on auf + *Akk.*)

repertoire /'repətwɑ:(r)/ *n.* Repertoire, *das*

repertory /'repətərɪ/ *n.* (Theatre) Repertoiretheater, *das*

'repertory company *n.* Repertoiretheater, *das*

repetition /repɪ'tɪʃn/ *n.* Wiederholung, *die*

repetitious /repɪ'tɪʃəs/ *adj.* sich immer wiederholend *attr.*

repetitive /rɪ'petɪtɪv/ *adj.* eintönig

repetitive 'strain injury *n.* chronisches Überlastungssyndrom

rephrase /ri:'freɪz/ *v.t.* umformulieren; **I'll ~ that** ich will es anders ausdrücken

replace /rɪ'pleɪs/ *v.t.* **(a)** (vertically) zurückstellen; (horizontally) zurücklegen
(b) (take place of) ersetzen; **~ A with** *or* **by B** A durch B ersetzen
(c) (exchange) austauschen, auswechseln ⟨*Maschinen[teile] usw.*⟩

re'placement *n.* **(a)** ▶ REPLACE A: Zurückstellen, *das;* Zurücklegen, *das*
(b) (provision of substitute for) Ersatz, *der; attrib.* Ersatz-
(c) (substitute) Ersatz, *der;* **~ [part]** Ersatzteil, *das*

replay ① /ri:'pleɪ/ *v.t.* wiederholen ⟨*Spiel*⟩; nochmals abspielen ⟨*Tonband usw.*⟩
② /'ri:pleɪ/ *n.* Wiederholung, *die;* (match) Wiederholungsspiel, *das*

replenish /rɪ'plenɪʃ/ *v.t.* auffüllen

replica /'replɪkə/ *n.* Nachbildung, *die*

reply /rɪ'plaɪ/ ①*v.i.* **~ [to sb./sth.]** [jmdm./ auf etw. (*Akk.*)] antworten
② *v.t.* **~ that** ...: antworten, dass ...
③ *n.* Antwort, *die* (**to** auf + *Akk.*)

r

re'ply-paid *adj.* ~-paid telegram
RP-Telegramm, *das;* ~-paid envelope
Freiumschlag, *der*

repopulate /riː'pɒpjʊleɪt/ *v.t.* neu
besiedeln

report /rɪ'pɔːt/ **1** *v.t.* (a) (relate) berichten/
(in writing) einen Bericht schreiben über
(+ *Akk.*); (state formally also) melden
(b) (name to authorities) melden (to *Dat.*); (for
prosecution) anzeigen (to bei)
2 *v.i.* (a) Bericht erstatten (on über + *Akk.*);
berichten (on über + *Akk.*)
(b) (present oneself) sich melden (to bei)
3 *n.* (a) (account) Bericht, *der* (on, about
über + *Akk.*)
(b) (Sch.) Zeugnis, *das*
(c) (of gun) Knall, *der*

reportedly /rɪ'pɔːtɪdlɪ/ *adv.* wie verlautet

reported 'speech *n.* indirekte Rede

re'porter *n.* Reporter, *der*/Reporterin, *die*

repossess /riːpə'zes/ *v.t.* wieder in Besitz
nehmen

reprehensible /reprɪ'hensɪbl/ *adj.*
tadelnswert

represent /reprɪ'zent/ *v.t.* (a) darstellen
(as als)
(b) (act for) vertreten

representation /reprɪzen'teɪʃn/ *n.* (a)
(depicting, image) Darstellung, *die*
(b) (acting for sb.) Vertretung, *die*
(c) make ~s to sb. bei jmdm. Protest
einlegen

representative /reprɪ'zentətɪv/ **1** *n.* (a)
(Commerc.) Vertreter, *der*/Vertreterin, *die*
(b) R~ (Amer. Polit.) Abgeordnete, *der/die*
2 *adj.* (typical) repräsentativ (of für)

repress /rɪ'pres/ *v.t.* (a) unterdrücken
⟨Aufruhr, Gefühle, Lachen usw.⟩
(b) (Psych.) verdrängen ⟨Gefühle⟩ (from aus)

repressed /rɪ'prest/ *adj.* unterdrückt;
(Psych.) verdrängt

repression /rɪ'preʃn/ *n.* Unterdrückung,
die

repressive /rɪ'presɪv/ *adj.* repressiv

reprieve /rɪ'priːv/ **1** *v.t.* ~ sb. (postpone
execution) jmdm. Strafaufschub gewähren;
(remit execution) jmdm. begnadigen
2 *n.* Strafaufschub, *der* (of für)/
Begnadigung, *die;* (fig.) Gnadenfrist, *die*

reprimand /'reprɪmɑːnd/ **1** *n.* Tadel, *der*
2 *v.t.* tadeln

reprint 1 /riː'prɪnt/ *v.t.* wieder abdrucken
2 /'riːprɪnt/ *n.* Nachdruck, *der*

reprisal /rɪ'praɪzl/ *n.* Vergeltungsakt, *der*
(for gegen)

reproach /rɪ'prəʊtʃ/ **1** *v.t.* ~ sb. jmdm.
Vorwürfe machen
2 *n.* Vorwurf, *der*

reproachful /rɪ'prəʊtʃfl/ *adv.* vorwurfsvoll

reproduce /riːprə'djuːs/ **1** *v.t.*
wiedergeben
2 *v.i.* (multiply) sich fortpflanzen

reproduction /riːprə'dʌkʃn/ *n.* (a)
Wiedergabe, *die*
(b) (producing offspring) Fortpflanzung, *die*
(c) (copy) Reproduktion, *die*

reproductive /riːprə'dʌktɪv/ *adj.*
Fortpflanzungs-

reprove /rɪ'pruːv/ *v.t.* tadeln

reptile /'reptaɪl/ *n.* Reptil, *das*

republic /rɪ'pʌblɪk/ *n.* Republik, *die*

republican /rɪ'pʌblɪkən/ **1** *adj.*
republikanisch
2 *n.* R~ (Amer. Polit.) Republikaner, *der*/
Republikanerin, *die*

repudiate /rɪ'pjuːdɪeɪt/ *v.t.* zurückweisen

repugnance /rɪ'pʌɡnəns/ *n.* Abscheu, *der*
(to[wards] vor + *Dat.*)

repugnant /rɪ'pʌɡnənt/ *adj.* widerlich (to
Dat.)

repulse /rɪ'pʌls/ *v.t.* abwehren

repulsion /rɪ'pʌlʃn/ *n.* (disgust) Widerwille,
der (towards gegen)

repulsive /rɪ'pʌlsɪv/ *adj.* abstoßend

reputable /'repjʊtəbl/ *adj.* angesehen
⟨Person, Beruf, Zeitung usw.⟩; anständig
⟨Verhalten⟩; seriös ⟨Firma⟩

reputably /'repjʊtəblɪ/ *adv.* anständig

reputation /repjʊ'teɪʃn/ *n.* (a) Ruf, *der;*
have a ~ for *or* of doing/being sth. in dem
Ruf stehen, etw. zu tun/sein
(b) (good name) Name, *der*

repute /rɪ'pjuːt/ **1** *v.t. in pass.* be ~d [to
be] sth. als etw. gelten; she is ~d to have/
make …: man sagt, dass sie … hat/macht
2 *n.* Ruf, *der*

reputed /rɪ'pjuːtɪd/ *adj.,* **re'putedly** *adv.*
angeblich

request /rɪ'kwest/ **1** *v.t.* bitten; ~ sth. of
or from sb. jmdn. um etw. bitten
2 *n.* Bitte, *die* (for um); at sb.'s ~: auf jmds.
Bitte (*Akk.*) [hin]

re'quest stop *n.* (Brit.) Bedarfshaltestelle,
die

require /rɪ'kwaɪə(r)/ *v.t.* (a) (need) brauchen
(b) (order, demand) verlangen (of von); be ~d
to do sth. etw. tun müssen

re'quirement *n.* (a) (need) Bedarf, *der*
(b) (condition) Erfordernis, *das*

requisite /'rekwɪzɪt/ **1** *adj.* notwendig (to,
for für)
2 *n. in pl.* toilet/travel ~s Toiletten-/
Reiseartikel *Pl.*

requisition /rekwɪ'zɪʃn/ **1** *n.* (order for sth.)
Anforderung, *die* (for *Gen.*)
2 *v.t.* anfordern

rescind /rɪ'sɪnd/ *v.t.* für ungültig erklären

rescue /'reskjuː/ **1** *v.t.* retten (from aus)
2 *n.* Rettung, *die; attrib.* Rettungs⟨dienst,
-mannschaft⟩; go/come to the/sb.'s ~: jmdm.
zu Hilfe kommen

rescuer /'reskjuːə(r)/ *n.* Retter, *der*/
Retterin, *die*

'**rescue worker** n. [Einsatz]helfer, der/ -helferin, die

research /rɪ'sɜːtʃ, 'riːsɜːtʃ/ ❶ n. Forschung, die (**into, on** über + Akk.)
❷ v.i. forschen; ∼ **into** sth. etw. erforschen

research as'sistant n. wissenschaftlicher Assistent/ wissenschaftliche Assistentin

researcher /-'--, '---/ n. Forscher, der/ Forscherin, die

research: ∼ **student** n. ≈ Doktorand, der/Doktorandin, die; ∼ **work** n. Recherchen Pl.; (medical, scientific) Forschungsarbeit, die; ∼ **worker** n. ≈ Rechercheur, der/Recherchêurin, die; (medical, scientific) Forscher, der/Forscherin, die

resell /riː'sel/ v.t., resold /riː'səʊld/ weiterverkaufen (**to** an + Akk.)

resemblance /rɪ'zembləns/ n. Ähnlichkeit, die (**to** mit)

resemble /rɪ'zembl/ v.t. ähneln, gleichen (+ Dat.)

resent /rɪ'zent/ v.t. übel nehmen

resentful /rɪ'zentfl/ adj. übelnehmerisch, nachtragend ⟨Person, Art⟩; **be** ∼ **of** or **feel** ∼ **about** sth. etw. übel nehmen

re'sentment n. Groll, der (geh.); **feel** ∼ **towards** or **against** sb. einen Groll auf jmdn. haben

reservation /rezə'veɪʃn/ n. (a) Reservierung, die; **have a** ∼ [**for a room**] ein Zimmer reserviert haben
(b) (doubt) Vorbehalt, der (**about** gegen); Bedenken (**about** bezüglich + Gen.); **without** ∼: ohne Vorbehalt

reserve /rɪ'zɜːv/ ❶ v.t. reservieren lassen ⟨Zimmer, Tisch, Platz⟩; (set aside) reservieren; ∼ **the right to do** sth. sich (Dat.) [das Recht] vorbehalten, etw. zu tun
❷ n. (a) (extra amount) Reserve, die (**of** an + Dat.) **have/hold** or **keep** sth. **in** ∼: etw. in Reserve haben/halten
(b) (place set apart) Reservat, das
(c) (Sport) Reservespieler, der/-spielerin, die; **the R**∼**s** die Reserve
(d) (reticence) Zurückhaltung, die

reserved /rɪ'zɜːvd/ adj. (reticent) reserviert

reservoir /'rezəvwɑː(r)/ n. ([artificial] lake) Reservoir, das

reshape /riː'ʃeɪp/ v.t. umgestalten

reshuffle /riː'ʃʌfl/ ❶ v.t. (a) umbilden ⟨Kabinett⟩
(b) (Cards) neu mischen
❷ n. Umbildung, die

reside /rɪ'zaɪd/ v.i. (formal) wohnen; wohnhaft sein (Amtsspr.)

residence /'rezɪdəns/ n. (a) (abode) Wohnsitz, der; (of ambassador etc.) Residenz, die
(b) (stay) Aufenthalt, der

'**residence permit** n. Aufenthaltsgenehmigung, die

resident /'rezɪdənt/ ❶ adj. wohnhaft; **be** ∼ **in England** seinen Wohnsitz in England haben
❷ n. (inhabitant) Bewohner, der/Bewohnerin, die; (at hotel) Hotelgast, der

residential /rezɪ'denʃl/ adj. Wohn⟨gebiet, -siedlung, -straße⟩; ∼ **hotel** Hotel für Dauergäste

residential 'care n. stationäre Pflege

resident's 'parking n. Parken nur für Anlieger

residual /rɪ'zɪdjʊəl/ adj. zurückgeblieben

residue /'rezɪdjuː/ n. (a) Rest, der
(b) (Chem.) Rückstand, der

resign /rɪ'zaɪn/ ❶ v.t. zurücktreten von ⟨Amt⟩
❷ v. refl. ∼ **oneself to** sth./**to doing** sth. sich mit etw. abfinden/sich damit abfinden, etw. zu tun
❸ v.i. ⟨Arbeitnehmer:⟩ kündigen; ⟨Regierungsbeamter:⟩ zurücktreten (**from** von)

resignation /rezɪg'neɪʃn/ n. (a) ▶ RESIGN 3: Kündigung, die; Rücktritt, der; **tender one's** ∼: seine Kündigung/seinen Rücktritt einreichen
(b) (being resigned) Resignation, die; **with** ∼: resigniert

resigned /rɪ'zaɪnd/ adj. resigniert; **be** ∼ **to** sth. sich mit etw. abgefunden haben

resilience /rɪ'zɪliəns/ n. (a) Elastizität, die
(b) (fig.) Unverwüstlichkeit, die

resilient /rɪ'zɪliənt/ adj. elastisch; (fig.) unverwüstlich

resin /'rezɪn/ n. Harz, das

resist /rɪ'zɪst/ ❶ v.t. (a) standhalten (+ Dat.) ⟨Frost, Hitze, Feuchtigkeit usw.⟩
(b) (oppose) sich widersetzen (+ Dat.); widerstehen (+ Dat.) ⟨Versuchung⟩
❷ v.i. ▶ 1B: sich widersetzen; widerstehen

resistance /rɪ'zɪstəns/ n. Widerstand, der (**to** gegen)

re'sistance movement n. Widerstandsbewegung, die

resistant /rɪ'zɪstənt/ adj. (a) (opposed) **be** ∼ **to** sich widersetzen (+ Dat.)
(b) (having power to resist) widerstandsfähig (**to** gegen)

reskill /riː'skɪl/ v.t. fort- od. weiterbilden; umschulen ⟨Arbeitslose⟩

resold ▶ RESELL

resolute /'rezəluːt/ adj. resolut, energisch ⟨Person⟩; entschlossen ⟨Tat⟩

resolution /rezə'luːʃn/ n. (a) (firmness) Entschlossenheit, die
(b) (decision) Entschließung, die; (Polit. also) Resolution, die
(c) (resolve) Vorsatz, der; **make a** ∼: einen Vorsatz fassen

resolve /rɪ'zɒlv/ ❶ v.t. (a) lösen ⟨Problem, Rätsel⟩; ausräumen ⟨Schwierigkeit⟩
(b) (decide) beschließen   ⋯⟶

(c) (settle) beilegen ⟨*Streit*⟩; regeln
⟨*Angelegenheit*⟩
2 *n.* **(a)** Vorsatz, *der*
(b) (resoluteness) Entschlossenheit, *die*
resolved /rɪˈzɒlvd/ *adj.* ~ **[to do sth.]**
entschlossen[, etw. zu tun]

resonant /ˈrezənənt/ *adj.* hallend ⟨*Ton,
Klang*⟩

resort /rɪˈzɔːt/ **1** *n.* **(a)** (place)
Aufenthalt[sort], *der;* [holiday] ~: Ferienort,
der; ski ~: Skiurlaubsort, *der;* seaside ~:
Seebad, *das*
(b) (recourse) as a last ~: als letzter Ausweg
2 *v.i.* ~ to sth./sb. zu etw. greifen/sich an
jmdn. wenden (for um)

resound /rɪˈzaʊnd/ *v.i.* widerhallen

re'sounding *adj.* hallend ⟨*Lärm*⟩;
überwältigend ⟨*Sieg, Erfolg*⟩

resource /rɪˈsɔːs, rɪˈzɔːs/ *n. usu. in pl.*
(stock) Mittel *Pl.*; Ressource, *die*

resourceful /rɪˈsɔːsfl, rɪˈzɔːsfl/ *adj.* findig
⟨*Person*⟩

respect /rɪˈspekt/ **1** *n.* **(a)** (esteem)
Respekt, *der,* Achtung, *die* (for vor + *Dat.*);
show ~ for sb./sth. Respekt vor jmdm./etw.
zeigen
(b) (aspect) Hinsicht, *die;* in some ~s in
mancher Hinsicht
(c) with ~ to ...: in Bezug auf ... (*Akk.*); was
... [an]betrifft
2 *v.t.* respektieren; achten

respectable /rɪˈspektəbl/ *adj.* angesehen
⟨*Bürger usw.*⟩; ehrenwert ⟨*Motive*⟩; (decent)
ehrbar (geh.) ⟨*Leute, Kaufmann*⟩; anständig,
respektabel ⟨*Beschäftigung usw.*⟩

respectful /rɪˈspektfl/ *adj.* respektvoll
(to[wards] gegenüber)

re'spectfully *adv.* respektvoll

respective /rɪˈspektɪv/ *adj.* jeweilig

re'spectively *adv.* beziehungsweise

respiration /respɪˈreɪʃn/ *n.* Atmung, *die*

respiratory /ˈrespərətərɪ/ *adj.*
Atmungs⟨*system, -organ, -funktion*⟩

respite /ˈrespaɪt/ *n.* Ruhepause, *die;* (delay)
Aufschub, *der;* without ~: ohne Pause

resplendent /rɪˈsplendənt/ *adj.* prächtig

respond /rɪˈspɒnd/ **1** *v.i.* **(a)** (answer)
antworten (to auf + *Akk.*)
(b) (react) reagieren (to auf + *Akk.*); ⟨*Patient,
Bremsen:*⟩ ansprechen (to auf + *Akk.*)
2 *v.t.* antworten; erwidern

response /rɪˈspɒns/ *n.* **(a)** (answer) Antwort,
die (to auf + *Akk.*); in ~ [to] als Antwort [auf
(+ *Akk.*)]
(b) (reaction) Reaktion, *die*

responsibility /rɪspɒnsɪˈbɪlɪtɪ/ *n.* **(a)** (being
responsible) Verantwortung, *die*
(b) (duty) Verpflichtung, *die*

responsible /rɪˈspɒnsɪbl/ *adj.* **(a)**
verantwortlich; be ~ to sb. jmdm.
gegenüber verantwortlich sein (for für)
(b) (trustworthy) verantwortungsvoll

responsibly /rɪˈspɒnsɪblɪ/ *adv.*
verantwortungsbewusst

responsive /rɪˈspɒnsɪv/ *adj.*
aufgeschlossen ⟨*Person*⟩; be ~ to sth. auf
etw. (*Akk.*) reagieren

rest¹ /rest/ **1** *v.i.* ruhen; ~ on ruhen auf
(+ *Dat.*); ~ from sth. sich von etw. ausruhen;
~ assured that ...: seien Sie versichert, dass
...; ~ with sb. ⟨*Verantwortung:*⟩ bei jmdm.
liegen
2 *v.t.* **(a)** ~ sth. against sth. etw. an etw.
(*Akk.*) lehnen
(b) ausruhen ⟨*Augen*⟩
3 *n.* **(a)** (repose) Ruhe, *die*
(b) (break, relaxation) Ruhe[pause], *die;*
Erholung, *die* (from von); take a ~: sich
ausruhen (from von); give it a ~! (coll.) hör
jetzt mal auf damit!
(c) (pause) have a ~: [eine] Pause machen;
~ period [Ruhe]pause, *die*

rest² *n.* the ~: der Rest; we'll do the ~:
alles Übrige erledigen wir

restaurant /ˈrestərɒnt/ *n.* Restaurant, *das*

'restaurant car *n.* (Brit. Railw.)
Speisewagen, *der*

rest: ~ **cure** *n.* Erholungskur, *die;* ~ **day**
n. Ruhetag, *der*

'rested *adj.* ausgeruht

restful /ˈrestfl/ *adj.* ruhig ⟨*Tag, Woche*⟩

'rest home *n.* Pflegeheim, *das*

restive /ˈrestɪv/ *adj.* unruhig

'restless *adj.* unruhig ⟨*Nacht, Schlaf,
Bewegung*⟩; ruhelos ⟨*Person*⟩

restoration /restəˈreɪʃn/ *n.* **(a)** (of peace,
health) Wiederherstellung, *die;* (of work of art,
building) Restaurierung, *die*
(b) the R~ (Brit. Hist.) die Restauration

restore /rɪˈstɔː(r)/ *v.t.* **(a)** (give back)
zurückgeben
(b) restaurieren ⟨*Bauwerk, Kunstwerk usw.*⟩;
~ sb. to health jmdn. wiederherstellen
(c) wiederherstellen ⟨*Ordnung, Ruhe*⟩

restrain /rɪˈstreɪn/ *v.t.* zurückhalten
⟨*Gefühl, Lachen, Person*⟩; bändigen
⟨*unartiges Kind, Tier*⟩; ~ sb./oneself from
doing sth. jmdn. davon abhalten/sich
zurückhalten, etw. zu tun

restrained /rɪˈstreɪnd/ *adj.* zurückhaltend
⟨*Wesen, Kritik*⟩; beherrscht ⟨*Reaktion, Worte*⟩

restraint /rɪˈstreɪnt/ *n.* **(a)** (restriction)
Einschränkung, *die*
(b) (reserve) Zurückhaltung, *die*
(c) (self-control) Selbstbeherrschung, *die*

restrict /rɪˈstrɪkt/ *v.t.* beschränken (to auf
+ *Akk.*)

re'stricted *adj.* beschränkt

restriction /rɪˈstrɪkʃn/ *n.* Beschränkung,
die (on *Gen.*)

restrictive /rɪˈstrɪktɪv/ *adj.* restriktiv

'rest room *n.* (esp. Amer.) Toilette, *die*

restyle /riːˈstaɪl/ *v.t.* neu stylen; ~ sb.'s
hair jmdm. eine neue Frisur machen

result /rɪ'zʌlt/ ① *v.i.* (a) (follow) ∼ **from sth.** die Folge einer Sache (*Gen.*) sein
(b) (end) ∼ **in sth.** in etw. (*Dat.*) resultieren
② *n.* Ergebnis, *das;* **be the** ∼ **of sth.** die Folge einer Sache (*Gen.*) sein; **as a** ∼ **[of this]** infolgedessen

re'sultant /rɪ'zʌltənt/ *attrib. adj.* daraus resultierend

resume /rɪ'zjuːm/ *v.t.* wieder aufnehmen; fortsetzen ⟨*Reise*⟩

résumé /'rezʊmeɪ/ *n.* (a) (summary) Zusammenfassung, *die*
(b) (Amer.: curriculum vitae) Lebenslauf, *der*

resumption /rɪ'zʌmpʃn/ *n.* Wiederaufnahme, *die*

resurface /riː'sɜːfɪs/ ① *v.t.* ∼ **a road** den Belag einer Straße erneuern
② *v.i.* (lit. or fig.) wieder auftauchen

resurgence /rɪ'sɜːdʒəns/ *n.* Wiederaufleben, *das*

resurrection /rezə'rekʃn/ *n.* Auferstehung, *die*

resuscitate /rɪ'sʌsɪteɪt/ *v.t.* wieder beleben

resuscitation /rɪsʌsɪ'teɪʃn/ *n.* Wiederbelebung, *die*

retail /'riːteɪl/ ① *adj.* Einzel⟨*handel*⟩; Einzelhandels⟨*geschäft, -preis*⟩
② *adv.* **buy/sell** ∼**:** en détail kaufen/ verkaufen

'retailer *n.* Einzelhändler, *der/*-händlerin, *die*

'retailing /'riːteɪlɪŋ/ *n., no art.* Einzelhandel, *der*

retail 'price index *n.* (Brit.) Preisindex des Einzelhandels

retain /rɪ'teɪn/ *v.t.* behalten; ein-, zurückbehalten ⟨*Gelder*⟩

retaining: ∼ **fee** *n.* Honorarvorschuss, *der;* ∼ **wall** *n.* Böschungsmauer, *die*

retaliate /rɪ'tælɪeɪt/ *v.i.* Vergeltung üben (**against** an + *Dat.*)

retaliation /rɪtælɪ'eɪʃn/ *n.* Vergeltung, *die;* **in** ∼ **for** als Vergeltung für

retarded /rɪ'tɑːdɪd/ *adj.* [mentally] ∼**:** [geistig] zurückgeblieben

retch /retʃ/ *v.i.* würgen

retentive /rɪ'tentɪv/ *adj.* gut ⟨*Gedächtnis*⟩

rethink /riː'θɪŋk/ *v.t.,* rethought /riː'θɔːt/ noch einmal überdenken

reticence /'retɪsəns/ *n.* Zurückhaltung, *die*

reticent /'retɪsənt/ *adj.* zurückhaltend (**on, about** in Bezug auf + *Akk.*)

retina /'retɪnə/ *n.* Netzhaut, *die*

retinue /'retɪnjuː/ *n.* Gefolge, *das*

retire /rɪ'taɪə(r)/ *v.i.* (a) ⟨*Angestellter, Arbeiter:*⟩ in Rente (*Akk.*) gehen; ⟨*Beamter, Militär:*⟩ in Pension *od.* den Ruhestand gehen
(b) (withdraw) sich zurückziehen (**to** in + *Akk.*)

retired /rɪ'taɪəd/ *adj.* aus dem Berufsleben ausgeschieden; ⟨*Beamter, Soldat*⟩ im Ruhestand, pensioniert

re'tirement *n.* Ruhestand, *der;* **take early** ∼ ⟨*Selbstständiger:*⟩ sich vorzeitig zur Ruhe setzen; ⟨*Angestellter, Arbeiter:*⟩ vorzeitig in Rente (*Akk.*) gehen; ⟨*Beamter, Militär:*⟩ sich vorzeitig pensionieren lassen

retirement: ∼ **age** *n.* Altersgrenze, *die;* ∼ **home** *n.* (a) (house, flat) Alters- *od.* Ruhesitz, *der;* (b) (institution) Alters- *od.* Altenheim, *das;* ∼ **pay,** ∼ **pension** *ns.* [Alters]rente, *die*

retiring /rɪ'taɪərɪŋ/ *adj.* (shy) zurückhaltend

retort /rɪ'tɔːt/ ① *n.* Entgegnung, *die* (**to** auf + *Akk.*)
② *v.t.* entgegnen

retrace /rɪ'treɪs/ *v.t.* zurückverfolgen; ∼ **one's steps** denselben Weg noch einmal zurückgehen

retract /rɪ'trækt/ *v.t.* zurücknehmen

retrain /riː'treɪn/ ① *v.i.* [sich] umschulen [lassen]
② *v.t.* umschulen

re'training *n.* Umschulung, *die*

retreat /rɪ'triːt/ ① *n.* (a) (withdrawal) Rückzug, *der;* **beat a** ∼ (fig.) das Feld räumen
(b) (place) Zufluchtsort, *der*
② *v.i.* sich zurückziehen

retribution /retrɪ'bjuːʃn/ *n.* Vergeltung, *die*

retrieval /rɪ'triːvl/ *n.* (a) (of situation) Rettung, *die;* **beyond** *or* **past** ∼**:** hoffnungslos
(b) (rescue) Rettung, *die;* (from wreckage) Bergung, *die*

retrieve /rɪ'triːv/ *v.t.* (a) (rescue) retten (**from** aus); (from wreckage) bergen (**from** aus)
(b) (recover) zurückholen ⟨*Brief*⟩; wiederholen ⟨*Ball*⟩; wiederbekommen ⟨*Geld*⟩
(c) (Comp.) wieder auffinden ⟨*Informationen*⟩
(d) ⟨*Hund:*⟩ apportieren
(e) retten ⟨*Situation*⟩

re'triever *n.* Apportierhund, *der;* (breed) Retriever, *der*

retrospect /'retrəspekt/ *n.* **in** ∼**:** im Nachhinein

retrospective /retrə'spektɪv/
① *adj.* retrospektiv (geh.)
② *n.* (Art) Retrospektive, *die* (geh.)

retrovirus /'retrəʊvaɪrəs/ *n.* Retrovirus, *das od. der*

returf /riː'tɜːf/ *v.t.* neuen Rasen verlegen auf (+ *Dat.*)

return /rɪ'tɜːn/ ① *v.i.* (come back) zurückkommen; (go back) zurückgehen; (by vehicle) zurückfahren
② *v.t.* (a) (bring back) zurückbringen; zurückgeben ⟨*geliehenen/gestohlenen Gegenstand*⟩; ∼**ed with thanks** mit Dank zurück ⋯⟫

(b) erwidern ⟨Besuch, Gruß, Liebe⟩; sich revanchieren für (ugs.) ⟨Freundlichkeit, Gefallen⟩
(c) (elect) wählen ⟨Kandidaten⟩
(d) ~ a verdict of guilty/not guilty ⟨Geschworene:⟩ auf „schuldig"/„nicht schuldig" erkennen
3 n. **(a)** Rückkehr, die; many happy ~s [of the day]! herzlichen Glückwunsch [zum Geburtstag]!
(b) by ~ [of post] postwendend
(c) (ticket) Rückfahrkarte, die; (for flight) Rückflugschein, der
(d) ~[s] (proceeds) Gewinn, der (on, from aus)
(e) (bringing back) Zurückbringen, das; (of property, goods, book) Rückgabe, die (to an + Akk.); receive/get sth. in ~ [for sth.] etw. [für etw.] bekommen
returnable /rɪˈtɜːnəbl/ adj. Mehrweg⟨behälter, -flasche usw.⟩; rückzahlbar ⟨Gebühr, Kaution⟩; ~ bottle Pfandflasche, die; ~ deposit Pfand, der
return: ~ ˈfare n. Preis für eine Rückfahrkarte/(for flight) einen Rückflugschein; ~ ˈflight n. Rückflug, der; ~ ˈjourney n. Rückreise, die; Rückfahrt, die; ~ ˈmatch n. Rückspiel, das; ~ ˈticket n. (Brit.) Rückfahrkarte, die; (for flight) Rückflugschein, der; ~ ˈtrip n. **(a)** (trip back) Rückweg, der; Rückfahrt, die; **(b)** (trip out and back) Hin- und Rückfahrt, die; Hin- und Rückreise, die
retype /riːˈtaɪp/ v.t. neu tippen
reunification /riːjuːnɪfɪˈkeɪʃn/ n. Wiedervereinigung, die
reunify /riːˈjuːnɪfaɪ/ v.t. wieder vereinigen
reunion /riːˈjuːnjən/ n. (gathering) Treffen, das
reunite /riːjʊˈnaɪt/ v.t. wieder zusammenführen
reusable /riːˈjuːzəbl/ adj. wieder verwendbar
reuse **1** /riːˈjuːz/ v.t. wieder verwenden **2** /riːˈjuːs/ n. Wiederverwendung, die
rev /rev/ (coll.) **1** n., usu. in pl. Umdrehung, die
2 v.i., -vv- hochtourig laufen **3** v.t., -vv- aufheulen lassen
■ **rev ˈup** v.t. aufheulen lassen
Rev. /ˈrevərənd, (coll.) rev/ abbr. = **Reverend** Rev.
reveal /rɪˈviːl/ v.t. enthüllen (geh.); be ~ed ⟨Wahrheit:⟩ ans Licht kommen
reˈvealing adj. aufschlussreich
revel /ˈrevl/ v.i., (Brit.) -ll- genießen (in Akk.); ~ in doing sth. es [richtig] genießen, etw. zu tun
revelation /revəˈleɪʃn/ n. **(a)** Enthüllung, die (geh.); be a ~: einem die Augen öffnen **(b)** (Relig.) Offenbarung, die
reveller /ˈrevələ(r)/ n. Feiernde, der/die
revelry /ˈrevəlrɪ/ n. Feiern, das

revenge /rɪˈvendʒ/ **1** v.t. rächen ⟨Person, Tat⟩
2 n. (action) Rache, die; take ~ or have one's ~ [on sb.] [for sth.] Rache [an jmdm.] [für etw.] nehmen; in ~ for sth. als Rache für etw
revengeful /rɪˈvendʒfl/ adj. rachsüchtig (geh.)
revenue /ˈrevənjuː/ n. ~[s] Einnahmen Pl.
revere /rɪˈvɪə(r)/ v.t. verehren
reverence /ˈrevərəns/ n. Ehrfurcht, die
Reverend /ˈrevərənd/ adj. the ~ John Wilson Hochwürden John Wilson
reverent /ˈrevərənt/ adj. ehrfürchtig
reverie /ˈrevərɪ/ n. Träumerei, die
reversal /rɪˈvɜːsl/ n. Umkehrung, die
reverse /rɪˈvɜːs/ **1** adj. entgegengesetzt ⟨Richtung⟩; Rück⟨seite⟩; umgekehrt ⟨Reihenfolge⟩
2 n. (contrary) Gegenteil, das **(b)** (Motor Veh.) Rückwärtsgang, der; put the car into ~, go into ~: den Rückwärtsgang einlegen
3 v.t. **(a)** umkehren ⟨Reihenfolge⟩; ~ the charge[s] (Brit.) ein R-Gespräch anmelden **(b)** zurücksetzen ⟨Fahrzeug⟩
4 v.i. zurücksetzen; rückwärts fahren
reverse: ~ˈcharge adj. (Brit.) make a ~charge call ein R-Gespräch führen; ~ ˈgear n. (Motor Veh.) Rückwärtsgang, der; see also GEAR 1A
reversible /rɪˈvɜːsɪbl/ adj. beidseitig tragbar ⟨Kleidungsstück⟩; Wende⟨mantel, -jacke⟩
reˈversing light n. Rückfahrscheinwerfer, der
revert /rɪˈvɜːt/ v.i. ~ to zurückkommen auf (+ Akk.) ⟨Thema, Frage⟩; ~ to savagery in den Zustand der Wildheit zurückfallen
review /rɪˈvjuː/ **1** n. **(a)** (survey) Überblick, der (of über + Akk.)
(b) (re-examination) [nochmalige] Überprüfung **(c)** (of book, play, etc.) Kritik, die; Rezension, die
2 v.t. **(a)** (survey) untersuchen; prüfen **(b)** (re-examine) überprüfen **(c)** (Mil.) inspizieren **(d)** (write a criticism of) rezensieren
reˈviewer n. Rezensent, der/Rezensentin, die
revile /rɪˈvaɪl/ v.t. schmähen (geh.)
revise /rɪˈvaɪz/ v.t. **(a)** (check over) durchsehen ⟨Manuskript⟩ **(b)** (for exam) wiederholen; abs. lernen
revision /rɪˈvɪʒn/ n. **(a)** (checking over) Durchsicht, die **(b)** (amended version) revidierte Fassung **(c)** (for exam) Wiederholung, die
revisit /riːˈvɪzɪt/ v.t. wieder besuchen
revitalize /riːˈvaɪtəlaɪz/ v.t. neu beleben
revival /rɪˈvaɪvl/ n. Neubelebung, die
revive /rɪˈvaɪv/ **1** v.i. (come back to consciousness) wieder zu sich kommen; (be reinvigorated) zu neuem Leben erwachen

2 *v.t.* (a) (restore to consciousness) wieder beleben; (reinvigorate) wieder zu Kräften kommen lassen
(b) wieder wecken ⟨*Lebensgeister, Interesse*⟩

revoke /rɪ'vəʊk/ *v.t.* aufheben ⟨*Entscheidung*⟩; widerrufen ⟨*Befehl, Erlaubnis, Genehmigung*⟩

revolt /rɪ'vəʊlt/ **1** *v.i.* revoltieren (**against** gegen)
2 *v.t.* mit Abscheu erfüllen
3 *n.* Revolte, *die* (auch fig.); Aufstand, *der*

re'volting *adj.* abscheulich; (unpleasant) widerlich

revolution /revə'luːʃn/ *n.* Revolution, *die*

revolutionary /revə'luːʃənərɪ/ **1** *adj.* revolutionär
2 *n.* Revolutionär, *der*/Revolutionärin, *die*

revolve /rɪ'vɒlv/ **1** *v.t.* drehen
2 *v.i.* sich drehen (**round, about, on** um)

revolver /rɪ'vɒlvə(r)/ *n.* [Trommel]revolver, *der*

revolving /rɪ'vɒlvɪŋ/ *attrib. adj.* Dreh⟨*bühne, -tür*⟩

revue /rɪ'vjuː/ *n.* Kabarett, *das;* (musical show) Revue, *die*

revulsion /rɪ'vʌlʃn/ *n.* Abscheu, *der* (**at** vor + *Dat.*, gegen)

reward /rɪ'wɔːd/ **1** *n.* Belohnung, *die*
2 *v.t.* belohnen

re'warding *adj.* lohnend; **be** ∼/**financially** ∼: sich lohnen/einträglich sein

rewind /riː'waɪnd/ *v.t.,* **rewound** /riː'waʊnd/
(a) wieder aufziehen ⟨*Uhr*⟩
(b) zurückspulen ⟨*Film, Band*⟩

'rewind button *n.* (on camera) Rückspulknopf, *der;* (on cassette recorder etc.) Rücklauftaste, *die*

reword /riː'wɜːd/ *v.t.* umformulieren

rewrite /riː'raɪt/ *v.t.,* **rewrote** /riː'rəʊt/, **rewritten** /riː'rɪtn/ noch einmal [neu] schreiben; (write differently) umschreiben

rhetoric /'retərɪk/ *n.* [**art of**] ∼: Redekunst, *die;* Rhetorik, *die*

rhetorical /rɪ'tɒrɪkl/ *adj.* rhetorisch

rheumatic /ruː'mætɪk/ *adj.* rheumatisch

rheumatism /'ruːmətɪzm/ *n.* Rheumatismus, *der;* Rheuma, *das* (ugs.)

Rhine /raɪn/ *pr. n.* Rhein, *der*

rhino /'raɪnəʊ/ *n., pl.* **same or** ∼**s** (coll.),
rhinoceros /raɪ'nɒsərəs/ *n., pl.* **same or** ∼**es** Nashorn, *das;* Rhinozeros, *das*

rhododendron /rəʊdə'dendrən/ *n.* Rhododendron, *der*

rhubarb /'ruːbɑːb/ *n.* Rhabarber, *der*

rhyme /raɪm/ **1** *n.* Reim, *der;* **without** ∼ **or reason** ohne Sinn und Verstand
2 *v.i.* sich reimen (**with** auf + *Akk.*)

rhythm /'rɪðm/ *n.* Rhythmus, *der*

rhythmic /'rɪðmɪk/, **rhythmical** /'rɪðmɪkl/ *adj.* rhythmisch

rib /rɪb/ **1** *n.* Rippe, *die*
2 *v.t.,* **-bb-** (coll.) aufziehen (ugs.)

ribald /'rɪbəld/ *adj.* zotig

ribbon /'rɪbn/ *n.* Band, *das;* (on typewriter) [Farb]band, *das*

'ribcage *n.* Brustkorb, *der*

rice /raɪs/ *n.* Reis, *der*

rice: ∼ **'pudding** *n.* Milchreis, *der;* ∼ **wine** *n.* Reiswein, *der*

rich /rɪtʃ/ **1** *adj.* (a) reich (**in** an + *Dat.*); (fertile) fruchtbar ⟨*Land, Boden*⟩
(b) (splendid) prachtvoll
(c) (containing much fat, oil, eggs, etc.) gehaltvoll
(d) (deep, full) voll[tönend] ⟨*Stimme*⟩; voll ⟨*Ton*⟩; satt ⟨*Farbe, Farbton*⟩
2 *n. pl.* **the** ∼: die Reichen *Pl.*; ∼ **and poor** Arm und Reich

riches /'rɪtʃɪz/ *n. pl.* Reichtum, *der*

'richly *adv.* (a) (splendidly) reich; üppig ⟨*ausgestattet*⟩; prächtig ⟨*gekleidet*⟩
(b) (fully) voll und ganz; ∼ **deserved** wohlverdient

'richness *n.* (a) (of food) Reichhaltigkeit, *die*
(b) (of voice) voller Klang; (of colour) Sattheit, *die*

rickets /'rɪkɪts/ *n.* Rachitis, *die*

rickety /'rɪkɪtɪ/ *adj.* wack[e]lig

ricochet /'rɪkəʃeɪ/ **1** *n.* (a) Abprallen, *das*
(b) (hit) Abpraller, *der*
2 *v.i.,* ∼**ed** /'rɪkəʃeɪd/ abprallen (**off** von)

rid /rɪd/ *v.t.,* **-dd-,** **rid:** ∼ **sth. of sth.** etw. von etw. befreien; ∼ **oneself of sb./sth.** sich von jmdm./etw. befreien; **be** ∼ **of sb./sth.** jmdn./etw. los sein (ugs.); **get** ∼ **of sb./sth.** jmdn./etw. loswerden

riddance /'rɪdəns/ *n.* **good** ∼! Gott sei Dank ist er/es *usw.* weg!

ridden ▶ RIDE 2, 3

riddle¹ /'rɪdl/ *n.* Rätsel, *das*

riddle² *v.t.* durchlöchern; ∼**d with bullets** von Kugeln durchsiebt

ride /raɪd/ **1** *n.* (on horseback) [Aus]ritt, *der;* (in vehicle, at fair) Fahrt, *die;* ∼ **in a train/coach** Zug-/Busfahrt, *die;* **go for a** ∼: ausreiten; **go for a [bi]cycle** ∼: Rad fahren; **go for a** ∼ **[in the car]** [mit dem Auto] wegfahren; **take sb. for a** ∼ (fig. coll.: deceive) jmdn. reinlegen (ugs.)
2 *v.i.,* **rode** /rəʊd/, **ridden** /'rɪdn/ (on horse) reiten; (on bicycle, in vehicle) fahren; ∼ **to town on one's bike/in one's car/on the train** mit dem Rad/Auto/Zug in die Stadt fahren
3 *v.t.,* **rode, ridden** reiten ⟨*Pferd usw.*⟩; fahren mit ⟨*Fahrrad*⟩
■ **ride a'way, ride 'off** *v.i.* wegreiten/-fahren

'rider *n.* (a) Reiter, *der*/Reiterin, *die;* (of cycle) Fahrer, *der*/Fahrerin, *die*
(b) (addition) Zusatz, *der*

ridge /rɪdʒ/ *n.* (a) (of roof) First, *der*
(b) (long hilltop) Grat, *der;* Kamm, *der*
(c) (Meteorol.) ∼ **[of high pressure]** lang gestrecktes Hoch

ridicule /'rɪdɪkjuːl/ **1** *n.* Spott, *der*   ···≻

2 *v.t.* verspotten

ridiculous /rɪˈdɪkjʊləs/ *adj.* lächerlich

riding /ˈraɪdɪŋ/ *n.* Reiten, *das*

riding: ~ lesson *n.* Reitstunde, *die;*
~ **school** *n.* Reitschule, *die*

rife /raɪf/ *pred. adj.* weit verbreitet

riff-raff /ˈrɪfræf/ *n.* Gesindel, *das*

rifle /ˈraɪfl/ 1 *n.* Gewehr, *das*
2 *v.t.* durchwühlen
3 *v.i.* ~ **through sth.** etw. durchwühlen

rift /rɪft/ *n.* Unstimmigkeit, *die*

rig[1] /rɪg/ *n.* (for oil well) [Öl]förderturm, *der;*
(off shore) Förderinsel, *die*
■ **rig 'out** *v.t.* ausstaffieren
■ **rig 'up** *v.t.* aufbauen

rig[2] *v.t.,* **-gg-** manipulieren ⟨*[Wahl]ergebnis⟩*;
fälschen ⟨*Wahl⟩*

rigging /ˈrɪgɪŋ/ *n.* Takelung, *die*

right /raɪt/ 1 *adj.* (a) (just, morally good,
sound) richtig
(b) (correct, true) richtig; **you're [quite]** ~: du
hast [völlig] recht; **be ~ in sth.** Recht mit
etw. haben; **is that clock ~?** geht die Uhr da
richtig?; **put** *or* **set** ~: richtig stellen
⟨*Irrtum, Behauptung⟩*; wieder gutmachen
⟨*Unrecht⟩*; berichtigen ⟨*Fehler⟩*; richtig
stellen ⟨*Uhr⟩*; **put** *or* **set sb.** ~: jmdn.
berichtigen; **that's** ~: ja[wohl]; so ist es; **is
that** ~? stimmt das?; (indeed?) aha!; **[am I]** ~?
nicht [wahr]?
(c) (preferable, most suitable) richtig; recht; **do
sth. the** ~ **way** etw. richtig machen
(d) (opposite of left) recht...; **on the** ~ **side**
rechts
(e) **R~** (Polit.) recht...
2 *v.t.* aus der Welt schaffen ⟨*Unrecht⟩*
3 *n.* (a) (fair claim, authority) Recht, *das;* **have
a/no** ~ **to sth.** ein/kein Anrecht *od.* Recht
auf etw. (*Akk.*) haben; **in one's own** ~: aus
eigenem Recht; ~ **of way** Vorfahrtsrecht,
das; **have** ~ **of way** Vorfahrt haben
(b) (what is just) Recht, *das;* **by** ~**[s]** von
Rechts wegen; **in the** ~: im Recht
(c) (~-hand side) rechte Seite; **on** *or* **to the**
~ **[of sb./sth.]** rechts [von jmdm./etw.]
(d) (Polit.) **the R~:** die Rechte
4 *adv.* (a) (correctly) richtig
(b) (to the ~-hand side) nach rechts
(c) (completely) ganz
(d) (exactly) genau; ~ '**now** im Moment; jetzt
sofort ⟨*handeln⟩*
(e) (straight) direkt

'**right angle** *n.* rechter Winkel; **at** ~**s to
sth.** rechtwinklig zu etw.

righteous /ˈraɪtʃəs/ *adj.* rechtschaffen

rightful /ˈraɪtfl/ *adj.* rechtmäßig ⟨*Besitzer,
Herrscher⟩*

right: ~-**hand** *adj.* recht...; ~-'**handed**
1 *adj.* rechtshändig; ⟨*Werkzeug⟩* für
Rechtshänder; **be** ~-**handed** ⟨*Person:⟩*
Rechtshänder/Rechtshänderin sein; 2 *adv.*
rechtshändig; ~-**hand** '**man** *n.* rechte
Hand

'**rightly** *adv.* zu Recht

right: ~-'**minded** *adj.* gerecht denkend;
~-**to-**'**life** *attrib. adj.* Recht-auf-Leben-;
~ '**wing** *n.* rechter Flügel; ~-**wing** *adj.*
(Polit.) rechtsgerichtet; Rechts⟨*extremist,
-intellektueller⟩*; ~-**winger** *n.* (a) (Sport)
Rechtsaußen, *der;* (b) (Polit.) Rechte, der/*die*

rigid /ˈrɪdʒɪd/ *adj.* (a) starr; (stiff) steif
(b) (strict) streng; unbeugsam ⟨*System⟩*

rigidity /rɪˈdʒɪtɪ/ *n.* ▶ RIGID: Starrheit, *die;*
Steifheit, *die;* Strenge, *die*

rigmarole /ˈrɪgmərəʊl/ *n.* (a) (talk)
langatmiges Geschwafel (ugs.)
(b) (procedure) Zirkus, *der*

rigor /ˈrɪgə(r)/ (Amer.) ▶ RIGOUR

rigor mortis /rɪgə ˈmɔːtɪs/ *n.* Totenstarre,
die

rigorous /ˈrɪgərəs/ *adj.* streng

rigour /ˈrɪgə(r)/ *n.* (Brit.) Strenge, *die*

rile /raɪl/ *v.t.* (coll.) ärgern

rim /rɪm/ *n.* Rand, *der;* (of wheel) Felge, *die*

rind /raɪnd/ *n.* (of fruit) Schale, *die;* (of cheese)
Rinde, *die;* (of bacon) Schwarte, *die*

ring[1] /rɪŋ/ 1 *n.* (a) Ring, *der*
(b) (Boxing) Ring, *der;* (in circus) Manege, *die*
2 *v.t.* (surround) umringen; einkreisen ⟨*Wort⟩*

ring[2] 1 *n.* (a) (act of sounding bell) Läuten,
das; Klingeln, *das*
(b) (Brit. coll.: telephone call) Anruf, *der;* **give sb.
a** ~: jmdn. anrufen
(c) (fig.: impression) **have the** ~ **of truth [about
it]** glaubhaft klingen
2 *v.i.,* **rang** /ræŋ/, **rung** /rʌŋ/ (a) (sound
clearly) [er]schallen; ⟨*Hammer:⟩* [er]dröhnen
(b) (be sounded) ⟨*Glocke, Klingel, Telefon:⟩*
läuten; ⟨*Wecker, Telefon, Kasse:⟩* klingeln; **the
doorbell rang** es klingelte
(c) (~ bell) läuten (**for** nach)
(d) (Brit.: make telephone call) anrufen
3 *v.t.,* **rang, rung** (a) läuten ⟨*Glocke⟩*; ~ **the
[door]bell** läuten; klingeln; **it** ~**s a bell** (fig.
coll.) es kommt mir [irgendwie] bekannt vor
(b) (Brit.: telephone) anrufen
■ **ring 'back** (Brit.) *v.t. & i.* (a) (again) wieder
anrufen
(b) (in return) zurückrufen
■ **ring 'off** *v.i.* (Brit.) auflegen
■ **ring 'out** *v.i.* ertönen
■ **ring 'up** *v.t.* (Brit.: telephone) anrufen

ring: ~ **binder** *n.* Ringbuch, *das;*
~ **finger** *n.* Ringfinger, *der*

ringing /ˈrɪŋɪŋ/ *n.* Läuten, *das;* (Brit. Teleph.)
~ **tone** Freiton, *der*

'**ringleader** *n.* Anführer, *der*/Anführerin,
die

ringlet /ˈrɪŋlɪt/ *n.* [Ringel]löckchen, *das*

ring: ~ **road** *n.* Ringstraße, *die;* ~**tone** *n.*
Klingelton *der*

rink /rɪŋk/ *n.* (for ice skating) Eisbahn, *die;* (for
roller skating) Rollschuhbahn, *die*

rinse /rɪns/ 1 *v.t.* (a) (wash out) ausspülen
⟨*Mund, Gefäß usw.⟩*
(b) [aus]spülen ⟨*Wäsche usw.⟩*; abspülen
⟨*Hände, Geschirr⟩*

r

2 *n.* Spülen, *das; give sth. a* [good/quick] ~: etw. [gut/schnell] ausspülen/abspülen/ spülen
■ **rinse 'out** *v.t.* ausspülen

riot /ˈraɪət/ 1 *n.* Aufruhr, *der;* ~s Unruhen *Pl.; run* ~: randalieren
2 *v.i.* randalieren

'rioter *n.* Randalierer, *der*

'riot gear *n.* Schutzkleidung *od.* -ausrüstung

riotous /ˈraɪətəs/ *adj.* (a) gewalttätig
(b) (unrestrained) wild

rip /rɪp/ 1 *n.* Riss, *der*
2 *v.t.,* -pp- zerreißen; ~ **open** aufreißen
■ **rip 'off** *v.t.* (a) (remove from) reißen von; (remove) abreißen
(b) (coll.: defraud) übers Ohr hauen (ugs.)
■ **rip 'out** *v.t.* herausreißen (of aus)

RIP *abbr.* = **rest in peace** R.I.P.

'ripcord *n.* Reißleine, *die*

ripe /raɪp/ *adj.* reif (for zu)

ripen /ˈraɪpn/ 1 *v.t.* zur Reife bringen
2 *v.i.* reifen

'ripeness *n.* Reife, *die*

'rip-off *n.* (coll.) Nepp, *der* (ugs.)

riposte /rɪˈpɒst/ 1 *n.* (retort) [rasche] Entgegnung
2 *v.i.* [rasch] antworten

ripple /ˈrɪpl/ 1 *n.* kleine Welle
2 *v.i.* ⟨See:⟩ sich kräuseln; ⟨Welle:⟩ plätschern
3 *v.t.* kräuseln

rise /raɪz/ 1 *n.* (a) (advancement) Aufstieg, *der*
(b) (in value, price, cost) Steigerung, *die;* (in population, temperature) Zunahme, *die*
(c) (Brit.) [pay] ~ (in wages) Lohnerhöhung, *die;* (in salary) Gehaltserhöhung, *die*
(d) (hill) Anhöhe, *die*
(e) *give* ~ *to* führen zu; Anlass geben zu ⟨Spekulation⟩
2 *v.i.,* rose /rəʊz/, risen /ˈrɪzn/ (a) (go up) aufsteigen
(b) ⟨Sonne, Mond:⟩ aufgehen
(c) (increase, reach higher level) steigen
(d) (advance) ⟨Person:⟩ aufsteigen
(e) ⟨Teig, Kuchen:⟩ aufgehen
(f) (Theatre) ⟨Vorhang:⟩ aufgehen
(g) ⟨Fluss:⟩ entspringen
■ **rise 'up** *v.i.* (a) ~ up [in revolt] aufbegehren (geh.)
(b) ⟨Berg:⟩ aufragen

risen ▶ RISE 2

'riser *n. early* ~: Frühaufsteher, *der/* Frühaufsteherin, *die*

rising /ˈraɪzɪŋ/ 1 *n.* (of sun, moon, etc.) Aufgang, *der*
2 *adj.* (a) aufgehend ⟨Sonne, Mond usw.⟩
(b) steigend ⟨Kosten, Temperatur, Wasser, Flut⟩
(c) (sloping upwards) ansteigend

risk /rɪsk/ 1 *n.* Gefahr, *die;* (chance taken) Risiko, *das; at one's own* ~: auf eigene

Gefahr *od.* eigenes Risiko; *take the* ~ *of doing sth.* es riskieren, etw. zu tun; *be at* ~ ⟨Zukunft, Plan:⟩ gefährdet sein
2 *v.t.* riskieren; *I'll* ~ *it* ich lasse es darauf ankommen

'risky *adj.* gefährlich; gewagt ⟨Experiment, Projekt⟩

risotto /rɪˈzɒtəʊ/ *n., pl.* ~s Risotto, *der od. das*

risqué /ˈrɪskeɪ/ *adj.* gewagt

rissole /ˈrɪsəʊl/ *n.* Frikadelle, *die*

rite /raɪt/ *n.* Ritus, *der*

ritual /ˈrɪtʃʊəl/ 1 *adj.* rituell; Ritual⟨mord, -tötung⟩
2 *n.* Ritual, *das*

rival /ˈraɪvl/ 1 *n.* (competitor) Rivale, *der/* Rivalin, *die; business* ~s Konkurrenten *Pl.*
2 *v.t.,* (Brit.) -ll- nicht nachstehen (+ *Dat.*)

rivalry /ˈraɪvlrɪ/ *n.* Rivalität, *die* (geh.)

river /ˈrɪvə(r)/ *n.* Fluss, *der*

river: ~ **bank** Flussufer, *der;* ~ **basin** *n.* Stromgebiet, *das;* ~ **bed** *n.* Flussbett, *das* ~**side** 1 *n.* Flussufer, *das;* 2 *attrib. adj.* am Fluss gelegen; am Fluss *nachgestellt*

rivet /ˈrɪvɪt/ 1 *n.* Niete, *die*
2 *v.t.* (a) [ver]nieten
(b) (fig.) fesseln

'riveting *adj.* fesselnd

rivulet /ˈrɪvjʊlɪt/ *n.* Bach, *der*

RN *abbr.* (Brit.) = **Royal Navy** Königl. Mar.

road /rəʊd/ *n.* Straße, *die; across or over the* ~ [from us] [bei uns] gegenüber; *by* ~ (by car/bus/lorry) per Auto/Bus/Lkw; *be on the* ~: auf Reisen *od.* unterwegs sein; ⟨Theaterensemble usw.:⟩ auf Tournee *od.* Tour sein

road: ~ **accident** *n.* Verkehrsunfall, *der;* ~ **atlas** *n.* Autoatlas, *der;* ~**block** *n.* Straßensperre, *die;* ~ **bridge** *n.* Straßenbrücke, *die;* ~ **haulage** *n.* Gütertransport auf der Straße; ~ **hog** *n.* Verkehrsrowdy, *der;* ~ **hump** ▶ SPEED BUMP

roadie /ˈrəʊdɪ/ *n.* (coll.) Roadie, *der*

road: ~ **manager** *n.* Roadmanager, *der;* ~ **map** *n.* Straßenkarte, *die;* ~**mender** *n.* Straßen[bau]arbeiter, *der/*-arbeiterin, *die;* ~ **rage** *n.* häufig zu gewalttätigen Ausbrüchen führende Wut eines Autofahrers; ~ **safety** *n.* Verkehrssicherheit, *die;* ~ **sense** *n.* Gespür für Verkehrssituationen; ~**side** *n.* Straßenrand, *der; at or by/along the* ~side am Straßenrand; ~ **sign** *n.* Verkehrszeichen, *das;* Straßenschild, *das* (ugs.); ~ **sweeper** *n.* Straßenkehrer, *der/* -kehrerin, *die;* ~ **tax** *n.* (Brit.) Kraftfahrzeugsteuer, *der;* Kfz-Steuer, *die;* ~ **transport** *n.* Personen- und Güterbeförderung auf der Straße; *form of* ~ *transport* Verkehrsmittel der Straße; ~ **user** *n.* Verkehrsteilnehmer, *der/*
⋯⟶

-teilnehmerin, *die;* ∼**way** *n.* Fahrbahn, *die;*
∼**works** *n. pl.* Straßenbauarbeiten *Pl.;*
∼**worthy** *adj.* fahrtüchtig

roam /rəʊm/ ① *v.i.* umherstreifen
② *v.t.* streifen durch

roaming /'rəʊmɪŋ/ *n.* (Teleph.) Roaming, *das*

roar /rɔ:(r)/ ① *n.* (of wild beast) Gebrüll, *das;*
(of applause) Tosen, *das;* (of engine, traffic)
Dröhnen, *das;* ∼s/a ∼ [of laughter]
dröhnendes Gelächter
② *v.i.* brüllen (**with** vor + *Dat.*); ⟨*Motor:*⟩
dröhnen

'**roaring** *adj.* (a) bullernd (ugs.) ⟨*Feuer*⟩
(b) a ∼ **success** ein Bombenerfolg; **do a**
∼ **trade** ein Bombengeschäft machen

roast /rəʊst/ ① *v.t.* braten; rösten
⟨*Kaffeebohnen, Kastanien*⟩
② *attrib. adj.* gebraten ⟨*Fleisch, Ente usw.*⟩;
Brat⟨*hähnchen, -kartoffeln*⟩; Röst⟨*kastanien*⟩;
∼ **beef** (sirloin) Roastbeef, *das*
③ *n.* Braten, *der*

rob /rɒb/ *v.t.,* -**bb**- ausrauben ⟨*Bank, Safe,*
Kasse⟩; berauben ⟨*Person*⟩

robber /'rɒbə(r)/ *n.* Räuber, *der*/Räuberin,
die

robbery /'rɒbərɪ/ *n.* Raub, *der;* **robberies**
Raubüberfälle *Pl.*

robe /rəʊb/ *n.* Gewand, *das* (geh.); (of judge,
vicar) Talar, *der*

robin /'rɒbɪn/ *n.* ∼ [**redbreast**] Rotkehlchen,
das

robot /'rəʊbɒt/ *n.* Roboter, *der*

robotics /rəʊ'bɒtɪks/ *n.* Robotertechnik,
die; Robotik, *die*

robust /rəʊ'bʌst/ *adj.* robust

rock¹ /rɒk/ *n.* (a) (piece of ∼) Fels, *der*
(b) (large ∼, hill) Felsen, *der*
(c) (substance) Fels, *der;* (esp. Geol.) Gestein,
das
(d) (boulder) Felsbrocken, *der;* (Amer.: stone)
Stein, *der*
(e) stick of ∼: Zuckerstange, *die*
(f) be on the ∼s (fig. coll.) ⟨*Ehe, Firma:*⟩
kaputt sein (ugs.)

rock² ① *v.t.* wiegen; (in cradle) schaukeln
② *v.i.* (a) schaukeln
(b) (sway) schwanken
③ *n.* (Mus.) Rock, *der; attrib.* Rock-; ∼ **and** *or*
'**n' roll** [**music**] Rock and Roll, *der*

rock: ∼-'**bottom** (coll.) ① *adj.* ∼-**bottom**
prices Schleuderpreise *Pl.* (ugs.); ② *n.* **reach**
or **touch** ∼-**bottom** ⟨*Handel, Preis:*⟩ in den
Keller fallen (ugs.); **her spirits reached**
∼-**bottom** ihre Stimmung war auf dem
Tiefpunkt; ∼ **climber** *n.* Kletterer, *der*/
Kletterin, *die;* ∼ **climbing** *n.*
[Fels]klettern, *das*

rocker /'rɒkə(r)/ *n.* **be off one's** ∼ (fig. coll.)
übergeschnappt *od.* durchgedreht sein (ugs.)

rockery /'rɒkərɪ/ *n.* Steingarten, *der*

rocket /'rɒkɪt/ ① *n.* Rakete, *die*
② *v.i.* ⟨*Preise:*⟩ in die Höhe schnellen

rocket: ∼ **base** *n.* (Mil.)
Raketen[abschuss]basis, *die;* ∼ **launcher**
n. Raketenwerfer, *der;* ∼-**propelled** *adj.*
raketengetrieben

rock: ∼ **face** *n.* Felswand, *die;* ∼**fall** *n.*
Steinschlag, *der;* ∼ **formation** *n.*
Gesteinsformation, *die;* ∼ **garden** *n.*
Steingarten, *der;* ∼-**hard** *adj.* steinhart

rocking: ∼ **chair** *n.* Schaukelstuhl, *der;*
∼ **horse** *n.* Schaukelpferd, *das*

rock: ∼ **plant** *n.* Felsenpflanze, *die;* (Hort.)
Steingartengewächs, *das;* ∼ **salt** *n.*
Steinsalz, *das*

'**rocky** *adj.* (a) felsig
(b) (coll.: unsteady) wackelig (ugs.)

rod /rɒd/ *n.* Stange, *die;* (for punishing) Rute,
die; (for fishing) [Angel]rute, *die*

rode ▶ RIDE 2, 3

rodent /'rəʊdənt/ *n.* Nagetier, *das*

rodeo /'rəʊdɪəʊ, rəʊ'deɪəʊ/ *n., pl.* ∼**s** Rodeo,
der od. das

roe¹ /rəʊ/ *n.* (of fish) [**hard**] ∼: Rogen, *der;*
[**soft**] ∼: Milch, *die*

roe² *n.* ∼ [**deer**] Reh, *das*

rogue /rəʊg/ *n.* Gauner, *der*

role, rôle /rəʊl/ *n.* Rolle, *die*

role: ∼ **model** *n.* Leitbild, *das;*
∼ **playing** *n.* Rollenspiel, *das;*
∼ **reversal** *n.* Rollentausch, *der*

róll¹ /rəʊl/ *n.* (a) Rolle, *die;* (of cloth etc.)
Ballen, *der;* ∼ **of film** Rolle Film
(b) [**bread**] ∼: Brötchen, *das*
(c) **be on a** ∼ (coll.) eine Glückssträhne
haben

roll² ① *n.* (of drum) Wirbel, *der*
② *v.t.* (a) rollen; (between surfaces) drehen
(b) (shape by ∼ing) rollen; drehen ⟨*Zigarette*⟩
(c) walzen ⟨*Rasen, Metall usw.*⟩; ausrollen
⟨*Teig*⟩
③ *v.i.* (a) rollen
(b) ⟨*Maschine:*⟩ laufen; **get sth.** ∼**ing** (fig.)
etw. ins Rollen bringen
(c) **be** ∼**ing in money** *or* **in it** (coll.) im Geld
schwimmen (ugs.)
■ **roll a'bout** *v.i.* herumrollen; ⟨*Schiff:*⟩
schlingern; ⟨*Kind, Hund:*⟩ sich wälzen
■ **roll 'back** *v.t.* zurückrollen
■ **roll 'by** *v.i.* ⟨*Zeit:*⟩ vergehen
■ **roll 'in** *v.i.* (coll.) ⟨*Briefe, Geldbeträge:*⟩
eingehen
■ **roll 'over** *v.i.* ⟨*Person:*⟩ sich umdrehen, (to
make room) sich zur Seite rollen
■ **roll 'up** ① *v.t.* aufrollen ⟨*Teppich*⟩;
zusammenrollen ⟨*Landkarte, Dokument*
usw.⟩; hochkrempeln ⟨*Ärmel*⟩
② *v.i.* (coll.: arrive) aufkreuzen (salopp)

'**roll-call** *n.* Ausrufen aller Namen; (Mil.)
Zählappell, *der*

rolled 'oats *n. pl.* Haferflocken *Pl.*

'**roller** *n.* (a) Rolle, *die;* (for lawn, road, etc.)
Walze, *die*
(b) (for hair) Lockenwickler, *der*

roller: R∼**blade** ® *n.* Rollerblade, *der;*

rollerblade ⋯⋗ rotary · · · ·

Inliner, der; **~blade** v.i. Rollerblades
fahren; **~ blind** n. Rouleau, das;
~ coaster n. Achterbahn, die; **~ skate**
n. Rollschuh, der; **~skate** v.i. Rollschuh
laufen; **~ skating** n. Rollschuhlaufen, das
'**roll film** n. Rollfilm, der
'**rolling** adj. wellig ⟨Gelände⟩; **~ hills** sanfte
Hügel Pl.
rolling: ~ pin n. Teigrolle, die; **~ stock**
n. (Brit. Railw.) Fahrzeugbestand, der
roll: ~neck 1 n. Rollkragen, der; 2 adj.
Rollkragen-; **~on ~off** adj. **~on ~off**
ship/ferry Roll-on-roll-off-Schiff, das/-Fähre,
die; **~over** n. (von Auslosung zu
Auslosung) aufgestockter Jackpot; **~up**
(Brit. coll.)**, ~your-own** (esp. Amer. coll.) ns.
Selbstgedrehte, die
ROM /rɒm/ abbr. (Comp.) = **read only
memory** ROM
Roman /'rəʊmən/ 1 n. Römer, der/
Römerin, die
2 adj. römisch
Roman 'Catholic 1 adj. römisch-
katholisch
2 n. Katholik, der/Katholikin, die; **sb. is a
~**: jmd. ist römisch-katholisch
romance /rə'mæns/ n. (a) (love affair)
Romanze, die
(b) (love story) [romantische]
Liebesgeschichte
Romania /rəʊ'meɪnɪə/ pr. n. Rumänien
(das)
Romanian /rəʊ'meɪnɪən/ 1 adj.
rumänisch; **sb. is ~**: jmd. ist Romäne/
Romänin
2 n. (a) (person) Rumäne, der/Rumänin, die
(b) (language) Rumänisch, das; see also
ENGLISH 2A
Roman 'numeral n. römische Ziffer
romantic /rəʊ'mæntɪk/ adj. romantisch
romanticism /rəʊ'mæntɪsɪzm/ n. (Lit., Art.,
Mus.) Romantik, die
romanticize /rəʊ'mæntɪsaɪz/ v.t.
romantisieren
'**roman type** n. (Printing) Antiquaschrift,
die
Romany /'rəʊmənɪ/ 1 (a) (person) Rom,
der
(b) (language) Romani, das
2 adj. Roma-; (Ling.) Romani-
Rome /rəʊm/ pr. n. Rom (das)
romp /rɒmp/ 1 v.i. (a) [herum]tollen
(b) **~ home** or **in** (coll.: win easily) spielend
gewinnen
2 n. Tollerei, die
rompers /'rɒmpəz/ n. pl. Spielhöschen, das
roof /ru:f/ 1 n. (a) Dach, das
(b) **~ of the mouth** Gaumen, der
2 v.t. bedachen
'**roof garden** Dachgarten, der
'**roofing** n. (material) Deckung, die
'**roof: ~ rack** n. Dachgepäckträger, der;
~top n. Dach, das

rook¹ /rʊk/ n. (Ornith.) Saatkrähe, die
rook² n. (Chess) Turm, der
rookery /'rʊkərɪ/ n. Saatkrähenkolonie, die
room /ru:m, rʊm/ n. (a) (in building) Zimmer,
das; (for function) Saal, der
(b) (space) Platz, der; **make ~ [for sb./sth.]**
[jmdm./einer Sache] Platz machen; **there is
still ~ for improvement in his work** seine
Arbeit ist noch verbesserungsfähig
room: ~-mate n. Zimmergenosse, der/
-genossin, die; **~ service** n.
Zimmerservice, der; **~ temperature** n.
Zimmertemperatur, die
roomy /'ru:mɪ/ adj. geräumig
roost /ru:st/ 1 n. [Sitz]stange, die
2 v.i. ⟨Vogel:⟩ sich [zum Schlafen]
niederlassen
root¹ /ru:t/ 1 n. Wurzel, die; **put down ~s/
take ~**: Wurzeln schlagen
2 v.i. ⟨Pflanze:⟩ wurzeln
3 v.t. **stand ~ed to the spot** wie
angewurzelt dastehen
■ **root 'out** v.t. ausrotten
root² v.i. (a) (turn up ground) wühlen (for
nach)
(b) (coll.) **~ for** (cheer) anfeuern
'**root crop[s]** n. [pl.] Hackfrüchte Pl.
'**rooted** adj. eingewurzelt
'**rootless** adj. wurzellos
'**root vegetable** n. Wurzelgemüse, das
rope /rəʊp/ 1 n. (a) (cord) Seil, das
(b) **know the ~s** sich auskennen
2 v.t. festbinden
■ **rope 'in** v.t. (fig.) einspannen (ugs.)
rope 'ladder n. Strickleiter, die
ro-ro /'rəʊrəʊ/ adj. Ro-Ro-⟨Schiff, Fähre⟩
rosary /'rəʊzərɪ/ n. Rosenkranz, der
rose¹ /rəʊz/ n. (a) (plant, flower) Rose, die
(b) (colour) Rosa, das
rose² ▶ RISE 2
rosé /rəʊ'zeɪ, 'rəʊzeɪ/ n. Rosé, der
rose: ~ bed n. Rosenbeet, das; **~bud** n.
Rosenknospe, die; **~ bush** n. Rosenstrauch,
der; **~ hip** n. Hagebutte, die
rosemary /'rəʊzmərɪ/ n. Rosmarin, der
'**rose petal** n. Rosen[blüten]blatt, das
rosette /rəʊ'zet/ n. Rosette, die
roster /'rɒstə(r)/ n. Dienstplan, der
rostrum /'rɒstrəm/ n., pl. **rostra** /'rɒstrə/
or **~s** Podium, das
rosy /'rəʊzɪ/ adj. rosig
rot /rɒt/ 1 n. (a) ▶ 2: Verrottung, die;
Fäulnis, die; (fig.: deterioration) Verfall, der;
stop the ~ (fig.) dem Verfall Einhalt gebieten
(b) (coll.: nonsense) Quark, der (salopp)
2 v.i. **-tt-** verrotten; ⟨Fleisch, Gemüse,
Obst:⟩ verfaulen
3 v.t. **-tt-** verrotten lassen; verfaulen lassen
⟨Fleisch, Gemüse, Obst⟩; zerstören ⟨Zähne⟩
rota /'rəʊtə/ n. (Brit.) (order of rotation) Turnus,
der; (list) Arbeitsplan, der
rotary /'rəʊtərɪ/ adj. rotierend

r

rotate /rəʊˈteɪt/ ① v.i. (revolve) rotieren; sich drehen

② v.t. in Rotation versetzen

rotation /rəʊˈteɪʃn/ n. (a) Rotation, die, Drehung, die (about um)

(b) (succession) turnusmäßiger Wechsel; **in** or **by** ∼: im Turnus

rote /rəʊt/ n. **by** ∼: auswendig

rotten /ˈrɒtn/ adj., ∼er /ˈrɒtnə(r)/, ∼est /ˈrɒtnɪst/ (a) (decayed) verrottet; verfault ⟨Obst, Gemüse⟩; faul ⟨Ei, Holz, Zähne⟩; ∼ **to the core** (fig.) verdorben bis ins Mark

(b) (corrupt) verdorben

(c) (coll.: bad) mies (ugs.)

rotund /rəʊˈtʌnd/ adj. (a) (round) rund

(b) (plump) rundlich

rouble /ˈruːbl/ n. Rubel, der

rouge /ruːʒ/ n. Rouge, das

rough /rʌf/ ① adj. (a) (coarse, uneven) rau; holp[e]rig ⟨Straße usw.⟩; uneben ⟨Gelände⟩; unruhig ⟨Überfahrt⟩

(b) (violent) grob ⟨Person, Worte, Behandlung⟩

(c) (trying) hart; **this is** ∼ **on him** das ist hart für ihn; **sth. is** ∼ **going** etw. ist nicht einfach

(d) (approximate) grob ⟨Skizze, Schätzung⟩; vag ⟨Vorstellung⟩; ∼ **paper/notebook** Konzeptpapier, das/Kladde, die

(e) (coll.: ill) angeschlagen (ugs.)

② n. **[be] in** ∼: [sich] im Rohzustand [befinden]

③ adv. rau ⟨spielen⟩; **sleep** ∼: im Freien schlafen

④ v.t. ∼ **it** primitiv leben

■ **rough 'out** v.t. grob entwerfen

■ **rough 'up** v.t. (coll.) zusammenschlagen

roughage /ˈrʌfɪdʒ/ n. Ballaststoffe Pl.

rough: ∼-**and-ready** adj. provisorisch; ∼ **and 'tumble** n. [milde] Rauferei; ∼ **copy,** ∼ **draft** ns. grobe Skizze; grober Entwurf; ∼ **'diamond** n. (fig.) ungehobelter, aber guter Mensch

roughen /ˈrʌfn/ v.t. aufrauen

rough: ∼ **'justice** n. ziemlich willkürliche Urteile Pl.; ∼ **'luck** n. Pech, das

'roughly adv. (a) (violently) roh; grob

(b) (crudely) leidlich; grob ⟨skizzieren, bearbeiten, bauen⟩

(c) (approximately) ungefähr; grob ⟨geschätzt⟩

'roughness n. (a) Rauheit, die; (unevenness) Unebenheit, die

(b) (violence) Rohheit, die

'roughshod adj. **ride** ∼ **over sb./sth.** jmdn./etw. mit Füßen treten

roulette /ruːˈlet/ n. Roulette, das

round /raʊnd/ ① adj. rund; **in** ∼ **figures** rund gerechnet

② n. (a) (recurring series) Serie, die; ∼ **of talks/ negotiations** Gesprächs-/Verhandlungsrunde, die; **the daily** ∼: der Alltag

(b) (of ammunition) Ladung, die; **50** ∼**s [of ammunition]** 50 Schuss Munition

(c) (of game or contest) Runde, die

(d) (burst) ∼ **of applause** Beifallssturm, der

(e) ∼ **[of drinks]** Runde, die

(f) (regular calls) Runde, die; Tour, die; **go [on]** or **make one's** ∼**s** seine Runden machen

(g) **a** ∼ **of toast/sandwiches** eine Scheibe Toast/eine Portion Sandwiches

③ adv. (a) **all the year** ∼: das ganze Jahr hindurch; **the third time** ∼: beim dritten Mal; **have a look** ∼: sich umsehen; **ask sb.** ∼ **[for a drink]** jmdn. [zu einem Gläschen zu sich] einladen

(b) (by indirect way) herum; **walk** ∼: außen herum gehen

(c) (here) hier; (there) dort; **I'll go** ∼ **tomorrow** ich gehe morgen hin

④ prep. (a) um [... herum]; **travel** ∼ **England** durch England reisen; **run** ∼ **the streets** durch die Straßen rennen; **walk** ∼ **and** ∼ **sth.** immer wieder um etw. herumgehen

(b) (in various directions from) um [... herum]; rund um ⟨einen Ort⟩

⑤ v.t. ∼ **a bend** um eine Kurve fahren/ gehen/kommen usw

■ **round 'off** v.t. abrunden

■ **round 'up** v.t. verhaften ⟨Verdächtige⟩; zusammentreiben ⟨Vieh⟩

round: ∼ **a'bout** adv. (on all sides) ringsum; ∼**about** ① n. (a) (Brit.: merry-go-round) Karussell, das; (b) (Brit.: road junction) Kreisverkehr, der. ② adj. umständlich; ∼ **'brackets** n. pl. runde Klammern Pl.

rounded /ˈraʊndɪd/ adj. (a) rund

(b) harmonisch ⟨Person⟩

rounders /ˈraʊndəz/ n. sing. (Brit.) Rounders, das; ≈ Schlagball, der

round: ∼ **'number** n. runde Zahl; ∼ **'robin** n. Petition, die; ∼**-shouldered** /raʊndˈʃəʊldəd/ adj. ⟨Person⟩ mit einem Rundrücken; ∼**-the-'clock** adj. rund um die Uhr nachgestellt; ∼ **'trip** n. Rundreise, die; ∼**-up** n. (a) (of animals) Zusammentreiben, das; (b) (summary) Zusammenfassung, die

rouse /raʊz/ v.t. wecken (from aus)

rousing /ˈraʊzɪŋ/ adj. mitreißend ⟨Lied⟩; leidenschaftlich ⟨Rede⟩

rout /raʊt/ ① n. [wilde] Flucht; (defeat) verheerende Niederlage

② v.t. aufreiben ⟨Feind, Truppen⟩; vernichtend schlagen ⟨Gegner⟩

route /ruːt/ n. Route, die; Weg, der

'route march n. (Mil.) Übungsmarsch, der

routine /ruːˈtiːn/ ① n. (a) Routine, die

(b) (coll.: set speech) Platte, die (ugs.)

(c) (Theatre) Nummer, die; (Dancing, Skating) Figur, die

② adj. routinemäßig; Routine⟨arbeit⟩

roux /ruː/ n. Mehlschwitze, die

row¹ /raʊ/ ① (coll.) n. (a) (noise) Krach, der; **make a** ∼: Krach machen

(b) (quarrel) Krach, der (ugs.); **have/start a** ∼: Krach haben/anfangen (ugs.)

② v.i. sich streiten

row² /rəʊ/ n. Reihe, die; **in a** ∼: in einer Reihe

row³ /rəʊ/ v.i. & t. (with oars) rudern

rowan /'rəʊən/ n. ~ [tree] Eberesche, die

rowboat /'rəʊbəʊt/ n. (Amer.) Ruderboot, das

rowdy /'raʊdɪ/ [1] adj. rowdyhaft; **the party was** ~: auf der Party ging es laut zu [2] n. Krawallmacher, der

rower /'rəʊə(r)/ n. Ruderer, der/Ruderin, die

rowing /'rəʊɪŋ/ n. Rudern, das

rowing: ~ **boat** n. (Brit.) Ruderboot, das; ~ **machine** n. Rudergerät, das

royal /'rɔɪəl/ adj. königlich

royal: R~ **'Air Force** n. (Brit.) Königliche Luftwaffe; ~ **'blue** n. (Brit.) Königsblau, das; ~ **'family** n. königliche Familie; **R**~ **'Navy** n. (Brit.) Königliche Kriegsmarine

royalty /'rɔɪəltɪ/ n. (a) (payment) Tantieme, die (on für) (b) collect. (royal persons) Mitglieder Pl. des Königshauses

RSI abbr. = **repetitive strain injury**

RSPCA abbr. (Brit.) = **Royal Society for the Prevention of Cruelty to Animals** britischer Tierschutzverein

rub /rʌb/ [1] v.t., -bb- reiben (**on, against** an + Dat.); (to remove dirt etc.) abreiben; (to dry) trockenreiben; ~ **sth. off sth.** etw. von etw. [ab]reiben [2] v.i., -bb- reiben ([up]**on, against** an + Dat.) [3] n. give it a ~: reib es ab; **there's the** ~ (fig.) da liegt der Haken [dabei] (ugs.)
■ **rub 'down** v.t. abreiben
■ **rub 'in** v.t. einreiben; **there's no need to** or don't ~ **it in** (fig.) reib es mir nicht [dauernd] unter die Nase
■ **rub 'off** v.t. wegreiben; wegwischen
■ **rub 'out** [1] v.t. ausreiben; (using eraser) ausradieren [2] v.i. sich ausreiben/sich ausradieren lassen

rubber /'rʌbə(r)/ n. (a) Gummi, das od. der (b) (eraser) Radiergummi, der

rubber: ~ **'band** n. Gummiband, das; ~ **'glove** n. Gummihandschuh, der; ~ **plant** n. Gummibaum, der; ~ **'stamp** n. Gummistempel, der; ~**-stamp** v.t. (fig.) absegnen (ugs.)

rubbery /'rʌbərɪ/ adj. gummiartig; (tough) zäh

rubbish /'rʌbɪʃ/ [1] n. (a) (refuse) Abfall, der; (to be collected and dumped) Müll, der (b) (worthless material) Plunder, der (ugs.); **be** ~: nichts taugen (c) (nonsense) Quatsch, der (ugs.) [2] int. Quatsch (ugs.)

rubbish: ~ **bin** n. Abfall-/Mülleimer, der; (in factory) Abfall-/Mülltonne, die; ~ **chute** n. Müllschlucker, der; ~ **collection** n. Müllabfuhr, die; ~ **dump** n. Müllkippe, die; ~ **heap** n. Müllhaufen, der; ~ **tip** n. Müllabladeplatz, der

rubbishy /'rʌbɪʃɪ/ adj. mies (ugs.)

rubble /'rʌbl/ n. Trümmer Pl.

rubella /ru'belə/ n. (Med.) Röteln Pl.

ruby /'ru:bɪ/ n. Rubin, der

ruby 'wedding n. Rubinhochzeit, die

rucksack /'rʌksæk, 'rʊksæk/ n. Rucksack, der

rudder /'rʌdə(r)/ n. [Steuer]ruder, das

ruddy /'rʌdɪ/ adj. (a) (reddish) rötlich (b) (Brit. coll.: bloody) verdammt (salopp)

rude /ruːd/ adj. (a) unhöflich; (stronger) rüde; **be** ~ **to sb.** zu jmdm. grob unhöflich sein/jmdn. rüde behandeln (b) (abrupt) unsanft; ~ **awakening** böses Erwachen

'rudely adv. (a) (impolitely) unhöflich; rüde (b) (abruptly) jäh (geh.)

'rudeness n. (bad manners) ungehöriges Benehmen

rudimentary /ruːdɪ'mentərɪ/ adj. elementar; primitiv ⟨Gebäude⟩

rudiments /'ruːdɪmənts/ n. pl. Grundlagen Pl.

rueful /'ruːfl/ adj. reumütig

ruffian /'rʌfɪən/ n. Rohling, der

ruffle /'rʌfl/ v.t. (a) kräuseln; ~ **sb.'s hair** jmdm. durch die Haare fahren (b) (upset) aus der Fassung bringen

rug /rʌg/ n. [kleiner, dicker] Teppich; **Persian** ~: Perserbrücke, die

rugby /'rʌgbɪ/ n. Rugby, das

rugby: ~ **ball** n. Rugbyball, der; ~ **tackle** n. tiefes Fassen; **the policeman brought him down with a** ~ **tackle** der Polizist warf sich auf ihn und riss ihn zu Boden

rugged /'rʌgɪd/ adj. (a) (uneven) zerklüftet; unwegsam ⟨Land⟩; zerfurcht ⟨Gesicht⟩ (b) (sturdy) robust

ruin /'ruːɪn/ [1] n. (a) in sing. or pl. (remains) Ruine, die; **in** ~s in Trümmern (b) (downfall) Ruin, der [2] v.t. ruinieren; verderben ⟨Urlaub, Abend⟩; ~**ed** (reduced to ruins) verfallen; **a** ~**ed castle/church** eine Burg-/Kirchenruine

ruinous /'ruːnəs/ adj. ruinös

rule /ruːl/ [1] n. (a) Regel, die; **the** ~s **of the game** die Spielregeln; **be against the** ~s regelwidrig sein; (fig.) gegen die Spielregeln verstoßen; **as a** ~: in der Regel; ~ **of thumb** Faustregel, die (b) no pl. (government) Herrschaft, die (**over** über + Akk.) [2] v.t. (a) (control) beherrschen (b) (be the ruler of) regieren; ⟨Monarch, Diktator usw.:⟩ herrschen über (+ Akk.) [3] v.i. (a) (govern) herrschen (b) (decide) entscheiden (**against** gegen; **in favour of** für)
■ **rule 'out** v.t. ausschließen; (prevent) unmöglich machen

'rule book n. Regeln

ruled /ruːld/ adj. liniert ⟨Papier⟩

ruler /'ruːlə(r)/ *n.* **(a)** (person) Herrscher, *der*/Herrscherin, *die*
(b) (for measuring) Lineal, *das*

ruling /'ruːlɪŋ/ **1** *adj.* herrschend ⟨*Klasse*⟩; regierend ⟨*Partei*⟩
2 *n.* Entscheidung, *die*

rum /rʌm/ *n.* Rum, *der*

Rumania etc. /ruːˈmeɪnɪə/ ▶ ROMANIA etc.

rumble /'rʌmbl/ **1** *n.* Grollen, *das*
2 *v.i.* **(a)** grollen; ⟨*Magen:*⟩ knurren
(b) ⟨*Fahrzeug:*⟩ rumpeln (ugs.)

ruminate /'ruːmɪneɪt/ *v.i.* ∼ **on** *or* **over sth.** über etw. (*Akk.*) grübeln

rummage /'rʌmɪdʒ/ *v.i.* wühlen; ∼ **through sth.** etw. durchwühlen (ugs.)

rummy /'rʌmɪ/ *n.* Rommé, *das*

rumour (*Brit.*; *Amer.*: **rumor**) /'ruːmə(r)/
1 *n.* Gerücht, *das;* **there is a** ∼ **that** ...: es geht das Gerücht, dass ...
2 *v.t.* **it is** ∼**ed that** ...: es geht das Gerücht, dass ...

rump /rʌmp/ *n.* **(a)** (buttocks) Hinterteil, *das* (ugs.)
(b) (remnant) Rest, *der*

rumple /'rʌmpl/ *v.t.* **(a)** (crease) zerknittern
(b) (tousle) zerzausen

'rump steak *n.* Rumpsteak, *das*

rumpus /'rʌmpəs/ *n.* (coll.) Krach, *der* (ugs.); **kick up** *or* **make a** ∼: einen Spektakel veranstalten (ugs.)

'rumpus room *n.* (Amer.) Spielzimmer, *das*

run /rʌn/ **1** *n.* **(a)** Lauf, *der;* **go for a** ∼: laufen gehen; **on the** ∼ (fleeing) auf der Flucht
(b) (trip in vehicle) Fahrt, *die;* (for pleasure) Ausflug, *der*
(c) (continuous stretch) Länge, *die*
(d) (spell) **she has had a long** ∼ **of success** sie war lange [Zeit] erfolgreich; **have a long** ∼ ⟨*Stück, Show:*⟩ viele Aufführungen erleben
(e) (succession) Serie, *die;* (Cards) Sequenz, *die;* **a** ∼ **of victories** eine Siegesserie
(f) (use) **have the** ∼ **of sth.** etw. zu seiner freien Verfügung haben
(g) (enclosure) Auslauf, *der*
(h) (in stocking etc.) Laufmasche, *die*
2 *v.i.*, **-nn-**, **ran** /ræn/, **run (a)** laufen; ∼ **for the bus** laufen, um den Bus zu kriegen (ugs.); ∼ **to help sb.** jmdm. zu Hilfe eilen
(b) (roll, slide) laufen; ⟨*Ball, Kugel:*⟩ rollen, laufen; ⟨*Schlitten, [Schiebe]tür:*⟩ gleiten
(c) ⟨*Rad, Maschine:*⟩ laufen
(d) (operate on a schedule) fahren; ∼ **between two places** ⟨*Zug, Bus:*⟩ zwischen zwei Orten verkehren
(e) (flow) laufen; ⟨*Fluss:*⟩ fließen; ⟨*Augen:*⟩ tränen; **his nose was** ∼**ning** ihm lief die Nase
(f) ⟨*Vertrag, Theaterstück:*⟩ laufen
(g) (have wording) lauten; ⟨*Geschichte:*⟩ gehen (fig.)
(h) ⟨*Butter, Eis:*⟩ zerlaufen; ⟨*Farben:*⟩ auslaufen

(i) (in election) kandidieren
3 *v.t.*, **-nn-**, **ran**, **run (a)** laufen lassen; (drive) fahren; ∼ **one's hand/fingers through/along** *or* **over sth.** mit der Hand/den Fingern durch etw. fahren/über etw. (*Akk.*) streichen; ∼ **an** *or* **one's eye along** *or* **down** *or* **over sth.** (fig.) etw. überfliegen
(b) (cause to flow) [ein]laufen lassen; ∼ **a bath** ein Bad einlaufen lassen
(c) (organize, manage) führen, leiten ⟨*Geschäft usw.*⟩; veranstalten ⟨*Wettbewerb*⟩
(d) (operate) bedienen ⟨*Maschine*⟩; verkehren lassen ⟨*Verkehrsmittel*⟩; einsetzen ⟨*Sonderbus, -zug*⟩; laufen lassen ⟨*Motor*⟩
(e) (own and use) sich (*Dat.*) halten ⟨*Auto*⟩
(f) ∼ **sb. into town** etc. jmdn. in die Stadt usw. fahren

■ **run a'cross** *v.t.* ∼ **across sb./sth.** jmdn. treffen/auf etw. (*Akk.*) stoßen

■ **run a'way** *v.i.* **(a)** (flee) weglaufen; fortlaufen
(b) (abscond) ∼ **away [from home]** [von zu Hause] weglaufen

■ **run 'down 1** *v.t.* **(a)** (collide with) überfahren
(b) (criticize) heruntermachen (ugs.)
(c) (reduce) abbauen
2 *v.i.* **(a)** hin-/herunterlaufen
(b) (decline) sich verringern
(c) ⟨*Uhr, Spielzeug:*⟩ ablaufen; ⟨*Batterie*⟩ leer werden

■ **'run into** *v.t.* **(a)** ∼ **into a tree** gegen einen Baum fahren
(b) (meet) ∼ **into sb.** jmdm. in die Arme laufen (ugs.)
(c) stoßen auf (+ *Akk.*) ⟨*Schwierigkeiten, Widerstand usw.*⟩
(d) (amount to) ∼ **into thousands** in die tausende gehen

■ **run 'off 1** *v.i.* weglaufen
2 *v.t.* abziehen ⟨*Kopien*⟩

■ **run 'out 1** *v.i.* **(a)** hin-/herauslaufen
(b) ⟨*Vorräte, Bestände:*⟩ zu Ende gehen

■ **run 'out of** *v.t.* **sb.** ∼**s out of sth.** jmdm. geht etw. aus; **I'm** ∼**ning out of patience** meine Geduld geht zu Ende

■ **run 'over 1** /'--/ *v.t.* (knock down) überfahren
2 /-'-/ *v.i.* überlaufen

■ **'run through** *v.t.* durchspielen ⟨*Theaterstück*⟩; durchgehen ⟨*Plan*⟩

■ **'run to** *v.t.* **(a)** (amount to) sich belaufen auf (*Akk.*)
(b) (be sufficient for) **sth. will** ∼ **to sth.** etw. reicht für etw.

■ **run 'up 1** *v.i.* hinlaufen; **come** ∼**ning up** hingelaufen kommen
2 *v.t.* **(a)** rasch nähen ⟨*Kleidungsstück*⟩
(b) zusammenkommen lassen ⟨*Schulden, Rechnung*⟩

■ **run 'up against** *v.t.* stoßen auf (+ *Akk.*) ⟨*Probleme, Widerstand usw.*⟩

run: ∼**about** *n.* (coll.) [little] ∼**about** Kleinwagen, *der;* ∼**around** *n.* (coll.) **give sb. the** ∼**around** jmdn. an der Nase herumführen (ugs.); ∼**away 1** *n.*

Ausreißer, *der*/Ausreißerin, *die* (ugs.);
2 *attrib. adj.* durchgegangen ⟨*Pferd*⟩; außer
Kontrolle geraten ⟨*Fahrzeug, Preise*⟩;
galoppierend ⟨*Inflation*⟩; **~down** /'--/ *n.*
(coll.: briefing) Übersicht, *die* (on über + *Akk.*);
~down /-'-/ *adj.* (tired) mitgenommen

rung¹ /rʌŋ/ *n.* Sprosse, *die*

rung² ▶ RING² 2, 3

'**runner** *n.* (a) Läufer, *der*/Läuferin, *die*
(b) (Bot.) Ausläufer, *der*
(c) (on sledge) Kufe, *die*

'**runner bean** *n.* (Brit.) Stangenbohne, *die*

runner-'up *n.* Zweite, *der*/*die;* the runners-
up die Platzierten *Pl.*

'**running** **1** *n.* (a) (management) Leitung, *die*
(b) (action) Laufen, *das;* in/out of the ~: im/
aus dem Rennen
2 *adj.* (in succession) hintereinander; **win for**
the third year ~: schon drei Jahre
hintereinander gewinnen

running: ~ 'commentary *n.*
(Broadcasting; also fig.) Livekommentar, *der;*
~ costs *n. pl.* Betriebskosten *Pl.;*
~ shoe *n.* Rennschuh, *der;* **~ 'total** *n.*
fortlaufende Summe; **~ track** *n.*
Aschenbahn, *die;* **~ 'water** *n.* hot and cold
~ water fließendes kaltes und warmes
Wasser

runny /'rʌnɪ/ *adj.* (a) laufend ⟨*Nase*⟩
(b) zu dünn ⟨*Farbe, Marmelade*⟩

run: ~-of-the-'mill *adj.* ganz gewöhnlich;
~-up *n.* (a) during *or* in the ~-up to an
event im Vorfeld eines Ereignisses; (b)
(Sport) Anlauf, *der;* **~way** *n.* (for take-off)
Startbahn, *die;* (for landing) Landebahn, *die*

rupture /'rʌptʃə(r)/ **1** *n.* Bruch, *der*
2 *v.t.* ~ oneself sich (*Dat.*) einen Bruch
zuziehen

rural /'rʊərl/ *adj.* ländlich

ruse /ruːz/ *n.* List, *die*

rush¹ /rʌʃ/ *n.* (Bot.) Binse, *die*

rush² **1** *n.* (a) (hurry) Eile, *die;* what's all the
~? wozu diese Hast?; **be in a [great] ~:** in
[großer] Eile sein

(c) (period of great activity) Hochbetrieb, *der;*
(~ hour) Stoßzeit, *die*
(c) **make a ~ for sth.** sich auf etw. (*Akk.*)
stürzen
2 *v.t.* (a) ~ sb./sth. somewhere jmdn./etw.
auf schnellstem Wege irgendwohin bringen;
be ~ed (have to hurry) in Eile sein; ~ sb. **into**
doing sth. jmdn. dazu drängen, etw. zu tun
(b) (perform quickly) auf die Schnelle
erledigen; ~ it zu schnell machen
3 *v.i.* (a) (move quickly) eilen; ⟨*Hund, Pferd:*⟩
laufen; ~ **to help sb.** jmdm. zu Hilfe eilen
(b) (hurry unduly) sich zu sehr beeilen; **don't**
~! nur keine Eile!

■ **rush a'bout, rush a'round** *v.i.*
herumhetzen

rush: ~ hour *n.* Stoßzeit, *die;* ~ **job** *n.*
eilige Arbeit

rusk /rʌsk/ *n.* Zwieback, *der*

Russia /'rʌʃə/ *pr. n.* Russland (*das*)

Russian /'rʌʃn/ **1** *adj.* russisch; **sb. is ~:**
jmd. ist Russe/Russin
2 *n.* (a) (person) Russe, *der*/Russin, *die*
(b) (language) Russisch, *das; see also* ENGLISH
2A

rust /rʌst/ **1** *n.* Rost, *der*
2 *v.i.* rosten

rustic /'rʌstɪk/ *adj.* (a) ländlich
(b) rustikal ⟨*Mobiliar*⟩

rustle /'rʌsl/ **1** *n.* Rascheln, *das*
2 *v.i.* rascheln
3 *v.t.* (a) rascheln lassen
(b) (Amer.: steal) stehlen

■ **rustle 'up** *v.t.* zusammenzaubern
⟨*Mahlzeit*⟩

'**rustproof** *adj.* rostfrei

'**rusty** *adj.* rostig

rut /rʌt/ *n.* Spurrille, *die;* be in a ~ (fig.) aus
dem [Alltags]trott nicht mehr
herauskommen

ruthless /'ruːθlɪs/ *adj.* rücksichtslos

RV *abbr.* (Amer.) = **recreational**
vehicle

rye /raɪ/ *n.* Roggen, *der*

'**rye bread** *n.* Roggenbrot, *das*

Ss

S, s /es/ *n.* S, s, *das*

S. *abbr.* (a) = **south** S
(b) = **southern** s.

sabbath /'sæbəθ/ *n.* Sabbat, *der*

sabbatical /sə'bætɪkl/ **1** *adj.* ~ term/year
Forschungssemester/-jahr, *das*
2 *n.* Forschungsurlaub, *der*

sabotage /'sæbətɑːʒ/ **1** *n.* Sabotage, *die*

2 *v.t.* einen Sabotageakt verüben auf
(+ *Akk.*); (fig.) sabotieren

saboteur /sæbə'tɜː(r)/ *n.* Saboteur, *der*

saccharin /'sækərɪn/ *n.* Saccharin, *das*

sachet /'sæʃeɪ/ *n.* Beutel, *der;* (cushion-
shaped) Kissen, *das*

sack /sæk/ **1** *n.* (a) Sack, *der*   ⸱⸱⸱❖

(b) (coll.: dismissal) Rausschmiss, *der* (ugs.); **get the ∼:** rausgeschmissen werden (ugs.); **give sb. the ∼:** jmdn. rausschmeißen (ugs.)
② *v.t.* (coll.) rausschmeißen (ugs.) **(for** wegen)

sacking /'sækɪŋ/ *n.* **(a)** (coll.: dismissal) Rausschmiss, *der* (ugs.)
(b) (coarse fabric) Sackleinen, *das*

sacrament /'sækrəmənt/ *n.* Sakrament, *das*

sacred /'seɪkrɪd/ *adj.* heilig

sacrifice /'sækrɪfaɪs/ ① *n.* Opfer, *das*
② *v.t.* opfern

sacrilege /'sækrɪlɪdʒ/ *n.* **[act of]** ∼: Sakrileg, *das*

sad /sæd/ *adj.* traurig **(at, about** über + *Akk.*); schmerzlich ⟨*Tod, Verlust*⟩; **feel ∼:** traurig sein

sadden /'sædn/ *v.t.* traurig stimmen

SAD *abbr.* = **seasonal affective disorder**

saddle /'sædl/ ① *n.* Sattel, *der*
② *v.t.* **(a)** satteln ⟨*Pferd usw.*⟩
(b) (fig.) ∼ **sb. with sth.** jmdm. etw. aufbürden (geh.)

'saddlebag *n.* Satteltasche, *die*

sadism /'seɪdɪzm/ *n.* Sadismus, *der*

sadist /'seɪdɪst/ *n.* Sadist, *der*/Sadistin, *die*

sadistic /sə'dɪstɪk/ *adj.,* **sa'distically** *adv.* sadistisch

'sadly *adv.* **(a)** (with sorrow) traurig
(b) (unfortunately) leider

'sadness *n.* Traurigkeit, *die*

sadomasochism /seɪdəʊ'mæsəkɪzm/ *n.* Sadomasochismus, *der*

s.a.e. /eseɪ'iː/ *abbr.* = **stamped addressed envelope** adressierter Freiumschlag

safari /sə'fɑːrɪ/ *n.* Safari, *die*; **on ∼:** auf Safari

safe /seɪf/ ① *n.* Safe, *der;* Geldschrank, *der*
② *adj.* **(a)** (out of danger) sicher **(from** vor + *Dat.*); **he's ∼:** er ist in Sicherheit; ∼ **and sound** sicher und wohlbehalten
(b) (free from danger) ungefährlich; sicher ⟨*Ort, Hafen*⟩; **wish sb. a ∼ journey** jmdm. eine gute Reise wünschen; **to be on the ∼ side** zur Sicherheit
(c) (reliable) sicher ⟨*Methode, Investition*⟩

safe: ∼**guard** ① *n.* Schutz, *der;* ② *v.t.* schützen; ∼ **'haven** *n.* **(a)** (safe place) Zuflucht, *die;* **(b)** (Polit.) Schutzzone, *die*

safely /'seɪflɪ/ *adv.* sicher; **did the parcel arrive ∼?** ist das Paket heil angekommen?

safe 'sex Safersex, *der*

safety: ∼ **belt** *n.* Sicherheitsgurt, *der;* ∼ **catch** *n.* (of gun) Sicherungshebel, *der;* ∼ **helmet** *n.* Schutzhelm, *der;* ∼ **margin** *n.* Spielraum, *der;* ∼ **pin** *n.* Sicherheitsnadel, *die;* ∼ **valve** *n.* Sicherheitsventil, *das;* (fig.) Ventil, *das*

'safe zone *n.* (Polit.) Schutzzone, *die*

saffron /'sæfrən/ *n.* Safran, *der*

sag /sæg/ *v.i.,* **-gg-** durchhängen; (sink) sich senken

saga /'sɑːgə/ *n.* **(a)** (story of adventure) Heldenepos, *das;* (medieval narrative) Saga, *die*
(b) (long involved story) [ganzer] Roman (fig.)

sage[1] /seɪdʒ/ *n.* (Bot.) Salbei, *der od. die*

sage[2] ① *adj.* weise
② *n.* Weise, *der*

Sagittarius /sædʒɪ'teərɪəs/ *n.* (Astrol; Astron.) der Schütze

Sahara /sə'hɑːrə/ *pr. n.* **the ∼ [Desert]** die [Wüste] Sahara

said ▶ SAY 1

sail /seɪl/ ① *n.* **(a)** Segelfahrt, *die*
(b) (piece of canvas) Segel, *das*
② *v.i.* **(a)** (travel on water) fahren; (in sailing boat) segeln
(b) (start voyage) auslaufen **(for** nach)
③ *v.t.* **(a)** steuern ⟨*Boot, Schiff*⟩; segeln mit ⟨*Segeljacht, -schiff*⟩
(b) durchfahren/⟨*Segelschiff:*⟩ durchsegeln ⟨*Meer*⟩

sail: ∼**board** *n.* Surfbrett, *das* (*zum Windsurfen*); ∼**boarding** *n.* Windsurfen, *das;* ∼**boat** *n.* (Amer.) Segelboot, *das*

'sailing *n.* Segeln, *das*

sailing: ∼ **boat** *n.* Segelboot, *das;* ∼ **ship** *n.* Segelschiff, *das*

sailor /'seɪlə(r)/ *n.* Seemann, *der;* (in navy) Matrose, *der*

saint ① /seɪk/ *n.* ≈ heilig S∼ **Michael** der heilige Michael; Sankt Michael
② /seɪnt/ *n.* Heilige, *der/die*

'saintly /'seɪntlɪ/ *adj.* heilig

sake /seɪk/ *n.* **for the ∼ of um … (***Gen.***)** willen; **for my** *etc.* ∼: um meinetwillen *usw.;* mir *usw.* zuliebe

salad /'sæləd/ *n.* Salat, *der*

salad: ∼ **cream** *n.* ≈ Mayonnaise, *die;* ∼ **dressing** *n.* Salatsoße, *die;* ∼ **servers** *n. pl.* Salatbesteck, *das*

salary /'sælərɪ/ *n.* Gehalt, *das*

sale /seɪl/ *n.* **(a)** Verkauf, *der;* (at reduced prices) Ausverkauf, *der;* (at end of season) Schlußverkauf, *der;* **[up] for ∼:** zu verkaufen
(b) ∼**s** (amount sold) Verkaufszahlen *Pl.* **(of** für); Absatz, *der*
(c) [jumble *or* rummage] ∼: [Wohltätigkeits]basar, *der*

'sale price *n.* **(a)** (retail price) Verkaufspreis, *der*
(b) (price in sale) Ausverkaufspreis, *der*

sales: ∼ **assistant** (Brit.), ∼ **clerk** (Amer.) *ns.* Verkäufer, *der*/Verkäuferin, *die;* ∼**man** /'seɪlzmən/ *n., pl.* ∼**men** /'seɪlzmən/ Verkäufer, *der*

'salesmanship *n.* Kunst des Verkaufens

sales: ∼ **rep** (coll.), ∼ **representative** *ns.* [Handels]vertreter, *der*/-vertreterin, *die;* ∼**woman** *n.* Verkäuferin, *die*

salient /'seɪlɪənt/ *adj.* auffallend

saliva /sə'laɪvə/ *n.* Speichel, *der*

sallow /'sæləʊ/ *adj.* blassgelb

salmon /'sæmən/ *n.* Lachs, *der*

saloon /sə'luːn/ *n.* **(a)** (Brit.) ~ [**bar**] *separater Teil eines Pubs mit mehr Komfort* **(b)** (Brit.) ~ [**car**] Limousine, *die*

salt /sɔːlt, sɒlt/ ❶ *n.* [**common**] ~: [Koch]salz, *das* ❷ *adj.* (containing or tasting of ~) salzig; (preserved with ~) gepökelt ⟨*Fleisch*⟩; gesalzen ⟨*Butter*⟩ ❸ *v.t.* **(a)** salzen **(b)** (cure) [ein]pökeln **(c)** ~ the roads Salz auf die Straßen streuen

salt: ~ **cellar** *n.* Salzfässchen, *das*; ~ '**water** *n.* Salzwasser, *das*

'**salty** *adj.* salzig

salute /sə'luːt/ ❶ *v.t.* grüßen ❷ *v.i.* (Mil., Navy) [militärisch] grüßen ❸ *n.* Salut, *der;* militärischer Gruß

salvage /'sælvɪdʒ/ ❶ *n.* Bergung, *die* ❷ *v.t.* bergen

salvation /sæl'veɪʃn/ *n.* Erlösung, *die*

Salvation 'Army *n.* Heilsarmee, *die*

salvo /'sælvəʊ/ *n.* Salve, *die*

Samaritan /sə'mærɪtən/ *n.* good ~: [barmherziger] Samariter; the ~s (organization) ≈ die Telefonseelsorge

same /seɪm/ ❶ *adj.* the ~: der/die/das gleiche; the ~ [**thing**] (identical) der-/die-/dasselbe ❷ *adv.* all *or* just the ~: trotzdem

sample /'sɑːmpl/ ❶ *n.* (example) [Muster]beispiel, *das;* (specimen) Probe, *die;* [**commercial**] ~: Muster, *das* ❷ *v.t.* probieren

'**sample letter** *n.* Musterbrief, *der*

sampler /'sɑːmplə(r)/ *n.* (trial pack) Probe[packung], *die*

sanatorium /sænə'tɔːrɪəm/ *n.* Sanatorium, *das*

sanctify /'sæŋktɪfaɪ/ *v.t.* heiligen

sanctimonious /sæŋktɪ'məʊnɪəs/ *adj.* scheinheilig

sanction /'sæŋkʃn/ ❶ *n.* Sanktion, *die* ❷ *v.t.* sanktionieren

sanctity /'sæŋktɪtɪ/ *n.* Heiligkeit, *die*

sanctuary /'sæŋktʃʊərɪ/ *n.* **(a)** (holy place) Heiligtum, *das* **(b)** (refuge) Zufluchtsort, *der* **(c)** (for animals) Naturschutzgebiet, *das*

sand /sænd/ ❶ *n.* Sand, *der* ❷ *v.t.* ~ sth. [down] etw. [ab]schmirgeln

sandal /'sændl/ *n.* Sandale, *die*

sand: ~**bag** ❶ *n.* Sandsack, *der;* ❷ *v.t.* mit Sandsäcken schützen; ~**bank** *n.* Sandbank, *die;* ~**castle** *n.* Sandburg, *die;* ~ **dune** *n.* Düne, *die;* ~**paper** ❶ *n.* Sandpapier, *das;* ❷ *v.t.* [mit Sandpapier] [ab]schmirgeln; ~**pit** *n.* Sandkasten, *der;* ~**stone** *n.* Sandstein, *der*

sandwich /'sænwɪdʒ/ ❶ *n.* Sandwich, *der od. das;* ≈ [zusammengeklapptes] belegtes Brot; **cheese** ~: Käsebrot, *das* ❷ *v.t.* einschieben (**between** zwischen + *Akk.;* **into** in + *Akk.*)

'**sandy** *adj.* **(a)** sandig; Sand⟨*boden, -strand*⟩ **(b)** rotblond ⟨*Haar*⟩

sane /seɪn/ *adj.* **(a)** geistig gesund **(b)** (sensible) vernünftig

sang ▸ SING

sanitary /'sænɪtərɪ/ *adj.* sanitär ⟨*Verhältnisse, Anlagen*⟩

'**sanitary napkin** (Amer.), '**sanitary towel** (Brit.) *ns.* Damenbinde, *die*

sanitation /sænɪ'teɪʃn/ *n.* Kanalisation und Abfallbeseitigung

sanitize (sanitise) /'sænɪtaɪz/ *v.t.* (fig.) entschärfen

sanity /'sænɪtɪ/ *n.* geistige Gesundheit; **lose one's** ~: den Verstand verlieren

sank ▸ SINK 2, 3

Santa Claus /'sæntə klɔːz/ *n.* der Weihnachtsmann

sap /sæp/ ❶ *n.* Saft, *der* ❷ *v.t.,* -**pp**- zehren an (+ *Dat.*)

sapling /'sæplɪŋ/ *n.* junger Baum

sapphire /'sæfaɪə(r)/ *n.* Saphir, *der*

sarcasm /'sɑːkæzm/ *n.* Sarkasmus, *der*

sarcastic /sɑː'kæstɪk/ *adj.* sarkastisch

sardine /sɑː'diːn/ *n.* Sardine, *die*

Sardinia /sɑː'dɪnɪə/ *pr. n.* Sardinien (*das*)

sardonic /sɑː'dɒnɪk/ *adj.* höhnisch; sardonisch ⟨*Lächeln*⟩

SARS /sɑːz/ *n.* SARS, *das*

sash /sæʃ/ *n.* Schärpe, *die*

sash 'window *n.* Schiebefenster, *das*

sat ▸ SIT

Sat. *abbr.* = **Saturday** Sa.

Satan /'seɪtən/ *pr. n.* Satan, *der*

satanic /sə'tænɪk/ *adj.* satanisch

satchel /'sætʃl/ *n.* [Schul]ranzen, *der*

satellite /'sætəlaɪt/ *n.* Satellit, *der*

satellite: ~ '**broadcasting** *n.* Satellitenfunk, *der;* ~ **dish** *n.* Satellitenschüssel, *die;* ~ **receiver** *n.* Satellitenempfänger, *der;* ~ **technology** *n.* Satellitentechnik, *die;* ~ '**television** *n.* Satellitenfernsehen, *das;* ~ **town** *n.* Satelliten- *od.* Trabantenstadt, *die*

satin /'sætɪn/ *n.* Satin, *der*

satire /'sætaɪə(r)/ *n.* Satire, *die* (on auf + *Akk.*)

satirical /sə'tɪrɪkl/ *adj.* satirisch

satisfaction /sætɪs'fækʃn/ *n.* Befriedigung, *die* (at, with über + *Akk.*); **meet with sb.'s [complete]** ~: jmdn. [in jeder Weise] zufrieden stellen

satisfactory /sætɪs'fæktərɪ/ *adj.* zufrieden stellend

satisfied /'sætɪsfaɪd/ *adj.* **(a)** (contented) zufrieden **(b)** (convinced) überzeugt (**of** von)

S

satisfy /ˈsætɪsfaɪ/ v.t. **(a)** befriedigen; zufrieden stellen ‹Kunden›; stillen ‹Hunger, Durst›
(b) (convince) ~ **sb. [of sth.]** jmdn. [von etw.] überzeugen

'satisfying adj. befriedigend; sättigend ‹Gericht, Speise›

satphone /ˈsætfəʊn/ n. Satellitentelefon, das

saturate /ˈsætʃəreɪt/ v.t. durchnässen; [mit Feuchtigkeit durch]tränken ‹Boden, Erde›

saturated /ˈsætʃəreɪtɪd/ adj. durchnässt

Saturday /ˈsætədeɪ, ˈsætədɪ/ n. Samstag, der; see also FRIDAY

'Saturday job n. Samstagsjob, der (ugs.)

Saturn /ˈsætən/ pr. n. (Astron.) Saturn, der

sauce /sɔːs/ n. **(a)** Soße, die
(b) (impudence) Frechheit, die

sauce: ~ **boat** n. Sauciere, die; ~**pan** /ˈsɔːspən/ n. Kochtopf, der; (with straight handle) [Stiel]kasserolle, die

saucer /ˈsɔːsə(r)/ n. Untertasse, die

saucy /ˈsɔːsɪ/ adj. **(a)** (rude) frech
(b) (pert, jaunty) keck

Saudi Arabia /saʊdɪ əˈreɪbɪə/ pr. n. Saudi-Arabien (das)

sauna /ˈsɔːnə, ˈsaʊnə/ n. Sauna, die

saunter /ˈsɔːntə(r)/ v.i. schlendern

sausage /ˈsɒsɪdʒ/ n. Wurst, die

sausage: ~ **meat** n. Wurstmasse, die; ~ **'roll** n.: Blätterteig mit Wurstfüllung

savage /ˈsævɪdʒ/ **1** adj. **(a)** (uncivilized) primitiv; wild ‹Volksstamm›; unzivilisiert ‹Land›
(b) (fierce) brutal; wild ‹Tier›
2 n. Wilde, der/die (veralt.)

savagery /ˈsævɪdʒrɪ/ n. Brutalität, die

save /seɪv/ **1** v.t. **(a)** (rescue) retten (from vor + Dat.); ~ **oneself from falling** sich [beim Hinfallen] fangen
(b) (put aside) aufheben; sparen ‹Geld›; sammeln ‹Briefmarken usw.›; (conserve) sparsam umgehen mit
(c) (make unnecessary) sparen ‹Geld, Zeit, Energie›; ~ **sb./oneself sth.** jmdm./sich etw. ersparen
(d) (Sport) abwehren ‹Schuss, Ball;›
(e) (Comp.) speichern; sichern; ~ **sth. on [to] a disk** etw. auf Diskette abspeichern
2 v.i. sparen (on Akk.)
3 n. (Sport) Abwehr, die
▪ **save 'up** **1** v.t. sparen
2 v.i. sparen (for für, auf + Akk.)

'saver n. Sparer, der/Sparerin, die

saving /ˈseɪvɪŋ/ **1** n. in pl. Ersparnisse Pl.
2 adj. ‹kosten-, benzin›sparend

savings: ~ **account** n. Sparkonto, das; ~ **bank** n. Sparkasse, die

saviour /ˈseɪvjə(r)/ n. **(a)** Retter, der/Retterin, die
(b) (Relig.) **the S~:** der Heiland

savor etc. (Amer.) ▶ SAVOUR etc.

savour /ˈseɪvə(r)/ (Brit.) **1** n. (flavour) Geschmack, der
2 v.t. genießen

savoury /ˈseɪvərɪ/ (Brit.) **1** adj. **(a)** pikant; salzig
(b) (appetizing) appetitanregend
2 n. [pikantes] Häppchen

saw[1] /sɔː/ **1** n. Säge, die
2 v.t., p.p. sawn /sɔːn/ or sawed [zer]sägen; ~ **in half** in der Mitte durchsägen
3 v.i., p.p. sawn or sawed sägen; ~ **through sth.** etw. durchsägen

saw[2] ▶ SEE

saw: ~**dust** n. Sägemehl, das; ~**mill** n. Sägemühle, die

sawn ▶ SAW[1] 2, 3

'sawn-off adj. (Brit.) ‹Gewehr› mit abgesägtem Lauf

saxophone /ˈsæksəfəʊn/ n. Saxophon, das

saxophonist /sækˈsɒfənɪst/ n. Saxophonist, der/Saxophonistin, die

say /seɪ/ **1** v.t. pres. t. **he says** /sez/, p.t. & p.p. **said** /sed/ **(a)** sagen; **that is to ~:** das heißt; **do as** or **what I ~:** tun Sie, was ich sage; **when all is said and done** letzten Endes; **go without ~ing** sich von selbst verstehen; **she is said to be clever/to have done it** man sagt, sie sei klug/habe es getan
(b) (recite) sprechen ‹Gebet, Text›
(c) (have specified wording or reading) sagen; ‹Zeitung:› schreiben; ‹Uhr:› zeigen ‹Uhrzeit›; **what does it ~ here?** was steht hier?
2 n. **have a** or **some ~:** ein Mitspracherecht haben (in bei); **have no ~:** nichts zu sagen haben; **have one's ~:** seine Meinung sagen

'saying n. Redensart, die

scab /skæb/ n. [Wund]schorf, der

scaffold /ˈskæfəld/ n. Schafott, das

'scaffolding n. Gerüst, das

'scaffolding pole n. Gerüststange, die

scald /skɔːld, skɒld/ **1** n. Verbrühung, die
2 v.t. verbrühen

scale[1] /skeɪl/ n. **(a)** (of fish, reptile, etc.) Schuppe, die
(b) (in kettle etc.) Kesselstein, der; (on teeth) Zahnstein, der

scale[2] n. **(a)** in sing. or pl. (weighing instrument) ~**[s]** Waage, die
(b) (dish of balance) Waagschale, die

scale[3] **1** n. **(a)** (series of degrees) Skala, die
(b) (Mus.) Tonleiter, die
(c) (dimensions) Ausmaß, das; **be on a small ~:** bescheidenen Umfang haben
(d) (ratio of reduction) Maßstab, der; **what is the ~ of the map?** welchen Maßstab hat diese Karte?
(e) (indication) (on map) Maßstab, der; (on thermometer) [Anzeige]skala, die
2 v.t. ersteigen ‹Mauer, Leiter, Gipfel›
▪ **scale 'down** v.t. [entsprechend] drosseln ‹Produktion›; Abstriche machen bei ‹Planungen›

scalp /skælp/ n. Kopfhaut, die

scalpel ⋯⬩ schizophrenia ⋯⬩

scalpel /'skælpl/ *n*. Skalpell, *das*

scam /skæm/ *n*. (coll.) Masche, *die* (ugs.)

scamper /'skæmpə(r)/ *v.i.* ⟨Person:⟩ flitzen; ⟨Tier:⟩ huschen

scampi /'skæmpɪ/ *n. pl.* Scampi *Pl.*

scan /skæn/ ⟨1⟩ *v.t.*, **-nn-:** **(a)** (search thoroughly) absuchen **(for** nach)
(b) (look over cursorily) flüchtig ansehen; überfliegen ⟨Zeitung, Liste usw.⟩ **(for** auf der Suche nach)
(c) (Med.) szintigraphisch untersuchen
(d) (Comp.) scannen
⟨2⟩ *v.i.*, **-nn-** ⟨Vers[zeile]:⟩ das richtige Versmaß haben
⟨3⟩ *n.* (Med.) szintigraphische Untersuchung, *die;* (image) Szintigramm, *das*

scandal /'skændl/ *n.* **(a)** Skandal, *der* **(about/of** um); (story) Skandalgeschichte, *die*
(b) (outrage) Empörung, *die*
(c) (gossip) Klatsch, *der* (ugs.)

scandalize /'skændəlaɪz/ *v.t.* schockieren

scandalous /'skændələs/ *adj.* skandalös; schockierend ⟨Bemerkung⟩

Scandinavia /skændɪ'neɪvɪə/ *pr. n.* Skandinavien (*das*)

Scandinavian /skændɪ'neɪvɪən/⟨1⟩ *adj.* skandinavisch; **sb. is ∼:** jmd. ist Skandinavier/Skandinavierin
⟨2⟩ *n.*(a) (person) Skandinavier, *der*/ Skandinavierin, *die*
(b) (Ling.) skandinavische Sprachen *Pl.*

scant /skænt/ *adj.* wenig

scanty /'skæntɪ/ *adj.* spärlich; knapp ⟨Bikini⟩

scapegoat /'skeɪpgəʊt/ *n.* Sündenbock, *der;* **make sb. a ∼:** jmdn. zum Sündenbock machen

scar /skɑː(r)/ ⟨1⟩ *n.* Narbe, *die*
⟨2⟩ *v.t.*, **-rr-:** ∼ **sb./sb.'s face** bei jmdm./in jmds. Gesicht (*Dat.*) Narben hinterlassen

scarce /skeəs/ *adj.* **(a)** (insufficient) knapp
(b) (rare) selten; **make oneself ∼** (coll.) sich aus dem Staub machen (ugs.)

'scarcely *adv.* kaum

scarcity /'skeəsɪtɪ/ *n.* Knappheit, *die* (**of** an + *Dat.*)

scare /skeə(r)/ ⟨1⟩ *n.* **(a)** (sensation of fear) Schreck[en], *der;* **give sb. a ∼:** jmdm. einen Schreck[en] einjagen
(b) (general alarm) [allgemeine] Hysterie; **bomb ∼:** Bombendrohung, *die*
⟨2⟩ *v.t.* (frighten) Angst machen (+ *Dat.*); (startle) erschrecken
■ **scare a'way, scare 'off** *v.t.* verscheuchen

'scarecrow *n.* Vogelscheuche, *die*

scared /skeəd/ *adj.* **be ∼ of sb./sth.** vor jmdm./etw. Angst haben; **be ∼ of doing/to do sth.** sich nicht [ge]trauen, etw. zu tun

scaremongering /'skeəmʌŋgərɪŋ/ *n.* Panikmache, *die*

scarf /skɑːf/ *n., pl.* ∼**s or scarves** /skɑːvz/ Schal, *der;* (square) Halstuch, *das;* (worn over hair) Kopftuch, *das*

scarlet /'skɑːlɪt/ ⟨1⟩ *n.* Scharlach, *der*
⟨2⟩ *adj.* scharlachrot

scarlet 'fever *n.* Scharlach, *der*

scarves ▶ SCARF

scary /'skeərɪ/ *adj.* Furcht erregend ⟨Anblick⟩; schaurig ⟨Film, Geschichte⟩

scathing /'skeɪðɪŋ/ *adj.* bissig ⟨Person, Humor, Bemerkung⟩

scatter /'skætə(r)/ ⟨1⟩ *v.t.* **(a)** vertreiben; auseinander treiben ⟨Menge⟩
(b) (distribute irregularly) verstreuen
⟨2⟩ *v.i.* sich auflösen; ⟨Menge:⟩ sich zerstreuen; (in fear) auseinander stieben

scattered /'skætəd/ *adj.* verstreut; vereinzelt ⟨Regenschauer⟩

scatty /'skætɪ/ *adj.* (Brit. coll.) dusslig (salopp)

scavenge /'skævɪndʒ/ *v.i.* ∼ **for sth.** nach etw. suchen

'scavenger *n.* (animal) Aasfresser, *der;* (fig. derog.: person) Aasgeier, *der* (ugs.)

scenario /sɪ'nɑːrɪəʊ/ *n., pl.* ∼**s** Szenario, *das*

scene /siːn/ *n.* **(a)** (place of event) Schauplatz, *der;* ∼ **of the crime** Tatort, *der*
(b) (division of act) Auftritt, *der*
(c) (view) Anblick, *der*
(d) behind the ∼s hinter den Kulissen
(e) the political/drug/artistic ∼: die politische/Drogen-/Kunstszene

scenery /'siːnərɪ/ *n.* **(a)** Landschaft, *die*
(b) (Theatre) Bühnenbild, *das*

scenic /'siːnɪk/ *adj.* landschaftlich schön

scent /sent/ ⟨1⟩ *n.* **(a)** (smell) Duft, *der*
(b) (Hunting; also fig.: trail) Fährte, *die;* **be on the ∼ of sb./sth.** (fig.) jmdm./einer Sache auf der Spur sein
(c) (Brit.: perfume) Parfüm, *das*
⟨2⟩ *v.t.* wittern

scented /'sentɪd/ *adj.*(a) (having smell) duftend
(b) (perfumed) parfümiert

sceptic /'skeptɪk/ *n.* Skeptiker, *der*/ Skeptikerin, *die*

sceptical /'skeptɪkl/ *adj.* skeptisch; **be ∼ about or of sb./sth.** jmdm./einer Sache skeptisch gegenüberstehen

scepticism /'skeptɪsɪzm/ *n.* Skepsis, *die*

schedule /'ʃedjuːl/ ⟨1⟩ *n.* **(a)** (list) Tabelle, *die;* (for event) Programm, *das*
(b) (of work) Zeitplan, *der*
(c) on ∼: plangemäß
⟨2⟩ *v.t.* zeitlich planen

'scheduled flight *n.* Linienflug, *der*

scheme /skiːm/ *n.* **(a)** (arrangement) Anordnung, *die*
(b) (plan) Programm, *das;* (project) Projekt, *das*
(c) (dishonest plan) Intrige, *die*

schizophrenia /skɪtsə'friːnɪə/ *n.* Schizophrenie, *die*

S

schizophrenic /ˌskɪtsəˈfrenɪk, ˌskɪtsəˈfriːnɪk/ *adj.* schizophren

scholar /ˈskɒlə(r)/ *n.* Gelehrte, *der/die*

'scholarly *adj.* wissenschaftlich; gelehrt ⟨*Person*⟩

'scholarship *n.* (a) (award) Stipendium, *das* (b) (scholarly work) Gelehrsamkeit, *die*

school /skuːl/ *n.* Schule, *die;* (Amer.: college) Hochschule, *die;* **be at** *or* **in** ∼: in der Schule sein; (attend ∼) zur Schule gehen; **go to** ∼: zur Schule gehen; ∼ **holidays/exchange** Schulferien *Pl.*/Schüleraustausch, *der*

school: ∼ **age** *n.* Schulalter, *das;* ∼**bag** *n.* Schultasche, *die;* ∼**boy** *n.* Schüler, *der;* ∼**child** *n.* Schulkind, *das;* ∼ **friend** *n.* Schulfreund, *der*/-freundin, *die;* ∼**girl** *n.* Schülerin, *die;* ∼ **'governor** *n.*: Mitglied des Schulbeirats; ∼**kid** *n.* (coll.) Schulkind, *das;* ∼ **leaver** *n.* (Brit.) Schulabgänger, *der*/-abgängerin, *die;* ∼**master** *n.* Lehrer, *der;* ∼**mistress** *n.* Lehrerin, *die;* ∼ **'rule** *n.* Schulvorschrift, *die;* Schulregel, *die;* **it is a** ∼ **rule that …**: an der Schule ist es Vorschrift, dass …; ∼**teacher** *n.* Lehrer, *der*/Lehrerin, *die;* ∼ **'uniform** *n.* Schuluniform, *die;* ∼ **work** *n.* Schularbeiten *Pl.;* ∼ **'year** *n.* Schuljahr, *das*

sciatica /saɪˈætɪkə/ *n.* Ischias, *der od. das*

science /ˈsaɪəns/ *n.* Wissenschaft, *die*

science 'fiction *n.* Sciencefiction, *die*

scientific /ˌsaɪənˈtɪfɪk/ *adj.* wissenschaftlich

scientist /ˈsaɪəntɪst/ *n.* Wissenschaftler, *der*/Wissenschaftlerin, *die*

sci-fi /ˈsaɪfaɪ/ *n.* (coll.) Sciencefiction, *die*

scintillating /ˈsɪntɪleɪtɪŋ/ *adj.* (fig.) geistsprühend

scissors /ˈsɪzəz/ *n. pl.* **[pair of]** ∼: Schere, *die*

scoff[1] /skɒf/ *v.i.* (mock) spotten; ∼ **at** sich lustig machen über (+ *Akk.*)

scoff[2] *v.t.* (coll.: eat greedily) verschlingen

scold /skəʊld/ *v.t.* ausschimpfen (**for** wegen); **she** ∼**ed him for being late** sie schimpfte ihn aus, weil er zu spät kam

scone /skɒn, skəʊn/ *n.: weicher, oft zum Tee gegessener kleiner Kuchen*

scoop /skuːp/ ① *n.* (a) Schaufel, *die;* (for ice cream etc.) Portionierer, *der* (b) (Journ.) Knüller, *der* (ugs.) ② *v.t.* schaufeln ⟨*Kohlen, Zucker*⟩; schöpfen ⟨*Flüssigkeit*⟩

■ **scoop 'out** *v.t.* (a) (hollow out) aushöhlen; schaufeln ⟨*Loch, Graben*⟩ (b) [her]ausschöpfen ⟨*Flüssigkeit*⟩; auslöffeln ⟨*Fruchtfleisch*⟩; (with a knife) herausschneiden ⟨*Gehäuse, Fruchtfleisch*⟩

■ **scoop 'up** *v.t.* schöpfen ⟨*Flüssigkeit, Suppe*⟩; schaufeln ⟨*Erde*⟩

scooter /ˈskuːtə(r)/ *n.* (a) (toy) Roller, *der* (b) [motor] ∼: [Motor]roller, *der*

scope /skəʊp/ *n.* (a) Bereich, *der;* (of discussion etc.) Rahmen, *der* (b) (opportunity) Entfaltungsmöglichkeiten *Pl.*

scorch /skɔːtʃ/ *v.t.* versengen

scorched 'earth policy *n.* Politik der verbrannten Erde

scorching /ˈskɔːtʃɪŋ/ *adj.* glühend heiß

score /skɔː(r)/ ① *n.* (a) (points) [Spiel]stand, *der;* (made by one player) Punktzahl, *die;* **keep [the]** ∼: zählen (b) (Mus.) Partitur, *die;* (Cinemat.) [Film]musik, *die* (c) *pl. same or* ∼**s** (group of 20) zwanzig (d) *in pl.* (great numbers) ∼**s [and** ∼**s] of** zig (ugs.); Dutzende [von] (e) **on that** ∼: was das betrifft (f) **pay off** *or* **settle an old** ∼ (fig.) eine alte Rechnung begleichen ② *v.t.* erzielen ⟨*Erfolg, Punkt usw.*⟩; ∼ **a goal** ein Tor schießen ③ *v.i.* (a) (make ∼) Punkte/einen Punkt erzielen; (∼ goal/goals) ein Tor/Tore schießen/werfen (b) (keep ∼) aufschreiben

'scoreboard *n.* Anzeigetafel, *die*

'scorer *n.* (a) (recorder) Anschreiber, *der*/Anschreiberin, *die* (b) (Footb.) Torschütze, *der*/-schützin, *die*

'scoresheet *n.* Anschreibebogen, *der*

scorn /skɔːn/ ① *n.* Verachtung, *die* ② *v.t.* verachten; in den Wind schlagen ⟨*Rat*⟩; ausschlagen ⟨*Angebot*⟩

scornful /ˈskɔːnfl/ *adj.* verächtlich ⟨*Lächeln, Blick*⟩; **be** ∼ **of sth.** für etw. nur Verachtung haben

Scorpio /ˈskɔːpɪəʊ/ *n.* (Astrol; Astron.) der Skorpion

scorpion /ˈskɔːpɪən/ *n.* Skorpion, *der*

Scot /skɒt/ *n.* Schotte, *der*/Schottin, *die*

scotch *v.t.* den Boden entziehen (+ *Dat.*) ⟨*Gerücht*⟩; zunichte machen ⟨*Plan*⟩

Scotch /skɒtʃ/ ① *adj.* ▶ SCOTTISH ② *n.* Scotch, *der;* schottischer Whisky

Scotch: ∼ **'egg** *n.: hart gekochtes Ei in Wurstbrät;* ∼ **'whisky** *n.* schottischer Whisky

scot-'free *adj.* **[get off/go]** ∼: ungeschoren [davonkommen *od.* bleiben]

Scotland /ˈskɒtlənd/ *pr. n.* Schottland (*das*)

Scots /skɒts/ ① *adj.* (esp. Scot.) schottisch; **sb. is** ∼: jmd. ist Schotte/Schottin ② *n.* (dialect) Schottisch, *das*

Scotsman /ˈskɒtsmən/ *n., pl.* **Scotsmen** /ˈskɒtsmən/ Schotte, *der*

'Scotswoman *n.* Schottin, *die*

Scottish /ˈskɒtɪʃ/ *adj.* schottisch; **sb. is** ∼: jmd. ist Schotte/Schottin

scoundrel /ˈskaʊndrl/ *n.* Schuft, *der*

scour[1] /ˈskaʊə(r)/ *v.t.* (search) durchkämmen (**for** nach)

scour[2] *v.t.* scheuern ⟨*Topf, Metall*⟩

'scourer *n.* Topfreiniger, *der*

scourge /skɜːdʒ/ *n.* Geißel, *die*

scout /skaʊt/ ①*n.* (a) [Boy] S~:
Pfadfinder, *der*
(b) (Mil.) Späher, *der*
②*v.i.* ~ **for** Ausschau halten nach

scowl /skaʊl/ ①*v.i.* ein mürrisches
Gesicht machen
②*n.* mürrischer [Gesichts]ausdruck

scram /skræm/ *v.i.*, **-mm-** (coll.) abhauen
(salopp)

scramble /ˈskræmbl/ ①*v.i.* (a) (clamber)
klettern; ~ **through a hedge** sich durch eine
Hecke zwängen
(b) (move hastily) rennen (ugs.); ~ **for sth.** um
etw. rangeln
②*v.t.* (Teleph., Radio) verschlüsseln

scrambled 'egg *n.* Rührei, *das*

scrap¹ /skræp/ ①*n.* (a) (of paper) Fetzen,
der; (of food) Bissen, *der*
(b) *in pl.* (*odds and ends*) (*of food*) Reste *Pl.*
(c) (smallest amount) **not a ~ of** kein bisschen;
(of sympathy, truth also) nicht ein Fünkchen;
not a ~ of evidence nicht die Spur eines
Beweises
(d) ~ **[metal]** Schrott, *der;* ~ **iron** Alteisen,
das
②*v.t.*, **-pp-** wegwerfen; (send for ~)
verschrotten; (fig.) aufgeben

scrap² (coll.) ①*n.* (fight) Rauferei, *die*
②*v.i.*, **-pp-** sich raufen

'scrapbook *n.* [Sammel]album, *das*

scrape /skreɪp/ ①*v.t.* (a) (make smooth)
schaben ⟨Häute, Möhren, Kartoffeln usw.⟩;
abziehen ⟨Holz⟩; (damage) verschrammen
⟨Fußboden, Auto⟩
(b) (remove) [ab]kratzen ⟨Farbe, Schmutz,
Rost⟩ (**off, from** von)
(c) (draw along) schleifen
(d) ~ **together** (raise) zusammenkratzen
(ugs.); (save up) zusammensparen
②*v.i.* (a) (move with sound) schleifen
(b) (emit scraping noise) ein schabendes
Geräusch machen
(c) (rub) streifen (**against, over** *Akk.*)
③*n.* (a) (act, sound) Kratzen, *das* (**against** an
+ *Dat.*)
(b) (predicament) Schwulitäten *Pl.* (ugs.)
■ **scrape 'by** *v.i.* (fig.) sich über Wasser
halten (**on** mit)
■ **scrape 'out** *v.t.* (a) (excavate) buddeln
(ugs.); scharren
(b) (clean) auskratzen
■ **scrape through** ① /'--/ *v.t.* sich
zwängen durch; (fig.) mit Hängen und
Würgen kommen durch ⟨Prüfung⟩
②/'-'-/ *v.i.* sich durchzwängen; (fig.: in
examination) mit Hängen und Würgen
durchkommen

'scraper *n.* (for shoes) Kratzeisen, *das;* (grid)
Abtreter, *der;* (tool, kitchen utensil) Schaber,
der; (for removing ice from car windows)
[Eis]kratzer, *der*

scrap: ~ **heap** *n.* Schrotthaufen, *der;*
~ **merchant** *n.* Schrotthändler, *der/*
-händlerin, *die;* ~ **'paper** *n.*
Schmierpapier, *das*

scrappy /ˈskræpɪ/ *adj.* lückenhaft

'scrapyard *n.* Schrottplatz, *der*

scratch /skrætʃ/ ①*v.t.* (a) (score surface of)
zerkratzen; (score skin of) kratzen
(b) (get scratch[es] on) ~ **oneself/one's hands**
etc. sich schrammen/sich (*Dat.*) die Hände
usw. zerkratzen
(c) (scrape without marking) kratzen; kratzen an
(+ *Dat.*) ⟨Insektenstich usw.⟩; ~ **oneself/**
one's arm sich kratzen/sich (*Dat.*) den Arm
od. am Arm kratzen
②*v.i.* kratzen; (~ oneself) sich kratzen
③*n.* (a) (mark, wound) Kratzer, *der* (ugs.);
Schramme, *die*
(b) (sound) Kratzen, *das*
(c) **have a [good]** ~: sich [ordentlich]
kratzen
(d) **start from** ~: bei Null anfangen (ugs.); **be**
up to ~ ⟨Arbeit, Leistung:⟩ nichts zu
wünschen übrig lassen; ⟨Person:⟩ den
Anforderungen genügen
■ **scratch a'bout, scratch a'round**
v.i. scharren; (fig.: search) suchen (**for** nach)

'scratch card *n.* Rubbellos, *das*

scrawl /skrɔːl/ ①*v.t.* hinkritzeln
②*v.i.* kritzeln
③*n.* Gekritzel, *das;* (handwriting) Klaue, *die*
(salopp)

scrawny /ˈskrɔːnɪ/ *adj.* hager; dürr

scream /skriːm/ ①*v.i.* schreien (**with** vor
+ *Dat.*)
②*v.t.* schreien
③*n.* Schrei, *der;* (of jet engine) Heulen, *das;*
~**s of pain** Schmerzensschreie *Pl.*

screech /skriːtʃ/ ①*v.i. & t.* kreischen
②*n.* Kreischen, *das*

screen /skriːn/ ①*n.* (a) (partition)
Trennwand, *die;* (piece of furniture)
Wandschirm, *der*
(b) (of trees, persons, fog) Wand, *die*
(c) (Cinemat.) Leinwand, *die;* [TV] ~:
Bildschirm, *der*
②*v.t.* (a) (shelter) schützen (**from** vor
+ *Dat.*); (conceal) verdecken
(b) vorführen ⟨Film⟩
(c) (for disease) untersuchen

screening /ˈskriːnɪŋ/ *n.* (a) (in cinema)
Vorführung, *die;* (on TV) Sendung, *die*
(b) (Med.) Untersuchung, *die*

screen: ~**play** *n.* Drehbuch, *das;*
~ **saver** *n.* (Comp.) Bildschirmschoner, *der;*
~**writer** *n.* Filmautor, *der/*-autorin, *die*

screw /skruː/ ①*n.* Schraube, *die;* **he has a**
~ **loose** (coll. joc.) bei ihm ist eine Schraube
locker *od.* lose (salopp)
②*v.t.* (a) schrauben (**to** an + *Akk.*);
~ **together** zusammenschrauben; ~ **down**
festschrauben
(b) ~ **you!** (coarse) leck mich am Arsch!
(salopp)

S

■ **screw 'up** *v.t.* (a) (crumple up) zusammenknüllen ⟨*Blatt Papier*⟩
(b) verziehen ⟨*Gesicht*⟩; zusammenkneifen ⟨*Augen, Mund*⟩
(c) (sl.: bungle) vermurksen (salopp); ∼ **it/ things up** Mist bauen (salopp)

screw: ∼ **cap** *n.* Schraubverschluss, *der;* ∼**driver** *n.* Schraubenzieher, *der*

'screwed-up *adj.* (fig. coll.) neurotisch

'screw top ▶ ∼ CAP

screwy /'skruːɪ/ *adj.* (coll.) spinnig (ugs.)

scribble /'skrɪbl/ ☐**1** *v.t.* hinkritzeln ☐**2** *v.i.* kritzeln ☐**3** *n.* Gekritzel, *das*

script /skrɪpt/ *n.* (a) (handwriting) Handschrift, *die*
(b) (of play) Regiebuch, *das;* (of film) [Dreh]buch, *das*
(c) (for broadcaster) Manuskript, *das*

scripture /'skrɪptʃə(r)/ *n.* (a) [Holy] S∼, the [Holy] S∼s die [Heilige] Schrift
(b) (Sch.) Religion, *die*

'scriptwriter *n.* (of film) Drehbuchautor, *der*/-autorin, *die*

scroll /skrəʊl/ ☐**1** *n.* (roll) Rolle, *die* ☐**2** *v.t.* (Comp.) scrollen
■ **scroll 'down** *v.i.* (Comp.) runterscrollen
■ **scroll 'up** *v.i.* (Comp.) hochscrollen
scrollable /'skrəʊləbl/ *adj.* (Comp.) scrollbar

'scroll bar *n.* (Comp.) Rollballen, *der*

scrounge /skraʊndʒ/ (coll.) ☐**1** *v.t.* schnorren (ugs.) (**off, from** von) ☐**2** *v.i.* schnorren (ugs.) (**from** bei)

'scrounger *n.* (coll.) Schnorrer, *der*/ Schnorrerin, *die* (ugs.)

scrub¹ /skrʌb/ ☐**1** *v.t.*, **-bb-:** (a) schrubben (ugs.); scheuern
(b) (coll.: cancel) zurücknehmen ⟨*Befehl*⟩; sausen lassen (ugs.) ⟨*Plan*⟩
☐**2** *v.i.*, **-bb-** schrubben (ugs.); scheuern
☐**3** *n.* **give sth. a** ∼**:** etw. schrubben (ugs.) *od.* scheuern

scrub² *n.* (brushwood) Buschwerk, *das;* (area) Buschland, *das*

scruff¹ /skrʌf/ *n.* **by the** ∼ **of the neck** beim Genick

scruff² *n.* (Brit. coll.) (man) vergammelter Typ (ugs.); (woman, girl) Schlampe, *die*

'scruffy *adj.* vergammelt (ugs.)

scrum /skrʌm/ *n.* Gedränge, *das*

scruple /'skruːpl/ *n.* Skrupel, *der;* **have no** ∼**s about doing sth.** keine Skrupel haben, etw. zu tun

scrupulous /'skruːpjʊləs/ *adj.* gewissenhaft ⟨*Person*⟩; unbedingt ⟨*Ehrlichkeit*⟩; peinlich ⟨*Sorgfalt*⟩

scrutinize /'skruːtɪnaɪz/ *v.t.* [genau] untersuchen ⟨[*Forschungs*]*gegenstand*⟩; [über]prüfen ⟨*Rechnung, Pass, Fahrkarte*⟩; mustern ⟨*Person*⟩

scrutiny /'skruːtɪnɪ/ *n.* (a) (critical gaze) musternder Blick

(b) (examination) (of recruit) Musterung, *die;* (of bill, passport, ticket) [Über]prüfung, *die*

scuff /skʌf/ ☐**1** *v.t.* streifen; verschrammen ⟨*Schuhe, Fußboden*⟩ ☐**2** *n.* Schramme, *die*

scuffle /'skʌfl/ ☐**1** *n.* Handgreiflichkeiten *Pl.* ☐**2** *v.i.* handgreiflich werden (**with** gegen)

scullery /'skʌlərɪ/ *n.* Spülküche, *die*

sculptor /'skʌlptə(r)/ *n.* Bildhauer, *der*/ -hauerin, *die*

sculpture /'skʌlptʃə(r)/ *n.* (a) (art) Bildhauerei, *die*
(b) (piece of work) Skulptur, *die;* Plastik, *die;* (pieces collectively) Skulpturen *Pl.*

scum /skʌm/ *n.* (a) Schmutzschicht, *die;* (film) Schmutzfilm, *der*
(b) (fig. derog.) Abschaum, *der*

'scumbag *n.* (sl. derog.) Schwein, *das* (salopp)

scurry /'skʌrɪ/ *v.i.* huschen

scuttle¹ /'skʌtl/ *n.* Kohlenfüller, *der*

scuttle² (Naut.) *v.t.* versenken

scuttle³ *v.i.* rennen; flitzen (ugs.); ⟨*Maus, Krabbe:*⟩ huschen

scythe /saɪð/ *n.* Sense, *die*

SE *abbr.* = **south-east** SO

sea /siː/ *n.* (a) Meer, *das;* **the** ∼**:** das Meer; **die See; by** ∼**:** mit dem Schiff; **by the** ∼**:** am Meer; **at** ∼**:** auf See (*Dat.*); **be all at** ∼ (fig.) nicht mehr weiter wissen; **put [out] to** ∼**:** in See (*Akk.*) gehen
(b) (specific tract of water) Meer, *das*

sea: ∼ **'air** *n.* Seeluft, *die;* ∼**bed** *n.* Meeresboden, *der;* ∼**bird** *n.* Seevogel, *der;* ∼ **breeze** *n.* Seewind, *der;* ∼**food** *n.* Meeresfrüchte *Pl.; attrib.* Fisch⟨*restaurant*⟩; ∼**gull** *n.* [See]möwe, *die*

seal¹ /siːl/ *n.* (Zool.) Robbe, *die;* [common] ∼**:** [Gemeiner] Seehund

seal² ☐**1** *n.* (wax etc., stamp, impression) Siegel, *das*
☐**2** *v.t.* (a) (stamp, affix ∼ to) siegeln ⟨*Dokument*⟩; (fasten with ∼) verplomben ⟨*Tür, Stromzähler*⟩
(b) (close securely) abdichten ⟨*Behälter, Rohr usw.*⟩; zukleben ⟨*Umschlag, Paket*⟩
(c) (stop up) verschließen; abdichten ⟨*Leck*⟩; verschmieren ⟨*Riss*⟩
■ **seal 'off** *v.t.* abriegeln

sea: ∼ **lane** *n.* See[schifffahrts]straße, *die;* ∼ **legs** *n. pl.* Seebeine *Pl.* (Seemannsspr.); **get** *or* **find one's** ∼ **legs** sich (*Dat.*) Seebeine wachsen lassen; ∼**level** *n.* Meeresspiegel, *der*

'sealing wax *n.* Siegellack, *der*

'sea lion *n.* Seelöwe, *der*

seam /siːm/ *n.* (a) Naht, *die*
(b) (of coal) Flöz, *das*

sea: ∼**man** /'siːmən/ *n., pl.* ∼**men** /'siːmən/ Matrose, *der;* ∼ **mist** *n.* Küstennebel, *der*

'seamless *adj.* nahtlos

seance /'seɪəns/**, séance** /'seɪãs/ *n.* Séance, *die*

sea: ~plane n. Wasserflugzeug, das; **~port** n. Seehafen, der; **~ power** n. Seemacht, die

sear /'sɪə(r)/ v.t. versengen

search /sɜ:tʃ/ **1** v.t. durchsuchen (for nach); absuchen ⟨Gebiet, Fläche⟩ (for nach); (fig.: probe) erforschen ⟨Herz, Gewissen⟩; suchen in (+ Dat.) ⟨Gedächtnis⟩ (for nach) **2** v.i. suchen (for nach) **3** n. Suche, die (for nach); (of building, room, etc.) Durchsuchung, die; in ~ of sb./sth. auf der Suche nach jmdm./etw

'search engine n. (Comp.) Suchmaschine, die

'searching adj. prüfend, forschend ⟨Blick⟩; bohrend ⟨Frage⟩

search: ~light n. Suchscheinwerfer, der; **~ party** n. Suchtrupp, der; **~ warrant** n. Durchsuchungsbefehl, der

sea: ~ salt n. Meersalz, das; Seesalz, das; **~shore** n. [Meeres]küste, die; (beach) Strand, der; **~sick** adj. seekrank; **~sickness** n. Seekrankheit, die; **~side** n. [Meeres]küste, die; by/to/at the ~side am/ ans/am Meer; **~side town** Seestadt, die

season /'si:zn/ **1** n. (a) Jahreszeit, die; nesting ~: Nistzeit, die (b) (period of social activity) [opera/football] ~: [Opern-/Fußball]saison, die; holiday or (Amer.) vacation ~: Urlaubszeit, die; tourist ~: Reisezeit, die (c) raspberries are in/out of or not in ~: jetzt ist die/nicht die Saison od. Zeit für Himbeeren; be in ~ (on heat) brünstig sein (d) ▶ SEASON TICKET **2** v.t. würzen ⟨Fleisch, Rede⟩

seasonable /'si:zənəbl/ adj. der Jahreszeit gemäß

seasonal /'si:zənl/ adj. Saison⟨arbeit, -geschäft⟩; saisonabhängig ⟨Preise⟩

seasonal affective disorder /si:zənl əˈfektɪv dɪsɔːdə(r)/ n. (Med.) saisonabhängige Depression

'seasoned adj. (fig.) erfahren

'seasoning n. Gewürze Pl.; Würze, die

'season ticket n. Dauerkarte, die

seat /si:t/ **1** n. (a) Sitzgelegenheit, die; (in vehicle, cinema, etc.) Sitz, der; (of toilet) [Klosett]brille, die (ugs.) (b) (place) Platz, der; (in vehicle) [Sitz]platz, der; have or take a ~: sich [hin]setzen (c) (part of chair) Sitzfläche, die (d) (buttocks) Gesäß, das; (part of clothing) Gesäßpartie, die; (of trousers) Sitz, der **2** v.t. (a) (cause to sit) setzen; ⟨Platzanweiser:⟩ einen Platz anweisen (+ Dat.); ~ oneself sich setzen (b) (have ~s for) Sitzplätze bieten (+ Dat.); ~ 500 people 500 Sitzplätze haben

'seat belt n. Sicherheitsgurt, der

'seat-belt tensioner /'tenʃnə(r)/n. Gurtstraffer, der

'seated adj. sitzend; remain ~: sitzen bleiben

'seating n. Sitzplätze Pl.; attrib. Sitz⟨ordnung, -plan⟩

sea: ~ urchin n. Seeigel, der; **~ wall** n. Strandmauer, die; **~ water** n. Meerwasser, das; **~weed** n. [See]tang, der; **~worthy** adj. seetüchtig

secateurs /sekə'tɜ:z/ n. pl. (Brit.) Gartenschere, die

secluded /sɪ'klu:dɪd/ adj. (hidden) versteckt; (isolated) abgelegen; zurückgezogen ⟨Leben⟩

seclusion /sɪ'klu:ʒn/ n. (remoteness) Abgelegenheit, die; (privacy) Zurückgezogenheit, die

second¹ /'sekənd/ **1** adj. zweit...; ~ largest/highest etc. zweitgrößt.../-höchst... usw.; come/be ~: Zweiter/Zweite werden/ sein **2** n. (a) (unit of time or angle) Sekunde, die (b) (coll.: moment) Sekunde, die (ugs.); wait a few ~s einen Moment warten; in a ~ (immediately) sofort (ugs.); (very quickly) im Nu (ugs.); just a ~! (coll.) einen Moment! (c) the ~ (in sequence, rank) der/die/das Zweite (d) in pl. (helping of food) zweite Portion **3** v.t. (support) unterstützen

second² /sɪ'kɒnd/ v.t. (transfer) vorübergehend versetzen

secondary /'sekəndərɪ/ adj. (of less importance) zweitrangig; Neben⟨sache⟩; be ~ to sth. einer Sache (Dat.) untergeordnet sein

'secondary school n. höhere Schule

second: ~-best /-'-/ **1** adj. zweitbest...; **2** /-'-/ n. Zweitbeste, der/die/das; **~-class 1** /-'-/ adj. (of lower class) zweiter Klasse nachgestellt; Zweite[r]-Klasse-⟨Fahrkarte, Abteil, Post, Brief usw.⟩; **~-class stamp** Briefmarke für einen Zweiter-Klasse-Brief; **2** /-'-/ adv. zweiter Klasse ⟨fahren⟩; **~ 'floor** ▶ FLOOR 1B; **~ hand** n. Sekundenzeiger, der; **~-hand 1** /'---/ adj. (a) gebraucht ⟨Kleidung, Auto usw.⟩; antiquarisch ⟨Buch⟩; (b) (selling used goods) Gebrauchtwaren-; Secondhand⟨laden⟩; (c) ⟨Nachrichten, Bericht⟩ aus zweiter Hand; **2** /-'-/ adv. aus zweiter Hand; **~ 'home** n. Zweitwohnung, die

'secondly adv. zweitens

second: ~ name n. Nachname, der; **~-'rate** adj. zweitklassig; **~ 'thoughts** n. pl. have ~ thoughts sich (Dat.) anders überlegen (about mit); we've had ~ thoughts about buying it wir wollen es nun doch nicht kaufen; but on ~ thoughts ...: wenn ich's mir [noch mal] überlege, ...

secrecy /'si:krɪsɪ/ n. (a) (keeping of secret) Geheimhaltung, die (b) (secretiveness) Heimlichtuerei, die (c) in ~: im Geheimen

secret /'si:krɪt/ **1** adj. geheim;   ···⋮

S

Geheim⟨*fach, -tür, -abkommen, -kode*⟩;
heimlich ⟨*Trinker, Liebhaber*⟩; **keep sth. ~:**
etw. geheim halten (**from** vor + *Dat.*)
2 *n.* **(a)** Geheimnis, *das;* **make no ~ of sth.**
kein Geheimnis aus etw. machen; (fig.)
keinen Hehl aus etw. machen; **keep ~s/ a ~:**
schweigen (fig.)
(b) in ~: im Geheimen

secret 'agent *n.* Geheimagent, *der/*
-agentin, *die*

secretarial /sekrə'teərɪəl/ *adj.*
Sekretärinnen⟨*kursus, -tätigkeit*⟩; ⟨*Arbeit*⟩ als
Sekretärin

secretary /'sekrətərɪ/ *n.* Sekretär, *der/*
Sekretärin, *die*

secret 'ballot *n.* geheime Abstimmung

secretive /'siːkrɪtɪv/ *adj.* verschlossen
⟨*Person*⟩: **be ~:** geheimnisvoll tun (**about**
mit)

'secretly *adv.* heimlich; insgeheim ⟨*etw.*
glauben⟩

sect /sekt/ *n.* Sekte, *die*

section /'sekʃn/ *n.* **(a)** (part cut off)
Abschnitt, *der;* Stück, *das;* (part of divided
whole) Teil, *der*
(b) (of firm) Abteilung, *die;* (of organization)
Sektion, *die*
(c) (of chapter, book) Abschnitt, *der;* (of statute
etc.) Paragraph, *der*

sector /'sektə(r)/ *n.* Sektor, *der*

secular /'sekjʊlə(r)/ *adj.* weltlich

secure /sɪ'kjʊə(r)/ **1** *adj.* sicher; (firmly
fastened) fest; **~ against burglars** gegen
Einbruch geschützt
2 *v.t.* **(a)** sichern (**for** *Dat.*); beschaffen
⟨*Auftrag*⟩ (**for** *Dat.*); (for oneself) sich (*Dat.*)
sichern
(b) (fasten) sichern

se'curely *adv.* (firmly) fest ⟨*verriegeln,*
zumachen⟩; sicher ⟨*befestigen, untergebracht*
sein⟩

security /sɪ'kjʊərɪtɪ/ *n.* **(a)** Sicherheit, *die;*
~ [measures] Sicherheitsmaßnahmen *Pl.*
(b) (Finance) **securities** *pl.* Wertpapiere *Pl.*

security: ~ check *n.*
Sicherheitskontrolle, *die;* **~ forces** *n. pl.*
Sicherheitskräfte *Pl.;* **~ guard** *n.* Wächter,
*der/*Wächterin, *die;* **~ risk** *n.*
Sicherheitsrisiko, *das;* **~ van** *n.*
gepanzerter Transporter; (for money)
Geldtransporter, *der*

sedan /sɪ'dæn/ *n.* (Amer. Motor Veh.)
Limousine, *die*

sedate /sɪ'deɪt/ **1** *adj.* bedächtig; gesetzt
⟨*alte Dame*⟩; gemächlich ⟨*Tempo, Leben*⟩
2 *v.t.* sedieren

sedation /sɪ'deɪʃn/ *n.* Sedation, *die;* **be**
under ~: sediert sein

sedative /'sedətɪv/ **1** *n.*
Beruhigungsmittel, *das*
2 *adj.* sedativ

sedentary /'sedəntərɪ/ *adj.* sitzend

sediment /'sedɪmənt/ *n.* Ablagerung, *die;*
(of tea, coffee, etc.) Bodensatz, *der*

seduce /sɪ'djuːs/ *v.t.* verführen

seduction /sɪ'dʌkʃn/ *n.* Verführung, *die*

seductive /sɪ'dʌktɪv/ *adj.* verführerisch;
verlockend ⟨*Angebot*⟩

see /siː/ **1** *v.t.,* **saw** /sɔː/, **seen** /siːn/ **(a)**
sehen; **I can ~ it's hard for you** ich verstehe,
dass es nicht leicht für dich ist; **I ~ what**
you mean ich verstehe[, was du meinst]
(b) (meet [with]) sehen; treffen; (meet socially)
sich treffen mit; **I'll ~ you there/at five** wir
sehen uns dort/um fünf; **~ you!, [I'll] be**
~ing you! (coll.) bis bald! (ugs.)
(c) (speak to) sprechen ⟨*Person*⟩ (**about**
wegen); (visit) gehen zu ⟨*Arzt, Anwalt usw.*⟩;
(receive) empfangen
(d) (find out) feststellen; (by looking) nachsehen
(e) (make sure) **~ [that]** ...: darauf achten,
dass ...
(f) (imagine) sich (*Dat.*) vorstellen
(g) (escort) begleiten
2 *v.i.,* **saw, seen (a)** sehen
(b) (make sure) nachsehen
(c) I ~: ich verstehe; **you ~:** weißt du/wisst
ihr/wissen Sie
■ **'see about** *v.t.* sich kümmern um
■ **see 'off** *v.t.* **(a)** (say goodbye to)
verabschieden
(b) (chase away) vertreiben
■ **see 'out** *v.t.* (escort) hinausbegleiten (**of**
aus); **~ oneself out** allein hinausfinden
■ **see through** *v.t.* **(a)** /'--/ hindurchsehen
durch; (fig.) durchschauen
(b) /-'-/ (not abandon) zu Ende bringen
■ **'see to** *v.t.* sich kümmern um

seed /siːd/ **1** *n.* **(a)** Samen, *der;* (of grape
etc.) Kern, *der*
(b) *no pl., no indef. art.* (**~s** collectively)
Samen[körner] *Pl.;* (as collected for sowing)
Saatgut, *das;* (for birds) Körner *Pl.;* **go** *or* **run**
to ~: Samen bilden; (fig.) herunterkommen
(ugs.)
(c) (Sport) gesetzter Spieler/gesetzte Spielerin
2 *v.t.* **(a)** (place **~**s in) besäen
(b) (Sport) setzen ⟨*Spieler*⟩; **be ~ed number**
one als Nummer eins gesetzt werden/sein

'seed bed *n.* [Saat]beet, *das*

'seedless *adj.* kernlos

seedling /'siːdlɪŋ/ *n.* Sämling, *der*

'seedy *adj.* **(a)** (coll.: unwell) **feel ~:** sich
[leicht] angeschlagen fühlen
(b) (shabby) schäbig, (ugs.) vergammelt
⟨*Aussehen*⟩; heruntergekommen ⟨*Stadtteil*⟩
(c) (disreputable) zweifelhaft

'seeing *conj.* **~ [that]** ...: in Anbetracht
dessen, dass ...

seek /siːk/ *v.t.,* **sought** /sɔːt/ suchen;
anstreben ⟨*Posten, Amt*⟩; sich bemühen um
⟨*Anerkennung, Interview, Einstellung*⟩; (try to
reach) aufsuchen

seem /siːm/ *v.i.* scheinen; **you ~ tired** du
wirkst müde; **she ~s nice** sie scheint nett zu
sein

'seeming *adj.* scheinbar

'seemingly *adv.* (a) (evidently) offensichtlich

(b) (to outward appearance) scheinbar

seemly /'siːmlɪ/ *adj.* schicklich

seen ▶ SEE

seep /siːp/ *v.i.* ~ [away] [ab]sickern

'see-saw *n.* Wippe, *die*

seethe /siːð/ *v.i.* (a) ~ [with anger/ inwardly] vor Wut/innerlich schäumen (b) ⟨Straßen usw.:⟩ wimmeln (with von)

'see-through *adj.* durchsichtig

segment /'segmənt/ *n.* (of orange, pineapple, etc.) Scheibe, *die*

segregate /'segrɪgeɪt/ *v.t.* trennen; (racially) absondern

segregation /segrɪ'geɪʃn/ *n.* Trennung, *die;* [racial] ~: Rassentrennung, *die*

seismic /'saɪzmɪk/ *adj.* seismisch

seize /siːz/ ① *v.t.* (a) ergreifen; ~ **power** die Macht ergreifen; ~ **sb. by the arm/collar** jmdn. am Arm/Kragen packen; ~ **the opportunity [to do sth.]** die Gelegenheit ergreifen [und etw. tun]; ~ **any/a** *or* **the chance [to do sth.]** jede/die Gelegenheit nutzen[, um etw. zu tun]; **be** ~**d with remorse/panic** von Gewissensbissen geplagt/ von Panik ergriffen werden

(b) (capture) gefangen nehmen ⟨Person⟩; kapern ⟨Schiff⟩; mit Gewalt übernehmen ⟨Flugzeug, Gebäude⟩; einnehmen ⟨Festung, Brücke⟩

(c) (confiscate) beschlagnahmen

② *v.i.* ▶ ~ UP

∎ **'seize on** *v.t.* sich (*Dat.*) vornehmen ⟨Einzelheit, Aspekt, Schwachpunkt⟩; aufgreifen ⟨Idee, Vorschlag⟩

∎ **seize 'up** *v.i.* sich festfressen

seizure /'siːʒə(r)/ *n.* (a) ▶ SEIZE 1B, C: Gefangennahme, *die;* Kapern, *das;* Übernahme, *die;* Einnahme, *die;* Beschlagnahme, *die*

(b) (Med.) Anfall, *der*

seldom /'seldəm/ *adv.* selten

select /sɪ'lekt/ ① *adj.* ausgewählt

② *v.t.* auswählen

selection /sɪ'lekʃn/ *n.* (a) (what is selected [from]) Auswahl, *die* (of an + *Dat.,* from aus) (b) (act of choosing) [Aus]wahl, *die*

selective /sɪ'lektɪv/ *adj.* (using selection) selektiv; (careful in one's choice) wählerisch

self /self/ *n., pl.* **selves** [selvz] Selbst, *das* (geh.); Ich, *das*

self- *pref.* selbst-/Selbst-

self: ~**ab'sorbed** *adj.* mit sich selbst beschäftigt; ~**ad'dressed** *adj.* ~**-addressed envelope** adressierter Rückumschlag; ~**ad'hesive** *adj.* selbstklebend; ~**ap'pointed** *adj.* selbst ernannt; ~**as'surance** *n.* Selbstsicherheit, *die;* ~**as'sured** *adj.* selbstsicher; ~**a'wareness** *n.* Selbsterkenntnis, *die;* ~**'catering** ① *adj.*

mit Selbstversorgung *nachgestellt;* ② *n.* Selbstversorgung, *die;* ~**'centred** *adj.* egozentrisch; ~**con'fessed** *adj.* erklärt; ~**'confidence** *n.* Selbstbewusstsein, *das;* ~**'confident** *adj.* selbstbewusst; ~**'conscious** *adj.* unsicher; ~**'consciousness** *n.* Unsicherheit, *die;* ~**con'tained** *adj.* abgeschlossen ⟨Wohnung⟩; ~**con'trol** *n.* Selbstbeherrschung, *die;* ~**con'trolled** *adj.* voller Selbstbeherrschung *nachgestellt;* ~**'critical** *adj.* selbstkritisch; ~**de'ception** *n.* Selbsttäuschung, *die;* ~**de'feating** *adj.* unsinnig; ~**de'fence** *n.* Notwehr, *die;* **in** ~**-defence** aus Notwehr; ~**de'lusion** *n.* Selbsttäuschung, *die;* ~**de'nial** *n.* Selbstverleugnung, *die;* ~**de'structive** *adj.* selbstzerstörerisch; ~**'discipline** *n.* Selbstdisziplin, *die;* ~**-drive** *adj.* ~**-drive hire** [company] Autovermietung, *die;* ~**-drive vehicle** Mietwagen, *der;* ~**em'ployed** *adj.* selbstständig; ~**-e'steem** *n.* Selbstachtung, *die;* ~**'evident** *adj.* offenkundig; ~**-ex'planatory** *adj.* ohne weiteres verständlich; **be** ~**-explanatory** für sich selbst sprechen; ~**ful'filling** *adj.* zur eigenen Bestätigung mit beitragend; ~**'help** *n.* Selbsthilfe, *die;* ~**-im'portant** *adj.* eingebildet; ~**-in'dulgent** *adj.* maßlos; ~**in'flicted** *adj.* selbst beigebracht ⟨Wunde⟩; selbst auferlegt ⟨Strafe⟩; ~**'interest** *n.* Eigeninteresse, *das*

'selfish *adj.,* **'selfishly** *adv.* selbstsüchtig

'selfishness *n.* Selbstsucht, *die*

self-'knowledge *n.* Selbsterkenntnis, *die*

selfless /'selflɪs/ *adj.* selbstlos

self: ~**-'motivated** *adj.* von sich aus motiviert; ~**ob'sessed** *adj.* ichbesessen; ~**o'pinionated** *adj.* eingebildet; ~**-'pity** *n.* Selbstmitleid, *das;* ~**-'portrait** *n.* Selbstporträt, *das;* ~**pos'sessed** *adj.* selbstbeherrscht; ~**preser'vation** *n.* Selbsterhaltung, *die;* ~**-'raising flour** *n.* (Brit.) mit Backpulver versetztes Mehl; ~**-re'liant** *adj.* selbstbewusst; ~**-re'spect** *n.* Selbstachtung, *die;* ~**-re'specting** *adj.* **no** ~**-respecting person** ...: niemand, der etwas auf sich hält, ...; ~**-'righteous** *adj.* selbstgerecht; ~**'sacrifice** *n.* Selbstaufopferung, *die;* ~**-'satisfied** *adj.* selbstzufrieden; (smug) selbstgefällig; ~**-'service** *n.* Selbstbedienung, *die; attrib.* Selbstbedienungs-; ~**-suf'ficient** *adj.* unabhängig; selbstständig ⟨Person⟩; ~**-'taught** *adj.* autodidaktisch; ~**-taught person** Autodidakt, *der*/Autodidaktin, *die;* ~**-'willed** *adj.* eigenwillig

sell /sel/ ① *v.t.,* **sold** /səʊld/ ~ **sth. to sb.,** ~ **sb. sth.** jmdm. etw. verkaufen; **be sold out** ausverkauft sein

② *v.i.,* **sold** sich verkaufen; ⟨Person:⟩ verkaufen

⋯❖

■ **sell 'off** *v.t.* verkaufen

■ **sell 'out** ① *v.t.* **(a)** ausverkaufen
(b) (coll.: betray) verraten
② *v.i.* **we have** *or* **are sold out** wir sind ausverkauft

'sell-by date *n.* ≈ Mindesthaltbarkeitsdatum, *das*

'seller *n.* **(a)** Verkäufer, *der*/Verkäuferin, *die*
(b) (product) **be a good/slow ~:** sich gut/nur langsam verkaufen

'selling point *n.* **a [good] ~ point** (fig.) ein Pluspunkt

'sellotape *v.t.* mit Tesafilm kleben

Sellotape ® /'seləteɪp/ *n.* ≈ Tesafilm, *der* ⓦ

'sell-out *n.* **be a ~:** ausverkauft sein; (coll.: betrayal) Verrat sein

selves *pl. of* SELF

semaphore /'seməfɔː(r)/ ① *n.* (system) Winken, *das*
② *v.i.* **~ to sb.** jmdm. ein Winksignal übermitteln

semblance /'sembləns/ *n.* Anschein, *der*

semen /'siːmən/ *n.* Samen, *der*

semester /sɪ'mestə(r)/ *n.* Semester, *das*

semi- /semɪ/ *pref.* halb-/Halb-

semi: ~bold *adj.* (Printing) halbfett; **~breve** *n.* (Brit. Mus.) ganze Note; **~circle** *n.* Halbkreis, *der;* **~circular** *adj.* halbkreisförmig; **~colon** *n.* Semikolon, *das;* **~de'tached** *adj. & n.* **~-detached [house]** Doppelhaushälfte, *die;* **~'final** *n.* Halbfinale, *das*

seminar /'semɪnɑː(r)/ *n.* Seminar, *das*

semi: ~'precious *adj.* **~-precious stone** Halbedelstein, *der;* **~skimmed** ① *adj.* teilentrahmt; ② *n.* teilentrahmte Milch; **~tone** *n.* (Mus.) Halbton, *der*

semolina /semə'liːnə/ *n.* Grieß, *der*

senate /'senət/ *n.* Senat, *der*

senator /'senətə(r)/ *n.* Senator, *der*

send /send/ *v.t.*, **sent** [sent] schicken; senden (geh.)

■ **send a'way** ① *v.t.* wegschicken
② *v.i.* **~ away [to sb.] for sth.** etw. [bei jmdm.] anfordern

■ **send 'back** *v.t.* zurückschicken

■ **'send for** *v.t.* **(a)** (tell to come) holen lassen; rufen ⟨Polizei, Arzt usw.⟩
(b) (order from elsewhere) anfordern

■ **send 'off** *v.t.* ① **(a)** (dispatch) abschicken ⟨Sache⟩
(b) (Sport) vom Platz stellen
② *v.i.* ▶ SEND AWAY 2

■ **send 'up** *v.t.* (Brit. coll.: parody) parodieren

'sender *n.* Absender, *der*

'send-off *n.* Verabschiedung, *die*

senile /'siːnaɪl/ *adj.* senil

senile de'mentia *n.* senile Demenz

senility /sɪ'nɪlɪtɪ/ *n.* Senilität, *die*

senior /'siːnɪə(r)/ ① *adj.* **(a)** (older) älter

(b) höher ⟨Rang, Beamter, Stellung⟩; leitend ⟨Angestellter, Stellung⟩; **~ manager** obere Führungskraft; **~ management** oberer Führungskreis
② *n.* (older) Ältere, *der/die;* (of higher rank) Vorgesetzte, *der/die*

senior 'citizen *n.* Senior, *der/*Seniorin, *die*

seniority /siːnɪ'ɒrɪtɪ/ *n.* (greater length of service) höheres Dienstalter; (higher rank) höherer Rang

senior 'partner *n.* Seniorpartner, *der/* -partnerin, *die*

sensation /sen'seɪʃn/ *n.* **(a)** (feeling) Gefühl, *das*
(b) (person, event, etc.) Sensation, *die*

sensational /sen'seɪʃənl/ *adj.* sensationell

sensationalise ▶ SENSATIONALIZE

sensationalism /sen'seɪʃənəlɪzm/ *n.* Sensationshascherei, *die*

sensationalist /sen'seɪʃənəlɪst/ *adj.* sensationslüstern

sensationalize /sen'seɪʃənəlaɪz/ *v.t.* **~ sth.** etw. zur Sensation aufbauschen

sense /sens/ ① *n.* **(a)** (faculty) Sinn, *der;* **~ of smell/touch/taste** Geruchs-/Tast-/Geschmackssinn, *der;* **come to one's ~s** das Bewusstsein wiedererlangen
(b) *in pl.* (normal state of mind) Verstand, *der;* **have taken leave of one's ~s** den Verstand verloren haben
(c) (consciousness) Gefühl, *das;* **~ of responsibility/guilt** Verantwortungs-/Schuldgefühl, *das*
(d) (practical wisdom) Verstand, *der;* **sound** *or* **good ~:** [gesunder Menschen]verstand; **not have the ~ to do sth.** nicht so schlau sein, etw. zu tun; **there is no ~ in doing that** es hat keinen Sinn, das zu tun
(e) (meaning) Sinn, *der;* (of word) Bedeutung, *die;* **make ~:** einen Sinn ergeben; **in a** *or* **one ~:** in gewisser Hinsicht; **make ~ of sth.** etw. verstehen
② *v.t.* spüren

'senseless *adj.* **(a)** (unconscious) bewusstlos
(b) (purposeless) sinnlos

sensible /'sensɪbl/ *adj.* **(a)** (reasonable) vernünftig
(b) (practical) zweckmäßig

sensibly /'sensɪblɪ/ *adv.* **(a)** (reasonably) vernünftig
(b) (practically) zweckmäßig

sensitive /'sensɪtɪv/ *adj.* empfindlich; **be ~ to sth.** empfindlich auf etw. (Akk.) reagieren

sensitivity /sensɪ'tɪvɪtɪ/ *n.* Empfindlichkeit, *die*

sensory /'sensərɪ/ *adj.* Sinnes-

sensual /'sensjʊəl/ *adj.* sinnlich

sensuous /'sensjʊəs/ *adj.* sinnlich

sent ▶ SEND

sentence /'sentəns/ ① *n.* **(a)** (Law) [Straf]urteil, *das*

(b) (Ling.) Satz, *der*
2 *v.t.* verurteilen (**to** zu)

sentiment /'sentɪmənt/ *n.* **(a)** Gefühl, *das*
(b) (sentimentality) Sentimentalität, *die*
(c) (thought) Gedanke, *der*

sentimental /sentɪ'mentl/ *adj.*
sentimental

sentimentality /sentɪmen'tælɪtɪ/ *n.*
Sentimentalität, *die*

sentimentalize /sentɪ'mentəlaɪz/ *v.t.*
sentimental darstellen

sentry /'sentrɪ/ *n.* Wache, *die*

separable /'sepərəbl/ *adj.* trennbar

separate 1 /'sepərət/ *adj.* verschieden
⟨Fragen, Probleme, Gelegenheiten⟩; gesondert
⟨Teil⟩; separat ⟨Eingang, Toilette, Blatt
Papier, Abteil⟩; (one's own, individual) eigen
⟨Zimmer, Identität, Organisation⟩; **keep two
things ~:** zwei Dinge auseinander halten
2 /'sepəreɪt/ *v.t.* trennen; **they are ~d** (no
longer live together) sie leben getrennt
3 *v.i.* **(a)** (disperse) sich trennen
(b) ⟨Ehepaar:⟩ sich trennen

separately /'sepərətlɪ/ *adv.* getrennt

separation /sepə'reɪʃn/ *n.* Trennung, *die*

Sept. *abbr.* = **September** Sept.

September /sep'tembə(r)/ *n.* September,
der; see also AUGUST

septic /'septɪk/ *adj.* septisch; **go ~:** eitrig
werden

sequel /'si:kwl/ *n.* **(a)** (consequence, result)
Folge, *die* (**to** von)
(b) (continuation) Fortsetzung, *die*

sequence /'si:kwəns/ *n.* **(a)** Reihenfolge,
die
(b) (part of film) Sequenz, *die*

sequin /'si:kwɪn/ *n.* Paillette, *die*

Serbia /'sɜːbɪə/ *pr. n.* Serbien, *das*

Serbian /'sɜːbɪən/ 1 *adj.* serbisch; **sb. is
~:** jmd. ist Serbe/Serbin
2 *n.* **(a)** (Ling.) serbischer Dialekt
(b) (person) Serbe, *der*/Serbin, *die.* See also
ENGLISH 2A

serenade /serə'neɪd/ 1 *n.* Ständchen, *das*
2 *v.t.* **~ sb.** jmdm. ein Ständchen bringen

serene /sɪ'ri:n/ *adj.* gelassen

serenity /sɪ'renɪtɪ/ *n.* Gelassenheit, *die*

sergeant /'sɑːdʒənt/ *n.* (Mil.) Unteroffizier,
der; (police officer) ≈ Polizeimeister, *der*

sergeant 'major *n.* ≈
[Ober]stabsfeldwebel, *der*

serial /'sɪərɪəl/ *n.* Fortsetzungsgeschichte,
die; (Radio, Telev.) Serie, *die*

serialize /'sɪərɪəlaɪz/ *v.t.* in Fortsetzungen
veröffentlichen; (Radio, Telev.) in
Fortsetzungen senden

'serial killer *n.* Serienmörder, *der*

series /'sɪəri:z, 'sɪərɪz/ *n., pl. same* **(a)**
(sequence) Reihe, *die;* (of events, misfortunes)
Folge, *die*
(b) (set of successive issues) Serie, *die;* **radio/TV
~:** Hörfunkreihe/Fernsehserie, *die*

(c) (set of books) Reihe, *die*

serious /'sɪərɪəs/ *adj.* **(a)** (earnest) ernst
(b) (important, grave) ernst ⟨Angelegenheit,
Lage, Problem, Zustand⟩; ernsthaft ⟨Frage,
Einwand, Kandidat⟩; schwer ⟨Krankheit,
Unfall, Fehler, Niederlage⟩; ernst zu
nehmend ⟨Rivale⟩; ernstlich ⟨Gefahr,
Bedrohung⟩; bedenklich ⟨Mangel⟩

'seriously *adv.* **(a)** (earnestly) ernst; **take
sth./sb. ~:** etw./jmdn. ernst nehmen
(b) (severely) ernstlich; schwer ⟨verletzt⟩

'seriousness *n.* Ernst, *der;* **in all ~:** ganz
im Ernst

sermon /'sɜːmən/ *n.* Predigt, *die*

serpent /'sɜːpənt/ *n.* Schlange, *die*

serrated /se'reɪtɪd/ *adj.* gezackt; **~ knife**
Sägemesser, *das*

serum /'sɪərəm/ *n.* Serum, *das*

servant /'sɜːvənt/ *n.* Diener, *der*/Dienerin,
die

serve /sɜːv/ 1 *v.t.* **(a)** (work for) dienen
(+ *Dat.*)
(b) (be useful to) dienlich sein (+ *Dat.*)
(c) (meet needs of) nutzen (+ *Dat.*); **~ a/no
purpose** einen Zweck erfüllen/keinen Zweck
haben
(d) durchlaufen ⟨Lehre⟩; verbüßen
⟨Haftstrafe⟩
(e) (dish up) servieren; (pour out) einschenken
(**to** *Dat.*)
(f) **~[s]** *or* **it ~s him right!** [das] geschieht
ihm recht!
2 *v.i.* **(a)** dienen; **~ as chairman** das Amt
des Vorsitzenden innehaben; **~ as a Member
of Parliament** Mitglied des Parlaments sein;
~ on a jury Geschworener/Geschworene
sein
(b) (be of use) **~ to do sth.** dazu dienen, etw.
zu tun; **~ to show sth.** etw. zeigen; **~ for** *or*
as dienen als
(c) (Sport) aufschlagen
3 *n.* ▶ SERVICE 1G
■ **serve 'up** *v.t.* **(a)** servieren
(b) (offer for consideration) auftischen (ugs.)

server /'sɜːvə(r)/ *n.* (Comp.) Server, *der*

service /'sɜːvɪs/ 1 *n.* **(a)** Dienst, *der;* **do
sb. a ~:** jmdm. einen guten Dienst erweisen
(b) (Eccl.) Gottesdienst, *der*
(c) (attending to customer) Service, *der;* (in shop,
garage, etc.) Bedienung, *die*
(d) (system of transport) Verbindung, *die;* **there
is no [bus] ~ on Sundays** sonntags
verkehren keine Busse
(e) (provision of maintenance) **[after-sale] ~:**
Kundendienst, *der;* **take one's car in for a ~:**
sein Auto zur Inspektion bringen
(f) (operation) Betrieb, *der;* **out of ~:** außer
Betrieb
(g) (Sport) Aufschlag, *der;* **whose ~ is it?**
wer hat Aufschlag?
(h) (crockery set) Service, *das*
(i) (assistance) **can I be of ~ [to you]?** kann
ich Ihnen behilflich sein?; **I'm at your ~:** ich
stehe zu Ihren Diensten ⸱⸱⸱⟶

S

(j) (Mil.) the [armed or fighting] ~s die
Streitkräfte *Pl.*; **in the** ~**s** beim Militär
(k) [motorway] ~**s** [Autobahn]raststätte, *die*
2 *v.t.* warten ⟨*Wagen, Waschmaschine,
Heizung*⟩

serviceable /'sɜːvɪsəbl/ *adj.* **(a)** (useful)
nützlich
(b) (durable) haltbar

service: ~ **area** *n.* Raststätte, *die;*
~ **charge** *n.* Bedienungsgeld, *das;*
~ **hatch** *n.* Durchreiche, *die;*
~ **industry** *n.* Dienstleistungsbetrieb, *der;*
~**man** *n.* /'sɜːvɪsmən/ *n., Pl.* ~**men**
/'sɜːvɪsmən/ Militärangehörige, *der;*
~ **provider** *n.* (Comp.) Provider, *der;*
Internet ~ **provider** Internetanbieter, *der;*
~ **station** *n.* Tankstelle, *die*

serviette /sɜːvɪ'et/ *n.* (Brit.) Serviette, *die*

servile /'sɜːvaɪl/ *adj.* unterwürfig

servility /sɜː'vɪlɪtɪ/ *n.* Unterwürfigkeit, *die*

serving /'sɜːvɪŋ/ *n.* Portion, *die*

'serving spoon *n.* Vorlegelöffel, *der*

servitude /'sɜːvɪtjuːd/ *n.* Knechtschaft, *die*

sesame /'sesəmɪ/ *n.* ~ [seed] Sesamkorn,
das

session /'seʃn/ *n.* (meeting) Sitzung, *die;* **be
in** ~: tagen

set /set/ **1** *v.t.*, **-tt-, set (a)** (put) (horizontally)
legen; (vertically) stellen; ~ **sb. ashore** jmdn.
an Land setzen; ~ **sth./things right** or **in
order** etw./die Dinge in Ordnung bringen
(b) (apply) setzen; ~ **a match to sth.** ein
Streichholz an etw. (*Akk.*) halten; *see also*
FIRE 1A; LIGHT¹ 1D
(c) (adjust) einstellen (**at** auf + *Akk.*);
aufstellen ⟨*Falle*⟩; stellen ⟨*Uhr*⟩; ~ **the alarm
for 5.30 a.m.** den Wecker auf 5.30 Uhr stellen
(d) **be** ~ ⟨*Buch, Film:*⟩ spielen (**in** in + *Dat.*)
(e) (specify) festlegen ⟨*Bedingungen*⟩;
festsetzen ⟨*Termin, Ort usw.*⟩ (**for** auf
+ *Akk.*); ~ **limits** Grenzen setzen
(f) ~ **sb. thinking that …**: jmdn. auf den
Gedanken bringen, dass …
(g) (put forward) stellen ⟨*Frage, Aufgabe*⟩;
aufgeben ⟨*Hausaufgabe*⟩; aufstellen ⟨*Rekord*⟩;
(compose) zusammenstellen ⟨*Rätsel, Fragen*⟩;
~ **sb. an example,** ~ **an example to sb.**
jmdm. ein Beispiel geben; ~ **sb. a task/
problem** jmdm. eine Aufgabe stellen/jmdn.
vor ein Problem stellen; ~ **[sb./oneself] a
target** [jmdm./sich] ein Ziel setzen
(h) (Med.: put into place) [ein]richten;
einrenken ⟨*verrenktes Gelenk*⟩
(i) legen ⟨*Haare*⟩
(j) decken ⟨*Tisch*⟩; auflegen ⟨*Gedeck*⟩
(k) fassen ⟨*Edelstein*⟩
2 *v.i.*, **-tt-, set (a)** (solidify) fest werden
(b) (go down) ⟨*Sonne, Mond:*⟩ untergehen
3 *n.* **(a)** (group) Satz, *der;* ~ **[of two]** Paar,
das; **a** ~ **of chairs** eine Sitzgruppe
(b) (radio, TV) Gerät, *das*
(c) (Tennis) Satz, *der*
(d) (of hair) Legen, *das*

(e) (Theatre: scenery) Bühnenbild, *das;* (area of
performance) (of film) Drehort, *der;* (of play)
Bühne, *die*
(f) (of people) Kreis, *der*
(g) (Math.) Menge, *die*
4 *adj.* **(a)** (fixed) fest ⟨*Absichten,
Zielvorstellungen, Zeitpunkt*⟩; **be** ~ **in one's
ways** or **habits** in seinen Gewohnheiten
festgefahren sein; ~ **meal** or **menu** Menü,
das
(b) (prescribed) vorgeschrieben ⟨*Buch, Lektüre*⟩
(c) (ready) **be** [all] ~ **for sth.** zu etw. bereit
sein; **be** [all] ~ **to do sth.** bereit sein, etw. zu
tun
(d) (determined) **be** ~ **on sth./doing sth.** zu
etw. entschlossen sein/entschlossen sein,
etw. zu tun
■ **'set about** *v.t.* ~ **about sth.** sich an etw.
(*Akk.*) machen; ~ **about doing sth.** sich
daranmachen, etw. zu tun
■ **set a'side** *v.t.* **(a)** beiseite legen
(b) aufheben ⟨*Urteil, Entscheidung*⟩
■ **set 'back** *v.t.* **(a)** aufhalten
⟨*Entwicklung*⟩; zurückwerfen ⟨*Projekt,
Programm*⟩
(b) (coll.: cost) kosten ⟨*Person*⟩
(c) (place at a distance) zurücksetzen
■ **set 'down** *v.t.* **(a)** absetzen ⟨*Fahrgast*⟩
(b) (record) niederschreiben
■ **set 'off** **1** *v.i.* (begin journey) aufbrechen;
(start to move) losgehen; ⟨*Fahrzeug:*⟩ losfahren
2 *v.t.* **(a)** (cause to explode) explodieren
lassen; abbrennen ⟨*Feuerwerk*⟩
(b) auslösen ⟨*Reaktion, Alarmanlage*⟩
■ **set 'out** **1** *v.i.* **(a)** (begin journey)
aufbrechen (**for** nach/zu)
(b) ~ **out to do sth.** sich (*Dat.*) vornehmen,
etw. zu tun
2 *v.t.* darlegen
■ **set 'up** **1** *v.t.* **(a)** errichten
⟨*Straßensperre, Denkmal*⟩; aufbauen ⟨*Zelt,
Klapptisch*⟩
(b) (establish) gründen ⟨*Firma, Organisation*⟩;
einrichten ⟨*Büro*⟩
2 *v.i.* ~ **up in business** ein Geschäft
aufmachen

'setback *n.* Rückschlag, *der*

settee /se'tiː/ *n.* Sofa, *das*

'setting *n.* **(a)** (Mus.) Vertonung, *die*
(b) (surroundings) Rahmen, *der;* (of novel etc.)
Schauplatz, *der*

'setting lotion *n.* Haarfestiger, *der*

settle /'setl/ **1** *v.t.* **(a)** (horizontally)
[sorgfältig] legen; (vertically) [sorgfältig]
stellen; (at an angle) [sorgfältig] lehnen
(b) (determine, resolve) sich einigen auf ⟨*Preis*⟩;
beilegen ⟨*Streit, Konflikt,
Meinungsverschiedenheit*⟩; ausräumen
⟨*Zweifel*⟩; entscheiden ⟨*Frage, Spiel*⟩
(c) (pay) bezahlen ⟨*Rechnung, Betrag*⟩; erfüllen
⟨*Forderung, Anspruch*⟩; ausgleichen ⟨*Konto*⟩
2 *v.i.* **(a)** (become established) sich
niederlassen; (as colonist) sich ansiedeln
(b) (pay) abrechnen
(c) (in chair, in front of fire, etc.) sich

niederlassen; (to work etc.) sich konzentrieren (**to** auf + *Akk.*); (into way of life, retirement, etc.) sich gewöhnen (**into** an + *Akk.*)
(**d**) (subside) ‹*Haus, Fundament, Boden:*› sich senken
(**e**) ‹*Schnee:*› liegen bleiben
■ **settle 'down** $\boxed{1}$ *v.i.* (**a**) (make oneself comfortable) sich niederlassen (**in** in + *Dat.*)
(**b**) (in town or house) heimisch werden
$\boxed{2}$ *v.t.* (**a**) ~ oneself down sich [gemütlich] hinsetzen
(**b**) (calm down) beruhigen
■ **'settle for** *v.t.* (agree to) sich zufrieden geben mit
■ **'settle 'in** *v.i.* (in new home) sich einleben
■ **'settle on** *v.t.* (decide on) sich entscheiden für
■ **settle 'up** *v.i.* abrechnen; **~ up with the waiter** beim Kellner bezahlen
'settlement *n.* (**a**) (of argument, conflict, dispute, differences) Beilegung, *die;* (of question) Klärung, *die;* (of bill, account) Bezahlung, *die;* (of court case) Vergleich, *der*
(**b**) (colony) Siedlung, *die*
settler /'setlə(r)/ *n.* Siedler, *der*/Siedlerin, *die*
set: **~-to** *n., pl.* **~-tos: have a ~-to** Streit haben; (with fists) sich prügeln; **~-up** *n.* System, *das*
seven /'sevn/ $\boxed{1}$ *adj.* sieben
$\boxed{2}$ *n.* Sieben, die. See also EIGHT
seventeen /sevn'ti:n/ $\boxed{1}$ *adj.* siebzehn
$\boxed{2}$ *n.* Siebzehn, die. See also EIGHT
seventeenth /sevn'ti:nθ/ $\boxed{1}$ *adj.* siebzehnt...
$\boxed{2}$ *n.* (fraction) Siebzehntel, *das. See also* EIGHTH
seventh /'sevnθ/ $\boxed{1}$ *adj.* sieb[en]t...
$\boxed{2}$ *n.* (in sequence, rank) Sieb[en]te, *der/die/ das;* (fraction) Sieb[en]tel, *das. See also* EIGHTH
seventieth /'sevntɪɪθ/ *adj.* siebzigst...
seventy /'sevntɪ/ $\boxed{1}$ *adj.* siebzig
$\boxed{2}$ *n.* Siebzig, die. See also EIGHT; EIGHTY 2
sever /'sevə(r)/ *v.t.* (**a**) (cut) durchtrennen; (fig.) abbrechen ‹*Beziehungen*›
(**b**) (separate) abtrennen; (with axe etc.) abhacken
several /'sevrl/ $\boxed{1}$ *adv.* mehrere; einige; **~ times** mehrmals
$\boxed{2}$ *pron.* einige; **~ of us** einige von uns; **~ of the buildings** einige od. mehrere [der] Gebäude
severe /sɪ'vɪə(r)/ *adj.,* **~r** /sɪ'vɪərə(r)/, **~st** /sɪ'vɪərɪst/ hart ‹*Urteil, Strafe, Kritik, Test, Prüfung*›; streng ‹*Frost, Stil, Schönheit*›; schwer ‹*Dürre, Verlust, Behinderung, Verletzung, Krankheit*›; rau ‹*Wetter*›; heftig ‹*Anfall, Schmerz*›; bedrohlich ‹*Mangel, Knappheit*›; stark ‹*Blutung*›
se'verely *adv.* hart; schwer ‹*verletzt, behindert*›

severity /sɪ'verɪtɪ/ *n.* Strenge, *die;* (of drought, shortage) großes Ausmaß; (of criticism) Schärfe, *die*
sew /səʊ/ *v.t. & i., p.p.* **sewn** /səʊn/ *or* **sewed** /səʊd/ nähen
■ **sew 'on** *v.t.* annähen ‹*Knopf*›; aufnähen ‹*Abzeichen, Band*›
■ **sew 'up** *v.t.* nähen ‹*Saum, Naht, Wunde*›
sewage /'sju:ɪdʒ/ *n.* Abwasser, *das*
'sewage disposal *n.* Abwasserbeseitigung, *die*
sewer /'sju:ə(r), 'su:ə(r)/ *n.* (tunnel) Abwasserkanal, *der;* (pipe) Abwasserleitung, *die*
'sewing *n.* Näharbeit, *die*
'sewing machine *n.* Nähmaschine, *die*
sewn ▶ SEW
sex /seks/ *n.* (**a**) Geschlecht, *das*
(**b**) (sexuality; coll.: intercourse) Sex, *der* (ugs.); **have ~ with sb.** (coll.) mit jmdm. schlafen; Sex mit jmdm. haben (salopp)
sex: **~ appeal** *n.* Sexappeal, *der;* **~ change** *n.* Geschlechtsumwandlung, *die;* **~ discrimination** *n.* sexuelle Diskriminierung; **~ education** *n.* Sexualerziehung, *die*
sexism /'seksɪzm/ *n.* Sexismus, *der*
sexist /'seksɪst/ *adj.* sexistisch
sex: **~ life** *n.* Geschlechtsleben, *das;* Sexualleben, *das;* **~ maniac** *n.* Triebverbrecher, *der;* **you ~ maniac!** (coll.) du geiler Bock! (ugs.); **~ offender** *n.* Sexual[straf]täter, *der*/-täterin, *die*
sexploitation /seksplɔr'teɪʃn/ *n.* [kommerzielle] Ausbeutung der Sexualität
sex: **~ shop** *n.* Sexshop, *der;* **~ symbol** *n.* Sexidol, *das*
sexual /'sekʃʊəl/ *adj.* sexuell
sexual: **~ a'buse** *n.* sexueller Missbrauch; **~ 'harassment** *n.* sexuelle Belästigung; **~ 'intercourse** *n.* Geschlechtsverkehr, *der*
sexuality /sekʃʊ'ælɪtɪ/ *n.* Sexualität, *die*
sexual: **~ 'organs** *n. pl.* Geschlechtsorgane *Pl.;* **~ 'partner** *n.* Sexualpartner, *der*/-partnerin, *die*
'sexy *adj.* sexy (ugs.)
sh /ʃ/ *int.* sch; pst
shabbily /'ʃæbɪlɪ/ *adv.,* **shabby** /'ʃæbɪ/ *adj.* schäbig
shack /ʃæk/ *n.* [armselige] Hütte
shackle /'ʃækl/ $\boxed{1}$ *n., usu. in pl.* Fessel, *die*
$\boxed{2}$ *v.t.* anketten (**to** an + *Akk.*)
shade /ʃeɪd/ $\boxed{1}$ *n.* (**a**) Schatten, *der*
(**b**) (colour) Ton, *der;* (fig.) Schattierung, *die*
(**c**) (lamp~) [Lampen]schirm, *der*
$\boxed{2}$ *v.t.* (**a**) (screen) beschatten
(**b**) (darken with lines) ~ **[in]** [ab]schattieren
$\boxed{3}$ *v.i.* übergehen (**into** in + *Akk.*)
shadow /'ʃædəʊ/ $\boxed{1}$ *n.* Schatten, *der*
$\boxed{2}$ *v.t.* (follow) beschatten

S

'shadowy *adj.* (indistinct) schattenhaft

shady /'ʃeɪdɪ/ *adj.* (a) schattig

(b) (disreputable) zwielichtig

shaft /ʃɑːft/ *n.* (a) (of tool, golf club) Schaft, *der*

(b) (Mech. Engin.) Welle, *die*

(c) (of mine, lift) Schacht, *der*

(d) (of light, lightning) Strahl, *der*

shaggy /'ʃægɪ/ *adj.* zottelig

shake /ʃeɪk/ ① *n.* Schütteln, *das;* give sb./ sth. a ~: jmdn./etw. schütteln

② *v.t.*, **shook** /ʃʊk/, **shaken** /'ʃeɪkn/ (a) (move violently) schütteln; ~ one's fist/a stick at sb. jmdm. mit der Faust/einem Stock drohen; ~ **hands** sich (*Dat.*) die Hand geben

(b) (cause to tremble) erschüttern ⟨*Gebäude usw.*⟩; ~ **one's head** den Kopf schütteln

(c) (shock) erschüttern

③ *v.i.*, **shook, shaken** wackeln; ⟨*Boden, Stimme:*⟩ beben; ⟨*Hand:*⟩ zittern

■ **shake 'off** *v.t.* abschütteln

■ **shake 'up** *v.t.* (a) (upset, shock) einen Schrecken einjagen (+ *Dat.*)

(b) (reorganize) umkrempeln (ugs.)

shaken ▶ SHAKE 2, 3

shaky /'ʃeɪkɪ/ *adj.* wack[e]lig ⟨*Möbelstück, Leiter*⟩; zittrig ⟨*Hand, Stimme, Greis*⟩; **feel** ~: sich zittrig fühlen

shall /ʃl, stressed ʃæl/ *v. aux. only in pres.* shall, *neg.* (coll.) **shan't** /ʃɑːnt/, *past* **should** /ʃəd, stressed ʃʊd/, *neg.* (coll.) **shouldn't** /'ʃʊdnt/ (a) (expr. simple future) werden

(b) should (expr. conditional) würde/würdest/ würden/würdet; **I should have been killed if I had let go** ich wäre getötet worden, wenn ich losgelassen hätte; **if we should be defeated** falls wir unterliegen [sollten]

(c) (expr. will or intention) **what** ~ **we do?** was sollen wir tun?; **let's go in,** ~ **we?** gehen wir doch hinein, oder?; **we should be safe by now** jetzt dürften wir in Sicherheit sein; **he shouldn't do things like that!** er sollte so etwas nicht tun!

shallot /ʃə'lɒt/ *n.* Schalotte, *die*

shallow /'ʃæləʊ/ *adj.* seicht ⟨*Wasser, Fluss*⟩; flach ⟨*Schüssel, Teller, Wasser*⟩; (fig.) flach ⟨*Person*⟩

sham /ʃæm/ ① *adj.* unecht; imitiert ⟨*Leder, Holz, Pelz*⟩

② *n.* (pretence) Heuchelei, *die;* (person) Heuchler, *der*/Heuchlerin, *die*

③ *v.t.*, -mm- vortäuschen

④ *v.i.*, -mm- simulieren

shambles /'ʃæmblz/ *n.* (coll.) Chaos, *das;* **the room was a** ~: das Zimmer glich einem Schlachtfeld

shambolic /ʃæm'bɒlɪk/ *adj.* (coll.) chaotisch

shame /ʃeɪm/ *n.* (a) Scham, *die*

(b) (state of disgrace) Schande, *die;* **put sb./sth. to** ~: jmdn. beschämen/etw. in den Schatten stellen

(c) **what a** ~! wie schade!

'shamefaced *adj.* betreten

shameful /'ʃeɪmfl/ *adj.* beschämend

'shameless *adj.* schamlos

shampoo /ʃæm'puː/ ① *v.t.* schamponieren

② *n.* Shampoo[n], *das*

shamrock /'ʃæmrɒk/ *n.* Klee, *der*

shandy /'ʃændɪ/ *n.* Bier mit Limonade; Radlermaß, *die* (bes. südd.)

shan't /ʃɑːnt/ (coll.) = **shall not**

shanty[1] /'ʃæntɪ/ *n.* (hut) [armselige] Hütte

shanty[2] *n.* (song) Shanty, *das*

'shanty town *n.* Bidonville, *das*

shape /ʃeɪp/ ① *v.t.* formen; bearbeiten ⟨*Holz, Stein*⟩ (into zu)

② *n.* Form, *die;* **take** ~: Gestalt annehmen

■ **shape 'up** *v.i.* sich entwickeln

'shapeless *adj.* formlos; unförmig ⟨*Kleid, Person*⟩

shapely /'ʃeɪplɪ/ *adj.* wohlgeformt ⟨*Beine, Busen*⟩; gut ⟨*Figur*⟩

share /ʃeə(r)/ ① *n.* (a) (portion) Teil, *der od. das;* [fair] ~: Anteil, *der;* **fair** ~**s** gerechte Teile; **do more than one's** [fair] ~ **of the work** mehr als seinen Teil zur Arbeit beitragen

(b) (Commerc.) Aktie, *die*

② *v.t.* teilen; gemeinsam tragen ⟨*Verantwortung*⟩

③ *v.i.* ~ **in** teilnehmen an (+ *Dat.*); beteiligt sein an (+ *Dat.*) ⟨*Gewinn*⟩; teilen ⟨*Freude, Erfahrung*⟩

■ **share 'out** *v.t.* aufteilen (**among** unter + *Akk.*)

share: ~ **certificate** *n.* Aktienurkunde, *die;* ~**holder** *n.* Aktionär, *der*/Aktionärin, *die;* ~ **index** *n.* Aktienindex, *der;* ~**out** *n.* Aufteilung, *die;* ~**ware** *n.* (Comp.) Shareware, *die*

shark /ʃɑːk/ *n.* Hai[fisch], *der*

sharp /ʃɑːp/ ① *adj.* (a) scharf; spitz ⟨*Nadel, Bleistift, Gipfel, Winkel*⟩; deutlich ⟨*Unterscheidung*⟩; sauer ⟨*Apfel*⟩; herb ⟨*Wein*⟩; (shrill, piercing) schrill ⟨*Schrei, Pfiff*⟩; heftig ⟨*Schmerz, Krampf, Kampf*⟩; begabt ⟨*Schüler, Student*⟩

(b) (derog.: dishonest) gerissen

(c) (Mus.) [um einen Halbton] erhöht ⟨*Note*⟩

② *adv.* (a) (punctually) **at six o'clock** ~: Punkt sechs Uhr

(b) **turn** ~ **right/left** scharf nach rechts/links abbiegen

(c) **look** ~! halt dich ran! (ugs.)

(d) (Mus.) zu hoch ⟨*singen, spielen*⟩

sharpen /'ʃɑːpn/ *v.t.* schärfen; [an]spitzen ⟨*Bleistift*⟩

'sharpener *n.* (for pencils) Spitzer, *der* (ugs.)

'sharp-eyed *adj.* scharfäugig; **be** ~: scharfe Augen haben

'sharpish *adv.* (coll.) (quickly) rasch; (promptly) unverzüglich; sofort

'sharply *adv.* scharf; in scharfem Ton ⟨*antworten*⟩

'sharpness *n.* Schärfe, *die;* (fineness of point) Spitzheit, *die*

'sharp-witted *adj.* scharfsinnig

shatter /'ʃætə(r)/ 1 *v.t.* zertrümmern; zerbrechen ‹Glas, Fenster›; zerschlagen ‹Hoffnungen› 2 *v.i.* zerbrechen

shattered /'ʃætəd/ *adj.* **(a)** zerbrochen ‹Glas, Fenster›; (fig.) zerstört ‹Hoffnungen›; zerrüttet ‹Nerven› **(b)** (coll.: greatly upset) she was ~ by the news die Nachricht hat sie schwer mitgenommen; I'm ~! ich bin ganz erschüttert!; (Brit. coll.: exhausted) ich bin kaputt! (ugs.)

'shattering *adj.* verheerend ‹Wirkung›; vernichtend ‹Schlag, Niederlage›

shave /ʃeɪv/ 1 *v.t.* rasieren; abrasieren ‹Haare› 2 *v.i.* sich rasieren 3 *n.* Rasur, *die;* **have a ~:** sich rasieren ■ **shave 'off** *v.t.* abrasieren

'shaven /'ʃeɪvn/ *adj.* rasiert; [kahl] geschoren ‹Kopf›

'shaver *n.* Rasierapparat, *der*

'shaver point *n.* Anschluss, *der* für den Rasierapparat

shaving /'ʃeɪvɪŋ/ *n.* **(a)** Rasieren, *das* **(b)** *in pl.* (of wood, metal, etc.) Späne *Pl.*

shaving: ~ **brush** *n.* Rasierpinsel, *der;* ~ **cream** *n.* Rasiercreme, *die;* ~ **foam** *n.* Rasierschaum, *der;* ~ **soap** *n.* Rasierseife, *die;* ~ **stick** *n.* Stangenrasierseife, *die*

shawl /ʃɔːl/ *n.* Schultertuch, *das*

she /ʃɪ, *stressed* ʃiː/ *pron.* sie

sheaf /ʃiːf/ *n., pl.* **sheaves** /ʃiːvz/ (of corn etc.) Garbe, *die;* (of paper, arrows, etc.) Bündel, *das*

shear /ʃɪə(r)/ *v.t., p.p.* **shorn** /ʃɔːn/ *or* **sheared** (clip) scheren

shears /ʃɪəz/ *n. pl.* **[pair of]** ~: Schere, *die;* **garden** ~: Gartenschere, *die*

sheath /ʃiːθ/ *n., pl.* ~**s** /ʃiːðz, ʃiːθs/ **(a)** (for knife, sword, etc.) Scheide, *die* **(b)** (condom) Gummischutz, *der*

sheaves *pl. of* SHEAF

shebang /ʃɪ'bæŋ/ *n.* (Amer. coll.) **the whole** ~: der ganze Kram (ugs.)

shed¹ /ʃed/ *v.t.,* **-dd-, shed (a)** verlieren; abwerfen ‹Laub, Geweih› **(b)** vergießen ‹Blut, Tränen› **(c)** verbreiten ‹Licht›

shed² *n.* Schuppen, *der*

she'd /ʃɪd, *stressed* ʃiːd/ **(a)** = **she had; (b)** = **she would**

sheen /ʃiːn/ *n.* Glanz, *der*

sheep /ʃiːp/ *n., pl. same* Schaf, *das*

sheep: ~ **dip** *n.* Desinfektionsbad für Schafe; ~**dog** *n.* Hütehund, *der;* Schäferhund, *der;* **Old English S~dog** Bobtail, *der*

sheepish /'ʃiːpɪʃ/ *adj.* verlegen

sheep: ~ **shearer** *n.* Schafscherer, *der;* ~**shearing** *n.* Schafschur, *die;* ~**skin** *n.* Schaffell, *das*

sheer /ʃɪə(r)/ *adj.* **(a)** rein; blank ‹Unsinn, Gewalt›; **by** ~ **chance** rein zufällig **(b)** schroff ‹Felsen, Abfall›

sheet /ʃiːt/ *n.* **(a)** Laken, *das* **(b)** (of thin metal or plastic) Folie, *die;* (of iron, tin) Blech, *das;* (of glass) Platte, *die;* (of paper) Bogen, *der;* Blatt, *das*

sheet: ~ **lightning** *n.* Flächenblitz, *der;* ~ **music** *n.* Notenblätter *Pl.*

sheik[h] /ʃeɪk, ʃiːk/ *n.* Scheich, *der*

shelf /ʃelf/ *n., pl.* **shelves** /ʃelvz/ Brett, *das;* Bord, *das;* **shelves** (set) Regal, *das*

'shelf life *n.* Lagerfähigkeit, *die*

shell /ʃel/ 1 *n.* **(a)** Schale, *die;* (of snail) Haus, *das;* (of turtle, tortoise) Panzer, *der;* (on beach) Muschel, *die* **(b)** (Mil.) (bomb) Granate, *die* 2 *v.t.* **(a)** (take out of ~) schälen **(b)** (Mil.) [mit Artillerie] beschießen ■ **shell 'out** *v.t. & i.* (coll.) blechen (ugs.) **(on** für)

she'll /ʃɪl, *stressed* ʃiːl/ = **she will**

shell: ~**fish** *n., pl. same* **(a)** Schal[en]tier, *das;* (oyster, clam) Muschel, *die;* (crustacean) Krebstier, *das;* **(b)** *in pl.* (Gastr.) Meeresfrüchte *Pl.;* ~ **shock** *n.* Kriegsneurose, *die;* ~ **suit** *n.* Trilobalanzug, *der*

shelter /'ʃeltə(r)/ 1 *n.* **(a)** (shield) Schutz, *der* **(against** vor + *Dat.,* gegen); **bomb** or **air-raid** ~: Luftschutzraum, *der;* **get under** ~: sich unterstellen **(b)** *no pl.* (place of safety) Zuflucht, *die* 2 *v.t.* schützen **(from** vor + *Dat.*); Unterschlupf gewähren (+ *Dat.*) ‹Flüchtling› 3 *v.i.* Schutz suchen **(from** vor + *Dat.*)

'sheltered /'ʃeltəd/ *adj.* geschützt; behütet ‹Leben;› **live in** ~ **housing** in einer Altenwohnung/in Altenwohnungen leben

shelve /ʃelv/ 1 *v.t.* (defer) auf Eis legen (ugs.) 2 *v.i.* (slope) abfallen

shelves *pl. of* SHELF

'shelving *n.* Regale *Pl.*

shepherd /'ʃepəd/ 1 *n.* Schäfer, *der* 2 *v.t.* führen

'shepherdess *n.* Schäferin, *die*

shepherd: ~'s **'crook** *n.* Schäferstock, *der;* ~'s **'pie** *n.: Auflauf aus Hackfleisch mit einer Schicht Kartoffelbrei darüber*

sheriff /'ʃerɪf/ *n.* Sheriff, *der*

sherry /'ʃerɪ/ *n.* Sherry, *der*

she's /ʃɪz, *stressed* ʃiːz/ **(a)** = **she is; (b)** = **she has**

Shia(h) /'ʃiːə/ *n.* (Muslim Relig.) Schia, *die*

shield /ʃiːld/ 1 *n.* Schild, *der* 2 *v.t.* schützen **(from** vor + *Dat.*)

shift /ʃɪft/ 1 *v.t.* **(a)** (move) umstellen ‹Möbel›; wegnehmen ‹Arm, Hand, Fuß›; wegräumen ‹Schutt›; entfernen ‹Schmutz, Fleck›; ~ **the responsibility/blame on to sb.** die Verantwortung/Schuld auf jmdn. schieben

····⫶·

S

(b) (Amer. Motor Veh.) ∼ **gears** schalten

2 *v.i.* (a) ⟨*Wind:*⟩ drehen (**to** nach); ⟨*Ladung:*⟩ verrutschen

(b) (coll.: move quickly) rasen

3 *n.* (a) **a** ∼ **in emphasis** eine Verlagerung des Akzents; **a** ∼ **in public opinion** ein Umschwung der öffentlichen Meinung

(b) (for work) Schicht, *die;* **eight-hour/late** ∼: Achtstunden-/Spätschicht, *die;* **do** *or* **work the late** ∼: Spätschicht haben

'**shift work** *n.* Schichtarbeit, *die*

shifty /'ʃɪftɪ/ *adj.* verschlagen

Shiite /'ʃiːaɪt/ (Muslim Relig.) **1** *n.* Schiit, *der*/Schiitin, *die*

2 *adj.* schiitisch

shilling /'ʃɪlɪŋ/ *n.* (Hist.) Shilling, *der*

shilly-shally /'ʃɪlɪʃælɪ/ *v.i.* zaudern; **stop** ∼**ing!** entschließ dich endlich!

shimmer /'ʃɪmə(r)/ **1** *v.i.* schimmern

2 *n.* Schimmer, *der*

shin /ʃɪn/ **1** *n.* Schienbein, *das*

2 *v.i.,* **-nn-:** ∼ **up/down a tree** *etc.* einen Baum *usw.* hinauf-/hinunterklettern

'**shin bone** *n.* Schienbein, *das*

shine /ʃaɪn/ **1** *v.i.,* **shone** /ʃɒn/ ⟨*Lampe, Licht, Stern:*⟩ leuchten; ⟨*Sonne, Mond:*⟩ scheinen; (reflect light) glänzen

2 *v.t.,* **shone:** ∼ **a light on sth./in sb.'s eyes** etw. anleuchten/jmdm. in die Augen leuchten

3 *n.* Glanz, *der*

shingle /'ʃɪŋgl/ *n.* (pebbles) Kies, *der*

'**shingles** *n.* (Med.) Gürtelrose, *die*

shin: ∼ **guard,** ∼ **pad** *ns.* Schienbeinschutz, *der*

shiny /'ʃaɪnɪ/ *adj.* glänzend

ship /ʃɪp/ **1** *n.* Schiff, *das*

2 *v.t.,* **-pp-** (transport by sea) verschiffen; (send by road, train, or air) verschicken ⟨*Waren*⟩

'**shipbuilding** *n.* Schiffbau, *der*

'**shipment** *n.* (a) Versand, *der;* (by sea) Verschiffung, *die*

(b) (amount) Sendung, *die*

'**shipowner** *n.* Schiffseigentümer, *der*/ -eigentümerin, *die;* (of several ships) Reeder, *der*/Reederin, *die*

'**shipper** *n.* Spediteur, *der*/Spediteurin, *die;* (company) Spedition, *die*

'**shipping** *n.* (a) (ships) Schiffe *Pl.;* (traffic) Schifffahrt, *die*

(b) (transporting) Versand, *der*

shipping: ∼ **agent** *n.* Schiffsagent, *der;* ∼ **forecast** *n.* Seewetterbericht, *der;* ∼ **lane** *n.* Schifffahrtsweg, *der*

ship: ∼**shape** *adj.* in bester Ordnung; ∼**wreck** **1** *n.* Schiffbruch, *der;* **2** *v.t.* **be** ∼**wrecked** Schiffbruch erleiden; ∼**yard** *n.* [Schiffs]werft, *die*

shirk /ʃɜːk/ *v.t.* sich drücken vor (+ *Dat.*)

'**shirker** *n.* Drückeberger, *der*/ Drückebergerin, *die* (ugs.)

shirt /ʃɜːt/ *n.* [man's] ∼: [Herren- *od.* Ober]hemd, *das*

'**shirtsleeve** *n.* Hemdsärmel, *der;* **in** ∼**s** in Hemdsärmeln

shit /ʃɪt/ (coarse) **1** *v.i.,* **-tt-, shitted** *or* **shit** scheißen (derb)

2 *n.* (a) Scheiße, *die* (derb); **have** (Brit.) *or* (Amer.) **take a** ∼: scheißen (derb)

(b) (person) Scheißkerl, *der* (derb)

(c) (nonsense) Scheiß, *der* (salopp)

shiver /'ʃɪvə(r)/ **1** *v.i.* zittern (**with** vor + *Dat.*)

2 *n.* Schau[d]er, *der* (geh.)

shoal /ʃəʊl/ *n.* (of fish) Schwarm, *der*

shock /ʃɒk/ **1** *n.* (a) Schock, *der;* **give sb. a** ∼: jmdm. einen Schock versetzen

(b) (violent impact) Erschütterung, *die* (**of** durch)

(c) (Electr.) Schlag, *der*

(d) (Med.) Schock, *der*

2 *v.t.* ∼ **sb.** [deeply] ein [schwerer] Schock für jmdn. sein; (scandalize) jmdn. schockieren

'**shock absorber** *n.* Stoßdämpfer, *der*

'**shocking** *adj.* (a) schockierend

(b) (coll.: very bad) fürchterlich (ugs.)

shock: ∼ **jock** *n.* (coll.) Skandal-DJ, *der;* ∼**proof** *adj.* stoßfest; ∼ **wave** *n.* Druckwelle, *die* (from *Gen.*); (of earthquake) Erschütterungswelle, *die* (from *Gen.*)

shod ▶ SHOE 2

shoddy /'ʃɒdɪ/ *adj.* schäbig; minderwertig ⟨*Arbeit, Stoff, Artikel*⟩

shoe /ʃuː/ **1** *n.* Schuh, *der;* (of horse) [Huf]eisen, *das;* **put oneself into sb.'s** ∼**s** (fig.) sich in jmds. Lage (*Akk.*) versetzen

2 *v.t.,* ∼**ing, shod** /ʃɒd/ beschlagen ⟨*Pferd*⟩

shoe: ∼**horn** *n.* Schuhlöffel, *der;* ∼**lace** *n.* Schnürsenkel, *der;* ∼**maker** *n.* Schuhmacher, *der;* ∼ **polish** *n.* Schuhcreme, *die;* ∼ **shop** *n.* Schuhgeschäft, *das;* ∼**string** *n.* **on a** ∼**string** (coll.) mit ganz wenig Geld

shone ▶ SHINE 1, 2

shoo /ʃuː/ **1** *int.* sch

2 *v.t.* scheuchen; ∼ **away** fortscheuchen

shook ▶ SHAKE 2, 3

shoot /ʃuːt/ **1** *v.i.,* **shot** /ʃɒt/ (a) schießen (**at** auf + *Akk.*)

(b) (move rapidly) schießen (ugs.)

2 *v.t.,* **shot** (a) (wound) anschießen; (kill) erschießen; (hunt) schießen; ∼ **sb. dead** jmdn. erschießen

(b) schießen mit ⟨*Bogen, Munition, Pistole*⟩; abschießen ⟨*Pfeil, Kugel*⟩ (**at** auf + *Akk.*)

(c) (Cinemat.) drehen ⟨*Film, Szene*⟩

3 *n.* (Bot.) Trieb, *der*

■ **shoot** '**down** *v.t.* niederschießen ⟨*Person*⟩; abschießen ⟨*Flugzeug*⟩

■ **shoot** '**out** *v.i.* hervorschießen

■ **shoot** '**up** *v.i.* in die Höhe schießen; ⟨*Preise, Kosten, Temperatur:*⟩ in die Höhe schnellen

shooting: ∼ **range** *n.* Schießstand, *der;* ∼ '**star** *n.* Sternschnuppe, *die*

'**shoot-out** *n.* Schießerei, *die*

shop /ʃɒp/ **1** *n.* Laden, *der;* Geschäft, *das;* go to the ~s einkaufen gehen; **talk ~:** fachsimpeln (ugs.)
2 *v.i.,* -pp- einkaufen; **go ~ping** einkaufen gehen
■ **shop a'round** *v.i.* sich umsehen (**for** nach)

shopaholic /ˈʃɒpəhɒlɪk/ *n.* Kaufsüchtige, *der/die*

shop: ~ **assistant** *n.* (Brit.) Verkäufer, *der/*Verkäuferin, *die;* ~**front** *n.* Schaufensterfront, *die;* ~**keeper** *n.* Ladenbesitzer, *der/*-besitzerin, *die;* ~**lifter** *n.* Ladendieb, *der/*-diebin, *die;* ~**lifting** *n.* Ladendiebstahl, *der;* ~**owner** ▶ ~KEEPER

'**shopper** *n.* Käufer, *der/*Käuferin, *die*

'**shopping** *n.* (a) Einkaufen, *das;* **do the/one's ~:** einkaufen/[seine] Einkäufe machen
(b) (items bought) Einkäufe *Pl.*

shopping: ~ **bag** *n.* Einkaufstasche, *die;* ~ **basket** *n.* Einkaufskorb, *der;* ~ **centre** *n.* Einkaufszentrum, *das;* ~ **list** *n.* Einkaufszettel, *der;* ~ **mall** /-mæl/ *n.* Einkaufszentrum, *das;* ~ **precinct** *n.* Einkaufs- od. Geschäftsviertel, *das;* ~ **street** *n.* Geschäftsstraße, *die;* ~ **trolley** *n.* (in supermarket) Einkaufswagen, *der;* (personal) Einkaufsroller, *der*

shop: ~-**soiled** *adj.* (Brit.) (slightly damaged) leicht beschädigt; (slightly dirty) angeschmutzt; ~ **steward** *n.* [gewerkschaftlicher] Vertrauensmann; ~ '**window** *n.* Schaufenster, *das*

shore /ʃɔː(r)/ *n.* Ufer, *das;* (beach) Strand, *der*
■ **shore 'up** *v.t.* abstützen ‹Mauer, Haus›; (fig.) stützen

shorn ▶ SHEAR

short /ʃɔːt/ **1** *adj.* (a) kurz; **in a ~ time** *or* **while** (soon) bald; in Kürze; **a ~ time** *or* **while ago/later** vor kurzem/kurze Zeit später; **in ~,** ...: kurz, ...
(b) klein ‹Person, Wuchs›
(c) (deficient, scanty) knapp; **go ~ [of sth.]** [an etw. (*Dat.*)] Mangel leiden; **sb. is ~ of sth.** jmdm. fehlt es an etw. (*Dat.*); **time is getting/is ~:** die Zeit wird/ist knapp; **be in ~ supply** knapp sein; **be ~ [of cash]** knapp [bei Kasse] sein (ugs.)
2 *adv.* (a) (abruptly) plötzlich; **stop ~:** plötzlich abbrechen; **stop sb. ~:** jmdm. ins Wort fallen
(b) **stop ~ of doing sth.** nicht so weit gehen, etw. zu tun

shortage /ˈʃɔːtɪdʒ/ *n.* Mangel, *der* (**of** an + *Dat.*); ~ **of fruit/teachers** Obstknappheit, *die*/Lehrermangel, *der*

short: ~**bread** *n.* Shortbread, *das;* Kekse aus Butterteig; ~ '**circuit** *n.* (Electr.) Kurzschluss, *der;* ~**coming** *n.,* usu. *in pl.* Unzulänglichkeit, *die;* ~ '**cut** *n.* (a)

Abkürzung, *die;* **take a ~ cut** den Weg abkürzen; (b) (Comp.) **[keyboard]** ~**cut** Shortcut, *der*

shorten /ˈʃɔːtn/ **1** *v.i.* kürzer werden
2 *v.t.* kürzen; verkürzen ‹Besuch, Wartezeit›

short: ~**fall** *n.* Fehlmenge, *die;* ~-**haired** *adj.* kurzhaarig; Kurzhaar‹dackel, -katze›; ~**hand** *n.* Stenografie, *die;* ~**hand typist** Stenotypist, *der/*-typistin, *die;* ~ **list** *n.* (Brit.) engere Auswahl; **be on/put sb. on the ~ list** in der engeren Auswahl sein/jmdn. in die engere Auswahl nehmen; ~-**list** *v.t.* in die engere Auswahl nehmen; ~-**lived** *adj.* kurzlebig

'**shortly** *adv.* in Kürze; demnächst; ~ **before/after sth.** kurz vor/nach etw.

short: ~ '**pastry** *n.* Mürbeteig, *der;* ~-**range** *adj.* (a) Kurzstrecken‹flugzeug, -rakete usw.›; (b) (relating to time) kurzfristig

shorts /ʃɔːts/ *n. pl.* (a) (trousers) kurze Hose[n *Pl.*]; Shorts *Pl.*
(b) (Amer.: underpants) Unterhose, *die*

short: ~-'**sighted** *adj.* kurzsichtig; ~-**sleeved** /-ˈsliːvd/ *adj.* kurzärm[e]lig; ~-**staffed** /-ˈstaːft/ *adj.* **be [very] ~-staffed** [viel] zu wenig Personal haben; ~ '**story** *n.* Kurzgeschichte, *die;* ~-'**tempered** *adj.* aufbrausend; ~-**term** *adj.* kurzfristig; (provisional) vorläufig ‹Lösung›; befristet ‹Vertrag›; ~ '**trousers** *n. pl.* kurze Hose[n *Pl.*]; ~ **wave** *n.* (Radio) Kurzwelle, *die*

shot /ʃɒt/ **1** *n.* (a) Schuss, *der;* **fire a ~:** einen Schuss abgeben (**at** auf + *Akk.*); **like a ~** (fig.) wie der Blitz (ugs.); **I'd do it like a ~:** ich würde es auf der Stelle tun
(b) (Athletics) **put the ~:** die Kugel stoßen; **[putting] the ~:** Kugelstoßen, *das*
(c) (Sport: stroke, kick, throw) Schuss, *der*
(d) (Photog.) Aufnahme, *die;* (Cinemat.) Einstellung, *die*
2 ▶ SHOOT 1, 2
3 *adj.* **be/get ~ of** (coll.) los sein/loswerden

'**shotgun** *n.* [Schrot]flinte, *die*

should ▶ SHALL

shoulder /ˈʃəʊldə(r)/ **1** *n.* Schulter, *die*
2 *v.t.* schultern; (fig.) übernehmen

shoulder: ~ **bag** *n.* Umhängetasche, *die;* ~ **blade** *n.* Schulterblatt, *das;* ~ **joint** *n.* Schultergelenk, *das;* ~-**length** *adj.* schulterlang; ~ **pad** *n.* Schulterpolster, *das;* ~ **strap** *n.* (on garment) Schulterklappe, *die;* (on bag) Trageriemen, *der*

shouldn't /ˈʃʊdnt/ (coll.) = should not;
▶ SHALL

shout /ʃaʊt/ **1** *n.* Ruf, *der;* (inarticulate) Schrei, *der*
2 *v.i. & t.* schreien
■ **shout 'down** *v.t.* niederschreien
■ **shout 'out** **1** *v.i.* aufschreien
2 *v.t.* [laut] rufen

'**shouting** *n.* Geschrei, *das*

shove /ʃʌv/ **1** *n.* Stoß, *der*
2 *v.t.* stoßen; schubsen (ugs.); (coll.: put) tun ⋯⟶

■ **shove a'way** v.t. (coll.) wegschubsen (ugs.)

■ **shove 'off** v.i. (coll.: leave) abschieben (ugs.)

shovel /'ʃʌvl/ **1** n. Schaufel, die **2** v.t., (Brit.) -ll- schaufeln

show /ʃəʊ/ **1** n. (a) (entertainment, performance) Show, die; (Theatre) Vorstellung, die; (Radio, Telev.) [Unterhaltungs]sendung, die (b) (exhibition) Ausstellung, die; Schau, die; put sth. on ∼: etw. ausstellen; be on ∼: ausgestellt sein (c) (appearance) Anschein, der; be for ∼: reine Angeberei sein (ugs.) **2** v.t., p.p. shown /ʃəʊn/ (a) zeigen; vorzeigen ⟨Pass, Fahrschein usw.⟩; ∼ sb. sth., ∼ sth. to sb. jmdm. etw. zeigen (b) beweisen ⟨Mut, Urteilsvermögen usw.⟩; ∼ sb. that ...: jmdm. beweisen, dass ...; ∼ [sb.] kindness/mercy freundlich [zu jmdm.] sein/Erbarmen [mit jmdm.] haben (c) ⟨Thermometer, Uhr usw.:⟩ anzeigen (d) (exhibit in a show) ausstellen; zeigen ⟨Film⟩ **3** v.i., p.p. shown (a) (be visible) sichtbar od. zu sehen sein; (come into sight) sich zeigen (b) (be ∼n) ⟨Film:⟩ laufen; ⟨Künstler:⟩ ausstellen

■ **show 'in** v.t. hinein-/hereinführen

■ **show 'off** v.i. angeben (ugs.); prahlen

■ **show 'out** v.t. hinausführen

■ **show 'round** v.t. herumführen

■ **show 'through** v.i. durchscheinen

■ **show 'up 1** v.t. (a) (make visible) [deutlich] sichtbar machen (b) (coll.: embarrass) blamieren **2** v.i. (a) (be visible) [deutlich] zu sehen sein (b) (coll.: arrive) sich blicken lassen (ugs.)

show: ∼ **biz** (coll.)**,** ∼ **business** ns., no art. Schaugeschäft, das; ∼**case** n. Vitrine, die; (fig.) Schaufenster, das; '∼**down** n. (fig.) Kraftprobe, die; have a ∼down [with sb.] sich [mit jmdm.] auseinander setzen

shower /'ʃaʊə(r)/ **1** n. (a) Schauer, der; ∼ of rain/hail Regen-/Hagelschauer, der (b) (for washing) Dusche, die; have or take a [cold/quick] ∼: [kalt/schnell] duschen **2** v.t. (lavish) ∼ sth. [up]on sb., ∼ sb. with sth. jmdn. mit etw. überhäufen **3** v.i. (have a ∼) duschen

shower: ∼ **cap** n. Duschhaube, die; ∼ **curtain** n. Duschvorhang, der; ∼ **gel** n. Duschgel, das; ∼**proof** adj. [bedingt] regendicht

'showery adj. it is ∼: es gibt immer wieder kurze Schauer; a ∼ day ein Tag mit Schauerwetter

'showjumping n. Springreiten, das

shown ▶ SHOW 2, 3

show: ∼**-off** n. (coll.) Angeber, der/ Angeberin, die; ∼**piece** n. (of exhibition, collection) Schaustück, das; (highlight) Paradestück, das; ∼**room** n. Ausstellungsraum, der; ∼ **trial** n. Schauprozess, der

'showy adj. protzig (ugs.)

shrank ▶ SHRINK

shred /ʃred/ **1** n. Fetzen, der; (fig.) Spur, die; tear sth. to ∼s etw. zerfetzen; (fig.) etw. zerpflücken **2** v.t., -dd- [im Reißwolf] zerkleinern

shredder /'ʃredə(r)/ n. (for paper) Reißwolf, der

shrew /ʃruː/ n. (Zool.) Spitzmaus, die

shrewd /ʃruːd/ adj. klug; genau ⟨[Ein]schätzung⟩

shriek /ʃriːk/ **1** n. [Auf]schrei, der **2** v.i. [auf]schreien **3** v.t. schreien

shrift /ʃrɪft/ n. give sb. short ∼: jmdn. kurz abfertigen (ugs.); get short ∼ kurz abgefertigt werden (ugs.)

shrill /ʃrɪl/ adj. schrill

shrimp /ʃrɪmp/ n. Garnele, die

shrine /ʃraɪn/ n. (tomb) Grab, das

shrink /ʃrɪŋk/ **1** v.i., shrank /ʃræŋk/, shrunk /ʃrʌŋk/ (a) schrumpfen; ⟨Kleidung, Stoff:⟩ einlaufen; ⟨Metall, Holz:⟩ sich zusammenziehen (b) (recoil) ∼ from sb./sth. vor jmdm. zurückweichen/vor etw. (Dat.) zurückschrecken; ∼ from doing sth. sich scheuen, etw. zu tun **2** v.t., shrank, shrunk einlaufen lassen ⟨Textilien⟩

shrinkage /'ʃrɪŋkɪdʒ/ n. (of clothing) Einlaufen, das

shrink: ∼**-proof, ∼-resistant** adjs. schrumpffrei; be ∼-proof nicht einlaufen; ∼**-wrap** v.t. in einer Schrumpffolie verpacken

shrivel /'ʃrɪvl/ v.i., (Brit.) -ll-: ∼ [up] verschrumpeln; ⟨Pflanze, Blume:⟩ welk werden

shroud /ʃraʊd/ **1** n. Leichentuch, das **2** v.t. ∼ sth. in sth. etw. in etw. (Akk.) hüllen

Shrove 'Tuesday /ʃrəʊv/ n. Fastnachtsdienstag, der

shrub /ʃrʌb/ n. Strauch, der

shrubbery /'ʃrʌbərɪ/ n. Gesträuch, das

shrug /ʃrʌg/ **1** v.t. & i., -gg-: ∼ [one's shoulders] die Achseln zucken **2** n. ∼ [of one's or the shoulders] Achselzucken, das

■ **shrug 'off** v.t. in den Wind schlagen

shrunk ▶ SHRINK

shrunken /'ʃrʌŋkn/ adj. verhutzelt (ugs.) ⟨Person⟩; schrump[el]lig ⟨Apfel⟩

shudder /'ʃʌdə(r)/ **1** v.i. zittern (with vor + Dat.) **2** n. Zittern, das

shuffle /'ʃʌfl/ **1** n. (a) Schlurfen, das; walk with a ∼: schlurfen (b) (Cards) Mischen, das; give the cards a [good] ∼: die Karten [gut] mischen **2** v.t. (a) (Cards) mischen

(b) ∼ **one's feet** von einem Fuß auf den anderen treten

shun /ʃʌn/ *v.t.,* **-nn-** meiden

shunt /ʃʌnt/ *v.t.* (Railw.) rangieren

shush /ʃʊʃ/ *int.* still

shut /ʃʌt/ **1** *v.t.,* **-tt-, shut** zumachen; schließen; zusammenklappen ⟨*Klappmesser, Fächer*⟩; ∼ **one's finger in the door** sich (*Dat.*) den Finger in der Tür einklemmen **2** *v.i.,* **-tt-, shut** schließen; ⟨*Blüte:*⟩ sich schließen

■ **shut 'down** **1** *v.t.* **(a)** schließen, zumachen ⟨*Deckel*⟩ **(b)** stilllegen ⟨*Fabrik*⟩; abschalten ⟨*Kernreaktor*⟩ **2** *v.i.* ⟨*Laden, Fabrik:*⟩ geschlossen werden

■ **shut 'out** *v.t.* aussperren

■ **shut 'up** **1** *v.t.* abschließen; einsperren ⟨*Tier, Person*⟩ **2** *v.i.* (coll.: be quiet) den Mund halten

shutter /'ʃʌtə(r)/ *n.* **(a)** [Fenster]laden, *der* **(b)** (Photog.) Verschluss, *der;* ∼ **release** Auslöser, *der;* ∼ **speed** Verschlusszeit, *die*

shuttle /'ʃʌtl/ **1** *n.* (in loom) Schiffchen, *das* **2** *v.i.* pendeln

shuttle: ∼**cock** *n.* Federball, *der;* '∼ **service** *n.* Pendelverkehr, *der*

shy /ʃaɪ/ *adj.,* ∼**er** *or* **shier** /'ʃaɪə(r)/, ∼**est** *or* **shiest** /'ʃaɪɪst/ scheu; (diffident) schüchtern

■ **shy a'way** *v.i.* ∼ **away from sth./doing sth.** etw. scheuen/sich scheuen, etw. zu tun

'**shyness** *n.* Scheuheit, *die;* (diffidence) Schüchternheit, *die*

Siamese /saɪə'miːz/: ∼ '**cat** *n.* Siamkatze, *die;* ∼ '**twins** *n. pl.* siamesische Zwillinge *Pl.*

Siberia /saɪ'bɪərɪə/ *pr. n.* Sibirien (*das*)

sibling /'sɪblɪŋ/ *n.* (male) Bruder, *der;* (female) Schwester, *die; in pl.* Geschwister *Pl.*

Sicily /'sɪsɪlɪ/ *pr. n.* Sizilien (*das*)

sick /sɪk/ **1** *adj.* **(a)** (ill) krank; **be off** ∼: krank [gemeldet] sein **(b)** (Brit.: vomiting or about to vomit) **be** ∼: sich erbrechen; **I'm going to be** ∼: ich muss mich erbrechen; **sb. gets/feels** ∼: jmdm. wird/ist [es] übel *od.* schlecht; **be/get** ∼ **of sb./sth.** (fig.) jmdn./etw. satt haben/ allmählich satt haben; **make sb.** ∼ (disgust) jmdn. anekeln **2** *n. pl.* **the** ∼: die Kranken *Pl.*

sick 'building syndrome *n.* Sickbuildingsyndrom, *das*

'**sicken** /'sɪkn/ **1** *v.i.* **be** ∼**ing for sth.** (Brit.) krank werden; etw. ausbrüten (ugs.) **2** *v.t.* (disgust) anwidern

'**sickening** *adj.* Ekel erregend, widerlich ⟨*Anblick, Geruch*⟩

sickle /'sɪkl/ *n.* Sichel, *die*

sick: ∼ **leave** *n.* Urlaub wegen Krankheit; **be on** ∼ ≈ krank geschrieben sein; ∼ **list** *n.* Liste der Kranken, *die;* **on the** ∼ **list:** krank [gemeldet/geschrieben]

'**sickly** *adj.* kränklich

'**sickness** *n.* Krankheit, *die;* (nausea) Übelkeit, *die*

sick: ∼ **pay** *n.* Entgeltfortzahlung im Krankheitsfalle; (paid by insurance) Krankengeld, *das;* ∼**room** *n.* Krankenzimmer, *das*

side /saɪd/ **1** *n.* **(a)** Seite, *die;* ∼ **of beef** Rinderhälfte, *die;* ∼ **of bacon** Speckseite, *die;* **walk/stand** ∼ **by** ∼: nebeneinander gehen/stehen; **work/fight** ∼ **by** ∼ **[with sb.]** Seite an Seite [mit jmdm.] arbeiten/ kämpfen; **live** ∼ **by** ∼ **[with sb.]** in [jmds.] unmittelbarer Nachbarschaft leben; **to one** ∼: zur Seite; **on one** ∼: an der Seite; **on the** ∼ (as ∼line) nebenbei; **take** ∼**s [with/against sb.]** [für/gegen jmdn.] Partei ergreifen **(b)** (Sport: team) Mannschaft, *die* **2** *v.i.* ∼ **with sb.** sich auf jmds. Seite (*Akk.*) stellen **3** *adj.* Seiten-

side: ∼**board** *n.* Anrichte, *die;* ∼**boards** (coll.), ∼**burns** *ns. pl.* (on cheeks) Backenbart, *der;* (in front of the ears) Koteletten *Pl.;* ∼**car** *n.* Beiwagen, *der;* ∼ **dish** *n.* Beilage, *die;* ∼ **door** *n.* Seitentür, *die;* ∼ **effect** *n.* Nebenwirkung, *die;* ∼ **entrance** *n.* Seiteneingang, *der;* ∼ **exit** *n.* Seitenausgang, *der;* ∼ **issue** *n.* Randproblem, *das;* ∼ **kick** *n.* (coll.) Kumpan, *der;* ∼**light** *n.* Begrenzungsleuchte, *die;* **drive on** ∼**lights** mit Standlicht fahren; ∼**line** *n.* (occupation) Nebenbeschäftigung, *die;* ∼**long** *adj.* **a** ∼**long look/glance** ein Seitenblick; ∼ **plate** *n.* kleiner Teller (neben dem Teller für das Hauptgericht); ∼ **road** *n.* Seitenstraße, *die;* ∼**saddle** *adv.* **ride** ∼**saddle** im Damensitz reiten; ∼ **salad** *n.* Salat [als Beilage]; **steak with chips and a** ∼ **salad** Steak mit Pommes frites und dazu ein Salat; ∼**show** *n.* Nebenattraktion, *die;* ∼**step** **1** *n.* Schritt zur Seite; **2** *v.t.* ausweichen (+ *Dat.*); ∼ **street** *n.* Seitenstraße, *die;* ∼ **table** *n.* Beistelltisch, *der;* ∼**track** *v.t.* **get** ∼**tracked** abgelenkt werden; ∼**walk** *n.* (Amer.) Bürgersteig, *der;* ∼**ways** /'saɪdweɪz/ **1** *adv.* **look at sb./sth.** ∼**ways** jmdn./etw. von der Seite ansehen; **2** *adj.* seitlich; ∼ **wind** *n.* Seitenwind, *der*

siding /'saɪdɪŋ/ *n.* Abstellgleis, *das*

sidle /'saɪdl/ *v.i.* schleichen [**up to** zu]

siege /siːdʒ/ *n.* Belagerung, *die;* (by police) Umstellung, *die;* **lay** ∼ **to sth.** etw. belagern

siesta /sɪ'estə/ *n.* Siesta, *die*

sieve /sɪv/ **1** *n.* Sieb, *das* **2** *v.t.* sieben

sift /sɪft/ *v.t.* sieben; ∼ **sth. from sth.** etw. von etw. trennen

■ **sift 'out** *v.t.* aussieben

sigh /saɪ/ **1** *n.* Seufzer, *der;* **breathe** *or* **give** *or* **heave a** ∼: einen Seufzer ausstoßen; ∼ **of relief/contentment** Seufzer der Erleichterung/Zufriedenheit **2** *v.i.* seufzen; ∼ **with relief/despair** erleichtert/verzweifelt seufzen

S

sight /saɪt/ ① n. **(a)** (faculty) Sehvermögen, *das;* **know sb. by** ∼: jmdn. vom Sehen kennen
(b) (act of seeing; spectacle) Anblick, *der;* **catch/lose** ∼ **of sb./sth.** jmdn./etw. erblicken/aus dem Auge verlieren; **at first** ∼: auf den ersten Blick
(c) *in pl.* ∼s (places of interest) Sehenswürdigkeiten *Pl.;* **see the** ∼s die Sehenswürdigkeiten besichtigen
(d) (range) Sichtweite, *die;* **in** ∼: in Sicht; **within** *or* **in** ∼ **of sb./sth.** (able to see) in jmds. Sichtweite (*Dat.*)/in Sichtweite einer Sache; **out of** ∼: außer Sicht
(e) (of gun) Visier, *das;* **set/have [set] one's** ∼s **on sth.** (fig.) etw. anpeilen
② *v.t.* sichten 〈*Land, Schiff, Flugzeug*〉; sehen 〈*Entflohenen, Vermissten*〉

sighted /'saɪtɪd/ *adj.* sehend; **partially** ∼: [hochgradig] sehbehindert

'sighting n. Beobachtung, *die*

sight-read (Mus.) *v.t. & i.* 〈*Pianist usw.:*〉 vom Blatt spielen; 〈*Sänger:*〉 vom Blatt singen

'sightseeing n. **go** ∼: Besichtigungen machen

sightseer /'saɪtsiːə(r)/ n. Tourist (*der die Sehenswürdigkeiten besichtigt*)

sign /saɪn/ ① n. **(a)** (symbol, signal, indication) Zeichen, *das;* (of future event) Anzeichen, *das;* **as a** ∼ **of** als Zeichen (+ *Gen.*)
(b) (Astrol.) ∼ **[of the zodiac]** Sternzeichen, *das*
(c) (notice; on shop etc.) Schild, *das*
② *v.t. & i.* unterschreiben; ∼ **one's name** [mit seinem Namen] unterschreiben

▪ **sign 'on** *v.i.* (as unemployed) sich arbeitslos melden

▪ **sign 'up** *v.i.* sich [vertraglich] verpflichten (**with** bei); (for course) sich einschreiben

signal /'sɪɡnl/ ① n. Signal, *das;* **a** ∼ **for sth./to do sth.** ein Zeichen zu etw./für jmdn
② *v.i.*, (Brit.) **-ll-** signalisieren; Signale geben; 〈*Kraftfahrer:*〉 blinken; (with hand) anzeigen; ∼ **to sb. [to do sth.]** jmdm. ein Zeichen geben[, etw. zu tun]

signal: ∼ **box** n. Stellwerk, *das;* ∼ **man** /-mən/ n. Bahnwärter, *der*

signature /'sɪɡnətʃə(r)/ n. Unterschrift, *die;* (on painting) Signatur, *die*

'signature tune n. Erkennungsmelodie, *die*

'signboard n. Schild, *das*

signet ring /'sɪɡnɪt rɪŋ/ n. Siegelring, *der*

significance /sɪɡ'nɪfɪkəns/ n. Bedeutung, *die;* **be of [no]** ∼: [nicht] von Bedeutung sein

significant /sɪɡ'nɪfɪkənt/ *adj.* **(a)** (noteworthy, important) bedeutend
(b) (full of meaning) bedeutsam

sig'nificantly *adv.* **(a)** (meaningfully) bedeutungsvoll; ∼ **[enough]** bedeutsamerweise
(b) (notably) bedeutend

signify /'sɪɡnɪfaɪ/ *v.t.* bedeuten

sign: ∼ **language** n. Zeichensprache, *die;* ∼**post** n. Wegweiser, *der;* ∼**writer** n. Schildermaler, *der*

Sikh /siːk, sɪk/ n. Sikh, *der*

silence /'saɪləns/ ① n. Schweigen, *das;* (keeping a secret) Verschwiegenheit, *die;* (stillness) Stille, *die;* **there was** ∼: es herrschte Schweigen/Stille; **in** ∼: schweigend
② *v.t.* zum Schweigen bringen; (fig.) ersticken 〈*Proteste*〉; mundtot machen 〈*Gegner*〉

'silencer n. (on gun; Brit. Motor Veh.) Schalldämpfer, *der*

silent /'saɪlənt/ *adj.* stumm; (noiseless) unhörbar; (still) still; **be** ∼ (say nothing) schweigen; ∼ **film** Stummfilm, *der*

'silently *adv.* schweigend; stumm 〈*weinen, beten*〉; (noiselessly) lautlos

silent ma'jority n. schweigende Mehrheit

silhouette /sɪlʊ'et/ ① n. **(a)** (picture) Schattenriss, *der*
(b) (appearance against the light) Silhouette, *die*
② *v.t.* **be** ∼**d against sth.** sich als Silhouette gegen etw. abheben

silicon /'sɪlɪkən/ n. Silicium, *das;* ∼ **chip** Siliciumchip, *der*

silicone /'sɪlɪkəʊn/ n. Silikon, *das;* ∼ **implant** Silikonimplantat, *das*

silk /sɪlk/ ① n. Seide, *die*
② *attrib. adj.* seiden; Seiden-

'silkworm n. Seidenraupe, *die*

'silky *adj.* seidig

sill /sɪl/ n. (of door) [Tür]schwelle, *die;* (of window) Fensterbank, *die*

silly /'sɪlɪ/ *adj.* dumm; (imprudent, unwise) töricht; (childish) albern

silo /'saɪləʊ/ n., *pl.* ∼s Silo, *der*

silt /sɪlt/ n. Schlamm, *der;* Schlick, *der*

silver /'sɪlvə(r)/ ① n. Silber, *das*
② *attrib. adj.* silbern; Silber〈*pokal, -münze*〉

silver: ∼ **'jubilee** n. silbernes Jubiläum; ∼ **'medal** n. Silbermedaille, *die;* ∼ **'paper** n. Silberpapier, *das;* ∼**-plated** *adj.* versilbert; ∼**smith** n. Silberschmied, *der*/-schmiedin, *die;* ∼ **'wedding** n. Silberhochzeit, *die*

SIM card /'sɪm kɑːd/ n. SIM-Karte, *die*

similar /'sɪmɪlə(r)/ *adj.* ähnlich (**to** *Dat.*)

similarity /sɪmɪ'lærɪtɪ/ n. Ähnlichkeit, *die* (to mit)

'similarly *adv.* ähnlich; (in exactly the same way) ebenso

simile /'sɪmɪlɪ/ n. Vergleich, *der*

simmer /'sɪmə(r)/ ① *v.i.* 〈*Flüssigkeit:*〉 sieden; ziehen
② *v.t.* köcheln *od.* ziehen lassen

▪ **simmer 'down** *v.i.* sich abregen (ugs.)

simper /'sɪmpə(r)/ *v.i.* affektiert *od.* gekünstelt lächeln

simple /'sɪmpl/ *adj.* einfach; (unsophisticated, not elaborate) schlicht 〈*Mobiliar, Schönheit,*

simple-minded ⋯⋗ siphon ⋯ ⋮

Kunstwerk, Kleidung⟩; **it was a**
∼ misunderstanding es war [ganz] einfach
ein Missverständnis

'simple-minded *adj.* (a) (unsophisticated)
schlicht
(b) (unintelligent) beschränkt

simpleton /'sɪmpltən/ *n.* Einfaltspinsel,
der (ugs.)

simplicity /sɪm'plɪsɪtɪ/ *n.* Einfachheit, *die;*
(unpretentiousness, lack of sophistication)
Schlichtheit, *die*

simplification /sɪmplɪfɪ'keɪʃn/ *n.*
Vereinfachung, *die*

simplify /'sɪmplɪfaɪ/ *v.t.* vereinfachen

simplistic /sɪm'plɪstɪk/ *adj.* [all]zu simpel

simply /'sɪmplɪ/ *adv.* einfach; (in an
unsophisticated manner) schlicht; (merely) nur; **it**
∼ isn't true es ist einfach nicht wahr; **I was**
∼ trying to help ich wollte nur helfen

simulate /'sɪmjʊleɪt/ *v.t.* (a) (feign)
vortäuschen
(b) simulieren ⟨*Bedingungen, Wetter usw.*⟩

simulation /sɪmjʊ'leɪʃn/ *n.* (a) (feigning)
Vortäuschung, *die*
(b) (imitation of conditions) Simulation, *die*
(c) (simulated object) Imitation, *die*

simulator /'sɪmjʊleɪtə(r)/ *n.* Simulator, *der*

simultaneous /sɪml'teɪnɪəs/ *adj.*,
simul'taneously *adv.* gleichzeitig

sin /sɪn/ ① *n.* Sünde, *die*
② *v.i.,* **-nn-** sündigen

since /sɪns/ ① *adv.* seitdem
② *prep.* seit; **I have/had been waiting ∼**
8 o'clock ich warte/wartete [schon] seit
8 Uhr; **he has lived here ∼ his childhood** er
wohnt seit seiner Kindheit hier; **∼ seeing**
you ...: seit ich dich gesehen habe; **∼ then/**
that time inzwischen
③ *conj.* (a) seit; **it is a long time/so long/not**
so long ∼ ...: es ist lange/so lange/gar nicht
lange her, dass ...
(b) (seeing that, as) da

sincere /sɪn'sɪə(r)/ *adj.,* **∼r** /sɪn'sɪərə(r)/,
∼st /sɪn'sɪərɪst/ aufrichtig; herzlich ⟨*Grüße,*
Glückwünsche usw.⟩

sin'cerely *adv.* aufrichtig; **yours ∼:** mit
freundlichen Grüßen

sincerity /sɪn'serɪtɪ/ *n.* Aufrichtigkeit, *die*

sinew /'sɪnjuː/ *n.* Sehne, *die*

sinful /'sɪnfl/ *adj.* sündig; (reprehensible)
sündhaft; **it is ∼ to** ...: es ist eine Sünde,
zu ...

sing /sɪŋ/ *v.i. & t.,* **sang** /sæŋ/, **sung** /sʌŋ/
singen
■ **sing 'up** *v.i.* lauter singen

singe /sɪndʒ/ *v.t. & i.,* **∼ing** versengen

singer /'sɪŋə(r)/ *n.* Sänger, *der*/Sängerin,
die

single /'sɪŋgl/ ① *adj.* (a) einfach; (sole)
einzig; (separate, individual, isolated) einzeln; **not**
a ∼ one kein Einziger/keine Einzige/kein

Einziges; **every ∼ one** jeder/jede/jedes
Einzelne; **every ∼ day** jeden Tag; **∼ ticket**
(Brit.) einfache Fahrkarte
(b) (for one person) Einzel⟨*bett, -zimmer*⟩
(c) (unmarried) ledig; **a ∼ man/woman** ein
Lediger/eine Ledige; **∼ people** Ledige *Pl.*;
∼ parent allein erziehender Elternteil;
∼ mother allein erziehende *od.* stehende
Mutter
② *n.* (a) (Brit.: ticket) einfache Fahrkarte; [a]
∼/two ∼s to Manchester, please einmal/
zweimal einfach nach Manchester, bitte
(b) (record) Single, *die*
(c) *in pl.* (Tennis etc.) Einzel, *das*
■ **single 'out** *v.t.* **∼ sb./sth. out as/for sth.**
jmdn./etw. als/für etw. auswählen

single: ∼ cream *n.* [einfache] Sahne;
∼ 'currency *n.* Einheitswährung, *die;*
∼-decker ① *n.* Bus/Straßenbahn mit nur
einem Deck; **be a ∼-decker** ⟨*Bus,*
Straßenbahn:⟩ nur ein Deck haben; ② *adj.*
∼-decker bus/tram Bus/Straßenbahn mit
[nur] einem Deck; **∼ [European]**
market *n.* [europäischer] Binnenmarkt;
∼-'handed *adv.* allein; **∼-lens 'reflex**
camera *n.* (Photog.) einäugige
Spiegelreflexkamera; **∼-minded** *adj.*
zielstrebig; **∼-mindedly** /sɪŋgl'maɪndɪdlɪ/
adv. zielstrebig; **∼-sex** *adj.* **∼ school** reine
Mädchen-/Jungenschule

'singles bar *n.* Singlekneipe, *die*

'single-storey *adj.* eingeschossig

singlet /'sɪŋglɪt/ *n.* (Brit.) (vest) Unterhemd,
das; (Sport) Trikot, *das*

singly /'sɪŋglɪ/ *adv.* einzeln

singular /'sɪŋgjʊlə(r)/ ① *adj.* (a) (Ling.)
singularisch; Singular-; **∼ noun** Substantiv
im Singular
(b) (extraordinary) einmalig
② *n.* (Ling.) Einzahl, *die;* Singular, *der*

'singularly *adv.* (extraordinarily)
außerordentlich

sinister /'sɪnɪstə(r)/ *adj.* finster; (of evil
omen) Unheil verkündend

sink /sɪŋk/ ① *n.* Spülbecken, *das*
② *v.i.,* **sank** /sæŋk/ *or* **sunk** /sʌŋk/, **sunk**
sinken
③ *v.t.,* **sank** *or* **sunk, sunk** (a) versenken
⟨*Schiff*⟩
(b) niederbringen ⟨*Schacht*⟩
■ **sink 'in** *v.i.* (fig.) jmdm. ins Bewusstsein
dringen; ⟨*Warnung, Lektion:*⟩ verstanden
werden

'sink unit *n.* Spüle, *die*

'sinner *n.* Sünder, *der*/Sünderin, *die*

sinus /'saɪnəs/ *n.* Nebenhöhle, *die*

sinusitis /saɪnə'saɪtɪs/ *n.*
Nebenhöhlenentzündung, *die*

sip /sɪp/ ① *v.t.,* **-pp-: ∼ [up]** schlürfen
② *v.i.,* **-pp-: ∼ at/from sth.** an etw. (*Dat.*)
nippen
③ *n.* Schlückchen, *das*

siphon /'saɪfn/ ① *n.* Siphon, *der* ⋯⋗

2 *v.t.* [durch einen Saugheber] laufen lassen

sir /sɜː(r)/ *n.* **(a)** (formal address) der Herr; (to teacher) Herr Meier/Schmidt *usw.* **(b)** (in letter) **Dear Sir** Sehr geehrter Herr; **Dear Sirs** Sehr geehrte [Damen und] Herren; **Dear Sir or Madam** Sehr geehrte Dame/Sehr geehrter Herr **(c) Sir** /sə(r)/ (title of knight etc.) Sir

siren /'saɪrən/ *n.* Sirene, *die*

sirloin /'sɜːlɔɪn/ *n.* **(a)** (Brit.) Roastbeef, *das;* ~ **steak** Rumpsteak, *das* **(b)** (Amer.) Rumpsteak, *das*

sissy /'sɪsɪ/ **1** *n.* Waschlappen, *der* **2** *adj.* feige

sister /'sɪstə(r)/ *n.* **(a)** Schwester, *die* **(b)** (Brit.: nurse) Oberschwester, *die*

'sister-in-law *n., pl.* **sisters-in-law** Schwägerin, *die*

sisterly /'sɪstəlɪ/ *adj.* schwesterlich

sit /sɪt/ **1** *v.i.,* **-tt-,** sat /sæt/ **(a)** (become seated) sich setzen; ~ **on** *or* **in a chair/in an armchair** sich auf einen Stuhl/in einen Sessel setzen **(b)** (be seated) sitzen **2** *v.t.,* **-tt-,** sat **(a)** setzen **(b)** (Brit.) machen ⟨*Prüfung*⟩

■ **sit 'back** *v.i.* sich zurücklehnen; (fig.) sich im Sessel zurücklehnen

■ **sit 'down** *v.i.* **(a)** (become seated) sich setzen (**on/in** auf/in + *Akk.*) **(b)** (be seated) sitzen

■ **sit 'up** **1** *v.i.* **(a)** (rise) sich aufsetzen **(b)** (be sitting erect) [aufrecht] sitzen **(c)** (stay up) aufbleiben **2** *v.t.* aufsetzen

sitcom /'sɪtkɒm/ (coll.) ▶ SITUATION COMEDY

site /saɪt/ **1** *n.* **(a)** (land) Grundstück, *das* **(b)** (location) Sitz, *der;* (of new factory etc.) Standort, *der* **2** *v.t.* stationieren ⟨*Raketen*⟩; ~ **a factory in London** London als Standort einer Fabrik wählen; **be** ~**d** gelegen sein

siting /'saɪtɪŋ/ *n.* Standortwahl, *die* (of für); (position) Lage, *die*

sitter /'sɪtə(r)/ ▶ BABYSITTER

'sitting *n.* Sitzung, *die;* **the first** ~ [for lunch] der erste Schub [zum Mittagessen]

sitting: ~ **'duck** *n.* (fig.) leichtes Ziel; ~ **room** *n.* Wohnzimmer, *das;* ~ **'target** ▶ ~ DUCK

situate /'sɪtjʊeɪt/ *v.t.* legen

'situated *adj.* gelegen; **be** ~: liegen

situation /sɪtjʊ'eɪʃn/ *n.* **(a)** (location) Lage, *die* **(b)** (circumstances) Situation, *die* **(c)** (job) Stelle, *die*

situation 'comedy *n.* Situationskomödie, *die*

six /sɪks/ **1** *adj.* sechs **2** *n.* Sechs, *die. See also* EIGHT

six: ~**-'footer** *n.* (person) Zweimetermann, *der*/-frau, *die;* ~**-pack** *n.* Sechserpack, *der*

sixteen /sɪks'tiːn/ **1** *adj.* sechzehn

2 *n.* Sechzehn, *die. See also* EIGHT

sixteenth /sɪks'tiːnθ/ **1** *adj.* sechzehnt... **2** *n.* (fraction) Sechzehntel, *das. See also* EIGHTH

sixth /sɪksθ/ **1** *adj.* sechst... **2** *n.* (in sequence, rank) Sechste, *der/die/das;* (fraction) Sechstel, *das. See also* EIGHTH

sixth: ~ **form** *n.* (Brit. Sch.) ≈ zwölfte/ dreizehnte Klasse; ~**-form college** *n.* (Brit. Sch.) ≈ Oberstufenzentrum, *das; College, das nur Schüler der zwölften/dreizehnten Klasse aufnimmt;* ~**-former** *n.* (Brit. Sch.) Schüler/Schülerin der zwölften/dreizehnten Klasse; ~ **'sense** *n.* sechster Sinn

sixtieth /'sɪkstɪθ/ *adj.* sechzigst...

sixty /'sɪkstɪ/ **1** *adj.* sechzig **2** *n.* Sechzig, *die. See also* EIGHT; EIGHTY 2

size /saɪz/ *n.* Größe, *die;* (of paper) Format, *das;* **be twice the** ~ **of sth.** zweimal so groß wie etw. sein; **a** ~ **8 dress** ein Kleid [in] Größe 8; **be** ~ **8** ⟨*Person.*⟩ Größe 8 haben

■ **size 'up** *v.t.* taxieren ⟨*Lage*⟩

sizeable /'saɪzəbl/ *adj.* ziemlich groß; beträchtlich ⟨*Summe, Einfluss*⟩

sizzle /'sɪzl/ *v.i.* zischen

skate **1** *n.* (ice ~) Schlittschuh, *der;* (roller ~) Rollschuh, *der* **2** *v.i.* (ice~) Schlittschuh laufen; (roller-~) Rollschuh laufen

'skateboard **1** *n.* Skateboard, *das;* Rollerbrett, *das* **2** *v.i.* Skateboard fahren

'skateboarder *n.* Skateboardfahrer, *der/* -fahrerin, *die*

'skateboarding *n.* Skateboardfahren, *das*

'skater *n.* (ice ~) Eisläufer, *der/*-läuferin, *die;* (roller ~) Rollschuhläufer, *der/*-läuferin, *die*

skating /'skeɪtɪŋ/ *n.* (ice ~) Schlittschuhlaufen, *das;* (roller ~) Rollschuhlaufen, *das*

'skating rink *n.* (ice) Eisbahn, *die;* (for roller skating) Rollschuhbahn, *die*

skeleton /'skelɪtn/ *n.* Skelett, *das*

skeleton: ~ **'key** *n.* Dietrich, *der;* ~ **'staff** *n.* Minimalbesetzung, *die*

skeptic *etc.* (Amer.) ▶ SCEPTIC *etc.*

sketch /sketʃ/ **1** *n.* **(a)** (drawing) Skizze, *die* **(b)** (play) Sketch, *der* **2** *v.t.* skizzieren

sketch: ~**book** *n.* Skizzenbuch, *das;* ~ **map** *n.* Faustskizze, *die*

'sketchy *adj.* skizzenhaft; lückenhaft ⟨*Informationen, Bericht*⟩

skew /skjuː/ **1** *adj.* schräg **2** *n.* **on the** ~: schief

skewer /'skjuːə(r)/ **1** *n.* Bratspieß, *der* **2** *v.t.* aufspießen

ski /skiː/ **1** *n.* **(a)** Ski, *der* **(b)** (on vehicle) Kufe, *die* **2** *v.i.* Ski laufen *od.* fahren

'ski boot *n.* Skistiefel, *der*

skid /skɪd/ **1** *v.i.*, **-dd-** schlittern; (from one side to the other; spinning round) schleudern **2** *n.* Schlittern/Schleudern, *das*

'skid marks *n. pl.* Schleuderspur, *die*

skier /'skiːə(r)/ *n.* Skiläufer, *der*/-läuferin, *die*

skiing /'skiːɪŋ/ *n.* Skilaufen, *das;* (Sport) Skisport, *der*

'ski jumping *n.* Skispringen, *das*

skilful /'skɪlfl/ *adj.* geschickt; gewandt ⟨Redner⟩; gut ⟨Beobachter, Lehrer⟩

'ski lift *n.* Skilift, *der*

skill /skɪl/ *n.* **(a)** (expertness) Geschick, *das;* (of artist) Können, *das* **(b)** (technique) Fertigkeit, *die;* (of weaving, bricklaying) Technik, *die*

skilled /'skɪld/ *adj.* **(a)** ▶ SKILFUL **(b)** qualifiziert ⟨Arbeit, Tätigkeit⟩; ~ **trade** Ausbildungsberuf, *der* **(c)** (trained) ausgebildet

'skillful (Amer.) ▶ SKILFUL

skim /skɪm/ *v.t.*, **-mm-:** **(a)** (remove) abschöpfen **(b)** abrahmen ⟨Milch⟩ **(c)** ▶ ~ THROUGH ■ **skim 'off** *v.t.* abschöpfen ■ **'skim through** *v.t.* überfliegen ⟨Buch, Zeitung⟩

skimmed 'milk *n.* entrahmte Milch

skimp /skɪmp/ **1** *v.t.* sparen an (+ *Dat.*) **2** *v.i.* sparen (with, on an + *Dat.*)

'skimpy *adj.* winzig ⟨Badeanzug⟩; spärlich ⟨Wissen⟩

skin /skɪn/ **1** *n.* **(a)** Haut, *die* **(b)** (fur) Fell, *das* **(c)** (peel) Schale, *die* **2** *v.t.*, **-nn-** häuten; schälen ⟨Frucht⟩ **skin:** ~ **cancer** *n.* Hautkrebs, *der;* ~ **colour** *n.* Hautfarbe, *die;* ~ **cream** *n.* Hautcreme, *die;* ~**-deep** *adj.* (fig.) oberflächlich; ~ **disease** *n.* Hautkrankheit, *die;* ~ **diver** *n.* Taucher, *der*/Taucherin, *die;* ~ **diving** *n.* Tauchen, *das;* ~**flint** *n.* Geizhals, *der;* ~ **graft** *n.* Hauttransplantation, *die;* ~**head** *n.* Skinhead, *der*

skinny /'skɪnɪ/ *adj.* mager

skint /skɪnt/ *adj.* (Brit. coll.) **be** ~: blank *od.* pleite sein (ugs.)

'skin-tight *adj.* hauteng

skip¹ /skɪp/ **1** *v.i.*, **-pp-:** **(a)** hüpfen **(b)** (with skipping rope) seilspringen **2** *v.t.*, **-pp-** (omit) überspringen; ~ **breakfast/ lunch** das Frühstück/Mittagessen auslassen **3** *n.* Hüpfer, *der*

skip² *n.* (Building) Container, *der*

ski: ~ **pass** *n.* Skipass, *der;* ~ **pole** *n.* Skistock, *der*

skipper /'skɪpə(r)/ *n.* Kapitän, *der*

'skipping rope (Brit.), **'skip rope** (Amer.) *ns.* Sprungseil, *das*

'ski resort *n.* Skiurlaubsort, *der*

skirmish /'skɜːmɪʃ/ *n.* (Mil.) Gefecht, *das*

skirt /skɜːt/ **1** *n.* Rock, *der* **2** *v.t.* herumgehen um ■ **skirt 'round** *v.t.* herumgehen um; (fig.) umgehen

'skirting *n.* ~ **[board]** (Brit.) Fußleiste, *die*

ski: ~ **run** *n.* Skihang, *der;* (prepared) [Ski]piste, *die;* ~**stick** *n.* Skistock, *der*

skittle /'skɪtl/ *n.* **(a)** Kegel, *der* **(b)** ~**s** *sing.* (game) Kegeln, *das*

skive /skaɪv/ *v.i.* (Brit. coll.) sich drücken (ugs.) ■ **skive 'off** (Brit. coll.) **1** *v.i.* sich verdrücken (ugs.) **2** *v.t.* schwänzen (ugs.)

skulk /skʌlk/ *v.i.* lauern

skull /skʌl/ *n.* Schädel, *der*

skunk /skʌŋk/ *n.* Stinktier, *das*

sky /skaɪ/ *n.* Himmel, *der;* **in the** ~: am Himmel

sky: ~**diving** *n.* Fallschirmspringen, *das* (als Sport); Fallschirmsport, *der;* ~**-high** **1** *adj.* himmelhoch; astronomisch (ugs.) ⟨Preise usw.⟩; **2** *adv.* **go** ~**-high** ⟨Preise usw.:⟩ in astronomische Höhen klettern (ugs.); ~**light** *n.* Dachfenster, *das;* ~**line** *n.* Silhouette, *die;* (characteristic of certain town) Skyline, *die;* ~ **marshal** *n.* Skymarshal, *der;* ~**scraper** *n.* Wolkenkratzer, *der*

slab /slæb/ *n.* **(a)** (flat stone etc.) Platte, *die* **(b)** (thick slice) [dicke] Scheibe; (of cake) [dickes] Stück; (of chocolate, toffee) Tafel, *die*

slack /slæk/ **1** *adj.* **(a)** (lax) nachlässig; schlampig (ugs.) **(b)** (loose) schlaff; locker ⟨Verband⟩ **2** *n.* **take in** *or* **up the** ~: das Seil/die Schnur *usw.* straffen **3** *v.i.* (coll.) bummeln (ugs.)

slacken /'slækn/ **1** *v.i.* **(a)** (loosen) sich lockern **(b)** (diminish) nachlassen; ⟨Geschwindigkeit:⟩ sich verringern **2** *v.t.* **(a)** (loosen) lockern **(b)** (diminish) verringern

slacker /'slækə(r)/ *n.* (derog.) Faulenzer, *der*/Faulenzerin, *die*

slacks /slæks/ *n. pl.* **[pair of]** ~: lange Hose; Slacks *Pl.*

slag /slæg/ *n.* Schlacke, *die*

slain ▶ SLAY

slake /sleɪk/ *v.t.* löschen, stillen ⟨Durst⟩

slam /slæm/ **1** *v.t.*, **-mm-:** **(a)** (shut) zuschlagen **(b)** (put violently) knallen (ugs.) **2** *v.i.*, **-mm-** zuschlagen

slander /'slɑːndə(r)/ **1** *n.* Verleumdung, *die* (on *Gen.*) **2** *v.t.* verleumden

slanderous /'slɑːndərəs/ *adj.* verleumderisch

slang /slæŋ/ n. Slang, der; ‹Theater-, Soldaten-, Juristen›jargon, der; attrib. Slang‹wort, -ausdruck›

'slanging match n. gegenseitige [lautstarke] Beschimpfung

slangy /'slæŋɪ/ adj. Slang‹ausdruck, -wort›; salopp ‹Wortwahl, Redeweise›

slant /slɑːnt/ 1 v.i. ‹Fläche:› sich neigen; ‹Linie:› schräg verlaufen
2 v.t. (a) abschrägen
(b) (fig.: bias) [so] hinbiegen (ugs.) ‹Meldung, Bemerkung›
3 n. Schräge, die; on the or a ~: schräg

slanting /'slɑːntɪŋ/ adj. schräg

slap /slæp/ 1 v.t., -pp-: (a) schlagen
(b) (put) knallen (ugs.)
2 v.i., -pp- schlagen; klatschen
3 n. Schlag, der
4 adv. voll; ~ in the middle genau in der Mitte

'slapdash adj. schludrig (ugs.)

'slap-up attrib. adj. (coll.) ‹Essen› mit allen Schikanen (ugs.)

slash /slæʃ/ 1 v.t. (a) aufschlitzen
(b) (fig.) [drastisch] reduzieren; [drastisch] kürzen ‹Gehalt, Umfang›
2 n. (a) (slit) Schlitz, der
(b) (~ing stroke) Hieb, der

slat /slæt/ n. Latte, die

slate /sleɪt/ 1 n. (a) (Geol.) Schiefer, der
(b) (Building) Schieferplatte, die
2 v.t. (Brit. coll.: criticize) in der Luft zerreißen (ugs.)

slaughter /'slɔːtə(r)/ 1 n. Schlachten, das; (massacre) Gemetzel, das
2 v.t. schlachten; (massacre) abschlachten

slave /sleɪv/ 1 n. Sklave, der/Sklavin, die
2 v.i. ~ [away] schuften (ugs.); sich abplagen (at mit)

'slave driver n. (fig.) Sklaventreiber, der/ -treiberin, die

slavery /'sleɪvərɪ/ n. Sklaverei, die

slavish /'sleɪvɪʃ/ adj. sklavisch

slay /sleɪ/ v.t., slew /sluː/, slain /sleɪn/ (literary) ermorden

sleaze /sliːz/ n. (derog.) Korruption, die

'sleazebag, 'sleazeball ns. (sl. derog.) Drecksack, der (derb abwertend)

sleazy /'sliːzɪ/ adj. schäbig; (disreputable) anrüchig

sled /sled/, **sledge** /sledʒ/ ns. Schlitten, der

'sledgehammer n. Vorschlaghammer, der

sleek /sliːk/ adj. (glossy) seidig

sleep /sliːp/ 1 n. Schlaf, der; get/go to ~: einschlafen; put to ~: einschläfern ‹Tier›
2 v.i., slept /slept/ schlafen
3 v.t. slept: the hotel ~s 80 das Hotel hat 80 Betten
■ **sleep a'round** v.i. (coll.) herumschlafen (ugs.)
■ **sleep 'in** v.i. im Bett bleiben

■ **sleep 'off** v.t. ausschlafen; ~ it off seinen Rausch ausschlafen
■ **sleep 'over** v.i. [auswärts] übernachten; our cousin was ~ing over unser Cousin übernachtete bei uns
■ **sleep together** v.i. (also coll. euphem.) miteinander schlafen
■ **sleep with** v.t. ~ with sb. (coll. euphem.) mit jmdm. schlafen

'sleeper n. (a) be a heavy/light ~: einen tiefen/leichten Schlaf haben
(b) (Brit. Railw.: support) Schwelle, die
(c) (Railw.) (coach) Schlafwagen, der; (train) [night] ~: Nachtzug mit Schlafwagen

sleeping: ~ **accommodation** n. Übernachtungsmöglichkeit, die; ~ **bag** n. Schlafsack, der; ~ **car** n. Schlafwagen, der; ~ **'partner** n. (Commerc.) stiller Teilhaber; ~ **pill,** ~ **tablet** ns. Schlaftablette, die

sleep: ~**less** adj. schlaflos; ~**walk** v.i. schlafwandeln; ~**walker** n. Schlafwandler, der/-wandlerin, die

'sleepover n. Übernachtung außer Haus od. bei anderen Leuten

'sleepy adj. schläfrig

sleet /sliːt/ 1 n. Schneeregen, der
2 v.i. impers. it is ~ing es gibt Schneeregen

sleeve /sliːv/ n. (a) Ärmel, der; (fig.) have sth. up one's ~: etw. in petto haben (ugs.); roll up one's ~s die Ärmel hochkrempeln (ugs.)
(b) (for record) Hülle, die

'sleeveless adj. ärmellos

sleigh /sleɪ/ n. Schlitten, der

sleight of 'hand /slaɪt/ n. Fingerfertigkeit, die

slender /'slendə(r)/ adj. (a) (slim) schlank; schmal ‹Buch, Band›
(b) gering ‹Chance, Mittel, Hoffnung›

slept ▶ SLEEP 2, 3

sleuth /sluːθ/ n. Detektiv, der

slew¹ /sluː/ v.i. & t. schwenken

slew² ▶ SLAY

slice /slaɪs/ 1 n. Scheibe, die; (of apple, melon, peach, cake, pie) Stück, das; a ~ of cake ein Stück Kuchen
2 v.t. in Scheiben schneiden; in Stücke schneiden ‹Bohnen, Apfel, Kuchen usw.›; ~d bread Schnittbrot, das

slick /slɪk/ 1 adj. (a) (dexterous) professionell
(b) (pretentiously dexterous) clever (ugs.)
2 n. [oil] ~: Ölteppich, der

slid ▶ SLIDE 1, 2

slide /slaɪd/ 1 v.i., slid /slɪd/ rutschen; ‹Kolben, Schublade, Feder:› gleiten
2 v.t., slid schieben
3 n. (a) (children's ~) Rutschbahn, die
(b) (Photog.) Dia[positiv], das

slide: ~ **film** n. Diafilm, der; ~ **projector** n. Diaprojektor, der; ~ **show** n. Diashow, die

sliding door /'slaɪdɪŋ/ n. Schiebetür, die

slight /slaɪt/ ① *adj.* leicht; schwach ⟨*Hoffnung, Aussichten, Wirkung*⟩; **not in the ~est** nicht im Geringsten
② *n.* Verunglimpfung, *die* (**on** *Gen.*); (lack of courtesy) Affront, *der* (**on** gegen)

'slightly *adv.* ein bisschen; leicht ⟨*verletzen, riechen nach, gewürzt sein, ansteigen*⟩; flüchtig ⟨*jmdn. kennen*⟩; oberflächlich ⟨*etw. kennen*⟩

slim /slɪm/ ① *adj.* schlank; schmal ⟨*Band, Buch*⟩; schwach ⟨*Aussicht, Hoffnung*⟩; gering ⟨*Gewinn, Chancen*⟩
② *v.i.,* **-mm-** abnehmen

slime /slaɪm/ *n.* Schleim, *der*

slimmer /'slɪmə(r)/ *n.* (Brit.) *jmd., der etwas für die schlanke Linie tut;* **advice/a diet for ~s** Ratschläge *Pl.*/eine Diät zum Abnehmen

slimming /'slɪmɪŋ/① *n.* Abnehmen, *das; attrib.* Schlankheits-
② *adj.* schlank machend.

slimy /'slaɪmɪ/ *adj.* schleimig

sling /slɪŋ/ ① *n.* (Med.) Schlinge, *die*
② *v.t.,* slung /slʌŋ/ (coll.: throw) schmeißen (ugs.)

sling 'out *v.t.* (coll.) wegschmeißen (ugs.); **~ sb. out** jmdn. rausschmeißen (ugs.)

slink /slɪŋk/ *v.i.,* slunk /slʌŋk/ schleichen
■ **slink a'way, slink 'off** *v.i.* davonschleichen

slip /slɪp/ ① *v.i.,* **-pp-:** (a) (slide) rutschen; ⟨*Messer:*⟩ abrutschen; (and fall) ausrutschen
(b) (escape) schlüpfen
(c) (go) **~ to the butcher's** *etc.* [rasch] zum Fleischer *usw.* rüberspringen (ugs.)
② *v.t.,* **-pp-:** (a) stecken; **~ the dress over one's head** das Kleid über den Kopf streifen
(b) **~ sb.'s mind** *or* **memory** jmdm. entfallen
③ *n.* (a) (fall) **after his ~:** nachdem er ausgerutscht [und gestürzt] war
(b) (mistake) Versehen, *das;* **~ of the tongue** Versprecher, *der*
(c) (underwear) Unterrock, *der*
(d) (piece of paper) Zettel, *der*
(e) **give sb. the ~:** jmdm. entwischen (ugs.)
■ **slip a'way** *v.i.* (a) ⟨*Person:*⟩ sich fortschleichen
(b) ⟨*Zeit:*⟩ verfliegen
■ **slip 'down** *v.i.* runterrutschen (ugs.)
■ **slip 'in** *v.i.* ⟨*Person:*⟩ sich hineinschleichen
■ **'slip into** *v.t.* schlüpfen in (+ *Akk.*) ⟨*Kleidungsstück*⟩
■ **slip 'off** ① *v.i.* (a) runterrutschen (ugs.)
(b) ▶ SLIP AWAY A
② *v.t.* abstreifen ⟨*Schmuck, Handschuh*⟩; schlüpfen aus ⟨*Kleid, Schuh*⟩
■ **slip 'on** *v.t.* überstreifen ⟨*Handschuh, Ring*⟩; schlüpfen in (+ *Akk.*) ⟨*Kleid, Schuh*⟩
■ **slip 'out** *v.i.* ⟨*Person:*⟩ sich hinausschleichen
■ **slip 'over** *v.i.* (fall) ausrutschen
■ **slip 'up** *v.i.* (coll.) einen Schnitzer machen (ugs.)

slipped 'disc /slɪpt/ *n.* Bandscheibenvorfall, *der*

'slipper *n.* Hausschuh, *der*

slippery /'slɪpərɪ/ *adj.* schlüpfrig

slippy /'slɪpɪ/ (coll.) ▶ SLIPPERY

slip: ~ road *n.* (Brit.) (to motorway) Auffahrt, *die;* (from motorway) Ausfahrt, *die;* **~shod** *adj.* schludrig (ugs.); **~-up** *n.* (coll.) Schnitzer, *der*

slit /slɪt/ ① *n.* Schlitz, *der*
② *v.t.,* **-tt-,** slit aufschlitzen; **~ sb.'s throat** jmdm. die Kehle durchschneiden

slither /'slɪðə(r)/ *v.i.* rutschen

sliver /'slɪvə(r)/ *n.* Splitter, *der*

slob /slɒb/ *n.* (coll.) Schwein, *das* (derb)

slobber /'slɒbə(r)/ *v.i.* sabbern (ugs.)

slog /slɒɡ/ ① *v.t.,* **-ɡɡ-** (in boxing, fight) voll treffen
② *v.i.,* **-ɡɡ-** (work) schuften (ugs.)
③ *n.* (a) (hit) wuchtiger Schlag
(b) (work) Plackerei, *die* (ugs.)

slogan /'sləʊɡən/ *n.* Slogan, *der;* (advertising ~) Werbeslogan, *der*

slop /slɒp/ ① *v.i.* schwappen (**out of, from** aus)
② *v.t.* schwappen; (intentionally) kippen
■ **slop 'over** *v.i.* überschwappen

slope /sləʊp/ ① *n.* (a) (slant) Neigung, *die*
(b) (slanting ground) Hang, *der*
② *v.i.* (slant) sich neigen; ⟨*Boden, Garten:*⟩ abschüssig sein; **~ downwards/upwards** ⟨*Straße:*⟩ abfallen/ansteigen
■ **slope a'way** *v.i.* abfallen
■ **slope 'off** *v.i.* (coll.) sich verdrücken (ugs.)

sloppy /'slɒpɪ/ *adj.* schludrig (ugs.)

slosh /slɒʃ/ *adj.* ① *v.i.* platschen (ugs.); ⟨*Flüssigkeit:*⟩ schwappen
② *v.t.* (coll.: pour clumsily) schwappen

sloshed /slɒʃt/ *adj.* (Brit. coll.) blau (ugs.)

slot /slɒt/ ① *n.* (a) (hole) Schlitz, *der*
(b) (groove) Nut, *die*
② *v.t.,* **-tt-:** **~ sth. into place/sth.** etw. einfügen/in etw. (*Akk.*) einfügen
■ **slot 'in** ① *v.t.* einfügen
② *v.i.* sich einfügen
■ **slot to'gether** ① *v.t.* zusammenfügen
② *v.i.* (lit. or fig.) sich zusammenfügen

sloth /sləʊθ/ *n.* (a) (lethargy) Trägheit, *die*
(b) (Zool.) Faultier, *das*

'slot machine *n.* Automat, *der;* (for gambling) Spielautomat, *der*

slouch /slaʊtʃ/ *v.i.* sich schlecht halten

Slovak /'sləʊvæk/ ① *adj.* slowakisch; **sb. is ~:** jmd. ist Slowake/Slowakin
② *n.* (a) (person) Slowake, *der*/Slowakin, *die*
(b) (language) Slowakisch, *das; see also* ENGLISH 2A

Slovakia /sləˈvɑːkɪə/ *pr. n.* Slowakei, *die*

Slovene /'sləʊviːn/ ① *adj.* slowenisch; **sb. is ~:** jmd. ist Slowene/Slowenin
② *n.* (a) (person) Slowene, *der*/Slowenin, *die*
(b) (language) Slowenisch, *das*

Slovenia /sləˈviːnɪə/ *pr. n.* Slowenien (*das*)

Slovenian /slə'viːnɪən/ ▶ SLOVENE

slovenly /'slʌvnlɪ/ adj. schlampig (ugs.)

slow /sləʊ/ ① adj. langsam; langwierig
⟨Arbeit⟩; be [ten minutes] ~ ⟨Uhr:⟩ [zehn
Minuten] nachgehen
② adv. langsam
③ v.i. langsamer werden; ~ to a halt
anhalten
∎ slow 'down, slow 'up v.i. langsamer
werden

'slowcoach n. Trödler, der/Trödlerin, die
(ugs.)

'slowly adv. langsam

slow 'motion n. in ~: in Zeitlupe

slowness n. Langsamkeit, die

slow: ~ 'puncture n. winziges Loch;
~ train n. Bummelzug, der (ugs.);
~-witted /sləʊ'wɪtɪd/ adj. [geistig]
schwerfällig

sludge /slʌdʒ/ n. Schlamm, der

slug /slʌg/ n. Nacktschnecke, die

sluggish /'slʌgɪʃ/ adj. träge; schleppend
⟨Nachfrage⟩

sluice /sluːs/ ① n. Schütz, das
② v.t. ~ [down] abspritzen

'sluice gate n. Schütz, das

slum /slʌm/ n. Slum, der; ⟨single house or
apartment⟩ Elendsquartier, das

slumber /'slʌmbə(r)/ (poet./rhet.) ① n. ~[s]
Schlummer, der (geh.)
② v.i. schlummern (geh.)

slump /slʌmp/ ① n. Sturz, der (fig.); ⟨in
demand, investment, sales⟩ starker Rückgang
(in Gen.); ⟨economic depression⟩ Depression, die
② v.i. (a) stark zurückgehen;
⟨Preise, Kurse:⟩ stürzen
(b) ⟨collapse⟩ ⟨Person:⟩ fallen; ~ed in a chair
in einem Sessel zusammengesunken

slung ▶ SLING 2

slunk ▶ SLINK

slur /slɜː(r)/ ① v.t., -rr-: ~ one's words/
speech undeutlich sprechen
② n. Beleidigung, die (on für)

slurp /slɜːp/ (coll.) ① v.t. ~ [up] schlürfen
② n. Schlürfen, das

slush /slʌʃ/ n. Schneematsch, der

'slush fund n. Fonds, der für
Bestechungsgelder

'slushy adj. (a) matschig
(b) ⟨sloppy⟩ sentimental

slut /slʌt/ n. Schlampe, die (ugs.)

sly /slaɪ/ ① adj. schlau; gerissen (ugs.)
⟨Geschäftsmann, Trick⟩; verschlagen ⟨Blick⟩
② n. on the ~: heimlich

smack¹ /smæk/ ① n. (a) ⟨sound⟩ Klatsch,
der
(b) ⟨blow⟩ Schlag, der; ⟨on child's bottom⟩ Klaps,
der (ugs.)
② v.t. (a) [mit der flachen Hand] schlagen
(b) ~ one's lips [mit den Lippen] schmatzen
③ adv. (coll.) direkt

smack² v.i. ~ of schmecken nach; (fig.)
riechen nach (ugs.)

small /smɔːl/ ① adj. klein; gering
⟨Wirkung, Appetit, Fähigkeit⟩; schmal
⟨Taille⟩; dünn ⟨Stimme⟩; make sb. feel ~:
jmdn. beschämen
② n. ~ of the back Kreuz, das
③ adv. klein

small: ~ ad n. (coll.) Kleinanzeige, die;
~ 'change n. Kleingeld, das; ~holding
n. landwirtschaftlicher Kleinbetrieb;
~-'minded adj. kleinlich; ~pox n.
Pocken Pl.; ~ 'print n. (lit. or fig.)
Kleingedruckte, das

smalls /smɔːlz/ n. pl. (Brit. coll.)
Unterwäsche, die

small: ~ 'screen n. (Telev.) Bildschirm,
der; ~ talk n. leichte Unterhaltung; (at
parties) Smalltalk, der; make ~ talk [with sb.]
[mit jmdm.] Konversation machen

smarmy /'smɑːmɪ/ adj. (coll.) kriecherisch

smart /smɑːt/ ① adj. (a) ⟨clever⟩ clever;
⟨ingenious⟩ raffiniert
(b) ⟨neat⟩ schick; schön ⟨Haus, Garten, Auto⟩
(c) attrib. ⟨fashionable⟩ elegant; smart
② v.i. schmerzen

smart: ~ alec[k] /smɑːt 'ælɪk/ n. (coll.)
Besserwisser, der/Besserwisserin, die;
~ bomb n. intelligente Bombe; ~ card n.
Chipkarte, die; ~ drug n. Nootropikum,
das

smarten /'smɑːtn/ v.t. herrichten;
~ oneself [up] auf sein Äußeres achten

'smartly adv. (a) ⟨cleverly⟩ clever
(b) ⟨neatly⟩ schmuck ⟨[an]gestrichen⟩; smart,
flott ⟨gekleidet, geschnitten⟩

'smart money n. the ~ is on ... Experten
setzen auf ...

smash /smæʃ/ ① v.t. (a) zerschlagen
(b) ~ sb. in the face/mouth jmdm. [hart] ins
Gesicht/auf den Mund schlagen
(c) ⟨Tennis etc.⟩ schmettern
② v.i. (a) zerbrechen
(b) ⟨crash⟩ krachen ⟨into gegen⟩
③ n. (a) ⟨sound⟩ Krachen, das
(b) ▶ SMASH-UP
(c) ⟨Tennis⟩ Schmetterball, der
∎ smash 'in v.t. zerschmettern; einschlagen
⟨Tür, Schädel⟩
∎ smash 'up v.t. zertrümmern

smash-and-'grab [raid] n. (coll.)
Schaufenstereinbruch, der

smashed /smæʃt/ adj. (sl.) (a) ⟨drunk⟩ get
~ on sth. von etw. besoffen werden (derb); be
~ out of one's head or mind or brains
sturzbetrunken (ugs.) od. (derb) sturzbesoffen
sein
(b) ⟨on drugs⟩ stoned (Drogenjargon)

'smashing adj. (coll.) toll (ugs.)

'smash-up n. schwerer Zusammenstoß

smattering /'smætərɪŋ/ n. [have] a ~ of
German etc. ein paar Brocken Deutsch usw.
[können]

smear /smɪə(r)/ 1 v.t. (a) (daub)
beschmieren; (put on or over) schmieren
(b) (smudge) verwischen
(c) (fig.) in den Schmutz ziehen
2 n. (a) (blotch) [Schmutz]fleck, der
(b) (fig.) Beschmutzung, die (on Gen.)
smear: ~ campaign n.
Schmutzkampagne, die; **~ tactics** n. pl.
schmutzige Mittel Pl.; **~ test** n. (Med.)
Abstrich, der

smell /smel/ 1 n. (a) have a good/bad
sense of ~: einen guten/schlechten
Geruchssinn haben
(b) (odour) Geruch, der (of nach); (pleasant
also) Duft, der (of nach); **a ~ of burning/gas**
ein Brand-/Gasgeruch
(c) (stink) Gestank, der
2 v.t., smelt /smelt/ or smelled /smeld/ (a)
(perceive) riechen
(b) (inhale ~ of) riechen an (+ Dat.)
3 v.i., smelt or smelled (a) (emit ~) riechen;
(pleasantly also) duften
(b) ~ **of sth.** (lit. or fig.) nach etw. riechen
(c) (stink) riechen

'smelly adj. stinkend; **be ~:** stinken

smelt ▶ SMELL 2, 3

smile /smaɪl/ 1 n. Lächeln, das; **give sb. a
~:** jmdn. anlächeln
2 v.i. lächeln; **~ at sb./sth.** jmdn.
anlächeln/über etw. (Akk.) lächeln

smirk /smɜːk/ 1 v.t. grinsen
2 n. Grinsen, das

smith /smɪθ/ n. Schmied, der

smithereens /smɪðə'riːnz/ n. pl. blow/
smash sth. to ~: etw. in tausend Stücke
sprengen/schlagen

smock /smɒk/ n. Kittel, der

smog /smɒg/ n. Smog, der

smoke /sməʊk/ 1 n. Rauch, der
2 v.i. & t. rauchen

smoked /sməʊkt/ adj. (Cookery) geräuchert

'smoke detector n. Rauchmelder, der

'smoke-free adj. rauchfrei

'smokeless adj. rauchlos; rauchfrei
〈Zone〉

smoker/'sməʊkə(r)/ n. Raucher, der/
Raucherin, die; **~'s cough** Raucherhusten,
der

'smokescreen n. [künstliche]
Nebelwand; (fig.) Vernebelung die (for Gen.)

smoking /'sməʊkɪŋ/ n. (a) Rauchen, das;
'no ~' „Rauchen verboten"
(b) (seating area) [do you want to sit in] ~ or
non-~? möchten Sie für Raucher oder
Nichtraucher?

'smoking compartment n. (Railw.)
Raucherabteil, das

smoky /'sməʊkɪ/ adj. (emitting smoke)
rauchend; (smoke-filled) verräuchert

smooth /smuːð/ 1 adj. (a) (even) glatt;
eben 〈Straße, Weg〉
(b) (mild) weich

(d) (not jerky) geschmeidig 〈Bewegung〉; ruhig
〈Fahrt, Flug〉; weich 〈Landung〉
(d) (without problems) reibungslos
2 v.t. glätten

smoothie /'smuːðɪ/ n. (coll. derog.)
aalglatter Typ (ugs.)

'smoothly adv. (a) (evenly) glatt
(b) (not jerkily) geschmeidig 〈sich bewegen〉;
weich 〈landen〉; reibungslos 〈funktionieren〉

smother /'smʌðə(r)/ v.t. ersticken; (fig.)
unterdrücken 〈Gähnen〉; ersticken
〈Gelächter, Schreie〉

smoulder /'sməʊldə(r)/ v.i. schwelen; **she
was ~ing with rage** Zorn schwelte in ihr

smudge /smʌdʒ/ 1 v.t. verwischen
2 v.i. schmieren
3 n. Fleck, der

smug /smʌg/ adj. selbstgefällig

smuggle /'smʌgl/ v.t. schmuggeln
■ **smuggle 'in** v.t. einschmuggeln; hinein-/
hereinschmuggeln 〈Person〉
■ **smuggle 'out** v.t. hinaus-/
herausschmuggeln

smuggler /'smʌglə(r)/ n. Schmuggler, der/
Schmugglerin, die

smuggling /'smʌglɪŋ/ n. Schmuggel, der

smutty /'smʌtɪ/ adj. (lewd) schmutzig

snack /snæk/ n. Imbiss, der

'snackbar n. Schnellimbiss, der

snag /snæg/ n. (problem) Haken, der; **what's
the ~?** wo klemmt es? (ugs.)

snail /sneɪl/ n. Schnecke, die; **at [a] ~'s
pace** im Schneckentempo (ugs.)

'snail mail n. (coll. joc.) Schneckenpost, die

snake /sneɪk/ n. Schlange, die

snap /snæp/ 1 v.t., -pp-: (a) (break)
zerbrechen; **~ sth. in two** or **in half** etw. in
zwei Stücke brechen
(b) **~ one's fingers** mit den Fingern
schnalzen
(c) **~ sth. home** or **into place** etw.
einschnappen lassen; **~ shut** zuschnappen
lassen 〈Portemonnaie, Schloss〉; zuklappen
〈Buch, Etui〉; **~ sth. open** etw. aufschnappen
lassen
(d) (take photograph of) knipsen
(e) (say sharply) fauchen; (speak crisply or curtly)
bellen
2 v.i., -pp-: (a) (break) brechen
(b) (fig.: give way under strain) ausrasten (ugs.);
my patience has finally ~ped nun ist mir
der Geduldsfaden aber gerissen
3 n. (Photog.) Schnappschuss, der
■ **'snap at** v.t. (speak sharply to) anfauchen
(ugs.)
■ **snap 'off** v.t. & i. abbrechen
■ **snap 'up** v.t. (fig. coll.) [sich (Dat.)]
schnappen (ugs.)

'snapshot n. Schnappschuss, der

snare /sneə(r)/ 1 n. Schlinge, die
2 v.t. [in einer Schlinge] fangen

snarl[1] /snɑːl/ 1 v.i. knurren
2 n. Knurren, das

S

snarl² n. (tangle) Knoten, der
■ **snarl 'up** v.t. (bring to a halt) zum Erliegen
bringen; **get ~ed up in the traffic** im Verkehr
stecken bleiben
'snarl-up n. Stau, der

snatch /snætʃ/ ① v.t. (a) (grab) schnappen;
~ **sth. from sb.** jmdm. etw. wegreißen;
~ **some sleep** ein bisschen schlafen
(b) (steal) klauen (ugs.)
② v.i. einfach zugreifen
③ n. ~**es of talk/conversation**
Gesprächsfetzen Pl.

snazzy /'snæzɪ/ adj. (coll.) [super]schick
(ugs.)

sneak /sniːk/ ① v.t. schmuggeln; ~ **a look**
at schielen nach
② v.i. (a) schleichen
(b) (Brit. Sch. coll.: tell tales) petzen (Schülerspr.)
③ n. (Brit. Sch. coll.) Petze, die (Schülerspr.)
■ **sneak 'out** v.i. [sich] hinausschleichen
'sneaker (Amer.) Turnschuh, der
'sneaking attrib. adj. heimlich; leise
‹Verdacht›
'sneak thief n. Einschleichdieb, der
'sneaky adj. (a) (underhand) hinterhältig
'(b) **have a ~ feeling that ...:** so ein leises
Gefühl haben, dass ...

sneer /snɪə(r)/ v.i. höhnisch lächeln/grinsen
■ **'sneer at** v.t. höhnisch anlächeln/
angrinsen; (scorn) verhöhnen

sneeze /sniːz/ ① v.i. niesen
② n. Niesen, das

snicker /'snɪkə(r)/ ▶ SNIGGER

snide /snaɪd/ adj. abfällig

sniff /snɪf/ ① n. Schnuppern, das; (with
running nose, while crying) Schniefen, das
② v.i. schniefen; (to detect a smell) schnuppern
③ v.t. riechen od. schnuppern an (+ Dat.);
~ **glue/cocaine** Klebstoff schnüffeln/Kokain
sniffen (Drogenjargon)
■ **'sniff at** v.t. (a) ▶ SNIFF 3
(b) (show contempt for) die Nase rümpfen über
sniffer dog /'snɪfə dɒɡ/ n. Spürhund, der
snigger /'snɪɡə(r)/ ① v.i. [boshaft] kichern
② n. [boshaftes] Kichern
snip /snɪp/ ① v.t. **-pp-** schnippeln (ugs.),
schneiden ‹Loch›; schnippeln (ugs.) od.
schneiden an (+ Dat.) ‹Tuch, Haaren, Hecke›;
(cut off) abschnippeln (ugs.); abschneiden
② n. (cut) Schnitt, der; Schnipser, der (ugs.)
snipe /snaɪp/ v.i. ~ **at** aus dem Hinterhalt
beschießen
'sniper n. Heckenschütze, der
snippet /'snɪpɪt/ n. (of information in newspaper)
Notiz, die; (of conversation) Gesprächsfetzen,
der; **useful ~s of information** nützliche
Hinweise
snivel /'snɪvl/ v.i., (Brit.) **-ll-** schniefen
'snivelling (Amer.: **sniveling**) (fig.) attrib.
adj. heulend
snob /snɒb/ n. Snob, der
snobbery /'snɒbərɪ/ n. Snobismus, der
snobbish /'snɒbɪʃ/ adj. snobistisch

snog /snɒɡ/ (Brit. coll.) ① v.i., **-gg-** knutschen
(ugs.)
② n. Knutschen, das (ugs.)
snooker /'snuːkə(r)/ n. Snooker, das
snoop /snuːp/ v.i. schnüffeln (ugs.)
snooty /'snuːtɪ/ adj. (coll.) hochnäsig (ugs.)
snooze /snuːz/ (coll.) ① v.i. dösen (ugs.)
② n. Nickerchen, das (fam.)
'snooze button n. Schlummertaste, die
snore /snɔː(r)/ ① v.i. schnarchen
② n. Schnarcher, der (ugs.); ~**s** Schnarchen,
das
snorkel /'snɔːkl/ n. Schnorchel, der
snort /snɔːt/ v.i. schnauben (**with**, in vor
+ Dat.); (sl.: take) ~ **[coke]** [Koks] sniffen
(Drogenjargon)
snot /snɒt/ n. (sl.) Rotz, der (derb)
snotty adj. rotznäsig (salopp); ~ **child/nose**
Rotznase, die (salopp)
snout /snaʊt/ n. Schnauze, die; (of pig)
Rüssel, der
snow /snəʊ/ ① n. Schnee, der
② v.i. impers. **it ~s/is ~ing** es schneit
■ **snow 'in** v.t. **they are ~ed in** sie sind
eingeschneit
■ **snow 'under** v.t. **be ~ed under** (with work)
erdrückt werden; (with gifts, mail) überschüttet
werden
snow: ~ball ① n. Schneeball, der; ② v.i.
(fig.) lawinenartig zunehmen; ~ **blindness**
n. Schneeblindheit, die; ~**board** ① n.
Snowboard, das; ② v.i. Snowboard fahren;
~**boarder** n. Snowboarder, der/
Snowboarderin, die; ~**boarding** n.
Snowboardfahren, das; Snowboarden, das;
~**bound** adj. eingeschneit; ~**-capped**
adj. schneebedeckt; ~ **chains** n. pl.
Schneeketten Pl.; ~**drift** n. Schneewehe,
die; ~**drop** n. Schneeglöckchen, das; ~**fall**
n. Schneefall, der; ~**flake** n. Schneeflocke,
die; ~**man** n. Schneemann, der; ~**plough**
n. Schneepflug, der; ~**storm** n.
Schneesturm, der
'snowy adj. schneereich ‹Gegend›;
schneebedeckt ‹Berge›
snub /snʌb/ ① v.t., **-bb-:** (a) (rebuff)
brüskieren
(b) (reject) ablehnen
② n. Abfuhr, die
snub-'nosed adj. stupsnasig
snuff¹ /snʌf/ n. Schnupftabak, der; **take a**
pinch of ~: eine Prise schnupfen
snuff² v.t. ~ **[out]** löschen ‹Kerze›
snuffle /'snʌfl/ v.i. schnüffeln
snug /snʌɡ/ adj. gemütlich; behaglich; **be a**
~ **fit** genau passen
snuggle /'snʌɡl/ v.i. ~ **up to sb.** sich an
jmdn. kuscheln; ~ **together** sich aneinander
kuscheln; ~ **up** or **down in bed** sich ins Bett
kuscheln
so /səʊ/ ① adv. (a) so; **as winter draws near,**
so it gets darker je näher der Winter rückt,
desto dunkler wird es; **so ... as so ...:** wie; **so**

far bis hierher; (until now) bisher; (to such a distance) so weit; **so much the better** um so besser; **so long!** bis dann! (ugs.); **and so on** [and so forth] und so weiter [und so fort]; **so as to** zu; **so** [that] damit; **I'm so glad/ tired!** ich bin ja so froh/müde!; **It's a rainbow!** – **So it is!** Es ist ein Regenbogen! – Ja, wirklich!; **'You suggested it.** – **So I did** Du hast es vorgeschlagen. – Das stimmt; **is that so?** so? (ugs.); wirklich?; **so am/have/ would/could/will/do I** ich auch

(b) *pron.* he suggested that I take the train, and if I had done so, ...: er riet mir, den Zug zu nehmen, und wenn ich es getan hätte, ...; **I'm afraid so** leider ja; **I told you so** ich habe es dir [ja] gesagt; **a week or so** etwa eine Woche; **very much so** in der Tat

② *conj.* (therefore) daher; **so there you 'are!** ich habe also recht!; **so 'there!** [und] fertig!; **so?** na und?; **so you see** ...: du siehst also ...; **so where have you been?** wo warst du denn?

soak /səʊk/ ① *v.t.* (a) einweichen ⟨*Wäsche in Lauge*⟩; eintauchen ⟨*Brot in Milch*⟩

(b) (wet) nass machen

② *v.i.* (a) (steep) **put sth. in sth. to ∼:** etw. in etw. (*Dat.*) einweichen

(b) (drain) ⟨*Feuchtigkeit, Nässe:*⟩ sickern

'soaking *adj. & adv.* **∼** [wet] völlig durchnässt

'so-and-so *n., pl.* **∼'s** (a) ⟨person not named⟩ [Herr/Frau] Soundso

(b) (coll.: disliked person) Biest, *das* (ugs.)

soap /səʊp/ *n.* (a) Seife, *die;* **with ∼ and water** mit Wasser und Seife

(b) (coll.) ▶ SOAP OPERA

soap: **∼ flakes** *n. pl.* Seifenflocken *Pl.;* **∼ opera** *n.* Seifenoper, *die* (ugs.); **∼ powder** *n.* Seifenpulver, *das;* **∼suds** *n. pl.* Seifenschaum, *der*

'soapy *adj.* seifig; **∼ water** Seifenlauge, *die*

soar /sɔː(r)/ *v.i.* aufsteigen; (fig.) ⟨*Preise, Kosten usw.:*⟩ in die Höhe schießen (ugs.)

sob /sɒb/ ① *v.i.,* **-bb-** schluchzen (**with** vor + *Dat.*)

② *n.* Schluchzer, *der*

sober /'səʊbə(r)/ *adj.* (a) (not drunk) nüchtern

(b) (serious) ernst

■ **sober 'up** ① *v.i.* nüchtern werden

② *v.t.* ausnüchtern

'sobering *adj.* ernüchternd

so-called /'səʊkɔːld/ *adj.* so genannt; (alleged) angeblich

soccer /'sɒkə(r)/ *n.* Fußball, *der*

sociable /'səʊʃəbl/ *adj.* gesellig

social /'səʊʃl/ *adj.* (a) sozial; gesellschaftlich

(b) (of ∼ life) gesellschaftlich; gesellig ⟨*Abend, Beisammensein*⟩

'social club *n.* Klub für geselliges Beisammensein

socialism /'səʊʃəlɪzm/ *n.* Sozialismus, *der*

socialist /'səʊʃəlɪst/ ① *n.* Sozialist, *der/* Sozialistin, *die*

② *adj.* sozialistisch

socialize /'səʊʃəlaɪz/ *v.i.* geselligen Umgang pflegen; **∼ with sb.** (chat) sich mit jmdm. unterhalten

'social life *n.* gesellschaftliches Leben; **not have much ∼** ⟨*Person:*⟩ nicht viel ausgehen

'socially *adv.* **meet ∼:** sich privat treffen; **∼ deprived** sozial benachteiligt

social: **∼ 'science** *n.* Sozialwissenschaften *Pl.;* Gesellschaftswissenschaften *Pl.;* **∼ se'curity** *n.* (a) (Brit.: benefit) Sozialhilfe, *die;* (b) (system) soziale Sicherheit; **∼ 'service** *n.* staatliche Sozialleistung; **∼ 'services** *n. pl.* Sozialdienste *Pl.;* **∼ work** *n.* Sozialarbeit, *die;* **∼ worker** *n.* Sozialarbeiter, *der/-*arbeiterin, *die*

society /sə'saɪətɪ/ *n.* (a) Gesellschaft, *die;* **high ∼:** Highsociety, *die*

(b) (club, association) Verein, *der*

socio-eco'nomic *adj.* sozioökonomisch

sociological /səʊsɪə'lɒdʒɪkl/ *adj.* soziologisch

sociologist /səʊsɪ'ɒlədʒɪst/ *n.* Soziologe, *der/*Soziologin, *die*

sociology /səʊsɪ'ɒlədʒɪ/ *n.* Soziologie, *die*

sock¹ /sɒk/ *n.* Socke, *die*

sock² *v.t.* (coll.: hit) hauen (ugs.)

socket /'sɒkɪt/ *n.* (a) (Anat.) (of eye) Höhle, *die;* (of joint) Pfanne, *die*

(b) (Electr.) Steckdose, *die*

soda /'səʊdə/ *n.* Soda, *das*

'soda water *n.* Soda[wasser], *das*

sodden /'sɒdn/ *adj.* durchnässt (**with** von)

sodium /'səʊdɪəm/ *n.* Natrium, *das*

sodium: **∼ bi'carbonate** *n.* doppeltkohlensaures Natrium; Natriumhydrogenkarbonat, *das;* **∼ 'chloride** *n.* Natriumchlorid, *das*

sofa /'səʊfə/ *n.* Sofa, *das*

soft /sɒft/ *adj.* weich; (quiet) leise; (gentle) sanft; **have a ∼ spot for sb.** eine Vorliebe für jmdn. haben

soft: **∼-boiled** *adj.* weich gekocht ⟨*Ei*⟩; **∼-centred** *adj.* ⟨*Praline usw.*⟩ mit weicher Füllung; **∼ copy** *n.* (Comp.) Softcopy, *die;* **∼ cover** *n.* **book with a ∼ cover** Buch mit einem Softcover (Verlagsw.) *od.* mit einem flexiblen Einband; **∼ drink** *n.* alkoholfreies Getränk; **∼ drug** *n.* weiche Droge

soften /'sɒfn/ ① *v.i.* weicher werden

② *v.t.* aufweichen ⟨*Boden*⟩; enthärten ⟨*Wasser*⟩; mildern ⟨*Farbe*⟩

soft: **∼ 'furnishings** *n. pl.* (Brit.) Raumtextilien *Pl.;* **∼-'hearted** /sɒft'hɑːtɪd/ *adj.* weichherzig

'softly *adv.* (quietly) leise; (gently) sanft

soft: **∼ option** *n.* Weg des geringsten Widerstandes; **∼ 'porn** (coll.), **∼ por'nography** *ns.* Softpornographie, ⋯⃗

die; **∼-spoken** *adj.* leise sprechend
⟨*Person*⟩; **∼ top** *n.* **(a)** (roof) Stoffverdeck,
das; **(b)** (car) Cabrio, *das;* **∼ 'toy** *n.*
Stoffspielzeug, *das;* (toy animal) Stofftier, *das;*
∼ verge *n.* (Brit.) Grünstreifen, *der;*
∼ware *n.* (Comp.) Software, *die*

soggy /'sɒgɪ/ *adj.* aufgeweicht

soil¹ /sɔɪl/ *n.* Erde, *die;* Boden, *der*

soil² *v.t.* beschmutzen

solace /'sɒləs/ *n.* Trost, *der;* **take** *or* **find**
∼ in sth. Trost in etw. (*Dat.*) finden

solar /'səʊlə(r)/ *adj.* Sonnen-

solar: ∼ e'clipse *n.* Sonnenfinsternis, *die;*
∼ 'energy *n.* Sonnenenergie, *die;*
∼ 'panel *n.* Sonnenkollektor, *der;* (on
satellite) Sonnensegel, *das;* **∼-powered** *adj.*
mit Sonnenenergie betrieben; **∼ system**
n. Sonnensystem, *das*

sold ▶ SELL

solder /'səʊldə(r)/ ① *n.* Lot, *das*
② *v.t.* löten

soldering iron /'səʊldərɪŋaɪən/ *n.*
Lötkolben, *der*

soldier /'səʊldʒə(r)/ *n.* Soldat, *der*

sole¹ /səʊl/ *n.* (of foot/shoe) Sohle, *die*

sole² *adj.* einzig; alleinig ⟨*Verantwortung,
Recht*⟩; Allein⟨*erbe, -eigentümer*⟩

'solely *adv.* einzig und allein

solemn /'sɒləm/ *adj.* feierlich; ernst
⟨*Anlass, Gespräch*⟩

solicitor /sə'lɪsɪtə(r)/ *n.* (Brit.: lawyer)
Rechtsanwalt, *der*/-anwältin, *die*

solid /'sɒlɪd/ ① *adj.* **(a)** (rigid) fest
(b) (of the same substance all through) massiv
(c) (well-built) stabil; solide gebaut ⟨*Haus,
Mauer usw.*⟩
(d) (complete) ganz; **a good ∼ meal** eine
kräftige Mahlzeit
② *n.* fester Körper

solidarity /sɒlɪ'dærɪtɪ/ *n.* Solidarität, *die*

solid: ∼ 'fuel *n.* fester Brennstoff; **∼-'fuel**
attrib. adj. Festbrennstoff-; **∼-fuel rocket**
Feststoffrakete, *die*

solidify /sə'lɪdɪfaɪ/ *v.i.* fest werden

solitary /'sɒlɪtərɪ/ *adj.* **(a)** einsam;
∼ confinement Einzelhaft, *die*
(b) (sole) einzig

solitude /'sɒlɪtjuːd/ *n.* Einsamkeit, *die*

solo /'səʊləʊ/ ① *n., pl.* **∼s** (Mus.) Solo, *das*
② *adj.* **(a)** (Mus.) Solo-
(b) **∼ flight** Alleinflug, *der*
③ *adv.* **(a)** (Mus.) solo
(b) **go/fly ∼** (Aeronaut.) einen Alleinflug
machen

soloist /'səʊləʊɪst/ *n.* (Mus.) Solist, *der*/
Solistin, *die*

solstice /'sɒlstɪs/ *n.* Sonnenwende, *die*

soluble /'sɒljʊbl/ *adj.* **(a)** (esp. Chem.) löslich
(b) (solvable) lösbar

solution /sə'luːʃn/ *n.* **(a)** (esp. Chem.)
Lösung, *die*

(b) ([result of] solving) Lösung, *die* (**to** *Gen.*);
find a ∼ to sth. eine Lösung für etw. finden;
etw. lösen

solvable /'sɒlvəbl/ *adj.* lösbar

solve /sɒlv/ *v.t.* lösen

solvent /'sɒlvənt/ ① *adj.* **(a)** (esp. Chem.)
lösend
(b) (Finance) solvent
② *n.* Lösungsmittel, *das*

sombre (*Amer.:* **somber**) /'sɒmbə(r)/ *adj.*
dunkel; düster ⟨*Stimmung, Atmosphäre*⟩

some /səm, *stressed* sʌm/ ① *adj.* **(a)** (one or
other) [irgend]ein; **∼ day** eines Tages
(b) (a considerable quantity of) einig...
(c) (a small quantity of) ein bisschen; **would you
like ∼ wine/cherries?** möchten Sie [etwas]
Wein/[ein paar] Kirschen?; **do ∼ shopping/
reading** einkaufen/lesen
(d) (to a certain extent) **∼ guide** eine gewisse
Orientierungshilfe
② *pron.* einig...; **would you like ∼?** möchtest
du etwas?/(plural) welche?; **∼ ..., others ...:**
manche ..., andere ...

somebody /'sʌmbədɪ/ *n. & pron.* jemand;
∼ or other irgendjemand

'somehow *adv.* **∼ [or other]** irgendwie

someone /'sʌmwʌn/ ▶ SOMEBODY

somersault /'sʌməsɔːlt/ *n.* Purzelbaum,
der (ugs.); Salto, *der* (Sport); **turn a ∼:** einen
Purzelbaum schlagen (ugs.)/einen Salto
springen

'something *n. & pron.* etwas; **∼ new** etwas
Neues; **∼ or other** irgendetwas; **see ∼ of sb.**
jmdn. sehen

'sometime ① *adj.* ehemalig
② *adv.* irgendwann

'sometimes *adv.* manchmal

'somewhat *adv.* ziemlich

'somewhere ① *adv.* **(a)** (in a place)
irgendwo
(b) (to a place) irgendwohin
② *n.* **look for ∼ to stay** sich nach einer
Unterkunft umsehen

son /sʌn/ *n.* Sohn, *der*

sonata /sə'nɑːtə/ *n.* Sonate, *die*

song /sɒŋ/ *n.* **(a)** Lied, *das*
(b) (bird cry) Gesang, *der*

song: ∼bird *n.* Singvogel, *der;* **∼book** *n.*
Liederbuch, *das*

sonic /'sɒnɪk/ *attrib. adj.* Schall-; **∼ bang** *or*
boom Überschallknall, *der*

'son-in-law *n., pl.* **sons-in-law**
Schwiegersohn, *der*

soon /suːn/ *adv.* **(a)** bald; (quickly) schnell
(b) (early) früh; **none too ∼:** keinen
Augenblick zu früh; **∼er or later** früher oder
später
(c) **we'll set off as ∼ as he arrives** sobald er
ankommt, machen wir uns auf den Weg; **as
∼ as possible** so bald wie möglich
(d) (willingly) **just as ∼ [as ...]** genauso gern
[wie ...]; **she would ∼er die than ...:** sie
würde lieber sterben, als ...

soot /sʊt/ n. Ruß, der

soothe /suːð/ v.t. (a) (calm) beruhigen
(b) lindern ⟨Schmerz⟩

soothing /ˈsuːðɪŋ/ adj. beruhigend;
wohltuend ⟨Bad, Creme, Massage⟩

'sooty adj. verrußt; rußig

sophisticated /səˈfɪstɪkeɪtɪd/ adj. (a)
(cultured) kultiviert
(b) (elaborate, complex) hoch entwickelt; subtil
⟨Argument, System⟩

soporific /sɒpəˈrɪfɪk/ adj. einschläfernd

sopping /ˈsɒpɪŋ/ adj. & adv. ~ [wet] völlig
durchnässt

soppy /ˈsɒpɪ/ adj. (Brit. coll.) rührselig;
sentimental ⟨Person⟩

soprano /səˈprɑːnəʊ/ n. Sopran, der; (female
also) Sopranistin, die

sorbet /ˈsɔːbɪt, ˈsɔːbeɪ/ n. Sorbet, das

sorcerer /ˈsɔːsərə(r)/ n. Zauberer, der

sorcery /ˈsɔːsərɪ/ n. Zauberei, die

sordid /ˈsɔːdɪd/ adj. dreckig; unerfreulich
⟨Detail, Geschichte⟩

sore /sɔː(r)/ ①️ adj. weh; (inflamed or injured)
wund; a ~ throat Halsschmerzen Pl.; sb. has
a ~ back/foot etc. jmdm. tut der Rücken/
Fuß usw. weh
②️ n. wunde Stelle

'sorely adv. sehr; dringend ⟨nötig⟩;
~ tempted stark versucht

sorrow /ˈsɒrəʊ/ n. Kummer, der

sorry /ˈsɒrɪ/ adj. (a) sb. is ~ that ...: es tut
jmdm. Leid, dass ...; sb. is ~ about sth.
jmdm. tut etwas Leid; I am or feel ~ for him
er tut mir Leid; sb. is or feels ~ for sth.
jmd. bedauert etw.; ~! Entschuldigung!; ~?
wie bitte?; I'm ~ to say leider; you'll be ~!
das wird dir noch Leid tun
(b) (wretched) traurig

sort /sɔːt/ ①️ n. (a) Art, die; (type) Sorte, die;
a new ~ of bicycle ein neuartiges Fahrrad;
all ~s of ...: alle möglichen ...; there are all
~s of things to do es gibt alles Mögliche od.
allerlei zu tun; ~ of (coll.: more or less) mehr
oder weniger; nothing of the ~: nichts
dergleichen
(b) be out of ~s nicht in Form sein
②️ v.t. sortieren
■ sort 'out v.t. (a) (settle) klären; schlichten
⟨Streit⟩; beenden ⟨Verwirrung⟩
(b) (select) aussuchen

'sort code n. Bankleitzahl, die

sortie /ˈsɔːtɪ/ n. Ausfall, der; (flight) Einsatz,
der

'sorting office n. Postverteilstelle, die

SOS n. SOS, das

'so so, 'so-so adj., adv. so lala (ugs.)

soufflé /ˈsuːfleɪ/ n. Soufflé, das

sought ▶ SEEK

soul /səʊl/ n. Seele, die; not a ~: keine
Menschenseele

'soul-destroying adj. (a) (boring)
nervtötend

(b) (depressing) deprimierend

soulful /ˈsəʊlfl/ adj. gefühlvoll; (sad)
schwermütig

soul: ~ mate n. Seelenverwandte, der/die;
~-searching n. Gewissenskampf, der

sound¹ /saʊnd/ ①️ adj. (a) (healthy) gesund;
intakt ⟨Gebäude, Mauerwerk⟩; of ~ mind im
Vollbesitz seiner geistigen Kräfte
(b) (well-founded) vernünftig ⟨Argument, Rat⟩;
klug ⟨Wahl⟩; it makes ~ sense es ist sehr
vernünftig
(c) (Finance: secure) gesund, solide ⟨Basis⟩;
klug ⟨Investition⟩
②️ adv. fest, tief ⟨schlafen⟩

sound² ①️ n. (a) (Phys.) Schall, der
(b) (noise) Laut, der; (of wind, sea, car, footsteps,
breaking glass or twigs) Geräusch, das; (of voices,
laughter, bell) Klang, der; do sth. without a ~:
etw. lautlos tun
(c) (Radio, Telev., Cinemat.) Ton, der
(d) (fig.: impression) I like the ~ of your plan
ich finde, Ihr Plan hört sich gut an; I don't
like the ~ of this das hört sich nicht gut an
②️ v.i. klingen; it ~s as if .../like ...: es
klingt, als .../wie ...; that ~s a good idea to
me ich finde, die Idee hört sich gut an; that
~s odd to me das hört sich seltsam an,
finde ich; ~s good to me! klingt gut! (ugs.)
③️ v.t. (a) ertönen lassen
(b) (utter) ~ a note of caution zur Vorsicht
mahnen
■ **sound 'off** v.i. tönen (ugs.),
schwadronieren (on, about, von)
■ **sound 'out** v.i. ausfragen ⟨Person⟩; ~ sb.
out on sth. bei jmdm. wegen etw. vorfühlen

sound: ~ barrier n. Schallmauer, die;
~ bite n. kurzes, prägnantes Zitat;
~ card n. (Comp.) Soundkarte, die;
~ effect n. Geräscheffekt, der;
~ engineer n. Toningenieur, der/
-ingenieurin, die

'sounding board n. (a) (Mus.) Decke, die
(b) (fig.: trial audience) ≈ Testgruppe, die

'soundless adj. lautlos

'soundly adv. (a) (solidly) stabil, solide
⟨bauen⟩
(b) (deeply) tief, fest ⟨schlafen⟩
(c) (thoroughly) ordentlich (ugs.) ⟨verhauen⟩;
vernichtend ⟨schlagen, besiegen⟩

sound: ~proof ①️ adj. schalldicht; ②️ v.t.
schalldicht machen; **~ system** n.
Tonanlage, die; **~track** n. Soundtrack, der;
~ wave n. Schallwelle, die

soup /suːp/ n. Suppe, die; be/land in the ~
(fig. coll.) in der Patsche sitzen/landen (ugs.)

souped-up /ˈsuːptʌp/ attrib. adj. (Motor Veh.
coll.) frisiert (ugs.)

soup: ~ plate n. Suppenteller, der;
~ spoon n. Suppenlöffel, der

sour /ˈsaʊə(r)/ adj. (a) sauer
(b) (morose) griesgrämig; säuerlich ⟨Blick⟩
(c) (unpleasant) bitter

source /sɔ:s/ n. Quelle, die; ~ of income/
infection Einkommensquelle, die/
Infektionsherd, der; at ~: an der Quelle

sour 'cream n. saure Sahne; Sauerrahm,
der

south /saʊθ/ ① n. (a) Süden, der; in/
to[wards]/from the ~: im/nach/von Süden; **to
the ~ of** südlich von
(b) usu. S~ (Geog., Polit.) Süden, der
② adj. südlich; Süd⟨küste, -wind, -grenze⟩
③ adv. nach Süden; ~ of südlich von

South: ~ 'Africa pr. n. Südafrika (das);
~ 'African adj. südafrikanisch;
~ A'merica pr. n. Südamerika (das);
~ A'merican adj. südamerikanisch;
s~bound adj. ⟨Zug, Verkehr usw.⟩ in
Richtung Süden; s~-'east ① n. Südosten,
der; ② adj. südöstlich; Südost⟨wind, -küste⟩;
③ adv. südostwärts; nach Südosten;
s~-'eastern adj. südöstlich

southerly /ˈsʌðəlɪ/ adj. südlich; ⟨Wind⟩ aus
südlichen Richtungen

southern /ˈsʌðən/ adj. südlich; Süd⟨grenze,
-hälfte, -seite⟩

Southern Europe pr. n. Südeuropa (das)

South: ~ 'Germany pr. n.
Süddeutschland (das); ~ 'Pole pr. n.
Südpol, der

southward[s] /ˈsaʊθwəd(s)/ adv. südwärts

south: ~-'west ① n. Südwesten, der;
② adj. südwestlich; Südwest⟨wind, -küste⟩;
③ adv. südwestwärts; nach Südwesten;
~-'western adj. südwestlich

souvenir /suːvəˈnɪə(r)/ n. Souvenir, das (of
aus); Andenken, das

sovereign /ˈsɒvrɪn/ n. (ruler) Souverän, der

sovereignty /ˈsɒvrɪntɪ/ n. Souveränität,
die

Soviet /ˈsəʊvɪət, ˈsɒvɪət/ adj. (Hist.)
sowjetisch; Sowjet⟨bürger, -literatur⟩

Soviet 'Union pr. n. (Hist.) Sowjetunion,
die

sow[1] /səʊ/ v.t., p.p. **sown** /səʊn/ or **sowed**
/səʊd/ (a) (plant) [aus]säen
(b) einsäen ⟨Feld, Boden⟩

sow[2] /saʊ/ n. (female pig) Sau, die

sown ▶ sow[1]

soya [bean] /ˈsɔɪə (biːn)/ n. Sojabohne, die

soy sauce /ˈsɔɪ sɔːs/ n. Sojasoße, die

sozzled /ˈsɒzld/ adj. (coll.) voll (ugs.)

spa /spɑː/ n. (a) (place) Bad, das; Badeort,
der
(b) (spring) Mineralquelle, die

space /speɪs/ n. (a) Raum, der
(b) (interval between points) Platz, der; **clear a ~:**
Platz schaffen
(c) **the wide open ~s** das weite, flache Land
(d) (Astron.) Weltraum, der
(e) (blank between words) Zwischenraum, der
(f) (interval of time) Zeitraum, der; **in the ~ of
a minute/an hour** innerhalb einer Minute/
Stunde; **in a short ~ of time he was back**
nach kurzer Zeit war er zurück

space 'out v.t. verteilen

space: ~ age n. [Welt]raumzeitalter, das;
~ bar n. Leertaste, die; ~craft n.
Raumfahrzeug, das; ~-saving adj. Platz
sparend; ~ship n. Raumschiff, das; ~suit
n. Raumanzug, der; ~ travel n. Raumfahrt,
die

spacious /ˈspeɪʃəs/ adj. geräumig

spade /speɪd/ n. (a) Spaten, der
(b) (Cards) Pik, das; see also CLUB 1C

spaghetti /spəˈɡetɪ/ n. Spaghetti Pl.

Spain /speɪn/ pr. n. Spanien (das)

spam /spæm/ n. (Comput.) Spam, der

span /spæn/ ① n. (a) Spanne, die;
Zeitspanne, die
(b) (of bridge) Spannweite, die
② v.t., -nn- überspannen ⟨Fluss⟩; umfassen
⟨Zeitraum⟩

Spaniard /ˈspænjəd/ n. Spanier, der/
Spanierin, die

Spanish /ˈspænɪʃ/ ① adj. spanisch; **sb. is
~:** jmd. ist Spanier/Spanierin
② n. (a) (language) Spanisch, das; see also
ENGLISH 2A
(b) the ~ pl. die Spanier Pl.

spank /spæŋk/ ① n. ≈ Klaps, der (ugs.)
② v.t. ~ sb. jmdm. einen Klaps geben (ugs.)

spanner /ˈspænə(r)/ n. (Brit.)
Schraubenschlüssel, der

spar /spɑː(r)/ v.i., -rr-: (a) (Boxing) sparren
(b) (fig.: argue) [sich] zanken

spare /speə(r)/ ① adj. (a) (not in use) übrig;
~ time/moment Freizeit, die/freier
Augenblick; **there is one ~ seat** ein Platz ist
noch frei
(b) (for use when needed) zusätzlich, Extra⟨bett,
-tasse⟩; ~ room Gästezimmer, das
② n. Ersatzteil, das/-reifen, der usw
③ v.t. (a) entbehren; **we arrived with ten
minutes to ~:** wir kamen zehn Minuten
früher an
(b) (not inflict on) ~ sb. sth. jmdm. etw.
ersparen
(c) (not hurt) [ver]schonen
(d) (fail to use) **not ~ any expense/pains** or
efforts keine Kosten/Mühe scheuen; **no
expense ~d** an nichts gespart

spare: ~ 'part n. Ersatzteil, das; ~ 'tyre
n. Reserve-, Ersatzreifen, der; ~ 'wheel n.
Ersatzrad, das

sparing /ˈspeərɪŋ/ adj., **sparingly** adv.
sparsam

spark /spɑːk/ ① n. (a) Funke, der; (fig.) a
~ of generosity/decency ein Funke[n]
Großzügigkeit/Anstand
(b) a bright ~ (coll.: person, also iron.) ein
schlauer Kopf
② v.t. ~ [off] zünden; (fig.) auslösen

sparkle /ˈspɑːkl/ ① v.i. ⟨Diamant:⟩
glitzern; ⟨Augen:⟩ funkeln
(b) (be lively) sprühen (with vor + Dat.)
② n. Funkeln, das

sparkling /'spɑːklɪŋ/ adj. glitzernd ⟨Diamant⟩; funkelnd ⟨Augen⟩

sparkling 'wine n. Schaumwein, der

'spark plug n. Zündkerze, die

sparrow /'spærəʊ/ n. Spatz, der

sparse /spɑːs/ adj. spärlich; dünn ⟨Besiedlung⟩

spasm /'spæzm/ n. Krampf, der

spasmodic /spæz'mɒdɪk/ adj. (a) (marked by spasms) krampfartig (b) (intermittent) sporadisch

spastic /'spæstɪk/ ⎣1⎦ n. Spastiker, der/ Spastikerin, die ⎣2⎦ adj. spastisch

spat ▶ SPIT 1, 2

spate /speɪt/ n. (a) the river is in [full] ∼: der Fluss führt Hochwasser (b) (fig.) a ∼ of sth. eine Flut von etw.; a ∼ of burglaries eine Einbruchsserie

spatial /'speɪʃl/ adj. räumlich

spatter /'spætə(r)/ v.t. spritzen; ∼ sb./sth. with sth. jmdn./etw. mit etw. bespritzen

spatula /'spætjʊlə/ n. Spachtel, der od. die

spawn /spɔːn/ ⎣1⎦ v.t. (fig.) hervorbringen ⎣2⎦ v.i. (Zool.) laichen ⎣3⎦ n. (Zool.) Laich, der

speak /spiːk/ ⎣1⎦ v.i., spoke /spəʊk/, spoken /'spəʊkn/ (a) sprechen; ∼ [with sb.] on or about sth. [mit jmdm.] über etw. (Akk.) sprechen; ∼ for/against sth. sich für/gegen etw. aussprechen (b) (on telephone) Is Mr Grant there? – S∼ing! Ist Mister Grant da? – Am Apparat!; who is ∼ing, please? wer ist am Apparat, bitte? ⎣2⎦ v.t., spoke, spoken sprechen ⟨Satz, Wort, Sprache⟩; sagen ⟨Wahrheit⟩; ∼ one's mind sagen, was man denkt

■ **'speak for** v.t. sprechen für; sth. is spoken for (reserved) etw. ist schon vergeben

■ **'speak of** v.t. sprechen von; ∼ing of Mary da wir gerade von Mary sprechen; nothing to ∼ of nichts Besonderes

■ **'speak to** v.t. sprechen od. reden mit

■ **speak 'up** v.i. lauter sprechen

'speaker n. (a) (in public) Redner, der/ Rednerin, die (b) (of a language) Sprecher der/Sprecherin, die; be a 'French ∼: Französisch sprechen (c) (loudspeaker) Lautsprecher, der

'speaking ⎣1⎦ n. Sprechen, das; ∼ clock (Brit.) telefonische Zeitansage ⎣2⎦ adv. strictly/generally ∼: genau genommen/im Allgemeinen

spear /spɪə(r)/ n. Speer, der

'spearhead ⎣1⎦ n. (fig.) Speerspitze, die ⎣2⎦ v.t. (fig.) anführen

'spearmint n. Grüne Minze; ∼ chewing gum Pfefferminzkaugummi, der od. das

spec[1] /spek/ (coll.) ▶ SPECIFICATION

spec[2] /spek/ n. (coll.: speculation) on ∼: auf gut Glück; auf Verdacht (ugs.)

special /'speʃl/ adj. speziell; besonder...; nobody ∼: niemand Besonderes

special de'livery n. (Post) Eilzustellung, die

special effects n. pl. (Cinemat.) Special effects Pl.

specialist /'speʃəlɪst/ n. (a) Spezialist, der/Spezialistin, die (in für) (b) (Med.) Facharzt, der/-ärztin, die

speciality /speʃɪ'rælɪtɪ/ n. Spezialität, die

specialization /speʃəlaɪ'zeɪʃn/ n. Spezialisierung, die

specialize /'speʃəlaɪz/ v.i. sich spezialisieren (in auf + Akk.)

specialized /'speʃəlaɪzd/ adj. (a) (requiring detailed knowledge) speziell; Spezial⟨kenntnisse, -gebiet⟩ (b) (concentrating on small area) spezialisiert

'specially adv. (a) speziell; make sth. ∼: etw. speziell od. extra anfertigen (b) (especially) besonders

special: ∼ 'needs n. children with ∼ needs Kinder, die besonders betreut werden müssen; ∼ needs teacher Förderlehrer, der/-lehrerin, die; ∼ 'offer n. Sonderangebot, das; on ∼ offer im Sonderangebot; ∼ **school** n. Sonderschule, die

specialty /'speʃltɪ/ (esp. Amer.) ▶ SPECIALITY

species /'spiːʃiːz/ n., pl. same Art, die; ∼ barrier Artenbarriere, die; Artengrenze, die

specific /sprɪ'sɪfɪk/ adj. bestimmt; could you be more ∼? kannst du dich genauer ausdrücken?

specifically /sprɪ'sɪfɪkəlɪ/ adv. ausdrücklich; eigens; extra (ugs.)

specification /spesɪfɪ'keɪʃn/ n., often pl. (details) technische Daten Pl.; (for building) Baubeschreibung, die

specify /'spesɪfaɪ/ v.t. ausdrücklich sagen; unless otherwise specified wenn nicht anders angegeben

specimen /'spesɪmən/ n. (a) (example) Exemplar, das (b) (sample) Probe, die

speck /spek/ n. (a) (spot) Fleck, der (b) (particle) Teilchen, das; ∼ of soot/dust Rußflocke, die/Staubkörnchen, das

specs /speks/ n. pl. (coll.: spectacles) Brille, die

spectacle /'spektəkl/ n. (a) in pl. [pair of] ∼s Brille, die (b) (public show) Spektakel, das

'spectacle case n. Brillenetui, das

spectacular /spek'tækjʊlə(r)/ adj. spektakulär

spectator /spek'teɪtə(r)/ n. Zuschauer, der/Zuschauerin, die

spec'tator sport n. Publikumssport, der

specter (Amer.) ▶ SPECTRE

spectra pl. of SPECTRUM

spectre /'spektə(r)/ n. (Brit.) (a) (ghost) Gespenst, das (b) (fig.) Schreckgespenst, das

S

spectrum /'spektrəm/ *n., pl.* **spectra**
/'spektrə/ Spektrum, *das*

speculate /'spekjʊleɪt/ *v.i.* spekulieren
(**about, on** über + *Akk.*)

speculation /spekjʊ'leɪʃn/ *n.* Spekulation,
die (**over** über + *Akk.*)

speculative /'spekjʊlətɪv/ *adj.* spekulativ

speculator /'spekjʊleɪtə(r)/ *n.* Spekulant,
der/Spekulantin, *die*

sped ▶ SPEED 2

speech /spiːtʃ/ *n.* (a) (public address) Rede,
die; **make** *or* **deliver** *or* **give a ~:** eine Rede
halten
(b) (faculty or manner of speaking) Sprache, *die*

'speechless *adj.* sprachlos (**with** vor
+ *Dat.*)

speed /spiːd/ **1** *n.* Geschwindigkeit, *die;*
Schnelligkeit, *die;* **at a ~ of ...:** mit einer
Geschwindigkeit von ...
2 *v.i.* (a) *p.t. & p.p.* **sped** /sped/ *or* **speeded**
schnell fahren; rasen (ugs.)
(b) *p.t.&p.p.* **speeded** (go too fast) zu schnell
fahren; rasen (ugs.)

speed: **~boat** *n.* Rennboot, *das;*
~ bump *n.* Bodenschwelle, *die;*
~ camera *n.*
Geschwindigkeitsüberwachungskamera, *die;*
~ dating *n.* Speeddating, *das*

'speeding *n.*
Geschwindigkeitsüberschreitung, *die*

'speed limit *n.*
Geschwindigkeitsbeschränkung, *die*

speedo /'spiːdəʊ/ *n., pl.* **~s** (Brit. coll.) Tacho,
der (ugs.)

speedometer /spiː'dɒmɪtə(r)/ *n.*
Tachometer, *der od. das*

speed: **~ ramp** *n.* Bodenschwelle, *die;*
~way *n.* Speedwayrennen, *das*

'speedy *adj.* schnell; umgehend, prompt
⟨Antwort⟩

spell[1] /spel/ **1** *v.t.* **spelt** /spelt/ (Brit.) *or*
spelled (a) schreiben; (aloud) buchstabieren
(b) (fig.: mean) bedeuten
2 *v.i.* **spelt** (Brit.) *or* **spelled** (say)
buchstabieren; (write) richtig schreiben

spell[2] *n.* (period) Weile, *die;* **a cold ~:** eine
Kälteperiode

spell[3] *n.* (a) (magic charm) Zauberspruch, *der;*
cast a ~ on sb. jmdn. verzaubern
(b) (fascination) Zauber, *der;* **break the ~:** den
Bann brechen

'spellbound *adj.* verzaubert

'spell checker ▶ SPELLING CHECKER

'spelling *n.* Rechtschreibung, *die*

spelling: **~ checker** *n.*
Rechtschreibprogramm, *das;* **~ mistake**
n. Rechtschreibfehler, *der*

spelt ▶ SPELL[1]

spend /spend/ *v.t.,* **spent** /spent/ (a) (pay
out) ausgeben; **~ a penny** (fig. coll.) mal
verschwinden (ugs.)
(b) verbringen ⟨Zeit⟩

'spendthrift *n.* Verschwender, *der*/
Verschwenderin, *die*

spent **1** ▶ SPEND
2 *adj.* (a) (used up) verbraucht
(b) (drained of energy) erschöpft

sperm /spɜːm/ *n. pl* **~s** *or same* Sperma,
der

sperm: **~ bank** *n.* Samenbank, *die;*
~ count *n.* Spermienzahl, *die;* **~ donor**
n. Samenspender, *der;* Spermaspender, *der*

spew /spjuː/ *v.t.* spucken

sphere /sfɪə(r)/ *n.* (a) (field of action) Bereich,
der; Sphäre, *die* (geh.)
(b) (Geom.) Kugel, *die*

spherical /'sferɪkl/ *adj.* kugelförmig

spice /spaɪs/ **1** *n.* Gewürz, *das;* (fig.) Würze,
die
2 *v.t.* würzen

'spice rack *n.* Gewürzregal, *das*

spicy /'spaɪsɪ/ *adj.* pikant; würzig

spider /'spaɪdə(r)/ *n.* Spinne, *die*

spider: **~ plant** *n.* Grünlilie, *die;* **~'s**
web (Amer.: **~ web**) Spinnennetz, *das*

spike /spaɪk/ *n.* Stachel, *der*

spiky /'spaɪkɪ/ *adj.* stachelig

spill /spɪl/ **1** *v.t.,* **spilt** /spɪlt/ *or* **spilled**
verschütten ⟨Flüssigkeit⟩; **~ sth. on sth.** etw.
auf etw. (*Akk.*) schütten; **~ the beans** aus
der Schule plaudern
2 *v.i.,* **spilt** *or* **spilled** überlaufen

spilt ▶ SPILL

spin /spɪn/ **1** *v.t.,* **-nn-, spun** /spʌn/ (a)
spinnen; **~ yarn** Garn spinnen
(b) (in washing machine etc.) schleudern
2 *v.i.,* **-nn-, spun** sich drehen; **my head is**
~ning (fig.) mir schwirrt der Kopf
■ **spin 'out** *v.t.* (prolong) in die Länge ziehen

spinach /'spɪnɪdʒ/ *n.* Spinat, *der*

spinal /'spaɪnl/ *adj.* Wirbelsäulen-;
Rückgrat[s]-

spinal: **~ 'column** *n.* Wirbelsäule, *die;*
~ 'cord *n.* Rückenmark, *das*

spindle /'spɪndl/ *n.* Spindel, *die*

spindly /'spɪndlɪ/ *adj.* spindeldürr

spin: **~ doctor** *n.* (coll.) Spin-Doktor, *der;*
~ 'drier *n.* Wäscheschleuder, *die;* **~-'dry**
v.t. schleudern

spine /spaɪn/ *n.* (a) (backbone) Wirbelsäule,
die
(b) (Bot., Zool.) Stachel, *der*

'spineless *adj.* (fig.) rückgratlos

'spin-off *n.* Nebenprodukt, *das*

spinster /'spɪnstə(r)/ *n.* ledige Frau

spiny /'spaɪnɪ/ *adj.* stachelig

spiral /'spaɪrl/ **1** *adj.* spiralförmig
2 *n.* Spirale, *die*
3 *v.i.,* (Brit.) **-ll-** ⟨Weg:⟩ sich hochwinden;
⟨Kosten:⟩ in die Höhe klettern; ⟨Rauch:⟩ in
einer Spirale aufsteigen

spiral 'staircase *n.* Wendeltreppe, *die*

spire /'spaɪə(r)/ *n.* Turmspitze, *die*

spirit /'spɪrɪt/ n. (a) in pl. (distilled liquor) Spirituosen Pl.
(b) (mental attitude) Geisteshaltung, die; in the right/wrong ∼: mit der richtigen/falschen Einstellung; take sth. in the wrong ∼: etw. falsch auffassen
(c) (courage) Mut, der
(d) (mental tendency) Geist, der; high ∼s gehobene Stimmung; in poor or low ∼s niedergedrückt

'spirited adj. beherzt

'spirit level n. Wasserwaage, die

spiritual /'spɪrɪtʃʊəl/ adj. spirituell (geh.)

spit /spɪt/ ① v.i., -tt-, spat /spæt/ or spit spucken
② v.t., -tt-, spat or spit spucken
③ n. Spucke, die
■ **spit 'out** v.t. ausspucken

spite /spaɪt/ ① n. (a) Boshaftigkeit, die
(b) in ∼ of trotz; in ∼ of oneself obwohl man es eigentlich nicht will
② v.t. ärgern

spiteful /'spaɪtfl/ adj. gehässig

spitting 'image n. be the ∼ of sb. jmdm. wie aus dem Gesicht geschnitten sein

spittle /'spɪtl/ n. Spucke, die

splash /splæʃ/ ① v.t. spritzen; ∼ sth. on [to] or over sb./sth. jmdn./etw. mit etw. bespritzen
② v.i. (a) spritzen
(b) (in water) platschen (ugs.)
③ n. (a) (liquid) Spritzer, der
(b) (noise) Plätschern, das
■ **splash 'out** vi. (coll.) ∼ out on sth. für etw. unbekümmert Geld ausgeben

splendid /'splendɪd/ adj. (excellent) großartig; (magnificent) prächtig

splendour (Brit.; Amer.: **splendor**) /'splendə(r)/ n. Pracht, die

splint /splɪnt/ n. Schiene, die

splinter /'splɪntə(r)/ n. Splitter, der

split /splɪt/ ① n. (a) (tear) Riss, der
(b) (division into parts) [Auf]teilung, die; (fig.) Spaltung, die
② adj. gespalten; be ∼ on a question [sich (Dat.] in einer Frage uneins sein
③ v.t., -tt-, split (a) (tear) zerreißen
(b) (divide) teilen
④ v.i., -tt-, split (a) ⟨Holz:⟩ splittern; ⟨Stoff, Seil:⟩ reißen; ∼ apart zersplittern
(b) (divide into parts) sich teilen
■ **split 'up** ① v.t. aufteilen
② v.i. (coll.) sich trennen; ∼ up with sb. sich von jmdm. trennen

split: ∼-**level** adj. mit Zwischengeschoss nachgestellt; auf zwei Ebenen nachgestellt; a ∼-**level lounge** ein Wohnraum auf zwei Ebenen; ∼-**level cooker** Einbauherd, bei dem Kochplatten und Backofen getrennt sind; ∼ '**pea** n. getrocknete [halbe] Erbse; ∼ **perso'nality** n. gespaltene Persönlichkeit; ∼ '**second** n. in a

∼ **second** im Bruchteil einer Sekunde; ∼-**second timing** [zeitliche] Abstimmung auf die Sekunde genau

splitting /'splɪtɪŋ/ adj. a ∼ **headache** rasende Kopfschmerzen Pl.

splutter /'splʌtə(r)/ v.i. ⟨Person:⟩ prusten; ⟨Motor:⟩ stottern

spoil /spɔɪl/ ① v.t., spoilt /spɔɪlt/ or spoiled
(a) (impair) verderben
(b) (pamper) verwöhnen; be ∼t for choice die Qual der Wahl haben
② v.i., spoilt or spoiled (a) verderben
(b) be ∼ing for a fight Streit suchen
③ n. ∼[s pl.] Beute, die

'spoiler n. (of car, aircraft) Spoiler, der

'spoilsport n. Spielverderber, der/ -verderberin, die

spoilt ▶ SPOIL 1, 2

spoke¹ /spəʊk/ n. Speiche, die

spoke², spoken ▶ SPEAK

spokesman /'spəʊksmən/ n., pl. **spokesmen** /'spəʊksmən/ Sprecher, der

sponge /spʌndʒ/ ① n. Schwamm, der
② v.t. mit einem Schwamm waschen
■ **'sponge on** v.t. ∼ on sb. bei od. von jmdm. schnorren (ugs.)

sponge: ∼ **bag** n. (Brit.) Kulturbeutel, der; ∼ **cake** n. Biskuitkuchen, der

sponger /'spʌndʒə(r)/ n. Schmarotzer, der/ Schmarotzerin, die

spongy /'spʌndʒɪ/ adj. schwammig

sponsor /'spɒnsə(r)/ ① n. Sponsor, der
② v.t. (a) sponsern
(b) (Polit.) ∼ sb. jmds. Kandidatur unterstützen

spontaneity /spɒntə'niːɪtɪ/ n. Spontaneität, die

spontaneous /spɒn'teɪnɪəs/ adj. spontan

spooky /'spuːkɪ/ adj. gespenstisch

spool /spuːl/ n. Spule, die

spoon /spuːn/ n. (a) Löffel, der
(b) (amount) ▶ SPOONFUL

'spoon-feed v.t. (fig.) ∼ sb. jmdm. alles vorkauen (ugs.)

spoonful /'spuːnfʊl/ n. a ∼ of sugar ein Löffel [voll] Zucker

sporadic /spə'rædɪk/ adj. sporadisch

sporadically /spə'rædɪkəlɪ/ adv. hin und wieder

spore /spɔː(r)/ n. Spore, die

sport /spɔːt/ ① n. (a) Sport, der; ∼s Sportarten Pl.; **water/indoor** ∼: Wasser-/ Hallensport, der
(b) (fun) Spaß, der
(c) be a [real] ∼ (coll.) ein prima Kerl sein (ugs.); be a ∼! sei kein Spielverderber!
② v.t. stolz tragen

'sporting adj. (a) sportlich
(b) give sb. a ∼ **chance** jmdm. eine [faire] Chance geben

sports: ∼ **bra** n. Sport-BH, der; ∼ **car** n. Sportwagen, der; ∼ **centre** n.   ···⟩

Sportzentrum, *das;* ~ **channel** *n.*
Sportkanal, *der;* ~ **commentator** *n.*
Sportberichterstatter, *der/*-berichterstatterin,
die; ~ **complex** *n.* Sportzentrum, *das;*
~ **field** *n.* Sportplatz, *der;* ~ **hall** *n.*
Sporthalle, *die;* ~ **jacket** *n.* sportlicher
Sakko; ~**man** /'spɔːtsmən/ *n., pl.* ~**men**
/'spɔːtsmən/ Sportler, *der;* ~**manship**
/'spɔːtsmənʃɪp/ *n.* (fairness) [sportliche]
Fairness; ~ **page** *n.* (Journ.) Sportseite, *die;*
~ **section** *n.* (Journ.) Sportteil, *der;*
~**wear** *n.* Sport[be]kleidung, *die;*
~**woman** *n.* Sportlerin, *die*

'**sporty** *adj.* sportlich

spot /spɒt/ **1** *n.* (a) (precise place) Stelle, *die;*
on this ~: an dieser Stelle; be in a tight ~
(fig. coll.) in der Klemme sitzen (ugs.); put sb.
on the ~ (fig. coll.) jmdn. in Verlegenheit
bringen
(b) (suitable area) Platz, *der*
(c) (dot) Tupfen, *der*
(d) (stain) ~ [of blood/grease/ink] [Blut-/Fett-/
Tinten]fleck, *der*
(e) (Brit. coll.: small amount) do a ~ of work/
sewing ein bisschen arbeiten/nähen
(f) (drop) a ~ or a few ~s of rain ein paar
Regentropfen
(g) (Med.) Pickel, *der*
2 *v.t.,* **-tt-** (detect) entdecken; erkennen
⟨*Gefahr*⟩

spot: ~ '**check** *n.* Stichprobe, *die;* ~**less**
adj. fleckenlos; her house is absolutely ~less
(fig.) ihr Haus ist makellos sauber; ~**light**
n. Scheinwerfer, *der;* be in the ~light (fig.) im
Rampenlicht stehen

spotted /'spɒtɪd/ *adj.* gepunktet

'**spotty** *adj.* (pimply) picklig

spouse /spaʊs/ *n.* [Ehe]gatte, *der/*-gattin,
die

spout /spaʊt/ **1** *n.* Schnabel, *der;* (of tap)
Ausflussrohr, *das*
2 *v.i.* (gush) schießen (from aus)

sprain /spreɪn/ **1** *v.t.* verstauchen
2 *n.* Verstauchung, *die*

sprang ▸ SPRING 2, 3

sprawl /sprɔːl/ *v.i.* (a) sich ausstrecken;
(fall) der Länge nach hinfallen
(b) (straggle) sich ausbreiten

'**sprawling** *attrib. adj.* wuchernd
⟨*Großstadt*⟩

spray[1] /spreɪ/ (bouquet) Strauß, *der*

spray[2] **1** *v.t.* spritzen; sprühen ⟨*Parfüm*⟩;
besprühen ⟨*Haar, Pflanze*⟩
2 *n.* (a) (drops) Sprühnebel, *der*
(b) (liquid) Spray, *der od. das*

spray: ~ **can** ▸ AEROSOL A; ~ **gun** *n.*
Spritzpistole, *die*

spread /spred/ **1** *v.t.,* **spread** (a)
ausbreiten ⟨*Tuch, Landkarte*⟩ (on auf
+ *Dat.*); streichen ⟨*Butter, Farbe, Marmelade*⟩
(b) (extend range of) verbreiten
(c) (distribute) verteilen
2 *v.i.,* **spread** sich ausbreiten

3 *n.* (a) Verbreitung, *die;* (of city, poverty)
Ausbreitung, *die*
(b) (coll.: meal) Festessen, *das*
(c) (paste) Brotaufstrich, *der*
(d) (Printing) the advertisement was a full-
page/double-page ~: die Anzeige war
ganzseitig/doppelseitig
■ **spread 'out** **1** *v.t.* ausbreiten
2 *v.i.* sich verteilen

'**spreadsheet** *n.* (Comp.) Arbeitsblatt, *das*

spree /spriː/ *n.* go on a shopping ~: ganz
groß einkaufen gehen

'**spree killer** *n.* Amokläufer, *der*

sprig /sprɪg/ *n.* Zweig, *der*

sprightly /'spraɪtlɪ/ *adj.* munter

spring /sprɪŋ/ **1** *n.* (a) (season) Frühling,
der; in [the] ~: im Frühling *od.* Frühjahr
(b) (water) Quelle, *die*
(c) (Mech.) Feder, *die*
(d) (jump) Sprung, *der*
2 *v.i.,* **sprang** /spræŋ/ *or* (Amer.) **sprung**
/sprʌŋ/, **sprung** (a) (jump) springen; ~ to life
(fig.) [plötzlich] zum Leben erwachen
(b) (arise) entspringen (from *Dat.*)
3 *v.t.,* **sprang** *or* (Amer.) **sprung,** **sprung:**
~ sth. on sb. jmdn. mit etw. überfallen

spring: ~**board** *n.* Sprungbrett, *das;*
~ '**chicken** *n.* be no ~ chicken nicht
mehr der/die Jüngste sein (ugs.); ~-'**clean**
1 *n.* Frühjahrsputz, *der;* **2** *v.t.*
Frühjahrsputz machen in (+ *Dat.*);
~**loaded** *adj.* mit Sprungfeder
nachgestellt; ~ '**onion** *n.* Frühlingszwiebel,
die; ~**time** *n.* Frühling, *der*

springy /'sprɪŋɪ/ *adj.* elastisch; federnd
⟨*Schritt, Brett, Boden*⟩

sprinkle /'sprɪŋkl/ *v.t.* streuen; sprengen
⟨*Flüssigkeit*⟩

sprinkler /'sprɪŋklə(r)/ *n.* (Hort.) Sprinkler,
der

sprinkling /'sprɪŋklɪŋ/ *n.* a ~ of snow/
sugar/dust eine dünne Schneedecke/Zucker-/
Staubschicht

sprint /sprɪnt/ **1** *v.t. & i.* rennen; sprinten
(bes. Sport)
2 *n.* Sprint, *der*

sprout /spraʊt/ **1** *n.* (a) Brussels ~s
Rosenkohl, *der*
(b) (Bot.) Trieb, *der*
2 *v.i.* sprießen (geh.)

spruce /spruːs/ **1** *adj.* gepflegt
2 *n.* Fichte, *die*

sprung /sprʌŋ/ **1** ▸ SPRING 2, 3
2 *attrib. adj.* gefedert

spry /spraɪ/ *adj.* rege

spud /spʌd/ *n.* (coll.) Kartoffel, *die*

spun ▸ SPIN

spunk /spʌŋk/ *n.* (coll.: courage) Mumm, *der*
(ugs.)

spur /spɜː(r)/ **1** *n.* Sporn, *der;* (fig.) Ansporn,
der; on the ~ of the moment ganz spontan
2 *v.t.,* **-rr-** (fig.) anspornen

spurious /'spjʊərɪəs/ *adj.* gespielt ⟨*Interesse*⟩; unberechtigt ⟨*Anspruch, Anklage*⟩

spurn /spɜːn/ *v.t.* zurückweisen

spurt¹ /spɜːt/ *n.* Spurt, *der;* **put on a ~**: einen Spurt einlegen

spurt² 1 *v.i.* **~ out** [**from** *or* **of**] herausspritzen [aus]
2 *n.* Strahl, *der*

spy /spaɪ/ 1 *n.* Spion, *der*/Spionin, *die*
2 *v.i.* spionieren; **~ on sb.** jmdm. nachspionieren

spy: ~master *n.* Chef, *der* eines Spionagerings; **~ ring** *n.* Spionagering, *der;* **~ story** *n.* Spionagegeschichte, *die*

squabble /'skwɒbl/ 1 *n.* Streit, *der*
2 *v.i.* sich zanken (**over, about** wegen)

squad /skwɒd/ *n.* (a) (Mil.) Gruppe, *die*
(b) (group) Mannschaft, *die*

squadron /'skwɒdrən/ *n.* (a) (Navy) Geschwader, *das*
(b) (Air Force) Staffel, *die*

squalid /'skwɒlɪd/ *adj.* (a) (dirty) schmutzig
(b) (poor) schäbig

squall /skwɔːl/ *n.* (gust) Bö, *die*

squalor /'skwɒlə(r)/ *n.* Schmutz, *der*

squander /'skwɒndə(r)/ *v.t.* vergeuden

square /skweə(r)/ 1 *n.* (a) (Geom.) Quadrat, *das*
(b) (open area) Platz, *der*
2 *adj.* (a) quadratisch
(b) **a ~ metre/mile** ein Quadratmeter/eine Quadratmeile
(c) **be all ~**: [völlig] quitt sein (*ugs.*)
3 *v.t.* (a) (Math.) quadrieren
(b) **~ it with sb.** es mit jmdm. klären
4 *v.i.* (agree) übereinstimmen
■ **square 'up** *v.i.* (settle up) abrechnen

square: ~ 'brackets *n. pl.* eckige Klammern *Pl.;* **~ 'meal** *n.* anständige Mahlzeit (ugs.); **~ 'root** *n.* Quadratwurzel, *die*

squash /skwɒʃ/ 1 *v.t.* (crush) zerquetschen; **~ sth. flat** etw. platt drücken
2 *n.* (a) Fruchtsaftgetränk, *das*
(b) (Sport) Squash, *das*

squash: ~ court *n.* Squashfeld, *das;* **~ racket** *n.* Squashschläger, *der*

squat /skwɒt/ *v.i.,* **-tt-:** (a) (crouch) hocken
(b) **~ in a house** ein Haus besetzen

'squatter *n.* Hausbesetzer, *der*/-besetzerin, *die*

squawk /skwɔːk/ *v.i.* ⟨*Krähe:*⟩ krähen; ⟨*Huhn:*⟩ kreischen

squeak /skwiːk/ 1 *n.* (a) (of animal) Quieken, *das*
(b) (of brakes, hinge, etc.) Quietschen, *das*
2 *v.i.* (a) ⟨*Tier:*⟩ quieken
(b) ⟨*Scharnier, Tür, Bremse, Schuh usw.:*⟩ quietschen

squeaky /'skwiːkɪ/ *adj.* quietschend

squeal /skwiːl/ 1 *v.i.* (a) **~ with pain/in**

fear ⟨*Person:*⟩ vor Schmerz/Angst aufschreien; ⟨*Tier:*⟩ vor Schmerz/Angst laut quieken
(b) ⟨*Bremsen, Räder:*⟩ kreischen; ⟨*Reifen:*⟩ quietschen
2 *n.* Kreischen, *das;* (of tyres) Quietschen, *das;* (of animal) Quieken, *das*

squeamish /'skwiːmɪʃ/ *adj.* **be ~**: zart besaitet sein

squeeze /skwiːz/ 1 *n.* Druck, *der;* **give sth. a small ~**: etw. [leicht] drücken
2 *v.t.* (a) (press) drücken; drücken auf (+ *Akk.*) ⟨*Tube, Plastikflasche*⟩; (to get juice) auspressen
(b) (extract) drücken (**out of** aus); **~ out sth.** etw. herausdrücken
(c) (force) zwängen

squelch /skweltʃ/ *v.i.* quatschen (ugs.)

squid /skwɪd/ *n.* Kalmar, *der*

squiggle /'skwɪgl/ *n.* Schnörkel, *der*

squint /skwɪnt/ 1 *n.* Schielen, *das*
2 *v.i.* (a) (Med.) schielen
(b) (with half-closed eyes) blinzeln

squire /'skwaɪə(r)/ *n.* ≈ Gutsherr, *der*

squirm /skwɜːm/ *v.i.* sich winden (**with** vor + *Dat.*)

squirrel /'skwɪrl/ *n.* Eichhörnchen, *das*

squirt /skwɜːt/ 1 *v.t.* spritzen; sprühen ⟨*Spray, Puder*⟩; **~ sth. at sb.** jmdm. mit etw. bespritzen/besprühen
2 *v.i.* spritzen
3 *n.* Spritzer, *der*

st. *abbr.* (Brit.: unit of weight) = **stone**

St *abbr.* = **Saint** St.

St. *abbr.* = **Street** Str.

stab /stæb/ 1 *v.t.,* **-bb-** stechen; **~ sb. in the chest** jmdm. in die Brust stechen
2 *v.i.,* **-bb-** stechen
3 *n.* (a) Stich, *der*
(b) (coll.: attempt) **make** *or* **have a ~** [**at it**] [es] probieren

stability /stə'bɪlɪtɪ/ *n.* Stabilität, *die*

stabilize /'steɪbɪlaɪz/ 1 *v.t.* stabilisieren
2 *v.i.* sich stabilisieren

stable¹ /'steɪbl/ *adj.* stabil; gefestigt ⟨*Person*⟩

stable² *n.* Stall, *der*

stack /stæk/ 1 *n.* (a) (pile) Stoß, *der;* Stapel, *der*
(b) (coll.: large amount) Haufen, *der* (ugs.)
(c) [chimney] **~**: Schornstein, *der*
2 *v.t.* **~ [up]** [auf]stapeln

stadium /'steɪdɪəm/ *n.* Stadion, *das*

staff /stɑːf/ 1 *n.* (a) (stick) Stock, *der*
(b) (personnel) Personal, *das;* (of school) Lehrerkollegium, *das*
2 *v.t.* mit Personal ausstatten

staff: ~ meeting *n.* [Lehrer]konferenz, *die;* **~room** *n.* Lehrerzimmer, *das*

stag /stæg/ *n.* Hirsch, *der*

stage /steɪdʒ/ 1 *n.* (a) (Theatre) Bühne, *die*
(b) (part of process) Stadium, *das;* **at this ~**: ···▷

in diesem Stadium; **do sth. by** ~**s** etw.
abschnittsweise tun; **in the final** ~**s** in der
Schlussphase
(c) (distance) Etappe, *die*
2 *v.t.* (a) (present) inszenieren
(b) (arrange) veranstalten
stage: ~**coach** *n.* Postkutsche, *die;*
~ **door** *n.* Bühneneingang, *der;* ~ **effect**
n. Bühneneffekt, *der;* ~ **fright** *n.*
Lampenfieber, *das;* ~**hand** *n.*
Bühnenarbeiter, *der/*-arbeiterin, *die;*
~**manage** *v.t.* (fig.) veranstalten;
~ **name** *n.* Künstlername, *der*
stagger /ˈstægə(r)/ 1 *v.i.* schwanken
2 *v.t.* (astonish) die Sprache verschlagen
(+ *Dat.*)
stagnant /ˈstægnənt/ *adj.* (a) stehend
⟨*Gewässer*⟩
(b) (Econ.) stagnierend
stagnate /stægˈneɪt/ *v.i.* (a) ⟨*Wasser:*⟩
abstehen
(b) ⟨*Wirtschaft, Geschäft:*⟩ stagnieren;
⟨*Person:*⟩ abstumpfen
stagnation /stægˈneɪʃn/ *n.* (a) (of water)
Stehen, *das*
(b) (Econ.) Stagnation, *die*
stag: ~ **night** *n.*: Zechabend des
*Bräutigams mit seinen Freunden kurz vor
seiner Hochzeit;* ~ **party** *n.* Herrenabend,
der
staid /steɪd/ *adj.* gesetzt
stain /steɪn/ 1 *v.t.* (a) verfärben; (make ~s
on) Flecken hinterlassen auf (+ *Dat.*)
(b) (colour) beizen ⟨*Holz*⟩
2 *n.* Fleck, *der*
stained 'glass *n.* farbiges Glas;
~ **'window** Fenster mit Glasmalerei
'stainless *adj.* fleckenlos
stainless 'steel *n.* Edelstahl, *der*
'stain remover *n.* Fleck[en]entferner, *der*
stair /steə(r)/ *n.* (step) [Treppen]stufe, *die;*
~s Treppe, *die*
stair: ~**case** *n.* Treppenhaus, *das;* ~**way**
n. Treppe, *die*
stake /steɪk/ *n.* (a) (pointed stick) Pfahl, *der*
(b) (wager) Einsatz, *der;* **be at** ~: auf dem
Spiel stehen
stale /steɪl/ *adj.* alt; muffig; abgestanden
⟨*Luft*⟩; alt[backen] ⟨*Brot*⟩; schal ⟨*Bier, Wein
usw.*⟩
'stalemate *n.* Patt, *das*
stalk[1] /stɔːk/ *v.t.* (a) sich heranpirschen an
(+ *Akk.*)
(b) (follow obsessively) ~ **sb.** jmdm. nachstellen
stalk[2] *n.* (Bot.) (main stem) Stängel, *der;* (of
leaf, flower, fruit) Stiel, *der*
stalker /ˈstɔːkə(r)/ *n.* (obsessive pursuer)
[lästiger] Verfolger
stall /stɔːl/ 1 *n.* (a) (stall) Stand, *der*
(b) (Brit. Theatre) ~s Parkett, *das*
2 *v.t.* abwürgen (ugs.) ⟨*Motor*⟩
3 *v.i.* ⟨*Motor:*⟩ stehen bleiben

'stallholder *n.* Standinhaber, *der/*
-inhaberin, *die*
stallion /ˈstæljən/ *n.* Hengst, *der*
stalwart /ˈstɔːlwət/ *adj.* (determined)
entschieden; (loyal) treu
stamen /ˈsteɪmen/ *n.* Staubblatt, *das*
stamina /ˈstæmɪnə/ *n.* Ausdauer, *die*
stammer /ˈstæmə(r)/ 1 *v.i.* stottern
2 *v.t.* stammeln
3 *n.* Stottern, *das*
stamp /stæmp/ 1 *v.t.* (a) (impress, imprint sth.
on) [ab]stempeln
(b) ~ **one's foot** mit dem Fuß stampfen
(c) (put postage ~ on) frankieren; ~**ed
addressed envelope** frankierter
Rückumschlag
(d) become *or* be ~**ed on sb.'s memory** *or*
mind sich jmdm. fest einprägen
2 *v.i.* aufstampfen
3 *n.* Marke, *die;* (postage ~) Briefmarke, *die;*
(instrument for ~ing) Stempel, *der*
■ **'stamp on** *v.t.* (a) zertreten ⟨*Insekt*⟩;
~ **on sb's foot** jmdm. auf den Fuß treten
(b) (suppress) durchgreifen gegen
■ **stamp 'out** *v.t.* [aus]stanzen; (fig.)
ausmerzen
stamp: ~ **album** *n.* Briefmarkenalbum,
das; ~ **collecting** *n.*
Briefmarkensammeln, *das;* ~ **collection**
n. Briefmarkensammlung, *die;* ~ **duty** *n.*
Stempelsteuer, *die*
stampede /stæmˈpiːd/ *n.* Stampede, *die*
stance /stɑːns/ *n.* (posture; fig.: attitude)
Haltung, *die*
stanch /stɑːnʃ/ *v.t.* stillen ⟨*Blut*⟩; abbinden
⟨*Wunde*⟩
stand /stænd/ 1 *v.i.,* stood /stʊd/ (a)
stehen
(b) **my offer/promise still** ~**s** mein Angebot/
Versprechen gilt nach wie vor; **as it** ~**s, as
things** ~: wie die Dinge [jetzt] liegen; **I'd like
to know where I** ~ (fig.) ich möchte wissen,
wo ich dran bin
(c) (be candidate) kandidieren
(d) [not] ~ **in sb.'s way** (fig.) jmdm. [keine]
Steine in den Weg legen
(e) (be likely) ~ **to win** *or* **gain/lose sth.** etw.
gewinnen/verlieren können
2 *v.t.,* stood (a) (set in position) stellen
(b) (endure) ertragen; **I cannot** ~ **[the sight of]
him/her** ich kann ihn/sie nicht ausstehen; **he
can't** ~ **the pressure/strain** er ist dem Druck/
den Strapazen nicht gewachsen; **I can't** ~ **it
any longer!** ich halte es nicht mehr aus!
(c) (buy) ~ **sb. sth.** jmdm. etw. spendieren
3 *n.* (a) (support) Ständer, *der*
(b) (stall; at exhibition) Stand, *der*
(c) (raised structure) Tribüne, *die*
■ **stand a'bout, stand a'round** *v.i.*
herumstehen
■ **stand a'side** *v.i.* zur Seite treten
■ **stand 'back** *v.i.* (a) ~ **[well] back [from
sth.]** [ein gutes Stück] [von etw.] entfernt
stehen

(b) (fig.: distance oneself) zurücktreten
■ **'stand between** *v.t.* sth. ~s between sb. and sth. (fig.) etw. steht jmdm. bei etw. im Wege
■ **stand by** 1 /-'-/ *v.i.* (a) (be near) daneben stehen
(b) (be ready) sich zur Verfügung halten
2 /'--/ *v.t.* (a) (support) ~ by sb./one another jmdn./sich [gegenseitig] beistehen
(b) (adhere to) ~ by sth. zu etw. stehen
■ **stand 'down** *v.i.* verzichten
■ **'stand for** *v.t.* (a) (signify) bedeuten
(b) (coll.: tolerate) sich (*Dat.*) bieten lassen
■ **stand 'in** *v.i.* aushelfen; ~ in for sb. für jmdn. einspringen
■ **stand 'out** *v.i.* (be prominent) herausragen; ~ out a mile (fig.) nicht zu übersehen sein
■ **'stand over** *v.t.* beaufsichtigen
■ **stand 'up** *v.i.* (a) aufstehen; ~ up straight sich aufrecht hinstellen
(b) ~ up well [in comparison with sb./sth.] [im Vergleich zu jmdm./etw.] gut abschneiden; ~ up for sb./sth. für jmdn./etw. Partei ergreifen; ~ up to sb. sich jmdm. entgegenstellen

stand-alone /stændə'ləʊn/ *adj.* (Comp.) selbstständig
standard /'stændəd/ 1 *n.* (a) Maßstab, *der;* safety ~s Sicherheitsnormen *Pl.;* above/below/up to ~: überdurchschnittlich [gut]/unter dem Durchschnitt/der Norm entsprechend
(b) (degree) Niveau, *das;* ~ of living Lebensstandard, *der*
(c) ~s (morals) Prinzipien *Pl.*
(d) (flag) Standarte, *die*
2 *adj.* Standard-; be ~ practice allgemein üblich sein
standardize /'stændədaɪz/ *v.t.* standardisieren
'standard lamp *n.* Stehlampe, *die*
stand: ~by 1 *n.* be on ~by einsatzbereit sein; 2 *adj.* Ersatz-; ~-in 1 *n.* Ersatz, *der;* 2 *adj.* Ersatz-
'standing 1 *n.* (a) (repute) Ansehen, *das*
(b) (duration) of long/short ~: von langer/kurzer Dauer
2 *adj.* (a) (erect) stehend
(b) fest ⟨Regel, Brauch⟩
standing: ~ 'order *n.* Dauerauftrag, *der;* ~ o'vation *n.* stürmischer Beifall; ~ room *n.* Stehplätze *Pl.*
stand-offish /stænd'ɒfɪʃ/ *adj.* reserviert
stand: ~pipe *n.* Standrohr, *das;* ~point *n.* (fig.) Standpunkt, *der;* ~still *n.* Stillstand, *der;* be at a ~still stillstehen; come to a ~still zum Stehen kommen
stank ▶ STINK 1
staple[1] /'steɪpl/ 1 *n.* [Heft]klammer, *die*
2 *v.t.* heften (on to an + *Akk.*)
staple[2] 1 *attrib. adj.* (a) Grund-; a ~ diet ein Grundnahrungsmittel
(b) (Commerc.) grundlegend; ~ goods Haupthandelsartikel *Pl.*

2 *n.* (Commerc.: major item) Haupterzeugnis, *das*
stapler /'steɪplə(r)/ *n.* [Draht]hefter, *der*
star /stɑː(r)/ 1 *n.* (a) Stern, *der*
(b) (prominent person) Star, *der*
2 *v.i.* ~ in a film in einem Film die Hauptrolle spielen
starboard /'stɑːbəd/ *n.* Steuerbord, *das*
starch /stɑːtʃ/ *n.* Stärke, *die*
starchy /'stɑːtʃɪ/ *adj.* stärkehaltig ⟨Nahrungsmittel⟩; (fig.: prim) steif
stardom /'stɑːdəm/ *n.* Starruhm, *der*
stare /steə(r)/ *v.i.* starren; ~ at sb./sth. jmdn./etw. anstarren
'starfish *n.* Seestern, *der*
stark /stɑːk/ 1 *adj.* scharf ⟨Kontrast, Umriss⟩
2 *adv.* völlig; ~ naked splitternackt (ugs.)
'starless *adj.* stern[en]los
starlet /'stɑːlɪt/ *n.* Starlet[t], *das*
starling /'stɑːlɪŋ/ *n.* Star, *der*
'starlit *adj.* sternhell
starry /'stɑːrɪ/ *adj.* sternklar
star: ~ sign *n.* Sternzeichen, *das;* ~-studded *adj.* ⟨Show, Film, Besetzung⟩ mit großem Staraufgebot
start /stɑːt/ 1 *v.i.* (a) (begin) anfangen; ~ on sth. etw. beginnen
(b) (set out) aufbrechen
(c) (begin to function) anlaufen; ⟨Auto, Motor usw.:⟩ anspringen
2 *v.t.* (a) (begin) beginnen [mit]; ~ doing or to do sth. [damit] anfangen, etw. zu tun
(b) (cause) auslösen; anfangen ⟨Streit, Schlägerei⟩; legen/(accidentally) verursachen ⟨Brand⟩
(c) (set up) ins Leben rufen ⟨Organisation, Projekt⟩
(d) (switch on) einschalten; anlassen ⟨Motor, Auto⟩
3 *n.* (a) Anfang, *der;* Beginn, *der;* (of race) Start, *der;* from the ~: von Anfang an; from ~ to finish von Anfang bis Ende; make a ~: anfangen (on mit); (on journey) aufbrechen
(b) (Sport: ~ing place) Start, *der*
'starter *n.* (a) (food) Vorspeise, *die*
(b) (Sport) Starter, *der*
starting /'stɑːtɪŋ/: ~ point *n.* (lit. or fig.) Ausgangspunkt, *der;* ~ post *n.* (Sport) Startpfosten, *der;* ~ salary *n.* Anfangsgehalt, *das*
startle /'stɑːtl/ *v.t.* erschrecken; be ~d by sth. über etw. (*Akk.*) erschrecken
startling /'stɑːtlɪŋ/ *adj.* erstaunlich
starvation /stɑː'veɪʃn/ *n.* Verhungern, *das*
starve /stɑːv/ *v.i.* ~ [to death] verhungern
stash /stæʃ/ (coll.) 1 *v.t.* ~ [away] verstecken
2 *n.* [geheimes] Lager
state /steɪt/ 1 *n.* (a) (condition) Zustand, *der*
(b) (nation) Staat, *der*
(c) be in a ~: aufgeregt sein
(d) lie in ~: aufgebahrt sein ⋯⋗

2 *v.t.* (express) erklären; angeben ⟨*Alter usw.*⟩

stately /'steɪtlɪ/ *adj.* majestätisch; stattlich ⟨*Körperbau, Gebäude*⟩

stately 'home *n.* Herrensitz, *der*

'**statement** *n.* (a) (stating, account) Aussage, *die;* (declaration) Erklärung, *die*
(b) [bank] ∼: Kontoauszug, *der*

state: ∼-of-the-'art *adj.* auf dem neuesten Stand der Technik *nachgestellt;* ∼ **school** *n.* (Brit.) staatliche Schule; ∼**-owned** *adj.* staatlich

statesman /'steɪtsmən/ *n., pl.* **statesmen** /'steɪtsmən/ Staatsmann, *der*

static /'stætɪk/ *adj.* statisch

static elec'tricity *n.* statische Elektrizität

station /'steɪʃn/ 1 *n.* (a) ▶ RAILWAY STATION
(b) (status) Rang, *der*
2 *v.t.* aufstellen ⟨*Wache*⟩

stationary /'steɪʃənərɪ/ *adj.* stehend; **be** ∼: stehen

stationer /'steɪʃənə(r)/ *n.* ∼'s [shop] Schreibwarengeschäft, *das*

stationery /'steɪʃənərɪ/ *n.* (a) (writing materials) Schreibwaren *Pl.*
(b) (writing paper) Briefpapier, *das*

'**station wagon** *n.* (Amer.) Kombiwagen, *der*

statistic /stə'tɪstɪk/ *n.* statistische Tatsache

statistical /stə'tɪstɪkl/ *attrib. adj.*, **statistically** /stə'tɪstɪkəlɪ/ *adv.* statistisch

statistics /stə'tɪstɪks/ *n.* Statistik, *die*

statue /'stætʃuː, 'stætjuː/ *n.* Statue, *die*

statuesque /stætjʊ'esk/ *adj.* statuenhaft; (imposing) stattlich

stature /'stætʃə(r)/ *n.* Statur, *die;* (fig.) Format, *das*

status /'steɪtəs/ *n.* Rang, *der;* **social** ∼: [gesellschaftlicher] Status

'**status symbol** *n.* Statussymbol, *das*

statute /'stætjuːt/ *n.* Gesetz, *das*

statutory /'stætjʊtərɪ/ *adj.* gesetzlich

staunch /stɔːntʃ/ *adj.* treu ⟨*Freund*⟩; überzeugt ⟨*Katholik usw.*⟩

stave /steɪv/ *v.t.* ∼ '**off** abwenden; stillen ⟨*Hunger*⟩

stay /steɪ/ 1 *n.* Aufenthalt, *der;* (visit) Besuch, *der;* **come/go for a short** ∼ **with sb.** jmdn. kurz besuchen
2 *v.i.* bleiben; ∼ **put** (coll.) ⟨*Person:*⟩ bleiben[, wo man ist]; ∼ **the night in a hotel** die Nacht in einem Hotel verbringen
3 *v.t.* ∼ **the course** (fig.) durchhalten
∎ **stay a'head** *v.i.* die Führung halten
∎ **stay a'way** *v.i.* wegbleiben
∎ **stay be'hind** *v.i.* zurückbleiben
∎ **stay 'in** *v.i.* zu Hause bleiben
∎ **stay 'out** *v.i.* (a) (not go home) wegbleiben (ugs.)
(b) (remain outside) draußen bleiben

∎ **stay 'over** *v.i.* (coll.) über Nacht bleiben
∎ **stay 'up** *v.i.* aufbleiben

'**staying power** *n.* Durchhaltevermögen, *das*

stead /sted/ *n.* (a) **in sb.'s** ∼: an jmds. Stelle (*Dat.*)
(b) **stand sb. in good** ∼: jmdm. zustatten kommen

steadfast /'stedfɑːst/ *adj.* standhaft; zuverlässig ⟨*Freund*⟩

steadily /'stedɪlɪ/ *adv.* (a) (stably) fest
(b) (continuously) stetig

steady /'stedɪ/ 1 *adj.* (a) (stable) stabil; (not wobbling) standfest
(b) (still) ruhig
(c) (regular, constant) stetig; gleichmäßig ⟨*Arbeit, Tempo*⟩; stabil ⟨*Preis, Lohn*⟩; gleich bleibend ⟨*Temperatur*⟩; **we had** ∼ **rain/drizzle** wir hatten Dauerregen/es nieselte [bei uns] ständig
(d) **a** ∼ **job** eine feste Stelle; **a** ∼ **boyfriend** ein fester Freund
2 *v.t.* festhalten ⟨*Leiter*⟩; beruhigen ⟨*Nerven*⟩

steak /steɪk/ *n.* Steak, *das*

'**steak knife** *n.* Messer mit Sägezahnung

steal /stiːl/ 1 *v.t.*, **stole** /stəʊl/, **stolen** /'stəʊln/ stehlen (**from** *Dat.*)
2 *v.i.*, **stole**, **stolen** (a) stehlen; ∼ **from sb.** jmdn. bestehlen
(b) ∼ **in/out** sich hinein-/hinausstehlen

stealth /stelθ/ *n.* Heimlichkeit, *die;* **by** ∼: heimlich

stealthy /'stelθɪ/ *adj.* heimlich

steam /stiːm/ 1 *n.* Dampf, *der;* **let off** ∼ (fig.) Dampf ablassen (ugs.); **run out of** ∼ (fig.) den Schwung verlieren; **under one's own** ∼ (fig.) aus eigener Kraft
2 *v.t.* (Cookery) dämpfen; dünsten
3 *v.i.* dämpfen; ∼**ing hot** dampfend heiß
∎ **steam a'head** *v.i.* (fig. coll.) rasche Fortschritte machen
∎ **steam 'up** *v.i.* beschlagen

steam: ∼boat *n.* Dampfschiff, *das;* (small) Dampfboot, *das;* ∼ **engine** *n.* Dampflok[omotive], *die;* (stationary) Dampfmaschine, *die*

'**steamer** *n.* Dämpfer, *der*

steam: ∼ iron *n.* Dampfbügeleisen, *das;* ∼**roller** *n.* Dampfwalze, *die;* ∼ **train** *n.* Dampfzug, *der*

'**steamy** *adj.* dunstig; beschlagen ⟨*Glas*⟩

steel /stiːl/ 1 *n.* Stahl, *der*
2 *attrib. adj.* stählern; Stahl⟨*helm, -block, -platte*⟩
3 *v.t.* ∼ **oneself for/against sth.** sich für/gegen etw. wappnen (geh.); ∼ **oneself to do sth.** allen Mut zusammennehmen, um etw. zu tun

steel: ∼ 'band *n.* (Mus.) Steelband, *die;* ∼ '**drum** *n.* (Mus.) Steeldrum, *die;* ∼ **industry** *n.* Stahlindustrie, *die;* ∼ '**wool** *n.* Stahlwolle, *die;* ∼**works** *n. sing. or pl.* Stahlwerk, *das*

S

steep¹ /stiːp/ adj. (a) steil
(b) (coll.: excessive) happig (ugs.); **the bill is [a bit] ~:** die Rechnung ist [ziemlich] gesalzen (ugs.)

steep² v.t. (soak) einweichen

steeped /stiːpt/ adj. durchdrungen (**in** von)

steeple /ˈstiːpl/ n. Kirchturm, der

steer /stɪə(r)/ ☐1 v.t. steuern; lenken
☐2 v.i. steuern; **~ clear of sb./sth.** (fig. coll.) jmdm./einer Sache aus dem Weg[e] gehen

'steering n. (Motor Veh.) Lenkung, die

steering: ~ column n. Lenksäule, die; **~ lock** n. Lenkradschloss, das; **~ wheel** n. Lenkrad, das

stem¹ /stem/ ☐1 n. (a) (Bot.) Stiel, der
(b) (Ling.) Stamm, der
☐2 v.i., -mm-: **~ from sth.** auf etw. (Akk.) zurückzuführen sein

stem² v.t., -mm- (check, dam up) aufhalten; eindämmen ⟨Flut⟩; stillen ⟨Blutung⟩

stench /stentʃ/ n. Gestank, der

stencil /ˈstensl/ n. Schablone, die; (for duplicating) Matrize, die

step /step/ ☐1 n. (a) Schritt, der; **take a ~ back/forwards** einen Schritt zurücktreten/ nach vorn treten
(b) (stair) Stufe, die; **a flight of ~s** eine Treppe; **[pair of] ~s** (ladder) Stehleiter, die
(c) **be in ~:** im Schritt sein; (with music) im Takt sein
(d) **take ~s to do sth.** Schritte unternehmen, um etw. zu tun
(e) (stage) **~ by ~:** Schritt für Schritt; **what is the next ~?** wie geht es weiter?
(f) (grade) Stufe, die
☐2 v.i., -pp- treten; **~ inside** eintreten; **~ into sb's shoes** (fig.) an jmds. Stelle treten; **~ over sb./sth.** über jmdn./etw. steigen
▪ **step 'back** v.i. zurücktreten
▪ **step 'in** v.i. (a) eintreten
(b) (fig.) (take sb.'s place) einspringen; (intervene) eingreifen
▪ **step 'up** ☐1 v.i. (ascend) hinaufsteigen
☐2 v.t. erhöhen; verstärken ⟨Anstrengungen⟩

step: ~ aerobics n. Stepaerobic, das; **~child** n. Stiefkind, das; **~daughter** n. Stieftochter, die; **~father** n. Stiefvater, der; **~ladder** n. Stehleiter, die; **~mother** n. Stiefmutter, die

'stepping stone n. Trittstein, der; (fig.) Sprungbrett, das (**to** für)

stereo /ˈsterɪəʊ/ ☐1 n. Stereo, das; (equipment) Stereoanlage, die
☐2 adj. stereo; Stereo⟨aufnahme, -platte⟩

stereophonic /sterɪəˈfɒnɪk/ adj. stereophon

stereotype /ˈsterɪətaɪp/ ☐1 n. Stereotyp, das
☐2 v.t. in ein Klischee zwängen; **~d** stereotyp

sterile /ˈsteraɪl/ adj. steril

sterility /stəˈrɪlɪtɪ/ n. Sterilität, die

sterilization /sterɪlaɪˈzeɪʃn/ n. Sterilisation, die

sterilize /ˈsterɪlaɪz/ v.t. sterilisieren

sterling /ˈstɜːlɪŋ/ ☐1 n. Sterling, der; **in ~:** in Pfund [Sterling]
☐2 attrib. adj. (a) **~ silver** Sterlingsilber, das
(b) (fig.) gediegen

stern¹ /stɜːn/ adj. streng; ernst ⟨Warnung⟩

stern² n. (Naut.) Heck, das

'sternly adv. streng

steroid /ˈsterɔɪd/ n. Steroid, das

stethoscope /ˈsteθəskəʊp/ n. Stethoskop, das

stew /stjuː/ ☐1 n. Eintopf, der
☐2 v.t. schmoren [lassen]

steward /ˈstjuːəd/ n. (a) (on ship, plane) Steward, der
(b) (at public meeting etc.) Ordner, der

'stewardess n. Stewardess, die

stewed /stjuːd/ adj. (Cookery) geschmort

'stewing steak n. [Rinder]schmorfleisch, das

stick /stɪk/ ☐1 v.t., **stuck** /stʌk/ (a) (thrust point of) stecken; **~ sth. in[to] sth.** mit etw. in etw. (Akk.) stechen
(b) (coll.: put) stecken; **~ a picture on the wall/a vase on the shelf** ein Bild an die Wand hängen/eine Vase aufs Regal stellen; **~ sth. in the kitchen** etw. in die Küche tun (ugs.)
(c) (with glue etc.) kleben
(d) **the car is stuck in the mud** das Auto ist im Schlamm stecken geblieben; **the door is stuck** die Tür klemmt [fest]
☐2 v.i., **stuck** (a) (be fixed by point) stecken
(b) (adhere) kleben; **~ to sth.** an etw. (Dat.) kleben
(c) (become immobile) ⟨Auto, Räder:⟩ stecken bleiben; ⟨Schublade, Tür, Griff, Bremse:⟩ klemmen; ⟨Schlüssel:⟩ feststecken
☐3 n. Stock, der; **a ~ of chalk** ein Stück Kreide; **a ~ of celery/rhubarb** eine Stange Sellerie/Rhabarber
▪ **stick a'bout, stick a'round** v.i. (coll.) dableiben; (wait) warten
▪ **'stick by** v.t. (fig.) stehen zu
▪ **stick 'on** v.t. (glue on) aufkleben
▪ **stick 'out** ☐1 v.t. (a) herausstrecken ⟨Zunge⟩
(b) **~ it out** (coll.) durchhalten
☐2 v.i. (a) ⟨Bauch:⟩ vorstehen; **his ears ~ out** er hat abstehende Ohren
(b) (be obvious) sich abheben; **~ out a mile** (coll.) [klar] auf der Hand liegen; **~ out like a sore thumb** (coll.) ins Auge springen
▪ **'stick to** v.t. (a) (be faithful to) halten ⟨Versprechen⟩; bleiben bei ⟨Entscheidung⟩
(b) **~ to the point** beim Thema bleiben
▪ **stick to'gether** v.i. zusammenkleben; (fig.) zusammenhalten
▪ **stick 'up** ☐1 v.t. (a) (coll.) anschlagen ⟨Poster⟩; **~ up one's hand** die Hand heben ┈┊

S

(b) (seal) zukleben
2 *v.i.* **~ up for sb./sth.** für jmdn./etw. eintreten; **~ up for yourself!** setz dich zur Wehr!

stick de'odorant *n.* Deo[dorant]stift, *der*

'sticker *n.* Aufkleber, *der*

'sticking plaster *n.* Heftpflaster, *das*

stickler /'stɪklə(r)/ *n.* **be a ~ for tidiness/ authority** es mit der Sauberkeit sehr genau nehmen/in puncto Autorität keinen Spaß verstehen

'stick-up *n.* (coll.) bewaffneter Raubüberfall

'sticky *adj.* **(a)** klebrig; **~ label** Aufkleber, *der*
(b) (humid) schwül ‹*Klima, Luft*›

stiff /stɪf/ *adj.* **(a)** (rigid) steif; hart ‹*Bürste, Stock*›; **be frozen ~:** steif vor Kälte sein
(b) (intense, severe) hartnäckig
(c) (formal) steif
(d) (difficult) hart ‹*Test*›; schwer ‹*Frage, Prüfung*›
(e) (coll.) **be bored/scared ~:** sich zu Tode langweilen/eine wahnsinnige Angst haben (ugs.)

stiffen /'stɪfn/ **1** *v.t.* steif machen
2 *v.i.* steifer werden; ‹*Person:*› erstarren

'stiffness *n.* Steifheit, *die*

stifle /'staɪfl/ **1** *v.t.* ersticken; (fig.) unterdrücken
2 *v.i.* ersticken

stifling /'staɪflɪŋ/ *adj.* stickig; drückend ‹*Hitze*›

stigma /'stɪgmə/ *n.* Stigma, *das* (geh.)

stile /staɪl/ *n.* Zauntritt, *der*

stiletto /stɪ'letəʊ/ *n.* **~ [heel]** Stöckelabsatz, *der*

still¹ /stɪl/ **1** *pred. adj.* still; **be ~:** [still] stehen; **hold sth. ~:** etw. ruhig halten; **keep or stay ~:** stillhalten; **stand ~:** stillstehen
2 *adv.* **(a)** (without change) noch; *expr. surprise or annoyance* immer noch
(b) (nevertheless) trotzdem
(c) *with comparative* (even) noch

still² *n.* Destillierapparat, *der*

still: ~ birth *n.* Totgeburt, *die;* **~born** *adj.* tot geboren; **~ 'life** *n.* (Art) Stillleben, *das*

stilt /stɪlt/ *n.* Stelze, *die*

'stilted *adj.* gestelzt

stimulant /'stɪmjʊlənt/ *n.* Stimulans, *das*

stimulate /'stɪmjʊleɪt/ *v.t.* anregen

stimulation /stɪmjʊ'leɪʃn/ *n.* Anregung, *die*

stimulus /'stɪmjʊləs/ *n., pl.* **stimuli** /'stɪmjʊlaɪ/ Ansporn, *der*

sting /stɪŋ/ **1** *n.* **(a)** (wounding) Stich, *der;* (by jellyfish, nettles) Verbrennung, *die*
(b) (from ointment, wind) Brennen, *das*
2 *v.t., stung* /stʌŋ/ stechen
3 *v.i., stung* brennen

'stinging nettle *n.* Brennnessel, *die*

stingy /'stɪndʒɪ/ *adj.* geizig; knaus[e]rig (ugs.)

stink /stɪŋk/ **1** *v.i.*, **stank** /stæŋk/ *or* **stunk** /stʌŋk/, **stunk** stinken (**of** nach)
2 *n.* Gestank, *der*

'stink bomb *n.* Stinkbombe, *die*

stint /stɪnt/ **1** *v.i.* **~ on sth.** an etw. (*Dat.*) sparen
2 *n.* [Arbeits]pensum, *das*

stipulate /'stɪpjʊleɪt/ *v.t.* (demand) fordern; (lay down) festlegen

stipulation /stɪpjʊ'leɪʃn/ *n.* (condition) Bedingung, *die*

stir /stɜː(r)/ **1** *v.t.,* **-rr-:** **(a)** (mix) rühren; umrühren ‹*Tee, Kaffee*›
(b) (move) bewegen
2 *v.i.,* **-rr-** (move) sich rühren
3 *n.* Aufregung, *die*
■ **stir 'in** *v.t.* einrühren
■ **stir 'up** *v.t.* **(a)** (disturb) aufrühren
(b) (fig.: arouse) wecken ‹*Interesse, Leidenschaft*›

stirring /'stɜːrɪŋ/ *adj.* bewegend ‹*Musik, Poesie*›; mitreißend ‹*Rede*›

stirrup /'stɪrəp/ *n.* Steigbügel, *der*

stitch /stɪtʃ/ **1** *n.* **(a)** (Sewing) Stich, *der;* (Knitting) Masche, *die*
(b) (pain) **have a ~:** Seitenstechen haben
2 *v.t.* nähen
■ **stitch 'up** *v.t.* **(a)** nähen; vernähen ‹*Loch, Riss, Wunde*›
(b) (Brit. fig. coll.: betray, cheat) reinlegen (ugs.); linken (salopp)

'stitching *n.* **(a)** Naht, *die*
(b) (ornamental stitches) Stickerei, *die*

stoat /stəʊt/ *n.* Hermelin, *das*

stock /stɒk/ **1** *n.* **(a)** (origin, family, breed) Abstammung, *die*
(b) (supply, store) Vorrat, *der;* (in shop etc.) Warenbestand, *der;* **be in/out of ~** ‹*Ware:*› vorrätig/nicht vorrätig sein; **have sth. in ~:** etw. auf Lager haben; **take ~ of sth.** (fig.) über etw. (*Akk.*) Bilanz ziehen
(c) (Cookery) Brühe, *die*
2 *v.t.* **(a)** (supply with ~) beliefern
(b) (Commerc.: keep in ~) auf Lager haben
3 *attrib. adj.* Standard-

stock: ~broker Effektenmakler, *der/*-maklerin, *die;* **~ cube** *n.* Brühwürfel, *der;* **~ exchange** *n.* Börse, *die*

stocking /'stɒkɪŋ/ *n.* Strumpf, *der*

'stockist *n.* Fachhändler, *der/*-händlerin, *die*

stock: ~ market *n.* **(a)** Börse, *die;* **(b)** (trading) Börsengeschäft, *das;* **~ market crash** Börsenkrach, *der;* **~pile** **1** *n.* Vorrat, *der;* (weapons) Arsenal, *das;* **2** *v.t.* horten; anhäufen ‹*Waffen*›; **~pot** *n.* Suppentopf, *der;* **~room** *n.* Lager, *das;* **~'still** *pred. adj.* bewegungslos; **~taking** *n.* Inventur, *die*

stocky /'stɒkɪ/ *adj.* stämmig

stodgy /'stɒdʒɪ/ *adj.* pappig

stoical /'stəʊɪkl/ adj. stoisch
stoicism /'stəʊɪsɪzm/ n. Stoizismus, der
stoke /stəʊk/ v.t. heizen ⟨Ofen, Kessel⟩; unterhalten ⟨Feuer⟩
stole ▶ STEAL
stolen /'stəʊln/ 1 ▶ STEAL
2 attrib. adj. heimlich ⟨Vergnügen, Kuss⟩
stolid /'stɒlɪd/ adj. stur (ugs.)
stomach /'stʌmək/ 1 n. (a) Magen, der
(b) (abdomen) Bauch, der
2 v.t. (fig.: tolerate) ausstehen
stomach: ∼ **ache** n. Magenschmerzen Pl.; **have a** ∼ **ache** Magenschmerzen haben; ∼ **upset** n. Magenverstimmung, die
stone /stəʊn/ 1 n. (a) Stein, der; **a** ∼'**s throw [away]** (fig.) nur einen Steinwurf weit entfernt; **be written** or **carved** or **set in** ∼ (fig.) unverrückbar sein
(b) (Brit.: weight unit) Gewicht von 6,35 kg
2 adj. steinern; Stein⟨mauer, -brücke⟩
3 v.t. mit Steinen bewerfen
stone: S∼ **Age** n. Steinzeit, die; ∼-**cold** adj. eiskalt
stoned /stəʊnd/ adj. (sl.) stoned (Drogenjargon); (drunk) voll zu (salopp)
stone: ∼-'**dead** pred. adj. mausetot (fam.); **kill sth.** ∼-**dead** (fig.) etw. völlig zunichte machen; ∼-'**deaf** adj. stocktaub (ugs.); ∼**mason** n. Steinmetz, der; ∼'**wall** (Brit.) v.i. mauern (fig.); ∼**ware** n., no pl. Steingut, das; attrib. ⟨Krug, Vase⟩ aus Steingut; ∼**washed** adj. mit Steinen ausgewaschen; ∼**work** n. Mauerwerk, das
stony /'stəʊnɪ/ adj. steinig
stood ▶ STAND 1, 2
stool /stu:l/ n. Hocker, der
stoop /stu:p/ 1 v.i. ∼ [**down**] sich bücken
2 n. **walk with a** ∼: gebeugt gehen
stop /stɒp/ 1 v.t., -**pp**-: (a) anhalten ⟨Person, Fahrzeug⟩; aufhalten ⟨Fortschritt, Verkehr, Feind⟩
(b) (not let continue) unterbrechen ⟨Redner, Spiel, Gespräch⟩; beenden ⟨Krieg, Arbeit⟩; stoppen ⟨Produktion, Uhr⟩; einstellen ⟨Zahlung, Lieferung⟩; ∼ **that!** hör damit auf!; ∼ **smoking/crying** aufhören zu rauchen/weinen
(c) (not let happen) verhindern ⟨Verbrechen, Unfall⟩; ∼ **sth. [from] happening** verhindern, dass etw. geschieht
(d) (switch off) abstellen ⟨Maschine⟩
(e) (block up) zustopfen ⟨Loch⟩; verschließen ⟨Wasserhahn, Flasche⟩
(f) ∼ **a cheque** einen Scheck sperren lassen
2 v.i., -**pp**-: (a) (not extend further) aufhören; ⟨Zahlungen, Lieferungen:⟩ eingestellt werden
(b) (not move further) ⟨Fahrzeug, Fahrer:⟩ halten; ⟨Maschine, Motor:⟩ stillstehen; ⟨Uhr, Fußgänger, Herz:⟩ stehen bleiben
3 n. (a) (halt) Halt, der; **bring to a** ∼: zum Stehen bringen ⟨Fahrzeug⟩; zum Erliegen bringen ⟨Verkehr⟩; unterbrechen ⟨Arbeit⟩; **come to a** ∼: stehen bleiben; ⟨Fahrzeug:⟩

zum Stehen kommen; ⟨Arbeit, Verkehr:⟩ zum Erliegen kommen; **put a** ∼ **to** abstellen ⟨Missstände, Unsinn⟩
(b) (place) Haltestelle, die
■ **stop 'by** v.i. (Amer.) vorbeischauen (ugs.)
■ **stop 'out** v.i. (coll.) draußen bleiben
■ **stop 'over** v.i. (coll.) übernachten (**at** bei)
■ **stop 'up** 1 v.t. zustopfen ⟨Loch, Öffnung⟩
2 v.i. (coll.) ▶ STAY UP
stop: ∼ **button** n. Stopptaste, die; ∼**cock** n. Abstellhahn, der; ∼**gap** n. Notlösung, die; ∼ **light** n. (traffic light) rotes Licht; ∼**over** n. Stopover, der
stoppage /'stɒpɪdʒ/ n. (a) (halt) Stillstand, der; (strike) Streik, der
(b) (deduction) Abzug, der
stopper /'stɒpə(r)/ n. Stöpsel, der
stopping /'stɒpɪŋ/: ∼ **distance** n. Anhalteweg, der; ∼ **place,** ∼ **point** ns. Station, die
stop: ∼**press** n. letzte Meldung/ Meldungen Pl.; ∼ **sign** n. Stoppschild, das; ∼ **signal** n. Haltesignal, das; ∼**watch** n. Stoppuhr, die
storage /'stɔ:rɪdʒ/ n. Lagerung, die; (of films, books, documents) Aufbewahrung, die; (of data, water, electricity) Speicherung, die
storage: ∼ **capacity** n. (Comp.) Speicherkapazität, die; ∼ **device** n. (Comp.) Speichermedium, das; ∼ **heater** n. [Nacht]speicherofen, der; ∼ **space** n. Lagerraum, der; (in house) Platz [zum Aufbewahren]; ∼ **tank** n. Sammelbehälter, der
store /stɔ:(r)/ 1 n. (a) (Amer.: shop) Laden, der
(b) (Brit.: large general shop) Kaufhaus, das
(c) (warehouse) Lager, das; **put sth. in** ∼: etw. einlagern
(d) (stock) Vorrat, der (**of** an + Dat.); **be** or **lie in** ∼ **for sb.** jmdn. erwarten
(e) **set [great]** ∼ **by** or **on sth.** [großen] Wert auf etw. (Akk.) legen
2 v.t. einlagern; speichern ⟨Getreide, Energie, Wissen, Daten⟩
■ **store 'up** v.t. speichern; ∼ **up provisions** sich (Dat.) Vorräte anlegen
store: ∼ **detective** n. Kaufhausdetektiv, der; ∼**house** n. Lager[haus], das; ∼**keeper** n. (Amer.: shopkeeper) Besitzer eines Einzelhandelsgeschäftes; ∼**room** n. Lagerraum, der
storey /'stɔ:rɪ/ n. Stockwerk, das
stork /stɔ:k/ n. Storch, der
storm /stɔ:m/ 1 n. Unwetter, das; (thunder∼) Gewitter, das
2 v.t. & i. stürmen
'**storm damage** n. Sturmschaden, der (meist Pl.)
'**stormy** adj. stürmisch
story[1] /'stɔ:rɪ/ n. (a) Geschichte, die
(b) (news item) Bericht, der
(c) (coll.: lie) Märchen, das
story[2] (Amer.) ▶ STOREY

S

'story book n. Geschichtenbuch, *das;* (with fairy tales) Märchenbuch, *das*

stout /staʊt/ adj. (a) (strong) fest (b) (fat) beleibt

stove /stəʊv/ n. Ofen, *der;* (for cooking) Herd, *der*

stow /stəʊ/ v.t. verstauen (**into** in + *Dat.*)

■ **stow a'way** ① v.t. verwahren
② v.i. als blinder Passagier reisen

straddle /'strædl/ v.t. ~ **a fence/chair** rittlings auf einem Zaun/Stuhl sitzen

straggle /'strægl/ v.i. ~ [**along**] **behind the others** den anderen hinterherzockeln (ugs.)

straggler /'stræglə(r)/ n. Nachzügler, *der*

straggly /'strægli/ zottig ‹Haar, Bart›

straight /streɪt/ ① adj. (a) gerade; glatt ‹Haar›; **in a** ~ **line** in gerader Linie
(b) (undiluted) **drink whisky** ~: Whisky pur trinken
(c) (direct) direkt ‹Blick, Schuss, Weg›; **be** ~ **with sb.** zu jmdm. offen sein; **get sth.** ~ (fig.) etw. genau verstehen; **put** *or* **set the record** ~: die Sache richtig stellen
② adv. (a) gerade
(b) (directly) geradewegs; ~ **after** sofort nach; **come** ~ **to the point** direkt zur Sache kommen; **look sb.** ~ **in the eye** jmdm. direkt in die Augen blicken; ~ **ahead** *or* **on** immer geradeaus
(c) (frankly) aufrichtig
(d) (clearly) klar ‹sehen, denken›

straight a'way adv. sofort

straighten /'streɪtn/ ① v.t. (a) gerade ziehen ‹Teppich›; glätten ‹Kleidung, Haare›
(b) (put in order) aufräumen
② v.i. gerade werden

■ **straighten 'out** ① v.t. (a) gerade biegen; glätten ‹Decke, Teppich›
(b) (clear up) klären
② v.i. gerade werden

■ **straighten 'up** ① v.t. ▶ TIDY UP
② v.i. sich aufrichten

straight: ~ **'face** n. **with a** ~ **face** ohne eine Miene zu verziehen; **keep a** ~ **face** keine Miene verziehen; ~**faced** adj. mit unbewegter Miene *nachgestellt;* ~**'forward** adj. (frank) freimütig; schlicht ‹Stil, Sprache, Bericht›; klar ‹Anweisung, Vorstellungen›; (b) (simple) einfach

strain /streɪn/ ① n. (a) (pull) Belastung, *die;* (on rope) Spannung, *die*
(b) (tension) Stress, *der;* **be under [a great deal of]** ~: unter großem Stress stehen
(c) (person, thing) **be a** ~ **on sb./sth.** jmdn./etw. belasten
(d) (muscular injury) Zerrung, *die*
② v.t. (a) (overexert) überanstrengen; zerren ‹Muskel›
(b) (stretch tightly) [fest] spannen
(c) (filter) durchseihen; seihen (**through** durch)
③ v.i. (strive intensely) sich anstrengen

strained /streɪnd/ adj. gezwungen ‹Lächeln›; ~ **relations** gespannte Beziehungen *Pl.*

'strainer n. Sieb, *das*

strait /streɪt/ n. (a) in sing. or pl. (Geog.) Meerenge, *die*
(b) *usu.* in pl. (distress, difficulty) Schwierigkeiten *Pl.*

strait: ~**jacket** n. Zwangsjacke, *die;* ~**-laced** /streɪt'leɪst/ adj. puritanisch

strand¹ /strænd/ n. (thread) Faden, *der;* (of beads) Kette, *die;* (of hair) Strähne, *die;* (of rope) Strang, *der*

strand² v.t. (leave behind) trockensetzen; **be [left]** ~**ed** festsitzen; (fig.) seinem Schicksal überlassen sein

strange /streɪndʒ/ adj. (peculiar) seltsam; sonderbar; ~ **to say** seltsamerweise; **feel** ~: sich komisch fühlen

strangely /'streɪndʒli/ adv. seltsam

stranger /'streɪndʒə(r)/ n. Fremde, *der/die;* **he is a** ~ **here/to the town** er ist hier/in der Stadt fremd; **be a/no** ~ **to sth.** etw. nicht gewöhnt/etw. gewöhnt sein

strangle /'stræŋgl/ v.t. erwürgen

'stranglehold n. Würgegriff, *der*

strangulation /stræŋgjʊ'leɪʃn/ n. Erwürgen, *das*

strap /stræp/ ① n. (a) (leather) Riemen, *der;* (textile) Band, *das;* (shoulder ~) Träger, *der;* (for watch) Armband, *das*
(b) (to grasp in vehicle) Halteriemen, *der*
② v.t., -pp-: ~ [**into position**]/**down** festschnallen; ~ **oneself in** sich anschnallen

'strapless adj. trägerlos

strapping /'stræpɪŋ/ adj. stramm

strata pl. of STRATUM

strategic /strə'tiːdʒɪk/ adj. strategisch

strategically /strə'tiːdʒɪkəli/ adv. strategisch

strategist /'strætɪdʒɪst/ n. Stratege, *der/* Strategin, *die*

strategy /'strætɪdʒi/ n. Strategie, *die*

stratosphere /'strætəsfɪə(r)/ n. Stratosphäre, *die*

stratum /'strɑːtəm/ n., pl. **strata** /'strɑːtə/ Schicht, *die*

straw /strɔː/ n. (a) no pl. Stroh, *das*
(b) (single stalk) Strohhalm, *der;* **that's the last** *or* **final** ~: jetzt reichts aber
(c) [drinking] ~: Strohhalm, *der*

strawberry /'strɔːbəri/ n. Erdbeere, *die*

stray /streɪ/ ① v.i. (a) (wander) streunen
(b) (deviate) abweichen (**from** von)
② n. (animal) streunendes Tier
③ adj. (a) streunend
(b) (occasional) vereinzelt

streak /striːk/ n. Streifen, *der;* (in hair) Strähne, *die;* **have a jealous/cruel** ~: zur Eifersucht/Grausamkeit neigen

'streaky adj. streifig; ~ **bacon** durchwachsener Speck

stream /striːm/ **1** *n.* (of water) Wasserlauf, *der;* (brook) Bach, *der*
2 *v.i.* strömen; ⟨Sonnenlicht:⟩ fluten; **have a** ∼ing **cold** einen schlimmen Schnupfen haben

streamer /ˈstriːmə(r)/ *n.* (ribbon) Band, *das;* (of paper) Luftschlange, *die*

'streamline *v.t.* [eine] Stromlinienform geben (+ *Dat.*); **be** ∼**lined** eine Stromlinienform haben

street /striːt/ *n.* Straße, *die;* **in the** ∼: auf der Straße; **in** (Brit.) *or* **on ... Street** in der ...straße

street: ∼**car** *n.* (Amer.) Straßenbahn, *die;* ∼ **cred** /ˈstriːt kred/ (coll.)**,** ∼ **credibility** *ns.* [glaubwürdiges] Image; ∼ **crime** *n., no indef. art.* Straßenkriminalität, *die;* ∼ **lamp** *n.* Straßenlaterne, *die;* ∼ **lighting** *n.* Straßenbeleuchtung, *die;* ∼ **map** *n.* Stadtplan, *der;* ∼ **market** *n.* Straßenmarkt, *der;* ∼ **plan** *n.* Stadtplan, *der;* ∼ **sweeper** *n.* (a) (person) Straßenfeger, *der/*-fegerin, *die* (bes. nordd.); Straßenkehrer, *der/*-kehrerin, *die* (bes. südd.); (b) (vehicle) Straßenkehrmaschine, *die;* ∼ **vendor** *n.* Straßenhändler, *der/* -händlerin, *die;* ∼**-wise** *adj.* (coll.) **be** ∼**-wise** wissen, wo es langgeht

strength /streŋθ/ *n.* (power) Kraft, *die;* (strong point, force, intensity, amount of ingredient) Stärke, *die;* (of poison, medicine) Wirksamkeit, *die;* **not know one's own** ∼: nicht wissen, wie stark man ist; **give sb.** ∼: jmdn. stärken; **go from** ∼ **to** ∼: immer erfolgreicher werden; **on the** ∼ **of sth./that** aufgrund einer Sache (*Gen.*)/dessen; **in full** ∼: in voller Stärke; **the police were there in** ∼: ein starkes Polizeiaufgebot war da

strengthen /ˈstreŋθən/ *v.t.* stärken; (reinforce, intensify) verstärken

strenuous /ˈstrenjʊəs/ *adj.* (a) (energetic) energisch; gewaltig ⟨Anstrengung⟩ (b) (requiring exertion) anstrengend

stress /stres/ **1** *n.* (a) (strain) Stress, *der;* **be under** ∼: unter Stress (*Dat.*) stehen (b) (emphasis) Betonung, *die* **2** *v.t.* (emphasize) betonen

'stressed out *adj.* (coll.) [völlig] gestresst

stressful /ˈstresfl/ *adj.* anstrengend

stress: ∼ **mark** *n.* Betonungszeichen, *das;* ∼**-related** *adj.* stressbedingt

stretch /stretʃ/ **1** *v.t.* (a) (lengthen) strecken ⟨Arm, Hand⟩; recken ⟨Hals⟩; dehnen ⟨Gummiband⟩; (tighten) spannen (b) (widen) dehnen **2** (a) *v.i.* (extend in length) sich dehnen (b) ∼ **to sth.** (be sufficient for) für etw. reichen **3** *v. refl.* sich strecken **4** *n.* (a) **have a** ∼: sich strecken (b) **at a** ∼ (fig.) wenn es sein muss (c) (expanse) Abschnitt, *der;* **a** ∼ **of road** ein Stück Straße

(d) (period) **a four-hour** ∼: eine [Zeit]spanne von vier Stunden; **at a** ∼: ohne Unterbrechung **5** *adj.* Stretch⟨hose, -gewebe⟩

stretcher /ˈstretʃə(r)/ *n.* [Trag]bahre, *die*

stretch: ∼ **marks** *n. pl.* Schwangerschaftsstreifen *Pl.;* ∼ **pants** *n. pl.* Stretchhose, *die*

stretchy /ˈstretʃɪ/ *adj.* (coll.) dehnbar

strew /struː/ *v.t., p.p.* **strewed** /struːd/ *or* **strewn** /struːn/ streuen

stricken /ˈstrɪkn/ *adj.* (afflicted) heimgesucht; havariert ⟨Schiff⟩; **be** ∼ **with** fear/grief angsterfüllt/grambeugt

strict /strɪkt/ *adj.* (a) (firm) streng; **in** ∼ **confidence** streng vertraulich (b) (precise) streng

'strictly *adv.* streng; ∼ **[speaking]** streng genommen

stride /straɪd/ **1** *n.* Schritt, *der;* **put sb. off his** ∼ (fig.) jmdn. aus dem Konzept bringen; **take sth. in one's** ∼ (fig.) mit etw. gut fertig werden **2** *v.i.,* **strode** /strəʊd/, **stridden** /ˈstrɪdn/ [mit großen Schritten] gehen

strident /ˈstraɪdənt/ *adj.* schrill

strife /straɪf/ *n.* Streit, *der*

strike /straɪk/ **1** *n.* (Industry) Streik, *der;* Ausstand, *der;* **be on/go [out]** *or* **come out on** ∼: in den Streik getreten sein/in den Streik treten **2** *v.t.,* **struck** /strʌk/ (a) (hit) schlagen; ⟨Schlag, Geschoss:⟩ treffen; ⟨Blitz:⟩ [ein]schlagen in (+ *Akk.*) (b) (delete) streichen (from, off aus) (c) (ignite) anzünden ⟨Streichholz⟩ (d) (chime) schlagen (e) (impress) beeindrucken; ∼ **sb. as [being] silly** jmdm. dumm erscheinen; **it** ∼**s sb. that** ...: es scheint jmdm., dass ... (f) (occur to) einfallen (+ *Dat.*) **3** *v.i.,* **struck** (a) (deliver a blow) zuschlagen; ⟨Blitz:⟩ einschlagen; ⟨Unheil, Katastrophe:⟩ hereinbrechen (geh.); (hit) schlagen (against gegen, [up]on auf + *Akk.*) (b) (ignite) zünden (c) (chime) schlagen (d) (Industry) streiken
■ **strike 'back** *v.i.* zurückschlagen
■ **strike 'off** *v.t.* (∼ off list) streichen ⟨Namen⟩; (from professional body) die Zulassung entziehen (+ *Dat.*)
■ **'strike through** *v.t.* durchstreichen ⟨Wort⟩; (on list also) ausstreichen
■ **'strike up** *v.t.* beginnen ⟨Unterhaltung⟩; schließen ⟨Freundschaft⟩

strike: ∼ **action** *n.* Streikaktionen *Pl.;* ∼ **pay** *n.* Streikgeld, *das*

'striker *n.* (a) (worker on strike) Streikende, *der/die* (b) (Footb.) Stürmer, der/Stürmerin, *die*

striking /ˈstraɪkɪŋ/ *adj.* auffallend; erstaunlich ⟨Ähnlichkeit⟩; schlagend ⟨Beispiel⟩

'striking distance n. Reichweite, die

string /strɪŋ/ ① n. (a) (thin cord) Schnur, die; (to tie up parcels etc. also) Bindfaden, der; **pull [a few** or **some]** ~s (fig.) seine Beziehungen spielen lassen; **with no** ~s **attached** ohne Bedingung[en]

(b) (of bow) Sehne, die; (of racket, musical instrument) Saite, die

② v.t., **strung** /strʌŋ/ (thread) auffädeln

■ **string a'long** v.t. (deceive) an der Nase herumführen (ugs.)

■ **string to'gether** v.t. auffädeln; miteinander verknüpfen ⟨Wörter⟩

■ **string 'up** v.t. aufhängen

string: ~ **bag** n. [Einkaufs]netz, das; ~ **'bean** n. (Amer.) Stangenbohne, die

stringed /strɪŋd/ attrib. adj. (Mus.) Saiten-

stringent /'strɪndʒənt/ adj. streng

string 'vest n. Netzhemd, das

strip¹ /strɪp/ ① v.t., **-pp-** ausziehen ⟨Person⟩
② v.i., **-pp-** sich ausziehen

strip² n. (narrow piece) Streifen, der

strip: ~ **cartoon** n. Comic[strip], der; ~ **club** n. Stripteaselokal, das

stripe /straɪp/ n. Streifen, der

striped /straɪpt/ adj. gestreift

strip: ~ **light** n. Neonröhre, die; ~ **lighting** n. Neonbeleuchtung, die

stripped pine /strɪpt 'paɪn/ n. abgebeizte Kiefer

stripper /'strɪpə(r)/ n. Stripper, der/ Stripperin, die (ugs.)

strip'tease n. Striptease, der

stripy /'straɪpɪ/ adj. gestreift; Streifen⟨muster⟩

strive /straɪv/ v.i., **strove** /strəʊv/, **striven** /'strɪvn/ sich bemühen; ~ **after** or **for sth.** nach etw. streben

strode ▶ STRIDE 2

stroke¹ /strəʊk/ n. (a) (act of striking) Schlag, der

(b) (Med.) Schlaganfall, der

(c) (sudden impact) ~ **of lightning** Blitzschlag, der; ~ **of [good] luck** Glücksfall, der

(d) **at a** or **one** ~: auf einen Schlag; **not do a** ~ **[of work]** keinen [Hand]schlag tun; ~ **of genius** genialer Einfall

(e) (in swimming) Zug, der

(f) (of clock) Schlag, der; **on the** ~ **of nine** Punkt neun [Uhr]

stroke² ① v.t. streicheln
② n. **give sb./sth. a** ~: jmdn./etw. streicheln

stroll /strəʊl/ ① v.i. spazieren gehen
② n. **go for a** ~: einen Spaziergang machen

strong /strɒŋ/ adj., ~**er** /'strɒŋgə(r)/, ~**est** /'strɒŋgɪst/ stark; fest ⟨Fundament, Schuhe⟩; robust ⟨Konstitution, Magen⟩; kräftig ⟨Arme, Muskeln, Tritt, Zähne⟩; leistungsfähig ⟨Wirtschaft⟩; gut, handfest ⟨Grund, Beispiel, Argument⟩; glühend ⟨Anhänger⟩; kräftig ⟨Geruch, Geschmack, Stimme⟩; **there is a**

~ **possibility that** ...: es ist sehr wahrscheinlich, dass ...; **take** ~ **measures/ action** energisch vorgehen

strong: ~**hold** n. Festung, die; (fig.) Hochburg, die; ~ **'language** n. derbe Ausdrucksweise

'strongly adv. stark; solide ⟨gearbeitet⟩; energisch ⟨protestieren, bestreiten⟩; nachdrücklich ⟨unterstützen⟩; dringend ⟨raten⟩; fest ⟨glauben⟩

strong: ~**man** n. Muskelmann, der (ugs.); ~**-'minded** adj. willensstark; ~**room** n. Tresorraum, der; ~**-'willed** adj. willensstark

stroppy /'strɒpɪ/ adj. (Brit. coll.) pampig (salopp)

strove ▶ STRIVE

struck ▶ STRIKE 2, 3

structural /'strʌktʃərl/ adj. baulich

structure /'strʌktʃə(r)/ n. (a) Struktur, die (b) (something constructed) Konstruktion, die; (building) Bauwerk, das

structured /'strʌktʃəd/ adj. strukturiert; geregelt ⟨Leben⟩

struggle /'strʌgl/ ① v.i. kämpfen; ~ **to do sth.** sich abmühen, etw. zu tun; ~ **against** or **with sb./sth.** mit jmdm./etw. od. gegen jmdn./ etw. kämpfen; ~ **with sth.** (try to cope) mit etw. kämpfen
② n. Kampf, der

strum /strʌm/ ① v.i., **-mm-** klimpern (ugs.) (**on** auf + Dat.)
② v.t., **-mm-** klimpern (ugs.) auf (+ Dat.)

strung ▶ STRING 2

strut¹ /strʌt/ ① v.i., **-tt-** stolzieren
② n. stolzierender Gang

strut² n. (support) Strebe, die

stub /stʌb/ ① n. (a) (remaining portion) Stummel, der; (of cigarette) Kippe, die
(b) (counterfoil) Abschnitt, der
② v.t., **-bb-**: (a) ~ **one's toe [against** or **on sth.]** sich (Dat.) den Zeh [an etw. (Dat.)] stoßen
(b) ausdrücken ⟨Zigarette⟩

■ **stub 'out** v.t. ausdrücken

stubble /'stʌbl/ n. Stoppeln Pl.

stubbly /'stʌblɪ/ adj. stopp[e]lig

stubborn /'stʌbən/ adj. (a) (obstinate) starrköpfig; störrisch ⟨Tier, Gesicht, Haltung⟩
(b) (resolute) hartnäckig

'stubbornness n. ▶ STUBBORN: Starrköpfigkeit, die; Hartnäckigkeit, die

stuck ▶ STICK 1, 2

'stuck up adj. (conceited) eingebildet

student /'stjuːdənt/ n. Student, der/ Studentin, die; (in school or training establishment) Schüler, der/Schülerin, die; **be a** ~ **of sth.** etw. studieren

studio /'stjuːdɪəʊ/ n., pl. ~**s (a)** (workroom) Atelier, das
(b) (Cinemat., Radio, Telev.) Studio, das

studio: ~ **apartment** (Amer.) ▶ ~ FLAT;

~ **'audience** n. (Radio, Telev.) Publikum im Studio; ~ **flat** n. (Brit.) **(a)** Atelier, das; **(b)** (one-room flat) Einzimmerwohnung, die

studious /'stjuːdɪəs/ adj. lerneifrig

study /'stʌdɪ/ 1 n. **(a)** Studium, das **(b)** (room) Arbeitszimmer, das 2 v.t. studieren; sich (Dat.) [sorgfältig] durchlesen ⟨Prüfungsfragen, Bericht⟩

'study group n. Arbeitsgruppe, die

stuff /stʌf/ 1 n. (material[s]) Zeug, das (ugs.) 2 v.t. **(a)** stopfen; zustopfen ⟨Loch, Ohren⟩; (Cookery) füllen; ~ sth. with or full of sth. etw. mit etw. voll stopfen (ugs.) **(b)** (sl.) ~ him! zum Teufel mit ihm!

stuffed 'shirt n. (coll. derog.) Spießer, der (ugs. abwertend)

'stuffing n. **(a)** (material) Füllmaterial, das **(b)** (Cookery) Füllung, die

stuffy /'stʌfɪ/ adj. stickig

stumble /'stʌmbl/ v.i. stolpern (over über + Akk.)

stumbling block /'stʌmblɪŋblɒk/ n. Stolperstein, der

stump /stʌmp/ 1 n. (of tree, branch, tooth) Stumpf, der; (of cigar, pencil) Stummel, der 2 v.t. verwirren; **be ~ed** ratlos sein

'stumpy adj. gedrungen; ~ **tail** Stummelschwanz, der

stun /stʌn/ v.t., **-nn-** (knock senseless) betäuben; **be ~ned at** or **by sth.** (fig.) von etw. wie betäubt sein

stung ▶ STING 2, 3

stunk ▶ STINK 1

stunner /'stʌnə(r)/ n. (coll.) **be a ~:** Spitze sein (ugs.)

stunning /'stʌnɪŋ/ adj. (coll.) **(a)** (splendid) hinreißend **(b)** (shocking) bestürzend ⟨Nachricht⟩; (amazing) sensationell

stunt¹ /stʌnt/ v.t. hemmen

stunt² n. halsbrecherisches Kunststück; (Cinemat.) Stunt, der

'stunt man n. Stuntman, der

stupefying /'stjuːpɪfaɪɪŋ/ adj. die Sinne betäubend ⟨Hitze⟩; (fig.: astonishing) unfassbar

stupendous /stjuːˈpendəs/ adj. gewaltig

stupid /'stjuːpɪd/ adj. dumm; (ridiculous) lächerlich; **it would be ~ to do sth.** es wäre töricht, etw. zu tun

stupidity /stjuːˈpɪdɪtɪ/ n. Dummheit, die

'stupidly adv. dumm

stupor /'stjuːpə(r)/ n. Benommenheit, die; **in a drunken ~:** sinnlos betrunken

sturdy /'stɜːdɪ/ adj. kräftig; stämmig ⟨Beine, Arme⟩

stutter /'stʌtə(r)/ 1 v.i. stottern 2 n. Stottern, das

sty¹ /staɪ/ ▶ PIGSTY

sty², stye /staɪ/ n. (Med.) Gerstenkorn, das

style /staɪl/ n. Stil, der; [hair]~: Frisur, die; **dress in the latest ~:** sich nach der neuesten Mode kleiden

styli pl. of STYLUS

stylish /'staɪlɪʃ/ adj. stilvoll; elegant ⟨Kleidung, Auto, Person⟩

stylist /'staɪlɪst/ n. (hair~) Haarstilist, der/ -stilistin, die

stylus /'staɪləs/ n., pl. **styli** /'staɪlaɪ/ or ~**es** [Abtast]nadel, die

suave /swɑːv/ adj. gewandt

sub- /sʌb/ pref. unter-; sub-

sub'conscious 1 adj. unterbewusst 2 n. Unterbewusstsein, das

sub'continent n. Subkontinent, der

'subcontract v.t. an einen Subunternehmer vergeben

subcon'tractor n. Subunternehmer, der/ -unternehmerin, die

'subculture n. Subkultur, die

subdivide /'---, --'-/ v.t. unterteilen

subdue /səbˈdjuː/ v.t. bändigen ⟨Kind, Tier⟩; dämpfen ⟨Zorn, Lärm, Licht⟩

subdued /səbˈdjuːd/ adj. gedämpft

'subgroup n. Untergruppe, die

'subheading n. Untertitel, der

sub'human adj. unmenschlich

subject 1 /'sʌbdʒɪkt/ n. **(a)** Staatsbürger, der/-bürgerin, die; (to monarch) Untertan, der/ Untertanin, die **(b)** (topic) Thema, das; (of study) Fach, das; **change the ~:** das Thema wechseln 2 /'sʌbdʒɪkt/ adj. **be ~ to sth.** von etw. abhängen 3 /səbˈdʒekt/ v.t. unterwerfen (to Dat.); (expose) ~ **sb./sth. to sth.** jmdn./etw. einer Sache (Dat.) aussetzen

subjective /səbˈdʒektɪv/ adj., **sub'jectively** adv. subjektiv

'subject matter n., no indef. art. Gegenstand, der

subjugate /'sʌbdʒʊgeɪt/ v.t. unterjochen (to unter + Akk.)

subjugation /sʌbdʒʊˈgeɪʃn/ n. Unterjochung, die

subjunctive /səbˈdʒʌŋktɪv/ n. Konjunktiv, der

sub'let v.t., **-tt-,** sublet untervermieten

sublime /səˈblaɪm/ adj. erhaben

submarine /sʌbməˈriːn/ n. Unterseeboot, das; U-Boot, das

submerge /səbˈmɜːdʒ/ v.t. **(a)** ~ **sth.** [in the water] etw. eintauchen **(b)** (flood) ⟨Wasser:⟩ überschwemmen; **be ~d** in water unter Wasser stehen

submerged /səbˈmɜːdʒd/ adj. versunken

submission /səbˈmɪʃn/ n. **(a)** (surrender, meekness) Unterwerfung, die **(b)** (presentation) Einreichung, die (to bei)

submissive /səbˈmɪsɪv/ adj. gehorsam

submit /səbˈmɪt/ v.t., **-tt-** (present) einreichen; vorbringen ⟨Vorschlag⟩; ~ **sth. to sb.** jmdm. etw. vorlegen

S

subordinate 1 /sə'bɔːdɪnət/ *adj.*
untergeordnet
2 /sə'bɔːdɪnət/ *n.* Untergebene, *der*/*die*
3 /sə'bɔːdɪneɪt/ *v.t.* unterordnen (**to** *Dat.*)

subscribe /səb'skraɪb/ *v.i.* (a) (support) ∼ **to**
sth. sich einer Sache anschließen
(b) (make contribution) ∼ **to** sth. eine Spende
für etw. zusichern
(c) ∼ **to a newspaper** eine Zeitung
abonnieren

sub'scriber *n.* (to newspaper etc.) Abonnent,
der/Abonnentin, *die* (**to** *Gen.*)

subscription /səb'skrɪpʃn/ *n.* (membership
fee) Mitgliedsbeitrag, *der* (**to** für); (to
newspaper etc.) Abonnement, *das*

subsequent /'sʌbsɪkwənt/ *adj.* folgend;
später ⟨*Gelegenheit*⟩

'subsequently *adv.* später; danach

subservient /səb'sɜːvɪənt/ *adj.*
untergeordnet (**to** *Dat.*); (servile) unterwürfig

subside /səb'saɪd/ *v.i.* (a) (sink lower) ⟨*Flut,
Fluss:*⟩ sinken; ⟨*Boden, Haus:*⟩ sich senken
(b) (abate) nachlassen

subsidence /səb'saɪdəns/ *n.* (of ground,
structure) Senkung, *die*

subsidiary /səb'sɪdɪərɪ/ 1 *adj.*
untergeordnet ⟨*Funktion, Stellung*⟩;
Neben⟨*fach, -aspekt*⟩
2 *n.* (Commerc.) Tochtergesellschaft, *die*

subsidize /'sʌbsɪdaɪz/ *v.t.* subventionieren

subsidy /'sʌbsɪdɪ/ *n.* Subvention, *die*

subsist /səb'sɪst/ *v.i.* ∼ **on sth.** von etw.
leben

subsistence /səb'sɪstəns/ *n.* [Über]leben,
das

'subsoil *n.* Untergrund, *der*

substance /'sʌbstəns/ *n.* (a) Stoff, *der*
(b) (solidity) Substanz, *die*
(c) (content) Inhalt, *der*

'substance abuse *n.* Drogen- und
Genussmittelmissbrauch, *der*

sub'standard *adj.* unzulänglich

substantial /səb'stænʃl/ *adj.* (a)
(considerable) beträchtlich
(b) gehaltvoll ⟨*Essen*⟩
(c) (solid) solide ⟨*Möbel, Haus*⟩; wesentlich
⟨*Unterschied*⟩

sub'stantially *adv.* (a) (considerably)
wesentlich
(b) (solidly) solide
(c) (essentially) im Wesentlichen

substitute /'sʌbstɪtjuːt/ 1 *n.* (a) ∼[s *pl.*]
Ersatz, *der*
(b) (Sport) Ersatzspieler, *der*/-spielerin, *die*
2 *v.t.* ∼ **A for B** B durch A ersetzen

substitution /sʌbstɪ'tjuːʃn/ *n.* Ersetzung,
die; **make a** ∼ (Sport) [einen Spieler]
auswechseln

subterfuge /'sʌbtəfjuːdʒ/ *n.*
Täuschungsmanöver *Pl.*

'subtitle *n.* Untertitel, *der*

subtle /'sʌtl/ *adj.* subtil (geh.); zart ⟨*Duft,
Parfüm, Hinweis*⟩; fein ⟨*Geschmack,
Unterschied, Humor*⟩

'subtotal *n.* Zwischensumme, *die*

subtract /səb'trækt/ *v.t.* abziehen

subtraction /səb'trækʃn/ *n.* Subtraktion,
die

sub'tropical *adj.* subtropisch

suburb /'sʌbɜːb/ *n.* Vorort, *der*

suburban /sə'bɜːbən/ *adj.* Vorort-; ⟨*Leben,
Haus*⟩ am Stadtrand

suburbia /sə'bɜːbɪə/ *n.* (derog.) die
[eintönigen] Vororte *Pl.*

subversive /səb'vɜːsɪv/ *adj.* subversiv

'subway *n.* (a) (passage) Unterführung, *die*
(b) (Amer.: railway) Untergrundbahn, *die;*
U-Bahn, *die*

sub-'zero *adj.* ∼ **temperatures/conditions**
Temperaturen unter Null

succeed /sək'siːd/ 1 *v.i.* (a) Erfolg haben;
sb. ∼s in sth. jmdm. gelingt etw.; jmd.
schafft etw.; **sb. ∼s in doing sth.** es gelingt
jmdm., etw. zu tun; jmd. schafft es, etw. zu
tun; ∼ **in business/college** geschäftlich/im
Studium erfolgreich sein; **I did not** ∼ **in
doing it** ich habe es nicht geschafft
(b) (come next) die Nachfolge antreten
2 *v.t.* (take place of) ablösen

success /sək'ses/ *n.* Erfolg, *der;* **make a**
∼ **of sth.** bei etw. Erfolg haben

successful /sək'sesfl/ *adj.* erfolgreich; **be**
∼ **in** sth./**doing sth.** Erfolg bei etw. haben/
dabei haben, etw. zu tun

suc'cessfully *adv.* erfolgreich

succession /sək'seʃn/ *n.* (a) Folge, *die;* **in**
∼: hintereinander
(b) (series) Serie, *die*
(c) (to throne) Erbfolge, *die*

successive /sək'sesɪv/ *adj.* aufeinander
folgend

suc'cessively *adv.* hintereinander

successor /sək'sesə(r)/ *n.* Nachfolger, *der*/
Nachfolgerin, *die*

suc'cess story *n.* Erfolgsstory, *die* (ugs.)

succinct /sək'sɪŋkt/ *adj.* (a) (terse) knapp
(b) (clear) prägnant

succulent /'sʌkjʊlənt/ *adj.* saftig

succumb /sə'kʌm/ *v.i.* unterliegen; ∼ **to**
sth. einer Sache (*Dat.*) erliegen

such /sʌtʃ/ 1 *adj.* (a) (of that kind) solch...;
∼ **a person** ein solcher Mensch; ∼ **a book**
ein solches Buch; ∼ **people** solche Leute;
∼ **things** so etwas; **I said no** ∼ **thing** ich
habe nichts dergleichen gesagt; **there is no**
∼ **bird** einen solchen Vogel gibt es nicht; **or
some** ∼ **thing** oder so etwas; **you'll do no**
∼ **thing** das wirst du nicht tun; **experiences**
∼ **as these** solche Erfahrungen
(b) (so great) solch...; derartig; **I got** ∼ **a fright
that ...:** ich bekam einen derartigen *od.* (ugs.)
so einen Schrecken, dass ...; ∼ **was the force
of the explosion that ...:** die Explosion war
so stark, dass ...; **to** ∼ **an extent** dermaßen

(c) *with adj.* so; ~ **a big house** ein so großes
Haus; ~ **a long time** so lange
② *pron.* **as ~:** als solcher/solche/solches;
(strictly speaking) im Grunde genommen; an
sich; ~ **as** wie [zum Beispiel]; ~ **is life** so ist
das Leben
such-and-such /ˈsʌtʃənsʌtʃ/ *adj.* **at ~ a
time** um die und die Zeit
'suchlike *pron.* derlei
suck /sʌk/ **①** *v.t.* saugen (**out of** aus);
lutschen ⟨Bonbon⟩
② *sth.* ~**s** (esp. Amer. sl.) etw. ist Scheiße
(derb)
▪ **suck 'up** **①** *v.t.* aufsaugen
② *v.i.* ~ **up to sb.** (coll.) jmdm. in den
Hintern kriechen (salopp)
'sucker *n.* **(a)** (suction pad) Saugfuß, *der;*
(Zool.) Saugnapf, *der*
(b) (coll.: dupe) Dumme, *der/die*
suckle /ˈsʌkl/ *v.t.* säugen
suction /ˈsʌkʃn/ *n.* Saugwirkung, *die*
Sudan /suːˈdɑːn/ *pr. n.* [**the**] ~: [der] Sudan
sudden /ˈsʌdn/ **①** *adj.* **(a)** (unexpected)
plötzlich
(b) (abrupt) jäh ⟨Abgrund, Übergang, Ruck⟩;
there was a ~ bend in the road plötzlich
machte die Straße eine Biegung
② *n.* **all of a ~:** plötzlich
'suddenly *adv.* plötzlich
'suddenness *n.* Plötzlichkeit, *die*
suds /sʌdz/ *n. pl.* [**soap**]~: [Seifen]lauge,
die; (froth) Schaum, *der*
sue /suː/ **①** *v.t.* verklagen (**for** auf + *Akk.*)
② *v.i.* klagen (**for** auf + *Akk.*)
suede /sweɪd/ *n.* Wildleder, *das*
suet /ˈsuːɪt/ *n.* Talg, *der*
Suez /ˈsuːɪz, ˈsjuːɪz/ *pr. n.* Suez (*das*);
~ **Canal** Suez-Kanal, *der*
suffer /ˈsʌfə(r)/ **①** *v.t.* erleiden;
durchmachen ⟨Schweres, Kummer⟩; dulden
⟨Unverschämtheit⟩
② *v.i.* leiden
▪ **'suffer from** *v.t.* leiden unter (+ *Dat.*);
leiden an (+ *Dat.*) ⟨Krankheit⟩
sufferance /ˈsʌfərəns/ *n.* Duldung, *die;* **he
remains here on ~ only** er ist hier bloß
geduldet
'suffering *n.* Leiden, *das*
suffice /səˈfaɪs/ **①** *v.i.* genügen; ~ **it to say
...:** nur so viel sei gesagt: ...
② *v.t.* genügen + *Dat.*)
sufficiency /səˈfɪʃənsɪ/ *n.* Zulänglichkeit,
die
sufficient /səˈfɪʃənt/ *adj.* genug; ~ **money/
food** genug Geld/genug zu essen; **be ~:**
genügen; ~ **reason** Grund genug; **have you
had ~?** (food, drink) haben Sie schon genug?
sufficiently *adv.* genug; (adequately)
ausreichend; ~ **large** groß genug; **a ~ large
number** eine genügend große Zahl
suffix /ˈsʌfɪks/ *n.* Nachsilbe, *die*

suffocate /ˈsʌfəkeɪt/ **①** *v.t.* ersticken; **he
was ~d by the smoke** der Rauch erstickte
ihn
② *v.i.* ersticken
suffocation /sʌfəˈkeɪʃn/ *n.* Erstickung,
die; **a feeling of ~:** das Gefühl, zu ersticken
sugar /ˈʃʊɡə(r)/ **①** *n.* Zucker, *der;* **two ~s,
please** (lumps) zwei Stück Zucker, bitte;
(spoonfuls) zwei Löffel Zucker, bitte
② *v.t.* zuckern
sugar: ~ **basin** ▶ ~ BOWL; ~ **beet** *n.*
Zuckerrübe, *die;* ~ **bowl** *n.* Zuckerschale,
die; (covered) Zuckerdose, *die;* ~ **cane** *n.*
Zuckerrohr, *das;* ~**-coated** *adj.* gezuckert;
mit Zucker überzogen ⟨Dragee usw.⟩;
~ **daddy** *n.* (coll.) spendabler älterer Mann,
der ein junges Mädchen aushält; ~ **lump** *n.*
Zuckerstück, *das;* (when counted) Stück
Zucker; ~ **tongs** *n. pl.* Zuckerzange, *die*
'sugary *adj.* süß; (fig.) süßlich
suggest /səˈdʒest/ *v.t.* **(a)** (propose)
vorschlagen; ~ **sth. to sb.** jmdm. etw.
vorschlagen; **he ~ed going to the cinema** er
schlug vor, ins Kino zu gehen
(b) (assert) **are you trying to ~ that he is
lying** wollen Sie damit sagen, dass er lügt?
(c) (make one think of) suggerieren;
⟨Symptome, Tatsachen:⟩ schließen lassen auf
(+ *Akk.*)
suggestion /səˈdʒestʃn/ *n.* **(a)** Vorschlag,
der; **at** or **on sb.'s ~:** auf jmds. Vorschlag
(*Akk.*)
(b) (insinuation) Andeutungen *Pl.*
(c) (fig.: trace) Spur, *die*
suggestive /səˈdʒestɪv/ *adj.* **(a)** **be ~ of
sth.** auf etw. (*Akk.*) schließen lassen
(b) (indecent) anzüglich
suicidal /suːɪˈsaɪdl/ *adj.* selbstmörderisch; **I
felt** or **was quite ~:** ich hätte mich am
liebsten gleich umgebracht
suicide /ˈsuːɪsaɪd/ *n.* Selbstmord, *der*
'suicide attempt *n.* Selbstmordversuch,
der
suit /suːt/ **①** *n.* **(a)** (for men) Anzug, *der;* (for
women) Kostüm, *das*
(b) (Law) ~ [**at law**] Prozess, *der*
(c) (Cards) Farbe, *die;* **follow ~** (fig.) das
Gleiche tun
② *v.t.* **(a)** anpassen (**to** *Dat.*)
(b) **be ~ed** [**to sth./one another**] [zu etw./
zueinander] passen
(c) (satisfy needs of) passen (+ *Dat.*); **will
Monday ~ you?** passt Ihnen Montag?; **does
the climate ~ you?** bekommt Ihnen das
Klima?
(d) (go well with) passen zu; **does this hat
~ me?** steht mir dieser Hut?; **black ~s her**
Schwarz steht ihr gut
③ *v. refl.* ~ **oneself** tun, was man will;
~ **yourself!** [ganz] wie du willst!
suitability /suːtəˈbɪlɪtɪ/ *n.* Eignung, *die* (**for**
für)
suitable /ˈsuːtəbl/ *adj.* geeignet;
angemessen ⟨Kleidung⟩; (convenient) passend; ⋯⋗

~ **for children** für Kinder geeignet; **Monday is the most ~ day [for me]** Montag passt [mir] am besten

suitably /'su:təblɪ/ adv. angemessen; entsprechend ⟨gekleidet⟩

'**suitcase** n. Koffer, der

suite /swiːt/ n. (a) (of furniture) Garnitur, die; **three-piece ~:** Polstergarnitur, die (b) (of rooms) Suite, die

suitor /'suːtə(r)/ n. Freier, der

sulfur, sulfuric (Amer.) ▶ SULPH-

sulk /sʌlk/ v.i. schmollen

'**sulky** adj. schmollend; eingeschnappt (ugs.)

sullen /'sʌlən/ adj. mürrisch

sulphur /'sʌlfə(r)/ n. Schwefel, der

sulphuric /sʌl'fjʊərɪk/ adj. ~ **acid** Schwefelsäure, die

sultan /'sʌltən/ n. Sultan, der

sultana /sʌl'tɑːnə/ n. Sultanine, die

sultry /'sʌltrɪ/ adj. schwül

sum /sʌm/ n. (a) Summe, die (of aus); ~ **[total]** Ergebnis, das (b) (Arithmetic) Rechenaufgabe, die; **do ~s** rechnen; **she is good at ~s** sie kann gut rechnen

■ **sum 'up** ① v.t. (a) zusammenfassen (b) (Brit.: assess) einschätzen ② v.i. ein Fazit ziehen

summarily /'sʌmərɪlɪ/ adv. summarisch; ~ **dismissed** fristlos entlassen

summarize /'sʌməraɪz/ v.t. zusammenfassen

summary /'sʌmərɪ/ ① adj. summarisch; fristlos ⟨Entlassung⟩ ② n. Zusammenfassung, die

summer /'sʌmə(r)/ n. Sommer, der; **in [the] ~:** im Sommer

summer: ~ **house** n. [Garten]laube, die; ~ **school** n. Sommerkurs, der; ~ **term** n. Sommerhalbjahr, das; ~**time** n. Sommer, der

'**summery** adj. sommerlich

summing 'up n. Zusammenfassung, die

summit /'sʌmɪt/ n. Gipfel, der; ~ **conference/meeting** Gipfelkonferenz, die/ -treffen, das

summon /'sʌmən/ v.t. (a) rufen (**to** zu); holen ⟨Hilfe⟩ (b) (Law) vorladen

■ **summon 'up** v.t. aufbringen

summons /'sʌmənz/ n. Vorladung, die

sump /sʌmp/ n. Ölwanne, die

sumptuous /'sʌmptjʊəs/ adj. üppig; luxuriös ⟨Möbel, Kleidung⟩

sun /sʌn/ ① n. Sonne, die; **catch the ~** (be in sunny position) viel Sonne abbekommen; (get ~burnt) einen Sonnenbrand bekommen ② v. refl., **-nn-** sich sonnen

Sun. abbr. = **Sunday** So.

sun: ~**baked** adj. an der Sonne getrocknet ⟨Ziegel⟩; ausgedörrt ⟨Landschaft, Prärie usw.⟩; ~**bathe** v.i. sonnenbaden;

~**bathing** n. Sonnenbaden, das; ~**beam** n. Sonnenstrahl, der; ~**bed** n. (with UV lamp) Sonnenbank, die; (in garden) Gartenliege, die; ~**block** n. Sonnenschutzcreme, die [mit hohem Lichtschutzfaktor]; ~**burn** n. Sonnenbrand, der; ~**burnt** adj. be/get ~burnt einen Sonnenbrand haben/ bekommen; ~**cream** n. Sonnencreme, die

sundae /'sʌndeɪ/ n. **[ice cream] ~:** Eisbecher, der

Sunday /'sʌndeɪ, 'sʌndɪ/ n. Sonntag, der; ~ **opening** die sonntägliche Öffnung; ~ **trading** sonntägliche Ladenöffnung; see also FRIDAY

sun: ~**deck** n. Sonnendeck, das; ~**dial** n. Sonnenuhr, die; ~**-dried** adj. an der Sonne getrocknet

sundry /'sʌndrɪ/ ① adj. verschieden ② n. in pl. Verschiedenes

'**sunflower** n. Sonnenblume, die

sung ▶ SING

sun: ~**glasses** n. pl. Sonnenbrille, die; ~**hat** n. Sonnenhut, der

sunk ▶ SINK 2, 3

sun: ~**lamp** n. Höhensonne, die; ~**lit** adj. sonnenbeschienen; ~**light** n. Sonnenlicht, das

Sunni /'sʌnɪ/ n. (Muslim Relig.) Sunnit, der/Sunnitin, die; attrib. sunnitisch

sunny /'sʌnɪ/ adj. sonnig; ~ **intervals** Aufheiterungen

sun: ~ **protection factor** n. Lichtschutzfaktor, der; ~**ray** n. Sonnenstrahl, der; ~**rise** n. Sonnenaufgang, der; ~**roof** n. (Motor Veh.) Schiebedach, das; ~**set** n. Sonnenuntergang, der; ~**shade** n. Sonnenschirm, der; ~**shine** n. Sonnenschein, der; ~**stroke** n. Sonnenstich, der; ~**tan** n. [Sonnen]bräune, die; get a ~tan braun werden; ~**tan lotion** n. Sonnencreme, die; ~**tanned** adj. braun [gebrannt]; ~**tan oil** n. Sonnenöl, das; ~**trap** n. sonniges Plätzchen; ~ **worshipper** n. (lit./joc.) Sonnenanbeter, der/-anbeterin, die

super /'suːpə(r)/ adj. (coll.) super (ugs.)

superb /suː'pɜːb/ adj. einzigartig; erstklassig ⟨Essen⟩

superbug /'suːpəbʌg/ n. multiresistenter Erreger

supercilious /suːpə'sɪlɪəs/ adj. hochnäsig

supercomputer /'suːpəkəmpjuːtə(r)/ n. Supercomputer, der

superficial /suːpə'fɪʃl/ adj. oberflächlich

superficiality /suːpəfɪʃɪ'ælɪtɪ/ n. Oberflächlichkeit, die

superfluous /suː'pɜːfluəs/ adj. überflüssig

super: ~**glue** n. Sekundenkleber, der; ~**human** adj. übermenschlich; ~**highway** n. (a) (Amer.) Autobahn, die; (b) (Comp.) Datenautobahn, die

superintendent /suːpərɪn'tendənt/ n. (Brit. Police) Kommissar, der/Kommissarin, die

superior /suːˈpɪərɪə(r)/ **1** adj. (a) (of higher quality) besonders gut ⟨Restaurant, Qualität, Stoff⟩; überlegen ⟨Technik, Intelligenz⟩; **he thinks he is ~ to us** er hält sich für besser als wir
(b) (having higher rank) höher…; **be ~ to sb.** einen höheren Rang als jmd. haben
2 n. Vorgesetzte, der/die
superiority /suːpɪərɪˈɒrɪtɪ/ n. Überlegenheit, die (to über + Akk.)
superlative /suːˈpɜːlətɪv/ **1** adj. (a) unübertrefflich
(b) (Ling.) **a ~ adjective/adverb** ein Adjektiv/ Adverb im Superlativ
2 n. (Ling.) Superlativ, der
super: **~market** n. Supermarkt, der; **~model** n. Supermodel, das; **~natural** adj. übernatürlich; **~power** n. (Polit.) Supermacht, die
supersede /suːpəˈsiːd/ v.t. ablösen (by durch)
supersonic /suːpəˈsɒnɪk/ adj. Überschall-
superstar /ˈsuːpəstɑː(r)/ n. Superstar, der
superstition /suːpəˈstɪʃn/ n. Aberglaube, der
superstitious /suːpəˈstɪʃəs/ adj. abergläubisch
superstore /ˈsuːpəstɔː(r)/ n. Großmarkt, der
supervise /ˈsuːpəvaɪz/ v.t. beaufsichtigen
supervision /suːpəˈvɪʒn/ n. Aufsicht, die
supervisor /ˈsuːpəvaɪzə(r)/ n. Aufseher, der/Aufseherin, die
supper /ˈsʌpə(r)/ n. Abendessen, das; **have [one's] ~:** zu Abend essen
'suppertime n. Abendbrotzeit, die; **it's ~:** es ist Zeit zum Abendessen
supplant /səˈplɑːnt/ v.t. ablösen, ersetzen (by durch)
supple /ˈsʌpl/ adj. geschmeidig
supplement /ˈsʌplɪmənt/ **1** n. (a) Ergänzung, die (to + Gen.); (addition) Zusatz, der
(b) (of book) Nachtrag, der; (of newspaper) Beilage, die
(c) (to fare) Zuschlag, der
2 v.t. ergänzen
supplementary /sʌplɪˈmentərɪ/ adj. zusätzlich; **~ fare/charge** Zuschlag, der
supplier /səˈplaɪə(r)/ n. (Commerc.) Lieferant, der/Lieferantin, die
supply /səˈplaɪ/ **1** v.t. liefern ⟨Waren usw.⟩; beliefern ⟨Kunden, Geschäft⟩; **~ sth. to sb., ~ sb. with sth.** jmdn. mit etw. versorgen/ (Commerc.) beliefern
2 n. Vorräte Pl.; **military/medical supplies** militärischer/medizinischer Nachschub; **~ and demand** (Econ.) Angebot und Nachfrage
sup'ply teacher n. Vertretung, die
support /səˈpɔːt/ **1** v.t. (a) (hold up) stützen ⟨Mauer, Verletzten⟩; (bear weight of) tragen

(b) unterstützen ⟨Politik, Verein⟩; (Footb.) **~ Spurs** Spurs-Fan sein
(c) (provide for) ernähren ⟨Familie, sich selbst⟩
(d) (speak in favour of) befürworten
2 n. (a) Unterstützung, die; **in ~:** zur Unterstützung; **speak in ~ of sb./sth.** jmdn. unterstützen/etw. befürworten
(b) (money) Unterhalt, der
(c) (sb./sth. that ~s) Stütze, die
sup'porter n. Anhänger, der/Anhängerin, die; **football ~:** Fußballfan, der
sup'porting adj. (Cinemat., Theatre) **~ role** Nebenrolle, die; **~ actor/actress** Schauspieler/-spielerin in einer Nebenrolle; **~ film** Vorfilm, der
supportive /səˈpɔːtɪv/ adj. hilfreich; **be very ~ [to sb.]** [jmdm.] eine große Hilfe od. Stütze sein
suppose /səˈpəʊz/ v.t. (a) (assume) annehmen; **~ or supposing [that] he …:** angenommen, [dass] er …
(b) (presume) vermuten; **I ~ so** (doubtfully) ja, vermutlich; (more confidently) ich glaube schon
(c) **be ~d to do/be sth.** (be generally believed to do/be sth.) etw. tun/sein sollen
(d) (allow) **you are not ~d to do that** das darfst du eigentlich nicht; **I'm not ~d to be here** ich dürfte eigentlich gar nicht hier sein
supposed /səˈpəʊzd/ attrib. adj. mutmaßlich
supposedly /səˈpəʊzɪdlɪ/ adv. angeblich
supposition /sʌpəˈzɪʃn/ n. Annahme, die; Vermutung, die
suppress /səˈpres/ v.t. unterdrücken
suppression /səˈpreʃn/ n. Unterdrückung, die
supremacy /suːˈpreməsɪ/ n. (a) (supreme authority) Souveränität, die
(b) (superiority) Überlegenheit, die
supreme /suːˈpriːm/ adj. höchst…
Supt. abbr. = **Superintendent**
surcharge /ˈsɜːtʃɑːdʒ/ n. Zuschlag, der
sure /ʃʊə(r)/ **1** adj. sicher; **be ~ of sth.** sich (Dat.) einer Sache (Gen.) sicher sein; **~ of oneself** selbstsicher; **don't be too ~:** da wäre ich mir nicht so sicher; **there is ~ to be a petrol station** es gibt bestimmt eine Tankstelle; **don't worry, it's ~ to turn out well** keine Sorge, es wird schon alles gut gehen; **for ~** (coll.) auf jeden Fall; **make ~ [of sth.]** sich [einer Sache] vergewissern; **make or be ~ you do it, be ~ to do it** (do not fail to do it) sieh zu, dass du es tust; (do not forget) vergiss nicht, es zu tun; **a ~ winner** ein todsicherer Tipp (ugs.)
2 adv. **~ enough** tatsächlich
3 int. **~!, ~ thing!** (Amer.) na klar! (ugs.)
sure: **~-fire** attrib. adj. (Amer. coll.) todsicher; **~-footed** adj. trittsicher
'surely **1** adv. (a) as sentence-modifier doch; **~ we've met before?** wir kennen uns doch, oder?

···⧽

(b) (steadily) sicher; **slowly but** ∼: langsam, aber sicher
(c) (certainly) sicherlich
2 *int.* (Amer.) natürlich

surf /sɜːf/ *n.* 1 Brandung, *die*
2 *v.i.* (a) surfen
(b) (Comp.) surfen; (TV) zappen (ugs.)
3 *v.t.* (Comp., TV) ∼ **the Internet** im Internet surfen; ∼ **the channels** sich durch die Kanäle zappen (ugs.)

surface /'sɜːfɪs/ 1 *n.* Oberfläche, *die;* **outer** ∼: Außenfläche, *die;* **the earth's** ∼: die Erdoberfläche; **on the** ∼: an der Oberfläche; (fig.) oberflächlich betrachtet
2 *v.i.* auftauchen; (fig.) hochkommen

surface: ∼ **area** *n.* Oberfläche, *die;* ∼ **mail** *n.* gewöhnliche Post

'surfboard *n.* Surfbrett, *das*

surfeit /'sɜːfɪt/ *n.* Übermaß, *das*

'surfer *n.* Surfer, *der*/Surferin, *die*

'surfing *n.* Surfen, *das*

surge /sɜːdʒ/ *v.i.* ⟨Wellen:⟩ branden; **the crowd** ∼**d forward** die Menschenmenge drängte nach vorn

surgeon /'sɜːdʒən/ *n.* Chirurg, *der*/Chirurgin, *die*

surgery /'sɜːdʒərɪ/ *n.* (a) Chirurgie, *die;* **undergo** ∼: sich einer Operation (*Dat.*) unterziehen
(b) (Brit.: place) Praxis, *die;* **doctor's/dental** ∼: Arzt-/Zahnarztpraxis, *die*
(c) (Brit.: time) Sprechstunde, *die*

surgical /'sɜːdʒɪkl/ *adj.* chirurgisch; ∼ **treatment** Operation, *die*/Operationen *Pl.*

surly /'sɜːlɪ/ *adj.* mürrisch

surmise /sə'maɪz/ 1 *n.* Vermutung, *die*
2 *v.t.* mutmaßen

surmount /sə'maʊnt/ *v.t.* überwinden

surmountable /sə'maʊntəbl/ *adj.* überwindbar

surname /'sɜːneɪm/ *n.* Nachname, *der;* Zuname, *der*

surpass /sə'pɑːs/ *v.t.* übertreffen; ∼ **oneself** sich selbst übertreffen

surplus /'sɜːpləs/ 1 *n.* Überschuss, *der* (**of** an + *Dat.*)
2 *adj.* überschüssig; **be** ∼ **to sb.'s requirements** von jmdm. nicht benötigt werden

surprise /sə'praɪz/ 1 *n.* (a) Überraschung, *die;* **take sb. by** ∼: jmdn. überrumpeln; **to my great** ∼, **much to my** ∼: zu meiner großen Überraschung; **it came as a** ∼ **to us** es war für uns eine Überraschung
(b) *attrib.* überraschend, unerwartet ⟨Besuch⟩; **a** ∼ **attack** ein Überraschungsangriff
2 *v.t.* überraschen; überrumpeln ⟨Feind⟩; **I shouldn't be** ∼**d if ...:** es würde mich nicht wundern, wenn ...; **be** ∼**d at sb./sth.** sich über jmdn./etw. wundern

surprising /sə'praɪzɪŋ/ *adj.* überraschend

surprisingly *adv.* überraschend; ∼ **[enough], he was ...:** überraschenderweise war er ...

surreal /sə'rɪəl/ *adj.* surrealistisch

surrealism /sə'rɪəlɪzm/ *n.* Surrealismus, *der*

surrender /sə'rendə(r)/ 1 *n.* (to enemy) Kapitulation, *die;* (of possession) Aufgabe, *die*
2 *v.i.* kapitulieren
3 *v.t.* aufgeben

surreptitious /sʌrəp'tɪʃəs/ *adj.* heimlich; verstohlen ⟨Blick⟩

surrogate /'sʌrəgət/ *n.* Ersatz, *der*

surrogate 'mother *n.* Leihmutter, *die*

surround /sə'raʊnd/ *v.t.* (a) (come or be all round) umringen; ⟨Truppen, Heer:⟩ umzingeln ⟨Stadt, Feind⟩
(b) (encircle) umgeben; **be** ∼**ed by** *or* **with sth.** von etw. umgeben sein

sur'rounding *adj.* umliegend; **the** ∼ **countryside** die [Landschaft in der] Umgebung

sur'roundings *n. pl.* Umgebung, *die*

surveillance /sə'veɪləns/ *n.* Überwachung, *die;* **be under** ∼: überwacht werden

survey 1 /sə'veɪ/ *v.t.* betrachten; überblicken ⟨Landschaft⟩; inspizieren ⟨Gebäude⟩; bewerten ⟨Situation⟩
2 /'sɜːveɪ/ *n.* Überblick, *der* (**of** über + *Akk.*); (poll) Umfrage, *die;* (Surv.) Vermessung, *die*

surveyor /sə'veɪə(r)/ *n.* (of building) Gutachter, *der*/Gutachterin, *die;* (of land) Landvermesser, *der*/-vermesserin, *die*

survival /sə'vaɪvl/ *n.* Überleben, *das;* **fight for** ∼: Existenzkampf, *der*

sur'vival kit *n.* Notausrüstung, *die*

survive /sə'vaɪv/ 1 *v.t.* überleben
2 *v.i.* ⟨Person:⟩ überleben; ⟨Schriften, Traditionen:⟩ erhalten bleiben

survivor /sə'vaɪvə(r)/ *n.* Überlebende, *der/die*

sus /sʌs/ (Brit. coll.) *v.t.,* **-ss-** spitzkriegen (ugs.); **get sb.** ∼**sed** jmdn. durchschauen
■ **sus 'out** *v.t.* (coll.) checken (ugs.); spannen (ugs.)

susceptible /sə'septɪbl/ *adj.* empfänglich (**to** für); (to illness) anfällig (**to** für)

suspect 1 /sə'spekt/ *v.t.* (a) (imagine to be likely) vermuten; ∼ **the worst** das Schlimmste befürchten; ∼ **sb. to be sth.,** ∼ **that sb. is sth.** glauben *od.* vermuten, dass jmd. etw. ist
(b) (mentally accuse) verdächtigen; ∼ **sb. of sth./of doing sth.** jmdn. einer Sache verdächtigen/jmdn. verdächtigen, etw. zu tun
2 /'sʌspekt/ *adj.* fragwürdig; verdächtig ⟨Stoff, Paket⟩
3 /'sʌspekt/ *n.* Verdächtige, *der/die*

suspend /sə'spend/ *v.t.* (a) (hang up) [auf]hängen
(b) (stop) suspendieren

(c) (from work) ausschließen (**from** von); sperren ‹*Sportler*›

suspended 'sentence *n.* (Law) Strafe mit Bewährung

suspender belt /sə'spendə belt/ *n.* (Brit.) Strumpfbandgürtel, *der*

suspenders /sə'spendəz/ *n. pl.* **(a)** (Brit.: for stockings) Strumpfbänder *Pl.* **(b)** (Amer.: for trousers) Hosenträger *Pl.*

suspense /sə'spens/ *n.* Spannung, *die;* **keep sb. in** ∼: jmdn. auf die Folter spannen

suspension /sə'spenʃn/ *n.* (Motor Veh.) Federung, *die*

su'spension bridge *n.* Hängebrücke, *die*

suspicion /sə'spɪʃn/ *n.* **(a)** (uneasy feeling) Misstrauen, *das* (unconfirmed belief) Verdacht, *der;* **have a** ∼ **that …:** den Verdacht haben, dass … **(b)** (suspecting) Verdacht, *der* (**of** auf + *Akk.*); **on** ∼ **of murder** wegen Mordverdachts; **be under** ∼: verdächtigt werden

suspicious /sə'spɪʃəs/ *adj.* **(a)** (tending to suspect) misstrauisch (of gegenüber); **be** ∼ **of sb./sth.** jmdm./einer Sache misstrauen **(b)** (arousing suspicion) verdächtig

sustain /sə'steɪn/ *v.t.* **(a)** (support) tragen ‹*Gewicht*›; (fig.) aufrechterhalten **(b)** erleiden ‹*Verlust, Verletzung*›

sustainable /sʌ'steɪnəbl/ *adj.* (Ecology) nachhaltig

sustenance /'sʌstməns/ *n.* Nahrung, *die*

SW *abbr.* **(a)** = **south-west** SW **(b)** (Radio) = **short wave** KW

swab /swɒb/ *n.* (Med.: pad) Tupfer, *der*

swagger /'swægə(r)/ *v.i.* großspurig stolzieren

swallow¹ /'swɒləʊ/ ① *v.t.* schlucken; (by mistake) verschlucken ② *v.i.* schlucken ③ *n.* Schluck, *der* ∎ **swallow 'up** *v.t.* verschlucken

swallow² *n.* Schwalbe, *die*

swam ▶ SWIM 1

swamp /swɒmp/ ① *n.* Sumpf, *der* ② *v.t.* überschwemmen

'swampy *adj.* sumpfig

swan /swɒn/ *n.* Schwan, *der*

'swansong *n.* (fig.) Schwanengesang, *der*

swap /swɒp/ ① *v.t.*, **-pp-** tauschen (**for** gegen) ② *v.i.*, **-pp-** tauschen ③ *n.* Tausch, *der*

swarm /swɔːm/ ① *n.* Schwarm, *der* ② *v.i.* schwärmen; (teem) wimmeln (**with** von)

swarthy /'swɔːðɪ/ *adj.* dunkel

swastika /'swɒstɪkə/ *n.* Hakenkreuz, *das*

swat /swɒt/ *v.t.*, **-tt-** totschlagen

sway /sweɪ/ ① *v.i.* [hin und her] schwanken; (gently) sich wiegen ② *v.t.* **(a)** wiegen **(b)** (influence) beeinflussen

③ *n.* (fig.) Herrschaft, *die;* **hold** ∼ **over sb.** über jmdn. herrschen

swear /sweə(r)/ ① *v.t.*, swore /swɔː(r)/, sworn /swɔːn/ schwören ‹*Eid usw.*› ② *v.i.*, swore, sworn **(a)** fluchen **(b)** ∼ **to sth.** etw. beschwören · ∎ **'swear at** *v.t.* beschimpfen ∎ **'swear by** *v.t.* (coll.) schwören auf (+ *Akk.*)

'swear word *n.* Kraftausdruck, *der*

sweat /swet/ ① *n.* Schweiß, *der* ② *v.i.* schwitzen

'sweatband *n.* Schweißband, *das*

sweater /'swetə(r)/ *n.* Pullover, *der*

sweat: ∼**shirt** *n.* Sweatshirt, *das;* ∼**shop** *n.* ausbeuterische [kleine] Klitsche (ugs.)

'sweaty *adj.* schweißig

swede *n.* Kohlrübe, *die*

Swede /swiːd/ *n.* Schwede, *der*/Schwedin, · *die*

Sweden /'swiːdn/ *pr. n.* Schweden (*das*)

Swedish /'swiːdɪʃ/ ① *adj.* schwedisch; **sb. is** ∼: jmd. ist Schwede/Schwedin ② *n.* Schwedisch, *das; see also* ENGLISH 2A

sweep /swiːp/ ① *v.t.*, swept /swept/ **(a)** fegen; kehren **(b)** ∼ **the country** ‹*Epidemie, Mode:*› das Land überrollen ② *v.i.*, swept **(a)** fegen; kehren **(b)** (go fast) ‹*Person, Auto:*› rauschen; ‹*Wind usw.:*› fegen ③ *n.* **(a)** give sth. a ∼: etw. fegen *od.* kehren **(b)** (curve) Bogen, *der* ∎ **sweep 'up** *v.t.* zusammenfegen; zusammenkehren

'sweeping *adj.* pauschal; weit reichend ‹*Einsparung*›; umwälzend ‹*Veränderung*›

sweet /swiːt/ ① *adj.* süß; reizend ‹*Wesen, Gesicht, Mädchen*›; **have a** ∼ **tooth** gern Süßes mögen; **how** ∼ **of you!** wie nett *od.* lieb von dir! ② *n.* (Brit.) **(a)** (candy) Bonbon, *das od. der* **(b)** (dessert) Nachtisch, *der*

sweet: ∼**and-'sour** *attrib. adj.* süßsauer; ∼ **corn** *n.* Zuckermais, *der*

sweeten /'swiːtn/ *v.t.* süßen

'sweetener *n.* Süßstoff, *der*

'sweetheart *n.* Schatz, *der*

'sweetness *n.* Süße, *die*

sweet: ∼ **'pea** *n.* Wicke, *die;* ∼ **po'tato** *n.* Batate, *die;* ∼**shop** *n.* (Brit.) Süßwarengeschäft, *das;* ∼ **talk** (Amer.) *n.* Süßholzgeraspel, *das* (ugs.); ∼**talk** *v.t.* ∼-talk sb. [into doing sth.] jmdn. beschwatzen[, etw. zu tun]

swell /swel/ ① *v.t.*, swelled, swollen /'swəʊlən/ *or* swelled anschwellen lassen ② *v.i.*, swelled, swollen *or* swelled **(a)** (expand) ‹*Körperteil:*› anschwellen; ‹*Segel:*› sich blähen; ‹*Material:*› aufquellen **(b)** ‹*Anzahl:*› zunehmen '**swelling** *n.* Schwellung, *die*

swelter /'sweltə(r)/ *v.i.* ~ **in the heat** in der Hitze schmoren (ugs.) ~**ing** glühend heiß ⟨*Tag, Wetter*⟩; ~**ing heat** Bruthitze, *die*

swept ▶ SWEEP 1, 2

swerve /swɜːv/ **1** *v.i.* einen Bogen machen; ~ **to the right/left** nach rechts/links [aus]schwenken
2 *n.* Bogen, *der*

swift /swɪft/ **1** *adj.* schnell
2 *n.* Mauersegler, *der*

'**swiftly** *adv.* schnell

swig /swɪg/ (coll.) Schluck, *der*

swill /swɪl/ *v.t.* ~ [**out**] [aus]spülen

swim /swɪm/ **1** *v.i.*, -mm-, **swam** /swæm/, **swum** /swʌm/ schwimmen; **my head was** ~**ming** mir war schwindelig
2 *n.* **have a/go for a** ~: schwimmen/ schwimmen gehen

'**swimmer** *n.* Schwimmer, *der*/ Schwimmerin, *die;* **be a good/poor** ~: gut/ schlecht schwimmen können

'**swimming** *n.* Schwimmen, *das*

swimming: ~ **baths** *n. pl.* Schwimmbad, *das;* ~ **costume** *n.* Badeanzug, *der;* ~ **lesson** *n.* Schwimmstunde, *die;* ~ **lessons** *n.* Schwimmunterricht, *der;* ~ **pool** *n.* Schwimmbecken, *das;* (building) Schwimmbad, *das;* ~ **trunks** *n. pl.* Badehose, *die*

'**swimsuit** *n.* Badeanzug, *der*

swindle /'swɪndl/ **1** *v.t.* betrügen; ~ **sb. out of sth.** jmdn. um etw. betrügen
2 *n.* Schwindel, *der;* Betrug, *der*

swindler /'swɪndlə(r)/ *n.* Schwindler, *der*/ Schwindlerin, *die*

swine /swaɪn/ *n.* Schwein, *das*

swing /swɪŋ/ **1** *n.* (a) Schaukel, *die*
(b) (~ing) Schaukeln, *das;* **in full** ~ (fig.) in vollem Gang[e]
2 *v.i.*, **swung** /swʌŋ/ (a) schwingen; (in wind) schaukeln
(b) (go in sweeping curve) schwenken
3 *v.t.*, **swung** schwingen

swing: ~**bin** *n.* Schwingdeckel[müll]eimer, *der;* ~ '**door** *n.* Pendeltür, *die*

swipe /swaɪp/ (coll.) **1** *v.t.* (a) (hit) knallen (ugs.)
(b) (coll.: steal) klauen (ugs.)
(c) ~ **the card through the swipe reader** die Karte durch das [Karten]lesegerät ziehen
2 *n.* (device) ~ [**reader**] [Karten]lesegerät, *das*

'**swipe card** *n.* Magnetkarte, *die*

swirl /swɜːl/ **1** *v.i.* wirbeln
2 *v.t.* umherwirbeln
3 *n.* Spirale, *die*

swish /swɪʃ/ **1** *v.i.* zischen
2 *n.* Zischen, *das*
3 *adj.* (coll.) schick (ugs.)

Swiss /swɪs/ **1** *adj.* Schweizer; schweizerisch; **sb. is** ~: jmd. ist Schweizer/ Schweizerin

2 *n.* Schweizer, *der*/Schweizerin, *die;* **the** ~ *pl.* die Schweizer *Pl.*

Swiss '**roll** *n.* Biskuitrolle, *die*

switch /swɪtʃ/ **1** *n.* (a) (esp. Electr.) Schalter, *der*
(b) (change) Wechsel, *der*
2 *v.t.* (a) (change) ~ **sth.** [**over**] **to sth.** etw. auf etw. (*Akk.*) umstellen *od.* (Electr.) umschalten
(b) (exchange) tauschen
3 *v.i.* wechseln; ~ [**over**] **to sth.** auf etw. (*Akk.*) umstellen *od.* (Electr.) umschalten
■ **switch** '**off** *v.t. & i.* ausschalten; (also fig. coll.) abschalten
■ **switch** '**on** **1** *v.t.* einschalten; anschalten
2 *v.i.* sich anschalten

switch: ~**back** *n.* Achterbahn, *die;* ~**blade** *n.* Springmesser, *das;* ~**board** *n.* [Telefon]zentrale, *die*

Switzerland /'swɪtsələnd/ *pr. n.* die Schweiz

swivel /'swɪvl/ **1** *v.i.*, -ll- sich drehen
2 *v.t.*, -ll- drehen

'**swivel chair** *n.* Drehstuhl, *der*

swollen /'swəʊlən/ **1** ▶ SWELL
2 *adj.* geschwollen; angeschwollen ⟨*Fluss*⟩

swoon /swuːn/ (literary) *v.i.* ohnmächtig werden

swoop /swuːp/ **1** *n.* (a) Sturzflug, *der*
(b) (coll.: raid) Razzia, *die*
2 *v.i.* herabstoßen; ~ **on sb.** sich auf jmdn. stürzen

swop ▶ SWAP

sword /sɔːd/ *n.* Schwert, *das*

'**swordfish** *n.* Schwertfisch, *der*

swore, sworn ▶ SWEAR

swot /swɒt/ (Brit. coll.) **1** *n.* Streber, *der*/ Streberin, *die*
2 *v.i.*, -tt- büffeln (ugs.)

swum ▶ SWIM 1

swung ▶ SWING 2, 3

'**swung dash** *n.* Tilde, *die*

sycamore /'sɪkəmɔː(r)/ *n.* Bergahorn, *der*

sycophant /'sɪkəfænt/ *n.* Kriecher, *der*

syllable /'sɪləbl/ *n.* Silbe, *die*

syllabus /'sɪləbəs/ *n.* Lehrplan, *der;* (for exam) Studienplan, *der*

symbol /'sɪmbl/ *n.* Symbol, *das* (of für)

symbolic /sɪm'bɒlɪk/**, symbolical** /sɪm'bɒlɪkl/ *adj.* symbolisch

symbolism /'sɪmbəlɪzm/ *n.* Symbolik, *die*

symbolize /'sɪmbəlaɪz/ *v.t.* symbolisieren

symmetrical /sɪ'metrɪkl/ *adj.* symmetrisch

symmetry /'sɪmɪtrɪ/ *n.* Symmetrie, *die*

sympathetic /sɪmpə'θetɪk/ *adj.* mitfühlend

sympathize /'sɪmpəθaɪz/ *v.i.* (a) ~ **with sb.** mit jmdm. [mit]fühlen
(b) ~ **with** (understand) Verständnis haben für

sympathy /'sɪmpəθɪ/ n. Mitgefühl, das; in deepest ∼: mit aufrichtigem Beileid

symphonic /sɪm'fɒnɪk/ adj. sinfonisch

symphony /'sɪmfənɪ/ n. Sinfonie, die

'symphony orchestra n. Sinfonieorchester, das

symposium /sɪm'pəʊzɪəm/ n., pl. **symposia** /sɪm'pəʊzɪə/ Symposion, das

symptom /'sɪmptəm/ n. Symptom, das

symptomatic /sɪmptə'mætɪk/ adj. symptomatisch (of für)

synagogue (Amer.: **synagog**) /'sɪnəgɒg/ n. Synagoge, die

sync /sɪŋk/ (coll.) n. be in ∼/out of ∼: harmonieren/nicht harmonieren (with mit)

synchromesh /'sɪŋkrəmeʃ/ n. (Motor Veh.) Synchrongetriebe, das

synchronize /'sɪŋkrənaɪz/ v.t. synchronisieren; gleichstellen ⟨Uhren⟩

syndicate /'sɪndɪkət/ n. Syndikat, das

syndrome /'sɪndrəʊm/ n. Syndrom, das

synonym /'sɪnənɪm/ n. Synonym, das

synonymous /sɪ'nɒnɪməs/ adj. (a) (Ling.) synonym (with mit)
(b) ∼ with (fig.) gleichbedeutend mit

synopsis /sɪ'nɒpsɪs/ n., pl. **synopses** /sɪ'nɒpsi:z/ Inhaltsangabe, die

syntactic /sɪn'tæktɪk/ adj. syntaktisch

syntax /'sɪntæks/ n. Syntax, die

synthesis /'sɪnθɪsɪs/ n., pl. **syntheses** /'sɪnθɪsi:z/ Synthese, die

synthesize /'sɪnθɪsaɪz/ v.t. zur Synthese bringen; (Chem.) synthetisieren

synthesizer /'sɪnθɪsaɪzə(r)/ n. (Mus.) Synthesizer, der

synthetic /sɪn'θetɪk/ adj. synthetisch

syphilis /'sɪfɪlɪs/ n. Syphilis, die

syphon ▶ SIPHON

Syria /'sɪrɪə/ pr. n. Syrien (das)

syringe /sɪ'rɪndʒ/ ☐1 n. Spritze, die ☐2 v.t. spritzen; ausspritzen ⟨Ohr⟩

syrup /'sɪrəp/ n. Sirup, der

system /'sɪstəm/ n. System, das

systematic /sɪstə'mætɪk/ adj., **systematically** /sɪstə'mætɪkəlɪ/ adv. systematisch

systematize /'sɪstəmətaɪz/ v.t. systematisieren

system: ∼ disk n. (Comp.) Systemdiskette, die; ∼ **error** n. (Comp.) Systemfehler, der; ∼**s analyst** n. Systemanalytiker, der/-analytikerin, die; ∼ **software** n. (Comp.) Systemsoftware, die

---

Tt

T, t /tiː/ n. T, t, das; **to a T** ganz genau; **T-junction** Einmündung, die; **T-bone steak** T-Bone-Steak, das; **T-shirt** T-Shirt, das

ta /tɑː/ int. (Brit. coll.) danke

tab /tæb/ ☐1 n. (a) (projecting flap) Zunge, die; (on clothing) Etikett, das; (with name) Namensschild, das
(b) pick up the ∼ (Amer. coll.) die Zeche bezahlen
(c) keep ∼s or a ∼ on (watch) [genau] beobachten
(d) (Comp.) Tabulator, der
☐2 v.t. (Comp.) tabellarisieren

tabby /'tæbɪ/ n. ∼ [cat] Tigerkatze, die

'tab key n. (Comp.) Tabulatortaste, die

table /'teɪbl/ ☐1 n. (a) Tisch, der
(b) (list) Tabelle, die; ∼ of contents Inhaltsverzeichnis, das
☐2 v.t. einbringen

tableau /'tæbləʊ/ n., pl. ∼x /'tæbləʊz/ Tableau, das

table: ∼cloth n. Tischdecke, die; ∼ **leg** n. Tischbein, das; ∼ **linen** n. Tischwäsche, die; ∼ **manners** n. pl. Tischmanieren Pl.; ∼ **mat** n. Set, das;

∼ **salt** n. Tafelsalz, das; ∼**spoon** n. Servierlöffel, der; ∼**spoonful** n. Servierlöffel [voll]

tablet /'tæblɪt/ n. (a) Tablette, die
(b) (of soap) Stück, das

table: ∼ **tennis** n. Tischtennis, das; ∼ **tennis bat** Tischtennisschläger, der; ∼ **wine** n. Tischwein, der

tabloid /'tæblɔɪd/ n. Boulevardzeitung, die; the ∼s (derog.) die Boulevardpresse; ∼ **journalism** Sensationsjournalismus, der

taboo, tabu /tə'buː/ ☐1 n. Tabu, das ☐2 adj. Tabu⟨wort⟩; be ∼: tabu sein

tabulate /'tæbjʊleɪt/ v.t. tabellarisch darstellen

tabulator /'tæbjʊleɪtə(r)/ n. Tabulator, der

tacit /'tæsɪt/ adj., **'tacitly** adv. stillschweigend

taciturn /'tæsɪtɜːn/ adj. schweigsam; wortkarg

tack /tæk/ ☐1 n. (a) (nail) kleiner Nagel
(b) (stitch) Heftstich, der
(c) (Naut., also fig.) Kurs, der
☐2 v.t. (a) (nail) festnageln
(b) (stitch) heften

⋯⫶

3 *v.i.* (Naut.) kreuzen

tackle /'tækl/ 1 *v.t.* (a) angehen ⟨*Problem usw.*⟩; ∼ **sb. about/on/over sth.** jmdn. auf etw. (*Akk.*) ansprechen; (ask for sth.) jmdn. um etw. angehen
(b) (Sport) angreifen ⟨*Spieler*⟩; (Amer. Footb.; Rugby) fassen
2 *n.* (a) (equipment) Ausrüstung, *die*
(b) (Sport) Angriff, *der;* (sliding ∼) Tackling, *das;* (Amer. Footb.; Rugby) Fassen und Halten

tacky /'tækɪ/ *adj.* (a) (sticky) klebrig
(b) (coll. derog.: tasteless) geschmacklos

tact /tækt/ *n.* Takt, *der; he has no* ∼: er hat kein Taktgefühl

tactful /'tæktfl/ *adj.,* '**tactfully** *adv.* taktvoll

tactical /'tæktɪkl/ *adj.* taktisch

tactics /'tæktɪks/ *n. pl.* Taktik, *die*

'**tactless** *adj.,* '**tactlessly** *adv.* taktlos

tadpole /'tædpəʊl/ *n.* Kaulquappe, *die*

tag¹ /tæg/ 1 *n.* (a) Schild, *das*
(b) (electronic device) (on person) elektronische Fessel; (on goods) Sicherungsetikett, *das*
(c) (Comp.) Tag, *das;* Markierung, *die*
2 *v.t.,* **-gg-:** (Comp.) taggen; markieren
■ **tag a'long** *v.i.* mitkommen

tag² *n.* (game) Fangen, *das*

tail /teɪl/ 1 *n.* (a) Schwanz, *der*
(b) *in pl.* (on coin) ∼**s [it is]** Zahl
2 *v.t.* (coll.: follow) beschatten
■ **tail 'back** *v.i.* sich stauen
■ **tail 'off** *v.i.* (a) zurückgehen
(b) (into silence) verstummen

tail: ∼**back** *n.* (Brit.) Rückstau, *der;* ∼ **end** *n.* Ende, *das;* ∼**gate** 1 *n.* (Motor Veh.) Heckklappe, *die;* 2 *v.i.* zu dicht auffahren; ∼ **light** *n.* Rücklicht, *das*

tailor /'teɪlə(r)/ *n.* Schneider, *der/* Schneiderin, *die*

tailored /'teɪləd/, '**tailor-made** *adjs.* maßgeschneidert

'**tail wind** *n.* Rückenwind, *der*

taint /teɪnt/ *v.t.* verderben; **be** ∼**ed with sth.** mit etw. behaftet sein (geh.)

Taiwan /taɪ'wɑːn/ *pr. n.* Taiwan (*das*)

take /teɪk/ 1 *v.t.,* **took** /tʊk/, **taken** /'teɪkn/
(a) (get hold of, grasp, seize) nehmen
(b) (capture) einnehmen ⟨*Stadt, Festung*⟩; machen ⟨*Gefangenen*⟩
(c) (gain, earn) ⟨*Laden:*⟩ einbringen; ⟨*Person:*⟩ einnehmen; ⟨*Film, Stück:*⟩ einspielen; (win) gewinnen ⟨*Satz, Spiel, Preis, Titel*⟩
(d) (∼ away with one) mitnehmen; (steal) mitnehmen (verhüll.); ∼ **place** stattfinden; (spontaneously) sich ereignen; ⟨*Wandlung:*⟩ sich vollziehen
(e) (avail oneself of, use) nehmen; machen ⟨*Pause, Ferien, Nickerchen*⟩; ∼ **the opportunity to do/of doing sth.** die Gelegenheit dazu benutzen, etw. zu tun
(f) (carry, guide, convey) bringen; ∼ **sb. to visit sb.** jmdn. zu Besuch bei jmdm. mitnehmen;

∼ **home** mit nach Hause nehmen; (earn) nach Hause bringen ⟨*Geld*⟩; (accompany) nach Hause bringen
(g) (remove) nehmen; (deduct) abziehen; ∼ **sth./sb. from sb.** jmdm. etw./jmdm. wegnehmen
(h) (make) machen ⟨*Foto, Kopie*⟩; (photograph) aufnehmen; aufnehmen ⟨*Brief, Diktat*⟩; machen ⟨*Prüfung, Sprung, Spaziergang, Reise*⟩; ablegen ⟨*Gelübde, Eid*⟩; treffen ⟨*Entscheidung*⟩
(i) (conduct) halten ⟨*Gottesdienst, Unterricht*⟩; **Ms X** ∼**s us for maths** in Mathe haben wir Frau X
(j) (eat, drink) nehmen ⟨*Zucker, Milch, Tabletten, Überdosis*⟩; trinken ⟨*Tee, Kaffee, Kognak usw.*⟩
(k) (need, require) brauchen ⟨*Platz, Zeit*⟩; haben ⟨*Objekt, Plural-s*⟩; gebraucht werden mit ⟨*Kasus*⟩; **sth.** ∼**s an hour/a year/all day** etw. dauert eine Stunde/ein Jahr/einen ganzen Tag
(l) (ascertain and record) notieren ⟨*Namen, Adresse, Autonummer usw.*⟩; fühlen ⟨*Puls*⟩; messen ⟨*Temperatur, Größe usw.*⟩
(m) (assume) ∼ **it [that]** ...: annehmen, dass ...; ∼ **sb./sth. for/to be sth.** jmdn./etw. für etw. halten
(n) (react to) aufnehmen; ∼ **sth. well/badly** etw. gut/nur schwer verkraften; ∼ **sth. calmly** *or* **coolly** etw. gelassen [auf]nehmen
(o) (accept) annehmen
(p) (adopt, choose) ergreifen ⟨*Maßnahmen*⟩; unternehmen ⟨*Schritte*⟩; ∼ **the wrong road** die falsche Straße fahren/gehen
(q) **be** ∼**n ill** krank werden
(r) ∼ **sth. to bits** *or* **pieces** etw. auseinander nehmen
2 *v.i.,* **took, taken** (a) ⟨*Transplantat:*⟩ vom Körper angenommen werden; ⟨*Sämling, Pflanze:*⟩ angehen
(b) (detract) ∼ **from sth.** etw. schmälern
■ '**take after** *v.t.* ∼ **after sb.** (resemble) jmdm. ähnlich sein; (∼ as one's example) es jmdm. gleichtun
■ **take a'way** *v.t.* (a) (remove) wegnehmen; (to a distance) mitnehmen; ∼ **sth. away from sb.** jmdm. etw. abnehmen; **to** ∼ **away** ⟨*Pizza, Snack usw.*⟩ zum Mitnehmen
(b) (Math.: deduct) abziehen
■ **take a'way from** *v.t.* schmälern
■ **take 'back** *v.t.* zurücknehmen; (return) zurückbringen
■ **take 'down** *v.t.* (a) (carry or lead down) hinunterbringen
(b) abnehmen ⟨*Bild, Ankündigung, Weihnachtsschmuck*⟩; herunterziehen ⟨*Hose*⟩; ∼ **sth. down from a shelf** etw. von einem Regal herunternehmen
(c) (write down) aufnehmen
■ **take 'in** *v.t.* (a) hineinbringen; (bring indoors) hereinholen
(b) enger machen ⟨*Kleidungsstück*⟩
(c) (understand) begreifen
(d) (cheat) hereinlegen (ugs.); (deceive) täuschen

■ **take 'off** 1 *v.t.* **(a)** abnehmen ‹Deckel, Hut, Tischtuch, Verband›; abziehen ‹Kissenbezug›; ausziehen ‹Schuhe, Handschuhe›; ablegen ‹Mantel, Schmuck›
(b) (deduct) abziehen; ∼ **sth. off sth.** etw. von etw. abziehen
(c) ∼ **a day** *etc.* **off** sich (*Dat.*) einen Tag *usw.* frei nehmen (ugs.)
(d) (mimic) nachahmen
2 *v.i.* (Aeronaut.) starten

■ **take 'on** *v.t.* **(a)** (undertake) übernehmen; auf sich (*Akk.*) nehmen ‹Bürde›
(b) (employ) einstellen
(c) (as opponent) es aufnehmen mit; (Sport: meet) antreten gegen

■ **take 'out** *v.t.* **(a)** (remove) herausnehmen; ziehen ‹Zahn›; ∼ **sth. out of sth.** etw. aus etw. [heraus]nehmen
(b) (withdraw) abheben ‹Geld›
(c) (go out with) ∼ **sb. out** mit jmdm. ausgehen; ∼ **sb. out to** *or* **for lunch** jmdn. zum Mittagessen einladen
(d) (get issued) abschließen ‹Versicherung›; ausleihen ‹Bücher›; ∼ **out a subscription to sth.** etw. abonnieren
(e) ∼ **it out on sb.** seine Wut an jmdm. auslassen

■ **take 'over** 1 *v.t.* übernehmen
2 *v.i.* übernehmen; ‹Manager, Firmenleiter:› die Geschäfte übernehmen; ‹Regierung, Präsident:› die Amtsgeschäfte übernehmen; ∼ **over from sb.** jmdn. ersetzen; (temporarily) jmdn. vertreten

■ **'take to** *v.t.* **(a)** (get into habit of) ∼ **to doing sth.** es sich (*Dat.*) angewöhnen, etw. zu tun
(b) (like) sich hingezogen fühlen zu ‹Person›; sich erwärmen für ‹Sache›

■ **take 'up** 1 *v.t.* **(a)** (lift up) hochheben; (pick up) aufheben; herausreißen ‹Dielen›; aufreißen ‹Straße›
(b) (carry or lead up) hinaufbringen
(c) in Anspruch nehmen ‹Zeit›; brauchen/ (undesirably) wegnehmen ‹Platz›
(d) (start) ergreifen ‹Beruf›; anfangen ‹Tennis, Schach, Gitarre usw.›; aufnehmen ‹Arbeit, Kampf›; antreten ‹Stelle›; ∼ **up a hobby** sich (*Dat.*) ein Hobby zulegen
(e) (pursue further) ∼ **sth. up with sb.** sich in einer Sache an jmdn. wenden
2 *v.i.* ∼ **up with sb.** (coll.) sich mit jmdm. einlassen

'takeaway *n.* (meal) Essen zum Mitnehmen; (restaurant) Restaurant mit Straßenverkauf

taken ▶ TAKE

take: ∼**-off** *n.* **(a)** (Aeronaut.) Start, *der;* **(b)** (coll.: caricature) Parodie, *die;* ∼**over** *n.* Übernahme, *die*

takings /'teɪkɪŋz/ *n. pl.* Einnahmen *Pl.*

talc /tælk/ *n.* Talkum, *das*

talcum /'tælkəm/ *n.* ∼ **[powder]** Körperpuder, *der*

tale /teɪl/ *n.* Erzählung, *die;* Geschichte, *die* (of von, about über + *Akk.*)

talent /'tælənt/ *n.* Talent, *das;* have [great/ no *etc.*] ∼ **[for sth.]** [viel/kein *usw.*] Talent [zu *od.* für etw.] haben

'talented *adj.* talentiert

'talent-spotting *n.* Talentsuche, *die*

talk /tɔːk/ 1 *n.* **(a)** (discussion) Gespräch, *das;* have a ∼ **[with sb.]** [about sth.] [mit jmdm.] [über etw. (*Akk.*)] sprechen; [mit jmdm.] ∼**s [with sb.]** [mit jmdm.] Gespräche führen; **there is [much/some]** ∼ **of …:** man hört [häufig/öfter] von …
(b) (speech, lecture) Vortrag, *der*
2 *v.i.* sprechen (**with, to** mit); (lecture) sprechen; (converse) sich unterhalten; (have ∼s) Gespräche führen; (gossip) reden; ∼ **on the phone** telefonieren
3 *v.t.* reden; ∼ **sb. into/out of sth.** jmdn. zu etw. überreden/jmdm. etw. ausreden

■ **talk 'over** *v.t.* besprechen

■ **talk 'round** *v.t.* ∼ **sb. round** jmdn. überreden

talkative /'tɔːkətɪv/ *adj.* gesprächig

talking: ∼ **point** *n.* Gesprächsthema, *das;* ∼**-to** *n.* (coll.) Standpauke, *die* (ugs.)

'talk show *n.* Talkshow, *die*

tall /tɔːl/ *adj.* hoch; groß ‹Person, Tier›; **that's a** ∼ **order** das ist ziemlich viel verlangt; ∼ **story** unglaubliche Geschichte

tally /'tælɪ/ 1 *n.* keep a ∼ **of sth.** über etw. (*Akk.*) Buch führen
2 *v.i.* übereinstimmen

talon /'tælən/ *n.* Klaue, *die*

tambourine /tæmbə'riːn/ *n.* Tamburin, *das*

tame /teɪm/ 1 *adj.* zahm; (fig.: spiritless) lahm (ugs.)
2 *v.t.* zähmen

tamper /'tæmpə(r)/ *v.i.* ∼ **with** sich (*Dat.*) zu schaffen machen an (+ *Dat.*)

tampon /'tæmpɒn/ *n.* Tampon, *der*

tan /tæn/ 1 *v.t.*, **-nn-** gerben ‹Tierhaut, Fell›
2 *v.i.*, **-nn-** braun werden
3 *n.* **(a)** (colour) Gelbbraun, *das*
(b) (sun∼) Bräune, *die;* have/get a ∼: braun sein/werden
4 *adj.* gelbbraun

tandem /'tændəm/ *n.* ∼ **[bicycle]** Tandem, *das*

tang /tæŋ/ *n.* (taste) Geschmack, *der;* (smell) Geruch, *der*

tangent /'tændʒənt/ *n.* Tangente, *die;* go off at a ∼ (fig.) plötzlich vom Thema abschweifen

tangerine /tændʒə'riːn/ *n.* (fruit) ∼ **[orange]** Tangerine, *die*

tangible /'tændʒɪbl/ *adj.* greifbar; spürbar ‹Unterschied, Verbesserung›; handfest ‹Beweis›

tangle /'tæŋgl/ 1 *n.* Gewirr, *das;* (in hair) Verfilzung, *die*
2 *v.t.* verheddern (ugs.); verfilzen ‹Haar›

■ **tangle 'up** *v.t.* verheddern (ugs.)

tango /'tæŋgəʊ/ n., pl. ~s Tango, der

tank /tæŋk/ n. (a) Tank, der

(b) (Mil.) Panzer, der

tankard /'tæŋkəd/ n. Krug, der

tanker /'tæŋkə(r)/ n. (ship) Tanker, der; (vehicle) Tank[last]wagen, der

tanned /tænd/ adj. braun gebrannt

tantalize /'tæntəlaɪz/ v.t. reizen

tantalizing /'tæntəlaɪzɪŋ/ adj. verlockend

tantamount /'tæntəmaʊnt/ adj. be ~ to sth. gleichbedeutend mit etw. sein

tantrum /'tæntrəm/ n. Wutanfall, der; (of child) Trotzanfall, der; throw a ~: einen Wutanfall/Trotzanfall bekommen

tap¹ /tæp/ **1** n. Hahn, der; hot/cold[-water] ~: Warm-/Kaltwasserhahn, der; be on ~ (fig.) zur Verfügung stehen

2 v.t., -pp-: (a) erschließen ⟨Reserven, Markt⟩

(b) (Teleph.) abhören; anzapfen (ugs.)

tap² **1** v.t., -pp- klopfen an (+ Akk.); (on upper surface) klopfen auf (+ Akk.)

2 v.i., -pp-: ~ at/on sth. an etw. (Akk.) klopfen; (on upper surface) auf etw. (Akk.) klopfen

3 n. Klopfen, das

'tap dance **1** n. Stepp[tanz], der

2 v.i. Stepp tanzen; steppen

tape /teɪp/ **1** n. (a) Band, das; adhesive or (coll.) sticky ~: Klebeband, das

(b) (for recording) [Ton]band, das (of mit); make a ~ of sth. etw. auf Band aufnehmen

2 v.t. (a) (record on ~) [auf Band] aufnehmen

(b) (bind with ~) [mit Klebeband] zukleben

(c) have got sb./sth. ~d (coll.) jmdn. durchschaut haben/etw. im Griff haben

tape: ~ cassette n. Tonbandkassette, die; **~ deck** n. Tapedeck, das; **~ measure** n. Bandmaß, das

taper /'teɪpə(r)/ **1** v.i. sich verjüngen; ~ [to a point] spitz zulaufen

2 n. [wax] ~: Wachsstock, der

tape: ~ recorder n. Tonbandgerät, das; **~ recording** n. Tonbandaufnahme, die

tapestry /'tæpɪstrɪ/ n. Gobelingewebe, das; (wall-hanging) Bildteppich, der

'tapeworm n. Bandwurm, der

'tap water n. Leitungswasser, das

tar /tɑ:(r)/ **1** n. Teer, der; high-~/low-~ cigarette Zigarette mit hohem/niedrigem Teergehalt

2 v.t., -rr- teeren

target /'tɑ:gɪt/ **1** n. (a) Ziel, das; hit/miss the/its ~: [das Ziel] treffen/das Ziel verfehlen; production/export/savings ~: Produktions-/Export-/Sparziel, das; be above/below ~ (fig.) das Ziel über-/unterschritten haben

(b) (Sport) Zielscheibe, die

2 v.t. (fig.) zielen auf ⟨Käufergruppe⟩

target: ~ date n. vorgesehener Termin; **~ figure** n. (esp. Commerc.) Ziel, das

tariff /'tærɪf/ n. (a) (tax) Zoll, der

(b) (list of charges) Tarif, der

tarnish /'tɑ:nɪʃ/ **1** v.t. stumpf werden lassen ⟨Metall⟩; (fig.) beflecken ⟨Ruf⟩

2 v.i. stumpf werden

tarpaulin /tɑ:'pɔ:lɪn/ n. Plane, die

tart¹ /tɑ:t/ adj. herb; sauer ⟨Obst⟩; (fig.) scharfzüngig

tart² n. (a) (Brit.) (filled pie) ≈ Obstkuchen, der; (small pastry) Obsttörtchen, das

(b) (sl.: prostitute) Nutte, die (salopp)

■ **tart 'up** v.t. (Brit. coll.) ~ oneself up, get ~ed up sich auftakeln (ugs.)

tartan /'tɑ:tən/ **1** n. Schotten[stoff], der

2 adj. Schotten⟨rock, -jacke⟩

tartar /'tɑ:tə(r)/ n. Zahnstein, der

tartar sauce /'tɑ:tə 'sɔ:s/ n. Remoulade[nsoße], die

task /tɑ:sk/ n. Aufgabe, die; take sb. to ~: jmdm. eine Lektion erteilen

task: ~bar n. (Comp.) Taskleiste, die; **~ force** n. Sonderkommando, das

tassel /'tæsl/ n. Quaste, die

taste /teɪst/ **1** v.t. (a) schmecken; (try a little) probieren

(b) (recognize flavour of) [heraus]schmecken

2 v.i. schmecken (of nach); not ~ of anything nach nichts schmecken

3 n. (a) (flavour) Geschmack, der; [sense of] ~: Geschmack[ssinn], der

(b) (discernment) Geschmack, der

(c) (sample) Kostprobe, die

tasteful /'teɪstfl/ adj., **'tastefully** adv. geschmackvoll

'tasteless adj. geschmacklos

tasty /'teɪstɪ/ adj. lecker

tat /tæt/ n. ▶ TIT²

tattered /'tætəd/ adj. zerlumpt ⟨Kleidung⟩; zerfleddert ⟨Buch⟩

tatters /'tætəz/ n. pl. Fetzen Pl.; be in ~: in Fetzen sein; (fig.) ruiniert sein

tattoo /tə'tu:/ **1** v.t. tätowieren

2 n. Tätowierung, die

tattooer /tə'tu:ə(r)/, **tattooist** /tə'tu:ɪst/ ns. Tätowierer, der/Tätowiererin, die

tatty /'tætɪ/ adj. (coll.) schäbig

taught ▶ TEACH

taunt /tɔ:nt/ **1** v.t. verspotten (about wegen)

2 n. spöttische Bemerkung

Taurus /'tɔ:rəs/ n. (Astrol., Astron.) der Stier

taut /tɔ:t/ adj. straff ⟨Seil, Kabel⟩; gespannt ⟨Muskel⟩

tavern /'tævən/ n. Schenke, die

tawny /'tɔ:nɪ/ adj. gelbbraun

tax /tæks/ **1** n. Steuer, die; before/after ~: vor Steuern/nach Abzug der Steuern; for ~ reasons aus steuerlichen Gründen

2 v.t. (a) besteuern; versteuern ⟨Einkommen⟩

(b) (fig.) strapazieren ⟨Kräfte, Geduld⟩

taxable /'tæksəbl/ adj. steuerpflichtig

tax: ∼ **allowance** n. Steuerfreibetrag, der; ∼ **assessment** n. Steuerbescheid, der

taxation /tæk'seɪʃn/ n. Besteuerung, die; (taxes payable) Steuern Pl.

tax: ∼ **avoidance** n. Steuerumgehung, die; ∼ **bill** n. Steuerbescheid, der; (amount) Steuerschuld, die; ∼ **bracket** n. Stufe im Steuertarif; ∼-**deductible** adj. steuerabzugsfähig; [steuerlich] absetzbar; ∼ **demand** n. Steuerforderung, die; ∼ **disc** n. (Motor Veh.) Steuerplakette, die; ∼ **evasion** n. Steuerhinterziehung, die; ∼ **exile** n. (person) Steuerflüchtling, der; ∼ **form** n. Steuerformular, das; ∼-**free** adj. steuerfrei; ∼ **haven** n. Steueroase, die (ugs.)

taxi /'tæksɪ/ [1] n. Taxi, das [2] v.i., ∼ing or taxying ⟨Flugzeug:⟩ rollen

'**taxi driver** n. Taxifahrer, der/-fahrerin, die

tax: ∼ **incentive** n. steuerlicher Anreiz; ∼ **inspector** n. Steuerinspektor, der/ -inspektorin, die

taxi: ∼ **rank** (Brit.), ∼ **stand** (Amer.) ns. Taxistand, der

tax: ∼**man** n. (coll.) Finanzbeamte, der/ -beamtin, die; ∼ **office** n. Finanzamt, das ∼**payer** n. Steuerzahler, der/-zahlerin, die; ∼ **return** n. Steuererklärung, die; ∼ **relief** n. Steuererleichterung, die; ∼ **year** n. Steuerjahr, das

TB abbr. = **tuberculosis** Tb, die

tbsp. abbr., pl. same or ∼s: **tablespoon**

tea /tiː/ n. **(a)** Tee, der **(b)** (meal) [high] ∼: Abendessen, das

tea: ∼ **bag** n. Teebeutel, der; ∼ **break** n. (Brit.) Teepause, die; ∼ **caddy** n. Teebüchse, die

teach /tiːtʃ/ [1] v.t., taught /tɔːt/ unterrichten; (at university) lehren; ∼ sb./ oneself/an animal sth. jmdm./sich/einem Tier etw. beibringen; ∼ sb. to ride jmdm. das Reiten beibringen [2] v.i., taught unterrichten

'**teacher** n. Lehrer, der/Lehrerin, die

teacher: ∼ **training** n. Lehrerausbildung, die; ∼-**training college** n. ≈ pädagogische Hochschule

'**teaching profession** n. Lehrberuf, der

tea: ∼ **cloth** n. Geschirrtuch, das; ∼ **cosy** n. Teewärmer, der; ∼**cup** n. Teetasse, die

teak /tiːk/ n. Teak[holz], das

'**tea leaf** n. Teeblatt, das

team /tiːm/ n. Team, das; (Sport also) Mannschaft, die
■ **team 'up** v.i. sich zusammentun (ugs.)

team: ∼ **effort** n. Team- od. Gemeinschaftsarbeit, die; ∼ **game** n. Mannschaftsspiel, das; ∼ **leader** n. Gruppenleiter, der/-leiterin, die; ∼**mate** n. Mannschaftskamerad, der/-kameradin, die;

∼ '**spirit** n. Teamgeist, der; (Sport also) Mannschaftsgeist, der; ∼**work** n. Teamarbeit, die

'**teapot** n. Teekanne, die

tear¹ /teə(r)/ [1] n. Riss, der [2] v.t., tore /tɔː(r)/, torn /tɔːn/ **(a)** (rip) zerreißen; (pull apart) auseinander reißen; (damage) aufreißen; ∼ **open** aufreißen ⟨Brief, Paket⟩ **(b)** ∼ sth. out of sb.'s hands jmdm. etw. aus der Hand reißen [3] v.i., tore, torn **(a)** (rip) [zer]reißen **(b)** (move hurriedly) rasen (ugs.)
■ **tear a'way** v.t. wegreißen; ∼ oneself away (fig.) sich losreißen
■ **tear 'up** v.t. zerreißen

tear² /tɪə(r)/ n. Träne, die

tearful /'tɪəfl/ adj. weinend

tear /tɪə(r)/: ∼**drop** n. Träne, die; ∼ **gas** n. Tränengas, das

tease /tiːz/ [1] v.t. necken (about wegen); aufziehen (ugs.) (about mit) [2] v.i. seine Späße machen

tea: ∼ **service,** ∼**set** ns. Teeservice, das; ∼ **shop** n. (Brit.) ≈ Café, das; ∼**spoon** n. Teelöffel, der; ∼ **strainer** n. Teesieb, das

teat /tiːt/ n. **(a)** Zitze, die **(b)** (of rubber or plastic) Sauger, der

tea: ∼**time** n. Teezeit, die; ∼ **towel** n. Geschirrtuch, das; ∼ **trolley** n. Teewagen, der; ∼ **urn** n. Teebehälter, der

techie /'tekɪ/ n. (coll.) Technikfreak, der; (computer expert) Computerfreak, der

technical /'teknɪkl/ adj. technisch ⟨Problem, Daten, Fortschritt⟩; Fach⟨kenntnis, -sprache, -begriff, -wörterbuch⟩; ∼ **college** Fachhochschule, die; ∼ **term** Fachbegriff, der; Fachausdruck, der

technicality /teknɪ'kælɪtɪ/ n. technisches Detail

technician /tek'nɪʃn/ n. Techniker, der/ Technikerin, die

technique /tek'niːk/ n. Technik, die; (procedure) Methode, die

techno /'teknəʊ/ [1] adj. Techno- [2] n. Techno, der od. das

technological /teknə'lɒdʒɪkl/ adj. technisch; technologisch

technology /tek'nɒlədʒɪ/ n. Technik, die; (application of science) Technologie, die

technophobe /'teknəʊfəʊb/ n. Mensch mit einer Technikphobie

teddy /'tedɪ/ n. ∼ [**bear**] Teddy[bär], der

tedious /'tiːdɪəs/ adj. langwierig ⟨Reise, Arbeit⟩; (uninteresting) langweilig

tee /tiː/ (Golf) Tee, das

teem /tiːm/ v.i. wimmeln (with von)

teen /tiːn/ adj. Teenager-

teenage[d] /'tiːneɪdʒ(d)/ attrib. adj. im Teenageralter nachgestellt

teenager /'ti:neɪdʒə(r)/ n. Teenager, der;
(loosely) Jugendliche, der/die

teens /ti:nz/ n. pl. Teenagerjahre Pl.

'tee shirt n. T-Shirt, das

teeter /'ti:tə(r)/ v.i. wanken; ~ on the edge
of sth. schwankend am Rande einer Sache
(Gen.) stehen

teeth pl. of TOOTH

teething troubles /'ti:ðɪŋ trʌblz/ n. pl.
have ~ (fig.) Anfangsschwierigkeiten haben

teetotal /ti:'təʊtl/ adj. abstinent lebend

teetotaller /ti:'təʊtələ(r)/ n. Abstinenzler,
der/Abstinenzlerin, die

TEFL /'tefl/ abbr. = **teaching of
English as a foreign language**

Teflon ® /'teflɒn/ n. Teflon (Wz), das

Tel., tel. abbr. = **telephone** Tel.

telebanking /'telɪbæŋkɪŋ/ n. Telebanking,
das

telecommunications
/telɪkəmju:nɪ'keɪʃnz/ n. pl. Fernmelde- od.
Nachrichtentechnik, die

telecommute /'telɪkəmju:t/ v.i. Telearbeit
verrichten

telecommuting /'telɪkəmju:tɪŋ/ n.
Telearbeit, die

teleconference /'telɪkɒnfərəns/ n.
Telekonferenz, die

telecottage /'telɪkɒtɪdʒ/ n.: jedermann
zugängliche Einrichtung, die
Telearbeitern Zugang zu einem ans Internet
angeschlossenen Computer bietet

telegram /'telɪgræm/ n. Telegramm, das

telegraph /'telɪgrɑ:f/ n. Telegraf, der;
~ pole Telegrafenmast, der

telemarketing /'telɪmɑ:kɪtɪŋ/ n.
Telefonmarketing, das

telepathy /tɪ'lepəθɪ/ n. Telepathie, die

telephone /'telɪfəʊn/ [1] n. Telefon, das;
attrib. Telefon-; **answer the ~:** Anrufe
entgegennehmen; (on one occasion) ans Telefon
gehen; (speak) sich melden; **be on the ~:**
Telefon haben; (be speaking) telefonieren (**to**
mit)
[2] v.t. anrufen
[3] v.i. anrufen; ~ **for a taxi** nach einem Taxi
telefonieren

telephone: ~ **'answering machine**
n. Anrufbeantworter, der; ~ **'banking** n.
Telefonbanking, das; ~ **book** n.
Telefonbuch, das; ~ **booth,** (Brit.) ~ **box**
ns. Telefonzelle, die; ~ **call** n.
Telefongespräch, das; ~ **connection** n.
Telefonverbindung, die; ~ **directory** n.
Telefonverzeichnis, das; ~ **exchange** n.
Fernmeldeamt, das; ~ **number** n.
Telefonnummer, die; ~ **operator** n.
Telefonist, der/Telefonistin, die

telephonist /tɪ'lefənɪst/ n. Telefonist, der/
Telefonistin, die

telephoto /telɪ'fəʊtəʊ/ adj. ~ **lens**
Teleobjektiv, das

teleprinter /'telɪprɪntə(r)/ n.
Fernschreiber, der

'telesales n. pl. Telefonverkauf, der;
Verkauf per Telefon

telescope /'telɪskəʊp/ n. Teleskop, das;
Fernrohr, das

telescopic /telɪ'skɒpɪk/ adj. (collapsible)
ausziehbar; Teleskop⟨antenne⟩

Teletex ® /'telɪteks/ n. Teletex, das

teletext /'telɪtekst/ n. Teletext, der

televise /'telɪvaɪz/ v.t. im Fernsehen
senden od. übertragen

television /'telɪvɪʒn, telɪ'vɪʒn/ n. (a) no art.
das Fernsehen; **on ~:** im Fernsehen; **watch
~:** fernsehen
(b) (~ set) Fernsehapparat, der; Fernseher,
der (ugs.)

television: ~ **aerial** n. Fernsehantenne,
die; ~ **channel** n. [Fernseh]kanal, der;
~ **coverage** n. Fernsehberichterstattung,
die; ~ **licence** n. (Brit.)
Fernsehgenehmigung, die (die jährlich gegen
Zahlen der Gebühren erneuert wird);
~ **licence fee** Fernsehgebühren Pl.;
~ **lounge** n. Fernsehraum, der;
~ **personality** n. Fernsehgröße, die (ugs.);
~ **picture** n. Fernsehbild, das;
~ **programme** n. Fernsehsendung, die;
~ **screen** n. Bildschirm, der; ~ **serial** n.
Fernsehserie, die; ~ **set** n. Fernsehgerät,
das; ~ **studio** n. Fernsehstudio, das;
~ **viewer** n. Fernsehzuschauer, der/
-zuschauerin, die

teleworking /'telɪwɜ:kɪŋ/ n. Telearbeit, die

telex /'teleks/ [1] n. Telex, das
[2] v.t. ein Telex schicken (+ Dat.); telexen
⟨Nachricht⟩

tell /tel/ [1] v.t., told /təʊld/ (a) (relate)
erzählen; (make known) sagen ⟨Name, Adresse⟩;
anvertrauen ⟨Geheimnis⟩; ~ **sb. sth. or sth.
to sb.** jmdm. etw. erzählen/sagen/
anvertrauen; ~ **sb. the way to the station**
jmdm. den Weg zum Bahnhof beschreiben;
~ **sb. the time** jmdm. die Uhrzeit sagen;
~ **tales** (lie) Lügengeschichten erzählen;
(gossip) tratschen (ugs.)
(b) (instruct) sagen; ~ **sb. [not] to do sth.**
jmdm. sagen, er soll[e] etw. [nicht] tun
(c) (determine) feststellen; (see, recognize)
erkennen (**by an** + Dat.); (with reference to the
future) [vorher]sagen
(d) (distinguish) unterscheiden
(e) **all told** insgesamt
[2] v.i., told (a) (determine) **how can you ~?**
wie kann man das feststellen od. wissen?;
you never can ~: man kann nie wissen
(b) (give information) erzählen (**of, about** von)
(c) (reveal secret) es verraten; **time will ~:** das
wird sich zeigen
(d) (produce an effect) sich auswirken
■ **tell a'part** v.t. auseinander halten
■ **tell 'off** v.t. (coll.) ~ **sb. off [for sth.]** jmdn.
[für od. wegen etw.] ausschimpfen

teller /'telə(r)/ n. (a) (in bank) ▶ CASHIER

(b) (counting votes) Stimmenzähler, *der/* -zählerin, *die*

telly /'telɪ/ *n.* (Brit. coll.) Fernseher, *der* (ugs.); **on ~:** im Fernsehen; **watch ~ :** Fernsehen gucken (ugs.)

temp /temp/ *n.* (Brit. coll.) Zeitarbeitskraft, *die*

temper /'tempə(r)/ ☐1 *n.* **(a)** Naturell, *das;* **be in a good/bad ~:** gute/schlechte Laune haben; **keep/lose one's ~:** sich beherrschen/die Beherrschung verlieren **(b)** (anger) **fit of ~:** Wutanfall, *der;* **have a ~:** jähzornig sein ☐2 *v.t.* mäßigen; mildern ⟨Kritik⟩

temperament /'tempramant/ *n.* (nature) Veranlagung, *die;* Natur, *die;* (disposition) Temperament, *das*

temperamental /tempra'mentl/ *adj.* launenhaft

temperate /'tempərat/ *adj.* gemäßigt

temperature /'temprɪtʃə(r)/ *n.* Temperatur, *die;* **have** *or* **run a ~** (coll.) Temperatur *od.* Fieber haben

template /'templɪt/ *n.* **(a)** Schablone, *die* **(b)** (Comp.) Schablone, *die;* Template, *das*

temple¹ /'templ/ *n.* Tempel, *der*

temple² *n.* (Anat.) Schläfe, *die*

tempo /'tempəʊ/ *n., pl.* **~s** *or* **tempi** /'tempiː/ Tempo, *das*

temporarily /'tempərərɪlɪ/ *adv.* vorübergehend

temporary /'tempərərɪ/ ☐1 *adj.* vorübergehend; provisorisch ⟨Gebäude, Büro;⟩ **~ job** Aushilfstätigkeit, *die* ☐2 *n.* Aushilfe, *die;* Aushilfskraft, *die*

tempt /tempt/ *v.t.* **(a) ~ sb. to do sth.** jmdn. geneigt machen, etw. zu tun; **be ~ed to do sth.** versucht sein, etw. zu tun; **~ sb. out** jmdn. hinauslocken **(b)** (provoke) herausfordern; **~ fate** das Schicksal herausfordern

temptation /temp'teɪʃn/ *n.* **(a)** *no pl.* (attracting) Verlockung, *die;* (being attracted) Versuchung, *die* **(b)** (thing) Verlockung, *die*

'tempting *adj.* verlockend

ten /ten/ ☐1 *adj.* zehn ☐2 *n.* Zehn, *die.* See also EIGHT

tenable /'tenəbl/ *adj.* haltbar ⟨Theorie⟩; vertretbar ⟨Standpunkt⟩

tenacious /tɪ'neɪʃəs/ *adj.* hartnäckig

tenacity /tɪ'næsɪtɪ/ *n.* Hartnäckigkeit, *die*

tenant /'tenənt/ *n.* (of flat, residential building) Mieter, *der/*Mieterin, *die;* (of farm, shop) Pächter, *der/*Pächterin, *die*

tend¹ /tend/ *v.i.* **~ to do sth.** dazu neigen *od.* tendieren, etw. zu tun; **~ to etw.** neigen; **he ~s to get upset if ...:** er regt sich leicht auf, wenn ...

tend² *v.t.* sich kümmern um; hüten ⟨Schafe⟩; bedienen ⟨Maschine⟩

tendency /'tendənsɪ/ *n.* (inclination) Tendenz, *die;* **have a ~ to do sth.** dazu neigen, etw. zu tun

tender¹ /'tendə(r)/ *adj.* **(a)** (not tough) zart **(b)** (loving) zärtlich **(c)** (sensitive) empfindlich

tender² ☐1 *v.t.* **(a)** (present) einreichen ⟨Rücktritt⟩; vorbringen ⟨Entschuldigung⟩ **(b)** (offer as payment) anbieten ☐2 *n.* Angebot, *das*

'tenderly *adv.* (gently) behutsam; (lovingly) zärtlich

'tenderness *n.* ▶ TENDER¹: Zartheit, *die;* Zärtlichkeit, *die;* Empfindlichkeit, *die*

tendon /'tendən/ *n.* (Anat.) Sehne, *die*

tenement /'tenɪmənt/ *n.* Mietshaus, *das*

tenet /'tenɪt/ *n.* Grundsatz, *der*

tenner /'tenə(r)/ *n.* (Brit. coll.) Zehnpfundschein, *der*

tennis /'tenɪs/ *n.* Tennis, *das*

tennis: ~ ball *n.* Tennisball, *der;* **~ club** *n.* Tennisverein, *der;* **~ court** *n.* (for lawn ~) Tennisplatz, *der;* (indoor) Tennishalle, *die;* **~ 'elbow** *n., no art.* (Med.) Tennisell[en]bogen, *der;* **~ match** *n.* Tennismatch, *das;* Tennisspiel, *das;* **~ racket** *n.* Tennisschläger, *der;* **~ shoe** *n.* Tennisschuh, *der*

tenor /'tenə(r)/ *n.* (Mus.) Tenor, *der*

tense¹ /tens/ *n.* (Ling.) Zeit, *die;* **in the present/future** *etc.* **~:** im Präsens/Futur *usw.*

tense² ☐1 *adj.* gespannt ☐2 *v.i.* **sb. ~s** jmds. Muskeln spannen sich an ☐3 *v.t.* anspannen

tension /'tenʃn/ *n.* **(a)** Spannung, *die* **(b)** (mental strain) Anspannung, *die*

tent /tent/ *n.* Zelt, *das*

tentacle /'tentəkl/ *n.* Tentakel, *der od. das*

tentative /'tentətɪv/ *adj.* **(a)** (not definite) vorläufig **(b)** (hesitant) zaghaft

tenterhooks /'tentəhʊks/ *n. pl.* **be on ~:** [wie] auf glühenden Kohlen sitzen

tenth /tenθ/ ☐1 *adj.* zehnt... ☐2 *n.* (in sequence, rank) Zehnte, *der/die/das;* (fraction) Zehntel, *das.* See also EIGHTH

tent: ~ peg *n.* Zeltpflock, *der;* **~ pole** *n.* Zeltstange, *die*

tenuous /'tenjʊəs/ *adj.* dünn ⟨Atmosphäre⟩; dürftig ⟨Argument⟩; unbegründet ⟨Anspruch⟩

tepid /'tepɪd/ *adj.* lauwarm

term /tɜːm/ *n.* **(a)** [Fach]begriff, *der* **(b)** *in pl.* (conditions) Bedingungen *Pl.;* **come to ~s with sth.** mit etw. zurechtkommen; (resign oneself to sth.) sich mit etw. abfinden **(c)** *in pl.* (charges) Konditionen *Pl.* **(d) in the short/long/medium ~:** kurz-/lang-/mittelfristig **(e)** (Sch.) Halbjahr, *das;* (Univ.: one of two/three divisions per year) Semester, *das/*Trimester, *das* ···⟶

t

(f) (limited period) Zeitraum, *der;* ~ [of office] Amtszeit, *die*

(g) *in pl.* (mode of expression) Worte *Pl.*

(h) *in pl.* (relations) be on good/bad ~s with sb. mit jmdm. auf gutem/schlechtem Fuß stehen

terminal /'tɜːmnl/ ① *n.* (a) (for train or bus) Bahnhof, *der;* (for airline passengers) Terminal, *der od. das*

(b) (Teleph., Comp.) Terminal, *das*

② *adj.* (Med.) unheilbar

terminally /'tɜːmnəlɪ/ *adv.* ~ ill unheilbar krank

terminate /'tɜːmneɪt/ *v.t.* (a) beenden; lösen ‹Vertrag›

(b) (Med.) unterbrechen ‹Schwangerschaft›

termini *pl. of* TERMINUS

terminology /tɜːmɪ'nɒlədʒɪ/ *n.* Terminologie, *die*

terminus /'tɜːmnəs/ *n., pl.* ~es *or* termini /'tɜːmnaɪ/ Endstation, *die*

terrace /'terəs, 'terɪs/ *n.* Terrasse, *die; (row of houses)* Häuserreihe, *die*

terraced house /'terəst haʊs, 'terɪst haʊs/ *n.* Reihenhaus, *das*

terracotta /terə'kɒtə/ *n., no indef. art.* Terrakotta, *die*

terrain /te'reɪn/ *n.* Gelände, *das*

terrestrial /tə'restrɪəl/ *adj.* terrestrisch ‹Raumschiff, Fernsehen, Bevölkerung›; Erd‹satellit, -bevölkerung›

terrible /'terɪbl/ *adj.* (a) (coll.: very great or bad) schrecklich (ugs.)

(b) (coll.: incompetent) schlecht

(c) (causing terror) furchtbar

terribly /'terɪblɪ/ *adv.* (a) (coll.: very) unheimlich (ugs.)

(b) (coll.: appallingly) furchtbar (ugs.)

(c) (coll.: incompetently) schlecht

(d) (fearfully) auf erschreckende Weise

terrier /'terɪə(r)/ *n.* Terrier, *der*

terrific /tə'rɪfɪk/ *adj.* (coll.) (a) (great, intense) irrsinnig (ugs.)

(b) (magnificent) sagenhaft (ugs.)

(c) (highly expert) klasse (ugs.)

terrify /'terɪfaɪ/ *v.t.* (a) Angst machen (+ *Dat.*); be terrified that ...: Angst haben, dass ...

(b) (scare) Angst einjagen (+ *Dat.*)

'terrifying *adj.* entsetzlich ‹Erlebnis, Buch›; Furcht erregend ‹Anblick›; beängstigend ‹Geschwindigkeit›

territorial /terɪ'tɔːrɪəl/ *adj.* territorial; Gebiets‹anspruch usw.›

territory /'terɪtrɪ/ *n.* Gebiet, *das*

terror /'terə(r)/ *n.* [panische] Angst; Schrecken, *der*

terrorism /'terərɪzm/ *n.* Terrorismus, *der;* (terrorist acts) Terror, *der*

'terrorist *n.* Terrorist, *der*/Terroristin, *die; attrib.* Terror‹gruppe, -organisation, -angriff, -netzwerk, -zelle›

terrorize /'terəraɪz/ *v.t.* (a) (frighten) in [Angst und] Schrecken versetzen

(b) (coerce) terrorisieren

terse /tɜːs/ *adj.* (a) (concise) kurz und bündig

(b) (curt) knapp

test /test/ ① *n.* (a) (Sch.) Klassenarbeit, *die;* (Univ.) Klausur, *die;* put sb./sth. to the ~: jmdn./etw. erproben

(b) (analysis) Test, *der*

② *v.t.* untersuchen ‹Wasser, Augen›; testen ‹Gehör, Augen›; prüfen ‹Schüler›; ~ sb. for Aids jmdn. auf Aids untersuchen

■ **'test out** *v.t.* ausprobieren ‹Produkte› (on an + *Dat.*); erproben ‹Theorie, Idee›

Testament /'testəmənt/ *n.* Old/New ~ (Bibl.) Altes/Neues Testament

test: ~ ban *n.* Atom[waffen]teststopp, *der;* ~ **ban treaty** *n.* [Atom]teststopp-Abkommen, *das;* ~ **drive** *n.* Probefahrt, *die;* ~**-drive** *v.t.* Probe fahren

testicle /'testɪkl/ *n.* Testikel, *der* (fachspr.); Hoden, *der*

testify /'testɪfaɪ/ ① *v.i.* (a) ~ to sth. etw. bezeugen

(b) (Law) ~ against sb. gegen jmdn. aussagen

② *v.t.* bestätigen

testimonial /testɪ'məʊnɪəl/ *n.* Zeugnis, *das;* Referenz, *die*

testimony /'testɪmənɪ/ *n.* Aussage, *die*

test: ~ pilot *n.* Testpilot, *der*/-pilotin, *die;* ~ **tube** *n.* Reagenzglas, *das;* ~**-tube baby** *n.* (coll.) Retortenbaby, *das* (ugs.)

testy /'testɪ/ *adj.* leicht reizbar ‹Person›; gereizt ‹Antwort›

tetanus /'tetənəs/ *n.* Tetanus, *der*

tetchy /'tetʃɪ/ *adj.* leicht reizbar; gereizt

tether /'teðə(r)/ ① *n.* be at the end of one's ~: am Ende [seiner Kraft] sein

② *v.t.* anbinden (to an + *Dat. od. Akk.*)

text /tekst/ ① *n.* Text, *der*

② *v.t.* ~ sb. jmdm. eine [Text]nachricht schicken

③ *v.i.* eine Textnachricht [ver]schicken; (to mobile phone) eine SMS [ver]schicken; simsen (ugs.)

text: ~book *n.* Lehrbuch, *das;* ~**book case** Paradefall, *der;* ~ **file** *n.* (Comp.) Textdatei, *die*

textile /'tekstaɪl/ *n.* Stoff, *der;* ~s Textilien *Pl.*

'textphone *n.* Texttelefon, *das*

'text processing *n.* (Comp.) Textverarbeitung, *die*

texture /'tekstʃə(r)/ *n.* Beschaffenheit, *die;* (of fabric) Struktur, *die*

Thai /taɪ/ ① *adj.* thailändisch; sb. is ~: jmd. ist Thai

② *n.* (a) *pl. same or* ~s Thai, *der/die*

(b) (language) Thai, *das*

Thailand /'taɪlænd/ *pr. n.* Thailand (*das*)

Thames /temz/ *pr. n.* Themse, *die*

than /ðən, *stressed* ðæn/ *conj.* als; I know you better ~ [I do] him ich kenne dich besser als ihn

thank /θæŋk/ *v.t.* ~ **sb. [for sth.]** jmdm. [für etw.] danken; ~ **God or goodness or heaven[s]** Gott sei Dank; [I] ~ **you** danke; **no,** ~ **you** nein, danke; **yes,** ~ **you** ja, bitte; ~ **you very much** vielen herzlichen Dank

thankful /'θæŋkfl/ *adj.* dankbar

thankfully /'θæŋkfəlɪ/ *adv.* **(a)** (gratefully) dankbar
(b) (as sentence-modifier: fortunately) glücklicherweise

'**thankless** *adj.* undankbar

thanks /θæŋks/ *n. pl.* **(a)** (gratitude) Dank, *der;* ~ **to** (with the help of) dank; (on account of the bad influence of) wegen
(b) (formula expr. gratitude) danke; **no,** ~: nein, danke; **yes,** ~: ja, bitte; **many** ~ (coll.) vielen Dank

thanksgiving /'θæŋksgɪvɪŋ/ *n.* T~ **[Day]** (Amer.) [amerikanisches] Erntedankfest; Thanksgiving Day, *der*

'**thank-you** *n.* (coll.) Dankeschön, *das*

that ⓵ /ðæt/ *adj., pl.* **those** /ðəʊz/ **(a)** dieser/diese/dieses
(b) (coupled or contrasted with 'this') der/die/das
⓶ /ðæt/ *pron., pl.* **those (a)** der/die/das; **what bird is** ~? was für ein Vogel ist das?; **like** ~: so; **[just] like** ~ (without effort, thought) einfach so; ~'**s right!** gut *od.* recht so; (iron.) nur so weiter!; ~ **will do** das reicht
(b) (Brit.) **who is** ~? wer ist da?; (on telephone) wer ist am Apparat?
⓷ /ðət/ *rel. pron., pl.* **same** der/die/das; **everyone** ~ **I know** jeder, den ich kenne; **this is all [the money]** ~ **I have** das ist alles [Geld], was ich habe
⓸ /ðæt/ *adv.* (coll.) so
⓹ /ðət/ *rel. adv.* der/die/das; **the day** ~ **I first met her** der Tag, an dem ich sie zum ersten Mal sah
⓺ /ðət, *stressed* ðæt/ *conj.* dass; [**in order**] ~: damit

thatch /θætʃ/ *n.* (of straw) Strohdach, *das;* (of reeds) Schilfdach, *das;* (roofing) Dachbedeckung, *die*

thatched /θætʃt/ *adj.* stroh-/schilfgedeckt

thaw /θɔː/ ⓵ *n.* Tauwetter, *das*
⓶ *v.i.* **(a)** tauen
(b) (melt) auftauen
⓷ *v.t.* auftauen
■ **thaw 'out** ▶ THAW 2, 3

the /before vowel ðɪ, before consonant ðə, when stressed ðiː/ ⓵ *def. art.* der/die/das
⓶ *adv.* ~ **more I practise** ~ **better I play** je mehr ich übe, desto *od.* umso besser spiele ich; **so much** ~ **worse for sb./sth.** umso schlimmer für jmdn./etw

theatre (*Amer.:* **theater**) /'θɪətə(r)/ *n.* **(a)** Theater, *das*
(b) (lecture ~) Hörsaal, *der*
(c) (Brit. Med.) ▶ OPERATING THEATRE

theatrical /θɪ'ætrɪkl/ *adj.* **(a)** schauspielerisch
(b) (showy) theatralisch

theft /θeft/ *n.* Diebstahl, *der*

their /ðeə(r)/ *poss. pron. attrib.* ihr

theirs /ðeəz/ *poss. pron. pred.* ihrer/ihre/ ihres

them /ðəm, *stressed* ðem/ *pron.* sie; (as indirect object) ihnen; *see also* HER[1]

theme /θiːm/ *n.* Thema, *das*

theme: ~ **music** *n.* Titelmelodie, *die;* ~ **park** *n.:* Freizeitpark, dessen Attraktionen und Einrichtungen auf ein bestimmtes Thema bezogen sind; ~ **song** *n.* Erkennungssong, *der;* ~ **tune** Erkennungsmelodie, *die*

themselves /ðəm'selvz/ *pron.* **(a)** *emphat.* selbst
(b) *refl.* sich ⟨waschen usw.⟩; sich selbst ⟨die Schuld geben, regieren⟩. See also HERSELF

then /ðen/ ⓵ *adv.* **(a)** (at that time) damals; ~ **and there** auf der Stelle
(b) (after that) dann; ~ **[again]** (and also) außerdem; **but** ~ (after all) aber schließlich
(c) (in that case) dann; **but** ~ **again** aber andererseits
⓶ *n.* **before** ~: vorher; davor; **from** ~ **on** von da an; **since** ~: seitdem
⓷ *adj.* damalig

theological /θiːə'lɒdʒɪkl/ *adj.* theologisch; Theologie⟨student⟩

theology /θɪ'ɒlədʒɪ/ *n.* Theologie, *die*

theoretical /θɪə'retɪkl/ *adj.* theoretisch

theory /'θɪərɪ/ *n.* Theorie, *die;* **in** ~: theoretisch

therapeutic /θerə'pjuːtɪk/ *adj.* therapeutisch

therapist /'θerəpɪst/ *n.* Therapeut, *der/* Therapeutin, *die*

therapy /'θerəpɪ/ *n.* Therapie, *die*

there /ðeə(r)/ ⓵ *adv.* **(a)** (in/at that place) da; dort; (fairly close) da; **be down/in/up** ~: da unten/drin/oben sein
(b) (calling attention) **hello or hi** ~! hallo!; **you** ~! Sie da!
(c) (in that respect) da; **so** ~: und damit basta (ugs.)
(d) (to that place) dahin, dorthin ⟨gehen, fahren, rücken⟩; **down/up** ~: dort hinunter/ hinauf
(e) /ðə(r), *stressed* ðeə(r)/ **was** ~ **anything in it?** war da irgendwas drin?; ~ **was once es** war einmal; ~ **is enough food** es gibt genug zu essen
⓶ *int.* ~, ~: na, na (ugs.); ~ **[you are]!** da, siehst du!
⓷ *n.* da; dort; **near** ~: da *od.* dort in der Nähe

thereabouts /'ðeərəbaʊts/ *adv.* **(a)** da [in der Nähe]
(b) (near that number) ungefähr

therefore /'ðeəfɔː(r)/ *adv.* deshalb; also

thermal /'θɜːml/ *adj.* thermisch; ~ **underwear** *n.* kälteisolierende Unterwäsche

thermal imaging /θɜːml 'ɪmɪdʒɪŋ/ *n.* Thermographie, *die*

t

thermometer /θə'mɒmɪtə(r)/ n.
Thermometer, *das*

Thermos, thermos ® /'θɜːməs/ n.
~ **[flask/jug/bottle]** Thermosflasche, *die* Ⓦ

thermostat /'θɜːməstæt/ n. Thermostat,
der

these pl. of THIS

thesis /'θiːsɪs/ n., pl. **theses** /'θiːsiːz/ **(a)**
(proposition) These, *die*
(b) (dissertation) Dissertation, *die* (on über
+ Akk.)

they /ðeɪ/ pron. **(a)** sie
(b) (people in general) man

they'd /ðeɪd/ **(a)** = they would
(b) = they had

they'll /ðeɪl/ = they will

they're /ðeə(r)/ = they are

they've /ðeɪv/ = they have

thick /θɪk/ ⒈ adj. **(a)** dick; a rope two
inches ~, a two-inch ~ rope ein zwei Zoll
starkes od. dickes Seil
(b) (dense) dicht ⟨Haar, Nebel, Wolken usw.⟩
(c) (filled) ~ **with** voll von
(d) dickflüssig ⟨Sahne⟩; dick ⟨Suppe,
Schlamm, Kleister⟩
(e) (stupid) dumm
⒉ n. **in the** ~ **of** mitten in (+ Dat.)

thick 'ear n. **give sb. a** ~ (Brit. coll.) jmdm.
ein paar hinter die Ohren geben (ugs.)

thicken /'θɪkn/ ⒈ v.t. dicker machen;
eindicken ⟨Sauce⟩
⒉ v.i. **(a)** dicker werden
(b) ⟨Nebel:⟩ dichter werden
(c) the plot ~**s** die Sache wird kompliziert

'thickly adv. **(a)** (in a thick layer) dick
(b) (densely) dicht

'thickness n. **(a)** Dicke, *die*; **be two metres
in** ~: zwei Meter dick sein
(b) (denseness) Dichte, *die*

thick: ~**set** adj. gedrungen; ~**-skinned**
adj. (fig.) dickfellig (ugs.)

thief /θiːf/ n., pl. **thieves** /θiːvz/ Dieb, *der*/
Diebin, *die*

thieve /θiːv/ v.i. stehlen

thieves pl. of THIEF

thigh /θaɪ/ n. Oberschenkel, *der*

thimble /'θɪmbl/ n. Fingerhut, *der*

thin /θɪn/ ⒈ adj. **(a)** dünn; a tall, ~ man ein
großer, hagerer Mann
(b) (sparse) dünn, schütter ⟨Haar⟩
⒉ adv. dünn
⒊ v.t., -nn-: **(a)** dünner machen
(b) (dilute) verdünnen
■ **thin 'out** v.i. ⟨Menschenmenge:⟩ sich
verlaufen; ⟨Verkehr:⟩ abnehmen

thing /θɪŋ/ n. **(a)** Sache, *die*; Ding, *das*;
what's that ~ in your hand? was hast du da
in der Hand?; be a rare ~: etwas Seltenes
sein
(b) (action) it was the right ~ to do es war das
einzig Richtige; that was a foolish/friendly
~ to do das war eine große Dummheit/das
war sehr freundlich

(c) (fact) [Tat]sache, *die*; it's a strange ~ that
...: es ist seltsam, dass ...; the best/worst
~ about her das Beste/Schlimmste an ihr
(d) (idea) say the first ~ that comes into
one's head das sagen, was einem gerade so
einfällt; what a ~ to say! wie kann man nur
so etwas sagen!
(e) (task) she has a reputation for getting ~s
done sie ist für ihre Tatkraft bekannt; a big
~ to undertake ein großes Unterfangen
(f) (affair) Sache, *die*; Angelegenheit, *die*
(g) (circumstance) take ~s too seriously alles
zu ernst nehmen; how are ~s? wie gehts
[dir]?
(h) (individual, creature) Ding, *das*
(i) in pl. (personal belongings, clothes) Sachen Pl.
(j) (product of work) Sache, *die*; the latest ~:
der letzte Schrei
(k) (what is important or proper) das Richtige; the
~ is ... (question) die Frage ist ...

thingamy /'θɪŋəmɪ/, **thingumabob**
/'θɪŋəməbɒb/, **thingumajig** /'θɪŋəmədʒɪg/,
thingummy /'θɪŋəmɪ/, **thingy** /'θɪŋɪ/ ns.
(coll.) Dings, *der*/*die*/*das* (salopp); Dingsbums,
der/*die*/*das* (ugs.)

think /θɪŋk/ ⒈ v.t., **thought** /θɔːt/ **(a)**
(consider) meinen; **we** ~ [that] he will come
wir denken od. glauben, dass er kommt;
what do you ~? was meinst du? do you
really ~ so? findest du wirklich?; what do
you ~ of him/it? was hältst du von ihm/
davon?; ..., don't you ~? ... , findest od.
meinst du nicht auch?; I ~ so/not ich glaube
schon/nicht; I ~ I'll try ich glaube, ich werde
es versuchen
(b) (imagine) sich (Dat.) vorstellen
⒉ v.i., **thought** [nach]denken; I need time to
~: ich muss es mir erst überlegen; I've been
~ing ich habe nachgedacht; ~ twice es sich
(Dat.) zweimal überlegen
■ **'think of** v.t. **(a)** denken an (+ Akk.); he
~s of everything er denkt einfach an alles
(b) (have as idea) we'll ~ of something wir
werden uns etwas einfallen lassen; can you
~ of anyone who ...? fällt dir jemand ein,
der ...?
(c) (remember) sich erinnern an (+ Akk.); I
just can't ~ of her name ich komme einfach
nicht auf ihren Namen
(d) ~ little/nothing of sb./sth. (consider
contemptible) wenig/nichts von jmdm./etw.
halten; not ~ much of sb./sth. nicht viel von
jmdm./etw. halten
■ **think 'over** v.t. sich (Dat.) überlegen
■ **think 'through** v.t. [gründlich]
durchdenken
■ **think 'up** v.t. (coll.) sich (Dat.) ausdenken
'thinker n. Denker, *der*/Denkerin, *die*
'think tank n. Beraterstab, *der*
'thin-skinned adj. (fig.) empfindlich;
dünnhäutig (geh.)

third /θɜːd/ ⒈ adj. dritt...
⒉ n. (in sequence, rank) Dritte, *der*/*die*/*das*;
(fraction) Drittel, *das*. See also EIGHTH

'thirdly adv. drittens

third: ~ **'party** n. attrib. ~**-party** insurance Haftpflichtversicherung, die; ~**-rate** adj. drittklassig; **T**~ **'World** n. Dritte Welt; **countries of the T**~ **World, T**~ **World countries** Länder der Dritten Welt

thirst /θɜːst/ **1** n. Durst, der; **die of** ~: verdursten
2 v.i. ~ **for revenge/knowledge** nach Rache/Wissen dürsten (geh.)

'thirsty adj. durstig; **be** ~: Durst haben

thirteen /θɜːˈtiːn/ **1** adj. dreizehn
2 n. Dreizehn, die. See also EIGHT

thirteenth /θɜːˈtiːnθ/ adj. dreizehnt... See also EIGHTH

thirtieth /ˈθɜːtɪɪθ/ **1** adj. dreißigst...
2 n. (fraction) Dreißigstel, das. See also EIGHTH

thirty /ˈθɜːtɪ/ **1** adj. dreißig
2 n. Dreißig, die. See also EIGHT; EIGHTY 2

'thirty-something **1** adj. **be** ~: in den Dreißigern sein
2 n. Dreißiger, der/-in, die

this /ðɪs/ **1** adj., pl. **these** /ðiːz/ dieser/ diese/dieses; (with less emphasis) der/die/das; **at** ~ **time** zu dieser Zeit; **by** ~ **time** inzwischen; mittlerweile; **these days** heut[zutage]; **before** ~ **time** vorher; zuvor; **all** ~ **week** die[se] ganze Woche; ~ **morning/ evening** etc. heute Morgen/Abend usw.; **these last three weeks** die letzten drei Wochen; ~ **Monday** (to come) nächsten Montag
2 pron., pl. **these** (a) **what's** ~? was ist [denn] das?; **fold it like** ~: falte es so! (b) (the present) **before** ~: bis jetzt (c) (Brit. Teleph.: person speaking) ~ **is Andy** hier [spricht od. ist] Andy; (Amer. Teleph.) **who did you say** ~ **was?** wer ist am Apparat? (d) ~ **and that** dies und das

thistle /ˈθɪsl/ n. Distel, die

thorn /θɔːn/ n. (a) (part of plant) Dorn, der (b) (plant) Dornenstrauch, der

'thorny adj. (a) dornig (b) (fig.) heikel

thorough /ˈθʌrə/ adj. gründlich

thorough: ~**bred** n. reinrassiges Tier; (horse) Rassepferd, das; ~**fare** n. Durchfahrtsstraße, die; **'no** ~**fare'** „Durchfahrt verboten"; (on foot) „kein Durchgang"

'thoroughly adv. gründlich ⟨untersuchen⟩; gehörig ⟨erschöpft⟩; so richtig ⟨genießen⟩; zutiefst ⟨beschämt⟩; total ⟨verdorben, verwöhnt⟩; **be** ~ **fed up with sth.** (coll.) von etw. die Nase gestrichen voll haben (ugs.)

'thoroughness n. Gründlichkeit, die

those ▶ THAT 1, 2

though /ðəʊ/ **1** conj. (a) (despite the fact that) obwohl; **late** ~ **it was** obwohl es so spät war;

the car, ~ **powerful, is also economical** der Wagen ist zwar stark, aber [zugleich] auch wirtschaftlich
(b) (but nevertheless) aber; **a slow** ~ **certain method** eine langsame, aber od. wenn auch sichere Methode
(c) (even if) [even] ~: auch wenn
(d) (and yet) ~ **you never know** obwohl man nie weiß
2 adv. (coll.) trotzdem

thought /θɔːt/ **1** ▶ THINK
2 n. (a) no pl. Denken, das (b) no pl., no art. (reflection) Überlegung, die; Nachdenken, das (c) (consideration) Rücksicht, die (**for** auf + Akk.) (d) (idea, conception) Gedanke, der; **it's the** ~ **that counts** der gute Wille zählt; **give up all** ~[s] **of sth.** sich (Dat.) etw. aus dem Kopf schlagen

thoughtful /ˈθɔːtfl/ adj. (a) nachdenklich (b) (considerate) rücksichtsvoll; (helpful) aufmerksam

'thoughtfully adv. (a) nachdenklich (b) (considerately) rücksichtsvollerweise

'thoughtless adj. (a) gedankenlos (b) (inconsiderate) rücksichtslos

'thoughtlessly adv. (a) gedankenlos (b) (inconsiderately) aus Rücksichtslosigkeit

thought: ~ **process** n. Denkprozess, der; ~**-provoking** adj. nachdenklich stimmend; **be** ~**-provoking** nachdenklich stimmen

thousand /ˈθaʊznd/ **1** adj. (a) tausend; **a** or **one** ~: eintausend; **two/several** ~: zweitausend/mehrere tausend; **a** or **one** ~ **and one** [ein]tausend[und]eins (b) **a** ~ **[and one]** (fig.: innumerable) tausend (ugs.)
2 n. (a) (number) tausend; **a** or **one/two** ~: ein-/zweitausend (b) (written figure; group) Tausend, das (c) (indefinite amount) ~**s** tausende

thousandth /ˈθaʊznθ/ **1** adj. tausendst...
2 n. (fraction) Tausendstel, das; (in sequence) Tausendste, der/die/das

thrash /θræʃ/ v.t. (a) verprügeln (b) (defeat) vernichtend schlagen
■ **thrash 'out** v.t. ausdiskutieren

thrashing /ˈθræʃɪŋ/ n. (beating) Prügel Pl.; **give sb. a** ~: jmdm. eine Tracht Prügel verpassen (ugs.)

thread /θred/ **1** n. (a) Faden, der (b) (of screw) Gewinde, das
2 v.t. (a) einfädeln; auffädeln ⟨Perlen⟩ (b) ~ **one's way through sth.** sich durch etw. schlängeln

'threadbare adj. abgenutzt; abgetragen ⟨Kleidung⟩; (fig.) abgedroschen ⟨Argument⟩

threat /θret/ n. Drohung, die

threaten /ˈθretn/ v.t. (a) bedrohen; ~ **sb. with sth.** jmdm. etw. androhen (b) ~ **to do sth.** damit drohen, etw. zu tun (c) drohen mit ⟨Gewalt, Rache usw.⟩

threatening /ˈθretnɪŋ/ adj. drohend

three /θriː/ ⓵ adj. drei

⓶ n. Drei, die. See also EIGHT

three: ~-dimensional /θriːdɪˈmenʃənl/ adj. dreidimensional; **~fold** adj., adv. dreifach; **a ~fold increase** ein Anstieg auf das Dreifache; **~-lane** adj. dreispurig; **~-pin** ▸ PIN 1 C; **~-quarters** ⓵ n. drei Viertel pl. (of + Gen.); **~-quarters of an hour** eine Dreiviertelstunde; ⓶ adv. drei viertel (voll); **~some** /ˈθriːsəm/ n. Dreigespann, das; Trio, das

thresh /θreʃ/ v.t. dreschen

threshold /ˈθreʃəʊld/ n. Schwelle, die

threw ▸ THROW 1

thrift /θrɪft/ n. Sparsamkeit, die

'thrifty adj. sparsam

thrill /θrɪl/ ⓵ v.t. (a) (excite) faszinieren (b) (delight) begeistern

⓶ n. (a) Erregung, die (b) (exciting experience) aufregendes Erlebnis

'thriller n. Thriller, der

'thrilling adj. aufregend; spannend (Buch, Film)

thrive /θraɪv/ v.i., thrived or throve /θrəʊv/, thrived or thriven /ˈθrɪvn/ (a) (Pflanze:) wachsen und gedeihen (b) (prosper) aufblühen (on bei)

throat /θrəʊt/ n. Hals, der; (esp. inside) Kehle, die; **a** [sore] **~:** Halsschmerzen Pl.

throb /θrɒb/ ⓵ v.i., -bb- pochen; (Motor:) dröhnen

⓶ n. Pochen, das; (of engine) Dröhnen, das

throes /θrəʊz/ n. pl. Qual, die; **be in the ~ of sth.** (fig.) mitten in etw. (Dat.) stecken (ugs.)

thrombosis /θrɒmˈbəʊsɪs/ n., pl. thromboses /θrɒmˈbəʊsiːz/ Thrombose, die

throne /θrəʊn/ n. Thron, der

throng /θrɒŋ/ n. [Menschen]menge, die

throttle /ˈθrɒtl/ v.t. erdrosseln

through /θruː/ ⓵ prep. (a) durch (b) (Amer.: up to and including) bis [einschließlich] (c) (by reason of) durch; infolge von (Vernachlässigung, Einflüssen)

⓶ adv. (a) let sb. **~:** jmdn. durchlassen (b) (Teleph.) be **~:** durch sein (ugs.); be **~ to** sb. mit jmdm. verbunden sein

⓷ attrib. adj. durchgehend (Zug)

through'out ⓵ prep. **~ the war/period** den ganzen Krieg/die ganze Zeit hindurch; **~ the country** im ganzen Land

⓶ adv. (entirely) ganz; (always) stets; die ganze Zeit [hindurch]

throve ▸ THRIVE

throw /θrəʊ/ ⓵ v.t., threw /θruː/, thrown /θrəʊn/ (a) werfen; **~ sth. to sb.** jmdm. etw. zuwerfen; **~ sth. at sb.** etw. nach jmdm. werfen (b) (bring to the ground) zu Boden werfen; abwerfen (Reiter)

(c) (coll.: disconcert) (Frage:) aus der Fassung bringen

⓶ n. Wurf, der

■ **throw a'way** v.t. (a) wegwerfen (b) (lose by neglect) verschenken (Vorteil, Spiel usw.)

■ **throw 'up** ⓵ v.t. (a) hochwerfen (Arme, Hände) (b) (produce) hervorbringen (Ideen usw.) ⓶ v.i. (coll.) brechen (ugs.)

'throwaway adj. (a) Wegwerf-; Einweg- (b) beiläufig (Bemerkung)

thrown ▸ THROW 1

thrush /θrʌʃ/ n. (Ornith.) Drossel, die

thrust /θrʌst/ ⓵ v.t., thrust stoßen; **~ aside** (fig.) beiseite schieben

⓶ n. Stoß, der

thud /θʌd/ n. dumpfer Schlag

thug /θʌg/ n. Schläger, der; **football ~s** Fußballrowdys Pl.

thuggish /ˈθʌgɪʃ/ adj. aggressiv (Verhalten, Fußballfan)

thumb /θʌm/ ⓵ n. Daumen, der; **get the ~s up** (Person, Projekt:) akzeptiert werden; **be under sb.'s ~:** unter jmds. Fuchtel stehen ⓶ v.t. **~ a lift** per Anhalter fahren

■ **'thumb through** v.t. durchblättern

thumb: ~ index n. Daumenregister, das; **~nail** n. Daumennagel, der; **~tack** n. (Amer.) Reißzwecke, die

thump /θʌmp/ ⓵ v.t. [mit Wucht] schlagen ⓶ v.i. (a) hämmern (at, on gegen) (b) (Herz:) heftig pochen ⓷ n. (blow) Schlag, der; (sound) Bums, der (ugs.); dumpfer Schlag

thunder /ˈθʌndə(r)/ ⓵ n. Donner, der ⓶ v.i. donnern

thunder: ~clap n. Donnerschlag, der; **~storm** n. Gewitter, das

thundery /ˈθʌndərɪ/ adj. gewittrig

Thurs. abbr. = **Thursday** Do.

Thursday /ˈθɜːzdeɪ, ˈθɜːzdɪ/ n. Donnerstag, der; see also FRIDAY

thus /ðʌs/ adv. so

thwart /θwɔːt/ v.t. durchkreuzen (Pläne); vereiteln (Versuch); **~ sb.** jmdm. einen Strich durch die Rechnung machen

thyme /taɪm/ n. Thymian, der

thyroid /ˈθaɪrɔɪd/ n. Schilddrüse, die

tiara /tɪˈɑːrə/ n. Diadem, das

tick /tɪk/ ⓵ v.i. ticken ⓶ v.t. (a) mit einem Häkchen versehen (b) ▸ **~ OFF** A ⓷ n. (a) (of clock etc.) Ticken, das (b) (mark) Häkchen, das

■ **tick 'off** v.t. (a) (cross off) abhaken (b) (coll.: reprimand) rüffeln (ugs.)

ticket /ˈtɪkɪt/ n. Karte, die; (for bus, train) Fahrschein, der; (for aeroplane) Flugschein, der; (for lottery, raffle) Los, das; (for library) Ausweis, der; **price ~:** Preisschild, das

ticket: ~ agency n. Kartenvorverkaufsstelle, die; **~ agent** n.

Inhaber/Inhaberin einer
Kartenvorverkaufsstelle; ~ **collector** n.
(on train) Schaffner, der/Schaffnerin, die; (on
station) Fahrkartenkontrolleur, der/
-kontrolleurin, die; ~ **dispenser** n.
Kartenautomat, der; (for train etc.) Fahrschein-
od. Fahrkartenautomat, der; ~ **holder** n.
Besitzer/Besitzerin einer Eintrittskarte;
~ **machine** ▶ ~ DISPENSER; ~ **office** n.
Fahrkartenschalter, der; (for advance booking)
Kartenvorverkaufsstelle, die

tickle /'tɪkl/ v.t. & i. kitzeln

ticklish /'tɪklɪʃ/ adj. kitzlig

tidal /'taɪdl/ adj. Gezeiten

'tidal wave n. Flutwelle, die

tiddlywinks /'tɪdlɪwɪŋks/ n. sing. (game)
Flohhüpfen, das

tide /taɪd/ [1] n. Tide, die (nordd.); **high ~:**
Flut, die; **low ~:** Ebbe, die; **the ~s** die
Gezeiten; **the ~ is in/out** es ist Flut/Ebbe
[2] v.t. ~ **sb. over** jmdm. über die Runden
helfen (ugs.)

tidiness /'taɪdɪnɪs/ n. Ordentlichkeit, die

tidy /'taɪdɪ/ [1] adj. ordentlich; aufgeräumt
⟨Zimmer, Schreibtisch⟩
[2] v.t. aufräumen; ~ **oneself** sich
zurechtmachen
■ **tidy 'up** v.i. aufräumen

tie /taɪ/ [1] v.t. **tying** /'taɪɪŋ/ binden (**to** an
+ Akk., **into** zu); ~ **a knot** einen Knoten
machen; (Sport) ~ **the match** unentschieden
spielen
[2] v.i., **tying (a)** (be fastened) **it ~s at the
back** es wird hinten gebunden
(b) (have equal scores) ~ **for second place** mit
gleicher Punktzahl den zweiten Platz
erreichen
[3] n. **(a)** Krawatte, die
(b) (bond) Band, das; (restriction) Bindung, die
(c) (equality of scores) Punktgleichheit, die
(d) (Sport: match) Begegnung, die
■ **tie 'in** v.i. ~ **in with sth.** zu etw. passen
■ **tie 'up** v.t. **(a)** festbinden; ~ **up a parcel**
ein Paket verschnüren
(b) (keep busy) beschäftigen

tier /tɪə(r)/ n. **(a)** Rang, der
(b) (unit) Stufe, die

tiger /'taɪgə(r)/ n. Tiger, der

tiger e'conomy n. Tigerstaat, der

tight /taɪt/ [1] adj. **(a)** (firm) fest; fest
angezogen ⟨Schraube, Mutter⟩; fest sitzend
⟨Deckel⟩
(b) (close-fitting) eng ⟨Kleid, Schuh usw.⟩
(c) (impermeable) ~ **seal/joint** dichter
Verschluss/dichte Fuge
(d) (taut) straff
(e) (difficult to negotiate) **a ~ corner** eine enge
Kurve; **be in a ~ corner** (fig.) in der Klemme
sein (ugs.)
(f) (strict) streng ⟨Kontrolle, Disziplin⟩
(g) (coll.: stingy) knauserig (ugs.)
(h) (coll.: drunk) voll (salopp)
[2] adv. fest; **hold ~!** halt dich fest!

[3] n. in pl. **(a)** (Brit.) **[pair of]** ~s
Strumpfhose, die
(b) (of dancer etc.) Trikothose, die

tighten /'taɪtn/ [1] v.t. **(a)** [fest] anziehen
⟨Knoten, Schraube⟩; straff ziehen ⟨Seil⟩
(b) verschärfen ⟨Kontrolle⟩
[2] v.i. sich spannen

tight-fisted /taɪt'fɪstɪd/ adj. geizig

'tightrope n. Drahtseil, das

tile /taɪl/ [1] n. (on roof) Ziegel, der; (on floor)
Fliese, die; (on wall) Kachel, die
[2] v.t. [mit Ziegeln] decken ⟨Dach⟩; fliesen
⟨Fußboden⟩; kacheln ⟨Wand⟩

till[1] /tɪl/ [1] prep. bis; (followed by article +
noun) bis zu; **not** [...] ~: erst
[2] conj. bis

till[2] n. Kasse, die

'till receipt n. Kassenzettel, der

tilt /tɪlt/ [1] v.i. kippen
[2] v.t. kippen; neigen ⟨Kopf⟩
[3] n. **(a)** Schräglage, die; **a 45° ~:** eine
Neigung von 45°
(b) [at] full ~: mit voller Wucht

timber /'tɪmbə(r)/ n. [Bau]holz, das

time /taɪm/ [1] n. **(a)** Zeit, die; **in [the
course of]** ~, **as** ~ **goes on/went on** mit der
Zeit; im Laufe der Zeit; **in** ~, **with** ~ (sooner
or later) mit der Zeit; **in [good]** ~ (not late)
rechtzeitig; **all the** or **this** ~: die ganze Zeit;
(without ceasing) ständig; **a short** ~ **ago** vor
kurzem; ~ **off** or **out** freie Zeit; **in 'no** ~: im
Handumdrehen; **in a week's/year's** ~: in
einer Woche/in einem Jahr; **harvest/
Christmas** ~: Ernte-/Weihnachtszeit, die; **on
~** (punctually) pünktlich; **ahead of** ~: zu früh
⟨ankommen⟩; vorzeitig ⟨fertig werden⟩; **have
a good** ~: sich amüsieren; Spaß haben
(ugs.); **have no** ~ **for sb./sth.** (fig.) für jmdn./
etw. ist einem seine Zeit zu schade
(b) (occasion) Mal, das; **for the first** ~: zum
ersten Mal; **at** ~**s** gelegentlich; ~ **and again,
~ after** ~: immer [und immer] wieder; **at
one** ~, **at [one and] the same** ~
(simultaneously) gleichzeitig; **one at a** ~:
einzeln; **two at a** ~: jeweils zwei
(c) (point in day etc.) [Uhr]zeit, die; **tell the** ~:
die Uhr lesen; **what** ~ **is it?, what is the** ~?
wie spät ist es?; **by this/that** ~: inzwischen;
by the ~ **[that] we arrived** bis wir hinkamen;
T~! (Brit.: in pub) Feierabend!; ~, **[ladies and]
gentlemen, please!** wir machen Feierabend,
meine [Damen und] Herren!
(d) (multiplication) mal; **three** ~**s four** drei mal
vier
(e) (Mus.) Takt, der; **in** ~: im Takt
[2] v.t. **(a)** zeitlich abstimmen; **be well** ~d
zur richtigen Zeit kommen
(b) (set to operate at correct ~) einstellen
(c) (measure ~ taken by) stoppen

time: ~ **bomb** n. Zeitbombe, die;
~**-consuming** adj. **(a)** (taking ~)
zeitaufwendig; **(b)** (wasteful of ~)
zeitraubend; ~ **lag** n. zeitliche
Verzögerung

timeless /ˈtaɪmlɪs/ adj. zeitlos

'**time limit** n. Frist, die

timely /ˈtaɪmlɪ/ adj. rechtzeitig

time: ~scale n. Zeitskala, die; **~ sheet** n. Stundenzettel, der; **~ switch** n. Zeitschalter, der; **~table** n. (a) (scheme of work) Zeitplan, der; (Educ.) Stundenplan, der; (b) (Transport) Fahrplan, der; **~ warp** n. Verwerfung im Raum-Zeit-Kontinuum; **~ zone** n. Zeitzone, die

timid /ˈtɪmɪd/ adj. (a) scheu ⟨Tier⟩ (b) zaghaft ⟨Mensch⟩; (shy) schüchtern

timing /ˈtaɪmɪŋ/ n. (a) that was perfect ~! du kommst gerade im richtigen Augenblick! (b) (Theatre, Sport) Timing, das

tin /tɪn/ ① n. (a) (metal) Zinn, das; ~[plate] Weißblech, das (b) (Brit.: for preserving) [Konserven]dose, die ② v.t., **-nn-** (Brit.) zu Konserven verarbeiten

tin 'foil n. Stanniol, das; Alufolie, die

tinge /tɪndʒ/ ① v.t., **~ing** /ˈtɪndʒɪŋ/ tönen ② n. [leichte] Färbung; (fig.) Hauch, der

tingle /ˈtɪŋgl/ v.i. kribbeln

tinker /ˈtɪŋkə(r)/ ① n. Kesselflicker, der ② v.i. ~ **with** sth. an etw. (Dat.) herumbasteln (ugs.)

tinkle /ˈtɪŋkl/ ① n. Klingeln, das ② v.i. klingeln

tinned /tɪnd/ adj. (Brit.) Dosen-

tin: ~opener n. (Brit.) Dosenöffner, der; **~pot** attrib. adj. (derog.) schäbig

tinsel /ˈtɪnsl/ n. Lametta, das

tint /tɪnt/ ① n. Farbton, der ② v.t. tönen; kolorieren ⟨Zeichnung⟩

tiny /ˈtaɪnɪ/ adj. winzig

tip¹ /tɪp/ n. (end, point) Spitze, die

tip² ① v.i., **-pp-** (lean, fall) kippen; ~ **over** umkippen ② v.t., **-pp-**: (a) (make tilt) kippen (b) (make overturn) umkippen; (Brit.: discharge) kippen (c) voraussagen ⟨Sieger⟩; ~ sb. to win auf jmds. Sieg tippen (d) (reward) ~ sb. jmdm. Trinkgeld geben ③ n. (a) (money) Trinkgeld, das (b) (special information) Hinweis, der; Tipp, der (ugs.) (c) (Brit.) Müllkippe, die ∎ **tip 'off** v.t. ~ sb. off jmdm. einen Hinweis od. (ugs.) Tipp geben

'**tip-off** n. Hinweis, der

tipsy /ˈtɪpsɪ/ adj. (coll.) angeheitert; beschwipst (ugs.)

tip: ~toe ① v.i. auf Zehenspitzen gehen; ② n. on ~toe[s] auf Zehenspitzen; **~top** adj. tipptopp (ugs.)

tire¹ /ˈtaɪə(r)/ (Amer.) ▶ TYRE

tire² ① v.t. ermüden ② v.i. müde werden; ermüden; ~ **of** sth./ doing sth. einer Sache (Gen.) überdrüssig werden ∎ **tire 'out** v.t. erschöpfen; ~ oneself out doing sth. etw. bis zur Erschöpfung tun

tired /ˈtaɪəd/ adj. (a) (weary) müde (b) (fed up) be ~ of sth./doing sth. etw. satt haben/es satt haben, etw. zu tun

tiredness /ˈtaɪədnɪs/ n. Müdigkeit, die

'**tireless** adj. unermüdlich

tiresome /ˈtaɪəsəm/ adj. (a) (wearisome) mühsam (b) (annoying) lästig

tiring /ˈtaɪərɪŋ/ adj. ermüdend

tissue /ˈtɪʃuː, ˈtɪsjuː/ n. (a) Gewebe, das (b) [paper] ~: Papiertuch, das; (handkerchief) Papiertaschentuch, das (c) ~ [paper] Seidenpapier, das

tit¹ /tɪt/ n. (Ornith.) Meise, die

tit² n. it's ~ for tat wie du mir, so ich dir

'**titbit** n. (a) (food) Häppchen, das (ugs.) (b) (piece of news) Neuigkeit, die

titchy /ˈtɪtʃɪ/ adj. (coll.) klitzeklein (ugs.)

titillate /ˈtɪtɪleɪt/ v.t. erregen

titillation /tɪtɪˈleɪʃn/ n. Kitzel, der

title /ˈtaɪtl/ n. Titel, der

title: ~ deed n. (Law) Eigentumsurkunde, die; **~holder** n. (Sport) Titelhalter, der/ -halterin, die; ~ **page** n. Titelseite, die; ~ **role** n. Titelrolle, die

tittle-tattle /ˈtɪtltætl/ n. Klatsch, der (ugs.)

'**T-junction** n. Einmündung, die

to ① /before vowel tʊ, before consonant tə, stressed tuː/ prep. (a) (in the direction of and reaching) zu; (with name of place) nach; **go to work/to the theatre** zur Arbeit/ins Theater gehen; **to France** nach Frankreich (b) (as far as) bis zu; **from London to Edinburgh** von London [bis] nach Edinburgh; **increase from 10% to 20%** von 10% auf 20% steigen (c) (introducing relationship or indirect object) **to sb./ sth.** jmdm./einer Sache (Dat.); **lend/explain** etc. sth. **to sb.** jmdm. etw. leihen/erklären usw.; **speak to sb.** mit jmdm. sprechen; **that's all there is to it** mehr ist dazu nicht zu sagen; **what's that to you?** was geht das dich an?; **to me** (in my opinion) meiner Meinung nach; **14 miles to the gallon** 14 Meilen auf eine Gallone (d) (until) bis; **to the end** bis zum Ende; **to this day** bis heute; **five [minutes] to eight** fünf [Minuten] vor acht (e) (with infinitive of a verb) zu; (expr. purpose, or after) **too um** [...] zu; **want to know** wissen wollen; **do sth. to annoy sb.** etw. tun, um jmdn. zu ärgern; **too hot to drink** zu heiß zum Trinken; **he would have phoned but forgot to** er hätte angerufen, aber er vergaß es ② adv. /tuː/ **to and fro** hin und her

toad /təʊd/ n. (also fig. derog.) Kröte, die

'**toadstool** n. Giftpilz, der

toast /təʊst/ ① n. (a) no pl. Toast, der; **a piece of ~**: eine Scheibe Toast (b) (call to drink) Toast, der; **drink a ~ to sb./ sth.** auf jmdn./etw. trinken ② v.t. (a) rösten; toasten ⟨Brot⟩

(b) (drink to) trinken auf (+ *Akk.*)

'toaster *n.* Toaster, *der*

'toast rack *n.* Toastständer, *der*

tobacco /təˈbækəʊ/ *n., pl.* ~s Tabak, *der*

tobacconist /təˈbækənɪst/ *n.* Tabak[waren]händler, *der*/-händlerin, *die*

toboggan /təˈbɒgən/ **1** *n.* Schlitten, *der* **2** *v.i.* Schlitten fahren

tod /tɒd/ *n.* (Brit. coll.) on one's ~: [ganz] allein

today /təˈdeɪ/ **1** *n.* heute; ~'s newspaper die Zeitung von heute **2** *adv.* heute

toddler /ˈtɒdlə(r)/ *n.* ≈ Kleinkind, *das*

to-do /təˈduː/ *n.* Getue, *das* (ugs.)

toe /təʊ/ **1** *n.* Zeh, *der;* Zehe, *die;* (of footwear) Spitze, *die* **2** *v.t.,* ~ing (fig.) ~ the line *or* (Amer.) mark sich einordnen

toenail *n.* Zeh[en]nagel, *der*

toffee /ˈtɒfɪ/ *n.* Karamell, *der;* (Brit.: piece) Toffee, *das;* Sahnebonbon, *das*

'toffee apple *n.* mit Karamell überzogener Apfel am Stiel

tofu /ˈtəʊfuː/ *n., no indef. art.* Tofu, *der*

together /təˈgeðə(r)/ *adv.* **(a)** (in or into company) zusammen **(b)** (simultaneously) gleichzeitig **(c)** (one with another) miteinander

toggle /ˈtɒgl/ **1** *n.* **(a)** (button) Knebelknopf, *der* **(b)** (Comp.) [Kipp]schalter, *der;* Umschalttaste, *die* **2** *v.i.* (Comp.) [hin und her] schalten

toil /tɔɪl/ **1** *v.i.* schwer arbeiten **2** *n.* [harte] Arbeit

toilet /ˈtɔɪlɪt/ *n.* Toilette, *die;* go to the ~: auf die Toilette gehen

toilet: ~ **bag** *n.* Kulturbeutel, *der;* ~ **brush** *n.* Klosettbürste, *die;* ~ **paper** *n.* Toilettenpapier, *das*

toiletries /ˈtɔɪlɪtrɪz/ *n. pl.* Körperpflegemittel *Pl.;* Toilettenartikel *Pl.*

toilet: ~ **roll** *n.* Rolle Toilettenpapier; ~ **seat** *n.* Klosettbrille, *die* (ugs.); Toilettensitz, *der;* ~ **tissue** ▶ ~ PAPER; ~ **water** *n.* Toilettenwasser, *das;* Eau de Toilette, *das*

token /ˈtəʊkn/ **1** *n.* **(a)** (voucher) Gutschein, *der* **(b)** (counter, disc) Marke, *die* **(c)** (sign) Zeichen, *das* **2** *attrib. adj.* symbolisch ‹*Preis*›

Tokyo /ˈtəʊkjəʊ/ *pr. n.* Tokio (*das*)

told ▶ TELL

tolerable /ˈtɒlərəbl/ *adj.* **(a)** (endurable) erträglich (**to, for** für) **(b)** (fairly good) leidlich; annehmbar

tolerance /ˈtɒlərəns/ *n.* Toleranz, *die*

tolerant /ˈtɒlərənt/ *adj.* tolerant (**of, towards** gegen[über])

tolerate /ˈtɒləreɪt/ *v.t.* dulden; (bear) ertragen ‹*Schmerzen*›

toleration /tɒləˈreɪʃn/ *n.* Tolerierung, *die* (geh.)

toll¹ /təʊl/ *n.* **(a)** (tax, duty) Gebühr, *die* **(b)** (damage etc.) Aufwand, *der;* take its ~ of sth. einen Tribut an etw. (*Dat.*) fordern (fig.)

toll² *v.i.* ‹*Glocke:*› läuten

toll: ~ **bridge** *n.* gebührenpflichtige Brücke; ~**road** *n.* gebührenpflichtige Straße; Mautstraße, *die* (bes. österr.)

tom /tɒm/ *n.* (cat) Kater, *der*

tomato /təˈmɑːtəʊ/ *n., pl.* ~es Tomate, *die*

tomato: ~ **juice** *n.* Tomatensaft, *der;* ~ **'ketchup** *n.* Tomatenketchup, *der od. das;* ~ **'purée** *n.* Tomatenmark, *das*

tomb /tuːm/ *n.* Grab, *das;* (monument) Grabmal, *das*

'tomboy *n.* Wildfang, *der*

'tombstone *n.* Grabstein, *der*

'tomcat *n.* Kater, *der*

tome /təʊm/ *n.* dicker Band; Wälzer, *der* (ugs.)

tomfoolery /tɒmˈfuːlərɪ/ *n.* Blödsinn, *der* (ugs.)

tomorrow /təˈmɒrəʊ/ **1** *n.* morgen; ~ morning/afternoon/evening/night morgen früh *od.* Vormittag/Nachmittag/Abend/ Nacht; ~'s newspaper die morgige Zeitung **2** *adv.* morgen; see you ~! (coll.) bis morgen!; the day after ~: übermorgen

ton /tʌn/ *n.* Tonne, *die*

tone /təʊn/ **1** *n.* **(a)** (sound) Klang, *der;* (Teleph.) Ton, *der* **(b)** (style of speaking) Ton, *der* **(c)** (tint, shade) [Farb]ton, *der* **(d)** (fig.: character) lower/raise the ~ of sth. das Niveau einer Sache (*Gen.*) senken/ erhöhen; set the ~: den Ton angeben **2** *v.t.* tönen; abtönen ‹*Farbe*› ▪ **tone 'down** *v.t.* [ab]dämpfen ‹*Farbe*›; (fig.) mäßigen ‹*Sprache*›

tone: ~-**'deaf** *adj.* ohne musikalisches Gehör; ~ **dialling** (Teleph.) *n.* Tonwahl, *die*

tongs /tɒŋz/ *n. pl.* [pair of] ~: Zange, *die*

tongue /tʌŋ/ *n.* Zunge, *die;* bite one's ~ (lit. or fig.) sich auf die Zunge beißen; find one's ~: seine Sprache wieder finden; hold one's ~: stillschweigen; he made the remark ~ in cheek (fig.) er meinte die Bemerkung nicht ernst

tongue: ~-**tied** *adj.* schüchtern; ~-**twister** *n.* Zungenbrecher, *der* (ugs.)

tonic /ˈtɒnɪk/ **1** *n.* **(a)** (Med.) Tonikum, *das* **(b)** (fig.: invigorating influence) Wohltat, *die* (geh.) **(c)** (~ water) Tonic, *das* **2** *attrib. adj.* kräftigend; (fig.) wohltuend ‹*Wirkung*›

'tonic water *n.* Tonic[wasser], *das*

tonight /təˈnaɪt/ **1** *n.* **(a)** (this evening) heute Abend; ~'s performance die heutige [Abend]vorstellung **(b)** (this or the coming night) heute Nacht

                                                 ⋯⋗

2 *adv.* **(a)** (this evening) heute Abend **(b)** (during this or the coming night) heute Nacht; [I'll] see you ~! bis heute Abend!

tonne /tʌn/ *n.* [metrische] Tonne

tonsil /ˈtɒnsl/ *n.* [Gaumen]mandel, *die;* have one's ~s out sich (*Dat.*) die Mandeln herausnehmen lassen

tonsillitis /tɒnsəˈlaɪtɪs/ *n.* Mandelentzündung, *die*

too /tuː/ *adv.* **(a)** (excessively) zu; ~ difficult a task eine zu schwierige Aufgabe **(b)** (also) auch **(c)** (coll.: very) besonders; not ~ pleased nicht gerade erfreut

took ▶ TAKE

tool /tuːl/ *n.* **(a)** (garden ~) Gerät, *das;* [set of] ~s Werkzeug, *das* **(b)** (Comp.) Tool, *das;* Werkzeug, *das* **(c)** (fig.: means) [Hilfs]mittel, *das*

tool: ~**bar** *n.* (Comp.) Werkzeugleiste, *die;* ~**box** *n.* Werkzeugkasten, *der;* ~ **kit** *n.* Werkzeug, *das*

toot /tuːt/ **1** *v.i.* (on car etc. horn) hupen **2** *n.* Tuten, *das*

tooth /tuːθ/ *n., pl.* teeth /tiːθ/ **(a)** Zahn, *der* **(b)** (of rake, fork, comb) Zinke, *die;* (of cogwheel, saw) Zahn, *der*

tooth: ~**ache** *n.* Zahnschmerzen *Pl.;* ~**brush** *n.* Zahnbürste, *die;* ~ **decay** *n.* Zahnverfall, *der;* ~**glass** *n.* Zahnputzglas, *das;* ~ **mug** *n.* Zahnputzbecher, *der;* ~**paste** *n.* Zahnpasta, *die;* ~**pick** *n.* Zahnstocher, *der;* ~ **powder** *n.* Zahnpulver, *das*

top¹ /tɒp/ **1** *n.* **(a)** (highest part) Spitze, *die;* (of table) Platte, *die;* (~ end) oberes Ende; (of tree) Wipfel, *der;* (~ floor) oberstes Stockwerk; (rim of glass) Rand, *der;* on ~ of one another aufeinander; on ~ of sth. (fig.: in addition) zusätzlich zu etw.; from ~ to bottom von oben bis unten; at the ~: oben; at the ~ of the building/hill/pile/stairs oben im Gebäude/ [oben] auf dem Hügel/[oben] auf dem Stapel/ oben an der Treppe **(b)** (highest rank) Spitze, *die;* ~ of the table (Sport) Tabellenspitze, *die;* be [at the] ~ of the class der/die Klassenbeste sein **(c)** (upper surface) Oberfläche, *die;* (of cupboard, chest) Oberseite, *die;* on ~ of sth. [oben] auf etw. (*position: Dat.; direction: Akk.*) **(d)** (folding roof) Verdeck, *das* **(e)** (upper deck of bus) Oberdeck, *das* **(f)** (cap of pen) [Verschluss]kappe, *die* **(g)** (upper garment) Oberteil, *das* **(h)** (lid) Deckel, *der;* (of bottle) Stöpsel, *der* **2** *adj.* oberst...; höchst... 〈*Ton, Preis*〉; ~ end oberes Ende; the ~ pupil der beste Schüler; ~ speed Spitzen- *od.* Höchstgeschwindigkeit, *die* **3** *v.t.* **(a)** (be taller than) überragen **(b)** (surpass) übertreffen

■ **top 'up** (Brit. coll.) *v.t.* auffüllen 〈*Tank, Flasche, Glas*〉

top² *n.* (toy) Kreisel, *der*

top: ~**-flight** *attrib. adj.* erstrangig; Spitzen〈*sportler, -politiker*〉; ~ **'hat** *n.* Zylinder[hut], *der;* ~**-heavy** *adj.* oberlastig

topic /ˈtɒpɪk/ *n.* Thema, *das*

topical /ˈtɒpɪkl/ *adj.* aktuell

'topless *adj.* a ~ dress/swimsuit ein busenfreies Kleid/ein Oben-ohne-Badeanzug; go/bathe ~: oben ohne gehen/baden

top-level *attrib. adj.* Gipfel〈*treffen, -konferenz*〉; ~-level negotiations/deals Verhandlungen/Vereinbarungen auf höchster Ebene

topmost /ˈtɒpməʊst, ˈtɒpməst/ *adj.* oberst...; höchst... 〈*Gipfel, Note*〉

top-'notch *adj.* (coll.) fantastisch (ugs.)

topple /ˈtɒpl/ **1** *v.i.* fallen **2** *v.t.* stürzen

■ **topple 'down** *v.i.* hinab-/herabfallen

■ **topple 'over** *v.i.* umfallen

top: ~**-quality** *adj.* [qualitativ] hochwertig; ~**-ranking** *attrib. adj.* Spitzen〈*funktionär, -beamter, -politiker, -sportler*〉; hochrangig 〈*Offizier*〉; ~ **'secret** *adj.* streng geheim; ~ **'soil** *n.* Mutterboden, *der*

topsy-turvy /tɒpsɪˈtɜːvɪ/ *adv.* verkehrtrum (ugs.)

'top-up *n.* (coll.) Auffüllung, *die;* I need a ~: ich muss mir noch mal nachgießen/ nachgießen lassen; ~ card (for mobile phone) Aufladekarte, *die*

torch /tɔːtʃ/ *n.* (Brit.) Taschenlampe, *die*

'torchlight *n.* Licht der/einer Taschenlampe; by ~light im Schein einer Taschenlampe

tore, torn ▶ TEAR¹ 2, 3

torment **1** /ˈtɔːment/ *n.* Qual, *die* **2** /tɔːˈment/ *v.t.* quälen

tornado /tɔːˈneɪdəʊ/ *n., pl.* ~es Wirbelsturm, *der;* (in North America) Tornado, *der*

torpedo /tɔːˈpiːdəʊ/ **1** *n., pl.* ~es Torpedo, *der* **2** *v.t.* torpedieren

torrent /ˈtɒrənt/ *n.* reißender Bach; (fig.) Flut, *die*

torrential /təˈrenʃl/ *adj.* wolkenbruchartig 〈*Regen*〉

torso /ˈtɔːsəʊ/ *n., pl.* ~s Rumpf, *der;* bare ~: nackter Oberkörper

tortoise /ˈtɔːtəs/ *n.* Schildkröte, *die*

tortoiseshell /ˈtɔːtəsʃel/ *n.* Schildpatt, *das*

tortuous /ˈtɔːtjʊəs/ *adj.* verschlungen; (fig.) umständlich

torture /ˈtɔːtʃə(r)/ **1** *n.* Folter, *die* **2** *v.t.* foltern; (fig.) quälen

Tory /ˈtɔːrɪ/ (Brit. Polit. coll.) *n.* Tory, *der*

toss /tɒs/ **1** *v.t.* **(a)** (throw upwards) hochwerfen; ~ a pancake einen Pfannkuchen [durch Hochwerfen] wenden **(b)** (throw casually) werfen; schmeißen (ugs.) **(c)** ~ a coin eine Münze werfen

(d) (Cookery: mix) wenden; mischen ‹*Salat*›
   2️⃣ *v.i.* **(a)** ∼ **and turn** sich [schlaflos] im
Bett wälzen
   (b) ‹*Schiff:*› hin und her geworfen werden
   (c) (∼ coin) eine Münze werfen; ∼ **for sth.**
mit einer Münze um etw. losen
   3️⃣ *n.* **(a)** ∼ **of a coin** Hochwerfen einer
Münze
   (b) (throw) Wurf, *der*
   (c) I couldn't give a ∼ (fig. Brit. sl.) es ist mir
scheißegal (salopp)
   ■ **toss 'up** *v.i.* eine Münze werfen; ∼ **up for
sth.** mit einer Münze um etw. losen

tot¹ /tɒt/ *n.* (coll.) **(a)** kleines Kind
   (b) (of liquor) Gläschen, *das*

tot² (coll.) *v.t.,* **-tt-:** ∼ **'up** zusammenziehen
(ugs.)

total /'təʊtl/ 1️⃣ *adj.* **(a)** gesamt;
Gesamt‹*gewicht, -wert, usw.*›
   (b) (absolute) völlig *nicht präd.;* **a** ∼ **beginner**
ein absoluter Anfänger
   2️⃣ *n.* (number) Gesamtzahl, *die;* (amount)
Gesamtbetrag, *der;* (result of addition) Summe,
die; **a** ∼ **of 200** insgesamt 200; **in** ∼:
insgesamt
   3️⃣ *v.t.,* (Brit.) ∼ **-ll-:** **(a)** addieren,
zusammenzählen ‹*Zahlen*›
   (b) (amount to) [insgesamt] betragen

total e'clipse *n.* (Astron.) totale Finsternis

totalitarian /təʊtælɪ'teərɪən/ *adj.* totalitär

'totally *adv.* völlig

totter /'tɒtə(r)/ *v.i.* wanken; taumeln

touch /tʌtʃ/ 1️⃣ *v.t.* **(a)** berühren
   (b) (harm) anrühren
   (c) (fig.: rival) ∼ **sth.** an etw. (*Akk.*)
heranreichen
   (d) (affect emotionally) rühren
   2️⃣ *v.i.* sich berühren; **don't** ∼**!** nicht
anfassen!
   3️⃣ *n.* **(a)** Berührung, *die*
   (b) *no art.* (faculty) **[sense of]** ∼: Tastsinn,
der
   (c) (small amount) **a** ∼ **of** salt/pepper *etc.* eine
Spur Salz/Pfeffer *usw.;* **a** ∼ **of irony** *etc.* ein
Anflug von Ironie *usw.*
   (d) (fig.) Detail, *das*
   (e) (communication) **be in/out of** ∼ **[with sb.]**
[mit jmdm.] Kontakt/keinen Kontakt haben;
get in ∼: mit jmdm. Kontakt aufnehmen
   ■ **touch 'down** *v.i.* ‹*Flugzeug:*› landen
   ■ **'touch on** *v.t.* (mention) ansprechen
   ■ **touch 'up** *v.t.* (improve) ausbessern

'touch: ∼**-and-go** *adj.* **it is** ∼**-and-go**
[whether...] es steht auf des Messers
Schneide [, ob...]; ∼**down** *n.* (Aeronaut.)
Landung, *die*

'touching *adj.* rührend

touch: ∼**line** *n.* (Footb., Rugby) Seitenlinie,
die; ∼**paper** *n.* Zündpapier, *das;* (on
firework) Papierlunte, *die;* ∼**-tone** *adj.* **a**
∼**-tone telephone** ein Telefon mit
Mehrfrequenzwahl; ∼**type** *v.i.* blind
schreiben; ∼**typing** *n.* Blindschreiben,
das

touchy /'tʌtʃɪ/ *adj.* empfindlich; heikel
‹*Thema*›

tough /tʌf/ *adj.* **(a)** fest ‹*Material, Stoff*›;
zäh ‹*Fleisch; fachspr.:* Werkstoff, Metall›;
widerstandsfähig ‹*Belag, Glas, Haut*›;
strapazierfähig ‹*Kleidung*›
   (b) (hardy) zäh ‹*Person*›
   (c) (difficult) schwierig
   (d) (severe, harsh) hart
   (e) (coll.) ∼ **luck** Pech, *das*

toughen /'tʌfn/ *v.t.* ∼ **[up]** abhärten
‹*Person*›; verschärfen ‹*Gesetz*›

toupee, toupet /'tu:peɪ/ *n.* Toupet, *das*

tour /tʊə(r)/ 1️⃣ *n.* **(a)** [Rund]reise, *die;* Tour,
die (ugs.)
   (b) (Theatre, Sport) Tournee, *die*
   (c) (of house etc.) Besichtigung, *die*
   (d) ∼ **[of duty]** Dienstzeit, *die*
   2️⃣ *v.i.* **(a)** ∼/go ∼ing in *or* through a
country eine Reise *od.* (ugs.) Tour durch ein
Land machen
   (b) (Theatre, Sport) eine Tournee machen
   3️⃣ *v.t.* **(a)** besichtigen ‹*Stadt, Gebäude*›; ∼ **a
country/region** eine Reise *od.* (ugs.) Tour
durch ein Land/Gebiet machen
   (b) (Theatre, Sport) ∼ **a country/the provinces**
eine Tournee durch das Land/die Provinz
machen

tour de force /tʊə də 'fɔ:s/ *n., pl.* **tours de
force** /tʊə də 'fɔ:s/ Glanzleistung, *die*

'tour guide *n.* Reiseführer, *der*/
Reiseführerin, *die;* (book) Reiseführer, *der*
(to, of von)

'touring holiday *n.* **have a** ∼ **in a country**
in den Ferien/im Urlaub durch ein Land
fahren

tourism /'tʊərɪzm/ *n.* **(a)** Tourismus, *der*
   (b) (operation of tours) Touristik, *die*

tourist /'tʊərɪst/ 1️⃣ *n.* Tourist, *der*/
Touristin, *die*
   2️⃣ *attrib. adj.* Touristen-

tourist: ∼ **agency** *n.* Reisebüro, *das;*
∼ **attraction** *n.* Touristenattraktion, *die;*
∼ **board** *n.* (Brit.) Amt für
Fremdenverkehrswesen; ∼ **class** *n.*
Touristenklasse, *die;* ∼ **hotel** *n.*
Touristenhotel, *das;* ∼ **industry** *n.*
Tourismusindustrie, *die;* ∼ **infor'mation
centre,** ∼ **office** *ns.*
Fremdenverkehrsbüro, *das;*
Touristeninformation, *die* (ugs.);
∼ **season** *n.* Touristensaison, *die;*
∼ **trade** ▶ ∼ INDUSTRY

touristy /'tʊərɪstɪ/ *adj.* (derog.) auf
Tourismus getrimmt (ugs.); Touristen‹*stadt,
-nest, -gegend*› (ugs. abwertend)

'tour leader *n.* Reiseleiter, *der*/-leiterin,
die

tournament /'tʊənəmənt/ *n.* (Hist.; Sport)
Turnier, *das*

tourniquet /'tʊənɪkeɪ/ *n.* (Med.)
Tourniquet, *das*

'tour operator *n.* Reiseveranstalter, *der*/
-veranstalterin, *die*

tousle /'taʊzl/ *v.t.* zerzausen

tout /taʊt/ **1** *v.i.* ~ **for customers** Kunden anreißen (ugs.) *od.* werben
2 *n.* Anreißer, *der*/Anreißerin, *die* (ugs.);
ticket ~: Kartenschwarzhändler, *der*/-händlerin, *die*

tow /təʊ/ **1** *v.t.* schleppen; ziehen ‹*Anhänger, Wasserskiläufer*›
2 *n.* Schleppen, *das;* **give a car a** ~: einen Wagen schleppen; **on** ~: im Schlepp[tau]
■ **tow a'way** *v.t.* abschleppen

toward /tə'wɔːd/, **towards** /tə'wɔːdz/ *prep.* **(a)** (in direction of) ~ **sb./sth.** auf jmdn./ etw. zu; **turn** ~ **sb.** sich zu jmdm. umdrehen **(b)** (in relation to) gegenüber; **feel sth.** ~ **sb.** jmdm. gegenüber etw. empfinden **(c)** (for) **a contribution** ~ **sth.** ein Beitrag zu etw.; **proposals** ~ **solving a problem** Vorschläge zur Lösung eines Problems **(d)** (near) gegen; ~ **the end of May** [gegen] Ende Mai

'tow bar *n.* (Motor Veh.) Anhängerkupplung, *die*

towel /'taʊəl/ *n.* Handtuch, *das*

towelling ⟨*Amer.:* **toweling**⟩ /'taʊəlɪŋ/ *n., no indef. art.* Frottierware, *die*

'towel rail *n.* Handtuchhalter, *der*

tower /'taʊə(r)/ **1** *n.* Turm, *der*
2 *v.i.* in die Höhe ragen
■ **'tower above** *v.t.* ~ **above sb./sth.** jmdn./etw. überragen

'tower block *n.* Hochhaus, *das*

'towering *attrib. adj.* hoch aufragend; (fig.) herausragend ⟨*Leistung*⟩

town /taʊn/ *n.* Stadt, *die;* **the** ~ **of Cambridge** die Stadt Cambridge; **in [the]** ~: in der Stadt; **the** ~ (people) die Stadt; **be in/ out of** ~: in der Stadt/nicht in der Stadt sein

town: ~ **'centre** *n.* Stadtmitte, *die;* Stadtzentrum, *das;* ~ **'council** *n.* (Brit.) Stadtrat, *der;* ~ **'councillor** *n.* (Brit.) Stadtrat, *der*/-rätin, *die;* ~ **'hall** *n.* Rathaus, *das;* ~ **house** *n.* (residence in ~) Stadthaus, *das;* (terrace house) Reihenhaus, *das*

townie /'taʊni:/ *n.* Stadtmensch, *der*

town: ~ **'planner** *n.* Stadtplaner, *der*/-planerin, *die;* ~ **'planning** *n.* Stadtplanung, *die*

tow: ~**path** *n.* Leinpfad, *der;* ~ **rope** *n.* Abschleppseil, *das*

toxic /'tɒksɪk/ *adj.* giftig

toxicity /tɒk'sɪsɪti/ *n.* Giftigkeit, *die*

toxic 'waste *n.* Giftmüll *der;* ~ **tip** *or* **dump** Giftmülldeponie, *die*

toxin /'tɒksɪn/ *n.* Toxin, *das*

toy /tɔɪ/ **1** *n.* Spielzeug, *das;* ~**s** Spielzeug, *das*
2 *adj.* Spielzeug-
3 *v.i.* ~ **with the idea of doing sth.** mit dem Gedanken spielen, etw. zu tun

toy: ~ **boy** *n.* (coll.) Gespiele, *der* (scherzh.); ~**shop** *n.* Spielwarengeschäft, *das*

trace /treɪs/ **1** *v.t.* **(a)** (copy) durchpausen; abpausen **(b)** zeichnen ⟨*Linie*⟩ **(c)** (follow track of) folgen (+ *Dat.*); verfolgen **(d)** (find) finden
2 *n.* Spur, *die*

'trace element *n.* (Chem.) Spurenelement, *das*

'tracing paper /'treɪsɪŋ peɪpə(r)/ *n.* Pauspapier, *das*

track /træk/ **1** *n.* **(a)** Spur, *die;* (of wild animal) Fährte, *die;* ~**s** (footprints) [Fuß]spuren; (of animal also) Fährte, *die;* **keep** ~ **of sb./sth.** jmdn./etw. im Auge behalten **(b)** (path) Weg, *der;* (footpath) Pfad, *der* **(c)** (Sport) Bahn, *die;* **cycling/greyhound** ~: Radrennbahn, *die*/Windhundrennbahn, *die* **(d)** (Railw.) Gleis, *das* **(e)** (course taken) Route, *die;* (of rocket, satellite) Bahn, *die*
2 *v.t.* ~ **an animal** die Spur/Fährte eines Tieres verfolgen; **the police** ~**ed him [to Paris]** die Polizei folgte seiner Spur [bis nach Paris]
■ **track 'down** *v.t.* aufspüren

'trackball, 'tracker ball *ns.* (Comp.) Rollball, *der*

'track events *n. pl.* Laufwettbewerbe *Pl.*

'tracking station *n.* (Astronaut.) Bahnverfolgungsstation, *die*

'track: ~**shoe** *n.* Rennschuh, *der;* ~**suit** *n.* Trainingsanzug, *der*

tract¹ /trækt/ *n.* (area) Gebiet, *das*

tract² *n.* (pamphlet) [Flug]schrift, *die*

tractor /'træktə(r)/ *n.* Traktor, *der*

trad /træd/ (Mus. coll.) *adj.* traditional (Jargon); ~ **jazz** Traditional Jazz, *der*

trade /treɪd/ **1** *n.* **(a)** (line of business) Gewerbe, *das;* **he's a butcher/lawyer** *etc.* **by** ~: er ist von Beruf Metzger/Rechtsanwalt *usw.* **(b)** *no indef. art.* (commerce) Handel, *der* **(c)** (craft) Handwerk, *das*
2 *v.i.* (buy and sell) Handel treiben
3 *v.t.* tauschen; austauschen ⟨*Waren, Grüße*⟩; sich ⟨*Dat.*⟩ sagen ⟨*Beleidigungen*⟩; ~ **sth. for sth.** etw. gegen etw. tauschen
■ **trade 'in** *v.t.* in Zahlung geben
■ **trade 'up** *v.i.* sich verbessern

trade: ~ **balance** *n.* Handelsbilanz, *die;* ~ **deficit** *n.* passive Handelsbilanz; Handelsbilanzdefizit, *das;* ~ **'discount** *n.* Branchenrabatt, *der;* ~ **fair** *n.* [Fach]messe, *die;* ~ **journal** *n.* Fachzeitschrift, *die;* ~ **mark** *n.* Warenzeichen, *das;* **leave one's** ~ **mark on sth.** (fig.) einer Sache ⟨*Dat.*⟩ seinen Stempel aufdrücken; ~ **name** *n.* Fachbezeichnung, *die;* (proprietary name) Markenname, *der;* ~ **price** *n.* Einkaufspreis, *der*

'trader *n.* Händler, *der*/Händlerin, *die*

trade: ~ **'secret** *n.* Geschäftsgeheimnis, *das;* ~**sman** /'treɪdzmən/ *n., pl.* ~**smen** /'treɪdzmən/ (shopkeeper) [Einzel]händler, *der;*

(craftsman) Handwerker, *der;* ~ **'union** *n.*
Gewerkschaft, *die; attrib.* Gewerkschafts-;
~ **'unionist** *n.* Gewerkschaft[l]er, *der/*
Gewerkschaft[l]erin, *die*

trading /'treɪdɪŋ/ *n.* Handel, *der*

trading: ~ **estate** *n.* (Brit.)
Gewerbegebiet, *das;* ~ **hours** *n. pl.*
Geschäftszeit, *die;* **during/outside** ~ **hours**
während/außerhalb der Geschäftszeit;
'Trading hours: …' „Geschäftszeiten: …";
~ **partner** *n.* Handelspartner, *der*

tradition /trə'dɪʃn/ *n.* Tradition, *die*

traditional /trə'dɪʃənl/ *adj.* traditionell;
herkömmlich ⟨*Erziehung, Methode*⟩

tra'ditionally *adv.* traditionell

traffic /'træfɪk/ **1** *n.* **(a)** *no indef. art.*
Verkehr, *der*
(b) (trade) Handel, *der*
2 *v.i.,* **-ck-:** ~ **in sth.** mit etw. handeln

traffic: ~ **calming** *n.*
Verkehrsberuhigung, *die;* ~ **circle** *n.*
(Amer.) Kreisverkehr, *der;* ~ **cone** *n.*
Pylon, *der;* Leitkegel, *der;* ~ **island** *n.*
Verkehrsinsel, *die;* ~ **jam** *n.*
[Verkehrs]stau, *der*

trafficker /'træfɪkə(r)/ *n.* Händler, *der/*
Händlerin, *die;* ~ **in drugs:** Drogenhändler,
der/-händlerin, *die*

traffic: ~ **lights** *n. pl.* [Verkehrs]ampel,
die; ~ **police** *n.* Verkehrspolizei, *die;*
~ **report** *n.* Verkehrsübersicht, *die;* (on
radio) Verkehrsservice, *der;* ~ **sign** *n.*
Verkehrszeichen, *das;* ~ **signals**
▶ ~ LIGHTS; ~ **warden** *n.* (Brit.)
Hilfspolizist, *der;* (woman) Hilfspolizistin, *die;*
Politesse, *die*

tragedy /'trædʒɪdɪ/ *n.* Tragödie, *die*

tragic /'trædʒɪk/ *adj.* tragisch

trail /treɪl/ **1** *n.* **(a)** Spur, *die;* ~ **of smoke/**
dust Rauch-/Staubfahne, *die*
(b) (Hunting) Spur, *die;* Fährte, *die*
(c) (path) Pfad, *der;* Weg, *der*
2 *v.t.* **(a)** (pursue) verfolgen
(b) (drag) ~ **sth.** [after *or* behind one] etw.
hinter sich ⟨*Dat.*⟩ herziehen
3 *v.i.* **(a)** (be dragged) schleifen
(b) (lag) hinterhertrotten
(c) ⟨*Pflanze:*⟩ kriechen

trailer /'treɪlə(r)/ *n.* **(a)** Anhänger, *der;*
(Amer.: caravan) Wohnanhänger, *der*
(b) (Cinemat., Telev.) Trailer, *der*

train /treɪn/ **1** *v.t.* **(a)** ausbilden (in in
+ *Dat.*); erziehen ⟨*Kind*⟩; abrichten ⟨*Hund*⟩;
dressieren ⟨*Tier*⟩
(b) (Sport) trainieren
(c) (Hort.) ziehen
2 *v.i.* **(a)** eine Ausbildung machen; **he is**
~**ing as** *or* **to be a doctor/engineer** er macht
eine Arzt-/Ingenieursausbildung
(b) (Sport) trainieren
3 *n.* **(a)** (Railw.) Zug, *der;* **on the** ~: im Zug
(b) (of skirt etc.) Schleppe, *die*
(c) ~ **of thought** Gedankengang, *der*

'train driver *n.* Lokomotivführer, *der/*
-führerin, *die*

trained /treɪnd/ *adj.* ausgebildet ⟨*Arbeiter,*
Lehrer, Arzt, Stimme⟩; abgerichtet ⟨*Hund*⟩;
dressiert ⟨*Tier*⟩; geschult ⟨*Geist, Auge, Ohr*⟩

trainee /treɪ'ni:/ *n.* Auszubildende, *der/die*

'trainer *n.* [Konditions]trainer, *der/*
-trainerin, *die*

'train fare *n.* Fahrpreis, *der*

'training *n.* **(a)** Ausbildung, *die*
(b) (Sport) Training, *das*

training: ~ **camp** *n.* (Sport)
Trainingslager, *das;* ~ **college** *n.*
berufsbildende Schule; ~ **course** *n.*
Lehrgang, *der;* ~ **scheme** *n.*
Ausbildungsprogramm, *das;* ~ **shoes** *n.*
pl. Trainingsschuhe *Pl.*

train: ~ **journey** *n.* Bahnfahrt, *die;* (long)
Bahnreise, *die;* ~ **service** *n.*
Zugverbindung, *die;* ~ **set** *n.*
[Modell]eisenbahn, *die;* ~**spotting** *n.:* das
Aufschreiben von Lokomotivnummern als
Hobby; ~ **station** *n.* (Amer.) Bahnhof, *der*

traipse /treɪps/ *v.i.* latschen (salopp)
▪ **traipse about, traipse around** *v.i.*
rumlatschen (salopp)

trait /treɪt/ *n.* Eigenschaft, *die*

traitor /'treɪtə(r)/ *n.* Verräter, *der/*
Verräterin, *die*

traitorous /'treɪtərəs/ *adj.* verräterisch

trajectory /trə'dʒektərɪ/ *n.* [Flug]bahn, *die*

tram /træm/ *n.* (Brit.) Straßenbahn, *die;*
~lines Straßenbahnschienen *Pl.*

tramp /træmp/ **1** *n.* Landstreicher, *der/*
-streicherin, *die;* (in city) Stadtstreicher, *der/*
-streicherin, *die*
2 *v.i.* **(a)** (tread heavily) trampeln
(b) (walk) marschieren

trample /'træmpl/ **1** *v.t.* zertrampeln
2 *v.i.* trampeln
▪ **'trample on** *v.t.* herumtrampeln auf
(+ *Dat.*)

trampoline /'træmpəli:n/ *n.* Trampolin,
das

'tram stop *n.* Straßenbahnhaltestelle, *die*

trance /trɑːns/ *n.* Trance, *die;* **be in a** ~: in
Trance sein

tranquil /'træŋkwɪl/ *adj.* ruhig

tranquillity /træŋ'kwɪlɪtɪ/ Ruhe, *die*

tranquillizer /'træŋkwɪlaɪzə(r)/ *n.*
Beruhigungsmittel, *das*

transact /træn'zækt/ *v.t.* ~ **business**
Geschäfte tätigen

transaction /træn'zækʃn/ *n.* Geschäft,
das; (financial) Transaktion, *die*

transatlantic /trænsət'læntɪk/ *adj.*
transatlantisch

transcend /træn'send/ *v.t.* übersteigen

transcript /'trænskrɪpt/ *n.* Abschrift, *die;*
(of trial) Protokoll, *das*

transfer **1** /træns'fɜː(r)/ *v.t.,* **-rr-:** ⋯⇒

(a) (move) verlegen (**to** nach); überweisen ⟨*Geld*⟩ (**to** auf + *Akk.*); übertragen ⟨*Befugnis, Macht*⟩ (**to** *Dat.*)
(b) übereignen ⟨*Gegenstand, Grundbesitz*⟩ (**to** *Dat.*)
(c) versetzen ⟨*Arbeiter, Angestellte*⟩; (Footb.) transferieren
2 /træns'fɜː(r)/ *v.i.*, **-rr-: (a)** (when travelling) umsteigen
(b) (change job etc.) wechseln
3 /'trænsfɜː(r)/ *n.* **(a)** (moving) Verlegung, *die;* (of powers) Übertragung, *die* (**to** an + *Akk.*); (of money) Überweisung, *die*
(b) (of employee etc.) Versetzung, *die;* (Footb.) Transfer, *der*
(c) (picture) Abziehbild, *das*

transferable /træns'fɜːrəbl/ *adj.* übertragbar

'transfer: ∼ fee *n.* (Footb.) Ablösesumme, *die;* Transfersumme, *die* (fachspr.); **∼ list** *n.* (Footb.) Transferliste, *die*

transform /træns'fɔːm/ *v.t.* verwandeln

transformation /trænsfə'meɪʃn/ *n.* Verwandlung, *die*

trans'former *n.* (Electr.) Transformator, *der*

transfusion /træns'fjuːʒn/ *n.* (Med.) Transfusion, *die*

transient /'trænzɪənt/ *adj.* kurzlebig; vergänglich

transistor /træn'zɪstə(r)/ *n.* Transistor, *der*

transit /'trænsɪt/ *n.* **in ∼:** auf der Durchreise; ⟨*Waren*⟩ auf dem Transport; **passengers in ∼:** Transitreisende *Pl.*

transition /træn'sɪʒn, træn'zɪʃn/ *n.* Übergang, *der;* Wechsel, *der*

transitional /træn'zɪʃənl/ *adj.* Übergangs-

transitive /'trænsɪtɪv/ *adj.* (Ling.) transitiv

'transit lounge *n.* Transithalle, *die*

transitory /'trænsɪtərɪ/ *adj.* vergänglich; (fleeting) flüchtig

'transit passenger *n.* Transitpassagier, *der*

translate /træns'leɪt/ *v.t.* übersetzen

translation /træns'leɪʃn/ *n.* Übersetzung, *die*

translator /træns'leɪtə(r)/ *n.* Übersetzer, *der/*Übersetzerin, *die*

translucent /træns'luːsənt/ *adj.* durchscheinend

transmission /træns'mɪʃn/ *n.* **(a)** Übertragung, *die*
(b) (Motor Veh.) Antrieb, *der;* (gearbox) Getriebe, *das*

transmit /træns'mɪt/ *v.t.*, **-tt-: (a)** (pass on) übersenden; übertragen
(b) durchlassen ⟨*Licht*⟩; leiten ⟨*Wärme*⟩

trans'mitter *n.* Sender, *der*

transparency /træns'pærənsɪ/ *n.* **(a)** Durchsichtigkeit, *die*
(b) (Photog.) Transparent, *das;* (slide) Dia, *das*

transparent /træns'pærənt/ *adj.* durchsichtig

transparently /træns'pærəntlɪ/ *adv.* offenkundig; **∼ obvious** ganz offenkundig

transpire /træn'spaɪə(r)/ *v.i.* sich herausstellen; (coll.: happen) passieren

transplant **1** /træns'plɑːnt/ *v.t.* **(a)** verpflanzen ⟨*Organ*⟩
(b) (plant in another place) umpflanzen
2 /'trænsplɑːnt/ *n.* (Med.) Transplantation, *die;* Verpflanzung, *die*

transport **1** /træns'pɔːt/ *v.t.* transportieren; befördern
2 /'trænspɔːt/ *n.* **(a)** Transport, *der;* Beförderung, *die; attrib.* Beförderungs-
(b) (means of conveyance) Verkehrsmittel, *das;* **be without ∼:** kein [eigenes] Fahrzeug haben

'transport café *n.* (Brit.) Fernfahrerlokal, *das*

transpose /træns'pəʊz/ *v.t.* vertauschen; umstellen

transsexual /træns'seksjʊəl/ **1** *adj.* transsexuell
2 *n.* Transsexuelle, *der/die*

transvestite /træns'vestaɪt/ *n.* Transvestit, *der*

trap /træp/ **1** *n.* **(a)** Falle, *die;* **set** *or* **lay a ∼ for an animal** eine Falle für ein Tier legen *od.* aufstellen; **set** *or* **lay a ∼ for sb.** (fig.) jmdm. eine Falle stellen; **fall into a/sb.'s ∼** (fig.) in die/jmdm. in die Falle gehen
(b) (sl.: mouth) Klappe, *die* (salopp)
2 *v.t.*, **-pp-: (a)** [in *od.* mit einer Falle] fangen ⟨*Tier*⟩; (fig.) in eine Falle locken ⟨*Person*⟩; **be ∼ped** (fig.) in eine Falle gehen/in der Falle sitzen; **be ∼ped in a cave/by the tide** in einer Höhle festsitzen/von der Flut abgeschnitten sein
(b) (confine) einschließen; einklemmen ⟨*Körperteil*⟩

trap'door *n.* Falltür, *die*

trapeze /trə'piːz/ *n.* Trapez, *das*

tra'peze artist *n.* Trapezkünstler, *der/* -künstlerin, *die*

trash /træʃ/ *n.* **(a)** (rubbish) Abfall, *der*
(b) (badly made thing) Mist, *der* (ugs.); (bad literature) Schund, *der* (ugs.)

trauma /'trɔːmə/ *n.*, *pl.* **∼ta** /'trɔːmətə/ *or* **∼s** Trauma, *das*

traumatic /trɔː'mætɪk/ *adj.* traumatisch

traumatize /'trɔːmətaɪz/ *v.t.* traumatisieren

travel /'trævl/ **1** *n.* Reisen, *das; attrib.* Reise-
2 *v.i.*, (Brit.) **-ll-** reisen; (go in vehicle) fahren
3 *v.t.*, (Brit.) **-ll-** zurücklegen ⟨*Strecke, Entfernung*⟩; benutzen ⟨*Weg, Straße*⟩; **we had ∼led 10 miles** wir waren 10 Meilen gefahren
■ **travel a'bout, travel a'round** *v.i.* umherreisen

travel: ∼ agency *n.* Reisebüro, *das;* **∼ agent** *n.* Reisebürokaufmann, *der/* -kauffrau, *die;* **∼ brochure** *n.* Reiseprospekt, *der;* **∼ bureau** *n.* Reisebüro, *das*

traveler, traveling (Amer.) ▶ TRAVELL-

'travel insurance n. Reiseversicherung, die

traveller /'trævlə(r)/ n. (Brit.) **(a)** Reisende, der/die
(b) in pl. (gypsies etc.) fahrendes Volk

'traveller's cheque n. Reisescheck, der

travelling /'trævlɪŋ/ attrib. adj. (Brit.) Wander⟨zirkus, -ausstellung⟩

travelling: ~ **clock** n. Reisewecker, der; ~ **'salesman** n. Vertreter, der

travel: ~**sick** adj. reisekrank; ~**sickness** n. Reisekrankheit, die; ~**sickness pill** n. Tablette gegen Reisekrankheit

trawler /'trɔːlə(r)/ n. [Fisch]trawler, der

tray /treɪ/ n. Tablett, das; (for correspondence) Ablagekorb, der

treacherous /'tretʃərəs/ adj. **(a)** treulos ⟨Person⟩
(b) (deceptive) tückisch

treachery /'tretʃərɪ/ n. Verrat, der

treacle /'triːkl/ n. (Brit.) Sirup, der

tread /tred/ ① n. **(a)** (of tyre, boot, etc.) Lauffläche, die; **2 millimetres of** ~ **on a tyre** 2 Millimeter Profil auf einem Reifen
(b) (sound of walking) Schritt, der
② v.i., **trod** /trɒd/, **trodden** /'trɒdn/ or **trod** treten (**in/on** in/auf + Akk.); (walk) gehen
③ v.t. **trod, trodden** or **trod** treten auf (+ Akk.); stampfen ⟨Weintrauben⟩

'treadmill n. (lit. or fig.) Tretmühle, die

treason /'triːzn/ n. [**high**] ~: Hochverrat, der

treasure /'treʒə(r)/ ① n. Schatz, der; Kostbarkeit, die; **art** ~**s** Kunstschätze Pl.
② v.t. in Ehren halten

treasure: ~ **house** n. [wahre] Fundgrube; ~ **hunt** n. Schatzsuche, die

treasurer /'treʒərə(r)/ n. Kassenwart, der/ -wartin, die

treasury /'treʒərɪ/ n. **the T**~: das Finanzministerium

treat /triːt/ ① n. **(a)** [besonderes] Vergnügen
(b) (entertainment) Vergnügen, für dessen Kosten jmd. anderes aufkommt; **lay on a special** ~ **for sb.** jmdm. etwas Besonderes bieten; **it's my** ~: ich lade ein
② v.t. **(a)** behandeln; ~ **sth. as a joke** etw. als Witz nehmen; ~ **sth. with contempt** für etw. nur Verachtung haben
(b) (Med.) behandeln; ~ **sb. for sth.** jmdn. wegen etw. behandeln; (before confirmation of diagnosis) jmdn. auf etw. (Akk.) behandeln
(c) klären ⟨Abwässer⟩
(d) (provide with at own expense) einladen; ~ **sb. to sth.** jmdm. etw. spendieren; ~ **oneself to a new hat** sich (Dat.) einen neuen Hut leisten

treatise /'triːtɪs, 'triːtɪz/ n. Abhandlung, die

'treatment n. Behandlung, die

treaty /'triːtɪ/ n. [Staats]vertrag, der

treble /'trebl/ ① adj. **(a)** dreifach
(b) (Brit. Mus.) ~ **voice** Sopranstimme, die
② n. **(a)** (~ quantity) Dreifache, das
(b) (Mus.) **he is a** ~: er singt Sopran
③ v.t. verdreifachen
④ v.i. sich verdreifachen

'treble clef n. (Mus.) Violinschlüssel, der

tree /triː/ n. Baum, der

'tree house n. Baumhaus, das

'treeless adj. baumlos

tree: ~**lined** adj. von Bäumen gesäumt; ~ **surgeon** n. Baumchirurg, der; ~ **surgery** n. Baumchirurgie, die; ~**top** n. [Baum]wipfel, der; ~ **trunk** n. Baumstamm, der

trek /trek/ ① v.i., **-kk-** ziehen (**across** durch)
② n. [schwierige] Reise

trellis /'trelɪs/ n. Gitter, das; (for plants) Spalier, das

tremble /'trembl/ v.i. zittern (**with** vor + Dat.)

trembling /'tremblɪŋ/ ① adj. zitternd
② n. Zittern, das

tremendous /trɪ'mendəs/ adj. gewaltig; (coll.: wonderful) großartig

tremor /'tremə(r)/ n. **(a)** Zittern, das
(b) [earth] ~: leichtes Erdbeben

trench /trentʃ/ n. Graben, der; (Mil.) Schützengraben, der

trench 'warfare n. Grabenkrieg, der

trend /trend/ n. **(a)** Trend, der; **upward** ~: steigende Tendenz
(b) (fashion) Mode, die; [Mode]trend, der

trendiness n. (Brit. coll.) modische Art

'trendsetter n. Trendsetter, der

'trendy adj. (Brit. coll.) modisch; Schickimicki⟨kneipe⟩ (ugs.)

trepidation /trepɪ'deɪʃn/ n. Beklommenheit, die

trespass /'trespəs/ v.i. ~ **on** unerlaubt betreten ⟨Grundstück⟩

'trespasser n. Unbefugte, der/die

trial /'traɪəl/ n. **(a)** (Law) [Gerichts]verfahren, das; **be on** ~ [**for murder**] [wegen Mordes] vor Gericht stehen
(b) (testing) Test, der; **employ sb. on** ~: jmdn. probeweise einstellen; [**by**] ~ **and error** [durch] Ausprobieren
(c) (trouble) Problem, das
(d) (Sport) (competition) Prüfung, die; (for selection) Testspiel, das

trial 'run n. (of car) Testfahrt, die; (fig.) Probelauf, der

triangle /'traɪæŋgl/ n. **(a)** Dreieck, das
(b) (Mus.) Triangel, der od. das

triangular /traɪ'æŋgjʊlə(r)/ adj. dreieckig

tribal /'traɪbl/ adj. Stammes-

tribalism /'traɪbəlɪzm/ n. Tribalismus, der (fachspr.)

t

tribe /traɪb/ *n.* Stamm, *der*

tribulation /trɪbjʊˈleɪʃn/ *n.* Kummer, *der*

tribunal /traɪˈbjuːnl/ *n.* Schiedsgericht, *das*

tributary /ˈtrɪbjʊtəri/ *n.* Nebenfluss, *der*

tribute /ˈtrɪbjuːt/ *n.* Tribut, *der* (**to** an + *Akk.*); **pay ~ to sb./sth.** jmdm./einer Sache den schuldigen Tribut zollen (geh.)

trice /traɪs/ *n.* **in a ~:** im Handumdrehen

trick /trɪk/ ①*n.* (**a**) Trick, *der;* **it was all a ~:** das war [alles] nur Bluff
(**b**) (feat of skill etc.) Kunststück, *das; that should do the ~* (coll.) damit dürfte es klappen (ugs.)
(**c**) (knack) **get** *or* **find the ~** [of doing sth.] den Dreh finden[, wie man etw. tut]
(**d**) (prank) Streich, *der;* **play a ~ on sb.** jmdm. einen Streich spielen
(**e**) (Cards) Stich, *der*
②*v.t.* täuschen; hereinlegen; **~ sb. out of/ into sth.** jmdm. etw. ablisten
③*adj.* **~ photograph** Trickaufnahme, *die;* **~ question** Fangfrage, *die*

trickery /ˈtrɪkəri/ *n.* [Hinter]list, *die*

trickle /ˈtrɪkl/ *v.i.* rinnen; (in drops) tröpfeln

trickster /ˈtrɪkstə(r)/ *n.* Schwindler, *der/* Schwindlerin, *die*

'tricky *adj.* verzwickt (ugs.)

tricycle /ˈtraɪsɪkl/ *n.* Dreirad, *das*

tried ▶ TRY 2, 3

trifle /ˈtraɪfl/ *n.* (**a**) (Brit. Gastron.) Trifle, *das*
(**b**) (thing of slight value) Kleinigkeit, *die*

trifling /ˈtraɪflɪŋ/ *adj.* unbedeutend ⟨*Angelegenheit*⟩; gering ⟨*Wert*⟩

trigger /ˈtrɪgə(r)/ ①*n.* (**a**) (of gun) Abzug, *der;* (of machine) Drücker, *der*
(**b**) (fig.) Auslöser, *der*
②*v.t.* **~ [off]** auslösen

trigonometry /trɪgəˈnɒmɪtri/ *n.* Trigonometrie, *die*

trilingual /traɪˈlɪŋgwəl/ *adj.* dreisprachig

trill /trɪl/ ①*n.* Trillern, *das;* (Mus.) Triller, *der*
②*v.i.* trillern

trillion /ˈtrɪljən/ *n.* (million million) Billion, *die*

trilogy /ˈtrɪlədʒi/ *n.* Trilogie, *die*

trim /trɪm/ ①*v.t.,* **-mm-:** (**a**) schneiden ⟨*Hecke*⟩; [nach]schneiden ⟨*Haar*⟩; beschneiden ⟨*Papier, Hecke, Budget*⟩
(**b**) (ornament) besetzen (with mit)
②*adj.* proper; gepflegt ⟨*Garten*⟩
③*n.* (**a**) **be in ~** (healthy) in Form *od.* fit sein
(**b**) (cut) Nachschneiden, *das*

'trimming *n.* (**a**) (decorations) Verzierung, *die*
(**b**) *in pl.* (coll.: accompaniments) Beilagen *Pl.;* **with all the ~s** mit allem Drum und Dran (ugs.)

Trinity /ˈtrɪnɪti/ *n.* (Theol.) **the [Holy] ~:** die Heilige Dreieinigkeit

trinket /ˈtrɪŋkɪt/ *n.* kleines, billiges Schmuckstück

trio /ˈtriːəʊ/ *n., pl.* **~s** Trio, *das*

trip /trɪp/ ①*n.* (**a**) Reise, *die;* (shorter) Ausflug, *der*
(**b**) (coll.: drug-induced hallucinations) Trip, *der*
②*v.i.,* **-pp-** stolpern (on über + *Akk.*)
■ **trip 'over** *v.t.* stolpern über (+ *Akk.*)
■ **trip 'up** ①*v.i.* (**a**) stolpern
(**b**) (fig.) einen Fehler machen
②*v.t.* (**a**) stolpern lassen
(**b**) (fig.) aufs Glatteis führen (fig.)

tripe /traɪp/ *n.* (**a**) Kaldaunen *Pl.*
(**b**) (coll.: rubbish) Quatsch, *der* (ugs.)

triple /ˈtrɪpl/ ①*adj.* (**a**) (threefold) dreifach
(**b**) (three times greater than) **~ the ...:** der/die/ das dreifache ...
②*n.* Dreifache, *das*
③*v.i.* sich verdreifachen
④*v.t.* verdreifachen

'triple jump *n.* (Sport) Dreisprung, *der*

triplet /ˈtrɪplɪt/ *n.* Drilling, *der*

triplicate /ˈtrɪplɪkət/ *n.* **in ~:** in dreifacher Ausfertigung

trip 'mileage recorder *n.* (Motor Veh.) Tageskilometerzähler, *der*

tripod /ˈtraɪpɒd/ *n.* Dreibein, *das*

'tripper *n.* (Brit.) Ausflügler, *der/* Ausflüglerin, *die*

'tripwire *n.* Stolperdraht, *der*

trite /traɪt/ *adj.* banal

triumph /ˈtraɪəmf, ˈtraɪʌmf/ ①*n.* Triumph, *der* (over über + *Akk.*)
②*v.i.* triumphieren (over über + *Akk.*)

triumphant /traɪˈʌmfənt/ *adj.* (**a**) siegreich
(**b**) triumphierend ⟨*Blick*⟩

trivia /ˈtrɪvɪə/ *n. pl.* Belanglosigkeiten *Pl.*

trivial /ˈtrɪvɪəl/ *adj.* belanglos

triviality /trɪvɪˈælɪti/ *n.* Belanglosigkeit, *die*

trivialize /ˈtrɪvɪəlaɪz/ *v.t.* auf eine belanglose Ebene bringen

trod, trodden ▶ TREAD 2, 3

trolley /ˈtrɒli/ *n.* (**a**) (for serving food) Servierwagen, *der*
(**b**) [supermarket] **~:** Einkaufswagen, *der*

trombone /trɒmˈbəʊn/ *n.* Posaune, *die*

troop /truːp/ ①*n.* (**a**) *in pl* Truppen *Pl.*
(**b**) (fig.) Schar, *die*
②*v.i.* **~ in/out** hinein-/hinausströmen

troop: ~ carrier *n.* Truppentransporter, *der;* **~ship** *n.* Truppentransporter, *der*

trophy /ˈtrəʊfi/ *n.* Trophäe, *die*

tropic /ˈtrɒpɪk/ *n.* **the T~s** (Geog.) die Tropen; **the ~ of Cancer/Capricorn** (Astron., Geog.) der Wendekreis des Krebses/ Steinbocks

tropical /ˈtrɒpɪkl/ *adj.* tropisch; Tropen⟨*krankheit, -kleidung*⟩

tropical: ~ 'medicine *n.* Tropenmedizin, *die;* **~ 'rainforest** *n.* tropischer Regenwald

trot /trɒt/ ①*n.* (coll.) **on the ~:** hintereinander; **be on the ~:** auf Trab sein (ugs.)
②*v.i.,* **-tt-** traben

trouble /'trʌbl/ 1 n. (a) Ärger, der; Schwierigkeiten Pl.; there'll be ~ [if ...] es wird Ärger geben, [wenn ...]; what's the ~? was ist denn?
(b) engine/brake ~: Probleme mit dem Motor/der Bremse; suffer from heart/liver ~: herz-/leberkrank sein
(c) (inconvenience) Mühe, die; take a lot of ~: sich (Dat.) sehr viel Mühe geben; it's more ~ than it's worth es lohnt sich nicht
(d) in sing. or pl. (unrest) Unruhen Pl.
2 v.t. (a) (agitate) beunruhigen; don't let it ~ you mach dir deswegen keine Sorgen
(b) (inconvenience) stören
3 v.i. (make an effort) sich bemühen

troubled /'trʌbld/ adj. (a) (worried) besorgt
(b) (restless) unruhig

trouble: ~-free adj. problemlos; ~maker n. Unruhestifter, der/-stifterin, die

troublesome /'trʌblsəm/ adj. schwierig; lästig ‹Krankheit›

trough /trɒf/ n. Trog, der

troupe /truːp/ n. Truppe, die

trouser /'traʊzə/: ~ leg n. Hosenbein, das; ~ press n. Bügelpresse, die; Hosenbügler, der

trousers /'traʊzəz/ n. pl. [pair of] ~: Hose, die

'trouser suit n. (Brit.) Hosenanzug, der

trousseau /'truːsəʊ/ n., pl. ~s or ~x /'truːsəʊz/ Aussteuer, die

trout /traʊt/ n., pl. same Forelle, die

trout: ~ farm n. Forellenzuchtbetrieb, der; ~-fishing n. Forellenfang, der

trowel /'traʊəl/ n. Kelle, die; (Hort.) Pflanzkelle, die

truant /'truːənt/ n. play ~: [die Schule] schwänzen (ugs.)

truce /truːs/ n. Waffenstillstand, der

truck /trʌk/ n. (a) Last[kraft]wagen, der; Lkw, der
(b) (Brit. Railw.) offener Güterwagen

'truck driver, trucker /'trʌkə(r)/ ns. Lastwagenfahrer, der/-fahrerin, die; (long-distance) Fernfahrer, der/-fahrerin, die

truculent /'trʌkjʊlənt/ adj. aufsässig

trudge /trʌdʒ/ v.i. trotten; (through snow etc.) stapfen

true /truː/ adj., ~r /'truːə(r)/, ~st /'truːɪst/
(a) wahr; wahrheitsgetreu ‹Bericht›; richtig ‹Vorteil›; (rightly so called) eigentlich; echt, wahr ‹Freund›; is it ~ that ...? stimmt es, dass ...?; ~ to life lebensecht
(b) (loyal) treu

truffle /'trʌfl/ n. Trüffel, die od. (ugs.) der

truism /'truːɪzm/ n. Binsenweisheit, die

truly /'truːlɪ/ adv. (a) wirklich
(b) (accurately) zutreffend; yours ~: mit freundlichen Grüßen

trump /trʌmp/ (Cards) 1 n. Trumpf, der
2 v.t. übertrumpfen

'trump card n. (lit. or fig.) Trumpf, der

trumped up /'trʌmpt ʌp/ adj. falsch ‹Beschuldigung usw.›

trumpet /'trʌmpɪt/ n. Trompete, die

'trumpeter n. Trompeter, der/ Trompeterin, die

truncheon /'trʌntʃn/ n. Schlagstock, der

trundle /'trʌndl/ v.t. & i. rollen

trunk /trʌŋk/ n. (a) (of elephant etc.) Rüssel, der
(b) (large box) Schrankkoffer, der
(c) (of tree) Stamm, der
(d) (of body) Rumpf, der
(e) (Amer.: of car) Kofferraum, der
(f) in pl. (Brit.) [swimming] ~s Badehose, die

truss /trʌs/ n. (Med.) Bruchband, das

trust /trʌst/ 1 n. (a) Vertrauen, das; place or put one's ~ in sb./sth. sein Vertrauen auf od. in jmdn./etw. setzen; take sth. on ~: etw. einfach glauben
(b) (organization managed by trustees) Treuhandgesellschaft, die; [charitable] ~: Stiftung, die; (association of companies) Trust, der
(c) (Law) hold in ~: treuhänderisch verwalten
2 v.t. (rely on) trauen (+ Dat.); vertrauen (+ Dat.) ‹Person›; ~ sb. with sth. jmdm. etw. anvertrauen
3 v.i. (a) ~ to sich verlassen auf (+ Akk.)
(b) (believe) ~ in sb./sth. auf jmdn./etw. vertrauen

trustee /trʌ'stiː/ n. Treuhänder, der/ Treuhänderin, die

trustful /'trʌstfl/, **trusting** adjs. vertrauensvoll

trust: ~ fund n. Treuhandvermögen, das; ~worthy adj. vertrauenswürdig

truth /truːθ/ n., pl. ~s /truːðz, truːθs/ Wahrheit, die; tell the [whole] ~: die [ganze] Wahrheit sagen

truthful /'truːθfl/ adj. ehrlich

try /traɪ/ 1 n. Versuch, der; have a ~ at sth./doing sth. etw. versuchen/versuchen, etw. zu tun; give it a ~, have a ~: es versuchen
2 v.t. (a) (attempt) versuchen
(b) (test usefulness of) probieren
(c) (test) auf die Probe stellen ‹Fähigkeit, Kraft, Geduld›
(d) (Law.: take to trial) ~ a case einen Fall verhandeln; ~ sb. [for sth.] jmdn. [wegen einer Sache] vor Gericht stellen
3 v.i. es versuchen; ~ hard/harder sich (Dat.) viel/mehr Mühe geben
■ **try 'on** v.t. anprobieren ‹Kleidungsstück›
■ **try 'out** v.t. ausprobieren

'trying adj. (a) (testing) schwierig
(b) (difficult to endure) anstrengend

tsar /zɑː(r)/ n. (Hist.) Zar, der

'T-shirt n. T-Shirt, das

tub /tʌb/ n. Kübel, der; (for ice cream etc.) Becher, der

tuba /'tjuːbə/ n. (Mus.) Tuba, die

tubby /'tʌbɪ/ *adj.* rundlich

tube /tju:b/ *n.* **(a)** (for conveying liquids etc.) Rohr, *das* **(b)** (small cylinder) Tube, *die;* (for sweets, tablets) Röhrchen, *das* **(c)** (Anat., Zool.) Röhre, *die* **(d)** (of TV etc.) Röhre, *die* **(e)** (Brit. coll.: underground railway) U-Bahn, *die*

tuber /'tju:bə(r)/ *n.* (Bot.) Knolle, *die*

tuberculosis /tju:bɜ:kjʊ'ləʊsɪs/ *n.* Tuberkulose, *die*

tube: ∼ station *n.* (Brit. coll.) U-Bahnhof, *der;* **∼ train** *n.* (Brit. coll.) U-bahn-Zug, *der*

tubing /'tju:bɪŋ/ *n.* Rohre *Pl.*

tubular /'tju:bjʊlə(r)/ *adj.* röhrenförmig

tuck /tʌk/ **1** *v.t.* stecken **2** *n.* (in fabric) (for decoration) Biese, *die;* (to tighten) Abnäher, *der* ■ **tuck 'in 1** *v.t.* hineinstecken **2** *v.i.* (coll.) zulangen (ugs.) ■ **tuck 'up** *v.t.* **(a)** hochkrempeln ⟨*Ärmel, Hose*⟩; hochnehmen ⟨*Rock*⟩ **(b)** (cover snugly) zudecken

Tue., Tues. *abbrs.* = **Tuesday** Di.

Tuesday /'tju:zdeɪ, 'tju:zdɪ/ *n.* Dienstag, *der; see also* FRIDAY

tuft /tʌft/ *n.* Büschel, *das*

tug /tʌg/ **1** *n.* **(a)** Ruck, *der;* ∼ **of war** Tauziehen, *das* **(b)** ∼ [boat] Schlepper, *der* **2** *v.t.,* **-gg-** ziehen **3** *v.i.,* **-gg-** zerren (**at** an + *Dat.*)

tuition /tju:'ɪʃn/ *n.* Unterricht, *der*

tulip /'tju:lɪp/ *n.* Tulpe, *die*

tumble /'tʌmbl/ **1** *v.i.* stürzen; fallen **2** *n.* Sturz, *der*

tumble: ∼down *adj.* verfallen; **∼-drier** *n.* Wäschetrockner, *der;* **∼-dry** *v.t.* im Automaten trocknen

tumbler /'tʌmblə(r)/ *n.* (short) Whiskyglas, *das;* (long) Wasserglas, *das*

tummy /'tʌmɪ/ *n.* (child lang./coll.) Bäuchlein, *das*

tummy: ∼ ache *n.* (child lang./coll.) Bauchweh, *das;* ∼ **button** *n.* (child lang./coll.) Bauchnabel, *der;* ∼ **upset** *n.* (child lang./coll.) Magenverstimmung, *die*

tumour (*Brit.; Amer.:* **tumor**) /'tju:mə(r)/ *n.* Tumor, *der*

tumult /'tju:məlt/ *n.* Tumult, *der*

tuna /'tju:nə/ *n., pl. same or* ∼s Thunfisch, *der*

tune /tju:n/ **1** *n.* **(a)** (melody) Melodie, *die;* **change one's** ∼ (fig.) sein Verhalten ändern; **call the** ∼: den Ton angeben **(b)** (correct pitch) **sing in/out of** ∼: richtig/ falsch singen; **be in/out of** ∼ ⟨*Instrument:*⟩ richtig gestimmt/verstimmt sein **2** *v.t.* **(a)** (Mus.: put in ∼) stimmen **(b)** (Radio, Telev.) einstellen (**to** auf + *Akk.*) **(c)** einstellen ⟨*Motor, Vergaser*⟩

tune 'in *v.i.* (Radio, Telev.) ∼ **to a station** einen Sender einstellen

tuneful /'tju:nfl/ *adj.* melodisch

tuner /'tju:nə(r)/ *n.* **(a)** (Mus.) Stimmer, *der/* Stimmerin, *die* **(b)** (radio) Tuner, *der*

tunic /'tju:nɪk/ *n.* (of soldier) Uniformjacke, *die;* (of schoolgirl) Kittel, *der*

'tuning fork /'tju:nɪŋfɔ:k/ *n.* Stimmgabel, *die*

Tunisia /tju:'nɪzɪə/ *pr. n.* Tunesien (*das*)

tunnel /'tʌnl/ **1** *n.* Tunnel, *der;* (dug by animal) Gang, *der* **2** *v.i.,* (Brit.) **-ll-** einen Tunnel graben

turban /'tɜ:bən/ *n.* Turban, *der*

turbine /'tɜ:baɪn/ *n.* Turbine, *die*

turbocharged /'tɜ:bəʊtʃɑ:dʒd/ *adj.* mit Turbolader *nachgestellt*

turbot /'tɜ:bət/ *n.* Steinbutt, *der*

turbulence /'tɜ:bjʊləns/ *n.* **(a)** Aufgewühltheit, *die;* (fig.) Aufruhr, *der* **(b)** (Phys.) Turbulenz, *die*

turbulent /'tɜ:bjʊlənt/ *adj.* **(a)** aufgewühlt **(b)** (Phys.) turbulent

turd /tɜ:d/ *n.* (coarse) Scheißhaufen, *der* (derb)

tureen /tjʊə'ri:n/ *n.* Terrine, *die*

turf /tɜ:f/ *n., pl.* ∼**s** or **turves** /tɜ:vz/ **(a)** *no pl.* Rasen, *der* **(b)** (segment) Rasenstück, *das* ■ **turf 'out** *v.t.* (coll.) rausschmeißen (ugs.)

Turk /tɜ:k/ *n.* Türke, *der/*Türkin, *die*

turkey *n.* Truthahn, *der/*Truthenne, *die;* (esp. as food) Puter, *der/*Pute, *die*

Turkey /'tɜ:kɪ/ *pr. n.* die Türkei

Turkish /'tɜ:kɪʃ/ **1** *adj.* türkisch; **sb. is** ∼: jmd. ist Türke/Türkin **2** *n.* Türkisch, *das; see also* ENGLISH 2A

turmoil /'tɜ:mɔɪl/ *n.* Aufruhr, *der*

turn /tɜ:n/ **1** *n.* **(a)** **it is sb.'s** ∼ **to do sth.** jmd. ist an der Reihe, etw. zu tun; **it's your** ∼ [next] du bist als Nächster/Nächste dran (ugs.) *od.* an der Reihe; **out of** ∼: außer der Reihe; (fig.) an der falschen Stelle ⟨*lachen*⟩; **take [it in]** ∼**s** sich abwechseln **(b)** (rotary motion) Drehung, *die* **(c)** (change of direction) Wende, *die;* **take a** ∼ **to the right/left, do** *or* **take a right/left** ∼: nach rechts/links abbiegen; (fig.) **take a favourable** ∼ sich zum Guten wenden; **the** ∼ **of the year/century** die Jahres-/Jahrhundertwende **(d)** (bend) Kurve, *die;* (corner) Ecke, *die* **(e)** (short performance) Nummer, *die* **(f)** (service) **do sb. a good** ∼: jmdm. einen guten Dienst erweisen **(g)** (coll.: fright) **give sb. quite a** ∼: jmdm. einen gehörigen Schrecken einjagen (ugs.) **2** *v.t.* **(a)** (make revolve) drehen **(b)** (reverse) umdrehen; wenden ⟨*Pfannkuchen, Auto, Heu*⟩; ∼ **sth. upside down** *or* **on its head** (lit. or fig.) etw. auf den Kopf stellen; ∼ **the page** umblättern **(c)** (give new direction to) drehen, wenden ⟨*Kopf*⟩; ∼ **a hose/gun on sb./sth.** einen

Schlauch/ein Gewehr auf jmdn./etw. richten; ∼ **one's attention/mind to sth.** sich/ seine Gedanken einer Sache (*Dat.*) zuwenden

(d) ∼ **sb. loose on sb./sth.** jmdn. auf jmdn./ etw. loslassen

(e) (cause to become) verwandeln; ∼ **the lights [down] low** das Licht dämpfen; ∼ **a play/ book into a film** ein Theaterstück/Buch verfilmen

(f) (shape in lathe) drechseln ⟨*Holz*⟩; drehen ⟨*Metall*⟩

(g) drehen ⟨*Pirouette*⟩; schlagen ⟨*Purzelbaum*⟩

3 *v.i.* **(a)** (revolve) sich drehen

(b) (reverse direction) ⟨*Person:*⟩ sich herumdrehen; ⟨*Auto:*⟩ wenden

(c) (take new direction) sich wenden; (∼ round) sich umdrehen; ∼ **to the left/right** nach links/rechts abbiegen

(d) (become) werden; ∼ **[in]to sth.** zu etw. werden; (be transformed) sich in etw. (*Akk.*) verwandeln

(e) (become sour) ⟨*Milch:*⟩ sauer werden

▪ **turn a'way** **1** *v.i.* sich abwenden

2 *v.t.* **(a)** (avert) abwenden

(b) (send away) wegschicken

▪ **turn 'down** *v.t.* **(a)** herunterschlagen ⟨*Kragen*⟩

(b) niedriger stellen ⟨*Heizung*⟩; herunterdrehen ⟨*Gas*⟩; leiser stellen ⟨*Ton, Radio, Fernseher*⟩

(c) (reject) ablehnen; abweisen ⟨*Kandidaten usw.*⟩

▪ **turn 'in** **1** *v.t.* **(a)** nach innen drehen

(b) (hand in) abgeben

2 *v.i.* **(a)** (enter) einbiegen

(b) (coll.: go to bed) in die Falle gehen (salopp)

▪ **turn 'off** **1** *v.t.* abschalten; abstellen ⟨*Wasser, Gas*⟩; zudrehen ⟨*Wasserhahn*⟩

2 *v.i.* abbiegen

▪ **turn on** *v.t.* **(a)** /-'-/ anschalten; aufdrehen ⟨*Wasserhahn, Gas*⟩

(b) /'--/ (attack) angreifen

▪ **turn 'out** **1** *v.t.* **(a)** (expel) hinauswerfen (ugs.)

(b) (switch off) ausschalten; abdrehen ⟨*Gas*⟩

(c) (produce) produzieren

(d) (Brit.) (empty) ausräumen; leeren; (get rid of) wegwerfen

2 *v.i.* **(a)** (prove to be) sb./sth. ∼**s out to be** sth. jmd./etw. stellt sich als jmd./etw. heraus; **everything** ∼**ed out well/all right in the end** alles endete gut

(b) (appear) ⟨*Fans usw.:*⟩ erscheinen

▪ **turn 'over** **1** *v.t.* umdrehen

2 *v.i.* **(a)** (tip over) umkippen; ⟨*Boot:*⟩ kentern; ⟨*Auto, Flugzeug:*⟩ sich überschlagen

(b) (from one side to the other) sich umdrehen

(c) (∼ a page) umblättern

▪ **turn 'round** *v.i.* sich umdrehen

▪ **'turn to** *v.t.* (fig.) ∼ **to sb.** sich an jmdn. wenden; ∼ **sb. for help/advice** bei jmdm. Hilfe/Rat suchen; ∼ **to drink** sich in den Alkohol flüchten

▪ **turn 'up** **1** *v.i.* **(a)** ⟨*Person:*⟩ erscheinen

(b) (present itself) auftauchen; ⟨*Gelegenheit:*⟩ sich bieten

2 *v.t.* **(a)** hochschlagen ⟨*Kragen*⟩

(b) lauter stellen ⟨*Ton, Radio, Fernseher*⟩; aufdrehen ⟨*Heizung, Gas*⟩; heller machen ⟨*Licht*⟩

'turnaround *n.* **(a)** (change) [Kehrt]wende, *die*

(b) (of aircraft, ship, vehicle) Abfertigung, *die*

turned-up /'tɜːndʌp/ *adj.* ∼ **nose** Stupsnase, *die* (ugs.)

'turning *n.* Abzweigung, *die*

'turning point *n.* Wendepunkt, *der*

turnip /'tɜːnɪp/ *n.* [weiße] Rübe

turn: ∼**out** *n.* (of people) Beteiligung, *die* (for an + *Dat.*); ∼**over** *n.* **(a)** (Commerc.) Umsatz, *der;* (of stock) Umschlag, *der;* **(b)** (of staff) Fluktuation, *die;* ∼**pike** *n.* (Amer.) gebührenpflichtige Autobahn; ∼**stile** *n.* Drehkreuz, *das;* ∼**table** *n.* Plattenteller, *der;* ∼**up** *n.* (Brit. Fashion) Aufschlag, *der*

turpentine /'tɜːpntaɪn/ *n.* Terpentin, *das*

turps /tɜːps/ *n.* (coll.) Terpentin, *das* (ugs.)

turquoise /'tɜːkwɔɪz/ **1** *n.* **(a)** Türkis, *der*

(b) (colour) Türkis, *das*

2 *adj.* türkis[farben]

turret /'tʌrɪt/ *n.* Türmchen, *das*

turreted /'tʌrɪtɪd/ *adj.* ⟨*Schloss*⟩ mit Mauertürmchen

turtle /'tɜːtl/ *n.* **(a)** Meeresschildkröte, *die*

(b) (Amer.: freshwater reptile) Wasserschildkröte, *die*

'turtleneck *n.* ∼**neck pullover** Pullover mit Stehbund

turves ▶ TURF B

tusk /tʌsk/ *n.* Stoßzahn, *der*

tussle /'tʌsl/ **1** *n.* Gerangel, *das* (ugs.)

2 *v.i.* sich balgen

tutor /'tjuːtə(r)/ *n.* [private] ∼: [Privat]lehrer, *der*/-lehrerin, *die*

tut[-tut] /tʌt('tʌt)/ **1** *int.* na[, na]

2 *v.i.,* -tt-: ∼ [with disapproval] [missbilligend] „na, na!" sagen

tutu /'tuːtuː/ *n.* Tutu, *das*

tuxedo /tʌk'siːdəʊ/ *n., pl.* ∼**s** *or* ∼**es** (Amer.) Smoking, *der*

TV /tiː'viː/ *n.* **(a)** Fernsehen, *das*

(b) (television set) Fernseher, *der* (ugs.)

twaddle /'twɒdl/ *n.* Gewäsch, *das* (ugs.)

twang /twæŋ/ **1** *v.t.* zupfen ⟨*Saite*⟩

2 *n.* [nasal] ∼: Näseln, *das*

tweed /twiːd/ *n.* Tweed, *der*

tweezers /'twiːzəz/ *n. pl.* [pair of] ∼: Pinzette, *die*

twelfth /twelfθ/ **1** *adj.* zwölft...

2 *n.* (fraction) Zwölftel, *das. See also* EIGHTH

twelve /twelv/ **1** *adj.* zwölf

2 *n.* Zwölf, *die. See also* SIX

twentieth /'twentɪθ/ **1** *adj.* zwanzigst...

2 *n.* (fraction) Zwanzigstel, *das. See also* EIGHTH

twenty /'twentɪ/ ① *adj.* zwanzig
② *n.* Zwanzig, *die.* See also EIGHT; EIGHTY 2

twice /twaɪs/ *adv.* **(a)** zweimal
(b) (doubly) doppelt

twiddle /'twɪdl/ *v.t.* herumdrehen an
(+ *Dat.*) (ugs.); ~ **one's thumbs** (lit. or fig.)
Däumchen drehen

twig¹ /twɪg/ *n.* Zweig, *der*

twig² (coll.) ① *v.t.*, **-gg-** kapieren (ugs.)
② *v.i.,* **-gg-** es kapieren (ugs.)

twilight /'twaɪlaɪt/ *n.* **(a)** (evening light)
Dämmerlicht, *das*
(b) (period of half-light) Dämmerung, *die*

twin /twɪn/ ① *attrib. adj.* **(a)** Zwillings-
(b) (forming a pair) Doppel-
② *n.* Zwilling, *der*
③ *v.t.* **Bottrop is ~ned with Blackpool**
Bottrop und Blackpool sind Partnerstädte

twin 'beds *n. pl.* zwei Einzelbetten *Pl.*

twine /twaɪn/ ① *n.* Bindfaden, *der*
② *v.i.* sich winden (**about, around** um)

twinge /twɪndʒ/ *n.* Stechen, *das;* ~[s] **of**
conscience (fig.) Gewissensbisse *Pl.*

twinkle /'twɪŋkl/ ① *v.i.* funkeln (**with** vor
+ *Dat.*)
② *n.* Funkeln, *das*

twinkling /'twɪŋklɪŋ/ *n.* **in a ~, in the ~ of**
an eye im Handumdrehen

'twin town *n.* (Brit.) Partnerstadt, *die*

twirl /twɜːl/ ① *v.t.* [schnell] drehen
② *v.i.* wirbeln (**around** über + *Akk.*)

twist /twɪst/ ① *v.t.* **(a)** verdrehen ‹*Worte,*
Bedeutung›; ~ **one's ankle** sich (*Dat.*) den
Knöchel verrenken; ~ **sb.'s arm** jmdm. den
Arm umdrehen; (fig.) jmdm. [die]
Daumenschrauben anlegen
(b) (rotate) drehen
② *v.i.* sich winden
③ *n.* **(a)** (motion) Drehung, *die*
(b) (unexpected occurrence) überraschende
Wendung

'twisted *adj.* verbogen; (fig.) verdreht (ugs.
abwertend) ‹*Geist*›; verquer ‹*Humor*›

twit /twɪt/ *n.* (Brit. coll.) Trottel, *der* (ugs.)

twitch /twɪtʃ/ ① *v.i.* ‹*Mund, Lippe:*› zucken
② *n.* Zucken, *das*

twitter /'twɪtə(r)/ ① *n.* Zwitschern, *das*
② *v.i.* zwitschern

two /tuː/ ① *adj.* zwei

② *n.* Zwei, *die.* See also EIGHT

two: ~**-bit** *adj.* (Amer.) (of poor quality) mies
(ugs.); ~**-faced** /'tuːfeɪst/ *adj.* (fig.) falsch;
~**fold** *adj., adv.* zweifach; **a ~fold increase**
ein Anstieg auf das Doppelte; ~**-lane** *adj.*
zweispurig; ~**-piece** ① *n.* Zweiteiler, *der;*
② *adj.* zweiteilig; ~**-seater** /-'--/ *n.*
Zweisitzer, *der;* ~**some** /'tuːsəm/ *n.* Paar,
das; ~**-storey** *adj.* zweigeschossig;
~**tone** *adj.* zweifarbig; ~**up** ~**-down** *n.*
kleines [Reihen]haus; ~**-way** *adj.* **(a)**
zweibahnig (Verkehrsw.); '~**-way traffic ahead**'
„Achtung Gegenverkehr"; **(b)** ~**-way mirror**
Einwegspiegel, *der*

tycoon /taɪ'kuːn/ *n.* Magnat, *der*

tying ▸ TIE 1, 2

type /taɪp/ ① *n.* **(a)** Art, *die;* (person) Typ,
der; **what ~ of car …?** was für ein Auto …?
(b) (Printing) Drucktype, *die*
② *v.t.* [mit der Maschine] schreiben; tippen
(ugs.)
③ *v.i.* Maschine schreiben
■ **type 'out** *v.t.* [mit der Schreibmaschine]
abschreiben; abtippen (ugs.)

type: ~**cast** *v.t.* [auf eine bestimmte Rolle]
festlegen; ~**face** *n.* Schriftbild, *das;*
~**script** *n.* maschine[n]geschriebene
Fassung; ~**setter** *n.* [Schrift]setzer, *der*/
-setzerin, *die;* ~**setting** *n.* [Schrift]setzen,
das; ~**writer** *n.* Schreibmaschine, *die;*
~**written** *adj.* maschine[n]geschrieben

typhoid /'taɪfɔɪd/ *n.* ~ **[fever]** Typhus, *der*

typhoon /taɪ'fuːn/ *n.* Taifun, *der*

typical /'tɪpɪkl/ *adj.* typisch (**of** für)

typify /'tɪpɪfaɪ/ *v.t.* ~ **sth.** als typisches
Beispiel für etw. dienen

typing /'taɪpɪŋ/ *n.* Maschineschreiben, *das*

'typing error *n.* Tippfehler, *der*

typist /'taɪpɪst/ *n.* Schreibkraft, *die*

typography /taɪ'pɒgrəfɪ/ *n.* Typographie,
die

tyrannical /tɪ'rænɪkl/ *adj.* tyrannisch

tyranny /'tɪrənɪ/ *n.* Tyrannei, *die*

tyrant /'taɪərənt/ *n.* Tyrann, *der*

tyre /'taɪə(r)/ *n.* Reifen, *der*

'tyre pressure *n.* Reifendruck, *der*

tzar *etc.* ▸ TSAR *etc.*

Uu

U, u /juː/ *n.* U, u, *das*

'U-bend *n.* U-Rohr, *das*

ubiquitous /juːˈbɪkwɪtəs/ *adj.*
allgegenwärtig

udder /ˈʌdə(r)/ *n.* Euter, *das*

UFO /ˈjuːfəʊ/ *n., pl.* ~s Ufo, *das*

ugh /ʌh, ʊh, ɜːh/ *int.* bah

ugliness /ˈʌɡlɪnɪs/ *n.* Hässlichkeit, *die*

ugly /ˈʌɡlɪ/ *adj.* (a) hässlich
(b) (nasty) übel ⟨*Wunde, Laune usw.*⟩

UHF *abbr.* = **ultra-high frequency**
UHF

UHT *abbr.* = **ultra heat-treated**
ultrahoch erhitzt

UK *abbr.* = **United Kingdom**

Ukraine /juːˈkreɪn/ *pr. n.* Ukraine, *die*

Ukrainian /juːˈkreɪnɪən/ ⓵ *adj.*
ukrainisch; **sb. is** ~: jmd. ist Ukrainer/
Ukrainerin
⓶ *n.* (a) (person) Ukrainer, *der*/Ukrainerin,
die
(b) (language) Ukrainisch, *das; see also*
ENGLISH 2 A

ulcer /ˈʌlsə(r)/ *n.* Geschwür, *das*

ulterior /ʌlˈtɪərɪə(r)/ *adj.* hintergründig;
~ **motive** Hintergedanke, *der*

ultimate /ˈʌltɪmət/ ⓵ *attrib. adj.* (a) (final)
letzt...; (eventual) endgültig ⟨*Sieg*⟩
(b) (fundamental) tiefst...
⓶ *n.* **the** ~ **in comfort/luxury** der Gipfel an
Bequemlichkeit/Luxus

'ultimately *adv.* (a) (in the end) schließlich
(b) (in the last analysis) letzten Endes

ultimatum /ʌltɪˈmeɪtəm/ *n., pl.* ~s *or*
ultimata /ʌltɪˈmeɪtə/ Ultimatum, *das*

ultra'sound *n.* Ultraschall, *der*

ultra'violet *adj.* (Phys.) ultraviolett; UV-
⟨*Lampe, Filter*⟩

umbilical cord /ʌmˈbɪlɪkl kɔːd/ *n.*
Nabelschnur, *die*

umbrage /ˈʌmbrɪdʒ/ *n.* **take** ~ **[at sth.]** [an
etw. (+ *Dat.*)] Anstoß nehmen

umbrella /ʌmˈbrelə/ *n.* [Regen]schirm, *der*

um'brella stand *n.* Schirmständer, *der*

umpire /ˈʌmpaɪə(r)/ *n.* Schiedsrichter, *der*/
-richterin, *die*

umpteen /ʌmpˈtiːn/ *adj.* (coll.) zig (ugs.); x
(ugs.)

unabashed /ʌnəˈbæʃt/ *adj.* ungeniert

unable /ʌnˈeɪbl/ *pred. adj.* **be** ~ **to do sth.**
etw. nicht tun können

unabridged /ʌnəˈbrɪdʒd/ *adj.* ungekürzt

unac'ceptable *adj.* unannehmbar

unaccompanied /ʌnəˈkʌmpənɪd/ *adj.*
ohne Begleitung *nachgestellt*

unac'countable *adj.* unerklärlich

unaccountably /ʌnəˈkaʊntəblɪ/ *adv.*
unerklärlicherweise

unac'customed *adj.* ungewohnt; **be** ~ **to**
sth. etw. (*Akk.*) nicht gewöhnt sein

unadulterated /ʌnəˈdʌltəreɪtɪd/ *adj.* (a)
(pure) unverfälscht
(b) (utter) völlig

unadventurous /ʌnədˈventʃərəs/ *adj.*
bieder ⟨*Person*⟩; ereignislos ⟨*Leben*⟩

unafraid /ʌnəˈfreɪd/ *adj.* **be** ~ **[of sb./sth.]**
keine Angst [vor jmdm./etw.] haben

unaided /ʌnˈeɪdɪd/ *adj.* ohne fremde Hilfe

unalike /ʌnəˈlaɪk/ *pred. adj.* unähnlich

unambiguous /ʌnæmˈbɪɡjʊəs/ *adj.*
unzweideutig

unambitious /ʌnæmˈbɪʃəs/ *adj.* ⟨*Person*⟩
ohne Ergeiz

unanimity /juːnəˈnɪmɪtɪ/ *n.* Einmütigkeit,
die

unanimous /juːˈnænɪməs/ *adj.*
einstimmig; **be** ~ **in doing sth.** etw.
einmütig tun

u'nanimously *adv.* einstimmig

unannounced /ʌnəˈnaʊnst/ *adj.*
unangemeldet

unappetizing /ʌnˈæpɪtaɪzɪŋ/ *adj.*
unappetitlich

unarmed /ʌnˈɑːmd/ *adj.* unbewaffnet;
~ **combat** Kampf ohne Waffen

unassuming /ʌnəˈsjuːmɪŋ/ *adj.*
bescheiden

unattached /ʌnəˈtætʃt/ *adj.* (a) nicht
befestigt
(b) (without a partner) ungebunden

unat'tended *adj.* (a) ~ **to** (not dealt with)
unerledigt; nicht bedient ⟨*Kunde*⟩; nicht
behandelt ⟨*Patient*⟩
(b) (not supervised) unbewacht ⟨*Parkplatz,
Gepäck*⟩

unat'tractive *adj.* unattraktiv

unauthorized /ʌnˈɔːθəraɪzd/ *adj.*
unbefugt; **no entry for** ~ **persons** Zutritt für
Unbefugte verboten

una'vailable *adj.* nicht erhältlich ⟨*Ware*⟩;
be ~ **for comment** zur Stellungnahme nicht
zur Verfügung stehen

una'voidable *adj.* unvermeidlich

unaware /ʌnəˈweə(r)/ *adj.* **be** ~ **of sth.**
sich (*Dat.*) einer Sache (*Gen.*) nicht bewusst
sein

unawares /ʌnəˈweəz/ *adv.* **catch sb.** ~:
jmdn. überraschen

unbalanced /ʌnˈbælənst/ *adj.* **(a)**
unausgewogen
(b) (mentally ∼) unausgeglichen
unˈbearable *adj.*, **unbearably**
/ʌnˈbeərəblɪ/ *adv.* unerträglich
unbeatable /ʌnˈbiːˈtəbl/ *adj.* unschlagbar
(ugs.)
unˈbeaten *adj.* **(a)** ungeschlagen
(b) (not surpassed) unerreicht; ungebrochen
⟨*Rekord*⟩
unbeˈlievable *adj.* **(a)** unglaublich
(b) (tremendous) unwahrscheinlich
unbiased, unbiassed /ʌnˈbaɪəst/ *adj.*
unvoreingenommen
unblemished /ʌnˈblemɪʃt/ *adj.* makellos
⟨*Haut, Ruf*⟩
unˈblock *v.t.* frei machen
unˈbolt *v.t.* aufriegeln ⟨*Tür*⟩
unborn /ʌnˈbɔːn, *attrib.* ˈʌnbɔːn/ *adj.*
ungeboren
unˈbreakable *adj.* unzerbrechlich
unburden /ʌnˈbɜːdn/ *v.t.* ∼ oneself sein
Herz ausschütten
unˈbutton *v.t.* aufknöpfen
uncalled-for /ʌnˈkɔːldfɔː(r)/ *adj.*
unangebracht
uncanny /ʌnˈkænɪ/ *adj.* unheimlich
uncared-for /ʌnˈkeədfɔː(r)/ *adj.*
vernachlässigt
unˈcaring /ʌnˈkeərɪŋ/ *adj.* gleichgültig
unˈceasing /ʌnˈsiːsɪŋ/ *adj.* unaufhörlich
unceremonious /ʌnserɪˈməʊnɪəs/ *adj.* **(a)**
(informal) formlos
(b) (abrupt) brüsk
unceˈremoniously *adv.* ohne
Umschweife
unˈcertain *adj.* **(a)** (not sure) be ∼ [whether
...] sich (*Dat.*) nicht sicher sein[, ob ...]
(b) (not clear) ungewiss ⟨*Ergebnis, Zukunft*⟩;
of ∼ age/origin unbestimmten Alters/
unbestimmter Herkunft
(c) (ambiguous) vage; in no ∼ terms ganz
eindeutig
uncertainty /ʌnˈsɜːtntɪ/ *n.* **(a)**
Ungewissheit, *die*
(b) (hesitation) Unsicherheit, *die*
unˈchanged /ʌnˈtʃeɪndʒd/ *adj.* unverändert
uncharacteristic /ʌnkærɪktəˈrɪstɪk/ *adj.*
uncharakteristisch (of für)
unˈcharitable *adj.*, **uncharitably**
/ʌnˈtʃærɪtəblɪ/ *adv.* lieblos
unˈcivil *adj.* unhöflich
uncle /ˈʌŋkl/ *n.* Onkel, *der*
unˈcomfortable *adj.* **(a)** unbequem
(b) (feeling discomfort) be ∼: sich unbehaglich
fühlen
(c) (uneasy, disconcerting) unangenehm;
peinlich ⟨*Stille*⟩
unˈcomfortably *adv.* unbequem; be
∼ aware of sth. sich (*Dat.*) einer Sache
peinlich bewusst sein
unˈcommon *adj.* ungewöhnlich

uncompliˈmentary *adj.* wenig
schmeichelhaft
uncompromising /ʌnˈkɒmprəmaɪzɪŋ/
adj. kompromisslos
unconˈditional *adj.* bedingungslos
⟨*Kapitulation*⟩; kategorisch ⟨*Ablehnung*⟩;
⟨*Versprechen*⟩ ohne Vorbehalte
unconfirmed /ʌnkənˈfɜːmd/ *adj.*
unbestätigt
unˈconscious ① *adj.* **(a)** (Med.) bewusstlos
(b) (unaware) be ∼ of sth. sich einer Sache
(*Gen.*) nicht bewusst sein
(c) (not intended; Psych.) unbewusst
② *n.* Unbewusste, *das*
unˈconsciously *adv.* unbewusst
uncontrollable /ʌnkənˈtrəʊləbl/ *adj.*
unkontrollierbar; the child is ∼: das Kind ist
nicht zu bändigen
unconˈventional *adj.*,
unconˈventionally *adv.*
unkonventionell
unconvinced /ʌnkənˈvɪnst/ *adj.* nicht
überzeugt; remain ∼: sich nicht überzeugen
lassen
uncooked /ʌnˈkʊkt/ *adj.* roh
uncoˈoperative *adj.* unkooperativ;
(unhelpful) wenig hilfsbereit
uncoordinated /ʌnkəʊˈɔːdmeɪtɪd/ *adj.*
unkoordiniert
unˈcork *v.t.* entkorken
uncouth /ʌnˈkuːθ/ *adj.* ungehobelt ⟨*Person,
Benehmen*⟩; grob ⟨*Bemerkung*⟩
unˈcover *v.t.* aufdecken
undaunted /ʌnˈdɔːntɪd/ *adj.* unverzagt
undecided /ʌndɪˈsaɪdɪd/ *adj.* **(a)** (not settled)
nicht entschieden
(b) (hesitant) unentschlossen
undeclared /ʌndɪˈkleəd/ *adj.* ∼ income (for
tax) nicht angegebenes Einkommen
ˈundelete *v.t.* (Comp.) wiederherstellen
undemanding /ʌndɪˈmɑːndɪŋ/ *adj.*
anspruchslos
undeˈniable *adj.*, **undeniably**
/ʌndɪˈnaɪəblɪ/ *adv.* unbestreitbar
under /ˈʌndə(r)/ ① *prep.* **(a)** (underneath,
below) unter (*position:* + *Dat.*; *motion:*
+ *Akk.*); from ∼ the table/bed unter dem
Tisch/Bett hervor
(b) (undergoing) ∼ treatment in Behandlung;
∼ repair in Reparatur; ∼ construction im
Bau
(c) (in conditions of) bei ⟨*Stress, hohen
Temperaturen usw.*⟩
(d) (subject to) unter (+ *Dat.*); ∼ the terms of
the contract nach den Bestimmungen des
Vertrags
(e) (with the use of) unter (+ *Dat.*); ∼ an
assumed name unter falschem Namen
(f) (less than) unter (+ *Dat.*)
② *adv.* **(a)** (in or to a lower or subordinate position)
darunter

(b) (in/into a state of unconsciousness) be ~/put **sb. ~:** in Narkose liegen/jmdn. in Narkose versetzen

under: ~a'chieve *v.i.* unter dem erreichbaren Leistungsniveau bleiben; **~-age** *adj.* minderjährig; **~carriage** *n.* Fahrwerk, *das;* **~clothes** *n. pl.,* **~clothing** *n.* ▶ UNDERWEAR; **~coat** *n.* (layer of paint) Grundierung, *die;* (paint) Grundierfarbe, *die;* **~'cover** *adj.* (disguised) getarnt; (secret) verdeckt; **~cover agent** Geheimagent, *der;* **~current** *n.* Unterströmung, *die;* (fig.) Unterton, *der;* **~'cut** *v.t.,* **~cut** unterbieten; **~dog** *n.* **(a)** (in fight) Unterlegene, *der/die;* **(b)** (fig.) Benachteiligte, *der/die;* **~'done** *adj.* halb gar; **~estimate** /ʌndər'estɪmeɪt/ ⒈ *v.t.* unterschätzen; ⒉ /ʌndər'estɪmət/ *n.* Unterschätzung, *die;* **~'fed** *adj.* unterernährt; **~'foot** *adv.* am Boden; **be trampled ~foot** mit Füßen zertrampelt werden; **~'go** *v.t., forms as* GO 1: durchmachen; **~go treatment** sich einer Behandlung unterziehen; **~go a change** sich verändern; **~'graduate** *n.* **~graduate** [**student**] Student/Studentin vor der ersten Prüfung; **~ground** ⒈ /'--'-/ *adv.* **(a)** unter der Erde; (Mining) unter Tage; **(b)** (fig.) (in hiding) im Untergrund; (into hiding) in den Untergrund; ⒉ /'---/ *adj.* unterirdisch ⟨*Höhle, See*⟩; **~ground railway** Untergrundbahn, *die;* U-Bahn, *die;* **~ground car park** Tiefgarage, *die;* ⒊ /'---/ *n.* (railway) U-Bahn, *die;* **~ground station/train** U-Bahnhof, *der/*U-Bahn-Zug, *der;* **~growth** *n.* Unterholz, *das;* **~hand, ~'handed** *adj.* **(a)** (secret) heimlich; **(b)** (crafty) hinterhältig; **~lay** *n.* Unterlage, *die;* **~'lie** *v.t., forms as* LIE²: **~lie sth.** (fig.) einer Sache (*Dat.*) zugrunde liegen; **~lying cause** eigentliche Ursache; **~'line** *v.t.* unterstreichen

underling /'ʌndəlɪŋ/ *n.* Untergebene, *der/die*

under: ~'lying ▶ UNDERLIE; **~'mine** *v.t.* **(a)** unterhöhlen; **(b)** (fig.) untergraben; unterminieren ⟨*Autorität*⟩

underneath /ʌndə'niːθ/ ⒈ *prep.* unter (*position: + Dat.; motion: + Akk.*) ⒉ *adv.* darunter

under: ~'nourished *adj.* unterernährt; **~'paid** *adj.* unterbezahlt; **~pants** *n. pl.* Unterhose, *die;* **~'pass** *n.* Unterführung, *die;* **~'play** *v.t.* herunterspielen; **~'privileged** *adj.* unterprivilegiert; **~'rate** *v.t.* unterschätzen; **~seal** *n.* Unterbodenschutz, *der;* **~signed** /ʌndə'saɪnd/ *adj.* (esp. Law) **the ~signed** der/ die Unterzeichnete/(pl.) die Unterzeichneten (Papierdt.); **~'staffed** *adj.* unterbesetzt; **be ~staffed** an Personalmangel leiden

understand /ʌndə'stænd/ ⒈ *v.t.,* **understood** /ʌndə'stʊd/ **(a)** verstehen; **make oneself understood** sich verständlich machen
(b) (have heard) gehört haben

(c) (take as implied) **it was understood that …:** es wurde allgemein angenommen, dass … ⒉ *v.i.,* **understood (a)** verstehen **(b)** (gather, hear) **if I ~ correctly** wenn ich mich nicht irre; **he is, I ~, no longer here** er ist, wie ich höre, nicht mehr hier

understandable /ʌndə'stændəbl/ *adj.* verständlich

understandably /ʌndə'stændəblɪ/ *adv.* verständlicherweise

under'standing ⒈ *adj.* verständnisvoll ⒉ *n.* **(a)** (agreement) Verständigung, *die;* **reach an ~ with sb.** sich mit jmdm. verständigen; **on the ~ that …:** unter der Voraussetzung, dass … **(b)** (intelligence) Verstand, *der* **(c)** (insight) Verständnis, *das* (of, for für)

under: ~statement *n.* Untertreibung, *die;* **~study** *n.* Ersatzspieler, *der/*-spielerin, *die;* **~'take** *v.t., forms as* TAKE 1: unternehmen; **~take a task** eine Aufgabe übernehmen; **~take to do sth.** sich verpflichten, etw. zu tun; **~taker** *n.* Leichenbestatter, *der/*-bestatterin, *die;* **~'taking** *n.* **(a)** (task) Aufgabe, *die;* **(b)** (pledge) Versprechen, *das;* **~tone** *n.* **in ~tones** *or* **an ~tone** mit gedämpfter Stimme; **~tone of criticism** kritischer Unterton; **~tow** *n.* Unterströmung, *die;* **~value** *v.t.* unterbewerten; **~water** ⒈ /'---/ *attrib.* Unterwasser-; ⒉ /--'--/ *adv.* unter Wasser; **~wear** *n.* Unterwäsche, *die;* **~'weight** *adj.* untergewichtig; **~world** *n.* Unterwelt, *die*

undeserved /ʌndɪ'zɜːvd/ *adj.* unverdient

unde'sirable *adj.* unerwünscht; **it is ~ that …:** es ist nicht wünschenswert, dass …

undeveloped /ʌndɪ'veləpt/ *adj.* **(a)** (immature) nicht voll ausgebildet **(b)** (not built on) nicht bebaut

undies /'ʌndɪz/ *n. pl.* (coll.) Unterwäsche, *die*

un'dignified *adj.* blamabel

undisciplined /ʌn'dɪsɪplɪnd/ *adj.* undiszipliniert

undiscovered /ʌndɪ'skʌvəd/ *adj.* unentdeckt

undisguised /ʌndɪs'gaɪzd/ *adj.* unverhohlen

undisturbed /ʌndɪ'stɜːbd/ *adj.* (not interrupted) ungestört

undo /ʌn'duː/ *v.t.,* **undoes** /ʌn'dʌz/, **undoing** /ʌn'duːɪŋ/, **undid** /ʌn'dɪd/, **undone** /ʌn'dʌn/ (unfasten) aufmachen

un'done *adj.* **(a)** (not accomplished) unerledigt **(b)** (not fastened) offen

undoubted /ʌn'daʊtɪd/ *adj.* unzweifelhaft

un'doubtedly *adv.* zweifellos

un'dress ⒈ *v.t.* ausziehen; **get ~ed** sich ausziehen ⒉ *v.i.* sich ausziehen

undrinkable /ʌnˈdrɪŋkəbl/ *adj.* nicht trinkbar; ungenießbar

un'due *attrib. adj.* übertrieben; übermäßig

undulating /ˈʌndjʊleɪtɪŋ/ *adj.* Wellen⟨linie⟩; ~ **country** sanfte Hügellandschaft

unduly /ʌnˈdjuːlɪ/ *adv.* übermäßig

undying /ʌnˈdaɪɪŋ/ *adj.* ewig; unsterblich ⟨Ruhm⟩

unearth /ʌnˈɜːθ/ *v.t.* **(a)** ausgraben
(b) (fig.: discover) aufdecken

unearthly /ʌnˈɜːθlɪ/ *adj.* unheimlich; **at an ~ hour** in aller Herrgottsfrühe

un'easy *adj.* **(a)** (anxious) besorgt; **he felt ~:** ihm war unbehaglich zumute
(b) (restless) unruhig

uneatable /ʌnˈiːtəbl/ *adj.* ungenießbar

uneco'nomic *adj.* unrentabel

uneco'nomical *adj.* ~ **[to run]** unwirtschaftlich

uneducated /ʌnˈedjʊkeɪtɪd/ *adj.* ungebildet

unemotional /ʌnɪˈməʊʃənl/ *adj.* emotionslos; nüchtern

unemployed /ʌnɪmˈplɔɪd/ ① *adj.* arbeitslos
② *n. pl.* **the ~:** die Arbeitslosen Pl.

unem'ployment *n.* Arbeitslosigkeit, *die*

unem'ployment benefit *n.* Arbeitslosengeld, *das*

un'ending *adj.* endlos

un'equal *adj.* unterschiedlich; ungleich ⟨Kampf⟩; **be ~ to sth.** einer Sache (*Dat.*) nicht gewachsen sein

unequalled (*Amer.:* **unequaled**) /ʌnˈiːkwld/ *adj.* unerreicht

une'quivocal *adj.* eindeutig

unerring /ʌnˈɜːrɪŋ/ *adj.* unfehlbar

un'ethical *adj.* unmoralisch

un'even *adj.* **(a)** (not smooth) uneben
(b) (not uniform) ungleichmäßig
(c) (odd) ungerade ⟨Zahl⟩

un'evenly *adv.* ungleichmäßig

uneventful /ʌnɪˈventfl/ *adj.* ereignislos

unexciting /ʌnɪkˈsaɪtɪŋ/ *adj.* wenig aufregend; (boring) langweilig

unex'pected *adj.* unerwartet

unexplained /ʌnɪkˈspleɪnd/ *adj.* ungeklärt

un'fair *adj.* unfair; ungerecht

un'fairly *adv.* **(a)** (unjustly) ungerecht; unfair ⟨spielen⟩
(b) (unreasonably) zu Unrecht

un'fairness *n.* Ungerechtigkeit, *die*

un'faithful *adj.* untreu

unfa'miliar *adj.* **(a)** (strange) unbekannt; ungewohnt ⟨Arbeit⟩
(b) be ~ with sth. sich mit etw. nicht auskennen

un'fasten *v.t.* **(a)** öffnen
(b) (detach) lösen

un'favourable *adj.* ungünstig

un'favourably *adv.* ungünstig; **be ~ disposed towards sb./sth.** jmdm./etw. gegenüber ablehnend eingestellt sein

un'feeling *adj.* gefühllos

unfinished /ʌnˈfɪnɪʃt/ *adj.* unvollendet ⟨Werk⟩; unerledigt ⟨Arbeit⟩

un'fit *adj.* **(a)** ungeeignet
(b) (not physically fit) nicht fit (ugs.); ~ **for military service** [wehrdienst]untauglich

un'flattering *adj.* wenig schmeichelhaft

un'flinching *adj.* unerschrocken

un'fold ① *v.t.* entfalten; ausbreiten ⟨Zeitung, Landkarte⟩
② *v.i.* sich entfalten; (develop) sich entwickeln

unfore'seen *adj.* unvorhergesehen

unforgettable /ʌnfəˈgetəbl/ *adj.* unvergesslich

unforgivable /ʌnfəˈgɪvəbl/ *adj.* unverzeihlich

un'fortunate *adj.* unglücklich

un'fortunately *adv.* leider

un'founded *adj.* (fig.) unbegründet

un'freeze *v.t. & i.*, **unfroze** /ʌnˈfrəʊz/, **unfrozen** /ʌnˈfrəʊzn/ auftauen

un'friendly *adj.* unfreundlich; feindlich ⟨Staat⟩

unfulfilled /ʌnfʊlˈfɪld/ *adj.* unerfüllt ⟨Person⟩

un'furl ① *v.t.* aufrollen; losmachen ⟨Segel⟩
② *v.i.* sich aufrollen

un'furnished *adj.* unmöbliert

ungainly /ʌnˈgeɪnlɪ/ *adj.* unbeholfen

ungram'matical *adj.* ungrammatisch

un'grateful *adj.* undankbar

un'happily *adv.* **(a)** unglücklich
(b) (unfortunately) leider

un'happiness *n.* Bekümmertheit, *die*

un'happy *adj.* unglücklich; (not content) unzufrieden (**about** with); **be** *or* **feel ~ about doing sth.** Bedenken haben, etw. zu tun

un'harmed *adj.* unbeschädigt; (uninjured) unverletzt

un'healthy *adj.* ungesund

unheard-of /ʌnˈhɜːdɒv/ *adj.* (unknown) [gänzlich] unbekannt; (unprecedented) beispiellos; (outrageous) unerhört

un'helpful *adj.* wenig hilfsbereit ⟨Person⟩; ⟨Bemerkung, Kritik⟩ die einem nicht weiterhilft

un'hook *v.t.* vom Haken nehmen; aufhaken ⟨Kleid⟩

un'hurt *adj.* unverletzt

unhy'gienic *adj.* unhygienisch

unicorn /ˈjuːnɪkɔːn/ *n.* Einhorn, *das*

uni'dentified *adj.* nicht identifiziert; ~ **flying object** unbekanntes Flugobjekt

unification /juːnɪfɪˈkeɪʃn/ *n.* Einigung, *die*

uniform /ˈjuːnɪfɔːm/ ① *adj.* einheitlich; **be ~ in shape/size** die gleiche Form/Größe haben

2 *n.* Uniform, *die; in/out of* ∼: in/ohne Uniform

uniformity /juːnɪˈfɔːmɪtɪ/ *n.* Einheitlichkeit, *die*

'uniformly *adv.* einheitlich

unify /ˈjuːnɪfaɪ/ *v.t.* einigen

unilateral /juːnɪˈlætərl/ *adj.* einseitig

uni'maginable *adj.* unvorstellbar

uni'maginative *adj.* fantasielos

unim'portant *adj.* unwichtig; bedeutungslos

unimpressed /ʌnɪmˈprest/ *adj.* nicht beeindruckt

unin'habitable *adj.* unbewohnbar

unin'habited *adj.* unbewohnt

un'injured *adj.* unverletzt

uninspired /ʌnɪnˈspaɪəd/ *adj.* einfallslos; I am/feel ∼: mir fehlt die Inspiration

uninspiring /ʌnɪnˈspaɪərɪŋ/ *adj.* langweilig

unin'telligent *adj.* nicht intelligent

unin'telligible *adj.* unverständlich

unin'tended *adj.* unbeabsichtigt

unin'tentional *adj.,* **unin'tentionally** *adv.* unabsichtlich

un'interested *adj.* desinteressiert (in an + *Dat.*)

un'interesting *adj.* uninteressant

uninterrupted /ʌnɪntəˈrʌptɪd/ *adj.* ununterbrochen

uninvited /ʌnɪnˈvaɪtɪd/ *adj.* ungeladen

union /ˈjuːnɪən/ *n.* (a) (trade ∼) Gewerkschaft, *die* (b) (Polit.) Union, *die*

Union 'Jack *n.* (Brit.) Union Jack, *der*

unique /juːˈniːk/ *adj.* einzigartig

unisex /ˈjuːnɪseks/ *adj.* Unisex⟨mantel, -kleidung⟩; ∼ **hairdresser** Damen-und-Herren-Frisör, *der*

unison /ˈjuːnɪsən/ *n.* Unisono, *das; in* ∼: einstimmig; **act in** ∼ (fig.) vereint handeln

unit /ˈjuːnɪt/ *n.* (a) (also Mil., Math.) Einheit, *die;* ∼ **of length/monetary** ∼: Längen-/Währungseinheit, *die* (b) (piece of furniture) Element, *das;* **kitchen** ∼: Küchenelement, *das*

unite /juːˈnaɪt/ 1 *v.t.* vereinigen; einen, einigen ⟨Partei, Mitglieder⟩ 2 *v.i.* sich vereinigen

u'nited *adj.* (a) (harmonious) einig (b) (combined) gemeinsam

United: ∼ **'Kingdom** *pr. n.* Vereinigtes Königreich [Großbritannien und Nordirland]; ∼ **'Nations** *pr. n. sing.* Vereinte Nationen *Pl.;* ∼ **States [of A'merica]** *pr. n. sing.* Vereinigte Staaten [von Amerika] *Pl.*

unit 'price *n.* Stückpreis, *der*

unity /ˈjuːnɪtɪ/ *n.* Einheit, *die*

universal /juːnɪˈvɜːsl/ *adj.,* **uni'versally** *adv.* allgemein

universe /ˈjuːnɪvɜːs/ *n.* Universum, *das*

university /juːnɪˈvɜːsɪtɪ/ *n.* Universität, *die; attrib.* Universitäts-

uni'versity place *n.* Studienplatz, *der*

un'just *adj.* ungerecht

unjustified /ʌnˈdʒʌstɪfaɪd/ *adj.* ungerechtfertigt

unkempt /ʌnˈkempt/ *adj.* ungepflegt

un'kind *adj.,* **un'kindly** *adv.* unfreundlich

un'kindness *n.* Unfreundlichkeit, *die*

un'known 1 *adj.* unbekannt 2 *adv.* ∼ **to sb.** ohne dass jmd. davon weiß/wusste

un'lawful *adj.* ungesetzlich

unleaded /ʌnˈledɪd/ *adj.* bleifrei ⟨Benzin⟩

unless /ənˈles/ *conj.* es sei denn; wenn ... nicht

un'like 1 *adj.* nicht ähnlich 2 *prep.* **be** ∼ **sb./sth.** jmdm./einer Sache nicht ähnlich sein; ∼ **him, ...:** im Gegensatz zu ihm ...

un'likely *adj.* unwahrscheinlich; **be** ∼ **to do sth.** etw. wahrscheinlich nicht tun

un'limited *adj.* unbegrenzt

un'load *v.t.* entladen ⟨Lastwagen, Waggon⟩; löschen ⟨Schiff, Schiffsladung⟩; ausladen ⟨Gepäck⟩

un'lock *v.t.* aufschließen

un'lucky *adj.* (a) unglücklich; (not successful) glücklos; **be [very]** ∼: [großes] Pech haben (b) (bringing bad luck) **an** ∼ **number** eine Unglückszahl; **be** ∼: Unglück bringen

unmanageable /ʌnˈmænɪdʒəbl/ *adj.* widerspenstig ⟨Kind, Pferd⟩; unkontrollierbar ⟨Situation⟩

un'manned *adj.* unbemannt

un'married *adj.* unverheiratet; ledig

un'mask *v.t.* (fig.) entlarven

unmi'stakable/ʌnmɪˈsteɪkəbl/ *adj.* deutlich; unverwechselbar ⟨Handschrift, Stimme⟩

unmistakably /ʌnmɪˈsteɪkəblɪ/ *adv.* unverkennbar

un'mitigated *adj.* vollkommen; **be an** ∼ **disaster** (coll.) eine einzige Katastrophe sein

unmotivated /ʌnˈməʊtɪveɪtɪd/ *adj.* unmotiviert

un'natural *adj.,* **un'naturally** *adv.* unnatürlich; (abnormal) nicht normal

un'necessarily *adv.,* **un'necessary** *adj.* unnötig

unnerve /ʌnˈnɜːv/ *v.t.* entnerven

unnerving /ʌnˈnɜːvɪŋ/ *adj.* entnervend

unnoticed /ʌnˈnəʊtɪst/ *adj.* unbemerkt

unobservant /ʌnəbˈzɜːvənt/ *adj.* unaufmerksam

unobserved /ʌnəbˈzɜːvd/ *adj.* unbeobachtet

unob'tainable *adj.* nicht erhältlich; **number ~** (Teleph.) kein Anschluss unter dieser Nummer

unofficial *adj.*, **unofficially** *adv.* inoffiziell

un'pack *v.t. & i.* auspacken

un'paid *adj.* unbezahlt; nicht bezahlt; **~ for** nicht bezahlt

unpalatable /ʌn'pælətəbl/ *adj.* ungenießbar

un'paralleled *adj.* beispiellos

un'pardonable *adj.* unverzeihlich

un'pleasant *adj.*, **un'pleasantly** *adv.* unangenehm

un'pleasantness *n.* (bad feeling) Verstimmung, *die*

un'plug *v.t.*, -gg-: **~ a lamp** den Stecker einer Lampe herausziehen

un'popular *adj.* unbeliebt ⟨*Lehrer, Regierung usw.*⟩; unpopulär ⟨*Maßnahme, Politik*⟩ (with bei)

un'precedented *adj.* beispiellos

unpre'dictable *adj.* unberechenbar

unpre'pared *adj.* unvorbereitet

unprepos'sessing *adj.* wenig attraktiv

unpre'tentious *adj.* einfach ⟨*Wein, Stil, Haus*⟩; bescheiden ⟨*Person*⟩

unprincipled /ʌn'prɪnsɪpld/ *adj.* skrupellos

unprintable /ʌn'prɪntəbl/ *adj.* nicht druckreif

unpro'ductive *adj.* fruchtlos ⟨*Diskussion, Nachforschung*⟩; unproduktiv ⟨*Zeit, Arbeit*⟩

unpro'fessional *adj.* (contrary to standards) standeswidrig

un'profitable *adj.* unrentabel

un'promising *adj.* nicht sehr viel versprechend

unpublished /ʌn'pʌblɪʃt/ *adj.* unveröffentlicht

un'qualified *adj.* (a) unqualifiziert (b) (absolute) uneingeschränkt; voll ⟨*Erfolg*⟩

un'questionable *adj.* unbezweifelbar ⟨*Tatsache*⟩; unbestreitbar ⟨*Recht, Ehrlichkeit*⟩

unquestionably /ʌn'kwestʃənəblɪ/ *adv.* ohne Frage

unquote /ʌn'kwəʊt/ *v.i.* …, **quote, …, ~:** …, Zitat, …, Ende des Zitats

unravel /ʌn'rævl/ **1** *v.t.*, (Brit.) -ll- entwirren; (undo) aufziehen; (fig.) **~ a mystery/the truth** ein Geheimnis enträtseln/ die Wahrheit aufdecken **2** *v.i.*, (Brit.) -ll- sich aufziehen

un'real *adj.* unwirklich

unrea'listic *adj.* unrealistisch

un'reasonable *adj.* unvernünftig; übertrieben ⟨*Ansprüche, Forderung, Preis, Kosten*⟩

unrecognizable /ʌn'rekəgnaɪzəbl/ *adj.* be [absolutely *or* quite] **~:** [überhaupt] nicht wieder zu erkennen sein

unre'lated *adj.* be **~:** nicht miteinander zusammenhängen; (by family) nicht verwandt sein

unrelenting /ʌnrɪ'lentɪŋ/ *adj.* unvermindert, nicht nachlassend ⟨*Hitze, Kälte*⟩

unre'liable *adj.* unzuverlässig

unrequited /ʌnrɪ'kwaɪtɪd/ *adj.* unerwidert

unreservedly /ʌnrɪ'zɜ:vɪdlɪ/ *adv.* uneingeschränkt

unresolved /ʌnrɪ'zɒlvd/ *adj.* (a) (not solved) ungelöst (b) (undecided) be **~:** sich [noch] nicht entschieden haben

un'rest *n.* Unruhen *Pl.*

unre'stricted *adj.* unbeschränkt; uneingeschränkt

un'ripe *adj.* unreif

un'rivalled (*Amer.:* **un'rivaled**) *adj.* unübertroffen

un'roll 1 *v.t.* aufrollen **2** *v.i.* sich aufrollen

unromantic /ʌnrə'mæntɪk/ *adj.* unromantisch

unruly /ʌn'ru:lɪ/ *adj.* ungebärdig

un'safe *adj.* nicht sicher; **feel ~:** sich unsicher fühlen

un'said *adj.* ungesagt

un'salted *adj.* ungesalzen

unsatis'factory *adj.* unbefriedigend

unsatisfying /ʌn'sætɪsfaɪɪŋ/ *adj.* unbefriedigend

un'savoury (*Amer.:* **un'savory**) *adj.* unangenehm; zweifelhaft ⟨*Angelegenheit*⟩; unerfreulich ⟨*Einzelheiten*⟩

unscathed /ʌn'skeɪðd/ *adj.* unversehrt

unscented /ʌn'sentɪd/ *adj.* nicht parfümiert ⟨*Seife, Shampoo*⟩

un'screw 1 *v.t.* abschrauben **2** *v.i.* sich abschrauben lassen

un'scrupulous *adj.* skrupellos

unsecured /ʌnsɪ'kjʊəd/ *adj.* (Finance) ohne Sicherheit[en] *nachgestellt*

un'seemly *adj.* unschicklich

unself'conscious *adj.* unbefangen

un'selfish *adj.* selbstlos

un'selfishness *n.* Selbstlosigkeit, *die*

un'settled *adj.* (changeable) wechselhaft; (fig.) ruhelos ⟨*Leben*⟩; unruhig ⟨*Zeit, Land*⟩

un'settling *adj.* störend

unshak[e]able /ʌn'ʃeɪkəbl/ *adj.* unerschütterlich

un'shaven *adj.* unrasiert

un'sightly *adj.* unschön

un'skilled *adj.* ungelernt ⟨*Arbeiter*⟩

un'skimmed *adj.* **~ milk** Vollmilch, *die*

un'sociable *adj.* ungesellig

unsolved /ʌn'sɒlvd/ *adj.* unaufgeklärt ⟨*Verbrechen*⟩

unso'phisticated *adj.* einfach

un'sound *adj.* **(a)** (diseased) nicht gesund; krank
(b) baufällig ⟨*Gebäude*⟩
(c) (ill-founded) wenig stichhaltig; nicht vertretbar ⟨*Ansicht, Methode*⟩
(d) of ~ mind unzurechnungsfähig

unspeakable /ʌn'spiːkəbl/ *adj.* unbeschreiblich; (very bad) unsäglich

unspecified /ʌn'spesɪfaɪd/ *adj.* nicht näher bezeichnet

unspoken /ʌn'spəʊkn/ *adj.* ungesagt

un'stable *adj.* nicht stabil; [mentally/emotionally] ~: [psychisch] labil

un'steadily *adv.* unsicher

un'steady *adj.* unsicher; wackelig ⟨*Leiter, Tisch*⟩

unstoppable /ʌn'stɒpəbl/ *adj.* unhaltbar ⟨*Schuss aufs Fußballtor*⟩; (fig.) unaufhaltsam

un'stuck *adj.* come ~: sich lösen; (fig. coll.: fail) ⟨*Person:*⟩ baden gehen (ugs.) (over mit)

unsuc'cessful *adj.* erfolglos; be ~: keinen Erfolg haben

unsuc'cessfully *adv.* erfolglos

un'suitable *adj.* ungeeignet

unsu'specting *adj.* nichtsahnend

un'sweetened *adj.* ungesüßt

unsympa'thetic *adj.* wenig mitfühlend; be ~: kein Mitgefühl zeigen

untalented /ʌn'tæləntɪd/ *adj.* untalentiert

untenable /ʌn'tenəbl/ *adj.* unhaltbar

unthinkable /ʌn'θɪŋkəbl/ *adj.* unvorstellbar

unthinking /ʌn'θɪŋkɪŋ/ *adj.*, **un'thinkingly** *adv.* gedankenlos

un'tidily *adv.* unordentlich

un'tidiness *n.* ▶ UNTIDY: Ungepflegtheit, *die;* Unaufgeräumtheit, *die*

un'tidy *adj.* ungepflegt ⟨*Äußeres, Person, Garten*⟩; unaufgeräumt ⟨*Zimmer*⟩

un'tie *v.t.* untying aufknüpfen ⟨*Seil, Paket*⟩; aufbinden ⟨*Knoten*⟩; losbinden ⟨*Pferd, Boot*⟩

until /ən'tɪl/ ① *prep.* bis; ~ [the] evening bis zum Abend; ~ then bis dahin; not ~ [Christmas/the summer] erst [Weihnachten/im Sommer]
② *conj.* bis

un'timely *adj.* **(a)** ungelegen
(b) (premature) vorzeitig

un'tiring *adj.* unermüdlich

un'told *adj.* unbeschreiblich; unermesslich ⟨*Reichtümer, Anzahl*⟩

untoward /ˌʌntə'wɔːd, ʌn'təʊəd/ *adj.* ungünstig; nothing ~ happened es gab keine Schwierigkeiten

untranslatable /ˌʌntræns'leɪtəbl/ *adj.* unübersetzbar

untreated /ʌn'triːtɪd/ *adj.* unbehandelt

un'true *adj.* unwahr; that's ~: das ist nicht wahr

un'trustworthy *adj.* unzuverlässig

un'truth *n.* Unwahrheit, *die*

un'truthful *adj.* verlogen

un'typical *adj.* untypisch (of für)

unusable /ʌn'juːzəbl/ *adj.* unbrauchbar

unused¹ /ʌn'juːzd/ *adj.* (new, fresh) unbenutzt; (not utilized) ungenutzt

unused² /ʌn'juːst/ *adj.* (unaccustomed) be ~ to sth./doing sth. etw. (Akk.) nicht gewohnt sein/nicht gewohnt sein, etw. zu tun

un'usual *adj.*, **un'usually** *adv.* ungewöhnlich

unvarnished /ʌn'vɑːnɪʃt/ *adj.* unlackiert; (fig.) ungeschminkt ⟨*Wahrheit*⟩

un'veil *v.t.* enthüllen; (fig.) vorstellen ⟨*Produkt*⟩; enthüllen ⟨*Plan*⟩

un'versed *adj.* nicht bewandert (in in + *Dat.*)

un'wanted *adj.* unerwünscht

un'warranted *adj.* ungerechtfertigt

un'welcome *adj.* unwillkommen

un'well *adj.* unwohl; look ~: nicht wohl od. gut aussehen; he feels ~ (poorly) er fühlt sich nicht wohl

un'wholesome *adj.* (lit. or fig.) ungesund

unwieldy /ʌn'wiːldɪ/ *adj.* sperrig

un'willing *adj.* widerwillig; be ~ to do sth. etw. nicht tun wollen

un'willingly *adv.* widerwillig

unwind /ʌn'waɪnd/ ① *v.t.*, unwound /ʌn'waʊnd/ abwickeln
② *v.i.*, unwound **(a)** sich abwickeln
(b) (coll.: relax) sich entspannen

un'wise *adj.* unklug

unwitting /ʌn'wɪtɪŋ/ *adj.*, **un'wittingly** *adv.* unwissentlich

un'workable *adj.* undurchführbar ⟨*Plan*⟩

un'worthy *adj.* unwürdig; be ~ of sth. einer Sache (Gen.) nicht würdig sein; be ~ of sb./sth. ⟨*Verhalten:*⟩ einer Person/Sache (Gen.) unwürdig sein

un'wrap *v.t.*, -pp- auswickeln

un'written *adj.* ungeschrieben

un'zip *v.t.*, -pp-: **(a)** ~ a dress/bag *etc.* den Reißverschluss eines Kleides/einer Tasche *usw.* öffnen
(b) (Comp.) entpacken ⟨*Datei*⟩

up /ʌp/ ① *adv.* **(a)** (to higher place) nach oben; (in lift) aufwärts; the bird flew up to the roof der Vogel flog aufs Dach [hinauf]; up into the air in die Luft [hinauf]; up here/there hier herauf/dort hinauf; higher/a little way up höher/ein kurzes Stück hinauf; come on up! komm [hier/weiter] herauf!
(b) (to upstairs) herauf/hinauf; nach oben
(c) (in higher place, upstairs) oben; up here/there hier/da oben; the next floor up ein Stockwerk höher
(d) (out of bed) be up auf sein
(e) (in price, value, amount) prices have gone up/are up die Preise sind gestiegen; butter is up [by …] Butter ist […] teurer ⋯⟿

u

(f) (as far as) **up to sth.** bis zu etw.; **up to here/there** bis hier[hin]/bis dorthin

(g) [not] **be/feel up to sth.** (capable of sth.) einer Sache (*Dat.*) [nicht] gewachsen sein/ sich einer Sache (*Dat.*) [nicht] gewachsen fühlen; [not] **be/have up to doing sth.** [nicht] in der Lage sein/sich [nicht] in der Lage fühlen, etw. zu tun

(h) be up to sth. (doing) etw. anstellen (ugs.); **it is [not] up to sb. to do sth.** (sb.'s duty) es ist [nicht] jmds. Sache, etw. zu tun

(i) be three points/games up mit drei Punkten/Spielen vorn liegen

(j) walk up and down auf und ab gehen

(k) time is up die Zeit ist abgelaufen

2 *prep.* herauf/hinauf; **walk up the hill/road** den Berg/die Straße hinaufgehen; **walk up and down the platform** auf dem Bahnsteig auf und ab gehen; **further up the ladder/coast** weiter oben auf der Leiter/an der Küste; **live just up the road** ein Stück weiter oben in der Straße wohnen

3 *adj.* (coll.: amiss) **what's up?** was ist los? (ugs.); **something is up** irgendwas ist los (ugs.)

4 *v.t.*, **-pp-** (coll.: increase) erhöhen

'up-and-coming *adj.* (coll.) aufstrebend

'up-and-up *n.* (coll.) **be on the ∼:** auf dem aufsteigenden Ast sein (ugs.)

'upbeat **1** *n.* (Mus.) Auftakt, *der*
2 *adj.* (coll.) (optimistic) optimistisch; (cheerful) fröhlich

'upbringing *n.* Erziehung, *die*

up'date *v.t.* auf den aktuellen Stand bringen

up 'front *adv.* (coll.: as down payment) im Voraus

upgrade **1** /-'-/ *v.t.* **(a)** aufwerten ⟨*Stellung*⟩
(b) (improve) verbessern
(c) (Comp.) aufrüsten, nachrüsten ⟨*Computer*⟩
2 /'--/ *n.* (Comp.) (act of upgrading) Nachrüsten, *die*; Erweiterung, *die*; (upgraded version) erweiterte Version; Upgrade, *der* (fachspr.)

upheaval /ʌp'hi:vl/ *n.* Aufruhr, *der*; (disturbance) Durcheinander, *das*

up'hill **1** *adj.* (fig.) **an ∼ task/struggle** eine mühselige Aufgabe/ein harter Kampf
2 *adv.* bergauf

uphold *v.t.*, **upheld** unterstützen; wahren ⟨*Tradition*⟩

upholster /ʌp'həʊlstə(r)/ *v.t.* polstern

up'holsterer *n.* Polsterer, *der*/Polsterin, *die*

up'holstery *n.* **(a)** (craft) Polster[er]handwerk, *das*
(b) (padding) Polsterung, *die*

'upkeep *n.* Unterhalt, *der*

up'lifting *adj.* erhebend

'uplighter *n.* Deckenfluter, *der*

up'load *v.t.* (Comp.) hinaufladen ⟨*Datei, Daten*⟩

'upmarket *adj.* exklusiv

upon /ə'pɒn/ *prep.* auf (*direction:* + *Akk.*; *position:* + *Dat.*)

upper /'ʌpə(r)/ **1** *compar. adj.* ober...; Ober⟨*grenze, -lippe, -arm usw.*⟩; **∼ circle** oberer Rang; **∼ class[es]** Oberschicht, *die*; **have/get/gain the ∼ hand** die Oberhand haben/gewinnen/erhalten
2 *n.* Oberteil, *das*

upper 'deck *n.* Oberdeck, *das*

'uppermost **1** *adj.* oberst...
2 *adv.* ganz oben

'upright *adj.* aufrecht

'uprising *n.* Aufstand, *der*

'uproar *n.* Aufruhr, *der*

up'root *v.t.* [her]ausreißen; ⟨*Sturm:*⟩ entwurzeln

upset **1** /ʌp'set/ *v.t.*, **-tt-**, **upset (a)** (overturn) umkippen; (accidentally) umstoßen ⟨*Tasse, Milch usw.*⟩
(b) (distress) erschüttern; (make angry) aufregen; **don't let it ∼ you** nimm es nicht so schwer
(c) (make ill) **sth. ∼s sb.** etw. bekommt jmdm. nicht
(d) durcheinander bringen ⟨*Plan*⟩
2 *v.i.*, **-tt-**, **upset** umkippen
3 *adj.* (distressed) bestürzt; (agitated) aufgeregt; **get ∼ [about/over sth.]** sich [über etw. (*Akk.*)] aufregen
4 /'ʌpset/ *n.* **(a)** (agitation) Aufregung, *die*; (annoyance) Verärgerung, *die*
(b) stomach ∼: Magenverstimmung, *die*
(c) (upheaval) Aufruhr, *der*

up'setting *adj.* erschütternd; (sad) traurig; (annoying) ärgerlich

'upshot *n.* Ergebnis, *das*

upside 'down **1** *adv.* verkehrt herum; **turn sth. ∼:** etw. auf den Kopf stellen
2 *adj.* auf dem Kopf stehend ⟨*Bild*⟩; **be ∼:** auf dem Kopf stehen

upstairs **1** /-'-/ *adv.* nach oben ⟨*gehen, kommen*⟩; oben ⟨*sein, wohnen*⟩
2 /'--/ *adj.* im Obergeschoss *nachgestellt*

'upstart *n.* Emporkömmling, *der*

up'stream *adv.* flussaufwärts

'uptake *n.* **be quick/slow on the ∼** (coll.) schnell begreifen/schwer von Begriff sein (ugs.)

uptight /-'-, '--/ *adj.* (coll.: tense) nervös (**about** wegen)

up to 'date *adj.* **be/keep ∼:** auf dem neuesten Stand sein/bleiben; **bring sth. ∼:** etw. auf den neuesten Stand bringen

up-to-'date *attrib. adj.* (current) aktuell; (modern) modern

up-to-the-'minute *adj.* hochaktuell

'upturn *n.* Aufschwung, *der* (**in** *Gen.*)

upturned /'ʌptɜ:nd/ *adj.* umgedreht; **∼ nose** Stupsnase, *die*

upward /'ʌpwəd/ **1** *adj.* nach oben gerichtet
2 *adv.* aufwärts ⟨*sich bewegen*⟩; nach oben ⟨*sehen, gehen*⟩

upwards /'ʌpwədz/ adv. (a) ▶ UPWARD 2
(b) ~ of über (+ Akk.)

uranium /jʊə'reɪnɪəm/ n. Uran, das

Uranus /'jʊərənəs, jʊə'reɪnəs/ pr. n.
(Astron.) Uranus, der

urban /'ɜ:bn/ adj. städtisch; Stadt‹gebiet,
-bevölkerung, -planung›

urbane /ɜ:'beɪn/ adj. weltmännisch

urchin /'ɜ:tʃɪn/ n. Strolch, der

urge /ɜ:dʒ/ **1** v.t. ~ sb. to do sth. jmdn.
drängen, etw. zu tun
2 n. Trieb, der
■ **urge 'on** v.t. antreiben; (encourage)
anfeuern

urgency /'ɜ:dʒənsɪ/ n. Dringlichkeit, die

urgent /'ɜ:dʒənt/ adj. dringend; (to be dealt
with immediately) eilig; **be in ~ need of sth.**
etw. dringend brauchen

'**urgently** adv. dringend; (immediately) eilig

urinal /jʊə'raɪnl/ n. [public] ~: [öffentliche]
Herrentoilette; Pissoir, das

urinary /'jʊərɪnərɪ/ adj. Harn-

urinate /'jʊərɪneɪt/ v.i. urinieren

urine /'jʊərɪn/ n. Urin, der; Harn, der

URL abbr. (Comp.) = **uniform resource
locator** URL, der

urn /ɜ:n/ n. (a) tea/coffee ~: Tee-/
Kaffeemaschine, die
(b) (vessel) Urne, die

Uruguay /'jʊərəgwaɪ/ pr. n. Uruguay (das)

us /əs, stressed ʌs/ pron. uns; **it's us** wir
sinds (ugs.)

US abbr. = **United States** USA

USA abbr. = **United States of
America** USA

usage /'ju:zɪdʒ, 'ju:sɪdʒ/ n. (a) Brauch, der
(b) (Ling.) Sprachgebrauch, der

use 1 /ju:s/ n. (a) Gebrauch, der; (of
dictionary, calculator, room) Benutzung, die; (of
word, pesticide, spice) Verwendung, die; [not] be
in ~: [nicht] in Gebrauch sein; be no longer
in ~: nicht mehr verwendet werden; make
~ of sb./sth. jmdn./etw. gebrauchen/(exploit)
ausnutzen; make good ~ of, turn or put to
good ~: gut nutzen ‹Zeit, Talent, Geld›; put
sth. to ~: etw. verwenden
(b) (usefulness) Nutzen, der; is it of [any] ~?
ist das [irgendwie] von Nutzen?; be [of] no
~ [to sb.] [jmdm.] nicht nützen; it's no
~ [doing that] es hat keinen Sinn[, das zu
tun]
(c) (purpose) Verwendung, die; have/find a
~ for sth./sb. für etw./jmdn. Verwendung
haben/finden; have no/not much ~ for sth./
sb. etw./jmdn. nicht/kaum brauchen
2 /ju:z/ v.t. (a) benutzen; nutzen
‹Gelegenheit›; anwenden ‹Gewalt›; in
Anspruch nehmen ‹Firma, Dienstleistung›;
nutzen ‹Zeit, Gelegenheit›; verwenden
‹Kraftstoff, Butter, Wort›
(b) ~d to /'ju:st tə/ **I ~d to live in London**
früher habe ich in London gelebt

■ **use 'up** v.t. aufbrauchen; verbrauchen
‹Geld, Energie›

use-by date /'ju:zbaɪ/ n. (esp. Brit.)
[Mindest]haltbarkeitsdatum, das

used 1 adj. (a) /ju:zd/ gebraucht;
gestempelt ‹Briefmarke›; ~ car
Gebrauchtwagen, der
(b) /ju:st/ ~ to sth. [an] etw. (Akk.) gewöhnt
2 /ju:st/ ▶ USE 2B

useful /'ju:sfl/ adj. nützlich; praktisch
‹Werkzeug›; hilfreich ‹Rat, Idee›

'**usefulness** n. Nützlichkeit, die

useless /'ju:slɪs/ adj. unbrauchbar
‹Werkzeug, Rat, Idee›; nutzlos ‹Wissen,
Information, Protest, Anstrengung, Kampf›;
zwecklos ‹Widerstand, Protest›

user /'ju:zə(r)/ n. Benutzer, der/Benutzerin,
die

user: ~-**friendly** adj. benutzerfreundlich;
~ **group** n. Benutzergruppe, die;
~ **interface** n. (Comp.)
Benutzerschnittstelle, die; ~ **name** n.
(Comp.) Benutzername, der

usher /'ʌʃə(r)/ **1** n. (in court)
Gerichtsdiener, der; (at cinema, church)
Platzanweiser, der
2 v.t. führen
■ **usher 'in** v.t. hineinführen; (fig.)
einläuten

usherette /ʌʃə'ret/ n. Platzanweiserin, die

USSR abbr. (Hist.) = **Union of Soviet
Socialist Republics** UdSSR, die

usual /'ju:ʒʊəl/ adj. üblich

usually /'ju:ʒʊəlɪ/ adv. gewöhnlich

usurp /ju:'zɜ:p/ v.t. sich (Dat.)
widerrechtlich aneignen

utensil /ju:'tensɪl/ n. Utensil, das; writing
~s Schreibutensilien Pl.; kitchen ~s
Küchengeräte Pl.

uterus /'ju:tərəs/ n. Gebärmutter, die

utilitarian /ju:tɪlɪ'teərɪən/ adj. funktionell

utility /ju:'tɪlɪtɪ/ n. (a) Nutzen, der
(b) [public] ~: öffentlicher
Versorgungsbetrieb

u'tility room n.: Raum, in dem [größere]
Haushaltsgeräte (z.B. Waschmaschine)
installiert sind

utilize /'ju:tɪlaɪz/ v.t. nutzen

utmost /'ʌtməʊst/ **1** adj. äußerst...;
größt... ‹Höflichkeit, Eleganz, Einfachheit,
Geschwindigkeit›
2 n. Äußerste, das; do or try one's ~ to do
sth. mit allen Mitteln versuchen, etw. zu tun

utter¹ /'ʌtə(r)/ adj. völlig; vollkommen;
~ fool Vollidiot, der (ugs.)

utter² v.t. (a) von sich geben ‹Schrei,
Seufzer›
(b) (say) sagen

utterance /'ʌtərəns/ n. Worte Pl.

'**utterly** adv. völlig; vollkommen; äußerst
‹dumm, lächerlich›

'U-turn *n.* Wende [um 180°]; (fig.)
Kehrtwendung, *die;* **make a** ∼: wenden; **'No**
∼**s'** „Wenden verboten"

UV *abbr.* = **ultraviolet** UV

Vv

V¹, v /vi:/ *n.* V, v, *das*

V² *abbr.* = **volt[s]** V

v. *abbr.* = **versus** gg.

vacancy /'veɪkənsɪ/ *n.* **(a)** (job) freie Stelle
(b) (room) freies Zimmer; **'vacancies'**
„Zimmer frei"; **'no vacancies'** „belegt"

vacant /'veɪkənt/ *adj.* **(a)** frei; **'situations**
∼**'** „Stellenangebote"
(b) (mentally) leer

vacate /və'keɪt/ *v.t.* räumen

vacation /və'keɪʃn/ *n.* **(a)** (Brit. Univ.) Ferien
Pl.
(b) (Amer.) ▶ HOLIDAY B

vaccinate /'væksɪneɪt/ *v.t.* impfen

vaccination /væksɪ'neɪʃn/ *n.* Impfung, *die;*
have a ∼: geimpft werden

vaccine /'væksi:n/ *n.* Impfstoff, *der*

vacillate /'væsɪleɪt/ *v.i.* schwanken

vacuum /'vækjʊəm/ **1** *n.* **(a)** Vakuum, *das;*
live in a ∼: im luftleeren Raum leben
(b) (coll.: ∼ cleaner) Staubsauger, *der* (ugs.)
2 *v.t. & i.* [staub]saugen

vacuum: ∼ **cleaner** *n.* Staubsauger, *der;*
∼ **flask** *n.* (Brit.) Thermosflasche, *die;*
∼**-packed** *adj.* vakuumverpackt

vagaries /'veɪɡərɪz/ *n. pl.* Launen *Pl.*

vagina /və'dʒaɪnə/ *n.* Scheide, *die*

vagrant /'veɪɡrənt/ *n.* Landstreicher, *der/*
-streicherin, *die;* (in cities) Stadtstreicher, *der/*
-streicherin, *die*

vague /veɪɡ/ *adj.* vage; verschwommen
⟨*Form, Umriss*⟩; (absent-minded)
geistesabwesend; **not have the** ∼**st idea** *or*
notion nicht die blasseste *od.* leiseste
Ahnung haben

'vaguely *adv.* vage; entfernt ⟨*bekannt sein,*
erinnern an⟩; schwach ⟨*sich erinnern*⟩

vain /veɪn/ *adj.* **(a)** (conceited) eitel
(b) (useless) leer; vergeblich ⟨*Hoffnung,*
Versuch⟩; **in** ∼: vergeblich

'vainly *adv.* vergebens

vale /veɪl/ *n.* (arch./poet.) Tal, *das*

valentine /'væləntaɪn/ *n.* ∼ **[card]**
Grußkarte zum Valentinstag; **St. V**∼**'s Day**
Valentinstag, *der*

valet /'væleɪ/ *n.* Kammerdiener, *der*

valiant /'vælɪənt/ *adj.,* **'valiantly** *adv.*
tapfer

valid /'vælɪd/ *adj.* **(a)** (legally acceptable)
gültig; berechtigt ⟨*Anspruch*⟩
(b) (justifiable) stichhaltig ⟨*Argument*⟩; triftig
⟨*Grund*⟩; begründet ⟨*Einwand,*
Entschuldigung⟩

validate /'vælɪdeɪt/ *v.t.* rechtskräftig
machen

validity /və'lɪdɪtɪ/ *n.* Gültigkeit, *die*

valley /'vælɪ/ *n.* Tal, *das*

valour (Amer.: **valor**) /'vælə(r)/ *n.*
Tapferkeit, *die*

valuable /'væljʊəbl/ **1** *adj.* wertvoll; **be**
∼ **to sb.** für jmdn. wertvoll sein
2 *n.* ∼**s** Wertsachen *Pl.*

valuation /væljʊ'eɪʃn/ *n.* Schätzung, *die*

value /'vælju:/ **1** *n.* Wert, *der;* **be of great/**
little/some/no ∼ **[to sb.]** [für jmdn.] von
großem/geringem/einigem/keinerlei Nutzen
sein; **know the** ∼ **of sth.** wissen, was etw.
wert ist; **something/nothing of** ∼: etwas/
nichts Wertvolles
2 *v.t.* schätzen

value added 'tax *n.* Mehrwertsteuer, *die*

valued /'vælju:d/ *adj.* geschätzt

'value judgement *n.* Werturteil, *das*

'valueless *adj.* wertlos

valuer /'væljʊə(r)/ *n.* Schätzer, *der;* Taxator,
der

valve /vælv/ *n.* **(a)** Ventil, *das*
(b) (Anat.) Klappe, *die*

vampire /'væmpaɪə(r)/ *n.* Vampir, *der*

van /væn/ *n.* [delivery] ∼: Lieferwagen, *der*

vandal /'vændl/ *n.* Rowdy, *der*

vandalism /'vændəlɪzm/ *n.* Wandalismus,
der

vandalize /'vændəlaɪz/ *v.t.* [mutwillig]
beschädigen

vanilla /və'nɪlə/ **1** *n.* Vanille, *die*
2 *adj.* Vanille-

vanish /'vænɪʃ/ *v.i.* verschwinden

vanity /'vænɪtɪ/ *n.* Eitelkeit, *die*

'vanity bag *n.* Kosmetiktäschchen, *das*

vantage point /'vɑ:ntɪdʒ pɔɪnt/ *n.*
Aussichtspunkt, *der*

vapour (Brit.; Amer.: **vapor**) /'veɪpə(r)/ *n.*
Dampf, *der*

'vapour trail *n.* (Aeronaut.) Kondensstreifen,
der

variable /'veərɪəbl/ *adj.* **(a)** (alterable) veränderbar; **be** ~: verändert werden können
(b) (inconsistent) unbeständig ⟨*Wetter, Wind, Leistung*⟩; wechselhaft ⟨*Wetter, Launen, Qualität*⟩
variance /'veərɪəns/ *n.* **be at** ~ **[with sth.]** [mit etw.] nicht übereinstimmen
variant /'veərɪənt/ *n.* Variante, *die*
variation /veərɪ'eɪʃn/ *n.* **(a)** (varying) Veränderung, *die;* (difference) Unterschied, *der*
(b) (variant) Variante, *die* (of, on *Gen.*)
varicose vein /værɪkəʊs 'veɪn/ *n.* Krampfader, *die*
varied /'veərɪd/ *adj.* unterschiedlich; abwechslungsreich ⟨*Leben*⟩
variety /və'raɪətɪ/ *n.* **(a)** (diversity) Vielfältigkeit, *die;* (in diet, routine) Abwechslung, *die;* **add** *or* **give** ~ **to sth.** etw. abwechslungsreicher gestalten
(b) (assortment) Auswahl, *die* (of an + *Dat.*, von); **for a** ~ **of reasons** aus verschiedenen Gründen
(c) (Theatre) Varietee, *das*
(d) (form) Art, *die;* (of fruit, vegetable) Sorte, *die;* (cultivated) Züchtung, *die*
various /'veərɪəs/ *adj.* **(a)** *pred.* (different) verschieden; unterschiedlich
(b) *attrib.* (several) verschiedene; **at** ~ **times** mehrere Male
'variously *adv.* unterschiedlich
varnish /'vɑːnɪʃ/ ⓵ *n.* Lasur, *die*
⓶ *v.t.* lasieren
vary /'veərɪ/ ⓵ *v.t.* verändern; ändern ⟨*Bestimmungen, Programm, Methode, Route*⟩; (add variety to) abwechslungsreicher gestalten
⓶ *v.i.* (become different) sich ändern; ⟨*Preis, Qualität:*⟩ schwanken; (be different) unterschiedlich sein
'varying *adj.* wechselnd; (different) unterschiedlich
vase /vɑːz/ *n.* Vase, *die*
vast /vɑːst/ *adj.* **(a)** (huge) riesig; weit ⟨*Fläche, Meer*⟩
(b) (coll.: great) enorm; Riesen⟨*menge, -summe*⟩
'vastly *adv.* (coll.) enorm; weitaus ⟨*besser*⟩; weit ⟨*überlegen, unterlegen*⟩
vat /væt/ *n.* Bottich, *der*
VAT /viːˈɛːtiː, væt/ *abbr.* = **value added tax** MwSt.
Vatican /'vætɪkən/ *pr. n.* Vatikan, *der*
vault¹ /vɔːlt, vɒlt/ *n.* **(a)** (Archit.) Gewölbe, *das*
(b) (in bank) Tresorraum, *der*
(c) (tomb) Gruft, *die*
vault² ⓵ *v.i.* sich schwingen
⓶ *v.t.* sich schwingen über (+ *Akk.*)
⓷ *n.* Sprung, *der*
VD *n.* Geschlechtskrankheit, *die*
VDU *abbr.* = **visual display unit**

veal /viːl/ *n.* Kalb[fleisch], *das; attrib.* Kalbs-
veer /vɪə(r)/ *v.i.* ⟨*Auto:*⟩ ausscheren
■ **veer a'way, veer 'off** *v.i.* ⟨*Auto:*⟩ ausscheren; ⟨*Fahrer, Straße:*⟩ abbiegen
veg /vedʒ/ *n., pl. same* (coll.) Gemüse, *das*
vegan /'viːgən/ ⓵ *n.* Veganer, *der/* Veganerin, *die*
⓶ *adj.* vegan
vegetable /'vedʒtəbl/ *n.* Gemüse, *das;* **fresh** ~**s** frisches Gemüse; *attrib.* Gemüse⟨*suppe, -extrakt, -garten*⟩
'vegetable oil *n.* Pflanzenöl, *das*
vegetarian /vedʒɪ'teərɪən/ ⓵ *n.* Vegetarier, *der/*Vegetarierin, *die*
⓶ *adj.* vegetarisch; **sb. is** ~: jmd. ist Vegetarier/Vegetarierin; **eat** ~ **[food]** vegetarisch essen
vegetarianism /vedʒɪ'teərɪənɪzm/ *n.* Vegetarismus, *der*
vegetate /'vedʒɪteɪt/ *v.i.* nur noch [dahin]vegetieren
vegetation /vedʒɪ'teɪʃn/ *n.* Vegetation, *die*
veggie /'vedʒɪ/ (coll.) ⓵ *adj.* vegetarisch; ~ **burger** Bratling, *der*
⓶ *n.* Vegetarier, *der/*Vegetarierin, *die*
vehement /'viːəmənt/ *adj.,*
'vehemently *adv.* heftig
vehicle /'viːɪkl/ *n.* **(a)** Fahrzeug, *das*
(b) (fig.: medium) Vehikel, *das*
vehicular /vɪ'hɪkjʊlə(r)/ *adj.* Fahrzeug-
veil /veɪl/ ⓵ *n.* Schleier, *der*
⓶ *v.t.* verschleiern
veiled /veɪld/ *adj.* verschleiert; (fig.) versteckt
vein /veɪn/ *n.* **(a)** Vene, *die;* (any blood vessel) Ader, *die*
(b) (fig.: mood) Stimmung, *die;* **in a similar** ~: vergleichbarer Art
Velcro ® /'velkrəʊ/ *n.* Klettverschluss, *der* Ⓦ
velocity /vɪ'lɒsɪtɪ/ *n.* Geschwindigkeit, *die*
velvet /'velvɪt/ ⓵ *n.* Samt, *der*
⓶ *adj.* aus Samt *nachgestellt;* Samt-
'velvety *adj.* samtig
vendetta /ven'detə/ *n.* Hetzkampagne, *die;* (feud) Fehde, *die*
vending machine /'vendɪŋ məʃiːn/ *n.* [Verkaufs]automat, *der*
vendor /'vendə(r)/ *n.* Verkäufer, *der/* Verkäuferin, *die*
veneer /vɪ'nɪə(r)/ *n.* Furnier, *das*
venerable /'venərəbl/ *adj.* ehrwürdig
venerate /'venəreɪt/ *v.t.* verehren
ve'nereal disease *n.* (Med.) Geschlechtskrankheit, *die*
venetian blind /vɪ'niːʃn blaɪnd/ *n.* Jalousie, *die*
Venezuela /venɪ'zweɪlə/ *pr. n.* Venezuela *(das)*

V

vengeance /'vendʒəns/ n. (a) Rache, die; take ~ [up]on sb. [for sth.] sich an jmdm. [für etw.] rächen
(b) with a ~ (coll.) gewaltig (ugs.)

Venice /'venɪs/ pr. n. Venedig (das)

venison /'venɪsn, 'venɪzn/ n. Hirsch, der; Hirschfleisch, das; (roe deer) Reh[fleisch], das

venom /'venəm/ n. Gift, das

venomous /'venəməs/ adj. giftig

vent¹ /vent/ 1 n. (a) Öffnung, die
(b) (fig.) Ventil, das (fig.); give ~ to Luft machen (+ Dat.)
2 v.t. (fig.) Luft machen (+ Dat.)

vent² n. (in garment) Schlitz, der

ventilate /'ventɪleɪt/ v.t. belüften

ventilation /ventɪ'leɪʃn/ n. Belüftung, die

ventilator /'ventɪleɪtə(r)/ n. (a) Ventilator, der
(b) (Med.) Beatmungsgerät, das

ventriloquist /ven'trɪləkwɪst/ n. Bauchredner, der/-rednerin, die

venture /'ventʃə(r)/ 1 n. Unternehmung, die
2 v.i. (a) (dare) wagen
(b) (dare to go) sich wagen
3 v.t. wagen
■ **venture 'out** v.i. sich hinauswagen

venue /'venju:/ n. (Sport) [Austragungs]ort, der; (Mus., Theatre) [Veranstaltungs]ort, der; (meeting place) Treffpunkt, der

Venus /'vi:nəs/ pr. n. (Astron.) Venus, die

veranda[h] /və'rændə/ n. Veranda, die

verb /vɜːb/ n. Verb, das

verbal /'vɜːbl/ adj., **verbally** /'vɜːbəlɪ/ adv. (a) (relating to words) sprachlich
(b) (oral[ly]) mündlich

verbatim /vɜː'beɪtɪm/ adj., adv. [wort]wörtlich

verbose /vɜː'bəʊs/ adj. weitschweifig ‹Roman, Autor›; langatmig ‹Rede, Redner›

verdict /'vɜːdɪkt/ n. Urteil, das; ~ of guilty/not guilty Schuld-/Freispruch, der; reach a ~: zu einem Urteil kommen

verge /vɜːdʒ/ n. (a) Rasensaum, der; (on road) Bankette, die
(b) (fig.) be on the ~ of war/tears am Rande des Krieges stehen/den Tränen nahe sein; be on the ~ of doing sth. kurz davor stehen, etw. zu tun
■ **'verge on** v.t. [an]grenzen an (+ Akk.)

verger /'vɜːdʒə(r)/ n. Küster, der

verifiable /'verɪfaɪəbl/ adj. nachprüfbar

verification /verɪfɪ'keɪʃn/ n. (a) (check) Überprüfung, die
(b) (confirmation) Bestätigung, die

verify /'verɪfaɪ/ v.t. (a) (check) überprüfen
(b) (confirm) bestätigen

veritable /'verɪtəbl/ adj. richtig

vermin /'vɜːmɪn/ n. Ungeziefer, das

vermouth /'vɜːməθ/ n. Wermut[wein], der

vernacular /və'nækjʊlə(r)/ n. Landessprache, die

versatile /'vɜːsətaɪl/ adj. vielseitig; (having many uses) vielseitig verwendbar

versatility /vɜːsə'tɪlɪtɪ/ n. Vielseitigkeit, die

verse /vɜːs/ n. (a) (stanza) Strophe, die
(b) (poetry) Lyrik, die; write some ~: einige Verse schreiben; piece of ~: Gedicht, das; written in ~: in Versform
(c) (in Bible) Vers, der

versed /vɜːst/ adj. be [well] ~ in sth. sich in etw. (Dat.) [gut] auskennen

version /'vɜːʃn/ n. Version, die; (in another language) Übersetzung, die; (of vehicle, machine, tool) Modell, das

versus /'vɜːsəs/ prep. gegen

vertebra /'vɜːtɪbrə/ n., pl. ~e /'vɜːtɪbriː/ Wirbel, der

vertebrate /'vɜːtɪbrət/ n. Wirbeltier, das

vertical /'vɜːtɪkl/ adj. senkrecht; be ~: senkrecht stehen

vertically /'vɜːtɪkəlɪ/ adv. senkrecht

vertigo /'vɜːtɪgəʊ/ n. Schwindel, der

verve /vɜːv/ n. Schwung, der

very /'verɪ/ 1 attrib. adj. (a) (precise, exact) genau; you're the ~ person I wanted to see genau dich wollte ich sehen; at the ~ moment when ...: im selben Augenblick, als ...; at the ~ centre genau in der Mitte; the ~ thing genau das Richtige
(b) (extreme) at the ~ back/front ganz hinten/vorn; at the ~ end/beginning ganz am Ende/Anfang; from the ~ beginning von Anfang an; only a ~ little nur ein ganz kleines bisschen
(c) (mere) bloß ‹Gedanke›
(d) (absolute) absolut ‹Minimum, Maximum›; the ~ most I can offer is ...: ich kann allerhöchstens ... anbieten; for the ~ last time zum allerletzten Mal
(e) emphat. before their ~ eyes vor ihren Augen
2 adv. (a) (extremely) sehr; it's ~ near es ist ganz in der Nähe; ~ probably höchstwahrscheinlich; not ~ much nicht sehr; ~ little [nur] sehr wenig ‹verstehen, essen›; thank you [~,] ~ much [vielen,] vielen Dank
(b) (absolutely) aller‹best..., -letzt..., -leichtest...›; at the ~ latest allerspätestens
(c) (precisely) the ~ same one genau der-/die-/dasselbe

vessel /'vesl/ n. (a) (receptacle) Gefäß, das; [drinking] ~: Trinkgefäß, das
(b) (Naut.) Schiff, das

vest /vest/ 1 n. (a) (Brit.) Unterhemd, das
(b) (Amer.: waistcoat) Weste, die
2 v.t. ~ sb. with sth., ~ sth. in sb. jmdm. etw. verleihen

'vested adj. have a ~ interest in sth. ein persönliches Interesse an etw. (Dat.) haben

vestige /'vestɪdʒ/ n. Spur, die; not a ~ of truth kein Fünkchen Wahrheit

vestment /'vestmənt/ n. [Priester]gewand, *das*

vestry /'vestrɪ/ n. Sakristei, *die*

vet /vet/ [1] n. Tierarzt, *der*/-ärztin, *die* [2] v.t., **-tt-** überprüfen

veteran /'vetərən/ n. Veteran, *der*/ Veteranin, *die*

veteran 'car n. (Brit.) Veteran, *der*

veterinarian /vetərɪ'neərɪən/ n. (Amer.) Tierarzt, *der*/-ärztin, *die*

veterinary /'vetərɪnərɪ/ adj. tiermedizinisch

veterinary 'surgeon n. (Brit.) Tierarzt, *der*/-ärztin, *die*

veto /'vi:təʊ/ [1] n., pl. **~es** Veto, *das* [2] v.t. sein Veto einlegen gegen

vex /veks/ v.t. [ver]ärgern; (cause to worry) beunruhigen; **be ~ed with sb.** sich über jmdn. ärgern

vexation /vek'seɪʃn/ n. Verärgerung, *die*

vexed /vekst/ adj. (a) verärgert **(b) ~ question** viel diskutierte Frage

VHF abbr. = **Very High Frequency** UKW

via /'vaɪə/ prep. über (+ Akk.) ⟨Ort, Sender, Telefon⟩; durch ⟨Eingang, Schornstein, Person⟩; per ⟨Post⟩

viability /vaɪə'bɪlɪtɪ/ n. (feasibility) Realisierbarkeit, *die*

viable /'vaɪəbl/ adj. (feasible) realisierbar

viaduct /'vaɪədʌkt/ n. Viadukt, *das od. der*

Viagra ® /vaɪ'ægrə/ n. Viagra, *das*

vibrant /'vaɪbrənt/ adj. lebensprühend ⟨Atmosphäre⟩; lebhaft ⟨Farbe⟩

vibrate /vaɪ'breɪt/ [1] v.i. vibrieren; (under strong impact) beben [2] v.t. vibrieren lassen

vibration /vaɪ'breɪʃn/ n. Vibrieren, *das;* (under strong import) Beben, *das*

vicar /'vɪkə(r)/ n. Pfarrer, *der*

vicarage /'vɪkərɪdʒ/ n. Pfarrhaus, *das*

vicarious /vɪ'keərɪəs/ adj. nachempfunden

vice¹ /vaɪs/ n. Laster, *das*

vice² n. (Brit.: tool) Schraubstock, *der*

vice: ~-'chairman n. stellvertretender Vorsitzender; **~'president** n. Vizepräsident, *der*/-präsidentin, *die;* **~ squad** n. Sittenpolizei, *die*

vice versa /vaɪsɪ 'vɜ:sə/ adv. umgekehrt

vicinity /vɪ'sɪnɪtɪ/ n. Umgebung, *die;* **in the ~ [of a place]** in der Nähe [eines Ortes]

vicious /'vɪʃəs/ adj. (a) (malicious) böse; bösartig ⟨Tier⟩ **(b)** (violent) brutal

vicious 'circle n. Teufelskreis, *der*

'viciously adv. (a) (maliciously) boshaft **(b)** (violently) brutal

victim /'vɪktɪm/ n. Opfer, *das;* (of sarcasm, abuse) Zielscheibe, *die* (fig.).

victimization /vɪktɪmaɪ'zeɪʃn/ n. Schikanierung, *die*

victimize /'vɪktɪmaɪz/ v.t. schikanieren

victor /'vɪktə(r)/ n. Sieger, *der*/Siegerin, *die*

victorious /vɪk'tɔ:rɪəs/ adj. siegreich

victory /'vɪktərɪ/ n. Sieg, *der* **(over** über + Akk.); attrib. Sieges-

video /'vɪdɪəʊ/ [1] adj. Video- [2] n., pl. **~s** (~ recorder) Videorekorder, *der;* (~tape, ~ recording) Video, *das* (ugs.) [3] v.t. ▶ VIDEOTAPE 2

video: ~ camera n. Videokamera, *die;* **~ cas'sette** n. Videokassette, *die;* **~ cas'sette recorder** n. Videokassettenrekorder, *der;* **~ clip** n. Videoclip, *der;* **~ film** n. Videofilm, *der;* **~ game** n. Videospiel, *das;* **~ library** n. Videothek, *die;* **~ machine** n. Videogerät, *das;* **~ 'nasty** n. Horrorvideo, *das;* **~-on-demand** n. Video-on-Demand, *das;* **~ player** n. Video-Player, *der;* **~ recorder** n. Videorekorder, *der;* **~ recording** n. Videoaufnahme, *die;* **~tape** [1] n. Videoband, *das;* [2] v.t. [auf Videoband (Akk.)] aufnehmen

vie /vaɪ/ v.i., vying /'vaɪɪŋ/ **~ [with sb.] for sth.** [mit jmdm.] um etw. wetteifern

Vienna /vɪ'enə/ [1] pr. n. Wien (*das*) [2] attrib. adj. Wiener

Viennese /vɪə'ni:z/ [1] adj. Wiener [2] n., pl. same Wiener, *der*/Wienerin, *die*

Vietnam /vɪet'næm/ pr. n. Vietnam (*das*)

Vietnamese /vɪetnə'mi:z/ [1] adj. vietnamesisch; **sb. is ~:** jmd. ist Vietnamese/Vietnamesin [2] n., pl. same **(a)** (person) Vietnamese, *der*/ Vietnamesin, *die* **(b)** (language) Vietnamesisch, *das*

view /vju:/ [1] n. **(a)** (range of vision) Sicht, *die;* **be out of/in ~:** nicht zu sehen/zu sehen sein **(b)** (what is seen) Aussicht, *die* **(c)** (picture) Ansicht, *die* **(d)** (opinion) Ansicht, *die;* **what is your ~ or are your ~s on this?** was meinst du dazu?; **hold or take the ~ that ...:** der Ansicht sein, dass ...; **in my ~:** meiner Ansicht nach **(e) be on ~:** besichtigt werden können; **in ~ of sth.** (fig.) angesichts einer Sache; **with a ~ to doing sth.** in der Absicht, etw. zu tun [2] v.t. **(a)** (look at) sich (Dat.) ansehen **(b)** (consider) betrachten **(c)** (inspect) besichtigen [3] v.i. (Telev.) fernsehen

viewdata /'vju:deɪtə/ n. Bildschirmtextsystem, *das*

'viewer n. **(a)** (Telev.) [Fernseh]zuschauer, *der*/-zuschauerin, *die;* **(b)** (for slides) Diabetrachter, *der*

viewfinder n. Sucher, *der*

viewing /'vju:ɪŋ/ n. (Telev.) Fernsehen, *das;* **~ figures** Einschaltquoten Pl.; **at peak ~ time** zur besten Sendezeit

'viewpoint n. Standpunkt, *der*

V

vigil /'vɪdʒɪl/ n. Wachen, das; **keep** ∼: wachen

vigilance /'vɪdʒɪləns/ n. Wachsamkeit, die

vigilant /'vɪdʒɪlənt/ adj. wachsam

vigilante /vɪdʒɪ'læntɪ/ n. Mitglied einer/der Bürgerwehr

vigor (Amer.) ▶ VIGOUR

vigorous /'vɪɡərəs/ adj. kräftig; heftig ⟨Attacke, Protest⟩; energisch ⟨Versuch, Anstrengung, Leugnen, Maßnahme⟩

'vigorously adv. heftig; kräftig ⟨schrubben, drücken⟩

vigour /'vɪɡə(r)/ n. (Brit.) (of person) Vitalität, die; (of body) Kraft, die; (of protest, attack) Heftigkeit, die

vile /vaɪl/ adj. gemein ⟨Verleumdung⟩; vulgär ⟨Sprache⟩; (repulsive) widerwärtig; (coll.: very unpleasant) scheußlich (ugs.)

villa /'vɪlə/ n. (a) [holiday] ∼: Ferienhaus, das
(b) [country] ∼: Landhaus, das

village /'vɪlɪdʒ/ n. Dorf, das; attrib. Dorf-

village: ∼ **'green** n. Dorfwiese, die; ∼ **'hall** n. Dorfgemeinschaftshaus, das

villager /'vɪlɪdʒə(r)/ n. Dorfbewohner, der/ -bewohnerin, die

villain /'vɪlən/ n. (a) Verbrecher, der
(b) (Theatre) Bösewicht, der

villainous /'vɪlənəs/ adj. gemein

vindicate /'vɪndɪkeɪt/ v.t. (a) (justify) rechtfertigen
(b) (clear) rehabilitieren

vindication /vɪndɪ'keɪʃn/ n. (a) (justification) Rechtfertigung, die
(b) (clearing) Rehabilitierung, die

vindictive /vɪn'dɪktɪv/ adj. nachtragend

vine /vaɪn/ n. Weinrebe, die

vinegar /'vɪnɪɡə(r)/ n. Essig, der

vinegary /'vɪnɪɡərɪ/ adj. sauer

vineyard /'vɪnjɑːd, 'vɪnjəd/ n. Weinberg, der

vintage /'vɪntɪdʒ/ ⓵ n. Jahrgang, der
⓶ adj. erlesen ⟨Wein⟩

vintage 'car n. (Brit.) Oldtimer, der

vintner /'vɪntnə(r)/ n. Weinhändler, der/ -händlerin, die

vinyl /'vaɪnɪl/ n. Vinyl, das

viola /vɪ'əʊlə/ n. Bratsche, die

violate /'vaɪəleɪt/ v.t. (a) (justify) verletzen; brechen ⟨Vertrag, Versprechen, Gesetz⟩
(b) (profane, rape) schänden

violation /vaɪə'leɪʃn/ n. ▶ VIOLATE: Verletzung, die; Bruch, der; Schändung, die

violence /'vaɪələns/ n. (a) (force) Heftigkeit, die; (of blow) Wucht, die
(b) (brutality) Gewalt, die; (at public event) Gewalttätigkeiten Pl.; **resort to** or **use** ∼: Gewalt anwenden

violent /'vaɪələnt/ adj. gewalttätig; (fig.) heftig; wuchtig ⟨Schlag, Stoß⟩; Gewalt⟨verbrecher, -tat⟩

'violently adv. brutal; (fig.) heftig

violet /'vaɪələt/ ⓵ n. (a) Veilchen, das
(b) (colour) Violett, das
⓶ adj. violett

violin /vaɪə'lɪn/ n. Violine, die; Geige, die

vio'linist n. Geiger, der/Geigerin, die

VIP /viːaɪ'piː/ n. Prominente, der/die; **the** ∼**s** die Prominenz

viper /'vaɪpə(r)/ n. Viper, die

virgin /'vɜːdʒɪn/ ⓵ n. (a) Jungfrau, die
(b) **the [Blessed] V**∼ **[Mary]** die [Heilige] Jungfrau [Maria]
⓶ adj. (unspoiled) unberührt; ∼ **olive oil** natives Olivenöl

virginity /və'dʒɪnɪtɪ/ n. Unschuld, die

Virgo /'vɜːɡəʊ/ n., pl. ∼**s** (Astrol., Astron.) die Jungfrau

virile /'vɪraɪl/ adj. männlich

virility /vɪ'rɪlɪtɪ/ n. Männlichkeit, die

virology /vaɪə'rɒlədʒɪ/ n. Virologie, die

virtual /'vɜːtjʊəl/ adj. **a** ∼ ...: so gut wie ein/eine ...; **the traffic came to a** ∼ **standstill** der Verkehr kam praktisch zum Stillstand (ugs.)

'virtually adv. so gut wie; praktisch (ugs.)

virtual re'ality n. (Comp.) virtuelle Realität

virtue /'vɜːtjuː/ n. (a) (moral excellence) Tugend, die
(b) (advantage) Vorteil, der
(c) **by** ∼ **of** aufgrund (+ Gen.)

virtuoso /vɜːtjʊ'əʊzəʊ/ n., pl. **virtuosi** /vɜːtjʊ'əʊziː/ or ∼**s** Virtuose, der/Virtuosin, die

virtuous /'vɜːtjʊəs/ adj. rechtschaffen ⟨Person⟩; tugendhaft ⟨Leben⟩

virulent /'vɪrʊlənt/ adj. (a) (Med.) virulent; stark wirkend ⟨Gift⟩
(b) (fig.) heftig; scharf ⟨Angriff⟩

virus /'vaɪərəs/ n. (a) Virus, das
(b) (Comp.) [Computer]virus, das od. der

visa /'viːzə/ n. Visum, das

vis-à-vis /viːzɑː'viː/ prep. (in relation to) bezüglich (+ Gen.)

viscosity /vɪs'kɒsɪtɪ/ n. Dickflüssigkeit, die

viscount /'vaɪkaʊnt/ n. Viscount, der

viscous /'vɪskəs/ adj. dickflüssig

visibility /vɪzɪ'bɪlɪtɪ/ n. (a) Sichtbarkeit, die
(b) (range of vision) Sicht, die; (Meteorol.) Sichtweite, die

visible /'vɪzɪbl/ adj. sichtbar

'visibly adv. sichtlich

vision /'vɪʒn/ n. (a) (sight) Sehkraft, die
(b) (dream) Vision, die
(c) usu. pl. (imaginings) Fantasien Pl.
(d) (insight, foresight) Weitblick, der

visit /'vɪzɪt/ ⓵ v.t. besuchen; aufsuchen ⟨Arzt⟩
⓶ v.i. einen Besuch/Besuche machen
⓷ n. Besuch, der; **pay** or **make a** ∼ **to sb.**, **pay sb. a** ∼: jmdm. einen Besuch abstatten (geh.)

'visiting: ∼ **card** n. Visitenkarte, die; ∼ **hours** n. pl. Besuchszeiten Pl.

visitor /'vɪzɪtə(r)/ n. Besucher, der/
Besucherin, die; (to hotel) Gast, der; **have ~s/
a ~:** Besuch haben

'visitors' book n. Gästebuch, das; **sign
the ~:** sich ins Gästebuch eintragen

visual /'vɪzjʊəl, 'vɪʒjʊəl/ adj. visuell;
optisch ⟨Eindruck, Darstellung⟩

visual: ~ aids n. pl.
Anschauungsmaterial, das; **~ dis'play
unit** n. Bildschirmgerät, das

visualization /vɪzjʊəlaɪ'zeɪʃn/ n.
Veranschaulichung, die; (imagining)
Sichvorstellen, das

visualize /'vɪzjʊəlaɪz, 'vɪʒjʊəlaɪz/ v.t. (a)
(imagine) sich (Dat.) vorstellen
(b) (envisage) voraussehen

'visually adv. bildlich

vital /'vaɪtl/ adj. (a) (essential to life)
lebenswichtig
(b) (essential) unbedingt notwendig
(c) (crucial) entscheidend (**to** für); **it is ~ that
you ...:** es ist von entscheidender
Bedeutung, dass Sie ...

vitality /vaɪ'tælɪtɪ/ n. Vitalität, die

'vitally adv. **~ important** von allergrößter
Wichtigkeit; (crucial) von entscheidender
Bedeutung

vitamin /'vɪtəmɪn, 'vaɪtəmɪn/ n. Vitamin,
das

vitamin pill n. Vitamintablette, die

vitriolic /vɪtrɪ'ɒlɪk/ adj. ätzend

vivacious /vɪ'veɪʃəs/ adj. lebhaft

vivacity /vɪ'væsɪtɪ/ n. Lebhaftigkeit, die

vivid /'vɪvɪd/ adj. lebhaft ⟨Farbe,
Erinnerung⟩; lebendig ⟨Schilderung⟩

'vividly adv. lebendig ⟨beschreiben⟩;
remember sth. ~: sich lebhaft an etw. (Akk.)
erinnern

vixen /'vɪksn/ n. Füchsin, die

vocabulary /və'kæbjʊlərɪ/ n. (a) (list)
Vokabelverzeichnis, das; **learn ~:** Vokabeln
lernen
(b) (range of language) Wortschatz, der

vocal /'vəʊkl/ adj. (a) (concerned with voice)
stimmlich
(b) lautstark ⟨Minderheit, Protest⟩

'vocal cords n. pl. Stimmbänder Pl.

vocalist /'vəʊkəlɪst/ n. Sänger, der/
Sängerin, die

vocation /və'keɪʃn/ n. Berufung, die

vocational /və'keɪʃənl/ adj. berufsbezogen

vocational: ~ college n. Berufsschule,
die; **~ guidance** n. Berufsberatung, die;
~ training n. berufliche Bildung

vociferous /və'sɪfərəs/ adj. laut; lautstark
⟨Forderung, Protest⟩

vodka /'vɒdkə/ n. Wodka, der

vogue /vəʊg/ n. Mode, die; **be in/come into
~:** in Mode sein/kommen

voice /vɔɪs/ 1 n. Stimme, die; **in a firm/
loud/soft ~:** mit fester/lauter/sanfter
Stimme

2 v.t. zum Ausdruck bringen

voice: ~mail n. Voicemail, die; **~-over**
n. Begleitkommentar, der;
~ recognition n. (Comp.)
Spracherkennung, die

void /vɔɪd/ 1 adj. (a) (empty) leer
(b) (invalid) ungültig
(c) **~ of** ohne [jeden/jedes/jede]
2 n. Nichts, das

vol. abbr. = **volume** Bd.

volatile /'vɒlətaɪl/ adj. (a) (Chem.) flüchtig
(b) (fig.) impulsiv; brisant ⟨Lage⟩

volcanic /vɒl'kænɪk/ adj. vulkanisch

volcano /vɒl'keɪnəʊ/ n., pl. **~es** Vulkan,
der

vole /vəʊl/ n. Wühlmaus, die

volition /və'lɪʃn/ n. Wille, der; **of one's own
~:** aus eigenem Willen

volley /'vɒlɪ/ n. (a) (of missiles) Salve, die; **a
~ of arrows** ein Hagel von Pfeilen
(b) (Tennis) Volley, der

'volleyball n. Volleyball, der

volt /vəʊlt/ n. Volt, das

voltage /'vəʊltɪdʒ/ n. Spannung, die

voluble /'vɒljʊbl/ adj. redselig

volume /'vɒljuːm/ n. (a) (book) Band, der
(b) (loudness) Lautstärke, die; (of voice)
Volumen, das
(c) (space) Rauminhalt, der; (amount of
substance) Teil, der

'volume control n. Lautstärkeregler, der

voluntarily /'vɒləntərɪlɪ/ adv.,
voluntary /'vɒləntərɪ/ adj. freiwillig

volunteer /vɒlən'tɪə(r)/ 1 n. Freiwillige,
der/die
2 v.t. anbieten ⟨Hilfe, Dienste⟩;
herausrücken mit ⟨Informationen⟩
3 v.i. sich [freiwillig] melden; **~ to do** or
~ for the shopping sich zum Einkaufen
bereit erklären

voluptuous /və'lʌptjʊəs/ adj. üppig

vomit /'vɒmɪt/ 1 v.t. erbrechen
2 v.i. sich übergeben
3 n. Erbrochene, das

voodoo /'vuːduː/ n. Wodu, der

voracious /və'reɪʃəs/ adj. gefräßig
⟨Person⟩; unbändig ⟨Appetit⟩

vote /vəʊt/ 1 n. (a) (individual ~) Stimme,
die
(b) (act of voting) Abstimmung, die; **take a
~ on sth.** über etw. (Akk.) abstimmen
(c) (right to ~) Stimmrecht, das
2 v.i. abstimmen; (in election) wählen; **~ for/
against** stimmen für/gegen; **~ to do sth.**
beschließen, etw. zu tun; **~ Labour/
Conservative** etc. Labour/die Konservativen
usw. wählen
3 v.t. **~ sb. Chairman/President** etc. jmdn.
zum Vorsitzenden/Präsidenten usw. wählen
■ **vote 'in** v.t. wählen

'voter n. Wähler, der/Wählerin, die

'vote-catching n. Stimmenfang, der

voting /'vəʊtɪŋ/ n. Abstimmen, das; (in election) Wählen, das

voting: ~ **age** n. Wahlalter, das; ~ **slip** n. Wahlzettel, der; Stimmzettel, der; ~ **system** n. Wahlsystem, das

vouch /vaʊtʃ/ 1 v.t. ~ **that** ...: sich dafür verbürgen, dass ...
2 v.i. ~ **for** sb./sth. sich für jmdn./etw. verbürgen

'voucher n. Gutschein, der

vow /vaʊ/ 1 n. Gelöbnis, das; (Relig.) Gelübde, das
2 v.t. geloben

vowel /'vaʊəl/ n. Vokal, der

voyage /'vɔɪɪdʒ/ 1 n. Reise, die; (sea ~) Seereise, die; outward/homeward ~, ~ out/ home Hin-/Rückreise, die; a ~ **to the moon** ein Mondflug
2 v.i. (literary) reisen

voyeur /vwɑːˈjɜː(r)/ n. Voyeur, der

voyeurism /vwɑːˈjɜːrɪzm/ n. Voyeurismus, der

vulgar /'vʌlɡə(r)/ adj. vulgär; ordinär ⟨Person, Benehmen, Witz⟩

vulgarity /vʌlˈɡærɪtɪ/ n. Vulgarität, die

vulnerable /'vʌlnərəbl/ adj. (a) (exposed to danger) angreifbar; be ~ **to** sth. für etw. anfällig sein; be ~ **to attack/in a** ~ **position** leicht angreifbar sein
(b) (without protection) schutzlos

vulture /'vʌltʃə(r)/ n. Geier, der

vying ▶ VIE

Ww

W¹, w /'dʌblju:/ n. W, w, das

W² abbr. = **watt[s]** W

W. abbr. (a) = **west** W.
(b) = **western** w.

wad /wɒd/ n. (a) Knäuel, das; (smaller) Pfropfen, der
(b) (of papers) Bündel, das

wadding /'wɒdɪŋ/ n. Futter, das

waddle /'wɒdl/ 1 v.i. watscheln
2 n. watschelnder Gang

wade /weɪd/ v.i. waten
■ **'wade through** v.t. (fig. coll.) durchackern (ugs.) ⟨Buch⟩

wafer /'weɪfə(r)/ n. Waffel, die

'wafer-thin adj. hauchdünn

waffle¹ /'wɒfl/ n. (Gastr.) Waffel, die

waffle² (Brit. coll.: talk) 1 v.i. schwafeln (ugs.)
2 n. Geschwafel, das (ugs.)

waft /wɒft, wɑːft/ 1 v.t. wehen
2 v.i. ziehen

wag /wæɡ/ 1 v.t., **-gg-** ⟨Hund:⟩ wedeln mit ⟨Schwanz⟩; ~ **one's finger at** sb. jmdm. mit dem Finger drohen
2 v.i., **-gg-** ⟨Schwanz:⟩ wedeln

wage /weɪdʒ/ 1 n. in sing. or pl. Lohn, der
2 v.t. führen ⟨Krieg⟩

wage: ~ **claim** n. Lohnforderung, die; ~ **earner** n. Lohnempfänger, der/ -empfängerin, die; be the ~ **earner of the family** der Ernährer/die Ernährerin der Familie sein; ~ **freeze** n. Lohnstopp, der; ~ **increase** n. Lohnerhöhung, die; ~ **packet** n. Lohntüte, die

wager /'weɪdʒə(r)/ (dated/formal) 1 n. Wette, die; lay a ~ **on** sth. auf etw. (Akk.) wetten
2 v.t. & i. wetten

wage: ~ **rise** n. Lohnerhöhung, die; ~ **scale** n. Tarif, der; ~ **slave** n. Lohnsklave, der

waggle /'wæɡl/ (coll.) 1 v.t. ~ **its tail** ⟨Hund:⟩ mit dem Schwanz wedeln
2 v.i. hin und her schlagen

waggon (Brit.), **wagon** /'wæɡən/ n. Wagen, der

waif /weɪf/ n. (child) verlassenes Kind

wail /weɪl/ 1 v.i. klagen (geh.) (for um); ⟨Kind:⟩ heulen
2 n. klagender Schrei; ~**s** Geheul, das

waist /weɪst/ n. Taille, die; tight round the ~: eng in der Taille

'waistband n. Gürtelbund, der; (of trousers) [Hosen]bund, der; (of skirt) [Rock]bund, der

waistcoat /'weɪskəʊt/ n. (Brit.) Weste, die

'waistline n. Taille, die; be bad for the ~: schlecht für die schlanke Linie sein

wait /weɪt/ 1 v.i. (a) (await) warten; ~ **[for] an hour** eine Stunde warten; ~ **a moment** Moment mal; keep sb. ~**ing**, make sb. ~: jmdn. warten lassen
(b) ~ **at table** servieren
2 v.t. (await) warten auf (+ Akk.); ~ **one's turn** warten, bis man drankommt
3 n. (a) after a long/short ~: nach langer/ kurzer Wartezeit
(b) lie in ~ **for** sb./sth. jmdm./einer Sache auflauern
■ **wait be'hind** v.i. noch dableiben
■ **'wait for** v.t. warten auf (+ Akk.); ~ **for** sb. **to do** sth. darauf warten, dass jmd. etw. tut; ~ **for the rain to stop** warten, bis der Regen aufhört
■ **'wait on** v.t. (serve) bedienen
■ **wait 'up** v.i. aufbleiben (for wegen)

'waiter *n.* Kellner, *der;* ∼! Herr Ober!

'waiting: ∼ **list** *n.* Warteliste, *die;*
∼ **room** *n.* Wartezimmer, *das;* (Railw.)
Warteraum, *der*

waitress /'weɪtrɪs/ *n.* Serviererin, *die;* ∼!
Fräulein! (veralt.)

waive /weɪv/ *v.t.* verzichten auf (+ *Akk.*)

wake¹ /weɪk/ 1 *v.i.*, woke /wəʊk/, woken
/'wəʊkn/ aufwachen
2 *v.t.*, woke, woken wecken
3 *n.* (by corpse) Totenwache, *die*
■ **wake 'up** 1 *v.i.* aufwachen; ∼ up to sth.
(fig.: realize) etw. erkennen
2 *v.t.* (a) wecken
(b) (fig.: enliven) wachrütteln

wake² *n.* Kielwasser, *das;* in the ∼ of sth.
(fig.) im Gefolge von etw.

waken /'weɪkn/ 1 *v.t.* wecken
2 *v.i.* aufwachen

'wake-up call (esp. Amer.) ▶ ALARM CALL

Wales /weɪlz/ *pr. n.* Wales (*das*)

'walk /wɔːk/ 1 *v.i.* (a) laufen; (not run)
gehen; (not drive) zu Fuß gehen; learn to ∼:
laufen lernen
(b) (exercise) gehen
2 *v.t.* (a) (lead) führen; ausführen ⟨Hund⟩
(b) (accompany) bringen
3 *n.* (a) Spaziergang, *der;* go [out] for *or*
take *or* have a ∼: einen Spaziergang
machen; ten minutes' ∼ from here zehn
Minuten zu Fuß von hier
(b) (gait) Gang, *der*
(c) (path) [Spazier]weg, *der*
■ **walk a'way with** *v.t.* (coll.: win easily)
spielend leicht gewinnen
■ **'walk into** *v.t.* (hit by accident) laufen
gegen ⟨Pfosten, Laternenpfahl⟩; ∼ into sb.
mit jmdm. zusammenstoßen; ∼ into a trap
in eine Falle gehen
■ **walk 'off with** *v.t.* sich davonmachen
mit
■ **walk 'out** *v.i.* (a) (leave in protest) aus
Protest den Saal verlassen
(b) (go on strike) in den Streik treten
■ **walk 'out of** *v.t.* (leave in protest) aus
Protest verlassen
■ **walk 'out on** *v.t.* verlassen

'walker *n.* (a) Spaziergänger, *der*/
-gängerin, *die;* (rambler) Wanderer, *der*/
Wanderin, *die*
(b) (baby-∼) Laufstuhl, *der*

walkie-talkie /wɔːkɪ'tɔːkɪ/ *n.* Walkie-
Talkie, *das*

'walking *n.* [Spazieren]gehen, *das;* at
∼ pace im Schritttempo; be within
∼ distance zu Fuß zu erreichen sein

walking: ∼ **frame** *n.* Gehbock, *der;*
Gehgestell, *das;* ∼ **holiday** *n.*
Wanderurlaub, *der;* ∼ **shoe** *n.*
Wanderschuh, *der;* ∼ **stick** *n.*
Spazierstock, *der;* ∼ **tour** *n.* Wanderung,
die

Walkman ® /'wɔːkmən/ *n., pl.* **Walkmans**
Walkman, *der* Ⓦ꜀

walk: ∼**out** *n.* Arbeitsniederlegung, *die;*
∼**over** *n.* (fig.: easy victory) Spaziergang, *der*
(ugs.); ∼**way** *n.* Fußweg, *der;* (over machinery
etc.) Laufsteg, *der*

wall /wɔːl/ *n.* Wand, *die;* (freestanding) Mauer,
die; **drive sb. up the** ∼ (fig. coll.) jmdn. auf die
Palme bringen (ugs.); **go to the** ∼ (fig.) an die
Wand gedrückt werden
■ **wall 'up** *v.t.* zumauern

wall: ∼**chart** *n.* Schautafel, *die;*
∼ **cupboard** *n.* Hängeschrank, *der*

wallet /'wɒlɪt/ *n.* Brieftasche, *die*

wall: ∼**flower** *n.* Goldlack, *der;*
∼ **hanging** *n.* Wandbehang, *der;* ∼ **light**
n. Wandlampe, *die*

wallop /'wɒləp/ (coll.) 1 *v.t.* schlagen
2 *n.* Schlag, *der*

wallow /'wɒləʊ/ *v.i.* (a) sich wälzen
(b) (fig.) schwelgen (in in + *Dat.*)

wall: ∼ **painting** *n.* Wandgemälde, *das;*
∼**paper** 1 *n.* (a) Tapete, *die;* (b) (Comp.)
Hintergrund, *der;* (pattern)
Hintergrundmuster, *das;* 2 *v.t.* tapezieren;
∼**-to-**∼ *adj.* ∼**-to-**∼ carpeting
Teppichboden, *der;* ∼ **unit** *n.*
Hängeelement, *das*

walnut /'wɔːlnʌt/ *n.* Walnuss, *die*

walrus /'wɔːlrəs/ *n.* Walross, *das*

waltz /wɔːlts, wɒls/ 1 *n.* Walzer, *der*
2 *v.i.* Walzer tanzen

wan /wɒn/ *adj.* bleich

wand /wɒnd/ *n.* Stab, *der*

wander /'wɒndə(r)/ 1 *v.i.* (go aimlessly)
umherirren; (walk slowly) bummeln
2 *v.t.* wandern durch
3 *n.* (coll.) Spaziergang, *der*
■ **wander a'bout** *v.i.* sich herumtreiben
■ **wander 'off** *v.i.* (stray) weggehen

wane /weɪn/ *v.i.* abnehmen

wangle /'wæŋgl/ *v.t.* (coll.) organisieren
(ugs.)

wannabe /'wɒnəbɪ/ *n.* (coll. derog.)
Möchtegern, *der; attrib.* Möchtegern-

want /wɒnt/ 1 *v.t.* (a) (desire) wollen; ∼ to
do sth. etw. tun wollen; I ∼ it done by
tonight ich will, dass es bis heute Abend
fertig wird
(b) (require, need) brauchen; 'W∼ed – cook'
„Koch/Köchin gesucht"; you're ∼ed on the
phone du wirst am Telefon verlangt; the
windows ∼ painting die Fenster müssten
gestrichen werden; you ∼ to be [more]
careful du solltest vorsichtig[er] sein
(c) ∼ed [by the police] [polizeilich] gesucht
2 *n.* (a) (lack) Mangel, *der* (of an + *Dat.*); for
∼ of sth. aus Mangel an etw. (*Dat.*)
(b) (need) Not, *der*
(c) (desire) Bedürfnis, *das*
■ **'want for** *v.t.* sb. ∼s for nothing *or*
doesn't ∼ for anything jmdm. fehlt es an
nichts

'wanting *adj.* be ∼: fehlen; sb./sth. is ∼ in ┈┈╎>

sth. jmdm./einer Sache fehlt es an etw.
(*Dat.*); be found ~: für unzureichend
befunden werden

wanton /'wɒntən/ *adj.*, **'wantonly** *adv.*
mutwillig

war /wɔː(r)/ *n.* Krieg, *der;* **between the** ~s
zwischen den Weltkriegen; **declare** ~: den
Krieg erklären (**on** *Dat.*); **be at** ~: sich im
Krieg befinden; **make** ~: Krieg führen (**on**
gegen)

warble /'wɔːbl/ *v.t. & i.* trällern

war: ~ **correspondent** *n.*
Kriegsberichterstatter, *der/*
-berichterstatterin, *die;* ~ **crime** *n.*
Kriegsverbrechen, *das;* ~ **criminal** *n.*
Kriegsverbrecher, *der/*-verbrecherin, *die*

ward /wɔːd/ *n.* (a) (in hospital) Station, *die;*
she's in W~ 3 sie liegt auf Station 3
(b) (child) Mündel, *das od. die*
(c) (electoral division) Wahlbezirk, *der*
■ **ward 'off** *v.t.* abwehren

'war damage *n.* Kriegsschäden *Pl.*

warden /'wɔːdn/ *n.* (a) (of hostel) Heimleiter,
der/-leiterin, *die;* (of youth hostel)
Herbergsvater, *der/*-mutter, *die*
(b) (supervisor) Aufseher, *der/*Aufseherin, *die*

'warder *n.* (Brit.) Wärter, *der*

wardrobe /'wɔːdrəʊb/ *n.* (a)
Kleiderschrank, *der*
(b) (clothes) Garderobe, *die*

warehouse /'weəhaʊs/ *n.* Lagerhaus, *das;*
(part of building) Lager, *das*

wares /weəz/ *n. pl.* Ware, *die*

warfare /'wɔːfeə(r)/ *n.* Krieg, *der*

war: ~ **game** *n.* Kriegsspiel, *das;*
~ **grave** *n.* Kriegs- *od.* Soldatengrab, *das;*
~head *n.* Sprengkopf, *der*

warily /'weərɪlɪ/ *adv.* vorsichtig; (suspiciously)
misstrauisch

'warlike *adj.* kriegerisch

warm /wɔːm/ 1 *adj.* (a) warm; I am [very]
~: mir ist [sehr] warm
(b) (enthusiastic) herzlich ‹*Grüße, Dank*›
2 *v.t.* wärmen; warm machen ‹*Flüssigkeit*›;
~ one's hands sich (*Dat.*) die Hände
wärmen
3 *v.i.* ~ to sb./sth. (come to like) sich für
jmdn./etw. erwärmen
■ **warm 'up** 1 *v.i.* warm werden;
‹*Sportler:*› sich aufwärmen
2 *v.t.* aufwärmen ‹*Speisen*›; erwärmen
‹*Raum, Zimmer*›

warm-blooded /'wɔːmblʌdɪd/ *adj.*
warmblütig;

'war memorial *n.* Kriegerdenkmal, *das*

warm-hearted /'wɔːmhɑːtɪd/ *adj.*
warmherzig ‹*Person*›

'warmly *adv.* (a) warm
(b) (fig.) herzlich ‹*willkommen heißen,
gratulieren, begrüßen, grüßen, danken*›

warmonger /'wɔːmʌŋgə(r)/ *n.*
Kriegshetzer, *der/*-hetzerin, *die*

warmth /wɔːmθ/ *n.* (a) Wärme, *die*

(b) (fig.) Herzlichkeit, *die*

'warm-up *n.* have a ~ (Sport) sich
aufwärmen; ~ [lap] (Motor Racing)
Aufwärmrunde, *die*

warn /wɔːn/ *v.t.* (a) (inform, give notice)
warnen (**against, of, about** vor + *Dat.*); ~ **sb.
that** ...: jmdn. darauf hinweisen, dass ...;
~ sb. not to do sth. jmdn. davor warnen,
etw. zu tun
(b) (admonish) ermahnen; (officially) abmahnen

warning 1 *n.* (a) (advance notice)
Vorwarnung, *die*
(b) (lesson) let that be a ~ to you lass dir das
eine Warnung sein
(c) (caution) Verwarnung, *die;* (less official)
Warnung, *die*
2 *adj.* Warn‹*schild, -signal usw.*›

'warning triangle *n.* Warndreieck, *das*

warp /wɔːp/ 1 *v.i.* sich verbiegen; ‹*Holz,
Schallplatte:*› sich verziehen
2 *v.t.* (a) verbiegen
(b) (fig.) a ~ed sense of humour ein
abartiger Humor

war: ~**path** *n.* be on the ~path (fig.) in
Rage sein; ~**plane** *n.* Kampfflugzeug, *das*

warrant /'wɒrənt/ 1 *n.* (for sb.'s arrest)
Haftbefehl, *der;* [search] ~:
Durchsuchungsbefehl, *der*
2 *v.t.* (a) (justify) rechtfertigen
(b) (guarantee) garantieren

'warranty *n.* Garantie, *die*

warrior /'wɒrɪə(r)/ *n.* (esp. literary) Krieger,
der (geh.)

Warsaw /'wɔːsɔː/ 1 *pr. n.* Warschau (*das*)
2 *attrib. adj.* Warschauer; ~ Pact (Hist.)
Warschauer Pakt

'warship *n.* Kriegsschiff, *das*

wart /wɔːt/ *n.* Warze, *die*

war: ~**time** *n.* (a) Kriegszeit, *die;* in or
during ~: im Krieg; (b) attrib.
Kriegs‹*rationierung, -evakuierung usw.*›
~-**torn** *adj.* kriegsgeschunden

wary /'weərɪ/ *adj.* vorsichtig; (suspicious)
misstrauisch (of gegenüber); be ~ of sb./sth.
sich vor jmdm./etw. in Acht nehmen

'war zone *n.* Kriegsgebiet, *das*

was ▶ BE

wash /wɒʃ/ 1 *v.t.* (a) waschen; ~ oneself
sich waschen; ~ one's hands/face/hair sich
(*Dat.*) die Hände/das Gesicht/die Haare
waschen; ~ the clothes Wäsche waschen;
~ the dishes [Geschirr] spülen; ~ the floor
den Fußboden aufwischen
(b) (remove) waschen ‹*Fleck*› (out of aus);
abwaschen ‹*Schmutz*› (off von)
(c) (carry along) spülen
2 *v.i.* (a) sich waschen
(b) ‹*Stoff, Kleidungsstück:*› sich waschen
lassen
3 *n.* (a) give sb./sth. a [good] ~: jmdn./etw.
[gründlich] waschen
(b) (laundering) Wäsche, *die*
(c) (of ship) Sog, *der*

■ **wash 'down** *v.t.* abspritzen ‹*Auto, Deck, Hof*›

■ **wash 'off** ⓵ *v.t.* ~ sth. off etw. abwaschen

⓶ *v.i.* abgehen; (from fabric etc.) herausgehen

■ **wash 'out** *v.t.* ausscheuern ‹*Topf*›; ausspülen ‹*Mund*›; ~ **dirt/marks out of clothes** Schmutz/Flecken aus Kleidern [her]auswaschen

■ **wash 'up** ⓵ *v.t.* (Brit.) ~ **the dishes up** das Geschirr spülen

⓶ *v.i.* abwaschen; spülen

washable /'wɒʃəbl/ *adj.* waschbar

'**washbasin** *n.* Waschbecken, *das*

washed-'out *adj.* verwaschen (fig.: exhausted) abgespannt

washed-'up *adj.* (coll.) kaputt (ugs.)

washer /'wɒʃə(r)/ *n.* (of tap) Dichtungsring, *der*

'**washing** *n.* Wäsche, *die;* **do the ~:** waschen

washing: ~ **machine** *n.* Waschmaschine, *die;* ~ **powder** *n.* Waschpulver, *das;* ~-'**up** *n.* (Brit.) Abwasch, *der;* **do the ~-up** abwaschen; spülen; ~-'**up liquid** *n.* Spülmittel, *das*

'**washtub** *n.* Waschbottich, *der*

wasn't /'wɒznt/ (coll.) **= was not;** ▶ BE

wasp *n.* Wespe, *die*

waste /weɪst/ ⓵ *n.* (a) (useless remains) Abfall, *der;* **kitchen ~:** Küchenabfälle *Pl.* (b) (extravagant use) Verschwendung, *die;* **it's a ~ of** time/money/energy das ist Zeit-/Geld-/Energieverschwendung

⓶ *v.t.* (squander) verschwenden; **all his efforts were ~d** all seine Mühe war umsonst; **don't ~ my time!** stehlen Sie mir nicht die Zeit!

⓷ *adj.* (a) ~ **material** Abfall, *der* (b) **lay sth. ~:** etw. verwüsten

■ **waste a'way** *v.i.* immer mehr abmagern

waste: ~**basket** ▶ WASTE-PAPER BASKET; ~ **disposal** *n.* Abfallbeseitigung, *die;* ~ **disposal site** *n.* [Müll]deponie *die;* ~ **disposal unit** *n.* Müllzerkleinerer, *der*

wasteful /'weɪstfl/ *adj.* (a) (extravagant) verschwenderisch (b) (causing waste) unwirtschaftlich

waste: ~**land** *n.* Ödland, *das;* ~ **management** *n.* Abfallmanagement, *das;* Müllmanagement, *das;* ~ '**paper** *n.* Papierabfall, *der;* ~-'**paper basket** *n.* Papierkorb, *der;* ~ **pipe** *n.* Abflussrohr, *das;* ~ **reduction** *n.* Abfallverminderung, *die;* Müllreduzierung, *die*

watch /wɒtʃ/ ⓵ *n.* (a) [wrist/pocket] ~: [Armband-/Taschen]uhr, *die* (b) **keep ~:** Wache halten; **keep [a] ~ for sb./sth.** auf jmdn./etw. achten (c) (Naut.) Wache, *der*

⓶ *v.i.* ~ **for sb./sth.** auf jmdn./etw. warten

⓷ *v.t.* (a) (observe) sich (*Dat.*) ansehen ‹*Sportveranstaltung, Fernsehsendung*›;

~ [the] television *or* TV fernsehen; ~ **sb. do** *or* **doing sth.** zusehen, wie jmd. etw. tut; **we are being ~ed** wir werden beobachtet (b) (be careful of, look after) achten auf (+ *Akk.*)

■ **watch 'out** *v.i.* (a) (be careful) aufpassen; ~ **out!** Vorsicht! (b) (look out) ~ **out for sb./sth.** auf jmdn./etw. achten

'**watchdog** *n.* Wachhund, *der;* (fig.) [public] ~: [*Leiter/Leiterin einer*] *Aufsichtsbehörde*

watchful /'wɒtʃfl/ *adj.* wachsam

watch: ~**maker** *n.* Uhrmacher, *der/*-macherin, *die;* ~**man** /'wɒtʃmən/ *n.*, *pl.* ~**men** /'wɒtʃmən/ Wachmann, *der;* ~ **strap** *n.* [Uhr]armband, *das;* ~**tower** *n.* Wachturm, *der*

water /'wɔːtə(r)/ ⓵ *n.* (a) Wasser, *das* (b) *in pl.* (part of the sea etc.) Gewässer *Pl.*

⓶ *v.t.* (a) bewässern ‹*Land*›; wässern ‹*Pflanzen*›; ~ **the flowers** die Blumen [be]gießen (b) verwässern ‹*Bier usw.*› (c) tränken ‹*Tier*›

⓷ *v.i.* ‹*Augen:*› tränen; **my mouth was ~ing** mir lief das Wasser im Munde zusammen

■ **water 'down** *v.t.* verwässern

water: ~**bed** *n.* Wasserbett, *das;* ~ **birth** *n.* Unterwassergeburt, *die;* ~ **biscuit** *n.* Cracker, *der;* ~ **bottle** *n.* Wasserflasche, *die;* ~ **butt** *n.* Regentonne, *die;* ~ **closet** *n.* Toilette, *die;* WC, *das;* Wasserklosett, *das* (veralt.); ~**colour** *n.* (a) (paint) Wasserfarbe, *die;* (b) (picture) Aquarell, *das;* ~**cress** *n.* Brunnenkresse, *die;* ~**fall** *n.* Wasserfall, *der;* ~**front** *n.* Ufer, *das;* **a ~front location** eine Gegend am Wasser; ~ **heater** *n.* Heißwassergerät, *das;* ~**hole** *n.* Wasserloch, *das*

watering: ~ **can** *n.* Gießkanne, *die;* ~ **place** *n.* (for animals) Wasserstelle, *die*

water: ~ **level** *n.* Wasserstand, *der;* ~**lily** *n.* Seerose, *die;* ~**line** *n.* (Naut.) Wasserlinie, *die;* ~**logged** /'wɔːtəlɒgd/ *adj.* nass ‹*Boden*›; aufgeweicht ‹*Sportplatz*›; ~ **main** *n.* Hauptwasserleitung, *die;* ~**mark** *n.* Wasserzeichen, *das;* ~**melon** *n.* Wassermelone, *die;* ~ **meter** *n.* Wasseruhr, *die;* ~ **pipe** *n.* Wasserrohr, *das;* ~ **pistol** *n.* Wasserpistole, *die;* ~ **polo** *n.* Wasserball, *der;* ~**proof** ⓵ *adj.* wasserdicht; wasserfest ‹*Farbe*›; ⓶ *v.t.* wasserdicht machen; imprägnieren ‹*Stoff*›; ~ **rates** *n. pl.* **the ~ rates** die Wassergebühren *Pl.;* ~-**repellent** *adj.* Wasser abstoßend; ~-**resistant** *adj.* wasserundurchlässig; wasserfest ‹*Farbe*›; ~**shed** *n.* (fig.) Wendepunkt, *der;* ~**ski** ⓵ *n.* Wasserski, *der;* ⓶ *v.i.* Wasserski laufen; ~**skiing** *n.* Wasserskilaufen, *das;* ~ **softener** /'sɒfnə(r)/ *n.* Wasserenthärter, *der;* ~-**soluble** *adj.* wasserlöslich; ~ **supply** *n.* Wasserversorgung, *die;* ~ **table** *n.* Grundwasserspiegel, *der;* ~ **tap** *n.* Wasserhahn, *der;* ~**tight** *adj.* wasserdicht;

W

∼ **tower** *n.* Wasserturm, *der;* ∼**way** *n.*
Wasserstraße, *die;* ∼ **vapour** *n.*
Wasserdampf, *der;* ∼**works** *n. sing., pl.
same* (establishment) Wasserwerk, *das;* (system)
Wasserversorgungssystem, *das*

'**watery** *adj.* wässrig

watt /wɒt/ *n.* Watt, *das*

wattage /'wɒtɪdʒ/ *n.* Wattzahl, *die*

wave /weɪv/ **1** *n.* (a) Welle, *die*
(b) (gesture) **give sb. a** ∼: jmdm. zuwinken;
with a ∼ **of one's hand** mit einem Winken
2 *v.i.* (a) ⟨*Fahne, Flagge, Wimpel:*⟩ wehen;
⟨*Baum, Gras, Korn:*⟩ sich wiegen
(b) (with hand) winken; ∼ **at** *or* **to sb.** jmdm.
zuwinken
3 *v.t.* schwenken; schwingen ⟨*Schwert*⟩;
∼ **one's hand at** *or* **to sb.** jmdm. zuwinken;
∼ **goodbye to sb.** jmdm. zum Abschied
zuwinken

■ **wave a**'**side** *v.t.* (a) abtun ⟨*Zweifel,
Einwand*⟩
(b) ∼ **sb. aside** [jmdm.] abwinken

wave: ∼**band** *n.* Wellenbereich, *der;*
∼**length** *n.* Wellenlänge, *die;* **be on the
same** ∼**length** [**as sb.**] (fig.) die gleiche
Wellenlänge [wie jmd.] haben

waver /'weɪvə(r)/ *v.i.* schwanken

wavy /'weɪvɪ/ *adj.* wellig; ∼ **line**
Schlangenlinie, *die*

wax[1] /wæks/ **1** *n.* (a) Wachs, *das*
(b) (in ear) Schmalz, *das*
2 *v.t.* wachsen

wax[2] *v.i.* (a) ⟨*Mond:*⟩ zunehmen
(b) (become) werden ·

wax '**crayon** *n.* Wachsmalstift, *der*

waxed /wækst/ *adj.* gewachst; ∼ **paper**
Wachspapier, *das*

wax: ∼**work** *n.* Wachsfigur, *die;* ∼**works**
n. sing., pl. same Wachsfigurenkabinett, *das*

'**waxy** *adj.* wachsweich

way /weɪ/ **1** *n.* (a) Weg, *der;* **ask the** *or*
one's ∼: nach dem Weg fragen; '**W**∼ **In/Out**'
„Ein-/Ausgang"; **by** ∼ **of Switzerland** über
die Schweiz; **lead the** ∼: vorausgehen; **go out
of one's** ∼: einen Umweg machen; (fig.)
keine Mühe scheuen
(b) (method) Art und Weise, *die;* **do it this** ∼:
mach es so
(c) (distance) Stück, *das;* **it's a long** ∼ **off** *or* **a
long** ∼ **from here** es ist weit weg von hier;
all the ∼: den ganzen Weg
(d) (direction) Richtung, *die;* **she went this/
that/the other** ∼: sie ist in diese/die/die
andere Richtung gegangen; **stand sth. the
right/wrong** ∼ **up** etw. richtig/falsch herum
stellen
(e) (respect) **in** [**exactly**] **the same** ∼: [ganz]
genauso; **in some** ∼**s** in gewisser Hinsicht;
in one ∼: auf eine Art; **in every** ∼: in jeder
Hinsicht; **in a** ∼: auf eine Art
(f) (custom) Art, *die*
(g) **get** *or* **have one's** [**own**] ∼, **have it one's**
[**own**] ∼: seinen Willen kriegen; **be in sb.'s**
or **the** ∼: [jmdm.] im Weg sein; **make** ∼ **for**

sth. für etw. Platz machen; (fig.) einer Sache
(*Dat.*) Platz machen; **in a bad** ∼: schlecht;
either ∼: so oder so; **by the** ∼: übrigens
2 *adv.* weit; ∼ **back** (coll.) vor langer Zeit

way: ∼**bill** *n.* Frachtbrief, *der;* ∼'**lay** *v.t.,
forms as* LAY[2] 1: (a) (ambush) überfallen; (b)
(stop for conversation) abfangen; ∼'**out** *adj.*
(coll.) extrem; verrückt; ∼**side** *n.* Wegrand,
der; **fall by the** ∼**side** (fig.) auf der Strecke
bleiben (ugs.)

wayward /'weɪwəd/ *adj.* eigenwillig

WC *abbr.* = **water closet** WC, *das*

we /wɪ, *stressed* wi:/ *pl. pron.* wir

weak /wi:k/ *adj.* (a) schwach; (easily led)
labil ⟨*Charakter, Person*⟩
(b) dünn ⟨*Getränk*⟩

weaken /'wi:kn/ **1** *v.t.* schwächen;
beeinträchtigen ⟨*Augen*⟩
2 *v.i.* ⟨*Entschlossenheit, Kraft:*⟩ nachlassen

weak-kneed /'wi:kni:d/ *adj.* (fig.) feige

weakling /'wi:klɪŋ/ *n.* Schwächling, *der*

'**weakly** *adv.* schwach

'**weakness** *n.* Schwäche, *die*

'**weak-willed** *adj.* willensschwach

wealth /welθ/ *n.* (a) (abundance) Fülle, *die*
(b) (riches, being rich) Reichtum, *der*

'**wealthy** **1** *adj.* reich
2 *n. pl.* **the** ∼: die Reichen Pl.

'**wealth tax** *n.* Vermögenssteuer, *die*

wean /wi:n/ *v.t.* abstillen; ∼ **sb.** [**away**] **from
sth.** (fig.) jmdm. etw. abgewöhnen

weapon /'wepən/ *n.* Waffe, *die;* ∼ **of mass
destruction** Massenvernichtungswaffe, *die*

weaponry /'wepənrɪ/ *n.* Waffen Pl.

wear /weə(r)/ **1** *n.* (a) ∼ [**and tear**]
Abnutzung, *die*
(b) (clothes) Kleidung, *die*
2 *v.t.,* **wore** /wɔː(r)/, **worn** /wɔːn/ (a) (have
on) tragen ⟨*Schmuck, Brille, Kleidung,
Perücke*⟩; **I haven't a thing to** ∼: ich habe
überhaupt nichts anzuziehen
(b) (rub) abtragen ⟨*Kleidungsstück*⟩; abnutzen
⟨*Teppich*⟩; **a** [**badly**] **worn tyre** ein [**stark**]
abgefahrener Reifen
3 *v.i.,* **wore, worn** (a) ⟨*Kleider:*⟩ sich
durchscheuern; ⟨*Absätze:*⟩ sich ablaufen;
⟨*Teppich:*⟩ sich abnutzen
(b) (endure rubbing) halten; ∼ **well/badly** sich
gut/schlecht tragen

■ **wear a**'**way** **1** *v.t.* abschleifen
2 *v.i.* sich abnutzen

■ **wear** '**down** *v.t.* (fig.) zermürben

■ **wear** '**off** *v.i.* ⟨*Schicht:*⟩ abgehen;
⟨*Wirkung, Schmerz:*⟩ nachlassen

■ **wear** '**out** **1** *v.t.* (a) aufbrauchen;
auftragen ⟨*Kleidungsstück*⟩
(b) (fig.: exhaust) kaputtmachen (ugs.); **be worn
out** kaputt sein (ugs.)
2 *v.i.* kaputtgehen (ugs.)

■ **wear** '**through** **1** *v.i.* sich
durchscheuern
2 *v.t.* durchscheuern

909

wearable ⋯◆ weird ⋯⋯

wearable /'weərəbl/ *adj.* sth. is [not] ∼: man kann etw. [nicht] anziehen

wearer /'weərə(r)/ *n.* Träger, *der*/Trägerin, *die*

wearily /'wɪərɪlɪ/ *adv.* müde

wearing /'weərɪŋ/ *adj.* ermüdend

wearisome /'wɪərɪsəm/ *adj.* ermüdend

weary /'wɪərɪ/ ① *adj.* (a) (tired) müde (b) be ∼ of sth. einer Sache (*Gen.*) überdrüssig sein
② *v.t.* be wearied by sth. durch etw. erschöpft sein
③ *v.i.* ∼ of sth./sb. einer Sache/jmds. überdrüssig werden

weasel /'wiːzl/ *n.* Wiesel, *das*

weather /'weðə(r)/ ① *n.* Wetter, *das;* what's the ∼ like? wie ist das Wetter?; in all ∼s bei jedem Wetter; he is feeling under the ∼ (fig.) er ist [zur Zeit] nicht ganz auf dem Posten
② *v.t.* abwettern ⟨*Sturm*⟩; (fig.) durchstehen ⟨*schwere Zeit*⟩

weather: ∼-beaten *adj.* wettergegerbt ⟨*Gesicht*⟩; verwittert ⟨*Felsen, Gebäude*⟩; **∼ chart** *n.* Wetterkarte, *die;* **∼cock** *n.* Wetterhahn, *der;* **∼ conditions** *n. pl.* Witterungsverhältnisse *Pl.;* **∼ forecast** *n.* Wettervorhersage, *die;* **∼ man** *n.* Meteorologe, *der;* **∼ map** *n.* Wetterkarte, *die;* **∼proof** *adj.* wetterfest; **∼ report** *n.* Wetterbericht, *der;* **∼ vane** *n.* Wetterfahne, *die*

weave¹ /wiːv/ ① *n.* Bindung, *die*
② *v.t.,* wove /wəʊv/, woven /'wəʊvn/ (a) weben; flechten ⟨*Korb, Kranz*⟩
(b) (fig.) einflechten ⟨*Thema usw.*⟩ (into in + *Akk.*)

weave² *v.i.* (take intricate course) sich schlängeln

weaver *n.* Weber, *der*/Weberin, *die*

web /web/ *n.* (a) Netz, *das;* spider's ∼: Spinnennetz, *das*
(b) the Web (Comp.) das Web (fachspr.); das Netz

web authoring *n.* Webauthoring, *das* (fachspr.) *attrib.* Webauthoring-⟨*Programm, Software, usw.*⟩

webbed feet /webd 'fiːt/ *n. pl.* Schwimmfüße *Pl.*

Web: ∼ browser *n.* (Comp.) Web-Browser, *der;* **∼ designer** *n.* Webdesigner, *der/*-designerin, *die;* **∼ page** *n.* (Comp.) Webseite, *die;* **∼ site** *n.* (Comp.) Website, *die*

we'd /wɪd, *stressed* wiːd/ (a) = we had; (b) = we would

Wed. *abbr.* = **Wednesday** Mi.

wedding /'wedɪŋ/ *n.* Hochzeit, *die*

wedding: ∼ anniversary *n.* Hochzeitstag, *der;* **∼ cake** *n.* Hochzeitskuchen, *der;* **∼ day** *n.* Hochzeitstag, *der;* **∼ dress** *n.* Brautkleid, *das;* **∼ present** *n.* Hochzeitsgeschenk, *das;* **∼ ring** *n.* Ehering, *der*

wedge /wedʒ/ ① *n.* Keil, *der*
② *v.t.* verkeilen; ∼ a door/window open eine Tür/ein Fenster festklemmen, damit sie/es offen bleibt

wedge-shaped *adj.* keilförmig

wedlock /'wedlɒk/ *n.* born in/out of ∼: ehelich/unehelich geboren

Wednesday /'wenzdeɪ, 'wenzdɪ/ *n.* Mittwoch, *der; see also* FRIDAY

wee¹ /wiː/ *adj.* (child lang./Scot.) klein

wee² ▶ WEE-WEE

weed /wiːd/ ① *n.* ∼[s] Unkraut, *das*
② *v.t.* jäten
■ **weed 'out** *v.t.* (fig.) aussieben

weedkiller *n.* Unkrautvertilgungsmittel, *das*

weedy *adj.* spillerig (ugs.) ⟨*Person*⟩

week /wiːk/ *n.* Woche, *die;* for several ∼s mehrere Wochen lang; once a ∼, every ∼: einmal in der Woche; three times a ∼: dreimal in der Woche; a two-∼ visit ein zweiwöchiger Besuch; a ∼ today/tomorrow heute/morgen in einer Woche; a ∼ on Monday, Monday ∼: Montag in einer Woche

weekday *n.* Wochentag, *der*

weekend /-'-, '--/ *n.* Wochenende, *das;* at the ∼: am Wochenende; go away for the ∼: übers Wochenende wegfahren

weekly /'wiːklɪ/ ① *adj.* wöchentlich; Wochen⟨*zeitung, -zeitschrift, -lohn*⟩
② *adv.* wöchentlich
③ *n.* (newspaper) Wochenzeitung, *die;* (magazine) Wochenzeitschrift, *die*

weep /wiːp/ *v.i. & t.,* wept /wept/ weinen

weepie /'wiːpɪ/ *n.* (coll.) Schmachtfetzen, *der* (salopp)

weeping 'willow *n.* Trauerweide, *die*

weepy /'wiːpɪ/ ① *adj.* weinerlich
② *n.* ▶ WEEPIE

wee-wee (coll.) ① *n.* Pipi, *das* (ugs.); do a ∼: Pipi machen (ugs.)
② *v.i.* Pipi machen (ugs.)

weigh /weɪ/ *v.t. & i.* wiegen
■ **weigh 'down** *v.t.* (fig.: depress) niederdrücken
■ **weigh 'up** *v.t.* abwägen

weighing machine *n.* Waage, *die*

weight /weɪt/ *n.* Gewicht, *das;* what is your ∼? wie viel wiegen Sie?; be under/over ∼: zu wenig/zu viel wiegen

weighting *n.* Zulage, *die*

weightlessness *n.* Schwerelosigkeit, *die*

weight: ∼lifter *n.* Gewichtheber, *der/* -heberin, *die;* **∼lifting** *n.* Gewichtheben, *das* **∼-train** *v.i.* mit Hanteln trainieren; **∼ training** *n.* Hanteltraining, *das;* **∼-watcher** *n.* Schlankheitsbewusste, *der/ die*

weighty *adj.* (a) (heavy) schwer (b) (important) gewichtig

weir /wɪə(r)/ *n.* Wehr, *das*

weird /wɪəd/ *adj.* (coll.: odd) bizarr

weirdo /'wɪədəʊ/ n., pl. ~s ▶ WEIRDIE

welcome /'welkəm/ [1] int. willkommen; ~ home/to England! willkommen zu Hause/ in England!
[2] n. (a) Willkommen, das
(b) (reception) Empfang, der
[3] v.t. begrüßen
[4] adj. (a) willkommen; gefällig ⟨Anblick⟩
(b) pred. you are ~ to take it du kannst es gern nehmen; you're ~: gern geschehen!

welcoming /'welkəmɪŋ/ adj. einladend

weld /weld/ v.t. (join) verschweißen; (repair, make, attach) schweißen (⟨on⟩ to an + Akk.)

'**welder** n. Schweißer, der/Schweißerin, die

'**welding** n. Schweißen, das

welfare /'welfeə(r)/ n. (a) (health and prosperity) Wohl, das
(b) (social work; payments etc.) Sozialhilfe, die; be on ~ (Amer.) Sozialhilfe bekommen

welfare: W~ '**State** n. Wohlfahrtsstaat, der; ~ **work** n. Sozialarbeit, die; ~ **worker** n. Sozialarbeiter, der/ -arbeiterin, die

well¹ /wel/ n. (a) Brunnen, der
(b) ▶ OIL WELL
(c) (stair~) Treppenloch, das

well² [1] int. ~! meine Güte!; ~, let's forget that na ja, lassen wir das; ~, who was it? nun od. und, wer war's?; oh ~[, never mind] na ja[, macht nichts]; ~? na?
[2] adv., better /'betə(r)/, best /best/ gut; gründlich ⟨trocknen, schütteln⟩; the business/ patient is doing ~: das Geschäft geht gut/ dem Patienten geht es gut; ~ done! großartig!; he is ~ over forty er ist weit über vierzig; as ~ (in addition) auch; A as ~ as B B und auch [noch] A
[3] adj. (in good health) How are you feeling now? – Quite ~, thank you Wie fühlen Sie sich jetzt? – Ganz gut, danke; look ~: gut aussehen; feel ~: sich wohl fühlen; he isn't [very] ~: es geht ihm nicht [sehr] gut; get ~ soon! gute Besserung!; make sb. ~: jmdn. gesund machen

we'll /wɪl, stressed wiːl/ = we will

well: ~-aimed adj. gezielt; **~-balanced** adj. ausgeglichen ⟨Person⟩; **~-behaved** ▶ BEHAVE 1; **~-being** n. Wohl, das; **~-bred** adj. anständig; **~-built** adj. ⟨Person⟩ mit guter Figur; be ~-built eine gute Figur haben; **~-chosen** adj. wohlgesetzt ⟨Worte⟩; **~-connected** adj. ⟨Person⟩ mit guten Beziehungen; ~ **done** adj. (Cookery) durchgebraten; **~-dressed** adj. gut gekleidet; **~-educated** adj. gebildet; **~-fed** adj. wohlgenährt; **~-founded** adj. [wohl] fundiert; **~-heeled** adj. (coll.) gut betucht (ugs.)

wellington /'welɪŋtən/ n. ~ [boot] Gummistiefel, der

well: ~-intentioned /'welɪntenʃənd/ adj. gut gemeint; **~-known** adj. bekannt; ~ **made** adj. gut [gearbeitet]; **~-mannered** adj. ⟨Person⟩ mit guten

Manieren; be ~-mannered gute Manieren haben; **~-meaning** adj. wohlmeinend; be **~-meaning** es gut meinen; **~-meant** adj. gut gemeint; ~ **off** adj. wohlhabend; sb. is ~ off jmdm. geht es [finanziell] gut; ~ **paid** adj. gut bezahlt; **~-read** /'welred/ adj. belesen; **~-spoken** adj. sprachlich gewandt; **~-timed** adj. zeitlich gut gewählt; **~-to-do** adj. wohlhabend; **~-tried** adj. bewährt; **~-wisher** n. Sympathisant, der/Sympathisantin, die

Welsh /welʃ/ [1] adj. walisisch; sb. is ~: jmd. ist Waliser/Waliserin
[2] n. (a) (language) Walisisch, das; see also ENGLISH 2A
(b) pl. the ~: die Waliser Pl.

Welsh: ~man /'welʃmən/ n., pl. ~men /'welʃmən/ Waliser, der; ~ '**rabbit,** ~ '**rarebit** /'reəbɪt/ ns. Käsetoast, der

went ▶ GO 1

wept ▶ WEEP

were ▶ BE

we're /wɪə(r)/ = we are; ▶ BE

weren't (coll.) = were not; ▶ BE

west /west/ [1] n. (a) Westen, der; in/ to[wards]/from the ~: im/nach/von Westen; to the ~ of westlich von
(b) usu. W~ (Geog., Polit.) Westen, der
[2] adj. westlich; West⟨küste, -wind, -grenze, -tor⟩
[3] adv. nach Westen; ~ of westlich von

West: ~ Ber'lin pr. n. (Hist.) West-Berlin (das); **w~bound** adj. ⟨Zug, Verkehr usw.⟩ in Richtung Westen; ~ **Country** n. (Brit.) Westengland, das; ~ '**End** n. (Brit.) Westend, das

westerly /'westəlɪ/ adj. westlich; ⟨Wind⟩ aus westlichen Richtungen

western /'westən/ [1] adj. westlich; West⟨grenze, -hälfte, -seite⟩; ~ **Germany** Westdeutschland, das
[2] n. Western, der

Western 'Europe pr. n. Westeuropa (das)

West: ~ 'German (Hist.) [1] adj. westdeutsch; he/she is ~ German er ist Westdeutscher/sie ist Westdeutsche; [2] n. Westdeutsche, der/die; ~ '**Germany** pr. n. (Hist.) Westdeutschland (das); ~ '**Indian** [1] adj. westindisch; sb. is ~ Indian jmd. ist Westinder/-inderin; [2] n. Westinder, der/ -inderin, die; ~ '**Indies** pr. n. pl. Westindische Inseln Pl.

westward[s] /'westwəd(z)/ adv. westwärts

wet /wet/ [1] adj. (a) nass
(b) (rainy) regnerisch; feucht ⟨Klima⟩
(c) frisch ⟨Farbe⟩; '~ paint„frisch gestrichen"
(d) (coll.: feeble) schlapp (ugs.)
[2] v.t., wet or wetted befeuchten
[3] n. (a) (moisture) Feuchtigkeit, die
(b) in the ~: im Regen

'**wetness** n. Nässe, die

'**wet suit** n. Tauchanzug, der

we've /wɪv, *stressed* wiːv/ = **we have**

whack /wæk/ (coll.) ① *v.t.* hauen (ugs.) ② *n.* Schlag, *der*

whacked /wækt/ *adj.* (Brit. coll.: tired out) erledigt (ugs.); kaputt (ugs.)

whale /weɪl/ *n.* **(a)** Wal, *der* **(b)** (coll.) **we had a ~ of a [good] time** wir haben uns bombig (ugs.) amüsiert

'whalebone *n.* Fischbein, *das*

whaler /'weɪlə(r)/ *n.* Walfänger, *der*

whaling /'weɪlɪŋ/ *n.* Walfang, *die*

wharf /wɔːf/ *n., pl.* **wharves** /wɔːvz/ *or* **~s** Kai, *der*

what /wɒt/ ① *adj.* welch...; **~ book?** welches Buch?; **~ time does it start?** um wie viel Uhr fängt es an?; **~ kind of man is he?** was für ein Mensch ist er?; **~ a fool you are!** was für ein Dummkopf du doch bist!; **~ cheek/luck!** was für eine Frechheit/ein Glück!; **I will give you ~ help I can** ich werde dir helfen, so gut ich kann ② *adv.* **~ do I care?** was kümmerts mich?; **~ does it matter?** was machts? ③ *pron.* was; **~?** wie?; was? (ugs.); **~ is your name?** wie heißt du/heißen Sie?; **~ about ...?** (**~ will become of ...?**) was ist mit ...?; **~ about a game of chess?** wie wärs mit einer Partie Schach?; **~'s-his/-her/-its-name** wie heißt er/sie/es noch; **~ for?** wozu?; **~ is it like?** wie ist es?; **so ~?** na und?; **do ~ I tell you** tu, was ich dir sage

whatever /wɒt'evə(r)/ ① *adj.* **~ problems you have** was für Probleme Sie auch haben; **nothing ~:** absolut nichts ② *pron.* **do ~ you like** mach, was du willst; **~ happens, ...:** was auch geschieht, ...; **or ~:** oder was auch immer; **~ does he want?** (coll.) was will er nur?

whatsit /'wɒtsɪt/ *n.* (coll.) (thing) Dingsbums, *das* (ugs.); (person) Dingsda, *der* (ugs.)

wheat /wiːt/ *n.* Weizen, *der*

wheedle /'wiːdl/ *v.t.* **~ sb. into doing sth.** jmdm. so lange gut zureden, bis er etw. tut; **~ sth. out of sb.** jmdm. etw. abschwatzen (ugs.)

wheel /wiːl/ ① *n.* **(a)** Rad, *das;* **[potter's] ~:** Töpferscheibe, *die* **(b)** (steering **~**) Lenkrad, *das;* (ship's **~**) Steuerrad, *das;* **at** *or* **behind the ~** (of car) am Steuer ② *v.t.* (push) schieben ③ *v.i.* **(a)** (turn round) kehrtmachen **(b)** (circle) kreisen

wheel: ~barrow *n.* Schubkarre, *die;* **~ brace** *n.* Radschlüssel, *der;* **~chair** *n.* Rollstuhl, *der;* **~ clamp** *n.* Parkkralle, *die*

wheeler-dealer /wiːlə'diːlə(r)/ *n.* Mauschler, *der*/Mauschlerin, *die;* (financial) Geschäftemacher, *der*/-macherin, *die*

'wheelie bin *n.* (Brit. coll.) Müllcontainer, *der* auf Rollen

'wheel reflector *n.* (on bicycle) Speichenreflektor, *der*

wheeze /wiːz/ *v.t.* schnaufen

whelk /welk/ *n.* Wellhornschnecke, *die*

when /wen/ ① *adv.* wann; **the time ~ ...:** die Zeit, zu der/(with past tense) als ...; **the day ~ ...:** der Tag, an dem/(with past tense) als ... ② *conj.* **(a)** (at the time that) als; (with present or future tense) wenn; **~ reading [a newspaper]** beim Lesen [einer Zeitung] **(b)** (whereas) **why do you go abroad ~ it's cheaper here?** warum fährst du ins Ausland, wo es doch hier billiger ist? ③ *pron.* **by/till ~ ...?;** bis wann ...?; **since ~ ...?** seit wann ...?

whence /wens/ *adv., conj.* (arch./literary) woher

whenever /wen'evə(r)/ ① *adv.* wann immer; **or ~:** oder wann immer; **~ did he do it?** (coll.) wann hat er es nur getan? ② *conj.* jedes Mal wenn

where /weə(r)/ ① *adv.* **(a)** (position) wo; **~ shall we sit?** wohin wollen wir uns setzen? **(b)** (to **~**) wohin ② *conj.* wo ③ *pron.* **near/not far from ~ it happened** nahe der Stelle/nicht weit von der Stelle, wo es passiert ist

whereabouts ① /weərə'baʊts/ *adv.* (where) wo; (to where) wohin ② /'weərəbaʊts/ *n., sing. or pl.* (of thing) Verbleib, *der;* (of person) Aufenthalt[sort], *der*

where: ~'as *conj.* während; **he is very quiet, ~as she is an extrovert** er ist sehr ruhig, sie dagegen ist eher extravertiert; **~'by** *adv.* mit dem/der/denen; **~upon** /weərə'pɒn/ *adv.* worauf

wherever /weər'evə(r)/ ① *adv.* **(a)** (position) wo immer; **sit ~ you like** setz dich, wohin du magst; **or ~:** oder wo immer **(b)** (direction) wohin immer; **or ~:** oder wohin immer **(c)** **~ have you been?** (coll.) wo hast du bloß gesteckt? ② *conj.* **(a)** (position) überall [da], wo; **~ possible** wo *od.* wenn [irgend] möglich **(b)** (direction) wohin auch; **~ he went** wohin er auch ging

wherewithal /'weəwɪðɔːl/ *n.* (coll.) **the ~:** das nötige Kleingeld (ugs.)

whet /wet/ *v.t.,* **-tt-: (a)** (sharpen) wetzen **(b)** (fig.) anregen ⟨*Appetit*⟩

whether /'weðə(r)/ *conj.* ob; **I don't know ~ to go [or not]** ich weiß nicht, ob ich gehen soll [oder nicht]

which /wɪtʃ/ ① *adj.* welch...; **~ one** welcher/welche/welches; **~ ones** welche; **~ way** (how) wie; (in **~** direction) wohin ② *pron.* **(a)** *interrog.* welcher/welche/welches; **~ of you?** wer von euch? **(b)** *rel.* der/die/das; **of ~:** dessen/deren; **after ~:** worauf[hin]

whichever /wɪtʃ'evə(r)/ ① *adj.* welcher/welche/welches ... auch ⋯⟶

W

2 *pron.* **(a)** welcher/welche/welches ... auch **(b)** (coll.) ~ could it be? welcher/welche/welches könnte das nur sein?

whiff /wɪf/ *n.* (puff; fig.: trace) Hauch, *der;* (smell) leichter Geruch

while /waɪl/ **1** *n.* Weile, *die;* [for] a ~: eine Weile; **a long** ~: lange; **for a little** *or* **short** ~: eine kleine Weile; [only] a little *or* short ~ ago [erst] kürzlich *od.* vor kurzem; **be worth sb.'s** ~: sich [für jmdn.] lohnen **2** *conj.* **(a)** während; (as long as) solange **(b)** (although) obgleich **(c)** (whereas) während

■ **while a'way** *v.t.* ~ away the time sich (*Dat.*) die Zeit vertreiben (**by, with** mit)

whilst /waɪlst/ (Brit.) ▶ WHILE 2

whim /wɪm/ *n.* Laune, *die*

whimper /'wɪmpə(r)/ **1** *n.* ~[s] Wimmern, *das;* (of dog etc.) Winseln, *das* **2** *v.i.* wimmern; ⟨Hund:⟩ winseln

whimsical /'wɪmzɪkl/ *adj.* launenhaft; (odd, fanciful) spleenig

whine /waɪn/ **1** *v.i.* **(a)** heulen; ⟨Hund:⟩ jaulen **(b)** (complain) jammern **2** *n.* **(a)** Heulen, *das;* (of dog) Jaulen, *das* **(b)** (complaint) ~[s] Gejammer, *das*

whip /wɪp/ **1** *n.* **(a)** Peitsche, *die* **(b)** (Brit. Parl.) Fraktionsgeschäftsführer, *der/* -führerin, *die* **2** *v.t.,* **-pp-: (a)** peitschen **(b)** (Cookery) schlagen **(c)** (move quickly) reißen **(d)** (coll.: steal) klauen (ugs.)

■ **whip 'out** *v.t.* [blitzschnell] herausziehen

■ **whip 'up** *v.t.* **(a)** (arouse) anheizen (ugs.) **(b)** (coll.: make quickly) schnell hinzaubern ⟨Gericht, Essen⟩

whiplash *n.* ~lash [injury] Peitschenschlagverletzung, *die*

whipped 'cream *n.* Schlagsahne, *die*

'whipping cream *n.* [flüssige] Schlagsahne

'whip-round *n.* (Brit. coll.) Sammlung, *die*

whirl /wɜːl/ **1** *v.t.* [im Kreis] herumwirbeln **2** *v.i.* wirbeln **3** *n.* **(a)** Wirbeln, *das;* she was *or* her thoughts were in a ~ (fig.) ihr schwirrte der Kopf **(b)** (bustle) Trubel, *der*

■ **whirl 'round** **1** *v.t.* [im Kreis] herumwirbeln **2** *v.i.* [im Kreis] herumwirbeln; ⟨Rad, Rotor:⟩ wirbeln

whirl: ~pool *n.* Strudel, *der;* (bathing pool) Whirlpool, *der;* **~wind** *n.* Wirbelwind, *der*

whirr /wɜː(r)/ **1** *v.i.* surren **2** *n.* Surren, *das*

whisk /wɪsk/ **1** *n.* (Cookery) Schneebesen, *der;* (part of mixer) Rührbesen, *der* **2** *v.t.* **(a)** (Cookery) [mit dem Schnee-/ Rührbesen] schlagen **(b)** (convey rapidly) in Windeseile bringen

■ **whisk a'way** *v.t.* **(a)** (remove suddenly) ~ **sth. away [from sb.]** [jmdm.] etw. [plötzlich] wegreißen **(b)** (convey rapidly) in Windeseile wegbringen

whisker /'wɪskə(r)/ *n.* **(a)** ~s (on man's cheek) Backenbart, *der* **(b)** (of cat, mouse, rat) Schnurrhaar, *das*

whiskey (Amer., Ir.)**, whisky** /'wɪskɪ/ *n.* Whisky, *der;* (American or Irish) Whiskey, *der*

whisper /'wɪspə(r)/ **1** *v.i.* flüstern; ~ **to sb.** jmdm. etwas zuflüstern **2** *v.t.* flüstern; ~ **sth. to sb.** jmdm. etw. zuflüstern **3** *n.* **(a)** Flüstern, *das;* in a ~, in ~s im Flüsterton **(b)** (rumour) Gerücht, *das*

whistle /'wɪsl/ **1** *v.i.* pfeifen; ~ **at sb.** (in disapproval) jmdn. auspfeifen **2** *v.t.* pfeifen **3** *n.* **(a)** (sound) Pfiff, *der;* (whistling) Pfeifen, *das* **(b)** (instrument) Pfeife, *die;* **blow a/one's** ~: pfeifen

whistling 'kettle *n.* Pfeifkessel, *der*

white /waɪt/ **1** *adj.* weiß **2** *n.* **(a)** (colour) Weiß, *das* **(b)** (of egg) Eiweiß, *das* **(c)** W~ (person) Weiße, *der/die*

white: ~ **bread** *n.* Weißbrot, *das;* ~ **cell** *n.* weißes Blutkörperchen; ~ **'coffee** *n.* (Brit.) Kaffee mit Milch; ~**'collar worker** *n.* Angestellte, *der/die;* ~ **corpuscle** ▶ ~ CELL; ~ **'elephant** ▶ ELEPHANT; **W~ House** *pr. n.* (Amer. Polit.) the W~ House das Weiße Haus; ~**-knuckle ride** *n.* Fahrt mit äußerstem Nervenkitzel; ~ **'lie** ▶ LIE[1] 1; ~ **'meat** *n.* weißes Fleisch [und Geflügel]

whiten /'waɪtn/ **1** *v.t.* weiß machen; weißen ⟨Wand, Schuhe⟩ **2** *v.i.* weiß werden

'whiteness *n.* Weiß, *das*

white: W~ 'Paper *n.* (Brit.) *öffentliches Diskussionspapier über Vorhaben der Regierung;* ~ **'sauce** *n.* weiße *od.* helle Soße; ~**wash** **1** *n.* [weiße] Tünche; (fig.) Schönfärberei, *die;* **2** *v.t.* [weiß] tünchen; ~ **'wedding** *n.* Hochzeit, *die* in Weiß; ~ **'wine** *n.* Weißwein, *der*

Whit 'Monday /wɪt/ *n.* Pfingstmontag, *der*

Whitsun /'wɪtsn/ *n.* Pfingsten, *das od. Pl.;* **at** ~: zu *od.* an Pfingsten

whittle /'wɪtl/**:** ~ **a'way** *v.t.* ~ away sb.'s rights/power jmdm. nach und nach alle Rechte/Macht nehmen; ~ **'down** *v.t.* allmählich reduzieren ⟨Anzahl, Gewinn⟩; verkürzen ⟨Liste⟩

whiz, whizz /wɪz/ **1** *v.i.* **-zz-** zischen **2** *n.* Zischen, *das*

'whiz[z]-kid *n.* (coll.) Senkrechtstarter, *der*

who /hʊ, *stressed* huː/ *pron.* **(a)** *interrog.* wer; (coll.: whom) wen; (coll.: to whom) wem **(b)** *rel.* der/die/das; *pl.* die; (coll.: whom) den/

die/das; (coll.: to whom) dem/der/denen;
anyone/those ∼ ...: wer ...; **everybody ∼ ...:**
jeder, der ...

whoa /wəʊ/ int. brr

who'd /hʊd, stressed huːd/ **(a)** = who had;
(b) = who would

whoever /huːˈevə(r)/ pron. **(a)** wer
[immer]
(b) (no matter who) wer ... auch
(c) (coll.) ∼ **could it be?** wer könnte das nur
sein?

whole /həʊl/ ① adj. ganz; **the ∼ lot** [of
them] [sie] alle
② n. Ganze, das; **the ∼:** das Ganze; **the ∼ of
my money/the village/London** mein ganzes
Geld/das ganze Dorf/ganz London; **as a ∼:**
als Ganzes; **on the ∼:** im Großen und
Ganzen

whole: ∼**food** n. Vollwertkost, die;
∼**hearted** /həʊlˈhɑːtɪd/ adj. herzlich
⟨Dank[barkeit]⟩; rückhaltlos
⟨Unterstützung⟩; ∼**meal** adj. Vollkorn-;
∼ **'milk** n. Vollmilch, die; ∼ **note** n.
(Amer. Mus.) ganze Note; ∼ **'number** n.
ganze Zahl; ∼**sale** ① adj. **(a)**
Großhandels-; **(b)** (fig.: on a large scale)
massenhaft; Massen-; ② adv. **(a)** en gros;
(b) (fig.: on a large scale) massenweise;
∼**saler** /ˈhəʊlseɪlə(r)/ n. Großhändler, der/
-händlerin, die

wholesome /ˈhəʊlsəm/ adj. gesund

who'll /hʊl, stressed huːl/ = who will

wholly /ˈhəʊllɪ/ adv. völlig

whom /huːm/ pron. **(a)** interrog. wen; as
indirect object wem
(b) rel. den/die/das; pl. die; as indirect object
dem/der/dem; pl. denen

whooping cough /ˈhuːpɪŋ kɒf/ n.
Keuchhusten, der

whopper /ˈwɒpə(r)/ n. (coll.) **(a)** Riese, der
(b) (lie) faustdicke Lüge

whopping /ˈwɒpɪŋ/ adj. riesig;
Riesen- (ugs.); faustdick ⟨Lüge⟩

whore /hɔː(r)/ n. Hure, die

who's /huːz/ **(a)** = who is
(b) = who has

whose /huːz/ pron. **(a)** interrog. wessen;
∼ [book] is that? wem gehört das [Buch]?
(b) rel. dessen/deren/dessen; pl. deren

who've /hʊv, stressed huːv/ = who have

why /waɪ/ ① adv. **(a)** (for what reason)
warum; (for what purpose) wozu; ∼ **is that?**
warum das?
(b) (on account of which) **the reason ∼ he did it**
der Grund, warum er es tat
② int. ∼, **certainly/of course!** aber sicher!

wick /wɪk/ n. Docht, der

wicked /ˈwɪkɪd/ adj. böse

'wickedness n. Bosheit, die

wicker /ˈwɪkə(r)/ n. Korbgeflecht, das;
attrib. Korb⟨waren, -stuhl⟩

'wickerwork n. **(a)** (material) Korbgeflecht,
das

(b) (articles) Korbwaren Pl.

wicket /ˈwɪkɪt/ n. (Cricket) Tor, das

'wicketkeeper n. (Cricket) Torwächter,
der/-wächterin, die

wide /waɪd/ ① adj. **(a)** (broad) breit; groß
⟨Abstand, Winkel⟩; **three feet ∼:** drei Fuß
breit
(b) (extensive) weit; umfassend ⟨Lektüre,
Wissen, Kenntnisse⟩; reichhaltig ⟨Auswahl,
Sortiment⟩
(c) (off target) **be ∼ of sth.** etw. verfehlen
② adv. **(a)** ∼ **awake** hellwach
(b) (off target) **shoot ∼:** danebenschießen; **go
∼:** das Ziel verfehlen

wide: ∼**angle 'lens** n. (Photog.)
Weitwinkelobjektiv, das; ∼**eyed** adj.
(surprised) mit großen Augen nachgestellt

'widely adv. **(a)** (over a wide area) weit
⟨verbreitet, gestreut⟩
(b) (by many people) weithin ⟨bekannt,
akzeptiert⟩; **a ∼ held view** eine weit
verbreitete Ansicht
(c) (greatly) erheblich ⟨sich unterscheiden⟩

widen /ˈwaɪdn/ ① v.t. verbreitern
② v.i. sich verbreitern

wide: ∼**open** attrib. adj., ∼ **'open** pred.
adj. weit geöffnet ⟨Fenster, Tür⟩; weit
aufgerissen ⟨Mund, Augen⟩; **be ∼ open**
⟨Fenster, Tür:⟩ weit offen stehen;
∼**ranging** /ˈwaɪdreɪndʒɪŋ/ adj. weit
gehend ⟨Maßnahme, Veränderung⟩;
ausführlich ⟨Diskussion, Gespräch⟩;
∼ **'screen** n. Breitwand, die; ∼**screen
television,** ∼**screen TV** ns.
Breitwandfernsehen, das; ∼**spread** adj.
weit verbreitet

widow /ˈwɪdəʊ/ n. Witwe, die

widowed /ˈwɪdəʊd/ adj. verwitwet

widower /ˈwɪdəʊə(r)/ n. Witwer, der

width /wɪdθ/ n. Breite, die; (of garment)
Weite, die

wield /wiːld/ v.t. schwingen; (fig.) ausüben
⟨Macht, Einfluss⟩

wife /waɪf/ n., pl. **wives** /waɪvz/ Frau, die

'wife battering n. Misshandlung, die der
[Ehe]frau

wig /wɪg/ n. Perücke, die

wiggle /ˈwɪgl/ (coll.) ① v.t. hin und her
bewegen
② v.i. wackeln

wild /waɪld/ ① adj. **(a)** wild lebend ⟨Tier⟩;
wild wachsend ⟨Pflanze⟩
(b) wild ⟨Landschaft⟩
(c) (unrestrained) wild ⟨Erregung⟩; **run ∼**
⟨Pferd, Hund:⟩ frei herumlaufen; ⟨Kind:⟩
herumtoben; **send or drive sb. ∼:** jmdn.
rasend vor Erregung machen
(d) (coll.: very keen) **be ∼ about sb./sth.** wild
auf jmdn./etw. sein
② n. **the ∼[s]** die Wildnis; **see an animal in
the ∼:** ein Tier in freier Wildbahn sehen

wild: ∼ '**boar** *n.* Wildschwein, *das;*
∼ **card** *n.* wilde Karte; ∼**cat** *n.* Wildkatze, *die*

wilderness /'wɪldənɪs/ *n.* Wildnis, *die;* (desert) Wüste, *die*

wild: ∼ '**goose chase** *n.* (fig.) aussichtslose Suche; ∼**life** *n.* die Tier- und Pflanzenwelt; ∼**life park/reserve/sanctuary** Naturpark, *der/*-reservat, *das/*-schutzgebiet, *das*

'**wildly** *adv.* wild; **be** ∼ **excited about sth.** über etw. (*Akk.*) ganz aus dem Häuschen sein (ugs.); ∼ **inaccurate** völlig ungenau

wilful /'wɪlfl/ *adj.,* **wilfully** /'wɪlfəlɪ/ *adv.*
(a) (deliberate[ly]) vorsätzlich
(b) (obstinate[ly]) starrsinnig

will¹ /wɪl/ *v. aux., only in: pres.* will, *neg.* (coll.) won't /wəʊnt/, *past* would /wʊd/, *neg.* (coll.) wouldn't /'wʊdnt/ He won't help me. W∼/Would you? Er will mir nicht helfen. Bist du bereit?; **the car won't start** das Auto springt nicht an; ∼/**would you pass the salt, please?** gibst du bitte mal das Salz rüber?/ würdest du bitte mal das Salz rübergeben?; ∼ **you be quiet!** willst du wohl ruhig sein!; **he** ∼ **sit there hour after hour** er pflegt dort stundenlang zu sitzen; **he '**∼ **insist on doing it** er besteht unbedingt darauf, es zu tun; ∼ **you have some more cake?** möchtest *od.* willst du noch etwas Kuchen?; **the box** ∼ **hold 5 lb. of tea** in die Kiste gehen 5 Pfund Tee; **tomorrow he** ∼ **be in Oxford** morgen ist er in Oxford; **I promise I won't do it again** ich verspreche, ich mach's nicht noch mal; **if he tried, he would succeed** wenn er es versuchen würde, würde er es schaffen; ∼ **you please tidy up** würdest du bitte aufräumen?

will² *n.* (a) (faculty) Wille, *der*
(b) (Law: testament) Testament, *das*
(c) (desire) **at** ∼: nach Belieben; ∼ **to live** Lebenswille, *der;* **against one's/sb.'s** ∼: gegen seinen/jmds. Willen

'**willing** *adj.* willig; **ready and** ∼: bereit; **be** ∼ **to do sth.** bereit sein, etw. zu tun

'**willingly** *adv.* (a) (with pleasure) gern[e]
(b) (voluntarily) freiwillig

'**willingness** *n.* Bereitschaft, *die*

willow /'wɪləʊ/ *n.* Weide, *die*

willowy /'wɪləʊɪ/ *adj.* gertenschlank

'**will power** *n.* Willenskraft, *die*

willy-nilly /wɪlɪ'nɪlɪ/ *adv.* wohl oder übel ‹etw. tun müssen›

wilt /wɪlt/ *v.i.* ‹Pflanze, Blumen:› welk werden, welken

wily /'waɪlɪ/ *adj.* listig; gewieft ‹Person›

wimp /wɪmp/ *n.* (coll.) Schlappschwanz, *der* (ugs.)

wimpish /'wɪmpɪʃ/ *adj.* (coll.) lahm (ugs.)

win /wɪn/ ① *v.t.,* **-nn-,** won /wʌn/ gewinnen; bekommen ‹Stipendium, Vertrag, Recht›; ∼ **sb. sth.** jmdm. etw. einbringen
② *v.i.,* **-nn-,** won gewinnen

③ *n.* Sieg, *der;* **have a** ∼: gewinnen
▪ **win 'over, win 'round** *v.t.* bekehren; (to one's side) auf seine Seite bringen; (convince) überzeugen
▪ **win 'through** *v.i.* Erfolg haben

wince /wɪns/ *v.i.* zusammenzucken (at bei)

winch /wɪntʃ/ ① *n.* Winde, *die*
② *v.t.* winden; ∼ **up** hochwinden

wind¹ /wɪnd/ ① *n.* Wind, *der;* (Med.) Blähungen *Pl.;* **get** ∼ **of sth.** (fig.) Wind von etw. bekommen; **be in the** ∼ (fig.) in der Luft liegen; **get/have the** ∼ **up** (coll.) Manschetten (ugs.) kriegen/haben
② *v.t.* **the blow** ∼ed **him** der Schlag nahm ihm den Atem

wind² /waɪnd/ ① *v.i.,* wound /waʊnd/ (a) (curve) sich winden; (move) sich schlängeln
(b) (coil) sich wickeln
② *v.t.,* wound (a) (coil) wickeln; ∼ **sth. on** [to] sth. etw. auf etw. (*Akk.*) [auf]wickeln
(b) aufziehen ‹Uhr›
▪ **wind 'down** *v.t.* (a) herunterdrehen ‹Autofenster›
(b) (fig.: reduce gradually) einschränken
▪ **wind 'up** ① *v.t.* (a) hochdrehen ‹Autofenster›
(b) (coil) aufwickeln
(c) aufziehen ‹Uhr›
(d) (coll.: annoy deliberately) auf die Palme bringen (ugs.)
(e) beschließen ‹Debatte›
(f) (Finance, Law) auflösen
② *v.i.* (a) (conclude) schließen
(b) (coll.: end up) ∼ **up in prison/hospital** [zum Schluss] im Gefängnis/Krankenhaus landen (ugs.)

wind /wɪnd/: ∼**-blown** *adj.* vom Wind zerzaust ‹Haar›; ∼**break** *n.* Windschutz, *der;* ∼**breaker** (Amer.), ∼**cheater** (Brit.) *ns.* Windjacke, *die;* ∼ **chill factor** *n.* Wind-chill-Index, *der*

winded /'wɪndɪd/ *adj.* **be** ∼: außer Atem sein

winder /'waɪndə(r)/ *n.* (of watch) Krone, *die;* (of clock, toy) Aufziehschraube, *die*

wind /wɪnd/: ∼**fall** *n.* (a) (fruit) ∼**falls** Fallobst, *das;* (b) (fig.) warmer Regen (ugs.); ∼**fall tax** (einmalige) Sondersteuer auf Privatisierungsgewinne; ∼ **farm** *n.* Windpark, *der;* ∼ **force** *n.* Windstärke, *die;* ∼ **instrument** *n.* Blasinstrument, *das;* ∼**mill** *n.* Windmühle, *die*

window /'wɪndəʊ/ *n.* (also Comp.) Fenster, *das;* (shop ∼) [Schau]fenster, *das;* **break a** ∼: eine Fensterscheibe zerbrechen

window: ∼ **box** *n.* Blumenkasten, *der;* ∼ **cleaner** *n.* Fensterputzer, *der/*-putzerin, *die;* ∼ **cleaning** *n.* Fensterputzen, *das;* ∼ **display** *n.* Schaufensterauslage, *die;* ∼ **dresser** *n.* Schaufensterdekorateur, *der/*-dekorateurin, *die;* ∼ **dressing** *n.* (fig.) Schönfärberei, *die;* ∼ **frame** *n.* Fensterrahmen, *der;* ∼ **ledge** *n.* (inside) Fensterbank, *die;* (outside) Fenstersims, *der*

od. das; ~ **pane** *n.* Fensterscheibe, *die;*
~ **shopping** *n.* Schaufensterbummeln,
das; go ~ shopping einen
Schaufensterbummel machen; ~ **sill** *n.*
(inside) Fensterbank, *die;* (outside)
Fenstersims, *der od. das*
wind /wɪnd/: ~**pipe** *n.* (Anat.) Luftröhre,
die; ~ **power** *n.* Windkraft, *die;* ~**proof**
adj. windabweisend; ~**proof jacket**
Windjacke, *die;* ~**screen,** (Amer.)
~**shield** *ns.* Windschutzscheibe, *die;*
~screen/~shield wiper Scheibenwischer,
der; ~screen/~shield washer
Scheibenwaschanlage, *die;* ~**surfer** *n.*
Windsurfer, *der;* ~**surfing** *n.* Windsurfen,
das; ~**swept** *adj.* windgepeitscht; vom
Wind zerzaust ⟨*Person, Haare*⟩; ~ **tunnel**
n. Windkanal, *der*
windward /'wɪndwəd/ *adj.* ~ side
Windseite, *die*
'**windy** *adj.* windig
wine /waɪn/ *n.* Wein, *der*
wine: ~ **bar** *n.* Weinstube, *die;* ~ **bottle**
n. Weinflasche, *die;* ~ **cellar** *n.*
[Wein]keller, *das;* ~ **cooler** *n.*
Weinkühler, *der;* ~**glass** *n.* Weinglas, *das;*
~**grower** *n.* Winzer, *der*/Winzerin, *die;*
~**growing** ①*n.* Weinbau, *der;* ②*adj.*
~-growing area Weingegend, *die;* ~ **list** *n.*
Weinkarte, *die;* ~ **merchant** *n.*
Weinhändler, *der*/-händlerin, *die;*
~ merchants (business) Weinhandlung, *die;*
~ **tasting** /'waɪnteɪstɪŋ/ *n.* Weinprobe,
die; ~ **vault** *n.* Weinkeller, *der;*
~ '**vinegar** *n.* Weinessig, *der*
wing /wɪŋ/ *n.* (a) (Ornith., Archit., Sport) Flügel,
der
(b) (Aeronaut.) Tragfläche, *die*
(c) (Brit. Motor. Veh.) Kotflügel, *der*
winged /wɪŋd/ *adj.* geflügelt
winger /'wɪŋə(r)/ *n.* (Sport) Außenstürmer,
der/-stürmerin, *die*
wing: ~ **mirror** *n.* (Brit. Motor Veh.)
Außenspiegel, *der;* ~**span** *n.*
[Flügel]spannweite, *die;* ~ **tip** *n.*
Flügelspitze, *die*
wink /wɪŋk/ ①*v.i.* (a) blinzeln; (as signal)
zwinkern; ~ at sb. jmdm. zuzwinkern
(b) (flash) blinken
②*n.* (a) Blinzeln, *das;* (signal) Zwinkern,
das; give sb. a ~: jmdm. zuzwinkern
(b) not sleep a ~: kein Auge zutun
'**winner** *n.* Sieger, *der*/Siegerin, *die;* (of
competition or prize) Gewinner, *der*/
Gewinnerin, *die*
'**winning** *adj.* (a) *attrib.* siegreich;
~ number Gewinnzahl, *die*
(b) (charming) einnehmend; gewinnend
⟨*Lächeln*⟩
'**winning post** *n.* Zielpfosten, *der*
'**winnings** *n. pl.* Gewinn, *der*
winter /'wɪntə(r)/ *n.* Winter, *der;* in [the] ~:
im Winter
winter 'sports *n. pl.* Wintersport, *der*

wintry /'wɪntrɪ/ *adj.* winterlich; ~ shower
Schneegestöber, *das*
wipe /waɪp/ ①*v.t.* (a) abwischen;
[auf]wischen ⟨*Fußboden*⟩; (dry) abtrocknen;
~ one's mouth/eyes/nose sich (*Dat.*) den
Mund/die Tränen/die Nase abwischen;
~ one's feet/shoes [sich (*Dat.*)] die Füße/
Schuhe abtreten
(b) (get rid of) [ab]wischen; ~ one's/sb.'s
tears sich/jmdm. die Tränen abwischen
②*n.* give sth. a ~: etw. abwischen
■ **wipe 'down** *v.t.* abwischen
■ **wipe 'off** *v.t.* (a) (remove) wegwischen;
löschen ⟨*Bandaufnahme*⟩
(b) (pay off) zurückzahlen ⟨*Schulden*⟩
■ **wipe 'out** *v.t.* (a) (remove) wegwischen;
(erase) auslöschen
(b) (cancel) tilgen; zunichte machen ⟨*Vorteil,
Gewinn usw.*⟩
(c) (destroy) ausrotten ⟨*Rasse, Tierart,
Feinde*⟩; ausmerzen ⟨*Seuche, Korruption*⟩
■ **wipe 'up** *v.t.* (a) aufwischen
(b) (dry) abtrocknen
'**wiper** *n.* (Motor Veh.) Wischer, *der*
wire /'waɪə(r)/ ①*n.* (a) Draht, *der*
(b) (Electr., Teleph.) Leitung, *die*
(c) (coll.: telegram) Telegramm, *das*
②*v.t.* (a) (fasten) ~ sth. together etw. mit
Draht verbinden
(b) (Electr.) ~ sth. to sth. etw. an etw. (*Akk.*)
anschließen; ~ a house in einem Haus die
Stromleitungen legen
wire: ~ '**brush** *n.* Drahtbürste, *die;*
~ **cutters** *n. pl.* Drahtschneider, *der*
'**wireless** ① *adj.* (Comp.) drahtlos
② *n.* (Brit. dated) Radio, *das*
wire: ~ '**netting** *n.* Maschendraht, *der;*
~ '**strippers** *n. pl.* Abisolierzange, *die;*
~ '**wool** *n.* Stahlwolle, *die*
wiring /'waɪərɪŋ/ *n.* [elektrische] Leitungen
Pl.
wisdom /'wɪzdəm/ *n.* (a) Weisheit, *die*
(b) (prudence) Klugheit, *die*
'**wisdom tooth** *n.* Weisheitszahn, *der*
wise /waɪz/ *adj.* (a) weise; vernünftig
⟨*Meinung*⟩
(b) (prudent) klug
(c) be none the ~r kein bisschen klüger als
vorher sein
wise: ~**crack** (coll.) *n.* witzige
Bemerkung; ~ **guy** *n.* (coll.) Klugscheißer,
der (salopp)
'**wisely** *adv.* weise; (prudently) klug
wish /wɪʃ/ ①*v.t.* wünschen; I ~ I was or
were rich ich wollte, ich wäre reich; I ~ to
go ich möchte gehen; ~ sb. luck/success
etc. jmdm. Glück/Erfolg *usw.* wünschen;
~ sb. well jmdm. alles Gute wünschen
②*v.i.* wünschen; ~ for sth. sich (*Dat.*) etw.
wünschen
③*n.* Wunsch, *der;* make a ~: sich (*Dat.*)
etwas wünschen; get *or* have one's ~:
seinen Wunsch erfüllt bekommen

W

wishful thinking /ˈwɪʃfl ˈθɪŋkɪŋ/ n. Wunschdenken, *das*

'wishing well n. Wunschbrunnen, *der*

wishy-washy /ˈwɪʃɪwɒʃɪ/ adj. labberig (ugs.); (fig.) lasch

wisp /wɪsp/ n. (of straw) Büschel, *das;* ~ of hair Haarsträhne, *die;* ~ of cloud/smoke Wolkenfetzen, *der*/Rauchfahne, *die*

wistful /ˈwɪstfl/ adj., wehmütig

wit /wɪt/ n. **(a)** (humour) Witz, *der* **(b)** (intelligence) Geist, *der;* be at one's ~'s *or* ~s' end sich (*Dat.*) keinen Rat mehr wissen; be frightened *or* scared out of one's ~s Todesangst haben; have/keep one's ~s about one auf Draht (ugs.) sein/nicht den Kopf verlieren **(c)** (person) geistreicher Mensch

witch /wɪtʃ/ n. Hexe, *die*

witch: ~**craft** n. Hexerei, *die;* ~ **doctor** n. Medizinmann, *der;* ~**-hunt** n. Hexenjagd, *die* (**for** auf + *Akk.*)

with /wɪð/ prep. mit; **put sth.** ~ **sth.** etw. zu etw. stellen/legen; **have nothing to write** ~: nichts zum Schreiben haben; **I'm not '**~ **you** (coll.) ich komme nicht mit; **tremble** ~ **fear** vor Angst zittern; **I have no money** ~ **me** ich habe kein Geld dabei *od.* bei mir; **sleep** ~ **the window open** bei offenem Fenster schlafen

with'draw ①️ v.t., *forms as* DRAW 1: zurückziehen; abziehen ⟨*Truppen*⟩; ~ **sth. from an account** etw. von einem Konto abheben ②️ v.i., *forms as* DRAW 1: sich zurückziehen

withdrawal /wɪðˈdrɔːəl/ n. **(a)** Zurücknahme, *die;* (of troops) Abzug, *der;* (of money) Abhebung, *die* **(b)** (from drugs) Entzug, *der;* ~ **symptoms** Entzugserscheinungen *Pl.*

with'drawn adj. (unsociable) verschlossen

wither /ˈwɪðə(r)/ ①️ v.t. verdorren lassen ②️ v.i. [ver]welken

◼ **wither a'way** v.i. dahinwelken (geh.)

withered /ˈwɪðəd/ adj. verwelkt ⟨*Gras, Pflanze*⟩; verkrüppelt ⟨*Gliedmaße*⟩

withering /ˈwɪðərɪŋ/ adj. vernichtend ⟨*Blick*⟩

with'hold v.t., *forms as* HOLD²: ~ **sth. from sb.** jmdm. etw. vorenthalten

within /wɪˈðɪn/ prep. innerhalb; **stay/be** ~ **the law** im Boden des Gesetzes nicht verlassen; ~ **eight miles of sth.** acht Meilen im Umkreis von etw.

without /wɪˈðaʊt/ prep. ohne; ~ **doing sth.** ohne etw. zu tun; ~ **his knowing** ohne dass er davon weiß/wusste

with'stand v.t., withstood /wɪθˈstʊd/ standhalten (+ *Dat.*); aushalten ⟨*Beanspruchung, hohe Temperaturen*⟩

witness /ˈwɪtnɪs/ ①️ n. Zeuge, *der*/Zeugin, *die* (**of, to** *Gen.*) ②️ v.t. **(a)** (see) ~ **sth.** Zeuge/Zeugin einer Sache (*Gen.*) sein

(b) bestätigen ⟨*Unterschrift*⟩

'witness box (Brit.), **'witness stand** (Amer.) ns. Zeugenstand, *der*

witticism /ˈwɪtɪsɪzm/ n. Witzelei, *die*

wittingly /ˈwɪtɪŋlɪ/ adv. wissentlich

witty /ˈwɪtɪ/ adj. witzig; geistreich ⟨*Person*⟩

wives pl. of WIFE

wizard /ˈwɪzəd/ n. Zauberer, *der*

wizardry /ˈwɪzədrɪ/ n. Zauberei, *die*

wizened /ˈwɪzənd/ adj. runz[e]lig

WMD abbr. = **weapon of mass destruction** MVW

wobble /ˈwɒbl/ v.i. wackeln

wobbly /ˈwɒblɪ/ adj. wack[e]lig

woe /wəʊ/ n. (arch./literary/joc.) ~[s] Jammer, *der;* ~ **betide you!** wehe dir!

woebegone /ˈwəʊbɪgɒn/ adj. jammervoll

woeful /ˈwəʊfl/ adj. (deplorable) beklagenswert; (distressed) jammervoll

wok /wɒk/ n. (Cookery) Wok, *der*

woke, woken ▶ WAKE¹ 1, 2

wolf /wʊlf/ ①️ n., pl. wolves /wʊlvz/ Wolf, *der* ②️ v.t. ~ [**down**] verschlingen

woman /ˈwʊmən/ n., pl. **women** /ˈwɪmɪn/ Frau, *die;* ~ **doctor** Ärztin, *die;* ~ **friend** Freundin, *die*

womanize /ˈwʊmənaɪz/ v.i. den Frauen nachstellen

womanizer /ˈwʊmənaɪzə(r)/ n. Schürzenjäger, *der*

'womanly adj. fraulich

womb /wuːm/ n. Gebärmutter, *die*

women pl. of WOMAN

women: ~**folk** n. pl. Frauen *Pl.;* **W**~**'s 'Lib** (coll.)**, W**~**'s Libe'ration** ns. die Frauenbewegung; ~**'s movement** n. Frauenbewegung, *die;* ~**'s 'prison** n. Frauengefängnis, *das;* ~**'s 'refuge** n. Frauenhaus, *das;* ~**'s 'rights** n. pl. die Rechte der Frau

won ▶ WIN 1, 2

wonder /ˈwʌndə(r)/ ①️ n. **(a)** (thing) Wunder, *das* **(b)** (feeling) Staunen, *das* ②️ adj. Wunder- ③️ v.i. sich wundern; staunen (**at** über + *Akk.*) ④️ v.t. sich fragen; **I** ~ **what the time is** wie viel Uhr mag es wohl sein?; **I** ~ **whether I might open the window** dürfte ich vielleicht das Fenster öffnen?

wonderful /ˈwʌndəfl/ adj., **wonderfully** /ˈwʌndəfəlɪ/ adv. wunderbar

wondering /ˈwʌndərɪŋ/ adj., **wonderingly** /ˈwʌndərɪŋlɪ/ adv. staunend

won't /wəʊnt/ (coll.) = will not; ▶ WILL¹

woo /wuː/ v.t. **(a)** (literary: court) ~ **sb.** um jmdn. werben (geh.) **(b)** umwerben ⟨*Kunden, Wähler*⟩

wood /wʊd/ n. **(a)** Holz, *das;* **touch** ~ (Brit.), **knock on** ~ (Amer.) unberufen!

(b) (trees) Wald, *der*
wood: ∼ carving *n.* (object)
Holzschnitzerei, *die;* ∼**craft** *n.* (∼work)
Holzschnitzerei, *die;* ∼**cut** *n.* Holzschnitt,
der; ∼**cutter** *n.* Holzfäller, *der*
'**wooded** *adj.* bewaldet
wooden /'wʊdn/ *adj.* **(a)** hölzern; Holz-
(b) (fig.: stiff) hölzern
wood: ∼land /'wʊdlənd/ *n.* Waldland, *das;*
∼**pecker** *n.* Specht, *der;* ∼ **pigeon** *n.*
Ringeltaube, *die;* ∼**wind** *n.* the ∼wind [section] die
Holzbläser *Pl.;* ∼**wind instrument**
Holzblasinstrument, *das;* ∼**work** *n.* **(a)**
(craft) Arbeiten mit Holz; **(b)** (things)
Holzarbeit[en *Pl.*]; ∼**worm** *n.* Holzwurm,
der; **it's got** ∼**worm** da ist der Holzwurm
drin (ugs.)
'**woody** *adj.* **(a)** (wooded) waldreich
(b) (consisting of wood) holzig
wool /wʊl/ *n.* Wolle, *die; attrib.* Woll-
woollen (*Amer.:* **woolen**) /'wʊlən/
[1] *adj.* wollen
[2] *n.* ∼s Wollsachen *Pl.*
'**woolly** *adj.* **(a)** wollig, Woll⟨pullover,
-mütze⟩
(b) (confused) verschwommen
woozy /'wuːzɪ/ *adj.* (coll.) **(a)** (dizzy) duselig
(ugs.)
(b) (drunk) angeduselt (salopp)
word /wɜːd/ [1] *n.* Wort, *das;* ∼s (of song or
actor) Text, *der;* **in other** ∼s mit anderen
Worten; ∼ **for** ∼: Wort für Wort; **too funny**
etc. **for** ∼s unsagbar komisch *usw.;* **have** ∼s
einen Wortwechsel haben; **have a** ∼ **[with**
sb.] about sth. [mit jmdm.] über etw. (*Akk.*)
sprechen; **could I have a** ∼ **[with you]?** kann
ich dich mal sprechen?; **say a few** ∼s ein
paar Worte sprechen; **keep/break one's** ∼:
sein Wort halten/brechen; **by** ∼ **of mouth**
durch mündliche Mitteilung; **send** ∼ **that**
…: Nachricht geben, dass …
[2] *v.t.* formulieren
'**wording** *n.* Formulierung, *die*
word: ∼ order *n.* Wortstellung, *die;*
∼**play** *n.* Wortspiel, *das;* ∼ **processing**
n. Textverarbeitung, *die;* ∼ **processor** *n.*
Textverarbeitungssystem, *das*
wordy /'wɜːdɪ/ *adj.* weitschweifig
wore ▶ WEAR 2, 3
work /wɜːk/ [1] *n.* **(a)** Arbeit, *die;* **at** ∼
(engaged in ∼ing) bei der Arbeit; (fig.: operating)
am Werk; (at job) auf der Arbeit; **out of** ∼:
arbeitslos; **be in** ∼: eine Stelle haben; **set to**
∼ ⟨*Person:*⟩ sich an die Arbeit machen; **go**
out to ∼: arbeiten gehen
(b) ∼s *sing. or pl.* (factory) Werk, *das*
(c) ∼s *pl.* (∼ing parts) Werk, *das;* (operations)
Arbeiten *Pl.*
(d) (thing made or achieved) Werk, *das;* **a** ∼ **of**
art/literature ein Kunstwerk/literarisches
Werk
[2] *v.i.* **(a)** arbeiten

(c) (function effectively) funktionieren; **make the**
television ∼: den Fernsehapparat in
Ordnung bringen
(c) (have an effect) wirken (**on** auf + *Akk.*)
(d) ∼ **loose** sich lockern
[3] *v.t.* **(a)** bedienen ⟨*Maschine*⟩; betätigen
⟨*Bremse*⟩
(b) (get labour from) arbeiten lassen
(c) ausbeuten ⟨Steinbruch, Grube⟩
(d) (cause to go gradually) führen; ∼ **one's way**
up/into sth. sich hocharbeiten/in etw.
hineinarbeiten
■ **work 'off** *v.t.* **(a)** (get rid of) loswerden;
abreagieren ⟨Wut⟩
(b) abarbeiten ⟨Schuld⟩
■ '**work on** *v.t.* **(a)** ∼ **on sth.** an etw. (*Dat.*)
arbeiten
(b) (try to persuade) ∼ **on sb.** jmdn. bearbeiten
(ugs.)
■ **work 'out** [1] *v.t.* **(a)** (calculate)
ausrechnen
(b) (solve) lösen
(c) (devise) ausarbeiten
[2] *v.i.* **(a)** sth. ∼s out at £2 etw. ergibt
2 Pfund
(b) (have result) laufen; **things** ∼**ed out [well]**
in the end es ist schließlich doch alles gut
gegangen
■ **work 'up** [1] *v.t.* (excite) aufpeitschen
⟨*Menge*⟩; **get** ∼**ed up** sich aufregen
[2] *v.i.* ∼ **up to sth.** ⟨*Musik:*⟩ sich zu etw.
steigern; ⟨Geschichte, Film:⟩ auf etw. (*Akk.*)
zusteuern
workable /'wɜːkəbl/ *adj.* (feasible)
durchführbar
workaholic /wɜːkə'hɒlɪk/ *n.* (coll.)
arbeitswütiger Mensch
work: ∼bench *n.* Werkbank, *die;* ∼**day**
n. Werktag, *der*
'**worker** *n.* Arbeiter, *der*/Arbeiterin, *die*
'**worker bee** *n.* Arbeiterbiene, *die*
work: ∼ ethic *n.* Arbeitsethos, *das;*
∼ **experience** *n.* (for schoolchildren)
Praktikum, *das;* ∼**force** *n.* Belegschaft,
die;
'**working** *adj.* **(a)** (in work) werktätig
(b) ∼ **model** funktionsfähiges Modell
working: ∼ 'capital *n.* Betriebskapital,
das; ∼ '**class** *n.* Arbeiterklasse, *die;*
∼**-class** *adj.* der Arbeiterklasse
nachgestellt; **sb. is** ∼**-class** jmd. gehört zur
Arbeiterklasse; ∼ **clothes** *n. pl.*
Arbeitskleidung, *die;* ∼ '**day** *n.* **(a)** (portion
of day) Arbeitstag, *der;* **(b)** (day when work is
done) Werktag, *der;* ∼ '**hours** *n. pl.*
Arbeitszeit, *die;* ∼ '**knowledge** *n.*
ausreichende Kenntnisse (**of** in + *Dat.*);
∼ '**mother** *n.* berufstätige Mutter;
∼ '**order** *n.* **be in [good]** ∼ **order**
betriebsbereit sein; ⟨*Auto:*⟩ fahrbereit sein;
∼**-'over** *n.* (sl.) Abreibung, *die* (ugs.);
∼ '**week** *n.* Arbeitswoche, *die;* **a 35-hour**
∼ **week** eine 35-Stunden-Woche; ∼ '**wife** *n.*
berufstätige Ehefrau
work: ∼load *n.* Arbeitslast, *die;* ∼**man** ····⟩

W

/'wɜːkmən/ *n., pl.* ∼men /'wɜːkmən/ Arbeiter, *der;* ∼**manship** /'wɜːkmənʃɪp/ *n.* (quality) Kunstfertigkeit, *die;* ∼**out** *n.* [Fitness]training, *das;* ∼ **permit** *n.* Arbeitserlaubnis, *die;* ∼**sheet** *n.* (a) (recording work done) Arbeitszettel, *der;* (b) (for student) Formular mit Prüfungsfragen; ∼**shop** *n.* (a) (room) Werkstatt, *die;* (b) (building) Werk, *das;* ∼**station** *n.* (Comp.) Workstation, *die;* ∼ **table** *n.* Arbeitstisch, *der;* ∼**-to-'rule** *n.* Dienst nach Vorschrift

world /wɜːld/ *n.* (a) Welt, *die;* in the ∼: auf der Welt; the tallest building in the ∼: das höchste Gebäude der Welt; all over the ∼: in *od.* auf der ganzen Welt
(b) (vast amount) it will do him a *or* the ∼ of good es wird ihm unendlich gut tun; a ∼ of difference ein weltweiter Unterschied

world: W∼ **'Bank** *n.* Weltbank, *die;* ∼ **'champion** *n.* Weltmeister, *der/* -meisterin, *die;* **W**∼ **'Cup** *n.* Worldcup, *der;* ∼**-famous** *adj.* weltberühmt; **W**∼ **'Heritage Site** *n.* Welterbestätte, *die*

'worldly *adj.* weltlich; weltlich eingestellt ⟨Person⟩

worldly 'wise *adj.* weltklug

world: ∼ **'music** *n.* Weltmusik, *die;* ∼ **'power** *n.* Weltmacht, *die;* ∼ **'record** *n.* Weltrekord, *der;* ∼**-record holder** Weltrekordhalter, *der/*-halterin, *die;* ∼**-shaking** *adj.* welterschütternd; **World 'Trade Organization** *n.* Welthandelsorganisation, *die;* ∼ **view** *n.* Weltsicht, *die;* ∼ **'war** *n.* Weltkrieg, *der;* the First/Second **W**∼ War, **W**∼ War **I/II** der Erste/Zweite Weltkrieg; der 1./2. Weltkrieg; ∼**wide** /'--/ *adj.* weltweit *nicht präd.;* **W**∼ **Wide 'Web** *n.* (Comp.) World Wide Web, *das*

worm /wɜːm/ **1** *n.* Wurm, *der* **2** *v.t.* ∼ oneself into sb.'s favour sich in jmds. Gunst (*Akk.*) schleichen

worn ▶ WEAR 2, 3

'worn-out *adj.* (a) abgetragen ⟨Kleidungsstück⟩; abgenutzt ⟨Teppich⟩
(b) erschöpft ⟨Person⟩

worried /'wʌrɪd/ *adj.* besorgt

worry /'wʌrɪ/ **1** *v.t.* (a) beunruhigen
(b) (bother) stören
2 *v.i.* sich (*Dat.*) Sorgen machen
3 *n.* Sorge, *die;* **sth. is the least of sb.'s worries** etw. ist jmds. geringste Sorge

'worrying *adj.* (a) (causing worry) beunruhigend
(b) (full of worry) sorgenvoll ⟨Zeit, Woche⟩

worse /wɜːs/ **1** *adj.* schlechter; schlimmer ⟨Schmerz, Krankheit, Benehmen⟩
2 *adv.* schlechter; schlimmer; schlechter ⟨sich benehmen⟩
3 *n.* Schlimmeres

worsen /'wɜːsn/ **1** *v.t.* verschlechtern
2 *v.i.* sich verschlechtern

worship /'wɜːʃɪp/ **1** *v.t.,* (Brit.) -pp-: (a) anbeten

(b) (idolize) abgöttisch verehren
2 *v.i.* (Brit.) -pp- am Gottesdienst teilnehmen
3 *n.* (a) Anbetung, *die;* (service) Gottesdienst, *der*
(b) Your/His **W**∼: ≈ Euer/seine Ehren

'worshipper (*Amer.:* **worshiper**) *n.* Gottesdienstbesucher, *der/*-besucherin, *die*

worst /wɜːst/ **1** *adj.* schlechtest...; schlimmst... ⟨Schmerz, Krankheit, Benehmen⟩
2 *adv.* am schlechtesten/schlimmsten
3 *n.* (a) the ∼: der/die/das Schlimmste; get *or* have the ∼ of it (suffer the most) am meisten zu leiden haben; if the ∼ comes to the ∼: wenn es zum Schlimmsten kommt
(b) (poorest in quality) Schlechteste, *der/die/das*

worsted /'wʊstɪd/ *n.* Kammgarn, *das*

worth /wɜːθ/ **1** *adj.* wert; it's ∼ £80 es ist 80 Pfund wert; is it ∼ hearing/the effort? ist es hörenswert/der Mühe wert?; is it ∼ doing? lohnt es sich?; it isn't ∼ it es lohnt sich nicht
2 *n.* Wert, *der;* ten pounds' ∼ of petrol Benzin für zehn Pfund

'worthless *adj.* (a) (valueless) wertlos
(b) (having bad qualities) nichtswürdig

'worthwhile *adj.* lohnend

worthy /'wɜːðɪ/ *adj.* würdig

wouldn't /'wʊdnt/ (coll.) = would not;
▶ WILL[1]

wound[1] /wuːnd/ **1** *n.* Wunde, *die*
2 *v.t.* verwunden; (fig.) verletzen

wound[2] ▶ WIND[2]

wove, woven ▶ WEAVE[1] 2

wrangle /'ræŋgl/ **1** *v.i.* [sich] streiten
2 *n.* Streit, *der*

wrap /ræp/ **1** *v.t.,* -pp- einwickeln; (fig.) hüllen; ∼ped abgepackt ⟨Brot usw.⟩; ∼ sth. [a]round sth. etw. um etw. wickeln
2 *n.* Umschlag[e]tuch, *das*
■ **wrap 'up** *v.t.* (a) einwickeln
(b) (conclude) abschließen
(c) be ∼ped up in one's work in seine Arbeit völlig versunken sein

'wrapper *n.* (a) sweet/toffee ∼[s] Bonbonpapier, *das*
(b) (of book) Schutzumschlag, *der*

'wrapping *n.* Verpackung, *die*

'wrapping paper *n.* (strong) Packpapier, *das;* (decorative) Geschenkpapier, *das*

wrath /rɒθ/ *n.* Zorn, *der*

wreak /riːk/ *v.t.* (a) (cause) anrichten
(b) ∼ vengeance on sb. an jmdm. Rache nehmen

wreath /riːθ/ *n., pl.* **wreaths** /riːðz, riːθs/ Kranz, *der*

wreck /rek/ **1** *n.* (a) Wrack, *das*
(b) (destruction of ship) Schiffbruch, *der*
2 *v.t.* (a) (destroy) ruinieren; zu Schrott fahren ⟨Auto⟩; be ∼ed (shipwrecked) Schiffbruch erleiden
(b) (fig.: ruin) zerstören; ruinieren ⟨Gesundheit, Urlaub⟩

wreckage /'rekɪdʒ/ n. Wrackteile Pl.; (fig.) Trümmer Pl.

wren n. Zaunkönig, der

wrench /rentʃ/ 1 n. (a) (esp. Amer.: spanner) Schraubenschlüssel, der (b) (violent twist) Verrenkung, die (c) (fig.) **be a great ∼ [for sb.]** sehr schmerzhaft für jmdn. sein 2 v.t. (a) reißen; **∼ sth. from sb.** jmdm. etw. entreißen (b) **∼ one's ankle** sich (Dat.) den Knöchel verrenken

wrest /rest/ v.t. **∼ sth. from sb.** jmdm. etw. entreißen

wrestle /'resl/ v.i. ringen

wrestler /'reslə(r)/ n. Ringer, der/ Ringerin, die

wrestling /'reslɪŋ/ n. Ringen, das

wretch /retʃ/ n. Kreatur, die

wretched /'retʃɪd/ adj. (a) (miserable) unglücklich (b) (coll.: damned) elend (c) (very bad) erbärmlich

wriggle /'rɪgl/ 1 v.i. (a) sich winden; ⟨Fisch:⟩ zappeln (b) (move) sich schlängeln 2 v.t. **∼ one's way** sich schlängeln 3 n. Windung, die

wring /rɪŋ/ v.t., wrung /rʌŋ/ (a) wringen; **∼ out** auswringen (b) **∼ sb.'s hand** jmdm. fest die Hand drücken; **∼ the neck of an animal** einem Tier den Hals umdrehen (c) **∼ sth. from or out of sb.** (fig.) jmdm. etw. abpressen

wringing 'wet adj. tropfnass

wrinkle /'rɪŋkl/ 1 n. Falte, die; (in paper) Knick, der 2 v.t. falten 3 v.i. sich in Falten legen

wrinkled /'rɪŋkld/ adj. runz[e]lig

wrinkly /'rɪŋklɪ/ 1 adj. runz[e]lig 2 n. (coll.) Grufti, der (ugs.)

wrist /rɪst/ n. Handgelenk, das

'wristwatch n. Armbanduhr, die

writ /rɪt/ n. (Law) Verfügung, die

write /raɪt/ 1 v.i., wrote /rəʊt/, written /'rɪtn/ schreiben; **∼ to sb./a firm** jmdm./an eine Firma schreiben 2 v.t., wrote, written schreiben; ausschreiben ⟨Scheck:⟩; **the written language** die Schriftsprache; **written applications** schriftliche Anträge Pl.

■ **write 'back** v.i. zurückschreiben

■ **write 'down** v.t. aufschreiben

■ **write 'off** 1 v.t. (a) abschreiben ⟨Schulden, Verlust⟩ (b) (destroy) zu Schrott fahren 2 v.i. **∼ off for sth.** etw. [schriftlich] anfordern

'write-off n. Totalschaden, der

write-pro'tect v.t. (Comp.) shreibschützen; mit einem Shreibschutz versehen

writer /'raɪtə(r)/ n. Schriftsteller, der/ Schriftstellerin, die; (of letter, article) Verfasser, der/Verfasserin, die

'write-up n. (by critic) Kritik, die

writhe /raɪð/ v.i. sich winden

writing /'raɪtɪŋ/ n. (a) Schreiben, das; **put sth. in ∼:** etw. schriftlich machen (ugs.) (b) (handwriting, something written) Schrift, die

'writing paper n. Schreibpapier, das

written ▶ WRITE

wrong /rɒŋ/ 1 adj. (a) (morally bad) unrecht (geh.); (unfair) ungerecht (b) (mistaken) falsch; **be ∼** ⟨Person:⟩ sich irren; **the clock is ∼:** die Uhr geht falsch (c) (not suitable) falsch; **give the ∼ answer** eine falsche Antwort geben; **[the] ∼ way round** verkehrt herum (d) (out of order) nicht in Ordnung; **what's ∼?** was ist los? 2 adv. falsch 3 n. Unrecht, das; **do ∼:** Unrecht tun 4 v.t. **∼ sb.** jmdn. ungerecht behandeln

'wrongdoer n. Übeltäter, der/-täterin, die; Missetäter, der/-täterin, die (geh.)

'wrongdoing n. no indef. art. Missetaten Pl. (geh.)

wrongful /'rɒŋfl/ adj. (a) (unfair) unrecht (geh.) (b) (unlawful) rechtswidrig

'wrongfully adv. (a) (unfairly) unrecht (geh.) ⟨handeln⟩; zu Unrecht ⟨beschuldigen⟩ (b) (unlawfully) rechtswidrig

'wrongly adv. (a) falsch (b) (mistakenly) zu Unrecht (c) ▶ WRONGFULLY A

wrote ▶ WRITE

wrought iron /rɔːt 'aɪən/ n. Schmiedeeisen, das; attrib. schmiedeeisern

wrung ▶ WRING

wry /raɪ/ adj., **∼er** or wrier /'raɪə(r)/, **∼est** or wriest /'raɪɪst/ ironisch ⟨Blick⟩; fein ⟨Humor, Witz⟩

WTO abbr. = WORLD TRADE ORGANISATION

WWW abbr. = **World Wide Web** WWW

W

Xx

X, x /eks/ *n.* X, x, *das*
xenophobia /zenə'fəʊbɪə/ *n.*
Fremdenfeindlichkeit, *die*
xenophobic /zenə'fəʊbɪk/ *adj.*
fremdenfeindlich
Xerox ®, **xerox** /'zɪərɒks/ ① *n.* (copy)
Xerokopie, *die*

② **xerox** *v.t.* xerokopieren

Xmas /'krɪsməs, 'eksməs/ *n.* (coll.)
Weihnachten, *das*

'X-ray ① *n.* (picture) Röntgenaufnahme, *die*
② *v.t.* röntgen; durchleuchten ‹*Gepäck*›

Yy

Y, y /waɪ/ *n.* Y, y, *das*
yacht /jɒt/ *n.* (a) (for racing) Segeljacht, *die*
(b) (for pleasure) Jacht, *die*
'yachting *n.* Segeln, *das*
yachtsman /'jɒtsmən/ *n., pl.* **yachtsmen**
/'jɒtsmən/ Segler, *der*
yank (coll.) ① *v.t.* reißen an (+ *Dat.*)
② *n.* Reißen, *das*
Yank /jæŋk/ *n.* (Brit. coll.: American) Ami, *der*
(ugs.)
yap /jæp/ *v.i.*, **-pp-** kläffen
yard¹ /jɑːd/ *n.* (measure) Yard, *das*
yard² *n.* (a) (attached to building) Hof, *der;* in
the ∼: auf dem Hof
(b) (for storage) Lager, *das*
(c) (Amer.: garden) Garten, *der*
'yardstick *n.* (fig.) Maßstab, *der*
yarn /jɑːn/ *n.* (a) (thread) Garn, *das*
(b) (coll.: story) Geschichte, *die*
yawn /jɔːn/ ① *n.* Gähnen, *das*
② *v.i.* gähnen
'yawning *adj.* gähnend
year /jɪə(r)/ *n.* (a) Jahr, *das;* for [many] ∼s
jahrelang; once a ∼, every ∼: einmal im
Jahr; a ten-∼-old ein Zehnjähriger/eine
Zehnjährige
(b) (group of students, vintage of wine) Jahrgang,
der
'yearbook *n.* Jahrbuch, *das*
'yearly ① *adj.* jährlich;
Einjahres‹*abonnement*›
② *adv.* jährlich
yearn /jɜːn/ *v.i.* ∼ for *or* after sth./for sb.
sich nach etw./jmdm. sehnen; ∼ to do sth.
sich danach sehnen, etw. zu tun
'yearning *n.* Sehnsucht, *die*
yeast /jiːst/ *n.* Hefe, *die*
yell /jel/ ① *n.* gellender Schrei

② *v.t. & i.* [gellend] schreien
yellow /'jeləʊ/ ① *adj.* gelb
② *n.* Gelb, *das*
yellow: ∼ **'card** *n.* (Footb.) gelbe Karte;
∼ **'fever** *n.* Gelbfieber, *das*
yellowish /'jeləʊɪʃ/ *adj.* gelblich
Yellow 'Pages *n. pl.* ® gelbe Seiten *Pl.*
yelp /jelp/ ① *v.i.* jaulen
② *n.* Jaulen, *das*
yen /jen/ *n.* (coll.: longing) **sb. has a** ∼ **to do
sth.** es drängt jmdn. danach, etw. zu tun
yes /jes/ ① *adv.* ja; (in contradiction) doch
② *n., pl.* ∼**es** Ja, *das*
'yes-man *n.* (coll. derog.) Jasager, *der*
(abwertend)
yesterday /'jestədeɪ, 'jestədɪ/ ① *n.*
gestern; **the day before** ∼: vorgestern; ∼**'s
paper** die gestrige Zeitung
② *adv.* gestern; **the day before** ∼:
vorgestern
yet /jet/ ① *adv.* (a) (still) noch; ∼ **again** noch
einmal
(b) (hitherto) bisher; **his best** ∼: sein bisher
bestes
(c) *neg.* **not [just]** ∼: [jetzt] noch nicht
(d) (before all is over) doch noch; **he could win**
∼: er könnte noch gewinnen
(e) *with compar.* (even) noch
(f) (nevertheless) doch
② *conj.* doch
yew /juː/ *n.* ∼ **tree** Eibe, *die*
Yiddish /'jɪdɪʃ/ ① *adj.* jiddisch
② *n.* Jiddisch, *das; see also* ENGLISH 2A
yield /jiːld/ ① *v.t.* (give) bringen;
hervorbringen ‹*Ernte*›; abwerfen ‹*Gewinn*›
② *v.i.* (a) sich unterwerfen
(b) (give right of way) Vorfahrt gewähren
③ *n.* Ertrag, *der*

yob /jɒb/ n. (Brit. coll.) Rowdy, der

yobbish /'jɒbɪʃ/ adj. (Brit. coll.) rowdyhaft

yobbo /'jɒbəʊ/ n. pl. ~s ▶ YOB

yodel /'jəʊdl/ v.i. & t., (Brit.) -ll- jodeln

yoga /'jəʊgə/ n. Joga, der od. das

yoghurt, yogurt /'jɒgət/ n. Joghurt, der od. das

yoke /jəʊk/ n. Joch, das

yokel /'jəʊkl/ n. [Bauern]tölpel, der

yolk /jəʊk/ n. Dotter, der od. das; Eigelb, das

yonder /'jɒndə(r)/ (literary) **1** adj. ~ tree jener Baum dort (geh.)
2 adv. dort drüben

Yorkshire 'pudding n. Yorkshirepudding, der

you /jʊ, stressed juː/ pron. **(a)** sing./pl. du/ihr; (polite) sing. or pl. Sie; as direct object dich/euch/Sie; as indirect object dir/euch/Ihnen; refl. dich/dir/euch; (polite) sich; it was ~: du warst/ihr wart/Sie waren es
(b) (one) man

you'd /jʊd, stressed juːd/ **(a)** = you had
(b) = you would

you'll /jʊl, stressed juːl/ **(a)** = you will
(b) = you shall

young /jʌŋ/ **1** adj., ~er /'jʌŋgə(r)/, ~est /'jʌŋgɪst/ jung
2 n. pl. (of animals) Junge Pl.; the ~ (~ people) die jungen Leute

youngish adj. ziemlich jung

youngster /'jʌŋstə(r)/ n. **(a)** (child) Kleine, der/die/das
(b) (young person) Jugendliche, der/die

your /jə(r), stressed jʊə(r), jɔː(r)/ poss. pron. attrib.: sing. dein; pl. euer; (polite) sing. or pl. Ihr

you're /jə(r), stressed jʊə(r), jɔː(r)/ = you are

yours /jʊəz, jɔːz/ poss. pron. pred.: sing. deiner/deine/dein[e]s; pl. eurer/eure/eures; (polite) sing. or pl. Ihrer/Ihre/Ihr[e]s; see also HERS

yourself /jə'self, jʊə'self, jɔː'self/ pron. **(a)** emphat. selbst
(b) refl. dich/dir/(polite) sich. See also HERSELF

yourselves /jə'selvz, jʊə'selvz, jɔː'selvz/ pron. **(a)** emphat. selbst
(b) refl. euch/(polite) sich. See also HERSELF

youth /juːθ/ n. **(a)** Jugend, die
(b) pl. ~s /juːðz/ (young man) Jugendliche, der

youth: ~ **centre** n. Jugendzentrum, das; ~ **club** n. Jugendklub, der

youthful /'juːθfl/ adj. jugendlich

'youth hostel n. Jugendherberge, die

you've /jʊv, stressed juːv/ = you have

yo-yo ® /'jəʊjəʊ/ n., pl. ~s Jo-Jo, das

Yugoslav /'juːgəslɑːv/ ▶ YUGOSLAVIAN

Yugoslavia /juːgə'slɑːvɪə/ pr. n. Jugoslawien (das); ex-~: Ex-Jugoslawien (das)

Yugoslavian /juːgə'slɑːvɪən/ **1** adj. jugoslawisch; sb. is ~: jmd. ist Jugoslawe/Jugoslawin
2 n. Jugoslawe, der/Jugoslawin, die

yuk /jʌk/ int. (coll.) bäh

yummy /'jʌmɪ/ (coll.) int. lecker

yuppie /'jʌpɪ/ n. (coll.) Yuppie, der

yuppie 'flu n. (coll.) Yuppie-Grippe, die

Zz

Z, z /zed, (Amer.) ziː/ n. Z, z, das

Zaire /zɑː'ɪə(r)/ pr. n. Zaire (das)

Zambia /'zæmbɪə/ pr. n. Sambia (das)

zany /'zeɪnɪ/ adj. irre komisch (ugs.); Wahnsinns⟨humor, -komiker⟩

zap /zæp/ (coll.) v.i. -pp- (Telev. coll.) zappen (ugs.)

zapper /'zæpə(r)/ n. (Telev. coll.) Drücker, der (ugs.)

zeal /ziːl/ n. Eifer, der

zealous /'zeləs/ adj. eifrig

zebra /'zebrə, 'ziːbrə/ n. Zebra, das

zebra 'crossing n. (Brit.) Zebrastreifen, der

zenith /'zenɪθ/ n. Zenit, der

zero /'zɪərəʊ/ n., pl. ~s Null, die

zero: ~-'rated adj. ~-rated goods nicht mehrwertsteuerpflichtige Güter; ~ 'tolerance n. Nulltoleranz, die (for, to, of gegenüber)

zest /zest/ n. (enthusiasm) Begeisterung, die; ~ for living Lebenslust, die

zigzag /'zɪgzæg/ **1** adj. zickzackförmig; Zickzack⟨muster, -anordnung⟩
2 n. Zickzacklinie, die

Zimbabwe /zɪm'bɑːbwɪ/ pr. n. Simbabwe (das)

zinc /zɪŋk/ n. Zink, das

zip /zɪp/ **1** n. Reißverschluss, der ···❖

② *v.t.*, -pp-: (a) ~ [up] sth. den Reißverschluss an etw. (*Dat.*) zuziehen
(b) (Comp.) ~ [up] packen ‹*Datei*›

'zip bag *n.* Tasche, *die* mit Reißverschluss

'Zip code *n.* (Amer.) Postleitzahl, *die*

zip fastener ▶ ZIP 1

zipper /ˈzɪpə(r)/ ▶ ZIP 1

zither /ˈzɪðə(r)/ *n.* Zither, *die*

zodiac /ˈzəʊdɪæk/ *n.* Tierkreis, *der;* **sign of the** ~: Tierkreiszeichen, *das*

zombie (*Amer.:* **zombi**) /ˈzɒmbɪ/ *n.* Zombie, *der*

zone /zəʊn/ *n.* Zone, *die*

zoo /zuː/ *n.* Zoo, *der*

'zookeeper *n.* Zoowärter, *der*/-wärterin, *die*

zoological /zuːəˈlɒdʒɪkl/ *adj.* zoologisch

zoologist /zuːˈɒlədʒɪst/ *n.* Zoologe, *der*/ Zoologin, *die*

zoology /zuːˈɒlədʒɪ/ *n.* Zoologie, *die*

zoom /zuːm/ *v.i.* rauschen

■ **zoom 'in on** *v.t.* zoomen auf (+ *Akk.*)

'zoom lens *n.* Zoomobjektiv, *das*

zucchini /zʊˈkiːnɪ/ *n.*, *pl. same or* ~**s** (esp. Amer.) Zucchino, *der*

Contents

Grammar Reference

925

Glossary of grammatical terms

Abbreviation A shortened form of a word or phrase: etc. = usw.

Absolute use The use of a transitive verb without an expressed object, as in: I didn't *realize*

Accusative The case of a direct object; some German prepositions take the accusative

Active In the active form the subject of the verb performs the action: he asked = er hat gefragt

Adjective A word describing a noun: a *red* pencil = ein *roter* Stift

Adverb A word that describes or changes the meaning of a verb, an adjective, or another adverb: she sings *beautifully* = sie singt schön

Article The definite article, the = der/die/das, and indefinite article, a/an = ein/eine/ein, used in front of a noun

Attributive An adjective or noun is attributive when it is used directly before a noun: the *black* dog = der *schwarze* Hund; *farewell* speech = Abschiedsrede

Auxiliary verb One of the verbs – as German haben, sein, werden - used to form the perfect or future tense: I *will* help = ich *werde* helfen

Cardinal number A whole number representing a quantity: one/two/three = eins/zwei/drei

Case The form of a noun, pronoun, adjective, or article that shows the part it plays in a sentence; there are four cases in German - nominative, accusative, genitive, and dative

Clause A self-contained section of a sentence that contains a subject and a verb

Collective noun A noun that is singular in form but refers to a group of individual persons or things, e.g. royalty, grain

Collocate A word that regularly occurs with another; in German, Buch is a typical collocate of the verb lesen.

Comparative The form of an adjective or adverb that makes it "more": smaller = kleiner, more clearly = klarer

Compound adjective An adjective formed from two or more separate words: selbstbewusst (selbst + bewusst) = self-confident

Compound noun A noun formed from two or more separate words: der Flughafen (Flug+ Hafen) = airport

Compound verb A verb formed by adding a prefix to a simple verb; in German, some compound verbs are separable (an|fangen), and some are inseparable (verlassen)

Conditional tense A tense of a verb that expresses what might happen if something else occurred: he would go = er würde gehen

Conjugation Variation of the form of a verb to show tense, person, mood, etc.

Conjunction A word used to join clauses together: and = und, because = weil

Consonant In German, all the letters of the alphabet other than a, e, i, o, u, ä, ö, ü

Copula A verb, such as be or become, which links a subject and predicate

Dative The case of an indirect object; many German prepositions take the dative

Declension The form of a noun, pronoun, or adjective that corresponds to a particular case, number, or gender; some German nouns decline like adjectives, e.g. Beamte, Taube

Definite article: the = der/die/das

Demonstrative adjective: an adjective indicating the person or thing referred to; *this* table = *dieser* Tisch

Demonstrative pronoun A pronoun indicating the person or thing referred to; *this* is my bicycle = *das* ist mein Fahrrad

Direct object The noun or pronoun directly affected by the verb: he caught *the ball* = er fing *den Ball*

Direct speech A speaker's actual words or the use of these in writing

Elliptical Having a word or words omitted, especially where the sense can be guessed from the context

Ending Letters added to the stem of verbs, as well as to nouns and adjectives, according to tense, case, etc.

Feminine One of the three noun genders in German: die Frau = the woman

Future tense The tense of a verb that refers to something that will happen in the future: I will go = ich werde gehen

Gender One of the three groups of nouns, pronouns, and adjectives in German: masculine, feminine, or neuter

Genitive The case that shows possession; some prepositions in German take the genitive

Imperative A form of a verb that expresses a command: **go away! = geh weg!**

Imperfect tense The tense of a verb that refers to an uncompleted or a habitual action in the past: **I went there every Friday = ich ging jeden Freitag dorthin**

Impersonal verb A verb in English used only with 'it', and in German only with '**es**': **it is raining = es regnet**

Indeclinable adjective An adjective that has no inflected forms, as German **klasse, Moskauer**

Indefinite article: a/an = **ein/eine/ein**

Indefinite pronoun A pronoun that does not identify a specific person or object: **one = man, something = etwas**

Indicative form The form of a verb used when making a statement of fact or asking questions of fact: **he is just coming = er kommt gleich**

Indirect object The noun or pronoun indirectly affected by the verb, at which the direct object is aimed: **I gave *him* the book = ich gab *ihm* das Buch**

Indirect speech A report of what someone has said which does not reproduce the exact words

Infinitive The basic part of a verb: **to play = spielen**

Inflect To change the ending or form of a word to show its tense or its grammatical relation to other words: **gehe** and **gehst** are inflected forms of the verb **gehen**

Inseparable verb A verb with a prefix that can never be separated from it: **verstehen, ich verstehe**

Interjection A sound, word, or remark expressing a strong feeling such as anger, fear, or joy: **oh! = ach!**

Interrogative pronoun A pronoun that asks a question: **who? = wer?**

Intransitive verb A verb that does not have a direct object: **he died suddenly = er ist plötzlich gestorben**

Irregular verb A verb that does not follow one of the set patterns and has its own individual forms

Masculine One of the three noun genders in German: **der Mann = the man, der Stuhl = the chair**

Modal verb A verb that is used with another verb (not a modal) to express permission, obligation, possibility, etc., as German **können, sollen**, English **might, should**

Negative expressing refusal or denial; there aren't any = **es gibt keine**

Neuter One of the three noun genders in German: **das Buch = the book, das Kind = the child**

Nominative The case of the subject of a sentence; in sentences with **sein** and **werden** the noun after the verb is in the nominative: **that is my car = das ist mein Auto**

Noun A word that names a person or a thing

Number The state of being either singular or plural

Object The word or words naming the person or thing acted upon by a verb or preposition, as 'Buch' in **er las das Buch** or 'ihm' in **ich traue ihm**

Ordinal number A number that shows a person's or thing's position in a series: **the *twenty-first* century = das *einundzwanzigste* Jahrhundert, the *second* door on the left = die *zweite* Tür links**

Part of speech A grammatical term for the function of a word; noun, verb, adjective, etc., are parts of speech.

Passive In the passive form the subject of the verb experiences the action rather than performs it: **he was asked = er wurde gefragt**

Past participle The part of a verb used to form past tenses: **she had gone, er hat gelogen**

Perfect tense The tense of a verb that refers to a completed action in the past or an action that started in the past and is still going on: **I have already eaten = ich habe schon gegessen; I have been reading all day = ich habe den ganzen Tag gelesen**

Person Any of the three groups of personal pronouns and forms taken by verbs; the **first person** (e.g. **I/ich**) refers to the person(s) speaking, the **second person** (e.g. **you**/du) refers to the person(s) spoken to; the **third person** (e.g. **he/er**) refers to the persons spoken about

Personal pronoun A pronoun that refers to a person or thing: **he/she/it = er/sie/es**

Phrasal verb A verb in English combined with a preposition or an adverb to have a particular meaning: **run away = weglaufen**

Phrase A self-contained section of a sentence that does not contain a full verb

Pluperfect tense The tense of a verb that refers to something that happened before a particular point in the past: **als ich ankam, *war* er schon *losgefahren*** = when I arrived, he *had* already *left*

Plural Of nouns etc., referring to more than one: **the trees = die Bäume**

Possessive adjective An adjective that shows possession, belonging to someone or something; **my = mein/meine/mein**

Possessive pronoun A pronoun that shows possession, belonging to someone or something: **mine = meiner/meine/meins**

Postpositive Placed after the word to which it relates, as **in stock** in the phrase **items in stock**

Predicate The part of a sentence that says something about the **subject**, e.g. **went home** in **John went home**

Predicative An adjective is predicative when it comes after a verb such as **be** or **become** in English, or after **sein** or **werden** in German: **she is beautiful = sie ist schön**

Prefix A letter or group of letters added to the beginning of a word to change its meaning; in German, the prefix can move from separable verbs (**an|fangen**), but stays fixed to inseparable verbs (**verlassen**)

Preposition A word that stands in front of a noun or pronoun, relating it to the rest of the sentence; in German prepositions are always followed by a particular case, usually either the accusative or dative, but occasionally the genitive: **with = mit (+ dative), for = für (+ accusative), because of = wegen (+ genitive)**

Present participle The part of a verb that in English ends in –ing, and in German adds –d to the infinitive: **asking = fragend**

Present tense The tense of a verb that refers to something happening now: **I make = ich mache**

Pronoun A word that stands instead of a noun: **he = er, she = sie, mine = meiner/meine/meins**

Proper noun A name of a person, place, institution, etc., in English written with a capital letter at the start; **Germany**, the **Atlantic**, **Karl**, **Europa** are all proper nouns

Reflexive pronoun A pronoun that goes with a reflexive verb: in German **mich, dich, sich, uns, euch, sich**

Reflexive verb A verb whose object is the same as its subject; in German, it is used with a reflexive pronoun: **du sollst dich waschen =** you should wash yourself

Regular verb A verb that follows a set pattern in its different forms

Relative pronoun A pronoun that introduces a subordinate clause, relating to a person or thing mentioned in the main clause: **the man *who* visited us = der Mann, *der* uns besucht hat**

Reported Speech Another name for Indirect speech

Root The part of a word to which inflections are added; **fahr-** is the root of the verb **fahren**

Sentence A sequence of words, with a subject and a verb, that can stand on their own to make a statement, ask a question, or give a command

Separable verb A verb with a prefix that can be separated from it in some tenses: **anfangen, anzufangen, angefangen**, but **ich fange an, du fingst an**

Singular Of nouns etc., referring to just one: **the tree = der Baum**

Stem The part of a verb to which endings are added; **fahr-** is the stem of **fahren**

Subject In a clause or sentence, the noun or pronoun that causes the action of the verb: *he* caught the ball = **er fing den Ball**

Subjunctive A verb form that is used to express doubt or unlikelihood: **if I were to tell you that ... = wenn ich dir sagen würde, dass ...**

Subordinate clause A clause which adds information to the main clause of a sentence but cannot be used as a sentence by itself

Suffix A letter or group of letters joined to the end of a word to make another word, as **-heit** in **Schönheit**

Superlative The form of an adjective or adverb that makes it "most": **the *smallest* house = das *kleinste* Haus, most clearly = am klarsten**

Syllable A division of a word that contains a vowel sound that is pronounced as a single unit: **Helikopter** has four syllables, he-li-kop-ter

Tense The form of a verb that tells when the action takes place: present, future, imperfect, perfect, pluperfect

Transitive verb A verb that is used with a direct object: **she read the book = sie las das Buch**

Verb A word or group of words that describes an action: **the children *are playing* = die Kinder *spielen***

Vowel In German, one of the following letters: a, e, i, o, u, ä, ö, ü

Summary of German grammar

1 Verbs

1.1 Regular verbs

Most German verbs are regular and add the same endings to their stem. You find the stem by taking away the **-en** (or sometimes just **-n**) from the end of the infinitive. The infinitive of the verb, for example the regular verb **machen**, is the form you look up in the dictionary. The stem of **machen** is **mach-**. There are six endings for each tense, to go with the different pronouns:

ich = *I*   du = *you*   er/sie/es = *he/she/it*
wir = *we*   ihr = *you*   sie/Sie = *they/you (polite form)*.

1.2 Irregular verbs

Some German verbs are irregular and change their stem or add different endings. All the irregular verbs that appear in the dictionary are given in the section *German irregular verbs* on pages 944–947.

1.3 Present tense

For example, *I make, I am making*, or *I do make*:

infinitive	ich	du	er/sie/es	wir	ihr	sie/Sie
machen	mache	machst	macht	machen	macht	machen

1.4 Imperfect tense

For example, *I made, I was making*, or *I used to make*:

infinitive	ich	du	er/sie/es	wir	ihr	sie/Sie
machen	machte	machtest	machte	machten	machtet	machten

1.5 Future tense

For example, *I will make* or *I shall make*. The future is formed by using the present tense of **werden**, which is the equivalent of *will* or *shall*, with the infinitive of the main verb: **ich werde machen**.

infinitive	ich	du	er/sie/es	wir	ihr	sie/Sie
werden	werde	wirst	wird	werden	werdet	werden

1.6 Perfect tense

For example, *I made* or *I have made*. Most German verbs form the perfect tense with the present tense of **haben**, which is the equivalent of *have*, plus the past participle: **ich habe gemacht**. Some verbs form the perfect tense with **sein** instead of **haben**, and these are all marked *(sein)* in the dictionary. They are either verbs expressing motion and involving a change of place:

> er ist heute nach Berlin gefahren = *he drove to Berlin today*
> *he went out* = er ist hinausgegangen

or, they express a change of state, and this includes verbs meaning to happen (**geschehen, passieren, vorkommen**):

> er ist aufgewacht = *he woke up*
> sie ist gestern gestorben = *she died yesterday*

infinitive	ich	du	er/sie/es	wir	ihr	sie/Sie
haben	habe	hast	hat	haben	habt	haben
sein	bin	bist	ist	sind	seid	sind

1.7 The subjunctive

This is a form of the verb that is used to express speculation, hope, and doubt, and in reported speech. (It is rarely used in English; one example is: *if I were you*, instead of *if I was you*.) The subjunctive is used in both written and spoken German.

> es könnte wahr sein = *it could be true*
> wenn ich du wäre, … = *if I were you, …*
> er sagt, dass er selten in die Stadt gehe = *he says he seldom goes into town*

Present subjunctive

infinitive	ich	du	er/sie/es	wir	ihr	sie/Sie
machen	mache	machest	mache	machen	machet	machen
sein	sei	sei(e)st	sei	seien	seid	seien

Imperfect subjunctive

For regular verbs this is the same as the normal imperfect forms, but irregular verbs vary.

infinitive	ich	du	er/sie/es	wir	ihr	sie/Sie
machen	machte	machtest	machte	machten	machtet	machten
werden	würde	würdest	würde	würden	würdet	würden
sein	wäre	wär(e)st	wäre	wären	wär(e)t	wären

1.8 Conditional tense

The conditional tense expresses what would happen if something else occurred. The imperfect subjunctive of **werden** (**würde, würdest**, etc) is used with the infinitive to form the conditional tense.

> er würde gehen = *he would go*
> das würde ich nicht machen = *I wouldn't do that*

1.9 Reflexive verbs

The object of a reflexive verb is the same as its subject. In German, the object is a reflexive pronoun. This is usually in the accusative (**ich wasche mich** = *I wash myself*). The reflexive pronouns of some verbs are in the dative (**ich stelle mir vor** = *I imagine*), and these are marked in both halves of the dictionary with the label (*Dat*).

infinitive	ich	du	er/sie/es	wir	ihr	sie/Sie
sich waschen	wasche mich	wäschst dich	wäscht sich	waschen uns	wascht euch	waschen sich
sich vorstellen	stelle mir vor	stellst dir vor	stellt sich vor	stellen uns vor	stellt euch vor	stellen sich vor

1.10 The passive

In the passive, the subject of the verb experiences the action rather than performs it: **er wurde gefragt** = *he was asked*. In German, the passive is formed as follows:

PRESENT PASSIVE	es wird gemacht (present tense of **werden** + past participle)	*it is done*
IMPERFECT PASSIVE	es wurde gemacht (imperfect tense of **werden** + past participle)	*it was done*
FUTURE PASSIVE	es wird gemacht werden (present tense of **werden** + past participle + **werden**)	*it will be done*
PERFECT PASSIVE	es ist gemacht worden (present tense of **sein** + past participle + **worden**)	*it has been done*

When forming the perfect passive, note that the past participle of **werden** used is **worden** rather than **geworden**.

1.11 Separable verbs

Some German verbs have stressed separable prefixes, such as **ab-**, **an-**, **aus-**, **her-**, **hin-**, **nach-**, **vor-**, **zu-**. These prefixes become detached from the main verb in the simple tenses: **hinausgehen: ich gehe hinaus**, **sie ging hinaus**. In compound tenses formed with the past participle, for example the perfect tense, the **ge-** of the past participle comes between the prefix and the verb:

er/sie/es hat angefangen = *he/she/it has begun*
er/sie/es ist angekommen = *he/she/it has arrived*

1.12 Inseparable verbs

The following unstressed prefixes are never separated from their verb in either simple or compound tenses and do not take **ge-** in the past participle:

be-, emp-, ent-, er-, ge-, ver-, zer-.
er begleitet seinen Bruder = *he is accompanying his brother*
er wurde nicht begleitet = *he was not accompanied*

2 Articles

The definite article (*the*) can be translated in the nominative case by **der**, **die** or **das** in German. Similarly the indefinite article (*a*) can be translated by **ein**, **eine**, or **ein**.

Summary of German grammar

There are three genders of nouns in German: masculine (**der Mann** = *the man*), feminine (**die Frau** = *the woman*), and neuter (**das Buch** = *the book*). There are two forms of number: singular (**der Baum** = *the tree*) and plural (**die Bäume** = *the trees*). And there are four cases, which show the part a noun plays in a sentence: nominative (for the subject), accusative (for the object), genitive (to show possession), and dative (for the indirect object). The plural forms of the definite article are the same for all three genders. More information on gender is given below.

2.1 Definite article: der/die/das, (*plural*) die = *the*

	SINGULAR masculine	feminine	neuter	PLURAL all genders
NOMINATIVE	**der** Mann	**die** Frau	**das** Buch	**die** Bäume
ACCUSATIVE	**den** Mann	**die** Frau	**das** Buch	**die** Bäume
GENITIVE	**des** Mannes	**der** Frau	**des** Buches	**der** Bäume
DATIVE	**dem** Mann	**der** Frau	**dem** Buch	**den** Bäumen

2.2 Indefinite article

ein/eine/ein = *a* or *an*. This article can only be singular.

	masculine	feminine	neuter
NOMINATIVE	**ein** Mann	**eine** Frau	**ein** Buch
ACCUSATIVE	**einen** Mann	**eine** Frau	**ein** Buch
GENITIVE	**eines** Mannes	**einer** Frau	**eines** Buches
DATIVE	**einem** Mann	**einer** Frau	**einem** Buch

3 Nouns

In German, all nouns take an initial capital letter wherever they appear in a sentence: **der Baum**, **die Schule**, **das Buch**.

3.1 Gender

All German nouns belong to one of the three genders: masculine (**der Mann** = *the man*), feminine (**die Frau** = *the woman*), and neuter (**das Buch** = *the book*). These three examples are logical, with masculine for a male person, feminine for a female person, and neuter for an object. But genders of German nouns do not always follow logic. For example, **der Fluss** (= *the river*), **die Menge** (= *the quantity/crowd*), **das Haus** (= *the house*). **Das Mädchen** (= *the girl*) is neuter and not feminine, because the ending **-chen** is always neuter.

The gender of German nouns is given in both sides of the dictionary by adding **der**, **die**, or **das** after each noun. There are some general rules regarding the gender of groups of nouns, but these cover only a small proportion of them and in many cases a noun's gender can only be established by looking it up.

3.2 Masculine nouns

- male persons and animals: **der Arbeiter** = *worker*; **der Bär** = *bear*

- 'doers' and 'doing' instruments ending in **-er** in German: **der Gärtner** = *gardener*; **der Computer** = *computer*

- days, months, and seasons: **(der) Montag** = *Monday*; **(der) März** = *March*; **der Frühling** = *spring*

- words ending in **-ich**, **-ig**, and **-ling**: **der Strich** = line; **der Honig** = *honey*; **der Lehrling** = *apprentice*

- words ending in **-ismus**, **-ist**, and **-ant**: **der Kapitalismus** = *capitalism*; **der Kriminalist** = *detective*; **der Diamant** = *diamond*

3.3 Feminine nouns

- female persons and animals: **die Schauspielerin** = *actress*; **die Henne** = *hen*. The feminine form of professions and animals is made by adding **-in** to the masculine: **der Schauspieler/die Schauspielerin** = *actor/actress*

- nouns ending in **-ei**, **-ie**, **-ik**, **-in**, **-ion**, **-heit**, **-keit**, **-schaft**, **-tät**, **-ung**, **-ur**: **die Gärtnerei** = *gardening*; **die Energie** = *energy*; **die Million** = *million*; **die Freiheit** = *freedom*; **die Freundlichkeit** = *friendliness*; **die Feindschaft** = *enmity*; **die Universität** = *university*; **die Verwaltung** = *management*; **die Natur** = *nature*

- many nouns ending in **-e**: **die Blume** = *flower*. Note that there are many common exceptions, including **der Name** = *name*; **der Käse** = *cheese*; **das Ende** = *end*

3.4 Neuter nouns

- names of continents, most countries, and towns: **(das) Europa** = *Europe*; **(das) Deutschland** = *Germany*; **(das) Köln** = *Cologne*

- nouns ending in **-chen** and **-lein** (diminutive suffixes): **das Mädchen**, **das Fräulein** = *girl*

- most (but not all) nouns beginning with **Ge-** or ending in **-nis**, **-tel**, or **-um**: **das Geheimnis** = *secret*; **das Viertel** = *quarter*; **das Zentrum** = *centre*

- infinitives of verbs used as nouns: **das Lachen** = *laughter*; **das Essen** = *food*

3.5 Compound nouns

When two nouns combine to make a compound noun, the gender of the compound is that of the second noun:

der Brief + die Marke = die Briefmarke (= *stamp*).

. . . .

3.6 Plural

There are no hard and fast rules for the the formation of plural nouns in German. An ending is generally added. Masculine nouns frequently add -e (**der Freund**, **die Freunde**). When the vowels -**a**- or -**u**- appear in the stem of a noun, they may add an umlaut to give: -**ä**-, -**ü**- as in: (**der Gast**, **die Gäste**; **das Haus**, **die Häuser**). Feminine words ending in -**heit**, -**keit**, and -**ung** always add -**en** to make the plural (**die Abbildung**, **die Abbildungen**).

The plurals of all nouns are shown in the German-English part of the dictionary.

3.7 Case

There are four cases, which show the part a noun plays in a sentence: nominative, accusative, genitive, and dative. The noun's article changes according to the case, and the ending of the noun changes in some cases:

| | SINGULAR | | |
	masculine	feminine	neuter
NOMINATIVE	der Mann	die Frau	das Buch
ACCUSATIVE	den Mann	die Frau	das Buch
GENITIVE	des **Mann(e)s**	der Frau	des **Buch(e)s**
DATIVE	dem Mann	der Frau	dem Buch

| | PLURAL | | |
	masculine	feminine	neuter
NOMINATIVE	die Männer	die Frauen	die Bücher
ACCUSATIVE	die Männer	die Frauen	die Bücher
GENITIVE	der Männer	der Frauen	der Bücher
DATIVE	den **Männern**	den Frauen	den **Büchern**

The nominative is used for the subject of a sentence. It is important to note that in sentences with **sein** (*to be*) and **werden** (*to become*), the noun after the verb is in the nominative.

der Hund bellte = *the dog barked*
das ist mein Wagen = *that is my car*

The accusative is used for the direct object and after some prepositions (listed on page 941):

sie hat einen Sohn = *she has a son*

The genitive shows possession, and is also used after some prepositions (listed on page 941):

der Hund meines Mannes = *my husband's dog*

The dative is used for the indirect object. Some German verbs, such as **helfen**, take the dative when you might have expected the accusative. This information is given in both halves of the dictionary. The dative is also used after some prepositions (listed on page 941):

sie gab den Kindern die Bücher = *she gave the books to the children*
er hilft der Frau = *he is helping the woman*

The following sentence combines all four cases:

der Mann gibt der Frau den Bleistift = *the man gives the woman the girl's pencil*
des Mädchens

der Mann *is the subject* (*in the nominative*)
gibt *is the verb*
der Frau *is the indirect object* (*in the dative*)
den Bleistift *is the direct object* (*in the accusative*)
des Mädchens *is in the genitive* (*showing possession*).

4 Adjectives

An adjective is a word qualifying a noun. In German, an adjective in front of a noun adds endings that vary with the noun's gender, number, and case. Adjectives that come after a noun do not add endings.

4.1 Adjectives following the definite article **der**, **die**, **das** take the following endings:

	SINGULAR			PLURAL
	masculine	feminine	neuter	all genders
NOMINATIVE	der rote Hut	die rote Lampe	das rote Buch	die roten Autos
ACCUSATIVE	den roten Hut	die rote Lampe	das rote Buch	die roten Autos
GENITIVE	des roten Hutes	der roten Lampe	des roten Buches	der roten Autos
DATIVE	dem roten Hut	der roten Lampe	dem roten Buch	den roten Autos

4.2 German demonstrative adjectives follow the pattern of the definite article, and adjectives after them change their endings in the same way as after **der/die/das**. For example, **dieser/diese/dieses** (= *this*):

	SINGULAR			PLURAL
	masculine	feminine	neuter	all genders
NOMINATIVE	dieser	diese	dieses	diese
ACCUSATIVE	diesen	diese	dieses	diese
GENITIVE	dieses	dieser	dieses	dieser
DATIVE	diesem	dieser	diesem	diesen

Other adjectives of this type are:

jeder, jede, jedes = *every, each*
jener, jene, jenes = *that*
mancher, manche, manches = *many a, some*

solcher, solche, solches = *such*
welcher, welche, welches = *which*

4.3 Adjectives following the indefinite article **ein**, **eine**, **ein** take the following endings:

Summary of German grammar

	SINGULAR		
	masculine	feminine	neuter
NOMINATIVE	ein roter Hut	eine rote Lampe	ein rotes Buch
ACCUSATIVE	einen roten Hut	eine rote Lampe	ein rotes Buch
GENITIVE	eines roten Hutes	einer roten Lampe	eines roten Buches
DATIVE	einem roten Hut	einer roten Lampe	einem roten Buch

Other German adjectives that follow the pattern of the indefinite article, and take the same endings as **ein**, **eine**, **ein**, are:

dein = *your*　　　ihr = *her/their*　　　mein = *my*　　　kein = *no*
euer = *your*　　　sein = *his/its*　　　unser = *our*
Ihr = *your*

These adjectives can also be used in the plural: **keine Autos** = *no cars*; **deine Eltern** = *your parents*; **unsere Lehrer** = *our teachers*, etc. The endings of adjectives that follow them are the same in the plural regardless of gender:

	PLURAL
	all genders
NOMINATIVE	keine roten Autos
ACCUSATIVE	keine roten Autos
GENITIVE	keiner roten Autos
DATIVE	keinen roten Autos

4.4 Adjectives in front of a noun, without an article, take the following endings:

	SINGULAR			PLURAL
	masculine	feminine	neuter	all genders
NOMINATIVE	guter Wein	frische Milch	kaltes Bier	alte Leute
ACCUSATIVE	guten Wein	frische Milch	kaltes Bier	alte Leute
GENITIVE	guten Weins	frischer Milch	kalten Biers	alter Leute
DATIVE	gutem Wein	frischer Milch	kaltem Bier	alten Leuten

4.5 Adjectives as nouns

In German, adjectives can be used as nouns, spelt with a capital letter: **alt** = *old*, **ein Alter** = *an old man*, **eine Alte** = *an old woman*.

With the definite article (**der**, **die**, **das**), these nouns take the following endings:

	SINGULAR			PLURAL
	masculine	feminine	neuter	all genders
NOMINATIVE	der Alte	die Alte	das Alte	die Alten
ACCUSATIVE	den Alten	die Alte	das Alte	die Alten
GENITIVE	des Alten	der Alten	des Alten	der Alten
DATIVE	dem Alten	der Alten	dem Alten	den Alten

Adjectives can be used in this way in the neuter, usually to express an abstract concept: **das Gute** = *the good* (nominative and accusative), **des Guten** (genitive), **dem Guten** (dative).

· ·

With the indefinite article (**ein, eine, ein**), these nouns take the following endings:

	SINGULAR masculine	feminine	neuter	PLURAL all genders without an article
NOMINATIVE	ein Alter	eine Alte	ein Altes	Alte
ACCUSATIVE	einen Alten	eine Alte	ein Altes	Alte
GENITIVE	eines Alten	einer Alten	eines Alten	Alter
DATIVE	einem Alten	einer Alten	einem Alten	Alten

4.6 Comparatives and superlatives of adjectives

In English, the comparative of the adjective *small* is *smaller*, and of *difficult* is *more difficult*. The superlatives are *smallest* and *most difficult*. In German, there is just one way to form the comparative and superlative: by adding the endings **-er** and **-(e)st**:

> klein, kleiner, der/die/das kleinste = *small, smaller, smallest*

Many adjectives whose stem vowel is **-a-, -o-,** or **-u-** take an umlaut to become **-ä-, -ö-** or **-ü-,** in the comparative and superlative:

> kalt, kälter, der/die/das kälteste = *cold, colder, coldest*
> grob, gröber, der/die/das gröbste = *rude, ruder, rudest*
> jung, jünger, der/die/das jüngste = *young, younger, youngest*

Some important adjectives are irregular:

> groß, größer, der/die/das größte = *big, bigger, biggest*
> gut, besser, der/die/das beste = *good, better, best*
> hoch, höher, der/die/das höchste = *high, higher, highest*
> viel, mehr, der/die/das meiste = *much, more, most*
> nah, näher, der/die/das nächste = *near, nearer, nearest*

Comparative and superlative adjectives take the same endings as basic adjectives:

> ein kleineres Kind = *a smaller child*
> ein billigerer Hut = *a cheaper hat*
> der kälteste Monat = *the coldest month*
> die nächste Bushaltestelle = *the nearest bus stop*

· ·

5 Adverbs

5.1 In German almost all adjectives can also be used as adverbs. Adverbs can modify a verb, an adjective, or another adverb.

> sie singt schön (adverb: schön + verb: singt) = *she sings beautifully*
> sie war schnell fertig (adverb: schnell + adjective: fertig) = *she was ready quickly*
> er fährt sehr langsam (adverb: sehr + adverb: langsam) = *he drives very slowly*

The following important adverbs are invariable: **auch** = *also*, **fast** = *almost*, **immer** = *always*, **sehr** = *very*, **leider** = *unfortunately*

> sie ist sehr klug = *she is very clever*

Summary of German grammar

5.2 Comparatives and superlatives of adverbs

The comparative is formed by adding **-er** to the basic adverb, and the superlative by adding the ending **-(e)sten** to the basic adverb and putting **am** in front:

klar, klarer, am klarsten = *clearly, more clearly, most clearly*

Some important adverbs are irregular:

bald, früher, am frühesten = *soon, earlier, at the earliest*
gut, besser, am besten = *well, better, best*
gern, lieber, am liebsten = *willingly, more willingly, most willingly*

5.3 Adverbs of time

There are many adverbs and adverbial expressions of time. They are invariable. Some common ones are:

morgens = *in the morning*	wochenlang, jahrelang *etc* = *for weeks, for years* etc
nachmittags = *in the afternoon*	montags, dienstags *etc* = *on Mondays, Tuesdays* etc
nachts = *in the night*	
bald = *soon*	jetzt = *now*
endlich = *in the end*	kürzlich = *recently*
immer, stets = *always*	wieder = *again*

5.4 Adverbs of order

The use of adverbs and adverbial expressions to convey order is frequent in German. Here are some common patterns of usage:

erstens = *firstly*	zum ersten Mal = *for the first time*
zweitens = *secondly*	zum zweiten Mal = *for the second time*
drittens = *thirdly*	zum dritten Mal = *for the third time*

6 Pronouns

Pronouns are words that can replace a noun. Examples in English are:
I, you, he, she, it, which, theirs, mine, yours.

6.1 Personal pronouns

These pronouns, such as **er**, **sie**, **es** = *he/she/it*, refer to people or things.

	I	you	he/it	she/it	it	we	you	they	you
NOMINATIVE	ich	du	er	sie	es	wir	ihr	sie	Sie
	me	you	him/it	her/it	it	us	you	them	you
ACCUSATIVE	mich	dich	ihn	sie	es	uns	euch	sie	Sie
DATIVE	mir	dir	ihm	ihr	ihm	uns	euch	ihnen	Ihnen

The genitive form is not given, because it is so rarely used.

Summary of German grammar

· ·

In German there are two forms for you, **du** and **Sie**. **Du** (plural **ihr**) is informal and is used when speaking to a child, a member of your family, or someone you know well. When speaking to a person or a group of people you do not know very well, use the polite form, **Sie**.

German pronouns agree in gender with the noun they refer to. In the nominative case, 'it' can be be translated by **er** or **sie**, as well as **es**:

> er (der Bleistift) ist rot = *it (the pencil) is red*
> sie (die Rose) ist schön = *it (the rose) is beautiful*
> es (das Auto) ist teuer = *it (the car) is expensive*

6.2 Possessive pronouns

The possessive pronouns are:

> meiner/meine/mein(e)s = *mine* unserer/unsere/unser(e)s = *ours*
> deiner/deine/dein(e)s = *yours* eurer/eure/eures = *yours*
> (informal singular) (informal plural)
> seiner/seine/sein(e)s = *his* ihrer/ihre/ihr(e)s = *theirs*
> ihrer/ihre/ihr(e)s = *hers* Ihrer, Ihre, Ihr(e)s = *yours* (polite)
> seiner/seine/sein(e)s = *its*

They all take endings like **meiner/meine/mein(e)s**, as follows:

	SINGULAR			PLURAL
	masculine	feminine	neuter	all genders
NOMINATIVE	meiner	meine	mein(e)s	meine
ACCUSATIVE	meinen	meine	mein(e)s	meine
GENITIVE	meines	meiner	meines	meine
DATIVE	meinem	meiner	meinem	meinen

As can be seen in the table, in the neuter form an **-e-** can be added (making **meines**). This applies to all the possessive pronouns, but the extra **-e-** is rare.

6.3 Relative pronouns

Relative pronouns link a main clause to a subordinate clause. In English they are *who, which, that*, and *what*. In German they are **der, die**, or **das**, depending on the noun referred to:

	SINGULAR			PLURAL
	masculine	feminine	neuter	all genders
NOMINATIVE	der	die	das	die
ACCUSATIVE	den	die	das	die
GENITIVE	dessen	deren	dessen	deren
DATIVE	dem	der	dem	denen

Relative pronouns can be left out in English, but never in German:

> das Buch, das ich lese = *the book (that) I'm reading*

They agree in gender and number with the noun they refer back to:

> der Mann, der uns besucht hat = *the man who visited us*

(**der** is masculine singular)

• •

der Mann, dessen Frau den Wagen = *the man, whose wife had rented the car,*
vermietet hatte, wusste es nicht   *did not know about it*

The case of the pronoun depends on its function in the clause it introduces:

der Bleistift, den ich gestern gekauft habe = *the pencil I bought yesterday*

(**den** is masculine singular, and accusative, because it is the object of the clause it introduces)

6.4 Interrogative pronouns

These pronouns are used to ask questions:

wer? = *who?*   was? = *what?*   welcher/welche/welches? = *which?*

Wer changes as follows:

NOMINATIVE wer?   ACCUSATIVE wen?   GENITIVE wessen?   DATIVE wem?

wer sprach? = *who was speaking?*
wen trafst du? = *who (whom) did you meet?*
wessen Buch ist das? = *whose book is that?*
mit wem spricht er? = *who is he talking to?*

Was? is invariable.

was ist das? = *what is that?*

Welcher: The forms are the same as those given for dieser on page 934.

welche Zeitung hast du gekauft? = *which newspaper have you bought?*

Was für ein … ? This expression means 'what kind or sort of …?' **Ein** takes the endings according to whether the noun qualified is the subject, object, or indirect object.

was für ein Mann/eine Frau ist das? (subject) = *what sort of a man/woman is that?*
was für ein Geschenk bekam er? (object) = *what sort of a present did he get?*
was für Zeitungen haben Sie? (plural object) = *what sort of newspapers do you have?*

6.5 Reflexive pronouns

The object of a reflexive verb is the same as its subject. In German, the object is a reflexive pronoun. This is usually in the accusative (**ich wasche mich** = *I wash myself*). The reflexive pronouns of some verbs are in the dative (**ich stelle mir vor** = *I imagine*).

The following table shows which accusative reflexive pronoun corresponds to the normal (nominative) personal pronoun.

ich	mich	wir	uns
du	dich	ihr	euch
er, sie, es, man	sich	sie, Sie	sich

sie erinnern sich daran = *they remember it*
es bewegt sich = *it's moving*

The dative forms are the same as the above, except for the **ich** and **du** forms: **ich: mir**; **du: dir**.

6.6 Indefinite pronouns

Some of these pronouns take endings according to whether they are the subject, object, or indirect object in the sentence. Among those that do are: **jemand** = *someone* or *somebody*, **niemand** = *no one* or *nobody*, **irgend jemand** = *anyone* or *anybody*.

	someone	no one	anyone
NOMINATIVE	jemand	niemand	irgend jemand
ACCUSATIVE	jemanden	niemanden	irgend jemanden
DATIVE	jemandem	niemandem	irgend jemandem

jemand hat mein Fahrrad genommen = *someone has taken my bicycle*
sie sah niemanden = *she saw no one*
er gab es jemandem = *he gave it to someone*

The genitive case is rarely used.

6.7 One

The pronoun *one* is translated by **einer**, **eine**, **eines** or **eins**, which take the endings already given on page 938 for singular possessive pronouns, according to their function in the sentence.

trinken wir ein(e)s? (ein Bier) = *shall we have one? (a beer)*
einer von uns muss es tun = *one of us must do it*

Similarly **keiner**, **keine**, **keines** or **keins** = *no one* or *nobody*, *nothing* (neuter) take the endings according to their function in the sentence.

keiner will ihn begleiten = *no one wants to go with him*

Indefinite pronouns which are invariable are:

something = etwas; *everything* = alles; *nothing* = nichts
gefällt noch etwas? = *would you like something else?*
sie nahm alles = *she took everything*
er weiss nichts = *he knows nothing*

Note that *something/everything/nothing good* is translated by **etwas/alles/nichts Gutes**

something good has happened = etwas Gutes ist geschehen

7 Prepositions

Prepositions are words like *above*, *in*, *under* that convey the idea of place and come in front of a noun or pronoun. In German, the noun following a preposition always has to be in one of three cases: dative, accusative, or genitive.

Prepositions can also be prefixes and form separable verbs:

die Straße entlanggehen = *to walk along the street*
er geht die Straße entlang = *he is walking along the street*

In the dictionary, the case governed by a preposition is given as follows:

mit 1 *Präp mit Dat.*

This means that **mit** always takes the dative case.

The following prepositions always take the dative:

aus   bei   mit   nach   seit   von   zu

The following prepositions always take the accusative:

bis   durch   entlang   für   gegen   ohne   um

The following prepositions always take the genitive:

anstatt   während   trotz   wegen

There is a group of prepositions that can take the dative or the accusative, depending on the sense of the sentence.

They are:

an   auf   außer   hinter   in   unter   neben   vor   über   zwischen

If the speaker wishes to convey the idea that someone or something is stationary, the dative case is used:

sie saß in der Küche = *she sat in the kitchen*
es liegt auf dem Tisch = *it's lying on the table*

But if the speaker wishes to convey the idea of movement the accusative case is used:

sie ging in die Küche = *she went into the kitchen*
er legte den Beutel auf den Tisch = *he put the bag on the table*

Note the expressions **nach Hause** and **zu Hause**: **nach Hause** = *home* (*homewards*), and **zu Hause** = *at home*.

Some forms of the definite article are usually shortened when used with certain prepositions:

am (an dem); **ans** (an das); **aufs** (auf das); **beim** (bei dem)
durchs (durch das); **fürs** (für das); **im** (in dem); **ins** (in das)
ums (um das); **vom** (von dem); **zum** (zu dem); **zur** (zu der)

8 Conjunctions

Conjunctions are words, such as **und** = *and*, **aber** = *but*, which link clauses in a sentence.

Some common conjunctions are:

aber = *but*   denn = *for*   oder = *or*   sondern = *but (on the contrary)*   und = *and*

These conjunctions do not change normal word order in the two clauses:

ich gehe und er kommt auch = *I am going and he is coming too*

This is because the clauses are of equal weight or importance.

• •

Conjunctions which introduce a subordinate clause make the verb in the subordinate clause appear at the end:

als = *when, = as*	bevor = *before*	bis = *until*	da = *since*	dass = *that*
ob = *whether*	während = *while*	wenn = *when, = if*	weil = *because*	

als er das erfuhr, wollte er nicht mitkommen	= *when he found out, he didn't want to come*
er konnte nicht in die Schule gehen, weil er krank war	= *he couldn't go to school, because he was ill*
wenn sie in die Stadt geht, nimmt sie immer ihre Handtasche	= *when she goes to town, she always takes her handbag*

• •

9 Word order

The basic rule for German word order is that the verb comes second in a sentence. The subject of the sentence usually comes before the verb:

meine Mutter fährt am Freitag nach Köln = *my mother is going to Cologne on Friday*

When the verb used is in a compound tense, such as the perfect and the future tenses, the auxiliary verb comes second in the sentence, while the past participle (in the perfect) or infinitive (in the future tense) goes to the end:

wir haben sehr lang gewartet = *we waited a very long time*
sie wird sicher bald kommen = *she is sure to come soon*

Infinitives go to the end in other sentences too, as when used with modal verbs or the verb **lassen**:

ich kann dieses Lied nicht leiden = *I can't stand this song*
du musst hier bleiben = *you must stay here*
ich lasse mir die Haare schneiden = *I'm going to have my hair cut*

In questions the normal order of the subject and the verb is inverted, as in English:

kommst du heute Abend? = *are you coming this evening?*

In commands the verb is placed first:

komm schnell rein! = *come in quickly!*

Subordinate clauses

A speaker or writer may start a sentence with a subordinate clause in order to introduce variety or for effect. In this case the verb stays in second place, after the subordinate clause, and the subject of the main clause follows the verb; **blieb** in the example below:

da ich kein Geld hatte, blieb ich zu Hause = *since I had no money, I stayed at home*

In the subordinate clause itself, the verb goes to the end; *cf.* **hatte** in the previous example and **war** in the following one:

er konnte nicht in die Schule gehen, weil er krank war

The relative pronouns **der**, **die**, and **das**, as well as conjunctions such as **als** = *when*, **dass** = *that*, **weil** = *because*, introduce subordinate clauses and therefore cause the verb to go to the end of the subordinate clause.

(See the section on Conjunctions for more examples.)

der Junge, der hier wohnt, ist in der Schule	= *the boy, who lives here, is at school*
die Soldaten, die gestern hier waren, haben nicht bezahlt	= *the soldiers, who were here yesterday, did not pay*

When separable verbs separate, the prefix goes to the end:

der Film fängt um acht Uhr an	= *the film starts at 8 o'clock*
wann kommt der Zug an?	= *when does the train arrive?*

When there are a number of phrases in a sentence, the usual order for the different elements is: 1 time, 2 manner, 3 place:

wir fahren heute mit dem Auto nach München = *we are driving to Munich today*

(*time* = heute; *manner* = mit dem Auto; *place* = nach München)

German irregular verbs / Deutsche unregelmäßige Verben

Irregular and partly irregular verbs are listed alphabetically by infinitive. 1st, 2nd, and 3rd person present and imperative forms are given after the infinitive, and preterite subjunctive forms after the preterite indicative, where they take an umlaut, change *e* to *i*, etc.

Verbs with a raised number in the German-English section of the Dictionary have the same number in this list.

Compound verbs (including verbs with prefixes) are only given if a) they do not take the same forms as the corresponding simple verb, e.g. *befehlen*, or b) there is no corresponding simple verb, e.g. *bewegen*.

An asterisk (*) indicates a verb which is also conjugated regularly.

Infinitive / Infinitiv	Preterite / Präteritum	Past Participle / 2. Partizip
abwägen	wog (wöge) ab	abgewogen
backen (du bäckst, er bäckt; *auch:* du backst, er backt)	backte, *älter:* buk (büke)	gebacken
befehlen (du befiehlst, er befiehlt; befiehl!)	befahl (beföhle, befähle)	befohlen
beginnen	begann (begänne, *seltener:* begönne)	begonnen
beißen	biss	gebissen
bergen (du birgst, er birgt; birg!)	barg (bärge)	geborgen
bersten (du birst, er birst; birst!)	barst (bärste)	geborsten
besinnen	besann (besänne)	besonnen
bewegen[2]	bewog (bewöge)	bewogen
biegen	bog (böge)	gebogen
bieten	bot (böte)	geboten
binden	band (bände)	gebunden
bitten	bat (bäte)	gebeten
blasen (du bläst, er bläst)	blies	geblasen
bleiben	blieb	geblieben
bleichen*	blich	geblichen
braten (du brätst, er brät)	briet	gebraten
brechen (du brichst, er bricht; brich!)	brach (bräche)	gebrochen
brennen	brannte (brennte)	gebrannt
bringen	brachte (brächte)	gebracht
denken	dachte (dächte)	gedacht
dreschen (du drischst, er drischt; drisch!)	drosch (drösche)	gedroschen
dringen	drang (dränge)	gedrungen
dürfen (ich darf, du darfst, er darf)	durfte (dürfte)	gedurft
empfehlen (du empfiehlst, er empfiehlt, empfiehl!)	empfahl (empföhle, *seltener:* empfähle)	empfohlen
erklimmen	erklomm (erklömme)	erklommen
erlöschen (du erlischst, er erlischt; erlisch!)	erlosch (erlösche)	erloschen

German irregular verbs

Infinitive	Preterite	Past Participle
Infinitiv	*Präteritum*	*2. Partizip*

erschallen*	erscholl (erschölle)	erschollen
erschrecken[1,3] (du erschrickst, er erschrickt; erschrick!)	erschrak (erschäke)	erschrocken
erwägen	erwog (erwöge)	erwogen
essen (du isst, er isst; iss!)	aß (äße)	gegessen
fahren (du fährst, er fährt)	fuhr (führe)	gefahren
fallen (du fällst, er fällt)	fiel	gefallen
fangen (du fängst, er fängt)	fing	gefangen
fechten (du fichtst, er ficht; ficht!)	focht (föchte)	gefochten
finden	fand (fände)	gefunden
flechten (du flichtst, er flicht; flicht!)	flocht (flöchte)	geflochten
fliegen	flog (flöge)	geflogen
fliehen	floh (flöhe)	geflohen
fließen	floss (flösse)	geflossen
fressen (du frisst, er frisst; friss!)	fraß (fräße)	gefressen
frieren	fror (fröre)	gefroren
gären*	gor (göre)	gegoren
gebären (*geh.*: du gebierst, sie gebiert; gebier!)	gebar (gebäre)	geboren
geben (du gibst, er gibt; gib!)	gab (gäbe)	gegeben
gedeihen	gedieh	gediehen
gehen	ging	gegangen
gelingen	gelang (gelänge)	gelungen
gelten (du giltst, er gilt; gilt!)	galt (gölte, gälte)	gegolten
genesen	genas (genäse)	genesen
genießen	genoss (genösse)	genossen
geschehen (es geschieht)	geschah (geschähe)	geschehen
gewinnen	gewann (gewönne, gewänne)	gewonnen
gießen	goss (gösse)	gegossen
gleichen	glich	geglichen
gleiten	glitt	geglitten
glimmen	glomm (glömme)	geglommen
graben (du gräbst, er gräbt)	grub (grübe)	gegraben
greifen	griff	gegriffen
haben (du hast, er hat)	hatte (hätte)	gehabt
halten (du hältst, er hält)	hielt	gehalten
hängen[1]	hing	gehangen
hauen	haute, *geh.*: hieb	gehauen
heben	hob (höbe)	gehoben
heißen	hieß	geheißen
helfen (du hilfst, er hilft; hilf!)	half (hülfe, *selten*: hälfe)	geholfen
kennen	kannte (kennte)	gekannt
klingen	klang (klänge)	geklungen
kneifen	kniff	gekniffen
kommen	kam (käme)	gekommen
können (ich kann, du kannst, er kann)	konnte (könnte)	gekonnt
kriechen	kroch (kröche)	gekrochen
laden[1,2] (du lädst, er lädt)	lud (lüde)	geladen
lassen (du lässt, er lässt)	ließ	gelassen
laufen (du läufst, er läuft)	lief	gelaufen
leiden	litt	gelitten
leihen	lieh	geliehen
lesen[1,2] (du liest, er liest; lies!)	las (läse)	gelesen
liegen	lag (läge)	gelegen
lügen	log (löge)	gelogen
mahlen	mahlte	gemahlen
meiden	mied	gemieden

German irregular verbs

Infinitive *Infinitiv*	Preterite *Präteritum*	Past Participle *2. Partizip*
melken* (du milkst, er milkt; milk!; du melkst, er melkt; melke!)	molk (mölke)	gemolken
messen (du misst, er misst; miss!)	maß (mäße)	gemessen
misslingen	misslang (misslänge)	misslungen
mögen (ich mag, du magst, er mag)	mochte (möchte)	gemocht
müssen (ich muss, du musst, er muss)	musste (müsste)	gemusst
nehmen (du nimmst, er nimmt; nimm!)	nahm (nähme)	genommen
nennen	nannte (nennte)	genannt
pfeifen	pfiff	gepfiffen
preisen	pries	gepriesen
quellen (du quillst, er quillt; quill!)	quoll (quölle)	gequollen
raten (du rätst, er rät)	riet	geraten
reiben	rieb	gerieben
reißen	riss	gerissen
reiten	ritt	geritten
rennen	rannte (rennte)	gerannt
riechen	roch (röche)	gerochen
ringen	rang (ränge)	gerungen
rinnen	rann (ränne, *seltener:* rönne)	geronnen
rufen	rief	gerufen
salzen*	salzte	gesalzen
saufen (du säufst, er säuft)	soff (söffe)	gesoffen
saugen*	sog (söge)	gesogen
schaffen*	schuf (schüfe)	geschaffen
schallen*	scholl (schölle)	geschallt
scheiden	schied	geschieden
scheinen	schien	geschienen
scheißen	schiss	geschissen
schelten (du schiltst, er schilt; schilt!)	schalt (schölte)	gescholten
scheren[1]	schor (schöre)	geschoren
schieben	schob (schöbe)	geschoben
schießen	schoss (schösse)	geschossen
schinden	schindete	geschunden
schlafen (du schläfst, er schläft)	schlief	geschlafen
schlagen (du schlägst, er schlägt)	schlug (schlüge)	geschlagen
schleichen	schlich	geschlichen
schleifen[1]	schliff	geschliffen
schließen	schloss (schlösse)	geschlossen
schlingen	schlang (schlänge)	geschlungen
schmeißen	schmiss	geschmissen
schmelzen (du schmilzt, er schmilzt; schmilz!)	schmolz	geschmolzen
schneiden	schnitt	geschnitten
schrecken* (du schrickst, er schrickt; schrick!)	schrak (schräke)	geschreckt
schreiben	schrieb	geschrieben
schreien	schrie	geschrie[e]n
schreiten	schritt	geschritten
schweigen	schwieg	geschwiegen
schwellen (du schwillst, er schwillt; schwill!)	schwoll (schwölle)	geschwollen
schwimmen	schwamm (schwömme, *seltener:* schwämme)	geschwommen
schwinden	schwand (schwände)	geschwunden

Infinitive / *Infinitiv*	Preterite / *Präteritum*	Past Participle / *2. Partizip*
schwingen	schwang (schwänge)	geschwungen
schwören	schwor (schwüre)	geschworen
sehen (du siehst, er sieht; sieh[e]!)	sah (sähe)	gesehen
sein (ich bin, du bist, er ist, wir sind, ihr seid, sie sind; sei!)	war (wäre)	gewesen
senden*	sandte (sendete)	gesandt
sieden*	sott (sötte)	gesotten
singen	sang (sänge)	gesungen
sinken	sank (sänke)	gesunken
sitzen	saß (säße)	gesessen
sollen (ich soll, du sollst, er soll)	sollte	gesollt
spalten*	spaltete	gespalten
speien	spie	gespie[e]n
spinnen	spann (spönne, spänne)	gesponnen
sprechen (du sprichst, er spricht; sprich!)	sprach (spräche)	gesprochen
sprießen	spross (sprösse)	gesprossen
springen	sprang	gesprungen
stechen (du stichst, er sticht; stich!)	stach (stäche)	gestochen
stehen	stand (stünde, *auch:* stände)	gestanden
stehlen (du stiehlst, er stiehlt; stiehl!)	stahl (stähle, *seltener:* stöhle)	gestohlen
steigen	stieg	gestiegen
sterben (du stirbst, er stirbt; stirb!)	starb (stürbe)	gestorben
stinken	stank (stänke)	gestunken
stoßen (du stößt, er stößt)	stieß	gestoßen
streichen	strich	gestrichen
streiten	stritt	gestritten
tragen (du trägst, er trägt)	trug (trüge)	getragen
treffen (du triffst, er trifft; triff!)	traf (träfe)	getroffen
treiben	trieb	getrieben
treten (du trittst, er tritt; tritt!)	trat (träte)	getreten
triefen*	troff (tröffe)	getroffen
trinken	trank (tränke)	getrunken
trügen	trog (tröge)	getrogen
tun	tat (täte)	getan
verderben (du verdirbst, er verdirbt; verdirb!)	verdarb (verdürbe)	verdorben
verdrießen	verdross (verdrösse)	verdrossen
vergessen (du vergisst, er vergisst, vergiss!)	vergaß (vergäße)	vergessen
verlieren	verlor (verlöre)	verloren
verschleißen*	verschliss	verschlissen
verzeihen	verzieh	verziehen
wachsen[1] (du wächst, er wächst)	wuchs (wüchse)	gewachsen
waschen (du wäschst, er wäscht)	wusch (wüsche)	gewaschen
weichen	wich	gewichen
weisen	wies	gewiesen
wenden[2]*	wandte (wendete)	gewandt
werben (du wirbst, er wirbt; wirb!)	warb (würbe)	geworben
werden (du wirst, er wird; werde!)	wurde, *dichter.:* ward (würde)	geworden; *als Hilfsv.:* worden
werfen (du wirfst, er wirft; wirf!)	warf (würfe)	geworfen
wiegen[1]	wog (wöge)	gewogen
winden	wand (wände)	gewunden
wissen (ich weiß, du weißt, er weiß)	wusste (wüsste)	gewusst

German irregular verbs

Infinitive *Infinitiv*	Preterite *Präteritum*	Past Participle *2. Partizip*
wollen (ich will, du willst, er will)	wollte	gewollt
wringen	wrang (wränge)	gewrungen
ziehen	zog (zöge)	gezogen
zwingen	zwang (zwänge)	gezwungen

English irregular verbs / Englische unregelmäßige Verben

Ein Sternchen (*) weist darauf hin, dass die korrekte Form von der jeweiligen Bedeutung abhängt.

Infinitive / Infinitiv	Past Tense / Präteritum	Past Participle / 2. Partizip
arise	arose	arisen
awake	awoke	awoken
be	was *sing.*, were *pl.*	been
bear	bore	borne
beat	beat	beaten
become	became	become
begin	began	begun
bend	bent	bent
bet	bet, betted	bet, betted
bid	*bade, bid	*bidden, bid
bind	bound	bound
bite	bit	bitten
bleed	bled	bled
blow	blew	blown
break	broke	broken
breed	bred	bred
bring	brought	brought
broadcast	broadcast	broadcast
build	built	built
burn	burnt, burned	burnt, burned
burst	burst	burst
bust	bust, busted	bust, busted
buy	bought	bought
cast	cast	cast
catch	caught	caught
choose	chose	chosen
cling	clung	clung
come	came	come
cost	*cost, costed	*cost, costed
creep	crept	crept
cut	cut	cut
deal	dealt	dealt
dig	dug	dug
dive	dived, (*Amer.*) dove	dived
do	did	done
draw	drew	drawn
dream	dreamt, dreamed	dreamt, dreamed
drink	drank	drunk
drive	drove	driven
dwell	dwelt	dwelt
eat	ate	eaten
fall	fell	fallen
feed	fed	fed
feel	felt	felt
fight	fought	fought

Infinitive / Infinitiv	Past Tense / Präteritum	Past Participle / 2. Partizip
find	found	found
flee	fled	fled
fling	flung	flung
floodlight	floodlit	floodlit
fly	flew	flown
forbid	forbade, forbad	forbidden
forecast	forecast, forecasted	forecast, forecasted
foretell	foretold	foretold
forget	forgot	forgotten
forgive	forgave	forgiven
forsake	forsook	forsaken
freeze	froze	frozen
get	got	got, (*Amer.*) gotten
give	gave	given
go	went	gone
grind	ground	ground
grow	grew	grown
hang	*hung, hanged	*hung, hanged
have	had	had
hear	heard	heard
hew	hewed	hewn, hewed
hide	hid	hidden
hit	hit	hit
hold	held	held
hurt	hurt	hurt
keep	kept	kept
kneel	knelt, (*esp. Amer.*) kneeled	knelt, (*esp. Amer.*) kneeled
know	knew	known
lay	laid	laid
lead	led	led
lean	leaned, (*Brit.*) leant	leaned, (*Brit.*) leant
leap	leapt, leaped	leapt, leaped
learn	learnt, learned	learnt, learned
leave	left	left
lend	lent	lent
let	let	let
lie[3]	lay	lain
light	lit, lighted	lit, lighted
lose	lost	lost
make	made	made

English irregular verbs

Infinitive *Infinitiv*	Past Tense *Präteritum*	Past Participle *2. Partizip*
mean	meant	meant
meet	met	met
mow	mowed	mown, mowed
overhang	overhung	overhung
pay	paid	paid
prove	proved	proved, proven
put	put	put
quit	quitted, (Amer.) quit	quitted, (Amer.) quit
read /riːd/	read /red/	read /red/
rid	rid	rid
ride	rode	ridden
ring[3]	rang	rung
rise	rose	risen
run	ran	run
saw	sawed	sawn, sawed
say	said	said
see	saw	seen
seek	sought	sought
sell	sold	sold
send	sent	sent
set	set	set
sew	sewed	sewn, sewed
shake	shook	shaken
shear	sheared	shorn, sheared
shed	shed	shed
shine	shone	shone
shit	shitted, shit	shitted, shit
shoe	shod	shod
shoot	shot	shot
show	showed	shown
shrink	shrank	shrunk
shut	shut	shut
sing	sang	sung
sink	sank, sunk	sunk
sit	sat	sat
slay	slew	slain
sleep	slept	slept
slide	slid	slid
sling	slung	slung
slink	slunk	slunk
slit	slit	slit
smell	smelt, smelled	smelt, smelled
sow	sowed	sown, sowed
speak	spoke	spoken
speed	*sped, speeded	*sped, speeded
spell	spelled, (Brit.) spelt	spelled, (Brit.) spelt
spend	spent	spent
spill	spilt, spilled	spilt, spilled
spin	spun	spun
spit	spat, spit	spat, spit
split	split	split
spoil	spoilt, spoiled	spoilt, spoiled
spread	spread	spread
spring	sprang, (Amer.) sprung	sprung
stand	stood	stood
steal	stole	stolen
stick	stuck	stuck
sting	stung	stung
stink	stank, stunk	stunk
strew	strewed	strewed, strewn
stride	strode	stridden
strike	struck	struck
string	strung	strung
strive	strove	striven
sublet	sublet	sublet
swear	swore	sworn
sweep	swept	swept
swell	swelled	swollen, swelled
swim	swam	swum
swing	swung	swung
take	took	taken
teach	taught	taught
tear	tore	torn
tell	told	told
think	thought	thought
thrive	thrived, throve	thrived, thriven
throw	threw	thrown
thrust	thrust	thrust
tread	trod	trodden, trod
understand	understood	understood
undo	undid	undone
wake	woke	woken
wear	wore	worn
weave[1]	wove	woven
weep	wept	wept
wet	wet, wetted	wet, wetted
win	won	won
wind[2] /waɪnd/	wound /waʊnd/	wound /waʊnd/
wring	wrung	wrung
write	wrote	written

Numbers / Zahlen

Cardinal numbers	Kardinalzahlen	Ordinal numbers	Ordinalzahlen
1 one	1 eins, ein...	1st first	1. erst...
2 two	2 zwei	2nd second	2. zweit...
3 three	3 drei	3rd third	3. dritt...
4 four	4 vier	4th fourth	4. viert...
5 five	5 fünf	5th fifth	5. fünft...
6 six	6 sechs	6th sixth	6. sechst...
7 seven	7 sieben	7th seventh	7. siebt..., siebent...
8 eight	8 acht	8th eighth	8. acht...
9 nine	9 neun	9th ninth	9. neunt...
10 ten	10 zehn	10th tenth	10. zehnt...
11 eleven	11 elf	11th eleventh	11. elft...
12 twelve	12 zwölf	12th twelfth	12. zwölft...
13 thirteen	13 dreizehn	13th thirteenth	13. dreizehnt...
14 fourteen	14 vierzehn	14th fourteenth	14. vierzehnt...
15 fifteen	15 fünfzehn	15th fifteenth	15. fünfzehnt...
16 sixteen	16 sechzehn	16th sixteenth	16. sechzehnt...
17 seventeen	17 siebzehn	17th seventeenth	17. siebzehnt...
18 eighteen	18 achtzehn	18th eighteenth	18. achtzehnt...
19 nineteen	19 neunzehn	19th nineteenth	19. neunzehnt...
20 twenty	20 zwanzig	20th twentieth	20. zwanzigst...
21 twenty-one	21 einundzwanzig	21st twenty-first	21. einundzwanzigst...
30 thirty	30 dreißig	30th thirtieth	30. dreißigst...
40 forty	40 vierzig	40th fortieth	40. vierzigst...
50 fifty	50 fünfzig	50th fiftieth	50. fünfzigst...
60 sixty	60 sechzig	60th sixtieth	60. sechzigst...
70 seventy	70 siebzig	70th seventieth	70. siebzigst...
80 eighty	80 achtzig	80th eightieth	80. achtzigst...
90 ninety	90 neunzig	90th ninetieth	90. neunzigst...
100 one hundred	100 [ein]hundert	100th [one] hundredth	100. [ein]hundertst...
101 one hundred and one	101 [ein]hundert[und]eins	101st [one] hundred and first	101. [ein]hundert[und]erst...
1,000 one thousand	1 000 [ein]tausend	1,000th [one] thousandth	1 000. [ein]tausendst...
1,001 one thousand and one	1 001 [ein]tausend[und]eins	1,001st one thousand and first	1 001. [ein]tausend[und]erst...
10,000 ten thousand	10 000 zehntausend	10,000th ten thousandth	10 000. zehntausendst...
13,438 thirteen thousand, four hundred and thirty-eight	13 438 dreizehntausendvierhundert[und]achtunddreißig	13,438th thirteen thousand, four hundred and thirty-eighth	13 438. dreizehntausendvierhundert[und]achtunddreißigst...
100,000 one hundred thousand	100 000 [ein]hunderttausend	100,000th [one] hundred thousandth	100 000. [ein]hunderttausendst...
1,000,000 one million	1 000 000 eine Million	1,000,000th [one] millionth	1 000 000. millionst...
2,000,000 two million	2 000 000 zwei Millionen	2,000,000th two millionth	2 000 000. zweimillionst...
1,000,000,000 one billion	1 000 000 000 eine Milliarde	1,000,000,000th one billionth	1 000 000 000. milliardst...

Numbers / Zahlen

- -

Vulgar fractions and mixed numbers / Brüche (gemeine Brüche) und gemischte Zahlen

in figures *in Zahlen*	in words	*in Worten*
$^1/_2$	a/one half	*ein halb*
$^1/_3$	a/one third	*ein drittel*
$^1/_4$	a/one quarter	*ein viertel*
$^1/_{10}$	a/one tenth	*ein zehntel*
$^2/_3$	two-thirds	*zwei drittel*
$^1/_1$	one over one	*ein eintel*
$^4/_1$	four over one	*vier eintel*
$^m/_n$	m over n	*m n-tel*
$^x/_6$	x over six	*x sechstel*
$1\,^1/_2$	one and a half	*ein[und]einhalb*

Decimal numbers / Dezimalzahlen

written as	*geschrieben*	spoken as	*gesprochen*
0.1	*0,1*	nought point one	*null Komma eins*
0.015	*0,015*	nought point nought one five	*null Komma null eins fünf*
1.40	*1,40*	one point four o [əʊ]	*eins Komma vier null*

Weights and Measures / Maße und Gewichte

Weight / Gewichte

1,000 milligrams (mg)	= 1 gram (g)	= 15.43 grains
1 000 Milligramm (mg)	= *1 Gramm (g)*	
1,000 grams	= 1 kilogram (kg)	= 2.205 pounds
1 000 Gramm	= *1 Kilogramm (kg)*	
1,000 kilograms	= 1 tonne (t)	= 19.684 hundredweight
1 000 Kilogramm	= *1 Tonne (t)*	
	1 ounce (oz.)	= 28.35 g
16 ounces	= 1 pound (lb.)	= 0.454 kg
14 pounds	= 1 stone (st.)	= 6.35 kg
112 pounds	= 1 hundredweight	= 50.8 kg
20 hundredweight	= 1 ton (t.)	= 1,016.05 kg

Length / Längenmaße

10 millimetres (mm)	= 1 centimetre (cm)	= 0.394 inch
10 Millimeter (mm)	= *1 Zentimeter (cm)*	
100 centimetres	= 1 metre (m)	= 39.4 inches/1.094 yards
100 Zentimeter	= *1 Meter (m)*	
1,000 metres	= 1 kilometre (km)	= 0.6214 mile/ $5/8$ mile
1 000 Meter	= *1 Kilometer (km)*	
	1 inch (in.)	= 25.4 mm
12 inches	= 1 foot (ft.)	= 30.48 cm
3 feet	= 1 yard (yd.)	= 0.914 m
220 yards	= 1 furlong	= 201.17 m
8 furlongs	= 1 mile (m.)	= 1.609 km
1,760 yards	= 1 mile	= 1.609 km

Square measure / Flächenmaße

100 square metres (sq. m)	= 1 are	= 0.025 acre
100 Quadratmeter (m^2)	= *1 Ar (a)*	
100 ares	= 1 hectare (ha)	= 2.471 acres
100 Ar	= *1 Hektar (ha)*	
100 hectares	= 1 square kilometre (sq.km)	= 0.386 square miles
100 hektar	= *1 Quadratkilometer (km^2)*	
	1 square inch	= 6.452cm^2
144 square inches	= 1 square foot	= 929.03 cm^2
9 square feet	= 1 square yard	= 0.836 m^2
4,840 square yards	= 1 acre	= 0.405 ha
640 acres	= 1 square mile	= 2.59k^2/259 ha

Cubic measure / Raummaße

1 cubic centimetre (cc) . . . . = 0.06 cubic inches
1 Kubikzentimeter (cm³)

1,000,000 cubic centimetres . . . . = 1 cubic metre (cu. m) . . . . = 35.714 cubic feet/
1 000 000 Kubikzentimeter . . . . = *1 Kubikmeter (m³)* . . . . 1.307 cubic yards

                                                   1 cubic inch . . . . = 16.4 cm³

1,728 cubic inches . . . . = 1 cubic foot . . . . = 0.028 m³

27 cubic feet . . . . = 1 cubic yard . . . . = 0.764 m³

Capacity / Hohlmaße

10 millilitres (ml) . . . . = 1 centilitre (cl)
10 Milliliter (ml) . . . . = *1 Zentiliter (cl)*

100 centilitres . . . . = 1 litre (l) . . . . = 1.76 pints (2.1 US pints)/
100 Zentiliter . . . . = *1 Liter (l)* . . . . 0.22 gallons (0.264 US gallons)

4 gills . . . . = 1 pint (pt.) (1.201 US pints) . . . = 0.568 l

2 pints . . . . = 1 quart (qt.) (1.201 US quarts) = 1.136 l

4 quarts . . . . = 1 gallon (gal) (1.201 US gallons) = 4.546 l

Also available from Oxford University Press

Oxford-Duden Dictionary

- Now in colour
- Over 800,000 words, phrases, and translations

978-0-19-860974-2

Concise Oxford-Duden German Dictionary

- Over 400,000 words, phrases, and translations

978-0-19-860976-0

Oxford Colour German Dictionary Plus

- 100,000 words, phrases, and translations

978-0-19-860901-8
978-0-19-860899-8
(US edition)

Oxford German Minidictionary

- Over 100,000 entries and translations

978-0-19-861044-1

Oxford Take Off in German

- Language learning course with almost 5 hours of audio

978-0-19-861294-1
(Book + 4 CD's)

Quick Take Off in German

- Language learning course with almost 3 hours of audio

978-0-19-860655-0
(Book + 2 CD's)

OXFORD
UNIVERSITY PRESS